A STUDENT'S GUIDE TO THE FEDERAL RULES OF CIVIL PROCEDURE

2013

By

Steven Baicker–McKee

Assistant Professor of Law
Duquesne University School of Law

William M. Janssen

Professor of Law
Charleston School of Law

John B. Corr

Professor of Law, American University
Washington College of Law

WEST®

Mat #41465902

ISBN 978–0–314–28848–6

PREFACE TO THE 2013 EDITION OF THE *STUDENT'S GUIDE*

We authors are grateful to you for choosing once again to add the *Student's Guide to the Federal Rules of Civil Procedure* to your law library. Few people have the opportunity to work and write about topics they enjoy, and our subscribers are the ones who provide that opportunity to us. Without regard to whether you have a long-standing relationship with us and our work, or if you are a first-time consumer of what we hope will be a useful companion in your journey through American law, welcome aboard.

The *Student's Guide* was created to meet a particular need—to bridge the gap we saw between, on the one extreme, expansive, multi-volume treatises on the Federal Rules of Civil Procedure and, on the other extreme, pamphlets that simply reprint the text of the Rules. Our hope was to develop a reliable, current, single-volume, readily "grabbed" and consulted, easily transported resource for understanding and applying the Rules.

Our unique format remains the same as it always has. The *Student's Guide* begins with an introduction to **General Concepts in Federal Practice** (including personal jurisdiction changes ushered in by recent Supreme Court opinions). Then, each Rule is discussed in turn, beginning with the **Current Rule Text**, followed immediately by our **Authors' Commentary** to that Rule and its subparts. Our Commentary distills each Rule's "**Purpose and Scope**," summarizes the "**Core Concept**," of each Rule's subsections, and follows with an extended textual discussion of the Rule in its "**Applications**," including helpful citations from the Supreme Court, the national Courts of Appeals, and the District Courts. The *Student's Guide* also contains an orienting summary to **federal appellate practice**. Often-consulted sections of the **federal Judiciary Code** (Title 28) are also supplied, as are complete sets of **official civil forms.** The *Student's Guide* also contains the text of the **Constitution** and an introduction to **federal multidistrict litigation** (MDL).

What's New in the 2013 Edition:

• Federal Courts Jurisdiction and Venue Clarification Act: This new statute took effect in January 2012. Although it became law with an absolute minimum of publicity, it applies in every federal district court. The Act extensively rewrote many portions of the federal venue laws, adjusted certain venue and jurisdictional concepts relating to aliens and corporations, and reconfigured portions of the federal removal procedures (codifying the unanimity requirement and resolving a national division on the 30–day removal period). These changes, and others implemented by the Act, are introduced and discussed in this edition of the *Student's Guide*. The as-amended text of the affected provisions appears in Part VII of this edition.

- **Almost 1,300 New Citations:** This edition contains nearly *1,300 new citations*, most to opinions from the Nation's federal courts decided between Fall 2011 and late Summer 2012.

- **Tracking the Changes to Federal Practice:** The past several years have seen major changes to federal practice–the Supreme Court's new personal jurisdiction changes, a new class action opinion, the 2010 expert amendments and summary judgment amendments, the 2009 time computation amendments and "indicative ruling" amendments, the 2007 and 2009 "plausibility"-in-pleading decisions, the 2007 "restyling" amendments and "e-government" privacy amendments, and the 2006 e-discovery amendments. This edition of the *Student's Guide* not only reflects and discusses these changes, but continues to track the evolving case law construing and applying the provisions.

We thank you, again, for a great many years together with the *Student's Guide*. We are, each year, graced by comments and suggestions for improving the product, and we welcome all of them. Your vigilance helps us keep the *Student's Guide* a current, useful, and responsive resource for the bench and bar. Thank you.

THE AUTHORS

June 2013

THE AUTHORS

STEVEN BAICKER–MCKEE, after more than 20 years as a litigator at Babst Calland in Pittsburgh, Pennsylvania, serving on the firm's Operating Committee and Board of Directors, has joined the faculty at the Duquesne University School of Law as an Assistant Professor teaching procedure and energy law. He remains associated with Babst Calland, and has been recognized as one of the Outstanding Lawyers of America and elected to the Academy of Trial Lawyers.

Mr. Baicker-McKee received his B.A. from Yale University, then spent the next several years building fine furniture and custom cabinets in Charlottesville, Virginia before attending law school. Mr. Baicker–McKee received his J.D. from Marshall-Wythe School of Law, College of William and Mary, where he was on the Board of Editors of the *William and Mary Law Review*. He served a two-year clerkship with the Honorable Glenn E. Mencer of the United States District Court for the Western District of Pennsylvania, to whom he is forever indebted. Mr. Baicker-McKee's tenure as Judge Mencer's law clerk provided the inspiration for this book.

Mr. Baicker-McKee resides in Pittsburgh, Pennsylvania with his wife, Carol, and their three children, Kyle, Eric, and Sara. Their love and support were instrumental in the development of this book. Mr. Baicker-McKee is also grateful for the support of his parents, Joe and Macky Baicker.

JOHN B. CORR is a Professor of Law at the American University, Washington College of Law, in Washington, D.C. As a specialist in civil procedure, conflict of laws, and bankruptcy, he has advised and consulted with private practitioners in a variety of litigation matters. The author of articles dealing with civil procedure and/or conflicts in a number of journals, Mr. Corr has also received numerous "outstanding professor" awards, based on student ballots.

As a member of the New York and District of Columbia Bars, Mr. Corr practiced in the litigation department of the Washington office of Fried, Frank, Harris, Shriver & Kampelman before he began a career in legal education.

Mr. Corr graduated from the Georgetown University Law Center, where he was an editor of the Georgetown Law Journal. Before receiving his J.D. degree, Mr. Corr earned M.A. and Ph.D. degrees in history. He also served for two years in the U.S. Army as a captain in military intelligence.

WILLIAM M. JANSSEN is an Associate Professor of Law at the Charleston School of Law in Charleston, South Carolina. Mr. Janssen teaches courses in civil procedure, products liability, and first amendment law. He has twice been honored by the students of the law school as "Professor of the Year." Before his appointment to the faculty in Charleston, Mr. Janssen was a litigation partner, the Chair of Life Sciences Practices, and a member of the Executive Committee at the Midatlantic law firm of Saul Ewing LLP, with whom he practiced for almost seventeen years. Mr. Janssen helped design and implement Saul Ewing's nationally recognized "We're All In!" pro bono initiative. He focused his private practice in pharmaceutical and medical device risk management and litigation. Mr. Janssen is a member of the International Association of Defense Counsel and its Drug, Device, & Biotech committee, and the Food and Drug Law Institute. He is admitted to practice law in the federal and State courts of Pennsylvania, the Federal Circuit, the Third Circuit, the Fourth Circuit, and the United States Supreme Court, and has practiced pro hac vice in various other jurisdictions. For five academic terms, Mr. Janssen served as an Adjunct Instructor at the Temple University School of Law.

Mr. Janssen graduated from Saint Joseph's University in Philadelphia and The American University, Washington College of Law, in Washington, D.C. He served as Executive Editor of the American University Law Review and as a member of the Moot Court Board. After law school, Mr. Janssen clerked for the Honorable James McGirr Kelly, on the United States District Court for the Eastern District of Pennsylvania, and for the Honorable Joseph F. Weis, Jr., on the United States Court of Appeals for the Third Circuit.

Mr. Janssen thanks his family and friends for teaching him that you have not truly lived until you've answered, for the thousandth time: "No, we're still not done with that book yet." Mr. Janssen dedicates this effort to his parents, Bill and Catherine, and to TMcP.

The authors welcome any comments, suggestions, or constructive criticisms of this book. Their telephone and telefax numbers and email addresses are provided below.

Steven Baicker–McKee
(412) 394-5499
(412) 394-6576 (fax)
sbaicker@bccz.com (email)

John B. Corr
(202) 274-4208
(202) 274-4130 (fax)
jbcorr@cox.net (email)

William M. Janssen
(843) 377-2442
(843) 853-2519 (fax)
wjanssen@charlestonlaw.edu (email)

Summary of Contents

Page

PART I   JUDICIAL RULEMAKING 1

PART II   GENERAL CONCEPTS IN FEDERAL PRACTICE—
PERSONAL JURISDICTION, NOTICE REQUIREMENTS,
FEDERAL SUBJECT MATTER JURISDICTION, VENUE,
FORUM NON CONVENIENS, REMOVAL, *ERIE*, RES JUDI-
CATA AND COLLATERAL ESTOPPEL 9

PART III–A   AN ORIENTATION TO FIVE YEARS OF MAJOR
RULE AMENDMENTS 183

PART III   FEDERAL RULES OF CIVIL PROCEDURE WITH
COMMENTARY AND PRACTICE POINTERS 185

PART IV   APPENDIX OF FORMS 1403

PART V   MULTIDISTRICT LITIGATION 1425

PART VI   APPELLATE PROCEDURE 1433

PART VII   TITLE 28, JUDICIARY AND JUDICIAL PROCE-
DURE—SELECTED PROVISIONS 1519

PART VIII   THE CONSTITUTION OF THE UNITED STATES 1585

Summary of Contents

Table of Contents

	Page
PART I. JUDICIAL RULEMAKING	1
PART II. GENERAL CONCEPTS IN FEDERAL PRACTICE— PERSONAL JURISDICTION, NOTICE REQUIREMENTS, FEDERAL SUBJECT MATTER JURISDICTION, VENUE, FORUM NON CONVENIENS, REMOVAL, *ERIE*, RES JUDI- CATA AND COLLATERAL ESTOPPEL	9
A. FEDERAL JURISDICTION, VENUE AND *ERIE*	10
§ 2.1 Introduction	10
§ 2.2 Jurisdiction Over Persons or Things—Introduction	10
§ 2.3 Jurisdiction Over Persons or Things—Requirements for Personal Jurisdiction	11
§ 2.4 Jurisdiction Over Persons or Things—Requirements for Personal Jurisdiction—Due Process: Consent, In-State Service, or Minimum Contacts	11
§ 2.5 Jurisdiction Over Persons or Things—Requirements for Personal Jurisdiction—State Limitations: Long-Arm Statutes	22
§ 2.6 Jurisdiction Over Persons or Things—Requirements for Personal Jurisdiction—Notice	24
§ 2.7 Jurisdiction Over Persons or Things—Requirements for Personal Jurisdiction—Special Considerations in Federal Court	26
§ 2.8 Jurisdiction Over Persons or Things—Special Requirements for Quasi in Rem Jurisdiction	30
§ 2.9 Jurisdiction Over Persons or Things—Requirements for in Rem Jurisdiction	34
§ 2.10 Subject Matter Jurisdiction in Federal District Courts—Intro- duction	37
§ 2.11 Subject Matter Jurisdiction in Federal District Courts—Federal Question Jurisdiction	40
§ 2.12 Subject Matter Jurisdiction in Federal District Courts—Require- ments for Diversity Jurisdiction	48
§ 2.13 Subject Matter Jurisdiction in Federal District Courts—Require- ments for Supplemental Jurisdiction	74
§ 2.14 Venue	85
§ 2.15 Forum Non Conveniens	96
§ 2.16 Removal	110
§ 2.17 Removal Procedure	120
§ 2.17a Procedure after Removal	131
§ 2.17b Removal of Class Actions	143
§ 2.18 The *Erie* Doctrine	147

                                                                    Page
B. RES JUDICATA AND COLLATERAL ESTOPPEL 164
§ 2.19   Introduction 164
§ 2.20   Res Judicata—Elements 167
§ 2.21   Res Judicata—Scope 172
§ 2.22   Res Judicata—Counterclaims: Rule 13(a) 173
§ 2.23   Res Judicata—Affirmative Defense: Rule 8(c) 174
§ 2.24   Res Judicata—Relationship to Full Faith and Credit 174
§ 2.24a Jurisdiction and Res Judicata 174
§ 2.24b Events That Postdate Filing 175
§ 2.25   Collateral Estoppel—Elements 175
§ 2.26   Collateral Estoppel—Mutuality v. Nonmutual Estoppel 178
§ 2.27   Collateral Estoppel—Application to Issues of Law and Fact 181
§ 2.28   Collateral Estoppel—Exceptions to Collateral Estoppel 181
§ 2.29   Collateral Estoppel—Affirmative Defense: Rule 8(c) 182
§ 2.30   Collateral Estoppel—Relationship to Full Faith and Credit 182

**PART III–A. AN ORIENTATION TO FIVE YEARS OF MAJOR
        RULE AMENDMENTS** 183

**PART III. FEDERAL RULES OF CIVIL PROCEDURE WITH
        COMMENTARY AND PRACTICE POINTERS** 185

I. SCOPE OF RULES—FORM OF ACTION 188
Rule 1.   Scope and Purpose 188
Rule 2.   One Form of Action 195

**II. COMMENCING AN ACTION; SERVICE OF PROCESS,
        PLEADINGS, MOTIONS, AND ORDERS** 198
Rule 3.   Commencing an Action 198
Rule 4.   Summons 206
Rule 4.1.   Serving Other Process 265
Rule 5.   Serving and Filing Pleadings and Other Papers 268
Rule 5.1.   Constitutional Challenge to a Statute—Notice, Certification,
    and Intervention 284
Rule 5.2.   Privacy Protection for Filings Made With the Court 290
Rule 6.   Computing and Extending Time; Time for Motion Papers 297

III. PLEADINGS AND MOTIONS 316
Rule 7.   Pleadings Allowed; Form of Motions and Other Papers 316
Rule 7.1.   Disclosure Statement 325
Rule 8.   General Rules of Pleading 329
Rule 9.   Pleading Special Matters 355
Rule 10.   Form of Pleadings 373
Rule 11.   Signing Pleadings, Motions, and Other Papers; Representa-
    tions the Court; Sanctions 384
Rule 12.   Defenses and Objections: When and How Presented; Motion
    for Judgment on the Pleadings; Consolidating Motions; Waiving De-
    fenses; Pretrial Hearing 413
Rule 13.   Counterclaim and Crossclaim 501
Rule 14.   Third–Party Practice 521
Rule 15.   Amended and Supplemental Pleadings 533
Rule 16.   Pretrial Conferences; Scheduling; Management 564

Page

IV. PARTIES 582
Rule 17. Plaintiff and Defendant; Capacity; Public Officers 582
Rule 18. Joinder of Claims 595
Rule 19. Required Joinder of Parties 599
Rule 20. Permissive Joinder of Parties 613
Rule 21. Misjoinder and Nonjoinder of Parties 620
Rule 22. Interpleader 624
Rule 23. Class Actions 634
Rule 23.1. Derivative Actions by Shareholders 694
Rule 23.2. Actions Relating to Unincorporated Associations 703
Rule 24. Intervention 706
Rule 25. Substitution of Parties 727

V. DEPOSITIONS AND DISCOVERY 735
Rule 26. Duty to Disclose; General Provisions Governing Discovery 735
Rule 27. Depositions to Perpetuate Testimony 799
Rule 28. Persons Before Whom Depositions May Be Taken 807
Rule 29. Stipulations About Discovery Procedure 812
Rule 30. Depositions by Oral Examination 814
Rule 31. Depositions by Written Questions 843
Rule 32. Using Depositions in Court Proceedings 848
Rule 33. Interrogatories to Parties 859
Rule 34. Producing Documents, Electronically Stored Information, and Tangible Things, or Entering Onto Land, for Inspection and Other Purposes 874
Rule 35. Physical and Mental Examinations 890
Rule 36. Requests for Admission 899
Rule 37. Failure to Make Disclosures or to Cooperate in Discovery; Sanctions 909

VI. TRIALS 933
Rule 38. Right to a Jury Trial; Demand 933
Rule 39. Trial by Jury or by the Court 940
Rule 40. Scheduling Cases for Trial 945
Rule 41. Dismissal of Actions 946
Rule 42. Consolidation; Separate Trials 959
Rule 43. Taking Testimony 964
Rule 44. Proving an Official Record 968
Rule 44.1. Determining Foreign Law 973
Rule 45. Subpoena 977
Rule 46. Objecting to a Ruling or Order 999
Rule 47. Selecting Jurors 1002
Rule 48. Number of Jurors; Verdict 1005
Rule 49. Special Verdict; General Verdict and Questions 1008
Rule 50. Judgment as a Matter of Law in a Jury Trial; Related Motion for a New Trial; Conditional Ruling 1015
Rule 51. Instructions to the Jury; Objections; Preserving a Claim of Error 1026
Rule 52. Findings and Conclusions by the Court; Judgment on Partial Findings 1033
Rule 53. Masters 1041

VII. JUDGMENT 1054
Rule 54. Judgment; Costs 1054

Page

Rule 55.   Default; Default Judgment _____ 1085
Rule 56.   Summary Judgment _____ 1102
Rule 57.   Declaratory Judgment _____ 1150
Rule 58.   Entering Judgment _____ 1160
Rule 59.   New Trial; Altering or Amending a Judgment _____ 1175
Rule 60.   Relief From a Judgment or Order _____ 1193
Rule 61.   Harmless Error _____ 1215
Rule 62.   Stay of Proceedings to Enforce a Judgment _____ 1222
Rule 62.1.   Indicative Ruling on a Motion for Relief That is Barred by a
   Pending Appeal _____ 1234
Rule 63.   Judge's Inability to Proceed _____ 1237

VIII.   PROVISIONAL AND FINAL REMEDIES _____ 1242
Rule 64.   Seizing a Person or Property _____ 1242
Rule 65.   Injunctions and Restraining Orders _____ 1246
Rule 65.1.   Proceedings Against a Surety _____ 1269
Rule 66.   Receivers _____ 1272
Rule 67.   Deposit Into Court _____ 1280
Rule 68.   Offer of Judgment _____ 1283
Rule 69.   Execution _____ 1294
Rule 70.   Enforcing a Judgment for a Specific Act _____ 1300
Rule 71.   Enforcing Relief for or Against a Nonparty _____ 1304

IX.   SPECIAL PROCEEDINGS _____ 1306
Rule 71.1.   Condemning Real or Personal Property _____ 1306
Rule 72.   Magistrate Judges: Pretrial Order _____ 1329
Rule 73.   Magistrate Judges: Trial by Consent; Appeal _____ 1337
Rule 74.   Method of Appeal From Magistrate to District Judge Under
   Title 28, U.S.C, § 636(C)(4) and Rule 73(D) _____ 1342
Rule 75.   Proceedings on Appeal From Magistrate to District Judge
   Under Rule 73(D) _____ 1343
Rule 76.   Judgment of the District Judge on the Appeal Under Rule
   73(D) and Costs _____ 1344

X.   DISTRICT COURTS AND CLERKS _____ 1345
Rule 77.   Conducting Business; Clerk's Authority; Notice of an Order
   or Judgment _____ 1345
Rule 78.   Hearing Motions; Submission on Briefs _____ 1349
Rule 79.   Records Kept by the Clerk _____ 1351
Rule 80.   Stenographic Transcript as Evidence _____ 1354

XI.   GENERAL PROVISIONS _____ 1355
Rule 81.   Applicability of the Rules in General; Removed Actions _____ 1355
Rule 82.   Jurisdiction and Venue Unaffected _____ 1363
Rule 83.   Rules by District Courts; Judged Directives _____ 1365
Rule 84.   Forms _____ 1370
Rule 85.   Title _____ 1371
Rule 86.   Effective Dates _____ 1372

SUPPLEMENTAL RULES FOR ADMIRALTY OR MARITIME
   CLAIMS AND ASSET FORFEITURE ACTIONS _____ 1374
Rule A.   Scope of Rules _____ 1374
Rule B.   In Personam Actions: Attachment and Garnishment _____ 1375
Rule C.   In Rem Actions: Special Provisions _____ 1378

                                                               Page
Rule D.   Possessory, Petitory, and Partition Actions ------------------ 1382
Rule E.   Actions In Rem and Quasi In Rem: General Provisions ---------- 1383
Rule F.   Limitation of Liability ------------------------------------- 1390
Rule G.   Forfeiture Actions in Rem------------------------------------ 1394

PART IV.   APPENDIX OF FORMS --------------------------------------- 1403
Form 1   Caption-- 1404
Form 2   Date, Signature, Address, E-mail Address, and Telephone
  Number -- 1405
Form 3   Summons--- 1405
Form 4   Summons on a Third–Party Complaint--------------------------- 1406
Form 5   Notice of a Lawsuit and Request to Waive Service of a Sum-
  mons -- 1406
Form 6   Waiver of the Service of Summons----------------------------- 1407
Form 7   Statement of Jurisdiction ----------------------------------- 1408
Form 8   Statement of Reasons for Omitting a Party ------------------- 1409
Form 9   Statement Noting a Party's Death ---------------------------- 1409
Form 10   Complaint to Recover a Sum Certain--------------------------- 1409
Form 11   Complaint for Negligence------------------------------------ 1410
Form 12   Complaint for Negligence When the Plaintiff Does Not Know
  Who Is responsible -- 1410
Form 13   Complaint for Negligence Under the Federal Employers' Lia-
  bility Act--- 1411
Form 14   Complaint for Damages Under the Merchant Marine Act ------- 1411
Form 15   Complaint for the Conversion of Property -------------------- 1412
Form 16   Third–Party Complaint -------------------------------------- 1412
Form 17   Complaint for Specific Performance of a Contract to Convey
  Land -- 1412
Form 18   Complaint for Patent Infringement --------------------------- 1413
Form 19   Complaint for Copyright Infringement and Unfair Competi-
  tion--- 1413
Form 20   Complaint for Interpleader and Declaratory Relief ----------- 1414
Form 21   Complaint on a Claim for a Debt and to Set Aside a Fraudu-
  lent Conveyance Under Rule 18(B) ------------------------------------ 1415
Form 30   Answer Presenting Defenses Under Rule 12(B)----------------- 1416
Form 31   Answer to a Complaint for Money Had and Received With a
  Counterclaim for Interpleader --------------------------------------- 1416
Form 40   Motion to Dismiss Under Rule 12(B) For Lack of Jurisdiction,
  Improper Venue, Insufficient Service of Process, or Failure to State a
  Claim --- 1417
Form 41   Motion to Bring in a Third–Party Defendant ------------------ 1418
Form 42   Motion to Intervene as a Defendant Under Rule 24 ------------ 1418
Form 50   Request to Produce Documents and Tangible Things, or to
  Enter Onto Land Under Rule 34 -------------------------------------- 1418
Form 51   Request for Admissions Under Rule 36 ----------------------- 1419
Form 52   Report of the Parties' Planning Meeting --------------------- 1419
Form 60   Notice of Condemnation ------------------------------------- 1420
Form 61   Complaint for Condemnation -------------------------------- 1421
Form 70   Judgment on a Jury Verdict---------------------------------- 1422
Form 71   Judgment by the Court Without a Jury ----------------------- 1422
Form 80   Notice of a Magistrate Judge's Availability ------------------ 1422
Form 81   Consent to an Assignment to a Magistrate Judge ------------- 1423
Form 82   Order of Assignment to a Magistrate Judge------------------- 1423

Page

PART V. MULTIDISTRICT LITIGATION 1425
§ 5.1   Introduction 1425
§ 5.2   The Federal Multidistrict Litigation Statute, 28 U.S.C.A. § 1407 .. 1430

PART VI. APPELLATE PROCEDURE 1433
§ 6.1   Introduction 1433
§ 6.2   Step One: Appealability 1433
§ 6.3   Step Two: Time for Taking an Appeal 1441
§ 6.4   Step Three: Procedure for Taking an Appeal 1449
§ 6.5   Step Four: Stays Pending Appeal 1453
§ 6.6   Step Five: the Appeal Process 1455
§ 6.7   Step Six: Appeals to the United States Supreme Court 1457
§ 6.8   *Federal Rules of Appellate Procedure* (Effective July 1, 1968;
amendments effective December 1, 2011) 1459

TITLE I. APPLICABILITY OF RULES 1460
Rule 1.   Scope of Rules; Definition; Title 1460
Rule 2.   Suspension of Rules 1461

**TITLE II. APPEAL FROM A JUDGMENT OR ORDER OF A
DISTRICT COURT** 1461
Rule 3.   Appeal as of Right—How Taken 1461
Rule 3.1.   Appeal From a Judgment of a Magistrate Judge in a Civil
Case [Abrogated] 1462
Rule 4.   Appeal as of Right—When Taken 1462
Rule 5.   Appeal by Permission 1467
Rule 5.1.   Appeal by Leave Under 28 U.S.C. § 636(c)(5) [Abrogated] 1468
Rule 6.   Appeal in a Bankruptcy Case From a Final Judgment, Order, or
Decree of a District Court or Bankruptcy Appellate Panel 1468
Rule 7.   Bond for Costs on Appeal in a Civil Case 1470
Rule 8.   Stay or Injunction Pending Appeal 1470
Rule 9.   Release in a Criminal Case 1471
Rule 10.   The Record on Appeal 1471
Rule 11.   Forwarding the Record 1473
Rule 12.   Docketing the Appeal; Filing a Representation Statement;
Filing the Record 1475
Rule 12.1.   Remand After an Indicative Ruling by the District Court on
a Motion for Relief That is Barred by a Pending Appeal 1475

**TITLE III. REVIEW OF A DECISION OF THE UNITED STATES
TAX COURT** 1476
Rule 13.   Review of a Decision of the Tax Court 1476
Rule 14.   Applicability of Other Rules to the Review of a Tax Court
Decision 1476

**TITLE IV. REVIEW OR ENFORCEMENT OF AN ORDER OF AN
ADMINISTRATIVE AGENCY, BOARD, COMMISSION, OR
OFFICER** 1477
Rule 15.   Review or Enforcement of an Agency Order How Obtained;
Intervention 1477
Rule 15.1.   Briefs and Oral Argument in a National Labor Relations
Board Proceeding 1478
Rule 16.   The Record on Review or Enforcement 1478
Rule 17.   Filing the Record 1478

Page

Rule 18. Stay Pending Review----- 1479
Rule 19. Settlement of a Judgment Enforcing an Agency Order in Part 1479
Rule 20. Applicability of Rules to the Review or Enforcement of an
Agency Order ----- 1480

TITLE V. EXTRAORDINARY WRITS ----- 1480
Rule 21. Writs of Mandamus and Prohibition, and Other Extraordinary
Writs----- 1480

**TITLE VI. HABEAS CORPUS; PROCEEDINGS IN FORMA
PAUPERIS**----- 1481
Rule 22. Habeas Corpus and Section 2255 Proceedings----- 1481
Rule 23. Custody or Release of a Prisoner in a Habeas Corpus Proceed-
ing----- 1482
Rule 24. Proceeding in Forma Pauperis----- 1482

TITLE VII. GENERAL PROVISIONS ----- 1484
Rule 25. Filing and Service----- 1484
Rule 26. Computing and Extending Time ----- 1486
Rule 26.1. Corporate Disclosure Statement----- 1487
Rule 27. Motions----- 1488
Rule 28. Briefs----- 1489
Rule 28.1. Cross–Appeals ----- 1492
Rule 29. Brief of an Amicus Curiae----- 1493
Rule 30. Appendix to the Briefs----- 1494
Rule 31. Serving and Filing Briefs ----- 1497
Rule 32. Form of Briefs, Appendices, and Other Papers ----- 1497
Rule 32.1. Citing Judicial Dispositions ----- 1499
Rule 33. Appeal Conferences----- 1500
Rule 34. Oral Argument----- 1500
Rule 35. En Banc Determination ----- 1501
Rule 36. Entry of Judgment; Notice ----- 1502
Rule 37. Interest on Judgment----- 1502
Rule 38. Frivolous Appeal—Damages and Costs ----- 1502
Rule 39. Costs ----- 1502
Rule 40. Petition for Panel Rehearing ----- 1503
Rule 41. Mandate: Contents; Issuance and Effective Date; Stay----- 1504
Rule 42. Voluntary Dismissal----- 1505
Rule 43. Substitution of Parties ----- 1505
Rule 44. Case Involving a Constitutional Question When the United
States or the Relevant State is Not a Party----- 1506
Rule 45. Clerk's Duties ----- 1506
Rule 46. Attorneys ----- 1507
Rule 47. Local Rules by Courts of Appeals ----- 1508
Rule 48. Masters----- 1509
§ 6.9 Appendix of Forms to the *Federal Rules of Appellate Procedure* ---- 1509
Form 1. Notice of Appeal to a Court of Appeals From a Judgment or
Order of a District Court----- 1509
Form 2. Notice of Appeal to a Court of Appeals From a Decision of the
United States Tax Court ----- 1510
Form 3. Petition for Review of Order of an Agency, Board, Commission
or Officer ----- 1511
Form 4. Affidavit Accompanying Motion for Permission to Appeal in
Forma Pauperis ----- 1511

Form 5. Notice of Appeal to a Court of Appeals from a Judgment or Order of a District Court or a Bankruptcy Appellate Panel ---------------- 1517
Form 6. Certificate of Compliance with Rule 32(a) ------------------------- 1518

PART VII. TITLE 28, JUDICIARY AND JUDICIAL PROCEDURE—SELECTED PROVISIONS ------------------------------ 1519

§ 144.   Bias or Prejudice of Judge ------------------------------------ 1521
§ 451.   Definitions -- 1521
§ 452.   Courts Always Open; Powers Unrestricted by Expiration of Sessions -- 1522
§ 455.   Disqualification of Justice, Judge, or Magistrate -------------------- 1522
§ 636   Jurisdiction, Powers, and Temporary Assignment------------------ 1524
§ 1251. Original Jurisdiction -------------------------------------- 1529
§ 1253. Direct Appeals from Decisions of Three-Judge Courts ------------ 1529
§ 1254. Courts of Appeals; Certiorari; Certified Questions -------------- 1529
§ 1257. State Courts; Certiorari ------------------------------------ 1530
§ 1291. Final Decisions of District Courts -------------------------- 1530
§ 1292. Interlocutory Decisions ------------------------------------ 1530
§ 1331. Federal Question -- 1532
§ 1332. Diversity of Citizenship; Amount in Controversy; Costs ---------- 1532
§ 1333. Admiralty, Maritime and Prize Cases ------------------------ 1537
§ 1334. Bankruptcy Cases and Proceedings -------------------------- 1537
§ 1335. Interpleader-- 1538
§ 1337. Commerce and Antitrust Regulations; Amount in Controversy, Costs -- 1538
§ 1338. Patents, Plant Variety Protection, Copyrights, Mask Works, Designs, Trademarks, and Unfair Competition ---------------- 1539
§ 1339. Postal Matters -- 1539
§ 1340. Internal Revenue; Customs Duties ------------------------- 1539
§ 1343. Civil Rights and Elective Franchise -------------------------- 1539
§ 1345. United States as Plaintiff--------------------------------- 1540
§ 1346. United States as Defendant------------------------------- 1540
§ 1349. Corporation Organized Under Federal Law As Party ------------- 1541
§ 1357. Injuries Under Federal Laws------------------------------- 1542
§ 1359. Parties Collusively Joined or Made------------------------- 1542
§ 1361. Action to Compel an Officer of the United States to Perform His Duty --- 1542
§ 1367. Supplemental Jurisdiction ----------------------------------- 1542
§ 1369. Multiparty, Multiforum Jurisdiction------------------------ 1543
§ 1390. Scope -- 1544
§ 1391. Venue Generally-- 1544
§ 1397. Interpleader-- 1546
§ 1400. Patents and Copyrights, Mask Works, and Designs -------------- 1546
§ 1401. Stockholder's Derivative Action --------------------------- 1547
§ 1402. United States as Defendant--------------------------------- 1547
§ 1404. Change of Venue -- 1547
§ 1406. Cure or Waiver of Defects --------------------------------- 1548
§ 1407. Multidistrict Litigation ----------------------------------- 1548
§ 1412. Change of Venue -- 1548
§ 1441. Removal of Civil Actions---------------------------------- 1548
§ 1442. Federal Officers or Agencies Sued or Prosecuted ------------- 1550
§ 1442a. Members of Armed Forces Sued or Prosecuted --------------- 1551
§ 1443. Civil Rights Cases-- 1551

Page

§ 1445. Nonremovable Actions -------------------------------------- 1552
§ 1446. Procedure for Removal of Civil Actions----------------------- 1552
§ 1447. Procedure After Removal Generally -------------------------- 1554
§ 1448. Process After Removal ------------------------------------- 1555
§ 1449. State Court Record Supplied -------------------------------- 1555
§ 1451. Definitions -- 1555
§ 1453. Removal of Class Actions----------------------------------- 1555
§ 1631. Transfer to Cure Want of Jurisdiction ---------------------- 1556
§ 1651. Writs --- 1557
§ 1652. State Laws as Rules of Decision----------------------------- 1557
§ 1653. Amendment of Pleadings to Show Jurisdiction --------------- 1557
§ 1654. Appearance Personally or by Counsel ---------------------- 1557
§ 1657. Priority of Civil Actions----------------------------------- 1557
§ 1658. Time Limitations on the Commencement of Civil Actions Arising under Acts of Congress---------------------------------- 1557
§ 1691. Seal and Teste of Process--------------------------------- 1558
§ 1692. Process and Orders Affecting Property in Different Districts ---- 1558
§ 1695. Stockholder's Derivative Action ------------------------- 1558
§ 1696. Service in Foreign and International Litigation -------------- 1558
§ 1697. Service in Multiparty, Multiforum Actions ------------------ 1558
§ 1731. Handwriting --- 1559
§ 1732. Record Made in Regular Course of Business; Photographic Copies -- 1559
§ 1733. Government Records and Papers; Copies-------------------- 1559
§ 1734. Court Record Lost or Destroyed, Generally ---------------- 1559
§ 1735. Court Record Lost or Destroyed Where United States Interested -- 1560
§ 1738. State and Territorial Statutes and Judicial Proceedings; Full Faith and Credit --- 1560
§ 1739. State and Territorial Nonjudicial Records; Full Faith and Credit--- 1561
§ 1746. Unsworn Declarations under Penalty of Perjury ------------- 1561
§ 1781. Transmittal of Letter Rogatory or Request------------------ 1562
§ 1782. Assistance to Foreign and International Tribunals and to Litigants before Such Tribunals ----------------------------------- 1562
§ 1783. Subpoena of Person in Foreign Country-------------------- 1563
§ 1784. Contempt -- 1563
§ 1785. Subpoenas in Multiparty, Multiforum Actions -------------- 1564
§ 1821. Per Diem and Mileage Generally; Subsistence-------------- 1564
§ 1826. Recalcitrant Witnesses ------------------------------------ 1565
§ 1914. District Court; Filing and Miscellaneous Fees; Rules of Court 1566
§ 1915. Proceedings in Forma Pauperis -------------------------- 1566
§ 1917. District Courts; Fee on Filing Notice of or Petition for Appeal 1568
§ 1920. Taxation of Costs --- 1569
§ 1924. Verification of Bill of Costs -------------------------------- 1569
§ 1927. Counsel's Liability for Excessive Costs--------------------- 1569
§ 1961. Interest--- 1569
§ 1963. Registration of Judgments for Enforcement in Other Districts-- 1570
§ 1964. Constructive Notice of Pending Actions ------------------- 1570
§ 2071. Rule-Making Power Generally------------------------------ 1571
§ 2072. Rules of Procedure and Evidence; Power to Prescribe ------------ 1571
§ 2101. Supreme Court; Time for Appeal or Certiorari; Docketing; Stay -- 1572

		Page
§ 2104.	Reviews of State Court Decisions	1573
§ 2106.	Determination	1573
§ 2107.	Time for Appeal to Court of Appeals	1573
§ 2111.	Harmless Error	1574
§ 2201.	Creation of Remedy	1574
§ 2202.	Further Relief	1574
§ 2283.	Stay of State Court Proceedings	1574
§ 2284.	Three-Judge Court; When Required; Composition; Procedure	1574
§ 2361.	Process and Procedure	1575
§ 2401.	Time for Commencing Action Against United States	1575
§ 2402.	Jury Trial in Actions Against United States	1576
§ 2403.	Intervention by United States or a State; Constitutional Question	1576
§ 2404.	Death of Defendant in Damage Action	1576
§ 2408.	Security Not Required of United States	1576
§ 2411.	Interest	1577
§ 2412.	Costs and Fees	1577
§ 2413.	Executions in Favor of United States	1581
§ 2414.	Payment of Judgments and Compromise Settlements	1581
§ 2415.	Time for Commencing Actions Brought by the United States	1581
§ 2416.	Time for Commencing Actions Brought by the United States— Exclusions	1584

PART VIII.   THE CONSTITUTION OF THE UNITED STATES 1585

PART I
JUDICIAL RULEMAKING
A. THE FEDERAL RULES OF PRACTICE AND PROCEDURE*

The federal rules govern procedure, practice, and evidence in the federal courts. They set forth the procedures for the conduct of court proceedings and serve as a pattern for the procedural rules adopted by many state court systems.

Authority

The Congress has authorized the federal judiciary to prescribe the rules of practice, procedure, and evidence for the federal courts, subject to the ultimate legislative right of the Congress to reject, modify, or defer any of the rules. The authority and procedures for promulgating rules are set forth in the Rules Enabling Act. 28 U.S.C. §§ 2071 to 2077.

The Judicial Conference of the United States is also required by statute to "carry on a continuous study of the operation and effect of the general rules of practice and procedure." 28 U.S.C. § 331. As part of this continuing obligation, the Conference is authorized to recommend amendments and additions to the rules to promote

- simplicity in procedure,
- fairness in administration,
- the just determination of litigation, and
- the elimination of unjustifiable expense and delay.

The Rules Committees

The Judicial Conference's responsibilities as to rules are coordinated by its Committee on Rules of Practice and Procedure, commonly referred to as the "Standing Committee." 28 U.S.C. § 2073(b). The Standing Committee has five advisory committees, dealing respectively with the appellate, bankruptcy, civil, criminal, and evidence rules. 28 U.S.C. § 2073(a)(2). The Standing Committee reviews and coordinates the recommendations of the five advisory committees, and it recommends to the Judicial Conference proposed rules changes "as may be necessary to maintain consistency and otherwise promote the interests of justice." 28 U.S.C. § 2073(b).

The Standing Committee and the advisory committees are

---

*This description of current procedures for federal judicial rulemaking is a summary prepared for the bench and bar by the Administrative Office of the U.S. Courts.

composed of federal judges, practicing lawyers, law professors, state chief justices, and representatives of the Department of Justice. Each committee has a reporter, a prominent law professor, who is responsible for coordinating the committee's agenda and drafting appropriate amendments to the rules and explanatory committee notes.

The Assistant Director for Judges Programs of the Administrative Office of the United States Courts currently serves as secretary to the Standing Committee, coordinates the operational aspects of the rules process, and maintains the records of the committees. The Rules Committee Support Office of the Administrative Office provides the day to day administrative and legal support for the secretary and the committees.

Open Meetings and Records

Meetings of the rules committees are open to the public and are widely announced. All records of the committees, including minutes of committee meetings, suggestions and comments submitted by the public, statements of witnesses, transcripts of public hearings, and memoranda prepared by the reporters, are public and are maintained by the secretary. Copies of the rules and proposed amendments are available from the Rules Committee Support Office. The proposed amendments are also published on the Judiciary's website <http:\\www.uscourts.gov>.

B. HOW THE RULES ARE AMENDED

The pervasive and substantial impact of the rules on the practice of law in the federal courts demands exacting and meticulous care in drafting rule changes. The rulemaking process is time-consuming and involves a minimum of seven stages of formal comment and review. From beginning to end, it usually takes two to three years for a suggestion to be enacted as a rule.

The process, however, may be expedited when there is an urgent need to enact an amendment to the rules.

All interested individuals and organizations are provided an opportunity to comment on proposed rules amendments and to recommend alternative proposals. The comments received from this extensive and thorough public examination are studied very carefully by the committees and generally improve the amendments. The committees actively encourage the submission of comments, both positive and negative, to ensure that proposed amendments have been considered by a broad segment of the bench and bar.

STEP 1 INITIAL CONSIDERATION BY THE ADVISORY COMMITTEE

Making suggestions for changes

Proposed changes in the rules are suggested by judges, clerks of court, lawyers, professors, government agencies, or other individuals and organizations. They are considered in the first instance by the appropriate advisory committees (appellate, bankruptcy, civil, criminal, or evidence). Suggestions for changes, additions, or deletions must be submitted in writing to the secretary, who acknowledges each letter and distributes it to the chair of the Standing Committee and the chair and reporter of the advisory committee.

The reporter normally analyzes the suggestions and makes appropriate recommendations to the advisory committee. The suggestions from the public and the recommendations of the reporter are placed on the advisory committee's agenda and are normally discussed at its next meeting. The advisory committees usually meet twice a year, and they also conduct business by telephone and correspondence.

Consideration of suggestions

In considering a suggestion for a change in the rules, the advisory committee may take several courses of action, including:

1. Accepting the suggestion, either completely or with modifications or limitations:
2. Deferring action on the suggestion or seeking additional information regarding its operation and impact;
3. Rejecting a suggestion because it does not have merit or would be inconsistent with other rules or a statute; or
4. Rejecting a suggestion because, although it may be meritorious, it simply is not necessary or important enough to warrant the significant step of an amendment to the federal rules.

The secretary is required, to the extent feasible, to advise the person making a suggestion of the action taken on it by the advisory committee.

Drafting Rules Changes

When an advisory committee decides initially that a particular change in the rules would be appropriate, it normally asks its reporter to prepare a draft amendment to the rules and an explanatory committee note. The draft amendment and committee note are discussed and voted upon at a committee meeting.

The Standing Committee has a style subcommittee that works with the respective advisory committees in reviewing proposed amendments to ensure that the rules are written in clear and consistent language. In addition, the reporter of the Standing Committee and the reporters of the five advisory committees are encouraged to work together to promote clarity and consistency among the various sets of federal rules.

STEP 2 PUBLICATION AND PUBLIC COMMENT

Once an advisory committee votes initially to recommend an amendment to the rules, it must obtain the approval of the Standing Committee, or its chair, to publish the proposed amendment for public comment. In seeking publication, the advisory committee must explain to the Standing Committee the reasons for its proposal, including any minority or separate views.

After publication is approved, the secretary arranges for printing and distribution of the proposed amendment to the bench and bar, to publishers, and to the general public. More than 10,000 persons and organizations are on the mailing list, including

- federal judges and other federal court officers,
- United States attorneys,
- other federal government agencies and officials,
- state chief justices,
- state attorneys general,
- legal publications,
- law schools,
- bar associations, and
- interested lawyers, individuals, and organizations requesting distribution.

In order to promote public comment, the proposed amendments are sent to points of contact that have been established with 53 state bar associations.

The public is normally given 6 months to comment in writing to the secretary regarding the proposed amendment. In an emergency, a shorter time period may be authorized by the Standing Committee.

During the 6-month comment period, the advisory committee schedules one or more public hearings on the proposed amendments. Persons who wish to appear and testify at the hearings are required to contact the secretary at least 30 days before the hearings.

STEP 3 CONSIDERATION OF THE PUBLIC COMMENTS AND FINAL APPROVAL BY THE ADVISORY COMMITTEE

At the conclusion of the public comment period, the reporter is required to prepare a summary of the written comments received from the public and the testimony presented at the hearings. The advisory committee then takes a fresh look at the proposed rule changes in light of the written comments and testimony.

If the advisory committee decides to make a substantial change in its proposal, it may provide a period for additional public notice and comment.

Once the advisory committee decides to proceed in final form, it submits the proposed amendment to the Standing Committee for approval. Each proposed amendment must be accompanied by a separate report summarizing the comments received from the public and explaining any changes made by the advisory committee following the original publication. The advisory committee's report must also include minority views of any members who wish to have their separate views recorded.

STEP 4 APPROVAL BY THE STANDING COMMITTEE

The Standing Committee considers the final recommendations of the advisory committee and may accept, reject, or modify them. If the Standing Committee approves a proposed rule change, it will transmit it to the Judicial Conference with a recommendation for approval, accompanied by the advisory committee's reports and the Standing Committee's own report explaining any modifications it made. If the Standing Committee makes a modification that constitutes a substantial change from the recommendation of the advisory committee, the proposal will normally be returned to the advisory committee with appropriate instructions.

STEP 5 JUDICIAL CONFERENCE APPROVAL

The Judicial Conference normally considers proposed amendments to the rules at its September session each year. If approved by the Conference, the amendments are transmitted promptly to the Supreme Court.

STEP 6 SUPREME COURT APPROVAL

The Supreme Court has the authority to prescribe the federal rules, subject to a statutory waiting period. 28 U.S.C. §§ 2072, 2075. The Court normally transmits proposed rules amendments to the Congress by May 1 of each year. 28 U.S.C. §§ 2074, 2075.

STEP 7 CONGRESSIONAL REVIEW

The Congress has a statutory period of at least 7 months to act on any rules prescribed by the Supreme Court. If the Congress does not enact legislation to reject, modify, or defer the rules, they take effect as a matter of law on December 1. 28 U.S.C. §§ 2074, 2075.

C. SUMMARY OF PROCEDURES

Action	Date
STEP 1	
• Suggestion for a change in the rules. (*Submitted in writing to the secretary.*)	At any time.
• Referred by the secretary to the appropriate advisory committee.	Promptly after receipt.
• Considered by the advisory committee.	Normally at the next committee meeting.

Action	Date
● If approved, the advisory committee seeks authority from the Standing Committee to circulate to bench and bar for comment.	Normally at the same meeting or the next committee meeting.

STEP 2
| ● Public comment period. | 6 months. |
| ● Public hearings. | During the public comment period. |

STEP 3
| ● Advisory committee considers the amendment afresh in light of public comments and testimony at the hearings. | About one or two months after the close of the comment period. |
| ● Advisory committee approves amendment in final form and transmits to the Standing Committee. | About one or two months after the close of the comment period. |

STEP 4
| ● Standing Committee approves amendment, with or without revisions, and recommends approval by the Judicial Conference. | Normally at its June meeting. |

STEP 5
| ● Judicial Conference approves amendment and transmits to the Supreme Court. | Normally at its September session. |

STEP 6
| ● The Supreme Court prescribes the amendment. | By May 1. |

STEP 7

Action	Date
• Congress has statutory time period in which to enact legislation to reject, modify, or defer the amendment.	By December 1.
• Absent Congressional action, the amendment becomes law.	December 1.

D. 2013 CIVIL RULE DEVELOPMENTS

The Advisory Committee on Civil Rules submitted proposed amendments to Rule 45, the subpoena rule, and a conforming amendment to Rule 37, the rule dealing with failure to cooperate in discovery, with a recommendation that they be approved and forwarded to the Supreme Court, then to Congress, in an expectation that they take effect on December 1, 2013.

The changes recommended to the Rule 45 package since publication are minor and are summarized below. The modified version of the amendment package also includes style changes recommended by the Committee's style consultant. The proposed amendments to Rule 45 result from a multi-year study of subpoena practice culminating in a decision by the advisory committee to adopt the most modest form of rule simplification considered and to adopt some but not all of the specific rule amendments proposed during the study of the rule. Four specific changes are being proposed. First, the amendments seek to simplify Rule 45 by making the court where an action is pending the issuing court, permitting service throughout the United States (as is currently authorized under Criminal Rule 17(e)), and combining all provisions on the place of compliance into a new Rule 45(c). It preserves the various place-of-compliance provisions of the current rule except its reference to state law. The "*Vioxx* issue" is addressed separately below.

A clarifying amendment to the proposed Committee Note on Rule 45(c) addresses concerns expressed in the comments that the amended rule might be read to require a subpoena for all depositions, even of parties or party officers, directors, or managing agents. The proposed Committee Note was clarified to remind readers that no subpoena is required for depositions of these witnesses, and that the geographical limitations applicable to subpoenas do not apply when such depositions are simply noticed. Another Committee Note clarification confirms that, when the issuing court has made an order for remote testimony under Rule 43(a), a subpoena may be used to command the distant witness to attend and testify within the geographical limits of Rule 45(c).

Second, the proposed amendments address the transfer of

subpoena-related motions. New Rule 45(c) essentially retains the existing rule requirement that motions to quash or enforce a subpoena be made in the district where compliance with the subpoena is required. The result is that the "enforcement court" may often be different from the "issuing court." Existing authority has recognized that some disputes over subpoena enforcement are better decided by the issuing court. The proposed amendments therefore add Rule 45(f), which explicitly authorizes transfer of subpoena-related motions from the enforcement court to the issuing court, including not only motions for a protective order but also motions to enforce the subpoena.

Third, the proposed amendments resolve conflicting interpretations of the current rule as to whether a party or party officer can be compelled by subpoena to travel more than 100 miles to attend trial. One interpretation is that the geographical limits applicable to other witnesses do not apply to a party or party officer. *See In re Vioxx Products Liability Litigation*, 438 F. Supp. 2d 664 (E.D. La. 2006) (requiring an officer of the defendant corporation, who lived and worked in New Jersey, to testify at trial in New Orleans even though he was not served within Louisiana under Rule 45(b)(2)). The alternative interpretation is that the rule sets forth the same geographical limits for all trial witnesses. *See Johnson v. Big Lots Stores, Inc.*, 251 F.R.D. 213 (E.D. La. 2008) (holding that opt-in plaintiffs in Fair Labor Standards Act action could not be compelled to travel long distances from outside the state to attend trial because they were not served with subpoenas within the state as required by Rule 45(b)(2)). The division in the caselaw resulted from differing interpretations of the 1991 amendments to Rule 45. The advisory committee concluded that those amendments were not intended to create the expanded subpoena power recognized in the *Vioxx* line of cases, and it decided to restore the original meaning of the rule. The proposed new amendments therefore provide in Rule 45(c)(1) that a subpoena may command any person to testify only within the limits that apply to all witnesses. As noted above, proposed Committee Note language was added to recognize that this provision does not affect existing law on the location for a deposition of a party or party's officer, director, or managing agent, for which a subpoena is not needed.

Finally, the 1991 amendments introduced the "documents only" subpoena, and added a requirement in Rule 45(b)(1) that each party be given notice of a subpoena that requires document production. In the 2007 restyling of the Civil Rules, the rule was clarified to direct that notice be provided before service of the subpoena, but experience has shown that many lawyers do not comply with the notice requirement. Therefore, the proposed amendments move the notice provision to a more prominent position, and also require that the notice include a copy of the subpoena.

PART II

General Concepts in Federal Practice—Personal Jurisdiction, Notice Requirements, Federal Subject Matter Jurisdiction, Venue, Forum Non Conveniens, Removal, *Erie*, Res Judicata and Collateral Estoppel

Table of Sections

A. FEDERAL JURISDICTION, VENUE AND *ERIE*

Sec.

2.1	Introduction.
2.2	Jurisdiction Over Persons or Things—Introduction.
2.3	—Requirements for Personal Jurisdiction.
2.4	— —Due Process: Consent, In-State Service, or Minimum Contacts.
2.5	— —State Limitations: Long-Arm Statutes.
2.6	— —Notice.
2.7	— —Special Considerations in Federal Court.
2.8	—Special Requirements for Quasi In Rem Jurisdiction.
2.9	—Requirements for In Rem Jurisdiction.
2.10	Subject Matter Jurisdiction in Federal District Courts—Introduction.
2.11	—Federal Question Jurisdiction.
2.12	—Requirements for Diversity Jurisdiction.
2.13	—Requirements for Supplemental Jurisdiction.
2.14	Venue.
2.15	Forum Non Conveniens.
2.16	Removal.
2.17	Removal Procedure.
2.17a	Procedure After Removal.
2.17b	Removal of Class Actions.
2.18	The *Erie* Doctrine.

B. RES JUDICATA AND COLLATERAL ESTOPPEL

2.19	Introduction.
2.20	Res Judicata—Elements.
2.21	—Scope.
2.22	—Counterclaims: Rule 13(a).
2.23	—Affirmative Defense: Rule 8(c).
2.24	—Relationship to Full Faith and Credit.
2.25	Collateral Estoppel—Elements.
2.26	—Mutuality v Nonmutual Estoppel.
2.27	—Application to Issues of Law and Fact.
2.28	—Exceptions to Collateral Estoppel.
2.29	—Affirmative Defense: Rule 8(c).
2.30	Relationship to Full Faith and Credit.

A. FEDERAL JURISDICTION, VENUE AND *ERIE*

§ 2.1 Introduction

Although the Federal Rules of Civil Procedure control many aspects of a civil suit in a district court, the Rules do not contain all the elements that must be satisfied before the suit can be prosecuted successfully. Of particular importance at the onset of litigation are the concepts of jurisdiction and venue. For the most part, these elements are not discussed in the Rules. In fact, Rule 82 provides that the Rules neither increase nor limit a district court's power and obligations in the areas of subject matter jurisdiction and venue. A claimant's failure to satisfy requirements of subject matter jurisdiction and venue, however, will usually assure failure in the suit.

Before a federal district court may hear a plaintiff's claim, it must satisfy three prerequisites. These are: (1) jurisdiction over persons or things (*i.e.,* the court's ability to drag an individual into its district); (2) subject matter jurisdiction (*i.e.,* the court's ability to hear a particular kind of claim);[1] and (3) venue.

Every cause of action sued upon in a case, irrespective of whether it is a count brought by the plaintiff, a counterclaim, crossclaim, or impleader, must satisfy one of the kinds of jurisdiction over persons or things, *as well as* some kind of subject matter jurisdiction.[2] However, requirements of venue, discussed below, apply only to the claims brought by a plaintiff. If, upon appropriate notice to the court, it is found that any of these requirements are lacking, the court will not hear the case.

§ 2.2 Jurisdiction Over Persons or Things—Introduction

There are three kinds of jurisdiction over persons or things: personal jurisdiction (the normal form of action against an individual, company, or other entity, also known as *in personam* jurisdiction); quasi in rem jurisdiction (actions in the nature of attachment); and in rem jurisdiction (where an object or piece of land is the subject of the lawsuit). Every count in a case must

---

[1]*Ruhrgas AG v. Marathon Oil Co.,* 526 U.S. 574, 119 S. Ct. 1563, 143 L. Ed. 2d 760 (1999) (while jurisdictional issues should generally be resolved before court addresses merits of a case, there is no rigid rule directing court to decide questions of subject matter jurisdiction before deciding questions of personal jurisdiction).

[2]*Insurance Corp. of Ireland, Ltd. v. Compagnie des Bauxites de Guinee,* 456 U.S. 694, 701, 102 S. Ct. 2099, 2103, 72 L. Ed. 2d 492 (1982) ("The validity of an order of a federal court depends upon that court's having jurisdiction over both the subject matter and the parties."). *See also, e.g., Conrad v. Ace Property Co.,* ____ F.3d ____ n.1 (9th Cir. 2008) ("Because the district court had subject matter jurisdiction under § 1332, we need not inquire whether it also had federal question jurisdiction under 28 U.S.C. § 1331.").

satisfy one or another of these jurisdictional standards.[1] There is no requirement that a count satisfy more than one. However, in cases where one kind of jurisdiction over persons or things is uncertain, it would be a wise tactic to try to satisfy another kind as well. In certain factual settings there may also be advantages if one particular kind or other is achieved.

Important: In the area of jurisdiction over persons or things, it should be kept in mind that in many circumstances the power of a federal court to hear cases is closely analogous to the power of a state court in the state where the federal court sits. Thus, jurisdiction over persons or things should not pose many new problems for practicing attorneys already familiar with similar jurisdictional concepts in state courts.

Important: If jurisdiction over persons or things is absent, and the court also has no quasi in rem jurisdiction or in rem jurisdiction, the typical remedy is to dismiss the claim.[2]

ADDITIONAL RESEARCH REFERENCES
C.J.S., Federal Courts §§ 4(1) to 6
West's Key Number Digest, Federal Courts ⌐3 to 5

§ 2.3 Jurisdiction Over Persons or Things—Requirements for Personal Jurisdiction

Two elements play important roles in determining the requirements for personal jurisdiction. These are notions of fair play, as developed under Due Process provisions of the Constitution, and state limitations on the authority of the state courts to exercise personal jurisdiction. Fair play, or due process, divides into two components: an evaluation of the contacts that exist between the defendant and the state where the court sits; and an evaluation of the quality of notice of the suit that the defendant received.

§ 2.4 Jurisdiction Over Persons or Things—Requirements for Personal Jurisdiction—Due Process: Consent, In-

---

[1]*See, e.g., Youn v. Track, Inc.,* 324 F.3d 409, 417 (6th Cir. 2003) ("The party seeking to assert personal jurisdiction bears the burden of demonstrating that such jurisdiction exists;" standard of proof is preponderance of evidence). *But cf., Burger King Corp. v. Rudzewicz,* 471 U.S. 462, 477–78, 105 S. Ct. 2174, 85 L. Ed. 2d 548 (1985) (if defendant purposefully made contact with forum and contacts are related to cause of action, burden of proof shifts to defendant to "present a compelling case that the presence of some other consideration would render jurisdiction unreasonable").

[2]*See* Rule 12(b)(2) (authorizing dismissal for lack of personal jurisdiction); *See, e.g., Swaim v. Moltan Co.,* 73 F.3d 711, 718 (7th Cir. 1996) ("If the district court finds itself without [personal] jurisdiction . . . then it is obligated to dismiss the case because it has no authority over the defendant.").

State Service, or Minimum Contacts

CORE CONCEPT

Before a federal trial court may exert personal jurisdiction over a defendant, it must satisfy the due process standard of the 5th or 14th Amendments of the Constitution.[1] This requirement must be met for each defendant.[2]

This requirement has meant primarily that the exercise of personal jurisdiction must not be fundamentally unfair to the defendant. The most common means of satisfying this fairness requirement are: (1) the defendant's consent to jurisdiction; (2) service of process on the defendant within the territorial confines of a state in which the district court sits; or (3) service of process on a non-consenting defendant not within a state, when such service is fair because the defendant has sufficient "contacts" with the state.

APPLICATIONS

Burden of Proof

In general, it is the duty of the party asserting a claim (usually the plaintiff) to demonstrate that the court has personal jurisdiction.[3] This burden is usually not onerous in the early phase of litigation.[4] Particularly in the absence of an evidentiary hearing, a plaintiff's burden can be met by a prima facie demonstration of jurisdiction.[5] Even when that prima facie case is opposed by affidavits, the court will typically resolve all factual

---

[1]*Dusenbery v. U.S.*, 534 U.S. 161, 167, 122 S. Ct. 694, 151 L. Ed. 2d 597 (2002) ("The Due Process Clause of the Fifth Amendment prohibits the United States, as the Due Process Clause of the Fourteenth Amendment prohibits the States, from depriving any person of property without 'due process of law.'").

[2]*Cf., Rush v. Savchuk*, 444 U.S. 320, 332, 100 S. Ct. 571, 572, 62 L. Ed. 2d 516 (1980) ("The requirements of *International Shoe* . . . must be met as to each defendant over whom a . . . court exercises jurisdiction." Acknowledging, however, that parties' relationships among themselves may be relevant to their relationships to the forum). *See also Patin v. Thoroughbred Power Boats Inc.*, 294 F.3d 640, 653 (5th Cir. 2002) (*Rush* "does not preclude us from imputing the jurisdictional contacts of a predecessor corporation to its successor corporation or individual alter ego.").

[3]*See, e.g., AST Sports Science, Inc. v. CLF Distribution Ltd.*, 514 F.3d 1054, 1056 (10th Cir. 2008) (where jurisdiction is contested, plaintiff has burden).

[4]*See, e.g., Doe v. National Medical Services*, 974 F.2d 143, 145 (10th Cir. 1992) (burden is light "in the preliminary stages of litigation").

[5]*See, e.g., Alpine View Co. Ltd. v. Atlas Copco AB*, 205 F.3d 208, 215 (5th Cir. 2000) ("When . . . the district court conducted no evidentiary hearing, the party seeking to assert jurisdiction must present sufficient facts as to make out only a prima facie case supporting jurisdiction."); *OMI Holdings, Inc. v. Royal Ins. Co. of Canada*, 149 F.3d 1086, 1091 (10th Cir. 1998) ("The plaintiff may make this prima facie showing by demonstrating, via affidavits or other written materials, facts that if true would support jurisdiction over the defendant.").

disputes in favor of the plaintiff.[6]

If the court is satisfied that a defendant had purposeful contacts with a state, the burden shifts to the defendant to make "a compelling case" demonstrating why the court's exercise of personal jurisdiction would be unjust.[7]

Consent to Jurisdiction

If a party consents to jurisdiction, the Due Process requirement of fairness is satisfied. Consent may occur in a variety of ways. The following examples are typical of circumstances where persons may have consented to personal jurisdiction:

(1) *By Contract:* If the parties, through a contract or agreement prior to the initiation of litigation, consent to the jurisdiction of a court, such agreements will generally be enforced even if the chosen court might not otherwise have been able to sustain its jurisdiction.[8] Exceptions arise when there was substantially unequal bargaining power between the parties that gave one side an unfair advantage in choosing the jurisdiction, or there was the absence of *any* rational link between the court chosen and the parties or cause of action.[9]

A related question that arises about forum selection clauses in contracts is whether such clauses may properly *exclude* the use of judicial fora not chosen in the clause (even if such courts could, in the absence of the clause, have exercised personal jurisdiction under, e.g., principles of minimum contacts, discussed elsewhere in this text), or whether forum selection clauses may only provide the potential to *expand* the available fora to include courts that might otherwise have not enjoyed jurisdiction over the parties. It is now settled that such clauses are to be construed according to–standard principles of contract law, which may result depending on the wording of specific clauses in individual cases in either restriction or expansion of the available fora.[10]

(2) *Waiver:* A party who does not object to personal jurisdic-

---

[6]*See, e.g., Wenz v. Memery Crystal,* 55 F.3d 1503, 1505 (10th Cir. 1995) (limiting this deferential approach to the facts of plaintiff's well-pled complaint, not to "mere conclusory allegations").

[7]*Burger King Corp. v. Rudzewicz,* 471 U.S. 462, 477, 105 S. Ct. 2174, 2185, 85 L. Ed. 2d 528, 544 (1985).

[8]*National Equipment Rental, Limited v. Szukhent,* 375 U.S. 311, 315–16, 84 S. Ct. 411, 414, 11 L. Ed. 2d 354 (1964). ("[I]t is settled. . . . that parties to a contract may agree in advance to submit to the jurisdiction of a given court."). *See also Burger King Corp. v. Rudzewicz,* 471 U.S. 462, 473, n. 14, 105 S. Ct. 2174, 85 L. Ed.

2d 528 (1985) ("[P]articularly in the commercial context, parties frequently stipulate in advance to submit their controversies for resolution within a particular jurisdiction.").

[9]*See, e.g., Shell v. R.W. Sturge, Ltd.,* 55 F.3d 1227 (6th Cir.1995) (forum selection clause is presumptively enforceable in the absence of fraud, overreaching, grave inconvenience, or violation of forum's public policy).

[10]*See, e.g., Dunne v. Libbra,* 330 F.3d 1062, 1063 (8th Cir. 2003) (applying general principles of contract construction). *But cf., M.B. Restaurants, Inc. v. CKE Restaurants, Inc.,* 183 F.3d 750, 752 n. 4 (8th Cir.

tion in a timely manner waives objections, and thereby consents.[11] In the federal courts, timely objections to personal jurisdiction are controlled by Rule 12(b)(2), (g), and (h)(1), and must be raised in the answer or before the answer is filed.

(3) *Counterclaims:* A plaintiff sued on a counterclaim may consent to personal jurisdiction on the counterclaim by filing the original complaint.[12] It is unclear if this consent to jurisdiction over the counterclaim is limited to countersuits closely related to plaintiff's original claims, or whether consent extends to unrelated counterclaims.[13]

On the other hand, most courts agree that if a defendant files *both* an objection to jurisdiction and a claim that is either a counterclaim, cross-claim, or third party impleader, the objection to jurisdiction is not waived[14]—provided that the new claim does not involve the joinder of new parties.[15] The conclusion is that an objection to jurisdiction may be preserved if it is filed with a claim asserted against someone who is already a party.

It is unsettled whether filing an in rem action constitutes

1999) (noting split among circuits as to whether forum selection clauses in diversity cases should be construed pursuant to federal or state law).

[11]*See, e.g., Gerber v. Riordan*, 649 F.3d 514, 519 (6th Cir. 2011) ("Only those submissions, appearances and filings that [demonstrate defendant's intention to] defend the suit on the merits or must cause the court to go to effort that would be wasted if personal jurisdiction is later found lacking . . . result in a waiver of a personal jurisdiction defense."); *Preferred RX, Inc. v. American Prescription Plan, Inc.*, 46 F.3d 535 (6th Cir.1995) (defendants objected to personal jurisdiction in their original answer; but when plaintiff filed amended complaint containing new count, defendants answered but did not challenge jurisdiction as to new count; held, as to new count, defendants waived defense of lack of personal jurisdiction).

[12]*Adam v. Saenger*, 303 U.S. 59, 58 S. Ct. 454, 82 L. Ed. 649 (1938). (By suing, a plaintiff submits to the court's jurisdiction over counterclaims). *Cf., General Contracting & Trading Co., LLC v. Interpole, Inc.*, 940 F.2d 20, 22 (1st Cir. 1991) (third-party defendant in first suit filed second, related suit against original defendant in same court; held, by filing second suit, third-party defendant submitted to personal jurisdiction in first suit).

[13]*But see, Threlkeld v. Tucker*, 496 F.2d 1101, 1103 (9th Cir. 1974) (action to enforce state court judgment; held, state court had jurisdiction to hear counterclaim because filing complaint meant plaintiff had submitted to jurisdiction as to *any* counterclaim). *See also Frank's Casing Crew & Rental Tools, Inc. v. PMR Technologies, Ltd.*, 292 F.3d 1363, 1372 (Fed. Cir. 2002) ("Where . . . a defendant seeks to bring into the same action new claims against new parties, not arising out of the same transaction or occurrence, such action is not authorized by the joinder rules, and we think that such an attempted joinder constitutes a waiver as to the claims then pending in the action against the party seeking to add the additional claims.").

[14]*Bayou Steel Corp. v. M/V Amstelvoorn*, 809 F.2d 1147, 1149 (5th Cir. 1987) (not distinguishing between compulsory and permissive counterclaims; holding that view is majority position).

[15]*See, e.g., Frank's Casing Crew & Rental Tools, Inc. v. PMR Technologies, Ltd.*, 292 F.3d 1363, 1372 (Fed. Cir. 2002) (counterclaims, cross-claims and impleader actions against persons already parties do not, by themselves, constitute a waiver of properly raised objections to jurisdiction; different result if claims do not arise from original transaction or occurrence and are brought against new parties).

consent to personal jurisdiction to a counterclaim.[16]

(4) *Consent to Determine Jurisdiction:* Perhaps the most subtle form of consent occurs when a defendant objects to personal jurisdiction, claiming that sufficient links between the defendant and the court do not exist. In that circumstance, the defendant, though preserving the objection to jurisdiction, has consented for the limited purpose of allowing the court to determine whether personal jurisdiction exists.[17]

Transient Jurisdiction ("Tag" Jurisdiction)

A defendant served with process while physically present within a state is normally subject to the personal jurisdiction of the trial courts within that state.[18] It is irrelevant whether the defendant lives within the state or was just passing through; personal jurisdiction is present in such cases simply because the defendant was properly served within the state.[19] One important exception to exercise of "tag" jurisdiction occurs when a defendant was either forced into a jurisdiction, or induced there by fraud. Enticing a defendant to come to a state for bogus reasons will vitiate personal jurisdiction.[20]

---

[16]*Compare, U.S. v. One Lear Jet Aircraft*, 836 F.2d 1571, 1576–77 (11th Cir. 1988) (en banc) (filing an in rem action does not usually equal consent to personal jurisdiction), *with U.S. v. 51 Pieces of Real Property Roswell, N.M.*, 17 F.3d 1306, 1313 (10th Cir. 1994) (rejecting *One Lear Jet Aircraft*; concluding that government submits to personal jurisdiction upon filing forfeiture action).

[17]*Insurance Corp. of Ireland, Ltd. v. Compagnie des Bauxites de Guinee*, 456 U.S. 694, 102 S. Ct. 2099, 72 L. Ed. 2d 492 (1982). *See also Transaero, Inc. v. La Fuerza Aerea Boliviana*, 162 F.3d 724, 729 (2d Cir. 1998) ("[W]hen a defendant appears and challenges jurisdiction, it agrees to be bound by the court's determination on the jurisdictional issue.").

[18]*See, e.g., North American Catholic Educational Programming Foundation, Inc., v. Cardinale*, 567 F.3d 8, 16 (1st Cir. 2009) (in-state presence of defendants is "the classic basis for general jurisdiction").

[19]*Burnham v. Superior Court of California, County of Marin*, 495 U.S. 604, 110 S. Ct. 2105, 109 L. Ed. 2d 631 (1990) (plurality opinion). *See generally* Fed. R. Civ. P. 4(e)(2). *See also, In re Edelman*, 295 F.3d 171 (2d Cir. 2002) (tag jurisdiction that is constitutional under *Burnham*, supra, is *a fortiori* applicable to personal service of a discovery subpoena on a non-party); *First American Corp. v. Price Waterhouse LLP*, 154 F.3d 16, 20 (2d Cir. 1998) (subpoena served on non-party witness; "We are satisfied that in light of *Burnham* . . . the assertion of personal jurisdiction . . . based upon service [within a state] satisfies due process."); *Kadic v. Karadzic*, 70 F.3d 232, 247 (2d Cir. 1995) ("Fed. R. Civ. P. 4(e)(2) specifically authorizes personal service of a summons and complaint upon an individual physically present within a judicial district of the United States, and such personal service comports with the requirements of due process for the assertion of personal jurisdiction." Citing *Burnham*, supra). *But cf., Conn v. Zakharov*, 667 F.3d 705, 715–16 (6th Cir. 2012) (expressing skepticism, but not deciding, that *Burnham* should be limited to its facts).

[20]*See, e.g., Amusement Equipment, Inc. v. Mordelt*, 779 F.3d 264, 271 (5th Cir. 1985) (where defendant's presence is obtained by fraud, service can be quashed).

Minimum Contacts

A defendant served with process outside the territorial confines of the state where a court sits may nonetheless be subject to the personal jurisdiction of courts within that state. Personal jurisdiction may be sustained even if the defendant does not consent to jurisdiction.[21] For such jurisdiction to be constitutional, the defendant has to have "contacts" with the state in which the court sits of such a quality and nature that exercise of personal jurisdiction would not offend "traditional notions of fair play and substantial justice."[22] It should be noted, however, that the "contacts" necessary to sustain personal jurisdiction need not always be physical contacts. In appropriate circumstances an intentional relationship with residents of a state can be a basis for sustaining personal jurisdiction.[23] By itself, however, a finding of minimum contacts is only a first step toward establishing personal jurisdiction. Additional requirements are discussed immediately below.

Purposeful Availment

In the past, once the minimum contacts described immediately above were identified, the court might normally proceed to determine the fairness and foreseeability of an assertion of personal jurisdiction over the defendant.[24] That older

---

[21]*International Shoe Co. v. State of Washington*, 326 U.S. 310, 317, 66 S. Ct. 154, 90 L. Ed 95 (1945) (noting that instant case did not address consent or appointment of agent to receive service of process).

[22]*International Shoe Co. v. State of Wash., Office of Unemployment Compensation and Placement*, 326 U.S. 310, 66 S. Ct. 154, 90 L. Ed. 95 (1945). *Cf., ALS Scan, Inc. v. Digital Service Consultants, Inc.*, 293 F.3d 707, 711 (4th Cir. 2002) ("However minimal the burden of defending in a foreign tribunal, a defendant may not be called upon to do so unless he has had the 'minimal contacts' with that State that are a prerequisite to its exercise of power over him."); *IMO Industries, Inc. v. Kiekert AG*, 155 F.3d 254, 259 (3d Cir. 1998) (where plaintiff has not met burden of demonstrating defendant's minimum contacts with forum, court need not reach question of whether exercise of jurisdiction would satisfy fair play and substantial justice).

[23]*Burger King Corp. v. Rudzewicz*, 471 U.S. 462, 476, 105 S. Ct. 2174, 2184, 85 L. Ed. 2d 528 (1985) ("So long as a commercial actor's efforts are 'purposefully directed' toward residents of another State, we have consistently rejected the notion that an absence of physical contacts can defeat personal jurisdiction there."). *See also, e.g., Oriental Trading Co., Inc. v. Firetti*, 236 F.3d 938, 943 (8th Cir. 2001) (in fraud case, "numerous" telephone calls, faxes and invoices sent to forum state should have caused defendants to understand that injury from fraud would be felt in forum-held, absence of physical contacts with forum may not necessarily defeat personal jurisdiction). *But see TruServ Corp. v. Flegles, Inc.*, 419 F.3d 584, 589 (7th Cir. 2005) ("[S]imply contracting with a party based in [a state] is not enough to establish the required minimum contacts.").

[24]*See, e.g., Bell Helicopter Textron, Inc. v. Heliqwest International, Ltd.*, 385 F.3d 1291, 1295 (10th Cir. 2004) ("In the context of products liability the minimum contacts requirement turns, in some measure, on foreseeability.").

approach, however, is now altered significantly.[25] In its place a new analysis begins with a second requirement following minimum contacts. This second question to be addresses is whether the defendant purposefully conducted activity within a jurisdiction, thereby triggering both the benefits and burdens of that jurisdiction's law.[26] Increasingly, the element of purposefulness has become the *sine qua non* when the constitutionality of an assertion of personal jurisdiction over a defendant served with process outside a state's borders is at issue.[27] Moreover, foreseeability that lesser contacts, such as a non-purposeful relationship with a jurisdiction, might lead to legal entanglements, is no longer a proper substitute for the requirement of purposefulness.[28]

With that background, the requirement of purposefulness in the context of cases in which defendants inject their products or services into the stream of commerce will now require fact-specific analyses of individual cases to determine whether the defendant's conduct was a purposeful entry into a forum state that constituted an invocation of the benefits and protections of the forum's laws.[29]

---

[25] *J. McIntyre Machinery, Ltd. v. Nicastro*, ___ U.S. ___, 131 S. Ct. 2780, 2787–89, 180 L. Ed. 2d 765, 774–76 (2011) (plurality opinion) ("Freeform notions of fundamental fairness" cannot sustain an assertion of personal jurisdiction; "[J]urisdiction is in the first instance a question of authority rather than fairness.").

[26] *J. McIntyre Machinery, Ltd. v. Nicastro*, ___ U.S. ___, 131 S. Ct. 2780, 2788, 180 L. Ed. 2d 765, 775 (2011) (plurality opinion).

[27] *J. McIntyre Machinery, Ltd. v. Nicastro*, ___ U.S. ___, 131 S. Ct. 2780, 2788, 180 L. Ed. 2d 765, 775 (2011) (plurality opinion). ("The defendant's transmission of goods permits the exercise of jurisdiction only where the defendant can be said to have targeted the forum; as a general rule, it is not enough that the defendant might have predicted that its goods will reach the forum State."); *Burger King Corp. v. Rudzewicz*, 471 U.S. 462, 474, 105 S. Ct. 2174, 2183, 85 L. Ed. 2d 528 (1985) ("[T]he constitutional touchstone remains whether the defendant purposefully established 'minimum contacts' in the forum State."); *(Hanson v. Denckla*, 357 U.S. 235, 253, 78 S. Ct. 1228, 2 L. Ed. 2d 1283 (1958) (requiring purposeful availment). *But*

cf., *Dole Food Co. v. Watts*, 303 F.3d 1104, 1114–15 (9th Cir. 2002) ("There may be circumstances under which the purposeful injection into the forum supports a finding of purposeful availment yet still weighs against the reasonableness of jurisdiction;" but not finding that situation in instant case).

[28] *J. Mcintyre Machinery, Ltd. v. Nicastro*, ___ U.S. ___, 131 S. Ct. 2780, 2790, 180 L. Ed. 2d 765, 777 (2011) (plurality opinion) ("[T]he authority to subject a defendant to judgment depends on purposeful availment;" neither foreseeability nore general fairness considerations are the touchstone of jurisdiction).

[29] *J. Mclntyre Machinery, Ltd, v. Nicastro*, ___ U.S. ___, 131 S. Ct. 2780, 2788, 180 L. Ed. 2d 765, 775 (2011) (plurality opinion) (in instant case, a distributor sold defendant's products in United States, defendant attended trade shows in United States but not in forum state; and four of defendant's machines "ended up" in forum; defendant had no office in forum, owned no property and paid no taxes in forum, and did not advertise or send employees to forum; held, though defendant may have purposefully entered United States, it had no purposeful contact with forum; thus,

Weighing Factors

Once purposefulness, as described above, is established, the final step to evaluate the constitutionality of an assertion of personal jurisdiction is to determine, on a case by case basis, whether it is appropriate for the forum to extend its power to particular cases.[30] The following factors are often considered when a court is determining whether a defendant's contacts with a state are sufficient to sustain personal jurisdiction. There is no requirement that all these factors be satisfied before personal jurisdiction attaches.[31] Moreover, other considerations, not yet identified, may arise and be more significant in the factual settings of other cases.[32]

(1) *Magnitude of Defendant's Contacts:* The greater the defendant's contacts with a state, the more likely it is that a court within that state will sustain personal jurisdiction.[33] Means of measuring magnitude may include the dollar value of defendant's activity or the nature and size of the wrong that defendant is alleged to have committed.

(2) *Systematic and Continuous Nature of Defendant's Contacts:* The longer a defendant's contacts with a state endure, the greater the possibility that such contacts may be used to sustain personal jurisdiction.[34] Thus, a defendant doing substantial business within a state for a prolonged period of

---

no personal jurisdiction); *Asahi Metal Industry Co. v. Superior Court*, 480 U.S. 102, 112, 107 S. Ct. 1026, 94 L. Ed. 2d 192 (1987) (plurality opinion) (Jurisdiction "must come about by an action of the defendant purposefully directed toward the forum State. The placement of a product into the stream of commerce, without more is an [inadequate] act.").

[30]*J. McIntyre Machinery, Ltd. v. Nicastro*, ___ U.S. ___, 131 S. Ct. 2780, 2789, 180 L. Ed. 2d 765, 776 (2011) (plurality opinion).

[31]*Cf., e.g., Northern Laminate Sales, Inc. v. Davis*, 403 F.3d 14, 25 (1st Cir. 2005) ("This circuit divides [the] minimum contacts analysis into three inquiries: relatedness, purposeful availment, and reasonableness.").

[32]*International Shoe Co. v. State of Wash., Office of Unemployment Compensation and Placement*, 326 U.S. 310, 66 S. Ct. 154, 90 L. Ed. 95 (1945). *See also Asahi Metal Industry Co., Ltd. v. Superior Court*, 480 U.S. 102, 113, 107 S. Ct. 1026, 1032, 94 L. Ed. 2d 92 (1987) (plurality opinion) (to determine reasonableness, "[a] court must consider the burden on the defendant, the interests of the forum

State, and the plaintiff's interest in obtaining relief. It must also weigh in its determination 'the interstate judicial system's interest in obtaining the most efficient resolution of controversies; and the shared interest of the several States in furthering fundamental substantive social policies.' ").

[33]*But cf., Burger King Corp. v. Rudzewicz*, 471 U.S. 462, 477–78, 105 S. Ct. 2174, 85 L. Ed. 2d 528 (1985) ("[R]equirements inherent in the concept of 'fair play and substantial justice' may defeat the reasonableness of jurisdiction even if [a] defendant has purposefully engaged in forum activities."). *See, e.g., Omeluk v. Langsten Slip & Batbyggeri A/S*, 52 F.3d 267, 270 (9th Cir. 1995) (if defendant's activities had been substantial, jurisdiction would have been good even if activities had been unrelated to cause of action).

[34]*See, e.g., Omeluk v. Langsten Slip & Batbyggeri A/S*, 52 F.3d 267 (9th Cir.1995) ("systematic and continuous" contacts usually equals good jurisdiction). *Cf., Streber v. Hunter*, 221 F.3d 701, 718 (5th Cir. 2000) (where defendant's contact with forum is not continuous, personal jurisdiction is satisfied only when defendant

time will be more vulnerable to personal jurisdiction within that state.[35] Similarly, a defendant domiciled in a state is very likely to be vulnerable to suit in that state (even if process is served outside the state), because domicile usually connotes a longstanding relationship with a state. Note, however, that a single contact for a short period of time may not be systematic or continuous, but could still sustain personal jurisdiction because the contact is large enough, purposeful enough, and sufficiently related to a cause of action so that the exercise of jurisdiction is not unfair.

(3) *Relation Between Defendant's Contacts and the Cause of Action:* If a defendant's contacts with a state have nothing to do with a cause of action, the burden of establishing personal jurisdiction based on such contacts will be more difficult to achieve.[36] If the contacts are closely related to the cause of action, it is more likely that jurisdiction based on such contacts will be upheld.[37]

(4) *Availability of Witnesses and Evidence:* If the plaintiff's choice of forum will make it burdensome or impossible for the defendant to produce relevant testimony and other evidence, personal jurisdiction will be more difficult to sustain.[38]

(5) *Forum Interest in a Suit:* Although not strictly a contact between a defendant and a state, the presence of a special state interest in a suit might help sustain personal jurisdiction.[39] A state's interest in title to land within its boundaries is such an interest.[40] In practice, however, special state interests are rarely identified, and even when identified, are not often significant in the weighing of factors of fairness.[41]

---

purposefully avails himself of protection of forum law through minimum contacts and where exercise of jurisdiction does not offend fair play and substantial justice).

[35]*See also, e.g., Boschetto v. Hansing*, 539 F.3d 1011, 1019 (9th Cir. 2008) (defendant's one-time use of eBay does not, of itself, establish jurisdiction over transaction for which eBay served as conduit; but serial use of eBay may help support finding of personal jurisdiction).

[36]*See, e.g., Glater v. Eli Lilly & Co.*, 744 F.2d 213, 216 (1st Cir. 1984) (if suit is unrelated to defendant's instate activities, the standard for satisfying jurisdiction is "considerably more stringent").

[37]*Cf., Inamed Corp. v. Kuzmak*, 249 F.3d 1356, 1362 (Fed. Cir. 2001) ("arise out of or related to" standard "has not been clearly delineated by the Supreme Court").

[38]*See, e.g., Terracom v. Valley Nat. Bank*, 49 F.3d 555, 561 (9th Cir. 1995) (availability of witnesses and evidence should be weighed).

[39]*Keeton v. Hustler Magazine, Inc.*, 465 U.S. 770, 776, 104 S. Ct. 1473, 1479, 79 L. Ed. 2d 790 (1984) (fairness of jurisdiction depends partially on whether state has "legitimate interest" in requiring defendant to answer claim related to defendant's activities).

[40]*Shaffer v. Heitner*, 433 U.S. 186, 206, 97 S. Ct. 2569, 2581, 53 L. Ed. 2d 683 (1977) (state has interest in marketability of property within its borders that may help support some form of jurisdiction).

[41]*See, e.g., Kulko v. Superior Court of California In and For City and County of San Francisco*, 436 U.S. 84, 98–101, 98 S. Ct. 1690, 1700–01, 56 L. Ed. 2d 132 (1978) (state's "substantial interests" in care of children do not sustain jurisdiction; interest can be

Jurisdictional Discovery

Sometimes a plaintiff will allege that the defendant has possession of facts demonstrating that the defendant has contacts with the state sufficient to support personal jurisdiction. In such circumstances a court may grant limited discovery to determine such jurisdictional facts. If such discovery is allowed, it will take place within the rules of discovery discussed elsewhere in this text and within any limits the court may impose.

Before authorizing such discovery, courts normally require that the plaintiff make a good faith showing that discovery might lead to facts demonstrating existence of personal jurisdiction over the defendant.[42]

Specific Jurisdiction v. General Jurisdiction

Frequently courts use the terms "specific jurisdiction" and "general jurisdiction." These terms may appear daunting, but in fact they are merely explanations for the application of personal jurisdiction to different sets of facts.[43] "Specific jurisdiction" is generally used to indicate that a defendant's contacts with a state may not be large or systematic and continuous.[44] However, the contact may still satisfy jurisdictional requirements if it is related to the cause of action and purposeful, and jurisdiction based on the contacts is otherwise reasonable.[45] By contrast, "general jurisdiction" may be found where the

---

vindicated through existing interstate means of cooperation). *But see AST Sports Science, Inc. v. CLF Distribution Ltd.*, 514 F.3d 1054, 1062 (10th Cir. 2008) (finding important state interest where plaintiff is forum resident and forum's law will be applied; also noting party's interest — where plaintiff has filed for bankruptcy and is suing foreign defendant, court may consider difficulty in finding foreign counsel willing and able to handle case in foreign forum that is partly controlled by United States bankruptcy law).

[42]*Cf., e.g., Caribbean Broadcasting System, Ltd. v. Cable & Wireless P.L.C.*, 148 F.3d 1080, 1089–90 (D.C. Cir. 1998) (plaintiff's failure to make good faith showing justifies refusal to grant jurisdictional discovery). *See also Phoenix Consulting Inc. v. Republic of Angola*, 216 F.3d 36, 40 (D.C. Cir. 2000) (jurisdictional discovery should not be permitted if defendant has raised other procedural defenses, such as forum non conveniens or other jurisdictional issues).

[43]*See generally, Helicopteros Nacionales de Colombia, S.A. v. Hall*, 466 U.S. 408, 414–15, 104 S. Ct. 1868, 1872, 80 L. Ed. 2d 404 nn. 8–9 (1984) (identifying "specific" and "general" jurisdiction, and distinguishing them). *See also, e.g., ALS Scan, Inc. v. Digital Service Consultants, Inc.*, 293 F.3d 707, 711 (4th Cir. 2002) (two approaches exist for *International Shoe*-"by finding specific jurisdiction based on conduct connected to the suit or by finding general jurisdiction"); *Alpine View Co. Ltd. v. Atlas Copco AB*, 205 F.3d 208, 215 (5th Cir. 2000) (" 'Minimum contacts' can be established either through contacts sufficient to assert specific jurisdiction, or contacts sufficient to assert general jurisdiction.").

[44]*See, e.g., Stroman Realty, Inc. v. Antt*, 528 F.3d 382, 385 (5th Cir. 2008) ("If the contacts are less pervasive, courts may exercise 'specific jurisdiction' in 'a suit arising out of or related to the defendant's contact with the forum.' ").

[45]*Goodyear Dunlop Tires Operations, S.A. v. Brown, U.S.*, 113 S. Ct. 2846, 2851, 180 L. Ed. 2d 796, 803

defendant's contacts with the state are unrelated to the cause of action, but are substantial, systematic and continuous.[46] However, it should be emphasized that when a plaintiff seeks to sustain a suit based on unrelated contacts, the contacts should indeed be substantial.[47]

Personal Jurisdiction Based on Plaintiffs Contacts

In general it is settled that personal jurisdiction over a defendant in a particular forum can never be based solely on a plaintiffs contacts with that forum.[48] However, if a defendant's acts outside the forum give rise to a cause of action within the forum, a plaintiffs contacts with the forum, *e.g.,* residence, may

---

(2011) ("Specific jurisdiction . . . depends on an 'affiliatio[n] between the forum and the underlying controversy;" bus accident in foreign country, tire made and sold by foreign subsidiaries abroad; defendant subsidiaries do no direct business in forum state; small numbers of tires of different design were sold in forum, but not by defendant subsidiaries; held, no general jurisdiction over these defendants); *Burger King Corp. v. Rudzewicz*, 471 U.S. 462, 472, 105 S. Ct. 2174, 85 L. Ed. 2d 528 (1985) (good personal jurisdiction where defendant has " 'purposefully directed' his activities at residents of the forum and the litigation results from alleged inquiries that 'arise out of or relate to those activities' "). *See, e.g., be2 LLC v. Ivanov*, 642 F.3d 555, 558 (7th Cir. 2011) (defendant not subject to personal jurisdiction "simply because the defendant owns or operates a website that is accessible in the forum state, even if that site is 'interactive;' " defendant did not deliberately exploit forum).

[46]*Goodyear Dunlop Tires Operations, S.A. v. Brown, U.S.*, 113 S. Ct. 2846, 2851, 180 L. Ed. 2d 796 (2011) ("A court may assert general jurisdiction over foreign (sister-state or foreign-country) corporations to hear any and all claims against them when their affiliations with the State are so 'continuous and systematic' as to render them essentially at home in the forum State;" but loose unrelated activity will not support personal jurisdiction, notwithstanding that such activity is continuous). *See, e.g., LSI*

Industries Inc. v. Hubbell Lighting, Inc., 232 F.3d 1369, 1375 (Fed. Cir. 2000) (patent dispute; defendant is subject to jurisdiction where defendant nets several million dollars in annual sales within forum; general jurisdiction exists, notwithstanding fact that disputed product itself was not sold within forum); *Phillips Exeter Academy v. Howard Phillips Fund*, 196 F.3d 284, 288 (1st Cir. 1999) ("[A] defendant who has maintained a continuous and systematic linkage with the forum state brings himself within the general jurisdiction of that state's courts in respect to all matters, even those that are unrelated to the defendant's contacts with the forum.").

[47]*See, e.g., Epps v. Stewart Information Services Corp.*, 327 F.3d 642, 648 (8th Cir. 2003) (general jurisdiction requires systematic and continuous contacts, plus other enumerated factors of fairness); *ALS Scan, Inc. v. Digital Service Consultants, Inc.*, 293 F.3d 707, 712 (4th Cir. 2002) ("To establish general jurisdiction over the defendant, the defendant's activities in the State must have been 'continuous and systematic,' a more demanding standard than is necessary for establishing specific jurisdiction."); *Chaiken v. VV Pub. Corp.*, 119 F.3d 1018, 1028 (2d Cir. 1997) (circulation of 183 copies of publication in state, creating annual gross revenues of $21,000, does not of itself satisfy general jurisdiction).

[48]*Goodyear Dunlop Tires Operations, S.A. v. Brown, ____ U.S. ____, 113 S. Ct. 2846, 180 L. Ed. 2d 796 (2011).*

add additional weight to the assertion of personal jurisdiction.[49]

ADDITIONAL RESEARCH REFERENCES

C.J.S., Constitutional Law § 1150
C.J.S., Constitutional Law § 1153
C.J.S., Federal Courts §§ 165(1) to 190 et seq.
West's Key Number Digest, Constitutional Law ☞305(4)
West's Key Number Digest, Federal Courts ☞76 to 76.35

§ 2.5 Jurisdiction Over Persons or Things—Requirements for Personal Jurisdiction—State Limitations: Long-Arm Statutes

CORE CONCEPT

Before a federal trial court may exert its personal jurisdiction over an out-of-state, non-consenting defendant, the court must usually satisfy requirements laid down by the legislature of the state in which it sits.[1] These requirements are found in the so-called "long-arm" statutes, which every state has enacted. Satisfying the long-arm requirements is a burden additional to the obligations of fairness imposed by the Constitution.[2]

The long-arm powers may not exceed the constitutional limits of due process, discussed above. In fact, some state long-arm statutes are drafted to allow trial courts to reach as far as due process will allow. However, it is possible that a state will choose not to permit an exercise of personal jurisdiction to the fullest extent permitted by the Constitution. In that circumstance, the court's ability to reach defendants outside the territory of the state may be constrained by the long-arm statute.[3] These distinctions between the long-arm statutes of particular states require

---

[49]*Goodyear Dunlop Tires Operations, S.A. v. Brown*, ___ U.S. ___, 113 S. Ct. 2846, 180 L. Ed. 2d 796, 809 (2011); *Calder v. Jones*, 465 U.S. 783, 788, 104 S. Ct. 1482, 79 L. Ed. 2d 804 (1984) ("The plaintiffs lack of 'contacts' will not defeat otherwise proper jurisdiction . . . but they may be so manifold as to permit jurisdiction when it would not exist in their absence.").

[1]*See, e.g., Penguin Group (USA) Inc. v. American Buddha*, 609 F.3d 30, 35 (2d Cir. 2010) ("In litigation arising under federal statutes that do not contain their own jurisdictional provisions . . . federal courts are to apply the personal jurisdiction rules of the forum state," assuming that those rules meet constitutional due process

standards).

[2]*See, e.g., GTE New Media Services Inc. v. BellSouth Corp.*, 199 F.3d 1343, 1347 (D.C. Cir. 2000), (even if long-arm statute is satisfied, requirement of due process must still be met); *Wenz v. Memery Crystal*, 55 F.3d 1503 (10th Cir.1995) (for jurisdiction over nonresident defendant, court must examine both the state long-arm statute and issues of due process).

[3]*See, e.g., Talbot v. Johnson Newspaper Corp.*, 71 N.Y.2d 827, 829–30, 527 N.Y.S.2d 729, 522 N.E.2d 1027, 1028–29 (1988) ("[T]he New York long-arm statute . . . does not provide for in personam jurisdiction in every case in which due process would permit it.").

attorneys to consult, and become familiar with, the long-arm statutes of individual states relevant to their practices.

APPLICATIONS

Consent

Where a defendant has already consented to the personal jurisdiction of the court, the need for application of a long-arm statute is eliminated.[4]

Service Within a State

Long-arm statutes authorize exercise of personal jurisdiction beyond the boundaries of the state in which a court sits. Thus if a defendant is properly served with process within a state, the long-arm statute of that state will have no application.

Overlap With Due Process

The long-arm statutes of many states permit their courts to exercise personal jurisdiction over out-of-state defendants to the full extent of Due Process limitations of the Constitution.[5] In such states there is thus no need to make separate analyses to determine if both the constitutional requirements of fairness and long-arm requirements are satisfied: if due process is satisfied, so is the long-arm statute.[6] However, in states that do not permit exercise of personal jurisdiction to the fullest constitutional extent, it is necessary to make two different analyses. Jurisdiction must satisfy due process, and it must also fit within the statutory scheme of the long-arm statute.[7] For purposes of the reach of the state long-arm statute, the inter-

---

[4]*See, e.g., General Contracting & Trading Co., LLC v. Interpole, Inc.,* 940 F.2d 20, 22 (1st Cir. 1991) (long-arm analysis is unnecessary if defendant has submitted to personal jurisdiction); *Knowlton v. Allied Van Lines, Inc.,* 900 F.2d 1196, 1197–99 (8th Cir. 1990) (existence of consent to jurisdiction, whether expressly or by waiver, eliminates need to satisfy state long-arm statute; appointment of agent to receive service of process is "[o]ne of the most solidly established ways of giving . . . consent").

[5]*See, e.g.,* Rhode Island General Laws Annotated § 9-5-33(a). *See also, e.g., Penguin Group (USA) Inc. v. American Buddha,* 609 F.3d 30, 35 (2d Cir. 2010) (most states outside New York extend long-arm statutes to the full extent of due process); *North American Catholic Educational Programming Foundation, Inc. v. Cardinale,* 567 F.3d 8, 16 (1st Cir. 2009) ("Rhode Island's long arm statute is designed to extend jurisdiction to the full constitutional reach."); *AST Sports Science, Inc. v. CLF Distribution Ltd.,* 514 F.3d 1054, 1057 (10th Cir. 2008) ("The Colorado Supreme Court has interpreted the Colorado's long-arm statute to extend jurisdiction to the fullest extent permitted by the Due Process Clause of the Fourteenth Amendment.").

[6]*See, e.g., Chan v. Society Expeditions, Inc.,* 39 F.3d 1398, 1405 (9th Cir. 1994) (when long-arm statute is "coextensive" with due process, court needs to examine only the due process requirement).

[7]*Cf., e.g., Best Van Lines, Inc. v. Walker,* 490 F.3d 239 (2d Cir. 2007) (district court properly looked first to New York law to determine if personal jurisdiction was satisfied; no need to look to 14th Amendment due process consideration unless court could determine that it had jurisdiction under New York law); *Mwani v. bin Laden,* 417 F.3d 1, 9 (D.C. Cir. 2005) (noting that some portions of District of Co-

pretation of the state's highest court is dispositive.[8]

Example

The New York long-arm statute permits exercise of personal jurisdiction in New York courts over many out-of-state defendants who commit tortious acts outside the state which create injury within the state.[9] However, that authority explicitly excludes cases where defendants are accused of defamatory acts outside New York that cause injury within the state. Thus a federal court in New York could not use the New York long-arm statute to exercise personal jurisdiction over a defendant who was accused of defamation outside New York that caused injury within the state. This would be true even if the due process requirements for personal jurisdiction, discussed above, were satisfied.

ADDITIONAL RESEARCH REFERENCES

C.J.S., Constitutional Law § 1150
C.J.S., Constitutional Law § 1153
C.J.S., Federal Courts §§ 165(1) to 190 et seq.
West's Key Number Digest, Constitutional Law ⟳305(4)
West's Key Number Digest, Federal Courts ⟳76 to 76.35

§ 2.6 Jurisdiction Over Persons or Things—Requirements for Personal Jurisdiction—Notice

CORE CONCEPT

The notice requirement for personal jurisdiction overlaps substantially with the fairness requirements. Both "notice" and "minimum contacts" are requirements derived from the Due Process clauses of the Constitution. Even so, there are a few distinctions to be made between notice and minimum contacts. For example, if a defendant had elaborate contacts with a state, but was never notified of the pendency of a lawsuit, the defendant would never have a fair opportunity to present a defense. Thus, personal jurisdiction would be lacking—even though minimum

---

lumbia long-arm statute reach as far as due process permits, but others do not; for application of the latter provisions court must be satisfied that more stringent requirements are met); *New Wellington Financial Corp. v. Flagship Resort Development Corp.*, 416 F.3d 290, 294 n.6 (4th Cir. 2005) ("It is nonetheless still possible for the contacts of a non-resident defendant to satisfy due process but not meet the specific grasp of a Virginia long-arm statute provision.").

[8]*See, e.g., Diamond Crystal Brands, Inc. v. Food Movers*

International, Inc., 593 F.3d 1249, 1258 (11th Cir. 2010) ("[W]e must interpret and apply Georgia's long-arm statute in the same way as would the Georgia Supreme Court."); *Touchcom, Inc. v. Bereskin & Parr*, 574 F.3d 1403 (Fed. Cir. 2009) (federal court defers to state supreme court's interpretation of state long-arm statute, but for purposes of due process analysis federal precedent controls).

[9]New York Civil Practice Law and Rules 302(a)(3).

contacts were present—because requirements of notice were not satisfied.[1]

APPLICATIONS

Due Process Standard

To satisfy Due Process requirements, notice to the defendant must be of a quality that is reasonably likely, in all the circumstances of the case, to apprise the defendant of the pending action and afford an opportunity to make a defense.[2] This standard is very fact-dependent.[3] Normally, notice by first-class mail is satisfactory for Due Process purposes[4] (*but see* Rule 4 for acceptable methods of service of original pleadings.) However, where the names or addresses of defendants are not known and cannot reasonably be known, less in the way of notice is required.[5] Thus, in a literal sense, it is entirely possible, if not commonplace, that the constitutional requirement of no-

---

[1]*Murphy Bros., Inc. v. Michetti Pipe Stringing, Inc.*, 526 U.S. 344, 350, 119 S. Ct. 1322, 1327, 143 L. Ed. 2d 448 (1999) ("In the absence of service of process (or waiver of service by the defendant), a court ordinarily may not exercise power over a party the complaint names as a defendant."). *See, e.g., Peay v. BellSouth Medical Assistance Plan*, 205 F.3d 1206, 1209 (10th Cir. 2000) ("While service of process and personal jurisdiction both must be satisfied before a suit can proceed, they are distinct concepts that require separate inquiries.").

[2]*Nelson v. Adams USA, Inc.*, 529 U.S. 460, 467, 120 S. Ct. 1579, 1585, 146 L. Ed. 2d 530 (2000) (amended complaint joining new party; held, where newly joined defendant is "adjudged liable the very first moment his personal liability was legally at issue" he is denied an opportunity to prepare a defense and is thereby denied due process).

[3]*Mennonite Bd. of Missions v. Adams*, 462 U.S. 791, 799, 103 S. Ct. 2706, 2711, 77 L. Ed. 2d 180 (1983) (heightened duty to provide notice where state knows of opponent's inexperience or incompetence). *See, e.g., U.S. v. Ligas*, 549 F.3d 497, 500 (7th Cir. 2008) (service requires more than defendant's awareness that he has been sued and has received copy of summons and complaint; requirements of Rule 4 must be met); *Lakeshore Broadcasting, Inc. v. F.C.C.*, 199 F.3d 468, 474 (D.C. Cir. 1999)

(publication notice of regulations gave party that had initiated administrative process sufficient notice; distinguishing *Mullane v. Central Hanover Bank & Trust* as applying to parties who had no reason to know a judicial proceeding was pending).

[4]But cf., *Robinson v. Hanrahan*, 409 U.S. 38, 93 S. Ct. 30, 34 L. Ed. 2d 47 (1972) (mail service of notice of forfeiture to home address of party government knows to be incarcerated does not meet constitutional requirement). *See, e.g., U.S. v. One Toshiba Color Television*, 213 F.3d 147 (3d Cir. 2000) (forfeiture case involving incarcerated party; held, while mailing is usually adequate notice, mailing is not "per se satisfaction of notice requirements"; noting differences among circuits, but holding that in providing mail service on prisoner held in state confinement, using proper address of jail, federal government need not prove actual notice; instead, government must demonstrate that methods of service used are reasonably calculated to result in actual notice).

[5]*Dusenbery v. U.S.*, 534 U.S. 161, 170, 122 S. Ct. 694, 701, 151 L. Ed. 2d 597 (2002) (Due process "does not say that the State *must provide* actual notice, but that it *must attempt to provide* actual notice"; and attempt need not involve "heroic efforts" by government); *Mullane v. Central Hanover Bank & Trust Co.*, 339 U.S. 306, 314, 70 S. Ct. 652, 94 L. Ed. 865 (1950). *But cf., Jones v. Flowers*, 547 U.S. 220, 126

tice will be met even where an interested party received no notice at all.[6]

Statutory Notice

In addition to satisfying constitutional requirements for notice, a party must also serve process in accordance with the
statute or rule of procedure governing service in a particular
court. For federal courts, Rule 4 (discussed elsewhere in this
text) governs service of process at the beginning of a suit. Rule
4 cannot establish standards for service that do not meet the
constitutional requirements for notice. However, Rule 4 could
prescribe requirements for service more rigorous than those
required by the Constitution.

ADDITIONAL RESEARCH REFERENCES

C.J.S., Constitutional Law § 1154
C.J.S., Federal Courts §§ 165(1) to 190 et seq.
West's Key Number Digest, Constitutional Law ⚷309
West's Key Number Digest, Federal Courts ⚷76 to 76.35

§ 2.7 Jurisdiction Over Persons or Things—Requirements for Personal Jurisdiction—Special Considerations in Federal Court

CORE CONCEPT

In matters of jurisdiction over persons and things, federal
courts generally behave in much the same way as state courts
sitting in the same state:[1] the jurisdictional authority is much
the same in the two systems. Rule 4(k), which generally governs
the territorial limit of service of process from a federal court,
makes that point explicitly. However, there are a few circumstances where a federal court may have a somewhat greater

---

S. Ct. 1708, 1713–14, 164 L. Ed. 2d
415 (2006) (notice of tax sale sent by
certified mail was returned unclaimed;
held, state "must take additional reasonable steps to attempt to provide notice to the property owner before selling his property, if it is practicable to
do so;" but still acknowledging that
actual notice is not required; distinguishing earlier cases as circumstances where government was unaware that attempt at service had
failed).

[6]*See, e.g., Juris v. Inamed Corp.,*
685 F.3d 1294, 1321 (11th Cir. 2012)
(due process does not require actual
notice, only " 'a good faith effort to
provide actual notice' "); *Baldwin v.
Credit Based Asset Servicing and*
Securitization, 516 F.3d 734, 737 (8th
Cir. 2008) ("The Due Process Clause
does not require that an interested
party actually receive notice.").

[1]*See, e.g., Ruiz de Molina v.
Merritt & Furman Ins. Agency, Inc.,*
207 F.3d 1351, 1355 (11th Cir. 2000)
("A federal court sitting in diversity
may exercise jurisdiction over a non-
resident defendant to the same extent
as a court of that state."). *Cf., Depre-
nyl Animal Health, Inc. v. University
of Toronto Innovations Foundation,*
297 F.3d 1343, 1350 (Fed. Cir. 2002)
(*International Shoe* applies to federal
courts through Fifth Amendment as it
applies to state courts through Fourteenth Amendment).

jurisdictional reach than its state counterpart. Rule 4(k) contains some of these exceptions. Others are creatures of Congressional legislation.

APPLICATIONS

Nationwide Personal Jurisdiction

For several federal causes of action, including suits under federal antitrust laws and the federal securities laws, Congress has authorized federal courts to exercise their personal jurisdiction throughout the United States.[2] Thus, in hearing an antitrust claim filed in Baltimore, a federal court in Maryland has personal jurisdiction over a defendant in Hawaii, Puerto Rico, Alaska, or some other distant jurisdiction, even if it could not otherwise reach that defendant under the considerations mentioned earlier in this section on personal jurisdiction.[3] These statutes, while not rare, are generally the exceptions to the normal practice. When such statutes come into play, it is possible that the court will make a minimum contacts analysis that may differ somewhat from the concept developed for domestic defendants. In the first place, a court evaluating personal jurisdiction in a case involving a federal cause of action that authorized nationwide jurisdiction will be less concerned with issues of state/federal relationships and more concerned about the federal policies underlying the federal right that has been asserted by the plaintiff.[4] Secondly, it is uncertain whether, in making a minimum contact analysis in the context of nationwide personal jurisdiction, the court should examine only whether minimum contacts exist[5] or whether the court should also look to whether an exercise of jurisdiction

---

[2] *J. McIntyre Machinery Ltd. v. Nicastro*, ___ U.S. ___, 131 S. Ct. 2780, 2789, 180 L. Ed. 2d 765, 776 (2011) (plurality opinion) ("[A] defendant may in principle be subject to the jurisdiction of the courts of the United States but not of any particular State.").

[3] *See, e.g.*, 15 U.S.C.A. § 22. *See also In re Federal Fountain, Inc.*, 165 F.3d 600, 601–02 (8th Cir. 1999) (en banc) (where Congress has authorized personal jurisdiction nationwide and defendant is found within territory of United States, federal courts may exercise personal jurisdiction over defendant; concluding that "virtually every . . . court" has reached same conclusion). *Accord, Board of Trustees, Sheet Metal Workers' Nat. Pension Fund v. Elite Erectors, Inc.*, 212 F.3d 1031, 1035 (7th Cir. 2000) (agreeing with *Federal Fountain*; rejecting *Peay*; "we have concluded that nationwide

service under [certain] statutes is proper, as long as the defendants have adequate contacts [within] the United States as a whole"). *But see Peay v. BellSouth Medical Assistance Plan*, 205 F.3d 1206, 1210 (10th Cir. 2000) (acknowledging disagreement with *Federal Fountain*; citing other cases in conflict; concluding that even where Congress has authorized nationwide service, plaintiff's choice of forum must still be "fair and reasonable"). *See also Republic of Panama v. BCCI Holdings (Luxembourg) S.A.*, 119 F.3d 935, 943–44 (11th Cir. 1997) (concluding that fairness and convenience are still relevant to analysis).

[4] *See, e.g., Pinker v. Roche Holdings Ltd.*, 292 F.3d 361 (3d Cir. 2002).

[5] *See, e.g., Securities Investor Protection Corp. v. Vigman*, 764 F.2d 1309, 1316 (9th Cir. 1985) (looking only to whether defendant has mini-

reasonable in a particular district.[6]

For many other federal causes of action, such as civil rights claims or truth-in-lending cases, the more conventional forms of obtaining personal jurisdiction must be followed.

Important: Nationwide personal jurisdiction should not be equated with personal jurisdiction throughout the world. If the defendant in the antitrust action filed in Baltimore was in Brazil, the Congressional grant of nationwide jurisdiction would not be effective to reach the Brazilian defendant. In such a circumstance the federal court would still have resort to the considerations of minimum contacts and either state long-arm statutes or the special provision of Rule 4(k)(2), discussed immediately below. But if those tools were insufficient, then personal jurisdiction could not be sustained.

Pendent Personal Jurisdiction

A district court's authority to exercise nationwide personal jurisdiction over causes of action arising under federal law raises a question as to the power of the court to exercise personal jurisdiction over state causes of action that are related to the federal claims. For such state claims, of course, there is normally no equivalent nationwide personal jurisdiction. In that circumstance, in the absence of some intervening theory of joinder, a plaintiff might be forced to split the causes of action between federal and state courts. Federal courts have responded to this problem by developing an approach they describe as pendent personal jurisdiction. The apparently settled rule is that in such cases the district court enjoys discretion to hear the state claims, provided that the federal claim is substantial and that it shares a common nucleus of operative fact with the state claims.[7]

Pendent personal jurisdiction has also been applied when a federal court enjoys good personal jurisdiction over a federal cause of action, but state law appears to prevent litigation of a

---

mum contacts with United States as a whole; not concerned with any potential absence of contacts with particular federal district).

[6]*See, e.g., Republic of Panama v. BCCI Holdings (Luxembourg) S.A.,* 119 F.3d 935, 945–46 (11th Cir. 1997) (district court should weigh fairness to defendant in particular district against "federal interest involved in the litigation;" asserting that other circuits follow this approach).

[7]*See, e.g., CE Distribution, LLC v. New Sensor Corp.,* 380 F.3d 1107, 1113 (9th Cir. 2004) ("[W]e have explicitly adopted the concept of pendent personal jurisdiction, provided there is a sufficient common nucleus of operative facts that the state and federal claims share.); *U.S. v. Botefuhr,* 309 F.3d 1263, 1272–75 (10th Cir. 2002) (observing that pendent personal jurisdiction gives district court discretion, not obligation, to hear state claims; collecting cases and noting that all circuits which have addressed issue, and most district courts, have upheld pendent personal jurisdiction). *See also Fiore v. Walden,* 659 F.3d 838, 858 (9th Cir. 2011) (facts supporting one claim do not have to be identical to claims for which personal jurisdiction is good, "so long as the core facts are the same"). *But cf., Administrators of Tulane Educational Fund v. Ipsen Pharma, S.A.S.,* 770 F.Supp.2d 24, 31 n.l (D.D.C. 2011) (where court lacks personal jurisdiction, there can be no pendent personal jurisdiction).

closely related state claim. For example, if a labor union is sued for an alleged violation of federal labor law, but otherwise cognizable claims under state law would be barred in state court because the union (an unincorporated association) cannot be sued under its common name, there is some authority permitting the federal court to hear the state claims under the theory of pendent personal jurisdiction.[8]

Special Considerations of Rule 4(k)

As is discussed elsewhere in this study, Rule 4(k) authorizes federal courts in certain circumstances to exercise personal jurisdiction over certain designated persons who may be served within 100 miles, measured in a straight line in any direction, from the federal courthouse. This Rule applies irrespective of how many state boundaries may intervene. Such designated persons include those who may be joined under the applicable state long-arm law, parties impleaded under Rule 14, parties joined under Rule 19, parties who can be served under federal statutory interpleader legislation, 28 U.S.C.A. § 1335, and parties subject to service authorized by any other applicable federal legislation. Note that Rule 4(k) does not provide the 100 mile bulge to plaintiffs seeking to initiate an action by serving a defendant.

This 100 mile rule applies only within the United States. A federal court in Detroit, Michigan, for example, could not use Rule 4(k) to serve a person in Windsor, Ontario, even though Windsor is much less than 100 miles from Detroit. If a federal court is located in the center of a state, more than 100 miles from its borders, Rule 4(k)'s 100-mile bulge has little utility. If, however, a federal court is located in a part of a state immediately adjacent to a neighboring state, Rule 4(k) may provide advantages not available in a state court.

Finally, Rule 4(k)(2) explicitly permits exercise of personal jurisdiction in federal causes of action where the defendant has sufficient contacts with the United States as a whole, but not with any particular state.[9]

---

[8]*See, e.g., Price v. United Mine Workers*, 336 F.2d 771, 775 (6th Cir. 1964) (if federal claims are substantial, and state claims are closely related, district court has "jurisdiction to fully determine [entire dispute] including its local aspects").

[9]*See also, e.g., Medical Mut. of Ohio v. deSoto*, 245 F.3d 561, 566–67 (6th Cir. 2001) (in case brought under Employee Retirement Income and Security Act, 29 U.S.C.A. § 1132 provided nationwide personal jurisdiction; court, therefore, could look to defendant's contacts with entire country, rather than only forum state; rejecting contrary approach of requiring plaintiff to demonstrate that defendant had sufficient contacts with both United States as a whole and forum state). *But see Bradford Co. v. Conteyor North America, Inc.*, 603 F.3d 1262, 1272 (Fed. Cir. 2010) ("[F]or a court to exercise personal jurisdiction [under Rule 4(k)(2)], the plaintiff's claim must arise under federal law, the defendant must not be subject to jurisdiction in any state's court of general jurisdiction, and exercise of jurisdiction must comport with due process."); *Peay v. BellSouth Medical Assistance Plan*, 205 F.3d 1206, 1210–12 (10th Cir. 2000) (29 U.S.C.A. § 1132 authorizes nation-

ADDITIONAL RESEARCH REFERENCES

C.J.S., Constitutional Law § 1154
C.J.S., Federal Civil Procedure §§ 204 to 221 et seq.
C.J.S., Federal Civil Procedure §§ 486 et seq.
C.J.S., Federal Courts §§ 16 et seq.
West's Key Number Digest, Constitutional Law ☞305
West's Key Number Digest, Federal Civil Procedure ☞461 to 505
West's Key Number Digest, Federal Courts ☞71

§ 2.8 Jurisdiction Over Persons or Things—Special Requirements for Quasi in Rem Jurisdiction

CORE CONCEPT

Quasi in rem jurisdiction is an alternative to personal jurisdiction. It is employed most commonly as a means of obtaining the presence of a defendant in a court by judicial attachment (i.e., seizure) of property belonging to the defendant. In order for the court to attach such property, the property must be located within the state in which the court sits.

APPLICATIONS

Prerequisites

A court may exercise quasi in rem jurisdiction when six elements are present: 1) thing of value; 2) territorial limit; 3) defendant's asset; 4) seizure or attachment; 5) notice; and 6) minimum contacts are satisfied. *All six* elements must be satisfied.[1]

(1) *Thing of Value:* Quasi in rem jurisdiction presupposes that the thing seized has value. Because a judgment in favor of a plaintiff will often be enforced through forced sale or forfeiture of the thing seized, quasi in rem jurisdiction would have little meaning if the asset had no value. Moreover, the value of the asset seized determines the monetary limit of the court's jurisdiction in quasi in rem cases.[2]

◆ *Example:* If a plaintiff's claim had a maximum value of one million dollars, that would normally be the

---

wide service of process, but requirement of personal jurisdiction requires separate due process analysis to determine whether plaintiff's choice of forum is fair and reasonable). *Cf., Merial, Ltd. v. Cipia Ltd.*, 681 F.3d 1283, 1294 (Fed. Cir. 2012) (Rule 4(k)(2) cannot successfully be avoided by a defendant's showing of a forum where palintiff could sue, but which plaintiff would have had "no basis for personal jurisdiction but for [defendant's] consent").

[1]*See, e.g., Winter Storm Shipping,*

Ltd. v. TPI, 310 F.3d 263, 269 (2d Cir. 2002) (due process requirements for quasi in rem jurisdiction similar to those for personal jurisdiction). For a fuller discussion of the requirements for quasi in rem jurisdiction, *see Shaffer v. Heitner*, 433 U.S. 186, 97 S. Ct. 2569, 53 L. Ed. 2d 683 (1977).

[2]*Shaffer v. Heitner*, 433 U.S. 186, 207, n. 23, 97 S. Ct. 2569, 53 L. Ed. 2d 683 (1977) (liability in an in rem action is limited to the value of the property).

amount for which the plaintiff would like to sue. If the court had personal jurisdiction over the defendant, normally the defendant would have potential liability (assuming a judgment for the plaintiff) up to the full amount of the claim. However, if the court's jurisdiction was based on quasi in rem jurisdiction, and the thing seized was a bank account with a value of $400,000, the limit of the court's quasi in rem jurisdiction would be $400,000—the value of the asset.[3] The plaintiff would retain a claim for $600,000, but normally could not prosecute it in that same court, unless additional assets could be seized, or jurisdiction could be established on the basis of personal jurisdiction.

Important: Although quasi in rem jurisdiction may sometimes be less advantageous from a plaintiff's point of view, historically it has also posed dilemmas for defendants. Consider again the example mentioned above. If the plaintiff cannot obtain personal jurisdiction, the limit of the court's jurisdiction will be $400,000. An out-of-state defendant will have the choice of appearing in court to defend on the merits, or staying outside the state and defaulting. A decision to default obviously forfeits defenses on the merits. If the defendant appears, however, the plaintiff may be able to serve process in-state that will satisfy personal jurisdiction. The court could then hear plaintiff's claim for the full amount of $1,000,000. Thus defendant would be faced with the hard choice of defaulting on $400,000, or appearing and risking exposure for an additional $600,000. Some courts—but by no means all—resolved this dilemma by allowing defendant to make a "limited appearance," in which defendant could contest the merits of the quasi in rem claim ($400,000), but remain immune from service of process for personal jurisdiction while the $400,000 claim was litigated.[4] Nowadays the sixth requirement for quasi in rem jurisdiction, minimum contacts, has substantially eased this problem.

(2) *Territorial Requirement:* Courts exercising quasi in rem jurisdiction have a definite territorial limit to their jurisdiction. For quasi in rem jurisdiction to be sustained, the asset must be seized while it is within the territorial confines of the state in which the court sits.[5] Where the asset is something as tangible and immoveable as realty, the territorial requirement is not a

---

[3]*Shaffer v. Heitner*, 433 U.S. 186, 209, 97 S. Ct. 2569, 53 L. Ed. 2d 683 (1977) ("the value of the property seized [serves] to limit the extent of possible liability."). *Cf., Teyseer Cement Co. v. Halla Maritime Corp.*, 794 F.2d 472, 477 (9th Cir. 1986) (certain kinds of maritime jurisdiction are actually quasi in rem, "because any judgment rendered is limited to the value of the attached property").

[4]*See, e.g., U.S. v. First Nat. City Bank*, 379 U.S. 378, 390, 85 S. Ct. 528, 13 L. Ed. 2d 365 (1965) (noting split of authority on availability of limited appearance).

[5]*See, e.g., Glencore Grain Rotterdam B.V. v. Shivnath Rai Harnarain Co.*, 284 F.3d 1114, 1127 (9th Cir. 2002) ("[T]he sine qua non of basing jurisdiction on a defendant's assets in the forum is the identification

substantial hurdle—if the land is within the state, the land is not going to change its location. More mobile assets, such as automobiles, present somewhat more significant problems because there is some risk that they will be moved before attachment can occur. The biggest questions of territoriality, however, arise when the asset is an intangible item. Things such as accounts receivable or stock ownership in a corporation certainly have value, but they have no definite situs comparable to that of land or automobiles. Courts have resolved these problems with rules arbitrary in their nature, but generally followed for lack of a better solution. Depending on the law of the state where a corporation is incorporated, for example, shares in a corporation are generally held to be located either where the certificate evidencing ownership is found, or in the state where the entity is incorporated.[6]

Important: Quasi in rem jurisdiction is always territorial in nature. Thus, there is no need to address long-arm statutes, because such statutes are applicable only when the court is attempting to reach outside its own state's territory.[7]

(3) *Defendant's Asset:* Because the purpose of quasi in rem jurisdiction is to sue a particular defendant or group of defendants, it would make little sense if a suit against one person was sustained by seizure of the asset of another person, who was not a party and had no connection to the case. Certainly, in that case, the true defendant would have no incentive to appear in court, and the person whose property was seized would be entitled to retain the asset. Thus, the third requirement for quasi in rem jurisdiction is that the asset seized must at least arguably belong to the defendant. The defendant's title need not be absolutely clear, however. If the purpose of the plaintiff's suit is to resolve a dispute between the parties as to title in the asset that was seized, this requirement of quasi in rem jurisdiction is satisfied if the defendant merely claims the property or will claim the property.

(4) *Seizure or Attachment:* The court's quasi in rem jurisdiction cannot begin until the court has effective control of the asset.[8] The nature of the seizure depends heavily on the nature of the property seized, but generally it is enough that the court has effectively interfered with the defendant's control, even if

---

of [such an] asset.").

[6] *See, e.g., Shaffer v. Heitner,* 433 U.S. 186, 191, 97 S. Ct. 2569, 2573, 53 L. Ed. 2d 683 (1977) (Delaware law makes Delaware the situs of stock ownership in Delaware corporations). *See also Office Depot Inc. v. Zuccarini,* 596 F.3d 696, 702 (9th Cir. 2010) (under California law, for purposes of quasi in rem jurisdiction, internet domain names are located where domain name registry is located).

[7] *See, e.g., Newhard, Cook & Co. v. Inspired Life Centers, Inc.,* 895 F.2d 1226, 1228 (8th Cir. 1990) (if case is based on quasi in rem jurisdiction, long-arm requirements generally need not be satisfied).

[8] *See, e.g., Transportes Navieros y Terrestes S.A. de C.V. v. Fairmount Heavy Transport N.V.,* 572 F.3d 96 (2d Cir. 2009) ("[W]hen a court either refuses to issue or vacates an attachment, the court deprives itself of jurisdiction.").

the court does not have actual possession. With land, for example, the court can simply order that title be frozen in the local records office pending the outcome of the suit. With stock shares, the same can be accomplished by ordering the appropriate authority to halt trading in the particular shares at issue. By contrast, if the asset was a rare diamond, or an automobile, the court might take physical custody of the property.

(5) *Notice:* As with personal jurisdiction, quasi in rem jurisdiction requires notice to the defendant that will satisfy both constitutional due process and the service of process requirements of Rule 4. Application of the due process requirement is similar to that imposed on personal jurisdiction, with allowance for the fact that quasi in rem cases may sometimes require less notice to the defendant. This may occur because sometimes the act of seizing a defendant's property may reasonably be assumed to notify a defendant of the pendency of the case.[9]

(6) *Requirements of Fair Play: Minimum Contacts:* The due process requirement of "traditional notions of fair play and substantial justice" applies to quasi in rem jurisdiction. In practice, this means quasi in rem jurisdiction is likely to be sustained only in circumstances where the assets seized bear a substantial relation to the cause of action on which plaintiff is suing,[10] or in circumstances where other facts suggest that exercise of quasi in rem jurisdiction would not be fundamentally unfair to defendant.[11] Both of those standards are highly fact-specific. An attorney uncertain whether, under due process, quasi in rem jurisdiction can be sustained, should research carefully the developing case law in this area.

Relation to Rule 4

Rule 4(n) limits the circumstances in which a federal court may assert quasi in rem or in rem jurisdiction, even if an assertion of such jurisdiction is constitutionally sound. Basically, there are two circumstances where a federal court may employ such jurisdiction. First, Rule 4(n) permits jurisdiction if a federal statute authorizes it. In that situation, notice to affected parties is governed by other applicable provisions of Rule 4, presumably including nationwide service when it is appropriate. Second, Rule 4(n) permits such jurisdiction even in the absence of a federal statute authorizing it, if the court is unable to obtain personal jurisdiction over the defendant(s). In that circumstance, Rule 4(n) provides that jurisdiction will be

---

[9]*Cf., S.E.C. v. Ross,* 504 F.3d 1130, 1139 n.9 (9th Cir. 2007) ("Exercising *in rem* jurisdiction would have served to give notice to [defendant], but it would not have given the court *in personam* jurisdiction over him.").

[10]*Rush v. Savchuk,* 444 U.S. 320, 328, 100 S. Ct. 571, 62 L. Ed. 2d 516 (1980) ("[T]he mere presence of property does not establish [jurisdiction];"

property ownership may indicate other contacts, but property by itself will usually be insufficient).

[11]*But see Shaffer v. Heitner,* 433 U.S. 186, 204, 97 S. Ct. 2569, 53 L. Ed. 2d 683 (1977) (normally "relationship among the defendant, forum, and the litigation" is fulcrum of quasi in rem jurisdiction).

obtained according to the process of the state in which the district court sits.

Enforcing Judgments

It should be noted that the "minimum contacts" requirement for quasi in rem jurisdiction is applicable only in cases in which the plaintiff has brought a cause of action that will be litigated (assuming good jurisdiction) on the merits. By contrast, if the plaintiff has already won a judgment and seeks only to enforce the judgment against a defendant's assets, the requirement that the asset must have some relationship to the underlying litigation does not apply.[12] All the other elements, however, must still be met.

ADDITIONAL RESEARCH REFERENCES

C.J.S., Constitutional Law § 1139
C.J.S., Courts §§ 54 to 60
C.J.S., Federal Courts § 25(1, 2)
West's Key Number Digest, Constitutional Law ⊕305
West's Key Number Digest, Courts ⊕21
West's Key Number Digest, Federal Courts ⊕93

§ 2.9 Jurisdiction Over Persons or Things—Requirements for in Rem Jurisdiction

CORE CONCEPT

As its name suggests, in rem jurisdiction is closely related to quasi in rem jurisdiction—so much so, in fact, that courts occasionally use the two terms interchangeably. The most important difference is that in rem jurisdiction usually involves trying title to property and, in theory, determining the rights of all people throughout the world in that property.[1] Quasi in rem jurisdiction, by contrast, usually involves a much more discrete group of defendants, whose claims are usually far less theoretical. In practice, federal courts use in rem jurisdiction in fairly discrete areas of litigation. Those areas in which in rem jurisdiction may most often be employed are actions in admiralty, involving shipping on navigable waters where the vessel is seized as the basis

---

[12]*Shaffer v. Heitner*, 433 U.S. 186, 210, 97 S. Ct. 2569, 53 L. Ed. 2d 683 (1977) ("Once it has been determined by a court of competent jurisdiction that the defendant is a debtor of the plaintiff, there would seem to be no unfairness in allowing an action to realize on that debt in a State where the defendant has property, whether or not that State would have jurisdiction to determine the existence of the debt as an original matter.").

[1]*See, e.g., U.S. v. Real Property Located at 475 Martin Lane*, 545 F.3d 1134, 1144 (9th Cir. 2008) ("In rem actions are generally considered proceedings 'against all the world.' ").

of jurisdiction;[2] bankruptcy cases;[3] child-custody proceedings;[4] and civil condemnation of property that was the instrumentality of a crime, which the government now seeks to keep as its own.[5]

Important: If in rem jurisdiction is lacking, and the court also lacks personal jurisdiction and quasi in rem jurisdiction, the typical remedy is to dismiss the claim.

APPLICATIONS

Prerequisites: There are five prerequisites for a court to exercise in rem jurisdiction.

(1) *Thing of Value:* If the property whose title is at issue had no value, there would be little point to the litigation itself. As might be expected, this element of in rem jurisdiction is usually not difficult to satisfy.

(2) *Territorial Requirement:* Like quasi in rem jurisdiction, in rem jurisdiction is territorial in nature. The property must be located within the state in which the court sits at the onset of the action.[6]

(3) *Seizure by the Court:* The court's in rem jurisdiction cannot begin until the court has effective control of the asset.[7] The nature of the seizure depends heavily on the nature of the property seized, but generally it is enough that the court has effectively interfered with the defendant's control, even if the court does not have actual possession. With land, for example, the court can simply order that title be frozen in the local records office pending the outcome of the suit. With stock shares, the same can be accomplished by ordering the appropriate authority to halt trading in the particular shares at issue. By contrast, if the asset was a rare diamond, or an automobile, the marshal might take physical custody of the property.

(4) *Notice Requirement:* As with personal jurisdiction and quasi in rem jurisdiction, in rem jurisdiction requires notice to the defendant that will satisfy both due process and the service of process requirements of Rule 4. Otherwise, this is an area where in rem jurisdiction differs somewhat from quasi in rem

---

[2] *See, e.g., The Belgenland,* 114 U.S. 355, 5 S. Ct. 860, 29 L. Ed. 152 (1885).

[3] *Central Virginia Community College v. Katz,* 546 U.S. 356, 126 S. Ct. 990, 1000, 163 L. Ed. 2d 945 (2006) ("Bankruptcy jurisdiction, as understood today and at the time of the framing, is principally in rem jurisdiction.").

[4] *Struck v. Cook County Public Guardian,* 508 F.3d 858, 859 (7th Cir. 2007).

[5] *See, e.g., U.S. v. U.S. Coin and Currency,* 401 U.S. 715, 91 S. Ct. 1041, 28 L. Ed. 2d 434 (1971). *See also, U.S. v. One Parcel of Real Estate at 10380 SW 28th Street, Miami, FL,* 214 F.3d 1291, 1294 (11th Cir.2000). ("The focus of an in rem narcotics forfeiture is not the guilt of any person or the attempt to punish a person, but the 'guilt' of the property, *i.e.,* whether the property had been used in connection with illicit drug activity.").

[6] *See, e.g., In re Gallo,* 573 F.3d 433 (7th Cir. 2009) ("An out-of-state court does not have in rem jurisdiction over property in Florida, although it may place a constructive trust on such property.").

[7] *See, e.g., Petroleos Mexicanos Refinancion v. M/T King A,* 554 F.3d 99, 102 (3d Cir. 2009) (in rem jurisdiction requires existence of lien).

jurisdiction. Because the nature of an in rem case—trying title as to potential claimants throughout the world—is much more diffuse than that of a typical quasi in rem case, notice that will satisfy constitutional requirements of due process will often be by publication in newspapers, etc., rather than some form of personal service on a defendant. In this area in rem requirements are probably substantially more relaxed than those of personal or quasi in rem jurisdiction. It is important to note, however, that if the identity and location of a particular claimant is known to the defendant, then the requirement of better notice, such as mail service, probably applies. Additionally, courts must satisfy their own rules on service, in addition to constitutional requirements. Under Rule 4(e)(2), governing in rem attachments, federal courts are authorized to use the service of process rules of the state in which they sit.

(5) *Requirements of Fair Play:* As with cases grounded upon personal jurisdiction or quasi in rem jurisdiction, cases founded on in rem jurisdiction must also satisfy requirements of due process.[8] Because in rem actions always involve suits closely related to the property seized, however, the fairness requirements of due process are usually met without difficulty.[9]

Continuing Nature of In Rem Jurisdiction

It is settled that once a district court acquires in rem jurisdiction over a res, it can retain in rem jurisdiction throughout the case even if it loses physical control of the res.[10]

No Competing Assertions of In Rem Jurisdiction

It appears settled that if one court has established in rem jurisdiction over an asset, "a second court will not assume *in rem* jurisdiction over the same *res.*"[11]

Relation to Rule 4

Rule 4(n) limits the circumstances in which a federal court may assert quasi in rem or in rem jurisdiction, even if an assertion of such jurisdiction is constitutionally sound. Basically, there are two circumstances where a federal court may employ such jurisdiction. First, Rule 4(n) permits jurisdiction if a federal statute authorizes it. In that situation, notice to affected parties is governed by other applicable provisions of Rule 4, presumably including nationwide service when it is appropriate. Second, Rule 4(n) permits such jurisdiction even in the absence of a federal statute authorizing it, if the court is

---

[8]*See, e.g., Harrods Ltd. v. Sixty Internet Domain Names*, 302 F.3d 214, 224 (4th Cir. 2002) (minimum contacts analysis of *International Shoe* also apply to in rem actions).

[9]*See, e.g., Porsche Cars North America, Inc. v. Porsche.net*, 302 F.3d 248, 260 (4th Cir. 2002) (in case based upon in rem jurisdiction, where property itself is cause of action, jurisdiction is good in state where property is located).

[10]*Republic Nat. Bank of Miami v. U.S.*, 506 U.S. 80, 88, 113 S. Ct. 554, 121 L. Ed. 2d 474 (1992) ("Stasis is not a general prerequisite to the maintenance of jurisdiction.").

[11]*Marshall v. Marshall*, 547 U.S. 293, 126 S. Ct. 1735, 1748, 164 L. Ed. 2d 480 (2006).

unable to obtain personal jurisdiction over the defendant(s). In that circumstance, Rule 4(n) provides that jurisdiction will be obtained according to the process of the state in which the district court sits.

ADDITIONAL RESEARCH REFERENCES

C.J.S., Constitutional Law § 1139
C.J.S., Courts §§ 54 to 60
C.J.S., Federal Courts § 25(1, 2)
West's Key Number Digest, Constitutional Law ☞305
West's Key Number Digest, Courts ☞21
West's Key Number Digest, Federal Courts ☞93

§ 2.10 Subject Matter Jurisdiction in Federal District Courts—Introduction

Attorneys unfamiliar with federal trial courts often have substantial difficulty with two points about federal subject matter jurisdiction. First, federal courts are courts of *limited* subject matter jurisdiction, and thus will be unable to hear certain types of cases that could be brought routinely in a state trial court, which often enjoys a broader scope of subject matter jurisdiction. Second, the need to meet standards of federal subject matter jurisdiction is an *additional* requirement, separate from jurisdiction over persons and things, that must be satisfied before a federal trial court will hear a case.[1] Both subject matter jurisdiction and jurisdiction over persons and things must be satisfied *as to each count in a case* before a federal court will hear a count.[2] Failure to satisfy either requirement as to any count creates a substantial risk that the count will be dismissed, even if other counts may proceed. These requirements apply irrespective of whether the count arises in plaintiff's complaint, a counterclaim, a crossclaim, an impleader, or under any other relevant rule.

Distinctions between jurisdiction over persons or things and subject matter jurisdiction are best understood by considering the limitations each kind of jurisdiction places on a federal court.

---

[1]*Bell v. Hood*, 327 U.S. 678, 682, 66 S. Ct. 773, 776, 90 L. Ed. 939 (1946) (issue of whether complaint states cause of action should be decided after court determines that it has jurisdiction). *See, e.g., Glencore Grain Rotterdam B.V. v. Shivnath Rai Harnarain Co.*, 284 F.3d 1114, 1128 (9th Cir. 2002) (existence of subject matter jurisdiction, but not also personal jurisdiction, requires dismissal of case); *Southern Cross Overseas Agencies, Inc. v. Wah Kwong Shipping Group Ltd.*, 181 F.3d 410, 414 (3d Cir. 1999) (courts should decide jurisdiction first "and then address other issues only if there is jurisdiction").

[2]*But cf., Goetzke v. Ferro Corp.*, 280 F.3d 766, 778–79 (7th Cir. 2002) (state statute providing that claim may be heard only by administrative board may operate to strip state courts of jurisdiction, but not federal courts; if jurisdiction meets standards set by Congress, state law cannot bar federal district court's jurisdiction).

Jurisdiction over persons or things defines the limits of a court's reach to take control of litigation affecting a specific person or piece of property. Subject matter jurisdiction, by contrast, limits the kind of cases a court may hear, irrespective of where the affected persons or pieces of property may be found. Thus, if a person is served with process within a state where a court sits, the personal jurisdiction of the court is probably satisfied. But if the cause of action is of a kind that a federal court cannot hear, the court would still lack subject matter jurisdiction and the case should be dismissed.

◆ *Example:* Subject to exceptions discussed below under supplemental jurisdiction, federal courts may not hear causes of action based on state law if the plaintiff and defendant are citizens of the same state. This particular difference between subject matter jurisdiction and jurisdiction over persons and things may be explained by the following case. If plaintiff and defendant are both citizens of New York, and if the cause of action is a tort under state law, personal jurisdiction will be satisfied if the defendant is served with process within New York. However, the federal court will not have subject matter jurisdiction because suits based on state law, where the parties are citizens of the same state, do not fall within any of the categories of suits a federal court can hear. Thus the case should be dismissed, even though personal jurisdiction is satisfactory.

Affirmative Duty to Plead Jurisdiction: The burden of demonstrating that the requirements of federal subject matter jurisdiction are met rests on the party asserting the claim.[3]

Dismissal if Subject Matter Jurisdiction Absent: As the foregoing example suggests, the standard remedy for failure to satisfy subject matter jurisdiction is dismissal of the claim.[4]

Consent: Unlike personal jurisdiction, subject matter

---

[3]*Kokkonen v. Guardian Life Insurance Co. of America*, 511 U.S. 375, 377, 114 S. Ct. 1673, 128 L. Ed. 2d 391 (1994) (presumption is against subject matter jurisdiction; burden of establishing subject matter jurisdiction lies on party asserting it); *Merrell Dow Pharmaceuticals Inc. v. Thompson*, 478 U.S. 804, 810, 106 S. Ct. 3229, 92 L. Ed. 2d 650 (1986) ("[J]urisdiction may not be sustained on a theory that the plaintiff has not advanced."). *See also* Fed.R.Civ.P. Form 7 (indicating that subject matter jurisdiction should be alleged in com-

plaint).

[4]*Arbaugh v. Y&H Corp.*, 546 U.S. 500, 126 S. Ct. 1235, 1237, 163 L. Ed. 2d 1097 (2006) ("[W]hen a federal court concludes that it lacks subject-matter jurisdiction, the complaint must be dismissed in its entirety."); *Steel Co. v. Citizens for a Better Environment*, 523 U.S. 83, 118 S. Ct. 1003, 140 L. Ed. 2d 210 (1998) (first responsibility of court is to determine jurisdiction; if jurisdiction is lacking, court should dismiss without addressing merits). *But cf., McCready v. eBay, Inc.*, 453 F.3d 882 (7th Cir.2006) (if

jurisdiction cannot be obtained through consent of the parties.[5] The rationale is that limits on a federal district court's subject matter jurisdiction are grounded in a proper balance of federal and state judicial power, and it is not the prerogative of the parties to enter into agreements that have the effect of upsetting that balance. Moreover, because the parties cannot by consent confer subject matter jurisdiction on the court, Rule 12(h) provides no time limit on objections to subject matter jurisdiction. Instead, Rule 12(h)(3) stipulates that objections to subject matter jurisdiction can be raised "[w]henever" they appear, and that the court can act on motion of either party or on its own motion.[6]

Comparison with Quasi in Rem Jurisdiction: Quasi in rem jurisdiction and subject matter jurisdiction are separate and distinct concepts. Quasi in rem jurisdiction permits a court to exercise power over a defendant, because the court has control of property belonging to the defendant. Subject matter jurisdiction defines the kind of cases the court may hear. In a case where the plaintiff and defendant were both New York citizens, for example, a federal court in California might have quasi in rem jurisdiction if it attached property in California belonging to defendant. If the cause of action was based on state law, however, subject matter jurisdiction would be lacking because the parties were not of diverse citizenship.

The three kinds of federal subject matter jurisdiction most frequently encountered are: (1) federal question ju-

---

practicable, prior to dismissal, plaintiff will typically be allowed to amend complaint to correct defect in allegation of jurisdiction).

[5]*Insurance Corp. of Ireland, Ltd. v. Compagnie des Bauxites de Guinee*, 456 U.S. 694, 702, 102 S. Ct. 2099, 2104, 72 L. Ed. 2d 492 (1982) ("[N]o action of the parties can confer subject-matter jurisdiction upon a federal court. Thus, the consent of the parties is irrelevant."). *See also, Days Inns Worldwide, Inc. v. Patel*, 445 F.3d 899, 904 (6th Cir. 2006) ("[T]he parties cannot confer subject matter jurisdiction where it does not otherwise exist."); *Smith v. Ashland, Inc.*, 250 F.3d 1167 (8th Cir.2001) (subject matter jurisdiction cannot be conferred on court by consent of parties; however, parties may stipulate to fact of diversity based on citizenship of party).

[6]*Bender v. Williamsport Area School Dist.*, 475 U.S. 534, 541, 106 S. Ct. 1326, 1331, 89 L. Ed. 2d 501 (1986) ("[E]very federal appellate court has a special obligation 'to satisfy itself not only of its own jurisdiction, but also that of the lower courts in a case under review,' even though the parties are prepared to concede it."). *See, e.g., International Union of Operating Engineers v. County of Plumas*, 559 F.3d 1041, ___ (9th Cir. 2009) (defendant who asserted federal subject matter jurisdiction for purposes of removal "is not precluded from challenging subject matter jurisdiction on appeal"); *Fax Telecommunicaciones Inc. v. AT & T*, 138 F.3d 479, 485 (2d Cir. 1998) ("[W]e have an obligation to determine *sua sponte* whether the district court had jurisdiction to hear the case."); *State Farm Mut. Auto. Ins. Co. v. Powell*, 87 F.3d 93 (3d Cir. 1996) (permitting challenge to diversity jurisdiction, notwithstanding that issue was raised only in appellate court).

risdiction; (2) jurisdiction based on diversity of citizenship; and (3) supplemental jurisdiction.

Hypothetical Jurisdiction

Normally a court will address questions of jurisdiction before
it proceeds to the merits.[7] However, if the jurisdictional question arises from a statute rather than the Constitution, some
courts permit consideration of a non-jurisdictional questions
before the jurisdictional problem is resolved.[8]

§ 2.11 Subject Matter Jurisdiction in Federal District Courts—Federal Question Jurisdiction

CORE CONCEPT

Congress authorized jurisdiction in federal district courts "of
all civil actions arising under the Constitution, laws, or treaties
of the United States." 28 U.S.C.A. § 1331.[1] In addition, Congress
has enacted specific statutes authorizing federal district courts to
hear causes of action relating to certain areas of federal law. For
example, 28 U.S.C.A. § 1337 authorizes federal courts to hear
civil actions arising under federal laws regulating commerce. In
the same fashion, 28 U.S.C.A. § 1338 provides subject matter jurisdiction over claims arising under federal patent law, and 28
U.S.C.A. § 1343 authorizes a federal court to hear claims alleging
violations of federally guaranteed civil rights.

APPLICATIONS

28 U.S.C.A. § 1331 and Specific Jurisdictional Statutes

The substantial overlap between the broad jurisdictional
grant of § 1331 and the more discrete grants mentioned above
does not necessarily make the specific jurisdictional statutes
superfluous. For example, 28 U.S.C.A. § 1333, conferring
subject matter jurisdiction over admiralty claims, preempts
§ 1331 when the case arises in admiralty. Thus the plaintiff
must sue under § 1333, not § 1331,[2] and that has several
important consequences.

---

[7]*Steel Co. v. Citizens for a Better
Environment,* 523 U.S. 83, 101, 118 S.
Ct. 1003, 140 L. Ed. 2d 210 (1998).

[8]*See, e.g., Fama v. Commissioner
of Correctional Services,* 235 F.3d 804,
816 n.11 (2d Cir. 2002).

[1]*See also Up State Federal Credit
Union v. Walker,* 198 F.3d 372, 375 (2d
Cir. 1999) (contract disputes with
federal government are controlled by
federal common law and are thus
federal questions within meaning of
§ 1331); *Sam L. Majors Jewelers v.
ABX, Inc.,* 117 F.3d 922, 926 (5th Cir.
1997) (§ 1331 also provides jurisdictional foundation for cases arising

under federal common law).

[2]*See, e.g., New York State
Waterways Ass'n, Inc. v. Diamond,* 469
F.2d 419 (2d Cir. 1972). *See also
Shalala v. Illinois Council on Long
Term Care, Inc.,* 529 U.S. 1, 4, 120 S.
Ct. 1084, 1089, 146 L. Ed. 2d 1 (2000)
(most claims under Medicare Act can-
not invoke federal question jurisdic-
tion under § 1331; such claims are
usually consigned by statute to a spe-
cial administrative review process);
*International Science & Technology
Institute, Inc. v. Inacom Communica-
tions, Inc.,* 106 F.3d 1146, 1154 (4th
Cir. 1997) ("It is clear . . . that § 1331
is a general federal-question statute,

(1) *Exclusive Subject Matter Jurisdiction:* Under § 1333, the jurisdiction of the federal district court is *exclusive,* i.e., the claim cannot be brought in a state court. Exclusive subject matter jurisdiction is characteristic of many of the specific jurisdictional statutes like § 1333. Federal jurisdiction under § 1331, by contrast, is usually concurrent with that of state courts, which means the claims could have been filed *either* in federal court *or* in state court.[3] It is settled that if a federal cause of action is silent as to whether it lies within exclusive federal jurisdiction, or instead is subject to the concurrent jurisdiction of federal and state trial courts, the jurisdiction is concurrent—not exclusive.[4]

(2) *Limitations in Specific Statute:* If a cause of action must be filed under a specific jurisdictional statute like § 1333, the limitations associated with that cause of action attach to the filing. In admiralty cases, for example, there is no right to a jury trial. Under § 1331, jury trials are available as they would be under the more general constraints of the Seventh Amendment to the Constitution.[5]

Additionally, if other federal law precludes a court's use of § 1331 to obtain jurisdiction over a case, § 1331 is simply not available as a source of jurisdiction.[6]

(3) *Jurisdiction to Determine Jurisdiction:* While parties cannot confer subject matter jurisdiction on the court through mutual consent, it is nevertheless settled that if subject matter jurisdiction is in question a district court has jurisdiction to

---

which gives the district courts original jurisdiction unless a specific statute assigns jurisdiction elsewhere.").

[3]*Grubb v. Public Utilities Commission of Ohio,* 281 U.S. 470, 50 S. Ct. 374, 74 L. Ed. 972 (1930). *See also Mims v. Arrow Financial Services, LLL,* ___ U.S. ___, 132 S. Ct. 140, 151, 181 L. Ed. 2d 881 (2012) (existence of state court jurisdiction does not by itself preclude federal subject matter jurisdiction under § 1331; "[J]urisdiction conferred by 28 U.S.C. § 1331 should hold firm against 'mere implication flowing from subsequent legislation.'").

[4]*Tafflin v. Levitt,* 493 U.S. 455, 458–59, 110 S. Ct. 792, 794–95, 107 L. Ed. 2d 887 (1990) (presumption is in favor of concurrent jurisdiction, not exclusive jurisdiction).

[5]*See also, e.g., McCarthy v. Apfel,* 221 F.3d 1119, 1123 (9th Cir. 2000) (jurisdiction based on 42 U.S.C.A. § 405(g) of Social Security Act, rather than on 28 U.S.C.A. § 1331, would alter, *inter alia,* standard of proof from preponderance of evidence (§ 1331) to substantial evidence (§ 405(g))).

[6]*Your Home Visiting Nurse Services, Inc. v. Shalala,* 525 U.S. 449, 456, 119 S. Ct. 930, 933, 142 L. Ed. 2d 919 (1999) (citing 42 U.S.C.A. § 405(h), providing that "no action against . . . the [Secretary] or any officer or employee thereof shall be brought under section 1331 . . . of title 28 to recover on any claim under" the Medicare Act). *See also, e.g., GTE North, Inc. v. Strand,* 209 F.3d 909, 916 (6th Cir. 2000) (subject matter jurisdiction under § 1331 requires showing that cause of action arose under federal law *and* that § 1331 is not preempted by a more specific statute that strips district courts of subject matter jurisdiction). *But cf,* Newpage Wisconsin System, Inc. v. United Steel, Paper & Forestry, Rubber, Manufacturing, AFL-CIO/CLC, ___ F.3d ___, (7th Cir. 2011) (where more specific statute does not supercede § 1331, § 1331 may serve as a basis for federal subject matter jurisdiction).

decide that question.[7]

(3) *Absence of Specific Statute:* For many federal causes of action, the only statute authorizing enforcement in a federal court is 28 U.S.C.A. § 1331.[8] That is, many federal causes of action do not enjoy their own specific grant of jurisdiction, equivalent to those of §§ 1333, 1337, 1338, and 1343.

(4) *Suits Based on Treaties:* 28 U.S.C.A. § 1331 is the only provision authorizing subject matter jurisdiction in a federal district court to enforce a cause of action arising under "treaties of the United States."

Well-Pleaded Complaint Rule

In general, subject matter jurisdiction based on a federal question requires that the federal question must appear on a fair reading of a well-pleaded complaint.[9] Federal questions raised in the answer do not create jurisdiction.[10] The significance of the rule is to restrict substantially federal question jurisdiction. It is always possible, and often happens, that important federal questions will arise on the defendant's side of the case, *i.e.,* as a federal defense to a state cause of action. Such defenses, though otherwise appropriate, and perhaps even central to the merits of a case, will not typically confer federal question jurisdiction on a federal district court[11]—not because there is no federal question, but because the federal question

---

[7]*United States v. Ruiz,* 536 U.S. 622, 628, 122 S. Ct. 2450, 153 L. Ed. 2d 586 (2007) ("[I]t is familiar law that a federal court always has jurisdiction to determine its own jurisdiction.").

[8]*Cf., Verizon Maryland, Incorporated v. Global NAPS, Inc.,* 377 F.3d 355, 369 (4th Cir. 2004) ("When a 'case's resolution depends on resolution of a federal question sufficiently substantial to arise under federal law within the meaning of 28 U.S.C. § 1331,' there is § 1331 jurisdiction even though the relevant statute does not explicitly or implicitly provide for a cause of action.").

[9]*Caterpillar Inc. v. Williams,* 482 U.S. 386, 392, 107 S. Ct. 2425, 96 L. Ed. 2d 318 (1987) (federal question must be "presented on the face of the plaintiffs properly pleaded complaint"). *Cf., Duke Power Co. v. Carolina Environmental Study Group, Inc.,* 438 U.S. 59, 98 S. Ct. 2620, 57 L. Ed. 2d 595 (1978) (test is not whether plaintiff can actually recover on cause of action; test is whether allegation of federal cause of action is patently without merit and thereby deserves dismissal); *Perpetual Securities, Inc. v. Tang,* 290 F.3d 132, 136–37 (2d Cir. 2002) (alle-

gation of federal question must be colorable; mere allegation of federal question, without more, "will not automatically confer federal question jurisdiction"); *Harris v. Owens,* 264 F.3d 1282, 1289 (10th Cir. 2001) ("If the federal claim is not wholly frivolous, it suffices to establish federal jurisdiction even if it ultimately is rejected on the merits.").

[10]*See, e.g., Chicago Tribune Co. v. Board of Trustees of the University of Illinois.,* 680 F.3d 1001, 1003 (7th Cir. 2012) ("[A] potential federal defense is not enough to create federal jurisdiction under 1331."); *Hansen v. Harper Excavating, Inc.,* 641 F.3d 1216, 1220 (10th Cir. 2011) ("[T]hat the defendant possesses a federal defense is not sufficient to invoke federal question jurisdiction.").

[11]*See, e.g., Penobscot Nation v. Georgia-Pacific Corp.,* 254 F.3d 317 (1st Cir. 2001) (fact that case involves federal issue does not, of itself, satisfy § 1331; Supreme Court "has, for some time, required that it be apparent from the fact of the plaintiff's complaint either that a cause of action arise under federal law . . . or at least (in some cases) that a traditional state-law

arises only in a defense and not in a well-pleaded complaint.[12]

It should be noted that the term "well pleaded complaint" is a term of art and does not require the plaintiff to plead with any particular special skill. For purposes of federal question jurisdiction under § 1331 it is only necessary that the facts alleged in the complaint establish a cause of action arising under the Constitution, law or treaties of the United States.[13]

"Hypothetical" Jurisdiction

In the ordinary course of events, district courts are instructed to address and resolve jurisdictional questions before addressing questions going to the merits of a case.[14] However, there

---

cause of action (e.g., a tort or contract claim) present an important federal issue;" also noting that second alternative is very narrow exception); *Gritchen v. Collier*, 254 F.3d 807 (9th Cir. 2001) ("Simply raising a constitutional argument in defense of an action that is brought in state court does not open the federal forum."); *Iowa Management & Consultants, Inc. v. Sac & Fox Tribe of Mississippi in Iowa*, 207 F.3d 488, 489 (8th Cir. 2000) (plaintiff's anticipation that defendant will raise federal law as defense in contract litigation does not create federal question jurisdiction).

[12]*See, e.g., Metropolitan Life Ins. Co. v. Taylor*, 481 U.S. 58, 63, 107 S. Ct. 1542, 1546, 95 L. Ed. 2d 55 (1987) ("It is long settled law that a cause of action arises under federal law only when the plaintiff's well-pleaded complaint raises issues of federal law."). *Louisville & N.R. Co. v. Mottley*, 211 U.S. 149, 29 S. Ct. 42, 53 L. Ed. 126 (1908); *Butero v. Royal Maccabees Life Ins. Co.*, 174 F.3d 1207, 1212 (11th Cir. 1999) ("As an affirmative defense, [federal] preemption does not furnish federal subject-matter jurisdiction under 28 U.S.C. § 1331."). *Cf., Club Comanche, Inc. v. Government of Virgin Islands*, 278 F.3d 250, 260 (3d Cir. 2002) (action to quiet title to land where defendant's claim to land is based on federal law does not satisfy federal question jurisdiction; noting, however, authority reaching opposite result if action is to remove cloud on title, not to quiet title); *McClelland v. Gronwaldt*, 155 F.3d 507, 512 (5th Cir. 1998) (overruled by, Arana v. Ochsner Health Plan, 338 F.3d 433 (5th Cir. 2003)) (accepting general rule that

federal preemption does not, of itself, create jurisdiction under § 1331; noting, however, that when federal law completely preempts an area, so that any "state" claim is actually a mislabeled federal claim, claim is a federal cause of action under § 1331; acknowledging that this principle of complete preemption has limited application).

[13]*Franchise Tax Bd. of State of Cal. v. Construction Laborers Vacation Trust for Southern California*, 463 U.S. 1, 27–28, 103 S. Ct. 2841, 2855–56, 77 L. Ed. 2d 420 (1983) (case arises under § 1331 if "a well-pleaded complaint establishes either that federal law creates the cause of action or that the plaintiff's right to relief necessarily depends on resolution of a substantial question of federal law"). *See, e.g., Radici v. Associated Ins. Companies*, 217 F.3d 737 (9th Cir. 2000) (complaint erroneously asserted diversity jurisdiction; where court could clearly find federal question jurisdiction, error was insignificant). *See also Flowers v. First Hawaiian Bank*, 295 F.3d 966 (9th Cir.2002) ("An appropriate allegation that a claim arises 'under the Constitution, laws, or treaties of the United States,' 28 U.S.C. § 1331, is sufficient to vest a federal district court with jurisdiction to determine whether or not the claim actually does so arise, and if it does, to decide the issue the claim presents.").

[14]*Steel Co. v. Citizens for a Better Environment*, 523 U.S. 83, 94, 118 S. Ct. 1003, 140 L. Ed. 2d 210 (1998) (noting long line of Supreme Court cases requiring resolution of jurisdictional questions first). *See also Ruhrgas AG v. Marathon Oil Co.*, 526 U.S. 574, 119 S. Ct. 1563, 143 L. Ed. 2d 760 (1999)

remains some authority in some federal circuits for the idea that the "jurisdiction first" approach is limited to jurisdictional issues raised by Article III of the Constitution.[15] Attorneys must consult local precedent and practice.

Congressionally Chartered Corporations

Most companies incorporated in the United States are created and organized under the law of a particular state. However, a small number of corporations are created through Congressional enactment. Such federally created corporations may sue or be sued under § 1331 without regard to whether claims at issue arise under federal or state law.[16]

Constitutional Torts

In a few unusual circumstances the Supreme Court has recognized a right to a private suit for a constitutional violation, notwithstanding that neither the relevant constitutional provision nor federal statutory law expressly recognizes such a right.[17] The authority to file such an implied constitutional tort in federal district court is derived from 28 U.S.C.A. § 1331.[18]

Refusing to Plead a Federal Claim: Complete Preemption

Ordinarily, the plaintiff has control of the counts in his complaint and may therefore avoid federal question jurisdiction simply by foregoing claims based on federal law.[19] However, in areas where federal law has completely preempted state law, a

---

jurisdiction should be resolved before addressing merits question, but there is no rule requiring inquiry into subject matter jurisdiction before personal jurisdiction).

[15]U.S. Const. art. III, § 2, cl. 1. *See, e.g., Greenwood ex rel. Estate of Greenwood v. New Hampshire Public Utilities Com'n*, 527 F.3d 8, 13 (1st Cir. 2008) ("This court has consistently interpreted the *Steel Co.* rule as applying in its strict form only to issues going to Article III requirements."); *Jan's Helicopter Service, Inc. v. F.A.A.*, 525 F.3d 1299, 1305 (Fed. Cir. 2008) (distinguishing *Steel Co.* because subject matter jurisdiction in instant case came from different clause of Article III than was at issue in *Steel Co.*); *McBee v. Delica Co., Ltd.*, 417 F.3d 107 (1st Cir. 2005) (notwithstanding *Steel Co.*, addressing trademark issues before resolving personal jurisdiction issues).

[16]*Union Pac. Ry. Co. v. Myers*, 115 U.S. 1, 5 S. Ct. 1113, 29 L. Ed. 319 (1885). *See also, e.g., Aliotta v. National R.R. Passenger Corp.*, 315 F.3d 756,

758 (7th Cir. 2003) ("Federal question jurisdiction exists for congressionally incorporated corporations under 28 U.S.C.A. § 1331.").

[17]*See, e.g., Bivens v. Six Unknown Named Agents of Federal Bureau of Narcotics*, 403 U.S. 388, 91 S. Ct. 1999, 29 L. Ed. 2d 619 (1971) (federal officers' alleged violation of Fourth Amendment gives rise to private cause of action).

[18]*Correctional Services Corp. v. Malesko*, 534 U.S. 61, 122 S. Ct. 515, 151 L. Ed. 2d 456 (2001) (also citing Supreme Court cases creating private rights of action under Fifth and Eighth Amendments, as well as cases refusing to recognize additional rights; refusing to extend *Bivens* principles to permit suit for damages by halfway-house inmate against private defendants).

[19]*Caterpillar Inc. v. Williams*, 482 U.S. 386, 389, 107 S. Ct. 2425, 2427, 96 L. Ed. 2d 318 (1987) (normally, non-diverse plaintiff who has federal cause of action but who prefers to avoid federal district court "may avoid

plaintiff cannot avoid the federal question by pleading only state law.[20] It should be noted, however, that assertion of federal question jurisdiction under this corollary to the well-pleaded complaint rule applies only where federal law has completely preempted an area.[21]

Preemption as a Cause of Action

As is discussed immediately above, preemption is normally a defense available when a plaintiff has pleaded only state law claims and thereby tried to avoid applicable federal law. However, it is settled that the doctrine also permits a cause of action on grounds of preemption when the plaintiff seeks "to enjoin state officials from interfering with federal rights."[22]

Claims Under Federal Common Law

Where a cause of action is based on federal common law, it is settled that § 1331 provides a basis for federal question subject matter jurisdiction.[23]

State Claims That Depend on Federal Law

There is another narrow exception to the general rule that jurisdiction under § 1331 may be based only upon an allegation of a federal question in a well-pleaded complaint. Where the plaintiff's cause of action arises from state law, but depends for its resolution on "a substantial question of federal law," it is possible that a district court will have federal question jurisdiction under § 1331.[24] However, attorneys are cautioned that this is indeed a narrow exception to the general rule, extending the

---

federal jurisdiction by exclusive reliance on state law"); *The Fair v. Kohler Die & Specialty Co.*, 228 U.S. 22, 25, 33 S. Ct. 410, 411, 57 L. Ed. 716 (1913) ("[T]he party who brings a suit is master to decide what law he will rely upon.").

[20]*Beneficial Nat. Bank v. Anderson*, 539 U.S. 1, 8, 123 S. Ct. 2058, 2063, 156 L. Ed. 2d 1 (2003) ("When the federal statute completely pre-empts the state-law cause of action, a claim which comes within the scope of that cause of action, even if pleaded in terms of state law, is in reality based on federal law."); *Avco Corp. v. Aero Lodge*, 390 U.S. 557, 88 S. Ct. 1235, 20 L. Ed. 2d 126 (1968) (plaintiff sued union for breach of no-strike clause in contract; plaintiff did not assert applicable federal labor law; held, union could remove case to district court, because case was controlled by federal law notwithstanding plaintiff's plea of state law).

[21]*Beneficial Nat. Bank v. Anderson*, 539 U.S. 1, 7, 123 S. Ct.

2058, 2063, 156 L. Ed. 2d 1 (2003) (test of complete preemption is whether federal statute "wholly displaces" otherwise relevant state claims).

[22]*Shaw v. Delta Air Lines, Inc.*, 463 U.S. 85, 96, 103 S. Ct. 2890, 77 L. Ed. 2d 490 (1983). *See also, e.g., Southwestern Bell Telephone, LP v. City of Houston*, 529 F.3d 257 (5th Cir. 2008) (complaint that city ordinance is preempted by federal law is a federal question under § 1331).

[23]*National Farmers Union Insurance Co. v. Crow Tribe of Indians*, 471 U.S. 845, 850, 105 S. Ct. 2447, 85 L. Ed. 2d 818 (1985) (federal common law falls within ambit of federal law as contemplated by § 1331).

[24]*Grable & Sons Metal Products, Inc. v. Darue Engineering & Mfg.*, 545 U.S. 308, 125 S. Ct. 2363, 2367, 162 L. Ed. 2d 257 (2005) (but doctrine requires that state-law claim "really and substantially involves a dispute or controversy respecting the validity, construction, or effect of [federal] law"). *See also Verizon Maryland*,

scope of jurisdiction under § 1331 only modestly.[25]

Declaratory Judgments

The well-pleaded complaint rule applies to declaratory judgments in the following fashion. For a declaratory judgment action to rest on federal question jurisdiction, the federal question must be found on the defendant's side of the case. In other words, federal question jurisdiction exists if, had the suit been brought as a conventional case, the pleading of the declaratory judgment defendant, as a conventional plaintiff, would have stated a federal question.[26]

Weak Federal Claims: "Insubstantiality"

It is settled that the probability of defeat on the merits does not, by itself, strip a plaintiff's claim of federal question jurisdiction.[27] However, where a plaintiff files a claim that superficially appears to be a federal question but is actually only a "dressed up" state claim offered to satisfy federal question jurisdiction, the court may dismiss the claim. This

---

Incorporated v. Global NAPS, Inc., 377 F.3d 355 (4th Cir. 2004) ("When a 'case's resolution depends on resolution of a federal question sufficiently substantial to arise under federal law within the meaning of 28 U.S.C. § 1331,' there is § 1331 jurisdiction even though the relevant statute does not explicitly or implicitly provide for a cause of action."). *But cf., Nevada v. Bank of America Corp.*, 672 F.3d 661, 675 (9th Cir. 2012) (even if state law claim necessarily turns on "substantial and disputed question of federal law," finding of § 1331 jurisdiction should be approached with great care).

[25]*Empire Healthchoice Assur., Inc. v. McVeigh*, 547 U.S. 677, 126 S. Ct. 2121, 165 L. Ed. 2d 131 (2006) (no subject matter jurisdiction where insurance carrier sought reimbursement for payment of federal government's health insurance costs for third parties; held, claim was based on state law contract rights, not federal law; existence of great interest of federal government in health and welfare of federal workforce is insufficient to convert contract cause of action into federal cause of action; noting that category of exceptions is "special and small"); *Merrell Dow Pharmaceuticals Inc. v. Thompson*, 478 U.S. 804, 813–14, 106 S. Ct. 3229, 3234, 92 L. Ed. 2d 650 (1986) ("[T]he mere presence of a federal issue in a state cause of action

does not automatically confer federal-question jurisdiction." Congressional determination that no federal remedy exists for violation of federal statute means that claimed violation of federal statute as element of state claim "is insufficiently 'substantial' to confer federal-question jurisdiction"). *But cf., Downey v. State Farm Fire & Cas. Co.*, 266 F.3d 675, 682 (7th Cir. 2001) (insurance contract between private parties fell within § 1331 for two reasons: first, on particular facts of case it implicated provisions of federal flood control program; second, if private insurer did not pay, federal funds were at risk).

[26]*Skelly Oil Co. v. Phillips Petroleum Co.*, 339 U.S. 667, 70 S. Ct. 876, 94 L. Ed. 1194 (1950) *See also, e.g., Heydon v. MediaOne of Southeast Michigan, Inc.*, 327 F.3d 466, 470 (6th Cir. 2003) ("The Declaratory Judgment Act does not create an independent basis for federal subject matter jurisdiction."); *State of Mo. ex rel. Missouri Highway and Transp. Com'n v. Cuffley*, 112 F.3d 1332, 1335 (8th Cir. 1997) (In a declaratory judgment suit, "we must consider whether a well-pleaded complaint in . . . a traditional action would present a federal issue.").

[27]*Bell v. Hood*, 327 U.S. 678, 66 S. Ct. 773, 90 L. Ed. 939 (1946).

"insubstantiality doctrine" is only employed rarely.[28]

Sovereign Immunity

Section 1331 may authorize subject matter jurisdiction over a cause of action, but it does not, by itself, defeat a well-founded assertion of sovereign immunity.[29]

No Jurisdiction to Review State Court Decisions

Even in circumstances where a federal question may be found in a well-pleaded complaint, it is settled that district courts have no authority under § 1331 to hear challenges to existing state court judgments based on the presence of that federal question. Parties who wish to challenge such a judgment may ultimately seek relief from the United States Supreme Court, but the original jurisdiction vested in federal district courts by § 1331 does not extend to appellate jurisdiction over state judgments.[30]

Post-Filing Events

In general, jurisdiction is evaluated on the basis of facts as they existed at the time the complaint was filed. Events that occur subsequent to filing of the complaint normally have no bearing on the court's jurisdictional decision.[31]

Amount in Controversy

Unlike diversity jurisdiction, there is usually no requirement that federal question cases satisfy any specific dollar amount.[32] Thus, if a case arose under the federal civil rights laws, and

---

[28]See, e.g., Dixon v. Coburg Dairy, Inc., 330 F.3d 250, 255–56 (4th Cir. 2003) (noting that pretextual motive for miscast claim or patently insubstantial and frivolous claim is ground for invocation of rarely used doctrine). See also Young v. Hosemann, 598 F.3d 184, 188 (5th Cir. 2010) (while frivolous or insubstantial claims — "a claim which has no plausible foundation or which is clearly foreclosed by a prior Supreme Court decision — may be dismissed, it is normally true that upon assertion of "a cognizable federal claim, dismissal for want of jurisdiction is disfavored as a matter of policy").

[29]See, e.g., High Country Citizens Alliance v. Clarke, 454 F.3d 1177, 1181 (10th Cir.2006) ("§ 1331 will only confer subject matter jurisdiction where some other statute provides such a waiver").

[30]District of Columbia Court of Appeals v. Feldman, 460 U.S. 462, 476, 103 S. Ct. 1303, 1311, 75 L. Ed. 2d 206 (1983); Rooker v. Fidelity Trust

Co., 263 U.S. 413, 416, 44 S. Ct. 149, 150, 68 L. Ed. 362 (1923). See also Verizon Maryland, Inc. v. Public Service Com'n of Maryland, 535 U.S. 635, 644 n.3, 122 S. Ct. 1753, 1759 n.3, 152 L. Ed. 2d 871 (2002) ("The Rooker-Feldman doctrine . . . recognizes that [§ 1331] is a grant of original jurisdiction, and does not authorize district courts to exercise appellate jurisdiction over state-court judgments, which Congress has reserved to this Court.").

[31]See, e.g., Sallen v. Corinthians Licenciamentos LTDA, 273 F.3d 14, 23 (1st Cir. 2001) (noting only very narrow exceptions to general rule). But cf., Connectu LLC v. Zuckerberg, 522 F.3d 82, 91 (1st Cir. 2008) (where complaint originally founded on diversity of citizenship is properly amended as of right under Rule 15(a) to plead a federal question, normal rule of testing subject matter jurisdiction at time of original filing is inapposite).

[32]Arbaugh v. Y&H Corp., 546 U.S. 500, 126 S. Ct. 1235, 1239, 163 L. Ed. 2d 1097 (2006) ("Congress amended 28

the amount at issue was only ten dollars, the case would still qualify for federal subject matter jurisdiction.

Citizenship

Unlike diversity jurisdiction, the citizenship of parties in federal question cases has no relevance to subject matter jurisdiction. It is irrelevant, for example, if both the plaintiff and the defendant are citizens of the same foreign country, or if both the plaintiff and the defendant are citizens of the same American state.

No Domestic Relations Exception for Federal Questions

Unlike cases based on diversity jurisdiction, a case based on federal question jurisdiction that also involves domestic relations issues may be heard in a federal district court.[33] This is a different result than would normally be achieved in a domestic relations case where jurisdiction is based on diversity of citizenship. Diversity jurisdiction is discussed elsewhere in this text.

ADDITIONAL RESEARCH REFERENCES

C.J.S., Federal Courts §§ 27 to 43 et seq.
West's Key Number Digest, Federal Courts ⏦161 to 247

§ 2.12 Subject Matter Jurisdiction in Federal District Courts—Requirements for Diversity Jurisdiction

CORE CONCEPT

Subject matter jurisdiction based on diversity of citizenship permits a federal district court to hear state causes of action[1] if two basic requirements are fulfilled: the plaintiff must be a citizen of a state or jurisdiction other than that in which the defendant is a citizen; and the amount in controversy must exceed $75,000, exclusive of interest and costs.[2] Such claims are within the concurrent jurisdiction of federal courts, which means that they can be filed in either state court or federal court. Between twenty and twenty-five percent of the cases in federal court are founded on diversity jurisdiction, but a larger percentage of jurisdictional difficulties arise in this area.

U.S.C. § 1331 . . . to eliminate the amount-in-controversy threshold.").

[33]See, e.g., Atwood v. Fort Peck Tribal Court Assiniboine, 513 F.3d 943, 945 (9th Cir. 2008) (domestic relations bar to lawsuit applicable only in diversity cases, not federal question cases); U.S. v. Bailey, 115 F.3d 1222, 1231 (5th Cir. 1997) (domestic relations exception applicable only in di-

versity cases).

[1]See, e.g., LaSala v. Bordier et Cie, 519 F.3d 121, 139 (3d Cir. 2008) (diversity jurisdiction encompasses " 'all civil actions' ", notwithstanding that they arise under law of foreign country, if diversity of citizenship and amount in controversy requirements are met).

[2]28 U.S.C.A. § 1332.

APPLICATIONS

Diverse Citizenship

28 U.S.C.A. § 1332 describes four different circumstances that satisfy diversity of citizenship:

(1) when the plaintiff is a citizen of an American state other than that of which the defendant is a citizen;[3]

(2) when the parties on one side are citizens of American states, and the opposing parties are citizens or subjects of foreign states;[4]

(3) when the parties are citizens of different American states, and additional parties are citizens or subjects of foreign states;[5] and

(4) when a foreign state is a plaintiff suing citizens of American states.[6]

Citizenship of an Individual

For purposes of diversity jurisdiction, 28 U.S.C.A. § 1332(a) defines citizenship for an individual in an American state as domiciled in the state. Domicile normally requires that the individual has both a physical presence in the state and an intent to reside in the state indefinitely.[7] An amendment in 2012 to § 1332(a)(2) effectively closed one possible loophole through

---

[3]*Cf, Medical Assurance Co., Inc. v. Hellman*, 610 F.3d 371 (7th Cir. 2010) ("naked declaration" of diversity is insufficient; affidavits alleging diversity based on "the best of my knowledge and belief" are insufficient when they stand alone).

[4]*Ruhrgas AG v. Marathon Oil Co.*, 526 U.S. 574, 580 n.2, 119 S. Ct. 1563, 143 L. Ed. 2d 760 (1999) (presence of foreign corporations on both sides of case means requirement of complete diversity is not met and jurisdiction cannot be invoked under § 1332(a)(2)). *Cf., Iraola & CIA, S.A. v. Kimberly-Clark Corp.*, 232 F.3d 854, 859 (11th Cir. 2000) (citizens of American states on one side of case may themselves be citizens of various American states; rejecting argument that § 1332(a)(2) requires American citizens to be citizens of only one American state).

[5]Under this provision it appears settled that citizens or subjects of foreign states may be "additional parties" on both sides of a case. *See, e.g., Dresser Industries, Inc. v. Underwriters at Lloyd's of London*, 106 F.3d 494, 497–98 (3d Cir. 1997) (so holding; citing other authority).

[6]*But cf., Olympia Exp., Inc. v. Linee Aeree Italiane, S.P.A.*, 509 F.3d 347, 349 (7th Cir. 2007) ("[A] suit against a foreign state is not within [diversity] jurisdiction.").

[7]*See, e.g., Kanter v. Warner-Lambert Co.*, 265 F.3d 853, 857 (9th Cir. 2001) (state citizenship is domicile, not mere residence; residence is only physical presence, while domicile is residence plus intention to make permanent abode); *Palazzo ex rel. Delmage v. Corio*, 232 F.3d 38, 41 (2d Cir. 2000) ("An individual's citizenship . . . is determined by his domicile;" a natural person "has but one domicile"). *See also Wachovia Bank v. Schmidt*, 546 U.S. 303, 318, 126 S. Ct. 941, 951, 163 L. Ed. 2d 797 (2006) (an individual with multiple residences is nevertheless a citizen of only one state); *Washington v. Hovensa LLC*, ___ F.3d___, ___ (3d Cir. 2011) (when two requirements for change of plaintiff s domicile are met, domicile changes "instantly"); *Preston v. Tenet Healthsystem Memorial Medical Center, Inc.*, 485 F.3d 793, 797–98 (5th Cir. 2007) ("A person's state of domicile presumptively continues unless rebutted with sufficient evidence of change."). *See also Hall v. Curran*, 599 F.3d 70, 72 (1st Cir. 2010) (per curiam) ("In cases involving prisoners, the courts presume that the prisoner re-

which diverse jurisdiction involving aliens legally resident in the United States and domiciled in an American state might have been broader than more conventional diversity jurisdiction involving citizens of different American states. As now written, § 1332(a)(2) forecloses the possibility of diversity jurisdiction in a suit between a citizen of an American state and a legal resident alien who is domiciled in the same state.[8]

Prior to 2012 the last sentence of § 1332(a) provided that an alien lawfully resident in the United States and permanently residing in an American state would be treated, for diversity purposes, as a citizen of the American state in which the alien was domiciled.[9] That sentence is now deleted, with the apparently intended effect of ensuring that aliens permanently resident in the United States and domiciled in different states may not use diversity jurisdiction to sue one another in a district court.

Finally, if an American citizen is also a citizen of a foreign state, the only citizenship that may be evaluated for purposes of diversity jurisdiction is the individual's United States citizenship.[10] Thus, consistent with the result in the paragraph immediately above, when such a person is domiciled outside the United States, the person may not sue or be sued in diversity.[11]

Citizenship of Indian Tribes and Tribal Corporations

Most courts have concluded that individual Indian tribes are not citizens of a state for the purposes of § 1332.[12] At the same time, however, tribal corporations are normally treated as equivalent to state corporations for purposes of diversity jurisdiction.[13] Unincorporated tribal associations, by contrast, are treated in similar fashion to other non-Indian unincorporated associations, i.e., they normally may not sue or be sued

---

mains a citizen of the state where he was domiciled before his incarceration, even if he is subsequently incarcerated in a different state." Presumption is rebuttable, though to do so requires more than prisoner's unsupported allegations); *McCormick v. Aderholt*, 293 F.3d 1254, 1257–58 (11th Cir. 2002) (change of domicile requires, concurrently, physical presence at new domicile and intention to reside there indefinitely).

[8]28 U.S.C. § 1332(a)(2).

[9]*See, e.g., Saadeh v. Faouki*, 107 F.3d 52, 58 (D.C. Cir. 1997).

[10]*See, e.g., Sanchez v. Aerovias de Mexico, S.A.*, 590 F.3d 1027, 1028 n.1 (9th Cir. 2010) ("[D]ual-citizenshp poses no jurisdictional problem."); *Swiger v. Allegheny Energy, Inc.*, 540 F.3d 179, 185 (3d Cir. 2008) (where party has dual United States and United

Kingdom citizenship, with domicile outside the United States, only applicable nationality is that of United States; thus no diversity jurisdiction).

[11]*See, e.g., Frett-Smith v. Vanterpool*, 511 F.3d 396, 400 (3d Cir. 2008) ("The only way that an American national, living abroad, can sue under § 1332 is under § 1332(a)(1) if that national is a citizen, i.e., domiciled, in one of the fifty U.S. states.").

[12]*See, e.g., Wells Fargo Bank, N.A. v. Lake of the Torches Economic Development Corp.*, 656 F.3d 684, 693 (7th Cir. 2011) (citing other circuits; but acknowledging that individual members of tribe are state citizens).

[13]*See, e.g., Cook v. AVI Casino Enterprises, Inc.*, 548 F.3d 718, 723 (9th Cir. 2008) (tribal corporations are citizens of state for diversity purposes).

on the basis of diversity jurisdiction.[14] The relationship of non-Indian unincorporated associations is addressed in greater detail later in this subsection.

Corporate Citizenship

28 U.S.C.A. § 1332(c) provides that for diversity purposes a corporation[15] is a citizen both of the state where it is incorporated and the state in which it has its principal place of business.[16] If a corporation is incorporated in more than one state, then it is a citizen of every state where incorporated.[17] However, a corporation will have only one principal place of business.[18] Thus, depending on the particular facts of incorporation and location of business operations, a corporation may be a citizen of one, two, or even more jurisdictions for diversity purposes.[19] Historically, the lower courts had developed different approaches to the determination of a principal place of

---

[14]*See, e.g., Miccosukee Tribe of Indians of Florida v. Kraus-Anderson Construction Co.*, 607 F.3d 1268, 1276 (11th Cir. 2010) (majority view does not permit unincorporated Indian tribes to sue in diversity).

[15]*Cf. Samantar v. Yousuf,* __ U.S. __, 130 S. Ct. 2278, 2287, 176 L. Ed. 2d 1047 (2010) (natural persons cannot be citizens under § 1332(c)).

[16]*See, e.g., MacGinnitie v. Hobbs Group, LLC*, 420 F.3d 1234, 1239 (11th Cir. 2005) ("For diversity purposes a corporation is a citizen of both the state where it is incorporated and the state where it has its principal place of business."). *But cf., MAS Capital, Inc. v. Biodelivery Sciences Intern., Inc.*, 524 F.3d 831, 832 (7th Cir. 2008) (where corporation is incorporated in American state but has principal place of business in foreign country, "foreign principal place of business does not count" for assessment of citizenship); *Torres v. Southern Peru Copper Corp.*, 113 F.3d 540, 543 (5th Cir. 1997) (reference in § 1332(c) to "State" is reference "only to the fifty states, Territories, District of Columbia, and Puerto Rico, but not to foreign states").

[17]*See, e.g., Freeman v. Northwest Acceptance Corp.*, 754 F.2d 553, 558 (5th Cir. 1985) (if parent and subsidiary are treated as a single corporation, then all states of incorporation are states in which the corporation is a citizen). *Cf., Wild v. Subscription Plus, Inc.*, 292 F.3d 526, 528–29 (7th Cir. 2002) (held, where corporate charter is revoked at time of filing but was later restored, revocation does not affect corporation's status for diversity purposes; noting that state law permitted corporation to sue and be sued in its own name until corporation was actually dissolved). *But see Universal Licensing Corp. v. Paola del Lungo S.p.A.*, 293 F.3d 579, 581 (2d Cir. 2002) (corporation "could not be considered to be incorporated in a state that had revoked its corporate charter").

[18]*Wachovia Bank v. Schmidt*, 546 U.S. 303, 126 S. Ct. 941, 951, 163 L. Ed. 2d 797 (2006) (ordinarily a corporation is a citizen "of at most 2 States;" "[A] corporation surely is not deemed a citizen of every State in which it maintains a business establishment."); *Cf., Cincinnati Ins. Co. v. Eastern Atlantic Ins. Co.*, 260 F.3d 742, 747 (7th Cir. 2001) (noting with some irritation that doing business is not the same as the rule that corporate citizenship may rest upon corporation's principal place of business).

[19]*See, e.g., Union Pacific R. Co. v. 174 Acres of Land Located in Crittenden County, Ark.*, 193 F.3d 944, 946 (8th Cir. 1999) (for purposes of diversity it is "long recognized that a corporation can be incorporated in more than one State"). *Cf., Wachovia Bank v. Schmidt*, 546 U.S. 303, 126 S. Ct. 941, 945, 163 L. Ed. 2d 797 (2006) (for purposes of diversity, nationally chartered bank is "located," pursuant to 28 U.S.C.A. § 1348, only in state where main office is located); *Lincoln Property Co. v.*

business, but it now seems settled that a corporation's principal place of business for purposes of diversity jurisdiction is the corporate "nerve center." That is, the principal place of business is the place from which the corporation's officers control its operation.[20]

Important: If a corporation has citizenship in more than one jurisdiction, the opposing party must be diverse from *all* the citizenships, or diversity is not established.[21]

Corporation with Foreign Contacts

Previously there was uncertainty as to whether the foreign contacts of some corporations were to be taken into account in determining corporate citizenship for diversity purposes. The legislative changes that took place at the beginning of 2012 have substantially resolved that issue. Under amended § 1332(c), the place(s) of incorporation and principal place of business of a corporation are to be taken into account in determining eligibility for diversity jurisdiction. Thus, for example, in a suit involving a citizen of an American state and a corporation incorporated under foreign law but with a principal place of business in the same American state, diversity jurisdiction would be lacking.[22]

Along a similar line of reasoning, an alien living abroad who sued an American corporation with its principal place of business abroad would also fail to meet the clarified requirements of diversity jurisdiction.[23]

Corporations No Longer Doing Business

In unusual cases it may occur that a corporation has *no* place of business at the time a lawsuit is filed. This situation can occur when a corporation remains incorporated but is simply not presently doing any business. Two differing approaches have been developed to deal with that situation. The first looks to the corporation's most recent place of business to help determine citizenship.[24] The second approach concludes that because a corporation ceased operations before the lawsuit was filed, it

---

Roche, 546 U.S. 81, 126 S. Ct. 606, 614–16, 163 L. Ed. 2d 415 (2005) (for purpose of diversity, corporation that is a real party in interest does not acquire citizenship of its affiliates).

[20]*Hertz Corp. v. Friend*, __ U.S. __, 130 S. Ct. 1181, 1191–92, 175 L. Ed. 2d 1029 (2010) (distinguishing an office where corporation holds, e.g., board meetings as not the principal place of business).

[21]*See, e.g., Hall v. Rental Associates, Inc.*, 833 F.2d 370 (D.C. Cir. 1987) (plaintiff must be diverse from both corporate citizenships).

[22]28 U.S.C. § 1332(c)(1).

[23]28 U.S.C. § 1331(c)(1).

[24]*See, e.g., Harris v. Black Clawson Co.*, 961 F.2d 547, 551 (5th Cir. 1992) (state where corporation last conducted business is relevant to inquiry); *Wm. Passalacqua Builders, Inc. v. Resnick Developers South, Inc.*, 933 F.2d 131, 141 (2d Cir. 1991) (diversity includes state where party "last transacted business"). *Cf., Athena Automotive, Inc. v. DiGregorio*, 166 F.3d 288, 291–92 (4th Cir. 1999) (where party had stopped doing business in state where lawsuit was later filed, but continued doing business in another state, party no longer had principal place of business in forum state and was therefore diverse from opposing party who was citizen of forum).

has no place of business for purposes of diversity jurisdiction.[25]

There is also some uncertainty as to the threshold issue of the kinds of facts necessary to establish whether a corporation has actually ceased business operations.[26] This entire area obviously requires that attorneys consult the local practice.

Unincorporated Associations

For diversity purposes, unincorporated associations such as partnerships, joint ventures, and labor unions are treated as citizens of every state in which one or more of their members is a citizen.[27] Thus, for very large unincorporated entities, such as national labor unions with members in every state, diversity of citizenship is unlikely to exist between the labor union and its opponent in a lawsuit.[28] It is also important to note that for purposes of diversity jurisdiction, limited liability companies are unincorporated associations, whose citizenship is therefore determined by the citizenship of all its members.[29]

Exception: When the case involves class litigation, a recent amendment to 28 U.S.C.A. § 1332 may produce a different result than was available under established case law. In the future, for class actions, the citizenship of an unincorporated association shall be both the state where it has its principal place of business and the state under whose laws it is organized.[30]

Trusts

It is settled that for purposes of § 1332(a), trusts take the citizenship of the trustee. The citizenship of beneficiaries of the

---

[25]*See, e.g., Midlantic Nat. Bank v. Hansen,* 48 F.3d 693, 696 (3d Cir. 1995) (inactive corporation has no principal place of business and therefore is citizen of state of incorporation).

[26]*See, e.g., Grand Union Supermarkets of the Virgin Islands, Inc. v. H.E. Lockhart Management, Inc.,* 316 F.3d 408, 409–11 (3d Cir. 2003) ("corporate trappings," such as paying franchise taxes, filing corporate reports, or the qualifications required to potentially conduct business in the future are not enough if company is not entering contracts, hiring employees, making sales, maintaining an address, possessing office equipment or owning property; "[A] corporation must actually conduct business for it to have a principal place of business.").

[27]*Carden v. Arkoma Associates,* 494 U.S. 185, 195–96, 110 S. Ct. 1015, 1021, 108 L. Ed. 2d 157 (1990) (in diversity cases a limited partnership has the citizenship of every general part-

ner and limited partner). *See, e.g., American Vantage Companies, Inc. v. Table Mountain Rancheria,* 292 F.3d 1091, 1093 (9th Cir. 2002) ("[A]n unincorporated Indian tribe . . . is not a 'citizen' of a state within the meaning of the federal diversity statute . . . and thus cannot sue or be sued in diversity."); *Riley v. Merrill Lynch, Pierce, Fenner & Smith, Inc.,* 292 F.3d 1334 (11th Cir. 2002) (business trust has citizenship of all its shareholders).

[28]*See, e.g., Belle View Apartments v. Realty ReFund Trust,* 602 F.2d 668 (4th Cir. 1979) (diversity fails because citizenships of unincorporated associations' memberships overlap).

[29]*See, e.g., Harvey v. Grey Wolf Drilling Co.,* 542 F.3d 1077, 1080 (5th Cir. 2008); *Pramco, LLC ex rel. CFSC Consortium, LLC v. San Juan Bay Marina, Inc.,* 435 F.3d 51 (1st Cir. 2006).

[30]28 U.S.C.A. § 1332(d)(10).

trust is irrelevant to an analysis of diversity jurisdiction.[31]

States of United States are Not Citizens

It is settled that for purposes of diversity jurisdiction, an American state is not a "citizen."[32]

Two results follow from that principle. First, a state cannot be used to create diversity jurisdiction when the opposing party is from another state.[33] Second, a state's presence in a suit where diversity jurisdiction is otherwise satisfied, *i.e.*, by the presence of other parties who are diverse, will normally not destroy that jurisdiction.[34]

"Stateless" Foreign Persons and Corporations

Section 1332(a)(2) confers diversity jurisdiction in suits between citizens of an American state and citizens or subjects of foreign states (assuming that the amount-in-controversy requirement is also satisfied). However, some parties, who are clearly not citizens of any American state, also may not enjoy the status of citizens of foreign states because they are citizens of some sort of governmental unit that does not possess the elements of sovereignty. Until recently there was substantial disagreement as to whether corporations who are not citizens of American states and do not enjoy full citizen status under a foreign sovereign could nevertheless be citizens or subjects of a foreign state for purposes of § 1332(a)(2). The disagreement is now resolved. Such a corporation is now treated as a citizen or subject of a foreign sovereign for purposes of diversity.[35]

Non-American Causes of Action

Assuming that the parties are appropriately diverse and the amount in controversy requirement is satisfied, subject matter jurisdiction under § 1332 normally extends to causes of action

---

[31]*Navarro Savings Assocation v. Lee*, 446 U.S. 458, 463, 100 S. Ct. 1779, 64 L. Ed. 2d 425 (1980). *See, e.g., Grede v. Bank of New York Mellon*, 598 F.3d 899, 901 (7th Cir. 2010) ("[A] trust's citizenship is that of the trustee, rather than the beneficiaries.").

[32]*Moor v. County of Alameda*, 411 U.S. 693, 717–18, 93 S. Ct. 1785, 366 L. Ed. 2d 596 (1973) ("There is no question that a State is not a 'citizen' for purposes of diversity jurisdiction," but a county may be a citizen because it is more than a mere "arm" of a State.).

[33]*Moor v. County of Alameda*, 414 U.S. 693, 93 S. Ct. 1785, 366 L. Ed. 2d 596 (1973).

[34]*Missouri, Kansas & Texas Railway Co. v. Hickman*, 183 U.S. 53, 59, 22 S. Ct. 18, 46 L. Ed. 78 (1901) (state's presence defeats diversity jurisdiction only if "the relief sought is that which inures to it alone, and in its favor the judgment or decree, if for the plaintiff, will effectively operate.").

[35]*JPMorgan Chase Bank v. Traffic Stream (BVI) Infrastructure Ltd.*, 536 U.S. 88, 122 S. Ct. 2054, 153 L. Ed. 2d 95 (2002) (British Virgin Islands corporation may appropriately be a citizen of United Kingdom for diversity purposes; issue is governed by construction of § 1332, not foreign law (although in instant case foreign law and § 1332 are harmonious); held, corporation may be a citizen of United Kingdom notwithstanding that it is organized under law of British Overseas Territory, not law of Britain itself). *See also Stiftung v. Plains Marketing, L.P.*, 603 F.3d 295, 298 (5th Cir. 2010) (foreign law determines whether foreign entity is a jurisdictional person for purposes of § 1332).

arising under the laws of foreign countries.[36]

Foreign Citizens Suing One Another

28 U.S.C.A. § 1332 contains no provision authorizing citizens or subjects of one foreign state to sue citizens or subjects of another foreign state in diversity. Thus if a subject of Great Britain sought to use a federal district court to sue a citizen of Brazil on a state cause of action, diversity jurisdiction would not exist.[37]

District of Columbia, Puerto Rico, and U.S. Territories

For purposes of diversity jurisdiction, 28 U.S.C.A. § 1332(e) treats jurisdictions such as the District of Columbia, Puerto Rico, the Virgin Islands, Guam, etc., as American states. Thus, persons domiciled in those jurisdictions will typically be treated as citizens of those "states" for diversity purposes.[38]

U.S. Citizens Domiciled in Foreign Countries

Americans domiciled abroad are obviously not domiciled in an American state. Thus, they cannot be citizens of an American state for diversity purposes. At the same time, American citizens domiciled abroad are not citizens or subjects of the foreign countries in which they reside. Thus they do not qualify for diversity jurisdiction as citizens or subjects of foreign states. The result, anomalous as it may seem, is that American citizens domiciled abroad do not qualify for diversity jurisdiction under any of the four categories of 28 U.S.C.A. § 1332, and thus may not sue or be sued in a federal district court on the basis of diversity jurisdiction.[39]

Note, however, that such persons may qualify for federal

---

[36]*See, e.g., LaSala v. Bordier et Cie*, 519 F.3d 121, 139 (3d Cir. 2008) ("Congress has the authority to counter-instruct district courts not to entertain particular categories of civil actions arising under foreign law, but we do not believe that we should readily imply such a result from statutory text that appears to direct otherwise.").

[37]*See, e.g., Franceskin v. Credit Suisse*, 214 F.3d 253, 258 (2d Cir. 2000) (if plaintiff is citizen of a foreign country and defendant is incorporated in a different foreign country but maintains principal place of business in United States, diversity is still lacking). *But see Universal Licensing Corp. v. Paola del Lungo S.p.A.*, 293 F.3d 579, 581 (2d Cir. 2002) ("[D]iversity is lacking . . . where the only parties are foreign entities, or where on one side there are citizens and aliens and on the opposite side there are only aliens."); *Saadeh v. Farouki*, 107 F.3d 52, 61 (D.C. Cir. 1997) (§ 1332 "did not confer diversity jurisdiction over a lawsuit between an alien on one side and an alien and a citizen on the other side, regardless of the residence status of the aliens").

[38]Until recently, the relevant provision was § 1332(d). However, that provision is now re-designated as § 1332(e). *See, e.g., U.S. v. Cirino*, 419 F.3d 1001, 1004 (9th Cir. 2005) ("Congress . . . has determined that Puerto Rico is to be treated as a 'state' for purposes of diversity jurisdiction."); *Brown v. Francis*, 75 F.3d 860, 865 (3d Cir. 1996) (for purposes of diversity jurisdiction, Virgin Islands is a state). *But cf., Barwood, Inc. v. District of Columbia*, 202 F.3d 290, 292 (D.C. Cir. 2000) (District of Columbia is treated as a state under § 1332, but it is "not a citizen of a state (or of itself)"; thus, where District of Columbia is a defendant, there is no diversity).

[39]*Newman-Green, Inc. v. Alfonzo-Larrain*, 490 U.S. 826, 828, 109 S. Ct.

court if the cause of action rests on a federal question, discussed above. It is also possible that such persons may sue or be sued in federal court if they fit within the description of supplemental jurisdiction, discussed below.

Suits Against the United States

Section 1332 does not create subject matter jurisdiction for suits against the United States.[40]

Form Selection Clauses

A forum selection clause in a contract choosing, e.g., a particular state trial court does not automatically oust a federal district court of its otherwise property diversity jurisdiction. However, assuming the clause is freely negotiated and unaffected by fraud or excessively unbalanced bargaining power, it will normally be enforced.[41]

Timing of Citizenship

The parties must be diverse at the time the suit is filed.[42] It is irrelevant that the parties may not have been diverse at the time the cause of action arose,[43] or that a party diverse at the time of filing acquires a non-diverse citizenship in the course of

---

2218, 104 L. Ed. 2d 893 (1989) (United States citizen domiciled abroad cannot meet diversity requirements of § 1332). *See, e.g., Coury v. Prot*, 85 F.3d 244, 248 (5th Cir. 1996) ("An American national, living abroad, cannot sue or be sued in federal court under diversity jurisdiction . . . unless that party is a citizen, *i.e.* domiciled, in a particular state of the United States."); *Sadat v. Mertes*, 615 F.2d 1176, 1183 (7th Cir. 1980) (An American citizen's domicile abroad does not thereby make him a citizen of a foreign state.).

[40]*See, e.g., U.S. v. Park Place Associates*, 563 F.3d 907, 919 (9th Cir. 2009) ("The United States . . . is neither a state nor a citizen of a state, and may neither sue nor be sued under § 1332.").

[41]*M/S Bremen v. Zapata Off-Shore Co.*, 407 U.S. 1, 13, 92 S. Ct. 1907, 32 L. Ed. 2d 513 (1972).

[42]*Grupo Dataflux v. Atlas Global Group, L.P.*, 541 U.S. 567, 124 S. Ct. 1920, 158 L. Ed. 2d 866 (2004) (party's post-filing change in citizenship cannot cure lack of subject matter jurisdiction that existed at time of filing); *Dole Food Co. v. Patrickson*, 538 U.S. 468, 477, 123 S. Ct. 1655, 1662, 155 L. Ed. 2d 643 (2003) ("It is well settled . . . that federal-diversity jurisdiction depends on the citizenship of the par-

ties at the time suit is filed."). *But see Wild v. Subscription Plus, Inc.*, 292 F.3d 526, 528 (7th Cir. 2002) (held, where corporate charter is revoked at time of filing but was later restored, revocation does not affect corporation's status for diversity purpose; noting that state law permitted corporation to sue and be sued in its own name until corporation was actually dissolved; citing this circumstances as exception to general rule); *Soberay Mach. & Equipment Co. v. MRF Ltd., Inc.*, 181 F.3d 759, 763 (6th Cir. 1999) ("Although we agree that a party may not create diversity by dropping a nondiverse and indispensable party, we note that it is appropriate to drop a nondiverse and dispensable party from litigation in order to achieve diversity.").

[43]*See, e.g., Associated Ins. Management Corp. v. Arkansas General Agency, Inc.*, 149 F.3d 794 (8th Cir.1998) ("[W]e determine diversity of citizenship at the time an action is filed; . . . the district court cannot retroactively create diversity jurisdiction if it did not exist when the complaint was filed."). *Rodriguez-Diaz v. Sierra-Martinez*, 853 F.2d 1027, 1029 (1st Cir. 1988) ("It is the domicile at the time suit is filed which controls, and the fact that the plaintiff has changed his domicile with the purpose

the lawsuit.[44] Thus, if a citizen of New York seeks to sue another New York citizen in federal district court over a state cause of action, the plaintiff could create diversity of citizenship by making a genuine change of domicile from New York to another jurisdiction prior to filing suit.

It should be noted that recent Congressional amendments to 28 U.S.C.A. § 1332, governing diversity jurisdiction, have tended to adopt the existing case law approach to the timing of diversity jurisdiction.[45]

Comparison with Timing of Jurisdiction Assessment in Removed Cases

As is discussed immediately above, when a case is filed originally in a federal district court, diversity jurisdiction is normally evaluated as of the date of the filing.[46] However, when a case arrives in federal district court through the process of removal,[47] the analysis of jurisdiction is made as of the date the removal petition was filed,[48] which will normally occur at some time after the case was originally filed. Jurisdiction in removed cases is discussed in greater detail later in this book.

Complete Diversity

To satisfy diversity jurisdiction, *all* plaintiffs must have citizenship different from that of *all* defendants.[49] There is no requirement that plaintiffs have citizenships different from one

---

of bringing a diversity action in federal court is irrelevant."). *See also Hartford Ins. Group v. Lou-Con Inc.*, 293 F.3d 908 (5th Cir. 2002) (facts underlying jurisdictional amount are judged as of filing complaint).

[44]*See, e.g., Bank One, Texas, N.A. v. Montle*, 964 F.2d 48, 49 (1st Cir. 1992) ("Domicile is determined as of the time the suit is filed, and once diversity jurisdiction is established, it is not lost by a later change in domicile."). *But cf., Dominium Austin Partners, L.L.C. v. Emerson*, 248 F.3d 720, 725 (8th Cir. 2001) (subject matter jurisdiction is usually evaluated at commencement of action; exception exists where nondiverse but indispensable party is later joined under Rule 19). *Cf., Meridian Sec. Ins. Co. v. Sadowski*, 441 F.3d 536, 538 (7th Cir. 2006) (if amount in controversy was met at outset, subsequent award of less than that amount does not terminate diversity jurisdiction).

[45]28 U.S.C.A. § 1332(d)(7) (citizenship in most class actions to be determined as of date of filing original or amended complaint, or, if case did not originally qualify for federal sub-

ject matter jurisdiction, as of date federal subject matter jurisdiction might have existed).

[46]*But cf., Dominium Austin Partners, L.L.C. v. Emerson*, 248 F.3d 720, 725 (8th Cir. 2001) (noting exception where nondiverse indispensable party is joined under Rule 19 subsequent to initial filing).

[47]*See* 28 U.S.C.A. §§ 1441, 1446.

[48]*Pullman Co. v. Jenkins*, 305 U.S. 534, 547, 59 S. Ct. 347, 349, 83 L. Ed. 334 (1939). *But see Ryan ex rel. Ryan v. Schneider National Carriers, Inc.*, 263 F.3d 816, 819 (8th Cir. 2001) ("In the case of a removed action, diversity [of citizenship] must exist both when the state action is filed and when the petition for removal is filed.").

[49]*Exxon Mobil Corp. v. Allapattah Services, Inc.*, 545 U.S. 546, 125 S. Ct. 2611, 2617, 162 L. Ed. 2d 502 (2005) (acknowledging that complete diversity is not a constitutional mandate, but "we have consistently interpreted § 1332 as requiring complete diversity: In a case with multiple plaintiffs and multiple defendants, the presence in the action of a single plaintiff from the same state as a single defendant de-

another, or that defendants have citizenships different from each other. Thus if a plaintiff was a citizen of Ohio, diversity jurisdiction would fail if any defendant was also a citizen of Ohio. However, if five plaintiffs were citizens of Ohio, diversity jurisdiction could still exist if all defendants were citizens of states other than Ohio.

Realignment of Parties

The requirement of complete diversity in cases governed by § 1332 means that the alignment of parties (i.e., as plaintiffs or defendants) may be crucial to a determination of the existence of federal subject matter jurisdiction. Normally it is a plaintiff who provides the initial alignment parties in the plaintiff's complaint. However, because a plaintiff is not a disinterested party, the court has authority to re-align the parties to reflect accurately, on the one hand, the parties whose interests coincide and, on the other hand, those parties whose interests conflict with the first group of parties.[50]

Diversity Jurisdiction in Class Actions

Congress recently enacted[51] major changes in the requirements for diversity jurisdiction in most cases involving class actions governed by Rule 23.[52] These changes are fairly complex, but their net effect will sometimes be to ease substantially the requirements for diversity jurisdiction in class actions from what had been the established requirements for such jurisdiction in class lawsuits. The changes, incorporated as an amendment to 28 U.S.C.A. § 1332,[53] provide that diversity jurisdiction shall be satisfied when the following new

---

prives the district court of original diversity jurisdiction over the entire action;" citing *Strawbridge, supra*); *Strawbridge v. Curtiss*, 7 U.S. 267, 2 L. Ed. 435 (1806). *See also Ravenswood Investment Co. v. Avalon Correctional Services*, ___ F.3d ___ (10th Cir. 2011) ("Jurisdiction based on diversity does not contemplate diversity of *claims,* but rather diversity of parties") ([emphasis in original]).

[50]*City of Indianapolis v. Chase National Bank of New York*, 314 U.S. 63, 69, 62 S. Ct. 15, 86 L. Ed. 47 (1941) (courts have "broad authority to look beyond pleadings and [realign] the parties according to their sides in the dispute"). *But cf., Scotts Co., LLC v. Seeds, Inc.*, ___ F.3d ___ (9th Cir. 2012) (but district court, making determination, looks to case at bar, not "claims made in a different case").

[51]*See, e.g., Bush v. Cheaptickets, Inc.*, 425 F.3d 683, 686 (9th Cir. 2005) (by its terms, new legislation applied

to all class actions "commenced on or after" February 18, 2005; for purpose of this law, action commences when it commenced in state court as defined by state law; date of removal is *not* date that action commenced); *Pritchett v. Office Depot, Inc.*, 420 F.3d 1090, 1094 (10th Cir. 2005) (same). *But cf., Knudsen v. Liberty Mut. Ins. Co.*, 435 F.3d 755, 758 (7th Cir. 2006) (original complaint filed in state court prior to effective date of legislation; amended complaint, involving new claims, was filed after effective date of new legislation; held, amended complaint did not relate back, and defendant was therefore entitled to benefit of new legislation's broader definition of subject matter jurisdiction; "[A] novel claim tacked on to an existing case commences new litigation for purposes of the Class Action Fairness Act.").

[52]*See* Fed.R.Civ.P. 23.

[53]As amended, the provision that is currently designated as § 1332(d) is

requirements are met. First, diversity jurisdiction for class actions will be satisfied when the amount in controversy exceeds $5,000,000, exclusive of interest and costs.[54] This amount in controversy need not be satisfied by every single individual member of the class. Instead, the individual claims of the class members will be aggregated to determine if the amount in controversy has been satisfied.[55] Second, diversity jurisdiction in most class actions now requires that one of three other requirements is met. Diversity is satisfied if, in addition to meeting the amount in controversy requirement: (a) any member of a class of plaintiffs is a citizen of an American state different from the American state of citizenship of any defendant; (b) any member of a class of plaintiffs is a foreign state or a citizen or subject of a foreign state and any defendant is a citizen of an American state; or (c) any member of a class of plaintiffs is a citizen of an American state and any defendant is a foreign state or a citizen or subject of a foreign state.[56] It is worth noting that *all* class actions based on diversity must satisfy the amount in controversy requirement. However, the additional requirement for diverse citizenship can be met by satisfying *any* of the three foregoing descriptions of diverse citizenship.[57]

It should be noted that recent legislation affecting jurisdiction in class actions did not, for the most part, change one settled rule. It remains true that, even in class actions, the party asserting federal jurisdiction through removal or an orig-

---

renamed § 1332(e). A new provision, governing jurisdiction in class actions, is inserted as 28 U.S.C.A. § 1332(d).

[54]*Cf., Frederick v. Hartford Underwriters Insurance Co.*, 683 F.3d 1242, 1245 (10th Cir. 2012) (test is not amount of plaintiff's recovery, but amount demanded in good faith; punitive damages may be part of amount in controversy, but they cannot simply be assumed).

[55]28 U.S.C.A. § 1332(d)(6). *Shady Grove Orthopedic Associates, P.A. v. Allstate Insurance Co.*, __ U.S. __, 130 S. Ct. 1431, 1437 n.3, 176 L. Ed. 2d 311 (2010) (section 1332 relaxes rule against aggregation if claims equal at least $5 million). *See, e.g., Pastor v. State Farm Mut. Auto. Ins. Co*, 487 F.3d 1042, 1044 (7th Cir. 2007) ("Although the class members' claims are small the Class Action Fairness Act authorized the aggregation of class members' claims to satisfy the minimum amount in controversy required in a diversity suit, which in the case of a suit governed by the Act is $5 million."); *Frazier v. Pioneer Americas*

LLC, 455 F.3d 542 (5th Cir. 2006) (new legislation "explicitly allows aggregation of each class member's claim"). *But cf., DiTolla v. Doral Dental IPA of New York*, 469 F.3d 271, 276–77 (2d Cir. 2006) (where total pool of funds is not in dispute, only that part of fund which is in controversy may be used to satisfy amount in controversy requirement; acknowledging that on instant facts calculation of amount in controversy is difficult).

[56]*See, e.g., Luther v. Countrywide Home Loans Servicing, LP*, ____ F.3d ____ (9th Cir. 2008) ("[C]omplete diversity is not required."); *Blockbuster, Inc. v. Galeno*, 472 F.3d 53, 56 (2d Cir. 2006) (noting minimal diversity requirement). *But see Dennison v. Carolina Payday Loans, Inc.*, 549 F.3d 941, 942 (4th Cir. 2008) (where all members of class are citizens of same state that incorporated defendant, minimal diversity is not satisfied by additional fact that defendant's principal place of business may be located in another state).

[57]28 U.S.C.A. § 1332(d)(2).

inal filing bears the burden of establishing such jurisdiction.[58] However, the enactment creates an exception to that general rule in one circumstance. When, in a case removed to federal court in which the removing defendants have already met their jurisdictional burdens, plaintiffs who seek remand to state court under the newly created "local controversy" exception[59] must bear the burden of proving that the "local controversy" exception applies.[60] The "local controversy" exception is discussed in greater detail in the pages immediately following.

Rejecting "Jurisdictional Gamesmanship"

In enacting the new provisions that extend diversity jurisdiction over many class actions, Congress made clear that the definition of a class action is to be construed liberally. Thus, Congress intended to discourage "jurisdictional gamesmanship" intended to prevent the exercise of federal subject matter jurisdiction over diversity class actions.[61]

Continuing Jurisdiction in Absence of Class Certification

If a case has satisfied diversity jurisdiction under the relaxed standards for class actions, jurisdiction will survive even if the case is not ultimately certified as a class action.[62]

Declining Diversity Jurisdiction in Class Actions

Notwithstanding the possibility that a class action has met the requirements for diversity jurisdiction discussed immediately above, the recent amendments to § 1332 also provide federal district courts with some substantial opportunities to refrain from hearing such a class lawsuit.[63] The first of these, governed by new § 1332(d)(3), provides the court with discre-

---

[58]*See, e.g., Blockbuster, Inc. v. Galeno*, 472 F.3d 53, 57 (2d Cir. 2006) (identifying settled rule); *see, e.g., Nevada v. Bank of America Corp.*, 672 F.3d 661, 667–68 (9th Cir. 2012) (noting that jurisdictional amount is found in § 1332(a)). *Cf., Back Doctors, Ltd., v. Metropolitan Property & Casualty Insurance Co.*, 637 F.3d 827, 830 (7th Cir. 2011) (defendant seeking removal "is entitled to present its own estimate of the stakes; it is not bound by the plaintiff's estimate").

[59]28 U.S.C.A. § 1332(d)(4).

[60]*See, e.g., Hart v. FedEx Ground Package System Inc.*, 457 F.3d 675, 680 (7th Cir. 2006); *Evans v. Walter Industries, Inc.*, 449 F.3d 1159, 1165 (11th Cir. 2006).

[61]S.Rep. No. 109-14, at 35 (2005). *See, e.g., Louisiana Ex Rel. Caldwell v. Allstate Ins. Co.*, 536 F.3d 418 (5th Cir. 2008).

[62]*See, e.g., In re Burlington Northern Santa Fe Railway Co.*, 606 F.3d 379, 381 (7th Cir. 2010) (where case is properly removed, jurisdiction survives when class certification is denied or even when plaintiff decides not to seek certification at all); *United Steel, Paper & Forestry, Rubber, Manufacturing, Energy, Allied Industrial & Service Workers International Union, AFL-CIO, CLC v. Shell Oil Co.*, 602 F.3d 1087, 1091–92 (9th Cir. 2010) (citing other cases; noting general rule that "post-filing developments do not defeat jurisdiction if jurisdiction was properly invoked as of the time of filing").

[63]*But cf., Knepper v. Rite Aid Corp.*, 675 F.3d 249, 261 (3d Cir. 2012) (authority to decline jurisdiction is limited to enumerated situations; court lacks authority "to invoke an extratextual supplement outside those exceptions").

tion to decline to exercise diversity jurisdiction when two requirements are met[64] and some other prudential considerations are weighed. The first of the two requirements is that more than one-third and less than two-thirds of the total membership of a plaintiff class is comprised of citizens of the state in which the action was originally filed. The second requirement is that the "primary" defendants are citizens of the state in which the action was originally filed.[65] In addition to the existence of those two requirements the court must also weigh the following factors.

(a) whether the claims in question involve matters of national or interstate interest;

(b) whether the claims will be controlled by the law of the state where the case was originally filed or by the law of another state or states;

(c) whether the plaintiffs have, through artful pleading, sought to avoid federal subject matter jurisdiction;

(d) whether the action was filed in a court with a clear relationship with the plaintiffs, the underlying events, or the defendants;

(e) whether the number of class plaintiffs who are citizens of the state in which the case was filed is substantially larger than the number of plaintiffs from any other state, and the citizenship of other plaintiffs is dispersed among a significant variety of other states; and

(f) whether during the three years prior to filing the instant action, some other class action has been filed asserting similar claims, without regard to whether the claims were asserted on behalf of the identical plaintiffs.[66]

Local Controversy Exception

Under this statutory exception, the district court is required to decline to exercise jurisdiction if all of the following elements are met: (1) more than two-thirds of class plaintiffs are citizens of the state of original filing; (2) at least one defendant is a citizen of the state where the suit was originally filed and is both a subject of "significant" relief sought by the plaintiff class and a party whose alleged conduct is a "significant" basis for the plaintiffs' cause of action; (3) principal injuries in the case were incurred in the state of original filing; and (4) there has been no filing of a lawsuit in the last three years based on the same or similar allegations by the same or other plaintiffs

---

[64]*See, e.g., Frazier v. Pioneer Americas LLC*, 455 F.3d 542 (5th Cir. 2006) (plaintiffs have burden of showing applicability of exceptions under § 1332(d)(3)); *Evans v. Walter Industries, Inc.*, 449 F.3d 1159, 1164 (11th Cir. 2006) (burden of showing jurisdictional basis of removal falls on defendant/opponent of class; but burden of showing applicability of exceptions to removal under new legislation falls on class members). *But see Miedema v. Maytag Corp.*, 450 F.3d 1322, 1327–28 (11th Cir. 2006) (placing burden on removing party); *Abrego Abrego v. The Dow Chemical Co.*, 443 F.3d 676, 685 (9th Cir. 2006) (same as *Miedema*).

[65]28 U.S.C.A. § 1332(d)(3).

[66]28 U.S.C.A. § 1332(d)(3).

against any of the same defendants.[67]

Home State Exception

Section 1332(d)(4)(B) requires a district court to refuse jurisdiction if two requirements are met: two-thirds or more of plaintiff class are citizens of state of original filing; *and* "primary defendants" are also citizens of that state.[68]

◆ **NOTE:** Unlike the provisions of the recent legislation that leave unchanged the pre-existing burdens of proof regarding subject matter jurisdiction, § 1332(d)(4) has been construed in removal cases to place the burden of proving the applicability of the "local controversy" exception on the plaintiffs. Thus, if the defendants have met their burden of proving the existence of diversity jurisdiction, the burden shifts to the plaintiffs to show that the "local controversy" exception should be invoked to block the exercise of federal subject matter jurisdiction.[69]

Class Actions Unaffected by Amendments

Notwithstanding the broad scope of the recent amendment to § 1332, certain fairly narrow categories of class actions are expressly excluded from the scope of the new provisions. Specifically, amended § 1332 does not apply to any class action in which the primary defendants are "States, State officials, or other governmental entities against whom the district court may be foreclosed from ordering relief."[70] Thus, for example, a suit against a state that was barred by the Eleventh Amendment of the Constitution[71] if it had been brought by an individual plaintiff does not somehow acquire subject matter jurisdiction because it has been brought by a class of plaintiffs pursuant to new § 1332. Additionally, the amendments to § 1332 may not be used to satisfy diversity jurisdiction when the aggregate number of class plaintiffs is less than 100.[72] It may, however, be possible to satisfy subject matter jurisdiction

---

[67]28 U.S.C. § 1132(d)(4)(A). *See, e.g., In re Sprint Nextel Corp.*, 593 F.3d 669, 672 (7th Cir. 2010).

[68]28 U.S.C. § 1332(d)(4)(B). *See, e.g., In re Sprint Nextel Corp.*, 593 F.3d 669, 672 (7th Cir. 2010). *See also In re Hannaford Bros. Co. Customer Data Security Breach Litigation*, 564 F.3d 75, 78 n.2 (1st Cir. 2009) (when home state exception under § 1332(d)(4) applies, it overrides a finding of diversity under § 1332(d)(2)).

[69]*See, e.g., Hart v. FedEx Ground Package System Inc.*, 457 F.3d 675, 680 (7th Cir. 2006); *Evans v. Walter Industries, Inc.*, 449 F.3d 1159, 1165 (11th Cir. 2006).

[70]28 U.S.C.A. § 1332(d)(5)(A). *See also Frazier v. Pioneer Americas LLC,* 455 F.3d 542 (5th Cir. 2006) (plaintiffs have burden of showing applicability of exceptions under § 1332(d)(5)); *Evans v. Walter Industries, Inc.*, 449 F.3d 1159, 1164 (11th Cir. 2006) (burden of showing jurisdictional basis of removal falls on defendant/opponent of class; but burden of showing applicability of exceptions to removal under new legislation falls on class members).

[71]U.S. Const., Amend. 11.

[72]28 U.S.C.A. § 1332(d)(5)(B). *See, e.g., Blockbuster, Inc. v. Galeno*, 472 F.3d 53, 56 (2d Cir. 2006) (applying requirement of at least 100 class members).

over classes that are comprised of less than 100 plaintiffs through application of the Supreme Court's recent holding on the use of supplemental jurisdiction[73] in certain class actions. This possibility is discussed at greater length in the treatment of both supplemental jurisdiction and Federal Rule of Civil Procedure 23 elsewhere in this book.

Finally, the new version of § 1332 does not apply to class actions that rest "solely" upon a claim arising under certain federal securities laws, the laws of a state involving the internal affairs of corporations or other business entities (provided that the corporation or entity is incorporated or organized in that state), or laws that relate to rights and duties, including fiduciary duties, created by any security or the federal Securities Act of 1933.[74] Where parties may seek to file such cases on the basis of diversity jurisdiction, case law requirements for subject matter jurisdiction will presumably be the applicable standard.[75]

Mass Actions

As amended by the Class Action Fairness Act of 2005, § 1332(d) treats many mass actions as the equivalent of class actions for purposes of diversity jurisdiction or removal from state court. The definition of a mass action, as provided in § 1332(d)(11)(B)(i), is a civil action in which one hundred or more persons each seek monetary relief and a joint trial because their claims involve a single event or occurrence that gave rise to the cause of action.[76] Section 1132(d)(11)(B)(i) also provides that mass actions which meet that definition are deemed eligible for treatment as class actions only if they meet the additional requirement that each plaintiff's individual claim meets the amount in controversy requirement established in § 1332(a),[77] governing more conventional non-class diversity actions. Because § 1332(a) requires an amount in controversy in excess of $75,000 for each plaintiff's claims, it establishes a

---

[73]*Exxon Mobil Corp. v. Allapattah Services, Inc.*, 545 U.S. 546, 125 S. Ct. 2611, 162 L. Ed. 2d 502 (2005) (overruling existing precedent; holding that in some circumstances district court's supplemental jurisdiction may extend to cases in which class members would not satisfy amount-in-controversy requirement for diversity jurisdiction).

[74]28 U.S.C.A. § 1332(d)(9). *See also Appert v. Morgan Stanley Dean Witter*, 673 F.3d 609, 618 (7th Cir. 2012) (in removed cases, party seeking remand has burden to prove applicability of § 1332(d)((9)).

[75]*See, e.g., Exxon Mobil Corp. v. Allapattah Services, Inc.*, 545 U.S. 546, 125 S. Ct. 2611, 162 L. Ed. 2d 502 (2005) (in some circumstances district court's

supplemental jurisdiction may extend to cases in which class members would not satisfy amount-in-controversy requirement for diversity jurisdiction); *Supreme Tribe of Ben Hur v. Cauble*, 255 U.S. 356, 41 S. Ct. 338, 65 L. Ed. 673 (1921) (in class actions based on diversity jurisdiction, citizenship of class representatives (not all members of class) should be compared to citizenship of opponents of class).

[76]28 U.S.C.A. § 1332(d)(11)(B)(i). *See, e.g., Anderson v. Bayer Corp.*, 610 F.3d 390 (7th Cir. 2010) (refusing to relax numerical requirement where less than 100 plaintiffs were involved).

[77]28 U.S.C.A. § 1332(d)(11)(B); *Louisiana Ex. Rel Caldwell v. Allstate Ins. Co.*, 536 F.3d 418 (5th Cir. 2008).

more rigorous standard that must be met before all of § 1332(d) can apply to a case.[78] By contrast, class action plaintiffs entitled to the full range of benefits of § 1332(d)(2) to (10) need meet only the often more modest requirement that the aggregate claim of the entire class exceeds $5,000,000.[79]

If a mass action falls within the scope of § 1332(d)(11), and is not excepted by provisions of § 1332(d)(11)(B)(ii), it will be treated like most class actions for purposes of diversity jurisdiction and removal.[80] Section 1332(d)(11)(B)(ii) is discussed immediately below.

Exceptions: Mass Actions Not Within the Scope of § 1332(d)

Section 1332(d)(11)(B)(ii) expressly provides that certain civil actions containing elements of mass actions shall nevertheless not be treated as mass actions for purposes of 1332(d) if those civil actions fall into any of several categories. The four enumerated exceptions are:

Local Events: A lawsuit is not a mass action for purposes of § 1332(d) if the claims involved arise from events that occurred in the state where the lawsuit was filed and the injuries from the event are found in that state or contiguous states.[81]

Joinder by Defendant: A lawsuit is not a mass action for purposes of § 1332(d) if the claims in question were joined by a motion of a defendant.[82]

Public Interest Claims / Private Attorneys General: Some

---

[78]*See, e.g., Nevada v. Bank of America Corp.*, 672 F.3d 661, 667–68 (9th Cir. 2012) (noting that jurisdictional amount is found in § 1332(a)).

[79]28 U.S.C.A. § 1332(d)(2). *But see Lowery v. Alabama Power Co.*, 483 F.3d 1184, 1201 (11th Cir. 2007) (suggesting that mass actions may only have to meet the aggregate amount in controversy requirement of $5,000,000). It is respectfully suggested that the 11th Circuit has made an error on this point, for it appears clear that for mass actions (as opposed to class actions), § 1332(d)(11)(B)(i) expressly provides that the amount in controversy is defined by § 1332(a), which requires more than $75,000 for each claim, making the $5,000,000 standard of § 1332(d)(2) inapplicable to mass actions. The error may only be an administrative error, for *Lowery* later quotes accurately the applicability of § 1332(a). 483 F.3d at 1202 (quoting without comment about earlier statement). See *also Pastor v.*

State Farm Mut. Auto. Ins. Co, 487 F.3d 1042, 1044 (7th Cir. 2007) ("Although the class members' claims are small, the Class Action Fairness Act authorized the aggregation of class members' claims to satisfy the amount in controversy required in a diversity suit, which in the case of a suit governed by the Act is $5 million."); *Frazier v. Pioneer Americas LLC*, 455 F.3d 542 n. 10 (5th Cir. 2006) (new legislation "explicitly allows aggregation of each class member's claim").

[80]*See, e.g., Lowery v. Alabama Power Co.*, 483 F.3d 1184, 1195 (11th Cir. 2007) (any lawsuit qualifying as a mass action is generally a class action for purposes of diversity jurisdiction and removal).

[81]28   U.S.C.A. § 1332(d)(11)(B)(ii)(I).

[82]28   U.S.C.A. § 1332(d)(11)(B)(ii)(II). *See, e.g., Anderson v. Bayer Corp.*, 610 F.3d 390 (7th Cir. 2010).

state laws authorize some lawsuits by private plaintiffs on behalf of the general public. These lawsuits are distinguishable from cases brought to assert rights belonging to individuals or classes of claimants. When such public interest claims form the entire basis of a lawsuit, the case cannot be a mass action for purposes of § 1332(d).[83]

Consolidation for Pretrial Proceedings Only: If the claims at issue have been consolidated for pretrial purposes only, the lawsuit cannot be a mass action within the meaning of § 1332(d).[84]

An additional exception to the treatment of mass claims as mass actions for purposes of § 1332(d) is implicit in the requirement that mass actions must involve individual claims for monetary relief in amounts greater than $75,000.[85] The requirement that claims for monetary relief be an element of a mass action necessarily means that cases involving claims only for non-monetary equitable relief cannot be treated as mass actions under § 1332(d).

Restrictions on Transfers of Mass Actions

In many cases 28 U.S.C.A. § 1407 authorizes transfer of cases involving common questions of fact so that they may be consolidated in a particular district.[86] One unusual feature of § 1332(d) is a provision prohibiting transfer under § 1407 unless a majority of the plaintiffs in an action request such transfer.[87] Thus, in mass actions, it may be possible to remove a case from state court to a federal district court that sits in the same state, but transfer to another federal district court will normally be unavailable to a defendant. An exception to this exceptional provision provides, however, that § 1332(d)(11)(C) does not apply to cases certified, or proposed to be certified, as class actions pursuant to Rule 23 of the Federal Rules of Civil Procedure.[88]

Mass Actions: Statutes of Limitations

Section 1332(d)(11)(D) tolls statutes of limitations for claims included in a mass action for the period that the action is in a federal court.[89]

State Constraints on Diversity Jurisdiction

It is settled that where the requirements of § 1332 are met, a state has no authority to deprive a district court of diversity

---

[83] 28 U.S.C.A. § 1332(d)(11)(B)(ii)(III). *See also LG Display Co. v. Madigan*, 665 F.3d 768, 772 (7th Cir. 2011) (claim by state attorney general on behalf of general public, not individual claimants, is not a mass action within meaning of § 1332(d)).

[84] 28 U.S.C.A. § 1332(d)(11)(B)(ii)(IV).

[85] 28 U.S.C.A. § 1332(d)(11)(B)(i).

[86] 28 U.S.C.A. § 1407(a).

[87] 28 U.S.C.A. § 1332(d)(11)(C).

[88] 28 U.S.C.A. § 1332(d)(11)(C)(ii).

[89] 28 U.S.C.A. § 1332(d)(11)(D).

jurisdiction.[90]

Exceptions for Domestic Relations and Probate Cases

Although § 1332 is silent on the issue, federal courts routinely do not exercise diversity jurisdiction over cases in which divorce, child custody or matters of probate are at issue.[91] However, these exceptions to the application of diversity jurisdiction are construed narrowly. Thus, if a case involved a dispute over property arising out of a divorce decree previously granted, the federal court might hear the case if the requirements of diversity jurisdiction were otherwise satisfied.[92]

Additionally, if the basis of federal subject matter jurisdiction is § 1331 (governing federal questions) and not diversity, the result can be very different. If, for example, a plaintiff files a child custody claim based on federal common law (as could happen if one parent was a native American), the basis of subject matter jurisdiction is a federal question. In that circumstance the domestic relations exception barring diversity jurisdiction is inapplicable, and a district court may hear the federal question.[93] Section 1331 is discussed elsewhere in this text.

---

[90]*See, e.g., Superior Beverage Co., Inc. v. Schieffelin & Co.*, 448 F.3d 910, 917 (6th Cir. 2006) ("[A] state may not deprive a federal court of jurisdiction merely by declaring in a statute that it holds exclusive jurisdiction."); *Dunlap v. Nestle USA, Inc.*, 431 F.3d 1015, 1017 (7th Cir. 2005) ("[S]tate law may not enlarge or contract federal jurisdiction. . . . The exclusivity provisions of Illinois' workers' compensation statute do not (indeed, may not) affect the scope of the jurisdictional authority granted to the federal courts by Congress."). *See also Chicago & N.W.R. Co. v. Whitton*, 80 U.S. 270, 20 L. Ed. 571 (1871) ("In all cases, where a general right is thus conferred, it can be enforced in any Federal court within the State having jurisdiction of the parties.").

[91]*Markham v. Allen*, 326 U.S. 490, 494, 66 S. Ct. 296, 298, 90 L. Ed. 256 (1946) ("[A] federal court has no jurisdiction to probate a will or administer an estate;" but the district court may hear a suit against an estate, provided it is only to establish the claim against the estate and does not interfere with the probate court's jurisdiction or proceedings). *See also Moser v. Pollin*, 294 F.3d 335, 338 (2d Cir. 2002) (probate matter is outside scope of diversity jurisdiction in either of two circumstances: when district court is asked "to directly probate a will or administer an estate;" or when hearing the action would cause district court to interfere with probate proceedings, disrupt state jurisdiction of probate court, or take control of property that was controlled by probate court).

[92]*Ankenbrandt v. Richards*, 504 U.S. 689, 112 S. Ct. 2206, 119 L. Ed. 2d 468 (1992) (domestic relations exception only prevents issuing divorce, alimony, or child custody decrees). *See, e.g., Rash v. Rash*, 173 F.3d 1376 (11th Cir. 1999) (rule of refusing jurisdiction is not absolute and is narrowly confined; court will not adjudicate parties' "domestic affairs," but will resolve dispute over assets).

[93]*See, e.g., Atwood v. Fort Peck Tribal Court Assiniboine*, 513 F.3d 943, 945 (9th Cir. 2008) (domestic relations bar to lawsuit applicable only in diversity cases, not federal question cases); *U.S. v. Bailey*, 115 F.3d 1222, 1231 (5th Cir. 1997) (domestic relations exception applicable only in diversity cases).

Insurance Companies and Direct Action Suits

A few states permit plaintiffs in tort actions to sue the defendant's insurance company directly, rather than proceeding first against the alleged tortfeasor. 28 U.S.C.A. § 1332(c)(1) takes account of that circumstance, providing that in such cases insurance companies will be treated as citizens of the state where the alleged tortfeasors have citizenship, in addition to the states where the insurance company has citizenship. When applicable, the practical effect of this provision is to reduce somewhat a plaintiff's possibilities for obtaining diversity jurisdiction.

The 2012 amendments to the diversity statute have clarified the status of foreign insured parties and foreign insurors in the context of direct action suits. It is now settled that in determining diversity jurisdiction the citizenship of insurors that are either incorporated outside the United States or have their principal place of business outside the United States will be taken into account. Similarly, the citizenship of insured parties, whether domestic or foreign, will also be evaluated in making the diversity determination.[94]

It should be noted that attribution of an insured's citizenship to the insured's own insuror applies only to circumstances where a plaintiff has a claim against the insured that may also properly be asserted against the insuror without necessarily first joining or suing the insured.[95] If the suit is a dispute between the insuror and the insured, conventional standards of diversity jurisdiction apply.[96]

Decedents, Infants, and Incompetents

28 U.S.C.A. § 1332(c)(2) provides that, for diversity purposes, parties acting as representatives of decedents' estates, infants, or incompetent persons shall be deemed to take the citizenship of the estate of persons whom they represent.[97] 28 U.S.C.A. § 1332(c)(2) was enacted to preclude creation of diversity in such cases simply by appointing a representative of different citizenship than the party the representative opposes.

Diversity Jurisdiction and Federal Causes of Action

In the ordinary course of events it would seem unnecessary to decide whether, if the requirements for diversity jurisdiction

---

[94]28 U.S.C. § 1332(c)(1).

[95]See, e.g., Searles v. Cincinnati Ins. Co., 998 F.2d 728, 729 (9th Cir. 1993).

[96]See, e.g., City of Vestavia Hills v. General Fidelity Insurance Co., 676 F.3d 1310, 1315 (11th Cir. 2012) (suit is not a direct action against insured if cause of action could not have been filed against party that was originally insured). Clark v. Chubb Group of Ins. Cos., 337 F.3d 687 (6th Cir. 2003) (Ohio insured sued insurer that was citizen of state other than Ohio; held, standard requirements for diversity apply because suit was not direct action suit governed by § 1332(c)(1)).

[97]See, e.g., Gustafson v. zumBrunnen, 546 F.3d 398, ___ (7th Cir. 2008) (party suing in behalf of estate is treated, for purposes of § 1332(c)(2), as representative of estate, notwithstanding that another representative of estate already exists); King v. Cessna Aircraft Co., 505 F.3d 1160, 1170 (11th Cir. 2007) ("Where an estate is a party, the citizenship that counts for diversity purposes is that of the decedent.").

are met, such jurisdiction could attach to a federally created cause of action. Such causes of action would, after all, normally be tested against the requirements for federal question jurisdiction.[98] However, in unusual circumstances where Congress has created a federal cause of action but has withheld federal question jurisdiction, there is some authority permitting district courts to use diversity jurisdiction if the requirements for diversity are met.[99]

Citizenship of Persons not Joined as Parties

It is now settled that the citizenship of a person not joined as a party cannot destroy diversity jurisdiction, notwithstanding that the absent person has an interest in the lawsuit.[100] Thus, if a plaintiff has a state claim against one potential defendant who is diverse and another potential defendant who is not diverse, and the non-diverse defendant is not an indispensable party under Rule 19,[101] the plaintiff may choose to sue only the diverse defendant and thereby satisfy diversity jurisdiction.

Nominal Parties

Diversity is not affected by the presence of nominal parties, i.e., individuals without an interest in the lawsuit.[102]

Collusive Invocation of Diversity Jurisdiction

The diversity provisions of 28 U.S.C.A. § 1332 are modified by 28 U.S.C.A. § 1359, governing collusive invocation of jurisdiction. Section 1359 provides that if a party, "by assignment or otherwise," has been "improperly or collusively . . . joined" to invoke jurisdiction, the federal district court will not have jurisdiction. Section 1359 prohibits invocation of diversity jurisdiction where a corporation, not diverse from the defendant, assigned its cause of action to another person for the primary purpose of creating diversity. This rule applies even if the assignment itself is lawful and valid under state law.[103] However, it is still reasonable to assume that an assignment

---

[98]28 U.S.C.A. § 1331.

[99]*See, e.g., Gottlieb v. Carnival Corp.*, 436 F.3d 335, 340 (2d Cir. 2006) (permitting use of § 1332 in case arising under Telephone Consumer Protection Act, 47 U.S.C.A. §§ 227 et seq.; "Nothing in § 1332 limits its application to state-law causes of action.").

[100]*Lincoln Property Co. v. Roche*, 546 U.S. 81, 126 S. Ct. 606, 615, 163 L. Ed. 2d 415 (2005) (noting that lower court "had no warrant . . . to inquire whether some other person might have been joined as an additional or substitute defendant").

[101]In some circumstances, Rule 19 may direct the joinder of a party not previously sued. If that provision of Rule 19 is applicable to a case, and

such a joinder destroys diversity, the district court may be obligated to dismiss the action for failure of subject matter jurisdiction. *See* Author's Commentary on Rule 19.

[102]*Salem Trust Co. v. Manufacturers' Finance Co.*, 262 U.S. 182, 190, 44 S. Ct. 266, 68 L. Ed. 628 (1924) (citizenship of nominal parties will not be considered). *See also Slater v. Republic-Vanguard Insurance Co.*, 650 F.3d 1132, 1134 (8th Cir. 2011) ("The presence of a nondiverse party who is 'nominal' may be ignored.").

[103]*Kramer v. Caribbean Mills, Inc.*, 394 U.S. 823, 827, 89 S. Ct. 1487, 1490, 23 L. Ed. 2d 9 (1969). (legality of assignment under state law does not necessarily equate to validity for purposes of federal jurisdiction).

lawful under state law, and made primarily for purposes other than to create diversity, may surmount this obstacle.[104]

Fraudulent Joinder and Removal

Fraudulent joinder occurs when a plaintiff who has sued in state court joins a nondiverse defendant against whom the plaintiff obviously has no cause of action under settled law.[105] The purpose of such joinder, of course, is to prevent removal of the real case, against a diverse defendant, to federal district court. When the true defendant nevertheless files a removal petition, the court, upon identifying a fraudulent joinder of the nondiverse defendant, will deny a motion to remand and retain jurisdiction over the removed case.[106]

Amount in Controversy

Diversity jurisdiction requires not only that the parties be citizens of different states or countries, but also that the matter in controversy exceed $75,000, exclusive of interest and costs.[107] The time at which the amount in controversy is measured is the date that the suit is filed. Later events that may reduce the amount recoverable do not nullify diversity jurisdiction that was proper at the time of filing.[108]

---

[104]*Cf. Yokeno v. Mafnas*, 973 F.2d 803, 811 (9th Cir. 1992) (even if jurisdictional motive is apparent, assignment may create jurisdiction if independent business motive is "sufficiently compelling").

[105]See, e.g., *Smallwood v. Illinois Central Railroad Co.*, 385 F.3d 568, 578 (5tth Cir. 2004) (improper joinder is either "(1) actual fraud in the pleading of jurisdictional facts, or (2) inability of the plaintiff to establish a cause of action against the non-diverse party in state court*").

[106]*Morris v. Princess Cruises, Inc.*, 236 F.3d 1061, 1067–68 (9th Cir. 2001).

[107]*See, e.g., Colavito v. New York Organ Donor Network, Inc.*, 438 F.3d 214, 221 (2d Cir. 2006) (plea for punitive damages may satisfy amount in controversy requirement even if plaintiff would only be entitled to compensatory damages that are nominal). *But cf., State Farm Mut. Auto. Ins. Co. v. Powell*, 87 F.3d 93 (3d Cir. 1996) (amount in controversy not satisfied by pleading exact amount identified in § 1332; amount pleaded must *exceed* amount identified in § 1332). *Cf., Missouri State Life Ins. Co. v. Jones*, 290 U.S. 199, 202, 54 S. Ct. 133, 134,

78 L. Ed. 267, 269 (1933) (attorney's fees may be counted toward amount in controversy when prevailing party may collect them as part of damages per, e.g., state statute; held, state characterization of such fees as "costs" is irrelevant to diversity jurisdiction). *See, e.g., Manguno v. Prudential Property and Cas. Ins. Co.*, 276 F.3d 720, 723 (5th Cir. 2002) ("If a state statute provides for attorney's fees, such fees are included as part of the amount in controversy."). *But see Martin v. Franklin Capital Corp.*, 251 F.3d 1284, 1292 (10th Cir. 2001) ("[A]ttorneys fees cannot be aggregated for purposes of diversity jurisdiction."); *Spielman v. Genzyme Corp.*, 251 F.3d 1 (1st Cir.2001) (denying aggregation of attorney's fees even where state statute authorizes such fees).

[108]*See, e.g., Yang Qin Luo v. Mikel*, 625 F.3d 772, 776 (2d Cir. 2010) ("[A] plaintiff cannot seek to deprive a federal court of jurisdiction by reducing her demand to $75,000 or less once the jurisdictional threshold has been satisfied."); *Hart v. Schering-Plough Corp.*, 253 F.3d 272 (7th Cir.2001) ("The amount in controversy is whatever is required to satisfy the plaintiff's demand in full, on the date suit began;" issue of $90,000 annual salary does

"Legal Certainty" Test

In the ordinary case, determination of the amount in controversy is made by reference to plaintiff's prayer for relief. Unliquidated claims for more than $75,000 will normally be taken at face value as satisfying the amount in controversy requirement.[109] Only in the unusual case, where it is certain—based on the liquidated nature of the claim, the manifestly frivolous nature of the prayer for relief, or an existing statutory limitation on damages recoverable—that the plaintiff cannot possibly recover the jurisdictional amount, will the court disregard the plaintiff's prayer.[110]

If the amount in controversy is at issue, it is normally the

---

not satisfy amount in controversy because defendant had paid plaintiff more than $17,000 in severance payments prior to suit); *Wolde-Meskel v. Vocational Instruction Project Community Services, Inc.*, 166 F.3d 59, 62 (2d Cir. 1999) (defendant obtained summary judgment on one count, resulting in decline in amount in controversy; held, trial court retained jurisdiction over other counts because once jurisdiction is obtained, a change in domicile or amount in controversy does not oust court's jurisdiction; summarizing cases and citing contrary minority view).

[109]*See, e.g.*, *Kroske v. U.S. Bank Corp.*, 432 F.3d 976, 980 (9th Cir. 2005) (where the amount sought is not clear in complaint, court may require "summary-judgment-type evidence" as to amount in controversy); *Zunamon v. Brown*, 418 F.2d 883, 885 (8th Cir. 1969) (Plaintiff's claim ordinarily decides amount in controversy.). *See also*, *Mitchell v. Brown & Williamson Tobacco Corp.*, 294 F.3d 1309, 1315 (11th Cir. 2002) (where plaintiff filed in state court and defendant removed, plaintiff's allegation of damages in state court that satisfy amount in controversy requirement should have "strong presumption" that pleading does not allege large amount simply to satisfy diversity); *Cohn v. Petsmart, Inc.*, 281 F.3d 837, 840 (9th Cir. 2002) ("A settlement letter is relevant evidence of the amount in controversy if that appears to reflect a reasonable estimate of the plaintiff's claim."); *U.S. Fire Ins. Co. v. Villegas*, 242 F.3d 279, 284 (5th Cir. 2001) (if applicable law

permits recovery of punitive damages, good-faith pleading of such damages may be included in determination of amount in controversy, notwithstanding that jury ultimately did not award such damages); *Massachusetts Cas. Ins. Co. v. Harmon*, 88 F.3d 415 (6th Cir. 1996) (where validity of disability insurance policy is at issue, assessment of amount in controversy may include future potential benefits). *But cf., Middleton v. City of Blue Springs, Mo.*, 145 F.3d 993 (8th Cir. 1998) (if amount in controversy is challenged by opponent or court, claimant must prove amount by preponderance of evidence; court must dismiss if it concludes to legal certainty that claimant cannot recover required amount); *Larkin v. Brown*, 41 F.3d 387, 388 (8th Cir. 1994) (if claim for punitive damages is necessary to satisfy amount in controversy requirement, the claim should get closer scrutiny than claim for compensatory damages.).

[110]*See, e.g.*, *Carton v. General Motors Acceptance Corp.*, 611 F.3d 451 (8th Cir. 2010) (where statutory cap on damages is $50,000 plaintiff cannot meet jurisdictional requirement of $75,000); *Chase Manhattan Bank, N.A. v. American Nat. Bank and Trust Co. of Chicago*, 93 F.3d 1064, 1070 (2d Cir. 1996) (where plaintiff suffered no damages, there is "a legal certainty" that jurisdictional amount is not satisfied); *Burns v. Anderson*, 502 F.2d 970, 972 (5th Cir. 1974) (broken thumb with no lingering pain or disability; only modest lost wages; held, jurisdictional amount not satisfied).

plaintiff's burden to demonstrate that the requirement is met.[111] An exception arises when a plaintiff originally files suit in state court and the defendant successfully removes the case to federal court. In that circumstance, if it is unclear whether the plaintiff's state claim met the amount in controversy requirement, the burden of proving the existence of the jurisdictional amount is shifted to the defendant who removed.[112]

Recovery of Less than $75,000

If a plaintiff initially seeks more than $75,000, but ultimately recovers less than that amount, 28 U.S.C.A. § 1332(b) provides that the court may deny recovery of costs to the plaintiff, and may assess costs against the plaintiff. However, jurisdiction that was proper at the outset is unaffected.[113] The calculation of the plaintiff's recovery under § 1332(b) is made solely on the basis of awards to plaintiff, and does not include deductions for the defendant's successful claims against the plaintiff. The court's authority under § 1332(b) is discretionary.[114] Moreover, "costs" do not include recovery of attorney fees.

Jurisdictional Amount in Equity Cases

Because suits seeking equitable relief are grounded in an allegation that traditional money damages are an inadequate remedy, federal courts have had to adjust the more-than $75,000 requirement to the peculiarities of such cases. Perhaps the most common approach is to try to measure the amount in controversy in equity cases by the value of the right the plaintiff

---

[111]*See, e.g., Marcus Food Co. v. DiPanfilo*, 6712 F.3d 1159, 1171 (10th Cir. 2011) (if amount in controversy is challenged, party asserting subject matter jurisdiction must demonstrate that mouns in controversy is achievable); *Woodmen of World Life Insurance Society v. Manganaro*, 342 F.3d 1213, 1216 (10th Cir. 2003) (plaintiff must show "it is not legally certain that the claim is less than the jurisdictional amount").

[112]*McNutt v. General Motors Acceptance Corp. of Indiana*, 298 U.S. 178, 189, 56 S. Ct. 780, 80 L. Ed. 1135 (1936) (burden of proving subject matter jurisdiction rests on party seeking to invoke federal subject matter jurisdiction). *See, e.g., Smith v. American General Life and Acc. Ins. Co., Inc.*, 337 F.3d 888 (7th Cir. 2003) (explaining general rule, but noting exception applies in removal cases because plaintiff is unlikely to have fabricated an amount in controversy when plaintiff originally filed in state court). *See generally Kokkonen v. Guardian Life Ins. Co. of America*, 511 U.S. 375, 377, 114

S. Ct. 1673, 1675, 128 L. Ed. 2d 391 (1994) ("[T]he burden of establishing [subject matter jurisdiction] rests upon the party asserting jurisdiction."). *See also TIG Ins. Co. v. Reliable Research Co.*, 334 F.3d 630 (7th Cir. 2003) (intervening plaintiff bears burden of establishing subject matter jurisdiction).

[113]*See, e.g., Meridian Sec. Ins. Co. v. Sadowski*, 441 F.3d 536, 538 (7th Cir. 2006) (if amount in controversy was met at outset, subsequent award of less than that amount does not terminate subject matter jurisdiction). *Pratt Central Park Ltd. Partnership v. Dames & Moore, Inc.*, 60 F.3d 350, 351 (7th Cir. 1995) ("The penalty for recovering less than [the jurisdictional amount] is the denial of costs . . . not the loss of the whole judgment.").

[114]*See, e.g., Coventry Sewage Associates v. Dworkin Realty Co.*, 71 F.3d 1, 8 n. 6 (1st Cir. 1995) ("The determination of whether or not to impose such cost sanctions is, of course, within the sound discretion of the district court.").

seeks to enforce.[115] A similar approach is to measure the amount in controversy by the value of vindication to the plaintiff.[116] A less favored approach is to measure the amount in controversy by the costs of compliance a defendant will face.[117] As these constructions suggest, there are a variety of techniques for attempting the evaluation, and lower courts enjoy substantial discretion in how they make their determinations.[118]

◆ *Example:* Assume a plaintiff owns a small plot of land worth less than $75,000 immediately below a large dam owned by the defendant. If the defendant intends to release water held by the dam, it may not do damage worth more than $75,000 to the plaintiff's property. Measuring the amount in controversy by the value to the plaintiff of an injunction preventing the release would therefore not satisfy the amount in controversy. However, the cost to the defendant of not releasing the water might be considerably more than $75,000. If so, measuring the amount in controversy by the cost to defendant of complying with the injunction would satisfy the jurisdictional requirement.

Arbitration Cases

In cases where district courts are asked to enforce arbitration awards, various circuit courts have adopted three distinct approaches to the amount in controversy requirement: (1) the "award approach," which is based on the amount the claimant was actually awarded, without regard to what the claimant actually sought;[119] (2) the "demand approach," which is based on the amount the claimant sought, not on the amount the

---

[115]*Glenwood Light & Water Co. v. Mutual Light, Heat & Power Co.*, 239 U.S. 121, 36 S. Ct. 30, 60 L. Ed. 174 (1915). *See also Hartford Ins. Group v. Lou-Con Inc.*, 293 F.3d 908, 911 (5th Cir. 2002) (in declaratory judgment action over validity of insurance policy, amount in controversy is usually measured by limits of policy; however, if issue is applicability of policy to particular occurrence, amount in controversy is usually not policy limit, but value of claim underlying the particular dispute).

[116]*See, e.g., Cohen v. Office Depot, Inc.*, 204 F.3d 1069, 1077 (11th Cir. 2000) ("When a plaintiff seeks injunctive or declaratory relief, the amount in controversy is the monetary value of the object of the litigation from the plaintiff's perspective.").

[117]*See, e.g., Justice v. Atchison, Topeka and Santa Fe Ry. Co.*, 927 F.2d 503, 505 (10th Cir. 1991) (looking to defendant's cost of compliance; noting authority for looking either to cost to defendant or value to plaintiff). *But see In re Ford Motor Co./Citibank (South Dakota), N.A.*, 264 F.3d 952, 960–61 (9th Cir. 2001) (refusing to measure jurisdictional amount by cost to defendant of complying with injunction).

[118]*See, e.g., JTH Tax, Inc. v. Frashier*, 624 F.3d 635, 639 (4th Cir. 2010) (court may use either worth of injunction to plaintiff or cost of injunction to defendant).

[119]*See, e.g., Ford v. Hamilton Investments, Inc.*, 29 F.3d 255, 260 (6th Cir. 1994).

claimant was actually awarded;[120] or (3) the "remand approach," in which, if a party seeks to remand the case to arbitration, the amount in controversy is determined by reference to the amount claimed in the arbitration.[121] Attorneys will find it necessary to consult the local practice.

Aggregation of Claims

If a plaintiff has more than one claim against a defendant, but no single claim exceeds $75,000 in value, questions arise as to whether the plaintiff may add the value of the claims together to satisfy the amount in controversy requirement. Case law indicates that a single plaintiff may aggregate claims against a single defendant, no matter how dissimilar the claims may be.[122] However, if each claim is merely an alternative theory for which only one recovery would be permitted, only the amount of that potential recovery may be considered when calculating the amount in controversy.

When multiple parties are involved, the case law is less liberal. It appears that two or more plaintiffs can add their claims together to satisfy the jurisdictional amount only if the claims are truly joint.[123] For example, if two plaintiffs each owned, as joint tenants, half of an automobile worth $80,000, and the suit alleged that the defendant had destroyed the automobile completely, the plaintiffs could probably add their individual $40,000 claims to satisfy the jurisdictional amount. But if the allegations were that the two plaintiffs each suffered $40,000 in personal injuries at the hands of the defendant, aggregation would not be permitted because the claims would be seen as distinct—even if the injuries occurred in the same accident.[124]

The precedent in cases where a single plaintiff seeks to sue

---

[120]See, e.g., American Guaranty Co. v. Caldwell, 72 F.2d 209, 211 (C.C.A. 9th Cir. 1934).

[121]See, e.g., Karsner v. Lothian, 532 F.3d 876 (D.C. Cir. 2008).

[122]See, e.g., Werwinski v. Ford Motor Co., 286 F.3d 661, 666 (3d Cir. 2002) ("Only claims, whether related or unrelated, of a single plaintiff against a single defendant may be aggregated."); Galt G/S v. JSS Scandinavia, 142 F.3d 1150 (9th Cir.1998) (upholding aggregation of statutorily authorized attorneys' fees with principal claim); Klepper v. First American Bank, 916 F.2d 337, 341 (6th Cir. 1990) ("It is well established that claims [brought by a single plaintiff against a single defendant] can be aggregated to satisfy the jurisdictional amount requirement."); But see In re Abbott Laboratories, 51 F.3d 524, 529

(5th Cir. 1995) (Congressional enactment of supplemental jurisdiction, 28 U.S.C.A. § 1367, obviated need for each plaintiff to satisfy independently the requisite amount in controversy in class actions).

[123]See, e.g., Snyder v. Harris, 394 U.S. 332, 334, 89 S. Ct. 1053, 1056, 22 L. Ed. 2d 319 (1969) (allowing multiple plaintiffs to aggregate where they have "common and undivided interest"). But cf. Ard v. Transcontinental Gas Pipe Line Corp., 138 F.3d 596 (5th Cir.1998) (acknowledging differences among appellate courts; holding that, generally, several plaintiffs may not aggregate their individual claims for punitive damages).

[124]See also Spielman v. Genzyme Corp., 251 F.3d 1 (1st Cir.2001) (denying aggregation of attorney's fees even where state statute authorizes such

more than one defendant follows a similar pattern. Aggregation is permitted only if the claims against the defendants involve joint liability.[125]

Counterclaims

If the plaintiff's complaint fails to meet requirements for subject matter jurisdiction, it is possible that counterclaims that satisfy diversity jurisdiction will still be heard.[126]

ADDITIONAL RESEARCH REFERENCES

C.J.S., Federal Courts §§ 44 to 73 et seq.
West's Key Number Digest, Federal Courts ☜261 to 319

§ 2.13 Subject Matter Jurisdiction in Federal District Courts—Requirements for Supplemental Jurisdiction

CORE CONCEPT

Supplemental jurisdiction, authorized by Congress at 28 U.S.C.A. § 1367, is the means by which parties may add state law counts in a federal court case, even though the state law counts could not have been brought by themselves because they cannot satisfy the requirements of either federal question or diversity jurisdiction.

◆ *Example:* Suppose that a New York plaintiff had two causes of action against a New York defendant: one arising under federal antitrust law, the other under state law. Federal antitrust claims are within the exclusive subject matter jurisdiction of federal district courts. The state claim, by contrast, does not qualify for diversity jurisdiction because both parties are New York citizens. Thus the plaintiff in a situation such as this might theoretically have to prosecute two separate suits, one in federal court and the other in state court, and incur all the extra expenditures in time and money such suits

---

fees). *Cf., e.g., Mehlenbacher v. Akzo Nobel Salt, Inc.,* 216 F.3d 291 (2d Cir.2000) (claims are separate and distinct where plaintiffs "seek recovery for their losses as individuals only, and not collectively"; thus no aggregation permitted in instant case); *Meritcare Inc. v. St. Paul Mercury Ins. Co.,* 166 F.3d 214, 218 (3d Cir. 1999) (plaintiffs claimed losses on similar insurance policies covering a single event; denying aggregation when "the plaintiffs have a community of interest, but fall short of establishing a single title or right in which they have a common and undivided interest").

[125]*See, e.g., Jewell v. Grain Dealers Mut. Ins. Co.,* 290 F.2d 11, 13 (5th Cir. 1961) (Permitting aggregation against multiple defendants only where they are jointly liable to plaintiff).

[126]*See, e.g., Barefoot Arthitect, Inv. v. Bunge,* 632 F.3d 8232, 836 (3d Cir. 2011) (dismissal of complaint will not bar adjudication of counterclaim that has independent jurisdictional foundation).

would entail for both the parties and the taxpayers. Supplemental jurisdiction is intended to reduce such diseconomies, and at the same time limit damage to federalism by limiting the circumstances in which nondiverse state claims may be prosecuted in federal district courts.

NOTE: 28 U.S.C.A. § 1367, governing supplemental jurisdiction only became effective in December 1990. Prior to that date the area was governed by two closely related doctrines of case law: pendent jurisdiction and ancillary jurisdiction. In creating supplemental jurisdiction, Congress combined much of those two doctrines.[1] However, Congress also overruled some previously existing features of the case law, so that judicial precedent prior to December 1990 should be approached with care.

APPLICATIONS

Limited Survival of Ancillary Jurisdiction

As is discussed immediately above, enactment of 28 U.S.C. § 1367 codified and reduced somewhat the scope of ancillary jurisdiction. However, there is still a small niche in which non-statutory ancillary jurisdiction may exist. For example, when a court has proper jurisdiction over a case, it has jurisdiction over the entire case - including jurisdiction to maintain control of proceedings required to enforce the court's judgment.[2] This jurisdiction exists even in situations where the court could not have exercised jurisdiction if the related issue had come before the court independently.[3]

Prerequisite for Supplemental Jurisdiction

As its name suggests, supplemental jurisdiction is not an independent basis for satisfying requirements of federal subject matter jurisdiction in the same way as federal question jurisdiction or diversity jurisdiction. Instead, counts based on

---

[1]*Peacock v. Thomas*, 516 U.S. 349, 355, 116 S. Ct. 862, 133 L. Ed. 2d 817 (1996). *See, e.g., Global NAPS, Inc. v. Verizon New England Inc.*, 603 F.3d 71, 76 (1st Cir. 2010) (section 1367 provides supplemental jurisdiction "over both compulsory and at least some permissive counterclaims," eliminating previous requirement of independent jurisdiction for permissive counterclaims); *IFC Interconsult, AG v. Safeguard Intern. Partners, LLC.*, 438 F.3d 298, 309 (3d Cir. 2006) ("We do not see the relevant inquiries for ancillary and supplemental jurisdiction as separate."). *But see Robb Evans & Associates, LLC v. Holibaugh*, 609 F.3d 359, 363 (4th Cir. 2010) (although § 1367 codified much of the common law of ancillary jurisdiction, it is still true that certain aspects of ancillary jurisdiction, such as jurisdiction over claims that are related but nonetheless not part of the original action, continue to exist; applying ancillary jurisdiction to circumstances in which court appointed receiver sought to recover property that fell within scope of receiver's authority).

[2]*Peacock v. Thomas*, 516 U.S. 349, 359, 116 S. Ct. 861, 133 L. Ed. 2d 817 (1996) ("Ancillary enforcement jurisdiction is . . . a creature of necessity.").

[3]*See, e.g., National City Mortgage Co. v. Stephen*, 647 F.3d 78, 85 (3d Cir. 2011) (federal courts need power to enforce their own judgments without reliance on state courts).

supplemental jurisdiction must be able to attach themselves to some other count already properly present in the lawsuit. Thus, before supplemental jurisdiction can be invoked, there must already exist at least one count that can satisfy federal subject matter jurisdiction through either, e.g., federal question jurisdiction, diversity jurisdiction, or a suit where the United States is a party.[4]

Prohibitions Contained in Other Federal Statutes

By its terms, § 1367(a) provides that the exercise of supplemental jurisdiction pursuant to § 1367 may be prohibited if another federal statute expressly creates that prohibition.[5]

Standing

In order for a court to hear a claim based on supplemental jurisdiction, there is an additional requirement that each cause of action satisfy requirements for standing. In the absence of standing, a district court may not hear a supplemental claim, notwithstanding that the elements of § 1367 are satisfied.[6]

Same Case or Controversy

28 U.S.C.A. § 1367(a) establishes that supplemental jurisdiction will be effective, if at all, only over non-diverse state claims that "form part of the same case or controversy" as another count or counts in the action. This requirement confirms the need for at least one count in the case that can independently satisfy one of the kinds of federal subject matter jurisdiction

---

[4]28 U.S.C.A. § 1367(a). See also, e.g., In re Aramark Leisure Services, 523 F.3d 1169, 1175 (10th Cir. 2008) ("Under [§ 1367(a)], a federal court may exercise supplemental jurisdiction over related third-party claims when the court has admiralty jurisdiction over the original claim."); Picciotto v. Continental Cas. Co., 512 F.3d 9, 21 (1st Cir. 2008))"[Section 1367(a)] incorporates [the] well established requirement that there be a viable action over which the district court has 'original jurisdiction' before supplemental jurisdiction may be considered."); Nowak v. Ironworkers Local 6 Pension Fund, 81 F.3d 1182, 1187 (2d Cir. 1996) (A court "cannot exercise supplemental jurisdiction unless there is first a proper basis for original federal jurisdiction.").

[5]28 U.S.C.A. § 1367(a). See also 42 U.S.C.A. § 13981(e)(4) (prohibiting use of § 1367 to establish jurisdiction over state law claims seeking divorce, alimony, equitable distribution of marital property, or child custody). See,

e.g., In re Literary Works in Electronic Databases Copyright Litigation, 509 F.3d 116, 127–28 (2d Cir. 2007) (no supplemental jurisdiction "over jurisdictionally-deficient federal claims" attached to claim that satisfied original subject matter jurisdiction); Handberry v. Thompson, 446 F.3d 335, 345–46 (2d Cir. 2006) (18 U.S.C.A. § 3626(a)(1)(A), governing civil suits for prospective relief regarding prison conditions, restricts use of § 1367; where legislative intent is clear, restriction on § 1367 applies notwithstanding that express language of prohibition is absent from statute).

[6]DaimlerChrysler Corp. v. Cuno, 547 U.S. 332, 352, 126 S. Ct. 1854, 164 L. Ed. 2d 589 (2006) (standing for each claim is an additional requirement). See, e.g., Dow Jones & Co. v. Ablaise Ltd., 606 F.3d 1338, 1348 (Fed. Cir. 2010) ("[E]ach of the claims over which a district court exercises its supplemental jurisdiction must have standing on its own.").

discussed above.[7] It goes further than that, however, in requiring some relationship between the supplemental count and the counts that already satisfy jurisdiction.[8] The pre-1990 case law concentrated on how much similarity existed between the witnesses and evidence relevant to the respective counts. Where substantial similarity existed, the court's power to hear non-diverse state claims could probably be established. Cases applying the "same case or controversy" standard of § 1367 are likely to employ much the same approach to determining whether the non-diverse state counts are sufficiently related to the other counts to satisfy supplemental jurisdiction.[9]

Sovereign Immunity

It appears settled that § 1367 does not contain a waiver of federal sovereign immunity. Thus, even if a particular claim would otherwise fall within a district court's supplemental jurisdiction, sovereign immunity could still be a bar to hearing an additional claim.[10]

Joined or Intervening Parties

28 U.S.C.A. § 1367(a) specifically provides that in appropri-

---

[7]See, e.g., Lindsay v. Government Employees Ins. Co., 448 F.3d 416, 423 (D.C. Cir. 2006) (§ 1367(a) "encompasses both diversity jurisdiction and federal question jurisdiction").

[8]See, e.g., Ammerman v. Sween, 54 F.3d 423, 424 (7th Cir. 1995) ("A loose factual connection between the claims" may satisfy the requirements of same case or controversy.). But see Serrano-Moran v. Grau-Gaztambide, 195 F.3d 68, 69 (1st Cir. 1999) (civil rights claim against police officers accused of beating deceased does not share common nucleus of facts with supplemental claim of malpractice against medical defendants).

[9]See, e.g., ABF Freight Systems v. International Brotherhood of Teamsters, 654 F.3d 954, 963 (8th Cir. 2011) (equating same case or controversy with common nucleus of operative fact; noting that test for both phrases is whether a party might be expected to try all claims in one proceeding); ABF Freight System, Inc. v. International Brotherhood of Teamsters, 645 F.3d 954, 963 (8th Cir. 2011) (equating same case or controversy with older terminology, i.e., common nucleus of operative fact; noting that test is whether claims are sufficiently similar so that normally plaintiff would bring them in same

case); Houskins v. Sheahan, 549 F.3d 480, 495 (7th Cir. 2008) ("A loose factual connection is generally sufficient."); Tamiami Partners, Ltd. ex rel. Tamiami Development Corp. v. Miccosukee Tribe of Indians of Fla., 177 F.3d 1212 (11th Cir. 1999) (all claims arose from defendant's actions relating to underlying agreement; holding requirement for commonality satisfied even though success of federal claims did not depend on success of state claims); see also 3D Systems, Inc. v. Aarotech Laboratories, Inc., 160 F.3d 1373, 1377 (Fed. Cir. 1998) (state claims of trade libel and unfair competition are "hand-in-hand" with federal claims of patent infringement when all claims arise out of defendant's sales activity for certain products in California); Itar-Tass Russian News Agency v. Russian Kurier, Inc., 140 F.3d 442, 445–48 (2d Cir. 1998) (state law motion for fees for plaintiff's attorney and expert witness are supplemental to underlying federal copyright claims).

[10]See, e.g., San Juan County, Utah v. U.S., 503 F.3d 1163, 1182 n. 4 (10th Cir. 2007) (en banc) (also expressing doubt that § 1367 could be used to defeat state sovereign immunity as such immunity is preserved in the Eleventh Amendment of the United States Constitution).

ate circumstances supplemental jurisdiction may be extended to include counts involving joined or intervening parties.[11] This provision overrides prior case law holding that courts could not extend their ancillary jurisdiction to persons not already parties to the case.[12] However, this provision is limited somewhat by § 1367(b), discussed below.

Nondiverse Pendent Parties and Claims

Closely related to some of the issues addressed by § 1367(b) is the question of nondiverse pendent parties. Prior to enactment of § 1367, it was fairly well settled that simply because one plaintiff could assert diversity jurisdiction, a nondiverse plaintiff could not attach a state claim to the first plaintiff's diverse count. That result applied even if the two claims were closely related.

Now, however, a different result may apply. The settled rule now is that where all the other requirements of supplemental jurisdiction are satisfied, and at least one plaintiff already named in the action satisfies the amount in controversy requirement, claims by other plaintiffs that fall short of the jurisdictional amount may be treated as supplemental to the claim that satisfies original jurisdiction.[13]

The result is different, however, if the presence of additional parties would violate the requirement of diverse citizenship. In that circumstance, § 1367 does not authorize supplemental jurisdiction.[14]

Claims under Foreign Law

If a cause of action arising under foreign law could be heard by a state court, it appears that such a claim could be a supplemental claim under § 1367.[15]

Sua Sponte Application

It is settled that federal courts may dismiss a case for lack of subject matter jurisdiction even when the parties have not

---

[11]*See, e.g., Ciambriello v. County of Nassau*, 292 F.3d 307, 325 (2d Cir. 2002) (federal claims against one defendant (but not others) dismissed; but state claims against defendant who obtained dismissal of federal claim remain in federal court under § 1367(a)); *Tamiami Partners, Ltd. ex rel. Tamiami Development Corp. v. Miccosukee Tribe of Indians of Fla.*, 177 F.3d 1212, 1223–24 (11th Cir. 1999) ("[T]he parties to the federal and supplemental claims need not be identical in order for supplemental jurisdiction to lie.").

[12]*See, e.g., Abbott Laboratories v. CVS Pharmacy, Inc.*, 290 F.3d 854, 858 (7th Cir. 2002) ("Ever since 28 U.S.C. § 1367(a) overturned [prior case law], the supplemental jurisdiction

has been capacious enough to include claims by or against third parties.").

[13]*Exxon Mobil Corp. v. Allapattah Services, Inc.*, 545 U.S. 546, 558–59, 125 S. Ct. 2611, 162 L. Ed. 2d 502 (2005).

[14]*See, e.g., Merrill Lynch & Co. Inc. v. Allegheny Energy, Inc.*, 500 F.3d 171, 179 (2d Cir. 2007) (explaining that expansive language of Supreme Court's explanation of § 1367 in *Exxon Mobil Corp. v. Allapattah Services, Inc.*, "does not extend to additional parties whose presence defeats diversity").

[15]*See, e.g., Voda v. Cordis Corp.*, 476 F.3d 887, 894 (Fed. Cir. 2007) (this result assumes that all requirements for supplemental jurisdiction are met).

raised the issue.[16] However, when a party asserting a nondiverse claim has not attempted to invoke supplemental jurisdiction, there is uncertainty as to whether courts should invoke such jurisdiction *sua sponte*.[17] Attorneys are encouraged to investigate the local practice.

Restrictions on Supplemental Jurisdiction

28 U.S.C.A. § 1367(b) eliminates the use of supplemental jurisdiction when certain facts are present. Thus, even if a nondiverse state count meets the "same case or controversy" requirement of § 1367(a), it may still not qualify for supplemental jurisdiction. This possibility occurs when the counts already satisfying federal subject matter jurisdiction are based solely on diversity jurisdiction under § 1332 and either of two other elements are present:

(1) the non-diverse counts are claims by plaintiffs[18] in the original action against persons made parties under Rule 14 (impleader), Rule 19 (joinder), Rule 20 (permissive joinder), or Rule 24 (intervention);[19] *or*

(2) the non-diverse counts are claims by persons who entered the case as plaintiffs under either Rule 19 (joinder) or Rule 24 (intervention).[20]

The exceptions in 28 U.S.C.A. § 1367(b) are a legislative

---

[16]*See, e.g., Pennsylvania Nurses Ass'n v. Pennsylvania State Educ. Ass'n*, 90 F.3d 797, 801 (3d Cir. 1996) ("[W]e must consider the jurisdictional question even where the parties are prepared to concede it.").

[17]*Compare, e.g., U.S. ex rel. Ramseyer v. Century Healthcare Corp.*, 90 F.3d 1514 (10th Cir. 1996) (declining to invoke supplemental jurisdiction where plaintiff failed to assert it in complaint), *with* Townsquare Media, Inc. v. Brill, ____ F.3d ____, ____ (7th Cir. 2011) (if case involved federal claim as well as non-diverse state law claims, plaintiff has no affirmative duty to cite § 1367 as basis of supplemental jurisdiction); *Rodriguez v. Doral Mortg. Corp.*, 57 F.3d 1168 (1st Cir. 1995) (holding that federal court, with proper notice to parties, may invoke supplemental jurisdiction on its own initiative over previously unpleaded nondiverse state claim that court identified for parties).

[18]*See, e.g., LM Insurance Corp. v. Spaulding Enterprises, Inc.*, 533 F.3d 542 (7th Cir. 2008) (no supplemental jurisdiction when plaintiff would be suing non-diverse defendant joined under Rule 20). *But cf., Kemper/Prime Indus. Partners v. Montgomery Watson*

Americas, Inc., 487 F.3d 1061, 1063 (7th Cir. 2007) ("[A] defendant's impleader under Fed. R. Civ. P. 14 of a party that is not diverse from the plaintiff does not destroy jurisdiction."). *United Capitol Ins. Co. v. Kapiloff*, 155 F.3d 488 (4th Cir.1998) (defendants in declaratory judgment action sought to use supplemental jurisdiction to join nondiverse parties on counterclaim; held, § 1367(b) does not bar such joinder).

[19]*See, e.g., Ryan ex rel. Ryan v. Schneider Nat. Carriers, Inc.*, 263 F.3d 816, 820 (8th Cir. 2001) (per curiam) (diversity claims by several plaintiffs; cross-claim by some plaintiffs against another plaintiff, who was not diverse from them; held, § 1367(b) does not prevent use of supplemental jurisdiction over cross-claim because original plaintiff sued on cross-claim was not made party by other plaintiffs under any of Rules 14, 19, 20 or 24); *Burka v. Aetna Life Ins. Co.*, 87 F.3d 478 n. 4 (D.C. Cir. 1996) (noting that § 1367(b) does not prevent use of supplemental jurisdiction over claims against parties added pursuant to Rule 25(c)).

[20]*See, e.g., Barefoot Architect, Inc. v. Bunge*, 632 F.3d 822, 836 (3d Cir. 2011) (denying use of supplemental ju-

adoption of existing case law. An example may demonstrate their operation.

◆ ***Example:*** If a plaintiff wanted to sue two defendants on a tort claim, but only one of the defendants was of citizenship diverse from that of the plaintiff, a claim against both defendants could not be filed in federal court. Instead, the plaintiff might sue only the diverse defendant, in which case (assuming other requirements of jurisdiction are satisfied), the federal court could hear the claim. In those circumstances it would often be predictable that the diverse defendant would use Rule 14 to implead the non-diverse defendant. Now that the non-diverse defendant is in the case, the plaintiff might seek to bring a new count against the non-diverse defendant. Requirements of § 1367(a) would be satisfied, because the count against the non-diverse defendant certainly forms part of the same case or controversy as the original count against the diverse defendant. Notice, however, what the effective result is, if this "supplemental" count against the non-diverse defendant is allowed. The plaintiff, by anticipating the impleader, will have achieved suit in federal district court against both defendants—even though diversity jurisdiction would have failed if plaintiff had sought to sue them both directly. However, § 1367(b) prohibits the plaintiff from using supplemental jurisdiction to sue a party joined under Rule 14. In fact, § 1367(b) usually precludes use of supplemental jurisdiction by a plaintiff if the original basis of federal subject matter jurisdiction is diversity jurisdiction under § 1332.

NOTE: Note that 28 U.S.C.A. § 1367(b) restricts a plaintiff's use of supplemental jurisdiction only when the original cause of action is based upon diversity jurisdiction under § 1332 and the exercise of supplemental jurisdiction would contradict the requirements of § 1332.[21] Thus, where the underlying facts do not conflict with the requirements of § 1332, the prohibition contained in § 1367(b) is inapplicable.[22] If the original basis for federal jurisdiction is a federal question, under § 1331, the restrictions

---

risdiction by plaintiffs seeking to intervene under Rule 24).

[21] 28 U.S.C.A. § 1367(b).

[22] *See, e.g., Mattel, Inc. v. Bryant,* 446 F.3d 1011, 1014 (9th Cir. 2006) ("Neither § 1332 nor § 1367 upset the long-established judge-made rule that the presence of a nondiverse and not indispensable defendant intervenor does not destroy complete diversity."); *Aurora Loan Services, Inc. v. Craddieth,* 442 F.3d 1018, 1025 (7th Cir. 2006)

("Section 1367(b)'s purpose of preventing plaintiffs who would have destroyed federal jurisdiction had they joined a suit at its outset from using Rule 24 to circumvent the requirement of complete diversity has no application to a party forced to intervene to protect an interest that arose during the course of a federal litigation in which he had no stake at the outset. Such a party has no say in deciding where the suit is brought and so cannot be gaming the system;" also not-

imposed by § 1367(b) on the use of supplemental jurisdiction simply do not apply.

Sovereign Immunity

It is settled that § 1367 does not create a waiver of the sovereign immunity of the United States.[23]

Criminal Cases

It appears settled that § 1367 has no applicability to the jurisdiction of federal courts when they exercise ancillary jurisdiction in criminal cases.[24]

Court's Discretion

Even if supplemental jurisdiction exists under 28 U.S.C.A. § 1367(a) and (b), § 1367(c) provides the court with substantial discretion to refuse to hear the supplemental counts.[25] When a district court dismisses state counts under any provision of § 1367(c), it will typically do so without prejudice to any refiling of those counts in state court.[26]

---

ing that federal jurisdiction is usually determined as of date complaint is filed).

[23]*See, e.g., Dunn & Black, P.S. v. U.S.*, 492 F.3d 1084, 1088 n.3, (9th Cir. 2007) ("§ 1367 merely grants federal court supplemental jurisdiction over state claims related to certain federal claims in any civil action of which the district court has original jurisdiction . . . and that section cannot 'operate as a waiver of the United States sovereign immunity.' ").

[24]*See, e.g., Garcia v. Teitler*, 443 F.3d 202, 207 (2d Cir. 2006) (noting that § 1367, by its terms, relates to "civil action").

[25]*Carlsbad Tech, Inc. v. HIF Bio, Inc.*, 556 U.S. 635, 639, 129 S. Ct. 1862, 1866, 173 L. Ed. 2d 843 (2009) ("A district court's decision whether to exercise [subject matter jurisdiction over state claims] after dismissing every claim over which it had original jurisdiction is purely discretionary."). *See, e.g., Estate of Amergi v. Palestinian Authority*, 611 F.3d 1350,1366 (11th Cir. 2010) (court may appropriately consider "inconvenience, expense, and fairness to the parties"); *Dargis v. Sheahan*, 526 F.3d 981, 990 (7th Cir. 2008) (district court should relinquish jurisdiction over state claims "unless any of the following three circumstances exist: (1) the state law claims may not be refiled because

a statute of limitations has expired, (2) substantial judicial resources have been expended on the state claims, or (3) it is clearly apparent how the state claims are to be decided"); *Palmer v. Hospital Authority of Randolph County*, 22 F.3d 1559, 1566 (11th Cir. 1994) (emphasizing that § 1367(c) permitted district court's rejection or retention of jurisdiction; court could refuse to hear case even when it had power to do so). *See also In re Repository Technologies, Inc.*, 601 F.3d 710, 721 (7th Cir. 2010) (power to remand under § 1367(c) "does not extend to claims over which the district court has original jurisdiction").

[26]*See, e.g., Gregory v. Dillard's, Inc.*, 565 F.3d 464, 477 (8th Cir. 2009) (en banc) (where federal claims were properly dismissed, state claims also properly dismissed as novel questions of state law should be dismissed without prejudice "so they may be decided by [state] courts"); *Horton v. Board of County Com'rs of Flagler County*, 202 F.3d 1297, 1300 n. 3 (11th Cir. 2000) (if district court dismisses under § 1367(c) plaintiff can refile in state court); *Bass v. Parkwood Hosp.*, 180 F.3d 234, 236 (5th Cir. 1999) ("When a court dismisses all federal claims before trial, the general rule is to dismiss any pendent claims. . . . However, the dismissal of the pendent claims should expressly be without prejudice so that the plaintiff may

The four circumstances[27] in which a federal court might choose to dismiss a count that otherwise qualifies for supplemental jurisdiction are:

(1) *Difficult Questions of State Law:* This provision of 28 U.S.C.A. § 1367(c)(1) codifies the common sense precedent permitting district courts to dismiss a non-diverse state count if it is clear state courts would be better able to untangle the uncertain questions of state law. However, it is likely that federal courts will employ § 1367(c)(1) only in unusual cases involving the greatest difficulty in applying state law.[28]

(2) *Non-Diverse State Claim Predominates:* The court may decline to exercise supplemental jurisdiction when the non-diverse state claim predominates over the claims which formed the original basis of the court's subject matter jurisdiction.[29] Such cases are probably fairly unusual.

(3) *Original Counts Dismissed:* Sometimes the court may decline to exercise supplemental jurisdiction when it has already dismissed the claims over which it has federal question or diversity jurisdiction.[30] Whether the court "may" dismiss, or "must" dismiss, the supplemental claims depends heavily on

---

refile his claims in the appropriate state court.").

[27]*See, e.g., Enochs v. Lampasas County,* 641 F.3d 155, 164(5th Cir. 2010) (suggesting that various considerations should not be evaluated as independent grounds for dismissal, but rather should be balanced with one another).

[28]*See, e.g., D.D. ex rel. V.D. v. New York City Bd. of Educ.,* 480 F.3d 138 (2d Cir. 2007) (supplemental jurisdiction inappropriate because "State and City regulatory schemes are intricate and difficulty to interpret"); *Houlton Citizens' Coalition v. Town of Houlton,* 175 F.3d 178 (1st Cir.1999) (federal claims resolved before trial; state claim was both difficult and novel question; held, district court should dismiss state claim without prejudice); *Edmondson & Gallagher v. Alban Towers Tenants Ass'n,* 48 F.3d 1260 (D.C. Cir. 1995) (justifying refusal to hear state claims because the applicable law has been the subject of conflicting decisions). *Cf., Parker v. Scrap Metal Processors, Inc.,* 468 F.3d 733, 743–44 (11th Cir. 2006) ("Generally, state tort claims are not considered novel or complex. . . . Moreover, negligence, nuisance, and property damage claims have been held as not raising novel or complex issues of state law.").

[29]*See, e.g., Diven v. Amalgamated Transit Union Intern. and Local 689,* 38 F.3d 598, 602 (D.C. Cir. 1994) (apparent primacy of state claim indicated by weakness of federal claim— "even before discovery"). *Cf., San Pedro Hotel Co., Inc. v. City of Los Angeles,* 159 F.3d 470, 478 (9th Cir. 1998) (if court dismisses under § 1367(c)(2), failure to state reasons for doing so is not abuse of discretion; nevertheless, suggesting that courts should provide explanation, and noting that statement of reasons is required for dismissal under § 1367(c)(4)); *Ervin v. OS Restaurant Services, Inc.,* 632 F.3d 971, 980 (7th Cir. 2011) ("A simple disparity in numbers [of parties] should not lead a court to the conclusion that a state claim 'substantially predominates' over the [federal] action.").

[30]*See, e.g., Campbell v. West Pittston Borough,* ___ F.3d ___, ___ (3d Cir. 2012) (early grant of summary judgment may also be ground to dismiss remaining state claims); *Roche v. John Hancock Mut. Life Ins. Co.,* 81 F.3d 249, 256–57 (1st Cir. 1996) (identifying factors of "comity, judicial economy, convenience, fairness, and the like" in deciding whether to dismiss under § 1367(c)(3)). *But cf., Goodson v. City of Corpus Christi,* 202 F.3d 730, 741 (5th Cir. 2000) (if district court erroneously dismisses claims

the reasoning that underlies the dismissal of the claims that asserted original subject matter jurisdiction. If the basis for dismissal of those claims is a finding that the court lacked original jurisdiction, the supplemental claims must be dismissed.[31] If, on the other hand, the basis for dismissal of the supplemental claims relates to the merits, the district court may have discretion to retain the supplemental claims under § 1367(c).[32]

Courts applying § 1367(c) also give substantial weight to the point in the case at which dismissal on the merits occurred. If the federal court was able to dismiss the federal question or diversity claims at the outset of the case, it would probably be appropriate to dismiss the supplemental claims immediately (or remand to state court if the case reached federal court through the process of removal).[33] If, however, the federal court proceeded through much of the litigation and had informed

---

that enjoyed original jurisdiction, it is abuse of discretion to dismiss state claims on ground that original jurisdiction is lacking).

[31]*Arbaugh v. Y&H Corp.*, 546 U.S. 500, 126 S. Ct. 1235, 1244, 163 L. Ed. 2d 1097 (2006) ("[W]hen a federal court concludes that it lacks subject-matter jurisdiction, the court must dismiss the complaint in its entirety."). *See, e.g., Scarfo v. Ginsberg*, 175 F.3d 957 (11th Cir. 1999) ("The federal courts of appeals . . . have uniformly held that once the district court determines that subject matter jurisdiction over a plaintiff's federal claims does not exist, courts must dismiss a plaintiff's [nondiverse] state law claims."). *But see Eastman v. Marine Mechanical Corp.*, 438 F.3d 544, 551 (6th Cir. 2006) (subject matter jurisdiction is evaluated as of date of removal of case from state court; "but if an amendment eliminates all the federal claims, remand becomes a discretionary decision.").

[32]*Arbaugh v. Y&H Corp.*, 546 U.S. 500, 126 S. Ct. 1235, 1244–45, 163 L. Ed. 2d 1097 (2006) ("[W]hen a court grants a motion to dismiss for failure to state a federal claim, the court generally retains discretion to exercise supplemental jurisdiction, pursuant to 28 U.S.C. § 1367, over pendent state-law claims."). *See, e.g., Beck v. Dobrowski*, 559 F.3d 680, 686 (7th Cir. 2009) (presumption in favor of dismissal "is strengthened when . . . an identical case is already pending in state court and is nearer final resolu-

tion than the claim in the federal suit"); *Herman Family Revocable Trust v. Teddy Bear*, 254 F.3d 802 (9th Cir.2001) ("A dismissal on the merits is different from a dismissal on jurisdictional grounds. If the district court dismisses all federal claims on the merits, it has discretion under § 1367(c) to adjudicate the remaining claims; if the court dismisses for lack of subject matter jurisdiction, it has no discretion and must dismiss all claims.")

[33]*Carnegie-Mellon University v. Cohill*, 484 U.S. 343, 350, 108 S. Ct. 614, 98 L. Ed. 2d 720 (1988) (noting absence of inflexible or mandatory rule, but "[i]n the usual case in which all federal-law claims are eliminated before trial, the balance of the factors to be considered under [supplemental jurisdiction]-judicial economy, convenience, fairness, and comity-will point toward declining to exercise jurisdiction over the remaining state-law claims"). *See, e.g., Hedges v. Musco*, 204 F.3d 109, 123 (3d Cir. 2000) (where claim that was basis for original jurisdiction is dismissed before trial, district court " 'must decline to decide [supplemental claims] unless consideration of judicial economy, convenience, and fairness to the parties provide an affirmative justification for doing so' "); *Annulli v. Panikkar*, 200 F.3d 189, 202–03 (3d Cir. 1999) (no abuse of discretion to dismiss state claims even though federal claims were on "eve of trial" when defendant filed motion for summary judgment; although federal court was site of two

itself of the merits of the supplemental claims, then dismissal of the other claims would probably not justify dismissing the supplemental claims.[34]

(4) *Other Exceptional Circumstances:* This provision of 28 U.S.C.A. § 1367(c) obviously provides the court with discretion in circumstances not anticipated by Congress.[35]

Important: It is important to note that if a non-diverse state claim fails to qualify for supplemental jurisdiction and is dismissed (or remanded to state court) by the court, the dismissal has no consequence for claims that qualify for the court's jurisdiction. Those latter claims may continue to be prosecuted.[36] It is possible, however, that for reasons of economy a claimant may choose to dismiss the qualifying claims and

---

years of litigation, fifteen pages of court docket, 1,800 pages of depositions, and 2,800 pages of discovery documents, plaintiff could still use evidence in state court; moreover, plaintiff assumed risk of dismissal of state claims when plaintiff filed in federal court and invoked § 1367).

[34]*See, e.g., Tomaiolo v. Mallinoff,* 281 F.3d 1, 11 (1st Cir. 2002) (retention of state claims was not abuse of discretion when "[t]he litigation was far advanced, the court had before it cross-motions for summary judgment, discovery had closed, [the plaintiff] had filed her sixth amended complaint, and all claims arose from the same core of facts"); *Miller Aviation v. Milwaukee County Bd. of Supervisors,* 273 F.3d 722, 731–32 (7th Cir. 2001) (abuse of discretion to dismiss state count when previous disposition of federal claim left nothing of state claim for state court to decide, or when substantial investment of judicial resources have already been expended and dismissal would therefore produce judicial efficiency). *Mizuna, Ltd. v. Crossland Federal Sav. Bank,* 90 F.3d 650 (2d Cir. 1996) (claim supporting original jurisdiction voluntarily dismissed; held, because court had properly acquired original jurisdiction, it enjoyed discretion to retain supplemental jurisdiction over related nondiverse claims; discretion to retain supplemental counts properly exercised where "three judicial officers had already expended substantial resources . . . over a year's time").

[35]*See, e.g., Gregory v. Shelby County, Tenn.,* 220 F.3d 433, 446 (6th Cir. 2000) (where state law provides that cause of action against state officer in his official capacity is within "exclusive original jurisdiction" of state trial court, state legislature's "clear preference" to have such claims tried in state court is exceptional circumstance within scope of § 1367(c)(4)); *Birchem v. Knights of Columbus,* 116 F.3d 310, n. 3, 22 A.D.D. 770 (8th Cir. 1997) (if plaintiff, who is entitled to jury trial, seeks to join federal claims with state claims, but state cause of action places burden of proof on defendant, trial court should consider dismissing state claim under § 1367(c)(4)); *Hays County Guardian v. Supple,* 969 F.2d 111 (5th Cir. 1992) (finding exceptional circumstances and compelling reasons where adjudicating state claims in federal court would parallel adjudication of identical claims in state court). *Cf., Treglia v. Town of Manlius,* 313 F.3d 713, 723 (2d Cir. 2002) (court has discretion to decline supplemental jurisdiction only if reason is based on at least one of four enumerated categories in § 1367(c)); *Executive Software North America, Inc. v. U.S. Dist. Court for Cent. Dist. of California,* 24 F.3d 1545, 1557 (9th Cir. 1994) (if court dismisses under § 1367(c)(4), it must identify the circumstances the court found "exceptional").

[36]*See, e.g., In re City of Mobile,* 75 F.3d 605, 607–08 (11th Cir. 1996) (although properly remanding nondiverse counts to state court, district court has no authority under § 1367(c) to remand counts within its original subject matter jurisdiction).

prosecute those claims, along with the dismissed claims, in state court.

Statutes of Limitations

28 U.S.C.A. § 1367(d) provides that actions filed in federal court under § 1367(a), and subsequently dismissed, will usually not be barred by a statute of limitations because of time lost in federal court.[37] Section 1367(d) accomplishes this end by tolling statutes of limitations while the claim is pending, and by providing a period of at least 30 days after dismissal in which the claim may be refiled in state court. Moreover, § 1367(d) provides that if state law will allow more than 30 days in which to refile, the claimant will enjoy the benefit of the longer period.[38] Section 1367(d) is a most unusual provision, in that it is a circumstance where federal law extends a state statute of limitations for a claim that arises under state law. However, it is now settled that the provision is constitutional.[39]

Tolling Other Claims

If a claim filed under 28 U.S.C.A. § 1367(a) is dismissed by the federal court, it is possible the claimant will want to dismiss other claims that qualify for federal subject matter jurisdiction, so that the entire case may be refiled in state court. To permit such a possibility free of the bar of statutes of limitations, § 1367(d)'s tolling provisions also extend to claims voluntarily dismissed in the aftermath of a denial of supplemental jurisdiction to one claim.

"State" Defined

28 U.S.C.A. § 1367(e) provides that whenever the term "State" is used in § 1367, it shall also include the District of Columbia, Puerto Rico, and United States Territories.

ADDITIONAL RESEARCH REFERENCES

C.J.S., Federal Courts §§ 11 to 26 et seq.
West's Key Number Digest, Federal Courts ⨂14 to 25

§ 2.14 Venue

---

[37]*But cf., Raygor v. Regents of University of Minnesota*, 534 U.S. 533, 122 S. Ct. 999, 152 L. Ed. 2d 27 (2002) (when state claims asserted under § 1367 are dismissed on Eleventh Amendment grounds, § 1367(d) does not toll statute of limitations for such claims against non-consenting defendants).

[38]*Myers v. County of Lake, Ind.*, 30 F.3d 847, 848 (7th Cir. 1994) (§ 1367(d) "removes the principal reason for retaining a case in federal court when the federal claim belatedly disappears.").

[39]*Jinks v. Richland County, S.C.*, 538 U.S. 456, 123 S. Ct. 1667, 155 L. Ed. 2d 631 (2003). *But cf., Raygor v. Regents of University of Minnesota*, 534 U.S. 533, 122 S. Ct. 999, 152 L. Ed. 2d 27 (2002) (§ 1367(d) does not toll limitations period when suit is dismissed because a State, as defendant, has asserted 11th Amendment immunity to suit against federal court).

CORE CONCEPT

The requirement of venue sets the appropriate federal districts in which a particular case should be heard. Requirements to satisfy venue are additional to the jurisdictional prerequisites. Thus, even if a plaintiff satisfied both kinds of jurisdiction, the case might still be dismissed if venue was lacking.[1] State courts are also subject to the venue requirements established by their respective legislatures, and such requirements may differ significantly from the federal venue statutes. For federal courts, however, the only venue requirements that must be met are those enacted by Congress.[2]

APPLICATIONS

Section 1390(a): Venue and Subjet Matter Jurisdiction

Section 1390 was added to Title 28 as part of the 2012 amendments. Section 1390(a) fulfills two purposes. First it provides a definition of venue as the proper geographic location(s) (i.e., the proper district court or courts) for a particular civil action that falls within the subject matter jurisdiction of a district court. Second, § 1390(a) also makes clear that venue requirements for federal district courts are separate and distinct from requirements of subject matter jurisdiction,[3] which are addressed in other portions of Title 28 and this text.

Section 1390(b): Not Applicable to Admiralty, Maritime or Prize Cases

New § 1390(b) makes clear that the general venue provisions of § 1391, discussed below, do not extend to cases in federal district court arising under § 1333, which governs cases arising under federal admiralty or maritime law.[4]

Section 1390(c): Venue, Removal and Transfer

Settled case law existing prior to the 2012 venue amendments provides that if a claim is removed from a state court to a federal district court § 1391, discussed below, does not apply. Thus, a removed claim is treated somewhat differently than a case originally filed in federal district court.[5] However, a party who sought removal of a claim does not thereby waive a chal-

---

[1] *Cf., e.g., U. S. ex rel. Rudick v. Laird*, 412 F.2d 16, 20 (2d Cir. 1969) ("[J]urisdiction must first be found over the subject matter and the persons involved in the cause before the question of venue can be properly reached.").

[2] *Cf, Leroy v. Great Western United Corp.*, 443 U.S. 173, 184, 99 S. Ct. 2710, 61 L. Ed. 2d 464 (1979) ("The desirability of consolidating similar claims in a single proceeding . . . does not justify reading [28 U.S.C. § 1391] to give the plaintiff the right to select the place of trial that best suits his convenience."); *SEC v. Johnson*, 650 F.3d 710, 716 (D.C. Cir. 2011) (venue should not be given "liberal" or "policy" construction).

[3] 28 U.S.C. § 1390(a).

[4] 28 U.S.C. § 1390(b).

[5] *Polizzi v. Cowles Magazines, Inc.*, 345 U.S. 663, 665, 73 S. Ct. 900, 902, 97 L. Ed. 2d 133) (1953) ("[T]he venue of removed actions is governed by . . . § 1441(a) (the basic federal removal statute)."). *See, e.g., PT United Can Co. v. Crown Cork & Seal Co.*, 138

lenge to the state court's venue. That challenged is preserved and may be raised in a federal court.[6]

New 1390(c) makes clear that the new venue provisions of Title 28 do not change existing law governing the location of a district court that will hear a civil action that has been removed from state court. However, new § 1390(c) adds a new wrinkle if a case has been removed and is now the subject of a possible transfer from the district court to which it had been removed to some other district court. In that circumstance 1390(c) expressly provides that if a case has been removed to a federal district court, venue provisions such as § 1391, discussed below, govern which districts and/or divisionss of federal district courts may hear the transferred case.[7]

Introduction to Venue

Section 1391 restricts the choice of federal district court in which a plaintiff may sue to those districts that Congress deems fair. This assessment of fairness is sometimes quite distinct from the concepts of constitutional fairness discussed under jurisdiction over persons or things. Thus, it is possible that a federal district court might have satisfactory personal jurisdiction over a defendant, but the action could still be dismissed for failure to meet venue requirements. For example, a defendant might be served with process within the state where the federal court sits, which would normally satisfy personal jurisdiction, but requirements of § 1391 might still not be met. In that sense, venue can be an additional trap for the unwary plaintiff.

Considerations of the relative merits of venue requirements aside, § 1391 can influence significantly the suitability of the particular federal district court a plaintiff has chosen. For that reason alone, the technical elements of venue are also important to successful prosecutions and defenses of civil claims in federal court.

Section 1391: Venue Generally

Section 1391 was amended substantially in 2012. One result is that much of the older case law is now displaced, so that older precedent must be used with care, if at all. In a few respects, however, the amended statute does not change older law. Section 1391(a), for example, still provides that § 1391 governs venue for all civil actions, except in circumstances where a special venue provision may apply to a particular cause of action.[8]

Local or Transitory Actions

As amended, § 1391(a)(2) makes no distinction between ac-

F.3d 65, 72 (2d Cir. 1998) (in a removed case "one may not challenge venue I the district court as of right according to that court's venue rules, as if the case had been originally brought there.").

[6]*PT United Can Co. v. Crown Cork & Seal Co.*, 138 F.3d 65, 73 (2d Cir. 1998).

[7]28 U.S.C. § 1390(c).

[8]28 U.S.C. § 1391(a)(1). *See also, e.g.,* 28 U.S.C. § 1401 (governing venue in shareholder's derivative actions).

tions that might previously have been deemed "local" or "transitory" in nature. Thus, older law that might have restrict certain causes of action dealing with disputes over land to the district in which the land is located is now ineffective.[9]

Venue in Diversity and Federal Question Cases

Amended § 1391(b) eliminates older distinctions between venue requirements for diversity lawsuits and venue for cases arising from federal questions. It should be noted that these new venue requirements are similar in substance to the older requirements for those causes of action, but the new provision eliminates relatively minor distinctions in wording that may have caused more confusion than they were worth.

As now written, § 1391(b) permits either of two options for satisfying the venue requirement, plus a third option that may be employed by a plaintiff *if* neither of the first two options is available. It is useful to keep in mind, therefore, that there are not necessarily three venue options. Instead, a plaintiff has only two options, with the third available only if the first two options can be used in the circumstances of a particular case.

Where Defendant Resides: in any judicial district where any defendant resides, provided that all defendants reside in the same state.[10]

Where Substantial Events or Omissions Occurred: in any judicial district in which a substantial part of the relevant events occurred,[11] or where a substantial part of the property that gave rise to the action is found, such as a district in which damage occurred in a tort case, or where performance was to have occurred in a contract action.[12] It should be noted that in pre-amendment cases, courts generally considered acts of both the plaintiff and the defendant.[13]

Where Any Defendant is Subject to Personal Jurisdiction: in any judicial district in which any defendant is subject to personal jurisdiction at the time a suit is filed. Note that for the purposes of new § 1391(b)(3), personal jurisdiction is measured by the boundaries of a federal judicial district. Thus, in

---

[9]28 U.S.C. § 1391(a)(2).

[10]*See, e.g., Algodonero De Las Cabezas, S.A. v. American Suisse Capital, Inc.*, 432 F.3d 1341, 1345 (11th Cir. 2005) (corporations that conduct business, receive correspondence, and are subject to service of process in a district are "residents" in that district; if such corporations are the only defendants, § 1391(b)(1) is satisfied).

[11]*See, e.g., Uffner v. La Reunion Francaise, S.A.*, 244 F.3d 38, 42 (1st Cir. 2001) (when events underlying claim occurred in different places, "venue may be proper in any number of districts;" but when single event supports allegation of venue in particular district, event must be substantial).

[12]*See, e.g., Voest-Alpine Tradiong USA Corp. v. Bank of China*, 288 F.3d 262, 265 (5th Cir. 2002) (dispute over validity of letter of credit that was issued in China; held, good venue in Houston where letter was accepted in Houston; letter was presented to correspondent bank in Houston; and payment was to be made to correspondent bank in Houston).

[13]*See, e.g., Uffner v. La Reunion Francoise, S.A.*, 244 F.3d 38, 43 n.6 (1st Cir. 2001) (collecting cases and adopting majority view).

states which have more than one judicial district, § 1391(b)(3) may be used to satisfy venue requirements only when a defendant is subject to personal jurisdiction in that portion of the state which comprises the federal judicial district. It should also be noted that § 1391(b)(3) may only be employed if a party is unable to satisfy venue requirements under either § 1391(b)(1) 0r (b)(2). If either of those options is available, the party may not employ 1391(b)(3).[14]

Federal Judicial Districts

State borders matter significantly in questions of jurisdiction. For venue questions, however, the important boundary is that which exists between federal judicial districts. In smaller states, the entire state may be a single district. In Rhode Island, for example, the United States District Court for the District of Rhode Island is the only federal district court within the state. Larger states may have as many as four federal judicial districts within them. New York, for example has four judicial districts: the Eastern, Western, Southern, and Northern Districts.

◆ **NOTE:** It is also possible that a federal judicial district will break itself down into still smaller components. For example, the United States District Court for the Eastern District of Virginia is one of two federal district courts within Virginia. The Eastern District, in turn, is subdivided into four divisions: the Alexandria Division; the Norfolk Division; the Richmond Division; and the Newport News Division. Local rules of a federal district court might supplement venue statutes by requiring that a case be filed not only within the proper judicial district, but also within the appropriate division within that district.[15]

Venue and Residence

Reference is frequently made throughout § 1391 to judicial districts or states in which a defendant resides. As amended in 2012, § 1391(c) establishes venue standards for both natural persons who are individual defendants as well as legal entities with the capacity to sue or be sued in their own names. As discussed below, § 11391(c) also provides that defendants not resident in the United States have no venue defense to a civil suit.

Venue for Natural Persons: Section 1391(b)(1), discussed above, provides a qualified opportunity for a plaintiff to satisfy a venue requirement by filing suit in a judicial district in which

---

[14]*See, e.g., Aldodonero De Las Cabezas, S.A. v. American Suisse Capital, Inc.,* 432 F.3d 1343, 1345 (11th Cir. 2005) ("[V]enue may be predicated on [§ 1391(b)(3)] only when neither § 1391(b)(1) or (2) are satisfied.").

[15]*See, e.g., Garus v. Rose Acre Farms, Inc.,* 839 F. Supp. 563, 566 n. 2 (N.D. Ind. 1993) (noting that local rule divides division into subdivision for venue purposes).

at least one defendant resides.[16] As amended, § 1391(c)(1) provides that venue for natural persons derives from the residence of such defendants. It should be noted that this use of the term "residence" can be considerably more restrictive than a layperson's use of the term. As provided in § 1391(c)(1), a natural person's residence is deemed to be the judicial district in which that person is domiciled.[17] Typically, a natural person has only one domicile (and thus, for venue purposes, only one residence), notwithstanding that the person in question may actually have homes in several different states.[18] It should be noted that this definition of residence applies to citizens as well as aliens lawfully admitted for permanent residence in the United States.[19]

Residence for Entities that May Sue or be Sued in Their Own Names: Section 1391(c)(2) provides two distinct definitions of residence for entities that may sue or be sued in their own names. The first definition of residence applies to such entities that are defendants. It provides that a defendant is residence in any judicial district in which that defendant would be subject to the personal jurisdiction of the federal court. This provision could obviously provide multiple venue opportunities for venue over such entities, which is a significant departure from venue for natural persons (where, typically, each person will have only one residence.[20]

The second definition of residence applies when the entity in question is a plaintiff. In that circumstance § 1391(c)(2) provides that residence (and therefore venue based on residence) may be found only in the judicial district encompassing the plaintiff's principal place of business.[21] This definition of residence has the obvious potential to involve fewer places of residence than might be found if an entity is a defendant.

Another point should be emphasized about the scope of an entity's residence under § 1391(c)(2). Under the predecessor provision to amended § 1391(c)(2), residence was defined only for use in the context of corporations. However, as currently written, § 1391(c)(2) applies to all entities, including (but not limited to) corporations that have the capacity to sue or be sued in their own name. That change represents a broadening of the applicability of the venue provisions in the context of "legal" persons.

Defendants Not Residence in the United States: As amended in 2012, § 1391(c)(3) provides that defendants not resident in the United States may be sued in any judicial district. Further,

---

[16]28 U.S.C. § 1391(b)(1) (qualification is that all other defendants must be residents of the state in which the federal district court is located).

[17]28 U.S.C § 1391(c)(1).

[18]*See, e.g., Manley v. Engram,* 755 F.2d 1463, 1468 (11th Cir. 1985) ("mere residence" in a state does not equal venue' "rather, it is the individual's 'permanent' residence - i.e., his domicile that is the benchmark for determining proper venue.").

[19]28 U.S.C. § 1391(c)(1).

[20]28 U.S.C. § 1391(c)(2). *See also* 28 U.S.C. § 1391(c)(1).

[21]28 U.S.C § 1391(c)(2).

if such non-resident defendants are co-defendants with parties who are resident in the United States, only the residence of the United States-based defendants may be taken into account in determining the appropriateness of venue.[22] The predecessor to this provision, no repealed, applied only to the absence of a venue requirement for suing aliens. As now written, § 1391(c)(3) applies to all non-residents, including both aliens and United States citizens whose residence is outside the United States.

Counterclaims and Crossclaims

Generally speaking, only plaintiffs have the burden of satisfying requirements of venue. Counterclaims, crossclaims, and similar actions normally do not raise venue questions.[23] This distinction is a significant departure from jurisdictional requirements, discussed above, for which every count in a case must satisfy some form of both jurisdiction over persons or things and subject matter jurisdiction.

Consent to Venue

If parties consent to personal jurisdiction in a particular district or state, it appears settled that they also consent to venue there.[24] Moreover, if the plaintiff files suit in a federal judicial district where venue is improper, the court may still hear that case if the defendant does not object to venue.[25] Rule 12(g) and (h), governing timing and waiver of certain motions to dismiss, identify the time frame in which a defendant must either raise objections to venue or forego them.[26]

Venue and Removal

If a claim is removed from a state court to a federal district court, § 1391 does not apply. Thus, a removed claim is treated somewhat differently than a case originally filed in federal court.[27] However, a party who sought removal of a claim does not thereby waive a challenge to the state court's venue. That

---

[22]28 U.S.C. § 1391(c)(3).

[23]*See, e.g., Bredberg v. Long,* 778 F.2d 1285, 1288 (8th Cir. 1985) (where venue is proper as to plaintiff's claims, it is improbable that an objection to venue will be heard as to counterclaims or cross-claims).

[24]*See, e.g., Doctor's Associates, Inc. v. Stuart,* 85 F.3d 975 (2d Cir. 1996) (party may consent to venue by consenting to personal jurisdiction).

[25]*See, e.g., Leroy v. Great Western United Corp.,* 443 U.S. 173, 99 S. Ct. 2710, 61 L. Ed. 2d 464 (1979) (both personal jurisdiction and venue may be waived). *See also Tri-State Employment Services, Inc. v. Mountbatten Sur. Co., Inc.,* 295 F.3d 256, 260 n. 2 (2d Cir. 2002) (defendant's failure to raise venue means defendant has waived issue); *King v. Russell,* 963 F.2d 1301 (9th Cir. 1992) (per curiam) (improper venue waived if defendant does not object to venue while raising other Rule 12 issues). *Cf., Algodonera De Las Cabezas, S.A. v. American Suisse Capital, Inc.,* 432 F.3d 1343, 1345 (11th Cir. 2005) (courts may dismiss sua sponte for lack of venue, but only after giving defendant a chance to waive venue requirement).

[26]*But see Costlow v. Weeks,* 790 F.2d 1486, 1488 (9th Cir. 1986) (where defendant has made no appearance whatever, court may dismiss for lack of venue *sua sponte*).

[27]*See, e.g., PT United Can Co. Ltd. v. Crown Cork & Seal Co., Inc.,* 138 F.3d 65, 72 (2d Cir. 1998) (In a removed case "one may not challenge venue in the district court as of right,

challenge is preserved and may be raised in federal court.[28] Another way of understanding the interplay of these two points is to recognize that for a removed claim the applicable venue standard is that which governed the state court in which the claim was originally filed.

Remedy

If the court, on timely objection of a party, finds venue to be deficient, the court may dismiss the action, allowing plaintiff to refile the claim elsewhere if the action is not otherwise barred.[29] This can raise significant statutes of limitations problems for a plaintiff. With limitations periods in mind, Congress enacted 28 U.S.C.A. § 1406, which allows a federal district court, on finding venue to be faulty, to *transfer* a cause of action to a judicial district or division where venue is proper. The court's discretion to employ this remedy is broad, constrained only by "the interest of justice." The practical consequence of transfer is that the court need not dismiss the action—which means the plaintiff will not run afoul of statutes of limitations.[30]

Corporate Residence in States with Multiple Districts

Most or all of our smaller states, and some of our middle-sized states, contain only one federal judicial district that comprises the territory of the entire state. However, in other, larger states such as Texas, California, or Florida, there is more than one judicial district. In such states it is possible for a corporation to have a presence in more than one judicial district that would give rise to personal jurisdiction, if each judicial district was a stand-alone state. Amended § 11391(d) provides two ways to determine venue in those judicial districts, depending on the applicability of certain key facts.

First, if the corporation in question has sufficient contacts so that it would be subject to personal jurisdiction in more than one district (if the districts were states), it is treated as resident for venue purposes in each such district. Alternatively, if the corporation is subject to personal jurisdiction in the state as a whole, but lacks contacts with any individual district sufficient to establish residence and venue in any district, § 1391(d), the corporation is treated as resident in (and subject to venue in) the judicial district with which the corporation has the most significant contacts.[31]

NOTE: The complexities of venue should not be allowed to ob-

---

according to that court's venue rules, as if the case had been originally brought there."). *See generally Polizzi v. Cowles Magazines, Inc.*, 345 U.S. 663, 665, 73 S. Ct. 900, 902, 97 L. Ed. 1331 (1953) ("[T]he venue of removed actions is governed by . . . § 1441(a) [the federal removal statute].").

[28]*See, e.g., PT United Can Co. Ltd. v. Crown Cork & Seal Co., Inc.*, 138 F.3d 65, 73 (2d Cir. 1998) (citing *Polizzi, supra*).

[29]*Polizzi v. Cowles Magazines, Inc.*, 345 U.S. 663, 73 S. Ct. 900, 97 L. Ed. 1331 (1953).

[30]*See, e.g., Smith v. Thompson*, 685 F. Supp. 177 (N.D. Ill. 1988) (where pro se inmate files in an improper venue, this court usually transfers in preference to a dismissal).

[31]28 U.S.C. § 1391(d).

scure the fact that for purposes of venue, as it relates to corporations, the important element is "residence," not domicile or citizenship. This is an important difference from venue for natural persons, where residence usually arises from domicile.[32] Thus, while 28 U.S.C.A. § 1391(c) bears some facial similarity to the statute governing diversity citizenship for corporations, the results of these two rules can be quite different. For example, assume that General Motors, a large company, is for diversity purposes a citizen of Delaware (place of incorporation) and of Michigan (principal place of business). This would mean that for a party to sue General Motors on a state claim in federal court on the basis of diversity of citizenship, the plaintiff would have to be a citizen of some state (or foreign country) other than Delaware and Michigan. For venue, however, the fact that General Motors is a large company doing business in many judicial districts means, first, that General Motors is probably subject to personal jurisdiction in all of those districts. That means, in turn, that General Motors has residence in many judicial districts, and venue may be appropriate in all of them. Thus the company's widespread business activity makes it subject to personal jurisdiction, as well as venue, in many places. But for purposes of diversity jurisdiction, it is a citizen of only two states, affording plaintiffs from other states and foreign countries substantial opportunities to sue in federal court on state claims involving more than $75,000. As these examples indicate, the interplay of venue, subject matter jurisdiction, and jurisdiction over persons or things can create major complexities for plaintiffs, as well as important opportunities for defendants to oppose plaintiff's initial choice of forum.

Unincorporated Associations

For venue purposes, the case law treats partnerships, sole proprietorships, and other unincorporated associations in much the same manner as corporations, so that unincorporated associations are probably deemed to reside in every judicial district where they are subject to personal jurisdiction, according to the same threefold analysis of 28 U.S.C.A. § 1391(c).[33]

Aliens

Section 1391(d) provides that aliens may be sued in any judicial district. Case law suggests that this provision applies equally to alien corporations as well as alien natural persons,[34] so venue requirements for most alien defendants are not dif-

---

[32]See *Manley v. Engram*, 755 F.2d 1463, 1466 (11th Cir. 1985) (for purposes of venue, "residence" for natural persons means "domicile.").

[33]*Denver & R. G. W. R. Co. v. Brotherhood of R. R. Trainmen*, 387 U.S. 556, 87 S. Ct. 1746, 18 L. Ed. 2d 954 (1967) (multi-state unincorporated association has residence, for venue purposes, wherever it does business).

[34]*See, e.g., Go-Video, Inc. v. Akai Elec. Co., Ltd.*, 885 F.2d 1406, 1413 (9th Cir. 1989) (permitting use of § 1391(d) to establish venue in suit against foreign corporations).

ficult to satisfy. It is uncertain whether a non-U.S. citizen
domiciled in an American state (and therefore a citizen of that
state for diversity purposes, under 28 U.S.C.A. § 1332(a)), is an
"alien" for purposes of § 1391(d). Assuming such a person is not
an alien, § 1391(d) would have no application in a suit where
that person was the defendant. Thus ordinary requirements for
venue, found in § 1391(a) and (b), would have to be satisfied.

The United States

Section 1391(e) expands venue possibilities if the United
States, a federal agency, or a federal officer acting in an official
capacity is a defendant. These provisions apply to the governmental defendant only, and only to governmental defendants
who are part of the executive branch of the federal
government.[35] A separate basis for venue must be found as to
other defendants. The three venue possibilities available under
§ 1391(e) are:

(1) *A Single Defendant's Residence:* in a judicial district
where a single defendant in the action resides. It is important
to note that the United States, its agencies or officers can
thereby be sued in a judicial district where some other defendant resides.[36] That would be true even if the federal officer, for
example, did not reside in that district and did no business
there; or

(2) *Location of Events or Property:* in a judicial district where
"a substantial part of the events or omissions giving rise to the
claim occurred, or a substantial part of property that is the
subject of the action is situated;"[37] or

(3) *Plaintiff's Residence:* in a judicial district where a single
plaintiff resides,[38] provided that the cause of action does not
involve real property.[39] Section 1391(e)(3), in particular, is a
major expansion of venue opportunities for suits against the
United States and its agents.

It is important to note that a plaintiff may obtain the benefit
of 28 U.S.C.A. § 1391(e) even if the suit also contains additional,
non-federal defendants. In fact, the presence of non-federal
defendants, and the use of their residences, creates the foundation for using § 1391(e)(1) to satisfy venue as to the United

---

[35]*See, e.g., Trackwell v. U.S.
Government,* 472 F.3d 1242, 1246
(10th Cir. 2007) (suggesting that
venue under § 1391(e) cannot be applied to legislative or judicial branches
or their officers).

[36]*See also Bartman v. Cheney,* 827
F. Supp. 1, 3 (D.D.C. 1993) (residence
for federal officer or agency exists in
any district where defendant performs
"significant amount" of official duties).

[37]*See, e.g., Andrean v. Secretary
of U.S. Army,* 840 F. Supp. 1414, 1422
(D. Kan. 1993) (for purposes of
§ 1391(e)(2), court is not restricted to

only events or activities involving
named defendant; court may examine
"all" events that gave rise to claim).

[38]*See, e.g., Sidney Coal Co., Inc.
v. Social Sec. Admin.,* 427 F.3d 336,
344–45 (6th Cir. 2005) ("§ 1391(e)(3)
contains no requirement that all plaintiffs must reside in the same district;"
noting unanimity of federal courts on
this view of § 1391(e)(3)).

[39]*See, e.g., Immigrant Assistance
Project of Los Angeles County Federa-
tion of Labor (AFL-CIO) v. I.N.S.,* 306
F.3d 842, 868 (9th Cir. 2002).

States, its agencies, and officers in judicial districts where venue as to the governmental defendant would not otherwise be possible.

NOTE: The additional venue possibilities of § 1391(e) are available *only against federal defendants in a case.*[40] Section 1391(e) specifically provides that if non-federal parties are also defendants, venue as to them must be satisfied under § 1391(a) or (b), or some other specific venue statute. Thus, § 1391(e) may permit a plaintiff to satisfy venue as to a federal officer in a judicial district where venue would not be available as to the federal defendant under § 1391(a) or (b), but as to non-federal defendants the normal requirements of other venue provisions would apply.

Nationwide Personal Jurisdiction Over Federal Agencies and Officers

To ensure that the broad venue authority of § 1391(e) is not nullified by problems of personal jurisdiction, § 1391(e) also provides that the federal district court shall be able, by certified mail, to obtain personal jurisdiction over federal agencies and officers not found within the state in which the court sits.

Personal Suits Against Federal Officers

The venue opportunities provided by 28 U.S.C.A. § 1391(e) as to federal officers are available only when the officers are sued in their official capacities. If they are sued personally for money damages, § 1391(e) is not applicable.[41] In such circumstances the provisions of § 1391(a) or (b), or some other more specific venue statute, would control.

Suits Against Foreign Countries

Section 1391(f) prescribes the venue when foreign countries, or their agencies, are defendants. Four possibilities for venue exist, depending on whether suit is against the foreign sovereign itself, its agency, or its shipping or cargo. These possibilities are:

(1) *Location of Events or Property:* in a judicial district where a substantial portion of the events giving rise to the claim occurred,[42] or where a substantial part of property that is the subject of the claim is located.

(2) *Location of Vessel or Cargo:* in any judicial district where a vessel or cargo belonging to a foreign state is located. This venue possibility is available only if the claim arose under 28 U.S.C.A. § 1605(b), governing suits in admiralty against foreign

---

[40]*See, e.g., King v. Russell*, 963 F.2d 1301, 1303 (9th Cir. 1992) (§ 1391(e) "only applies to suits against officers of the executive branch").

[41]*Stafford v. Briggs*, 444 U.S. 527, 100 S. Ct. 774, 63 L. Ed. 2d 1 (1980) (§ 1391(e) unavailable where suit is for money damages against federal employees individually).

[42]*See, e.g., U.S. Titan, Inc. v. Guangzhou Zhen Hua Shipping Co., Ltd.*, 241 F.3d 135, 153–54 (2d Cir. 2001) (noting parallel language of § 1391(b)(2) and (f)(1); requirement of substantial events satisfied by fact that defendant directed relevant communications to plaintiff in form district).

states; or

(3) *Location of Agency That is Doing Business:* if the defendant is an agency or instrumentality of the foreign state, as described in 28 U.S.C.A. § 1603(b), in any judicial district in which the agency is licensed to do business or doing business. It is important to note that privately owned non-American corporations do not fit within the description of a foreign state's instrumentality as defined by § 1603(b). For § 1603(b) to apply, the foreign state itself, not merely its citizens, must be the majority owner of an instrumentality;[43] or

(4) *Venue in the District of Columbia:* if the defendant is a foreign state itself, or a political subdivision of a foreign state, venue may be satisfied in the United States District Court for the District of Columbia.[44]

Sovereign Immunity

Nothing in § 1391(f) waives whatever immunity a foreign state, or its agencies or instrumentalities, may have. Instead, § 1391(f) provides venue possibilities only on the assumption that the suit is otherwise permitted by law, and that immunities either do not apply or have been waived for the purposes of the suit.

ADDITIONAL RESEARCH REFERENCES

C.J.S., Federal Courts §§ 16 to 21 et seq.
C.J.S., Federal Courts §§ 165 to 190 et seq.
West's Key Number Digest, Federal Courts ⬤━71 to 157

§ 2.15 Forum Non Conveniens

CORE CONCEPT

The forum non conveniens doctrine provides that a court selected by the claimant will not hear a cause of action if the court is an "inappropriate" forum. A trial court enjoys substantial discretion to determine whether it is an appropriate forum for a case, but that discretion is qualified by some important requirements, discussed below, that must be satisfied before a court's determination receives such deference.

APPLICATIONS

Relationship to Jurisdiction and Venue

Forum non conveniens shares some characteristics with jurisdiction and venue, but operates independently of those

---

[43]*See, e.g., Transaero, Inc. v. La Fuerza Aerea Boliviana*, 30 F.3d 148, 152 (D.C. Cir. 1994) (limiting venue under § 1391(f)(3) to commercial enterprise that is agent or instrumentality of foreign state).

[44]*See, e.g., Telcordia Tech Inc. v. Telkom SA Ltd.*, 458 F.3d 172, 176 (3d Cir. 2006) (where majority owner of company is foreign country, district court in District of Columbia is an additional option for venue).

requirements. Thus, even if a plaintiff has chosen a court that enjoys: personal jurisdiction or quasi in rem jurisdiction over the defendant; subject matter jurisdiction over the kind of case at issue; and satisfactory venue, the court may refuse to hear the case if it determines that the court is an inappropriate forum.[1] At the same time, the court will typically not address the question of forum non conveniens until it first determines whether requirements of jurisdiction and venue are satisfied.[2]

Timing

In the ordinary course of events a motion to dismiss under the doctrine of forum non conveniens or a motion to transfer a case under 28 U.S.C.A. § 1404 (discussed below) will normally be made early in the litigation.[3] A motion made after judgment will not be granted.[4]

Moreover, even a motion made earlier in a case is substantially less likely to prevail on appeal once the case has proceeded through trial to judgment.[5]

---

[1]*Sinochem Intern. Co. Ltd. v. Malaysia Intern. Shipping Corp.*, 549 U.S. 422, 127 S. Ct. 1184, 167 L. Ed. 2d 15 (2007) ("A district court . . . may dispose of an action by a forum non conveniens dismissal, bypassing questions of subject-matter and personal jurisdiction, when considerations of convenience, fairness, and judicial economy so warrant."); *American Dredging Co. v. Miller*, 510 U.S. 443, 453, 114 S. Ct. 981, 127 L. Ed. 2d 285 (1994) (Forum non conveniens is "a supervening venue provision, permitting displacement of the ordinary rules of venue when, in light of certain conditions, the trial court thinks that jurisdiction ought to be declined."). *See, e.g., Wiwa v. Royal Dutch Petroleum Co.*, 226 F.3d 88, 100 (2d Cir. 2000) (forum non conveniens is "a discretionary device permitting a court in rare instances to dismiss claims even if the court is a permissible venue with proper jurisdiction over the claim.").

[2]*Gulf Oil Corp. v. Gilbert*, 330 U.S. 501, 504, 67 S. Ct. 839, 840, 91 L. Ed. 1055 (1947) ("[T]he doctrine of forum non conveniens can never apply if there is absence of jurisdiction or venue."); *Baris v. Sulpicio Lines, Inc.*, 932 F.2d 1540, 1542 (5th Cir. 1991) (court should typically address issue of forum non conveniens only after determining that jurisdiction exists). *See also Albion v. YMCA Camp Letts*, 171 F.3d 1, 2 (1st Cir. 1999) (transfer under 28 U.S.C.A. § 1404 also inappropriate where court lacked personal jurisdiction over defendant). *But see Sinochem International Co., Ltd. v. Malaysian International Shipping Corp.*, 549 U.S. 422, 127 S. Ct. 1184, 167 L. Ed. 2d 15 (2007) (court has authority, where appropriate, to dismiss on grounds of forum non conveniens without addressing issues of personal or subject matter jurisdiction); *In re Arbitration between Monegasque De Reassurances S.A.M. v. Nak Naftogaz of Ukraine*, 311 F.3d 488, 498 (2d Cir. 2002) (sometimes acceptable for district court to decide forum non conveniens prior to addressing jurisdiction).

[3]*But see Yavuz v. 61 MM Ltd.*, 576 F.3d 1166, 1173 (10th Cir. 2009) (forum non conveniens is not waived by failing to raise it in original responsive pleading).

[4]*See, e.g., Ortiz v. Gaston County Dyeing Machine Co.*, 277 F.3d 594, 597–98 (1st Cir. 2002) ("Once the court entered judgment . . . it was too late to request a transfer.").

[5]*See, e.g., Zelinski v. Columbia 300, Inc.*, 335 F.3d 633 (7th Cir. 2003) (once trial was finished, public interest in favor of not moving case may arise from policy of not wasting judicial resources already expended on case); *McLennan v. American Eurocopter Corp., Inc.*, 245 F.3d 403, 423–24

Timing: Relationship to Jurisdiction

In the ordinary course of most lawsuits where jurisdiction and forum non conveniens are at issue, courts will normally address jurisdictional issues first.[6] However, it is also permissible for courts to address forum non conveniens problems prior to solving jurisdictional issues if individual circumstances would make that approach preferable.[7]

Forum Selection Clauses

In circumstances where the parties have agreed in advance to a forum selection clause, that choice of forum will normally be resistant an attack on grounds of forum non conveniens.[8] Other factors of public and private interest may still be examined, but they will normally not prevail over an otherwise valid forum selection clause.[9]

A different problem can arise if a plaintiff ignores a forum selection clause that requires the plaintiff to sue in some jurisdiction other than the forum the plaintiff actually chose. In that circumstance a district court has the option to dismiss the case under Rule 12(b) or to grant a motion to transfer when § 1404 is available.[10]

(5th Cir. 2001) (when case is tried to conclusion, denial of motion is strengthened; to prevail on appeal, moving party must show "great prejudice").

[6]See, e.g., Figueiredo Ferraz e Engenharia de Projeto LTDA v. Republic of Peru, 665 F.3d 384, 389 (2d Cir. 2011).

[7]In re Arbitration Between Monogasque de Reassurances S.A.M. v. NAK Naftogaz of Ukraine, 311 F.3d 488, 497–98 (2d Cir. 2002) (permissible to address forum non conveniens prior to subject matter jurisdiction where jurisdiction is based on statute, not Constitution).

[8]Stewart Organization, Inc. v. Ricoh Corp., 487 U.S. 22, 29, 108 S. Ct. 2239, 2243, 101 L. Ed. 2d 22 (1988) ("The presence of a forum-selection clause . . . will be a significant factor that figures centrally in the district court's calculus."). See, e.g., P & S Business Machines, Inc. v. Canon USA, Inc., 331 F.3d 804, 807–08 (11th Cir. 2003) (choice made in forum selection clause will rarely be disturbed).

[9]See, e.g., Wong v. PartyGaming Ltd., 589 F.3d 821, 833 (6th Cir. 2009) (in determining forum non conveniens motion in the context of valid forum

selection clause, courts give less deference to plaintiff's choice of home forum); Bonny v. Society of Lloyd's, 3 F.3d 156, 160 n. 11 (7th Cir. 1993) ("[A] party's financial status at any given time in the course of litigation cannot be the basis for enforcing or not enforcing a valid forum selection clause."); Moses v. Business Card Exp., Inc., 929 F.2d 1131, 1138–39 (6th Cir. 1991) (economic disparity between parties and one party's claim of financial hardship cannot overcome valid forum selection clause). But see Aguas Lenders Recovery Group LLC v. Suez, S.A., 585 F.3d 696, 700 (2d Cir. 2009) (permissive forum selection clause, i.e., "one that designates a forum in advance, but does not preclude a different choice," does not bar application of forum non conveniens analysis).

[10]28 U.S.C. § 1404 (authorizing change of venue in some circumstances). See, e.g., TradeComet.com v. Google, Inc., 647 F.3d 472, 475 (2d Cir. 2011) (§ 1404 is not exclusive vehicle for enforcing forum selection clause; applying Fed. R. Civ. P. 12(b)). But cf., Slater v. Energy Services Group International Inc., 634 F.3d 1326, 1333 (11th Cir. 2011) (§ 1404 is proper means to transfer to enforce forum selection clause, but Rule 12(b)(3) is

Requirement of an Adequate Alternative Forum

An important limit on a trial court's discretion to dismiss a case on forum non conveniens grounds arises from the requirement that, before the court employs its discretion in the matter, it must first determine that an adequate alternative forum exists.[11] The defendant has the burden of demonstrating the availability of such a forum.[12] Even if the plaintiff's choice of forum seems strained, that choice will not be overruled (assuming no problems with jurisdiction and venue) until the trial court makes that determination.[13] If there is no other such forum, the court will retain the case.

Evaluating the adequacy of an alternative forum requires a determination as to whether the defendants are subject to service of process in the alternative forum,[14] and whether the alternative forum will hear the case.[15] For other American jurisdictions this analysis tends to focus on the question of ju-

---

means of dismissal due to violation of forum selection clause).

[11]*Gulf Oil Corp. v. Gilbert*, 330 U.S. 501, 506–07, 67 S. Ct. 839, 91 L. Ed. 1055 (1947) ("[F]orum non conveniens . . . presupposes at least two forums in which the defendant is amenable to process."). *See, e.g., Chang v. Baxter Healthcare Corp.*, 599 F.3d 728, 736 (7th Cir. 2010) (if suit would be time-barred in alternative forum, alternative forum is inadequate); *Galustian v. Peter*, 591 F.3d 724, 731 (4th Cir. 2010) (requirement for forum non coveniens dismissal is that alternative forum is available for *all defendants*); *Iragorri v. International Elevator, Inc.*, 203 F.3d 8, 13 (1st Cir. 2000) (district court should determine adequacy of alternative forum before weighing factors of private and public interest). *Compare Naviera Joanna SA v. Koninklijke Boskalis Westminster NV*, 569 F.3d 189, 202–03 (4th Cir. 2009) (if plaintiff intentionally waits to file suit until statute of limitations in alternative forum has expired, plaintiff cannot defeat forum non conveniens by arguing lack of adequate alternative forum) *with Chang v. Baxter Healthcare Corp.*, 599 F.3d 728, 736 (7th Cir. 2010) (describing different situation if untimeliness is due merely to "delays inherent in litigation").

[12]*See, e.g., In re Ford Motor Co.*, 591 F.3d 406, 412 (5th Cir. 2009) (if defendant submits to jurisdiction of alternative forum, that forum is available for purposes of forum non conve-

niens analysis); *Duha v. Agrium, Inc.*, 448 F.3d 867, 873 (6th Cir. 2006) (first requirement is that defendant show "available and adequate alternative forum"); *Jones v. GNC Franchising, Inc.*, 211 F.3d 495, 499 n. 22 (9th Cir. 2000) (defendant has burden of proving existence of "adequate alternative forum").

[13]*Piper Aircraft Co. v. Reyno*, 454 U.S. 235, 255, 102 S. Ct. 252, 70 L. Ed. 2d 419 (1981) ("At the outset of any forum non conveniens inquiry, the court must determine whether there exists an alternative forum."). *See also Norex Petroleum Ltd. v. Access Industries, Inc.*, 416 F.3d 146 (2d Cir. 2005) (if movant fails to identify adequate alternative forum, "the forum non conveniens motion must be denied regardless of the degree of deference accorded plaintiff's forum choice").

[14]*See, e.g., Gutierrez v. Advanced Medical Optics, Inc.*, 640 F.3d 1025, 1029 (9th Cir. 2011) (alternative forum is adequate if " 'defendants are amenable to service of process' . . . and 'when the entire case and all parties can come within the jurisdiction of that forum' ").

[15]*See, e.g., Gutierrez v. Advanced Medical Optics, Inc.*, 640 F.3d 1025, 1029 (9th Cir. 2011) (if court grants forum non conveniens motion but developments in foreign jurisdiction could leave plaintiffs without an adequate forum, court could reconsider original decision); *Abdullahi v. Pfizer, Inc.*, 562 F.3d 163, 172 (2d Cir. 2009)

risdiction over the defendant.[16] If there is some question about jurisdiction in the proposed alternative forum, a defendant can usually eliminate the issue by stipulating to jurisdiction in that forum.[17]

A development in some foreign jurisdictions has added a new wrinkle to the question of the availability of an alternative forum in foreign countries. Some countries, apparently concerned about the use of foreign non conveniens in United States courts,[18] have enacted legislation providing that if one of their citizens files a suit in, e.g., a United States court, the courts of the plaintiff's home country are closed to that plaintiff on that cause of action. These laws apply to circumstances where, prior to the filing in the United States, the plaintiff's home court would otherwise have had concurrent jurisdiction.[19]

In such circumstances it is possible to conclude that the foreign court, in the most literal sense, is no longer an available forum.[20] Whether this practice of closing foreign courts should invariably be treated as rendering them "unavailable" for purposes of a federal foreign non conveniens analysis will require further case law development in the United States. In the meantime, attorneys will have to try to identify the local practice.

(where "tectonic change" occurs in foreign political landscape, court could revisit original decision on forum non conveniens); *In re Bridgestone/ Firestone, Inc.*, 420 F.3d 702, 705 (7th Cir. 2005) (where Mexican court held it lacked personal jurisdiction over defendants, foreign forum was not available); *Canales Martinez v. Dow Chemical Co.*, 219 F. Supp. 2d 719, 728 (E.D. La. 2002) (foreign forum not available where foreign court would not hear case if another sovereign's court had previously dismissed on ground of forum non conveniens).

[16]*Piper Aircraft Co. v. Reyno*, 454 U.S. 235, 255, n. 22, 102 S. Ct. 252, 70 L. Ed. 2d 419 (1981) ("Ordinarily, this requirement [of an adequate alternative forum] will be satisfied when the defendant is 'amenable to process' in the other jurisdiction.").

[17]*See, e.g., Ravelo Monegro v. Rosa*, 211 F.3d 509, 514 (9th Cir. 2000) (abuse of discretion where, *inter alia*, district court did not condition dismissal on defendant's participation in judicial proceedings in Dominican Republic; case also had significant relation with plaintiff's chosen forum and evidence was at least as likely to be available in United States); *Gschwind v. Cessna Aircraft Co.*, 161 F.3d 602,

606 (10th Cir. 1998) ("Defendants agreed to be subject to suit in France. That concession is generally enough to make the alternative forum available."). *See also Alpine View Co. Ltd. v. Atlas Copco AB*, 205 F.3d 208, 221 (5th Cir. 2000) (foreign court is available if " 'entire case and all parties' " are subject to its jurisdiction). *But cf., Wild v. Subscription Plus, Inc.*, 292 F.3d 526, 531 (7th Cir. 2002) ("[T]here is no absolute bar to the transfer of a multidefendant suit to a district in which one of the defendants cannot be served." Treating § 1404 as closely analogous to § 1406 for this purpose).

[18]It appears that many countries do not recognize the doctrine of foreign non conveniens and have no equivalent to it. *See, e.g., Canales Martinez v. Dow Chemical Co.*, 219 F.Supp.2d 719, 730 (E.D. La. 2002) ("As a general rule, civilian [sic] legal systems . . . simply do not recognize the doctrine of foreign non conveniens.").

[19]*See, e.g.,* Costa Rico Codigo Procesal Civil art. 31 (CCP 31).

[20]*See, e.g., Canales Martinze v. Dow Chemical Co.*, 219 F.Supp.2d 719, 728 (E.D. La. 2002) (treating Costa Rican courts as closed to case at bar).

If the proposed alternative forum is found in another country, the trial court hearing the forum non conveniens motion will, in addition to questions of jurisdiction and service of process, also examine whether the foreign court has the capacity to provide an adequate remedy.[21] In extreme cases, there may also be questions about the integrity of a particular foreign court.[22] When the court believes that another forum would be more appropriate but still retains some concern over whether a case will actually be heard in the foreign court, the appropriate practice is to include a clause in the dismissal order providing that parties may return to the dismissing court to resume their case.[23]

The probability that a foreign court will not apply American substantive law is usually not weighed heavily in determining

---

[21]*Piper Aircraft Co. v. Reyno*, 454 U.S. 235, 254, 102 S. Ct. 252, 70 L. Ed. 2d 419 (1981) (dismissal inappropriate "if the remedy provided by the alternative forum is so clearly inadequate or unsatisfactory that it is no remedy at all"). *See, e.g., Nemariam v. Federal Democratic Republic of Ethiopia*, 315 F.3d 390, 394 (D.C. Cir. 2003) (alleged alternative forum is inadequate where foreign tribunal cannot make award directly to plaintiff, and government that would be claimant in place of plaintiff has no duty to send any award to her); *Gonzalez v. Chrysler Corp.*, 301 F.3d 377, 382 (5th Cir. 2002) (Mexico's low cap on tort damages does not make Mexico an inappropriate forum); *Leon v. Millon Air, Inc.*, 251 F.3d 1305, 1311 (11th Cir. 2001) ("Courts have been strict about requiring that defendants demonstrate that the alternative forum offers at least some relief."); *Satz v. McDonnell Douglas Corp.*, 244 F.3d 1279, 1283 (11th Cir. 2001) ("An adequate forum need not be a perfect forum;" concerns about filing fees, lack of discovery, and delay do not automatically render foreign forum inadequate; noting that, in instant case, defendant agreed to use of discovery rules of American federal courts); *DiRienzo v. Philip Services Corp.*, 232 F.3d 49, 58 (2d Cir. 2000) (procedural differences, such as possibility that foreign court will not certify a class action, do not make foreign forum inadequate); *El-Fadl v. Central Bank of Jordan*, 75 F.3d 668, 678 (D.C. Cir. 1996) (Jordanian courts unsuitable in part because recently enacted Jordanian law immunized defendants from liability for actions in question).

[22]*See, e.g., BP Chemicals Ltd. v. Jiangsu Sopo Corp.*, 285 F.3d 677, 688 (8th Cir. 2002) ("[P]roper resolution of the forum non conveniens argument will depend heavily upon whether [plaintiff] could receive a fair hearing in the Chinese courts."). *Cf., In re Arbitration between Monegasque De Reassurances S.A.M. v. Nak Naftogaz of Ukraine*, 311 F.3d 488, 499 (2d Cir. 2002) ("We have been reluctant to find foreign courts 'corrupt' or 'biased.' "); *Leon v. Millon Air, Inc.*, 251 F.3d 1305 (11th Cir. 2001) (plaintiff's assertion that foreign court is too corrupt to be fair usually does not prevail; significant evidence of severe problems of partiality or years of delay needed to upset presumption that foreign forum is adequate); *Iragorri v. International Elevator, Inc.*, 203 F.3d 8, 13 (1st Cir. 2000) (notwithstanding State Department advisory on danger of traveling in Columbia, native Columbians who are naturalized United States citizens face less danger and are more familiar with culture and language of Columbia than other Americans).

[23]*See, e.g., Vasquez v. Bridgestone/Firestone, Inc.*, 325 F.3d 665, 675 (5th Cir. 2003) (if foreign forum may not be open or defendant may not submit to jurisdiction there, it is abuse of discretion to fail to include "return jurisdiction" clause in dismissal order; remedy for such abuse of discretion is to remand to insert clause).

the adequacy of an alternative forum.[24] However, the result may be different in cases where distinctions in procedural law preclude a reasonable opportunity for the plaintiff to present a case.[25]

Deference to Plaintiff's Choice of Forum: Exceptions and Modification

Normally, the court will give substantial deference to a plaintiff's choice of forum.[26] Thus, for a defendant to prevail on

---

[24]*Piper Aircraft Co. v. Reyno*, 454 U.S. 235, 247, 102 S. Ct. 252, 261, 70 L. Ed. 2d 419 (1981) ("The possibility of a change in substantive law should ordinarily not be given conclusive or even substantial weight in the forum non conveniens inquiry."). *See, e.g., Dickson Marine Inc. v. Panalpina, Inc.*, 179 F.3d 331, 342 (5th Cir. 1999) ("[D]ifferences in substantive law should not be given conclusive weight in a forum non conveniens inquiry."). *Cf., Boosey & Hawkes Music Publishers, Ltd. v. Walt Disney Co.*, 145 F.3d 481, 492 (2d Cir. 1998) (noting that refusal to dismiss case on grounds of forum non conveniens will require trial court to apply foreign law, but also noting that "[w]hile reluctance to apply foreign law is a valid factor favoring dismissal, . . . standing alone it does not justify dismissal.").*But cf., Gschwind v. Cessna Aircraft Co.*, 161 F.3d 602, 606 (10th Cir. 1998) (in 10th Cir. There is an additional threshold requirement beyond existence of alternative forum; court should also determine whether foreign law applies; only if both thresholds are met should court weigh public and private interests).

[25]*See, e.g., Lacey v. Cessna Aircraft Co.*, 932 F.2d 170, 185 n. 12 (3d Cir. 1991) (Canadian forum inadequate because plaintiff would face "serious impediments" to obtaining sources of proof). *But see Stroitelstvo Bulgaria Ltd. v. Bulgarian-American Enterprise Fund*, 589 F.3d 417, 484 (7th Cir. 2009) (foreign forum's four percent filing fee does not render that forum inadequate); *Alpha Therapeutic Corp. v. Nippon Hoso Kyokai*, 199 F.3d 1078, 1090 (9th Cir. 1999) (fact that Japan's civil procedure rules "are not friendly to plaintiffs" did not by itself make erroneous district court's finding that Japan was adequate alternative fo-

rum); *Alfadda v. Fenn*, 159 F.3d 41, 48 (2d Cir. 1998) (inability of plaintiff to use materials obtained through U.S. discovery in a French court is a relevant factor, but not necessarily dispositive).

[26]*Koster v. (American) Lumbermens Mut. Cas. Co.*, 330 U.S. 518, 524, 67 S. Ct. 828, 831, 91 L. Ed. 1067 (1947) (plaintiff's choice of forum gets great deference when suit is in plaintiff's home forum); *Gulf Oil Corp. v. Gilbert*, 330 U.S. 501, 508, 67 S. Ct. 839, 843, 91 L. Ed. 1055 (1947) ("[U]nless the balance is strongly in favor of the defendant, the plaintiff's choice of forum should rarely be disturbed."). *See also Iragorri v. United Technologies Corp.*, 274 F.3d 65, 71–72 (2d Cir. 2001) (noting sliding scale of deference involving several factors, but beginning with high deference for plaintiff's choice of home forum and sliding to less deference for foreign plaintiff; "the more it appears that a domestic or foreign plaintiff's choice of forum has been dictated by reasons that the law recognizes as valid, the greater the deference that will be given to the plaintiff's forum choice"). Moreover, in a case where the plaintiff is a United States citizen and one or more defendants are non-Americans, the plaintiff's decision to sue in a judicial district other than the one in which the plaintiff resides does not nullify the deference to which the plaintiff's choice is entitled. *See, e.g., Wiwa v. Royal Dutch Petroleum Co.*, 226 F.3d 88, 103 (2d Cir. 2000) ("The benefit for a U.S. resident plaintiff of suing in a U.S. forum is not limited to suits in the very district where the plaintiff resides, especially considering that the defendant may not be amenable to suit in the plaintiff's district of residence."); *Reid-Walen v. Hansen*, 933 F.2d 1390, 1394 (8th Cir. 1991) (assuming plaintiff has not

a forum non conveniens motion, the defendant must demonstrate that the plaintiff's choice of forum was significantly inappropriate, notwithstanding the existence of satisfactory jurisdiction and venue. As applied to the facts of particular cases, this deference means that when the court is weighing the public and private interests discussed below, the plaintiff's choice of forum will not be defeated by a mere preponderance of interests favoring dismissal. In fact, in most cases the forum non conveniens motion will not be granted unless the weighing factors discussed below "weigh heavily in favor of trial in the alternative forum."[27] In all cases the trial court's discretion in weighing factors may not be used to nullify the deference to which a plaintiff's choice of forum is entitled.[28]

Additionally, it should be clear that the entire question of the amount of deference due to the plaintiff's choice of forum does not even arise until the defendant establishes the existence of an adequate alternative forum. If there is no such forum, the motion to dismiss will simply be denied.[29]

Exception: Plaintiff Does Not Reside in District: If the plaintiff does not reside in the judicial district where the case was filed, the plaintiffs choice of forum receives less deference.[30]

Exception: Non-American Plaintiffs: In federal courts it is settled that American plaintiffs receive substantially more deference in their choices of fora than do non-American plaintiffs.[31] However, "less deference" is not the same as no deference at all, and a foreign plaintiff's choice of forum is still entitled to

---

selected the forum to harass or vex the defendant, "the 'home' forum for the plaintiff is any federal district in the United States, not the particular district where the plaintiff lives").

[27] *R. Maganlal & Co. v. M.G. Chemical Co., Inc.*, 942 F.2d 164, 167 (2d Cir. 1991).

[28] *See also DiRienzo v. Philip Services Corp.*, 232 F.3d 49, 60 (2d Cir. 2000) (presumption in favor of home forum not weakened by fact that case is class action; acknowledging, however, that such weakening exists in shareholder's derivative suit, per *Koster v. (American) Lumbermens Mut. Cas. Co.*, 330 U.S. 518, 525, 67 S. Ct. 828, 832, 91 L. Ed. 1067 (1947)); *Wiwa v. Royal Dutch Petroleum Co.*, 226 F.3d 88, 101 (2d Cir. 2000) (deference to plaintiff's choice of forum "increases as the plaintiff's ties to the forum increase"); *Guidi v. Inter-Continental Hotels Corp.*, 224 F.3d 142 (2d Cir.2000) (failure to give American plaintiffs choice of forum "significant deference" is "unsound").

[29] *Norex Petroleum Ltd. v. Access Industries, Inc.*, 416 F.3d 146 (2d Cir. 2005).

[30] *See, e.g., Employers Mutual Casualty Co. v. Bartile Roofs, Inc.*, 618 F.3d 1153, 1168 (10th Cir. 2010).

[31] *Piper Aircraft Co. v. Reyno*, 454 U.S. 235, 256, 102 S. Ct. 252, 266, 70 L. Ed. 2d 419 (1981) ("Because the central purpose of any forum non conveniens inquiry is to ensure that the trial is convenient, a foreign plaintiff's choice deserves less deference."). *See also Pollux Holding Ltd. v. Chase Manhattan Bank*, 329 F.3d 64, 73 (2d Cir. 2003) ("Even assuming that, by treaty, plaintiffs were entitled to access American courts on the same terms as American citizens . . ., our case law does not support plaintiffs' assertion that such a treaty would require their choice of law forum be afforded the same deference afforded to a United States citizen bringing suit in his or her home forum.").

some respect.[32] Additionally, a foreign plaintiff may be entitled to somewhat greater deference if it can establish that the selected forum is highly convenient.[33]

Exception: Certain Declaratory Judgment Plaintiffs: If the plaintiff who has chosen the forum has sought relief in the form of a declaratory judgment, with a "bad faith" motive of taking advantage of the true plaintiff in a race to the forum, it appears that the declaratory judgment plaintiff's choice of forum is not entitled any deference.[34]

Exception: Identical Suits in Different Venues: If an unusual case involves identical lawsuits that were filed in different venues, there is no deference to either plaintiff's choice of forum.[35]

Modification: Corporate Plaintiffs in International Business: If the plaintiff is an American corporation with substantial experience in international business transactions and is suing on a cause of action that arose outside the United States, it appears that such a plaintiff will receive less deference than would, *e.g.,* an individual American plaintiff suing on a personal injury incurred while on vacation outside the United States.[36]

---

[32]*See, e.g., Bigio v. Coca-Cola Co.,* 448 F.3d 176, 179 (2d Cir. 2006) (even a foreign plaintiff's choice of forum is entitled to some deference; moreover, deference should increase if choice of forum has legitimate foundation); *Lacey v. Cessna Aircraft Co.,* 862 F.2d 38, 45–46 (3d Cir. 1988) (Less deference for foreign plaintiffs "is 'not an invitation to accord a foreign plaintiff's selection of an American forum no deference.' "). *Cf., Windt v. Qwest Communications Intern., Inc.,* 529 F.3d 183 (3d Cir. 2008) (abuse of discretion to fail to determine amount of deference due to foreign plaintiff's choice of forum).

[33]*See, e.g., Lony v. E.I. Du Pont de Nemours & Co.,* 886 F.2d 628, 634 (3d Cir. 1989) ("Because the reason for giving a foreign plaintiff's choice less deference is not xenophobia, but merely a reluctance to assume that the choice is a convenient one, that reluctance can readily be overcome by a strong showing of convenience."). *See also Veba-Chemie A.G. v. M/V Getafix,* 711 F.2d 1243, 1248 (5th Cir. 1983) ("The forum non conveniens analysis has never asked the courts to reconstruct and weight the relative conveniences as they existed when plaintiff brought suit. Instead, the forum non conveniens inquiry — including the

convenience, availability and adequacy elements — has always been conducted in the present tense.").

[34]*See, e.g., Hyatt Intern. Corp. v. Coco,* 302 F.3d 707, 718 (7th Cir. 2002) (plaintiff's choice of forum normally gets deference, but "[w]e have wariness at the prospect of 'a suit for declaratory judgment aimed solely at wrestling the choice of forum from the natural plaintiff.' "); *NSI Corp. v. Showco, Inc.,* 843 F. Supp. 642, 645 (D. Or. 1994) (using declaratory judgment proceeding to obtain unfair advantage in choice of forum is ground for dismissal). *See also Interface Partners International, Ltd., v. Hananel,* 575 F.3d 97, 102 n.9 (1st Cir. 2009) (if plaintiff chose a forum to forum shop, e.g., "to win a tactical advantage resulting from local laws that favor the plaintiff's case," plaintiff's choice of forum should get less deference).

[35]*See, e.g., Research Automation, Inc. v. Schrader-Bridgeport International, Inc.,* 626 F.3d 973, 979 (7th Cir. 2010).

[36]*See, e.g., Pollux Holding Ltd. v. Chase Manhattan Bank,* 329 F.3d 64, 70–71 (2d Cir. 2003) (corporations with status of United States citizen residing abroad receives deference only to extent that corporations have

Weighing Factors: Judicial Discretion

Once a trial court has identified an adequate alternative forum in which the defendants will be subject to jurisdiction, it is authorized to weigh, on a case by case basis,[37] the important factors of public and private interest in determining whether to grant a defendant's forum non conveniens motion.[38] In doing so, the court enjoys significant discretion that will not lightly be overturned on appeal, including the power to impose conditions on its decisions.[39] However, failure to weigh all the factors of public or private interest that arise in a particular case may be abuse of discretion.[40]

---

significant connections with forum; otherwise, corporations get less deference); *Guidi v. Inter-Continental Hotels Corp.*, 224 F.3d 142 (2d Cir. 2000) (because plaintiffs are "ordinary American citizens," they face significant inconvenience in litigating in Egypt; corporate defendant with principal place of business in forum faces no comparable hardship in defending in United States); *Kamel v. Hill-Rom Co., Inc.*, 108 F.3d 799, 804 (7th Cir. 1997) (suggesting that sophisticated American corporate plaintiff suing on foreign cause of action receives "somewhat discounted" deference). *See also Koster v. Lumbermens Mutual Casualty Co.*, 330 U.S. 518, 527, 67 S. Ct. 828, 91 L. Ed.1067 (1947) (where corporation is incorporated in a state where it otherwise does little or no business, the "[p]lace of corporate domicile . . . might be entitled to little consideration").

[37]*Van Cauwenberghe v. Biard*, 486 U.S. 517, 529, 108 S. Ct. 1945, 100 L. Ed. 2d 517 (1988) (" '[T]he district court is accorded substantial flexibility in evaluating a *forum non conveniens* motion,' . . . and 'each case turns on its facts.' ").

[38]*But cf., Aldana v. Del Monte Fresh Produce N.A., Inc.*, 578 F.3d 1283, 1298 (11th Cir. 2009) ("[I]t is only when the private interest factors are 'at or near equipoise' that a district court is obliged to consider the public interests at stake in a suit.").

[39]*See, e.g., MSC Mediterranean Shipping Co. v. Koninklijke Boskalis Westminster NV*, 569 F.3d 189, ____ (4th Cir. 2009) (granting forum non conveniens motion provided that statute of limitations defense will not be raised in foreign proceeding); *Bank of Credit and Commerce International (OVERSEAS) Ltd. v. State Bank of Pakistan*, 273 F.3d 241, 244–48 (2d Cir. 2001) (in granting motion, court has discretion to require party prevailing on motion to: waive statute of limitation defense; agree that if opponent obtains final judgment on in foreign court, it may be enforced elsewhere; and to waive forum non conveniens defense if foreign court refused to hear case on statute of limitations grounds).

[40]*See, e.g., EFCO Corp. v. Aluma Systems USA, Inc.*, 268 F.3d 601, 603 (8th Cir. 2001) ("Abuse of discretion occurs when the district court does not hold the defendants to their burden of persuasion on all the elements of the forum non conveniens analysis, fails to consider the relevant public and private interest factors established in *Piper Aircraft* . . . or clearly errs in weighing the *Piper Aircraft* factors."); *Dickson Marine Inc. v. Panalpina, Inc.*, 179 F.3d 331, 341 (5th Cir. 1999) ("[A] district court abuses its discretion when it grants a motion to dismiss without oral or written reasons or when it fails to address and balance the relevant principles and factors."); *Reid-Walen v. Hansen*, 933 F.2d 1390, 1393 (8th Cir. 1991) ("An abuse of discretion may occur when the district court fails to consider one or more of the important private or public interest factors, does not hold the defendants to their burden of persuasion on all elements of the forum non conveniens analysis, or has clearly erred in weighing the factors the court must consider.").

Public Interest Factors

The public interest factors may differ somewhat from one case to another, but it is settled that they include: "(1) having local disputes settled locally; (2) avoiding problems of applying foreign law; and (3) avoiding burdening jurors with cases that have no impact on their community."[41] In some cases there may also be questions about the enforceability of a judgment that the court would render if it retained the case.

Local Disputes: The desire to settle local disputes locally (or, alternatively, the desire to avoid imposing distant disputes on a local court) takes into account questions such as local court congestion or burdens on jurors.[42]

Application of Foreign Law: Courts may be reluctant to take cases in which they will be obligated to apply the law of another jurisdiction. However, in a weighing of factors related to forum non conveniens, this consideration normally carries only limited weight.[43]

Burdening Jurors with Cases of No Local Interest: This factor contains two parts: whether local citizens should have to carry the burden of trying a case unrelated to their community; and whether the citizenry of another area has a greater interest in the outcome of a case.[44]

Enforceability of a Judgment: If enforcement of a prospective judgment could require further litigation outside the United States, the court may weigh that factor in determining whether the case should be heard in the United States in the first instance.[45] This consideration would carry particular weight if there was a significant possibility that the judgment would be unenforceable, thus potentially reducing the American judicial proceeding to a waste of time and judicial resources. However, this "enforceability" factor normally plays no role in forum non conveniens determinations if enforcement will occur in the

---

[41]*Alfadda v. Fenn*, 159 F.3d 41, 46 (2d Cir. 1998) (citing *Piper Aircraft* and *Gulf Oil*). *See also Zelinski v. Columbia 300, Inc.*, 335 F.3d 633 (7th Cir. 2003) (once trial was finished, public interest in favor of not moving case may arise from policy of not wasting judicial resources already expended on case).

[42]*Gulf Oil Corp. v. Gilbert*, 330 U.S. 501, 67 S. Ct. 839, 91 L. Ed. 1055 (1947). *But cf., Guidi v. Inter-Continental Hotels Corp.*, 224 F.3d 142 (2d Cir.2000) (district court's finding that it is " 'heavily overburdened' " is of "little or no significance" where all judicial vacancies have recently been filled; moreover, while the existence of related litigation in another forum may sometimes justify dismissal so that judicial efficiency is served by permitting consolidation of cases, this

consideration usually arises only when the parties in both lawsuits are substantially identical).

[43]*See, e.g., Boosey & Hawkes Music Publishers, Ltd. v. Walt Disney Co.*, 145 F.3d 481, 492 (2d Cir. 1998) (by itself, burden of applying foreign law does not justify dismissal).

[44]*Gulf Oil Corp. v. Gilbert*, 330 U.S. 501, 67 S. Ct. 839, 91 L. Ed. 1055 (1947). *But cf., P & S Business Machines, Inc. v. Canon USA, Inc.*, 331 F.3d 804, 808 (11th Cir. 2003) (docket congestion is an appropriate consideration, but "case law does not suggest that docket congestion is, by itself, a dispositive factor").

[45]*Gulf Oil Corp. v. Gilbert*, 330 U.S. 501, 67 S. Ct. 839, 91 L. Ed. 1055 (1947).

United States, because the Full Faith and Credit clause of the Constitution generally requires an American court to enforce the final judgment of another American court.

Public Policy: In unusual cases, courts may retain a particular lawsuit because public policy favors an American forum for such a suit.[46]

Pending Litigation in a Foreign Forum: The existence of concurrent litigation in a foreign court is *not* a factor arguing in favor of dismissing a case on forum non conveniens grounds.[47]

Private Interest Factors

Private interest factors include: "(1) ease of access to evidence;[48] (2) the cost for witnesses to attend trial;[49] (3) the availability of compulsory process;[50] and (4) other factors that might shorten trial or make it less expensive."[51] For the most part, these factors revolve around the impact of forum selection on the ability of parties to prove their case. If a plaintiff's choice of forum-or the defendant's proposed alternative-substantially affects a party's ability to put forward witnesses and evidence,

[46]*See, e.g., DiRienzo v. Philip Services Corp.*, 294 F.3d 21, 29–31 (2d Cir. 2002) (private interest factors: documents in Canada, but no particular problems of transport; most witnesses in Canada, but all within a few hours of New York forum by automobile and air travel; some third-party witnesses in Canada cannot be forced to testify in New York, but videotaped depositions arranged through letters rogatory may be suitable substitute; public interest factors: most tend not to weigh heavily on instant facts, but United States has strong interest in hearing cases arising under federal securities laws, and this factor strongly supports plaintiff's choice of forum); *Wiwa v. Royal Dutch Petroleum Co.*, 226 F.3d 88, 105 (2d Cir. 2000) (federal law reflects policy in favor of hearing claims of torture under color of foreign law). *But cf., Allstate Life Ins. Co. v. Linter Group Ltd.*, 994 F.2d 996, 1002 (2d Cir. 1993) ("While . . . United States courts have an interest in enforcing United States securities laws, this alone does not prohibit them from dismissing a securities action on the ground of forum non conveniens.").

[47]*See, e.g., Adelson v. Hananel*, 510 F.3d 43, 54 (1st Cir. 2007) (error to focus "on the existence of parallel proceedings in a foreign court").

[48]*See, e.g., Duha v. Agrium, Inc.*, 448 F.3d 867, 876 (6th Cir. 2006) (where courts are dealing with "cases involving foreign language documents," they "normally consider their impact and perhaps the cost of translation in the balance of convenience").

[49]*See, e.g., Gates Learjet Corp. v. Jensen*, 743 F.2d 1325, 1335–36 (9th Cir. 1984) (issue is not number of witnesses in each location, but access and convenience to forum and cost of travel).

[50]*See, e.g., Duha v. Agrium, Inc.*, 448 F.3d 867, 877 (6th Cir. 2006) (availability of compulsory process carries weight only where it appears that important witnesses would be unwilling to testify).

[51]*Alfadda v. Fenn*, 159 F.3d 41, 46 (2d Cir. 1998) (citing *Piper Aircraft* and *Gulf Oil*). *See also Leon v. Millon Air, Inc.*, 251 F.3d 1305 (11th Cir. 2001) (private interest factors generally considered more significant than public factors, but both kinds of facts should be weighed); *Guidi v. Inter-Continental Hotels Corp.*, 224 F.3d 142 (2d Cir. 2000) (abuse of discretion for district court not to consider emotional burden of litigating in Egypt, where plaintiff's or their relatives were attacked by terrorists and where plaintiffs justifiably fear for their safety).

the court will be inclined to weigh that consideration heavily.[52]

Application of Doctrine *Sua Sponte*

Normally, a forum non conveniens issue is raised by a party. At the same time, parties are free to waive the issue, and such waiver may occur in a variety of circumstances.[53] However, a party's decision to waive the issue is subject to the court's authority to raise the issue *sua sponte*.[54] For example, the court might do so if the convenience of non-party witnesses was an important issue.

Transfer

Congress has provided a special remedy for forum non conveniens cases originally filed in federal district courts. 28 U.S.C.A. § 1404 provides that a federal court that is an inappropriate forum may *transfer* the case to another federal district court in which the case "might have been brought."[55] Because a transferred case is not dismissed, transfer creates no statute of

---

[52]*Piper Aircraft Co. v. Reyno*, 454 U.S. 235, 102 S. Ct. 252, 70 L. Ed. 2d 419 (1981) (large proportion of relevant evidence in foreign country is factor weighing in favor of dismissal). *See also, e.g., Alpine View Co. Ltd. v. Atlas Copco AB*, 205 F.3d 208, 222 (5th Cir. 2000) (upholding district court's assessment of private factors where no witness was identified in United States who would be needed for "general discovery" and documents existed mostly outside United States; private interest factors favor dismissal sufficiently so that circuit court need not address factors of public interest). *But see DiRienzo v. Philip Services Corp.*, 294 F.3d 21 (2d Cir. 2002) (private interest factors: documents in Canada, but no particular problems of transport; most witnesses in Canada, but all within a few hours of New York forum by automobile and air travel; some third-party witnesses in Canada cannot be forced to testify in New York, but videotaped depositions arranged through letters rogatory may be suitable substitute; public interest factors: most tend not to weigh heavily on instant facts, but United States has strong interest in hearing cases arising under federal securities laws, and this factor strongly supports plaintiff's choice of forum).

[53]*See, e.g., Corporacion Mexicana de Servicios Maritimos, S.A. de C.V. v. M/T Respect*, 89 F.3d 650, 656 n. 1 (9th Cir. 1996) (by intervening, party

waived forum non conveniens); *Heller Financial, Inc. v. Midwhey Powder Co., Inc.*, 883 F.2d 1286, 1293 (7th Cir. 1989) (valid forum-selection clause waives defense of forum non conveniens).

[54]*See, e.g., Wong v. PartyGaming, Ltd*, 589 F.3d 821, 830 (6th Cir. 2009) (agreeing with existence of district court's *sua sponte* authority). *Corporacion Mexicana de Servicios Maritimos, S.A. de C.V. v. M/T Respect*, 89 F.3d 650, 656 n. 1 (9th Cir. 1996). *But cf, Tazoe v. Airbus S.A.S.*, 631 F.3d 1321, 1336 (11th Cir. 2011) (court may act *sua sponte,* but parties must have a chance to be heard; show cause order is minimum to which they are entitled).

[55]*See, e.g., Ecker v. United States*, 575 F.3d 70, 76 (1st Cir. 2009) (noting limitation on transfer only to districts where case might have been brought); *In re Genentech, Inc.*, 566 F.3d 1338, 1343 (Fed. Cir. 2009) (suggesting that convenience of witnesses and cost of attendance for witnesses may be most important factors for transfer analysis). *But cf., Wild v. Subscription Plus, Inc.*, 292 F.3d 526, 531 (7th Cir. 2002) ("[T]here is no absolute bar to the transfer of a multidefendant suit to a district in which one of the defendants cannot be served." Treating § 1404 as closely analogous to § 1406 for this purpose).

limitations problems.[56] Transfer is now the standard remedy in cases where it can be applied.[57]

Limits on Transfer

Federal district courts may use § 1404 only to transfer cases to other federal district courts. If a federal court recognizes that the appropriate forum for an action is outside the United States, the only remedy available is dismissal of the action, with permission to the plaintiff to file the cause of action elsewhere. This remedy can create practical problems for plaintiffs, so courts often condition a grant of a defendant's motion to dismiss for forum non conveniens on understandings that the defendant will submit to jurisdiction in another country and will not challenge the suit on statute of limitations grounds.[58]

Partial Transfers

It is uncertain whether § 1404 requires transfer of an entire case or, alternatively, whether a district court may choose to transfer only a portion of a case.[59] Attorneys must consult the local precedent.

Before 2012, § 1404(d) expressly permitted transfers of caes

---

[56]*Ferens v. John Deere Co.*, 494 U.S. 516, 110 S. Ct. 1274, 108 L. Ed. 2d 443 (1990) (transfer to state where applicable statute of limitations will bar suit has no ill consequence for suit, because statute of limitations of transferor jurisdiction remains in effect). *See also In re LimitNone, LLC*, 551 F.3d 572, 577 (7th Cir. 2008) (" § 1404(a) is nothing more than a codification of the traditional forum non conveniens rules without the attendant disadvantages of outright dismissal."). *But see In re Volkswagen of America, Inc.*, 545 F.3d 304, 309–10 (5th Cir. 2008) (plaintiff's choice of forum in forum non conveniens context "is weightier than a plaintiff's choice of venue under § 1404(a).").

[57]*Quackenbush v. Allstate Ins. Co.*, 517 U.S. 706, 116 S. Ct. 1712, 135 L. Ed. 2d 1 (1996) (for federal courts, transfer pursuant to § 1404 is preferred remedy for problems arising from forum non conveniens; dismissal appropriate "only in 'cases where the alternative forum is abroad' "). *Sinochem Intern. Co. Ltd. v. Malaysia Intern. Shipping Corp.*, 549 U.S. 422, 127 S. Ct. 1184, 167 L. Ed. 2d 15 (2007) (also acknowledging use of common-law doctrine of forum non conveniens "in rare instances where a state or territorial court serves litigation conve-

nience best"). *See, e.g., In re Volkswagen of America, Inc.*, 545 F.3d 304, 314 (5th Cir. 2008) (using relevant factors of forum non conveniens to decide transfer motion; also noting, however, that burden of proving existence of "substantially more convenient alternative" that is so important to forum non conveniens does not apply to transfer). *But see New York Marine and General Insurance Co. v. Lafarge North America, Inc.*, 599 F.3d 102, 113–14 (2d Cir. 2010) (affirming use of clear and convincing evidence standard to determine whether defendant made out a sufficiently strong case for transfer).

[58]*See, e.g., Leon v. Million Air, Inc.*, 251 F.3d 1305 (11th Cir.2001) (affirming dismissal, subject to following conditions: (1) admission of liability for damage caused by plane crash; (2) acceptance of service of process and jurisdiction in appropriate foreign court; (3) waiver of statute of limitations; (4) payment of final judgments of foreign court; and (5) case may be reinstated if foreign court rejects jurisdiction).

[59]*See, e.g., D'Jamoos v. Pilatus Aircraft, Ltd.*, 566 F.3d 94, 110 (3d Cir. 2009) (collecting contrary authority).

to or from the district courts for Guam, the Northern Marianas, and the Virgin Islands if other requirements of § 1404 were satisfied. However, as now amended, § 1404(d) expressly excludes those courts from possibilities to participate in transfers under § 1404.[60]

ADDITIONAL RESEARCH REFERENCES

C.J.S., Federal Courts §§ 10(1) et seq.
West's Key Number Digest, Federal Courts ☞45

§ 2.16 Removal

CORE CONCEPT

Removal permits a defendant to move a case from a state trial court to a federal district court. The process is controlled by federal law.

28 U.S.C.A. § 1441 identifies most of the kinds of lawsuits that may be removed from a state court to federal district court. These include most diversity suits, most federal question suits, non-diverse state claims which are joined with federal questions, and suits against foreign states.[1] Section 1441 also contains a provision permitting removal even in circumstances where a state court lacked jurisdiction over the case when it was originally filed.

APPLICATIONS

Removal Statutes

The most important removal provisions are 28 U.S.C.A. § 1441 (governing removal for diversity cases, most federal questions, and non-diverse claims joined with federal questions), 28 U.S.C.A. § 1446 (establishing the procedure for accomplishing removal), and § 1447 (governing procedure after removal). Specific statutes provide for removal in particular circumstances, such as suits against federal officers or agencies (28 U.S.C.A. §§ 1442, 1442a, and 1444), and suits where a defendant might not be able to assert a federal civil right in a state court (28 U.S.C.A. § 1443). Additionally, 28 U.S.C.A. § 1445 provides that certain kinds of cases (*e.g.,* suits against railroads under the Federal Employers' Liability Act and suits arising under state workers' compensation laws) may not be removed. If a case has been removed, 28 U.S.C.A. §§ 1447 to 49 establish the procedures a court will follow after a case has been removed. Finally, Congress recently enacted 28 U.S.C.A.

---

[60]28 U.S.C. § 1404(d).

[1]*Cf. City of Chicago v. International College of Surgeons,* 522 U.S. 156, 163, 118 S. Ct. 523, 529, 139 L. Ed. 2d 525 (1997) ("The propriety of removal . . . depends on whether the case originally could have been filed in federal court.").

§ 1453, which now governs removal of class actions.

Exceptions to § 1441(a)

Section 1441(a) provides that the general right of removal is subject to such exceptions as Congress may create.[2] Congress has preserved some exceptions in 28 U.S.C.A. § 1445, such as cases arising under state workers' compensation statutes.

Jurisdictional Requirement

Removal is permissible only when at least one claim filed by the plaintiff falls within the original subject matter jurisdiction of the federal district court.[3]

Burden of Proof: Presumption Against Removal

It is settled that the party seeking removal must meet the burden of establishing that the jurisdictional requirements for removal are met.[4] It is also settled that the statutory right to remove is narrowly construed.[5] Where a doubt exists, a district court will resolve it by remanding the case.[6]

---

[2]*Breuer v. Jim's Concrete of Brevard, Inc.*, 538 U.S. 691, 123 S. Ct. 1882, 155 L. Ed. 2d 923 (2003) (if federal subject matter jurisdiction is satisfied, statutory prohibition against removal must be express). Cf., e.g., *Nevada v. Hicks*, 533 U.S. 353, 121 S. Ct. 2304, 150 L. Ed. 2d 398 (2001) (federal civil rights claims governed by 42 U.S.C.A. § 1983 may not be filed in tribal courts, partly because § 1441 does not authorize removal of federal claims from such courts; only claims in state courts might qualify for removal under § 1441).

[3]*Beneficial Nat. Bank v. Anderson*, 539 U.S. 1, 8, 123 S. Ct. 2058, 2063, 156 L. Ed. 2d 1 (2003) ("[A] state claim may be removed to federal court in only two circumstances-when Congress expressly so provides . . . or when a federal statute wholly displaces the state-law cause of action through complete pre-emption."); *Jefferson County, Ala. v. Acker*, 527 U.S. 423, 430, 119 S. Ct. 2069, 2074, 144 L. Ed. 2d 408 (1999) ("It is the general rule that an action may be removed from state court to federal court only if a federal district court would have original jurisdiction over the claim in suit."). Cf. *Wisconsin Dept. of Corrections v. Schacht*, 524 U.S. 381, 118 S. Ct. 2047, 141 L. Ed. 2d 364 (1998) (presence of one claim that is barred by Eleventh Amendment immunity does not prevent removal of other claims that meet jurisdictional requirements); *K2 America Corp. v. Roland Oil & Gas, LLC*, 653 F.3d 1024, 1029 n.6 (9th Cir. 2011) (defense of complete federal preemption of state-law claim cannot be basis for removal); *Charvat v. EchoStar Satellite, LLC*, 630 F.3d 459, 464 (6th Cir. 2010) ("Statutory permission to litigate a federal claim in state court does not expressly remove a district court's federal-question (or for that matter diversity) jurisdiction." Citing § 1441).

[4]*See, e.g., Geographic Expeditions, Inc. v. Estate of Lhotka*, 599 F.3d 1102, 1107 (9th Cir. 2010) (proponent of removal must prove, by preponderance of evidence, right to remove).

[5]*See, e.g., Geographic Expeditions, Inc. v. Estate of Lhotka*, 599 F.3d 1102, 1107 (9th Cir. 2010) (strong presumption against removal jurisdiction).

[6]*See, e.g., Central Iowa Power Cooperative v. Midwest Independent Transmission System Operator, Inc.*, 561 F.3d 904, 912 (8th Cir. 2009) ("Critically, the party seeking removal has the burden to establish federal subject matter jurisdiction."); *Dahl v. R.J. Reynolds Tobacco Co.*, 478 F.3d 965, 968 (8th Cir. 2007) (all doubts should be resolved in favor of remand).

Timing of Evaluation of Subject Matter Jurisdiction

In removal cases the presence or absence of federal subject matter jurisdiction is evaluated at the time a petition for removal is filed.[7] This approach differs from that applied when a case was originally filed in a district court. In that circumstance subject matter jurisdiction is evaluated as of the date of the filing of the case.[8]

An exception to the "good jurisdiction at time of removal" mandate may arise when a case that lacked subject matter jurisdiction at the time of removal subsequently acquires jurisdiction later in the litigation. Thus, if a plaintiff in a removed case subsequently amends the complaint in a way that establishes good subject matter jurisdiction, the defect that existed at the time of removal will be ignored.[9]

Removal from State Court Only

For removal to be effective under § 1441, the case must have been in state court at the time the removal petition was filed. Section 1441 provides no authority to remove a case from a state administrative agency to a federal district court.[10]

Defendant's Right

Section 1441(a) restricts the right of removal to parties who are defendants to the plaintiff's case in chief. The majority view appears to be that defendants on counterclaims, cross-claims, or third-party impleaders have no right to remove cases from state court.[11] However, these defendants may find claims affecting them removed if a defendant on an original count files

---

[7]*Caterpillar Inc. v. Lewis*, 519 U.S. 61, 73, 117 S. Ct. 467, 136 L. Ed. 2d 437 (1996) (case must "be fit for federal adjudication at the time the removal petition is filed"). *See, e.g., Harper v. AutoAlliance Intern., Inc.*, 392 F.3d 195, 210 (6th Cir. 2004) ("The existence of subject matter jurisdiction is determined by examining the complaint as it existed at the time of removal.").

[8]*Dole Food Co. v. Patrickson*, 538 U.S. 468, 477, 123 S. Ct. 1655, 155 L. Ed. 2d 643 (2003) ("It is well settled . . . that federal-diversity jurisdiction depends on the citizenship of the parties at the time suit is filed.").

[9]*Caterpillar Inc. v. Lewis*, 519 U.S. 61, 64, 117 S. Ct. 467, 136 L. Ed. 2d 437 (1996) (defect not "fatal to federal-court adjudication" where defect is later cured). *See, e.g., Moffitt v. Residential Funding Co., LLC*, 604 F.3d 156, 159 (4th Cir. 2010) ("[I]f a plaintiff voluntarily amends his complaint to allege a basis for federal ju-

risdiction, a federal court may exercise jurisdiction even if the case was improperly removed."). *See also Pegram v. Herdrich*, 530 U.S. 211, 216 n.2, 120 S. Ct. 2143, 147 L. Ed. 2d 164 (2000) (where plaintiff later added federal claims "we therefore have jurisdiction regardless of the correctness of the removal").

[10]*See, e.g., Porter Trust v. Rural Water Sewer & Solid Waste Management District No. 1*, 607 F.3d 1251, 1253 (10th Cir. 2010) (removal available only from state court; even a state board that exercises a judicial function may not meet "plain language" requirement for a state court; rejecting some district court precedent permitting removal from state agency); *Oregon Bureau of Labor and Industries ex rel. Richardson v. U.S. West Communications, Inc.*, 288 F.3d 414, 415 (9th Cir. 2002) ("§ 1441(a) authorizes removal only from a 'state court,'" not an administrative agency).

[11]*See, e.g., First Nat. Bank of*

a notice of removal. This possibility is discussed below, under *Joinder of "Non-Removable" Claims*. Further, if the basis of removal is a third-party claim against a foreign state, § 1441(d) (governing removal of claims against foreign states) will permit removal, notwithstanding the different result reached in cases governed by § 1441(a) or (b).[12]

Forum Selection Clauses

A valid forum selection clause that limits jurisdiction exclusively to a non-federal court is apparently enforceable, notwithstanding that the parties would otherwise be eligible for federal diversity jurisdiction.[13] However, it does not follow that the same result would be reached in a case involving potential federal question jurisdiction (particularly exclusive federal question jurisdiction). In that situation attorneys should consult local practice.

Geography of Removal

Cases removed from state court are removed to the federal court of the district (or division) that includes the location in which the state court sits.[14] Thus, a case removed from a Pennsylvania state trial court in Harrisburg, Pennsylvania would be sent to the United States District Court for the Middle District of Pennsylvania, the federal district court that includes Harrisburg.

Pulaski v. Curry, 301 F.3d 456, 461 (6th Cir. 2002) ("[N]either § 1441(a) nor § 1441(c) provides third-party defendants with the right to remove a case to federal court."); *Lewis v. Windsor Door Co., a Div. of Ceco Corp.*, 926 F.2d 729, 733 (8th Cir. 1991) (removal cannot be based on third-party claim that may be within original jurisdiction of federal court); *Thomas v. Shelton*, 740 F.2d 478, 487–88 (7th Cir. 1984) (third party defendants may not remove). *But see In re Wilson Industries, Inc.*, 886 F.2d 93, 96 (5th Cir. 1989) (removal "can be based on a third-party claim where a separate and independent controversy is stated"; apparent minority view).

[12]*See, e.g., Davis v. McCourt*, 226 F.3d 506 (6th Cir.2000) (collecting cases; also noting that entire lawsuit, not merely third-party complaint against foreign entity, is removed).

[13]*See, e.g., Florida Polk County v. Prison Health Services, Inc.*, 170 F.3d 1081, 1083–84 (11th Cir. 1999) (applying principles of contract law to determine whether to enforce forum selection clause). *But cf. Yakin v. Tyler Hill Corp.*, 566 F.3d 72, 76 (2d Cir. 2009)

("[O]bligatory venue language," standing alone limits case to county court only if a federal court was not located in the same county); *Kerobo v. Southwestern Clean Fuels Corp.*, 285 F.3d 531, 534–35 (6th Cir. 2002) (suit in Michigan state court; parties had forum clause selection choosing California venue; holding such a clause could not prevent removal to Michigan federal court).

[14]28 U.S.C.A. § 1441(a). *Global Satellite Communication Co. v. Starmill U.K. Ltd.*, 378 F.3d 1269, 1271 (11th Cir. 2004) (in venue issues relating to removal, the controlling statute is § 1441(a), not the general venue statute, 28 U.S.C.A. § 1391); *See, e.g., Kerobo v. Southwestern Clean Fuels, Corp.*, 285 F.3d 531, 534 (6th Cir. 2002) (removal from state court within area embraced by Eastern District of Michigan could only be to Eastern District of Michigan). *But cf. Peterson v. BMI Refractories*, 124 F.3d 1386, 1394 (11th Cir. 1997) (removal to "wrong" district court is procedural error that is waivable; issue is not jurisdictional in nature).

Fictitious Names Disregarded

When determining whether the federal court has diversity jurisdiction over a removed case, § 1441(a) provides that if state procedure allows suits against defendants under fictitious names (*e.g. General Motors v. John Doe, Mary Roe, and Jane Coe*), the citizenship of such defendants will be disregarded.[15] This provision was previously located in § 1441(a), but as part of the 2012 amendments to § 1441 it has been relocated to § 1441(b)(1). This relocation did not involve a substantive change in law. This change, in turn, required that § 1441(b) be reorganized into distinct parts. The first part of the reorganization was the re-designation of the "fictitious names" provision as new § 1441(b)(1), and the second part was the re-designation of former § 1441(b) as § 1441(b)(2). However, no substantial change was made in § 1441(b)(2). Finally, § 1441(b)(3) continues to permit removal of federal question cases, a point discussed a few pages earlier in this text.

Federal Question Cases

Section 1441(b) authorizes a defendant to remove any cause of action based upon the Constitution, laws or treaties of the United States, if the federal court has original jurisdiction over the claim.[16] In general, this provision is treated as authorizing removal of cases that could have been filed originally in federal district court pursuant to 28 U.S.C.A. § 1331 (governing federal subject matter jurisdiction over federal questions).[17] 28 U.S.C.A. § 1445(a) creates an exception to this general right of removal by prohibiting removal of suits against railroads based upon the Federal Employers' Liability Act.

Diversity Cases

Section 1441(b) also authorizes removal of cases where the parties meet requirements of diversity jurisdiction, subject to one significant exception. If any defendant sued on a diversity count is a citizen of the state in which the claim was filed, that count is not eligible for removal to federal district court.[18]

Congress recently enacted § 1453, which eliminated the ap-

---

[15]*See, e.g., Howell by Goerdt v. Tribune Entertainment Co.*, 106 F.3d 215, 218 (7th Cir. 1997) ("[N]aming a John Doe defendant will not defeat the named defendants' right to remove a diversity case if their citizenship is diverse from that of the plaintiffs.").

[16]*Rivet v. Regions Bank of Louisiana*, 522 U.S. 470, 118 S. Ct. 921, 139 L. Ed. 2d 912 (1998) (basis for removal of federal question claim must appear on face of well-pleaded complaint; "a defendant cannot remove on the basis of a federal defense," *e.g.*, res judicata). *But cf., Romero v. International Terminal Operating Co.*, 358 U.S. 354, 368–69, 79 S. Ct. 468, 478, 3 L. Ed. 2d 368 (1959) (admiralty case filed in state court may not be removed to federal court as federal question; thus, if removal was possible at all, it would have to rest on some other ground, e.g., diversity jurisdiction).

[17]*See, e.g., Eastman v. Marine Mechanical Corp.*, 438 F.3d 544, 549 (6th Cir. 2006) (scope of § 1441(b) "is considered to be identical to the scope of federal question jurisdiction under § 1331.").

[18]*Lincoln Property Co. v. Roche*, 546 U.S. 81, 126 S. Ct. 606, 613, 163 L. Ed. 2d 415 (2005); *See, e.g., Tillman*

plicability of this exception to removal of cases that are class actions. For such class actions, the exception contained in § 1441(b) is replaced by an express provision making removal possible "without regard to whether any defendant is a citizen of the State in which the action is brought."[19] Section 1453 is discussed at greater length elsewhere in this text.

It should also be noted that removal cannot be defeated simply by joining defendants with no real interest in the claim. In such cases of "fraudulent joinder," the court will dismiss the unnecessary parties and uphold removal.[20]

Fraudulent Joinder

It is possible that a plaintiff will join a nondiverse defendant for the purpose of preventing removal of an otherwise diverse claim. Such a tactic is permissible if there is a legitimate basis for the joinder. It is not always easy to identify the standard for fraudulent joinder.[21] However, if there is no colorable basis for the claim against the nondiverse defendant, federal case law provides that the court will disregard the nondiverse defendant when ruling on a motion for remand to state court.[22] Where relevant, this doctrine is an important exception to the requirement of complete diversity. Fraudulent joinder may also

---

v. R.J. Reynolds Tobacco, 253 F.3d 1302 (11th Cir.2001) ("no defendant can be a citizen of the state in which the action was brought;" one narrow exception arises if a defendant is such a citizen but "there is no possibility that the plaintiff can establish any cause of action against that defendant;" in that circumstance, court may dismiss that defendant and retain diversity jurisdiction). But cf. McCall v. Scott, 239 F.3d 808, 813 (6th Cir. 2001) ("[T]he inclusion of an unserved resident defendant in the action does not defeat removal."); Blackburn v. United Parcel Service, Inc., 179 F.3d 81 n. 3 (3d Cir. 1999) (suit against defendant in defendant's home state court that would meet requirements for diversity jurisdiction is nevertheless not eligible for removal; however, defect is waivable under 28 U.S.C.A. § 1447(c) if not raised within 30 days of filing of notice of removal).

[19]28 U.S.C.A. § 1453(b). See also Abrego Abrego v. The Dow Chemical Co., 443 F.3d 676, 681 (9th Cir. 2006) (noting that § 1453 "overrides the judge-created requirement that each defendant consent to removal"). It should be noted that the exceptions created by § 1453 for class actions are themselves subject to an exception.

Specifically, § 1453(d) provides that § 1453 is inapplicable to any class action "solely" involving: (1) a claim concerning a covered security under certain federal securities laws; (2) a claim relating to the internal affairs or governance of a corporation or other business entity arising under the laws of the state that incorporated or organized the enterprise; or (3) a claim relating to the rights and duties, including fiduciary duties, created by the Securities Act of 1933.

[20]See e.g., Pampillonia v. RJR Nabisco, Inc., 138 F.3d 459, 461 (2d Cir. 1998) (so holding; but noting that defendant bears heavy burden of proof on "fraudulent joinder").

[21]See, e.g., Travis v. Irby, 326 F.3d 644, 647 (5th Cir. 2003) ("Neither our circuit nor other circuits have been clear in describing the fraudulent joinder standard;" collecting cases). But cf., In re Briscoe, 448 F.3d 201, 218 (3d Cir. 2006) ("Unless the claims against the non-diverse defendant could be deemed 'wholly insubstantial and frivolous,' . . . the joinder could not be considered fraudulent.").

[22]See, e.g., Jerome-Duncan, Inc. v. Auto-By-Tel, L.L.C., 176 F.3d 904 (6th Cir. 1999).

be found when a plaintiff engages in "outright fraud" in pleading jurisdictional allegations.[23] A third type of fraudulent joinder may arise when the plaintiff joins a nondiverse defendant who has no joint, several or alternative liability with a diverse defendant, and there is no connection between the claims against the diverse and nondiverse defendants.[24]

Post-Removal Events Affecting Jurisdiction

It is unclear whether a case that was properly removed on the basis of diversity jurisdiction must or should be remanded to state court when events occurring after removal would have defeated removal had those events occurred prior to removal. The circuits are in conflict,[25] and attorneys must consult local precedent.

Joinder of "Non-Removable" Claims

Section 1441(c) governs circumstances in which many counts, including counts removable under § 1441(b) and counts that do not qualify for removal underf that section, are filed in the same case. The 2012 amendments to § 1441 have changed subsection (c) considerably. Previously, if a defendant sought to remove one or more separate and independent counts arising under federal question jurisdiction,[26] § 1441(c) provided that a notice of removal would cause *all* counts to be removed to

---

[23]*See, e.g., Triggs v. John Crump Toyota, Inc.*, 154 F.3d 1284, 1287 (11th Cir. 1998).

[24]*See, e.g., Tapscott v. MS Dealer Service Corp.*, 77 F.3d 1353, 1360 (11th Cir. 1996).

[25]*Compare, e.g., Spencer v. U.S. Dist. Court for Northern Dist. of Ca.*, 393 F.3d 867, 870–71 (9th Cir. 2004) (in instant case, removal appropriate at time it occurred; after removal, defendant who was diverse but was also a local resident was joined; held, district court was not obligated to remand case to state court; refusing to decide whether district court had discretion to remand); *Poore v. American-Amicable Life Ins. Co. of Texas*, 218 F.3d 1287, 1290–91 (11th Cir. 2000) (post-removal reduction in amount in controversy does not destroy district court's subject matter jurisdiction); *Van Meter v. State Farm Fire and Cas. Co.*, 1 F.3d 445, 450 (6th Cir. 1993) (overruled by, Blackburn v. Oaktree Capital Management, LLC, 511 F.3d 633 (6th Cir. 2008)) (removal that was valid when it occurred need not be upset by post-removal events that would otherwise destroy subject mat-

ter jurisdiction); *Matter of Shell Oil Co.*, 966 F.2d 1130, 1133 (7th Cir. 1992) (jurisdiction valid at time of removal "is unaffected by subsequent acts"); *with, e.g., Mayes v. Rapoport*, 198 F.3d 457, 461 (4th Cir. 1999) (post-removal joinder of non-diverse defendant requires remand to state court; only alternative would be to deny joinder, if that is appropriate); *Cobb v. Delta Exports, Inc.*, 186 F.3d 675, 677 (5th Cir. 1999) ("[P]ost-removal joinder of non-diverse defendants pursuant to Fed.R.Civ.P. 19 destroys diversity for jurisdictional purposes and requires remand, even when the newly joined defendants are not indispensable."); *Casas Office Machines, Inc. v. Mita Copystar America, Inc.*, 42 F.3d 668, 673 (1st Cir. 1994) (post-removal substitution of real parties in place of fictitious names destroyed diversity, and thereby also defeated subject matter jurisdiction); *In re Merrimack Mut. Fire Ins. Co.*, 587 F.2d 642, 646 (5th Cir. 1978) (requiring remand upon post-removal joinder of indispensable parties).

[26]28 U.S.C. § 1331.

federal district court.[27] The federal judge would then decide which non-removable counts would remain in the federal proceeding and which would be remanded to state court.[28]

Under the recently amended versions of § 1441(c), however, the situation is somewhat different. Section § 1441(c) still authorizes removal of non-removable claims when they accompany claims that fall within federal question jurisdiction,[29] but as amended the provision now directs that claims not within the original or supplemental jurisdiction of the federal district court *shall* be severed and remanded to the state court from which they were removed.[30] The result is to limit a district court's discretion (if, indeed, it ever properly existed) to retain non-removable claims that were not within the scope of the case or controversy of the federal questions upon which removal was originally based.

By contrast, there is no authority in § 1441(c), or anywhere else in § 1441, to remove nondiverse state claims to federal court when the basis for removal is a diverse count. Little or no authority exists on the topic, but it appears that in such circumstances the diverse claim may be removed under § 1441(b), and the nondiverse claims must remain in state court.

Additionally, there is a modest trend in courts to permit remand under § 1441(c) of both federal and state claims if state claims predominate.[31] Whether this view of a court's authority under § 1441(c) will prevail is currently uncertain.

Defendant's Consent to Removal in Cases Controlled by § 1441(c)

The 2012 amendments to removal provide generally that all defendants properly joined and served must consent to the removal of the action.[32] This point is discussed in greater detail when 28 U.S.C. § 1446 is addressed later in this text. It is worth noting at this point, however, that for the purpose of removing an entire case under § 1441(c), that contains both federal questions and non-removable counts, only the consent

---

[27]*Carlsbad Technologies, Inc. v. HIF Bio, Inc.*, 556 U.S. 635, 129 S. Ct. 1862, 1865 (2009) (§ 1441(c) "allows removal of an entire case when it includes at least one claim over which the federal district court has original jurisdiction.").

[28]*See, e.g., Justice v. Atchison, Topeka and Sante Fe Ry. Co.*, 927 F.2d 503, 504 (10th Cir. 1991) (remand of non-diverse state claims is within court's discretion).

[29]28 U.S.C. § 1331.

[30]28 U.S.C. § 1441(c)(2).

[31]*See, e.g., Wirtz Corp. v. United Distilleries & Vintners North America, Inc.*, 224 F.3d 708, 713 (7th Cir. 2000) (state interest in administration of alcoholic beverage program outweighs diversity jurisdiction; reversing denial of motion to remand); *Eastus v. Blue Bell Creameries, L.P.*, 97 F.3d 1200, 106 (5th Cir. 1996) (collecting cases). *See also Metro Ford Truck Sales, Inc. v. Ford Motor Co.*, 145 F.3d 320 (5th Cir. 1998) (permitting remand of federal claims within concurrent jurisdiction of federal and state courts; noting different result if federal court's jurisdiction is exclusive).

[32]28 U.S.C. § 1446(a).

of defendants sued on the federal questions must be obtained.[33] Consent of defendants sued only on the non-removable counts is not required.

Suits Against Foreign States

Section 1441(d) authorizes removal of suits filed in state court[34] against foreign countries or their agents,[35] without regard to whether the suit was based on a federal question or state law.[36]

The right to remove under § 1441(d) is substantially unqualified.[37] Moreover, the time limit for filing a removal petition under § 1441(d) may be extended, for good cause shown, beyond the thirty-day limit established by § 1446(b) and imposed routinely on more conventional removal petitions.[38] It should be noted, however, that while a foreign state's right to remove is unrestricted if filed within the thirty-day limit, a removal petition filed outside that time limit is subject to the discretion of the district court. It is the defendant's burden to demonstrate good cause for the delay in filing such a petition.[39]

Foreign States—Jury Trials

In any suit where removal was based upon § 1441(d), the court must try the case without a jury.[40]

---

[33]28 U.S.C. § 1441(c)(2).

[34]*Cf., Attorney General of Guam v. Torres*, 419 F.3d 1017, 1025 (9th Cir. 2005) (for purposes of § 1441(d), territorial courts of Guam are state courts).

[35]*Dole Food Co. v. Patrickson*, 538 U.S. 468, 477, 123 S. Ct. 1655, 1662, 155 L. Ed. 2d 643 (2003) (for a corporation to remove on ground it is instrumentality of foreign state, the foreign state must own a majority of the corporation's shares; mere control of corporation is not enough; such majority ownership must exist at time lawsuit is filed).

[36]*See, e.g., Hanil Bank v. PT. Bank Negara Indonesia (Persero)*, 148 F.3d 127 (2d Cir. 1998) (noting removal of breach of contract claim against bank owned by Indonesian government). *See also Davis v. McCourt*, 226 F.3d 506 (6th Cir. 2000) (noting that § 1441(d) authorizes removal even where count against foreign entity is third-party complaint; further, where removal occurs under § 1441(d), entire lawsuit, not merely third-party complaint against foreign entity, is removed); *Alonzi v. Budget Const. Co.*, 55 F.3d 331, 332–33 (7th

Cir. 1995) (noting that § 1441(d) allows removal by foreign states; also noting that under majority view, § 1441(d) permits removal of entire case, including otherwise non-removable claims against citizens of American states; but also citing contrary authority).

[37]28 U.S.C.A. § 1441(d) (foreign state may remove any state court civil action to district court).

[38]*See, e.g., Suter v. Munich Reinsurance Co.*, 223 F.3d 150, 159 n.4 (3d Cir. 2000) (removal outside time limits of § 1446(b) permitted "for cause shown").

[39]*See, e.g., Big Sky Network Canada, Ltd., v. Sichuan Provincial Government*, 533 F.3d 1183, 1187 (10th Cir. 2008) (noting defendant's burden; identifying (1) prejudice to opposing party, (2) length of delay and its likely impact on future proceedings, (3) reason for delay, and (4) whether defendant acted in good faith).

[40]*See, e.g., Olympia Exp., Inc. v. Linee Aeree Italiane, S.P.A.*, 509 F.3d 347, 350 (7th Cir. 2007) ("[T]he power conferred by § 1441(d) does not include the power to conduct a jury trial.").

Time: Cases Involving Foreign Counties

If a defendant seeks removal because a suit is against a foreign country, § 1441(d) authorizes the court to extend the provisions in § 1446(b) that normally govern time limits for filing a removal notice. However, extensions are granted only "for cause shown."[41]

Removal of Multiparty, Multidistrict Wrongful Death Actions

Title 28 U.S.C.A. § 1369 governs district court subject matter jurisdiction over multiparty, multiforum litigation in cases in which the deaths of 75 or more natural persons occurred in the same location.[42] Recently enacted § 1441(e) governs the circumstances in which a case that could have been filed under § 1369 may be removed to a district court. New § 1441(e) expressly provides that the provisions of § 1441(b), usually applicable to removal petitions, are inapplicable to removal petitions addressed to cases under § 1369.[43] The procedure for removal, however, is still subject to 28 U.S.C.A. § 1446, which is discussed in greater detail elsewhere in this text.

The addition of new § 1441(e) required redesignation of old § 1441(e) (governing district court jurisdiction over cases removed from a state court that may have lacked jurisdiction) as § 1441(f).[44]

State Court Jurisdiction

Section 1441(f) permits a federal district court to hear a removed case even if the state court in which the case was originally filed lacked jurisdiction.[45] Section 1441(f) was added in December 1990, and renders obsolete prior case law on the matter. However, nothing in § 1441(e) excuses a federal court from its own obligation to satisfy federal jurisdictional requirements, which generally means that at least one count in the removed case must satisfy requirements for federal question jurisdiction or diversity jurisdiction.[46]

Venue

Section 1441(f), governing the authority of a federal court to retain a case where a state court lacked jurisdiction, does not address the additional question of venue. However, case law indicates that while a removed claim does not have to satisfy

---

[41]See, e.g., Big Sky Network Canada v. Sichuan Provincial Government, 533 F.3d 1183, 1187 (10th Cir. 2008) ("cause shown" must be justification beyond extended pleading period that foreign state automatically enjoys).

[42]28 U.S.C.A. § 1369.

[43]28 U.S.C.A. § 1441(e)(1).

[44]See, e.g., Palmer v. City Nat. Bank, of West Virginia, 498 F.3d 236 (4th Cir. 2007) (explaining redesigna-tion).

[45]See, e.g., In re Brand Name Prescription Drugs Antitrust Litigation, 123 F.3d 599, 611 (7th Cir. 1997) (case is removable even where state court could not hear it because case is within exclusive federal jurisdiction).

[46]See, e.g., In re CSX Transp., Inc., 151 F.3d 164 (4th Cir. 1998) ("While state court jurisdiction is not ordinarily a prerequisite for removability . . . jurisdiction in the district court is.").

the federal venue statute, 28 U.S.C.A. § 1391, it must have satisfied the venue rules governing the state court from which it was removed.[47]

ADDITIONAL RESEARCH REFERENCES

C.J.S., Removal of Causes §§ 1 to 46 et seq.
C.J.S., Removal of Causes §§ 52 to 101 et seq.
C.J.S., Removal of Causes §§ 126 to 171 et seq.
C.J.S., Removal of Causes §§ 177 to 226 et seq.
C.J.S., Removal of Causes §§ 235 to 275 et seq.
C.J.S., Removal of Causes §§ 297 to 310 et seq.
West's Key Number Digest, Removal of Cases ☞1 to 120

§ 2.17 Removal Procedure

CORE CONCEPT

Defendants eligible for removal from state court to federal district court should file a notice of removal with the appropriate federal court[1] within 30 days of some kind of notice, whether a pleading, motion or otherwise, indicating that a case is eligible for removal. Filing the notice automatically removes the case from the jurisdiction of the state court, and the federal court will make decisions as to how the case will thereafter be processed. If the federal court determines that removal was erroneous, the remedy is remand to the state court from which the case was originally removed.

APPLICATIONS

Contents of Notice

The notice of removal should contain a concise statement of the grounds upon which removal is based.[2] The notice should be accompanied by copies of "all process, pleadings, and orders

---

[47]*See, e.g., PT United Can Co. Ltd. v. Crown Cork & Seal Co., Inc.*, 138 F.3d 65, 72 (2d Cir. 1998) (citing other cases). *But see Hollis v. Florida State University*, 259 F.3d 1295, 1296 (11th Cir. 2001) ("We conclude that state-law venue deficiencies cannot be the basis for dismissal of a removed action because 28 U.S.C. § 1441(f) . . . abrogated the theory of derivative jurisdiction. Upon removal the question of venue is governed by federal law, not state law, and under § 1441(a) a properly removed action necessarily fixes venue in the district where the state court action was pending." Suggesting that if defendant dislikes federal venue, motion to transfer to an-

other division or district is appropriate).

[1]*See, e.g., Global Satellite Communication Co. v. Starmill U.K. Ltd.*, 378 F.3d 1269 (11th Cir.2004) (appropriate court is district court in district and division where case is pending).

[2]*See, e.g., Strawn v. AT&T Mobility, LLC*, 530 F.3d 293 (4th Cir. 2008) (removal petition need only allege federal subject matter jurisdiction; however, if removal is then challenged, party seeking removal must demonstrate existence of jurisdiction). *Cf., Williams v. Costco Wholesale Corp.*, 471 F.3d 975, 976 (9th Cir. 2006) ("The civil removal statute, unlike the re-

served upon" the defendant seeking removal.[3]

Unanimous Consent: Complications

The 2012 amendments include a requirement in new 28 U.S.C. § 1446(a)(2)(A) providing that to sustain removal solely under § 1441[4] all defendants must "join in or consent to the removal."[5] Thus, if two defendants are sued on a single count that might qualify for removal, but only one seeks to remove, the case is not eligible for removal and will be remanded to state court. This rule of unanimity was previously well established in case law,[6] so this particular amendment to § 1446(a) has no practical effect beyond confirming what was already settled.

It should be noted that some district courts extended the requirement for unanimous consent a step further. There is a substantial body of precedent in district courts holding that the petition for removal must not only reflect the unanimous agreement of the defendants, but that each individual defendant must personally, or through that defendant's own counsel, confirm to the court that the individual defendant has consented to the removal petition. In other words, an attorney for one defendant cannot sign on this matter for defendants the attorney does not represent. Any attempt to do so may result in rejection of the removal petition and remand to state court. District courts holding this view do not consider the obligations of an attorney under Rule 11 (governing representations to the court) to be controlling in this area, notwithstanding the express admonition of 28 U.S.C. § 1446(a) (governing removal procedure)

---

moval statute for criminal cases, has no requirement that all grounds for removal be listed in the notice." Noting that if removal could be sustained on both diversity jurisdiction and federal question jurisdiction, defendant did not have to list both grounds in notice).

[3]*See, e.g., Cook v. Randolph County, Ga.*, 573 F.3d 1143 (11th Cir. 2009) ("[F]ailure to include all state court pleadings and process with the notice of removal is procedurally incorrect but is not a jurisdictional defect;" also, defendants need file only those pleadings and orders served on defendants, not necessarily all pleadings); *Usatorres v. Marina Mercante Nicaraguenses, S.A.*, 768 F.2d 1285, 1286 (11th Cir. 1985) (defendant filed motion to dismiss in state court, then filed removal petition; held, defendant had no duty to file copy of motion to dismiss with removal petition, because motion was not "served upon" defen-

dant within meaning of § 1446(a)). *See also 'Asociacion Nacional de Pescadores a Pequena Escala O Artesanales de Colombia (ANPAC) v. Dow Quimica de Colombia S.A.*, 988 F.2d 559, 565 (5th Cir. 1993) (removal petitions are more persuasive when defendant has, *inter alia*, jurisdictional facts at hand.).

[4]Provisions of Title 28 other than § 1441 amy not be addressed in this portion of the text but may also permit removal. For example, 28 U.S.C. § 1442 may authorize removal of claims against federal officers, and 28 U.S.C. § 1453 governs removal of class actions. New § 1446(a)(2)(A) does not apply to either of those sections.

[5]28 U.S.C. § 1446(a)(2)(A).

[6]*Cf., Townsquare Media, Inc. v. Brill*, ___ F.3d ___, ___ (7th Cir. 2011) (applying settled case law, but noting that failure to make timely objection vitiates lack of unanimity).

that Rule 11 applies to removal petitions.[7]

Though it has not yet disappeared, this line of thinking appears to be in retreat. Another line of cases, led by circuit courts, holds that whil unanimity is required, the means of consenting is not limited to personal approval by individuals, directly or through counsel.[8] The result is that attorneys must consult local practice and precedent.

It should also be noted that Congress recently enacted 28 U.S.C. § 1453, governing removal of class actions from state court to federal district court. One of the provisions of new 1453 eliminates the case law requirement for unanimous consent among the class action defendants before removal is appropriate. Instead, § 1453 provides that in cases involving class actions eligible for removal, *any* defendant may seek removal "without consent of all defendants."[9] Thus, the requirement in some district courts that each defendant express individually a consent to removal, discussed immediately above, will presumably not be applicable to most class actions. Section 1453 is discussed in greater detail elsewhere in this text.

Filing Equals Removal

Removal occurs as soon as the defendant files an appropriate notice of removal with the federal district court.[10] The federal court may then make decisions on the sustainability of the removal.

Rule 11

Section 1446(a) explicitly provides that notices of removal are subject to the provisions of Rule 11, which permits the

---

[7]*See, e.g., Landman v. Borough of Bristol*, 896 F.Supp. 406, 408 (E.D. Pa. 1995) ("[O]ne defendant's attempt to speak on behalf of another defendant will not suffice."); *Creekmore v. Food Lion, Inc.*, 797 F.Supp. 505, 509 (E.D. Va. 1992) (1446 "requires all defendants, individually, or through their counsel, to voice their consent before the court, not through another party's attorney").

[8]*See, e.g., Esposito v. Home Depot U.S.A., Inc.*, 590 F.3d 72, 76 (1st Cir. 2009) ("[C]onduct less explicit than joining the notice will suffice."): *Proctor v. Vishay Technology, Inc.*, 584 F.3d 1208, 1225 (9th Cir. 2009) ("Filing of a notice of removal can be effective without individual consent documents on behalf of each defendant"); *Pritchett v. Cottrell, Inc.*, 512 F.3d 1057, 1062 (8th Cir. 2008) ("[E]ach defendant need not necessarily sign the notice of removal.").

[9]28 U.S.C. § 1453(b). The exceptions created by § 1453 for class actions are themselves subject to exceptions. Specifically, § 1453(d) provides that § 1453 is inapplicable to any class action "solely" involving: (1) a claim concerning a covered security under certain federal securities laws; (2) a claim relating to the internal affairs or governance of a corporation or other business entity arising under the laws of the state that incorporated or organized the enterprise; or (3) a claim relating to the rights and duties, including fiduciary duties, created by the Securities Act of 1933.

[10]*See, e.g., Speiser, Krause & Madole P.C. v. Ortiz*, 271 F.3d 884, 887 (9th Cir. 2001) (removal is automatic upon proper filing and service of papers; thereafter, case is controlled by rules of federal district court); *Yarnevic v. Brink's, Inc.*, 102 F.3d 753, 754 (4th Cir. 1996) ("A proper filing of a notice of removal immediately strips the state court of its jurisdiction.").

court to impose sanctions for inappropriate pleadings and motions. However, there is no rule prohibiting a party from filing more than one petition for removal, provided that each petition meets the requirements of Rule 11 and is timely.[11]

Time

In general, § 1446 provides that a defendant eligible for removal has thirty days in which to file a notice of removal.[12] That apparently innocuous time limit, however, has produced uncertainty as to its application in a variety of different circumstances. As a reader progresses through the tangles arising in this area, an effort to keep in mind a few considerations may help the reader understand the complexities of the issue and the need to apply the time limit to a number of different factual settings. Perhaps the most important consideration to grasp is that because the case at issue will have been filed originally in a state trial court, state rules governing service of initial pleadings in that court will have a significant impact on the determination of when the 30-day period begins to run. Second, because the presence or absence of federal question jurisdiction or diversity jurisdiction is a federal matter that may often be of no importance to a state court, documents filed in state court or served on defendants while a case is in its early stages may make no reference whatsoever to such concepts as, e.g., the presence of a federal cause of action, the amount in controversy between the parties, or the citizenship of the parties. Thus, facts crucial to a determination of federal subject matter jurisdiction, and therefore to a determination of eligibility for removal, may simply be glossed over in state pleadings or not appear at all. Third, even in cases where, for some reason, it is apparent early on that a particular case filed in state court may qualify for removal to federal district court, it is nevertheless possible that service of process on all defendants may not occur simultaneously. Thus, if the case involves more than one defendant, it is possible that months will elapse between the date when the first defendant gets notice of the possibility of removal and the date when the last-served defendant obtains similar information. All of these issues carry great potential for confusing the question of when the thirty day period identified

---

[11]*See, e.g., Benson v. SI Handling Systems, Inc.*, 188 F.3d 780, 782 (7th Cir. 1999) ("Nothing in § 1446 forecloses multiple petitions for removal." Rejecting per se rule that a party may seek removal only once). *Cf., Amoche v. Guarantee Trust Life Insurance Co.*, 556 F.3d 41, 53 (1st Cir. 2009) ("Successive attempts at removal are permissible where the grounds for removal become apparent only later in the litigation.").

[12]28 U.S.C.A. § 1446(b). *See also In re Methyl Tertiary Butyl Ether* ("MTBE") *Products Liability Litigation*, 522 F. Supp. 2d 557, 567–68 (S.D. N.Y. 2007) ("Nothing in the statute allows the thirty-day limitation to be restarted based on subsequent case law."). *But see Calderon v. Pathmark Stores, Inc.*, 101 F.Supp.2d 246, 247 (S.D.N.Y. 2000) ("[W]here service is made on a statutory agent . . . a defendant's time to remove runs, not from the date of service on the statutory agent, but from the date on which the defendant receives the notice that such service has been made.").

in § 1446(b) begins to run.

To avoid making the problem of determining when the thirty day period begins to run more difficult than it has to be, it is important to recognize that some issues, at least, are settled and may be addressed without undue difficulty by a diligent attorney. In cases where the initial documents filed or served in a case (summons and/or complaint) make clear that a case is eligible for removal, the rules are fairly clear as to the running of the time limit. In particular, it is now settled that in circumstances where any of four possible scenarios for service of process may be imposed by state rules, there are the following answers: (1) if state law provides for service of the summons and complaint simultaneously and that requirement is met, the thirty day limitation begins to run upon receipt of that service; (2) if, as permitted or required by state law, a summons is served on the defendant, but the complaint is not "furnished" until a later date, the thirty day period begins to run from the date the defendant received the complaint;[13] (3) if a defendant is served with a summons, but the complaint is filed in court under a state rule that does not mandate service of the complaint, the limitation on removal starts to run on the date that the complaint is available to the defendant through filing; and (4) if a complaint is filed in state court before any service on the defendant, the removal limitation period begins to run from the date of service of the summons on the defendant.[14]

In all the scenarios laid out above, it is important to note that, subject to an exception discussed immediately below, the time limit in which a defendant must file a notice of removal does not begin to run until some form of formal service, as directed by state law, has been accomplished on the defendant.[15] The exception is that if a defendant has, pursuant to applicable state law, voluntarily waived the formal requirements of service of process, there is of course no formal service and therefore the thirty day limitation period will begin to run on

---

[13]*Murphy Bros., Inc. v. Michetti Pipe Stringing, Inc.*, 526 U.S. 344, 354, 119 S. Ct. 1322, 1328, 143 L. Ed. 2d 448 (1999) (apparently equating a "furnished" complaint with a served complaint).

[14]*Murphy Bros., Inc. v. Michetti Pipe Stringing, Inc.*, 526 U.S. 344, 354, 119 S. Ct. 1322, 1328, 143 L. Ed. 2d 448 (1999). *See, e.g., Sikirica v. Nationwide Ins. Co.*, 416 F.3d 214 (3d Cir. 2005) (in instant case plaintiff served summons but not complaint; "a writ of summons alone [cannot] be the 'initial pleading' that triggers the 30-day period for removal"). *Cf., Whitaker v. American Telecasting, Inc.*, 261 F.3d 196, 204–05 (2d Cir. 2001) (defendant was served with copy of summons with notice; complaint was served more than two months later, at which time defendant sought removal; held, removal was untimely because "initial pleading" is not necessarily complaint; summons with notice could trigger running of time; noting that in New York, summons is broad document that includes statement of nature of action and relief sought).

[15]*Murphy Bros., Inc. v. Michetti Pipe Stringing, Inc.*, 526 U.S. 344, 356, 119 S. Ct. 1322, 1329, 143 L. Ed. 2d 448 (1999) (rejecting informal service through fax delivery of a "courtesy copy" of complaint as starting the running of the thirty day limitation period).

the occurrence of some other event,[16] such as the date waiver of service becomes effective.

As amended in 2012, § 1446(b) provides that each defendant shall have 30 days "after receipt by service on" that defendant to file a notion of removal.[17] Thus later served defendants have a later running time in which to file their notices.

Further, amended § 1446(b)(2)(C) complements new § 1446(b)(2)(B) by making allowance for an earlier served defendant who did not file a notice of removal within that defendant's own thirty-day limit. Under § 1446(b)(2), an earlier served defendant has authority to consent to the notice of removal filed by a later served defendant, without regard to whether the earlier served defendant had previously filed a notice of removal.[18] This provision clarifies some uncertainty in the previous version of § 1446(b) and also affords some degree of flexibility to an earlier served defendant's options to seek removal.

Subject to one important provision, discussed below under § 1446(c), amended § 1446(b) retains an important provision from the previous version of this subsection. If the original pleading in a case does not disclose a basis for removal, the beginning of the 30-day limitation period does not run from service of a summons and/or the original complaint. Instead, the 30-day limitation begins to run when the defendant receives, "through service or otherwise,"[19] Thus, if the defendant learns about eligibility for removal for the first time from, e.g., an amended pleading, a motion, answers obtained in discovery, or information contained in a post-filing settlement proposal, the 30-day period apparently begins to run on the date of receipt of that information.[20]

At least two other questions remain. First, when should the thirty day limit begin to run if a defendant is aware of the possibility of removal before a case has even been filed? If such a defendant files a notice of removal after the case is filed, but

[16]*Murphy Bros., Inc. v. Michetti Pipe Stringing, Inc.*, 526 U.S. 344, 350, 119 S. Ct. 1322, 1326, 143 L. Ed. 2d 448 (1999) ("Unless a named defendant agrees to waive service, the summons continues to function as the *sine qua non* directing an individual or entity to participate in a civil action or forgo procedural or substantive rights."). *But cf., Kundson v. Systems Painters, Inc.*, 634 F.3d 968, 974 (8th Cir. 2011) (if original state complaint did not disclose amount in controversy, that pleading alone cannot trigger running of 30 day time limit).

[17]28 U.S.C. § 1446(b)(2)(B).

[18]28 U.S.C. § 1446(b)(2)(C).

[19]28 U.S.C. § 1446(b)(3).

[20]*See, e.g., Babosa v. LensCrafters, Inc.*, 498 F.3d 972, 975 (9th Cir. 2007) (letter from opposing counsel identifying amount in controversy is notice of removal eligibility); *Peters v. Lincoln Electric Co.*, 285 F.3d 456, 466 (6th Cir. 2002) (information obtained through plaintiff's response to deposition questions is "other paper" for purpose of § 1446(b); *Addo v. Globe Life and Accident Insurance Co.*, 230 F.3d 759, 761 (5th Cir. 2000) ("post-complaint letter concerning settlement terms my constitute an 'other paper' under § 1446(b)"). *See also* 28 U.S.C. § 1446(c)(3)(A) (information acquired about the amount in controversy subsequent to the initial filing may be used to meet the eligibility requirements for § 1445(b)(3)).

before formal service on the defendant, and then takes no further action on removal after being served, what is the result when more than thirty days elapses after service? This problem, which could be called an issue of premature removal, may be answered by distinguishing the solutions provided in this discussion, above. Those solutions apply to situations in which some form of service, or filing and service, occurred under state law, and a notice of removal was filed at a later date. The instant problem, involving filing of a notice of removal before service, has been treated as unrelated to those solutions. Instead, it appears that such a removal prior to service can be a timely removal.[21]

Second, it will be obvious to all attorneys that sometimes a pleading filed in state court may not fall within one of only two possibilities—removable or not. That is, while sometimes a state complaint will be clear on its face that removal is possible, or be totally unclear as to a removal possibility, a third contingency exists and may even be commonplace. It is entirely possible that a state pleading will hint at, but not confirm, the possibility of removal. In such a circumstance, the common practice is to relieve the defendant of guessing at removal eligibility or investigating the question further. Instead, the defendant's time limit for removal begins to run only where it is clear, from a reading of the state court document itself, that removal is possible. Thus, the defendant generally has no burden to make an independent investigation or to fear running of the limitation period when the state document's meaning for removal is ambiguous.[22]

Differing Sources of Evidence

As is apparent from the immediately preceding text, there are important but sometimes subtle distinctions between the applications of the first and second paragraphs of § 1446(b). Moreover, the distinction can sometimes reach further than the differences in timing that have already been discussed. In particular, the first paragraph of § 1446(b), governing removal shortly after the commencement of a case, permits a defendant to use both a plaintiff's initial filings as well as additional evidence the defendant is able to develop independently of those

---

[21]See, e.g., Delgado v. Shell Oil Co., 231 F.3d 165, 177 (5th Cir. 2000) (formal service of process "is not an absolute prerequisite to removal;" requirement exists that suit be commenced before removal, but defendant need only have receipt of a document, through service or otherwise, that case is eligible for removal; distinguishing Murphy Brothers). But cf., Carvalho v. Equifax Information Services, LLC, 629 F.3d 876, 885 (9th Cir. 2010) ("It is axiomatic that a case cannot be removed before its inception.").

[22]See, e.g., Harris v. Bankers Life and Cas. Co., 425 F.3d 689, 695 (9th Cir. 2005) (where it is unclear from complaint whether case is removable, time limit does not begin to run against defendant; only where basis for removal is "revealed affirmatively" does time begin to run; further, defendant has no duty to investigate ambiguity).

filings to establish a case's eligibility for removal.[23]

By contrast, if a defendant seeks removal under the second paragraph of § 1446(b), the defendant's evidence supporting removal must be derived only from a plaintiff's subsequent filings in a case. In that circumstance the defendant is not permitted to offer evidence that the defendant is able to develop independently of the plaintiff's later filings. Thus, this second avenue to removal may be more difficult for a defendant to use.[24]

Defendants Which are Foreign Sovereigns

Where the defendant desiring to remove a case is a foreign sovereign within the meaning of the Foreign Sovereign Immunities Act,[25] the thirty-day time limit for filing a removal notice may be more elastic. 28 U.S.C.A. § 1441(d) provides that the district court may, for cause shown, permit such a defendant to file a removal petition after the thirty-day time limit has expired.[26] Section 1441(d) is discussed in greater detail elsewhere in this text.

"After-Acquired" Eligibility for Removal

If a case does not qualify for removal at the time of receipt of the original process on a defendant, the defendant will have 30 days to file a notice of removal from the time an amended pleading motion, order, or other paper giving notice of eligibility for removal is served.[27] However, if the basis for removal is subject matter jurisdiction based on diversity of citizenship, the period

---

[23]*See, e.g., Pretka v. Kolter City Plaza II, Inc.*, 608 F.3d 744, 759 (11th Cir. 2010) (for removal under first paragraph of § 1446(b), defendants may "offer their own evidence in support of removals at the commencement of the case;" noting that same opportunity to use defendant's own evidence, separate from or in addition to evidence from a plaintiff's own initial filings, is not available for removal attempts for which a notice of removal is filed later in a case under the second paragraph of § 1446(b)).

[24]*See, e.g., Pretka v. Kolter City Plaza II, Inc.*, 608 F.3d 744, 760(11th Cir. 2010) (noting difference between two paragraphs; while second paragraph "offers an additional avenue for removal, that road is not an easy one for defendants to travel"); *Bosky v. Kroger Texas, LP*, 288 F.3d 208, 211 (5th Cir. 2002) (first paragraph permits use of broader range of information).

[25]28 U.S.C.A. § 1605.

[26]*See, e.g., Big Sky Network Canada, Ltd., v. Sichuan Provincial Government*, 533 F.3d 1183 (10th Cir. 2008) (explaining factors relevant to court's decision to extend time period).

[27]*See, e.g., Durham v. Lockheed Martin Corp.*, 445 F.3d 1247, 1250 (9th Cir. 2006) (thirty-day time limit starts from receipt of original pleading that " 'affirmatively reveals on its face the facts necessary for federal court jurisdiction.' . . . Otherwise, the thirty-day clock doesn't begin ticking until a defendant receives 'a copy of an amended pleading, motion, order or other paper' from which it can be determined that the case is removable.' "); *Knudsen v. Liberty Mut. Ins. Co.*, 411 F.3d 805, 807 (7th Cir. 2005) ("[A]n amendment to the pleadings that adds a claim under federal law (where only state law claims had been framed before) or adds a new defendant, opens a new window of removal."); *Peters v. Lincoln Elec. Co.*, 285 F.3d 456, 466 (6th Cir. 2002) (adapting majority rule that plaintiff's response to deposition questions may constitute an "other paper" for purposes of § 1446(b)); *Green v. R.J. Reynolds Tobacco Co.*, 274 F.3d 263,

of time for "after-acquired" eligibility will normally be no more than one year after the initiation of the lawsuit.[28] For purposes of the one-year limitation, courts usually measure "commencement" of the case under the rules governing commencement in the relevant state court.[29]

Amended § 1446(c)(1) contains an important exception to its general rule that removal in diversity cases normally cannot take place after the expiration of one year following commencement of the lawsuit. The exception arises in circumstances where a plaintiff acted in "bad faith" to prevent a defendant's removal.[30] This provision displaces older case law rulings that permitted extension of the one-year limitation where a plaintiff behaved inequitably. Presumably the result of the amendment will be somewhat more uniform application of this exception, but it will still be necessary for the courts to work out the meaning of "bad faith" in this circumstance. However, § 1446(c)(3)(B) provides one circumstance in which district courts are directed to find bad faith. If a plaintiff deliberately failed to disclose the true amount in controversy in order to block removal, a finding to that effect is *ipso facto* bad faith.[31]

Congress recently enacted § 1453, which eliminated the one year time limit for removal of cases based on "after-acquired"

---

266 (5th Cir. 2001) (appellate decision in unrelated but similar case can be "order" for purposes of triggering application of second paragraph of § 1446(b); collecting cases, acknowledging that holding is minority view); *Huffman v. Saul Holdings Ltd. Partnership*, 194 F.3d 1072, 1078–79 (10th Cir. 1999) (adopting majority rule that for purpose of § 1446(b) a discovery deposition is treated as equivalent to receipt of "an actual written document"; combination of "petition setting out the factual premise of plaintiff's lawsuit; financial documents produced in discovery; and, most importantly, the voluntary and unequivocal testimony of [one plaintiff] that plaintiffs were seeking $300,000 in damages" gave defendant notice-no later than date of plaintiff's deposition testimony-that jurisdictional amount was satisfied).

[28]*Cf., e.g., In re Burns & Wilcox, Ltd.*, 54 F.3d 475, 476 (8th Cir. 1995) (noting that diversity case may not be removed if one year has elapsed since commencement of suit; but issue waived when claimant failed to raise it). *But cf. Braud v. Transport Service Co. of Illinois*, 445 F.3d 801, 806 (5th Cir. 2006) (where new defendant is added more than one year after initial filing, and case is now eligible for removal, removal clock starts to run again notwithstanding passage of more than one year); *Brierly v. Alusuisse Flexible Packaging, Inc.*, 184 F.3d 527 (6th Cir. 1999) (plaintiff sued two defendants on state diversity claim; after lengthy delay, second defendant was finally served; thereupon both defendants sought removal; because of delay in service of second defendant, more than one year passed before both defendants sought removal together; held, one year time limit is inapplicable to cases that were removable from their inception; time limit "applies only to those [diversity cases] that were not initially removable").

[29]*See, e.g., Bush v. Cheaptickets, Inc.*, 425 F.3d 683, 688 (9th Cir. 2005) (for purposes of one year limitation, "great majority" of federal courts look to state court rules controlling commencement of action; rejecting minority approach of invariably starting running of one year from date of service).

[30]28 U.S.C. § 1446(c)(1).

[31]28 U.S.C. § 1446(c)(3)(B).

diversity jurisdiction if the case is a class action.[32] Thus, while it is still necessary for a defendant seeking removal to do so within 30 days of notice of eligibility of removal, there is no requirement in class action lawsuits for such a defendant to have sought removal within the one year period for seeking removal in non-class action suits that are based on diversity. Section 1453 is discussed in greater detail elsewhere in this text.

Diversity Cases and Amount in Controversy

As amended, § 1446(c) has resolved some uncertainty about amount in controversy requirements for removal of diversity cases. In the first instance, § 1446(c)(2) defers to the amount in controversy raised in the initial pleading in the case.[33] However, additional provisions permit exceptions to that rule where circumstances warrant. First, if the initial pleading seeks only nonmonetary relief, the notice of removal may assert a suitable amount in controversy.[34] Second, even if the initial pleading seeks monetary relief, but state procedure does not permit a plea for a sum certain or, alternatively, permits recovery of damages greater than the amount sought in the initial pleading, the notice of removal may assert a suitable amount in controversy.[35] Third, if the initial pleading contains a request for monetary relief in an amount less than the jurisdictional requirement, removal may still be appropriate if the district court finds that the amount in controversy is actually satisfied, notwithstanding the apparent shortfall in the initial pleading. Section 1446(c)(2)(B) provides that the standard of proof the court will apply is a preponderance of the evidence.[36] The fourth exception arises where the initial pleading does not disclose a sufficient amount in controversy, but subsequent information comes to light demonstrating that the amount in controversy is satisfied. In such a circumstance the subsequent information may be used to establish eligibility for removal.[37] This last provision harmonizes with § 1446(b)(3), governing establishment of a right to removal using information obtained subsequent to an initial pleading that erroneously suggested the absence of a right to removal.

---

[32]28 U.S.C.A. § 1453(b). *See, e.g., Miedema v. Maytag Corp.*, 450 F.3d 1322, 1327 n.3 (11th Cir. 2006) (§ 1453(b) eliminates the one-year limitation of § 1446(b)); *Abrego Abrego v. The Dow Chemical Co.*, 443 F.3d 676, 681 (9th Cir. 2006) (same). It should be noted that the exceptions created by § 1453 for class actions are themselves subject to an exception. Specifically, § 1453(d) provides that § 1453 is inapplicable to any class action "solely" involving: (1) a claim concerning a covered security under certain federal securities laws; (2) a claim relating to the internal affairs or governance of a corporation or other business entity arising under the laws of the state that incorporated or organized the enterprise; or (3) a claim relating to the rights and duties, including fiduciary duties, created by the Securities Act of 1933.

[33]28 U.S.C. § 1446(c)(2).

[34]28 U.S.C. § 1446(c)(2)(A)(i).

[35]28 U.S.C. § 1446(c)(2)(A)(ii).

[36]28 U.S.C. § 1446(c)(2)(B).

[37]28 U.S.C. § 1446(c)(3)(A).

Criminal Matters

Removal is also available for a narrow range of criminal actions. Section 1446(c) governs procedure in such matters, but has no relevance to removal in civil cases.

Notification to State Court and Other Parties

Section 1446(d) requires that the defendants seeking removal "promptly" notify the state court and other parties, through filing and service of copies of the notice of removal.

State Court Jurisdiction

Section 1446(d) also directs the state court, upon receipt of notice of removal, to take no further action in a removed case. The state court may only re-acquire jurisdiction if the federal court remands one or more counts.[38]

Bond, Rule 11 and Sanctions

Until 1991, § 1446 required that a defendant seeking removal post a bond to cover the plaintiff's costs if the federal court determined that removal was inappropriate. Congress amended the removal statutes in 1991 to remove that requirement, and case law addressing the issue of bonds is obsolete. However, there are still two provisions that may provide reimbursement to a plaintiff whose case has been wrongly removed. Section 1446(a) explicitly provides that notices of removal are subject to the provisions of Federal Rule of Civil Procedure 11, which permits the court to impose sanctions for inappropriate pleadings and motions. Additionally, 28 U.S.C.A. § 1447(c) authorizes a district court that has decided to remand a case to impose costs and actual expenses, "including attorney fees," as part of an order remanding a case to a state court.[39]

Remedy for Inappropriate Removal

If the federal court determines that removal was inappropriate, it may remand part or all of the case to the state court. Dismissal is *not* an appropriate remedy.[40]

---

[38]*See, e.g., California ex rel. Sacramento Metropolitan Air Quality Management Dist. v. U.S.*, 215 F.3d 1005 (9th Cir. 2000) ("The removal of an action to federal court necessarily divests state and local courts of their jurisdiction over a particular dispute."); *Kansas Public Employees Retirement System v. Reimer & Koger Associates, Inc.*, 77 F.3d 1063, 1069 (8th Cir. 1996) (§ 1446(d) is "express authorization to stay state court proceedings"). *But see Lawrence v. Chancery Court of Tennessee*, 188 F.3d 687, 693 (6th Cir. 1999) (§ 1446(d) does not prohibit state court from taking "ministerial steps that do not affect the adjudication of the parties' dispute," such as collection of accrued costs from state-court party who signed cost bond).

[39]*See, e.g., Maguire Oil Co. v. City of Houston*, 143 F.3d 205, 207 (5th Cir. 1998).

[40]*See, e.g., University of South Alabama v. American Tobacco Co.*, 168 F.3d 405, 411 (11th Cir. 1999) ("[A] federal court must remand for lack of subject matter jurisdiction notwithstanding the presence of other motions pending before the court."); *Ondis v. Barrows*, 538 F.2d 904, 908 (1st Cir. 1976) (dismissal is inappropriate; remand is appropriate remedy). *But cf. Caterpillar Inc. v. Lewis*, 519 U.S. 61, 77, 117 S. Ct. 467, 477, 136 L. Ed.

ADDITIONAL RESEARCH REFERENCES

C.J.S., Removal of Causes § 8
C.J.S., Removal of Causes §§ 182 to 230 et seq.
C.J.S., Removal of Causes §§ 235 to 275 et seq.
C.J.S., Removal of Causes §§ 297 to 310 et seq.
West's Key Number Digest, Removal of Cases ⟿77 to 120

§ 2.17a Procedure after Removal

CORE CONCEPT

Once a case has been removed to a federal district court, 28 U.S.C.A. §§ 1447 to 49 provide much of the direction for decisions that the court may be required to make in the initial processing of the removed case. The areas governed by these sections include: authority to issue orders and process; acquisition of the record of the case during the period that the case was in state court; timing of remand motions; appeals of remand decisions; and joinder after removal.

APPLICATIONS

Authority to Issue Orders and Process

Section 1447(a) supplies the district court with authority to issue orders and process necessary to bring parties within the jurisdiction of the court. This authority is supplemental to process that may already have been served under the authority of the state court before the case was removed. Section 1447(a) has been the source of very few reported decisions in the past two decades.

Obtaining Case Record

Section 1447(b) authorizes the district court to obtain all records of a removed case in either of two ways. The court may require the party who sought removal to provide such copies, or the court may, through writ of certiorari to the state court, obtain the records directly. If the district court chooses to impose the burden on the party who sought removal, a party's failure to comply may be a consideration in a decision to remand the case to state court.[1]

Timing of Motion to Remand

Section 1447(c) provides two different time limits on motions to remand cases to state court. If the ground for remand is any basis other than the federal court's lack of subject matter jurisdiction, a party seeking remand must file an appropriate mo-

---

2d 437 (1996) (if district court denies motion to remand removed case, and denial of motion is subsequently found to be error on appeal, "the judgment must be vacated").

[1]*See, e.g., Patel v. Moore*, 968 F. Supp. 587, 591 (D. Kan. 1997) ("[C]ompliance with section 1446(a) does not satisfy the additional requirement authorized by section 1447(b).").

tion within 30 days of the date of the petition to remove required by § 1446(a).[2] However, if the basis for seeking remand is an allegation that the federal court lacks subject matter jurisdiction over the case, § 1447(c) provides that the motion to remand may be made at any time prior to final judgment in the case.[3]

Remand *Sua Sponte*

If the federal district court notices its own lack of subject matter jurisdiction, § 1447(c) provides that the court need not wait for a motion to remand from a party. Instead, the court can and must remand the case on its own initiative. Such action must be taken if the court notices its lack of subject matter jurisdiction at any time prior to final judgment.[4]

However, if the basis for remand is not a lack of subject matter jurisdiction but only a procedural defect, it is error for the district court to remand *sua sponte*.[5]

Partial Remand

If a district court lacks subject matter jurisdiction over a single count in a case, but enjoys jurisdiction over other claims, the court will remand the count lacking subject matter jurisdiction but may hear the other claims.[6]

No Discretion to Dismiss

While § 1447(c) directs a district court to remand a case that was removed without a basis in subject matter jurisdiction, there is no authority to dismiss such a case.[7]

---

[2]*See, e.g., Vasquez v. North County Transit Dist.*, 292 F.3d 1049 (9th Cir. 2002) (failure to make timely objection to erroneously removed workers' compensation claim waives right to remand); *Handelsman v. Bedford Village Associates Ltd. Partnership*, 213 F.3d 48, 50 n. 2 (2d Cir. 2000) (procedural defect—in case based on diversity jurisdiction, defendant was citizen of forum state—was waived when plaintiff failed to object within 30 days of removal).

[3]*Wisconsin Dept. of Corrections v. Schacht*, 524 U.S. 381, 391, 118 S. Ct. 2047, 2054, 141 L. Ed. 2d 364 (1998) ("[Section 1447(c)] differentiates between removals that are defective because of lack of subject matter jurisdiction and removals that are defective for some other reason, *e.g.*, because the removal took place after relevant time limits had expired. For the latter kind of case, there must be a motion to remand no later than 30 days after the filing of the removal no-

tice. . . . For the former kind of case, remand may take place without such a motion and at any time.").

[4]*Id.* (Whenever the district court concludes that it lacks subject matter jurisdiction, "remand may take place without . . . a motion and at any time.").

[5]*See, e.g., In re FMC Corporation Packaging Systems Div.*, 208 F.3d 445, 451 (3d Cir. 2000) (citing other circuit courts).

[6]*Wisconsin Department of Corrections v. Schacht*, 524 U.S. 381, 392, 118 S. Ct. 2047, 141 L. Ed. 2d 364 (1998) (if district court lacks subject matter jurisdiction over a single count due to Eleventh Amendment considerations, it does not, *ipso facto*, lack subject matter jurisdiction over other claims).

[7]*See, e.g., Hudson Savings Bank v. Austin*, 479 F.3d 102, 108–09 (1st Cir. 2007) ("This command [to remand] is obligatory and does not affect district courts leeway to dismiss rather

Section 1447(c) and Non-Jurisdictional Grounds for Remand

Although lack of subject matter jurisdiction is probably the most common reason alleged for seeking remand, a number of other possibilities exist. Because these other possible grounds for remand do not address the district court's subject matter jurisdiction, motions for remand on these grounds may fall within the 30 day time limit established by § 1447(c).[8]

An example of such a ground is failure to comply with the time limits of § 1446(b), which mandates that a petition for removal must be filed within 30 days of receipt of the "pleading, motion, order or other paper" which put the defendant on notice that the case is removable. Additionally, § 1446(b) requires that if the original basis for subject matter jurisdiction is diversity of citizenship under 28 U.S.C.A. § 1332, no petition for removal is allowable if it is filed more than one year after commencement of the action. If the party seeking removal did not comply with either of these time limits when they are applicable, there is authority that the opposing party's motion to remand must be filed within the 30 day limit imposed by § 1447(c).[9]

Less certain is whether an objection to removal because one of the defendants on a state claim was a citizen of the state in which the case was filed falls within the time limit of § 1447(c). On the one hand, if the parties are diverse from one another and the amount in controversy was satisfied, the federal court would have had subject matter jurisdiction over any case originally filed in the district court. On the other hand, removal is prohibited notwithstanding the presence of diversity jurisdiction if a defendant is sued in the defendant's home state court (§ 1441(b)).[10]

It should also be noted that although § 1447(c) itself is held

---

than remand.").

[8] See, e.g., Hudson Savings Bank v. Austin, 479 F.3d 102, 108–09 (1st Cir. 2007) (when removal is defective on grounds other than lack of subject matter jurisdiction, motion to remand must be made within 30 day time limit of § 1447(c)). But cf., Graphic Communications Local 1B Health & Welfare Fund "A" v. CVS Caremark Corp., 636 F.3d 971, 975 (8th Cir. 2011) (not all grounds for remand are "defects" within meaning of § 1447(c); therefore 30 day limit for remand motions may not apply to such non-"defect" situations; in such circumstances applicable standard is a "reasonable" time, which could be same as, or more or less than, 30 day limit).

[9] See, e.g., Huffman v. Saul Holdings Ltd. Partnership, 183 F.3d 1180 n. 3 (10th Cir. 1999) (although time limits of § 1446 are mandatory, defect may be waived by failing to file motion to remand within time limit of § 1447(c)).

[10] Compare, e.g., Handelsman v. Bedford Village Associates Ltd. Partnership, 213 F.3d 48, 50 n. 2 (2d Cir. 2000) (erroneous removal of case based on diversity jurisdiction where defendant was citizen of forum state; held, error was procedural defect, waived when plaintiff failed to object within 30 days of removal); Blackburn v. United Parcel Service, Inc., 179 F.3d 81 n. 3 (3d Cir. 1999) (although complete diversity existed in case, removal was inappropriate because one defendant was a citizen of state in which case was filed; however, defect in removal waived when motion to remand

to specify only two grounds for remand (lack of subject matter jurisdiction and defects in removal procedure),[11] other grounds for remand may exist, such as an exercise of the district court's discretion to abstain from deciding a question.[12] Such grounds are certainly not jurisdictional and they also do not necessarily indicate a defect in removal procedure. In that sense, they are not specified by § 1447(c), and it is unclear whether they are subject to the 30 day time limit § 1447(c) provides for filing remand motions on grounds other than jurisdiction. However, as is discussed further below, the fact that these grounds are not specified in § 1447(c) has an impact on the ability of a party to seek review of a district court's decision to remand on such grounds.

Discretion to Impose Costs and Fees

As is discussed above, § 1446(a) imposes the signature requirements of Federal Rule of Civil Procedure 11 to notices of removal. Additionally, § 1447(c) expressly authorizes the district court, when remanding a case, to impose costs and actual expenses, "including attorney fees," where such action would be appropriate.[13] The authority to consider a motion for costs and fees continues even if the underlying case has al-

---

was not made within 30 days, as provided in § 1447(c) *with, e.g., Hurt v. Dow Chemical Co.*, 963 F.2d 1142, 1145 (8th Cir. 1992) (original jurisdiction present if plaintiff has originally filed in federal court; however, removal authority was lacking under § 1441(b); held, plaintiff did not waive objection to removal by waiting more than 30 days to file motion to remand, because lack of removal authority under § 1441(b) should be treated as jurisdictional defect).

[11]*Quackenbush v. Allstate Ins. Co.*, 517 U.S. 706, 712, 116 S. Ct. 1712, 1718, 135 L. Ed. 2d 1 (1996) (section 1447(c) specifies only two grounds for remand; however, other grounds not specified in § 1447(c) may conceivably arise).

[12]As an example, consider the effect of 28 U.S.C.A. § 1441(c). Section 1441(c) provides that if the basis for removal of a case is the presence of a separate and independent federal question, as defined in 28 U.S.C.A. § 1331, the entire case, including "otherwise non-removable claims" may be removed at the same time. Presumably these non-removable claims would typically be claims where diversity jurisdiction was lacking or, perhaps, situations in which the parties

were diverse but the defendant had been sued in a state court of a state in which the defendant is a citizen. Section 1441(c) provides not only that such claims may be removed, but also that the district court shall decide whether to retain or remand such "non-removable" claims in which state law predominates. The meaning of § 1441(c), when considered in light of § 1447(c), is that certain claims may be remanded to state court even when there was no defect in removal procedure and the requirement of federal subject matter jurisdiction is satisfied (assuming, *e.g.,* that non-diverse state claims fall within the supplemental jurisdiction of the district court under 28 U.S.C.A. § 1367). A district court's decision to remand non-diverse supplemental claims is not subject to the ban on judicial review established by § 1447(d), *see, e.g., Eastus v. Blue Bell Creameries, L.P.*, 97 F.3d 100, 103 (5th Cir. 1996) (§ 1447(d) does not bar review of remand based on district court's discretionary authority under § 1441(c)), but it is unclear whether the time limit of § 1447(c) is applicable to a motion to remand on such discretionary grounds.

[13]*Martin v. Franklin Capital Corp.*, 546 U.S. 132, 126 S. Ct. 704, 711, 163 L. Ed. 2d 547 (2005) ("Absent

ready been remanded to state court.[14]

Notice of Remand: Termination of Federal Jurisdiction

When the district court decides to remand a case to state court, § 1447(c) directs the clerk of court to send a certified copy of the notice of remand to the clerk of the relevant state court. This mailing has significance beyond its value as notification to the state court. In addition to fulfilling the purpose of notice, it is generally held that mailing of the notice of remand divests the federal district court of its jurisdiction over the case.[15]

If remand is based on a failure of federal subject matter jurisdiction or a shortcoming in the process of removal, the remand becomes effective even earlier, *i.e.,* at the time the order is entered.[16]

Once remand is effective, jurisdiction vests in the state court.

Appeal or Reconsideration of Remand Order

Section 1447(d) governs the circumstances in which a district court's decision to remand a case to state court may be reviewed, either by that court or upon appeal. It will probably come as a significant surprise to many attorneys to learn that, subject to some exceptions, remand orders are not reviewable by any court whatsoever.[17] In fact, § 1447(d) provides that subject to exceptions once remand orders based on either

---

unusual circumstances, courts may award attorney's fees under § 1447(c) only where the removing party lacked an objectively reasonable basis for seeking removal. Conversely, when an objectively reasonable basis exists, fees should be denied."). *Cf., e.g., Wisconsin v. Hotline Industries, Inc.,* 236 F.3d 363, 364 (7th Cir. 2000) (recovery for expenditures on salaried government attorneys is limited to "actual outlays," not prevailing market rates for private attorneys). *But see Circle Industries USA, Inc. v. Parke Const. Group, Inc.,* 183 F.3d 105, 109 (2d Cir. 1999) (§ 1447(c) does not authorize award of fees if defendant successfully opposes remand; fee award possible under § 1447(c) only if remand granted).

[14]*Bryant v. Britt,* 420 F.3d 161 (2d Cir. 2005). *See also MB Financial, N.A. v. Stevens,* 678 F.3d 497, 500 (7th Cir. 2012) (parties who receive fee award under § 1447(c) also are entitled to reimbursement for expenses incurred defending award on appeal).

[15]*See, e.g., Bryan v. BellSouth Communications, Inc.,* 492 F.3d 231, 235 n.1 (4th Cir. 2007) ("A remand is

effective when the district court mails a certified copy of the remand order to the state court, . . . or, if the remand is based on lack of subject-matter jurisdiction or a defect in the removal process, when the remand order is entered."). *See, e.g., Arnold v. Garlock, Inc.,* 278 F.3d 426, 438 (5th Cir. 2001) ("Once the remand order is certified and mailed . . . the matter remanded is removed from federal jurisdiction.").

[16]*See, e.g., Bryan v. BellSouth Communications, Inc.,* 492 F.3d 231, 235 n.1 (4th Cir. 2007).

[17]*Powerex Corp. v. Reliant Energy Services, Inc.,* 551 U.S. 224, 234, 127 S. Ct. 2411, 2418, 168 L. Ed. 2d 112 (2007) ("[W]hen . . . the District Court relied upon a ground that is colorable characterized as subject-matter jurisdiction, appellate review is barred by § 1447(d)."); *Kircher v. Putnam Funds Trust,* 547 U.S. 633, 640, 126 S. Ct. 2145, 2152, 165 L. Ed. 2d 92 (2006) ("[W]e have relentlessly repeated that 'any remand order issued on the grounds specified in § 1447(c) [is immunized from all forms of appellate review], whether or not that order might be deemed erroneous by an ap-

procedural defects raised within thirty days of removal or lack of subject matter jurisdiction are certified to the appropriate state court, they "are not reviewable on appeal or otherwise." The "or otherwise" provision has been construed to mean that even the district court may not look again at a final remand order, because the effect of entering the order (as is discussed immediately above) divests the district court of jurisdiction.[18] Further, if this prohibition on review of a certified remand order is applicable, it usually acts as a bar to a second effort at removal by the same parties on similar grounds.[19]

Exceptions to § 1447(d)

The impact of the prohibition in § 1447(d) on review of a certified remand order is difficult to overstate. Moreover, the exceptions to the general rule of § 1447(d) are varied.[20] The most important of these exceptions are discussed immediately below.

(1) *Statutory Exception:* Section 1447(d) expressly provides that if the original ground for removal was found in § 1443 (removal of civil rights cases), the prohibition on review of the remand order found in § 1447(d) does not apply.[21]

(2) *Remand Not Based on § 1447(c):* Section 1447(c),

---

pellate court."). *See, e.g., In re Blackwater Securities Consulting, LLC*, 460 F.3d 578, 582 (4th Cir. 2006) (limitation on review applies even when remand is "inarguably erroneous"); *In re WTC Disaster Site*, 414 F.3d 352 (2d Cir. 2005) (neither appeal nor mandamus is available). See also, *Things Remembered, Inc. v. Petrarca*, 516 U.S. 124, 116 S. Ct. 494, 133 L. Ed. 2d 461 (1995) (§ 1447(d)'s proscription on review also applies to bankruptcy cases; holding § 1447(d) applicable to 28 U.S.C.A. § 1452, governing remand of federal bankruptcy case to state court).

[18]*See, e.g., Doe v. American Red Cross*, 14 F.3d 196, 199 (3d Cir. 1993) ("Courts have construed Section 1447(d) as prohibiting appeals of remand orders as well as reviews by district courts of their own remands based on the same grounds as the initial removals."); *Seedman v. U.S. Dist. Court for Cent. Dist. of California*, 837 F.2d 413, 414 (9th Cir. 1988) (per curiam) (Section 1447(d) "has been universally construed to preclude not only appellate review but also reconsideration by the district court. Once a district court certifies a remand order to state court it is divested of ju-

risdiction and can take no further action on the case."). *But see Roe v. O'Donohue*, 38 F.3d 298, 301 (7th Cir. 1994) (noting that Northern District of Illinois "automatically delays remands to afford time for reconsideration").

[19]*See, e.g., Hunt v. Acromed Corp.*, 961 F.2d 1079, 1081 (3d Cir. 1992) (court may not reconsider remand through device of second removal effort based on same reasoning as original removal effort). *But cf., Benson v. SI Handling Systems, Inc.*, 188 F.3d 780, 783 (7th Cir. 1999) (second effort to remove not prohibited if allegations of jurisdictional facts had changed after initial remand).

[20]*See generally Adkins v. Illinois Cent. R. Co.*, 326 F.3d 828, 831 (7th Cir. 2003) ("The naïve reader might think that [§ 1447(d)] meant no appellate consideration by appeal, by writ of mandamus, or by any other device that lawyers might serve up, but that reader would be wrong.").

[21]*See, e.g., Patel v. Del Taco, Inc.*, 446 F.3d 996, 998 (9th Cir. 2006) (remand, based on lack of jurisdiction, of removal under § 1441 not reviewable; but where removal was based on § 1443, appellate review of remand is permissible). See generally *Dudley-*

discussed above, identifies two grounds for remanding removed cases: defects in removal procedure, and lack of federal subject matter jurisdiction.[22] It appears settled that when the district court has remanded a case based on either of these grounds, § 1447(d) almost always prohibits review of the decision.[23] However, when the ground for remand falls outside the scope of §§ 1443 and 1447(c), review of the remand decision is possible either in the district court that granted it or upon appellate review.[24] Examples of such grounds for remand that have been subjected to review include: a

---

Barton v. Service Corp. International, 633 F.3d 1151, 1152 (10th Cir. 2011) (federal statute must "specifically" permit appeal, "and those instances are rare").

[22]*Quackenbush v. Allstate Ins. Co.*, 517 U.S. 706, 712, 116 S. Ct. 1712, 1718, 135 L. Ed. 2d 1 (1996). *Cf., Carlson v. Arrowhead Concrete Works, Inc.*, 445 F.3d 1046, 1051 (8th Cir. 2006) (scope of judicial review of remand order under § 1447(d) is limited to verification that lack of subject matter jurisdiction was "actual basis for remand").

[23]*Powerex Corp. v. Reliant Energy Services, Inc.*, 127 S. Ct. 2411, 168 L. Ed. 2d 112 (U.S. 2007) ("[R]eview of the District Court's characterization of its remand as resting upon lack of subject-matter jurisdiction, to the extent that it is permissible at all, should be limited to confirming that characterization was colorable." Also holding that a district court's decision to remand a properly removed case because a subject matter jurisdiction problem arose is unreviewable under § 1447(d)). *See, e.g., Carlson v. Arrowhead Concrete Works, Inc.*, 445 F.3d 1046, 1053–54 (8th Cir. 2006) (collateral order rule does not create exception to ban on reviews of remand orders under § 1447(c)). *But see American Soda, LLP v. U.S. Filter Wastewater Group, Inc.*, 428 F.3d 921, 924 (10th Cir. 2005) (permitting review of remand based on forum selection clause; using collateral order doctrine as vehicle for review); *Heaton v. Monogram Credit Card Bank of Georgia*, 297 F.3d 416 (5th Cir.2002) (remand based on lack of jurisdiction is normally not appealable, but 12 U.S.C. § 1819(b)(2)(C) creates excep-

tion to § 1447(d) for Federal Deposit Insurance Corporation); *Poore v. American-Amicable Life Ins. Co. of Texas*, 218 F.3d 1287, 1291 (11th Cir. 2000) (notwithstanding § 1447(d), finding of lack of subject matter jurisdiction was reviewable where district court exceeded its authority by erroneously relying on post-removal amendment to complaint); *Carr v. American Red Cross*, 17 F.3d 671, 680 (3d Cir. 1994) (district court dismissed crossclaim against one defendant and remanded remainder of case on jurisdictional grounds; held, bar to appellate review of jurisdictionally motivated remand did not apply because district court's dismissal of cross-claim meant that cross-claim would not be heard in state court; thus, where that order triggered the removal, both the dismissal and the remand must be subject to appellate review).

[24]*Quackenbush v. Allstate Ins. Co.*, 517 U.S. 706, 712, 116 S. Ct. 1712, 1718, 135 L. Ed. 2d 1 (1996). *See also, e.g., City of Tucson v. U.S. West Communications, Inc.*, 284 F.3d 1128, 1131 (9th Cir. 2002) ("[I]t is clear that non-jurisdictional, discretionary remands are not barred from appellate review."); *Snodgrass v. Provident Life and Acc. Ins. Co.*, 147 F.3d 1163, 1165 (9th Cir. 1998) (" 'Exceptional' remand orders, entered pursuant to some doctrine or authority other than § 1447(c), are not subject to § 1447(d)'s prohibition."). *But see Stevens v. Brink's Home Security, Inc.*, 378 F.3d 944, 949 (9th Cir. 2004) (appeal based on district court's obligation to remand under § 1447(e) after joinder of non-diverse parties is immunized from appellate review under § 1447(d)).

remand order based on either a motion of a party or the court's own motion that asserts a procedural defect, but which does so more than thirty days after removal;[25] a district court's decision to abstain from deciding state questions;[26] a *sua sponte* remand by the district court based only on a procedural defect in removal (not a defect in subject matter jurisdiction);[27] a remand based on the discretionary jurisdiction of the Declaratory Judgment Act;[28] a magistrate judge's remand order;[29] a remand based on the district court's discretionary authority under § 1441(c);[30] a discretionary remand of claims within a district court's supplemental jurisdiction under 28 U.S.C.A. § 1367(c);[31] situations where the Supreme Court has clarified a party's right to remove in the period between the original remand decision and a party's second attempt to remove;[32] circumstances in which, if a federal court did not review an order that determines a claim for attorney fees, no court would be able to review it because the state court would lack jurisdiction to do so;[33] a remand based on defendants' waiver of their arbitra-

---

[25]*See, e.g., Mitskovski v. Buffalo and Fort Erie Public Bridge Authority*, 435 F.3d 127, 131–32 (2d Cir. 2006).

[26]*Quackenbush v. Allstate Insurance Co.*, 517 U.S. 706, 712, 116 S. Ct. 1712 (1996) (remand based on abstention is appealable).

[27]*See, e.g., Whole Health Chiropractic & Wellness, Inc. v. Humana Medical Plan, Inc.*, 254 F.3d 1317 (11th Cir.2001) (noting that all circuits addressing this issue agree).

[28]*See, e.g., Snodgrass v. Provident Life and Acc. Ins. Co.*, 147 F.3d 1163, 1165 (9th Cir. 1998). *See also Xiong v. State*, 195 F.3d 424, 426 (8th Cir. 1999) (district court ignored clear circuit court precedent in remanding on ground of lack of jurisdiction; thus, "there was simply no jurisdictional question" to be resolved in district court, and circuit court could hear appeal of remand).

[29]*See, e.g., Vogel v. U.S. Office Products Co.*, 258 F.3d 509, 517–18 (6th Cir. 2001) (remand order is dispositive matter, which magistrate judge cannot enter; instead, magistrate judge must submit findings and recommendations to district judge for review and approval; thus, § 1447(d)'s prohibition on appellate review of

remand order does not apply to magistrate judge's attempted remand order, which itself is invalid and subject to review by both district court and appellate court; noting some disagreement, collecting cases).

[30]*See, e.g., Niehaus v. Greyhound Lines, Inc.*, 173 F.3d 1207, 1210 (9th Cir. 1999) (asserting authority to review district court's remand of pendant state claims); *Eastus v. Blue Bell Creameries, L.P.*, 97 F.3d 100, 103 (5th Cir. 1996).

[31]*Carlsbad Technology, Inc. v. HIF Bio, Inc.*, 556 U.S. 635, 640, 129 S. Ct. 1862, 1866–67 (2009) (remand based on § 1367(c) is appealable).

[32]*See, e.g., Baker v. Kingsley*, 387 F.3d 649, 654 (7th Cir. 2004) (basis for remand was discretionary power to decline jurisdiction under § 1367, governing supplemental jurisdiction; held, § 1447(d) does not bar appellate review); *Doe v. American Red Cross*, 14 F.3d 196 (3d Cir.1993) (Red Cross had attempted to remove, but district court remanded; after Supreme Court upheld right of Red Cross to remove in unrelated case, appellate court approved second effort at removal in instant case).

[33]*See, e.g., Hornbuckle v. State*

tion rights;[34] an erroneous holding that multiple efforts to remove are barred even where changed allegations of fact demonstrate that subject matter jurisdiction is now satisfied;[35] a remand order issued after the district judge erroneously refused to recuse himself;[36] and a remand granted as enforcement of a valid forum selection clause.[37] Finally, the circuit court may properly look at the "objective merits" of the remand order to determine the appropriateness of an award of costs and fees under § 1447(c).[38] As these examples indicate, however, the exceptions to the general rule that remand orders are not reviewable are themselves fairly limited. In particular, remands on the grounds of defects in removal procedure or lack of subject matter jurisdiction remain almost entirely beyond the scope of any review, even if they are mixed with considerations that appear to fall outside the scope of the prohibition of § 1447(d).[39]

Farm Lloyds, 385 F.3d 538, 541 (5th Cir. 2004) ("Although this Court may not review a district court's remand for lack of subject matter jurisdiction, we may review the district court's award of attorney fees."); *Garbie v. DaimlerChrysler Corp.*, 211 F.3d 407, 409 (7th Cir. 2000) (award of attorney's fees for wrongful removal is "independently appealable order").

[34]*See, e.g., Restoration Preservation Masonry, Inc. v. Grove Europe Ltd.*, 325 F.3d 54, 59 (1st Cir. 2003) (appellate court is not engaging in prohibited review of jurisdictional issue where its review of waiver of arbitration may be made separately from jurisdiction).

[35]*See, e.g., Benson v. SI Handling Systems, Inc.*, 188 F.3d 780, 783 (7th Cir. 1999) (§ 1447(d) does not bar review of remand of second effort to remove—on second effort district court acknowledged that subject matter jurisdiction was now satisfied, but remanded on ground that multiple efforts to remove are not permitted).

[36]*See, e.g., Republic of Panama v. American Tobacco Co. Inc.*, 217 F.3d 343, 345–46 (5th Cir. 2000) (remand order that was issued after district judge denied recusal motion may technically be insulated from review by § 1447(d); however, when recusal was appropriate, erroneous failure to recuse means that all orders issued af-

ter that failure should be vacated; in such circumstances, vacating remand order is " 'ministerial task' unrelated to the remand itself, and thus not prohibited by § 1447(d)").

[37]*See, e.g., Yakin v. Tyler Hill Corp.*, 566 F.3d 72, 75 (2d Cir. 2009) (remand based on forum-selection clause is appealable); *Global Satellite Communication Co. v. Starmill U.K. Ltd.*, 378 F.3d 1269 (11th Cir.2004) (" § 1447(d) does not bar review of remand order based upon a forum selection clause").

[38]*See, e.g., Dahl v. Rosenfeld*, 316 F.3d 1074, 1079 (9th Cir. 2003) (although remand was error that cannot be reversed, award of attorneys' fees based on such error is reviewable and may be reversed); *Roxbury Condominium Ass'n, Inc. v. Anthony S. Cupo Agency*, 316 F.3d 224, 227 (3d Cir. 2003) (when court examines attorney's fees, it may not reverse remand order but it may evaluate merits of order to help determine whether fee award is appropriate); *Stuart v. UNUM Life Ins. Co. of America*, 217 F.3d 1145, 1148 (9th Cir. 2000) (acknowledging, however, that remand order itself may not be reviewed with any view to reversing it).

[39]*See, e.g., Yakama Indian Nation v. State of Wash. Dept. of Revenue*, 176 F.3d 1241 (9th Cir. 1999) (treating

It should be noted that *denial* of remand does not implicate § 1447(d). Thus, such a denial is reviewable on appeal.[40]

New Exception: Appeal of Grant or Denial of Remand in Class Actions

Congress recently created an exception to the general rule that, pursuant to § 1447(d), remand of a case removed from state court is not appealable. Pursuant to 28 U.S.C.A. 1453(c), in a case involving class action litigation, district court decisions granting or denying remand may be appealed to the appropriate court of appeals.[41] Such an appeal must be made within seven days of entry of the original order.[42]

The appellate court must decide such an appeal within 60 days of the filing of the appeal,[43] unless one of two circumstances arises. First, the time may be extended for any amount of time if all parties consent to the extension.[44] Alternatively, the time may be extended for up to ten days, for good cause shown.[45] If the appellate court does not act within the specified time limits, including any applicable extensions, the appeal is automatically denied.[46] Section 1453 is discussed at greater length elsewhere in this text.

Joinder After Removal

If a district court retains jurisdiction of a removed case, § 1447(e) vests the court with considerable discretion to

---

remand order based primarily, but not entirely, on jurisdictional issues as not reviewable). *But cf. In re U.S. Healthcare*, 159 F.3d 142, 146 (3d Cir. 1998) (where magistrate judge issues remand order and lacks authority to do so under § 1447(c), prohibitions on review under § 1447(d) do not apply).

[40]*See, e.g., In re Seven Fields Development Corp.*, 505 F.3d 237, 245 (3d Cir. 2007) (§ 1447(d) controls remand under either "general removal provision" or "bankruptcy removal provision;" but § 1447(d) is inapplicable when court is "not dealing with an order remanding the case."); *City & County of San Francisco v. PG & E Corp.*, 433 F.3d 1115, 1121 (9th Cir. 2006) (prohibition on appellate review inapplicable where district court denies remand motion); *Bracken v. Matgouranis*, 296 F.3d 160 (3d Cir.2002) ("[A]ppellate review of District Court orders denying remand is not prohibited.").

[41]*See, e.g., Anderson v. Bayer Corp.*, 610 F.3d 390 (7th Cir. 2010)

(noting exception permitting appeal of order granting or denying motion to remand class action). *See also Hertz Corp. v. Friend*, __ U.S. __, 130 S. Ct. 1181, 1187, 175 L. Ed. 2d 1029 (2010) (although § 1453 expressly authorizes appeals only to a "court of appeals" and does not mention Supreme Court, § 1453 is not a barrier to appeal to Supreme Court).

[42]28 U.S.C.A. § 1435(c)(1). *See, e.g., Miedema v. Maytag Corp.*, 450 F.3d 1322, 1326 (11th Cir. 2006) (notwithstanding § 1447(d), § 1453(c)(1) provides that circuit court may review remand order if removal took place under 28 U.S.C.A. § 1332(d) (jurisdictional portion of Class Action Fairness Act)); *Prime Care of Northeast Kan., LLC v. Humana Ins. Co.*, 447 F.3d 1284, 1285 (10th Cir. 2006) (same).

[43]28 U.S.C.A. § 1453(c)(2).

[44]28 U.S.C.A. § 1453(c)(3).

[45]28 U.S.C.A. § 1453(c)(3)(B).

[46]28 U.S.C.A. § 1453(c)(4).

determine whether to permit joinder of additional parties.[47] This discretion includes authority to join parties whose participation in the case destroys subject matter jurisdiction.[48] However, if such non-diverse parties are joined, the court must remand the case to state court. In other words, the district court has discretion to refuse to join parties whose presence destroys subject matter jurisdiction.[49] If, on the other hand, such parties are joined, the court may not retain the case, and must remand because it lacks jurisdiction.[50]

Appellate Review of Remand Pursuant to § 1447(e)

As has been discussed earlier, § 1447(d) often prevents appellate review of a district court's decision under § 1447(c) to remand a case to state court based on lack of subject matter jurisdiction. A question that remains is whether a remand order pursuant to § 1447(e) is subject to the same limitations on review. To this date it appears that a § 1447(e) decision to remand based on lack of subject matter jurisdiction is similarly non-reviewable.[51] It should be noted, however, that when a district court decides to retain a case and *not* remand under

---

[47]*See also Casas Office Machines, Inc. v. Mita Copystar America, Inc.*, 42 F.3d 668, 673–75 (1st Cir. 1994) (§ 1441(e) also applies to replacement of "John Doe" defendants with real defendants).

[48]*Cf., Kabakjian v. U.S.*, 267 F.3d 208, 212 (3d Cir. 2001) (§ 1447(e) is exception to general rule, particularly applicable to diversity cases, that jurisdiction is determined at time of filing); *Ryan ex rel. Ryan v. Schneider Nat. Carriers, Inc.*, 263 F.3d 816, 819 (8th Cir. 2001) ("In the case of a removed action diversity must exist both when the state petition is filed and when the petition for removal is filed.").

[49]*See, e.g., Mayes v. Rapoport*, 198 F.3d 457, 462 (4th Cir. 1999) (where plaintiff joined new non-diverse defendant without leave of court (using provision of Rule 15(a) permitting plaintiff one amended complaint as of right), district court still retains authority under § 1447(e) to reject joinder of new defendant; where purpose of joinder is to defeat diversity jurisdiction, decision to reject joinder is within court's discretion); *Newcombe v. Adolf Coors Co.*, 157 F.3d 686, 691 (9th Cir. 1998) (affirming district court's decision not to join non-diverse party under § 1447(e)). *See also Casas Office Machines, Inc. v. Mita Copystar*

America, Inc., 42 F.3d 668, 674 (1st Cir. 1994) (§ 1447(e) also gives court discretion to add or reject later-named fictitious parties, with similar results).

[50]*See, e.g., Mayes v. Rapoport*, 198 F.3d 457, 461 (4th Cir. 1999) ("[T]he statute does not allow a district court to retain jurisdiction once it permits a nondiverse defendant to be joined in the case."); *Ingram v. CSX Transp., Inc.*, 146 F.3d 858, 863 (11th Cir. 1998) ("Because § 1447(e) was applicable here, the district court was left with only two options: (1) deny joinder; or (2) permit joinder and remand [the] case to state court. The district court chose to permit the diversity-destroying joinder and, as a result, it should have remanded this action to [state] court.").

[51]*See, e.g., Stevens v. Brink's Home Security, Inc.*, 378 F.3d 944 (9th Cir.2004) (applying proscription of § 1447(d) to remand under § 1447(e)); *Matter of Florida Wire & Cable Co.*, 102 F.3d 866, 868–69 (7th Cir. 1996) (no jurisdiction to review, by mandamus or otherwise); *Washington Suburban Sanitary Com'n v. CRS/Sirrine, Inc.*, 917 F.2d 834, 836 n. 5 (4th Cir. 1990) (remand under § 1447(e) should be treated similarly to remand under § 1447(c)—no appellate review of remand based on lack of subject matter jurisdiction).

§ 1447(e), that decision is reviewable.[52]

Serving Defendants After Removal Has Occurred

It is possible that in a case involving several defendants, the first defendant served with process will be eligible to petition for removal. Such a defendant might promptly seek removal in order to avoid the time limit on removal petitions (30 days from service) established in § 1446. That might mean that some defendants remain unserved after removal. To correct that situation, 28 U.S.C.A. § 1448 addresses two points. First, § 1448 expressly authorizes the district court to permit completion of service initiated in the state proceeding or to issue its own service on unserved defendants.[53] Second, once such defendants have been served, § 1448 permits them to make a decision either to challenge the removal by seeking remand or to accept the removal that has already occurred.[54] In establishing this potential right for later-served defendants to seek remand or removal, § 1448 does not affect in any way whatever rights a plaintiff might have to file a motion to remand.[55]

Failure of State Court to Supply Record

In the unusual circumstance where a state court does not supply the federal court with the record of proceedings that occurred before the case was removed, 28 U.S.C.A. § 1449 provides the district court with authority to re-create the record "by affidavit or otherwise." Such authority under § 1449 exists only where the state court's failure to provide the record is inappropriate. If, for example, the party seeking use of the record failed to pay appropriate legal fees to the state court, a district court would not have authority under § 1449 to re-create the record. Section 1449 has not been the subject of sig-

---

[52]*See, e.g., Ingram v. CSX Transp., Inc.*, 146 F.3d 858, 863 (11th Cir. 1998) ("Because § 1447(e) was applicable here, the district court was left with only two options: (1) deny joinder; or (2) permit joinder and remand [the] case to state court. The district court chose to permit the diversity-destroying joinder and, as a result, it should have remanded this action to [state] court.").

[53]*Murphy Bros., Inc. v. Michetti Pipe Stringing, Inc.*, 526 U.S. 344, 354, 119 S. Ct. 1322, 1329, 143 L. Ed. 2d 448 n. 6 (1999) ("[Section 1448] allows the plaintiff to serve an unserved defendant or to perfect flawed service once the action has been removed.").

[54]*Id.* (second paragraph of § 1448 "explicitly reserves the unserved defendant's right to take action (move to remand) after service is perfected"). *See also, e.g., McKinney v. Board of*

Trustees of Mayland Community College, 955 F.2d 924, 926 n. 3 (4th Cir. 1992) (if second defendant is served more than 30 days after first defendant is served, the first defendant can file for, and obtain, removal, and the second defendant can use authority of § 1448 to seek remand); *Getty Oil Corp., a Div. of Texaco, Inc. v. Insurance Co. of North America*, 841 F.2d 1254, 1263 (5th Cir. 1988) ("[I]f a removal petition is filed by a served defendant and another defendant is served after the case is thus removed, the latter defendant may still either accept the removal or exercise its right to choose the state forum by making a motion to remand.").

[55]*See, e.g., Lewis v. Rego Co.*, 757 F.2d 66, 69 (3d Cir. 1985) ("The right which the statute gives to such a defendant to move to remand the case confers no rights upon a plaintiff.").

nificant reported precedent in the past two decades.

§ 2.17b Removal of Class Actions

CORE CONCEPT

In 2005 Congress enacted the Class Action Fairness Act, which has been encoded in 28 U.S.C.A. §§ 1332, 1453, and 1711–15. Section 1453 governs circumstances in which a class action that was filed in state court may be removed to a federal district court. The most important features of § 1453 are two: first, most class actions are now generally much less difficult to remove to district court than more conventional civil actions; and second, if a district court decides to remand to state court a class action that had been removed, § 1453 generally affords the defendant who removed the action significantly better access to an appeal of that district court decision. The most important exception to the two foregoing generalizations is also contained in § 1453.

APPLICATIONS

Definitions

Section 1453(a) defines four terms (class, class action, class certification order, and class member) by incorporating the definitions of these terms found in § 1332(d)(1), which is another portion of the newly enacted Class Action Fairness Act. Section 1332 is discussed at greater length elsewhere in this text.

Standard Removal Requirements: Exceptions

Sections 1332, 1441 and 1446, discussed elsewhere in this text, govern many of the requirements applicable to removal of cases from state court to federal court, including class actions. However, when a case falls within the scope of the Class Action Fairness Act, a number of provisions of §§ 1332, 1441, 1446, and case law are inapplicable to removal of a class action. Most of these exceptions to removal of class actions are identified in § 1453(b), but two of them are located in § 1332(d)(2). All of these exceptions are identified immediately below.

Exception: Diversity of Citizenship. In the ordinary course of events, a party seeking to establish subject matter jurisdiction in a federal district court based on diversity of citizenship must establish complete diversity between all plaintiffs and all defendants.[1] However, § 1332(d)(2) expressly provides that for purposes of class actions within the scope of the Class Action Fairness Act, diversity jurisdiction may be satisfied simply by establishing that a single class member is diverse from the class opponents.[2]

Exception: Amount in Controversy. In civil cases that do not

---

[1]*Exxon Mobil Corp. v. Allapattah Services, Inc.*, 545 U.S. 546, 125 S. Ct. 2611, 2617, 162 L. Ed. 2d 502 (2005) ("[W]e have consistently interpreted § 1332 as requiring complete diversity.").

[2]28 U.S.C.A. § 1332(d)(2). *See also Miedema v. Maytag Corp.*, 450

involve class actions, diversity jurisdiction is not established unless the amount in controversy for each plaintiff exceeds $75,000, exclusive of interest and costs.[3] However, in cases controlled by the Class Action Fairness Act, the amount in controversy in most class actions must exceed $5,000,000, exclusive of interest and costs.[4] This figure is obviously larger than the more traditional monetary requirement for individual parties in cases not involving class actions, but it will often be easier to achieve in class actions because the total amount in dispute in many cases often exceeds $5,000,000, even where the claims of individual participants are for amounts that may be less than the $75,000 requirement.[5]

Exception: One-Year Limitation on Removal of Diversity Cases. In cases not controlled by the Class Action Fairness Act, § 1446(b) permits removal on the basis of diversity jurisdiction only within the first year after commencement of the action in state court.[6] By contrast, § 1453(b) expressly provides that "the 1-year limitation under § 1446(b) shall not apply."[7]

Exception: Citizenship of Defendants. Section 1441 provides that in cases where a defendant is a citizen of the state where the case is filed, removal may not be based on diversity of citizenship—even if the diversity requirements themselves are satisfied.[8] However, in cases controlled by the Class Action Fairness Act, the citizenship of a defendant in the forum state is not an impediment to removal.[9]

Exception: Unanimous Consent. For more conventional cases, case law has long imposed a requirement that *all* defendants join in the removal petition.[10] However, cases controlled by the Class Action Fairness Act may be removed by a single defen-

---

F.3d 1322, 1327 (11th Cir. 2006) (§ 1332(d) establishes requirement of only minimal diversity in Class Action Fairness Cases).

[3]28 U.S.C.A. § 1332(a).

[4]28 U.S.C.A. § 1332(d). *See also Miedema v. Maytag Corp.*, 450 F.3d 1322, 1327 (11th Cir. 2006) (noting requirement of more than $5,000,000).

[5]*But cf., Marple v. T-Mobile Central, LLC*, 639 F.3d 1109, 1110 (8th Cir. 2011) (no authority to aggregate amounts sought in separate class actions to achieve amount in controversy). *See also Frederick v. Hartford Underwriters Insurance Co.*, 683 F.3d 1242, 1244 (10th Cir 2012) (defendant may present his own estimate of amount in controversy).

[6]28 U.S.C.A. § 1446(b).

[7]28 U.S.C.A. § 1446(b). *See, e.g., Lowery v. Alabama Power Co.*, 483 F.3d 1184, 1195 (11th Cir. 2007)

(§ 1453 eliminates one-year limitation on removal of class action diversity suits); *Miedema v. Maytag Corp.*, 450 F.3d 1322, 1327 n. 3 (11th Cir. 2006) (also noting that § 1446(b)'s one year limitation is not applicable). *But cf., Babasa v. LensCrafters, Inc.*, 498 F.3d 972, 974 (9th Cir. 2007) (thirty day time limit of § 1446(b), which starts to run on date that defendant received notice that case is removable, still applies in cases controlled by § 1453).

[8]28 U.S.C.A. § 1441(b). *Lincoln Property Co. v. Roche*, 546 U.S. 81, 126 S. Ct. 606, 613, 163 L. Ed. 2d 415 (2005).

[9]28 U.S.C.A. § 1453(b).

[10]*Chicago, R. I. & P. Ry. Co. v. Martin*, 178 U.S. 245, 248, 20 S. Ct. 854, 855, 44 L. Ed. 1055 (1900) ("[I]t was well settled that a removal could not be effected unless all the parties on the same side of the controversy united in the petition.").

dant, without the need for unanimous consent among defendants.[11]

Original Defendants Only

Section 1453 does not change the established rule that only an original defendant may seek removal.[12] Thus, in most circuits it is still true that counter-defendants, cross-claim defendants, and third-party defendants cannot remove.[13]

Appellate Review

In conventional removal cases, § 1447(d) imposes a broad general prohibition on appellate review or reconsideration of remand orders based on procedural defects in the removal petition or lack of subject matter jurisdiction.[14] In cases controlled by the Class Action Fairness Act, however, § 1453(c)(1) provides that, while § 1447 itself generally applies to removal of class actions, the prohibition in § 1447(d) does not.[15]

Discretionary Appeal

There is no right to appeal a district court's order granting or denying remand of a class action to a state court. Instead, § 1453(c)(1) gives the circuit court discretion to hear such an appeal.[16]

---

[11]28 U.S.C.A. § 1453(b). *See also Farina v. Nokia, Inc.*, 625 F.3d 97, 113 (3d Cir. 2010) (not only may a single defendant remove the case; that lone defendant can remove entire case, "not just the claims asserted against that particular defendant").

[12]*See, e.g., First Bank v. DJL Properties, LLC*, 598 F.3d 915, 916 (7th Cir. 2010) (plaintiffs who became counterclaim defendants may not remove under § 1453); *Palisades Collections LLC v. Shorts*, 552 F.3d 327, 336 (4th Cir. 2008) (restricting right of removal to parties joined as original defendants).

[13]*See, e.g., Palisades Collections LLC v. Shorts*, 552 F.3d 327, 336 (4th Cir. 2008) (prohibiting removal by those categories of non-original defendants); *Progressive West Insurance Co. v. Preciado*, 479 F.3d 1014, 1017 (9th Cir. 2007) (§ 1453 does not change "longstanding rule that a plaintiff/ cross-defendant cannot remove an action to federal court"). *But see In re Wilson Industries, Inc.*, 886 F.2d 93, 96 (5th Cir. 1989) (in conventional removal cases, third-party defendant may seek removal).

[14]*See, e.g., In re WTC Disaster Site*, 414 F.3d 352, 364 (2d Cir. 2005) (neither appeal nor mandamus is available). Section 1447(d), and its exceptions, are discussed in greater detail elsewhere in this text.

[15]28 U.S.C.A. § 1453(c)(1). *See, e.g., Lowery v. Alabama Power Co.*, 483 F.3d 1184, 1193 (11th Cir. 2007) (§ 1453(c) permits review de novo of district court's decision to remand case that was removed pursuant to Class Action Fairness Act); *Miedema v. Maytag Corp.*, 450 F.3d 1322, 1326 (11th Cir. 2006) (notwithstanding § 1447(d), remand orders in cases that were removed pursuant to Class Action Fairness Act may be reviewed by appellate court). *But cf., Saab v. Home Depot U.S.A., Inc.*, 469 F.3d 758, 759 (8th Cir. 2006) (where removal of class action was based on "traditional diversity jurisdiction," § 1453(c) exception to non-appe/ability of remand orders does not apply).

[16]28 U.S.C.A. § 1453(c)(1) ("[A] court of appeals *may* accept an appeal." (italics added)). *See also, e.g., Evans v. Walter Industries, Inc.*, 449 F.3d 1159, 1162 (11th Cir. 2006) (§ 1453(c)(1) makes acceptance of petition discretionary). *See also Hertz Corp. v. Friend*, __ U.S. __, 130 S. Ct.

Time Limit for Application to Appeal

Although the literal language of § 1453(c)(1) is a bit confused, most courts are in accord in holding that parties seeking review of a decision on remand must apply to the circuit court within seven days of the order granting or denying the motion to remand.[17]

Time Limit for Circuit Court to Decide

If the court of appeals accepts an application to appeal, § 1453(c)(2) directs the appellate court to decide the issue within sixty days,[18] subject to extensions of that time (discussed immediately below). The 60-day time limit begins to run from the date that the court of appeals granted the petition to appeal.[19]

Extension of Time Limit to Decide

Section 1453(c)(2) authorizes the circuit court to extend the sixty days in which it must decide an appeal in either of two circumstances.[20] First, if all parties consent to an extension, the court may extend the sixty days "for any period of time."[21] Second, without regard to the consent of parties, the court may

---

1181, 1187, 175 L. Ed. 2d 1029 (2010) (authorization for "court of appeals" to hear an appeal, without any mention of Supreme Court, does not deprive Supreme Court of its appellate jurisdiction).

[17]*See, e.g., Miedema v. Maytag Corp.*, 450 F.3d 1322 (11th Cir.2006) (appeal must be made within seven days of date of remand order; acknowledging that § 1453(c)(1) requires application within "not less than 7 days," but holding that literal application of that language would produce "absurd result;" noting agreement with other circuits); *Pritchett v. Office Depot, Inc.*, 420 F.3d 1090, 1093 n. 2 (10th Cir. 2005) ("The statute should read that an appeal is permissible if filed 'not more than' seven days after entry of the remand order."). *See also Patterson v. Dean Morris, L.L.P.*, 444 F.3d 365, 368 n.1 (5th Cir. 2006) (also excluding weekends and holidays from calculation of seven days). *But see Spivey v. Vertrue, Inc.*, 528 F.3d 982, 983–84 (7th Cir. 2008) (acknowledging that Congress probably intended § 1453(c)(1) to require petition to be filed within seven days; noting consensus of other circuits that "less" should be read to mean "more," but criticizing notion that Congressional wording can so easily be disregarded; holding instead that literal language creates no

time limit for appeal, thus triggering application of Fed.R.App.P. 4(a)(1)(A) and 5(a)(2) (which, taken together, provide that if no time limit is specified by statute, appeal must be filed within 30 days after judgment or entry of order appealed from).

[18]28 U.S.C.A. § 1453(c)(2). *See, e.g., United Steel, Paper & Forestry, Rubber, Manufacturing Energy, Allied Industrial & Service Workers International Union, AFL-CIO, CLC v. ConocoPhillips Co.*, 593 F.3d 802, 806 n.6 (9th Cir. 2010) (appellate court must " 'complete all action . . . including rendering judgment' "). *Braud v. Transport Service Co. of Illinois*, 445 F.3d 801, 803 n. 2 (5th Cir. 2006) (60 days begin to run "from the date on which [the court] granted application for leave to appeal").

[19]*See, e.g., Evans v. Walter Industries, Inc.*, 449 F.3d 1159, 1162–63 (11th Cir. 2006) (rejecting start of running of sixty days as of date petition to appeal is filed).

[20]*See, e.g., Bush v. Cheaptickets, Inc.*, 425 F.3d 683, 686 n. 2 (9th Cir. 2005) (noting alternative grounds for extension of time).

[21]28 U.S.C.A. § 1453(c)(3)(A). *See also, e.g., Prime Care of Northeast Kan., LLC v. Humana Ins. Co.*, 447 F.3d 1284, 1285 n. 1 (10th Cir. 2006)

extend the time "for good cause shown and in the interests of justice."[22] If an extension is granted for good cause and without the consent of all parties, § 1453(c)(3)(B) limits the extension to a maximum of ten days.[23]

Failure to Decide Appeal Within Time Limit

Section 1453(c)(4) governs the result if an appellate court does not decide an appeal within the time limit (including extensions, if any). If no decision is forthcoming, the appeal is denied.[24]

Cases Outside Scope of § 1453

Section 1453(d) establishes several categories of actions not within the scope of removal provisions of the Class Action Fairness Act, even if the cases in question are in fact potential class actions. These exceptions are: (1) cases involving "solely" claims under federal securities laws;[25] and (2) cases involving "solely" claims arising under state corporate laws governing the internal affairs or governance of state chartered corporations.[26]

§ 2.18 The *Erie* Doctrine

I. THE PROBLEM

Federal district courts are sometimes called upon to hear state law disputes—that is, disputes arising under a state's constitution, statutes, or common law, rather than under federal law. The two most frequent circumstances when federal courts hear state disputes arise when the court's jurisdiction is based on diversity of citizenship[1] or supplemental jurisdiction.[2] When a federal court is confronted with a state law dispute, what substantive law should it apply: federal law or state law? In adjudicating state law disputes, should federal or state procedural rules apply? Efforts to determine when federal or state substantive or procedural law applies have bewitched federal courts

---

(noting extension of sixty days by consent of parties).

[22] 28 U.S.C.A. § 1453(c)(3)(B). *See also, e.g., Braud v. Transport Service Co. of Illinois*, 445 F.3d 801, 803 n. 2 (5th Cir. 2006) (noting standard for extension to which parties did not consent).

[23] *See, e.g., Braud v. Transport Service Co. of Illinois*, 445 F.3d 801, 803 n. 2 (5th Cir. 2006) (noting limit of ten days).

[24] 28 U.S.C.A. § 1453(c)(4) (in such circumstances "the appeal shall be denied"). *See also, e.g., Miedema v. Maytag Corp.*, 450 F.3d 1322, 1327 n. 2 (11th Cir. 2006) (failure to decide is denial of petition).

[25] *See, e.g., Greenwich Financial Services Distressed Mortgage Fund 3 LLC v. Countrywide Financial Corp.*, 603 F.3d 23, 30 (2d Cir. 2010) (noting this exception).

[26] *See, e.g., First Bank v. DJL Properties, LLC*, 598 F.3d 915, 916 (7th Cir. 2010) (plaintiffs who became counterclaim defendants may not remove under § 1453); *Brill v. Countrywide Home Loans, Inc.*, 427 F.3d 446, 450 (7th Cir. 2005) (citing 28 U.S.C.A. § 1453(d) for the "list of claims to which [the Class Action Fairness Act's] removal provisions are inapplicable").

[1] 28 U.S.C.A. § 1332.

[2] 28 U.S.C.A. § 1367.

almost since the founding of the Republic.

Questions of the subject matter jurisdiction of federal district courts over state causes of action (that is, when federal courts are even entitled to hear state claims) are difficult enough in their own right. However, even after jurisdictional questions are resolved, a party's ability to file a state cause of action in a federal district court gives rise to another set of difficult questions, going to the law that the court should apply to the state claim. As will become evident below, the answers to such questions are still a source of some uncertainty. For that reason alone, it is important not to make the investigation of this problem more difficult than it needs to be.

With that consideration in mind, it should be clear at the outset that the question of identifying the appropriate law a federal district court should apply to a state cause of action is not a matter of jurisdiction. Generally, before a court reaches this question, usually it will have addressed and resolved jurisdictional issues in the case. In other words, if the court lacks jurisdiction to hear the case, normally it will dismiss the action. When that happens, the court need not concern itself with identifying the law that would apply if the court could hear the case. Therefore, the court usually will address questions of the appropriate law to apply to a case only after determining that the court has jurisdiction to hear the claims.[3]

II. *ERIE R.R. CO. v. TOMPKINS*[4]

The current approach to identifying the proper law to apply to a state cause of action in a federal court[5] is based on the *Erie* doctrine. *Erie* rests on two important premises: (1) a claimant should not be encouraged to shop for a federal forum because doing so might result in application of federal law that would affect the outcome of the case; and (2) federal courts hearing state claims lack Constitutional authority to create substantive common law independent of the law that state courts would apply to those claims. Thus, the established approach prior to *Erie*, which permitted federal courts to create so-called "federal general common law" that might be at odds with state law, was

---

[3]It sometimes happens that a court may take an objection to its jurisdiction under advisement and render a decision only after hearing other portions of the case. This approach is an exception to the more typical practice. Moreover, it means that at least tentatively the court has assumed that it possesses jurisdiction to hear the case, subject to the possibility of a different decision later.

[4]*Erie R. Co. v. Tompkins*, 304 U.S. 64, 58 S. Ct. 817, 82 L. Ed. 1188 (1938).

[5]It should be noted that while the original *Erie* doctrine developed in the context of cases based on the diversity jurisdiction of federal district courts, it appears now to be applied also to cases in which district courts have supplemental jurisdiction over non-diverse state claims. *Felder v. Casey*, 487 U.S. 131, 151, 108 S. Ct. 2302, 2313, 101 L. Ed. 2d 123 (1988) (*Erie* also applies to claims based on predecessors to supplemental jurisdiction).

unconstitutional.

The case arose out of an injury that Tompkins suffered while walking alongside a railroad track. When Tompkins sued, the possibility of recovery rested on a determination of his legal status while he was walking on what was clearly railroad property. Under state common law, Tompkins was a trespasser, to whom the railroad owed at most a minimal duty of care. If state law was applied, Tompkins was entitled to no damages. Federal general common law, developed prior to *Erie*, offered the plaintiff greater possibilities. By placing less emphasis on Tompkins' status as an individual not invited onto railroad property, and more emphasis on the railroad's duty of care to individuals who were on its property, federal general common law afforded Tompkins substantial possibilities for a sizeable award of damages.[6]

However, when the Supreme Court got the case, it abolished the body of law that existed prior to *Erie*. At one stroke the Court overruled older precedent and held that in the future there would be no federal general common law. Instead, federal trial courts hearing diversity cases were directed to apply the same state law that a state court hearing the same case would have used.[7]

Part of the impact was immediate and lasting. Federal courts would, in the future, defer to state common law as well as to state statutes. If this rule had been in effect at the time that Tompkins was injured, his lawyer would have known that state law, identifying Tompkins as a trespasser, would have given him little in the way of a claim against the railroad. That result—the federal court's use of state law to determine if the plaintiff has a cognizable cause of action, and to determine if any applicable substantive defenses block the suit—continues to be the law of *Erie* to the present day.

Abolition of federal general common law also meant that the Constitutional concern that the Court expressed in *Erie* was resolved. Recognition of the requirement to apply state substantive law meant that the Constitutionally questionable practice of creating a body of federal substantive law in competition with state law was at an end.

Finally, the temptation to engage in forum shopping was reduced, though not eliminated. Once federal general common law was no more, lawyers lost an important reason to file in federal district courts (*i.e.,* to get different substantive law than a state court would apply). The transformation was radical and, in some respects, complete.

But some new and knotty problems emerged in the wake of

---

[6]*Erie R.R. Co. v. Tompkins,* 304 U.S. 64, 68, 58 S. Ct. 817, 818, 82 L. Ed. 1188 (1938).

[7]*Erie R.R. Co. v. Tompkins,* 304 U.S. 64, 71, 58 S. Ct. 817, 823, 82 L. Ed. 1188 (1938).

Erie. It is those problems which continue to cluster around the *Erie* doctrine to the current day, and which are the subject of the remainder of this section.

III. SUBSTANCE v. PROCEDURE: GUARANTY TRUST CO. v. YORK[8]

A clue to the central problem arising in the aftermath of *Erie* can be found in a concurring opinion. One justice agreed with the central holding of *Erie*, *i.e.*, that federal general common law should be abolished and that federal district courts should apply state substantive law. At the same time, he also commented that it was obvious federal courts would remain free to apply their own procedural law—even in diversity cases.[9] But what seemed obvious at the time the Court decided *Erie* proved to be somewhat less clear as additional time passed.

Courts have long identified differences between substantive law and procedural law. Usually substantive law is described as the law that determines whether a party has a claim cognizable in a court, and whether the defendant has a legal defense that bars such a claim on the merits. For example, if a plaintiff sued on a claim of negligence, most states would permit recovery only if the plaintiff could demonstrate that: (1) the defendant owed the plaintiff a duty of care; (2) the defendant breached that duty; and (3) the breach proximately caused injury to the plaintiff or damage to the plaintiff's property. Those are the substantive elements of the tort of negligence.[10] In a state that recognized the defense of contributory negligence, a defendant could defeat the claim by demonstrating that the plaintiff had been contributorily negligent in the event that led to the plaintiff's injury. This assertion of contributory negligence is a substantive defense.

By contrast, procedural law does not address whether the plaintiff has a cause of action or whether the defendant necessarily has a defense. Instead, procedure governs the way in which both plaintiff and defendant must present their sides of the case to the court. At its simplest level, procedural law will control the length of paper on which pleadings must be filed (*e.g.*, letter size or legal size) or whether the complaint may be written out by hand. More complex problems arise over procedure regulating the joining of additional parties, the conduct of discovery, or the admissibility of evidence. These procedural rules help direct the course of a lawsuit and, pragmatically, can often determine the

---

[8]*Guaranty Trust Co. of N.Y. v. York*, 326 U.S. 99, 65 S. Ct. 1464, 89 L. Ed. 2079 (1945).

[9]*Erie*, 304 U.S. at 90, 58 S. Ct. at 828 (Reed, J., concurring) ("No one doubts federal power over procedure."). But cf., *Jinks v. Richland County, S.C.*, 538 U.S. 456, 123 S. Ct. 1667, 155 L. Ed. 2d 631 (2003) (implying that courts cannot always easily untangle the relationship between substance and procedure, no matter what the purpose may be for trying to do so).

[10]These elements may be stated somewhat differently in different states, but the basic requirements are usually very similar.

outcome of a case. At the same time, they do not directly address the substantive legal standard a plaintiff must meet in order to demonstrate negligence to the satisfaction of the court.

In the context of the *Erie* doctrine, the ability of federal courts to apply their own procedure (or not) remains the central unresolved question that *Erie* produced. On the one hand, there is no serious question about the Constitutional authority of federal courts and Congress to create procedural law that governs federal courts. In that sense, the decision of a federal district court to apply its own procedure to a case involving a state cause of action does not raise the same Constitutional doubts that application of federal general common law had raised in the era prior to *Erie*.

At the same time, in many cases procedure can alter the outcome of a case as surely as substantive law. For example, a case can easily be lost when a party is unprepared to cross-examine effectively an opponent's expert. In some states, preparation to cross-examine an expert is impaired by rules of procedure limiting or prohibiting deposition of opposing experts. By contrast, Federal Rule of Civil Procedure 26 generally permits such depositions. Therefore, to the extent that a federal court's procedure might be different than that of a state court, lawyers might still choose to file cases in federal court (when, *e.g.,* diversity requirements are satisfied) in order to obtain the benefit of federal procedure. Potential problems of forum shopping thus remain when federal courts are able to apply their own procedure.

After *Erie*, the Supreme Court returned to the problem of determining when, if at all, federal courts may use their own procedure in diversity cases. One of the most important early decisions was *Guaranty Trust Co. v. York*,[11] in which the Court had to choose between application of a federal doctrine limiting the time in which a case had to be filed or a state statute of limitations that set a different time limit. Under the state statute, the plaintiff's claim was barred. Under the federal doctrine, the plaintiff's case could proceed.

In its own way, *Guaranty Trust* was more difficult than *Erie*. *Guaranty Trust* involved an arguably procedural issue, and there could be no question that federal courts are authorized to apply their own procedure in many of the cases they hear. For example, when a cause of action arises out of federal law, a federal court must have procedure with which to process the case. The federal court cannot be bound to the application of the procedure of the state in which the federal court sits, because that would mean the procedure applied to federal questions would differ from one state to another. The result would be an unacceptable lack of uniformity in the way federal claims were heard across the

---

[11]*Guaranty Trust Co. of N.Y. v. York*, 326 U.S. 99, 65 S. Ct. 1464, 89 L. Ed. 2079 (1945).

United States. Additionally, the Court could not simply order lower federal courts to apply federal procedure when hearing federal claims and state procedure when hearing state claims. In the first place, that approach would require federal judges to learn, and apply, two different bodies of procedure on a regular basis. Secondly, when cases appeared on the federal docket involving both federal and state claims, an attempt to apply federal procedure to federal claims and state procedure to state claims might often produce unacceptable confusion. Consider, for example, what would happen if federal rules of evidence treated a piece of testimony as inadmissible, while state rules of evidence would admit the testimony.

Guaranty Trust took a tentative step toward resolving the problem by directing federal courts to use state procedure whenever the choice of procedure would determine the outcome of the case. As applied to the facts of *Guaranty Trust*, this approach meant that the federal court should use the state statute of limitations.[12] The reasoning was that under the state rule, the plaintiff's claim was time barred. Application of the federal limitation period would permit the plaintiff to pursue the claim. While it was still possible that the plaintiff might lose the case on the merits, the difference between certain defeat for the plaintiff under the state law and a possibility of victory under the federal law is a sufficient difference in outcome to justify barring the use of federal procedure.

IV. CONTINUING DEVELOPMENT: SOURCES OF FEDERAL PROCEDURE

The underpinning of the decision in *Guaranty Trust* was a concern that a sufficiently large potential difference in outcome caused by the application of federal procedure would create unacceptable levels of forum shopping of the kind that *Erie* originally sought to prevent. This linkage between outcome determination and forum shopping was an important step in extending the *Erie* doctrine to procedural issues as well as matters of substantive law. However, at the same time, an emphasis on "outcome determination" as the basis for choosing between federal procedure and state procedure can easily be an overly broad assessment.[13] In a given case, even the most modest differences in procedure,

---

[12]This result still applies in the context of statutes of limitations. *Jinks v. Richland County, S.C.*, 538 U.S. 456, 123 S. Ct. 1667, 155 L. Ed. 2d 631 (2003) (dicta) ("For *Erie* purposes . . . statutes of limitation are treated as substantive;" citing *Guaranty Trust*). *See also Shady Grove Orthopedic Associates, P.A. v. Allstate Insurance Co.*, ___ U.S. ___, 130 S. Ct. 1431, 176 L. Ed. 2d 311 (2010) (Stevens, J., concurring) (some state procedure is applicable because it is part of state's "substantive rights and remedies"). *But cf., Utica Lloyd's of Texas v. Mitchell*, 138 F.3d 208, 210 (5th Cir. 1998) (refusing to apply attorney's fee provision of Texas Declaratory Judgment Act because "it functions solely as a procedural mechanism").

[13]*Schipani v. McLeod*, 541 F.3d 158, 164–65 (2d Cir. 2008) ("[S]tate

e.g., page limitations in different courts on the length of briefs, can produce a significantly different outcome. For example, conforming to such page limitations might force an attorney to abandon arguments of potential value. Moreover, because sensible lawyers will litigate only issues that could have a bearing on the outcome of a case, a test that considered only outcome determination might require application of state procedure for almost every state claim filed in federal court—including claims filed in conjunction with federal causes of action.

For that reason, the continuing evolution of the *Erie* doctrine has included the identification of other factors to weigh in a determination as to the applicability of state or federal procedure. Perhaps the most significant factor identified in later cases is the importance of identifying the source of the federal procedure that is arguably applicable to a state cause of action. Over time, the Supreme Court has addressed the relationship of *Erie* to three different sources of federal procedure somewhat differently, as follows.

A. Federal Case Law Procedure.

In instances where the pertinent federal procedure develops through case law, and not through statutes or rules, the choice between federal and state procedure depends heavily on a weighing of interests. In *Byrd v. Blue Ridge Rural Electric Cooperative, Inc.,*[14] a worker's compensation case, one key issue was whether the injured plaintiff was an employee, for purposes of the worker's compensation statute, of the defendant. A second issue, and the one that raised the *Erie* question, was whether the jury or the judge should decide the plaintiff's employment relationship (if any) with the defendant. Under state procedure the judge was authorized to make that decision, while the established federal practice was to leave the question to the jury.

The Supreme Court acknowledged that if the only *Erie* measurement was outcome determination, identification of the proper role of judge and jury might well require application of state procedure. However, the Court concluded that other factors, in addition to outcome determination, were also relevant to the case. In particular, the Court extended the *Erie* analysis to include consideration of the competing state and federal interests in applying state and federal procedure, respectively. These considerations, along with an evaluation of the possibility that application of federal procedure might significantly affect the outcome of the case, were to be weighed to determine whether state or federal procedure should control.[15] In other words, a strong state interest in application of state procedure weighs in

---

law governs the award of prejudgment interest [but] postjudgment interest is governed by federal statute.").

[14]*Byrd v. Blue Ridge Rural Elec.*

Co-op., Inc., 356 U.S. 525, 78 S. Ct. 893, 2 L. Ed. 2d 953 (1958).

[15]*Id.* at 533–539, 78 S. Ct. at 899–902.

favor of applying state procedure, while a weak state interest reduces the argument for using state procedure. A strong federal interest in applying federal procedure supports use of federal procedure, while a weak federal interest reduces the argument for using federal procedure. And if the use of federal procedure might significantly affect the outcome of the case, such a prospect argues in favor of using state procedure.[16]

A major difficulty in applying *Byrd* arises when the court tries to identify state and federal interests and to weigh their relative importance in a particular case. Additionally, an assessment of the impact that application of federal procedure might have on the outcome of a case can also be uncertain.[17] The only way attorneys can approach this question is to research the policies behind the competing state and federal procedures and then see how those policies measure up against one another.[18] For assessing prospects of outcome determination, the inquiry is more nearly a pragmatic evaluation of the way in which application of federal procedure might affect the course of the litigation.

Thus, when the federal procedure potentially applicable to a case is procedure developed by judicial practice (*i.e.*, case law procedure), courts typically weigh the three factors identifies in *Byrd*: (1) relative strength of state interests behind state procedure; (2) relative strength of federal interests behind federal procedure;

---

[16]*Id.* at 539, 78 S. Ct. at 902.

[17]*Id.* (noting uncertainty of effect of difference between judge and jury on outcome of case). *See also, e.g., Esfeld v. Costa Crociere, S.P.A.*, 289 F.3d 1300, 1306–09 (11th Cir. 2002) (noting that "vast majority" of federal appellate courts use federal law of forum non conveniens; holding that while forum non conveniens will often be outcome-determinative, federal interest in controlling its own process in a way that is uniform across the country outweighed the outcome-determinative factor; holding that federal law of forum non conveniens should control; citing other cases).

[18]This suggestion is not meant to indicate that thorough research alone will yield an answer upon which diligent attorneys may confidently rely. Indeed, continuing developments in the Supreme Court indicate that *Byrd* does not identify a single true path with the clarity and precision of a laser. In *Gasperini v. Center for Humanities, Inc.*, 518 U.S. 415, 116 S. Ct. 2211, 135 L. Ed. 2d 659 (1996), a jury awarded a large verdict to the plaintiff. Under New York law, a state appellate court has authority to order a new trial when the jury's verdict "deviates materially" from reasonable compensation. Federal procedure differs from that standard in two important respects. First, a federal district judge normally has less discretion to modify a jury's verdict than the New York law allows. Second, New York vests this power in an appellate court. By contrast, the Seventh Amendment to the United States constitution normally imposes much stricter limits on the authority of federal appellate courts to modify jury verdicts.

The Supreme Court grappled with this cluster of problems in the following manner. First, in diversity cases federal district courts—not circuit courts—will apply the New York statute's standard for modifying jury verdicts. This practice, of course, is not directly consistent with the New York mandate to provide such review in appellate courts. Second, in a bow to the Seventh Amendment, federal circuit courts will review the district court's application of the New York law under the existing federal standard for circuit courts, *i.e.,* an abuse of discretion.

and (3) likelihood that application of federal procedure will significantly alter the outcome of the case.[19]

B. Rules Enabling Act:[20] Federal Rules of Procedure.

Case law is not the only source of federal procedure. In fact, only a few years before the Supreme Court decided *Erie*, Congress enacted legislation creating a process by which federal rules of procedure could be enacted without necessarily involving direct participation in each rule by Congress. The Rules Enabling Act was the source of, *inter alia*, the current Federal Rules of Civil Procedure, which are so important to the processing of civil cases in federal courts.

Interplay between the *Erie* doctrine and federal rules developed under the authority of the Rules Enabling Act was inevitable. For example, in a case where state procedure required a plaintiff to post a bond before proceeding with a suit, but Federal Rule of Civil Procedure 23.1 required no bond, the Court had to decide whether the state bond requirement prevailed over a federal rule that otherwise appeared to be relevant to the case.[21] In another case, state procedure provided that an applicable statute of limitations continued to run after a case was filed with the court until the defendant was served. By contrast, Federal Rule of Civil Procedure 3 provides that a federal case is "commenced" by filing a complaint with the federal district court. A possible construction of Rule 3 is that once the case is filed, the statute of limitations is tolled. The case before the Supreme Court was one in which the plaintiff had filed the complaint in federal district court before the statute of limitations had expired, but service of process on the defendant did not occur until after the statute of limitations would have expired.[22] Under state procedure, therefore, the plaintiff's suit was untimely. Under the apparent literal language of Federal Rule 3, the plaintiff's filing was timely, and the case could proceed.

In both cases, the Supreme Court concluded that the applicable procedure was state procedure, but the reasoning was insufficiently persuasive to lay to rest concerns about the impact of the *Erie* doctrine on cases involving rules of procedure developed under the authority of the Rules Enabling Act. Some, but by no means all, of this uneasiness was laid to rest when the Supreme Court decided *Hanna v. Plumer*.[23]

In *Hanna* a plaintiff served the defendant by leaving a copy of

---

[19]It should be noted that the *Byrd* analysis does not assess directly the possible impact that application of state procedure will have on the outcome of a case.

[20]28 U.S.C.A. § 2072.

[21]*Cohen v. Beneficial Indus. Loan Corp.*, 337 U.S. 541, 69 S. Ct. 1221, 93 L. Ed. 1528 (1949).

[22]*Ragan v. Merchants Transfer & Warehouse Co.*, 337 U.S. 530, 69 S. Ct. 1233, 93 L. Ed. 1520 (1949).

[23]*Hanna v. Plumer*, 380 U.S. 460, 85 S. Ct. 1136, 14 L. Ed. 2d 8 (1965).

the summons and complaint with the defendant's spouse at the defendant's residence. This was lawful service under Federal Rule of Civil Procedure 4. However, under state procedure, service was not satisfactory unless the defendant was served personally. The Supreme Court re-examined its growing body of precedent under the *Erie* doctrine and concluded that service was satisfactory because Rule 4 applied, not the state procedure.[24]

The reasoning of the Court's majority was that the relation of *Erie* to the Rules Enabling Act required a two-step analysis of the possible application of a federal rule of civil procedure to a state cause of action. The first step was to determine if the rule at issue could lawfully be made. Because the Rules Enabling Act only permitted creation of federal rules which were purely procedural, and which did not alter substantive rights, the first inquiry was to determine if the rule in question in a particular case was procedural. In the case at bar Rule 4, governing the means of making service of process on a defendant, affected no substantive rights and clearly passed this "pure procedure" requirement.

The second step was to determine if the federal rule (such as Rule 4) could be harmonized with state procedure, or whether the federal and state procedures were locked in conflict. The Court explained that if the two could be harmonized because, *e.g.,* they did not address the same concerns, no choice between them was necessary. However, if they actually collided, then a federal rule of civil procedure lawfully created under the Rules Enabling Act should be applied over the state procedure.[25]

The literal rule of *Hanna* appears to be that if a federal rule of civil procedure is a lawful exercise of rule-making power under the Rules Enabling Act, and the rule conflicts directly with state procedure, the federal rule applies.[26] That approach appears to leave little room for considerations of outcome determination, which had been so important to the Supreme Court in both *Erie* and *Guaranty Trust*.[27] However, an important concurring opinion in *Hanna* helps explain the interplay between the federal rules of civil procedure and concerns about outcome determination under *Erie*.

While agreeing with the result in *Hanna* (application of Rule 4 over conflicting state procedure), Justice Harlan added that a de-

---

[24]*Id.* at 462, 85 S. Ct. at 1140.

[25]*Id.* at 468, 85 S. Ct. at 1143.

[26]*Shady Grove Orthopedic Associates, P.A. v. Allstate Insurance Co.,* __ U.S. __, 130 S. Ct. 1431, 1441–42, 176 L. Ed. 2d 311 (2010) (plurality opinion) (state law prohibiting class litigation as to particular cause of action "flatly contradict(s)" Rule 23, which autho-

rizes class actions if certain requirements are met; holding Rule 23 controls; also noting "we have rejected every statutory challenge to a Federal Rule that has come before us").

[27]*See, e.g., Morel v. Daimler-Chrysler AG,* 565 F.3d 20, 24 (1st Cir. 2009) (in situation controlled by *Hanna,* the approaches of both *Erie* and *Guaranty Trust* are inapplicable).

termination of the applicability of a federal rule to a case arising under state law should also take into account whether the possible application of federal procedure would have influenced an attorney's decision to choose the federal court in order to avoid the application of state procedure.[28] Where such a decision might reasonably have been made, and where the application of federal procedure would impinge on a significant state policy, Justice Harlan believed the state procedure should apply—even if, under the majority's test, state procedure conflicted with a valid federal rule of procedure.[29] When applied, Justice Harlan's approach refined the "outcome-determinative" test for procedure that had been so important at least since *Guaranty Trust*. In essence, Justice Harlan avoided the possibility that a difference in procedure could always determine the outcome by concentrating his analysis on the estimated importance of procedure at the time an attorney was choosing the court in which the case would be heard. Put another way, if a reasonable attorney, upon noticing that federal procedure offered a significant advantage not available under state procedure, would choose the federal court in order to obtain the benefit of federal procedure, the federal procedure would be sufficiently outcome determinative to justify displacing it with state procedure. While Justice Harlan made these observations in the context of federal rules of procedure, they appear to have applicability also to the circumstances governed by *Byrd, i.e.,* situations in which federal procedure arising purely from case law may conflict with state procedure.

Understanding *Hanna* can be difficult enough. However, the difficulty is sometimes compounded when *Hanna* is applied in particular cases. In *Walker v. Armco Steel Corp.*,[30] for example, the Supreme Court returned to a question it had originally addressed a generation earlier. *Walker* involved a plaintiff who had sued on a state claim in federal district court. The claim was filed before the statute of limitations expired, but the complaint was not served on the defendant until after the statute would have expired. Applicable state law provided that the statute continued to run until service on the defendant. The plaintiff argued that Federal Rule of Civil Procedure 3, describing an action as "commenced" when filed with the district court, meant that the statute of limitations was tolled by the plaintiff's timely filing with the clerk's office.

Walker was a reprise of *Ragan v. Merchants Transfer & Warehouse Co.*,[31] in which the Court had held that state procedure controlled, and Rule 3 did not apply. Many observers believed that the intervening decision in *Hanna* had nullified the

---

[28] *Id.* at 474, 85 S. Ct. at 1146 (Harlan, J., concurring).

[29] *Id.*

[30] *Walker v. Armco Steel Corp.*, 446 U.S. 740, 100 S. Ct. 1978, 64 L. Ed. 2d 659 (1980).

[31] *Ragan v. Merchants Transfer & Warehouse Co.*, 337 U.S. 530, 69 S. Ct. 1233, 93 L. Ed. 1520 (1949).

result in *Ragan*. A unanimous Supreme Court, applying *Hanna*, concluded otherwise. The Court recognized that under the *Hanna* analysis, Rule 3 was a lawful rule of procedure, enacted within the authority of the Rules Enabling Act. However, the Court also concluded that Rule 3, at least in diversity cases, was not intended to toll state statutes of limitations. The Court was a bit vague as to the precise purpose of Rule 3 when state claims were before a federal district court.[32] However, its conclusion was that state procedure for tolling a statute of limitation (service on the defendant) controlled because there was "no direct conflict" between the state law and Rule 3.[33] Thus, the requirement of *Hanna* that, before a lawful federal rule can apply to a diversity case it must first be in direct conflict with state procedure was not met, and state law applied.

Walker suggests that there can be grave uncertainty as to the circumstances when a federal rule conflicts to a substantial degree with state procedure. To that extent, *Walker* casts doubt on the predictability of the *Hanna* test as it applies to cases concerning the applicability of federal rules of procedure enacted under the Rules Enabling Act. The Supreme Court appears to be sensitive to this problem, and in the aftermath of *Walker* the Court emphasized that the analysis enunciated in *Hanna* continues to govern in most circumstances.[34] Nevertheless, *Walker* serves as a caution to attorneys that, before assuming a federal rule of procedure displaces state procedure, one must first establish not only that the federal rule is authorized by the Rules Enabling Act, but also that the federal rule truly clashes with otherwise applicable state procedure.

C. Procedure Enacted Directly by Congress.

Although Congress enacted the Rules Enabling Act to authorize a process for creating rules of procedure in which Congress itself did not have to be actively involved, Congress has also created other important procedural provisions independent of the Rules Enabling Act. These provisions are codified at Title 28 of the United States Code.

When one of these statutory procedures is arguably applicable in a diversity case, considerations related to *Erie* arise again. In this circumstance, as with case law controlled by *Byrd* or rules of procedure controlled by *Hanna*, the federal district court must decide whether federal statutory procedure may be applied, or whether it must defer to state procedure. The Supreme Court ad-

---

[32]*Walker*, 446 U.S. at 750, 100 S. Ct. at 1985 ("Rule 3 governs the date from which various timing requirements of the Federal Rules begin to run, but does not affect state statutes of limitations.").

[33]*Id.* at 751, 100 S. Ct. at 1986.

[34]*See, e.g., Burlington Northern R. Co. v. Woods*, 480 U.S. 1, 107 S. Ct. 967, 94 L. Ed. 2d 1 (1987) (applying *Hanna* test, finding Federal Rule of Appellate Procedure 38 applicable in place of state procedure).

dressed this question in *Stewart Organization, Inc. v. Ricoh Corp.*[35] *Stewart* addressed whether a motion to transfer a case pursuant to a contractual forum selection clause was enforceable under 28 U.S.C.A. § 1404(a) or unenforceable because state procedure disfavored such clauses.

The Supreme Court held that the standards for transfer of venue under the federal statute controlled. In a straightforward opinion the Court concluded that federal courts are bound to apply procedure enacted by Congress, provided only that Congress was within its Constitutional authority and that the statute was relevant to the issue before the district court.[36] *Stewart* may have left some modest room for questioning when an attorney can be certain that the federal statutory procedure controls. However, it appears that this question can be answered with somewhat more confidence than the question posed by *Hanna* when a federal rule is at issue, *i.e.,* does the rule conflict sufficiently with state procedure?

V. IDENTIFYING STATE LAW

In cases where a federal district court recognizes that it is obligated to apply state law on an issue, a question remains as to how to identify the state law. Of course, if the relevant state supreme court has addressed the matter clearly, its word on state law is normally final. The question becomes more difficult, however, if state law is not entirely clear.[37]

Federal judges hear many cases where state law is implicated. However, they still lack the experience with state law that state judges will typically have. Moreover, when a state judge decides a difficult question of state law, a party has the ability to seek review of that decision by state appellate judges, who presumably are also familiar with state law. By contrast, if a federal district judge applies state law in a potentially erroneous way, the challenge to that decision is heard by other federal judges. Those federal appellate judges, in turn, may not even be from the state whose law is at issue.

To address the problems raised by this situation, three distinct approaches have evolved. The first is simply to recognize that difficult questions of state law are best handled in the state court system, and to abstain from deciding the case. This approach has the advantage of ensuring that a decision will not be made by a

---

[35]*Stewart Organization, Inc. v. Ricoh Corp.*, 487 U.S. 22, 108 S. Ct. 2239, 101 L. Ed. 2d 22 (1988).

[36]*Id.* at 26, 108 S. Ct. at 2242.

[37]*Klaxon Co. v. Stentor Electric Mfg. Co.*, 313 U.S. 487, 497, 61 S. Ct. 1020, 85 L. Ed. 1477 (1941) ("[T]he proper function of the . . . federal court is to ascertain what the state law is, not what it ought to be."); *West v. American Tel. & Tel. Co.*, 311 U.S. 223, 236, 61 S. Ct. 179, 183, 85 L. Ed. 139 (1940) ("The highest court of the state is the final arbiter of what is state law." Citing *Erie*. Possible exception if state supreme court has made clear its previous view has changed.).

federal court. However, it imposes on the parties all the delay and additional expense involved in re-starting the case in state court. For this reason and others, federal courts have not employed the abstention option frequently.[38]

The second option is to certify the difficult question to the high court of the state whose law is at issue. In states whose legislatures have enacted certification legislation, federal courts may apply to state supreme courts for resolution of difficult questions of state law. Certification carries with it the prospect of a definitive answer to a hard question, but its promise has always been limited by some real-world obstacles. In the first place, certification is expensive for litigants, involving a possible need to brief and argue an issue before yet another court. Second, certification is almost certain to produce delay in obtaining a final judgment in the federal case, for the federal litigation must be held in abeyance pending the decision in the state supreme court.[39] Finally, a certification statute does not necessarily require a state supreme court to answer a question from a federal court. In circumstances where state high courts already feel overburdened by their own dockets, it is sometimes possible that in the end no answer will be forthcoming. Thus, while certification is used more frequently than abstention, it has been much less than a universal solution to the problem of getting a good answer to a hard question of state law.

The third option available to federal courts is the course followed most frequently. Federal courts simply address the difficult question directly, and try to resolve it themselves with the tools available.[40] To undertake this effort, federal courts look to a variety of sources, including: analogous decisions by the state high court; reported decisions from lower state courts;[41] trends in neighboring states; and even "scholarly treatises, the Restate-

---

[38]*Meredith v. City of Winter Haven*, 320 U.S. 228, 234, 64 S. Ct. 7, 11, 88 L. Ed. 9 (1943) (abstention should be employed only in "exceptional circumstances"). *See also Minot v. Eckardt-Minot*, 13 F.3d 590, 593 (2d Cir. 1994) (in some limited circumstances, abstention may be appropriate basis to remand case previously removed to federal court, but "courts should be wary of using judicially-crafted abstention doctrines to deny out-of-state litigants a federal forum that they prefer").

[39]*See, e.g., West American Ins. Co. v. Bank of Isle of Wight*, 673 F. Supp. 760, 764 (E.D. Va. 1987) (certification imposes on time and resources of both state supreme court and parties).

[40]*See, e.g., First National Bank of Durant v. Trans Terra Corp. International*, 142 F.3d 802, 806–10 (5th Cir. 1998) (duty is to try to ascertain what state supreme court would do; choosing approach of more recent intermediate court over older cases). *But cf., David v. Tanksley*, 218 F.3d 928, 930 (8th Cir. 2000) ("[O]ur duty is to 'ascertain and apply' Arkansas law, 'not to formulate the legal mind of the state.' "). *See also Blankenship v. USA Truck, Inc.*, 601 F.3d 852, 860 (8th Cir. 2010) ("The district court ran afoul of *Erie* when, instead of grappling with Arkansas Supreme Court precedent, the district court relied on 'presuasive' cases from other jurisdictions.").

[41]*See, e.g., Leonard v. Dorsey & Whitney LLP*, 553 F.3d 609, 618 (8th Cir. 2009) ("If the state's highest court

ment of Law, and germane law review articles."[42] This approach has the greatest potential for producing analyses of state law that are later established to be incorrect.[43] At the same time, it provides the best answer a federal court can achieve without forcing the parties into the delay and expense that may attend abstention or certification.

VI. THE JOB IS NOT DONE

As difficult as it may be to follow the evolution of the *Erie* doctrine on these pages, the reader should understand that *Erie* and some related issues have still other ramifications. Many of these questions are outside the scope of the current discussion, but their importance in cases where they arise cannot be overstated. Consider, for example, the following two issues.

A. Using the Law the State Court Would Use.

The heart of *Erie* is a rule directing federal district courts to apply the substantive law that a state court would use. In *Erie* itself, application of that rule meant that a federal district court sitting in New York would apply the same substantive law that a New York state trial court would use.

That application may seem straightforward enough, but it contains a subtle distinction. *Erie* does not direct a federal district court sitting in New York to use New York substantive law in every single case controlled by *Erie*. Instead, it directs the federal district court to defer to the state courts in two different ways: first, to use the same substantive law that the state court would use; and second, to use the same system for determining which state's substantive law the state court would actually apply. The second point is complicated, but can be seen more clearly using *Erie* itself as an example.

The injury to Tompkins that gave rise to the *Erie* case occurred in Pennsylvania. The lawsuit was heard in a federal district court in New York. If the case had been heard in a state court in New York, the state court would have had to decide whether to use

---

has not clearly spoken, we may rely on the decision of intermediate state courts, unless we are convinced by persuasive data that the highest state court would decide the issue differently."); *State Farm Mut. Auto. Ins. Co. v. Pate*, 275 F.3d 666, 669 (7th Cir. 2001) ("When the state Supreme Court has not decided the issue, the rulings of the state intermediate appellate courts must be accorded great weight, unless there are persuasive indications that the state's highest court would decide the case differently.").

[42]*McKenna v. Ortho Pharmaceutical Corp.*, 622 F.2d 657, 662 (3d Cir.

1980).

[43]*See, e.g., Bogy v. Ford Motor Co.*, 538 F.3d 352, 355 (5th Cir. 2008) (when state law is unclear, federal court "must make an *Erie* guess"). *See also Ticknor v. Choice Hotels International, Inc.*, 265 F.3d 931, 939 (9th Cir. 2001) (courts should "approximate state law as closely as possible in order to make sure that the vindication of the state right is without discrimination because of the federal forum").

New York substantive law (the law of the state where the case was heard), Pennsylvania substantive law (the law of the state where the incident took place), or the substantive law of some other state. On the facts of *Erie*, it was clear at the time the case was heard that a New York state court would have applied the substantive law of Pennsylvania on the ground that the accident giving rise to the suit occurred in Pennsylvania.[44] Because a New York court would have used Pennsylvania law, the duty of the federal district court in New York under the *Erie* doctrine—to apply the same law that a state court would use—was also to use Pennsylvania law.

An entire body of law (called either "conflict of laws" or "choice of law") is devoted to determining when a state trial court should use its own law or the law of another state. While the study of conflict of laws is not immediately within the scope of *Erie*, it is probably apparent how important conflict of laws can be for cases to which the *Erie* doctrine applies.

B. A Residue of Federal Common Law.

Although *Erie* abolished federal general common law, another form of federal common law continues to exist on the margin of *Erie*. The Supreme Court has held that such common law may apply to cases nominally involving state law, but in which the United States has such a strong interest in a uniform body of law applied across the country that *Erie* must defer to other considerations. It should be emphasized that the federal common law at issue is not the kind of federal general common law that the older rule of *Swift v. Tyson* imposed on most state causes of action in federal courts.[45] At the same time, this surviving body of federal common law can be substantive law, notwithstanding *Erie*. For example, in *Clearfield Trust Co. v. United States*,[46] the Supreme Court concluded that federal law controlled whether the federal government was liable to an innocent party that had cashed a stolen federal payroll check. The need for uniform treatment of federal checks throughout the country was held to require

---

[44]This point was so thoroughly settled at the time of *Erie* that the discussion of applicable law centered solely on whether federal general common law or Pennsylvania law controlled the case. There was, in short, no suggestion that a federal district court in New York would apply New York substantive law to the facts of *Erie*. That same result might not be quite as clear today, but it was eminently clear when *Erie* was decided.

[45]*Cf., American Electric Power Co. v. Connecticut*, ___ U.S. ___, 131 S.

Ct. 2527, 2535, 180 L. Ed. 2d 435 2d (2011) (more recent, "keener" understanding of *Erie* recognizes limited existence of federal common law where Congress has directed or where "basic scheme of the Constitution so demands;" Holding that environmental protection falls within Congressional legislative reach, and courts may fill in statutory interstices).

[46]*Clearfield Trust Co. v. U.S.*, 318 U.S. 363, 63 S. Ct. 573, 87 L. Ed. 838 (1943).

the application of federal common law on this substantive issue.[47]

The number of circumstances in which federal common law may, notwithstanding *Erie*, displace state substantive law is uncertain but probably quite limited.[48] In any event, the question arises only infrequently, and is therefore not central to an understanding of the problems raised more frequently by *Erie*. However, in the occasional case where precedent like *Clearfield Trust* may displace *Erie*, an awareness of the continuing vitality of this pocket of surviving federal common law can be crucial.

VII. SUMMARY

The following summary addresses the central points of *Erie*. If a reader appreciates the reasoning underlying these summary points, the reader will probably have a working understanding of this challenging doctrine.

    A. *Erie* resolved that federal courts hearing most state causes of action will apply state substantive law.[49]

    B. *Erie* impact on the possible application of federal procedure is more complicated. It is clear that *Guaranty Trust* was an important starting point for this matter, but over time more sophisticated approaches have developed. In particular, determining whether federal or state procedure applies depends heavily on the source from which federal procedure emanates.[50]

        1. If the source of federal procedure is federal case law, *Byrd v. Blue Ridge Rural Electric Co-op., Inc.* provides the analytical framework. *Byrd* requires identification and weighing of the purpose behind the state's procedure, the purpose behind federal procedure, and the prospect that application of federal procedure might

---

[47]*Clearfield Trust Co. v. United States*, 318 U.S. 363, 365, 63 S. Ct. 573, 87 L. Ed. 838 (1943). *But see American Electric Power Co. v. Connecticut*, ___ U.S. ___, ___ S. Ct. ___, 180 L. Ed. 2d 435 (2011) (acknowledging cases like *Clearfield*, but holding that where Congress actually displaced federal common law, *e.g.*, where environmental legislation has been enacted to authorize containment of carbon dioxide emissions, federal common law is no longer applicable; result holds even if regulatory agency (EPA) has not yet created statutorily authorized regulations).

[48]*See, e.g., Empire Healthchoice Assur., Inc. v. McVeigh*, 547 U.S. 677, 126 S. Ct. 2121, 2131–32, 165 L. Ed. 2d 131 (2006) (acknowledging *Clearfield* as "a pathmarking precedent on the authority of federal courts to fashion uniform federal common law on issues of national concern," but noting

that such common law is still unusual); *Boyle v. United Technologies Corp.*, 487 U.S. 500, 507, 108 S. Ct. 2510, 2515, 101 L. Ed. 2d 442 (1988) (noting that presence of "an area of uniquely federal interest . . . establishes a necessary, not a sufficient, condition for the displacement of state law"); *Bank of America Nat. Trust & Sav. Ass'n v. Parnell*, 352 U.S. 29, 77 S. Ct. 119, 1 L. Ed. 2d 93 (1956) (applying state law to determine who had burden of proof on issue of defendants' good faith; refusing to extend rule of *Clearfield Trust*).

[49]*C.I.R. v. Bosch's Estate*, 387 U.S. 456, 465, 87 S. Ct. 1776, 1782, 18 L. Ed. 2d 886, 893–94 (1967) ("[S]tate law as announced by the highest court of the State is to be followed.").

[50]The source of state procedure, it should be noted, is not relevant.

encourage litigants to shop for the federal forum in order to obtain a more favorable outcome.

2. If the source of federal procedure is one of the Federal Rules of Civil Procedure, or another rule promulgated under the Rules Enabling Act (or a case construing such a rule), *Hanna v. Plumer* provides the framework. First, it will be important to determine if the rule at issue is a lawful rule of procedure within the scope of the Rules Enabling Act. Second, if the rule is legitimately procedural, it will be necessary to determine if the rule conflicts with otherwise applicable state procedure, or if it is possible to harmonize the rule with state procedure. If federal and state procedure conflict, federal law will apply. However, there remains the question as to whether the federal law actually conflicts with state procedure. Additionally, there is uncertainty as to whether federal procedure will apply if a litigant chose the federal court in order to obtain a more favorable outcome in the case through application of the federal rule.

3. If the source of federal procedure is Title 28 of the United States Code, *Stewart Organization, Inc. v. Ricoh Corp.* directs the application of federal procedure if: (1) the federal statute is on point, and; (2) is a Constitutional exercise of power by Congress.

C. If the federal district court decides that it should apply state law (whether substantive or procedural), but the state law to be applied is uncertain, the court may have three options to consider: (1) abstain from deciding the issue; (2) certify the question to the state supreme court, if a certification statute is available; or (3) attempt, from available sources, to predict how the state supreme court would have decided the matter.

B. RES JUDICATA AND COLLATERAL ESTOPPEL

§ 2.19 Introduction

Generally

Res judicata and collateral estoppel are related doctrines that address the consequences of an entry of judgment in one lawsuit on subsequent cases that are related to the original case.[1] Subject to some important exceptions, these judicial doctrines establish

---

[1]Importantly, it is the second court — not the court that first heard the case and entered a judgment — that will decide the applicability of the first judgment to other cases. *See Phillips Petroleum Co. v. Shutts*, 472 U.S. 797, 805, 105 S. Ct. 2965, 86 L. Ed. 2d 628 (1985) ("[A] court adjudicating a dispute may not be able to predetermine the res judicata effect of its own judgment.").

the rule that once a case has reached a final judgment, many claims or issues related to that case should be treated as finally decided, once and for all. Thus, if res judicata applies to a case, a plaintiff who lost a lawsuit will often be precluded from raising claims which were raised (or perhaps, which could have been raised) in that lawsuit. In a roughly analogous way, collateral estoppel provides that once an issue has been decided in litigation, that issue may be treated as decided—without further proof—in any subsequent litigation in which the issue is relevant.

The policies behind these related doctrines are judicial economy and finality in litigation. At the same time, when these doctrines are potentially applicable to a case they can create the possibility of substantial risk or opportunity for opposing parties. For example, under the doctrine of res judicata, a plaintiff who has several related claims against the same defendant may often find it necessary to raise both claims in the same litigation, or risk foregoing any claims that are not asserted.

Case Law Doctrine

Res judicata and collateral estoppel owe their existence almost entirely to development in the courts.[2] Legislative influence on these doctrines is limited, and constitutional considerations arise only in circumstances where res judicata or collateral estoppel might have the potential to limit the due process right of an interested party to a fair hearing. Thus, if res judicata was applied to preclude a claim by a party that had not yet had a fair opportunity to be heard in court, it is possible that res judicata would run afoul of due process and the claim would have to be heard.[3] The due process limitation on these doctrines is therefore important. However, as is discussed below, due process can sometimes be satisfied even in circumstances where an interested person was not, literally, a party to a case.

Because res judicata and collateral estoppel are not constitutional in nature, the influence of the Supreme Court on these doctrines is somewhat limited. The Court can and does establish the standards for these two doctrines when they are used in federal courts, but the states are free to accept or reject federal views of these doctrines. Supreme Court cases may therefore be an important source of influence on the application of res judicata or collateral estoppel in state courts, but such decisions are not

---

[2]*Taylor v. Sturgell*, 128 S. Ct. 2161, 171 L. Ed. 2d 155 (U.S. 2008) ("The preclusive effect of a federal-court judgment is determined by federal common law.").

[3]*See, e.g., South Central Bell Telephone Co. v. Alabama*, 526 U.S. 160, 168, 119 S. Ct. 1180, 1185, 143 L. Ed. 2d 258 (1999) (due process prevents application of res judicata to bar litigation by parties who did not participate in prior action, either personally, through concept of privity, or through membership in a class).

necessarily the final word.[4]

Basic Terminology

Two basic areas of terminology can produce some confusion in application of these doctrines, but the confusion can be clarified without difficulty. The first source of confusion arises from the fact that some older cases apply the term "res judicata" indiscriminately to circumstances involving either res judicata or collateral estoppel. The doctrines certainly share some common attributes, but they are also different enough to deserve the distinctive names that have come to be applied to them. Thus, when using an older case that describes what appears to be an application of collateral estoppel as "res judicata," a reader should simply be cautioned to remember the now generally discarded habit of using "res judicata" as an umbrella term covering both doctrines.[5]

The second source of confusion may arise from more recent efforts to replace the terms "res judicata" and "collateral estoppel" with labels that are more descriptive of what the underlying doctrines try to do. Thus, "res judicata" is sometimes described as "claim preclusion," and "collateral estoppel" may be called "issue preclusion."[6] Reception of these newer terms has been mixed over the past generation or so of judicial decisions,[7] but enough cases use the terms so that a reader must be familiar with them. However, for purposes of reducing confusion in this section, the terms "res judicata" and "collateral estoppel" will be used exclusively.

These two areas are not the only sources of difficulty with terms that attach to the two doctrines. Case law developments in collateral estoppel, especially, have produced a few terms that will be discussed in greater detail below.

---

[4]Because state courts often develop their own case law in this area, federal courts hearing diversity claims must sometimes determine whether to apply state procedure or federal procedure. In other words, federal courts must make an analysis under the rule of *Erie v. Tompkins*, discussed in § 2.18. As a general rule, federal courts have concluded that where state and federal views of res judicata differ, state views should be applied in a diversity case. See, e.g., *Xantech Corp. v. Ramco Industries, Inc.*, 159 F.3d 1089, 1092 (7th Cir. 1998) ("[W]e look to the law of Indiana in this diversity action to determine whether the claims that [the plaintiff] makes in this suit are barred on res judicata grounds.").

[5]*Migra v. Warren City School Dist. Bd. of Educ.*, 465 U.S. 75, 77 n. 1, 104 S. Ct. 892, 79 L. Ed. 2d 56 (1984) (noting older practice of using res judicata as term describing both res judicata and collateral estoppel; also noting Court's more recent tendency to apply label of res judicata only to matters of claim preclusion).

[6]*See, e.g., Yeager v. U.S.*, ___ U.S. ___, 129 S. Ct. 2360, 2367 n. 4, 174 L. Ed. 2d 78 (2009) ("Currently, the more descriptive term 'issue preclusion' is often used in lieu of 'collateral estoppel.'").

[7]*Kircher v. Putnam Funds Trust*, 547 U.S. 633 n. 14, 126 S. Ct. 2145, 2157, 165 L. Ed. 2d 92 (2006) ("Modern usage calls for the descriptive term, 'issue preclusion,' in place of 'collateral estoppel.' But we are backsliders out of pity for the tired reader; 'preclusion' by statutory fiat is enough preclusion for one opinion.").

§ 2.20 Res Judicata—Elements

Elements

Before a court will apply res judicata to a claim, ordinarily three elements must be satisfied. First, there must have been prior litigation in which "identical" claims were raised, or at least could have been raised. Second, the parties in the second litigation must be "identical" in some manner to the parties in the original litigation. Third, there must have been a final judgment on the merits in the original litigation.[1]

As may already be obvious, these three seemingly straightforward requirements contain within them some important ambiguities, which will be examined in turn. Immediately before doing so, however, it would be useful to keep in mind an underlying feature of res judicata that is also a useful means of spotting potential res judicata issues. Res judicata may potentially apply to a case only in circumstances where that case bears some relationship to a prior lawsuit that has already been decided. In the absence of previous litigation, a court in a pending case would have no prior decision to which to refer. Thus, while the existence of prior litigation does not necessarily establish the existence of res judicata questions, the absence of prior litigation means there is no possibility of res judicata problems in a pending case.

"Identical Claims"; Same Transaction or Occurrence

If the claims at issue in pending litigation bear no relationship to claims that were raised in prior litigation, the instant claims will not be barred by res judicata. For example, if a plaintiff now suing a defendant on a contract claim that arose six weeks ago had previously brought a lawsuit against the same defendant for an utterly unrelated claim that occurred a decade before the breach claim arose, the claims in the two cases would not be identical and res judicata would not be applied. However, if a plaintiff had two claims against a defendant arising out of the same event—and had previously sued on one claim, but not the other—there is a substantial possibility that the requirement for identical claims would be satisfied. Thus, if the defendant was a state police officer who allegedly beat and injured a citizen for motives arising from religious bias, the plaintiff might have at least two civil causes of actions against the police officer, such as: (1) a federal civil rights claim under 42 U.S.C.A. § 1983 (deprivation of a federal civil right by a person acting under color of state law); and (2) a state law claim of battery. If we assume that the plaintiff sued on the state battery claim in previous litigation, and then tried to sue on the federal claim in the pending litigation, it is likely that the requirement of "identical" claims between the two lawsuits would be satisfied.

---

[1]*Cromwell v. Sac County*, 94 U.S. 351, 24 L. Ed. 195 (1876).

It is important to note that the claims need not be literally identical to satisfy this requirement for res judicata. In the example above, the federal claim shares much in common with the state claim that was previously litigated, but to prevail on the merits of the federal claim the plaintiff would have to demonstrate additional evidence not necessary to win on the state lawsuit. For the state battery claim, the plaintiff would have to demonstrate only the elements of the common law tort of battery. However, for the federal cause of action, the plaintiff would also have to demonstrate that the defendant was acting under color of state law (*i.e.*, a police officer) and that there was some intent to violate the plaintiff's federal civil rights (religious discrimination). These elements would be additional to the requirements for common law battery, and in a particular case they might require proof that the plaintiff does not possess. In that sense, the two claims in the example are not literally "identical," because they rest on distinct theories of recovery.

Courts once struggled to develop rules to determine when two claims share enough in common to satisfy the requirement that the claims are "identical" for purposes of res judicata. However, many years ago most courts abandoned the notion that claims based on the same facts, but different theories of recovery, were insufficiently "identical" to satisfy this requirement. Today, most courts have accepted the proposition that two claims are "identical" if their "underlying facts are 'related in time, space, origin, or motivation, whether they form a convenient trial unit, and whether their treatment as a unit conforms to the parties' expectations or business understanding or usage.' "[2] Put another way, the claim in the second suit is sufficiently "identical" to the claim that was or could have been litigated in the first suit if both claims share a common "nucleus of operative fact."[3] This language shares much in common with judicial commentary about the requirement in supplemental jurisdiction, 28 U.S.C.A. § 1367(a), for the "same case or controversy."[4] It is also related to the idea in Federal Rule of Civil Procedure 13(a) that counterclaims may be compulsory if they arise out of the same "transac-

---

[2]*Interoceanica Corp. v. Sound Pilots, Inc.*, 107 F.3d 86, 90 (2d Cir. 1997) (quoting Restatement (Second) of Judgments § 24(b) (1982)).

[3]*Apparel Art Intern., Inc. v. Amertex Enterprises Ltd.*, 48 F.3d 576, 583 (1st Cir. 1995) ("Under this approach, a cause of action is defined as a set of facts which can be characterized as a single transaction or a series of related transactions."). *See also, e.g., Lane v. Peterson*, 899 F.2d 737, 742

(8th Cir. 1990) (standard for measuring same cause of action is whether both claims derive from "same nucleus of operative facts").

[4]*See, e.g., United Mine Workers of America v. Gibbs*, 383 U.S. 715, 86 S. Ct. 1130, 16 L. Ed. 2d 218 (1966) (developing the concept of "common nucleus of operative fact" in the context of judicial predecessor of supplemental jurisdiction).

tion or occurrence" as the opposing party's claim.[5]

Applying this transactional test to the claims in the case involving the alleged beating inflicted by the police officer, most courts would almost certainly conclude that the state battery claims and the federal civil rights claim share enough common features to satisfy this requirement of "identical" claims for res judicata. The primary reason courts would likely reach that conclusion is that the two claims, though based on somewhat differing legal theories, arose from the same occurrence, at the same time, and would require substantially overlapping items of proof.[6]

At the same time, the transactional test for "identical" claims should not be pushed too far. If the transactions or events at issue took place at significantly different points in time, claims arising from those different times will generally not be treated as "identical."[7] Thus, in a circumstance where ship pilots had sued to recover fees owed by a shipping company under a state statute, the judgment in that case would not preclude subsequent claims for fees arising from voyages that had not yet taken place at the time of the first litigation.[8]

"Identical" Parties; Privity

The second requirement for res judicata is that the parties in the second action must be identical to the parties in the first action, or in privity with parties in the first action. Thus, if two pedestrians walking along a sidewalk were injured by a motorist whose automobile went out of control and struck them, the outcome of a suit involving only the first pedestrian as a plaintiff would not be a bar to a second and independent suit by the second pedestrian. Even though the claims of both pedestrians arose from the same occurrence, the obvious difference between the parties would preclude application of res judicata.

For purposes of this second requirement for res judicata, par-

---

[5]Fed.R.Civ.P. 13(a). *See also, e.g.*, Fed.R.Civ.P. 15(c)(2) (permitting relation back of amended pleading if, inter alia, "the claim or defense asserted in the amended pleading arose out of the conduct, transaction, or occurrence set forth or attempted to be set forth in the original pleading"); Fed.R.Civ.P. 20(a) (permitting joinder of parties as plaintiffs if, inter alia, their claims arise from "the same transaction, occurrence, or series of transactions or occurrences").

[6]*See, e.g., N.L.R.B. v. United Technologies Corp.*, 706 F.2d 1254, 1260 (2d Cir. 1983) (for res judicata, test is whether "same evidence is needed to support both claims, and [whether] the facts essential to the

second were present in the first").

[7]*See, e.g., S.E.C. v. First Jersey Securities, Inc.*, 101 F.3d 1450, 1464 (2d Cir. 1996) ("If the second litigation involved different transactions, and especially subsequent transactions, there generally is no claim preclusion;" presence of same parties or even overlapping facts need not be dispositive to prove "identical" claims).

[8]*See, e.g., Interoceanica Corp. v. Sound Pilots, Inc.*, 107 F.3d 86, 91 (2d Cir. 1997) ("While the subsequent voyages represent wrongs that are the 'same' in legal theory, they are not related in time, space, or origin to the wrongs litigated [earlier].").

ties who are literally the same persons or business entities are clearly "identical." The question that may arise, however, is whether persons who are different but who share a common interest may be treated as "identical." The issue raised here is a concept of privity of interest between two distinct individuals or business entities.

In general, there are several circumstances in which someone not literally a party to the first action may nevertheless be treated as in privity with a person or entity that was a party: (1) where the nonparty succeeded to the interest of a party, for example, by purchasing whatever interest the party may have had after completion of the first litigation; (2) where the nonparty, though technically not participating in the first suit, nevertheless controlled one party's litigation in that suit—where, for example, the nonparty is an insurance company for a party; (3) where the nonparty shares a property interest with the party;[9] (4) where the party and nonparty have an agent-principal relationship; (5) where the party otherwise "adequately represented" the interest of the nonparty[10]; or (6) where a person agrees to be bound by the outcome of a case.[11]

These categories may superficially appear straightforward. However, it appears that privity is applied only after careful scrutiny of the nuances of particular cases, and perhaps not always with consistency. For example, where one entity holds a twenty percent interest in another entity's lawsuit, the two interests were deemed "completely identical" with one another and the entities were held to be in privity.[12] However, defendants sued individually may not be in privity with their employers.[13] A general rule is that while privity may in some circumstances substitute adequately for the requirement that the parties in both lawsuits be identical, there should be no assumption that a court will support an assertion of privity without a careful examination of the facts underlying the assertion.

It should be noted that in this requirement of identical parties

---

[9]See, e.g., Hart v. Yamaha-Parts Distributors, Inc., 787 F.2d 1468, 1472 (11th Cir. 1986) (citing these examples). See also, e.g., Nero v. Ferris, 222 Va. 807, 813, 284 S.E.2d 828, 831 (1981) ("[P]rivity generally involves a party so identical in interest with another that he represents the same legal right [but making this determination requires] a careful examination into the circumstances of each case.").

[10]Howell Hydrocarbons, Inc. v. Adams, 897 F.2d 183, 188 (5th Cir. 1990).

[11]Taylor v. Sturgell, 128 S. Ct. 2161, 171 L. Ed. 2d 155 (U.S. 2008).

[12]Virginia Sur. Co. v. Northrop Grumman Corp., 144 F.3d 1243, 1247 (9th Cir. 1998).

[13]See, e.g., Willner v. Budig, 848 F.2d 1032, 1034 (10th Cir. 1988) ("Res judicata does not bar [plaintiff's] claims against the defendants in their individual capacities because the defendants are not in privity with the University."); Headley v. Bacon, 828 F.2d 1272, 1277–79 (8th Cir. 1987) (distinguishing privity between principal and agent from privity between a governmental entity and officials sued in their individual capacities).

(or privity), the doctrine of res judicata differs in an important respect from case law addressing the doctrine of collateral estoppel. As is discussed later in this analysis, courts do not invariably require that the parties be identical before applying collateral estoppel to issues in a case. However, this distinction comes with several important qualifications, which are addressed under the discussion of collateral estoppel.

Final Judgment "On the Merits"

The third and final prerequisite for application of res judicata is the requirement that the first litigation has proceeded to a final judgment on the merits of the case. When considering application of this prerequisite there are two points to keep in mind. First, not all judicial decisions are "final." Second, not all final judgments are based on the merits of the case.

It is generally well settled that when a trial judge enters judgment, so that the parties are now in a position to enforce or appeal the judgment, finality has been achieved and this element of res judicata has been satisfied.[14] By contrast, one obvious example of litigation that does not constitute a final judgment arises when the parties settle their case. A settlement that does not involve action by the court does not constitute a judgment. The result may be different, however, if the parties seek to have their settlement entered by the court as a judgment or decree. Such action may convert a settlement into a final judgment, which therefore may qualify as res judicata for subsequent litigation.[15]

Res judicata also may not apply to situations in which a judge makes an important decision which is, nevertheless, less than a final judgment. For example, in a case in which plaintiffs seek certification of their lawsuit as a class action, denial of such certification may not necessarily be a final judgment, even though the reality of the situation is that denial of class status is often a punishing blow to the parties seeking certification.[16]

For res judicata to apply, a judgment must also be on the merits of a case. Litigation that goes through to a jury verdict obviously

---

[14]*Clay v. U.S.*, 537 U.S. 522, 526, 123 S. Ct. 1072, 1076, 155 L. Ed. 2d 88 (2003) ("[A] federal judgment becomes final for appellate review and claim preclusion purposes when the district court disassociates itself from the case, leaving nothing to be done at the court of first instance save execution of the judgment.").

[15]*See, e.g., Richardson v. Alabama State Bd. of Educ.*, 935 F.2d 1240, 1244 (11th Cir. 1991) ("We specifically have held that res judicata applies to Title VII consent decrees."). *But cf. Keith v. Aldridge*, 900 F.2d 736, 740 (4th Cir. 1990) (where parties consent to resolution of one portion of a case but expressly reserve right to continue litigating other claims, res judicata will not block continuation of unresolved litigation).

[16]*See, e.g., In re General Motors Corp. Pick-Up Truck Fuel Tank Products Liability Litigation*, 134 F.3d 133, 146 (3d Cir. 1998) ("Denial of class certification is not a 'judgment' for the purposes of the Anti-Injunction Act while the underlying litigation remains pending.").

meets this requirement. However, the applicability of res judicata to litigation terminated under, for example, a subsection of Federal Rule of Civil Procedure 12(b) may depend on both the particular subsection employed as well as the facts of a particular case. In general, cases dismissed for failure to state a claim for which relief may be granted—e.g., Rule 12(b)(6)—are judgments on the merits for purposes of res judicata.[17] By contrast, cases dismissed on jurisdictional grounds, such as Rule 12(b)(1) (lack of subject matter jurisdiction) have res judicata effect only to the extent that the jurisdictional issue is foreclosed. If the claimant subsequently files a second suit alleging a different theory of recovery, or files in a different, appropriate forum, the original dismissal will normally not block the second suit because the jurisdictional dismissal was not on the merits of the case.[18]

There are even situations where a final judgment on the merits may not have res judicata effect because application of res judicata would conflict with some other, even more important, legal principle. For example, if a district court heard a case involving legal and equitable claims with common facts, and erroneously dismissed all the legal claims, entry of a final ruling on the equitable claims might have no res judicata effect. Instead, if the equitable ruling rested on findings of facts that were common to both legal and equitable claims, the equitable ruling would be vacated, because the parties have a right under the Seventh Amendment[19] to the Constitution to a jury determination of facts relating to legal claims.[20] At the same time, however, it should be noted that this analysis applies to a relatively uncommon situation, and most equitable decisions are entitled to res judicata effect even if later changes in facts might otherwise permit the district court to modify its own equitable decree.

§ 2.21 Res Judicata—Scope

When it is applicable to a case, res judicata bars re-litigation of claims which have previously been litigated—or which could have been litigated in a prior lawsuit. This scope of res judicata differs significantly from the requirement for collateral estoppel, because

---

[17]*Federated Dept. Stores, Inc. v. Moitie*, 452 U.S. 394, 399 n. 3, 101 S. Ct. 2424, 69 L. Ed. 2d 103 (1981) (dismissal under Rule 12(b)(6) is final judgment for purposes of res judicata). *Cf., New Haven Inclusion Cases*, 399 U.S. 392, 481, 90 S. Ct. 2054, 2104, 26 L. Ed. 2d 691 (1970) (failure to appeal adverse decision makes that decision a matter of res judicata).

[18]*Semtek Intern. Inc. v. Lockheed Martin Corp.*, 531 U.S. 497, 121 S. Ct. 1021, 149 L. Ed. 2d 32 (2001) (judgment "on the merits" does not always

trigger application of claim preclusion in subsequent lawsuit). *See, e.g., Costner v. URS Consultants, Inc.*, 153 F.3d 667, 673 (8th Cir. 1998) (distinguishing between application of res judicata for jurisdictional issue in first case and inapplicability of res judicata to different theory of recovery, even where second suit arises from same facts as first claim).

[19]U.S. Const. Amend VII.

[20]*Lytle v. Household Mfg., Inc.*, 494 U.S. 545, 555–56, 110 S. Ct. 1331, 108 L. Ed. 2d 504 (1990).

collateral estoppel applies only to claims which were actually litigated—not claims that could have been litigated but were not.

When applied to claims that were not actually raised, but which could have been raised, the scope of res judicata is rather broad. Thus, where a police officer allegedly attacked and beat a citizen in circumstances that give rise to both a state battery claim and a federal civil rights claim, a plaintiff's decision to sue only on the state claim may preclude assertion of the federal claim at a later date. Provided that the federal claim and the state claim could have been raised concurrently in the court in which the plaintiff filed and provided that the other elements of res judicata are satisfied, the claim not raised would be barred because it could have been raised.[1] This corollary of res judicata should strongly encourage attorneys to consider carefully all their potential theories of recovery in the first litigation.

By contrast, if a claim could not have been raised in the first lawsuit, assertion of that claim in later litigation is not barred by res judicata. Thus, if the first court lacked jurisdiction to hear a particular kind of claim, that claim may be asserted later in a court of competent jurisdiction.[2] This circumstance may most commonly arise when a plaintiff has both a state cause of action and a federal claim which is within the exclusive subject matter jurisdiction of a federal court. If the plaintiff files first in a state court, the outcome of that case will not serve as a bar, under res judicata, to a subsequent filing on the federal claim in a federal court. However, if the plaintiff filed first in a federal district court which had jurisdiction (either diversity or supplemental jurisdiction) over the state claim, failure to file both claims at once would probably create a situation in which the unasserted claim will be barred in later litigation.

§ 2.22 Res Judicata—Counterclaims: Rule 13(a)

In the federal system, res judicata is not generally applied to potential counterclaims by defendants. Thus, when a defendant does not assert counterclaims, res judicata does not bar their assertion in subsequent litigation. However, the fact that the case law doctrine of res judicata is generally inapplicable to potential counterclaims in federal court does not mean defendants are free to raise or withhold all of their counterclaims. Instead, Federal Rule of Civil Procedure 13(a) provides that counterclaims deemed

---

[1]*Cromwell v. Sac County*, 94 U.S. 351, 24 L. Ed. 195 (1876) (when applicable, res judicata bars claims actually raised and which might have been raised).

[2]*Marrese v. American Academy of Orthopaedic Surgeons*, 470 U.S. 373, 382, 105 S. Ct. 1327, 1333, 84 L. Ed. 2d 274 (1985) ("With respect to matters that were not decided in the state proceedings . . . claim preclusion generally does not apply where 'the plaintiff was unable to . . . seek a remedy because of the limitations on the subject matter jurisdiction of the courts.'").

"compulsory" must be asserted.[1] Failure to do so usually results in judicial refusal to hear the claim in subsequent litigation.[2]

Some state court systems have no compulsory counterclaim rule comparable to Rule 13(a). In such states, the use of res judicata to bar a claim that was not raised as a counterclaim in prior litigation may vary significantly from the federal practice.

§ 2.23 Res Judicata—Affirmative Defense: Rule 8(c)

In the federal system, res judicata is specifically listed within Federal Rule of Civil Procedure 8(c) as an affirmative defense.[1] That means a defendant seeking to use res judicata to preclude a plaintiff's claim must affirmatively raise the defense. Subject to some important exceptions, failure to raise the defense means that it is waived.[2]

§ 2.24 Res Judicata—Relationship to Full Faith and Credit

Full faith and credit is a constitutional provision[1] controlling the circumstances when courts of one state must enforce the judicial decisions of another state. This constitutional provision relies on res judicata in the following manner. If the res judicata doctrine of the state in which a judgment was rendered would require other courts in that same state to treat the judgment as final and preclusive, full faith and credit will generally require the courts of other states to give the same effect to the judgement as would be given in the state that rendered the judgment. Analogous rules usually require federal courts to give similar deference to the final judgments of state courts of competent jurisdiction.[2]

§ 2.24a Jurisdiction and Res Judicata

---

[1]*See generally*, Fed.R.Civ.P. 13(a).

[2]*See, e.g., New York Life Ins. Co. v. Deshotel*, 142 F.3d 873, 882 (5th Cir. 1998) ("It is well settled that a failure to plead a compulsory counterclaim bars a party from bringing a later independent action on that claim.").

[1]*Taylor v. Sturgell*, 128 S. Ct. 2161, 171 L. Ed. 2d 155 (U.S. 2008) ("Claim preclusion, like issue preclusion, is an affirmative defense.").

[2]*See, e.g., McKinnon v. Kwong Wah Restaurant*, 83 F.3d 498, 505 (1st Cir. 1996) ("To avoid waiver, a defendant must assert all affirmative defenses in the answer."). *But cf. Jakobsen v. Massachusetts Port Authority*, 520 F.2d 810, 813 (1st Cir. 1975) (no waiver where failure to plead affirmative defense does not unfairly preju-

dice opposing party).

[1]U.S. Const. Art. IV § 1.

[2]*Durfee v. Duke*, 375 U.S. 106, 84 S. Ct. 242, 11 L. Ed. 2d 186 (1963) (where Nebraska had considered, inter alia, jurisdictional issues and would treat the judgment as res judicata, federal district court in Missouri had duty under full faith and credit provisions to give the same effect to judgement as Nebraska would give it). *See also, e.g., Community Bank of Homestead v. Torcise*, 162 F.3d 1084 n. 5 (11th Cir. 1998) ("Under the Full Faith and Credit Act, 28 U.S.C. § 1738 (1994), state court judgments are to be given the same preclusive effect in federal court that they would have in the state in which judgment was rendered.").

In general, when a court erroneously hears a case over which it lacks jurisdiction, a timely and proper challenge to the resulting judgment may render that judgment a nullity.[1] However, res judicata often creates an important exception to that generality. If a judgment has become final, either because no appeal was taken or because appeals have been exhausted, res judicata will normally bar consideration of any later challenge to the judgment, without regard to whether the court that originally heard the case did so erroneously.[2] The circumstances in which res judicata does not prevail over a belated jurisdictional challenge are very narrow.[3]

§ 2.24b Events That Postdate Filing

It appears settled that res judicata is inapplicable to events that arise after a lawsuit has been filed.[1]

§ 2.25 Collateral Estoppel—Elements

As will be explained in greater detail below, the requirements for the application of collateral estoppel (or "issue preclusion")[1] vary more significantly among the jurisdictions than does the application of res judicata. Nevertheless, there are several requirements for collateral estoppel that are applied fairly consistently throughout the United States. First, there must have been a prior litigation in which the identical issue was before the court.[2] Second, the issue must have been actually litigated in the first judicial proceeding.[3] Third, the issue must necessarily have been decided in a case in which a final judgment was entered.[4]

On the surface there is an apparent overlap between the

---

[1]For a more comprehensive discussion of some of the more significant kinds of jurisdictional requirements applicable to federal district courts *see* §§ 2.1 to 2.12 of this text.

[2]*Kontrick v. Ryan*, 540 U.S. 443, 456 n.9, 124 S. Ct. 906, 916, 157 L. Ed. 2d 867 (2007) ("Even subject-matter jurisdiction . . . may not be attacked collaterally.").

[3]*Travelers Indemnity Co. v. Bailey*, ___ U.S. ___, 129 S. Ct. 2195, 2206, 174 L. Ed. 2d 99 (2009) (subject to narrow exceptions judgments are protected from collateral attack by res judicata; collecting some exceptions).

[1]*See, e.g., Morgan v. Covington Township*, ___ F.3d ___, ___ (3d Cir. 2011) (citing five other circuits with same view, and no dissenting circuits).

[1]*See, e.g., Dodd v. Hood River County*, 136 F.3d 1219, 1224 (9th Cir. 1998) (acknowledging that most courts still use "collateral estoppel" as appropriate term, but noting that the Ninth Circuit prefers to use "issue preclusion").

[2]See, e.g., *U.S. v. Shanbaum*, 10 F.3d 305, 311 (5th Cir. 1994) ("[T]he issue under consideration in a subsequent action must be identical to the issue litigated in a prior action.").

[3]*Regions Hosp. v. Shalala*, 522 U.S. 448, 461, 118 S. Ct. 909, 918, 139 L. Ed. 2d 895 (1998) ("Absent actual and adversarial litigation . . . principles of issue preclusion do not hold fast.").

[4]*Cf., Arizona v. California*, 530 U.S. 392, 120 S. Ct. 2304, 147 L. Ed. 2d 374 (2000) ("[S]ettlements ordinarily occasion no issue preclusion . . . unless it is clear . . . that the parties intend their agreement to have such an effect."). See, e.g., *Murdock v. Ute*

requirements for collateral estoppel and the requirements, discussed earlier, for res judicata. However, while there is reason to recognize the two bodies of case law as related, the similarities can easily be overstated, with resulting unfavorable consequences. As is explained immediately below, some of the superficial similarities actually conceal differences between res judicata and collateral estoppel that can affect the outcome of a particular case.

Identical Issues

The standard for determining whether, for purposes of applying collateral estoppel, an issue in a prior lawsuit is the same as an issue in pending litigation is very different from the standard for identical claims in matters of res judicata. As discussed earlier, most courts conclude that two claims are identical for purposes of res judicata if they arise from the same transaction or occurrence. By contrast, in determining whether two issues are identical, most courts require that the issues track each other more closely than that. However, once such a substantial amount of similarity is identified, it is unimportant whether claims in one case bear any significant relationship to claims in another case.[5]

Actually, Vigorously Litigated

The requirement in collateral estoppel for actual litigation of an issue in a prior proceeding differs in at least two important respects from the possibility under res judicata that claims which were not litigated, but which could have been litigated, may be barred in later litigation. First, it is settled that collateral estoppel will not bar litigation of any issue that was not actually raised in a prior proceeding, regardless of whether the issue could have been raised. For example, in a breach of contract suit, it is possible that a defendant would make a tactical decision not to raise questions about whether the contract was unenforceable for a failure of consideration. If the plaintiff sued to enforce another obligation on the contract that only became due after the first suit was resolved, collateral estoppel would not prevent the defendant from raising the consideration simply because it could have been (but was not) raised in the first litigation. An even simpler example would arise if, in the first suit, the defendant chose to default and not enter any defense. The plaintiff would thereby win, but when the second cause of action arose all issues about consideration would still be available for the defendant to raise.[6]

Similarly, for collateral estoppel to apply an issue must have

---

Indian Tribe of Uintah and Ouray Reservation, 975 F.2d 683, 687 (10th Cir. 1992) (to apply collateral estoppel, "the prior action [must have] finally adjudicated on the merits").

[5]*U.S. v. Shanbaum*, 10 F.3d 305,

311 (5th Cir. 1994) ("[U]nder issue preclusion, unlike claim preclusion, the subject matter of the later suit need not have any relationship to the subject matter of the prior suit.").

[6]*Cromwell v. Sac County*, 94 U.S.

been litigated with some vigor. Thus, if an issue was raised in a passing way but did not engage the attention of the litigants significantly, the issue may not be estopped in later litigation because it was not litigated vigorously. To permit collateral estoppel to apply to issues raised in such a casual manner, perhaps because their importance to subsequent litigation was not yet foreseen, would produce unfair surprise for litigants.[7] It might also force needless complexity on the first litigation, as parties jockeyed to ensure that they would not be estopped collaterally in subsequent litigation.

Necessarily Decided on the Merits

This requirement has two parts, and courts sometimes treat them as distinct requirements. However, a decision to do so does not alter the analysis of this standard.

The first part of this requirement is that for collateral estoppel to apply, the issue decided in the first suit must have been decided in a way that is consistent with the judgment in the first suit. Thus, in the contract example used above, assume that the defendant was not found liable in the first suit because the plaintiff was found to have been in breach. If the jury also found that the consideration underlying the contract was good consideration, that finding would, in a literal sense, be unnecessary to the judgment that vindicated the defendant. Thus, if the same contract later gave rise to another cause of action not available at the time of the first lawsuit, the defendant would not be precluded from asserting lack of consideration as a defense. Keep in mind, of course, that permission to relitigate the issue does not mean the defendant will prevail on the consideration issue. Refusal to apply collateral estoppel does not, of itself, guarantee victory for anyone. Instead, it only provides that the issue will be fought over again.

Similarly, if a jury finds for a plaintiff without explaining which of two distinct grounds (or both) is the basis for the verdict, a defendant retains the right to challenge those same grounds if they arise as issues in subsequent litigation.[8] Conversely, if a jury expressly finds for a plaintiff on two distinct grounds, both of

---

351, 24 L. Ed. 195 (1876) (default judgments not eligible for collateral estoppel).

[7]Id. at 356 ("Various considerations, other than the actual merits, may govern a party in bringing forward grounds of recovery or defence in one action, which may not exist in another action upon a different demand, such as the smallness of the amount or the value of the property in controversy, the difficulty of obtaining the necessary evidence, the expense of the litigation, and his own situation at the time."). *But cf. Community Bank of Homestead v. Torcise*, 162 F.3d 1084 (11th Cir.1998) (observing that this requirement does not examine the quality or quantity of evidence or argument presented, only that fair opportunity to present the issue arose in a context where party understood potential adverse consequences).

[8]*Cf., e.g., Matter of Caton*, 157 F.3d 1026, 1029 (5th Cir. 1998) ("We only require that the record introduced

which were vigorously litigated and which were decided in the plaintiff's favor, both may be treated as eligible for collateral estoppel in subsequent lawsuits.[9]

The second part of this requirement is that collateral estoppel applies only to issues resolved in cases decided on the merits.[10] Often, this will mean that cases which were dismissed on, for example, jurisdictional grounds will not develop issues in ways that qualify for collateral estoppel in subsequent cases. However, if the issues for which collateral estoppel treatment is sought are the procedural issues on which the original case was actually decided, then the requirement that the prior judgment "on the merits" is satisfied, at least for the procedural issues.[11]

§ 2.26 Collateral Estoppel—Mutuality v. Nonmutual Estoppel

As discussed previously under the law of res judicata, there is a requirement that the parties in the second suit must be identical to (or in privity with) parties in the first suit before any claims may be precluded. At one time, a similar requirement of identical parties also applied to situations involving collateral estoppel. In the context of collateral estoppel, this requirement has been referred to as the "mutuality requirement,"[1] meaning that estoppel could not apply unless it applied mutually to all parties in a lawsuit. However, that requirement has experienced substantial erosion over the past half century. Today most jurisdictions (but not all)[2] have substantially abandoned this requirement.

The replacement for the mutuality requirement—the require-

---

have sufficient detail to allow the use of collateral estoppel.").

[9]But cf., National Satellite Sports, Inc. v. Eliadis, Inc., 253 F.3d 900, 909–10 (6th Cir. 2001) (if prior decision involved resolution of two issues, either of which could have supported prior decision, prior judgment is not conclusive as to either issue standing alone; collecting substantial authority on both sides of question).

[10]See, e.g., Yeager v. U.S., ___ U.S. ___, 129 S. Ct. 2360, 2368, 174 L. Ed. 2d 78 (2009) ("[C]onsideration of hung counts has no place in the issue-preclusion analysis."); Arizona v. California, 530 U.S. 392, 120 S. Ct. 2304, 147 L. Ed. 2d 374 (2000) (noting that while settlement entered by court as judgment can have res judicata effect, such a settlement normally does not have collateral estoppel effect).

[11]See, e.g., Transaero, Inc. v. La Fuerza Aerea Boliviana, 162 F.3d 724,

731 (2d Cir. 1998) ("[T]he service of process and personal jurisdiction issues were necessary to support the D.C. Circuit's final judgment—indeed, these issues were the subject of that judgment.").

[1]See, e.g., Blonder-Tongue Laboratories, Inc. v. University of Illinois Foundation, 402 U.S. 313, 91 S. Ct. 1434, 28 L. Ed. 2d 788 (1971).

[2]See, e.g., State Farm Fire & Cas. Co. v. Mabry, 255 Va. 286, 289, 497 S.E.2d 844, 846 (1998) (imposing requirement that parties in current litigation be identical with parties in prior litigation or in privity with such parties). It should also be noted that collateral estoppel may be invoked against the federal government when the United States is a party to litigation and the elements of collateral estoppel (including requirements of mutuality) are established. U.S. v. Stauffer Chemical Co., 464 U.S. 165, 104 S. Ct. 575, 78 L. Ed. 2d 388 (1984).

ment that parties in the second suit be identical to or in privity with parties in the first suit—is an assessment of fairness that, when satisfied, is ground for permitting application of nonmutual collateral estoppel.

The terminology of this area of the law of collateral estoppel can be awkward and initially difficult to grasp. However, because courts tend to use the terms that have been created for this area, it is essential that they be understood before proceeding any further. First, to repeat, a "mutuality" requirement means merely that a court will not apply collateral estoppel unless the parties in the second action are identical to (or in privity with) the parties in the original case. Second, when a court says it follows an approach of "nonmutuality," the court merely means that it may not always impose a requirement that the parties in the second lawsuit be identical to the parties in the first suit. Thus, subject to the requirements discussed below, an application of "nonmutual" collateral estoppel means that the court found collateral estoppel appropriate even though the parties in both suits were not identical. Third, "defensive" nonmutual collateral estoppel means that the court is being asked to apply collateral estoppel in a circumstance where the defendant in the second lawsuit is trying to use nonmutual collateral estoppel defensively—as a shield—to ward off the plaintiff's attack. Fourth, "offensive" nonmutual collateral estoppel means that the court is being asked to apply collateral estoppel to prevent a defendant from raising an issue that was (allegedly) litigated in a prior lawsuit. Thus, the plaintiff is trying to use nonmutual collateral estoppel as a sword, to strike down a defense raised by a defendant. The distinction between defensive and offensive nonmutual collateral estoppel is important, because it is distinctly possible that the requirements for defensive nonmutual collateral estoppel might be less difficult to meet than the requirements for offensive nonmutual collateral estoppel.

Defensive Nonmutual Collateral Estoppel

Suppose a plaintiff sues a defendant for patent infringement. Suppose further that the essence of the defense is that the patent on which the plaintiff's claim is based is not a valid patent. If the defendant wins the case on that ground, the matter is obviously res judicata between the two parties. But if the plaintiff later files a second lawsuit, against a different defendant, asserting that the same patent was infringed, it is clear that the parties in the second suit are not identical with the parties in the first suit. Additionally, it will often be true that the defendant in the second suit will not be in privity with the defendant in the first suit. In those circumstances, if the mutuality requirement is imposed,

---

However, it is also settled that nonmutual collateral estoppel may not be invoked against the federal govern-

ment. *U.S. v. Mendoza*, 464 U.S. 154, 104 S. Ct. 568, 78 L. Ed. 2d 379 (1984).

the plaintiff will not be estopped from asserting (in the second suit) the validity of the patent that was found to be invalid in the first suit. This is inefficient for the courts, and also creates the possibility that a finding of a valid patent in the second suit will create an unacceptable situation for other parties trying to discern the validity of the patent. Thus, the majority of judicial systems facing such problems now permit a party in the position of the defendant in the second suit to assert the defense of collateral estoppel, provided only that the plaintiff had a full and fair opportunity to litigate the patent validity issue in the first lawsuit.[3]

Offensive Nonmutual Collateral Estoppel

A more problematic use of nonmutual collateral estoppel arises when a party seeks to use the rule as more than a defense to an action. In a well known case decided by the Supreme Court,[4] the defendants had previously been sued by the Securities and Exchange Commission for making false proxy statements. The Commission sought an injunction, and the defendants lost that lawsuit. Subsequently a class of shareholders sued the defendants on the same grounds and sought collateral estoppel for the previous court's finding that the proxy statements had been false and misleading. In contrast to defensive nonmutual collateral estoppel, where collateral estoppel is used as a shield to ward off a subsequent claim by a plaintiff who had lost a prior lawsuit, this case was an attempt to use the defendants' prior loss as a sword with which to produce a second unfavorable result for those defendants.

The Supreme Court concluded that, at least sometimes, nonmutual collateral estoppel could be used offensively as well as defensively. However, for collateral estoppel to be applied offensively, the Court directed lower federal courts to examine all the circumstances of a case to ensure that application of collateral estoppel is fair. Specifically, the Court suggested that lower courts examine: (1) whether the plaintiff seeking offensive nonmutual collateral estoppel could have participated in the previous suit; (2) whether the defendant had a fair chance to litigate the issue with knowledge of the fact that the same issue might arise in subsequent litigation; (3) whether the judgment in the litigation for which collateral estoppel is sought was inconsistent with results in any litigation which had taken place still earlier;[5] and (4) whether, in the previous suit, procedural limitations had prevented the defendant from offering some evidence or

---

[3]*See, e.g., Blonder-Tongue Laboratories, Inc. v. University of Illinois Foundation*, 402 U.S. 313, 91 S. Ct. 1434, 28 L. Ed. 2d 788 (1971).

[4]*Parklane Hosiery Co., Inc. v. Shore*, 439 U.S. 322, 99 S. Ct. 645, 58 L. Ed. 2d 552 (1979).

[5]An example of how this situation could occur arises if one posits a one-car automobile accident in which three passengers in the car are injured. If the first passenger sues the

otherwise defending himself in ways now open in the later litigation.[6]

Nonmutuality and the United States

Although the United States is as vulnerable as any party to the application of collateral estoppel when the requirement of mutuality is satisfied, it is settled that nonmutual collateral estoppel (defensive or offensive) may not be applied against the United States.[7]

§ 2.27 Collateral Estoppel—Application to Issues of Law and Fact

Older cases expressed doubt that collateral estoppel was applicable to issues of law as well as fact. While some jurisdictions may still follow that rule, the clear trend in most circumstances is to apply collateral estoppel to issues of both law and fact.[1]

§ 2.28 Collateral Estoppel—Exceptions to Collateral Estoppel

Even in situations where all the requirements of collateral estoppel are satisfied, it is still possible that additional considerations may make application of estoppel unfair in a particular case. For example, as has already been discussed above, courts are reluctant to impose collateral estoppel in circumstances where the affected party might not reasonably have appreciated the risk of collateral estoppel in subsequent cases. Additionally, if the law or facts of a situation undergo material change between the first lawsuit and the second one, it might be unfair to impose collat-

---

driver and alleges that the driver was intoxicated at the time of the accident, the driver might win by introducing into evidence a police report showing that the driver was free of intoxicants. That finding, of course, would not bind the two passengers who had not yet sued. If the second passenger then sued, making the same allegation about intoxication, that passenger might win by demonstrating that the police test for intoxicants in the driver's blood was administered improperly. Thus, if the third passenger waited to sue until he/she was sufficiently healed to participate actively in a lawsuit, offensive nonmutual collateral estoppel might apply to the victory of the second passenger over the driver. Given the fact that the driver had both a prior victory and a prior defeat on the issue of intoxication, it might seem unfair to treat the issue as estopped against the driver in the third lawsuit. Thus, the Supreme Court's approach suggests that in such circumstances no party should be able to claim estoppel, and the parties in the third suit should relitigate the issue of intoxication again.

[6]*Parklane Hosiery Co., Inc. v. Shore*, 439 U.S. 322, 99 S. Ct. 645, 58 L. Ed. 2d 552 (1979).

[7]*U.S. v. Mendoza*, 464 U.S. 154, 162, 104 S. Ct. 568, 573, 78 L. Ed. 2d 379 (1984).

[1]*Montana v. U. S.*, 440 U.S. 147, 162, 99 S. Ct. 970, 978, 59 L. Ed. 2d 210 (1979) (normal rules of collateral estoppel apply to questions of law, provided that both lawsuits involve substantially related claims).

eral estoppel on issues decided in the first suit.[1] Finally, collateral estoppel will typically be inapplicable to situations where a district court judgment is not appealable.[2]

§ 2.29 Collateral Estoppel—Affirmative Defense: Rule 8(c)

Collateral estoppel, like res judicata, is listed as an affirmative defense under Federal Rule of Civil Procedure 8(c).[1] In theory, affirmative defenses must be raised or waived.[2] However, if a party is seeking to apply nonmutual collateral estoppel offensively, so as to preclude a defendant from relitigating an issue previously decided, such use of collateral estoppel is obviously not a "defense" to a claim and therefore raises no issues that would be governed by Rule 8(c).

§ 2.30 Collateral Estoppel—Relationship to Full Faith and Credit

The command that courts of one jurisdiction must give full faith and credit[1] to the judgments of another jurisdiction applies to matters of collateral estoppel. Thus, if the courts of a jurisdiction where a case was decided would treat an issue in that case as controlled by collateral estoppel, other courts have a duty to give the issue the same status of collateral estoppel as would be accorded by the court that decided the case.[2]

---

[1]*Montana v. U. S.*, 440 U.S. 147, 159, 99 S. Ct. 970, 976, 59 L. Ed. 2d 210 (1979) ("[C]hanges in facts essential to a judgment will render collateral estoppel inapplicable in a subsequent action raising the same issues."); *C.I.R. v. Sunnen*, 333 U.S. 591, 601, 68 S. Ct. 715, 721, 92 L. Ed. 898 (1948) (collateral estoppel inapplicable where relevant law changed between first and second proceeding). *But cf. Hickerson v. City of New York*, 146 F.3d 99, 105 (2d Cir. 1998) (failure to offer evidence already available in first suit is not a defense to collateral estoppel in second suit).

[2]*Kircher v. Putnam Funds Trust*, 547 U.S. 633, 126 S. Ct. 2145, 2156–57, 165 L. Ed. 2d 92 (2006) (28 U.S.C.A. § 1447(d) makes unreviewable, as a matter of law, many district court decisions to remand removed cases; in such cases there is no collateral estoppel result barring a state court from re-examining the reasoning underlying the decision of the district court-even though the state court should treat the remand decision itself as final).

[1]*See also Blonder-Tongue Laboratories, Inc. v. University of Illinois Foundation*, 402 U.S. 313, 91 S. Ct. 1434, 28 L. Ed. 2d 788 (1971).

[2]*But cf., e.g., Petrocelli v. Daniel Woodhead Co., a Subsidiary of Woodhead Industries, Inc.*, 993 F.2d 27, 29 n. 1 (3d Cir. 1993) (affirmative defense not raised in original pleading is not waived if it can be properly raised under Rule 15, governing amendments to pleadings).

[1]U.S. Const. Art. IV § 1. See also, 28 U.S.C.A. § 1738.

[2]*See, e.g., Community Bank of Homestead v. Torcise*, 162 F.3d 1084, 1087 n. 5 (11th Cir. 1998) (noting obligation to use Florida standard for collateral estoppel because prior judgment was rendered in Florida).

PART III-A
AN ORIENTATION TO FIVE YEARS OF MAJOR RULE AMENDMENTS

The Federal Rules of Civil Procedure have undergone significant revisions since 2006, creating uncertainties in application. This edition of the *Federal Civil Rules Handbook* reprints the current – as amended – language of each Rule. Broad summaries of the various revisions appear below. Discussions of how particular amendments affect each individual Rule will be found in the *Authors' Commentary* that follow that Rule.

***

Summary Judgment Amendments (2010). Effective December 2010, Rule 56 was entirely rebuilt. Although the summary judgment standard remains essentially unchanged (*i.e.*, no genuine dispute as to any material fact and entitled to judgment as a matter of law), the revised Rule 56 now: (a) restores the verb "shall" to the summary judgment command; (b) verifies that parties moving for or opposing summary judgment have a duty of "factual support" and then sets out the manner in which that duty may be discharged; (c) approves summary judgment declarations, as well as affidavits, in introducing that support; (d) permits objections to improper support; (e) elaborates on the district judge's discretion when positions lack the required support; (f) verifies that motions can be filed immediately, without waiting for discovery; (g) deletes national "default" time periods for summary judgment opposition and reply briefs; (h) confirms that district judges need only consider the formal summary judgment record in their rulings; (i) explicitly allows "partial" summary judgments; (j) codifies the court's right to enter judgment in favor of the *non-moving* party, on grounds not requested by the moving party, and *sua sponte*; (k) emphasizes the trial judge's discretion in treating facts as established for purposes of trial; (l) requires trial courts to explain the reasons for their Rule 56 rulings; and (m) expands the available discretionary sanctions for bad faith summary judgment affidavits and declarations.

Expert Amendments (2010). Also effective December 2010, the Rules governing disclosure and discovery of experts was altered. Rule 26(b)(4)(B) now protects draft expert reports from disclosure as trial preparation material. Rule 26(b)(4)(C) broadens the trial-preparation-material protection for communications between counsel and expert witnesses unless the communications pertain to expert compensation, or to facts, data, or assumptions provided by counsel which the experts considered in forming their opinions. Rule 26(a)(2)(C) requires that, for testifying experts who are not specially retained, parties must now disclose the subject matter of their expected testimony and a summary of the facts and opinions on which they are expected to testify.

Time Computation Amendments (2009). Effective December 2009, the procedures for computing time were adjusted and the hodge-podge of varying time periods was normalized. No time period was shortened. Most time periods were standardized into multiples of 7 (except those of 30 days and longer). The confusing "*less-than-11-day*" rule was eliminated. New hourly time period procedures were added, as were procedures for how time periods begin and end. Most post-trial motion periods were expanded from 10 to 28 days.

"Restyling" Amendments (2007). Effective December 2007, the Rules were all "restyled". This complete, top-to-bottom rewrite was not intended to effect any substantive change in the Rules or their operation, but to clean up the text. Some (but not many) Rule subparts were repositioned. Language inconsistencies were removed, antiquated and unnecessary references were pruned, needless prose "intensifiers" were deleted, passive voice was rephrased, sentences were simplified, and graphically orienting restructurings (new labels, headings, indentations) was added.

Privacy Amendments (2007). Effective December 2007, the Rules implemented the E-Government Act of 2002 by the adoption of new Rule 5.2 which directs the redaction of certain personal-identifying information, and permits the redaction of other such information filings under seal.

Discovery of Electronic Data Amendments (2006). Effective December 2006, the Rules formalized a national approach for disclosure and discovery of electronically-stored information, through amendments to the Rules governing pretrial conferences (Rule 16), initial disclosures (Rule 26), interrogatories (Rule 33), document requests (Rule 34), subpoenas (Rule 45), and sanctions (Rule 37). The amendments also prescribed the form in which electronic data is to be produced, with attendant procedures for objections and motion practice regarding producing electronic data from particularly burdensome sources or in particularly onerous forms. The amendments also create a safe harbor for electronic data destroyed during routine computer operations.

Two Other New Rules. New **Rule 5.1** was adopted in 2006 to gather in a single place the provisions requiring notice, certification, and a right of intervention for constitutional challenges to federal or state laws. New **Rule 7.1** was adopted in 2002 to require the filing of a disclosure statement by nongovernmental corporate parties.

PART III
FEDERAL RULES OF CIVIL PROCEDURE WITH COMMENTARY AND PRACTICE POINTERS

Rules Effective September 16, 1938

Including Amendments Effective December 1, 2010

Research Note

Rule requirements, case law applications, commentary, and references to treatises and law reviews are available in Wright, Miller, et al., Federal Practice and Procedure, *Volumes 4 to 20.*

Use WESTLAW ® *to find cases citing or applying rules.* WESTLAW *may also be used to search for terms in court rules or to update court rules. See the US-RULES and US-ORDERS SCOPE screens for detailed descriptive information and search tips.*

Table of Rules

I. SCOPE OF RULES—FORM OF ACTION

Rule

1.   Scope and Purpose.
2.   One Form of Action.

II. COMMENCING AN ACTION; SERVICE OF PROCESS, PLEADINGS, MOTIONS, AND ORDERS

3.   Commencing An Action.
4.   Summons.
4.1.   Serving Other Process.
5.   Serving and Filing Pleadings and Other Papers.
5.1.   Constitutional Challenge to a Statute—Notice, Certification, and Intervention.
5.2.   Privacy Protection for Filings Made With the Court.
6.   Computing and Extending Time; Time for Motion Papers.

III. PLEADINGS AND MOTIONS

7.   Pleadings Allowed; Form of Motions and Other Papers.
7.1.   Disclosure Statement.
8.   General Rules of Pleading.
9.   Pleading Special Matters.
10.   Form of Pleadings.
11.   Signing Pleadings, Motions, and Other Papers; Representations to Court; Sanctions.
12.   Defenses and Objections: When and How Presented; Motion for Judgment on the Pleadings; Consolidating Motions; Waiving Defenses; Pretrial Hearing.
13.   Counterclaim and Crossclaim.

14.   Third-Party Practice.

15.   Amended and Supplemental Pleadings.

16.   Pretrial Conferences; Scheduling; Management.

IV. PARTIES

17.   Plaintiff and Defendant; Capacity; Public Officers.

18.   Joinder of Claims.

19.   Required Joinder of Parties.

20.   Permissive Joinder of Parties.

21.   Misjoinder and Nonjoinder of Parties.

22.   Interpleader.

23.   Class Actions.

23.1.   Derivative Actions By Shareholders.

23.2.   Actions Relating to Unincorporated Associations.

24.   Intervention.

25.   Substitution of Parties.

V. DEPOSITIONS AND DISCOVERY

26.   Duty to Disclose; General Provisions Governing Discovery.

27.   Depositions to Perpetuate Testimony.

28.   Persons Before Whom Depositions May Be Taken.

29.   Stipulations About Discovery Procedure.

30.   Depositions By Oral Examination.

31.   Depositions By Written Questions.

32.   Using Depositions in Court Proceedings.

33.   Interrogatories to Parties.

34.   Producing Documents, Electronically Stored Information, and Tangible Things, or Entering Onto Land, for Inspection and Other Purposes.

35.   Physical and Mental Examinations.

36.   Requests for Admission.

37.   Failure to Make Disclosures or to Cooperate In Discovery; Sanctions.

VI. TRIALS

38.   Right to a Jury Trial; Demand.

39.   Trial By Jury or By the Court.

40.   Scheduling Cases for Trial.

41.   Dismissal of Actions.

42.   Consolidation; Separate Trials.

43.   Taking Testimony.

44.   Proving an Official Record.

44.1.   Determining Foreign Law.

45.   Subpoena.

46.   Objecting to a Ruling or Order.

47.   Selecting Jurors.

48.   Number of Jurors; Verdict.

49.   Special Verdict; General Verdict and Questions.

50.   Judgment as a Matter of Law In a Jury Trial; Related Motion for a New Trial; Conditional Ruling.

51.   Instructions to the Jury; Objections; Preserving a Claim of Error.

52.   Findings and Conclusions By the Court; Judgment on Partial Findings.

53.   Masters.

VII. JUDGMENT

54.   Judgment; Costs.

55.   Default; Default Judgment.

56.   Summary Judgment.

57.   Declaratory Judgment.

58.   Entering Judgment.

59.   New Trial; Altering Or Amending a Judgment.

60.   Relief From a Judgment Or Order.

61.   Harmless Error.

62.   Stay of Proceedings to Enforce a Judgment.

62.1   Indicative Ruling on a Motion for Relief That is Barred by a Pending Appeal

63.   Judge's Inability to Proceed.

VIII. PROVISIONAL AND FINAL REMEDIES

64.   Seizing a Person Or Property.

65.   Injunctions and Restraining Orders.

65.1.   Proceedings Against a Surety.

66.   Receivers.

67.   Deposit Into Court.

68.   offer of Judgment.

69.   Execution.

70.   Enforcing a Judgment for a Specific Act.

71.   Enforcing Relief for Or Against a Nonparty.

IX. SPECIAL PROCEEDINGS

71.1.   Condemning Real Or Personal Property.

72.   Magistrate Judges; Pretrial Orders.

73.   Magistrate Judges; Trial By Consent and Appeal.

74.   Method of Appeal From Magistrate to District Judge Under Title 28, U.S.C. § 636(C)(4) and 73(D).

75.   Proceedings on Appeal From Magistrate to District Judge Under Rule 73(D).

76.   Judgment of the District Judge on the Appeal Under Rule 73(D) and Costs.

X. DISTRICT COURTS AND CLERKS

77.   Conducting Business; Clerk's Authority; Notice of An Order Or Judgment.

78.   Hearing Motions; Submission on Briefs.

79.   Records Kept By the Clerk.

80.   Stenographic Transcript as Evidence.

XI. GENERAL PROVISIONS

81.   Applicability of the Rules In General; Removed Actions.

82.   Jurisdiction and Venue Unaffected.

83.   Rules By District Courts; Judge's Directives.

84.   Forms.

85.   Title.

86.   Effective Dates.

APPENDIX OF FORMS

[The Appendix of Forms is reproduced in Part IV, below.]

I. SCOPE OF RULES—FORM OF ACTION

RULE 1
SCOPE AND PURPOSE

These rules govern the procedure in all civil actions and proceedings in the United States district courts, except as stated in Rule 81. They should be construed and administered to secure the just, speedy, and inexpensive determination of every action and proceeding.

[Amended December 29, 1948, effective October 20, 1949; February 28, 1966, effective July 1, 1966; April 22, 1993, effective December 1, 1993; April 30, 2007, effective December 1, 2007.]

AUTHORS' COMMENTARY ON RULE 1

PURPOSE AND SCOPE

The Federal Rules apply generally to all civil actions in the district courts of the United States. Federal courts, and the attorneys who appear before them, are required to construe and administer the Rules in a manner that achieves the just, speedy, and inexpensive determination of each civil action.

APPLICATIONS

Creation, Status, and Validity of the Federal Rules

Under the authority vested by the Rules Enabling Act of 1934,[1] the United States Supreme Court promulgated the original Federal Rules of Civil Procedure in December 1937. The original Rules became effective in September 1938, and have been amended on numerous occasions since. The Rules have the force and effect of law. They superseded inconsistent statutes enacted prior to their effective date.

The Federal Rules enjoy "presumptive validity".[2] Nevertheless, although promulgated by the United States Supreme Court, a Federal Rule may still be challenged as inconsistent with the rulemaking power delegated by Congress to the

---

[1]Act of June 19, 1934, ch. 651, 48 Stat. 1064, codified in current form at 28 U.S.C.A. §§ 2071 to 77.

[2]*See Exxon Corp. v. Burglin*, 42 F.3d 948, 950 (5th Cir. 1995).

Supreme Court under the Rules Enabling Act.[3] To date, no Rule has ever been declared invalid.[4]

The Advisory Committee and Its Committee Notes

To help draft the original Federal Rules, the Supreme Court appointed an Advisory Committee on Rules comprising a panel of judges, attorneys, and law professors. This consultative tradition continues today, in the form of the Judicial Conference of the United States' Advisory Committee on Civil Rules, which investigates and recommends amendments to the Rules. The members of the Advisory Committee have included federal and State judges, practicing attorneys, law professors, and Department of Justice representatives.[5]

Both the original Advisory Committee and its successors have published "Notes" as an aid in construing and interpreting the particular purpose and intent of each Rule and its amendments. The Committee Notes are only guides; the Notes neither are a part of the Rules nor have they been approved by the Supreme Court. However, in practice, the Notes have assumed the force of a veritable legislative history to the Rules and their amendments. The Notes can be cited as formidable (though non-binding) authority for construing the Rules.[6]

Where the Rules Apply

Rule 1 implements Article III, Section 2 of the Constitution which extends the judicial power of the United States "to all Cases, in Law and Equity, arising under this Constitution, the Laws of the United States, and [its] Treaties . . . [and] to all Cases of admiralty and maritime Jurisdiction."[7] The Rules apply to all civil cases[8] in all district courts of the United States, and "automatically" so.[9] By special congressional enactments, the Rules have been extended to the United States District

---

[3]*See Mississippi Pub. Corp. v. Murphree*, 326 U.S. 438, 444, 66 S. Ct. 242, 246, 90 L. Ed. 185 (1946) ("The fact that this Court promulgated the rules as formulated and recommended by the Advisory Committee does not foreclose consideration of their validity, meaning or consistency"). *See also Hanna v. Plumer*, 380 U.S. 460, 471, 85 S. Ct. 1136, 1143, 14 L. Ed. 2d 8 (1965) (when situation is covered by Federal Rules, court must apply them unless "the Rule in question transgresses [ ] the terms of the [Rules] Enabling Act [or the Constitution]").

[4]*See Exxon Corp. v. Burglin*, 42 F.3d 948, 950 (5th Cir. 1995).

[5]The procedure for amending the Federal Rules is more specifically described in Part I of this text.

[6]A discussion of the history behind and the legal effect of the Advisory Committee Notes, the collected case law discussing the interpretative value and weight of the Notes, and the full text of the original and amending Notes appears in Part VIII of this text.

[7]*See Vodusek v. Bayliner Marine Corp.*, 71 F.3d 148, 153 (4th Cir. 1995) (citing U.S. Const. art. III, § 2).

[8]*See Ashcroft v. Iqbal*, 556 U.S. 662, 684, 129 S.Ct. 1937, 1953, 73 L.Ed.2d 868 (2009).

[9]*See Shady Grove Orthopedic Assocs., P.A. v. Allstate Ins. Co.*, __ U.S. __, __, 130 S.Ct. 1431, 1438, 176 L.Ed.2d 311 (2010).

Court for the District of Columbia,[10] and to the territorial and insular courts of Guam,[11] the Northern Mariana Islands,[12] Puerto Rico,[13] and the Virgin Islands.[14] Because it is not a "district court", the Rules do not apply to the United States Tax Court.[15] Unless a Rule requires or permits the application of State procedure, the federal courts do not apply State procedures that conflict with the Rules.[16]

Civil Rules and the Courts of Appeals

By their terms the Federal Rules of Civil Procedure apply only to the federal District Courts. However, the policies that underlie the Rules may apply equally to the Courts of Appeals.[17]

Civil Rules and Criminal Cases

Likewise, the Federal Rules of Civil Procedure apply only in civil disputes, and do not govern criminal cases.[18]

Specialized Proceedings

Specialized proceedings are governed by the Rules,[19] unless they are expressly included in Rule 81's list of those to which

---

[10]*See* 28 U.S.C.A. § 88 (officially confirming that the District of Columbia is a judicial district of the United States). *See also* Rule 81(d)(2) (applying law of District of Columbia, where appropriate, when word "state" is used).

[11]*See* 48 U.S.C.A. § 1424 (creating district court of Guam and vesting it with the jurisdiction of a district court of the United States).

[12]*See* 48 U.S.C.A. §§ 1821 & 1822 (creating district court of the Northern Mariana Islands and vesting it with the jurisdiction of a district court of the United States).

[13]*See* 28 U.S.C.A. § 119 (creating Puerto Rico as a judicial district).

[14]*See* 48 U.S.C.A. §§ 1611 & 1612 (creating district court of the Virgin Islands and vesting it with the jurisdiction of a district court of the United States).

[15]*See Michaels v. C.I.R.*, 144 F.3d 495, 497 (7th Cir. 1998) (commenting that although the Rules are not binding on the Tax Court, they "provide a source of persuasive authority to that court in filling any gaps in its own rules of procedure"). *See generally* 26 U.S.C.A. § 7453 (authorizing promulgation of Tax Court Rules of Practice & Procedure); Tax Ct. R. 1(b) (provid-

ing that "These Rules shall be construed to secure the just, speedy, and inexpensive determination of every case").

[16]*See Shady Grove Orthopedic Assocs., P.A. v. Allstate Ins. Co.*, __ U.S. __, __, 130 S.Ct. 1431, 1437, 176 L.Ed.2d 311 (2010) (if Federal Rule answers procedural question in issue, "it governs" unless it is invalid); *Gasperini v. Ctr. for Humanities, Inc.*, 518 U.S. 415, 427 n.7, 116 S.Ct. 2211, 135 L.Ed.2d 659 (1996) (declaring it "settled" that a valid, on-point Federal Rule "applies regardless of contrary state law").

[17]*See Newman-Green, Inc. v. Alfonzo-Larrain*, 490 U.S. 826, 832, 109 S. Ct. 2218, 2223, 104 L. Ed. 2d 893 (1989); *Rosenfeld v. Oceania Cruises, Inc.*, 682 F.3d 1320, 1332 n.14 (11th Cir. 2012); *Wilson v. Maritime Overseas Corp.*, 150 F.3d 1, 6 n.4 (1st Cir.1998).

[18]*See United States v. McCalister*, 601 F.3d 1086, 1087–88 (10th Cir. 2010).

[19]*See S.J. v. Issaquah Sch. Dist. No. 411*, 470 F.3d 1288, 1292 (9th Cir. 2006) (citing Rule 1 to reject claim that IDEA actions, because of their "appellate flavor", are not controlled by the Rules).

the Rules do not apply.[20] Under Rule 81, for example, the Rules apply in bankruptcy proceedings, but only to the extent prescribed by the Federal Rules of Bankruptcy Procedure.[21] Although the Rules apply generally to admiralty proceedings,[22] they do *not* apply to prize proceedings in admiralty.[23] In the absence of federal law providing otherwise, the Rules also apply to, among other proceedings: admission to citizenship proceedings[24] (but not to the Board of Immigration Appeals and deportation proceedings[25]), habeas corpus and quo warranto proceedings,[26] federal arbitrations, and to proceedings to review orders by the Secretaries of Agriculture and Interior, proceedings to enforce National Labor Relations Board orders and Longshore and Harbor Workers' Compensation Act compensation orders, reviewing orders denying a certificate of clearance, and reviewing railway labor dispute arbitration awards.[27]

Likewise, the Rules also apply generally to de novo immigration proceedings,[28] civil contempt proceedings (when the original proceeding was governed by the Rules), civil actions for forfeiture and penalty actions by the United States,[29] patent cases, removed cases,[30] civil actions in which the United States or one of its officers or agencies is a party,[31] and proceedings to compel compliance with a subpoena to testify or to produce documents, as issued by an officer or agency of the United States pursuant to federal statute.[32]

Rules to be Harmonized Together

The Rules were designed to be "interdependent".[33] Thus, in interpreting them, courts seek to "harmonize" the Rules with one another, and will only allow one Rule to take precedence

---

[20]Rule 81 was amended in 2001 to omit references that had formerly excluded the Rules from Copyright cases and from mental health proceedings in the United States District Court for the District of Columbia. With the abrogation of the separate Copyright Rules, the Rules now apply in copyright cases, and because Congress has now transferred such proceedings to local courts in the District of Columbia, the mental health proceedings provision was eliminated as superfluous.

[21]See Rule 81(a)(2).

[22]See *Blanchard v. Cortes-Molina*, 453 F.3d 40 (1st Cir.2006).

[23]See Rule 81(a)(1).

[24]See Rule 81(a)(3).

[25]See *Poole v. Mukasey*, 522 F.3d 259, 263 (2d Cir. 2008).

[26]See Rule 81(a)(4).

[27]See Rule 81(a)(6).

[28]See *Alvear v. Kirk*, 87 F. Supp. 2d 1241, 1243 (D.N.M. 2000) (holding that Rules 12 and 56 governed de novo immigration proceedings pursuant to 8 U.S.C. § 1421(c)).

[29]*Cf. U.S. v. Mosavi*, 138 F.3d 1365 (11th Cir. 1998) (Rules do not apply to criminal forfeitures).

[30]See Rule 81(c)(1).

[31]The Rules were not designed to extend the jurisdiction of the federal courts. Consequently, the Rules' references to procedures for suing or being sued by the United States does not constitute a waiver of sovereign immunity.

[32]See Rule 81(a)(5).

[33]See *Weiss v. Regal Collections*, 385 F.3d 337, 342 (3d Cir. 2004).

over another where truly irreconcilable conflicts arise.[34]

"Just", "Speedy", and "Inexpensive" Mandate

Aside from defining when the Rules apply, Rule 1 also fixes the broad objectives of the Federal Rules of Civil Procedure: they are to be construed and administered so as to achieve the "just, speedy, and inexpensive determination of every action".[35] This admonition applies also to Local Rules, promulgated to supplement the National Rules.[36]

Often cited, these goals have been heralded by the Supreme Court as "the touchstones of federal procedure".[37] The text of Rule 1 emphasizes the trial courts' affirmative duty to exercise the procedural authority the Rules bestow so as to resolve civil litigation fairly and without undue cost or delay.[38] This affirmative duty is shared by practicing attorneys, as officers of the court.[39] To realize Rule 1's goals of "just, speedy, and inexpensive" determinations of federal cases, the parties are expected to work diligently to follow the Rules and the courts are called upon to resolutely enforce the Rules, otherwise the Rules—and the laudable objectives they seek—will become illusory.[40]

The courts have quoted these touchstones as guidance for construing and interpreting the Rules. In finding a Rule's meaning, the touchstones of Rule 1 disfavor any interpretation that will cause confusion[41] or which "lays traps for the unwary".[42] So pervasive is the Rule 1 mission that it has been cited as author-

---

[34]*See Weiss v. Regal Collections,* 385 F.3d 337, 342 (3d Cir. 2004).

[35]*See Wood v. GCC Bend, LLC,* 422 F.3d 873, 882–83 (9th Cir. 2005) (noting that the "first of the Federal Rules of Civil Procedure mandates construing the rest" to achieve the Rule 1 touchstones).

[36]*See Stevo v. Frasor,* 662 F.3d 880, 887 (7th Cir. 2011).

[37]*Brown Shoe Co. v. U.S.,* 370 U.S. 294, 306, 82 S. Ct. 1502, 1513, 8 L. Ed. 2d 510 (1962). *See In re Bayer AG,* 146 F.3d 188, 189 (3d Cir. 1998) (commenting that the Rules and Rule 1's touchstones "initiated a revolution in the litigation process in the federal courts in this country" and, ultimately, influenced foreign litigation as well).

[38]*See* Rule 1 advisory committee notes 1993. *See also Johnson v. Board of County Com'rs for County of Fremont,* 868 F. Supp. 1226 (D. Colo. 1994) (commenting that public interest demands a seemly and efficient use of judicial resources to achieve Rule 1 goals, and courts are thus obligated to raise perceived dangers to these objec-

tives even if parties do not).

[39]*See Reebok Int'l Ltd. v. Sebelen,* 959 F. Supp. 553, 558 n. 1 (D.P.R. 1997) (citing Herman Melville's fable, *Bartleby the Scrivener,* as a valuable reminder that "the lawyer's role extends beyond filing motions and be an unquestioning mouthpiece for his client. His role is to engage in the adversarial process in good faith and in accordance with" the precepts of Rule 1); *Hill v. MacMillan McGraw-Hill Sch. Publ'g Co.,* 1995 WL 317054 (N.D. Cal. 1995) (noting that litigants have obligation to court to refrain from conduct that frustrates the aims of Rule 1), *appeal dismissed,* 102 F.3d 422 (9th Cir.1996).

[40]*See Mused v. U.S. Dept. of Agriculture Food and Nutrition Service,* 169 F.R.D. 28, 35 (W.D. N.Y. 1996).

[41]*See Rodriguez v. Our Lady of Lourdes Med. Ctr.,* 552 F.3d 297, 302 (3d Cir. 2008).

[42]*See U.S. ex rel. Russell v. Epic Healthcare Mgmt. Group,* 193 F.3d 304, 307–08 (5th Cir. 1999).

ity for preventing a litigant from flouting the "spirit" of the Rules, even where the litigant's conduct might otherwise comport with the Rule's literal meaning.[43]

Examples of the courts' reliance on Rule 1 to achieve these objectives are legion. A few samples are illustrative. The U.S. Supreme Court cited Rule 1's mandate to justify a broadening of the long-cramped reach of the summary judgment rule.[44] The U.S. Courts of Appeals have cited Rule 1 to eschew an "unduly rigid application" of local rules,[45] to overrule prior precedent that had rigidly commanded at least one chance to amend a dismissed complaint (even where no such leave was sought),[46] to approve the "filing" *instanter* of a pleading attached to a motion for leave but never separately filed,[47] to reverse a trial judge's refusal to grant a modest extension of time to respond to a summary judgment motion,[48] to justify entertaining successive summary judgment motions,[49] and to forbid the "ambushing" of a trial court with belatedly raised objections,[50] in regulating "Rambo"-style litigation tactics.[51] Likewise, the U.S. District Courts have cited Rule 1 in permitting defendants' removal of a case before it had been served,[52] in allowing successive Rule 12(b)(6) motions to dismiss,[53] in permitting "predictive coding"

---

[43]*See U.S. v. High Country Broad. Co.*, 3 F.3d 1244, 1245 (9th Cir. 1993). *But see Central States, Southeast & Southwest Areas Pension Fund v. Central Cartage Co.*, 69 F.3d 1312, 1314–15 (7th Cir. 1995) (cautioning that "the need to consider the objectives in Fed.R.Civ.P. 1 when construing all of the rules does not justify disregarding limitations explicitly built into them").

[44]*See Celotex Corp. v. Catrett*, 477 U.S. 317, 327, 106 S. Ct. 2548, 2555, 91 L. Ed. 2d 265 (1986) (commenting how summary judgment constitutes an integral role in implementing the Federal Rules' task of a just, speedy, and inexpensive resolution of litigation).

[45]*See Mitskovski v. Buffalo and Fort Erie Public Bridge Authority*, 435 F.3d 127, 133 (2d Cir. 2006).

[46]*See Wagner v. Daewoo Heavy Indus. America Corp.*, 314 F.3d 541, 542–43 (11th Cir. 2002).

[47]*See A. Bauer Mech., Inc. v. Joint Arbitration Bd. of Plumbing Contractors' Ass'n & Chicago Journeymen Plumbers' Local Union 130*, 562 F.3d 784, 791 (7th Cir. 2009).

[48]*See Ahanchian v. Xenon Pictures, Inc.*, 624 F.3d 1253, 1255 & 1259 (9th Cir. 2010).

[49]*See Hoffman v. Tonnemacher*, 593 F.3d 908, 911 (9th Cir. 2010).

[50]*See Celle v. Filipino Reporter Enters. Inc.*, 209 F.3d 163, 175–76 (2d Cir. 2000) (rejecting maneuver that "would permit a losing party to lead a trial court into error and then to profit on appeal from the misguidance").

[51]*See In re Amezaga*, 195 B.R. 221 (Bankr. D. P.R. 1996) (noting that "Rambo Litigation" is not tolerated because, although it may project zealous advocacy, it does not promote Rule 1's goals); *Applied Telematics, Inc. v. Sprint Corp.*, 1995 WL 79237 (E.D. Pa. 1995) (decrying counsel's "Rambo Litigation" deposition defense tactics as failing to promote goals of Rule 1).

[52]*See Valido-Shade v. WYETH, LLC*, __ F. Supp. 2d __, __, 2012 WL 2861113, at *1–*4 (E.D.Pa. July 11, 2012).

[53]*See Allstate Ins. Co. v. Countrywide Fin. Corp.*, 824 F.Supp.2d 1164, 1175 (C.D.Cal. 2011).

while preparing responses to discovery production requests,[54] in forcing disclosure of the identity of "confidential informants" in a private securities case,[55] in approving the videotaping of discovery depositions,[56] in refusing to tolerate deposition errata sheets that alter substance of a witness' testimony (rather than merely correct transcription errors),[57] and in limiting the number of testifying experts[58] and excusing the need for a full *Daubert* hearing to assess their reliability.[59]

In the words of one court, this "simple" Rule is a reminder that form should not be exalted over substance.[60] Yet, the Rules' flexibility is certainly not unbounded. Rule 1's touchstones cannot be cited, for example, to distort a clearly pleaded claim into alleging something that it certainly does not under the banner of liberality.[61]

Additional Research References

Wright & Miller, *Federal Practice and Procedure* §§ 1011 to 1040
C.J.S., Federal Civil Procedure §§ 5 et seq.; Federal Courts § 284
West's Key Number Digest, Federal Civil Procedure ⊶21; ⊶31 to 44; Federal Courts ⊶522

---

[54]*See Moore v. Publicis Groupe*, __ F.R.D. __, __, 2012 WL 607412, at *1 (S.D.N.Y. 2012), *adopted by*, 2012 WL 1446534 (S.D.N.Y. Apr. 26, 2012).

[55]*See Plumbers & Pipefitters Local Union No. 630 Pension-Annuity Trust Fund v. Arbitron, Inc.*, 278 F.R.D. 335, 342 (S.D.N.Y. 2011).

[56]*See Fanelli v. Centenary College*, 211 F.R.D. 268, 271 (D.N.J. 2002) (because it may foster careful assessment of the strengths and weaknesses of trial testimony of witnesses (including how a jury might view that testimony), videotaped discovery depositions may lead to more prompt settlements).

[57]*See E.I. du Pont de Nemours & Co. v. Kolon Indus., Inc.*, 277 F.R.D. 286, 297–98 (E.D.Va. 2011).

[58]*See Planned Parenthood of Cent. New Jersey v. Verniero*, 22 F. Supp. 2d 331, 339 (D.N.J. 1998).

[59]*See Lanni v. State of N.J.*, 177 F.R.D. 295, 303 (D.N.J. 1998).

[60]*See Hall v. Sullivan*, 229 F.R.D. 501, 504 (D. Md. 2005).

[61]*See Lee v. MBNA Long Term Disability & Benefit Plan*, 136 Fed. Appx. 734 (6th Cir. 2005) (although Rule 1 directs liberal construction of pleadings, it will not justify finding a State claim in a complaint pleaded as an ERISA case).

RULE 2
ONE FORM OF ACTION

There is one form of action—the civil action.

[Amended April 30, 2007, effective December 1, 2007.]

AUTHORS' COMMENTARY ON RULE 2

PURPOSE AND SCOPE

The Rules have merged the law and equity sides of the federal courts, providing a single procedural framework for all claims and defenses. All relief may now be obtained in the same action, whether the case seeks legal remedies, equitable remedies, or both.

APPLICATIONS

Merger of Law and Equity Courts

Upon the arrival of Rule 2, the actions at law and suits in equity were merged together in the federal courts, with only one "form of action" remaining — the "civil action".[1]

Civil Action Defined

For civil claims, the Rules establish only one form of proceeding, known as a "civil action". This term refers to the entire civil proceeding, including all component "claims" and "cases" within that proceeding,[2] and notwithstanding how the lawsuit might be labeled or titled.[3] Accordingly, for example, a party may not remove to federal court only a portion of lawsuit

---

[1]See *Federal Reserve Bank of Atlanta v. Thomas*, 220 F.3d 1235, 1242 n.5 (11th Cir. 2000); *Cablevision of the Midwest, Inc. v. City of Brunswick*, 117 F. Supp. 2d 658, 661 (N.D. Ohio 2000).

[2]See *Nolan v. Boeing Co.*, 919 F.2d 1058, 1066 (5th Cir. 1990) (ruling that "case" and "action" refer to the same thing—the entirety of a civil proceeding, including third party claims). See also *Fogg v. Ashcroft*, 254 F.3d 103, 107 (D.C. Cir. 2001) (citing Rule 2 as support for holding that statutory cap on damages in "an action brought" under the Civil Rights Act of 1964 applies to entire lawsuit, not just to individual claims within

lawsuit); *Hudson v. Reno*, 130 F.3d 1193, 1199 (6th Cir. 1997) (same); *U.S. v. NL Indus., Inc.*, 2005 WL 1267419 at *5 (S.D. Ill. 2005) (citing *Federal Civil Rules Handbook*, noting that all component claims are encompassed in "civil action"); *U.S. v. Barcroft*, 2008 WL 901198 (E.D. Tex. 2008) (notice of intent to levy was not a "civil action" under Rule 2 because it was not commenced with the filing of a Rule 3 complaint); *Matter of Hinote*, 179 F.R.D. 335, 336 (S.D. Ala. 1998) (same result, pre-commencement discovery in likely ERISA case).

[3]See *Wade v. Ogden*, 2009 WL 2423535, at *3 (D.Utah Aug. 4, 2009) (rejecting argument that "petition" is distinguishable from "suit" or "com-

filed in State court.[4]

Joinder of All Claims and Defenses

Without a separate law-side and equity-side to the federal courts, a party may now join all claims and defenses (legal and equitable) against all opposing parties in one action.[5] Note, however, that the Rules and certain judiciary title statutes may limit such joinder.[6]

Determining Form of Action

Although the federal courts no longer recognize a distinction in procedure between cases on the "law-side" and suits in "equity", this distinction still persists in some limited contexts in which the federal courts may yet be called upon to discern the substantive "form" of the litigation (*i.e.*, legal or equitable).[7] This inquiry may arise when the court has to decide whether a litigant enjoys a right to a trial by jury,[8] or when, in diversity cases, the controlling State law retains the law / equity distinction as to substantive issues (like the applicable statute of limitations).

Equity Principles Applicable

Although the Rules have fused law and equity into a single procedural framework, the federal courts still apply equity principles in appropriate cases.[9]

---

plaint").

[4]*See, e.g., Clark Const. Group, Inc. v. Hellmuth, Obata & Kassabaum, Inc.*, 286 F. Supp. 2d 1348, 1348–52 (M.D. Fla. 2003) (litigant's attempt to remove less than whole civil action, and "unilaterally sever . . . claims and remove only part of the State Court Action", was foreclosed by Rules and deprived Court of subject matter jurisdiction).

[5]*See U.S. ex rel. Rahman v. Oncology Assocs., P.C.*, 198 F.3d 502, 508–09 (4th Cir. 1999) (citing Rule 2 as support for the proposition that mandamus relief can be sought in same lawsuit that involved other, unrelated relief because "the modern trend in civil pleading has been to encourage that all claims for relief be brought in a single suit").

[6]*See, e.g.,* 28 U.S.C.A. § 1367 (enumerating the federal court's supplemental jurisdiction over state law claims); Rule 18 (joinder of claims and remedies); Rule 19 (joinder of parties).

[7]*See Burlington Northern R. Co. v. Nebraska Public Power Dist.*, 931 F. Supp. 1470, 1479 (D. Neb. 1996).

[8]*See Wooddell v. Int'l Bhd. of Elec. Workers, Local 71*, 502 U.S. 93, 97, 112 S. Ct. 494, 497, 116 L. Ed. 2d 419 (1991) (to decide whether a particular lawsuit would resolve "legal" rights, and thus entitle the litigants to a trial by jury, the courts: (1) compare the action to 18th Century claims brought in English courts; and (2) determine whether the remedy sought is legal or equitable in nature). *See also* Rule 38 (discussing effect of action "in equity" in assessing a party's Seventh Amendment right to a jury trial).

[9]*See Stainback v. Mo Hock Ke Lok Po*, 336 U.S. 368, 382, 69 S. Ct. 606, 93 L. Ed. 741 (1949) (noting that Rules' merger of law and equity did not affect the substantive principles of equity); *Matter of U.S. Brass Corp.*, 110 F.3d 1261, 1267 (7th Cir. 1997) (commenting that since law and equity were merged in the federal courts, judges have freely imported equitable defenses into suits at law).

Complete Relief

When granting final judgment, a court may grant all the relief to which a party is entitled (legal and equitable), regardless of the relief demanded in the pleadings.[10] Note, however, that many judicial districts require parties to list in a pretrial memorandum the specific relief they intend to seek and, thereafter, to remain bound by that listing at trial.[11]

Additional Research References

Wright & Miller, *Federal Practice and Procedure* §§ 1041 to 1050
C.J.S., Federal Civil Procedure § 4, §§ 37 et seq.
West's Key Number Digest, Federal Civil Procedure ☞5 to 7; ☞71 to 73; ☞81 to 86

---

[10]*See* Rule 54(c).

[11]*See, e.g.*, E.D. Pa. Loc. R. 16.1(c)(3) & (d)(2)(b)(3) (requiring party seeking relief to identify the precise monetary and non-monetary relief requested).

II. COMMENCING AN ACTION; SERVICE OF PROCESS, PLEADINGS, MOTIONS, AND ORDERS

RULE 3

COMMENCING AN ACTION

A civil action is commenced by filing a complaint with the court.

[Amended April 30, 2007, effective December 1, 2007.]

AUTHORS' COMMENTARY ON RULE 3

PURPOSE AND SCOPE

A civil action is commenced under Rule 3 on the date on which a complaint is filed, *not* the date of service. This dating function is important for many purposes, including the tolling of the statute of limitations in federal question cases. That tolling effect will *not* exist in diversity cases when contrary State tolling rules apply, nor in cases where a specific federal statute provides a different tolling rule. If commencement does trigger a tolling, that tolling will only benefit plaintiffs who successfully serve their summons and complaints within 120 days thereafter (or show good cause for not doing so).[1]

APPLICATIONS

Action "Commences" When Complaint is Filed

An action becomes "pending" when the complaint is delivered for filing to a court officer authorized to receive it.[2] Prior to filing, the federal district court lacks authority to act in the dispute.[3] Moreover, the filing must constitute a genuine com-

---

[1] *See* Rule 4(m).

[2] *See U.S. v. $8,221,877.16 in U.S. Currency*, 330 F.3d 141, 159 (3d Cir. 2003) (noting that the word "commence" is term of art with only one unambiguous meaning—it does not "encompass broad concepts, but rather requires 'invocation of the judicial process' "). *See also Local Union No. 38, Sheet Metal Workers' Intern. Ass'n, AFL-CIO v. Pelella*, 350 F.3d 73, 82 (2d Cir. 2003) (an action is instituted in federal court when "a plaintiff files

a complaint as that constitutes the first step invoking the judicial process").

[3] *See S.E.C. v. Ross*, 504 F.3d 1130, 1140–41 (9th Cir. 2007) (court would not proceed on motion for disgorgement of gains without complaint naming motion's respondent as party); *U.S. v. Barcroft*, 2008 WL 901198 at *1 (E.D. Tex. 2008) (notice of intent to levy not removable because no accompanying complaint was filed); *Adair v. England*, 193 F. Supp. 2d 196, 200

plaint for the action to commence.[4]

Service Generally Not Required for Commencement

Service of process is generally not required for the lawsuit to "commence". So long as service is completed within 120 days after the complaint is filed with the court, the litigants become "plaintiff" and "defendant" when the complaint is filed, not when it is served.[5]

"Commencement" is Provisional—Without Service, Action Dismissed in 120 Days

Although an action becomes "pending" when the complaint is delivered for filing, Rule 4(m) authorizes the district court to dismiss the action, without prejudice, if service of both the summons and the complaint is not made within 120 days of commencement (unless good cause is shown why service was not accomplished during that period).[6]

"Commencement" is Provisional — Action Dismissed for Later Lack of Diligent Prosecution

Once a plaintiff files the complaint, the plaintiff must prosecute the action with due diligence. Rule 3 does not relieve plaintiffs of their obligation to prosecute the complaint after filing. The court may dismiss any action for lack of due diligence in proceeding with the lawsuit.[7]

Uses of Rule 3's Dating Function

Rule 3's function of "dating" the commencement of a lawsuit as of the day the complaint is filed with the court is useful in many contexts. This dating function may be used to evaluate:

- The timeliness of the action, under the applicable statute of limitations and/or laches (see discussions below);
- Ripeness;
- Personal Jurisdiction, which generally vests at the time

(D.D.C. 2002) (if no complaint filed, federal court lacks jurisdiction to hear petition for injunctive relief).

[4]*See Radin v. Jersey City Med. Ctr.*, 375 Fed. Appx. 205, 206–07 (3d Cir. 2010) (per curiam) (blank piece of paper containing only a caption does not qualify); *Powell v. Rios*, 241 Fed. Appx. 500 (10th Cir. 2007) (intimating that filing a TRO, without a complaint, would not be sufficient to commence a federal action); *Greene v. Philadelphia Housing Auth.*, 789 F. Supp. 2d 582, 585 (E.D.Pa. 2011) (filing motion for TRO, without also filing complaint, does not quality).

[5]*See Howell by Goerdt v. Tribune*

Entertainment Co., 106 F.3d 215, 217 (7th Cir. 1997). *See also Clay v. U.S.*, 199 F.3d 876, 880 (6th Cir. 1999) ("A person becomes 'a party' only by beginning a lawsuit, Fed. R. Civ. P. 3, or by being joined as a party after a suit has been instituted").

[6]*See* Rule 4(m). Note, however, that Rule 4(m) does not apply to service within a foreign country, *see* Rule 4(m) (referencing Rule 4(f)); or to service upon a foreign state and its political subdivisions, agencies, and instrumentalities, *see* Rule 4(m) (referencing Rule 4(j)(1)).

[7]*See* Rule 41(b).

an action is commenced;[8]
- Diversity Jurisdiction, which also generally vests at the time an action is commenced;[9]
- Venue, which likewise is generally assessed as of the date the action is commenced;[10]
- Procedural Timing Deadlines, such as the earliest moment for propounding discovery and filing summary judgment motions;
- Competing Jurisdiction Issues, when complaints involving the same parties and issues are filed in two different courts and the law provides that the first court to obtain jurisdiction should proceed and the second court should dismiss the case or abstain from exercising jurisdiction;
- Litigation of Claims Accruing After the Filing of the Complaint, where new claims usually cannot be litigated in the same case absent an amendment to the complaint;[11] and
- Compulsory Counterclaims, which must be filed or are deemed waived unless they are already the subject of another "pending" action.[12]

"Commencement" in Federal Question Cases

Ordinarily, in cases involving federal question jurisdiction, Rule 3 will govern when a lawsuit "commences" and will, typically, serve to toll the statute of limitations upon the filing of the complaint.[13] One exception exists—where the federal question is based on a statute that, itself, contains a separate "commencement" provision, the terms of that statute will control. In neither event will State law apply to the issue of

---

[8]*See U.S. v. Certain Real and Personal Property Belonging to Hayes*, 943 F.2d 1292 (11th Cir. 1991) (court's in rem jurisdiction depends upon court's continued control over property; if property is sold or removed from the court's jurisdiction, the forum is divested of jurisdiction).

[9]*See Freeport-McMoRan, Inc. v. K N Energy, Inc.*, 498 U.S. 426, 428, 111 S. Ct. 858, 859, 112 L. Ed. 2d 951 (1991) (if diversity jurisdiction exists at the time the lawsuit is filed, jurisdiction will not be divested by subsequent events). *Cf. Stevens v. Nichols*, 130 U.S. 230, 231–32, 9 S. Ct. 518, 518–19, 32 L. Ed. 914 (1889) (case may be removed to federal court only if diversity exists both at the time the action is commenced and at the time removal is sought).

[10]*See Daughetee v. CHR Hansen, Inc.*, 2011 WL 1113868, at *3–*4 (N.D. Iowa Mar. 25, 2011) (collecting cases showing division on issue, but noting majority view is to test venue as of time of filing).

[11]*See Rule 15. See also Altseimer v. Bell Helicopter Textron Inc.*, 919 F. Supp. 340, 342–43 (E.D. Cal. 1996) (citing Rule 3's "commencement" dating function in refusing to apply new federal statute to existing civil action, where new Act expressly did not apply to lawsuits "commenced" before the date of the Act's enactment).

[12]*See Rule 13(a)(2)(A).*

[13]*See Henderson v. U.S.*, 517 U.S. 654, 657 n.2, 116 S. Ct. 1638, 1641 n.2, 134 L. Ed. 2d 880 (1996). *See also Iran Air v. Kugelman*, 996 F.2d 1253, 1257 (D.C. Cir. 1993) (applying Rule 3 to toll statute of limitations on federally-created right even though service not accomplished until after period had expired).

"commencement". Even where the federal law lacks a specific statute of limitations, and the applicable limitations period is "borrowed" either from another federal law[14] or from State law,[15] Rule 3's commencement function will govern, and the filing of the complaint will generally toll the limitations period.

"Commencement" in Diversity Cases

In diversity cases, Rule 3 will apply for the purposes of evaluating uniquely federal issues, such as the presence or absence of diverse citizenship and the computation of time under the Federal Rules.[16]

However, Rule 3 will not always toll the applicable State law statute of limitations upon the mere filing of a diversity complaint. The *Erie* doctrine[17] compels that, where State law provides a contrary tolling requirement or tolling limitation, Rule 3 cannot be permitted to give the State law cause of action a longer life in a federal court than it would otherwise have in the State courts.[18] Thus, if under State law the limitations period would not be tolled until service is accomplished or the filing fee is paid, Rule 3 will not act to toll the limitations period merely upon filing.[19] Similarly, where State law requires the issuance of a summons before the applicable statute of limita-

---

[14]*See West v. Conrail*, 481 U.S. 35, 107 S. Ct. 1538, 95 L. Ed. 2d 32 (1987) (in action under Railway Labor Act, which lacked specific statute of limitations or commencement period, Rule 3 tolled the applicable statute of limitations upon filing).

[15]*See Sain v. City of Bend*, 309 F.3d 1134, 1135–38 (9th Cir. 2002) (joining other federal circuits in ruling that Rule 3 provides tolling function for limitations period borrowed from State law in Section 1983 case).

[16]*See Jenkins v. Village of Maywood*, 506 F.3d 622, 624 (7th Cir. 2007) (although federal courts borrow statute of limitations and coordinate tolling rules from State, federal procedural rules govern determination of when action was voluntarily dismissed).

[17]*Erie R. Co. v. Tompkins*, 304 U.S. 64, 58 S. Ct. 817, 82 L. Ed. 1188 (1938). The *Erie* doctrine may obligate the federal courts to apply State law as the substantive law of decision in diversity cases.

[18]*See Walker v. Armco Steel Corp.*, 446 U.S. 740, 100 S. Ct. 1978, 64 L. Ed. 2d 659 (1980); *Ragan v. Merchants Transfer & Warehouse Co.*, 337 U.S.

530, 69 S. Ct. 1233, 93 L. Ed. 1520 (1949).

[19]*See Henderson v. U.S.*, 517 U.S. 654, 657 n. 2, 116 S. Ct. 1638, 1641 n. 2, 134 L. Ed. 2d 880 (1996) (commenting that in a federal court action upon a right created by State law, the plaintiff must serve process before the statute of limitations has expired, if the law of that State so requires); *Walker v. Armco Steel Corp.*, 446 U.S. 740, 100 S. Ct. 1978, 64 L. Ed. 2d 659 (1980) (holding that Oklahoma law, which tolls the statute of limitations only upon service, supersedes Rule 3's tolling effect); *Ragan v. Merchants Transfer & Warehouse Co.*, 337 U.S. 530, 69 S. Ct. 1233, 93 L. Ed. 1520 (1949) (same conclusion under Kansas law); *Johnson v. Carroll*, 658 F.3d 819, 828–29 (8th Cir. 2011) (holding that Minnesota's commencement rule applies, which dates commencement by service); *Habermehl v. Potter*, 153 F.3d 1137, 1139 (10th Cir. 1998) (ruling that case was time-barred under Wyoming law, where limitations periods are only tolled 60 days for service, and service was not completed in time). *But cf. Hart v. Bates*, 897 F. Supp. 710 (E.D. N.Y. 1995) (applying federal, rather than Pennsylvania, time limita-

tions is tolled, the federal courts will honor that requirement: until the summons is issued, the limitations period will continue to run.[20]

"Commencement" in Supplemental Jurisdiction Cases

Where a complaint, invoking the federal courts' supplemental jurisdiction, pleads both federal claims and State law claims, the courts will likely follow the same rules as they do in diversity cases. Rule 3 will not give a State law cause of action longer life in a federal forum than that same cause of action would enjoy in State court.[21]

Commencement and Proper Pleading

There is some authority for the proposition that a complaint which is defectively pleaded under Rule 8 may not qualify as a proper commencement under Rule 3 (and, therefore, may not serve to toll an applicable limitations period).[22]

Commencement and Removed Cases

Ordinarily, a case is not considered "re"-commenced if it is removed to federal court. Instead, the general federal approach holds that a lawsuit is deemed "commenced" at one, discrete moment in time—typically, when the original lawsuit is filed in a court of competent jurisdiction.[23] Nevertheless, if an applicable State law requires effective service in order for "commencement" to be complete, the time for removal might be postponed; in such cases, the lawsuit might not be considered "commenced" (and, thus, eligible for removal) until the defendants are actually served.[24]

Commencement and Amended Complaints

Because an amended complaint often cannot be filed until leave of court has first been granted,[25] many courts have ruled that the amended complaint is deemed filed, for "commence-

---

tion for proper service of process where Pennsylvania did not condition the "commencement" of a civil action upon effective service, and did not deem service as integral to the tolling of its statute of limitations).

[20] See Eades v. Clark Distributing Co., Inc., 70 F.3d 441 (6th Cir. 1995).

[21] See Anderson v. Unisys Corp., 47 F.3d 302, 309 (8th Cir. 1995) (affirming dismissal of State law claims where, under Minnesota law, an action is not "commenced" until the initial process is served); Appletree Square I, Ltd. Partnership v. W.R. Grace & Co., 29 F.3d 1283, 1286 (8th Cir. 1994) (same).

[22] See Male v. Tops Friendly Markets, 2008 WL 1836948 (W.D. N.Y.

2008) (ruling that because contested complaint failed to satisfy the Twomby pleading standard, it did not "commence" an action under Rule 3, which denied a later amendment's claim for relation-back status, thus rendering the amending claims untimely).

[23] See Pritchett v. Office Depot, Inc., 420 F.3d 1090, 1094 (10th Cir. 2005). But see Wasserman v. Rodacker, 557 F.3d 635, 639 (D.C.Cir. 2009) (removed actions are "commenced" when removal is effected and clerk receives complaint).

[24] See, e.g., Dinkel v. General Motors Corp., 400 F. Supp. 2d 289, 293 (D. Me. 2005).

[25] See Rule 15.

ment" and statute of limitations purposes, as of the date that the motion for leave to amend is filed.[26] Practitioners should rely on this principle with great care, however. Whether this treatment applies to all cases (or just those where an earlier amendment was made impossible by circumstances), whether this treatment applies where the motion neither attaches the proposed amended complaint nor properly describes it, and whether this treatment has any effect where the leave is denied, are each unclear.

Commencement and Counterclaims

Only complaints are "commenced" (and, thus, implicated by Rule 3). A counterclaim is not a "civil action" and, therefore, is typically not deemed to "commence" within the meaning of Rule 3.[27]

Unique Prerequisites for Commencement

Certain federal statutes contain special prerequisites for commencing a civil action, such as receiving a right-to-sue letter or exhausting administrative remedies.[28] Thus, merely filing a complaint pursuant to Rule 3 might not toll the statute of limitations if such prerequisites are not met. Particular statutes should be consulted carefully for such prerequisites.

Filing By Mail

The "mailbox" rule generally will not apply in Rule 3 circumstances. If original papers are mailed to the Clerk's Office for filing, filing is only complete—and the lawsuit only "commences"—upon the Clerk's receipt of the complaint.[29]

Filing By Electronic Means

Where the district court operates an electronic filing system, a civil action may be deemed commenced upon the electronic filing itself, even though the filing fee is not yet paid.[30]

Filing After Business Hours

Rule 77 prescribes that the District Courts are "always

---

[26]See, e.g., Mayes v. AT & T Information Systems, Inc., 867 F.2d 1172, 1173 (8th Cir. 1989); Koch v. Shell Oil Co., 8 F. Supp. 2d 1264, 1267–68 (D. Kan. 1998); Massachusetts Public Interest Research Group v. ICI Americas Inc., 777 F. Supp. 1032, 1036 (D. Mass. 1991). See also Nett v. Bellucci, 437 Mass. 630, 630–47, 774 N.E.2d 130, 130–42 (2002) (on certified question from the First Circuit Court of Appeals, citing cases, and extensively discussing "commencement" effect of motion for leave to amend); The Children's Store v. Cody Enterprises, Inc., 154 Vt. 634, 640–42, 580 A.2d 1206, 1209–11 (1990) (same

effect).

[27]See Jonathan H. v. Souderton Area Sch. Dist., 562 F.3d 527, 529–30 (3d Cir. 2009).

[28]See, e.g., Truitt v. County of Wayne, 148 F.3d 644 (6th Cir.1998) (discussing EEOC right-to-sue letter procedure).

[29]See McIntosh v. Antonino, 71 F.3d 29, 36–37 (1st Cir. 1995); Cooper v. City of Ashland, 871 F.2d 104, 105 (9th Cir. 1989).

[30]See Searcy v. County of Oakland, 735 F.Supp.2d 759, 761 (E.D.Mich. 2010).

open". Accordingly, a complaint will often be deemed to be filed as of the time it was delivered to the Clerk's Office, even if delivered after the Clerk's business hours.[31] Likewise, a complaint transmitted for electronic filing with the court will still be deemed filed, even if the receiving computer rejected it.[32]

Filing Fees

The federal courts are divided over whether the payment of filing fees is required prior to commencing an action (and tolling the limitations period).[33] To avoid any risk on this point, fees should be paid properly at the time the complaint is delivered to the court.

Pauper and Prisoner Plaintiffs

The federal courts have an *in forma pauperis* procedure for plaintiffs who lack the ability to pay filing fees. A plaintiff proposing to proceed *in forma pauperis* can toll the statute of limitations by filing a proper motion for leave to proceed *in forma pauperis*.[34] However, if the petition to proceed *in forma pauperis* is denied, the plaintiff must promptly pay the court filing fees or risk losing the limitations period tolling benefit of having "commenced" the lawsuit.[35]

In complaints prepared by *pro se* prisoner plaintiffs, the courts have generally followed a variation of the "mailbox" rule

---

[31]*See Turner v. City of Newport*, 887 F. Supp. 149 (E.D. Ky. 1995) (holding that complaint was timely filed when delivered to the Clerk's post office box, after the office had closed, on last day before statute of limitations ran).

[32]*See Farzana K. v. Indiana Dept. of Educ.*, 473 F.3d 703, 706–07 (7th Cir. 2007).

[33]*See Searcy v. County of Oakland*, 735 F.Supp.2d 759, 765–68 (E.D.Mich. 2010) (noting national division on question, and that weight of authority favors view that payment of fee is not required for commencement). *Compare Robinson v. America's Best Contacts and Eyeglasses*, 876 F.2d 596 (7th Cir. 1989) (in Rule 4 context, construing local court rule to require payment of fee as prerequisite for filing) *with McDowell v. Delaware State Police*, 88 F.3d 188, 191 (3d Cir. 1996) (filing fee is not jurisdictional; although complaint is not deemed to be formally filed until fee is paid, it is constructively filed when the Clerk receives it, so long as the plaintiff ultimately pays the fee or is granted leave to proceed *in forma pauperis*); *Cintron v. Union*

Pacific R. Co., 813 F.2d 917, 920–21 (9th Cir. 1987) (filing fee is not jurisdictional); *Rodgers on Behalf of Jones v. Bowen*, 790 F.2d 1550 (11th Cir.1986) (dismissal was inappropriate sanction for non-payment of filing fees); *Wrenn v. American Cast Iron Pipe Co.*, 575 F.2d 544, 547 (5th Cir. 1978) (timely payment of filing fee is not jurisdictional).

[34]*See Powell v. Jacor Commc'ns Corp.*, 320 F.3d 599, 602–03 (6th Cir. 2003) (ruling that complaint, which would have been timely filed under Kentucky law had the acceptance of the complaint not been delayed by the *in forma pauperis* petition, was deemed timely filed under Rule 3).

[35]*See Truitt v. County of Wayne*, 148 F.3d 644 (6th Cir.1998) (pauper litigant must pay filing fee within applicable limitations period, as tolled during the pendency of the *in forma pauperis* application); *Williams-Guice v. Board of Educ. of City of Chicago*, 45 F.3d 161 (7th Cir. 1995) (limitations period resumes running once *in forma pauperis* application is denied); *Jarrett v. US Sprint Commc'ns Co.*, 22 F.3d 256 (10th Cir. 1994) (same).

that deems a lawsuit as "commenced" upon delivery of the complaint to the prison officials.[36]

Additional Research References

Wright & Miller, *Federal Practice and Procedure* §§ 1051 to 57
C.J.S., Federal Civil Procedure § 3
West's Key Number Digest, Federal Civil Procedure ☞4

---

[36]*See Cooper v. Brookshire*, 70 F.3d 377 (5th Cir.1995); *Dory v. Ryan*, 999 F.2d 679 (2d Cir.1993); *Garvey v. Vaughn*, 993 F.2d 776 (11th Cir.1993). *Cf. Houston v. Lack*, 487 U.S. 266, 108 S. Ct. 2379, 101 L. Ed. 2d 245 (1988) (holding that notice of appeal is "filed" within the meaning of the Federal Rules of Appellate Procedure when delivered by a *pro se* prisoner to the prison authorities). *But see Jackson v. Nicoletti*, 875 F. Supp. 1107 (E.D. Pa. 1994) (after recounting six reasons for refusing to extend the Supreme Court's *Houston v. Lack* appeal-period mailbox rule to assessing "commencement" of a *pro se* prisoner's lawsuit under Rule 3, the district court dismissed the lawsuit as time-barred where the complaint was not delivered to the clerk of court within two years after the prisoner's claim accrued).

RULE 4
SUMMONS

(a) Contents; Amendments.

(1) *Contents.* A summons must:

(A) name the court and the parties;

(B) be directed to the defendant;

(C) state the name and address of the plaintiff's attorney or—if unrepresented—of the plaintiff;

(D) state the time within which the defendant must appear and defend;

(E) notify the defendant that a failure to appear and defend will result in a default judgment against the defendant for the relief demanded in the complaint;

(F) be signed by the clerk; and

(G) bear the court's seal.

(2) *Amendments.* The court may permit a summons to be amended.

(b) Issuance.
On or after filing the complaint, the plaintiff may present a summons to the clerk for signature and seal. If the summons is properly completed, the clerk must sign, seal, and issue it to the plaintiff for service on the defendant. A summons—or a copy of a summons that is addressed to multiple defendants—must be issued for each defendant to be served.

(c) Service.

(1) *In General.* A summons must be served with a copy of the complaint. The plaintiff is responsible for having the summons and complaint served within the time allowed by Rule 4(m) and must furnish the necessary copies to the person who makes service.

(2) *By Whom.* Any person who is at least 18 years old and not a party may serve a summons and complaint.

(3) *By a Marshal or Someone Specially Appointed.*

At the plaintiff's request, the court may order that service be made by a United States marshal or deputy marshal or by a person specially appointed by the court. The court must so order if the plaintiff is authorized to proceed in forma pauperis under 28 U.S.C. § 1915 or as a seaman under 28 U.S.C. § 1916.

(d) Waiving Service.

    (1) *Requesting a Waiver.* An individual, corporation, or association that is subject to service under Rule 4(e), (f), or (h) has a duty to avoid unnecessary expenses of serving the summons. The plaintiff may notify such a defendant that an action has been commenced and request that the defendant waive service of a summons. The notice and request must:

    (A) be in writing and be addressed:

        (i) to the individual defendant; or

        (ii) for a defendant subject to service under Rule 4(h), to an officer, a managing or general agent, or any other agent authorized by appointment or by law to receive service of process;

    (B) name the court where the complaint was filed;

    (C) be accompanied by a copy of the complaint, two copies of a waiver form, and a prepaid means for returning the form;

    (D) inform the defendant, using text prescribed in Form 5, of the consequences of waiving and not waiving service;

    (E) state the date when the request is sent;

    (F) give the defendant a reasonable time of at least 30 days after the request was sent—or at least 60 days if sent to the defendant outside any judicial district of the United States—to return the waiver; and

    (G) be sent by first-class mail or other reliable means.

    (2) *Failure to Waive.* If a defendant located within the United States fails, without good cause, to sign and return a waiver requested by a plaintiff

located within the United States, the court must impose on the defendant:

    (A) the expenses later incurred in making service; and

    (B) the reasonable expenses, including attorney's fees, of any motion required to collect those service expenses.

(3) *Time to Answer After a Waiver.* A defendant who, before being served with process, timely returns a waiver need not serve an answer to the complaint until 60 days after the request was sent—or until 90 days after it was sent to the defendant outside any judicial district of the United States.

(4) *Results of Filing a Waiver.* When the plaintiff files a waiver, proof of service is not required and these rules apply as if a summons and complaint had been served at the time of filing the waiver.

(5) *Jurisdiction and Venue Not Waived.* Waiving service of a summons does not waive any objection to personal jurisdiction or to venue.

(e) Serving an Individual Within a Judicial District of the United States. Unless federal law provides otherwise, an individual—other than a minor, an incompetent person, or a person whose waiver has been filed—may be served in a judicial district of the United States by:

(1) following state law for serving a summons in an action brought in courts of general jurisdiction in the state where the district court is located or where service is made; or

(2) doing any of the following:

    (A) delivering a copy of the summons and of the complaint to the individual personally;

    (B) leaving a copy of each at the individual's dwelling or usual place of abode with someone of suitable age and discretion who resides there; or

    (C) delivering a copy of each to an agent authorized by appointment or by law to receive service of process.

(f) **Serving an Individual in a Foreign Country.** Unless federal law provides otherwise, an individual—other than a minor, an incompetent person, or a person whose waiver has been filed—may be served at a place not within any judicial district of the United States:

  (1) by any internationally agreed means of service that is reasonably calculated to give notice, such as those authorized by the Hague Convention on the Service Abroad of Judicial and Extrajudicial Documents;

  (2) if there is no internationally agreed means, or if an international agreement allows but does not specify other means, by a method that is reasonably calculated to give notice:

    (A) as prescribed by the foreign country's law for service in that country in an action in its courts of general jurisdiction;

    (B) as the foreign authority directs in response to a letter rogatory or letter of request; or

    (C) unless prohibited by the foreign country's law, by:

      (i) delivering a copy of the summons and of the complaint to the individual personally; or

      (ii) using any form of mail that the clerk addresses and sends to the individual and that requires a signed receipt; or

  (3) by other means not prohibited by international agreement, as the court orders.

(g) **Serving a Minor or an Incompetent Person.** A minor or an incompetent person in a judicial district of the United States must be served by following state law for serving a summons or like process on such a defendant in an action brought in the courts of general jurisdiction of the state where service is made. A minor or an incompetent person who is not within any judicial district of the United States must be served in the manner prescribed by Rule 4(f)(2)(A), (f)(2)(B), or (f)(3).

(h) **Serving a Corporation, Partnership, or Association.** Unless federal law provides other-

wise or the defendant's waiver has been filed, a domestic or foreign corporation, or a partnership or
other unincorporated association that is subject to
suit under a common name, must be served:

(1) in a judicial district of the United States:

   (A) in the manner prescribed by Rule 4(e)(1) for
        serving an individual; or

   (B) by delivering a copy of the summons and of
        the complaint to an officer, a managing or gen-
        eral agent, or any other agent authorized by
        appointment or by law to receive service of
        process and—if the agent is one authorized by
        statute and the statute so requires—by also
        mailing a copy of each to the defendant; or

(2) at a place not within any judicial district of the
     United States, in any manner prescribed by Rule
     4(f) for serving an individual, except personal
     delivery under (f)(2)(C)(i).

**(i) Serving the United States and Its Agencies,
Corporations, Officers, or Employees.**

(1) *United States.* To serve the United States, a
     party must:

   (A) (i) deliver a copy of the summons and of the
            complaint to the United States attorney for
            the district where the action is brought—or
            to an assistant United States attorney or
            clerical employee whom the United States
            attorney designates in a writing filed with
            the court clerk—or

       (ii) send a copy of each by registered or certi-
             fied mail to the civil-process clerk at the
             United States attorney's office;

   (B) send a copy of each by registered or certified
        mail to the Attorney General of the United
        States at Washington, D.C.; and

   (C) if the action challenges an order of a nonparty
        agency or officer of the United States, send a
        copy of each by registered or certified mail to
        the agency or officer.

(2) *Agency; Corporation; Officer or Employee Sued in
     an Official Capacity.* To serve a United States
     agency or corporation, or a United States officer

or employee sued only in an official capacity, a party must serve the United States and also send a copy of the summons and of the complaint by registered or certified mail to the agency, corporation, officer, or employee.

(3) *Officer or Employee Sued Individually.* To serve a United States officer or employee sued in an individual capacity for an act or omission occurring in connection with duties performed on the United States' behalf (whether or not the officer or employee is also sued in an official capacity), a party must serve the United States and also serve the officer or employee under Rule 4(e), (f), or (g).

(4) *Extending Time.* The court must allow a party a reasonable time to cure its failure to:

(A) serve a person required to be served under Rule 4(i)(2), if the party has served either the United States attorney or the Attorney General of the United States; or

(B) serve the United States under Rule 4(i)(3), if the party has served the United States officer or employee.

(j) Serving a Foreign, State, or Local Government.

(1) *Foreign State.* A foreign state or its political subdivision, agency, or instrumentality must be served in accordance with 28 U.S.C. § 1608.

(2) *State or Local Government.* A state, a municipal corporation, or any other state-created governmental organization that is subject to suit must be served by:

(A) delivering a copy of the summons and of the complaint to its chief executive officer; or

(B) serving a copy of each in the manner prescribed by that state's law for serving a summons or like process on such a defendant.

(k) Territorial Limits of Effective Service.

(1) *In General.* Serving a summons or filing a waiver of service establishes personal jurisdiction over a defendant:

(A) who is subject to the jurisdiction of a court of

general jurisdiction in the state where the district court is located;

    (B) who is a party joined under Rule 14 or 19 and is served within a judicial district of the United States and not more than 100 miles from where the summons was issued;

    (C) when authorized by a federal statute.

(2) *Federal Claim Outside State-Court Jurisdiction.* For a claim that arises under federal law, serving a summons or filing a waiver of service establishes personal jurisdiction over a defendant if:

    (A) the defendant is not subject to jurisdiction in any state's courts of general jurisdiction; and

    (B) exercising jurisdiction is consistent with the United States Constitution and laws.

(*l*) Proving Service.

(1) *Affidavit Required.* Unless service is waived, proof of service must be made to the court. Except for service by a United States marshal or deputy marshal, proof must be by the server's affidavit.

(2) *Service Outside the United States.* Service not within any judicial district of the United States must be proved as follows:

    (A) if made under Rule 4(f)(1), as provided in the applicable treaty or convention; or

    (B) if made under Rule 4(f)(2) or (f)(3), by a receipt signed by the addressee, or by other evidence satisfying the court that the summons and complaint were delivered to the addressee.

(3) *Validity of Service; Amending Proof.* Failure to prove service does not affect the validity of service. The court may permit proof of service to be amended.

(m) Time Limit for Service. If a defendant is not served within 120 days after the complaint is filed, the court—on motion or on its own after notice to the plaintiff—must dismiss the action without prejudice against that defendant or order that service be made within a specified time. But if the plaintiff shows good cause for the failure, the court must extend the time for service for an appropriate period. This subdivision (m) does not apply to service in a foreign country under Rule 4(f) or 4(j)(1).

(n) Asserting Jurisdiction over Property or Assets.

(1) *Federal Law.* The court may assert jurisdiction over property if authorized by a federal statute. Notice to claimants of the property must be given as provided in the statute or by serving a summons under this rule.

(2) *State Law.* On a showing that personal jurisdiction over a defendant cannot be obtained in the district where the action is brought by reasonable efforts to serve a summons under this rule, the court may assert jurisdiction over the defendant's assets found in the district. Jurisdiction is acquired by seizing the assets under the circumstances and in the manner provided by state law in that district.

[Amended January 21, 1963, effective July 1, 1963; February 28, 1966, effective July 1, 1966; April 29, 1980, effective August 1, 1980; amended by Pub.L. 97-462, § 2, January 12, 1983, 96 Stat. 2527, effective 45 days after January 12, 1983; amended March 2, 1987, effective August 1, 1987; April 22, 1993, effective December 1, 1993; April 17, 2000, effective December 1, 2000; April 30, 2007, effective December 1, 2007.]

AUTHORS' COMMENTARY ON RULE 4

PURPOSE AND SCOPE

Rule 4 sets forth the procedure for notifying defendants that a federal civil lawsuit has been filed against them. This procedure requires that the defendants be served with "original process"—a copy of a summons and complaint. Rule 4 does *not* address whether a defendant is amenable to jurisdiction within the particular judicial district, or whether service on a defendant is consistent with the Due Process Clause of the United States Constitution. Instead, Rule 4 simply sets forth the procedure for serving the summons and complaint, *assuming* the defendant can be served properly and constitutionally.

GENERAL COMMENTARY ON SERVICE

"Constitutional" *versus* "Rule 4" Service

The U.S. Constitution's Due Process Clause requires that service be completed in a manner that is "reasonably calculated," under the circumstances, to apprise the defendant of the pending lawsuit and to afford a reasonable opportunity to make a defense.[1] Meeting this constitutional standard, however, is not sufficient. The manner of service must *also* comport with the procedural requirements set by Rule 4.[2] Together, the goal of service is provide such notice that the opposing party may fairly respond to the lawsuit.[3]

Actual Notice Is Not *Required*

The mere fact that a defendant did not receive actual notice of the lawsuit does not necessarily render service of process defective or personal jurisdiction improper.[4] So long as the constitutional "reasonably calculated" standard is satisfied, lack of actual notice does not offend the Due Process Clause.[5] Due process will require, however, that if a plaintiff comes to learn that an attempted service failed to reach the defendant, additional efforts to re-attempt service will be required if they would be reasonable under the circumstances.[6]

Actual Notice Alone is Not *Enough*

Although the core goal of service is to ensure that the defendants are aware of the lawsuit pending against them, simply proving their actual, subjective awareness is unlikely to be sufficient. Actual receipt of notice likely will satisfy the Constitution's due process requirements,[7] but formal compli-

---

[1]*See Jones v. Flowers*, 547 U.S. 220, 226 (2006); *Mullane v. Central Hanover Bank & Trust Co.*, 339 U.S. 306, 314 (1950).

[2]*See Williams v. GEICO Corp.*, 792 F.Supp.2d 58, 65 (D.D.C. 2011) (satisfying constitutional requirements for notice does not necessarily satisfy the notice requirements imposed by the Rules). *See also Omni Capital Int'l, Ltd. v. Rudolf Wolff & Co., Ltd.*, 484 U.S. 97, 104 (1987); *S.E.C. v. Ross*, 504 F.3d 1130, 1140 (9th Cir. 2007); *Albra v. Advan, Inc.*, 490 F.3d 826, 828 (11th Cir. 2007); *Bridgeport Music, Inc. v. Rhyme Syndicate Music*, 376 F.3d 615, 623 (6th Cir. 2004); *McMasters v. U.S.*, 260 F.3d 814, 817–18 (7th Cir. 2001).

[3]*See Henderson v. U.S.*, 517 U.S. 654, 672, 116 S. Ct. 1638, 1648, 134 L. Ed. 2d 880 (1996).

[4]*See Dusenbery v. United States*, 534 U.S. 161, 171, 122 S.Ct. 694, 151 L.Ed.2d 597 (2002) (noting that Court has never required actual notice (*i.e.*, receipt of notice) as inexorable requirement for satisfying due process).

[5]*See Jones v. Flowers*, 547 U.S. 220, 226 (2006); *Mullane v. Central Hanover Bank & Trust Co.*, 339 U.S. 306, 314 (1950).

[6]*See Jones v. Flowers*, 547 U.S. 220, 226–39 (2006).

[7]*See United Student Aid Funds, Inc. v. Espinosa*, __ U.S. __, __, 130 S.Ct. 1367, 1378, 176 L.Ed.2d 158 (2010) (actual notice satisfies due process rights to notice).

ance with Rule 4 is required as well.[8] However, if actual notice occurred, Rule 4 will likely be given a liberal construction.[9]

Distinguishing *Service* from *Jurisdiction* and *Venue*

Service of the summons and complaint (or waiver of service) is a prerequisite to the district court's exercise of jurisdiction over a defendant.[10] But complying with the federal service rules does not mean that proper jurisdiction and proper venue exists. Though impacted by service,[11] those concepts (jurisdiction and venue) are distinct from service and must be separately satisfied.[12] All of these requirements — proper service, proper jurisdiction, and proper venue — are prerequisites to the exercise of federal judicial power.

Jurisdiction over the Subject Matter: Federal courts are courts of limited jurisdiction. They may hear only those cases over which the Constitution and Congress give them authority. Such authority has been given to federal courts to hear disputes over "federal questions," such as those involving federal laws, federal constitutional rights, admiralty, bankruptcy, patents, copyrights, and postal matters.[13] Federal courts also may hear "diversity" disputes of more than $75,000, such as those between citizens of different States, or between American citizens and foreign nationals or foreign countries.[14] And when federal question or federal diversity jurisdiction exists, federal courts may hear some accompanying State claims that, though not independently qualifying for federal jurisdiction, are so related to claims that do qualify that the interests of judicial economy permit the exercise of "supplemental" jurisdiction.[15]

Jurisdiction over the Person (or Thing): Like all courts, federal courts must also possess the legal right to exercise coercive authority over (and issue a judgment binding upon) the particular parties to a lawsuit. Plaintiffs consent to such authority when they file their lawsuits in the forum. Although defendants, too, may consent to such authority, when they re-

---

[8]*See Williams v. GEICO Corp.*, 792 F. Supp. 2d 58, 65 (D.D.C. 2011) (satisfying constitutional requirements for notice does not necessarily satisfy the notice requirements imposed by the Rules). *See also Omni Capital Int'l, Ltd. v. Rudolf Wolff & Co., Ltd.*, 484 U.S. 97, 104 (1987); *Mann v. Castiel*, 681 F.3d 368, 372 (D.C.Cir. 2012); *S.E.C. v. Ross*, 504 F.3d 1130, 1140 (9th Cir. 2007).

[9]*See Direct Mail Specialists, Inc. v. Eclat Computerized Techs., Inc.*, 840 F.2d 685, 688 (9th Cir. 1988); *Armco, Inc. v. Penrod-Stauffer Bldg. Sys., Inc.*, 733 F.2d 1087, 1089 (4th Cir. 1984).

[10]*See Omni Capital Intern., Ltd. v. Rudolf Wolff & Co., Ltd.*, 484 U.S.

97, 103, 108 S. Ct. 404, 409, 98 L. Ed. 2d 415 (1987).

[11]*See Mississippi Publishing Corp. v. Murphree*, 326 U.S. 438, 444–45, 66 S.Ct. 242, 90 L.Ed. 185 (1946) ("service of summons is the procedure by which a court having venue and jurisdiction of the subject matter of the suit asserts jurisdiction over the person of the party served").

[12]*See Henderson v. U.S.*, 517 U.S. 654, 670, 116 S. Ct. 1638, 1647, 134 L. Ed. 2d 880 (1996).

[13]*See* 28 U.S.C.A. §§ 1331, 1333 to 1367.

[14]*See* 28 U.S.C.A. § 1332.

[15]*See* 28 U.S.C.A. § 1367.

fuse, federal courts still may possess such authority if those defendants have such sufficient contacts with the forum that requiring them to travel to that forum and defend there will not offend the "traditional notions of fair play and substantial justice" demanded by constitutional due process.[16]

Venue: Finally, venue defines which, among the various potential judicial districts, is most logically and conveniently the proper site for the lawsuit.[17]

The nuances of federal jurisdiction and venue are discussed in greater detail in Part II of this text (*General Concepts In Federal Practice*).

Immunity from Service

In certain circumstances, a defendant who might otherwise be properly served with a summons and complaint may be deemed to be "immune" from service. Immunity from service is governed by federal case law, and exists where the due administration of justice demands it.[18] Whether to confer the immunity is vested in the discretion of the district court; the purpose of the immunity is *not* primarily to protect the defendant who is seeking to avoid service, but instead to aid the court in its judicial administration.[19] Persons are generally immune from service when they are present in the jurisdiction to attend court, give a deposition, or conduct settlement discussions in connection with another, unrelated lawsuit, or when they enter the jurisdiction to participate in a legislative or administrative hearing process.[20] This immunity generally encompasses not only the time when the person is actually present in court or attending other formal proceedings, but also typically extends for a reasonable period before and after the proceedings to allow the person to enter and then freely leave the jurisdiction.[21]

Persons may also be immune from service when they are lured by fraud or trickery into the jurisdiction by the plaintiff who then attempts to serve them.[22] Indeed, some courts have even adopted a bright line rule for in-State negotiations: these

---

[16]*See International Shoe Co. v. Washington,* 326 U.S. 310, 316, 66 S. Ct. 154, 158, 90 L. Ed. 95 (1945).

[17]*See* 28 U.S.C.A. §§ 1391 to 1412.

[18]*See Stewart v. Ramsay,* 242 U.S. 128, 37 S. Ct. 44, 61 L. Ed. 192 (1916). *See also ARW Exploration Corp. v. Aguirre,* 45 F.3d 1455 (10th Cir.1995) (noting that immunity from service is a procedural, not substantive, rule, and *Erie* concerns do not dictate that State law apply).

[19]*See Northern Light Technology, Inc. v. Northern Lights Club,* 236 F.3d 57, 62 (1st Cir. 2001); *Estate of Ungar*

v. Palestinian Authority, 396 F. Supp. 2d 376, 381 (S.D. N.Y. 2005).

[20]*See Lamb v. Schmitt,* 285 U.S. 222, 52 S. Ct. 317, 76 L. Ed. 720 (1932); *Page Co. v. MacDonald,* 261 U.S. 446, 43 S. Ct. 416, 67 L. Ed. 737 (1923).

[21]*See Cabiri v. Assasie-Gyimah,* 921 F. Supp. 1189, 1193 (S.D. N.Y. 1996).

[22]*See Fitzgerald & Mallory Const. Co. v. Fitzgerald,* 137 U.S. 98, 104, 11 S. Ct. 36, 34 L. Ed. 608 (1890); *Gudavadze v. Kay,* 556 F. Supp. 2d 299, 304 (S.D. N.Y. 2008); *May Dept.*

courts hold that when a plaintiff invites a defendant to enter the foreign jurisdiction for settlement discussions, the plaintiff may not, during those discussions, serve the defendant with process unless defendants are either cautioned that they may be served while present or, after having entered the jurisdiction, they are first given an opportunity to depart immediately after the discussions fail.[23]

This immunity, however, can be waived. A defendant who fails to timely assert immunity may be deemed to have waived it.[24] Likewise, a defendant who is immune for the purposes of attending court or a deposition may waive the immunity by arriving in the jurisdiction prematurely, by conducting other business while in the jurisdiction, or by failing to leave the jurisdiction promptly.[25] Some courts have held that defendants may also lack immunity if they enter the forum to defend against criminal charges,[26] to attend proceedings as a mere "spectator" with no obligation to be there,[27] or when the service involves the same case or a case arising out of or involving the same subject matter as the one for which the defendants are already appearing.[28]

Service in Removed Cases

Once a case has been removed from State court to federal

Stores Co. v. Wilansky, 900 F. Supp. 1154, 1163–64 (E.D. Mo. 1995); *Henkel Corp. v. Degremont, S.A.*, 136 F.R.D. 88, 91 (E.D. Pa. 1991).

[23]*See May Dept. Stores Co. v. Wilansky*, 900 F. Supp. 1154, 1164–65 (E.D. Mo. 1995) (collecting cases).

[24]*See Republic Productions, Inc v. American Federation of Musicians of U S and Canada*, 173 F. Supp. 330 (S.D. N.Y. 1959). *See also Fitzgerald & Mallory Const. Co. v. Fitzgerald*, 137 U.S. 98, 104, 11 S. Ct. 36, 34 L. Ed. 608 (1890) (noting opportunity for a motion challenging service, but observing that no such motion had been filed).

[25]*See Uniroyal, Inc. v. Sperberg*, 63 F.R.D. 55 (S.D. N.Y. 1973) (applying the "dual purpose rule", which forfeits service immunity when a person, present in a foreign jurisdiction for the purpose of the administration of justice, engages in unrelated business dealings or social activity while present in the foreign jurisdiction). *Cf. Fun-Damental Too, Ltd. v. Hwung*, 1997 WL 289712 (S.D. N.Y. 1997) (immunity not waived where nonresident defendant traveled to the forum for a

deposition and, on the night before his deposition, visited a showroom for one hour and had dinner; such activities were "trivial and insubstantial"). *See generally Willbros Int'l, Inc. v. Hydrodive Int'l, Ltd.*, 2008 WL 4178339, at *2 (S.D.Tex. Sept. 5, 2008) (noting that waiver view is "not widely recognized", and in any event is based not on whether other activities occurred but on their degree and proportion).

[26]*See Garibay v. Sullivan*, 2010 WL 4509826, at *2 (D.Ariz. Oct. 28, 2010).

[27]*See Northern Light Technology, Inc. v. Northern Lights Club*, 236 F.3d 57, 63 (1st Cir. 2001). *But see Norex Petroleum Ltd. v. Access Indus., Inc.*, 620 F.Supp.2d 587, 590 (S.D.N.Y. 2009) (voluntary or involuntary character of witness' appearance should not govern availability of privilege).

[28]*See ARW Exploration Corp. v. Aguirre*, 45 F.3d 1455 (10th Cir.1995); *Sullivan v. Sullivan*, 2003 WL 22218166, at *1 (D. Conn. 2003); *Cabiri v. Assasie-Gyimah*, 921 F. Supp. 1189 (S.D. N.Y. 1996); *In re Aluminum Phosphide Antitrust Litigation*, 160 F.R.D. 629 (D. Kan. 1995).

court, service of process can be completed (or, if defective, new process can issue) as though the lawsuit had been filed originally in federal court.[29] Prior to removal, the applicable State laws will typically govern the propriety of service and process; following removal, the federal Rules will govern.[30]

Service When "Federal Law Provides Otherwise"

Congress has, on occasion, written laws that contain their own, particular service of process provisions. In such contexts, various parts of Rule 4 confirm that service of process can be accomplished on individuals, corporations, associations, and other non-governmental entities by following those law-specific provisions.[31]

- *Multiparty, Multiforum Jurisdiction Statute:* Where federal jurisdiction is based, in whole or in part, upon the federal multiparty, multijurisdictional statute,[32] service can be made at any place within the United States or, if otherwise permitted by law, anywhere outside the United States.[33]

Serving Amended Complaints

Generally, amended complaints are served under Rule 5, and the rigors of proper Rule 4 service are not implicated.[34] However, Rule 4 service could nevertheless still be required for the amended complaint if new defendants are added, if the claims contained there differ significantly from those in the original pleading, if circumstances persuade the court that Rule 5 service on the attorney is unlikely to ensure notice to the party, if extraterritorial service was made originally and the amendment contains claims unrelated to the original dispute, or if the precepts of Due Process otherwise require it.[35]

---

[29]*See* 28 U.S.C.A. § 1448.

[30]*See Norsyn, Inc. v. Desai,* 351 F.3d 825, 829 n.4 (8th Cir. 2003).

[31]*See* Rule 4(e) (permitting service on individuals within the United States with a federal law that "provides otherwise"); Rule 4(f) (same, for individuals in a foreign country); Rule 4(h) (same, for corporations and associations). *But see* Rule 4(g) (service on infants and incompetents contains no such provision); Rule 4(i) (same, for United States, its agencies, corporations, officers, or employees); Rule 4(j) (same, for foreign, state, or local governments).

[32]*See* 28 U.S.C.A. § 1369.

[33]*See* 28 U.S.C.A. § 1697.

[34]*See Employee Painters' Trust v. Ethan Enterprises, Inc.,* 480 F.3d 993, 999 (9th Cir. 2007); *Mach v. Florida Casino Cruise, Inc.,* 187 F.R.D. 15, 17 (D. Mass. 1999).

[35]*See Brait Builders Corp. v. Massachusetts, Div. of Capital Asset Mgmt.,* 644 F.3d 5, 9–10 (1st Cir. 2011); *Employee Painters' Trust v. Ethan Enterprises, Inc.,* 480 F.3d 993, 999 (9th Cir. 2007). *See also* Authors' Commentary to Rule 5(a) (**"Pleadings Asserting Claims Against Existing Parties"**).

Burden of Proving Service of Process

The party attempting service generally bears the burden of establishing that the service is proper.[36] This burden may shift, however, if the opposing party does not promptly move to challenge the purported service. If a default judgment is entered against such a party, that party may bear the burden of proving that the purported service was defective.[37]

RULE 4(a)—CONTENTS OF AND AMENDING SUMMONS

CORE CONCEPT

The form of a federal summons is the same in all federal cases. The earlier practice of permitting the use of State forms of summons has been abandoned. A standardized federal summons form has been approved by the United States Supreme Court.[38] The summons must:

- *Issue from the Clerk:* The summons must be issued by the clerk of court, and must bear the court's seal and the clerk's signature.
- *Identify the Case:* The summons must also identify the district court, name the parties to the lawsuit, and list the name and address of plaintiff or plaintiff's attorney.
- *Be Directed to the Defendant:* The summons must be directed specifically to the defendant.
- *Note Time to Appear:* The summons must state the time within which the defendant must appear and defend.
- *Warn Against Default:* The summons must caution the defendant that a failure to appear and defend will result in the entry of a default judgment for the relief requested in the complaint.

APPLICATIONS

Purpose of Summons

The purpose of the summons is to alert the defendants that a lawsuit is pending against them and that they have a limited time in which to respond. The summons is not required to advise the defendant of every conceivable response one could make to the lawsuit.[39]

Invalid Summons

A summons that has not been issued, signed, and sealed by

---

[36]*See Mann v. Castiel*, 681 F.3d 368, 372 (D.C.Cir. 2012); *Grand Entertainment Group, Ltd. v. Star Media Sales, Inc.*, 988 F.2d 476, 488 (3d Cir. 1993).

[37]*See Burda Media, Inc. v. Viertel*, 417 F.3d 292, 299 (2d Cir. 2005).

[38]*See* Form 1 ("Summons"), in-cluded with the Appendix of Forms as reprinted in this text.

[39]*See Frye v. Bowman, Heintz, Boscia, Vician, P.C.*, 193 F. Supp. 2d 1070, 1080 (S.D. Ind. 2002) (noting the "inherent difficulties in attempting to provide all potentially helpful information in a summons", the court wrote

the clerk of court is a nullity and cannot confer personal jurisdiction over the defendant; this defect is fundamental and,
ordinarily, cannot be waived.[40]

Form of Summons Otherwise Liberally Examined

If the summons omits one of the requirements for proper
form, but otherwise generally complies with the Rule's requirements, the court may choose not to dismiss the lawsuit but
instead may permit an amendment to the summons or grant
some other cure.[41] For example, a summons that is properly
"directed" to the defendant, but prints a wrong address, or
contains an otherwise inconsequential defect, will generally not
be dismissed for this mistake.[42] Similar inconsequential fail-
ings may be ignored as well.[43] Where the summons more
fundamentally fails to comply with the Rule, the court may
enter a dismissal.[44]

---

that it "would hardly seem practical to
attach to a summons a copy of the
Federal Rules of Civil Procedure and
portions of the United States Code").

[40]*See Ayres v. Jacobs & Crumplar,
P.A.*, 99 F.3d 565, 568–70 (3d Cir.
1996); *McKibben v. Credit Lyonnais*,
1999 WL 604883, at *2 (S.D.N.Y. Aug.
10, 1999). *See also Harper v. City of
New York*, 424 Fed. Appx. 36, 40 (2d
Cir. 2011) (summons improper when
not issued by clerk and lacking court's
seal); *Macaluso v. N.Y. State Dep't of
Envt'l Conservation*, 115 F.R.D. 16,
17–18 (E.D.N.Y. 1986) (dismissing
without leave to replead). *But see Clark
v. Goodwill Indus. of Hawaii, Inc.*,
2009 WL 3050277, at *4–*5 (D.Haw.
Sept. 21, 2009) (although "not perfect",
service of summons lacking clerk's
signature and seal was still "substantial compliance" with Rule 4).

[41]*See George W. v. U.S. Dept. of
Educ.*, 149 F. Supp. 2d 1195, 1200–02
(E.D. Cal. 2000) (noting that Rule 4 is
"flexible" and "should be liberally
construed so long as a party receives
sufficient notice of the complaint").

[42]*See Spiess v. Meyers*, 483 F.
Supp. 2d 1082, 1093 (D. Kan. 2007);
Sullivan v. Potter, 2006 WL 785289,
at *2 (D.D.C. 2006).

[43]*See Doe v. Constant*, 354
Fed.Appx. 543, 546 (2d Cir. 2009)
(rejecting Rule 4(b) error where defendant received actual notice, and summons' defects (misstating full business
name, labeling party as "commander")
were "purely clerical"); *Wortham v.
American Family Ins. Co.*, 2002 WL
31128057, at *2–3 (N.D. Iowa 2002)
(dismissal denied, and leave to amend
summons granted, where only one
defendant's name appeared on summons, although other defendants were
clearly identified in caption of both
summons and complaint); *GMAC
Mortg. Corp. of PA v. Weisman*, 1997
WL 83416 (S.D. N.Y. 1997) (although
summons failed to state the time for
response, because defendant did not
immediately object to the defect and
even reached stipulation on time for
response, court would not dismiss the
complaint). *But see Sene v. MBNA
America, Inc.*, 2005 WL 2304181 (D.
Del. 2005) (summons contained neither seal of court nor signature of
clerk, and court dismissed lawsuit).

[44]*See Wasson v. Riverside County*,
237 F.R.D. 423 (C.D. Cal. 2006)
(quashing service on party not named
in complaint and for whom no summons was issued by the Clerk);
Schroeder v. Kochanowski, 311 F.
Supp. 2d 1241, 1256 (D. Kan. 2004)
(dismissal granted where served summons was copy, lacking court seal, and
omitted plaintiff's name and address).

RULE 4(b)—ISSUANCE OF SUMMONS

CORE CONCEPT

Once the complaint is filed, the plaintiff is responsible for preparing the summons in an appropriate form, and submitting it to the clerk of court for signing and sealing. If the plaintiff's summons is proper, the clerk will sign and seal the form, and issue it to the plaintiff for service. Copies of the summons must be issued for each defendant.

APPLICATIONS

Form of Summons Liberally Examined

Courts liberally construe the issuance requirements of Rule 4(b).[45] If the summons is sufficiently accurate to provide proper notice, and any alleged defect in form has not prejudiced the defendant, a defect in the form of summons as issued will be discounted as harmless and the plaintiff will be afforded an opportunity to amend the summons to cure the error.[46]

Photocopies of Summons in Multi-Defendant Cases

An original summons—containing a raised seal-of-the-court and a pen-signed signature of the clerk—may not be necessary in cases involving multiple defendants. In such cases, copies of the original summons (that bear the name of the served defendant) may be used.[47] But each defendant in a multi-defendant case must receive both a summons and complaint, or the service fails.[48]

RULE 4(c)—SERVICE

CORE CONCEPT

A summons and complaint are served together. The plaintiff is responsible for effective service. A U.S. Marshal will serve process, but only if ordered to do so by the court.

APPLICATIONS

Both Summons and Complaint Must Be Served

In order for Rule 4 service to be proper, *both* the summons and complaint must be served. Neglecting either one entitles the defendant to a dismissal for improper service.[49] Serving an

---

[45]*But cf. Authors' Commentary to Rule 4(a) supra,* "**Invalid Summons**".

[46]*See Time Products v. J. Tiras Classic Handbags, Inc.*, 1994 WL 363930 (S.D. N.Y. 1994).

[47]*See New York Transp., Inc. v. Naples Transp., Inc.*, 116 F. Supp. 2d 382, 386 (E.D. N.Y. 2000).

[48]*See Harper v. City of New York*, 424 Fed. Appx. 36, 39–40 (2d Cir. 2011); *Cherry v. Spence*, 249 F.R.D. 226, 229 (E.D. N.C. 2008); *Gant v. Kant*, 314 F. Supp. 2d 532, 533 (D. Md. 2004) ("Each defendant, whether there be one or many, and whether they be members of the same family or strangers, must be served as provided by statute or rule").

[49]*See Cardenas v. City of Chicago*, 646 F.3d 1001 (7th Cir. 2011); *Albra v. Advan, Inc.*, 490 F.3d 826, 828 (11th Cir. 2007); *Blackmon v. U.S.D. 259 School Dist.*, 769 F.Supp.2d 1267,

incomplete copy of the complaint is likewise vulnerable to a dismissal.[50]

Plaintiff Selects the Process Server

Except in certain cases, such as those involving pauper plaintiffs or seamen plaintiffs, the plaintiff generally is responsible for selecting an appropriate person to serve all defendants with copies of the summons and complaint. Typically, the plaintiff appoints a commercial process server who accomplishes the service task for a fee.[51]

Service Only by Adult Non-Party

Any person over the age of 18 who is not a party to the lawsuit may serve original process. Because they are "parties" to the lawsuit, plaintiffs may not serve process themselves.[52] This bar against permitting a party to serve original process applies to service by certified mail (in those instances where such service is permitted). If the party mails that party's own certified letter, the service is improper.[53] However, the attorneys for a party may serve process for their clients, although such service is not the "most preferable method".[54]

Service by Commercial Overnight Courier Service

It remains an unresolved question whether original process that is delivered by a commercial overnight courier service (such as FedEx, UPS, DHL, or the like) can ever be considered as "personal" service or dwelling-house service.[55]

1273–74 (D.Kan. 2011).

[50]*See Cherry v. Spence*, 249 F.R.D. 226, 228–29 (E.D. N.C. 2008) (delivering only first page of complaint is failure of service: "defendants cannot admit or deny each allegation in the complaint when they only possess one page of it").

[51]*See Byrd v. Stone*, 94 F.3d 217, 219 (6th Cir. 1996).

[52]*See Walker v. University of Colorado Board of Regents*, 139 F.3d 913 (10th Cir. 1998) (Table; text available on Westlaw at 1998 WL 67321, at **1) (although disfavored, the Tenth Circuit permits this opinion to be cited if it has persuasive value on a material issue and copies are supplied to the court) (holding that plaintiff's attempt to effect service of process himself was not effective); *Boltes v. Entex*, 158 F.R.D. 110 (S.D. Tex. 1994) (commenting that plaintiff, as a party, is expressly prohibited from serving process upon a defendant).

[53]*See Constien v. United States*, 628 F.3d 1207, 1213–17 (10th Cir. 2010); *Williams v. Court Servs. & Offender Supervision Agency for D.C.*, 840 F.Supp.2d 192, 199 n.3 (D.D.C. 2012). *But cf. N.C. State Univ.*, 2009 WL 2869927, at *1-*2 (E.D.N.C. Sept. 2, 2009) (if state law permits service by party, Rule 4(e)(1) may override Rule 4(c)(2)), *aff'd*, 2010 WL 1017940 (4th Cir. Mar. 19, 2010). *But see Clark v. Goodwill Indus. of Hawaii, Inc.*, 2009 WL 3050277, at *4-*5 (D.Haw. Sept. 21, 2009) (although "not perfect", service by party was still "substantial compliance" with Rule 4).

[54]*See Trustees of Local Union No. 727 Pension Fund v. Perfect Parking, Inc.*, 126 F.R.D. 48, 51–52 (N.D. Ill. 1989). *Accord Commodity Futures Trading Com'n v. American Metals Exchange Corp.*, 693 F. Supp. 168, 186 (D.N.J. 1988); *Jugolinija v. Blue Heaven Mills, Inc.*, 115 F.R.D. 13, 15 (S.D. Ga. 1986).

[55]*See Cambridge Holdings Group, Inc. v. Federal Ins. Co.*, 489 F.3d 1356, 1362 (D.C. Cir. 2007) (noting, but failing to rule upon this "novel and unlikely theory").

Service by U.S. Marshal or Others Specially Appointed

The court, upon a plaintiff's request, may direct that the United States Marshal or some other specially-appointed person serve process. Such court-appointed service is required, however, in the cases of pauper plaintiffs[56] or seamen plaintiffs.[57] If such an appointment is made, and as long as the plaintiff was entitled to Marshal service in the first instance, and cooperated with the Marshal in accomplishing service, the plaintiff is permitted to rely on the Marshal to complete service.[58]

Service Must Occur *After* the Complaint is Filed

Service is not effective unless the complaint that is served has first been filed with the court. Thus, the practice of informally presenting an adversary with a copy of a complaint before it is filed with the clerk of court will not satisfy the requirements for service of process under Rule 4.[59]

RULE 4(d)—WAIVING SERVICE

CORE CONCEPT

A defendant is duty-bound to avoid the unnecessary costs of formal personal service of process, or risk being taxed with the costs of service and associated attorney's fees. The waiver-of-service procedure enforces this duty.

APPLICATIONS

Precaution In Citing Pre–December 1993 Cases

Formerly, Rule 4 permitted "service by mail" in limited circumstances. On December 1, 1993, this "service by mail" provision was replaced with the current Rule 4(d) waiver-of-service procedure. This provision, with its formal and obligatory acknowledgment form, was designed to resolve the "sandbagging" and "blindsiding" risks associated with the former approach.[60]

---

[56]28 U.S.C.A. § 1915(c). *See Lindsey v. U.S. R.R. Retirement Bd.*, 101 F.3d 444, 447–48 (5th Cir. 1996); *Byrd v. Stone*, 94 F.3d 217, 219 (6th Cir. 1996).

[57]28 U.S.C.A. § 1916.

[58]*See Robinson v. Clipse*, 602 F.3d 605, 608 (4th Cir. 2010) (time for service should be tolled while trial court considers whether to order Marshal to effect service); *Olsen v. Mapes*, 333 F.3d 1199, 1204–05 (10th Cir. 2003) (finding that plaintiffs were not culpable for failing to comply with Rules or court orders when they relied on

Marshal to complete service).

[59]*See J.O. Alvarez, Inc. v. Rainbow Textiles, Inc.*, 168 F.R.D. 201 (S.D. Tex. 1996) (default judgment not proper against defendants who failed to answer a complaint that was served before it was filed; defendants' actual or constructive notice of lawsuit does not satisfy the Rule 4 service requirements).

[60]*See Carimi v. Royal Carribean Cruise Line, Inc.*, 959 F.2d 1344, 1348 (5th Cir. 1992) (commenting that service-by-mail provisions were intended to provide a convenient way to

Constitutionality

The constitutionality of the waiver-of-service rule has been addressed only cursorily (and upheld).[61]

Certain Defendants Exempt From Rule

By its terms, the waiver-of-service procedure applies only to individuals, corporations, or associations served under Rule 4(e), (f), or (h). Accordingly, the procedure is usually not available for serving: (1) the United States as defendant;[62] (2) agencies, corporations, or officers[63] of the United States as defendants; (3) other governments and government-related entities as defendants;[64] or (4) minors and incompetent persons as defendants.[65] Note, however, that although federal workers are exempt from the waiver-of-service provisions when sued in their official capacities, they are *not* exempt when sued as individuals.[66]

Applies to Defendants Outside the United States, But Without Penalties

Although Rule 4 emphasizes a preference for proceeding under international service treaty agreements (such as the Hague Service Convention), the waiver-of-service procedure is intended to permit waiver of service by foreign (nongovernmental) defendants because of the cost savings to both plaintiff and defendant.[67] Note, however, that the penalties for refusing to waive formal service of process do *not* apply to

---

eliminate the costly and time consuming traditional methods of service, but were "a less dependable and less formal alternative to conventional service").

[61]*See U.S. v. Hafner*, 421 F. Supp. 2d 1220, 1224 (D.N.D. 2006) (rejecting constitutional challenge in case where defendant signed waiver-of-service form, commenting that the challenge was rejected for "obvious reasons").

[62]*See Constien v. United States*, 628 F.3d 1207, 1213 (10th Cir. 2010). *See also Robinson v. Turner*, 886 F. Supp. 1460, 1465 (S.D. Ind. 1995) (commenting that unreliability caused United States to be exempted from Rule 4(d) waiver provisions).

[63]*See Emuchay v. Catron*, 2000 WL 303223, at *2 (D. Conn. 2000) (confirming that Rule does not authorize waiver of service in lawsuits against federal employees sued in their official capacities).

[64]*See Libertarian Party v. Dardenne*, 595 F.3d 215, 218–19 (5th Cir. 2010) (not applicable to State of-

ficials sued in official capacity); *Lepone-Dempsey v. Carroll County Com'rs*, 476 F.3d 1277, 1281 (11th Cir. 2007) (not applicable to local governments); *Chapman v. New York State Div. for Youth*, 227 F.R.D. 175, 180 (N.D. N.Y. 2005) (not applicable to State, State agency, or State official).

[65]*See* Rule 4(d)(1).

[66]*See Mosley v. Douglas County Correctional Center*, 192 F.R.D. 282, 283 (D. Neb. 2000). *See also* Rule 4(i)(3) (noting that federal officers and employees sued in their individual capacity are served in the manners prescribed by Rule 4(e), (f), or (g)). *See also* Rule 4(i)(2) advisory committee notes to 2000 amendments ("Invocation of the individual service provisions of subdivisions (e), (f), and (g) invokes also the waiver-of-service provisions of subdivision (d)").

[67]*See* Rule 4(d) advisory committee rule (noting specifically the cost-saving nature of the waiver procedure for defendants who otherwise would be served under an international service of process convention, which costs

foreign defendants.[68]

Venue and Jurisdiction Defenses Preserved

A defendant who waives formal service of process does not lose the right to contest venue and jurisdiction.[69] The defendant does, however, waive any objection to service and to the form of process.

Plaintiff's Choice

A plaintiff is not required to seek a waiver of service. The plaintiff may choose to seek a waiver, or may instead immediately proceed to traditional formal service of process.[70] But a plaintiff who does *both* simultaneously (seek a waiver and formally serve) will likely lose the right to recover service costs.[71]

Defendant's Response Options

Waiver of service can only occur if the defendant actually signs and returns the waiver form,[72] and only becomes effective when the signed waiver form is filed.[73] Oral waivers are not proper.[74] The Rule does not *require* the defendant to waive,[75] (although the defendant may confront financial consequences for failing to waive, see below). If the defendant ignores the request or otherwise refuses to waive, the plaintiff must proceed with formal service under another provision of Rule 4.[76]

---

might include "the sometimes substantial expense of translation that may be wholly unnecessary for defendants fluent in English").

[68]*See* Rule 4(d)(2). *See also Quilling v. Shaw*, 2001 WL 611147, at *1 (N.D. Tex. 2001) (cost provisions of Rule 4(d) do not apply to defendants located outside United States). Note that at least one district court has rejected the argument that a foreign defendant should be considered "located" in the United States within the meaning of Rule 4(d) when that defendant has such significant contacts with the forum that it is susceptible to personal jurisdiction in the United States. *See Hoffman-La Roche, Inc. v. Invamed, Inc.*, 183 F.R.D. 157 (D.N.J. 1998).

[69]*See* Rule 4(d)(5). *See also Mann v. Castiel*, 681 F.3d 368, 373 (D.C.Cir. 2012).

[70]*See Budget Rent A Car System Inc. v. Miles*, 2005 WL 1106335, at *3 (S.D. Ohio 2005).

[71]*See Koellen v. Pollard*, 2010 WL 2330270, at *2 (E.D.Wis. June 7, 2010)

(denying reimbursement because plaintiff chose to incur service costs before time for defendants' return of waiver form had expired).

[72]*See Moss v. Wyeth, Inc.*, __ F. Supp. 2d __, __, 2012 WL 1802445, at *3 (D.Conn. 2012); *Convergence Techs. (USA), LLC v. Microloops Corp.*, 711 F. Supp. 2d 626, 629–33 (E.D.Va. 2010).

[73]*See Davis v. Liese*, 353 Fed.Appx. 95, 98 (10th Cir. 2009); *Moss v. Wyeth, Inc.*, __ F. Supp. 2d __, __, 2012 WL 1802445, at *3 (D.Conn. 2012).

[74]*See Kopacz v. Hopkinsville Surface & Storm Water Utility*, 2010 WL 2541170, at *1 (W.D. Ky. June 18, 2010).

[75]*See Tann v. Fisher*, 276 F.R.D. 190, 192 (D.Md. 2011); *Manuel v. City of Bangor*, 691 F.Supp.2d 212, 230 (D.Me. 2010).

[76]*See Cambridge Holdings Group, Inc. v. Federal Ins. Co.*, 489 F.3d 1356 (D.C. Cir. 2007); *Lepone-Dempsey v. Carroll County Com'rs*, 476 F.3d 1277, 1281 (11th Cir. 2007); *O.J. Distribut-*

Incentives for Waiving

By agreeing to waive formal service of process, a defendant's time for responding to the complaint is nearly tripled—from 21 days (following personal service) to 60 days (following request for waiver).[77] For defendants who are addressed outside the United States, the extension is even longer: a defendant addressed outside the United States who agrees to waive formal service has 90 days to respond to the complaint.[78]

Consequences of Not Waiving

If the defendant lacks "good cause" for refusing to waive service, the court must tax costs against the defendant.[79] These costs include the expenses incurred in formally serving process on the defendant, as well as a reasonable attorney's fee for any motion practice required to collect those service costs.[80] Before any costs and attorney's fees will be taxed, the prescribed time for the defendant to waive service must first have expired.[81]

> *"Good Cause" Defined:* The type of "good cause" necessary for refusing to waive formal service of process will be rare.[82] This "good cause" test is not satisfied by a belief that the claim is unjust or that the court lacks jurisdiction,[83] or by counsel's claim that he or she was busy or otherwise preoccupied,[84] or by nonprejudicial waiver form

---

ing, Inc. v. Hornell Brewing Co., Inc., 340 F.3d 345, 354 (6th Cir. 2003).

[77]*See* Rule 4(d)(3). One district court extended the 60-day period to 63 days, citing the 3-day addition for mailed service under Rule 6(d), formerly Rule 6(e). *See Petrousky v. Civil Air Patrol, Inc.,* 1998 WL 213726 (N.D. N.Y. 1998).

[78]*See* Rule 4(d)(3).

[79]*See Rollin v. Cook,* 466 Fed.Appx. 665, 667 (9th Cir. 2012); *Marcello v. Maine,* 238 F.R.D. 113, 115 (D. Me. 2006); *U.S. v. Butterfield,* 91 F. Supp. 2d 704, 706 (D. Vt. 2000). See also *Mathon v. Marine Midland Bank, N.A.,* 875 F. Supp. 986 (E.D. N.Y. 1995) (effect of Rule 4(d) is to shift cost of service to defendant who refuses to agree to waive formal service).

[80]*See* Rule 4(d)(2). *See Tann v. Fisher,* 276 F.R.D. 190, 192 (D.Md. 2011) (expenses include reasonable attorney's fees for preparing motion); *U.S. Engine Prod., Inc. v. AGCS Marine Ins. Co.,* 769 F.Supp.2d 626, 629 (S.D.N.Y. 2011) (same); *Graves v. Church of the Lord Jesus Christ of the Apostalic Faith, Inc.,* 2003 WL

21659168, at *1 (E.D. Pa. 2003) (costs for process server, courier, and photocopying, and motion expenses).

[81]*See* Rule 4(d) advisory committee note. *See also Andrew v. Clark,* 561 F.3d 261, 271–72 (4th Cir. 2009) (because "reasonable" time for return of waiver had not expired, no costs awarded).

[82]*See* Rule 4(d) advisory committee note to 1993 amendments. *See also Neal v. Cochran, Cherry, Givens & Smith, P.C.,* 589 F.Supp.2d 1363, 1364 (N.D.Ga. 2008).

[83]*See Marcello v. Maine,* 238 F.R.D. 113, 115–16 (D. Me. 2006) (rejecting "good cause" claim that lawsuit was frivolous, motion was premature, and pending motion to dismiss would require cost shift in the other direction); *Morales v. SI Diamond Technology, Inc.,* 1999 WL 144469, at *2 (S.D. N.Y. 1999) (defendants' belief that the complaint lacks merit and desire to increase plaintiff's costs do not constitute "good cause").

[84]*See D'Agostine v. United Hosp. Supply Corp.,* 1996 WL 417266, at *5 (E.D. Pa. 1996) (rejecting as "good

defects.[85] However, non-receipt of the waiver request,[86] a failure to otherwise comply with all the prerequisites of Rule 4(d),[87] a good faith belief that, as a matter of law, the waiver-of-service provisions would not apply,[88] an illiteracy in English, or defects in the waiver form would likely satisfy the "good cause" test.[89]

Waiver Procedure

The waiver-of-service procedure is triggered when (but only when) a plaintiff formally requests a defendant to waive formal service of process. The mere fact that the defendants come to learn that a complaint has been filed against them does not excuse compliance with the formal waiver procedures set in Rule 4(d).[90] To the contrary, a failure to meet—literally—each

---

cause" defendants' counsel's assertion that "he was in the process of relocating his practice and was in the middle of various litigations").

[85]*See Neal v. Cochran, Cherry, Givens & Smith, P.C.*, 589 F.Supp.2d 1363, 1365 (N.D.Ga. 2008) (non-misleading error in stating defendant's formal business name is not good cause to refuse waiver).

[86]*See Hy Cite Corp. v. badbusinessbureau.com, L.L.C.*, 418 F. Supp. 2d 1142, 1153–54 (D. Ariz. 2005) (no expenses where defendant was never mailed a request for waiver, even if defendant informed plaintiff that the process was futile); *Hausmann v. Roscher*, 2001 WL 115462, at *2 (E.D. Pa. 2001) (physically absent from residence is "good cause"). *But see Double S Truck Line, Inc. v. Frozen Food Exp.*, 171 F.R.D. 251, 253–54 (D. Minn. 1997) (service costs taxed against defendant, notwithstanding defendant's claim that it did not receive sufficient time to respond to waiver form; form had been delivered to defendant's agent but was delayed in reaching defendant because agent lacked defendant's accurate address).

[87]*See McGann v. State of N.Y.*, 77 F.3d 672 (2d Cir. 1996) (waiver-of-service procedure not effective where plaintiff failed to include acknowledgment form along with the mailed summons and complaint); *Jones v. Int'l Ass'n of Bridge Structural Ornamental & Reinforcing Iron Workers*, __ F. Supp. 2d __, __, 2012 WL 1067154, at

*12–*13 (E.D. Wis. 2012) (service failed since waiver form lacked plaintiff's signature and contact information); *Perez v. County of Westchester*, 83 F. Supp. 2d 435, 441 (S.D. N.Y. 2000), aff'd, 242 F.3d 367 (2d Cir. 2000) (denying reimbursement where notice and request were not addressed directly to the defendant, were not accompanied by a copy of the complaint, and lacked a prepaid means for compliance in writing); *Mason Tenders Dist. Council Pension Fund v. Messera*, 1997 WL 221200, at *6 (S.D. N.Y. 1997) (no costs taxed where plaintiffs sent acknowledgment form with self-addressed return envelope, but did not stamp the return envelope); *Spivey v. Board of Church Extension and Home Mission of Church of God*, 160 F.R.D. 660 (M.D. Fla. 1995) (refusing to award costs where waiver form was sent errantly addressed to "Edwin Ross" rather than "R. Edward Ross", and was mailed to corporate defendant generally, rather than addressed to an officer or managing general agent of the corporation).

[88]*See Mosley v. Douglas County Correctional Center*, 192 F.R.D. 282, 283 (D. Neb. 2000) (finding good cause for failure to waive service because no legal authority addressed whether employees of a municipal corporation were susceptible to this procedure).

[89]*See* Rule 4(d) advisory committee note to 1993 amendments.

[90]*See Mann v. Castiel*, 681 F.3d 368, 373 (D.C.Cir. 2012).

of these prerequisites may result in defective service[91] and/or a refusal by the court to impose the penalties for a refusal to waive service.[92] The waiver-of-service procedure follows:

    (1) *Request For Waiver:* The plaintiff must formally and unequivocally request a defendant to waive formal service of process.[93] The request must:

- Actually be sent (even if the defendant tells the plaintiff in advance that requesting a waiver is "futile");[94]
- Be in writing;[95]
- Conform to the federal "Notice Of A Lawsuit & Request For A Waiver" form, which will list: (a) the date on which the plaintiff's request was sent; (b) the date by which the defendant's waiver is due; (c) the identity of the court; and (d) the consequences of both waiver and a refusal to waive;[96]
- Contain two (2) copies of a waiver form and a prepaid means to return it to the plaintiff;[97] [*Note:* Although Rule 4(d) does not compel the use of the

---

[91]*See Larsen v. Mayo Medical Center*, 218 F.3d 863 (8th Cir. 2000) (where Rule 4(d) provisions not complied with strictly, waiver not satisfied and personal service must be obtained); *McGann v. State of N.Y.*, 77 F.3d 672 (2d Cir. 1996) (waiver not effective where plaintiff failed to include acknowledgment form along with the mailed summons and complaint).

[92]*See Green v. Benden*, 2000 WL 1468764 (N.D. Ill. 2000) (service costs denied where waiver request failed to contain copies of commencement notice, request for waiver, or prepaid means of compliance), aff'd in part, vac'd in part on other grounds, 281 F.3d 661 (7th Cir. 2002); *Perez v. County of Westchester*, 83 F. Supp. 2d 435, 441 (S.D. N.Y. 2000), aff'd, 242 F.3d 367 (2d Cir. 2000) (denying reimbursement, where notice and request were not addressed directly to the defendant, were not accompanied by a copy of the complaint, and lacked a prepaid means for compliance).

[93]*See Mann v. Castiel*, 681 F.3d 368, 373 (D.C.Cir. 2012).

[94]*See* Rule 4(d)(1)(G). *See also Hy Cite Corp. v. badbusinessbureau.com, L.L.C.*, 418 F. Supp. 2d 1142, 1153–54 (D. Ariz. 2005) (holding that defendant cannot be ordered to pay Rule 4(d) expenses if he was never mailed a request for waiver, even if defendant informed plaintiff that the process was futile).

[95]*See* Rule 4(d)(1)(A). *Cf. Kopacz v. Hopkinsville Surface & Storm Water Utility*, 2010 WL 2541170, at *1 (W.D. Ky. June 18, 2010) ("verbal" waiver not effective).

[96]*See* Rule 4(d)(1)(B), (D), (E), & (F). *Cf. Shell v. American Family Rights Ass'n*, 2009 WL 3837890, at *2 (D.Colo. Nov. 13, 2009) (notice effective even though date-sent was missing from form); *Trevino v. D.H. Kim Enterprises, Inc.*, 168 F.R.D. 181, 182–83 (D. Md. 1996) (notice effective even though plaintiffs did not use the official Notice form, but did advise of consequences); *Dymits v. American Brands, Inc.*, 1996 WL 751111 (N.D. Cal. 1996) (notice effective even though plaintiff omitted a small portion of the official form warning).

[97]*See* Rule 4(d)(1)(C). *See also McGann v. State of N.Y.*, 77 F.3d 672 (2d Cir. 1996) (waiver-of-service procedure not effective where plaintiff failed to include an acknowledgment form along with the mailed summons and complaint); *Mason Tenders Dist. Council Pension Fund v. Messera*, 1997 WL 221200, at *6 (S.D. N.Y. 1997) (waiver-of-service procedure found to be defective where plaintiffs sent to

officially-approved federal Notice form[98] and Waiver form,[99] prudent practitioners are wise to use both in order to ensure that all necessary information is correctly included.]

- Contain a copy of the complaint[100] (although a copy of a summons is *not* required);[101]
- Be sent by first-class mail or by "other reliable means", including private hand delivery and facsimile transmission;[102] and [*Note:* If electronic means are used for requesting a waiver, the plaintiff should maintain proof of transmission.]
- Be addressed directly to the individual defendant or, if the defendant is a corporation or association, to the individual subject to, or authorized to accept, service.[103] [*Note:* Merely mailing "blind" to a business address will not constitute proper delivery.]

    (2) *Response Time:* After the request is sent, the defendant must be given at least 30 days (60 days if outside the United States) to respond by returning the waiver.[104]

- *120-Day Warning:* Rule 4(m)'s 120-day period for completing service continues to run while the waiver-of-service request is outstanding. This 120-day period does *not* toll while the defendant

---

defendant the acknowledgment form with self-addressed return envelope, but failed to stamp the return envelope).

[98]*See* Form 5 ("Notice of a Lawsuit and Request to Waive Service of a Summons"), included in Appendix of Forms, reprinted in this text at Part IV.

[99]*See* Form 6 ("Waiver of the Service of Summons"), included in Appendix of Forms, reprinted in this text at Part IV.

[100]*See* Rule 4(d)(1)(C). *See Cammack New Liberty, LLC v. Int'l Greetings USA, Inc.*, 2009 WL 4807401, at *1–*2 (E.D.Ky. Dec. 5, 2009) (waiver request improper because complaint not included).

[101]*See Ecret v. Diamond*, 2007 WL 2743432, at *2 n. 1 (W.D. Wash. 2007). *See also* Rule 4(d) advisory committee note 1993 ("transmission of the notice and waiver forms is a private nonjudicial act, does not purport to effect service, and is not accompanied by any summons or directive from a court").

[102]*See* Rule 4(d)(1)(G). *See also* Rule 4(d) advisory committee note (describing availability of and procedure for electronic communications, such as facsimile transmission).

[103]*See* Rule 4(d)(1)(A). *See also Spivey v. Board of Church Extension and Home Mission of Church of God,* 160 F.R.D. 660 (M.D. Fla. 1995) (to comply with Rule 4(d) waiver procedure, waiver form must be accurately addressed to individual defendants and must be addressed to an authorized agent of corporate defendants).

[104]*See* Rule 4(d)(1)(F). *See also Andrew v. Clark*, 561 F.3d 261, 271–72 (4th Cir. 2009) (30-days might not be sufficiently "reasonable", if circumstances suggest that waiver might yet have been returned). *But cf. Koellen v. Pollard*, 2010 WL 2330270, at *2 (E.D.Wis. June 7, 2010) (denying reimbursement because plaintiff chose to incur service costs before time for defendants' return of waiver form had expired).

considers whether to waive.[105] Either waiver of service or, alternatively, formal service must be accomplished within the 120-day period.[106]

- *Limitations Period Warning:* In some jurisdictions, the statutes of limitation are not tolled in diversity or supplemental jurisdiction cases until actual service is made. Thus, in such jurisdictions, this waiver-of-service procedure should not be used if the limitations period is close to expiring.

Dating the "Waived" Service

If the defendant agrees to waive service by returning the waiver, the date of service is deemed to be the date the plaintiff files the waiver form with the court.[107] This dating function does *not* set the time for the defendant's responsive pleading; other rules set that period.[108] Instead, this dating function is important for those States where limitations periods are only tolled upon service, and not mere commencement.[109]

Motion to Recover Service Expenses

Where a defendant refuses, without good cause, to waive formal service of process, a motion to collect the costs and expenses of actual service can be filed promptly after the actual, formal service is completed. The plaintiff need not wait until the bill of costs process at the litigation's end.[110] A defendant's obligation to reimburse these costs is *not* affected by who eventually becomes the prevailing party in the litigation; rather, this obligation remains even if the defendant is otherwise entitled to its bill of costs at the end of the case.[111] Reimbursable expenses may include a reasonable attorney's fee for prosecuting the motion to collect costs, but may *not* include any attorney's fee associated with arranging for formal service

---

[105]*See* Rule 4(d) advisory committee note to 1993 amendment. *See also Weldon v. Electronic Data Systems Corp.*, 138 Fed. Appx. 136 (11th Cir. 2005) (per curiam) (refusing to apply equitable tolling to claim that plaintiff was "misled" by defendant's failure to timely respond to request for waiver of service) (unpublished decision).

[106]*See Chicago Dist. Council of Carpenters Pension Fund v. Wright Erectors, Inc.*, 1994 WL 592068 (N.D. Ill. 1994).

[107]*See* Rule 4(d)(4). *See also Davis v. Liese*, 353 Fed.Appx. 95, 98 (10th Cir. 2009); *Moss v. Wyeth, Inc.*, ___ F. Supp. 2d ___, ___, 2012 WL 1802445, at *3 (D.Conn. 2012).

[108]*See* Rules 4(d)(3) and 12(a)(1)(A)

(ii).

[109]*See* Rule 4(d)(4) advisory committee note to 1993 amendments. *See also, e.g., Corporex Cos., LLC v. Proskauer Rose, LLP*, 713 F.Supp.2d 678, 688 (E.D.Ky. 2010) (under Kentucky law, limitations tolled only upon issuance of summons).

[110]*See Double S Truck Line, Inc. v. Frozen Food Exp.*, 171 F.R.D. 251, 253–54 (D. Minn. 1997).

[111]*See Estate of Darulis v. Garate*, 401 F.3d 1060, 1063–64 (9th Cir. 2005) (commenting that Rule 4(d)'s policy "would be undermined if a defendant who creates unnecessary costs can gamble that he or she will be able to sidestep Rule 4(d)(2) via Rule 54(d)(1) ").

after the defendant's refusal to waive.[112] Attorney's fees might not be reimbursed when the plaintiff proceeds *pro se*.[113] The courts scrutinize carefully the requested fees and costs to guard against overreaching by counsel in their requests for reimbursement.[114]

U.S. Marshal's Use of Waiver-of-Service Procedure

When the Rules authorize service by the U.S. Marshal, the Marshal may mail the waiver-of-service forms to the defendants, prior to attempting to serve process personally.[115]

RULE 4(e)—SERVING INDIVIDUALS WITHIN A JUDICIAL DISTRICT OF THE UNITED STATES

CORE CONCEPT

Original process may be served upon any competent, adult individual found within the United States in the following manners:

(1) ***Specific Federal Law***: In any manner specifically authorized by federal law for such service, where Congress has determined that a particular type of service is necessary or proper;[116] or

(2) ***Waiver***: Under the waiver-of-service provisions of Rule 4(d); or

(3) ***State Law***: In the manner authorized by the State in which the district court sits, or by the State in which the service is to be accomplished; or

(4) ***Personal Service***: By personally delivering the summons and complaint to the individual being served; or

(5) ***Left at Dwelling House***: By leaving the summons and complaint at the individual's dwelling house or

---

[112]*See Graves v. Church of the Lord Jesus Christ of the Apostolic Faith, Inc.*, 2003 WL 21659168, at *1 (E.D. Pa. 2003) (denying plaintiff's request for reimbursement for attorney's fees spent arranging formal service on defendant after waiver was refused).

[113]*See Marcello v. Maine*, 238 F.R.D. 113, 117–18 (D. Me. 2006).

[114]*See, e.g., Ahern v. Northern Techs. Int'l. Corp.*, 206 F. Supp. 2d 418, 422 (W.D.N.Y. 2002) (finding request for $1,845 in attorney's fees "unreasonable", and granting a reduced fee award of $80 instead); *Donaghue v. CT Holdings, Inc.*, 2001 WL 1543816 (S.D. N.Y. 2001) (granting motion, and awarding plaintiff reasonably fee of $406.25 for the preparation, service, and filing of motion, and

costs of $140.00 for effecting service).

[115]*See Hairston v. Falano*, 1999 WL 412440, at *3 (N.D. Ill. 1999); *Rose v. Garbs*, 1999 WL 299892, at *3 (N.D. Ill. 1999).

[116]*See, e.g., Commodity Futures Trading Com'n v. Worldwide Commodity Corp.*, 366 F. Supp. 2d 276, 280 (E.D. Pa. 2005) (noting that because Commodities Exchange Act has its own specific service provisions, statute governs proper execution of service of summons); *Green v. William Mason & Co.*, 996 F. Supp. 394, 395–96 (D.N.J. 1998) (noting that ERISA contains just such a jurisdictional provision, permitting breach of fiduciary duty claims to be served in any district court where the defendants reside or may be found) (citing 29 U.S.C.A. § 1132(e)(2)).

231

usual place of abode with a person of suitable age and discretion residing there; or

(6) *Agent*: By delivering the summons and complaint to an agent appointed by the individual to receive service, or to an agent authorized by law to receive service.

APPLICATIONS

Service Upon Individuals, Generally

This Rule applies whenever service is made upon individual persons. Thus, the individual service Rule will apply when the served defendant is the unincorporated business trade name by which a natural individual conducts his or her business.[117]

Service by Personal Delivery

Personal delivery may not always require that the recipient walk away from the encounter holding the summons and complaint. The service documents must be "tendered" to the recipient. Thereafter, once the recipient is physically confronted with service, and refuses to take personal possession of the service documents, service by personal delivery may still, under certain circumstances, be accomplished by leaving the documents near the recipient (such as on a nearby table or on the floor near the person).[118]

Service on Non-Resident Individual's Agent

A non-resident person, not otherwise present in the forum, may be served properly with process by serving that individual's agent for service. The recipient "agent", however, must be authorized to accept service either by appointment or by operation of law.[119] This ordinarily requires appointment for the

---

[117]*See, e.g., Bridgeport Music, Inc. v. Rhyme Syndicate Music*, 376 F.3d 615, 624–25 (6th Cir. 2004) ("Service on Carrumba Music, the d/b/a for Jorge Hinojosa, is governed by Fed.R. Civ.P. 4(e), the provision for service of process on individuals").

[118]*See Travelers Cas. & Sur. Co. of America v. Brenneke*, 551 F.3d 1132, 1136 (9th Cir. 2009) (service sufficient when process placed within defendant's immediate proximity and further compliance defeated only by defendant's knowing, intentional act to evade service); *Novak v. World Bank*, 703 F.2d 1305, 1310 n.14 (D.C. Cir. 1983) ("When a person refuses to accept service, service may be effected by leaving the papers at a location, such as on a table or on the floor, near that person"); *American Indoor Football Ass'n, Inc. v. Lockwood*, 267

F.R.D. 663, 667 (M.D.Ala. 2010) (noting that "touch-and-leave" or leaving in defendant's physical proximity may be adequate); *Republic Credit Corp. I v. Rance*, 172 F. Supp. 2d 1178, 1181 (S.D. Iowa 2001) (service effected by leaving summons and complaint at front gate, when process server encountered defendant, advised defendant of service papers, and defendant turned and entered residence without speaking; "This Court has no interest in forcing process servers to chase down defendants and jam court papers into their hands in order to effect personal service, as depicted on television").

[119]*See* Rule 4(e)(2)(C). *See also Silvious v. Pharaon*, 54 F.3d 697, 701–02 (11th Cir. 1995); *Moody v. Finander*, 2010 WL 5535703, at *2 (S.D.Cal. Dec. 1, 2010). *Compare Nazareth Nat'l Bank & Trust Co. v.*

express purpose of receiving process.[120] Some States have provided, by statute, that service on non-residents (who are otherwise amenable to jurisdiction within the State) may be accomplished by serving the secretary of State or some similar State law official; in such States, service in this manner may be appropriate service under federal law as well.[121]

Service on Implied-in-Fact Agents

Courts have, in appropriate contexts, permitted service upon "implied" agents where the factual circumstances support that implication.[122]

Service on Individual's Attorney

Service upon an individual is proper by serving the individual's attorney *only* when the attorney has been specifically authorized to accept service on the individual's behalf.[123]

Service at Individual's Dwelling House

An individual can be served with process by delivering the summons and complaint to a "person of suitable age and discretion" residing at the defendant's dwelling house or usual place of abode. In such cases, the process need not be handed directly to the served defendant.[124] Moreover, the recipient need not necessarily be an adult, so long as the court reaches the case-by-case, fact-specific determination that the recipient was of "suitable age and discretion". Nevertheless, the recipient ordinarily must be "residing" at the home;[125] service upon a

---

E.A. Intern. Trust, 1999 WL 549036 (W.D. Pa. 1999) (holding service proper because summons and complaint "were left with a specified security guard at defendant's residence who was 'instructed by [defendant] to accept service' "), *with Staudinger v. Hoelscher, Inc.*, 166 F. Supp. 2d 1335, 1339 (D. Kan. 2001) (holding service improper because plant manager (on whom service was made) was not authorized by virtue of that position to accept service for president and owner of plant).

[120]*See Nyholm v. Pryce*, 259 F.R.D. 101, 104 (D.N.J. 2009) (also, describing criteria for assessing appointment).

[121]*See, e.g., Goktepe v. Lawrence*, 220 F.R.D. 8, 8–12 (D. Conn. 2004) (Connecticut statute).

[122]*See, e.g., U.S. v. Ziegler Bolt and Parts Co.*, 111 F.3d 878, 881 (Fed.Cir. 1997); *U.S. v. Balanovski*, 236 F.2d 298, 303 (2d Cir. 1956); *Sikhs for Justice v. Nath*, 850 F. Supp. 435, 440 (S.D.N.Y. 2012). *See also In re*

Focus Media Inc., 387 F.3d 1077, 1082–83 (9th Cir. 2004) (recognizing implied authority to receive service in bankruptcy context).

[123]*See United States v. Ziegler Bolt & Parts Co.*, 111 F.3d 878, 881 (Fed. Cir.1997); *Santos v. State Farm Fire & Cas. Co.*, 902 F.2d 1092, 1094 (2d Cir.1990); *Tindle v. Xenos*, 2010 WL 4739787, at *2 (E.D.Mich. Nov. 16, 2010).

[124]*See Limon-Hernandez v. Lumbreras*, 171 F.R.D. 271 (D. Or. 1997).

[125]*See U.S. v. Rose*, 437 F. Supp. 2d 1166 (S.D. Cal. 2006) (dwelling-house service requires that address be defendant's usual place of abode *and* that papers be left with someone actually residing there); *Srein v. Silverman*, 2001 WL 366620, at *2 (E.D. Pa. 2001) (dwelling-house service only complete when papers left with person who actually resides at defendant's home, not merely present at the time of service).

non-resident maid or landlady will likely be ineffective.[126] Likewise, service on an apartment complex's security guard will not suffice, at least absent proof of the guard's obligation to notify the served persons.[127]

- *Transient Defendants:* Service at a "dwelling house" or "usual place of abode" may not always be an available option. In certain circumstances, there may be no acceptable "dwelling house" service location for transient defendants, such as those living aboard ships or those who are homeless, living on the streets or in shelters.[128]

- *Traveling Defendants:* A traveling defendant's "usual place of abode" is likely to include either the place where that person is actually living at the time of service or the place that person recognizes as his legal residence, even if business takes him away on a regular basis.[129]

- *Hotels and Motels:* In certain circumstances, particularly during long, extended stays, service can be appropriate at a hotel or motel where the defendant is residing.[130]

- *Multiple "Usual Abodes":* A person may have two or more "usual places of abode" (and may be properly served at any one of them), so long as each contains sufficient indicia of the permanence of the person's residence there.[131]

---

[126]*Compare Franklin America, Inc. v. Franklin Cast Products, Inc.*, 94 F.R.D. 645 (E.D. Mich. 1982) (service on part-time housekeeper deemed insufficient), *with Barclays Bank of New York v. Goldman*, 517 F. Supp. 403 (S.D. N.Y. 1981) (service on resident maid deemed sufficient). *See also Jaffe and Asher v. Van Brunt*, 158 F.R.D. 278 (S.D. N.Y. 1994) (although defendant was not staying at his parents' home when service was made there, service ruled proper where defendant resided at that address when in the area, maintained private bedroom, clothes, phone line, and fax there, received mail there (which mother forwarded to him), and represented to plaintiff that this was his residence); *TRW, Inc. v. Derbyshire*, 157 F.R.D. 59 (D. Colo. 1994) (holding that service on defendant's mother, at address defendant represented to be his current forwarding address, was proper).

[127]*See Kolker v. Hurwitz*, 269 F.R.D. 119, 123–24 (D.P.R. 2010).

[128]*See Cox v. Quigley*, 141 F.R.D. 222 (D. Me. 1992) (young college graduate, who left home and was serving on board a ship, had no "dwelling house" or "usual place of abode", other than his ship); *see id.* at 226 ("The last shelter at which a homeless person slept will often not furnish reasonable assurance that process will reach the defendant. For such defendants service at the dwelling house or place of abode is unavailable; personal service may be a plaintiff's only option then, no matter how difficult").

[129]*See S.E.C. v. Marino*, 29 Fed. Appx. 538, 540–41 (10th Cir. 2002) (citation restricted—not selected for publication in Federal Reporter) (finding service proper because, even though defendant's vocation took him on extended trips abroad, he maintained his home and family in service location).

[130]*See Howard Johnson Intern., Inc. v. Wang*, 7 F. Supp. 2d 336 (S.D. N.Y. 1998), aff'd, 181 F.3d 82 (2d Cir. 1999) (finding hotel to be defendant's dwelling place or usual place of abode).

[131]*See National Development Co. v. Triad Holding Corp.*, 930 F.2d 253, 257–58 (2d Cir. 1991); *craigslist, Inc.*

- *Relatives, Family, and Friends:* Unless it is also the defendant's dwelling house or usual place of abode, service on the home of the defendant's relatives, family, or friends is usually not sufficient.[132]

State Law Service Generally

The Rules permit service in any manner authorized by *either* the State in which the district court sits *or* the State in which the service is to be accomplished.[133] If service is accomplished in accordance with either of those State's service laws, Rule 4(e) is satisfied.[134]

State Law Service—Serving at Place of Business

The Federal Rules do *not* specifically authorize serving individuals by leaving a copy of the summons and complaint at the individual's regular place of business.[135] This type of service is, nevertheless, often still available to a plaintiff because many States authorize service at business addresses.[136]

RULE 4(f)—SERVING INDIVIDUALS IN A FOREIGN COUNTRY

CORE CONCEPT

Original process may be served upon any competent, adult defendant outside the United States, who is both amenable to service and subject to the court's personal jurisdiction, as follows:

(1) *Specific Federal Law*: In any manner specifically authorized by federal law for such service, where Congress has determined that a particular type of service is necessary or proper; or

---

v. Hubert, 278 F.R.D. 510, 515 (N.D.Cal. 2011).

[132]*See Levine v. Duchacova*, 2010 WL 4941951, at *2 (S.D.Cal. Nov. 30, 2010) (even if defendant occasionally visits or vacations there). Compare *Howard v. Shelton*, 277 F.R.D. 168, 170 (S.D.Miss. 2011) (finding apartment of boyfriend to be a usual place of abode).

[133]*See* Rule 4(e)(1). *See also Grayson v. Hsin*, 413 Fed.Appx. 596, 597–99 (4th Cir. 2011); *Colleton Preparatory Academy, Inc. v. Hoover Universal, Inc.*, 616 F.3d 413, 421 n.9 (4th Cir. 2010).

[134]*See Vax-D Medical Technologies, LLC v. Texas Spine Medical Center*, 485 F.3d 593, 596 (11th Cir. 2007) (service complied with Texas case law regarding individuals who conduct business under assumed name); *Homer v. Jones-Bey*, 415 F.3d

748, 754 (7th Cir. 2005) (noting that effectiveness of service in such circumstances turns on relevant provisions of State law); *In re Subpoena to Huawei Techs. Co.*, 720 F.Supp.2d 969, 976 (N.D.Ill. 2010) (service proper under Illinois law because service on "administrator manager" qualified as service on any agent); *Estate of Klieman v. Palestinian Auth.*, 467 F. Supp. 2d 107, 112–14 (D.D.C. 2006) (serving researcher employed by PLO was insufficient without proof that he was PLO's authorized agent for service of process).

[135]*See Melkaz Intern. Inc. v. Flavor Innovation Inc.*, 167 F.R.D. 634 (E.D.N.Y. 1996). *See also Boateng v. Inter American Univ. of P.R.*, 188 F.R.D. 26 (D.P.R. 1999) (holding that place of employment is not "dwelling place" or "usual place of abode").

[136]*See* Rule 4(e)(1).

(2) ***Waiver***: Under the waiver-of-service provisions of Rule 4(d), if not prohibited by the law of the foreign country of service;[137] or

(3) ***International Agreement***: Where Congress has not established otherwise, and where the waiver-of-service provisions either are prohibited by foreign law or are not honored by an executed acknowledgment of service, service may be completed in any internationally agreed upon manner that is reasonably calculated to give notice, such as the *Hague Convention on the Service Abroad of Judicial and Extrajudicial Documents in Civil or Commercial Matters*;[138] or

(4) ***Court Order***: In any other manner directed by the court, so long as the chosen method is not prohibited by international agreement.

If no international agreement exists, or if the agreement permits service by other means, then original process may be served upon any competent, adult defendant outside the United States, who is both amenable to service and subject to the court's personal jurisdiction, as follows:

(5) ***Foreign Law***: In the manner prescribed by the law of the foreign country; or

(6) ***Letters Rogatory***: In the manner directed in response to a letter rogatory or letter of request; or

(7) ***Personal Service / Mail Delivery***: Unless prohibited by the foreign country's law: (a) by personally delivering the summons and complaint to the individual defendant, or (b) by the clerk of court mailing process in a manner requiring a signed receipt; or

(8) ***Court Order***: In any other manner directed by the court, so long as the chosen method is not prohibited by international agreement.

APPLICATIONS

Applies to Foreign Service, Not to Foreign Citizens

The provisions of Rule 4(f) are not triggered merely because the defendant is a citizen of a foreign country. Foreign nationals living, traveling, or conducting business within the United States generally may be served with process domestically under Rule 4(e), just as any other individual may. Instead, Rule 4(f) is triggered only when the defendant—whether an American

---

[137]*See R. Griggs Group Ltd. v. Filanto Spa*, 920 F. Supp. 1100, 1103 (D. Nev. 1996).

[138]Nov. 15, 1965, 20 U.S.T. 361, T.I.A.S. No. 6638, 658 U.N.T.S. 163. The text of the Convention on the Service Abroad of Judicial and Extrajudicial Documents in Civil or Commercial Matters is reprinted in the Supplement to 28 U.S.C.A. following Rule 4 (WESTLAW: USCA database, **ci(frcp/2 4) & treaties**).

national or a citizen of another country—is served outside the United States.[139]

Hague Service Is Required, If Available

The Supreme Court has ruled that service in accordance with the Hague Service Convention is mandatory, wherever that Convention applies.[140] The Convention obviously will not apply when the foreign Nation is not a signatory to that treaty,[141] nor will it apply if the a signatory Nation refuses to comply with the treaty's provisions.[142] Service under the Convention may require the federal court to issue a formal request for service directly to the foreign Nation's designated authority.[143] Alternatively, service by mail under the Convention may be proper, but the courts are divided on this question.[144]

Internationally Agreed Upon Service Details

Process served pursuant to an international agreement must comport with all specific, peculiar requirements imposed by the host country, such as the translation of process into the local language.[145]

Service on United States Agent

When formally serving an individual located in a foreign country, a plaintiff has two options: service in the foreign country, pursuant to the various provisions of this Rule 4(f); or service within the United States on the individual's authorized

---

[139]*See Stars' Desert Inn Hotel & Country Club, Inc. v. Hwang*, 105 F.3d 521, 524 (9th Cir. 1997).

[140]*See Volkswagenwerk Aktiengesellschaft v. Schlunk*, 486 U.S. 694, 108 S. Ct. 2104, 100 L. Ed. 2d 722 (1988). *See also U.S. ex rel. Thomas v. Siemens AG*, 708 F.Supp.2d 505, 517–18 (E.D.Pa. 2010); *Marcantonio v. Primorsk Shipping Corp.*, 206 F. Supp. 2d 54, 57 (D. Mass. 2002). *Cf. Brown v. Bandai America, Inc.*, 2002 WL 1285265, at *3 (N.D. Tex. 2002) (because Japan is signatory to Hague Convention, court must determine whether defendant was properly served in accordance with Convention requirements).

[141]*See Nuance Commc'ns, Inc. v. Abbyy Software House*, 626 F.3d 1222, 1237–38 (Fed. Cir. 2010) (Russia); *Marks v. Alfa Group*, 615 F.Supp.2d 375, 377 (E.D.Pa. 2009) (Liechtenstein).

[142]*See In re Potash Antitrust Litig.*, 667 F.Supp.2d 907, 929–30 (N.D.Ill. 2009).

[143]*See Tracfone Wireless, Inc. v. Bequator Corp., Ltd.*, 717 F.Supp.2d 1307, 1308 (S.D.Fla. 2010).

[144]*See infra* Authors' Commentary to Rule 4(f) ("**Service Internationally Through the Mails**").

[145]*See Friedman v. Israel Labour Party*, 1997 WL 379181 (E.D. Pa. 1997) (holding service improper on Israeli defendant where plaintiff failed to send complaint directly to Israeli Director of Courts, as Israel required in its adoption of the Hague Service Convention); *Pennsylvania Orthopedic Ass'n v. Mercedes-Benz A.G.*, 160 F.R.D. 58 (E.D. Pa. 1995) (ruling that service attempted under the Hague Convention on a German corporate defendant was ineffective because the complaint had not been translated into German).

agent (if one exists), pursuant to Rule 4(e).[146]

Service Internationally through the Mails

The effectiveness of international postal service can vary widely depending on the forum court and the Nation where such service is attempted:

- *First,* many Nations are signatories to the Hague Convention, and some (but not all) Circuits hold that international mail service can be permitted by the Convention to non-objecting Nations.[147]

- *Second,* international mail service may be accomplished if the Nation of service does not forbid it *and* if it is dispatched by the American clerk of court with a signed receipt required *and* if there is no applicable international agreement in place (*e.g.*, the Nation of service is not a Hague signatory) or, if in place, any agreement permits such service.[148] Exacting compliance with these requirements is essential: such mailed service is *not* effective if it is performed by someone other than the court clerk,[149] or if the serving party fails to prove affirmatively that service by mail is not prohibited by the foreign country's law.[150]

- *Third,* such service may be expressly ordered by the American court, provided, too, that it is not forbidden by the Nation of service *and* there in no applicable international agreement or the applicable agreement permits such service.[151]

- *Fourth,* the Rule broadly permitting service in a manner "prescribed by the law of the foreign country for service in that country" probably will not suffice to authorize international mail service.[152]

---

[146]*See Silvious v. Pharaon*, 54 F.3d 697 (11th Cir.1995) (per curiam); *Brown v. China Integrated Energy, Inc.*, __ F.R.D. __, __, 2012 WL 2913537, at *3 (C.D.Cal. 2012).

[147]*Compare Nuovo Pignone, SpA v. STORMAN ASIA M/V*, 310 F.3d 374, 384 (5th Cir. 2002) (Federal Express service not permitted by Hague Convention), *and Bankston v. Toyota Motor Corp.*, 889 F.2d 172, 173–74 (8th Cir. 1989) (mail service not permitted by Hague Convention), *with Brockmeyer v. May*, 383 F.3d 798, 801–03 (9th Cir. 2004) (permitting mail service under Hague Convention), *and Ackermann v. Levine*, 788 F.2d 830, 838 (2d Cir. 1986) (same).

[148]*See* Rule 4(f)(2)(C)(ii). *See also Brockmeyer v. May*, 383 F.3d 798, 806–08 (9th Cir. 2004) (discussing such service); *SignalQuest, Inc. v.*

Tien-Ming Chou, __ F.R.D. __, __, 2012 WL 1859656, at *1–*5 (D.N.H. 2012) (same).

[149]*See Hyundai Merchant Marine Co. Ltd. v. Grand China Shipping (Hong Kong) Co.*, __ F. Supp. 2d __, __, 2012 WL 2870703, at *7–*8 (S.D.Ala. 2012); *Russell Brands, LLC v. GVD Int'l Trading, SA*, 282 F.R.D. 21, 23 (D.Mass. 2012).

[150]*See Nabulsi v. Nahyan*, 2008 WL 1924235, at *4 (S.D. Tex. 2008). *See also S.E.C. v. Alexander*, 248 F.R.D. 108, 111–14 (E.D. N.Y. 2007).

[151]*See* Rule 4(f)(3). *See also Brockmeyer v. May*, 383 F.3d 798, 806–08 (9th Cir. 2004) (discussing such service).

[152]*See* Rule 4(f)(2)(A). *See also Brockmeyer v. May*, 383 F.3d 798, 806–08 (9th Cir. 2004) (rejecting mail service to United Kingdom under this

"Court-Ordered" Type of Service, Generally

So long as the method of service is not prohibited by "international agreement", the plaintiff can request and the district court can order a means of service specifically tailored to achieve service upon individuals in a foreign country.[153] In an appropriate case, such an order might even be entered retroactively, *nunc pro tunc*.[154]

This type of "court-ordered" service has been particularly useful to the courts when encountering elusive international defendants, especially those striving to evade service of process.[155] Few restrictions restrain the district court's creativity in crafting an alternate means of service.[156] So long as the alternative service is (1) ordered by the court, (2) not prohibited by applicable international agreement, and (3) reasonably calculated, under the circumstances, to apprise the defendant of the pendency of the action and afford an opportunity to respond, the courts enjoy wide discretion.[157] Indeed, this "court-ordered" service option may even be employed where service could otherwise be accomplished through the various options set forth in Rule 4(f)(2).[158] The "court-ordered" service option has been applied by the courts to authorize service by publica-

---

provision); *Prewitt Enterprises, Inc. v. Organization of Petroleum Exporting Countries*, 353 F.3d 916, 925 (11th Cir. 2003) (same, mail to Austria); *Hyundai Merchant Marine Co. Ltd. v. Grand China Shipping (Hong Kong) Co.*, — F. Supp. 2d —, —, 2012 WL 2870703, at *8 (S.D.Ala. 2012) (same, FedEx to Hong Kong).

[153]*See Forum Financial Group, LLC v. President, Fellows of Harvard College*, 199 F.R.D. 22, 23–24 (D. Me. 2001) (authorizing service upon foreign defendant by certified mail sent to his American attorney).

[154]*Compare Marks v. Alfa Group*, 615 F.Supp.2d 375, 379–80 (E.D.Pa. 2009) (permitting *nunc pro tunc* order) *and Igloo Prods. Corp. v. Thai Welltex Int'l Co.*, 379 F.Supp.2d 18, 20 (D.Mass. 2005) (same), *with Brockmeyer v. May*, 383 F.3d 798, 806 (9th Cir.2004) (denying *nunc pro tunc* order), *with Klein v. United States*, 278 F.R.D. 94, 96–97 (W.D.N.Y. 2011) (same).

[155]*See Rio Properties, Inc. v. Rio Intern. Interlink*, 284 F.3d 1007, 1018 (9th Cir. 2002) (justifying alternate service because plaintiff was "faced with an international e-business scofflaw, playing hide-and-seek with the federal court"). *See also Smith v.*

Islamic Emirate of Afghanistan, 2001 WL 1658211, at *3 (S.D. N.Y. 2001) (permitting alternative service on Osama Bin Laden and Al Qaeda terrorist network).

[156]*See Rio Props., Inc. v. Rio Int'l Interlink*, 284 F.3d 1007, 1016 (9th Cir. 2002) (listing alternative service authorizations by other courts).

[157]*See Rio Properties, Inc. v. Rio Intern. Interlink*, 284 F.3d 1007, 1014–18 (9th Cir. 2002) (discussing analysis for crafting alternative service under Rule 4(f)). *But see id.* at 1014 (briefly discussing controversy over whether court's discretion to craft alternative service includes methods in violation of foreign country's internal laws).

[158]*See Nuance Commc'ns, Inc. v. Abbyy Software House*, 626 F.3d 1222, 1239 (Fed. Cir. 2010) (court-ordered service stands alone, and may be appropriate even if other means of service could succeed); *Rio Properties, Inc. v. Rio Intern. Interlink*, 284 F.3d 1007, 1014–15 (9th Cir. 2002) (expressly rejecting argument that Rule creates "a hierarchy of preferred methods of service of process" that first requires failed service under each of the Rule 4(f)(2) options before resorting to

tion,[159] ordinary mail, mail to a last known address, e-mail,[160] delivery to certain members of the defendant's family,[161] delivery to an affiliated business address,[162] delivery to the defendant's attorney,[163] facsimile transmission and telex,[164] and by private overnight courier.[165]

"Court-Ordered" Service by E-Mail

Recently, and cautiously, courts have, on occasion, ordered alternate service of process by electronic mail (e-mail) in cases involving international defendants with a known e-mail address, who engaged in internet activities, and who attempt to evade service by other means.[166] Noting the many complications with e-mail service (*e.g.*, an inability to confirm actual receipt of an e-mail message, system compatibility issues, possible failure of attachments (such as exhibits) to transmit, be received, or be "opened" in comprehensible form, etc.), courts have granted e-mail service only on a case-by-case basis, upon a proper balancing of these limitations against the corresponding benefits of such service in particular circumstances.[167] More recently, courts have shown even greater liberality in permit-

---

court-ordered service). *But see Fujitsu Ltd. v. Belkin Int'l, Inc.*, 782 F. Supp. 2d 868, 878–80 (N.D.Cal. 2011) (court refuses to order special service absent showing why service under Taiwanese law is inadequate); *FMAC Loan Receivables v. Dagra*, 228 F.R.D. 531, 534 (E.D. Va. 2005) (court may require showing of reasonable effort to serve otherwise or why court-ordered service is necessary).

[159] See *Smith v. Islamic Emirate of Afghanistan*, 2001 WL 1658211, at *3 (S.D.N.Y. 2001) (permitting service on Osama Bin Laden and Al Qaeda by publication in Afghani newspapers, Pakistani newspaper where Bin Laden published Fatwahs, and broadcast advertising on local television networks).

[160] See *supra* Authors' Commentary to Rule 4(f) ("**Court-Ordered Service by E-Mail**").

[161] See *U.S. v. Padilla*, 2002 WL 471838, at *1 (E.D. Cal. 2002) (service via delivery to both daughter and attorney of defendant, with letter requesting that recipients forward to defendant, and offering to send copies directly to defendant's residence if the recipients provided the address).

[162] See *Rio Props., Inc. v. Rio Int'l Interlink*, 284 F.3d 1007, 1016 (9th Cir. 2002) (service on local affiliate);

Guifu Li v. A Perfect Day Franchise, Inc, 281 F.R.D. 373, 388–89 (N.D.Cal. 2012) (service on franchise).

[163] See *Rio Props., Inc. v. Rio Int'l Interlink*, 284 F.3d 1007, 1016 (9th Cir. 2002); *Russell Brands, LLC v. GVD Int'l Trading, SA*, 282 F.R.D. 21, 26 (D.Mass. 2012); *U.S. Commodity Futures Trading Comm'n v. Aliaga*, 272 F.R.D. 617, 620–21 (S.D. Fla. 2011).

[164] See *Studio A. Entm't, Inc. v. Active Distribs., Inc.*, 2008 WL 162785, at *4 (N.D. Ohio 2008) (collecting cases approving service by fax).

[165] *Russell Brands, LLC v. GVD Int'l Trading, SA*, 282 F.R.D. 21, 26 (D.Mass. 2012) (service by Federal Express); *TracFone Wireless, Inc. v. Bitton*, 278 F.R.D. 687, 692-93 (S.D.Fla. 2012) (same).

[166] See *Rio Properties, Inc. v. Rio Intern. Interlink*, 284 F.3d 1007, 1017–18 (9th Cir. 2002).

[167] See *Rio Properties, Inc. v. Rio Intern. Interlink*, 284 F.3d 1007, 1017–18 (9th Cir. 2002) (discussing e-mail option, and finding that e-mail service was perhaps most likely method to notify defendant of summons and complaint); *Popular Enterprises, LLC v. Webcom Media Group, Inc.*, 225 F.R.D. 560, 560–63 (E.D. Tenn. 2004) (permitting e-mail

ting substituted service by email.[168]

Return of Service

Once service abroad is complete, the proof of service can be made in the manner provided by Rule 4(*l*), by the law of the foreign country, or by order of court.[169] If service was accomplished by mail, the proof of service should include a signed return receipt.

Effect of Foreign Service

Foreign countries are not parties to the U.S. Constitution's Full Faith and Credit Clause, and thus the enforcement abroad of a judgment entered by an American federal court is dependent on comity and international treaties. Moreover, in certain foreign countries, failure to adhere to the host nation's service regulations could even subject the unwary process server to criminal penalties.[170]

RULE 4(g)—SERVING MINORS AND INCOMPETENT PERSONS

CORE CONCEPT

Original process may be served upon any minor or incompetent person in the following manners:

- *Service Inside the United States:* In any manner authorized for the service of process on minors or incompetent persons by the State in which service is to be made.

- *Service Outside the United States:* In any manner: (1) prescribed by the law of the foreign country; (2) directed in response to a letter rogatory or letter of request; or (3) by such other means as the court may direct.

APPLICATIONS

State Law Dictates Proper Service

For domestic service of process to be effective upon a minor or incompetent person, the service must comply with the requirements for such service as promulgated by the State in

---

service as most likely to apprise defendant of lawsuit).

[168]*See Fraserside IP LLC v. Letyagin*, 280 F.R.D. 630, 630 (N.D. Iowa); *TracFone Wireless, Inc. v. Bitton*, 278 F.R.D. 687, 693 (S.D.Fla. 2012); *Gurung v. Malhotra*, 279 F.R.D. 215, 219–20 (S.D.N.Y. 2011).

[169]*See Tracfone Wireless, Inc. v. Bequator Corp., Ltd.*, 717 F.Supp.2d 1307, 1309–10 (S.D.Fla. 2010) (authorizing filing of FedEx proof-of-

signature as return of service).

[170]*See Volkswagenwerk Aktiengesellschaft v. Schlunk*, 486 U.S. 694, 108 S. Ct. 2104, 100 L. Ed. 2d 722 (1988) (commenting on possible adverse consequences of failing to comply with applicable international treaties). *See generally* Joseph F. Weis, Jr., *The Federal Rules and the Hague Conventions: Concerns of Conformity and Comity*, 50 U. Pitt. L. Rev. 903 (1989).

which service is attempted.[171]

RULE 4(h)—SERVING CORPORATIONS, PARTNERSHIPS, AND ASSOCIATIONS

CORE CONCEPT

Original process may be served upon any domestic or foreign corporation, partnership, or unincorporated association subject to suit under a common name, in the following manners:

(1) **Specific Federal Law**: In any manner specifically authorized by federal law for such service, where Congress has determined that a particular type of service is necessary or proper; or

(2) **Waiver**: Under the waiver-of-service provisions of Rule 4(d); or

(3) **SERVICE INSIDE THE UNITED STATES**:

    (a) **State Law**: In the manner authorized by the State in which the district court sits, or by the State in which the service is to be accomplished; or

    (b) **Officer, Managing Agent, or General Agent**: By delivering the summons and complaint to an officer, managing agent, or general agent; or

    (c) **Agent**: By delivering the summons and complaint to an agent appointed to receive service or authorized by law to receive service; and if required by statute, by also mailing the summons and complaint to the defendant; or

(4) **SERVICE OUTSIDE THE UNITED STATES**:

    In any manner provided for service upon individuals in a foreign country, except personal service.[172]

APPLICATIONS

Service on Domestic Company's Officer, Manager, or General Agent

To effectively serve a corporation, partnership, or association through an officer, manager, or general agent, the summons and complaint must be directed to and delivered to that person. Simply addressing the mail to the company generally, or to its legal department, will generally not suffice.[173] Whether a particular person qualifies as an officer, managing agent, or

---

[171]*See Seibels, Bruce & Co. v. Nicke*, 168 F.R.D. 542, 545 (M.D. N.C. 1996) (mailing complaint to minor's last place of residence was defective service because Indiana law required service on both minor and the minor's custodial parent).

[172]*See* Rule 4(f); *but see* Rule 4(f)(2)

(C)(i) (no personal service).

[173]*See Larsen v. Mayo Medical Center*, 218 F.3d 863 (8th Cir. 2000) (holding that papers mailed to "Medical/Legal Department, Mayo Clinic" was ineffective service under Rule 4(h)).

general agent of the company will depend upon the person's organizational authority: a person qualifying for this status will typically hold a position of broad executive responsibility with some continuity.[174] This is a highly factually-sensitive inquiry.[175] This service need not occur at the company's headquarters, however; proper service could be proper anywhere the officer, manager, or general agent may be found.[176] Note, however, that delivering service papers to a corporate employee or representative is not sufficient, unless that person is a corporate officer, managing agent, or general agent.[177] Accordingly, service on one of the corporation's owners[178] or its in-house counsel[179] will not, without more, qualify as proper service.

Service on Authorized Agent

In addition to delivery to an officer, managing agent, or general agent, corporations, partnerships, and associations can also be served by delivering the summons and complaint to any other agent specially authorized to receive service, either by appointment or by operation of law.[180] Such person or entity must have been actually (or impliedly) appointed or autho-

---

[174]See Gottlieb v. Sandia Am. Corp., 452 F.2d 510, 513 (3d Cir. 1971). See also Baade v. Price, 175 F.R.D. 403, 405 (D.D.C. 1997) (person must have "some measure of discretion in operating some phase of the defendant's business or in the management of a given office", must have "such status that common sense would expect the recipient to see that the summons promptly gets into the hands of the appropriate personnel", and must be working for the company at the time of service).

[175]See, e.g., Vax-D Med. Technologies, LLC v. Texas Spine Medical Center, 485 F.3d 593, 596 (11th Cir. 2007) (service on company's manager sufficient); Ayres v. Jacobs & Crumplar, P.A., 99 F.3d 565, 567–68 (3d Cir. 1996) (service on office manager was insufficient); Adams v. AlliedSignal General Aviation Avionics, 74 F.3d 882, 885 (8th Cir. 1996) (service on officer of subsidiary insufficient service on parent corporation, absent probative evidence that subsidiary and parent are not independently operated); Malcolm v. Honeoye Falls-Lima Educ. Ass'n, 678 F.Supp.2d 100, 104–05 (W.D.N.Y. 2010) (service on company's general

counsel insufficient); Battie v. Freeman Decorating, 2001 WL 1345927 (E.D. La. 2001) (service on receptionist sufficient); Estates of Ungar ex rel. Strachman v. Palestinian Authority, 153 F. Supp. 2d 76, 89-91 (D.R.I. 2001) (service on Chief PA and PLO Representative in United States and to PLO's Deputy Permanent Observer to United Nations sufficient); Romand v. Zimmerman, 881 F. Supp. 806 (N.D. N.Y. 1995) (service on chairperson of board of trustees insufficient); Cf. Schollenberger v. Sears, Roebuck and Co., 876 F. Supp. 153 (E.D. Mich. 1995) (service on insurance claims representative insufficient).

[176]See Mommaerts v. Hartford Life and Acc. Ins. Co., 472 F.3d 967, 967–68 (7th Cir. 2007).

[177]See Williams v. GEICO Corp., 792 F.Supp. 2d 58, 65 (D.D.C. 2011).

[178]See Reynolds Innovations, Inc. v. E-CigaretteDirect, LLC, 851 F. Supp. 2d 961, 963 (M.D.N.C. 2012).

[179]See Waldner v. North American Truck & Trailer, Inc., 277 F.R.D. 401, 415 (D.S.D. 2011).

[180]See Rule 4(h)(1)(B).

rized,[181] and the serving party bears the burden of establishing that fact.[182]

Service at Domestic Company Headquarters

The Rules do *not* specifically authorize service by leaving a copy of the summons and complaint at the company's headquarters.[183] This type of service, however, may still be permitted. Rule 4(h) authorizes service in the federal courts in any manner permitted by the forum's State law.[184] For example, some States permit service on corporations by certified mail,[185] and others forgive service on the wrong corporate person so long as service is made at the corporate offices following the instructions of corporate employees found there.[186]

Service on Foreign Company

If served within the United States, a foreign corporation, partnership, or association can be served like domestic corporations — by delivering the summons and complaint to its officer, managing agent, general agent, or other agent authorized to receive service by appointment or by law.[187] If served outside the United States, the foreign company can be served like internationally-served individuals, under Rule 4(f),[188] except personal service.[189] Failure to comply with those provisions will

---

[181]*See In re Game Tracker, Inc.*, 746 F.Supp.2d 207, 214–15 (D.Me. 2010). *See also U.S. ex rel. Thomas v. Siemens AG*, 708 F.Supp.2d 505, 519 (E.D.Pa. 2010) (mere delivery is not sufficient, nor is service on a parent automatically proper as service on the subsidiary and vice versa).

[182]*See Nature's First Inc. v. Nature's First Law, Inc.*, 436 F. Supp. 2d 368 (D. Conn. 2006).

[183]*See Melkaz Intern. Inc. v. Flavor Innovation Inc.*, 167 F.R.D. 634 (E.D. N.Y. 1996).

[184]*See* Rule 4(h)(1)(A) (incorporating Rule 4(e)(1)).

[185]*See Alfa Corp. v. Alfagres, S.A.*, 385 F. Supp. 2d 1230, 1238 (M.D. Ala. 2005) (Alabama law).

[186]*See M'Baye v. World Boxing Ass'n*, 429 F. Supp. 2d 652, 656–57 (S.D. N.Y. 2006) (New York law). *See also Dailey v. R & J Commercial Contracting*, 2002 WL 484988, at *3 (S.D.Ohio 2002) ("When a corporation holds itself out to the public as receiving mail at a particular address, it must take some minimal steps to in-

sure that when certified mail service is directed to that address, it receives actual notice, and its failure to do so cannot be attributed to the plaintiff, who is entitled to rely upon the address in requesting certified mail service"); *Battie v. Freeman Decorating*, 2001 WL 1345927, at *1 (E.D. La. 2001) (commenting the delivery of summons and complaint to corporation's receptionist may be sufficient service).

[187]*See U.S. ex rel. Thomas v. Siemens AG*, 708 F.Supp.2d 505, 519 (E.D.Pa. 2010); *Madu, Edozie & Madu, P.C. v. SocketWorks Ltd. Nigeria*, 265 F.R.D. 106, 118–19 (S.D.N.Y. 2010).

[188]*See Nuance Commc'ns, Inc. v. Abbyy Software House*, 626 F.3d 1222, 1237 (Fed. Cir. 2010); *TracFone Wireless, Inc. v. Distelec Distribuciones Electronicas, S.A. de DV*, 268 F.R.D. 687, 689 (S.D.Fla. Aug 23, 2010).

[189]*But see Nuance Commc'ns, Inc. v. Abbyy Software House*, 626 F.3d 1222, 1238 (Fed. Cir. 2010) (personal delivery may be appropriate if made pursuant to applicable foreign law).

render the service ineffective.[190]

RULE 4(i)—SERVING THE UNITED STATES, ITS AGENCIES, CORPORATIONS, AND OFFICERS

CORE CONCEPT

To properly serve the United States, its agencies, corporations, or officers with original process, the summons and complaint must be served at several different locations.

APPLICATIONS

Multiple Service Is Mandatory, Not Discretionary

When serving the United States, its agencies, corporations, or officers, the multiple service requirements of Rule 4(i) are obligatory; failing to comply with these obligations will defeat proper service and prevent the court from acquiring jurisdiction over the federal defendants.[191]

The United States as Defendant

Original process must be served upon the United States as follows:

(1) ***United States Attorney***: By *either* (a) personally delivering the summons and complaint to the United States Attorney for the judicial district in which the action is brought, or her designee, *or* (b) sending the summons and complaint by registered or certified mail to the civil process clerk at the office of the United States Attorney; *and*

- *Warning:* If service is made under option (b), the mailing has to be addressed to the "Civil Process Clerk" and not the U.S. Attorney; misaddressing the mailed service in this manner renders the service improper.[192]

(2) ***Attorney General***: By *also* sending a copy of the summons and complaint by registered or certified mail to the United States Attorney General in Washington, D.C.; *and*

(3) ***Federal Officer or Agency***: In lawsuits attacking the validity of an order of a non-party officer or agency of the United States, by *also* sending a copy of the summons and complaint by registered or certified mail to

---

[190]*See Emery v. Wood Indus., Inc.*, 2001 WL 274747, at * 3 (D.N.H. 2001) (hand-delivery of complaint and summons to Assistant Manager for Public Relations in Taiwan failed to comply with procedures authorized by Rule 4).

[191]*See Marcus v. Postmaster General, U.S. Postal Serv. Southeast Area*, 461 Fed. Appx. 820, 822–23 (11th Cir. 2011); *Hutto v. U.S. Gov't*, 2010 WL 2854685, at *3 (N.D.Okla. July 16, 2010).

[192]*See Vargas v. Potter*, 792 F.Supp.2d 214, 217 (D.P.R. 2011).

such officer or agency.

Federal Officers, Agencies, or Corporations as Defendants

Original process may be served upon an officer, agency, or corporation of the United States as follows:

(1) ***United States***: By serving the United States (see above); *and*

(2) ***Federal Officer, Agency, or Corporation***: By *also* sending a copy of the summons and complaint by registered or certified mail to the federal officer, agency, or corporation named as a defendant.[193]

Federal Officers/Employees Sued in their Individual Capacities

In certain instances, federal officers and employees may be sued in their individual—rather than official—capacities.[194] In such cases, the type of service required will depend on the allegations of the pleading:

- *On-the-Job Claims:* If the federal officers or employees are sued in their individual capacities for acts or omissions occurring in connection with the performance of their federal duties, then proper service requires (1) service upon the United States *and* (2) service upon the officer or employee under Rule 4(e), (f), or (g).[195]

- *Claims Unrelated to the Job:* If the federal officers or employees are sued in their individual capacities for any other acts or omissions (that is, for conduct unrelated to the performance of their federal duties), then proper service requires only service under Rule 4(e), (f), or (g). Service on the United States is not required.[196]

These procedures apply to former federal officers and employees, as well as current personnel.[197]

If the plaintiff intends to sue the federal officials in *both* their individual and official capacities, the plaintiff must: (1)

---

[193]*See* Rule 4(i)(2). *See also Cleveland v. Williams*, 874 F. Supp. 270 (E.D. Cal. 1994) (where United States was not also served in lawsuit against IRS agents sued in their official capacities, complaint was dismissed as to all defendants).

[194]*See Bivens v. Six Unknown Named Agents of Federal Bureau of Narcotics*, 403 U.S. 388, 91 S. Ct. 1999, 29 L. Ed. 2d 619 (1971) (permitting action for money damages against federal officers acting under color of their official authority for injuries caused by the officers' unconstitutional conduct).

[195]*See* Rule 4(i)(3).

[196]*See* Rule 4(i)(2)(B) advisory committee note to 2000 amendments ("Many actions are brought against individual federal officers or employees of the United States for acts or omissions that have no connection whatever to their government roles. There is no reason to require service on the United States in these actions").

[197]*See* Rule 4(i)(2)(B) advisory committee notes to 2000 amendments (noting that an action against former federal personnel "is covered by paragraph (2)(B) in the same way as an action against a present officer or employee").

individually serve the officials under Rule 4(e), (f), or (g); *and* (2) serve the United States as well under Rule 4(i).[198] The plaintiff generally does not need to serve the official twice personally, however (*i.e.*, one service for each capacity).[199]

Serving "Copies" on Federal Defendants

One court has ruled that the requirement to serve a "copy" of summons and complaints may be met by photocopies of the originals.[200]

Careful! Name the Correct Federal Defendant

Practitioners should take special care to ensure that the proper defendant is named. A lawsuit may be dismissed if it mistakenly names a federal officer or agency as a defendant when the proper defendant is the United States, or mistakenly names the United States as a defendant when the proper defendant is a federal agency or officer, or mistakenly names federal officers as defendants in their official rather than individual capacities.[201]

Curing Incomplete Service on Federal Defendants

In view of the complexity of these multiple service obligations, Rule 4(i) establishes a "cure" for incomplete service in cases requiring service on officers, agencies, or federal corporations. So long as either the United States Attorney or the Attorney General has been properly served in such cases, the court must allow a plaintiff a reasonable period of time to fulfill the multiple service obligations at all other locations.[202]

- *"Cure" is Opportunity for Extension, Not an Excuse of Obligation:* The "cure" provision in Rule 4(i) does not excuse or forgive an incomplete service. To the contrary, the "cure" provision only authorizes an extension of time to complete the plaintiff's obligations—the full, required

---

[198]*See McCaslin v. Cornhusker State Industries*, 952 F. Supp. 652, 658–59 (D. Neb. 1996) (construing Rule 4(j), holding that service delivered directly to government employees conferred jurisdiction over them only in their individual capacities; to sue the government itself, service on the chief executive officer or the State attorney general's office was required).

[199]*See* Rule 4(i)(2) advisory committee notes to 2000 amendments (commenting that amendments are intended "to ensure that no one would read the seemingly independent provisions of paragraphs 2(A) and 2(B) to mean that service must be made twice both on the United States and on the United States employee when the em-ployee is sued in both official and individual capacities"). *See also Buttler v. Keller*, 169 F.R.D. 9, 10 (N.D. N.Y. 1996) (under applicable State law, a single service upon an individual, named in both his individual and representative capacities, suffices to confer jurisdiction).

[200]*See Marmolejos v. United States*, — F. Supp. 2d —, —, 2012 WL 2122196, at *2–*4 (D.P.R. 2012).

[201]*See, e.g.,* 28 U.S.C.A. § 2671 (under Federal Torts Claims Act, actions to recover for the torts of a federal agency must name the United States as a defendant).

[202]Rule 4(i)(4).

service under Rule 4(i) must still be accomplished.[203]

- *"Cure" in Federal Agency, Corporation, & Official Capacity Lawsuits:* If the plaintiff succeeds in serving either the United States Attorney or the Attorney General in a lawsuit asserting Rule 4(i)(2) claims (claims against a federal agency or corporation, or official capacity claims against federal officers of employees), but the plaintiff neglects to serve other required parties, the courts will allow the plaintiff a "reasonable time" to perfect proper service.[204] Note, however, that this "cure" provision applies *only* when proper service has already been achieved on the United States Attorney or the Attorney General.[205]

- *"Cure" in On-the-Job Individual Capacity Lawsuits:* In a lawsuit against federal officers or employees sued for Rule 4(i)(3) claims (individual capacity, "on-the-job" claims), a plaintiff who successfully serves the officer or employee will be granted a "reasonable time" to serve the United States as well.[206]

- *"Cure" Not General Extension of Time:* The extension is not unlimited; the "cure" must be accomplished within a "reasonable time" after the original, incomplete service is made.[207]

RULE 4(j)—SERVING FOREIGN, STATE, OR LOCAL GOVERNMENTS

CORE CONCEPT

The methods for serving process on a foreign, State, or local

---

[203]*See McMasters v. U.S.*, 260 F.3d 814, 817–18 (7th Cir. 2001).

[204]*See* Rule 4(i)(4)(A).

[205]*But see Gargano v. I.R.S.*, 207 F.R.D. 22, 23 (D. Mass. 2002) (commenting that some courts, confronted by a failure to serve the U.S. Attorney or Attorney General, "see room for a grant of equitable relief where overly strict adherence to the literal wording of the Rule appears to elevate form over substance", and have applied a four-part analysis that could grant such relief where: (1) all necessary governmental parties have actual notice of the lawsuit; (2) the government has suffered no prejudice from the service defect; (3) the plaintiff had a justifiable excuse for the failure to make proper service; and (4) the plaintiff would be severely prejudiced by a dismissal).

[206]*See* Rule 4(i)(4)(B).

[207]*See Kurzberg v. Ashcroft*, 619 F.3d 176, 184–86 (2d Cir. 2010) (cure not reasonable where plaintiffs failed to serve during 120-day period after being notified of deficient service by defendant); *Tuke v. U.S.*, 76 F.3d 155, 158 (7th Cir. 1996) (cure not reasonable where plaintiff failed to serve "for months" and, after being notified by the United States of the deficiency, failed to act promptly or properly); *Mused v. U.S. Dept. of Agriculture Food and Nutrition Service*, 169 F.R.D. 28, 35–36 (W.D. N.Y. 1996) (cure not reasonable where plaintiff waited nearly a year to cure service defect). *See also Mused v. U.S. Dept. of Agriculture Food and Nutrition Service*, 169 F.R.D. 28, 36 (W.D. N.Y. 1996) (rejecting argument that duration of defect be marked from date defect was "discovered", rather than when defect actually occurred).

government vary depending upon the type of government served and the application of other laws.

APPLICATIONS

Applicability of the Waiver-of-Service Procedure

The Rule 4(d) waiver-of-service procedure is *not* authorized for serving foreign, State, or local governments.[208] Whether the waiver procedure may be used to serve employees of a foreign, State, or local government in their official capacities remains unclear.[209]

Serving Foreign Governments, Their Political Subdivisions, Agencies, or Instrumentalities, Generally

Original process on these defendants must be served in accordance with the federal Foreign Sovereign Immunities Act.[210] The FSIA permits four types of service, listed in order of required preference (*i.e.*, the plaintiff must use method one, unless it is unavailable, in which case the plaintiff must use method two, unless it is unavailable, and so on).[211] The provisions of the Act demand "strict adherence".[212]

Serving Foreign Governments

The four permitted methods for serving a foreign government, as prescribed by the FSIA, are, in descending order of preference:

(1) ***Agreed-Method:*** In any manner arranged between the plaintiff and the foreign State, but if not then:

(2) ***International Agreement:*** In accordance with an applicable international treaty or convention, such as the *Hague Convention on the Service Abroad of Judicial and Extrajudicial Documents in Civil or Commercial Matters*,[213] but if not then:

(3) ***Ministry of Foreign Affairs:*** By the clerk of court

---

[208]*See* Rule 4(d)(1) (Rule 4(j) defendants absent from list of permitted waiver defendants). *See also Cupe v. Lantz*, 470 F. Supp. 2d 136, 138 (D. Conn. 2007). *But see Ecret v. Diamond*, 2007 WL 2743432, at *2–*3 (W.D. Wash. 2007) (though not authorized by Rule 4(j), waiver that was sought and then granted by local government enforced by court).

[209]*Compare Cupe v. Lantz*, 470 F. Supp. 2d 136, 138 (D. Conn. 2007) (Rule 4(d) inapplicable to state employees sued in their official capacities), *with Marcello v. Maine*, 238 F.R.D. 113, 115 (D. Me. 2006) (serving public employees in their official capacities is done through Rule 4(e) which, in turn, permits Rule 4(d) waiver-of-service

procedure).

[210]28 U.S.C.A. § 1608. *See generally Argentine Republic v. Amerada Hess Shipping Corp.*, 488 U.S. 428, 434, 109 S.Ct. 683, 102 L.Ed.2d 818 (1989); *Angellino v. Royal Family Al-Saud*, 688 F.3d 771, 776 (D.C.Cir. 2012).

[211]*See Murphy v. Islamic Republic of Iran*, 740 F.Supp.2d 51, 66 (D.D.C. 2010).

[212]*See Transaero, Inc. v. La Fuerza Aerea Boliviana*, 30 F.3d 148, 154 (D.C. Cir. 1994).

[213]Nov. 15, 1965, 20 U.S.T. 361, T.I.A.S. No. 6638, 658 U.N.T.S. 163. The text of the Convention on the Service Abroad of Judicial and Extrajudi-

mailing a copy of the summons and complaint and a notice of suit, along with translations thereof, in a manner requiring a signed receipt, to the head of the ministry of foreign affairs, but if such service is not available within 30 days, then:

(4) *Special Consular Services:* By the clerk of court mailing a copy of the summons and complaint and a notice of suit, along with translations thereof, in a manner requiring a signed receipt, to the United States Director of Special Consular Services, for transmittal to the foreign State through diplomatic channels.

Serving Non-Governmental Foreign Entities

The four permitted methods for serving foreign agencies and instrumentalities, as prescribed by the FISA, are, in descending order of preference:

(1) *Agreed-Method:* By serving process in any manner arranged between the plaintiff and the foreign agency or instrumentality,[214] but if not then:

(2) *Agent or International Agreement: Either* (a) by delivering process to an officer, managing agent, or general agent of the foreign agency or instrumentality, or to an agent appointed by the foreign agent or instrumentality to receive service of process or authorized by law to receive such service; *or* (b) by serving process in accordance with an applicable international treaty or convention, such as the *Hague Convention on the Service Abroad of Judicial and Extrajudicial Documents in Civil or Commercial Matters*,[215] but if not then:

(3) *Letter Rogatory, Clerk Mailing, or Court Order:* In one of the following manners: (a) by delivering process (together with a translation thereof) as directed in response to a letter rogatory or letter of request; *or* (b) by the clerk of court mailing process (along with translations thereof) in a manner requiring a signed receipt, to the agency or instrumentality; *or* (c) by order of court consistent with the law of the place where service is to be accomplished.

---

cial Documents in Civil or Commercial Matters is reprinted in the Supplement to 28 U.S.C.A. following Fed.R. Civ.P. 4 (WESTLAW: USCA database, **ci(frcp/2 4) & treaties).**

[214]*See Matter of Arbitration Between Trans Chem. Ltd. & China Nat. Machinery Import & Export Corp.,* 978 F. Supp. 266 (S.D. Tex. 1997), aff'd, 161 F.3d 314 (5th Cir. 1998) (service upon foreign agency was proper because it was made in accordance with the terms of the contract between the agency and the plaintiff).

[215]Nov. 15, 1965, 20 U.S.T. 361, T.I.A.S. No. 6638, 658 U.N.T.S. 163. The text of the Convention on the Service Abroad of Judicial and Extrajudicial Documents in Civil or Commercial Matters is reprinted in the Supplement to 28 U.S.C.A. following Fed.R. Civ.P. 4 (WESTLAW: USCA database, **ci(frcp/2 4) & treaties).**

Serving State and Local Governments, Generally

A State, municipal corporation, or other government organization may be served with original process in either of two ways, service under either of which will be deemed sufficient:[216]

(1) ***Chief Executive Officer:*** By personally delivering the summons and complaint to the chief executive officer of the State, municipal corporation, or governmental organization[217] (note that "delivery", in this provision, has been interpreted to exclude service by mail);[218] or

(2) ***State Law:*** By serving the summons and complaint in the manner authorized by the State in which the service is to be accomplished (which may permit mailing).[219] Note, the phrase "that state's law" refers to the State where the served entity is physically located and of which it is a citizen.[220] Some State laws require service on *multiple* officials in order to be proper.[221] Personal service on an official while traveling outside the State or local territory is unlikely to confer jurisdiction on the official's government.[222]

Serving State and Local Governments, Eleventh Amendment Concerns

The Eleventh Amendment to the U.S. Constitution restricts the authority of the federal courts to hear lawsuits against States.[223] Additionally, individual State and municipal sovereign immunity laws limit the federal courts' ability to enter

---

[216]*See Lawver v. Department of Corrections, State of Neb.*, 2007 WL 3376742, at *4 (D. Neb. 2007) (successful delivery under first method qualified as proper service, even though that delivery would have been found to be improper under second method).

[217]*See Coleman v. Milwaukee Bd. of School Directors*, 290 F.3d 932, 933–34 (7th Cir. 2002) (where school board had no "chief executive officer", only option for plaintiff was to serve as prescribed by State law); *McCaslin v. Cornhusker State Industries*, 952 F. Supp. 652, 658–59 (D. Neb. 1996) (holding that service delivered directly to government employees conferred jurisdiction over them only in their individual capacities; to sue the government itself, service on the chief executive officer or the State attorney general's office was required).

[218]*See Yates v. Baldwin*, 633 F.3d 669, 672 (8th Cir. 2011); *Morris v. City of Orlando*, 2010 WL 2836623, at *2 (M.D.Fla. July 19, 2010).

[219]*See Patterson v. Whitlock*, 392 Fed.Appx. 185, 188 n.7 (4th Cir. 2010) (noting State law option, and that North Carolina law permits mailing); *Holmes v. Gonzalez*, 2010 WL 1408436, at *2 (E.D.Tenn. Apr. 2, 2010) (Tennessee permits certain certified mail service).

[220]*See Rocky Mountain Chipseal, LLC v. Sherman County*, 841 F.Supp.2d 1224, 1228 (D.Colo. 2012).

[221]*See Peak v. District of Columbia*, 236 F.R.D. 13, 16 (D.D.C. 2006) (proper service upon the District of Columbia requires service on both the District's Attorney General and Mayor).

[222]*See Rocky Mountain Chipseal, LLC v. Sherman County*, 841 F.Supp.2d 1224, 1228–30 (D.Colo. 2012) (serving Kansas county commissioner while in Colorado for personal reasons did not vest Colorado with jurisdiction over Kansas county).

[223]*See Pennhurst State School & Hosp. v. Halderman*, 465 U.S. 89, 104 S. Ct. 900, 79 L. Ed. 2d 67 (1984) (noting that Eleventh Amendment pre-

awards against States, municipalities, and governmental entities.

RULE 4(k)—TERRITORIAL LIMITS OF EFFECTIVE SERVICE

CORE CONCEPT

Serving a summons and complaint (or filing an executed waiver of service) will vest a federal court with jurisdiction over that defendant if: the defendant is amenable to service under the forum State's jurisdictional laws; the defendant was joined to the lawsuit by impleader or necessary party practice within the "bulge" region; a federal statute permits it; or the defendant is not subject to any particular State's jurisdiction but possesses sufficient contacts with the U.S. to be sued here.

APPLICATIONS

Exercise of Federal Personal Jurisdiction

There is no broad, general federal long-arm statute,[224] but a schedule setting out the federal courts' "long-arm" jurisdictional reach exists in Rule 4(k). It provides that the federal courts acquire personal jurisdiction, upon effective service of process or a filed waiver of formal service, over:

- *State Long-Arm Statutes:* Defendants who are amenable to suit in the State where the district court is sitting in accordance with the provisions of that State's long-arm statute;[225]

- *100-Mile "Bulge" Rule:* Defendants joined as impleaded third-parties or necessary parties and who are served within 100 miles of the place where the summons issues;[226] and

  > *Note:* The bulge rule does *not* apply to service on the original parties to the lawsuit, nor does it constrict the range for service if a State or federal statute authorizes broader (or unlimited) service of process.

- *Federal Long-Arm Statutes:* Defendants who are amenable to suit in the district court pursuant to a federal statute providing for national or worldwide service of process (such as, for example, the federal interpleader

---

vents federal courts from hearing suits for damages filed by citizens against States, unless the defending State first consents). *See also Florida Dept. of State v. Treasure Salvors, Inc.*, 458 U.S. 670, 102 S. Ct. 3304, 73 L. Ed. 2d 1057 (1982) (confirming that Eleventh Amendment extends to bar suits by citizens against their own State of residence, in the absence of that State's consent to suit).

[224]*See S.E.C. v. Ross*, 504 F.3d 1130, 1138 (9th Cir. 2007).

[225]Rule 4(k)(1)(A). *See Felland v. Clifton*, 682 F.3d 665, 672 (7th Cir. 2012); *ITL Int'l, Inc. v. Constenla, S.A.*, 669 F.3d 493, 497 (5th Cir. 2012).

[226]Rule 4(k)(1)(B).

statute, 28 U.S.C. § 1335.)[227]

Asserting "National" Jurisdiction

The federal courts also have personal jurisdiction over non-resident defendants who have sufficient contacts with the United States as a Nation to warrant the application of federal law, yet who lack sufficient contacts with any single, particular State to support personal jurisdiction under State law long-arm statutes.[228] This special jurisdiction will apply in only rare cases.[229] In assessing whether contacts are sufficient for "national" personal jurisdiction, courts may apply the traditional general and specific jurisdiction inquiries.[230] Thus, if a defendant's contacts with the United States nationally (1) relate to or give rise to plaintiff's cause of action, (2) involve an act by which the defendant purposefully availed itself of the privilege of conducting activities within the Nation, and (3) allowed the defendant to reasonably foresee the possibility of being haled into court here, then Rule 4(k)(2) jurisdiction may be proper.[231] Actual, physical contacts with the United States are therefore not always required, so long as the requisite constitutional foreseeability is present.[232] This inquiry helps ensure that such defendants are afforded "fair warning" before

---

[227]Rule 4(k)(1)(C). *See Wultz v. Islamic Republic of Iran*, 755 F.Supp.2d 1, 31 (D.D.C. 2010) (service in Antiterrorism Act claim); *Flynn v. R.D. Masonry, Inc.*, 736 F.Supp.2d 54, 59 (D.D.C. 2010) (service in ERISA claim). *See generally U.S. S.E.C. v. Carrillo*, 115 F.3d 1540 (11th Cir. 1997) (where federal statute authorizes nationwide or worldwide service, the requisite "minimum contacts" analysis tests for contacts with the United States as a Nation).

[228]*See* Rule 4(k)(2). *See also Omni Capital Intern., Ltd. v. Rudolf Wolff & Co., Ltd.*, 484 U.S. 97, 111, 108 S. Ct. 404, 413, 98 L. Ed. 2d 415 (1987). *See generally Eskofot A/S v. E.I. Du Pont De Nemours & Co.*, 872 F. Supp. 81 (S.D. N.Y. 1995) (defendants have sufficient contacts with United States generally so that due process concerns are not offended where the defendants transact business in the United States, perform an act within the United States, or have an effect in the United States by an act done elsewhere).

[229]*See EcoDisc Tech. AG v. DVD Format/Logo Licensing Corp.*, 711 F. Supp. 2d 1074, 1086 n.6 (C.D.Cal. 2010).

[230]*See Submersible Systems, Inc.*

v. Perforadora Central, S.A. de C.V., 249 F.3d 413, 420–21 (5th Cir. 2001); *BP Chemicals Ltd. v. Formosa Chemical & Fibre Corp.*, 229 F.3d 254, 258–63 (3d Cir. 2000). *See also Base Metal Trading, Ltd. v. OJSC "Novokuznetsky Aluminum Factory"*, 283 F.3d 208, 216 (4th Cir. 2002) (rejecting Rule 4(k)(2) jurisdiction because alleged contacts with United States "appear sparse and limited to a few shipments of aluminum arriving in American ports", and refusing to commit "the limited resources of the federal courts . . . [to] resolving disputes between two foreign corporations with little or no connection to our country").

[231]*See Associated Transport Line, Inc. v. Productos Fitosanitarios Proficol El Carmen, S.A.*, 197 F.3d 1070, 1074 (11th Cir. 1999). *Cf. Consolidated Development Corp. v. Sherritt, Inc.*, 216 F.3d 1286 (11th Cir. 2000) (holding that personal jurisdiction will not lie where foreign corporation, that does not engage in general business in the forum, simply negotiates a contract there or has a subsidiary that markets defendant's products).

[232]*See Mwani v. bin Laden*, 417 F.3d 1, 13–14 (D.C. Cir. 2005) (permitting exercise of jurisdiction over international terrorist who orchestrated

being subjected to the coercive power of the federal courts.[233]

Prerequisites for Asserting "National" Jurisdiction

To qualify for this type of national-contacts service of process, three conditions (in addition to proper service or waiver of service[234]) are required:[235]

> *(1) Federal Claims:* Plaintiff's claims against the No-State-Resident defendant must arise under federal law;[236]
>
> *(2) No Conventional Jurisdiction Possible:* The defendant is beyond the jurisdictional reach of any individual State court and no situation-specific federal statute applies to confer jurisdiction;[237] *and*
>
> *(3) Exercise of Personal Jurisdiction is Constitutional:* The exercise of personal jurisdiction over the defendant would not offend the Constitution or other federal law.[238]

Burden of Proof in "National" Jurisdiction Cases

The plaintiff bears the burden of establishing that the prerequisites exist for Rule 4(k)(2) national-contacts service,[239] and limited jurisdictional discovery may be granted to help with that burden.[240] The courts are divided, however, on how that burden is discharged. The majority approach requires the plaintiff to make three prima facia showings: (1) the claim arises under federal law; (2) no situation-specific federal statute confers jurisdiction; and (3) the defendant's contacts with the United States nationally satisfy due process concerns.[241] Once the plaintiff makes these showings, the burden then shifts

---

bombing abroad that killed Americans, intended to "cause pain and sow terror" back in the United States, and participated in an ongoing conspiracy to attack the United States, with local overt acts).

[233]*See Saudi v. Northrop Grumman Corp.*, 427 F.3d 271, 275 (4th Cir. 2005).

[234]*See Merial Ltd. v. Cipla Ltd.*, 681 F.3d 1283, 1295 (Fed.Cir. 2012).

[235]*See Merial Ltd. v. Cipla Ltd.*, 681 F.3d 1283, 1294 (Fed.Cir. 2012) (listing elements); *Porina v. Marward Shipping Co., Ltd.*, 521 F.3d 122, 127 (2d Cir. 2008) (same).

[236]*See Getz v. The Boeing Co.*, 654 F.3d 852, 858-60 (9th Cir. 2011) (describing "substantive federal law" requirement, and surveying case law). *See also Bradford Co. v. Conteyor North America, Inc.*, 603 F.3d 1262, 1272 (Fed.Cir. 2010).

[237]*See Merial Ltd. v. Cipla Ltd.*,

681 F.3d 1283, 1294 (Fed.Cir. 2012); *Fraser v. Smith*, 594 F.3d 842, 848–49 (11th Cir. 2010).

[238]*See Bradford Co. v. Conteyor North America, Inc.*, 603 F.3d 1262, 1272 (Fed.Cir. 2010); *Fraser v. Smith*, 594 F.3d 842, 848–49 (11th Cir. 2010); *Holland America Line Inc. v. Wärtsilä North America, Inc.*, 485 F.3d 450, 461 (9th Cir. 2007).

[239]*See U.S. v. Swiss American Bank, Ltd.*, 191 F.3d 30, 38 (1st Cir. 1999).

[240]*See Toys "R" Us, Inc. v. Step Two, S.A.*, 318 F.3d 446, 458 (3d Cir. 2003) (allowing jurisdictional discovery on limited issue of defendant's business activities in United States, including business plans, marketing strategies, sales, and other commercial interactions); *Dardana Ltd. v. Yugansknefttegaz*, 317 F.3d 202, 208 (2d Cir. 2003) (remanding for discovery).

[241]*See ISI Int'l, Inc. v. Borden Ladner Gervais LLP*, 256 F.3d 548,

to the defendant to show that some specific State does indeed possess jurisdiction.[242] If the defendant does so, the plaintiff may (a) seek a transfer to a State where proper jurisdiction exists, (b) discontinue the lawsuit and re-file it, or (c) challenge the defendant's assertions.[243] This burden-shifting technique invests the defendant with the ability to "knock out" Rule 4(k)(2) by actually consenting to personal jurisdiction in some other State. Conversely, failing to so consent will permit the federal court to proceed with the Rule 4(k)(2) analysis without the accompanying burden of a 50-State constitutional analysis.[244]

The minority approach adds one further, more onerous requirement: that the plaintiff certify, based on information readily available to party and counsel, that the defendant is not subject to the jurisdiction of any U.S. State.[245] This requires the type of 50-State constitutional analysis that the majority approach rejects.

Default Judgments and "National" Jurisdiction

In denying relief from a default judgment, a court may consider whether personal jurisdiction could have been proper under Rule 4(k)(2), even though jurisdiction had been errantly premised on other grounds originally.[246] Moreover, a defaulting defendant will not be relieved of a default entered in the exercise of Rule 4(k)(2) jurisdiction by an *ex post facto* consent to personal jurisdiction in a different U.S. forum, unless that different forum would have possessed personal jurisdiction absent the consent.[247]

---

552 (7th Cir. 2001). *See also Touchcom, Inc. v. Bereskin & Parr*, 574 F.3d 1403, 1414–15, (Fed.Cir. 2009) (joining Fifth, Ninth, Eleventh, and D.C. Circuits in following the *ISI Int'l* approach).

[242]*See Haines v. Selendang Ayu M/V*, 403 Fed.Appx. 194, 195 (9th Cir. 2010) (Rule 4(k)(2) unavailable because defendants concede amenability in Alaska).

[243]*See ISI Intern., Inc. v. Borden Ladner Gervais LLP*, 256 F.3d 548, 552 (7th Cir. 2001).

[244]*See Merial Ltd. v. Cipla Ltd.*, 681 F.3d 1283, 1294 (Fed.Cir. 2012) (avoids "saddl[ing]" the plaintiff with an extraordinary challenge"); *Adams v. Unione Mediterranea Di Sicurta*, 364 F.3d 646, 651 (5th Cir. 2004) (agreeing that "a piecemeal analysis of the existence *vel non* of jurisdiction in

all fifty states is not necessary"); *ISI Intern., Inc. v. Borden Ladner Gervais LLP*, 256 F.3d 548, 552 (7th Cir. 2001) ("This procedure makes it unnecessary to traipse through the 50 states, asking whether each could entertain the suit").

[245]*See U.S. v. Swiss Am. Bank*, 191 F.3d 30, 38–41 (1st Cir. 1999). *See also Base Metal Trading, Ltd. v. OJSC "Novokuznetsky Aluminum Factory,"* 283 F.3d 208, 215 (4th Cir.2002) (applying First Circuit approach); *In re South African Apartheid Litig.*, 643 F.Supp.2d 423, 428–29, (S.D.N.Y. 2009) (same).

[246]*See Merial Ltd. v. Cipla Ltd.*, 681 F.3d 1283, 1296–98 (Fed.Cir. 2012).

[247]*See Merial Ltd. v. Cipla Ltd.*, 681 F.3d 1283, 1294–95 (Fed.Cir. 2012).

RULE 4(*l*)—PROVING SERVICE

CORE CONCEPT

Where formal service has not been waived, the process server must present proof of service to the court.

APPLICATIONS

Effect of Proof of Service

A filed proof of service is recognized as prima facie evidence that service was properly accomplished.[248] But, the presumption of validity is rebuttable.[249] For example, the courts often accept an affidavit from a purported agent who denies authority to accept service as sufficient to rebut the presumption.[250] If the presumption is rebutted, the burden of proving proper service of process returns to the plaintiff.[251] However, a naked allegation denying service (without any further evidentiary showing) is usually insufficient to rebut a proper affidavit of service.[252]

Nature of Proof

The proof of service should contain sufficient facts to confirm that valid service has been accomplished (*e.g.,* the dwelling place where process was left, the name of the receiving agent). Where service was made by someone other than a United States Marshal, an affidavit of service is required,[253] although proof by other means may, under proper circumstances, be acceptable.[254]

Service Outside the United States

If service is made under treaty or other international agreement, proof of service must be in accordance with that treaty or agreement. If service is made in any other manner, proof of service must include a receipt signed by the addressee or other satisfactory evidence of delivery.

---

[248]*See Blair v. City of Worcester,* 522 F.3d 105, 111 (1st Cir. 2008); *O'Brien v. R.J. O'Brien & Associates, Inc.,* 998 F.2d 1394, 1398 (7th Cir. 1993).

[249]*See Blair v. City of Worcester,* 522 F.3d 105, 111–12 (1st Cir. 2008). *See also Gottlieb v. Sandia Am. Corp.,* 452 F.2d 510, 514 (3d Cir. 1971) (return from U.S. Marshal "is not conclusive on the question of service on an agent, it will stand in the absence of proof to the contrary").

[250]*See Blair v. City of Worcester,* 522 F.3d 105, 112 (1st Cir. 2008) (collecting cases).

[251]*See Blair v. City of Worcester,* 522 F.3d 105, 112 (1st Cir. 2008).

[252]*See Economy Stone Midstream Fuel, LLC v. M/V A.M. THOMPSON,* 2009 WL 973441, at *1 (N.D.Miss. Apr. 9, 2009).

[253]*See Patterson v. Brown,* 2008 WL 219965, at *12 (W.D. N.C. 2008), rev'd in part on other grounds, 2010 WL 3303749 (4th Cir. 2010) (unsworn attorney's assertion of service not sufficient).

[254]*See Udoinyion v. Guardian Sec.,* 440 Fed.Appx. 731, 735 (11th Cir. 2011) (unsworn statement under penalty of perjury permitted); *TracFone Wireless, Inc. v. Unlimited PCS Inc.,* 279 F.R.D. 626, 631 (S.D.Fla. 2012) (copy of FedEx proof-of-signature form permitted in Rule 4(f)(2) international service case).

Failure to Present Proof of Service

The plaintiff "must" make a proof of service to the court.[255] However, so long as the plaintiff demonstrates that the defendant was properly served, the process server's technical failure to present proof of service will not affect the validity of the service.[256] This liberality does *not* mean that a plaintiff enjoys similar liberality in the discharging the duty of *completing* service of process; to the contrary, the provisions of Rule 4(*l*) do not in any way alter the 120-day time period for accomplishing service set out in Rule 4(m).[257]

Amendment to Proof of Service

Where an amendment would cure the defect in the proof of service, the courts generally will grant leave to so amend.[258]

RULE 4(m)—TIME LIMIT FOR SERVICE

CORE CONCEPT

The summons and complaint must be served within 120 days after the complaint is filed, unless the plaintiff is able to show "good cause" why process could not be served within that time. If "good cause" is not shown, the district court must either dismiss the lawsuit without prejudice or, in its discretion, direct that service be accomplished within a new specified time.

APPLICATIONS

The 120-Day Service Period

A federal lawsuit is "commenced" by filing the complaint,[259] and then remains pending for 120 days to enable the claimant to accomplish a valid service of process upon (or obtain a waiver from) every defendant. Failure to complete service within that 120-day window exposes the lawsuit to dismissal.

Dismissals for Failing to Serve Within 120 Days

Dismissals under this Rule for failure to timely serve process are made without prejudice.[260] If, however, a re-filed complaint would be beyond the applicable statute of limitations, the Rule 4(m) dismissal "without prejudice" will not defeat an

---

[255]*See Mann v. Castiel*, 681 F.3d 368, 373 (D.C.Cir. 2012).

[256]*See* Rule 4(*l*)(3). *See also Colony Ins. Co. v. Ropers of Hattiesburg, LLC*, 2011 WL 1226095, at *4 (S.D. Miss. Mar. 29, 2011) (citing authorities confirming "the Rules means what it says").

[257]*See Chhaparwal v. West Virginia University Hospitals, Inc.*, 2008 WL 2543429, at *3 (N.D. W. Va. 2008).

[258]*See Nolan v. City of Yonkers*, 168 F.R.D. 140, 143 (S.D. N.Y. 1996) (noting that request to amend proof of service should rarely be refused, and then granting leave to do so).

[259]*See* Rule 3.

[260]*See Mack v. Dillon*, 594 F.3d 620, 622 (8th Cir. 2010); *Lemoge v. U.S.*, 587 F.3d 1188, 1195–98 (9th Cir. 2009); *Betty K Agencies, Ltd. v. M/V MONADA*, 432 F.3d 1333, 1342 n.5 (11th Cir. 2005).

affirmative defense asserting time-bar.[261] Moreover, a Rule 4(m) dismissal is generally considered an abandoned claim, and is accorded no interruptive effect on the running of the statute of limitations; thus, the dismissal is the equivalent (for these purposes) of the claim having never been filed at all.[262]

Extensions of Time to Complete Service

Under the pre-December 1, 1993 version of Rule 4,[263] unless the plaintiff could demonstrate "good cause" for failing to serve process within 120 days of filing, the district court had no alternative but to dismiss the lawsuit without prejudice. Now, under current Rule 4(m), courts distinguish between justified delay ("good cause") and excusable neglect.[264] As to the former (justified delay), the district court *must* grant a plaintiff an extension for "an appropriate period".[265] When good cause is not shown, the district court has the option of either dismissing the lawsuit without prejudice or, in the exercise of its discretion, excusing the delay by issuing an order that directs that service be completed within a specified additional period of time.[266]

Mandatory "Good Cause" Extensions

The plaintiff bears the burden of proving that "good cause" exists to excuse a delay in service of process.[267] No fixed

---

[261]*See Conover v. Lein*, 87 F.3d 905, 908–09 (7th Cir. 1996) (commenting that dismissals "without prejudice" under Rule 4(m) are not necessarily dismissals "without consequence," if the pertinent statutes of limitations have run); *Hawkins v. McHugh*, 46 F.3d 10 (5th Cir.1995) (applying Louisiana law and holding that dismissal does not interrupt prescription or toll the prescription period). *See also Cardenas v. City of Chicago*, 646 F.3d 1001, 1008 (7th Cir. 2011) (although ordinarily without prejudice, Rule 4(m) dismissals may be made with prejudice if limitations period has expired).

[262]*See Cruz v. Louisiana ex rel. Dept. of Public Safety and Corrections*, 528 F.3d 375, 379 (5th Cir. 2008).

[263]The prior practice, former Rule 4(j), provided: "If a service of the summons and complaint is not made upon a defendant within 120 days after the filing of the complaint and the party on whose behalf such service was required cannot show good cause why such service was not made within that period, the action shall be dismissed

as to that defendant without prejudice upon the court's own initiative with notice to such party or upon motion".

[264]*See Coleman v. Milwaukee Bd. of School Directors*, 290 F.3d 932, 934 (7th Cir. 2002).

[265]*See Robinson v. Clipse*, 602 F.3d 605, 608 (4th Cir.2010); *Lemoge v. U.S.*, 587 F.3d 1188, 1198 (9th Cir. 2009); *Laurence v. Wall*, 551 F.3d 92, 94 (1st Cir. 2008). *Cf. Bogle-Assegai v. Connecticut*, 470 F.3d 498, 508–09 (2d Cir. 2006) (extension denied where no showing of good cause was made and extension would have spanned more than 600 days, a delay not consistent with "an appropriate period").

[266]*See Meilleur v. Strong*, 682 F.3d 56, 61 (2d Cir. 2012); *Lemoge v. U.S.*, 587 F.3d 1188, 1198 (9th Cir. 2009); *Lepone-Dempsey v. Carroll County Com'rs*, 476 F.3d 1277, 1282 (11th Cir. 2007).

[267]*See Lepone-Dempsey v. Carroll County Com'rs*, 476 F.3d 1277, 1281 (11th Cir. 2007); *Nafziger v. McDermott Intern., Inc.*, 467 F.3d 514, 521 (6th Cir. 2006); *Habib v. General*

guidelines define "good cause",[268] and it remains an exercise of discretion.[269] Minimally, good cause requires a showing of good faith and a reasonable basis, beyond the plaintiff's control, for failing to comply with the Rules,[270] such as a service-evading defendant,[271] a pending bankruptcy stay,[272] or, in some cases, a sudden illness or natural catastrophe.[273] This standard is a demanding one,[274] and is ordinarily applied narrowly to protect only those litigants who have exercised meticulous care in attempting to complete service.[275] As one court has aptly warned: "The lesson to the federal plaintiff's lawyer is not to take any chances. Treat the 120 days with the respect reserved for a time bomb."[276]

Motors Corp., 15 F.3d 72, 73 (6th Cir. 1994).

[268]*See Kurka v. Iowa County*, 628 F.3d 953, 957 (8th Cir. 2010).

[269]*See Zapata v. City of New York*, 502 F.3d 192, 197 (2d Cir. 2007); *Byrd v. Stone*, 94 F.3d 217, 219 (6th Cir. 1996).

[270]*See Mann v. Castiel*, 681 F.3d 368, 374–75 (D.C.Cir. 2012); *Kurka v. Iowa County*, 628 F.3d 953, 957 (8th Cir. 2010); *Rance v. Rocksolid Granit USA, Inc.*, 583 F.3d 1284, 1286 (11th Cir. 2009).

[271]*See Mann v. Castiel*, 681 F.3d 368, 374 (D.C.Cir. 2012); *Coleman v. Milwaukee Bd. of Sch. Dtrs.*, 290 F.3d 932, 934 (7th Cir. 2002).

[272]*See De Tie v. Orange County*, 152 F.3d 1109 (9th Cir. 1998).

[273]*See Matasareanu v. Williams*, 183 F.R.D. 242, 246 (C.D. Cal. 1998); *Gambino v. Village of Oakbrook*, 164 F.R.D. 271, 274 (M.D. Fla. 1995).

[274]*See Lemoge v. U.S.*, 587 F.3d 1188, 1198 (9th Cir. 2009) (to show "good cause", plaintiff may be required to prove (a) excusable neglect, (b) defendant's personal, actual notice of the pending lawsuit, (c) defendant's lack of prejudice, and (d) plaintiff's severe prejudice if lawsuit were dismissed).

[275]*See Despain v. Salt Lake Area Metro Gang Unit*, 13 F.3d 1436, 1438 (10th Cir. 1994). *Accord Lepone-Dempsey v. Carroll County Com'rs*, 476 F.3d 1277, 1281–82 (11th Cir. 2007) (noting that good cause exists when outside factors, other than inadvertence or negligence, defeated service); *Hamilton v. Endell*, 981 F.2d 1062, 1065 (9th Cir. 1992) (inadvertent error or ignorance of governing rules will not excuse a failure to timely serve process). *Compare Lepone-Dempsey v. Carroll County Com'rs*, 476 F.3d 1277, 1282 (11th Cir. 2007) (relying on defendant's assertion that he would sign waiver form was not good faith) *and Despain v. Salt Lake Area Metro Gang Unit*, 13 F.3d 1436, 1438 (10th Cir. 1994) (neither mere absence of prejudice nor mistake of counsel constitutes "good cause") *and Powell v. Starwalt*, 866 F.2d 964 (7th Cir.1989) (attorney inadvertence will not constitute "good cause") *and Matasareanu v. Williams*, 183 F.R.D. 242, 246 (C.D. Cal. 1998) (lack of legal training and attorney guidance does not constitute "good cause") *and Braithwaite v. Johns Hopkins Hosp.*, 160 F.R.D. 75 (D. Md. 1995) (delay resulting from the psychological distress caused by the murder of plaintiff's only daughter during 120-day service period did not constitute "good cause") *with Habib v. General Motors Corp.*, 15 F.3d 72, 73 (6th Cir. 1994) (*pro se* litigant's medical conditions, combined with diligent efforts to complete service, satisfies "good cause" test).

[276]*Braxton v. U.S.*, 817 F.2d 238, 241 (3d Cir. 1987) (quoting *Siegel, Practice Commentary on Amendment of Federal Rule 4 (Eff. Feb. 26, 1983) with Special Statute of Limitations Precautions*, 96 F.R.D. 88, 103 (1983)).

"Good Cause" and U.S. Marshal Service Delays

Ordinarily, *pro se* litigants for whom the United States Marshal's Service may be directed to serve process will be granted a "good cause" extension of the 120-day period where a delay in service is attributable to the Marshal's service,[277] although some courts require more of *pro se* litigants to invoke this type of extension (such as pre-expiration notification and request for anticipated extension).[278]

Permissive Extensions

When "good cause" is not shown, the decision whether to dismiss or grant a further extension is committed to the district court's discretion[279] (essentially, plaintiffs throw themselves "on the mercy of the district court"[280]). Although Rule 4(m) lists no criteria for making this determination,[281] the district court is nevertheless still obligated to consider whether circumstances exist to warrant an extension of the 120-day service period.[282] (Although encouraged to do, the Rule does not require district judges to detail the reasoning for their ruling.[283]) In making this evaluation, the court may examine, among other factors, the length of and reasons for the delay, whether the delay was within the plaintiff's control, good faith, prejudice to the defendants, whether the applicable statute of limitations would bar a re-filing, whether the failure to timely serve was due to a difficulty in serving government officials, whether the offending party is proceeding *pro se*, whether the unserved defendant has been evading service or concealing a defect in service, and whether service was eventually accomplished and, if so, how far beyond the 120-day period actual, effective service occurred.[284] Moreover, a defendant's admission of liability will prove an important factor tilting in favor of granting a permissive extension.[285] The courts of appeals review such decisions under an abuse of discretion standard, and can be expected to often affirm any reasoned and principled decision by the trial

---

[277]*See Mann v. Castiel*, 681 F.3d 368, 374–75 (D.C.Cir. 2012); *Robinson v. Clipse*, 602 F.3d 605, 608 (4th Cir. 2010); *Rance v. Rocksolid Granit USA, Inc.*, 583 F.3d 1284, 1287–88 (11th Cir. 2009).

[278]*See Meilleur v. Strong*, 682 F.3d 56, 63 (2d Cir. 2012).

[279]*See Cardenas v. City of Chicago*, 646 F.3d 1001, 1006 (7th Cir. 2011); *Gerena v. Korb*, 617 F.3d 197, 201 (2d Cir. 2010).

[280]*See U.S. v. McLaughlin*, 470 F.3d 698, 700 (7th Cir. 2006).

[281]*See U.S. v. McLaughlin*, 470 F.3d 698, 700 (7th Cir. 2006).

[282]*See Rance v. Rocksolid Granit USA, Inc.*, 583 F.3d 1284, 1286 (11th Cir. 2009); *Panaras v. Liquid Carbonic Industries Corp.*, 94 F.3d 338, 341 (7th Cir. 1996).

[283]*See Cardenas v. City of Chicago*, 646 F.3d 1001, 1007 (7th Cir. 2011).

[284]*See, e.g., Cardenas v. City of Chicago*, 646 F.3d 1001, 1006 (7th Cir. 2011); *Kurka v. Iowa County*, 628 F.3d 953, 959 (8th Cir. 2010); *Lemoge v. U.S.*, 587 F.3d 1188, 1195 (9th Cir. 2009); *Millan v. USAA General Indem. Co.*, 546 F.3d 321, 325–26 (5th Cir. 2008).

[285]*See U.S. v. McLaughlin*, 470 F.3d 698, 701 (7th Cir. 2006).

court.[286]

> *Note:* Although the effect of the statute of limitations may be considered by the court in evaluating whether to grant a permissive extension,[287] this does not mean that a permissive extension is mandatory whenever a dismissal would result in a time-bar.[288] Instead, the district court must assess whether all criteria, in addition to time-bar, warrant the permissive extension.

Substantive State Law Can Impact 120-Day Period

The substantive laws of some States provide that merely filing a complaint does not toll the applicable statutes of limitations. In those instances, Rule 4(m) will not prevent a cause of action from becoming time-barred during the 120-day service period, if State law would so dictate.[289]

Defendants Can Waive 120-Day Period

Although Rule 4(m) contains mandatory-sounding dismissal language, defendants may still waive the 120-day service period by filing an omnibus Rule 12 motion and omitting from that motion the claim that process was served beyond Rule 4(m)'s 120-day time period.[290]

Sua Sponte Dismissals

When service has not been effected within the 120-day service period, the action may be dismissed upon motion, or upon

---

[286]*See Kurka v. Iowa County*, 628 F.3d 953, 959–60 (8th Cir. 2010) (although factors "favored" extension, no abuse of discretion to deny one); *Coleman v. Milwaukee Bd. of School Directors*, 290 F.3d 932, 934 (7th Cir. 2002) (although most judges "would exercise lenity and allow a late service," no abuse of discretion to deny it). *Compare U.S. v. McLaughlin*, 470 F.3d 698, 701 (7th Cir. 2006) (where service delay causes "zero prejudice" to any party or the court, granting permissive extension "cannot be an abuse of discretion").

[287]*See Lemoge v. U.S.*, 587 F.3d 1188, 1195 (9th Cir. 2009); *Mann v. American Airlines*, 324 F.3d 1088, 1090–91 (9th Cir. 2003).

[288]*See Kurka v. Iowa County*, 628 F.3d 953, 959–60 (8th Cir. 2010); *Lepone-Dempsey v. Carroll County Com'rs*, 476 F.3d 1277, 1282 (11th Cir. 2007). *See also Boley v. Kaymark*, 123 F.3d 756, 759 (3d Cir. 1997) ("it is not a factor that standing alone supports a finding of prejudice to the defendant"). *But cf. Millan v. USAA General Indem. Co.*, 546 F.3d 321, 326 (5th Cir. 2008) (if timebar would result, court may only dismiss upon clear record of delay or contumacious conduct by plaintiff, the absence of a lesser but better sanction, *and* presence of aggravating factor (*e.g.*, delay by client not lawyer, actual prejudice to defendant, delay caused intentionally)).

[289]*See Torre v. Brickey*, 278 F.3d 917, 919–20 (9th Cir. 2002) (holding that Rule 4(m) did not preserve claims for 120-day period where substantive law of forum State, Oregon, does not toll statute of limitations until service is effected); *Larsen v. Mayo Medical Center*, 218 F.3d 863 (8th Cir. 2000) (same, under Minnesota law); *Habermehl v. Potter*, 153 F.3d 1137, 1139 (10th Cir. 1998) (same, under Wyoming law). *See also* Authors' Commentary to Rule 3 ("**Diversity Jurisdiction Cases**" and "**Supplemental Jurisdiction Cases**").

[290]*See McCurdy v. American Bd. of Plastic Surgery*, 157 F.3d 191, 195 (3d Cir. 1998) (citing cases).

the court's own initiative.[291] Such *sua sponte* dismissals under Rule 4(m) require prior "notice to the plaintiff".[292]

120-Day Period Does Not Apply to Foreign Service

The 120-day service rule does not apply to service within a foreign country,[293] or to service upon a foreign state and its political subdivisions, agencies, and instrumentalities.[294] However, the time allowable for accomplishing foreign service is not unlimited, as district courts must retain the ability to control their dockets.[295] Some courts have conditioned this foreign service "exemption" upon a showing that good faith attempts were made to serve within the 120-day period; if no such attempts were made, these courts hold that the exemption will not apply and the passage of 120 days can justify a dismissal.[296]

New 120-Day Period For Newly Added Parties

When a complaint is amended to add new parties, the plaintiff is given 120 days from the date of amendment to serve the new defendants.[297] Note, however, that this new 120-day clock will apply only to the newly-added parties; amendments will ordinarily not extend the time for serving parties who were named earlier.[298]

---

[291] *See* Rule 4(m).

[292] *See Sanders v. Southwestern Bell Tel., L.P.*, 544 F.3d 1101, 1111 (10th Cir. 2008); *Brown v. District of Columbia*, 514 F.3d 1279, 1286–87 (D.C. Cir. 2008); *Nagy v. Dwyer*, 507 F.3d 161, 164 (2d Cir. 2007).

[293] *See* Fed.R.Civ.P. 4(m) (referencing Fed. R. Civ. P. 4(f))(providing for service upon individuals in foreign countries). *See Guifu Li v. A Perfect Day Franchise, Inc*, 281 F.R.D. 373, 388 (N.D.Cal. 2012); *Lutsenko v. Pshnka*, 282 F.R.D. 5, 7 (D.D.C. 2012). *See generally Sang Young Kim v. Frank Mohn A/S*, 909 F. Supp. 474, 479–80 (S.D. Tex. 1995) (noting that exclusion of foreign service from the 120-day limit "helps to counterbalance the complex and time-consuming nature of foreign service of process"); *Pennsylvania Orthopedic Ass'n v. Mercedes-Benz A.G.*, 160 F.R.D. 58 (E.D. Pa. 1995) (commenting that, to compensate for the possibility of very complex and time-consuming service, Rule 4(m) acts to remove all deadlines for serving a complaint in a foreign country). *But cf. Goodstein v. Bombardier Capital, Inc.*, 167 F.R.D. 662, 665–66 (D. Vt. 1996) (holding that Rule 4(m)'s timeliness requirement is only excused where service is attempted in a foreign country).

[294] *See* Fed.R.Civ.P. 4(m) (referencing Fed.R.Civ.P. 4(j)(1)) (providing for service upon foreign States and their political subdivisions, agencies, and instrumentalities).

[295] *See Nylok Corp. v. Fastener World Inc.*, 396 F.3d 805, 807 (7th Cir. 2005).

[296] *See USHA (India), Ltd. v. Honeywell Intern., Inc.*, 421 F.3d 129, 134 (2d Cir. 2005); *Nylok Corp. v. Fastener World Inc.*, 396 F.3d 805, 807 (7th Cir. 2005); *Allstate Ins. Co. v. Funai Corp.*, 249 F.R.D. 157 (M.D. Pa. 2008). *See also Montalbano v. Easco Hand Tools, Inc.*, 766 F.2d 737, 740 (2d Cir. 1985) (same holding, construing former Rule 4(j) (predecessor to Rule 4(m))).

[297] *See City of Merced v. Fields*, 997 F. Supp. 1326, 1338 (E.D. Cal. 1998); *Del Raine v. Carlson*, 153 F.R.D. 622, 628 (S.D. Ill. 1994), rev'd in part on other grounds, 77 F.3d 484 (7th Cir. 1996) (Table).

[298] *See Lindley v. City of Birmingham*, 452 Fed.Appx. 878, 880 (11th Cir. 2011); *Brait Builders Corp. v.*

In Forma Pauperis Motions and 120-Day Period

Because the statute of limitations is ordinarily tolled during the pendency of a motion for leave to proceed *in forma pauperis*, the Rule 4(m) 120-day period for service will not begin to run until the complaint is stamped "filed" (either when the *in forma pauperis* motion is granted without a fee or the filing fee is actually paid).[299]

RULE 4(n)—ASSERTING JURISDICTION OVER PROPERTY OR ASSETS

CORE CONCEPT

If authorized by federal statute, the district court may exercise jurisdiction over property. Moreover, if personal jurisdiction over a particular defendant is not possible, the district court may exercise jurisdiction over that defendant's property by seizing the property as permitted under State law.

APPLICATIONS

Effect

A federal court may exercise jurisdiction over property located within its geographic territory.[300] However, a judgment in a *quasi-in-rem* or *in-rem* lawsuit acts only upon the seized property; it has no *in personam* effect. Thus, a plaintiff cannot enforce a *quasi-in-rem* or *in-rem* judgment against property of the defendant located outside the forum State.[301]

Amount in Controversy

A *quasi-in-rem* or *in-rem* action only permits execution of the seized property; the courts, however, are divided on the proper method for computing the amount in controversy—either by the value of the seized property or the sum stated in the complaint's demand clause.[302]

> *Note:* If the plaintiff's claim exceeds the value of seized property, the plaintiff is free to sue elsewhere for the remaining, unrecovered amount of the claim.

Due Process

Just as in the personal jurisdiction context, a federal court can ordinarily hear a *quasi-in-rem* action only if the Due Pro-

---

Mass. Div. of Capital Asset Mgmt., 644 F.3d 5, 9 (1st Cir. 2011).

[299] *See Scary v. Philadelphia Gas Works*, 202 F.R.D. 148 (E.D. Pa. 2001).

[300] *See Office Depot Inc. v. Zuccarini*, 596 F.3d 696, 700 (9th Cir. 2010).

[301] *See Sara Lee Corp. v. Gregg*, 2002 WL 1925703, at *2 (M.D. N.C. 2002) (noting that quasi in rem jurisdiction over defendant's property is limited to the property located within forum). The effect of quasi-in-rem and in-rem actions are discussed in greater depth in Part II of this text, §§ 2.8 to 2.9.

[302] *See Great Am. Ins. Co. v. Louis Lesser Enterprises, Inc.*, 353 F.2d 997 (8th Cir. 1965) (noting disagreement among courts).

cess test is satisfied.[303]

Additional Research References

Wright & Miller, *Federal Practice and Procedure* §§ 1061 to 1137
C.J.S., Federal Civil Procedure §§ 187 to 223
West's Key Number Digest, Federal Civil Procedure ⇒403, ⇒404, ⇒411 to 427, ⇒441 to 446, ⇒461 to 505, ⇒511 to 518, ⇒531 to 540

---

[303]*See Shaffer v. Heitner*, 433 U.S. 186, 97 S. Ct. 2569, 53 L. Ed. 2d 683 (1977); *Office Depot Inc. v. Zuccarini*, 596 F.3d 696, 700 (9th Cir. 2010).

RULE 4.1
SERVING OTHER PROCESS

(a) **In General.** Process—other than a summons under Rule 4 or a subpoena under Rule 45—must be served by a United States marshal or deputy marshal or by a person specially appointed for that purpose. It may be served anywhere within the territorial limits of the state where the district court is located and, if authorized by a federal statute, beyond those limits. Proof of service must be made under Rule 4(l).

(b) **Enforcing Orders: Committing for Civil Contempt.** An order committing a person for civil contempt of a decree or injunction issued to enforce federal law may be served and enforced in any district. Any other order in a civil-contempt proceeding may be served only in the state where the issuing court is located or elsewhere in the United States within 100 miles from where the order was issued.

[Adopted April 22, 1993, effective December 1, 1993; April 30, 2007, effective December 1, 2007.]

AUTHORS' COMMENTARY ON RULE 4.1

PURPOSE AND SCOPE

Rule 4.1 sets the procedure for service of types of process other than a civil summons or a subpoena. Such process is served either by a United States Marshal or by an individual specially appointed by the court.

APPLICATIONS

What Is "Other Process"

Service of original process is governed by Rule 4, and service of a subpoena is governed by Rule 45. Any "other process" is governed by this Rule 4.1. Such "other process" thus includes execution orders,[1] orders of civil commitment,[2] orders to show cause,[3] and orders for injunctions, attachments, arrests, and judicial sales.[4] Rule 4.1 does not apply to orders of criminal commitment.

Process Server

"Other process" must be served either by the United States Marshal, a deputy Marshal, or some other person specially appointed for the purpose by the court.[5] (Whether to appoint a Marshall or some other person is left to the court's discretion, unless the plaintiff is a pauper or seaman.[6]) Service performed by anyone else is defective.[7] To date, the only case law exception to this requirement appears in the context of process to enforce a judgment for the payment of money. Such enforcement proceedings are governed by Rule 69(a), which provides that the "procedure on execution" must follow State practice. At least one court has held that, notwithstanding the broad, general language of Rule 4.1, the provisions of Rule 69(a) compel that State practice govern the service of process in such execution proceedings.[8]

Limits of Service

"Other process" may be served either within the State in which the district court is sitting or as otherwise provided by federal statute.[9] Special procedures, however, guide serving and enforcing orders of civil commitment. Proper service and enforcement in those proceedings will depend on whether the law to be enforced is federal or State. If federal law, the order may be served and enforced in any federal district. If State law (as in diversity cases), the order may be served only within the

---

[1] *See Schneider v. National R.R. Passenger Corp.*, 72 F.3d 17 (2d Cir. 1995).

[2] *See F.T.C. v. Verity Intern., Ltd.*, 140 F. Supp. 2d 313, 318 (S.D. N.Y. 2001) (applying Rule 4.1 to civil commitment order which directed that defendants, who had willfully disobeyed court order, were to be arrested and detained if they enter the United States, until such time as they complied with court order), order vacated, 443 F.3d 48 (2d Cir.2006); *Spectacular Venture, L.P. v. World Star Intern., Inc.*, 927 F. Supp. 683 (S.D. N.Y. 1996) (applying Rule 4.1 to civil contempt orders).

[3] *See Fidelity Nat'l Fin., Inc. v. Friedman*, 2010 WL 960420, at *6 (D.Ariz. Mar. 15, 2010).

[4] *See JTH Tax Inc. v. Lee*, 2007 WL 1320505, at *2 n.2 (C.D. Ill. 2007).

[5] *See Fidelity Nat'l Fin., Inc. v. Friedman*, 2010 WL 960420, at *6 (D.Ariz. Mar. 15, 2010).

[6] *See JTH Tax Inc. v. Lee*, 2007 WL 1320505, at *2 (C.D. Ill. 2007).

[7] *See Schneider v. National R.R. Passenger Corp.*, 72 F.3d 17 (2d Cir.1995) (State sheriff who had "seized" Amtrak locomotives in the course of executing upon a $1.8 million plaintiff's personal injury judgment was not a Marshal, deputy Marshal, or specially appointed process server, and thus process was defective under Rule 4.1 and the sheriff was not entitled to his service fee for executing upon the trains).

[8] *See Apostolic Pentecostal Church v. Colbert*, 169 F.3d 409, 414 (6th Cir. 1999).

[9] *See Hoult v. Hoult*, 373 F.3d 47, 53 (1st Cir. 2004).

State of the issuing court or elsewhere in the United States within 100 miles of the of where the order was issued.[10]

Proof of Service

The process server—the Marshal, deputy Marshal, or specially appointed person—must file a proof of service with the court as provided in Rule 4(l).[11]

---

[10]*See SD Protection, Inc. v. Del Rio,* 587 F.Supp.2d 429, 435 (E.D.N.Y. 2008); *Spectacular Venture, L.P. v. World Star Int'l,* 927 F.Supp. 683, 685–86 (S.D.N.Y.1996).

[11]*See* Rule 4.1(a).

RULE 5
SERVING AND FILING PLEADINGS AND OTHER PAPERS

(a) Service: When Required.

(1) *In General.* Unless these rules provide otherwise, each of the following papers must be served on every party:

(A) an order stating that service is required;

(B) a pleading filed after the original complaint, unless the court orders otherwise under Rule 5(c) because there are numerous defendants;

(C) a discovery paper required to be served on a party, unless the court orders otherwise;

(D) a written motion, except one that may be heard ex parte; and

(E) a written notice, appearance, demand, or offer of judgment, or any similar paper.

(2) *If a Party Fails to Appear.* No service is required on a party who is in default for failing to appear. But a pleading that asserts a new claim for relief against such a party must be served on that party under Rule 4.

(3) *Seizing Property.* If an action is begun by seizing property and no person is or need be named as a defendant, any service required before the filing of an appearance, answer, or claim must be made on the person who had custody or possession of the property when it was seized.

(b) Service: How Made.

(1) *Serving an Attorney.* If a party is represented by an attorney, service under this rule must be made on the attorney unless the court orders service on the party.

(2) *Service in General.* A paper is served under this rule by:

(A) handing it to the person;

(B) leaving it:

      (i)   at the person's office with a clerk or other person in charge or, if no one is in charge, in a conspicuous place in the office; or

     (ii)   if the person has no office or the office is closed, at the person's dwelling or usual place of abode with someone of suitable age and discretion who resides there;

  (C) mailing it to the person's last known address—in which event service is complete upon mailing;

  (D) leaving it with the court clerk if the person has no known address;

  (E) sending it by electronic means if the person consented in writing—in which event service is complete upon transmission, but is not effective if the serving party learns that it did not reach the person to be served; or

  (F) delivering it by any other means that the person consented to in writing—in which event service is complete when the person making service delivers it to the agency designated to make delivery.

 (3) *Using Court Facilities.* If a local rule so authorizes, a party may use the court's transmission facilities to make service under Rule 5(b)(2)(E).

(c) Serving Numerous Defendants.

 (1) *In General.* If an action involves an unusually large number of defendants, the court may, on motion or on its own, order that:

  (A) defendants' pleadings and replies to them need not be served on other defendants;

  (B) any crossclaim, counterclaim, avoidance, or affirmative defense in those pleadings and replies to them will be treated as denied or avoided by all other parties; and

  (C) filing any such pleading and serving it on the plaintiff constitutes notice of the pleading to all parties.

 (2) *Notifying Parties.* A copy of every such order must be served on the parties as the court directs.

(d) Filing.

(1) *Required Filings; Certificate of Service.* Any paper after the complaint that is required to be served—together with a certificate of service—must be filed within a reasonable time after service. But disclosures under Rule 26(a)(1) or (2) and the following discovery requests and responses must not be filed until they are used in the proceeding or the court orders filing: depositions, interrogatories, requests for documents or tangible things or to permit entry onto land, and requests for admission.

(2) *How Filing Is Made—In General.* A paper is filed by delivering it:

   (A) to the clerk; or

   (B) to a judge who agrees to accept it for filing, and who must then note the filing date on the paper and promptly send it to the clerk.

(3) *Electronic Filing, Signing, or Verification.* A court may, by local rule, allow papers to be filed, signed, or verified by electronic means that are consistent with any technical standards established by the Judicial Conference of the United States. A local rule may require electronic filing only if reasonable exceptions are allowed. A paper filed electronically in compliance with a local rule is a written paper for purposes of these rules.

(4) *Acceptance by the Clerk.* The clerk must not refuse to file a paper solely because it is not in the form prescribed by these rules or by a local rule or practice.

[Amended January 21, 1963, effective July 1, 1963; March 30, 1970, effective July 1, 1970; April 29, 1980, effective August 1, 1980; March 2, 1987, effective August 1, 1987; April 30, 1991, effective December 1, 1991; April 22, 1993, effective December 1, 1993; April 23, 1996, effective December 1, 1996; April 17, 2000, effective December 1, 2000; April 23, 2001, effective December 1, 2001; April 12, 2006, effective December 1, 2006; April 30, 2007, effective December 1, 2007.]

AUTHORS' COMMENTARY ON RULE 5

PURPOSE AND SCOPE

Rule 5 sets forth the general filing requirements for all pleadings and other papers, and the general service requirements for all pleadings and other papers *except* the complaint and summons. The provisions of Rule 5 are designed to achieve two objectives: to ensure that each party to a civil action obtains a copy of all documents formally used in prosecuting and defending the case, and to create a rationally-assembled record with the clerk.

This is a general service and filing rule. Other Rules establish separate requirements crafted for particular circumstances (*e.g.,* Rule 4, governing service of complaint and summons; Rule 45(b), governing service of subpoenas). Likewise, many federal district courts have developed specific local service and filing requirements that supplement the provisions of Rule 5.

RULE 5(a)—SERVICE REQUIRED

CORE CONCEPT

Unless specifically excused by the Court, every party who has entered an appearance must be served with a copy of the following:

- *All Orders required by their terms to be served (i.e.,* Rule 77(d) notices of entry of orders);
- *All Pleadings After the Original Complaint,* generally including amended complaints;
- *All Discovery Papers;*
- *All Written Motions* (except *ex parte* motions); and
- *All Other Appropriate Legal Papers* (such as written notices, appearances, demands, offers of judgment,[1] and similar papers).

APPLICATIONS

Broadly Construed

Courts expansively construe Rule 5's inventory of legal papers that must be served.[2]

Pleadings Asserting Claims Against New Parties

Pleadings asserting claims against new parties (*e.g.,* third-party claims) must always be served formally, as original pro-

---

[1] *See Magnuson v. Video Yesteryear,* 85 F.3d 1424, 1429 (9th Cir. 1996) (service of Rule 68 offers must comply with Rule 5).

[2] *See, e.g., Elborough v. Evansville Comty. Sch. Dist.,* 636 F. Supp. 2d 812, 826 (W.D. Wis. 2009) (Rule 5 applies to papers by all parties, including involuntary plaintiffs).

cess, pursuant to Rule 4.[3]

Pleadings Asserting Claims Against Existing Parties

Pleadings modifying pending claims or asserting new claims against existing parties (*i.e.*, by amending an original pleading) are usually served under the less demanding methods of Rule 5[4] — provided, of course, original service of process has already been accomplished.[5] However, formal service under Rule 4 may be required if:

- New claims are asserted against parties who have defaulted;[6]
- Circumstances persuade the court that service on the attorney is unlikely to ensure notice to the party;
- Extraterritorial service of process was used in the original pleading and a new claim is unrelated to the initial claim; or
- Due Process requires Rule 4 service (*i.e.*, federal jurisdiction was premised on a particular injury-causing event, and the complaint was amended to assert a different claim which could not otherwise be brought in that district).

New Pleadings/Other Papers Against Defaulting Parties

Once proper service of original process is accomplished under Rule 4, it is expected that the served party will appear and defend the case. If, instead, that party defaults, future pleadings and other papers in the lawsuit ordinarily do not need to be served on that party.[7] To this rule, there is one exception and one clarification. If a later pleading asserts a "new" claim for relief against the non-appearing party, that later pleading[8] must be served upon the non-appearing party

---

[3]*See* Rule 14(a)(1). *See also In re Tax Indebtedness of Townley*, 2002 WL 32026154, at *2 (E.D.Wash. Nov. 15, 2002); *Holland v. Washington Metro. Area Transit Auth.*, 1987 WL 9039, at *1 (D.D.C. Mar. 19, 1987).

[4]*See Vax-D Medical Technologies, LLC v. Texas Spine Medical Center*, 485 F.3d 593, 597 (11th Cir. 2007); *Employee Painters' Trust v. Ethan Enterprises, Inc.*, 480 F.3d 993, 995–99 (9th Cir. 2007).

[5]*See PNC Bank, N.A. v. Twin Tier Dev't Group, Inc.*, 2010 WL 5300819, at *1 (M.D.Pa. Dec. 20, 2010) (when amendment made after service of original process, Rule 5 applies; when before, Rule 4 applies).

[6]*See* Rule 5(a)(2). *See also Employee Painters' Trust v. Ethan Enters., Inc.*, 480 F.3d 993, 999 (9th Cir. 2007). *See infra* Authors' Commentary to Rule 5(a) ("**New Pleadings Against Defaulting Parties**").

[7]*See* Rule 5(a)(2). *See also Belkin v. Islamic Republic of Iran*, 667 F.Supp.2d 8, 19–20 (D.D.C. 2009); *Trustees of the St. Paul Elec. Const. Industry Fringe Benefit Funds v. Martens Elec. Co.*, 485 F. Supp. 2d 1063, 1066 (D. Minn. 2007).

[8]*See Peterson v. Islamic Republic of Iran*, 627 F.3d 1117, 1130 n.5 (9th Cir. 2010) (noting that exception applies only to new claims asserted in pleading (not in motions)).

pursuant to Rule 4, *as original process.*[9] This is intended to ensure that a party, once served, is enabled to make a prudent decision, informed of all consequences, of whether to answer or default.[10] A claim is considered "new" when it differs substantially from the original pleading.[11] This, however, does not necessarily mean that, following a default, the original pleading can be amended less substantially and a default judgment thereafter entered on the basis of that revised — but unserved — pleading; such a result would seem to offend the prudent decision-making goal of this Rule.[12]

General Exceptions to the Service Requirement

The service requirements set by Rule 5 do *not* apply to the service of:

- *Original complaints* (governed by Rule 4);
- *Ex parte motions;*[13]
- *Pleadings between numerous defendants* (if service is excused by court order under Rule 5(c));
- *Papers governed by special service procedures.*[14]

Common Law Exception to Service Requirement

In the unusual instance where a non-defaulting party is not properly served with a pleading or paper that must be served, but that party receives actual notice of it and is not prejudiced by the lack of service, a court may accept and act on the unserved paper.[15]

Seizure Actions

Actions begun by the seizure of property (arrest, attachment, garnishment) are subject to Rule 5. In these cases, any paper required to be served before filing an answer, claim, or

---

[9]*See Peterson v. Islamic Republic of Iran,* 627 F.3d 1117, 1130 n.5 (9th Cir. 2010); *Blair v. City of Worcester,* 522 F.3d 105, 109–10 (1st Cir. 2008).

[10]*See Blair v. City of Worcester,* 522 F.3d 105, 109 (1st Cir. 2008).

[11]*See Belkin v. Islamic Republic of Iran,* 667 F.Supp.2d 8, 20 (D.D.C. 2008); *Poitevint v. Dynamic Recovery Servs., Inc.,* 2011 WL 201493, at *1-*2 (M.D.Fla. Jan. 20, 2011).

[12]*See IBEW Local 595 Health & Welfare Trust Fund v. Givens Elec., Inc.,* 2011 WL 2414346, at *1-*2 (N.D.Cal. June 15, 2011); *O'Callaghan v. Sifre,* 242 F.R.D. 69, 73 (S.D.N.Y. 2007).

[13]But the basis for entering such an *ex parte* motion must be provided. *See Johnson v. Lamas,* 2011 WL 2982692, at *3 n.4 (E.D.Pa. July 21, 2011).

[14]*See, e.g.,* Rule 45(b) (service procedures for subpoenas); *Gates v. Syrian Arab Republic,* 646 F.3d 2, 5–6 (D.C.Cir. 2011) (when specific federal statute sets service procedures, statute likely supersedes Rule 5(a)).

[15]*See McKinnie v. Roadway Express, Inc.,* 341 F.3d 554, 557–59 (6th Cir. 2003) (holding that where party is not properly served with summary judgment motion, but has actual notice of the motion prior to disposition, a court's decision to grant the motion will not be reversed on appeal for this reason unless the affected party demonstrates a genuine issue of material fact that would defeat summary judgment). *But see Magnuson v. Video Yesteryear,* 85 F.3d 1424, 1431 (9th Cir. 1996) (rejecting actual notice view, absent "exceptional good cause").

appearance must be served on the person with custody or possession of the property at the time of seizure.

Effect of Unserved Pleadings and Other Papers

A pleading or other paper that must be served (either under Rule 4 or Rule 5) but is not served will ordinarily be given no legal effect.[16] Thus, amended complaints that are filed but not served are ineffective and usually will not supersede the original,[17] and motion exhibits that are filed but not served may not be relied upon to support or oppose the motion.[18]

RULE 5(b)—METHOD OF SERVICE

CORE CONCEPT

Service is ordinarily made on each party's attorney, not on the party directly. Service may be accomplished in several ways:

SERVICE BY PERSONAL DELIVERY:

(1) **Hand Delivery**: The served document is handed either to the attorney or, if unrepresented or if the court orders otherwise, to the party; *or*

(2) **Office**: The served document is left at the recipient's office with the person "in charge" of the office or, if no one is "in charge" of the office, at the recipient's office in a conspicuous place; *or*

(3) **Home**: If hand delivery and office service are unavailable, the served document may be left at the recipient's residence with a person of suitable age and discretion residing there.

SERVICE BY MAIL:

Last Known Address: The served document is mailed to the recipient's last known address.

SERVICE BY OTHER AGREED MEANS:

Electronic Transmission or Otherwise: The served document is delivered or transmitted by "any other means" to which the person served has agreed, in writing.

SERVICE WHERE NO ADDRESS IS KNOWN:

Clerk of Court: If the recipient's last known address is unavailable, the served document may be left with the clerk of court.

---

[16]*See McNally v. O'Flynn*, 2010 WL 891151, at *2 (W.D.N.Y. Mar. 10, 2010) (failure to serve on every party prompts dismissal without prejudice).

[17]*See International Controls Corp. v. Vesco*, 556 F.2d 665, 669 (2d Cir. 1977) (amended complaint remains inchoate until served under Rule 5(a)).

[18]*See Thorne v. Steubenville Police Officer*, 463 F. Supp. 2d 760, 770 (S.D. Ohio 2006).

APPLICATIONS

Service on Attorney, Not Party

Pleadings and other papers generally must be served on the party's attorney, and not on the party directly.[19] However, service may be made on the party directly if a specific Rule so requires, if the party is unrepresented, or if the court so requires.

Parties Represented by Multiple Attorneys

Service is complete upon serving one attorney for each represented party. If a party is represented by multiple counsel, multiple service is ordinarily not required.[20]

Service by Mail

Service by mail is complete at the moment a properly posted envelope is deposited with the Post Office.[21] The Post Office's failure to postmark the envelope on the day of deposit does not alter this effect.[22] Non-receipt or non-acceptance usually does not affect the validity of service.[23]

- *Note:* Rule 6(d) gives the recipient of mailed service 3 extra days to respond. Accordingly, if a quick response is preferred, personal service will eliminate this additional 3 day response period.

Service By Electronic Transmission

Service by electronic transmission may be made, but only if the person served has expressly consented to such service.[24] This limitation applies to court-served orders as well.[25] The consent must be in writing; consent may not be implied from conduct (such as an e-mail address on a defendant's letterhead or a mere failure to object).[26] Thus, service by facsimile remains

---

[19]*See Rushing v. Bd. of Supervisors of Univ. of La. Sys.*, 270 F.R.D. 259, 260 (M.D.La. 2010).

[20]*See Buchanan v. Sherrill*, 51 F.3d 227, 228 (10th Cir. 1995); *Daniel Intern. Corp. v. Fischbach & Moore, Inc.*, 916 F.2d 1061, 1063 (5th Cir. 1990).

[21]*See* Rule 5(b)(2)(C). *See also U.S. v. Clingman*, 288 F.3d 1183, 1185 (10th Cir. 2002); *U.S. v. Novaton*, 271 F.3d 968, 1015–16 (11th Cir. 2001).

[22]*See Larez v. Holcomb*, 16 F.3d 1513, 1515 (9th Cir. 1994) (noting that document placed in the mail on the last day for service was timely served, even though Post Office did not postmark the envelope until the next day).

[23]*Dunlap v. Transamerica Occidental Life Ins. Co.*, 858 F.2d 629 (11th Cir.1988).

[24]*See* Rule 5(b)(2)(E). *See also Smith v. Psychiatric Solutions, Inc.*, __ F. Supp. 2d __, __, 2012 WL 1071956, at *25 (N.D.Fla. 2012); *Baldwin v. United States*, 823 F.Supp.2d 1087, 1109–11 (D.N.Mar.I. 2011).

[25]*See Calderon v. IBEW Local 47*, 508 F.3d 883, 884 (9th Cir. 2007).

[26]*See* Rule 5(b)(2)(D) advisory committee note to 2001 amendments. *See also RFR Industries, Inc. v. Century Steps, Inc.*, 477 F.3d 1348, 1352 (Fed. Cir. 2007) (rejecting argument that a showing of "exceptional good cause" could excuse noncompliance with the consent-in-writing requirement); *Ortiz-Moss v. New York City Dept. of Transp.*, 623 F.Supp. 2d 404, 407 (S.D. N.Y. 2008) (failure to earlier object is not consent, which cannot be implied from

ineffective, absent this written consent.[27] Parties are "encouraged" to reach specific agreement on the specific scope of the written consent, including (1) the name of the person to whom service should be made, (2) the appropriate address (fax number, e-mail address, etc.) for such service, (3) the format to be used for attachments, and (4) the duration of the consent.[28]

When consent has been obtained, service by electronic transmission (including both direct transmission of the document and transmission of a notice that the document is available through a certain electronic link) is deemed complete upon transmission.[29] (Each district may, by local rule, authorize the making of such transmissions from common court facilities.[30])

- *Failed Transmission:* If the serving party learns, after the electronic transmission is attempted, that the transmission failed and did not reach the person to be served, the service is not considered effective.[31] Such a transmission failure can be a mechanical one (*e.g.*, an "incomplete" or "failed" fax message) or one relating to a change in the recipient's profile (*e.g.*, original counsel consents to the District's electronic filing service, but a change in counsel renders this consent ineffective).[32]

Even when consent to electronic service has been granted, parties often may still serve traditionally by mail.[33]

Service By "Other Means"

Service by some "other means" is also approved, provided that the recipient has consented, in writing, to the alternative method of service.[34] When permitted, such service by "other means" is deemed complete when the person making the service delivers the document to the entity engaged to make the delivery.[35]

Private Overnight Courier Services

Private overnight courier services (such as FedEx) are not the Post Office, and they do not provide "mail" service. Thus, handing legal papers to a private courier service might not constitute service by mail under Rule 5(b)(2)(C), and therefore might not entitle the sender to completed service upon mailing.

---

conduct).

[27]*See Magnuson v. Video Yesteryear*, 85 F.3d 1424, 1430 (9th Cir. 1996); *Mandarino v. Mandarino*, 257 F.R.D. 394, 395–96 (S.D.N.Y. 2009); *U.S. v. Galiczynski*, 44 F. Supp. 2d 707, 713 (E.D. Pa. 1999), aff'd, 203 F.3d 818 (3d Cir. 1999).

[28]*See* Rule 5(b)(2)(D) advisory committee note to 2001 amendments.

[29]*See* Rule 5(b)(2)(D). *See also* Rule 5(b)(2)(E) advisory committee note to 2001 amendments.

[30]*See* Rule 5(b)(3).

[31]*See* Rule 5(b)(2)(E). *See also Freeman v. City of Detroit*, 274 F.R.D. 610, 612 (E.D. Mich. 2011).

[32]*See McKinnie v. Roadway Express, Inc.*, 341 F.3d 554, 557 (6th Cir. 2003).

[33]*See Wolters Kluwer Fin. Servs., Inc. v. Scivantage*, 564 F.3d 110, 116 (2d Cir. 2009).

[34]*See* Rule 5(b)(2)(F).

[35]*See* Rule 5(b)(2)(F).

Rather, service by a courier service is more likely to be deemed a type of personal service, complete only upon the courier's delivery of the document to the ultimate recipient.[36] If, however, service by private overnight courier has been consented to, it will qualify as effective service by "other means".[37] (Overnight courier services provided by the U.S. Post Office, however, are likely still considered mail service.)[38]

Service At Home

Service can be accomplished at the recipient's home, if hand delivery or office service are unavailable.[39] Presumably, this Rule will be interpreted by the courts in the same manner as Rule 4. Thus, the recipient of service need not necessarily be an adult, so long as the court reaches the case-by-case factual determination that the recipient is of "suitable age and discretion". Generally, service must be made on a person "residing" at the home; service on a maid, a landlady, or some other non-resident might be ineffective.[40]

Prisoner Plaintiffs

For documents served by *pro se* prisoners, the courts generally recognize a "mailbox" rule that deems documents as served upon delivery of those documents to the prison officials.[41]

---

[36]*See Transco Leasing Corp. v. U.S.*, 992 F.2d 552, 554 (5th Cir. 1993) (commenting, without deciding, that service by overnight courier might not qualify as service by mail under Rule 5). *Compare Schudel v. General Elec. Co.*, 120 F.3d 991 (9th Cir. 1997) (noting that personal delivery or delivery to U.S. Postal Service could have satisfied service requirement, delivery to Federal Express did not), *and Magnuson v. Video Yesteryear*, 85 F.3d 1424, 1430–31 (9th Cir. 1996) (holding that delivery by Federal Express is not "mail", noting that drafters in 1937 could not have intended to authorize service by private delivery services), *and Audio Enterprises, Inc. v. B & W Loudspeakers of America, a Div. of Equity Intern. Inc.*, 957 F.2d 406, 409 (7th Cir. 1992) (noting that Federal Express is not first class mail within the meaning of Rule 4), *and Prince v. Poulos*, 876 F.2d 30, 32 (5th Cir. 1989) (in construing Federal Rule of Appellate Procedure 25, the court held that Federal Express is not a "public authority" and is not a form of "mail"), *and Chudasama v. Mazda Motor Corp.*, 1995 WL 641984, at *16 n. 20 (M.D. Ga. 1995) (holding that service by private courier is not complete under Rule until the paper is handed to counsel or delivered to counsel's office), vacated on other grounds, 123 F.3d 1353 (11th Cir.1997), *and Edmond v. U.S. Postal Service*, 727 F. Supp. 7 (D.D.C. 1989), aff'd in part, rev'd in part, 949 F.2d 415 (D.C. Cir. 1991) (holding that service via Federal Express was effective when delivered to litigant's home), *with U.S. v. Certain Real Property and Premises Known as 63–29 Trimble Road, Woodside, N.Y.*, 812 F. Supp. 332, 334 (E.D. N.Y. 1992) (service via Federal Express "mail" is valid because Rule 5(b) does not require that "mailing" occur through the United States Postal Service).

[37]*See* Rule 5(b)(2)(F).

[38]*See Danger v. Wachovia Corp.*, 2011 WL 1743763, at *3 (S.D.Fla. May 6, 2011).

[39]*See* Rule 5(b)(2)(B).

[40]*See supra* Authors' Commentary to Rule 4(e) ("**Service at Individual's Dwelling House**") (discussing service on maid and landlady).

[41]*See Schroeder v. McDonald*, 55 F.3d 454, 459 (9th Cir.1995) (noting that incarcerated *pro se* litigants effect

RULE 5(c)—SERVING NUMEROUS DEFENDANTS

CORE CONCEPT

Where an unusually large number of defendants are sued, the court may order that the defendants need not serve every other defendant with pleadings and responses, and that cross-claims, counterclaims, and affirmative defenses are deemed automatically denied or avoided as between the numerous defendants.

APPLICATIONS

Court Order

Rule 5(c) is seldom used. It is effective only upon court order.[42] The court's enabling order must be served on all parties.

Plaintiff Must Be Served

Rule 5(c) does not excuse service on the plaintiff of all papers. Even if the action involves a large number of plaintiffs (*e.g.,* a mass tort case), service must still be made on each plaintiff.

Court Filing Still Required

Rule 5(c) also does not excuse the pleader's obligation to *file* the pleading with the Court.[43]

Only Pleadings/Responses

This limitation applies only to pleadings and responses; all papers other than pleadings and responses must be served.

RULE 5(d)—FILING WITH THE COURT

CORE CONCEPT

Any paper required to be served must also be filed with the court within a reasonable time after service, accompanied by a certificate of service. Papers are to be filed with the clerk of court, unless the court permits filing with the judge personally. Where so provided by proper local rules (but *only* where so provided), papers may also be filed by electronic means, including by facsimile transmission. The clerk of court may not refuse to accept a paper for filing simply because the paper does not conform to these Rules or the district's local rules.

---

service under Rule 5(b) by submitting their documents to prison authorities); *cf.* Fed.R.App.P. 4(c) (document deemed "filed" by prisoner when deposited into prison's internal mail system).

[42]*See Kuklachev v. Gelfman,* 2009

WL 497576, at *4 n.5 (E.D.N.Y. Feb. 26, 2009) (parties may not rely on Rule 5(c) in absence of court order).

[43]*See U.S. v. Atlas Lederer Co.,* 282 F. Supp. 2d 687, 701–03 (S.D. Ohio 2001).

APPLICATIONS

Impact of 2007 "Restyling" Amendments

Rule 5(d) was significantly restructured during the 2007 Federal Civil Rules "Restyling" Project, by folding former Rule 5(e) into Rule 5(d). Current Rule 5(d) now retains the content of both subparts. In researching current Rule 5(d), practitioners should be mindful of this repositioning.

"Reasonable" Time For Filing Defined

Whether the time between service and filing is "reasonable" is a matter left to the discretion of the district court.[44] Consequently, practitioners should file their papers simultaneously with service, or as soon thereafter as possible. Moreover, this Rule only sets the ordinary procedure to be followed. Where, for example, the court fixes a specific time for filing a particular paper, that Order must be obeyed (not the more general "reasonable time" procedure of Rule 5(d)).[45]

Certificate of Service

A party's certificate of service must accompany every filed copy of a document,[46] and should identify the document served, the date of service, and the manner of delivery.[47] Nevertheless, because the principal purpose of a certificate of service is to verify for the court that proper service has been accomplished, the court will likely not invalidate a legal filing that lacks a certificate of service, so long as proper service is not contested.[48]

Document Itself Must Be Filed

A document will not be deemed "filed" unless it is separately and formally filed with the court. Thus, attaching a document as an exhibit to another paper will not constitute a "filing" of

---

[44] See Chesson v. Jaquez, 986 F.2d 363, 365 (10th Cir. 1993) (holding that filing within six days after service is "reasonable", particularly because a weekend fell within that period); Baldwin v. United States, 823 F.Supp.2d 1087, 1110 (D.N.Mar.I. 2011) (filing within five days of service deemed reasonable); Biocore Medical Technologies, Inc. v. Khosrowshahi, 181 F.R.D. 660, 668 (D. Kan. 1998), aff'd, 348 F.3d 1163 (10th Cir. 2003) (noting that courts have decided that documents filed up to six days after service are filed within a "reasonable time" under Rule 5(d); holding that filing almost two months after service is not "reasonable"); Ives v. Guilford Mills, Inc., 3 F. Supp. 2d 191, 194 (N.D. N.Y. 1998) (finding three weeks reasonable under the circumstances).

[45] See Raymond v. Ameritech Corp., 442 F.3d 600, 605–06 (7th Cir. 2006).

[46] See Horowitch v. Diamond Aircraft Indus., Inc., 645 F.3d 1254, 1258–59 (11th Cir. 2011) (certificate must be supplied at time of filing, not service).

[47] See Golden v. McCaughtry, 915 F. Supp. 77, 79 (E.D. Wis. 1995) (noting certificate of service filing obligation).

[48] See Russell v. City of Milwaukee, 338 F.3d 662, 665–67 (7th Cir. 2003) (finding that failure to include certificate of service with suggestion of death did not defeat court's finding that service had, in fact, been made); Ives v. Guilford Mills, Inc., 3 F. Supp. 2d 191 (N.D. N.Y. 1998) (concluding that an invalidation under such circumstances "would seem to serve no purpose except to fruitlessly extend the length of this litigation").

the attachment.[49]

Actual Possession by Clerk Is Required

Documents are only filed when placed in the clerk's possession.[50] Thus, leaving a document lying against the clerk's office door or slipping a document underneath the clerk's office door will generally *not* be considered an effective filing until the day the clerk actually receives the document. However, placing a document in a box designated by the clerk as an after-hours depository should constitute effective filing as of the time of deposit.[51]

Filing by Mail

Because documents are only deemed to be filed when they come into the clerk's possession, a document will *not* be deemed "filed" when it is placed in the United States Mail, addressed to the clerk. Instead, except for prisoner plaintiffs,[52] mailed documents are "filed" on the date they are actually received by the clerk.[53]

Filing by Electronic Means, Including By Fax

Electronic filing is *not* permitted in every district. Instead, the Rules permit each federal district to provide for such filing in its rules.[54] Attempting to file by facsimile or by other electronic means in a district that has not adopted such a procedure may not constitute effective, or timely, filing.[55] But a

---

[49]*See Orsini v. Kugel*, 9 F.3d 1042, 1045 (2d Cir. 1993) (holding that a stipulation had not been "filed" merely because it was attached as an exhibit to another court paper). *But see A. Bauer Mech., Inc. v. Joint Arbitration Bd. of Plumbing Contractors' Ass'n & Chicago Journeymen Plumbers' Local Union 130*, 562 F.3d 784, 791 (7th Cir. 2009) (approving the deemed "filing" *instanter* of pleading attached to motion for leave but never separately filed).

[50]*See Trepanier v. City of Blue Island*, 364 Fed.Appx. 260, 262 (7th Cir. 2010); *Riordan v. State Farm Mut. Auto. Ins. Co.*, 589 F.3d 999, 1003 (9th Cir. 2009); *McIntosh v. Antonino*, 71 F.3d 29, 36–37 (1st Cir. 1995).

[51]*See* Rule 77(a) ("When Court Is Open"). *See also Greenwood v. State of N.Y., Office of Mental Health (OMH)*, 842 F.2d 636, 639 (2d Cir. 1988) (document placed in night depository box operated by Clerk's Office, and bearing date/time stamp imprinted on document by device also operated by

Clerk's Office, was deemed to have been "filed" as of the date and time stamped on document); *Turner v. City of Newport*, 887 F. Supp. 149, 151 (E.D. Ky. 1995) (holding that complaint was timely filed when placed in the Clerk's post office box at 11:30 p.m. on the final day of the statute of limitations).

[52]*See infra* Authors' Commentary to Rule 5(d) ("**Prisoner Plaintiffs**").

[53]*See Trepanier v. City of Blue Island*, 364 Fed.Appx. 260, 261–62 (7th Cir. 2010); *McIntosh v. Antonino*, 71 F.3d 29, 36–37 (1st Cir. 1995); *Salcedo v. Town of Dudley*, 629 F.Supp.2d 86, 97 (D.Mass. 2009).

[54]*See Riordan v. State Farm Mut. Auto. Ins. Co.*, 589 F.3d 999, 1003 n.1 (9th Cir. 2009).

[55]*See McIntosh v. Antonino*, 71 F.3d 29, 34–35 (1st Cir. 1995) (litigant's claim that a facsimile "filing" was effective, when such filing was not expressly authorized under the local rules, "is whistling past the graveyard"—without a local rule permitting

district may, if it chooses, permit (or even *require*)[56] electronic filing, signing, and/or verifying of documents. If so permitted, a document electronically filed in conformity with the local rules is deemed a "written paper" within the meaning of the Rules.

Filing With the Judge

Where the judge so permits,[57] papers may be "filed" with the judge directly, after which the judge is required to transmit the papers "forthwith" to the clerk's office.[58]

Other Rules

Certain Rules and the district's local rules may prescribe specific other service and filing guidelines.

Enforcing the Rule

Ordinary, in the absence of contumacious behavior, a failure to timely file a properly-served pleading will be remedied by an order compelling the filing, and not with a dismissal.[59] Practitioners should, however, be wary of relying on such liberality; the practice of merely compelling compliance, rather than dismissing, is not expressly guaranteed by the Rules.

Effect of Unpaid Fees

There is a division among courts as to whether filing is effective prior to the payment of any applicable filing fees.[60] Thus, prudence dictates that all filing fees be paid at the time a docu-

---

such transmissions, "facsimile filings in a federal court are dead on arrival"); *In re Fisherman's Wharf Fillet, Inc.*, 83 F. Supp. 2d 651, 657 (E.D. Va. 1999) (absent local rule permitting such filings, facsimile transmission "filings" are "deemed null and of no legal effect"); *Johnson v. United Steel Workers of America*, 172 F.R.D. 185, 187 (W.D. Va. 1997) (refusing to consider faxed copy of affidavit because it was a not an original, and no local rule permitted filing of facsimile papers in lieu of originals). *But see U.S. v. Harvey*, 516 F.3d 553, 556 (7th Cir. 2008) (relying on what is now Rule 5(d)(4), ruling that electronically filed document, though improper, should still have been accepted).

[56]If *required* by local rules, reasonable exceptions must be made for those for whom such electronic filing would be a hardship. *See* Rule 5(d)(3). *See also* Rule 5(e) advisory committee note to 2006 amendments.

[57]*See Riordan v. State Farm Mut. Auto. Ins. Co.*, 589 F.3d 999, 1003 (9th Cir. 2009). *See also Tran v. Minnesota Dept. of Transp.*, 2006 WL 2917037, at

*2 (D. Minn. 2006), aff'd, 259 Fed. Appx. 901 (8th Cir. 2008) (noting that no judge is under an obligation to permit a filing in this way).

[58]*See Life Ins. Co. of North America v. Von Valtier*, 116 F.3d 279, 282–83 (7th Cir. 1997) (disapproving of trial judge's delay in transmitting motion to the clerk's office, noting that "the system will break down unless the judge scrupulously follows the directions to note the date and transmit the documents immediately to the clerk. Less than perfect adherence to these instructions will mean that actual filing dates will become as uncertain as the former dates of service were, and something as important as the jurisdictional time limit for taking an appeal will once again be subject to factual disputes").

[59]*See Betty K Agencies, Ltd. v. M/V MONADA*, 432 F.3d 1333, 1340 (11th Cir. 2005).

[60]*Compare Farzana K. v. Indiana Dep't of Educ.*, 473 F.3d 703, 707–08 (7th Cir. 2007) (filing proper, but dismissal possible if fees remain unpaid) *and Searcy v. County of Oakland*, 735

ment is filed with the court.

Refusal by Clerk to Accept For Filing

A paper is considered "filed" upon the completion of the act of delivering it to the clerk of court; procedural flaws in the paper will not impede the "filing".[61] Although neither the clerk of court (nor the clerk's computer system) may refuse to file a paper that does not conform to the Rules or to the district's local rules,[62] the clerk may advise the filing party or attorney of the paper's deficiencies. A local rule may also instruct the clerk to inform the judge of the paper's defect. The task of enforcing rules concerning procedure and form are reserved exclusively for the district judge,[63] and sanctions of a lesser nature can be imposed for local rule violations.[64]

Discovery Papers

To conserve the physical resources of the clerk's office and federal courthouses, discovery requests and discovery responses are *not* to be filed with the court unless and until (a) they are actually "used" in court proceedings or (b) the trial court so orders.[65] This prohibition applies to requests, responses, and objections made under the Rules governing depositions, interrogatories, admissions, production demands, and entry upon land demands,[66] as well as to deposition transcripts themselves.[67] Local rules prescribing different filing requirements are superseded by this uniform, national approach.[68] There is, therefore, no implied right of public access to this sort of unfiled discovery.[69]

The phrase "used in the proceeding" is interpreted broadly to include those discovery materials used in connection with motions, pretrial conferences, and otherwise.[70] However, a party who "uses" discovery materials while interrogating witnesses

---

F.Supp.2d 759 (E.D.Mich. Aug 30, 2010) (same) *with Truitt v. County of Wayne*, 148 F.3d 644, 648 (6th Cir.1998) (filing proper only when fees are paid).

[61]*See Transportes Navieros y Terrestres S.A. de C.V. v. Fairmount Heavy Transport, N.V.*, 572 F.3d 96, 100 (2d Cir. 2009); *Royall v. National Ass'n of Letter Carriers, AFL-CIO*, 548 F.3d 137, 140–43 (D.C.Cir. 2008); *Klemm v. Astrue*, 543 F.3d 1139, 1143 (9th Cir. 2008).

[62]*See Vince v. Rock County*, 604 F.3d 391, 392 (7th Cir. 2010); *Transportes Navieros y Terrestres S.A. de C.V. v. Fairmount Heavy Transport, N.V.*, 572 F.3d 96. 100 (2d Cir. 2009); *Klemm v. Astrue*, 543 F.3d 1139, 1143 (9th Cir. 2008).

[63]*See Jones v. Warden of Stateville Correctional Center*, 918 F. Supp. 1142, 1151 (N.D. Ill. 1995).

[64]*See Klemm v. Astrue*, 543 F.3d 1139, 1143 (9th Cir. 2008).

[65]*See* Rule 5(d)(1). *See also* Rule 5(d) advisory committee note to 2000 amendments (discussing resource conservation objective).

[66]*See* Rule 5(d) advisory committee note to 2000 amendments.

[67]*See Rohrbough v. Harris*, 549 F.3d 1313, 1318 (10th Cir. 2008).

[68]*See* Rule 5(d) advisory committee note to 2000 amendments.

[69]*See Bond v. Utreras*, 585 F.3d 1061, 1076 (7th Cir. 2009).

[70]*See* Rule 5(d) advisory committee note to 2000 amendments.

during depositions need not file those materials with the court.[71] Moreover, if a party "uses" only a portion of a voluminous discovery document, only the "used" portion need be filed with the court (although any other party would be free to file other relevant portions used).[72]

Prisoner Plaintiffs

As with service under Rule 5(b), a *pro se* prisoner's papers are usually deemed "filed" under Rule 5(d) upon delivery of those documents to the prison officials.[73]

Additional Resource Sources

Wright & Miller, *Federal Practice and Procedure* §§ 1141 to 53
C.J.S., Federal Civil Procedure § 261, § 349
West's Key Number Digest, Federal Civil Procedure ☞664, ☞665

---

[71]*See* Rule 5(d) advisory committee note to 2000 amendments.

[72]*See* Rule 5(d) advisory committee note to 2000 amendments.

[73]*See Gibson v. City Municipality of New York*, 692 F.3d 198, 201 n.3 (2d Cir. 2012); *Trepanier v. City of Blue Island*, 364 Fed.Appx. 260, 261–62 (7th Cir. 2010); *Cooper v. Brookshire*, 70 F.3d 377 (5th Cir.1995). *Cf. Houston v. Lack*, 487 U.S. 266, 108 S. Ct. 2379, 101 L. Ed. 2d 245 (1988) (holding that a *pro se* prisoner's notice of appeal was "filed" within the meaning of the Federal Rules of Appellate Procedure when the notice was delivered to the prison authorities).

RULE 5.1
CONSTITUTIONAL CHALLENGE TO A STATUTE—NOTICE, CERTIFICATION, AND INTERVENTION

(a) Notice by a Party. A party that files a pleading, written motion, or other paper drawing into question the constitutionality of a federal or state statute must promptly:

(1) file a notice of constitutional question stating the question and identifying the paper that raises it, if:

(A) a federal statute is questioned and the parties do not include the United States, one of its agencies, or one of its officers or employees in an official capacity; or

(B) a state statute is questioned and the parties do not include the state, one of its agencies, or one of its officers or employees in an official capacity; and

(2) serve the notice and paper on the Attorney General of the United States if a federal statute is questioned—or on the state attorney general if a state statute is questioned—either by certified or registered mail or by sending it to an electronic address designated by the attorney general for this purpose.

(b) Certification by the Court. The court must, under 28 U.S.C. § 2403, certify to the appropriate attorney general that a statute has been questioned.

(c) Intervention; Final Decision on the Merits. Unless the court sets a later time, the attorney general may intervene within 60 days after the notice is filed or after the court certifies the challenge, whichever is earlier. Before the time to intervene expires, the court may reject the constitutional challenge, but may not enter a final judgment holding the statute unconstitutional.

(d) No Forfeiture. A party's failure to file and serve the notice, or the court's failure to certify, does not forfeit a constitutional claim or defense that is otherwise timely asserted.

[Adopted April 12, 2006, effective December 1, 2006; amended April 30, 2007, effective December 1, 2007.]

AUTHORS' COMMENTARY ON RULE 5.1

PURPOSE AND SCOPE

Rule 5.1 was added in 2006, and is the repositioning of the former final three sentences of old Rule 24(c). The Rule is designed to ensure that an affected federal or State official is given notice and the opportunity to intervene in a case that litigates the constitutionality of a federal or State statute. The Rule compels a party challenging constitutionality to promptly notify the appropriate attorney general, and directs the district court to make a certification of the challenge to the appropriate attorney general.

RULE 5.1(a)—NOTICE BY A PARTY

CORE CONCEPT

Any party who draws into question the constitutionality of a federal or State statute must ensure that the appropriate attorney general is informed of the pending litigation challenge.

APPLICATIONS

Prior Precedent

Because portions of Rule 5.1 track rather closely the now abrogated last three sentences of Rule 24(c), it is likely that courts will look to existing precedent construing those sentences of old Rule 24(c) where such precedent does not contradict the slightly different language of Rule 5.1.

Goal of Certification

The goal of the certification requirement is to protect the public interest by ensuring that the executive branch of the government is alerted of the filing, and then afforded the opportunity to make its views heard, any time a law is challenged constitutionally.[1] The government has standing to defend its

---

[1]*See Oklahoma ex rel Edmondson v. Pope*, 516 F.3d 1214, 1216 (10th Cir. 2008); *Virginia ex rel. Cuccinelli v. Sebelius*, 702 F.Supp.2d 598, 605–06 & 606 n.4 (E.D.Va. 2010), *rev'd on other grounds*, 656 F.3d 253 (4th Cir. 2011).

laws' constitutionality.[2]

Only Statute Challenges Trigger Notice / Certification

By its terms, the Rule 5.1 notice and certification obligation is implicated only by constitutional challenges to federal or State statutes.[3]

Notice and Service by a Party

With one exception (see below), Rule 5.1(a) requires a party who files a writing (whether a pleading, written motion, or other paper) that challenges the constitutionality of a federal or State statute to file a notice of the challenge with the district court. The contents of the notice must state the nature of the challenge and identify the document that contains the challenge. Both the notice and the challenge document must then be served on the affected attorney general (federal or State).[4]

Method of Service

Service of the notice on the affected federal or State attorney general must be made via certified or registered mail, or by electronic service through any electronic address established by the attorney general for this purpose.[5]

Exception to Notice and Service Requirement

Rule 5.1(a) contains one exception to the notice and service requirement it normally mandates. If a federal or State statute is challenged, but the United States or the affected State is already a party itself or through agencies or officers sued in an official capacity, there is obviously no need for the special notice requirement of Rule 5.1(a). Such notice is therefore not required in those circumstances.[6]

Elimination of Requirement of "Affecting the Public Interest"

The former language of Rule 24(c) limited this notify-and-serve obligation to situations in which the constitutional challenge to a statute affected the public interest. Rule 5.1(a) intentionally omits this limiting language.[7]

---

[2]See *Diamond v. Charles*, 476 U.S. 54, 62, 106 S.Ct. 1697, 90 L.Ed.2d 48 (1986).

[3]See *Arnold v. Melwani*, 2011 WL 3861682, at *4–*5 (D.Guam Aug. 31, 2011) (certification not required in lawsuit challenging constitutionality of local court rule).

[4]See Rule 5.1(a)(1).

[5]See Rule 5.1(a)(2).

[6]See Rule 5.1(a)(1)(A) to (1)(B). See also *Shah v. Danberg*, 855 F. Supp. 2d 215, 225 (D.Del. 2012); *American Charities for Reasonable Fundraising Regulation, Inc.*, 2010 WL 2802497, at *7 (D.Utah July 15, 2010); *Lee v. U.S.*, 2007 WL 1111250, at *2 n.1 (S.D. Fla. 2007).

[7]See Rule 5.1 Advisory Committee Note to 2006 amendments ("It is better to assure, through notice, that the attorney general is able to determine whether to seek intervention on the ground that the act or statute affects a public interest.").

No New Claim or Right

This Rule is not intended to create a new or independent cause of action or basis for relief; it is, instead, merely a vehicle to help ensure that notice to the affected federal or State attorney general will occur.[8]

RULE 5.1(b)—CERTIFICATION BY THE COURT

CORE CONCEPT

The district court must, additionally, certify to the appropriate federal or State attorney general the presence of a constitutional challenge. This requirement supplements a party's duty as described in Rule 5.1(a).

APPLICATION

Court's Duty to Certify

The district court, independent of and in addition to the duties of notice and service imposed on parties by Rule 5.1(a), must certify to the affected federal or State attorney general that a party has made a constitutional challenge to a federal or State statute.[9] This certification obligation is imposed on the court by 28 U.S.C.A. § 2403 for two reasons. First, if the constitutional challenge was not raised by a party's pleading, written motion, or other paper, the court's certification is the only means of assuring that the interested federal or State attorney general will receive notice of the challenge.[10] Second, because Rule 5.1(d) prohibits a forfeiture of a properly asserted constitutional claim or defense for a party's failure to serve notice of a written challenge to the interested federal or State attorney general, or for the court's failure to certify[11] (and judicial precedent derived from old Rule 24(c) seems to hold that no lesser sanction exists),[12] the judicial certification requirement of Rule 5.1(b) is the only means of assuring that notice actually reaches the federal or State attorney general when the United

---

[8]*See Latta v. Cuomo*, 2010 WL 4607523, at *1 (E.D.N.Y. Nov. 5, 2010); *Lee v. U.S.*, 2007 WL 1111250, at *2 n.1 (S.D. Fla. 2007).

[9]*See* Rule 5.1(b).

[10]*See* Rule 5.1 Advisory Committee Note to 2006 amendments ("The court's certification obligation remains, and is the only notice" when the challenge was not raised in a manner identified in Rule 5.1(a)).

[11]*See* Rule 5.1(d).

[12]*See, e.g., Tonya K. by Diane K. v. Board of Educ. of City of Chicago*, 847 F.2d 1243, 1247 (7th Cir. 1988) ("Failure to notify the Attorney Gen-

eral is not a jurisdictional defect."); *Merrill v. Town of Addison*, 763 F.2d 80, 83 (2d Cir. 1985) ("Absent indication of harm, or prejudice to the government's opportunity to fully present its views, belated certification, while not ideal, is sufficient to honor the purpose of section 2403."). *Cf. In re Young*, 82 F.3d 1407, 1412 (8th Cir. 1996) (temporarily removing case from argument calendar so that appellate court can certify constitutional question and give United States time to intervene; "Certification has occurred even after judgment at the appellate level.").

States or a State is not a party to a case.

RULE 5.1(c)—INTERVENTION; FINAL DECISION ON THE MERITS

CORE CONCEPT

Rule 5.1(c) creates a right of intervention for the federal or State attorney general potentially affected by a constitutional challenge. It also establishes the rather flexible time limits within which the affected attorney general must act. Rule 5.1(c) also provides that the court may continue to process the case while the attorney general is contemplating intervention, but the court may not enter a final judgment holding the statute unconstitutional.

APPLICATIONS

Time to Intervene

An attorney general may intervene of right within 60 days of filing of the notice of constitutional challenge or certification of the challenge, whichever is earlier. However, the court is authorized to extend the 60 day limit.[13] Such an extension may granted by motion or the court's *sua sponte* act.[14]

Other Activity

While an attorney general is contemplating intervention, Rule 5.1 envisages that most of the routine activity of the court will continue in the case.[15]

Intervention Only Permitted, Not Required

The attorney general is not *required* to exercise the right to intervene; the decision whether to intervene or not is a matter left to the attorney general's discretion.[16] Thus, an attorney general's choice not to intervene does not preclude an opposition to a constitutional challenge raised in a later case.[17]

Dismissal Without Allowing Intervention Is Permitted

Until the time for intervention expires, a court may not enter a final judgment declaring a federal or State law unconstitutional; it may, however, reject the constitutional challenge

---

[13]*See* Rule 5.1(c).

[14]*See* Rule 5.1 Advisory Committee Note to 2006 amendments ("The court may extend the 60-day period on its own or on motion.").

[15]*See* Rule 5.1 Advisory Committee Note to 2006 amendments ("Pretrial activities may continue without interruption during the intervention period, and the court retains authority to grant interlocutory relief.").

[16]*See Kuroiwa v. Lingle*, 2008 WL 2622816, at *4 (D. Haw. 2008).

[17]*See Flying J, Inc. v. Van Hollen*, 597 F.Supp.2d 848, 855 (E.D.Wis. 2009), *judgment rev'd on other grounds*, 621 F.3d 658 (7th Cir. 2010). *See also Estate of Kunkel v. U.S.*, 689 F.2d 408, 420 (3d Cir.1982) (Becker, J., concurring) (such a construction is "plainly wrong").

at any time.[18] In practice, courts tend to either postpone a ruling on constitutionality until the government intervenes[19] or, if obviously unmeritorious, deny the constitutional challenge with a right of reconsideration (should the government intervene to object).[20]

RULE 5.1(d)—NO FORFEITURE

CORE CONCEPT

Failure by a party or a court to fulfill the requirements of Rule 5.1 does not work a forfeiture of any constitutional claim or defense that is asserted in a timely manner.[21]

APPLICATIONS

Other Consequences for a Failure to Notify or Certify

Although a forfeiture of a constitutional claim or defense is prohibited, the Rule and its predecessor are silent as to other consequences of a party's failure to notify or a court's failure to certify. Such failures have not been considered a jurisdictional defect.[22] But, to allow time for the executive branch's views to be aired and considered, courts have removed cases from an oral argument calendar,[23] permitted post-oral argument notification and an accompanying permission to intervene,[24] and vacated and remanded to facilitate a trial-level opportunity to intervene.[25] Likewise, the remedy for a belatedly issued notice or certification may, provided no prejudice befalls the executive branch, merely be an invitation for rehearing.[26]

---

[18]*See* Rule 5.1(c). *See also Burghart v. Corrections Corp. of America*, 2008 WL 820178, at *1 n.* (W.D. Okla. 2008); *Delaplaine v. United Airlines, Inc.*, 518 F. Supp. 2d 1275, 1278 n.3 (W.D. Wash. 2007).

[19]*See Hunter v. Hamilton County Bd. of Elections*, 850 F. Supp. 2d 795, 842 (S.D.Ohio 2012).

[20]*See Satkar Hospitality Inc. v. Cook County Bd. of Rev.*, 2011 WL 4431029, at *2 (N.D.Ill. Sept. 21, 2011); *Postell v. Woods*, 2011 WL 3417137, at *2–*3 (W.D.Mich. Aug. 4, 2011).

[21]*See* Rule 5.1(d). *But see Mardis v. Hannibal Pub. Sch. Dist. #60*, 2009 WL 1140037, at *5 n.8 (E.D.Mo. Apr. 28, 2009) (party's failure to comply meant constitutional issue "not properly before" the court); *Gundaker/ Jordan American Holdings, Inc. v. Clark*, 2008 WL 4550540, at *3 (E.D.Ky. Oct. 9, 2008) (same); *Citizens For A Better Lawnside, Inc. v. Bryant*, 2006 WL 3825145, at *8 (D.N.J. 2006) (finding that plaintiffs failed, pursuant to Rule 5.1, to file and serve written notice and, thus, their constitutional challenge was dismissed without prejudice).

[22]*See Tonya K. by Diane K. v. Board of Educ. of City of Chicago*, 847 F.2d 1243, 1247 (7th Cir. 1988).

[23]*See In re Young*, 82 F.3d 1407, 1412–13 (8th Cir. 1996).

[24]*See Merrill v. Town of Addison*, 763 F.2d 80, 83 (2d Cir. 1985).

[25]*See Oklahoma ex rel Edmondson v. Pope*, 516 F.3d 1214, 1216 (10th Cir. 2008).

[26]*See Buchanan County, Virginia v. Blankenship*, 545 F. Supp. 2d 553, 555 n.3 (W.D. Va. 2008). *See also Merrill v. Town of Addison*, 763 F.2d 80, 83 (2d Cir. 1985); *Thatcher v. Tennessee Gas Transmission Co.*, 180 F.2d 644, 648 (5th Cir. 1950).

RULE 5.2
PRIVACY PROTECTION FOR FILINGS MADE WITH THE COURT

(a) **Redacted Filings.** Unless the court orders otherwise, in an electronic or paper filing with the court that contains an individual's social-security number, taxpayer-identification number, or birth date, the name of an individual known to be a minor, or a financial-account number, a party or nonparty making the filing may include only:

  (1) the last four digits of the social-security number and taxpayer-identification number;

  (2) the year of the individual's birth;

  (3) the minor's initials; and

  (4) the last four digits of the financial-account number.

(b) **Exemptions from the Redaction Requirement.** The redaction requirement does not apply to the following:

  (1) a financial-account number that identifies the property allegedly subject to forfeiture in a forfeiture proceeding;

  (2) the record of an administrative or agency proceeding;

  (3) the official record of a state-court proceeding;

  (4) the record of a court or tribunal, if that record was not subject to the redaction requirement when originally filed;

  (5) a filing covered by Rule 5.2(c) or (d); and

  (6) a pro se filing in an action brought under 28 U.S.C. §§ 2241, 2254, or 2255.

(c) **Limitations on Remote Access to Electronic Files; Social-Security Appeals and Immigration Cases.** Unless the court orders otherwise, in an action for benefits under the Social Security Act, and in an action or proceeding relating to an order of removal, to relief from removal, or to immigration benefits or detention, access to an electronic file is authorized as follows:

(1) the parties and their attorneys may have remote electronic access to any part of the case file, including the administrative record;

(2) any other person may have electronic access to the full record at the courthouse, but may have remote electronic access only to:

(A) the docket maintained by the court; and

(B) an opinion, order, judgment, or other disposition of the court, but not any other part of the case file or the administrative record.

(d) Filings Made Under Seal. The court may order that a filing be made under seal without redaction. The court may later unseal the filing or order the person who made the filing to file a redacted version for the public record.

(e) Protective Orders. For good cause, the court may by order in a case:

(1) require redaction of additional information; or

(2) limit or prohibit a nonparty's remote electronic access to a document filed with the court.

(f) Option for Additional Unredacted Filing Under Seal. A person making a redacted filing may also file an unredacted copy under seal. The court must retain the unredacted copy as part of the record.

(g) Option for Filing a Reference List. A filing that contains redacted information may be filed together with a reference list that identifies each item of redacted information and specifies an appropriate identifier that uniquely corresponds to each item listed. The list must be filed under seal and may be amended as of right. Any reference in the case to a listed identifier will be construed to refer to the corresponding item of information.

(h) Waiver of Protection of Identifiers. A person waives the protection of Rule 5.2(a) as to the person's own information by filing it without redaction and not under seal.

[Adopted April 30, 2007, effective December 1, 2007.]

AUTHORS' COMMENTARY ON RULE 5.2

PURPOSE AND SCOPE

The vulnerability of electronically-accessible court files to privacy and security mischief prompted the adoption in 2007 of Rule 5.2. The Rule allows for a heightened measure of protection for certain personal data identifiers, with additional protections in social security and immigration cases. Invoking these benefits is a burden placed on parties and their counsel.

CORE CONCEPT

From many categories of court filings, parties may redact or seal certain personal data identifiers. In social security and immigration cases (where such identifiers are likely to be both especially relevant and peculiarly vulnerable), the redaction right does not generally apply, but electronic access to those files will now be restricted. For good cause, parties may seek enhanced protections beyond those set forth in Rule 5.2. The right to claim these protections (and the duty of doing so) lies with parties and their counsel.

APPLICATIONS

Privacy and Security Objectives

Rule 5.2 is the federal courts' implementation of the E-Government Act of 2002.[1] It is intended to protect the privacy and security interests implicated by electronic filing of (and the consequent public access to) court papers.[2]

The Redaction Right

Both parties and nonparties who are making a filing with the court may redact, as of right, the following information from their court filings:

- *Social Security Number / Taxpayer ID Number:* In lieu thereof, the filer may include only the last four digits of those numbers;
- *Birth Year:* The filer may omit entirely;
- *Minor's Name:* In lieu thereof, the filer may include only the minor's initials; and
- *Financial Account Numbers:* In lieu thereof, the filer

---

[1] Pub.L. No. 107-347, § 205(c)(3), 116 Stat. 2899, 2914 (2002) (codified at 44 U.S.C. § 3501 note, as amended 2004).

[2] *See* Rule 5.2 advisory committee note.

may include only the last four digits of those numbers.[3]
In order to facilitate the ready use of the redacted information, the filer may, if he or she wishes, choose among two supplementation alternatives. The filer may supplement the redacted version of the materials with an unredacted copy filed under seal.[4] Or the filer may supplement the redacted version by filing, under seal, a "reference list" that allows the redactions to be decoded.[5]

The Sealing Right

In addition to the sealing options to which a filer is entitled as a supplement to redacted filings, the court may withdraw the right of redaction, in favor of a filing under seal, which the court may later unseal or order a replacement redaction.[6]

Applies to Paper Filings (and Trial Exhibits), As Well As Electronic Filings

Rule 5.2 applies broadly to all filings, whether made electronically or in paper form. Many judicial districts scan materials filed in paper format into their electronic case files, thus rendering those materials electronically accessible to the public in much the same way as they would have been had they been filed electronically in the first instance.[7] Trial exhibits, if filed with the court, are likewise encompassed within the reach of Rule 5.2.[8]

Unfiled Materials Not Protected

Although other Rules may authorize confidentiality protections in other contexts, Rule 5.2 likely has no application where the materials at issue are not filed.[9]

Exceptions to the Redaction Right

The right of redaction does *not* apply in the following circumstances: (a) when the court orders otherwise,[10] (b) in a forfeiture proceeding, if the financial account number identifies property claimed to be subject to forfeiture,[11] (c) to the record of

---

[3]*See* Rule 5.2(a).

[4]*See* Rule 5.2(f). *See also Crossman v. Astrue*, 714 F. Supp. 2d 284, 289 (D.Conn. 2009).

[5]*See* Rule 5.2(g).

[6]*See* Rule 5.2(d).

[7]*See* Rule 5.2 advisory committee note ("It is electronic availability, not the form of the initial filing, that raises the privacy and security concerns addressed in the E-Government Act.").

[8]*See* Rule 5.2 advisory committee note.

[9]*See Kremen v. Cohen*, 2012 WL 2277857, at *2 (N.D.Cal. June 18, 2012) (protection applies only to publically filed materials, not subpoenas).

[10]*See* Rule 5.2(a). *See also Dawn L. v. Greater Johnstown Sch. Dist.*, 586 F.Supp.2d 332, 339 n.3 (W.D.Pa. 2008) (because minor's birth date is necessary to case, general redaction requirement is exempted).

[11]*See* Rule 5.2(b)(1).

an administrative or agency proceeding,[12] (d) to the official record of a State court proceeding,[13] (e) to the record of a court or tribunal where the record was not subject to the redaction requirement when originally filed,[14] (f) to social security and immigration cases,[15] (g) to cases where the court orders that filings not be redacted but, instead, be filed under seal,[16] and (h) to *pro se* filings in actions brought under 28 U.S.C.A. §§ 2241, 2254, or 2255.[17] There is unlikely to be an exception to the redaction duty merely because the document or information might be otherwise publicly accessible.[18]

The Burden of Redacting / Sealing

The burden of exercising this right of redaction or sealing rests with the filer of the materials, and not with the courts or otherwise.[19] Consequently, if a party intends to take advantage of the privacy and security benefits of this right, either the party or counsel must remember to perform the redaction or seek the sealing. The drafters urged counsel to remind their clients that personal data identifiers that could have been, but were not, protected will be publicly accessible over the internet.[20] The court may, however, order a redaction or sealing *sua sponte*.[21]

Intended (and Inadvertent) Waivers

Parties may, balancing costs against benefits, waive their entitlement to Rule 5.2's protection by filing their information without redaction and not under seal.[22] An inadvertent failure

---

[12]*See* Rule 5.2(b)(2).

[13]*See* Rule 5.2(b)(3).

[14]*See* Rule 5.2(b)(4).

[15]*See* Rule 5.2(b)(5).

[16]*See* Rule 5.2(b)(5).

[17]*See* Rule 5.2(b)(6).

[18]*See Coleman v. Zaccari*, 2011 WL 2607941, at *1 (D.N.H. June 30, 2011).

[19]*See* Rule 5.2(h). *See also* Rule 5.2 advisory committee note. *See also Crossman v. Astrue*, 714 F.Supp.2d 284, 290 (D.Conn. 2009).

[20]*See* Rule 5.2 advisory committee note ("Parties must remember that any personal information not otherwise protected by sealing or redaction will be made available over the internet. Counsel should notify clients of this fact so that an informed decision may be made on what information is to be included in a document filed with the court.").

[21]*See Garner v. U.S. Gov't/Fed. Bureau of Investigation*, 2010 WL 1688483, at *1 (S.D.Ga. Jan. 5, 2010); *Online Payment Solutions Inc. v. Svenska Handelsbanken AB*, 638 F.Supp.2d 375, 383 n.4 (S.D.N.Y. 2009); *Brown v. McConnell*, 2009 WL 2338001, at *2 n.3 (S.D.Ga. July 27, 2009); *Robinson v. Hicks*, 2009 WL 82479, at *1 n.4 (M.D.Pa. Jan. 9, 2009).

[22]*See* Rule 5.2(h). *See also* Rule 5.2 advisory committee note ("One may wish to waive the protection if it is determined that the costs of redaction outweigh the benefits to privacy."). *See also Kremen v. Cohen*, 2012 WL 2277857, at *2 (N.D.Cal. June 18, 2012); *Wells v. EMF Corp.*, 757 F.Supp.2d 791, 798 (N.D.Ind. 2010); *Patterson v. Prudential Ins. Co.*, 693 F.Supp.2d 642, 643 n.1 (S.D.Tex. 2010).

to redact or seal may be remedied upon motion to the court.[23]

Additional Privacy / Security Protections

The denomination in Rule 5.2 of certain categories of personal data identifiers is not intended to give rise to a negative presumption that *only* those categories of data are entitled to protection or that the abbreviated identifiers (*e.g.*, last four digits, minor's initials) are not themselves, in an appropriate case, entitled to be shielded entirely.[24] For "good cause", the court may grant protective orders allowing the redaction of additional information, or either limiting or barring remote electronic access by a nonparty to a filed document.[25]

Social Security and Immigration Cases

Citing the "prevalence of sensitive information and the volume of filings", the drafters singled out certain social security and immigration cases for special treatment.[26] These cases are *not* entitled to the automatic right of redaction.[27] Although parties and their counsel enjoy unrestricted access to such filings, nonparties are entitled to remote electronic access only to case docket numbers and court disposition documents; to gain full access to the files, nonparties must access them in-person at the courthouse (and may do so, at the courthouse, electronically).[28]

---

[23]*See* Rule 5.2 advisory committee note ("If a person files an unredacted identifier by mistake, that person may seek relief from the court.").

[24]*See* Rule 5.2 advisory committee note (noting that, in certain cases, all parts of an account number or social security number may need protection, or that protection should extend to other identifiers, like driver's license numbers and alien registration numbers).

[25]*See* Rule 5.2(e). *See also In re Roman Catholic Archbishop of Portland*, 661 F.3d 417, 425–26 (9th Cir. 2011) (refusing to fashion a presumptively-protected approach for personnel records); *P.D. ex rel. C.D. v. Carroll Consol. Sch. Corp.*, 820 F.Supp.2d 907, 908–10 (N.D.Ind. 2011) (questioning litigation anonymity for parents of minor parties based on risk that disclosure of parents' identities will disclose minors' identities); *Nash v. Life Ins. Co. of North America*, 2010 WL 2044935, at *1 (S.D.Cal. May 18, 2010) (finding "compelling reason" standard not satisfied for further sealing); *Online Payment Solutions Inc. v. Svenska Handelsbanken AB*, 638 F.Supp. 2d 375, 383 n.4 (S.D.N.Y. 2009) (sealing names, e-mail addresses, phone numbers, and IP addresses).

[26]*See* Rule 5.2 advisory committee note. *See also Crossman v. Astrue*, 714 F.Supp.2d 284, 288–89 (D.Conn. 2009). This Rule applies to actions for benefits under the Social Security Act, and actions or proceedings relating to orders of removal, relief from removal, or immigration benefits or detention. *See* Rule 5.2(c).

[27]*See* Rule 5.2(b)(5).

[28]*See* Rule 5.2(c). *See also Crossman v. Astrue*, 714 F.Supp.2d 284, 288–90 (D.Conn. 2009).

No New Claim or Right

This Rule does not create a new or independent claim or right of action for its violation.[29]

Enforcement and Sanctions

Courts enforce the redaction obligations by orders of redaction,[30] public admonishment,[31] and, in appropriate cases, by sanction awards of many varieties.[32]

Privacy Protection and "Particularized" Pleading

Certain federal claims require enhanced detail in pleading (such as fraud, governed by Rule 9(b)), and the redaction/sealing procedures may be used to properly balance privacy with this command for additional pleading specificity.[33]

---

[29] *See Good v. Khosrowshahi*, 296 Fed.Appx. 676, 680 (10th Cir.2008) (unpublished opinion); *Dunbar v. O'Neill*, 2010 WL 5158534, at *2 (D.S.C. Nov. 23, 2010), *adopted*, 2010 WL 5157136 (D.S.C. Dec. 14, 2010).

[30] *See Dawson v. Pelican Mgmt., Inc.*, 2012 WL 2357308, at *2 n.2 (E.D.N.Y. June 1, 2012), *adopted*, 2012 WL 2344663 (E.D.N.Y. June 19, 2012).

[31] *See Hanks v. Shinseki*, 2010 WL 3000835, at *4 (N.D.Tex. July 28, 2010) (admonishing, rather than sanctioning, where error caught within one business day and corrected within hours).

[32] *See Reed v. AMCO Ins. Co.*, 2012 WL 846475, at *3 (D.Nev. Mar. 9, 2012) (even in the absence of bad faith, awarding attorney fees related to motion to seal and sanctions motion); *Taitz v. Astrue*, 2011 WL 3039167, at *1-*2 (D.D.C. July 25, 2011) (striking violative opposition papers and exhibits in summary judgment proceeding); *Weakley v. Redline Recovery Servs.,*

LLC, 2011 WL 1522413, at *2 (S.D.Cal. Apr. 20, 2011) (imposing costs for 5 years of credit monitoring, and noting potential for later damages lawsuit); *Allstate Ins. Co. v. Linea Latina De Accidentes, Inc.*, 2010 WL 5014386, at *1–*4 (D.Minn. Nov. 24, 2010) (imposing costs for 1 year of credit monitoring, written notice to all affected persons, and charitable donation); *Engeseth v. County of Isanti, Minn.*, 665 F.Supp.2d 1047, 1048 (D. Minn. 2009) (imposing costs for credit reports and credit monitoring, notice to all affected persons, and charitable donation). *But cf. Richards v. Great Western Ins. Co.*, 2012 WL 695991, at *12 (D.Minn. Jan. 13, 2012) (denying sanctions due to quick remedial action), *adopted*, 2012 WL 718715 (D.Minn. Mar. 5, 2012).

[33] *See Exergen Corp. v. Wal-Mart Stores, Inc.*, 575 F.3d 1312, 1329 n.6 (Fed.Cir. 2009) (noting Rule 5.2's value in Rule 9(b) fraud cases, where courts endeavor to protect defendants against reputational harm).

RULE 6
COMPUTING AND EXTENDING TIME; TIME FOR MOTION PAPERS

(a) Computing Time. The following rules apply in computing any time period specified in these rules, in any local rule or court order, or in any statute that does not specify a method of computing time.

(1) *Period Stated in Days or a Longer Unit.* When the period is stated in days or a longer unit of time:

   (A) exclude the day of the event that triggers the period;

   (B) count every day, including intermediate Saturdays, Sundays, and legal holidays; and

   (C) include the last day of the period, but if the last day is a Saturday, Sunday, or legal holiday, the period continues to run until the end of the next day that is not a Saturday, Sunday, or legal holiday.

(2) *Period Stated in Hours.* When the period is stated in hours:

   (A) begin counting immediately on the occurrence of the event that triggers the period;

   (B) count every hour, including hours during intermediate Saturdays, Sundays, and legal holidays; and

   (C) if the period would end on a Saturday, Sunday, or legal holiday, the period continues to run until the same time on the next day that is not a Saturday, Sunday, or legal holiday.

(3) *Inaccessibility of the Clerk's Office.* Unless the court orders otherwise, if the clerk's office is inaccessible:

   (A) on the last day for filing under Rule 6(a)(1), then the time for filing is extended to the first accessible day that is not a Saturday, Sunday, or legal holiday; or

   (B) during the last hour for filing under Rule

6(a)(2), then the time for filing is extended to the same time on the first accessible day that is not a Saturday, Sunday, or legal holiday.

(4) *"Last Day" Defined.* Unless a different time is set by a statute, local rule, or court order, the last day ends:

   (A) for electronic filing, at midnight in the court's time zone; and

   (B) for filing by other means, when the clerk's office is scheduled to close.

(5) *"Next Day" Defined.* The "next day" is determined by continuing to count forward when the period is measured after an event and backward when measured before an event.

(6) *"Legal Holiday" Defined.* "Legal holiday" means:

   (A) the day set aside by statute for observing New Year's Day, Martin Luther King Jr.'s Birthday, Washington's Birthday, Memorial Day, Independence Day, Labor Day, Columbus Day, Veterans' Day, Thanksgiving Day, or Christmas Day;

   (B) any day declared a holiday by the President or Congress; and

   (C) for periods that are measured after an event, any other day declared a holiday by the state where the district court is located.

(b) Extending Time.

(1) *In General.* When an act may or must be done within a specified time, the court may, for good cause, extend the time:

   (A) with or without motion or notice if the court acts, or if a request is made, before the original time or its extension expires; or

   (B) on motion made after the time has expired if the party failed to act because of excusable neglect.

(2) *Exceptions.* A court must not extend the time to act under Rules 50(b) and (d), 52(b), 59(b), (d), and (e), and 60(b).

(c) Motions, Notices of Hearing, and Affidavits.

(1) *In General.* A written motion and notice of the

hearing must be served at least 14 days before the time specified for the hearing, with the following exceptions:

(A) when the motion may be heard ex parte;

(B) when these rules set a different time; or

(C) when a court order—which a party may, for good cause, apply for ex parte—sets a different time.

(2) *Supporting Affidavit.* Any affidavit supporting a motion must be served with the motion. Except as Rule 59(c) provides otherwise, any opposing affidavit must be served at least 7 days before the hearing, unless the court permits service at another time.

(d) Additional Time After Certain Kinds of Service. When a party may or must act within a specified time after service and service is made under Rule 5(b)(2)(C), (D), (E), or (F), 3 days are added after the period would otherwise expire under Rule 6(a).

[Amended effective March 19, 1948; July 1, 1963; July 1, 1966; July 1, 1968; July 1, 1971; August 1, 1983; August 1, 1985; August 1, 1987; December 1, 1999; April 23, 2001, effective December 1, 2001; April 25, 2005, effective December 1, 2005; April 30, 2007, effective December 1, 2007; March 26, 2009, effective December 1, 2009.]

AUTHORS' COMMENTARY ON RULE 6

PURPOSE AND SCOPE

Rule 6 sets the procedure for computing the passage of time under the Rules. Although other, substantive Rules define the length of allowable time for such acts as answering pleadings or filing motions, Rule 6 dictates how those defined time periods are to be calculated. Rule 6 also authorizes the district court to enlarge the time periods fixed in the Rules.

Note: A perpetual calendar can be found in Part X of this text.

RULE 6(a)—COMPUTING OF TIME

CORE CONCEPT

All time periods set by the Rules, by local rules, by court orders, or by statutes are governed by the computation instructions of

Rule 6(a), unless the source itself specifies a different method (or sets a time certain). No Rule 6 time period can end on a weekend, a legal holiday, or a day when the courthouse is inaccessible. In such instances, a brief extension is supplied.

APPLICATIONS

Impact of 2009 "Time Computation" Amendments

Rule 6(a) was the template for the Time Computation Amendments of 2009, which endeavored to simplify the task of computing time in federal court. The current Rule 6(a) deletes the old *less-than-11-day* counting rule, standardizes most time periods into multiples of 7-days, includes a method for computing hourly time periods, adds ending-time and backwards-counting instructions, and enlarges certain unrealistically short periods.

No Effect on Times Certain

When the court sets a "time certain" for an act or a filing, Rule 6(a) will *not* automatically extend that date if it falls on a Saturday, Sunday, or holiday[1] (although a court may still grant such extensions in its discretion).[2]

Periods Set in Days or Longer

In counting periods stated in units of time measured in days or longer (*e.g.,* days, months, or years), the day that triggers the period is excluded and then every other day is included. If the period ends on a weekend, a legal holiday, or a day when the clerk's office is inaccessible, the period is extended to the end of the next day that is not a weekend, a legal holiday, or a clerk's-office-inaccessible day. Thus, for example, if a Rule period was due to expire on Saturday, February 21 (and assuming Monday, February 23 was Washington's Birthday), that Rule period would actually expire at the end of the day on Tuesday, February 24.

- *Triggering Event:* What starts a time period running will depend on the implicated statute, rule, regulation, or other law.[3]
- *When A Day "Ends":* Unless otherwise specified, a day "ends" for electronic filing at midnight in the court's time zone, and for all other filings when the clerk's office

---

[1] *See* Rule 6(a) advisory committee note to 2009 amendment ("They do not apply when a fixed time to act is set."). *See also Violette v. P.A. Days, Inc.,* 427 F.3d 1015, 1016–20 (6th Cir. 2005) (Rule 6(a) does not apply to extend a date-certain, set by the court, which expired on a Saturday of a long, federal holiday weekend).

[2] *See Scanlon v. Greenberg Traurig, LLP,* 778 F.Supp.2d 56, 59 (D.D.C. 2011).

[3] *See Tiberio v. Allergy Asthma Immunology of Rochester,* 664 F.3d 35, 37–38 (2d Cir. 2011) (EEOC 90-day limitations period begins on date right-to-sue letter is received by *either* claimant or counsel).

is scheduled to close.[4]

Periods Set in Hours

In counting periods stated in units of time measured in hours, the period begins immediately upon the triggering event and includes every hour thereafter. If the period ends on a weekend, a legal holiday, or during an hour when the clerk's office is inaccessible, the period is extended to the same time on the next day that is not a weekend, a legal holiday, or a clerk's-office-inaccessible day.

- *Inaccessible Final "Hour":* No extensions are automatically provided on days when the clerk's office is inaccessible *unless* that inaccessibility continues into the final hour of the time period.[5]
- *No Rounding-Up:* There is no "rounding" of hourly time periods. They will expire at the precise minute that the computation method produces (*e.g.,* 2:17 p.m.), and not be "rounded-up" to the next whole hour.[6]
- *Crossing Daylight Savings Time:* Because *every* hour is counted, a time period that straddles the shift from daylight savings time to standard time will not produce an extra hour for the time period.[7]

Legal Holidays — Federal

The term "legal holiday" includes any day so declared by the President or Congress. There are currently ten standing federal holidays:

1. New Year's Day
2. Dr. Martin Luther King, Jr.'s Birthday
3. Washington's Birthday
4. Memorial Day
5. Independence Day
6. Labor Day
7. Columbus Day
8. Veterans' Day
9. Thanksgiving Day
10. Christmas Day

Legal Holidays — State

A special rule governs holidays that are declared by States. For "forward-looking" time periods (*i.e.,* acts to be taken within a time *after* a triggering event), State holidays are considered

---

[4]*See* Rule 6(a)(4). *See also Justice v. Town of Cicero*, 682 F.3d 662, 664–65 (7th Cir. 2012) (late-night electronic filing accessibility does not excuse failure to e-file before 11:59 p.m. on due-date - "A document entered into the electronic system at 12:01 AM on a Thursday has been filed on Thursday, not on 'virtual Wednesday.' ").

[5]*See* Rule 6(a)(3) advisory committee note to 2009 amendment.

[6]*See* Rule 6(a)(2) advisory committee note to 2009 amendment.

[7]*See* Rule 6(a)(2) advisory committee note to 2009 amendment.

"legal holidays" under Rule 6(a). Time periods typically cannot end on such days. However, for "backward-looking" time periods (*i.e.*, acts to be taken no later than a certain time *before* an event), State holidays are *not* considered "legal holidays" under Rule 6(a). In such instances (like with Rule 26(f), which requires an attorney's meeting at least 21 days before a scheduling conference), the 21st day *can* fall on a State holiday and that day will *not* be excluded from the computation.

Legal Holidays — Identifying When There Is One

From time to time, special federal holidays have been recognized.[8] Likewise, States are free to recognize their own holidays, even if the federal judiciary is otherwise open.[9] Occasionally, identifying whether a particular day qualifies as a "legal holiday" under Rule 6(a) can prove difficult. On those occasions, the courts note that the Rule provides "reasonable flexibility", and is intended to abate the "hardship" of permitting "days of rest to shorten already tight deadlines".[10] One court has adopted a "simplicity" rule, which holds that any day the President closes the federal government for celebratory or commemorative reasons, a snow emergency, a terrorist act, or some other *force majeure*, a rebuttable presumption is created that a federal holiday was declared.[11] Days when the clerk's office is declared closed by the Chief Judge might not, however, qualify for this extension.[12]

Clerk's Office Inaccessibility

What causes the clerk's office to be considered "inaccessible" is not defined by the Rules, although the drafters emphasize

---

[8]*See, e.g., Reyes-Cardona v. J. C. Penney Co., Inc.*, 690 F.2d 1 (1st Cir. 1982) (legal holiday in Puerto Rico honoring Eugenio Maria de Hostos was properly excluded from computation of time under Rule 6(a)).

[9]*See Yepremyan v. Holder*, 614 F.3d 1042, 1044 (9th Cir. 2010) (finding day after Thanksgiving to be legal holiday in California); *Tamez v. Manthey*, 589 F.3d 764, 769 (5th Cir. 2009) (finding Texas Independence Day to be a legal holiday in Texas); *Dietrich v. John Ascuaga's Nugget*, 548 F.3d 892, 896 n.3 (9th Cir. 2008) (finding Nevada Day to be legal holiday in Nevada); *Wright v. Trinity Catering, Inc.*, 2007 WL 2155728, at *1–*3 (E.D. La. 2007) (finding Mardi Gras to be legal holiday in Louisiana, implemented parish by parish); *Seacor by Seacor v. Secretary of Dept. of Health and Human Services*, 34 Fed. Cl. 141, 143–44 (1995) (finding Patriot's Day to be a legal holiday in Massachusetts).

[10]*See Mashpee Wampanoag Tribal Council, Inc. v. Norton*, 336 F.3d 1094, 1098–99 (D.C. Cir. 2003) (recognizing Christmas Eve 2001 as qualifying holiday for federal litigators, where President gave all Executive Branch employees that day off).

[11]*See Hart v. Sheahan*, 396 F.3d 887, 891 (7th Cir. 2005).

[12]*See Garcia-Velazquez v. Frito Lay Snacks Caribbean*, 358 F.3d 6, 9–11 (1st Cir. 2004) (New Year's Eve not excluded, even though Chief Judge declared clerk's office closed); *In re Cascade Oil Co.*, 848 F.2d 1062, 1064 (10th Cir. 1988) (day after Thanksgiving not excluded, same reasoning); *Kirby v. General Elec. Co.*, 2000 WL 33917974, at *2 (W.D. N.C. 2000), aff'd, 20 Fed. Appx. 167 (4th Cir. 2001) (Christmas Eve and New Year's Eve not excluded, same reasoning, per curiam).

that bad weather is not the only qualifying cause (an "outage" of the clerk's electronic filing system is given as one example).[13] The Rule contemplates that "inaccessibility" will continue to evolve through caselaw.[14] To date, that caselaw has found "inaccessibility" when the clerk's office is closed *officially* for any reason[15] (including inclement weather closures),[16] when local weather conditions near the courthouse make travelling to the clerk's office dangerous, difficult, or impossible,[17] or when other circumstances make the courthouse inaccessible as a practical matter.[18] An individual's own, personal weather-related difficulties, which do not also cause the clerk's office to close, close early, or be otherwise dangerous to reach, generally will not qualify for this extension.[19]

Time Periods of Less than 11 Days

Under the pre-2009 amendment version of Rule 6(a), time periods of less than 11 days were given a special computation method (*i.e.*, intervening weekends and legal holidays were excluded). To simplify time computation, this approach has been abandoned.[20] Effective December 1, 2009, time periods that were formerly less than 11 days have been expanded to

---

[13]*See* Rule 6(a)(3) advisory committee note to 2009 amendment. *Accord Chao Lin v. U.S. Attorney Gen.*, 677 F.3d 1043, 1045 (11th Cir. 2012).

[14]*See* Rule 6(a)(3) advisory committee note to 2009 amendment.

[15]*See Chao Lin v. U.S. Attorney Gen.*, 677 F.3d 1043, 1045 (11th Cir. 2012).

[16]*See Telephone and Data Systems, Inc. v. Amcell F Atlantic City, Inc.*, 20 F.3d 501 (D.C. Cir. 1994) (clerk's office is "inaccessible" within the meaning of Rule 6(a) when inclement weather forces office to close, notwithstanding that clerk's office's 24-hour "drop box" was still available).

[17]The courthouse need not be physically closed in order for the clerk's office to be deemed "inaccessible". *See U.S. Leather, Inc. v. H & W Partnership*, 60 F.3d 222 (5th Cir. 1995) ("An ice storm that temporarily knocks out an area's power and telephone service and makes travelling dangerous, difficult or impossible, thereby rendering the federal courthouse inaccessible to those in the area of the courthouse, is enough to come within Rule 6(a)'s weather exception").

[18]*See Latham v. Dominick's Finer Foods*, 149 F.3d 673 (7th Cir.1998) (holding that district court was "inaccessible as a practical matter without heroic measures" on December 26, 1997 because chief judge ordered the court closed, in recognition of President's executive order closing executive branch of federal government on that day).

[19]*See Chao Lin v. U.S. Attorney Gen.*, 677 F.3d 1043, 1045–46 (11th Cir. 2012) (untimely delivery by FedEx is not courthouse inaccessibility, and now-untimely deportation review petition is rejected); *O'Malley v. Town of Egremont*, 453 F. Supp. 2d 240, 246–47 (D. Mass. 2006). *See generally* William G. Phelps, *When is office of clerk of court inaccessible due to weather or other conditions for purpose of computing time period for filing papers under Rule 6(a) of Federal Rules of Civil Procedure*, 135 A.L.R. Fed. 259.

[20]*See Yost v. Stout*, 607 F.3d 1239, 1241 n.3 (10th Cir. 2010) (noting deletion of less-than-11-day procedure which had made calculating deadlines "unnecessarily complicated" and caused "counterintuitive results")

compensate.[21]

Effect on Rule 23(f) Applications

Rule 23(f) permits a court of appeals to allow an appeal from a grant or denial of class action certification if an application is made for the appeal within 14 days of the trial court's order. Rule 6 applies to such applications.[22]

Effect on Time Periods Set by Private Contracts

Ordinarily, the computation procedures embodied in Rule 6 do *not* apply to time periods set in private contracts.[23]

Effect on Federal Statutes

The Rule 6(a) computation instructions apply to "any statute" that does not specify a different approach.[24] Previously, the courts were divided as to whether Rule 6(a) would extend a statutory deadline (especially a limitations deadline) that otherwise expired on a weekend, legal holiday, or clerk's-office-inaccessiblity day.[25] It now seems clear that Rule 6(a) *does* apply to all federal statutes (absent a different computation method supplied in the statute itself).[26]

Effect on State Statutes of Limitation

In diversity cases, the federal courts typically apply the

---

[21]*See* Rule 6(a)(1) advisory committee note to 2009 amendment.

[22]*See Beck v. Boeing Co.*, 320 F.3d 1021, 1021–23 (9th Cir. 2003); *In re Veneman*, 309 F.3d 789, 793 (D.C. Cir. 2002); *Sumitomo Copper Litigation v. Credit Lyonnais Rouse, Ltd.*, 262 F.3d 134, 137 n.1 (2d Cir. 2001).

[23]*See J. Aron & Co., Inc. v. S/S Olga Jacob*, 527 F.2d 416, 417 (5th Cir. 1976).

[24]*See* Rule 6(a) ("The following rules apply in computing any time period specified in . . . any statute that does not specify a method of computing time."). *See also Windland v. Quarterman*, 578 F.3d 314, 317 (5th Cir. 2009) (Rule 6(a)'s general approach supplanted when statute provides different direction).

[25]*Compare Bartlik v. U.S. Dept. of Labor*, 62 F.3d 163 (6th Cir. 1995) (en banc) (majority view: holding that petition for review of agency decision due on Saturday, Sunday, federal holiday, or courthouse-inaccessible day is timely if filed on the next day courthouse is open for business). *with Scanio v. U.S.*, 37 F.3d 858, 860–61 (2d Cir. 1994) (minority view: holding that

final filing day is not extended when statutory last day is a Saturday, Sunday, holiday, or a day on which the clerk's office is inaccessible). *See also Union Nat. Bank of Wichita, Kan. v. Lamb*, 337 U.S. 38, 40–41, 69 S. Ct. 911, 912–13, 93 L. Ed. 1190 (1949) (holding that a petition for review of State supreme court decision filed on Monday—the ninety-first day of the statutory ninety-day filing period, was timely filed: "[s]ince [Rule 6(a)] had the concurrence of Congress and since no contrary policy is expressed in the statute governing this review, we think that the considerations of liberality and leniency which find expression in Rule 6(a) are equally applicable").

[26]*See* Rule 6(a) advisory committee note to 2009 amendment ("does not apply when computing a time period set by a statute if the statute specifies a method of computing time."). *See also American Canoe Ass'n, Inc. v. City Of Attalla*, 363 F.3d 1085, 1086 (11th Cir. 2004). *Cf. F.D.I.C. v. Enventure V*, 77 F.3d 123, 125–26 (5th Cir. 1996) (Rule 6(a) counting procedure does not apply when Congress' statute of limitations expressly states otherwise).

time computation methods set by State law.[27] If, however, the applicable State law is silent on the computation question, the courts may apply Rule 6.

RULE 6(b)—EXTENDING TIME

CORE CONCEPT

The district courts may extend many of the time periods set by the Rules. Extensions sought before a time period expires may be granted for "good cause". Extensions sought after a time period expires may be granted only "on motion" and if both "good cause" and "excusable neglect" are proven. Time periods for many post-trial motions may not be extended at all.

APPLICATIONS

No Stipulated Extensions

Ordinarily, parties may not extend the time periods set in the Rules by simply stipulating to the extension.[28] Court approval is required.[29] In several contexts, the Rules themselves (and local and chambers rules) include standing grants of such authority,[30] and courts always anticipate the civility and mutual respect among members of the bar that ought to encourage attorney consent to one another's reasonable, non-prejudicial, good faith extension requests.[31]

Sua Sponte Extensions

The case law is divided on whether, absent a party's motion, a court may extend a time period.[32]

Extensions Before the Time Period Expires

If the extension request is made *before* the time period expires, the district court, in its discretion,[33] may grant an extension for "good cause".[34] Neither notice to the adversary nor a formal motion is required by the Rule, although ap-

---

[27]*See Walker v. Armco Steel Corp.*, 446 U.S. 740, 100 S. Ct. 1978, 64 L. Ed. 2d 659 (1980).

[28]*See Orange Theatre Corp. v. Rayherstz Amusement Corp.*, 130 F.2d 185 (3d Cir. 1942).

[29]*See Gray v. Lewis & Clark Expeditions, Inc.*, 12 F. Supp. 2d 993 (D. Neb. 1998); *Allstate Ins. Co. v. Administratia Asigurarilor De Stat*, 163 F.R.D. 196, 199 (S.D. N.Y. 1995).

[30]*See, e.g.*, Rule 29(b) (permitting unapproved stipulated extensions of time in discovery unless the extended time would interfere with the discovery schedule, a motion hearing, or trial).

[31]*See Ahanchian v. Xenon*

Pictures, Inc., 624 F.3d 1253, 1263 (9th Cir. 2010).

[32]*Compare Smith v. District of Columbia*, 430 F.3d 450, 456–57 (D.C.Cir.2005) (noting no-extension view) *with Mitchell-Tracey v. United General Title Ins. Co.*, 839 F.Supp.2d 821, 826 (D.Md. 2012) (noting that *sua sponte* extensions are proper).

[33]*See Hetzel v. Bethlehem Steel Corp.*, 50 F.3d 360, 367 (5th Cir. 1995) (observing that district courts are granted "broad discretion" under Rule 6(b) to expand filing deadlines).

[34]*See Lujan v. National Wildlife Federation*, 497 U.S. 871, 896, 110 S. Ct. 3177, 3192, 111 L. Ed. 2d 695 (1990) (noting that cause must be shown before an enlargement of time is

plicable local rules may establish a more specific extension procedure. "Good cause" is not an especially rigorous standard, and has been interpreted broadly.[35] Pre-expiration extensions are granted routinely if they are sought in good faith and do not prejudice the adversary[36] (but the court's discretion is broad).[37] In an appropriate case, the district court may convene an evidentiary hearing to explore the issues of good faith and prejudice.[38]

Extensions After the Time Period Expires

If the extension request is made *after* the time period expires, the district court's discretion is more restricted. The district court may grant such an extension if: (1) "good cause" is shown, *and* (2) the failure to act was the result of "excusable neglect".[39] The courts have tested carefully a litigant's claim of excusable neglect; general unfamiliarity with the Rules or a crowded professional schedule will not constitute excusable neglect,[40] nor will a delay taken for strategic reasons.[41] In fact, demonstrating excusable neglect is not easily done, and was not intended to be.[42] As one court aptly wrote: "When parties wait until the last minute to comply with a deadline, they are playing with fire."[43] A formal request for an excusable neglect extension is required; trial courts abuse their discretion in granting such relief in the absence of a motion by the affected litigant.[44]

The Supreme Court has noted that excusable neglect is a "somewhat elastic concept", not limited exclusively to omissions caused by circumstances outside the moving party's control, but which must be assessed in view of all relevant circumstances

---

[35]See *Ahanchian v. Xenon Pictures, Inc.*, 624 F.3d 1253, 1259 (9th Cir. 2010); *Stark-Romero v. National R.R. Passenger Co. (AMTRAK)*, 275 F.R.D. 544, 547 (D.N.M. 2011).

[36]See *Ahanchian v. Xenon Pictures, Inc.*, 624 F.3d 1253, 1259–60 (9th Cir. 2010).

[37]See *Yancick v. Hanna Steel Corp.*, 653 F.3d 532, 537–39 (7th Cir. 2011) (no abuse of discretion in refusing to permit late filing of attorney who waited until last minute).

[38]See *Ahanchian v. Xenon Pictures, Inc.*, 624 F.3d 1253, 1260 (9th Cir. 2010).

[39]See *Murphy v. Eddie Murphy Productions, Inc.*, 611 F.3d 322, 324 (7th Cir. 2010); *Staley v. Owens*, 367

Fed.Appx. 102, 105 (11th Cir. 2010).

[40]See *Ragguette v. Premier Wines & Spirits*, 691 F.3d 315, 317–33 (3d Cir. 2012); *Keeton v. Morningstar, Inc.*, 667 F.3d 877, 882–84 (7th Cir. 2012); *Hawks v. J.P. Morgan Chase Bank*, 591 F.3d 1043, 1048 (8th Cir. 2010).

[41]See *Huggins v. FedEx Ground Package Sys., Inc.*, 592 F.3d 853, 856–57 (8th Cir. 2010).

[42]See *Thompson v. E.I. DuPont de Nemours & Co., Inc.*, 76 F.3d 530, 534 (4th Cir. 1996).

[43]*Spears v. City of Indianapolis*, 74 F.3d 153, 157 (7th Cir. 1996).

[44]See *Drippe v. Tobelinski*, 604 F.3d 778, 784–85 (3d Cir. 2010); *Smith v. District of Columbia*, 430 F.3d 450, 456–57 (D.C. Cir. 2005).

surrounding the omission.[45] Negligent oversight (if that oversight is deemed excusable) is encompassed in this standard.[46] For example, an attorney's inexplicable failure to read and apply "crystal clear" legal rules will not be deemed excusable neglect, but an attorney's "plausible misinterpretation" of an ambiguous legal rule may be.[47] Likewise, an inadvertent, good faith, and understandable calendaring error may qualify,[48] though unexceptional, ordinary calendaring oversights likely will not.[49] Malfunctioning of the court's electronic filing systems will likely qualify,[50] but technical difficulties experienced by counsel likely will not.[51] The fact that the error lies with the attorney, and not with the attorney's client, is *not* dispositive on whether "excusable neglect" exists. Clients are held responsible for the omissions of their attorneys, even if the clients are not separately culpable for the error.[52] The Court considers this excusable neglect hurdle as the "greatest" substantive obstacle of all.[53] In testing whether the neglect was excusable, courts have considered some or all of the following factors:

1. The prejudice to the opponent;
2. The length of the delay and its potential impact on the course of the judicial proceedings;
3. The causes for the delay, and whether those causes were within the reasonable control of the moving party;
4. The moving party's good faith;
5. Whether the omission reflected professional incompetence, such as an ignorance of the procedural rules;
6. Whether the omission reflected an easily manufactured

---

[45] *See Pioneer Inv. Services Co. v. Brunswick Associates Ltd. Partnership*, 507 U.S. 380, 390–95, 113 S. Ct. 1489, 1496–98, 123 L. Ed. 2d 74 (1993) (construing excusable neglect in the context of Bankruptcy Rule 9006(b), which was patterned after Rule 6(b)).

[46] *See Mommaerts v. Hartford Life and Acc. Ins. Co.*, 472 F.3d 967, 968 (7th Cir. 2007) (quoting *Pioneer Inv. Services Co. v. Brunswick Associates Ltd. Partnership*, 507 U.S. 380, 395, 113 S. Ct. 1489, 123 L. Ed. 2d 74 (1993)).

[47] *See Lewis v. School Dist. #70*, 523 F.3d 730, 740 (7th Cir. 2008); *Pryor v. Aerotek Scientific, LLC*, 278 F.R.D. 516, 522 (C.D.Cal. 2011).

[48] *See Kirkland v. Guardian Life Ins. Co.*, 352 Fed.Appx. 293, 295 (11th Cir. 2009) (counsel calendared proper date, but then filed notice of removal a day earlier than planned).

[49] *See Ragguette v. Premier Wines & Spirits*, 691 F.3d 315, 317–33 (3d Cir. 2012) (no excusable neglect for busy calendar, imprecise instructions to subordinates, inaction by subordinates).

[50] *See Salts v. Epps*, 676 F.3d 468, 474–75 (5th Cir. 2012).

[51] *See Schoenman v. F.B.I.*, 857 F. Supp. 2d 76, 78–83 (D.D.C. 2012) ("malfunctioning scanner" not sufficient); *Phillips v. Seattle Times Co.*, 818 F.Supp.2d 1277, 1281–82 (W.D.Wash. 2011) (lightning strike that disabled internet connection might excuse one-day delay but not three).

[52] *See Allen v. Murph*, 194 F.3d 722, 724 (6th Cir. 1999).

[53] *Lujan v. National Wildlife Federation*, 497 U.S. 871, 897, 110 S. Ct. 3177, 3193, 111 L. Ed. 2d 695 (1990).

excuse that the court could not verify;

7. Whether the moving party had failed to provide for a consequence that was readily foreseeable; and

8. Whether the omission constituted a complete lack of diligence.[54]

Ordinarily, opponents are not deemed "prejudiced" merely because granting an extension would require them to respond to (and litigate) an otherwise untimely pleading or motion.[55] However, courts are reluctant to approve extensions of time after prior extensions have been granted and ignored.[56]

No Extensions

Rule 6(b)(2) prohibits the district court from extending the following post-trial motion time periods:[57]

(1) Time for seeking a judgment as a matter of law or new trial, under Rules 50(b) or 50(d);

(2) Time for requesting an amendment or expansion of the court's findings in a non-jury case, under Rule 52(b);

(3) Time for granting a new trial or proposing to alter or amend the judgment, under Rule 59(b), (d), or (e); and

(4) Time for requesting relief from judgment, under Rule 60(b).

As to these post-trial motions, the court may not rescue a party's failure to act within the designated time period.[58] For years, these time periods were an alarmingly brief 10 days. Effective December 2009, most of the periods were extended to a more sensible 28 days.[59]

Notwithstanding the prohibitory language of Rule 6(b)(2), two caselaw caveats are noteworthy. First, several courts have declared this prohibition a non-jurisdictional "claim-processing"

---

[54]*See Pioneer Inv. Services Co. v. Brunswick Associates Ltd. Partnership*, 507 U.S. 380, 390–95, 113 S. Ct. 1489, 1496–98, 123 L. Ed. 2d 74 (1993); *Drippe v. Tobelinski*, 604 F.3d 778, 785 (3d Cir. 2010); *Chorosevic v. MetLife Choices*, 600 F.3d 934, 946 (8th Cir. 2010); *Staley v. Owens*, 367 Fed.Appx. 102, 105 (11th Cir. 2010).

[55]*See Kimberg v. University of Scranton*, 411 Fed.Appx. 473, 479 (3d Cir. 2010).

[56]*See Spears v. City of Indianapolis*, 74 F.3d 153 (7th Cir.1996) (finding no abuse of discretion where the district court refused to grant a 24-hour extension, after having previously granted several, earlier extensions); *McIntosh v. Antonino*, 71 F.3d 29 (1st Cir.1995) (finding no abuse of discretion in court's "exasperated denial" of

a third extension).

[57]Although not listed specifically as a non-extending Rule, the courts have construed Rule 71A as prohibiting the district court from enlarging the time to answer in a condemnation proceeding.

[58]*See Browder v. Director, Dept. of Corrections of Illinois*, 434 U.S. 257, 261–62, 98 S. Ct. 556, 54 L. Ed. 2d 521 (1978). *See also Blue v. Int'l Bhd. of Elec. Workers Local Union 159*, 676 F.3d 579, 582–84 (7th Cir. 2012); *Green v. Drug Enforcement Admin.*, 606 F.3d 1296, 1300 (11th Cir. 2010).

[59]*See Yost v. Stout*, 607 F.3d 1239, 1241 n.3 (10th Cir. 2010) ("[e]xperience has proved that in many cases it is not possible to prepare a satisfactory post-judgment motion in 10 days") (citation omitted).

rule that will be deemed waived if not asserted in opposition to an untimely post-trial motion[60] (though the courts are divided whether such a backdoor maneuver to file an otherwise untimely motion extends the time for taking an appeal).[61] Second, a forty-year old case law exemption from the Seventh Circuit Court of Appeals held that in "unique circumstances" these periods could be extended, provided there was a genuine ambiguity in the Rule language to begin with and the district court took action that gave the parties the specific assurance (albeit improperly) that an extension had been granted.[62] The validity of this exemption has been often questioned, and always limited tightly,[63] and the Supreme Court has rejected its application in a related context.[64]

Other Enlargement Rules

Several other Rules authorize the district court to grant extensions of time in particular circumstances.[65]

Time Periods Set by Statute

The pre-2007 language was clear that extensions under Rule 6(b) could only be granted to time periods set by the Rules

---

[60]*See Advanced Bodycare Solutions, LLC v. Thione Int'l, Inc.*, 615 F.3d 1352, 1359 n.15 (11th Cir. 2010); *Dill v. General American Life Ins. Co.*, 525 F.3d 612, 618–20 (8th Cir. 2008). *See also Eberhart v. U.S.*, 546 U.S. 12, 19, 126 S. Ct. 403, 163 L. Ed. 2d 14 (2005) (applying "nonjurisdictional claim processing" rule concept in context of Federal Rules of Criminal Procedure).

[61]*See Advanced Bodycare Solutions, LLC v. Thione Int'l, Inc.*, 615 F.3d 1352, 1359 n.15 (11th Cir. 2010) (appeal proper, but only from ruling on untimely post-trial motions, not from underlying judgment itself); *Lizardo v. United States*, 619 F.3d 273, 278–80 (3d Cir. 2010) (although district court may rule on untimely motion, time for appeal is not extended). *Accord Blue v. Int'l Bhd. of Elec. Workers Local Union 159*, 676 F.3d 579, 582–84 (7th Cir. 2012); *Green v. Drug Enforcement Admin.*, 606 F.3d 1296, 1301–02 (11th Cir. 2010) (same). *But see Obaydullah v. Obama*, 688 F.3d 784, 786–93 (D.C.Cir. 2012) (appellee's intentional waiver of objection to modestly late filing of Rule 59(e) motion triggers appellate tolling); *National Ecological Found. v. Alexander*, 496 F.3d 466, 474–75 (6th Cir.

2007) (untimely but unobjected to post-trial motion tolls appeal period).

[62]*See Eady v. Foerder*, 381 F.2d 980 (7th Cir. 1967). *See also Varhol v. National R.R. Passenger Corp.*, 909 F.2d 1557 (7th Cir. 1990) (equally divided en banc court considered but refused to overrule *Eady*).

[63]*See Robinson v. City of Harvey*, 489 F.3d 864, 870–71 (7th Cir. 2007).

[64]*See Bowles v. Russell*, 551 U.S. 205, 213–14, 127 S. Ct. 2360, 2366, 168 L. Ed. 2d 96 (U.S. 2007) (denouncing doctrine as "illegitimate", overruling prior case law, and emphasizing "that the timely filing of a notice of appeal in a civil case is a jurisdictional requirement").

[65]*See, e.g.*, Rule 4(m) (extensions to serve summons and complaint); Rule 30(d)(1) (extensions for oral depositions); Rule 31(a)(5) (extensions for depositions on written interrogatories); Rule 33(b)(2) (extensions to answer interrogatories); Rule 34(b)(2) (extensions to respond to production requests); Rule 36(a)(3) (extensions to answer requests for admission); Rule 39(b) (extensions to demand jury trial); Rule 59(c) (extensions to submit affidavits in opposition to new trial motion).

themselves or by court orders.[66] Statutory time periods could not be extended under Rule 6(b).[67] The restyled version of Rule 6(b) omits this expressly limiting language.[68] Although the 2007 changes to Rule 6 were "intended to be stylistic only",[69] the effect of this restyling omission remains uncertain. The few courts that have addressed the issue have ruled that restyled Rule 6(b), like its predecessor, does not authorize extensions to statutory time periods.[70]

Scope of Extension

The language of a party's proposed extension order should be chosen carefully. An order extending the time for a defendant to "answer" the complaint does not necessarily extend the time for "moving" to dismiss the complaint. Therefore, broad language is advised: *e.g.,* requesting an extension to "answer, move, or otherwise plead".

RULE 6(c)—MOTIONS, NOTICES OF HEARING, AFFIDAVITS

CORE CONCEPT

A written motion and notice of hearing must be served on the non-moving party at least 14 days before a motion hearing date, unless the district court specifies otherwise.

APPLICATIONS

Impact of 2009 "Time Computation" Amendments

In 2009, the time period set in Rule 6(c)(1), formerly 5 days long, was enlarged to 14 days, and the period set in Rule 6(c)(2), formerly 1 day long, was enlarged to 7 days.

Impact of 2007 "Restyling" Amendments

The 2007 amendments deleted former Rule 6(c) (which had been empty of content since 1966), and moved up the remaining two subparts of Rule 6. Current Rule 6(c) now retains the content of former Rule 6(d). In researching current Rule 6(c), practitioners should be mindful of this repositioning.

---

[66]*See* Fed. R. Civ. P. 6(b) (pre-restyling) ("When by these rules or by a notice given thereunder or by order of court an act is required or allowed to be done at or within a specified time, the court" may grant an enlargement).

[67]*See Kreutzer v. Bowersox,* 231 F.3d 460, 463 n.2 (8th Cir. 2000) ("Rule 6(b), by its own terms, only applies to time limits set by the Federal Rules of Civil Procedure, or to limits set by the court. . . . It cannot be used to extend

a statutory limit.").

[68]*See* Rule 6(b) ("When an act may or must be done within a specified time, the court may, for good cause, extend the time . . . ").

[69]*See* Rule 6 advisory committee note to 2007 amendment.

[70]*See Argentine Republic v. Nat'l Grid Plc,* 637 F.3d 365, 368 (D.C.Cir. 2011); *Potter v. Astrue,* 2008 WL 4610234, at *1–*2 (E.D.N.C. Oct. 16, 2008).

Motion Days

This 14-day notice procedure applies to those district courts with "motion days" or the equivalent (where all motions are heard orally). The Rule provides that the non-moving party must be served with notice of all motions at least 14 days before the hearing day, unless the court directs otherwise.[71]

Special Timing

This 14-day notice requirement is a default rule of general application. Any Rule that contains a specific, different time period supersedes this default rule, as does any court order fixing a different time period.[72]

Motion Affidavits

When a motion is supported with affidavits, the supporting affidavits must be served simultaneously with the motion. When an opposition to a motion is supported with affidavits, the opposing affidavits must be served not less than 7 days before the hearing. These service requirements do not apply to affidavits submitted in support of reply briefs;[73] but many courts will accept a reply affidavit if filed simultaneously with the reply brief and addresses matters raised in the adversary's opposition brief.[74] The district court may modify these service requirements.[75] Untimely affidavits may be stricken.[76]

> *Exception:* Affidavits opposing a motion for new trial must be served within 14 days after service of the motion.[77]

Time Period May Be Extended

The provisions of Rule 6(b) apply to Rule 6(c), and the 14-day period may be extended if the requisites for extension in

---

[71]*See Stewart Title Guar. Co. v. Cadle Co.*, 74 F.3d 835, 837 (7th Cir. 1996) (noting that judicial district adopted a different schedule by local rule, permitting written motions to be filed just two days before hearing).

[72]*See Ciena Corp. v. Jarrard*, 203 F.3d 312, 319–20 (4th Cir. 2000) (permitting different time periods in the context of interlocutory injunctions).

[73]*See McGinnis v. Southeast Anesthesia Associates, P.A.*, 161 F.R.D. 41 (W.D. N.C. 1995) (ruling that affidavits submitted with reply brief during a motion to dismiss briefing were not governed by Rule 6).

[74]*See Robinson v. Empire Equity Group, Inc.*, 2009 WL 4018560, at *2 (D.Md. Nov. 18, 2009); *Doolittle v. Structured Invs. Co.*, 2008 WL 5121591, at *3 (D.Idaho Dec. 4, 2008); *Cardenas*

v. Dorel Juvenile Group, Inc., 230 F.R.D. 635, 636 (D. Kan. 2005). Cf. *Smith v. Lab. Corp. of America, Inc.*, 2009 WL 3872042, at *3 (D.Idaho Nov. 17, 2009) (reply affidavit stricken where no reasonable justification offered for failing to file affidavit with original motion papers).

[75]*See Lovelace v. Lee*, 472 F.3d 174, 204 (4th Cir. 2006) (district court has discretion to accept untimely affidavit); *Orsi v. Kirkwood*, 999 F.2d 86, 91–92 (4th Cir. 1993) (although district court may enlarge time period of this Rule, such enlargements should generally be granted only if cause or excusable neglect is shown).

[76]*See S.D. v. St. Johns County Sch. Dist.*, 632 F.Supp.2d 1085, 1100 n.15 (M.D.Fla. 2009).

[77]*See* Rule 59.

Rule 6(b) are satisfied.[78]

RULE 6(d)—ADDITIONAL TIME AFTER CERTAIN KINDS OF SERVICE

CORE CONCEPT

A party is given 3 extra days in which to act, if that party is to act within a specified time after service of a document and that document was served by mail, by other pre-agreed means (such as electronically), or by leaving it with the clerk (if permitted).

APPLICATIONS

Impact of 2007 "Restyling" Amendments

The 2007 amendments repositioned the content of former Rule 6(e) to its current location, in Rule 6(d). In researching current Rule 6(d), practitioners should be mindful of this repositioning.

Purpose

The Rules permit service of papers, under certain circumstances, to be made by mail, by other pre-agreed means (such as electronically), and by leaving the papers with the court clerk.[79] Such service is generally considered complete at the time of mailing or other transmission; completed service does *not* await actual receipt. To compensate for time lapses caused by these special means of delivery, Rule 6(d) adds 3 extra days to certain time periods. Rule 6(b) thus assumes that postal deliveries will typically arrive at their destinations within 3 days of mailing.[80] Similarly, when service is made electronically or by other means, this additional 3-day period is added to offset possible transmission delays.[81]

Applies to "After-Service" Deadlines Only

This 3-day extension applies only to responses due within a certain time after "service" of a preceding document.

No 3-Day Extension to "After-Filing" Deadlines

There is *no* 3-day extension when responses are due within a prescribed time after the "filing" of a document, even if that document is subsequently served through the mails (or through

---

[78]*See Savage v. Liberty Mut. Fire Ins. Co.*, 2009 WL 2245133, at *2 (D.Idaho July 24, 2009); *Laroque v. Domino's Pizza, LLC*, 557 F. Supp. 2d 346, 350–51 (E.D. N.Y. 2008).

[79]*See* Rule 5(b)(2)(C), (D), (E), (F).

[80]*See Sherlock v. Montefiore Medical Center*, 84 F.3d 522, 525–26 (2d Cir. 1996) (noting "assumption" that mailed documents are received 3 days after mailing).

[81]*See* Rule 6(d). *See also* Rule 6(e) advisory committee note to 2001 amendments (noting that electronic transmission is not always instantaneous, and may not arrive in a readable format, causing further delays). *But cf. Love v. Commissioner of Social Sec.*, 605 F.Supp.2d 893, 895–96 (W.D.Mich. 2009) (applying 3-days to electronic transmission service, but criticizing extension as a "vestige" of pre-electronic age).

the special service means provided in Rules 5(b)(2)(C), (D), (E), and (F)).[82] Nor is a 3-day extension self-acquired by the act of mailing a document that must otherwise be filed by a particular date,[83] or self-acquired by electronically delivering a document from which a time period is to be dated.[84]

- *Post-Trial Motions Caution:* Because most post-trial motions must be *"filed"* (not "served") within 28-days "after the entry of judgment" or "after the jury was discharged", there are *no* 3-day extensions to these periods.[85]

No 3-Day Extension to "After-Receipt" Deadlines

There generally is also *no* 3-day extension where responses are due within a prescribed period after actual "receipt" of a document, even though the received document was served through the mails (or through the special service means provided in Rules 5(b)(2)(C), (D), (E), and (F)).[86] However, a party may receive additional "mail" time when a party receives notice that the delivery of a letter was attempted, unsuccessfully, and is now ready to be picked up. In such cases, the courts may choose to extend the time period so as to allow that party a few extra days to retrieve the letter.[87]

No 3-Day Extension to "Date-Certain" Deadlines

There is no 3-day extension for date-specific deadlines fixed by the court.[88]

No 3-Day Extension to Most Statutes of Limitation

The prevailing view among the courts is that the 3-day extension period does not apply to extend statutes of

---

[82]*See McCarty v. Astrue*, 528 F.3d 541, 545 (7th Cir. 2008); *Delta Airlines v. Butler*, 383 F.3d 1143, 1145 (10th Cir. 2004); *Jackson v. Crosby*, 375 F.3d 1291, 1293 n.5 (11th Cir. 2004); *Rouse v. Lee*, 339 F.3d 238, 245–46 (4th Cir. 2003). *Compare Ramos v. Quien*, 631 F.Supp.2d 601, 608–09 (E.D.Pa. 2008) (refusing to add 3-days to 30-day removal time because it is an "after-filing" period), *with N.J. Dep't of Envt'l Prot. v. Exxon Mobil Corp.*, 381 F.Supp.2d 398, 402 (D.N.J.2005) (adding 3 days to 30-day removal period if notice was served by mail).

[83]*See Johnson v. McBride*, 381 F.3d 587 (7th Cir. 2004).

[84]*See Lewis v. School Dist. #70*, 523 F.3d 730, 739–40 (7th Cir. 2008).

[85]*See* Rules 50(b), 50(d), 52(b), 59(b), 59(d), 59(e), 60(c)(1). *See also Albright v. Virtue*, 273 F.3d 564, 570–71 (3d Cir. 2001) (motions for reconsideration under Rule 59(e) cannot be enlarged by this Rule); *Parker v. Board of Public Utilities of Kansas City, Kan.*, 77 F.3d 1289, 1291 (10th Cir. 1996) (same).

[86]*See Begay v. St. Joseph's Indian School*, 922 F. Supp. 270, 272–73 (D.S.D. 1996) (Rule 6(e) does not provide an additional 3-days for responses to mailed right-to-sue letter, where response period begins to run only from date of receipt of the letter).

[87]*See Zillyette v. Capital One Financial Corp.*, 179 F.3d 1337, 1341–42 (11th Cir. 1999); *Sousa v. N.L.R.B.*, 817 F.2d 10, 11 (2d Cir. 1987).

[88]*See Bacon v. Stiefel Labs., Inc.*, 714 F.Supp.2d 1186, 1189 n.1 (S.D.Fla. 2010) (ruling Rule 6(d) inapplicable, but granting extension to accept late filing).

limitation.[89]

Applies to No-Known-Address Service

The 3-day extension also applies in those cases where, aware of a defendant's last known address, the serving party delivers the documents to the clerk of court.[90]

Periods of 11-Days or Less

Under the pre-2009 amendment version of Rule 6(a), time periods of less than 11 days were given a special computation method (*i.e.*, intervening weekends and legal holidays were excluded). This, in turn, created uncertainty as to how (and when) the 3-day mail extension should properly be added if an "after-service" time period were involved. The 2009 "Time Computation" amendments ended this confusion. To simplify time computation, effective December 1, 2009, the former "*less-than-11-days*" special computation method has been deleted in its entirety, and time periods that were formerly less than 11 days have been expanded to compensate.[91]

Additional 3-Day Period Applies to Objections to Magistrate Judge Rulings

A district judge may direct a magistrate judge to consider and decide nondispositive pretrial matters, and to consider and submit a recommendation on dispositive motions.[92] The parties, thereafter, have 14 days from service to file objections to the magistrate judge's order or recommendation.[93] If the magistrate judge's order or recommendation is served upon the parties by mail, the additional 3-day period of Rule 6(d) applies to extend this 14-day objection period.[94]

Additional Research References

Wright & Miller, *Federal Practice and Procedure* §§ 1161 to 71
C.J.S., Federal Civil Procedure § 194, § 250, § 302, § 331, §§ 354 to 369, §§ 394 to 436, § 569, § 571§ 701, § 732, §§ 764 to 789 et seq., §§ 933 to 934; Time §§ 2 to 17 et seq.
West's Key Number Digest, Federal Civil Procedure ☞417, ☞624, ☞734 to 735, ☞824, ☞865, ☞868, ☞923, ☞956, ☞1033, ☞1051, ☞1143, ☞1342 to 1343, ☞1612, ☞1679 to 1680, ☞1701 to 1705, ☞1991 to

---

[89]*See Velez-Diaz v. U.S.*, 507 F.3d 717, 719–20 (1st Cir. 2007) (noting prevailing rule); *Donovan v. Maine*, 276 F.3d 87, 91 (1st Cir. 2002) (same).

[90]*See* Rule 6(d); *see also* Rule 5(b)(2)(D). *See also* Rule 6(e) advisory committee note to 2001 amendments.

[91]*See* Rule 6(a)(1) advisory committee note to 2009 amendment.

[92]*See* 28 U.S.C. § 636(b)(1); Rule 72(a) to (b).

[93]*See* 28 U.S.C. § 636(b)(1); Rule

72(a) to (b). *Note:* formerly this period was 10 days, but was enlarged to 14 days in 2009 as part of the "Time Computation" Project. *See* Statutory Time-Periods Tech. Amts. Act of 2009, Pub. L. No. 111-16, § 6(1), 123 Stat. 1607, 1608 (2009).

[94]*See* Rule 72(b) advisory committee's note 1983 Addition; *Vanderberg v. Donaldson*, 259 F.3d 1321, 1325 (11th Cir. 2001); *Lerro v. Quaker Oats Co.*, 84 F.3d 239, 241–42 (7th Cir. 1996).

1998; Time ⊗2 to 15

III. PLEADINGS AND MOTIONS

RULE 7
PLEADINGS ALLOWED; FORM OF MOTIONS AND OTHER PAPERS

(a) Pleadings. Only these pleadings are allowed:

  (1) a complaint;

  (2) an answer to a complaint;

  (3) an answer to a counterclaim designated as a counterclaim;

  (4) an answer to a crossclaim;

  (5) a third-party complaint;

  (6) an answer to a third-party complaint; and

  (7) if the court orders one, a reply to an answer.

(b) Motions and Other Papers.

  (1) *In General.* A request for a court order must be made by motion. The motion must:

    (A) be in writing unless made during a hearing or trial;

    (B) state with particularity the grounds for seeking the order; and

    (C) state the relief sought.

  (2) *Form.* The rules governing captions and other matters of form in pleadings apply to motions and other papers.

[Amended effective March 19, 1948; July 1, 1963; August 1, 1983; April 30, 2007, effective December 1, 2007.]

AUTHORS' COMMENTARY ON RULE 7

—— PURPOSE AND SCOPE ——

Rule 7 lists the pleadings permitted in federal court, and sets forth the general requirements for the form of motions. The provisions of this Rule are often supplemented extensively by local rules, which practitioners should consult carefully.

Impact of the 2007 "Restyling" Amendments

Former Rule 7(c), which noted the abolition of demurrers, pleas, and exceptions, was deleted as no longer necessary. Researchers searching for Rule 7(c) and its interpretative caselaw should note this deletion.

RULE 7(a)—PLEADINGS PERMITTED AND REPLIES

CORE CONCEPT

Rule 7(a) lists the six types of pleadings that may be filed in federal court: (1) a complaint; (2) an answer to a complaint; (3) a reply to a counterclaim, if the counterclaim is so designated; (4) an answer to a crossclaim; (5) a third-party complaint; and (6) a third-party answer. In addition to these six pleadings, the court may, in its discretion, order a reply to an answer, a third-party answer, or a counterclaim answer.

APPLICATIONS

Not Pleadings

The list in Rule 7(a) is exhaustive.[1] Assuming no counterclaim or crossclaim is filed, the pleadings in a typical case are considered closed once a complaint and answer have been filed.[2] Consequently, the following documents—which do not appear in the Rule 7(a) list—are *not* "pleadings": a writ, a motion to dismiss,[3] a motion for summary judgment,[4] a motion for reconsideration,[5] a motion for sanctions,[6] a motion to stay,[7] an "informative" motion,[8] a response to a motion,[9] a "suggestion" under Rule 12(h)(3) of a lack of subject matter jurisdiction, a brief or memorandum,[10] a reply brief or memorandum,[11] a supplemental

---

[1]See *A. Bauer Mech., Inc. v. Joint Arbitration Bd. of Plumbing Contractors' Ass'n & Chicago Journeymen Plumbers' Local Union 130*, 562 F.3d 784, 790 (7th Cir. 2009); *Yuhasz v. Brush Wellman, Inc.*, 341 F.3d 559, 569 (6th Cir. 2003).

[2]See *Doe v. U.S.*, 419 F.3d 1058, 1061 (9th Cir. 2005); *Wedgewood Ltd. P'ship I. v. Township of Liberty, Ohio*, 456 F. Supp. 2d 904, 917 (S.D. Ohio 2006).

[3]See *Richardson v. Stanley Works, Inc.*, 597 F.3d 1288, 1297 (Fed.Cir. 2010); *Merritt v. Fogel*, 349 Fed.Appx. 742, 745 (3d Cir. 2009).

[4]See *Principal Health Care of Louisiana, Inc. v. Lewer Agency, Inc.*, 38 F.3d 240, 244 (5th Cir. 1994); *Circle Group, L.L.C. v. Southeastern Carpenters Reg'l Council*, 836 F.Supp.2d 1327, 1347 (N.D.Ga. 2011).

[5]See *Schneller v. Fox Subacute at Clara Burke*, 368 Fed.Appx. 275, 278 (3d Cir. 2010).

[6]See *Phinney v. Paulshock*, 181 F.R.D. 185 (D.N.H. 1998), aff'd, 199 F.3d 1 (1st Cir. 1999).

[7]See *Nanosolutions, LLC v. Prajza*, 793 F.Supp. 2d 46, 52 (D.D.C. 2011).

[8]See *Colon v. Blades*, 268 F.R.D. 143, 146 (D.P.R. 2010).

[9]See *Deegan v. Strategic Azimuth LLC*, 768 F.Supp.2d 107, 112 (D.D.C. 2011); *Crisco v. Lockheed Martin Corp.*, 2010 WL 3119170, at *2 n.2 (N.D.Tex. Aug. 4, 2010).

[10]See *Gibson v. United Airlines*,

brief,[12] exhibits to briefs,[13] "freestanding" or "stand-alone" counterclaims and crossclaims not included in an answer,[14] summary judgment statements,[15] discovery papers,[16] a notice of appeal,[17] a notice of removal,[18] affidavits,[19] declarations,[20] expert reports and testimony,[21] a certificate or affidavit of merit,[22] and court-ordered "reports".[23]

Definitions

(1) *Complaint:* A complaint is the document that sets forth either the initial plaintiff's claim for relief or a third-party plaintiff's claim for relief. There can be only one operative version of a complaint in a federal civil action; amended complaints supplant their predecessors.[24]

(2) *Answer:* An answer is the document that sets forth a defendant's opposition to a complaint, a counterclaim, a crossclaim, or a third-party complaint.[25]

(3) *Counterclaim:* A counterclaim is that portion of an answer that sets forth a defendant's or third-party defendant's claims against the original plaintiff or third-party plaintiff.

Inc., 783 F. Supp. 2d 983, 994 (E.D.Mich. 2011); *Chase Manhattan Bank v. BCE Mobile Comm'cns Inc.*, 722 F.Supp.2d 505, 506 (D.Del. 2010).

[11] *See Nwachukwu v. Rooney*, 362 F. Supp. 2d 183, 190 (D.D.C. 2005).

[12] *See Dassault Systemes, S.A. v. Childress*, 2010 WL 2854339, at *2 (E.D.Mich. July 20, 2010), *vacated on other grounds*, 663 F.3d 832 (6th Cir. 2011).

[13] *See Albertson v. Fremont County*, 834 F.Supp.2d 1117, 1123 n.3 (D.Idaho 2011); *Gibson v. United Airlines, Inc.*, 783 F. Supp. 2d 983, 994 (E.D.Mich. 2011).

[14] *See Columbia Gas Transmission LLC v. Crawford*, 267 F.R.D. 227 (N.D.Ohio 2010) (freestanding counterclaims); *State Farm Mut. Auto. Ins. Co. v. Mathis*, 2009 WL 5065685, at *1 (N.D.Okla. Dec. 16, 2009) (standalone crossclaims).

[15] *See DeSouza v. EGL Eagle Global Logistics LP*, 596 F.Supp.2d 456, 459 (D.Conn. 2009).

[16] *See Carlson v. Reed*, 249 F.3d 876, 878 n.1 (9th Cir. 2001) (interrogatories are not pleadings).

[17] *See Adkins v. Safeway, Inc.*, 985 F.2d 1101, 1102 (D.C. Cir. 1993).

[18] *See Ellenburg v. Spartan Motors Chassis, Inc.*, 519 F.3d 192, 199 (4th Cir. 2008).

[19] *See Ojeda v. Louisville Ladder Inc.*, 410 Fed.Appx. 213, 216 (11th Cir. 2010); *Gibson v. United Airlines, Inc.*, 783 F. Supp. 2d 983, 994 (E.D.Mich. 2011).

[20] *See Granger v. Gill Abstract Corp.*, 566 F. Supp. 2d 323, 334–35 (S.D. N.Y. 2008); *Finke v. Kirtland Community College Bd. of Trustees*, 359 F. Supp. 2d 593, 596–97 (E.D. Mich. 2005).

[21] *See MJ Harbor Hotel, LLC v. McCormick & Schmick Restaurant Corp.*, 599 F.Supp.2d 612, 623 (D.Md. 2009).

[22] *See Liggon-Redding v. Estate of Sugarman*, 659 F.3d 258, 265 n.5 (3d Cir. 2011).

[23] *See Burns v. Lawther*, 53 F.3d 1237 (11th Cir.1995) (in prisoner civil rights case, special, pre-answer reports).

[24] *See, e.g., In re Wireless Telephone Federal Cost Recovery Fees Litigation*, 396 F.3d 922, 928 (8th Cir. 2005); *Pintando v. Miami-Dade Housing Agency*, 501 F.3d 1241, 1243 (11th Cir. 2007).

[25] *See LeBoeuf, Lamb, Greene & MacRae, L.L.P. v. Worsham*, 185 F.3d 61, 66–67 (2d Cir. 1999) (noting that responsive pleading (an answer) is required to a complaint).

(4) *Crossclaim:* A crossclaim is that portion of an answer that sets forth one defendant's claims against one or more co-defendants. In many cases, defendants crossclaim against one another for indemnification or contribution. [*Note:* although answers to crossclaims (like answers to counterclaims) are listed as pleadings, the crossclaims themselves (and counterclaims as well) are *not* pleadings — this is because both crossclaims and counterclaims are usually included in the answer.][26]

(5) *Reply:* A reply is the pleading by which a party responds to an answer, a counterclaim answer, a crossclaim answer, or a third-party answer.[27] Replies are not permitted as of right; a court order is required before a party may file a reply.[28] New matter pleaded in an answer (to which a reply would typically respond) is deemed automatically denied or avoided under the Rules.[29]

Note: Practitioners may encounter answers that include an averment designated as a "counterclaim" but which, in reality, is actually only an affirmative defense. Although responses are only required to bona fide counterclaims, practitioners should reply to all labeled "counterclaims"—whether they appear facially proper or not—to avoid any risk that the averments might be deemed admitted.

Motion to Permit or Compel a Reply

To be granted leave to file a reply, or to compel such a filing by another litigant, the moving party must make a clear and convincing showing that substantial reason or extraordinary circumstances require a reply.[30] Courts may permit or compel a reply to an answer for several reasons: when a type of new matter is pleaded in the answer that might affect the outcome of the trial or might otherwise greatly broaden the issues in the case, when the information sought through the reply cannot be acquired through discovery, when a misdesignated affirmative defense must be answered or clarified, or when the case otherwise should not proceed without a reply.

Note: More recently, courts have required that plaintiffs in federal civil rights cases file specific and particularized replies when the defendants are public officials and assert

---

[26]*See In re Cessna Distrib'ship Antitrust Litig.*, 532 F.2d 64, 67 (8th Cir. 1976).

[27]*See* Rule 7(a)(7). *See also* Rule 7 advisory committee note from 2007.

[28]*See, e.g., Mihos v. Swift*, 358 F.3d 91, 106 (1st Cir. 2004); *U.S. v. Shanbaum*, 10 F.3d 305, 312 n. 4 (5th Cir. 1994); *Sevcik v. Unlimited Const. Services, Inc.*, 462 F. Supp. 2d 1140, 1143 n.1 (D. Haw. 2006).

[29]*See* Rule 8(b)(6). *See also United States v. Clayton*, 465 B.R. 72, 80–81 (M.D.N.C. 2011); *In re Enron Corp. Secs., Derivative & "'ERISA" Litig.*, 540 F. Supp. 2d 759, 795–96 (S.D. Tex. 2007).

[30]*See Moviecolor Limited v. Eastman Kodak Co.*, 24 F.R.D. 325 (S.D. N.Y. 1959).

qualified immunity as an affirmative defense.[31]

RULE 7(b)—MOTIONS AND OTHER PAPERS

CORE CONCEPT

Rule 7(b) sets the broad, national procedures for motion practice in the federal courts.

APPLICATIONS

Motion Defined

A motion is a request to the court, usually submitted in writing, that seeks an order.[32] A letter to the court ordinarily does not qualify as a motion.[33]

WARNING: Consult the Local Rules

Nearly every district has promulgated local rules governing motion practice before their courts and, in some instances, individual judges have issued "standing orders" for their chambers or case-specific orders regulating such particulars as the time for and method of responding to motions, page limitations for motions and responses, the proper form for such filings, the acceptability of "reply briefs", chambers' policies on courtesy copies for the judge, the number of motion copies that must be submitted, and the scheduling of oral arguments. Practitioners should always consult the local rules of court and chambers' standing orders to locate any unique procedures for motion practice within a specific district.

Rules Governing Pleading Forms Also Apply to Motions

The Rules that govern the styling of captions and the form of pleadings also apply to motions.[34]

---

[31]*See Crawford-El v. Britton*, 523 U.S. 574, 118 S. Ct. 1584, 140 L. Ed. 2d 759 (1998) (commenting that trial court may order a reply to an answer that asserts a public official's qualified immunity, to protect the substance of the defense by compelling the plaintiff to aver some "specific, nonconclusory factual allegations" that demonstrate improper motive); *Reyes v. Sazan*, 168 F.3d 158, 161 (5th Cir. 1999) (commenting that trial courts, when faced with sparse details of claimed wrongdoing alleged against public officials, should routinely require plaintiffs to file a reply under Rule 7(a) to qualified immunity defenses).

[32]*See U.S. ex rel. Atkins v. McInteer*, 470 F.3d 1350, 1361 (11th Cir. 2006); *In re Vogel Van & Storage, Inc.*, 59 F.3d 9, 12 (2d Cir. 1995).

[33]*See Mortensen v. Nevens*, 2011 WL 772885, at *1 (D.Nev. Feb. 25, 2011). *See also Keith v. Mayes*, 2010 WL 3339041, at *2 n.2 (S.D.Ga. Aug. 23, 2010) ("This is a Court of record, not a pen pal. Such requests must be made by motion.").

[34]This directive is not a license for creative lawyering designed to evade either the requirements of other Rules or the express instructions of the court. *See Swanson v. U.S. Forest Service*, 87 F.3d 339, 345 (9th Cir. 1996) (when court denied counsel the right to file an overlength motion brief, counsel could not escape this ruling by relying on Rule 7(b)(2) to justify the "incorporation by reference" under Rule 10(c) of an additional 69 pages of argument contained in earlier filings).

Formal Requirements for Motions

All motions must be in writing, unless they are presented during a hearing or trial.[35] A written "notice of hearing" on the motion will satisfy this requirement.

Form: Written motions must comply with the requirements of Rule 10—they must include a caption listing the name of the court, the title of the action, the docket number, and the title of the motion.

Contents: Written motions must set forth "with particularity" the grounds for seeking the order and the relief sought.[36] This particularity requirement ensures that the court and the adversary receive ample notice of both the relief sought and the moving party's reasoning, so that the court fully understands the motion and the adversary has a meaningful opportunity to respond.[37] The Rule is given liberal application,[38] and "ritualistic detail" is not required.[39] But the court expects reasonable particularity,[40] and will examine the supporting memoranda in making that determination.[41] In fact, if the motion is insufficiently particularized, but references another filed document, the court may examine that document in assessing particularity[42] (but the court will not weigh materials submitted after the filing period, since to do so would defeat the Rule's notice goal).[43] In making this particularity assessment, the court will consider whether any party is prejudiced by the motion's form and whether it can rule fairly on the motion.[44] Requests for relief made in a passing comment, a stray sentence to a brief, or a footnote

---

[35]*See Contech Const. Prods., Inc. v. Heierli,* 764 F.Supp.2d 96, 106 (D.D.C. 2011).

[36]*See Contech Const. Prods., Inc. v. Heierli,* 764 F.Supp.2d 96, 106 (D.D.C. 2011).

[37]*See Elustra v. Mineo,* 595 F.3d 699, 708 (7th Cir. 2010); *Hinz v. Neuroscience, Inc.,* 538 F.3d 979, 983 (8th Cir. 2008); *Feldberg v. Quechee Lakes Corp.,* 463 F.3d 195, 197 (2d Cir. 2006).

[38]*See Hinz v. Neuroscience, Inc.,* 538 F.3d 979, 983 (8th Cir. 2008); *Intera Corp. v. Henderson,* 428 F.3d 605, 612–14 (6th Cir. 2005).

[39]*See Kelly v. Moore,* 376 F.3d 481, 484 (5th Cir. 2004). *See also Elustra v. Mineo,* 595 F.3d 699, 707–08 (7th Cir. 2010) (handwritten note, reading: "I never aggred [sic] to settlement vacate order Dec 11-08 and reinstate case", though simple, complied

with each requirement of Rule 7(b)).

[40]*See Fort James Corp. v. Solo Cup Co.,* 412 F.3d 1340, 1347 (Fed. Cir. 2005); *Talano v. Northwestern Medical Faculty Found., Inc.,* 273 F.3d 757, 760 (7th Cir. 2001). *See also Allender v. Raytheon Aircraft Co.,* 439 F.3d 1236, 1240 (10th Cir. 2006) ("reasonable specification" required).

[41]*See Lac Du Flambeau Band of Lake Superior Chippewa Indians v. State of Wis.,* 957 F.2d 515, 516 (7th Cir. 1992) (simultaneously filed brief satisfied Rule 7(b)'s particularity requirement).

[42]*See Fort James Corp. v. Solo Cup Co.,* 412 F.3d 1340, 1347 (Fed. Cir. 2005).

[43]*See Hinz v. Neuroscience, Inc.,* 538 F.3d 979, 983 (8th Cir. 2008).

[44]*See Cambridge Plating Co., Inc. v. Napco, Inc.,* 85 F.3d 752, 760 (1st Cir. 1996).

are likely to fail the particularity test.[45] A motion that fails that test may be dismissed or denied.[46]

- *Consequences:* A motion that fails to satisfy these requirements may be deemed a nullity, with disastrous consequences.[47]

- *Motions to Amend:* When a party submits a motion to amend, the particularity requirement may require the party to attach to the motion a copy of the proposed amended pleading, unless the motion sets forth the substance of or otherwise adequately describes the contemplated revision.[48] Informal amendment requests—unaccompanied by the proposed amended pleading itself or a summary of its substance—do not conform to Rule 7(b) and may be refused for that reason.[49]

Supporting Memorandum or Brief: Rule 7 does not expressly require a party to submit a supporting memorandum or brief along with motions or oppositions to motions.[50] Note, however, that many districts have promulgated local rules requiring supporting memoranda, and providing that a motion lacking such support may be dismissed.

Form of Order: Many local rules obligate the moving party to attach a form of order to the motion which, if signed and entered, would grant the relief requested in the motion. Similarly, the party opposing a motion may be required to attach a form of order which would deny the requested relief.

---

[45]*See Cozzarelli v. Inspire Pharms. Inc.*, 549 F.3d 618, 630–31 (4th Cir. 2008) (request in footnote and final sentence not sufficient); *Gray v. Evercore Restructuring L.L.C.*, 544 F.3d 320, 327 (1st Cir. 2008) (concluding comment, requesting other relief in the alternative, not sufficient); *Frees v. Duby*, 2010 WL 4923535, at *2 (W.D.Mich. Nov. 29, 2010) ("Judges are not like pigs, hunting for truffles buried in briefs.") (quotation omitted).

[46]*See, e.g., Evans v. Pearson Enterprises, Inc.*, 434 F.3d 839, 853 (6th Cir. 2006); *Butler v. Coral Volkswagen, Inc.*, 804 F.2d 612, 614–15 (11th Cir. 1986). Cf. *Hopkins v. Bowen*, 850 F.2d 417, 420 (8th Cir. 1988) (memorandum in support of summary judgment considered a "motion" for summary judgment where it described particular grounds for the motion, prayed for specific relief, provided the opponent sufficient opportunity to respond, and caused no prejudice).

[47]*See Elustra v. Mineo*, 595 F.3d 699, 707 (7th Cir. 2010) (improperly skeletal post-trial motions do not

postpone time for taking an appeal); *Moore v. American Family Mut. Ins. Co.*, 576 F.3d 781, 785 (8th Cir. 2009) (insufficiently particularized post-trial motion preserves nothing for appellate review).

[48]*See DelRio-Mocci v. Connolly Props. Inc.*, 672 F.3d 241, 251 (3d Cir. 2012); *Rosenberg v. Gould*, 554 F.3d 962, 967 (11th Cir. 2009).

[49]*See Benoit v. U.S. Dep't of Agriculture*, 608 F.3d 17, 21 (D.C.Cir. 2010) (unwritten, one-sentence, conditional suggestion not sufficient); *Cozzarelli v. Inspire Pharms. Inc.*, 549 F.3d 618, 630–31 (4th Cir. 2008) (request in footnote and closing sentence not sufficient); *Gray v. Evercore Restructuring L.L.C.*, 544 F.3d 320, 327 (1st Cir. 2008) (conclusory, passing request with no particular grounds not sufficient).

[50]*See Star Mark Mgmt., Inc. v. Koon Chun Hing Kee Soy & Sauce Factory, Ltd.*, 682 F.3d 170, 176–77 (2d Cir. 2012) (noting that "motion" is different than a memorandum).

Attaching Affidavits and Other Exhibits: A party may support a motion with affidavits or other materials. Practitioners are cautioned, however, that such attachments can have substantial procedural consequences.[51]

Signing: The written motion must be signed in accordance with Rule 11 by the party's counsel or, if unrepresented, by the party herself. If the motion is not signed after the omission is called to the attention of the party or the party's counsel, the court may strike the document.

Service: A signed copy of the motion or "notice of hearing" must be served upon counsel for represented parties or, if unrepresented, upon the party herself. Unless the court directs otherwise, service must be accomplished not later than 14 days prior to the hearing on the motion.[52]

- *Certificate of Service:* The motion must contain a certificate of service verifying that the document was served.[53]

Filing: The written motion or "notice of hearing" must be filed within a reasonable time after service.[54] Note, however, that local rules may prescribe other, supplemental filing requirements.

Opposing Written Motions

Rule 7 contains no requirement that an opponent file an "answer" to any motion and, absent local rule requirements to the contrary, a motion can be opposed solely by filing a brief or memorandum. The form, signing, filing, and service requirements for motions are generally applicable to oppositions as well.

Withdrawing Written Motions

A written motion should ordinarily be withdrawn with the same formality with which it was filed. Consequently, written motions should be withdrawn in writing.[55]

Hearings and Arguments on Written Motions

The court may, in its discretion, schedule a motion for a hearing or oral argument. Neither is expressly required under the Rules, although local rule provisions may specify additional hearing and argument requirements. Hearings held *ex parte* (without notice to the opponent) are generally discouraged and are permitted only in exceptional circumstances, such as ap-

---

[51]*See, e.g.,* Rule 12(d) (if matters outside the pleadings are presented to, and considered by, the court on a Rule 12(b)(6) motion to dismiss or Rule 12(c) motion for judgment on the pleadings, court must convert motion into Rule 56 motion for summary judgment).

[52]*See* Rule 5 and Rule 6(c).

[53]*See* Rule 5(d)(1).

[54]*See* Rule 5(d)(1).

[55]*See United Coin Meter Co., Inc. v. Seaboard Coastline RR.,* 705 F.2d 839, 843 (6th Cir. 1983).

plications for temporary restraining orders.[56]

Oral Motions

Oral motions may be made, so long as they are raised in open court at a hearing or trial.[57] This presentation will satisfy the writing requirement of Rule 7 if the oral motion is transcribed or otherwise recorded.[58] This "writing" requirement for oral motions functions to ensure that the motion is accurately memorialized and that both the court and the opponent have sufficient opportunity to prepare for the motion.[59]

Amendments to Motions

A party may seek leave to amend a motion. Leave is generally granted if the amendment is sought before the opponent has filed the opposition memorandum or brief, before the court has entertained oral argument, and before a ruling has been issued. Motions are amended, rather than just refiled, where a new, replacement motion would be improper or out of time.[60]

Additional Research References

Wright & Miller, *Federal Practice and Procedure* §§ 1181 to 1200
C.J.S., Federal Civil Procedure § 124, §§ 247 to 280 et seq., §§ 301 to 319 et seq., §§ 363 to 375 et seq.
West's Key Number Digest, Federal Civil Procedure ☞295, ☞621 to 665, ☞671 to 680, ☞731 to 745, ☞771 to 786, ☞903, ☞921 to 928

---

[56]*See* Rule 65(b).

[57]*See Meriwether v. Coughlin*, 879 F.2d 1037, 1042 (2d Cir. 1989) (noting that, because oral motion was asserted in open court, written document not required). *See also Kerry Steel, Inc. v. Paragon Industries, Inc.*, 106 F.3d 147, 154 (6th Cir. 1997) (noting that Rules allow motions at hearings, and refusing to hold as significant the attorney's omission of the utterance: "I move").

[58]*See Atchison, Topeka & Santa Fe Ry. Co. v. California State Bd. of Equalization*, 102 F.3d 425, 427 (9th Cir. 1996); *People of State of Ill. ex rel.*

Hartigan v. Peters, 871 F.2d 1336, 1341 (7th Cir. 1989).

[59]*See Taragan v. Eli Lilly and Co., Inc.*, 838 F.2d 1337, 1340–41 (D.C. Cir. 1988) (requirement of adequate opportunity to prepare and respond satisfied by oral motions if they are germane to hearing or trial).

[60]*See, e.g.,* Rule 12(g) and 12(h) (providing that defenses of improper personal jurisdiction, lack of venue, insufficient process, or inadequate service of process are deemed waived if not asserted in original Rule 12(b) motion).

RULE 7.1
DISCLOSURE STATEMENT

(a) Who Must File; Contents. A nongovernmental corporate party must file two copies of a disclosure statement that:

    (1) identifies any parent corporation and any publicly held corporation owning 10% or more of its stock; or

    (2) states that there is no such corporation.

(b) Time to File; Supplemental Filing. A party must:

    (1) file the disclosure statement with its first appearance, pleading, petition, motion, response, or other request addressed to the court; and

    (2) promptly file a supplemental statement if any required information changes.

[Added April 29, 2002, effective December 1, 2002; April 30, 2007, effective December 1, 2007.]

AUTHORS' COMMENTARY ON RULE 7.1

PURPOSE AND SCOPE

Rule 7.1 was added to the Rules in 2002 to help assist district judges in making properly informed decisions on whether certain financial interests require their disqualification in particular cases.

CORE CONCEPT

Rule 7.1 is modeled after Rule 26.1 of the Federal Rules of Appellate Procedure,[1] and requires specific financial disclosures by all non-governmental corporate parties to an action or proceeding in district court.[2] The Rule is intended to provide the appropriate level of financial disclosures necessary to allow for properly informed judicial recusal decisions in those circumstances where

---

[1] *See* Rule 7.1 advisory committee note to 2002 amendments. *See also* Fed. R. App. P. 26.1 (setting forth filing requirements for "Corporate Disclosure Statements").

[2] Rule 7.1(a).

automatic financial interest disqualification is compelled.[3]

APPLICATIONS

Automatic Financial Interest Disqualifications

Rule 7.1 was not designed to cover all circumstances that might call for a district judge's recusal.[4] Instead, the information compelled by Rule 7.1 reflects the financial interest standard for automatic disqualification under the Code of Conduct for United States Judges.[5]

Disclosure Procedures

The disclosure obligation applies to non-governmental corporate litigants. (Parties who are not corporations have no disclosure duty under this Rule.)[6] Disclosing parties must file with the court a written statement that either (1) identifies each parent corporation and publicly held corporation owning 10% or more of their stock, *or* (2) states that no such corporation exists.[7] Two copies of the statement must be filed.[8]

Timing

The disclosure is due when a party files its first appearance, pleading, petition, motion, response, or other request addressed to the court[9] (although at least one court has ruled that the disclosure is not an absolute precondition for filing a disposi-

---

[3] *See* Rule 7.1 advisory committee note to 2002 amendments (explaining that Rule strikes balance between requiring adequate amount of financial information and more detailed disclosures that "will be difficult", would unnecessarily "place a burden on the parties and on the courts", and "create a risk that a judge will overlook the one bit of information that might require disqualification, and also may create a risk that unnecessary disqualifications will be made rather than attempt to unravel a potentially difficult question"). *See also Rubio v. BNSF Railway Co.*, 548 F. Supp. 2d 1220, 1227 (D.N.M. 2008) (purpose of statement "is to allow judges to determine whether they should recuse themselves"); *Gebhart v. Raytheon Aircraft Co.*, 2004 WL 1212047, at *2 n.13 (D. Kan. 2004) (statement is required "so that the assigned judge can ascertain whether he or she has a financial interest in the party or associated entities, which would require recusal").

[4] *See* Rule 7.1 advisory committee note to 2002 amendments.

[5] *See* Rule 7.1 advisory committee note to 2002 amendments. *See also* Code of Conduct for United States Judges at Canon 3C(1)(c) ("A judge shall disqualify himself or herself in a proceeding in which the judge's impartiality might reasonably be questioned, including but not limited to instances in which . . . (c) the judge knows that the judge, individually or as a fiduciary, or the judge's spouse or minor child residing in the judge's household, has a financial interest in the subject matter in controversy or in a party to the proceeding, or any other interest that could be affected substantially by the outcome of the proceeding").

[6] *See Bardfield v. Chisholm Props. Circuit Events, LLC*, 2010 WL 2278461, at *5 (N.D.Fla. May 4, 2010), *recommendation adopted*, 2010 WL 2278459 (N.D.Fla. June 4, 2010) (individuals have no Rule 7.1 duty).

[7] *See* Rule 7.1(a).

[8] *See* Rule 7.1(a).

[9] *See* Rule 7.1(b)(1).

tive motion).[10] Whether the statement must also be served on the parties is unclear; nothing in the Rule directly addresses this question.[11]

Supplementing the Statement

Parties are also obligated under the Rule to "promptly" file a supplemental statement when any change in the required information occurs.[12]

More Extensive Disclosures Under Local Rules

Local rules may require additional disclosures (and those regional experiences along with advances in electronic technology may one day justify additional National disclosures and an amendment to this Rule).[13]

Effect of Non-Filing

Courts have excused a party's failure to file, or timely file, its Rule 7.1 disclosure statement, especially when the omission causes no prejudice and is promptly corrected.[14] However, a persistent failure to file the disclosure statement (particularly when pressed by the court) could result in contempt,[15] dismissal,[16] striking appearance and jury demand,[17] or other sanctions.[18]

Collateral Effects of Statement

Both litigants and the courts have used disclosure statements and the information they contain for various collateral purposes. Content from the statements has been offered for the

---

[10]*See Feller v. Indymac Mortg. Servs.*, 2010 WL 342187, at *2 (W.D.Wash. Jan. 26, 2010).

[11]*See Plotzker v. Lamberth*, 2008 WL 4706255, at *12 (W.D.Va. 2008) (holding that service is not required because statements are only "intended to be used by judges in determining whether disqualification is necessary").

[12]*See* Rule 7.1(b)(2).

[13]*See* Rule 7.1 advisory committee note to 2002 amendments.

[14]*See Ameriprise Fin. Servs., Inc. v. Koenig*, 2012 WL 379940, at *8 n.9 (D.N.J. Feb. 6, 2012) (refusing to deny injunction because of missing disclosure); *Russell v. BAC Home Loans Servicing, LP*, 2011 WL 3861526, at *3 (D.Haw. Aug. 10, 2011) (refusing to "dismiss" notice of removal because of missing disclosure), *adopted*, 2011 WL 3861432 (D.Haw. Aug. 30, 2011); *Ferro Corp. v. Continental Cas. Co.*, 2007 WL 120761, at *1–*2 (N.D. Ohio. Jan. 10, 2007) (refusing to remand because

of missing disclosure); *Smith v. Argent Mortg. Co., LLC*, 2006 WL 581157, at *1 (D.Colo. Mar. 7, 2006) (refusing to strike motion to dismiss because of missing disclosure).

[15]*See American Gen. Life Ins. Co. v. Lawson Bros. Trucking Co.*, 2008 WL 4899425, at *1 (S.D.Ill. 2008) (holding attorney-of-record in contempt and directing $100 per day fine to accrue against him until disclosure statement filed).

[16]*See Medmarc Cas. Ins. Co. v. Sterling & Dowling PC*, 2010 WL 3747754, at *1 (S.D.Ill. Sept. 20, 2010) (threatening non-compliant party with dismissal).

[17]*See Hanratty v. Watson*, 2010 WL 3522996, at *1 (S.D.Ill. Sept. 2, 2010) (threatening non-compliant party with these strikes).

[18]*See Feezor v. Big 5 Corp.*, 2010 WL 308751, at *1–*3 (E.D.Cal. Jan. 15, 2010) (imposing modest monetary sanction on non-disclosing defendant).

court's consideration in ruling on remand motions[19] and on motions to dismiss.[20] One court used a disclosure statement to resolve a dispute concerning a draft settlement agreement,[21] and another court ordered that a plaintiff be judicially estopped from substituting another party-plaintiff due, in part, to confusion created by a delinquent Statement.[22] But other courts have been more reluctant to give disclosure statements broad collateral use. They have refused to rely on a disclosure statement for the substitution of parties or an amendment to a complaint,[23] and have rejected a disclosure statement as consent to removal.[24]

---

[19] *See Modern Indus. Firebrick Corp. v. Shenango Inc.*, 2012 WL 2405236, at *2 (W.D.N.Y. June 25, 2012); *Mazzolin v. Lehman Bros. Real Estate Fund III, L.P.*, 2011 WL 4435649, at *2 (N.D.Ill. Sept. 23, 2011).

[20] *See Little v. Stock Bldg. Supply, LLC*, 2011 WL 5149145, at *7 (E.D.N.C. Oct. 28, 2011).

[21] *See Ha v. Deutsche Bank New Jersey Services, Inc.*, 2005 WL 589408, at *2 (S.D. N.Y. 2005).

[22] *See Engines Southwest, Inc. v. Kohler Co.*, 2006 WL 1896071 (W.D. La. 2006).

[23] *See Gebhart v. Raytheon Aircraft Co.*, 2004 WL 1212047, at *2 (D. Kan. 2004).

[24] *See Royal v. Fontenot*, 2010 WL 4068868, at *3–*4 (W.D.La. Oct. 14, 2010).

RULE 8
GENERAL RULES OF PLEADING

(a) Claim for Relief. A pleading that states a claim for relief must contain:

   (1) a short and plain statement of the grounds for the court's jurisdiction, unless the court already has jurisdiction and the claim needs no new jurisdictional support;

   (2) a short and plain statement of the claim showing that the pleader is entitled to relief; and

   (3) a demand for the relief sought, which may include relief in the alternative or different types of relief.

(b) Defenses; Admissions and Denials.

   (1) *In General.* In responding to a pleading, a party must:

     (A) state in short and plain terms its defenses to each claim asserted against it; and

     (B) admit or deny the allegations asserted against it by an opposing party.

   (2) *Denials—Responding to the Substance.* A denial must fairly respond to the substance of the allegation.

   (3) *General and Specific Denials.* A party that intends in good faith to deny all the allegations of a pleading—including the jurisdictional grounds—may do so by a general denial. A party that does not intend to deny all the allegations must either specifically deny designated allegations or generally deny all except those specifically admitted.

   (4) *Denying Part of an Allegation.* A party that intends in good faith to deny only part of an allegation must admit the part that is true and deny the rest.

   (5) *Lacking Knowledge or Information.* A party that lacks knowledge or information sufficient to form a belief about the truth of an allegation must so

state, and the statement has the effect of a denial.

    (6) *Effect of Failing to Deny.* An allegation—other than one relating to the amount of damages—is admitted if a responsive pleading is required and the allegation is not denied. If a responsive pleading is not required, an allegation is considered denied or avoided.

(c) Affirmative Defenses.

    (1) *In General.* In responding to a pleading, a party must affirmatively state any avoidance or affirmative defense, including:

- accord and satisfaction;
- arbitration and award;
- assumption of risk;
- contributory negligence;
- duress;
- estoppel;
- failure of consideration;
- fraud;
- illegality;
- injury by fellow servant;
- laches;
- license;
- payment;
- release;
- res judicata;
- statute of frauds;
- statute of limitations; and
- waiver.

    (2) *Mistaken Designation.* If a party mistakenly designates a defense as a counterclaim, or a counterclaim as a defense, the court must, if justice requires, treat the pleading as though it were correctly designated, and may impose terms for doing so.

(d) Pleading to Be Concise and Direct; Alternative Statements; Inconsistency.

    (1) *In General.* Each allegation must be simple, concise, and direct. No technical form is required.

(2) *Alternative Statements of a Claim or Defense.* A party may set out two or more statements of a claim or defense alternatively or hypothetically, either in a single count or defense or in separate ones. If a party makes alternative statements, the pleading is sufficient if any one of them is sufficient.

(3) *Inconsistent Claims or Defenses.* A party may state as many separate claims or defenses as it has, regardless of consistency.

(e) Construing Pleadings. Pleadings must be construed so as to do justice.

[Amended effective July 1, 1966; August 1, 1987; April 30, 2007, effective December 1, 2007; April 28, 2010 effective December 1, 2010.]

AUTHORS' COMMENTARY ON RULE 8

PURPOSE AND SCOPE

Rule 8 establishes the "notice" pleading protocol for the federal courts. It sets the requirements for pleading claims and defenses, and outlines both the procedures for proper denials and the consequences for failing to deny. Rule 8 entitles pleaders to allege claims or defenses alternatively, hypothetically, or inconsistently—provided the pleading complies with the requirements of Rule 11. In federal court, pleadings are construed liberally so as to do justice.

RULE 8(a)—CLAIMS FOR RELIEF

CORE CONCEPT

In a "short" and "plain" statement, a party asserting a claim must include: (1) the grounds for the court's jurisdiction; (2) a statement of a claim showing that the pleader is entitled to relief; and (3) a demand for relief.

APPLICATIONS

Element 1: Grounds for Jurisdiction

A party filing a claim in a complaint, counterclaim, cross-claim, or third-party complaint must state in short and plain terms the basis for the court's subject matter jurisdiction for each count.[1]

- *Diversity Jurisdiction:* When jurisdiction is based on diversity of citizenship,[2] the plaintiff must allege: (1) the citizenship of each party (*e.g.,* for individuals, their State of citizenship; for corporations, their State of incorporation *and* their principal place of business); and (2) that the amount in controversy—exclusive of interest and costs—exceeds $75,000. Although the recent "plausibility" pleading standard has injected uncertainty elsewhere, it appears that properly pleading jurisdiction may still be accomplished by following one or more of the options set in Official Form 7.[3]

- *Federal Question Jurisdiction:* When jurisdiction is based on the presence of a federal question,[4] the claimant must identify the Constitutional provisions, laws, or treaties that create such jurisdiction.

- *Admiralty Jurisdiction:* A claim that has both an admiralty or maritime basis for jurisdiction and another basis for jurisdiction may be brought under either the federal court's specific admiralty jurisdiction or its ordinary jurisdiction. A party wishing to proceed under the rules governing admiralty or maritime claims must include a statement in the complaint that the action is an admiralty or maritime claim within the meaning of Rule 9(h).[5]

- *Supplemental Jurisdiction:* When diversity, federal question, or admiralty/maritime jurisdiction exists as to one or more claims in the complaint, the pleader may allege the right to litigate certain other State-law claims in the same case when those claims are so related to qualifying claims that they form part of the same "case or controversy".[6]

- *Personal Jurisdiction:* Ordinarily, plaintiffs need not allege personal jurisdiction in their complaint; Rule 8(a) requires only that subject matter jurisdiction be alleged.[7]

---

[1]For a discussion of jurisdiction in the federal courts, see §§ 2.1 to 2.13 of this text. *See McNutt v. General Motors Acceptance Corp. of Indiana,* 298 U.S. 178, 189, 56 S. Ct. 780, 785, 80 L. Ed. 1135 (1936) (commenting that pleader "must allege in his pleading the facts essential to show jurisdiction"); *Underwriters at Lloyd's, London v. Osting-Schwinn,* 613 F.3d 1079, 1085–86 (11th Cir. 2010) (party commencing suit has burden of establishing facts supporting federal jurisdiction); *U.S. v. Bustillos,* 31 F.3d 931, 933 (10th Cir. 1994) (must affirmatively allege facts supporting jurisdiction and, if challenged, bear ￪he burden of proving that).

[2]28 U.S.C.A. § 1332.

[3]*See* Form 7—Statement of Jurisdiction (reprinted in Part IV of this text). *See also Harris v. Rand,* 682 F.3d 846, 849–51 (9th Cir. 2012) (ruling that even after *Twombly, Iqbal,* and *Hertz,* following Official Form 7(a) meets the pleader's obligation for alleging a corporation's citizenship for diversity purposes).

[4]28 U.S.C.A. § 1331.

[5]28 U.S.C.A. § 1333.

[6]28 U.S.C.A. § 1367.

[7]*See Merial Ltd. v. Cipla Ltd.,* 681 F.3d 1283, 1296 (Fed.Cir. 2012) (no specific assertion of basis for court's personal jurisdiction over de-

Element 2: Short and Plain Statement of the Claim

The pleader must next state, in short and plain terms, a claim showing an entitlement to relief. This requires pleaders to give their opponents fair notice of their claim and the grounds upon which it rests.[8] Intricately detailed factual allegations are not necessary,[9] nor need pleaders always set out their legal theories[10] (even asserting an incorrect legal theory will not always be fatal).[11] The Rules rely on discovery and summary judgment, rather than pleadings, to flesh out the disputed facts and cull unmeritorious cases.[12] Thus, the Rules generally[13] impose a more lenient pleading obligation than do many State courts.[14]

Although encouraging brevity, the federal pleading duty is far from trivial; the pleading must still contain "enough" to give defendants fair notice of a complaint's claims and the grounds for them.[15] Merely incanting labels, legal conclusions, and the

---

fendant is required); *Caribbean Broadcasting System, Ltd. v. Cable & Wireless P.L.C.*, 148 F.3d 1080, 1090 (D.C. Cir. 1998) (because lack of personal jurisdiction is an affirmative defense, complaint was not required to make specific personal jurisdiction allegations). *See also Purdue Research Foundation v. Sanofi-Synthelabo, S.A.*, 338 F.3d 773, 781–82 (7th Cir. 2003) (complaints need not set forth facts alleging personal jurisdiction).

[8]*See Tellabs, Inc. v. Makor Issues & Rights, Ltd.*, 551 U.S. 308, 319, 127 S. Ct. 2499, 2507, 168 L. Ed. 2d 179 (2007); *Erickson v. Pardus*, 551 U.S. 89, 93, 127 S. Ct. 2197, 2200, 167 L. Ed. 2d 1081 (2007) (per curiam); *Bell Atlantic Corp. v. Twombly*, 550 U.S. 544, 555, 127 S. Ct. 1955, 1964, 167 L. Ed. 2d 929 (2007); *Jones v. Bock*, 549 U.S. 199, 212, 127 S. Ct. 910, 919, 166 L. Ed. 2d 798 (2007).

[9]*See Ashcroft v. Iqbal*, 556 U.S. 662, 678, 129 S.Ct. 1937, 1949, 173 L.Ed.2d 868 (2009); *Bell Atlantic Corp. v. Twombly*, 550 U.S. 544, 555 & 555 n.3, 127 S. Ct. 1955, 1964, 167 L. Ed. 2d 929 (2007).

[10]*See Skinner v. Switzer*, __ U.S. __, __, 131 S.Ct. 1289, 1296 (2011) ("a complaint need not pin plaintiff's claim for relief to a precise legal theory").

[11]*See Williams v. Seniff*, 342 F.3d 774 (7th Cir.2003).

[12]*See Swierkiewicz v. Sorema N.*

A., 534 U.S. 506, 512, 122 S. Ct. 992, 998, 152 L. Ed. 2d 1 (2002).

[13]Note, however, that this liberality is qualified in certain cases (see *Exceptions*, below).

[14]*See Dura Pharmaceuticals, Inc. v. Broudo*, 544 U.S. 336, 347, 125 S. Ct. 1627, 1634, 161 L. Ed. 2d 577 (2005) ("ordinary pleading rules are not meant to impose a great burden upon a plaintiff"); *Fanning v. Potter*, 614 F.3d 845, 851 (8th Cir. 2010) ("not a demanding standard"). *See also Hamilton v. Palm*, 621 F.3d 816, 817 (8th Cir. 2010) (notice pleading standard not abrogated).

[15]*See Tellabs, Inc. v. Makor Issues & Rights, Ltd.*, 551 U.S. 308, 319, 127 S. Ct. 2499, 2507, 168 L. Ed. 2d 179 (2007) ("Although the rule encourages brevity, the complaint must say enough to give the defendant 'fair notice of what the plaintiff's claim is and the grounds upon which it rests' "); *Dura Pharmaceuticals, Inc. v. Broudo*, 544 U.S. 336, 346–47, 125 S. Ct. 1627, 161 L. Ed. 2d 577 (2005) ("We concede that ordinary pleading rules are not meant to impose a great burden upon a plaintiff", but allegations must still give fair notice); *Amron v. Morgan Stanley Inv. Advisors Inc.*, 464 F.3d 338, 343–44 (2d Cir. 2006) ("we stop well short of saying that Plaintiffs bear no burden at the pleading stage", because they must allege "those facts *necessary* to a finding of liability").

formulaic elements of a cause of action is not sufficient.[16] Instead, a claim's allegations must "possess enough heft" to show an entitlement to relief (thus justifying that the costly process of litigation continue).[17] Pleaders must therefore allege sufficient facts to move beyond the level of speculation, to "nudge[] their claims across the line from conceivable to plausible".[18] This "plausibility" line, however, does not require that the claims appear "likely" or "probably" true".[19] Yet, it will bar claims resting on a mere "thread-bare" recital of elements, naked legal conclusions, and "unadorned, the-defendant-unlawfully-harmed-me" accusations.[20] "Plausibility" may also be absent when equivocal factual allegations are equally consistent with both culpable and innocent conduct.[21] In such cases, important factual material is omitted at the pleader's peril.[22]

- *"Plausible" Pleadings:* In *Bell Atlantic Corp. v. Twombly,* the Supreme Court announced the "plausibility" pleading standard (discussed above).[23] In so doing, the Court expressly overruled the oft-quoted, very forgiving pleading mantra from its 1957 decision in *Conley v. Gibson* (namely, that no complaint should be dismissed for failing to properly state a claim "unless it appears beyond

---

[16]*See Ashcroft v. Iqbal,* 556 U.S. 662, 678, 129 S.Ct. 1937, 1949, 173 L.Ed.2d 868 (2009); *Bell Atlantic Corp. v. Twombly,* 550 U.S. 544, 555, 127 S. Ct. 1955, 1964–65, 167 L. Ed. 2d 929 (2007).

[17]*See Bell Atlantic Corp. v. Twombly,* 550 U.S. 544, 557, 127 S. Ct. 1955, 1966, 167 L. Ed. 2d 929 (2007). *See also id.* at 558–59, 127 S.Ct. at 1967 (noting enormous costs of modern discovery).

[18]*See Bell Atlantic Corp. v. Twombly,* 550 U.S. 544, 570, 127 S. Ct. 1955, 1974, 167 L. Ed. 2d 929 (2007). To cross into "the realm of plausible liability", the allegations must be factual (not conclusory) and suggestive (not neutral). *See id.* at 557 n.5, 127 S.Ct. at 1966 n.5. *See also Ocasio-Hernandez v. Fortuno-Burset,* 640 F.3d 1, 13 (1st Cir. 2011) (proper plausibility inquiry is "the reasonableness of the inference of liability that the plaintiff is asking the court to draw from the facts alleged in the complaint").

[19]*See Ashcroft v. Iqbal,* 556 U.S. 662, 696, 129 S.Ct. 1937, 1949, 173 L.Ed.2d 868 (2009); *Bell Atlantic Corp. v. Twombly,* 550 U.S. 544, 556, 127 S.Ct. 1955, 1965, 167 L.Ed.2d 929 (2007). *See also Sepulveda-Villarini v.*

Dep't of Educ. of Puerto Rico, 628 F.3d 25, 30 (1st Cir. 2010) (Soutor, J.) ("A plausible but inconclusive inference from pleaded facts will survive a motion to dismiss . . .").

[20]*See Ashcroft v. Iqbal,* 556 U.S. 662, 678, 129 S.Ct. 1937, 1949, 173 L.Ed.2d 868 (2009). *See also Anderson v. U.S. Dep't of Housing & Urban Dev't,* 554 F.3d 525, 528–29 (5th Cir. 2008) (complaint must do more than name laws allegedly violated; they must put defendant on notice of what conduct is being called for defense).

[21]*See Ashcroft v. Iqbal,* 556 U.S. 662, 678, 129 S.Ct. 1937, 1949, 173 L.Ed.2d 868 (2009); *See Davis v. Coca-Cola Bottling Co. Consol.,* 516 F.3d 955, 974 n.43 (11th Cir. 2008) (standard is whether pleading plausibly suggests, and is not merely consistent with, a cognizable legal claim). *But see Hamilton v. Palm,* 621 F.3d 816, 819 (8th Cir. 2010) (dismissal improper where complaint raises plausible inferences supporting and rejecting liability).

[22]*See Bryson v. Gonzales,* 534 F.3d 1282, 1286 (10th Cir. 2008).

[23]550 U.S. 544, 127 S. Ct. 1955, 167 L.Ed.2d 929 (2007).

doubt that the plaintiff can prove no set of facts in support of his claim which could entitle him to relief").[24] The *Conley* language, wrote the Court, "earned its retirement" because it might, incorrectly, preserve a conclusorily pleaded claim on the mere theoretical chance that it might later find support.[25] The Court has now confirmed that *Twombly*'s "plausibility" standard is not limited only to antitrust cases (as *Twombly* was).[26] But precisely how this "plausibility" line is to be drawn remains uncertain,[27] and it seems sometimes to impose a pleading burden that may be impossible to discharge absent discovery (which, of course, comes only if the complaint survives).[28] But the Court has confirmed that notice pleading remains the broad objective.[29] It is clear that the standard is a "refined" one—somewhere between

---

[24]*See Bell Atlantic Corp. v. Twombly*, 550 U.S. 544, 554–63, 127 S. Ct. 1955, 1964–65, 167 L. Ed. 2d 929 (2007) (abrogating language in *Conley v. Gibson*, 355 U.S. 41, 45–46, 78 S. Ct. 99, 2 L. Ed. 2d 80 (1957)). This abrogation was not new rulemaking, but rather an interpretation of the existing language. *See In re Ins. Brokerage Antitrust Litig.*, 618 F.3d 300, 320 (3d Cir. 2010). Moreover, it is likely that *Conley*'s language had already been effectively abandoned in practice. *See Khalik v. United Air Lines*, 671 F.3d 1188, 1194 n.4 (10th Cir.2012) (commenting that "[e]ven before *Twombly/Iqbal*, cases that survived a motion to dismiss showed a higher level of detail"); *U.S. ex rel. Garst v. Lockheed-Martin Corp.*, 328 F.3d 374, 378 (7th Cir. 2003) (sufficient pleading requires that judges and parties "need not try to fish a gold coin from a bucket of mud"); *Mann v. Boatright*, 477 F.3d 1140, 1148 (10th Cir. 2007) (not court's job "to stitch together cognizable claims for relief from the wholly deficient pleading").

[25]*See Bell Atlantic Corp. v. Twombly*, 550 U.S. 544, 562–63, 127 S. Ct. 1955, 1969, 167 L. Ed. 2d 929 (2007). *See also Moss v. U.S. Secret Serv.*, 572 F.3d 962, 968 (9th Cir. 2009) (*Conley*, "read literally, set the bar too low").

[26]*See Ashcroft v. Iqbal*, 556 U.S. 662, 684, 129 S.Ct. 1937, 1953, 173 L.Ed.2d 868 (2009).

[27]*See Pruell v. Caritas Christi*,

678 F.3d 10, 14 (1st Cir. 2012) ("Adequacy is not always a clear line"); *Khalik v. United Air Lines*, 671 F.3d 1188, 1191 (10th Cir.2012) (noting uncertainty whether "plausibility" signals "minimal change" or "a significantly heightened fact-pleading standard"); *Starr v. Baca*, 652 F.3d 1202, 1215 (9th Cir. 2011) (noting "perplexing" difficulty in discerning how to apply standard).

[28]*See Khalik v. United Air Lines*, 671 F.3d 1188, 1191 (10th Cir.2012); *New Albany Tractor, Inc. v. Louisville Tractor, Inc.*, 650 F.3d 1046, 1050 (6th Cir. 2011).

[29]*See Ashcroft v. Iqbal*, 556 U.S. 662, 678–79, 129 S.Ct. 1937, 173 L.Ed.2d 868 (2009) ("Rule 8 marks a notable and generous departure from the hyper-technical, code-pleading regime of a prior era, but it does not unlock the doors of discovery for a plaintiff armed with nothing more than conclusions."); *Erickson v. Pardus*, 551 U.S. 89, 93, 127 S.Ct. 2197, 167 L.Ed.2d 1081 (2007) ("Specific facts are not necessary; the statement need only "give the defendant fair notice of what the . . . claim is and the grounds upon which it rests.' "). *See also HDC, LLC v. City of Ann Arbor*, 675 F.3d 608, 614 (6th Cir. 2012) (finding it "inaccurate" to read Supreme Court's cases "so narrowly as to be the death of notice pleading"); *Khalik v. United Air Lines*, 671 F.3d 1188, 1191 (10th Cir.2012) ("Rule 8(a)(2) still lives. There is no indication the Supreme Court intended a return to the more stringent

fact pleading and conclusory recitations of elements[30]—which is influenced greatly by context.[31] Indeed, this standard is best understood as a flexible pleading benchmark that varies depending on the type of claim chosen and the type of allegations pleaded: a "plausible" auto accident case may be very concisely pleaded, whereas a "plausible" antitrust or RICO case may demand a far fuller factual presentation.[32] As summarized by one court, plausibility requires only that the pleader supply those case details necessary "to present a story that holds together," and that courts will ask only "*could* these things have happened, not *did* they happen."[33]

- *"Information-and-Belief" Pleading:* The viability of pleading upon information and belief remains unclear after *Twombly*, *Iqbal*, and the arrival of "plausibility" pleadings. One court has predicted that such pleading remains proper at least where the facts lie only in the defendants' possession or where the belief is premised on factual information that makes an inference of liability plausible.[34]

- *Pleading With Excessive Factual Detail:* Practitioners debate the wisdom of pleading in more detail than the Rules require.[35] Some believe that added detail helps educate the judge and coax a favorable early impression. Others reject that view as unrealistic. In any event, an excessively detailed pleading is risky. It invites a pre-answer motion to dismiss premised on the very detail so gratuitously supplied.[36] It restricts the case in discovery and case management. And in extreme circumstances,

---

pre-Rule 8 pleading requirements").

[30]*See Khalik v. United Air Lines*, 671 F.3d 1188, 1191 (10th Cir.2012). *See also Keys v. Humana, Inc.*, 684 F.3d 605, 610 (6th Cir. 2012) (" 'plausibility' occupies that wide space between 'possibility' and 'probability' ").

[31]*See Ashcroft v. Iqbal*, 556 U.S. 662, 679, 129 S. Ct. 1937, 1950, 173 L. Ed. 2d 868 (2009); *Gee v. Pacheco*, 627 F.3d 1178, 1185 (10th Cir. 2010); *In re Ins. Brokerage Antitrust Litig.*, 618 F.3d 300, 320 n.18 (3d Cir. 2010)

[32]*See Swanson v. Citibank, N.A.*, 614 F.3d 400, 404–05 (7th Cir. 2010) (observing that in "many straightforward cases" the pleading burden is no different than before, though more complex cases "will require more detail" to give notice and to show how the pleading theory's "dots should be

connected"); *Arista Records, LLC v. Doe 3*, 604 F.3d 110, 120 (2d Cir. 2010) ("factual amplification" required only when needed "to render a claim plausible").

[33]*Swanson v. Citibank, N.A.*, 614 F.3d 400, 404 (7th Cir. 2010) (emphasis in original).

[34]*See Arista Records, LLC v. Doe 3*, 604 F.3d 110, 120 (2d Cir. 2010); *Trustees of the Auto. Mechanics' Industry Welfare and Pension Funds Local 701 v. Elmhurst Lincoln Mercury*, 677 F.Supp.2d 1053, 1054–55 (N.D.Ill. 2010).

[35]*See, e.g., Chaveriat v. Williams Pipe Line Co.*, 11 F.3d 1420, 1430 (7th Cir. 1993) (noting increasing trend toward greater specificity in complaints).

[36]*See, e.g., Tamayo v. Blagojevich*, 526 F.3d 1074, 1086 (7th Cir. 2008)

it may even warrant a dismissal for excessive verbosity (which is, itself, a violation of Rule 8(a)'s "short and plain" requirement).[37]

- *Relying On Federal Forms:* Rule 84 provides that the official federal form models contained in the Appendix of Forms[38] are sufficient to meet the notice pleading requirements of Rule 8.[39] It may be, however, that because those forms are only samples, a pleading that just narrowly satisfies an Official Form might not satisfy the "plausibility" standard, which will depend on the specificity required by the Form, the particular elements of the claim, and the pleading's phrasing.[40]

- *Enhanced Pleading Exceptions:* In certain types of claims, these Rules or the underlying law itself impose on the pleader an enhanced obligation of additional claim detail. For example, claims must be alleged with particularity when: (1) pleading fraud and mistake, under Rule 9(b); (2) pleading demand futility in a

(party may plead itself out of court by alleging facts that establish impenetrable defenses); *Sparrow v. United Air Lines, Inc.*, 216 F.3d 1111, 1116 (D.C. Cir. 2000) (same); *Jackson v. Marion County*, 66 F.3d 151, 153–54 (7th Cir. 1995) (same, noting "[w]e have expressed our puzzlement that lawyers insist on risking dismissal by filing prolix complaints").

[37]*See, e.g., Cafasso, U.S. ex rel. v. General Dynamics C4 Sys., Inc.*, 637 F.3d 1047, 1058–59 (9th Cir. 2011) (dismissal without leave to amend proper because "district courts are busy enough without having to penetrate a tome approaching the magnitude of *War and Peace* to discern a plaintiff's claims and allegations"); *Mann v. Boatright*, 477 F.3d 1140, 1147–48 (10th Cir. 2007) (99-page, single-spaced pleading failed to meet "a short and plain statement" standard, justifying dismissal); *U.S. ex rel. Garst v. Lockheed-Martin Corp.*, 328 F.3d 374, 378 (7th Cir. 2003) (finding no error when trial judge, after "wading through" four complaints and an ensuing statement, properly dismissed plaintiff's "distended" 400-paragraph, 155-page pleading accompanied by 99 attachments); *Magluta v. Samples*, 256 F.3d 1282, 1284 (11th Cir. 2001) (vacating judgment and directing that plaintiff replead because 58-page, group-pleaded "complaint is a quintes-

sential 'shotgun' pleading of the kind we have condemned repeatedly" where "any allegations that are material are buried beneath innumerable pages of rambling irrelevancies"). *But see Hearns v. San Bernardino Police Dept.*, 530 F.3d 1124, 129–133 (9th Cir. 2008) (claim will not be dismissed solely for excessive length, but may be if otherwise improper); *U.S. ex rel. Garst v. Lockheed-Martin Corp.*, 328 F.3d 374, 378 (7th Cir. 2003) (surplusage in "windy but understandable" pleadings should be ignored).

[38]*See* Official Forms 1-82 (reprinted in Part IV of this text).

[39]*See* Rule 84 (noting that Appendix forms "suffice" to "illustrate the simplicity and brevity that these rules contemplate"). *See also Swierkiewicz v. Sorema N. A.*, 534 U.S. 506, 512 n.4, 122 S. Ct. 992, 998 n.4, 152 L. Ed. 2d 1 (2002) (same); *In re Bill of Lading Transmission & Processing Sys. Patent Litig.*, 681 F.3d 1323, 1334 (Fed.Cir. 2012) (if interpretation of *Twombly* and example set by Official Forms conflict, "the Forms control"); *Hamilton v. Palm*, 621 F.3d 816, 818 (8th Cir. 2010) (satisfying forms will satisfy pleading obligation).

[40]*See In re Bill of Lading Transmission & Processing Sys. Patent Litig.*, 681 F.3d 1323, 1334 n.6 (Fed.Cir. 2012).

shareholder derivative action, under Rule 23.1; and (3) pleading scienter under the Private Securities Litigation Reform Act of 1995, 15 U.S.C.A. § 78U-4(b).[41] Moreover, where those special categories are inseparably intertwined with the essential allegations of other elements of a claim, those elements might be held to this "particularity" requirement as well.[42]

- *Rule 9(b) and RICO Case Statements:* Many Districts require that pleaders alleging violations of the federal Racketeer Influenced and Corrupt Organizations Act ("RICO") submit "RICO Case Statements", to flesh out the factual predicates and legal theory underlying such claims.[43] Such Statements have been approved, unless they would obligate the pleader to allege more information than Rule 8(a) and Rule 9(b) would otherwise require.[44]

- *Case Law Exceptions:* Although courts occasionally have tried to impose more elaborate pleading standards in certain categories of cases, it now appears settled that the only permissible exceptions to the "notice" pleading standard of Rule 8(a) are those contained in other Rules themselves.[45]

- *Pleading in Anticipation of Defenses:* Ordinarily, a

---

[41]*See Kanter v. Barella*, 489 F.3d 170, 175–76 (3d Cir. 2007) (listing exceptions). *See also Eternity Global Master Fund Ltd. v. Morgan Guar. Trust Co. of N.Y.*, 375 F.3d 168, 177 (2d Cir. 2004) (liberal notice pleading provides standard for judging complaints, except in claims for fraud and mistake, which Rule 9(b) requires be pleaded with particularity); *Credit Suisse First Boston Corp., In re*, 431 F.3d 36, 46 (1st Cir. 2005) (noting that PSLRA imposed pleading obligations beyond Rule 8(a)).

[42]*See Lachmund v. ADM Investor Services, Inc.*, 191 F.3d 777 (7th Cir. 1999) (holding that general allegations of agency do not suffice where the substantive fraud allegations offered by plaintiff are necessary to establish the agency relationship).

[43]*See Northland Ins. Co. v. Shell Oil Co.*, 930 F. Supp. 1069, 1074 (D.N.J. 1996). Many judicial districts require, by Standing Order, chambers policy, or otherwise, that the pleader answer a series of questions that supplement the RICO allegations of the complaint. *See, e.g.*, S.D. Cal. Rule 11.1; W.D. N.Y. Rule 5.1; *National Organization*

for Women, Inc. v. Scheidler, 510 U.S. 249, 249, 114 S. Ct. 798, 800, 127 L. Ed. 2d 99 (1994) (noting local rule). This pleading obligation is especially important where the facts noted in the RICO Case Statement are deemed to be pleading averments, properly considered in ruling upon a motion to dismiss. *See Glessner v. Kenny*, 952 F.2d 702, 712 (3d Cir. 1991) (collecting cases so holding).

[44]*See Wagh v. Metris Direct, Inc.*, 363 F.3d 821, 826–28 (9th Cir. 2003).

[45]*See, e.g., Swierkiewicz v. Sorema N. A.*, 534 U.S. 506, 512–15, 122 S. Ct. 992, 152 L. Ed. 2d 1 (2002) (no enhanced "prima facie case of discrimination" standard required in employment discrimination cases); *Leatherman v. Tarrant County Narcotics Intelligence & Coordination Unit*, 507 U.S. 163, 113 S. Ct. 1160, 122 L. Ed. 2d 517 (1993) (no "heightened pleading standard" in civil rights cases filed under 42 U.S.C.A. § 1983); *Pratt v. Tarr*, 464 F.3d 730, 731 (7th Cir. 2006) (noting that it is now "emphatically clear" that courts may not supplement Rule 9(b)'s list of claims that must be pleaded with particularity).

pleader need not anticipate defenses, nor preemptively include averments to "plead around" an expected defense.[46]

Element 3: Demand for Judgment

The pleader must also make a demand for judgment that identifies the remedies desired and the parties against whom relief is sought.[47] A party is not required to plead a specific sum certain in the demand.

- *Diversity of Citizenship Cases:* In cases based upon diversity of citizenship jurisdiction, a claimant must demand an amount in excess of $75,000, exclusive of interest and costs.[48] [In federal question cases, no such monetary limit is generally required.]

- *Pleading Damages Claim:* Although pleaders are not required to do more than state "the relief sought", the Rules *do* require pleaders to identify the type of relief they seek.[49] Thus, a pleading for equitable relief that does not include a demand for damages might not permit the pleader to later insist upon a damages award.[50]

- *Pleading Unliquidated Damages:* By local rule, certain Districts expressly forbid a plaintiff to plead a specific sum of unliquidated damages; instead, the pleader in those jurisdictions is permitted only to demand unliquidated damages generally.[51] Practitioners should consult the local rules.

- *Equitable and Declaratory Relief:* A party seeking equita-

---

[46]*See Richards v. Mitcheff,* __ F.3d __, __, 2012 WL 3217627, at *2 (7th Cir. 2012); *Cataldo v. U.S. Steel Corp.,* 676 F.3d 542, 547 (6th Cir. 2012); *Barry Aviation Inc. v. Land O'Lakes Municipal Airport Com'n,* 377 F.3d 682 (7th Cir. 2004).

[47]*See, e.g., Goldsmith v. City of Atmore,* 996 F.2d 1155, 1161 (11th Cir. 1993) (requirement of demand for judgment easily met by identifying requested remedies and parties from whom remedies are sought).

[48]*See St. Paul Mercury Indem. Co. v. Red Cab Co.,* 303 U.S. 283, 58 S. Ct. 586, 82 L. Ed. 845 (1938).

[49]*See* Rule 8(a)(3). *See also Seven Words LLC v. Network Solutions,* 260 F.3d 1089, 1098 (9th Cir. 2001) ("Surely a simple request 'for damages' would satisfy the notice requirement without imposing any undue burden on the drafter").

[50]*See Seven Words LLC v. Network Solutions,* 260 F.3d 1089, 1098 (9th Cir. 2001) (where damages claim was

made years into litigation, after various representations that only declaratory and injunctive relief was sought, after a motion to dismiss, and only days before oral argument on appeal, court joins other Courts of Appeals in declining to read a damages claim into complaint as improper under Rule 8(a)).

[51]*See, e.g.,* D. Del. Loc. R. 9.4 ("A pleading which sets forth a claim for relief in the nature of unliquidated money damages shall state in the ad damnum clause a demand specifying the nature of the damages claimed, e.g., 'compensatory,' 'punitive,' or both, but shall not claim any specific sum"); D. N.J. Loc. R. 8.1 ("A pleading which sets forth a claim for relief in the nature of unliquidated money damages shall state in the ad damnum clause a demand for damages generally without specifying the amount"); E.D. Pa. Loc. R. 5.1.1 ("No pleading asserting a claim for unliquidated damages shall contain any allegation as to the specific dollar amount

ble relief must plead the specific act to be prohibited or compelled. A party seeking declaratory relief must plead the specific declaration sought.

- *Special Damages:* A claimant must plead special damages with specificity, as provided by Rule 9(g).

- *Default Judgment:* In cases of default judgment, a claimant is limited to the specific amount of the demand, as provided by Rule 54(c).

- *Jury Demand:* A jury demand may be part of the original pleading. Rule 38 controls the circumstances in which a party may request trial by jury.

- *Alternative, Hypothetical, and Cumulative Demands:* A party may assert all demands for legal or equitable relief alternatively, hypothetically, and/or cumulatively. Rule 8 protects a party's right to plead inconsistently; under this Rule, portions of a pleading cannot be offered as admissions against other portions containing inconsistent or alternative averments.[52]

Rule 8's Rules Supplant Inconsistent State Rules

Some States impose by statute specialized pleading obligations for the courts in their jurisdiction. Where such pleading provisions conflict with Rule 8, those inconsistent State requirements will not apply in the federal courts of that State.[53]

Pleadings from *Pro Se* Litigants

Pleadings filed by *pro se* litigants are held to a less stringent standard than those prepared by attorneys.[54] Nevertheless, although construed liberally, *pro se* pleadings are not relieved of the obligation to allege sufficient facts to support a proper legal claim,[55] and to do so under the "plausibility" standard.[56]

---

claimed"); M.D. Pa. Loc. R. 8.1 ("The demand for judgment . . . shall not claim any specific sum where unliquidated damages are involved"); W.D. Pa. Loc. R. 8.1 ("any pleading demanding general damages unliquidated in amount shall, without claiming any specific sum, set forth only that money damages are claimed").

[52]*See Rodriguez-Suris v. Montesinos*, 123 F.3d 10, 20 (1st Cir. 1997); *Independent Enterprises Inc. v. Pittsburgh Water and Sewer Authority*, 103 F.3d 1165, 1175 (3d Cir. 1997); *Henry v. Daytop Village, Inc.*, 42 F.3d 89, 95 (2d Cir. 1994).

[53]*See Cohen v. Office Depot, Inc.*, 184 F.3d 1292 (11th Cir. 1999) (finding that Florida statute, which requires plaintiffs to obtain leave from

court before including punitive damages prayer, "conflicted" with Rule 8's requirement of concise statement identifying pleader's remedies; because federal rule occupied field in this regard, Florida statute could not apply to federal district court), opinion vacated in part, 204 F.3d 1069 (11th Cir. 2000) (Rule 8(a) discussion expressly reaffirmed).

[54]*See Erickson v. Pardus*, 551 U.S. 89, 94, 127 S. Ct. 2197, 2200, 167 L. Ed. 2d 1081 (2007) (per curiam); *Estelle v. Gamble*, 429 U.S. 97, 106, 97 S. Ct. 285, 50 L. Ed. 2d 251 (1976).

[55]*See Taylor v. Books A Million, Inc.*, 296 F.3d 376, 378 (5th Cir. 2002); *Riddle v. Mondragon*, 83 F.3d 1197, 1202 (10th Cir. 1996).

RULE 8(b)—DEFENSES; ADMISSIONS AND DENIALS

CORE CONCEPT

To respond to a pleading, parties must state their defenses (in short and plain terms) and admit or deny the allegations asserted against them. Denials must fairly respond to the substance of the allegations. If a responsive pleading is required, parties are deemed to have admitted all allegations they do not deny (except for allegations relating to the amount of damages).

APPLICATIONS

Impact of 2007 "Restyling" Amendments

In 2007, the content of former Rule 8(b) and 8(d) were combined together in current Rule 8(b). In researching current Rule 8(b), practitioners should be mindful of this repositioning.

"Notice" Pleading of Defenses

Rule 8(b) contemplates that defenses, like claims for relief under Rule 8(a), must be short and concise.[57] The purpose of such pleading is to provide reasonable notice to the adversary (and the court) of the allegations that the defending party proposes to place in issue.[58] Courts are divided on what effect *Twombly* and the Rule 8(a) "plausible" pleading mandate may have on defenses.[59] Some courts have ruled that defenses (like claims) must be asserted with sufficient detail to be "plausible," while others reject that view.[60]

Responsive Pleading Options

The purpose of responsive pleadings is to supply the opponent with fair notice of the defense.[61] When an allegation has been asserted against them, and a responsive pleading is required, pleaders have only three options: (1) admit, (2) deny,

---

[56]*See Atherton v. District of Columbia Office of Mayor*, 567 F.3d 672, 681–82 (D.C.Cir. 2009).

[57]*See* Rule 8(b)(1)(A). *See also Montgomery v. Wyeth*, 580 F.3d 455, 467–68 (6th Cir. 2009) (no "heightened" pleading for defense, only "short and plain" response required).

[58]*See U.S. v. 1866.75 Board Feet, 11 Doors And Casings, More of Less of Dipteryx Panamensis Imported from Nicaragua*, 2008 WL 839792, at *3 (E.D. Va. 2008).

[59]*See Francisco v. Verizon South, Inc.*, 2010 WL 2990159, at *6–*9 (E.D. Va. July 29, 2010) (surveying split).

[60]*See Montgomery v. Wyeth*, 580 F.3d 455, 467–68 (6th Cir. 2009) (in a brief discussion, ruling that no height-ened pleading standard applies to defenses). *Compare Francisco v. Verizon South, Inc.*, 2010 WL 2990159, at *6–*9 (E.D. Va. July 29, 2010) (applying "plausibility" to defenses) *with Loucks v. Shorest, LLC*, __ F. Supp. 2d __, __, 2012 WL 2126956, at *1 (M.D.Ala. 2012) (refusing to demand more of answers than "short and plain") *and Bank of Beaver City v. Southwest Feeders, L.L.C.*, 2011 WL 4632887, at *7 (D.Neb. Oct. 4, 2011) (refusing to apply "plausibility" to either Rules 8(b) or 8(c)); *and Bennett v. Sprint Nextl Corp.*, 2011 WL 4553055, at *1–*2 (D.Kan. Sept. 29, 2011) (refusing to apply "plausibility" to answers).

[61]*See Barnes & Noble, Inc. v. LSI Corp.*, 849 F.Supp.2d 925, 929 (N.D.Cal. 2012).

341

or (3) state a lack of knowledge or information necessary to admit or deny.[62] The Rules do not approve or permit other types of responses, and choosing to answer in other ways is a dangerous practice. An averment in a pleading that is not properly denied is deemed to be admitted,[63] thus failing to properly counter-plead could be catastrophic. One court has gone to great lengths to caution responsive pleaders away from antiquated (and perhaps now meaningless) pleading practices, such as "denied as a conclusion of law",[64] no response is required because the written document "speaks for itself",[65] or neither admitted nor denied, but "strict proof" demanded at trial.[66] Finding such pleading responses to be inconsistent with Rule 8(b), this court ordered a re-pleading with specific instructions to counsel *not* to bill the client for "correcting" the "counsel's errors"[67] and, in some instances, has even deemed paragraphs containing such responses to be admissions, bind-

---

[62]*See Lane v. Page*, 272 F.R.D. 581, 602 (D.N.M. 2011).

[63]*See* Rule 8(b)(6).

[64]*See Lane v. Page*, 272 F.R.D. 581, 603 (D.N.M. 2011) (must plead to legal conclusions); *Farrell v. Pike*, 342 F. Supp. 2d 433, 440–41 (M.D. N.C. 2004) (same); *Gracedale Sports and Entertainment, Inc. v. Ticket Inlet, LLC*, 1999 WL 618991 (N.D. Ill. 1999) (refusing to answer "legal conclusions" "flies in the face of the established doctrine that legal conclusions are a proper part of federal pleading, to which Rule 8(b) also compels a response"); *Saldana v. Riddle*, 1998 WL 373413 (N.D. Ill. 1998) (dismissing as "nonsense" the claim that legal conclusions need not be admitted or denied); *Pessler v. CBS, Inc. / WBBM-TV*, 1998 WL 246138 (N.D. Ill. 1998) ("Rule 8(b) does not confer on any pleader a right of self-determination as to any allegation that the pleader believes does not require a response"). *See generally Neitzke v. Williams*, 490 U.S. 319, 324, 109 S. Ct. 1827, 1831, 104 L. Ed. 2d 338 (1989) (observing that federal civil complaints "contain[] . . . both factual allegations and legal conclusions").

[65]*See Chicago Dist. Council of Carpenters Pension Fund v. Balmoral Racing Club, Inc.*, 2000 WL 876921, at *1 (N.D. Ill. 2000) (deriding "speaks for itself" responses, commenting that "[t]his Court has been attempting to listen to such written materials for years (in the forlorn hope that one will

indeed give voice)—but until some such writing does break its silence, this Court will continue to require pleaders to employ one of the three alternatives that are permitted by Rule 8(b)"). *See also Lane v. Page*, 272 F.R.D. 581, 603 (D.N.M. 2011) (improper response); *Continental Cas. Co. v. Duckson*, 2011 WL 2293873, at *2 (N.D.Ill. June 9, 2011) (dismissing "speaks-for-itself" response). *But see Scott v. Harris*, 550 U.S. 372, 378 n.5, 127 S. Ct. 1769, 1775 n.5, 167 L. Ed. 2d 686 (2007) (Supreme Court majority notes that they "are happy to allow the videotape to speak for itself").

[66]*See Gracedale Sports and Entertainment, Inc. v. Ticket Inlet, LLC*, 1999 WL 618991 (N.D. Ill. 1999) (demand for "strict proof" is meaningless); *King Vision Pay Per View, Ltd. v. J.C. Dimitri's Restaurant, Inc.*, 180 F.R.D. 332 (N.D. Ill. 1998) ("strict proof" demand improper). *See also Bond v. U.S. Mfg. Corp.*, 2010 WL 3037942, at *2 n.4 (E.D.Mich. July 30, 2010) (such responses "operate as admissions"); *United States v. Vehicle 2007 Mack 600 Dump Truck*, 680 F.Supp.2d 816, 826–28 (E.D.Mich. 2010) (same).

[67]*See Bobbitt v. Freeman Companies*, 2000 WL 1131948, at *1–*2 & *2 n. 2 (N.D. Ill. 2000); *Chicago Dist. Council of Carpenters Pension Fund v. Balmoral Racing Club, Inc.*, 2000 WL 876921 (N.D. Ill. 2000).

ing the party throughout the trial.[68]

Failure to Deny Factual Allegations

A failure to deny the factual allegations of a complaint will deem them admitted (although, in assessing the consequence of such admissions, the court may not enter judgment against the defaulting party without first assessing whether the uncontested-and-admitted facts actually state a cognizable cause of action).[69] The court will not deem admitted conclusions of law or facts that were not well-pleaded.[70]

Failure to Deny Amount of Damages

Although a failure to deny usually causes the allegation to be deemed admitted, this result does not occur with allegations relating to the amount of damages.[71]

General Denial

A party makes a general denial by denying each and every averment of the pleading. There is no required magic language for denying generally, as long as the intent to deny generally is clear.[72]

Qualified General Denial

A party may also assert a qualified general denial when the party wishes to deny all of the averments in the complaint except certain specific averments.

Specific Denial

A specific denial more narrowly denies a particular paragraph or portion of a claim. The most common denial is the specific denial.

Fairly Meeting the Substance of the Allegation

In a denial, the responding party must fairly meet the substance of the allegation.[73] Although the party may qualify the response (by, for example, admitting part and denying

---

[68]*See King Vision Pay Per View, Ltd. v. J.C. Dimitri's Restaurant, Inc.*, 180 F.R.D. 332 (N.D. Ill. 1998) (Shadur, J.) (deeming "strict proof" paragraphs to be admitted, and commenting that "this action will proceed on that basis").

[69]*See Marshall v. Baggett*, 616 F.3d 849, 852 (8th Cir. 2010); *Ryan v. Homecomings Fin. Network*, 253 F.3d 778, 780 (4th Cir.2001). *See also Ohio Cent. R. Co. v. Central Trust Co.*, 133 U.S. 83, 91, 10 S.Ct. 235, 33 L.Ed. 561 (1890).

[70]*See Wecosign, Inc. v. IFG Holdings, Inc.*, 845 F.Supp.2d 1072, 1078 (C.D.Cal. 2012).

[71]*See* Rule 8(b)(6). *See also Vevelstad v. Flynn*, 230 F.2d 695, 703 (9th Cir. 1956) (noting that "allegations as to amounts of damages are never admitted through failure to deny"); *Wecosign, Inc. v. IFG Holdings, Inc.*, 845 F.Supp.2d 1072, 1078–79 (C.D.Cal. 2012); *Pineda v. Masonry Const., Inc.*, 831 F.Supp.2d 666, 675 (S.D.N.Y. 2011); *Tweedy v. RCAM Title Loans, LLC*, 611 F.Supp.2d 603, 606 (W.D.Va. 2009) (averments as to damages need not be taken as true).

[72]*See In re Sterten*, 546 F.3d 278, 283 (3d Cir. 2008).

[73]*See* Rule 8(b)(2).

part[74]), the response may not improperly equivocate or confuse the issues.[75] The purpose of the answer is to assist the court and the opposing parties in clarifying the issues in dispute.[76]

Denials Based Upon Lack of Knowledge or Information

(1) *Substance of Denial:* A party may deny by pleading a lack of knowledge or information. But to do so, the party must plead *both* lack of knowledge *and* lack of information.[77] A party pleading lack of knowledge and information is also bound by the obligation of honesty in pleading; an allegation that is obviously within the responding party's knowledge or information cannot be avoided, and averring lack of knowledge or information in such circumstances may have the unintended effect of *admitting* the allegation.[78] However, in certain circumstances, lack of information may be asserted where the information at issue may exist but has proven to be difficult to uncover.[79]

(2) *Duty of Investigation:* A party denying based upon a lack of knowledge and information has the duty to reasonably investigate whether the information exists and how difficult it would be to find.[80]

(3) *Effect:* A pleading properly based upon a lack of knowledge and information is not an admission of the adverse party's averments, but a denial.

No Duty to Respond to Allegations Against Others

The 2007 amendments to Rule 8(b) seem to make express what was long understood in practice, namely that a pleader need not responsively plead to allegations directed solely at someone else.[81] If, however, the allegations directly or inferentially target the responsive pleader, a response is required.[82]

---

[74]*See* Rule 8(b)(3) to (b)(4).

[75]*See Reis Robotics USA, Inc. v. Concept Industries, Inc.*, 462 F. Supp. 2d 897, 907–08 (N.D. Ill. 2006) (striking improperly qualified answer, and ordering repleading).

[76]*See Hill v. Blue Cross and Blue Shield of Michigan*, 237 F.R.D. 613, 616 (E.D. Mich. 2006).

[77]*See Bobbitt v. Freeman Companies*, 2000 WL 1131948 (N.D. Ill. 2000).

[78]*See Harvey Aluminum (Inc.) v. N.L.R.B.*, 335 F.2d 749, 757 (9th Cir. 1964); *Dawkins v. Williams*, 511 F. Supp. 2d 248, 271 n.53 (N.D. N.Y. 2007); *Djourabchi v. Self*, 240 F.R.D. 5, 12 (D.D.C. 2006) (citing lack of knowledge, pleader denied allegation that he lacked a license to perform

general contracting work in the forum; court found that pleader should have known the answer and deemed the allegation admitted). *In re TCW/Camil Holding L.L.C.*, 2004 WL 1151562 (D. Del. 2004).

[79]*See Clay v. District of Columbia*, 831 F.Supp.2d 36, 46–47 (D.D.C. 2011).

[80]*See U.S. v. 1866.75 Board Feet, 11 Doors And Casings, More of Less of Dipteryx Panamensis Imported from Nicaragua*, 2008 WL 839792, at *3 (E.D. Va. 2008); *Greenbaum v. U.S.*, 360 F. Supp. 784, 787 (E.D. Pa. 1973).

[81]*See* Rule 8(b)(1)(B) (in a counter-pleading, party must "admit or deny the allegations asserted *against it* by an opposing party") (emphasis added).

[82]*See Griffin v. Fairman*, 1989 WL

Special Matters

Rule 9 requires that certain matters be denied specifically, such as the capacity of a party to sue or be sued, the legal existence of a party, the authority of a party to sue or be sued in a representative capacity, the occurrence or performance of conditions precedent, the issuance of a judgment, or the legality of a document or act.[83]

Affirmative Defenses

Affirmative defenses are automatically denied and do not need to be answered, unless required by court order.[84]

Fifth Amendment

Where an answer would subject a party to criminal charges or be used as evidence or a link in the evidence in a criminal proceeding, the pleader may refuse to answer by claiming the privilege to be free from self-incrimination, founded in the Fifth Amendment to the United States Constitution.[85]

RULE 8(c)—AFFIRMATIVE DEFENSES

CORE CONCEPT

An affirmative defense is any *fact* asserted by the respondent that vitiates the opposing party's claim. Rule 8(c) provides for the pleading of affirmative defenses, and also provides that misdesignated counterclaims will be deemed affirmative defenses. A party must raise all affirmative defenses as affirmative defenses or they are waived. In practice, courts may excuse this rule in appropriate cases.

APPLICATIONS

2010 Amendments — *Discharge in Bankruptcy*

Effective December 1, 2010, "discharge in bankruptcy" was removed from the list of affirmative defenses as "confusing", since discharges under the Bankruptcy Code actually void the underlying judgment that had fixed the debtor's personal li-

---

153556, at *1 (N.D. Ill. 1989) ("Though a party is of course excused from responding to a separate claim brought only against other parties to the litigation, there is simply no room for the quoted nonresponse to an allegation made in the midst of a claim that does target the responsive pleader.").

[83]*See* Rule 9(a), (c), (d), & (e).

[84]*See United States v. Clayton*, 465 B.R. 72, 80–81 (M.D.N.C. 2011); *Tyco Fire Prods. LP v. Victaulic Co.*, 777 F.Supp.2d 893, 903 (E.D.Pa. 2011). *See also* Rule 8(b)(6) ("If a responsive pleading is not required, an allegation is considered denied or avoided."); Rule

7(a) (absent court order, no counter-pleading to an answer (where affirmative defenses are ordinarily contained) is permitted).

[85]*See, e.g., LaSalle Bank Lake View v. Seguban*, 54 F.3d 387, 389–91 (7th Cir. 1995) (complaint cannot be deemed admitted when defendant invokes Fifth Amendment; complainant must produce evidence to support allegations); *In re Enron Corp. Secs., Derivative & Erisa Litig.*, 762 F.Supp.2d 942, 961 (S.D.Tex. 2010) (proper, timely invocation of privilege precludes deemed-admission).

ability on the discharged debt.[86]

Definition of Affirmative Defense

An affirmative defense is a defensive assertion of new facts or arguments that, if true, would defeat the asserted claim even if all of the claim's allegations are proven true.[87]

Duty to Plead Affirmative Defenses

Affirmative defenses must be asserted in a party's response to a preceding pleading.[88] The goal of this requirement, consistent with federal pleading practice generally, is to provide notice to the opponent, avoid surprise and undue prejudice, and afford the opponent a chance to argue, if able, why the defense is unfounded.[89]

"Notice" Pleading of Affirmative Defenses

The pleaders' duty is to "affirmatively state" their avoidances and affirmative defenses in their responsive pleading.[90] Prudent practice dictates that they be labeled as affirmative defenses/avoidances and pleaded in separate paragraphs. Unlike claims, Rule 8(c) does not require that affirmative defenses or avoidances make an entitlement "showing".[91] Consequently, the courts are divided on whether the *Twombly* "plausibility" standard governs the pleading of affirmative defenses.[92] In a debate that remains largely at the district court level,[93] some courts have ruled that defenses (like claims) must be asserted

---

[86]*See* Rule 8(c)(1) advisory committee note to 2010 amendment.

[87]*See Emergency One, Inc. v. American Fire Eagle Engine Co., Inc.*, 332 F.3d 264, 271 (4th Cir. 2003); *Saks v. Franklin Covey Co.*, 316 F.3d 337, 350 (2d Cir. 2003). *See also Estate of Hamilton v. City of New York*, 627 F.3d 50, 57 (2d Cir. 2010) (when defendants wish to make a point about something that is not an element of the claim, they must plead it as affirmative defense).

[88]*See Taylor v. Sturgell*, 553 U.S. 880, 907 128 S. Ct. 2161, 2179–80, 171 L. Ed. 2d 155 (2008); *John R. Sand & Gravel Co. v. U.S.*, 552 U.S. 130, 133, 128 S. Ct. 750, 753, 169 L. Ed. 2d 591 (2008).

[89]*See Blonder-Tongue Laboratories, Inc. v. University of Illinois Foundation*, 402 U.S. 313, 350, 91 S. Ct. 1434, 1453, 28 L. Ed. 2d 788 (1971); *Simmons v. Navajo County*, 609 F.3d 1011, 1023 (9th Cir. 2010); *Creative Consumer Concepts, Inc. v. Kreisler*, 563 F.3d 1070, 1076–77 (10th Cir. 2009).

[90]*See* Rule 8(c)(1).

[91]*Cf.* Rule 8(a)(2). Depending upon whether Rule 8(c) is properly read as an elaboration of, or wholly independent from, Rule 8(b)(1)(A), it may also be that even a "short and plain" statement is not required for affirmative defenses.

[92]*See Weed v. Ally Fin. Inc.*, 2012 WL 2469544, at *3 (E.D.Pa. June 28, 2012) (collecting cases); *Cottle v. Falcon Holdings Mgmt., LLC*, 2012 WL 266968, at *1 (N.D.Ind. Jan. 30, 2012) (same); *Paducah River Painting, Inc. v. McNational Inc.*, 2011 WL 5525938, at *2 (W.D.Ky. Nov. 14, 2011) (same); *Bennett v. Sprint Nextl Corp.*, 2011 WL 4553055, at *1–*2 (D.Kan. Sept. 29, 2011) (same).

[93]*See Herrera v. Churchill McGee, LLC*, 680 F.3d 539, 547 n.6 (6th Cir. 2012) (sidestepping the issue, noting panel had "no occasion to address" and, therefore, "express[ed] no view" on the impact of *Twombly* and *Iqbal* on affirmative defenses). *But see Montgomery v. Wyeth*, 580 F.3d 455,

with sufficient detail to be "plausible,"[94] while others reject that view.[95] Courts that have required "plausibly"-pleaded affirmative defenses have found that some affirmative defenses may be pleaded quite simply while still imparting the necessary notice, while other affirmative defenses need a further description.[96] Bald, laundry lists of affirmative defenses are always vulnerable.[97]

But No Duty to Respond to Affirmative Defenses

Although the party asserting them must plead affirmative defenses, there is no general duty (absent court order) on the party opposing an affirmative defense to answer or otherwise counter-plead to them. Instead, the Rules deem any affirmative defenses automatically denied or avoided.[98]

Enumerated Affirmative Defenses

Rule 8(c) contains a *non-exhaustive*[99] list of defenses that must be pleaded affirmatively: accord and satisfaction, arbitration and award, assumption of risk, contributory negligence, discharge in bankruptcy, duress, estoppel, failure of consideration, fraud, illegality, injury by fellow servant, laches, license, payment, release, res judicata, statute of frauds, statute of limitations, and waiver.

Unenumerated Affirmative Defenses

In addition to the matters enumerated as affirmative defenses, parties are generally required under Rule 8(c) to plead as affirmative defenses any new factual matter that would come

---

467–68 (6th Cir. 2009) (in a brief discussion, ruling that no heightened pleading standard applies to defenses).

[94]*See, e.g., J & J Sports Prods., Inc. v. Martinez,* 2011 WL 4373960, at *2 (E.D.Cal. Sept. 19, 2011); *E.E.O.C. v. Kelley Drye & Warren, LLP,* 2011 WL 3163443, at *2 (S.D.N.Y. July 25, 2011); *Racick v. Dominion Law Assocs.,* 270 F.R.D. 228, 233–34 (E.D.N.C. 2010).

[95]*See, e.g., Cape Flattery Ltd. v. Titan Maritime LLC,* 2012 WL 3113168, at *9–*10 (D.Haw. July 31, 2012); *Weed v. Ally Fin. Inc.,* 2012 WL 2469544, at *3–*4 (E.D.Pa. June 28, 2012); *Drury v. Wendy's Old Fashioned Hamburgers of New York, Inc.,* 2012 WL 2339747, at *2–*3 (D.Kan. June 19, 2012).

[96]*See Long v. Howard Univ.,* 550 F.3d 21, 24 (D.C.Cir. 2008) ("claims are barred by the applicable statute of limitations" is sufficient). *See also Mag Instrument, Inc. v. JS Prods., Inc.,* 595 F.Supp.2d 1102, 1107–08 (C.D.Cal.

2008) (noting that, if it gives fair notice of the defense, an affirmative defense pleaded in general terms will be proper).

[97]*See Shechter v. Comptroller of City of New York,* 79 F.3d 265, 270 (2d Cir.1996) (bald assertions of affirmative defenses may be stricken); *Dann v. Lincoln Nat'l Corp.,* 274 F.R.D. 139, 145–47 (E.D.Pa. 2011) (bare bones affirmative defenses violate fair notice requirement of Rule 8).

[98]*See United States v. Clayton,* 465 B.R. 72, 80–81 (M.D.N.C. 2011). *See also* Rule 7(a) (absent court order, there is no duty to counter-plead to an answer, the place where affirmative defenses are typically contained); Rule 8(b)(6) ("If a responsive pleading is not required, an allegation is considered denied or avoided.").

[99]*See Jones v. Bock,* 549 U.S. 199, 212, 127 S. Ct. 910, 919, 166 L. Ed. 2d 798 (2007) (noting that list is nonexhaustive).

as a surprise at trial.[100] Whether a defense is an affirmative one is not always clear. Courts have developed several tests for identifying an affirmative defense: whether the defendant would bear the burden of proving it;[101] whether the defense involves an element necessary or extrinsic to plaintiff's cause of action[102] or would controvert the plaintiff's proof,[103] whether the defense would bar the right to relief even if the plaintiff's allegations were admitted,[104] or whether a failure to plead it affirmatively would deprive the plaintiff of an opportunity to rebut the defense or adjust litigation strategy to meet it.[105]

Burden of Proof

The party raising an affirmative defense has the burden of proving it.[106]

Special Matters

When asserting an affirmative defense that contains special matters, such as the capacity of a party to sue or be sued, fraud or mistake, the performance of conditions precedent, the authority of a party to sue or be sued in a representative capacity, the legal existence of a party, the legality of an official document or act, or the issuance of a judgment, the party must plead with particularity, as provided in Rule 9.[107]

---

[100]*See, e.g., Proctor v. Fluor Enterprises, Inc.*, 494 F.3d 1337, 1350 (11th Cir. 2007) (borrowed servant doctrine is affirmative defense under State law); *Frederick v. Kirby Tankships, Inc.*, 205 F.3d 1277, 1286–87 (11th Cir. 2000) (failure to mitigate is affirmative defense); *Brinkley v. Harbour Recreation Club*, 180 F.3d 598, 612 (4th Cir. 1999) ("factor-other-than-sex" defense to Equal Pay Act claims is affirmative defense); *Ringuette v. City of Fall River*, 146 F.3d 1 (1st Cir.1998) (qualified immunity is an affirmative defense); *Gray v. Bicknell*, 86 F.3d 1472, 1480 (8th Cir. 1996) (merger is an affirmative defense); *F.D.I.C. v. Calhoun*, 34 F.3d 1291, 1299 (5th Cir. 1994) ("ratification" is an affirmative defense recognized by State law); *Union Mut. Life Ins. Co. v. Chrysler Corp.*, 793 F.2d 1, 13 (1st Cir. 1986) ("novation" is an affirmative defense); *Red Deer v. Cherokee County, Iowa*, 183 F.R.D. 642 (N.D. Iowa 1999) ("after-acquired evidence" is an affirmative defense).

[101]*See Winforge, Inc. v. Coachmen Indus., Inc.*, 691 F.3d 856, 869 (7th Cir. 2012); *National Market Share, Inc. v. Sterling Nat. Bank*, 392 F.3d 520, 526–27 (2d Cir. 2004).

[102]*See Ingraham v. U.S.*, 808 F.2d 1075, 1079 (5th Cir.1987).

[103]*See Winforge, Inc. v. Coachmen Indus., Inc.*, 691 F.3d 856, 869 (7th Cir. 2012).

[104]*See Wolf v. Reliance Standard Life Ins. Co.*, 71 F.3d 444, 449 (1st Cir. 1995).

[105]*See In re Sterten*, 546 F.3d 278, 285 (3d Cir. 2008); *National Market Share, Inc. v. Sterling Nat. Bank*, 392 F.3d 520, 526–27 (2d Cir. 2004); *Oden v. Oktibbeha County, Miss.*, 246 F.3d 458, 467 (5th Cir. 2001).

[106]*See Surles v. Andison*, 678 F.3d 452, 458 (6th Cir. 2012); *Sharp v. Johnson*, 669 F.3d 144, 158 (3d Cir. 2012); *Gonzalez v. Hasty*, 651 F.3d 318, 322 (2d Cir. 2011).

[107]*See Rule 9(a), (c), (d), & (e).

Misdesignated Affirmative Defenses

Misdesignated counterclaims will be deemed affirmative defenses, and vice versa.[108] Affirmative defenses labeled as denials will be treated as affirmative defenses and will not be deemed waived where their proper assertion will promote a disposition of the case on the merits and will not prejudice the adverse parties.[109] Where, however, the claimed error is more than a mere mislabeling and instead proposes to assert a new claim, the party may seek leave to amend.[110]

Waiver

An affirmative defense that is not timely pleaded may be deemed waived.[111] But waiver does not follow inexorably.[112] Waiver may be excused where the unpleaded affirmative defense is later raised without prejudice to any other party (or otherwise comes to the notice of the other party),[113] where it is actually tried with the parties' implied consent,[114] or where the law on the topic at issue remains unsettled.[115] Waiver may also be excused where "peculiar facts" and the "interests of justice" so warrant,[116] and where the defense was raised at a "pragmatically sufficient time".[117] Thus, for example, in an appropriate case, an affirmative defense asserted for the first time by motion for summary judgment may be considered by the court a motion to amend the defendant's answer, which would prevent

---

[108]See *Hatco Corp. v. W.R. Grace & Co. Conn.*, 59 F.3d 400, 411 n.8 (3d Cir. 1995); *Rabin v. Fidelity Nat'l Prop. & Cas. Ins. Co.*, 2012 WL 1884507, at *13 (D.Colo. May 23, 2012); *Multibank 2009-1 RES-ADC Venture, LLC v. PineCrest at Neskowin, LLC*, 857 F. Supp. 2d 1072, 1079 (D.Or. 2012).

[109]See *Reiter v. Cooper*, 507 U.S. 258, 113 S. Ct. 1213, 122 L. Ed. 2d 604 (1993). *See also Giles v. General Elec. Co.*, 245 F.3d 474, 491–92 (5th Cir. 2001) (affirmative defense not waived if asserted "at a pragmatically sufficient time" and did not prejudice the opponent).

[110]See *Rocheux Int'l of N.J., Inc. v. U.S. Merchants Fin. Group, Inc.*, 741 F.Supp.2d 651, 660 (D.N.J. 2010).

[111]See, e.g., *Day v. McDonough*, 547 U.S. 198, 202, 126 S. Ct. 1675, 1679, 164 L. Ed. 2d 376 (2006); *Society of the Holy Transfiguration Monastery, Inc. v. Gregory*, 689 F.3d 29, 58 (1st Cir. 2012); *Pensacola Motor Sales Inc. v. Eastern Shore Toyota, LLC*, 684 F.3d 1211, 1221–22 (11th Cir. 2012); *Kapche v. Holder*, 677 F.3d 454, 465 (D.C.Cir. 2012).

[112]See *Seals v. General Motors Corp.*, 546 F.3d 766, 770 (6th Cir. 2008); *Rose v. AmSouth Bank of Florida*, 391 F.3d 63, 65 (2d Cir. 2004).

[113]See *Pensacola Motor Sales Inc. v. Eastern Shore Toyota, LLC*, 684 F.3d 1211, 1221–22 (11th Cir. 2012); *Standard Waste Systems Ltd. v. Mid-Continent Cas. Co.*, 612 F.3d 394, 398 (5th Cir. 2010); *Schmidt v. Eagle Waste & Recycling, Inc.*, 599 F.3d 626, 632 (7th Cir. 2010).

[114]See *Society of the Holy Transfiguration Monastery, Inc. v. Archbishop Gregory*, 754 F.Supp.2d 219, 228 (D.Mass. 2010).

[115]See *Pasco ex rel. Pasco v. Knoblauch*, 566 F.3d 572, 577 (5th Cir. 2009).

[116]See *Shell Rocky Mountain Production, LLC v. Ultra Resources, Inc.*, 415 F.3d 1158, 1164 (10th Cir. 2005).

[117]See *Standard Waste Sys. Ltd. v. Mid-Continent Cas. Co.*, 612 F.3d 394, 398 (5th Cir. 2010).

waiver.[118] Notwithstanding this possible liberality, the trial court enjoys broad discretion, and its decision will likely not be disturbed unless it is completely unreasonable.[119] In exercising their discretion, the courts remain vigilant to protect the plaintiff against being "ambushed" by an unpleaded affirmative defense; a naked "failure-to-state-a-claim" defense, therefore, is unlikely to be considered by the court a preservation of an otherwise unpleaded affirmative defense.[120] If deemed waived, an affirmative defense ordinarily cannot be later revived by asserting it during subsequent motion practice.[121]

Raising Affirmative Defenses *Sua Sponte*

Some courts have held that certain defenses—such as *res judicata* and collateral estoppel—may, in certain instances, be raised by the court *sua sponte*, even when they had not been properly pleaded, mindful of the strong public interest in conserving scarce judicial resources by avoiding improper relitigations.[122] Otherwise, courts will usually refuse to raise affirmative defenses *sua sponte*.[123]

RULE 8(d)—PLEADING TO BE CONCISE AND DIRECT; ALTERNATIVE STATEMENTS; INCONSISTENCY

CORE CONCEPT

Parties must plead claims and defenses in a simple, direct, and concise manner consistent with the federal notice pleading standard. They may do so alternatively, hypothetically, and inconsistently (subject, of course, to their Rule 11 duty of honest pleading). No technical pleading forms are necessary. Parties should set forth the averments in general terms and should omit evidentiary material.

---

[118]*See Anthony v. City of New York*, 339 F.3d 129, n.5 (2d Cir. 2003). *But cf. Gilbert v. Napolitano*, 670 F.3d 258, 260–61 (D.C.Cir. 2012) (raising affirmative defense in motion to dismiss ruled to be too late).

[119]*See Old Line Life Ins. Co. of America v. Garcia*, 418 F.3d 546 (6th Cir.2005); *Castro v. Chicago Housing Authority*, 360 F.3d 721, 735 (7th Cir. 2004). *But see Pasco ex rel. Pasco v. Knoblauch*, 566 F.3d 572, 577 (5th Cir. 2009) (district court erred in simply presuming prejudice from 52-month delay in asserting defense).

[120]*See Saks v. Franklin Covey Co.*, 316 F.3d 337, 350 (2d Cir. 2003).

[121]*See Lebouef v. Island Operating Co.*, 342 Fed.Appx. 983, 984 (5th Cir. 2009).

[122]*See LaCroix v. Marshall County*, 409 Fed.Appx. 794, 798–99 (5th Cir. 2011); *Shurick v. Boeing Co.*, 623 F.3d 1114, 1116 n.2 (11th Cir. 2010); *Curry v. City of Syracuse*, 316 F.3d 324, 330 (2d Cir. 2003). *But cf. Arizona v. California*, 530 U.S. 392, 412–13, 120 S. Ct. 2304, 2317–18, 147 L. Ed. 2d 374 (2000) (cautioning that *sua sponte* consideration of statute of limitations affirmative defenses should be allowed only sparingly).

[123]*See Latimer v. Roaring Toyz, Inc.*, 601 F.3d 1224, 1239 (11th Cir. 2010); *Lebouef v. Island Operating Co.*, 342 Fed.Appx. 983, 984 (5th Cir. 2009).

APPLICATIONS

Impact of 2007 "Restyling" Amendments

In 2007, the content of former Rule 8(b) and 8(d) were combined together in current Rule 8(b). Former Rule 8(e) was moved up and now is current Rule 8(d). In researching current Rule 8(d), practitioners should be mindful of this repositioning.

Improper Pleadings

Although liberally construed, when pleadings are not simple, concise, and direct, but instead are so convoluted and difficult to understand that it is impossible to assess whether the pleader has alleged a meritorious claim, the trial court may either grant a motion to dismiss for violating Rule 8 or, alternatively, grant a motion for a more definite statement.[124] Where the improper pleading is not subsequently remedied, the pleading can even be dismissed with prejudice and without further right of re-pleading.[125] Note, however, that mere verbosity or excessive length is unlikely to warrant a dismissal.[126]

Incorporation by Reference

A party may adopt by reference paragraphs of previous counts rather than repleading each alternative or hypothetical claim or defense, as provided by Rule 10(c).

Alternative, Hypothetical, And Inconsistent Pleadings

Statements of claims or defenses may be asserted in the alternative, hypothetically, and even inconsistently.[127] But such inconsistent pleading may only occur when legitimate doubt as

---

[124]*See Stanard v. Nygren*, 658 F.3d 792, 797–801 (7th Cir. 2011) (second amended complaint properly denied where its length, rampant grammatical, syntactical, and typographical errors, and vague, confusing, and conclusory nature made it unintelligible); *Mann v. Boatright*, 477 F.3d 1140, 1147–48 (10th Cir. 2007) (99-page, single-spaced pleading failed to meet "a short and plain statement" standard, justifying dismissal); *Desardouin v. United Parcel Service, Inc.*, 285 F. Supp. 2d 153, 157 (D. Conn. 2003) (noting that dismissal is permitted where complaint "is so confused, ambiguous, vague, or otherwise unintelligible that its true substance, if any, is well disguised"). *Cf. Mendiondo v. Centinela Hosp. Medical Center*, 521 F.3d 1097, 1105 n.4 (9th Cir. 2008) (such dismissals are appropriate only where complaint is "patently verbose, confusing, and rambling").

[125]*See Chennareddy v. Dodaro*, 282 F.R.D. 9, 16 (D.D.C. 2012).

[126]*See Hearns v. San Bernardino Police Dep't*, 530 F.3d 1124, 1131–32 (9th Cir. 2008) (collecting cases).

[127]*See* Rule 8(d)(2) to (d)(3). *See also Cleveland v. Policy Management Systems Corp.*, 526 U.S. 795, 805, 119 S. Ct. 1597, 1603, 143 L. Ed. 2d 966 (1999) ("Our ordinary Rules recognize that a person may not be sure in advance upon which legal theory she will succeed, and so permit parties to 'set forth two or more statements of a claim or defense alternately or hypothetically,' and to 'state as many separate claims or defenses as the party has regardless of consistency' "). *See generally Elena v. Municipality of San Juan*, 677 F.3d 1, 8 (1st Cir. 2012); *Brown v. Cassens Transport Co.*, 675 F.3d 946, 968 (6th Cir. 2012); *Huffman v. Union Pac. R.R.*, 675 F.3d 412, 418 (5th Cir. 2012).

to the true facts exists.[128] After all, every pleading, including alternative, hypothetical, and inconsistent ones, must abide by the obligations set in Rule 11.[129] Thus, for example, a pleader often may allege an unjust enrichment claim as an alternative to a breach of contract claim,[130] unless the existence of a valid, enforceable contract is uncontested[131] or the equity claim is foreclosed for other reasons.[132] Of course, the pleader cannot recover on both inconsistent theories.[133] Moreover, the court must be able to readily identify claims or defenses that are pleaded alternatively, hypothetically, or inconsistently. Although no "magic words" are required, it must be reasonably obvious from the pleading itself that these types of claims or defenses are being asserted.[134] While separate inconsistent *claims* and *defenses* are permitted under the Rules, the factual allegations *within* each claim or defense cannot be inconsistent with the alleged right of recovery, or else the claim or defense could defeat itself.[135]

Inconsistent Pleadings As Admissions

Because Rule 8(d) protects a party's right to plead inconsistent claims and defenses, statements made in claims or defenses cannot generally be offered as admissions against other claims or defenses within the same pleading that contain inconsistent or alternative averments.[136] However, unequivocal averments of fact, made *within* a particular claim or defense,

---

[128]*See American Int'l Adjustment Co. v. Galvin*, 86 F.3d 1455, 1461 (7th Cir. 1996); *Koch v. I-Flow Corp.*, 715 F.Supp.2d 297, 301–03 (D.R.I. 2010).

[129]*See Harris v. Koenig*, 722 F.Supp.2d 44, 54 (D.D.C. 2010).

[130]*See Stockton East Water Dist. v. United States*, 583 F.3d 1344, 1368 (Fed.Cir. 2009); *In re Light Cigarettes Mktg. Sales Practices Litig.*, 751 F.Supp.2d 183, 191 (D.Me. 2010); *Daigle v. Ford Motor Co.*, 713 F.Supp.2d 822, 828 (D.Minn. 2010).

[131]*See Gunther v. Capital One, N.A.*, 703 F.Supp.2d 264, 276 (E.D.N.Y. 2010); *Baumgardner v. Bimbo Food Bakeries Distrib., Inc.*, 697 F.Supp.2d 801, 816–17 (N.D.Ohio 2010).

[132]*See In re Light Cigarettes Mktg. Sales Practices Litig.*, 751 F.Supp.2d 183, 192 (D.Me. 2010) (such as where the legal claim provides an exclusive remedy).

[133]*In re Checking Account Overdraft Litig.*, 694 F.Supp.2d 1302, 1321 (S.D.Fla. 2010).

[134]*See Holman v. Indiana*, 211 F.3d 399, 407 (7th Cir. 2000) ("While the [pleaders] need not use particular words to plead in the alternative, they must use a formulation from which it can be reasonably inferred that this is what they were doing").

[135]*See In re Livent, Inc. Noteholders Securities Litigation*, 151 F. Supp. 2d 371 (S.D. N.Y. 2001) (commenting that Rule 8(e) does not "grant[] plaintiffs license to plead inconsistent assertions of facts within the allegations that serve as the factual predicates for an independent, unitary claim. Internally conflicting factual assertions that constitute integral components of a claim must be distinguished from a permissible alternative statement embodying a theory of a whole sufficient claim") (citation omitted). *See also Aetna Cas. and Sur. Co. v. Aniero Concrete Co., Inc.*, 404 F.3d 566, 585–86 (2d Cir. 2005) (affirming on basis of district court's opinion, from which quotation comes) (noting that claim that is "at war with itself" cannot survive summary judgment).

[136]*See Aholelei v. Department of Public Safety*, 488 F.3d 1144, 1149

may constitute judicial admissions that conclusively bind the pleader throughout the litigation.[137] Additionally, if the positions taken by the pleader are accepted by the court, the pleader may be foreclosed by judicial estoppel from taking an inconsistent, contrary position in later proceedings.[138]

RULE 8(e)—CONSTRUING PLEADINGS

CORE CONCEPT

Courts must construe pleadings "so as to do justice." Consequently, so long as the pleading provides the adverse party with proper notice of claims and defenses, it will not be construed hypertechnically.

APPLICATIONS

Impact of 2007 "Restyling" Amendments

Because another Rule subpart was repositioned, the content of current Rule 8(e) contains what formerly was Rule 8(f). In researching current Rule 8(e), practitioners should be mindful of this repositioning.

All Pleadings Construed Liberally

One fundamental tenor and philosophy of the Rules is liberality over technicality.[139] Because Rule 8(e) requires the courts to construe pleadings "as to do justice", all pleadings are construed liberally.[140] In federal practice, form is never exalted over substance.[141] Likewise, the familiar contract law tenet of construing documents against their drafter is not applied in reviewing federal pleadings.[142] Courts will not rely solely on the labels used by the pleader to describe claims or defenses, but may reach deeper and seek out the true substance of the

---

(9th Cir. 2007); *Rodriguez-Suris v. Montesinos*, 123 F.3d 10, 20 (1st Cir. 1997); *Independent Enterprises Inc. v. Pittsburgh Water and Sewer Authority*, 103 F.3d 1165, 1175 (3d Cir. 1997); *Henry v. Daytop Village, Inc.*, 42 F.3d 89, 95 (2d Cir. 1994). *See also American Intern. Adjustment Co. v. Galvin*, 86 F.3d 1455, 1460 (7th Cir. 1996) (noting that, in pleading context, Rules abolish doctrine of election of remedies).

[137] *See Astroworks, Inc. v. Astroexhibit, Inc.*, 257 F. Supp. 2d 609, 615 n.10 (S.D. N.Y. 2003); *Friedmann v. U.S.*, 107 F. Supp. 2d 502, 510–11 (D.N.J. 2000).

[138] *Cf. Montrose Medical Group Participating Savings Plan v. Bulger*, 243 F.3d 773, 782 (3d Cir. 2001) (judicial estoppel will not apply to the as-

sertion of contrary positions in different proceedings when the initial claim was never accepted or adopted by the court).

[139] *See Minger v. Green*, 239 F.3d 793, 799 (6th Cir. 2001).

[140] *See, e.g., Skaff v. Meridien North America Beverly Hills, LLC*, 506 F.3d 832, 839 (9th Cir. 2007); *Rodriguez v. Doral Mortg. Corp.*, 57 F.3d 1168, 1171 (1st Cir. 1995).

[141] *See Phillips v. Girdich*, 408 F.3d 124, 128 (2d Cir. 2005).

[142] *See Miller v. Philadelphia Geriatric Center*, 463 F.3d 266, 272 (3d Cir. 2006) ("Pleadings need not be construed most strongly against the pleader, rather we should make a determined effort to understand what she is attempting to set forth.").

allegations.[143] Where those allegations, so construed, would state a cognizable claim or defense, the requirements of Rule 8 are usually satisfied.

But No Unwarranted Constructions

Although pleadings are liberally construed, the court must still always "do justice". A pleading will not be given so broadly generous a reading that it prejudices another party or denies a party fair notice of a claim or defense.[144] Courts are, thus, not obligated to invent for the pleader a claim or defense not fairly included within the pleading,[145] nor need they grant a pleader a type of relief not fairly demanded within the pleading (especially where to do so will cause prejudice).[146]

Pleadings Drafted by Laypersons

Courts generally apply less stringent standards to pleadings drafted by laypersons, such as *pro se habeas corpus* petitions and social security applications.[147]

Additional Research References

Wright & Miller, *Federal Practice and Procedure* §§ 1201 to 1290
C.J.S., Federal Civil Procedure §§ 252 to 280 et seq., §§ 301 to 308
West's Key Number Digest, Federal Civil Procedure ☞631 to 653, ☞654 to 657, ☞671 to 680, ☞731 to 745, ☞751 to 759

---

[143]*See Mead Corp. v. ABB Power Generation, Inc.*, 319 F.3d 790, 795 (6th Cir. 2003) (noting that courts do "not rely solely on labels", but "probe deeper and examine the substance of the complaint"). *See also Minger v. Green*, 239 F.3d 793, 799 (6th Cir. 2001) (construing claim labeled as "negligent misrepresentation" (which would have been barred by discretionary function doctrine) as one for intentional misrepresentation (which could go forward)).

[144]*See Zokari v. Gates*, 561 F.3d 1076, 1084–88 (10th Cir. 2009).

[145]*See Smith v. Aztec Well Servicing Co.*, 462 F.3d 1274, 1284 (10th Cir. 2006).

[146]*See Seven Words LLC v. Network Solutions*, 260 F.3d 1089, 1098 (9th Cir. 2001) (where damages claim was made years into litigation, after various representations that only declaratory and injunctive relief was sought, after a motion to dismiss, and only days before oral argument on appeal, court joins other Courts of Appeals in declining to read a damages claim into complaint).

[147]*See Erickson v. Pardus*, 551 U.S. 89, 94, 127 S. Ct. 2197, 2200, 167 L. Ed. 2d 1081 (2007) (per curiam); *Hughes v. Rowe*, 449 U.S. 5, 101 S. Ct. 173, 66 L. Ed. 2d 163 (1980); *Haines v. Kerner*, 404 U.S. 519, 92 S. Ct. 594, 30 L. Ed. 2d 652 (1972); *Estelle v. Gamble*, 429 U.S. 97, 106, 97 S. Ct. 285, 50 L. Ed. 2d 251 (1976).

RULE 9
PLEADING SPECIAL MATTERS

(a) Capacity or Authority to Sue; Legal Existence.

   (1) *In General.* Except when required to show that the court has jurisdiction, a pleading need not allege:

      (A) a party's capacity to sue or be sued;

      (B) a party's authority to sue or be sued in a representative capacity; or

      (C) the legal existence of an organized association of persons that is made a party.

   (2) *Raising Those Issues.* To raise any of those issues, a party must do so by a specific denial, which must state any supporting facts that are peculiarly within the party's knowledge.

(b) Fraud or Mistake; Conditions of Mind. In alleging fraud or mistake, a party must state with particularity the circumstances constituting fraud or mistake. Malice, intent, knowledge, and other conditions of a person's mind may be alleged generally.

(c) Conditions Precedent. In pleading conditions precedent, it suffices to allege generally that all conditions precedent have occurred or been performed. But when denying that a condition precedent has occurred or been performed, a party must do so with particularity.

(d) Official Document or Act. In pleading an official document or official act, it suffices to allege that the document was legally issued or the act legally done.

(e) Judgment. In pleading a judgment or decision of a domestic or foreign court, a judicial or quasi-judicial tribunal, or a board or officer, it suffices to plead the judgment or decision without showing jurisdiction to render it.

(f) Time and Place. An allegation of time or place is material when testing the sufficiency of a pleading.

(g) Special Damages. If an item of special damage is claimed, it must be specifically stated.

(h) Admiralty or Maritime Claim.

(1) *How Designated.* If a claim for relief is within the admiralty or maritime jurisdiction and also within the court's subject-matter jurisdiction on some other ground, the pleading may designate the claim as an admiralty or maritime claim for purposes of Rules 14(c), 38(e), and 82 and the Supplemental Rules for Admiralty or Maritime Claims and Asset Forfeiture Actions. A claim cognizable only in the admiralty or maritime jurisdiction is an admiralty or maritime claim for those purposes, whether or not so designated.

(2) *Designation for Appeal.* A case that includes an admiralty or maritime claim within this subdivision (h) is an admiralty case within 28 U.S.C. § 1292(a)(3).

[Amended effective July 1, 1966; July 1, 1968; July 1, 1970; August 1, 1987, April 11, 1997, effective December 1, 1997; April 12, 2006, effective December 1, 2006; April 30, 2007, effective December 1, 2007.]

AUTHORS' COMMENTARY ON RULE 9

PURPOSE AND SCOPE

Special requirements apply for pleading capacity and authority, fraud, mistake, conditions precedent, official documents or acts, judgments, time and place, special damages, and admiralty and maritime claims.

RULE 9(a)—CAPACITY OR AUTHORITY TO SUE; LEGAL EXISTENCE

CORE CONCEPT

Unless necessary to establish the court's subject matter jurisdiction, a pleading need not aver capacity or authority to sue, or an association's legal existence. A defendant may challenge these issues, but must do so by specific denial in a responsive pleading or motion.

APPLICATIONS

Pleading Capacity Only When Jurisdictional

Unless it is necessary to establish the subject matter jurisdiction of the federal courts, a party's capacity or authority to sue, or an association's legal existence need not be pleaded. When necessary to establish jurisdiction, however, these defenses must be averred.[1]

Procedure For *Challenging* Capacity

Ordinarily, a litigant seeking to challenge (a) a party's legal existence, (b) a party's capacity to sue or be sued, or (c) a party's authority to sue or be sued in a representative capacity must raise the issue by specific denial in a responsive pleading or pre-answer motion.[2] Failure to do so likely waives that defense.[3] The required "specific denial" does not always obligate the pleader to "spell out in detail" why capacity is lacking;[4] but the pleader must include all specific facts that are "peculiarly within the party's knowledge".[5] The purpose of this pleading duty is to place the adversary on appropriate notice of the capacity defense.[6] Once pleaded, there is no further duty on the party challenging capacity to file an early dispositive motion on the issue.[7]

Note: Prior to the 2007 amendments, Rule 9(a) used the language "specific negative averment" in place of the current (and simpler) "specific denial".

Liberal Construction

Under appropriate circumstances, courts have given Rule 9(a)'s pleading duty a liberal interpretation. Thus, a pleader who reasonably delays in asserting lack of capacity may be forgiven the untimely assertion,[8] as may the pleader who mislabels a capacity defense as a challenge to standing may be excused the error.[9]

---

[1] *See Moore v. City of Harriman,* 272 F.3d 769, 772–74 (6th Cir. 2001) (noting division among appellate courts as to whether, given limitations of Eleventh Amendment, a Section 1983 defendant's "capacity" must be formally alleged in the complaint, and ruling that such capacity may be pleaded or, in certain circumstances, discerned under "course of proceedings" test).

[2] *See* Rule 9(a)(1). *See also F.D.I.C. v. Calhoun,* 34 F.3d 1291, 1299 (5th Cir. 1994); *Brown v. Williamson,* 134 F. Supp. 2d 1286, 1291 (M.D. Ala. 2001).

[3] *See De Saracho v. Custom Food Mach., Inc.,* 206 F.3d 874, 878 (9th Cir. 2000).

[4] *See Pugh v. Kobelco Const. Mach. America, LLC,* 413 Fed.Appx. 134, 136 (11th Cir. 2011).

[5] *See* Rule 9(a)(2). *See also DDR Hendon Nassau Park II LP v. RadioShack Corp.,* 2010 WL 723776, at *6 (N.D.Ohio Feb. 24, 2010) (facts are "peculiarly within a party's knowledge" when only that party knows them).

[6] *See AmeriPride Servs., Inc. v. Valley Indus. Serv., Inc.,* 2008 WL 5068672, at *5 (E.D.Cal. Nov. 25, 2008).

[7] *See AmeriPride Servs., Inc. v. Valley Indus. Serv., Inc.,* 2008 WL 5068672, at *5 (E.D.Cal. Nov. 25, 2008).

[8] *See Miller v. City of Cincinnati,* ___ F. Supp. 2d ___, ___, 2012 WL 1623526, at *5 (S.D.Ohio 2012).

[9] *See Masood v. Saleemi,* 2007 WL 2069853, at *4 (W.D. Wash. 2007).

Waiver By Failing to Plead Lack of Capacity

The defense of lack of capacity or authority to sue or be sued, or an association's legal existence, is usually waived if not timely and specifically pleaded.[10] Waiver may be excused if the defense is affirmatively apparent from the face of the complaint and a specific denial is found to be unnecessary,[11] where the defense (though late) was raised at the pragmatically earliest time,[12] or where the court finds a lack of prejudice under the circumstances of the delay.[13] If, however, the defense affects the court's subject matter jurisdiction, a party may assert that defense at any time and the court may raise it *sua sponte*.[14]

RULE 9(b)—FRAUD, MISTAKE, CONDITION OF MIND

CORE CONCEPT

A party must plead fraud and mistake with particularity, but may plead malice, intent, knowledge, and other conditions of a person's mind generally.

APPLICATIONS

Goal of Pleading With Particularity

Some claims—like fraud—may have an *in terrorem* or stigmatizing effect on defendants and their reputations,[15] and are often easily fabricated (because the evidence is frequently circumstantial).[16] The courts expect pleaders to perform a greater pre-complaint investigation in such cases, to ensure that any such claim is "responsible and supported, rather than defamatory and extortionate".[17] This practice also allows an early and informed response from the party defending against

---

[10]*See, e.g., RK Co. v. See*, 622 F.3d 846, 849 n.2 (7th Cir. 2010); *De Saracho v. Custom Food Machinery, Inc.*, 206 F.3d 874, 878 (9th Cir. 2000).

[11]*See Brown v. Williamson*, 134 F. Supp. 2d 1286, 1291 (M.D. Ala. 2001). *But cf. Srock v. U.S.*, 2006 WL 2460769, at *4–*5 (E.D. Mich. 2006) (collecting cases and scholarship on late assertion of Rule 9(a) defenses, and ruling that these defenses should be subject to an early waiver rule).

[12]*See Wiwa v. Royal Dutch Petroleum Co.*, 2009 WL 464946, at *3–*6 (S.D.N.Y. Feb. 25, 2009).

[13]*See AmeriPride Servs., Inc. v. Valley Indus. Serv., Inc.*, 2008 WL 5068672, at *5–*8 (E.D.Cal. Nov. 25, 2008).

[14]*See E.R. Squibb & Sons, Inc. v. Accident & Cas. Ins. Co.*, 160 F.3d 925, 935–36 (2d Cir. 1998) (if party with capacity defense is strategically not asserting it in order to preserve federal jurisdiction, court may assess the capacity of the parties *sua sponte*).

[15]*See U.S. ex rel. Marlar v. BWXT Y-12, L.L.C.*, 525 F.3d 439, 445 (6th Cir. 2008); *U.S. ex rel. Fowler v. Caremark RX, L.L.C.*, 496 F.3d 730, 740 (7th Cir. 2007); *Vess v. Ciba-Geigy Corp. USA*, 317 F.3d 1097, 1104 (9th Cir. 2003).

[16]*See Bennett v. MIS Corp.*, 607 F.3d 1076, 1101 (6th Cir. 2010).

[17]*See Borsellino v. Goldman Sachs Group, Inc.*, 477 F.3d 502, 507 (7th Cir. 2007) (internal citation omitted).

such accusations,[18] and guards against lawsuits filed in the unsubstantiated hope of discovering an unknown wrong.[19] It helps to ensure that only viable claims of fraud or mistake are permitted to proceed to discovery.[20] Thus, requiring that such claims be pleaded with particularity (1) ensures that the defendants have fair notice of the plaintiff's claim, (2) helps safeguard the defendants against spurious accusations, and the resulting reputational harm, (3) reduces the possibility that a meritless fraud claim can remain in the case, by ensuring that the full and complete factual allegation is not postponed until discovery, and (4) protects defendants against "strike" suits.[21]

No Common Law Additions to Rule 9(b)'s List

Rule 9(b) requires that only fraud and mistake be pleaded with particularity. It is now "emphatically clear" that courts are not permitted to add to this list and require, by common law, that other claims be pleaded with particularity.[22]

Amount of Particularity Required

The amount of particularity or specificity required for pleading fraud or mistake will differ from case to case,[23] but generally depends upon the amount of access the pleader has to the specific facts,[24] considering the complexity of the claim, the relationship of the parties, the context in which the alleged fraud

---

[18]See *BJC Health System v. Columbia Cas. Co.*, 478 F.3d 908, 917 (8th Cir. 2007); *Swartz v. KPMG LLP*, 476 F.3d 756, 764 (9th Cir. 2007).

[19]See *Kearns v. Ford Motor Co.*, 567 F.3d 1120, 1125 (9th Cir. 2009). *See also Grubbs v. Kanneganti*, 565 F.3d 180, 190 (5th Cir. 2009) (describing Rule 9(b) inquiry as "what is required for a ticket to the federal discovery apparatus").

[20]See *In re BP Lubricants USA Inc.*, 637 F.3d 1307, 1310 (Fed.Cir. 2011).

[21]See *Chesbrough v. VPA, P.C.*, 655 F.3d 461, 466–67 (6th Cir. 2011); *Kearns v. Ford Motor Co.*, 567 F.3d 1120, 1125 (9th Cir. 2009); *U.S. ex rel. Grubbs v. Kanneganti*, 565 F.3d 180, 190 (5th Cir. 2009). The term "strike suit" is "professional slang" to refer to litigation that is not brought to redress genuine wrongs, but to inflict a nuisance upon the defendant. *See Cohen v. Beneficial Indus. Loan Corp.*, 337 U.S. 541, 548, 69 S. Ct. 1221, 1226, 93 L. Ed. 1528 (1949).

[22]See *Hutchison v. Deutsche Bank Secs. Inc.*, 647 F.3d 479, 484 (2d Cir. 2011) (Rule 9(b) does not apply to negligence claims). *See also Swierkiewicz v. Sorema N. A.*, 534 U.S. 506, 512–15, 122 S. Ct. 992, 152 L. Ed. 2d 1 (2002); *Leatherman v. Tarrant County Narcotics Intelligence and Coordination Unit*, 507 U.S. 163, 168, 113 S. Ct. 1160, 122 L. Ed. 2d 517 (1993).

[23]See *E-Shops Corp. v. U.S. Bank Nat'l Ass'n*, 678 F.3d 659, 663 (8th Cir. 2012); *U.S. ex rel. Grubbs v. Kanneganti*, 565 F.3d 180, 188 (5th Cir. 2009.

[24]See, e.g., *Ebeid ex rel. U.S. v. Lungwitz*, 616 F.3d 993, 999 (9th Cir. 2010) (relaxed where evidence exclusively within defendant's possession); *In re Rockefeller Ctr. Props., Inc. Secs. Litig.*, 311 F.3d 198, 216 (3d Cir. 2002) (noting that rigidity of pleading requirements may be relaxed in situations where requisite factual information is peculiarly within defendant's knowledge or control).

or mistake occurs,[25] and the amount of specificity necessary for the adverse party to prepare a responsive pleading.[26] The particularity requirement of Rule 9 is not, however, intended to abrogate or mute the Rule 8 "notice" pleading standard that applies in federal courts, and the two Rules must be read in harmony with one another.[27] Plaintiffs are still obligated to plead only "notice" of a fraud or mistake claim (viewed, as are all pleadings, through the *Twombly* "plausibility" lens).[28] But Rule 9(b) plainly compels a higher degree of that notice.[29] Thus, in fraud and mistake claims, pleaders usually must supply the "newspaper-first-paragraph" — the "who, what, when, where, and how" of the alleged scheme or mistake.[30] This "newspaper-paragraph" requirement, however, is not to be applied with too much rigidity — so long as precision and substantiation are somehow injected into the pleading.[31] "Omniscience" is not required,[32] but nor is conclusory pleading acceptable.[33] The particularity requirement must be met in the pleading itself; generally, courts will not consider after-the-fact elaborations in briefs and memoranda when testing particularity.[34]

Rule 9(b) Particularity and *Twombly*'s "Plausibility"

Pleaders alleging fraud or mistake must not only do so with particularity, they must remember to also meet the general threshold of Rule 8(a): all allegations must be pleaded in a

---

[25]*See, e.g., Craftmatic Secs. Litig. v. Kraftsow*, 890 F.2d 628, 645 (3d Cir. 1989) ("[I]n the case of corporate fraud, plaintiff cannot be expected to have personal knowledge of the details of corporate internal affairs."). *See also In re GlenFed, Inc. Secs. Litig.*, 60 F.3d 591, 593 (9th Cir. 1995) ("In cases of corporate fraud where the false and misleading information is conveyed in prospectuses, registration statements, annual reports, press releases, or other 'group-published information,' it is reasonable to presume that these are collective actions of the officers. [Thus,] a plaintiff fulfills the particularity requirement of Rule 9(b) by pleading the misrepresentations with particularity and where possible the roles of the individual defendants in the misrepresentations.").

[26]*See Dudley v. Southeastern Factor & Finance Corp.*, 446 F.2d 303 (5th Cir. 1971).

[27]*See U.S. ex rel. Grubbs v. Kanneganti*, 565 F.3d 180, 185–86 (5th Cir. 2009); *U.S. v. Ford Motor Co.*, 532 F.3d 496, 504 (6th Cir. 2008); *BJC*

Health System v. Columbia Cas. Co., 478 F.3d 908, 917 (8th Cir. 2007).

[28]*See U.S. ex rel. Grubbs v. Kanneganti*, 565 F.3d 180, 185–86 (5th Cir. 2009).

[29]*See Schaller Tel. Co. v. Golden Sky Systems, Inc.*, 298 F.3d 736, 746 (8th Cir. 2002).

[30]*See E-Shops Corp. v. U.S. Bank Nat'l Ass'n*, 678 F.3d 659, 663 (8th Cir. 2012); *Wigod v. Wells Fargo Bank, N.A.*, 673 F.3d 547, 569 (7th Cir. 2012); *Illinois Nat'l Ins. Co. v. Wyndham Worldwide Operations, Inc.*, 653 F.3d 225, 232–33 (3d Cir. 2011).

[31]*See Pirelli Armstrong Tire Corp. Retiree Med. Benefits Trust v. Walgreen Co.*, 631 F.3d 436, 441–42 (7th Cir. 2011).

[32]*See Williams v. Duke Energy Int'l, Inc.*, 681 F.3d 788, 803 (6th Cir. 2012).

[33]*See E-Shops Corp. v. U.S. Bank Nat'l Ass'n*, 678 F.3d 659, 663 (8th Cir. 2012).

[34]*See Frederico v. Home Depot*, 507 F.3d 188, 201–02 (3d Cir. 2007).

manner that shows a "plausible" claim for relief.[35]

Fraud

Pleaders are obligated to place fraud defendants on notice of the "precise misconduct" with which they are accused.[36] Each of the elements of the alleged fraud must be pleaded with particularity;[37] more is required than mere conclusory allegations of plans or schemes, or a bald recitation of the technical elements of fraud.[38] Many courts require the pleader to allege (1) the time, place, and contents of the false representations or omissions, and explain how they were fraudulent, (2) the identity of the person making the misrepresentations, (3) how the misrepresentations misled the plaintiff, and (4) what the speaker gained from the fraud.[39] In the end, the pleaded facts must give rise to a "strong inference" of fraud to comport with Rule 9(b).[40] (Ordinarily, however, it is only the *circumstances* of the fraud that must be pleaded with particularity; as for all other facts, the less demanding standard of Rule 8 applies.[41]) Any fraud averment that does not meet this standard will be "stripped" from the pleading and discounted.[42]

- *Claims "Grounded" in Fraud:* The "particularity" requirement of Rule 9(b) applies not only to claims expressly denominated as "fraud" allegations, but also to claims that are "grounded" in fraud or that "sound" in fraud,[43] including misrepresentation (if under the governing law that claim "sounds" in fraud)[44] and aiding and abetting,[45] as well as other claims involving decep-

---

[35]*See Republic Bank & Trust Co. v. Bear Stearns & Co.,* 683 F.3d 239, 247–48 (6th Cir. 2012); *Mayfield v. Nat'l Ass'n for Stock Car Auto Racing, Inc.,* 674 F.3d 369, 377 (4th Cir. 2012); *Schatz v. Republican State Leadership Comm.,* 669 F.3d 50, 58 (1st Cir. 2012).

[36]*See Frederico v. Home Depot,* 507 F.3d 188, 200 (3d Cir. 2007). *See also U.S. v. Ford Motor Co.,* 532 F.3d 496, 504 (6th Cir. 2008).

[37]*See, e.g., Shushany v. Allwaste, Inc.,* 992 F.2d 517, 521 (5th Cir. 1993).

[38]*See U.S. ex rel. Rost v. Pfizer, Inc.,* 507 F.3d 720, 731 (1st Cir. 2007); *BJC Health System v. Columbia Cas. Co.,* 478 F.3d 908, 917 (8th Cir. 2007); *In re Burlington Coat Factory Secs. Litig.,* 114 F.3d 1410, 1418 (3d Cir. 1997).

[39]*See, Anschutz Corp. v. Merrill Lynch & Co.,* 690 F.3d 98, 105 (2d Cir. 2012); *Republic Bank & Trust Co. v. Bear Stearns & Co.,* 683 F.3d 239, 247

(6th Cir. 2012); *U.S. ex rel. Matheny v. Medco Health Solutions, Inc.,* 671 F.3d 1217, 1222 (11th Cir. 2012).

[40]*See Lerner v. Fleet Bank, N.A.,* 459 F.3d 273 (2d Cir.2006).

[41]*See United States v. Corinthian Colleges,* 655 F.3d 984, 992 (9th Cir. 2011).

[42]*See Sanford v. MemberWorks, Inc.,* 625 F.3d 550, 558 (9th Cir. 2010).

[43]*See Pirelli Armstrong Tire Corp. Retiree Med. Benefits Trust v. Walgreen Co.,* 631 F.3d 436, 446–47 (7th Cir. 2011); *Vess v. Ciba-Geigy Corp. USA,* 317 F.3d 1097, 1103–04 (9th Cir. 2003).

[44]*See Republic Bank & Trust Co. v. Bear Stearns & Co.,* 683 F.3d 239, 247–48 (6th Cir. 2012).

[45]*See E-Shops Corp. v. U.S. Bank Nat'l Ass'n,* 678 F.3d 659, 663 (8th Cir. 2012).

tive conduct.[46] If the claim does not "sound" in fraud, it need not be alleged with particularity, even if it alleges an enhanced level of misconduct.[47]

- *Federal Statutory Fraud Claims:* Generally, the "particularity" requirement of Rule 9(b) also applies to federal statutory fraud claims as well as federal common law fraud claims.[48] In fact, pleading in federal securities fraud claims is even further enhanced by yet additional pleading obligations.[49]
- *State Law Fraud Claims:* The "particularity" requirement applies to both federal and State-law fraud claims.[50]
- *Fraud As An Alternative Claim:* If the pleader alleges both fraud and non-fraud claims, only the fraud claims need to satisfy the particularity requirement (unless the same facts form the basis for both claims).[51]

Mistake

A party must also plead mistake with particularity. This obligates the pleader to plead with particularity the circumstances constituting the mistake — the "who, what, when, where, and how" of the mistake.[52]

Pleading on Information and Belief

Although Rule 9(b) generally prohibits allegations made on mere information and belief,[53] pleading in this fashion may be permitted if the pleader can show both that the essential information is exclusively within another party's control and specific facts upon which the information-and-belief is based.[54] This relaxation of Rule 9(b) reflects the practical inability of a pleader

---

[46]*See Exergen Corp. v. Wal-Mart Stores, Inc.*, 575 F.3d 1312, 1326–27 (Fed.Cir. 2009) ("inequitable conduct" claim in patent litigation must satisfy Rule 9(b)).

[47]*See Bayerische Landesbank v. Aladdin Capital Mgmt. LLC*, __ F.3d __, __, 2012 WL 3156441, at *19 (2d Cir. 2012) (neither gross negligence nor breach of contract trigger Rule 9(b)).

[48]*See, e.g., United States ex rel. Matheny v. Medco Health Solutions, Inc.*, 671 F.3d 1217, 1222 (11th Cir. 2012) (applies in federal False Claims Act lawsuits); *American Dental Ass'n v. Cigna Corp.*, 605 F.3d 1283, 1291 (11th Cir. 2010) (applies in mail/wire fraud RICO lawsuits).

[49]*See, e.g., Anschutz Corp. v. Merrill Lynch & Co.*, 690 F.3d 98, 105 (2d Cir. 2012) (noting how provisions of the Private Securities Litigation Act of 1995 further enhance Rule 9(b)'s pleading obligations)..

[50]*See Republic Bank & Trust Co. v. Bear Stearns & Co.*, 683 F.3d 239, 247–48 (6th Cir. 2012); *Sullivan v. Leor Energy, LLC*, 600 F.3d 542, 550–51 (5th Cir. 2010); *U.S. ex rel. Rost v. Pfizer, Inc.*, 507 F.3d 720, 731 n.8 (1st Cir. 2007).

[51]*See Kearns v. Ford Motor Co.*, 567 F.3d 1120, 1124 (9th Cir. 2009); *Liquidation Com'n of Banco Intercontinental, S.A. v. Renta*, 530 F.3d 1339, 1355–56 (11th Cir. 2008).

[52]*See Illinois Nat'l Ins. Co. v. Wyndham Worldwide Operations, Inc.*, 653 F.3d 225, 232–33 (3d Cir. 2011).

[53]*See Drobnak v. Andersen Corp.*, 561 F.3d 778, 783 (8th Cir. 2009).

[54]*See Pirelli Armstrong Tire Corp. Retiree Med. Benefits Trust v. Walgreen*

to allege factual details that are not accessible prior to discovery.[55] Nonetheless, mindful of the often *in terrorem* effect of such claims, this approach never grants the pleader a license to speculate.[56] The prerequisites for the relaxation must first be shown to exist.[57]

Malice, Intent, Knowledge, and Condition of Mind

A party may allege malice, intent, knowledge, and condition of mind generally, as with any ordinary allegation under Rule 8.[58] But this concept of tolerable "generality" is a relative one: pleaders are excused from the elevated pleading demands of Rule 9(b), but remain obligated to meet the less strict but still meaningful Rule 8 demands of *Twombly* plausibility.[59]

Pleading Tensions Between Fraud and Intent

There is some internal tension between Rule 9(b)'s requirement that fraud—which ordinarily requires an intent to deceive—be pleaded with particularity, and Rule 9(b)'s companion provision that intent itself may be pleaded generally. Courts usually resolve this apparent inconsistency by requiring that when the claim is based upon allegations of fraud, the party has a duty to follow the requirement to plead fraud with particularity, and intent generally.[60] But the facts, as pleaded, must give rise to a "strong inference of fraudulent

---

Co., 631 F.3d 436, 442–43 (7th Cir. 2011); *Shroyer v. New Cingular Wireless Servs., Inc.*, 606 F.3d 658, 665 (9th Cir. 2010); *Exergen Corp. v. Wal-Mart Stores, Inc.*, 575 F.3d 1312, 1330 (Fed.Cir. 2009).

[55] *See, e.g., In re Rockefeller Ctr. Props., Inc. Secs. Litig.*, 311 F.3d 198, 216 (3d Cir. 2002) (rigidity of pleading requirements may be relaxed where requisite factual information is peculiarly within defendant's knowledge or control); *Corley v. Rosewood Care Ctr., Inc.*, 142 F.3d 1041, 1051 (7th Cir. 1998) (particularity requirement "must be relaxed where the plaintiff lacks access to all facts necessary to detail his claim"); *In re Burlington Coat Factory Secs. Litig.*, 114 F.3d 1410, 1418 (3d Cir. 1997) (strict application of particularity rule prior to discovery could permit sophisticated defrauders to conceal their fraud).

[56] *See Tuchman v. DSC Commc'ns Corp.*, 14 F.3d 1061, 1068 (5th Cir. 1994).

[57] *See In re Rockefeller Ctr. Props., Inc. Secs. Litig.*, 311 F.3d 198, 216 (3d Cir. 2002) (even if defendant retains control over information, "boilerplate

and conclusory allegations" are not sufficient, and pleaders must still include "factual allegations that make their theoretically viable claim plausible"). *See also U.S. ex rel. Karvelas v. Melrose-Wakefield Hosp.*, 360 F.3d 220, 226 (1st Cir. 2004) (noting that relaxed pleading must later be amended, following discovery, with details).

[58] *See Mayfield v. Nat'l Ass'n for Stock Car Auto Racing, Inc.*, 674 F.3d 369, 377 (4th Cir. 2012); *Republic Bank & Trust Co. v. Bear Stearns & Co.*, 683 F.3d 239, 247–48 (6th Cir. 2012); *Schatz v. Republican State Leadership Comm.*, 669 F.3d 50, 58 (1st Cir. 2012).

[59] *See Ashcroft v. Iqbal*, 556 U.S. 662, 686–87, 129 S.Ct. 1937, 1954, 173 L.Ed.2d 868 (2009). *See also id.* ("Rule 8 does not empower [a pleader] to plead the bare elements of his cause of action, affix the label 'general allegation,' and expect his complaint to survive a motion to dismiss.").

[60] *See, e.g., Mayfield v. Nat'l Ass'n for Stock Car Auto Racing, Inc.*, 674 F.3d 369, 377 (4th Cir. 2012); *Wigod v. Wells Fargo Bank, N.A.*, 673 F.3d 547,

intent".[61]

Group Pleading

The particularized pleading requirement is designed to notify each defendant of his, her, or its purported role in the alleged misconduct. Lumping multiple defendants together in a group pleading (*e.g.*, "defendants misled the plaintiff by stating . . .") may defeat this notice objective and, thus, may be found to be improper under Rule 9(b).[62] Although the courts might not require a pleader to parse each fact and attribute every false statement to a particular defendant (especially in cases alleging conspiracy), the pleader will be obligated, at the very least, to notify each defendant as to how he or she is alleged to have participated in the fraud.[63]

Counterclaims and Affirmative Defenses

When asserting fraud or mistake in counterclaims or affirmative defenses, the pleader must assert fraud or mistake there with particularity.

Non-Party Fraud or Mistake

Where fraud or mistake was caused by non-parties[64] or when alleging that non-parties were defrauded,[65] a party may plead fraud or mistake more generally.

Opposing an Insufficiently Particular Pleading

A party may oppose a pleading that fails to plead fraud or

---

569 (7th Cir. 2012); *Wright v. BankAmerica Corp.*, 219 F.3d 79, 91 (2d Cir. 2000). *See also Chill v. General Elec. Co.*, 101 F.3d 263, 267 (2d Cir. 1996) (speaker's intent need not be pleaded with specificity because plaintiff realistically cannot be held to allege a defendant's actual state of mind).

[61]*See Heinrich v. Waiting Angels Adoption Servs, Inc.*, 668 F.3d 393, 406 (6th Cir. 2012); *In re DDAVP Direct Purchaser Antitrust Litig.*, 585 F.3d 677, 695 (2d Cir. 2009); *Exergen Corp. v. Wal-Mart Stores, Inc.*, 575 F.3d 1312, 1327 (Fed.Cir. 2009). *See also In re Burlington Coat Factory Secs. Litig.*, 114 F.3d 1410, 1418 (3d Cir. 1997) (quoting authority, that requisite inference of fraud may be shown either (a) by alleging facts to show that defendants had both motive and opportunity to commit fraud, or (b) by alleging facts that constitute strong circumstantial evidence of conscious misbehavior or recklessness). *But see In re GlenFed, Inc. Secs. Litig.*, 42 F.3d 1541, 1545–47 (9th Cir. 1994) (in banc) (rejecting such requirement, holding that plaintiff need not allege facts from

which intent to commit fraud may be inferred).

[62]*See United States v. Corinthian Colleges*, 655 F.3d 984, 997–98 (9th Cir. 2011); *Brooks v. Blue Cross and Blue Shield of Florida, Inc.*, 116 F.3d 1364, 1381 (11th Cir. 1997). *But see Phillips v. Scientific-Atlanta, Inc.*, 374 F.3d 1015, 1018–19 (11th Cir. 2004) (noting permissive "group pleading doctrine" in securities cases, which allows presumption of group responsibility for statements and omissions).

[63]*See United States v. Corinthian Colleges*, 655 F.3d 984, 998 (9th Cir. 2011).

[64]*See, e.g., Uni*Quality, Inc. v. Infotronx, Inc.*, 974 F.2d 918, 923 (7th Cir. 1992) "([W]here a plaintiff is alleging fraud against a third party, less detail may be required.").

[65]*See, e.g., Segal v. Gordon*, 467 F.2d 602, 607 (2d Cir. 1972) ("When the pleader is asserting that third persons have been defrauded, he may be unable to detail the claim and less specificity should be required.").

mistake with particularity by filing a Rule 12(e) motion for a more definite statement,[66] a Rule 12(f) motion to strike, or a Rule 12(b) motion to dismiss.[67] Often, parties assert these motions in the alternative.

Granting Leave to Amend

Where a complaint is dismissed for failing to allege with particularity, leave to amend should generally be granted freely.[68] Leave to amend may be denied, however, where an amendment is "futile" and could never offer the requisite particularity.[69]

Constitutionality of Enhanced Pleading

Any enhanced pleading duty necessarily carries with it the risk that, on occasion, it might cause the dismissal of a valid claim which, had the claim been permitted to reach discovery, could have found sound evidentiary support. The Supreme Court considered this possibility and, citing the authority of Congress and the Rules' drafters to adopt special pleading procedures, found no Seventh Amendment (jury right) impediment.[70]

Sealing or Redacting, to Further Protect Defendant Reputations

Because reputational harm is one concern of Rule 9(b), courts may require that fraud pleadings be filed under seal, be redacted of individual names, or otherwise safeguarded.[71]

RULE 9(c)—CONDITIONS PRECEDENT

CORE CONCEPT

Where applicable to the cause of action pleaded (such as in contract cases and in certain exhaustion contexts), a plaintiff may aver *generally* that all conditions precedent have been performed or have occurred. Conversely, a response alleging that a requisite condition precedent has *not* been performed or has not occurred must be set forth *specifically* and with particularity.

---

[66]*See, e.g., Coffey v. Foamex L.P.,* 2 F.3d 157, 162 (6th Cir. 1993) (approving use of Rule 12(e) to force correction of complaint defective under Rule 9(b)).

[67]*See, e.g., Kowal v. MCI Commc'ns Corp.,* 16 F.3d 1271, 1279 (D.C. Cir. 1994) (affirming dismissal under Rule 12(b)(6) for failure to meet requirements of Rule 9(b)).

[68]*See United States v. Corinthian Colleges,* 655 F.3d 984, 998 (9th Cir. 2011); *U.S. ex rel. Willard v. Humana Health Plan of Texas Inc.,* 336 F.3d 375, 387 (5th Cir. 2003). *See also U.S. ex rel. Williams v. Bell Helicopter*

Textron Inc., 417 F.3d 450, 454–55 (5th Cir. 2005) (reversing dismissal with prejudice as improperly circumventing one purpose of Rule 9(b)— avoiding unnecessary, preliminary litigation).

[69]*See Chill v. General Elec. Co.,* 101 F.3d 263, 271–72 (2d Cir. 1996).

[70]*See Tellabs, Inc. v. Makor Issues & Rights, Ltd.,* 551 U.S. 308, 327 n. 9, 127 S. Ct. 2499, 2519 n.9, 168 L. Ed. 2d 179 (2007).

[71]*See Exergen Corp. v. Wal-Mart Stores, Inc.,* 575 F.3d 1312, 1329 n.6 (Fed.Cir. 2009).

APPLICATION

Applies to Both Contractual And Statutory Conditions

The pleading practice set forth in Rule 9(c) for conditions precedent applies whether the conditions precedent are contractual or statutory in nature.[72]

Rule Sets Procedure Only

Rule 9(c) does *not* require that conditions precedent be alleged; rather, the Rule simply provides the procedure for doing so.[73]

General Allegations Sufficient To *Plead* Conditions

The complaint does not need to allege in detail how each condition was performed; the allegations are sufficient if they aver generally that all conditions precedent have been performed.[74] Such a pleading would be very brief, simply tracking the text of Rule 9(c).[75] Other courts require modestly more, such as pleading those facts from which an inference arises that all conditions precedent have been performed.[76] If the pleading of conditions precedent is required under the applicable law, a failure to generally plead the conditions may prompt a dismissal of the federal complaint (usually without prejudice).[77]

- *"Plausibility" Pleading:* There is no definitive answer to how the post-*Twombly* "plausible" pleading standard has impacted Rule 9(c)'s instruction that the performance of conditions precedent may be pleaded generally. Some courts have ruled that Rule 9(c) is undisturbed by the advent of the "plausibility" standard,[78] while others now demand only non-conclusory, factually-specific pleading of performance.[79]

---

[72]*See Walton v. Nalco Chemical Co.*, 272 F.3d 13, 21 n.13 (1st Cir. 2001).

[73]*See Kiernan v. Zurich Companies*, 150 F.3d 1120, 1123–24 (9th Cir. 1998); *Mendez v. Bank of America Home Loans Servicing, LP*, 840 F.Supp.2d 639, 647–48 (E.D.N.Y. 2012).

[74]*See, e.g., Wyatt v. Terhune*, 315 F.3d 1108, 1118 n.12 (9th Cir. 2003); *Walton v. Nalco Chemical Co.*, 272 F.3d 13, 22 (1st Cir. 2001); *Anderson v. United Telephone Co. of Kansas*, 933 F.2d 1500, 1505 (10th Cir. 1991).

[75]*See Mendez v. Bank of America Home Loans Servicing, LP*, 840 F.Supp.2d 639, 647–48 (E.D.N.Y. 2012) (citing *Moore's Federal Practice*, that

"all conditions precedent have occurred or been performed" would suffice).

[76]*See Floorcoverings, Intern., Ltd v. Swan*, 2000 WL 528480 (N.D. Ill. 2000).

[77]*See Rojas v. Don King Prods., Inc.*, 2012 WL 760336, at *2 (S.D.N.Y. Mar. 6, 2012).

[78]*See E.E.O.C. v. Bass Pro Outdoor World, LLC*, __ F. Supp. 2d __, __, 2012 WL 1965685, at *18 (S.D.Tex. 2012); *Sovereign Bank v. Sturgis*, __ F. Supp. 2d __, __, 2012 WL 1014607, at *3 (D.Mass. 2012).

[79]*See Napster, LLC v. Rounder Records Corp.*, 761 F.Supp.2d 200, 208–09 (S.D.N.Y. 2011); *Restrepo v. Wells Fargo Bank, N.A.*, 2010 WL

Specific Allegations Necessary To *Challenge* Conditions

Where a defendant seeks to challenge a plaintiff's allegation that a condition precedent has been fulfilled, the denial must be pleaded with specificity and particularity.[80] A failure to so plead deems admitted the allegation that conditions precedent were satisfied.[81] Once the issue is joined in this way, the burden returns to plaintiff to prove that the condition precedent contested by the defendant has been met.[82]

RULE 9(d)—OFFICIAL DOCUMENT OR ACT

CORE CONCEPT

A party asserting the existence or legality of an official document need only assert that the official document was issued legally or the official act was performed legally. Conversely, a party opposing the official document or act must specifically assert the defect in the official document or the illegality of the official act.

RULE 9(e)—JUDGMENT

CORE CONCEPT

When pleading the issuance of a judgment, a party need not also set forth matter showing the jurisdictional authority of the tribunal issuing the judgment.

APPLICATION

Pleading Issuance of Judgment

When pleading the issuance of a judgment or a decision of any court, judicial or quasi-judicial tribunal, board, or officer, a party should specifically identify the judicial body issuing the judgment, the date of the judgment, the parties participating in the proceeding, and the character or effect of the judgment. A party challenging the judgment in the answer cannot deny generally, but must specifically state the defect in the judgment.

RULE 9(f)—TIME AND PLACE

CORE CONCEPT

Time and place averments are material allegations and can, if

---

374771, at *3 (S.D.Fla. Feb.3, 2010). *Cf. Tessera, Inc. v. UTAC (Taiwan) Corp.*, 2012 WL 1067672, at *2 n.4 (N.D.Cal. Mar. 28, 2012) (noting that precedent that conditions precedent need not always be pleaded pre-dated the "plausibility" standard).

[80]*See Myers v. Central Fla. Invs., Inc.*, 592 F.3d 1201, 1224 (11th Cir. 2010); *E.E.O.C. v. Serv. Temps Inc.*, 679 F.3d 323, 331 (5th Cir. 2012).

[81]*See Myers v. Central Fla. Invs., Inc.*, 592 F.3d 1201, 1224 (11th Cir. 2010).

[82]*See Myers v. Central Fla. Invs., Inc.*, 592 F.3d 1201, 1224 (11th Cir. 2010); *Runnemede Owners, Inc. v. Crest Mortg. Corp.*, 861 F.2d 1053, 1057–58 (7th Cir. 1988); *APR Energy, LLC v. Pakistan Power Resources, LLC*, 653 F.Supp.2d 1227, 1233 & 1241–41 (M.D.Fla. 2009).

appropriate, support a dismissal of a claim or defense.

APPLICATION

Specificity *Not* Required, But If Made, Averments Are Material

Rule 9(f) does *not* require that averments of time and place be pleaded specifically.[83] Instead, Rule 9(f) simply confirms that, if pleaded, averments of time and place are material and can be considered in testing the sufficiency of a pleading.[84] Thus, if the averments of time and place establish an obvious defense (such as time-bar), the inclusion of those averments can support a dismissal,[85] or, in an appropriate case, a motion for a more definite statement.[86]

RULE 9(g)—SPECIAL DAMAGES

CORE CONCEPT

Special damages must be pleaded with particularity.

APPLICATIONS

Purpose

The obligation to plead special damages with specificity is designed to alert the defending parties to the nature of the claimed damages (thus avoiding trial surprise by the extent or character of the claim) and to ensure the court is advised of the claim.[87]

Defined

Identifying special damages (which must be specially pleaded) is not always clear.[88] Special damages are those damages that are proximately caused by the defendant's alleged wrongdoing, but which were unforeseeable or which might not come to the defendant's attention unless pleaded with specificity.[89] In other words, special damages are those that are

---

[83]*See Matthew v. U.S.*, 452 F. Supp. 2d 433, 446 (S.D. N.Y. 2006).

[84]*See Grosz v. Museum of Modern Art*, 772 F.Supp.2d 473, 477 (S.D.N.Y. 2010); *In re Maxim Integrated Prods., Inc. Secs. Litig.*, 639 F.Supp.2d 1038, 1051 (N.D.Cal. 2009).

[85]*See Grosz v. Museum of Modern Art*, 772 F.Supp.2d 473, 477 (S.D.N.Y. 2010); *In re Maxim Integrated Prods., Inc. Secs. Litig.*, 639 F.Supp.2d 1038, 1051 (N.D.Cal. 2009).

[86]*See Meyer v. United Airlines, Inc.*, 624 F.Supp.2d 923, 932 (N.D.Ill. 2008).

[87]*See Bowles v. Osmose Utilities Services, Inc.*, 443 F.3d 671, 675 (8th Cir. 2006); *Great Am. Indem. Co. v. Brown*, 307 F.2d 306, 308 (5th Cir. 1962); *Adams v. United States*, 823 F.Supp.2d 1074, 1086 (D.Idaho 2011).

[88]*See 44 Liquormart, Inc. v. State of R.I.*, 940 F. Supp. 437, 438–39 (D.R.I. 1996).

[89]*See, e.g., Weyerhaeuser Co. v. Brantley*, 510 F.3d 1256, 1267 (10th Cir. 2007); *LINC Finance Corp. v. Onwuteaka*, 129 F.3d 917, 922 (7th Cir. 1997). *See also Figgins v. Advance America Cash Advance Ctrs. of Mich., Inc.*, 482 F. Supp. 2d 861, 869 (E.D. Mich. 2007) (surveying definitions).

unusual for the particular type of claim pleaded.[90] Emotional distress damages,[91] attorney's fees,[92] punitive damages,[93] defamation damages,[94] and damages flowing from trade disparagement[95] are often examples of special damages that must be pleaded with specificity. Whether prejudgment interest is an item of special damages is unclear.[96] Liquidated damages typically are not special damages.[97] In diversity cases, special damages are defined by the pertinent State's law.[98]

Specificity

A party must plead special damages by alleging the claimed actual damages with particularity and by averring how those damages were the natural and direct result of the defendant's conduct.[99] A pleading is sufficiently specific if the opposing party can respond to the allegations of special damages.[100] This obligation is not "reducible to formula", and will depend on the nature of the claim at issue, the alleged injury, and the causal connection between the two.[101] Vague, conclusory catch-all allegations (such as "including but not limited to") are likely to

---

[90]See Tipton v. Mill Creek Gravel, Inc., 373 F.3d 913, 922 n. 10 (8th Cir. 2004); Adams v. United States, 823 F.Supp.2d 1074, 1086 (D.Idaho 2011); Walton v. Nova Information Systems, 514 F. Supp. 2d 1031, 1034 (E.D. Tenn. 2007).

[91]See Botosan v. Fitzhugh, 13 F. Supp. 2d 1047, 1053 (S.D. Cal. 1998).

[92]See, e.g., United Industries, Inc. v. Simon-Hartley, Ltd., 91 F.3d 762 (5th Cir. 1996); Perry v. Serenity Behavioral Health Sys., 2009 WL 1259367, at *2 (S.D.Ga. May 6, 2009) (collecting cases); Magpie Telecom Insiders, Inc. v. MPhase Techs., Inc., 2008 WL 5068836, at *1 (D.Colo. Nov. 24, 2008).

[93]See Capital Solutions, LLC v. Konica Minolta Bus. Solutions U.S.A., Inc., 2009 WL 1635894, at *8 (D.Kan. June 11, 2009); Teel v. United Technologies Pratt & Whitney, 953 F. Supp. 1534, 1537 (S.D. Fla. 1997). But see Dowdy v. Coleman Co., 2011 WL 6151432, at *5 (D.Utah Dec. 12, 2011) (ruling that punitive damages are not special damages); Figgins v. Advance America Cash Advance Centers of Michigan, Inc., 482 F. Supp. 2d 861, 869–70 (E.D. Mich. 2007) (same).

[94]See Muzikowski v. Paramount Pictures Corp., 322 F.3d 918, 924–27 (7th Cir. 2003); 3M Co. v. Boulter, 842 F.Supp.2d 85, 118 (D.D.C. 2012).

[95]See KBT Corp., Inc. v. Ceridian Corp., 966 F. Supp. 369 (E.D. Pa. 1997).

[96]See U.S. v. All Meat and Poultry Products Stored at Lagrou Cold Storage, 470 F. Supp. 2d 823, 834–35 (N.D. Ill. 2007) (noting, but not resolving, question).

[97]See Local 705 Bhd. of Teamsters Pension Fund v. Special Serv. Co., 2009 WL 1956720, at *2 (N.D.Ill. July 8, 2009).

[98]See Diggs v. Comcast, 2012 WL 2872874, at *4 (E.D.Cal. July 11, 2012).

[99]See Browning v. Clinton, 292 F.3d 235, 245–46 (D.C. Cir. 2002).

[100]See, e.g., Suarez Matos v. Ashford Presbyterian Community Hosp., Inc., 4 F.3d 47, 52 (1st Cir. 1993) ("the more natural are the damages, the less the pleading is needed."); Morton Grove Pharms, Inc. v. National Pediculosis Ass'n, Inc., 494 F. Supp. 2d 934, 941 (N.D. Ill. 2007) (allegation sufficient when it notifies defendant of nature of claimed damages); Italiano v. Jones Chemicals, Inc., 908 F. Supp. 904, 907 (M.D. Fla. 1995) (Rule 9(g) requires specific statement permitting defendants to prepare responsive pleading and begin their defense).

[101]See Marseilles Hydro Power, LLC. v. Marseilles Land & Water Co., 2003 WL 259142 (N.D. Ill. 2003).

be insufficient under Rule 9(g).[102] An appropriate statement of special damages will generally include an estimate of the total damages, along with a listing of the specific items that comprise that sum.[103] Conversely, a conclusory declaration that a party was "damaged" and that "business" was "curtail[ed]" will generally be found inadequate.[104]

Consequences of Failing to Plead Special Damages

A party's failure to plead special damages with specificity may bar that party's recovery of special damages.[105] However, because there is no timing requirement in the Rule, a party can seek leave from the court to amend to include further items of special damages in the pleading.[106] Moreover, because the goal is to protect against unfair surprise, the court may excuse (or at least liberally construe) a weakly pleaded special damages allegation if those damages were not an essential element of the underlying claim[107] or where the opponent was not actually prejudiced by the absence of further specificity.[108]

RULE 9(h)—ADMIRALTY AND MARITIME CLAIMS

CORE CONCEPT

Special rules apply to admiralty and maritime claims.[109] A claimant wishing to proceed under those special rules must designate the claim as an admiralty or maritime one.

APPLICATIONS

Election to Proceed in Admiralty/Maritime

When the only basis for the federal forum is admiralty jurisdiction, there is no need for an election; admiralty procedures

---

[102]*See Marseilles Hydro Power, LLC. v. Marseilles Land & Water Co.,* 2003 WL 259142 (N.D. Ill. 2003) (holding that court would not require answer to such "including but not limited to" allegation, and would not permit an unpleaded damages item to reach trial).

[103]*See City and County of San Francisco v. Tutor-Saliba Corp.,* 2005 WL 645389 (N.D. Cal. 2005). *But see Luxpro Corp. v. Apple, Inc.,* 658 F.Supp.2d 921, 935–36 (W.D.Ark. 2009) (specificity does not always require pleader to allege a specific dollar amount); *Marseilles Hydro Power, LLC. v. Marseilles Land & Water Co.,* 2003 WL 259142 (N.D. Ill. 2003) (commenting that estimates of final lost dollar amounts may be unnecessary).

[104]*See Artista Records, Inc. v. Flea World, Inc.,* 356 F. Supp. 2d 411, 428 (D.N.J. 2005).

[105]*See, e.g., Lott v. Levitt,* 556 F.3d 564, 570 (7th Cir. 2009); *United Industries, Inc. v. Simon-Hartley, Ltd.,* 91 F.3d 762, 764 (5th Cir. 1996); *44 Liquormart, Inc. v. State of R.I.,* 940 F. Supp. 437, 439 (D.R.I. 1996).

[106]*See Jones v. Krautheim,* 208 F. Supp. 2d 1173, 1178 (D. Colo. 2002).

[107]*See Adams v. United States,* 823 F.Supp.2d 1074, 1086 (D.Idaho 2011).

[108]*See Bowles v. Osmose Utilities Services, Inc.,* 443 F.3d 671, 675 (8th Cir. 2006).

[109]The full text of the *Supplemental Rules For Certain Admiralty And Maritime Claims* appears at the end of Part III of this text.

apply automatically.[110] When an admiralty dispute also has another basis for federal jurisdiction (*e.g.*, diversity), the claimant has a right to elect how to proceed (either under the admiralty rules or not).[111] If a claimant asserts both admiralty and another basis for jurisdiction, the claim will likely proceed in admiralty.[112] This right of election, however, is determined claim-by-claim; non-admiralty claims are not converted into admiralty claims merely by being joined with admiralty claims,[113] nor will a claim cognizable in both admiralty and diversity jurisdiction lose its ability to proceed in diversity merely by being joined with an admiralty-only claim (provided that claim has invoked only a non-admiralty basis for jurisdiction).[114] Nor is an admiralty election necessarily irrevocable; a claimant can always request the court for leave to amend (on such a motion, the court will consider whether the claimant took an unfair advantage of the original election or otherwise prejudiced the other parties).[115]

Significance of Election: Admiralty Procedures

A claim proceeding in admiralty is subject to those procedures that have, historically, attached to actions in admiralty; a claim proceeding in diversity, on the other hand, is subject to the Federal Rules of Civil Procedure.[116]

Significance of Election: No Jury Trial

Ordinarily, choosing to proceed in admiralty means that the claims in the case are decided by the court, and not by a jury.[117] This is true even where a defendant counterclaims for common law relief and asserts what would otherwise be a timely jury demand.[118] If, however, an admiralty case has a second, independent basis for federal jurisdiction, a jury demand will be honored so long as the claimant has not made an election to

---

[110]*See Luera v. M/V Alberta*, 635 F.3d 181, 188 (5th Cir. 2011).

[111]*See Luera v. M/V Alberta*, 635 F.3d 181, 188 (5th Cir. 2011); *St. Paul Fire & Marine Ins. Co. v. Lago Canyon, Inc.*, 561 F.3d 1181, 1184 (11th Cir. 2009); *Fedorczyk v. Caribbean Cruise Lines, Ltd.*, 82 F.3d 69, 73 (3d Cir. 1996).

[112]*See Luera v. M/V Alberta*, 635 F.3d 181, 188–89 (5th Cir. 2011). *But cf. Miles v. M/V HANSA CALEDONIA*, 245 F. Supp. 2d 1261, 1263 (S.D. Ga. 2002) (noting division among courts on question in jury context).

[113]*See Maersk, Inc. v. Neewra, Inc.*, 687 F.Supp.2d 300, 340 (S.D.N.Y. 2009).

[114]*See Luera v. M/V Alberta*, 635 F.3d 181, 189–93 (5th Cir. 2011).

[115]*See Luera v. M/V Alberta*, 635 F.3d 181, 187 (5th Cir. 2011); *Miller v. Orion Const., L.P.*, 2007 WL 4206210, at *1–*2 (S.D. Tex. 2007) (noting procedure, and denying amendment).

[116]*See Luera v. M/V Alberta*, 635 F.3d 181, 188 (5th Cir. 2011).

[117]*See Luera v. M/V Alberta*, 635 F.3d 181, 188 (5th Cir. 2011); *Wingerter v. Chester Quarry Co.*, 185 F.3d 657 (7th Cir.1998); *Concordia Co., Inc. v. Panek*, 115 F.3d 67, 70–71 (1st Cir. 1997).

[118]*See American S.S. Owners Mut. Protection and Indem. Ass'n, Inc. v. Lafarge North America, Inc.*, 2008 WL 2980919, at *2–*5 (S.D. N.Y. 2008) (so holding, following majority rule); *Great Lakes Reinsurance (UK) PLC v. Masters*, 2008 WL 619342, at *1–*2 (M.D. Fla. 2008) (same). *But cf. Markel*

proceed in admiralty.[119]

Type of Designation Required

To invoke the federal courts' admiralty jurisdiction, a plaintiff must include an affirmative statement in the pleadings identifying the proceeding as an admiralty or maritime claim.[120] Failing to so identify the claim means that it is not one.[121] However, a plaintiff need not specifically incant a citation to Rule 9(h), although that is certainly the preferred practice; instead, a simple statement asserting claims in admiralty or maritime law is sufficient.[122] The absence of a jury demand is one indication that the party intends to proceed in admiralty.[123]

Appellate Review

Admiralty claims enjoy a right of immediate interlocutory appeal, including admiralty claims contained in cases having non-admiralty claims as well.[124]

Additional Research References

Wright & Miller, *Federal Practice and Procedure* §§ 1291 to 1320
C.J.S., Federal Civil Procedure §§ 252 to 257 et seq.
West's Key Number Digest, Federal Civil Procedure ⟜633 to 651

American Ins. Co. v. Linhart, 2012 WL 2930207, at *3–*4 (E.D.N.Y. July 11, 2012) (noting dispute among some courts on the issue).

[119]*See Apache Corp. v. Global SantaFe Drilling Co.*, 832 F.Supp 2d 678, 698 (W.D.La. 2010); *Muhs v. River Rats, Inc.*, 586 F.Supp.2d 1364, 1371 (S.D.Ga. 2008).

[120]*See Fedorczyk v. Caribbean Cruise Lines, Ltd.*, 82 F.3d 69, 73 (3d Cir. 1996).

[121]*See Murphy v. Florida Keys Elec. Co-op. Ass'n, Inc.*, 329 F.3d 1311, 1319 (11th Cir. 2003).

[122]*See Luera v. M/V Alberta*, 635 F.3d 181, 188–89 (5th Cir. 2011) (mere assertion of admiralty jurisdiction is sufficient); *Foulk v. Donjon Marine Co., Inc.*, 144 F.3d 252, 256 (3d Cir. 1998) (direct citation to Rule 9(h) is unambiguous and may be preferable, but it is not required); *Concordia Co., Inc. v. Panek*, 115 F.3d 67, 72 (1st Cir. 1997) (although preferred technique is to expressly invoke Rule 9(h), including the phrase "In Admiralty" in the caption, with no accompanying demand for a jury trial, found sufficient).

[123]*See Concordia Co., Inc. v. Panek*, 115 F.3d 67, 72 (1st Cir. 1997).

[124]*See* 28 U.S.C.A. § 1292(a)(3).

RULE 10
FORM OF PLEADINGS

(a) Caption; Names of Parties. Every pleading must have a caption with the court's name, a title, a file number, and a Rule 7(a) designation. The title of the complaint must name all the parties; the title of other pleadings, after naming the first party on each side, may refer generally to other parties.

(b) Paragraphs; Separate Statements. A party must state its claims or defenses in numbered paragraphs, each limited as far as practicable to a single set of circumstances. A later pleading may refer by number to a paragraph in an earlier pleading. If doing so would promote clarity, each claim founded on a separate transaction or occurrence—and each defense other than a denial—must be stated in a separate count or defense.

(c) Adoption by Reference; Exhibits. A statement in a pleading may be adopted by reference elsewhere in the same pleading or in any other pleading or motion. A copy of a written instrument that is an exhibit to a pleading is a part of the pleading for all purposes.

[April 30, 2007, effective December 1, 2007.]

AUTHORS' COMMENTARY ON RULE 10

PURPOSE AND SCOPE

Rule 10 establishes the form generally required for pleadings and motions. Pleadings and motions must contain a caption. Claims and defenses must be set forth in numbered paragraphs, with each paragraph limited to a single set of circumstances. When doing so would promote clarity, separate counts must be pleaded for each claim or defense premised on a separate transaction or occurrence. Earlier paragraphs may be adopted by reference to avoid repetition, and exhibits may be attached to pleadings.

RULE 10(a)—CAPTION; NAMES OF PARTIES

CORE CONCEPT

Every pleading and motion must contain a caption. In the original complaint, the names of all parties must be listed in the caption. For later pleadings (except notices of appeal), listing the first named party on each side is sufficient.

APPLICATIONS

Contents of Caption

Captions must contain: (a) the name of the court; (b) the title of the action (including all party names); (c) the file or docket number; and (d) the document's designation (*e.g.*, complaint, answer, reply to counterclaim).

Party Names

The title of a lawsuit properly includes the names of all parties, and these names must be listed in the original complaint.[1] Ordinarily, persons and entities not listed in the original complaint's caption are not parties to the lawsuit.[2] In all pleadings subsequent to the complaint, however, the court and the parties may shorten the caption to include only the names of the first plaintiff, the first defendant, and (where necessary) an indication that others are parties to the case (*e.g.*, "et al.").[3]

- *Warning for Notices of Appeal:* The parties to an appeal must be individually named. Omitting party names with the use of "et al." or similar phrases on a notice of appeal may be fatally deficient. The courts of appeals may disregard these shortened phrases and may accept the appeal *only* as to those parties individually named in the notice of appeal or those parties who make their intent to appeal objectively clear.[4]

- *Actual Names:* The caption must state the parties' actual

---

[1] *See Myles v. U.S.*, 416 F.3d 551, 551 (7th Cir. 2005) ("to make someone a party the plaintiff must specify him in the caption and arrange for service of process"). *Cf. Ferdik v. Bonzelet*, 963 F.2d 1258, 1263 (9th Cir. 1992) (striking original complaint that listed parties-defendant as "et al.").

[2] *See Trackwell v. U.S. Government*, 472 F.3d 1242, 1243–44 (10th Cir. 2007) (even in *pro se* case, failure to name person in caption or even in text of complaint violates Rule); *W.N.J. v. Yocom*, 257 F.3d 1171, 1172 (10th Cir. 2001) (federal courts lack jurisdiction over unnamed parties since a case has not been commenced with respect to them); *Harris v. Auxilium Pharms.,*

Inc., 664 F.Supp.2d 711, 722 (S.D.Tex. 2009) (entity not named in caption is not a party to the lawsuit). *But cf. Williams v. Bradshaw*, 459 F.3d 846, 849 (8th Cir. 2006) (holding that caption is not determinative as to who are parties to lawsuit, but is entitled to "considerable weight" on the question).

[3] *See Spivey v. Board of Church Extension and Home Mission of Church of God*, 160 F.R.D. 660, 662 (M.D. Fla. 1995) (requesting counsel to use short form captioning of case in all future court documents).

[4] *See* Fed.R.App.P. 3(c) (modifying *Torres v. Oakland Scavenger Co.*, 487 U.S. 312, 108 S. Ct. 2405, 101 L. Ed. 2d 285 (1988) (holding that use of

names. Descriptive titles are appropriate only where they clearly identify the party.[5] False names (such as an alias) are not permitted, and pleading under a false name will justify a dismissal.[6]

Fictitious Name and Pseudonym Litigation

Parties have a limited entitlement to the redaction of certain "personal data identifiers".[7] Minors, for example, are now permitted by right to litigate using only their initials, instead of their full names.[8] Parties may also seek protective orders to grant the redaction of additional personally identifying information when "good cause" exists.[9]

In very unusual circumstances, the courts also permit parties to identify themselves throughout the lawsuit by a fictitious name or pseudonym (*e.g.* "Jane Doe").[10] Such permission is extraordinary and conflicts with the public's right to open access to the judiciary,[11] a concern of constitutional dimension,[12] and with the right of private litigants to confront their accusers.[13] In fact, some courts have written that a presump-

---

"et al." phrase did not constitute an effective appeal as to parties not specifically named)).

[5]*See Mitchell v. Maynard*, 80 F.3d 1433, 1441 (10th Cir. 1996) (commenting that a party not properly named in caption may still be deemed in the case if the allegations in the text of the complaint make plain that the party is intended as a defendant, although simply mentioning the party's name in a brief will not suffice). *Compare Abelesz v. Magyar Nemzeti Bank*, 692 F.3d 661, 661 (7th Cir. 2012) ("Holocaust Victims of Bank Theft" was insufficient identification of plaintiffs and improperly "presume[d]" the merits of their claims), *and OTR Drivers at Topeka Frito-Lay, Inc.'s Distribution Center v. Frito-Lay, Inc.*, 988 F.2d 1059 (10th Cir. 1993) ("Over-The-Road Drivers" was insufficient identification of plaintiffs in the lawsuit), *with Dean v. Barber*, 951 F.2d 1210 (11th Cir.1992) (naming "Chief Deputy of County Jail" was sufficient identification of defendant), *and English v. Cowell*, 969 F.2d 465 (7th Cir.1992) (use of alleged pseudonym permitted where party may have legally changed name to adopt pseudonym and where no claim of confusion or prejudice was asserted).

[6]*See Zocaras v. Castro*, 465 F.3d

479, 481–84 (11th Cir. 2006) ("A trial is not a masquerade party nor is it a game of judicial hide-n-seek where the plaintiff may offer the defendant the added challenge of uncovering his real name.").

[7]*See* Rule 5.2, and Authors' Commentary to Rule 5.2.

[8]*See* Rule 5.2(a)(3).

[9]*See* Rule 5.2(e).

[10]*See Doe v. Megless*, 654 F.3d 404, 408 (3d Cir. 2011) (although not expressly authorized by Rule 10(a), anonymity permitted in exceptional cases); *Roe v. Aware Woman Ctr. for Choice, Inc.*, 253 F.3d 678, 684–85 (11th Cir. 2001) (reversing trial court's refusal to permit pseudonym litigation in abortion case).

[11]*See Doe v. Megless*, 654 F.3d 404, 408 (3d Cir. 2011); *Doe v. Kamehameha Schs./Bernice Pauahi Bishop Estate*, 596 F.3d 1036, 1042 (9th Cir. 2010). *See also Doe v. Frank*, 951 F.2d 320, 324 (11th Cir. 1992) ("[l]awsuits are public events").

[12]*See Rose v. Beaumont Indep. School Dist.*, 240 F.R.D. 264, 265–66 (E.D. Tex. 2007); *Doe v. Del Rio*, 241 F.R.D. 154, 156 (S.D. N.Y. 2006).

[13]*See Doe v. Megless*, 654 F.3d 404, 409 (3d Cir. 2011); *Plaintiff B v. Francis*, 631 F.3d 1310, 1315 (11th

tion exists against such pleading,[14] and others have emphasized that parties in civil cases, bringing lawsuits of their own volition to vindicate their own interests, must be prepared to stand publicly behind their allegations.[15] The practice is, therefore, often denied even in cases involving issues of great intimacy and sensitivity.[16]

There are no "hard and fast" rules that the courts apply in judging whether to permit pseudonym litigation.[17] Instead, the courts balance the plaintiff's interest in anonymity against the public's interest in disclosure and the prejudice that may befall the defendant.[18] In performing this balance, many factors may be considered, including whether the anonymous plaintiffs are challenging governmental activity, whether pressing the lawsuit will compel the plaintiffs to reveal highly intimate information or disclose an intention or desire to engage in illegal activity, and whether a child plaintiff is involved.[19] Other factors that may be considered include risks to innocent nonparties and possible mitigation (both of prejudice to the defendant and injury to the plaintiff),[20] as well as whether the litigant's identity has remained confidential, whether the litigant is a public figure, the bases for fearing and avoiding disclosure, and the magnitude of the public interest — among other factors.[21] The courts may also examine whether disclosure of identities would create a risk of retaliatory physical or mental

---

Cir. 2011); *Doe v. Kamehameha Schs./ Bernice Pauahi Bishop Estate*, 596 F.3d 1036, 1042 (9th Cir. 2010).

[14]*See Plaintiff B v. Francis*, 631 F.3d 1310, 1315 (11th Cir. 2011); *Doe v. Kamehameha Schs./Bernice Pauahi Bishop Estate*, 596 F.3d 1036, 1042 (9th Cir. 2010).

[15]*See Rose v. Beaumont Indep. School Dist.*, 240 F.R.D. 264, 267–68 (E.D. Tex. 2007); *Doe v. Bell Atlantic Business Systems Services, Inc.*, 162 F.R.D. 418 (D. Mass. 1995).

[16]*See Rose v. Beaumont Indep. School Dist.*, 240 F.R.D. 264, 265–66 (E.D. Tex. 2007) (denying pseudonym status for young girl in case concerning her involvement in school sex club); *Doe v. Bell Atlantic Business Systems Services, Inc.*, 162 F.R.D. 418 (D. Mass. 1995) (denying pseudonym status to alleged victim of sexual harassment who claimed her traditional Chinese family would react negatively if the allegations became public).

[17]*See Rose v. Beaumont Indep. School Dist.*, 240 F.R.D. 264, 266 (E.D.

Tex. 2007).

[18]*See Doe v. Megless*, 654 F.3d 404, 408 (3d Cir. 2011); *Plaintiff B v. Francis*, 631 F.3d 1310, 1315–16 (11th Cir. 2011); *Sealed Plaintiff v. Sealed Defendant*, 537 F.3d 185, 189 (2d Cir. 2008).

[19]*See Plaintiff B v. Francis*, 631 F.3d 1310, 1316 (11th Cir. 2011); *Sealed Plaintiff v. Sealed Defendant*, 537 F.3d 185, 189–90 (2d Cir. 2008); *Doe v. Porter*, 370 F.3d 558, 560 (6th Cir. 2004); *W.N.J. v. Yocom*, 257 F.3d 1171 (10th Cir.2001).

[20]*See Sealed Plaintiff v. Sealed Defendant*, 537 F.3d 185, 190 (2d Cir. 2008) (listing 10 factors for consideration).

[21]*See Doe v. Megless*, 654 F.3d 404, 408–12 (3d Cir. 2011) (discussing different approaches). *See also Doe v. Kamehameha Schs./Bernice Pauahi Bishop Estate*, 596 F.3d 1036, 1042–46 (9th Cir. 2010) (weighing 5 factors: severity of threatened harm; reasonableness of fears; vulnerability to retaliation; prejudice to opponent; public interest).

harm.[22] To proceed by pseudonym, the party must petition the court for permission.[23] Specific procedures vary among the Circuits.[24] Permission, if granted, may be accompanied by a requirement that the true names of the parties be disclosed to the defendants and the court, but sealed to the general public.[25] More narrowly, a party may temporarily identify an opponent with a fictional name so long as the identities of the opponents are clear and their actual names will be uncovered through discovery.[26]

Alterations to the Caption

Rule 10(a) specifically encourages parties and the court to shorten the case caption in all documents subsequent to the complaint by listing only the first named plaintiff and defendant. Other immaterial alterations to the caption, such as changes in capitalization, fonts, or typefaces, are generally not improper and will not require remedy by the court.[27]

Pro Se Pleadings

In reviewing *pro se* pleadings, courts may scavenge the documents with greater vigor to discern whether the identities of parties are clear from the text of the allegations (if not so in the captions), but even in those instances, if the identities of the intended parties are not clear, the pleading is subject to dismissal.[28]

RULE 10(b)—PARAGRAPHS; SEPARATE STATEMENTS

CORE CONCEPT

Pleadings should contain separately-numbered paragraphs, each of which, as far as practicable, should contain a single set of circumstances. Pleadings should contain separate counts for claims arising from different transactions or occurrences, if doing

---

[22]*See Sealed Plaintiff v. Sealed Defendant*, 537 F.3d 185, 190 (2d Cir. 2008). *See also Does I thru XXIII v. Advanced Textile Corp.*, 214 F.3d 1058, 1068 (9th Cir. 2000) (in retaliation-case petitions, district court should weigh (1) severity of threatened harm, (2) reasonableness of fear of harm, (3) plaintiff's vulnerability to harm, (4) prejudice, at each stage of the proceedings, to the defendants and how that prejudice could be mitigated, and (5) whether public's interest would be best served by requiring disclosure of identities).

[23]*See W.N.J. v. Yocom*, 257 F.3d 1171 (10th Cir.2001).

[24]*See Doe v. Megless*, 654 F.3d 404, 408–12 (3d Cir. 2011) (discussing different approaches); *E.E.O.C. v. ABM Industries Inc.*, 249 F.R.D. 588, 592 (E.D. Cal. 2008) (describing procedural variations).

[25]*See W.N.J. v. Yocom*, 257 F.3d 1171 (10th Cir.2001).

[26]*See Dean v. Barber*, 951 F.2d 1210 (11th Cir.1992).

[27]*See Jaeger v. Dubuque County*, 880 F. Supp. 640 (N.D. Iowa 1995) (finding no Rule 10 violation by capitalization of party names or other alterations of fonts, type faces, ink types, printer types, or printing methods).

[28]*See Trackwell v. U.S. Government*, 472 F.3d 1242, 1243–44 (10th Cir. 2007).

so adds clarity. Defenses (other than denials) should be set forth in separate counts as well. In all other instances, separate counts are permitted, though not required.

APPLICATIONS

Paragraphing a Pleading's Facts

As far as practicable, a party should set forth each distinct allegation of fact in a separate paragraph, and each paragraph should be numbered.[29] The purpose of this requirement is to ensure a pleading that is easily understood by both the opponent and the court.[30]

"Group" Pleading

"Group" pleading allegations (*e.g.*, accusing the "defendants" generally of engaging in certain misconduct, without particularizing which defendant committed what act) are generally inappropriate. Such "group" pleading techniques may defeat the clarity objectives of the separate-paragraph requirement by failing to specify what each party is alleged to have done wrong.[31] This is particularly true with claims that must be alleged with particularity.[32]

Pleading in Separate Counts

A party may include in a single count all theories of recovery, so long as those theories are all premised on the same facts.[33] The better practice, however, is to plead distinct claims

---

[29]*See Politico v. Promus Hotels, Inc.*, 184 F.R.D. 232, 234 (E.D. N.Y. 1999) (as far as possible, complaint should avoid multiple allegations per paragraph); *Bieros v. Nicola*, 851 F. Supp. 683 (E.D. Pa. 1994) (commenting that each factual allegation should be pleaded in a separate paragraph).

[30]*See City of Fort Lauderdale v. Scott*, 773 F.Supp.2d 1355, 1358–59 (S.D.Fla. 2011); *Allen v. Life Ins. Co. of North America*, 267 F.R.D. 407, 409 (N.D.Ga. 2009). *See also O'Donnell v. Elgin, J. & E. Ry. Co.*, 338 U.S. 384, 392, 70 S. Ct. 200, 205, 94 L. Ed. 187 (1949) (chastising that "the unfortunately prolonged course" of trial was due, in part, to counsel's failure to separate issues in counsel's pleading, preparation, and thinking).

[31]*See Veltmann v. Walpole Pharmacy, Inc.*, 928 F. Supp. 1161, 1164 (M.D. Fla. 1996) (finding pleading insufficient where complaint made it impossible to determine which defendant committed which alleged act);

Gen-Probe, Inc. v. Amoco Corp., Inc., 926 F. Supp. 948, 962 (S.D. Cal. 1996) (counts must identify which averments relate to which claims and to which defendants). *See also Magluta v. Samples*, 256 F.3d 1282, 1284 (11th Cir. 2001) (vacating judgment and directing that plaintiff replead because 58-page, group-pleaded "complaint is a quintessential 'shotgun' pleading of the kind we have condemned repeatedly"). *Cf. In re GlenFed, Inc. Securities Litigation*, 60 F.3d 591, 592–93 (9th Cir. 1995) (noting that "group" pleading might be appropriate if complaint alleged that outside directors either participated in day-to-day activities of business, or had special relationship with business, such as participating in preparing or communicating group information).

[32]*See supra* Authors' Commentary to Rule 9(b) ("**Group Pleading**").

[33]*See Smith v. Computer Task Group, Inc.*, 568 F.Supp.2d 603, 612 n. 6 (M.D. N.C. 2008) (separate counts

and theories in separate counts.[34] In any event, where the claims and theories rest on different facts[35] or where clarity otherwise requires it,[36] distinct claims and theories must be pleaded in separate counts.[37] Separate counts help to ensure that the pleadings achieve their goals of framing the issues (through useful and productive pleadings), providing a platform for informed pretrial proceedings and discovery management, and facilitating evidentiary admissibility decisions at trial.[38] The practice also enables a court to grant dispositive relief with respect to an entire count, and not just part of one.[39] Thus, the dictates of Rule 10 are not intended to be exceptions to the federal practice against technical forms of pleading, but instead provide the guidelines that help ensure that pleadings are "simple, concise, and direct".[40]

Violations and Remedy

Improper paragraph numbering or conciseness will not defeat a pleading, unless the violations interfere with the ability to understand the claims or otherwise cause prejudice.[41] However, when a party's pleading provides insufficient notice of the claims because of its confusing structure, the absence of numbered paragraphs, or the improper combination of multiple claims in a single count, the opposing party may move for a

---

not strictly required where claims arise from same transaction or occurrence); *Woodburn v. Florida Dep't of Children & Family Servs.*, 859 F. Supp. 2d 1305, 1310 (S.D.Fla. 2012) (same).

[34]*See Stone Mountain Game Ranch, Inc. v. Hunt*, 746 F.2d 761, 763 (11th Cir. 1984); *Selep v. City of Chicago*, 842 F. Supp. 1068 (N.D. Ill. 1993). *But see Miller UK Ltd. v. Caterpillar Inc.*, 859 F. Supp. 2d 941, 942 (N.D.Ill. 2012) (using separate counts to plead distinct legal theories for the same claim, though "almost universally employed," is "a conceptually improper federal pleading technique").

[35]*See Resolution Trust Corp. v. Hess*, 820 F. Supp. 1359 (D. Utah 1993) (granting motion for more definite statement where multiple transactions were included within a single count).

[36]*See Pelletier v. Zweifel*, 921 F.2d 1465, 1479 n.29 (11th Cir. 1991) (pendent State claim discounted where no separate court was pleaded); *Dodge v. Susquehanna University*, 796 F. Supp. 829 (M.D. Pa. 1992) (because failure to separate into distinct counts gave defendant the impression that no breach of contract claim was being pressed, the belatedly asserted breach of contract theory was dismissed from the complaint). *But cf. Gardunio v. Town of Cicero*, 674 F.Supp.2d 976, 983–83 (N.D.Ill. 2009) (separate counts are required only when necessary to clarify claims); *Gilbert v. Feld*, 788 F. Supp. 854 (E.D. Pa. 1992) (separate counts not required where such practice would not enhance the clarity of the presentation of an already clear pleading).

[37]*See Bautista v. Los Angeles County*, 216 F.3d 837, 840–41 (9th Cir. 2000).

[38]*See Davis v. Coca-Cola Bottling Co. Consol.*, 516 F.3d 955, 980 n.57 (11th Cir. 2008); *Bautista v. Los Angeles County*, 216 F.3d 837, 840–41 (9th Cir. 2000).

[39]*See Savin v. Robinson*, 2001 WL 1191192 (N.D. Ill. 2001).

[40]*See Phillips v. Girdich*, 408 F.3d 124, 128 (2d Cir. 2005).

[41]*See Phillips v. Girdich*, 408 F.3d 124, 128 (2d Cir. 2005); *Patrick Patterson Custom Homes, Inc. v. Bach*, 586 F.Supp.2d 1026, 1038 (N.D.Ill. 2008).

more definite statement or to strike the pleading,[42] or a dismissal.[43] Such a motion must be made before filing a response. The typical remedy granted by the court is an order directing the party to replead, or a dismissal without prejudice and with leave to amend within a short period of time.[44]

RULE 10(c)—ADOPTION BY REFERENCE; EXHIBITS

CORE CONCEPT

A party may adopt by reference statements from the same pleading, or from a different pleading or motion filed in the same case. A party may also attach exhibits or writings to the pleading, thereby making the exhibits part of the pleading for all purposes.

APPLICATIONS

Adopting Paragraphs by Reference

By specifically cross-referencing earlier paragraphs, a party may incorporate the allegations contained there without having to repeat them. But this practice must be used with care. Thoughtlessly adopting wholesale prior sections of a pleading, including portions not germane to the count being pleaded, violates this Rule.[45]

Adopting Documents or Pleadings by Reference

A party may adopt documents or pleadings (in whole or in part) by reference so long as the adopted document or pleading is expressly named. Generally, this practice is limited to documents and pleadings that are already before the court. Documents or pleadings filed in another lawsuit usually cannot be

---

[42]*See Corbitt v. Home Depot U.S.A., Inc.*, 573 F.3d 1223, 1252–53 (11th Cir. 2009) (faulting "shotgun" pleading that failed to divide counts and to properly incorporate by reference); *Rogler v. U.S. Dep't of Health & Human Servs.*, 620 F.Supp.2d 123, 128 (D.D.C. 2009) (dismissing complaint as "too long, too convoluted, and too confusing to require" response); *Gonzales v. Wing*, 167 F.R.D. 352, 354–355 (N.D. N.Y. 1996) (dismissing plaintiff's 287-page, numberless complaint because it presented a "far too . . . heavy burden" upon the defendants to frame a comprehensive defense and provided the court with no meaningful basis to assess the claims' sufficiency).

[43]*See Stanard v. Nygren*, 658 F.3d 792, 797–801 (7th Cir. 2011) (second amended complaint properly denied where its length, rampant grammatical, syntactical, and typographical errors, and vague, confusing, and conclusory nature made it unintelligible).

[44]*See, e.g., Phillips v. Girdich*, 408 F.3d 124, 128 (2d Cir. 2005); *U.S. ex rel. Carpenter v. Abbott Labs., Inc.*, 723 F.Supp.2d 395, 411 n.27 (D.Mass. 2010). *But cf. Frederiksen v. City of Lockport*, 384 F.3d 437, 439 (7th Cir. 2004) (affirming dismissal with prejudice for failure to comply with Rule 10(b) after four chances over more than two years).

[45]*See Corbitt v. Home Depot U.S.A., Inc.*, 573 F.3d 1223, 1253 (11th Cir. 2009).

adopted by reference,[46] nor may parts of an abandoned pleading.[47]

Attaching Exhibits

A party may (but is not required to) attach copies of written instruments as exhibits to a pleading. Generally, newspaper articles, commentaries, and cartoons,[48] photographs and x-rays,[49] certain federal investigative reports,[50] affidavits,[51] and copies of superseded pleadings[52] do not qualify for attachment as exhibits. A videotape recording, however, may qualify.[53]

- *Attachments by Opponent:* If the pleader does *not* attach, but instead merely refers to, a written instrument in the pleading, the opponent may usually still attach that instrument to the responsive pleading, so long as the instrument is referred to in the first pleading, is indisputably authentic, and is "central" to the pleader's claim.[54] The same result may follow where the unattached exhibit is not referenced by the original pleader, but is unquestionably integral to the dispute.[55]

Effect of Attaching Exhibits

Exhibits attached to a pleading are made a part of that pleading for all purposes.[56]

- *Ruling on Motions to Dismiss:* The court may consider

---

[46]*See Constellation Energy Commodities Group Inc. v. Transfield ER Cape Ltd.*, 801 F.Supp. 2d 211, 223 (S.D.N.Y. 2011).

[47]*See Galloway v. City of Abbeville,* __ F. Supp. 2d __, __, 2012 WL 2527066, at *5 (M.D.Ala. 2012).

[48]*See Perkins v. Silverstein,* 939 F.2d 463, 467 (7th Cir. 1991). *But cf. Geinosky v. City of Chicago,* 675 F.3d 743, 745 & n.1 (7th Cir. 2012) (permitting party opposing a dismissal motion to "elaborate on his factual allegations", which may include, in a proper case, referencing a newspaper story).

[49]*See Nkemakolam v. St. John's Military Sch.,* __ F. Supp. 2d __, __, 2012 WL 2449841, at *4–*5 (D.Kan. 2012) (stricken because they were not included to be assertions of fact).

[50]*See Dichter-Mad Family Partners, LLP v. U.S.,* 707 F.Supp.2d 1016, 1019 (C.D.Cal. 2010) (factual allegations and decisions in report by SEC inspector general not properly incorporated).

[51]*See Rose v. Bartle,* 871 F.2d 331, 339 (3d Cir. 1989) (noting that affidavits are not Rule 10(c) materials).

[52]*See Hinton v. Trans Union, LLC,* 654 F.Supp.2d 440, 446–48 (E.D.Va. 2009) (rejecting attempt by amended complaint to incorporate original complaint), *aff'd,* 382 Fed. Appx. 256 (4th Cir. 2010).

[53]*See Howell by Goerdt v. Tribune Entertainment Co.,* 106 F.3d 215, 218–19 (7th Cir. 1997) (citing Rule 10(c) in treating videotape as "appended" to the complaint, where plaintiff's counsel urged the court to view it).

[54]*See U.S. v. Ritchie,* 342 F.3d 903, 908 (9th Cir. 2003); *Beddall v. State Street Bank and Trust Co.,* 137 F.3d 12, 17 (1st Cir. 1998); *Weiner v. Klais and Co., Inc.,* 108 F.3d 86, 89 (6th Cir. 1997).

[55]*See L-7 Designs, Inc. v. Old Navy, LLC,* 647 F.3d 419, 422 (2d Cir. 2011).

[56]*See Gburek v. Litton Loan Servicing LP,* 614 F.3d 380, 384 (7th Cir. 2010); *Park Univ. Enters., Inc. v. American Cas. Co. Of Reading, PA,* 442 F.3d 1239, 1244 (10th Cir. 2006).

attachments in ruling on dismissal motions,[57] and if an inconsistency exists between the attachment and the pleaded allegations, the attachment will control.[58] Similarly, where an attachment reveals a "built-in" defense that bars recovery as a matter of law, the court may grant a dismissal.[59]

- *Evaluating Particularity:* The court may consult attachments in evaluating whether an allegation of fraud or mistake meets the particularity requirement of Rule 9(b).[60]

- *"Vouching" Risk:* By adopting by reference a portion of an attached document, the pleader does not necessarily "vouch" for the truth of all the contents of the document. The attached document will be read in conjunction with the pleading that adopts it. Thus, a defamation plaintiff may safely attach an allegedly libelous writing without being deemed to have admitted as true all the asserted libels contained in the writing, just as a commercial plaintiff, alleging the non-receipt of goods, may attach an allegedly forged receipt without admitting that the document truthfully recounts that the goods were received.[61] Likewise, an aggrieved litigant can attach a copy of an appealed-from ruling without being deemed to have thereby "vouched" for the very reasoning or result that litigant is in the process of challenging.[62]

---

[57]*See Wigod v. Wells Fargo Bank, N.A.*, 673 F.3d 547, 556 (7th Cir. 2012); *Reynolds v. Dormire*, 636 F.3d 976, 979 (8th Cir. 2011); *Philips v. Pitt County Mem'l Hosp.*, 572 F.3d 176, 180 (4th Cir. 2009).

[58]*See Polzin v. Gage*, 636 F.3d 834, 838 (7th Cir. 2011); *Coos County Board of County Com'rs v. Kempthorne*, 531 F.3d 792, 811 n.14 (9th Cir. 2008); *General Elec. Capital Corp. v. Posey*, 415 F.3d 391, 398 n.8 (5th Cir. 2005).

[59]*See Hamilton v. O'Leary*, 976 F.2d 341 (7th Cir.1992).

[60]*See Adams Respiratory Therapeutics, Inc. v. Perrigo Co.*, 255 F.R.D. 443, 446 (W.D.Mich. 2009).

[61]*See Guzell v. Hiller*, 223 F.3d 518, 519 (7th Cir. 2000) (giving examples); *Gant v. Wallingford Bd. of Educ.*, 69 F.3d 669, 674–75 (2d Cir. 1995) (giving these examples). *See also Jones v. City of Cincinnati*, 521 F.3d 555, 561 (6th Cir. 2008) (attaching interview transcript may vouch that

statements were made, but not that they were true); *Pinder v. Knorowski*, 660 F.Supp.2d 726 (E.D.Va. 2009) (same).

[62]In fact, one Court of Appeals harshly derided this sort of "vouching" argument as "beyond nonsensical" and "unworthy" of the attorneys who asserted it. *See Carroll v. Yates*, 362 F.3d 984, 986 (7th Cir. 2004) ("The logic of the . . . argument is that an appellant, required by the appellate rules to append to his brief the decision of the district court or administrative agency that he is appealing, . . . by doing so kills the appeal because appending amounts to vouching for the truth of the propositions in the appended decision. The argument if accepted would do wonders for our workload, but is beyond nonsensical and unworthy of the office of the Attorney General of Illinois."). The Court, then, directed the filing attorneys to show cause why they should not be sanctioned for briefing "frivolous argumentation". *Id.*

Additional Research References

Wright & Miller, *Federal Practice and Procedure* §§ 1321 to 1330
C.J.S., Federal Civil Procedure § 251
West's Key Number Digest, Federal Civil Procedure ⟜625 to 629

RULE 11
SIGNING PLEADINGS, MOTIONS, AND OTHER PAPERS; REPRESENTATIONS TO THE COURT; SANCTIONS

(a) Signature. Every pleading, written motion, and other paper must be signed by at least one attorney of record in the attorney's name—or by a party personally if the party is unrepresented. The paper must state the signer's address, e-mail address, and telephone number. Unless a rule or statute specifically states otherwise, a pleading need not be verified or accompanied by an affidavit. The court must strike an unsigned paper unless the omission is promptly corrected after being called to the attorney's or party's attention.

(b) Representations to the Court. By presenting to the court a pleading, written motion, or other paper—whether by signing, filing, submitting, or later advocating it—an attorney or unrepresented party certifies that to the best of the person's knowledge, information, and belief, formed after an inquiry reasonable under the circumstances:

   (1) it is not being presented for any improper purpose, such as to harass, cause unnecessary delay, or needlessly increase the cost of litigation;

   (2) the claims, defenses, and other legal contentions are warranted by existing law or by a nonfrivolous argument for extending, modifying, or reversing existing law or for establishing new law;

   (3) the factual contentions have evidentiary support or, if specifically so identified, will likely have evidentiary support after a reasonable opportunity for further investigation or discovery; and

   (4) the denials of factual contentions are warranted on the evidence or, if specifically so identified, are reasonably based on belief or a lack of

information.

(c) Sanctions.

(1) *In General.* If, after notice and a reasonable opportunity to respond, the court determines that
Rule 11(b) has been violated, the court may
impose an appropriate sanction on any attorney,
law firm, or party that violated the rule or is
responsible for the violation. Absent exceptional
circumstances, a law firm must be held jointly
responsible for a violation committed by its
partner, associate, or employee.

(2) *Motion for Sanctions.* A motion for sanctions
must be made separately from any other motion
and must describe the specific conduct that allegedly violates Rule 11(b). The motion must be
served under Rule 5, but it must not be filed or
be presented to the court if the challenged paper,
claim, defense, contention, or denial is withdrawn or appropriately corrected within 21 days
after service or within another time the court
sets. If warranted, the court may award to the
prevailing party the reasonable expenses, including attorney's fees, incurred for the motion.

(3) *On the Court's Initiative.* On its own, the court
may order an attorney, law firm, or party to show
cause why conduct specifically described in the
order has not violated Rule 11(b).

(4) *Nature of a Sanction.* A sanction imposed under
this rule must be limited to what suffices to deter repetition of the conduct or comparable
conduct by others similarly situated. The sanction may include nonmonetary directives; an order to pay a penalty into court; or, if imposed on
motion and warranted for effective deterrence,
an order directing payment to the movant of part
or all of the reasonable attorney's fees and other
expenses directly resulting from the violation.

(5) *Limitations on Monetary Sanctions.* The court
must not impose a monetary sanction:

  (A) against a represented party for violating Rule
11(b)(2); or

  (B) on its own, unless it issued the show-cause order under Rule 11(c)(3) before voluntary dismissal or settlement of the claims made by or against the party that is, or whose attorneys are, to be sanctioned.

(6) *Requirements for an Order.* An order imposing a sanction must describe the sanctioned conduct and explain the basis for the sanction.

(d) Inapplicability to Discovery. This rule does not apply to disclosures and discovery requests, responses, objections, and motions under Rules 26 through 37.

[Amended April 28, 1983, effective August 1, 1983; March 2, 1987, effective August 1, 1987; April 22, 1993, effective December 1, 1993; April 30, 2007, effective December 1, 2007.]

AUTHORS' COMMENTARY ON RULE 11

PURPOSE AND SCOPE

Rule 11 establishes the standards attorneys and parties must meet when filing pleadings, motions, or other documents in court. It also regulates the circumstances in which sanctions may be imposed if the standards of Rule 11 are not met.

APPLICATIONS

Scope

Rule 11 applies to every pleading, written motion, or other paper filed or served[1] in the course of litigation, as well as to advocacy of documents previously filed.[2] Rule 11 does not apply to misconduct unrelated to signed motions, pleadings or other

---

[1] *See, e.g., Antonious v. Spalding & Evenflo Companies, Inc.*, 281 F.3d 1258, 1261 (Fed. Cir. 2002) (court ordered filing of document; through apparent inadvertence document was served but not filed; held, party which served offending document falls within scope of Rule 11 notwithstanding that document was never actually filed with court; acknowledging general principle that Rule 11 does not apply to documents not filed with court).

[2] *See, e.g., Legault v. Zambarano*, 105 F.3d 24, 27–28 (1st Cir. 1997) (let-

ter is within scope of Rule 11 only where letter was motion in disguise that was intended to affect judicial decision on such matter as whether to issue a preliminary injunction; acknowledging general rule that letter is outside scope of Rule 11); *O'Brien v. Alexander*, 101 F.3d 1479, 1489 (2d Cir. 1996) (oral advocacy flowing directly from documents filed with court fall within scope of Rule 11; other oral statements are not controlled by Rule 11).

papers.[3] Rule 11 is also inapplicable to state-court filings.[4]

Purpose of Rule 11

The purposes of Rule 11 are to deter baseless filings[5] and "streamline the administration and procedure of the federal courts."[6] Rule 11 sanctions are intended to facilitate case management, not to increase caseload by requiring a district court to analyze the reasonableness of legal and factual contentions that it would otherwise not have to ascertain.[7]

Rule 11 and Appellate Jurisdiction

In general, Rule 11 is applicable only to lawsuits in district courts.[8] Federal Rule of Appellate Procedure 38 usually controls sanctions for groundless appeals to circuit courts.[9] However, an exception to that delineation of authority occurs when a party

---

[3]*See, e.g., Ali v. Tolbert*, 636 F.3d 622, 626–27 (D.C. Cir. 2011) (actions intended to evade service of process and four-year delay in filing answer did not violate Rule 11 as they were not related to representations in court); *Lamboy-Ortiz v. Ortiz-Velez*, 630 F.3d 228, 245 (1st Cir. 2010) ("[N]o matter how vexatious or disruptive counsel's conduct was during trial, Rule 11 cannot reach such misconduct."); *Christian v. Mattel, Inc.*, 286 F.3d 1118, 1130–1131 (9th Cir. 2002) (Rule 11 inapplicable to discovery abuses or oral misrepresentations unrelated to document filings); *Milltex Industries Corp. v. Jacquard Lace Co., Ltd.*, 55 F.3d 34, 37 (2d Cir. 1995) (Rule 11 applicable only to circumstances involving pleadings, motions, or other papers; Rule 11 inapplicable to attorney's defiance of judicial order). *But see, Antonious v. Spalding & Evenflo Companies, Inc.*, 281 F.3d 1258, 1261 (Fed. Cir. 2002) (court ordered filing of document; through apparent inadvertence document was served but not filed; held, party which served offending document falls within scope of Rule 11 notwithstanding that document was never actually filed with court; however, acknowledging general principle that Rule 11 does not apply to documents not filed with court). *Turner v. Sungard Business Systems, Inc.*, 91 F.3d 1418, 1421 (11th Cir. 1996) (attorney whose only written document was notice of appearance was nevertheless subject to sanctions for later oral advocacy).

[4]*See, e.g., Lamboy-Ortiz v. Ortiz-Velez*, 630 F.3d 228, 245 (1st Cir. 2010) ("[I]t is Federal Rule of Appellate Procedure 38, not Federal Rule of Civil Procedure 11, that authorizes sanctions for the filing of frivolous appeals."); *Edwards v. General Motors Corp.*, 153 F.3d 242, 245 (5th Cir. 1998) (Rule 11 inapplicable to filing made in state court before case was removed to federal court; sanctions may be imposed on post-removal filings; noting general agreement among circuit courts); *Bisciglia v. Kenosha Unified School Dist. No. 1*, 45 F.3d 223, 226 (7th Cir. 1995) (filing in state court not sanctionable under Rule 11).

[5]*CQ Intern. Co., Inc. v. Rochem Intern., Inc., USA*, 659 F.3d 53, 62 (1st Cir. 2011); *Strom v. U.S.*, 641 F.3d 1051, 1059 (9th Cir. 2011). *See also In re Taylor*, 655 F.3d 274 (3d Cir. 2011). ("[T]he prime goal [of Rule 11 sanctions] should be deterrence of repetition of improper conduct", citing *Waltz v. County of Lycoming*, 974 F.2d 387, 390 (3d Cir. 1992).

[6]*Cooter & Gell v. Hartmarx Corp.*, 496 U.S. 384, 393, 110 S.Ct. 2447, 2462, 110 L.Ed.2d 359 (1990).

[7]*CQ Intern. Co., Inc. v. Rochem Intern., Inc., USA*, 659 F.3d 53, 62 (1st Cir.2011).

[8]*See Fengling Liu*, 664 F.3d 367, 373 n. 5 (2d Cir. 2011) and Fed. R. Civ. P. 1.

[9]*See, e.g., In re 60 East 80th Street Equities, Inc.*, 218 F.3d 109, 118–19 n. 3 (2d Cir. 2000) (Rule 11 inapplicable to appellate litigation).

files a notice of appeal. In that circumstance it is Rule 11 that requires the appellant to sign the notice of appeal. Thus, a failure to sign the notice is an error, which may be correctable under Rule 11(a), and an appellate court does not lose jurisdiction of an appeal if the appellant corrects the original failure to sign.[10]

Administrative Litigation

Normally Rule 11 is not applicable in proceedings before administrative agencies. Application of Rule 11 occurs in such cases only when the case becomes a lawsuit in a federal court.[11]

Documents Filed in State Court

If a document was filed when a case was pending in state court, Rule 11 cannot be used to sanction the signer of the document in federal district court. Thus, a failure to update or amend a state complaint, by itself, is not sanctionable in federal court.[12]

Party v. Attorney

Rule 11 does not authorize actions in favor of a party against the party's attorney.[13]

Pro Se Litigants

Rule 11 applies to pro se litigants. Thus, a pro se litigant may be sanctioned for violating Rule 11. However, a party's pro se status is a factor that is weighed in determining whether the party's behavior was reasonable under the standard of Rule 11.[14]

---

[10]*Becker v. Montgomery*, 532 U.S. 757, 121 S. Ct. 1801, 149 L. Ed. 2d 983 (2001) (distinguishing Rule 11 from jurisdictional requirements of Rules 3 and 4; also suggesting that appropriate means of adjusting signature requirement of Rule 11 "to keep pace with technological advances" is through process of rule amendment, not judicial decision). *See also Countryman v. Farmers Ins. Exchange*, 639 F.3d 1270, 1272 (10th Cir. 2010).

[11]*See, e.g., Santa Maria v. Pacific Bell*, 202 F.3d 1170, 1179 (9th Cir. 2000) ("The obligations of Rule 11 extend only to suits filed in federal court, not to such administrative procedures as filing a charge with the EEOC. . . . In fact, the very nature of an EEOC charge makes this clear: the charge serves as an allegation of wrongdoing which the EEOC investigates to determine if it has merit.").

[12]*See, e.g., Bisciglia v. Kenosha*

Unified School Dist. No. 1, 45 F.3d 223, 226–27 (7th Cir. 1995).

[13]*See, e.g., Mark Industries, Ltd. v. Sea Captain's Choice, Inc.*, 50 F.3d 730 (9th Cir.1995) (purpose of Rule 11 is to deter abuses that harm the opponent, not the client).

[14]*See, e.g., In re Nosek*, 609 F.3d 6, 9 (1st Cir. 2010) (citing factors listed by the 1993 Advisory Committee notes to Rule 11 for determining when liability is appropriate, including "whether the responsible person is trained in the law"); *Kennedy v. National Juvenile Detention Ass'n*, 187 F.3d 690, 696 (7th Cir. 1999) (affirming conclusion that claim was not frivolous, "especially considering the plaintiff's lack of legal representation"); *Moore v. Time, Inc.*, 180 F.3d 463, 463 (2d Cir. 1999) (affirming district court's denial of Rule 11 sanctions on attorney who appeared pro se where district court had reasoned that

Lack of Subject Matter Jurisdiction

Rule 11 applies even in cases where it is subsequently determined that the district court lacked subject matter jurisdiction.[15]

Voluntary Dismissal: Rule 41

It appears that a district court retains jurisdiction to impose Rule 11 sanctions even after a case has been voluntarily dismissed without prejudice under Rule 41.[16]

RULE 11(a)—SIGNATURE

CORE CONCEPT

Rule 11(a) requires that documents be signed by an attorney or (if there is no attorney) the party. It abolishes old verification requirements, unless they have been preserved by rule or statute.

Signature of Attorney

If a party has retained counsel, at least one attorney must sign the document and provide the attorney's address and telephone number.[17] Rule 11 requires that an individual attorney must sign the document. Under older law that is probably still good precedent, a signature that purports to be on behalf of an entire law firm does not satisfy the signature requirement of Rule 11.[18]

Signature of Party

A party must sign the document if the party is not repre-

---

attorney was "not sophisticated"; however, also imposing sanctions under Federal Rule of Appellate Procedure 38 for frivolous appeal; attorney had received "clear warning" from district court and had previously brought other frivolous appeals to appellate court).

[15]*Willy v. Coastal Corp.*, 503 U.S. 131, 112 S. Ct. 1076, 117 L. Ed. 2d 280 (1992). *See also, e.g., Tropf v. Fidelity Nat. Title Ins. Co.*, 289 F.3d 929, 938 (6th Cir. 2002) (citing *Willy, supra;* noting that sanctions in such circumstances do not violate Article III of Constitution); *Perpetual Securities, Inc. v. Tang*, 290 F.3d 132, 141 (2d Cir. 2002) (same result); *Branson v. Nott*, 62 F.3d 287, 293 (9th Cir. 1995) (absence of subject matter jurisdiction does not preclude application of Rule 11 sanctions).

[16]*See, e.g., Nelson v. Napolitan*, 657 F.3d 586, 589 (7th Cir. 2011) (citing *Cooter & Gell v. Hartmarx Corp.*, 496 U.S. 384, 397, 110 S.Ct. 2447, 110 L.Ed.2d 359 (1990)); *In re Schaefer Salt Recovery, Inc.*, 542 F.3d 90, 98 (3d Cir. 2008) ("[W]e have held that a district court has jurisdiction to impose sanctions under Rule 11 even though the motion seeking the sanctions was filed after the filing of a notice of voluntary dismissal under Rule 41.").

[17]*See, e.g., In re Lothian Oil Inc.*, 650 F.3d 539, 544 (5th Cir. 2011) (dismissed appeals of litigants who failed to sign notice of appeal and failed to correct pleadings after notice from clerk); *Duran v. Carris*, 238 F.3d 1268, 1271 (10th Cir. 2001) (attorney's failure to disclose that brief submitted by allegedly pro se party was actually ghostwritten by attorney, who did not enter appearance, is violation of Rule 11(a)).

[18]*Pavelic & LeFlore v. Marvel Entertainment Group*, 493 U.S. 120, 110 S. Ct. 456, 107 L. Ed. 2d 438 (1989).

sented by counsel.[19] The party must also provide an address and telephone number, if any. Although courts may be more lenient with pro se litigants, it should not be assumed that they are immune from Rule 11 sanctions.[20]

Verification and Affidavits

Rule 11 abolishes requirements of verification and affidavits for documents filed or served in the course of litigation, except where such a requirement is expressly preserved by another rule or statute.[21] The signature of a party or counsel is the substitute for prior verification practices. Continuing requirements for verification are most commonly encountered in suits at state law. Occasionally, however, a federal rule or statute may also require verification. For example, Rule 23.1, governing derivative actions by shareholders, requires verification of a plaintiff-shareholder's complaint.[22]

Failure to Sign

If a document subject to Rule 11 is not signed, the court has power to strike the document unless the proponent signs it promptly upon notification of the missing signature.[23]

RULE 11(b)—REPRESENTATIONS TO COURT

CORE CONCEPT

Rule 11(b) establishes the standards that documents which are regulated by Rule 11 must meet. It also specifically provides that the standards are applicable to later advocacy of such documents, as well as to the initial submission of the documents.

APPLICATIONS

Unsuccessful Pleadings and Motions

Mere failure to prevail on a particular pleading or motion

---

[19]*Maxwell v. Snow*, 409 F.3d 354, 356 (D.C. Cir. 2005) ("[A]ll pleadings by a *pro se* plaintiff must be signed by the party."). *Cf., Business Guides, Inc. v. Chromatic Communications Enterprises, Inc.*, 498 U.S. 533, 111 S. Ct. 922, 112 L. Ed. 2d 1140 (1991).

[20]*Maxwell v. Snow*, 409 F.3d 354, 356 (D.C. Cir. 2005) (failure of pro se plaintiff to sign complaint must, upon notification of defect, be corrected promptly or pleading must be stricken). *Warren v. Guelker*, 29 F.3d 1386, 1390 (9th Cir. 1994) (Rule 11 "explicitly applies to parties not represented by attorneys.").

[21]*See, e.g., Cobell v. Norton*, 391 F.3d 251, 255 (D.C. Cir. 2004) (subject to exceptions, Rule 11 eliminates the need for verification).

[22]*See also, e.g.,* 15 U.S.C.A. § 78u-4 (requiring sworn certification by proposed class representative in cases within scope of Private Securities Litigation Reform Act of 1995).

[23]*See, e.g., de Aza-Paez v. U.S.*, 343 F.3d 552, 552 (1st Cir. 2003) (per curiam) ("Rule 11(a) provides that an unsigned paper will not be stricken for lack of signature if it is corrected promptly"); *Kovilic Const. Co., Inc. v. Missbrenner*, 106 F.3d 768, 772 (7th Cir. 1997) ("[D]ocuments should be struck only where the failure to sign severely prejudiced the opposing party.").

does not, of itself, establish a violation of Rule 11.[24] Rule 11 is not a provision based on strict liability, and a violation may be found only when some significant carelessness is identified.[25] To find a violation, two elements must be met: "(1) whether the [relevant document] is legally or factually 'baseless' from an objective perspective, and (2) if the attorney has conducted 'a reasonable and competent inquiry' before signing and filing it.' "[26]

Claims Evaluated Individually

Although the literal language of Rule 11 might seem to address whether entire documents meet the Rule's requirements, it is settled that portions of a document might be in violation of Rule 11, notwithstanding that other portions of the same document are satisfactory.[27]

Improper Rule 11 Motions

Attorneys are cautioned that because Rule 11 violations may be raised by motions, such motions themselves are subject to review under Rule 11, and can be the subject of additional

---

[24]*Altran Corp. v. Ford Motor Co.*, 502 U.S. 939, 112 S. Ct. 373, 116 L. Ed. 2d 324 (1991) (if party's position is reasonable, a loss on the merits does not trigger Rule 11 sanctions). *See, e.g., Morris v. Wachovia Securities, Inc.*, 448 F.3d 268, 278 (4th Cir. 2006) (Rule 11(b) violation triggers sanctions only when violation renders the entire complaint a "substantial failure."); *Obert v. Republic Western Ins. Co.*, 398 F.3d 138, 146 (1st Cir. 2005) (objectively hopeless motion, filed in good faith, need not invariably be basis for sanctions; to impose sanctions in such cases on a routine basis "would tie courts and counsel in knots"); *Hartmarx Corp. v. Abboud*, 326 F.3d 862, 868 (7th Cir. 2003) (reasonable position on close question under new rule is not sanctionable even if other position is superior). *But cf., Holgate v. Baldwin*, 425 F.3d 671, 677 (9th Cir. 2005) (presence of one non-frivolous claim does not immunize entire complaint from Rule 11).

[25]*Citibank Global Markets, Inc. v. Rodriguez Santana*, 573 F.3d 17 (1st Cir. 2009) (citing other authority).

[26]*ICU Medical, Inc. v. Alaris Medical Systems, Inc.*, 558 F.3d 1368, 1381 (Fed. Cir. 2009). *See also In re Nosek*, 609 F.3d 6, 9 (1st Cir. 2010) (citing the 1993 Advisory Committee

notes to Rule 11 for determining when liability is appropriate: "Whether the improper conduct was willful, or negligent; whether it was part of a pattern of activity, or an isolated event; whether it infected the entire pleading, or only one particular count or defense; whether the person has engaged in similar conduct in other litigation; whether it was intended to injure; what effect it had on the litigation process in time or expense; whether the responsible person is trained in the law; what amount, given the financial resources of the responsible person, is needed to deter that person from repetition in the same case; [and] what amount is needed to deter similar activity by other litigants.").

[27]*See, e.g., Ledford v. Peeples*, 568 F.3d 1258, 1307 (11th Cir. 2009) (error for court to fail to isolate claims of each plaintiff in determining whether securities fraud claims were frivolous); *Perez v. Posse Comitatus*, 373 F.3d 321 (2d Cir.2004) ("A complaint challenged under Rule 11(b) is not ordinarily analyzed as an individual unit. . . . [T]he fact that a claim is properly asserted against one defendant does not mean that the same claim may properly be asserted against a different defendant.").

allegations of violations of Rule 11.[28]

Reasonable Inquiry

Rule 11(b) provides that persons who sign, file, submit or later advocate documents are certifying to the court that the document or advocacy is based upon the person's best knowledge, information or belief, which is in turn based upon an inquiry that was reasonable in the circumstances of the particular case.[29] This is a change in language from the previous Rule 11 standard, and is intended to lower the burden on the proponent of a document.[30] However, an attorney operates under a "continuous obligation to make inquiries."[31] While an attorney may rely on information provided by a client, such information must be obtained through reasonable inquiry.[32] The duty of reasonable inquiry applies to *pro se* parties, represented parties and attorneys, and is an objective standard of reason-

---

[28]*But see, Blue v. U.S. Dept. of Army*, 914 F.2d 525, 548 (4th Cir. 1990) ("Litigants should be able to defend themselves from the imposition of sanctions without incurring further sanctions.").

[29]*See, e.g., Eon-Net LP v. Flagstar Bancorp.*, 653 F.3d 1314, 1328 (Fed. Cir. 2011) (counsel failed to perform a reasonable pre-filing investigation and position taken during litigation unsupportable); *Ruth v. Unifund CCR Partners*, 604 F.3d 908, 911 (6th Cir. 2010) (sanctions proper when "minimal effort into searching public sources . . . would have discovered all she needed to know"); *Merritt v. International Ass'n of Machinists and Aerospace Workers*, 613 F.3d 609 (6th Cir. 2010) (sanctions upheld when "clerical error" would not have occurred "had Plaintiffs' counsel adequately researched the factual basis" for claims); *U.S. Bank Nat. Ass'n, N.D. v. Sullivan-Moore*, 406 F.3d 465, 470 (7th Cir. 2005) (empty head but pure heart is no excuse); *Antonious v. Spalding & Evenflo Companies, Inc.*, 275 F.3d 1066, 1072 (Fed. Cir. 2002) ("Rule 11 requires that the attorney not rely solely on the client's claim interpretation, but instead perform an independent claim analysis."); *Hernandez v. Joliet Police Dept.*, 197 F.3d 256, 264 (7th Cir. 1999) (failure to perform basic legal research to learn that suit against state's attorney's office was barred by 11th Amendment to federal

constitution). *But see Commercial Cleaning Services, L.L.C. v. Colin Service Systems, Inc.*, 271 F.3d 374, 386 (2d Cir. 2001) (error for district court not to provide sanctioned plaintiff with opportunity to conduct discovery to fill deficiencies in information; Rule 11(b) does not require plaintiff "to know at the time of pleading all facts necessary to establish the claim"); *Dubois v. U.S. Dept. of Agriculture*, 270 F.3d 77, 82 (1st Cir. 2001) (duty to investigate need not be pursued until absolute certainty is achieved); *Garr v. U.S. Healthcare, Inc.*, 22 F.3d 1274, 1278 (3d Cir. 1994) (the "obligation personally to comply with the requirements of Rule 11 clearly does not preclude the signer from any reliance on information from other persons").

[30]*Hadges v. Yonkers Racing Corp.*, 48 F.3d 1320, 1329–30 (2d Cir. 1995) (amended Rule 11 permits attorney to rely on objectively reasonable representation of client; thus, duty of attorney to make inquiry is relaxed). *See also Strom v. U.S.*, 641 F.3d 1051, 1059 (9th Cir. 2011) ("Rule 11 sets a low bar." Citing cases).

[31]*Battles v. City of Ft. Myers*, 127 F.3d 1298, 1300 (11th Cir. 1997) (failure to do so may be sanctionable if attorney advocates position that has become untenable).

[32]*In re Taylor*, 655 F.3d 274, 284 (3d Cir. 2011).

ableness under the circumstances.[33] Moreover, although the matter is still uncertain, the unwillingness of a party's opponent to cooperate in a pre-litigation examination of facts might not justify a party's failure to undertake a reasonable inquiry.[34]

Standard of Culpability

Rule 11(b)(1) provides that by presenting a document or arguing on its behalf, a person certifies that the document has no improper purpose, such as harassment[35] or undue delay or expense. This language carries over from the previous version of Rule 11, and is intended to regulate bad faith filings.[36] It should already be clear, of course, that while bad faith may indeed trigger sanctions under Rule 11, conduct that does not involve bad faith may also be sanctionable.[37]

The standard for imposing Rule 11 sanctions can change

---

[33]*Business Guides, Inc. v. Chromatic Communications Enterprises, Inc.*, 498 U.S. 533, 111 S. Ct. 922, 923–924, 112 L. Ed 1140 (1991).

[34]*Compare View Engineering, Inc. v. Robotic Vision Systems, Inc.*, 208 F.3d 981, 986 (Fed. Cir. 2000) (an opponent "is not required to allow pre-litigation discovery" and lack of such an opportunity is not a defense to sanctions for failure to make reasonable inquiry), *with Hoffmann-La Roche Inc. v. Invamed Inc.*, 213 F.3d 1359 (Fed. Cir. 2000) (reasonable inquiry met where claimants sought information from opponent prior to litigation, but were rejected; opponent was bound by confidentiality agreement with third party, but had not sought any sort of release; opponent released samples of drug at issue, but claimants were unable to reverse engineer samples to determine if patent infringement had occurred).

[35]*See, e.g., F.D.I.C. v. Maxxam, Inc.*, 523 F.3d 566, 584 (5th Cir. 2008) (legitimate tactics, not independently improper, considered collectively, caused harassment and delay and therefore violated Rule 11); *Whitehead v. Food Max of Mississippi, Inc.*, 332 F.3d 796 (5th Cir. 2003) (en banc) (even a nonfrivolous submission to court may be sanctionable when document was submitted for improper purpose; noting that excessive motions can constitute harassment, and even legitimate documents that also "use

abusive language toward opposing counsel" can trigger sanction). *But see Building and Const. Trades Council of Buffalo, New York and Vicinity v. Downtown Development, Inc.*, 448 F.3d 138 (2d Cir. 2006) (Rule 11(b) not triggered simply because otherwise proper lawsuit was motivated in substantial part by "interests unrelated to the subject matter of the action").

[36]*See, e.g., Cuna Mut. Ins. Soc. v. Office and Professional Employees Intern. Union, Local 39*, 443 F.3d 556, 561 (7th Cir. 2006) (in Seventh Circuit, meritless challenges to arbitration awards are particularly vulnerable to Rule 11 sanctions); *American Intern. Adjustment Co. v. Galvin*, 86 F.3d 1455 (7th Cir. 1996) ("[A] pleader may assert contradictory statements of fact only when legitimately in doubt about the facts in question;" citing Rule 11). *But cf., In re Pennie & Edmonds LLP*, 323 F.3d 86, 87 (2d Cir. 2003) (where court decides to impose sanctions sua sponte, law firm did not have benefit of "safe harbor" provision; thus sanctions were only appropriate for subjective bad faith, not for unreasonable but genuine subjective good faith).

[37]*See, e.g., Young v. City of Providence ex rel. Napolitano*, 404 F.3d 33 (1st Cir. 2005) (no bad faith requirement for sanctions under Rule 11). *Cf. PAE Government Services, Inc. v. MPRI, Inc.*, 514 F.3d 856, 859–60 (9th Cir. 2007) (holding that nothing in the Rules prevents a party from filing inconsistent and contradictory pleadings

depending on whether the accused is an attorney or party,[38] and whether the motion for sanctions is by a party or *sua sponte* by the court.[39] The standard has been variously stated as whether the legal position has "no chance of success,"[40] whether there is "no reasonable argument to extend, modify, or reverse the law as it stands,"[41] whether the pleading or position is culpably careless,[42] whether a reasonable attorney in like circumstances could not have believed his actions legally justified,[43] whether the frivolous nature of the claims-at-issue is unequivocal,[44] whether the actions "compromise standards of professional integrity and competence",[45] whether the actions show objective unreasonableness,[46] and whether the actions are "akin to contempt".[47] Rule 11 liability may be found where an

---

unless there is a showing of bad faith; reversing district court's order "striking" inconsistent pleadings as not authorized under current Rule 11; in addition, court had not followed procedural requirements of Rule 11).

[38]*In re Nosek*, 609 F.3d 6, 9 (1st Cir. 2010) (citing factors listed by the 1993 Advisory Committee notes to Rule 11 for determining when liability is appropriate, including "whether the responsible person is trained in the law").

[39]*ATSI Communications, Inc. v. Shaar Fund, Ltd.*, 579 F.3d 143, 150–152 (2nd Cir. 2009) (objective unreasonableness standard is replaced by subjective bad faith standard for *sua sponte* motion; however standard would not apply in Private Securities Litigation Reform Act case as that Act required court to make Rule 11 finding at the conclusion of the case).

[40]*Fishoff v. Coty, Inc.*, 634 F.3d 647, 654 (2d Cir. 2011) (citing *Morley v. Ciba-Geigy Corp.*, 66 F.3d 21, 25 (2d Cir. 1995)).

[41]*Id.*

[42]*Roger Edwards, LLC v. Fiddes & Son Ltd.*, 437 F.3d 140, 142 (1st Cir. 2006) ("To support a finding of frivolousness, some decree of fault is required, but the fault need not be a wicked or subjectively reckless state of mind; rather an individual 'must, at the very least, be culpably careless to commit a violation,'").

[43]*Burns v. George Basilikas Trust*, 599 F.3d 673, 677 (DC Cir. 2010) (citing *In re Sargent*, 136 F.3d 349, 352

(4th Cir.1998)).

[44]*Carter v. ALK Holdings, Inc.*, 605 F.3d 1319, 1324–1325 (Fed. Cir. 2010) (sanctions imposed for attempt to bring state court action into federal court improper when court found substantial question of federal patent law in action). *See also CQ Intern. Co., Inc. v. Rochem Intern., Inc., USA*, 659 F.3d 53, 61 (1st Cir. 2011) (claims although "belatedly and insufficiently developed" were not frivolous and did not warrant sanctions).

[45]*In re Crescent City Estates, LLC*, 588 F.3d 822, 830 (4th Cir. 2009) (dicta in case decided under 28 U.S.C.A. § 1447(c) declining to impose costs on attorney who erroneously removed case from state to federal court).

[46]*ATSI Communications, Inc. v. Shaar Fund, Ltd.*, 579 F.3d 143, 150 (2nd Cir. 2009) ("Since the inquiry must be 'reasonable under the circumstances,' liability for Rule 11 violations 'requires only a showing of objective unreasonableness on the part of the attorney or client signing the papers' citing *Ted Lapidus, S.A. v. Vann*, 112 F.3d 91, 96 (2d Cir.1997)); *Doe v. Fulton-Dekalb Hosp. Authority*, 628 F.3d 1325, 1340–1341 (11th Cir. 2010) (violated objective reasonableness when attorney provided no legal authority for position).

[47]*See Lucas v. Duncan*, 574 F.3d 772, 775 (D.C. Cir. 2009) and cases cited therein (acknowledging "the unusual position of the trial court in such circumstances, serving at once as both prosecutor and judge" but declining to choose between the "akin to

attorney files multiple identical claims rather than one suit against multiple parties.[48]

Rule 11 sanctions are reserved for correcting litigation abuse[49] and should not be "applied to adventuresome, though responsible, lawyering which advocates creative legal theories."[50]

Standard for Attorney's Motion v. Judicial Show Cause Order

It is clear that the means by which a Rule 11 issue is raised differ, depending on whether an attorney or the court raises the issue. In particular, an attorney or party seeking a sanction under Rule 11 must first comply with the "safe harbor" requirement of Rule 11(c)(1)(A), while a judicially initiated "show cause" order need not. However, it is less clear whether the objective standard for imposition of a Rule 11 sanction also differs, depending on whether the issue arises from an attorney's motion or a judge's order.[51] Attorneys must consult local precedent on this point.

Advocating Changes in Law

Rule 11(b)(2) provides that by presenting a document or arguing on its behalf, a person certifies that the arguments in the document are either justified by existing law or are "nonfrivolous" arguments for alteration in existing law.[52] Rule 11(b)(2) is a change from the previous version of Rule 11, and

---

contempt" and "objective reasonableness" standards, as both had been violated in that case).

[48]*See, e.g., De Dios v. International Realty & Investments*, 641 F.3d 1071, 1076 (9th Cir. 2011).

[49]*Ario v. Underwriting Members of Syndicate 53 at Lloyds for 1998 Year of Account*, 618 F.3d 277, 297 (3d Cir. 2010) (sanctions not warranted "since the cited cases did not expressly foreclose attorney's argument, and there was no basis in existing law" against it).

[50]*Mary Ann Pensiero, Inc. v. Lingle*, 847 F.2d 90, 94 (3d Cir. 1988).

[51]*Compare, e.g., Kaplan v. DaimlerChrysler, A.G.*, 331 F.3d 1251, 1255–56 (11th Cir. 2003) (court-initiated sanction requires finding of more serious misconduct); *In re Pennie & Edmonds LLP*, 323 F.3d 86, 90–93 (2d Cir. 2003) (standard is analogous to contempt of court standard); *and* United National Insurance Co. v. R & D Latex Corp., 242 F.3d 1102, 1115 (9th Cir.2001) (higher standard re-

quired for judicially imposed sanctions) *with Young v. City of Providence ex rel. Napolitano*, 404 F.3d 33, 39 (1st Cir. 2005) (specifically rejecting foregoing precedent; holding that standard is the same for sanctions sought by attorney or initiated by judge).

[52]*See, e.g., Matrix IV, Inc. v. American National Bank and Trust Co. of Chicago*, 649 F.3d 539, 542 (7th Cir. 2011) ("Based on the conflict in our caselaw, we cannot say that . . . claims were frivolous or designed to harass."); *Ario v. Underwriting Members of Syndicate 53 at Lloyds for 1998 Year of Account*, 618 F.3d 277, 297 (3d Cir. 3010) (sanctions not warranted even though there was no basis for argument in existing law, since the cited cases did not expressly foreclose attorney's argument, and there was no basis in existing law against him). *Brunt v. Service Employees Intern. Union*, 284 F.3d 715, 721 (7th Cir. 2002) (although parties' claims "were barred by existing Supreme Court and Seventh Circuit case law," district court could still properly find that complaint

is intended to be a lesser burden on an advocate than the former standard of "good faith" arguments.[53]

Foundation for Factual Allegations

Rule 11(b)(3) requires persons alleging facts to do so with "evidentiary support" or, when specifically stated, to believe they can develop evidentiary support through further investigation. Rule 11(b)(3) thus establishes a lesser standard than the former requirement that allegations be "well grounded" in fact.[54]

Rule 11 (b)(3) requires an attorney to certify that the factual contentions in a pleading "have evidentiary support." Rule 11 sanctions may not be imposed against an attorney if there is evidence to support the lawyer's assertions[55]; however, speculation and conclusory allegations coupled with general careless-

---

was not frivolous under rule 11); *In re Sargent*, 136 F.3d 349, 352 (4th Cir. 1998) (standard of Rule 11(b)(2) is "objective reasonableness. . . .[P]ut differently, a legal position violates Rule 11 if it 'has absolutely no chance of success under the existing precedent.' "). *Cf. McCarty v. Verizon New England, Inc.*, 674 F.3d 119, 125–126 (1st Cir. 2012) (tort claim clearly barred by state workers compensation exclusivity clause and pursued after warning of the court warranted sanctions; "Persistence on the part of counsel is often an admirable virtue; but in this instance it was overdone.").

[53]*See, e.g., Independent Lift Truck Builders Union v. NACCO Materials Handling Group, Inc.*, 202 F.3d 965, 968 (7th Cir. 2000) (no sanction for advocating position in conflict with two controlling decisions where position was " 'not totally baseless' " and " 'had some logical and practical appeal' "); *Protective Life Ins. Co. v. Dignity Viatical Settlement Partners, L.P.*, 171 F.3d 52, 57 (1st Cir. 1999) (party's attempt "to squeeze too much from [prior case law] . . . though aggressive, did not justify the imposition of Rule 11 sanctions;" using analogous case law as "building block" may not be persuasive to court, but can still be good faith). *Cf., Holgate v. Baldwin*, 425 F.3d 671, 680 (9th Cir. 2005) (failure to cite adverse authority does not by itself trigger Rule 11 sanctions). *But see, e.g., Margo v. Weiss*, 213 F.3d 55 (2d Cir.2000) (Rule 11(b)(2) "establishes

an objective standard, intended to eliminate any 'empty-head pure-heart' justification for patently frivolous arguments").

[54]*Rotella v. Wood*, 528 U.S. 549, 120 S. Ct. 1075, 145 L. Ed. 2d 1047 (2000) (Rule 11(b)(3) provides flexibility by "allowing pleadings based on evidence reasonably anticipated after further investigation or discovery"). *See, e.g., Tennessee Valley Authority v. Whitman*, 336 F.3d 1236 (11th Cir. 2003) (when EPA files suit, it need not possess evidence sufficient for victory at trial; instead, it need only meet equivalent of "probable cause" standard of criminal law, and not even "more rigorous 'substantial evidence' " standard of administrative law). *But cf., Morris v. Wachovia Securities, Inc.*, 448 F.3d 268, 277 (4th Cir. 2006) ("Factual allegations fail to satisfy Rule 11(b)(3) when they are 'unsupported by *any* information obtained prior to filing.' "); *Macken ex rel. Macken v. Jensen*, 333 F.3d 797 (7th Cir. 2003) (Rule 11(b)(3) requires plaintiff "to establish evidentiary support [of amount in controversy], or at least a likelihood of obtaining that support, *before* filing suit in federal court.").

[55]*Kiobel v. Millson*, 592 F.3d 78, 81 (2nd Cir. 2010) (overturning imposition of sanctions against attorney based on his claim that "witnesses are giving testimony that counsel knows to be false").

ness warrant sanctions.[56] There is no requirement under Rule 11 that the attorney distinguish fact from inference.[57]

Foundation for Denials

Rule 11(b)(4) requires denials of factual allegations to be warranted by the evidence unless a person specifically states that the denial is reasonably based upon a lack of information or on belief. Like Rule 11(b)(3), this provision also establishes a lesser standard than the former version of Rule 11.[58]

Conduct not a "Representation to the Court"

Conduct not involving a document submitted to the court, including the failure to submit a document, is not sanctionable under Rule 11.[59] Likewise, disregard of a court order,[60] attorney misconduct during trial,[61] and oral statements made during argument,[62] not included in written submissions to the court, do not fall under Rule 11.

RULE 11(c)—SANCTIONS

CORE CONCEPT

Rule 11(c) regulates who may be sanctioned for violations of Rule 11(b), as well as how the sanction process may be initiated. Rule 11(c) also governs the extent and limitations of the court's sanctioning power.

APPLICATIONS

Applicability to Rule 11(a)

By its terms, Rule 11(c) applies only to violations of Rule 11(b), not Rule 11(a). It is unnecessary to apply Rule 11(c) to Rule 11(a) because the last sentence of Rule 11(a) contains its

---

[56]*Mendez-Aponte v. Bonilla*, 645 F.3d 60, 68 (1st Cir. 2011) (sanctions upheld where opposition to summary judgment contained "speculation and conclusory allegations," was "incomprehensible," included irrelevant material and was generally "slopy and careless").

[57]*See Lucas v. Duncan*, 574 F.3d 772, 777 (D.C.Cir. 2009) ("The Rule merely requires an attorney to certify that the factual contentions in a paper he presents to the court "have evidentiary support").

[58]*But see, e.g., Attwood v. Singletary*, 105 F.3d 610, 613 (11th Cir. 1997) (actions based on arguably good faith belief are sanctionable where party failed to make reasonable inquiry into accuracy of information).

[59]*Ali v. Tolbert*, 636 F.3d 622, 626–27 (D.C. Cir. 2011) (citing cases

and holding actions intended to evade service of process and four-year delay in filing an answer did not violate Rule 11 as such conduct was not related to representations to court).

[60]*Metz v. Unizan Bank*, 655 F.3d 485, 491 (6th Cir. 2011) (Rule 11 does not directly cover the disregard of court orders).

[61]*Lamboy-Ortiz v. Ortiz-Velez*, 630 F.3d 228, 245 (1st Cir. 2010) ("[N]o matter how vexations or disruptive counsel's conduct during the trial, Rule 11 cannot reach such misconduct.").

[62]*See, e.g., In re Bees*, 562 F. 3d 284, 288–89 (4th Cir. 2009) (oral statement may form basis of Rule 11 sanctions only if it advocates a contention previously contained in a written submission.)

own sanction.

Persons Sanctioned

Rule 11(c) provides that in appropriate circumstances the court may sanction attorneys, law firms, or parties.[63] This is a change from the former provision, which was construed as not permitting sanctions against an entire law firm.

"Snapshot Rule"

Rule 11 liability, as to whether sanctions are appropriate and the date from which sanctions can be assessed, is determined at the time a document is filed.[64] However, Rule 11 also imposes a duty of continuing diligence, and is violated when a party continues to maintain a position despite discovery or other evidence that the position has no merit.[65]

Sovereign Immunity

It appears that government attorneys and their clients are subject to sanctions, including monetary sanctions, notwithstanding considerations of sovereign immunity.[66]

---

[63]*See, e.g., Union Planters Bank v. L & J Development Co., Inc.*, 115 F.3d 378, 384 (6th Cir. 1997) ("Rule 11 explicitly allows for the imposition of sanctions upon a party responsible for the rule's violation, provided that a represented party is not sanctioned for a violation of subsection (b)(2) involving unwarranted legal contentions."). *See also Holgate v. Baldwin*, 425 F.3d 671, 677 (9th Cir. 2005) (even lawyer who withdraws from case due to conflict of interest is not immune from Rule 11 sanctions for conduct prior to withdrawal). *See generally United Stars Industries, Inc. v. Plastech Engineered Products, Inc.*, 525 F.3d 605, 610 (7th Cir. 2008) (affirmed sanctions against law firm advancing position with no evidentiary support; district court awarded sanctions against firm under 28 U.S.C. § 1927 which only provides for sanctions against individual lawyers; court found that sanctions against firm were appropriate under Rule 11); *In re Cardizem CD Antitrust Litigation*, 481 F.3d 355, 360 (6th Cir. 2007) (court does not have power to impose costs on attorney absent express power granted by statute such as Rule 11 or 28 U.S.C. § 1927).

[64]*See, e.g., CQ Intern. Co., Inc. v. Rochem Intern., Inc., USA*, 659 F.3d 53, 63 (1st Cir. 2011); *Marlin v. Moody Nat. Bank, N.A.*, 533 F.3d 374, 380 (5th Cir. 2008) ("snapshot rule" applies when deciding whether sanctions are appropriate, as well as the date from which sanctions, if any, should be imposed); *Skidmore Energy, Inc. v. KPMG*, 455 F.3d 564, 570 (5th Cir. 2006) (the rule "ensures that Rule 11 liability is assessed only for a violation existing at the moment of filing"); *Salkil v. Mount Sterling Tp. Police Dept.*, 458 F.3d 520, 530 (6th Cir. 2006) (court should avoid using hindsight in assessing whether counsel's conduct was reasonable under the circumstances).

[65]*Fabriko Acquisition Corporation v. Prokos*, 536 F.3d 605, 610 (7th Cir.2008) (in determining Rule 11 liability, court does not focus only on the knowledge a party had as of the date of its filing; violation found in continuing to advocate a claim that has no legal basis and refusing to alter or withdraw it when the deficiency is pointed out); *B & H Medical, L.L.C. v. ABP Admin., Inc.*, 526 F.3d 257, 269 (6th Cir. 2008) (affirmed sanctions for obviously meritless antitrust lawsuit maintained "long beyond the time at which discovery demonstrated that the claims lacked support.")

[66]*See, e.g., Mattingly v. U.S.*, 939 F.2d 816, 817–18 (9th Cir. 1991) (affirming monetary sanctions; held, government is not immune from Rule

Magistrate Judges

It appears that magistrate judges do not have independent authority to order sanctions under Rule 11.[67] However, the issue is sufficiently unsettled so that attorneys should investigate local practice.

Judicial Discretion

The denial of a motion for sanctions is reviewed under the abuse-of-discretion standard.[68] In close cases the district court should provide an explanation of its reasons for denying sanctions,[69] and a circuit may remand close questions regarding a motion for sanctions where a district court denies sanctions without explanation.[70] Due to the highly deferential abuse-of-

---

11). *Cf., King v. Cooke*, 26 F.3d 720, 722 (7th Cir. 1994) (noting with approval imposition of Rule 11 sanctions on Indiana Office of the Attorney General; however, no discussion of sovereign immunity).

[67]*See, e.g., Rajaratnam v. Moyer*, 47 F.3d 922, 923 (7th Cir. 1995) (Congress has restricted independent authority of magistrate judges to three areas, none of which includes Rule 11 matters); *Bennett v. General Caster Service of N. Gordon Co., Inc.*, 976 F.2d 995, 998 (6th Cir. 1992) (magistrate judge may not order sanctions pursuant to Rule 11). *But see, Maisonville v. F2 America, Inc.*, 902 F.2d 746 (9th Cir. 1990) (permitting Rule 11 sanction by magistrate judge).

[68]*Cooter & Gell v. Hartmarx Corp.*, 496 U.S. 384, 405, 110 S. Ct. 2447, 110 L. Ed. 2d 359 (1990). *See also CQ Intern. Co., Inc. v. Rochem Intern., Inc., USA*, 659 F.3d 53, 59–62 (1st Cir. 2011) (appeals court will give "extraordinary deference" to denial of sanctions where it finds no legal or clear factual error); *Matrix IV, Inc. v. American National Bank and Trust Co. of Chicago*, 649 F.3d 539, 552 (7th Cir. 2011); *Reinhardt v. Gulf Ins. Co.*, 489 F.3d 405, 416 (1st Cir. 2007) ("A district court's decision to impose Rule 11 sanctions is reviewed for abuse of discretion, and any findings of fact supporting that decision are reviewed for clear error."); *Yokoyama v. Midland Nat. Life Ins. Co.*, 594 F.3d 1087, 1091 (9th Cir. 2010) (automatic abuse of discretion when district court errs as a matter of law in imposing sanctions). *But cf. Indah v. U.S. S.E.C.*, 661 F.3d 914, 926–929 (6th Cir. 2011) (applied plain error standard); *F.D.I.C. v. Maxxam, Inc.*, 523 F.3d 566, 576–77 (5th Cir. 2008) (whether litigation is frivolous is mixed question of fact and law; facts are reviewed for clear error and conclusions of law are reviewed *de novo*).

[69]*Willhite v. Collins*, 459 F.3d 866, 870 (8th Cir. 2006) (district courts should state the authority for each sanction imposed "as different sources of authority require different standards of proof and permit different types of sanctions against different parties."); *Thompson v. RelationServe Media, Inc.*, 610 F.3d 628, 637–638 (11th Cir. 2010) (remanded denial of Rule 11 sanctions in Private Securities Litigation Reform Act case where court did not explain basis of ruling or include specific findings required under PSLRA). *But see CQ Intern. Co., Inc. v. Rochem Intern., Inc., USA*, 659 F.3d 53, 62 (1st Cir. 2011) (not an abuse of discretion for court to decline to analyze every contention on Rule 11 motion); *DiPonio Const. Co., Inc. v. International Union of Bricklayers and Allied Craftworkers, Local 9*, 687 F.3d 744 (6th Cir. 2012) (no requirement of full evidentiary hearing before imposing sanctions in 6th Circuit).

[70]*See, e.g., Fuqua Homes, Inc. v. Beattie*, 388 F.3d 618, 623 (8th Cir. 2004) (remanding for failure to identify the source of authority for the sanctions imposed). *See also S. Bravo Systems, Inc. v. Containment Technologies Corp.*, 96 F.3d 1372, 1375 (Fed. Cir. 1996) ("When the requesting party makes a strong showing that Rule 11

discretion standard of review,[71] an appellate court which finds an abuse of discretion in denying Rule 11 sanctions will not impose the sanctions in the first instance, but will remand to the district court for further proceedings.[72] Congress, of course, retains authority to reduce judicial discretion, and has occasionally done so.[73]

Some courts have taken the position that appellate courts should hold trial judges to a higher standard and should only impose sanctions for conduct analogous to contempt when reviewing sanctions imposed *sua sponte*.[74]

Of course, Rule 11 does not authorize a judge to impose sanc-

---

violations may have occurred, however, the district court should provide some explanation for disregarding the proffered showing."). *Compare Moross Ltd. Partnership v. Fleckenstein Capital, Inc.*, 466 F.3d 508, 520 (6th Cir. 2006) (finding that the issue of sanctions was not so close that the district court's lack of explanation constituted abuse of discretion).

[71] *Bryant v. Military Department of Mississippi*, 597 F.3d 678, 694 (5th Cir. 2010) ("an abuse of discretion only occurs where no reasonable person could take the view adopted by the trial court", citing unpublished case, and affirming denial of sanctions in whistle blower and civil rights claims "where suit was not totally meritless and there was no evidence of improper purpose").

[72] *Michigan Division-Monument Builders of North America v. Michigan Cemetery Ass'n*, 524 F.3d 726, 739 (6th Cir. 2008); *See also Gary v. Braddock Cemetery*, 517 F.3d 195, 202–3 (3d Cir. 2008) (motions under Rule 11 must be decided in the first instance by the trial court absent extraordinary circumstances). *But cf. Ledford v. Peeples*, 568 F.3d 1258, 1307 (11th Cir. 2009) (district court's findings of fact inadequate, but remand unnecessary as court was compelled to find that counsel violated Rule 11 in filing patently frivolous securities fraud claims); *United Stars Industries, Inc. v. Plastech Engineered Products, Inc.*, 525 F.3d 605, 610 (7th Cir. 2008) (affirmed sanctions erroneously awarded by district court under 28 U.S.C. § 1927 holding that they were appropriate under Rule 11).

[73] *See, e.g., Simon DeBartolo*

Group, L.P. v. Richard E. Jacobs Group, Inc., 186 F.3d 157, 166–67 (2d Cir. 1999) ("Ordinarily, courts are under no particular obligation to make findings with regard to the compliance of litigants and their counsel with Rule 11 or to impose sanctions once a violation is found." However, the Private Securities Litigation Reform Act of 1995 requires courts, at the conclusion of all private lawsuits arising under the Securities Exchange Act of 1934 to make specific findings as to compliance with Rule 11. If a violation occurs in such cases, the court has no discretion and must impose sanctions, which are rebuttably presumed to be attorneys' fees and other expenses incurred in the lawsuit. The standard for determining whether a Rule 11 violation has occurred, however, remains unchanged by this legislation). *See also Rombach v. Chang*, 355 F.3d 164, 178 (2d Cir. 2004) (PSLRA requires court to make findings as to each party's and attorney's compliance with every element of Rule 11(b); where violations are found, court must impose sanctions; no discretion, as is normally the case with Rule 11 issues).

[74] *See e.g., ATSI Communications, Inc. v. Shaar Fund, Ltd.*, 579 F.3d 143, 150–152 (2nd Cir. 2009) (objective unreasonableness standard is replaced by subjective bad faith standard for *sua sponte* motion; however standard would not apply in Private Securities Litigation Reform Act case as that Act required court to make Rule 11 finding at the conclusion of the case); *Lucas v. Duncan*, 574 F.3d 772, 775 (D.C.Cir. 2009) (acknowledging "the unusual position of the trial court in such circumstances, serving at once as both prosecutor and judge" but declining to

tions in a case in another court unless the case merely originated there and was removed to his court.[75] Rule 11 does not deprive district courts of the ability to impose sanctions under their inherent powers.[76]

Appellate Procedure

An attorney who wishes to appeal the imposition of Rule 11 sanctions cannot rely on the client's notice of appeal. A notice of appeal filed on behalf of a client will not suffice as the client does not have standing to appeal the Rule 11 ruling.[77]

A district court's decision on a post-judgment Rule 11 motion is a separate judgment that requires the filing of a separate notice of appeal.[78]

(1) HOW INITIATED

(A) BY MOTION

Specificity

Motions for sanctions under Rule 11(c) must be made separately from other motions[79] and must allege with specificity the alleged violation of Rule 11(b).[80]

Service and Due Process

Rule 11(c)(2) provides that motions for sanctions must be served as required under Rule 5. Of course, any entity who may be subjected to Rule 11 sanctions, whether on a party's

---

choose between the "akin to contempt" and "objective reasonableness" standards, as both had been violated in that case).

[75]*World Outreach Conference Center v. City of Chicago*, 591 F.3d 531, 538 (7th Cir. 2009).

[76]*Mach v. Will County Sheriff*, 580 F.3d 495, 502 (7th Cir. 2009) (citing *Methode Elecs. Inc. v. Adam Techs., Inc.*, 371 F.3d 923, 927 (7th Cir. 2004).

[77]*See Halim v. Great Gatsby's Auction Gallery, Inc.*, 516 F.3d 557, 564 (7th Cir. 2008).

[78]*Keck Garrett & Associates, Inc. v. Nextel Communications, Inc.*, 517 F.3d 476, 488 (7th Cir. 2008).

[79]*See also Star Mark Management, Inc. v. Koon Chun Hing Kee Soy & Sauce Factory, Ltd*, 682 F.3d 170, 179 (2d Cir. 2012) (letter with motion was sufficient, no requirement of supporting affidavits or memorandum of law); *Williamson v. Recovery Ltd. Partnership*, 542 F.3d 43, 51–52 (2d Cir. 2008) (court properly denied request for attorneys' fees, costs, and

damages where no separate motion for sanctions was filed); *Perpetual Securities, Inc. v. Tang*, 290 F.3d 132, 142 (2d Cir. 2002) (abuse of discretion to grant party's motion for sanctions which was not made separately, and was only included in memorandum addressing other issues before court); *Johnson v. Waddell & Reed, Inc.*, 74 F.3d 147, 150 (7th Cir. 1996) (current version of Rule 11 requires "that a motion for sanctions . . . shall be made separately from other motions"). *But see Nisenbaum v. Milwaukee County*, 333 F.3d 804 (7th Cir.2003) (sending "letter" or "demand" to opposing party's lawyer instead of "motion" is nonetheless substantial compliance with Rule 11(c)(1)(A)).

[80]*See, e.g., Johnson v. Cherry*, 422 F.3d 540, 551–52 (7th Cir. 2005) ("A general notice that the court is contemplating sanctions is insufficient; rather, the offending party must be on notice of the specific conduct for which she is potentially subject to sanctions.").

motion or on the court's initiative, has a due process right to present a defense before any sanction is imposed.[81] In practice, the quality and nature of hearings is controlled by the specific factual circumstances in which the alleged Rule 11 violation occurs.[82]

"Safe Harbor"

Rule 11(c)(2) does not permit sanctions motions to be filed with the court until 21 days after service of the motion, or within any other time frame the court provides.[83] If the document challenged by the sanctions motion is withdrawn or corrected within that time frame, the motion may not be filed with the court, and thus no sanctions will be imposed.[84]

---

[81]*See, e.g., Marlin v. Moody Nat. Bank, N.A.*, 533 F.3d 374, 380 (5th Cir.2008) (vacated court's *sua sponte* award for failure to follow mandatory procedures under Rule 11, holding "compliance with Rule 11 is not optional."); *Perpetual Securities, Inc. v. Tang*, 290 F.3d 132, 141 (2d Cir. 2002) (whether on motion of party or on court's initiative, award of sanctions is inappropriate if party to be sanctioned has no opportunity to respond; when court initiates Rule 11 matter *sua sponte,* it must issue "show cause" order); *Vollmer v. Publishers Clearing House*, 248 F.3d 698 (7th Cir. 2001) (evidence of violation "must be stated with some specificity in the record" and there must be a full and fair opportunity to respond; also noting that court may consider past record of questionable conduct); *Tompkins v. Cyr*, 202 F.3d 770, 788 (5th Cir. 2000) (where motion is served after trial had concluded, opponents of motion had no opportunity to defend or correct complaint).

[82]*See, e.g., Spiller v. Ella Smithers Geriatric Center*, 919 F.2d 339, 346 (5th Cir. 1990) (in Rule 11 cases, Due Process is usually satisfied if the accused has a chance to respond with a brief); *Union Planters Bank v. L & J Development Co., Inc.*, 115 F.3d 378, 385 (6th Cir. 1997) (evidentiary hearing not required where sanctioned parties had "ample" notice and "meaningful" opportunity to be heard).

[83]*See, e.g., Lamboy-Ortiz v. Ortiz-Velez*, 630 F.3d 228, 244 (1st Cir. 2010) (failure to satisfy procedural require-

ments of 21-day notice and separate motion); *Winterrowd v. American General Annuity Insurance Co.*, 556 F.3d 815, 826 (9th Cir. 2009) (failure to provide required notice precludes an award of Rule 11 sanctions); *Grober v. Mako Products, Inc.*, __ F.3d __ (Fed. Cir. 2012) (Rule 11 motion dismissed as procedurally improper when filed after summary judgment); *Rector v. Approved Federal Sav. Bank*, 265 F.3d 248, 252–53 (4th Cir. 2001) (movant must serve Rule 11 motion at least 21 days before filing it with court; however, sanctioned party's failure to enter timely objection to movant's untimely service waives issue). A letter specifying the intent to seek sanctions and the basis of those sanctions will sometimes satisfy this requirement. *See, e.g., Matrix IV, Inc. v. American National Bank and Trust Co. of Chicago*, 649 F.3d 539, 552–53 (7th Cir. 2011) (letter sent two weeks after initial filing and two years before Rule 11 motion informing party of intent both to seek sanctions and basis for those sanctions held sufficient); *Nisenbaum v. Milwaukee County*, 333 F.3d 804, 808 (7th Cir. 2003) (awarded sanctions under Rule 11 when the defendant had sent the respondent only a letter and not a copy of the motion for sanctions). *But see Roth v. Green*, 466 F.3d 1179, 1192 (10th Cir. 2006) (warning letters sent months in advance of motion did not satisfy safe harbor requirement).

[84]*See, e.g., Lawrence v. Richman Group of CT LLC*, 620 F.3d 153 (2d Cir. 2010) (overturned sanctions when defendants gave 21-day notice of Rule

Costs of Presenting or Opposing Sanctions Motion

Rule 11(c)(2) provides the court with discretion to award costs, including attorney's fees, associated with presenting or opposing a sanctions motion.[85] The court will explain the basis for any fee award and specify who, as between the parties and their lawyers, is to pay the award.[86]

It should be noted that if a party arguably entitled to attorneys' fees pursuant to Rule 11 asks for an exorbitant amount, such a request may itself be an abuse of process and therefore may be grounds for denial of an award.[87]

Law Firm's Liability: Presumptions

When a sanction is to be imposed, Rule 11(c)(2) creates a strong presumption in favor of imposing it upon an entire law firm, in addition to whatever sanction may be imposed upon an individual attorney.[88] This provision changes the old rule, which was construed to apply only to individual attorneys, not to their firms.

---

11 filing, plaintiff re-filed amended complaint, and defendants filed for sanctions without 21-day safe harbor); *Sneller v. City of Bainbridge Island*, 606 F.3d 636, 639 (9th Cir. 2010) (Rule 11 sanctions against party which filed a motion to amend within the 21-day safe harbor period reversed, no requirement that the party dismiss offending claims with prejudice); *Brickwood Contractors, Inc. v. Datanet Engineering, Inc.*, 369 F.3d 385, 389 (4th Cir. 2004) (en banc) (safe harbor is mandatory condition precedent to sanctions); *Barber v. Miller*, 146 F.3d 707, 710–11 (9th Cir. 1998) (motion served and filed after offending complaint was dismissed does not meet safe harbor requirement because no opportunity existed to withdraw complaint); *AeroTech, Inc. v. Estes*, 110 F.3d 1523 (10th Cir.1997) (where offending party dismissed its claim before Rule 11 motion was filed, sanctions were not possible because offending party had no opportunity to cure offense within time limit provided by safe harbor provision). *But see Truesdell v. Southern California Permanente Medical Group*, 293 F.3d 1146 (9th Cir.2002) (district court dismissed complaint, with leave to amend, on twentieth day after service of motion for sanctions; held, full 21-day period was provided because: (1) moving party had provided informal written notice of Rule 11 motion 27 days prior to actually filing motion; and (2) dismissal with leave to amend left offending party with additional time to withdraw complaint); *Norelus v. Denny's, Inc.*, 628 F.3d 1270, 1298 (11th Cir. 2010).

[85] *See, e.g., Margolis v. Ryan*, 140 F.3d 850 (9th Cir.1998) (also observing that this provision alters earlier case law prohibiting award of fees and costs relating to filing sanctions motions).

[86] *Boim v. Holy Land Foundation for Relief and Development*, 511 F.3d 707, 749–50 (7th Cir. 2007).

[87] *See, e.g., Budget Rent-A-Car System, Inc. v. Consolidated Equity LLC*, 428 F.3d 717, 718 (7th Cir. 2005) (but to trigger this response, request must be exorbitant, not "merely excessive").

[88] *But see Rentz v. Dynasty Apparel Indus., Inc.*, 556 F.3d 389, 397 (6th Cir. 2009) (affirmed sanctions against attorney but not against law firm or party where sanctionable conduct was continued allegations with no supporting evidence, and where attorney signed his name individually and did not identify himself on pleading as a member of law firm and there was no evidence other attorneys were involved in sanctionable conduct).

Standing: Non-Parties

In general, persons who are not parties to litigation have no standing to bring a Rule 11 motion.[89] Exceptions to that general rule arise in narrow circumstances where a non-party is affected directly by otherwise sanctionable conduct.[90]

(B) ON COURT'S INITIATIVE

Show Cause Orders

When the court believes there may have been a violation of Rule 11(b), it may initiate the sanction process without waiting for a party to make a motion.[91] This is done by issuing an order directing the attorney, law firm, or party to show cause why it has not violated a provision of Rule 11(b). Rule 11(c)(3) requires the court to identify the potentially offending conduct with reasonable specificity,[92] and guarantees an affected party both notice and an opportunity to defend against the proposed sanction.[93] Normally, a "show cause" order will be issued only

---

[89]*See, e.g., New York News, Inc. v. Kheel*, 972 F.2d 482, 488–89 (2d Cir. 1992) (person who had not met intervention requirements of Rule 24 lacked standing to seek sanctions; moreover, such a person may not intervene solely to seek sanctions).

[90]*See, e.g., Nyer v. Winterthur Intern.*, 290 F.3d 456 (1st Cir. 2002) (person not made party because judge reserved judgment on motion to amend complaint nevertheless had standing to seek Rule 11 sanctions because he had to prepare possible defense against pending amended complaint); *Greenberg v. Sala*, 822 F.2d 882 (9th Cir.1987) (individuals named in frivolous complaint, but not served, incurred costs and attorney fees and had Rule 11 standing); *Westmoreland v. CBS, Inc.*, 770 F.2d 1168 (D.C. Cir. 1985) (non-party is entitled to Rule 11 after party's attorney commenced contempt proceedings against him).

[91]*But cf., Perpetual Securities, Inc. v. Tang*, 290 F.3d 132, 141 (2d Cir. 2002) (when court initiates Rule 11 matter *sua sponte*, it must issue "show cause" order).

[92]*See, e.g., Clark v. United Parcel Service, Inc.*, 460 F.3d 1004, 1007–1009 (8th Cir. 2006) (court notified attorney of six specific paragraphs in 480-page pleading that the court viewed as exemplary of widespread flaws and im-

posed sanctions based on length of document, numerous misstatements and mischaracterizations of the record, which "had a cumulative effect which [the] Court found to be repugnant to the very concept of judicial economy."); *Thornton v. General Motors Corp.*, 136 F.3d 450, 455 (5th Cir. 1998) (per curiam) (order that does not identify specific offending conduct does not afford adequate notice and constitutes abuse of district court's discretion).

[93]*See, e.g., Marlin v. Moody Nat. Bank, N.A.*, 533 F.3d 374, 378 (5th Cir.2008) (failure to comply with mandatory Rule 11 procedures was abuse of discretion when district court did not issue show cause but ordered plaintiffs to pay defendants' attorney fees and costs through summary judgment, and later ruled that award was under Rule 11); *Foster v. Wilson*, 504 F.3d 1046, 1052–53 (9th Cir. 2007) (imposition of sanctions reversed for lack of notice and opportunity to respond); *Johnson v. Waddell & Reed, Inc.*, 74 F.3d 147, 151 (7th Cir. 1996) (noting court's duty, when considering Rule 11 sanctions *sua sponte*, to identify offending contact specifically, and to provide adequate notice). *See also Brunig v. Clark*, 560 F.3d 292, 297–98 (5th Cir. 2009) (notice sufficient where magistrate judge's report recommending sanctions and directing party to show cause was filed two months be-

in circumstances analogous to contempt of court.[94]

The court may choose to exercise its inherent power to sanction even if Rule 11 would apply.[95]

No Formal "Safe Harbor"

Rule 11(c)(3) contains no explicit "safe harbor" provision such as is found in Rule 11(c)(2), although the court in its discretion may afford an offending party substantial leeway.[96]

The requirement under Rule 11(c)(5)(B) that the court issue a "show cause" order before imposing monetary sanctions affords parties an opportunity to explain their conduct.[97]

(2) NATURE OF SANCTION; LIMITATIONS

Policy of Deterrence

For the most part, sanctions for violations of Rule 11(b) are to be imposed primarily to deter similar violations by the offender or "others similarly situated."[98] This policy represents a substantial change from previous versions of Rule 11, which included a substantially stronger interest in compensating parties who had been damaged by Rule 11 violations.[99]

---

fore sanctions were ordered);

[94]*See, e.g., Kaplan v. Daimler-Chrysler, A.G.*, 331 F.3d 1251, 1255 (11th Cir. 2003) (Because Rule 11(c)(1)(B) does not provide safe harbor, court must provide notice and opportunity to be heard and "a higher standard ('akin to contempt') than in the case of party-initiated sanctions."). *Lucas v. Duncan*, 574 F.3d 772, 775 (D.C.Cir. 2009) (acknowledging "the unusual position of the trial court in such circumstances, serving at once as both prosecutor and judge" but declining to choose between the "akin to contempt" and "objective reasonableness" standards, as both had been violated in that case).

[95]*See, e.g., Metz v. Unizan Bank*, 655 F.3d 485, 491 (6th Cir. 2011) (rejecting argument to contrary); *Starski v. Kirzhnev*, 682 F.3d 51, 55 (1st Cir. 2012) (Rule 11 motion rejected for failure to offer "safe harbor" but court sanctioned behavior under inherent powers).

[96]*See, e.g., Elliott v. Tilton*, 64 F.3d 213, 216 (5th Cir. 1995) (noting contrast between "safe harbor" provision applicable when parties seek Rule 11 sanctions, and absence of "safe harbor" when court acts *sua sponte*). *See also In re Pennie & Edmonds LLP*,

323 F.3d 86, 87 (2d Cir. 2003) (where court decides to impose sanctions sua sponte, law firm did not have benefit of "safe harbor" provision; thus sanctions were only appropriate for subjective bad faith, not for unreasonable but genuine good faith).

[97]*Jones v. Illinois Central R. Co.*, 617 F.3d 843, 856 (6th Cir. 2010) (court should not impose sanctions *sua sponte* without first ordering defense counsel "to show cause why conduct specifically described in the order has not violated Rule 11(b)").

[98]*See, e.g., DiPaolo v. Moran*, 407 F.3d 140 (3d Cir.2005) ("Although monetary sanctions are not encouraged under Rule 11, they are not forbidden. . . . We have emphasized that the main purpose of Rule 11 is to deter, not to compensate."); *Hamilton v. Boise Cascade Exp.*, 519 F.3d 1197, 1205 (10th Cir. 2008) (dicta, contrasting 28 U.S.C.A. § 1927 sanction policy of compensating wronged party against Rule 11 policy of deterrence). *But cf., Union Planters Bank v. L & J Development Co., Inc.*, 115 F.3d 378 (6th Cir. 1997) (acknowledging general rule, but authorizing payment to injured party where sanctionable conduct was produced by bad motive).

[99]*But see* 15 U.S.C.A. § 78u-4

Sanctions Available

Rule 11(c)(4) authorizes the court to issue nonmonetary orders,[100] to require payment of a penalty into court, to require payment of some or all of an opposing party's attorney's fees[101] and expenses, or any combination thereof.[102] Payment to an opposing party requires a motion by a party,[103] and is unlikely to occur unless the court believes such payment serves a deterrent purpose.[104] Generally, any monetary sanction must flow directly from the conduct described in the Rule 11 motion. This

---

(subject to some exceptions, when party or attorney violates Rule 11(b) in litigation controlled by Private Securities Litigation Reform Act of 1995, there is a rebuttable presumption that appropriate sanction is reasonable attorney's fees and expenses directly resulting from violation). *See also Gurary v. Nu-Tech Bio-Med, Inc.*, 303 F.3d 212, 221–22 (2d Cir. 2002) (under P.S.L.R.A., substantial violation of Rule 11 requires sanction of repayment of full cost of violation to victim unless such a sanction would either be unreasonable burden or violation was de minimus; held, violation is not de minimus simply because offending complaint contains both frivolous and nonfrivolous allegations).

[100]Nonmonetary sanctions may include dismissal of the action, *see, e.g., Liggon-Redding v. Estate of Sugarman*, 659 F.3d 258, 263 (3d Cir. 2011), or injunctions governing future filings, *see, e.g., Ortman v. Thomas*, 99 F.3d 807, 811 (6th Cir. 1996) (rejecting permanent injunction on filing federal court lawsuit that arises out of claims alleged in, or underlying, case at bar; imposing, however, prefiling requirement mandating that, in future, sanctioned party would be required to satisfy magistrate judge that proposed claims were not frivolous or asserted for an improper purpose). *But see Tropf v. Fidelity Nat. Title Ins. Co.*, 289 F.3d 929, 940–41 (6th Cir. 2002) (approving permanent injunction against future lawsuit arising out of claims underlying instant case; applying injunction to federal and state filings as well as administrative proceedings; distinguishing *Ortman, supra*); *Villar v. Crowley Maritime Corp.*, 990 F.2d 1489, 1498–99 (5th Cir. 1993) (permanent injunction against similar lawsuits in both federal and state court).

[101]*See, e.g., Eon-Net LP v. Flagstar Bancorp.*, 653 F.3d 1314, 1320 (Fed. Cir. 2011) (failure to perform reasonable pre-filing investigation resulting in unsupportable position taken during litigation; upheld full attorney's fees and costs of $131,984.70 under Rule 11); *Claiborne v. Wisdom*, 414 F.3d 715 (7th Cir.2005) ("[S]anctions may include appropriate attorneys' fees incurred as a direct result of the violation."). *But cf., Massengale v. Ray*, 267 F.3d 1298, 1302 (11th Cir. 2001) (per curiam) (pro se litigant who is also a lawyer is not entitled to attorney's fees because pro se parties, by definition, have no such fees).

[102]*See, e.g., Riccard v. Prudential Ins. Co.*, 307 F.3d 1277, 1295 (11th Cir. 2002) (order enjoining new actions without first obtaining leave of court was reasonable where monetary sanction would not prevent further harassment of opposing party or clogging of judicial machinery).

[103]*See, e.g., Brunig v. Clark*, 560 F.3d 292, 298 (5th Cir. 2009) (where parties filed Rule 11 motion but did not comply with safe harbor provisions, sanction was on court's own initiative and would not support award of attorney's fees); *Methode Electronics, Inc. v. Adam Technologies, Inc.*, 371 F.3d 923, 926 (7th Cir. 2004) (if sanction is not imposed as result of motion by party but instead on court's initiative, attorney fees cannot be imposed); *Baffa v. Donaldson, Lufkin & Jenrette Securities Corp.*, 222 F.3d 52, 57 (2d Cir. 2000) (attorneys' fees may be awarded only pursuant to motion; such fees may not be awarded by court on its own initiative).

[104]*See, e.g., Barber v. Miller*, 146 F.3d 707 (9th Cir.1998) (if court initiates sanction, payment must be to court, not to party; payment to party

is consistent with the safe harbor goal of allowing the party an opportunity to correct behavior before it is sanctioned.[105] All of the monetary sanctions listed in Rule 11(c)(4) are subject to additional significant limitations, discussed below.

Attorney's Fees

If a sanction includes payment of an opposing party's attorney's fees or associated costs, courts generally use a "lodestar" method of calculating the appropriate amount. "The lodestar is determined by multiplying the number of hours reasonably expended by the reasonable hourly rate."[106] It should be noted, however, that the amount of fees recoverable from the offending party is limited to fees "incurred as a direct result of the [violation]."[107] Fees for government attorneys are calculated on the same basis as prevailing rates in the private sector.[108]

Rule 11 is a sanctions statute and not a fee shifting provision. The sanctions of Rule 11 are not tied to the outcome of the litigation, and instead depend on whether a specific filing is well founded. In addition, Rule 11 sanctions shift the cost of only a portion of the litigation, not the cost of the litigation as a

---

appropriate only when sanction initiated by motion and only to serve deterrent purpose).

[105]*See, e.g., Indah v. U.S. S.E.C.*, 661 F.3d 914, 927–929 (6th Cir. 2011) (reversed sanctions when the district court awarded the cost of the entire suit and the Rule 11 motion had only requested sanctions based on a Third Amended Complaint); *Giganti v. Gen-X Strategies, Inc.*, 222 F.R.D. 299, 314 (E.D.Va. 2004) (Rule 11 does not permit an award of attorney fees that were not incurred in responding to the sanctionable conduct); *but see Kendrick v. Zanides*, 609 F.Supp. 1162, 1173 (N.D.Cal. 1985) (holding that an opposing party may receive attorney fees under Rule 11 for fees that were not incurred in responding to the sanctionable conduct).

[106]*View Engineering, Inc. v. Robotic Vision Systems, Inc.*, 208 F.3d 981, 987 (Fed. Cir. 2000). *Skidmore Energy, Inc. v. KPMG*, 455 F.3d 564, 568 (5th Cir. 2006) (upheld lodestar analysis which multiplied the reasonable number of hours expended in defending the suit by the reasonable hourly rates; reasonableness of the hours expended was supported by the complexity of the litigation, the number of individual and foreign defendants, and the number of

claims asserted).

[107]*Divane v. Krull Elec. Co., Inc.*, 200 F.3d 1020, 1030 (7th Cir. 1999) (error to impose all fees incurred in litigation where at least some of such expenses are unrelated to violations of Rule 11); *Rentz v. Dynasty Apparel Industries, Inc.*, 556 F.3d 389, 400 (6th Cir. 2009) (where no dispute existed as to attorneys' fees incurred due to sanctionable conduct, it was error for court to award lesser amount). *Cf. B & H Medical, L.L.C. v. ABP Admin., Inc.*, 534 F.3d 801 (6th Cir.2008) (awarded $10,000 in attorneys fees for baselessly opposing summary judgment rather than $152,846 requested; district court opined "Plaintiff's claims suffered from fundamental and rather glaring evidentiary defects . . . it should not have been an especially onerous or time-consuming task to prepare a summary judgment motion that pointed out these deficiencies").

[108]*See, e.g., Napier v. Thirty or More Unidentified Federal Agents, Employees or Officers*, 855 F.2d 1080, 1092–93 (3d Cir. 1988) (assistant United States attorney should be billed at appropriate market rate in private sector, even in the absence of a regular billing rate for government lawyers).

407

whole.[109]

The court may not award attorney's fees under Rule 11 when sanctions are imposed sua sponte,[110] but may award attorney's fees under its inherent powers if the person being sanctioned has acted in bad faith.[111]

Nonmonetary Sanctions

Nonmonetary sanctions include dismissal unfavorable to the offender[112] or court-ordered pro bono service.[113] Under previous versions of Rule 11, nonmonetary sanctions included reprimands and suspension of an attorney.[114] Presumably these sanctions are available under the current version of Rule 11.

Punitive Damages

The previous version of Rule 11 was construed to permit punitive damages when the court found that sanction appropriate.[115] It appears that under the current version of

---

[109]*In re Southern California Sunbelt Developers, Inc.*, 608 F.3d 456, 462 (9th Cir. 2010) (citing *Business Guides, Inc. v. Chromatic Communications Enterprises, Inc.*, 498 U.S. 533, 111 S.Ct. 922, 112 L. Ed 1140 (1991). *See also Golden v. Helen Sigman & Associates, Ltd.*, 611 F.3d 356 (7th Cir. 2010) (sanctions calculated under "count-counting" methodology, adding fees clearly attributable to claims resulting in sanctions, and for fees not traceable to a specific claim, divided the total dollar amount of those fees by the number of claims brought against an individual defendant and then multiplying by the number of counts resulting in sanctions).

[110]*MHC Inv. Co. v. Racom Corp.*, 323 F.3d 620, 627 (8th Cir. 2003).

[111]*See, e.g., Willhite v. Collins*, 459 F.3d 866, 869–870 (8th Cir. 2006) (upheld sanction of one half of plaintiff's attorney's fees, amounting to $66,698.30, when district court had said sanctions were under both Rule 11 and its inherent authority but did not state authority for each sanction imposed).

[112]*See, e.g., Liggon-Redding v. Estate of Sugarman*, 659 F.3d 258, 263 (3d Cir. 2011); *Zocaras v. Castro*, 465 F.3d 479, 484 (11th Cir. 2006).

[113]*Reinhardt v. Gulf Ins. Co.*, 489 F.3d 405, 416 (1st Cir. 2007) (court imposed 10 hours of pro bono service based on attorney's refusal to enter into negotiations).

[114]*Matter of Dragoo*, 186 F.3d 614, 615–16 (5th Cir. 1999) (husband and wife attorneys suspended from practice before bankruptcy court for four years; readmission conditioned upon (1) 15 hours of continuing legal education in consumer bankruptcy law, (2) submission of records of all grievance and malpractice claims brought against attorneys, and disposition of such claims, and (3) evidence of mental stability of husband, who had used depression as defense against Rule 11 sanctions; however, rejecting requirement that wife, who had indicated no mental instability, must also demonstrate mental stability). *But see, Hutchinson v. Pfeil*, 208 F.3d 1180, 1186 (10th Cir. 2000) (sanctions should not be used to drive attorneys out of practice; when district court believes such remedies are appropriate, referral should be made to appropriate authorities who will ensure that attorneys receive due process); *Thornton v. General Motors Corp.*, 136 F.3d 450, 455 (5th Cir. 1998) (suspension from practice before court is inappropriate sanction under Rule 11(c)(1)(B); "[W]hen a district court finds that a disciplinary sanction more severe than admonition, reprimand or censure under Rule 11 is warranted, it should refer the matter to the appropriate disciplinary authorities.").

[115]*See, e.g., Robeson Defense Committee v. Britt*, 132 F.R.D. 650

Rule 11, punitive damage payments to parties are inappropriate.

Financial Status of Offender

In assessing monetary sanctions, courts take into account the financial status of the offender.[116] However, if the offender wants the court to know of the offender's limited ability to pay sanctions, the burden is on the offender to bring the relevant facts before the court.[117]

Alternative Remedies

Rule 11 is in addition to whatever remedies, such as censure or reprimand,[118] contempt, disciplinary complaints to a bar, Federal Rule of Appellate Procedure 38 (frivolous appeals), state claims such as abuse of process,[119] 28 U.S.C.A. § 1447(c) (expenses, including attorney's fees, for improper removal),[120] 28 U.S.C.A. § 1915(a) and (d) (frivolous filings *in forma pauperis*), and 28 U.S.C.A. § 1927 (unreasonable and vexatious multiplication of proceedings), the court or other persons may have.[121]

Duty to Mitigate

Under the previous version of Rule 11, a party seeking damages under Rule 11 must have made reasonable efforts to miti-

---

(E.D. N.C. 1989), affirmed in part, vacated in part on other grounds, 914 F.2d 505 (4th Cir. 1990).

[116]*See, e.g., Shales v. General Chauffeurs, Sales Drivers and Helpers Local Union*, 557 F.3d 746, 748–49 (7th Cir. 2009) ("The poorer the lawyer, the lower the sanction can be and still deter repetition by the lawyer or anyone similarly situated."). *See also Star Mark Management, Inc. v. Koon Chun Hing Kee Soy & Sauce Factory, Ltd*, 682 F.3d 170, 179 (2d Cir. 2012) (court did not err in reducing financial sanction from the $105,037 to $10,000 based on financial hardship).

[117]*See, e.g., Silva v. Witschen*, 19 F.3d 725 (1st Cir.1994) (if the offender presents no such facts, the court has no duty to inquire into them).

[118]*See, e.g., Thomas v. Tenneco Packaging Co., Inc.*, 293 F.3d 1306 (11th Cir. 2002) (per curiam) (separate from Rule 11, district court has inherent power to sanction attorney for documents that were rude and demeaning, with no purpose except harassment and intimidation of opposing counsel). *See also In re DeVille*, 361 F.3d 539, 548 (9th Cir. 2004) (noting that sanctions under court's inherent power require finding of bad faith, while imposition of Rule 11 sanctions "requires only a showing of objectively unreasonable conduct").

[119]*See, e.g., U.S. Express Lines Ltd. v. Higgins*, 281 F.3d 383, 393 (3d Cir. 2002) (Federal Rules do not preempt abuse of process and similar state torts).

[120]*See, e.g., Wisconsin v. Hotline Industries, Inc.*, 236 F.3d 363, 366 (7th Cir. 2000) (§ 1447(c) is alternative to Rule 11, which " 'can be used to impose a more severe sanction when appropriate.' ").

[121]*Clinton v. Jones*, 520 U.S. 681, 709, 117 S. Ct. 1636, 137 L. Ed. 2d 945 (1997) (court may apply broad array of authority, including Rule 11, 28 U.S.C.A. § 1927, and/or its inherent powers). *See also Xantech Corp. v. Ramco Industries, Inc.*, 159 F.3d 1089, 1094 (7th Cir. 1998) ("[F]ee requests made under Rule 11 do not pose a res judicata bar to subsequent actions for claims akin to malicious prosecution.").

gate its losses.[122] Presumably that requirement carries over to the current Rule 11, at least as to those unusual circumstances where a party may be entitled to compensation for a violation.

Monetary Sanctions: Frivolous Arguments of Law

Rule 11(c)(5)(A) explicitly prohibits application of monetary sanctions against a represented party for violations of Rule 11(b)(2), governing requirements that arguments for changes in law be nonfrivolous.[123] Monetary sanctions obviously remain available against attorneys or non-represented parties who violate Rule 11(b)(2).

Court-Initiated Monetary Sanctions: Settlement

If the court seeks to impose monetary sanctions on its own initiative, it may not do so if its show cause order was not issued before the parties voluntarily dismissed or settled the claims. However, Rule 11(c)(5)(B) provides no similar protection if the case goes to judgment.

Motions for Sanctions: Timing

The duty to offer an offending party a "safe harbor" apparently precludes an injured party from moving for sanctions after a case has ended,[124] or where the offending attorney has

---

[122]*See, e.g., Pollution Control Industries of America, Inc. v. Van Gundy*, 21 F.3d 152, 156 (7th Cir. 1994) (aggrieved party has duty to mitigate its costs "by resolving frivolous issues quickly and efficiently"). *See also Andretti v. Borla Performance Industries, Inc.*, 426 F.3d 824, 834 (6th Cir. 2005) (where both parties contributed to waste of judicial resources, no abuse of discretion to refuse to award sanctions).

[123]*See, e.g., Marlin v. Moody Nat. Bank, N.A.*, 533 F.3d 374, 378 (5th Cir.2008) ("Monetary sanctions may *not* be imposed against a *represented party*, as are Plaintiffs, for violation of Rule 11(b)(2) (requiring *legal contentions* to be warranted, *inter alia*, by existing law)."); *Janky v. Lake County Convention And Visitors Bureau*, 576 F.3d 356, 363–364 (7th Cir. 2009) (attorney's attempt to have his client's award reduced by the amount of Rule 11 sanction imposed against him violated 11(c)(5)(A)).

[124]*See, e.g., ResQNet.com, Inc. v. Lansa, Inc.*, 594 F.3d 860, 875 (Fed. Cir. 2010) ("general practice is that the motion must be filed before the offending contention has been withdrawn or

resolved" and finding sanction not appropriate when Rule 11 motion filed more than 2 years after offending claim withdrawn). *Roth v. Green*, 466 F.3d 1179, 1193 (10th Cir. 2006) (motion for sanctions filed after district court dismissed complaint should have been denied). *Tompkins v. Cyr*, 202 F.3d 770, 787–88 (5th Cir. 2000) (rejecting sanctions where Rule 11 motion was not filed until after conclusion of trial); *Ridder v. City of Springfield*, 109 F.3d 288 (6th Cir. 1997). *But cf., Divane v. Krull Elec. Co., Inc.*, 200 F.3d 1020, 1025–26 (7th Cir. 1999) (initial Rule 11 motion was premature, but gave clear notice to offending party that appropriateness of motion could not be determined until, after trial, lack of evidentiary support for offending claims might be clear; result was that trial court extended period of safe harbor for duration of trial; additionally appellate court notes that "Rule 11(c)(1)(A) does not specify any time period when a motion for sanctions must be filed, and we see no need to establish one. . . . By themselves, the purposes of Rule 11(c)(1)(A) do not justify a broad rule that sanctions cannot be imposed as a result of a motion properly submitted

withdrawn from the case.[125] Under the previous version of Rule 11 courts were divided as to whether motions could be filed after the case concluded.[126] While a party must file before the conclusion of the case, the court may retain jurisdiction to decide the Rule 11 motion after the conclusion of the principal matter.[127]

By contrast, when the court initiates a sanctions process by issuing a show cause order before a plaintiff voluntarily dismisses a case, the court retains power to impose sanctions even after dismissal.[128]

(3) ORDER

Order Imposing Sanctions

Rule 11(c)(6) provides that if the court imposes sanctions, it will describe the offending conduct and explain the basis for the sanction the court imposed.[129]

---

to the court after a judgment.")

[125]*Peer v. Lewis*, 606 F.3d 1306, 1315 (11th Cir. 2010).

[126]*See, e.g., Hunter v. Earthgrains Co. Bakery*, 281 F.3d 144, 152 (4th Cir. 2002) (delay of 14 months in moving for sanctions is unacceptable, even where opponent of sanctions has not alleged prejudice or lack of notice).

[127]*Samsung Electronics Co., Ltd. v. Rambus, Inc.*, 523 F.3d 1374, 1379 (Fed. Cir. 2008) (collecting cases and holding that a federal trial court enjoys discretion to postpone collateral issues, including Rule 11 motions); *Matrix IV, Inc. v. American National Bank and Trust Co. of Chicago*, 649 F.3d 539, 553 (7th Cir. 2011) ("Postjudgment motions for sanctions are permissible so long as the moving party substantially complies with Rule 11's safe-harbor requirement."); *In re Schaefer Salt Recovery, Inc.*, 542 F.3d 90, 97–98 (3d Cir. 2008) (motions for Rule 11 sanction must be filed "before the entry of a final judgment where such motions arise out of conduct that occurred prior to the final judgment" but "after the entry of final judgment and the filing of a notice of appeal, [the court] retains the power to adjudicate collateral matters such as sanctions under Rule 11"). *But see Gary v. Braddock Cemetery*, 517 F.3d 195, 201 (3d Cir. 2008) (when a Rule 11 motion

has been made by a party, a district court must respond to that issue prior to entry of a final judgment).

[128]*Cooter & Gell v. Hartmarx Corp.*, 496 U.S. 384, 110 S. Ct. 2447, 110 L. Ed. 2d 359 (1990). *But cf., Woodard v. STP Corp.*, 170 F.3d 1043, 1045 (11th Cir. 1999) (error for court to enter order retaining jurisdiction to impose sanctions under Rule 11 if plaintiff's attorneys bring a subsequent lawsuit in another forum; only court hearing subsequent lawsuit could impose such sanctions).

[129]*See, e.g., Vollmer v. Publishers Clearing House*, 248 F.3d 698, 711 (7th Cir. 2001) (failure to explain imposition of $50,000 sanction requires remand for explanation). *But cf., McLane, Graf, Raulerson & Middleton, P.A. v. Rechberger*, 280 F.3d 26, 44–45 (1st Cir. 2002) (district court encouraged, but not required, to give reasons for denying sanctions); *Anderson v. Boston School Committee*, 105 F.3d 762, 769 (1st Cir. 1997) (no requirement for explicit findings explaining denial of sanctions "where the record itself, evidence or colloquy, clearly indicates one or more sufficient supporting reasons. The occasional statements referring to an inflexible requirement for explicit findings in every case do not reflect our present considered judgment.").

Rule 11(d)—INAPPLICABILITY TO DISCOVERY

CORE CONCEPT

Rules 26 through 37, governing the discovery process, control the circumstances when sanctions may be imposed for inappropriate behavior in discovery. For that reason, Rule 11(d) provides that Rule 11(a), (b) and (c) have no applicability to discovery issues.[130]

Additional Research References

Wright & Miller, *Federal Practice and Procedure* §§ 1331 to 39
C.J.S. Federal Civil Procedure § 260
West's Key Number Digest, Federal Civil Procedure ⌖660 to 661, ⌖2750 to 2848

---

[130]*See, e.g., Patelco Credit Union v. Sahni*, 262 F.3d 897, 913 (9th Cir. 2001) ("Rule 11(d) specifically exempts discovery motions and objections from its procedural requirements."); *Baffa v. Donaldson, Lufkin & Jenrette Securities Corp.*, 222 F.3d 52, 57 (2d Cir. 2000) (failure to answer interrogatories fully is not sanctionable under Rule 11); *Jones v. Illinois Central R. Co.*, 617 F.3d 843, 856 (6th Cir. 2010) (documents were discovery and therefore outside scope of Rule 11 pursuant to Rule 11(d)). *But cf., Semien v. Life Ins. Co. of North America*, 436 F.3d 805, 814–15 (7th Cir. 2006) (ERISA case; circuit court notes that in such cases discovery is "normally disfavored," but where it is appropriate "the district court should employ all available tools, including the imposition of Rule 11 sanctions against those who would abuse the discovery process").

RULE 12

DEFENSES AND OBJECTIONS: WHEN AND HOW PRESENTED; MOTION FOR JUDGMENT ON THE PLEADINGS; CONSOLIDATING MOTIONS; WAIVING DEFENSES; PRETRIAL HEARING

(a) Time to Serve a Responsive Pleading.

(1) *In General.* Unless another time is specified by this rule or a federal statute, the time for serving a responsive pleading is as follows:

(A) A defendant must serve an answer:

(i) within 21 days after being served with the summons and complaint; or

(ii) if it has timely waived service under Rule 4(d), within 60 days after the request for a waiver was sent, or within 90 days after it was sent to the defendant outside any judicial district of the United States.

(B) A party must serve an answer to a counterclaim or crossclaim within 21 days after being served with the pleading that states the counterclaim or crossclaim.

(C) A party must serve a reply to an answer within 21 days after being served with an order to reply, unless the order specifies a different time.

(2) *United States and Its Agencies, Officers, or Employees Sued in an Official Capacity.* The United States, a United States agency, or a United States officer or employee sued only in an official capacity must serve an answer to a complaint, counterclaim, or crossclaim within 60 days after service on the United States attorney.

(3) *United States Officers or Employees Sued in an Individual Capacity.* A United States officer or employee sued in an individual capacity for an act or omission occurring in connection with

duties performed on the United States' behalf must serve an answer to a complaint, counter-claim, or crossclaim within 60 days after service on the officer or employee or service on the United States attorney, whichever is later.

(4) *Effect of a Motion.* Unless the court sets a differ-ent time, serving a motion under this rule alters these periods as follows:

    (A) if the court denies the motion or postpones its disposition until trial, the responsive pleading must be served within 14 days after notice of the court's action; or

    (B) if the court grants a motion for a more definite statement, the responsive pleading must be served within 14 days after the more definite statement is served.

(b) How to Present Defenses. Every defense to a claim for relief in any pleading must be asserted in the responsive pleading if one is required. But a party may assert the following defenses by motion:

(1) lack of subject-matter jurisdiction;

(2) lack of personal jurisdiction;

(3) improper venue;

(4) insufficient process;

(5) insufficient service of process;

(6) failure to state a claim upon which relief can be granted; and

(7) failure to join a party under Rule 19.

A motion asserting any of these defenses must be made before pleading if a responsive pleading is allowed. If a pleading sets out a claim for relief that does not require a responsive pleading, an opposing party may assert at trial any defense to that claim. No defense or objection is waived by joining it with one or more other defenses or objections in a respon-sive pleading or in a motion.

(c) Motion for Judgment on the Pleadings. After the pleadings are closed—but early enough not to delay trial—a party may move for judgment on the pleadings.

(d) Result of Presenting Matters Outside the

Pleadings. If, on a motion under Rule 12(b)(6) or 12(c), matters outside the pleadings are presented to and not excluded by the court, the motion must be treated as one for summary judgment under Rule 56. All parties must be given a reasonable opportunity to present all the material that is pertinent to the motion.

(e) Motion for a More Definite Statement. A party may move for a more definite statement of a pleading to which a responsive pleading is allowed but which is so vague or ambiguous that the party cannot reasonably prepare a response. The motion must be made before filing a responsive pleading and must point out the defects complained of and the details desired. If the court orders a more definite statement and the order is not obeyed within 14 days after notice of the order or within the time the court sets, the court may strike the pleading or issue any other appropriate order.

(f) Motion to Strike. The court may strike from a pleading an insufficient defense or any redundant, immaterial, impertinent, or scandalous matter. The court may act:

(1) on its own; or

(2) on motion made by a party either before responding to the pleading or, if a response is not allowed, within 21 days after being served with the pleading.

(g) Joining Motions.

(1) *Right to Join.* A motion under this rule may be joined with any other motion allowed by this rule.

(2) *Limitation on Further Motions.* Except as provided in Rule 12(h)(2) or (3), a party that makes a motion under this rule must not make another motion under this rule raising a defense or objection that was available to the party but omitted from its earlier motion.

(h) Waiving and Preserving Certain Defenses.

(1) *When Some Are Waived.* A party waives any defense listed in Rule 12(b)(2) to (5) by:

(A) omitting it from a motion in the circumstances

       described in Rule 12(g)(2); or

    (B) failing to either:

       (i)   make it by motion under this rule; or

      (ii)   include it in a responsive pleading or in an amendment allowed by Rule 15(a)(1) as a matter of course.

  (2) *When to Raise Others.* Failure to state a claim upon which relief can be granted, to join a person required by Rule 19(b), or to state a legal defense to a claim may be raised:

    (A) in any pleading allowed or ordered under Rule 7(a);

    (B) by a motion under Rule 12(c); or

    (C) at trial.

  (3) *Lack of Subject-Matter Jurisdiction.* If the court determines at any time that it lacks subject-matter jurisdiction, the court must dismiss the action.

(i) **Hearing Before Trial.** If a party so moves, any defense listed in Rule 12(b)(1) to (7)—whether made in a pleading or by motion—and a motion under Rule 12(c) must be heard and decided before trial unless the court orders a deferral until trial.

[Amended December 27, 1946, effective March 19, 1948; January 21, 1963, effective July 1, 1963; February 28, 1966, effective July 1, 1966; March 2, 1987, effective August 1, 1987; April 22, 1993, effective December 1, 1993; April 17, 2000, December 1, 2000; April 30, 2007, effective December 1, 2007; March 26, 2009, effective December 1, 2009.]

AUTHORS' COMMENTARY ON RULE 12

PURPOSE AND SCOPE

Rule 12 sets the time and procedures for serving responsive pleadings, for asserting factual and legal defenses and objections, and for making preliminary motions and motions for judgment on the pleadings.

Answers to complaints generally must be served within 21 days after service of process. If a defendant waives formal service of process, the answer is due within 60 days. Answers to crossclaims and counterclaims must be served within 21 days of service. Longer periods apply to service made on the United States and federal employees or when service is made outside the country. These response periods may be modified by court-approved stipulation, by court order, or by the defendant's filing of a Rule 12 motion.

Parties generally must assert their defenses and objections in their first responsive pleadings. However, certain enumerated defenses and objections may, at the party's discretion, be raised earlier by motion. If the party chooses to file such a motion, the party must assert all enumerated defenses and objections in the same motion.

A failure to assert all defenses and objections in the responsive pleading, or alternatively, a failure to include all enumerated defenses and objections when making a Rule 12 motion, results in a waiver of certain unasserted defenses and objections.

RULE 12(a)—TIME FOR SERVING RESPONSIVE PLEADINGS

CORE CONCEPT

Answers to a complaint must be served within 21 days after service. By waiving formal service of process, a responding party's time for answering is extended to 60 days. Service made outside the United States or on the federal government, its agencies, and its officers have different response times. Answers to counterclaims and crossclaims, as well as court-ordered replies to an answer, must be served within 21 days.

APPLICATIONS

Answers and Replies

Unless a Rule 12 motion is filed, a party generally must serve an answer within 21 calendar days after being served with a summons and complaint, a counterclaim, or a crossclaim. A party must serve a reply within 21 calendar days after being served with a court order directing a reply. These 21-day response periods apply even when service is made abroad.[1]

Note: These time periods run from the date of *service*, not the date of *filing*.

Impact of 2009 "Time Computation" Amendments

Effective December 2009, the Rule 12(a) time period was extended from 20 days to 21 days, to conform to the new multiples-of-7-days standard for federal civil time periods.

---

[1]*See TracFone Wireless, Inc. v. Technopark Co.*, 281 F.R.D. 683, 687 (S.D.Fla. 2012).

Exception: When Formal Service of Process is Waived

Waiving formal service of process is strongly encouraged through extensions of these response times.[2] A defendant who agrees to waive formal service receives 60 days to respond (if the waiver request was mailed to a U.S. address) and 90 days to respond (if mailed to an address outside the U.S.). These extensions apply only to service of original process, and not to counterclaims or crossclaims.

Exception: Serving the United States, Its Officers and Agencies

Responsive pleadings must be served within 60 days by the United States, by its agencies, and by those federal officers and employees who are *either* sued in their "official" capacities or sued in their "individual" capacities for acts or omissions occurring in connection with the performance of their federal duties.[3] In "individual" capacity, "on-the-job" claim lawsuits against federal personnel, this 60-day period begins to run when the individual is served or when the United States Attorney is served, whichever is later.[4] In all other cases (lawsuits against the United States, a federal agency, or a federal officer or employee sued in an official capacity), the 60-day period begins to run when the United States Attorney is served.[5] This pleading timetable applies to both current and former federal officers and employees.[6]

Note: When a pleading names as defendants both a governmental party and a non-governmental party, only the governmental party has 60 days in which to serve a responsive pleading. The non-governmental party's time for serving a responsive pleading remains 21 days.

Exception: Extensions by the Court

The time for serving responsive pleadings (like most other time periods set by the Rules) may be extended by court order.[7] Similarly, were the parties to agree to an extension of time for serving responsive pleadings, and were that agreement approved by the court, the time could be extended.

Exception: Tolling Effect of Rule 12(b) Motion

Rule 12(b) motions must be filed before a responsive pleading (because, by their nature, the relief sought by such motions is a pre-answer dismissal of the claim).[8] The act of serving a Rule 12(b) motion ordinarily suspends the party's time for serv-

---

[2]*See* Rule 4(d).

[3]*See* Rule 12(a)(2).

[4]*See* Rule 12(a)(3).

[5]*See* Rule 12(a)(2)(A).

[6]*See* Rule 12(a)(3) advisory com-

mittee notes to 2000 amendments.

[7]*See* Rule 6(b).

[8]*See* 12(b) (noting that Rule 12(b) motions "must be made before pleading if a responsive pleading is allowed").

ing a responsive pleading,[9] and that tolling will usually continue to run until the court has ruled on the pending motion.[10] Thereafter, the time for the delayed responsive pleading is as follows:

- If the court's order on the motion denies relief or postpones resolving the motion until trial, the responsive pleading must be served within 14 days after "notice" of the court's action,[11]
- If the court's order resolves a motion for more definite statement (Rule 12(e)) by requiring a clearer claim, the responsive pleading to the more definite statement must be served within 14 days after service of the more definite statement.[12]

If service is made on a party by mail or by any of Rule 5's service-by-consent methods, these 14-day periods are extended further by 3 extra days.[13] The court may, however, deviate from these timing rules entirely by setting a different schedule of its own, in which case the court-set schedule will control.[14]

Exceptions to Tolling Effect Rule

The tolling effect of a pending Rule 12(b) motion may be altered (or eliminated completely) in the following circumstances:

- *Motion by Other Defendant:* The tolling effect of a pending Rule 12(b) motion does not inure to the benefit of all defendants; only those defendants who file a Rule 12(b) motion receive the tolling.[15]
- *Motions Filed Against Amended Pleadings:* It is not clear whether a party who files a Rule 12(b) motion to an

---

[9]*See* Rule 12(a)(4).

[10]*See Butler v. Broward County Cent. Examining Bd.*, 367 Fed.Appx. 991, 992 (11th Cir. 2010). *But cf. Hill v. Blue Cross and Blue Shield of Michigan*, 237 F.R.D. 613, 616–17 (E.D. Mich. 2006) (to resolve longstanding delays in case, court strikes motion to dismiss, without prejudice, and orders defendant to file its answer).

[11]*See* Rule 12(a)(4)(A). Neither the Advisory Committee Notes nor published case law have expositively defined when a party is deemed to have received "notice" of such a court order within the meaning of Rule 12(a)(4)(A) (*e.g.*, when the order is docketed, when it arrives at counsel's office or the party's home, when counsel or the party actually sees it, etc.). The sparse case law references to this section either offer no substantive guidance at all or use language that appears directly inconsistent with the

plain terms of the Rule itself. *See, e.g., U.S. v. $57,960.00 in U.S. Currency*, 58 F. Supp. 2d 660, 668 (D.S.C. 1999) (dated from "being served" with denial order); *Ziegler v. Ziegler*, 28 F. Supp. 2d 601, 620 (E.D. Wash. 1998) (dated from "after receipt" of denial order); *U.S. v. Ware*, 172 F.R.D. 458, 459 (D. Kan. 1997) (dated from "after the court's denial" of motion); *Johnson-Medland v. Bethanna*, 1996 WL 612467 (E.D. Pa. 1996) (dated from "the date of this order").

[12]*See* Rule 12(a)(4)(B).

[13]*See* Rule 6(d).

[14]*See* 12(a)(4). *See also U.S. v. Elmes*, 532 F.3d 1138, 1145–46 (11th Cir. 2008) (alternate time set by court order prevails over general time period).

[15]*See Hanley v. Volpe*, 48 F.R.D. 387, 387–88 (E.D. Wis. 1970).

amended pleading is entitled automatically to a new Rule 12(a) tolling period. Some authority rejects such a tolling as a misreading of Rule 12(a);[16] others summarily acknowledge the tolling.[17]

- *Motions Converted to Summary Judgment Motions:* When materials outside the pleadings are presented with a Rule 12(b) motion (and not excluded by the court), the Rule 12(b) motion generally must be converted to a Rule 56 motion for summary judgment.[18] Rule 12(b) motions receive the tolling effect; Rule 56 motions do not. One court has decided that when a Rule 12(b) motion converts under these circumstances, the tolling effect will still apply.[19]

- *Partial Motions:* It now seems fairly settled that a party who files a Rule 12(b) motion to a portion, but not all, of a pending pleading (*e.g.*, motion to dismiss counts I, III, and VI) will have a tolling of its entire responsive pleading obligation. The substantial majority of the courts to have considered the question favor a complete tolling,[20] although a minority and some practitioner commentary

---

[16]*See General Mills, Inc. v. Kraft Foods Global, Inc.*, 487 F.3d 1368, 1376–77 (Fed. Cir. 2007), *clarified by*, 495 F.3d 1378, 1378–81 (Fed. Cir. 2007).

[17]*See, e.g., Sweetwater Investors, LLC v. Sweetwater Apartments Loan, LLC*, 2011 WL 1545076, at *1 & *4 (M.D.Ala. Apr. 25, 2011) (answer to amended complaint tolled by Rule 12(a)(4)); *American Orthodontics Corp. v. Epicor Software Corp.*, 746 F.Supp.2d 996, 1000 (E.D.Wis. 2010) (same); *McKenzie v. AAA Auto Family Ins. Co.*, 2010 WL 3718861, at *6 (D.Kan. Sept. 13, 2010) (same).

[18]*See* Rule 12(d).

[19]*See Marquez v. Cable One, Inc.*, 463 F.3d 1118, 1120–21 (10th Cir. 2006).

[20]*See Ideal Instruments, Inc. v. Rivard Instruments, Inc.*, 434 F. Supp. 2d 598, 637–40 (N.D. Iowa 2006) (following majority approach, and holding that motion to dismiss suspends time for responding to all portions of complaint, even unchallenged ones). *Accord, e.g., Talbot v. Sentinel Ins. Co., Ltd.*, 2012 WL 1068763, at *4–*5 (D.Nev. Mar. 29, 2012); *ThermoLife Int'l, LLC v. Gaspari Nutrition, Inc.*, 2011 WL 6296833, at *5 (D.Ariz. Dec. 16, 2011); *Aslani v. Sparrow Health*

Sys., 2009 WL 736654, at *4 n.10 (W.D.Mich. Mar. 12, 2009); *Gortat v. Capala Bros.*, 257 F.R.D. 353, 366 (E.D.N.Y. 2009); *Bd. of County Com'rs County of La Plata v. Brown Group Retail, Inc.*, 2008 WL 4527736, at *1–*2 (D.Colo. Oct. 3, 2008); *Beaulieu v. Bd. of Trs. of Univ. of West Florida*, 2007 WL 2020161, at *2 (N.D.Fla. July 9, 2007); *Godlewski v. Affiliated Computer Services, Inc.*, 210 F.R.D. 571, 572–73 (E.D. Va. 2002); *Rosa v. California Bd of Accountancy*, 2005 WL 1899515 (E.D. Cal. 2005), *aff'd*, 259 Fed. Appx. 918 (9th Cir. 2007); *Batdorf v. Trans Union*, 2000 WL 635455 (N.D. Cal. 2000); *Finnegan v. University of Rochester Medical Center*, 180 F.R.D. 247, 249–50 (W.D. N.Y. 1998); *Schwartz v. Berry College, Inc.*, 1997 WL 579166 (N.D. Ga. 1997); *Alex. Brown & Sons Inc. v. Marine Midland Banks, Inc.*, 1997 WL 97837 (S.D. N.Y. 1997); *Porter v. U.S. Dept. of Army*, 1995 WL 461898, at *4 (N.D. Ill. 1995), *aff'd*, 99 F.3d 1142 (7th Cir. 1996); *Circuit City Stores, Inc. v. Citgo Petroleum Corp. v. Mobil Oil Corp.*, 1994 WL 483463 (E.D. Pa. 1994); *Brocksopp Engineering, Inc. v. Bach-Simpson Ltd.*, 136 F.R.D. 485, 486–87 (E.D. Wis. 1991); *Baker v. Universal Die Casting, Inc.*, 725 F. Supp. 416, 420–21 (W.D. Ark. 1989); *Business Incentives Co., Inc. v. Sony Corp. of America*, 397

favor the view that the responding party must serve an interim responsive pleading to all unchallenged portions.[21]

- *Appellate Remands:* It is also not clear how much time a defendant has to responsively plead if an appellate court reverses a Rule 12(b) motion the trial court had granted.

Manipulative Motions and Tolling Effect

Courts will not tolerate the use of this Rule 12 tolling feature in attempts to frivolously manipulate the time period for responsive pleading. Thus, for example, the tolling rule will not apply where a motion for summary judgment is deliberately mislabeled as a Rule 12 motion solely to avoid the obligation to file an answer.[22]

State Court Rules Do Not Apply

Federal procedure governs the time for responding to a federal complaint, answer (if a response is ordered), counterclaim, or crossclaim. This is true even if the defendant is served pursuant to a State law that would have provided a longer response period.[23]

RULE 12(b)—DEFENSES AND OBJECTIONS

CORE CONCEPT

All legal and factual defenses to a claim for relief must be asserted in the responsive pleading to the claim. However, seven enumerated defenses may alternatively be asserted by motion served before the responsive pleading is due.

APPLICATIONS

Enumerated Defenses

As to the following seven defenses, a party may assert the defense either in the responsive pleading or by motion served

---

F. Supp. 63, 70 (S.D. N.Y. 1975).

[21]*See Gerlach v. Michigan Bell Tel. Co.*, 448 F. Supp. 1168 (E.D. Mich. 1978) (holding that responsive pleading was required to unchallenged counts, refusing to enter default, but awarding plaintiffs attorney fees for filing for default). *See also Okaya (USA), Inc. v. U.S.*, 27 Ct. Int'l Trade 1509, 2003 WL 22284567 (2003) (noting that that motion to dismiss part of a complaint did not extend time to answer remainder). *See generally* Scott L. Cagan, *A "Partial" Motion to Dismiss Under Federal Rule of Civil Procedure 12: You Had Better Answer*, 39 Fed.B.J. 202 (1992) (advocating same result). *But see Tingley Systems, Inc. v. CSC Consulting, Inc.*, 152 F. Supp. 2d 95,

122 (D. Mass. 2001) (noting that "no court has relied on [*Gerlach*'s] reasoning or followed its ruling" and that "one court explicitly rejected its reasoning").

[22]*See Ricke v. Armco, Inc.*, 158 F.R.D. 149, 150 (D. Minn. 1994) ("Such an attempt to manipulate the Federal Rules of Civil Procedure should not be condoned or encouraged by the Court"). *See also Resolution Trust Corp. v. Ruggiero*, 994 F.2d 1221, 1227 (7th Cir. 1993) (holding that frivolous motion under Rule 12 buys the movant no additional time within which to serve a responsive pleading).

[23]*See Beller & Keller v. Tyler*, 120 F.3d 21, 25–26 (2d Cir. 1997).

before the responsive pleading is due:

- Lack of Subject Matter Jurisdiction, Rule 12(b)(1).
- Lack of Personal Jurisdiction, Rule 12(b)(2).
- Improper Venue, Rule 12(b)(3).
- Insufficient Process, Rule 12(b)(4).
- Insufficient Service of Process, Rule 12(b)(5).
- Failure to State a Claim for which Relief Can Be Granted, Rule 12(b)(6).
- Failure to Join a Party Under Rule 19 (persons needed for just adjudication), Rule 12(b)(7).

Waived Defenses and Objections

If a party chooses to assert a Rule 12 motion, the party must join all Rule 12 defenses and objections in that motion. If the party makes a Rule 12 motion but omits a potential Rule 12 objection to (2) personal jurisdiction, (3) venue, (4) process, or (5) service, that objection is waived and cannot be asserted later in the responsive pleading or in a subsequent motion or trial objection.[24]

Time for Making Motion

A party who intends to assert a Rule 12 defense or objection in a pre-answer motion must do so before the responsive pleading is due. This requires Rule 12 motions to be served generally within 21 calendar days after service of the complaint, cross claim, or counterclaim to which the motions are directed; a defendant who waives formal service of process is given 60 calendar days in which to respond.[25] The parties can, upon court approval, stipulate to an extension of time. Moreover, although the time for filing a Rule 12 motion is logistically tied to the time for filing an answer, a delay in filing such a motion may, under certain circumstances, still be permitted.[26]

Note: Where a responsive pleading is not required, the responding party's defenses and objections can be asserted at trial.[27]

Amended Pleadings

When litigants amend their pleadings, the responding parties may withdraw their answers or replies, and replead. If an amendment adds new matter that gives rise to a new, previously inapplicable Rule 12 motion, the responding party may assert the new Rule 12 defense by motion or responsive pleading.[28]

Note: An amendment does not give the responding party

---

[24]*See* Rule 12(h).

[25]*See* Rule 12(a).

[26]*See Luv N' Care, Ltd. v. Babelito, S.A.*, 306 F. Supp. 2d 468, 468–73 (S.D. N.Y. 2004) (ruling that motion was not waived where delay was ex-

plained by settlement discussions and certain service complications).

[27]*See* Rule 12(b).

[28]*But see supra* Authors' Commentary to Rule 12(a) ("**Exceptions to Tolling Effect Rule**") (such motions

an entirely new opportunity to assert Rule 12 defenses. A possible Rule 12 defense that was not asserted to the original pleading (and, thus, was waived) cannot be revived and asserted to the amended pleading unless it relates to new matter added by the amendment.[29]

Preliminary Motions Not Listed in Rule 12

Rule 12 does not provide an exhaustive list of all possible preliminary motions.[30] For example, motions for extensions of time, to amend a pleading, to intervene, to substitute parties, or for the entering of a stay or an order commanding the posting of security may all be raised as preliminary motions. The court's broad discretion and the federal policy against unwarranted, dilatory motions are the principal limitations on such unenumerated motions.

Form of Motion

Rule 12 provides only sparse guidance on the form and procedure for federal motion practice.[31] The other Rules provide some additional detail. For example, Rule 7 requires that motions generally be in writing, include a caption, state with particularity the basis for the motion, and request specific relief.[32] Rule 5 requires that motions be served upon each party to the litigation and be filed within a reasonable time after service.[33] Rule 11 mandates that all motions be signed and be presented for only proper, legally-warranted, factually-warranted purposes.[34] Rule 78 provides for the hearing and disposition of motions, and provides that the district court, by rule or order, may permit motions to be submitted and determined on the papers only, without oral argument.[35]

Most of the other details of federal motion practice and procedure are governed by local court rules.[36] Practitioners are strongly cautioned: these details often vary greatly from one judicial district to another. For example:

- *Pre-Filing Consultation:* Some districts require that the moving party meet and confer with the adversary prior

---

to amended pleadings might *not* entitle the moving party to tolling).

[29]*See Sohns v. Dahl*, 392 F. Supp. 1208, 1220 (W.D. Va. 1975).

[30]*See Custom Vehicles, Inc. v. Forest River, Inc.*, 464 F.3d 725, 727 (7th Cir. 2006) ("Motions may be proper despite the lack of a specific rule"); *International Ass'n of Entrepreneurs of America v. Angoff*, 58 F.3d 1266, 1271 (8th Cir. 1995) (commenting that although Rule 12(b) ostensibly enumerates available pre-answer motions, the district courts have discretion to permit other, un-

enumerated pre-answer motions).

[31]*See, e.g.*, Rule 12(b) (enumerating types of pre-answer motions; requiring motion before answer; permitting extrinsic materials to be submitted on converted motions).

[32]*See* Rule 7(b)(1).

[33]*See* Rule 5(a) to (b) (duty to serve); Rule 5(d) (duty to file).

[34]*See* Rule 11.

[35]*See* Rule 78.

[36]*See* Rule 83(a) (authorizing districts to establish local rules of practice).

to filing any motion, and then certify that good faith attempts to resolve the motion before filing have failed.[37]

- *Form of Order Required:* Some districts require that the moving party include with the motion a proposed blank form of order.[38]
- *Legal Memorandum Required:* Some districts require that a brief or legal memorandum accompany the motion.[39]
- *Page Limits:* Many districts set formal page limits that must be followed strictly, unless leave of court is sought and granted for the filing of a longer document.[40]
- *Oral Argument:* Some districts establish a formal procedure for seeking oral argument on a motion.[41]
- *Miscellaneous Requirements:* Local rules provide a myriad of other requirements, varying from district to district.[42]

Because these types of significant differences abound, practitioners must carefully consult their district's local rules before engaging in motion practice.

Time for / Form of Response to Motion

Likewise, the Federal Rules provide very little guidance on the practice and procedure for responding to motions. This detail is also almost always governed by the district's local rules of practice, which may establish requirements regarding:

- *Time for Responding:* Many districts require non-moving parties to file their opposition papers within a certain number of days after *either* the filing of or service of the motion.[43]
- *Forms of Order:* Some districts require that the non-

---

[37]*See, e.g.,* D. Colo. Loc. R. 7.1.A. (pre-filing meet and confer duty); E.D. Mich. Loc. R. 7.1(a) (duty to seek concurrence in motion); D. Or. Loc. R. 7.1(a) (good faith certification requirement); M.D. Pa. Loc. R. 7.1 (certification of concurrence / non-concurrence obligation).

[38]*See, e.g.,* D. Idaho Loc. R. 7.1(a) (1) (requiring proposed order under certain circumstances); E.D. Pa. Loc. R. 7.1(a) (every motion must be accompanied by form of order); W.D. Pa. Loc. R. 7.1(B) (motion improper if proposed order is not included); W.D. Tenn. Loc. R. 7.2(a)(1)(A) (all motions must be accompanied by form of order).

[39]*See, e.g.,* E.D. Pa. Loc. R. 7.1(c); D.R.I. Loc. R. 7(a); D.S.C. Loc. R. 7.04.

[40]*See, e.g.,* M.D. Pa. Loc. R. 7.8(b)

(requiring double-spaced briefs limited to 15 pages); D.S.C. Loc. R. 7.05(B)(1) (35 page limit for initial brief); E.D. Tenn. Loc. R. 7.1(b) (25 page limit for initial brief).

[41]*See, e.g.,* D.Az. Loc. R. 7.2(f) (request made by notation directly on motion or response); D.S.D. Loc. R. 7.1 (request made either in conclusion of motion or by separate pleading); D. Utah Loc. R. 7.1(f) (oral argument only granted for "good cause shown").

[42]*See, e.g.,* M.D. Pa. Loc. R. 7.8(a) (memoranda must state legal question presented).

[43]*See, e.g.,* Alaska Loc. R. 7.1(e) (opposition due within 15 days after service of motion); D.S.C. Loc. R. 7.06 (opposition due within 14 days after motion is served); E.D. Tenn. Loc. R. 7.1(a) (opposition to dispositive motion

moving party include a proposed form of order.[44]

- *Page Limits:* Many districts establish page limits for opposition papers.[45]
- *Reply Briefs:* Some districts permit the moving party to file a reply brief, so long as the reply is filed within a prescribed period after filing or service of the opposition papers.[46] Local rules may also set reply brief page limits.[47]

Because these response provisions vary so greatly from judicial district to judicial district, non-moving parties must also take care to consult the district's local rules before responding to a pending motion.

Liberal Reading of Motions

Liberality applies to motions to dismiss. A motion to dismiss will not generally be rejected merely because it fails to specify which particular Rule it invokes.[48] Nevertheless, careful practitioners will ensure that the court is accurately focused on the precise nature of the motion's attack.

RULE 12(b)(1)—DISMISSAL FOR LACK OF SUBJECT MATTER JURISDICTION

CORE CONCEPT

A case will be dismissed under this provision if the court lacks jurisdictional authority over the subject matter of the dispute.

APPLICATIONS

Types of Challenges

A claim can be challenged under this provision both facially and substantively.[49] On a *facial* challenge, the defendant

---

due within 21 days of service); E.D. Va. Loc. R. 7(F)(1) (opposition due within 11 days of service).

[44] *See, e.g.,* E.D. Pa. Loc. R. 7.1(a); W.D. Tenn. Loc. R. 7.2(a)(2).

[45] *See, e.g.,* D. Az. Loc. R. 7.2(e) (opposition brief limited to 15 pages); M.D. Fla. Loc. R. 3.01(b) (opposition brief limited to 20 pages); D. Vt. Loc. R. 7(a)(4) (opposition to dispositive motions limited to 25 pages); D. Wyo. Loc. R. 7.1(b)(2)(B) (same).

[46] *See, e.g.,* D. Neb. Loc. R. 7.0.1(c) (reply briefs must be filed within 7 days after opposition brief is filed and served); D.S.C. Loc. R. 7.07 (reply briefs are "discouraged", but may be filed within 7 days after service of the opposition); N.D. Tex. Loc. R. 7.1(f)

(reply briefs must be filed within 14 days after opposition is filed). *But see* M.D. Fla. Loc. R. 3.01(b) (no reply briefs permitted absent leave of court); D.N.H. Loc. R. 7.1(e)(2) (no reply briefs to nondispositive motions).

[47] *See, e.g.,* E.D. Mich. Loc. R. 7.1(c) (reply briefs limited to 5 pages); N.D. Tex. Loc. R. 7.2(c) (reply briefs limited to 10 pages); D. Utah Loc. R. 7.1(b)(3) (same).

[48] *See Travel All Over the World, Inc. v. Kingdom of Saudi Arabia,* 73 F.3d 1423, 1429 (7th Cir. 1996).

[49] *See Carrier Corp. v. Outokumpu Oyj,* 673 F.3d 430, 440 (6th Cir. 2012); *Apex Digital, Inc. v. Sears, Roebuck & Co.,* 572 F.3d 440, 443–44 (7th Cir. 2009); *See also Arbaugh v. Y&H Corp.,*

contests the adequacy of the language used in the pleading.[50] The pleader is required to formally aver the basis for jurisdiction in federal court; if the pleader fails to do so, the pleading can be dismissed.[51] On a *substantive* (or *factual*) challenge, the defendant objects to the factual merits of the asserted federal jurisdiction.[52] In such a challenge, the pleading itself may have adequately alleged the presence of federal subject matter jurisdiction, but the actual facts and allegations before the court may belie that averment, confirming that federal jurisdiction is absent and, thus, compelling the case's dismissal.[53]

Legal Test

The legal test for assessing whether a federal lawsuit, challenged under Rule 12(b)(1), may continue or must be dismissed depends on the type of challenge posed:

- *Facial (or "Technical") Challenges:* In examining facial (or technical) challenges to federal subject matter jurisdiction, the court will construe the complaint liberally, accept all uncontroverted, well-pleaded factual allegations as true, and view all reasonable inferences in plaintiff's favor.[54] But legal conclusions (even those couched as factual allegations) will not be assumed true.[55] The court views the allegations as a whole; if a conclusory averment of subject matter jurisdiction is contradicted by other allegations in the pleading, the case may be dismissed.[56] This approach mirrors the procedure (and safeguards for the nonmoving party) of Rule 12(b)(6).[57] The adequacy of the pleading will be tested under the "short and plain" standard of Rule 8, as sharpened by the

---

546 U.S. 500, 126 S. Ct. 1235, 1240, 163 L. Ed. 2d 1097 (2006).

[50]*See Muscogee (Creek) Nation v. Oklahoma Tax Com'n*, 611 F.3d 1222, 1227 (10th Cir. 2010); *Apex Digital, Inc. v. Sears, Roebuck & Co.*, 572 F.3d 440, 443–44 (7th Cir. 2009); *O'Bryan v. Holy See*, 556 F.3d 361, 375–76 (6th Cir. 2009).

[51]*See Gibbs v. Buck*, 307 U.S. 66, 77, 59 S. Ct. 725, 83 L. Ed. 1111 (1939). *See also Valentin v. Hospital Bella Vista*, 254 F.3d 358, 363–64 (1st Cir. 2001).

[52]*See Memphis Biofuels, LLC v. Chickasaw Nation Indus., Inc.*, 585 F.3d 917, 919 (6th Cir. 2009); *Stalley ex rel. U.S. v. Orlando Regional Healthcare System, Inc.*, 524 F.3d 1229, 1232–33 (11th Cir. 2008); *Torres-Negron v. J & N Records, LLC*, 504 F.3d 151, 162 (1st Cir. 2007).

[53]*See Gibbs v. Buck*, 307 U.S. 66, 59 S. Ct. 725, 83 L. Ed. 1111 (1939); *Apex Digital, Inc. v. Sears, Roebuck &*

Co., 572 F.3d 440, 443–44 (7th Cir. 2009).

[54]*See Scheuer v. Rhodes*, 416 U.S. 232, 234–37, 94 S. Ct. 1683, 40 L. Ed. 2d 90 (1974); *USAA Cas. Ins. Co. v. Permanent Mission of Republic of Namibia*, 681 F.3d 103, 109 n.29 (2d Cir. 2012); *In re Schering Plough Corp. Intron/Temodar Consumer Class Action*, 678 F.3d 235, 243 (3d Cir. 2012); *Benson v. JPMorgan Chase Bank, N.A.*, 673 F.3d 1207, 1211 (9th Cir. 2012).

[55]*See Conyers v. Rossides*, 558 F.3d 137, 143 (2d Cir. 2009); *O'Bryan v. Holy See*, 556 F.3d 361, 376 (6th Cir. 2009).

[56]*See Gibbs v. Buck*, 307 U.S. 66, 59 S. Ct. 725, 83 L. Ed. 1111 (1939); *New Mexicans for Bill Richardson v. Gonzales*, 64 F.3d 1495, 1499 (10th Cir. 1995).

[57]*See Muscogee (Creek) Nation v. Oklahoma Tax Com'n*, 611 F.3d 1222, 1227 n.1 (10th Cir. 2010); *Hastings v.*

"plausibility" benchmark established in *Twombly*.[58] Whether subject matter jurisdiction exists is tested as of the date the lawsuit was filed.[59]

● *Factual (or "Substantive") Challenges:* In factual (or substantive) subject matter jurisdiction attacks, the court will *not* presume that plaintiff's controverted factual allegations are true,[60] but may instead weigh the evidence before it and find the facts, so long as this factfinding does not involve the merits of the dispute.[61] In doing so, the court enjoys broad discretion. The court may receive and consider extrinsic evidence.[62] The court must permit the pleader to respond with supporting evidence and, where necessary, may convene a limited evidentiary hearing or plenary trial to find the facts.[63] Whether a hearing *must* be held or not depends on the circumstances, and whether the parties have otherwise received notice and a fair opportunity to be heard.[64] A central consideration in whether to convene such a hearing is whether any of the parties have requested it.[65] Moreover, if a material fact concerning jurisdiction is disputed, a plenary hearing may be necessary to resolve the contested issue.[66]

● *"Intertwined" Merits:* If the merits are so intertwined with the jurisdiction issue that the two cannot be separated,[67] most courts will treat the motion like any other substantive

---

Wilson, 516 F.3d 1055, 1058 (8th Cir. 2008).

[58]*See In re Schering Plough Corp. Intron/Temodar Consumer Class Action*, 678 F.3d 235, 244 (3d Cir. 2012); *In re Mirant Corp.*, 675 F.3d 530, 533 (5th Cir. 2012); *Absolute Activist Value Master Fund Ltd. v. Ficeto*, 677 F.3d 60, 65 (2d Cir. 2012). *But see Maya v. Centex Corp.*, 658 F.3d 1060, 1068 (9th Cir. 2011) (*Twombly* not proper approach for testing jurisdictional questions of standing). *See generally Bell Atlantic Corp. v. Twombly*, 550 U.S. 544, 556–57, 127 S. Ct. 1955, 1974, 167 L. Ed. 2d 929 (2007). Note: the *Twombly* standard is discussed in the Authors' Commentary to Rule 8(a) *supra* and Rule 12(b)(6) *infra*.

[59]*See Grupo Dataflux v. Atlas Global Group, L.P.*, 541 U.S. 567, 574, 124 S. Ct. 1920, 1925, 158 L. Ed. 2d 866 (2004); *Conolly v. Taylor*, 27 U.S. 556, 7 L. Ed. 518, 1829 WL 3192 (1829) (Marshall, C.J.); *Rosa v. Resolution Trust Corp.*, 938 F.2d 383, 392 (3d Cir. 1991).

[60]*See Carrier Corp. v. Outokumpu Oyj*, 673 F.3d 430, 440 (6th Cir. 2012); *Shoshone Indian Tribe of Wind River*

Reservation v. United States, 672 F.3d 1021, 1030 (Fed.Cir. 2012); *Odyssey Marine Exploration, Inc. v. Unidentified Shipwrecked Vessel*, 657 F.3d 1159, 1169–70 (11th Cir. 2011).

[61]*See Arbaugh v. Y&H Corp.*, 546 U.S. 500, 514, 126 S. Ct. 1235, 1244, 163 L. Ed. 2d 1097 (2006); *Carrier Corp. v. Outokumpu Oyj*, 673 F.3d 430, 440 (6th Cir. 2012); *Arena v. Graybar Elec. Co.*, 669 F.3d 214, 223 (5th Cir. 2012).

[62]*See infra* Authors' Commentary to Rule 12(b)(1) ("**Extrinsic Materials**").

[63]*See Sharkey v. Quarantillo*, 541 F.3d 75, 83 (2d Cir. 2008); *Johnson v. U.S.*, 534 F.3d 958, 964 (8th Cir. 2008); *McCann v. Newman Irrevocable Trust*, 458 F.3d 281, 290 (3d Cir. 2006).

[64]*See Johnson v. U.S.*, 534 F.3d 958, 964 (8th Cir. 2008); *McCann v. Newman Irrevocable Trust*, 458 F.3d 281 (3d Cir.2006).

[65]*McCann v. Newman Irrevocable Trust*, 458 F.3d 281, 290 (3d Cir.2006).

[66]*McCann v. Newman Irrevocable Trust*, 458 F.3d 281, 290 (3d Cir.2006).

[67]*See Torres-Negron v. J & N Records, LLC*, 504 F.3d 151, 163 (1st

merits challenge, constrained by summary judgment principles that reserve the resolution of general disputes as to material facts for the ultimate factfinder.[68] Other courts differ, and instead simply impose a relaxed standard on resolving such motions.[69]

Burden of Proof

When a defendant challenges subject matter jurisdiction, the plaintiff (as the party asserting the existence of jurisdiction) must bear the burden of establishing jurisdiction.[70] The plaintiff must carry this burden by a preponderance of the evidence.[71] The burden, however, is generally not a heavy one.[72] In federal question cases, the party must demonstrate a nonfrivolous claim based on federal law,[73] and must meet all other

---

Cir. 2007); *Paper, Allied-Industrial, Chem. & Energy Workers Int'l Union v. Continental Carbon Co.*, 428 F.3d 1285, 1292 (10th Cir. 2005); *Autery v. U.S.*, 424 F.3d 944, 956 (9th Cir. 2005).

[68]*See Arbaugh v. Y&H Corp.*, 546 U.S. 500, 514, 126 S. Ct. 1235, 1244, 163 L. Ed. 2d 1097 (2006); *Carrier Corp. v. Outokumpu Oyj*, 673 F.3d 430, 443–44 (6th Cir. 2012); *Odyssey Marine Exploration, Inc. v. Unidentified Shipwrecked Vessel*, 657 F.3d 1159, 1169–70 (11th Cir. 2011). *But see Ord v. District of Columbia*, 587 F.3d 1136, 1140 (D.C.Cir. 2009) ("well-settled" that Rule 12(b)(1) motions do not convert to summary judgment motions upon review of extrinsic materials).

[69]*See S.R.P. ex rel. Abunabba v. United States*, 676 F.3d 329, 344 & n.7 (3d Cir. 2012) (noting approach, and disagreement among Circuits).

[70]*See Thomson v. Gaskill*, 315 U.S. 442, 446, 62 S. Ct. 673, 86 L. Ed. 951 (1942); *Lujan v. Defenders of Wildlife*, 504 U.S. 555, 561, 112 S. Ct. 2130, 2136, 119 L. Ed. 2d 351 (1992); *Taylor v. KeyCorp*, 680 F.3d 609, 612 (6th Cir. 2012); *Arena v. Graybar Elec. Co.*, 669 F.3d 214, 219 (5th Cir. 2012).

[71]*See Vantage Trailers, Inc. v. Beall Corp.*, 567 F.3d 745, 748 (5th Cir. 2009); *Hamm v. U.S.*, 483 F.3d 135, 137 (2d Cir. 2007).

[72]*See Garcia v. Copenhaver, Bell & Associates, M.D.'s, P.A.*, 104 F.3d 1256, 1260–61 (11th Cir. 1997) ("extremely difficult" to dismiss claim for lacking subject matter jurisdiction); *Musson Theatrical, Inc. v. Federal*

Exp. Corp., 89 F.3d 1244, 1248 (6th Cir. 1996) (plaintiff's burden not onerous). *See also Michigan Southern R.R. Co. v. Branch & St. Joseph Counties Rail Users Ass'n., Inc.*, 287 F.3d 568, 573 (6th Cir. 2002) (commenting that claim will survive motion to dismiss if plaintiff shows "any arguable basis in law" for claims alleged).

[73]*See Neitzke v. Williams*, 490 U.S. 319, 327, 109 S. Ct. 1827, 104 L. Ed. 2d 338 (1989) (noting that a patently insubstantial complaint may be dismissed for want of subject matter jurisdiction); *Hagans v. Lavine*, 415 U.S. 528, 536–37, 94 S. Ct. 1372, 1378–79, 39 L. Ed. 2d 577 (1974) (commenting that federal courts lack power to hear cases otherwise within their jurisdiction but which are "so attenuated and unsubstantial" as to be clearly devoid of merit); *Bell v. Hood*, 327 U.S. 678, 682–83, 66 S. Ct. 773, 776, 90 L. Ed. 939 (1946) (observing that actions may sometimes be dismissed for lack of jurisdiction where the federal claim "clearly appears to be immaterial and made solely for the purpose of obtaining jurisdiction or where such a claim is wholly insubstantial and frivolous"). *Cf. Holloway v. Pagan River Dockside Seafood, Inc.*, 669 F.3d 448, 452 (4th Cir. 2012) (Rule 12(b)(1) dismissal for deficit federal case is proper only claim is so insubstantial, implausible, precedentially foreclosed, or otherwise completely devoid of merit); *Boock v. Shalala*, 48 F.3d 348, 353 (8th Cir. 1995) (holding that federal claims, although "clearly meritless", were not so patently frivolous that they failed to confer subject

statutory prerequisites for litigating the federal claim (such as exhaustion of administrative remedies and compliance with all claims-filing limitations and requirements).[74] In diversity cases, the party must demonstrate complete diversity of citizenship[75] and a claim that in good faith exceeds $75,000, exclusive of interest and costs.[76] In all cases, the party must demonstrate standing[77] and a live "case or controversy" subject to the federal courts' judicial power under Article III of the Constitution.[78]

Timing & Waiver

Verifying its subject matter jurisdiction is a federal court's "first duty" in every case.[79] Consequently, challenges to subject matter jurisdiction may be raised at any time, by any party, or by the court.[80] Such challenges can even be raised after final judgment is entered.[81] A party cannot waive or forfeit the requirement of subject matter jurisdiction,[82] nor can the parties consent to have a case heard in federal court where subject matter jurisdiction is absent.[83] A Rule 12(b) motion challenging subject matter jurisdiction questions the "very power" of the

---

matter jurisdiction). Allegations that fail to meet the "frivolous" test warranting dismissal under Rule 12(b)(1) may nevertheless still be dismissed under Rule 12(b)(6) for failing to state a cognizable claim for relief.

[74] *See Hart v. Dep't of Labor ex rel. U.S.*, 116 F.3d 1338 (10th Cir. 1997) (analyzing under Rule 12(b)(1) the defense that plaintiff failed to file timely claim with proper agency as required by the Federal Tort Claims Act).

[75] *See City of Indianapolis v. Chase Nat'l Bank of New York*, 314 U.S. 63, 69, 62 S. Ct. 15, 86 L. Ed. 47 (1941).

[76] *See St. Paul Mercury Indem. Co. v. Red Cab Co.*, 303 U.S. 283, 289, 58 S. Ct. 586, 82 L. Ed. 845 (1938) (ruling that dismissal only proper where it appears, to a "legal certainty", that claim is truly for less than the jurisdictional amount); *NLFC, Inc. v. Devcom Mid-America, Inc.*, 45 F.3d 231, 237 (7th Cir. 1995) (noting that amount in controversy alleged, in good faith, by plaintiff is decisive as to jurisdictional amount, unless it appears to a legal certainty that the true claim falls below the [then-applicable] $50,000 threshold).

[77] *See In re Schering Plough Corp. Intron/Temodar Consumer Class Action*, 678 F.3d 235, 243 (3d Cir. 2012); *Amidax Trading Group v. S.W.I.*

F.T. SCRL, 671 F.3d 140, 145 (2d Cir. 2011).

[78] *See Bateman v. City of West Bountiful*, 89 F.3d 704, 706 (10th Cir. 1996) (ripeness challenges are examined under Rule 12(b)(1)); *Super Sack Mfg. Corp. v. Chase Packaging Corp.*, 57 F.3d 1054, 1056 (Fed. Cir. 1995) (Rule 12(b)(1) motion granted where actual controversy had been removed and the remaining issues had been rendered moot).

[79] *See McCready v. White*, 417 F.3d 700, 702 (7th Cir. 2005).

[80] *See Arena v. Graybar Elec. Co.*, 669 F.3d 214, 223 (5th Cir. 2012); *American Telecom Co., L.L.C. v. Republic of Lebanon*, 501 F.3d 534, 539 (6th Cir. 2007).

[81] *See Arbaugh v. Y&H Corp.*, 546 U.S. 500, 506, 126 S. Ct. 1235, 1240, 163 L. Ed. 2d 1097 (2006). *See also* Rule 60(b)(4).

[82] *See Arbaugh v. Y&H Corp.*, 546 U.S. 500, 514, 126 S. Ct. 1235, 1244, 163 L. Ed. 2d 1097 (2006); *Ledford v. Peeples*, 605 F.3d 871, 902 n.85 (11th Cir. 2010); *Sucampo Pharms., Inc. v. Astellas Pharma, Inc.*, 471 F.3d 544, 548–49 (4th Cir. 2006).

[83] *See Neirbo Co. v. Bethlehem Shipbuilding Corporation*, 308 U.S. 165, 60 S. Ct. 153, 84 L. Ed. 167 (1939); *Laughlin v. Kmart Corp.*, 50 F.3d 871, 873 (10th Cir. 1995).

court to hear the case.[84] Such motions should be heard before turning to any merits attacks.[85]

Extrinsic Materials

The appropriate role for extrinsic materials depends on the type of Rule 12(b)(1) challenge the parties make. In a facial (or technical) attack, the court is limited to considering the complaint alone (supplemented only by its exhibits).[86] In a factual (or substantive) attack, the parties may produce affidavits and other materials to support their positions on subject matter jurisdiction.[87] The court may also consider matters of public record.[88]

Allowing Pre-Ruling Jurisdictional Discovery

When a defendant moves to dismiss for lack of subject matter jurisdiction, discovery of the factual issues implicated by the motion may be permitted.[89] This is especially true where the discovery seeks information peculiarly within the knowledge of the adversary.[90] The party seeking the discovery carries the burden of showing its need.[91] Although the trial judge enjoys broad discretion in resolving such motions,[92] a refusal to grant jurisdictional discovery may constitute an abuse of discretion if it prejudices the plaintiff.[93]

Mislabeled Motions

Provided no prejudice is caused, courts often excuse a mislabeling of a Rule 12(b)(1) motion as a Rule 12(b)(6) failure

---

[84]*See Petruska v. Gannon University*, 462 F.3d 294, 302 (3d Cir. 2006).

[85]*See In re FEMA Trailer Formaldehyde Prods. Liab. Litig. (Miss. Plaintiffs)*, 668 F.3d 281, 286–87 (5th Cir. 2012).

[86]*See In re Schering Plough Corp. Intron/Temodar Consumer Class Action*, 678 F.3d 235, 243 (3d Cir. 2012); *Apex Digital, Inc. v. Sears, Roebuck & Co.*, 572 F.3d 440, 444 (7th Cir. 2009); *Carmichael v. Kellogg, Brown & Root Servs., Inc.*, 572 F.3d 1271, 1279–80 (11th Cir. 2009).

[87]*See Taylor v. KeyCorp*, 680 F.3d 609, 612 (6th Cir. 2012); *Shoshone Indian Tribe of Wind River Reservation v. United States*, 672 F.3d 1021, 1030 (Fed.Cir. 2012); *Downing/Salt Pond Partners, L.P. v. Rhode Island & Providence Plantations*, 643 F.3d 16, 17 (1st Cir. 2011). *See also Ord v. District of Columbia*, 587 F.3d 1136, 1140 (D.C.Cir. 2009) ("well-settled" that Rule 12(b)(1) motions do not convert to summary judgment motions

upon review of extrinsic materials).

[88]*See White v. Lee*, 227 F.3d 1214, 1242 (9th Cir. 2000).

[89]*See Breakthrough Mgmt. Group, Inc. v. Chukchansi Gold Casino & Resort*, 629 F.3d 1173, 1189 (10th Cir. 2010); *Skwira v. U.S.*, 344 F.3d 64, 71–72 (1st Cir. 2003).

[90]*See Gualandi v. Adams*, 385 F.3d 236, 244 (2d Cir. 2004).

[91]*See Breakthrough Mgmt. Group, Inc. v. Chukchansi Gold Casino & Resort*, 629 F.3d 1173, 1189 n.11 (10th Cir. 2010); *Freeman v. U.S.*, 556 F.3d 326, 341–42 (5th Cir. 2009).

[92]*See Freeman v. U.S.*, 556 F.3d 326, 341 (5th Cir. 2009).

[93]*See Sizova v. Nat. Institute of Standards & Technology*, 282 F.3d 1320, 1326 (10th Cir. 2002) (noting that such prejudice exists if "pertinent facts bearing on the question of jurisdiction are controverted . . . or where a more satisfactory showing of the facts is necessary").

to state a claim motion, and *vice versa*. In such an instance, the court will merely apply the appropriate legal standard and rule accordingly.[94]

Oral Hearing on Motion

Although a court must afford the plaintiff an opportunity to be heard before dismissing under Rule 12(b)(1), an oral hearing is not always necessary.[95]

Sua Sponte **Dismissals**

It is well established that dismissals for lack of subject matter jurisdiction may be ordered *sua sponte* by the trial court or even by a subsequent appeals court.[96] Indeed, courts have an independent obligation to confirm that subject matter jurisdiction is present, whether an objection on that ground is made or not.[97]

Ruling Deferred

Although the question of subject matter jurisdiction is resolved by the court, not the jury, the court may defer ruling on the challenge until after further materials are presented, after discovery is conducted, or after evidence is received at trial.[98] The court may *not*, however, defer ruling upon a subject matter jurisdictional challenge so as to rule instead upon a potentially simpler dispositive motion attacking the underlying merits of the lawsuit.[99] Because the judicial power of the United States is limited, jurisdiction must be established as a threshold matter before any merits ruling is possible.

Remedy

Generally, the court will permit a party to amend unless it

---

[94]*See Corrie v. Caterpillar, Inc.*, 503 F.3d 974, 980 (9th Cir. 2007); *Jarrard v. CDI Telecommcins Inc.*, 408 F.3d 905, 909 n.3 (7th Cir. 2005). *See also Zimmerman v. Cambridge Credit Counseling Corp.*, 409 F.3d 473, 475 n.4 (1st Cir. 2005) (discounting as "immaterial" dispute as to whether Rule 12(b)(1) or Rule 12(b)(6) was correct form for motion).

[95]*See In re Eckstein Marine Serv. L.L.C.*, 672 F.3d 310, 319–20 (5th Cir.2012), *petition for cert. filed*, 81 U.S.L.W. 3007 (U.S. June 25, 2012) (Nos. 11-1538 & 11-1253); *Odyssey Marine Exploration, Inc. v. Unidentified Shipwrecked Vessel*, 657 F.3d 1159, 1170 (11th Cir. 2011).

[96]*See Arbaugh v. Y&H Corp.*, 546 U.S. 500, 506, 126 S. Ct. 1235, 1240, 163 L. Ed. 2d 1097 (2006).

[97]*See Arbaugh v. Y&H Corp.*, 546 U.S. 500, 514, 126 S. Ct. 1235, 1244, 163 L. Ed. 2d 1097 (2006).

[98]*See Land v. Dollar*, 330 U.S. 731, 67 S. Ct. 1009, 91 L. Ed. 1209 (1947); *Valentin v. Hospital Bella Vista*, 254 F.3d 358, 364 n.3 (1st Cir. 2001).

[99]*See Steel Co. v. Citizens for a Better Env't*, 523 U.S. 83, 118 S. Ct. 1003, 140 L. Ed. 2d 210 (1998) (rejecting the so-called doctrine of "hypothetical" or "assumed" jurisdiction). *See also In re Great Lakes Dredge & Dock Co. LLC*, 624 F.3d 201, 209 (5th Cir. 2010) (should resolve jurisdictional motions before any merits attack). But the Supreme Court has confirmed that there is no "unyielding hierarchy" *among* jurisdictional requirements, and courts are free to resolve *personal* jurisdiction challenges before reaching potentially more difficult questions of *subject* matter jurisdiction. *See generally Ruhrgas AG v. Marathon Oil Co.*, 526 U.S. 574, 119 S. Ct. 1563, 143 L. Ed. 2d 760 (1999).

is clear that subject matter jurisdiction cannot be truthfully averred.[100] When the court lacks subject matter jurisdiction, it must dismiss the case in its entirety.[101]

Prejudice on Dismissal

A dismissal for lack of subject matter jurisdiction is usually not a decision on the merits, and generally will not preclude the plaintiff from filing the claim in a court that may properly hear the dispute.[102]

Dismissal's Effect on Supplemental Jurisdiction Claims

If a lawsuit's federal claims are dismissed for lack of subject matter jurisdiction, then all supplemental jurisdiction claims must ordinarily be dismissed as well.[103]

Appealability

A dismissal premised upon a lack of subject matter jurisdiction is ordinarily considered a "final order", subject to immediate review by the court of appeals.[104] However, denying a motion to dismiss for lack of subject matter jurisdiction generally is interlocutory and not immediately appealable.[105]

RULE 12(b)(2)—DISMISSAL FOR LACK OF PERSONAL JURISDICTION

CORE CONCEPT

A particular defendant may be dismissed from the lawsuit if personal jurisdiction over that defendant is absent.

---

[100]*See Leaf v. Supreme Court of State of Wis.*, 979 F.2d 589, 595 (7th Cir. 1992) (noting that leave to amend defective allegations of subject matter jurisdiction should be freely given).

[101]*See Arbaugh v. Y&H Corp.*, 546 U.S. 500, 514, 126 S. Ct. 1235, 1244, 163 L. Ed. 2d 1097 (2006).

[102]*See Stalley ex rel. U.S. v. Orlando Reg'l Healthcare System, Inc.*, 524 F.3d 1229, 1232 (11th Cir. 2008); *Mitchell v. Chapman*, 343 F.3d 811, 820 (6th Cir. 2003); *Ramming v. U.S.*, 281 F.3d 158, 161 (5th Cir. 2001). *But cf. Frigard v. U.S.*, 862 F.2d 201, 204 (9th Cir. 1988) (noting that although Rule 12(b)(1) dismissals are ordinarily without prejudice to a re-filing in a court of competent jurisdiction, some dismissals (such as those premised on sovereign immunity) are absolute such that no court could hear the case and no re-drafting of the pleadings could cure

the defect).

[103]*See Arena v. Graybar Elec. Co.*, 669 F.3d 214, 223–24 (5th Cir. 2012); *Musson Theatrical, Inc. v. Federal Exp. Corp.*, 89 F.3d 1244, 1255 (6th Cir. 1996).

[104]*See Carson Harbor Village Ltd. v. City of Carson*, 37 F.3d 468, 471 (9th Cir. 1994) (overruled on other grounds by, WMX Techs., Inc. v. Miller, 104 F.3d 1133 (9th Cir. 1997)). Note, however, that the Circuits are divided as to whether such a dismissal "without prejudice" and with leave to file an amendment is immediately appealable. *See WMX Techs., Inc. v. Miller*, 104 F.3d 1136 (9th Cir. 1997) (surveying Circuits, and ruling that such appeals are interlocutory).

[105]*See Harrison v. Nissan Motor Corp. in U.S.A.*, 111 F.3d 343, 347–48 (3d Cir. 1997).

APPLICATIONS

In Personam and *In Rem* Actions

Motions under this Rule may be used to challenge any asserted personal jurisdiction by the court, whether *in personam*, *in rem*, or *quasi in rem*.[106] The exercise of personal jurisdiction by a federal court must comport with both local requirements (*e.g.*, "tag" or long-arm statute) and federal constitutional requirements established by the Due Process Clause.[107]

Special Appearances

The Rules have abandoned the concepts of "special" and "general" appearances.[108] Now, a defendant can assert jurisdictional defenses, venue defenses, and even substantive defenses under Rule 12 without impliedly consenting to the court's personal jurisdiction.[109]

Types of Challenges

A defendant can challenge personal jurisdiction theoretically or factually (a both).[110] Theoretical challenges contest the plaintiff's theory of jurisdiction (*e.g.*, that the defendant subjected itself to jurisdiction in the forum by engaging in a particular set of actions). If the court determines that those facts, if proven to be true, would subject the defendant to personal jurisdiction in the forum, no hearing or factual resolution is required and the theoretical challenge fails.[111] Alternatively (or additionally), the defendant may challenge personal jurisdiction factually by disputing the facts the plaintiff has averred. When jurisdiction is challenged factually, the court or the factfinder must resolve the factual dispute.[112]

Legal Test

The nature of the court's inquiry on a Rule 12(b)(2) challenge depends on the type of challenge made (and, relatedly, how the motion is supported).[113] If the motion rests on the pleadings and allegations alone (typically, a theoretical chal-

---

[106]*See Newhard, Cook & Co. v. Inspired Life Centers, Inc.*, 895 F.2d 1226, 1228 (8th Cir. 1990).

[107]For a detailed discussion of personal jurisdiction, *see* Part II of this text.

[108]*See In re Hijazi*, 589 F.3d 401, 413 (7th Cir. 2009); *S.E.C. v. Ross*, 504 F.3d 1130, 1149 (9th Cir. 2007); *Chase v. Pan-Pacific Broadcasting, Inc.*, 750 F.2d 131, 133 (D.C. Cir. 1984). *See also Orange Theatre Corp. v. Rayherstz Amusement Corp.*, 139 F.2d 871, 874 (C.C.A. 3d Cir. 1944) (writing that a defendant "is no longer required at the door of the federal courthouse to intone that ancient abracadabra of the law,

de bene esse, in order by its magic power himself to remain outside even while he steps within").

[109]*See In re Hijazi*, 589 F.3d 401, 413 (7th Cir. 2009).

[110]*See Credit Lyonnais Securities (USA), Inc. v. Alcantara*, 183 F.3d 151, 153–54 (2d Cir. 1999).

[111]*See In re Magnetic Audiotape Antitrust Litigation*, 334 F.3d 204, 206 (2d Cir. 2003).

[112]*See Credit Lyonnais Securities (USA), Inc. v. Alcantara*, 183 F.3d 151, 153 (2d Cir. 1999).

[113]*See Foster-Miller, Inc. v. Babcock & Wilcox Canada*, 46 F.3d 138 (1st

lenge), the plaintiff only has to present a *prima facie* showing of jurisdiction — namely, factual allegations that, if credited by the factfinder, would be sufficient to confer personal jurisdiction.[114] In this posture, the uncontroverted allegations in the complaint are accepted as true, and factual disputes are resolved in the pleader's favor.[115] But allegations that are contradicted by affidavit are not assumed true.[116] Moreover, uncontradicted facts offered by the defendant are also considered.[117] For all of these reasons, this burden on plaintiff is considered "relatively slight".[118] But this burden is also only a preliminary one; if the jurisdictional challenge is renewed, the plaintiff will later have to prove the jurisdictional facts (so far, adequately alleged) at trial by a preponderance of the evidence.[119]

If the defendant goes beyond a theoretical challenge and contests the jurisdictional facts, or if the court finds that it would be unfair under the circumstances to make only a tentative, preliminary ruling, the court may convene a pretrial evidentiary hearing on personal jurisdiction. At the hearing, the plaintiff bears the full preponderance burden[120] and the court can find the jurisdictional facts.[121] If, however, such factfinding would be intertwined with the underlying merits, the court will often defer a final jurisdictional ruling until trial, allowing the jury to resolve the factual dispute (for both jurisdictional and

---

Cir.1995) (discussing three levels of inquiry under Rule 12(b)(2)). *See also Oldfield v. Pueblo De Bahia Lora, S.A.*, 558 F.3d 1210, 1219 n.19 (11th Cir. 2009) (same effect).

[114]*See Pervasive Software Inc. v. Lexware GmbH & Co. KG*, 688 F.3d 214, 219 (5th Cir. 2012); *Schneider v. Hardesty*, 669 F.3d 693, 697 (6th Cir. 2012); *CollegeSource, Inc. v. AcademyOne, Inc.*, 653 F.3d 1066, 1073 (9th Cir. 2011). *Cf. Nationwide Mut. Ins. Co. v. Tryg Intern. Ins. Co., Ltd.*, 91 F.3d 790 (6th Cir. 1996) (surmising that Circuit would apply the *prima facie* inquiry where trial judge permits limited discovery jurisdictional but does not convene an evidentiary hearing).

[115]*See Pervasive Software Inc. v. Lexware GmbH & Co. KG*, 688 F.3d 214, 219 (5th Cir. 2012); *Carrier Corp. v. Outokumpu Oyj*, 673 F.3d 430, 449 (6th Cir. 2012); *CollegeSource, Inc. v. AcademyOne, Inc.*, 653 F.3d 1066, 1073 (9th Cir. 2011).

[116]*See CollegeSource, Inc. v. AcademyOne, Inc.*, 653 F.3d 1066,

1073 (9th Cir. 2011).

[117]*See Astro-Med, Inc. v. Nihon Kohden America, Inc.*, 591 F.3d 1, 8 (1st Cir. 2009).

[118]*See Carrier Corp. v. Outokumpu Oyj*, 673 F.3d 430, 449 (6th Cir. 2012). *See also Johnson v. Arden*, 614 F.3d 785, 794 (8th Cir. 2010) ("minimal" required showing). *But cf. Massachusetts School of Law at Andover, Inc. v. American Bar Ass'n*, 142 F.3d 26, 34 (1st Cir. 1998) (cautioning that despite Rule 12(b)(2)'s liberal approach, "the law does not require us struthiously to 'credit conclusory allegations or draw far-fetched inferences' ").

[119]*See Mullins v. TestAmerica, Inc.*, 564 F.3d 386, 399 (5th Cir. 2009).

[120]*See Schneider v. Hardesty*, 669 F.3d 693, 697 (6th Cir. 2012); *Purdue Research Foundation v. Sanofi-Synthelabo, S.A.*, 338 F.3d 773, 782–83 (7th Cir. 2003).

[121]*See Walk Haydel & Associates, Inc. v. Coastal Power Production Co.*, 517 F.3d 235, 241–42 (5th Cir. 2008).

merits purposes).[122]

In an appropriate case, the court can opt for a middle course, requiring more from the plaintiff (*e.g.*, a more fulsome, factual showing of a "likelihood" of personal jurisdiction) before allowing the lawsuit to continue, yet making no final, conclusive pretrial ruling on the jurisdictional question.[123]

Burden of Proof

The burden lies with the party invoking the court's jurisdiction to establish the existence of that jurisdiction.[124]

Timing and Waiver

Challenges to personal jurisdiction are waived, unless raised by motion (if there is one) or in the responsive pleading.[125] Even if properly raised, the defense may later be deemed waived if the defendant fails to press the court for a ruling and, instead, chooses to participate in the litigation as though jurisdiction existed.[126] But there generally is no waiver (at least under the approach followed by a majority of the Circuits) merely because a defendant's responsive pleading includes a claim for affirmative relief (*e.g.*, filing a counterclaim, cross-claim, or third-party claim), provided the defendant asserts a timely objection to jurisdiction.[127]

Waiting for Default to Raise Personal Jurisdiction Objections

Ordinarily, defendants must raise objections to personal ju-

---

[122]*See Walk Haydel & Associates, Inc. v. Coastal Power Production Co.*, 517 F.3d 235, 242 (5th Cir. 2008).

[123]*See Foster-Miller, Inc. v. Babcock & Wilcox Canada*, 46 F.3d 138 (1st Cir.1995). *See also Purdue Research Foundation v. Sanofi-Synthelabo, S.A.*, 338 F.3d 773, 782–83 (7th Cir. 2003) (noting national precedent that once defendant submits affidavits or other evidence in opposition to jurisdiction, plaintiff must go beyond pleadings and submit affirmative evidence supporting jurisdiction).

[124]*See Pervasive Software Inc. v. Lexware GmbH & Co. KG*, 688 F.3d 214, 219 (5th Cir. 2012); *Carrier Corp. v. Outokumpu Oyj*, 673 F.3d 430, 449 (6th Cir. 2012); *CollegeSource, Inc. v. AcademyOne, Inc.*, 653 F.3d 1066, 1073 (9th Cir. 2011).

[125]*See Ins. Corp. of Ireland v. Compagnie des Bauxites de Guinee*, 456 U.S. 694, 703, 102 S.Ct. 2099, 72 L.Ed.2d 492 (1982); *City of New York v. Mickalis Pawn Shop, LLC*, 645 F.3d 114, 133 (2d Cir. 2011).

[126]*See Rates Technology Inc. v. Nortel Networks Corp.*, 399 F.3d 1302, 1308–09 (Fed. Cir. 2005) (noting waiver authority, but finding defendant did not "dally" but moved to dismiss at its "earliest opportunity"). *Cf. Hamilton v. Atlas Turner, Inc.*, 197 F.3d 58, 62 (2d Cir. 1999) (defense "forfeited" by failing to move to dismiss during four-year period following inclusion of defense in party's answer); *Trustees of Cent. Laborers' Welfare Fund v. Lowery*, 924 F.2d 731, 732–33 (7th Cir. 1991) (same, six-year period).

[127]*See S.E.C. v. Ross*, 504 F.3d 1130, 1149 (9th Cir. 2007); *Rates Technology Inc. v. Nortel Networks Corp.*, 399 F.3d 1302, 1307–08 (Fed. Cir. 2005); *Chase v. Pan-Pacific Broadcasting, Inc.*, 750 F.2d 131, 132 (D.C. Cir. 1984); *Neifeld v. Steinberg*, 438 F.2d 423, 428–29 (3d Cir. 1971). *See also Bayou Steel Corp. v. M/V Amstelvoorn*, 809 F.2d 1147 (5th Cir. 1987) (discussing divergent views, and adopting majority approach).

risdiction either in their omnibus Rule 12 motion or in their answer (if no Rule 12 motion is filed). But defendants have one further option: they may default and then resist the resulting judgment collaterally. But defendants choose this strategy at their peril; if their collateral attack on jurisdiction fails, they almost certainly will be held to have abandoned their right to defend on the merits.[128]

"Renewed" Motion at Trial

A Rule 12(b)(2) ruling can be tentative and preliminary (especially when made under the predictive *prima facie* standard). At trial, the defendant can renew the motion and insist that the plaintiff actually prove, by a preponderance of the evidence, all the alleged jurisdictional facts.[129] The defendant must actually renew the motion to do so.[130] Although the trial court may *sua sponte* return to the earlier jurisdictional objection, it is not required to do so, and in such cases is entitled to apply a mere reconsideration standard (essentially, revisiting the same forgiving *prima facie* analysis performed earlier).[131]

Summary Judgment Challenges

The appropriate procedural vehicle for contesting personal jurisdiction is a motion to dismiss under Rule 12(b)(2). Seeking a summary judgment under Rule 56 for a personal jurisdiction defect is neither theoretically proper nor practically wise.[132]

Extrinsic Materials

The parties may produce affidavits, interrogatories, depositions, oral testimony (if an evidentiary hearing is convened), and other materials to support their positions on personal jurisdiction.[133]

---

[128]*See Ins. Corp. of Ireland, Ltd. v. Compagnie des Bauxites de Guinee*, 456 U.S. 694, 706, 102 S.Ct. 2099, 72 L.Ed.2d 492 (1982); *Baldwin v. Iowa State Traveling Men's Ass'n*, 283 U.S. 522, 525, 51 S.Ct. 517, 75 L.Ed. 1244 (1931); *Merial Ltd. v. Cipla Ltd.*, 681 F.3d 1283, 1297 (Fed.Cir. 2012).

[129]*See Mullins v. TestAmerica, Inc.*, 564 F.3d 386, 399 (5th Cir. 2009); *United Techs. Corp. v. Mazer*, 556 F.3d 1260, 1274 (11th Cir. 2009); *Northern Laminate Sales, Inc. v. Davis*, 403 F.3d 14, 23 (1st Cir. 2005).

[130]*See Mullins v. TestAmerica, Inc.*, 564 F.3d 386, 399 & 399 n.7 (5th Cir. 2009) (absent special circumstances, failure to renew forecloses defendant's right to insist on preponderance burden at trial or waives defense entirely).

[131]*See Northern Laminate Sales, Inc. v. Davis*, 403 F.3d 14, 23 (1st Cir. 2005).

[132]*See Marten v. Godwin*, 499 F.3d 290, 295 n.2 (3d Cir. 2007).

[133]*See Walk Haydel & Associates, Inc. v. Coastal Power Production Co.*, 517 F.3d 235, 241 (5th Cir. 2008); *Negron-Torres v. Verizon Communications, Inc.*, 478 F.3d 19, 23 (1st Cir. 2007); *Schwarzenegger v. Fred Martin Motor Co.*, 374 F.3d 797, 800 (9th Cir. 2004).

Allowing Pre-Ruling Jurisdictional Discovery

Generally, discovery is available to aid the pleader in establishing the existence of personal jurisdiction.[134] Consequently, courts may grant limited jurisdictional discovery before ruling on a Rule 12(b)(2) motion to dismiss for lack of personal jurisdiction.[135] Whether, and under what constraints, to permit jurisdictional discovery are matters typically reserved for the trial judge's discretion,[136] which will not be overturned absent a showing of actual and substantial prejudice.[137] Jurisdictional discovery will generally be allowed where a "colorable" case for jurisdiction has been made, where the material facts that bear on jurisdiction are controverted, where a more satisfactory development of those facts is necessary, and where plaintiff has demonstrated that discovery will permit a supplementation of the jurisdictional allegations.[138] Conversely, such discovery may be properly refused when it is untimely sought,[139] where the request is improperly supported[140] or based on mere hunches and conjecture,[141] where the claim is "attenu-

---

[134]*See Oppenheimer Fund, Inc. v. Sanders*, 437 U.S. 340, 351, 98 S. Ct. 2380, 57 L. Ed. 2d 253 (1978) ("discovery is available to ascertain the facts bearing on [jurisdictional] issues"). *See generally Metcalfe v. Renaissance Marine, Inc.*, 566 F.3d 324, 336 (3d Cir. 2009); *Doe v. Unocal Corp.*, 248 F.3d 915, 922 (9th Cir. 2001); Note, *The Use of Discovery to Obtain Jurisdictional Facts*, 59 Va. L. Rev. 533 (1973).

[135]*See U.S. v. Swiss American Bank, Ltd.*, 274 F.3d 610, 625 (1st Cir. 2001) (noting that a "timely and properly supported" motion for jurisdictional discovery "merits solicitous attention"). *See, e.g., GTE New Media Services Inc. v. BellSouth Corp.*, 199 F.3d 1343, 1351–52 (D.C. Cir. 2000); *U.S. v. Swiss American Bank, Ltd.*, 191 F.3d 30, 45–46 (1st Cir. 1999).

[136]*See Walk Haydel & Associates, Inc. v. Coastal Power Production Co.*, 517 F.3d 235, 241–42 (5th Cir. 2008); *Best Van Lines, Inc. v. Walker*, 490 F.3d 239, 255 (2d Cir. 2007); *Negron-Torres v. Verizon Communications, Inc.*, 478 F.3d 19, 23 (1st Cir. 2007).

[137]*See Nuance Cmmc'ns, Inc. v. Abbyy Software House*, 626 F.3d 1222, 1236 (Fed.Cir. 2010) (defining prejudice as reasonable probability that outcome would have been different with new discovery).

[138]*See Nuance Cmmc'ns, Inc. v. Abbyy Software House*, 626 F.3d 1222, 1235–36 (Fed.Cir. 2010); *Metcalfe v. Renaissance Marine, Inc.*, 566 F.3d 324, 336 (3d Cir. 2009). *See also Eurofins Pharma US Holdings v. BioAlliance Pharma SA*, 623 F.3d 147, 157 (3d Cir. 2010) (permitted upon showing with reasonable particularity that jurisdiction exists).

[139]*See Platten v. HG Bermuda Exempted Ltd.*, 437 F.3d 118, 139–40 (1st Cir. 2006); *Massachusetts School of Law at Andover, Inc. v. American Bar Ass'n*, 142 F.3d 26, 37 (1st Cir. 1998).

[140]*See Carefirst Of Maryland, Inc. v. Carefirst Pregnancy Centers, Inc.*, 334 F.3d 390, 402–03 (4th Cir. 2003) ("only speculation or conclusory assertions about contacts with a forum state"); *Terracom v. Valley Nat. Bank*, 49 F.3d 555 (9th Cir. 1995) (plaintiff failed to demonstrate how further discovery could establish jurisdiction). *Cf. U.S. v. Swiss American Bank, Ltd.*, 191 F.3d 30, 45–46 (1st Cir. 1999) (timely, properly supported motion for jurisdictional discovery "merits solicitous attention").

[141]*See Viasystems, Inc. v. EBM-Papst St. Georgen GmbH & Co., KG*, 646 F.3d 589, 598 (8th Cir. 2011); *Nuance Cmmc'ns, Inc. v. Abbyy Software House*, 626 F.3d 1222, 1236

ated" and based on bare allegations that are specifically denied,[142] where a colorable case for jurisdiction has not been made,[143] where the plaintiff's claim is "clearly frivolous"[144] or otherwise based on alleged facts that, even if true, would not support jurisdiction,[145] or where the plaintiff lacks a good faith belief that such discovery could support the jurisdictional allegations.[146] Jurisdictional discovery is often dependent on the specific circumstances presented. Thus, jurisdictional discovery into whether a corporate defendant is adequately "doing business" within the forum may be granted more liberally[147] than such discovery of an individual[148] or a foreign sovereign.[149]

- *Foreign Discovery:* Generally, a party may (but is not necessarily obligated to) pursue foreign discovery through the Hague Evidence Convention.[150] When personal jurisdic-

---

(Fed.Cir. 2010). *See also Eurofins Pharma US Holdings v. BioAlliance Pharma SA,* 623 F.3d 147, 157 (3d Cir. 2010) (no fishing expeditions permitted).

[142]*See Getz v. The Boeing Co.,* 654 F.3d 852, 860 (9th Cir. 2011).

[143]*See Negron-Torres v. Verizon Communications, Inc.,* 478 F.3d 19, 27 (1st Cir. 2007) (no colorable case). *See also Best Van Lines, Inc. v. Walker,* 490 F.3d 239, 255 (2d Cir. 2007) (no prima facie case).

[144]*See Massachusetts School of Law at Andover, Inc. v. American Bar Ass'n,* 107 F.3d 1026, 1042 (3d Cir. 1997).

[145]*See Viasystems, Inc. v. EBM-Papst St. Georgen GmbH & Co., KG,* 646 F.3d 589, 598 (8th Cir. 2011); *Nuance Cmmc'ns, Inc. v. Abbyy Software House,* 626 F.3d 1222, 1236 (Fed.Cir. 2010).

[146]*See Caribbean Broadcasting System, Ltd. v. Cable & Wireless P.L.C.,* 148 F.3d 1080, 1090 (D.C. Cir. 1998) (discussing good faith belief requirement). *See also Kelly v. Syria Shell Petroleum Development B.V.,* 213 F.3d 841, 855–56 (5th Cir. 2000) (discovery may be denied where the discovery sought could not have added any significant facts); *Terracom v. Valley Nat. Bank,* 49 F.3d 555 (9th Cir. 1995) (denial of jurisdictional discovery where plaintiff failed to demonstrate how further discovery could establish jurisdiction); *Poe v. Babcock Intern.,*

plc, 662 F. Supp. 4, 7 (M.D. Pa. 1985) (jurisdictional discovery denied where plaintiff responded to motion with "mere speculation"). *Cf. GTE New Media Services Inc. v. BellSouth Corp.,* 199 F.3d 1343, 1351–52 (D.C. Cir. 2000) (jurisdictional discovery is justified if party demonstrates that discovery can supplement jurisdictional allegations).

[147]*See Massachusetts School of Law at Andover, Inc. v. American Bar Ass'n,* 107 F.3d 1026, 1042 (3d Cir. 1997) (noting that jurisdictional discovery often relates to "doing business" inquiry). *See also Metcalfe v. Renaissance Marine, Inc.,* 566 F.3d 324, 336 (3d Cir. 2009) (such discovery "particularly appropriate" where defendant is a corporation).

[148]*See Massachusetts School of Law at Andover, Inc. v. American Bar Ass'n,* 107 F.3d 1026, 1042 (3d Cir. 1997) (observing that presumption in favor of jurisdictional discovery is reduced when defendant is an individual).

[149]*See Alpha Therapeutic Corp. v. Nippon Hoso Kyokai,* 199 F.3d 1078, 1087–88 (9th Cir. 1999) (discussing the circumspection under which jurisdictional discovery from foreign sovereign should be ordered).

[150]Hague Convention on the Taking of Evidence Abroad in Civil or Commercial Matters, opened for signature, Mar. 18, 1970, 23 U.S.T. 2555, T.I.A.S. No. 7444, *reprinted in* 28 U.S.C. § 1781 Note. *See Societe Nationale Industrielle Aerospatiale v.*

tion over the foreign party is contested, the courts are divided as to whether discovery can proceed simply under the Rules or whether Convention discovery is required until the question of jurisdiction is resolved.[151]

Sua Sponte Dismissals

Several Circuits forbid *sua sponte* dismissals for lack of personal jurisdiction, reasoning that the objection is a waivable defense that must be properly asserted or else it is lost.[152] Other Circuits permit *sua sponte* personal jurisdiction dismissals, provided the plaintiffs are afforded the opportunity to contest the issue and to introduce new supporting evidence (sometimes even as late as on appeal).[153] Still others permit (or require) *sua sponte* examinations of personal jurisdiction when the defendants have not appeared to defend, and a default judgment against them is being sought.[154]

Ruling Deferred

The court may defer ruling on the challenge until after further materials are presented or after jurisdictional discovery is conducted.[155] But a court generally must resolve personal jurisdiction issues before reaching merits issues.[156]

U.S. Dist. Court for Southern Dist. of Iowa, 482 U.S. 522, 533–36, 107 S. Ct. 2542, 2550–51, 96 L. Ed. 2d 461 (1987) (first resort to Convention discovery is not required).

[151]*See In re Automotive Refinishing Paint Antitrust Litigation*, 358 F.3d 288, 299–305 (3d Cir. 2004) (ruling that Convention discovery is not required, but citing case law split).

[152]*See, e.g., City of New York v. Mickalis Pawn Shop, LLC*, 645 F.3d 114, 133 (2d Cir. 2011); *Pakootas v. Teck Cominco Metals, Ltd.*, 452 F.3d 1066, 1076 (9th Cir. 2006).

[153]*See Buchanan v. Manley*, 145 F.3d 386, 388–89 (D.C. Cir. 1998). *Cf. Trujillo v. Williams*, 465 F.3d 1210, 1217 (10th Cir. 2006) (*sua sponte* rulings on personal jurisdiction are proper under 28 U.S.C.A. § 1915 where defense is obvious from complaint's face and no further factual record is necessary).

[154]*See, e.g., Sinoying Logistics Pte Ltd. v. Yi Da Xin Trading Corp.*, 619 F.3d 207, 213 (2d Cir. 2010); *Mwani v. bin Laden*, 417 F.3d 1, 6 (D.C.Cir. 2005); *System Pipe & Supply, Inc. v. M/ V Viktor Kurnatovskiy*, 242 F.3d 322, 324 (5th Cir. 2001).

[155]*See Theunissen v. Matthews*, 935 F.2d 1454 (6th Cir.1991); *Data Disc, Inc. v. Systems Technology Associates, Inc.*, 557 F.2d 1280 (9th Cir. 1977); *Klockner-Pentaplast of America, Inc. v. Roth Display Corp.*, 860 F. Supp. 1119, 1121–22 (W.D. Va. 1994) (holding that factually intensive inquiry into personal jurisdiction would be deferred until trial, because a jurisdictional ruling would translate into a ruling on the merits).

[156]*See OMI Holdings, Inc. v. Royal Ins. Co. of Canada*, 149 F.3d 1086, 1090 (10th Cir. 1998); *Republic of Panama v. BCCI Holdings (Luxembourg) S.A.*, 119 F.3d 935, 940 (11th Cir. 1997). *See also Chudasama v. Mazda Motor Corp.*, 123 F.3d 1353, 1367–68 (11th Cir. 1997) (commenting that motions to dismiss should be resolved before full discovery is permitted). *See generally Steel Co. v. Citizens for a Better Env't*, 523 U.S. 83, 118 S. Ct. 1003, 140 L. Ed. 2d 210 (1998) (rejecting so-called "hypothetical" or "assumed" jurisdiction theory, and prohibiting federal courts from postponing subject matter jurisdiction challenge in preference to an easier, and also potentially dispositive, merits challenge). *But see Ruhrgas AG v.*

Effect of Denial of Motion

If a party's Rule 12(b)(2) motion is denied, that party's active participation in the ensuing trial will not constitute a waiver of *either* the party's ability to renew the motion before the district judge at time *or* the party's right to contest personal jurisdiction on appeal.[157]

Prejudice on Dismissal

A dismissal for lack of personal jurisdiction generally does not preclude the plaintiff from refiling the lawsuit against the defendant in a forum where that defendant is amenable to jurisdiction.[158]

Appealability

A dismissal as to all defendants for lack of personal jurisdiction is generally considered an appealable "final order".[159] Conversely, a dismissal as to less than all defendants[160] or a denial of the motion to dismiss is not a final order and ordinarily cannot be immediately appealed.[161]

RULE 12(b)(3)—DISMISSAL FOR IMPROPER VENUE

CORE CONCEPT

A case will be dismissed or transferred if venue is improper or inconvenient in the chosen forum.

APPLICATIONS

Proper Scope of Rule 12(b)(3)

Venue protects defendants against the risk that the plaintiff will select an unfair or unduly inconvenient place for trial.[162] Rule 12(b)(3) is the proper mechanism for asserting that the action should be dismissed either for lack of proper venue or under the common law doctrine of *forum non conveniens*.[163] Although the courts are divided on the question, a majority

---

Marathon Oil Co., 526 U.S. 574, 119 S. Ct. 1563, 143 L. Ed. 2d 760 (1999) (holding that there is no "unyielding hierarchy" *among* jurisdictional requirements, and courts are free to resolve simpler personal jurisdiction challenges before reaching potentially more difficult questions of subject matter jurisdiction).

[157]*See Northern Laminate Sales, Inc. v. Davis*, 403 F.3d 14, 23 (1st Cir. 2005). *See also Mullins v. TestAmerica, Inc.*, 564 F.3d 386, 398–99 (5th Cir. 2009).

[158]*See Kendall v. Overseas Dev't Corp.*, 700 F.2d 536 (9th Cir. 1983).

[159]*See Carteret Sav. Bank, F.A. v.*

Shushan, 919 F.2d 225, 230 (3d Cir. 1990) (noting that dismissal as to all defendants for lack of personal jurisdiction is appealable under the final order doctrine).

[160]*See Morton Int'l., Inc. v. A.E. Staley Mfg. Co.*, 460 F.3d 470, 476 (3d Cir. 2006).

[161]*See Northern Laminate Sales, Inc. v. Davis*, 403 F.3d 14, 23 (1st Cir. 2005); *S.E.C. v. Blazon Corp.*, 609 F.2d 960 (9th Cir. 1979).

[162]*See Belden Techs., Inc. v. LS Corp.*, 626 F.Supp.2d 448, 454 (D.Del. 2009).

[163]*See Gulf Oil Corp. v. Gilbert*, 330 U.S. 501, 67 S. Ct. 839, 91 L. Ed.

permit venue objections based on forum selection clauses to be raised by motion under this Rule.[164]

Rule 12(b)(3) and Venue *Transfers*

A request for a *transfer* of venue (rather than a *dismissal* for improper or inconvenient venue) is made under federal statute, not under Rule 12(b)(3).[165] However, if the trial court grants a Rule 12(b)(3) motion for improper venue, it enjoys the discretion, in lieu of a dismissal, to transfer the matter to a forum where venue is proper.[166]

Legal Test

The procedure for resolving a Rule 12(b)(3) motion is the same as the procedure used for testing challenges to personal jurisdiction.[167] The court may resolve the motion on the basis of the written submissions alone, or may convene an evidentiary hearing.[168] Without a hearing, a challenge to venue will be defeated if plaintiff sets forth sufficient facts which, if proven true, would confer venue.[169] Under this standard, plaintiff's well-pleaded factual allegations regarding venue are accepted as true, all reasonable inferences are drawn in plaintiff's favor, and factual conflicts are resolved in plaintiff's favor.[170] No such deference, however, will be given to legal conclusions,[171] and at least one court will not defer to allegations once they are controverted.[172] Alternatively, if the court holds an evidentiary hearing, the allegations are not presumed true, and plaintiff

---

1055 (1947).

[164]*See Slater v. Energy Servs. Group Int'l, Inc.*, 634 F.3d 1326, 1332–33 (11th Cir. 2011) (noting division; finding Rule 12(b)(3) proper vehicle for enforcing forum-selection clauses). *See also Doe 1 v. AOL LLC*, 552 F.3d 1077, 1081 (9th Cir. 2009); *Automobile Mechanics Local 701 Welfare and Pension Funds v. Vanguard Car Rental USA, Inc.*, 502 F.3d 740, 746 (7th Cir. 2007); *Lim v. Offshore Specialty Fabricators, Inc.*, 404 F.3d 898, 902 (5th Cir. 2005).

[165]*See* 28 U.S.C.A. § 1404 (authorizing transfer to more convenient district); 28 U.S.C.A. § 1406 (authorizing transfer to proper district).

[166]*See, e.g., Meteoro Amusement Corp. v. Six Flags*, 267 F. Supp. 2d 263, 266 (N.D. N.Y. 2003); *Audi AG & Volkswagen of America, Inc. v. Izumi*, 204 F. Supp. 2d 1014, 1017 (E.D. Mich. 2002).

[167]*See Gulf Ins. Co. v. Glasbrenner*, 417 F.3d 353, 355 (2d Cir. 2005); *Cold Spring Harbor Lab. v. Ropes & Gray*

LLP, 762 F.Supp.2d 543, 551 (E.D.N.Y. 2011).

[168]*See Centerville ALF, Inc. v. Balanced Care Corp.*, 197 F. Supp. 2d 1039, 1046 (S.D. Ohio 2002).

[169]*See Langton v. Cbeyond Communication, L.L.C.*, 282 F. Supp. 2d 504, 508 (E.D. Tex. 2003); *Darby v. U.S. Dept. of Energy*, 231 F. Supp. 2d 274, 276–77 (D.D.C. 2002).

[170]*See Faulkenberg v. CB Tax Franchise Sys., LP*, 637 F.3d 801, 806 (7th Cir. 2011); *Ambraco, Inc. v. Bossclip B.V.*, 570 F.3d 233, 238 (5th Cir. 2009); *Murphy v. Schneider National, Inc.*, 362 F.3d 1133, 1137 (9th Cir. 2004); *Coltrane v. Lappin*, __ F. Supp. 2d __, __, 2012 WL 3344223, at *2 (D.D.C. 2012); *Martinez v. Bloomberg LP*, __ F. Supp. 2d __, __, 2012 WL 3263921, at *1 (S.D.N.Y. 2012).

[171]*See Ellis-Smith v. Secretary of Army*, 793 F.Supp 2d 173, 175 (D.D.C. 2011).

[172]*See Kimmel v. Phelan Hallinan & Schmieg, PC*, 847 F.Supp.2d 753,

must instead establish venue by a preponderance of the evidence.[173] But, in resolving factual disputes on a venue motion to dismiss, the court will generally avoid factfinding that encroaches into the merits of the case.[174]

Burden of Proof

The case law is fractured as to who bears the burden of proof on a Rule 12(b)(3) challenge.[175] One approach (the majority view) vests the plaintiff with the burden of proving a *prima facie* showing[176] that the chosen forum is proper;[177] the minority approach requires that the defendant, as the party challenging venue, bear this burden.[178]

Timing and Waiver

Venue challenges are waived unless raised by motion (if there is one) or in the responsive pleading.[179] Once the Rule 12 motion period and the responsive pleading time have passed, an otherwise "waived" venue defense cannot ordinarily be raised by the court on its own initiative; *sua sponte* venue dismissals are ordinarily improper.[180] A defaulting defendant, thus, generally is deemed to have waived any objections to

---

759–60 (E.D.Pa. 2012).

[173]*See Gulf Ins. Co. v. Glasbrenner*, 417 F.3d 353, 355 (2d Cir. 2005).

[174]*See Belcher-Robinson, L.L.C. v. Linamar Corp.*, 699 F.Supp.2d 1329, 1333–34 (M.D.Ala. 2010).

[175]*See Zamora Entm't, Inc. v. William Morris Endeavor Entm'ts, L.L.C.*, 667 F.Supp.2d 1032, 1036 n.3 (S.D.Iowa 2009) (noting division); *Turnley v. Banc of America Inv. Servs.*, 576 F.Supp.2d 204, 211 n.6 (D.Mass. 2008) (same).

[176]*See McPhearson v. Anderson*, __ F. Supp. 2d __, __, 2012 WL 2819273, at *3 (E.D.Va. 2012); *Sepanski v. Janiking, Inc.*, 822 F.Supp.2d 309, 313 (W.D.N.Y. 2011).

[177]*See, e.g., Gulf Ins. Co. v. Glasbrenner*, 417 F.3d 353, 355 (2d Cir. 2005); *Bartholomew v. Virginia Chiropractors Ass'n, Inc.*, 612 F.2d 812, 816 (4th Cir. 1979); *Cohen v. Newsweek, Inc.*, 312 F.2d 76, 78 (8th Cir. 1963); *Coltrane v. Lappin*, __ F. Supp. 2d __, __, 2012 WL 3344223, at *2 (D.D.C. 2012); *Allchem Performance Prods., Inc. v. Aqualine Warehouse, LLC*, __ F. Supp. 2d __, __, 2012 WL 2886714, at *6 (S.D.Tex. 2012).

[178]*See Myers v. American Dental*

Ass'n, 695 F.2d 716, 724 (3d Cir. 1982); *Kimmel v. Phelan Hallinan & Schmieg, PC*, 847 F.Supp.2d 753, 759–60 (E.D.Pa. 2012); *Rimkus Consulting Group, Inc. v. Balentine*, 693 F.Supp.2d 681, 689 (S.D.Tex. 2010); *Noell Crane Sys. GmbH v. Noell Crane & Serv., Inc.*, 677 F.Supp.2d 852, 861 (E.D. Va. 2009).

[179]*See* Rule 12(h)(1). *See also Wachovia Bank v. Schmidt*, 546 U.S. 303, 316, 126 S. Ct. 941, 950, 163 L. Ed. 2d 797 (2006); *Automobile Mechanics Local 701 Welfare and Pension Funds v. Vanguard Car Rental USA, Inc.*, 502 F.3d 740, 746 (7th Cir. 2007).

[180]*See Automobile Mechanics Local 701 Welfare and Pension Funds v. Vanguard Car Rental USA, Inc.*, 502 F.3d 740, 746–47 (7th Cir. 2007) (noting and following majority rule). *But see Wong v. PartyGaming Ltd.*, 589 F.3d 821, 830 (6th Cir. 2009) (*sua sponte* dismissal can be proper under *forum non conveniens* doctrine); *Stjernholm v. Peterson*, 83 F.3d 347, 349 (10th Cir. 1996) (until defendants waive their venue defense, courts may raise *sua sponte* defective venue, although the case may not be dismissed without affording the parties an opportunity to present their views).

venue.[181] When properly asserted and preserved, a venue objection is unlikely to be deemed waived by a defendant who also asserts a counterclaim.[182]

Cases Involving Multiple Defendants Or Claims

Where a case involves more than one defendant, or more than one claim against a defendant, venue must be proper as to each defendant and as to each claim.[183]

Extrinsic Materials

The parties may submit affidavits and other materials to support their positions on improper venue.[184]

Pre-Ruling Venue Discovery

The court may permit limited discovery to aid in resolving the motion.[185]

Remedy

Ordinarily, a court may either dismiss for improper venue or transfer to a forum where venue would be proper.[186]

Ruling Deferred

The court may defer ruling on a venue challenge pending further factual development.[187]

Prejudice on Dismissal

A dismissal for improper venue generally does not preclude the plaintiff from re-filing the claim in a forum where venue is proper.[188]

---

[181]See Union Planters Bank, N.A. v. EMC Mortg. Corp., 67 F. Supp. 2d 915, 920 (W.D. Tenn. 1999).

[182]See Hillis v. Heineman, 626 F.3d 1014, 1016–19 (9th Cir. 2010).

[183]See Multi-Media Intern., LLC v. Promag Retail Services, 343 F. Supp. 2d 1024, 1033 (D. Kan. 2004); Centerville ALF, Inc. v. Balanced Care Corp., 197 F. Supp. 2d 1039, 1046 (S.D. Ohio 2002).

[184]See Liles v. Ginn-La West End, Ltd., 631 F.3d 1242, 1244 n.5 (11th Cir. 2011); Ambraco, Inc. v. Bossclip B.V., 570 F.3d 233, 238 (5th Cir. 2009); Doe 1 v. AOL LLC, 552 F.3d 1077, 1081 (9th Cir. 2009); Continental Cas. Co. v. American Nat. Ins. Co., 417 F.3d 727, 733 (7th Cir. 2005); Martinez v. Bloomberg LP, __ F. Supp. 2d __, __, 2012 WL 3263921, at *1 (S.D.N.Y. 2012); McLaughlin v. Holder, __ F. Supp. 2d __, __, 2012 WL 1893627, at *2 (D.D.C. 2012).

[185]See Oppenheimer Fund, Inc. v. Sanders, 437 U.S. 340, 351 n.13, 98 S.Ct. 2380, 2389 n.13, 57 L.Ed.2d 253 (1978) ("discovery is available to ascertain the facts bearing on [venue]"). See also Centerville ALF, Inc. v. Balanced Care Corp., 197 F. Supp. 2d 1039, 1046 (S.D. Ohio 2002).

[186]See Coltrane v. Lappin, __ F. Supp. 2d __, __, 2012 WL 3344223, at *2 (D.D.C. 2012); Allchem Performance Prods., Inc. v. Aqualine Warehouse, LLC, __ F. Supp. 2d __, __, 2012 WL 2886714, at *6 (S.D.Tex. 2012); Smithfield Packing Co. v. V. Suarez & Co., 857 F. Supp. 2d 581, 584 (E.D.Va. 2012).

[187]See Tenpenny v. U.S., 285 F.2d 213 (6th Cir. 1960).

[188]See In re Hall, Bayoutree Associates, Ltd., 939 F.2d 802, 804 (9th Cir. 1991) ("A determination of improper venue does not go to the merits of the case and therefore must be without prejudice").

Appealability

Ordinarily, a dismissal for improper venue or forum non conveniens is immediately appealable as a "final order".[189] Conversely, a denial of a motion to dismiss for lack of venue or forum non conveniens is interlocutory and not immediately appealable.[190]

RULES 12(b)(4)–(5)—DISMISSAL FOR (OR QUASHING OF) INSUFFICIENT PROCESS OR SERVICE

CORE CONCEPT

Process or service (or both) may be quashed or dismissed if improper.

APPLICATIONS

Insufficient Process—Rule 12(b)(4)

The process (summons and complaint) may be insufficient if the forms are technically deficient[191] (*e.g.*, wrong name[192]) or not sealed by the clerk.[193] Because dismissals for defects in the forms of summons are generally disfavored, courts often overlook minor technical defects (particularly where they can be cured), unless the complaining party is able to demonstrate actual prejudice.[194]

Insufficient Service—Rule 12(b)(5)

Service of the process may be insufficient if, for example, the mode of delivery is invalid, service is made on an improper

---

[189]*See Young Properties Corp. v. United Equity Corp.*, 534 F.2d 847, 852 (9th Cir. 1976) (noting general rule that order dismissing for improper venue or under the doctrine of forum non conveniens is final and appealable).

[190]*See Hohn v. U.S.*, 524 U.S. 236, 248, 118 S. Ct. 1969, 1976, 141 L. Ed. 2d 242 (1998); *United Disaster Response, LLC v. Omni Pinnacle, LLC*, 511 F.3d 476, 482 (5th Cir. 2007); *Rux v. Republic of Sudan*, 461 F.3d 461, 476 (4th Cir. 2006).

[191]*See In re Potash Antitrust Litig.*, 667 F.Supp.2d 907, 928 (N.D.Ill. 2009); *Olson v. Federal Election Comm'n*, 256 F.R.D. 8, 10 n.3 (D.D.C. 2009).

[192]*See Naranjo v. Universal Sur. of America*, 679 F.Supp.2d 787, 795 (S.D.Tex. 2010); *Austin v. Spaulding*, 2001 WL 345602 (D.R.I. 2001); *Ericson v. Pollack*, 110 F. Supp. 2d 582, 584 (E.D. Mich. 2000).

[193]*See Ayres v. Jacobs & Crumplar, P.A.*, 99 F.3d 565, 569 (3d Cir. 1996).

[194]*See U.S.A. Nutrasource, Inc. v. CNA Ins. Co.*, 140 F. Supp. 2d 1049, 1052–53 (N.D. Cal. 2001) (refusing to dismiss where summons used service mark / tradename, rather than formal corporate name, where technical error caused no prejudice and where complaint could be amended to insert "doing-business-as" designation for clarity); *Louisiana Acorn Fair Housing v. Quarter House*, 952 F. Supp. 352, 355 (E.D. La. 1997) (refusing to dismiss for insufficient process where summons served on "Quarter House Owners' Association" incorrectly identified the party as "Quarter House Homeowners Association, Inc.", absent showing that defendant did not receive notice or had suffered any prejudice from the technical error). *See also DeLuca v. AccessIT Group, Inc.*, 695 F.Supp.2d 54, 65 (S.D.N.Y. 2010).

person,[195] or delivery is either never accomplished or not accomplished within 120 days after commencement.[196]

Distinguishing Between Rules 12(b)(4) and 12(b)(5)

Courts have noted that, although distinct, the differences between motions under Rules 12(b)(4) and 12(b)(5) have not always been clear or observed in practice.[197] A mislabeling of a Rule 12(b)(4) or 12(b)(5) motion, particularly if that confusion does not prejudice the non-moving party, may well be overlooked by the courts.[198]

Legal Test

A motion to dismiss under these Rules must be made with specificity, must describe any prejudice suffered by the defendant, and must specify the manner in which the process or service failed to meet the requirements of Rule 4.[199] Once a proper motion is made, the plaintiff must make a *prima facie* demonstration of proper service through specific factual averments and other supporting materials; conclusory statements will usually not overcome a defendant's sworn representation controverting good service.[200] The plaintiff will usually be given the benefit of any factual doubts in resolving a service challenge,[201] and the requisites for Rule 4 service are liberally construed.[202] Courts may resolve any disputed questions of fact by considering affidavits, depositions, and oral testimony.[203]

- *No "Implied" Companion Motions:* A challenge to personal jurisdiction does not imply (or avoid the waiver

---

[195]*See Naranjo v. Universal Sur. of America*, 679 F.Supp.2d 787, 795 (S.D.Tex. 2010); *Olson v. Federal Election Comm'n*, 256 F.R.D. 8, 10 n.3 (D.D.C. 2009). *See also Schaeffer v. Village of Ossining*, 58 F.3d 48 (2d Cir.1995) (service quashed where process served on clerk not authorized to accept service on municipality defendant's behalf).

[196]*See Rzayeva v. U.S.*, 492 F. Supp. 2d 60, 74-75 (D. Conn. 2007); *Smith v. U.S.*, 475 F. Supp. 2d 1, 7 (D.D.C. 2006); *Wasson v. Riverside County*, 237 F.R.D. 423, 424 (C.D. Cal. 2006).

[197]*See Wasson v. Riverside County*, 237 F.R.D. 423, 424 (C.D. Cal. 2006). *See also Davies v. Jobs & Adverts Online, Gmbh*, 94 F. Supp. 4d 719, 721 (E.D. Va. 2000) (noting difference between Rules); *Richardson v. Alliance Tire and Rubber Co., Ltd.*, 158 F.R.D. 475, 477 (D. Kan. 1994) (same).

[198]*See Richardson v. Alliance Tire and Rubber Co., Ltd.*, 158 F.R.D. 475, 477–78 (D. Kan. 1994).

[199]*See O'Brien v. R.J. O'Brien & Associates, Inc.*, 998 F.2d 1394, 1400 (7th Cir. 1993) (objections must be specific); *Photolab Corp. v. Simplex Specialty Co.*, 806 F.2d 807, 810 (8th Cir. 1986) (same); *Fly Brazil Group, Inc. v. Gov't of Gabon, Africa*, 709 F.Supp.2d 1274, 1279 (S.D.Fla. 2010); *Davis v. Mara*, 587 F.Supp.2d 422, 428–29 (D.Conn. 2008).

[200]*See TAGC Mgmt., LLC v. Lehman*, 842 F.Supp.2d 575, 580–81 (S.D.N.Y. 2012).

[201]*See McClellan v. Board of County Com'rs of Tulsa County*, 261 F.R.D. 595, 603 (N.D.Okla. 2009).

[202]*See Waldner v. North Am. Truck & Trailer, Inc.*, 277 F.R.D. 401, 414–15 (D.S.D. 2011).

[203]*See Travelers Cas. & Sur. Co. of America v. Telstar Const. Co., Inc.*, 252 F. Supp. 2d 917, 923 (D. Ariz. 2003); *Mende v. Milestone Technology, Inc.*, 269 F. Supp. 2d 246, 251 (S.D. N.Y. 2003).

of) an unfiled, "companion" challenge to process or service; rather, process and service challenges must be asserted expressly.[204]

Burden of Proof

Most courts[205] hold that the burden lies with the plaintiff to demonstrate sufficient process and service; when process or service is challenged, the plaintiff must make a *prima facie* showing that the court's personal jurisdiction is properly exercised.[206] The process server's return is *prima facie* evidence—but not conclusive proof—of good service.[207] A conclusory representation that the defendant was properly served will not overcome a defendant's sworn affidavit otherwise.[208]

Timing and Waiver

Service and process challenges are waived unless raised by pre-answer motion (if there is one) or in the responsive pleading.[209] Thus, a defendant may not move for such a dismissal under these Rules *after* filing an answer that omitted that defense[210] or *after* filing an earlier Rule 12 motion that

---

[204]*See Hemispherx Biopharma, Inc. v. Johannesburg Consol. Invs.*, 553 F.3d 1351, 1360–61 (11th Cir. 2008).

[205]*But see Molinelli-Freytes v. Univ. of Puerto Rico*, 727 F.Supp.2d 60, 63 (D.P.R. 2010) (party seeking dismissal bears burden of showing failed service).

[206]*See Quinn v. Miller*, 470 Fed.Appx. 321, 323 (5th Cir. 2012); *Cardenas v. City of Chicago*, 646 F.3d 1001, 1005 (7th Cir. 2011); *Dickerson v. Napolitano*, 604 F.3d 732, 752 (2d Cir. 2010); *Grand Entertainment Group, Ltd. v. Star Media Sales, Inc.*, 988 F.2d 476, 488 (3d Cir. 1993); *McAlister v. Potter*, 843 F.Supp.2d 117, 119 (D.D.C. 2012); *LNV Corp. v. Robb*, 843 F.Supp.2d 1002, 1003 (W.D.Mo. 2012).

[207]*See Blair v. City of Worcester*, 522 F.3d 105, 111–12 (1st Cir. 2008); *Thomas v. New Leaders for New Schs.*, 278 F.R.D. 347, 351 (E.D.La. 2011). *See also O'Brien v. R.J. O'Brien & Associates, Inc.*, 998 F.2d 1394, 1398 (7th Cir. 1993) (signed return constitutes prima facie evidence of valid service that can be overcome by only "strong and convincing evidence"); *Gottlieb v. Sandia Am. Corp.*, 452 F.2d 510, 514 (3d Cir. 1971) (return from

U.S. Marshal "is not conclusive on the question of service on an agent, it will stand in the absence of proof to the contrary"); *Oltremari by McDaniel v. Kansas Social & Rehabilitative Service*, 871 F. Supp. 1331, 1350 (D. Kan. 1994) (noting that once plaintiff files return of service, Rule 12(b)(5) dismissal requires strong and convincing evidence that service was improper).

[208]*See Koulkina v. City of New York*, 559 F. Supp. 2d 300, 311 (S.D. N.Y. 2008); *Cooper v. Connecticut Public Defender's Office*, 480 F. Supp. 2d 536, 538 n.1 (D. Conn. 2007), aff'd, 280 Fed. Appx. 24 (2d Cir. 2008).

[209]*See Williams v. Jones*, 11 F.3d 247, 251 (1st Cir. 1993); *Hammann v. 1-800 Ideas.com, Inc.*, 455 F. Supp. 2d 942, 959 (D. Minn. 2006).

[210]*See* Rule 12(h)(1)(B). Practitioners should note that at least one court has interpreted the Rules to foreclose a litigant's right to contest objections to service or process if an answer is filed before the motion. *See Green v. City of Bessemer, Alabama*, 202 F. Supp. 2d 1272, 1273–74 (N.D. Ala. 2002) (finding Rule 12(b)(5) motion untimely because it was filed three days after party answered the complaint).

omitted that defense.[211] Such challenges generally may not be raised by the court on its own.[212] A defendant, of course, does *not* waive service and process objections by appearing in the case to object on those grounds.[213] Nor does the defendant waive the objection by failing to give the plaintiff early, pre-filing notice of an intent to object.[214]

Waiting for Default to Raise Service Objections

Although defendants must raise their objections to process and service either in their omnibus Rule 12 motion or in their answer (if no Rule 12 motion is filed), these defenses are *not* waived where the defendants never knew about the attempted service in time to object[215] or where they choose not to object and intend to contest the service later in a collateral attack to the entry, or enforcement, of a default.[216] But defendants act at their peril if, after receiving actual notice of a pleading, they choose to ignore the lawsuit in reliance on their own, untested belief that either the process or service was faulty. They must guess correctly. If they received actual, timely notice of the lawsuit and simply make technical objections to a strict compliance with Rule 4,[217] or otherwise appeared and defended the

---

[211]*See Chute v. Walker*, 281 F.3d 314, 319 (1st Cir. 2002) (because defendant omitted Rule 12(b)(5) defense from Rule 12(b)(6) motion to dismiss, it was waived).

[212]*See Chute v. Walker*, 281 F.3d 314, 319–20 & 320 n.6 (1st Cir. 2002) (collecting cases). *Accord Nuance Commc'ns, Inc. v. Abbyy Software House*, 626 F.3d 1222, 1240–41 (Fed. Cir. 2010). *But see Cardenas v. City of Chicago*, 646 F.3d 1001, 1005 (7th Cir. 2011) (suggesting court may dismiss on its own motion).

[213]*See Cataldo v. U.S. Dept. of Justice*, 2000 WL 760960 (D. Me. 2000).

[214]*See Davis v. Mara*, 587 F.Supp.2d 422, 428–29 (D.Conn. 2008) ("No Rule specifies any duty of a defendant to notify a plaintiff of its intention to raise either of these defenses").

[215]*See Corestates Leasing, Inc. v. Wright-Way Exp., Inc.*, 190 F.R.D. 356, 358 (E.D. Pa. 2000).

[216]*See Insurance Corp. of Ireland, Ltd. v. Compagnie des Bauxites de Guinee*, 456 U.S. 694, 706, 102 S. Ct. 2099, 72 L. Ed. 2d 492 (1982) ("A defendant is always free to ignore the judicial proceedings, risk a default judgment, and then challenge that judgment on jurisdictional grounds."); *Baldwin v. Iowa State Traveling Men's Ass'n*, 283 U.S. 522, 525, 51 S. Ct. 517, 75 L. Ed. 1244 (1931) (same). *See also Trustees of the St. Paul Elec. Const. Industry Fringe Benefit Funds v. Martens Elec. Co.*, 485 F. Supp. 2d 1063, 1065 (D. Minn. 2007) (noting that defendants who are not properly served are protected against default).

[217]*See O'Meara v. Waters*, 464 F. Supp. 2d 474, 476 (D. Md. 2006) (if defendants receive actual notice, failure to comply strictly with Rule 4 might be excused and service deemed valid); *Corestates Leasing, Inc. v. Wright-Way Exp., Inc.*, 190 F.R.D. 356, 358 (E.D. Pa. 2000). *See generally* 5A Charles Alan Wright & Arthur R. Miller, *Federal Practice & Procedure* § 1391, at 755 to 56 (1990) ("But when the party has received actual notice of the suit there is no due process problem in requiring him to object to the ineffective service within the period prescribed by Rule 12(h)(1) and the defense is one that he certainly can waive if he wishes to do so. This is because the defendant has failed to do what the rule says he must do if he is to avoid a waiver.").

lawsuit,[218] the defense might well be lost. Moreover, because in such collateral attacks the defendant is often the moving party, the defendant will likely bear the affirmative burden of proving deficient service.[219]

Extrinsic Materials

The parties may produce affidavits and other materials to support their positions on insufficient process or service.[220] The court may properly receive and consider such materials in deciding the motion,[221] and may even convene an evidentiary hearing[222]—all without converting the motion to dismiss into a motion for summary judgment.[223]

Remedy

A party may request that the case be dismissed under this Rule or, alternatively, that service be quashed and re-attempted.[224] If service or process is found to be ineffective, the court has discretion to either dismiss or quash.[225] The courts will generally prefer to quash, rather than dismiss, where there is a reasonable prospect that the defendant can be properly served with sufficient process.[226] Although the dismissal option

---

[218]*See In re Worldwide Web Sys. Inc.*, 328 F.3d 1291, 1300 (11th Cir. 2003) (service objections waived if Rule 60(b) voidness challenge to default judgment is made but claim of improper service is not "squarely raised"); *Broadcast Music, Inc. v. M.T.S. Enters., Inc.*, 811 F.2d 278, 281 (5th Cir. 1987) (service objections waived when parties gave impression of having been served then, later, tried to "pull failure of service out of the hat like a rabbit").

[219]*See "R" Best Produce, Inc. v. DiSapio*, 540 F.3d 115, 126 (2d Cir. 2008).

[220]*See SignalQuest, Inc. v. Tien-Ming Chou*, __ F.R.D. __, __, 2012 WL 1859656, at *1 (D.N.H. 2012); *TAGC Mgmt., LLC v. Lehman*, 842 F.Supp.2d 575, 581 (S.D.N.Y. 2012).

[221]*See Hahn v. Bauer*, 2010 WL 396228, at *5 (D.Minn. 2010); *Fagan v. Deutsche Bundesbank*, 438 F. Supp. 2d 376 (S.D. N.Y. 2006); *Metropolitan Alloys Corp. v. State Metals Industries, Inc.*, 416 F. Supp. 2d 561, 563 (E.D. Mich. 2006).

[222]*See SignalQuest, Inc. v. Tien-Ming Chou*, __ F.R.D. __, __, 2012 WL 1859656, at *1 (D.N.H. 2012).

[223]*See BPA Intern., Inc. v. Kingdom of Sweden*, 281 F. Supp. 2d 73, 80 (D.D.C. 2003); *Travelers Cas. & Sur. Co. of America v. Telstar Const. Co., Inc.*, 252 F. Supp. 2d 917, 923 (D. Ariz. 2003). *But see Cubero Valderama v. Delta Air Lines, Inc.*, 931 F. Supp. 119, 120 (D.P.R. 1996) (because court considered documents filed by party challenging service of process, it applied summary judgment standards to motion).

[224]*See TAGC Mgmt., LLC v. Lehman*, 842 F.Supp.2d 575, 580–81 (S.D.N.Y. 2012); *Boateng v. Inter American University of P.R.*, 188 F.R.D. 26, 27 (D.P.R. 1999). *See generally R. Griggs Group Ltd. v. Filanto Spa*, 920 F. Supp. 1100, 1102 (D. Nev. 1996) (noting that federal courts possess the authority to quash improper service of process, rather than dismissing the complaint, even though the Rules technically do not provide for a "Motion to Quash").

[225]*See Cardenas v. City of Chicago*, 646 F.3d 1001, 1005 (7th Cir. 2011); *Hilaturas Miel, S.L. v. Republic of Iraq*, 573 F.Supp.2d 781, 796 (S.D.N.Y. 2008); *Ramirez De Arellano v. Colloides Naturels Intern.*, 236 F.R.D. 83, 85 (D.P.R. 2006).

[226]*See Umbenhauer v. Woog*, 969 F.2d 25, 30–31 (3d Cir. 1992); *Pell v.*

remains available to the courts,[227] they will typically dismiss only when the failure of process or service prejudices the defendant or where proper service is unlikely to be accomplished.[228]

Prejudice on Dismissal

A dismissal for insufficient process or service is generally without prejudice and will not usually preclude the plaintiff from attempting to re-serve properly.[229] Where, however, the applicable limitations period has expired, it likely is not error to grant an insufficient process or service dismissal with prejudice.[230]

RULE 12(b)(6)—DISMISSAL FOR FAILURE TO STATE A CLAIM UPON WHICH RELIEF CAN BE GRANTED

CORE CONCEPT

A motion to dismiss for failure to state a claim is the descendant of the common law demurrer.[231] It tests the legal sufficiency of a party's claim for relief. The Rule allows trial courts to terminate lawsuits "that are fatally flawed in their legal premises and destined to fail, and thus to spare litigants the burdens of unnecessary pretrial and trial activity."[232]

APPLICATIONS

Legal Test

Rule 12(b)(6) motions test the sufficiency of a pleading.[233] Consequently, they compel an examination of whether the

---

Azar Nut Co., Inc., 711 F.2d 949, 950 (10th Cir. 1983); *Thomas v. New Leaders for New Schs.*, 278 F.R.D. 347, 352 (E.D.La. 2011); *Molinelli-Freytes v. Univ. of Puerto Rico*, 727 F.Supp.2d 60, 63 (D.P.R. 2010).

[227]*See McAlister v. Potter*, 843 F.Supp.2d 117, 119 (D.D.C. 2012).

[228]*See Gonzalez v. Ritz Carlton Hotel Co. of Puerto Rico*, 241 F. Supp. 2d 142, 147–48 (D.P.R. 2003); *Oltremari by McDaniel v. Kansas Social & Rehabilitative Service*, 871 F. Supp. 1331, 1349 (D. Kan. 1994).

[229]*See Umbenhauer v. Woog*, 969 F.2d 25, 30 (3d Cir. 1992); *Hammond v. Federal Bureau of Prisons*, 740 F.Supp.2d 105, 109 (D.D.C. 2010); *In re South African Apartheid Litig.*, 643 F. Supp. 2d 423, 431–32 (S.D.N.Y. 2009). *But cf. Coffin v. Ingersoll*, 1993 WL 208806 (E.D. Pa. 1993) (noting general rule that dismissal is without prejudice, but observing that where

statute of limitations has lapsed, dismissal effectively bars plaintiff from court).

[230]*See Cardenas v. City of Chicago*, 646 F.3d 1001, 1007–08 (7th Cir. 2011).

[231]*See De Sole v. U.S.*, 947 F.2d 1169, 1178 (4th Cir. 1991); *Podell v. Citicorp Diners Club, Inc.*, 859 F. Supp. 701, 704 (S.D. N.Y. 1994).

[232]*Advanced Cardiovascular Systems, Inc. v. Scimed Life Systems, Inc.*, 988 F.2d 1157, 1160 (Fed. Cir. 1993). *See Port Authority of New York and New Jersey v. Arcadian Corp.*, 189 F.3d 305 (3d Cir. 1999) (noting that Rule is designed to "screen out cases" where no remedy exists for the wrong alleged or where no relief could possibly be granted).

[233]*See Smith v. Frye*, 488 F.3d 263, 274 (4th Cir. 2007); *Christensen v. County of Boone, IL*, 483 F.3d 454, 458 (7th Cir. 2007); *Petruska v. Gannon*

pleaders did what they were obligated to do under the federal pleading Rules, Rule 8 and Rule 9.[234] Under Rule 12(b)(6), a claim may be dismissed either because it asserts a legal theory that is not cognizable as a matter of law or because the factual tale alleged is implausible.[235] When a claim is challenged under this Rule, the court construes the pleading liberally in the pleader's favor.[236] The court presumes that all well-pleaded allegations are true, resolves all reasonable doubts and inferences in the pleader's favor, and views the pleading in the light most favorable to the non-moving party.[237] No claim will be dismissed merely because the trial judge disbelieves the allegations or feels that recovery is remote or unlikely.[238]

Yet, although encouraging brevity, the federal pleading duty is far from trivial;[239] to satisfy the federal pleading requirements (Rules 8 and 9), the pleading must still contain "enough" to give defendants fair notice of both the complaint's claims and the grounds for those claims.[240] Although neither "detail factual

---

University, 462 F.3d 294, 302 (3d Cir. 2006).

[234]*See U.S. ex rel. Lemmon v. Envirocare of Utah, Inc.*, 614 F.3d 1163, 1171 (10th Cir. 2010) (Rule 8(a) and Rule 9(b) "join" to form pleading requirements); *Hefferman v. Bass*, 467 F.3d 596, 599–600 (7th Cir. 2006) (noting that Rule 12(b)(6) "does not stand alone", but implicates Rules 8 and 9).

[235]*See Bell Atlantic Corp. v. Twombly*, 550 U.S. 544, 555 & 570, 127 S. Ct. 1955, 1965 & 1974, 167 L. Ed. 2d 929 (2007); *Laguna Hermosa Corp. v. United States*, 671 F.3d 1284, 1288 (Fed.Cir. 2012).

[236]*See Kaltenbach v. Richards*, 464 F.3d 524, 526–27 (5th Cir. 2006).

[237]*See Fitzgerald v. Barnstable Sch. Comm.*, 555 U.S. 246, 249, 129 S.Ct. 788, 792, 172 L.Ed.2d 582 (2009); *Tellabs, Inc. v. Makor Issues & Rights, Ltd.*, 551 U.S. 308, 322, 127 S. Ct. 2499, 2509, 168 L. Ed. 2d 179 (2007); *Bell Atlantic Corp. v. Twombly*, 550 U.S. 544, 555, 127 S. Ct. 1955, 1965, 167 L. Ed. 2d 929 (2007); *Jackson v. Birmingham Bd. of Educ.*, 544 U.S. 167, 170–71, 125 S. Ct. 1497, 1502–03, 161 L. Ed. 2d 361 (2005); *Albright v. Oliver*, 510 U.S. 266, 267, 114 S. Ct. 807, 810, 127 L. Ed. 2d 114 (1994); *Scheuer v. Rhodes*, 416 U.S. 232, 94 S. Ct. 1683, 40 L. Ed. 2d 90 (1974).

[238]*See Bell Atlantic Corp. v.*

Twombly, 550 U.S. 544, 555–56, 127 S. Ct. 1955, 1965, 167 L. Ed. 2d 929 (2007); *Swierkiewicz v. Sorema N. A.*, 534 U.S. 506, 508, 122 S. Ct. 992, 152 L. Ed. 2d 1 (2002); *Neitzke v. Williams*, 490 U.S. 319, 327, 109 S. Ct. 1827, 104 L. Ed. 2d 338 (1989).

[239]*See Ashcroft v. Iqbal*, 556 U.S. 662, 678–79, 129 S.Ct. 1937, 1950, 173 L.Ed.2d 868 (2009) (though a generous departure from bygone era's hypertechnical pleading regime, Rule 8 still "does not unlock the doors of discovery for a plaintiff armed with nothing more than conclusions."); *Doyle v. Hasbro, Inc.*, 103 F.3d 186, 190 (1st Cir. 1996) (pleading requirement "is real" and "not entirely a toothless tiger").

[240]*See Tellabs, Inc. v. Makor Issues & Rights, Ltd.*, 551 U.S. 308, 319, 127 S. Ct. 2499, 2507, 168 L. Ed. 2d 179 (2007) ("Although the rule encourages brevity, the complaint must say enough to give the defendant 'fair notice of what the plaintiff's claim is and the grounds upon which it rests' "); *Dura Pharmaceuticals, Inc. v. Broudo*, 544 U.S. 336, 346–47, 125 S. Ct. 1627, 161 L. Ed. 2d 577 (2005) ("We concede that ordinary pleading rules are not meant to impose a great burden upon a plaintiff", but allegations must still give fair notice); *Calvi v. Knox County*, 470 F.3d 422, 430 (1st Cir. 2006) ("Notice pleading rules do not relieve a

allegations"[241] nor evidentiary-level factual showings[242] are required, and the pleader still enjoys "the benefit of imagination,"[243] an adequate "showing" by the pleader is required.[244] A pleader must do more than merely incant labels, conclusions, and the formulaic elements of a cause of action.[245] Likewise, the court will not accept as true bald assertions, conclusions, or inferences,[246] legal conclusions "couched" or "masquerading" as facts,[247] or conclusions contradicted by the complaint's own exhibits or other documents of which the court may take proper notice.[248]

Rather, pleaders must show that their allegations "possess enough heft" to establish an *entitlement to relief* (and, thereby, are sufficient to allow the costly process of litigation to continue).[249] Pleaders must allege enough facts to raise their claims beyond the level of speculation,[250] and must "nudge[]

---

plaintiff of responsibility for identifying the nature of her claim"); *Amron v. Morgan Stanley Inv. Advisors Inc.*, 464 F.3d 338, 343–44 (2d Cir. 2006) ("we stop well short of saying that Plaintiffs bear no burden at the pleading stage", because they must allege "those facts *necessary* to a finding of liability").

[241] *See Ashcroft v. Iqbal*, 556 U.S. 662, 678, 129 S.Ct. 1937, 1949, 173 L.Ed.2d 868 (2009); *Bell Atlantic Corp. v. Twombly*, 550 U.S. 544, 555, 127 S.Ct. 1955, 167 L.Ed.2d 929 (2007).

[242] *See Fowler v. UPMC Shadyside*, 578 F.3d 203, 213 (3d Cir. 2009).

[243] *See Bissessur v. Indiana Univ. Bd. of Trustees*, 581 F.3d 599, 602–03 (7th Cir. 2009)

[244] *See Bell Atlantic Corp. v. Twombly*, 550 U.S. 544, 555 & 555 n.3, 127 S. Ct. 1955, 1964–65, 167 L. Ed. 2d 929 (2007).

[245] *See Ashcroft v. Iqbal*, 556 U.S. 662, 678, 129 S.Ct. 1937, 1949, 173 L.Ed.2d 868 (2009); *Bell Atlantic Corp. v. Twombly*, 550 U.S. 544, 555, 127 S. Ct. 1955, 1964–65, 167 L. Ed. 2d 929 (2007).

[246] *See Ashcroft v. Iqbal*, 556 U.S. 662, 678–79, 129 S.Ct. 1937, 1949–50, 173 L.Ed.2d 868 (2009). *See also Bissessur v. Indiana Univ. Bd. of Trustees*, 581 F.3d 599, 603 (7th Cir. 2009) ("A plaintiff may not escape dismissal on a contract claim, for example, by stating that he had a contract with the de-

fendant, gave the defendant consideration, and the defendant breached the contract. What was the contract? The promises made? The consideration? The nature of the breach?"); *Aulson v. Blanchard*, 83 F.3d 1, 3 (1st Cir. 1996) (commenting that Rule's deferential standard does not obligate a court "to swallow the plaintiff's invective hook, line, and sinker; bald assertions, unsupportable conclusions, periphrastic circumlocutions, and the like need not be credited").

[247] *See Bell Atlantic Corp. v. Twombly*, 550 U.S. 544, 555, 127 S. Ct. 1955, 1965, 167 L. Ed. 2d 929 (2007) (quoting *Papasan v. Allain*, 478 U.S. 265, 286, 106 S. Ct. 2932, 92 L. Ed. 2d 209 (1986)). *See also Bishop v. Lucent Technologies, Inc.*, 520 F.3d 516, 519 (6th Cir. 2008); *Ashley v. U.S. Dept. of Interior*, 408 F.3d 997, 1000 (8th Cir. 2005).

[248] *See Lazy Y Ranch Ltd. v. Behrens*, 546 F.3d 580, 588 (9th Cir. 2008).

[249] *See Bell Atlantic Corp. v. Twombly*, 550 U.S. 544, 557, 127 S. Ct. 1955, 1966, 167 L. Ed. 2d 929 (2007). *See also Bissessur v. Indiana Univ. Bd. of Trustees*, 581 F.3d 599, 604 (7th Cir. Sept. 2009) (allowing pure conclusory pleadings to survive "would sanction a fishing expedition costing both parties, and the court, valuable time and resources.").

[250] *See Ashcroft v. Iqbal*, 556 U.S. 662, 678, 129 S.Ct. 1937, 1949, 173

their claims across the line from conceivable to plausible".[251] The facts they plead must be sufficient to give rise to a "reasonably founded hope that the discovery process will reveal relevant evidence" in support of their claims.[252] Pleaders must met their pleading burden for each element required for a recovery under some actionable theory[253] (although when tested, a pleading is not parsed, part by part, but will be read as a whole).[254]

Ergo, courts will test for comportment with Rule 12(b)(6) by performing a two-step inquiry — first, legal conclusions will be isolated, so as to uncover the pleading's purely factual allegations, and second, those factual allegations will be presumed true and then examined for plausibility.[255] Pleadings that are unable to "show" the requisite plausible entitlement to relief are thereby exposed by Rule 12(b)(6) at an early stage in the litigation so as to minimize the costs of time and money by the litigants and the courts.[256]

Rule 12(b)(6) After *Bell Atlantic v. Twombly*

In this May 2007 antitrust opinion, the Supreme Court announced the "plausibility" pleading standard discussed above.[257] In so doing, the Court expressly overruled the oft-quoted, very forgiving pleading mantra from its 1957 decision in *Conley v. Gibson* (namely, that no complaint should be dismissed for failing to properly state a claim "unless it appears beyond doubt that the plaintiff can prove no set of facts in support of his claim which could entitle him to relief").[258] The *Conley* language, wrote the Court, "earned its retirement" because it might, incorrectly, preserve a conclusorily pleaded claim on the

---

L.Ed.2d 868 (2009); *Bell Atlantic Corp. v. Twombly*, 550 U.S. 544, 555, 127 S. Ct. 1955, 1965, 167 L. Ed. 2d 929 (2007).

[251]*See Bell Atlantic Corp. v. Twombly*, 550 U.S. 544, 570, 127 S. Ct. 1955, 1974, 167 L. Ed. 2d 929 (2007). To cross into "the realm of plausible liability", the allegations must be factual (not conclusory) and suggestive (not neutral). *See id.* at 557 n.5, 127 S.Ct. at 1966 n.5.

[252]*See Bell Atlantic Corp. v. Twombly*, 550 U.S. 544, 559, 127 S. Ct. 1955, 1967, 167 L. Ed. 2d 929 (2007) (citations omitted).

[253]*See Bishop v. Lucent Technologies, Inc.*, 520 F.3d 516, 519 (6th Cir. 2008).

[254]*See Braden v. Wal-Mart Stores, Inc.*, 588 F.3d 585, 594 (8th Cir. 2009).

[255]*See Ashcroft v. Iqbal*, 556 U.S. 662, 678–79, 129 S.Ct. 1937, 1949–50, 173 L.Ed.2d 868 (2009).

[256]*See Bell Atlantic Corp. v. Twombly*, 550 U.S. 544, 558, 127 S. Ct. 1955, 1966, 167 L. Ed. 2d 929 (2007) (citations omitted).

[257]*Bell Atlantic Corp. v. Twombly*, 550 U.S. 544, 127 S.Ct. 1955, 167 L.Ed.2d 929 (2007).

[258]*See Bell Atlantic Corp. v. Twombly*, 550 U.S. 544, 554–63, 127 S.Ct. 1955, 167 L.Ed.2d 929 (2007) (abrogating language in *Conley v. Gibson*, 355 U.S. 41, 45–46, 78 S.Ct. 99, 2 L.Ed.2d 80 (1957)). It is likely that *Conley's* language had already been effectively abandoned in practice. *See U.S. ex rel. Garst v. Lockheed-Martin Corp.*, 328 F.3d 374, 378 (7th Cir. 2003) (sufficient pleading requires that judges and parties "need not try to fish a gold coin from a bucket of mud"); *Mann v. Boatright*, 477 F.3d 1140, 1148 (10th Cir. 2007) (not court's job "to stitch together cognizable claims for relief from the wholly deficient pleading").

mere theoretical chance that it might later find support.[259] In *Ashcroft v. Iqbal*, decided in May 2009, the Court confirmed that *Twombly*'s "plausibility" standard is not limited only to antitrust cases (as *Twombly* was).[260]

The full import of *Twombly* is still being assessed,[261] with courts reluctant to stake out broad predictions about *Twombly*'s application at the margins[262] and other courts suggesting that *Twombly* might still not apply in all contexts.[263] Nevertheless, the courts have generally read the decision as effecting a meaningful[264] (though perhaps not seismic)[265] change in direction in federal pleading (prompted principally, it is believed, by the

---

[259]*See Bell Atlantic Corp. v. Twombly*, 550 U.S. 544, 562–63, 127 S.Ct. 1955, 167 L.Ed.2d 929 (2007). *See also Moss v. U.S. Secret Serv.*, 572 F.3d 962, 968 (9th Cir. 2009) (*Conley*, "read literally, set the bar too low"); *McGovern v. City of Philadelphia*, 554 F.3d 114, 121 n.5 (3d Cir. 2009) (assertion that discovery be permitted to marshal facts necessary to support alleged theory is "misguided" understanding of federal pleading).

[260]*See Ashcroft v. Iqbal*, 556 U.S. 662, 684, 129 S.Ct. 1937, 1953, 173 L.Ed.2d 868 (2009).

[261]*See Courie v. Alcoa Wheel & Forged Prods.*, 577 F.3d 625, 630 (6th Cir. 2009) ("Exactly how implausible is "implausible" remains to be seen . . ."). *Cf. Watison v. Carter*, 668 F.3d 1108, 1112 (9th Cir. 2012) (still quoting "retired" *Conley* language); *Ritchie Capital Mgmt., L.L.C. v. Jeffries*, 653 F.3d 755, 764 (8th Cir. 2011) (same).

[262]*See, e.g., Phillips v. County of Allegheny*, 515 F.3d 224, 234 (3d Cir. 2008) (*Twombly* raises issues "not easily resolved" and is likely source of controversy "for years to come"); *Goldstein v. Pataki*, 516 F.3d 50, 56 (2d Cir. 2008) ("we need not take this occasion to contemplate the outer limits" of *Twombly*).

[263]*See Smith v. Duffey*, 576 F.3d 336, 340 (7th Cir. 2009) (Posner, J.) (musing that standard might not govern where case imposes low pretrial discovery burden); *Gunasekera v. Irwin*, 551 F.3d 461, 466 (6th Cir. 2009) (same effect).

[264]*See Khalik v. United Air Lines*, 671 F.3d 1188, 1191–92 (10th Cir. 2012) (*Twombly* is a "middle ground" between heightened pleading and mere labels, and the notice pleading regime of Rule 8(a) "still lives"); *Phillips v. Bell*, 365 Fed.Appx. 133, 138 (10th Cir. 2010) (recognizing that plausibility test overrules prior Circuit precedent that a complaint with only conclusory allegations could survive); *Courie v. Alcoa Wheel & Forged Prods.*, 577 F.3d 625, 629–30 (6th Cir. 2009) ("while this new *Iqbal/Twombly* standard screens out the 'little green men' cases just as *Conley* did, it is designed to also screen out cases that, while not utterly impossible, are 'implausible.'); *Tamayo v. Blagojevich*, 526 F.3d 1074, 1083 (7th Cir. 2008) (*Twombly* "retooled federal pleading standards").

[265]*See In re Insurance Brokerage Antitrust Litig.*, 618 F.3d 300, 319 n.17 (3d Cir. 2010) (although originally believing the plausibility standard "repudiated" earlier Supreme Court precedent, now "we are not so sure"); *Arista Records, LLC v. Doe 3*, 604 F.3d 110, 119 (2d Cir. 2010) (the *Twombly* opinion itself "belied" the notion that a heightened pleading standard is required); *Bissessur v. Indiana Univ. Bd. of Trustees*, 581 F.3d 599, 603 (7th Cir. 2009) ("Our system operates on a notice pleading standard; *Twombly* and its progeny do not change this fact."). *See generally* William M. Janssen, *Iqbal "Plausibility" in Pharmaceutical and Medical Device Litigation*, 71 LA. L. REV. 541 (2011) (discussing impact across pharmaceutical and medical device litigation sector).

burgeoning costs of discovery).[266] Precisely how *Twombly* applies depends on the specific context and type of claim alleged.[267] Under this new regime, much of the pre-*Twombly* pleading mandate survives. The basic "notice" pleading standard remains the rule in federal courts,[268] and it often is not an "onerous" burden.[269] The pleading of tediously detailed factual allegations is still not required,[270] nor the pleading of every fact necessary to sustain the plaintiff's burden.[271] It is also still not the courts' role to weigh its subjective assessment of whether the pleader's ultimate success on the merits is probable or unlikely.[272] The requisite "plausibility", therefore, is *not* measured by a likelihood of success.[273]

But what is required to satisfy this basic "notice" pleading standard has now evolved. It used to be that, abiding by *Conley*'s lenient mandate, courts might not have dismissed a complaint, even after rejecting a pleader's asserted legal theory, if the court were unable to positively confirm that there was no other theoretically possible claim that the pleader could have.[274] In other words, unless the pleaded allegations actually *denied* the pleader any possible avenue for recovery, the complaint might not have been dismissed. After *Twombly*, the required inquiry seems to be an inverted version of the former one: now, a proper complaint must do more than merely *avoid foreclosing* all possible bases for recovery; it must instead affirmatively *suggest* an actual *entitlement to relief* by supplying allegations that

---

[266]Judge Posner's eloquent assessment of this motivation is noteworthy. *See Swanson v. Citibank, N.A.*, 614 F.3d 400, 411–12 (7th Cir. 2010) (Posner, J., dissenting).

[267]*See Ashcroft v. Iqbal*, 556 U.S. 662, 679, 129 S.Ct. 1937, 1950, 173 L.Ed.2d 868 (2009) (assessing plausibility is "context-specific task"). *See also Phillips v. County of Allegheny*, 515 F.3d 224, 231 (3d Cir. 2008) ("Context matters in notice pleading.").

[268]*See Bissessur v. Indiana Univ. Bd. of Trustees*, 581 F.3d 599, 603 (7th Cir. 2009); *Aktieselskabet AF 21. November 2001 v. Fame Jeans Inc.*, 525 F.3d 8, 15 (D.C. Cir. 2008); *Phillips v. County of Allegheny*, 515 F.3d 224, 231 (3d Cir. 2008).

[269]*See Johnson v. Riverside Healthcare System, LP*, 534 F.3d 1116, 1122 (9th Cir. 2008).

[270]*See Ashcroft v. Iqbal*, 556 U.S. 662, 678, 129 S.Ct. 1937, 1949, 678 173 L.Ed.2d 868 (2009); *Bell Atlantic Corp. v. Twombly*, 550 U.S. 544, 555 & n.3, 127 S. Ct. 1955, 1964–65, 167 L. Ed. 2d 929 (2007).

[271]*See al-Kidd v. Ashcroft*, 580 F.3d 949, 977 (9th Cir. 2009), *petition for cert. filed*, 79 U.S.L.W. 3062 (U.S. July 16, 2010) (No. 10-98).

[272]*See Aktieselskabet AF 21. November 2001 v. Fame Jeans Inc.*, 525 F.3d 8, 17 (D.C. Cir. 2008); *Phillips v. County of Allegheny*, 515 F.3d 224, 234 (3d Cir. 2008).

[273]*See Anderson News, L.L.C. v. American Media, Inc.*, 680 F.3d 162, 189–90 (2d Cir. 2012) (proper *Twombly* inquiry does not choose between competing plausible interpretations of evidence, but asks simply if sufficient factual allegations exist to make plaintiff's claim plausible); *Mediacom Southeast LLC v. BellSouth Telecomms., Inc.*, 672 F.3d 396, 400 (6th Cir. 2012) (district court is not to choose between crediting defendant's, rather than plaintiff's, version of facts).

[274]*See Phillips v. County of Allegheny*, 515 F.3d 224, 231 (3d Cir. 2008) (*Conley* formulation could be viewed as obligating judges to speculate about undisclosed facts).

push the claim above the level of mere speculation.[275] And this "plausibility" must now appear affirmatively, on the face of the pleading.[276] In practice, the *Twombly* standard erects a flexible pleading benchmark that varies depending on the type of claim chosen and the type of allegations pleaded: a "plausible" auto accident case may be very concisely pleaded, whereas a "plausible" antitrust or RICO case (often built on inferences from facts that might be either innocent or culpable) may demand a far fuller factual presentation.[277]

Burden of Proof

The burden lies with the moving party.[278] In fact, even a failure by the non-moving party to oppose the motion will not necessarily justify an automatic dismissal.[279] The trial court must still determine whether a dismissal is appropriate.

Timing

The defense of failure to state a claim may be asserted at any time, even at trial,[280] but is waived if not asserted during trial.[281] Rule 12(b)(6) *motions* seeking dismissal of such claims, however, must ordinarily be filed before a responsive pleading is served. Once the pleadings are closed, the defense may be pressed on a Rule 12(c) motion for judgment on the pleadings

---

[275]*See Windy City Metal Fabricators & Supply, Inc. v. CIT Technical Financing Services, Inc.*, 536 F.3d 663, 667–68 (7th Cir. 2008); *Tamayo v. Blagojevich*, 526 F.3d 1074, 1084 (7th Cir. 2008). *See also Bishop v. Lucent Technologies, Inc.*, 520 F.3d 516, 519 (6th Cir. 2008).

[276]*See Johnson v. Riverside Healthcare System, LP*, 534 F.3d 1116, 1122 (9th Cir. 2008); *Bishop v. Lucent Technologies, Inc.*, 520 F.3d 516, 519 (6th Cir. 2008). *See also Morales-Tañón v. Puerto Rico Elec. Power Authority*, 524 F.3d 15, 18 (1st Cir. 2008) (assertion that pleader merely needs to plead enough facts for *the court* to find him a cognizable claim is now "simply wrong").

[277]*See Kansas Penn Gaming, LLC v. Collins*, 656 F.3d 1210, 1215 (10th Cir. 2011) (required nature and specificity of claim "will vary based on context"); *In re Insurance Brokerage Antitrust Litig.*, 618 F.3d 300, 319 n.18 (3d Cir. 2010) ("Some claims will demand relatively more factual detail to satisfy this standard, while others require less."); *Tamayo v. Blagojevich*,

526 F.3d 1074, 1083–85 (7th Cir. 2008) (same effect). This shifting-scale view of Rule 8(a)'s demands may well have predated *Twombly*. *See Tyco Fire Prods. LP v. Victaulic Co.*, 777 F.Supp.2d 893, 989 (E.D.Pa. 2011) (noting dictate, from pre-*Twombly* precedent, that "the more substantively complex the cause of action, the greater the mandate for detail under [Rule 8(a)].").

[278]*See Total Benefits Planning Agency, Inc. v. Anthem Blue Cross & Blue Shield*, 552 F.3d 430, 434 (6th Cir. 2008); *Ragin v. New York Times Co.*, 923 F.2d 995, 999 (2d Cir. 1991); *Yeksigian v. Nappi*, 900 F.2d 101, 104–05 (7th Cir. 1990).

[279]*See Goldberg v. Danaher*, 599 F.3d 181, 181–84 (2d Cir. 2010); *Pomerleau v. West Springfield Public Schools*, 362 F.3d 143, 145 (1st Cir. 2004).

[280]*See* Rule 12(h)(2).

[281]*See Arbaugh v. Y&H Corp.*, 546 U.S. 500, 507 126 S. Ct. 1235, 1240, 163 L. Ed. 2d 1097 (2006) (Rule 12(b)(6) objection "endures up to, but not beyond, trial on the merits").

or a Rule 56 motion for summary judgment.[282] A post-pleadings / pre-discovery motion that mistakenly asserts this defense under Rule 12(b)(6) will typically, absent prejudice to the nonmoving party, be treated as a Rule 12(c) motion.[283]

Waiver

A party generally does not waive the right to challenge a lawsuit for failing to state a claim,[284] provided the defense is asserted at some point before the conclusion of trial.[285]

"Clarifying" the Complaint with Briefs and Oral Argument

Although the factual averments in the *pleading* are deemed true on a motion to dismiss, the court will likely refuse to accept as true the pleader's statements made for the first time in a legal memorandum or brief that forms no part of the official pleadings.[286] However, the pleader's memorandum or brief can be used to "clarify" allegations of the pleading,[287] as can "factual elaborations" supplied by pleaders[288] and statements made by the pleaders during oral argument.[289]

Pleading in Anticipation of Affirmative Defenses

Ordinarily, plaintiffs need not anticipate the defendants' likely affirmative defenses,[290] nor attempt to preemptively "plead around" them in the complaint.[291] Whether the complaint states a claim upon which relief can be granted is generally not dependent on whether the defendant has a defense.[292]

---

[282]*See McGlone v. Bell*, 681 F.3d 718, 728 n.2 (6th Cir. 2012); *Patel v. Contemporary Classics of Beverly Hills*, 259 F.3d 123, at 125–26 (2d Cir. 2001).

[283]*See MacDonald v. Grace Church Seattle*, 457 F.3d 1079 (9th Cir.2006); *McMillan v. Collection Professionals Inc.*, 455 F.3d 754, 757 (7th Cir. 2006).

[284]*See* Rule 12(h)(2). *See also McIntosh v. Antonino*, 71 F.3d 29, 38 (1st Cir. 1995) (refusing to find waiver of statute of limitations defense, asserted as an affirmative defense, where defendant chose not to move for judgment earlier in the proceedings: "This assertion has no foothold in the law").

[285]*See Arbaugh v. Y&H Corp.*, 546 U.S. 500, 507, 126 S. Ct. 1235, 1240, 163 L. Ed. 2d 1097 (2006) (Rule 12(b)(6) objection "endures up to, but not beyond, trial on the merits").

[286]*See E.I. du Pont de Nemours & Co. v. Kolon Indus., Inc.*, 637 F.3d 435, 449 (4th Cir. 2011); *Dorsey v. Portfolio Equities, Inc.*, 540 F.3d 333, 338 (5th Cir. 2008); *Frederico v. Home Depot*, 507 F.3d 188, 201–02 (3d Cir. 2007).

[287]*See Pegram v. Herdrich*, 530 U.S. 211, 229, 120 S. Ct. 2143, 2155, 147 L. Ed. 2d 164 (2000); *Vance v. Rumsfeld*, 653 F.3d 591, 602 n.6 (7th Cir. 2011).

[288]*See Geinosky v. City of Chicago*, 675 F.3d 743, 745 & n.1 (7th Cir. 2012).

[289]*See Maio v. Aetna, Inc.*, 221 F.3d 472, 485 (3d Cir. 2000).

[290]*See Richards v. Mitcheff*, __ F.3d __, __, 2012 WL 3217627, at *1–*2 (7th Cir. 2012); *Memphis, Tennessee Area Local, American Postal Workers Union, AFL-CIO v. City of Memphis*, 361 F.3d 898, 902 (6th Cir. 2004).

[291]*See Xechem, Inc. v. Bristol-Myers Squibb Co.*, 372 F.3d 899, 901 (7th Cir. 2004).

[292]*See U.S. v. Northern Trust Co.*, 372 F.3d 886, 888 (7th Cir. 2004).

"Built-In" Defenses

The court will dismiss for failing to state a claim where the face of the complaint reveals patent, "built-in" affirmative defenses, such as statute of limitations, res judicata, exhaustion of administrative remedies, or statute of frauds.[293] Parties can "plead themselves out of court" in two ways. First, they can allege facts that (perhaps inadvertently) establish an affirmative defense[294] or otherwise demonstrate that success on the merits is not possible.[295] Second, they can attach extrinsic materials to their pleadings which reveal the presence of the same sort of "built-in" defenses.[296] "Built-in" defense dismissals are proper only were the damning facts are readily ascertainable from the complaint, the public record, or other allowable sources of judicial notice, *and* those facts conclusively demonstrate the defense.[297]

- *Best Resolved Under Rule 12(c):* Although courts have dismissed claims based on such such "built-in" defenses, the preferred practice seems to be to seek a judgment on the pleadings under Rule 12(c) once the pleadings have closed.[298]

Sua Sponte Motions

Provided it adopts a fair procedure for doing so, the trial court may, on its own initiative, and without an adversary's motion, dismiss a pleading for failing to state a claim upon which relief may be granted.[299] Such dismissals, however, are

---

[293]*See, e.g., Cataldo v. U.S. Steel Corp.*, 676 F.3d 542, 547 (6th Cir. 2012) (limitations); *Muhammad v. Oliver*, 547 F.3d 874, 878 (7th Cir. 2008) (res judicata); *Bryant v. Rich*, 530 F.3d 1368, 1380 n.2 (11th Cir. 2008) (exhaustion); *EPCO Carbon Dioxide Products, Inc. v. JP Morgan Chase Bank, NA*, 467 F.3d 466, 470 (5th Cir. 2006) (statute of frauds).

[294]*See Brownmark Films, LLC v. Comedy Partners*, 682 F.3d 687, 690 (7th Cir. 2012); *Cataldo v. U.S. Steel Corp.*, 676 F.3d 542, 547 (6th Cir. 2012); *Joyce v. Armstrong Teasdale, LLP*, 635 F.3d 364, 367 (8th Cir. 2011).

[295]*See San Geronimo Caribe Project, Inc. v. Acevedo-Vila*, 687 F.3d 465, 492 (1st Cir. 2012); *Trudeau v. Federal Trade Com'n.*, 456 F.3d 178 (D.C. Cir. 2006).

[296]*See Thompson v. Illinois Dept. of Professional Regulation*, 300 F.3d 750, 754 (7th Cir. 2002) ("where a plaintiff attaches documents and relies upon the documents to form the basis for a claim or part of a claim, dismissal is appropriate if the document negates the claim"); *Jacobsen v. Deseret Book Co.*, 287 F.3d 936, 941–42 (10th Cir. 2002) (in deciding Rule 12(b)(6) motion in copyright cases, "the legal effect of the works are determined by the works themselves rather than by allegations in the complaint" if the works are attached as exhibits). *See also infra* Authors' Commentary to Rule 12(b)(6) (**"Extrinsic Materials"**).

[297]*See Nisselson v. Lernout*, 469 F.3d 143, 150 (1st Cir. 2006).

[298]*See Richards v. Mitcheff*, __ F.3d __, __, 2012 WL 3217627, at *1–*2 (7th Cir. 2012); *Brownmark Films, LLC v. Comedy Partners*, 682 F.3d 687, 690 & n.1 (7th Cir. 2012).

[299]*See Taylor v. Acxiom Corp.*, 612 F.3d 325, 340 (5th Cir. 2010); *Martinez-Rivera v. Sanchez Ramos*, 498 F.3d 3, 7 (1st Cir. 2007). *But cf. Blue Cross & Blue Shield of Alabama v. Sanders*,

"strong medicine, and should be dispensed sparingly."[300] Generally, fair procedure requires that the trial court notify the pleader of its intention to grant a *sua sponte* dismissal and permit an opportunity to amend or otherwise respond.[301] One court forbids *sua sponte* dismissals (1) if no responsive pleading has been filed and an amendment as of right would still be timely, (2) if the complaint was filed in good faith, and (3) if the plaintiff has not been given notice of the *sua sponte* intent to dismiss coupled with a right to respond.[302] Nevertheless, a *sua sponte* dismissal entered without forewarning to the plaintiff may still be affirmed if the pleading's allegations are "patently meritless" and without any hope of cure.[303] In such a case, the party defending the dismissal carries the burden of demonstrating that the allegations, drawn most favorably to the pleader, are beyond all hope.[304]

Pro Se Litigants

Courts are particularly cautious while inspecting pleadings prepared by plaintiffs who lack counsel and are proceeding *pro se*. Often inartful, and rarely composed to the standards expected of practicing attorneys, *pro se* pleadings are viewed with considerable liberality and are held to less stringent standards than those expected of pleadings drafted by lawyers[305] (a relaxation that persists after *Twombly*).[306] Nevertheless, unrepresented plaintiffs are not relieved of their obligation to allege sufficient facts to support a cognizable legal claim.[307] Indeed, even *in forma pauperis* claims may be dismissed if found legally frivolous.[308] But dismissals of *pro se* pleaders are ordinarily accompanied by leave to replead (unless it is clear

---

138 F.3d 1347, 1354 (11th Cir. 1998) (because "failure to state a claim" is not a jurisdictional issue, court may not *sua sponte* decide the question unless plaintiff has preserved it); *Baker v. Cuomo*, 58 F.3d 814, 818 (2d Cir. 1995) (*sua sponte* dismissals without service of process and a responsive filing by the opponent are disfavored).

[300] *Chute v. Walker*, 281 F.3d 314, 319 (1st Cir. 2002).

[301] *See Martinez-Rivera v. Sanchez Ramos*, 498 F.3d 3, 7 (1st Cir. 2007); *Lee v. City of Los Angeles*, 250 F.3d 668, 683 (9th Cir. 2001).

[302] *See American United Life Ins. Co. v. Martinez*, 480 F.3d 1043, 1057 (11th Cir. 2007).

[303] *See Christiansen v. West Branch Cmty. Sch. Dist.*, 674 F.3d 927, 938 (8th Cir. 2012); *Chute v. Walker*, 281 F.3d 314, 319 (1st Cir. 2002).

[304] *Martinez-Rivera v. Sanchez*

Ramos, 498 F.3d 3, 7 (1st Cir. 2007).

[305] *See Erickson v. Pardus*, 551 U.S. 89, 94, 127 S. Ct. 2197, 2200, 167 L. Ed. 2d 1081 (2007) (per curiam); *Estelle v. Gamble*, 429 U.S. 97, 106, 97 S. Ct. 285, 50 L. Ed. 2d 251 (1976); *Haines v. Kerner*, 404 U.S. 519, 520–21, 92 S. Ct. 594, 595–96, 30 L. Ed. 2d 652 (1972).

[306] *See Ahlers v. Rabinowitz*, 684 F.3d 53, 60 (2d Cir. 2012); *Arnett v. Webster*, 658 F.3d 742, 751–52 (7th Cir.2011).

[307] *See Hall v. Witteman*, 584 F.3d 859, 863–64 (10th Cir. 2009); *Taylor v. Books A Million, Inc.*, 296 F.3d 376, 378 (5th Cir. 2002).

[308] *See* 28 U.S.C.A. § 1915(e)(2)(B); 28 U.S.C.A. § 1915A. *See also Neitzke v. Williams*, 490 U.S. 319, 109 S. Ct. 1827, 104 L. Ed. 2d 338 (1989) (describing standards for dismissals of *in forma pauperis* pleadings as frivolous).

that the best possible case has been pleaded).[309]

Extrinsic Materials

In ruling on a Rule 12(b)(6) motion, the court focuses principally on the complaint itself, but often may also consider a small category of additional materials:[310] exhibits attached to the complaint (unless their authenticity is questioned);[311] documents that the complaint incorporates by reference or are otherwise integral to the claim (provided they are undisputed);[312] information subject to judicial notice;[313] matters of public record (such as orders and other materials in the record of the case);[314] and concessions by plaintiffs made in their response to the motion.[315] The parties *may* submit (and the court *may* consider) further materials, but with a consequence—the motion will be re-cast. If the court, in its discretion,[316] considers such additional extrinsic evidence, the motion must be converted into a request for summary judgment under Rule 56.[317]

Oral Argument

The trial judge may, but is not obligated to, convene oral argument on a Rule 12(b)(6) motion to dismiss.[318]

---

[309]*See Hale v. King*, 642 F.3d 492, 503 (5th Cir. 2011).

[310]*See Daniels-Hall v. Nat'l Educ. Ass'n*, 629 F.3d 992, 998 (9th Cir. 2010); *Gee v. Pacheco*, 627 F.3d 1178, 1186 (10th Cir. 2010); *Winget v. JP Morgan Chase Bank, N.A.*, 537 F.3d 565, 576 (6th Cir. 2008).

[311]*See Rosenfield v. HSBC Bank, USA*, 681 F.3d 1172, 1178 (10th Cir. 2012); *Building Indus. Elec. Contractors Ass'n v. City of New York*, 678 F.3d 184, 187 (2d Cir. 2012); *Wigod v. Wells Fargo Bank, N.A.*, 673 F.3d 547, 556 (7th Cir. 2012).

[312]*See Rosenfield v. HSBC Bank, USA*, 681 F.3d 1172, 1178 (10th Cir. 2012); *Brownmark Films, LLC v. Comedy Partners*, 682 F.3d 687, 690 (7th Cir. 2012); *Building Indus. Elec. Contractors Ass'n v. City of New York*, 678 F.3d 184, 187 (2d Cir. 2012).

[313]*See Schatz v. Republican State Leadership Comm.*, 669 F.3d 50, 55–56 (1st Cir. 2012); *Skilstaf, Inc. v. CVS Caremark Corp.*, 669 F.3d 1005, 1016 n.9 (9th Cir. 2012); *Gee v. Pacheco*, 627 F.3d 1178, 1186 (10th Cir. 2010).

[314]*See Miller v. Redwood Toxicology Lab., Inc.*, 688 F.3d 928, 931 n.3 (8th Cir. 2012).

[315]*See Schatz v. Republican State Leadership Comm.*, 669 F.3d 50, 55–56 (1st Cir. 2012).

[316]*See Trans-Spec Truck Service, Inc. v. Caterpillar Inc.*, 524 F.3d 315, 321 (1st Cir. 2008); *Pueschel v. U.S.*, 369 F.3d 345, 353 n.3 (4th Cir. 2004); *Stahl v. U.S. Dept. of Agriculture*, 327 F.3d 697, 701 (8th Cir. 2003).

[317]For a more extensive discussion of this conversion process, see *infra* Authors' Commentary to Rule 12(d).

[318]*See* Rule 78 ("By rule or order, the court may provide for submitting and determining motions on briefs, without oral hearings."); *Greene v. WCI Holdings Corp.*, 136 F.3d 313, 316 (2d Cir. 1998) ("Every circuit to consider the issue has determined that the 'hearing' requirements of Rule 12 . . . do not mean that an oral hearing is necessary, but only require that a party be given the opportunity to present its views to the court"). *See also Pueschel v. U.S.*, 369 F.3d 345, 354 (4th Cir. 2004); *Cline v. Rogers*, 87 F.3d 176, 184 (6th Cir. 1996); *Riddle v. Mondragon*, 83 F.3d 1197, 1208 (10th Cir. 1996).

Postponing Discovery

Some courts permit a postponement of discovery after a Rule 12(b)(6) motion is filed, and then continuing for so long as it remains pending.[319]

Voluntary Dismissals While Motion is Pending

Plaintiffs may voluntarily dismiss a lawsuit at any time prior to the point where their adversaries serve an answer or a motion for summary judgment.[320] Consequently, plaintiffs are generally permitted to voluntarily dismiss their lawsuits during the pendency of a Rule 12(b)(6) motion to dismiss. This entitlement is *not* automatically lost when a defendant serves a motion to dismiss that is accompanied improperly by extrinsic materials (which could require that the motion be converted to a summary judgment proceeding); rather, until such a motion is formally converted by the court, the plaintiffs should still be permitted to voluntarily dismiss.[321]

Manner of Ruling

Although no detailed written opinion is required, the practice preferred by the appellate courts is that a dismissal be accompanied by some explanation for the decision, so as to supply both the parties and any reviewing court with the benefit of the trial court's reasoning.[322]

Ruling Deferred

Where circumstances persuade the court that claims should not be dismissed until further factual development is accomplished, the court may deny the Rule 12(b)(6) motion and revisit the merits of claims on a Rule 12(c) motion for judgment on the pleadings or a Rule 56 motion for summary judgment.[323] One court has further suggested that, in light of *Twombly*, a

---

[319]*See Mitchell v. McNeil*, 487 F.3d 374, 379 (6th Cir. 2007) (because plaintiffs failed to state a cognizable claim, there was no error in denying discovery); *Tucker v. Union of Needletrades, Industrial and Textile Employees*, 407 F.3d 784, 787–88 (6th Cir. 2005) (noting that "very purpose" of Rule 12(b)(6) is to permit challenge to legal sufficiency of complaints without subjecting party to discovery); *Rutman Wine Co. v. E. & J. Gallo Winery*, 829 F.2d 729, 738 (9th Cir. 1987) (same, noting that it is "sounder practice to determine whether there is any reasonable likelihood that plaintiffs can construct a claim before forcing the parties to undergo the expense of discovery").

[320]*See* Rule 41(a)(1)(A)(i).

[321]*See In re Bath and Kitchen Fixtures Antitrust Litigation*, 535 F.3d 161, 166 (3d Cir. 2008); *Swedberg v. Marotzke*, 339 F.3d 1139, 1142–45 (9th Cir. 2003).

[322]*See Metzler Inv. GMBH v. Corinthian Colleges, Inc.*, 540 F.3d 1049, 1061 n.5 (9th Cir. 2008).

[323]*See Keys Jet Ski, Inc. v. Kays*, 893 F.2d 1225, 1230 (11th Cir. 1990) (refusing to affirm district court's dismissal ruling in the absence of further factual development to support the claims); *Flue-Cured Tobacco Co-op. Stabilization Corp. v. U.S. E.P.A.*, 857 F. Supp. 1137, 1145 (M.D. N.C. 1994) (deferring determination of legal sufficiency of due process claim where adjudication on that issue can be more accurately accomplished after a factual record is developed); *Evello Investments, N.V. v. Printed Media Services, Inc.*, 158 F.R.D. 172, 173 (D. Kan. 1994)

period of pre-ruling discovery might be available.[324]

Post-Ruling Amendments to the Pleadings

The court will generally permit the pleader an opportunity to amend unless an amendment would be futile or inequitable.[325] Even when the court doubts the pleading defects can be overcome[326] or when the pleader neglects to request leave to do so,[327] plaintiffs are typically permitted to amend their dismissed pleading at least once (unless the exercise would be plainly futile).

NOTE: A plaintiff who is otherwise entitled to file an amended complaint following a Rule 12(b)(6) dismissal may choose instead to stand on the original complaint and appeal the dismissal.[328]

Prejudice on Dismissal

Unless the ruling is premised on mere technical pleading defects or the court directs otherwise (or permits an amended pleading), a dismissal for failing to state a claim is deemed to be a ruling on the merits, and, once final, is accorded full res judicata effect.[329] Conversely, an order denying dismissal under Rule 12(b)(6) does not conclusively resolve anything,[330] nor does it somehow forecast who will prevail at trial (or even whether

---

(citing Rule 12(d), court elected to defer consideration of Rule 12(b)(6) motion in "highly contentious and complicated case" where dismissal motion hinged on "complicated factual and legal questions"). *But see First Commercial Trust Co., N.A. v. Colt's Mfg. Co., Inc.*, 77 F.3d 1081, 1083 (8th Cir. 1996) (noting that litigants have no entitlement to discovery in the absence of a plausible legal theory).

[324]*See McCauley v. City of Chicago*, 671 F.3d 611, 619–20 (7th Cir. 2011) (intimating, without deciding, general availability of pre-ruling discovery).

[325]*See Anderson News, L.L.C. v. American Media, Inc.*, 680 F.3d 162, 185–86 (2d Cir. 2012); *Bausch v. Stryker Corp.*, 630 F.3d 546, 561–63 (7th Cir. 2010); *Great Western Mining & Mineral Co. v. Fox Rothschild LLP*, 615 F.3d 159, 175 (3d Cir. 2010). *Cf. Rosenfield v. HSBC Bank, USA*, 681 F.3d 1172, 1189–90 (10th Cir. 2012) (denying leave to amend is proper where such leave would be futile); *Wood v. City of San Diego*, 678 F.3d 1075, 1082 (9th Cir. 2012) (same).

[326]*See Ostrzenski v. Seigel*, 177 F.3d 245, 252–53 (4th Cir. 1999).

[327]*See In re New Jersey Title Ins. Litig.*, 683 F.3d 451, 462 (3d Cir. 2012). *But see Burtch v. Milberg Factors, Inc.*, 662 F.3d 212, 230 (3d Cir. 2011) (holding that court may enter final judgment upon dismissal where plaintiff has not properly requested leave to amend).

[328]*See Alston v. Parker*, 363 F.3d 229, 235 (3d Cir. 2004) ("If the plaintiff does not desire to amend, he may file an appropriate notice with the district court asserting his intent to stand on the complaint, at which time an order to dismiss the action would be appropriate"). *See also WMX Technologies, Inc. v. Miller*, 104 F.3d 1133 (9th Cir. 1997) (holding that plaintiff must obtain final judgment from district court before "standing" on original complaint and taking immediate appeal).

[329]*See Federated Dept. Stores, Inc. v. Moitie*, 452 U.S. 394, 399, 101 S. Ct. 2424, 69 L. Ed. 2d 103 (1981); *Pope v. Secretary for Dep't of Corrections*, 680 F.3d 1271, 1285–86 (11th Cir. 2012); *McLean v. U.S.*, 566 F.3d 391, 396 (4th Cir. 2009).

[330]*See PA Prison Soc. v. Cortes*,

the case can survive summary judgment).[331]

Appealability

Whether Rule 12(b)(6) rulings are appealable (immediately or otherwise) can be a challenging inquiry and merits careful research and study. A ruling that grants a Rule 12(b)(6) motion in its entirety and with prejudice, thus terminating the litigation, will almost certainly be a final order and immediately appealable.[332] However, the ruling might not be immediately appealable if it grants the motion but allows repleading,[333] or if it grants the motion only in part.[334] If the ruling denies the motion, the ruling might not be immediately appealable,[335] or, if the plaintiff has prevailed at trial, appealable at all.[336] Moreover, exceptions exist. For example, a ruling that denies a dismissal on certain immunity grounds may be immediately appealed,[337] as may denials that are "inextricably intertwined" with another order that is immediately appealable.[338]

RULE 12(b)(7)—DISMISSAL FOR FAILURE TO JOIN A RULE 19 PARTY

CORE CONCEPT

A case will be dismissed if there is an absent party without whom complete relief cannot be granted or whose interest in the dispute is of such a nature that to proceed without that party

---

622 F.3d 215, 247 (3d Cir. 2010).

[331]See Davis v. Davis, 526 F.2d 1286, 1290 (5th Cir. 1976).

[332]See ALA, Inc. v. CCAIR, Inc., 29 F.3d 855 (3d Cir.1994). See also Borden v. Allen, 646 F.3d 785 (11th Cir. 2011) (Rule 12(b)(6) is a ruling on the merits).

[333]See Eberhardt v. O'Malley, 17 F.3d 1023, 1024 (7th Cir. 1994). The pleader may, however, notify the court of an intent to stand on the dismissed pleading, and then appeal. See Alston v. Parker, 363 F.3d 229, 235 (3d Cir. 2004).

[334]Such partial grants might be made immediately appealable upon court order. See, e.g., Rule 54(b); 28 U.S.C. § 1292(b).

[335]See Ridpath v. Board of Governors Marshall University, 447 F.3d 292, 304 (4th Cir. 2006); Hill v. City of New York, 45 F.3d 653, 659 (2d Cir. 1995); Foster Wheeler Energy Corp. v. Metropolitan Knox Solid Waste Authority, Inc., 970 F.2d 199, 202 (6th Cir. 1992).

[336]See ClearOne Commc'ns, Inc. v. Biamp Systems, 653 F.3d 1163, 1172 (10th Cir. 2011) (no right to appeal from Rule 12(b)(6) ruling; appeal must be from motion for judgment as a matter of law); Bennett v. Pippin, 74 F.3d 578, 585 (5th Cir.1996) (same).

[337]See, e.g., Puerto Rico Aqueduct and Sewer Authority v. Metcalf & Eddy, Inc., 506 U.S. 139, 113 S. Ct. 684, 121 L. Ed. 2d 605 (1993) (holding that denial of Eleventh Amendment immunity was immediately appealable collateral order); Mitchell v. Forsyth, 472 U.S. 511, 105 S. Ct. 2806, 86 L. Ed. 2d 411 (1985) (holding that ruling denying qualified immunity was an immediately appealable collateral order); Zamani v. Carnes, 491 F.3d 990, 994 (9th Cir. 2007) (denial of anti-SLAPP motion immediately appealable under collateral order doctrine); Goldstein v. City of Long Beach, 481 F.3d 1170, 1172 (9th Cir. 2007) (denial of absolute immunity motion immediately appealable).

[338]See Hilton v. Hallmark Cards, 599 F.3d 894, 900 (9th Cir. 2010).

could prejudice either that party or others.

APPLICATIONS

Legal Test

The courts are hesitant to dismiss for failure to join absent parties, and will not do so on a vague possibility that unjoined persons may have an interest affected by the litigation.[339] The test is not mechanically formalistic, but hinges on the peculiar factual circumstances each case presents.[340] When a Rule 12(b)(7) motion is filed, the court will conduct a two-step assessment. The court will, first, apply the standards of Rule 19(a) to determine whether there is an absent party who must be joined to the litigation and, if so, second, whether such joinder is feasible (and, if joinder is not feasible, how under Rule 19(b) the court must proceed).[341] The court conducts this inquiry on the basis of the pleadings as they appear at the time the joinder is proposed.[342] The court will accept all of the pleader's well-pleaded factual allegations as true, and will draw all reasonable inferences in the pleader's favor.[343] However, legal conclusions and conclusorily-supported "threadbare recitals" of elements will not be accepted as true.[344] The ultimate decision is committed to the trial court's sound discretion.[345]

Timing and Waiver

An objection to the absence of a Rule 19 indispensable party may be asserted by motion filed before a responsive pleading, in the responsive pleading itself, by motion for judgment on the

---

[339]See *Direct Supply, Inc. v. Specialty Hosps. of Am., LLC*, __ F. Supp. 2d __, __, 2012 WL 2914361, at *6 (D.D.C. 2012); *Sever v. Glickman*, 298 F. Supp. 2d 267, 275 (D. Conn. 2004).

[340]See *Schlumberger Industries, Inc. v. National Sur. Corp.*, 36 F.3d 1274, 1286 (4th Cir. 1994); *Collegiate Licensing Co. v. American Cas. Co.*, 842 F.Supp.2d 1360, 1365 n.3 (N.D.Ga. 2012); *In re Chinese Manufactured Drywall Prods. Liab. Litig.*, 273 F.R.D. 380, 385 (E.D.La. 2011).

[341]See *Paiute-Shoshone Indians of Bishop Cmty. of Bishop Colony v. City of Los Angeles*, 637 F.3d 993, 996 n.1 (9th Cir. 2011); *HS Res., Inc. v. Wingate*, 327 F.3d 432, 439 (5th Cir. 2003); *Boulevard Bank Nat. Ass'n v. Philips Med. Sys. Int'l B.V.*, 15 F.3d 1419, 1422 (7th Cir. 1994).

[342]See *Register v. Cameron &*

Barkley Co., 467 F. Supp. 2d 519, 530 (D.S.C. 2006).

[343]See *Paiute-Shoshone Indians of Bishop Cmty. of Bishop Colony v. City of Los Angeles*, 637 F.3d 993, 996 n.1 (9th Cir. 2011); *Direct Supply, Inc. v. Specialty Hosps. of Am., LLC*, __ F. Supp. 2d __, __, 2012 WL 2914361, at *6 (D.D.C. 2012); *Estate of Eiteljorg ex rel. Eiteljorg v. Eiteljorg*, 813 F.Supp.2d 1069, 1074 (S.D.Ind. 2011).

[344]See *Pittsburgh Logistics Sys., Inc. v. C.R. England, Inc.*, 669 F.Supp.2d 613, 618 (W.D.Pa. 2009).

[345]See *Begay v. Public Serv. Co. of N.M.*, 710 F.Supp.2d 1161, 1181 (D.N.M. 2010); *R-Delight Holding LLC v. Anders*, 246 F.R.D. 496, 499 (D. Md. 2007) (citing *Provident Tradesmens Bank & Trust Co. v. Patterson*, 390 U.S. 102, 119, 88 S. Ct. 733, 19 L. Ed. 2d 936 (1968)).

pleadings, or during the trial on the merits.[346] Several courts hold that the trial judge enjoys the discretion to reject such a motion as untimely if the motion is found to have been submitted intentionally late to serve a litigant's own defensive purposes, rather than to protect the interests of the absent party.[347]

Burden of Proof

The burden lies with the person seeking the dismissal to demonstrate the "indispensable" nature of the absent party.[348] Some courts, however, shift the burden to the party opposing joinder once a *prima facie* case of required party status has been made.[349]

Sua Sponte Motions

Although the absence of a Rule 19 party is not a jurisdictional defect, the court may, on its own initiative, raise the absence of a Rule 19 party.[350]

Remedy

The court will, if possible, order that the absent party be joined in the lawsuit. If joinder is not possible, the court will consider whether in equity and good conscience the lawsuit should continue without the absent party.[351] Dismissals are disfavored, however.[352]

Extrinsic Materials

The parties may produce affidavits and other materials to

---

[346]*See Legal Aid Soc'y v. City of New York*, 114 F. Supp. 2d 204, 219 (S.D. N.Y. 2000) (noting that failure to join indispensable party is not a "threshold defense"; instead, defendant may raise this challenge through end of trial).

[347]*See, e.g., Judwin Props., Inc. v. U.S. Fire Ins. Co.*, 973 F.2d 432, 434 (5th Cir. 1992); *Ilan-Gat Engineers, Ltd. v. Antigua Intern. Bank*, 659 F.2d 234, 242 (D.C. Cir. 1981); *Fireman's Fund Ins. Co. v. Nat'l Bank of Cooperatives*, 103 F.3d 888, 896 (9th Cir. 1996); *Dore Energy Corp. v. Prospective Inv. & Trading Co., Ltd.*, 2008 WL 152119, at *1–*2 (W.D. La. 2008).

[348]*See Citizen Band Potawatomi Indian Tribe of Oklahoma v. Collier*, 17 F.3d 1292, 1293 (10th Cir. 1994); *Ilan-Gat Engineers, Ltd. v. Antigua Intern. Bank*, 659 F.2d 234 (D.C. Cir. 1981); *Center for Biological Diversity v. Pizarchik*, 858 F. Supp. 2d 1221, 1223 (D.Colo. 2012); *Tonasket v. Sargent*, 830 F.Supp.2d 1078, 1081 (E.D.Wash. 2011).

[349]*See Abbott v. BP Exploration & Prod. Inc.*, 781 F. Supp. 2d 453, 461 (S.D.Tex. 2011); *In re Chinese Manufactured Drywall Prods. Liab. Litig.*, 273 F.R.D. 380, 384–85 (E.D.La. 2011). *See generally Advanced Cardiology Ctr. Corp. v. Rodriguez*, 675 F. Supp. 2d 245, 250 (D.P.R. 2009) (surveying case law).

[350]*See Provident Tradesmens Bank & Trust Co. v. Patterson*, 390 U.S. 102, 111, 88 S.Ct. 733, 738–39, 19 L.Ed.2d 936 (1968); *Pickle v. Int'l Oilfield Divers, Inc.*, 791 F.2d 1237, 1242 (5th Cir. 1986).

[351]*See Rule 19(b). See also U.S. v. White*, 893 F. Supp. 1423 (C.D. Cal. 1995) (dismissal under Rule 12(b)(7) will be granted only where the unjoined party is "indispensable", and not just "necessary", and the party cannot otherwise be joined).

[352]*See Gorsuch v. Fireman's Fund Ins. Co.*, 360 F.2d 23 (9th Cir.1966).

support their positions on the absence of a Rule 19 party.[353] The courts differ on the legal effect of such extrinsic materials. Some courts hold that those materials can be considered freely without converting the motion into a summary judgment analysis,[354] while others hold that a conversion is required.[355]

Ruling Deferred

The court may defer ruling on the challenge until after discovery is conducted.[356]

Prejudice on Dismissal

A dismissal for lack of a Rule 19 party is proper only when the defect cannot be cured.[357] Moreover, such a dismissal generally does not preclude the plaintiff from re-instituting the claim in a court that can join the "indispensable" absent party.[358]

Appealability

The district court's denial of a Rule 12(b)(7) motion is usually interlocutory and not immediately appealable.[359]

RULE 12(c)—JUDGMENT ON THE PLEADINGS

CORE CONCEPT

After the pleadings are closed, a party may move for judgment on the pleadings if no material facts remain at issue and the parties' dispute can be resolved on both the pleadings and those facts of which the court can take judicial notice.

APPLICATIONS

Less Frequently Used

Rule 12(c)'s usefulness has been displaced in many instances

---

[353]See Davis Companies v. Emerald Casino, Inc., 268 F.3d 477, 480 n.4 (7th Cir. 2001); Citizen Band Potawatomi Indian Tribe of Oklahoma v. Collier, 17 F.3d 1292, 1293 (10th Cir. 1994); Direct Supply, Inc. v. Specialty Hosps. of Am., LLC, ___ F. Supp. 2d ___, ___, 2012 WL 2914361, at *6 (D.D.C. 2012); Tonasket v. Sargent, 830 F.Supp.2d 1078, 1081 (E.D.Wash. 2011).

[354]See 16th & K Hotel, LP v. Commonwealth Land Title Ins. Co., 276 F.Supp.2d 8, 12–13 (D.D.C. 2011).

[355]See Raytheon Co. v. Continental Cas. Co., 123 F. Supp. 2d 22, 32 (D. Mass. 2000); Steward v. Gwaltney of Smithfield, Ltd., 954 F. Supp. 1118, 1121 (E.D. Va. 1996), aff'd, 103 F.3d 120 (4th Cir. 1996).

[356]See Raytheon Co. v. Continental Cas. Co., 123 F. Supp. 2d 22, 32 (D.

Mass. 2000); Mije Associates v. Halliburton Services, 552 F. Supp. 418 (S.D. N.Y. 1982).

[357]See Sever v. Glickman, 298 F. Supp. 2d 267, 275 (D. Conn. 2004).

[358]See University of Pittsburgh v. Varian Med. Sys., Inc., 569 F.3d 1328, 1332 (Fed.Cir. 2009); Dredge Corp. v. Penny, 338 F.2d 456 (9th Cir.1964); Raytheon Co. v. Continental Cas. Co., 123 F. Supp. 2d 22, 33 n.9 (D. Mass. 2000). See De Wit v. Firstar Corp., 879 F. Supp. 947, 992 (N.D. Iowa 1995) (dismissals with prejudice appropriate only where the court first orders joinder of party and joinder is not accomplished).

[359]See PepsiCo., Inc. v. F. T. C., 472 F.2d 179 (2d Cir. 1972) (noting general principle that denial of any motion to dismiss is not a "final order" is applicable to Rule 12(b)(7) rulings).

by the more prevalent use of pre-answer Rule 12(b) motions to dismiss and post-answer / post-discovery Rule 56 motions for summary judgment.

Purpose

A motion for judgment on the pleadings may be used either to press Rule 12(b) defenses against the pleading's procedural defects or to seek a substantive disposition of the case on the basis of its underlying merits.[360] It remains a pleading attack, and therefore is concerned principally with the adequacy of the allegations it challenges,[361] although the motion, by definition, implicates the pleadings in their entirety.[362]

Legal Test

Because the motion represents a challenge at an embryonic stage in the litigation,[363] the court will construe the pleadings liberally,[364] and will not resolve contested facts.[365] Instead, the court will accept all well-pleaded material allegations of the nonmoving party as true, and view all facts and inferences in a light most favorable to the pleader.[366] A pleading's legal conclusions, however, will not be deemed admitted.[367] Likewise, unwarranted factual inferences will not be drawn to aid the plaintiff,[368] nor need pleaded allegations that undermine plaintiff's claim be ignored.[369]

The courts have articulated three seemingly different formulations for deciding Rule 12(c) motions. One group of courts, declaring Rule 12(b)(6) and Rule 12(c) to be functionally identical, defaults back to the typical Rule 12(b)(6) / *Twombly* search, asking whether the pleaders have "nudged their claims across the line from conceivable to plausible."[370] This *Twombly*

---

[360]*See Alexander v. City of Chicago*, 994 F.2d 333 (7th Cir.1993).

[361]*See Barany-Snyder v. Weiner*, 539 F.3d 327, 332 (6th Cir. 2008).

[362]*See Curran v. Cousins*, 509 F.3d 36, 44 (1st Cir. 2007).

[363]*See Perez-Acevedo v. Rivero-Cubano*, 520 F.3d 26, 29 (1st Cir. 2008).

[364]*See Brittan Commc'ns Int'l Corp. v. Southwestern Bell Tel. Co.*, 313 F.3d 899, 904 (5th Cir. 2002).

[365]*See Aponte-Torres v. University of Puerto Rico*, 445 F.3d 50, 54 (1st Cir. 2006).

[366]*Grajales v. Puerto Rico Ports Auth.*, 682 F.3d 40, 44-45 (1st Cir. 2012); *McGlone v. Bell*, 681 F.3d 718, 728 (6th Cir. 2012); *Morris v. City of Colorado Springs*, 666 F.3d 654, 660 (10th Cir. 2012).

[367]*See Fritz v. Charter Twp. of Comstock*, 592 F.3d 718, 722 (6th Cir. 2010); *Jebaco, Inc. v. Harrah's Operating Co.*, 587 F.3d 314, 318 (5th Cir. 2009). *See also Northern Indiana Gun & Outdoor Shows, Inc. v. City of South Bend*, 163 F.3d 449, 452 (7th Cir. 1998) (commenting that court is not required to ignore facts in complaint that undermine plaintiff's claim or to give weight to unsupported conclusions of law).

[368]*See JPMorgan Chase Bank, N.A. v. Winget*, 510 F.3d 577, 581–82 (6th Cir. 2007).

[369]*See Buchanan-Moore v. County of Milwaukee*, 570 F.3d 824, 827 (7th Cir. 2009).

[370]*See Grajales v. Puerto Rico Ports Auth.*, 682 F.3d 40, 44–45 (1st Cir. 2012); *HDC, LLC v. City of Ann Arbor*, 675 F.3d 608, 611 (6th Cir. 2012).

"plausibility" standard is discussed earlier.[371] A second group of courts applies an inquiry more akin—in language—to the summary judgment test, asking whether there is any material factual dispute and if the movant is entitled to judgment as a matter of law.[372] While this language may be read like Rule 56, the scope of the search is certainly far different; a Rule 12(c) examination is limited to the pleadings and a few other modest categories of extrinsic materials.[373] Finally, a last group of courts fashions a test somewhere in the middle, citing the Rule 12(b)(6) test as governing but then also adding the "no-material-factual-dispute" language as well.[374] Adding to this confusion, one Circuit even appears to straddle the line between different formulations, as different panels cite competing standards.[375]

- *Different Standard With Discovery?:* One court has mused that yet a different test for Rule 12(c) must be appropriate if discovery is already underway or completed by the time of the motion.[376]

- *No Implied "Admissions":* A party who for the purposes of Rule 12(c), presumes all of an opponent's well-pleaded facts as true, is not bound by any "admission" of this kind at trial. The party is free at trial to disprove or contradict the opponent's facts if the Rule 12(c) motion is denied.[377]

Timing

A motion for judgment on the pleadings can be made any time after the pleadings are closed.[378] Such a motion need *not* await discovery.[379] A Rule 12(c) motion is premature if made

---

[371]*See supra* Authors' Commentary to Rule 12(b)(6) ("**Legal Test**" and "**Rule 12(b)(6) After Bell Atlantic v. Twombly**").

[372]*See Sanders v. Mountain Am. Fed. Credit Union*, 689 F.3d 1138, 1140 (10th Cir. 2012); *Knepper v. Rite Aid Corp.*, 675 F.3d 249, 257 (3d Cir. 2012); *Thach v. Tiger Corp.*, 609 F.3d 955, 957 (8th Cir. 2010).

[373]*See* Rule 12(d).

[374]*See McGlone v. Bell*, 681 F.3d 718, 728 (6th Cir. 2012).

[375]*See Harris v. County of Orange*, 682 F.3d 1126, 1131 (9th Cir. 2012) (citing Rule 12(b)(6) test and *Twombly*); *Marshall Naify Revocable Trust v. United States*, 672 F.3d 620, 623 (9th Cir. 2012) (citing "no-material-factual-dispute" test); *Chavez v. United States*, 683 F.3d 1102, 1108 (9th Cir. 2012) (citing both).

[376]*See Grajales v. Puerto Rico Ports Auth.*, 682 F.3d 40, 44–46 (1st Cir. 2012) (musing that it is an "obvious anomaly" to test for plausibility in a pleading (so as to avoid unwarranted, costly discovery) when discovery has occurred).

[377]*See Wyman v. Wyman*, 109 F.2d 473 (C.C.A. 9th Cir. 1940).

[378]*See Buchanan-Moore v. County of Milwaukee*, 570 F.3d 824, 827 (7th Cir. 2009); *Hughes v. Tobacco Institute, Inc.*, 278 F.3d 417, 420 (5th Cir. 2001). *See also Warzon v. Drew*, 60 F.3d 1234, 1237 (7th Cir. 1995) (where answer had already been filed, district court converted defendants' Rule 12(b)(6) motion for dismissal into a Rule 12(c) motion for judgment on the pleadings).

[379]*See Carlson v. Reed*, 249 F.3d 876, 878 n.1 (9th Cir. 2001) (rejecting as "frivolous" an argument that a Rule 12(c) motion was granted prematurely

before an answer is filed.[380] An unlabeled or mislabeled Rule 12(b)(6) motion to dismiss submitted after an answer is filed will be treated as a Rule 12(c) motion.[381] However, a motion filed too long after the pleadings are closed may be refused as untimely.[382] Although filed first, a Rule 12(c) motion need not necessarily be decided before ruling on an also-pending summary judgment motion.[383]

Waiver

A motion for judgment on the pleadings cannot assert defenses and objections that a party has waived by failing to timely assert in a preliminary Rule 12(b) motion or in the responsive pleading.

"Built-In" Defenses

As in Rule 12(b)(6) practice, the court may grant judgment on the pleadings if the allegations themselves (or the content of properly-considered extrinsic materials) reveal an affirmative defense that fatally defeats the pleader's claim.[384] Indeed, some courts hold that "built-in" defenses are only properly raised by Rule 12(c) (or Rule 56) motions, and not under Rule 12(b)(6).[385]

Civil Rights Cases

Several courts view Rule 12(c) motions as "disfavored" in civil rights cases,[386] and hold that such motions should be applied with "particular strictness"[387] and in a manner that tests

---

where discovery had not yet been completed).

[380] *See Doe v. U.S.*, 419 F.3d 1058 (9th Cir. 2005) (premature and should have been denied); *Progressive Cas. Ins. Co. v. Estate of Crone*, 894 F. Supp. 383 (D. Kan. 1995). *But see Resolution Trust Corp. v. Wood*, 870 F. Supp. 797, 804 (W.D. Tenn. 1994) (ruling that, even where pleadings were not yet closed at the time the motions were filed, court would nevertheless consider the pleadings where plaintiff does not object to the motions as premature). However, the courts may agree to choose to treat premature, pre-answer Rule 12(c) motions as motions to dismiss under Rule 12(b)(6). *See also Warzon v. Drew*, 60 F.3d 1234 (7th Cir.1995); *Seber v. Unger*, 881 F. Supp. 323, 325 (N.D. Ill. 1995) (same).

[381] *See Brown v. Montoya*, 662 F.3d 1152, 1160 n.4 (10th Cir. 2011); *McGlone v. Bell*, 681 F.3d 718, 728 n.2 (6th Cir. 2012); *Alioto v. Town of Lisbon*, 651 F.3d 715, 718 (7th Cir. 2011).

[382] *See* Rule 12(c) (motion must be made "[a]fter the pleadings are closed" yet "early enough not to delay trial"). *See General Elec. Co. v. Sargent & Lundy*, 916 F.2d 1119, 1131 (6th Cir. 1990) (reversing "timeliness" denial of Rule 12(c) motion where no allegation of prejudice was pressed and where the basis for any alleged prejudice was not articulated).

[383] *See S.E.C. v. Wolfson*, 539 F.3d 1249, 1264–65 (10th Cir. 2008).

[384] *See Gray v. Evercore Restructuring L.L.C.*, 544 F.3d 320, 324 (1st Cir. 2008). *See also supra* Authors' Commentary to Rule 12(b)(6) ("**Built-In Defenses**").

[385] *See Richards v. Mitcheff*, __ F.3d __, __, 2012 WL 3217627, at *2 (7th Cir. 2012); *Brownmark Films, LLC v. Comedy Partners*, 682 F.3d 687, 690 & n.1 (7th Cir. 2012).

[386] *See McGlone v. Bell*, 681 F.3d 718, 728 (6th Cir. 2012).

[387] *See Cleveland v. Caplaw Enters.*, 448 F.3d 518, 521 (2d Cir. 2006); *Irish*

pleadings under a "very lenient, even de minimis" standard.[388]

Extrinsic Materials

In ruling on a Rule 12(c) motion, the court may consider the pleaded allegations, exhibits attached to the complaint, and matters of public record.[389] If the court, in its discretion, considers (or does not exclude[390]) any other extrinsic evidence presented by the parties on a Rule 12(c) motion, the court must convert the motion into a request for summary judgment under Rule 56.[391] Nonetheless, given the liberality of federal amendments, courts might allow extrinsic materials generated during pre-ruling discovery to fill gaps in a pleading,[392] and may otherwise affirm the use of extrinsic materials in a Rule 12(c) context when doing so is harmless error.[393]

New Factual Allegations Asserted on Appeal

Ordinarily, new arguments and allegations may not be raised on an appeal from a Rule 12(c) ruling unless they had first been made to the trial judge.[394] In very unusual instances, however, new allegations that were not raised below (but are consistent with the pleading) may be heard on appeal.[395]

Remedy

If the Rule 12(c) motion is granted, the prevailing parties obtain a final judgment in their favor.[396]

Prejudice on Dismissal

Granting a Rule 12(c) motion for judgment on the pleadings would terminate the case with prejudice, and courts tend to

---

Lesbian & Gay Organization v. Giuliani, 143 F.3d 638, 644 (2d Cir. 1998).

[388]See Deravin v. Kerik, 335 F.3d 195, 200 (2d Cir. 2003).

[389]See Grajales v. Puerto Rico Ports Auth., 682 F.3d 40, 44–45 (1st Cir. 2012); Barany-Snyder v. Weiner, 539 F.3d 327, 332 (6th Cir. 2008).

[390]There is a division among the Circuits as to when the conversion obligation is triggered. There are three approaches. Some courts require conversion anytime extrinsic evidence is not expressly excluded, others require conversion only if the court "considers" the extrinsic evidence, and still others require conversion only if, after considering the extrinsic evidence, the court chooses to "rely" on it. See Max Arnold & Sons, LLC v. W.L. Hailey & Co., Inc., 452 F.3d 494, 502–03 (6th Cir. 2006) (collecting cases, and electing first approach).

[391]See Rule 12(d). See also North-ville Downs v. Granholm, 622 F.3d 579, 585 (6th Cir. 2010); Cleveland v. Caplaw Enters., 448 F.3d 518, 521 (2d Cir. 2006); McCord v. Horace Mann Ins. Co., 390 F.3d 138, 141–42 (1st Cir. 2004). For a more extensive discussion of this conversion process, see infra Authors' Commentary to Rule 12(d).

[392]See Ideal Steel Supply Corp. v. Anza, 652 F.3d 310, 324–26 (2d Cir. 2011).

[393]See Ginsburg v. InBev NV/SA, 623 F.3d 1229, 1236 (8th Cir. 2010); Northville Downs v. Granholm, 622 F.3d 579, 585 (6th Cir. 2010).

[394]See Alioto v. Town of Lisbon, 615 F.3d 715, 721 (7th Cir. 2011).

[395]See Guise v. BWM Mortg., LLC, 377 F.3d 795, 798 (7th Cir. 2004).

[396]See Republic Steel Corp. v. Pennsylvania Eng'g Corp., 785 F.2d 174, 178 (7th Cir. 1986) (commenting that Rule 12(c) motions are directed towards obtaining final judgments on the merits).

permit leave to amend before final resolution (unless it is clear that no amendment could save the pleading).[397]

Appealability

For the same reasons noted in Rule 12(b)(6)'s discussion of appealability, practitioners must proceed with care in analyzing appeals from Rule 12(c) motions for judgment on the pleadings.[398] Generally, a decision granting such a motion is considered a "final order", and is immediately appealable, but a decision denying such a motion is deemed "interlocutory" and must await a final disposition on the merits.[399]

RULE 12(d)—PRESENTING MATTERS OUTSIDE THE PLEADINGS

CORE CONCEPT

Motions under Rule 12(b)(6) and Rule 12(c) are designed to test the pleadings. Consequently, with a few narrow exceptions, courts may not consider materials outside the pleadings when ruling on these motions. If, in deciding one of these motions, a court is presented with, and does not exclude, matters outside the pleadings, that court must (with a few narrow exceptions) "convert" the motion to one for summary judgment under Rule 56, and then allow the parties a reasonable opportunity to present all materials pertinent to such a motion.

APPLICATIONS

Impact of 2007 "Restyling" Amendments

Rule 12(d) was significantly restructured in 2007. The current content of Rule 12(d) is an amalgam of the closing sentences of former Rules 12(b) and 12(c); the former content of Rule 12(d) is now found in current Rule 12(i). In researching Rule 12(d), practitioners should be mindful of these changes.

Now, A Single Rule for "Conversion"

Before the 2007 "restyling" amendments took effect, the conversion procedure appeared separately in the former closing sentence of Rule 12(b)(6) and again in the former closing sentence of Rule 12(c). A single conversion procedure, now in Rule 12(d), consolidated that language.[400]

---

[397]See *Harris v. County of Orange*, 682 F.3d 1126, 1131 (9th Cir. 2012).

[398]See *supra* Authors' Commentary to Rule 12(b)(6) ("**Appealability**").

[399]See *Paskvan v. City of Cleveland Civil Service Com'n*, 946 F.2d 1233 (6th Cir. 1991). *But see Estate of Drayton v. Nelson*, 53 F.3d 165, 166 (7th Cir. 1994) (holding that order granting judgment on the pleadings was not final, appealable order because the lawsuit remained pending against other defendants).

[400]See *Ashanti v. City of Golden Valley*, 666 F.3d 1148, 1150–51 (8th Cir. 2012) (applies to Rule 12(b)(6) motions); *General Ins. Co. of Am. v. Clark Mall Corp.*, 644 F.3d 375, 378 (7th Cir.

Purpose

Both motions to dismiss and motions for judgment on the pleadings are vehicles to test the adequacy of pleadings. Consequently, expanding the inquiry to include a consideration of materials outside the pleadings would be inconsistent with those Rules' goals.[401]

Mechanics of "Conversion"

When, while considering a Rule 12(b)(6) or 12(c) motion, a court is presented with materials outside the pleadings, and does not exclude them, the court is obligated to "convert" the pleadings challenge into a summary judgment motion.[402] To do so, the court must give all parties notice of the conversion and an opportunity to both be heard and to present further materials in support of their positions on the motion.[403] Following conversion, and upon a proper request by the parties, the court typically ensures that the parties have a reasonable opportunity for discovery prior to ruling on the converted motion.[404] The court then proceeds to evaluate the motion as a request for summary judgment under Rule 56.[405] Conversion ensures that the distinct policies of pleadings challenges (*i.e.*, testing the adequacy of the allegations) and factual challenges (*i.e.*, testing the availability of supporting facts) are respected.[406]

Triggering "Conversion"

The conversion does not occur automatically.[407] The court retains the discretion to ignore the extra-pleading materials and resolve the motion solely on the basis of the pleading itself, in which case no conversion is necessary.[408] In fact, even when the court fails to expressly exclude the extra-pleading materi-

---

2011) (applies to Rule 12(c) motions).

[401] *See Rivera v. Centro Medico de Turabo, Inc.*, 575 F.3d 10, 15 (1st Cir. 2009); *Winget v. JP Morgan Chase Bank, N.A.*, 537 F.3d 565, 576 (6th Cir. 2008).

[402] *See Geinosky v. City of Chicago*, 675 F.3d 743, 745 n.1 (7th Cir. 2012); *Heinrich v. Waiting Angels Adoption Servs., Inc.*, 668 F.3d 393, 405 (6th Cir. 2012); *Ashanti v. City of Golden Valley*, 666 F.3d 1148, 1150–51 (8th Cir. 2012).

[403] *See Josendis v. Wall to Wall Residence Repairs, Inc.*, 662 F.3d 1292, 1296–97 (11th Cir. 2011); *Brooks v. Midwest Heart Group*, 655 F.3d 796, 800–01 (8th Cir. 2011).

[404] *See E.I. du Pont de Nemours & Co. v. Kolon Indus., Inc.*, 637 F.3d 435, 448–49 (4th Cir. 2011).

[405] *See infra* Authors' Commentary to Rule 56.

[406] *See Global Network Commc'ns., Inc. v. City of New York*, 458 F.3d 150 (2d Cir. 2006). *See also id.* (conversion directs "a pretrial motion to the vehicle most appropriate for its resolution, ensuring that the motion is governed by the rule specifically designed for the fair resolution of the parties' competing interests at a particular stage of the litigation.").

[407] *See Swedberg v. Marotzke*, 339 F.3d 1139, 1142–45 (9th Cir. 2003); *Casazza v. Kiser*, 313 F.3d 414, 417–18 (8th Cir. 2002).

[408] *See Heinrich v. Waiting Angels Adoption Servs., Inc.*, 668 F.3d 393, 405 (6th Cir. 2012); *Yakima Valley Mem. Hosp. v. Washington State Dep't of Health*, 654 F.3d 919, 925 n.6 (9th

471

als,[409] a conversion may not be necessary if the materials were, in fact, ignored by the court or otherwise irrelevant to the court's resolution of the motion.[410]

Type of Required Notice of "Conversion"

The required notice of conversion may be either actual or constructive.[411] Actual, formal notice might not be necessary if the non-moving party should have reasonably anticipated the conversion, was not taken by surprise, and was not deprived a reasonable opportunity to respond to the extra-pleading materials.[412] Thus, for example, the non-moving party's act of submitting extra-pleading materials in its own filing may be considered notice enough,[413] as may the act of dual-labeling the motion to dismiss as a motion for summary judgment "in the alternative".[414]

Exceptions to the "Conversion" Requirement

Various exceptions to the conversion procedure have been recognized. First, no conversion is required when the court considers exhibits attached to the complaint (unless their authenticity is questioned);[415] documents that the complaint incorporates by reference or are otherwise integral to the claim (provided they are undisputed);[416] information subject to judicial notice;[417] matters of public record (such as orders and

---

[409]There is a division among the Circuits as to when the conversion obligation is triggered. There are three approaches. Some courts require conversion anytime extrinsic evidence is not expressly excluded, others require conversion only if the court "considers" the extrinsic evidence, and still others require conversion only if, after considering the extrinsic evidence, the court chooses to "rely" on it. *See Max Arnold & Sons, LLC v. W.L. Hailey & Co., Inc.*, 452 F.3d 494, 502–03 (6th Cir. 2006) (collecting cases, and electing first approach).

[410]*See Stahl v. U.S. Dept. of Agriculture*, 327 F.3d 697, 701 (8th Cir. 2003); *Terracom v. Valley Nat. Bank*, 49 F.3d 555 (9th Cir. 1995).

[411]*See Barron ex rel. D.B. v. South Dakota Bd. of Regents*, 655 F.3d 787, 791–92 (8th Cir. 2011).

[412]*See Hernandez v. Coffey*, 582 F.3d 303, 307 (2d Cir. 2009).

[413]*See McCord v. Horace Mann Ins. Co.*, 390 F.3d 138, 141–42 (1st Cir. 2004); *Sira v. Morton*, 380 F.3d 57 (2d

Cir.2004); *Olsen v. Idaho State Bd. of Medicine*, 363 F.3d 916, 921–22 (9th Cir. 2004); *Trustmark Ins. Co. v. ESLU, Inc.*, 299 F.3d 1265, 1267–68 (11th Cir. 2002). *But cf.Sahu v. Union Carbide Corp.*, 548 F.3d 59, 69 (2d Cir. 2008) (noting principle, but finding notice inadequate on facts).

[414]*See Miller v. Herman*, 600 F.3d 726, 733 (7th Cir. 2010); *Riehm v. Engelking*, 538 F.3d 952, 962 n.5 (8th Cir. 2008). *But cf. Sahu v. Union Carbide Corp.*, 548 F.3d 59, 69 (2d Cir. 2008) (noting principle, but finding notice inadequate on facts).

[415]*See Geinosky v. City of Chicago*, 675 F.3d 743, 745 n.1 (7th Cir. 2012); *Rose v. Utah State Bar*, 471 Fed.Appx. 818, 820 (10th Cir. 2012).

[416]*See Geinosky v. City of Chicago*, 675 F.3d 743, 745 n.1 (7th Cir. 2012); *Ashanti v. City of Golden Valley*, 666 F.3d 1148, 1150–51 (8th Cir. 2012).

[417]*See Geinosky v. City of Chicago*, 675 F.3d 743, 745 n.1 (7th Cir. 2012); *Rose v. Utah State Bar*, 471 Fed.Appx. 818, 820 (10th Cir. 2012).

other materials in the record of the case);[418] and concessions by plaintiffs made in their response to the motion.[419] Note, however, that parties cannot escape this conversion rule in a Rule 12(c) context simply by attaching to their answer whatever extrinsic materials might be helpful to their later motion.[420]

Second, no conversion is usually required if only a portion of a document is attached as an exhibit to the complaint, and the moving party submits remaining portions with the motion.[421]

Third, a party may waive any objection to a failure to properly convert by failing to timely contest it.[422]

Fourth, even if not waived, a failure to properly convert may be deemed harmless if the non-moving party had an adequate opportunity to respond and was not otherwise prejudiced.[423]

Notifying *Pro Se* Litigants of Conversion

Because they are unlikely to appreciate the consequence of a conversion to summary judgment procedures, *pro se* litigants will ordinarily be entitled to unequivocal notice of that conversion and its meaning.[424]

RULE 12(e)—MOTION FOR MORE DEFINITE STATEMENT

CORE CONCEPT

If a pleading is so vague or ambiguous that a responsive pleading cannot be prepared, the responding party need not serve a response, but may instead move the court for an order directing the pleader to serve a more definite statement.

APPLICATIONS

Distinct from Rule 12(b)(6) Motions

Motions to dismiss and motions for more definite statements are not interchangeable. A motion to dismiss under Rule 12(b)(6) attacks a pleading for failing to allege a cognizable

---

[418]*See Ennenga v. Starns*, 677 F.3d 766, 773 (7th Cir. 2012).

[419]*See Schatz v. Republican State Leadership Comm.*, 669 F.3d 50, 55–56 (1st Cir. 2012).

[420]*See Horsley v. Feldt*, 304 F.3d 1125, 1134–35 (11th Cir. 2002) ("Otherwise, the conversion clause of Rule 12(c) would be too easily circumvented and disputed documents attached to an answer would have to be taken as true at the pleadings stage. The written instrument provision of Rule 10(c) does not require that.").

[421]*See Cooper v. Pickett*, 137 F.3d 616, 622–23 (9th Cir. 1997); *In re Stac Electronics Securities Litigation*, 89 F.3d 1399, 1405 (9th Cir. 1996).

[422]*See Abner v. Illinois Dep't of Transp.*, 674 F.3d 716, 719 n.1 (7th Cir. 2012).

[423]*See Ashanti v. City of Golden Valley*, 666 F.3d 1148, 1150–51 (8th Cir. 2012); *Atkins v. Salazar*, 677 F.3d 667, 678–81 (5th Cir. 2011); *Edgenet, Inc. v. Home Depot U.S.A., Inc.*, 658 F.3d 662, 664–65 (7th Cir. 2011).

[424]*See Renchenski v. Williams*, 622 F.3d 315, 339–41 (3d Cir. 2010); *Bruce v. Correctional Med. Servs., Inc.*, 389 Fed.Appx. 462, 465 (6th Cir. 2010); *Hernandez v. Coffey*, 582 F.3d 303, 307–08 (2d Cir. 2009).

claim eligible for some type of relief. In contrast, a Rule 12(e) motion for more definite statements attacks pleadings that do, in fact, state cognizable legal claims, yet those pleadings are so unclear that drafting a response to them is impossible.[425] Where the defending party is unable to frame a fair response to a pleading because the pleading's meaning is unclear, the proper remedy is ordinarily not a motion to dismiss but instead a motion for a more definite statement.[426]

- *Mislabeled Motions:* A motion to dismiss under Rule 12(b)(6) that, more correctly, is a motion for a more definite statement may be so converted by the court in its discretion.[427]

- *Filing Both Motions:* A party may file a motion to dismiss and a motion for more definite statement at the same time. In an appropriate case, the court may consider the motion for more definite statement first and hold the motion to dismiss in abeyance.[428]

Disfavored Motion

The Rules require the pleader to serve only a short, plain statement showing an entitlement to relief.[429] Due to these liberal pleading requirements in federal court, motions for a more definite statement are disfavored and granted only sparingly.[430] They are not a substitute for discovery,[431] and ordinarily will not be granted where the level and nature of the detail sought is a proper role for discovery.[432]

---

[425]*See Gregory Village Partners, L.P. v. Chevron U.S.A., Inc.*, 805 F.Supp. 2d 888, 896 (N.D.Cal. 2011); *Country Classics at Morgan Hill Homeowners' Ass'n, Inc. v. Country Classics at Morgan Hill, LLC*, 780 F. Supp. 2d 367, 370–71 (E.D.Pa. 2011).

[426]*See American Nurses' Ass'n v. State of Ill.*, 783 F.2d 716, 725 (7th Cir. 1986). *See also McClellon v. Lone Star Gas Co.*, 66 F.3d 98, 103 (5th Cir. 1995) (vacating court's dismissal of deficient complaint, without first permitting the pleader an opportunity to replead).

[427]*See Carter v. Newland*, 441 F. Supp. 2d 208, 214 (D. Mass. 2006); *Untracht v. Fikri*, 368 F. Supp. 2d 409, 412 n.6 (W.D. Pa. 2005); *Hall v. Tyco Intern. Ltd.*, 223 F.R.D. 219 (M.D. N.C. 2004).

[428]*See Thomas v. Independence Tp.*, 463 F.3d 285, 301 (3d Cir. 2006).

[429]*See Rule 8. See also Natomas Gardens Inv. Group, LLC v. Sinadinos*, 710 F.Supp.2d 1008, 1015 (E.D.Cal. 2010); *Perma-Liner Indus., Inc. v. U.S. Sewer & Drain, Inc.*, 630 F.Supp.2d 516, 526 (E.D.Pa. 2008) (same effect).

[430]*See U.S. E.E.O.C. v. Alia Corp.*, 842 F.Supp.2d 1243, 1250 (E.D.Cal. 2012); *SV Int'l, Inc. v. Fu Jian Quanyu Indus. Co.*, 820 F.Supp.2d 677, 693 (M.D.N.C. 2011); *Defined Space, Inc. v. Lakeshore East, LLC*, 797 F.Supp.2d 896, 903 (N.D.Ill. 2011).

[431]*See Commodity Futures Trading Com'n v. Sterling Trading Group, Inc.*, 605 F.Supp.2d 1245, 1326 (S.D.Fla. 2009).

[432]*See U.S. E.E.O.C. v. Alia Corp.*, 842 F.Supp.2d 1243, 1250 (E.D.Cal. 2012); *Epos Tech. Ltd. v. Pegasus Techs. Ltd.*, 636 F.Supp. 2d 57, 63 (D.D.C. 2009); *Flentye v. Kathrein*, 485 F. Supp. 2d 903, 911 (N.D. Ill. 2007). *See also Cross Timbers Concerned Citizens v. Saginaw*, 991 F. Supp. 563, 572–73 (N.D. Tex. 1997) (quoting Local Rule 12.1, which provides that "[e]xcept for motions complaining of

Legal Test

Motions for a more definite statement will ordinarily only be granted where the pleading is "unintelligible": so hopelessly vague and ambiguous that a defendant cannot fairly be expected to frame a response or denial, at least not without risking prejudice.[433] Such motions are particularly ill-suited to situations where the information sought is already within the defendant's knowledge, and the motion merely seeks a formal particularization of known facts.[434] Nevertheless, courts continue to grant these motions, even though disfavored, where the federal "notice pleading" standards are not met.[435] Just as Rule 12(e) motions are not legitimate substitutes for discovery, discovery is not a fair substitute for proper pleading.[436] Both the court and the litigants are entitled to know, at the pleading stage, who is being sued, why, and for what.[437] Courts have also used Rule 12(e) for various other purposes:

- *Special Pleading Obligations:* The motion may be used to seek facts that must be specially pleaded, such as fraud, mistake, denial of performance or occurrence,

---

failure to plead fraud or mistake with particularity pursuant to Fed.R.Civ.P. 9(b), a motion for more definite statement may only be filed where the information sought cannot be obtained by discovery").

[433]*See U.S. E.E.O.C. v. Alia Corp.*, 842 F.Supp.2d 1243, 1250 (E.D.Cal. 2012); *Premier Payments Online, Inc. v. Payment Sys. Worldwide*, 848 F.Supp.2d 513 (E.D.Pa. 2012); *SV Int'l, Inc. v. Fu Jian Quanyu Indus. Co.*, 820 F.Supp.2d 677, 693 (M.D.N.C. 2011).

[434]*See Babcock & Wilcox Co. v. McGriff, Seibels & Williams, Inc.*, 235 F.R.D. 632, 633 (E.D. La. 2006).

[435]*See Swierkiewicz v. Sorema N. A.*, 534 U.S. 506, 512, 122 S. Ct. 992, 998, 152 L. Ed. 2d 1 (2002) (noting that if pleading "fails to specify the allegations in a manner that provides sufficient notice", defendant can move for more definite statement before responding).

[436]*Cf. Eisenach v. Miller-Dwan Medical Center*, 162 F.R.D. 346, 348 (D. Minn. 1995) ("any current view that the deficiencies in pleading may be cured through liberalized discovery is at increasingly mounting odds with the public's dissatisfaction with exorbitantly expansive discovery, and the

impact that the public outcry has had upon our discovery Rules").

[437]*See McHenry v. Renne*, 84 F.3d 1172, 1179–80 (9th Cir. 1996) (writing that "[p]rolix, confusing complaints such as the ones plaintiffs filed in this case impose unfair burdens on litigants and judges. As a practical matter, the judge and opposing counsel, in order to perform their responsibilities, cannot use a complaint such as the one plaintiffs filed, and must prepare outlines to determine who is being sued for what. Defendants are then put at risk that their outline differs from the judge's, that plaintiffs will surprise them with something new at trial which they reasonably did not understand to be in the case at all, and that res judicata effects of settlement or judgment will be different from what they reasonably expected. . . . The judge wastes half a day in chambers preparing the 'short and plain statement' which Rule 8 obligated plaintiffs to submit. He then must manage the litigation without knowing what claims are made against whom. This leads to discovery disputes and lengthy trials, prejudicing litigants in other case who follow the rules, as well as defendants in the case in which the prolix pleading is filed.").

and special damages.[438]

- *Threshold Defenses:* The motion may also be used where the pleading fails to provide facts necessary to determine whether threshold defenses exist, such as statute of limitations (when claim arose) or statute of frauds (whether contract was written or oral, term for performance).[439]

- *Rule 10 Violations:* The motion is used to seek a re-pleading of a complaint or claim that is confusingly consolidated in a single count (when multiple counts would be proper), fails to properly paragraph, or otherwise violates the presentation dictates of Rule 10.[440]

- *RICO Case Statements*: The motion may also be used to compel the filing of "RICO Case Statements", required in many judicial districts to flesh out the factual predicates and legal theory underlying federal civil racketeering claims.[441] Such Statements have been approved, unless they would obligate the pleader to allege more information than Rule 8(a) and Rule 9(b) would otherwise require.[442]

Burden of Proof

The burden lies with the moving party to demonstrate that the challenged pleading is too vague or ambiguous to permit a response. The moving party must identify the deficiencies in the pleading, list the details sought to be provided, and assert

---

[438]*See* Rule 9. *See also Wagner v. First Horizon Pharmaceutical Corp.*, 464 F.3d 1273, 1280 (11th Cir. 2006).

[439]*See Thomas v. Independence Tp.*, 463 F.3d 285, 289 (3d Cir. 2006) (noting motion's usefulness in immunity cases); *Doe v. Bayer Corp.*, 367 F. Supp. 2d 904, 917 (M.D. N.C. 2005) (courts generally willing to demand more definite statement of dates where they are definite, but not where uncertain or where events occur over periods of time). *See also Rose v. Kinevan*, 115 F.R.D. 250 (D. Colo. 1987).

[440]*See Davis v. Coca-Cola Bottling Co. Consol.*, 516 F.3d 955, 983–84 (11th Cir. 2008).

[441]*See Northland Ins. Co. v. Shell Oil Co.*, 930 F. Supp. 1069, 1074 (D.N.J. 1996). Where claims are asserted under the federal Racketeer Influenced and Corrupt Organizations Act ("RICO"), 18 U.S.C.A. §§ 1961 to 68, many judicial districts now require, by Standing Order, chambers policy, or otherwise, that the pleader answer a series of questions that supplement the RICO allegations of the complaint. *See, e.g.*, S.D. Cal. Rule 11.1; W.D. N.Y. Rule 5.1; *National Organization for Women, Inc. v. Scheidler*, 510 U.S. 249, 249, 114 S. Ct. 798, 800, 127 L. Ed. 2d 99 (1994) (noting local rule in force in Northern District of Illinois); *O'Ferral v. Trebol Motors Corp.*, 45 F.3d 561, 562 (1st Cir. 1995) (same, District of Puerto Rico); *Frank v. D'Ambrosi*, 4 F.3d 1378, 1381 (6th Cir. 1993) (same, Northern District of Ohio); *Boogaerts v. Bank of Bradley*, 961 F.2d 765, 767 (8th Cir. 1992) (same, Western District of Arkansas). This pleading obligation is especially important where the facts noted in the RICO Case Statement are deemed to be pleading averments, properly considered in ruling upon a motion to dismiss. *See Glessner v. Kenny*, 952 F.2d 702, 712 (3d Cir. 1991) (collecting cases so holding).

[442]*See Wagh v. Metris Direct, Inc.*, 363 F.3d 821, 826–28 (9th Cir. 2003).

an inability to frame a response.[443]

Timing

Obviously, a motion for more definite statement must be filed before the party serves a response to the pleading claimed to be too vague or ambiguous.[444] Additionally, the moving party should appreciate the significance of moving for Rule 12(e) relief—once a Rule 12 motion is made, any waivable defense that should have been joined in that Rule 12 motion may be lost.[445] To abate the harshness of this result, the court may permit the moving party to withdraw the Rule 12(e) motion so as to permit a larger Rule 12 filing.[446]

Applies only to Pleadings

By its terms, Rule 12(e) is available to compel more definite statements only in pleadings. It cannot be used to require added detail in motions.[447]

May Be Used By Claimants, Too

When an answer pleads an unintelligible defense, a claimant can use Rule 12(e) to force the repleading of defenses.[448]

Sua Sponte Motions

The district court may, on its own initiative, strike a deficient pleading and direct the pleader to file a more definite statement.[449] This *sua sponte* option is especially valuable to resolve "shotgun pleading" deficiencies,[450] or when a motion to dismiss is pending but the more appropriate relief is re-

---

[443]*See Premier Payments Online, Inc. v. Payment Sys. Worldwide*, 848 F.Supp.2d 513 (E.D.Pa. 2012); *Defined Space, Inc. v. Lakeshore East, LLC*, 797 F.Supp.2d 896, 898 (N.D.Ill. 2011); *Young v. Wells Fargo & Co.*, 671 F.Supp.2d 1006, 1015 (S.D. Iowa 2009).

[444]*See Marx v. Gumbinner*, 855 F.2d 783, 792 (11th Cir. 1988); *U.S. E.E.O.C. v. Alia Corp.*, 842 F.Supp.2d 1243, 1250 (E.D.Cal. 2012). *See generally Santana Products, Inc. v. Sylvester & Associates, Ltd.*, 121 F. Supp. 2d 729, 738 (E.D.N.Y. 1999) (because Rule 12(e) motions must be presented before filing a responsive pleading, defendants' decision to file an answer precluded relief under motion).

[445]*See* Rules 12(g) & 12(h). *See also Caldwell-Baker Co. v. Southern Illinois Railcar Co.*, 225 F. Supp. 2d 1243, 1259, (D. Kan. 2002) (noting substantial number of courts that had ruled that a party moving for more definite statement may not later assert by mo-

tion another Rule 12(b) defense that was then available).

[446]*See Caldwell-Baker Co. v. Southern Illinois Railcar Co.*, 225 F. Supp. 2d 1243, 1259 (D. Kan. 2002) (holding that party's withdrawal of Rule 12(e) motion abated possible waiver of motion to dismiss for lack of personal jurisdiction).

[447]*See Brown v. F.B.I.*, 793 F.Supp. 2d 368, 382 (D.D.C. 2011); *Marcello v. Maine*, 489 F. Supp. 2d 82, 85 (D. Me. 2007).

[448]*See Exhibit Icons, LLC v. XP Cos., LLC*, 609 F.Supp.2d 1282, 1300 (S.D.Fla. 2009).

[449]*See Cesnik v. Edgewood Baptist Church*, 88 F.3d 902, 907 (11th Cir. 1996); *Fikes v. City of Daphne*, 79 F.3d 1079, 1083 (11th Cir. 1996).

[450]*See Wagner v. First Horizon Pharmaceutical Corp.*, 464 F.3d 1273, 1275 (11th Cir. 2006); *Jovine v. Abbott Labs., Inc.*, 795 F. Supp. 2d 1331, 1336 (S.D.Fla. 2011).

pleading with a more definite statement.[451]

Discretion of Trial Court

The decision to grant or deny a motion for a more definite statement is committed to the district court's sound discretion.[452]

Tolling Effect

While the motion is pending, the party's time for serving a responsive pleading is tolled. Once the court rules on the motion, a new (but shortened) response time begins. If the motion is granted, the party must serve a responsive pleading within 14 days after the more definite statement is served or within such other time as the court may direct. If the motion is denied, the party must serve a responsive pleading within 14 days of the court's order.

- ***2009 Amendments Note:*** Effective December 2009, the Rule 12(e) time period was extended from 10 days to 14 days, to conform to the new multiples-of-7-days standard for federal civil time periods.

Remedy

To comply with a Rule 12(e) order for a more definite statement, the pleader must amend the pleading to add sufficient detail to satisfy the court and to meet the adversary's objections.[453] If the pleader fails to serve the more definite statement, or fails to do so within the designated time period, the court may strike the pleading or make such other order as it deems just.[454]

RULE 12(f)—MOTION TO STRIKE

CORE CONCEPT

On its own initiative or upon motion, the court may strike from a pleading any insufficient defense or any redundant, immaterial, impertinent, or scandalous matter.

APPLICATIONS

Purpose

Both insufficient defenses and redundant, immaterial, impertinent, or scandalous matter are properly stricken from a pleading in order to avoid the time, effort, and expense neces-

---

[451]*See Thomas v. Independence Tp.*, 463 F.3d 285, 289 (3d Cir. 2006).

[452]*See Griffin v. Cedar Fair, L.P.*, 817 F.Supp.2d 1152, 1154 (N.D.Cal. 2011); *Holmes v. Fischer*, 764 F.Supp.2d 523, 531–32 (W.D.N.Y. 2011); *Woodard v. FedEx Freight East, Inc.*, 250 F.R.D. 178, 182 (M.D. Pa. 2008).

[453]*See Chennareddy v. Dodaro*, 282 F.R.D. 9, 14 (D.D.C. 2012); *Sefton v. Jew*, 204 F.R.D. 104, 106 (W.D. Tex. 2000).

[454]*See Chennareddy v. Dodaro*, 282 F.R.D. 9, 14 (D.D.C. 2012); *Sefton v. Jew*, 204 F.R.D. 104, 106 (W.D. Tex. 2000).

sary to litigate spurious issues.[455] Such motions may be granted when necessary to clean up the pleadings, streamline the litigation, or sidestep unnecessary efforts on immaterial issues.[456] They are not available to generally cull pleadings of "inappropriately hyperbolic allegations, ill-conceived attempts at levity, and other similar manifestations of bad judgment in drafting".[457]

General Test

Motions to strike are disfavored by the courts,[458] and especially so when they delay the litigation with little corresponding benefit.[459] In considering a motion to strike, courts will generally apply the same test used to determine a Rule 12(b)(6) motion[460]—the courts will deem as admitted all of the non-moving party's well-pleaded facts, draw all reasonable inferences in the pleader's favor, and resolve all doubts in favor of denying the motion to strike.[461] But the court will not accept as true the non-moving party's conclusions of law.[462] If disputed questions of fact or law remain as to the challenged material or defense, the motion to strike must be denied.[463] Likewise, if any doubt remains as to the potential later relevance of the contested allegations, the motion will be denied.[464]

---

[455]See Whittlestone, Inc. v. Handi-Craft Co., 618 F.3d 970, 973 (9th Cir. 2010); Armijo v. Yakima HMA, LLC, __ F. Supp. 2d __, __, 2012 WL 1205867, at 2 n.1 (E.D.Wash. 2012); Scott v. Durham, 772 F.Supp.2d 978, 980 (N.D.Ind. 2011).

[456]See E.E.O.C. v. Product Fabricators, Inc., __ F. Supp. 2d __, __, 2012 WL 2775009, at *1–*2 (D.Minn. 2012); Goode v. LexisNexis Risk & Info. Analytics Group, Inc., __ F. Supp. 2d __, __, 2012 WL 2400883, at *5 (E.D.Pa. 2012); McDowell v. Morgan Stanley & Co., 645 F. Supp. 2d 690, 693 (N.D.Ill. 2009).

[457]See Saylavee LLC v. Hockler, 228 F.R.D. 425, 426 (D. Conn. 2005).

[458]See BJC Health System v. Columbia Cas. Co., 478 F.3d 908 (8th Cir. 2007); Boreri v. Fiat S.p.A., 763 F.2d 17 (1st Cir. 2007); E.E.O.C. v. Joe Ryan Enters., Inc., 281 F.R.D. 660 (M.D.Ala. 2012); Aoki v. Benihana, Inc., 839 F.Supp.2d 759, 764 (D.Del. 2012).

[459]See Rosales v. FitFlop USA, LLC, __ F.Supp.2d __, __, 2012 WL 3224311, at *7 (S.D.Cal. 2012); Deep9 Corp. v. Barnes & Noble, Inc., 772 F.Supp.2d 1349, 1350 (W.D.Wash. 2011); Powell

v. West Asset Mgmt., Inc., 773 F.Supp.2d 761, 763 (N.D.Ill. 2011).

[460]See Johnson Outdoors Inc. v. Navico, Inc., 774 F.Supp.2d 1191, 1195 (M.D.Ala. 2011); Starnes Family Office, LLC v. McCullar, 765 F.Supp.2d 1036, 1047 (W.D.Tenn. 2011); Coach, Inc. v. Kmart Corps., 756 F.Supp.2d 421, 425 (S.D.N.Y. 2010).

[461]See E.E.O.C. v. Product Fabricators, Inc., __ F. Supp. 2d __, __, 2012 WL 2775009, at *1–*2 (D.Minn. 2012); Freeman v. ABC Legal Servs., Inc., __ F. Supp. 2d __, __, 2012 WL 2589965, at *2 (N.D.Cal. 2012); Haley Paint Co. v. E.I. Du Pont De Nemours & Co., 279 F.R.D. 331, 335–36 (D.Md. 2012).

[462]See U.S. v. Rohm and Haas Co., 939 F. Supp. 1142, 1151 (D.N.J. 1996).

[463]See Riemer v. Chase Bank, N.A., 275 F.R.D. 492, 494 (N.D.Ill. 2011); Dann v. Lincoln Nat'l Corp., 274 F.R.D. 139, 143 (E.D.Pa. 2011); Robinson v. Managed Accounts Receivables Corp., 654 F. Supp. 2d 1051, 1064–65 (C.D.Cal. 2009).

[464]See Beatie and Osborn LLP v. Patriot Scientific Corp., 431 F. Supp. 2d 367, 398 (S.D. N.Y. 2006); Montecino v. Spherion Corp., 427 F. Supp.

Burden of Proof

The burden lies with the party moving to strike.[465] Given the disfavored nature of the relief, the burden on the moving party is "formidable".[466] The moving party must state the basis for the motion with particularity and identify specifically the relief sought.[467] The moving party must generally make at least two showings: first, the challenged allegations must be clearly unrelated to the pleader's claims,[468] *and*, second, the moving party must be prejudiced by permitting those allegations to remain in the pleading.[469] This prejudice requirement remains controversial among the courts. Rule 12(f) does not, by its terms, require any showing of prejudice, and for this reason some courts have refused to impose that obligation on the movant.[470] A great many other courts, however, test for prejudice, citing the disfavor with which Rule 12(f) relief is viewed as support.[471] If considered in ruling on the motion, the requisite prejudice will exist when the contested allegation would confuse the issues or, by its length and complexity, would place an undue burden on the respondent, inject the possibility of unnecessarily extensive and burdensome discovery, improperly increase the time, expense, and complexity of the trial, or

2d 965, 966–67 (C.D. Cal. 2006).

[465] *See Bond v. U.S. Dep't of Justice*, 828 F.Supp.2d 60, 71–72 (D.D.C. 2011); *Haught v. The Louis Berkman, LLC*, 377 F. Supp. 2d 543 (N.D. W. Va. 2005); *Canadian St. Regis Band of Mohawk Indians ex rel. Francis v. New York*, 278 F. Supp. 2d 313, 325 (N.D. N.Y. 2003).

[466] *See U.S. ex rel. Pogue v. Diabetes Treatment Centers of America*, 474 F. Supp. 2d 75, 79 (D.D.C. 2007).

[467] *See Anderson v. Davis Polk & Wardwell LLP*, 850 F.Supp.2d 392, 409 (S.D.N.Y. 2012); *Credit General Ins. Co. v. Midwest Indem. Corp.*, 916 F. Supp. 766, 771 (N.D. Ill. 1996).

[468] *See Goode v. LexisNexis Risk & Info. Analytics Group, Inc.*, __ F. Supp. 2d __, __, 2012 WL 2400883, at *5 (E.D.Pa. 2012); *Loucks v. Shorest, LLC*, __ F. Supp. 2d __, __, 2012 WL 2126956, at *1 (M.D.Ala. 2012); *Rosales v. FitFlop USA, LLC*, __ F.Supp.2d __, __, 2012 WL 3224311, at *7 (S.D.Cal. 2012).

[469] *See Aoki v. Benihana, Inc.*, 839 F.Supp.2d 759, 764 (D.Del. 2012); *Olayan v. Holder*, 833 F.Supp.2d 1052,

1059 (S.D.Ind. 2011); *Frank v. Shell Oil Co.*, 828 F.Supp.2d 835, 852 (E.D.La. 2011).

[470] *See Lane v. Page*, 272 F.R.D. 581, 598–600 (D.N.M. 2011) (discussing controversy, listing cases, and refusing to require showing of prejudice).

[471] *See, e.g., Zurich American Ins. Co. v. Watts Regulator Co.*, 796 F.Supp.2d 240, 246 (D.Mass. 2011) (motions rarely granted absent showing of prejudice); *DDR Const. Servs., Inc. v. Siemens Indus., Inc.*, 770 F.Supp.2d 627, 664 (S.D.N.Y. 2011) (must show prejudice to prevail); *F.T.C. v. Cantkier*, 767 F.Supp.2d 147, 159–60 (D.D.C. 2011) (although not required by Rule 12(f), most courts require that challenged material be prejudicial or scandalous); *Dann v. Lincoln Nat'l Corp.*, 274 F.R.D. 139, 142–43 (E.D.Pa. 2011) (not granted absent prejudice or risk of issue confusion); *Shefts v. Petrakis*, 758 F.Supp.2d 620, 635–36 (C.D.Ill. 2010) (courts strike only after movant shows prejudice); *M.D. v. United States*, 745 F.Supp.2d 1274, 1275 (M.D.Fla. 2010) (usually denied unless prejudice shown).

otherwise unduly burden the moving party.[472]

Test For Striking Defenses

A motion to strike is the pleader's parallel to a Rule 12(b)(6) motion to dismiss. The court may strike any defense that is legally insufficient under the controlling substantive law,[473] or that contains matters that would confuse the issues in the case.[474] An insufficient defense is one that fails to meet the federal pleading standards imposed by Rules 8 and 9[475] (as tested under the plausibility inquiry[476]), fails to give fair notice to the opponent,[477] or is otherwise so deficient that no evidence in support of that defense would be admissible at trial.[478] The objective of such strikes is to eliminate irrelevant and frivolous defenses, the trial of which would otherwise unnecessarily waste time and money.[479] For example, a defense that is invalid under the facts alleged, and which would confuse the issues in the case, should be stricken.[480] Thus, to strike a defense, the moving party must show (a) there is no question of fact or law which might allow the challenged defense to succeed, (b) it appears to a certainty that the defense will fail regardless of what evidence is marshalled to support it, and (c) prejudice if the defense remains in the case.[481] In conducting this analysis, the court will construe the pleadings liberally in the favor of

---

[472]*See Coach, Inc. v. Kmart Corps.*, 756 F.Supp.2d 421, 425–26 (S.D.N.Y. 2010); *Hart v. Baca*, 204 F.R.D. 456, 457 (C.D. Cal. 2001).

[473]*See E.E.O.C. v. Product Fabricators, Inc.*, __ F. Supp. 2d __, __, 2012 WL 2775009, at *1–*2 (D.Minn. 2012); *S.E.C. v. Cuban*, 798 F.Supp. 2d 783, 787 (N.D.Tex 2011).

[474]*See Waste Management Holdings, Inc. v. Gilmore*, 252 F.3d 316, 347 (4th Cir. 2001); *Kaiser Aluminum & Chemical Sales, Inc. v. Avondale Shipyards, Inc.*, 677 F.2d 1045 (5th Cir. 1982); *United States v. Honeywell Int'l, Inc.*, 841 F.Supp.2d 112, 113 (D.D.C. 2012).

[475]*See Haley Paint Co. v. E.I. Du Pont De Nemours & Co.*, 279 F.R.D. 331, 335–36 (D.Md. 2012); *Mid-Continent Casualty Co. v. Active Drywall South, Inc.*, 765 F.Supp.2d 1360, 1361 (S.D.Fla. 2011).

[476]*See Mid-Continent Casualty Co. v. Active Drywall South, Inc.*, 765 F.Supp.2d 1360, 1361 (S.D.Fla. 2011).

[477]*See Kohler v. Islands Restaurants, LP*, 280 F.R.D. 560, 564 (S.D.Cal. 2012); *Starnes Family Office,*

LLC v. McCullar, 765 F.Supp.2d 1036, 1047 (W.D.Tenn. 2011); *Coach, Inc. v. Kmart Corps.*, 756 F.Supp.2d 421, 425 (S.D.N.Y. 2010).

[478]*See Openshaw v. Cohen, Klingenstein & Marks, Inc.*, 320 F. Supp. 2d 357, 364 (D. Md. 2004); *Microsoft Corp. v. Jesse's Computers & Repair, Inc.*, 211 F.R.D. 681, 683 (M.D. Fla. 2002).

[479]*See E.E.O.C. v. Bay Ridge Toyota, Inc.*, 327 F. Supp. 2d 167 (E.D. N.Y. 2004); *In re Complaint of J.A.R. Barge Lines, L.P.*, 307 F. Supp. 2d 668, 670 (W.D. Pa. 2004);

[480]*See Allapattah Services, Inc. v. Exxon Corp.*, 372 F. Supp. 2d 1344, 1371 (S.D. Fla. 2005).

[481]*See Coach, Inc. v. Kmart Corps.*, 756 F.Supp.2d 421, 425 (S.D.N.Y. 2010); *UMG Recordings, Inc. v. Lindor*, 531 F. Supp. 2d 453, 458 (E.D. N.Y. 2007). *See also Chao v. Linder*, 421 F. Supp. 2d 1129, 1133 (N.D. Ill. 2006) (to be sufficient, defense must (a) be properly pleaded, (b) comply with Rules 8 and 9, and (c) withstand a Rule 12(b)(6) analysis).

the defendant (the non-moving party).[482] However, the court is not obligated to accept naked, conclusory defenses, and inadequately pleaded defenses may be stricken.[483] Ordinarily, if the motion has merit, the court will strike the insufficient defense in its entirety, and will not attempt to carve the defense in portions.[484] Moreover, if the defense is stricken, the pleader will generally be granted leave to file an amended answer unless the amendment would be futile.[485]

- *Strikes Involving Inference-Drawing*: Defenses will not be stricken on a motion to strike if the court would be required to draw factual inferences or decided disputed questions of fact in a manner that favors the moving party.[486]
- *Strikes Involving Substantial and Disputed Questions:* Motions to strike are generally not intended to resolve substantial and disputed questions of law: legal issues on which courts are divided, confused or unsettled legal areas, or issues involving close or new questions of law.[487]
- *Strikes Involving Admissibility:* Motions to strike are ordinarily improper tools for making anticipatory evidentiary and admissibility judgments.[488]
- *Strikes Before Discovery:* Although motions to strike must generally be filed before a responsive pleading is served, some courts have noted their reluctance to strike defenses where there has been "no significant discovery".[489]

Test For Striking Redundant, Immaterial, Impertinent, or Scandalous Matter

Absent a "strong reason for so doing", courts will generally

---

[482]*See E.E.O.C. v. Product Fabricators, Inc.*, __ F. Supp. 2d __, __, 2012 WL 2775009, at *1–*2 (D.Minn. 2012); *Employers Ins. Co. of Wausau v. Crouse-Community Center, Inc.*, 489 F. Supp. 2d 176, 179 (N.D. N.Y. 2007); *Taylor v. Quall*, 471 F. Supp. 2d 1053, 1058–59 (C.D. Cal. 2007).

[483]*See Fesnak & Assocs., LLP v. U.S. Bank Nat'l Ass'n*, 722 F.Supp.2d 496, 502 (D.Del. 2010); *Sloan Valve Co. v. Zurn Indus., Inc.*, 712 F.Supp.2d 743, 749 (N.D.Ill. 2010).

[484]*See Stowe Woodward, L.L.C. v. Sensor Products, Inc.*, 230 F.R.D. 463, 468–69 (W.D. Va. 2005).

[485]*See U.S. v. Green*, 33 F. Supp. 2d 203, 212 (W.D. N.Y. 1998); *See U.S. v. 416.81 Acres of Land*, 514 F.2d 627 (7th Cir. 1975).

[486]*See Augustus v. Board of Public Instruction of Escambia County, Fla.*, 306 F.2d 862 (5th Cir. 1962); *Ammirati v. Bonati*, 1994 WL 34175 (M.D. Fla. 1994).

[487]*See Wausau Bus. Ins. Co. v. Horizon Admin. Servs. LLC*, 803 F.Supp. 2d 209, 213 (E.D.N.Y. 2011). *See also Canadian St. Regis Band of Mohawk Indians ex rel. Francis v. New York*, 278 F. Supp. 2d 313, 324 (N.D. N.Y. 2003) (noting that, otherwise, courts would risk "offering an advisory opinion on an abstract and hypothetical set of facts").

[488]*See Aoki v. Benihana, Inc.*, 839 F.Supp.2d 759, 764 (D.Del. 2012).

[489]*See Canadian St. Regis Band of Mohawk Indians ex rel. Francis v. New York*, 278 F. Supp. 2d 313, 324–25 (N.D. N.Y. 2003).

"not tamper with pleadings".[490] The court will not strike such matter unless it bears no possible relation to the parties' dispute, or could confuse the issues.[491] Moreover, mere redundancy, immateriality, impertinence, or scandalousness is not sufficient to justify striking an allegation—the allegation must also be shown to be prejudicial to the moving party.[492] If any doubt exists whether the contested matter should be stricken, the motion should be denied.[493] Consequently, to prevail on such a motion, the moving party must establish that: (1) no evidence in support of the contested allegations would be admissible at trial; (2) the allegations have no bearing on the relevant issues in the case; and (3) denying the strike would prejudice the moving party.[494] The court will also be disinclined to strike matter where the case will be tried without a jury.

If granted, the court's order will typically describe in detail the precise matter that must be stricken.[495]

- *Redundant Matter:* A redundant allegation is a needless repetition of other averments.[496]

- *Immaterial Matter:* Immaterial allegations are those

---

[490]*See McCrae Associates, LLC v. Universal Capital Management, Inc.*, 554 F. Supp. 2d 249, 254 (D. Conn. 2008); *Black v. Long Term Disability Ins.*, 373 F. Supp. 2d 897, 904 (E.D. Wis. 2005); *Lazar v. Trans Union LLC*, 195 F.R.D. 665, 668 (C.D. Cal. 2000).

[491]*See Salahuddin v. Cuomo*, 861 F.2d 40, 42 (2d Cir. 1988) (Rule 12(f) reserved for instances where the pleading "is so confused, ambiguous, vague, or otherwise unintelligible that its true substance, if any, is well disguised"); *Lipsky v. Commonwealth United Corp.*, 551 F.2d 887 (2d Cir. 1976); *Walters v. Fidelity Mortg. of Cal.*, 730 F.Supp.2d 1185, 1195–96 (E.D.Cal. 2010); *Lane v. Page*, 727 F.Supp.2d 1214, 1223 (D.N.M. 2010); *Tracfone Wireless, Inc. v. Zip Wireless Prods., Inc.*, 716 F.Supp.2d 1275, 1290 (N.D.Ga. 2010). *Cf. Delaware Health Care, Inc. v. MCD Holding Co.*, 893 F. Supp. 1279, 1291–92 (D. Del. 1995) (allegations that might create better understanding of plaintiff's claims or perform some other useful purpose in the dispute's just disposition will not be stricken).

[492]*See Greenwich Ins. Co. v. Rodgers*, 729 F.Supp.2d 1158, 1162 (C.D.Cal. 2010); *Fesnak & Assocs., LLP v. U.S. Bank Nat'l Ass'n*, 722 F.Supp.2d 496, 502 (D.Del. 2010); *Lane v. Page*, 727 F.Supp.2d 1214, 1223–24

(D.N.M. 2010).

[493]*See Southwestern Bell Telephone, L.P. v. Missouri Public Service Com'n*, 461 F. Supp. 2d 1055, 1064 (E.D. Mo. 2006), aff'd, 530 F.3d 676 (8th Cir. 2008).

[494]*See Lundy v. Town of Brighton*, 521 F. Supp. 2d 259, 265 (W.D. N.Y. 2007).

[495]*See Salahuddin v. Cuomo*, 861 F.2d 40, 43 (2d Cir. 1988) (noting that court would strike only so much of pleading as is redundant or immaterial).

[496]*See Black & Veatch Corp. v. Modesto Irrigation Dist.*, 827 F.Supp.2d 1130, 1136 (E.D.Cal. 2011); *Zurich American Ins. Co. v. Watts Regulator Co.*, 796 F.Supp.2d 240, 246 (D.Mass. 2011); *Germaine Music v. Universal Songs of Polygram*, 275 F. Supp. 2d 1288, 1299 (D. Nev. 2003). *See also Sorosky v. Burroughs Corp.*, 826 F.2d 794, 802 (9th Cir. 1987) (where no arguments were presented in support of theory, it was vulnerable to dismissal as redundant). *But cf. Dethmers Mfg. Co., Inc. v. Automatic Equipment Mfg. Co.*, 23 F. Supp. 2d 974, 1008–09 (N.D. Iowa 1998) (mere duplicative remedies do not necessarily make claims "redundant" if those claims require proof of different elements, but claim that simply recasts same elements under the guise of different the-

that either bear no essential or important relationship to the pleader's claim for relief or contain a statement of unnecessary particulars.[497] Allegations are immaterial if no evidence to support them would be admissible at trial.[498]

- *Impertinent Matter:* An impertinent allegation is an averment that does not pertain to, or is unnecessary to, the issues in dispute.[499] If the pleader would not be permitted to offer evidence at trial in support of the allegation, the allegation is likely impertinent.[500]

- *Scandalous Matter:* Scandalous matter does not merely offend someone's sensibilities; it must improperly cast a person or entity in a derogatory light.[501] Moreover, such matter will not be stricken if it describes acts or events relevant to the parties' dispute, unless the descriptions contain unnecessary detail.[502]

---

ory may be stricken as redundant).

[497]*See Whittlestone, Inc. v. Handi-Craft Co.*, 618 F.3d 970, 974 (9th Cir. 2010); *Aoki v. Benihana, Inc.*, 839 F.Supp.2d 759, 764 (D.Del. 2012); *Anderson v. Davis Polk & Wardwell LLP*, 850 F.Supp.2d 392, 409 (S.D.N.Y. 2012). *See also Bureerong v. Uvawas*, 922 F. Supp. 1450, 1478 (C.D. Cal. 1996) (striking Complaint's reference to "Slave Sweatshop").

[498]*See Holmes v. Fischer*, 764 F.Supp.2d 523, 532 (W.D.N.Y. 2011); *Johnson v. M & M Communications, Inc.*, 242 F.R.D. 187, 189 (D. Conn. 2007).

[499]*See Whittlestone, Inc. v. Handi-Craft Co.*, 618 F.3d 970, 974 (9th Cir. 2010); *Aoki v. Benihana, Inc.*, 839 F.Supp.2d 759, 764 (D.Del. 2012); *Anderson v. Davis Polk & Wardwell LLP*, 850 F.Supp.2d 392, 409 (S.D.N.Y. 2012); *Deep9 Corp. v. Barnes & Noble, Inc.*, 772 F.Supp.2d 1349, 1350 (W.D.Wash. 2011).

[500]*See Fantasy, Inc. v. Fogerty*, 984 F.2d 1524, 1527 (9th Cir. 1993), rev'd on other grounds, 510 U.S. 517, 114 S. Ct. 1023, 127 L. Ed. 2d 455 (1994); *Holmes v. Fischer*, 764 F.Supp.2d 523, 532 (W.D.N.Y. 2011); *Nevada Fair Housing Center, Inc. v. Clark County*, 565 F. Supp. 2d 1178, 1187 (D. Nev. 2008).

[501]*See Aoki v. Benihana, Inc.*, 839 F.Supp.2d 759, 764 (D.Del. 2012). *See,*

e.g., Alvarado-Morales v. Digital Equipment Corp., 843 F.2d 613 (1st Cir. 1988) (striking as "scandalous" references to "concentration camp", "brainwash", and "torture" which impugned the characters of the defendant); *Righthaven LLC v. Democratic Underground, LLC*, 791 F.Supp. 2d 968, 977 (D.Nev. 2011) (casts person in "cruelly derogatory light"); *Florance v. Buchmeyer*, 500 F. Supp. 2d 618, 645 (N.D. Tex. 2007) ("unnecessarily reflect[] on the moral character of an individual or state[] anything in repulsive language that detracts from the dignity of the court"); *Global View Ltd. Venture Capital v. Great Central Basin Exploration, L.L.C.*, 288 F. Supp. 2d 473, 481 (S.D. N.Y. 2003) (it "amounts to nothing more than name calling, and does not contribute to [the] . . . substantive claims"); *Sierra Club v. Tri-State Generation and Transmission Ass'n, Inc.*, 173 F.R.D. 275 (D. Colo. 1997) (degrade the defendants' moral character, contain repulsive language, or detract from the court's dignity).

[502]*See United States v. Coney*, 689 F.3d 365, 379–80 (5th Cir. 2012) (mere risk of offending someone's sensibilities does not justify a strike if pleadings are directly relevant and minimally supported); *Talbot v. Robert Matthews Distributing Co.*, 961 F.2d 654, 664–65 (7th Cir. 1992) (matter is "scandalous" if it bears no possible relation to the controversy); *Begay v.*

Striking Prayers For Relief

The courts are unclear whether Rule 12(f) motions are properly used to strike prayers seeking relief that are precluded as a matter of law. Some courts hold such use improper (reasoning that Rule 12(b)(6) or Rule 12(c) motions are the appropriate vehicles for such a remedy).[503]

Striking Improper Jury Demands

Rule 12(f) is a proper vehicle for striking an improper demand for trial by jury.[504]

Striking Documents Other Than Pleadings

As defined in Rule 12(f), motions to strike are directed to "pleadings" only. Consequently, these motions are technically not available to strike material contained in motions, briefs, memoranda, or affidavits.[505] Some courts, however, have permitted Rule 12(f) motions to strike affidavits and other materials that support pleadings.[506] Of those courts, some reason that Rule 12(f) offers the "only viable method" for challenging the materiality and pertinence of the documents under attack.[507] Others treat this technically improper use of Rule 12(f) as an "invitation" to adjudicate the admissibility of the contested materials.[508] Not all courts, however, will accept these uses of

Public Serv. Co. of N.M., 710 F.Supp.2d 1161, 1185 (D.N.M. 2010) (irrelevant allegations stricken as scandalous if they degrade defendants' moral character, contain repulsive language, or detract from court's dignity; relevant allegations stricken if they contain and go into unnecessary detail); *Consumer Solutions REO, LLC v. Hillery*, 658 F.Supp.2d 1002, 1020–21 (N.D.Cal. 2009) (scandalous matters reflect on moral character or detracts from court's dignity); *Javier H. v. Garcia-Botello*, 239 F.R.D. 342, 350 (W.D.N.Y. 2006) (inclusion of criminal pleas not stricken if factual basis for allegations).

[503] *See Whittlestone, Inc. v. Handi-Craft Co.*, 618 F.3d 970, 974 (9th Cir. 2010).

[504] *See Starnes Family Office, LLC v. McCullar*, 765 F.Supp.2d 1036, 1055 (W.D.Tenn. 2011).

[505] *See Pilgrim v. Trustees of Tufts College*, 118 F.3d 864 (1st Cir.1997) (not for motion papers or supporting affidavits); *Circle Group, L.L.C. v. Southeastern Carpenters Reg'l Council*, 836 F.Supp.2d 1327, 1349 (N.D.Ga.

2011) (not for briefs); *Albertson v. Fremont County*, 834 F.Supp.2d 1117, 1123 n.3 (D.Idaho 2011) (not for affidavits and other exhibits to motion response); *Ely v. Dolgencorp, LLC*, 827 F.Supp.2d 872, 878–79 (E.D.Ark. 2011) (not for motions); *MJ Harbor Hotel, LLC v. McCormick & Schmick Restaurant Corp.*, 599 F.Supp.2d 612, 623 (D.Md. 2009) (not for expert report or testimony); *Dragon v. I.C. System, Inc.*, 241 F.R.D. 424, 425–26 (D. Conn. 2007) (not for summary judgment statements).

[506] *See Kuntzman v. Wal-Mart*, 673 F.Supp.2d 690, 695–96 (N.D.Ind. 2009) (proper to strike inadmissible summary judgment materials). *See also Moret v. Geren*, 494 F. Supp. 2d 329, 336 (D. Md. 2007); *U.S. ex rel. Pogue v. Diabetes Treatment Centers of America*, 474 F. Supp. 2d 75, 79 n.4 (D.D.C. 2007).

[507] *See Judicial Watch, Inc. v. U.S. Dept. of Commerce*, 224 F.R.D. 261, 263 (D.D.C. 2004).

[508] *See Natural Resources Defense Council v. Kempthorne*, 539 F. Supp. 2d 1155, 1161–61 (E.D. Cal. 2008).

the motion.[509] court as an invitation to adjudicate the admissibility of certain material. Note, however, that local rules may permit courts to "strike" a document that violates a properly promulgated local requirement (such as no surreply briefs without prior approval).[510]

Timing

A motion to strike must be made before a responsive pleading is served or, if no responsive pleading is required, within 21 days after service of the preceding pleading.[511] In view of the court's authority to strike on its own initiative, this 21-day period is often not applied strictly when the proposal to strike has merit.[512]

- ***2009 Amendments Note:*** Effective December 2009, the Rule 12(f) time period was extended from 20 days to 21 days, to conform to the new multiples-of-7-days standard for federal civil time periods.

Discretion of Trial Court

The decision to grant or deny a motion to strike is vested in the trial judge's sound discretion.[513]

Sua Sponte Strikes

At any time, the court may, on its own initiative, strike matter from a pleading.[514] Thus, the court may properly consider a party's untimely motion or "suggestion" under Rule 12(f) to strike matter from the pleading.[515]

---

[509]*See Martin v. Town of Westport,* 558 F. Supp. 2d 228, 230–31 (D. Conn. 2008) (recounting, and adopting, view that Rule 12(f) should not be used for documents other than pleadings).

[510]*See Ysais v. New Mexico Jud. Standard Com'n,* 616 F.Supp.2d 1176, 1184 (D.N.M. 2009).

[511]*See U.S. v. $38,000.00 Dollars in U.S. Currency,* 816 F.2d 1538, 1547 (11th Cir. 1987); *Culinary and Service Employees Union, AFL-CIO Local 555 v. Hawaii Employee Ben. Admin., Inc.,* 688 F.2d 1228 (9th Cir. 1982); *Taylor v. Quall,* 471 F. Supp. 2d 1053, 1058–59 (C.D. Cal. 2007). *See also Circuit Systems, Inc. v. Mescalero Sales, Inc.,* 925 F. Supp. 546, 548 (N.D. Ill. 1996) (motion made beyond 20-day period is untimely and subject to denial).

[512]*See Osei v. Countrywide Home Loans,* 692 F.Supp.2d 1240, 1247 (E.D.Cal. 2010); *UMG Recordings, Inc. v. Lindor,* 531 F. Supp. 2d 453, 458 (E.D. N.Y. 2007); *In re Complaint of*

Rationis Enterprises, Inc. of Pananma, 210 F. Supp. 2d 421, 424–25 (S.D. N.Y. 2002).

[513]*See Delta Consulting Group, Inc. v. R. Randle Const., Inc.,* 554 F.3d 1133, 1141 (7th Cir. 2009); *BJC Health System v. Columbia Cas. Co.,* 478 F.3d 908, 917 (8th Cir. 2007); *Aoki v. Benihana, Inc.,* 839 F.Supp.2d 759, 764 (D.Del. 2012); *NCB Mgmt. Servs., Inc. v. F.D.I.C.,* 843 F.Supp.2d 62, 72 (D.D.C. 2012).

[514]*See Delta Consulting Group, Inc. v. R. Randle Const., Inc.,* 554 F.3d 1133, 1141 (7th Cir. 2009); *Kohler v. Islands Restaurants, LP,* 280 F.R.D. 560, 565 (S.D.Cal. 2012); *Thompson v. Hartford Life & Acc. Ins. Co.,* 270 F.R.D. 277, 279 (W.D.Ky. 2010).

[515]*See U.S. v. Lot 65 Pine Meadow,* 976 F.2d 1155, 1157 (8th Cir. 1992); *In re Complaint of Rationis Enterprises, Inc. of Pananma,* 210 F. Supp. 2d 421, 424–25 (S.D. N.Y. 2002).

Extrinsic Materials

Generally, the court will not consider extrinsic materials on a motion to strike.[516] Instead, the grounds supporting the motion to strike must be readily apparent from the face of the pleadings themselves or from materials that may be judicially noticed.[517] If the court does consider extrinsic materials, the motion to strike must ordinarily be converted into a motion for summary judgment.[518]

Converting Mislabeled Rule 12(f) Motions

The appropriate vehicle for testing the factual sufficiency of a pleading is usually not a motion to strike, but a Rule 12(b)(6) motion to dismiss or a Rule 12(c) motion for judgment on the pleadings.[519] Ordinarily, a mislabeled motion to strike that challenges factual sufficiency will simply be treated as a motion to dismiss.[520]

Prejudice on Dismissal

Where an allegation or defense is stricken as technically deficient, the dismissal is generally without prejudice to refile with a technically correct pleading.[521]

RULE 12(g)—JOINING MOTIONS

CORE CONCEPT

If a party chooses to make a motion under Rule 12, the party must include all Rule 12 defenses and objections then available in a single, omnibus motion. Rule 12(g) must be read in conjunction with Rule 12(h), concerning waiver of certain defenses.

---

[516]See Simmons v. Nationwide Mut. Fire Ins. Co., 788 F.Supp.2d 404, 407 (W.D.Pa. 2011); U.S. v. Sensient Colors, Inc., 580 F.Supp.2d 369, 374 (D.N.J. 2008). See also Diamond Scientific Co. v. Ambico, Inc., 848 F.2d 1220, 1226 (Fed. Cir. 1988) (noting that although extrinsic materials are generally not considered on a motion to strike, they may be accepted by the court where they present uncontested factual matters); Oneida Indian Nation of New York v. New York, 194 F. Supp. 2d 104, 117 (N.D. N.Y. 2002). But see Fantasy, Inc. v. Fogerty, 984 F.2d 1524, 1528–29 (9th Cir. 1993), rev'd on other grounds, 510 U.S. 517, 114 S. Ct. 1023, 127 L. Ed. 2d 455 (1994).

[517]See Illinois Nat'l Ins. Co. v. Nordic PCL Const., Inc., __ F. Supp. 2d __, __, 2012 WL 1492399, at *19 (D.Haw. 2012); In re Toyota Motor Corp. Unintended Acceleration Mktg.,

Sales Practices, & Prods. Liab. Litig., 754 F.Supp.2d 1145, 1169 (C.D.Cal. 2010); Coach, Inc. v. Kmart Corps., 756 F.Supp.2d 421, 425 (S.D.N.Y. 2010).

[518]See Liberty Mut. Ins. Co. v. Precision Valve Corp., 402 F. Supp. 2d 481, 484 (S.D. N.Y. 2005).

[519]See U.S. E.E.O.C. v. Global Horizons, Inc., 860 F.Supp.2d 1172, 1181 (D.Haw. 2012) (not proper use of Rule 12(f)).

[520]See Kelley v. Corrections Corp. of America, 750 F.Supp.2d 1132, 1146 (E.D.Cal. 2010).

[521]See Kohler v. Islands Restaurants, LP, 280 F.R.D. 560, 564 (S.D.Cal. 2012); Haley Paint Co. v. E.I. Du Pont De Nemours & Co., 279 F.R.D. 331, 335–36 (D.Md. 2012); Racick v. Dominion Law Assocs., 270 F.R.D. 228, 232 (E.D.N.C. 2010).

APPLICATIONS

Rule and Its Consequences

Any Rule 12 motion may be joined with any other Rule 12 motion.[522] The consequences of making a Rule 12 motion are two-fold. *First*, a party is generally permitted to make only one Rule 12 motion; thus, a party must consolidate all Rule 12 motion claims together, or risk losing the right to have them decided by pre-answer motion later.[523] *Second*, a party waives several Rule 12 defenses (namely, objections to personal jurisdiction, venue, form of process, and service of process) if they are not asserted in any Rule 12 motion that is made.[524] The intent behind these consequences is to avoid piecemeal litigating tactics, where defendants seek dismissal on one ground, lose there, and then seek dismissal anew on a different ground.[525]

Exception—Prohibition Applies Only to Defenses "Then Available"

A party is required to assert in an omnibus motion only those defenses and objections "then available" to that party.[526] Thus, new defenses and objections may be later asserted if they are triggered by an amended pleading or a more definite statement,[527] by a change in the law occurring while the motion is pending,[528] or by other interim developments.[529] But parties must act promptly. An unnecessarily lengthy delay in asserting a latent Rule 12 objection may, itself, be deemed a waiver.[530]

---

[522]*See* Rule 12(g)(1).

[523]*See* Rule 12(g)(2). *See McCurdy v. American Bd. of Plastic Surgery*, 157 F.3d 191, 194 (3d Cir. 1998). *See also Skrtich v. Thornton*, 280 F.3d 1295, 1306 (11th Cir.2002) (affirming dismissal of untimely asserted qualified immunity defense because Rule 12(g) prohibits party from filing a second pre-answer motion to dismiss raising omitted defense that could have been presented in earlier motion).

[524]*See* Rule 12(h)(1). *See also Crispin-Taveras v. Municipality of Carolina*, 647 F.3d 1, 6–7 (1st Cir. 2011) (objection to manner of service waived when party earlier objected only to service timeliness); *Pusey v. Dallas Corp.*, 938 F.2d 498, 501 n.4 (4th Cir.1991) (trial court *prohibited* from dismissing on basis of waived defense).

[525]*See Ennenga v. Starns*, 677 F.3d 766, 773 (7th Cir. 2012).

[526]*See Nattah v. Bush*, 770 F.Supp.2d 193, 201 (D.D.C. 2011).

[527]*See McCurdy v. American Bd. of Plastic Surgery*, 157 F.3d 191, 196 (3d Cir. 1998); *Glater v. Eli Lilly & Co.*, 712 F.2d 735, 738–39 (1st Cir. 1983); *Chatman-Bey v. Thornburgh*, 864 F.2d 804 (D.C. Cir. 1988).

[528]*See Holzsager v. Valley Hospital*, 646 F.2d 792, 796 (2d Cir. 1981) (courts will not demand clairvoyance from litigants; parties not deemed to have waived defenses or objections not then known to them); *Engel v. CBS, Inc.*, 886 F. Supp. 728, 728–730 (C.D. Cal. 1995) (holding that Rule 12(g) will not fault defendants for failing to press a defense they did not then know was available to them).

[529]*See Shropshire v. Canning*, 2012 WL 13658, at *4 (N.D.Cal. Jan. 4, 2012).

[530]*See Overseas Partners, Inc. v. PROGEN Musavirlik ve Yonetim Hizmetleri, Ltd. Sikerti*, 15 F. Supp. 2d 47 (D.D.C. 1998) (holding that, al-

Exception—Prior Motions to Stay/Dismiss/Abstain

Some courts have ruled that this preclusion of successive Rule 12 motions to dismiss will not apply where the preceding motion to dismiss or to stay was based on an alleged lack of federal jurisdiction under some abstention principle.[531]

Exception—No Unnecessary Delay

Even where other exceptions do not apply, the prohibition on successive Rule 12 motions is not absolute. Some courts have permitted a second motion where it would not result in unnecessary delay, expense, or inconvenience and would promote a more expeditious resolution of the case.[532]

Exception—Objections to Subject Matter Jurisdiction

Objections to subject matter jurisdiction concern the court's authority to hear and decide the case. Consequently, such objections cannot generally be lost through waiver.[533]

"Amending" a Rule 12 Motion

To avoid waiving Rule 12 defenses that were omitted inadvertently from a Rule 12 motion, parties may seek leave of court to "amend" or supplement their Rule 12 motions to include the omitted defenses or objections.[534] In considering such amendments, the court may examine whether the amendment request was filed before the Rule 12 motion was heard, the time interval between the original Rule 12 motion and the attempted correction, the moving party's good faith, and the likelihood that the omission was intentional and tactical, or merely inadvertent.[535]

Applies Only to Rule 12 Motions

This omnibus "consolidation" provision applies only to Rule 12 motions and only to defenses that may be asserted under

---

though service objections were not "available" at the time a first motion to dismiss was filed, litigants delayed in raising the new defense and this failure to promptly amend the motion constituted a waiver of the defense).

[531]See Aetna Life Ins. Co. v. Alla Medical Services, Inc., 855 F.2d 1470, 1475 (9th Cir. 1988); Ciolli v. Iravani, 625 F.Supp.2d 276, 290 n.7 (E.D.Pa. 2009); Bacardi, U.S.A., Inc. v. Premier Beverage, Inc., 352 F. Supp. 2d 1188, 1194 (D. Kan. 2005).

[532]See Clark St. Wine & Spirits v. Emporos Sys. Corp., 754 F.Supp.2d 474, 480 (E.D.N.Y. 2010); Lindsey v. U.S., 448 F. Supp. 2d 37, 55-57 (D.D.C. 2006); Stoffels ex rel., SBC Concession Plan v. SBC Communications, Inc., 430 F. Supp. 2d 642, 646–50 (W.D. Tex. 2006).

[533]See Rule 12(h)(3). See also Williams v. Roche, 2002 WL 1585568 (E.D. La. 2002).

[534]See Chatman-Bey v. Thornburgh, 864 F.2d 804 (D.C. Cir. 1988); Glater v. Eli Lilly & Co., 712 F.2d 735, 738 (1st Cir. 1983); Gray v. Snow King Resort, Inc., 889 F. Supp. 1473 (D. Wyo. 1995).

[535]See Thomas v. Bank, 2009 WL 481349, at *1 (M.D.Ga. Feb. 25, 2009) (denying amendment sought tactically); Nycal Corp. v. Inoco PLC, 949 F. Supp. 1115, 1119–20 (S.D. N.Y. 1997) (same). See also Maxtena, Inc. v. Marks, 2012 WL 113386, at *11 (D.Md. Jan. 12, 2012) (rejecting, seemingly categorically, such amendments as "an end run around both Rule 12(g)(2) and settled law).

Rule 12. This encompasses not only the Rule 12(b) defenses (*e.g.*, lack of personal jurisdiction, improper venue, improper service), but likely also Rule 12(e) motions for more definite statements and Rule 12(f) motions to strike.[536] but this rule does not apply to motions allowed under other Rules or laws,[537] nor does it apply to affirmative defenses (which remain preserved, even after a Rule 12 motion, if timely asserted in the responsive pleading).[538] Moreover, certain Rule 12 defenses and objections, even though not raised in the Rule 12 motion, are not deemed forever waived.[539]

Successive Rule 12 Motions to Dismiss

The plain language of Rule 12(g) protects the defense of failure to state a claim from the risk of waiver.[540] Some courts have interpreted this language so as to permit multiple, successive pre-answer Rule 12(b)(6) motions (at least where the successive motions are not prejudicing the opponent or adversely impacting efficiency or judicial economy).[541] Other courts have taken the opposite approach, holding that a defen-

---

[536]*See BAC Home Loans Servicing LP v. Fall Oaks Farm LLC*, 848 F.Supp.2d 818, 823–24 (S.D.Ohio 2012); *Lemanski v. Regents of Univ. of Cal.*, 2008 WL 3916021, at *3 & *3 n.1 (2008).

[537]*See Conrad v. Phone Directories Co.*, 585 F.3d 1376, 1383 n.2 (10th Cir. 2009) (not to motion to compel arbitration under FAA); *Yavuz v. 61 MM, Ltd.*, 576 F.3d 1166,1173 (10th Cir. 2009) (not to forum non conveniens motions); *Aetna Life Ins. Co. v. Alla Medical Services, Inc.*, 855 F.2d 1470 (9th Cir. 1988). *See also Wright v. Linebarger Googan Blair & Sampson, LLP*, 782 F. Supp. 2d 593, 614–16 (W.D.Tenn. 2011) (not to motions under Rule 17 challenging real party in interest status); *Dwyer v. Bicoy*, 2008 WL 5381485, at *4 (D.Colo. Dec. 22, 2008) (not to motions to transfer venue); *American Med. Ass'n v. United Healthcare Corp.*, 588 F.Supp.2d 432, 439 (S.D.N.Y. 2008) (not to motions to amend); *Baranof Fisheries Ltd. Partnership v. Elsey*, 1996 WL 467323 (D. Or. 1996) (not to motions for voluntary dismissal).

[538]*See Parker v. U.S.*, 110 F.3d 678, 682 (9th Cir. 1997). *See also Tahoe-Sierra Preservation Council, Inc. v. Tahoe Regional Planning Agency*, 992 F. Supp. 1218, 1225–26 (D. Nev. 1998), *aff'd in part, rev'd in part*, 216 F.3d 764 (9th Cir. 2000), aff'd, 535 U.S. 302,

122 S. Ct. 1465, 152 L. Ed. 2d 517 (2002) (holding that omitting statute of limitations defense from pre-answer motion is not a waiver).

[539]*See* Rule 12(h)(2) (lack of subject matter jurisdiction, failure to state a claim, failure to join an indispensable party, and failure to state a cognizable defense all preserved even if omitted from original Rule 12(b) motion). *See also U.S. ex rel. S. Prawer & Co. v. Verrill & Dana*, 962 F. Supp. 206, 209 (D. Me. 1997) (noting that Rule 12(b)(6) motions are not encompassed in Rule 12(g), and can be considered even after the Rule 12 motion is ruled upon).

[540]*See* Rule 12(g)(2). *See also Ennenga v. Starns*, 677 F.3d 766, 773 (7th Cir. 2012) (confirming that Rule 12(g) does not preclude a new Rule 12(b)(6) argument made in a later motion).

[541]*See MMB Dev't Group, Ltd. v. Westernbank P.R.*, 762 F.Supp.2d 356, 365 (D.P.R. 2010); *F.T.C. v. Innovative Mktg., Inc.*, 654 F.Supp.2d 378, 383–84 (D.Md. 2009); *In re Parmalat Securities Litigation*, 497 F. Supp. 2d 526, 530 (S.D. N.Y. 2007). *See generally Styles v. Triple Crown Publ'ns, LLC*, 2012 WL 1964443, at *3 (D.Md. May 30, 2012) (collecting cases); *Global Healing Ctr., LP v. Powell*, 2012 WL 1709144, at *3–*4 (S.D.Tex. May 15, 2012) (same).

dant is generally precluded from filing successive pre-answer motions to dismiss to raise arguments that the defendant could have raised, but did not, in the first motion.[542] This prohibition ordinarily applies even after an amended complaint is filed; if the basis for the motion to dismiss was available to the defendant at the time of the original complaint, the filing of an amended complaint will not trigger a new opportunity to assert the motion.[543]

Later Rule 12(c) Motion on Same Grounds

Rule 12(g) and Rule 12(h) seem to specifically preserve a party's right to file a pre-answer motion to dismiss for failure to state a claim *and* then, later, assert a failure to state a claim by motion for judgment on the pleadings.[544] Although some courts interpret this preservation broadly to permit such dual motions,[545] others question whether a party ought to be able to raise in a Rule 12(c) motion for judgment on the pleadings arguments that could have been (or were actually) raised in an earlier Rule 12(b)(6) motion to dismiss.[546]

Effect of Same Counsel for Multiple Defendants

Where the same attorney represents multiple defendants and files a consolidated Rule 12(b) motion jointly on their behalf, there is some uncertainty as to the effect of the attorney's decision to assert certain Rule 12(b) defenses by motion as to some, but not all, defendants. One view, emphasizing the goal of avoiding the dilatory effect of successive Rule 12(b) motions, would preclude a later Rule 12(b) filing by the other

---

[542]*See BAC Home Loans Servicing LP v. Fall Oaks Farm LLC*, 848 F.Supp.2d 818, 823–24 (S.D.Ohio 2012); *Candido v. District of Columbia*, 242 F.R.D. 151 (D.D.C. 2007); *766347 Ontario Ltd. v. Zurich Capital Markets, Inc.*, 274 F. Supp. 2d 926, 930 (N.D. Ill. 2003).

[543]*See Albany Ins. Co. v. Almacenadora Somex, S.A.*, 5 F.3d 907, 909 (5th Cir. 1993); *Gilmore v. Shearson/American Exp. Inc.*, 811 F.2d 108, 112 (2d Cir. 1987); *Pruco Life Ins. Co. v. Wilmington Trust Co.*, 616 F.Supp.2d 210, 214–16 (D.R.I. 2009) ("in law, as in life, do-overs are a rare commodity, and Rule 12 does not provide one here"). *But cf. American Medical Ass'n v. United Healthcare Corp.*, 588 F.Supp. 2d 432 (S.D. N.Y. 2008) (arguments that could have been (but were not) asserted to oppose a motion for leave to amend, were properly asserted on motion to dismiss).

[544]*See* Rule 12(g)(2) (failure to state claim is exception to bar on later motions); Rule 12(h)(2)(B) (permitting failure to state a claim to be raised on later Rule 12(c) motion). *See also Clark St. Wine & Spirits v. Emporos Sys. Corp.*, 754 F.Supp.2d 474, 480 (E.D.N.Y. 2010).

[545]*See Alexander v. City of Greensboro*, 801 F.Supp. 2d 429, 434 (M.D.N.C. 2011) (no Rule 12(c) bar where party could have raised argument during earlier Rule 12(b)(6) motion).

[546]*See Sprint Telephony PCS, L.P. v. County of San Diego*, 311 F. Supp. 2d 898, 904–05 (S.D. Cal. 2004) (although permitting Rule 12(c) motion asserting same arguments raised in earlier Rule 12(b)(6) motion, court noted the "tension" between Rule 12(g)'s consolidation policy and this sort of practice).

defendants.[547] An opposing, more recent, and more authorita-tive (and perhaps better reasoned) view rejects this result, cit-ing the absence of any such consolidated defendant provision in Rule 12(g).[548]

RULE 12(h)—WAIVING AND PRESERVING CERTAIN DEFENSES

CORE CONCEPT

Rule 12(h) sets forth the defenses and objections that are waived if not timely asserted, and lists the defenses and objec-tions that are not waivable.

APPLICATIONS

Basic Rule: Waived Defenses and Objections

Defenses and objections to personal jurisdiction (Rule 12(b)(2)), improper venue (Rule 12(b)(3)), insufficient process (Rule 12(b)(4)), and insufficient service (Rule 12(b)(5)), are waived[549] unless they are *either*:

- *Asserted By Motion*: In an omnibus Rule 12(b) motion, if one is filed, *or*
- *Asserted By Responsive Pleading:* If an omnibus Rule 12(b) motion is not filed.

Purpose

Judicial economy underlies this waiver provision. Automatic waiver is designed to prevent the delaying effect of the piece-meal assertion of Rule 12 objections and defenses through multiple motions, and to permit the early dismissal of inap-propriate claims before the court devotes unnecessary time and resources to adjudication.[550]

Waiver is Mandatory, Not Discretionary

The waiver provision of Rule 12(h) imposes a mandatory, not discretionary, obligation upon the district court.[551]

---

[547]*See Church of Scientology of California v. Linberg*, 529 F. Supp. 945, 966–67 (C.D. Cal. 1981).

[548]*See Schnabel v. Lui*, 302 F.3d 1023, 1034 (9th Cir. 2002).

[549]*See, e.g., Wachovia Bank v. Schmidt*, 546 U.S. 303, 316, 126 S. Ct. 941, 950, 163 L. Ed. 2d 797 (2006) (venue waived if not timely raised); *Ennenga v. Starns*, 677 F.3d 766, 773 (7th Cir. 2012) (untimely raised per-sonal jurisdiction, venue, process, or service objections are waived); *Hawknet, Ltd. v. Overseas Shipping Agencies*, 590 F.3d 87, 91 n.8 (2d Cir.

2009) (personal jurisdiction waived if not timely asserted); *Rates Tech. Inc. v. Nortel Networks Corp.*, 399 F.3d 1302, 1307 (Fed. Cir. 2005) (caution-ing "great diligence" in challenging personal jurisdiction, venue, and ser-vice).

[550]*See Ennenga v. Starns*, 677 F.3d 766, 773 (7th Cir. 2012); *Flory v. U.S.*, 79 F.3d 24, 25 (5th Cir. 1996).

[551]*See Pusey v. Dallas Corp.*, 938 F.2d 498, 501 n.4 (4th Cir.1991) (trial court *prohibited* from dismissing on basis of waived defense); *Polaroid Corp. v. Feely*, 889 F. Supp. 21 (D.

Waiver By Improper Assertion

A Rule 12(h) waivable defense may be lost by asserting it too obscurely or indirectly,[552] by asserting it incompletely,[553] or by asserting it too late in the applicable pleading or motion process.[554]

Waiver By Implication

By the very act of suing, a plaintiff impliedly waives any personal jurisdiction and venue objections.[555] Defendants, too, by their conduct, may impliedly waive objections to personal jurisdiction, venue, insufficient process, or insufficient service of process, even though those defenses were set forth in a timely motion to dismiss or in a responsive pleading. For example, a defendant who timely objects to personal jurisdiction, but then fails to timely bring the defense to the court for a ruling, choosing instead to participate actively in the litigation as though jurisdiction, venue, and proper service existed, may be deemed to have waived the jurisdictional objection.[556]

● *Waiver and Asserting Affirmative Claims:* Although some contrary authority persists,[557] the developing trend seems to suggest that a party does *not* waive a properly, timely asserted objection to jurisdiction by pressing an affirmative claim for relief,[558] or by filing ancillary motions (*e.g.,* for stay or injunction pending appeal) premised on the as-

---

Mass. 1995).

[552]*See, e.g., Hemispherx Biopharma, Inc. v. Johannesburg Consol. Invs.,* 553 F.3d 1351, 1360–61 (11th Cir. 2008) (personal jurisdiction challenge does not imply a companion (but unasserted) service challenge).

[553]*See Crispin-Taveras v. Municipality of Carolina,* 647 F.3d 1, 7 (1st Cir. 2011) (objection to manner of service waived when party earlier objected only to service timeliness).

[554]*See Ramer v. U.S.,* 620 F.Supp.2d 90, 102 (D.D.C. 2009) (defense waived when asserted in motion reply brief, not opening brief).

[555]*See Adam v. Saenger,* 303 U.S. 59, 67–68, 58 S. Ct. 454, 458, 82 L. Ed. 649 (1938).

[556]*see City of New York v. Mickalis Pawn Shop, LLC,* 645 F.3d 114, 134 (2d Cir. 2011); *Blockowicz v. Williams,* 630 F.3d 563, 566 (7th Cir. 2010); *Hamilton v. Atlas Turner, Inc.,* 197 F.3d 58, 62 (2d Cir. 1999). *See also White v. National Football League,* 41 F.3d 402, 407 (8th Cir. 1994). *Cf. Rates Technology Inc. v. Nortel Networks Corp.,* 399 F.3d 1302, 1308–09 (Fed.

Cir. 2005) (noting waiver authority, but finding defendant did not "dally" but moved to dismiss at its "earliest opportunity").

[557]*See Frank's Casing Crew & Rental Tools, Inc. v. PMR Technologies, Ltd.,* 292 F.3d 1363, 1372 (Fed. Cir. 2002) (holding that non-resident defendant in patent noninfringement declaratory judgment action waived personal jurisdiction objection when it filed class action counterclaim asserting unrelated infringements of patent by others).

[558]*See Hillis v. Heineman,* 626 F.3d 1014, 1017–19 (9th Cir. 2010) (filing of counterclaim and third-party complaint did not waive properly pleaded venue or personal jurisdiction defense); *Bayou Steel Corp. v. M/V Amstelvoorn,* 809 F.2d 1147, 1149 (5th Cir.1987) (discussing divergent views, but holding that filing of counterclaim, crossclaim, or third-party claim does not waive properly preserved objection to personal jurisdiction); *Rates Tech. Inc. v. Nortel Networks Corp.,* 399 F.3d 1302, 1307–08 (Fed.Cir. 2005) (same effect, personal jurisdiction).

serted jurisdictional defense.[559] This trend construes such affirmative claims for relief as simply contingent on the court's denial of the party's jurisdictional objections.[560]

Avoiding Waiver By Answering Only (No Motion)

Notwithstanding a language anomaly in Rule 12,[561] parties have the option of asserting their defenses *either* by motion *or* in their responsive pleading.[562] Thus, unless a waiver by implication later occurs (see above), parties who elect not to file a Rule 12 motion at all still dutifully preserve their defenses and objections by asserting them in their responsive pleading.[563]

Avoiding Waiver Through Amendment

A party's failure to assert a timely defense or objection can be cured if the court grants the delinquent party leave to amend the pleading or the Rule 12 motion.[564] Before granting such a waiver-rescuing amendment, the court may examine the timeliness of the amendment request (*e.g.*, if filed before the motion was heard), the time interval between the original filing and the attempted correction, the movant's good faith, and the likelihood the omission was inadvertent rather than intentional and tactical.[565]

Preserved Defenses and Objections

Defenses and objections to a failure to state a claim upon which relief can be granted (Rule 12(b)(6)), failure to join an indispensable party (Rule 12(b)(7)), and failure to state a legal defense (Rule 12(f)) are waived *only* if not asserted before the close of trial.[566] There is also authority for the proposition that the filing of a Rule 12(b)(6) motion on certain grounds will not be deemed a waiver of other grounds not asserted then, but

[559]*See PaineWebber Inc. v. Chase Manhattan Private Bank (Switzerland)*, 260 F.3d 453, 461 (5th Cir. 2001) (defendant who timely and properly asserted personal jurisdiction objection by motion, and engaged in no counterclaim or third-party practice, did not waive defense by filing motion for stay and injunction pending appeal premised on the jurisdictional defense).

[560]*See Bayou Steel Corp. v. M/V Amstelvoorn*, 809 F.2d 1147, 1149 (5th Cir. 1987).

[561]*See Pope v. Elabo GmbH*, 588 F.Supp.2d 1008, 1012–13 (D.Minn. 2008) (noting anomaly).

[562]*See* Rule 12(h)(1)(B).

[563]*See Argentine Republic v. National Grid Plc*, 637 F.3d 365, 367

(D.C.Cir. 2011); *Coons v. Industrial Knife Co.*, 620 F.3d 38, 41 (1st Cir. 2010); *Great Western Mining & Mineral Co. v. Fox Rothschild LLP*, 615 F.3d 159, 173 (3d Cir.2010).

[564]*See* Rule 12(h)(1)(B)(ii); Rule 15. *See also Gray v. Snow King Resort, Inc.*, 889 F. Supp. 1473 (D. Wyo. 1995).

[565]*See Thomas v. Bank*, 2009 WL 481349, at *1 (M.D.Ga. Feb. 25, 2009) (denying amendment sought tactically); *Nycal Corp. v. Inoco PLC*, 949 F. Supp. 1115, 1119–20 (S.D. N.Y. 1997) (same).

[566]*See Arbaugh v. Y&H Corp.*, 546 U.S. 500, 507, 126 S. Ct. 1235, 1236, 163 L. Ed. 2d 1097 (2006); *Ennenga v. Starns*, 677 F.3d 766, 773 (7th Cir. 2012); *Ideal Steel Supply Corp. v. Anza*, 652 F.3d 310, 325 (2d Cir. 2011).

raised later.[567] These defenses, though generally preserved throughout the lawsuit, may not be raised for the first time in post-trial motions or on appeal.[568]

- *Only One Pre-Answer Rule 12(b)(6) Motion:* Although the Rule 12(b)(6) defense of failure to state a claim is generally not waived (so long as it is asserted before the time of trial), some (but not all) courts have ruled that successive, pre-answer Rule 12(b)(6) motions are prohibited by Rule 12(g)'s requirement that all Rule 12 defenses (including failure to state a claim) be raised in a single, omnibus, pre-answer motion—if the party chooses to file a motion at all.[569]

- *Non-Waiver Applies to "Indispensable" Parties Only:* Rule 12(h) preserves only the defense of dismissal for failing to join an "indispensable" party. Where a party is necessary for proper adjudication under Rule 19, but can be joined as a party in the lawsuit, a motion for joinder may not be made if omitted from an omnibus Rule 12 motion or, alternatively, from the responsive pleading.[570]

Objections to Subject Matter Jurisdiction

Because objections to the court's subject matter jurisdiction concern the court's authority to hear and decide the parties' dispute, no one can waive such an objection, be estopped from raising the objection, or cure such a problem by consenting to jurisdiction where none exists.[571]

- *Asserted At Any Time:* Objections to subject matter jurisdiction may be made in the omnibus Rule 12 motion, in the responsive pleading, in subsequent pretrial motions, in a motion for relief from final judgment, or on appeal.[572] There is some authority that this liberality might not be unbounded; one court has ruled that the

---

[567]*See Peltz ex rel. Estate of Peltz v. Sears, Roebuck & Co.*, 367 F. Supp. 2d 711, 721 (E.D. Pa. 2005).

[568]*Brown v. Trustees of Boston University*, 891 F.2d 337 (1st Cir. 1989).

[569]*See supra* Authors' Commentary to Rule 12(g) ("**Successive Rule 12 Motions to Dismiss**").

[570]*See Citibank, N.A. v. Oxford Properties & Finance Ltd.*, 688 F.2d 1259 (9th Cir. 1982).

[571]*See* Rule 12(b)(1)'s *Wachovia Bank v. Schmidt*, 546 U.S. 303, 316, 126 S.Ct. 941, 950, 163 L.Ed.2d 797 (2006) (subject matter jurisdiction must be considered by court, even if parties do not raise it). *See also Ledford*

v. Peeples, 605 F.3d 871, 902 n.85 (11th Cir. 2010); *CNA v. U.S.*, 535 F.3d 132, 145–46 (3d Cir. 2008); *Auster v. Ghana Airways Ltd.*, 514 F.3d 44, 48 (D.C. Cir. 2008). *Cf. Moravian School Advisory Bd. of St. Thomas, V.I. v. Rawlins*, 70 F.3d 270 (3d Cir. 1995) (where district court lacked subject matter jurisdiction to hear the case, it also lacked jurisdiction to transfer it; the only remedy for lack of subject matter jurisdiction is dismissal).

[572]*See Arbaugh v. Y&H Corp.*, 546 U.S. 500, 506, 126 S. Ct. 1235, 1236, 163 L. Ed. 2d 1097 (2006); *Wachovia Bank v. Schmidt*, 546 U.S. 303, 316, 126 S. Ct. 941, 950, 163 L. Ed. 2d 797 (2006).

objection must be made while the case is still pending (*e.g.*, before trial, at trial, or on appeal); it cannot be raised for the first time as a collateral attack on the earlier judgment.[573]

- *"Suggestions":* Although a motion to dismiss for lack of subject matter jurisdiction is technically untimely if filed after the pleadings are closed, the courts will typically treat such a belated motion as a "suggestion" to the court that it lacks subject matter jurisdiction, and will then proceed to consider it on its merits.[574]

- *Raised By Court:* The trial court or the court of appeals may raise an objection to subject matter jurisdiction on its own initiative.[575]

Waiting for Default, Then Collaterally Attacking

Although the Rules require defendants to raise their objections to process, service, and personal jurisdiction in either an omnibus Rule 12 motion or the answer (if no motion is filed), these defenses are not necessarily lost where the defendants neither appear nor defend, but default.[576] In that instance, the constitutional protections of due process should permit those defendants to raise those objections in opposition to the motion for default[577] or collaterally.[578] But defendants act at their peril if they actually receive notice of the pending lawsuit and choose to ignore it, in reliance on their own, untested belief that process, service, or personal jurisdiction was faulty. Minimally, they must guess correctly. If they've guessed wrong, they likely

---

[573]*See City of South Pasadena v. Mineta*, 284 F.3d 1154, 1156–57 (9th Cir. 2002).

[574]*See S.J. v. Hamilton County, Ohio*, 374 F.3d 416, 418 n.1 (6th Cir. 2004).

[575]*See Insurance Corp. of Ireland, Ltd. v. Compagnie des Bauxites de Guinee*, 456 U.S. 694, 704, 102 S. Ct. 2099, 2105, 72 L. Ed. 2d 492 (1982); *Oregon v. Legal Servs. Corp.*, 552 F.3d 965, 969 (9th Cir. 2009); *Craig v. Ontario Corp.*, 543 F.3d 872 (7th Cir. 2008). *See also Ward v. Brown*, 22 F.3d 516 (2d Cir.1994) ("it has been the rule since nearly the inception of our republic that subject matter jurisdiction may be raised any time").

[576]*See Wong v. PartyGaming Ltd.*, 589 F.3d 821, 826 n.3 (6th Cir. 2009) (party does not waive Rule 12(b) defense simply by failing to respond timely). *Cf. In re Teknek, LLC*, 512 F.3d 342, 346 (7th Cir. 2007) (party not properly served who chooses to appear, without raising personal juris-

diction defense, waives it).

[577]*See Stinecipher v. U.S.*, 239 F.R.D. 282, 283 (D.D.C. 2006) (unless proper service is satisfied, court lacks power to assert personal jurisdiction). *See also Trustees of the St. Paul Elec. Const. Industry Fringe Benefit Funds v. Martens Elec. Co.*, 485 F. Supp. 2d 1063, 1065 (D. Minn. 2007) (noting that defendants who are not properly served are protected against default).

[578]*See Insurance Corp. of Ireland, Ltd. v. Compagnie des Bauxites de Guinee*, 456 U.S. 694, 706, 102 S.Ct. 2099, 72 L.Ed.2d 492, 34 Fed.R.Serv.2d 1 (1982) ("A defendant is always free to ignore the judicial proceedings, risk a default judgment, and then challenge that judgment on jurisdictional grounds in a collateral proceeding."); *Baldwin v. Iowa State Traveling Men's Ass'n*, 283 U.S. 522, 525, 51 S.Ct. 517, 75 L.Ed. 1244 (1931) (defendant objecting to personal jurisdiction has "the election not to appear at all," and then to attack collaterally).

forfeit their right to defend on the merits.[579] Conversely, if they timely raise these objections (and thus avoid a default), they have assented to the forum's jurisdiction to determine its own jurisdiction, and are thereby barred from attacking collaterally and, instead, must take any resulting jurisdictional grievance up on a direct appeal.[580]

- *Actual Notice:* Defendants who seek to object on service grounds, but who received actual notice of the lawsuit, may be found to have waived their service objections[581] or to have had those objections otherwise materially compromised.[582]

- *Appearing to Defend Default:* Appearing to participate in proceedings following entry of default will likely waive service and personal jurisdiction objections, unless, upon appearing, the defaulting party promptly asserts them.[583]

- *Appearing and Abandoning:* Likewise, those objections may also be waived if the defendant begins to assert them and then abandons them.[584]

- *Burden of Proof:* In a direct challenge, the party invoking the court's jurisdiction bears the burden of proving it; in a collateral challenge, the party contesting the original court's jurisdiction has the burden of disproving it.[585]

---

[579]*See* Rule 12(h)(1) (if court *has* jurisdiction, failure to properly assert process, service, and personal jurisdiction defense waives them); Rule 8(b)(6) (any allegation not timely denied is admitted, if response was required).

[580]*See Philos Techs., Inc. v. Philos & D, Inc.*, 645 F.3d 851 (7th Cir. 2011).

[581]*See Corestates Leasing, Inc. v. Wright-Way Exp., Inc.*, 190 F.R.D. 356, 358 (E.D. Pa. 2000); *see also O'Meara v. Waters*, 464 F. Supp. 2d 474, 476 (D. Md. 2006) (if defendants receive actual notice, failure to comply strictly with Rule 4 might be excused and service deemed valid). *See also* 5A Charles Alan Wright & Arthur R. Miller, *Federal Practice & Procedure* § 1391, at 755 to 56 (1990) ("But when the party has received actual notice of the suit there is no due process problem in requiring him to object to the ineffective service within the period prescribed by Rule 12(h)(1) and the defense is one that he certainly can

waive if he wishes to do so. This is because the defendant has failed to do what the rule says he must do if he is to avoid a waiver.").

[582]*See Burda Media, Inc. v. Viertel*, 417 F.3d 292 (2d Cir.2005) (ruling that where defaulting defendant had actual knowledge of proceeding, but delayed challenging allegedly improper service of process, that defendant will, in subsequent motion to vacate default, bear burden of proving that contested service did *not* occur).

[583]*See Democratic Republic of Congo v. FG Hemisphere Associates, LLC*, 508 F.3d 1062, 1064–65 (D.C. Cir. 2007).

[584]*See City of New York v. Mickalis Pawn Shop, LLC*, 645 F.3d 114, 134–36 (2d Cir. 2011).

[585]*See Philos Techs., Inc. v. Philos & D, Inc.*, 645 F.3d 851, 856–57 (7th Cir. 2011).

RULE 12(i)—HEARING BEFORE TRIAL

CORE CONCEPT

Unless the court orders that such motions are deferred until trial, the court may, *sua sponte* or upon a party's request, schedule Rule 12(b) and Rule 12(c) motions for a pretrial hearing and resolution.

APPLICATIONS

Impact of 2007 "Restyling" Amendments

Rule 12(i) was repositioned in 2007. The current content of Rule 12(i) was formerly found in Rule 12(d). In researching Rule 12(i), practitioners should be mindful of this change.

Rule 12(b) Defenses Asserted by Motion

When a Rule 12(b) defense or objection is asserted on a Rule 12(b) or Rule 12(c) motion, the moving papers themselves should include a "notice of hearing" or similar references following the practice dictated by the specific judicial district's local rules. As a matter of usual practice, the court will ordinarily resolve Rule 12(b) and Rule 12(c) motions by issuing a pretrial Memorandum and Order.

Rule 12(b) Defenses Asserted by Responsive Pleading

When a Rule 12(b) defense or objection is asserted only in the responsive pleading (*i.e.*, where no pre-answer Rule 12(b) motion for dismissal is filed), a Rule 12(i) application for preliminary hearing is necessary to obtain a pretrial determination from the court on those defenses and objections.[586]

When Pretrial Determinations are Proper

Even in the presence of a genuine factual dispute, the court may nevertheless decide, *pretrial*, challenges affecting subject matter jurisdiction, personal jurisdiction, standing, venue, and certain threshold defenses (like preclusion).[587] Such hearings have also proved useful in assessing pleadings against the new *Twombly* standard.[588] In deciding whether these types of issues should be determined preliminarily (or should, instead, await resolution at trial), the court weighs the need to test these defenses and the litigants' interest in having the objections resolved promptly, against the expense and delay of a preliminary hearing, the court's difficulty in deciding the issues preliminarily, and the likelihood that the issues will become so interconnected with the merits that deferring them until trial

---

[586]*See Rivera-Gomez v. de Castro*, 900 F.2d 1, 2 (1st Cir. 1990) (noting that Rule is "perhaps too infrequently invoked and too often overlooked"; it can, in appropriate instances, "be an excellent device for conserving time, expenses, and scarce judicial resources by targeting early resolution of thresh-old issues").

[587]*See Cameron v. Children's Hosp. Medical Center*, 131 F.3d 1167, 1170 (6th Cir. 1997).

[588]*See Kregler v. City of New York*, 646 F.Supp.2d 570 (S.D.N.Y. 2009), *vacated on other grounds*, 2010 WL 1740806 (2d Cir. May 3, 2010).

would be preferable.[589]

Resolving Personal Jurisdiction Challenges

When the Rule 12(b)(2) defense of lack of personal jurisdiction is raised, the court has three options for resolving the motion:

(1) The court may hear and resolve the motion before trial, by applying the preponderance-of-the-evidence standard;

(2) The court may defer the motion until time of trial, provided the plaintiff has offered a prima facie showing of jurisdiction; or

(3) The court may apply an intermediate scrutiny in circumstances where it would be unfair to require a defendant to incur the expenses and burden of a trial on the merits in view of a substantial jurisdictional question. In those instances, the court will defer the motion until trial only if the plaintiff first demonstrates a likelihood that personal jurisdiction exists over the defendant.[590]

On Motion or *Sua Sponte*

A hearing may be ordered upon a party's request or by the court *sua sponte*.[591]

When Pretrial Determinations are Properly Deferred

This Rule confirms that a district court's *pretrial* review and disposition of Rule 12(b) defenses and Rule 12(c) motions is discretionary, not mandatory. In appropriate cases, involving peculiarly complicated factual and legal issues, or where further factual development is necessary, the court may defer resolving Rule 12(b) defenses until time of trial.[592]

Oral Argument and Hearing

The moving party is generally not *entitled* to oral argument or an evidentiary hearing on the motion; instead, the right of "hearing" is ordinarily satisfied upon permitting a party the opportunity to, in some manner, present its views and arguments to the court.[593] Moreover, the court enjoys discretion on what type of hearing to allow: a hearing only on briefs, an oral argu-

---

[589]*See Cameron v. Children's Hosp. Medical Center*, 131 F.3d 1167, 1170–71 (6th Cir. 1997).

[590]*See Foster-Miller, Inc. v. Babcock & Wilcox Canada*, 46 F.3d 138 (1st Cir.1995); *Boit v. Gar-Tec Products, Inc.*, 967 F.2d 671 (1st Cir. 1992).

[591]*See Beltre v. Lititz Healthcare Staffing Solutions LLC*, 757 F.Supp.2d 373, 376 (S.D.N.Y. 2010).

[592]*See Nissim Corp. v. ClearPlay,*

Inc., 351 F. Supp. 2d 1343, 1346 (S.D. Fla. 2004); *Evello Investments, N.V. v. Printed Media Services, Inc.*, 158 F.R.D. 172, 173 (D. Kan. 1994).

[593]*See Greene v. WCI Holdings Corp.*, 136 F.3d 313, 316 (2d Cir. 1998). *See also In re Eckstein Marine Serv. L.L.C.*, 672 F.3d 310, 319–20 (5th Cir.2012), *petition for cert. filed*, 81 U.S.L.W. 3007 (U.S. June 25, 2012) (Nos. 11-1538 & 11-1253); *Odyssey Marine Exploration, Inc. v. Unidenti-*

ment,[594] or a full evidentiary hearing.[595]

Additional Research References

C.J.S., Federal Civil Procedure § 302, §§ 376 to 409 et seq., §§ 413 to 440 et seq., §§ 796 et seq., §§ 842 et seq.

West's Key Number Digest, Federal Civil Procedure ⚷734 to 735, ⚷941 to 1020, ⚷1031 to 1033, ⚷1041 to 1068, ⚷1101 to 1150, ⚷1721 to 1842

---

fied Shipwrecked Vessel, 657 F.3d 1159, 1170 (11th Cir. 2011).

[594]*See Obert v. Republic Western Ins. Co.*, 398 F.3d 138, 143 (1st Cir. 2005).

[595]*See Kregler v. City of New York*, 646 F.Supp.2d 570, 578 (S.D.N.Y. 2009), *vacated on other grounds*, 2010 WL 1740806 (2d Cir. May 3, 2010).

RULE 13
COUNTERCLAIM AND CROSSCLAIM

(a) Compulsory Counterclaim.

    (1) *In General.* A pleading must state as a counterclaim any claim that—at the time of its service—the pleader has against an opposing party if the claim:

        (A) arises out of the transaction or occurrence that is the subject matter of the opposing party's claim; and

        (B) does not require adding another party over whom the court cannot acquire jurisdiction.

    (2) *Exceptions.* The pleader need not state the claim if:

        (A) when the action was commenced, the claim was the subject of another pending action; or

        (B) the opposing party sued on its claim by attachment or other process that did not establish personal jurisdiction over the pleader on that claim, and the pleader does not assert any counterclaim under this rule

(b) Permissive Counterclaim. A pleading may state as a counterclaim against an opposing party any claim that is not compulsory.

(c) Relief Sought in a Counterclaim. A counterclaim need not diminish or defeat the recovery sought by the opposing party. It may request relief that exceeds in amount or differs in kind from the relief sought by the opposing party.

(d) Counterclaim Against the United States. These rules do not expand the right to assert a counterclaim—or to claim a credit—against the United States or a United States officer or agency.

(e) Counterclaim Maturing or Acquired After Pleading. The court may permit a party to file a supplemental pleading asserting a counterclaim that matured or was acquired by the party after serving an earlier pleading.

(f) [Abrogated]

(g) Crossclaim Against a Coparty. A pleading may state as a crossclaim any claim by one party against a coparty if the claim arises out of the transaction or occurrence that is the subject matter of the original action or of a counter-claim, or if the claim relates to any property that is the subject matter of the original action. The crossclaim may include a claim that the coparty is or may be liable to the crossclaimant for all or part of a claim asserted in the action against the cross-claimant.

(h) Joining Additional Parties. Rules 19 and 20 govern the addition of a person as a party to a counterclaim or crossclaim.

(i) Separate Trials; Separate Judgments. If the court orders separate trials under Rule 42(b), it may enter judgment on a counterclaim or cross-claim under Rule 54(b) when it has jurisdiction to do so, even if the opposing party's claims have been dismissed or otherwise resolved.

[Amended effective March 19, 1948; July 1, 1963; July 1, 1966; August 1, 1987; April 30, 2007, effective December 1, 2007; March 26, 2009, effective December 1, 2009.]

AUTHORS' COMMENTARY ON RULE 13

PURPOSE AND SCOPE

Rule 13 authorizes persons who are already parties to an action to assert counterclaims against an opposing party. The Rule distinguishes between counterclaims that must be raised in pending litigation, and counterclaims that may either be raised in the pending litigation or retained for subsequent litigation.[1] Rule 13 also controls the circumstances in which cross-claims against co-parties—*i.e.*, against persons who are aligned on the same side of the case as the cross-claimant—may be maintained in a pending action.

RULE 13(a)—COMPULSORY COUNTERCLAIM

---

[1] *Cf., Tank Insulation Intern., Inc. v. Insultherm, Inc.*, 104 F.3d 83, 88 (5th Cir. 1997) ("[U]nder rule 13 a counterclaim is either compulsory or permissive—it cannot be both.").

CORE CONCEPT

Subject to some exceptions discussed below, compulsory counterclaims are those counterclaims arising from the same transaction or occurrence that gave rise to the plaintiff's complaint. Such counterclaims are so closely related to claims already raised by a plaintiff that they can be adjudicated in the same action without creating confusion for a trier of fact or undue prejudice to the plaintiff. Consequently, Rule 13(a) generally requires that compulsory counterclaims must be asserted in the pending litigation or they are waived.

APPLICATIONS

Procedure

Compulsory counterclaims are asserted by pleading them in the answer to a complaint or a reply to a previously asserted counterclaim.[2]

Same Transaction or Occurrence

Courts generally agree that this standard for identifying compulsory counterclaims should be construed liberally, so as to further the goal of judicial economy.[3] However, courts differ in the way they actually apply the standard to specific facts. One application holds that the standard should be based on four inquiries: (1) whether the issues of law and fact in the various claims are essentially the same; (2) whether, in the absence of the compulsory counterclaim rule, res judicata would bar a subsequent suit on the counterclaim; (3) whether the same evidence could be used to support or refute the claim and counterclaim; and (4) whether a logical relationship exists between claim and counterclaim.[4] However, this approach does not require that all the questions be answered affirmatively before a counterclaim may be deemed compulsory.[5] Other courts are even more liberal in the way they apply the "same transaction or occurrence" standard, sometimes finding a compulsory counterclaim when there is any significant logical relationship between the plaintiff's claim and the counterclaim.[6] Thus, if a plaintiff sued on a contract, and the defendant had a

---

[2]*See, e.g., Shelter Mut. Ins. Co. v. Public Water Supply Dist. No. 7 of Jefferson County, Mo.*, 747 F.2d 1195 (8th Cir. 1984).

[3]*See, e.g., Transamerica Occidental Life Ins. Co. v. Aviation Office of America, Inc.*, 292 F.3d 384, 390 (3d Cir. 2002) ("[T]he objective of Rule 13(a) is to promote judicial economy, so the term 'transaction or occurrence' is construed generously to further this purpose.").

[4]*See, e.g., Q Intern. Courier Inc.*

v. Smoak, 441 F.3d 214, 219 (4th Cir. 2006) (citing line of cases using this approach). Cf., *Nasalok Coating Corp. v. Nylok Corp.*, 522 F.3d 1320, 1325–26 (Fed. Cir. 2008) (recites three part test, rejecting question of res judicata bar as "circular").

[5]*See, e.g., Painter v. Harvey*, 863 F.2d 329, 331 (4th Cir. 1988) (inquiries are not a "litmus test"; better analogy is to a "guideline").

[6]*See, e.g., Mitchell v. CB Richard Ellis Long Term Disability Plan*, 611

counterclaim resting on an assertion that the contract was a violation of federal antitrust law, the "logical relationship" test would probably treat the counterclaim as compulsory.[7]

Other, less broad, applications of the standard may require substantial overlap in all elements of the claims before a counterclaim is deemed compulsory.[8]

Exceptions to "Same Transaction" Standard

As stated immediately above, a counterclaim is not compulsory unless it arises from the same transaction or occurrence as one of the claims filed by an opposing party. However, the converse—that counterclaims arising from the same transaction or occurrence are compulsory—is not always true. Listed below are the circumstances in which a counterclaim need not be asserted even though it shares the same transaction or occurrence as a claim filed by an opposing party.[9]

(1) *Exception: Immature Claims:* A counterclaim that does not mature until after the party has served a pleading is not a compulsory counterclaim, even if it arises from the same transaction or occurrence as a claim filed by an opposing party.[10] Rule 13(e) provides that such a claim may be asserted as a

---

F.3d 1192 (9th Cir. 2010) (claim by MetLife insurance company that UNUM insurance company was liable for disability benefits of insured was compulsory counterclaim to insured's suit for benefits against MetLife, and so was lost when MetLife failed to file a cross-claim in insured's case); *In re Eldercare Properties, Ltd.*, 568 F.3d 506, 519 (5th Cir. 2009) (requiring only a logical relationship between claim and counterclaim). *See also Ross ex rel. Ross v. Board of Educ. of Tp. High School Dist. 211*, 486 F.3d 279, 284 (7th Cir. 2007) (there is no formalistic test for determining whether suits arise out of the same transaction or occurrence; courts should consider the totality of the claims). *But see, e.g., Nasalok Coating Corp. v. Nylok Corp.*, 522 F.3d 1320, 1326 (Fed. Cir. 2008) (claim of invalidity of patent is not a compulsory counterclaim in an action for infringement, holding "the question is the extent of factual overlap between what the plaintiff *must* establish to prove its claim and what the defendant *must* establish to prove its counterclaim").

[7]*See, e.g., Berrey v. Asarco Inc.*, 439 F.3d 636, 645–46 (10th Cir. 2006) (where Indian tribe sued mining company and others for environmental contamination of tribal lands, counterclaims for common law contribution and indemnity sounded in recoupment and were compulsory counterclaims under Rule 13 (a)).

[8]*See, e.g., In re Pegasus Gold Corp.*, 394 F.3d 1189, 1196 (9th Cir. 2005) (claims shared similar facts, but bankruptcy claim was not barred as a compulsory counterclaim that should have been raised in original proceeding because bankruptcy claim arose subsequent to original proceeding).

[9]*See, e.g., Kane v. Magna Mixer Co.*, 71 F.3d 555, 561–62 (6th Cir. 1995) ("If the claim does arise out of the same transaction or occurrence, it is not a permissive counterclaim, although . . . it may not be required to be asserted.").

[10]*See, e.g., Allan Block Corp. v. County Materials Corp.*, 512 F.3d 912, 920 (7th Cir. 2008) ("Rule 13(a) does not require the defendant to file as a compulsory counterclaim a claim that hasn't accrued yet (case citations omitted) either because it has not yet come into being or, though it has, the plaintiff could not have discovered it."); *In re Kaiser Group Intern. Inc.*, 399 F.3d 558, 568 (3d Cir. 2005) ("maturity" requirement of Rule 13(a) is a separate and additional requirement for

permissive counterclaim by filing a supplemental pleading, as provided by Rule 15(d), or it may be retained for future litigation, at the discretion of the party who holds the claim.

(2) *Exception: Rule 13(a) Inapplicable to Claims Until Service of Pleading:* Even if a counterclaim arises from the same transaction or occurrence as a plaintiff's claim, Rule 13(a) provides that it does not become a compulsory counterclaim until the time when the party holding the counterclaim is required to file a responsive pleading. Thus, if a defendant initially filed a motion to dismiss under Rule 12(b), that rule provides that no pleading need be filed until the court decides the Rule 12(b) motion. If the court granted the motion to dismiss, the defendant never had an obligation to file a responsive pleading. In that circumstance, any claim the defendant had against the plaintiff would not be deemed a compulsory counterclaim, and would be preserved for assertion in subsequent litigation. Similarly, if a plaintiff and defendant settle the plaintiff's claim before expiration of the time in which the defendant must answer, any counterclaim the defendant might have is not compulsory.[11]

(3) *Exception: Lack of Jurisdiction Over Third Parties:* If a counterclaim requires joinder of some additional person not subject to the court's jurisdiction, the counterclaim will not be deemed compulsory, irrespective of the amount of overlap it shares with the plaintiff's claim.[12]

(4) *Exception: Pending Lawsuits:* A counterclaim is not compulsory within the meaning of Rule 13(a) if it has already been sued upon in other litigation. Thus, if one person filed suit in a state court, and the opponent of that claim then sued in federal court, the original state claim would not be a compulsory counterclaim in federal court because it is already the subject of pending litigation.[13]

(5) *Exception: Quasi in Rem/In Rem Jurisdiction:* Where

---

compulsory counterclaims; it exists independently from "same transaction" requirement of Rule 13).

[11]*See, e.g., Bluegrass Hosiery, Inc. v. Speizman Industries, Inc.*, 214 F.3d 770 (6th Cir. 2000) (permitting claims not raised as counterclaims in prior lawsuit in state court; claims not barred as compulsory counterclaims because prior suit was settled before party had a duty to file an answer; "Rule 13(a) . . . only requires a compulsory counterclaim if the party who desires to assert a claim has served a pleading. . . . In other words, Rule 13(a) does not apply unless there has been some form of pleading."); *Carteret Sav. & Loan Ass'n v. Jackson*, 812 F.2d 36,

38 (1st Cir. 1987) (Rule 13(a) does not apply "if a pleading had never been required, as for example, if 'the time of serving, had never been reached.' ").

[12]*See, e.g., Landmark Bank v. Machera*, 736 F. Supp. 375, 379 (D. Mass. 1990) ("Rule 13(a) specifically precludes compulsory counterclaims that require for adjudication the presence of third parties over whom 'the court cannot acquire jurisdiction.' ").

[13]*See, e.g., Canon Latin America, Inc. v. Lantech (CR), S.A.*, 508 F.3d 597, 602 (11th Cir. 2007) (claim which was the subject of a Costa Rican suit pending when district court suit filed was not a compulsory counterclaim); *In re Piper Aircraft Corp.*, 244 F.3d

the plaintiff's complaint rests on the court's quasi in rem or in rem jurisdiction, a counterclaim will not be compulsory,[14] so long as the defendant refrains from raising any counterclaims under Rule 13. If, however, the defendant raises a Rule 13 counterclaim, then all other counterclaims that fall within the same transaction or occurrence as the plaintiff's claim—and not exempted by other exceptions, discussed above—are compulsory counterclaims and must be asserted.

(6) *Exception: Injunction / Declaratory Judgment Actions:* In some circumstances, defendants who have been sued only on equity claims may not be required to assert claims for money damages as counterclaims.[15]

"Opposing Party"

When a party seeks to use Rule 13(a) to bar a claim in a later lawsuit because the claim should have been raised as a compulsory counterclaim against the plaintiff in the original litigation, a question may arise as to the applicability of the Rule when the party seeking to bar the claim shares a close identity with the original plaintiff but is not literally identical to that plaintiff. Precedent on the issue is not plentiful, but in general it appears that the term "opposing party" is read rather broadly. Thus, a party who is sufficiently closely related to a plaintiff who should have been sued on a compulsory counterclaim in previous litigation is entitled to raise Rule 13(a) as a defense when that counterclaim is finally raised in a subsequent lawsuit.[16]

Of course, a party who sues in a representative capacity is

1289, 1296 (11th Cir. 2001) (for a counterclaim to fit within this exception to the compulsory counterclaim requirement "Rule 13(a) literally requires that the [counterclaim] be pending before the other action was commenced"). *See also, U.S. v. Dico, Inc.,* 136 F.3d 572, 577 (8th Cir. 1998) (pending administrative claim is not a compulsory counterclaim; "[Rule 13] does not require that the action be pending before another court, to the exclusion of an administrative tribunal of competent jurisdiction.").

[14]*Baker v. Gold Seal Liquors, Inc.,* 417 U.S. 467, 469, 94 S. Ct. 2504, 2506, 41 L. Ed. 2d 243 (1974) ("The claim is not compulsory . . . if the opposing party brought his suit by attachment or other process not resulting in personal jurisdiction but only in rem or quasi in rem jurisdiction.").

[15]*See, e.g., Allan Block Corp. v. County Materials Corp.,* 512 F.3d 912, 916 (7th Cir. 2008) (declaratory judg-

ment exception to res judicata is consistent with Rule 13 as rule is "in effect a procedural implementation of" the doctrine of res judicata); *Duane Reade, Inc. v. St. Paul Fire and Marine Ins. Co.,* 600 F.3d 190, 197 (2nd Cir. 2010) (where prior actions involved both declaratory relief and breach of contract claims, the declaratory judgment exception to Rule 13 was not available); *U.S. v. Snider,* 779 F.2d 1151, 1156 (6th Cir. 1985) (plaintiff sought only declaratory and injunctive relief; then sought preliminary injunction; court, pursuant to Rule 65, held trial on merits simultaneously with preliminary injunction hearing; held, defendant was not obligated to file counterclaim for money damages).

[16]*See, e.g., Transamerica Occidental Life Ins. Co. v. Aviation Office of America, Inc.,* 292 F.3d 384 (3d Cir. 2002) (successor in interest to party in prior litigation is "opposing party" under Rule 13(a) and therefore can raise bar to claim that should have

not subject to counterclaims against him in his individual capacity.[17]

Subject Matter Jurisdiction

Compulsory counterclaims must satisfy subject matter jurisdiction. They do so by satisfying the requirements of either federal question jurisdiction or diversity jurisdiction, or by qualifying for supplemental jurisdiction. Because compulsory counterclaims must arise from the same transaction or occurrence as the plaintiff's claim, counterclaims that do not qualify for federal question jurisdiction or diversity jurisdiction nevertheless usually meet the requirements for supplemental jurisdiction.[18]

It should be noted that the party asserting a counterclaim must include an allegation of facts demonstrating that the requirement of subject matter jurisdiction is met.[19] Subject matter jurisdiction is discussed elsewhere in this text.

---

been raised as counterclaim against predecessors in previously filed litigation); *Banco Nacional de Cuba v. First Nat. City Bank of New York*, 478 F.2d 191, 193 (2d Cir. 1973) (counterclaim against Republic of Cuba is proper, notwithstanding that named plaintiff is Cuban national bank; held, bank and government are one and the same and thus government is proper "opposing party" within scope of Rule 13(a)).

[17]*See Pioche Mines Consol., Inc. v. Fidelity-Philadelphia Trust Co.*, 206 F.2d 336, 337 (9th Cir. 1953). *Cited in In re Adbox, Inc.*, 488 F.3d 836, 840 (9th Cir. 2007). ("The question presented here, however, is whether the trustee is an 'opposing party' when he has brought a preference action that belongs to the bankruptcy estate and not to the debtor, but the counterclaim alleges causes of action that could have been brought against the debtor prior to its bankruptcy filing. We hold that he is not.")

[18]*Baker v. Gold Seal Liquors, Inc.*, 417 U.S. 467, 94 S. Ct. 2504, 41 L. Ed. 2d 243 (1974). *See, e.g., Barefoot Architect, Inc. v. Bunge*, 632 F.3d 822, 826 (3d Cir. 2011) (compulsory counterclaims erroneously dismissed by district court after grant of summary judgment on original federal claim; despite lack of diversity between parties, court had supplemental jurisdiction over counterclaim where diverse de-

fendants were forced to file their breach of contract claims as compulsory counterclaims); *St. Jude Medical, Inc. v. Lifecare Intern., Inc.*, 250 F.3d 587 (8th Cir. 2001) ("Because [defendant's] claims were compulsory counterclaims, there was supplemental jurisdiction to hear them in federal court."). *See also Columbia Gas Transmission Corp. v. Drain*, 191 F.3d 552, 559 (4th Cir. 1999) (where party raised counterclaims only to comply with Rule 13(a), and otherwise vigorously and successfully challenged district court's subject matter jurisdiction over original complaint, justice requires adherence to counterclaimant's request to dismiss counterclaim without prejudice).

[19]*McNutt v. General Motors Acceptance Corp. of Indiana*, 298 U.S. 178, 189, 56 S. Ct. 780, 785, 80 L. Ed. 1135 (1936) ("[P]rerequisites to the exercise of jurisdiction . . . are conditions which must be met by the party who seeks the exercise of jurisdiction in his favor. He must allege in his pleading the facts essential to show jurisdiction."). *Cf., e.g., Martin v. Franklin Capital Corp.*, 251 F.3d 1284 (10th Cir.2001) (removal case; "As the parties invoking the federal court's jurisdiction in this case, defendants bear the burden of establishing that the requirements for the exercise of diversity jurisdiction are present.").

Personal Jurisdiction Over Plaintiffs

Assertion of a compulsory counterclaim usually involves very few problems with personal jurisdiction over the plaintiff. By instituting an action, a plaintiff is held to have consented to the court's jurisdiction to adjudicate related claims,[20] and by definition, a compulsory counterclaim is closely related to the plaintiff's claim. Consent to personal jurisdiction is discussed at § 2.4.

Venue

Most courts hold that compulsory counterclaims need not satisfy venue requirements.[21]

Failure to Assert a Compulsory Counterclaim

Defendants who do not assert compulsory counterclaims are usually barred from raising the counterclaims in subsequent litigation.[22] The harshness of this result is mitigated by Rule 13(f), authorizing the court to permit amended pleadings that

---

[20]*Adam v. Saenger*, 303 U.S. 59, 58 S. Ct. 454, 82 L. Ed. 649 (1938). *See e.g., Schnabel v. Lui*, 302 F.3d 1023, 1037 (9th Cir. 2002) ("[P]laintiffs who avail themselves of the district court consent to personal jurisdiction" over counterclaims.) *See also In re Charter Oak Associates*, 361 F.3d 760, 768 (2d Cir. 2004) (most circuits agree that state's decision to file bankruptcy claim is waiver of immunity as to compulsory counterclaims).

[21]*See, e.g., Schoot v. U.S.*, 664 F. Supp. 293, 295 (N.D. Ill. 1987) ("[I]n the case of compulsory counterclaims, the venue statutes have been construed to apply only to the original claim, and not to the compulsory counterclaims.").

[22]*Baker v. Gold Seal Liquors, Inc.*, 417 U.S. 467, 469, 94 S. Ct. 2504, 41 L. Ed. 2d 243 (1974) ("A counterclaim which is compulsory but is not brought is thereafter barred."). *See, e.g., Mitchell v. CB Richard Ellis Long Term Disability Plan*, 611 F.3d 1192 (9th Cir. 2010) (claim by MetLife insurance company that UNUM insurance company was liable for disability benefits of insured was compulsory counterclaim to insured's suit for benefits against MetLife, and so was lost when MetLife failed to file a cross-claim in insured's case). *Polymer Industrial Products Co. v. Bridgestone/Firestone, Inc.*, 347 F.3d 935, 938 (Fed. Cir. 2003) ("Rule 13(a) makes [a patent] infringe-

ment counterclaim to a declaratory judgment action for noninfringement compulsory"); *New York Life Ins. Co. v. Deshotel*, 142 F.3d 873, 882 (5th Cir. 1998) ("It is well settled that a failure to plead a compulsory counterclaim bars a party from bringing a later independent action on that claim."). *See also Q Intern. Courier Inc. v. Smoak*, 441 F.3d 214, 220 (4th Cir. 2006) (corporation's action against shareholders following district court judgment in favor of corporation reversed and remanded for district court to decide whether claims constituted compulsory counter-claims under Rule 13(a) in the first action). *But see Handy v. Shaw, Bransford, Veilleux & Roth*, 325 F.3d 346, 350–53 (D.C. Cir. 2003) (practice of barring counterclaim in subsequent litigation "is usually applied in subsequent litigation on res judicata or collateral estoppel principles;" where district court has good subject matter jurisdiction, determination to proceed with claim not raised as counterclaim in previously filed lawsuit is matter of discretion which should take into account value of proceeding with related claims in one case and importance of exercising subject matter jurisdiction when it exists; held, where initial suit in state court had already been dismissed, no substantial proceedings had occurred in state court, and statute of limitations had in the meantime become a bar if instant litigation was dismissed,

include counterclaims, when the court believes such permission serves the interest of justice. Rule 13(a) is also limited by Rule 15(a), which permits a party to amend a pleading once as of right within certain designated time frames. Thus, a party who failed to include a compulsory counterclaim within an initial answer might be able to use Rule 15(a) to amend the answer of right or, if the time in which to amend of right has already passed, to seek leave of opposing counsel or leave of court to amend. However, once judgment is entered on a plaintiff's claim, compulsory counterclaims that were not raised are effectively barred, unless they can fit within the stricter standards of Rule 60(b), governing relief from judgments.

Exception: Class Actions

The normal requirement that a compulsory counterclaim must be timely raised is generally inapplicable to claims held by class action defendants.[23]

Mislabelled Counterclaims

Parties sometimes mistakenly identify counterclaims as cross-claims, and *vice versa*. They may also mislabel a counterclaim as a defense. Courts usually attach no significance to such errors, unless somehow they unfairly prejudice an opposing party.[24]

Statutes of Limitations

Courts are substantially divided as to the effect that a complaint has on statutes of limitations applicable to compulsory counterclaims. Most agree that if the counterclaim was still timely at the time the complaint was filed, the limitation period on the counterclaim is tolled by the filing of the complaint.[25]

RULE 13(b)—PERMISSIVE COUNTERCLAIM

CORE CONCEPT

Permissive counterclaims include those counterclaims that do not arise out of the same transaction or occurrence as the opposing party's claim. Although not stated expressly in Rule 13(b),

---

it is possible that district court should hear claim notwithstanding apparent mandate of Rule 13(a)).

[23]*See, e.g., Allapattah Services, Inc. v. Exxon Corp.*, 333 F.3d 1248 (11th Cir. 2003), aff'd, 545 U.S. 546, 125 S. Ct. 2611, 162 L. Ed. 2d 502 (2005) (normal practice is to wait until liability is established and individual class members file damage claims; at that point setoffs and counterclaims can properly be adjudicated on an individual basis).

[24]*Reiter v. Cooper*, 507 U.S. 258, 262, 113 S. Ct. 1213, 1217, 122 L. Ed.

2d 604 (1993) (holding that counterclaim mislabelled as defense should simply be treated as counterclaim).

[25]*See, e.g., Kirkpatrick v. Lenoir County Bd. of Educ.*, 216 F.3d 380, 388 (4th Cir. 2000) ("Because [plaintiffs] timely filed [their] actions, [defendant's] counterclaim relates back to the date of the original filing. Therefore, the counterclaim was timely regardless of whether the statute of limitations governing the matter was thirty days or three years.").

permissive counterclaims also include counterclaims arising out of the same transaction or occurrence as the opposing party's claims, but which fall within one or more of the exceptions to Rule 13(a) compulsory counterclaims, discussed above. Counterclaims denoted as permissive may be filed in the pending action, but they may also be asserted in a separate action. However, parties often encounter substantially greater difficulties with jurisdiction over permissive counterclaims than they normally encounter with compulsory counterclaims.

APPLICATIONS

Procedure
Permissive counterclaims are filed in answers to complaints or replies to counterclaims.[26]

Different Transaction or Occurrence
The standard for measuring whether a permissive counterclaim arises from a transaction or occurrence dissimilar from that underlying the complaint is the mirror image of the same transaction or occurrence test of compulsory counterclaims. For dissimilarity, courts usually look for the absence of a logical relationship between the complaint and counterclaim.[27] Thus, if a plaintiff sued on a contract, and the defendant had a counterclaim resting on a tort that had allegedly occurred at a different place and time, and had no relationship to the contract claim beyond the happenstance that the parties to both claims were identical, the counterclaim would probably be deemed permissive.

Subject Matter Jurisdiction
Permissive counterclaims must satisfy requirements for subject matter jurisdiction. Subject matter jurisdiction can be satisfied through any of three routes: federal question jurisdiction; diversity jurisdiction; or supplemental jurisdiction. However, as is discussed immediately below, it is uncertain whether supplemental jurisdiction is available in cases involving permissive counterclaims. Jurisdiction is discussed more elsewhere in this text.

(1) *Restrictions on Use of Supplemental Jurisdiction:* Generally, most permissive counterclaims do not arise from the same transaction or occurrence as the claim of the opposing party. Thus there is some question as to whether permissive counterclaims that do not meet the requirements for original subject matter jurisdiction (usually diversity or a federal question) and also do not arise from the same transaction or occurrence as

---

[26]*See, e.g., Shelter Mut. Ins. Co. v. Public Water Supply Dist. No. 7 of Jefferson County, Mo.,* 747 F.2d 1195 (8th Cir. 1984).

[27]*See, e.g., Warshawsky & Co. v.*

Arcata Nat. Corp., 552 F.2d 1257, 1261 (7th Cir. 1977) ("[A] counterclaim that has its roots in a separate transaction or occurrence is permissive.").

the opponent's initial claims may either qualify for supplemental jurisdiction or may nevertheless be heard by a federal district court notwithstanding these deficiencies. The established view is that such permissive counterclaims cannot use supplemental jurisdiction. Therefore a lack of original subject matter jurisdiction would mandate dismissal of the claims.[28] A more recent view, however, is that the established view is either incorrect[29] or, if it was ever correct, enactment of 28 U.S.C.A. § 1367 (governing supplemental jurisdiction) renders it obsolete.[30] Resolution of this question will probably require a decision by the Supreme Court. In the meantime attorneys must consult local precedent. Section 1367 is discussed in greater detail elsewhere in this text.

(2) *Supplemental Jurisdiction: Exceptional Circumstances:* The foregoing discussion of uncertainty about the jurisdictional foundation of permissive counterclaims not arising from the same transaction or occurrence as the opponent's initial claims should not obscure one fact. Permissive counterclaims that arise from the same transaction or occurrence but which are not for some reason compulsory may nevertheless satisfy subject matter jurisdiction through the requirements of federal question jurisdiction, diversity jurisdiction, or supplemental jurisdiction.[31]

It should be noted that the party asserting a permissive counterclaim must include an allegation of facts demonstrating

[28]*See, e.g., Oak Park Trust and Sav. Bank v. Therkildsen*, 209 F.3d 648, 651 (7th Cir. 2000) (counterclaim arose from events unrelated to plaintiff's claim; "a permissive counterclaim . . . is outside the supplemental jurisdiction . . . and requires an independent basis of federal jurisdiction"); *Unique Concepts, Inc. v. Manuel*, 930 F.2d 573, 574 (7th Cir. 1991) (compulsory counterclaims are eligible for supplemental jurisdiction, but permissive counterclaims "require their own jurisdictional basis").

[29]*See, e.g., Jones v. Ford Motor Credit Co.*, 358 F.3d 205, 212–13 (2d Cir. 2004) ("[I]t is no longer sufficient for courts to assert, without any reason other than dicta or even holdings from the era of judge-created ancillary jurisdiction, that permissive counterclaims require independent jurisdiction.").

[30]*See, e.g., Jones v. Ford Motor Credit Co.*, 358 F.3d 205, 213 (2d Cir. 2004) ("We share the view that section

1367 has displaced, rather than codified, whatever validity inhered in the earlier view that a permissive counterclaim requires independent jurisdiction (in the sense of federal question or diversity jurisdiction)."); *Channell v. Citicorp Nat. Services, Inc.*, 89 F.3d 379, 385 (7th Cir. 1996) (holding that § 1367 broadened the power of courts to hear non-diverse permissive counterclaims that are based on state law).

[31]*See, e.g., Leipzig v. AIG Life Ins. Co.*, 362 F.3d 406, 410 (7th Cir. 2004) ("Even a permissive counterclaim, if part of the same case or controversy, . . . may be brought under the supplemental jurisdiction statute, 28 U.S.C. § 1367(a), without an independent basis of jurisdiction."); *Crosby Yacht Yard, Inc. v. Yacht Chardonnay*, 164 F.R.D. 135 (D. Mass. 1996) (permissive counterclaim arising from same case or controversy—but not compulsory for unrelated reasons—may nevertheless satisfy requirements for supplemental jurisdiction).

that the requirement of subject matter jurisdiction is met.[32]

Personal Jurisdiction: Waiver of Defense

The objection to personal jurisdiction is waived where a defendant seeks affirmative relief in the form of a permissive counterclaim. This may be true even where those defenses were set forth in a timely motion to dismiss or in a responsive pleading.[33]

Venue

It is unclear whether permissive counterclaims must satisfy venue requirements.[34]

Failure to Assert a Permissive Counterclaim

No sanction attaches if a party holding a permissive counterclaim chooses not to assert it in pending litigation. The claim is not treated as barred, and may be asserted at a later date.[35]

Mislabelled Counterclaims

Parties sometimes mistakenly identify counterclaims as cross-claims, and *vice versa*. They may also mislabel a counterclaim as a defense. Courts usually attach no significance to such errors, unless somehow they unfairly prejudice an opposing party.[36]

Statutes of Limitations

An opposing party's decision to file a claim does not toll the time in which a permissive counterclaim not arising from the

---

[32]*McNutt v. General Motors Acceptance Corp. of Indiana*, 298 U.S. 178, 189, 56 S. Ct. 780, 785, 80 L. Ed. 1135 (1936) ("[P]rerequisites to the exercise of jurisdiction . . . are conditions which must be met by the party who seeks the exercise of jurisdiction in his favor. He must allege in his pleading the facts essential to show jurisdiction."). *Cf., e.g., Martin v. Franklin Capital Corp.*, 251 F.3d 1284 (10th Cir.2001) (removal case; "As the parties invoking the federal court's jurisdiction in this case, defendants bear the burden of establishing that the requirements for the exercise of diversity jurisdiction are present.").

[33]*See* Author's Commentary to Rule 12 (h), *supra*, "Implied Waiver."

[34]*See, e.g., Hansen v. Shearson/American Exp., Inc.*, 116 F.R.D. 246, 251 (E.D. Pa. 1987) (suggesting that "in some circumstances" permissive counterclaims must satisfy venue requirements; but rejecting challenge to venue in instant case).

[35]*See, e.g., U.S. Philips Corp. v. Sears Roebuck & Co.*, 55 F.3d 592, 599 (Fed. Cir. 1995) (permissive counterclaim not asserted is not thereby barred in subsequent litigation). *But see Capitol Hill Group v. Pillsbury, Winthrop, Shaw, Pittman, LLC*, 569 F.3d 485, 492 (D.C. Cir. 2009) (declining to determine whether claims were permissive or compulsory; holding that "if allowing a permissive counterclaim to go forward would nullify the earlier judgment or impair rights established in the earlier action, even a permissive counterclaim can be barred").

[36]*Reiter v. Cooper*, 507 U.S. 258, 262, 113 S. Ct. 1213, 1217, 122 L. Ed. 2d 604 (1993) (holding that counterclaim mislabelled as defense should simply be treated as counterclaim).

same transaction or occurrence must be filed.[37]

Counterclaims Maturing After Pleading

Rule 13(b) should be read in conjunction with Rule 13(e), which provides that counterclaims maturing or acquired after pleading are permissive counterclaims that may be filed in the pending action, subject to the court's discretion.

Separate Trials

Permissive counterclaims not arising from the same transaction or occurrence as the opposing party's claim may contain substantial potential for confusing the trier of fact or delaying adjudication of the original claims. Thus, Rule 13(i) authorizes the court to order separate proceedings.

RULE 13(c)—RELIEF SOUGHT IN A COUNTERCLAIM

CORE CONCEPT

Rule 13(c) provides that: (1) counterclaims may be for any amount, irrespective of whether the amount sought in the counterclaim exceeds the amount sought in the other party's claim; and (2) counterclaims may seek kinds of relief not sought in the opposing party's claim. For example, if the opposing party's claim sought money damages only, the counterclaim could seek either money damages, equitable relief, or both money damages and equitable relief.

RULE 13(d)—COUNTERCLAIM AGAINST THE UNITED STATES

CORE CONCEPT

As a general rule, the United States and its officers and agencies are immune from suits in federal courts, unless the United States waives that sovereign immunity. Rule 13(d) expressly provides that the counterclaim provisions of Rule 13(a) and (b) do not alter the current law of sovereign immunity.[38]

APPLICATIONS

Waiver of Immunity

A decision by the United States to sue on a claim generally does not constitute a waiver of sovereign immunity as to

---

[37] *See, e.g., Employers Ins. of Wausau v. U.S.*, 764 F.2d 1572, 1576 (Fed. Cir. 1985) ("[A] permissive counterclaim does not generate a . . . tolling period.").

[38] *See, e.g., In re Armstrong*, 206 F.3d 465, 473 (5th Cir. 2000) ("[T]he law is clear that a compulsory counterclaim shall not be used to expand claims against the United States beyond their limits as already established by law. See Fed.R.Civ.P. 13(d) ."); *U.S. ex rel. Fallon v. Accudyne Corp.*, 921 F. Supp. 611 (W.D. Wis. 1995) (limitations on waivers of sovereign immunity are enforceable against counterclaims; citing Rule 13(d)).

counterclaims for amounts above those sums for which the United States is suing. This result applies even if the counterclaims arise from the same transaction or occurrence as the complaint brought by the United States.[39] By contrast, a State which voluntarily joins litigation waives sovereign immunity for all compulsory counterclaims.[40]

Setoffs

Some courts have permitted counterclaims against the United States where: the claim and counterclaim arise from the same transaction or occurrence; and the money sought is a setoff against the government's claim that will only reduce the government's recovery.[41]

RULE 13(e)—COUNTERCLAIM MATURING OR ACQUIRED AFTER PLEADING

CORE CONCEPT

Rule 13(e) provides that if counterclaims mature or are acquired after a party has pleaded, the party may choose to assert them in a supplemental pleading, subject to the court's discretion.

APPLICATIONS

Procedure

A party seeking to assert a Rule 13(e) counterclaim must file a motion and supporting materials explaining the circumstances in which the counterclaim matured or was acquired.[42]

Party's Discretion

Rule 13(e) is permissive in nature, even if it arises from the same transaction or occurrence as the opposing party's claim. Thus, a party holding a counterclaim of the kind controlled by Rule 13(e) may assert it, subject to the court's permission, but is under no obligation to do so.[43]

---

[39]*See, e.g., U.S. v. Johnson*, 853 F.2d 619, 621 (8th Cir. 1988).

[40]*Board Of Regents of University Of Wisconsin System v. Phoenix Intern. Software, Inc.*, 653 F.3d 448, 463–69 (7th Cir. 2011) citing *Gardner v. New Jersey*, 329 U.S. 565, 574, 67 S.Ct. 467, 91 L.Ed. 504 (1947).

[41]*See, e.g., U.S. v. Forma*, 42 F.3d 759, 765 (2d Cir. 1994) (counterclaim permissible only to extent of reducing government's claim; barring affirmative relief). *Compare Berrey v. Asarco Inc.*, 439 F.3d 636, 643 (10th Cir. 2006) (Indian tribal immunity which is deemed coextensive with the immunity of the United States did not preclude counterclaim sounding in recoupment).

[42]*See, e.g., All West Pet Supply Co. v. Hill's Pet Products Div., Colgate-Palmolive Co.*, 152 F.R.D. 202, 204 (D. Kan. 1993) (court has discretion to permit or reject supplemental counterclaim).

[43]*Stone v. Department of Aviation*, 453 F.3d 1271 (10th Cir.2006) (where plaintiff had not received his right-to-sue letter at time of initial filing, claim has not matured and was not barred as a compulsory counterclaim under Rule 13(e)).

Judicial Discretion

If a party seeks to raise a Rule 13(e) counterclaim, the court retains discretion to refuse to hear the counterclaim in the pending action.[44] Generally, courts permit Rule 13(e) counterclaims where they will not confuse the trier of fact or where they will not unfairly prejudice other parties, particularly through excessively delaying the litigation.[45] Additionally, Rule 13(e) counterclaims that arise out of the same transaction or occurrence as the opposing party's claim are more likely to be heard in the pending litigation, than are claims that arise out of dissimilar transactions or occurrences.

Regardless of whether a counterclaim is compulsory or permissive, a district court does not abuse its discretion in dismissing a counterclaim in deference to state court litigation which involves the same matters. The common-law doctrine of abstention is not subservient to Rule 13 and the compulsory-permissive distinction does not limit a district court's power to abstain in a given case.[46]

Jurisdiction

Rule 13(e) counterclaims must meet one of the bases of subject matter jurisdiction, such as federal question jurisdiction, diversity jurisdiction, or supplemental jurisdiction. If the Rule 13(e) counterclaim arises out of the same transaction or occurrence as the original claim, then it will likely satisfy supplemental jurisdiction. If not, the counterclaim will need an independent basis of jurisdiction. For a more detailed discussion of subject matter jurisdiction, see §§ 2.10 to 2.13.

Venue

There is no venue requirement for Rule 13(e) counterclaims.

RULE 13(f) — OMITTED COUNTERCLAIM PROVISION (DELETED)

Rule 13(f) provided for filing of a counterclaim omitted through "oversight, inadvertence, or exclusable neglect, or when justice requires." The subsection was deleted from the Rules in 2009. The Civil Rules Advisory Committee of the Judicial Conference concluded that this subsection potentially conflicted with Rule 15 and was, in any case, redundant. The filing of an omitted counterclaim is now governed by Rule 15.[47]

---

[44] *See, e.g., id.*

[45] *See, e.g., id.* (noting that in absence of factors indicating unfair prejudice to opponent, policy of liberally granting leave to file supplemental claims also applies to Rule 13(e) counterclaims).

[46] *See American Home Assur. Co.* *v. Pope*, 487 F.3d 590, 604 (8th Cir. 2007).

[47] Civil Rules Advisory Committee Meeting, April 7–8 2008, Congressional Information Service Records of the U.S. Judicial Conference, p. 36; Civil Rules Advisory Committee Meeting, April 19–20, 2007, Congressional Infor-

RULE 13(g)—CROSSCLAIM AGAINST CO-PARTY

CORE CONCEPT

Rule 13(g) permits persons who are already parties to a suit to bring related claims against persons on the same side of the litigation. An essential difference between a cross-claim and a counterclaim is that crossclaims are suits against persons who had not, until the crossclaim was filed, been opponents of the person asserting the crossclaim. Counterclaims, by contrast, are suits against persons who have already sued the person asserting the counterclaim.

APPLICATIONS

Procedure

Crossclaims are typically raised in a responsive pleading.

Crossclaims Are Always Permissive

Unlike compulsory counterclaims under Rule 13(a), Rule 13(g) does not create a category of compulsory crossclaims. Instead, under Rule 13(g), all crossclaims are permissive, and may therefore be asserted in the pending litigation or in a separate action.[48]

Same Transaction or Occurrence

Crossclaims must arise out of the same transaction or occurrence as the original action, or relate to the same property that is in dispute in the original action.[49] In this important sense crossclaims, though permissive, are fundamentally different from permissive counterclaims, which often arise from a transaction or occurrence that is different than the original action. The standard of same transaction or occurrence varies from court to court. The most liberal interpretation requires a logical relation between the cross-claim and the original action.[50] Other courts look to the degree of overlap between the evidence to be used in the crossclaim and the evidence relevant

---

mation Service Records of the U.S. Judicial Conference, p.2; Civil Rules Advisory Committee Meeting, September 7–8, 2006, Congressional Information Service Records of the U.S. Judicial Conference, p.3.

[48]*See, e.g., U.S. v. Confederate Acres Sanitary Sewage and Drainage System, Inc.*, 935 F.2d 796, 799 (6th Cir. 1991) (Rule 13(g) makes cross-claims permissive). *But cf., Paramount Aviation Corp. v. Agusta*, 178 F.3d 132 (3d Cir. 1999) (observing that while cross-claims themselves are never compulsory, filing a cross-claim may make co-defendants into opposing par-

ties, which might make a counterclaim on the cross-claim compulsory; not deciding, but suggesting that such counterclaims might never be compulsory if they were responses to cross-claims that merely sought contribution or indemnity).

[49]*See, e.g., Federal Land Bank of St. Louis v. Cupples Bro.*, 116 F.R.D. 63, 65 (E.D. Ark. 1987).

[50]*See, e.g., Seattle Audubon Soc. v. Lyons*, 871 F. Supp. 1286, 1290 (W.D. Wash. 1994) (treating same transaction or occurrence as synonymous with "logical relationship" test).

to the original action.[51]

Crossclaims Against Co-Parties; Other Parties

Rule 13(g) provides that crossclaims may be brought only if at least one crossclaim defendant is a person already party to an action.[52] However, if a single crossclaim defendant is a party to the original action, additional persons may also be sued on the crossclaim, as provided by Rule 13(h) (discussed below).

Comparison With Impleader

A key difference between Rule 13(g) and Rule 14 impleader is that Rule 13(g) requires that at least one crossclaim defendant be a party. Rule 14, by contrast, provides a means of joining persons who were not previously parties to a pending suit.[53]

Derivative Liability

A crossclaimant may seek either affirmative relief or compensation for any liability the crossclaimant may have as a result of claims already filed against the crossclaimant.

Subject Matter Jurisdiction

Crossclaims must meet the standards of either federal question jurisdiction, diversity jurisdiction, or supplemental jurisdiction. Moreover, the party asserting a counterclaim must include an allegation of facts demonstrating that the requirement of subject matter jurisdiction is met.[54] However, subject matter jurisdiction is usually not a problem with crossclaims; because Rule 13(g) requires that crossclaims arise out of the same transaction or occurrence as the original action, crossclaims that cannot meet the standards of federal question jurisdiction or diversity jurisdiction usually will nevertheless

---

[51]*See, e.g., Danner v. Anskis*, 256 F.2d 123 (3d Cir.1958).

[52]*See, e.g., In re Oil Spill by Amoco Cadiz off Coast of France on March 16, 1978*, 699 F.2d 909, 913 (7th Cir. 1983) ("[A] Rule 13(g) cross-claim will lie only against an existing defendant."); *Mauney v. Imperial Delivery Services, Inc.*, 865 F. Supp. 142, 153 (S.D. N.Y. 1994) (cross-claim cannot be filed against third-party defendant because cross-claims are filed between co-parties). *See generally Polimaster Ltd. v. RAE Systems, Inc.*, 623 F.3d 832, 839 (9th Cir. 2010) (counterclaim defendants were "defendants" for purposes of arbitration agreement).

[53]*See, e.g., Ambraco, Inc. v. Bossclip B.V.*, 570 F.3d 233, 242 (5th Cir. 2009) (claim properly brought under Rule 14 impleader rather than

Rule 13(g) when crossclaimant had been dismissed as a party to the underlying suit before crossclaim under Rule 13(g) had been asserted).

[54]*McNutt v. General Motors Acceptance Corp. of Indiana*, 298 U.S. 178, 189, 56 S. Ct. 780, 785, 80 L. Ed. 1135 (1936) ("[P]rerequisites to the exercise of jurisdiction . . . are conditions which must be met by the party who seeks the exercise of jurisdiction in his favor. He must allege in his pleading the facts essential to show jurisdiction."). *Cf., e.g., Martin v. Franklin Capital Corp.*, 251 F.3d 1284 (10th Cir. 2001) (removal case; "As the parties invoking the federal court's jurisdiction in this case, defendants bear the burden of establishing that the requirements for the exercise of diversity jurisdiction are present.").

satisfy the requirements of supplemental jurisdiction.[55]

Personal Jurisdiction

Crossclaims must meet the requirements of personal jurisdiction. If the court in the original action has already acquired jurisdiction over the parties, it will normally also have jurisdiction over crossclaim defendants. If, however, jurisdiction is defective in the original action, it is possible that the crossclaim will suffer from similar jurisdictional defects. For a further discussion of jurisdiction over persons or things, see §§ 2.2 to 2.9.

Venue

Crossclaims need not satisfy venue requirements.[56]

Mislabelled Cross-Claims

Parties sometimes mistakenly identify cross-claims as counterclaims, and *vice versa*. Courts usually attach no significance to such errors, unless somehow they unfairly prejudice an opposing party.[57]

Statutes of Limitations: "Relation Back"

The precedent addressing whether statutes of limitations for crossclaims are tolled by the filing of the original action is unsettled, but some generalizations are possible. Crossclaims seeking "affirmative and independent relief" do not relate back to the original complaint. By contrast, crossclaims "in the nature of recoupment, indemnity, or contribution" will typically enjoy the benefit of relation back to the date of the filing of the original action.[58]

RULE 13(h)—JOINING ADDITIONAL PARTIES

CORE CONCEPT

Many times a counterclaim or crossclaim will require, for the just adjudication of the case, the joinder of persons who are not yet parties. Rule 13(h) expressly authorizes the use of Rules 19 and 20, governing joinder of persons, to achieve that end.

---

[55]*See, e.g., Ryan ex rel. Ryan v. Schneider Nat. Carriers, Inc.*, 263 F.3d 816, 819, (8th Cir. 2001) (per curiam) (addition of cross-claim against co-plaintiff that satisfies requirements of Rule 13(g) satisfies supplemental jurisdiction); *Meritor Sav. Bank v. Camelback Canyon Investors*, 783 F. Supp. 455, 457 (D. Ariz. 1991) (permitting supplemental jurisdiction over cross-claim).

[56]*See, e.g., Bredberg v. Long*, 778 F.2d 1285, 1288 (8th Cir. 1985) (if venue is proper on original claims, there may be no venue objection to cross-claims).

[57]*See, e.g., Schwab v. Erie Lackawanna R. Co.*, 438 F.2d 62, 64 (3d Cir. 1971) (mislabelling need not be fatal).

[58]*See, e.g., Kansa Reinsurance Co., Ltd. v. Congressional Mortg. Corp. of Texas*, 20 F.3d 1362, 1367–68 (5th Cir. 1994) (making distinction between two categories of cross-claims; noting also that Rule 15(c), governing relation back of pleadings, does not automatically permit an untimely cross-claim to relate back simply because the cross-claim arose from the same transaction or occurrence).

APPLICATIONS

Procedure

Although the law is not entirely settled, it appears that when counterclaimants or crossclaimants seek to join additional parties under Rule 13(h), they may simply make appropriate service on the parties to be joined and provide notice to those already parties. There appears to be no need to file a motion requesting leave to join the parties.[59]

Prerequisite of One Party

Rule 13(a), (b), and (g) provide that counterclaims and crossclaims cannot be sued upon unless at least one person being sued is already a party to the action. However, once one such person is sued on a counterclaim or crossclaim, Rule 13(h) permits joinder of other persons on that counterclaim or crossclaim, subject to the authority of Rules 19 and 20.[60]

Subject Matter Jurisdiction

Rule 13(h) claims must satisfy either federal question jurisdiction, diversity jurisdiction, or supplemental jurisdiction.[61] For a further discussion of subject matter jurisdiction, see §§ 2.10 to 2.13.

(1) *Claims by Original Plaintiff:* If the counterclaim or crossclaim is part of a case based solely on diversity of citizenship, and was filed by someone who was a plaintiff on the original claim, supplemental jurisdiction is not available as to new parties joined under either Rule 19 or Rule 20.[62]

(2) *Dissimilar Claims or Occurrences:* If a counterclaim does not arise from the same transaction or occurrence as the original action, Rule 13(h) may usually be employed only where the court has federal question jurisdiction or diversity jurisdiction over the counterclaim.[63] For a further discussion of subject matter jurisdiction, see §§ 2.10 to 2.13.

---

[59]*See, e.g., Northfield Ins. Co. v. Bender Shipbuilding & Repair Co., Inc.,* 122 F.R.D. 30 (S.D. Ala. 1988) (1966 amendment to Rule 13(h) eliminated requirement to obtain judicial approval for joinder); *but see, Mountain States Sports, Inc. v. Sharman,* 353 F. Supp. 613, 618 (D. Utah 1972), aff'd, 548 F.2d 905 (10th Cir. 1977) (general practice is to seek an order joining additional parties).

[60]*See, e.g., Asset Allocation and Management Co. v. Western Employers Ins. Co.,* 892 F.2d 566, 574 (7th Cir. 1989) (noting interplay of Rules 13(h) and 20). *See also Westwood Apex v. Contreras,* 644 F.3d 799, 802 n.1 (9th Cir. 2011) (defendant filed counterclaim against plaintiff and also against plaintiff's parent corporation and affiliated entities; held, parent corporation and affiliated entities were properly termed "*additional* counterclaim defendants").

[61]*But see, Rayman v. Peoples Sav. Corp.,* 735 F. Supp. 842, 854 (N.D. Ill. 1990) (noting, however, that compulsory counterclaims or cross-claims will usually satisfy supplemental jurisdiction).

[62]28 U.S.C.A. § 1367(b).

[63]*See, e.g., Federal Deposit Ins. Corp. v. La Rambla Shopping Center, Inc.,* 791 F.2d 215, 220 (1st Cir. 1986) (noting that counterclaims arising from unrelated transactions do not usually qualify for supplemental jurisdiction, and must have independent

Personal Jurisdiction

Additional parties may be joined under Rule 13(h) only if they are subject to the jurisdiction of the court.[64] For a further discussion of personal jurisdiction, see §§ 2.3 to 2.7.

Venue

Venue requirements do not apply to counterclaims or cross-claims in which Rule 13(h) joinder is sought.[65]

RULE 13(i)—SEPARATE TRIALS; SEPARATE JUDGMENTS

CORE CONCEPT

Because additional claims added to a case through Rule 13(a), (b), and (g) have substantial potential for confusing the trier of fact or delaying adjudication of the original claims, Rule 13(i) authorizes the court to hold separate hearings, as provided by Rule 42(b), and/or enter separate judgments, as provided by Rule 54(b).

APPLICATIONS

Judicial Discretion

Courts have substantial discretion to order separate trials and enter separate judgments, and the decision to process claims separately is not normally disturbed on appeal.[66]

Jurisdiction

Rule 13(i) is subject to the prerequisite that the court have jurisdiction over the claims and parties before it.[67]

Additional Research References

Wright & Miller, *Federal Practice and Procedure* §§ 1401 to 37
C.J.S., Federal Civil Procedure §§ 309 to 319 et seq.
West's Key Number Digest, Federal Civil Procedure ☞771 to 786

---

[64]*See, e.g., Cordner v. Metropolitan Life Ins. Co.*, 234 F. Supp. 765, 769 (S.D. N.Y. 1964) (Rule 13(h) requires jurisdiction over parties to be joined).

[65]*See, e.g., Lesnik v. Public Industrials Corporation*, 144 F.2d 968, 977 (C.C.A. 2d Cir. 1944) (so holding).

[66]*See, e.g., McLaughlin v. State Farm Mut. Auto. Ins. Co.*, 30 F.3d 861, 870 (7th Cir. 1994) (noting discretion of trial court in deciding whether to bifurcate trial).

[67]*See, e.g., Chattanooga Corp. v. Klingler*, 621 F. Supp. 756 (E.D. Tenn. 1985).

RULE 14
THIRD-PARTY PRACTICE

(a) When a Defending Party May Bring in a Third Party.

(1) *Timing of the Summons and Complaint.* A defending party may, as third-party plaintiff, serve a summons and complaint on a nonparty who is or may be liable to it for all or part of the claim against it. But the third-party plaintiff must, by motion, obtain the court's leave if it files the third-party complaint more than 14 days after serving its original answer.

(2) *Third-Party Defendant's Claims and Defenses.* The person served with the summons and third-party complaint—the "third-party defendant":

   (A) must assert any defense against the third-party plaintiff's claim under Rule 12;

   (B) must assert any counterclaim against the third-party plaintiff under Rule 13(a), and may assert any counterclaim against the third-party plaintiff under Rule 13(b) or any cross-claim against another third-party defendant under Rule 13(g);

   (C) may assert against the plaintiff any defense that the third-party plaintiff has to the plaintiff's claim; and

   (D) may also assert against the plaintiff any claim arising out of the transaction or occurrence that is the subject matter of the plaintiff's claim against the third-party plaintiff.

(3) *Plaintiff's Claims Against a Third-Party Defendant.* The plaintiff may assert against the third-party defendant any claim arising out of the transaction or occurrence that is the subject matter of the plaintiff's claim against the third-party plaintiff. The third-party defendant must then assert any defense under Rule 12 and any counterclaim under Rule 13(a), and may assert

521

any counterclaim under Rule 13(b) or any cross-claim under Rule 13(g).

(4) *Motion to Strike, Sever, or Try Separately.* Any party may move to strike the third-party claim, to sever it, or to try it separately.

(5) *Third-Party Defendant's Claim Against a Nonparty.* A third-party defendant may proceed under this rule against a nonparty who is or may be liable to the third-party defendant for all or part of any claim against it.

(6) *Third-Party Complaint In Rem.* If it is within the admiralty or maritime jurisdiction, a third-party complaint may be in rem. In that event, a reference in this rule to the "summons" includes the warrant of arrest, and a reference to the defendant or third-party plaintiff includes, when appropriate, a person who asserts a right under Supplemental Rule C(6)(a)(i) in the property arrested.

(b) When a Plaintiff May Bring in a Third Party. When a claim is asserted against a plaintiff, the plaintiff may bring in a third party if this rule would allow a defendant to do so.

(c) Admiralty or Maritime Claim.

(1) *Scope of Impleader.* If a plaintiff asserts an admiralty or maritime claim under Rule 9(h), the defendant or a person who asserts a right under Supplemental Rule C(6)(a)(i) may, as a third-party plaintiff, bring in a third-party defendant who may be wholly or partly liable—either to the plaintiff or to the third-party plaintiff—for remedy over, contribution, or otherwise on account of the same transaction, occurrence, or series of transactions or occurrences.

(2) *Defending Against a Demand for Judgment for the Plaintiff.* The third-party plaintiff may demand judgment in the plaintiff's favor against the third-party defendant. In that event, the third-party defendant must defend under Rule 12 against the plaintiff's claim as well as the third-party plaintiff's claim; and the action proceeds as if the plaintiff had sued both the

third-party defendant and the third-party plaintiff.

[Amended effective March 19, 1948; July 1, 1963; July 1, 1966; August 1, 1987; April 17, 2000, effective December 1, 2000; April 12, 2006, effective December 1, 2006; April 30, 2007, effective December 1, 2007; March 26, 2009, effective December 1, 2009.]

AUTHORS' COMMENTARY ON RULE 14

PURPOSE AND SCOPE

Rule 14 permits parties who are defending against claims to join other persons, not yet parties, who may be obligated to reimburse the party defending the claim for some or all of that party's liability. The decision to seek joinder, or to hold the claim for assertion in later litigation, belongs to the party defending on the claim: Rule 14 contains no requirement similar to Rule 13(a), which makes compulsory the assertion of certain counterclaims. Typically, a person is joined because that person, as a guarantor of some transaction, has an obligation to indemnify a party if the party is forced to pay on a claim. Third-party practice is also commonly employed when an alleged tortfeasor seeks contribution from others who may also be liable but whom the plaintiff has not sued. The Rule also describes the rights of persons who are joined as third-party defendants to claim and defend against the original plaintiffs and defendants, as well as to join still other persons who may be liable to the third parties.

NOTE: The labels necessitated by Rule 14 are superficially complex, but follow a consistent pattern. A party who seeks to join another person under Rule 14 is called a third-party plaintiff. The person joined is called a third-party defendant. Thus, if a defendant in a pending action sought to join someone not yet a party under Rule 14, the defendant would carry the additional title of third-party plaintiff, and the person joined would be a third-party defendant. If the third-party defendant sought, in turn, to join someone else, the person joined would be a fourth-party defendant, and the third-party defendant would carry the additional title of fourth-party plaintiff.

RULE 14(a)—A DEFENDING PARTY MAY BRING IN THIRD PARTY

CORE CONCEPT

Rule 14(a) describes the power of defendants to implead third parties. The Rule also describes the defenses available to third-party defendants, as well as the circumstances in which third-party defendants may claim against plaintiffs and defendants.

Finally, Rule 14(a) authorizes third-party defendants to implead potential fourth-party defendants who may be liable for some or all of any claim the third-party defendants might have to pay.

APPLICATIONS

Purpose

The purpose of Rule 14 is to permit additional parties whose rights may be affected by the decision in the original action to be joined so as to expedite the final determination of the rights and liabilities of all the interested parties in one suit.[1]

Third-Party Plaintiff's Discretion

Where applicable, a party's right to implead under Rule 14 is optional. There is no obligation to implead third parties.[2]

Who May Be Impleaded

Only persons not already parties may be impleaded.[3] This provision of Rule 14 stands in contrast to provisions of Rule 13, governing counterclaims and cross-claims, in which at least one of the persons sued on a counterclaim or cross-claim must already be a party to the case.

Procedure

A third-party defendant is joined upon service of a proper summons and third-party complaint.[4] For purposes of impleader under Rule 14, Rule 4(k) permits service on a third-party defendant found within 100 miles of the place from where the summons issued-without regard to whether such service takes place within another state.[5] This is a small but sometimes crucial expansion of personal jurisdiction in the context of Rule 14.

Time; Leave of Court

Rule 14(a) permits service of a third-party complaint "at any time." However, a party may file a third-party complaint without obtaining leave of court only in the fourteen-day period

---

[1]*American Zurich Ins. Co. v. Cooper Tire & Rubber Co.*, 512 F.3d 800, 805 (6th Cir. 2008).

[2]*See, e.g., Fernandez v. Corporacion Insular De Seguros*, 79 F.3d 207 (1st Cir.1996) (no obligation to implead; decision to forego impleader does not require instruction that jury is authorized to draw adverse inference).

[3]*See, e.g., Cutting Underwater Technologies USA, Inc. v. Eni U.S. Operating Co.*, 671 F.3d 512, 514, n. 2 (5th Cir. 2012) (claim asserted against non-parties were third-party claims and not counterclaims); *Mauney v. Imperial Delivery Services, Inc.*, 865 F. Supp. 142, 153 (S.D. N.Y. 1994) (under Rule 14, third-party suit cannot be filed against a third-party defendant who is already a party).

[4]*See, e.g., Jackson v. Southeastern Pennsylvania Transp. Authority*, 727 F. Supp. 965, 966 (E.D. Pa. 1990) (by its terms, Rule 14(a) authorizes service of third-party complaints).

[5]Fed.R.Civ.P. 4(k).

following that party's service of an answer to a claim.[6] Thereafter, a third-party complaint may be filed only upon motion, served on all parties, and after obtaining leave of court.[7] Generally, courts permit assertion of impleader claims unless they are raised so late in a pending suit that they unreasonably prejudice persons who are already parties.[8]

Relationship to Pending Claims

Rule 14(a) explicitly provides that claims against third-party defendants must relate to claims pending against the third-party plaintiff and must depend in some degree on the outcome of the original action. Rule 14(a) provides no authorization to assert claims against third-party plaintiffs that are unrelated to claims already pending.[9]

In addition, if the claims in the original, underlying action are settled, a court may properly dismiss the Rule 14 claim.[10]

Affirmative Relief; Derivative Liability and Rule 18

Although Rule 14(a)'s literal language might seem to limit third-party practice to claims for reimbursement or compensation,[11] a minority of courts have used Rule 18(a), governing

---

[6]*See, e.g., Smith v. Local 819 I.B.T. Pension Plan*, 291 F.3d 236 (2d Cir. 2002) (defendant's third-party complaint filed within fourteen days of serving answer, so no need to obtain leave of court).

[7]*See, e.g., Raytheon Aircraft Credit Corp. v. Pal Air Intern., Inc.*, 923 F. Supp. 1408 (D. Kan. 1996) (no obligation to obtain leave of court when impleader is brought within 10 days of answer).

[8]*See, e.g., State of N.Y. v. Solvent Chemical Co., Inc.*, 875 F. Supp. 1015 (W.D. N.Y. 1995) (impleader allowed more than 10 years after original complaint was filed; case was still in discovery, and third-party defendant still had good opportunity to prepare case). *See also Marseilles Hydro Power, LLC v. Marseilles Land and Water Co.*, 299 F.3d 643, 650 (7th Cir. 2002) (suit filed in February; counterclaim and third-party complaint filed in June; held, "clearly wrong" for district court to assert that third-party plaintiff waited too long to file third-party complaint; "We cannot for the life of us see what procedural economy could be gained by forcing [third-party plaintiff] to sue [third-party defendant] in a separate action or how the plaintiff could be prejudiced."). *But see Lexington Insur-*

ance Co. v. S.H.R.M. Catering Services, Inc.*, 567 F.3d 182, 187 (5th Cir. 2009) (Rule 14(c) motion dismissed as untimely where plaintiff filed motion two months prior to trial date).

[9]*See, e.g., American Zurich Ins. Co. v. Cooper Tire & Rubber Co.*, 512 F.3d 800, 805 (6th Cir. 2008) ("A defendant attempting to transfer the liability asserted against him by the original plaintiff to the third-party defendant is therefore the essential criterion of a third-party claim."); *U.S. v. Olavarrieta*, 812 F.2d 640, 643 (11th Cir. 1987) (Rule 14 requires that outcome of impleader must at least partly depend on outcome of original suit; "Rule 14(a) does not allow the defendant to assert a separate and independent claim even though the claim arises out of the same general set of facts as the main claim.").

[10]*American Zurich Ins. Co. v. Cooper Tire & Rubber Co.*, 512 F.3d 800, 805–6 (6th Cir. 2008) (court upheld dismissal of insured's third-party complaint seeking declaratory judgment after settlement and dismissal of original action seeing declaration regarding scope of insurance coverage).

[11]*See, e.g., F.D.I.C. v. Bathgate*, 27 F.3d 850, 872 (3d Cir. 1994) (limit-

joinder of claims, to permit third-party claims even when the amount sought is greater than that for which the third-party plaintiff might be liable on the original claim.[12] However, it appears settled that once a party is properly impleaded under Rule 14, that party may also be sued for affirmative relief under Rule 18.[13]

Defenses Available

Third-party defendants are entitled to raise their own defenses against the third-party plaintiff.[14] The explicit language of Rule 14(a) also authorizes third-party defendants to assert defenses that the third-party plaintiff may have against the original claim.[15]

Counterclaims by Third-Party Defendants

Rule 14(a) authorizes third-party defendants to file claims against third-party plaintiffs,[16] consistent with the requirements of Rule 13. Applying Rule 13 to such claims means that, when the counterclaims satisfy the requirements of Rule 13(a), governing compulsory counterclaims, they must be filed in the pending action or they are waived.

Cross-Claims by Third-Party Defendants

If more than one third-party defendant has been impleaded, Rule 14(a) authorizes the third-party defendants to file claims against one another, subject to the requirements of Rule 13. Because Rule 13(g) is permissive, such claims may be filed or may be retained for subsequent litigation. Additionally, because Rule 13(g) only permits cross-claims that arise out of the same transaction or occurrence as the original claims, third-party claims must relate to the transaction or occurrence underlying the original claims by the third-party plaintiff.

Claims Against Plaintiffs

Rule 14(a) permits a third-party defendant to make claims against an original plaintiff that arise out of the same transaction or occurrence as the claims originally filed by the plaintiff. Such claims are permissive, in that they may either be raised or retained for subsequent litigation. Note, however, that if an original plaintiff has already sued the third-party defendant in

---

ing Rule 14(a) to claims based on derivative liability).

[12]*See, e.g., King Fisher Marine Service, Inc. v. 21st Phoenix Corp.*, 893 F.2d 1155, 1158 (10th Cir. 1990) (permitting joinder of unrelated third-party claims, provided that jurisdiction and Rule 14 are already satisfied).

[13]*Id.*

[14]*See, e.g., Coons v. Industrial Knife Co.*, 620 F.3d 38, 43 (1st Cir. 2010) (court's leave to file third-party

complaint does not prevent the third party-defendant from asserting statute of limitations defense).

[15]Fed.R.Civ.P. 14(a).

[16]*Cf., Thomas v. Barton Lodge II, Ltd.*, 174 F.3d 636 (5th Cir.1999) (observing that some courts prohibit third-party defendants' suits against original defendants who are not third-party plaintiffs; concluding that such prohibitions are erroneous, and permitting such claims).

the litigation, the third-party defendant's claims against the plaintiff may be compulsory counterclaims subject to Rule 13(a). In such a circumstance, a third-party defendant's claims against a plaintiff are not permissive. Counterclaims against plaintiffs are discussed below.

Plaintiffs' Claims Against Third-Party Defendants

Rule 14(a) also permits plaintiffs to sue persons joined as third-party defendants, provided that the claim arises out of the same transaction or occurrence as the original claims against the defendants.[17] The language of Rule 14(a) makes clear that assertion of such claims is discretionary, and a plaintiff may choose to retain the claims for subsequent litigation.[18]

Third-Party Defendants' Counterclaims Against Plaintiffs

If a plaintiff sues a third-party defendant, any counterclaims the third-party defendant may have are governed by Rule 13.

Third-Party Defendants' Cross-Claims Upon Suit by Plaintiffs

Just as Rule 14(a) permits third-party defendants to cross-claim against one another after being joined by a third-party plaintiff, the Rule also permits third-party defendants to cross-claim against one another if one or more third-party defendant is sued by a plaintiff. Rule 14(a) expressly provides that such cross-claims are regulated by Rule 13.

Severance; Separate Trials

Third-party practice has obvious potential for complexity and for confusing a trier of fact. Rule 14(a) therefore provides that *any* party to the litigation may move to strike or sever the claims. Courts have substantial discretion when deciding such

---

[17]*U.S. ex rel. S. Prawer and Co. v. Fleet Bank of Maine*, 24 F.3d 320, 328 (1st Cir. 1994) (Rule 14(a) requires that plaintiff's claim against third-party defendant arose from same transaction or occurrence as claim against original defendant). *See also International Fidelity Ins. Co. v. Sweet Little Mexico Corp.*, 665 F.3d 671, 675 (5th Cir. 2011) (plaintiff could not bring claim against third party when no claim had been asserted against the plaintiff; decided under Court of International Trade Rule 14 which mirrors Federal Rule 14). *Cf., Project Hope v. M/V IBN SINA*, 250 F.3d 67 (2d Cir. 2001) (apparent dicta; if third-party defendant "is effectively on notice that it will be held liable on the plaintiff's claims and the two proceed against one another in an adverse manner," plaintiff need not formally amend complaint to include causes of action against impleaded party).

[18]*See, e.g., Atchison, Topeka and Santa Fe Ry. Co. v. Hercules Inc.*, 146 F.3d 1071, 1073 (9th Cir. 1998) ("Rule 14 makes claims by a plaintiff against a third-party defendant permissive, not compulsory."). *See also Luera v. M/V Alberta*, 635 F.3d 181, 185 n.3 (5th Cir. 2011) (under Rule 14(a), as contrasted with Admiralty Rule 14(c), plaintiff not required to assert claims against third-party defendant).

motions.[19] Courts weigh numerous factors in determining whether third-party claims should be severed.[20]

Fourth-Party Practice

Rule 14(a) grants third-party defendants the same power to implead as is enjoyed by the defendants. Thus, third-party defendants may join persons not yet parties who may be liable to the third-party defendants for part or all of the liability the third-party defendants may have to the third-party plaintiffs.

Rights of Fourth-Party Defendants

Although not explicitly addressed in Rule 14(a), it seems settled that fourth-party defendants enjoy all the rights and authority the Rule provides to third-party defendants, including availability of defenses, counterclaims, cross-claims, and impleader of additional persons.[21]

Admiralty and Maritime Cases; In Rem Jurisdiction

Rule 14(a) provides that third-party complaints arising under the admiralty jurisdiction of the court may be in rem actions against maritime property. In such cases, the summons used in conventional litigation may be supplanted by admiralty process, and the terminology for third-party plaintiffs and defendants may conform to admiralty practice.

Subject Matter Jurisdiction

Every third-party claim must fall within at least one of the forms of subject matter jurisdiction: *e.g.*, federal question jurisdiction; diversity jurisdiction; or supplemental jurisdiction. Because third-party claims of necessity are closely related to the original claims between the plaintiff and defendant, subject matter jurisdiction can usually be obtained under supplemental jurisdiction even in the absence of federal question jurisdiction or diversity jurisdiction.[22] However, an important exception to that generalization exists when the third-party claim is as-

---

[19]*See, e.g., First Nat. Bank of Nocona v. Duncan Sav. and Loan Ass'n*, 957 F.2d 775, 777 (10th Cir. 1992) ("The granting of leave for a defendant to prosecute a third party proceeding under Rule 14 rests in the sound discretion of the trial court."). *Williams v. Ford Motor Credit Co.*, 627 F.2d 158 (8th Cir.1980) (noting that trial court has substantial, but not unlimited, discretion to dismiss a third-party complaint).

[20]*See, e.g., Oklahoma ex rel. Edmondson v. Tyson Foods, Inc.*, 237 F.R.D. 679, 681 (N.D. Okla. 2006) (listing factors considered by courts in deciding whether to sever and granting plaintiff's motion to sever ap-proximately 160 third-party defendants with a myriad of third-party claims).

[21]*See, e.g., Garnay, Inc. v. M/V Lindo Maersk*, 816 F. Supp. 888 (S.D. N.Y. 1993) (processing fourth-party complaint under same jurisdictional standards as any third-party complaint).

[22]*See, e.g., Grimes v. Mazda North American Operations*, 355 F.3d 566, 572 (6th Cir. 2004) (third-party claim for contribution falls within scope of supplemental jurisdiction if "common nucleus" requirement is met). *See also Kemper/Prime Indus. Partners v. Montgomery Watson Americas, Inc.*, 487 F.3d 1061, 1063 (7th Cir. 2007)

serted by a plaintiff. 28 U.S.C.A. § 1367(b), governing restrictions on supplemental jurisdiction, expressly provides that when the original claims in the case are based solely on diversity jurisdiction, suits by plaintiffs against persons made parties under Rule 14 may not be founded on supplemental jurisdiction.[23] For a further discussion of subject matter jurisdiction, see §§ 2.10 to 2.13.

Personal Jurisdiction; Service of Process

Every third-party claim must also satisfy requirements of jurisdiction over persons and things.[24] For a further discussion of such jurisdiction, see §§ 2.2 to 2.9. For service of process on parties joined under Rule 14, a special provision in Rule 4(k)(1)(B) provides a sometimes useful extension of normal limits on service.[25] Rule 4 is discussed elsewhere in this text.

Venue

Requirements of venue do not apply to claims asserted under Rule 14.[26]

RULE 14(b)—WHEN A PLAINTIFF MAY BRING IN A THIRD PARTY

CORE CONCEPT

Rule 14(b) provides that if a plaintiff is the subject of a counterclaim, the plaintiff may join third parties who may be liable for part or all of that claim, in the same manner that Rule 14(a) authorizes defendants to join third parties.

APPLICATIONS

When Plaintiff is Sued

A plaintiff may not join persons under Rule 14 until the

(defendant's impleader under Rule 14 of a party that is not diverse from the plaintiff does not destroy jurisdiction); *Spring City Corp. v. American Bldgs. Co.*, 193 F.3d 165, 169 (3d Cir. 1999) ("[A] third-party defendant joined under [Rule 14] does not become a defendant as against the original plaintiff, so that federal jurisdiction is not destroyed where those parties are citizens of the same state.").

[23]*See, e.g., State Nat. Ins. Co. Inc. v. Yates*, 391 F.3d 577, 579 (5th Cir. 2004) ("Where . . . the district court's original jurisdiction is based solely on diversity the district court does *not* have supplemental jurisdiction" over Rule 14 claims asserted by a plaintiff); *Grimes v. Mazda North American Operations*, 355 F.3d 566, 572 (6th Cir. 2004) (§ 1367(b) is intended to prevent original plaintiffs, "but not defendants

or third parties - from circumventing the requirements of diversity"). *But see Ryan ex rel. Ryan v. Schneider Nat. Carriers, Inc.*, 263 F.3d 816, 820 (8th Cir. 2001) (permitting supplemental jurisdiction over third-party complaint brought by some plaintiffs against co-plaintiff; holding that co-plaintiff was not made party by other plaintiffs under, *inter alia*, Rule 20).

[24]*See, e.g., Rodd v. Region Const. Co.*, 783 F.2d 89 (7th Cir. 1986).

[25]*See, e.g., ESAB Group, Inc. v. Centricut, Inc.*, 126 F.3d 617, 622 (4th Cir. 1997).

[26]*See, e.g., Gundle Lining Const. Corp. v. Adams County Asphalt, Inc.*, 85 F.3d 201 (5th Cir. 1996) (Rule 14 claims are not subject to venue requirements).

plaintiff has been sued, and then only on third-party claims related to the counterclaim.[27] Thus, if a plaintiff sued a defendant on a single count, and the defendant counterclaimed on an unrelated count, the plaintiff would be entitled to employ Rule 14 to implead third-party defendants.[28]

Applicability of Rule 14(a) to Plaintiff's Third-Party Claims

Once a plaintiff has been served with a counterclaim, Rule 14(b) provides that the plaintiff may employ third-party practice as to that counterclaim in the same manner that Rule 14(a) makes third-party practice available to a defendant.[29]

Subject Matter Jurisdiction; Restraints on Supplemental Jurisdiction

If the original cause of action in the case is based solely on diversity of citizenship, a plaintiff's third-party claims must satisfy either federal question jurisdiction or diversity jurisdiction. Title 28 U.S.C.A. § 1367(b), governing restraints on the use of supplemental jurisdiction, expressly provides that the court has no supplemental jurisdiction over claims by plaintiffs against persons made parties under Rule 14.[30] For a further discussion of subject matter jurisdiction, see §§ 2.10 to 2.13.

Personal Jurisdiction

A plaintiff's third-party claims must satisfy requirements of jurisdiction over persons and things. For a further discussion of such jurisdiction, see §§ 2.2 to 2.9.

RULE 14(c)—ADMIRALTY OR MARITIME CLAIM

CORE CONCEPT

Rule 14(c) provides that when the original cause of action arose under the court's admiralty jurisdiction, the defendant may join third persons by alleging either that: they are liable to reimburse the defendant for some or all of the defendant's liability, or that

---

[27]*See, e.g., International Fidelity Ins. Co. v. Sweet Little Mexico Corp.*, 665 F.3d 671, 675 (5th Cir. 2011) (plaintiff could not bring claim against third party when no claim had been asserted against the plaintiff; decided under Court of International Trade Rule 14 which mirrors Federal Rule 14).

[28]*See, e.g., Chase Manhattan Bank, N.A. v. Aldridge*, 906 F. Supp. 866, 867 (S.D. N.Y. 1995) (once plaintiff is sued on a counterclaim, Rule 14(b) affords plaintiff same impleader powers provided to defendant by Rule 14(a)).

[29]*See, e.g., Powell, Inc. v. Abney*, 83 F.R.D. 482, 485 (S.D. Tex. 1979) ("Rule 14(b) . . . places a plaintiff in the same position as a defendant under Rule 14(a) when a counterclaim is filed.").

[30]*See, e.g., Guaranteed Systems, Inc. v. American Nat. Can Co.*, 842 F. Supp. 855 (M.D. N.C. 1994) (clear language of § 1367(b) prohibits use of supplemental jurisdiction by plaintiff, where original suit is based on diversity).

the third persons are liable directly to the plaintiff. This expands the general practice of impleader under Rule 14(a), where a defendant may implead only to establish that the person joined is liable to the defendant, and may not implead by alleging that the person to be joined is liable directly to the plaintiff.[31] The practical result of this feature of Rule 14(c) is that the third person becomes a co-defendant in the original action, rather than a third-party defendant.[32]

APPLICATIONS

Demand for Judgment

In order to designate an impleaded third-party defendant as a defendant to the plaintiff's original complaint, the literal language of Rule 14(c) appears to require that the third-party complaint "demand judgment against the third-party defendant in favor of the plaintiff." The precise meaning of this language is not entirely free from doubt. However, while there is some authority indicating that the third-party complaint must specifically demand judgment in that precise way, the greater weight of authority is that the requirement of Rule 14(c) should be liberally construed. Thus, clear language intending to implead third-party defendants as co-defendants to the original complaint satisfies the requirement of Rule 14(c).[33]

Applicability of Rule 14(a)

Beyond the special provision of Rule 14(c) that may make the third party a co-defendant, Rule 14(c) impleader actions generally proceed as though controlled by relevant provisions

---

[31]*See, e.g., Spring City Corp. v. American Bldgs. Co.*, 193 F.3d 165, 169 (3d Cir. 1999) ("[A] third-party defendant joined under [Rule 14(a)] does not become a defendant as against the original plaintiff.").

[32]*See, e.g., Royal & Sun Alliance Ins., PLC v. Ocean World Lines, Inc.*, 612 F.3d 138 (2nd Cir. 2010) (defendant impleaded third party requesting contribution and indemnification, and demanding judgment against third party in favor of plaintiff); *LeBlanc v. Cleveland*, 198 F.3d 353, 355 (2d Cir. 1999) ("Pursuant to Rule 14(c) . . . third-party complaints allowed the case to proceed as if [plaintiffs] had sued [the impleaded third party] as well as [the original defendants]."); *Galt G/S v. Hapag-Lloyd A.G.*, 60 F.3d 1370, 1374 (9th Cir. 1995) (not-

ing distinction between Rule 14(a) and (c)). *But see Texaco Exploration and Production Co. v. AmClyde Engineered Products Co., Inc.*, 243 F.3d 906, 910 (5th Cir. 2001) (statutory right to enforce contractual arbitration provision overrides liberal joinder provision of Rule 14(c) when the two provisions are in conflict).

[33]*See, e.g., Royal Ins. Co. of America v. Southwest Marine*, 194 F.3d 1009, 1018 (9th Cir. 1999) (collecting cases; also noting that while third-party complaints in instant case did not specifically demand judgment against third parties in favor of plaintiff, both complaints made specific and repeated references to Rule 14(c) and to defendants' alleged liability to plaintiff).

of Rule 14(a).[34]

Prerequisite of Rule 9(h)

By its terms, Rule 14(c) is available only when the plaintiff has asserted a claim "within the meaning of Rule 9(h)."[35]

Subject Matter Jurisdiction

Persons impleaded under the special provision of Rule 14(c) will generally be subject to the admiralty jurisdiction of the court.[36]

Personal Jurisdiction

Persons impleaded under Rule 14(c) must be within either the personal jurisdiction, quasi in rem jurisdiction, or in rem jurisdiction of the court. Because in rem jurisdiction is generally available in admiralty practice, however, jurisdictional requirements may usually be satisfied without difficulty.

Venue

Venue requirements do not generally apply to claims asserted under Rule 14.[37]

Additional Research References

Wright & Miller, *Federal Practice and Procedure* §§ 1441 to 65
C.J.S., Federal Civil Procedure §§ 117 to 126 et seq., § 318
West's Key Number Digest, Federal Civil Procedure ☞281 to 293

---

[34]*See, e.g., Rosario v. American Export-Isbrandtsen Lines, Inc.*, 531 F.2d 1227, 1231–32 (3d Cir. 1976), (noting that apart from special provision, Rule 14(c) does not operate exclusive of Rule 14(a)). *See also Greenwell v. Aztar Indiana Gaming Corp.*, 268 F.3d 486, 493–94 (7th Cir. 2001) (if plaintiff does not choose to notify opponent and court that plaintiff chooses to prosecute a claim as an admiralty claim that qualifies for both admiralty jurisdiction and ordinary civil jurisdiction, case will proceed under ordinary civil rules, and special admiralty provisions will not apply). *Luera v. M/V Alberta*, 635 F.3d 181, 185 n.3 (5th Cir. 2011) (in contrast to Rule 14(a), Admiralty Rule 14(c) requires that the plaintiff assert claims directly against third-party defendant). *Royal Ins. Co. of America v. Southwest Marine*, 194 F.3d 1009, 1019 (9th Cir. 1999) (once a direct relationship exists between plaintiff and third-party defendants pursuant to Rule 14(c), plaintiff must assert its claims directly against third-party defendants and they must answer the complaint; however, where third-party defendants have sufficient notice of lawsuit from original complaint, plaintiff had no duty to amend original complaint to assert claim against them).

[35]*See, e.g., Ambraco, Inc. v. Bossclip B.V.*, 570 F.3d 233, 243 (5th Cir. 2009) (requirements for impleading third-party defendant under Rule 14(c) include "an action sounding in admiralty or maritime").

[36]*See, e.g., Harrison v. Glendel Drilling Co.*, 679 F. Supp. 1413, 1417 (W.D. La. 1988) (Rule 14(c) can be invoked only in admiralty cases).

[37]*See, e.g., Gundle Lining Const. Corp. v. Adams County Asphalt, Inc.*, 85 F.3d 201 (5th Cir. 1996) (Rule 14 claims are not subject to venue requirements).

RULE 15
AMENDED AND SUPPLEMENTAL PLEADINGS

(a) Amendments Before Trial.

(1) *Amending as a Matter of Course.* A party may amend its pleading once as a matter of course within:

(A) 21 days after serving it, or

(B) if the pleading is one to which a responsive pleading is required, 21 days after service of a responsive pleading or 21 days after service of a motion under Rule 12(b), (e), or (f), whichever is earlier.

(2) *Other Amendments.* In all other cases, a party may amend its pleading only with the opposing party's written consent or the court's leave. The court should freely give leave when justice so requires.

(3) *Time to Respond.* Unless the court orders otherwise, any required response to an amended pleading must be made within the time remaining to respond to the original pleading or within 14 days after service of the amended pleading, whichever is later.

(b) Amendments During and After Trial.

(1) *Based on an Objection at Trial.* If, at trial, a party objects that evidence is not within the issues raised in the pleadings, the court may permit the pleadings to be amended. The court should freely permit an amendment when doing so will aid in presenting the merits and the objecting party fails to satisfy the court that the evidence would prejudice that party's action or defense on the merits. The court may grant a continuance to enable the objecting party to meet the evidence.

(2) *For Issues Tried by Consent.* When an issue not raised by the pleadings is tried by the parties'

533

express or implied consent, it must be treated in all respects as if raised in the pleadings. A party may move—at any time, even after judgment—to amend the pleadings to conform them to the evidence and to raise an unpleaded issue. But failure to amend does not affect the result of the trial of that issue.

(c) Relation Back of Amendments.

   (1) *When an Amendment Relates Back.* An amendment to a pleading relates back to the date of the original pleading when:

     (A) the law that provides the applicable statute of limitations allows relation back;

     (B) the amendment asserts a claim or defense that arose out of the conduct, transaction, or occurrence set out—or attempted to be set out—in the original pleading; or

     (C) the amendment changes the party or the naming of the party against whom a claim is asserted, if Rule 15(c)(1)(B) is satisfied and if, within the period provided by Rule 4(m) for serving the summons and complaint, the party to be brought in by amendment:

       (i) received such notice of the action that it will not be prejudiced in defending on the merits; and

       (ii) knew or should have known that the action would have been brought against it, but for a mistake concerning the proper party's identity.

   (2) *Notice to the United States.* When the United States or a United States officer or agency is added as a defendant by amendment, the notice requirements of Rule 15(c)(1)(C)(i) and (ii) are satisfied if, during the stated period, process was delivered or mailed to the United States attorney or the United States attorney's designee, to the Attorney General of the United States, or to the officer or agency.

(d) Supplemental Pleadings. On motion and reasonable notice, the court may, on just terms, permit a party to serve a supplemental pleading setting out any transaction, occurrence, or event that happened after the date of the pleading to be supplemented. The court may permit supplementation even though the original pleading is defective in stating a claim or defense. The court may order that the opposing party plead to the supplemental pleading within a specified time.

[Amended January 21, 1963, effective July 1, 1963; February 28, 1966, effective July 1, 1966; March 2, 1987, effective August 1, 1987; April 30, 1991, effective December 1, 1991; amended by Pub.L. 102-198, § 11, December 9, 1991, 105 Stat. 1626; amended April 22, 1993, effective December 1, 1993; April 30, 2007, effective December 1, 2007; March 26, 2009, effective December 1, 2009.]

AUTHORS' COMMENTARY ON RULE 15

PURPOSE AND SCOPE

Rule 15 governs the circumstances in which parties who have already pleaded in a case will be permitted to amend such pleadings. The Rule also provides the circumstances in which parties will be allowed to file new pleadings describing events that have occurred since the original pleadings were filed.

RULE 15(a)—AMENDMENTS BEFORE TRIAL

CORE CONCEPT

Rule 15(a) provides an automatic right to amend pleadings a single time within 21 days after serving it. Alternatively, if the pleading is one that requires a responsive pleading, the pleading may be amended of right once within "21 days after service of either a responsive pleading or a motion under Rule 12(b), (e), or (f), whichever is earlier."[1]

NOTE: On some occasions an amended pleading may be feasible under Rule 15(a), but the effects of the pleading will be restricted by Rule 15(c). Rule 15(c) determines whether an amended pleading will be treated as though it was filed on the date of the original pleading or on the date of filing. When the timing of a pleading (particularly a claim for relief) is at issue, attorneys should consult both Rule 15(a) and Rule 15(c).

APPLICATIONS

Amendment of Right

A party may amend a pleading without leave of court or

---

[1]*Vanguard Outdoor, LLC v. City of Los Angeles*, 648 F.3d 737 (9th Cir. 2011).

consent of opposing parties once, under either of two circumstances. First, a pleading may be amended of right if the amendment is filed within 21 days after serving it.[2] Alternatively, if the pleading to be amended requires a responsive pleading, it may be amended of right within 21 days of service of a responsive pleading or 21 days after service of a motion under Rule 12(b), (e), or (f) (whichever is earlier).

Motions, Pleadings, and Rule 15(a)

Motions are not pleadings, as Rule 7(a) and (b) makes clear. However, as provided in Rule 15(a)(1)(B), motions governed by Rule 12(b), (e), or (f) also provide the opposing party with a right to amend a pleading, provided that the amendment is made within 21 days after service of the motion.[3]

Right to Amend: Futility

When a party has no right to amend and must obtain leave of court to do so, it is proper for a court to deny such leave if an amendment would be futile.[4] However, if a party still has a right to amend, it is unclear whether the court can reject the amendment because it would be futile.[5] It is possible, of course, that such an amendment would fall within the scope of Rule 11, governing sanctions for certain acts related to, inter alia, pleading.[6]

Cases Removed from State Court: 28 U.S.C. § 1447(e)

Section 1447(e) of Title 28 of the United States Code provides that if, after a case is removed, a plaintiff seeks to join non-diverse defendants whose joinder would destroy diversity, the district may permit or deny joinder. If joinder is denied, the court continues to have jurisdiction over the case. However, if joinder is permitted, diversity jurisdiction no longer exists and (in the absence of some other basis for subject matter jurisdiction) the court must then remand the case to state court.

That situation gets more complicated if, after removal but

---

[2]*Mayle v. Felix*, 545 U.S. 644, 125 S. Ct. 2562, 2569, 162 L. Ed. 2d 582 (2005).

[3]*Alioto v. Town of Lisbon*, 651 F.3d 715 (7th Cir. 2011) (Rule 12(b)(6) motion is not a responsive pleading, which means "plaintiff ordinarily retains the ability to amend his complaint once as a matter of right, even after a court grants a motion to dismiss").

[4]*See* Authors' Commentary on Rule 15(a), "Futile Amendments."

[5]*See, e.g., Williams v. Board of Regents of University System of Georgia*, 441 F.3d 1287, 1296 (11th Cir. 2006) (In that circumstance "the plain language of Rule 15(a) shows that the court lacks the discretion to reject the amended complaint based on its alleged futility."). *But see Nattah v. Bush*, 605 F.3d 1052, 1056 (D.C. Cir. 2010) (if proposed amended pleading would "fail as a matter of law," court may reject it notwithstanding party's nominal right to amend); *Johnson v. Dossey*, 515 F.3d 778, 780 (7th Cir. 2008) ("A district court need not allow the filing of an amended complaint, even when no responsive pleading has been filed, if it is clear that the proposed amended complaint is deficient and would not survive a motion to dismiss.").

[6]*See* Authors' Commentary on Rule 11.

before a responsive pleading has been filed, a plaintiff exercises the right to amend a pleading and joins a non-diverse defendant under Rule 15(a) without needing leave of court. If Rule 15(a) could be used in that manner, it would undermine the district court's discretion under § 1447(e) to retain the removed case by denying joinder. Courts have resolved this conflict by concluding that they have authority to deny joinder under Rule 15(a), notwithstanding the plaintiff's apparent right under that Rule.[7]

Removal and § 1447(e) are discussed at greater length elsewhere in this text.

Rights of Joined Parties

If a party is served with an amended pleading permitted under Rule 15, that party normally enjoys a minimum of 14 days from the date of service of the amended pleading to respond to it.[8] Rule 15(a) expressly provides the district court with authority to modify that time limit.

Termination of Right to Amend

Many courts hold that once the court has entered an order of final judgment, a party's ability to amend of right terminates.[9] Thus if the court grants a motion to dismiss, and enters judgment, the dismissed party's right to amend expires.[10]

---

[7]*See, e.g., Mayes v. Rapoport*, 198 F.3d 457, 461 (4th Cir. 1999) ("[A] district court has the authority to reject a post-removal joinder that implicates 28 U.S.C. § 1447(e), even if the joinder was without leave of court.").

[8]*Nelson v. Adams USA, Inc.*, 529 U.S. 460, 465, 120 S. Ct. 1579, 1584, 146 L. Ed. 2d 530 (2000) ("This opportunity to respond, fundamental to due process, is the echo of the opportunity to respond to original pleadings secured by Rule 12." Held, where grant of leave to amend occurred simultaneously with entry of judgment against joined party, due process has been denied).

[9]*See, e.g., Jacobs v. Tempur-Pedic International, Inc.*, 626 F.3d 1327,1344 (11th Cir. 2010) (Rule 15(a) "has no application *after* judgment is entered."); *Ahmed v. Dragovich*, 297 F.3d 201 (3d Cir.2002) (once final judgment is entered, Rule 15 is inapplicable unless a party obtains relief under Rule 59 or Rule 60; unless judgment is set aside, party cannot use Rule 15 to amend). Cf., *Morse v. McWhorter*,

290 F.3d 795, 799 (6th Cir. 2002) ("Where a timely motion to amend judgment is filed under Rule 59(e), the Rule 15 and Rule 59 inquiries turn on the same factors."). *But cf., Camp v. Gregory*, 67 F.3d 1286 (7th Cir. 1995) (if complaint is dismissed but judgment is not yet entered, Rule 15(a) may still be available).

[10]*See, e.g., Gates v. Syrian Arab Republic*, 646 F.3d 1 (D.C. Cir. 2011) (*[P]leadings* cannot be amended on appeal."); *Hawks v. J.P. Morgan Chase Bank*, 591 F.3d 1043, 1050 (8th Cir. 2010) (right to amend terminates after complaint is dismissed; leave to amend may still be available); *Lewis v. Fresne*, 252 F.3d 352 (5th Cir. 2001) (noting termination of right to amend; also noting that leave to amend may still be available, but court has substantial discretion to refuse leave). *But cf. Fisher v. Kadant*, 589 F.3d 505, 508 (1st Cir. 2009) ("If . . . a motion to amend is filed *after* the entry of judgment, the district court lacks authority to consider the motion under Rule 15(a) unless and until the judgment is set aside.").

Requirement of Motion: Particularity and Rule 7(b)

Rule 15(a) amendments must be submitted to the court by motion. Attempts to amend a pleading through some other mechanism run a high risk of rejection by the district court.[11]

When a party submits a motion to amend, the particularity requirement of Rule 7(b) may require the party to attach to the motion a copy of the proposed amended pleading, unless the motion adequately describes the contemplated revision.[12]

Multiple Opposing Parties

If some opposing parties have already filed responsive pleadings and others have not, courts generally hold that the original pleading may be amended as of right, at least as to those parties that have not yet pleaded.[13]

Relation to Joinder Rules

It should be noted that when a party seeks to amend a complaint under Rule 15(a) to join additional claims or parties, the joinder will not be permitted simply because the requirements of Rule 15 have been met. In addition, the applicable joinder rules must also be satisfied.[14]

Relation to Rule 41(a)

When a party moves to amend a complaint to dismiss one of

---

[11]*See, e.g., Cozzarelli v. Inspire Pharmaceuticals, Inc.*, 549 F.3d 618, 630–31 (4th Cir. 2008) (request for leave to amend "only in a footnote of . . . response to defendants' motion to dismiss, and again in the final sentence of [a party's] objections to the recommendation of the magistrate judge . . . do not qualify as motions for leave to amend" and may therefore be disregarded by district court). *Cf. Gallop v. Cheney*, 642 F.3d 364, 369 (2d Cir. 2011) ("[N]o court can be said to have erred in failing to grant a request that was not made.").

[12]*See, e.g., U.S. ex rel. Atkins v. McInteer*, 470 F.3d 1350, 1362 (11th Cir. 2006) (noting requirement that movant submit copy of proposed amendment "or set forth the substance thereof"). *Moore v. State of Ind.*, 999 F.2d 1125, 1131 (7th Cir. 1993) (noting that courts may require submission of copy of proposed amended complaint, and commenting that motion alone might be adequate if it places adversary on proper notice of amendment's content). *See also In re Tamoxifen Citrate Antitrust Litigation*, 429 F.3d 370, 404 (2d Cir. 2005) ("It is within the court's discretion to deny leave to amend implicitly by not ad-

dressing the request when leave is requested informally in a brief filed in opposition to a motion to dismiss."); *Long v. Satz*, 181 F.3d 1275, 1279 (11th Cir. 1999) (plaintiff did not file motion for leave to amend; request for leave to amend was found only in memorandum opposing defendant's motion to dismiss; held, district court could deny leave to amend for failure to request leave properly).

[13]*See, e.g., Williams v. Board of Regents of University System of Georgia*, 441 F.3d 1287, 1296 (11th Cir. 2006) ("If the case has more than one defendant, and not all have filed responsive pleadings, the plaintiff may amend the complaint as a matter of course with regard to those defendants that have yet to answer.").

[14]*See, e.g., Hinson v. Norwest Financial South Carolina, Inc.*, 239 F.3d 611, 618 (4th Cir. 2001) (joinder of additional plaintiffs triggers application of Rule 20 requirements). *But see Bibbs v. Early*, 541 F.3d 267, 275 n. 39 (5th Cir. 2008) (if a party seeks to amend a pleading to drop or add parties, Rule 15 takes precedence over Rule 21).

its pending counts, it may appear that the motion may be made pursuant to either Rule 15(a) or Rule 41(a)(2). The appearance may often be reflective of reality, particularly if the complaint contains only a single count.[15] However, there is precedent for a clear distinction between the rules when a complaint contains more than one count and the plaintiff seeks dismissal of less than all the counts. In that circumstance the applicable rule is Rule 15(a), not Rule 41. By contrast, if all the counts are to be dismissed, the motion should be filed under Rule 41(a).[16]

In either case, however, dismissal is ordinarily granted without prejudice to a possible subsequent refilling of the dismissed counts.[17]

Relation With Rule 81(c)

If a case is removed from state court, it is possible that a party will be ordered under Rule 81(c) to file a repleading that conforms to federal practice. Generally, such a mandated repleading will not deprive a party of a one-time right to amend that may be available under Rule 15(a).[18]

Adverse Party's Consent

If a party's proposed amendment falls outside the time limits described above, it is often practical to ask the opposing party to consent to the amendment. When their duties to their own clients are not at issue, attorneys often cooperate in such matters as a matter of professional courtesy, and/or because they recognize that withholding consent will only force the party trying to amend to seek leave of court. If the opposing party consents to an amendment, there is no need to obtain court approval.[19] Rule 15(a) requires that consent of other parties be in writing,[20] which is usually filed with the court in the form of a praecipe.

---

[15]*See, e.g., Jet, Inc. v. Sewage Aeration Systems,* 223 F.3d 1360, 1364 (Fed. Cir. 2000) (in case at bar the Rules are "functionally interchangeable," although Rule 15(a) is preferred).

[16]*See, e.g., Sneller v. City of Bainbridge Island,* 606 F.3d 636, 639 (9th Cir. 2010) (Rule 41 applies to dismissal of total case; but Rule 15 "is the only procedure . . . to withdraw individual challenged claims"); *Klay v. United Healthgroup, Inc.,* 376 F.3d 1092, 1106 (11th Cir. 2004) (plaintiff who wishes to dispose of only part of a claim should normally cite Rule 15; Rule 41(a) should normally be used to dismiss an entire action).

[17]*Klay v. United Healthgroup, Inc.,* 376 F.3d 1092, 1107 (11th Cir. 2004) (under either Rule 15 or Rule 41, dismissal is normally without prejudice); *Jet, Inc. v. Sewage Aeration Systems,* 223 F.3d 1360, 1364 (Fed. Cir. 2000) (dismissal under either rule is typically without prejudice).

[18]*See, e.g., Kuehl v. F.D.I.C.,* 8 F.3d 905, 907 (1st Cir. 1993) (but where party engages in dilatory conduct in meeting Rule 81(c) requirements, Rule 15(a) right to amend may be treated as exhausted).

[19]*See, e.g., American States Ins. Co. v. Dastar Corp.,* 318 F.3d 881, 888 (9th Cir. 2003) (parties who obtain consent to amendment need not obtain court's approval).

[20]*See, e.g., Minter v. Prime Equipment Co.,* 451 F.3d 1196, 1204 (10th Cir. 2006) (noting writing requirement). *But cf., Mooney v. City of New York,* 219 F.3d 123 (2d Cir. 2000)

Leave of Court

If a proposed amendment cannot be filed as of right, and the opposing party will not consent, a motion may be filed with the court seeking leave to amend. In that circumstance, permission to amend rests within the discretion of the court. However, Rule 15(a) directs the court to grant leave to amend "when justice so requires," and in practice the burden is usually on the party opposing the amendment to demonstrate why the amendment should not be permitted.[21] Moreover, at least some courts hold that where a complaint's deficiency could be cured by an amendment, leave to amend must be given—and where a party has not sought such leave, district courts are expected to notify parties of the opportunity to amend within whatever

---

(plaintiff's response on merits to defense raised on motion rather than by responsive pleading is construed "as an implied grant of leave to amend the answer").

[21]*Foman v. Davis*, 371 U.S. 178, 83 S. Ct. 227, 9 L. Ed. 2d 222 (1962). *See, e.g., C.F. v. Capistrano Unified School District*, 654 F.3d 975, 985 (9th Cir. 2011) (policy should be applied with "'extreme liberality'"); *Lyn-Lea Travel Corp. v. American Airlines, Inc.*, 283 F.3d 282, 286 (5th Cir. 2002) (no error to permit defendants' amended pleadings to raise affirmative defense of preemption when new issue is question of law based on undisputed facts in instant case; also noting that no new discovery was necessary in this case); *Bryant v. Dupree*, 252 F.3d 1161 (11th Cir. 2001) (plaintiffs' previous amendment, filed as of right under Rule 15(a), should not be counted as a prior opportunity to amend with leave of court when defendants later file a motion to dismiss); *Pangburn v. Culbertson*, 200 F.3d 65, 70 (2d Cir. 1999) (liberal approach to leave to amend "applies with particular force to pro se litigants"); *Martin's Herend Imports, Inc. v. Diamond & Gem Trading United States of America Co.*, 195 F.3d 765, 770 (5th Cir. 1999) (Rule 15(a) "'evinces a bias in favor of granting leave to amend.'"). *See also Rose v. Hartford Underwriters Ins. Co.*, 203 F.3d 417, 420 (6th Cir. 2000) (marginal entry order denying leave to amend, without explanation, is abuse of discretion; but error is harmless if

amendment would be futile; proposed amendment is futile if it cannot withstand motion to dismiss under Rule 12(b)(6)); *Firestone v. Firestone*, 76 F.3d 1205, 1209 (D.C. Cir. 1996) (per curiam) (criticizing district court's "complete failure" to explain grounds for denying leave to amend). *But see, Minneapolis Firefighters' Relief Association v. MEMC Electronic Materials, Inc.*, 641 F.3d 1023, 1030 (8th Cir. 2011) (acknowledging that leave to amend should be freely given, but "placing a footnote in a resistance to a motion to dismiss requesting leave to amend in the event of dismissal is insufficient"); *Miller v. Champion Enterprises Inc.*, 346 F.3d 660, 690 (6th Cir. 2003) (in cases involving Private Securities Litigation Reform Act, 15 U.S.C.A. § 78u-4(b)(2) and (3), heightened pleading requirements of that law restrict liberal amendment standard of Rule 15(a); thus, failure to allege fraud with particularity may result in dismissal rather than leave to amend); *Lake v. Arnold*, 232 F.3d 360, 374 (3d Cir. 2000) (failure to provide draft amended complaint to district court is ground for denying leave to amend even where court did not provide reasons for denial); *Doe v. Howe Military School*, 227 F.3d 981, 989 (7th Cir. 2000) (proper exercise of discretion to deny motion to amend where plaintiffs did not state specifically what amended pleadings would allege; motion to amend or supplement complaint is held to higher standard of specificity than original complaint).

time limits are appropriate.[22]

Requirement to Submit Proposed Amendment

A party seeking leave to amend must, inter alia, submit a proposed amendment to the court.[23]

Termination of Leave to Amend; Rules 59 and 60

Some courts hold that once a case has been dismissed—with or without prejudice—leave to file subsequent amendments to pleadings lapses.[24] The situation may change if a plaintiff can meet the requirements of Rule 59(e) (governing motions to alter or amend judgments) or Rule 60(b) (governing motions to vacate judgments).[25] Otherwise, only if a district court dismisses without prejudice *and* expressly grants leave to amend will the possibility of amending a pleading still exist.[26] However, at least one circuit court treats dismissal without

---

[22]*Shane v. Fauver*, 213 F.3d 113 (3d Cir. 2000). *But see Myles v. U.S.*, 416 F.3d 551 (7th Cir. 2005) (no need for district judge to tell *pro se* plaintiff "he *ought* to amend; even *pro se* litigants are masters of their own complaints. . . . Fomenting litigation is not part of the judicial function.").

[23]*See, e.g., Pet Quarters, Inc. v. Depository Trust & Clearing Corp.*, 559 F.3d 772, 782 (8th Cir. 2009) (leave to amend inappropriate "where the plaintiff has not indicated how it would make the complaint viable, either by submitting a proposed amendment or indicating somewhere in its court filings what an amended complaint would have contained"); *Spadafore v. Gardner*, 330 F.3d 849, 853 (6th Cir. 2003) (otherwise court is unable to determine whether to grant leave to amend); *Gilmour v. Gates, McDonald and Co.*, 382 F.3d 1312, 1315 (11th Cir. 2004) ("A plaintiff may not amend her complaint through argument in a brief opposing summary judgment.").

[24]*See, e.g., Feliciano-Hernandez v. Pereira-Castillo*, 663 F.3d 527, 538 (1st Cir. 2011) (in absence of post-judgment relief, district court lacks authority to amend complaint).

[25]*See, e.g., Crestview Village Apartments v. U.S. Dept. of Housing and Urban Development*, 383 F.3d 552, 557–58 (7th Cir. 2004) (entry of final judgment terminates right to amend; plaintiff must then meet requirements of Rule 59 or Rule 60); *Ciralsky v. C.I.A.*, 355 F.3d 661, 672 (D.C. Cir.

2004) (once judgment is entered, ability to amend is terminated unless party can re-open judgment pursuant to Rule 59(e)); *Morse v. McWhorter*, 290 F.3d 795, 799 (6th Cir. 2002) ("Following entry of final judgment, a party may not seek to amend their complaint without first moving to alter, set aside or vacate judgment pursuant to either Rule 59 or Rule 60."). *See also Summers v. Earth Island Institute*, 555 U.S. 488, 129 S.Ct. 1142, 1153, 173 L.Ed.2d 1, 13 (2009) ("If Rule 15(b) allows additional facts to be inserted into the record after appeal has been filed, we are at the threshold of a brave new world of trail practice in which Rule 60 has been swallowed whole by Rule 15(b).").

[26]*Mirpuri v. ACT Mfg., Inc.*, 212 F.3d 624 (1st Cir. 2000). *See also Rodriguez v. U.S.*, 286 F.3d 972, 980 (7th Cir. 2002) (after judgment is entered, presumption in favor of leave to amend is inapplicable, and party must pursue relief under Rule 59 or Rule 60); *Building Industry Ass'n of Superior California v. Norton*, 247 F.3d 1241, 1245 (D.C. Cir. 2001) ("Ordinarily post-judgment amendment of a complaint under Rule 15(a) requires reopening of the judgment pursuant to Rule 59(e) or 60(b)."); *The Tool Box, Inc. v. Ogden City Corp.*, 419 F.3d 1084, 1087 (10th Cir. 2005) ("[E]ven though Rule 15(a) states that 'leave [to amend] shall be freely given when justice so requires,' this presumption is reversed in cases . . . where a plaintiff seeks to amend a complaint after judgment has been

prejudice, by itself, as an opportunity to amend a defective pleading.[27] Attorneys are advised to consult the local precedent.

Rule 16 and Case Management

While, as a general rule, leave to amend may be granted freely in the interest of justice, the likelihood of obtaining permission to amend diminishes drastically after the court enters a scheduling order and the scheduling deadlines have passed.[28] The same is true when the court enters a pretrial order limiting trial issues.[29] The converse, however, is probably not true. That is, compliance with a court order's time limits for filing motions to amend does not thereby enhance the probability that the motion will be granted.

A pretrial order under Rule 16 also affects pleadings-amended or not amended-in another important way. When a final pretrial order is entered, it supersedes all prior pleadings.[30]

---

entered and a case has been dismissed.").

[27]*Silva v. Di Vittorio*, 658 F.3d 1090, 1105 (9th Cir. 2011) (pro se plaintiff; absent futility, court should give plaintiff leave to amend even if plaintiff has not sought leave); *Borelli v. City of Reading*, 532 F.2d 950, 951 (3d Cir. 1976) (per curiam) ("Although the district court did not mention amendment, an implicit invitation to amplify the complaint is found in the phrase 'without prejudice.' " Also encouraging district courts to state expressly whether party has leave to amend).

[28]*See, e.g., Alioto v. Town of Lisbon*, 651 F.3d 715 (7th Cir. 2011) (noting that circuit courts generally impose heightened "good-cause" requirements under Rule 16(b) after a scheduling order has been issued); *O'Connell v. Hyatt Hotels of Puerto Rico*, 357 F.3d 152, 154–55 (1st Cir. 2004) ("good cause" standard of Rule 16(b) is "more stringent" than standard of Rule 15(a); bad faith and unfair prejudice considerations of Rule 15 may still be considered, but Rule 16 emphasizes evaluation of a party's diligence in seeking the amendment); *Leary v. Daeschner*, 349 F.3d 888, 909 (6th Cir. 2003) (once deadline for scheduling order has passed, requirement for good cause under Rule 16(b) must be satisfied; but district court must also evaluate potential of prejudice to opposing party). *But cf., Clark*

v. Martinez, 295 F.3d 809 (8th Cir.2002) ("[W]hen an issue is tried by consent [pursuant to Rule 15(b), discussed infra], it becomes of little moment whether it was encompassed in the pretrial order."); *In re Papio Keno Club, Inc.*, 262 F.3d 725, 729 (8th Cir. 2001) (noting that pretrial orders should be 'construed liberally' to include theories that might fit within order; also holding that notwithstanding pretrial order, issue tried with consent of parties may properly be heard).

[29]*See, e.g., In re Milk Products Antitrust Litigation*, 195 F.3d 430, 437 (8th Cir. 1999); *Rainy Lake One Stop, Inc. v. Marigold Foods, Inc.*, 529 U.S. 1038, 120 S. Ct. 1534, 146 L. Ed. 2d 348 (2000) ("When the district court has filed a Rule 16 pretrial scheduling order, it may properly require that good cause be shown for leave to file an amended pleading that is substantially out of time under that order."). *Byrd v. Guess*, 137 F.3d 1126, 1131–32 (9th Cir. 1998) ("Once the district court enters a scheduling order setting forth a deadline for the amendment of pleadings, modifications are allowed only upon showing of 'good cause.' . . . And once a pretrial order has been entered pursuant to rule 16(e) setting forth the parties and issues for trial, modifications are allowed 'only to prevent manifest injustice.' ").

[30]*Rockwell Intern. Corp. v. U.S.*, 549 U.S. 457, 127 S. Ct. 1397, 167 L. Ed. 2d 190 (2007) ("[W]e look to the

Standard of Discretion

Generally, leave to amend is granted unless a weighing of several factors suggests that leave would be inappropriate.[31] In particular, if leave to amend is denied, it will often occur because an amendment would create unfair prejudice to another party.[32] Prejudice is most commonly found when there has been substantial unjustified delay in moving to amend that creates an unfair disadvantage for an opposing party.[33] By contrast, no unfair prejudice exists simply because a party has

---

allegations as amended-here, the statement of claims in the final pretrial order.") *See, e.g., Wilson v. Muckala*, 303 F.3d 1207, 1215 (10th Cir. 2002) ("Claims, issues, defenses, or theories of damages not included in the pretrial order are waived even if they appeared in the complaint and, conversely, the inclusion of a claim in the pretrial order is deemed to amend any previous pleadings which did not include that claim.").

[31]*See, e.g., Benson v. St. Joseph Regional Health Center*, 575 F.3d 542, 550 (5th Cir. 2009) (district court has almost unlimited discretion to allow amendments prior to judgment, but "that discretion narrows considerably after entry of judgment"). *Jackson v. Rockford Housing Authority*, 213 F.3d 389 (7th Cir.2000) ("The general rule that amendment is allowed absent undue surprise or prejudice to the plaintiff is widely adhered to by our sister courts of appeals."). *Cf., U.S. ex rel. Lee v. SmithKline Beecham, Inc.*, 245 F.3d 1048, 1052 (9th Cir. 2001) (citing same factors, but noting they do not get equal weight; futility of amendment, by itself, can be ground for denying leave to amend).

[32]*See, e.g., Eminence Capital, LLC v. Aspeon, Inc.*, 316 F.3d 1048, 1052 (9th Cir. 2003) ("[I]t is the consideration of prejudice to the opposing party that carries the greatest weight."). *See also Thornton v. McClatchy Newspapers, Inc.*, 261 F.3d 789, 799 (9th Cir. 2001) (finding of bad faith in party's history of dilatory tactics and "doubtful value of proposed amendment" may also justify denial of leave to amend). *But see Kenda Corp., Inc. v. Pot O'Gold Money Leagues, Inc.*, 329 F.3d 216, 232 (1st Cir. 2003) (absence of prejudice to nonmoving party is not always dispositive of is-

sue; court may consider other factors and still deny motion to amend; failure to explain lengthy delay in making motion to amend can be fatal to proposed amendment).

[33]*See, e.g., Jin v. Metropolitan Life Ins. Co.*, 295 F.3d 335 (2d Cir. 2002) (no abuse of discretion to find undue delay in filing motion to amend over four years after original filing; more than three years after close of discovery; and nearly three months after ruling on summary judgment motions); *U.S. ex.rel. Bernard v. Casino Magic Corp.*, 293 F.3d 419 (8th Cir. 2002) (no abuse of discretion to deny leave to amend "two and a half years into the litigation," especially when plaintiff can obtain desired information without joining company as party); *Owens Corning v. National Union Fire Ins. Co. of Pittsburgh, PA*, 257 F.3d 484, 496–97 (6th Cir. 2001) (unfair prejudice when amendments "suddenly appear" as opponent "was preparing to litigate the remaining issues by motion for summary judgment"). *But compare Dennis v. Dillard Dept. Stores, Inc.*, 207 F.3d 523, 526 (8th Cir. 2000) (discovery had closed, but no unfair prejudice to opposing party where three months remained before trial date which could be used to reopen limited discovery-and district court could impose costs of new discovery on party seeking amendment), *and Bowles v. Reade*, 198 F.3d 752, 758 (9th Cir. 1999) ("Undue delay by itself . . . is insufficient to justify denying a motion to amend." Such delay justifies denial of leave to amend only when accompanied by unfair prejudice, bad faith, or futility), *with Jennings v. BIC Corp.*, 181 F.3d 1250, 1258 (11th Cir. 1999) ("The U.S. Supreme Court has held that undue delay is an adequate basis for denying leave to amend.").

to defend against new or better pleaded claims.[34] However, while Rule 15(a) imposes no time limits on motions for leave to amend pleadings, substantial unexplained and unjustified delays in seeking leave to amend generally reduce the prospects for obtaining leave to amend.[35]

Additionally, proposed amendments that contain a strong hint of sharp practice, unaccompanied by some justifying explanation, may also be rejected.[36]

Abuse of Discretion

Failure by the district court to explain its reasons for denying leave to amend may by itself be abuse of the court's discretion, unless the reason for the court's decision is apparent on the record.[37]

It is not abuse of discretion for a district court to fail to invite a party to amend a pleading.[38]

Futile Amendments

Amended pleadings that would clearly not prevail or

---

[34]*See, e.g., Popp Telcom v. American Sharecom, Inc.*, 210 F.3d 928, 943 (8th Cir. 2000) ("The inclusion of a claim based on facts already known or available to both sides does not prejudice the non-moving party."); *Busam Motor Sales v. Ford Motor Co.*, 203 F.2d 469, 472 (6th Cir. 1953) (Rule 15 amendment is not barred simply because it raises new issue of law).

[35]*Krupski v. Costa Crociere, S.p.A.*, __ U.S. __, 130 S.Ct. 2485, 177 L. Ed. 2d 48 (2010) (district court may consider "undue delay" or "dilatory motive" when considering whether to grant leave to amend pursuant to Rule 15(a); but no such discretion exists when court is considering relation back under Rule 15(c)). *See, e.g., Waldron v. Adams & Leese, L.L.P.*, 676 F.3d 455, 467 (5th Cir. 2012 (unexplained delay weighs in favor of denying leave); *Prater v. Ohio Educ. Ass'n*, 505 F.3d 437, 445 (6th Cir. 2007) (Sixth Circuit requires "at least some significant showing of prejudice" to deny motion otherwise based solely on delay); *Harrison v. Rubin*, 174 F.3d 249 (D.C. Cir. 1999) (undue delay where plaintiff sought to change factual allegations is ground for denying leave to amend; but where "amendment would do no more than clarify legal theories or make corrections" undue delay without prejudice to opposing party does not justify denial of

leave to amend). *See also California Public Employees' Retirement System v. Chubb Corp.*, 394 F.3d 126 (3d Cir.2004) (failure to follow district court's instructions on meeting heightened pleading requirements of Rule 9 justifies denial of leave to amend).

[36]*See, e.g., Hayes v. Whitman*, 264 F.3d 1017, 1027 (10th Cir. 2001) (rejecting proposed amendment that attempted to "salvage a lost case by untimely suggestion of new theories of recovery"); *Viernow v. Euripides Development Corp.*, 157 F.3d 785, 800 (10th Cir. 1998) (rejecting dubious effort to employ complaint as "moving target"); *Pallottino v. City of Rio Rancho*, 31 F.3d 1023, 1027 (10th Cir. 1994) (rejecting offers of "theories seriatim" to try to fend off dismissal).

[37]*Foman v. Davis*, 371 U.S. 178, 182, 83 S. Ct. 227, 230, 9 L. Ed. 2d 222 (1962). *Grayson v. Mayview State Hosp.*, 293 F.3d 103 (3d Cir. 2002) (when plaintiff does not seek leave to amend deficient complaint after defendant has moved to dismiss, court must inform plaintiff of leave to amend and provide time to do so; however, court has no such duty if amendment would be futile or inequitable).

[38]*See, e.g., Gomez v. Wells Fargo Bank, N.A.*, 676 F.3d 655, 665 (8th Cir. 2012).

improve the position of a party will be rejected.[39] For example, if the proposed amendment would not survive a motion to dismiss, it will be rejected.[40]

Imposition of Costs

Rule 15 does not address issues of costs arising from amended pleadings. However, it appears settled that, as a condition of granting leave to amend, a court may require an amending party to pay the opponent's costs caused by the amendment.[41]

Effect of Amendment

If an amendment is appropriate under Rule 15(a), it displaces the earlier pleading to which it is directed.[42] If a party filing an amendment wishes to preserve some portions of the original pleading, the party should incorporate those portions by specific reference in the amended pleading.

Responding to Amended Pleadings

Rule 15(a) provides that if the pleading amended is one to which a responsive pleading is appropriate, the opposing party will have either the time remaining before a response to the unamended version was due, or fourteen days—whichever is longer—in which to respond.[43] However, the court has authority to alter those time limits as may be appropriate in the cir-

---

[39]*Foman v. Davis*, 371 U.S. 178, 83 S. Ct. 227, 9 L. Ed. 2d 222 (1962); *Jefferson County School Dist. No. R-1 v. Moody's Investor's Services, Inc.*, 175 F.3d 848 (10th Cir. 1999) ("[T]he district court may deny leave to amend where amendment would be futile."); *Wisdom v. First Midwest Bank, of Poplar Bluff*, 167 F.3d 402, 409 (8th Cir. 1999) ("[P]arties should not be allowed to amend their complaint without showing how the complaint could be amended to save the meritless claim."). *But see, Van Le v. Five Fathoms, Inc.*, 792 F. Supp. 372 (D.N.J. 1992) (opponent of proposed amendment carries burden of clearly establishing futility).

[40]*See, e.g., In re NVE Corp. Securities Litigation*, 527 F.3d 749, 752 (8th Cir. 2008) (denying leave to amend when "appellants have not articulated any changes they wish to make, much less demonstrated how revision would address the numerous pleading deficiencies identified by the district court."); *Rodriguez v. U.S.*, 286 F.3d 972, 980 (7th Cir. 2002) ("A district court may properly deny a motion to amend as futile if the proposed amend-

ment would be barred by the statute of limitations."); *Rose v. Hartford Underwriters Ins. Co.*, 203 F.3d 417, 420 (6th Cir. 2000) (proposed amendment is futile if it cannot withstand motion to dismiss under Rule 12(b)(6)).

[41]*See, e.g., Valadez-Lopez v. Chertoff*, 656 F.3d 851, 857 (9th Cir. 2011) (noting "well-established" law that amended complaint replaces original complaint, which becomes a nullity).

[42]*See, e.g., In re Wireless Telephone Federal Cost Recovery Fees Litigation*, 396 F.3d 922, 928 (8th Cir. 2005) ("It is well-established that an amended complaint supercedes an original complaint and renders the original complaint without legal effect."); *King v. Dogan*, 31 F.3d 344, 346 (5th Cir. 1994) (same, "unless the amended complaint specifically refers to and adopts or incorporates by reference the earlier pleading").

[43]*See, e.g., General Mills, Inc. v. Kraft Foods Global, Inc.*, 495 F.3d 1378, 1379 (Fed. Cir. 2007) (explaining interplay between Rules 12(a)(1) to (4) and 15(a)(3).

cumstances of the case.[44]

Relationship to Rule 15(b)

Technically, a motion for leave of court to amend a pleading may be made at any time under Rule 15(a). However, if a suit has advanced to trial or post-trial motions, Rule 15(b), pertaining to amendments to conform to the evidence, is probably a more appropriate vehicle for amendments to pleadings. However, the difference between Rule 15(a) and (b) is not a bright line, and generally courts are liberal in granting permission for substantive amendments under either provision provided that no unfair prejudice thereby accrues to other parties.[45]

RULE 15(b)—AMENDMENTS DURING AND AFTER TRIAL

CORE CONCEPT

Rule 15(b) permits amendments to pleadings in two circumstances. The first situation arises when an issue not raised in the original pleadings is tried[46] by consent of the parties. The second occurs when an issue not raised in the pleadings is objected to, but the proposed amendment will either not create unfair prejudice, or such prejudice as may result can be cured by other judicial action.

APPLICATIONS

Timing; Relationship to Rule 15(a)

Motions to amend under Rule 15(b) may theoretically be made at any time. The language of the Rule, however, speaks to matters raised at trial, suggesting that the Rule should not generally be used at early stages of litigation.[47] Instead, early in the litigation it is more appropriate to seek to amend a pleading under the authority of Rule 15(a). Generally speaking, mo-

---

[44]*See also California Public Employees' Retirement System v. Chubb Corp.*, 394 F.3d 126 (3d Cir.2004) (failure to follow district court's instructions on meeting heightened pleading requirements of Rule 9 justifies denial of leave to amend).

[45]*See, e.g., U.S. for Use and Benefit of Seminole Sheet Metal Co. v. SCI, Inc.*, 828 F.2d 671 (11th Cir. 1987) (applying Rule 15(b) standards to amending dismissed complaint).

[46]*Cf., Marsh v. Butler County, Ala.*, 268 F.3d 1014, 1024 (11th Cir. 2001) (although Rule 15(b) discusses cases that have been "tried" by consent, "we accept Rule 15(b) as a guide by way of analogy, at the appellate level for

cases never tried, but litigated on motions").

[47]*See, e.g., Cook v. City of Bella Villa*, 582 F.3d 840, 852 (8th Cir. 2009) (Rule 15(b) not applicable to amendments prior to trial); *Gold v. Local 7 United Food and Commercial Workers Union*, 159 F.3d 1307, 1309 (10th Cir. 1998) ("Rule 15(b) seems a totally inappropriate vehicle for a motion to amend prior to trial."). *But see Ahmad v. Furlong*, 435 F.3d 1196, 1203 (10th Cir. 2006) (noting extensive split of authority as to whether Rule 15(b) should be applied to issues raised in a motion for summary judgment on the eve of trial; collecting cites).

tions to amend under Rule 15(b) are made at trial or in the immediate aftermath of a trial.[48]

However, while Rule 15(b) motions are generally made at trial or in the immediate aftermath of a trial,[49] there is authority permitting application of Rule 15(b) to some pre-trial situations "to address discrepancies."[50] Contrary authority is also available, so attorneys are advised to consult local authority and practice.

Relationship to Rule 15(c)

If a new claim is asserted through a pleading amended pursuant to Rule 15(b), there may still be questions about the timeliness of the claim. While Rule 15(b) may permit the amended pleading, Rule 15(c) controls whether the amended pleading is deemed to have been filed on the date of the original pleading or the date of the amendment. The distinction is significant when questions of statutes of limitations are raised.

Claims for Relief

Rule 15(b) may be employed to assert claims for affirmative relief, even after a trial is ended. Thus, for example, a counterclaim may be asserted through a Rule 15(b) amendment where the evidence on the counterclaim was heard at trial.[51]

Failure to Object

Rule 15(b) provides that an opposing party's consent to an amendment may be express or implied.[52] Thus, the court may find that parties who fail to object to the litigation of matters

---

[48]*See, e.g., United States v. 5443 Suffield Terrace*, 607 F.3d 504 (7th Cir. 2010) (in appropriate circumstance party may amend "even after judgment has been entered"); *Triple Five of Minnesota, Inc. v. Simon*, 404 F.3d 1088, 1095 (8th Cir. 2005) (Rule 15(b) "motion may be made at any time, even after judgment."). *See also Oneida Indian Nation v. County of Oneida*, 617 F.3d 114, 142 n.3 (2d Cir. 2010) (Rule 15(b) technically inapplicable on appeal, but nonetheless sometimes used by analogy when amendment will reflect more accurately what happened in trial court).

[49]*See, e.g., United States v. 5443 Suffield Trrace*, 607 F.3d 504 (7th Cir. 2010 (in appropriate circumstances party may amend after entry of judgment).

[50]*See, e.g., Liberty Lincoln-Mercury, Inc. v. Ford Motor Co.*, 676 F.3d 318, 327 n.7 (3d Cir. 2012) (not deciding issue, but collecting conflict-

ing authorities).

[51]*See, e.g., In re Meyertech Corp.*, 831 F.2d 410, 421 (3d Cir. 1987) (approving use of Rule 15(b) to raise a counterclaim).

[52]*See, e.g., U.S. ex rel. Modern Elec., Inc. v. Ideal Electronic Sec. Co., Inc.*, 81 F.3d 240 (D.C. Cir. 1996) (noting that express or implied consent is "a condition for treating unpled issues as though they were raised in the pleadings"); *Rodriguez v. Doral Mortg. Corp.*, 57 F.3d 1168, 1172 (1st Cir. 1995) (implied consent may be found where claim not mentioned in complaint is addressed "by means of a sufficiently pointed interrogatory answer or in a pretrial memorandum" to which opponent responds by engaging claim or by " 'silent acquiescence;' " alternatively, " 'consent to the trial of an issue may be implied if, during the trial, a party acquiesces in the introduction of evidence which is relevant only to that issue' "). *But see Dream Games of*

not within the four corners of the original pleadings have impliedly consented to adjudication of those matters.[53] In those circumstances, the court will permit an amended pleading that reflects the issues actually litigated.[54]

Failure to File an Amended Pleading; Motions to Amend

Rule 15(b) expressly provides that if parties are found to have consented to litigation of issues outside the original pleadings, there is no requirement that a formal amended pleading be filed. Instead, the result in the case will stand, irrespective of the presence or absence of amendments.[55]

However, if an opposing party makes a proper objection to evidence going to a new claim, the party seeking relief under Rule 15(b) must make an appropriate motion to amend.[56]

Amendments Over Objections to Evidence

If a party objects to the use of evidence on the ground that it does not address issues raised in the original pleadings, Rule 15(b) authorizes the court to allow amendments that encompass

---

Arizona, Inc. v. PC Onsite, 561 F.3d 983, 995 (9th Cir. 2009) (no amendment permitted under Rule 15(b) where evidence as to unpleaded issue was also relevant to previously pleaded issue and trial record did not disclose intent to raise new issue); *Koch v. Koch Industries, Inc.*, 203 F.3d 1202, 1217 (10th Cir. 2000) (no implied consent to new issue where testimony was relevant to issues already at trial).

[53] *See, e.g., Eich v. Board of Regents for Cent. Missouri State University*, 350 F.3d 752, 762 (8th Cir. 2003) (failure to object to jury instructions on economic damages means issue was tried by consent). *But see Sasse v. U.S. Dept. of Labor*, 409 F.3d 773, 781 (6th Cir. 2005) (no implied consent if issue was tried inadvertently; evidence going to both pleaded issue and unpleaded issue is not notice of new unpleaded issue's presence in case); *Kenda Corp., Inc. v. Pot O'Gold Money Leagues, Inc.*, 329 F.3d 216, 232 (1st Cir. 2003) (evidence directly relevant to pleaded issue cannot be used to imply consent to litigation of non-pleaded issue); *Kovacevich v. Kent State University*, 224 F.3d 806, 831 (6th Cir. 2000) (" 'Implied consent' " requires considerable litigation of a matter—"it must appear that the parties understood the evidence to be aimed at the unpleaded issue.' "). *But*

cf., IES Industries, Inc. v. U.S., 349 F.3d 574, 579 (8th Cir. 2003) ("It is axiomatic that evidence bearing on both claims and the defenses to those claims may well overlap in a given case. Such an inevitability does not foreclose amendment under Rule 15(b).").

[54] *See, e.g., House of Flavors, Inc. v. TFG Michigan, L.P.*, 643 F.3d 35, 41 (1st Cir. 2011) ("fair warning" of new direction in case justifies amendment under Rule 15(b)).

[55] *See, e.g., People for Ethical Treatment of Animals v. Doughney*, 263 F.3d 359, 367 (4th Cir. 2001) ("Even without a formal amendment, 'a district court may amend the pleadings merely by entering findings on the unpleaded issues.' "). *See also, Creative Demos, Inc. v. Wal-Mart Stores, Inc.*, 142 F.3d 367, 371–72 (7th Cir. 1998) (approving district court's amendment to conform to "what the parties were arguing about at trial, although they did not use the magic words").

[56] *See, e.g., Green Country Food Market, Inc. v. Bottling Group, LLC*, 371 F.3d 1275, 1281 (10th Cir. 2004) (where proper objection was made but advocate of amendment made no motion, "the lack of prejudice to a party does not provide a basis for amendment.").

such evidence.[57] Such amendments may be permitted on either of two grounds: the absence of unfair prejudice to the objecting party,[58] or the ability of the court to cure such prejudice.[59]

Grounds for Denying Rule 15(b) Amendments

Courts deny Rule 15(b) amendments on any of four grounds: bad faith; undue delay; unfair prejudice to an opponent; or futility of a proposed amendment.[60] It should be noted, however, that if an issue is tried with the express or implied consent of the parties, the district court must accept the amended pleading. In such circumstances, the court has no discretion, and acceptance of the amendment is mandatory.[61]

Unfair Prejudice

Determinations of unfair prejudice are highly fact specific. The most likely circumstance in which such prejudice will be found occurs when the objecting party is surprised by the evidence and has no reasonable opportunity to meet it.[62]

Curing Unfair Prejudice

If the source of unfair prejudice is surprise, courts may at-

---

[57]*Cf., Moncrief v. Williston Basin Interstate Pipeline Co.*, 174 F.3d 1150 (10th Cir.1999) (after objection has been made and ruled on, party seeking amendment under Rule 15(b) must make motion to amend; court cannot make amendment *sua sponte*).

[58]*See, e.g., New York State Elec. & Gas Corp. v. Secretary of Labor*, 88 F.3d 98 (2d Cir. 1996) ("In assessing whether the pleadings should conform to the proof, the pivotal question is whether prejudice would result.").

[59]*See, e.g., Green Country Food Market, Inc. v. Bottling Group, LLC*, 371 F.3d 1275, 1280 (10th Cir. 2004) ("The court may grant a continuance to enable the objecting party to meet such evidence.").

[60]*See, e.g., FilmTec Corp. v. Hydranautics*, 67 F.3d 931, 935 (Fed. Cir. 1995) (listing grounds). *But cf., Kenda Corp., Inc. v. Pot O'Gold Money Leagues, Inc.*, 329 F.3d 216, 232 (1st Cir. 2003) (absence of prejudice to nonmoving party is not always dispositive of issue; court may consider other factors and still deny motion to amend; failure to explain lengthy delay in making motion to amend can be fatal to proposed amendment).

[61]*See, e.g., Net Moneyin, Inc. v. VeriSign, Inc.*, 545 F.3d 1359, 1372 (Fed. Cir. 2008) (distinguishing discre-

tion of court under Rule 15(a)); *Wallin v. Fuller*, 476 F.2d 1204, 1210 (5th Cir. 1973) ("Amendment is thus not merely discretionary but mandatory in such a case.").

[62]*See, e.g., Walton v. Nalco Chemical Co.*, 272 F.3d 13, 20 (1st Cir. 2001) (implied consent found only if there is acquiescence to introduction of evidence relevant only to proposed new issue; if evidence also addresses existing issues, there is no implied consent); *Deere & Co. v. Johnson*, 271 F.3d 613, 622 (5th Cir. 2001) (same reasoning; also noting that jury's verdict form never mentioned new theory, which is something to which advocate of new theory would have objected if it believed both parties had implicitly accepted new theory); *Gussack Realty Co. v. Xerox Corp.*, 224 F.3d 85, 94 (2d Cir. 2000) ("Generally, introducing new claims for liability on the last day of the trial will prejudice the defendant;" prejudice found where plaintiffs moved to amend pleadings at close of their evidence after district court dismissed their nuisance claim). *But see IES Industries, Inc. v. U.S.*, 349 F.3d 574, 579 (8th Cir. 2003) (rejecting view that overlap of evidence vitiates consent; "It is axiomatic that evidence bearing on both claims and the defenses to those claims may well overlap in a given case.").

tempt to cure the problem by using their authority under Rule 15(b) to grant a continuance, so that the objecting party can prepare for the new evidence.[63] Such an order may include re-opening opportunities for discovery.

Resisting Rule 15(b) Motions to Amend

An attorney seeking to resist introduction of new issues at trial that are outside the original pleadings is substantially handicapped by the liberal approach of Rule 15(b) to intra-trial and post-trial amendments. If no challenge to the new issues is made, the attorney will often be deemed to have consented to the insertion of the new issues at trial.[64] If an objection is made, the attorney may be granted only the limited relief of a continuance. It is an unusual circumstance when claims, issues, or evidence relevant to a case is precluded from the trial entirely because its admission, through an amended pleading, creates incurable, unfair prejudice.[65] Such cases occur most commonly where a party seeks to amend after judgment has been entered.[66]

Relation to Rule 16

Rule 16 governs pre-trial conferences, including, *inter alia,* determination of issues that will be omitted from the trial. However, if an issue omitted under Rule 16 is actually tried, and if the issue arose with the express or implied consent of the parties pursuant to Rule 15(b), then the issue is properly before the court. In other words, in that circumstance Rule 15(b) governs.[67]

---

[63]*See, e.g., Menendez v. Perishable Distributors, Inc.*, 763 F.2d 1374, 1379 (11th Cir. 1985) (approving amendment, but noting need to give opponent opportunity to collect evidence). *But cf., Kenda Corp., Inc. v. Pot O'Gold Money Leagues, Inc.*, 329 F.3d 216, 232 (1st Cir. 2003) (absence of prejudice to nonmoving party is not always dispositive of issue; court may consider other factors and still deny motion to amend; failure to explain lengthy delay in making motion to amend can be fatal to proposed amendment).

[64]*See, e.g., Winger v. Winger*, 82 F.3d 140 (7th Cir.1996) (failure to object, along with other factors, "demonstrates that the issue was tried by implied consent"); *Estate of Dietrich v. Burrows*, 167 F.3d 1007, 1013 (6th Cir. 1999) (amended complaint never filed with court but nevertheless accepted because, *inter alia,* defendants

"treated the amendment as filed by specifically asking the district court to grant . . . summary judgment on the [amended] claim").

[65]*But see Pinkley, Inc. v. City of Frederick, MD.*, 191 F.3d 394, 401 (4th Cir. 1999) (amendment improper under rule 15(b) "where the defendant never conceded implicitly or explicitly that a conversion claim was at issue").

[66]*See, e.g., DCPB, Inc. v. City of Lebanon*, 957 F.2d 913, 917–18 (1st Cir. 1992) (where plaintiff, without good cause, did not raise claim until after judgment, court should deny "injection of new and different theory of liability at the very stroke of midnight").

[67]*See, e.g., Clark v. Martinez*, 295 F.3d 809 (8th Cir.2002) ("[W]hen an issue is tried by consent [pursuant to Rule 15(b), . . ., it becomes of little moment whether it was encompassed in the pretrial order."); *Kirkland v.*

Relation to Rule 56

Rule 15(b) questions usually arise in situations where a case has gone to trial and a dispute has arisen as to whether an issue or claim has been "tried by express or implied consent." Whether the principles underlying Rule 15(b) apply to cases decided on summary judgment, pursuant to Rule 56, appears to be an open question. Attorneys are advised to consult local precedent.[68]

Relation to Rule 60

Rule 60 governs motions to vacate judgments. It appears settled that, while a pleading may be amended under Rule 15 if a motion to vacate a judgment has been granted,[69] there is no authority in Rule 15(b) to amend a pleading prior to the grant of such a motion.[70]

RULE 15(c)—RELATION BACK OF AMENDMENTS

CORE CONCEPT

Assuming that an amended pleading will be permitted under the standards of either Rule 15(a) or (b), Rule 15(c) governs the circumstances in which the amendment will be treated as though it was filed on the date of the original pleading. This determination is highly relevant to the applicability of statutes of limitations to claims raised or parties joined in amended pleadings.

APPLICATIONS

Prerequisite of Right to Amend

Rule 15(c) deals only with whether an amendment will be treated as though it was filed at an earlier date rather than the

---

District of Columbia, 70 F.3d 629, 633–34 (D.C. Cir. 1995) (noting that if Rule 16 controlled, amendment by implied consent under Rule 15(b) would be "dead letter").

[68]*See, e.g., Independent Petroleum Ass'n of America v. Babbitt*, 235 F.3d 588, 596 (D.C. Cir. 2001) ("It is an open question whether the Federal Rules permit parties to impliedly consent to 'try' issues not raised in their pleadings through summary judgment motions;" citing cases). *See also Eddy v. Virgin Islands Water and Power Auth.*, 256 F.3d 204, 209 (3d Cir. 2001) (suggesting disapproval of raising affirmative defense for first time in motion for summary judgment, but permitting such amendment if opponent is not prejudiced); *Whitaker v. T.J. Snow Co.*, 151 F.3d 661, 663 (7th Cir. 1998) ("Because both parties squarely addressed the strict liability theory in their summary judgment briefs, the complaint was constructively amended to include that claim.").

[69]*Cf., e.g., Morse v. McWhorter*, 290 F.3d 795, 799 (6th Cir. 2002) ("Following entry of final judgment, a party may not seek to amend their complaint without first moving to alter, set aside or vacate judgment pursuant to either Rule 59 or Rule 60.").

[70]*Summers v. Earth Island Institute*, 555 U.S. 488, 129 S.Ct. 1142, 1153, 173 L.Ed.2d 1, 13 (2009) ("If rule 15(b) allows additional facts to be inserted into the record after appeal has been filed, we are at the threshold of a brave new world of trial practice in which Rule 60 has been swallowed whole by Rule 15(b).").

actual date of filing—whether the amendment, in the words of Rule 15(c), "relates back" to the date the original pleading was filed. Before such relation back is contemplated, however, the proponent of the amended pleading must first persuade the court that an amended pleading should be permitted at all.[71] The standards governing authority to file an amended pleading are discussed in Rule 15(a) and (b).[72]

Inapplicability to Separate Actions

Rule 15(c) applies, if at all, only to proposed amendments to existing pleadings. It is inapplicable to a situation where a party has filed a new lawsuit and seeks "relation back" status for the claim in that case.[73]

Right to Amend Not Restricted to "Pleadings"

Although Rule 15(c) itself refers only to amendments of pleadings, it is also appropriately applied to amendments of some other documents filed in district court.[74] However, Rule 15(c) does not apply to permit relation back of an untimely notice of appeal.[75]

Relation Back Permitted

Rule 15(c) permits an amended pleading to relate back to the date of the original pleading in any of three circumstances: (1) when the statute of limitations governing the cause of action permits relation back; (2) when the claim or defense in the amended pleading arose from the same transaction or occurrence as that set forth in the original pleading; or (3) when a new party is joined and it is not unfair, as defined in Rule 15(c), for the claim against that party to be treated as if it was raised on the date the original pleading was filed. Each of these circumstances is discussed in greater detail below.

There is no discussion in Rule 15(c) of the possibility of applying relation back to permit correction of formal defects in a pleading. However, it appears clear that such a correction will

---

[71]*Cf., Williams v. Lampe*, 399 F.3d 867 (7th Cir. 2005) ("In order to benefit from [Rule 15(c)'s] 'relation back' doctrine, the original complaint must have been timely filed.").

[72]*See, e.g., Ellzey v. U.S.*, 324 F.3d 521, 527 (7th Cir. 2003) (before relation back occurs, proposed "amendment still must be appropriate under the criteria of Rule 15(a)"); *Caban-Wheeler v. Elsea*, 71 F.3d 837, 841 (11th Cir. 1996) (noting difference in standards between permission to amend complaint and whether amended claim should relate back to original complaint).

[73]*See, e.g., Neverson v. Bissonnette*, 261 F.3d 120, 126 (1st Cir. 2001)

("Rule 15(c) simply does not apply where . . . the party bringing suit did not seek to 'amend' or 'supplement' his original pleading, but, rather, opted to file an entirely new [action] at a subsequent date.").

[74]*Scarborough v. Principi*, 541 U.S. 401, 416–18, 124 S. Ct. 1856, 1867–68, 158 L. Ed. 2d 674 (2004) (applying Rule 15(c) to application for award of attorney fees; noting previous decisions to apply Rule 15 to notice of appeal and EEOC discrimination charge).

[75]*See, e.g., Cruz v. International Collection Corp.*, 673 F.3d 991, 1002 (9th Cir. 2012).

usually relate back.[76]

Statutes of Limitations

Rule 15(c)(1)(A) provides that if the statute of limitations governing a particular cause of action permits relation back of amended pleadings, relation back is permitted. The purpose of Rule 15(c)(1)(A) is to ensure that the Rule is not used to contravene statutes of limitations specifically permitting relation back, if a statute is more generous to the amended pleading.[77] Rule 15(c)(1)(A) defers to a statute of limitations only if the statute is more generous on relation back. By its own terms, Rule 15(c)(1)(A) does not apply if the statute is more restrictive. In that circumstance the provisions of Rule 15(c)(1)(B) or (C) would determine whether an amended pleading would relate back.[78]

Same Transaction or Occurrence

Rule 15(c)(1)(B) permits an amended pleading to relate back if the amended claim or defense arose out of the same transaction or occurrence as the original pleading.[79] The standard of "same transaction or occurrence" has heretofore varied substantially within the circuits, with the broadest description encompassing all events that bear a logical relationship to the original transaction.[80] Other courts have looked to the degree of overlap of evidence between the occurrences raised in the

---

[76]*See, e.g., In re IFC Credit Corp.*, 663 F.3d 315, 321 (7th Cir. 2011) (lawyer inadvertently failed to sign document).

[77]*See, e.g., Morel v. Daimler-Chrysler AG*, 565 F.3d 20, 26 (1st Cir. 2009) (Rule 15(c) "cements a one-way ratchet; less restrictive state relation-back rules will displace federal relation-back rules, but more restrictive state relation-back rules will not.").

[78]*See, e.g., Morel v. Daimler-Chrysler AG*, 565 F.3d 20, 26 (1st Cir. 2009) (Rule 15(c) "cements a one-way ratchet; less restrictive state relation-back rules will displace federal relation-back rules, but more restrictive state relation-back rules will not.").

[79]*But cf., Slayton v. American Exp. Co.*, 460 F.3d 215, 227 (2d Cir. 2006) (no exercise of discretion when application of only Rule 15(c)(1)(B) is at issue; instead, if requirements of Rule 15(c)(2) are met, proposed amendments relate back; however, questions may remain under Rule 15(a), which would require use of judicial discretion). *See also Rasberry v. Garcia*, 448 F.3d 1150 (9th Cir.2006) (Rule 15(c)(1) (B) applies to habeas petitions; however, if original petition is dismissed, second petition cannot relate back to first).

[80]*See, e.g., Wilson v. Fairchild Republic Co., Inc.*, 143 F.3d 733, 738 (2d Cir. 1998) (overruled on other grounds by, Slayton v. American Exp. Co., 460 F.3d 215 (2d Cir. 2006)) ("The pertinent inquiry . . . is whether the original complaint gave the defendant fair notice of the newly alleged claims."); *Alpern v. UtiliCorp United, Inc.*, 84 F.3d 1525, 1543 (8th Cir. 1996) ("The basic inquiry is whether the amended complaint is related to the general fact situation alleged in the original pleading."). See also *Stevelman v. Alias Research Inc.*, 174 F.3d 79 (2d Cir. 1999) (new allegations added specificity but did not add new counts; held, "same transaction" requirement clearly satisfied; "Where no new cause of action is alleged, as here, this Court liberally grants relation back under Rule 15(c).").

amended pleading and the original pleading.[81] However, the Supreme Court recently held that the somewhat more restrictive construction of the "same transaction or occurrence" standard previously applied by a majority of the circuit courts is now the applicable law.[82] Thus, the broadest description appears to be available no longer.

It should be noted that this standard is measured by the facts pleaded. It does not depend on the legal theory offered. Thus, an amendment may relate back notwithstanding that the proffered amendment offers a new legal theory.[83]

Proving Lack of Notice

It appears that in determining whether relation back should be permitted under Rule 15(c)(2), a district court may consider relevant extrinsic evidence, and is not confined to examination of the pleadings themselves.[84]

Amendments That Add a Party or Change a Party's Name

To obtain the benefits of relation back when a new party is named[85] or a party's name is changed, the amended pleading must satisfy the elements of Rule 15(c)(1)(C): (1) it must arise from the same transaction or occurrence as the original pleading, as provided by Rule 15(c)(1)(B); and (2) within the 120-day period after filing of the original pleading that Rule 4(m) provides for service of process, the party named in the amended pleading must have both received sufficient notice of the pendency of the action so as not to be prejudiced in preparing a defense, and have known or should have known that but for a mistake of identity the party would have been named in the original pleading. The first element—same transaction or occurrence—follows the discussion of Rule 15(c)(1)(B), above. The other element has two parts—fair notice and awareness of a mistake in identity—that are explained immediately below. In addition to the requirement of same transaction or occurrence,

---

[81]See, e.g., Martell v. Trilogy Ltd., 872 F.2d 322, 325 (9th Cir. 1989) (noting that original and amended pleadings share "a common nucleus of operative facts").

[82]Mayle v. Felix, 545 U.S. 644, 125 S. Ct. 2562, 2569–75, 162 L. Ed. 2d 582 (2005).

[83]See, e.g., Maegdlin v. International Ass'n of Machinists and Aerospace Workers, Dist. 949, 309 F.3d 1051, 1053 (8th Cir. 2002). Cf., Johnson v. Crown Enterprises, Inc., 398 F.3d 339, 342 (5th Cir. 2005) (focus is not on caption of count, but underlying facts).

[84]U.S. ex rel. Bledsoe v. Community Health Systems, Inc., 501 F.3d 493, 517 (6th Cir. 2007) (permitting use of documents outside the formal pleadings).

[85]See, e.g., Gallas v. Supreme Court of Pennsylvania, 211 F.3d 760, 777 (3d Cir. 2000) (replacing "John Doe" with real name of party changes a party within meaning of Rule 15(c) (3)). See also Moore v. City of Harriman, 272 F.3d 769, 774 (6th Cir. 2001) (applying Rule 15(c)(1)(C), rather than Rule 15(c)(1)(B) to permit plaintiff to amend complaint to clarify that same defendants were being sued in their personal capacities).

both fair notice and awareness of a mistake concerning identity, must be satisfied before an amended pleading may relate back under Rule 15(c)(1)(C).

(1) *Notice:* The kind of notice Rule 15(c)(1)(C) requires is that which, in the particular circumstances of a case, ensures that the party joined is not unfairly prejudiced by an amended pleading that relates back to an earlier date.[86] If a party to be joined in an amended complaint learned of a suit within the 120-day period provided by Rule 4(m) for service of the original complaint,[87] and that party's opportunity to prepare a defense was not hindered by the time lag between the original pleading and the amended pleading, Rule 15(c)(1)(C)'s requirement of notice generally would be satisfied.[88] For example, corporations in a parent-subsidiary relationship with an entity sued in the original complaint would probably be held to have notice of the original action.[89] Similarly, if the proposed change merely corrects a "misnomer," the complaint may relate back.[90] However, where the original complaint cited only aliases of police officer defendants and not their actual names, the issue of notice is a more serious problem.[91] Finally, a person who had not been named as a defendant in the original complaint, but who was

---

[86]*See, e.g., Garvin v. City of Phila-delphia,* 354 F.3d 215, 222 (3d Cir. 2003) (prejudice is that which might be caused, for lack of notice, by difficulty in gathering evidence and preparing defense in case that became stale).

[87]*See, e.g., Jones v. Bernanke,* 557 F.3d 670, 675 (D.C. Cir. 2009) (original complaint, "not some other earlier filing or document," must provide notice of amended claim). *See also Robinson v. Clipse,* 602 F.3d 605, 609 (4th Cir. 2010) (if use of Rule 4(m) is tolled for unrelated reasons not within control of party, running of 120 day period is similarly tolled for application of Rule 15(c)(3)).

[88]*See, e.g., Singletary v. Pennsylvania Dept. of Corrections,* 266 F.3d 186, 189 (3d Cir. 2001) (in absence of actual notice to potential new party, identifying two means of imputing notice received by original defendants to party sought to be added: (1) through sharing same attorney; or (2) identity of interest between original parties and party sought to be added). *Cf., e.g., Atchinson v. District of Columbia,* 73 F.3d 418, 427 (D.C. Cir. 1996) (noting, *inter alia,* prejudice because individual defendant would probably

have adopted different discovery and defense tactics if he had received adequate notice of claim of his individual liability).

[89]*See, e.g., Andrews v. Lakeshore Rehabilitation Hosp.,* 140 F.3d 1405, 1408 (11th Cir. 1998) (if subsidiary had notice of suit, parent holding 100% of subsidiary "is deemed to have had notice"); *G.F. Co. v. Pan Ocean Shipping Co., Ltd.,* 23 F.3d 1498, 1503 (9th Cir. 1994) (original defendant was claims agent for new party and both parties shared the same attorney; held, good notice to new party).

[90]*See, e.g., Datskow v. Teledyne, Inc., Continental Products Div.,* 899 F.2d 1298, 1301–02 (2d Cir. 1990) (complaint properly served, but correct name of defendant was "Teledyne Industries, Inc.;" held, defendant had adequate notice of suit and thus "case may be categorized as one of mislabeling").

[91]*See, e.g., Eison v. McCoy,* 146 F.3d 468 (7th Cir.1998) (complaint's listing of "T.C., Cronie, Pac Man, and Crater Face" does not provide notice where police department has more than 17,000 employees). *But cf. Moore v. City of Harriman,* 272 F.3d 769, 774 (6th Cir. 2001) (police officers sued on

impleaded under Rule 14 by the original defendant, would probably be held to have had fair notice under Rule 15(c)(1)(C), if the impleader was served on that person within the 120-day period provided by Rule 4(m).

(2) *Knowledge of Mistaken Identity*: Before an amended pleading may relate back under Rule 15(c)(1)(C), the proponent of the pleading must also establish that within the 120-day period provided by Rule 4(m) the person to be joined knew, or should have known, that the person would have been sued under the original pleading but for some mistake in identity.[92] Thus, if a subsidiary corporation was sued when the claim should have been against its parent, and was served within the period provided by Rule 4(m), the parent might be charged with timely knowledge of the fact that the proper defendant should have been the parent.[93] With natural persons, the requirement may be satisfied when the name of the proper defendant is similar to the name of the person originally designated as a defendant, *and* the proper defendant knew of the mistake within the time limit established by Rule 4(m).[94]

Rule 15(c)(1)(C)(ii): Requirement of "Mistake"

Relation back under Rule 15(c)(1)(C)(ii) is permitted only if the party joined by amendment knew or should have known that it would have been sued originally but for a mistake. It is unclear whether the mistake may be one of either fact or law,[95] but in other respects this requirement has been construed rather strictly. Thus if the party seeking to amend made no mistake, relation back is not permitted under Rule 15(c)(1)(C).[96]

Moreover, addition of a new defendant will generally not

---

state tort claims as well as federal civil rights claims have "clear notice" from state claims and federal claim under 42 U.S.C.A. § 1983 that "they faced individual liability of some sort").

[92]*Krupski v. Costa Crociere, S.p.A.*, __ U.S. __, 130 S.Ct. 2485, 177 L. Ed. 2d 48 (2010) (issue is not whether amending party knew or should have known identity of proposed defendant, but whether defendant understood or should have understood that it was the proper defendant).

[93]*Krupski v. Costa Crociere, S.p.A.*, __ U.S. __, 130 S.Ct. 2485, 177 L. Ed. 2d 48 (2010). *See, e.g., Peterson v. Sealed Air Corp.*, 902 F.2d 1232 (7th Cir.1990) (service was on agent of both parent and subsidiary).

[94]*See, e.g., Brown v. Shaner*, 172 F.3d 927, 933 (6th Cir. 1999) (police officers sued in civil rights case; plaintiff's complaint identified individual

wrongful acts but did not state whether defendants were sued in their official capacity or individually; held, failure to identify allegation of individual liability satisfies "mistake" requirement, and defendants should have known that but for mistake they were being sued individually).

[95]*Compare, e.g., Woods v. Indiana University-Purdue University at Indianapolis*, 996 F.2d 880, 887 (7th Cir. 1993) (indicating that mistake may be of fact or law), *with Rendall-Speranza v. Nassim*, 107 F.3d 913, 918 (D.C. Cir. 1997) (amendment permitted, if at all, only for mistake of fact).

[96]*See, e.g., Gomez v. Randle*, ___ F.3d ___, ___ n.1 (7th Cir. 2012) (plaintiff's lack of knowledge of defendant's identity is not "mistake" that would permit relation back under Rule 15(c); *Garrett v. Fleming*, 362 F.3d 692 (10th Cir.2004) (lack of knowledge of relationship between entities does not

relate back if the new defendant is not being substituted for someone who is already a defendant.[97]

Relation Back of New Plaintiffs' Claims Under Rule 15(c)(1)(C)

In general, Rule 15(c)(1)(C) is not available to permit late-added plaintiffs to obtain the benefit of relation back to the date of the complaint by the original plaintiffs.[98] Exceptions to this prohibition on relation back by new plaintiffs arise when new plaintiffs share a great deal of overlapping interest with original plaintiffs or to correct a misnomer or misidentification.[99]

Undue Delay and Relation Back

Under Rule 15(a), a court may sometimes properly deny leave to amend a pleading when a party has delayed excessively and without good cause in seeking leave.[100] However, undue delay plays no role in an evaluation of relation back under Rule 15(c).[101]

---

satisfy requirement of error as to identity of proper party); *Jacobsen v. Osborne*, 133 F.3d 315, 321 (5th Cir. 1998) (relation back denied when proposed amendment would substitute named party for John Doe; no "mistake" present within meaning of Rule 15(c)(1)(C)(ii)); *Louisiana-Pacific Corp. v. ASARCO, Inc.*, 5 F.3d 431, 434 (9th Cir. 1993) (mistake in choosing who is vulnerable to suit does not meet mistake of identity requirement of Rule 15(c)(1)(C)(ii)). *But see, Arthur v. Maersk, Inc.*, 434 F.3d 196, 208 (3d Cir. 2006) (rejecting majority view that only a "misnomer or misidentification" may be a Rule 15(c)(3) mistake; "A mistake is no less a 'mistake' when it flows from lack of knowledge as opposed to an inaccurate description."); *Brown v. Shaner*, 172 F.3d 927, 933 (6th Cir. 1999) (police officers sued in civil rights case; plaintiff's complaint identified individual wrongful acts but did not state whether defendants were sued in their official capacity or individually; held, failure to identify allegation of individual liability satisfies "mistake" requirement). *See also, Alston v. Parker*, 363 F.3d 229, 236 (3d Cir. 2004) (considering possibility that civil rights plaintiffs may have unusual problem of not knowing precisely who "relevant actors" were, and should therefore perhaps have access to "some initial discovery"); *Woods v. Indiana University-Purdue University at India-*

napolis, 996 F.2d 880, 887 (7th Cir. 1993) (suit originally named police department rather than individual officers; held, police should have known that police department had sovereign immunity, and thus should have known of mistake; relation back permitted).

[97]*See, e.g., Braud v. Transport Service Co. of Illinois*, 445 F.3d 801, 807 (5th Cir. 2006) (distinguishing between misnomer that should be corrected and mere addition of party).

[98]*See, e.g., Asher v. Unarco Material Handling, Inc.*, 596 F.3d 313, 318 (6th Cir. 2010) (Rule 15(c)(1)(C) usually available only to add defendants).

[99]*See, e.g., Young v. Lepone*, 305 F.3d 1, 14 (1st Cir. 2002) (relation back of new plaintiffs' claims "theoretically available," but there must be, *inter alia,* an identity of interest with claims of original plaintiffs); *In re Kent Holland Die Casting & Plating, Inc.*, 928 F.2d 1448, 1450 (6th Cir. 1991) (noting relation back to correct misnomers as an exception to general prohibition of relation back for new plaintiffs).

[100]*See* Authors' Commentary on Rule 15(a).

[101]*Krupski v. Costa Crociere, S.p.A.* __ U.S. __, 130 S.Ct. 2485, 177 L. Ed. 2d 48 (2010) "([T]he speed with which a plaintiff moves to amend her com-

Relation to Laches

Laches is a case law doctrine that may be raised by a defendant where the plaintiff unreasonably delays in bringing a lawsuit, and thereby unfairly harms the defendant. Rule 15(c) governs circumstances where application of the Rule might avoid unfairness arising from strict application of a statute of limitations. Because laches applies, if at all, only in the absence of a relevant statute of limitations, Rule 15 "has no controlling force where . . . a defendant's remedy is provided by the equitable doctrine of laches."[102]

Rule 17: Amendments Changing or Adding Plaintiffs

Rule 15(c)(1)(C) discusses adding parties who are the subject of claims. Its applicability when the proposed amendment seeks to add a plaintiff is not entirely clear. On the one hand, there is precedent citing language in the Advisory Committee Notes to Rule 15(c) indicating that Rule 15(c) also governs that circumstance.[103] At the same time, Rule 17(a), governing requirements to prosecute a case in the name of the real party in interest, expressly provides that joinder or substitution of the real party in interest automatically relates back to the original filing date, apparently without regard to the requirements of Rule 15. Although the matter is not free of doubt, it appears that in such circumstances Rule 17(a), and not Rule 15, should control.[104]

Commencement and Amended Complaints

Because an amended complaint often cannot be filed until leave of court has first been granted, many courts have ruled that the amended complaint is deemed filed, for "commence-

---

plaint or files an amended complaint after obtaining leave to do so has no bearing on whether the amended complaint relates back." Noting contrast with Rule 15(a)). *See, e.g., Arthur v. Maersk, Inc.*, 434 F.3d 196, 203 (3d Cir. 2006) ("There is no allowance in Rule 15(c) for inquiry into a party's delay in moving for leave to amend.").

[102]*Brzozowski v. Correctional Physician Services, Inc.*, 360 F.3d 173, 182 (3d Cir. 2004).

[103]*See, e.g., McCabe v. Trombley*, 867 F. Supp. 120, 127 (N.D. N.Y. 1994) (citing Advisory Committee notes for application of Rule 15(c) to situations where a party seeks to add a plaintiff). *See also Immigrant Assistance Project of Los Angeles County Federation of Labor (AFL-CIO) v. I.N.S.*, 306 F.3d 842, 857 (9th Cir. 2002) (relation back should be measured by whether: (1) defendant already had notice of claim

of new plaintiff; (2) presence of new plaintiff creates unfair prejudice for defendant; and (3) new plaintiff shares identity of interest with original plaintiff); *Young v. Lepone*, 305 F.3d 1, 14 (1st Cir. 2002) (Rule 15(c)(1)(C) "can be applied to amendments that change the identity of plaintiffs").

[104]*See, e.g., Scheufler v. General Host Corp.*, 126 F.3d 1261, 1271 (10th Cir. 1997) (noting uncertainty; applying relation-back provisions of Rule 17(a)). *But cf., Plubell v. Merck & Co.*, 434 F.3d 1070, 1072 (8th Cir. 2006) (acknowledging that Rule 15(c) does not "expressly" address issues of changing amendments, but concluding that Rule 15(c) applies to such situations by analogy); *Cliff v. Payco General American Credits, Inc.*, 363 F.3d 1113, 1132 (11th Cir. 2004) (concluding that use of Rule 15(c)(1)(C) "rests on solid ground;" no discussion of Rule 17).

ment" and statute of limitations purposes, as of the date that the motion for leave to amend is filed.[105] Practitioners should rely on this principle with great care, however. Whether this treatment applies to all cases (or just those where an earlier amendment was made impossible by circumstances), whether this treatment applies where the motion neither attaches the proposed amended complaint nor properly describes it, and whether this treatment has any effect where the leave is denied, are each unclear.

Relation Back Against the United States

When the United States is a defendant, Rule 15(c)(2) provides that the requirements of timely notice of the action and knowledge of a mistake in identity, discussed immediately above, are satisfied if the original pleading was served on the United States Attorney (or designee), the Attorney General, or an agency or officer who would have been a proper defendant if named in the original complaint.[106] This express provision cuts through much of what might otherwise have been substantial technical obstacles to use of relation back against the United States under Rule 15(c)(1)(C).[107] However, even when the United States is a defendant, the amended pleading must still arise out of the same transaction or occurrence as the original pleading, and service of the original pleading upon the federal officers identified above must occur within the 120-day period provided by Rule 4(m).

RULE 15(d)—SUPPLEMENTAL PLEADINGS

CORE CONCEPT

Rule 15(d) governs circumstances in which parties are permitted to supplement previous pleadings to encompass events that have occurred since the earlier pleadings were filed.

APPLICATIONS

Leave of Court

There is no unqualified right to file a supplemental pleading.[108] Authority to file a supplemental pleading is

---

[105]*See, e.g., Mayes v. AT & T Information Systems, Inc.*, 867 F.2d 1172, 1173 (8th Cir. 1989).

[106]*See, e.g., Roman v. Townsend*, 224 F.3d 24, 28 (1st Cir. 2000).

[107]*See, e.g., Delgado-Brunet v. Clark*, 93 F.3d 339, 344 (7th Cir. 1996) (so noting; but also noting that notice to government officers who are sued personally cannot be inferred from service on another government officer).

[108]*Zenith Radio Corp. v. Hazeltine Research, Inc.*, 401 U.S. 321, 91 S. Ct. 795, 28 L. Ed. 2d 77 (1971). See, e.g., *Chicago Regional Council of Carpenters v. Village of Schaumburg*, 644 F.3d 353, 356 (7th Cir. 2011) ("no absolute right to expand the case;" district court has substantial discretion to grant or deny motion to supplement pleadings); *Burns v. Exxon Corp.*, 158 F.3d 336, 343 (5th Cir. 1998) ("While the text of Rule 15(a) provides that leave should

obtained by filing a motion.[109] Courts grant such leave when the supplemental pleadings will not unfairly prejudice other parties.[110]

Party's Discretion

Supplemental pleadings are optional. Thus, if a party acquires a claim as a result of facts arising after the original pleading was filed, and the requirements of Rule 15(d) are satisfied, there is an opportunity but not a duty to file a supplemental claim.[111]

Same Transaction or Occurrence

If the issues addressed in a proposed supplemental pleading are related to the transaction or occurrence that gave rise to the original pleadings, and no other considerations of fairness weigh against hearing the supplemental pleading, courts generally permit the supplemental pleading.[112] A supplemental pleading may be permitted even if it arises from a separate transaction, but totally unrelated supplemental pleadings are disfavored.[113]

Relation to Rule 15(a)

Judicial decisions to grant or deny Rule 15(d) motions to supplement pleadings are generally based on the same factors of fairness courts weigh when considering motions to amend pleadings under Rule 15(a).[114]

---

be freely granted, the text of Rule 15(d) does not similarly provide." Also noting that plaintiffs had failed to allege that an event had occurred since filing of complaint).

[109]*See, e.g., Bornholdt v. Brady*, 869 F.2d 57, 68 (2d Cir. 1989) (noting that Rule 15(d) requires a motion). *But see Cabrera v. City of Huntington Park*, 159 F.3d 374, 382 (9th Cir. 1998) (per curiam) (Plaintiff's "failure formally to plead a malicious prosecution claim either in an amended or supplemental pleading does not preclude the district court from considering the claim.").

[110]*See, e.g., Quaratino v. Tiffany & Co.*, 71 F.3d 58, 66 (2d Cir. 1995) ("Leave is normally granted, especially when the opposing party is not prejudiced."). *See also Glatt v. Chicago Park Dist.*, 87 F.3d 190, 194 (7th Cir. 1996) (motion to amend or supplement original complaint is held to higher standard of specificity than original complaint).

[111]*See, e.g., Lundquist v. Rice Memorial Hosp.*, 238 F.3d 975, 977

(8th Cir. 2001) (decision not to file supplemental claim does not prevent assertion of that claim in later separate proceeding; doctrine of res judicata does not apply).

[112]*City of Hawthorne v. Wright*, 493 U.S. 813, 110 S. Ct. 61, 107 L. Ed. 2d 28 (1989) (noting that use of Rule 15(d) is "favored"). *See also Weeks v. New York State (Div. of Parole)*, 273 F.3d 76, 88 (2d Cir. 2001) (although other factors may be crucial, "[t]he threshhold consideration . . . is whether 'the supplemental facts connect [the supplemental pleadings] to the original pleadings' ").

[113]*See, e.g., Id.* at 474 (noting that Rule 15(d) does not require "same transaction," but does require "some relationship").

[114]*See, e.g., Glatt v. Chicago Park Dist.*, 87 F.3d 190 (7th Cir. 1996) (under both Rule 15(a) and (d), court has authority to require substantiation of proposed amended or supplemental complaint, to ensure that motive is not simply to harass opponent).

Time to File

Rule 15(d) contains no restriction on the time in which a supplemental pleading may be filed. However, the court may consider inappropriate delay in attempting to assert supplemental claims as grounds for refusing to grant permission to file the supplemental pleading.[115] Additionally, a supplemental pleading is normally inappropriate if it attempts to introduce a new and distinct cause of action after the original case has gone to final judgment.[116]

Scope of Supplemental Pleadings

Supplemental pleadings should be restricted to events occurring since initiation of the suit.[117] If the issues raised predate the original pleadings, supplemental pleadings are not the appropriate mechanism for raising them. Instead, a party should consider amending the original pleadings, pursuant to Rule 15(a) or (b).[118]

Intervening Judicial Decisions

It appears that intervening judicial decisions that change the applicable law are not the sort of "occurrences or events" that might implicate Rule 15(d).[119]

Additional Parties

In general, supplemental pleadings may join additional parties, subject to the normal requirements of jurisdiction. However, where such joinder might confuse the trier of fact or unduly distract attention from the original claims, proposals to

---

[115]*See, e.g., Quaratino v. Tiffany & Co.*, 71 F.3d 58, 66 (2d Cir. 1995) (undue delay may be ground for denying supplemental pleading).

[116]*Summers v. Earth Island Institute*, 555 U.S. 488, 129 S.Ct. 1142, 1153, 173 L.Ed.2d 1, 13 (2009) (no authority in Rule 15(d) to supplement pleadings *"after the trial is over, judgment has been entered, and a notice of appeal has been filed"* [emphasis in original].) *See, e.g., Planned Parenthood of Southern Arizona v. Neely*, 130 F.3d 400, 402–03 (9th Cir. 1997) (per curiam) (final judgment divested district court of jurisdiction; noting possible exception in circumstances where district court retained jurisdiction or where plaintiff's supplemental allegation is that defendant was attempting to thwart original judgment; held, normal remedy after judgment is entered is to bring the "supplemental" allegations in a separate lawsuit).

[117]*See Haggard v. Bank of the Ozarks, Inc.*, 668 F.3d 196, 202 (5th Cir. 2012); *Chicago Regional Council of Carpenters v. Village of Schaumburg*, 644 F.3d 353, 356 (7th Cir. 2011).

[118]*See, e.g., Flaherty v. Lang*, 199 F.3d 607, 613 (2d Cir. 1999) (Rule 15(d) applies to events that arise subsequent to a pleading; Rule 15(a) applies to efforts to replead facts that occurred prior to original pleadings.). *But see Connectu LLC v. Zuckerberg*, 522 F.3d 82, 90 (1st Cir. 2008) ("There is an open question as to whether an amended complaint asserting a cause of action that arose only after the prior complaint was filed should be regarded as 'supplemental' rather than an 'amended' complaint. The difference is modest." Noting that amended complaints may sometimes be filed as a matter of right, but supplemental complains require permission of court).

[119]*See, e.g., United States v. Hicks*, 283 F.3d 380, 385 (D.C. Cir. 2002) (Rule 15(d) is addressed to relevant new facts, not changes in law).

add new parties may reduce the prospects for obtaining permission from the court to file a supplemental pleading.[120]

Relationship to Original Pleadings

Unlike amended pleadings, supplemental pleadings do not displace the original pleadings. Thus, there is no necessity to incorporate portions of the original pleadings in a supplemental pleading simply to preserve the original pleadings. However, it may often be convenient to incorporate portions of original pleadings and thereby avoid possible duplication.

Mislabelled Pleadings

If a party inadvertently mislabels a supplemental pleading as an amended pleading, the court will disregard the error if it does not unfairly prejudice an opposing party.[121]

Defective Original Pleadings

Rule 15(d) explicitly provides that defects in the original pleadings have no effect on a party's ability to file a supplemental pleading. Thus, even an uncorrectable defect in the original pleading, requiring dismissal of the counts that pleading contains, does not necessarily bar filing of a supplemental pleading, if the supplemental pleading itself is free from substantial defects.

Responses to Supplemental Pleadings

Rule 15(d) does not create either a right or duty to respond to a supplemental pleading. Instead, the Rule vests the court with authority to order a response when appropriate in the circumstances of a case. Typically, an opportunity to respond will be permitted when the supplemental pleading asserts a new cause of action.

Relation Back of Supplemental Pleadings

Because supplemental pleadings address only events that have occurred since the original pleadings were filed, no question normally arises as to whether supplemental pleadings relate back to the date the original pleadings were filed.[122] However, where relation back is important to the supplemental pleadings, courts tend to apply the standards of Rule 15(c) to determine whether relation back should be permitted.[123]

---

[120]*See, e.g., Planned Parenthood of Southern Arizona v. Neely*, 130 F.3d 400, 402 (9th Cir. 1997) (supplemental pleading cannot be used to introduce new and distinct claim).

[121]*See, e.g., Cabrera v. City of Huntington Park*, 159 F.3d 374, 382 (9th Cir. 1998) (per curiam) (erroneously characterizing supplemental pleading as amended pleading is im-

material).

[122]*But see Innovative Therapies, Inc. v. Kinetic Concepts, Inc.*, 599 F.3d 1377, 1384 (Fed. Cir. 2010) (Rule 15(c) "does not treat events that post-date the original pleading as if they had occurred at an earlier time.").

[123]*See, e.g., F.D.I.C. v. Knostman*, 966 F.2d 1133, 1138 (7th Cir. 1992). (using standards of Rule 15(c)).

Additional Research References

Wright & Miller, *Federal Practice and Procedure* §§ 1471 to 1510

C.J.S., Federal Civil Procedure §§ 322 to 356 et seq.

West's Key Number Digest, Federal Civil Procedure ⚷821 to 853, ⚷861 to 871

RULE 16
PRETRIAL CONFERENCES;
SCHEDULING; MANAGEMENT

(a) Purposes of a Pretrial Conference. In any action, the court may order the attorneys and any unrepresented parties to appear for one or more pretrial conferences for such purposes as:

   (1) expediting disposition of the action;

   (2) establishing early and continuing control so that the case will not be protracted because of lack of management;

   (3) discouraging wasteful pretrial activities;

   (4) improving the quality of the trial through more thorough preparation; and

   (5) facilitating settlement.

(b) Scheduling.

   (1) *Scheduling Order.* Except in categories of actions exempted by local rule, the district judge—or a magistrate judge when authorized by local rule—must issue a scheduling order:

    (A) after receiving the parties' report under Rule 26(f); or

    (B) after consulting with the parties' attorneys and any unrepresented parties at a scheduling conference or by telephone, mail, or other means.

   (2) *Time to Issue.* The judge must issue the scheduling order as soon as practicable, but in any event within the earlier of 120 days after any defendant has been served with the complaint or 90 days after any defendant has appeared.

   (3) *Contents of the Order.*

    (A) *Required Contents.* The scheduling order must limit the time to join other parties, amend the pleadings, complete discovery, and file motions.

    (B) *Permitted Contents.* The scheduling order may:

     (i)   modify the timing of disclosures under Rules 26(a) and 26(e)(1);

     (ii) modify the extent of discovery;

     (iii) provide for disclosure or discovery of electronically stored information;

     (iv) include any agreements the parties reach for asserting claims of privilege or of protection as trial-preparation material after information is produced;

     (v)   set dates for pretrial conferences and for trial; and

     (vi) include other appropriate matters.

  (4) *Modifying a Schedule.* A schedule may be modified only for good cause and with the judge's consent.

(c) Attendance and Matters for Consideration at a Pretrial Conference.

  (1) *Attendance.* A represented party must authorize at least one of its attorneys to make stipulations and admissions about all matters that can reasonably be anticipated for discussion at a pretrial conference. If appropriate, the court may require that a party or its representative be present or reasonably available by other means to consider possible settlement.

  (2) *Matters for Consideration.* At any pretrial conference, the court may consider and take appropriate action on the following matters:

    (A) formulating and simplifying the issues, and eliminating frivolous claims or defenses;

    (B) amending the pleadings if necessary or desirable;

    (C) obtaining admissions and stipulations about facts and documents to avoid unnecessary proof, and ruling in advance on the admissibility of evidence;

    (D) avoiding unnecessary proof and cumulative evidence, and limiting the use of testimony under Federal Rule of Evidence 702;

    (E) determining the appropriateness and timing of summary adjudication under Rule 56;

    (F) controlling and scheduling discovery, including orders affecting disclosures and discovery under Rule 26 and Rules 29 through 37;

    (G) identifying witnesses and documents, scheduling the filing and exchange of any pretrial briefs, and setting dates for further conferences and for trial;

    (H) referring matters to a magistrate judge or a master;

    (I) settling the case and using special procedures to assist in resolving the dispute when authorized by statute or local rule;

    (J) determining the form and content of the pretrial order;

    (K) disposing of pending motions;

    (L) adopting special procedures for managing potentially difficult or protracted actions that may involve complex issues, multiple parties, difficult legal questions, or unusual proof problems;

    (M) ordering a separate trial under Rule 42(b) of a claim, counterclaim, crossclaim, third-party claim, or particular issue;

    (N) ordering the presentation of evidence early in the trial on a manageable issue that might, on the evidence, be the basis for a judgment as a matter of law under Rule 50(a) or a judgment on partial findings under Rule 52(c);

    (O) establishing a reasonable limit on the time allowed to present evidence; and

    (P) facilitating in other ways the just, speedy, and inexpensive disposition of the action.

(d) Pretrial Orders. After any conference under this rule, the court should issue an order reciting the action taken. This order controls the course of the action unless the court modifies it.

(e) Final Pretrial Conference and Orders. The court may hold a final pretrial conference to formulate a trial plan, including a plan to facilitate the admission of evidence. The conference must be held as close to the start of trial as is reasonable, and must be attended by at least one attorney who will conduct the trial for each party and by any unrepresented party. The court may modify the order issued after a final pretrial conference only to prevent manifest injustice.

(f) Sanctions.

(1) *In General.* On motion or on its own, the court may issue any just orders, including those authorized by Rule 37(b)(2)(A)(ii)–(vii), if a party or its attorney:

(A) fails to appear at a scheduling or other pretrial conference;

(B) is substantially unprepared to participate—or does not participate in good faith—in the conference; or

(C) fails to obey a scheduling or other pretrial order.

(2) *Imposing Fees and Costs.* Instead of or in addition to any other sanction, the court must order the party, its attorney, or both to pay the reasonable expenses—including attorney's fees—incurred because of any noncompliance with this rule, unless the noncompliance was substantially justified or other circumstances make an award of expenses unjust.

[Amended April 28, 1983, effective August 1, 1983; March 2, 1987, effective August 1, 1987; April 22, 1993, effective December 1, 1993; April 12, 2006, effective December 1, 2006; April 30, 2007, effective December 1, 2007.]

AUTHORS' COMMENTARY ON RULE 16

PURPOSE AND SCOPE

Rule 16 authorizes the district court to convene pretrial conferences with the purpose of processing a case efficiently. While the court has discretion to hold such pretrial conferences, Rule 16 *requires* the court to issue a scheduling order setting procedures for discovery and trial, unless the case falls into a category which the court, by local rule, has exempted from the requirement for a scheduling order. Further, if a pretrial conference is held, Rule 16 also requires the court to issue a pretrial order after such a pretrial conference detailing the action at the conference and establishing the course of action to be followed. The order is binding unless subsequently modified by the court.

RULE 16(a)—PRETRIAL CONFERENCES

CORE CONCEPT

Rule 16(a) outlines the parameters and objectives for the court's pretrial conferences with the parties. When preparing for a pretrial conference, the litigants should consult both Rule 16(c) and the local rules concerning the subjects to be discussed at a pretrial conference.

APPLICATIONS

Pretrial Conferences

(1) *Initial or First Conference:* The court may convene the first pretrial conference as soon as all of the parties have been served with the complaint. Typically, the court will delay the pretrial conference until after an answer is filed or preliminary motions to dismiss are resolved. The first pretrial conference permits the parties to familiarize the court with the issues in the case and to propose a discovery schedule. After the conference, the court will issue an order detailing the decisions reached and action taken. Typically, the initial conference will address issues of scope and timing of discovery, filing of parties' pretrial narrative statements, the timing for filing of motions, alternative dispute resolution, and possibly an anticipated date for trial.

(2) *Subsequent and Final Pretrial Conferences:* Ordinarily, the court holds a final pretrial conference after the close of discovery, after ruling on dispositive pretrial motions and after the filing of the pretrial narrative statements.[1] At this conference, the court sets a trial date, seeks to further clarify the issues, discusses any extraneous matters, sets a schedule for any remaining motions, and encourages settlement discussions.

(3) *Other Pretrial Conferences:* Local rule may require the court to hold one pretrial conference, but the court may hold as many pretrial conferences as it deems necessary to apprise the court of the progress of the case.

Pretrial Orders

The court is required to issue a pretrial order detailing the action taken at any pretrial conference conducted pursuant to Rule 16, as provided by Rule 16(e).

Who Must Attend

Rule 16(a) authorizes the court to order attorneys and

---

[1]*But see Mizwicki v. Helwig,* 196 F.3d 828, 833 (7th Cir. 1999) (there is no requirement that the court conduct a final pretrial conference).

unrepresented parties to attend pretrial conferences,[2] and makes no reference to represented parties. Courts have held that represented parties (in contrast to their attorneys) may also be directed to attend.[3] Additionally, at least one court has held that the judge must also attend, and cannot delegate that function to a law clerk.[4]

Motion for Pretrial Conference

Generally, the court will set the time for pretrial conferences. However, the parties may seek a pretrial conference either by informal request or by motion.[5] The court has discretion to order additional pretrial conferences.

RULE 16(b)—SCHEDULING

CORE CONCEPT

After receiving the discovery report required under Rule 26(f) or after conducting a scheduling conference under Rule 16(a), the court will issue a scheduling order setting timetables for pretrial matters. This scheduling order must be issued within 90 days after the appearance of a defendant and within 120 days of the service of the complaint.[6] The district judge may prepare the scheduling order or may refer this task to a magistrate judge.

APPLICATIONS

Mandatory Topics

Rule 16(b) requires the court's order to include time limits for: joining parties[7] and amending pleadings;[8] filing motions;[9]

---

[2] *Royal Palace Hotel Associates, Inc. v. International Resort Classics, Inc.*, 178 F.R.D. 595, 597 (M.D. Fla. 1998) (local rule requiring attendance of lead trial counsel is enforceable).

[3] *See, e.g., Matter of Sargeant Farms, Inc.*, 224 B.R. 842, 845 (Bankr. M.D. Fla. 1998) (requiring party representative with settlement authority to attend Rule 16 conference).

[4] *Connolly v. National School Bus Service, Inc.*, 177 F.3d 593 (7th Cir. 1999).

[5] *See, e.g., Garcia-Perez v. Hospital Metropolitano*, 597 F.3d 6, 9 (1st Cir. 2010) (district court's failure to issue initial scheduling order may be grounds to vacate dismissal that was originally ordered because plaintiff allegedly did not prosecute case).

[6] *O'Connell v. Hyatt Hotels of Puerto Rico*, 357 F.3d 152, 154 (1st Cir. 2004).

[7] *Johnson v. Mammoth Recreations, Inc.*, 975 F.2d 604, 608 (9th Cir. 1992) (noting mandatory nature of Rule 16(b) as to time limit on party joinder).

[8] *See, e.g., Millennium Partners, L.P. v. Colmar Storage, LLC*, 494 F.3d 1293 (11th Cir. 2007) (Rule 16(b) scheduling orders and their underlying "good cause" requirement would be meaningless if Rule 15(a) was applied without considering impact of Rule 16(b)); *AmerisourceBergen Corp. v. Dialysist West, Inc.*, 445 F.3d 1132, 1141 (9th Cir. 2006) ("where a motion to amend the pleadings is made within the time established by the pretrial scheduling order for the making of such motions, the motion is presumptively timely"); *O'Connell v. Hyatt Hotels of Puerto Rico*, 357 F.3d 152, 154 (1st Cir. 2004) (the purpose of limiting the period for amending the pleadings is to assure that at some

and completing discovery.[10]

Optional Topics

At the court's discretion, the scheduling order may also include: modifications of time limits for disclosures under Rule 26(a) and (e)(1) and of the amount of discovery parties shall be permitted; the disclosure or discovery of electronic data;[11] provisions for recalling privileged documents after production;[12] dates for pretrial conferences and for trial; and other matters the court deems appropriate.[13]

Modification of Scheduling Order Deadlines

For good cause shown,[14] the court may grant a motion modifying or enlarging the deadlines in the scheduling order.[15] The Advisory Committee Notes provide that good cause is shown when the schedule cannot reasonably be met despite the diligence of the party seeking the extension.[16]

---

point both the parties and the pleadings will be fixed).

[9]*Rosario-Diaz v. Gonzalez*, 140 F.3d 312 (1st Cir.1998) (Rule 16 mandates that the court set a deadline for pretrial motions); *Lozada v. Dale Baker Oldsmobile, Inc.*, 145 F. Supp. 2d 878 (W.D. Mich. 2001).

[10]*Suntrust Bank v. Blue Water Fiber, L.P.*, 210 F.R.D. 196, 199 (E.D. Mich. 2002). *But see Dodson v. Runyon*, 86 F.3d 37, 41 (2d Cir. 1996) (explaining that a judge's failure to enter a scheduling order does not relieve counsel of the duty to his client to move forward with litigation).

[11]See the discussion in the commentary to Rule 26 for a discussion of the aspects of the discovery of electronic data that the parties may want to discuss in the Rule 16 conference and include in the Rule 26(f) report.

[12]See the discussion in the commentary to Rule 26(b)(5) and the Advisory Committee Note to the 2006 Amendment to Rule 26(b)(5) for discussions of the method for recalling produced privileged information prescribed by Rule 26(b)(5) and for alternative procedures.

[13]*Does I thru XXIII v. Advanced Textile Corp.*, 214 F.3d 1058, 1068 (9th Cir. 2000) (the court may use its powers under Rule 16 to address a party's need for anonymity).

[14]*Hussain v. Nicholson*, 435 F.3d 359, 368 (D.C. Cir. 2006) (attorney error generally does not constitute good cause, but may in extreme circumstances); *Andretti v. Borla Performance Industries, Inc.*, 426 F.3d 824, 830 (6th Cir. 2005) (court should consider possible prejudice to party opposing a motion to amend the schedule); *Leary v. Daeschner*, 349 F.3d 888, 906 (6th Cir. 2003) (a court choosing to modify the schedule upon a showing of good cause may do so only if the schedule cannot reasonably be met despite the diligence of the party seeking the extension).

[15]*See, e.g., O'Connell v. Hyatt Hotels of Puerto Rico*, 357 F.3d 152, 154 (1st Cir. 2004) (Rule 16(b)'s "good cause" standard, rather than Rule 15(a)'s "freely given" standard, governs motions to amend filed after scheduling order deadlines); *Parker v. Columbia Pictures Industries*, 204 F.3d 326, 339–40 (2d Cir. 2000).

[16]Advisory Committee Notes to Rule 16 (1983 amendments). *See also Southern Grouts & Mortars, Inc. v. 3M Co.*, 575 F.3d 1235, 1241 (11th Cir. 2009) (lack of good cause may be found where party already has full knowledge of information it seeks or where party fails diligently to seek information); *Hussain v. Nicholson*, 435 F.3d 359, 368 (D.C. Cir. 2006) (attorney error does not equal good cause, except in extreme circumstances). *But see Coleman v. Quaker Oats Co.*, 232 F.3d 1271, 1295 (9th Cir. 2000) (existence

Relation to Rule 15

Rule 15 governs amended and supplemental pleadings. The relationship between Rule 15 and Rule 16(b) is complex, partly because the two rules can be entangled at different points in a case.

Normally, if a party seeks to amend a pleading before the district court enters a Rule 16(b) scheduling order (or before the time limit of a scheduling order expires), the proposed amended pleading will be evaluated under the liberal amendment standard of Rule 15(a). Rule 15(a) will often confer a right to amend or, if the time to amend as of right has passed, will permit the proposed amendment through the consent of opposing parties or with leave of court.[17] Moreover, Rule 15(a) expressly provides that judicial leave to amend will often be granted in the interest of justice,[18] and the burden is usually on the party opposing the amendment to explain why it should be rejected.[19]

However, once the court enters a scheduling order under Rule 16(b), the situation can change significantly. Rule 16(b) mandates, *inter alia,* that the scheduling order include a time limit on amended pleadings.[20] Once that time limit passes, it appears that a party must demonstrate good cause to modify the scheduling order.[21] Unless the court agrees that the "good cause" standard of Rule 16(b) for modifying the scheduling order is met, a party may not invoke the liberal amendment standard of Rule 15(a).[22]

The complexity of the relationship between Rule 15 and Rule 16(b) does not end there, for Rule 15(b) has a different relation-

---

of good cause overcome by undue delay in moving to amend, combined with need to reopen summary judgment motion).

[17]Fed.R.Civ.P. 15(a).

[18]*See, e.g., Pangburn v. Culbertson*, 200 F.3d 65, 70 (2d Cir. 1999) (liberal approach to amend "applies with particular force to pro se litigants").

[19]*See, e.g., Laurie v. Alabama Court of Criminal Appeals*, 256 F.3d 1266, 1274 (11th Cir. 2001) ("There must be a substantial reason to deny a motion to amend.").

[20]Fed.R.Civ.P. 16(b).

[21]*EEOC v. Service Temps, Inc.*, ___ F.3d ___, ___ (5th Cir. 2012) (four factors to be evaluated for good cause: " '(1) the explanation for the failure to timely move for leave to amend; (2) the importance of the amendment; (3) potential prejudice in allowing the amendment; and (4) the availability of a continuance to cure such prejudice' ").

[22]*See, e.g., Pressure Products Medical Supplies, Inc. v. Greatbatch, Ltd.*, 599 F.3d 1308, 1315 (Fed. Cir. 2010) ("As to post-deadline amendments, a party 'must show good cause for not meeting the deadline before the more liberal standard of Rule 15(a) will apply."); *Trim Fit, LLC v. Dickey*, 607 F.3d 528 (8th Cir. 2010) (good cause to amend not found where amendment would unduly prejudice opposing party; opposing party's discovery and evidence would have been different if lawsuit had originally been litigated under proposed amentment); *Leary v. Daeschner*, 349 F.3d 888, 909 (6th Cir. 2003) ("Once the scheduling order's deadline passes, a plaintiff must first show good cause under Rule 16(b) for failure earlier to seek leave to amend before a court will consider whether amendment is proper under Rule 15(a)."). *But cf., U.S. ex rel. Ritchie v. Lockheed Martin Corp.*, 558 F.3d 1161, 1166 (10th Cir. 2009) (declining to decide whether Rule 16(b)(4) governs when motion to amend plead-

ship with Rule 16(b) than is described above for Rule 15(a). Rule 15(b) generally governs amendments of pleadings that arise during the court of a trial with the express or implied consent of the parties.[23] Thus, almost by definition, a pleading amended pursuant to Rule 15(b) will be amended well after the time limit set by a district court's scheduling order under Rule 16(b) has expired. This is obviously a different circumstance than the situation that arises under Rule 15(a), and it produces a different result. If Rule 15(b) is to have any meaning it must govern amendments occurring at or after trial. To do so, it must be applied notwithstanding the expiration of time limits for amendments imposed by Rule 16(b).[24]

To summarize, Rule 15(a) usually governs amended pleadings until the day that a time limit for amendments imposed by Rule 16(b) expires. At that point, the good cause standard for modifying the Rule 16(b) scheduling order must be met before the court will even evaluate the proposed amendment under Rule 15(a). However, once the trial begins and there is a possibility of amendment under the very different approach of Rule 15(b), other time limits imposed by the Rule 16(b) scheduling order have no relevance and the situation is governed solely by Rule 15(b).

RULE 16(c)—ATTENDANCE AND MATTERS FOR CONSIDERATION AT PRETRIAL CONFERENCES

CORE CONCEPT

Rule 16(c) contains a list of topics that the court may consider at Rule 16 conferences. Rule 16(c) also allows for the consideration of any other matters that may facilitate the "just, speedy, and inexpensive disposition of the action."

APPLICATIONS

Topics for Conferences

During a pretrial conference, the court may seek to define and simplify the contested facts, theories, and issues,[25] eliminate frivolous claims or defenses,[26] determine whether an amendment of the pleadings is necessary, address disclosure

---

ings would require alteration of scheduling orders).

[23]Fed.R.Civ.P. 15(b).

[24]See, e.g., Clark v. Martinez, 295 F.3d 809, 815 (8th Cir. 2002) ("[W]hen an issue is tried by consent [pursuant to Rule 15(b)] it becomes of little moment whether it was encompassed in the pretrial order.").

[25]See Kemin Foods, L.C. v.

Pigmentos Vegetales del Centro S.A. de C.V., 384 F. Supp. 2d 1334, 1352 (S.D. Iowa 2005), aff'd, 464 F.3d 1339 (Fed. Cir. 2006) (Rule 16 imposes a duty on each party to assist the court in defining the issues for trial); Castillo v. Norton, 219 F.R.D. 155, 163 (D. Ariz. 2003).

[26]See, e.g., MacArthur v. San Juan County, 495 F.3d 1157, 1161–62 (10th Cir. 2007) ("Rule 16(c) clearly permits

and discovery issues, seek the admission or denial of facts or documents, make advance rulings on the admissibility of evidence[27] and the appropriateness of expert witnesses,[28] require parties to file lists identifying witnesses[29] and documents, entertain requests to limit witnesses,[30] govern the order of proof at trial,[31] and discuss pretrial narrative statements, pending motions, stipulations limiting the issues for trial,[32] and scheduling matters. The court may consider stays, consolidations, or separate trials.[33] The court may also require parties to schedule presentation of evidence so that, if judgment as a matter of law or judgment on partial findings is appropriate, the court may reach those questions early in the trial. The court will also likely pursue the potential for settlement.[34] At the pretrial conference in a non-jury case, the court may decide to refer certain matters to another district judge, a magistrate judge, or a master.

Authority of Representatives

At the appropriate pretrial conference, which is usually the final pretrial conference, an attorney or party representative with the authority to enter stipulations and make admissions (not settlement) must be present. Rule 16(c) also authorizes the court, if appropriate, to require that an attorney or party

---

the district court to dismiss claims that do not present a genuine issue for trial at the pretrial conference."). *But cf., Rogan v. Menino*, 175 F.3d 75 (1st Cir. 1999) (district court cannot ignore procedural safeguards of Rule 56 summary judgment by dismissing defendants at pretrial conference).

[27]*Skydive Arizona, Inc. v. Quattrocchi*, 673 F.3d 1105, 1113 (9th Cir. 2012) (issue of admissibility may be challenged either before or during trial).

[28]*See, e.g., Avila v. Willits Environmental Remediation Trust*, 633 F.3d 828, 833–34 (9th Cir. 2011) (Rule 16(c)(2)(L) authorizes district court to use special procedures in managing especially difficult cases, including pre-trial determination of a potential expert witness' actual expertise).

[29]*Hollander v. Sandoz Pharmaceuticals Corp.*, 289 F.3d 1193 (10th Cir. 2002).

[30]*Planned Parenthood of Cent. New Jersey v. Verniero*, 22 F. Supp. 2d 331, 339 (D.N.J. 1998).

[31]*Dick v. Department of Veterans Affairs*, 290 F.3d 1356 (Fed. Cir. 2002)

(overruled on other grounds by, Garcia v. Department of Homeland Security, 437 F.3d 1322 (Fed. Cir. 2006)).

[32]*In re Air Crash Over Taiwan Straits on May 25, 2002*, 331 F. Supp. 2d 1176, 1194 (C.D. Cal. 2004) (discussing the split in authority over whether a court can require a party to stipulate as to uncontested facts); *Briggs v. Dalkon Shield*, 174 F.R.D. 369, 373 (D. Md. 1997) (stating that the trial court may have "authority to order one party to accept a stipulation offered by the opposing party.").

[33]*Dick v. Department of Veterans Affairs*, 290 F.3d 1356 (Fed. Cir. 2002) (overruled on other grounds by, Garcia v. Department of Homeland Security, 437 F.3d 1322 (Fed. Cir. 2006)).

[34]*F.T.C. v. Freecom Communications, Inc.*, 401 F.3d 1192, 1208 (10th Cir. 2005) (the court may require that a party or its representative be present or available by telephone in order to consider settlement); *Sloan v. State Farm Mut. Auto. Ins. Co.*, 360 F.3d 1220, 1227 (10th Cir. 2004) (while settlement is an appropriate topic for a pretrial conference, some cases cannot be settled and the parties' desire for a trial must be respected).

representative with authority to settle the case be present or available by telephone.

Memorializing Pretrial Conference

A court reporter generally will be present whenever the court expects to discuss and rule on issues at pretrial conference. In unusual circumstances, parties may bring their own stenographers if the court does not order a court reporter.

Settlement

It has been held that the court may order parties to attend a conference where settlement will be discussed[35] but may not coerce those parties into settlement.[36] However, a bankruptcy court may bar non-settling parties from bringing contribution claims against settling parties in an effort to facilitate a settlement.[37]

Rulings on Motions

At the pretrial conference, the court may rule on discovery motions, jurisdictional challenges, Rule 12(b) defenses preserved under Rule 12(g) and 12(h), other Rule 12 motions if those motions were not decided previously, motions for summary judgment,[38] or motions in limine.[39]

Binding Effect of Statements at Pretrial Conference

A party is held at trial to admissions and stipulations made at a pretrial conference. However, the court may permit a party in certain circumstances to withdraw its stipulations.

Pretrial Memorandum or Narrative Statement

(1) *Time:* At the first pretrial conference and in its scheduling order the court will usually provide a date on which the parties must file a pretrial memorandum or pretrial narrative statement. The court usually orders the plaintiff's pretrial narrative statement to be filed several weeks after the close of discovery and the defendant's pretrial narrative statement several weeks after the filing of the plaintiff's statement.

(2) *Contents:* Local rule or court order will define the information parties are required to include in their pretrial narrative statements. Ordinarily, the parties must state their legal theories or defenses, provide a list of witnesses and documents to be presented at trial, detail the intended use of expert wit-

---

[35]*In re Patenaude*, 210 F.3d 135, 144 (3d Cir. 2000).

[36]*Goss Graphics Systems, Inc. v. DEV Industries, Inc.*, 267 F.3d 624, 627 (7th Cir. 2001).

[37]*Matter of Munford, Inc.*, 97 F.3d 449, 455 (11th Cir. 1996).

[38]*Pine Ridge Coal Co. v. Local 8377, United Mine Workers of America*, 187 F.3d 415, 419 (4th Cir. 1999); *but*

see Rogan v. Menino, 175 F.3d 75, 80 (1st Cir. 1999) (court may not deprive a party of the procedural protections of Rule 56 by granting summary judgment under Rule 16).

[39]*Tucker v. Ohtsu Tire & Rubber Co., Ltd.*, 49 F. Supp. 2d 456, 462–63 (D. Md. 1999) (motions in limine may be presented at pretrial conferences).

nesses, and describe any exceptional legal or evidentiary questions that will be asserted at trial.

(3) *Effect and Amendment of:* The pretrial narrative statements are generally binding on the parties at trial, and failure to raise a legal issue may constitute waiver of that issue.[40] However, the court may permit the amendment of a pretrial narrative statement to include evidence not available at the time of filing the statement or for other legitimate reasons.[41]

(4) *Failure to File:* When a party fails to file a pretrial narrative statement required by local rule or court order, the court may impose sanctions under Rule 16(f).

RULE 16(d)—PRETRIAL ORDERS

CORE CONCEPT

Rule 16(d) requires the court to issue a pretrial order memorializing the action taken at any pretrial conference.[42] Once a pretrial order has been entered,[43] it supersedes all pleadings and controls the subsequent course of the case.[44] A pretrial order may include amendments to the pleadings,[45] stipulations, a statement of the issues for trial, the defenses available, the date for the filing of pretrial narrative statements, evidentiary or witness lists, and the date set for trial. The court may order a party to draft the order on the court's behalf.

APPLICATIONS

Pretrial Order Binding on Parties

All matters mentioned in the pretrial order are binding on the parties at trial.[46] Evidence or legal theories that are not at least implicitly raised in the pretrial order will be barred at trial unless admitted without objection.[47] Pretrial orders may

---

[40]*See McLean Contracting Co. v. Waterman Steamship Corp.*, 277 F.3d 477 (4th Cir.2002); *Olsen v. American S.S. Co.*, 176 F.3d 891 (6th Cir. 1999).

[41]*Payne v. S. S. Nabob*, 302 F.2d 803, 807 (3d Cir. 1962).

[42]*Athridge v. Rivas*, 141 F.3d 357, 362 (D.C. Cir. 1998).

[43]*Wall v. County of Orange*, 364 F.3d 1107, 1111 (9th Cir. 2004) (a pretrial order that was lodged but not entered is not controlling).

[44]*Rockwell Intern. Corp. v. U.S.*, 549 U.S. 457, 127 S. Ct. 1397, 167 L. Ed. 2d 190 (2007) (final pretrial order supercedes all prior pleadings).

[45]*Deere v. Goodyear Tire and Rubber Co.*, 175 F.R.D. 157, 164–65

(N.D. N.Y. 1997); *but see Wilson v. Muckala*, 303 F.3d 1207, 1215 (10th Cir. 2002) (amendment to pleading not necessary if issue is addressed in a pretrial order, because the pretrial order supersedes the pleadings).

[46]*Friedman & Friedman, Ltd. v. Tim McCandless, Inc.*, 606 F.3d 494 (8th Cir. 2010) (issues identified in final pretrial order control subsequent litigation; unplead affirmative defense that was identified in final pretrial order may therefore be asserted as a defense at trial).

[47]*Arsement v. Spinnaker Exploration Co., LLC*, 400 F.3d 238, 245 (5th Cir. 2005); *DP Aviation v. Smiths Industries Aerospace and Defense Systems Ltd.*, 268 F.3d 829, 841 (9th

not, however, be binding in retrials of the matter[48] or in subsequent litigation.[49] Because the purpose of Rule 16 is to clarify the real nature of the dispute,[50] a claim or theory not raised in the pretrial order should not be considered by the factfinder.[51] The court may impose sanctions under Rule 16(f) for a party's failure to comply with the order.

Objection to Pretrial Order and Preservation of Right to Appeal

In order to preserve a party's rights on appeal, a party should object to a pretrial order at the time it is issued or at the commencement of trial by asserting a motion to amend the order.

Modification of Pretrial Order

Where its modification will not unduly prejudice the opposing party, the court has discretion to modify a pretrial order to prevent manifest injustice.[52] The court may also modify a pretrial order when evidence not raised in the pretrial statement is discovered after the pretrial order has been issued,[53] or is introduced at trial.[54]

Appeal of Pretrial Order

Prior to the entry of judgment, a party has no right to a direct appeal from a pretrial order.[55] Ultimately, the pretrial order will be reviewed for abuse of discretion.[56]

Cir. 2001).

[48]*Johns Hopkins University v. CellPro, Inc.*, 152 F.3d 1342, 1357 (Fed. Cir. 1998) (rulings in pretrial order are controlling at trial, but may not control the scope of a retrial).

[49]*Atchison, Topeka and Santa Fe Ry. Co. v. Hercules Inc.*, 146 F.3d 1071, 1074 (9th Cir. 1998) (pretrial order limiting joinder of additional parties did not preclude a separate action against such additional parties).

[50]*See, e.g., Doe v. Tangipahoa Parish School Bd.*, 478 F.3d 679 (5th Cir. 2007) ("One purpose of the pretrial order is to put the parties on notice as to the evidence they must be prepared to present.").

[51]*Kona Technology Corp. v. Southern Pacific Transp. Co.*, 225 F.3d 595, 604 (5th Cir. 2000) (if a claim or issue is omitted from the pretrial order, it is waived, even if it appeared in the complaint); *Elvis Presley Enterprises, Inc. v. Capece*, 141 F.3d 188, 206 (5th Cir. 1998).

[52]*Galdamez v. Potter*, 415 F.3d 1015, 1020 (9th Cir. 2005) (setting forth a four part test for determination of whether to modify a pretrial order); *In re El Paso Refinery, L P,* 171 F.3d 249, 255 (5th Cir. 1999) (trial court has broad discretion in determining whether a pretrial order should be modified).

[53]*Ross v. Garner Printing Co.*, 285 F.3d 1106, 1114 (8th Cir. 2002).

[54]*See United Phosphorus, Ltd. v. Midland Fumigant, Inc.*, 205 F.3d 1219, 1236 (10th Cir. 2000).

[55]*Bradley v. Milliken*, 468 F.2d 902 (6th Cir. 1972).

[56]*Harper v. Albert*, 400 F.3d 1052, 1063 (7th Cir. 2005); *Koch v. Koch Industries, Inc.*, 203 F.3d 1202, 1222 (10th Cir. 2000); *Gorlikowski v. Tolbert*, 52 F.3d 1439 (7th Cir.1995).

RULE 16(e)—FINAL PRETRIAL CONFERENCE AND ORDERS

CORE CONCEPT

The court will usually conduct the final pretrial conference after the pretrial narrative statements have been filed and as close to trial as possible.[57] At the final pretrial conference, the court will make a schedule for any remaining motions and set a trial date.[58] An attorney who will conduct the trial or an unrepresented party must attend the conference with the authority to enter stipulations and make admissions (not settlement).[59]

RULE 16(f)—SANCTIONS

CORE CONCEPT

Upon motion or on the court's own initiative, the court will impose sanctions to force parties to comply with scheduling and pretrial orders and to compensate parties for expenses caused by an opposing party's noncompliance.[60] Sanctions may also attach to incorrect or incomplete pretrial statements,[61] or the failure to participate in a settlement conference in good faith.[62]

APPLICATIONS

Procedural and Substantive Errors

When a party commits a procedural error, courts generally will not impose sanctions that compromise the merits of the case.[63] Instead the court should impose costs and fees.[64] When a party commits a substantive error the court may impose sanc-

---

[57]*See Matter of Rhone-Poulenc Rorer Pharmaceuticals, Inc.*, 138 F.3d 695, 697 (7th Cir. 1998) (in multidistrict litigation, transferee court will normally issue final pretrial order).

[58]*See, e.g., Dream Games of Arizona, Inc. v. PC Onsite*, 561 F.3d 983, 996 (9th Cir. 2009) ("[T]o prevent prejudice, parties are typically considered bound by the statements of claims made in their pretrial order."); *Doe v. Tangipahoa Parish School Bd.*, 494 F.3d 494, 511 (5th Cir. 2007) (final pretrial order will control the case going forward, unless later modified; "One purpose of the pretrial order is to put the parties on notice as to the evidence they must be prepared to present."). *But cf. Hoffman v. Tonnemacher*, 593 F.3d 908, 913 (9th Cir. 2010) (district court may modify pretrial order solely to prevent manifest injustice; decision to permit summary judgment motion after entry of final pretrial order would be permissible if district court found "it would be a manifest injustice to require a party to defend itself in a second trial with-

out the opportunity to move first for summary judgment").

[59]*But cf., eg., Briscoe v. Klaus*, 538 F.3d 252, 260 (3d Cir. 2008) (pro se litigant with no history of dilatoriness should not be disciplined for violation of Rule 16(e) without first having opportunity to be heard).

[60]*Garlepied v. Main*, 2001 WL 305264 (E.D. La. 2001).

[61]*Bronk v. Ineichen*, 54 F.3d 425, 10 A.D.D. 143 (7th Cir. 1995) (excluding testimony of witness not named in pretrial statement).

[62]*Smith v. Northwest Financial Acceptance, Inc.*, 129 F.3d 1408, 1419 (10th Cir. 1997); *Landmark Legal Foundation v. E.P.A.*, 272 F. Supp. 2d 70, 88 (D.D.C. 2003) (Rule 16(f) sanctions apply only to actions related to pretrial conferences and orders, not to other potential violations).

[63]*Rice v. City of Chicago*, 333 F.3d 780, 786 (7th Cir. 2003) (a judge should consider punishing the lawyer through sanctions rather than the plaintiff through dismissal of the suit);

tions which compromise the merits of a party's case.[65]

Sanctions Imposed on Party's Motion

A party may file a motion for sanctions when a party or a party's attorney does not obey a scheduling[66] or pretrial order, when a party does not appear at a pretrial conference,[67] when a party is unprepared at a pretrial conference, or when a party does not act in good faith at a pretrial conference. The motion should be asserted as soon as possible after the sanctionable activity. Unless made during a hearing or trial, a party must file a written motion stating the reasons for the sanctions with particularity and the relief or order sought.

Sanctions Imposed Sua Sponte

When the court seeks to impose sanctions on its own initiative, the court must first provide notice and an opportunity to be heard to the sanctionable party.[68]

Purposes of Sanctions

Sanctions may be assessed to punish for improper conduct,[69] for purposes of deterrence, or to compensate the party injured by the improper conduct.[70]

Finding of Sanctionable Activity

The court will examine the record and any materials submitted by the parties. The court must make a specific finding of sanctionable activity. When it finds that a party has committed sanctionable activities, the court has discretion to impose sanctions, even in the absence of bad faith.[71] The court will not impose sanctions when the party can substantially justify its

---

John v. State of La., 828 F.2d 1129 (5th Cir. 1987).

[64]*Sanders v. Union Pacific R. Co.*, 154 F.3d 1037, 1042 (9th Cir. 1998) (imposing monetary sanctions on attorney can appropriately punish the one responsible for the harm), rehearing granted, opinion withdrawn, 179 F.3d 1244 (9th Cir. 1999).

[65]*See, e.g., Lucien v. Breweur*, 9 F.3d 26, 29 (7th Cir. 1993) (willful failure to attend final pretrial conference can be cause for dismissal with prejudice). *But see, Ball v. City of Chicago*, 2 F.3d 752, 758 (7th Cir. 1993) (punishing a lawyer through monetary sanctions preferable to punishing plaintiff through dismissal when fault lies with lawyer).

[66]*Lucas Automotive Engineering, Inc. v. Bridgestone/Firestone, Inc.*, 275 F.3d 762 (9th Cir. 2001) (sanctioning a party for failing to appear for a scheduled mediation); *Engineered Products*

Co. v. Donaldson Co., Inc., 313 F. Supp. 2d 951 (N.D. Iowa 2004) (sanctions imposed for failure to meet deadline for expert reports).

[67]*Templet v. HydroChem Inc.*, 367 F.3d 473, 481 (5th Cir. 2004); *Lititz Mut. Ins. Co. v. Royal Ins. Co. of America*, 58 F. Supp. 2d 1287, 1292 (D. Kan. 1999).

[68]*Ford v. Alfaro*, 785 F.2d 835 (9th Cir. 1986); *Newton v. A.C. & S., Inc.*, 918 F.2d 1121 (3d Cir. 1990).

[69]*U.S. v. Samaniego*, 345 F.3d 1280, 1284 (11th Cir. 2003).

[70]*See, e.g., Media Duplication Services, Ltd. v. HDG Software, Inc.*, 928 F.2d 1228, 1242 (1st Cir. 1991) (court may consider deterrence when assessing sanctions under Rule 16(f)); *Royal Palace Hotel Associates, Inc. v. International Resort Classics, Inc.*, 178 F.R.D. 588, 591 (M.D. Fla. 1997).

[71]*Rice v. Barnes*, 201 F.R.D. 549, 551 (M.D. Ala. 2001) (the court does

violation[72] or where the award of expenses would be unjust.

(1) *Against Whom:* The court may impose sanctions against the party and/or any attorney of the party.[73] Where a represented party has no knowledge of the sanctionable activity, the court may order sanctions against the attorney alone and preclude reimbursement from the client.

(2) *Notice and Hearing:* Before imposing sanctions, the court must provide the alleged sanctionable party with notice and an opportunity to be heard either orally or in writing.[74]

Nature of Sanctions

The court will design a sanction that appropriately matches the violation.[75] The court can impose any sanctions it deems appropriate,[76] including but not limited to the following:[77]

(1) *Discovery Sanctions:* Rule 16(f) incorporates the discovery sanctions found in Rule 37(b)(2)(B),[78] (C),[79] and (D), such as refusing to allow a party to support or oppose designated claims or defenses,[80] striking pleadings or parts thereof, precluding witnesses not properly disclosed,[81] or treating the conduct as contempt of court.[82]

(2) *Reasonable Expenses:* The court must require the

---

not need to find that the violation was willful); *Martin Family Trust v. Heco/Nostalgia Enterprises Co.,* 186 F.R.D. 601, 604 (E.D. Cal. 1999).

[72]*Firefighter's Institute for Racial Equality ex rel. Anderson v. City of St. Louis,* 220 F.3d 898, 902 (8th Cir. 2000).

[73]*Nick v. Morgan's Foods, Inc.,* 270 F.3d 590, 597 (8th Cir. 2001); *Republic of Philippines v. Westinghouse Elec. Corp.,* 43 F.3d 65 (3d Cir. 1994).

[74]*Ford v. Alfaro,* 785 F.2d 835 (9th Cir. 1986).

[75]*Republic of Philippines v. Westinghouse Elec. Corp.,* 43 F.3d 65 (3d Cir. 1994); *Smith v. Rowe,* 761 F.2d 360 (7th Cir. 1985).

[76]*Young v. Gordon,* 330 F.3d 76 (1st Cir. 2003); *Arnold v. Krause, Inc.,* 233 F.R.D. 126, 129 (W.D. N.Y. 2005) (Rule 16(f) allows the court to impose sanctions it deems just).

[77]*Nick v. Morgan's Foods, Inc.,* 270 F.3d 590, 595–96 (8th Cir. 2001).

[78]*Velez v. Awning Windows, Inc.,* 375 F.3d 35, 44 (1st Cir. 2004).

[79]*In re Orthopedic "Bone Screw" Products Liability Litigation,* 132 F.3d 152, 154 (3d Cir. 1997).

[80]*Velez v. Awning Windows, Inc.,* 375 F.3d 35, 42 (1st Cir. 2004).

[81]*Potomac Elec. Power Co. v. Electric Motor Supply, Inc.,* 190 F.R.D. 372 (D. Md. 1999) (setting forth factors for determining whether to exclude a witness); *Trost v. Trek Bicycle Corp.,* 162 F.3d 1004, 1008 (8th Cir. 1998) (court may exclude untimely expert evidence because failure to disclose timely was neither harmless nor substantially justified); *but see Lory v. General Elec. Co.,* 179 F.R.D. 86, 89 (N.D. N.Y. 1998) (exclusion of expert witness too severe a sanction where late disclosure was sole transgression and did not prejudice the defendant).

[82]*Trilogy Communications, Inc. v. Times Fiber Communications, Inc.,* 109 F.3d 739, 745 (Fed. Cir. 1997) (striking expert's reports from record when submitted after due date); *Bronk v. Ineichen,* 54 F.3d 425, 10 A.D.D. 143 (7th Cir. 1995) (excluding testimony of witness not named in pretrial statement); *Hathcock v. Navistar Intern. Transp. Corp.,* 53 F.3d 36 (4th Cir. 1995) (default can be appropriate sanction for failure to obey a scheduling order).

sanctionable person to pay reasonable expenses,[83] including attorney fees caused by noncompliance with Rule 16, unless the court finds that the noncompliance was "substantially justified" or that an award of expenses would be "unjust."[84] These expenses may be the only sanctions ordered or in addition to another sanction.

(3) *Court Costs:* The court may impose court costs on a party who causes court expense by the sanctionable activities.

(4) *Fines and Disciplinary Action:* In lieu of or in addition to other sanctions, the court may impose a fine[85] upon or seek disciplinary action against the sanctionable party.[86]

(5) *Dismissal:* The court may even dismiss a case[87] or enter default judgment[88] for failure to obey pretrial orders.[89] However, a trial court must apply lesser sanctions than dismissal except in an extreme situation were there is a clear record of delay or disobedience.[90] Some pertinent factors considered by the courts are the severity of the violation, the legitimacy of the party's excuse, repetition of violations, the deliberateness of the misconduct, mitigating excuses, prejudice to the court or opponent, and the adequacy of lesser sanctions.[91]

---

[83]*See, e.g., Tracinda Corp. v. DaimlerChrysler AG*, 502 F.3d 212, 214 (3d Cir. 2007) ("[M]onetary sanctions for noncompliance with Rule 16 pretrial orders are required and appropriate absent a showing that the violation was 'substantially justified' or the award of expenses is 'unjust' under the circumstances of the case."); *Former Employees of Tyco Electronics, Fiber Optics Div. v. U.S. Dept. of Labor*, 27 Ct. Int'l Trade 380, 259 F. Supp. 2d 1246 (2003) (attorney fees can be reduced even if reasonable for the tasks at issue); *Lithuanian Commerce Corp., Ltd. v. Sara Lee Hosiery*, 177 F.R.D. 205, 214–15 (D.N.J. 1997) (reasonableness is to be determined outside of opposing party's actual expenses).

[84]*Richardson v. Nassau County*, 184 F.R.D. 497 (E.D. N.Y. 1999).

[85]*Nick v. Morgan's Foods, Inc.*, 270 F.3d 590, 595–96 (8th Cir. 2001).

[86]*See Legault v. Zambarano*, 105 F.3d 24, 28–29 (1st Cir. 1997).

[87]*See, e.g., Nascimento v. Dummer*, 508 F.3d 905, 909 (9th Cir. 2007) (affirming dismissal without prejudice for party's "failure to appear or to explain that he would not be appearing be-

cause of his pending appeal, at the scheduled pretrial conference").

[88]*DIRECTV, Inc. v. Huynh*, 318 F. Supp. 2d 1122 (M.D. Ala. 2004)

[89]*Bay Fireworks, Inc. v. Frenkel & Co., Inc.*, 359 F. Supp. 2d 257, 262 (E.D. N.Y. 2005) (dismissal for failure to file a timely third party complaint deemed not on the merits).

[90]*Tower Ventures, Inc. v. City of Westfield*, 296 F.3d 43, 45–46 (1st Cir. 2002) (court may impose dismissal of action as a sanction for violation of court orders without consideration of lesser sanctions because disobedience of court orders constitutes extreme conduct); *Tunica-Biloxi Indians of Louisiana v. Pecot*, 227 F.R.D. 271, 278 (W.D. La. 2005) (district court is bound to impose the least severe sanction available).

[91]*Gripe v. City of Enid, Okl.*, 312 F.3d 1184, 1188 (10th Cir. 2002). *See also Ehrenhaus v. Reynolds*, 965 F.2d 916, 921 (10th Cir. 1992) (prior to dismissal, court must consider: degree of prejudice to opposing party; quantum of interference with judicial process; party's culpability; whether court had previously warned party of possibility of dismissal as sanction; and suit-

Appeal

An order imposing sanctions for failing to obey a Rule 16 scheduling or pretrial order is appealable only after final judgment has been entered in the underlying action.[92] "A district court's imposition of sanctions will be upheld unless an abuse of discretion or clearly erroneous."[93]

Additional Research References

Wright & Miller, *Federal Practice and Procedure* §§ 1521 to 1540
C.J.S., Federal Civil Procedure §§ 905 to 914
West's Key Number Digest, Federal Civil Procedure ⊕1921 to 1943

---

ability of lesser sanctions).

[92]*Cato v. Fresno City*, 220 F.3d 1073, 1074 (9th Cir. 2000).

[93]*See, e.g., Blakeley v. USAA Casualty Insurance Co.*, 633 F.3d 944, 949 (10th Cir. 2011) (review of dismissal based on frivolity is for abuse of discretion); *U.S. v. Samaniego*, 345 F.3d 1280, 1284 (11th Cir. 2003); *Young v. Gordon*, 330 F.3d 76 (1st Cir. 2003); *Spain v. Board of Educ. of Meridian Community Unit School Dist. No. 101*, 214 F.3d 925 (7th Cir.2000).

IV. PARTIES

RULE 17
PLAINTIFF AND DEFENDANT; CAPACITY; PUBLIC OFFICERS

(a) Real Party in Interest.

(1) *Designation in General.* An action must be prosecuted in the name of the real party in interest. The following may sue in their own names without joining the person for whose benefit the action is brought:

(A) an executor;

(B) an administrator;

(C) a guardian;

(D) a bailee;

(E) a trustee of an express trust;

(F) a party with whom or in whose name a contract has been made for another's benefit; and

(G) a party authorized by statute.

(2) *Action in the Name of the United States for Another's Use or Benefit.* When a federal statute so provides, an action for another's use or benefit must be brought in the name of the United States.

(3) *Joinder of the Real Party in Interest.* The court may not dismiss an action for failure to prosecute in the name of the real party in interest until, after an objection, a reasonable time has been allowed for the real party in interest to ratify, join, or be substituted into the action. After ratification, joinder, or substitution, the action proceeds as if it had been originally commenced by the real party in interest.

(b) Capacity to Sue or Be Sued. Capacity to sue or be sued is determined as follows:

(1) for an individual who is not acting in a representative capacity, by the law of the individual's domicile;

(2) for a corporation, by the law under which it was organized; and

(3) for all other parties, by the law of the state where the court is located, except that:

    (A) a partnership or other unincorporated association with no such capacity under that state's law may sue or be sued in its common name to enforce a substantive right existing under the United States Constitution or laws; and

    (B) 28 U.S.C. §§ 754 and 959(a) govern the capacity of a receiver appointed by a United States court to sue or be sued in a United States court.

(c) Minor or Incompetent Person.

(1) *With a Representative.* The following representatives may sue or defend on behalf of a minor or an incompetent person:

    (A) a general guardian;

    (B) a committee;

    (C) a conservator; or

    (D) a like fiduciary.

(2) *Without a Representative.* A minor or an incompetent person who does not have a duly appointed representative may sue by a next friend or by a guardian ad litem. The court must appoint a guardian ad litem—or issue another appropriate order—to protect a minor or incompetent person who is unrepresented in an action.

(d) Public Officer's Title and Name. A public officer who sues or is sued in an official capacity may be designated by official title rather than by name, but the court may order that the officer's name be added.

[Amended effective March 19, 1948; October 20, 1949; July 1, 1966; August 1, 1987; August 1, 1988; November 18, 1988; April 30, 2007, effective December 1, 2007.]

AUTHORS' COMMENTARY ON RULE 17

PURPOSE AND SCOPE

Rule 17 controls the determination of who may prosecute an action, or defend against one, in federal court. The standards are mandatory, but they can usually be satisfied without fundamentally altering the litigation.

RULE 17(a)—REAL PARTY IN INTEREST

CORE CONCEPT

The only parties on whose behalf suits may be initiated are those persons whose interests will be materially affected by the outcome.[1] Such persons should be the named plaintiffs, except that Rule 17(a) permits certain exceptions. This requirement is imposed on plaintiffs so that defendants will only have to face one suit over the same interest.[2]

APPLICATIONS

Naming the Interested Party

Subject to exceptions discussed below, the suit must be commenced not only on behalf of the real party in interest but also in the name of the real party in interest.[3] Thus, the real party in interest generally must be named in the caption.[4]

Relation to Rules 5.2 and 10

Rule 10 governs the form in which a pleading must be presented to the court. The requirement that, e.g., a complaint must include the names of all the plaintiffs is mandated by

---

[1]See, e.g., United HealthCare Corp. v. American Trade Ins. Co., Ltd., 88 F.3d 563, 569 (8th Cir. 1996) (Rule 17(a) "requires that the party who brings an action actually possess, under the substantive law, the right sought to be enforced."). See also Rawoof v. Texor Petroleum Co., Inc., 521 F.3d 750, 757 (7th Cir. 2008) (noting that Rule 17(a) is sometimes equated with nonconstitutional, prudential limitations on standing).

[2]See, e.g., Curtis Lumber Co. v. Louisiana Pacific Corp., 618 F.3d 762, 771 (8th Cir. 2010) (purpose of Rule 17(a) is to ensure that defendant will face only one suit and will obtain benefit of res judicata; Marina Management Services, Inc. v. Vessel My Girls, 202 F.3d 315, 318 (D.C. Cir. 2000) ("Rule 17(a) protects a defendant against a subsequent claim for the same debt underlying a previously entered judgment.").

[3]But cf., Sealed Plaintiff v. Sealed Defendant, 537 F.3d 185, 191 n.3 (2d Cir. 2008) (use of pseudonym does not conflict with Rule 17(a); requirement of real party in interest ensures only that lawsuit be prosecuted by party possessing substantive right at issue).

[4]Lincoln Property Co. v. Roche, 546 U.S. 81, 126 S. Ct. 606, 163 L. Ed. 2d 415 (2005) (Rule 17(a) mandates joinder of parties who assert claims that are pending before the court). See, e.g., Ross v. Marshall, 426 F.3d 745, 757 (5th Cir. 2005) (Rule 17(a) applicable only to those asserting claims, usually plaintiffs); Green v. Daimler Benz, AG, 157 F.R.D. 340, 344 (E.D. Pa. 1994) (ordering change in caption after substituting party). But cf., HB General Corp. v. Manchester Partners, L.P., 95 F.3d 1185, 1196 (3d Cir. 1996) ("[I]f the plaintiffs are real parties in interest, Rule 17(a) does not require the addition of other parties also fitting that description.").

Rule 10(a).[5] However, Rule 5.2 authorizes the court, for good cause, to redact certain information or place it under seal.[6] Thus, in limited circumstances Rule 5.2 may be used to modify the application of Rule 10(a). Rule 17(a)'s requirement that a real party in interest prosecute a lawsuit has little or no relation to this interplay of Rules 5.2 and 10. Instead, Rule 17 only ensures that a lawsuit is not prosecuted by someone who has no real interest in the cases, without regard to the formalities of a lawsuit's captioning.[7]

Mandatory Joinder of All Plaintiffs: Rule 19

Rule 17(a) requires that the plaintiff (or claimant) must generally be a real party in interest. However, once the requirements of Rule 17(a) are satisfied, there is no need to join all other persons who are real parties in interest with similar claims.[8] It may still be true, of course, that a non-party's absence could trigger dismissal of the action pursuant to Rule 19.[9]

Rule 17(a) and Defendants

Rule 17(a) governs circumstances in which plaintiffs (or persons asserting claims) must be added. It does not address whether defendants must be joined.[10]

Standing v. Real Party in Interest

While the requirements of standing and Rule 17(a) may differ in some respects, it is clear that both share the requirement that the plaintiff has a personal interest in the case.[11]

---

[5]Fed.R.Civ.P. 10(a).

[6]Fed.R.Civ.P. 5.2(e) and (f).

[7]*See, e.g., Sealed Plaintiff v. Sealed Defendant*, 537 F.3d 185, 191 n.3 (through Rule 17 "'defendants [are thus protected] against indiscriminate litigation by those lacking a real interest'").

[8]*See, e.g., Excimer Associates, Inc. v. LCA Vision, Inc.*, 292 F.3d 134, 140 (2d Cir. 2002) (If "plaintiff's injury is direct, the fact that another party may also have been injured and could assert its own claim does not preclude the plaintiff from asserting its claim directly."); *HB General Corp. v. Manchester Partners, L.P.*, 95 F.3d 1185, 1196 (3d Cir. 1996) ("[I]f the plaintiffs are real parties in interest, Rule 17(a) does not require the addition of other parties also fitting that description.").

[9]*See, e.g., Tifford v. Tandem Energy Corp.*, 562 F.3d 699, 707 (5th Cir. 2009) (in Rule 17 context, "if an indispensable party cannot be joined . . . dismissal may be appropriate"). *See also* Authors' Commentary on Rule 19.

[10]*Lincoln Property Co. v. Roche*, 546 U.S. 81, 90, 126 S. Ct. 606, 614, 163 L. Ed. 2d 415 (2005) ("Rule 17(a) . . . as its text displays, speaks to joinder of *plaintiffs*, not defendants."). *See, e.g., Salazar v. Allstate Texas Lloyd's, Inc.*, 455 F.3d 571, 573 (5th Cir. 2006) ("By its terms . . . Rule 17(a) applies only to plaintiffs.").

[11]*See, e.g., APCC Services, Inc. v. Sprint Communications Co.*, 418 F.3d 1238 (D.C. Cir. 2005) (also noting that Rule 17(a) may be satisfied by valid assignment of interest). *But cf. RMA Ventures California v. SunAmerica Life Insurance Co.*, 576 F.3d 1070, 1073 (10th Cir. 2009) (noting similarity between standing and real party in interest).

Raising a Rule 17 Defense

The manner in which a party may invoke Rule 17(a) is not clear.[12] Some courts indicate that the appropriate way to raise Rule 17 is through a pleading,[13] while other authority indicates it might be the appropriate subject of a motion.[14] Attorneys are encouraged to examine carefully the local practice.

Invoking Rule 17(a) Sua Sponte

Most courts hold that the district court, as well as the parties, may raise a Rule 17(a) issue.[15]

Timing; Waiver

Rule 17(a) does not provide an express time limit within which an objection must be made. However, if the objection is not made with reasonable promptness, in the circumstances of a particular case, it is waived.[16]

Exceptions to Naming Interested Party

Rule 17(a) explicitly exempts certain categories of persons from the general principal that the named party be the real party in interest. The most important of these enumerated exceptions are executors, administrators, guardians, trustees,[17] persons who have made contracts on behalf of third parties,[18] and circumstances where a statute authorizes suit in the name

---

[12]*See, e.g., Whelan v. Abell*, 953 F.2d 663, 672 n. 7 (D.C. Cir. 1992) ("We note that the question of how a Rule 17(a) defense is raised (as a 12(b)(6) motion or as a Rule 8(c) affirmative defense) remains unsettled.").

[13]*See, e.g., Weissman v. Weener*, 12 F.3d 84, 85 (7th Cir. 1993) (citing older authority indicating that preferred method is by raising Rule 17 in a defendant's answer); *Howerton v. Designer Homes by Georges, Inc.*, 950 F.2d 281, 283 (5th Cir. 1992) ("The issue of capacity is subject to waiver if not specifically raised by negative averment.").

[14]*See, e.g., In re Signal Intern., LLC*, 579 F.3d 478, 490 n.8 (5th Cir. 2009) ("pleading is not required to raise a real party in interest challenge," but challenge must nonetheless be timely). *Cf., e.g., Lans v. Digital Equipment Corp.*, 252 F.3d 1320 (Fed. Cir. 2001) (affirming grant of defendant's motion for summary judgment on ground of lack of Rule 17-related standing).

[15]*See, e.g., Weissman v. Weener*, 12 F.3d 84 (7th Cir. 1993) (no recent

decisions overrule district courts that invoke Rule 17(a) *sua sponte*).

[16]*See, e.g., School Board of Avoyelles Parish v. Department of Interior*, 647 F.3d 570, 577–78 (5th Cir. 2011) (failure to raise Rule 17(a)(1) in a timely manner may result in waiver of issue); *Rogers v. Samedan Oil Corp.*, 308 F.3d 477, 483 (5th Cir. 2002) ("[T]he defense is waived when it is not timely asserted.").

[17]*See, e.g., Lenon v. St. Paul Mercury Ins. Co.*, 136 F.3d 1365, 1370 n. 2 (10th Cir. 1998) (per curiam) (noting that trustee of express trust is real party in interest for purposes of Rule 17(a)).

[18]*See, e.g., Local 538 United Broth. of Carpenters and Joiners of America v. U.S. Fidelity and Guar. Co.*, 70 F.3d 741, 743 (2d Cir. 1995) (noting general principle that named party to contract may sue in own name without joining third-party beneficiary; but refusing to extend Rule 17(a) to permit labor union to sue employer on behalf of welfare fund without first joining the fund).

of a representative party.[19]

Subject Matter Jurisdiction

Rule 17(a) has some similarity with the requirements for diversity jurisdiction found in 28 U.S.C.A. § 1332. However, the two requirements can also diverge significantly from one another, with important consequences.[20] For example, Rule 17(a) permits, *inter alia,* an executor of a decedent's estate to be a real party in interest. However, such a person's status as a real party in interest under Rule 17(a) does not mean that person's citizenship is used for purposes of establishing diversity jurisdiction under 28 U.S.C.A. § 1332. Instead, § 1332(c)(2) provides that for purposes of diversity jurisdiction in an action brought on behalf of a decedent, infant, or incompetent person, the relevant citizenship is that of the deceased, infant, or incompetent person. Thus, under Rule 17(a) the executor may initiate the suit, but diversity is dependent on the citizenship of the represented person.[21]

Suits in the Name of the United States

If a statute allows the United States to sue on behalf of a real party in interest, Rule 17(a) also permits the United States to be the named plaintiff.

Intervenors under Rule 24

If a person seeks to intervene in an action under Rule 24 in order to assert a claim, that potential party must meet the requirements of Rule 17(a).[22]

Relation to Rule 25

Both Rules 17 and 25 govern who should be a party to a

---

[19]*See, e.g., U.S. ex rel. Long v. SCS Business & Technical Institute, Inc.,* 173 F.3d 870 (D.C. Cir. 1999) (in *qui tam* action under False Claims Act, 31 U.S.C.A. § 3730(b) provides that both the United States and the relator are real parties in interest). *Cf., Femedeer v. Haun,* 227 F.3d 1244, 1246 (10th Cir. 2000) (acknowledging possibility that some exceptional circumstances may require anonymity in unusual cases, but holding that previously convicted sex offender who is challenging state law requiring his registration as a sex offender must sue under his real name). *Marina Management Services, Inc. v. Vessel My Girls,* 202 F.3d 315, 318 (D.C. Cir. 2000) (noting lack of judicial consensus as to whether "an agent authorized to sue based solely on a power of attorney is a real party in interest under Rule 17(a)").

[20]*Navarro Sav. Ass'n v. Lee,* 446 U.S. 458, 463, n. 9, 100 S. Ct. 1779, 64 L. Ed. 2d 425 (1980) ("There is a 'rough symmetry' between the 'real party in interest' standard of Rule 17(a) and the rule that diversity jurisdiction depends upon the citizenship of real parties to the controversy. But the two rules serve different purposes and need not produce identical outcomes in all cases. . . . In appropriate circumstances, for example, a labor union may file suit in its own name as a real party in interest under Rule 17(a). To establish diversity, however, the union must rely upon the citizenship of each of its members.").

[21]*See, e.g., Airlines Reporting Corp. v. S and N Travel, Inc.,* 58 F.3d 857, 862 (2d Cir. 1995).

[22]*See, e.g., Ross v. Marshall,* 426 F.3d 745, 757 (5th Cir. 2005) (Rule 17(a) applicable to intervenors who assert claims).

suit. However, Rule 17 applies to transfers of interest prior to initiation of the suit, while Rule 25(c) controls transfers occurring after the suit is filed.[23]

Moreover, if a party becomes incompetent in the course of litigation, the case may not proceed without a real party in interest,[24] unless a Rule 25(b) motion for substitution has been made.[25]

Remedy

The preferred remedy is to allow the party an opportunity to amend so that the action can thereafter be prosecuted by the real party in interest.[26] Dismissal is a disfavored remedy for violation of the requirement to name the real party in interest as plaintiff.[27] Before a court grants a motion to dismiss, it must allow a real party in interest a reasonable opportunity to correct the defect by joining the action, or, if permitted as an exception to Rule 17(a), to ratify continuation of the action in the name of the original plaintiff. If the real party in interest takes such action, it is effective as if the joinder or ratification had occurred at the onset of the litigation.[28]

Relation to Rule 15

If an existing party must be replaced for failure to meet the requirements of rule 17, the real party in interest would

---

[23]*See, e.g., F.D.I.C. v. Deglau*, 207 F.3d 153, 159 (3d Cir. 2000) (Rule 17(a) governs who may bring a suit at time of filing; thus it considers transfers of interest that occur prior to filing; however, once case is filed, the impact of a post-filing transfer is governed by Rule 25(c)).

[24]Fed R. Civ. P. 17(a).

[25]*See, e.g., Kuelbs v. Hill*, 615 F.3d 1037 (8th Cir. 2010).

[26]*See, e.g., Esposito v. U.S.*, 368 F.3d 1271, 1272 (10th Cir. 2004) (party bringing action is entitled, after objections, to reasonable time to substitute real party in interest; such a right requires only that party's original mistake was "honest"); *Dunmore v. U.S.*, 358 F.3d 1107, 1112 (9th Cir. 2004) (purpose behind allowing plaintiff to cure defect without dismissal is to prevent plaintiff from being time-barred for "understandable mistake").

[27]*See, e.g., Wieburg v. GTE Southwest Inc.*, 272 F.3d 302, 308–09 (5th Cir. 2001) (where plaintiff lacks standing because civil causes of action are property of plaintiff's bankruptcy estate, case should not be dismissed

until bankruptcy trustee has opportunity to substitute himself for plaintiff); *Intown Properties Management, Inc. v. Wheaton Van Lines, Inc.*, 271 F.3d 164, 170 (4th Cir. 2001) (Rule 17 expressly provides that case shall not be dismissed until real party in interest has reasonable opportunity to join litigation). *But see Consul General of Republic of Indonesia v. Bill's Rentals, Inc.*, 330 F.3d 1041, 1047–48 (8th Cir. 2003) (dismissal with prejudice appropriate when Consul General did not act to cure defect within 18 months).

[28]*See, e.g., O'Hara v. District No. 1-PCD*, 56 F.3d 1514, 1519 (D.C. Cir. 1995) ("substitution of real party in interest for party prosecuting a suit has same effect as if action had been commenced in the name of real party in interest"). *See also, Scheufler v. General Host Corp.*, 126 F.3d 1261, 1270 (10th Cir. 1997) (when parties are joined as real parties in interest under Rule 17(a), joinder falls under "mandatory relation-back" authority of rule 17(a) and is not governed by Rule 15(c); thus claims of such parties automatically relate back to commencement of litigation).

normally join the litigation through the amendment process of rule 15.[29]

RULE 17(b)—CAPACITY TO SUE OR BE SUED

CORE CONCEPT

This provision chooses the law that will govern the capacity of a person to prosecute or defend a suit in federal court.

APPLICATIONS

Natural Persons

For individuals, the law which determines their capacity to sue or be sued is the law of their domicile.[30] Domicile is generally defined as the jurisdiction where a person has established a physical presence and has the intent to remain for an indefinite period.[31] Thus, a person's home is generally that person's domicile. For many persons, the state of domicile will not be the same state in which the case is heard. Particularly in diversity cases, at least one party will be domiciled outside the state where the case is heard.

Natural Persons as Representatives of Others

Natural persons suing on behalf of another, such as guardians or executors of estates, are governed by the law of the state in which the court sits.[32]

Pro Se Litigants

While a non-attorney parent may bring an action on behalf of a child, such a parent must be represented by an attorney.[33]

Corporations

The capacity of a corporation to sue or be sued is governed by the law of the jurisdiction in which the corporation is

---

[29]*See, e.g., Intown Properties Management, Inc. v. Wheaton Van Lines, Inc.*, 271 F.3d 164, 170 (4th Cir. 2001) (Rule 17 expressly provides that case shall not be dismissed until real party in interest has reasonable opportunity to join litigation). *See also* Advisory Committee Note to Rule 15 (1966).

[30]*See, e.g., Johns v. County of San Diego*, 114 F.3d 874 (9th Cir.1997).

[31]*See, e.g., Stifel v. Hopkins*, 477 F.2d 1116, 1120 (6th Cir. 1973) (using definition and discussing relationship to Rule 17(b)).

[32]*See, e.g., Maroni v. Pemi-Baker Regional School Dist.*, 346 F.3d 247,

249 n. 2 (1st Cir. 2003) ("State law is used to determine the age of majority," citing Rule 17(b)); *Gibbs ex rel. Gibbs v. Carnival Cruise Lines*, 314 F.3d 125, 135 (3d Cir. 2002) (state law controls whether representative has been duly appointed to litigate on behalf of infant); *Davis v. Piper Aircraft Corp.*, 615 F.2d 606, 609 (4th Cir. 1980) (citing Rule 17(b); state law controls capacity to bring wrongful death suit).

[33]*See, e.g., Cheung v. Youth Orchestra Foundation of Buffalo, Inc.*, 906 F.2d 59, 61 (2d Cir. 1990) ("The choice to appear pro se is not a true choice for minors who under state law, see Fed.R.Civ.P. 17(b), cannot determine their own legal actions.").

incorporated.[34]

Unincorporated Associations

If the cause of action is based on a federal question, Rule 17(b) provides that unincorporated associations have capacity to sue or be sued.[35]

Receivers

Rule 17(b) provides that the capacity of receivers appointed by a federal court to litigate in a federal court is governed by 28 U.S.C.A. §§ 754 (appointment of receivers in different federal judicial districts) and 959(a) (suits against receivers).

Capacity in All Other Cases

Notwithstanding the numerous specific provisions for capacity in Rule 17(b), there are other circumstances not addressed by those provisions. For example, when a partnership or other unincorporated association sues, or is sued, on a state cause of action in federal court, the law governing capacity is that of the state in which the court sits.[36]

Capacity Distinguished from Real Party in Interest

There are two important differences between capacity (Rule 17(b)) and real parties in interest (Rule 17(a)) and the concerns they address. The first is that satisfying real party in interest requirements is the duty of those who file claims, most typically plaintiffs. Capacity, by contrast, measures the ability of both plaintiffs and defendants to participate in a suit, even if the defendant has not filed a counterclaim or a crossclaim. The second difference is in the concepts underlying the respective provisions of Rule 17. Individuals may, because they are individuals, have capacity to sue. Capacity alone, however, does not permit those individuals to initiate a suit or to defend one. Unless they also have a material interest in the outcome of a cause of action, they may not bring a suit (or defend against a suit) because they are not also the real parties in interest.[37] Thus, to bring a suit, a party must have both "capacity," under the applicable law chosen by Rule 17(b), as well as a real stake

---

[34]*See, e.g., Citizens Elec. Corp. v. Bituminous Fire & Marine Ins. Co.,* 68 F.3d 1016, 1019 (7th Cir. 1995) (approving application of state law under Rule 17(b)).

[35]*See, e.g., Curley v. Brignoli, Curley & Roberts Associates,* 915 F.2d 81, 87 (2d Cir. 1990) (observing that Rule 17(b) grants "association capacity in federal question cases".)

[36]*See, e.g., Kauffman v. Anglo-American School of Sofia,* 28 F.3d 1223, 1225 (D.C. Cir. 1994) (cause of action based on state law means capacity of unincorporated association is

also based on state law). *See also Streit v. County of Los Angeles,* 236 F.3d 552, 565 (9th Cir. 2001) (in federal civil rights suit against county sheriff's department, Rule 17(b) deferred to state law to determine capacity of defendant to be sued).

[37]*See, e.g., Lans v. Digital Equipment Corp.,* 252 F.3d 1320 (Fed. Cir. 2001) (no right to amend complaint to name proper plaintiff where currently named plaintiff lacked standing to sue; original misrepresentation was apparently intentional).

in the outcome, as defined by Rule 17(a). To be sued, a defendant need only satisfy the law of capacity selected by Rule 17(b).

RULE 17(c)—MINOR OR INCOMPETENT PERSONS

CORE CONCEPT

This portion of Rule 17 controls the manner in which infants and other persons unable to represent their own interests will be represented in suits in federal court.[38] The provisions apply irrespective of whether the infant or incompetent person is participating in the suit as a plaintiff or defendant.

APPLICATIONS

Infants and Incompetents Already Represented

Where persons unable to care for their own interests already have others charged with the duty to care for them outside of litigation, such as guardians, Rule 17(c) grants such guardians authority to sue on behalf of the persons in their care.[39]

Infants and Incompetents Not Already Represented

Where persons unable to care for their own interests are not already within the legal authority of others, they may be represented in litigation by persons chosen to protect their interests. The court has power to appoint such guardians *ad litem* (persons who will represent the interest of others in litigation),[40] and to make other orders consistent with the best

---

[38]*See, e.g., Baloco ex rel. Tapia v. Drummond Co.*, 640 F.3d 1338, 1350 (11th Cir. 2011) (minor may sue or be sued only through a representative).

[39]*See, e.g., Fernandez-Vargas v. Pfizer*, 522 F.3d 55, 67 (1st Cir. 2008) (noting that where no wrongdoing or conflict of interest is present, parent will often be suitable representative of minor). *Cf., Gonzalez v. Reno*, 212 F.3d 1338 (11th Cir. 2000) (where child-plaintiff is "ably represented" by next friend, court need not appoint guardian ad litem); *Neilson v. Colgate-Palmolive Co.*, 199 F.3d 642, 650 (2d Cir. 1999) ("[O]nly one party may act in a representative capacity with respect to an infant or incompetent who comes before the court."). *See generally, In the Matter of Chicago, Rock Island and Pacific R. Co.*, 788 F.2d 1280, 1282 (7th Cir. 1986) (in circum-

stances where an infant or incompetent person is only a potential party, or whose interest is already represented, court has no duty to appoint a guardian ad litem; but may do so at its discretion; but if interest is not represented adequately, court has duty to appoint a representative).

[40]*See, e.g., Gibbs ex rel. Gibbs v. Carnival Cruise Lines*, 314 F.3d 125, 135–36 (3d Cir. 2002) (where infant is unrepresented, Rule 17(c) authorizes court to appoint guardian ad litem; unlike Rule 17(b), Rule 17(c) does not defer to state standards for appointment; instead Rule 17(c) directs court to look to best interests of infant); *T.W. by Enk v. Brophy*, 124 F.3d 893, 895 (7th Cir. 1997) ("next friend" usually appointed for plaintiff, while guardian ad litem usually appointed for defendant; but terms are not controlling).

interests of infants and incompetents in litigation.[41]

In the absence of "actual documentation or testimony by a mental health professional, a court of record, or a relevant public agency," the district court has no duty to make a sua sponte inquiry into a pro se party's lack of mental capacity.[42]

However, if it is settled that an unrepresented party is an infant or an incompetent person, the district court has an affirmative duty to appoint a guardian ad litem or to take other appropriate action.[43] On the other hand, if a district court receives "verifiable evidence of incompetence" it is required to make a *sua sponte* inquiry.[44]

Comparing Standing with Lack of Capacity

Standing is a jurisdictional requirement. Where standing is lacking, it cannot be waived or cured. Lack of capacity, by contrast, is not jurisdictional, and a defect in appointment of a guardian can be cured if there is a timely objection and notice of the defect.[45]

Prior Determination of Incompetence

There is no prerequisite that a state authority determine incompetence before a district court appoints a guardian ad litem.[46]

Incompetence: Delay of Trial

A criminal defendant who suffers from significant mental impairment may be entitled to a delay in trial proceedings until the impairment eases. However, in civil litigation mental incompetence may not have the same result. Instead, the court

---

[41]*See, e.g., Berrios v. New York City Housing Authority*, 564 F.3d 130, 134 (2d Cir. 2009) ("[A]s to a claim on behalf of an unrepresented minor or incompetent person, the court is not to reach the merits without appointing a suitable representative."); *Krain v. Smallwood*, 880 F.2d 1119, 1121 (9th Cir. 1989) (if infant or incompetent is unrepresented, "the court should not enter . . . a judgment on the merits without complying with Rule 17(c)"). *See also, Wenger v. Canastota Cent. School Dist.*, 146 F.3d 123 (2d Cir. 1998) (under Rule 17(c) court may act *sua sponte* to protect interests of infants and incompetent persons).

[42]*See, e.g., Ferrelli v. River Manor Health Care Center*, 323 F.3d 196, 202 (2d Cir. 2003) ("bizarre behavior" by itself does not require examination of competence).

[43]*See, e.g., Ferrelli v. River Manor Health Care Center*, 323 F.3d 196, 202 (2d Cir. 2003) (Rule 17(c) inquiry is mandatory "if there has been an adjudication of incompetence by an appropriate court of record or a relevant public agency").

[44]*See, e.g., Powell v. Symons*, ____ F.3d ____, ____ (3d Cir. 2012) (bizarre behavior of a prison inmate, standing alone, will not trigger evaluation of competence).

[45]*See, e.g., Lewis v. Ascension Parish School Board*, 662 F.3d 343, 347 (5th Cir. 2011).

[46]*See, e.g., Fonner v. Fairfax County, VA*, 415 F.3d 325 (4th Cir. 2005) ("Nothing in the rule prohibits the district court from appointing a guardian ad litem to represent a person not previously adjudicated as incompetent through a state proceeding.").

may employ Rule 17(c) to appoint a guardian ad litem.[47]

Authority of Representative

When a representative is appointed under Rule 17(c), that person has most of the authority that a competent client would have. However, Rule 17(c) does not by itself give the appointed person the right to serve as legal counsel for the infant or incompetent person.[48]

Other Orders

Section 17(c) expressly authorizes the district court to issue other orders necessary to protect infants and incompetents.[49] This authority includes the power to determine rates of compensation for guardians ad litem and to determine which party shall bear the cost of such expenses.[50]

RULE 17(d)—PUBLIC OFFICER'S TITLE AND NAME

CORE CONCEPT

Rule 17(d) was added in 2007. It continues a provision previously found under Rule 25(d). It allows suit by or against a public officer under either that person's official title or personal name. The court, however, may add the individual's name in cases where the official title alone has been used. The primary advantage of suing a public officer by title, rather than individual name, is that departure of the person from office thereby does not require consideration of a substitution of names under Rule 25.

---

[47]*See, e.g., U.S. v. Mandycz,* 351 F.3d 222, 225 n. 1 (6th Cir. 2003) (explaining application of Rule 17(c); "a civil defendant's mental incompetence does not trigger an abatement of trial as it does in the criminal context").

[48]*See, e.g., Tindall v. Poultney High School Dist.,* 414 F.3d 281 (2d Cir. 2005) (right to proceed *pro se* does not apply to non-attorney parents who are guardians ad litem of minor children); *Cavanaugh ex rel. Cavanaugh v. Cardinal Local School Dist.,* 409 F.3d 753, 755 (6th Cir. 2005) (Rule 17(c) does not authorize parents "to serve as legal counsel for their minor children's cause of action;" ordinary *pro se* rules do not apply); *Devine v. Indian River County School Bd.,* 121 F.3d 576, 581, 24 A.D.D. 807 (11th Cir. 1997) (Rule 17(c) "permits authorized repre-sentatives, including parents, to sue on behalf of minors, but does not confer any right upon such representatives to serve as legal counsel."). *But cf. Machadio v. Apfel,* 276 F.3d 103, 106 (2d Cir. 2002) (acknowledging general rule, but noting statutory exception permitting, *inter alia,* non-lawyer parents to bring Social Security claims on behalf of their children).

[49]*See, e.g., Robidowc v. Rosengren,* 638 F.3d 1177, 1181 (9th Cir. 2011) (judicial inquiry under Rule 17(c) focuses on fairness of net recovery to minors, not amounts allocated to adults or attorneys).

[50]*Gaddis v. U.S.,* 381 F.3d 444, 453 (5th Cir. 2004) (en banc) (court may apportion guardian ad litem fees as court costs).

Additional Research References

Wright & Miller, *Federal Practice and Procedure* §§ 1541 to 73
C.J.S., Federal Civil Procedure §§ 46 to 62 et seq.
West's Key Number Digest, Federal Civil Procedure ⚎111 to 116, ⚎131 to 149

RULE 18
JOINDER OF CLAIMS

(a) In General. A party asserting a claim, counter-claim, crossclaim, or third-party claim may join, as independent or alternative claims, as many claims as it has against an opposing party.

(b) Joinder of Contingent Claims. A party may join two claims even though one of them is contingent on the disposition of the other; but the court may grant relief only in accordance with the parties' relative substantive rights. In particular, a plaintiff may state a claim for money and a claim to set aside a conveyance that is fraudulent as to that plaintiff, without first obtaining a judgment for the money.

[Amended effective July 1, 1966; August 1, 1987; April 30, 2007, effective December 1, 2007.]

AUTHORS' COMMENTARY ON RULE 18

PURPOSE AND SCOPE

Rule 18 permits claimants to bring all claims they may have against persons already parties to a case, notwithstanding the fact that the claims may be unrelated to one another.[1]

CORE CONCEPT

Rule 18(a) abolishes prohibitions against bringing unrelated claims against the same defendant(s) in a single action. The origin of the claims, whether equitable, legal, or originating in admiralty, is irrelevant to the right to plead claims in a single action.[2]

---

[1]*See, e.g., Deajess Medical Imaging, P.C. v. Allstate Ins. Co.*, 381 F. Supp. 2d 307, 310 (S.D. N.Y. 2005) (Rule 18 "does not require that the aggregated claims be factually related.").

[2]*See, e.g., Dodoo v. Seagate Technology, Inc.*, 235 F.3d 522, 529 (10th Cir. 2000) (joinder of claims is "common and preferred method"); *Vodusek v. Bayliner Marine Corp.*, 71 F.3d 148, 154 (4th Cir. 1995) (Rule 18 permits "joinder of claims at law, in equity, and in admiralty"). *But see George v. Smith*, 507 F.3d 605, 607 (7th Cir. 2007) (Rule 18 provides no authority to bring an unrelated claim

APPLICATIONS

Parties Who May Join Claims

The right to join claims is available to any claimant who is a party to the case, irrespective of whether the claims filed will be counterclaims, crossclaims, third-party claims, or original claims filed by the plaintiff.[3]

Rule 18(a) is Permissive, Not Compulsory

A party choosing not to bring unrelated claims is free to file them in separate actions.[4] This assumes the claim is not otherwise barred by considerations such as a statute of limitations.

NOTE: Notwithstanding the permissive nature of Rule 18(a), there may be problems in subsequent litigation if the claims not filed in the initial litigation were related to the claims actually raised. In that circumstance, suits filed later may be subject to the bar of res judicata or collateral estoppel.

Separate Trials

Notwithstanding the liberal nature of this joinder provision, the trial court may still exercise its discretion to order separate trials on different claims pursuant to Rule 42(b).[5]

Relation to Rule 14

Rule 18 provides that a party properly asserting a third-party claim may join all claims that party has against a third-party defendant. However, it is still true that Rule 14, governing third-party practice, must first be applied to determine whether a third-party claim is permitted. If one of the claims does not meet the requirements of Rule 14, *e.g.,* if none of the asserted third-party claims relate to the claims against the third-party plaintiff, then impleader is not permissible. In that circumstance, there can be no joinder of third-party claims pursuant to Rule 18.[6]

---

against a second defendant; "Thus multiple claims against a single party are fine, but Claim A against Defendant 1 should not be joined with unrelated Claim B against Defendant 2.").

[3]*See, e.g., First Nat. Bank of Cincinnati v. Pepper*, 454 F.2d 626, 635 (2d Cir. 1972) (party asserting cross-claim that meets requirements of Rule 13(g) may also join unrelated claims pursuant to Rule 18(a)).

[4]*See, e.g., Perkins v. Board of Trustees of University of Illinois*, 116 F.3d 235 (7th Cir. 1997) ("Rule 18(a) permits rather than compels the joinder of distinct claims against one adversary.")

[5]*See, e.g., Parmer v. National Cash Register Co.*, 503 F.2d 275, 277 (6th Cir. 1974) (per curiam)(separation is within trial court's discretion).

[6]*See, e.g., Lehman v. Revolution Portfolio L.L.C.*, 166 F.3d 389, 394 (1st Cir. 1999) (once defendant, in role of third-party plaintiff, properly impleaded a third-party defendant, Rule 18(a) permits joinder of all claims that third-party plaintiff has against third-party defendant); *Tietz v. Blackner*, 157 F.R.D. 510, 512 (D. Utah 1994) ("Rule 18(a) would apply only after a suitable joinder under Rule 14 has been allowed.").

Relation to Rule 15

Rule 18 identifies the circumstances in which a party may, in the party's original pleading, join more than one claim against other parties. However, if an additional claim is asserted after an original claim has been filed, the additional claim must also meet the requirements of Rule 15, governing amendments to pleadings.[7]

Jurisdiction and Venue

Joinder under Rule 18(a) is subject to requirements of jurisdiction and venue. Thus, Rule 18(a) permits joinder of claims only where the claims independently satisfy such requirements.[8] For a further discussion of jurisdiction and venue, see §§ 2.1 to 2.14.

Joinder of Parties

Rule 18(a) authorizes only joinder of claims, not the addition of parties.[9] If joining a particular claim also requires joining additional parties, such parties may be added only as permitted under other applicable Rules.[10]

RULE 18(b)—JOINDER OF CONTINGENT CLAIMS

CORE CONCEPT

This portion of Rule 18 permits joining two claims in a single action, even if the situation is one in which the court must decide the first claim before the second claim can be determined. For example, a plaintiff may sue on a personal injury and add a count accusing a defendant of fraudulently transferring assets to the defendant's spouse as a means of frustrating enforcement of a judgment the plaintiff might obtain.

APPLICATION

Timing

In the example cited above, a plaintiff can present evidence on both claims at the same time, even though recovery on the allegation of fraudulent conveyance would first require that the

---

[7] See, e.g., Mackensworth v. S.S. American Merchant, 28 F.3d 246, 251 (2d Cir. 1994) (adding claim to existing complaint requires compliance with Rule 15; Rule 18 "deals only with pleading requirements").

[8] See, e.g., King Fisher Marine Service, Inc. v. 21st Phoenix Corp., 893 F.2d 1155, 1158 (10th Cir. 1990) ("[A] court may decide claims joined under Rule 18(a) only if independent jurisdiction and venue requirements are satisfied."). It should be noted that

where two counts are sufficiently related, courts may use supplemental jurisdiction as an "independent" source of subject matter jurisdiction.

[9] See, e.g., Bradbury Co., Inc. v. Teissier-duCros, 231 F.R.D. 413, 415 (D. Kan. 2005) ("The text of this rule clearly relates to the joinder of claims not parties.").

[10] See Rule 20, concerning joinder of parties.

defendant be held liable on the personal injury claim.[11]

NOTE: Rule 18(b) may afford a plaintiff substantial opportunity to gain advantage with a jury by using evidence of a fraudulent conveyance to color the jury's view of the personal injury claim. In theory, the court's authority under Rule 42(b) to separate the claims is a safeguard against the risk of such inappropriate prejudice to the defendant. In practice, the need to separate the claims may not be sufficiently obvious at the outset of the trial, when Rule 42(b) is most likely to be employed.

Additional Research References

Wright & Miller, *Federal Practice and Procedure* §§ 1581 to 94
C.J.S., Federal Civil Procedure §§ 40 to 41, § 301;
Fraudulent Conveyances § 331, § 494
West's Key Number Digest, Federal Civil Procedure ☞81 to 86, ☞733; Fraudulent Conveyances ☞241(2)

---

[11]*See, e.g., Huntress v. Huntress' Estate*, 235 F.2d 205, 207–08 (7th Cir. 1956) (noting that Rule 18(b) permits joinder of such counts).

RULE 19
REQUIRED JOINDER OF PARTIES

(a) Persons Required to Be Joined if Feasible.

  (1) *Required Party.* A person who is subject to service of process and whose joinder will not deprive the court of subject-matter jurisdiction must be joined as a party if:

    (A) in that person's absence, the court cannot accord complete relief among existing parties; or

    (B) that person claims an interest relating to the subject of the action and is so situated that disposing of the action in the person's absence may:

      (i) as a practical matter impair or impede the person's ability to protect the interest; or

      (ii) leave an existing party subject to a substantial risk of incurring double, multiple, or otherwise inconsistent obligations because of the interest.

  (2) *Joinder by Court Order.* If a person has not been joined as required, the court must order that the person be made a party. A person who refuses to join as a plaintiff may be made either a defendant or, in a proper case, an involuntary plaintiff.

  (3) *Venue.* If a joined party objects to venue and the joinder would make venue improper, the court must dismiss that party.

(b) When Joinder Is Not Feasible. If a person who is required to be joined if feasible cannot be joined, the court must determine whether, in equity and good conscience, the action should proceed among the existing parties or should be dismissed. The factors for the court to consider include:

  (1) the extent to which a judgment rendered in the person's absence might prejudice that person or the existing parties;

  (2) the extent to which any prejudice could be lessened or avoided by:

    (A) protective provisions in the judgment;

    (B) shaping the relief; or

    (C) other measures;

  (3) whether a judgment rendered in the person's absence would be adequate; and

  (4) whether the plaintiff would have an adequate remedy if the action were dismissed for nonjoinder.

(c) Pleading the Reasons for Nonjoinder. When asserting a claim for relief, a party must state:

  (1) the name, if known, of any person who is required to be joined if feasible but is not joined; and

  (2) the reasons for not joining that person.

(d) Exception for Class Actions. This rule is subject to Rule 23.

[Amended effective July 1, 1966; August 1, 1987; April 30, 2007, effective December 1, 2007.]

AUTHORS' COMMENTARY ON RULE 19

PURPOSE AND SCOPE

Rule 19 addresses distinct but related questions concerning joinder of parties. Rule 19(a) describes when a court should order the joinder of a person who is not yet a party to the case. If such a person should be joined, the court will then evaluate whether, under principles of jurisdiction and venue, the person can be joined.[1] If joinder is not feasible, Rule 19(b) addresses whether the court should dismiss the case or continue without that person. Application of Rule 19 typically arises when a defendant makes a motion to dismiss the action under Rule 12(b)(7), alleging that the plaintiff failed to join a person whose presence is "indispensable" to the action.

RULE 19(a)—PERSONS REQUIRED TO BE JOINED IF FEASIBLE

CORE CONCEPT

When feasible, persons should be joined when their absence

---

[1]*See, e.g., Keweenaw Bay Indian Community v. State*, 11 F.3d 1341, 1347 (6th Cir. 1993) (describing Rule 19 as a "three-step" analysis, including the jurisdiction/venue analysis).

will either materially reduce the likelihood that the court can provide justice for those already parties or be detrimental to the non-parties themselves.[2]

NOTE: More than most Rules, the application of Rule 19 is highly fact specific.[3] Thus, when the court addresses questions of impairment of interest, the court will examine both legal and actual, real-world, impairment.

APPLICATIONS

Analytical Sequence Under Rule 19

Use of Rule 19 requires a district court to consider up to three questions. First, the court must determine whether the person should be joined under the standard of Rule 19(a). If the court concludes there is no need to join the person, the analysis will end at that point. If, on the other hand, the court concludes that the person ought to be joined under a provision of Rule 19(a), the court will then determine whether the person may feasibly be joined. This second question implicates the issues of jurisdiction and venue, which are discussed at greater length elsewhere in this text. If a person who ought to be joined (under Rule 19(a)) is eligible to be joined, the court will order joinder, and the case will proceed with the addition of the joined party. However, if under this second analysis the person cannot be joined, the court will proceed to the third question, which requires application of the requirements of Rule 19(b). Using Rule 19(b), the court will determine whether the action may appropriately proceed without the unjoined person or whether the case must be dismissed because the court cannot administer justice in the person's absence.[4]

Joinder of Parties Necessary

The court may join necessary parties in the following cases:[5]

(1) The court may order joinder of a person in whose absence

---

[2]*See, e.g., Hammond v. Clayton,* 83 F.3d 191, 195 (7th Cir. 1996) ("Rule 19 is designed to protect the interests of absent persons, as well as those already before the court, from duplicative litigation, inconsistent judicial determinations, or other practical impairment of their legal interests.").

[3]*See, e.g., Gonzalez v. Metropolitan Transp. Authority,* 174 F.3d 1016, 1019 (9th Cir. 1999) ("Whether a party is necessary and indispensable is a pragmatic and equitable judgment, not a jurisdictional one."); *U.S. ex rel. Hall v. Tribal Development Corp.,* 100 F.3d 476, 481 (7th Cir. 1996) (Rule 19 analysis is pragmatic and fact specific).

[4]*EEOC v. Peabody Western Coal Co.,* 610 F.3d 1070 (9th Cir. 2010).

[5]*Cf., Johnson v. Smithsonian Inst.,* 189 F.3d 180, 188 (2d Cir. 1999) (error to find party necessary under Rule 19(a) because in party's absence district court " 'could not begin to determine whether [that party] unlawfully retained pieces of . . . art in 1946, or which pieces of the art were kept, or how [others] came to learn of this tortious act.' . . . The question of whether or not an entity or individual should be a party to an action is something quite different from the questions and problems associated with obtaining evidence from such an entity or individual." The need to obtain evidence is not a factor under Rule 19(a)).

complete relief cannot be granted to those already parties to the case.[6] For example, when an Indian group sues a state for exclusive fishing rights, and does not join other competing Indian groups, the state potentially is denied complete relief.[7]

(2) The court may order joinder of a party whose interest[8] may be impaired either practically or legally.[9] For example, when a plaintiff seeks to recover from a limited fund controlled by the defendant, and a non-party has a claim against the fund, the court may join the non-party so as to protect that person's possibility of sharing in the fund before it is exhausted.[10] By contrast, when the interests of an absent group

---

[6]*See, e.g., Disabled Rights Action Committee v. Las Vegas Events, Inc.*, 375 F.3d 861 (9th Cir.2004) (party is "necessary" if in its absence meaningful relief cannot be afforded to those who are already joined, thus risking multiple lawsuits on same issue).

[7]*See, e.g., Citizen Potawatomi Nation v. Norton*, 248 F.3d 993, 998 (10th Cir. 2001) (Rule 19(a) does not require possession of "actual" interest, but only a claimed interest where the claim is not "patently frivolous"). *Cf., Salt River Project Agricultural Improvement & Power District v. Lee*, ___ F.3d ___, ___ (10th Cir. 2012) (suit for injunction against officials of Indian tribe in their official capacity means tribe is not necessary party, because injunction would also bind future officers of tribe); *Manybeads v. U.S.*, 209 F.3d 1164, 1165 (9th Cir. 2000) (plaintiff cannot be provided complete relief without damage to prior settlement with rival Indian tribe; held, rival tribe is necessary party under Rule 19(a)(1)). *But see, Angst v. Royal Maccabees Life Ins. Co.*, 77 F.3d 701, 705 (3d Cir. 1996) (risk that successful party in instant lawsuit might face challenge to rights by receiver in later suit does not equal a lack of complete relief).

[8]*Cf., National Union Fire Ins. Co. of Pittsburgh, PA v. Rite Aid of South Carolina, Inc.*, 210 F.3d 246, 250–51 (4th Cir. 2000) ("A court should hesitate to conclude . . . that a litigant can serve as a proxy for an absent party unless the interests of the two are identical.").

[9]*Samantar v. Yousuf*, ___ U.S. ___, 130 S.Ct. 2278, 2292, 176 L.Ed2d 1047, 1066 (2010) (under common law of foreign sovereign immunity, "[e]ven if a suit is not governed by the [Foreign Sovereign Immunities] Act, . . . it may be the case that the foreign state itself . . . is a required party" because it has an interest potentially subject to impairment under Rule 19(a)(1)(B)). *See, e.g., Davis v. U.S.*, 192 F.3d 951, 958 (10th Cir. 1999) ("Rule 19 . . . does not require the absent party to actually possess an interest; it only requires the movant to show that the absent party 'claims an interest relating to the subject of the action.' "); *International Paper Co. v. Denkmann Associates*, 116 F.3d 134, 137 (5th Cir. 1997) (party held indispensable where it owned parcels of land "interspersed" among land parcels held by other party—adjudication of some parcels will be affected by other land). *But see, Rishell v. Jane Phillips Episcopal Memorial Medical Center*, 94 F.3d 1407, 1411 (10th Cir. 1996) (non-party husband's loss of consortium dependent on outcome of wife's right to recover on injury claim; but husband's interest is adequately represented by wife's guardian).

[10]*See, e.g., In re Torcise*, 116 F.3d 860, 865 (11th Cir. 1997) ("It is well established under Rule 19 that all claimants to a fund must be joined to determine the disposition of that fund."); *Angst v. Royal Maccabees Life Ins. Co.*, 77 F.3d 701, 705 (3d Cir. 1996) (where defendant insurance company is sued in both state and federal court and will have to pay into escrow account for same policy in two cases, plaintiff in state suit should be joined under Rule 19(a)(2)(ii)). *But see HS Resources, Inc. v. Wingate*, 327 F.3d

are adequately represented by existing parties, the absent group is not a necessary party under Rule 19(a)(1)(B)(i).[11]

(3) Where several persons have overlapping interests in a defendant's property, the court may order their joinder to preclude the possibility of inconsistent obligations. For example, if a tenant seeks an injunction to enforce a lease against a landlord, complications can arise if the property is also subject to a potentially conflicting lease held by another person. In that circumstance, joinder of the second tenant will prevent the risk that the landlord will be subject to inconsistent duties to the two tenants.[12]

As a general rule, courts construing contracts require that parties to the contract be joined.[13] Additionally, a shareholder's

---

432, 439 (5th Cir. 2003) (in dispute over landowner's right to royalty payments on natural gas well, case between instant landowner and gas company could be decided without joinder of other landowners whose leases were not affected); *National Union Fire Ins. Co. of Pittsburgh, PA v. Rite Aid of South Carolina, Inc.*, 210 F.3d 246, 252 (4th Cir. 2000) ("[A] contracting party is the paradigm of an indispensable party."). *See also U.S. v. Bowen*, 172 F.3d 682, 689 (9th Cir. 1999) (if absent party knows of litigation and does not claim a legally protected interest, joinder is unnecessary).

[11]*See, e.g., Salt River Project Agricultural Improvement & Power District v. Lee*, ___ F.3d ___, ___ (10th Cir. 2012) (adequate representation determined by three factors: (1) (whether interests of present and absent parties are sufficiently close so that existing parties will make all of absent party's arguments; (2) willingness of existing parties to make such arguments; and (3) whether absent party would add a factor that existing parties would neglect).

[12]*See, e.g., Helzberg's Diamond Shops, Inc. v. Valley West Des Moines Shopping Center, Inc.*, 564 F.2d 816 (8th Cir.1977). *See also, Dawavendewa v. Salt River Project Agr. Imp. and Power Dist.*, 276 F.3d 1150, 1157–58 (9th Cir. 2002) (absence of Navajo tribe, due to tribal sovereign immunity, leaves defendant, who is contracting party with tribe on lease that is challenged by plaintiff, vulnerable to later suit by tribe to enforce agree-

ment); *National Union Fire Ins. Co. of Pittsburgh, PA v. Rite Aid of South Carolina, Inc.*, 210 F.3d 246, 252 (4th Cir. 2000) ("[A] contracting party is the paradigm of an indispensable party."). *See also Ravenswood Investment Co. L.P., v. Avalon Correctional Services*, 651 F.3d 1219, 1225 (10th Cir. 2011) (in shareholder derivative action a corporation is an indispensable party). *But cf., Temple v. Synthes Corp., Ltd.*, 498 U.S. 5, 7, 111 S. Ct. 315, 316, 112 L. Ed. 2d 263 (1990) (per curiam) ("It has long been the rule that it is not necessary for all joint tortfeasors to be named as defendants in a single lawsuit."); *Lomando v. United States*, 667 F.3d 363, 384 (3d Cir. 2011) (no requirement to join joint tortfeasors or principle and agent).

[13]*See, e.g., Dawavendewa v. Salt River Project Agr. Imp. and Power Dist.*, 276 F.3d 1150, 1156–57 (9th Cir. 2002) (action to set aside lease or contract threatens non-party's interest in lease, thereby raising Rule 19(a)(2)); *Harris Trust and Sav. Bank v. Energy Assets Intern. Corp.*, 124 F.R.D. 115, 117 (E.D. La. 1989) ("[W]here interpretation of a contract is involved, parties to that contract must be joined."). *But cf., Extra Equipamentos E Exportacao Ltda. v. Case Corp.*, 361 F.3d 359, 363–64 (7th Cir. 2004) (litigation over settlement agreement may not require presence of corporate subsidiary whose parent is already a party and whose parent is sole owner of subsidiary; in such a circumstance the "complete identity" of interest between parent and subsidiary means absence of subsidiary may not be harmful to subsid-

derivative suit against a corporation typically makes the corporation itself an indispensable party.[14]

Procedure

Only a party may make a Rule 19 motion. However, while non-parties may not file Rule 19 joinder motions, the court may raise the issue *sua sponte*.[15] In the ordinary course of events, use of Rule 19 is triggered when a claimant has not joined everyone potentially affected by a claim. The party claimed against may then file a motion to dismiss the claim under Rule 12(b)(7), governing dismissals for failure to join a person who should be a party.[16] To determine whether the motion should be granted, the court will apply the standards of Rule 19. Typically, the court will either: (1) order the person joined, and deny the motion to dismiss; (2) refuse to order joinder, and deny the motion to dismiss; or (3) acknowledge that the person crucial to the action cannot (for reasons of jurisdiction or venue) be joined, and grant the motion to dismiss.

Service on Non-parties

If the court determines that a person should be joined in pending litigation, it will direct that service be made upon that person.[17] It should be noted that such service may properly employ the "bulge" provision of Rule 4(k), permitting service within 100 miles of the place where the service issued without regard to normal limitations that may be imposed by otherwise applicable law.[18]

Prerequisite that Non-Party to be Joined as Defendant be Subject to Cause of Action

It is not clear whether the person whose joinder as a defen-

---

iary).

[14]*Gabriel v. Preble*, 396 F.3d 10, 13 (1st Cir. 2005).

[15]*Republic of Philippines v. Pimentel*, 553 U.S. 851, 128 S. Ct. 2180, 171 L. Ed. 2d 131 (2008) ("A court with proper jurisdiction may also consider *sua sponte* the absence of a required person and dismiss for failure to join."). *See also Disabled in Action of Pennsylvania v. Southeastern Pennsylvania Transportation Authority*, 635 F.3d 87, 98 (3d Cir. 2011) (issue may be raised sua sponte by appellate court, even where not raised in trial court or by parties on appeal; but probably appropriate only in circumstance where absent party had no chance to raise issue; *MasterCard International, Inc. v. Visa International Service Association*, 471 F.3d 377, 382 (2d Cir. 2006) ("Because Rule 19 pro-

tects the rights of an absentee party, both trial courts and appellate courts may consider this issue *sua sponte*").

[16]*See, e.g., HS Resources, Inc. v. Wingate*, 327 F.3d 432, 438–39 (5th Cir. 2003) (describing relationship of rule 12(b)(7) to Rule 19).

[17]*See, e.g., PaineWebber, Inc. v. Cohen*, 276 F.3d 197, 200 (6th Cir. 2001) ("If the party is deemed necessary for the reasons enumerated in Rule 19(a), the court must next consider whether the party is subject to personal jurisdiction and can be joined without eliminating the basis for subject matter jurisdiction.").

[18]Fed.R.Civ.P. 4(k). *See also Quinones v. Pennsylvania General Ins. Co.*, 804 F.2d 1167, 1173–74 (10th Cir. 1986) (minimum contacts in bulge area made person amenable to service of process therein).

dant is sought must, as a prerequisite to joinder, be subject to a cause of action. The judicial precedent appears to be in conflict.[19] Attorneys are therefore forced to consult local precedent and practice.

Time

Rule 19 contains no express time limit within which a party seeking joinder must file a motion. However, undue delay in filing can be grounds for denying a motion,[20] particularly if absent persons will not be prejudiced by nonjoinder.[21]

Joinder of Plaintiffs

When a person should join as a plaintiff but refuses to do so, the court may join the person as an involuntary plaintiff or even a defendant.[22]

Joinder in Diversity Cases

In diversity cases joining an additional party may adversely affect jurisdiction. Courts have limited ability to avoid the problem, depending on whether the person to be joined should be joined as a plaintiff or a defendant. If the person to be joined could be made either an involuntary plaintiff or a defendant, the court may preserve jurisdiction simply by aligning the joined person in a way that maintains diversity.[23] However, if the person can only be joined as a defendant, and that joinder

---

[19]*Compare, e.g., Vieux Carre Property Owners, Residents & Associates, Inc. v. Brown*, 875 F.2d 453, 457 (5th Cir. 1989) ("[I]t is implicit in Rule 19(a) itself that before a party . . . will be joined as a defendant the plaintiff must have a cause of action against it."); *Davenport v. International Broth. of Teamsters, AFL-CIO*, 166 F.3d 356, 366 (D.C. Cir. 1999) (same), *with E.E.O.C. v. Peabody Western Coal Co.*, 400 F.3d 774, 783 (9th Cir. 2005) (permitting joinder notwithstanding lack of cause of action against third person where joinder will help effect complete relief between parties; citing, *inter alia, International Broth. of Teamsters v. U.S.*, 431 U.S. 324, 356 n. 43, 97 S. Ct. 1843, 52 L. Ed. 2d 396 (1977), and attempting to distinguish *Vieux* and *Davenport, supra*).

[20]*See, e.g., National Association of Chain Drug Stores v. New England Carpenters Health Benefit Fund*, 582 F.3d 30, 43 (1st Cir. 2009) ("Rule 19 dismissals are rarely appropriate when the objection is first made at the end of the case."); *Northeast Drilling, Inc. v. Inner Space Services, Inc.*, 243 F.3d 25, 36–37 (1st Cir. 2001) (affirm-ing denial of joinder when motion was made "well after" time limit set in scheduling order, with no explanation for delay); *Gil Enterprises, Inc. v. Delvy*, 79 F.3d 241, 247 (2d Cir. 1996) (citing excessive delay in raising Rule 19 issue as ground to deny motion).

[21]*See, e.g., Sierra Club v. Hathaway*, 579 F.2d 1162, 1166 (9th Cir. 1978) (because absent persons were not prejudiced by judgment, parties' failure to raise Rule 19 issue did not undermine judgment).

[22]*Independent Wireless Telegraph Co. v. Radio Corporation of America*, 269 U.S. 459, 46 S. Ct. 166, 70 L. Ed. 357 (1926). *But see, Eikel v. States Marine Lines, Inc.*, 473 F.2d 959, 962 (5th Cir. 1973) ("involuntary" plaintiffs should not be joined freely; such joinder should occur only in unusual cases where the person has an obligation to participate).

[23]*Koster v. (American) Lumbermens Mut. Cas. Co.*, 330 U.S. 518, 67 S. Ct. 828, 91 L. Ed. 1067 (1947). *Cf., Mayes v. Rapoport*, 198 F.3d 457, 462 (4th Cir. 1999) (in cases removed from state court, 28 U.S.C. § 1447(e) provides district courts with considerable

would destroy diversity, the court has no room to maneuver. In this situation, the court must apply Rule 19(b) to determine whether to proceed without the non-joined party.[24]

Venue

Joined persons retain the right to object to venue within the time frame provided in Rule 12(h)(1), governing preservation of certain defenses. When venue is inappropriate, the court must deny the motion to join a party. In that circumstance the court must consult Rule 19(b) to determine whether to proceed without the non-joined party.

RULE 19(b)—WHEN JOINDER IS NOT FEASIBLE

CORE CONCEPT

Rule 19(b) governs whether the court should proceed without persons who should be joined, but who cannot be joined because their joinder would defeat jurisdiction or venue. The court has substantial discretion to determine, under the considerations listed in Rule 19(b), whether to continue the litigation without the person or to dismiss the action because a party cannot be joined.[25]

NOTE: In most cases under Rule 19(b) the court attempts to continue the suit rather than dismiss it.[26] Thus a defendant who has filed a motion under Rule 12(b)(7) should contemplate ways

---

discretion to permit or deny post-removal joinder; however, if court permits joinder of non-diverse party and thereby destroys diversity jurisdiction, § 1447(e) requires court to remand case to state court; in any event, decision to permit or deny joinder in such removed cases is not controlled by Rule 19).

[24]*Cf., Cobb v. Delta Exports, Inc.*, 186 F.3d 675, 677 (5th Cir. 1999) ("[P]ost-removal joinder of non-diverse defendants pursuant to [Rule 19] destroys diversity for jurisdictional purposes and requires remand, even when the newly joined defendants are not indispensable."). *See also Ravenswood Investment Co., v. Avalon Correctional Services*, ___ F.3d ___ (10th Cir. 2011) ("[O]nly a party who is dispensable . . . may be dismissed to achieve complete diversity.").

[25]*See, e.g., Dore Energy Corp. v. Prospective Investment & Trading Co.*, 570 F.3d 219 (5th Cir. 2009) ("The factors under Rule 19(b) are concerned with whether actual harm to anyone's interest will occur if the case proceeds absent certain parties."); *Soberay Mach. & Equipment Co. v. MRF Ltd., Inc.*, 181 F.3d 759, 765 (6th Cir. 1999) (determination under Rule 19(b) should be made on case by case assessment; "there is no prescribed formula for determining whether a party is indispensable").

[26]*Republic of Philippines v. Pimentel*, 553 U.S. 851, 128 S. Ct. 2180, 171 L. Ed. 2d 131 (2008) ("The Rule instructs that nonjoinder even of a required person does not always result in dismissal."). *See, e.g., Teamsters Local Union No. 171 v. Keal Driveaway Co.*, 173 F.3d 915, 918 (4th Cir. 1999) ("Dismissal of a case is a drastic remedy . . . which should be employed only sparingly."). *Jaser v. New York Property Ins. Underwriting Ass'n*, 815 F.2d 240, 242 (2d Cir. 1987) ("[V]ery few cases should be terminated due to the absence of nondiverse parties unless there has been a reasoned determination that their nonjoinder makes just resolution of the action impossible.").

to reach a compromise with the court and opposing counsel that continues the suit on terms more favorable to the defendant. Shaping appropriate remedies is one area that might offer particularly good prospects for such terms.

APPLICATIONS

Relation to Rule 19(a)

If joinder is not required under Rule 19(a), the court will proceed without joinder. In such cases, the court does not have to evaluate the applicability of Rule 19(b).[27]

Who May Raise Rule 19(b)

The parties may raise Rule 19 issues. Additionally, the court may raise Rule 19(b) issues *sua sponte*.[28]

Relative Weight of Factors in Rule 19(b)

The considerations listed in Rule 19(b) are factors to be weighed, so that in a given case one might be more important than others.[29] The list is not one where every consideration must be satisfied before dismissal is ordered, or before the case may proceed.[30] Additionally, it is possible that in a particular case other factors not listed in Rule 19(b) could be important.[31]

Factors

(1) *Adverse Consequences of Proceeding Without a Person:* The court will examine whether adverse consequences such as legal or practical damage may result by proceeding without a party.[32] For example, persons already parties may be damaged if the suit creates the potential for inconsistent judgments

---

[27]*See, e.g., Snap-on Tools Corp. v. Mason*, 18 F.3d 1261, 1267 (5th Cir. 1994) (no need to apply Rule 19(b) standards when joinder is not mandated under Rule 19(a)).

[28]*See, e.g., Manning v. Energy Conversion Devices, Inc.*, 13 F.3d 606, 609 (2d Cir. 1994) (even if parties make no Rule 19(a) objections, the court is "obliged" to raise Rule 19(b) issues if they are present).

[29]*See, e.g., Delgado v. Plaza Las Americas, Inc.*, 139 F.3d 1 (1st Cir.1998) (referring to elements of Rule 19(b) as "gestalt factors").

[30]*See, e.g., Universal Reinsurance Co., Ltd. v. St. Paul Fire and Marine Ins. Co.*, 312 F.3d 82, 88–89 (2d Cir. 2002) ("Rule 19(b) . . . does not require that every factor support the district court's determination."); *Rhone-Poulenc Inc. v. International Ins. Co.*, 71 F.3d 1299, 1301 (7th Cir. 1995) ("Rule 19(b) sets forth a standard, not a rigid rule."); *Glenny v. American Metal Climax, Inc.*, 494 F.2d 651, 653 (10th Cir. 1974) (each factor should be evaluated for its significance in the particular case).

[31]*See, e.g., Gardiner v. Virgin Islands Water & Power Authority*, 145 F.3d 635, 640 (3d Cir. 1998) (listed factors "are not exhaustive, but they are the most important considerations"). *Cf., Davis v. U.S.*, 192 F.3d 951, 960 (10th Cir. 1999) (inability of court to join Indian tribe shielded by sovereign immunity may also be weighed, but presence of this additional factor does not eliminate application of factors listed in Rule 19(b)).

[32]*Cf., HB General Corp. v. Manchester Partners, L.P.*, 95 F.3d 1185, 1193 (3d Cir. 1996) (if all partners are parties, partnership itself may not be indispensable because its interests are represented adequately).

discussed in Rule 19(a).[33] Similarly, a person not joined may be harmed if the suit proceeds to judgment and exhausts a fund from which compensation might otherwise have been anticipated.[34] Finally, if there is a risk of collateral estoppel for the absent person, that factor weighs in favor of dismissing the action.[35] By contrast, if a potential party shows no interest in a case, its interests probably are not significantly affected by the outcome of the case.[36]

If the interest at risk is that of the absent party, and that interest is adequately represented by someone already in the case, it is possible that a court will consider the risk of impairment to be nullified.[37] However, courts are cautious in reaching the conclusion that an interest is adequately represented by existing parties.[38]

(2) *Avoiding Adverse Consequences:* The second consider-

---

[33]*See, e.g., Estate of Alvarez v. Donaldson Co., Inc.*, 213 F.3d 993 (7th Cir. 2000) (finding prejudice to plaintiff by proceeding in case without absent persons where, after potential favorable judgment, plaintiff would have to sue absent persons in state court); *National Union Fire Ins. Co. of Pittsburgh, PA v. Rite Aid of South Carolina, Inc.*, 210 F.3d 246, 252 (4th Cir. 2000) (first factor of Rule 19(b) "addresses many of the same concerns as Rule 19(a)(2)").

[34]*See, e.g., In re Torcise*, 116 F.3d 860, 865 (11th Cir. 1997) ("It is well established under Rule 19 that all claimants to a fund must be joined to determine the disposition of that fund.").

[35]*See, e.g., Schulman v. J.P. Morgan Inv. Management, Inc.*, 35 F.3d 799, 806 (3d Cir. 1994) ("Prejudice under Rule 19(b) . . . implicates principles of collateral estoppel."). *See also B. Fernandez & HNOS, Inc. v. Kellogg USA, Inc.*, 516 F.3d 18, 24 (1st Cir. 2008) (even in absence of possible collateral estoppel effect, non-party could be injured by potential "persuasive precedent").

[36]*See, e.g., Gardiner v. Virgin Islands Water & Power Authority*, 145 F.3d 635 (3d Cir.1998) (moreover, a party's right to contribution or indemnity from a person not joined "does not render that absentee indispensable"). *But cf., Tell v. Trustees of Dartmouth College*, 145 F.3d 417 (1st Cir.1998) (fact that potential party is silent does

not mean it does not claim an interest; language of Rule 19 merely means potential party "appears to have such an interest;" however, it is a different situation where potential party disclaimed an interest).

[37]*See, e.g., Hooper v. Wolfe*, 396 F.3d 744, 749 (6th Cir. 2005) ("When assessing prejudice, the court must consider whether the interests of an absent party are adequately represented by those already a party to the litigation."); *Dainippon Screen Mfg. Co., Ltd. v. CFMT, Inc.*, 142 F.3d 1266 (Fed. Cir. 1998) (presence of parent corporation in suit assures adequate representation of absent subsidiary).

[38]*See, e.g., Tell v. Trustees of Dartmouth College*, 145 F.3d 417 (1st Cir.1998) ("[W]ithout a perfect identity of interests, a court must be very cautious in concluding that a litigant will serve as a proxy for an absent party."). *See also Citizen Potawatomi Nation v. Norton*, 248 F.3d 993, 999 (10th Cir. 2001) (where some tribes will win and others will lose in litigation, federal government's presence in suit cannot adequately represent interests of all tribes). *But cf., Dixon v. Edwards*, 290 F.3d 699, 714 (4th Cir. 2002) (plaintiff faces no substantial risk of inconsistent obligation because, *inter alia,* non-parties support plaintiff's case and have stated that plaintiff represents overlapping interests they share with plaintiff); *Kansas v. U.S.*, 249 F.3d 1213 (10th Cir. 2001) (when interests of existing defendants are "substantially similar, if not identical," to

ation directs the court to determine if means are available to the court for minimizing potential damage. When applying this factor, the court should make a fact-specific analysis. For example, as illustrated in the discussion of Rule 19(a), if a tenant sought injunctive relief against a landlord, and the tenant agreed to a damage remedy rather than an injunction, the risk to the landlord of mutually inconsistent injunctions is minimized, and the case may be allowed to proceed.[39]

(3) *Adequacy of a Judgment:* This consideration addresses "adequacy" primarily from the point of view of the public interest in efficient and final disposition of legal disputes. Thus a judgment in a person's absence that will leave related claims by or against that person undecided, may be deemed an "inadequate" judgment.[40]

(4) *Availability of Another Forum:* The court will examine whether another forum is available in which the claimant may sue existing defendants as well as the person who cannot be joined.[41] When another forum is not available to the claimant,

---

absent party, potential for prejudice to absent party is "largely nonexistent").

[39]*See, e.g., Smith v. United Brotherhood of Carpenters & Joiners of America*, 685 F.2d 164, 166 (6th Cir. 1982) ("[S]imply because some form of relief might not be available due to the absence of certain parties, the entire suit should not be dismissed if meaningful relief can still be accorded."). *See also Jota v. Texaco, Inc.*, 157 F.3d 153, 162 (2d Cir. 1998) (absent party asserted sovereign immunity; without absent party, some aspects of equitable relief, such as environmental cleanup of polluted area, would be impossible; but dismissal was error because current defendant could provide all of legal relief and some of equitable relief plaintiff demanded; thus, relief could be shaped to diminish prejudice caused by inability to join absent party). *But see Laker Airways, Inc. v. British Airways, PLC*, 182 F.3d 843, 849 (11th Cir. 1999) (although plaintiff no longer seeks injunctive relief, prejudice to absent entity would still be significant because finding in favor of plaintiff would still require court to find that absent entity acted improperly, which might damage that entity's relationship with British government).

[40]*Republic of Philippines v. Pimentel*, 553 U.S. 851, 128 S.Ct. 2180, 2193, 171 L.Ed.2d 131 (2008) (third factor

addresses "social interest in the efficient administration of justice and the avoidance of multiple litigation"). *See, e.g., Estate of Alvarez v. Donaldson Co., Inc.*, 213 F.3d 993 (7th Cir. 2000) (judgment is inadequate when plaintiff would have to relitigate in state court to recover against absent persons). *But see Universal Reinsurance Co., Ltd. v. St. Paul Fire and Marine Ins. Co.*, 312 F.3d 82, 89–90 (2d Cir. 2002) (party had already won on merits; thus judgment can be "adequate" because resolution of issue on merits means time and expense of trying issues has already been expended); *Sac and Fox Nation of Missouri v. Pierce*, 213 F.3d 566 n. 11 (10th Cir. 2000) (where joinder is addressed for first time on appeal, "the preference for joinder . . . on efficiency grounds has all but disappeared at this late date"; thus, possibility that judgment in case will not settle whole controversy is not compelling).

[41]*Cf., City of Marietta v. CSX Transp., Inc.*, 196 F.3d 1300, 1307 (11th Cir. 1999) (where case has been pending for three years, and remand to state court would cause more delay, court may take such facts into account in determining whether plaintiff's possible alternative form is truly adequate); *Laker Airways, Inc. v. British Airways, PLC*, 182 F.3d 843, 849 (11th Cir. 1999) (plaintiff has adequate rem-

the court in most cases will proceed with the action.[42]

Public Interest Exception

In some cases where a public right is to be litigated, but some persons cannot be joined, courts have fashioned a "public interest exception" to Rule 19. When applicable, this exception means that such absent persons are not deemed crucial, without regard to whatever a Rule 19 analysis might have concluded. The scope of this exception seems unclear, and attorneys are advised to consult local precedent.[43]

Failure to Intervene

If a person who would practically be affected by a judgment nevertheless refuses to intervene, it might seem that a court would not weigh that person's interests as heavily. However, in some circumstances it appears that the interests of such a person may still be taken into account in determining whether to proceed in the person's absence.[44]

Relation to Rule 14

It is settled that if an absent person whose joinder is important can be added by impleader under Rule 14, dismissal under Rule 19(b) is not available.[45]

---

edy in right to file complaints with administrative agencies of United States or British governments).

[42]*Cf., e.g., Estate of Alvarez v. Donaldson Co., Inc.*, 213 F.3d 993 (7th Cir. 2000) (dismissal appropriate in part because plaintiff can sue all parties in state court); *Angst v. Royal Maccabees Life Ins. Co.*, 77 F.3d 701, 706 (3d Cir. 1996) (because plaintiff may assert claims in pending state action, case should be dismissed); *Manybeads v. U.S.*, 209 F.3d 1164, 1166 (9th Cir. 2000) (where first three factors of Rule 19(b) weigh against continuing case, fact that plaintiff will have no other forum in which to pursue First Amendment claim does not prevent dismissal when continuation of case would cause "a sovereign, not a party to the case, [to] suffer substantially from [plaintiff's] vindication"). But cf., *Dawavendewa v. Salt River Project Agr. Imp. and Power Dist.*, 276 F.3d 1150, 1161 (9th Cir. 2002) ("If no alternative forum exists, we should be 'extra cautious' before dismissing the suit." Concluding, however, that instant case should be dismissed).

[43]*See, e.g., Kickapoo Tribe of Indians of Kickapoo Reservation in Kansas v. Babbitt*, 43 F.3d 1491, 1500 (D.C. Cir. 1995) (explaining exception, collecting cases addressing it). *Cf., Kettle Range Conservation Group v. U.S. Bureau of Land Management*, 150 F.3d 1083, 1087 (9th Cir. 1998) (exception applicable, if at all, where absent parties' private interests will not be destroyed by continuation of litigation).

[44]*See, e.g., Kickapoo Tribe of Indians of Kickapoo Reservation in Kansas v. Babbitt*, 43 F.3d 1491, 1497 (D.C. Cir. 1995) ("Failure to intervene is not a component of the prejudice analysis where intervention would require the absent party to waive sovereign immunity."). *But see, Thunder Basin Coal Co. v. Southwestern Public Service Co.*, 104 F.3d 1205, 1208 (10th Cir. 1997) ("We specifically hold that an entity or individual subject to impleader under Fed. R. Civ. P. 14 and entitled to intervene under Fed. R. Civ. P. 24 is never an indispensable party." But the court did not decide whether availability of impleader or intervention, "standing alone," makes a party not indispensable.).

[45]*See, e.g., EEOC v. Peabody*

Comparison with Rule 20

Rule 20 governs, *inter alia,* circumstances in which a plaintiff has authority to join other persons as parties when they share an interest in a lawsuit.[46] Rule 19, by contrast, requires joinder when a person's presence is central to the administration of justice in the case. Thus application of Rule 19 will normally occur only when the interest of the absent person is particularly strong.[47]

Removed Cases

In circumstances where a lawsuit was removed from state court, the inability of a district court to join a person crucial to the case due to, e.g., a jurisdictional defect, may not inevitably force the court to choose between dismissal and continuation of the case without the absent person. Instead, the court has statutory discretion to permit joinder, followed by remand to the state court.[48]

Effect of Dismissal: Relation to Rule 41(b)

Rule 41 governs the effects of dismissals. In cases that have been dismissed for failure to join a party under Rule 19, Rule 41(b) provides that the dismissal is without prejudice to re-filing unless the order of dismissal provides otherwise.[49]

RULE 19(c)—PLEADING THE REASONS FOR NONJOINDER

CORE CONCEPT

Rule 19(c) places an affirmative duty on parties seeking relief to identify in their pleadings potentially interested persons who have not been joined. A court may use such information to notify these persons, so that they may join on their own initiative.

APPLICATIONS

Motions to Dismiss

The defendant may use the names provided by the plaintiff as a basis for a motion to dismiss the action for failure to join necessary parties under Rule 12(b)(7). In addition, defendants may make similar use of any such knowledge they possess independently of the pleadings.

RULE 19(d)—EXCEPTION FOR CLASS AC-

Western Coal Co., 610 F.3d 1070 (9th Cir. 2010) (collecting authority).

[46]Fed.R.Civ.P. 20(a).

[47]*See, e.g., Field v. Volkswagenwerk AG,* 626 F.2d 293, 299 (3d Cir. 1980) (explaining why Rule 19 joinder requires evidence of greater interest).

[48]28 U.S.C. § 1447(e). *See, e.g., Bailey v. Bayer CropScience L.P.,* 563 F.3d 302, 308 (8th Cir. 2009) (noting alternative of joinder/remand).

[49]Fed.R.Civ.P. 41(b). *See also University of Pittsburgh v. Varian Medical Systems, Inc.,* 569 F.3d 1328 (Fed. Cir. 2009) (Rule 19 dismissal is without prejudice; without citing Rule 41).

TIONS

CORE CONCEPT

When Rule 19 and Rule 23, governing class actions, both apply to a case, and they are in conflict, Rule 23 controls.

Additional Research References

Wright & Miller, *Federal Practice and Procedure* §§ 1601 to 26
C.J.S., Federal Civil Procedure §§ 95 to 112 et seq.
West's Key Number Digest, Federal Civil Procedure ☞201 to 233

RULE 20
PERMISSIVE JOINDER OF PARTIES

(a) Persons Who May Join or Be Joined.

(1) *Plaintiffs.* Persons may join in one action as plaintiffs if:

    (A) they assert any right to relief jointly, severally, or in the alternative with respect to or arising out of the same transaction, occurrence, or series of transactions or occurrences; and

    (B) any question of law or fact common to all plaintiffs will arise in the action.

(2) *Defendants.* Persons—as well as a vessel, cargo, or other property subject to admiralty process in rem—may be joined in one action as defendants if:

    (A) any right to relief is asserted against them jointly, severally, or in the alternative with respect to or arising out of the same transaction, occurrence, or series of transactions or occurrences; and

    (B) any question of law or fact common to all defendants will arise in the action.

(3) *Extent of Relief.* Neither a plaintiff nor a defendant need be interested in obtaining or defending against all the relief demanded. The court may grant judgment to one or more plaintiffs according to their rights, and against one or more defendants according to their liabilities.

(b) Protective Measures.
The court may issue orders—including an order for separate trials—to protect a party against embarrassment, delay, expense, or other prejudice that arises from including a person against whom the party asserts no claim and who asserts no claim against the party.

[Amended effective July 1, 1966; August 1, 1987; April 30, 2007, effective December 1, 2007.]

AUTHORS' COMMENTARY ON RULE 20

——————— PURPOSE AND SCOPE ———————

Rule 20 describes the circumstances in which a plaintiff may join with other plaintiffs against a single defendant, or join several defendants in a single action. It is permissive only, allowing joinder in many situations, but not requiring it.[1] However, if plaintiffs do not voluntarily join, the court retains discretion to consolidate actions that were brought separately under Rule 42(a). Rule 20 also gives the court authority to sever claims for separate trials against parties already joined. In addition, Rule 21 provides that a court may, in appropriate circumstances, dismiss parties joined under Rule 20.

RULE 20(a)—PERSONS WHO MAY JOIN OR BE JOINED

CORE CONCEPT

Joinder of parties is generally encouraged in the interest of judicial economy, subject to fulfillment of two prerequisites: the persons who join as plaintiffs or who are joined as defendants must be interested in claims that arise out of the same transaction or occurrence, or series of transactions or occurrences; and all the parties joined must share in common at least one question of law or fact.[2]

APPLICATIONS

"Same Transaction or Occurrence" Test

The courts have adopted various standards for determining whether a claim arises out of the same transaction or occurrence. The assessment is very specific to the facts of the particular case, but in general this requirement is satisfied if there is a substantial logical relationship between the transactions or occurrences at issue.[3]

---

[1]See, e.g., Applewhite v. Reichhold Chemicals, Inc., 67 F.3d 571, 574 (5th Cir. 1995) (Rule 20(a) is a plaintiff's option, once requirements are met). Cf., In re Cotton Yarn Antitrust Litigation, 505 F.3d 274, 284 (4th Cir. 2007) ("[A] plaintiff can prove the existence of a conspiracy in an action against just one of the members of the conspiracy.").

[2]See, e.g., Alexander v. Fulton County, Ga., 207 F.3d 1303, 1323 (11th

Cir. 2000) (identifying both requirements).

[3]See, e.g., Mosley v. General Motors Corp., 497 F.2d 1330, 1333 (8th Cir. 1974); ("[A]ll reasonably related claims for relief by or against different parties [should] be tried in a single proceeding."). See also Alexander v. Fulton County, Ga., 207 F.3d 1303, 1323 (11th Cir. 2000) (noting that courts use precedent construing rule 13(a) to determine existence of "same

Duty to Explain Analysis

Before the district court reaches a conclusion on the appropriateness of joinder under Rule 20(a), it is obligated to explain its analysis of the "same transaction or occurrence" test. Failure to do so is error.[4]

Common Question of Fact or Law

Rule 20(a) requires only that the joined parties share a single common question of fact or law. There is no requirement that the actions involving various parties overlap with one another to any greater degree.[5] Thus, for example, defendants who are allegedly jointly liable will almost invariably be subject to Rule 20 joinder.[6]

Denial of Joinder

Rule 20(a) is intended to afford broad opportunities for joinder of parties who have—or are the subject of—substantially related claims. However, the trial court retains substantial discretion to deny joinder in circumstances where joinder might produce jury confusion or undue delay in resolving a case.[7]

Improper Joinder v. Fraudulent Joinder

Rule 20(a) governs whether parties are properly joined. Presumably a fraudulent joinder will be improper joinder under Rule 20. However, for joinder to be improper, it is not necessary that it always be fraudulent. Simple failure to meet the requirements of Rule 20(a) will render joinder improper

---

transaction or occurrence" under Rule 20(a)); *Hensgens v. Deere & Co.*, 833 F.2d 1179, 1182 (5th Cir. 1987) (Rule 20 evaluation should weigh "the extent to which the purpose of the amendment is to defeat federal jurisdiction, whether the plaintiff has been dilatory in asking for amendment, whether plaintiff will be significantly injured if amendment is not allowed, and any other factors bearing on the equities.").

[4] *Moore v. Rohm & Haas Co.*, 446 F.3d 643, 647 (6th Cir. 2006).

[5] *See, e.g., Lee v. Cook County*, 635 F.3d 969, 971 (7th Cir. 2011) ("The common question need not predominate; that is a requirement for class actions, not for permissive joinder."). *See also Dougherty v. Mieczkowski*, 661 F. Supp. 267, 278 (D. Del. 1987) ("By its terms, Rule 20(a) only requires a single basis for commonality, in either law or fact, for the joinder to be acceptable.").

[6] *See, e.g., In re EMC Corp.*, ___ F.3d ___ (Fed. Cir. 2012) (however, joint liability is not prerequisite to joinder; "independent actions" may be joined if the claims against defendants arise out of same transaction or occurrence).

[7] *See, e.g., Chavez v. Illinois State Police*, 251 F.3d 612 (7th Cir.2001) (affirming denial of rule 20 joinder when discovery had already been terminated two years earlier and defendants would be unfairly prejudiced by need to reopen discovery); *Thompson v. Boggs*, 33 F.3d 847, 858 (7th Cir. 1994) (in civil rights case against police officer, joinder of second party properly denied where the following factors would create jury confusion; the two alleged incidents were separated by two years; the injury claims were separate and distinct; and the second complaint would require joinder of additional police officers as defendants).

without regard to whether it is also fraudulent.[8]

Admiralty Actions

Under Rule 20(a) a party may join parties, vessels, and other property subject to admiralty jurisdiction[9] (typically, admiralty actions are not based on personal jurisdiction over a vessel's owner, but upon the court's jurisdiction over the vessel, which is normally exercised when the vessel is served within the territorial confines of the jurisdiction in which the court sits).

Prisoners' Lawsuits

When a prison inmate files a civil suit *in forma pauperis,* the Prison Litigation Reform Act requires, *inter alia,* the prisoner to pay the full filing fee.[10] The effect of this legislation when multiple inmates seek to join their claims under Rule 20 is to require each such plaintiff to file a separate complaint and to pay separately the full filing fee, rather than pro-rate a single filing fee among all the plaintiffs. To the extent that joinder of multiple plaintiffs is permitted under Rule 20, the question that arises in inmate cases is whether such plaintiffs may file together and pay only a single fee. The appellate courts have so far reached different results on this issue.[11]

Complete Relief Unnecessary

Joinder of parties is feasible even if the court may not grant complete relief to each plaintiff or defendant. Thus, it is possible that two plaintiffs would join in a suit, even if the court could anticipate at the time of joinder that the judgment, if favorable, will satisfy the claim of one plaintiff completely, but will leave the other plaintiff with only partial satisfaction.[12]

---

[8]*See, e.g., Crockett v. R.J. Reynolds Tobacco Co.*, 436 F.3d 529, 533 (5th Cir. 2006) ("If [Rule 20] requirements are not met, joinder is improper even if there is no fraud in the pleadings."). *See also Coalition to Defend Affirmative Action v. Regents of University of Michigan*, ___ F.3d ___ (6th Cir. 2011) (if no claim is asserted against a defendant, that party is misjoined).

[9]*See, e.g., Luera v. M/V Alberta*, 635 F.3d 181, 194 (5th Cir. 2011) (Rule 20 permits "hybrid proceedings," involving admiralty and non-admiralty claims.).

[10]28 U.S.C.A. § 1915(b). *See, e.g., Abdul-Akbar v. McKelvie*, 239 F.3d 307, 331 (3d Cir. 2001) (legislative intent was to deter frivolous prisoner litigation).

[11]*See Hagan v. Rogers*, 570 F.3d 146 (3d Cir. 2009) (prisoners' *in forma pauperis* lawsuits "are not categorically barred," but each prisoner must pay full filing fee); *Hubbard v. Haley*, 262 F.3d 1194, 1198 (11th Cir. 2001) (28 U.S.C.A. § 1915(b)(1) requires each inmate to pay a full filing fee and, if relevant, a full appellate filing fee). *But see Boriboune v. Berge*, 391 F.3d 852, 853–55 (7th Cir. 2004) (permitting allocation of fees across all plaintiffs); *Talley-Bey v. Knebl*, 168 F.3d 884, 887 (6th Cir. 1999) (permitting pro-rated assessment of fees).

[12]*See, e.g., Triggs v. John Crump Toyota, Inc.*, 154 F.3d 1284, 1290 (11th Cir. 1998) ("[T]he express language of Rule 20 indicates that all plaintiffs need not seek relief against all defendants.").

Right to Relief Still Judged Separately

Notwithstanding joinder, parties still receive judgment according to the respective merits of their individual cases. Though important, this concept means no more than this: the victory of one of the joined parties in a case does not necessarily guarantee victory (or defeat) to another joined party.[13]

Jurisdiction: Relation to 28 U.S.C. § 1367

It is settled that for each party joined under Rule 20 the requirements of subject matter jurisdiction must be satisfied.[14] In circumstances where neither diversity jurisdiction or federal question jurisdiction can be used to satisfy subject matter jurisdiction for one or more parties joined under Rule 20, it may be possible to satisfy the jurisdictional requirement through the use of supplemental jurisdiction.

The supplemental jurisdiction of district courts is governed by 28 U.S.C. § 1367. In general, § 1367(a) authorizes courts to exercise supplemental jurisdiction over non-diverse state claims that arise from the same case or controversy as other claims that satisfy the original subject matter jurisdiction of district courts. However, § 1367(b) and (c) create some exceptions to the application of § 1367(a). In particular, § 1367(b) prohibits exercise of supplemental jurisdiction when: (1) the basis for original jurisdiction is diversity; (2) the supplemental claim is asserted by a plaintiff; and (3) the person who is the target of the claim was joined under, *inter alia,* Rule 20. It is settled that in a case based on diversity jurisdiction, § 1367 and Rule 20 may not be used to join non-diverse defendants.[15] However, until recently it was unclear whether § 1367(b) also prohibited joinder of non-diverse plaintiffs. That question is now settled: § 1367(b) is not a barrier to joinder of most non-diverse plaintiffs.[16] Supplemental jurisdiction is discussed at greater length elsewhere in this text.

---

[13]*See, e.g., Id.* at 1288 ("[T]he fact that a great many members of the putative plaintiff class can seek no relief against one of the defendants . . . would be no obstacle to the permissive joinder of [that defendant] under Rule 20."). *Cf., U.S. v. Real Property Known as 22249 Dolorosa Street, Woodland Hills, Cal.*, 190 F.3d 977, 982 (9th Cir. 1999) (claims in forfeiture proceeding joined under Rule 20; held, where government won most claims but lost others, government's liability for attorneys' fees in unsuccessful case cannot be shielded by fact that government prevailed on related claims; government liability for each forfeiture claim must be decided separately).

[14]*See, e.g., Merrill Lynch & Co. Inc. v. Allegheny Energy, Inc.*, 500 F.3d 171, 179 (2d Cir. 2007) (citing treatise, "'parties that are joined under Rules 19 and 20 . . . must independently satisfy the jurisdictional requirement.").

[15]*See, e.g., Stromberg Metal Works, Inc. v. Press Mechanical, Inc.*, 77 F.3d 928, 932 (7th Cir. 1996) ("Claims *against* persons made parties under Rule 20 are forbidden.").

[16]*Exxon Mobil Corp. v. Allapattah Services, Inc.*, 545 U.S. 546, 125 S. Ct. 2611, 162 L. Ed. 2d 502 (2005) (where other elements of diversity jurisdiction are met, plaintiffs permissively joined under Rule 20 with a plaintiff who meets amount in controversy require-

Relation to Rule 15

Rule 15 generally governs the circumstances when a party may amend a pleading, including amendments to add new parties. However, because Rule 20 also regulates whether parties may be joined, a proposed amended pleading to add a party must meet the requirements of both Rules 15 and 20.[17]

Compare With Rule 18

Though Rule 20(a) is quite liberal in permitting joinder of parties, it is still somewhat more restrictive than Rule 18, which governs joinder of *claims* by a single plaintiff against a single defendant. Rule 18 does not require that the claims arise from a common transaction or occurrence, and the claims need not share even a single question of law or fact in common.[18]

RULE 20(b)—PROTECTIVE MEASURES

CORE CONCEPT

Although Rule 20(a) may permit plaintiffs to join together, or to join several defendants together, the court retains discretion to order separate trials or other proceedings if necessary in the interest of justice.

APPLICATIONS

Embarrassment, Expense, or Delay

Primary factors considered by the court in determining whether to order separate trials are unreasonable embarrassment, expense or delay. These broad standards afford the trial court significant discretion in determining whether to separate the parties.

Source of Embarrassment, Expense or Delay

Rule 20(b) appears to permit relief in the form of separate trials if the source of the embarrassment, expense, or delay is someone not adverse to the affected party. It does not apply to circumstances where a party's embarrassment is produced by addition of an adverse party. In actuality, this distinction is not a substantial impingement on a court's discretion to separate. The rule's language is construed to be broad enough to permit separation when injustice would occur.[19] Moreover, the court has discretion to order separate proceedings of any

---

ment may enjoy supplemental jurisdiction under § 1367).

[17]*See, e.g., Hinson v. Norwest Financial South Carolina, Inc.*, 239 F.3d 611, 618 (4th Cir. 2001).

[18]*See, e.g., Intercon Research Associates, Ltd. v. Dresser Industries, Inc.*, 696 F.2d 53, 57 (7th Cir. 1982) ("[J]oinder of claims under Rule 18 becomes relevant only after the re-

quirements of Rule 20 . . . has [sic] been met.").

[19]*See, e.g., Coleman v. Quaker Oats Co.*, 232 F.3d 1271, 1296 (9th Cir. 2000) (although joinder was proper under Rule 20(a), separate trials under Rule 20(b) were also appropriate where ten plaintiffs, alleging age discrimination, might have confused jury as to individual facts; defendant would

claim in the interest of justice or convenience under Rules 21 and 42(b).

Additional Research References

Wright & Miller, *Federal Practice and Procedure* §§ 1651 to 60
C.J.S., Federal Civil Procedure §§ 94 to 116
C.J.S., Federal Civil Procedure § 318, § 917, § 918
West's Key Number Digest, Federal Civil Procedure ⟲241 to 267, ⟲1956

---

also have faced risk of prejudice from having "all ten plaintiffs testify in one trial"); *Avitia v. Metropolitan Club of Chicago, Inc.*, 49 F.3d 1219, 1224 (7th Cir. 1995) (Rule 20(b) permits court to weigh embarrassment to defendant from multiple claims of labor law violations, against cost to other parties and to courts of having more than one trial; denying motion for separate trials).

RULE 21
MISJOINDER AND NONJOINDER OF PARTIES

Misjoinder of parties is not a ground for dismissing an action. On motion or on its own, the court may at any time, on just terms, add or drop a party. The court may also sever any claim against a party.

[April 30, 2007, effective December 1, 2007.]

AUTHORS' COMMENTARY ON RULE 21

PURPOSE AND SCOPE

Rule 21 contains the remedy for misjoinder or nonjoinder that violates other Rules governing multiparty litigation. It ensures that inappropriate joinder of a party, or failure to join a party that should have been joined, need not result in dismissal of the action. It also provides the court with discretion to sever claims against a party for separate trials, or to order separate trials for joined parties, even if the joinder was otherwise appropriate.

APPLICATIONS

What Constitutes Inappropriate Joinder

Joinder may be inappropriate for a variety of reasons, including situations in which joinder of parties produces defects in jurisdiction or venue.[1] Additionally, joinder that does not meet the requirements of Rule 20(a) is inappropriate, and may necessitate the use of Rule 21.[2]

Inappropriate Joinder: Consequences

The consequence of an inappropriate joinder will not be dismissal of the entire action.[3] Instead, the court will order the inappropriately joined party dismissed, so that the remainder

---

[1]See, e.g., Whitaker v. American Telecasting, Inc., 261 F.3d 196, 206–07 (2d Cir. 2001) (approving use of rule 21 to dismiss non-diverse defendant who had no real connection to litigation).

[2]See, e.g., Acevedo v. Allsup's

Convenience Stores, Inc., 600 F.3d 516, 521 (5th Cir. 2010) ("Since Rule 21 does not provide any standards by which district courts can determine if parties are misjoined, courts have looked to Rule 20 for guidance.").

[3]See, e.g., Alvarez v. City of

of the action may continue.[4]

Failure to Join

If a party should have been joined but was not, the court will simply order appropriate service of process.[5]

Relationship to Rule 15

If parties seek to add a party under Rule 21, courts generally use the standard of Rule 15, governing amendments to pleadings, to determine whether to allow the addition.[6]

Relation to Rule 19: Diversity Jurisdiction

The authority of a district court to protect its diversity jurisdiction by dismissing a party under Rule 21 is subject to the restriction of Rule 19, which requires the presence of parties deemed indispensable to the action. In practice, that relationship means that if an indispensable party is also not diverse, the court cannot simply dismiss the party but must consider dismissing the action under Rule 19.[7]

Additionally, and notwithstanding the broad language of Rule 21, it appears settled that Rule 21 cannot be used to create diversity by substituting a diverse party for a non-diverse party.[8]

Chicago, 605 F.3d 445, 450 (7th Cir. 2010) ("[M]isjoinder of parties is never a ground for dismissing an action."); *Fowler v. UMPC Shadyside,* 578 F.3d 203, 209 (3d Cir. 2009) ("To remedy misjoinder . . . a court may not simply dismiss a suit altogether.").

[4] *Newman-Green, Inc. v. Alfonzo-Larrain,* 490 U.S. 826, 832, 109 S. Ct. 2218, 2222, 104 L. Ed. 2d 893 (1989) ("[I]t is well settled that Rule 21 invests district courts with authority to allow a dispensable nondiverse party to be dropped at any time, even after judgment has been rendered;" suggesting that federal appellate courts have similar authority). *But cf., DirecTV, Inc. v. Leto,* 467 F.3d 842, 846 (3d Cir. 2006) ("Although a district court has discretion to choose either severance or dismissal in remedying misjoinder, it is permitted under Rule 21 to opt for the latter only if 'just' - that is, if doing so 'will not prejudice any substantial right.' "). *Elmore v. Henderson,* 227 F.3d 1009, 1012 (7th Cir. 2000) (where party was inappropriately joined, Rule 21 permits district court to sever that party and hear that case separately rather than dismiss it, if dismissal would produce harsh result

under applicable statute of limitations). *See also McLaughlin v. Mississippi Power Co.,* 376 F.3d 344 (5th Cir.2004) (Rule 21 permits dismissal of misjoined parties, but not misjoined properties).

[5] *See, e.g., Teamsters Local Union No. 116 v. Fargo-Moorhead Auto. Dealers Ass'n,* 620 F.2d 204 (8th Cir. 1980).

[6] *See, e.g., Galustian v. Peter,* 591 F.3d 724, 730 (4th Cir. 2010) (acknowledging that some courts do not use Rule 15(a), but concluding that most courts do); *Frank v. U.S. West, Inc.,* 3 F.3d 1357, 1365 (10th Cir. 1993) ("A motion to add a party is governed by [Rule] 15(a).").

[7] *See, e.g., Investment Co. v. Avalon Correctional Services,* ___ F.3d ___ (10th Cir. 2011) (noting that in shareholder derivative action corporation is indispensable party); *Kirkland v. Legion Ins. Co.,* 343 F.3d 1135, 1142 (9th Cir. 2003).

[8] *See, e.g., Salazar v. Allstate Texas Lloyd's, Inc.,* 455 F.3d 571 (5th Cir.2006) ("Rule 21 does not allow for substitution of parties to create jurisdiction."); *Northern Trust Co. v. Bunge*

Relation to Rule 25

Rule 25 governs substitution of parties in any of the specific sections addressed by that Rule. By contrast, Rule 21 governs substitution "in the discretion of the court in situations not covered by Rule 25."[9]

Relation to Rule 42(b)

When a claim is severed under Rule 21, it ceases to be part of the same suit.[10] By contrast, if an issue is separated under Rule 42(b), it will be tried separately but remain part of the same lawsuit. The most important result of this distinction is that severed proceedings under Rule 21 become final as each proceeding goes to judgment, and may be appealed individually. Separate trials under Rule 42(b), by contrast, are typically *not* ready for appeal until all claims and issues are decided.[11]

Timing

The court may order dismissal or the addition of a party at any time in the action, subject only to the need to protect all parties from unfair prejudice.[12]

Motion

Adding or dropping a party may be done upon motion of someone already a party, or upon the court's own initiative.[13]

Corp., 899 F.2d 591, 597 (7th Cir. 1990) ("We have found no case in which Rule 21 has been used to add parties to cure a defect in statutory jurisdiction.").

[9]*Mathis v. Bess*, 761 F. Supp. 1023, 1026 (S.D. N.Y. 1991).

[10]*See, e.g., Rice v. Sunrise Express, Inc.*, 209 F.3d 1008, 1013 (7th Cir. 2000) ("Under Rule 21 . . . severance creates two separate actions where previously there was but one.").

[11]*See, e.g., Acevedo-Garcia v. Monroig*, 351 F.3d 547, 559–60 (1st Cir. 2003) (observing that courts sometimes confuse the two rules; noting that important practical difference is that under Rule 21 a judgment entered is final and appealable without regard to whether other severed portions of original case have proceeded to judgment; under Rule 42(b), however, separate trials do not usually become appealable until all of the trials have been decided); *Rice v. Sunrise Express, Inc.*, 209 F.3d 1008, 1013 (7th Cir. 2000) ("Under Rule 21 . . . severance creates two separate actions where previously there was but one").

[12]*Newman-Green, Inc. v. Alfonzo-Larrain*, 490 U.S. 826, 832, 109 S. Ct. 2218, 2223, 104 L. Ed. 2d 893 (1989) ("It is well-settled that Rule 21 invests district courts with authority to allow a dispensable nondiverse party to be dropped at any time [to preserve diversity jurisdiction], even after judgment has been rendered." However, while appellate courts also possess such authority, they should probably exercise it much more sparingly.). See, e.g., *Galt G/S v. JSS Scandinavia*, 142 F.3d 1150, 1154 (9th Cir. 1998) ("Rule 21 specifically allows for the dismissal of parties at any stage of the action. There is no requirement that diversity exist at the time of the filing of the complaint."). *But cf., Summers v. Earth Island Institute, 555 U.S. 488, 500, 129 S.Ct. 1142, 1153 173 L.Ed.2d 1* (Rule 21 does not permit joinder "*after the trial is over, judgment has been entered, and a notice of appeal has been filed.*") (Emphasis in original).

[13]*See, e.g., Delgado v. Plaza Las Americas, Inc.*, 139 F.3d 1 (1st Cir.1998) (court may raise nonjoinder *sua sponte*).

Preserving Diversity Jurisdiction

Even where a party is appropriately joined, circumstances can arise where the court can apply Rule 21 to drop a party. A notable example arises when a court dismisses a nondiverse party in order to obtain diversity jurisdiction over the remaining parties.[14]

Relation Back

If non-diverse parties are dismissed under Rule 21 in order to protect diversity jurisdiction, the dismissal will be treated as relating back to the date the complaint was filed.[15]

Severance of Claims or Parties

Even if parties or claims have been appropriately joined, the court may nonetheless use this Rule to order separate trials in the interest of justice.[16]

Additional Research References

Wright & Miller, *Federal Practice and Procedure* §§ 1681 to 89
C.J.S., Federal Civil Procedure §§ 117 to 126 et seq., §§ 171 to 177 et seq., §§ 318, §§ 343, §§ 803 to 809
West's Key Number Digest, Federal Civil Procedure ☞281 to 297, ☞384 to 386, ☞387 to 388, ☞1747 to 1750

---

[14]*See, e.g., Newman-Green, Inc. v. Alfonzo-Larrain*, 490 U.S. 826, 832–33, 109 S. Ct. 2218, 2222–23, 104 L. Ed. 2d 893 (1989) (Rule 21 permits dismissal of "dispensable" non-diverse defendants to cure jurisdictional defects; such dismissal can occur "even after judgment" and even by appellate court). *See, e.g., Fielder v. Credit Acceptance Corp.*, 188 F.3d 1031, 1039 (8th Cir. 1999) ("Rule 21 is often used to allow federal courts to escape a multi-party jurisdictional quandry.").

[15]*See, e.g., In re Lorazepam & Clorazepate Antitrust Litigation*, 631 F.3d 537, 542 (D.C. Cir. 2011) (doing so "allows the district court to save its prior rulings, and the jury's findings, which otherwise were entered without jurisdiction"); *Dexia Credit Local v. Rogan*, 629 F.3d 612, 621 (7th Cir. 2010) ("Rule 21 dismissals are retroactive.").

[16]*See, e.g., Rice v. Sunrise Express, Inc.*, 209 F.3d 1008, 1016 (7th Cir. 2000) (noting district courts' "broad discretion" under Rule 21; "[a]s long as there is a discrete and separate claim, the district court may exercise its discretion and sever it"); *Old Colony Ventures I, Inc. v. SMWNPF Holdings, Inc.*, 918 F. Supp. 343 (D. Kan. 1996) (in employing Rule 21, court should consider convenience of parties, avoidance of prejudice, and judicial efficiency.). *See also In re High Fructose Corn Syrup Antitrust Litigation*, 361 F.3d 439, 441 (7th Cir. 2004) (in the course of applying Rule 21, district court has authority to empanel separate juries in appropriate circumstances).

RULE 22
INTERPLEADER

(a) Grounds.

(1) *By a Plaintiff.* Persons with claims that may expose a plaintiff to double or multiple liability may be joined as defendants and required to interplead. Joinder for interpleader is proper even though:

(A) the claims of the several claimants, or the titles on which their claims depend, lack a common origin or are adverse and independent rather than identical; or

(B) the plaintiff denies liability in whole or in part to any or all of the claimants.

(2) *By a Defendant.* A defendant exposed to similar liability may seek interpleader through a cross-claim or counterclaim.

(b) Relation to Other Rules and Statutes.
This rule supplements—and does not limit—the joinder of parties allowed by Rule 20. The remedy this rule provides is in addition to—and does not supersede or limit—the remedy provided by 28 U.S.C. §§ 1335, 1397, and 2361. An action under those statutes must be conducted under these rules.

[Amended effective October 20, 1949; August 1, 1987; April 30, 2007, effective December 1, 2007.]

AUTHORS' COMMENTARY ON RULE 22

PURPOSE AND SCOPE

Rule 22 permits a person who may be subject to multiple liability by claimants with overlapping or inconsistent claims to interplead or join such claimants as defendants in a single action. In the ordinary procedure, once claimants are joined they will compete with one another to establish the validity and priority of their claims against the interpleader plaintiff.

RULE 22(a)—GROUNDS

CORE CONCEPT

Interpleader complements liberal joinder of parties under Rule 20 by allowing a stakeholder to join multiple, mutually inconsistent claims of various parties, and thereby determine rights in the asset (the "stake") in a single proceeding.

NOTE: Rule 22 interpleader is not the only kind of federal interpleader available. Statutory interpleader, found at 28 U.S.C.A. §§ 1335, 1397, and 2361, discussed below, is at least as important a source of interpleader authority as Rule 22. Although the two kinds of interpleader may often be employed in the same action, the differing characteristics of the two interpleaders sometimes make one more desirable, or available when the other is unavailable.[1] Thus, both versions should be considered when contemplating an interpleader action.

APPLICATIONS

Stakeholder as Claimant

The interpleader plaintiff may also be a claimant, as for example where a limited insurance fund is subject to claims exceeding the value of the fund. The insurance company may in appropriate circumstances be permitted to initiate the interpleader action, and then to participate as a claimant, if it contends that the other claims against the insurance fund are without merit.[2]

Claims Against the Stake

The only requirement under Rule 22 is that the interpleader plaintiff plead that the competing claims are at least partly inconsistent with one another, *e.g.,* where the claims against a fund exceed the value of the fund.[3] Interpleader actions need not be based on identical competing claims, or claims with a common origin, nor must the claims be totally incompatible

---

[1]*See, e.g., Federal Insurance Company v. Tyco International Ltd.,* 422 F. Supp. 2d 357 (S.D. N.Y. 2006) (explaining distinction between two kinds of interpleader).

[2]*Cf., Nationwide Mut. Fire Ins. Co. v. Eason,* 736 F.2d 130, 133 (4th Cir. 1984) (stakeholder is "not precluded" from making a claim on the asset).

[3]*See, e.g., Rhoades v. Casey,* 196 F.3d 592, 600 (5th Cir. 1999) ("A prerequisite to filing an interpleader action is that there must be a single, identifiable, fund."). *Pan Am. Fire & Cas. Co. v. Revere,* 188 F. Supp. 474 (E.D. La. 1960) (adversity requirement satisfied if claims against stake

amount to more than stakeholder's maximum liability). *See also, Hussain v. Boston Old Colony Ins. Co.,* 311 F.3d 623, 634 (5th Cir. 2002) ("[I]t is well settle that claims to the stake need not be mutually exclusive. . . . We and other courts have also found that adversity of claims is also satisfied when additional claims to a fund are derivative of one particular claimant's right to the fund."); *Hebel v. Ebersole,* 543 F.2d 14, 17 (7th Cir. 1976) (adversity requirement satisfied by "the risk of a double payment on single liability;" additional independent stakeholder liability does not defeat right to relief through interpleader).

with one another. In establishing this standard, Rule 22 eases significantly the requirements previously imposed on common law interpleader actions.

Defendants May Employ Interpleader

Sometimes a stakeholder will already have been sued by a claimant, but other claimants are not parties to the action. In such circumstances the stakeholder is entitled to initiate the interpleader action through a counterclaim or cross-claim, and then join the other claimants in the action.[4]

Subject Matter Jurisdiction

This Rule does not create jurisdiction in interpleader actions. Instead, it only authorizes interpleader *if* jurisdictional requirements in the federal courts are met. Federal subject matter jurisdiction is still required.[5] If the underlying cause of action is a federal question, subject matter jurisdiction for an interpleader is usually satisfied without difficulty. More commonly, however, the interpleader will arise from a state cause of action, and then the standard requirements for diversity jurisdiction must also be satisfied. The citizenship of the stakeholder must be diverse from that of the claimants, and the amount in controversy must exceed $75,000. The claimants need not be diverse among themselves.[6]

Personal Jurisdiction

Interpleader actions are actions against individuals, not against the asset, and so must satisfy requirements of personal jurisdiction. This means that service of process on claimants must satisfy Rule 4 service requirements as well as constitutional Due Process protections discussed in the section on personal jurisdiction.[7]

---

[4]*Grubbs v. General Elec. Credit Corp.*, 405 U.S. 699, 92 S. Ct. 1344, 31 L. Ed. 2d 612 (1972). *See, e.g., Aaron v. Mahl*, 550 F.3d 659, 663 (7th Cir. 2008) (defendant insurer faced with competing claims to the proceeds of a life insurance policy has standing to assert interpleader).

[5]*See, e.g., Aetna Life Ins. Co. v. Bayona*, 223 F.3d 1030, 1033 (9th Cir. 2000) ("Rule 22 interpleader is only a procedural device . . . -the rule does not convey [sic] jurisdiction on the courts"); *Commercial Nat. Bank of Chicago v. Demos*, 18 F.3d 485, 487 (7th Cir. 1994) ("Rule 22(1) provides a procedural framework for interpleader actions, but it does not confer subject matter jurisdiction.").

[6]*See, e.g., Hussain v. Boston Old Colony Ins. Co.*, 311 F.3d 623, 635 n. 46 (5th Cir. 2002) (diversity met when amount in controversy is satisfied and stakeholder is diverse from all claimants "even if citizenship of the claimants is not diverse"); *State Street Bank and Trust Co. v. Denman Tire Corp.*, 240 F.3d 83, 89 n. 4 (1st Cir. 2001) (statutory interpleader not available in diversity case "because the potential claimants are not diverse;" only Rule 22 is available); *Commercial Union Ins. Co. v. U.S.*, 999 F.2d 581, 584 (D.C. Cir. 1993) (Rule 22 looks to diversity between stakeholder and claimants; in contrast, statutory interpleader looks to diversity between claimants).

[7]*See, e.g., Metropolitan Life Ins. Co. v. Chase*, 294 F.2d 500, 502 (3d Cir. 1961) (interpleader under Rule 22

Venue Requirements

Rule 22 interpleader actions are subject to the general venue requirements contained in 28 U.S.C.A. § 1391.[8] These requirements are discussed earlier in this text.

Disinterested Stakeholders: Attorney's Fees

It appears settled that a disinterested stakeholder is entitled to recover attorney's fees.[9]

Payment into Court: Relation to Rule 67

Rule 22 does not require that the stakeholder turn the asset in dispute over to the custody of the court.[10] However, in practice, payment into court occurs in many Rule 22 cases.[11] It should be noted that Rule 67 authorizes a party, with leave of court, to pay a sum of money in dispute into court pending the outcome of the case. Rule 67 is sometimes the mechanism cited for payment of the stake into court in Rule 22 cases.[12]

Inconsistent Actions

Rule 22 interpleader contains no authority for the court to enjoin individual actions brought by claimants against the stakeholder in state courts. This is one of the important disadvantages of Rule 22 interpleader,[13] as compared with statutory interpleader, discussed immediately below.

Costs and Attorneys' Fees

In Rule 22 interpleader cases the district court has power to award both costs and attorneys' fees.[14]

---

requires personal jurisdiction over the claimants).

[8]*See, e.g., Leader Nat. Ins. Co. v. Shaw*, 901 F. Supp. 316, 320 (W.D. Okla. 1995) ("In cases of 'Rule' interpleader, venue is determined by reference to . . . § 1391.").

[9]*See, e.g., Perkins State Bank v. Connolly*, 632 F.2d 1306, 1311 (5th Cir. 1980) ("[C]osts and attorney's fees are generally awarded by federal courts to the plaintiff who initiates the interpleader as a mere stakeholder.").

[10]*See, e.g., Aaron v. Mahl*, 550 F.3d 659, 663 (7th Cir. 2008) (Rule 22 interpleaders do not require payment into court).

[11]*See, e.g., Matter of Bohart*, 743 F.2d 313, 317 (5th Cir. 1984) (in Rule 22 case, stakeholder turned fund over to court); *Kurland v. U.S.*, 919 F. Supp. 419 (M.D. Fla. 1996) (noting that Rule 22 does not require payment into court, but ordering such payment with consent of all parties).

[12]*See, e.g., Southtrust Bank of Florida, N.A. v. Wilson*, 971 F. Supp. 539, 542 (M.D. Fla. 1997) (using Rule 67 in a Rule 22 interpleader case).

[13]If the Rule 22 interpleader action has gone to judgment, a district court has authority to issue an injunction to protect the integrity of the judgment. *See, e.g., New York Life Ins. Co. v. Deshotel*, 142 F.3d 873 (5th Cir. 1998) (if judgment has been entered in interpleader case, court may act under authority of All Writs Statute, 28 U.S.C.A. § 1651, to prevent relitigation of issues precluded by res judicata or collateral estoppel; injunction applies to other federal proceedings). This authority, however, falls short of the authority federal courts enjoy in statutory interpleader cases to enjoin litigation that may compete with a pending interpleader action. This distinction is discussed again under statutory interpleader, below.

[14]*See, e.g., Sun Life Assurance Co. of Canada v. Sampson*, 556 F.3d 6, 8

RULE 22(b)—RELATION TO OTHER RULES AND STATUTES

CORE CONCEPT

Rule 22 explicitly states that interpleader under the Rule exists alongside and complements, rather than supercedes, statutory interpleader, discussed below.[15]

Additional Research References

Wright & Miller, *Federal Practice and Procedure* §§ 1701 to 21

STATUTORY INTERPLEADER

PURPOSE AND SCOPE

The sections of 28 U.S.C.A. that together comprise the federal interpleader statute share much in common with Rule 22. Like the Rule, the interpleader statute permits a stakeholder plaintiff to file an action against two or more adverse claimants to a stake that the plaintiff holds.[16] Once joined, the statute also contemplates that the claimants will then litigate against one another to determine the best disposition of the stake. However, the federal statute differs significantly from Rule 22 in a number of important respects. Thus there may be circumstances where both sources of interpleader authority should be employed, or where only one source and not the other will suffice.

The three specific sections of 28 U.S.C.A. that govern statutory interpleader are §§ 1335, 1397, and 2361. Section 1335 establishes the elements of a statutory interpleader action. Section 1397 establishes the special venue provisions governing statutory interpleader. Section 2361 establishes the broad personal juris-

---

(1st Cir. 2009) (acknowledging that Rule 22 contains no express authority, but holding that authority has long been part of court's equity power in interpleader cases). *But cf., Gelfgren v. Republic National Life Insurance Co.*, 680 F.2d 79, 81 (9th Cir. 1982) (in Rule 22 case court had discretion to award costs to stakeholder; but costs should not be awarded against stakeholder, "at least where the stakeholder has not been dilatory or otherwise guilty of bad faith").

[15] *See, e.g., Metropolitan Life Ins. Co. v. Price*, 501 F.3d 271, 275 (3d Cir. 2007) ("Unlike its statutory counterpart, rule interpleader is no more than a procedural device; the plaintiff must plead and prove an independent basis for subject matter jurisdiction.").

[16] *Cf., Airborne Freight Corp. v. U.S.*, 195 F.3d 238, 240 (5th Cir. 1999) ("central prerequisite" for interpleader is that the "plaintiff-stakeholder runs the risk but for determination in interpleader of multiple liability when several claimants assert rights to a single stake"); *Minnesota Mut. Life Ins. Co. v. Ensley*, 174 F.3d 977 (9th Cir. 1999) (held, it is not necessary, prior to initiation of the interpleader action, that more than one claimant has actually filed on the stake; "The court's jurisdiction under the interpleader statute extends to potential, as well as actual, claims.").

diction of a court hearing an interpleader action, and also authorizes the court to enjoin other federal or state judicial actions that may interfere with the interpleader.

---

28 U.S.C.A. § 1335. INTERPLEADER

CORE CONCEPT

The interpleader statute allows a stakeholder to join multiple, mutually inconsistent claims of various parties, and thereby determine rights in the asset (the "stake") in a single proceeding.[17]

APPLICATIONS

Stakeholder as Claimant
The interpleader plaintiff may also be a claimant,[18] as is the case with Rule 22 interpleader.

Claims Need Not Be Identical
Like Rule 22, the federal interpleader statute requires that the interpleader plaintiff plead that the claims are independent of, and at least partly inconsistent with, one another, e.g., where the claims against a fund exceed the value of the fund. Interpleader actions need not be based on identical competing claims, or claims with a common origin, nor must the claims be totally incompatible with one another.[19] These provisions are similar to those contained in Rule 22 interpleader.

Defendants May Employ Interpleader
Unlike Rule 22, the federal interpleader statute contains no *explicit* authority for defendants to initiate interpleader actions through a counterclaim or crossclaim. However, it appears settled that defendants may employ the interpleader statute in a manner parallel to that explicitly authorized by Rule 22.[20]

Subject Matter Jurisdiction
As with Rule 22, a federal court must have subject matter jurisdiction before it can hear interpleader claims. However, in

---

[17]*See, e.g., Rhoades v. Casey*, 196 F.3d 592, 600 (5th Cir. 1999) ("A prerequisite to filing an interpleader action is that there must be a single, identifiable, fund.").

[18]*State Farm Fire & Cas. Co. v. Tashire*, 386 U.S. 523, 533, 87 S. Ct. 1199, 1205, 18 L. Ed. 2d 270 (1967) (stakeholder need not be a disinterested party).

[19]*See, e.g., Metropolitan Property and Cas. Ins. Co. v. Shan Trac, Inc.*, 324 F.3d 20, 23 (1st Cir. 2003) (state law duty of insurers to settle legiti-

mate claims promptly in good faith creates potential obligation greater than value of stake; thus there "may" be sufficiently adverse claims within the meaning of § 1335); *Abex Corp. v. ABC Rail Corp.*, 158 F.R.D. 75, 76 (W.D. Pa. 1994) (citing requirement that conflicting claims need only be adverse to one another).

[20]*See, e.g., Ellis Nat. Bank of Jacksonville v. Irving Trust Co.*, 786 F.2d 466, 467 (2d Cir. 1986) (noting without comment use of statutory interpleader as a counterclaim).

diversity cases the requirements for subject matter jurisdiction in statutory interpleader are considerably more relaxed when compared to those which Rule 22 actions must satisfy. In diversity cases, statutory interpleader actions satisfy subject matter jurisdiction if the stake at issue is worth $500 or more,[21] and if the citizenship of only one of the claimants is diverse from that of any other claimant (not including the stakeholder).[22] Interpleader cases involving federal questions are unusual,[23] but not unheard of.[24]

Payment Into Court

The interpleader statute requires that the plaintiff deposit the asset at issue with the court.[25] This requirement is relaxed only if the plaintiff provides a bond in an amount subject to the court's discretion.[26] There is no similar explicit requirement for a bond in a Rule 22 action, but courts often require similar per-

---

[21]*See, e.g., Metropolitan Life Ins. Co. v. Price*, 501 F.3d 271, 275 (3d Cir. 2007) ("Unlike its statutory counterpart, rule interpleader is no more than a procedural device; the plaintiff must plead and prove an independent basis for subject matter jurisdiction.").

[22]*See, e.g., First Trust Corp. v. Bryant*, 410 F.3d 842, 852 (6th Cir. 2005) ("[O]nly two or more claimants need to be of diverse citizenship."); *State Street Bank and Trust Co. v. Denman Tire Corp.*, 240 F.3d 83, 89 n. 4 (1st Cir. 2001) (statutory interpleader not available in diversity case "because the potential claimants are not diverse;" only Rule 22 is available); *Franceskin v. Credit Suisse*, 214 F.3d 253 (2d Cir.2000) (requirement of diversity for statutory interpleader is that two or more claimants must be diverse from one another; where all claimants are citizens of Argentina, this requirement is not met; for Rule 22, diverse citizenship is satisfied if stakeholder is diverse from every claimant; thus, where stakeholder and claimants are all aliens, diversity requirement as defined by 28 U.S.C. § 1332 is not met); *Commercial Union Ins. Co. v. U.S.*, 999 F.2d 581, 584 (D.C. Cir. 1993) (for diversity in statutory interpleader cases, the focus is on diversity of claimant-defendants; citizenship of stakeholder is irrelevant in statutory interpleader). *But cf., Forcier v. Metropolitan Life Ins. Co.*, 469 F.3d 178, 182 n. 2 (1st Cir. 2006) (where all claimants are citizens of same state,

subject matter jurisdiction for statutory interpleader is unavailable; however, it is possible that the case will meet the differing requirements for subject matter jurisdiction that apply in Rule 22 cases).

[23]*See, e.g., Metropolitan Life Ins. Co. v. Price*, 501 F.3d 271, 275 (3d Cir. 2007) ("A federal question interpleader is a rarity.").

[24]Cf., *Metropolitan Life Ins. Co. v. Price*, 501 F.3d 271, 276 (3d Cir. 2007) ("Some interpleader actions do raise federal questions.").

[25]*Republic of Philippines v. Pimentel*, 553 U.S. 851, 128 S. Ct. 2180, 171 L. Ed. 2d 131 (U.S. 2008) (money or property, or a bond or surety equivalent, must be paid into court). *See, also, Federal Insurance Company v. Tyco International Ltd.*, 422 F. Supp. 2d 357, 395 (S.D. N.Y. 2006) ("The deposit of such funds is a jurisdictional requirement."); *Schneider v. Cate*, 405 F. Supp. 2d 1254, 1267 (D. Colo. 2005) ("The statute makes clear that 'the making of the deposit or the giving of the bond is a condition precedent to the acquisition of jurisdiction.'").

[26]*See e.g., U.S. Fire Ins. Co. v. Asbestospray, Inc.*, 182 F.3d 201, 210 (3d Cir. 1999) ("A proper deposit or bond is a jurisdictional prerequisite to bringing an interpleader [under § 1335]. The stakeholder invoking interpleader must deposit the largest amount for which it may be liable in view of the subject matter of the con-

formance by plaintiffs in Rule 22 cases anyway.

Costs and Attorneys' Fees

In statutory interpleader cases the district court has power to award both costs and attorneys' fees.[27]

28 U.S.C.A. § 1397. INTERPLEADER

CORE CONCEPT

Section 1397 provides that venue in a statutory interpleader action may be found in any judicial district in which one of the claimants resides.[28] This requirement differs from the traditional federal court venue requirements for Rule 22 interpleader. *See* 28 U.S.C.A. § 1391.

28 U.S.C.A. § 2361. PROCESS AND PROCEDURE

CORE CONCEPT

Section 2361 provides substantially expanded personal jurisdiction over the claimants. These powers often provide the plaintiff with a major advantage over analogous provisions governing Rule 22 actions. Section 2361 also authorizes the district court to enter final judgment discharging the stakeholder from further liability, thereby making the injunction permanent.[29]

APPLICATIONS

Process and Personal Jurisdiction

Statutory interpleader provides for nationwide personal jurisdiction and service of process.[30] Rule 22 actions, by contrast, must satisfy standard requirements for personal jurisdiction and service of process.

---

troversy." However, the amount to be deposited or bonded is measured by the realistic scope of the interpleader, not an "uncritical" assessment of "the highest amount claimed by the adverse claimants."). *Cf., Gaines v. Sunray Oil Co.*, 539 F.2d 1136, 1141 (8th Cir. 1976) ("The subject matter of an interpleader action is defined by the fund deposited by the stakeholder."). See also *Prudential Ins. Co. of America v. Bank of Commerce*, 857 F. Supp. 62, 64 (D. Kan. 1994) (when plaintiff seeks to post bond "the bond . . . should contain an obligor other than plaintiff as surety").

[27]*See, e.g., Sun Life Assurance Co. of Canada v. Sampson*, 556 F.3d 6, 8 (1st Cir. 2009) (acknowledging that § 1335 contains no express authority, but holding that authority has long

been part of court's equity power in interpleader cases; also noting authority under 28 U.S.C. § 2361 to "make all appropriate orders").

[28]*See, e.g., First Trust Corp. v. Bryant*, 410 F.3d 842, 853 n.7 (6th Cir. 2005).

[29]*Advantage Title Agency, Inc. v. Rosen*, 297 F. Supp. 2d 536, 539 (E.D. N.Y. 2003).

[30]*See, e.g., NYLife Distributors, Inc. v. Adherence Group, Inc.*, 72 F.3d 371, 375 (3d Cir. 1995) (noting availability of nationwide service on all claimants); *Carolina Cas. Ins. Co. v. Mares*, 826 F. Supp. 149, 154 (E.D. Va. 1993) (nationwide service of process under § 2361 available only in statutory interpleader actions).

Relief for Disinterested Stakeholders

When the district court is satisfied that interpleader has been invoked properly, § 2361 expressly authorizes the district court, in appropriate circumstances, to discharge a disinterested stakeholder.[31] The scope of such a discharge, however, extends to potential liability arising from multiple claims relating to distribution of the property in dispute. Unless all parties have received adequate notice and an opportunity to be heard, the discharge will not normally extend to the stakeholder's potential liability for, e.g., damage to the property while the stakeholder had custody.[32]

Injunctive Powers

In statutory interpleader cases, the federal court has authority to enjoin other federal or state proceedings that may affect the assets that are the subject of the interpleader action.[33] No comparable authority exists in Rule 22 actions.[34]

All Appropriate Orders: Attorneys' Fees

The crucial powers conferred by § 2361 — to serve process nationwide and to enjoin conflicting actions — are reinforced by an additional provision authorizing the court to "make all appropriate orders to enforce its judgment." This provision has been construed, *inter alia,* to authorize awards of costs and attorneys' fees.[35]

---

[31]*U.S. v. High Technology Products, Inc.,* 497 F.3d 637, 641 (6th Cir. 2007).

[32]*U.S. v. High Technology Products, Inc.,* 497 F.3d 637, 643–44 (6th Cir. 2007).

[33]*See, e.g., Lorillard Tobacco Co. v. Chester,* 589 F.3d 835, 844 (6th Cir. 2009) (noting that statutory interpleader is a " 'recognized exception to the Anti-Injunction Act' "). *But cf., First Trust Corp. v. Bryant,* 410 F.3d 842, 856 n.11 (6th Cir. 2005) (rejecting assertion that § 2361 could be statutory basis for award of attorney's fees in absence of more explicit authority); *U.S. Fire Ins. Co. v. Asbestospray, Inc.,* 182 F.3d 201, 211 (3d Cir. 1999) (injunction extends only to portion of fund that is subject matter of interpleader action; injunction does not extend to portions beyond reach of interpleader dispute; moreover, district courts should ensure that parallel proceedings in state court that predate interpleader action are treated with deference, especially if state ac-tions have resulted in judgments "or settlements in principle").

[34]*Cf., New York Life Ins. Co. v. Deshotel,* 142 F.3d 873 (5th Cir. 1998) (All Writs Statute, 28 U.S.C.A. § 1651, authorizes district court, after entry of judgment in Rule 22 action, to enter injunction against proceedings in other federal courts that would relitigate issues precluded by judgment). Note, however, that injunctive authority here applies only to cases decided, not to pending cases; to that extent the injunctive authority that a court enjoys under statutory interpleader is much broader, including both pre-judgment and post-judgment orders. *See, e.g., General Elec. Capital Assur. v. Van Norman,* 209 F. Supp. 2d 668, 670 (S.D. Tex. 2002) (judicial authority under § 2361 includes power to enter appropriate orders to ensure that judgments can be enforced).

[35]*See, e.g., Sun Life Assurance Co. of Canada v. Sampson,* 556 F.3d 6, 8 (1st Cir. 2009) (construing § 2361 as express authority for such awards).

Additional Research References

Wright & Miller, *Federal Practice and Procedure* §§ 1701 to 21
C.J.S., Interpleader §§ 2 to 52, §§ 53 to 57
West's Key Number Digest, Interpleader ⚷1 to 43

RULE 23
CLASS ACTIONS

(a) Prerequisites. One or more members of a class may sue or be sued as representative parties on behalf of all members only if:

(1) the class is so numerous that joinder of all members is impracticable;

(2) there are questions of law or fact common to the class;

(3) the claims or defenses of the representative parties are typical of the claims or defenses of the class; and

(4) the representative parties will fairly and adequately protect the interests of the class.

(b) Types of Class Actions. A class action may be maintained if Rule 23(a) is satisfied and if:

(1) prosecuting separate actions by or against individual class members would create a risk of:

(A) inconsistent or varying adjudications with respect to individual class members that would establish incompatible standards of conduct for the party opposing the class; or

(B) adjudications with respect to individual class members that, as a practical matter, would be dispositive of the interests of the other members not parties to the individual adjudications or would substantially impair or impede their ability to protect their interests;

(2) the party opposing the class has acted or refused to act on grounds that apply generally to the class, so that final injunctive relief or corresponding declaratory relief is appropriate respecting the class as a whole; or

(3) the court finds that the questions of law or fact common to class members predominate over any questions affecting only individual members, and that a class action is superior to other available methods for fairly and efficiently adjudicating

the controversy. The matters pertinent to these findings include:

  (A) the class members' interests in individually controlling the prosecution or defense of separate actions;

  (B) the extent and nature of any litigation concerning the controversy already begun by or against class members;

  (C) the desirability or undesirability of concentrating the litigation of the claims in the particular forum; and

  (D) the likely difficulties in managing a class action.

(c) Certification Order; Notice to Class Members; Judgment; Issues Classes; Subclasses.

  (1) *Certification Order.*

    (A) *Time to Issue.* At an early practicable time after a person sues or is sued as a class representative, the court must determine by order whether to certify the action as a class action.

    (B) *Defining the Class; Appointing Class Counsel.* An order that certifies a class action must define the class and the class claims, issues, or defenses, and must appoint class counsel under Rule 23(g).

    (C) *Altering or Amending the Order.* An order that grants or denies class certification may be altered or amended before final judgment.

  (2) *Notice.*

    (A) *For (b)(1) or (b)(2) Classes.* For any class certified under Rule 23(b)(1) or (b)(2), the court may direct appropriate notice to the class.

    (B) *For (b)(3) Classes.* For any class certified under Rule 23(b)(3), the court must direct to class members the best notice that is practicable under the circumstances, including individual notice to all members who can be identified through reasonable effort. The notice must clearly and concisely state in plain, easily understood language:

      (i)   the nature of the action;

      (ii)   the definition of the class certified;

      (iii) the class claims, issues, or defenses;

      (iv) that a class member may enter an appearance through an attorney if the member so desires;

      (v)   that the court will exclude from the class any member who requests exclusion;

      (vi) the time and manner for requesting exclusion; and

      (vii) the binding effect of a class judgment on members under Rule 23(c)(3).

(3) *Judgment.* Whether or not favorable to the class, the judgment in a class action must:

    (A) for any class certified under Rule 23(b)(1) or (b)(2), include and describe those whom the court finds to be class members; and

    (B) for any class certified under Rule 23(b)(3), include and specify or describe those to whom the Rule 23(c)(2) notice was directed, who have not requested exclusion, and whom the court finds to be class members.

(4) *Particular Issues.* When appropriate, an action may be brought or maintained as a class action with respect to particular issues.

(5) *Subclasses.* When appropriate, a class may be divided into subclasses that are each treated as a class under this rule.

(d) Conducting the Action.

(1) *In General.* In conducting an action under this rule, the court may issue orders that:

    (A) determine the course of proceedings or prescribe measures to prevent undue repetition or complication in presenting evidence or argument;

    (B) require—to protect class members and fairly conduct the action—giving appropriate notice to some or all class members of:

      (i)   any step in the action;

      (ii) the proposed extent of the judgment; or

      (iii) the members' opportunity to signify whether they consider the representation fair and adequate, to intervene and present claims or defenses, or to otherwise come into the action;

(C) impose conditions on the representative parties or on intervenors;

(D) require that the pleadings be amended to eliminate allegations about representation of absent persons and that the action proceed accordingly; or

(E) deal with similar procedural matters.

(2) *Combining and Amending Orders.* An order under Rule 23(d)(1) may be altered or amended from time to time and may be combined with an order under Rule 16.

(e) Settlement, Voluntary Dismissal, or Compromise. The claims, issues, or defenses of a certified class may be settled, voluntarily dismissed, or compromised only with the court's approval. The following procedures apply to a proposed settlement, voluntary dismissal, or compromise:

(1) The court must direct notice in a reasonable manner to all class members who would be bound by the proposal.

(2) If the proposal would bind class members, the court may approve it only after a hearing and on finding that it is fair, reasonable, and adequate.

(3) The parties seeking approval must file a statement identifying any agreement made in connection with the proposal.

(4) If the class action was previously certified under Rule 23(b)(3), the court may refuse to approve a settlement unless it affords a new opportunity to request exclusion to individual class members who had an earlier opportunity to request exclusion but did not do so.

(5) Any class member may object to the proposal if it requires court approval under this subdivision (e); the objection may be withdrawn only with the court's approval.

(f) Appeals. A court of appeals may permit an appeal from an order granting or denying class-action certification under this rule if a petition for permission to appeal is filed with the circuit clerk within 14 days after the order is entered. An appeal does not stay proceedings in the district court unless the district judge or the court of appeals so orders.

(g) Class Counsel.

(1) *Appointing Class Counsel.* Unless a statute provides otherwise, a court that certifies a class must appoint class counsel. In appointing class counsel, the court:

(A) must consider:

(i)   the work counsel has done in identifying or investigating potential claims in the action;

(ii) counsel's experience in handling class actions, other complex litigation, and the types of claims asserted in the action;

(iii) counsel's knowledge of the applicable law; and

(iv) the resources that counsel will commit to representing the class;

(B) may consider any other matter pertinent to counsel's ability to fairly and adequately represent the interests of the class;

(C) may order potential class counsel to provide information on any subject pertinent to the appointment and to propose terms for attorney's fees and nontaxable costs;

(D) may include in the appointing order provisions about the award of attorney's fees or nontaxable costs under Rule 23(h); and

(E) may make further orders in connection with the appointment.

(2) *Standard for Appointing Class Counsel.* When one applicant seeks appointment as class counsel, the court may appoint that applicant only if the applicant is adequate under Rule 23(g)(1) and (4). If more than one adequate applicant seeks appointment, the court must appoint the applicant best able to represent the interests of the class.

(3) *Interim Counsel.* The court may designate in-

terim counsel to act on behalf of a putative class before determining whether to certify the action as a class action.

(4) *Duty of Class Counsel.* Class counsel must fairly and adequately represent the interests of the class.

(h) Attorney's Fees and Nontaxable Costs. In a certified class action, the court may award reasonable attorney's fees and nontaxable costs that are authorized by law or by the parties' agreement. The following procedures apply:

(1) A claim for an award must be made by motion under Rule 54(d)(2), subject to the provisions of this subdivision (h), at a time the court sets. Notice of the motion must be served on all parties and, for motions by class counsel, directed to class members in a reasonable manner.

(2) A class member, or a party from whom payment is sought, may object to the motion.

(3) The court may hold a hearing and must find the facts and state its legal conclusions under Rule 52(a).

(4) The court may refer issues related to the amount of the award to a special master or a magistrate judge, as provided in Rule 54(d)(2)(D).

[Amended effective July 1, 1966; August 1, 1987; April 24, 1998, effective December 1, 1998; March 27, 2003, effective December 1, 2003; April 30, 2007, effective December 1, 2007; March 26, 2009, effective December 1, 2009.]

AUTHORS' COMMENTARY ON RULE 23

PURPOSE AND SCOPE

Rule 23 provides a means of joining parties in situations where the number of parties is sufficiently large so that it is impractical or inefficient for the parties to pursue their claims individually or through more conventional methods of joinder. Class actions are distinct from typical joinder situations in both the number of litigants involved and in the manner in which most class members participate in the case. Rule 23 contemplates that the class of litigants will be represented both by counsel and by "class representatives," *i.e.,* active members of the class who make many decisions for the entire class. Because there is potential for abusing the large number of class members who are not representatives and who therefore do not participate fully in many decisions, the court is charged with the obligation to monitor carefully important steps in the litigation process, such as approval of class litigation at the onset and potential settlements at the end. Class actions also present special problems of case management for the courts, so Rule 23 provides the trial judge with substantial additional authority to supervise progress in the case.

RULE 23(a)—PREREQUISITES

CORE CONCEPT

The specialized purpose of class actions—handling large numbers of litigants through class representatives—makes necessary a series of requirements intended to ensure that the opportunity to bring a class action is not misused or abused.[1] Two of these requirements have developed in case law. Others are listed in Rule 23(a). *All* requirements, whether in Rule 23(a) or developed in case law, must be satisfied before the court will certify a case as a class action.[2] Once the requirements are satisfied, however, the court is authorized to certify a class action without regard to whether state law attempts to impose additional requirements or an outright prohibition on class litigation.[3]

NOTE: In addition to the requirements of case law and Rule 23(a), a class action will not be certified unless it fits within some provision of Rule 23(b) as well.[4] Class actions must also meet the requirements of both personal jurisdiction and federal subject matter jurisdiction, and these requirements apply somewhat differently to class actions. Thus, while Rule 23(a) must be satisfied, meeting the requirements of Rule 23(a) alone will not produce a court-certified class action. With the exception of Rule 23(b), discussed separately, the additional prerequisites not mentioned in Rule 23(a), including case law requirements, venue and special questions of jurisdiction, are discussed immediately below. Ad-

---

[1]*Taylor v. Sturgell*, 128 S. Ct. 2161, 171 L. Ed. 2d 155 (U.S. 2008) (procedural safeguards of Rule 23 have overriding purpose of safeguarding interests of passive class members).

[2]*Wal-Mart Stores, Inc. v. Dukes*, ___ U.S. ___, 131 S.Ct. 2541, ___ L.Ed.2d ___ (2011). *See, e.g., Berger v. Compaq Computer Corp.*, 257 F.3d 475, 481 (5th Cir. 2001) ("[T]he party seeking certification bears the burden of establishing that *all* requirements of rule 23(a) have been satisfied.").

[3]*Shady Grove Orthopedic Associates, P.A. v. Allstate Insurance Co.*, ___ U.S. ___. 130 S.Ct. 1431, 1457, 176 L.Ed.2d 311 (2010).

[4]*Wal-Mart Stores, Inc. v. Dukes*, ___ U.S. ___, 131 S.Ct. 2541, ___ L.Ed.2d ___ (2011); *Shady Grove Orthopedic Associates, P.A. v. Allstate Insurance Co.*, ___ U.S. ___, 130 S.Ct. 1431, 1437, 176 L.Ed.2d 311 (2010) (class actions must meet two conditions: "The suit must satisfy the criteria set forth in subdivision (a) . . . and it also must fit into one of the three categories described in subdivision (b).").

ditionally, it should be understood that even if a proposed class meets all the requirements mentioned above, the district court may still retain discretion not to certify the class action.

APPLICATIONS

Burden of Proof

It is settled that the party who chooses to seek certification[5] has the burden of proving that the requirements for class certification are satisfied.[6]

Case Law Requirement for a Class

At least initially, the class representative must be a member of the class.[7] The purpose of this requirement is part of the courts' determination that class representatives will reflect the interests of the class. If a class representative was once a member but ceases to be a member of the class, the proper remedy is to select a new, suitable member of the class as a replacement representative.[8]

"Implicit" or "Implied" Classes

Rule 23 establishes a rigorous procedure to be followed before a case will be certified as a class action.[9] However, it is possible (though unusual) that in some circuits, classwide relief

---

[5]*Sprint Communications v. APCC Services, Inc.*, 554 U.S. 269, 128 S. Ct. 2531, 171 L. Ed. 2d 424 (2008) ("[C]lass actions are permissive, not mandatory.").

[6]*See, e.g., Novella v. Westchester County*, 661 F.3d 128, 149 (2d Cir. 2011) ("[A] plaintiff must satisfy all of the requirements of Rule 23 by a preponderance of the evidence.").

[7]*East Texas Motor Freight System Inc. v. Rodriguez*, 431 U.S. 395, 403, 97 S. Ct. 1891, 1896, 52 L. Ed. 2d 453 (1977) (error to certify class where named representatives are not members of class). *See, e.g., Holmes v. Pension Plan of Bethlehem Steel Corp.*, 213 F.3d 124, 135 (3d Cir. 2000) ("[A] plaintiff who lacks the personalized, redressable injury required for standing to assert claims on his own behalf would also lack standing to assert claims on behalf of a class."); *Great Rivers Co-op. of Southeastern Iowa v. Farmland Industries, Inc.*, 120 F.3d 893, 899 (8th Cir. 1997) ("Inherent in Rule 23 is the requirement that the class representatives be members of the class.").

[8]*See, e.g., Holmes v. Pension Plan of Bethlehem Steel Corp.*, 213 F.3d

124, 135–36 (3d Cir. 2000) (if class representative has "live claim" at time of motion for class certification, "neither a pending motion nor a certified class action need be dismissed if his individual claim subsequently becomes moot"; but if claim became moot prior to motion for class certification, motion will be denied and case will be dismissed); *Hardy v. City Optical Inc.*, 39 F.3d 765, 770 (7th Cir. 1994) (party dismissed "can no longer be the class representative"). *But see Kifer v. Ellsworth*, 346 F.3d 1155, 1156 (7th Cir. 2003) (initially, class representative was prison inmate who was subsequently released from jail; because class sought prospective relief through an injunction, class representative's personal claim had therefore become moot; "but the mooting of the class representative's personal claim does not bar him from continuing to represent the class, . . . as otherwise defendants might delay the grant of relief in class actions indefinitely by buying off the class representatives in succession.").

[9]*See, e.g., Garcia v. Johanns*, 444 F.3d 625, 631 (D.C. Cir. 2006) (plaintiff seeking class certification must meet all requirements of Rule 23(a) and one

may be obtained notwithstanding the fact that the district court failed to follow the Rule 23 requirements for class certification.[10] Other courts have been generally reluctant to embrace this concept,[11] and to reject it where the de facto finding of class certification was not embraced (at least tacitly) by the actions of all parties and the court.[12] On this point attorneys must consult both the local precedent as well as the facts of individual cases.

Settlement Classes

It appears settled that a class may be certified for purposes of settlement only. However, it is also settled that certification of such classes must fully satisfy the relevant requirements of Rule 23.[13]

---

requirement of Rule 23(b)).

[10]*See, e.g., Doe, 1-13 ex rel. Doe Sr. 1-13 v. Bush*, 261 F.3d 1037, 1050 (11th Cir. 2001) (case was filed as class action and plaintiffs made timely motion for class certification; magistrate judge recommended certification; parties and district court all behaved as though classwide relief might be appropriate; failure to certify formally was court's error, not caused by plaintiffs; no administrative problems will arise by treating case as class action; held, implied class appropriate; also citing several older cases); *Navarro-Ayala v. Hernandez-Colon*, 951 F.2d 1325, 1334 (1st Cir. 1991) (approving implied class "because this case was instituted by a complaint seeking class relief, implicitly granted class relief, and was conducted for years as a de facto class action").

[11]*See, e.g., Partington v. American Intern. Specialty Lines Ins. Co.*, 443 F.3d 334, 341 (4th Cir. 2006) ("the Fourth Circuit has never allowed the rigorous Rule 23 analysis to be accomplished implicitly;" noting that implicit certification has been approved "only in the context of contested actions where the parties and the court acted at all times as though a class existed").

[12]*See, e.g., Davis v. Hutchins*, 321 F.3d 641, 649 (7th Cir. 2003) (plaintiff had filed for class certification and defendant had not responded to complaint or motion; default was properly entered, but court had independent duty to address Rule 23 issues before

it granted classwide relief; held, no default certification).

[13]*Amchem Products, Inc. v. Windsor*, 521 U.S. 591, 117 S. Ct. 2231, 138 L. Ed. 2d 689 (1997) (certification of settlement class requires "heightened attention" of trial court; affirming denial of certification for failure to satisfy Rule 23(a)(4) and (b)(3); but noting that consideration of trial management is irrelevant to settlement class; also holding that court's authority to approve settlement under Rule 23(e) does not authorize court to disregard requirements of Rule 23(a) and (b)). *See, e.g., Denney v. Deutsche Bank AG*, 443 F.3d 253, 270 (2d Cir. 2006) ("Before certification is proper for any purpose-settlement, litigation, or otherwise-a court must ensure that the requirements of Rule 23(a) and (b) have been met. These requirements should not be watered down by virtue of the fact that the settlement is fair or equitable."). *See also, Ortiz v. Fibreboard Corp.*, 527 U.S. 815, 119 S. Ct. 2295, 144 L. Ed. 2d 715 (1999) (holding that ruling of *Amchem* requiring settlement classes for which certification is sought under rule 23(b)(3) to meet requirements of Rule 23(a) applies equally to settlement classes for which certification is sought under Rule 23(b)(1)(B)). *But cf., Smith v. Sprint Communications Co., L.P.*, 387 F.3d 612, 614 (7th Cir. 2004) (if settlement has been reached, "a district court need not inquire whether the case, if tried, would present intractable management problems, for the proposal is that there be no trial;" citing *Amchem*,

Arbitration

In general, contractual provisions that require arbitration of disputes are enforceable under the Federal Arbitration Act.[14] In the context of class actions, it is now apparently settled that an arbitration provision precluding class arbitration or class litigation is enforceable, notwithstanding state law to the contrary.[15]

Relation to Rule 68

Rule 68 governs offers of judgment. Circuit courts have identified at least two points of overlap between Rule 23 and Rule 68.

The first problem can arise because a defendant has made an offer of judgment for the full amount that a plaintiff may lawfully collect if the plaintiff's claim prevailed on the merits. This situation may occur most commonly when there is a statutory cap on the plaintiff's claim. When such an offer of judgment is made, courts normally use Rule 68 to impose an end to the litigation, without regard to any preference the plaintiff may have.[16] Whatever the merit this approach may have in ordinary civil litigation, it can produce a complication in a case that has been or may be certified as a class action. For example, if a defendant made an offer of judgment to an individual litigant for a full statutory amount, a court's decision to use a default judgment to effectively force a settlement of the case could preclude litigation of issues that were appropriate for treatment as a class action. Courts recognize this potential problem, and have held that a Rule 68 offer of judgment to an individual plaintiff cannot be used to render a putative class action moot.[17]

The second problem arises because Rule 68 provides that if a proper offer of judgment is made, followed by a filing with the

---

supra; however, other elements of Rule 23 must still be met).

[14]9 U.S.C. § 2 (arbitration agreements are "valid, irrevocable, and enforceable" except in circumstances where standard contract law would create exception).

[15]*AT&T Mobility LLC v. Concepcion*, ___ U.S. ___, 131 S.Ct. 1740, 179 L.Ed.2d 742 (2011) (Federal Arbitration Act overrides state law nullifying arbitration clause that contains waiver of class actions).

[16]*See, e.g., McCauley v. Trans Union, L.L.C.*, 402 F.3d 340, 341–42 (2d Cir. 2005) (where plaintiff rejects such offer, proper remedy is to enter default judgment for full dollar amount, plus costs).

[17]*See, e.g., Lucero v. Bureau of Collection Recovery, Inc.*, 639 F.3d 1239, 1249 (10th Cir. 2011) (citing numerous cases and noting "some tension in the legal concepts," but concluding that Rule 68 is inapplicable to Rule 23 class actions); *Carroll v. United Compucred Collections, Inc.*, 399 F.3d 620, 625 (6th Cir. 2005) (in instant case motion for class certification was pending but not yet decided when offer of judgment was made; if complaint could be rendered moot by use of Rule 68, court could never reach class action even in cases where class certification would be appropriate); *Weiss v. Regal Collections*, 385 F.3d 337, 348 (3d Cir. 2004) (same, but making exception for "undue delay" in filing motion for class certification).

district court of the offer, notice of proper acceptance, and proof of service, the court has no discretion in the matter, and must enter judgment.[18] Rule 23, by contrast, affords the court substantial authority to review and approve (or veto) a proposed settlement of a class action. Courts have resolved this apparent conflict by treating the authority of a district court under Rule 23 as an exception to the general requirement of Rule 68, controlling most offers of judgment outside the context of class litigation.[19]

Rule 23(a) Requirements for a Class

(1) *Numerosity:* Rule 23(a)(1) requires that the class membership be sufficiently large to warrant a class action because the alternative of joinder is "impracticable".[20] There is no threshold number of class members guaranteed to satisfy the "numerosity" requirement of Rule 23(a).[21] A class comprised of many hundreds, or thousands, of members will almost surely meet this test.[22] Classes of ten litigants or less will almost

---

[18]Fed.R.Civ.P. 68. *See, e.g, Webb v. James*, 147 F.3d 617, 621 (7th Cir. 1998) (noting that Rule 68 mandates entry of judgment on an offer that meets the requirements of Rule 68).

[19]*See, e.g., Ramming v. Natural Gas Pipeline Co. of America*, 390 F.3d 366, 371 (5th Cir. 2004) (duty of court to review settlement of class action under Rule 23 provides exception to Rule 68; same result, slightly different reasoning, when case involves plea for injunctive relief).

[20]*See, e.g., Central States Southeast and Southwest Areas Health and Welfare Fund v. Merck-Medco Managed Care, L.L.C.*, 504 F.3d 229, 244–45 (2d Cir. 2007) ("The numerosity requirement . . . does not mandate that joinder of all parties be impossible — only that the difficulty or inconvenience of joining all members of the class make use of the class action appropriate."). *Mullen v. Treasure Chest Casino, LLC*, 186 F.3d 620, 624 (5th Cir. 1999) (class of 100 to 150 members sufficient; additional factors supporting finding of adequate numerosity are reluctance of current employees to sue individually for fear of retaliation and possibility that transient nature of employment in gambling business would tend to make joinder difficult because members of potential class would tend to disperse geographically);

Robidoux v. Celani, 987 F.2d 931, 935 (2d Cir. 1993) (emphasizing that for certification, joinder need only be impracticable, not necessarily impossible).

[21]*See, e.g., Trevizo v. Adams*, 455 F.3d 1155 (10th Cir.2006) (holding that there is no set formula or number for determining numerosity; concluding that 84 potential class members is insufficient where joinder is not difficult); *Bittinger v. Tecumseh Products Co.*, 123 F.3d 877, 884 n. 1 (6th Cir. 1997) (noting that Rule 23(a)(1) is not a "strict numerical test;" holding, however, that where class comprises over 1,100 persons, suggestion that joinder is not impractical is "frivolous"); *Robidoux v. Celani*, 987 F.2d 931, 935 (2d Cir. 1993) (numerosity does not require exact estimate of class size, but only a reasonable estimate). *But see Vega v. T-Mobile USA, Inc.*, 564 F.3d 1256, 1257 (11th Cir. 2009) ("[A] plaintiff still bears the burden of making some showing, affording the district court the means to make a supported factual finding, that the class actually certified meets the numerosity requirement."); *Consolidated Rail Corp. v. Town of Hyde Park*, 47 F.3d 473, 483 (2d Cir. 1995) ("[N]umerosity is presumed at a level of 40 members.").

[22]*See, e.g., Bacon v. Honda of*

certainly not meet this test,[23] and will instead be consigned to joinder of parties under Rule 20. When the number of members falls between, approximately, twenty-five and one hundred, the probability of meeting the numerosity requirement varies from one judicial district to another.[24]

While the numerosity requirement is very fact specific, the requirement of impracticability of joinder must be affirmatively and specifically addressed in the certification motion.[25] It is not necessary that joinder of all parties is impossible, only that difficulty or inconvenience of joining all parties make a class action inappropriate.[26]

(2) *Common Questions of Law or Fact:* Rule 23(a)(2) requires the existence of common questions of law or fact among the class members before the case will be certified as a class action. To satisfy the requirement of Rule 23(a)(2), the common questions need not predominate. Historically, courts have generally had a liberal attitude toward this requirement, and close questions as to the existence of sufficient commonality tended to be resolved in favor of finding common questions.[27] That approach, however, has been modified recently, at least to the extent that it is now clear that failure to meet the commonality requirement of Rule 23(a)(2) is, by itself, sufficient ground to deny certification.[28] Moreover, mere allegations that class members have suffered common injuries is no longer enough to satisfy the commonality requirement. Instead, Rule 23(a)(2) as now construed requires not only common allegations but also that

America Mfg., Inc., 370 F.3d 565, 570 (6th Cir. 2004) ("There is no automatic cut-off point at which the number of plaintiffs makes joinder impracticable, [but] sheer number of potential litigants in a class, especially if it is more than several hundred, can be the only factor needed to satisfy Rule 23(a)(1).").

[23] *General Tel. Co. of the Northwest, Inc. v. Equal Employment Opportunity Commission*, 446 U.S. 318, 330, 100 S. Ct. 1698, 1706, 64 L. Ed. 2d 319 (1980) (classes of 15 members will often be too small). *See, e.g., National Ass'n of Government Employees v. City Public Service Bd. of San Antonio, Tex.*, 40 F.3d 698, 715 (5th Cir. 1994) (affirming that class of 11 members does not satisfy requirement of numerosity). *But cf., Grant v. Sullivan*, 131 F.R.D. 436, 446 (M.D. Pa. 1990) (approving certification of class of 14 members).

[24] *See, e.g., Stewart v. Abraham*, 275 F.3d 220, 226–27 (3d Cir. 2001)

(no minimum number required but more than 40 is generally sufficient). *But cf., Pruitt v. City of Chicago, Illinois*, 472 F.3d 925, 926 (7th Cir. 2006) (if joinder is practicable "then the other criteria don't matter;" acknowledging that sometimes a class of 40 is unmanageable, but not in instant case).

[25] *Golden v. City of Columbus*, 404 F.3d 950, 965 (6th Cir. 2005).

[26] *See, e.g., Novella v. Westchester County*, 661 F.3d 128, 143 (2d Cir. 2011).

[27] *See, e.g., Stewart v. Abraham*, 275 F.3d 220, 227 (3d Cir. 2001) (commonality can be satisfied if class representatives share a single question of fact or law with class members); *Mullen v. Treasure Chest Casino, LLC*, 186 F.3d 620, 625 (5th Cir. 1999) ("The test for commonality is not demanding.").

[28] *Wal-Mart Stores, Inc. v. Dukes*, ___ U.S. ___, 131 S.Ct. 2541, ___, ___ L.Ed.2d ___ (2011).

class litigation will resolve at least one issue common to the l class.[29]

Particularly in class actions involving fraud, there is now somewhat greater harmony between commonality for purposes of Rule 23(a) and the more stringent requirements for pleading fraud with particularity under Rule 9(b). For example, in securities cases controlled by the Private Securities Litigation Reform Act of 1995,[30] it is settled that a plaintiff seeking to serve as a class representative must plead with particularity sufficient to satisfy the requirements of Rule 9(b).[31]

In class actions based on allegations of employment discrimination there are at least two ways by which a plaintiff may successfully assert that a class of claimants shares a common question of law or fact with the plaintiff. The first is to demonstrate that some sort of testing procedure applicable to the group unfairly prejudiced the group in hiring or promotion. The second means of satisfying Rule 23(a)(2) is to provide significant evidence that the defendant had a general policy of discrimination.[32]

> **NOTE:** Although Rule 23(a) may be satisfied even if the common questions of law or fact do not predominate in the case, a class seeking certification under Rule 23(b)(3) must nevertheless include common questions of law or fact that *do* predominate over other questions. The interplay between Rule 23(a) and Rule 23(b) is discussed further below.

(3) *Class Representatives' Claims Must Be Typical:* Rule 23(a)(3) requires that the claims of class representatives be typical of the class as a whole, not merely some portion thereof.[33] Generally the class representatives need not have claims identical in all respects with those of other members of the class.[34] Substantial commonality appears to be sufficient, even if differences among the claims, *e.g.,* issues of

---

[29]*Wal-Mart Stores, Inc. v. Dukes,* ___ U.S. ___, 131 S.Ct. 2541, 2551, 180 L.Ed.2d 274 (2011). (Rule 23(a)(2) mandates that resolution of common issue in question "will resolve an issue that is central to the validity of [all of one common claim] in one stroke.").

[30]15 U.S.C. § 78u.

[31]*See, e.g., Berger v. Compaq Computer Corp.,* 257 F.3d 475, 478 (5tth Cir. 2001) (explaining statutory requirement to plead scienter with particularity).

[32]*Wal-Mart Stores, Inc. v. Dukes,* ___ U.S. ___, 131 S.Ct. 2541, ___ L. Ed. 2d ___ (2011) (in instant case, defendant had no testing or evaluating procedure at all, and had an announced policy, including penalties, in opposition to sex discrimination).

[33]*See, e.g., Rector v. City and County of Denver,* 348 F.3d 935, 950 (10th Cir. 2003) ("By definition, class representatives who do not have Article III standing to pursue the class claims fail to meet the typicality requirements of Rule 23."); *Schachner v. Blue Cross and Blue Shield of Ohio,* 77 F.3d 889, 896 n. 8 (6th Cir. 1996) (representative holding federal claim does not adequately represent certain class members who hold only state claims).

[34]*See, e.g., Lightbourn v. County of El Paso, Tex.,* 118 F.3d 421, 426, 22 A.D.D. 618 (5th Cir. 1997) ("The test for typicality, like the test for commonality, is not demanding."); *Paxton v. Union Nat. Bank,* 688 F.2d 552, 561

damages, also exist.[35] This requirement is intended to ensure that class representatives will represent the best interests of class members who take a less active part in managing the litigation. It also overlaps considerably the case law requirement that class representatives be members of the class.[36]

(4) *Representatives Must Fairly Protect the Class:* Because class actions vest authority over the interests of passive members of the class in the hands of class activists, Rule 23(a)(4) requires the court to ensure that class representatives will include individuals who will meet those responsibilities fully.[37] However, this "adequacy" requirement does not necessarily mean that all class representatives must be adequate. In a situation where there is more than one named representative, the requirement may be satisfied when only one representative is adequate.[38]

There is no "bright line" establishing when Rule 23(a)(4) is satisfied.[39] Nevertheless, courts tend to be particularly

---

(8th Cir. 1982) ("The Rule does not require that every question of law or fact be common to every member of the class."). *Cf., Wagner v. NutraSweet Co.,* 95 F.3d 527, 534 (7th Cir. 1996) ("[T]ypicality under Rule 23(a)(3) should be determined with reference to the [defendant's] actions, not with respect to particularized defenses it might have against certain class members.").

[35] *See, e.g., Ball v. Union Carbide Corp.,* 376 F.3d 554 (6th Cir.2004) (requirements of Rule 23(a)(2) and (3) "tend to merge"); *Mullen v. Treasure Chest Casino, LLC,* 186 F.3d 620, 625 (5th Cir. 1999) ("Like commonality, the test for typicality is not demanding."); *Alpern v. UtiliCorp United, Inc.,* 84 F.3d 1525, 1540 (8th Cir. 1996) ("Factual variations in the individual claims will not normally preclude class certification if the claim arises from the same event or course of conduct as the class claims, and gives rise to the same legal or remedial theory." Variations in damages do not necessarily undermine typicality.). *But see Stirman v. Exxon Corp.,* 280 F.3d 554, 562 (5th Cir. 2002) (although typicality is not normally a demanding test, finding insufficient typicality where class is based on implied lease covenant, and leases vary between market-value leases and proceeds leases under one

state's law, and other states have even greater range of differences in law); *Armstrong v. Davis,* 275 F.3d 849, 868–69 (9th Cir. 2001) (typicality satisfied by comparing type of injury alleged by named plaintiff with injuries of other class members; injuries must be similar but need not be identical; but class representatives should include parties who together have suffered the entire range of injuries alleged, from kidney disability to hearing impairment).

[36] *See, e.g., Robinson v. Sheriff of Cook County,* 167 F.3d 1155, 1157 (7th Cir. 1999) (Rule 23(a)(3) "is really an aspect of [Rule 23(a)(2)]; if [the representative's] claim is atypical, he is not likely to be an adequate representative.").

[37] *But cf. Ward v. Dixie National Life Insurance Co.,* 595 F.3d 164, 180 (4th Cir. 2010) ("[F]or conflict of interest to defeat the adequacy requirement, 'that conflict must be fundamental.' ").

[38] *See, e.g., Rodriguze v. West Publishing Corp.,* 563 F.3d 948, 961 (9th Cir. 2009) (" '[T]he adequacy-of-representation' requirement is satisfied as long as one of the class representatives is an adequate class representative.").

[39] *But cf., Denney v. Deutsche Bank*

sensitive to this requirement.[40] Potential conflicts of interest may disqualify applicants,[41] as can a suggestion that the proposed class representative lacks integrity.[42] If in the course of litigation the trial court finds that class representatives previously approved have become inadequate, the court retains authority to order appointment of new representatives.[43]

(5) *Adequacy of Counsel:* Rule 23(a)(4) contains no express language addressing the issue of whether it authorizes the court to examine the ability of the class' legal counsel to represent the class. Nevertheless, courts have heretofore

---

AG, 443 F.3d 253, 268 (2d Cir. 2006) ("Adequacy is twofold: the proposed class representative must have an interest in vigorously pursuing the claims of the class, and must have no interests antagonistic to the interests of other class members."); *Wolfert ex rel. Estate of Wolfert v. Transamerica Home First, Inc.*, 439 F.3d 165, 173 (2d Cir. 2006) ("There is no litmus test for determining when interests of one or more absent class members are sufficiently distinct from those of the class representatives to render those representatives inadequate.").

[40]*See, e.g., Stirman v. Exxon Corp.*, 280 F.3d 554, 563 (5th Cir. 2002) (error not to examine adequacy of class representatives as well as counsel; questioning adequacy of class representatives where leases may be dissimilar to those of class; and where representative may have waived statute of limitations issue unimportant to her individually but potentially significant to others in class; noting, inter alia, that adequacy of class representative often overlaps typicality requirement). *Cf., Dechert v. Cadle Co.*, 333 F.3d 801 (7th Cir.2003) (bankruptcy trustee is not per se unsuitable as class representative, but trustee's duty to protect interest of bankruptcy creditors may often conflict with interest of class members).

[41]*Ortiz v. Fibreboard Corp.*, 527 U.S. 815, 119 S. Ct. 2295, 144 L. Ed. 2d 715 (1999) (class comprised of holders of both present and future tort claims should be divided into subclasses with different counsel for each subclass; failure to provide different counsel means requirements of Rule 23(a)(4) are not met). *See, e.g., Randall v. Rolls-Royce Corp.*, 637 F.3d 818, 824

(7th Cir. 2011) (named plaintiffs who are vulnerable to defense that would not defeat unnamed plaintiffs do not meet requirement of Rule 23(a)(4)); *London v. Wal-Mart Stores, Inc.*, 340 F.3d 1246, 1255–56 (11th Cir. 2003) (personal friendship between class representative and lawyer, plus fact that class representative had been lawyer's stockbroker and might resume that role in future, meant class representative "cannot fairly and adequately represent the class"); *Pickett v. Iowa Beef Processors*, 209 F.3d 1276, 1280–81 (11th Cir. 2000) (acknowledging that requirements of rule 23(a)(4) can be satisfied unless conflict "is a fundamental one, going to the specific issues in controversy"; finding such conflict where plaintiffs are challenging contracts and marketing agreements that harmed some class members but benefited others). *Cf., Cordes & Co. Financial Services, Inc. v. A.G. Edwards & Sons, Inc.*, 502 F.3d 91, 103 (2d Cir. 2007) (parties are not precluded from serving as class representatives simply because they acquired their individual claims through assignment); *Fymbo v. State Farm Fire and Cas. Co.*, 213 F.3d 1320 (10th Cir. 2000) (where class members each have "a sufficiently large stake to be able to litigate" separately, that factor weighs against certifying class).

[42]*See, e.g., Savino v. Computer Credit, Inc.*, 164 F.3d 81, 87 (2d Cir. 1998) ("To judge the adequacy of representation, courts may consider the honesty and trustworthiness of the named plaintiff.").

[43]*See, e.g., Swanson v. Wabash, Inc.*, 577 F. Supp. 1308, 1326 (N.D. Ill. 1983) (citing cases).

routinely cited Rule 23(a)(4) for their authority to examine the ability of the class' legal counsel to represent the class.[44] With the introduction of Rule 23(g) in 2003, however, it is no longer necessary for courts to rely on Rule 23(a)(4) for supervision of class counsel. Instead, Rule 23(g) expressly grants a district court the right and responsibility to appoint suitable counsel. Until enough time has elapsed to permit the courts to develop their authority and duties under Rule 23(g), it is likely that much of the case law originally developed under the authority of Rule 23(a)(4) will continue to guide courts in this work. Rule 23(g) is discussed at greater length elsewhere in this text.

(6) *The "Most Sophisticated" Investor:* When a class action also falls within the scope of the Private Securities Litigation Reform Act of 1995[45] the court is obligated to appoint as lead plaintiff the "most adequate plaintiff." Such a person is identified as that member of the class who is most capable of representing the class. This requirement, however, has been held not to require that the chosen person possess unique advantages of experience, expertise, wealth or intellect.[46]

General Considerations

(1) *Diversity Jurisdiction:* In most class actions, federal subject matter jurisdiction based on diversity of citizenship is now governed by a recent addition to 28 U.S.C.A. § 1332. In 2005 Congress amended § 1332 to include special provisions applicable only to class actions. These provisions are found in § 1332(d). Subject to a few exceptions, § 1332(d)(2) provides that the amount in controversy requirement for class actions is a sum that exceeds $5,000,000, exclusive of interest and costs.[47] This requirement is often easier to meet than the standard for non-class litigation of more than $75,000 for each plaintiff, exclusive of interest and costs.[48] The reason is that the figure of more than $5,000,000 may be met by adding all the claims of the class members together,[49] whereas the amount of more than $75,000 is normally a requirement that each plaintiff

---

[44]Some courts continue to cite Rule 23(a)(4) as authority for a court to evaluate adequacy of class counsel. *See, e.g., Dewey v. Volkswagen Aktien Gesellschaft,* ___ F.3d ___ (3d Cir. 2012).

[45]15 U.S.C.A. § 78u-4(a)(3)(B).

[46]*Berger v. Compaq Computer Corp.,* 279 F.3d 313 (5th Cir.2002). *See also In re Cavanaugh,* 306 F.3d 726, 729 (9th Cir. 2002) (party with largest financial stake in litigation presumptively is most adequate party and, assuming requirements of Rule 23 are suming requirements of Rule 23 are

met, will typically be lead plaintiff).

[47]28 U.S.C.A. § 1332(d)(2). *See also, e.g., Frazier v. Pioneer Americas LLC,* 455 F.3d 542 (5th Cir. 2006) ("Unlike § 1332(a), [§ 1332(d)(6)] explicitly allows aggregation of each class member's claim.").

[48]28 U.S.C.A. § 1332(a).

[49]28 U.S.C.A. § 1332(d)(6). *See also, e.g., Frazier v. Pioneer Americas LLC,* 455 F.3d 542 (5th Cir. 2006) ("Unlike § 1332(a), [§ 1332(d)(6)] explicitly allows aggregation of each class member's claim.").

must meet individually.

Section 1332(d)(2) permits the requirement of diversity of citizenship in most class actions to be met in any of three ways: (A) a single member of the class may be a citizen of an American state that is different from the citizenship of any defendant; (B) a single member of the class may be a citizen or subject of a foreign state and any defendant is a citizen of an American state; or (C) a single member of a class may be a citizen of an American state and any defendant is either a foreign state or a citizen or subject of a foreign state.[50] It should be noted that this requirement permits the diversity of citizenship requirement to be satisfied even where some members of the class might not be of diverse citizenship from one or more defendants, which is a very different standard from the requirement for diverse citizenship in non-class litigation.[51]

Section 1332(d) also contains a number of exceptions to the special jurisdictional standards for class actions. Together, however, these exceptions probably constitute a relatively small proportion of the total number of class actions that are now otherwise jurisdictionally eligible to be filed in federal district court. The first potential exception arises when more than one-third, but less than two-thirds, of the class members as well as the primary defendants are citizens of the same state in which the action was originally filed. In that circumstance, § 1332(d) affords the district court discretion to decline to exercise its jurisdiction, after considering six factors: whether the claims involve matters of national or interstate interest; whether the claims will be subject to the law of the forum state or the laws of other states; whether the original pleading in the class action was pleaded in a manner intended to avoid federal jurisdiction; whether the action was filed in a forum with a "distinct" nexus with the class, the alleged wrong, or the defendants; whether the forum is the place of citizenship of a disproportionate number of class members, and the remaining class members are dispersed among a substantial number of other states; and whether, during the previous three years, other class actions asserting similar claims were filed on behalf of the same persons.[52]

Another exception, found in 28 U.S.C.A. § 1332(d)(4), requires the district court to decline jurisdiction if the following elements are met: more than two-thirds of the class members are citizens of the forum state; at least one significant defendant is a citizen of the forum state; principal injuries giving rise to the cause of action occurred in the forum state; and dur-

---

[50] 28 U.S.C.A. § 1332(d)(2)(A) to (C).

[51] *See, e.g., Evans v. Walter Industries, Inc.*, 449 F.3d 1159, 1163 (11th Cir. 2006) (noting that requirement is only minimal diversity); *Abrego*

Abrego v. The Dow Chemical Co., 443 F.3d 676, 680 (9th Cir. 2006) (§ 1332(d) "abandons the complete diversity rule for covered class actions.").

[52] 28 U.S.C.A. § 1332(d)(3).

ing the previous three years, no similar class action involving essentially the same parties has been filed.[53]

Additionally, the more generous jurisdictional standards of § 1332(d) do not apply if the primary defendants are states, state agencies, or state officials, or if the membership of the proposed class is less than one hundred.[54] Finally, these new jurisdictional standards do not apply to three distinct categories of class actions: lawsuits arising under designated federal securities laws; lawsuits relating to the internal affairs of corporations arising under the laws of the states where such corporations are incorporated; and lawsuits relating to the rights, duties, and obligations pursuant to a security as defined by federal law.[55]

Where the new § 1332(d) does not apply, it is probably safe to assume that pre-existing standards for determining diversity jurisdiction remain in place. In such circumstances, diversity of citizenship is probably satisfied if the class representatives are diverse from the party opposing the class.[56] Additionally, the amount in controversy requirement for class actions that do not fall within the more generous jurisdictional provisions of § 1332(d) is probably still controlled by the standard for non-class litigation. However, this standard has been loosened considerably, as is discussed under *Supplemental Jurisdiction*, immediately below.

There is an important exception to the general rule that conventional jurisdictional standards apply to a case if § 1332(d) does not apply. If a case was properly removed from state court but class certification is later denied, the district court nevertheless retains jurisdiction of such a case.[57]

For purposes of § 1332(d), an unincorporated association is deemed a citizen of the state in which its principal place of business is located as well as the state in which it was organized.[58] This new provision for affected class actions differs from the treatment of unincorporated associations in non-class litigation.

It should be noted that § 1332(d)(11) provides that most mass actions will, for jurisdictional purposes, be treated in a manner similar to the way other provisions of § 1332(d) address most class actions.

2) *Supplemental Jurisdiction:* The Supreme Court recently

---

[53]28 U.S.C.A. § 1332(d)(4).

[54]28 U.S.C.A. § 1332(d)(5).

[55]28 U.S.C.A. § 1332(d)(9).

[56]*Supreme Tribe of Ben Hur v. Cauble*, 255 U.S. 356, 41 S. Ct. 338, 65 L. Ed. 673 (1921) (overruled in part on other grounds by, *Toucey v. New York Life Ins. Co.*, 314 U.S. 118, 62 S. Ct. 139, 86 L. Ed. 100 (1941)).

[57]*See, e.g., United Steel, Paper & Forestry, Rubber, Manufacturing, Energy, Allied Industrial & Service Workers International Union v. Shell Oil Co.*, 602 F.3d 1087, 1091 (9th Cir. 2010); *Cunningham Charter Corp. v. Learjet, Inc.*, 592 F.3d 805, 806–07 (7th Cir. 2010); *Vega v. T-Mobile USA, Inc.*, 564 F.3d 1256, 1268 n. 12 (11th Cir. 2009).

[58]28 U.S.C.A. § 1332(d)(10).

resolved substantial uncertainty as to whether plaintiffs certified as members of a Rule 23 class had to satisfy the amount in
controversy requirement individually. The Court held that
when Congress enacted 28 U.S.C.A. § 1367 (governing supplemental jurisdiction), it effectively provided that if a single
member of the class meets the amount in controversy requirement for diversity jurisdiction, all other members whose claims
fall short of the requirement amount may nonetheless qualify
for supplemental jurisdiction if the other elements of § 1367
are satisfied.[59] This holding is applicable to classes governed by
Rule 23, but usually not to parties intervening in a class pursuant to Rule 24. Section 1367 is discussed in greater detail
elsewhere in this text.

(3) *Federal Question Suits:* Federal courts have subject matter jurisdiction over class actions involving federal questions in
the same manner as conventional litigation.

(4) *Personal Jurisdiction:* Jurisdiction over a defendant in a
class action is obtained in the same manner, and subject to the
same requirements, as jurisdiction over any defendant in
conventional litigation. The same is true for personal jurisdiction over a class of defendants, *i.e.,* each individual must be
subject to the jurisdiction of the court before that individual is
subject to the judgment. For a class of plaintiffs, however, class
members may be included in the suit even if they have no link
with the state where the case is being heard. This holding applies only to cases where members of the plaintiff class were afforded an opportunity to drop out of the class early in the litigation, and chose not to do so.[60] The Supreme Court has not yet
ruled on a circumstance where members of a plaintiff class
have no contact with the state in which the case is being heard,
and had no opportunity to drop out of the suit.

(5) *Venue:* Venue in class actions does not generally differ
from venue in conventional litigation. One potential exception
should be noted. If venue is based on the residence of the class,
the residences of the class representatives are examined, not
those of the entire class.[61]

(6) *Choice of Law:* In class actions based on state law, the
court can only apply the law of a jurisdiction that has a sufficient relationship with an individual litigant. Thus individual
litigants from states other than the forum may be entitled to
have the law of some other state applied to their claims. In a
class action, therefore, it is possible that the court may have to

---

[59]*Exxon Mobil Corp. v. Allapattah Services, Inc.*, 545 U.S. 546, 125 S. Ct. 2611, 2621–25, 162 L. Ed. 2d 502 (2005).

[60]*Phillips Petroleum Co. v. Shutts*, 472 U.S. 797, 105 S. Ct. 2965, 86 L. Ed. 2d 628 (1985).

[61]*See, e.g., Appleton Elec. Co. v. Advance-United Expressways*, 494 F.2d 126, 140 (7th Cir. 1974) (looking only to venue of named representa-tives).

apply the laws of a variety of states to different class members.[62]

(7) *Defendant Classes:* Most class action cases are suits in which the class is the plaintiff. However, it is possible that a class may be a defendant.[63] In that unusual circumstance, the provisions of Rule 23 apply in much the same fashion as they apply to plaintiff classes, with only a few differences. One difference is that members of a defendant class are entitled to constitutional protections of notice, as well as any protections provided within Rule 23. This difference tends to have little practical impact, however, because class representatives are obligated to protect the interests of passive class members, including appropriate notice, discussed elsewhere. A more significant potential distinction between a plaintiff class and a defendant class is heightened concern to ensure that the representatives of a defendant class adequately represent the interests of the class. The concern is greater with defendant classes because, at least initially, the representatives of a defendant class are chosen by the plaintiff who is suing the class.[64]

Certification and the Merits

The question whether a district court may properly consider the merits of the case when deciding a certification motion has long been unresolved.[65] However, it now appears settled that the analysis necessary for certification may often properly overlap with assessment of the merits of the plaintiffs claim.[66] Further, if an expert witness' evidence is "critical to class certi-

---

[62]*Phillips Petroleum Co. v. Shutts,* 472 U.S. 797, 105 S. Ct. 2965, 86 L. Ed. 2d 628 (1985).

[63]*See, e.g., Consolidated Rail Corp. v. Town of Hyde Park,* 47 F.3d 473 (2d Cir. 1995) (approving a defendant class and noting Rule 23 "does not require a willing representative, merely an adequate one"). *But see Henson v. East Lincoln Township,* 814 F.2d 410, 415–17 (7th Cir. 1987) (defendant classes may not be certified under Rule 23(b)(2)); *Bazemore v. Friday,* 751 F.2d 662, 669–700 (4th Cir. 1984), *affirmed in relevant part,* 478 U.S. 385, 387, 106 S.Ct. 3000, 92 L.Ed.2d 315 (1986) (Rule 23(b)(2) defendant classes generally prohibited, except where there is a challenge to "a statewide [government] rule or practice so that relief is available if the rule or practice is invalid").

[64]*See, e.g., Ameritech Ben. Plan Committee v. Communication Workers of America,* 220 F.3d 814, 819 (7th Cir. 2000) (defendant classes require special attention because they are "initi-

ated by those opposed to the interests of the class").

[65]*Compare Eisen v. Carlisle and Jacquelin,* 417 U.S. 156, 177, 94 S.Ct. 2140, 40 L.Ed.2d 732 (1974) ("We find nothing in either the language or history of Rule 23 that gives a court any authority to conduct a preliminary inquiry into the merits of a suit in order to determine whether it may be maintained as a class action.") *with General Telephone Co. of Southwest v. Falcon,* 457 U.S. 147, 160, 102 S.Ct. 2364, 72 L.Ed.2d 740 (1982) ("[S]ometimes it may be necessary for the court to probe behind the pleadings before coming to rest on the certification question.") *and Coopers and Lybrand v. Livesay,* 437 U.S. 463, 469 n.12, 98 S.Ct. 2454, 57 L.Ed.2d 351 (1978) (determination of class action may be "intimately involved with the merits of the claim").

[66]*Wal-Mart Stores, Inc. v. Dukes,* ___ U.S. ___, 131 S.Ct. 2541, ___ L.Ed.2d ___ (2011) (overlap between certification and merits "cannot be

fication," the district court must rule on challenges to the expert's qualifications or conclusions prior to deciding a motion for certification.[67]

It should be noted, however, that there is clear agreement authorizing dismissal of a case without deciding a motion for certification because the plaintiff cannot, e.g., state a cognizable claim or satisfy jurisdiction. In such circumstances the dismissal may address some feature of the merits of the case but does not address certification at all.[68]

Statutes of Limitation: Equitable Tolling

In a case based on federal question jurisdiction, it is settled that institution of the class action tolls applicable statutes of limitations for the class.[69] The statute remains in suspension until the district court denies certification.[70] If the statute resumes running, it does so from the point at which it was tolled.[71] This protection applies to parties who subsequently

---

helped"). *See also Ellis v. Costco Wholesale Corp.*, 657 F.3d 970, 981 (9th Cir. 2011) (where merits overlap with certification, "a district court *must* consider the merits"). *But cf., Gooch v. Life Insurance Co. of America*, 672 F.3d 402, 417 (6th Cir. 2011) (*Wal-Mart* does not apply in all circumstances; in the absence of disputes of fact or law that affect certification, district court should not examine merits).

[67]*See, e.g., AmeRican Honda Motor Co. v. Allen*, 600 F.3d 813, 815–16 (7th Cir. 2010) (per curiam) (both Federal Rule of Evidence 702 and *Daubert v. Merrill Dow Pharmaceuticals, Inc.*, 509 U.S. 579, 113 S.Ct. 2768, 125 L.Ed.2d 469 (1993), governing admissibility of expert evidence, apply to expert evidence use for purposes of class certification).

[68]*See, e.g., Boulware v. Crossland Mortg. Corp.*, 291 F.3d 261, 268 n. 4 (4th Cir. 2002) ("Because [plaintiff] failed to state a claim as the purported named plaintiff, and because all other similarly situated plaintiffs would likewise fail to state a claim, the district court necessarily acted within its discretion in denying class certification."); *Curtin v. United Airlines, Inc.*, 275 F.3d 88, 92 (D.C. Cir. 2001) (approving resolution of straightforward summary judgment motion without addressing more difficult and unnecessary question of class certification). *Cf.,*

Todd v. Exxon Corp., 275 F.3d 191, 202 n. 5 (2d Cir. 2001) ("[D]ifficulty meeting the predominance and typicality requirements for Rule 23 certification . . . does not indicate that plaintiff fails to state a claim upon which relief can be granted.").

[69]*American Pipe & Const. Co. v. Utah*, 414 U.S. 538, 550–51, 94 S. Ct. 756, 764–65, 38 L. Ed. 2d 713 (1974).

[70]*See, e.g., Taylor v. United Parcel Service, Inc.*, 554 F.3d 510, 519 (5th Cir. 2008) ("[I]f the district court denies class certification under Rule 23, tolling of the statute of limitation ends. . . . [A]n appeal of the denial of class certification does not extend the tolling period."). *Cf., Bridges v. Department of Maryland State Police*, 441 F.3d 197, 212–13 (4th Cir. 2006) (statute begins to run again when court enters order denying class certification, not when representative parties abandon class through inaction); *In re Copper Antitrust Litigation*, 436 F.3d 782, 793 (7th Cir. 2006) (statute of limitation resumes running when class certification is denied or party opts out of class). *See also Vinole v. Countrywide Home Loans, Inc.*, 571 F.3d 935 (9th Cir. 2009) ("[N]o rule or decisional authority prohibited [Defendant] from filing its motion to deny certification before Plaintiffs filed their motion to certify.").

[71]*American Pipe & Const. Co. v. Utah*, 414 U.S. 538, 542–43, 94 S. Ct.

seek to intervene in the suit after certification has been denied.[72] Further, if the class was certified under Rule 23(b)(3) and some members of the class exercise their right to opt out of the class under Rule 23(c)(2), the statute remains tolled as to those individuals until they exercise the right to opt out.[73] This protection applies even to members of the class who were unaware of the pendency of the class litigation.[74] Moreover, equitable tolling applies to "all members of the putative class until class certification has been denied."[75]

If following denial of class certification due to a deficiency in the class itself, e.g., failure to meet the requirement of numerosity/impractability of joinder, class members who seek to file a subsequent class action will be denied the benefits of equitable tolling.[76] However, where certification is denied solely due to a deficiency in the class representatives (and not in the class itself), the cases are in conflict.[77] Attorneys must consult the local precedent and practice.

It is uncertain whether plaintiffs who file individual actions while a motion to certify is pending should get the benefit of tolling.[78] Attorneys will be forced to consult local precedent and practice.

It should be noted that this doctrine of equitable tolling, though applicable to cases based on federal question jurisdiction, applies to class actions arising from state claims only when state law also provides for equitable tolling. Courts reach this conclusion through application of the *Erie* doctrine,[79] discussed elsewhere in this text.

756, 760–61, 38 L. Ed. 2d 713 (1974) (class action filed eleven days before running of statute; six months later certification was denied; held, individual claims filed eight days after entry of order denying class status were timely).

[72]*Id.* at 553.

[73]*Id.* at 550–51 (statute begins to run against individuals at time they opt out).

[74]*Id.* at 551. *See, e.g., Sawyer v. Atlas Heating & Sheet Metal Works, Inc.,* 642 F.3d 560, 561 (7th Cir. 2011) (*American Pipe* applicable to circumstances where dismissed suit affects third persons, but potentially inapplicable where original suit was voluntarily dismissed and subsequent suit is filed by same plaintiff).

[75]*Crown, Cork & Seal Co., Inc. v. Parker,* 462 U.S. 345, 354, 103 S. Ct. 2392, 2397, 76 L. Ed. 2d 628 (1983) (expanding *American Pipe* to apply to plaintiffs who file separate suits, not

just those who intervene in the original suit).

[76]*Yang v. Odom,* 392 F.3d 97, 104 (3d Cir. 2004).

[77]*Yang v. Odom,* 392 F.3d 97, 104–08 (3d Cir. 2004) (collecting cases).

[78]Compare *In re Hanford Nuclear Reservation Litigation,* 521 F.3d 1028 (9th Cir. 2008) (permitting tolling) *and In re WorldCom Securities Litigation,* 496 F.3d 245, 256 (2d Cir. 2007) (denial of tolling might force individual into inappropriate early decision on individual lawsuit versus class action) *with Wyser-Pratte Management Co., Inc. v. Telxon Corp.,* 413 F.3d 553, 569 (6th Cir. 2005) (purpose of tolling is undercut by premature individual lawsuit prior to class certification decision).

[79]*See, e.g., Wade v. Danek Medical, Inc.,* 182 F.3d 281, 286–87 (4th Cir. 1999) (under principles of *Erie,* state law controls; in instant case, Virginia

It should also be noted that for mass actions within the scope of the Class Action Fairness Act, encoded in part in § 1332(d)(11), the existing case law doctrine is now mandated by legislation.[80]

RULE 23(b)—TYPES OF CLASS ACTIONS

CORE CONCEPT

Before a class action will be certified, all the requirements of case law, jurisdiction, and Rule 23(a) must be satisfied. In addition, a class will not be certified unless it also fits within one of the types of classes described in Rule 23(b).[81] Unlike the requirement that all elements of Rule 23(a) be satisfied, however, Rule 23(b) is satisfied if only one of the kinds of classes described is present.[82]

NOTE: Although a class may be certified if it fits within only one of the Rule 23(b) categories, there are sometimes advantages to fitting within more than one of the categories. This analysis is discussed more fully immediately below and under Rule 23(c).

APPLICATIONS

Risk of Incompatible Duties for Class Opponent

A class will be certified if the opposing party will otherwise be at risk of being subjected to incompatible duties.[83] Rule 23(b)(1)(A) was invoked when the class opponent was sued by employees who, in the absence of a class action, might have obtained employment benefits for themselves that were inconsistent with the employer's obligations to other employees.[84]

Risk of Practical Impairment of Non-Parties' Interests

Rule 23(b)(1)(B) permits certification of a class if piecemeal litigation involving individual class members may as a practi-

---

does not provide for equitable tolling).

[80]28 U.S.C.A. § 1332(d)(11)(D).

[81]*See, e.g., Puffer v. Allstate Insurance Co.*, 675 F.3d 709, 716 (7th Cir. 2012) ("A plaintiff who moves for class certification must satisfy the numerosity, commonality, typicality, and adequacy of representation requirements of Rule 23(a), as well as at least one other subsection of Rule 23(b).").

[82]*See, e.g., Messner v. Northshore University Health System*, 669 F.3d 802, 811 (7th Cir. 2012).

[83]*Cf., In re Integra Realty Resources, Inc.*, 354 F.3d 1246, 1263–64 (10th Cir. 2004) ("A widely recognized limitation on (b)(1)(A) certification requires that there be 'more than the mere possibility that inconsistent judgments and resolution of identical questions of law would result if numerous actions are conducted instead of one class action;' " mere fact that class opponent might win some individual cases and lose others does not meet requirements of Rule 23(b)(1)(A)).

[84]*Mungin v. Florida East Coast Ry. Co.*, 318 F. Supp. 720 (M.D. Fla. 1970). *See also Zinser v. Accufix Research Institute, Inc.*, 253 F.3d 1180 (9th Cir. 2001) (where possible relief is a fund, which would be created by defendant, to pay for future medical monitoring of plaintiffs, relief sought is primarily monetary damages-not relief that imposes inconsistent obligations on defendant-and therefore case is not suitable for certification under Rule 23(b)(1)(A)).

cal matter produce injustice for class members who are not parties to the individual litigation.[85] One of the most common applications of Rule 23(b)(1)(B) occurs when numerous claimants may seek relief from a limited fund and, in the absence of class certification, individual lawsuits might deplete the fund before all worthy claimants had a chance to obtain some share of the fund.[86] However, to obtain certification under Rule 23(b)(1)(B) in such circumstances, it is settled that the "limited" fund must be "limited by more than the agreement of the parties."[87]

"Incompatible Duties" Contrasted with "Risk of Practical Impairment"

Rule 23(b)(1)(A), establishing the "incompatible duties" standard, has the primary purpose of protecting the opponent of the class from the possibility of inconsistent obligations. In a situation where Rule 23(b)(1)(A) is suitable, there is less concern about the potential class members, because even if no class is certified individual members of the class can still bring their claims individually without loss to themselves. In a Rule 23(b)(1)(B) situation involving potential "practical impairment," however, failure to certify a class creates the probability that individual members will not be able to share recovery in limited resources in a proportional manner, fair to all.[88]

---

[85]*Flanagan v. McDonnell Douglas Corp.*, 425 U.S. 911, 96 S. Ct. 1506, 47 L. Ed. 2d 761 (1976) (class certification appropriate to ensure "equitable distribution of the refund program"). *See, e.g., In re Integra Realty Resources, Inc.*, 354 F.3d 1246, 1264 (10th Cir. 2004) (Rule 23(b)(1)(B) is satisfied when resolution of first individual case could be dispositive of factual and legal issues that would resolve subsequent individual cases before those litigants had a chance to pursue their claims). *But cf., Tilley v. TJX Companies, Inc.*, 345 F.3d 34, 42 (1st Cir. 2003) (certification under Rule 23(b)(1)(B) "cannot rest solely on an anticipated stare decisis effect").

[86]*See, e.g., Trautz v. Weisman*, 846 F. Supp. 1160, 4 A.D.D. 955 (S.D. N.Y. 1994) (classic Rule 23(b)(1)(B) case occurs when multiple claims of individuals exceed value of limited fund, and early individual suits would exhaust fund before later-filing claimants can share).

[87]*Ortiz v. Fibreboard Corp.*, 527 U.S. 815, 119 S. Ct. 2295, 144 L. Ed. 2d 715 (1999) (error for district court to treat fund as limited only because parties agreed to limit claims to specified amount; before certifying class under Rule 23(b)(1)(B) district court should have examined grand total of funds actually available in event of success by plaintiffs; additionally, Supreme Court refuses to decide "whether Rule 23(b)(1)(B) may ever be used to aggregate individual tort claims"). *See also In re Simon II Litigation*, 407 F.3d 125, 138 (2d Cir. 2005) (inability of class plaintiffs to identify upper limit or insufficiency of fund means plaintiffs cannot meet Rule 23(b)(1)(B) requirement that individual plaintiffs would be prejudiced by separate lawsuits); *Zinser v. Accufix Research Institute, Inc.*, 253 F.3d 1180 (9th Cir. 2001) (for certification under Rule 23(b)(1)(B) plaintiffs must prove that fund is actually limited to amount less than that for which defendant might be liable).

[88]*Ortiz v. Fibreboard Corp.*, 527 U.S. 815, 834, 119 S.Ct. 2295, 144 L.Ed.2d 715 (1999).

Classes Seeking Final Injunctive or Declaratory Relief

Rule 23(b)(2) permits certification of class actions where the primary relief sought is injunctive or declaratory in nature.[89] There are two elements to satisfy before a class may be certified under Rule 23(b)(2): the class must share a general claim against the non-class party;[90] and the class must seek either final injunctive or declaratory relief.[91] Unlike claims for which class certification is sought under, e.g., Rule 23(b)(3), a determination to certify a class under Rule 23(b)(2) does not rest on considerations of manageability or judicial economy.[92] Race and gender discrimination class actions, seeking an alteration in the future behavior of the opponent of the class, are typical of the class actions certified under Rule 23(b)(2).[93]

Obtaining Damages in Class Actions

Certification of a class under Rule 23(b)(2) requires that the relief sought in the case is primarily declaratory or injunctive in nature. It may not always be disabling to attach a plea for damages to a Rule 23(b)(2) certification, but it is now clear that

---

[89]*Wal-Mart Stores, Inc. v. Dukes,* ___ U.S. ___, 131 S.Ct. 2541, ___ L.Ed.2d ___ (2011) (Rule 23(b)(2) addresses only injunctive relief, not other equitable relief such as back pay. *See, e.g., Thorn v. Jefferson-Pilot Life Ins. Co.,* 445 F.3d 311, 331 (4th Cir. 2006) (Rule 23(b)(2) applies only to case involving primarily injunctive or declaratory relief, not all forms of equitable relief; "if the Rule's drafters had intended the Rule to extend to all forms of equitable relief, the text of the Rule would say so"); *In re Allstate Ins. Co.,* 400 F.3d 505 (7th Cir. 2005) (refusing certification under Rule 23(b)(2) notwithstanding that relief sought is exclusively injunctive or declaratory; noting that if certification is appropriate, Rule 23(b)(3) is preferred when individual hearings for class members may be necessary to determine causation and liability).

[90]*Cf., e.g., Heffner v. Blue Cross and Blue Shield of Alabama, Inc.,* 443 F.3d 1330, 1344 (11th Cir. 2006) (where each plaintiff must demonstrate individual reliance on representations in documents that are central to case, commonality that is necessary for classwide equitable relief under Rule 23(b)(2) is lacking).

[91]*Wal-Mart Stores, Inc. v. Dukes,* ___ U.S. ___, 131 S.Ct. 2541, ___ L.Ed.2d ___ (2011). *See, e.g., Vallario*

v. Vandehey, 554 F.3d 1259, 1268 (10th Cir. 2009) ("Under Rule 23(b)(2), the injuries sustained by the class must be 'sufficiently similar that they can be addressed in a single injunction that need not differentiate between class members.'"); *Gooch v. Life Insurance Co. of America,* 672 F.3d 402, 417 (6th Cir. 2012) (declaratory relief often appropriate to ascertain meaning of contract). *Cf., Christ v. Beneficial Corp.,* 547 F.3d 1292 (11th Cir. 2008) (absence of underlying statutory authority to grant injunctive relief makes certification under Rule 23(b)(2) improper).

[92]*See, e.g., Rodriguez v. Hayes,* 578 F.3d 1032, 1051 (9th Cir. 2010) (citing other cases). *But see Kartman v. State Farm Mutual Automobile Insurance Co.,* 634 F.3d 883, 893 (7th Cir. 2011) (denying certification where injunction would be "administratively challenging," requiring a judge "to write an insurance-adjustment code").

[93]*See, e.g., Vallario v. Vandehey,* 554 F.3d 1259, 1269 (10th Cir. 2009) ("No doubt exists that Rule 23(b)(2) was intended, in large part, 'to enable civil rights actions.'"); *Comer v. Cisneros,* 37 F.3d 775, 796 (2d Cir. 1994) ("[p]attern of racial discrimination cases for injunctions against state or local officials are the 'paradigm' of [Rule 23(b)(2)] cases." [sic]).

seeking damages in a Rule 23(b)(2) case could damage the prospects for certification under that provision.[94]

NOTE: If damages are more important in the case than equitable remedies, it is likely that the suit will be certified under some provision other than Rule 23(b)(2) or not certified at all.[95] Alternatively, if a class is certified based on the predominance of common legal or factual questions under Rule 23(b)(3), substantial difficulties could follow. Rule 23(b)(3) class representatives may be burdened with substantial expenses in notifying other class members of the litigation.[96] Thus in seeking damages in a Rule 23(b)(2) class, the benefits of obtaining damages should be weighed against the possibility that the case might be certified under Rule 23(b)(3). If notification expenses in a particular case are likely to be substantial, it might be prudent to consider whether the class should seek damages at all.[97] Notification duties for a Rule 23(b)(3) class are discussed in Rule 23(c)(2), below. For other notification obligations the court may impose, see Rule 23(d)(2) and (e).

---

[94]*Wal-Mart Stores, Inc. v. Dukes,* ____ U.S. ____, 131 S.Ct. 2541, ____ L.Ed.2d ____ (2011) (absence of procedural protections of notice and right to opt out that are found in Rule 23(b)(3) are reasons to curtail use of Rule 23(b)(2) in cases involving monetary claims). *See, e.g., Kanter v. Warner-Lambert Co.,* 265 F.3d 853, 860 (9th Cir. 2001) ("In Rule 23(b)(2) cases, monetary damage requests are generally allowable only if they are merely incidental to the litigation."); *Lemon v. International Union of Operating Engineers, Local No. 139, AFL-CIO,* 216 F.3d 577 (7th Cir. 2000) (where compensatory damages would require examination of each individual's magnitude of injury, and punitive damages would require finding that defendant was recklessly indifferent to each plaintiff's federal rights, damages are not "incidental" within meaning of Rule 23(b)(2)).

[95]*Wal-Mart Stores, Inc. v. Dukes,* ____ U.S. ____, 131 S.Ct. 2541, ____ L.Ed.2d ____ (2011) (monetary damages not incidental to injunction or declaratory relief may not be certified under Rule 23(b)(2)); *Allison v. Citgo Petroleum Corp.,* 151 F.3d 402 (5th Cir.1998) (denying Rule 23(b)(2) because equitable remedies do not outweigh importance of money damages; holding that key to determination of "predomination" issue is whether request for monetary relief makes class

so disparate in makeup that notice and opt-out provisions are necessary). *But see Berger v. Xerox Corp. Retirement Income Guarantee Plan,* 338 F.3d 755 (7th Cir.2003) (declaratory judgment actions are usually preludes to requests for other relief (injunctive or monetary); likelihood that successful litigants may subsequently seek damages is not, of itself, fatal to effort to obtain certification under Rule 23(b)(2)).

[96]*See also In re Monumental Life Ins. Co.,* 365 F.3d 408, 417 (5th Cir. 2004) ("[D]ue process requires the provision of notice where a Rule 23(b)(2) class seeks monetary damages."); *Jefferson v. Ingersoll Intern. Inc.,* 195 F.3d 894, 896–97 (7th Cir. 1999) (judgments and settlements in cases certified under rule 23(b)(2) are more susceptible to collateral attack by class members than cases controlled by Rule 23(b)(3); defendants who need finality prefer Rule 23(b)(3), whose provisions for notice and opt out make judgments and settlements less vulnerable to collateral attacks).

[97]*Cf., Allen v. International Truck and Engine Corp.,* 358 F.3d 469, 470 (7th Cir. 2004) (suggesting that when case involving both equitable relief and money damages is certified under Rule 23(b)(2), notice and right to opt out may still be required for damages issues).

No "Predominance" Requirement in Rule 23(b)(2)

Technically, Rule 23(b)(2) contains no requirement that questions common to the class must predominate over non-common questions, such as is found among the requirements for certifying a class under Rule 23(b)(3). However, the requirement for cohesiveness in Rule 23(b)(2) classes — such as an issue of race or gender — will involve a closer bond between members of a (b)(2) class than typically exists in a (b)(3) class.[98]

Requirement of Finality

A class cannot be certified under Rule 23(b)(2) if the relief obtained, whether injunctive or declaratory, is not final.[99]

Supervisory Problems

Certification under Rule 23(b)(2) may be denied because the injunctive relief necessary would place an undue administrative burden on the court.[100]

Rule 23(b)(2) and Jury Trials

The Seventh Amendment to the United States Constitution normally provides a right to trial by jury in federal district courts in civil litigation where money damages are sought.[101] At the same time, in class actions certified under Rule 23(b)(2), the case must be based primarily on claims, which do not normally qualify to be heard by a jury. When the occasional Rule 23(b)(2) class action also contains a plea for money damages, the combination of circumstances might seem to create a problem. However, the solution appears to be readily available. In such cases, issues relating to damages alone or to both damages and injunctive or declaratory relief may require trial by jury, but issues going to the injunctive or declaratory claims alone should be heard by the judge.[102]

Predominance of Common Legal or Factual Questions

The final possibility for certifying a class action is a deter-

---

[98]*See, e.g., Holmes v. Continental Can Co.*, 706 F.2d 1144, 1155 n.8 (11th Cir. 1983)("[T]he (b)(2) class is distinguished from the (b)(3) class by class cohesiveness."). *See also Avritt v. Reliastar Life Insurance Co.*, 615 F.3d 1023,1035 (8th Cir. 2010) (cohesiveness even more important in (b)(2) class because there is no opportunity to opt out).

[99]*See, e.g., Kartman v. State Farm Mutual Automobile Insurance Co.*, 634 F.3d 883, 893(7th Cir. 2011) ("[I]njunction is not a final remedy if it would merely lay an evidentiary foundation for subsequent determination of liability."); *Bolin v. Sears, Roebuck & Co.*, 231 F.3d 970, 978 (5th Cir. 2000)

(denying class certification "where the declaratory relief . . . serves only to facilitate the award of damages").

[100]*See, e.g., Kartman v. State Farm Mutual Automobile Insurance Co.*, 634 F.3d 883, 893 (7th Cir. 2011) (denying certification where injunctive relief would be "administratively challenging" requiring a judge "to write an insurance-adjustment code").

[101]*Beacon Theatres, Inc. v. Westover*, 359 U.S. 500, 510, 79 S. Ct. 948, 956, 3 L. Ed. 2d 988 (1959).

[102]*Allen v. International Truck and Engine Corp.*, 358 F.3d 469, 471 (7th Cir. 2004).

mination that the questions of law or fact common to the members of the class predominate over other questions. Rule 23(b)(3) certification is often a last resort for litigants who cannot be certified under any other portion of Rule 23(b).[103] Two special requirements exist for Rule 23(b)(3) classes. Both must be satisfied to achieve certification under Rule 23(b)(3). First among these is the requirement that common questions *predominate* over individual interests.[104] As can be seen from cites contained in the immediately preceding footnote, resolution of the "predominance" analysis rests heavily on the facts of par-

---

[103]*See, e.g., DeBoer v. Mellon Mortg. Co.*, 64 F.3d 1171, 1175 (8th Cir. 1995) (where certification is appropriate under either Rule 23(b)(1) or (2), certification under Rule 23(b)(3) is inappropriate). *See also Murray v. GMAC Mortg. Corp.*, 434 F.3d 948, 953 (7th Cir. 2006) ("Rule 23(b)(3) was designed for situations . . . in which the potential recovery is too slight to support individual suits, but injury is substantial in the aggregate.").

[104]*Amchem Products, Inc. v. Windsor*, 521 U.S. 591, 623, 117 S. Ct. 2231, 2250, 138 L. Ed. 2d 689 (1997) (predominance issues require a "close look" at, among other factors, "difficulties likely to be encountered in the management of a class action;" predominance not satisfied if there are a number of significant questions peculiar to different categories within class or to individuals within class; exposure to different asbestos products, at different times, in different ways, for different periods of time, with differing results ranging from no injury through only symptoms of injury to grave illnesses of several different kinds, all complicated by differences in cigarette use among class members where use of cigarettes complicates injury, defeats allegation of predominance). *See, e.g., Gintis v. Bouchard Transportation Co.*, 596 F.3d 64, 66 (1st Cir. 2010) (rejecting general rule that pollution torts are ineligible for (b)(3) certification; explaining that different injuries, causes and amounts of damages are not fatal to certification; acknowledging division of authority); *In re Scrap Metal Antitrust Litigation*, 527 F.3d 517, 535 (6th Cir. 2008) (in antitrust cases, predominance can often be met by proof of conspiracy; in such cases

difference in amounts of damages is not inevitably a barrier to certification); *Tardiff v. Knox County*, 365 F.3d 1, 5 (1st Cir. 2004) (county policy of strip searching most or all categories of persons arrested satisfies "predominance," notwithstanding differences between cases of individual persons within those categories). *But see In re New Motor Vehicles Canadian Export Antitrust Litigation*, 522 F.3d 6, 20 (1st Cir. 2008) ("In antitrust class actions, common issues do not predominate if the fact of antitrust violation and the fact of antitrust impact cannot be established through common proof."); *Stirman v. Exxon Corp.*, 280 F.3d 554, 564 (5th Cir. 2002) ("[S]ignificant variations in state law . . . defeat predominance."); *Johnston v. HBO Film Management, Inc.*, 265 F.3d 178, 190 (3d Cir. 2001) ("[I]t has become well-settled that, as a general rule, an action based substantially on oral rather than written communications is inappropriate for treatment as a class action."); *Castano v. American Tobacco Co.*, 84 F.3d 734, 745 (5th Cir. 1996) ("[A] fraud class action cannot be certified when individual reliance will be an issue;" moreover, where laws of different states will apply to different class members, "variations in state law may swamp any common issues and defeat predominance"). *See also, Mullen v. Treasure Chest Casino, LLC*, 186 F.3d 620, 626–27 (5th Cir. 1999) (common issues of negligence and seaworthiness of vessel are "pivotal"; case invokes only federal law, so no choice of law issues; non-common issue of causation of illness will be left to second phase of litigation involving individual trials; held, requirement of predominance is satisfied).

ticular cases.[105] Individual damages issues are a potential complication when the district court addresses the question of predominance, but the court has some flexibility in considering ways to address this point.[106]

There is also an important unresolved question as to whose version of the "facts"—plaintiff's or defendant's—courts should use when addressing the predominance problem. On this particular point the cases are significantly divided, and attorneys are compelled to consult the local precedent.[107]

In other Rule 23(b) classes, by contrast, because the classes themselves will necessarily be more cohesive than a class certified under Rule 23(b)(3),[108] there is only the requirement, stated in Rule 23(a)(2), that common questions of law or fact exist among the class members, with no requirement that the common questions predominate.[109]

---

[105]*See also Tardiff v. Knox County*, 365 F.3d 1, 4 (1st Cir. 2004) (noting that in the context of class actions relating to strip searches of arrested persons, lower courts have reached opposite conclusions on questions of predominance). *But see Erica P. John Fund, Inc. v. Halliburton Co.*, U.S., 131 S.Ct. 2179, 180 L.Ed.2d 24 (2011) (in federal securities fraud lawsuits, proof of loss causation is not required for certification of a Rule 23(b)(3) class; such a requirement would almost always result in individual issues predominating over common issues).

[106]*See, e.g., Carnegie v. Household International, Inc.*, 376 F.3d 656, 661 (7th Cir. 2004) (appointing a magistrate judge or special master to address damage issue separately; letting class action proceed through liability and then decertifying class so that each class member can proceed separately on damages; creation of subclasses; or amending the class).

[107]*Tardiff v. Knox County*, 365 F.3d 1, 4 (1st Cir. 2004) ("It is sometimes taken for granted that the complaint's allegations are necessarily controlling; but class action machinery is expensive and in our view a court has the power to test disputed premises early on if and when the class action would be proper on one premise but not another;" collecting various appellate decisions on point). *See also Alaska Electrical Pension Fund v. Flowserve Corp.*, 572 F.3d 221 (5th Cir. 2009) (when loss causation is is-

sue going to predominance under Rule 23(b)(3), district court must itself find facts based on predominance of evidence; rejecting assertion that finding should be based on what a reasonable trier of fact would do; noting, however, that if same issue later goes to merits of case, trier of fact determines merits). *But cf., In re Initial Public Offering Securities Litigation*, 471 F.3d 24, 39 (2d Cir. 2006) ("A trial judge's finding on a merits issue *for purposes of a Rule 23 requirement* no more binds the court to rule for the plaintiff on the ultimate merits of that issue than does a finding that the plaintiff has shown a probability of success for purposes of a preliminary injunction.").

[108]*See, e.g., Holmes v. Continental Can Co.*, 706 F.2d 1144, 1155 n.8 (11th Cir. 1983) ("[T]he (b)(2) class is distinguished from the (b)(3) class by class cohesiveness."). *See also Avritt v. Reliastar Life Insurance Co.*, 615 F.3d 1023, 1035 (8th Cir. 2010) (cohesiveness even more important in (b)(2) class because there is no opportunity to opt out).

[109]*Amchem Products, Inc. v. Windsor*, 521 U.S. 591, 623, 117 S. Ct. 2231, 2250, 138 L. Ed. 2d 689 (1997) (for purposes of Rule 23(b)(3), predominance requirement is "far more demanding" than commonality requirement of Rule 23(a)). *See also, Walters v. Reno*, 145 F.3d 1032 (9th Cir. 1998) (no requirement under Rule 23(b)(2) that common issues predominate).

Certification Requirements for Classes Where Common Questions Predominate: Superiority

The second requirement for certification under Rule 23(b)(3) is a finding that a class action is the superior means of adjudicating the controversy.[110] A finding that common questions predominate will have significant additional influence on the court's determination of superiority, for the existence of predominant common issues will often support a conclusion that a class action is a superior means of adjudicating individual claims.[111] In reaching the "superiority" determination, a court is required to make four findings described in Rule 23(b)(3). The court may also address other issues that, in particular cases, are relevant to determining whether certification of a class action is the best way to process a case.[112] The court's determination of those points will ordinarily be dispositive of a Rule 23(b)(3) class certification. It should be noted that while the court is required to make findings on the four points listed, there is no requirement that before a class is certified, all four findings must be resolved in favor of certification. Instead, the court has discretion to weigh its findings in determining whether class certification is the superior method of litigating the controversy.

(1) *Rule 23(b)(3)(A)—Individual Interests in Separate Actions:* The court will evaluate the desire, if any, of individual litigants to pursue their own separate actions, and the net balance of interests between such individuals and the class as a whole.[113] Because individual litigants who feel the need to control their own cases may exercise their right under Rule

---

[110]*See, e.g., Gregory v. Finova Capital Corp.*, 442 F.3d 188, 191 n.3 (4th Cir. 2006) ("A necessary condition to certification under Rule 23(b)(3) is the class action's superiority to all other methods for the fair and efficient adjudication of the controversy. Thus, a class cannot be certified under Rule 23(b)(3) if there is a method to which the class action is not superior.").

[111]*See, e.g., Gintis v. Bouchard Transportation Co.*, 596 F.3d 64, 67–68 (1st Cir. 2010) (superiority is a "separate base to be touched," but many of the considerations relevant to predominance will also affect superiority analysis); *Klay v. Humana, Inc.*, 382 F.3d 1241, 1269 (11th Cir. 2004) ("In many respects the predominance analysis . . . has a tremendous impact on the superiority analysis . . . for the simple reason that, the more common issues predominate over individual issues, the more desirable a class action

lawsuit will be as a vehicle for adjudicating the plaintiffs' claims.").

[112]*See, e.g., Castano v. American Tobacco Co.*, 84 F.3d 734 (5th Cir.1996) (court may consider whether class action will preserve judicial resources). *See also, Hanlon v. Chrysler Corp.*, 150 F.3d 1011, 1022–23 (9th Cir. 1998) (individual suits would be ineffective for members of potential class).

[113]*See, e.g., Zinser v. Accufix Research Institute, Inc.*, 253 F.3d 1180 (9th Cir. 2001) ("Where damages suffered by each putative class member are not large, this factor weighs in favor of certifying a class action;" holding claims in excess of $50,000 each—the jurisdictional amount then in effect for diversity cases—tends to undermine an allegation that the claims are small); *In re Northern Dist. of California, Dalkon Shield IUD Products Liability Litigation*, 693 F.2d 847, 856 (9th Cir. 1982) (where class

23(c) to "opt out" of a Rule 23(b)(3) class, it is usually possible to certify the class and still accommodate most of the needs of such individuals. Harmonizing individual interests with class certification would be more difficult if it was likely that so many individuals would opt out that the "class" no longer represented the bulk of its potential members. In that circumstance, the evidence of such strong interest in individual litigation would argue strongly against certifying a Rule 23(b)(3) class.

(2) *Rule 23(b)(3)(B)—Pending Litigation:* The court will also consider the effects of any other pending litigation on the proposed class action. If individual class members have already begun to pursue their own cases, it may be difficult to justify certification of a Rule 23(b)(3) class on grounds of judicial economy.[114] Indeed, it is possible that such pending litigation will reach judgment before the class action, and many of the contested issues in the class action might then be resolved through application of principles of stare decisis or collateral estoppel.

(3) *Rule 23(b)(3)(C)—Progress in Class Litigation:* If the court hearing the class action has already invested enough resources in the case so that dismissal or refusal to certify the action would be inefficient, a strong argument exists in favor of certifying the class so that the action can be concentrated in the chosen forum.[115]

(4) *Rule 23(b)(3)(C)—Geography:* Another consideration that may bear on the wisdom of proceeding with the class action in the chosen forum is geography. If the case is being heard in an area of the country where the class or the evidence is concentrated, this may be an argument for continuing in the chosen forum.[116]

(5) *Rule 23(b)(3)(D)—Difficulties in Managing a Class*

---

members have a strong interest in individual suits, court should incline toward refusal to certify). *See also, Heaven v. Trust Co. Bank*, 118 F.3d 735, 738 (11th Cir. 1997) (counterclaims against individual class members is a factor to consider in evaluating whether, under Rule 23(b)(3)(A), individual members might have interest in controlling their own cases).

[114]*See, e.g., City of Inglewood v. City of Los Angeles*, 451 F.2d 948, 952 n. 4 (9th Cir. 1971) (directing that if party seeks a Rule 23(b)(3) class, "the court should note the fact that some 2,350 members of the class are already involved in suits against the same defendant"). *But cf., Hanlon v. Chrysler Corp.*, 150 F.3d 1011 (9th Cir.1998) (no bar to class certification where

only a few pending lawsuits may be difficult to merge into class action).

[115]*Cf., e.g., In re Mid-Atlantic Toyota Antitrust Litigation*, 564 F. Supp. 1379, 1391 (D. Md. 1983) ("The fact that the panel on multi-district litigation has transferred all actions [to the court] indicates the desirability [of the forum].")

[116]*See, e.g., Zinser v. Accufix Research Institute, Inc.*, 253 F.3d 1180 (9th Cir. 2001) (where potential plaintiffs, witnesses and evidence are spread across country, it is undesirable to concentrate litigation in instant forum unless plaintiff can demonstrate adequate justification); *Langley v. Coughlin*, 715 F. Supp. 522, 561 (S.D. N.Y. 1989) (location of "most relevant evidence" in forum is factor favoring

Action: Courts can refuse to certify if too many administrative difficulties exist in class actions. In exercising this discretion, courts consider a wide variety of factors affecting ease of administration of a case. Examples of problems in managing a class include internal disputes within a class and problems of notification of class members,[117] as well as the impact that state law variations can have on management in a multi-state case.[118]

Affirmative Defenses

The "predominance" requirement is obviously a substantial obstacle to class certification under Rule 23(b)(3). However, it appears settled that a defendant's possible affirmative defenses against claims by individual class members will not, of themselves, prevent the parties seeking class certification from meeting the requirement.[119]

RULE 23(c)—CERTIFICATION ORDER; NOTICE TO CLASS MEMBERS; JUDGMENT; ISSUES CLASSES; SUBCLASSES

CORE CONCEPT

Rules 23(a) and (b) contain most of the requirements that must be satisfied before a class may be certified. Rule 23(c), by contrast, concentrates on the procedure and timing of motions to certify and the process to be followed once a decision to certify has been made.

---

certification under Rule 23(b)(3)(C)).

[117]*See, e.g., Zinser v. Accufix Research Institute, Inc.,* 253 F.3d 1180 (9th Cir. 2001) (where pacemaker leads were implanted in different patients by different doctors in different states, producing different injuries at different times, there are too many individual issues and case management would be too difficult, notwithstanding common nucleus of facts about defendant's conduct). (proper to consider problems of notifying class members in deciding whether to certify class). *But cf., Williams v. Chartwell Financial Services, Ltd.,* 204 F.3d 748, 760 (7th Cir. 2000) (possible need for subclasses, by itself, is insufficient ground for denying certification because a class action would be unmanageable).

[118]*See, e.g., Castano v. American Tobacco Co.,* 84 F.3d 734 (5th Cir. 1996). *See also, Heaven v. Trust Co.*

Bank, 118 F.3d 735, 738 (11th Cir. 1997) (counterclaims against individual members of class with potential liability greater than original claims might create case management problems under Rule 23(b)(3)(D)). *But cf., Sullivan v. DB Investments, Inc.,* 667 F.3d 273, ___ (3d Cir. 2011) (differences in laws of fifty states do not, *ipso facto,* prevent class certification); *Mullen v. Treasure Chest Casino, LLC,* 186 F.3d 620, 627 (5th Cir. 1999) (superiority requirement satisfied by: lack of complex choice-of-law or *Erie* problems; modest number of class members ("hundreds instead of millions"); bifurcated-trial plan; and likelihood that trial would focus on secondhand smoke as both result of poor ventilation and cause of illnesses).

[119]*See, e.g., Smilow v. Southwestern Bell Mobile Systems, Inc.,* 323 F.3d 32, 39–40 (1st Cir. 2003).

APPLICATIONS

Motion or Court Initiative

A party may seek certification by motion, or the court may on its own initiative make the certification decision. It should be noted that the lack of a motion to certify does not relieve the district court of its duty to make this determination, and the lack of such a motion cannot be the basis for denial of class certification.[120]

Presumptions

For purposes of ruling on a Rule 23(c) certification motion, the district court will normally treat the factual allegations contained in the complaint as true.[121] However, if an expert's evidence is necessary for certification, a district court must first rule on expert's qualifications or evidence before ruling on class certification.[122]

"Implied" Classes

Rule 23(c)(1), by its express terms, appears to require that the district court "must" determine whether a class should be certified. However, there is authority that a court's failure to make a formal certification ruling does not mean the case at bar cannot be a class action. If the elements required for class certification are satisfied, an "implied" class may exist notwithstanding a lack of formal certification by the district court.[123]

---

[120]*See, e.g., Trevizo v. Adams*, 455 F.3d 1155 (10th Cir.2006) ("Rule 23(c)(1) places the onus on the court to make a determination irrespective of whether the parties have requested class action status."); *McGowan v. Faulkner Concrete Pipe Co.*, 659 F.2d 554, 559 (5th Cir. 1981) (trial court has duty to decide suitability of class action, even if no party makes a motion).

[121]*See, e.g., Vallario v. Vandehey*, 554 F.3d 1259, 1265 (10th Cir. 2009) ("[A]t the class certification stage a district court must generally accept the substantive, non-conclusory allegations of the complaint as true.").

[122]*See, e.g., American Honda Motor Co. v. Allen*, 600 F.3d 813, 816 (7th Cir. 2010) (per curiam) (court must perform full analysis required by *Daubert v. Merrill Dow Pharmaceuticals, Inc.*, 509 U.S. 579, 113 S.Ct. 2786, 125 L.Ed.2d 469 (1993)).

[123]*See, e.g., Doe, 1-13 ex rel. Doe Sr. 1-13 v. Bush*, 261 F.3d 1037, 1048–49 (11th Cir. 2001) ("[T]he fact that the district court failed to properly certify a class does not necessarily establish that no class exists, or that the defendants cannot be held in contempt for failing to provide class-wide relief."); *Navarro-Ayala v. Hernandez-Colon*, 951 F.2d 1325, 1333 (1st Cir. 1991) (no notice ever provided to class members, but "because this case was instituted by a complaint seeking class relief, implicitly granted class relief, and was conducted for years as a de facto class, it should and may be recognized as such"). *But see Brown v. Philadelphia Housing Authority*, 350 F.3d 338, 344 (3d Cir. 2003) (rejecting doctrine of implied class certification); *Martinez-Mendoza v. Champion Intern. Corp.*, 340 F.3d 1200 n. 37 (11th Cir. 2003) (Rule 23(c)(1) requires courts to determine independently whether case should be class action, even where no party seeks a ruling on class certification); *Davis v. Hutchins*, 321 F.3d 641, 648 (7th Cir. 2003) ("Class damages cannot be awarded if no class is certi-

Timing

Rule 23(c) provides no rigid timetable for resolving the certification issue, but courts are directed to make the decision "at an early practicable time."[124]

Preemptive Motion to Deny Certification

There is apparently no that would prevent the opponent of a class from moving to deny certification, even where the proponent of a class has not yet sought certification.[125]

Conditional Certification

In the past Rule 23(c)(1) permitted the court to make certification conditional upon later developments in the case. Even if the court had not expressly reserved the power, it retained authority to amend its order as events require.[126] However, Rule 23(c)(1) was amended in 2003 to remove the language

---

fied.").

[124]*See, e.g., Kerkhof v. MCI World-Com, Inc.*, 282 F.3d 44, 55 (1st Cir. 2002) (post-judgment certification should usually be discouraged because it "would frustrate the opt-out mechanisms for Rule 23(b)(3) classes provided in Rules 23(c)(2) and (c)(3), which were intended to avoid situations in which class members could choose to join only when judgment favored the class"); *Grandson v. University of Minnesota*, 272 F.3d 568, 574 (8th Cir. 2001) (failure to seek class certification before expiration of deadline for such motions and failure to seek extension of time constitute grounds for striking class allegations); *Prado-Steiman ex rel. Prado v. Bush*, 221 F.3d 1266, 1273 (11th Cir. 2000) ("Rule 23 contemplates that the class certification decision will be made prior to the close of discovery."); *Philip Morris Inc. v. National Asbestos Workers Medical Fund*, 214 F.3d 132 (2d Cir. 2000) (per curiam) (district court does not have "unfettered discretion" to delay decision on class certification; usually decision will be made somewhere between end of pleadings and end of discovery (depending on facts of individual cases), but only rarely should decision be delayed until after hearing on merits). *But cf., Miami University Wrestling Club v. Miami University*, 302 F.3d 608, 616 (6th Cir. 2002) ("We have consistently held that a district court is not required to rule on a motion for class certification before ruling on the merits of the

case."). *See also Alaska Electrical Pension Fund v. Flowserve Corp.*, 572 F.3d 221 (5th Cir. 2009) (when loss causation is issue going to predominance under Rule 23(b)(3), district court must itself find facts based on predominance of evidence; rejecting assertion that finding should be based on what a reasonable trier of fact would do; noting, however, that if same issue later goes to merits of case, trier of fact determines merits). *But cf., In re Initial Public Offering Securities Litigation*, 471 F.3d 24, 39 (2d Cir. 2006) ("A trial judge's finding on a merits issue *for purposes of a Rule 23 requirement* no more binds the court to rule for the plaintiff on the ultimate merits of that issue than does a finding that the plaintiff has shown a probability of success for purposes of a preliminary injunction.").

[125]*See, e.g., Kasalo v. Harris & Harris, Ltd.*, 656 F.3d 557, 563 (7th Cir. 2011) ("[A] court may deny class certification even before the plaintiff files a motion requesting certification.").

[126]*See, e.g., Lyons v. Georgia-Pacific Corp. Salaried Employees Retirement Plan*, 221 F.3d 1235, 1253 (11th Cir. 2000) ("Rule 23(a) is not immutable;" court retains power under Rule 23(c) and (d) to change prior order if subsequent events make that step appropriate); *Forehand v. Florida State Hosp. at Chattahoochee*, 89 F.3d 1562, 1566 (11th Cir. 1996) (court may decertify class previously certified even when case was filed ten years earlier and

authorizing conditional certification.[127] Instead, courts are encouraged to withhold certification until the requirements of Rule 23 are met. At the same time, courts are given latitude to make a decision on certification at all times up to the time of final judgment.[128]

Defining Claims, Issues or Defenses

If a class is certified, Rule 23(c)(1)(B) directs the district court to define the class, *i.e.,* to include in the certification order a clear and complete summary of the claims, issues, and defenses subject to class treatment. The definition should describe the class in a way that makes clear what the scope of the litigation and the breadth of the res judicata effect may be.[129] However, there is some reason to believe that district courts do not always fulfill this requirement completely.[130]

Amending a Certification Order

Rule 23(c)(1)(C) authorizes a district court to alter or amend its original certification order at any time prior to final judgment on the merits.[131]

Notice

As amended in 2003, Rule 23(c)(2) establishes various notice options and/or requirements for cases certified under Rule 23. For classes certified pursuant to Rule 23(b)(1) or (2), Rule 23(c)(2)(A) authorizes - but does not require - the district court to order notice to such classes.[132] This authority is intended to supplement the court's already existing power under Rule 23(d)(2) to issue notice in some circumstances to class members.[133] This change in Rule 23(c)(2) leaves unaltered the assumption that courts will be cautious in their use of notice to

---

had proceeded through trial).

[127]*See, e.g., Hohider v. United Parcel Service, Inc.,* 574 F.3d 169, 202 (3d Cir. 2009) (while district court retains authority to alter or amend its order, it must initially make a "definitive determination" that requirements of Rule 23 are met; court may no longer make a "conditional" certification and then await events).

[128]*See* Rule 23(c)(1) advisory committee notes to 2003 amendments.

[129]*Spano v. Boeing Co.,* 633 F.3d 574, 584 (7th Cir. 2011). *See also Mullen v. Treasure Chest Casino, LLC,* 186 F.3d 620, 624 n.l (5th Cir. 1999) (class of employees alleging illness caused by defective ventilation system is not deficient because allegation of defective system or injury from it has yet to be proven on merits); *Simer v. Rios,* 661 F.2d 655, 669 (7th Cir. 1981)

("It is axiomatic that for a class action to be certified a 'class' must exist.").

[130]*See, e.g., Wachtel ex rel. Jesse v. Guardian Life Ins. Co. of America,* 453 F.3d 179, 184 (3d Cir. 2006) (observing that district courts often do not fulfill this requirement adequately).

[131]*See, e.g., Voss v. Rolland,* 592 F.3d 242, 251 (1st Cir. 2010) (court has authority to modify certification order as events develop); *Culpepper v. Irwin Mortg. Corp.,* 491 F.3d 1260 (11th Cir. 2007) (district court thereby retains flexibility "in light of subsequent developments in the case").

[132]*See, e.g., Randall v. Rolls-Royce Corp.,* 637 F.3d 818, 820 (7th Cir. 2011) (in classes under Rule 23(b)(2) "notice to unnamed class members is optional").

[133]*See* Rule 23(c)(2) advisory committee notes to 2003 amendments. *See*

Rule 23(b)(1) and (2) classes so as, *inter alia,* not to burden the class representatives with unnecessary costs of notice.[134]

Because absent class members in a Rule 23(b)(2) class do not receive notice and are not permitted to opt out of the class, it is settled that such class members cannot challenge certification of the class.[135] This apparently harsh result is mitigated by other authority permitting absent class members to challenge imposition of res judicata or collateral estoppel. The alternative grounds for such a challenge would be either inadequate representation in the prior litigation[136] or lack of constitutionally required notice.[137]

Rule 23(c)(2) also establishes special requirements for notifying class members of pending Rule 23(b)(3) actions. The reason for this provision arises from the special nature of Rule 23(b)(3) suits, in which common questions must predominate and the class suit must be superior to alternative methods of adjudication. Such suits tend to involve the least homogeneous classes. Lack of homogeneity increases the risk that informal notice of the class action may not flow freely within the class. To correct this problem, Rule 23(c)(2) provides that individual members must receive the "best notice practicable," which will often be mail service on all class members whose identities and addresses are known.[138]

Finally, amended Rule 23(c)(2) also requires that if a class action requires certification under both Rule 23(b)(2) and (b)(3), the usually more burdensome notice requirements required for

---

also Eubanks v. Billington, 110 F.3d 87, 96 (D.C. Cir. 1997) (Rule 23(d) authorizes court to permit party to opt out of class certified under Rule 23(b)(1) or (2) "on a selective basis").

[134]*See* Rule 23(c)(2) advisory committee notes to 2003 amendments (noting that classes certified under Rule 23(b)(1) or (2) have no right to opt out, reducing need for notice on that point). *Cf.,* Rahman v. Chertoff, 530 F.3d 622, 626 (7th Cir. 2008) ("Members of a Rule 23(b)(2) class do not receive notice and can't opt out."). *See also* 15 U.S.C.A. § 78u-4 (in litigation within scope of Private Securities Litigation Reform Act of 1995, lead plaintiff must, within twenty days of filing complaint, provide publication notice in "widely circulated national business-oriented publication or wire service" of pending action and potential opportunity to serve as lead plaintiff).

[135]*Ticor Title Insurance Co. v. Brown,* 511 U.S. 117, 121, 114 S.Ct. 1359, 128 L.Ed.2d 33 (1994) (per curiam).

[136]*Hansberry v. Lee,* 311 U.S. 32, 42–43, 61 S.Ct. 115, 85 L.Ed.2d 22 (1940).

[137]*Wal-Mart Stores, Inc. v. Dukes,* ___ U.S. ___, 131 S.Ct. 2541, 2549, 180 L.Ed.2d 374 (2011).

[138]*See generally Schwarzschild v. Tse,* 69 F.3d 293, 295 (9th Cir. 1995) (in general, Rule 23(c)(2) requires notice to class members before merits are adjudicated; in unusual case where summary judgment is granted prior to certification, plaintiff no longer has duty of notification). *Cf., Mirfasihi v. Fleet Mortg. Corp.,* 356 F.3d 781, 786 (7th Cir. 2004) ("When individual notice is infeasible, notice by publication in a newspaper of national circulation . . . is an acceptable substitute.").

a (b)(3) class must be satisfied for the (b)(3) class.[139]

Elements of Notice to Rule 23(b)(3) Classes

Rule 23(c)(2) specifies that notification will include the following pieces of advice: (1) "the nature of the action, (2) the definition of the class certified, (3) the class claims, issues, or defenses," (4) the right of individual members of the class to appear through counsel if they choose, (5) the right to opt out of the class and not be bound by any judgment,[140] and (6) the binding effect of a class judgment on members of the class who do not opt out.[141]

Opting Out of Rule 23(b)(1) and (b)(2) Classes

The opt-out provision of Rule 23(c)(2) literally applies to Rule 23(b)(3) classes only. However, there is substantial support for the proposition that a district court has discretionary authority to permit opting out of Rule 23(b)(1) and (b)(2) classes.[142]

Expense of Notice

The financial burden of notification in Rule 23(b)(3) cases is generally borne by the class representatives.[143] Thus, in some cases class representatives should be selected with an eye to their financial resources as well as their dedication to the litigation. When the burden of Rule 23(b)(3) notification is onerous, the possibility of certification under another portion of Rule 23(b) should be explored.

---

[139]*See* Rule 23(c)(2) advisory committee notes to 2003 amendments.

[140]*See, e.g., Abbott Laboratories v. CVS Pharmacy, Inc.*, 290 F.3d 854, 859 (7th Cir. 2002) (if party opts out, party is not bound by judgment; moreover, party cannot be "dragged back in under . . . supplemental jurisdiction"); *Sperling v. Hoffmann-La Roche, Inc.*, 24 F.3d 463, 470 (3d Cir. 1994) ("Members of a Rule 23(b)(3) class are automatically included . . . unless they make a timely election to opt-out.").

[141]*See generally Eisen v. Carlisle and Jacquelin*, 417 U.S. 156, 94 S. Ct. 2140, 40 L. Ed. 2d 732 (1974).

[142]*See, e.g., McReynolds v. Richards-Cantave*, 588 F.3d 790, 800 (2d Cir. 2009) (acknowledging that right to opt out of (b)(1) and (b)(2) classes is "not obvious" but is never-

theless within the scope of Rule 23); *Eubanks v. Billington*, 110 F.3d 87, 94 (D.C. Cir. 1997); *Penson v. Terminal Transport Co., Inc.*, 634 F.2d 989, 993 (5th Cir. 1981) ("[A]lthough a member of a class certified under Rule 23(b)(2) has no absolute right to opt out of the class, a district court may mandate such a right pursuant to its discretionary power under Rule 23."). *But cf. Rahman v. Chertoff*, 530 F.3d 622, 626 (7th Cir. 2008) ("Members of a Rule 23(b)(2) class . . . can't opt out.").

[143]*Oppenheimer Fund, Inc. v. Sanders*, 437 U.S. 340, 356–59, 98 S. Ct. 2380, 2392–93, 57 L. Ed. 2d 253 (1978) (but if defendant could perform task more efficiently, burden may be shifted to defendant; also suggesting that other circumstances, not enumerated, may justify shifting cost from class representatives to defendant).

No Requirement to "Opt In"

There is no provision in Rule 23(c) requiring class members to "opt in" or be excluded from a class.[144] Rule 23(c) contains only an "opt out" provision.

Parties Bound by Judgment

Rule 23(c)(3) affords the court substantial discretion to determine the binding effect of a class action. Class actions certified under either Rule 23(b)(1) or (b)(2) (described above) have binding effect on whomever the court finds to be within the membership of the class.[145] There is no requirement that the class members receive notice of the action.[146] Rule 23(b)(3) actions bind class members who did not opt out under Rule 23(c)(2) and whom the court defines as members.[147] Thus it is possible that persons in a (b)(3) class might not get actual notice under Rule 23(c)(2) because their names and/or addresses are unknown, yet be bound because the court found them to be members of the class.

It is settled that if a class action is not certified, its result is not binding on nonparties.[148]

Subclasses

Rule 23(c)(4) authorizes the court to create classes only as to particular issues.[149] Rule 23(c)(5) authorizes the court to create subclasses within an action.[150] If subclasses are certified, each subclass is treated as an independent class for purposes of

---

[144]*Phillips Petroleum Co. v. Shutts*, 472 U.S. 797, 105 S. Ct. 2965, 86 L. Ed. 2d 628 (1985) (no due process requirement to "opt in"); *Kern v. Siemens Corp.*, 393 F.3d 120, 124 (2d Cir. 2004) (Rule 23(e) contains no "opt in" provision).

[145]*Taylor v. Sturgell*, 128 S. Ct. 2161, 171 L. Ed. 2d 155 (U.S. 2008) ("Representative suits with preclusive effect on nonparties include properly conducted class actions.").

[146]*See, e.g., Payne v. Travenol Laboratories, Inc.*, 673 F.2d 798, 812 (5th Cir. 1982) (notice required only in Rule 23(b)(3) classes and at time of dismissal or settlement). *Cf., Langbecker v. Electronic Data Systems Corp.*, 476 F.3d 299, 306 (5th Cir. 2007) ("Neither a Rule 23(b)(1) or (2) class action requires notice to class members or the option to opt-out.").

[147]*Eisen v. Carlisle and Jacquelin*, 417 U.S. 156, 94 S. Ct. 2140, 40 L. Ed. 2d 732 (1974) (Rule 23(c)(2) requirement of notice binds all members of Rule 23(b)(3) class who do not opt out).

See also Smentek v. Dart, ____ F.3d ____ (7th Cir. 2012) (if class certification is denied in first case, but different parties seek certification in a parallel case, district court? may use "comity" to deny certification of class in parallel case, but is not obligated to do so).

[148]*Smith v. Bayer Corp.*, ____ U.S. ____, 131 S.Ct. 2368, 2380, 180 L.Ed.2d 341 (2011).

[149]*See, e.g., Castano v. American Tobacco Co.*, 84 F.3d 734, 745 n.21 (5th Cir. 1996) (distinguishing "predominance" requirement of Rule 23(b)(3) from Rule 23(c)(4), where the latter is only "a housekeeping rule that allows courts to sever the common issues for a class trial").

[150]*In re Visa Check/MasterMoney Antitrust Litigation*, 280 F.3d 124, 141 (2d Cir. 2001) (Individualized damages issues may be handled by "(1) bifurcating liability and damage trials with the same or different juries; (2) appointing a magistrate judge or special master to preside over individual dam-

the action.

The circumstances in which the court is most likely to create subclasses occur when the class members share a cause of action against a class opponent, but also experience differing interests among themselves.[151] The most common use of subclasses is to help simplify the manageability of the primary class action. Occasionally, however, subclasses can help the overarching class meet the certification requirements of Rule 23. Moreover, even if a global class cannot be certified, some plaintiffs have attempted to replace the global class with multiple subclasses that may be certifiable by themselves. The state of the law as to this last use of Rule 23(c)(5) is currently unsettled, and attorneys should consul local precedent and practice.[152]

Classes for Settlement

Courts have certified classes created for purposes of settlement only. In such a circumstance, the court may notify potential class members of the possibility of class certification at the time the court notifies class members of the proposed settlement.[153]

Persons who may wish to contest settlements in class ac-

---

ages proceedings; (3) decertifying the class after the liability trial and providing notice to class members concerning how they may proceed to prove damages; (4) creating subclasses; or (5) altering or amending the class.").

[151]*Ortiz v. Fibreboard Corp.*, 527 U.S. 815, 119 S. Ct. 2295, 144 L. Ed. 2d 715 (1999) (class comprised of holders of both present and future claims "requires subdivision into homogenous subclasses"). *See, e.g., Hawkins v. Comparet-Cassani*, 251 F.3d 1230 (9th Cir.2001) (convict can represent other convicts on Eighth Amendment claim; however, Fourth Amendment claim can be raised only by individuals not already convicted, and convict/class representative therefore lacks standing; suggesting possibility of subclasses with different subclass representatives under Rule 23(c)(4)); *Marisol A. v. Giuliani*, 126 F.3d 372, 379 (2d Cir. 1997) (court emphasizes need to locate appropriate representatives for each subclass and to establish that each subclass of instant case meet requirements of Rule 23(b)(2); otherwise, describing value of subclasses as: (1) helping to focus discovery; (2) identifying claims for which there is no adequate representative, so that

such claims can be dismissed; and (3) opportunity for notice to defendants of specific charges).

[152]*Compare, e.g., Klay v. Humana, Inc.*, 382 F.3d 1241, 1261–62 (11th Cir. 2004 (subclasses may be used this way) *with Sprague v. General Motors Corp.*, 133 F.3d 388, 396–99 & n.9 (6th Cir. 1998) (en banc) (if global class is uncertifiable, subclasses are unavailable). The authors of this text are grateful to Professor Scott Dodson, who appears to be the first commentator to identify this issue and who generously provided us with both his research and suggested language for this point. *See* Scott Dodson, *Subclassing*, 27 Cardozo L. Rev. 2351 (2006).

[153]*See, e.g., In re General Motors Corp. Pick-Up Truck Fuel Tank Products Liability Litigation*, 55 F.3d 768 (3d Cir. 1995) (standard requirements of Rule 23(a) and (b) must be met; class is typically certified formally at same time court approves settlement). *But cf., Ortiz v. Fibreboard Corp.*, 527 U.S. 815, 119 S. Ct. 2295, 144 L. Ed. 2d 715 (1999) (trial court is obligated to ensure that requirements of Rule 23(a) and (b) are met; "A fairness hearing under subdivision (e) can no more swallow the preceding protec-

tions are generally free to intervene.[154]

RULE 23(d)—CONDUCTING THE ACTION

CORE CONCEPT

Rule 23(d) provides the court explicit authority to craft orders governing class suits. Central to class actions is a need to protect the interests of parties who are less active than persons engaged in more conventional litigation. At the same time, the potential administrative complexity of class actions requires that the court have tools immediately at hand to ensure that the litigation remains manageable.

APPLICATIONS

Undue Repetition of Evidence

Rule 23(d) explicitly vests the court with broad discretion to limit cumulative or repetitive evidence.

Relation to Rule 16

As amended in 2007, Rule 23(d)(2) contains two provisions. First, it authorizes alteration or amendment of any order previously issued under Rule 23(d)(1). Second, it provides that such an alteration or amendment may be combined with a pretrial order issued under Rule 16. However, even in circumstances in which orders under Rules 16 and 23(d)(2) are combined, it is settled that applications for Rule 23(d)(2) relief will be judged by a less exacting standard than the more stringent requirements for relief from a pretrial order under Rule 16.[155]

Additional Notice to Class Members

Rule 23(d)(1)(B) allows the court to order additional notice to class members to ensure fair treatment of passive members of the class.[156] The court's authority under this provision is very broad, and encompasses discretion to order notice to the class of almost any important event in the litigation.[157] The court may use its power in a variety of circumstances, including: no-

---

tive requirements of Rule 23 in a subdivision (b)(1)(B) action than in one under subdivision (b)(3).").

[154] *See, e.g., Crawford v. Equifax Payment Services, Inc.*, 201 F.3d 877, 881 (7th Cir. 2000).

[155] Advisory Note, Fed.R.Civ.P. 23 (2007).

[156] *See, e.g., Southern Ute Indian Tribe v. Amoco Production Co.*, 2 F.3d 1023 (10th Cir.1993) (using Rule 23(d) to order representatives of defendant class—not plaintiff—to notify passive members of defendant class of pending litigation).

[157] *See, e.g., Jefferson v. Ingersoll Intern. Inc.*, 195 F.3d 894, 898 (7th Cir. 1999) (suggesting possible certification under Rule 23(b)(2), but with use of Rule 23(d)(2) and (5) to notify members of class seeking both money and equitable relief and to provide opportunity to opt out). *But see Cobell v. Kempthorne*, 455 F.3d 317, 324 (D.C. Cir. 2006) (Rule 23(d)(2) authorizes orders affecting notice of procedural matters, but provides no authority to issue orders relating to substantive relief); *Cruz v. American Airlines, Inc.*, 356 F.3d 320, 331 (D.C. Cir. 2004) (expressing doubt that Rule 23(d)(2)

tice to a class of pending litigation; discussion of proposed judgments; identification of class representatives to the whole class; and informing the class of key decision points in the suit so the class can participate in decisions, or evaluate opportunities to seek to participate more actively as class representatives.

Supervision of Class Representatives and Intervenors

Rule 23(d)(1)(C) provides explicit authority for the court to monitor class representatives and intervenors, and thereby supports both fair representation for the class and expeditious processing of the entire case.[158]

Rejecting Class Certification

Rule 23(d)(1)(D) allows the court to enter an order stripping a case of allegations concerning class representation. This provision is typically employed when the court has already refused, under Rule 23(c)(1), to certify the case as a class action. It may also be used if the court originally certified a class, but later altered its decision and refused certification. In either circumstance, Rule 23(d)(1)(D) contemplates that a suit denied class certification may still proceed as conventional litigation, assuming that the requirements of such litigation are satisfied.

Other Procedural Matters

Rule 23(d)(1)(E) makes explicit that the authority of the court to issue orders to process a class suit expeditiously and fairly is not limited to the other provisions of Rule 23(d).[159] In so doing, Rule 23(d)(1)(E) re-emphasizes the broad discretion a trial court enjoys in class litigation. However, in regulating communications between class lawyers or class representatives to potential class members, the court will explain with particularity the need for such regulation.[160]

Alteration of Prior Rulings

As a practical matter, Rule 23(d)'s declaration that the court may alter prior orders as necessary to the conduct of the suit means the court is not bound by its own interlocutory decisions in class actions. Thus the court enjoys almost complete flexibility to adjust class litigation as events may require. In particular, courts are prepared to change earlier orders appointing class representatives if events show that the representatives are not protecting adequately the interests of the whole class.

---

grants authority to order notice to a class that has not been certified).

[158]*But see Cobell v. Kempthorne*, 455 F.3d 317, 323 (D.C. Cir. 2006) (Rule 23(d)(3) cannot be used to impose a condition on non-class defendant).

[159]*See, e.g., Molski v. Gleich*, 318 F.3d 937, 947 (9th Cir. 2003) (even with class certified under rule 23(b)(2), "a district court may require no-

tice and the right to opt-out under its discretionary authority provided in Rule 23(d)[(1)(C)]").

[160]*Gulf Oil Co. v. Bernard*, 452 U.S. 89, 101 S. Ct. 2193, 68 L. Ed. 2d 693 (1981) (requiring district court to explain the abuse such regulations are intended to address; reversing such regulations in the absence of explanation).

RULE 23(e)—SETTLEMENT, VOLUNTARY DISMISSAL OR COMPROMISE

CORE CONCEPT

Rule 23(e) requires court approval of voluntary dismissal or compromise, and requires that proposals to settle the case be submitted to the entire class for approval. This requirement of court supervision recognizes the fact that class actions are especially vulnerable to the possibility that the class representatives or the class attorneys may be placed in circumstances where their personal interests conflict with the interests of passive class members. The risk of inappropriate collaboration between class representatives, or class counsel, and the class opponent is probably greatest when questions of settlement or voluntary dismissal are at issue.[161] Rule 23(e) attempts to suppress the possibility of such conflicts by imposing a series of obligations on both the court and the parties seeking approval of the proposed settlement.

APPLICATIONS

Authority to Settle: Judicial Approval

As amended in 2003, Rule 23(e)(1)(A) expressly authorizes class representatives to settle claims, issues or defenses as appropriate.[162] However, this authority is subject to other provisions in Rule 23(e) that have the effect of giving the power to approve or veto settlement to the district court, which in turn must solicit the views of class members before making its decision. Additionally, in many circumstances a district court's approval of a settlement is subject to challenge on appeal by non-named class members.[163]

Comparison With Conventional Litigation

Rule 23(e) is an exception to the standard practice that parties may normally settle their disputes without the approval of the court.[164]

---

[161]*See, e.g., In re Vitamins Antitrust Class Actions*, 215 F.3d 26 (D.C. Cir.2000) (noting that "settlement dynamics" can cause even well-intentioned parties to give insufficient weight to interests of class as a whole).

[162]*See* Rule 23(e)(1)(A) advisory committee notes to 2003 amendments.

[163]*Devin v. Scardelletti*, 536 U.S. 1, 14, 122 S.Ct. 2005, 153 L.Ed.2d 27 (2002) (non-named member of mandatory class under Rule 23(b)(1) who makes timely objection to settlement may appeal without intervening first); *Fidel v. Farley*, 534 F.3d 508, 513 (6th Cir. 2008) (notwithstanding existence

of "opt out" right in Rule 23(b)(3) case non-named plaintiff who has claim for only modest damages can appeal settlement).

[164]*See, e.g., In re Cendant Corp. Litigation*, 264 F.3d 201, 231 (3d Cir. 2001) ("Under Rule 23(e), the District Court acts as a fiduciary guarding the rights of absent class members and must determine that the proffered settlement is 'fair, reasonable, and adequate.' "); *In re Painewebber Limited Partnerships Litigation*, 147 F.3d 132, 137 (2d Cir. 1998) (plaintiff's authority to dismiss an action voluntarily under Rule 41(a)(1) is expressly subject to court's authority under Rule 23(e)). *See*

All Class Actions

Rule 23(e) applies to all actions certified under any portion of Rule 23(b).[165] There is also authority that the notice requirement of Rule 23(e) applies even in some situations where the class was decertified or never certified at all.[166]

Effect on Individual Claims

The power of the court to approve or reject settlements of class litigation does not extend to individual claims which members of the class may possess separate from the class claims. By its terms, the approval power of Rule 23(e)(1)(A) is limited to class litigation only.[167]

Notice of Proposed Settlement

As amended, Rule 23(e)(1) expressly requires the district court to hold a hearing and make findings before approving a class settlement or voluntary dismissal.[168] The findings must include a determination that the proposed course of resolution for the class action is "fair, reasonable, and adequate."[169] Within the limits of due process, courts may treat the requirements of Rule 23(e) as satisfied by less notice than, for example, the requirement of first-class mail that may accompany notice obligations under Rule 23(c)(2) (governing notice in Rule 23(b)(3) "predominance of common questions" classes).[170] Moreover, because the litigation has moved toward settlement and

---

also, Matter of Cook, 49 F.3d 263 (7th Cir. 1995) (in a class action settlement involving a common fund, Rule 23(e) provides court with authority to monitor closely attorneys' fees).

[165]*See, e.g., Grimes v. Vitalink Communications Corp.*, 17 F.3d 1553, 1557 (3d Cir. 1994) (duty to monitor fairness of settlement is "particularly acute" in Rule 23(b)(1) and (2) class actions, because members of those classes cannot opt out of the class litigation).

[166]*See, e.g., Culver v. City of Milwaukee*, 277 F.3d 908, 914–15 (7th Cir. 2002) (acknowledging issue is "not yet definitively settled," but holding that all classes, without regard to status of certification, need notice to enable them to protect against, e.g, statute of limitations problems; but accepting contrary result if violation of Rule 23(e) is harmless). *See also Doe v. Lexington-Fayette Urban County Government*, 407 F.3d 755, 761 (6th Cir. 2005) (noting that *Culver's* requirement of notice to all classes is clear majority rule). *Cf., Shelton v. Pargo, Inc.*, 582 F.2d 1298, 1315 (4th

Cir. 1978) (no automatic requirement of notice to non-certified class members in the absence of collusion or unfair prejudice).

[167]*See* Rule 23(e)(1)(A) advisory committee notes to 2003 amendments.

[168]*See, e.g., In re Syncor ERISA Litigation*, 516 F.3d 1095, 1097 (9th Cir. 2008) ("Failure to [hold hearing] — even when the district court has already drafted a summary judgment order — is an abuse of discretion.").

[169]*See, e.g., International Union, United Auto., Aerospace, and Agr. Implement Workers of America v. General Motors Corp.*, 497 F.3d 615, 629 (6th Cir. 2007) (no requirement that proposed settlement offer pro rata distribution to individual members of class; settlement need only be fair, reasonable and adequate). *See also* Rule 23(e)(1)(C) advisory committee notes to 2003 amendments.

[170]*See, e.g., Denney v. Deutsche Bank AG*, 443 F.3d 253, 271 (2d Cir. 2006) (Rule 23(e) authorizes court to require additional notice where appropriate, *e.g.,* where information class members should have in order to make

the class representatives can now see what the potential outcome of the suit might be, the burdens of notice when Rule 23(e) is relevant are sometimes much less onerous than the burdens established by Rule 23(c)(2).[171]

Disclosure

As amended, Rule 23(e)(2) requires the proponents of a proposed settlement or voluntary dismissal to disclose any agreements that have been made that relate to the proposal.[172]

Settlement

The power to approve settlement of a class action lies within the court's discretion, and such decisions are rarely disturbed on appeal.[173] However, some important considerations may restrict judicial discretion. First, while the court is authorized to determine whether the settlement is fair to passive members of

---

a decision has changed; but court is under no blanket mandate to provide a second opt-out period under Rule 23(e)).

[171]*See, e.g., Faught v. American Home Shield Corp.*, 668 F.3d 1233, 1239 (11th Cir. 2011) ("The standard for the adequacy of a settlement notice is measured by reasonableness."); *Rodriguez v. West Publishing Corp.*, 563 F.3d 948, 961 n. 7 (9th Cir. 2009) ("Rule 23(e) does not require the notice to set forth every ground on which class members might object to the settlement."); *Gottlieb v. Wiles*, 11 F.3d 1004, 1013 (10th Cir. 1993) (suggesting that notice requirements of Rule 23(e) are less rigorous than those of Rule 23(b)(3) and (c)(2)). *But see, In re Katrina Canal Breaches Litigation*, 628 F.3d 185, 199 (5th Cir. 2010) ("[N]otice should at a minimum generally apprise class members that fees will be sought and awarded by the court at the settlement hearing or a subsequent hearing and indicate whether the defendants or the settlement fund will bear such costs."); *White v. State of Ala.*, 74 F.3d 1058, 1066 (11th Cir. 1996) (newspaper ads in small type, using "legalese" that attorneys might not fully understand, did not satisfy Rule 23(e) notice requirements). *See also* 15 U.S.C.A. § 78u-4 (in litigation controlled by Private Securities Litigation Reform Act of 1995, notice must include, inter alia, disclosure of recovery to class members; reason for settlement; agreements or disagreements as to damages

individual class members would potentially recover if class had achieved victory rather than settlement; and likely payments to lawyers); *In re Nissan Motor Corp. Antitrust Litigation*, 552 F.2d 1088, 1004–05 (5th Cir. 1977) (settlement notice need not be "overly detailed").

[172]*See* Rule 23(e)(2) advisory committee notes to 2003 amendments.

[173]*See, e.g., Durkin v. Shea & Gould*, 92 F.3d 1510, 1512 (9th Cir. 1996) (standard for approving settlement is whether it is "fundamentally fair, adequate, and reasonable"). *See also, Hanlon v. Chrysler Corp.*, 150 F.3d 1011 (9th Cir.1998) (for settlement approval prior to formal certification, court should make a "more probing inquiry" into terms of proposed settlement). *But see, In re Painewebber Limited Partnerships Litigation*, 147 F.3d 132 (2d Cir.1998) (notwithstanding Rule 23(e), members of potential class that is not yet certified are free to settle individual claims without court supervision; but Rule 23(e) applies once a class is certified). *But cf., Devlin v. Scardelletti*, 536 U.S. 1, 122 S. Ct. 2005, 153 L. Ed. 2d 27 (2002) (class member who was not named party and who objects to settlement has right to appeal without first intervening in case; where class member has no choice to opt out of litigation, as when class was certified under, e.g., Rule 23(b)(1), the right of class members to appeal settlement has even greater force).

the class,[174] the court must still give substantial deference to a consensus of class members on the wisdom of the settlement.[175] Disregarding such a consensus is not automatically abuse of discretion, but is likely to enhance the chances that the trial court's decision will be overturned on appeal. Second, while the court must pass on the fairness of the proposal, it may not rewrite the settlement to make it conform to the court's view of a satisfactory settlement.[176] Third, notwithstanding a request from both sides of a lawsuit, a district court has no authority under Rule 23(e) to take up the task of distributing residual funds.[177] Fourth, the court's duty is primarily to the members of the class.[178] If persons have previously opted out of the class, the court has no power or duty to use the settlement process to address their interests.[179] Fifth, at least in class actions af-

---

[174]*See, e.g., Hanlon v. Chrysler Corp.*, 150 F.3d 1011, 1026 (9th Cir. 1998) (court should consider: "the strengths of the plaintiff's case; the risk, expense, complexity, and likely duration of further litigation; the risk of maintaining a class action status throughout the trial; the amount offered in settlement; the extent of discovery completed and the stage of the proceedings; the experience and views of counsel; . . . and the reaction of the class members to the proposed settlement").

[175]*See, e.g., County of Suffolk v. Alcorn*, 266 F.3d 131, 135 (2d Cir. 2001) (notice provided to nearly one million class members; four hearings held in various places; audience numbered in hundreds; time for briefing was extended; class expert testified that settlement was fair; all expert testimony was subject to cross-examination); *Paradise v. Wells*, 686 F. Supp. 1442, 1444 (M.D. Ala. 1988) (first place court should look is to views of class).

[176]*Evans v. Jeff D.*, 475 U.S. 717, 726, 106 S. Ct. 1531, 1537, 89 L. Ed. 2d 747 (1986) (under rule 23(e), court has authority to approve or reject settlement, but cannot impose a settlement on unwilling parties). See, e.g., *In re Wireless Telephone Federal Cost Recovery Fees Litigation*, 396 F.3d 922, 934 (8th Cir. 2005) ("Rule 23(e) requires the court to intrude on that private consensual agreement merely to ensure that the agreement is not the product of fraud or collusion and

that, taken as a whole, it is fair, adequate and reasonable to all concerned.").

[177]*See, e.g., In re Lupron Marketing & Sales Practices Litigation*, 677 F.3d 21, 38 (1st Cir. 2012) (task is better left to adversarial process).

[178]*See, e.g., In re Cendant Corp. Litigation*, 264 F.3d 286, 295 (3d Cir. 2001) (district court has no duty to assess fairness of settlement to corporate opponent of class; such issues are more properly the subject of separate shareholder derivative litigation); *Tennessee Ass'n of Health Maintenance Organizations, Inc. v. Grier*, 262 F.3d 559, 566 (6th Cir. 2001) ("[U]nder Rule 23(e), non-class members have no standing to object to a lack of notice."). But cf., *Local No. 93, Intern. Ass'n of Firefighters, AFL-CIO C.L.C. v. City of Cleveland*, 478 U.S. 501, 106 S. Ct. 3063, 92 L. Ed. 2d 405 (1986) (intervenors are entitled to heard, but they have no right to a "quasi-trial" or to block the settlement by refusing to agree).

[179]*See, e.g., In re Vitamins Antitrust Class Actions*, 215 F.3d 26 (D.C. Cir.2000) (non-parties "fall outside the zone of interests protected by Rule 23(e)"). *But see In re Heritage Bond Litigation*, 546 F.3d 667, 677 (9th Cir. 2008) (in litigation controlled by Private Securities Litigation Reform Act, if a settlement satisfies the requirements of Rule 23(e)(2) but is rejected by some defendants, district court has authority to impose prohibition on non-settling defendants' future

fected by fee shifting provisions in civil rights cases, the court has the authority and duty to review waivers of attorneys' fees that are part of a proposed settlement.[180] Finally, the court's authority to certify a class created for purposes of settlement and to approve the proposed settlement is subject to a determination that the proposed class meets the requirements of Rule 23(a) and (b).[181]

Standard for Reviewing Settlement

Courts evaluating the fairness of a proposed settlement consider a number of factors, including: (1) possibility of fraud; (2) complexity and expense; (3) amount of discovery undertaken; (4) likelihood of success; (5) views of lawyers on both sides; (6) views of class members; and (7) the public interest.[182]

Legislation Authorizing Judicial Review of Settlements Involving "Coupons"

Congress has authorized district courts, when reviewing proposed settlements of class actions that involve an award of coupons, on motion of a party, to obtain expert testimony on the issue of the actual value to class members of coupons that are redeemed.[183] Moreover, in such cases, the court must hold a hearing and determine, in a written finding, that the settlement is fair, reasonable, and adequate to class members.[184] Finally, the court has discretion to require that a settlement provide for distribution of some portion of the value of

---

claims for contribution and indemnity).

[180]*Evans v. Jeff D.*, 475 U.S. 717, 728, 106 S. Ct. 1531, 1538, 89 L. Ed. 2d 747 (1986). *See also In re High Sulfur Content Gasoline Products Liability Litigation*, 517 F.3d 220, 227 (5th Cir. 2008) (state law cause of action not involving civil rights claims; "In a class action settlement, the district court has an independent duty under Federal Rules of Civil Procedure 23 to the class and the public to ensure that attorneys' fees are reasonable and divided up fairly among plaintiffs' counsel.").

[181]*Amchem Products, Inc. v. Windsor*, 521 U.S. 591, 117 S. Ct. 2231, 138 L. Ed. 2d 689 (1997). *See also Ortiz v. Fibreboard Corp.*, 527 U.S. 815, 119 S. Ct. 2295, 144 L. Ed. 2d 715 (1999) (fairness hearing under Rule 23(e) cannot adequately substitute for failure of class certification movants to demonstrate that certification requirements of Rule 23(a) and (b) are met). *In re Community Bank of Northern Virginia*, 418 F.3d 277, 299 (3d Cir. 2005) (mere fact that settle-

ment is "fair" does not relieve district court of duty to ensure that requirements of Rule 23(a) and (b) are met; an exception is that because settlement will not require a trial, district court may properly disregard issue of whether case will involve intractable management problems, as otherwise required by Rule 23(b)(3)(D)).

[182]*See, e.g., Poplar Creek Development Co. v. Chesapeake Applachia, L.L.C.*, 636 F.3d 235, 244 (6th Cir. 2011); *National Association of Chain Drug Stores v. New England Carpenters Health Benefits Fund*, 582 F.3d 30, 44 (1st Cir. 2009) (noting "laundry lists" of factors that case law provides; but "usually, the ultimate decision by the judge involves balancing the advantages and disadvantages of the proposed settlement as against the consequences of going to trial or other possible but perhaps unattainable variations on the proffered settlement").

[183]28 U.S.C.A. § 1712(d).

[184]28 U.S.C.A. § 1712(e).

unredeemed coupons to charitable or governmental organizations, per an agreement by the parties.[185] However, such a distribution may not be included as part of the basis for calculating attorney's fees.[186]

Protection against Loss by Class Members

In 28 U.S.C.A. § 1713, Congress provided the district court with authority to approve a proposed settlement involving a payment by members of the class to class counsel that would be a net loss to the class members. However, that authority is restricted to cases in which the court, by a written finding, concludes that nonmonetary benefits to the class "substantially" outweigh the monetary loss.[187] This provision of § 1713 is not restricted to cases involving "coupon" settlements, and appears to apply to class action settlements generally.

Protection against Geographic Discrimination

Congress has prohibited approval of proposed settlements in which some members of the class receive greater amounts of value than others based "solely" on their closer geographic ties to the location of the court hearing the case.[188] This provision appears to apply not only to "coupon" settlements but to class action settlements generally.

Additional Opportunity to Opt Out of Class

As amended, Rule 23(e)(4) provides members of classes previously certified under Rule 23(b)(3) with an additional opportunity to opt out of the proposed settlement or voluntary dismissal.[189] The notification obligations attendant on this opportunity will be the same as those required for initial certification of a Rule 23(b)(3) class under Rule 23(c)(2)(B). There are some restrictions on this new opportunity to opt out. First, it applies only to classes certified under Rule 23(b)(3). Second, only individual class members may exercise the option to opt out if they choose. No one has standing to attempt to opt out for other members of the class.[190]

Special Provisions for "Coupon" Settlements

Congress has enacted a number of provisions that are effective in class actions in which some or all members of the class will receive their award in the form of coupons. Title 28 U.S.C.A. § 1712(a) provides that when the attorney will receive a contingency fee based on the value of the coupons, the fee shall be based on the value to class members of the coupons

---

[185]28 U.S.C.A § 1712(e).

[186]28 U.S.C.A. § 1712(e).

[187]28 U.S.C.A. § 1713.

[188]28 U.S.C.A. § 1714.

[189]*See, e.g., Moulton v. United* *States Steel Corp.*, 581 F.3d 344, 354 (6th Cir. 2009) (Rule 23(e)(4) vests district court with discretion to provide opportunity to opt out).

[190]*See* Rule 23(e)(3) advisory committee notes to 2003 amendments.

that are actually redeemed.[191] The effect of this provision is to reduce at least somewhat any apparent disparities between the award of contingency fees to class counsel and the nominal value of coupons to class members.

Additionally, if a proposed settlement will provide the class with coupons, but the attorney's fee is not measured solely as a contingency award, § 1712(b) provides that the additional portion of the attorney's fee shall be based on the reasonable amount of time the lawyer expended on the case.[192]

The foregoing provisions are subject to review and approval by the court. They include authorization for an appropriate fee in cases involving equitable relief. Moreover, in making calculations as to the appropriate amount to be awarded as an attorney's fee, § 1712 expressly authorizes (but does not require) the use of a lodestar/multiplier method of determining fees.[193] This method of calculation is discussed at greater length on preceding pages.

If the proposed settlement contains both coupons and equitable relief, § 1712(c) provides that § 1712(a) shall govern the calculation of that portion of the attorney's fees applicable to the award of coupons, and 1712(b) shall govern the calculation of that portion of the attorney's fee attributable to considerations other than the award of coupons.[194]

Section 1712(d) provides the court with authority, upon motion of one of the parties, to obtain expert testimony on the issue of the actual value to class members of the coupons that are redeemed.[195] This provision appears to be relevant not only to calculation of an attorney's fee, but also the value and appropriateness of the settlement to the class. Judicial review of the appropriateness of a settlement to the class is discussed elsewhere in the analysis of Rule 23 and related material.

Finally, § 1712(e) authorizes the court to require that a portion of the value of unclaimed coupons be distributed to charitable or governmental organizations, as the parties choose. Such a distribution, however, cannot be used to calculate attorney's fees under § 1712.[196]

Objections to Settlement

Rule 23(e)(4) affords standing to any member of a class who wants to object to a proposed settlement or voluntary dismissal of a kind that requires judicial approval under Rule 23(e).[197] Once such an objection has been made, it can be withdrawn

---

[191]28 U.S.C.A. § 1712(a).

[192]28 U.S.C.A. § 1712(b)(1).

[193]28 U.S.C.A. § 1712(b)(2).

[194]28 U.S.C.A. § 1712(c).

[195]28 U.S.C.A. 1712(d).

[196]28 U.S.C.A. § 1712(e).

[197]*In re Rite Aid Corp. Securities Litigation*, 396 F.3d 294, 299 (3d Cir. 2005) (any class member may object to a settlement governed by Rule 23(e)).

only with the court's approval.[198]

NOTE: Limitations on the court's discretion notwithstanding, judicial control of settlements in class litigation is still profound.[199] To ensure that the court will approve settlements the parties reach, it is probably wise to invite the court to participate in settlement discussions whenever that is practical.

Legislative Expansion of Notice Requirements for Settlement

Congress enacted a series of additional notice requirements for proposed settlements of class actions. First, within ten days of the filing of a proposed settlement with the district court, each defendant participating in the proposed settlement must serve notice of the proposed settlement, to include the following documents on both the appropriate federal official and the appropriate state official in each state in which any class member resides: (1) the complaint, amended complaint (if any), and material filed with such pleadings (unless such documents are available electronically, in which case an appropriate explanation of access to the documents will suffice); (2) notice of any scheduled hearing in the case; (3) notice of any proposed or final notification to class members of their right to seek exclusion from the case, or a statement that no such right exists, as well as a copy of the proposed settlement; (4) a copy of the final settlement; (5) a copy of any contemporaneous agreement reached between class counsel and defendants' counsel; (6) any final judgment or notice of dismissal; (7) if feasible, names of the class members residing in each state and an estimate of the proportion of the settlement likely to be distributed in each state, or if that information is not reasonably available, a reasonable estimate of such information; and (8) any written judicial opinions relating to items three through six.[200]

For purposes of this provision, the appropriate federal official is the Attorney General of the United States. The appropriate state official is that person with primary regulatory authority over the business in which the defendant engages. If there is no such person, the appropriate state official is the state attorney general. If the defendant is a federal or state depositary institution, a foreign bank, or a subsidiary of any such institution, the appropriate federal official is not the Attorney General, but the person who has primary federal regulatory authority over such an entity. The appropriate state official also becomes the corresponding state official with similar regulatory

---

[198]*See* Rule 23(e)(5) advisory committee notes to 2003 amendments (also providing examples of circumstances in which approval of withdrawal of objection may be obtained).

[199]*See, e.g., In re BankAmerica*

Corp. Securities Litigation, 350 F.3d 747, 751 (8th Cir. 2003) (Rule 23(e) makes district court "fiduciary" and "guardian" of rights of passive members of class).

[200]28 U.S.C.A. § 1715(b).

authority when a defendant is a state financial institution.[201]

Presumably so that appropriate federal or state officials may participate in the settlement process, § 1715(d) provides that a final order approving a settlement may not issue until at least 90 days after the latest date of notification to federal or state officials required under § 1715(b).[202] If a class member is able to establish that the requirements of § 1715(b) were not met, the class member has the option to refuse to comply with the settlement agreement. No such option exists if the defendants have complied with § 1715(b).[203]

RULE 23(f)—APPEALS

CORE CONCEPT

Rule 23(f) creates the possibility that a district court's decision granting or denying class certification could be appealed on an interlocutory basis. That is, the parties might not have to wait until the end of the litigation in the district court to learn whether the decision to certify (or not) would be upheld.

APPLICATIONS

Appellate Discretion

Rule 23(f) vests discretion in appellate courts to permit or deny an appeal granting or denying class certification, and circuit courts have begun to develop standards for determining whether to permit an appeal. Although their discretion is substantially uncurbed,[204] there seems to be general agreement that review under Rule 23(f) should not be a commonplace event.[205] Nevertheless, several situations arise where a circuit court is more likely than not to permit Rule 23(f) interlocutory appellate review of a class certification decision. These situations may sometimes be found together in the same case, but each by itself may justify review. First, if a denial of class certification would probably preclude any realistic chance that individual claims could be prosecuted and the district court's decision was questionable, circuits are inclined to grant review.[206] Second, if a district court's grant of class certification puts

---

[201]28 U.S.C.A. § 1715(a).

[202]28 U.S.C.A. § 1715(d).

[203]28 U.S.C.A. 1715(e).

[204]*See, e.g., Gutierrez v. Johnson & Johnson*, 523 F.3d 187, 192 (3d Cir. 2008) (comparing decision to Supreme Court's authority to act on petition for certiorari); *Shin v. Cobb County Bd. of Educ.*, 248 F.3d 1061, 1063–65 (11th Cir. 2001) (discretion is "unfettered").

[205]*See, e.g., In re Lorazepam & Clorazepate Antitrust Litigation*, 289 F.3d 98, 105 (D.C. Cir. 2002) ("As is

true for all the circuits, we are of the view that Rule 23(f) review should be granted rarely where a case does not fall within one of these . . . categories."); *Waste Management Holdings, Inc. v. Mowbray*, 208 F.3d 288, 294 (1st Cir. 2000) (court will "exercise discretion judiciously").

[206]*See, e.g., Sumitomo Copper Litigation v. Credit Lyonnais Rouse, Ltd.*, 262 F.3d 134, 140 (2d Cir. 2001) (review likely if certification denial is death knell for case, and certification decision was questionable). *See also*

substantial pressure on a defendant to settle without regard to the merits of a case and the certification grant was questionable, review is appropriate.[207] Third, circuits generally agree that review is appropriate if it will help develop law regarding class actions.[208] For this last possibility to apply, some circuit courts do not require that there be evidence of some error by the district court,[209] but other courts have imposed additional caveats that the development of law must be both important to the instant litigation and class action law generally, as well as unlikely to be subject to review at the termination of the case in the district court.[210]

Another possibility for obtaining review under Rule 23(f) arises if a party can demonstrate that the district court's certification decision is clear error. In that circumstance some circuits have held that review should normally occur without regard to whether other factors, such as those discussed immediately above, are present.[211]

Circuit courts that emphasize the appropriateness of appellate review in the circumstance of clear error have also adopted a slightly different characterization of the factors that other courts have used. Instead of identifying the three independent circumstances in which appellate review may be appropriate, these circuits have melded the factors together in a way that

---

McReynolds v. Merrill Lynch, Pierce, Fenner & Smith, Inc., 672 F.3d 482, 484 (7th Cir. 2012) (death knell can apply to either plaintiffs or defendant; for plaintiff, because individual damages are too small to justify piecemeal litigation, or defendant, if certification will produce risk of even more damages that force defendant to settle); *Marisol A. v. Giuliani*, 126 F.3d 372, 375 (2d Cir. 1997) (per curiam) (appellate court exercises "even greater deference when the district court has certified a class than when it has declined to do so.").

[207]*See, e.g., Tardiff v. Knox County*, 365 F.3d 1, 3 (1st Cir. 2004) ("One reason for review is a threat of liability so large as to place on the defendant an 'irresistible pressure to settle.' ").

[208]*See, e.g., Carnegie v. Household Intern., Inc.*, 376 F.3d 656 (7th Cir. 2004) ("the more important the resolution of the issue is either to the particular litigation or to the general development of class action law," the greater is the likelihood that appeal will be heard).

[209]*See, e.g., Blair v. Equifax Check Services, Inc.*, 181 F.3d 832, 835 (7th Cir. 1999).

[210]*See, e.g, Vallario v. Vandehey*, 554 F.3d 1259, 1263 (10th Cir. 2009) (noting narrowness of this category; "a certification decision must involve an unresolved issue of law relating to class actions that is likely to evade end-of-case review, and this issue must be significant to the case at hand, as well as to class action cases generally"); *In re Lorazepam & Clorazepate Antitrust Litigation*, 289 F.3d 98, 105 (D.C. Cir. 2002) (same).

[211]*See, e.g., Prado-Steiman ex rel. Prado v. Bush*, 221 F.3d 1266, 1275 (11th Cir. 2000) (clear error means review could be appropriate "even if none of the other factors supports granting the Rule 23(f) petition"). *See also Lienhart v. Dryvit Systems, Inc.*, 255 F.3d 138, 145–46 (4th Cir. 2001) (manifest error justifies review even where other factors are not met). *Cf., Carnegie v. Household Intern., Inc.*, 376 F.3d 656 (7th Cir. 2004) ("the more novel the issue presented by the appeal and so the less likely that the district court's resolution of it will stand . . . the stronger the case for allowing the appeal").

weighs all of them, plus one or two others. In such circuits Rule 23(f) petitions may be granted if consideration of these factors—taken together, not independently—justify review: (1) the "death knell" consideration, discussed above; (2) potential abuse of discretion by the district court in making its certification decision; (3) whether the appeal presents an unsettled legal question of general importance and importance in the instant litigation that might not be susceptible to review at a later point in the case; (4) the status of the case in the district court, including consideration of progress in discovery, other unresolved motions, and the passage of time since initiation of the case; and (5) the possibility that at some future time it will be clear that prompt review now was appropriate.[212] Courts that follow this approach weigh most heavily the presence of manifest error in the district court's decision. When such error is found it may be unnecessary for the appellate court to find that the other factors favor review before granting a Rule 23(f) petition.[213]

Yet another court has adopted the three independent factors discussed above, plus the additional independent ground for review when a decision is clearly erroneous.[214]

Role of District Court; Relation to 28 U.S.C.A. § 1292

As is suggested immediately above, a determination to grant or deny an application to appeal under Rule 23(f) is vested in the court of appeals. Once a district court has granted or denied the motion for certification, its role under Rule 23(f) is minor. The district court's entry of the order on class certification starts the running of the ten days in which an application to appeal must be filed (discussed below).[215] Additionally, filing a motion for reconsideration within fourteen days of the district court's entry of its order tolls the running of the Rule 23(f) time limit.[216]

The extremely truncated role of district courts in Rule 23(f) cases highlights the difference between that Rule and 28 U.S.C.A. § 1292, which governs many other circumstances in which an interlocutory appeal may be sought on grounds outside the scope of Rule 23(f). In particular, § 1292 provides that the district court must agree to certify a question before it

---

[212]*See, e.g., Prado-Steiman ex rel. Prado v. Bush*, 221 F.3d 1266, 1274–75 (11th Cir. 2000). *See also Lienhart v. Dryvit Systems, Inc.*, 255 F.3d 138, 146 (4th Cir. 2001) (same).

[213]*Lienhart v. Dryvit Systems, Inc.*, 255 F.3d 138, 146 (4th Cir. 2001); *Prado-Steiman ex rel. Prado v. Bush*, 221 F.3d 1266, 1275 (11th Cir. 2000).

[214]*Newton v. Merrill Lynch, Pierce, Fenner & Smith, Inc.*, 259 F.3d 154, 165 (3d Cir. 2001).

[215]Fed. R. Civ. P. 23(f).

[216]*See, e.g., Shin v. Cobb County Bd. of Educ.*, 248 F.3d 1061, 1064–65 (11th Cir. 2001) ("[T]he fourteen-day period to file a Rule 23(f) petition does not start to run until the district judge rules on the motion for reconsideration."). *But cf., Gary v. Sheahan*, 188 F.3d 891, 893 (7th Cir. 1999) (late or successive motions to reconsider the district court's certification decision do not toll the time limits of Rule 23(f)).

can be put before a circuit court on an interlocutory basis.[217] Further, § 1292(b) requires that the district court's certification of an interlocutory appeal includes determinations as to the importance of the appeal and the need for an expeditious ruling by the circuit court on the questions at hand. Only after the district court has made that certification may the circuit court exercise its own discretion in determining whether to accept the appeal.[218]

Time

By its terms, Rule 23(f) requires that any application for such an appeal be made to the circuit court within 14 days after the district court has entered its order granting or denying class certification.[219] It appears settled that the computation of time for Rule 23(f) is governed by Rule 6(a), which is discussed elsewhere in this text.[220]

Raising Other Issues

Rule 23(f) authorizes appeal of class certification only. In general, other issues will not be considered when the basis for appeal is Rule 23(f).[221] Two exceptions to that practice are standing and subject matter jurisdiction, which appellate courts are willing to consider on an appeal under Rule 23(f).[222]

---

[217]28 U.S.C.A. § 1292(b).

[218]28 U.S.C.A. § 1292(b). *See, e.g., Jenkins v. BellSouth Corp.*, 491 F.3d 1288 (11th Cir. 2007) ("[S]ection 1292(b) does not guide our interpretation of Rule 23(f)."). *See also McNamara v. Felderhof*, 410 F.3d 277, 281 (5th Cir. 2005) (time limit of Rule 23(f) cannot be extended through untimely motion in district court for reconsideration of certification order). *Cf., Delta Airlines v. Butler*, 383 F.3d 1143, 1145 (10th Cir. 2004) (district court cannot extend time limit of Rule 23(f)).

[219]*See, e.g., Gutierrez v. Johnson & Johnson*, 523 F.3d 187, 192 (3d Cir. 2008) ("This 14-day limit . . . is strict and mandatory."). *Compare Chevron USA Inc. v. School Bd. Vermilion Parish*, 294 F.3d 716 (5th Cir. 2002) (limit of Rule 23(f) is jurisdictional and may not be waived); *Gary v. Sheahan*, 188 F.3d 891, 892 (7th Cir. 1999) (failure to seek appellate review within time limit of Rule 23(f) means "appeal must wait until the final judgment") *with McReynolds v. Merrill Lynch, Pierce, Fenner & Smith, Inc.*, 672 F.3d 482, 485 (7th Cir. 2012) (Rule 23(f) time limit is not jurisdictional).

[220]*See, e.g., In re Veneman*, 309 F.3d 789, 793 (D.C. Cir. 2002) (appellate courts have held unanimously that Rule 6(a) controls). *See also Fleischman v. Albany Medical Center*, 639 F.3d 28, 31 (2d Cir. 2011) (time to appeal runs from date of original order, not from later order denying amendment to order, "at least when the motion to amend is filed more than fourteen days after the original order"). *But cf., Gutierrez v. Johnson & Johnson*, 523 F.3d 187, 192 (3d Cir. 2008) (timely motion to reconsider tolls time limit).

[221]*See, e.g., Asher v. Baxter Intern. Inc.*, 505 F.3d 736, 738 (7th Cir. 2007) ("Rule 23(f) does not allow interlocutory appeals from orders designating (or not designating) lead plaintiffs.").

[222]*See, e.g., Rivera v. Wyeth-Ayerst Laboratories*, 283 F.3d 315, 319 (5th Cir. 2002) ("[S]tanding may—indeed must—be addressed even under the limits of a Rule 23(f) appeal."); *Bertulli v. Independent Ass'n of Continental Pilots*, 242 F.3d 290, 294 (5th Cir. 2001) (enunciating this general rule, but deciding that issues of standing are an exception and may be heard on a Rule

Relation to 28 U.S.C. § 1292

Section 1292(b) governs some of the circumstances in which a party may seek authorization for an interlocutory appeal from the decision of a district court. Section 1292(b) provides no fixed time limit for seeking such an appeal. However, it appears that when an interlocutory appeal might lie under Rule 23(f), neither district courts nor potential appellants should seek interlocutory relief under § 1292(b).[223]

Stay of District Court Proceedings

If the circuit court allows an appeal under Rule 23(f), the appeal does not automatically stay proceedings in the district court.[224] Instead, a party seeking such a stay must apply to either the district court or the court of appeals.

23(f) appeal); *Carter v. West Pub. Co.,* 225 F.3d 1258, 1262 (11th Cir. 2000) (under Rule 23(f) court may also evaluate standing, but not merits of case); *Prado-Steiman ex rel. Prado v. Bush,* 221 F.3d 1266, 1273 (11th Cir. 2000) ("Rule 23(f) should not be a vehicle for courts of appeals to micro-manage complex class action litigation as it unfolds in the district court."). *But see Mims v. Stewart Title Guaranty Co.,* 590 F.3d 298, 304 (5th Cir. 2009) (if issue is relevant to both certification and merits of case, court may examine issue to help determine appropriateness of certification); *McKowan Lowe & Co., Ltd. v. Jasmine, Ltd.,* 295 F.3d 380 (3d Cir. 2002) (refusing to review dismissal of plaintiff's underlying claims when hearing Rule 23(f) appeal of denial of class certification; Rule 23(f) does not extend to any other type order, "even where that order has some impact on another portion of Rule 23"); *In re Lorazepam & Clorazepate Antitrust Litigation,* 289 F.3d 98, 107–08 (D.C. Cir. 2002) (refusing to consider antitrust standing under Rule 23(f). "The fact that [defendant's] challenge would be dispositive of the class action is not unlike a variety of issues of law on the merits of a class action," but review of such issues "would inappropriately mix the issue of class certification with the merits of a case." However, acknowledging authority for evaluating constitutional standing under Rule 23(f); but distinguishing

such cases because such standing goes to court's jurisdiction, while antitrust standing does not). *See also Lindsay v. Government Employees Ins. Co.,* 448 F.3d 416, 420 (D.C. Cir. 2006) ("Because subject matter jurisdiction is a prerequisite to class certification, it is properly reviewed in a Rule 23(f) interlocutory appeal.").

[223]*Richardson Electronics, Ltd. v. Panache Broadcasting of Pennsylvania, Inc.,* 202 F.3d 957, 959 (7th Cir. 2000) (When issue "is an arguable candidate for a rule 23(f) appeal, the appellants may not use § 1292(b) to circumvent the 14-day limitation in Rule 23(f). . . . Should a case arise in which a class-certification order is appealable under [§] 1292(b) but not under [Rule] 23(f), perhaps because it presents an issue that while it satisfies the criteria of the statute does not involve the merits of class certification, the appellant can protect himself by seeking the district judge's permission to take a [§]1292(b) appeal at the same time that the appellant asks us to entertain his appeal under [Rule] 23(f).").

[224]*See, e.g., Prado-Steiman ex rel. Prado v. Bush,* 221 F.3d 1266, 1273 (11th Cir. 2000) ("Rule 23(f) contemplates that in most cases discovery (at the very least, merits discovery) will continue notwithstanding the pendency of an appeal of the class certification order.").

RULE 23(g)—CLASS COUNSEL

CORE CONCEPT

Rule 23(g) is an amendment to Rule 23, effective in late 2003. It governs the manner in which a court will supervise the appointment of counsel to represent the class. Previously there was no precise counterpart to Rule 23(g), but courts had previously used authority derived from Rule 23(a)(4) to develop substantial precedent guiding decisions courts had to make in this area. Additionally, the precepts adopted for class litigation in the area of securities law,[225] themselves heavily borrowed from case law, will also undoubtedly provide guidance to federal courts as they attempt to flesh out the requirements of new Rule 23(g).

2007 Amendments

The 2007 Style Project amended Rule 23(g) by transferring provisions within various subparts of subsection (g). Specifically, former Rule 23(g)(1)(B), addressing class counsel's duty of fair and adequate representation of the interests of the class, is now Rule 23(g)(4). Further, old Rule 23(g)(2)(C), addressing the inclusion of provisions about attorneys fees and nontaxable costs in the order appointing class counsel, is now Rule 23(g)(1)(D). These are not substantive changes, but they may require attorneys to be cautious to cite accurately to cases decided prior to the 2007 amendments.

APPLICATIONS

Prerequisite: Certification of a Class

A decision to appoint class counsel should not occur until the court first certifies a class.[226]

Relationship of Rule 23(a)(4) to Rule 23(g)

Until the addition of Rule 23(g), courts had routinely employed Rule 23(a)(4) (governing evaluation of whether class representatives would adequately protect class interests) to examine the adequacy of class counsel.[227] The standards developed by that case law[228] have been incorporated almost in their entirety into new Rule 23(g), giving courts broad discretion to

---

[225] 15 U.S.C.A. § 78u-4(a)(3)(B).

[226] See, e.g., Sheinberg v. Sorensen, 606 F.3d 130, 132 (3d Cir. 2010) (pursuant to Rule 23(g)(1), "A district court's decision to certify a class must *precede* the appointment of class counsel.").

[227] Amchem Products, Inc. v. Windsor, 521 U.S. 591, 626, 117 S. Ct. 2231, 138 L. Ed. 2d 689 (1997) ("The adequacy heading also factors in competency and conflicts of class counsel."). See, e.g., Sheinberg v. Sorensen, 606 F.3d 130, __ (3d Cir. 2010) (traditional analysis under Rule 23(a)(4) now takes place under Rule 23(g)).

[228] See, e.g., Fymbo v. State Farm Fire and Cas. Co., 213 F.3d 1320, 1320–21 (10th Cir. 2000) (Rule 23(a)(4) prevents non-attorney from serving as pro se class representative; plaintiff's pleadings were also evidence of lack of competence); Hanlon v. Chrysler Corp., 150 F.3d 1011, 1021 (9th Cir. 1998) (Rule 23(a)(4) requires evaluation of counsel's ability; also, in settlement class, court must also examine "rationale for not pursuing further litigation"); In re Fine Paper Antitrust Litigation, 617 F.2d 22, 27 (3d Cir. 1980) (trial judge has "constant duty" to

inquire and evaluate the appropriateness of permitting any particular lawyers' representation of the class.

Applicable Standards

Rule 23(g) identifies four factors the court must evaluate in appointing class counsel: the work an attorney has already done on the case; the attorney's experience in other class actions and complex litigation;[229] the attorney's familiarity with law applicable to the case; and resources.[230]

At the end of its evaluation, the court should be able to satisfy itself that the potential class counsel will "fairly and adequately represent the interests of the class."[231] In this process the court may consider the costs and fees a proposed attorney expects to get from the case.[232]

Ultimately, the court has a duty to select from among the potential attorneys the lawyer(s) who will best represent the class."[233]

Reverse Auctions

Historically, courts have discouraged reverse auctions-"the practice whereby the defendant in a series of class actions picks the most ineffectual class lawyers to negotiate a settlement with in the hope that the district court will approve a weak settlement that will preclude other claims against the defendant."[234] Rule 23(g)(1)(C)(iii) and (g)(2)(C) now provide the court with express authority to examine and propose appropriate terms for compensation and to include those requirements as part of the order appointing class counsel. The result should be to control attorneys' fees and costs while ensuring that the class opponent is not in a position to choose, unilaterally, the lawyers who will cost the least and who may not do the best work. These portions of Rule 23(g) harmonize closely with Rule 23(h), governing awards of attorney fees. Rule 23(h) is discussed immediately below.

RULE 23(h)—ATTORNEY'S FEES AND NONTAXABLE COSTS

CORE CONCEPT

Rule 23(h) governs the award of attorneys' fees in class actions. Heretofore this issue was controlled by case law as well as statutes applicable to particular kinds of class actions, such as

---

monitor "professional competency and behavior of class counsel").

[229]Fed.R.Civ.P. 23(g). *See also Sheinberg v. Sorensen*, 606 F.3d 130, 132 (3d Cir. 2010).

[230]Fed.R.Civ.P. 23(g)(1)(C) and (E).

[231]Fed.R.Civ.P. 23(g)(4).

[232]Fed.R.Civ.P. 23(g)(1)(C) to (D).

[233]Fed.R.Civ.P. 23(g)(2).

[234]*Reynolds v. Beneficial Nat. Bank*, 288 F.3d 277, 282 (7th Cir. 2002). *See also In re Cendant Corp. Litigation*, 264 F.3d 201 (3d Cir. 2001) (disapproving choice of lead counsel by reverse auction in case controlled by Private Securities Litigation Reform Act).

the Private Securities Litigation Reform Act of 1995.[235] New Rule 23(h) establishes no substantive standards for determining the appropriateness of a particular fee award. Instead, it establishes a procedure by which a fee application may be made and objections to that application may be heard.

APPLICATIONS

Existing Case Law

Outside of the area of class actions, and subject to some other important exceptional, the general American approach to attorney's fees is to require each party to bear its own burden. However, class actions present a special problem, because the nature of such litigation is that the work of attorneys may enrich an entire group of people. In such a situation it would be unfair to require that the attorneys be compensated, if at all, only by those few individuals who began the litigation.[236] New Rule 23(h) recognizes that principle by permitting attorneys to petition for fees that are taxable, in appropriate cases, against the entire class.

The basis and source of such fees has depended partly on the nature of the cause of action and the judgment or settlement obtained. For example, fees might have been available from the defendant when authorized under an applicable statute.[237] When such a statute was not applicable (and usually even when it was), the district court had substantial authority to determine the method of calculating fees and the amount that would be awarded. Rule 24(h), in essence, codifies that existing practice. Thus, it is likely that for at least the near future courts will rely on precedent developed prior to enactment of Rule 24(h) to determine the appropriateness of a fee award in a particular case.

Independent Assessment

A court's duty to assess the reasonableness of an award of fees is an independent obligation, even where parties have reached agreement on a dollar amount.[238]

Methods of Calculation

Measurement of the appropriate amount of a fee has usually been determined through one of two methods. If a fund was available, courts have awarded the lawyers a percentage

---

[235]15 U.S.C.A. § 78u-4(a)(6).

[236]*See, e.g, Savoie v. Merchants Bank*, 166 F.3d 456, 460 (2d Cir. 1999) ("A party whose initiative confers a benefit upon a class of people is entitled to recover its costs-including attorneys' fees-from the common fund."). *See also In re Synthroid Marketing Litigation*, 264 F.3d 712, 717 (7th Cir. 2001) ("Unless a class contracts privately over attorneys' fees, lawyers in class-fund cases must petition the court for their compensation.").

[237]*See, e.g.,* 42 U.S.C.A. § 1988 (governing attorneys' fees in civil rights litigation).

[238]*See, e.g., In re: Bluetooth Headset Products Liability Litigation*, 654 F.3d 935, ___ (9th Cir. 2011).

of the money available.[239] In circumstances where the court believed another approach was appropriate or where no fund was available, *e.g.,* where the class sought injunctive relief, courts typically measured the appropriate fee through a "lodestar" approach.[240] In the context of a class action, this calculation begins by determining appropriate hourly rates for individual lawyers, which are then multiplied by the number of hours actually and reasonably expended on the project. Finally, factors such as difficulty of the case, quality of legal work, risk of failure, etc., may be used in some cases to modify the result (up or down) reached by the simple multiplication of hours and rates.[241] It should be noted that while the lodestar method has been available in many class actions, the use of so-called "risk multipliers," *e.g.,* difficulty of the case, etc., has *not* been available in class actions where a fee is imposed based on a fee shifting statute. In such cases it appears that district courts have made their lodestar calculation based only on the reasonable hourly rate multiplied by the reasonable number of hours devoted to the case.[242]

---

[239]*Blum v. Stenson*, 465 U.S. 886, 900, 104 S. Ct. 1541, 1550 n. 16, 79 L. Ed. 2d 891 (1984) (approving calculation based on percentage of fund). *See, e.g., Hanlon v. Chrysler Corp.*, 150 F.3d 1011, 1029 (9th Cir. 1998) (approving approximately 4.5% of very large fund as appropriate compensation).

[240]*See, e.g.,* 28 U.S.C.A. § 1712(b) (expressly authorizing, but not mandating, use of lodestar method to calculate attorney's fees). *In re Synthroid Marketing Litigation*, 264 F.3d 712, 718 (7th Cir. 2001) ("We have held repeatedly that, when deciding on appropriate fee levels in common-fund cases, courts must do their best to award counsel the market price for legal services, in light of the risk of nonpayment and the normal rate of compensation in the market at the time."); *In re Cendant Corp. PRIDES Litigation*, 243 F.3d 722, 732 (3d Cir. 2001) (lodestar applicable when anticipated relief is too small to justify use of percentage-of-recovery method but case still has potential social benefit). *Compare, e.g., Savoie v. Merchants Bank*, 166 F.3d 456, 460 (2d Cir. 1999) (suggesting that Second Circuit will use only lodestar method to determine compensation, even in cases involving common fund) *with Goldberger v.*

Integrated Resources, Inc., 209 F.3d 43, 50 (2d Cir. 2000) (acknowledging that lodestar method is approved, but is not "exclusive methodology in common fund cases").

[241]*See, e.g., Gunter v. Ridgewood Energy Corp.*, 223 F.3d 190, 195 n. 1 (3d Cir. 2000) (factors to consider "include: (1) the size of the fund created and the number of persons benefited; (2) the presence or absence of substantial objection by members of the class to the settlement terms and/or fees requested by counsel; (3) the skill and efficiency of the attorneys involved; (4) the complexity and duration of the litigation; (5) the risk of nonpayment; (6) the amount of time devoted to the case by plaintiff's counsel; and (7) the awards in similar cases"); *Goldberger v. Integrated Resources, Inc.*, 209 F.3d 43, 53 (2d Cir. 2000) (lodestar case: "[o]f course contingency risk and quality of representation must be considered in settling a reasonable fee").

[242]*City of Burlington v. Dague*, 505 U.S. 557, 565–66, 112 S. Ct. 2638, 2642–43, 120 L. Ed. 2d 449 (1992) (rejecting use of risk multipliers in cases using lodestar method to calculate attorneys' fees under federal fee-shifting statutes).

Motion Required

Rule 23(h) requires that an application for attorneys' fees must be made by motion, subject to Rule 54(d) (governing taxation of costs).[243]

Notice

Rule 23(h) requires that the motion for fees must be served on all parties. If the motion is made by class counsel, as it typically will be, it must also "[be] directed to class members in a reasonable manner."[244]

Objections, Hearing and Findings

Rule 23(h) provides that both class members and the party who may have to pay the fees have standing to object to the motion. The court has discretion—not an obligation[245]—to hold a hearing on the motion. The court must make findings of fact and conclusions of law in a manner consistent with the requirements of Rule 52(a) (governing the court's duty in such matters when issues are tried to the court).

If the court approves a lump-sum attorneys' fee, it may be appropriate to permit attorneys to divide the fee among themselves by agreement.[246]

Special Masters and Magistrate Judges

Rule 23(h) permits the district court to refer matters relating to fees to special masters or magistrate judges.

Protection against Loss by Class Members

In 28 U.S.C.A. § 1713, Congress provided the district court with authority to approve a proposed settlement involving a payment by members of the class to class counsel that would be a net loss to the class members. However, that authority is restricted to cases in which the court, by a written finding, concludes that nonmonetary benefits to the class "substantially" outweigh the monetary loss.[247] This provision of § 1713 is not restricted to cases involving "coupon" settlements, and appears to apply to class action settlements generally.

---

[243]*See, e.g., Feldman v. Olin Corp.,* 673 F.3d 515, 517 (7th Cir. 2012).

[244]*In re Delphi Corp. Securities, Derivative & "ERISA" Litigation,* 248 F.R.D. 483, 506 (E.D. Mich. 2008).

[245]*But cf., In re High Sulfur Content Gasoline Products Liability Litigation,* 517 F.3d 220, 231–32 (5th Cir. 2008) (while district court is not required to hold hearing on motion for attorneys' fees in class action, a determination to hold such a hearing triggers requirements of notice and opportunity to be heard; rejecting *ex parte* hearing).

[246]*See, e.g., In re High Sulfur Content Gasoline Products Liability Litigation,* 517 F.3d 220, 234 (5th Cir. 2008) (but disapproving district court's approval of agreement among five attorneys to divide fee among themselves and seventy-four other attorneys without opportunity for other attorneys or district court to participate in decision).

[247]28 U.S.C.A. § 1713.

Additional Research References

Wright & Miller, *Federal Practice and Procedure* §§ 1751 to 1805
C.J.S., Federal Civil Procedure §§ 63 to 92, § 170
West's Key Number Digest, Federal Civil Procedure ⚷161 to 189

RULE 23.1
DERIVATIVE ACTIONS BY SHAREHOLDERS

(a) Prerequisites. This rule applies when one or more shareholders or members of a corporation or an unincorporated association bring a derivative action to enforce a right that the corporation or association may properly assert but has failed to enforce. The derivative action may not be maintained if it appears that the plaintiff does not fairly and adequately represent the interests of shareholders or members who are similarly situated in enforcing the right of the corporation or association.

(b) Pleading Requirements. The complaint must be verified and must:

  (1) allege that the plaintiff was a shareholder or member at the time of the transaction complained of, or that the plaintiff's share or membership later devolved on it by operation of law;

  (2) allege that the action is not a collusive one to confer jurisdiction that the court would otherwise lack; and

  (3) state with particularity:

    (A) any effort by the plaintiff to obtain the desired action from the directors or comparable authority and, if necessary, from the shareholders or members; and

    (B) the reasons for not obtaining the action or not making the effort.

(c) Settlement, Dismissal, and Compromise. A derivative action may be settled, voluntarily dismissed, or compromised only with the court's approval. Notice of a proposed settlement, voluntary dismissal, or compromise must be given to shareholders or members in the manner that the court orders.

[Added effective July 1, 1966; amended effective August 1, 1987; April 30, 2007, effective December 1, 2007.]

AUTHORS' COMMENTARY ON RULE 23.1

PURPOSE AND SCOPE

In a shareholder derivative suit, a shareholder sues on behalf of a corporation and/or its shareholders by alleging that the officers and directors who control the corporation will not institute the suit. In fact, often the officers and directors are themselves defendants in the derivative suit. The utility of shareholder derivative suits is balanced by the risk that this type of litigation can be used to harass corporate officers and directors into settlements favorable to the plaintiffs, at the expense of degrading corporate assets that are the common property of all shareholders. Through a series of procedural requirements not normally imposed on other kinds of litigation, Rule 23.1 attempts to preserve the social value of derivative suits, while reducing the risk of inappropriate harassment. Some of these requirements bear substantial similarity to elements of Rule 23, governing class actions.

RULE 23.1(a)—DERIVATIVE ACTION

CORE CONCEPT

Rule 23.1(a) provides that shareholders or members of a corporation may bring an action on behalf of a corporation that the corporation has not asserted. Only persons who will fairly and adequately represent the interests of other shareholders or members, and who will represent the interests of other similarly situated shareholders or members, may enforce the corporation's rights.

APPLICATIONS

Applicability

For the requirements of Rule 23.1 to apply to a case, a plaintiff must be a "shareholder" or "member" seeking to enforce a right of a corporation or unincorporated association.[1] Other types of derivative claims need not meet the standards of Rule 23.1.[2]

---

[1]*See, e.g., Lefkovitz v. Wagner*, 395 F.3d 773, 776 (7th Cir. 2005) ("Although most derivative suits are brought on behalf of corporations, a derivative suit can be brought on behalf of a partnership or other unincorporated form.").

[2]*Daily Income Fund, Inc. v. Fox*, 464 U.S. 523, 528, 104 S. Ct. 831, 834, 78 L. Ed. 2d 645 (1984) (Rule 23.1 applies only when "a shareholder claims a right that could have been, but was not, 'asserted' by the corporation."); *see also, Kayes v. Pacific Lumber Co.*, 51

Subject Matter Jurisdiction

If the cause of action is based exclusively on state law, the requirements of diversity jurisdiction must be satisfied. Diversity jurisdiction and other kinds of subject matter jurisdiction are discussed at §§ 2.10 to 2.13. Because the corporation is normally treated as an indispensable party needed for just adjudication, alignment of the corporate entity as a plaintiff or defendant can have significant consequences for jurisdiction. Although there is no absolute rule governing this issue, it is likely that the court will not align the corporation in a way that defeats diversity jurisdiction. The courts still retain discretion in this area, however, and have on occasion aligned the corporation in a way that defeats diversity.[3]

Personal Jurisdiction

Personal jurisdiction over defendants who are natural persons is obtained in derivative suits in the same manner as in other litigation. For corporations aligned as defendants, however, Congress has enacted a special service of process provision. 28 U.S.C.A. § 1695 allows plaintiffs in shareholder derivative suits to serve process on such corporate defendants "in any district where [they are] organized or licensed to do business or . . . doing business."

Venue

A special statute for derivative suits, 28 U.S.C.A. § 1401, provides that the plaintiff may sue in any judicial district where the corporation might have sued the same defendants. As a practical matter, this means § 1401 should be read in conjunction with § 1391(a) and (b), governing the venue requirements for diversity suits and many claims based on federal questions.

RULE 23.1(b)—PLEADING REQUIREMENTS

CORE CONCEPT

Rule 23.1(b) identifies the special pleading requirements for derivative actions governed by Rule 23.1 and also provide that a pleading governed by Rule 23.1 must be verified.

Verification of Complaint

Complaints that initiate shareholders' derivative actions must be sworn to and notarized. This is a departure from the

---

F.3d 1449, 1462–63 (9th Cir. 1995). (Rule 23.1 applies narrowly; it is not applicable to "plan beneficiaries" seeking "to enforce the right of the plan against its fiduciaries").

[3]*See, e.g., Liddy v. Urbanek*, 707 F.2d 1222, 1224 (11th Cir. 1983) ([F]inal alignment of the parties should reflect the actual antagonisms between the plaintiffs, the corporation, and the directors; held, corporation should be joined where appropriate, even when joinder will destroy diversity); *Frank v. Hadesman and Frank, Inc.*, 83 F.3d 158 (7th Cir.1996) (in derivative suit, corporation is aligned as plaintiff if shareholders have suffered harm in common; citing state law; dismissing because corporation is not diverse from defendant).

general practice in federal civil procedure, which usually imposes no federal requirement for verification of a complaint. The practical impact of a verification requirement in derivative suits may be limited, however, because it is not applied in a way that prohibits a layperson from relying on competent information in bringing a derivative suit.[4] Thus, any shareholder who has undertaken a reasonable investigation, in person or through the advice of qualified persons, of the allegations in the complaint, should be able to satisfy the verification requirement without undue difficulty.[5]

Standing: Continuous Ownership Requirement

Under Rule 23.1(b)(1), the complaint must state that the derivative suit is initiated on behalf of a person who: (1) was a shareholder at the time the cause of action arose, or who became a shareholder by operation of law from someone who had been a shareholder at that time; and (2) who remained a shareholder at the time the suit was filed.[6] If the plaintiff is divested of ownership while the suit is pending, the suit will usually be dismissed.[7] In diversity suits, these standing requirements of rule 23.1 will apparently apply even if state law might be less strict. The matter is not entirely free from doubt, however, and attorneys should consult the local practice.[8]

Collusive Attempts to Invoke Federal Jurisdiction

Rule 23.1(b)(2) requires that the plaintiff swear that a

---

[4]*Surowitz v. Hilton Hotels Corp.*, 383 U.S. 363, 86 S. Ct. 845, 15 L. Ed. 2d 807 (1966).

[5]*See, e.g., Lewis v. Curtis*, 671 F.2d 779, 788 (3d Cir. 1982) (reliance on Wall Street Journal article satisfies requirement).

[6]*See, e.g., In re Bank of New York Derivative Litigation*, 320 F.3d 291, 298 (2d Cir. 2003) (requiring plaintiff to own stock "*throughout* the course of the activities that constitute the *primary basis* of the complaint;" rejecting use of continuing wrong doctrine to expand definition of transaction; holding that plaintiff need not have owned stock during "the entire course of all relevants," but plaintiff must have owned stock "before the case of the allegedly wrongful conduct transpired"); *Rosenbaum v. MacAllister*, 64 F.3d 1439, 1443 (10th Cir. 1995) (explaining requirements of contemporaneous ownership and continuing ownership; also identifying one exception to those requirements).

[7]*See, e.g., Johnson v. U.S.*, 317 F.3d 1331, 1333–34 (Fed. Cir. 2003) (plaintiff who loses shareholder status through bankruptcy proceeding while instant lawsuit was pending loses standing upon cancellation of shares); *Schilling v. Belcher*, 582 F.2d 995, 999 (5th Cir. 1978) ("It is generally held that the ownership requirement continues throughout the life of the suit and that the action will abate if the plaintiff ceases to be a shareholder before the litigation ends.").

[8]*See, e.g., Kona Enterprises, Inc. v. Estate of Bishop*, 179 F.3d 767, 769 (9th Cir. 1999) (holding that standing requirement of Rule 23.1 "is procedural in nature and thus applicable in diversity actions"). *But see Fagin v. Gilmartin*, 432 F.3d 276, 285 (3d Cir. 2005) ("The question of whether the plaintiff is a 'shareholder' is determined by state law."); *Batchelder v. Kawamoto*, 147 F.3d 915, 917–18 (9th Cir. 1998) (where choice of law clause provided that Japanese law governed rights of interest holders, neither Rule 23.1 nor state law applied).

shareholder derivative suit based on diversity jurisdiction was not brought to manufacture federal court jurisdiction on behalf of the corporation. The possibility of manipulation may arise from a determination of the corporation's status as a plaintiff or defendant. In most cases it is probable that the corporation on whose behalf the derivative lawsuit was filed will be aligned as a plaintiff.[9] This alignment is usually of no consequence, provided that the corporation's citizenship is diverse from that of the defendants. However, if a corporate plaintiff is not diverse from all of the defendants, there is obviously a jurisdictional problem.[10] The solution lies in realignment of the corporation as a defendant — a solution permissible when the corporation is controlled by persons antagonistic to the interests of the stockholder plaintiffs.[11] Antagonism of this nature may be found where the corporate managers are simply opposed to the lawsuit.[12] In such circumstances, if the court realigns the corporation as a defendant, the problem with diversity jurisdiction may be resolved.

Pleading With Particularity

Rule 23.1 requires that certain allegations of the shareholder derivative complaint be pleaded with particularity. This means that the plaintiff must provide additional factual detail that is not normally required under the "notice pleading" policy of the Federal Rules. The requirement of particularity is usually satisfied without difficulty by plaintiffs who simply explain the facts behind their conclusory allegation.[13]

---

[9]*Koster v. Lumbermens Mutual Casualty Co.*, 330 U.S. 518, 522–23, 67 S.Ct. 828, 91 L.Ed. 1067 (1947) (derivative lawsuit does not belong to individual plaintiffs but to corporation, which is "the real party in interest").

[10]*See* 28 U.S.C. § 1332 (establishing requirements for subject matter jurisdiction based on diversity of citizenship).

[11]*Smith v. Sperling*, 354 U.S. 91, 95–96 n. 3, 77 S.Ct. 1112, 1 L.Ed.2d 1205 (1957) ("The ultimate interest of the corporation made defendant may be the same as that of the stockholder made plaintiff, but the corporation may be under a control antagonistic to him, and made to act in a way detrimental to his rights."). *See, e.g., In re Digimarc Corp. Derivative Litigation*, 549 F.3d 1223, 1234 (9th Cir. 2008) (exception applies "when a corporation's officers or directors are 'antagonistic' to those of the shareholder plaintiff(s)").

[12]*Swanson v. Traer*, 354 U.S. 114, 116, 77 S.Ct. 1116, 1 L.Ed.2d 1221 (1957). *Cf., In re Digimarc Corp. Derivative Litigation*, 549 F.3d 1223, 1235 (9th Cir. 2008) (antagonism determined on face of pleadings and nature of dispute; noting that some other courts find antagonism where complaint alleges that defendants who control corporation are engaged in fraud or malfeasance).

[13]*See, e.g., Halebian v. Berv*, 590 F.3d 195, 206 n. 7 (2d Cir. 2009) (adequacy of underlying claim is controlled by state law, but pleading requirements are controlled by Rule 23.1); *In re Abbott Laboratories Derivative Shareholders Litigation*, 325 F.3d 795, 804 (7th Cir. 2003) (holding requirement satisfied when "[a]lthough plaintiffs have a conclusory paragraph in their claim of demand futility, they have also incorporated all of the detailed factual allegations"); *Stepak v. Addison*, 20 F.3d 398, 400 (11th Cir. 1994) (mere allegation that law firm

Explanation of Efforts to Encourage Corporation to Protect Its Own Interest

Rule 23.1 requires that a plaintiff allege in the complaint, "with particularity," the following facts: (1) the efforts plaintiff made, if any, to encourage those who control the corporation—shareholders, officers and/or directors—to take action; and (2) the reasons why the efforts were unsuccessful, or reasons why no effort was made.[14]

Demand: Futility

Rule 23.1 requires the plaintiff to make a demand on the corporate officers to pursue the suit.[15] The facts of this demand must be pleaded with particularity.[16] However, plaintiffs are not entitled to discovery to establish the particular facts underlying an allegation of futility.[17]

The requirement that the plaintiff demand that the corporation bring the lawsuit may be waived, however, if it is clear from the facts of a case that such a demand would be clearly futile. Rule 23.1 requires the plaintiff to plead with particularity the facts establishing futility, but the standard by which the facts are evaluated is a matter of state law.[18]

---

was "conflicted" did not satisfy requirement of particularity in Rule 23.1; but allegations that law firm defended corporate officers in criminal matters related to plaintiff's demand, and then gave advice to board about demand, satisfied requirement).

[14]*Stepak v. Addison*, 20 F.3d 398, 402 (11th Cir. 1994); (Rule 23.1 imposes "more stringent pleading requirements" than Rules 8 and 12(b)(6)). *See, e.g., Frank v. Hadesman and Frank, Inc.*, 83 F.3d 158 (7th Cir.1996) (noting plaintiff's duty to make demand on corporate board to pursue claim).

[15]*See, e.g., Santomenno ex rel. John Hancock Trust v. John Hancock Life Insurance Co.*, 677 F.3d 178, 184 (3d Cir. 2012) (demand requirement applies to all claims that corporation could have brought on its own behalf). *But cf., Daily Income Fund, Inc. v. Fox*, 464 U.S. 523, 528, 104 S.Ct. 831, 78 L.Ed.2d 645 (1984) (Rule 23.1 demand requirement applicable only to corporation or other association eligible to enforce rights in their own name, not to, e.g., funds that may not sue in their own name).

[16]*See, e.g., Potter v. Hughes*, 546 F.3d 1051, 1055 (9th Cir. 2008) (find-

ing of proper demand is prerequisite to determination of subject matter jurisdiction); *In re Abbott Laboratories Derivative Shareholders Litigation*, 325 F.3d 795, 804 (7th Cir. 2003) (holding requirement satisfied when "[a]lthough plaintiffs have a conclusory paragraph in their claim of demand futility, they have also incorporated all of the detailed factual allegations").

[17]*See, e.g., In re Merck & Co., Inc. Securities, Derivative & ERISA Litigation*, 493 F.3d 393 (3d Cir. 2007) (if discovery was allowed, "shareholder plaintiffs [would] have incentive to make baseless allegations and then engage in discovery fishing expeditions").

[18]*Kamen v. Kemper Financial Services, Inc.*, 500 U.S. 90, 111 S. Ct. 1711, 114 L. Ed. 2d 152 (1991) (Rule 23.1 controls adequacy of pleadings. State law controls substantive standard). *See, e.g., In re Ferro Corp. Derivative Litigation*, 511 F.3d 611, 617 (6th Cir. 2008) ("Even when the derivative claims are brought under federal law, we apply the substantive law of the state of incorporation . . . to determine whether Plaintiffs' failure to make a demand is excused."); *McCall v. Scott*, 239 F.3d 808, 816 (6th Cir. 2001) (demand may be excused

Special Litigation Committees

When officers of a business entity are faced with a Rule 23.1 demand to pursue a lawsuit, a typical response has been to appoint a special litigation committee to investigate the matter. In that circumstance courts will usually grant a request to stay proceedings in the derivative action until the committee can make a report recommending a course of action, *e.g.,* terminate the litigation, take it over, or authorize the original plaintiff to continue it. The court has authority to accept or reject the recommendation.[19]

Adequacy of Representation

The plaintiff in a shareholder derivative suit must be a person who will adequately represent the best interests of those—the corporation and other shareholders—on whose behalf the suit is prosecuted.[20] Perhaps because Rule 23.1 derivative suits present fewer of the case management problems associated with Rule 23 class actions, the courts seem less concerned in derivative suits with the quality and experience of the plaintiff's counsel.[21]

RULE 23.1(c)—SETTLEMENT, DISMISSAL, AND COMPROMISE

CORE CONCEPT

Rule 23.1(c) provides that any settlement of a derivative action is subject to the court's approval. It also establishes a notice requirement for such settlements.[22]

"because either the directors were incapable of making an impartial decision, or the directors wrongfully refused a demand to sue").

[19]*See, e.g., Strougo on Behalf of Brazil Fund, Inc. v. Padegs*, 986 F. Supp. 812, 814 (S.D. N.Y. 1997) (explaining process and noting courts' awareness of special litigation committee's potential bias toward protecting corporate board and officers).

[20]*But see Powers v. Eichen*, 229 F.3d 1249, 1254 (9th Cir. 2000) (concluding that Rule 23.1 does not offer as much protection as Rule 23; "Unlike . . . Rule 23, in shareholder derivative suits under Rule 23.1, a preliminary affirmative determination that the named plaintiffs will fairly and adequately represent the interests of the other class members is not a prerequisite to the maintenance of the action.").

[21]*Cf., In re Sonus Networks, Inc. Shareholder Derivative Litigation*, 422 F. Supp. 2d 281, 292 (D. Mass. 2006), aff'd, 499 F.3d 47 (1st Cir. 2007) (inadequate representation, including fraud or collusion, will vitiate attempt to impose res judicata; however, allegation of mere failure to raise additional facts does not, by itself, constitute inadequate representation).

[22]*See, e.g., In re UnitedHealth Group Shareholder Derivative Litigation*, 631 F.3d 913, 917 (8th Cir. 2011) (noting that notice requirements for class actions are usually more extensive than notice requirements under Rule 23.1(c)).

Settlement Subject to Court Approval

Derivative suits may not be dismissed or settled without prior judicial approval.[23] The district court enjoys broad, but not totally unfettered, discretion to evaluate a proposed settlement.[24] In determining whether to approve a settlement, the court may consider the reaction of persons, such as other shareholders, who will be affected by the outcome of the case.[25] In theory, the court should not re-write a proposed settlement, but should limit itself to approving or disapproving the proposal.[26] In practice, courts have substantial ability to influence the contents of a settlement by indicating what the court deems a satisfactory compromise. In any event, persons who wish to oppose a proposed settlement or appeal a settlement must first intervene in the case.[27]

Notice of Settlement

Rule 23.1 requires that the court will order notice of voluntary dismissals or proposed settlements to interested persons. The court has substantial discretion, within the circumstances of the particular case, to determine the manner in which notification will occur.[28]

Bond Requirements

Many states require that plaintiffs in derivative suits post bonds, from which the defendants will be compensated for litigation expenses if the defendants prevail. Rule 23.1 contains no such requirement. In diversity suits, however, it is settled that federal courts will enforce requirements established under state law.[29]

---

[23]*Burks v. Lasker*, 441 U.S. 471, 485 n. 16, 99 S. Ct. 1831, 60 L. Ed. 2d 404 (1979) (provision applies "only to voluntary settlements between derivative plaintiffs and defendants. [Rule 23.1 provision does] not apply where the plaintiffs' action is involuntarily dismissed by a court."). *But cf., In re Sonus Networks, Inc, Shareholder Derivative Litigation*, 499 F.3d 47, 65 (1st Cir. 2007) (noting *Burks*, but also noting that "some involuntary dismissals have been held to be the functional equivalent of a voluntary dismissal and thus are subject to the notice-before-dismissal requirement.").

[24]*See, e.g., McDannold v. Star Bank, N.A.*, 261 F.3d 478, 488 (6th Cir. 2001) (district court "enjoys wide discretion in evaluating the settlement of derivative actions").

[25]*See, e.g., Bell Atlantic Corp. v. Bolger*, 2 F.3d 1304 (3d Cir.1993) ("We also consider the response of other shareholders to the lawsuit.").

[26]*See, e.g., United Founders Life Ins. Co. v. Consumers Nat. Life Ins. Co.*, 447 F.2d 647, 655 (7th Cir. 1971) ("The business judgment of the court is not to be substituted for that of the parties.").

[27]*See, e.g., Robert F. Booth Trust v. Crowley*, ____ F.3d ____, ____ (7th Cir. 2012) (intervention should be granted freely).

[28]*See, e.g., Robert F. Booth Trust v. Crowley*, ____ F.3d ____, ____ (7th Cir. 2012) (settlement requires notice, followed by judicial approval); *Kyriazi v. Western Elec. Co.*, 647 F.2d 388, 395 (3d Cir. 1981) (manner of notification within court's discretion, provided notice satisfies dues process).

[29]*Cohen v. Beneficial Indus. Loan Corp.*, 337 U.S. 541, 69 S. Ct. 1221, 93 L. Ed. 1528 (1949) (state bond require-

Numerosity Requirements

Rule 23.1 does not require that the plaintiff represent any number of similarly situated persons. Thus it will often be to the advantage of a shareholder who is one among a small group of similarly situated people to file a derivative action, rather than try to file a class action, which requires a greater number of plaintiffs.

Additional Research References

Wright & Miller, *Federal Practice and Procedure* §§ 1821 to 41
C.J.S., Corporations §§ 397 to 413
Federal Civil Procedure §§ 84 to 91, §§ 139, §§ 149, §§ 298; Corporations ☞202 to 214

---

ment applicable to diversity suit);   (3d Cir. 2005) (same).
Fagin v. Gilmartin, 432 F.3d 276, 285

RULE 23.2
ACTIONS RELATING TO
UNINCORPORATED ASSOCIATIONS

This rule applies to an action brought by or against the members of an unincorporated association as a class by naming certain members as representative parties. The action may be maintained only if it appears that those parties will fairly and adequately protect the interests of the association and its members. In conducting the action, the court may issue any appropriate orders corresponding with those in Rule 23(d), and the procedure for settlement, voluntary dismissal, or compromise must correspond with the procedure in Rule 23(e).

[Added effective July 1, 1966; April 30, 2007, effective December 1, 2007.]

AUTHORS' COMMENTARY ON RULE 23.2

PURPOSE AND SCOPE

Rule 23.2 extends some of the procedural protections of class actions under Rule 23 and shareholder derivative suits under Rule 23.1 to members of unincorporated associations who are sued through representatives, or on whose behalf representatives have initiated suit. The three rules all address situations where persons will be affected by the outcome of suits without necessarily having an opportunity to participate fully in litigation. Rule 23.2 is devoted to ensuring that representatives of the unincorporated association's membership adequately represent the interest of the entire membership.

NOTE: Rule 23.2 does not *create* a right for representatives of an unincorporated association to sue or be sued. Rather, it governs such a suit when the applicable state or federal law provides a cause of action by or against the unincorporated association, but does not permit suit by or against the association as an entity.[1]

---

[1] *See, e.g., Northbrook Excess and Surplus Ins. Co. v. Medical Malpractice Joint Underwriting Ass'n of Massachusetts*, 900 F.2d 476, 477 (1st Cir. 1990) ("Rule 23.2 provides a mechanism by which an association may sue or be sued through a representative where state law prevents the as-

APPLICATIONS

Requirement of Membership in Unincorporated Association: Rule 17

Before a plaintiff may represent the interests of an unincorporated association, the plaintiff must prove that an association exists and the plaintiff is a member. Rule 17(b) provides that the legal existence of an unincorporated association is controlled by the law of the forum state.[2]

Fair and Adequate Representation

The court's first concern is to ascertain whether the interests of the unincorporated association's representatives conflict with those of the association or its membership. However, the case law is divided as to whether an association's representatives in a Rule 23.2 case must meet the standards developed for adequate class representation in Rule 23(a), governing class actions.[3]

Orders Regulating Proceedings

Rule 23.2 explicitly incorporates Rule 23(d), governing the court's power to issue orders in the course of class action litigation. Because the court's authority under Rule 23(d) is broad, the effect of this incorporation is to give the trial court greater discretion to issue orders ensuring both the efficient processing of the case and substantial protection for passive members of the unincorporated association. Elements of Rule 23(d) should therefore also be consulted in the course of applying Rule 23.2.

Approval of Settlement

Rule 23.2 also explicitly incorporates Rule 23(e), which provides a court substantial authority to approve or disapprove settlements in class actions. As a practical matter, the effect is to require not only consultation of Rule 23(e), but also strong consideration of the possibility of inviting the trial judge to participate in settlement discussions whenever the discussions have advanced sufficiently to make participation practicable.

Numerosity

Rule 23.2 contains no requirement that the membership of the unincorporated association rise above some minimum

---

sociation from doing so in its own name."). *Cf., Benn v. Seventh-Day Adventist Church*, 304 F. Supp. 2d 716, 723 (D. Md. 2004) (most courts hold that where state law permits suit by unincorporated association as an entity, "Rule 23.2 is unavailable.").

[2]Fed.R.Civ.P. 17(b).

[3]*Compare Gravenstein v. Campion*, 96 F.R.D. 137, 140 (D. Alaska 1982) (Rule 23 requirements applied to Rule 23.2 lawsuit) *with* [*Curley v. Brignoli, Curley & Roberts Associates*, 915 F.2d 81, 86 (2d Cir. 1990) (requirements of Rule 23(a) do not apply to cases proceeding under Rule 23.2)].

number.[4] Nevertheless, counsel should investigate local precedent before proceeding with a Rule 23.2 action.

Citizenship for Diversity Jurisdiction

Where an unincorporated association may sue or be sued through representatives, the established practice is to determine diversity by examining the citizenship of the representatives.[5] Thus, an unincorporated association often can create diversity jurisdiction by selecting a representative who is a citizen of a different state from the defendants (provided that the amount in controversy exceeds $75,000, exclusive of interest and costs).

Amount in Controversy

The prevailing practice in federal district courts is to determine the amount in controversy by examining the individual claims of the membership of the unincorporated association. This approach creates a substantial hurdle to achieving diversity jurisdiction. Thus, if an unincorporated association has a claim for $1,000,000, the claim would appear to exceed the more-than-$75,000 requirement by a safe margin. If, however, the association has 10,000 members, and each member has an equal share in the aggregate claim of $1,000,000, the value of the suit to each member is only one hundred dollars—well short of the threshold for diversity jurisdiction.

Additional Research References

Wright & Miller, *Federal Practice and Procedure* § 1861

C.J.S., Associations § 8, §§ 40 to 48, §§ 51 to 53; Federal Civil Procedure §§ 76 to 93

West's Key Number Digest, Associations ☞20(1); Federal Civil Procedure ☞186.5

---

[4]*See, e.g., Curley v. Brignoli, Curley & Roberts Associates*, 915 F.2d 81, 86 (2d Cir. 1990) (numerosity and other prerequisites of Rule 23(a) inapplicable in Rule 23.2 case).

[5]*See, e.g., Aetna Cas. & Sur. Co. v. Iso-Tex, Inc.*, 75 F.3d 216, 218 (5th Cir. 1996) (diversity tested by looking to citizenship of named representatives); *Murray v. Scott*, 176 F. Supp. 2d 1249 (M.D. Ala. 2001) (same).

RULE 24
INTERVENTION

(a) Intervention of Right. On timely motion, the court must permit anyone to intervene who:

   (1) is given an unconditional right to intervene by a federal statute; or

   (2) claims an interest relating to the property or transaction that is the subject of the action, and is so situated that disposing of the action may as a practical matter impair or impede the movant's ability to protect its interest, unless existing parties adequately represent that interest.

(b) Permissive Intervention.

   (1) *In General.* On timely motion, the court may permit anyone to intervene who:

      (A) is given a conditional right to intervene by a federal statute; or

      (B) has a claim or defense that shares with the main action a common question of law or fact.

   (2) *By a Government Officer or Agency.* On timely motion, the court may permit a federal or state governmental officer or agency to intervene if a party's claim or defense is based on:

      (A) a statute or executive order administered by the officer or agency; or

      (B) any regulation, order, requirement, or agreement issued or made under the statute or executive order.

   (3) *Delay or Prejudice.* In exercising its discretion, the court must consider whether the intervention will unduly delay or prejudice the adjudication of the original parties' rights.

(c) Notice and Pleading Required. A motion to intervene must be served on the parties as provided in Rule 5. The motion must state the grounds for intervention and be accompanied by a pleading that sets out the claim or defense for which intervention is sought.

[Amended effective March 19, 1948; October 20, 1949; July 1, 1963; July 1, 1966; August 1, 1987; December 1, 1991; April 12, 2006, effective December 1, 2006; April 30, 2007, effective December 1, 2007.]

AUTHORS' COMMENTARY ON RULE 24

PURPOSE AND SCOPE

Rule 24 governs situations in which persons not already parties may intervene in existing litigation. Unlike most Rule 19 situations, where persons who are already parties seek to serve process on non-parties and conscript them into the litigation, in most Rule 24 situations the non-party seeks to join in litigation to which the non-party was not previously invited. Rule 24 attempts to balance the interest of the person seeking intervention with the burdens such intervention may impose on parties to pending suits. The Rule divides intervenors into two basic groups: those seeking intervention as of right under Rule 24(a); and those who seek the court's permission to intervene under Rule 24(b). Notwithstanding the terminology of those two portions of Rule 24, the court enjoys substantial discretion when deciding whether to permit intervention under either Rule 24(a) or Rule 24(b). There remain, however, important distinctions in the factors courts consider in exercising discretion under Rule 24(a) and Rule 24(b). Finally, while cases granting applications to intervene often declare that intervention provisions are to be construed liberally,[1] the application of Rule 24 to particular motions is not always as generous as such general statements might suggest.

RULE 24(a)—INTERVENTION OF RIGHT

CORE CONCEPT

Rule 24(a) identifies two distinct circumstances in which a person may be entitled to intervene in pending litigation: where a federal statute confers a right to intervene; and where the intervenor is able to satisfy all elements for intervention as of right.[2]

---

[1] *See, e.g., South Dakota ex rel Barnett v. U.S. Dept. of Interior*, 317 F.3d 783, 785 (8th Cir. 2003) (". . . Rule 24 should be liberally construed with all doubts resolved in favor of the proposed intervenor.").

[2] *See, e.g., Wilderness Society v. U.S. Forest Service*, 630 F.3d 1173, 1177 (9th Cir. 2011) ("(1) the motion must be timely; (2) the applicant must claim a 'significantly protectable' interest relating to the property or transaction which is the subject of the action; (3) the applicant must be so situated that the disposition of the action may as a practical matter impair or impede its ability to protect that interest; and (4) the applicant's interest must be

APPLICATIONS

Intervenor's Choice

There is no obligation to intervene. If the requirements of intervention are met, the decision to intervene rests with the potential intervenor.[3]

Timing

Rule 24(a) explicitly imposes a "timeliness" requirement on motions to intervene.[4] However, unlike timing elements in some other Federal Rules, the actual time limits are not set out in Rule 24(a).[5] Generally speaking, courts weigh four factors[6] in determining timeliness: (1) length of delay in seeking intervention;[7] (2) prejudicial impact of such delay on existing parties;[8] (3) prejudice to intervenor if intervention is denied; and (4)

---

inadequately represented by the parties to the action."); *League of United Latin American Citizens, Dist. 19 v. City of Boerne*, 659 F.3d 433 (5th Cir. 2011); *U.S. v. City of New York*, 198 F.3d 360, 364 (2d Cir. 1999) (movant must satisfy timeliness plus three elements enumerated in Rule 23(a)(2)).

[3]*Martin v. Wilks*, 490 U.S. 755, 109 S.Ct. 2180 (1989) (Rule 24 does not require intervention; it is permissive, not mandatory; drawing contrast with Rule 19). *See also Kourtis v. Cameron*, 419 F.3d 989 (9th Cir.2005) ("There is no duty of mandatory intervention imposed upon nonparties, and the decision not to intervene thus does not expose a nonparty to the earlier proceedings' preclusive effects."),

[4]*See, e.g., Associated Builders and Contractors, Inc. v. Herman*, 166 F.3d 1248, 1257 (D.C. Cir. 1999) ("If the motion was not timely, there is no need for the court to address the other factors that enter into an intervention analysis.").

[5]*See, e.g., Heaton v. Monogram Credit Card Bank of Georgia*, 297 F.3d 416 (5th Cir.2002) ("There are no absolute measures of timeliness; it is determined from all the circumstances."); *U.S. v. State of Wash.*, 86 F.3d 1499, 1503 (9th Cir. 1996) ("[A]ny substantial lapse of time weighs heavily against intervention."); *Atlantic Mut. Ins. Co. v. Northwest Airlines, Inc.*, 24 F.3d 958, 961 (7th Cir. 1994) (timeliness means intervenor applicant must "act with dispatch").

[6]Although substantially the same, the factors are sometimes stated differently. *See Geiger v. Foley Hoag LLP Retirement Plan*, 521 F.3d 60, 65 (1st Cir. 2008) (factors are (1) progress of case; (2) length of time intervenor knew her interest was imperiled; (3) foreseeable prejudice to existing parties if intervention is granted, or to intervenor if it is denied; and (4) any idiosyncratic circumstances that weigh for or against intervention).

[7]*See, e.g., U.S. v. Ritchie Special Credit Investments, Ltd.*, 620 F.3d 824, 831 (8th Cir. 2010) (intervention untimely where there was six-month delay between the entry of injunction freezing assets and filing of motion to intervene by secured creditor); *Zbaraz v. Madigan*, 572 F.3d 370 (7th Cir. 2009) (holding motion to intervene untimely where court had denied two motions to reconsider, defendants has filed notice of appeal, and nearly twenty-five years after initiation of litigation); *League of United Latin American Citizens v. Wilson*, 131 F.3d 1297, 1302 (9th Cir. 1997) (27 month delay in moving to intervene makes intervention motion "an uphill battle").

[8]*Cf., Effjohn Intern. Cruise Holdings, Inc. v. A&L Sales, Inc.*, 346 F.3d 552, 561 (5th Cir. 2003) (noting prejudice factor, but explaining, "[t]he inquiry for this factor is whether other parties were prejudiced *by the delay*, not whether they would be prejudiced *by the addition of the claim* (obviously, in the sense that they may obtain less, existing parties are always prejudiced by new claims) [emphasis in original]").

other factors affecting fairness in an individual case,[9] and requests for intervention during the pendency of the case from post-judgment or post-settlement requests.[10] The timeliness of a motion to intervene is frequently measured from the time the petitioner should have known his interest was not adequately represented.[11]

In this analysis, courts frequently distinguish intervention during a district court case from intervention on appeal.[12] An initial decision to reject intervention on grounds of lack of

---

[9]*See, e.g., Disability Advocates, Inc. v. New York Coalition for Quality Assisted Living, Inc.*, 675 F.3d 149, 160–161 (2d Cir. 2012) (intervention denied six years into litigation and after five week hearing where court found original plaintiff's lacked standing; "the District Court decided important questions of fact and law based entirely on the presentation of a plaintiff who lacked standing. The fact that the United States later "adopted" those findings and conclusions cannot remedy the absence of jurisdiction at trial."); *American Civil Liberties Union of Minnesota v. Tarek ibn Ziyad Academy*, 643 F.3d 1088 (8th Cir. 2011) (motion filed fourteen months after original suit untimely; no adequate explanation offered for lengthy delay which would prejudice existing parties); *Negron-Almeda v. Santiago*, 528 F.3d 15, 22–24 (1st Cir. 2008) (reviewing the factors and vacating district court's denial of intervention as untimely where lower court had misinterpreted an order relevant to would-be intervenor's knowledge of stake in the litigation); *U.S. v. Covington County School Dist.*, 499 F.3d 464, 466 (5th Cir. 2007) (applying factors and finding motion filed decades after action initiated and 15 weeks after the district court entered consent decree untimely). *See also, Associated Builders and Contractors, Inc. v. Herman*, 166 F.3d 1248, 1257 (D.C. Cir. 1999) (unexplained failure to take clear opportunity to intervene at trial is ground for denying intervention after judgment). *But cf., Associated Builders and Contractors, Saginaw Valley Area Chapter v. Perry*, 115 F.3d 386 (6th Cir.1997) (original party's decision not to appeal may create grounds for intervention even after trial court's decision).

[10]See, e.g., *Bond v. Utreras*, 585 F.3d 1061, 1071 (7th Cir. 2009) (Rule 24(b)(3) has been interpreted to suggest "that intervention postjudgment-which necessarily disturbs the final adjudication of the parties' rights-should generally be disfavored."); *R & G Mortg. Corp. v. Federal Home Loan Mortg. Corp.*, 584 F.3d 1, 10 (1st Cir. 2009) ("Requests for post-settlement intervention are rarely granted.").

[11]*See, e.g., League of United Latin American Citizens, Dist. 19 v. City of Boerne*, 659 F.3d 421, 434 (5th Cir. 2011) (motion timely when filed four weeks after filing of case); *Disability Advocates, Inc. v. New York Planned Parenthood of the Heartland v. Heineman*, 664 F.3d 716, 718 (8th Cir. 2011) (would-be intervenor failed to justify its delay in light of its prior knowledge of the case; the parties would be prejudiced because final judgment on their settlement had already been entered"); *Oklahoma ex rel. Edmondson v. Tyson Foods, Inc.*, 619 F.3d 1223, 1234–35 (10th Cir. 2010) (motion denied where "nothing had happened in the four-plus years since the State filed its complaint that would indicated that the State could no longer adequately represent" the petitioner's interest; collecting circuit cases).

[12]*Negron-Almeda v. Santiago*, 528 F.3d 15, 22 (1st Cir. 2008) (where "the proposed intervention post-dates the entry of judgment, timeliness is a crucial element in the Rule 24(a)(2) calculus"); *Elliott Industries Limited Partnership v. BP American Production Co.*, 407 F.3d 1091, 1103 (10th Cir.2005) ("[I]ntervention on appeal will be permitted 'only in exceptional case for imperative reasons.' "). Contra, *Carter v. Welles-Bowen Realty, Inc.*, 628 F.3d 790 (6th Cir. 2010) (holding without discussion that government's

timeliness is rarely disturbed on appeal.[13] This is probably the most important kind of discretion courts possess when considering applications to intervene under Rule 24(a).

"Collateral Purpose" Exception

Some courts modify the timeliness requirement of Rule 24(a) when the purpose of the intervention application is only to modify, e.g., an existing protective order.[14] This view has not been adopted in all circuits,[15] and lawyers must consult the local precedent.

Subject Matter Jurisdiction

When a person seeks to intervene as of right, subject matter jurisdiction may be established either through an independent basis of jurisdiction (such as diversity of citizenship[16] or federal question jurisdiction[17]) or through supplemental jurisdiction.[18] However, in circumstances where the basis for subject matter jurisdiction in the underlying case is diversity of citizenship and the intervening person is not diverse from the parties on the other side of the case, the availability of supplemental jurisdiction depends on whether the would-be intervenor will be aligned as a plaintiff or a defendant. If the intervenor will be a plaintiff, it is probable that the intervenor will not be able to employ supplemental jurisdiction.[19] If, on the other hand, the intervenor will be aligned as a defendant, supplemental juris-

---

motion to intervene on appeal was timely); *Flying J, Inc. v. Van Hollen*, 578 F.3d 569, 572 (7th Cir. 2009) (motion to intervene filed after final judgment found timely whereas motion during case would have been denied; party defendant to case presumed to be representing intervenor's interest during case but had chosen not to appeal). *Compare Taylor v. KeyCorp*, 680 F.3d 609, 616 (6th Cir. 2012) (motion to intervene after filing of notice of appeal denied; district court divested of jurisdiction by notice of appeal).

[13]*See, e.g., Negron-Almeda v. Santiago*, 528 F.3d 15, 21 (1st Cir. 2008) (applying abuse of discretion standard to district court's ruling regarding timeliness of motion for intervention as of right, holding "abuse of discretion is a relatively deferential standard of review" but not a "rubber stamp"). *Caterino v. Barry*, 922 F.2d 37, 40 (1st Cir. 1990) (trial court entitled to "substantive deference" on timeliness). *Cf., League of United Latin American Citizens, Dist. 19 v. City of Boerne*, 659 F.3d 421, 433 (5th Cir. 2011) (*de novo* standard applied

to timeliness when the district court makes no finding on the issue); *Puerto Rico Telephone Co. v. Sistema de Retiro de los Empleados del Gobiern y la Judicatura, et al.*, 637 F.3d 10, 14–15 (1st Cir. 2011) (remanding for reconsideration of timeliness issue where district court gave no explanation for denial).

[14]*See, e.g., United Nuclear Corp. v. Cranford Ins. Co.*, 905 F.2d 1424, 1427 (10th Cir. 1990). *See also Pansy v. Borough of Stroudsburg*, 23 F.3d 772, 780 n. 9 (3d Cir. 1994).

[15]*See, e.g., Empire Blue Cross and Blue Shield v. Janet Greeson's A Place For Us, Inc.*, 62 F.3d 1217, 1221 (9th Cir. 1995); *Banco Popular de Puerto Rico v. Greenblatt*, 964 F.2d 1227, 1230–34 (1st Cir. 1992) (refusing to modify timeliness requirement for limited purpose motion).

[16]28 U.S.C.A. § 1332.

[17]28 U.S.C.A. § 1331.

[18]28 U.S.C.A. § 1367.

[19]28 U.S.C.A. § 1367(b) (in cases where original basis of jurisdiction is diversity and person intervening un-

diction will normally be available.[20] Where a party who is dispensable under Rule 19 and is also nondiverse seeks to intervene under Rule 24, diversity jurisdiction is not necessarily defeated.[21]

Where the original basis for jurisdiction in the underlying case is a federal question, the problem resolves itself in a more straightforward manner. In those situations, supplemental jurisdiction is routinely available without regard to the intervenor's status as a plaintiff or defendant.[22]

Intervention cannot be used to establish jurisdiction for the underlying suit. If the court does not have competent jurisdiction, intervention cannot be used to cure as Rule 24 does not provide a basis for jurisdiction.[23] However, a "curative approach" has been recognized that allows the court to treat the pleading of an intervenor as a separate action even if the underlying claim is jurisdictionally deficient where the intervention is sought before any action has been taken by the defendants.[24]

der Rule 24 will be aligned as a plaintiff, supplemental jurisdiction is not available). *Exxon Mobil Corp. v. Allapattah Services, Inc.*, 545 U.S. 546, 125 S. Ct. 2611, 2621, 162 L. Ed. 2d 502 (2005) ("Section 1367(b) withholds supplemental jurisdiction over the claims of plaintiffs who seek to intervene pursuant to Rule 24."). *Griffin v. Lee*, 621 F.3d 380, 388–89 (5th Cir. 2010) (district court lacked supplemental jurisdiction over attorney's claim in intervention seeking attorney's fees accrued prior to his withdrawal from the case, where complete diversity of citizenship, on which district court's original jurisdiction was founded, was lacking; court charged with looking beyond pleadings to ensure that parties are aligned properly before determining whether intervention appropriate). *But cf., Aurora Loan Services, Inc. v. Craddieth*, 442 F.3d 1018, 1025 (7th Cir. 2006) (in diversity cases supplemental jurisdiction normally not available to intervenor plaintiffs; but prohibition on use of supplemental jurisdiction inapplicable where a person is "forced to intervene to protect an interest that arose during the course of a federal litigation in which he had no stake at the outset").

[20]*Exxon Mobil Corp. v. Allapattah Services, Inc.*, 545 U.S. 546, 125 S. Ct. 2611, 2621, 162 L. Ed. 2d 502 (2005) (noting that 28 U.S.C.A. § 1367(b) does not prohibit use of supplemental juris-

diction in such circumstances).

[21]*In re Olympic Mills Corp.*, 477 F.3d 1, 12 (1st Cir. 2007) (in bankruptcy case, court reviewed case law and concluded "the weight of authority holds that claims launched by necessary but dispensable, nondiverse defendant-intervenors do not defeat the original jurisdiction (diversity) that obtained at the commencement of the action").

[22]*See, e.g., Grace United Methodist Church v. City Of Cheyenne*, 451 F.3d 643, 672–73 (10th Cir. 2006) (for intervention of right in case originally based on federal question jurisdiction, supplemental jurisdiction is sufficient and no independent basis of jurisdiction is require).

[23]*Disability Advocates, Inc. v. New York Coalition for Quality Assisted Living, Inc.*, 675 F.3d 149, 160–161 (2d Cir. 2012) (intervention denied six years into litigation and after five week hearing where court found original plaintiff's lacked standing).

[24]*See, e.g., Miller & Miller Auctioneers, Inc. v. G.W. Murphy Indus., Inc.*, 472 F.2d 893, 895–96 (10th Cir. 1973) (upheld interpleader where intervenor had separate and independent basis for jurisdiction despite lack of jurisdiction for underlying case); *Hackner v. Guar. Trust Co.*, 117 F.2d 95, 98 (2d Cir. 1941) (Amendment to Complaint adding plaintiff

Subject matter jurisdiction is discussed at greater length elsewhere in this text.

Personal Jurisdiction

When a person attempts to intervene under Rule 24, that person submits to the jurisdiction of the court.[25] However, where the would-be intervenor simultaneously objects to personal jurisdiction, the court may find he has not consented.[26]

Statutory Right Narrowly Construed

Rule 24(a)(1) explicitly defers to any other federal statute that confers on qualifying persons an unconditional right to intervene in pending litigation. If applicants for statutory intervention demonstrate a right to intervene under Rule 24(a)(1), they "need not show inadequacy of representation or that their interests may be impaired if not allowed to intervene" as is required for intervention under Rule 24(a)(2).[27] However, the case law demonstrates a clear judicial tendency to construe statutory intervention rights narrowly.[28] As a practical result, persons seeking to intervene under Rule 24(a) should routinely consider arguing for intervention under the "interest" test of Rule 24(a)(2)—even in circumstances where they believe they might qualify for intervention as a statutory right under Rule 24(a)(1).[29]

Amicus Curiae Briefs

There may appear to be a superficial similarity between the

---

filed twenty-two days after initial complaint and before any action by the defendants).

[25]*See, e.g., County Sec. Agency v. Ohio Dept. of Commerce*, 296 F.3d 477 (6th Cir. 2002) (refusing to permit reservation of objections to jurisdiction made by petitioning intervenor; "a motion to intervene is fundamentally incompatible with an objection to personal jurisdiction").

[26]*S.E.C. v. Ross*, 504 F.3d 1130, 1149–50 (9th Cir. 2007) (reviews cases and acknowledges that courts have generally concluded that a party who intervenes consents to jurisdiction as a matter of law, but declines to find such consent where intervenor objected to court's exercise of personal jurisdiction, sufficiency of process, and venue).

[27]*Ruiz v. Estelle*, 161 F.3d 814, 828 (5th Cir. 1998) ("Under Rule 24(a)(1), intervenors need not even prove a 'sufficient' interest relating to the subject matter of the controversy, since *Congress* has already declared that interest sufficient by granting the statutory right to intervene." However, statutory intervention is still subject to a determination of timeliness, over which the district court enjoys substantial discretion.). *See also Newdow v. U.S. Congress*, 313 F.3d 495, 497 (9th Cir. 2002) (statute granting right to intervene in instant case also imposes requirement of timely application).

[28]*See, e.g., Phar-Mor, Inc. v. Coopers & Lybrand*, 22 F.3d 1228, 1232 (3d Cir. 1994) ("[C]ourts have construed Rule 24(a)(1) narrowly; these courts have been reluctant to interpret statutes to grant an unconditional right to intervene to private parties."); *Compare Schultz v. U.S.*, 594 F.3d 1120, 1123 (9th Cir. 2010) (where Mandatory Victims Restitution Act provided for exclusive remedy, no intervention as of right would be allowed).

[29]*Cf., Yorkshire v. U.S. I.R.S.*, 26 F.3d 942, 944 (9th Cir. 1994) (Rule 24(a)(2) "is construed broadly in favor of the applicants").

process of intervention and the opportunity to file an amicus curiae brief. However, courts do not equate amicus status with the rights and responsibilities of a party joined through intervention.[30]

Right to Intervene Generally

The right to intervene under Rule 24(a)(2) exists only when the court holds that a person seeking intervention has established three elements: (1) an interest in the subject matter of the pending litigation; (2) a substantial risk that the litigation will impair the interest; and (3) existing parties do not adequately protect that interest. Courts sometimes add timeliness to these factors.[31] These elements are *not* weighing factors. *All* must be satisfied before an applicant may exercise a right to intervene under Rule 24(a)(2).[32] Not all courts give the three factors equal weight.[33]

Once intervention is granted the intervening party must continue to meet these requirements throughout the duration of the litigation, or is subject to being dismissed from the case.[34]

Interest in the Subject Matter

The definition of an "interest" that satisfies Rule 24(a)(2) is

---

[30]*See, e.g., U.S. v. City of Los Angeles, Cal.*, 288 F.3d 391, 400 (9th Cir. 2002) ("[A]micus status is insufficient to protect the [petitioner for intervention's] rights because such status does not allow the [petitioner] to raise issues or arguments formally and gives it no right of appeal."); *Coalition of Arizona/New Mexico Counties for Stable Economic Growth v. Department of Interior*, 100 F.3d 837, 844 (10th Cir. 1996) ("[T]he right to file a brief as amicus curiae is no substitute for the right to intervene as a party in the action under Rule 24(a)(2)."). Courts sometimes agree to consider the filings of a failed intervenor as they would the filings of amicus curiae. *See, e.g., Coalition to Defend Affirmative Action v. Regents of University of Michigan*, 652 F.3d 607, 633 (6th Cir. 2011) (while party was rejected as intervenor, judges "nonetheless have considered his filings as we would those of amicus curiae"); *Brandt v. Goodling*, 636 F.3d 124, 131 (4th Cir. 2011) (same).

[31]*See, e.g., League of United Latin American Citizens, Dist. 19 v. City of Boerne*, 659 F.3d 421, 433 (5th Cir. 2011); *Negron-Almeda v. Santiago*, 528 F.3d 15, 22 (1st Cir. 2008); *Fox v.*

Tyson Foods, Inc., 519 F.3d 1298, 1302–3 (11th Cir. 2008); *Coalition to Defend Affirmative Action v. Granholm*, 501 F.3d 775, 779 (6th Cir. 2007).

[32]*See, e.g., Americans United for Separation of Church and State v. City of Grand Rapids*, 922 F.2d 303, 305 (6th Cir. 1990) (intervenor must satisfy all elements). *But cf., Ross v. Marshall*, 426 F.3d 745, 753 (5th Cir. 2005) (acknowledging that all elements must be met, but examination should be flexible and non-technical; "Intervention should generally be allowed where 'no one would be hurt and greater justice could be attained.' ").

[33]*See WildEarth Guardians v. National Park Service*, 604 F.3d 1192, 1199–1200 (10th Cir. 2010) (impairment of interest and inadequate representation were both minimal burdens).

[34]*Coalition to Defend Affirmative Action v. Regents of University of Michigan*, ___ F.3d __ (6th Cir. 2011) (dismissing party after he entered stipulation with defendant effectively aligning their interests and making his "presence in the litigation . . . a mere makeweight"; collecting cases).

unclear.[35] It is at least reasonably clear that a person who has an interest that by itself could be a case or controversy will meet the requirement of Rule 24(a)(2).[36] However, it is not necessary that the intervenor be a party with the right to bring the cause of action independently.[37] An economic interest in the subject matter of the litigation may satisfy this element of the Rule;[38] however, a property interest is not essential.[39] A

---

[35]*See, e.g., Utahns for Better Transp. v. U.S. Dept. of Transp.*, 295 F.3d 1111 (10th Cir. 2002) ("The sufficiency of an applicant's interest is a highly fact-specific determination." Also noting that "[t]here is some value in having the parties before the court so that they will be bound by the result."); *Daggett v. Commission on Governmental Ethics and Election Practices*, 172 F.3d 104, 110 (1st Cir. 1999) (noting that narrow reading of interest is disfavored, "although clear outer boundaries have yet to be developed").

[36]*See, e.g., Aurora Loan Services, Inc. v. Craddieth*, 442 F.3d 1018, 1022 (7th Cir. 2006) ("[T]he applicant's interest must be one on which an independent federal suit could be based, consistent with Article III's requirement that only a case or controversy can be litigated in a federal court at any stage of the proceeding.").

[37]*See, e.g., U.S. v. Philip Morris USA Inc.*, 566 F.3d 1095, 1145 (D.C. Cir. 2009) (public health organizations which could not have instituted RICO suit were nevertheless entitled to intervene in government's RICO prosecution); *Solid Waste Agency of Northern Cook County v. U.S. Army Corps of Engineers*, 101 F.3d 503, 507 (7th Cir. 1996) ("The strongest case for intervention is not where the aspirant for intervention could file an independent suit, but where the intervenor-aspirant has no claim against the defendant yet a legally protected interest that could be impaired by the suit.").

[38]*See, e.g., Flying J, Inc. v. Van Hollen*, 578 F.3d 569, 572 (7th Cir. 2009) (gasoline retailers who sought to intervene in suit to invalidate state law setting minimum price for gasoline had sufficient interest to intervene as of right as they would be "directly rather than remotely harmed by the

invalidation of the statute", loosing business to more efficient competitors); *In re Estate of Ferdinand E. Marcos Human Rights Litigation*, 536 F.3d 980, 987 (9th Cir. 2008) (Texas landowners had significant protectable interest to intervene in proceeding brought by judgment creditors to extend an expired judgment allowing foreclosure proceedings upon the landowners' property); *Fund For Animals, Inc. v. Norton*, 322 F.3d 728, 733 (D.C. Cir. 2003) (interest of foreign government agency in protecting flow of tourist dollars meets interest requirement of Rule 24(a)); *Utahns for Better Transp. v. U.S. Dept. of Transp.*, 295 F.3d 1111 (10th Cir. 2002) ("The threat of economic injury from the outcome of the litigation undoubtedly gives a petitioner the requisite interest."); *U.S. v. Peoples Benefit Life Ins. Co.*, 271 F.3d 411, 416 (2d Cir. 2001) (constructive trust may sometimes be sufficient interest to support intervention in forfeiture case.) *But see, Medical Liability Mut. Ins. Co. v. Alan Curtis LLC*, 485 F.3d 1006, 1008 (8th Cir. 2007) (held that an economic interest in the outcome of the litigation was not itself sufficient to warrant mandatory intervention and denied intervention where only interest was to ensure sufficient resources to satisfy would-be intervenor's claim); *Mt. Hawley Ins. Co. v. Sandy Lake Properties, Inc.*, 425 F.3d 1308, 1311 (11th Cir. 2005) ("legally protectable interest" is "more than an economic interest"); *State of Montana v. U.S. E.P.A.*, 137 F.3d 1135, 1142 (9th Cir. 1998) ("[A] speculative and purely economic interest does not create a protectable interest in litigation concerning a statute that regulates environmental, not economic interests.");

[39]*See, e.g., U.S. v. Brennan*, 650 F.3d 65, 81 (2d Cir. 2011) (white intervenors seeking to protect seniority

substantial privacy interest has also been found sufficient.[40] Also, if the intervening party will be legally bound by the judgment in the pending litigation, an "interest" exists that satisfies Rule 24(a)(2).[41] A desire to add to the factual record has been found insufficient.[42] Other cases construe the concept of "interest" more broadly.[43]

---

rights had sufficient interest to intervene in Title VII action alleging discriminatory hiring practices by school board); *WildEarth Guardians v. National Park Service*, 604 F.3d 1192, 1198–1201 (10th Cir. 2010) (hunting and conservation organization allowed to intervene as of right in suit brought by environmental organization challenging National Park Service's proposal to cull elk population; groups interest in culling of elk was sufficient interest to intervene, and impairment of interest and inadequate representation were both minimal burdens); *U.S. v. Carpenter*, 526 F.3d 1237, 1241 (9th Cir. 2008) (environmental groups' interest in seeing wilderness area preserved was sufficient to allow them to intervene in Quiet Title Act action even though they did not have a property interest).

[40]*Doe v. Oberweis Dairy*, 456 F.3d 704, 718 (7th Cir. 2006) (mother and sister of plaintiff asserting Title VII sexual harassment were entitled to intervene to contest trial court's grant of employer's motion for access to the plaintiff's psychiatric records, where mother and sister were present and participated in some of the sessions). Cf. *In re Request from United Kingdom Pursuant to Treaty Between Government of U.S. and Government of United . . .*, 685 F.3d 1, 22 (1st Cir. 2012) (academic researchers did not have a legally-significant protectable interest to intervene in criminal proceeding attempting to subpoena information from their institution despite intention of donator that information be kept confidential).

[41]*See, e.g., Stauffer v. Brooks Brothers, Inc.*, 619 F.3d 1321, 1329 (Fed. Cir. 2010) (intervention allowed where res judicata would prevent government from recovering fine for violation of patent); *City of Emeryville v. Robinson*, 621 F.3d 1251 (9th Cir.

2010) (property owners in CERCLA case has sufficient interest to intervene when facing imminent extinction of their state law rights of contribution for site clean-up costs, even though the interest was contingent upon the outcome of the litigation); *Triax Co. v. TRW, Inc.*, 724 F.2d 1224, 1227 (6th Cir. 1984) (collateral estoppel).

[42]*Brandt v. Gooding*, 636 F.3d 124, 131 (4th Cir. 2011) (upheld denial of intervention as of right to attorney who sought to intervene in former client's habeas proceeding; attorney "sought 'to add to the factual record' . . . this interest failed 'to satisfy the requirements for intervention of right or permissive intervention' ").

[43]*See, e.g., Bridgeport Guardians, Inc. v. Delmonte*, 602 F.3d 469, 474 (2nd Cir. 2010) (White and Hispanic police officers allowed to intervene as of right in city challenge to 1982 order intended to remedy civil rights violations against minorities when officers claimed proposed settlement permitted illegal race-norming of tests required for promotions; intervenors had sufficient interest in their employers' employment practices); *Roeder v. Islamic Republic of Iran*, 333 F.3d 228, 233 (D.C. Cir. 2003) (interest in protecting diplomatic agreement with foreign sovereign that might be affected by litigation gave United States interest that met intervention requirement); *In re Grand Jury Subpoena*, 274 F.3d 563, 570 (1st Cir. 2001) (appropriate intervention by attorney and corporate officers to attempt to quash grand jury subpoena; "[c]olorable claims of attorney-client and work product privilege qualify as sufficient interests to ground intervention as of right"); *Cotter v. Massachusetts Ass'n of Minority Law Enforcement Officers*, 219 F.3d 31, 34–36 (1st Cir. 2000) (black police officers previously promoted have interest in intervening in

Impairment of Interest

Rule 24(a)(2) declares that risk of impairment to an applicant's interest may include legal impairment, such as a risk that principles of stare decisis may apply.[44] At the same time, other practical consequences of litigation may also satisfy the "impairment" element. For example, even though a party may not, through res judicata or collateral estoppel, be bound by the judgment, a substantial risk of practical impairments can sometimes constitute sufficient risk of "impairment" to a party seeking to intervene.[45]

Adequate Representation by Existing Parties

Even if the person seeking intervention demonstrates that

---

suit alleging racial discrimination in promotions harmful to white officers; interest is in protecting promotions of black officers; organization of officers also has interest in intervening to protect interests of black officers who are not parties to suit); *Loyd v. Alabama Dept. of Corrections*, 176 F.3d 1336, 1339 (11th Cir. 1999) (state attorney general need not demonstrate standing before intervening in lawsuit over prisoners' rights, provided that existing parties have satisfied requirement of justiciable case or controversy); *Coalition of Arizona/New Mexico Counties for Stable Economic Growth v. Department of Interior*, 100 F.3d 837, 841 (10th Cir. 1996) (granting intervention where there is little economic interest, but intervenor has interest based on involvement with issue and record of advocacy of protection of affected wildlife); *but cf., Kootenai Tribe of Idaho v. Veneman*, 313 F.3d 1094, 1108 (9th Cir. 2002) (where statute creates liability only for government, private party cannot meet rigorous standard of interest that justifies intervention; however, permissive intervention under Rule 24(b) may still be possible, because lower standard of common question of law or fact may still be met). *But see League of United Latin American Citizens, Dist. 19 v. City of Boerne*, 659 F.3d 421, 434–35 (5th Cir. 2011) (voter had sufficient interest to intervene where outcome impacted his right to vote and he had no other procedural vehicle to protect his interest); *Perry v. Schwarzenegger*, 630 F.3d 898, 903–04 (9th Cir. 2011) (intervention in suit challenging constitutionality of law prohib-

iting same-sex marriages denied; deputy county clerk's desire to avoid "legal uncertainty and confusion" not a "significant protectable interest"); *Coalition to Defend Affirmative Action v. Granholm*, 501 F.3d 775, 781–83 (6th Cir. 2007) (finding that organizations that favored constitutional amendment had a "general ideological interest" and not a "substantial legal interest" and therefore could not intervene as of right in action challenging validity of amendment);

[44]*See, e.g., Sierra Club v. Espy*, 18 F.3d 1202, 1207 (5th Cir. 1994) (stare decisis effect of decision is sufficient potential impairment to satisfy requirements of Rule 24(a)(2)). *See also U.S. v. City of Los Angeles, Cal.*, 288 F.3d 391, 401 (9th Cir. 2002) (potential impairment is sufficient; no requirement that outcome will necessarily impair interest).

[45]*See, e.g., City of Chicago v. Federal Emergency Management Agency*, 660 F.3d 980, 986 (7th Cir. 2011) (ability of would-be intervenor to litigate claim in future not automatic bar to intervention); *Utah Ass'n of Counties v. Clinton*, 255 F.3d 1246, 1253 (10th Cir. 2001) (question of impairment cannot be separated from question of existence of interest; moreover, " 'the court is not limited to consequences of a strictly legal nature' "); *Grutter v. Bollinger*, 188 F.3d 394, 400 (6th Cir. 1999) ("minimal requirements" of impairment satisfied by likely prospect that access of minority students to university will be impaired if university stops using race as criterion in admissions).

the elements of "interest" and "impairment" are satisfied, intervention under Rule 24(a)(2) will be denied if the interest at risk is represented adequately by persons already parties to the action.[46] The burden of establishing inadequate representation is on the applicant for intervention but is minimal.[47] Typically, a potential intervenor will not have great difficulty establishing a lack of adequate representation by existing parties,[48] unless the intervenor and an existing party share identical objectives.[49]

Lack of adequate representation is most easily demonstrated if the interest is not currently represented at all, or if the persons already parties have positions clearly adverse to those of the intervention applicant.[50] Moreover, a difference in tactics does not of itself necessarily indicate a lack of adequate

---

[46]*See, e.g., Daggett v. Commission on Governmental Ethics and Election Practices*, 172 F.3d 104, 111 (1st Cir. 1999) (rebuttable presumption that government's defense of validity of statute adequately represents interests of citizens who support statute); *Clark v. Putnam County*, 168 F.3d 458, 461 (11th Cir. 1999) ("weak" presumption of adequate representation when "existing party seeks the same objectives as the would-be intervenor").

[47]*Haspel & Davis Milling & Planting Co. Ltd. v. Board Of Levee Commissioners of The Orleans Levee Dist. and State Of Louisiana*, 493 F.3d 570 (5th Cir. 2007) (State of Louisiana could not intervene as it did not satisfy burden of showing inadequate representing by existing party; levee board could adequately defend Louisiana's anti-seizure provisions). *See also Kane County, Utah v. U.S.*, 597 F.3d 1129, 1135 (10th Cir. 2010) (no intervention as of right when environmental group failed to show U.S. would not adequately protect its interest in action to quiet titled to roads crossing federal public lands); *Sierra Club, Inc. v. Leavitt*, 488 F.3d 904, 910 (11th Cir. 2007) (The Florida Department of Environmental Protection could not intervene in suit alleging Clean Water Act violations as its interests were adequately represented by the Sierra Club; no evidence presented to refute "weak" presumption of adequate representation when existing party seeks the same objectives as the would-be intervenors.)

[48]*Trbovich v. United Mine Workers of America*, 404 U.S. 528, 538 n.10, 92 S. Ct. 630, 636, 30 L. Ed. 2d 686 (1972) ("The requirement of the Rule is satisfied if the applicant shows that representation of his interest 'may be' inadequate; and the burden of making that showing should be treated as minimal."). *But see Southern Utah Wilderness Alliance v. Kempthorne*, 525 F.3d 966, 970 (10th Cir. 2008) (denied intervention of lessees in suit brought by environmental organizations challenging Bureau of Land Management's (BLM) sale of oil and gas leases on public land, ruling that BLM adequately represented lessees interest, and any damage to them was speculative).

[49]*See, e.g., B. Fernandez & Hnos., Inc. v. Kellogg USA, Inc.*, 440 F.3d 541, 546 (1st Cir. 2006) ("[I]n cases where the intervenor's ultimate objective matches that of the named party, a rebuttable presumption of adequate representation applies.").

[50]*See, e.g., City of Chicago v. Federal Emergency Management Agency*, 660 F.3d 980, 986–87 (7th Cir. 2011) (intervention of right appropriate when original party does not advance ground that would confer a tangible benefit on intervenor); *Perry v. Brown*, 671 F.3d 1052, 1068 (9th Cir. 2012) (proponents of state constitutional amendment outlawing gay marriage allowed to intervene in suit challenging constitutionality of amendment where existing defendants refused to argue for amendment's constitutionality); *Citizens for Balanced Use v. Montana Wilderness*

representation.[51] Adequate representation is generally presumed where a state represents its citizens, citizens seek to intervene as of right, and the state shares the same interest as the citizens.[52] There must continue to be a lack of adequate rep-

---

Association, 647 F.3d 893, 899 (9th Cir. 2011) (U.S. Forest Service did not adequately represent interests of conservation groups in action challenging order limiting motorized vehicles in wilderness study area; Service acted under compulsion of district court decision gained by previous litigation and Service was appealing that prior decision; appeal "demonstrates the fundamentally differing points of view between Applicants and the Forest Service on the litigation as a whole"); *Twelve John Does v. District of Columbia*, 117 F.3d 571 (D.C. Cir. 1997) (existing representation is generally adequate where there is no conflicting interest between representative and would-be intervenor and where representative has ability to litigate the issues with vigor); *Freedom from Religion Foundation, Inc. v. Geithner*, 644 F.3d 836 (9th Cir. 2011) (presumption of adequate representation not rebutted by ministers attempting to intervene in suit challenging constitutionality of tax exemptions; no showing defendants U.S. Treasury Department and California Tax Board construed statute differently from ministers). But see *Jordan v. Michigan Conference of Teamsters Welfare Fund*, 207 F.3d 854, 863 (6th Cir. 2000) (movant's burden is only to show that representation "may be" inadequate, not that representation "will in fact be inadequate".

[51]*See, e.g., U.S. v. City of Miami*, 278 F.3d 1174, 1179 (11th Cir. 2002) (police associations concerned with advancement of blacks and women is adequately represented by government interest in ending discrimination for all minorities); *Grutter v. Bollinger*, 188 F.3d 394, 401 (6th Cir. 1999) (prospect that university, in defending against challenge to admissions program based partly on race, may not present evidence of its own past discrimination; minority students have therefore demonstrated that existing representation by university is inade-

quate); *B.H. v. McDonald*, 49 F.3d 294 (7th Cir.1995) (party's preference to in-chamber conferences as opposed to open court hearings does not constitute inadequate representation). *But see B. Fernandez & Hnos., Inc. v. Kellogg USA, Inc.*, 440 F.3d 541, 546 (1st Cir. 2006) (presumption of adequate representation not established solely by fact that existing party and intervenor are subsidiaries of same parent); *Utahns for Better Transp. v. U.S. Dept. of Transp.*, 295 F.3d 1111 (10th Cir. 2002) (burden of showing inadequacy of representation is minimal; relying on government creates potential conflict between government's duty to protect public interest and private interests of private intervention petitioners; also, private parties have expertise that government lacks; finally, government's silence on its intent to protect private parties is "deafening"); *U.S. v. City of Los Angeles, Cal.*, 288 F.3d 391, 401–02 (9th Cir. 2002) (presumption that government will adequately represent interests "arises when the government is acting on behalf of a constituency that it represents. . . . The situation is different when the government acts as an employer, as here. . . . The presumption has not been applied to parties who are antagonists in the collective bargaining process.").

[52]*Department of Fair Employment and Housing v. Lucent Technologies, Inc.*, 642 F.3d 728, 740 (9th Cir. 2011) ("In the absence of a very compelling showing to the contrary, it will be presumed that a state adequately represents its citizens when the applicant shares the same interest."). *See also San Juan County v. U.S.*, 503 F.3d 1163, 1204–05 (10th Cir. 2007) (distinguishing between cases that implicate private rights and those that raise issue of public interest, and denying intervention despite protectable interest when government is a party pursuing a single objective which is aligned with petitioner).

resentation by other parties throughout the litigation or the intervenor risks being dismissed from the case.[53]

Judicial Discretion

The grant or denial of a motion to intervene as of right is generally reviewed under the abuse-of-discretion standard.[54]

Burden of Proof

While an applicant seeking to intervene as of right has the burden to show that requirements for intervention are met, those requirements are broadly interpreted in favor of intervention.[55]

Status of Intervenor: Standing

Assuming that an intervenor applicant satisfies the requirements of Rule 24(a)(2), the intervenor may participate as a party. However, left open is whether the intervenor, like a party, must satisfy the requirement of independent standing.[56] The courts are divided on this issue. Attorneys must consult local precedent.[57] In considering the issue, the 11th Circuit concluded that the failure to require standing by intervenors

---

[53]*Coalition to Defend Affirmative Action v. Regents of University of Michigan*, 652 F.3d 607, 633 (6th Cir. 2011) (dismissing intervening party after he entered stipulation with defendant effectively aligning their interests; "courts must be able to ensure that parties maintain a live interest in a case," citing authority).

[54]*See, e.g., Ungar v. Arafat*, 634 F.3d 46 (1st Cir. 2011); *Stauffer v. Brooks Brothers, Inc.*, 619 F.3d 1321, 1329 (Fed. Cir. 2010). The Ninth Circuit applies a "de novo" standard to the motion generally and an "abuse-of-discretion" standard to the timeliness prong. *See, e.g., Citizens for Balanced Use v. Montana Wilderness Association*, 647 F.3d 893 896 (9th Cir. 2011).

[55]*Citizens for Balanced Use v. Montana Wilderness Association*, 647 F.3d 893 897 (9th Cir. 2011). *See also U.S. v. Ritchie Special Credit Investments, Ltd.*, 620 F.3d 824, 831 (8th Cir. 2010) (court construes the federal rule of civil procedure governing intervention liberally and resolves any doubts in favor of the proposed intervenors).

[56]*See, e.g., City of Chicago v. Federal Emergency Management Agency*, 660 F.3d 980, 986–87 (7th Cir. 2011) (discussing conflict among cir-

cuits); *American Auto. Ins. Co. v. Murray*, 658 F.3d 311, 318 n. 4 (3d Cir. 2011) (neither this Court nor the Supreme Court has determined whether a potential intervenor must have Article III standing); *Diamond v. Charles*, 476 U.S. 54, 68–69, 106 S. Ct. 1697, 90 L. Ed. 2d 48 (1986) (leaving undecided the question whether every intervenor must demonstrate standing in addition to the requirements of Rule 24).

[57]Compare, *e.g., City of Chicago v. Federal Emergency Management Agency*, 660 F.3d 980, 984–85 (7th Cir. 2011); *American Civil Liberties Union of Minnesota v. Tarek ibn Ziyad Academy*, 643 F.3d 1088, 1092 (8th Cir. 2011) ("When a party opposes a motion to intervene on the basis of standing, the prospective intervenor must allege facts showing the familiar elements of Article III standing."); *DSI Associates LLC v. U.S.*, 496 F.3d 175 (2d Cir. 2007) (party who lacked standing could not reframe to intervene) *with, e.g., League of United Latin American Citizens, Dist. 19 v. City of Boerne*, 659 F.3d 421, 428 (5th Cir. 2011) (intervenor must establish standing if not seeking any relief that is also being sought by an original party with standing); *City of Colorado Springs v. Climax Molybdenum Co.*,

would make intervention of right too easy and thus "clutter too many lawsuits with too many parties."[58]

Class Actions

A class member seeking intervention as of right must satisfy the same requirements as other intervenors.[59] It is settled that if a non-named class member objects in a timely manner to a proposed settlement, that member need not intervene in order to appeal the settlement.[60] In a class action lawsuit, the timeliness clock does not start running until the putative intervenor knows that the class representative will not represent his interest.[61]

Conditional Intervention

It appears that if a court permits intervention as of right, it may impose conditions on such intervention.[62]

RULE 24(b)—PERMISSIVE INTERVENTION

CORE CONCEPT

Rule 24(b) contains provisions under which a person may move to intervene, but does not confer a right to intervene. Rule 24(b) applies a substantially more relaxed approach to motions to intervene. A person seeking permission to intervene under Rule 24(b) need not demonstrate the sort of interest required for intervention under Rule 24(a)(2). The court's discretion to reject

---

587 F.3d 1071, 1079 (10th Cir. 2009) (parties seeking to intervene as of right or permissively need not have independent standing so long as another party with constitutional standing on the same side as the intervenor remains in the case); *Dillard v. Chilton County Commission*, 495 F.3d 1324, 1336–37 (11th Cir. 2007) (intervenor can "piggyback" on the standing of the original parties); *Newby v. Enron Corp.*, 443 F.3d 416, 422 (5th Cir. 2006) ("this requirement has been construed liberally"); *United States v. Tennessee*, 260 F.3d 587, 595 (6th Cir. 2001) (an intervenor need not have the same standing necessary to initiate a lawsuit).

[58]*City of Chicago v. Federal Emergency Management Agency*, 660 F.3d 980, 984–85 (7th Cir. 2011).

[59]*In re Pet Foods Products Liability Litigation*, 629 F.3d 333, 349 (3d Cir. 2010).

[60]*Devlin v. Scardelletti*, 536 U.S. 1, 122 S. Ct. 2005, 153 L. Ed. 2d 27 (2002) (held, such a party easily satisfies standing requirement, and right to appeal is not restricted to named

parties).

[61]*See, e.g., In re Lease Oil Antitrust Litigation*, 570 F.3d 244, 248 (5th Cir. 2009). *See also Sierra Club v. Espy*, 18 F.3d 1202, 1206 (5th Cir. 1994) (noting alacrity with which would-be intervenor acted when it became aware that its interest would no longer be protected by original parties).

[62]*See, e.g., United States v. Albert Inv. Co., Inc.*, 585 F.3d 1386, 1396 (10th Cir. 2009) (the district court has the ability to lessen any potential delay by denying discovery or by denying an evidentiary hearing); *Walsh v. Walsh*, 221 F.3d 204, 213 (1st Cir. 2000) ("[I]t was well within the district court's discretion to limit [a person's] intervention, which took place long after trial and judgment, to a distinct legal issue that required no additional factfinding."); *Beauregard, Inc. v. Sword Services L.L.C.*, 107 F.3d 351, 352 (5th Cir. 1997) (permitting intervention provided, *inter alia,* that intervenor agreed to seize asset and help pay cost of maintaining asset; noting contrary scholarly authority).

Rule 24(b)(2) intervention applications, however, is substantially greater than its capacity to reject a Rule 24(a)(2) application.[63]

APPLICATIONS

Common Question of Law or Fact

The bedrock requirement for Rule 24(b)(2) permissive intervention is a demonstration by the person seeking intervention that there exists a common question of law or fact between that person's claim or defense and the pending litigation.[64]

Discretion

The standard of review for permissive intervention is clear abuse of discretion.[65] The district court must, of course, apply the correct legal standard to be entitled to this deference.[66] A district court's decision to deny permissive intervention is almost never overturned on appeal.[67]

---

[63]*United States v. Albert Inv. Co., Inc.*, 585 F.3d 1386, 1390 (10th Cir. 2009) (court of appeals reviews the denial of motion to intervene as of right de novo and denial of motion for permissive intervention for abuse of discretion).

[64]*See, e.g., Kootenai Tribe of Idaho v. Veneman*, 313 F.3d 1094, 1108 (9th Cir. 2002) (standard for permissive intervention under rule 24(b) is common question of law or fact, not more rigorous standard of interest that may be impaired); *Griffith v. University Hosp., L.L.C.*, 249 F.3d 658, 661 (7th Cir. 2001) (Rule 24(b) is appropriate way for third party to challenge protective order); *E.E.O.C. v. National Children's Center, Inc.*, 146 F.3d 1042, 1045 (D.C. Cir. 1998) (same; collecting circuit decisions).

[65]*See, e.g., Freedom from Religion Foundation, Inc. v. Geithner*, 644 F.3d 836 (9th Cir. 2011); *Blount-Hill v. Zelman*, 636 F.3d 278, 287 (6th Cir. 2011).

[66]*See Coffey v. C.I.R.*, 663 F.3d 947, 951 (8th Cir. 2011) (reversed denial of permissive intervention where district court considered, whether the proposed intervenor's participation was "necessary to advocate for an unaddressed issue" rather than the correct standard, "whether the intervention will cause 'undue

delay' or 'prejudice the adjudication of the original parties' rights', citing Rule 24 (b)(3)); *Freedom from Religion Foundation, Inc. v. Geithner*, 644 F.3d 836 (9th Cir. 2011) (reversed denial of permissive intervention where district court rejected the motion opining that intervention would destroy diversity jurisdiction; the jurisdiction in question was actually based on a federal question).

[67]*See, e.g., Northland Family Planning Clinic, Inc. v. Cox*, 487 F.3d 323, 346 (6th Cir. 2007) (denial of permissive intervention is reversed only for clear abuse of discretion by trial judge); *Purcell v. BankAtlantic Financial Corp.*, 85 F.3d 1508, 1513 (11th Cir. 1996) (Rule 24(b) intervention is "wholly discretionary" even where the requirements of Rule 24(b) are satisfied); *Shea v. Angulo*, 19 F.3d 343, 346 (7th Cir. 1994) (reversal of district court's decision denying permissive intervention " 'is a very rare bird indeed, so seldom seen as to be unique.' "). *But see Freedom from Religion Foundation, Inc. v. Geithner*, 644 F.3d 836, 844 (9th Cir. 2011) (reversed denial of permissive intervention where district court rejected the motion opining that intervention would destroy diversity jurisdiction; the jurisdiction in question was actually based on a federal question).

Subject Matter Jurisdiction

Persons attempting to intervene under Rule 24(b)(2) must establish an independent basis for subject matter jurisdiction. Supplemental jurisdiction is not available to would-be permissive intervenors.[68]

Timing

Applications to intervene under Rule 24(b) must be "timely". The determination of what constitutes a timely application rests within the court's discretion in the context of the facts in a particular case.[69] Because Rule 24(b) intervention questions do not typically affect the interests of non-parties as importantly as Rule 24(a) cases, courts tend to hold motions for permissive intervention to a more rigorous standard of timeliness than would be applied to motions for intervention of right.[70]

Delay or Prejudice

Rule 24(b) expressly authorizes the court to deny permissive intervention if intervention will unduly delay or prejudice the pending litigation. The provision permits denial of intervention if undue delay to existing parties will result even from an arguably timely application. That might occur if the complexity added by an intervenor would prolong the litigation

---

[68]*See, e.g., E.E.O.C. v. National Children's Center, Inc.*, 146 F.3d 1042, 1046 (D.C. Cir. 1998) ("Permissive intervention . . . has always required an independent basis for jurisdiction."). *See generally Barefoot Architect, Inc. v. Bunge*, 632 F.3d 822, 836 (3d Cir. 2011) (dicta; discussion of use of supplemental jurisdiction pursuant to 28 U.S.C. § 1367(b) for counterclaim by defendant, but questioning available for similar use of supplemental jurisdiction for intervention by plaintiffs).

[69]*See, e.g., Randall v. Rolls-Royce Corp.*, 637 F.3d 818, 827 (7th Cir. 2011) (permissive intervention denied when motion filed "almost four years after the suit had begun and long after it was plain that there were substantial doubts about the typicality of the named plaintiffs' claims and the adequacy of their representation of the class"); *Igartua v. U.S.*, 636 F.3d 18, 19 (1st Cir. 2011) (intervention by Commonwealth of Puerto Rico denied as untimely when filed after appeal heard by circuit court panel and prior to rehearing en banc); *Fox v. Tyson Foods, Inc.*, 519 F.3d 1298, 1304–1305

(11th Cir. 2008) (district court did not clearly abuse discretion in denying permissive intervention of 161 petitioners where action had been filed several years earlier and employer would need at least one additional year to depose the petitioners); *Caterino v. Barry*, 922 F.2d 37, 40 (1st Cir. 1990) (trial court entitled to "substantial deference"); *Medical Liability Mut. Ins. Co. v. Alan Curtis LLC*, 485 F.3d 1006, 1009 (8th Cir. 2007) (not abuse of discretion for district court to deny permissive intervention where motion for intervention filed more than a year after underlying suit filed and shortly before discovery deadline).

[70]*See, e.g., Banco Popular de Puerto Rico v. Greenblatt*, 964 F.2d 1227, 1230 (1st Cir. 1992) (timeliness standard more strict for Rule 24(a) than Rule 24(b)); *But cf. R & G Mortg. Corp. v. Federal Home Loan Mortg. Corp.*, 584 F.3d 1, 11 (1st Cir. 2009) (when intervenor seeks both as of right and permissive intervention, a finding of untimeliness with respect to the former normally applies to the latter).

excessively.[71] Similarly, inappropriate prejudice to existing parties might occur if the presence of the intervenor might shift the focus of the litigation from the pending issues to those introduced by the intervenor.[72] Rule 24(b)(3) has been interpreted to suggest "that intervention postjudgment-which necessarily disturbs the final adjudication of the parties' rights-should generally be disfavored."[73]

There is authority for the position that the "prejudice" evaluation of Rule 24(b)(3) should include an evaluation of the merits of the proposed party's claim. To the extent that the claim is duplicative or weak on its merits, the court will be inclined to give greater weight to concerns about delay or prejudice.[74]

Permissive Statutory Intervention

Fewer cases deal with permissive statutory intervention. Such statutes as exist, and which clearly contemplate permissive statutory intervention, generally accord the court authority to allow intervention by some public official such as the United States Attorney General.[75] In other circumstances it is less clear whether the statute is intended to allow intervention as of right or permissive intervention. Although the paucity of case law makes conclusions difficult, the inclination of courts to construe narrowly statutes that clearly contemplate intervention as of right may suggest that courts will be inclined to construe the uncertain statutes as authorizing permissive statutory intervention under Rule 24(b)(1) rather than statutory intervention as of right under Rule 24(a)(1). As a practical matter, that inclination provides the courts with greater opportunities to use discretion to reject an application for permissive intervention.

Standing for Non-statutory Permissive Intervention

Although a person seeking intervention under Rule 24(b)(2) need not demonstrate an "interest" within the kinds contem-

---

[71]*See, e.g., McHenry v. C.I.R.*, 677 F.3d 214, 216 (4th Cir. 2012) (permissive intervention by the Government of the United States Virgin Islands denied where it would "introduce redundancy into the proceedings"; Virgin Islands sought to intervene in tax case claiming interpretation of law could discourage entrepreneurs from coming to the Virgin Islands); *Massachusetts v. Microsoft Corp.*, 373 F.3d 1199 (D.C. Cir.2004) (prejudice evaluation "captures all the possible drawbacks of piling on parties," including extra cost and increased risk of error). *See also Farmland Dairies v. Commissioner of New York State Dept. of Agriculture and Markets*, 847 F.2d 1038, 1044 (2d Cir. 1988) (post-judgment intervention

is disfavored).

[72]*See, e.g., Alaniz v. Tillie Lewis Foods*, 572 F.2d 657, 659 (9th Cir. 1978), (per curiam). *See also Beaver v. Alaniz*, 439 U.S. 837, 99 S. Ct. 123, 58 L. Ed. 2d 134 (1978) (post-resolution intervention often unfairly hard on existing parties).

[73]*Bond v. Utreras*, 585 F.3d 1061, 1071 (7th Cir. 2009).

[74]*See, e.g., Massachusetts v. Microsoft Corp.*, 373 F.3d 1199 (D.C. Cir.2004) (but in instant case intervention is appropriate because concerns about delay or prejudice are minimal).

[75]*See, e.g.,* 42 U.S.C.A. § 2000a-3(a).

plated by Rule 24(a)(2), the person seeking permissive intervention must nonetheless have a sufficient stake in the litigation
to satisfy ordinary requirements for standing.[76] Whether standing is required for permissive intervention may depend on the
type of case and the status of the case at the time.[77]

Permissive Intervention for Public Officials

Rule 24(b) authorizes intervention by officers or agencies if
the pending litigation raises questions of law administered by
the officer or agency, or questions of regulations issued by the
officer or agency.[78]

Conditional Permissive Intervention

If intervention is permitted under Rule 24(b), the court has
substantial authority to impose conditions on the intervention.[79]

RULE 24(c)—NOTICE AND PLEADING REQUIRED

CORE CONCEPT

Rule 24(c) contains the provisions for notice and service of process of the motion to intervene. It also requires that the motion
to intervene be accompanied by a pleading that identifies the
claim or defense which is the basis of the attempt to intervene.

APPLICATIONS

Service of Process

The motion to intervene should be filed with the court and
served on all persons already parties to the pending litigation,
as provided in Rule 5.

Service of Proposed Pleading

In addition to the motion to intervene, Rule 24(c) also

---

[76]*See, e.g., U.S. v. Napper*, 887
F.2d 1528, 1532 (11th Cir. 1989)
(standing is required for both intervenors of right and permissive intervenors). *Cf. City of Herriman v. Bell*, 590
F.3d 1176, 1184 (10th Cir. 2010) (while
would-be intervenor need not have
standing in the Tenth Circuit, the
claimant must "have a claim or defense that shares at least some aspect
with a claim or defense presented",
and the City of Herriman, as a political subdivision, lacked authority to
bring equal protection challenge
against another political subdivision
and therefore could not intervene in
equal protection suit brought by vot-
ers). *But cf., In re Vitamins Antitrust
Class Actions*, 215 F.3d 26 (D.C.
Cir.2000) (expressing uncertainty as
to whether standing is required).

[77]*Bond v. Utreras*, 585 F.3d 1061,
1069–70 (7th Cir. 2009) (setting aside
questions of whether a permissive
intervenor must establish standing to
challenge a protective order in an
ongoing case, but holding that an
intervenor must establish standing to
challenge a protective order after the
case has been dismissed).

[78]*See, e.g., Harris v. Amoco
Production Co.*, 768 F.2d 669, 680 (5th
Cir. 1985) (citing federal law authorizing permissive intervention for federal
agency).

[79]*See, e.g., Beauregard, Inc. v.
Sword Services L.L.C.*, 107 F.3d 351,
352 (5th Cir. 1997) ("It is undisputed
that virtually any condition may be attached to a grant of permissive intervention.").

requires that the applicant for intervention file and serve a proposed pleading explaining the claim or defense that is the purpose of the intervention.[80] This proposed pleading should also be served consistent with the requirements of Rule 5, governing service on persons already parties.

Failure to Meet Rule 24(c) Motion and Pleading Requirements

There is a split of authority as to the consequences an intervenor should experience for failure to meet the motion and pleading requirements of Rule 24(c). An apparent majority of circuits has held that failure to comply with Rule 24(c) should not of itself disqualify the attempt to intervene.[81] A smaller number of circuits has applied the requirements more rigorously.[82]

---

[80]*See, e.g., Bridges v. Department of Maryland State Police*, 441 F.3d 197, 208 (4th Cir. 2006) (pleading gives existing parties notice of claim or defense for which intervention is sought); *Retired Chicago Police Ass'n v. City of Chicago*, 7 F.3d 584, 595 (7th Cir. 1993) (for purposes of Rule 24(c), intervenor should provide an original pleading, not merely an adoption by reference of prior pleadings; Rule 10(c), permitting adoption by reference in other situations, does not apply to pleadings required under Rule 24(c)).

[81]*See, e.g.,Westchester Fire Ins. Co. v. Mendez*, 585 F.3d 1183, 1189 (9th Cir. 2009) (allowed intervention despite failure to file a pleading, holding that interest did not disappear because of a "procedural misstep"); *U.S. v. Metropolitan St. Louis Sewer District*, 569 F.3d 829, 834 (8th Cir. 2009) ("statement of interest" provided sufficient notice and thereby satisfied requirement); *Providence Baptist Church v. Hillandale Committee, Ltd.*, 425 F.3d 309, 314 (6th Cir. 2005) (abuse of discretion to reject motion to intervene for failure to include pleading); *Massachusetts v. Microsoft Corp.*, 373 F.3d 1199, 1236 (D.C. Cir. 2004) (failure to include pleading with motion-procedural defects should generally be excused); *Piambino v. Bailey*, 757 F.2d 1112, 1121 (11th Cir. 1985) (same failure—such "nonprejudicial technical defects" may be disregarded); *Spring Const. Co., Inc. v. Harris*, 614 F.2d 374, 376–77 (4th Cir. 1980) (same); *Farina v. Mission Inv. Trust*, 615 F.2d 1068, 1074 (5th Cir. 1980) (objection that intervenor made no "formal petition to intervene" rejected as "excessively technical").

[82]*See, e.g, See also King v. University Healthcare System, L.C.*, 645 F.3d 713, 727 (5th Cir. 2011) (would-be intervenor/law firm attempted to attach judgment to former client through "a largely unexplained motion asking us to enforce a statutory privilege in its favor;" court denied motion to amend and to intervene); *Hollywood Mobile Estates Ltd. v. Seminole Tribe of Florida*, 641 F.3d 1259 (11th Cir. 2011) (would-be intervenor failed to attach copy of pleading to motion and so did not establish constitutional standing; motion to amend complaint denied as "futile" after conclusion that intervenors did not have standing in any case). *Public Service Co. of New Hampshire v. Patch*, 136 F.3d 197, 205 n. 6 (1st Cir. 1998) (failure to include pleading "ordinarily would warrant dismissal" of motion, but such result unnecessary in instant case because lower court rejected motion on other grounds); *Shevlin v. Schewe*, 809 F.2d 447, 450 (7th Cir. 1987) (pleading must accompany motion; defect may be excusable where intervenor later remedied defect, but not in case where pleading was never filed); *Abramson v. Pennwood Inv. Corp.*, 392 F.2d 759, 761 (2d Cir. 1968) (reference in motion to allegations of original complaint does not meet Rule 24(c) requirement). *See also Thompson*

Additional Research References

Wright & Miller, *Federal Practice and Procedure* §§ 1900 to 23
C.J.S., Federal Civil Procedure §§ 128 to 155
West's Key Number Digest, Federal Civil Procedure ⚷311 to 345

---

v. Boggs, 33 F.3d 847, 858 n. 10 (7th Cir. 1994) (Rule 24 motion by non-party to intervene is "proper course;" by contrast, courts do not grant motions to join when motion is made by non-party).

RULE 25
SUBSTITUTION OF PARTIES

(a) Death.

    (1) *Substitution if the Claim Is Not Extinguished.* If a party dies and the claim is not extinguished, the court may order substitution of the proper party. A motion for substitution may be made by any party or by the decedent's successor or representative. If the motion is not made within 90 days after service of a statement noting the death, the action by or against the decedent must be dismissed.

    (2) *Continuation Among the Remaining Parties.* After a party's death, if the right sought to be enforced survives only to or against the remaining parties, the action does not abate, but proceeds in favor of or against the remaining parties. The death should be noted on the record.

    (3) *Service.* A motion to substitute, together with a notice of hearing, must be served on the parties as provided in Rule 5 and on nonparties as provided in Rule 4. A statement noting death must be served in the same manner. Service may be made in any judicial district.

(b) Incompetency. If a party becomes incompetent, the court may, on motion, permit the action to be continued by or against the party's representative. The motion must be served as provided in Rule 25(a)(3).

(c) Transfer of Interest. If an interest is transferred, the action may be continued by or against the original party unless the court, on motion, orders the transferee to be substituted in the action or joined with the original party. The motion must be served as provided in Rule 25(a)(3).

(d) Public Officers; Death or Separation from Office. An action does not abate when a public officer who is a party in an official capacity dies, resigns, or otherwise ceases to hold office while the action is pending. The officer's successor is automatically substituted as a party. Later proceedings should be in the substituted party's name, but any misnomer not affecting the parties' substantial rights must be disregarded. The court may order substitution at any time, but the absence of such an order does not affect the substitution.

[Amended effective October 20, 1949; July 19, 1961; July 1, 1963; August 1, 1987; April 30, 2007, effective December 1, 2007.]

AUTHORS' COMMENTARY ON RULE 25

PURPOSE AND SCOPE

Rule 25 prescribes the steps to employ when, in any of four distinct circumstances described in the Rule, it becomes necessary to substitute a party in a case. Rule 25 applies only to cases already pending when the substitution becomes necessary. It does not apply to substitutions in circumstances where suit has not already commenced. Such circumstances are more likely to be controlled by Rule 17, governing a person's capacity to initiate a suit.

RULE 25(a)—DEATH

CORE CONCEPT

Rule 25(a) prescribes the procedure to follow for substituting a party when a plaintiff or defendant in pending litigation dies during the course of the proceedings. The Rule expressly defers to state or federal substantive law to determine whether the cause of action survives the death of the party, and is only applicable if the suit is not extinguished by the death.

APPLICATIONS

Motion for Substitution

Rule 25(a)(1) provides that any party, or the persons affiliated with the deceased party, may make a motion for substitution.[1] It is important to note that until a motion for substitution has been made and granted, the court has no

---

[1] *See, e.g., In re Baycol Products Litigation*, 616 F.3d 778, 785 (8th Cir. 2010) ("successor" can include persons, apart from administrator or executor of estate, who may move for substitution; persons eligible for status of successor include: primary distributee of estate that has been distributed; named executor of estate, "even if the will is not probated;" "primary beneficiary of an unprobated intestate, which need not be probated;" acknowl-

authority to proceed with the deceased party's case.[2]

Service

The motion should be filed and served on all parties consistent with the requirements of Rule 5. If the circumstances are such that service on non-parties is also appropriate, the non-parties shall be served consistent with the requirements for service of a summons under Rule 4, which controls service at the beginning of a suit. Rule 25(a)(3) authorizes service of such process in any federal judicial district.

Hearing

If there is a dispute as to the appropriateness of the proposed substituted party, the court has a duty to resolve the issue and may hold a hearing before ruling on the motion.[3] The notice of hearing should be filed and served on all parties in the manner provided by Rule 5.

Time

The time in which the motion for substitution must be made is 90 days from when the death of the party is "suggested" on the record of the case. Thus, a party may have been deceased for a substantial period before a suggestion of death is made, and that fact will have no consequence for the 90-day limitation.[4]

Suggestion of Death

Death of a party is suggested by written notice on the record, which should be filed and served on all parties pursuant to Rule 5.[5] Non-party representatives of the deceased should be served pursuant to Rule 4.[6]

---

edging that state law governs who may be a successor); *Atkins v. City of Chicago*, 547 F.3d 869, 872 (7th Cir. 2008) (attorney for deceased party may not file motion on his own behalf or on behalf of deceased client, but may file motion if estate is not represented by executor or administrator); *Unicorn Tales, Inc. v. Banerjee*, 138 F.3d 467 (2d Cir.1998) (suggestion can be made by widow who is not a party, and need not be made by formally appointed representative of estate).

[2]*See, e.g., Younts v. Fremont County, Iowa*, 370 F.3d 748, 752 (8th Cir. 2004) ("Because the deceased . . . is not a proper party on appeal and no proper party has been substituted for her, we cannot address the merits of the appeal raised on [her] behalf.").

[3]*See, e.g., Escareno v. Noltina Crucible and Refractory Corp.*, 139 F.3d 1456 (11th Cir.1998) (court has duty to determine whether substitute party-here an administrator of estate-was properly appointed; issue in instant case was whether probate court had jurisdiction to appoint administrator).

[4]*See, e.g., Grandbouche v. Lovell*, 913 F.2d 835 (10th Cir.1990). *But see, Miles, Inc. v. Scripps Clinic and Research Foundation*, 810 F. Supp. 1091, 1102 (S.D. Cal. 1993) (party who delays unreasonably in filing suggestion of death may be denied permission to substitute a party).

[5]*See, e.g., Barlow v. Ground*, 39 F.3d 231, 233–34 (9th Cir. 1994) (90 days does not start to run until representative of estate is properly served).

[6]See, e.g., id. at 233 (requiring service on non-party representatives under Rule 4).

Failure to Move for Substitution Within 90 Days

If more than 90 days elapses following the suggestion of death without a motion for substitution, Rule 25(a)(1) provides that the suit will be dismissed as to the deceased party. However, notwithstanding the apparently mandatory language of the Rule, the cases generally hold that the courts have discretion to extend the time in which a party may move for substitution.[7]

Status of Successor

A party who replaces a deceased party receives the status the deceased party possessed at the time of death. For example, if the deceased party had already consented to trial by a magistrate judge, the successor is bound by that consent.[8]

Death of a Party for Whom Substitution Cannot Be Made

Before Rule 25(a) can be employed to substitute a new party for a deceased party, the substantive law controlling the suit must allow survival of the cause of action. If the cause of action does not survive the death of a party, there can be no substitution for that party under Rule 25(a).[9] In multi-party litigation, however, it is possible that substantive law would extinguish the cause of action as to a deceased party, but that sufficient parties would remain to continue the action. In that circumstance, Rule 25(a)(2) directs that the action may continue as to surviving parties, with appropriate record made of the death.

RULE 25(b)—INCOMPETENCY

CORE CONCEPT

Rule 25(b) addresses the possibility of substitution for parties who become incompetent in the course of litigation. It requires a motion to substitute a representative for the incompetent party, and it expressly adopts the same service provisions applicable to substitution for deceased parties found in Rule 25(a).

---

[7]*See, e.g., Atkins v. City of Chicago*, 547 F.3d 869, 872 (7th Cir. 2008) (time does not start to run until all parties and interested non-parties have been served); *Continental Bank, N.A. v. Meyer*, 10 F.3d 1293, 1297 (7th Cir. 1993) (extensions of 90-day time period may be granted liberally). *But see, Kaubisch v. Weber*, 408 F.3d 540, 543 (8th Cir. 2005) (acknowledging district court's discretion; but "the misapplication or misreading of the plain language of Rule 25 does not establish excusable neglect"); *Russell v. City of Milwaukee*, 338 F.3d 662, 668 (7th Cir. 2003) (affirming dismissal where counsel failed to demonstrate excusable neglect).

[8]*See, e.g., Brook, Weiner, Sered, Kreger & Weinberg v. Coreq, Inc.*, 53 F.3d 851, 852 (7th Cir. 1995) ("A successor takes over without any other change in the status of the case," and therefore decedent's consent to trial by magistrate judge binds successor.).

[9]*See, e.g., Asklar v. Honeywell, Inc.*, 95 F.R.D. 419, 422 (D. Conn. 1982) (substantive law, not Rule 25(a), determines whether case may proceed after death of party).

APPLICATIONS

Survival of the Action
Incompetency will not extinguish a cause of action.

Timing
Rule 25(b) contains no reference to time limitations for motions to substitute parties. There is little or no case law on the point.[10]

RULE 25(c)—TRANSFER OF INTEREST

CORE CONCEPT
Rule 25(c) addresses substitution in circumstances in which, during the course of the litigation, an interest is transferred from a party to another entity. It also controls the procedure for substitution when one corporate entity loses its identity through dissolution or merger with another corporate entity.

APPLICATIONS

Option to Substitute Parties
Rule 25(c) does not require that the person now holding the interest transferred be substituted for the transferor-party.[11] Instead, the Rule allows the action to continue in the name of the transferor unless the court chooses to order substitution, or joinder, of the transferee.[12] Thus the case may go to judgment without any substitution of parties having occurred, and the absence of a formal substitution will have no consequence.[13] If it is appropriate in the circumstances of the particular case, both the transferor and transferee will be bound by the court's judgment.[14]

Personal Jurisdiction
Courts generally hold that when successors in interest are

---

[10]*But cf., Kuelbs v. Hill*, 615 F.3d 1037, 1042 (8th Cir. 2010) (if party becomes incompetent during pendency of case, Rule 25(b) motion for substitution must take place in reasonable period of time; otherwise action may be dismissed under Rule 17(a)).

[11]*See, e.g., In re Bernal*, 207 F.3d 595, 598 (9th Cir. 2000) (Rule 25(c) requires no action by anyone after a transfer of interest; judgment binds successor in interest even if successor is not named).

[12]*See, e.g., Burka v. Aetna Life Ins. Co.*, 87 F.3d 478 (D.C. Cir. 1996) (noting that Rule 25(c) affords option of replacing one party with another, or joining a person with original party).

[13]*See, e.g., Arnold Graphics*

Industries, Inc. v. Independent Agent Center, Inc., 775 F.2d 38, 40 (2d Cir. 1985) (enforcing judgment against successor corporation where substitution was made only after judgment).

[14]*See, e.g., Luxliner P.L. Export, Co. v. RDI/Luxliner, Inc.*, 13 F.3d 69, 71 (3d Cir. 1993) (even if no substitution is sought, judgment against original defendant can bind successor). *But cf., Organic Cow, LLC v. Center For New England Dairy Compact Research*, 335 F.3d 66, 72 (2d Cir. 2003) ("Where . . . a government entity terminates with no provision for naming a successor and with no appropriate governmental body to stand in its shoes for purposes of litigation . . . there can be no substitution of parties under Rule 25.").

joined under Rule 25(c), they are subject to the personal jurisdiction of the court simply because they are successors in interest, "without regard to whether they had any other minimum contacts."[15]

Timing

Rule 25(c) contains no time limit in which substitution must take place.

Subject Matter Jurisdiction: Relation to Rule 19

Joinder of a nondiverse party under rule 25(c) does not usually destroy diversity jurisdiction.[16] However, if the joined party was someone who would have been indispensable under Rule 19 at the time the case was filed, joinder of a nondiverse party destroys diversity jurisdiction.[17]

Extinguishing Corporate Causes of Action

Rule 25(c) is subordinate to substantive law on the issue of survival of a cause of action after corporate reorganizations. Thus if substantive law directs that dissolution of a corporation also extinguishes the corporation's causes of action, Rule 25(c) will not save the cause of action.[18]

Status of Successor

A party who enters a case as the legal successor of a corporation receives the status which the predecessor corporation possessed at the time the successor entered the case. For example, if the predecessor corporation had already consented to trial by a magistrate judge, the successor is bound by that consent.[19]

---

[15]*LiButti v. U.S.*, 178 F.3d 114 (2d Cir. 1999) (collecting other case authority).

[16]*Freeport-McMoRan, Inc. v. K N Energy, Inc.*, 498 U.S. 426, 428, 111 S. Ct. 858, 859, 112 L. Ed. 2d 951 (1991) (per curiam) (any other result would impede "normal business transactions during the pendency of what might be lengthy litigation").

[17]*Freeport-McMoRan, Inc. v. K N Energy, Inc.*, 498 U.S. 426, 111 S. Ct. 858, 112 L. Ed. 2d 951 (1991) (per curiam).

[18]*See, e.g., Citibank v. Grupo Cupey, Inc.*, 382 F.3d 29, 32–33 (1st Cir. 2004) ("Rule 25 does not substantively determine what actions survive the transfer of an interest."); *ELCA Enterprises, Inc. v. Sisco Equipment Rental & Sales, Inc.*, 53 F.3d 186, 190 (8th Cir. 1995) ("Rule 25 does not substantively determine what actions survive the transfer of an interest;

rather, it provides substitution procedures for an action that does survive."). *See also Organic Cow, LLC v. Center For New England Dairy Compact Research*, 335 F.3d 66 (2d Cir. 2003) (when mandate of commission created by Congress to administer dairy compact expired without renewal, private entity could not be substituted under Rule 25(c) because private entity had no authority to perform role of commission).

[19]*See, e.g., Andrews v. Lakeshore Rehabilitation Hosp.*, 140 F.3d 1405, 1408 (11th Cir. 1998) (where transfer of interest occurs prior to trial, Rule 25(c) is not applicable and therefore "does not save plaintiff's amendments from the statute of limitations"). *Brook, Weiner, Sered, Kreger & Weinberg v. Coreq, Inc.*, 53 F.3d 851, 852 (7th Cir. 1995) ("A successor takes over without any other change in the status of the case," and therefore a successor to a corporation is bound by the corpora-

Service of Process

If a motion to substitute parties is made under Rule 25(c), service should meet the requirements established in Rule 25(a) for motions to make substitutions for deceased parties.

Relation to Rule 17

Rule 25(c) governs transfers of interest during the pendency of a case. Rule 17(a), by contrast, governs situations in which an interest is transferred before the suit is filed.[20]

RULE 25(d)—PUBLIC OFFICERS; DEATH OR SEPARATION FROM OFFICE

CORE CONCEPT

Rule 25(d) governs substitution in which public officers are named parties to actions in their official capacities. It does not control substitution in suits where parties, who also happen to be public officers, are suing or being sued personally.[21] Rule 25(d) provides that if substitution of a successor to a public officer is necessary in a pending suit, the substitution shall be automatic. Rule 25(d) applies to circumstances involving death of a public officer or departure from public office for any reason.

APPLICATIONS

Motions

Because the substitution under Rule 25(d) occurs automatically, there is no need to file or serve a motion seeking the substitution.[22]

Timing

For the same reason that no motion is necessary under Rule 25(d), Rule 25(d) imposes no time requirements.

Survival of the Action

Rule 25(d) provides expressly that a suit by or against a

---

tion's previous consent to trial by a magistrate judge.).

[20]*See, e.g., F.D.I.C. v. Deglau,* 207 F.3d 153, 159 (3d Cir. 2000) (Rule 17 governs transfers prior to filing of lawsuit; after lawsuit begins, Rule 25 governs).

[21]*See, e.g., Society of Separationists v. Pleasant Grove City,* 416 F.3d 1239 (10th Cir.2005) (absence of claims against defendants personally makes substitution of successors proper, because suit was brought against elected officials in their official capacity). *Bunn v. Conley,* 309 F.3d 1002, 1009 (7th Cir. 2002) (*Bivens* claim is suit against government of-

ficer in individual (not official) capacity; thus newly appointed officer cannot be substituted for officer originally sued in individual capacity).

[22]*Cheney v. U.S. Dist. Court for Dist. of Columbia,* 541 U.S. 913, 916, 124 S. Ct. 1391, 1395, 158 L. Ed. 2d 225 (2004) (substitution is automatic). *See, e.g., King v. McMillan,* 594 F.3d 301, 308 (4th Cir. 2010) (state law cannot cut off substitution under Rule 25(d)); *Negron Gaztambide v. Hernandez Torres,* 145 F.3d 410 (1st Cir. 1998) (per curiam) (new officeholders are substituted automatically for their predecessors and automatically have same standing to litigate case).

public officer does not abate when a substitution occurs.[23]

Events Prior to Substitution: Stipulations, Admissions, Etc.

It appears settled that substitution of an official for a predecessor in office binds the successor to the results of previous events in the case as surely as if no substitution had been made.[24]

Substitutions in the Style of the Case

Rule 25(d) directs that proceedings subsequent to the substitution shall be in the name of the substituted party. However, this provision is usually no more than a formality, for no consequence attaches to erroneous use of the name of the original party—unless such error somehow has an adverse effect on the case.[25]

Order of Substitution

The court has discretion to order that a new public officer be substituted for a predecessor, but need not do so. Whatever the court decides, Rule 25(d) provides that the presence or absence of such an order does not alter the fact that the automatic substitution has already occurred.[26]

Additional Research References

Wright & Miller, *Federal Practice and Procedure* §§ 1951 to 62
C.J.S., Federal Civil Procedure §§ 156 to 168 et seq.
West's Key Number Digest, Federal Civil Procedure ⟜351 to 366, 391

---

[23]*See, e.g., Saldana-Sanchez v. Lopez-Gerena*, 256 F.3d 1, 10, (1st Cir. 2001) ("As Fed. R. Civ. P. 25(d)(1) makes clear, the substitution of a public official by his or her successor in an official capacity suit does not affect the underlying action.").

[24]*See, e.g., Morales Feliciano v. Rullan*, 303 F.3d 1, 7–8 (1st Cir. 2002) (holding that substituted party cannot repudiate stipulations to which predecessor agreed).

[25]*See, e.g., Cable v. Ivy Tech State College*, 200 F.3d 467, 475 (7th Cir. 1999) (Rule 17(d) "expressly directs that any misnomer of the parties that does not affect their substantive rights shall be disregarded even without a motion or order for substitution"); *Presbytery of New Jersey of Orthodox Presbyterian Church v. Florio*, 40 F.3d 1454, 1458 (3d Cir. 1994) (failure to amend caption to reflect election of new governor/defendant does not affect case).

[26]*See, e.g., Shakman v. Democratic Organization of Cook County*, 919 F.2d 455, 456 (7th Cir. 1990) (challenger who wins election against official defendant "automatically became a party to . . . consent decree").

V. DEPOSITIONS AND DISCOVERY

RULE 26
DUTY TO DISCLOSE; GENERAL PROVISIONS GOVERNING DISCOVERY

(a) Required Disclosures.

(1) *Initial Disclosure.*

(A) *In General.* Except as exempted by Rule 26(a)(1)(B) or as otherwise stipulated or ordered by the court, a party must, without awaiting a discovery request, provide to the other parties:

   (i)   the name and, if known, the address and telephone number of each individual likely to have discoverable information—along with the subjects of that information—that the disclosing party may use to support its claims or defenses, unless the use would be solely for impeachment;

   (ii) a copy—or a description by category and location—of all documents, electronically stored information, and tangible things that the disclosing party has in its possession, custody, or control and may use to support its claims or defenses, unless the use would be solely for impeachment;

   (iii) a computation of each category of damages claimed by the disclosing party—who must also make available for inspection and copying as under Rule 34 the documents or other evidentiary material, unless privileged or protected from disclosure, on which each computation is based, including materials bearing on the nature and extent of injuries suffered; and

   (iv) for inspection and copying as under Rule 34, any insurance agreement under which an insurance business may be liable to satisfy all or part of a possible judgment in the action or to indemnify or reimburse for payments made to satisfy the judgment.

(B) *Proceedings Exempt from Initial Disclosure.* The following proceedings are exempt from initial disclosure:

    (i)   an action for review on an administrative record;

    (ii)   a forfeiture action in rem arising from a federal statute;

    (iii)   a petition for habeas corpus or any other proceeding to challenge a criminal conviction or sentence;

    (iv)   an action brought without an attorney by a person in the custody of the United States, a state, or a state subdivision;

    (v)   an action to enforce or quash an administrative summons or subpoena;

    (vi)   an action by the United States to recover benefit payments;

    (vii)   an action by the United States to collect on a student loan guaranteed by the United States;

    (viii) a proceeding ancillary to a proceeding in another court; and

    (ix)   an action to enforce an arbitration award.

(C) *Time for Initial Disclosures—In General.* A party must make the initial disclosures at or within 14 days after the parties' Rule 26(f) conference unless a different time is set by stipulation or court order, or unless a party objects during the conference that initial disclosures are not appropriate in this action and states the objection in the proposed discovery plan. In ruling on the objection, the court must determine what disclosures, if any, are to be made and must set the time for disclosure.

(D) *Time for Initial Disclosures—For Parties Served or Joined Later.* A party that is first served or otherwise joined after the Rule 26(f) conference must make the initial disclosures within 30 days after being served or joined, unless a different time is set by stipulation or court order.

  (E) *Basis for Initial Disclosure; Unacceptable Excuses.* A party must make its initial disclosures based on the information then reasonably available to it. A party is not excused from making its disclosures because it has not fully investigated the case or because it challenges the sufficiency of another party's disclosures or because another party has not made its disclosures.

(2) *Disclosure of Expert Testimony.*

  (A) *In General.* In addition to the disclosures required by Rule 26(a)(1), a party must disclose to the other parties the identity of any witness it may use at trial to present evidence under Federal Rule of Evidence 702, 703, or 705.

  (B) *Witnesses Who Must Provide a Written Report.* Unless otherwise stipulated or ordered by the court, this disclosure must be accompanied by a written report--prepared and signed by the witness--if the witness is one retained or specially employed to provide expert testimony in the case or one whose duties as the party's employee regularly involve giving expert testimony. The report must contain:

    (i)   a complete statement of all opinions the witness will express and the basis and reasons for them;

    (ii)   the facts or data considered by the witness in forming them;

    (iii)   any exhibits that will be used to summarize or support them;

    (iv)   the witness's qualifications, including a list of all publications authored in the previous 10 years;

    (v)   a list of all other cases in which, during the previous 4 years, the witness testified as an expert at trial or by deposition; and

   (vi) a statement of the compensation to be paid for the study and testimony in the case.

(C) *Witnesses Who Do Not Provide a Written Report.* Unless otherwise stipulated or ordered by the court, if the witness is not required to provide a written report, this disclosure must state:

   (i) the subject matter on which the witness is expected to present evidence under Federal Rule of Evidence 702, 703, or 705; and

   (ii) a summary of the facts and opinions to which the witness is expected to testify.

(D) *Time to Disclose Expert Testimony.* A party must make these disclosures at the times and in the sequence that the court orders. Absent a stipulation or a court order, the disclosures must be made:

   (i) at least 90 days before the date set for trial or for the case to be ready for trial; or

   (ii) if the evidence is intended solely to contradict or rebut evidence on the same subject matter identified by another party under Rule 26(a)(2)(B) or (C), within 30 days after the other party's disclosure.

(E) *Supplementing the Disclosure.* The parties must supplement these disclosures when required under Rule 26(e).

(3) *Pretrial Disclosures.*

(A) *In General.* In addition to the disclosures required by Rule 26(a)(1) and (2), a party must provide to the other parties and promptly file the following information about the evidence that it may present at trial other than solely for impeachment:

   (i) the name and, if not previously provided, the address and telephone number of each witness—separately identifying those the party expects to present and those it may call if the need arises;

   (ii) the designation of those witnesses whose

testimony the party expects to present by deposition and, if not taken stenographically, a transcript of the pertinent parts of the deposition; and

(iii) an identification of each document or other exhibit, including summaries of other evidence—separately identifying those items the party expects to offer and those it may offer if the need arises.

(B) *Time for Pretrial Disclosures; Objections.* Unless the court orders otherwise, these disclosures must be made at least 30 days before trial. Within 14 days after they are made, unless the court sets a different time, a party may serve and promptly file a list of the following objections: any objections to the use under Rule 32(a) of a deposition designated by another party under Rule 26(a)(3)(A)(ii); and any objection, together with the grounds for it, that may be made to the admissibility of materials identified under Rule 26(a)(3)(A)(iii). An objection not so made—except for one under Federal Rule of Evidence 402 or 403—is waived unless excused by the court for good cause.

(4) *Form of Disclosures.* Unless the court orders otherwise, all disclosures under Rule 26(a) must be in writing, signed, and served.

(b) Discovery Scope and Limits.

(1) *Scope in General.* Unless otherwise limited by court order, the scope of discovery is as follows: Parties may obtain discovery regarding any nonprivileged matter that is relevant to any party's claim or defense—including the existence, description, nature, custody, condition, and location of any documents or other tangible things and the identity and location of persons who know of any discoverable matter. For good cause, the court may order discovery of any matter relevant to the subject matter involved in the action. Relevant information need not be admissible at the trial if the discovery appears reason-

ably calculated to lead to the discovery of admissible evidence. All discovery is subject to the limitations imposed by Rule 26(b)(2)(C).

(2) *Limitations on Frequency and Extent.*

    (A) *When Permitted.* By order, the court may alter the limits in these rules on the number of depositions and interrogatories or on the length of depositions under Rule 30. By order or local rule, the court may also limit the number of requests under Rule 36.

    (B) *Specific Limitations on Electronically Stored Information.* A party need not provide discovery of electronically stored information from sources that the party identifies as not reasonably accessible because of undue burden or cost. On motion to compel discovery or for a protective order, the party from whom discovery is sought must show that the information is not reasonably accessible because of undue burden or cost. If that showing is made, the court may nonetheless order discovery from such sources if the requesting party shows good cause, considering the limitations of Rule 26(b)(2)(C). The court may specify conditions for the discovery.

    (C) *When Required.* On motion or on its own, the court must limit the frequency or extent of discovery otherwise allowed by these rules or by local rule if it determines that:

        (i) the discovery sought is unreasonably cumulative or duplicative, or can be obtained from some other source that is more convenient, less burdensome, or less expensive;

        (ii) the party seeking discovery has had ample opportunity to obtain the information by discovery in the action; or

        (iii) the burden or expense of the proposed discovery outweighs its likely benefit, considering the needs of the case, the amount in controversy, the parties' resources, the importance of the issues at stake in the action, and the importance of the discovery in resolving the issues.

(3) *Trial Preparation: Materials.*

  (A) *Documents and Tangible Things.* Ordinarily, a party may not discover documents and tangible things that are prepared in anticipation of litigation or for trial by or for another party or its representative (including the other party's attorney, consultant, surety, indemnitor, insurer, or agent). But, subject to Rule 26(b)(4), those materials may be discovered if:

    (i)   they are otherwise discoverable under Rule 26(b)(1); and

    (ii) the party shows that it has substantial need for the materials to prepare its case and cannot, without undue hardship, obtain their substantial equivalent by other means.

  (B) *Protection Against Disclosure.* If the court orders discovery of those materials, it must protect against disclosure of the mental impressions, conclusions, opinions, or legal theories of a party's attorney or other representative concerning the litigation.

  (C) *Previous Statement.* Any party or other person may, on request and without the required showing, obtain the person's own previous statement about the action or its subject matter. If the request is refused, the person may move for a court order, and Rule 37(a)(5) applies to the award of expenses. A previous statement is either:

    (i)   a written statement that the person has signed or otherwise adopted or approved; or

    (ii) a contemporaneous stenographic, mechanical, electrical, or other recording—or a transcription of it—that recites substantially verbatim the person's oral statement.

(4) *Trial Preparation: Experts.*

  (A) *Deposition of an Expert Who May Testify.* A party may depose any person who has been identified as an expert whose opinions may be presented at trial. If Rule 26(a)(2)(B) requires a report from the expert, the deposition may be conducted only after the report is provided.

(B) *Trial–Preparation Protection for Draft Reports or Disclosures.* Rules 26(b)(3)(A) and (B) protect drafts of any report or disclosure required under Rule 26(a)(2), regardless of the form in which the draft is recorded.

(C) *Trial–Preparation Protection for Communications Between a Party's Attorney and Expert Witnesses.* Rules 26(b)(3)(A) and (B) protect communications between the party's attorney and any witness required to provide a report under Rule 26(a)(2)(B), regardless of the form of the communications, except to the extent that the communications:

   (i) relate to compensation for the expert's study or testimony;

   (ii) identify facts or data that the party's attorney provided and that the expert considered in forming the opinions to be expressed; or

   (iii) identify assumptions that the party's attorney provided and that the expert relied on in forming the opinions to be expressed.

(D) *Expert Employed Only for Trial Preparation.* Ordinarily, a party may not, by interrogatories or deposition, discover facts known or opinions held by an expert who has been retained or specially employed by another party in anticipation of litigation or to prepare for trial and who is not expected to be called as a witness at trial. But a party may do so only:

   (i) as provided in Rule 35(b); or

   (ii) on showing exceptional circumstances under which it is impracticable for the party to obtain facts or opinions on the same subject by other means.

(E) *Payment.* Unless manifest injustice would result, the court must require that the party seeking discovery:

    (i)   pay the expert a reasonable fee for time spent in responding to discovery under Rule 26(b)(4)(A) or (D); and

    (ii)   for discovery under (D), also pay the other party a fair portion of the fees and expenses it reasonably incurred in obtaining the expert's facts and opinions.

(5) *Claiming Privilege or Protecting Trial-Preparation Materials.*

    (A) *Information Withheld.* When a party withholds information otherwise discoverable by claiming that the information is privileged or subject to protection as trial-preparation material, the party must:

        (i)   expressly make the claim; and

        (ii)   describe the nature of the documents, communications, or tangible things not produced or disclosed—and do so in a manner that, without revealing information itself privileged or protected, will enable other parties to assess the claim.

    (B) *Information Produced.* If information produced in discovery is subject to a claim of privilege or of protection as trial-preparation material, the party making the claim may notify any party that received the information of the claim and the basis for it. After being notified, a party must promptly return, sequester, or destroy the specified information and any copies it has; must not use or disclose the information until the claim is resolved; must take reasonable steps to retrieve the information if the party disclosed it before being notified; and may promptly present the information to the court under seal for a determination of the claim. The producing party must preserve the information until the claim is resolved.

(c) Protective Orders.

(1) *In General.* A party or any person from whom discovery is sought may move for a protective order in the court where the action is pending—or as an alternative on matters relating to a deposi-

tion, in the court for the district where the deposition will be taken. The motion must include a certification that the movant has in good faith conferred or attempted to confer with other affected parties in an effort to resolve the dispute without court action. The court may, for good cause, issue an order to protect a party or person from annoyance, embarrassment, oppression, or undue burden or expense, including one or more of the following:

(A) forbidding the disclosure or discovery;

(B) specifying terms, including time and place, for the disclosure or discovery;

(C) prescribing a discovery method other than the one selected by the party seeking discovery;

(D) forbidding inquiry into certain matters, or limiting the scope of disclosure or discovery to certain matters;

(E) designating the persons who may be present while the discovery is conducted;

(F) requiring that a deposition be sealed and opened only on court order;

(G) requiring that a trade secret or other confidential research, development, or commercial information not be revealed or be revealed only in a specified way; and

(H) requiring that the parties simultaneously file specified documents or information in sealed envelopes, to be opened as the court directs.

(2) *Ordering Discovery.* If a motion for a protective order is wholly or partly denied, the court may, on just terms, order that any party or person provide or permit discovery.

(3) *Awarding Expenses.* Rule 37(a)(5) applies to the award of expenses.

(d) Timing and Sequence of Discovery.

(1) *Timing.* A party may not seek discovery from any source before the parties have conferred as required by Rule 26(f), except in a proceeding exempted from initial disclosure under Rule 26(a)(1)(B), or when authorized by these rules,

by stipulation, or by court order.

(2) *Sequence.* Unless, on motion, the court orders otherwise for the parties' and witnesses' convenience and in the interests of justice:

(A) methods of discovery may be used in any sequence; and

(B) discovery by one party does not require any other party to delay its discovery.

(e) Supplementing Disclosures and Responses.

(1) *In General.* A party who has made a disclosure under Rule 26(a)—or who has responded to an interrogatory, request for production, or request for admission—must supplement or correct its disclosure or response:

(A) in a timely manner if the party learns that in some material respect the disclosure or response is incomplete or incorrect, and if the additional or corrective information has not otherwise been made known to the other parties during the discovery process or in writing; or

(B) as ordered by the court.

(2) *Expert Witness.* For an expert whose report must be disclosed under Rule 26(a)(2)(B), the party's duty to supplement extends both to information included in the report and to information given during the expert's deposition. Any additions or changes to this information must be disclosed by the time the party's pretrial disclosures under Rule 26(a)(3) are due.

(f) Conference of the Parties; Planning for Discovery.

(1) *Conference Timing.* Except in a proceeding exempted from initial disclosure under Rule 26(a)(1)(B) or when the court orders otherwise, the parties must confer as soon as practicable—and in any event at least 21 days before a scheduling conference is to be held or a scheduling order is due under Rule 16(b).

(2) *Conference Content; Parties' Responsibilities.* In conferring, the parties must consider the nature and basis of their claims and defenses and the

possibilities for promptly settling or resolving the case; make or arrange for the disclosures required by Rule 26(a)(1); discuss any issues about preserving discoverable information; and develop a proposed discovery plan. The attorneys of record and all unrepresented parties that have appeared in the case are jointly responsible for arranging the conference, for attempting in good faith to agree on the proposed discovery plan, and for submitting to the court within 14 days after the conference a written report outlining the plan. The court may order the parties or attorneys to attend the conference in person.

(3) *Discovery Plan.* A discovery plan must state the parties' views and proposals on:

    (A) what changes should be made in the timing, form, or requirement for disclosures under Rule 26(a), including a statement of when initial disclosures were made or will be made;

    (B) the subjects on which discovery may be needed, when discovery should be completed, and whether discovery should be conducted in phases or be limited to or focused on particular issues;

    (C) any issues about disclosure or discovery of electronically stored information, including the form or forms in which it should be produced;

    (D) any issues about claims of privilege or of protection as trial-preparation materials, including—if the parties agree on a procedure to assert these claims after production— whether to ask the court to include their agreement in an order;

    (E) what changes should be made in the limitations on discovery imposed under these rules or by local rule, and what other limitations should be imposed; and

    (F) any other orders that the court should issue under Rule 26(c) or under Rule 16(b) and (c).

(4) *Expedited Schedule.* If necessary to comply with its expedited schedule for Rule 16(b) conferences,

a court may by local rule:

(A) require the parties' conference to occur less than 21 days before the scheduling conference is held or a scheduling order is due under Rule 16(b); and

(B) require the written report outlining the discovery plan to be filed less than 14 days after the parties' conference, or excuse the parties from submitting a written report and permit them to report orally on their discovery plan at the Rule 16(b) conference.

(g) Signing Disclosures and Discovery Requests, Responses, and Objections.

(1) *Signature Required; Effect of Signature.* Every disclosure under Rule 26(a)(1) or (a)(3) and every discovery request, response, or objection must be signed by at least one attorney of record in the attorney's own name—or by the party personally, if unrepresented—and must state the signer's address, e-mail address, and telephone number. By signing, an attorney or party certifies that to the best of the person's knowledge, information, and belief formed after a reasonable inquiry:

(A) with respect to a disclosure, it is complete and correct as of the time it is made; and

(B) with respect to a discovery request, response, or objection, it is:

(i) consistent with these rules and warranted by existing law or by a nonfrivolous argument for extending, modifying, or reversing existing law, or for establishing new law;

(ii) not interposed for any improper purpose, such as to harass, cause unnecessary delay, or needlessly increase the cost of litigation; and

(iii) neither unreasonable nor unduly burdensome or expensive, considering the needs of the case, prior discovery in the case, the amount in controversy, and the importance of the issues at stake in the action.

(2) *Failure to Sign.* Other parties have no duty to

act on an unsigned disclosure, request, response, or objection until it is signed, and the court must strike it unless a signature is promptly supplied after the omission is called to the attorney's or party's attention.

(3) *Sanction for Improper Certification.* If a certification violates this rule without substantial justification, the court, on motion or on its own, must impose an appropriate sanction on the signer, the party on whose behalf the signer was acting, or both. The sanction may include an order to pay the reasonable expenses, including attorney's fees, caused by the violation.

[Amended December 27, 1946, effective March 19, 1948; January 21, 1963, effective July 1, 1963; February 28, 1966, effective July 1, 1966; March 30, 1970, effective July 1, 1970; April 29, 1980, effective August 1, 1980; April 28, 1983, effective August 1, 1983; March 2, 1987, effective August 1, 1987; April 22, 1993, effective December 1, 1993; April 17, 2000, effective December 1, 2000; April 12, 2006, effective December 1, 2006; April 30, 2007, effective December 1, 2007; April 28, 2010, effective December 1, 2010.]

AUTHORS' COMMENTARY ON RULE 26

PURPOSE AND SCOPE

Rule 26 contains the general provisions governing discovery. It sets forth the general discovery procedures, controls the scope of inquiry allowed, provides for protective orders, and imposes a duty to supplement discovery responses. The general provisions in Rule 26 apply to the specific discovery devices in Rules 27 through 37.

NOTE: Rule 26 and the other discovery rules were substantially revised in 1970, 1993, 2000, 2006, 2007, and 2010. Therefore, great care should be exercised when citing or relying on decisions pertaining to Rule 26.

Expert Discovery Amendments: Rule 26 was amended as of December 1, 2010. The amendments, discussed in more detail in the commentary below, address discovery of experts. New Rule 26(a)(2)(C) provides that, with respect to experts who are not specially retained, and therefore who do not have to provide an expert report, the party's disclosure must set forth the subject matter on which the expert is expected to present evidence and a summary of the facts and opinions to which the witness is expected to testify. New Rule 26(b)(4)(B) protects draft expert reports from disclosure as trial preparation materials. New Rule 26(b)(4(C) protects communications between counsel and expert witnesses from disclosure as trial preparation materials unless they pertain to: (i) compensation for the expert; (ii) the facts or data that counsel provided and the expert considered in forming the opinions to be expressed; or (iii) the assumptions that counsel provided and the expert relied on in forming the opinions to be expressed.

RULE 26(a)—REQUIRED DISCLOSURES

CORE CONCEPT

Rule 26(a) requires that parties disclose certain information automatically, without the need for discovery requests, at three points during the litigation. First, all parties must make broad initial disclosures at or shortly after they conduct the discovery meeting under Rule 26(f). Second, Rule 26(a) requires disclosures about expert testimony 90 days before trial. Third, Rule 26(a) specifies the pretrial disclosures to be made 30 days before trial. Rule 26(a) also establishes the exclusive list of available discovery methods to supplement the automatic disclosures. In general, the only discovery devices that parties may use are: depositions upon oral examination (Rules 30, 27, 28, and 32); depositions upon written questions (Rules 31, 27, 28, and 32); written interrogatories (Rule 33); production of documents and things and entry onto land for inspection (Rule 34); physical and mental inspections (Rule 35); and requests for admission (Rule 36).

RULE 26(a)(1)—INITIAL DISCLOSURE

CORE CONCEPT

At the commencement of discovery, each party must disclose the identity of witnesses, a description of documents by category and location, a computation of each category of damages, and insurance information.

APPLICATIONS

Impact of 2007 "Restyling" Amendments

Current Rule 26(a) contains subsections that were regrouped and numbered as part of the 2007 "Restyling" Project. In researching current Rules 26(a), practitioners should be mindful of this repositioning.

Time for Initial Disclosure

Parties must make their initial disclosures at or within 14 days after the discovery meeting required by Rule 26(f), unless a different time is set by court order or stipulation.[1] Thus, Rule 26 establishes the following typical sequence for the early

---

[1] *R & R Sails, Inc. v. Ins. Co. of Pennsylvania*, 673 F.3d 1240, 1246 (9th Cir. 2012).

discovery events: first, the court schedules an initial scheduling conference; second, the parties conduct a discovery meeting at least 21 days before the court's initial scheduling conference; third, the parties make their voluntary disclosures; and fourth, the parties meet with the judge for the scheduling conference, where the timetable for the balance of the discovery events will be established. Parties joined or served after the Rule 26(f) conference must make the initial disclosures within 30 days after being joined or served, unless a different time is set by stipulation or court order.

Content of Initial Disclosure

Rule 26(a)(1) requires automatic initial disclosure of four categories of information:

(A) *Witnesses*: Parties must disclose the name, and if known the address and telephone number,[2] of each individual likely to have discoverable information that the disclosing party may use to support its claims or defenses.[3] Parties must also identify the subjects of such information.[4]

(B) *Documents*: Parties must provide a copy of, or a description by category and location of, all documents, electronically stored information, and tangible things that the disclosing party may use to support its claims or defenses.[5] Except in cases with very few documents, most parties will disclose categories and locations rather than producing all the documents. Parties must provide or describe all disclosable documents in their possession, control, or custody.[6]

(C) *Damages Computations*: Each party must provide a computation of any category of damages claimed by that party.[7] Each party must also produce the non-privileged documents supporting the computation, including documents

---

[2]*Scaife v. Boenne*, 191 F.R.D. 590, 594 (N.D. Ind. 2000) (Rule 26(a)(1) contemplates disclosure of address and telephone number so the other party can contact the witnesses, if appropriate).

[3]*Doe v. Young*, 664 F.3d 727, 734 (8th Cir. 2011); *Cummings v. General Motors Corp.*, 365 F.3d 944, 954 (10th Cir. 2004) (a party is not obligated to disclose witnesses or documents, whether favorable or unfavorable, that it does not intend to use).

[4]*Harriman v. Hancock County*, 627 F.3d 22, 29 (1st Cir. 2010).

[5]*Lovato v. Burlington Northern and Santa Fe Ry. Co.*, 200 F.R.D. 448 (D. Colo. 2001), rev'd on other grounds, 201 F.R.D. 509 (D. Colo. 2001) (medi-

cal records must be disclosed).

[6]See Rule 34(a) for an explanation of the scope of documents within a party's possession, custody, or control. *See also Nance v. Wayne County*, 264 F.R.D. 331, 338 (M.D.Tenn. 2009).

[7]*MGE UPS Systems, Inc. v. GE Consumer and Indus., Inc.*, 622 F.3d 361, 368 (5th Cir. 2010) (damages limited to categories disclosed); *Bessemer & Lake Erie R.R. Co. v. Seaway Marine Transport*, 596 F.3d 357, 366, 67 (6th Cir. 2010) (claim for lost profits excluded because not properly disclosed); *Williams v. Trader Pub. Co.*, 218 F.3d 481, 487 (5th Cir. 2000) (damages for emotional distress are not susceptible to the type of calculation contemplated by Rule 26(a)(1)).

bearing on the nature and extent of injuries suffered.[8]

(D) *Insurance*: Each party must provide all insurance policies that may provide coverage for part or all of any judgment that might be entered in the action.[9]

Additional disclosures may be required by directive.

Information to Support Claims or Defenses

Rule 26(a)(1) requires disclosure only of information and documents that the disclosing party may use to support its claims or defenses.[10] This provision dovetails with the exclusionary sanction of Rule 37(c)(1), so that a party may not use information or documents not disclosed initially or by supplement.[11] Note that this restriction to information that a party may use to support its claims or defenses does not apply to affirmative discovery such as interrogatories or document requests, which may seek information that is relevant to the claims or defenses in the case, regardless of whether the responding party may use the information to support its positions.[12]

Impeachment

Information and documents that a party may use solely for impeachment need not be disclosed.[13]

Electronic Data

Rule 26(a)(1)(A)(ii) specifically requires the disclosure of the "electronically stored information"[14] that it may use to support its claims or defenses. If electronic data is very costly or burdensome to disclose, a party may invoke the procedure under Rule 26(b)(2) (under which a party may notify the other parties that it is not collecting and disclosing certain electronic

---

[8]*R & R Sails, Inc. v. Ins. Co. of Pennsylvania*, 673 F.3d 1240, 1246 (9th Cir. 2012) (party must make the documents supporting the computation available for inspection); *E.E.O.C. v. Serv. Temps Inc.*, 679 F.3d 323, 334 (5th Cir. 2012) (no error in refusing to allow the plaintiff to claim a specific amount of damages when the plaintiff failed to disclose damages calculations).

[9]*Wickens v. Shell Oil Co.*, 620 F.3d 747, 759 (7th Cir. 2010); *Excelsior College v. Frye*, 233 F.R.D. 583, 585–86 (S.D. Cal. 2006) ("Rule 26(a)(1)(D), merely requires the disclosure of an insurance policy or other agreement that gives rise to an insurer's obligation to indemnify or hold its insured harmless for a judgment, and does not require the production of all agreements relating to insurance").

[10]*Krause v. Buffalo and Erie County Workforce Development Consortium, Inc.*, 425 F. Supp. 2d 352 (W.D. N.Y. 2006).

[11]The 2000 Amendment to the Advisory Committee Note to Rule 26(a)(1).

[12]*Allen v. Mill-Tel, Inc.*, __ F.R.D. __ (D.Kan. 2012).

[13]*Hammel v. Eau Galle Cheese Factory*, 407 F.3d 852, 869 (7th Cir. 2005); *Searles v. Van Bebber*, 251 F.3d 869 (10th Cir. 2001); *Lomascolo v. Otto Oldsmobile-Cadillac, Inc.*, 253 F. Supp. 2d 354, 359 (N.D. N.Y. 2003) (documents must be used *solely* for impeachment).

[14]The Advisory Committee Notes to the 2006 Amendments indicate that the term "electronically stored information" is consistent with the prior case law requiring the production of electronic documents and "data compilations."

data, and then either party may ask the court to determine whether the data need be disclosed).

Excluded Proceedings

Rule 26(a)(1)(B) excludes 8 categories of proceedings from the initial disclosures:

(1) appeals from administrative proceedings;

(2) petitions for habeas corpus or like challenges to criminal convictions or sentences;

(3) pro se prisoner actions;

(4) actions to enforce or quash an administrative summons or subpoena;

(5) actions by the United States to recover benefit payments;

(6) actions by the United States to collect on student loans guaranteed by the United States;

(7) proceedings ancillary to proceedings in other courts; and

(8) actions to enforce arbitration awards.

Disclose Information "Reasonably Available"

The parties must make their initial disclosures based on the information then "reasonably available."[15] A party may not avoid the initial disclosure requirements claiming that its investigation is not yet complete.[16]

Failure to Disclose

Failure to make the initial disclosures required by Rule 26(a)(1) can result in the exclusion of the undisclosed witness or information,[17] unless the party failing to make the disclosure can demonstrate that the failure was harmless or there was substantial justification.[18] Generally, providing the identity of a witness or producing the documents in discovery will not excuse failure to disclose under Rule 26(a)(1), because that does not put the other party on notice that the producing party may use that witness or those documents to support its claims or defenses.[19]

---

[15]*San Francisco Baykeeper v. West Bay Sanitary Dist.*, __ F.Supp.2d __ (N.D.Cal. 2011) (defining "reasonably available").

[16]*Wallace v. U.S.A.A. Life Gen. Agency, Inc.*, __ F.Supp.2d __ (D.Nev. 2012).

[17]*Wilson v. AM General Corp.*, 167 F.3d 1114 (7th Cir.1999) (rejecting claim that the witnesses were impeachment witnesses and excluding their testimony); *Quesenberry v. Volvo Group North America, Inc.*, __ F.R.D.

__ (W.D.Va. 2010) (no need to show that bad faith was the cause of the nondisclosure).

[18]*Hoyle v. Freightliner, LLC*, __ F.3d __ (4th Cir. 2011) (listing factors for determining whether a violation was harmless or justified); *Davis v. U.S. Bancorp*, 383 F.3d 761, 765 (8th Cir. 2004).

[19]*See Wallace v. U.S.A.A. Life Gen. Agency, Inc.*, __ F.Supp.2d __ (D.Nev. 2012).

Other Party's Failure to Disclose

A party may not refuse to make the Rule 26(a) disclosures because another party has also failed to do so.[20] Likewise, a party believing that another party's disclosure was not sufficient must nonetheless make its own disclosures.

Disclosures Automatic

The initial disclosures are automatically required, without any need for a request or demand.

Stipulations Not to Disclose

The parties may stipulate to the elimination or modification of the initial disclosures, unless precluded from doing so by local rule or court order.

Form of Disclosures

The initial disclosures should be in writing, signed, and served on other parties unless otherwise directed by local rule or court order.[21] The signature constitutes a certification that the disclosure is complete and accurate under Rule 26(g)(1).

Objections

A party believing that Rule 26(a)(1) initial disclosures are "not appropriate in the circumstances of the action" may object during the Rule 26(f) discovery conference. The objection should then be stated in the Rule 26(f) discovery plan filed with the court. Disclosures are not required thereafter except as ordered by the court.[22] In ruling on the objection, the court must determine what disclosures, if any, will be made and set the time for such disclosures.

New or Late Served Parties

Parties that have not been joined or served at the time of the initial disclosures or the Rule 26(f) discovery conference must still make initial disclosures. The time for their disclosures will be 30 days from when they are served or joined, unless modified by stipulation or order. The scope of such parties' disclosures will be similar to the original parties with respect to any stipulations or court orders.[23]

RULE 26(a)(2)—DISCLOSURE OF EXPERT TESTIMONY

CORE CONCEPT

Each party must disclose the identity of its testifying expert

---

[20]*See Jacobsen v. Deseret Book Co.,* 287 F.3d 936, 954 (10th Cir. 2002).

[21]*See S.E.C. v. TheStreet.Com,* 273 F.3d 222, 233 (2d Cir. 2001) (initial disclosures under Rule 26(a)(1) are not filed unless ordered by the court or used in a subsequent stage of the proceedings).

[22]The 2000 Amendment to the Advisory Committee Note to Rule 26(a)(1).

[23]The Advisory Committee Note to the 2000 Amendment to Rule 26(a)(1).

witnesses and produce an expert report for certain categories of testifying experts.

APPLICATIONS

2010 Amendments

Rule 26 has been amended as of December 1, 2010. The amendments, discussed in more detail in the commentary below, address discovery of experts. New Rule 26(a)(2)(C) provides that, with respect to experts who are not specially retained, and therefore who do not have to provide an expert report, the party's disclosure must set forth the subject matter on which the expert is expected to present evidence and a summary of the facts and opinions to which the witness is expected to testify.[24]

Which Experts

Rule 26(a)(2)(A) requires the disclosure of the identity of any person who "may be used at trial to present evidence" under the Federal Rules of Evidence governing expert testimony.[25]

Time for Expert Disclosure

The time for expert disclosures can be set by the court or stipulated by the parties.[26] In the absence of a court order or stipulation, the expert disclosures must be made 90 days before the trial date.[27] If the expert testimony is purely to contradict or rebut testimony disclosed by another party, then the disclosure must be made within 30 days after the disclosure by the other party.[28] Leave may be obtained to disclose an expert report for a rebuttal expert witness after the time for expert disclosures under Rule 26(a)(2).[29]

---

[24]*See Civix-DDI, LLC v. Metropolitan Regional Information Systems, Inc.*, __ F.R.D. __ (E.D.Va. 2011) (applying the amended Rule to a pending case).

[25]*Tribble v. Evangelides*, 670 F.3d 753, 758 (7th Cir. 2012).

[26]*See Goodman v. Staples The Office Superstore, LLC*, __ F.3d __ (9th Cir. 2011) (expert reports must be disclosed at the time and in the sequence ordered by the court); *Avila v. Willits Environmental Remediation Trust*, 633 F.3d 828, 834 (9th Cir. 2011) (court may set deadline for expert disclosures).

[27]*Lutz v. Glendale Union High School*, 403 F.3d 1061, 1071 (9th Cir. 2005) (the 90 day period applies only in the absence of a court established

deadline); *School Bd. of Collier County, Fla. v. K.C.*, 285 F.3d 977, 981 (11th Cir. 2002).

[28]*U.S. v. $231,930.00 in U.S. Currency*, 614 F.3d 837, 841 (8th Cir. 2010) (discussing the difference between rebuttal and impeachment testimony); *Wegener v. Johnson*, 527 F.3d 687, 690–91 (8th Cir. 2008) (impeachment evidence must be disclosed under Rule 26(a)(2)(C)(ii)); *Callahan v. A.E.V., Inc.*, 182 F.3d 237, 259 (3d Cir. 1999) (expert witness designated as "rebuttal expert" allowed to testify during case-in-chief).

[29]*See Wegener v. Johnson*, 527 F.3d 687, 692 (8th Cir. 2008) (the court has discretion to exclude the untimely report when allowing it would require another continuance of the trial); *Nyama v. Ashcroft*, 357 F.3d 812, 816

Impeachment Testimony

The courts are divided about whether expert impeachment evidence must be disclosed.[30]

Content of Disclosure

The disclosure must contain the identity of any witness who may provide expert testimony under the Federal Rules of Evidence governing expert testimony.[31] For witnesses who were retained or specially employed to provide expert testimony, the disclosure must include an expert report.[32] For all other experts, the disclosure must contain:

- the subject matter on which the expert is expected to present evidence; and
- a summary of the facts and opinions to which the witness is expected to testify.[33]

Expert Report

Each expert report must be in writing and signed by the expert,[34] and must contain: a complete statement of all the expert's opinions and the basis and reasons therefor;[35] the facts or data considered by the expert,[36] including documents provided by counsel;[37] any exhibits to be used as support for or a summary of the opinions; the qualifications of the expert and

---

(8th Cir. 2004).

[30]*See U.S. v. $231,930.00 in U.S. Currency*, 614 F.3d 837, 841 (8th Cir. 2010) (impeachment evidence need not be disclosed); *Wegener v. Johnson*, 527 F.3d 687, 690–91 (8th Cir. 2008) (impeachment evidence must be disclosed).

[31]*Hamburger v. State Farm Mut. Auto. Ins. Co.*, 361 F.3d 875, 883 n. 4 (5th Cir. 2004); *Coleman v. American Family Mut. Ins. Co.*, __ F.Supp.2d __ (N.D.Ind. 2011).

[32]*Goodman v. Staples The Office Superstore, LLC*, __ F.3d __ (9th Cir. 2011); *Smith v. Pfizer Inc.*, __ F.Supp.2d __ (M.D.Tenn. 2010).

[33]*Ingram v. Novartis Pharms. Corp.*, __ F.R.D. __ (W.D.Okla. 2012); *Sara Lee Corp. v. Kraft Foods Inc.*, __ F.R.D. __ (N.D.Ill. 2011).

[34]*Neiberger v. Fed Ex Ground Package System, Inc.*, 566 F.3d 1184, 1191 (10th Cir. 2009); *U.S. v. Kalymon*, 541 F.3d 624, 638 (6th Cir. 2008) (the attorney may provide assistance to the expert, or even draft the report, so long as it contains the expert's opinions); *Phipps v. Sheriff of Cook County*, 681 F.Supp.2d 899, 915 (N.D.Ill. 2009)

(report must be signed by the expert, but need not be signed by counsel); *but see Jenkins v. Bartlett*, 487 F.3d 482 (7th Cir. 2007) (allowing experts to adopt a letter written by another doctor as their report).

[35]*R.C. Olmstead, Inc., v. CU Interface, LLC*, __ F.3d __ (6th Cir. 2010) (report should contain enough detail such that the party does not have to depose the expert to avoid ambush); *Romero v. Drummond Co., Inc.*, 552 F.3d 1303, 1323 (11th Cir. 2008) (reports that "merely recite the general subject matter of their expected testimony" are insufficient).

[36]*Sara Lee Corp. v. Kraft Foods Inc.*, __ F.R.D. __ (N.D.Ill. 2011) (discussing the narrower scope of expert discovery under the 2010 amendments); *Iacangelo v. Georgetown University*, 560 F.Supp.2d 53 (D.D.C. 2008).

[37]*Fidelity Nat. Title Ins. Co. of New York v. Intercounty Nat. Title Ins. Co.*, 412 F.3d 745 (7th Cir.2005) (party must disclose all documents "considered" by the expert, without regard to the expert's document retention policy); *Synthes Spine Co., L.P. v. Walden*, 232 F.R.D. 460, 461–62 (E.D.

all publications authored by the expert in the past 10 years; the expert's compensation for his review and testimony; and a list of all other cases in which the expert has testified at trial or at deposition in the past 4 years.[38] The report itself should contain all the required information with considerable detail,[39] and may not satisfy Rule 26(a)(2)(B) by incorporating other material.[40]

Failure to Disclose Report

The failure to disclose a report meeting the requirements of Rule 26(a)(2)(B) may preclude the party from introducing the testimony as evidence on a motion, at a hearing, or at trial, either altogether[41] or as to specific opinions not disclosed in the report.[42] Such sanctions are "automatic and mandatory"[43] unless the party failing to disclose can show the failure was justified or harmless.[44] A party who believes that an opposing party has disclosed an inadequate expert report should file a motion

---

Pa. 2005) (the rule requires the disclosure of all information provided to the expert, including privileged information); *Colindres v. Quietflex Mfg.*, 228 F.R.D. 567 (S.D. Tex. 2005) (documents "considered" by the expert must be disclosed, even if not ultimately relied upon).

[38] *Doblar v. Unverferth Mfg. Co., Inc.*, 1999 DSD 12, 185 F.R.D. 258 (D.S.D. 1999) (awarding sanctions against the expert because many instances of prior testimony were not disclosed); *Coleman v. Dydula*, 190 F.R.D. 316, 318 (W.D. N.Y. 1999) (the list of cases should, at a minimum, include the name of the court where the testimony occurred, the names of the parties, the case number, and whether the testimony was given at a deposition or trial); *Zic v. Italian Government Travel Office*, 130 F. Supp. 2d 991, 1001 (N.D. Ill. 2001) (names of the parties in other cases in which the expert has testified is sufficient, although not ideal). *Cf. Trunk v. Midwest Rubber and Supply Co.*, 175 F.R.D. 664, 665 (D. Colo. 1997) (Rule 26(a)(2)(B) report does not require a party to produce reports offered by its expert witness in unrelated litigation).

[39] *Walter Intern. Prods., Inc. v. Salinas*, 650 F.3d 1402, 1410 (11th Cir. 2011) (short letter deemed inadequate); *Krischel v. Hennessy*, 533 F. Supp. 2d 790, 797–98 (N.D. Ill. 2008) (the report may not be "sketchy and vague").

[40] *Ingram v. Novartis Pharms. Corp.*, _ F.R.D. _ (W.D.Okla. 2012) (references to other reports and testimony improper); *U.S. v. Alabama Power Co.*, _ F.Supp.2d _ (N.D.Ala. 2011) (expert cannot rely on documents identified by other experts); *Smith v. State Farm Fire and Cas. Co.*, 164 F.R.D. 49 (S.D. W. Va. 1995) (report may not incorporate interrogatory answers).

[41] *Pena-Crespo v. Puerto Rico*, 408 F.3d 10, 13–14 (1st Cir. 2005); *Ortiz-Lopez v. Sociedad Espanola de Auxilio Mutuo Y Beneficiencia de Puerto Rico*, 248 F.3d 29 (1st Cir.2001).

[42] *Boston Gas Co. v. Century Indem. Co.*, 529 F.3d 8 (1st Cir. 2008); *Dairy Farmers of America, Inc. v. Travelers Ins. Co.*, 391 F.3d 936, 943–44 (8th Cir. 2004); *Salgado by Salgado v. General Motors Corp.*, 150 F.3d 735, 742 (7th Cir. 1998) (expert report must contain a detailed description of expert opinions and bases therefore).

[43] *But see S.E.C. v. Jasper*, 678 F.3d 1116, 1124 (9th Cir. 2012) (no error in admitting document prepared by undisclosed expert where the opposing party did not object under Rule 26(a)(2)).

[44] *Goodman v. Staples The Office Superstore, LLC*, _ F.3d _ (9th Cir. 2011) (treating physician who did not prepare an expert report allowed to testify because rule was murky as to treating physicians); *Gicla v. U.S.*, 572 F.3d 407, 411 (7th Cir. 2009) (failure

to compel a more complete report or a motion to exclude the expert promptly, as waiting until trial to raise the issue may result in waiver.[45] The courts are divided as to whether disclosure of the expert opinions or required information in deposition is a substitute for inclusion in the expert disclosure.[46]

Stipulations Not to Disclose Expert Reports

The parties may stipulate to the elimination or modification of the expert report disclosures, unless precluded from doing so by local rule or court order.

Testimony is Measure, Not Witness Qualification

The expert disclosures are required if the testimony is expert in nature, not factual; expert disclosures are not required if an expert is being called to give percipient factual testimony.[47]

Experts Employed by a Party

A party must produce an expert report for an employee only if the employee's duties regularly involve giving expert testimony or the employee was specially employed to provide expert testimony.[48] This requirement will only apply, however, if the employee is giving expert testimony.[49] Likewise, an individual party who intends to present expert testimony must list him or herself as an expert and disclose the information required by Rule 26(a)(2)(C), but need not produce an expert report.[50]

---

to disclose document reviewed by expert harmless where document did not change the expert's opinion).

[45]*Rodrick v. Wal-Mart Stores East, L.P.*, 666 F.3d 1093, 1096 (8th Cir. 2012).

[46]*See Walter Intern. Prods., Inc. v. Salinas*, 650 F.3d 1402, 1410 (11th Cir. 2011) (a report is necessary to effectively take an expert deposition); *Smith v. Tenet Healthsystem SL, Inc.*, 436 F.3d 879, 889 (8th Cir. 2006) (expert could rely on x-rays disclosed at the deposition because failure to disclose in the report was harmless); *In re Sulfuric Acid Antitrust Litigation*, 432 F. Supp. 2d 794 (N.D. Ill. 2006) (asking about additional opinions at deposition may open the door for admission of those opinions at trial).

[47]*Gomez v. Rivera Rodriguez*, 344 F.3d 103, 113 (1st Cir. 2003) (Rule 26(a)(2) does not encompass a percipient witness who happens to be an expert); *Gonzalez v. Executive Airlines, Inc.*, 236 F.R.D. 73 (D.P.R. 2006) (the

term expert pertains to those who will testify under Rule 702 of the Federal Rules of Evidence); *Indemnity Ins. Co. of North America v. American Eurocopter LLC*, 227 F.R.D. 421, 423 (M.D. N.C. 2005).

[48]*Tokai Corp. v. Easton Enterprises, Inc.*, 632 F.3d 1358, 1364–65 (Fed.Cir. 2011) (party seeking to use an employee expert bears the burden of showing that the expert is specially employed or regularly testifies); *Prieto v. Malgor*, 361 F.3d 1313, 1318 (11th Cir. 2004).

[49]*Watson v. U.S.*, 485 F.3d 1100 (10th Cir. 2007) (employee allowed to give expert testimony without expert report because he did not regularly give expert testimony); *Long v. Cottrell, Inc.*, 265 F.3d 663, 668 (8th Cir. 2001) (expert report not required even though employee regularly testified for the party as an expert witness because the testimony at issue was fact testimony, not expert testimony).

[50]*U.S. ex rel. Jones v. Brigham &*

757

Treating Physicians

An expert report is generally not required for a treating physician to testify regarding the treatment,[51] although a number of courts require an expert report when the treating physician will offer testimony beyond the scope of the treatment rendered.[52] However, parties must disclose the subject matter and a summary of the facts and opinions as to which a treating physician is expected to testify under Rule 26(a)(2)(C).[53] A physician conducting an Independent Medical Examination will generally be considered an expert for purposes of Rule 26(a)(2),[54] but the obligation to produce a report for a physician conducting an examination under Rule 35 is governed by Rule 35, not by Rule 26(a)(2).[55] When the attorney has referred the client to the physician, the physician is more likely to be treated as a specially retained expert.[56]

Disclosures Automatic

The expert disclosures are automatically required, without any need for a request or demand.

Form of Disclosures

The expert disclosures should be in writing, signed, and served on other parties, unless otherwise directed by local rule or court order.[57] The signature constitutes a certification that the disclosure is complete and accurate under Rule 26(g)(1).

Objections to Disclosures

The court's case management order may designate a period for filing objections to the sufficiency of expert disclosures, in which case such objections are waived if not timely raised.[58] Otherwise, sanctions for an insufficient disclosure are governed by the sanctions provisions in Rule 37(c)(1).

Duty to Supplement

Rule 26(a)(2) (governing expert disclosures) and Rule 26(e) (providing the duty to supplement) require parties to supplement their expert disclosures if the party learns that the infor-

---

Women's Hosp., 678 F.3d 72, 90 (1st Cir. 2012).

[51]*See Goodman v. Staples The Office Superstore, LLC*, __ F.3d __ (9th Cir. 2011); *Fielden v. CSX Transp., Inc.*, 482 F.3d 866, 869 (6th Cir. 2007).

[52]*See Goodman v. Staples The Office Superstore, LLC*, __ F.3d __ (9th Cir. 2011); *Musser v. Gentiva Health Services*, 356 F.3d 751, 757 (7th Cir. 2004).

[53]*Coleman v. American Family Mut. Ins. Co.*, __ F.Supp.2d __ (N.D.Ind. 2011).

[54]*Whitney v. U.S.*, 251 F.R.D. 1 (D.D.C. 2008).

[55]*Diaz v. Con-Way Truckload, Inc.*, 279 F.R.D. 412, 418 (S.D.Tex. 2012).

[56]*Perkins v. U.S.*, 626 F.Supp.2d 587 (E.D.Va. 2009).

[57]*See S.E.C. v. TheStreet.Com*, 273 F.3d 222, 233 (2d Cir. 2001) (initial disclosures under Rule 26(a)(2) are not filed unless ordered by the court or used in a subsequent stage of the proceedings).

[58]*McCoy v. Whirlpool Corp.*, 214 F.R.D. 646, 648–49 (D. Kan. 2003).

mation disclosed was incomplete or incorrect.[59] Supplemental expert information should be disclosed by the time the pretrial disclosures are made under Rule 26(a)(3), 30 days before trial unless otherwise set by the court.[60]

RULE 26(a)(3)—PRETRIAL DISCLOSURES

CORE CONCEPT

Prior to trial, each party must disclose the witnesses that may testify at trial, the deposition testimony that may be offered at trial, and the exhibits that may be offered at trial.

APPLICATIONS

Impact of 2007 "Restyling" Amendments

The 2007 "Restyling" Project reorganized Rule 26(a)(3), grouping former subsections (A) through (C) into subsections (i) through (iii) of new Rule 26(a)(3)(A). The trailing text at the end of Rule 26(a)(3) was made Rule 26(a)(3)(B). In researching current Rule 26(a), practitioners should be mindful of this repositioning.

Time for Pretrial Disclosure

The time for pretrial disclosures is often set by the court. In the absence of a court order, the expert disclosures must be made 30 days before the trial date.[61] Parties will not be required to respond to discovery requests seeking the information covered by Rule 26(a)(3) at an earlier stage in the litigation.[62]

Content of Pretrial Disclosure

Rule 26(a)(3) requires a pretrial disclosure of the following information:

(A) *Witnesses*: Each party must disclose the name and, unless already disclosed, the address and phone number of each witness that may testify at trial. The disclosure should indicate those witnesses who are expected to testify and those who may be called if needed.[63]

(B) *Depositions*: Each party must designate the testimony that the party intends to introduce in the form of a deposition. If the deposition was recorded other than stenographically, then the party must provide a transcript of the pertinent

---

[59]*David E. Watson, P.C. v. U.S.*, 668 F.3d 1008, 1014 (8th Cir. 2012); *Brainard v. American Skandia Life Assur. Corp.*, 432 F.3d 655, 664 (6th Cir. 2005).

[60]*U.S. S.E.C. v. Maxxon, Inc.*, 465 F.3d 1174, 1182 (10th Cir.2006); *Bixby v. KBR, Inc.*, __ F.R.D. __, (D.Or. 2011).

[61]*Trafton v. Sunbury Primary Care, P.A.*, __ F.Supp.2d __ (D.Me. 2010).

[62]*Banks v. Office of Senate Sergeant-at-Arms*, 222 F.R.D. 7, 15 (D.D.C. 2004).

[63]*But see Walter Intern. Prods., Inc. v. Salinas*, 650 F.3d 1402, 1415 (11th Cir. 2011) (court may require the parties to submit a list of witnesses they will actually call, not those that they "may" call).

parts of the testimony.[64]

(C) *Exhibits*: Each party must identify all exhibits, including demonstrative or summary exhibits. The disclosure should indicate those exhibits that the party expects to introduce and those that the party may introduce if needed.

Impeachment

The pretrial disclosure is not required to include documents or testimony to be introduced solely for impeachment.[65]

Failure to Disclose

Any witnesses, depositions, or exhibits not properly disclosed under Rule 26(a)(3) may be excluded from use at trial.[66]

Objections to Deposition Testimony or Exhibits

Any objections to the use of a deposition or exhibit must be served and filed within 14 days of the disclosure of the intent to use the deposition or exhibit. The statement of the objections should state the grounds for the objections. Failure to disclose such an objection is a waiver of the objection,[67] except for objections to relevancy under Rules 402 and 403 of the Federal Rules of Evidence. Note that the disclosure of the objection is not the same as making the objection; a party must still object when the deposition or exhibit is offered at trial.[68]

Disclosures Automatic

The pretrial disclosures are automatically required, without any need for a request or demand.

Form of Disclosures

The pretrial disclosures should be in writing, signed, served on other parties, and filed with the court, unless otherwise directed by local rule or court order. The signature constitutes a certification that the disclosure is complete and accurate under Rule 26(g)(1).

RULE 26(a)(4)—FORM OF DISCLOSURES

CORE CONCEPT

The automatic disclosures under Rule 26(a) should be in writing, signed, served on other parties, unless otherwise directed by

---

[64]*Tilton v. Capital Cities/ABC, Inc.*, 115 F.3d 1471, 1478 (10th Cir. 1997).

[65]*Hammel v. Eau Galle Cheese Factory*, 407 F.3d 852, 869 (7th Cir. 2005); *Bearint ex rel. Bearint v. Dorell Juvenile Group, Inc.*, 389 F.3d 1339 (11th Cir. 2004) (party cannot admit just the rebuttal parts of an expert's testimony if no report was disclosed); *U.S. v. Hawley*, 562 F.Supp.2d 1017

(N.D.Iowa 2008); *Halbasch v. Med-Data, Inc.*, 192 F.R.D. 641 (D. Or. 2000) (discussing the various interpretations of "solely for impeachment").

[66]The Advisory Committee Note to the 1993 Amendment to Rule 26.

[67]*Martin v. Harris*, 560 F.3d 210, 219 (4th Cir. 2009).

[68]The Advisory Committee Note to the 1993 Amendment to Rule 26.

local rule or court order. Only the pretrial disclosure under Rule 26(a)(3) must be filed. The signature constitutes a certification that the disclosure is complete and accurate under Rule 26(g)(1).

RULE 26(b)(1)—DISCOVERY SCOPE AND LIMITS—SCOPE IN GENERAL

CORE CONCEPT

In general, discovery is allowed of any matter that is relevant to the claim or defense of any party in the pending action and is not privileged.[69] Discovery is more limited with respect to trial preparation materials, non-testifying expert witnesses, and physical or mental examinations.

APPLICATIONS

Covered Actions

The discovery rules apply to all civil actions in federal court, except for the narrow exceptions listed in Rule 81 (such as certain admiralty matters and matters in arbitration pursuant to federal statute). The Rules apply in bankruptcy proceedings, patent actions, and civil contempt proceedings. They apply in habeas corpus actions if the court grants leave to conduct discovery.

"Relevant" Defined

The term "relevant" is not defined by the Rules, but was extremely broad prior to the 2000 Amendments.[70] Courts have defined "relevant" to encompass "any matter that bears on, or that reasonably could lead to other matters that could bear on, any issue that is or may be in the case."[71] Courts also have defined "relevant" as "germane."[72] However, although Rule 26(b)(1) continues to use the word "relevant" after the 2000 Amendments, the scope of discovery has been narrowed.[73]

Claim or Defense vs. Subject Matter

The 2000 Amendments changed the scope of discovery from

[69]*Gov't of Ghana v. ProEnergy Servs., LLC*, 677 F.3d 340, 342 (8th Cir. 2012); *WWP, Inc. v. Wounded Warriors Family Support, Inc.*, 628 F.3d 1032, 1039 (8th Cir. 2011).

[70]*United Oil Co., Inc. v. Parts Associates, Inc.*, 227 F.R.D. 404 (D. Md. 2005); *but see Food Lion, Inc. v. United Food and Commercial Workers Intern. Union, AFL-CIO-CLC*, 103 F.3d 1007, 1012–14 (D.C. Cir. 1997) (finding that "relevant" did not extend to third and fourth party documents).

[71]*Oil, Chemical & Atomic Workers Local Union No. 6-418, AFL-CIO v. N.L.R.B.*, 711 F.2d 348, 360 (D.C. Cir.

1983); *Coleman v. American Family Mut. Ins. Co.*, __ F.Supp.2d __ (N.D.Ind. 2011).

[72]*Oppenheimer Fund, Inc. v. Sanders*, 437 U.S. 340, 351, 98 S. Ct. 2380, 2389–90, 57 L. Ed. 2d 253 (1978).

[73]*See In re PE Corp. Securities Litigation*, 221 F.R.D. 20, 24 (D. Conn. 2003); *Behler v. Hanlon*, 199 F.R.D. 553, 555 (D. Md. 2001) (amended Rule 26 is more narrow); *but see United Oil Co., Inc. v. Parts Associates, Inc.*, 227 F.R.D. 404 (D. Md. 2005) (the new standard is still a broad one).

matters "relevant to the subject matter involved in the pending action" to matters "relevant to the claim or defense of any party."[74] The Advisory Committee did not define the distinction, but indicated that it wants the focus of discovery to be the actual claims and defenses in the action, and does not want discovery to be used to develop new claims or defenses not already pleaded.[75] However, information such as other incidents of the same type or involving the same product or information about a party's organizational structure may be relevant to the claims in the action.[76]

Motion to Expand the Scope

For "good cause," the court may expand discovery to include matters relevant to the subject matter involved in the action.[77] This determination might be made in the context of a motion to compel a more broad response to particular discovery requests, or possibly could be raised in the Rule 26(f) discovery report and addressed during the initial status conference with the court.[78] The "good cause" standard is meant to be flexible, giving broad discretion to the court.[79]

Relevant to Potential Claims

A party may discover any matter that is relevant to any claim, issue, or defense that is pleaded in the case, regardless of which party raises the claim, issue, or defense. Discovery is not permitted as to potential additional claims or defenses, absent a court order expanding the scope of discovery.[80] Thus, discovery is permitted with respect to claims that have been challenged by a motion to dismiss or motion for summary judgment. However, if a claim has been dismissed, further discovery that is relevant to that claim only will not be allowed.[81]

---

[74]*See In re Cooper Tire & Rubber Co.*, 568 F.3d 1180, 1188 (10th Cir. 2009); *Sallis v. University of Minn.*, 408 F.3d 470, 477–78 (8th Cir. 2005).

[75]The Advisory Committee Note to the 2000 Amendment to Rule 26(b)(1). *See also In re Cooper Tire & Rubber Co.*, 568 F.3d 1180 (10th Cir. 2009) (the focus of discovery should be the actual claims and defenses in the action); *Sallis v. University of Minn.*, 408 F.3d 470, 477 (8th Cir. 2005) (advisory committee wanted courts to be more involved in controlling discovery).

[76]The Advisory Committee Note to the 2000 Amendment to Rule 26(b)(1).

[77]*In re Cooper Tire & Rubber Co.*, 568 F.3d 1180 (10th Cir. 2009); *Lynn v. Monarch Recovery Mgmt., Inc.*, __ F.Supp.2d __ (D.Md. 2012).

[78]The Advisory Committee Note to the 2000 Amendment to Rule 26(b)(1). *See also In re Cooper Tire & Rubber Co.*, 568 F.3d 1180 (10th Cir. 2009) (expanding discovery to include matters relevant to the subject matter involved in the action requires court involvement).

[79]The Advisory Committee Note to the 2000 Amendment to Rule 26(b)(1).

[80]The Advisory Committee Note to the 2000 Amendment to Rule 26(b)(1).

[81]*Oppenheimer Fund, Inc. v. Sanders*, 437 U.S. 340, 351, 98 S. Ct. 2380, 2389–90, 57 L. Ed. 2d 253

Relevant vs. Admissible

Evidence need not be admissible to be relevant, and thus discoverable.[82] Relevant inadmissible evidence is discoverable if it is "reasonably calculated to lead to the discovery of admissible evidence."[83] Conversely, admissible evidence is almost always discoverable.[84]

Limitations on Discovery

The broad scope of discovery under Rule 26(b)(1) must be read in conjunction with the three limitations in Rule 26(b)(2) relating to discovery that is cumulative or unduly burdensome.[85]

Duty to Preserve

It is well recognized that parties and attorneys have a duty to preserve relevant evidence once litigation has been commenced or is reasonably anticipated. Some courts find this duty arises in part under Rule 26(b)(1).[86]

Jurisdictional Issues

Discovery is allowed with respect to jurisdictional issues.[87] Thus, parties may conduct discovery pertaining to other parties' citizenship, the amount in controversy, a party's contacts with the forum state, and other jurisdictional issues.

Location of Evidence

Rule 26(b)(1) explicitly authorizes discovery about the location and existence of documents and other evidence and about the identity and location of persons having knowledge of discoverable matters. The latter provision includes the identity of investigators hired by a party.

Matters Known to Others

A party must provide information and documents it possesses, regardless of who else possesses that information. Thus, it generally is not proper to object on the basis that the party already has the information it is requesting or that information is in the public record[88] or is otherwise available to the party[89] (although the court might curtail such requests as unduly

---

(1978).

[82]*Seattle Times Co. v. Rhinehart*, 467 U.S. 20, 104 S. Ct. 2199, 81 L. Ed. 2d 17 (1984); *In re Cooper Tire & Rubber Co.*, 568 F.3d 1180 (10th Cir. 2009).

[83]*Perry v. Schwarzenegger*, 591 F.3d 1126, 1143–44 (9th Cir. 2009); *U.S. v. R&F Properties of Lake County, Inc.*, 433 F.3d 1349, 1359 (11th Cir. 2005).

[84]*Terwilliger v. York Intern. Corp.*, 176 F.R.D. 214, 218 (W.D. Va. 1997).

[85]*In re Cooper Tire & Rubber Co.*,

568 F.3d 1180 (10th Cir. 2009).

[86]*See Yelton v. PHI, Inc.*, 279 F.R.D. 377, 384 (E.D.La. 2011).

[87]*Oppenheimer Fund, Inc. v. Sanders*, 437 U.S. 340, 351, 98 S. Ct. 2380, 57 L. Ed. 2d 253 (1978).

[88]*Mid-Atlantic Recycling Technologies, Inc. v. City of Vineland*, 222 F.R.D. 81 (D.N.J. 2004); *Petruska v. Johns-Manville*, 83 F.R.D. 32, 35 (E.D. Pa. 1979).

[89]*Abrahamsen v. Trans-State Exp., Inc.*, 92 F.3d 425, 428 (6th Cir. 1996).

burdensome in some circumstances).

Impeachment

Discovery is generally allowed of matters that would be used to impeach other parties' witnesses.[90] Thus, one normally may ask whether the responding party has any criminal convictions and may inquire as to prior statements.[91] It is less clear whether one may inquire as to what other parties will use for impeachment. The courts are divided as to whether a party may ask whether opponents are aware of any prior injuries of the party or whether opponents have surveillance movies of the party.

Discovery of Attorneys

Attorneys with discoverable facts not covered by attorney-client privilege or work product protection are subject to discovery despite being retained by one of the parties to represent it in the litigation.[92]

Privileges

Privileged matters are protected from discovery.[93] Privileges in federal court depend upon whether the action involves a state law issue before the court under diversity or supplemental jurisdiction, or whether the action involves a federal cause of action. If a state's substantive laws are being applied, that state's laws of privilege also apply,[94] except as to the attorney work product protection, which is governed by federal common law.[95] If the action is governed by federal law, then Rule 501 of the Federal Rules of Evidence applies. Essentially, Rule 501 instructs the federal courts to develop a body of federal common law privileges. When a deposition is taken in a state other than the state in which the action is pending, the analysis becomes very complicated, and depends upon each state's choice of law provisions.

Raising Claim of Privilege

The normal manner for raising a privilege is by objecting to a particular request or inquiry. For example, at a deposition, a

---

[90]*Hickman v. Taylor*, 329 U.S. 495, 511, 67 S. Ct. 385, 394, 91 L. Ed. 451 (1947); *Varga v. Rockwell Intern. Corp.*, 242 F.3d 693, 697 (6th Cir. 2001) (a party may not hold back materials responsive to a proper discovery request because it prefers to use the evidence as surprise impeachment evidence at trial).

[91]*See Curro v. Watson*, 884 F. Supp. 708 (E.D. N.Y. 1995), aff'd, 100 F.3d 942 (2d Cir. 1996) (limiting impeachment discovery to areas related to expected testimony).

[92]*United Phosphorus, Ltd. v. Midland Fumigant, Inc.*, 164 F.R.D. 245 (D. Kan. 1995).

[93]*Perry v. Schwarzenegger*, 591 F.3d 1126, 1140 (9th Cir. 2009) (communications protected by the First Amendment are privileged); *In re Lott*, 424 F.3d 446, 452 (6th Cir. 2005) (privileged material, even if relevant, is not discoverable).

[94]*Brown v. Waco Fire & Cas. Co.*, 73 F.R.D. 297 (S.D. Miss. 1976).

[95]*Tompkins v. R.J. Reynolds Tobacco Co.*, 92 F. Supp. 2d 70 (N.D. N.Y. 2000).

party may orally raise an objection to an individual question, then refuse to provide the privileged information (by counsel instructing the witness not to answer). In response to interrogatories, document requests, or requests for admission, a party may make a written objection to individual questions or requests and withhold the privileged information. The objection must include sufficient information so that the court and opposing counsel can assess the applicability of the privilege.[96]

Who May Assert

Usually, a privilege may only be asserted by the person holding the privilege. Certainly, one party may not assert a privilege of a non-party witness or another party. When an attorney or doctor is deposed it is unclear who may assert the privilege—the privilege technically belongs to the client, but courts allow the attorney to assert the privilege if asked about the attorney-client communication.[97]

Waiver of Privilege

Privileges generally are waived by voluntary disclosure,[98] either during discovery or elsewhere.[99] Thus, caution should be exercised in discussing or responding to discovery requests pertaining to privileged matters.

Recalling Privileged Information

Rule 26(b)(5)(B) establishes a procedure to recall privileged information that has already been produced. A party believing that it has produced privileged information may provide a notification to the parties who have received the information. The notification should be in writing (unless circumstances do not so allow, such as in a deposition) and should be sufficiently detailed to allow the receiving parties to evaluate the claim of privilege[100] After receiving such a notification, the receiving parties must return, sequester, or destroy the specified information and all copies (including taking reasonable steps to retrieve any information that the receiving party had already disclosed to other persons). If they do not agree with the privilege assertion, they can present the information to the court under seal for a determination of the privilege claim. During the pendency of the court's review of the privilege claim, the receiving parties are prohibited from using the information and the producing party must preserve it. Alternatively, the parties

---

[96]Rule 26(b)(5); *Burns v. Imagine Films Entertainment, Inc.*, 164 F.R.D. 589 (W.D. N.Y. 1996).

[97]*See Martin Marietta Materials, Inc. v. Bedford Reinforced Plastics, Inc.*, 227 F.R.D. 382, 390 (W.D. Pa. 2005) (privilege belongs to the client, not to the attorney).

[98]*In re Grand Jury Proceedings*

Subpoena to Testify to: Wine, 841 F.2d 230, 234 (8th Cir. 1988).

[99]*See In re Lott*, 424 F.3d 446, 452 (6th Cir. 2005) (attorney client privilege is waived when the legal advice is placed at issue).

[100]The 2006 Amendment to the Advisory Committee Note to Rule 26(b)(2).

can propose their own procedures for privileged information that has been produced or disclosed.

Documents Containing Privileged and Non-privileged Matters

If part of a document contains privileged matters and part does not, a party must provide the non-privileged matter, but may redact the privileged matter.

Privileged Matters to be Introduced at Trial

A majority of courts hold that a party cannot assert a privilege at the discovery stage, then introduce the privileged matter at trial.[101] Consequently, any matter intended to be introduced at trial should be produced during discovery if requested.

Particular Privileges

A detailed analysis of every potential privilege is beyond the scope of this book. The following is an overview of the most commonly asserted privileges:

- *Attorney-Client:* The attorney-client privilege applies to all confidential communications between a client and the client's attorney that occur in connection with legal representation or in the process of obtaining legal representation.[102] It applies to communications to an in-house attorney if the attorney is providing legal services. The privilege does not protect communications between one party and the attorney for another party. It does not protect documents or other physical evidence provided to the attorney (other than written communications to the attorney) or the underlying facts,[103] nor does it protect information or evidence gathered by the attorney from other sources or notes and memoranda prepared by the attorney (but see the discussion of attorney-work product under Rule 26(b)(3)).

- *Self-Incrimination:* The Fifth Amendment to the United States Constitution provides all persons (whether or not parties to a litigation) with a privilege against testifying in a manner that would tend to incriminate them.[104] The privilege applies at depositions,[105] interrogatories, requests for admission, and production of documents,[106] as well as at trial. Corporations may not assert the priv-

---

[101]*Doe v. Eli Lilly & Co., Inc.*, 99 F.R.D. 126, 127 (D.D.C. 1983).

[102]*Diversified Industries, Inc. v. Meredith*, 572 F.2d 596, 612 (8th Cir. 1977); *Martin Marietta Materials, Inc. v. Bedford Reinforced Plastics, Inc.*, 227 F.R.D. 382, 392 (W.D. Pa. 2005).

[103]*Martin Marietta Materials, Inc. v. Bedford Reinforced Plastics, Inc.*, 227 F.R.D. 382, 392 (W.D. Pa. 2005).

[104]*De Vita v. Sills*, 422 F.2d 1172 (3d Cir.1970).

[105]*In re Folding Carton Antitrust Litigation*, 609 F.2d 867 (7th Cir. 1979).

[106]*Gordon v. Federal Deposit Ins. Corp.*, 427 F.2d 578, 580 (D.C. Cir. 1970).

ilege, but corporate representatives may assert it if their testimony would incriminate them personally, regardless of whether they are testifying in their individual or representative capacities.[107] There can be no penalties or sanctions for properly exercising the Fifth Amendment privilege. However, in a civil proceeding it appears that opposing parties may comment on a party's exercise of the Fifth Amendment (in contrast to the prohibition on such comments in a criminal proceeding).[108]

- *Governmental Privileges:* The United States and the individual States must produce all relevant, non-privileged matter, just as any other party.[109] However, the United States has some extra privileges:

  - *Governmental Informer Privilege:* The United States has a qualified privilege to refuse to reveal the identity of an informer.[110] When the privilege is asserted, the court will balance the litigant's need for the information against the government's interest in protecting its informer's identity. The privilege belongs to the government, and protects only the identity of the informer, not the information provided by the informer. The government may not assert the privilege if it intends for the informer to testify at trial.

  - *Government's Privilege for Military or State Secrets:* The United States has a qualified privilege for matters that involve military or state secrets.[111] In order to assert the privilege, the head of the department that has control over the matter must lodge a formal claim of privilege. The court will then rule on the privilege by balancing the litigant's need against the government's interest in keeping the matter secret.[112]

  - *Government's Statutory Privilege:* Some statutes require governmental agencies and other entities to file certain documents or reports, and designate the submissions as confidential. Under these statutes, the privilege is generally absolute. A common example is income tax returns. Under

---

[107]*U.S. v. Kordel*, 397 U.S. 1, 8, 90 S. Ct. 763, 767, 25 L. Ed. 2d 1 (1970).

[108]*Baxter v. Palmigiano*, 425 U.S. 308, 96 S. Ct. 1551, 47 L. Ed. 2d 810 (1976).

[109]*U. S. v. Procter & Gamble Co.*, 356 U.S. 677, 681, 78 S. Ct. 983, 986, 2 L. Ed. 2d 1077 (1958).

[110]*Roviaro v. U.S.*, 353 U.S. 53, 59, 77 S. Ct. 623, 627, 1 L. Ed. 2d 639 (1957).

[111]*See General Dynamics Corp. v. U.S.*, __ U.S. __, 131 S.Ct. 1900, 1905 (2011).

[112]*U.S. v. Reynolds*, 345 U.S. 1, 73 S. Ct. 528, 97 L. Ed. 727 (1953).

the regulation,[113] the United States receives and keeps tax returns, but is not required to produce them to private litigants. Note that the privilege belongs to the United States only—the individual filing the return may be required to produce it (although other objections, such as relevance, might apply).

- *Executive Privilege:* The Executive branch of the United States government has a general qualified privilege, grounded in the need for the executive branch to gather information. The privilege generally must be asserted by the head of the relevant department. The court will then balance the litigant's need against the governmental interest asserted.[114]

- *Other Privileges:* In some states, communications with spouses, physicians, clergy, journalists,[115] accountants, and social workers are privileged.

Burden of Proof

The party raising a privilege has the burden of establishing the existence of the privilege.[116] The party challenging relevance has the burden of establishing non-relevance, unless the request is overly broad on its face or relevance is not readily apparent.[117]

RULE 26(b)(2)—LIMITATIONS ON FREQUENCY AND EXTENT

CORE CONCEPT

Rule 26(b)(2) requires the court to limit discovery that is unreasonably cumulative or duplicative,[118] is obtainable from another source more conveniently, or if the burden[119] or expense of

---

[113]26 C.F.R. § 301.6103(a-1)(c)).

[114]*U.S. v. Nixon*, 418 U.S. 683, 94 S. Ct. 3090, 41 L. Ed. 2d 1039 (1974).

[115]*In re Madden*, 151 F.3d 125, 128 (3d Cir. 1998) (recognizing qualified journalists' privilege); *Gonzales v. National Broadcasting Co., Inc.*, 155 F.3d 618, 626–27 (2d Cir. 1998) (journalists' privilege applies only to confidential information).

[116]*Heathman v. U.S. Dist. Court for Central Dist. of California*, 503 F.2d 1032, 1033 (9th Cir. 1974); *Hobart v. City of Stafford*, ___ F.Supp.2d ___ (S.D.Tex. 2011); *Martin Marietta Materials, Inc. v. Bedford Reinforced Plastics, Inc.*, 227 F.R.D. 382, 389

(W.D. Pa. 2005) (party asserting the privilege has the initial burden, then the burden shifts to the opposing party to establish waiver).

[117]*Moss v. Blue Cross and Blue Shield of Kansas, Inc.*, 241 F.R.D. 683 (D. Kan. 2007) (when the discovery sought appears relevant, the party opposing production has the burden to establish lack of relevance; when the discovery does not appear relevant, the party seeking production has the burden to demonstrate relevance).

[118]*Bayer AG v. Betachem, Inc.*, 173 F.3d 188 (3d Cir.1999).

[119]*In re Microcrystalline Cellulose Antitrust Litigation*, 221 F.R.D. 428

the proposed discovery outweighs the likely benefit.[120] The court must also limit discovery if the party seeking the discovery has had "ample opportunity" to obtain the information during prior discovery. Rule 26(b)(2)(B) also establishes a procedure for limiting the need to search for and produce electronic data if it would be unreasonably burdensome or costly to do so.

APPLICATIONS

Objections to Specific Requests
One method of asserting the limitations in Rule 26(b)(2) is by making an objection to a discovery request, such as objecting to an interrogatory or request for production as cumulative or overly burdensome.

Motion for Protective Order
A party seeking to have the use of certain discovery procedures limited should make a motion for a protective order under Rule 26(c).

Required Limitations
Rule 26(b)(2)(C) requires that the court limit discovery in 3 circumstances:

(i)   if the discovery is unreasonably cumulative or duplicative, or can be obtained from another source that is more convenient, less burdensome, or less expensive;[121]

(ii)   if the party seeking the discovery has already had ample opportunity to obtain the information in discovery; or

(iii)   if the burden or expense of the discovery outweighs the likely benefit, considering all the circumstances of the case.[122]

Limits Established by Other Rules
Other Rules place limits on the duration of depositions and on the number of interrogatories and depositions, which may be altered by court order.[123] These limits may also be altered by stipulation under Rule 29. The Rules do not contain any limit on the number of requests for admission, but such limits can be set by local rule, court order, or stipulation.

(E.D. Pa. 2004).

[120]*See Patterson v. Avery Dennison Corp.*, 281 F.3d 676, 681–82 (7th Cir. 2002) (before restricting discovery, the court should consider the totality of the circumstances, weighing the value of the material sought against the burden of providing it, and taking into account society's interest in furthering the truthseeking function); *Koch v. Koch Industries, Inc.*, 203 F.3d 1202, 1238 (10th Cir. 2000) (parties are not entitled to conduct a "fishing expedition").

[121]*U.S. E.E.O.C. v. Pinal County*, __ F.Supp.2d __ (S.D.Cal. 2010).

[122]*U.S. v. Jicarilla Apache Nation*, __ U.S. __, __ S.Ct. __ (2011) (authorizing courts to set limits on discovery based on equitable concerns); *In re MSTG, Inc.*, 675 F.3d 1337, 1346 (Fed. Cir. 2012).

[123]*Andamiro U.S.A. v. Konami Amusement of America, Inc.*, 2001 WL 535667 (C.D. Cal. 2001) (setting forth the factors for a motion to take more than 10 depositions).

Electronic Data

Rule 26(b)(2)(B) establishes a procedure to provide protections when a party believes that the production of "electronically stored information" will result in unreasonable burden or cost.[124] In such cases, the party invoking the protection must identify the sources of information that it is neither searching nor producing with sufficient particularity that the requesting party can evaluate the burden and cost of producing the information.[125] If the requesting party still believes that the information should be produced, the parties must confer to see if they can resolve the issue without court intervention.[126] If an informal conference does not resolve the issue, the requesting party may file a motion to compel or the responding party may file a motion for a protective order. In either type of motion, the responding party bears the burden of showing that the information is not reasonably accessible, in terms of undue burden or cost. Even following such a showing, the court may require production of the information upon good cause shown.[127] The good cause analysis examines whether the need for the discovery outweighs the burdens and costs of production.[128] Relevant factors include the specificity of the request, the information that is or should be available from other sources, predictions of the importance of the information, the importance of the issues at stake, and the parties' resources.[129]

RULE 26(b)(3)—TRIAL PREPARATION: MATERIALS

CORE CONCEPT

Rule 26(b)(3) provides limited protection to otherwise discoverable[130] trial preparation and work product materials.[131] Such materials must be produced in discovery *only* when the informa-

---

[124]*See Rodriguez-Torres v. Government Development Bank of Puerto Rico,* 265 F.R.D. 40, 43 (D.Puerto Rico 2010); *Disability Rights Council of Greater Washington v. Washington Metropolitan Transit Authority,* 242 F.R.D. 139 (D.D.C. 2007) (questioning whether a party who failed to maintain the data properly should be heard to complain that it is too burdensome to retrieve the data).

[125]The 2006 Amendment to the Advisory Committee Note to Rule 26(b)(2).

[126]The 2006 Amendment to the Advisory Committee Note to Rule 26(b)(2).

[127]*Rodriguez-Torres v. Government Development Bank of Puerto Rico,* 265

F.R.D. 40, 44 (D.Puerto Rico 2010); *Covad Communications Co. v. Revonet, Inc.,* 267 F.R.D. 14 (D.D.C. 2009).

[128]*Covad Communications Co. v. Revonet, Inc.,* 267 F.R.D. 14 (D.D.C. 2009) (forensic analysis by necessity implicates the balancing of need to burden).

[129]The 2006 Amendment to the Advisory Committee Note to Rule 26(b)(2); *Disability Rights Council of Greater Washington v. Washington Metropolitan Transit Authority,* 242 F.R.D. 139 (D.D.C. 2007).

[130]*Stoffels v. SBC Communications, Inc.,* 263 F.R.D. 406, 411–12 (W.D.Tex. 2009) (first step is to determine if materials are attorney-client communications, because work product

tion contained there is not reasonably available from any other source.[132] Note that the work product protection is broader than the attorney-client privilege, but is less absolute.[133]

APPLICATIONS

Documents Only (and Intangible Mental Impressions)

The work product protection applies only to documents.[134] However, some courts allow a party to assert the work product protection at a deposition when questions go to the party's trial strategy or counsel's mental impressions or "intangible work product."[135] It does not apply to facts known or gathered relating to the litigation, which generally are discoverable,[136] although it may apply to documents that summarize the facts.[137] It is unsettled whether the work product protection applies to compilations of documents, such as documents selected for deposition preparation.[138] The protection has been held not to apply to electronic images of documents created for use in the litigation.[139]

---

protection only applies to documents that are otherwise discoverable).

[131]See In re Perrigo Co., 128 F.3d 430, 437 (6th Cir. 1997) (noting that the work product doctrine creates a qualified immunity rather than a privilege).

[132]Rule 26(b)(3) is essentially a codification of the principles announced by the Supreme Court in Hickman v. Taylor, 329 U.S. 495, 67 S. Ct. 385, 91 L. Ed. 451 (1947), which contains an excellent discussion of the work product protection. See also In re Ford Motor Co., 110 F.3d 954 (3d Cir. 1997).

[133]See In re Sealed Case, 107 F.3d 46, 51 (D.C. Cir. 1997); Stopka v. Am. Family Mut. Ins. Co., Inc., 816 F.Supp.2d 516, 524 (N.D.Ill. 2011).

[134]In re Professionals Direct Ins. Co., 578 F.3d 432, 438 (6th Cir. 2009); In re EchoStar Communications Corp., 448 F.3d 1294 (Fed. Cir. 2006).

[135]Bear Republic Brewing Co. v. Central City Brewing Co., __ F.R.D. __ (D.Mass. 2011) (work product doctrine may be asserted at the deposition of a party's investigator); US Airline Pilots Ass'n v. Pension Ben. Guar. Corp., __

F.R.D. __ (D.D.C. 2011).

[136]See In re Cendant Corp. Securities Litigation, 343 F.3d 658, 662 (3d Cir. 2003); Ford Motor Co. v. Edgewood Properties, Inc., 257 F.R.D. 418 (D.N.J. 2009) (factual affidavits from witnesses not work product, even if the attorney had a role in its preparation); but see In re Grand Jury Subpoena Dated Oct. 22, 2001, 282 F.3d 156, 161 (2d Cir. 2002) (we see no reason why work product cannot encompass facts as well as opinions and strategy); Miller v. U.S. Dept. of Justice, 562 F.Supp.2d 82 (D.D.C. 2008) (the privilege covers factual materials prepared in anticipation of litigation).

[137]US Airline Pilots Ass'n v. Pension Ben. Guar. Corp., __ F.R.D. __ (D.D.C. 2011); Concepcion v. F.B.I., 606 F.Supp.2d 14, 34 (D.D.C. 2009)

[138]In re Grand Jury Subpoenas Dated March 19, 2002 and August 2, 2002, 318 F.3d 379, 385 (2d Cir. 2003); Nutramax Laboratories, Inc. v. Twin Laboratories Inc., 183 F.R.D. 458 (D. Md. 1998) (containing a detailed analysis of this issue).

[139]Hines v. Widnall, 183 F.R.D. 596 (N.D. Fla. 1998).

Prepared in Anticipation of Litigation

The work product protection applies only to documents prepared in anticipation of litigation.[140] Most courts apply the protection to documents prepared when litigation is expected but has not yet been commenced;[141] the timing of the preparation of the documents is not critical, as long as they were primarily concerned with the litigation.[142] Conversely, the protection does not apply to documents prepared in the regular course of business while litigation is pending.[143] The trend seems to be to apply the protection to documents prepared in anticipation of any litigation, not just the pending action.[144]

Parties and Their Agents

The work product protection applies to parties and their agents.[145] Thus, the work product protection applies to reports prepared by investigators on behalf of a party.[146] Unlike the at-

---

[140]*N.L.R.B. v. Interbake Foods, LLC*, 637 F.3d 492, 502 (4th Cir. 2011); *In re Professionals Direct Ins. Co.*, 578 F.3d 432, 439 (6th Cir. 2009) (the court will look at the subjective anticipation and the objective reasonableness of the anticipation); *In re Apollo Group, Inc. Securities Litigation*, 251 F.R.D. 12, 19 (D.D.C. 2008) ("litigation" includes administrative proceedings); *ReedHycalog UK, Ltd. v. Baker Hughes Oilfield Operations Inc.*, 242 F.R.D. 357 (E.D. Tex. 2007) (litigation need not be imminent, but litigation must have been the *"primary motivating purpose"*).

[141]*E.E.O.C. v. Lutheran Social Services*, 186 F.3d 959 (D.C. Cir. 1999); *Binks Mfg. Co. v. National Presto Industries, Inc.*, 709 F.2d 1109, 1119 (7th Cir. 1983); *Tom v. S.B., Inc.*, 280 F.R.D. 603, 615 (D.N.M. 2012).

[142]*In re Professionals Direct Ins. Co.*, 578 F.3d 432, 439 (6th Cir. 2009) (the party must demonstrate that litigation was the "driving force" behind the preparation of the document); *In re Ford Motor Co.*, 110 F.3d 954 (3d Cir.1997) (materials deemed to be prepared in anticipation of litigation for purposes of work product protection did not necessarily include legal advice).

[143]*Simon v. G.D. Searle & Co.*, 816 F.2d 397, 401 (8th Cir. 1987); *but see Mississippi Pub. Emps. Ret. Sys. v. Boston Scientific Corp.*, 649 F.3d 5, 31, n.24 (1st Cir. 2011) (an attorney's work product does not lose protection

because it is intended to inform a business decision influenced by the prospects of the litigation).

[144]*See Hobley v. Burge*, 433 F.3d 946, 949 (7th Cir. 2006) ("A majority of courts have held . . . that the privilege endures after termination of the proceedings for which the documents were created, especially if the old and new matters are related."); *In re Ford Motor Co.*, 110 F.3d 954 (3d Cir.1997) (looking to literal language of the Rule); *but see In re Grand Jury Subpoena*, 220 F.R.D. 130, 148 (D. Mass. 2004) (containing a detailed discussion of this issue); *Burton v. R.J. Reynolds Tobacco Co.*, 177 F.R.D. 491 (D. Kan. 1997) (documents must pertain to a specific claim or potential litigation, particularly for an insurance company whose entire business involves claims).

[145]*McKinley v. Board of Governors of Federal Reserve System*, __ F.3d __ (D.C.Cir. 2011) (consultant deemed to be party's agent); *Roe v. Catholic Health Initiatives Colorado*, 281 F.R.D. 632, 639-40 (D.Colo. 2012); *In re Grand Jury Subpoena*, 220 F.R.D. 130, 144 (D. Mass. 2004) (courts typically do not extend work product protection to documents prepared by non-parties or their agents).

[146]*See In re Grand Jury Subpoena (Mark Torf/Torf Environmental Management)*, 357 F.3d 900, 907 (9th Cir. 2004) (the work product doctrine applies to documents created by inves-

torney client privilege, work product does not require any involvement by an attorney, so long as the document is prepared by a party or a party's agent in anticipation of litigation.[147] If a non-party witness prepares a document for the witness's own purposes, it is generally not work product.[148] However, when an insurance company is defending a party, the protection may extend to documents prepared by or on behalf of the insurance company.[149]

Who May Assert

The work product protection may be invoked by the party or the party's attorney.[150]

Obtaining Work Product

Work product is discoverable if the attorney makes a sufficient showing that there is no reasonable alternative source for the same or substantially equivalent information,[151] and that the attorney has a *substantial* need for the information.[152] For example, a party may obtain a written statement in opposing counsel's files if the witness is no longer available.[153] Similarly, there may be no substitute for photographs or statements taken shortly after an incident. Work product is also discoverable in an action where the work product is directly at issue, such as in an action for legal malpractice.[154]

Mental and Legal Impressions

The mental impressions and legal evaluations of an attorney, investigator, or claims agent (sometimes referred to as "core" or "opinion" work product) enjoy an almost absolute priv-

---

tigators working for attorneys, provided the documents were created in anticipation of litigation); *In re Grand Jury Subpoena Dated Oct. 22, 2001,* 282 F.3d 156, 161 (2d Cir. 2002).

[147] *Kandel v. Brother Intern. Corp.,* 683 F.Supp.2d 1076, 1084 (C.D.Cal. 2010); *Boyer v. Gildea,* 257 F.R.D. 488 (N.D.Ind. 2009).

[148] *See Duck v. Warren,* 160 F.R.D. 80 (E.D. Va. 1995) (police internal affairs investigation documents were not prepared by the party police officer being sued, and thus were not work product).

[149] *See Tayler v. Travelers Ins. Co.,* 183 F.R.D. 67, 69 (N.D. N.Y. 1998).

[150] *Hobley v. Burge,* 433 F.3d 946, 949 (7th Cir. 2006); *Stoffels v. SBC Communications, Inc.,* 263 F.R.D. 406, 412 (W.D.Tex. 2009).

[151] *United Kingdom v. U.S.,* 238 F.3d 1312, 1322 (11th Cir. 2001); *U.S. v. Dish Network, L.L.C.,* __ F.Supp.2d __ (C.D.Ill. 2012); *Hendrick v. Avis Rent A Car System, Inc.,* 916 F. Supp. 256, 261 (W.D. N.Y. 1996) (expense in obtaining the information independently is a factor which may be considered by a court in determining whether to order disclosure of work product).

[152] *Leviton Mfg. Co., Inc. v. Universal Sec. Instruments, Inc.,* 606 F.3d 1353, 1365 (Fed.Cir. 2010) (obtaining work product should be very rare); *In re EchoStar Communications Corp.,* 448 F.3d 1294 (Fed. Cir. 2006).

[153] *McCoo v. Denny's Inc.,* 192 F.R.D. 675 (D. Kan. 2000) (statements from witnesses who failed to appear for their depositions must be produced).

[154] *Rutgard v. Haynes,* 61 F. Supp. 2d 1082 (S.D. Cal. 1999), aff'd, 11 Fed. Appx. 818 (9th Cir. 2001).

ilege from disclosure.[155] Thus, an attorney may redact statements reflecting mental and legal impressions from work product that must be disclosed under Rule 26(b)(3).[156] Note, however, that the protections in Rule 26(b)(3) do not apply to interrogatories, which may require the respondent to make legal conclusions requiring the application of law to facts (in other words, the responding attorney may not interpose an objection on the basis that such a legal conclusion is the attorney's work product).

Statement of a Party

A party may always obtain a copy of the party's own statement, whether a signed written statement or a recording of an oral statement.[157] A party may similarly obtain a copy of a statement by the party's agent or representative.[158] To obtain a copy of a party's statement, the party does not need to use the document request procedures in Rule 34, but instead may simply make a request under Rule 26(b)(3).[159] A statement can either be a written statement that the party has signed or otherwise adopted or approved, or a contemporaneous verbatim recording of the person's oral statement.

Statement of a Witness

A non-party witness has a right to a copy of the witness's own statement, whether a signed written statement or a recording of an oral statement. If a party refuses to provide a witness with a copy of the witness's statement, the witness may move to compel and for sanctions under Rule 37(a)(4). Parties, in contrast, do not have an absolute right to a copy of a non-party witness's statement.[160] A party can attempt to get a copy of a witness's statement directly from the witness or by making the showing of necessity required to obtain attorney-

---

[155]*In re Grand Jury Subpoena Dated July 6, 2005*, 510 F.3d 180 (2d Cir. 2007) (fact work product required to be produced in grand jury proceeding); *Mattenson v. Baxter Healthcare Corp.*, 438 F.3d 763, 768 (7th Cir. 2006); *but see Hager v. Bluefield Regional Medical Center, Inc.*, 170 F.R.D. 70, 78 (D.D.C. 1997) ("near absolute protection given by courts to opinion work product must give way" when attorney is designated as an expert witness).

[156]*See In re EchoStar Communications Corp.*, 448 F.3d 1294 (Fed. Cir. 2006).

[157]*Corley v. Rosewood Care Center, Inc.*, 142 F.3d 1041, 1052 (7th Cir. 1998); *Fausto v. Credigy Services Corp.*, 251 F.R.D. 436 (N.D.Cal. 2008) (noting that Rule 26(b)(3) does not provide the time frame in which the statement must be produced).

[158]*Woodard v. Nabors Offshore Corp.*, 2001 WL 13339 (E.D. La. 2001).

[159]*Manske v. UPS Cartage Services, Inc.*, __ F.Supp.2d __ (D.Me. 2011) (discussing the timing for production of a statement under Rule 26(b)(3)); *Rofail v. U.S.*, 227 F.R.D. 53, 55 (E.D. N.Y. 2005) (a party is entitled to obtain a copy of the statement it made, merely upon request and without any showing of any kind).

[160]*Garcia v. City of El Centro*, 214 F.R.D. 587, 594–95 (S.D. Cal. 2003).

work product.[161] A statement can either be a written statement that the party has signed or otherwise adopted or approved, or a contemporaneous verbatim recording of the person's oral statement.

Controlling Law

Unlike most privileges, the work product doctrine is controlled by federal common law, even in diversity cases.[162]

Burden of Proof

The party asserting the work product doctrine has the burden of demonstrating that the subject documents are work product.[163] The party seeking the opponent's work product then has the burden of showing the necessity of obtaining the work product.[164]

Waiver

Evaluating waiver of the work product doctrine entails an evaluation of FRE 502 as well as Rule 26(b)(3).[165] Generally, disclosure of documents to an adverse party, or in a manner such that an adverse party may see the documents,[166] constitutes a waiver of the work product protection with respect to those documents.[167] Disclosure of documents to a non-adverse party,[168] such as a co-defendant or a consultant,[169] may not con-

---

[161]*Garcia v. City of El Centro*, 214 F.R.D. 587, 594–95 (S.D. Cal. 2003) (there is a split as to whether the mere passage of time creates a substantial need for a witness statement).

[162]*360 Const. Co., Inc. v. Atsalis Bros. Painting Co.*, 280 F.R.D. 347, 353 (E.D.Mich. 2012); *Kandel v. Brother Intern. Corp.*, 683 F.Supp.2d 1076, 1083 (C.D.Cal. 2010).

[163]*Biegas v. Quickway Carriers, Inc.*, 573 F.3d 365, 381 (6th Cir. 2009) (conclusory affidavit not sufficient to carry burden of proof); *Roe v. Catholic Health Initiatives Colorado*, 281 F.R.D. 632, 639-40 (D.Colo. 2012).

[164]*Roe v. Catholic Health Initiatives Colorado*, 281 F.R.D. 632, 639-40 (D.Colo. 2012); *Ferko v. National Ass'n For Stock Car Auto Racing, Inc.*, 219 F.R.D. 396, 400 (E.D. Tex. 2003).

[165]*Bear Republic Brewing Co. v. Central City Brewing Co.*, __ F.R.D. __ (D.Mass. 2011).

[166]*Goodrich Corp. v. U.S. E.P.A.*, 593 F.Supp.2d 184, 190–92 (D.D.C. 2009) (disclosure to a 3rd party who

discloses to the opposing party deemed a waiver); *U.S. ex rel. Bagley v. TRW, Inc.*, 212 F.R.D. 554, 560 (C.D. Cal. 2003) (required disclosure of a document to the United States does not waive the attorney work product doctrine).

[167]*U.S. v. Massachusetts Institute of Technology*, 129 F.3d 681, 687 (1st Cir. 1997) (disclosure of a contractor's documents to a Defense Contract Audit Agency constitutes disclosure to a potential adversary which forfeits work product protection for disclosed documents); *Elkins v. District of Columbia*, 250 F.R.D. 20 (D.D.C. 2008) (disclosure waives the protection for documents disclosed and other documents relating to the same subject matter).

[168]*U.S. v. Duke Energy Corp.*, 214 F.R.D. 383, 389 (M.D. N.C. 2003) (but note that disclosure to a third party may require a joint defense agreement to preserve the work product protection).

[169]*U.S. v. Deloitte & Touche USA LLP*, 623 F.Supp.2d 39 (D.D.C. 2009).

stitute a waiver of the work product protection.[170] Disclosure of fact work product to a testifying expert or court appointed expert[171] may constitute waiver.[172] Disclosure to a third-party who does not share a common interest in developing legal theories and analyses of documents may or may not constitute a waiver.[173] Note that this differs from most privileges, which are waived by disclosure to anyone, not just parties.[174] The courts are divided as to which party has the burden of proving non-waiver.[175]

Recalling Trial Preparation Materials

Rule 26(b)(5)(B) establishes a procedure to recall attorney work product that has already been produced. A party believing that it has produced work product may provide a notification to the parties who have received the work product. The notification should be in writing (unless circumstances do not so allow, such as in a deposition) and should be sufficiently detailed to allow the receiving parties to evaluate the claim of work product protection[176] After receiving such a notification, the receiving parties must return, sequester, or destroy the specified work product and all copies (including taking reasonable steps to retrieve any work product that the receiving party had already disclosed to other persons). If they do not agree with the work product assertion, they can present the work product to the court under seal for a determination of the claim. During the pendency of the court's review of the claim, the receiving parties are prohibited from using the work product and the producing party must preserve it. Alternatively, the parties can propose their own procedures for work product that has been produced or disclosed.

Discovery Stage Only

Work product may be withheld as privileged during discov-

---

[170]*Trustees of Elec. Workers Local No. 26 Pension Trust Fund v. Trust Fund Advisors, Inc.*, 266 F.R.D. 1, 14 (D.D.C. 2010).

[171]*Ecuadorian Plaintiffs v. Chevron Corp.*, 619 F.3d 373, 378 (5th Cir. 2010).

[172]*Ecuadorian Plaintiffs v. Chevron Corp.*, 619 F.3d 373, 378, n.8 (5th Cir. 2010); *South Yuba River Citizens League v. National Marine Fisheries Service*, __ F.R.D. __ (E.D.Cal. 2009) (emails from counsel contained information considered by the expert, and thus were discoverable).

[173]*Broushet v. Target Corp.*, __ F.R.D. __ (E.D.N.Y. 2011) (disclosure of investigation results to the media prior to the commencement of the litigation not waiver); *Judicial Watch,*

Inc. v. U.S. Postal Service, 297 F. Supp. 2d 252, 268 (D.D.C. 2004) (disclosure to third party deemed waiver).

[174]*See In re Columbia / HCA Healthcare Corp. Billing Practices Litigation*, 293 F.3d 289, 314 (6th Cir. 2002) (disclosure to third parties does not waive the work product protection).

[175]*See Granite Partners v. Bear, Stearns & Co., Inc.*, 184 F.R.D. 49, 54 (S.D. N.Y. 1999) (party making work product claim has the burden of proving non-waiver); *Johnson v. Gmeinder*, 191 F.R.D. 638, 643 (D. Kan. 2000) (party claiming waiver must prove waiver).

[176]The 2006 Amendment to the Advisory Committee Note to Rule 26(b)(2).

ery, then used at trial. Note the contrast with most other privileges, which cannot be asserted during discovery then waived at trial.

RULE 26(b)(4)—TRIAL PREPARATION: EXPERTS

CORE CONCEPT

Parties may depose expert witnesses who may testify at trial.[177] Draft expert reports and most communications with experts are protected as trial preparation materials. Rule 26(b)(4) allows only very limited discovery with respect to non-testifying experts.[178]

APPLICATIONS

2010 Amendments

Rule 26 has been amended as of December 1, 2010. The amendments, discussed in more detail in the commentary below, address discovery of communications with experts. New Rule 26(b)(4)(B) protects draft expert reports from disclosure as trial preparation materials. New Rule 26(b)(4)(C) protects communications between counsel and expert witnesses from disclosure as trial preparation materials unless they pertain to: (i) compensation for the expert; (ii) the facts or data that counsel provided and the expert considered in forming the opinions to be expressed; or (iii) the assumptions that counsel provided and the expert relied on in forming the opinions to be expressed.[179]

Depositions of Experts

Parties may take the deposition of any expert witness that may testify at trial.[180]

Time for Expert Depositions

If an expert report is to be disclosed for the witness, then the deposition may not occur before the report is disclosed.

Experts Specially Retained but Not Expected to Testify

A party may obtain discovery pertaining to experts not expected to testify only upon a showing of exceptional circumstances rendering it impracticable to obtain facts or opinions

---

[177]FRCP 26(b)(4)(A). See also *Colindres v. Quietflex Mfg.*, 228 F.R.D. 567 (S.D. Tex. 2005) (the work product privilege does not apply to experts).

[178]*Employer's Reinsurance Corp. v. Clarendon Nat. Ins. Co.*, 213 F.R.D. 422 (D. Kan. 2003); *Agron v. Trustees of Columbia University in City of New York*, 176 F.R.D. 445, 449 (S.D. N.Y. 1997) (limitation on discovery is virtu-

ally inapplicable where adverse party has not objected to discovery of its expert).

[179]*Republic of Ecuador v. Bjorkman*, 801 F.Supp.2d 1121, 1125 (D.Colo. 2011).

[180]*R.C. Olmstead, Inc., v. CU Interface, LLC*, __ F.3d __ (6th Cir. 2010); *Broushet v. Target Corp.*, __ F.R.D. __ (E.D.N.Y. 2011).

on the same subject by other means.[181] Such further discovery might be allowed when the particular consulting expert was the only expert to examine evidence that is no longer available (such as a blood sample).[182] Some courts hold that a non-testifying expert loses the protections from discovery if the expert consults with the testifying experts.[183] If a non-testifying expert is to be shown classified or confidential information, the expert can be required to submit to a background check or sign a confidentiality acknowledgment.[184]

Discovery of Examining Physician

Discovery pertaining to treating or examining health professionals is available under Rule 35(b).[185] There is a split of authority as to whether a treating physician is a fact witness or an expert witness for purposes of the provisions of Rule 26(b)(4).[186]

Experts Informally Consulted

No discovery is permitted of experts informally consulted but not retained.[187]

Experts Generally Retained

Full discovery is permitted regarding an expert who is a full-time employee of a party, or who was retained generally, rather than in connection with pending or anticipated litigation.[188] No expert fees are awarded in connection with such discovery.

---

[181]*R.C. Olmstead, Inc., v. CU Interface, LLC*, __ F.3d __ (6th Cir. 2010); *Lowery v. Circuit City Stores, Inc.*, 158 F.3d 742, 765 (4th Cir. 1998). *But see American Crop Protection Ass'n v. U.S. E.P.A.*, 182 F. Supp. 2d 89, 93 (D.D.C. 2002) (non-testifying experts are shielded from discovery only in the action with respect to which they are consulted; full discovery is permitted of their writings and opinions in subsequent matters).

[182]*See, e.g., Spearman Industries, Inc. v. St. Paul Fire and Marine Ins. Co.*, 128 F. Supp. 2d 1148 (N.D. Ill. 2001) (describing circumstances where a party might obtain discovery from a non-testifying expert).

[183]*See In re Chevron Corp.*, 633 F.3d 153, 164, n.17 (3rd Cir. 2011).

[184]*See Ibrahim v. Dep't of Homeland Sec.*, 669 F.3d 983, 999 (9th Cir. 2012) (requiring non-testifying expert to undergo a background check).

[185]*But see Coleman v. Dydula*, 190 F.R.D. 320, 321–24 (W.D. N.Y. 1999) (awarding deposition attendance fees to treating physicians under Rule 26(b) (4)).

[186]*See, e.g., Kirkham v. Societe Air France*, 236 F.R.D. 9 (D.D.C. 2006). *Demar v. U.S.*, 199 F.R.D. 617 (N.D. Ill. 2001) (treating physician not entitled to expert fees from the party noticing the physician's deposition); *Grant v. Otis Elevator Co.*, 199 F.R.D. 673, 675–76 (N.D. Okla. 2001) (treating physician entitled to expert fee compensation for deposition testimony).

[187]*Eisai Co., Ltd. v. Teva Pharmaceuticals USA, Inc.*, 247 F.R.D. 440, 442 (D.N.J. 2007); *West Tennessee Chapter of Associated Builders and Contractors, Inc. v. City of Memphis*, 219 F.R.D. 587, 591 (W.D. Tenn. 2004).

[188]*Dunn v. Sears, Roebuck & Co.*, 639 F.2d 1171, 1174 (5th Cir. 1981); *Essex Builders Group, Inc. v. Amerisure Ins. Co.*, 235 F.R.D. 703 (M.D. Fla. 2006).

Experts Who Witnessed or Participated in Events

Discovery pertaining to an expert who acquired his knowledge and facts through witnessing or participating in the events that form the basis for the complaint is not covered by Rule 26(b)(4), which is limited to information acquired or developed in anticipation of litigation.[189] Thus, full fact discovery is allowed regarding such experts, and no expert fees are awarded.[190]

Party Who Is an Expert

A party cannot avoid discovery or obtain expert fees by claiming to be an expert witness.

Drafts of Expert Reports and Disclosures

A party is not required to disclose or produce a draft of an expert report or an expert disclosure, regardless of the form in which the draft is recorded.[191]

Communications with Experts

Communications between counsel and experts who are required to provide an expert report (*i.e.*, those retained or specially employed to testify) are protected as trial preparation materials unless they pertain to: (i) compensation for the expert; (ii) the facts or data that counsel provided and the expert considered in forming the opinions to be expressed; or (iii) the assumptions that counsel provided and the expert relied on in forming the opinions to be expressed.[192] Communications with experts who are not required to provide expert reports (i.e., treating physicians and other experts not retained or specially employed) are not protected under Rule 26(b)(4) — but they may be protected under other doctrines or privileges.[193]

Ex Parte Communications with Experts

All communications with an opposing party's expert should be through the procedures set forth in Rule 26, such as a Rule 26(b)(4) deposition; a party should not have *ex parte* communications with an expert for another party.[194]

Testifying Expert Fees

The court must impose on the party seeking expert discovery

---

[189]*Battle ex rel. Battle v. Memorial Hosp. at Gulfport*, 228 F.3d 544, 551 (5th Cir. 2000); *Essex Builders Group, Inc. v. Amerisure Ins. Co.*, 235 F.R.D. 703 (M.D. Fla. 2006).

[190]The Advisory Committee Note to Rule 26(b)(4); *Paquin v. Federal Nat. Mortg. Ass'n*, 119 F.3d 23, 33 (D.C. Cir. 1997) (denying payment of fees for alleged experts with personal knowledge).

[191]*GenOn Mid-Atlantic, LLC v. Stone & Webster, Inc.*, __ F.R.D. __ (S.D.N.Y. 2012).

[192]*GenOn Mid-Atlantic, LLC v. Stone & Webster, Inc.*, __ F.R.D. __ (S.D.N.Y. 2012); *Sara Lee Corp. v. Kraft Foods Inc.*, __ F.R.D. __ (N.D.Ill. 2011).

[193]Advisory Committee Notes to the 2010 Amendments to Rule 26(b)(4) (C).

[194]*See Sanderson v. Boddie-Noell Enterprises, Inc.*, 227 F.R.D. 448 (E.D. Va. 2005); *Sewell v. Maryland Dept. of Transp.*, 206 F.R.D. 545 (D. Md. 2002).

of a testifying expert the reasonable expert fees incurred in responding to the discovery[195] unless manifest injustice would result.[196] For a deposition, the fee normally includes compensation for time testifying and may or may not include preparation time.[197] However, if the expert charges more than a "reasonable" fee, the party retaining that expert must pay over and above the "reasonable" rate for that witness' deposition by an adversary.[198] Courts are split as to whether and when treating physicians are entitled to an expert witness fee.[199]

Non-testifying Expert Fees

If discovery is sought of non-testifying experts, the court must also require the party to pay a fair share of the expenses already expended for the experts to form their opinions, in addition to the experts' fees for the time testifying or responding to the discovery.

RULE 26(b)(5)—CLAIMING PRIVILEGE OR PROTECTING TRIAL-PREPARATION MATERIALS

CORE CONCEPT

A party who withholds information based on a claim of privilege or attorney work product protection must state the claim expressly and describe the nature of the documents or information so withheld in a manner that will enable other parties to assess the claim of privilege or protection.[200] If privileged information is inadvertently produced in discovery, the producing party

---

[195]*Gwin v. American River Transp. Co.*, 482 F.3d 969, 975 (7th Cir. 2007) (abuse of discretion not to award fees); *Knight v. Kirby Inland Marine Inc.*, 482 F.3d 347, 356 (5th Cir. 2007) (fees for testimony at a *Daubert* hearing are not discovery fees recoverable under Rule 26); *Trepel v. Roadway Express, Inc.*, 266 F.3d 418, 426–27 (6th Cir. 2001); *Haarhuis v. Kunnan Enterprises, Ltd.*, 177 F.3d 1007 (D.C. Cir. 1999) ($300 per hour for deposition, including time traveling to and from deposition, was reasonable).

[196]*Nilssen v. Osram Sylvania, Inc.*, 528 F.3d 1352 (Fed.Cir. 2008) (injustice is not limited to indigence, and can be based on the conduct of the party seeking fees; the decision not to award fees is reviewed for abuse of discretion); *Research Systems Corp. v. IPSOS Publicite*, 276 F.3d 914, 920 (7th Cir. 2002).

[197]*Knight v. Kirby Inland Marine Inc.*, 482 F.3d 347, 356 (5th Cir. 2007)

(fees for testimony are mandatory, but fees for other discovery are within the court's discretion); *Frydman v. Department of Justice*, 852 F. Supp. 1497 (D. Kan. 1994), aff'd, 57 F.3d 1080 (10th Cir. 1995) (holding that a large lapse of time can warrant compensation for preparation time); *Fiber Optic Designs, Inc. v. New England Pottery, LLC*, 262 F.R.D. 586, 591–94 (D.Colo. 2009) (expert time to prepare for deposition deemed excessive).

[198]*Fiber Optic Designs, Inc. v. New England Pottery, LLC*, 262 F.R.D. 586, 590–91 (D.Colo. 2009) (declining to impose surcharge by expert agency); *Frederick v. Columbia University*, 212 F.R.D. 176, 177 (S.D. N.Y. 2003) (setting forth a test for reasonableness of expert fees).

[199]*See Wirtz v. Kansas Farm Bureau Services, Inc.*, 355 F. Supp. 2d 1190, 1212–13 (D. Kan. 2005).

[200]*N.L.R.B. v. Interbake Foods, LLC*, 637 F.3d 492, 501 (4th Cir. 2011);

may notify the parties that received the information. The receiving parties must then either return the information or present the information to the court.

APPLICATIONS

Failure to State Claim of Privilege with Sufficient Specificity

If a party withholds information without properly disclosing the basis, the party may be subject to sanctions under Rule 37(b)(2), and may have waived the privilege.[201]

Privilege Log

Many courts read Rule 26(b)(5) to require a party asserting a privilege to produce a privilege log describing the documents withheld.[202] The log must set forth the facts that establish the privilege in sufficient detail that other parties and the court can assess the privilege assertion.[203] The Rules do not specify the time for production of a privilege log, and the case law varies.[204] Some courts hold that the log must be produced immediately,[205] some allow a reasonable time, and some hold that the respondent may wait until the court rules upon pending objections before generating the privilege log if the objections pertain to the allegedly privileged documents.[206] Privileges may be waived broadly for failure to produce a privilege log[207] or to produce a sufficiently detailed log,[208] or specifically for any documents omitted from the privilege log.[209] The courts are divided as to how to handle email (and particularly email chains) on a

---

N.L.R.B. v. Jackson Hosp. Corp., 557 F.3d 301 (D.D.C. 2009).

[201]*Hobley v. Burge*, 433 F.3d 946, 951 (7th Cir. 2006); *ePlus Inc. v. Lawson Software, Inc.*, 280 F.R.D. 247, 252 (E.D.Va. 2012) (failure to disclose author and recipients results in waiver).

[202]*Perry v. Schwarzenegger*, 591 F.3d 1126, 1133, n.1 (9th Cir. 2009) (privilege log is required and does not impose an unconstitutional burden); *Smith v. Cafe Asia*, 256 F.R.D. 247, 250 (D.D.C. 2009) (a privilege log has become the universally accepted means of asserting privileges in discovery in the federal courts). *But see Burlington Northern & Santa Fe Ry. Co. v. U.S. Dist. Court for Dist. of Mont.*, 408 F.3d 1142, 1147 (9th Cir. 2005) (rejecting a per se rule that failure to provide a timely privilege log is a waiver of the privilege); *Graham v. Mukasey*, 247 F.R.D. 205, 207 (D.D.C. 2008) (no need to create log of docu-

ments from which privileged information was redacted).

[203]*See N.L.R.B. v. Interbake Foods, LLC*, 637 F.3d 492, 502 (4th Cir. 2011).

[204]*Banks v. Office of the Senate Sergeant-at-Arms and Doorkeeper*, 226 F.R.D. 113 (D.D.C. 2005).

[205]*See, e.g, Covington v. Sailormen Inc.*, __ F.R.D. __ (N.D.Fla. 2011).

[206]*U.S. v. Philip Morris Inc.*, 314 F.3d 612, 621 (D.C. Cir. 2003).

[207]*Tom v. S.B., Inc.*, 280 F.R.D. 603, 614 (D.N.M. 2012); *Banks v. Office of Senate Sergeant-at-Arms*, 222 F.R.D. 7, 15 (D.D.C. 2004).

[208]*ePlus Inc. v. Lawson Software, Inc.*, 280 F.R.D. 247, 252 (E.D.Va. 2012); *Novelty, Inc. v. Mountain View Marketing, Inc.*, 265 F.R.D. 370, 380–81 (S.D.Ind. 2009).

[209]*Robinson v. Texas Auto. Dealers Ass'n*, 214 F.R.D. 432, 456 (E.D. Tex. 2003).

privilege log.[210] Parties may not be required to log communications with counsel after the litigation has commenced, and counsel often agree to omit such communications.[211]

Challenging Privilege Assertions

A party may challenge the privilege assertion for documents listed on a privilege log by filing a motion to compel, which places the burden on the party asserting the privilege of establishing an evidentiary basis, by affidavit, deposition transcript, or other evidence, for each element of the privilege.[212]

Recalling Privileged Information

Rule 26(b)(5)(B) establishes a procedure to recall privileged information that has already been produced.[213] A party believing that it has produced privileged information may provide a notification to the parties who have received the information. The notification should be in writing (unless circumstances do not so allow, such as in a deposition) and should be sufficiently detailed to allow the receiving parties to evaluate the claim of privilege[214] After receiving such a notification, the receiving parties must return, sequester, or destroy the specified information and all copies (including taking reasonable steps to retrieve any information that the receiving party had already disclosed to other persons).[215] If they do not agree with the privilege assertion, they can present the information to the court under seal for a determination of the privilege claim. During the pendency of the court's review of the privilege claim, the receiving parties are prohibited from using the information and the producing party must preserve it. Alternatively, the parties can propose their own procedures for privileged information that has been produced or disclosed.

Waiver of the Privilege for Recalled Information

Rule 26(b)(5)(B) does not address whether the privilege or protection is preserved for information that was disclosed and then recalled. There is substantial case law addressing this topic that is unaffected by the procedures in Rule 26(b)(5)(B).[216]

RULE 26(c)—PROTECTIVE ORDERS

CORE CONCEPT

The court may enter orders designed to protect the parties and

---

[210]*Muro v. Target Corp.*, 250 F.R.D. 350 (N.D. Ill. 2007).

[211]*Grider v. Keystone Health Plan Central, Inc.*, 580 F.3d 119, 140, n.22 (3rd Cir. 2009).

[212]*See N.L.R.B. v. Interbake Foods, LLC*, 637 F.3d 492, 501 (4th Cir. 2011).

[213]*See Briese Lichttechnik Vertriebs GmbH v. Langton*, 272 F.R.D. 369, 372 (S.D.N.Y. 2011); *Edelen v. Campbell*

Soup Co., 265 F.R.D. 676, 698 (N.D.Ga. 2010).

[214]The 2006 Amendment to the Advisory Committee Note to Rule 26(b)(2).

[215]*See Edelen v. Campbell Soup Co.*, 265 F.R.D. 676, 698 (N.D.Ga. 2010).

[216]The 2006 Amendment to the Advisory Committee Note to Rule 26(b)(2).

witnesses during the discovery process.

APPLICATIONS

Impact of 2007 "Restyling" Amendments

Rule 26(c) was significantly restructured during the 2007 Federal Civil Rules "Restyling" Project. The original 8 subsections are now subsections of Rule 26(c)(1), and the trailing text at the end was moved into new subsections 26(c)(2) and 26(c)(3). In researching current Rule 26(c), practitioners should be mindful of this repositioning.

Motion

Protective orders are obtained by motion filed in the district where the action is pending.[217] In the case of a deposition that is to occur in a different district, a motion may also be filed where the deposition is to occur.[218]

Certificate of Conference

A motion for protective order must include a certification that the movant has in good faith conferred or attempted to confer with the other party in an effort to resolve the dispute without court action.[219]

Timing

Normally, the motion must be filed before the discovery is to occur, unless there is no opportunity to do so.[220]

Who May File

A motion may be made by a party or by a witness from whom discovery is sought.[221] The motion must be brought by the individual whose interests are affected. Thus, a party may not move for a protective order to protect the interests of another, but may move to protect the party's own interests when discovery is sought from another.

Purpose of Protective Order

Rule 26(c) specifically instructs the court to limit the frequency or extent of discovery if justice so requires to protect a party or witness from annoyance, embarrassment,[222] oppres-

---

[217]Victor Stanley, Inc. v. Creative Pipe, Inc., 250 F.R.D. 251 (D.Md. 2008).

[218]In re Sealed Case, 141 F.3d 337 (D.C. Cir. 1998) (non-party witness has a right to have a motion for protective order heard in the district where the deposition is to occur); The Advisory Committee Note to Rule 26(c).

[219]Gov't of Ghana v. ProEnergy Services, LLC, 677 F.3d 340, 342 (8th Cir. 2012) (denying motion where the movant had not conferred); Allen v. Mill-Tel, Inc., __ F.R.D. __ (D.Kan. 2012).

[220]Mims v. Central Mfrs. Mut. Ins. Co., 178 F.2d 56 (5th Cir.1949); Drexel Heritage Furnishings, Inc. v. Furniture USA, Inc., 200 F.R.D. 255 (M.D. N.C. 2001).

[221]Silkwood v. Kerr-McGee Corp., 563 F.2d 433 (10th Cir.1977).

[222]Seattle Times Co. v. Rhinehart, 467 U.S. 20, 35 n. 21, 104 S.Ct. 2199,

sion, or undue burden[223] or expense.[224] Rule 26(b)(1) instructs the court to limit the frequency or extent of discovery if: (i) the discovery sought is unreasonably cumulative or is obtainable from a more convenient or less burdensome or expensive source; (ii) the party seeking the discovery has had ample opportunity to obtain the information; or (iii) the discovery is unduly burdensome[225] or expensive[226] taking into account the circumstances of the particular case. A court may grant a protective order prohibiting the taking of a deposition when it believes the information sought is wholly irrelevant to the issues or to prospective relief.[227]

Good Cause

Protective orders are entered for "good cause."[228] The court has almost complete discretion in determining what constitutes good cause,[229] and such determinations are rarely disturbed on appeal.[230] In general, the court will balance the need of the party seeking the discovery against the burden on the party responding.[231]

Burden of Proof

The party seeking the protective order has the burden of showing that good cause exists by stating particular and

---

81 L.Ed.2d 17 (1984) (the rule serves in part to protect parties' privacy interests); *Miscellaneous Docket Matter No. 1 v. Miscellaneous Docket Matter No. 2*, 197 F.3d 922, 925 (8th Cir. 1999).

[223]*Mitchell v. Fishbein*, 227 F.R.D. 239 (S.D. N.Y. 2005) (discussing the meaning of "burden").

[224]*Stagman v. Ryan*, 176 F.3d 986 (7th Cir. 1999).

[225]*Cummings v. General Motors Corp.*, 365 F.3d 944, 954 (10th Cir. 2004) (it is not enough that the discovery be burdensome, that burden must be "undue").

[226]*See Race Tires Am., Inc. v. Hoosier Racing Tire Corp.*, 674 F.3d 158, 171 (3d Cir. 2012).

[227]*Pintos v. Pacific Creditors Ass'n*, 504 F.3d 792, 801 (9th Cir. 2007) (balancing the need for the discovery against the need for confidentiality); *Minter v. Wells Fargo Bank, N.A.*, 258 F.R.D. 118 (D.Md. 2009) (motions to prohibit depositions are viewed unfavorably).

[228]*In re Violation of Rule 28(D)*, 635 F.3d 1352, 1357 (Fed.Cir. 2011);

Chicago Tribune Co. v. Bridgestone/Firestone, Inc., 263 F.3d 1304, 1310 (11th Cir. 2001) (applying the good cause standard, and rejecting the press' argument that a compelling interest was required to keep documents from the press).

[229]*Seattle Times Co. v. Rhinehart*, 467 U.S. 20, 104 S.Ct. 2199, 81 L.Ed.2d 17 (1984); *Salmeron v. Enterprise Recovery Systems, Inc.*, 579 F.3d 787, 795 (7th Cir. 2009) (court must independently make a good cause analysis before entering a protective order); *Rohrbough v. Harris*, 549 F.3d 1313, 1322 (10th Cir. 2008) (the good cause standard is highly flexible, having been designed to accommodate all relevant interests).

[230]*But see Citizens First Nat. Bank of Princeton v. Cincinnati Ins. Co.*, 178 F.3d 943, 944 (7th Cir. 1999) (court must make an actual determination of good cause, and may not allow the parties to seal whatever portions of the record they choose).

[231]*In re Sealed Case (Medical Records)*, 381 F.3d 1205, 1215–16 (D.C. Cir. 2004); *In re Wilson*, 149 F.3d 249, 252 (4th Cir. 1998).

specific facts.[232]

Depositions

Motions for protective orders are most common in connection with depositions, because such motions are the only mechanism for challenging a deposition in advance of its occurrence. With interrogatories, document requests, and requests for admission, a party can make objections to individual requests without providing a substantive response. The onus then shifts to the party seeking the discovery to move to compel an answer under Rule 37(a).

Types of Protective Order

Rule 26(c) lists eight kinds of protective orders, which are discussed immediately below. The list is not exclusive, however, and the court may make any type of protective order required by justice.[233] The specifically enumerated categories are:

(1) *Order that Disclosure or Discovery Not be Had:* Rule 26(c)(1)(A) allows the court to order that the automatic disclosure or requested discovery not occur.[234] Such orders are occasionally entered with respect to interrogatories or document requests, since the court can examine the requests. Such orders are rarely granted with respect to depositions.[235]

(2) *Specified Terms and Conditions:* The court can impose terms and conditions on the automatic disclosure or the taking of discovery under Rule 26(c)(1)(B).[236] The court may designate the time and location of a deposition,[237] or the time to respond to interrogatories, document requests, requests for admission, or other discovery activities.[238] The court may order the party seeking discovery to pay the responding party's resulting expenses.[239] The court may set deadlines for the completion of various phases of discovery or order that

---

[232]*Gulf Oil Co. v. Bernard*, 452 U.S. 89, 102, 101 S. Ct. 2193, 2201, 68 L. Ed. 2d 693 (1981); *In re Violation of Rule 28(D)*, 635 F.3d 1352, 1357 (Fed.Cir. 2011); *Kamakana v. City and County of Honolulu*, 447 F.3d 1172 (9th Cir.2006) (recognizing a heightened standard of "compelling reasons" necessary to keep documents to be attached to a dispositive motion secret).

[233]*Chicago Mercantile Exch., Inc. v. Tech. Research Grp., LLC*, 276 F.R.D. 237, 239 (N.D.Ill. 2011); *Kuhns v. City of Allentown*, 264 F.R.D. 223, 228 (E.D.Pa. 2010).

[234]*CineTel Films, Inc. v. Does 1-1,052*, __ F.Supp.2d __ (D.Md. 2012).

[235]*Simmons Foods, Inc. v. Willis*, 191 F.R.D. 625, 630 (D. Kan. 2000) (although courts rarely grant a protective order which totally prohibits a deposition, a request to take the deposition of the opposing party's counsel may justify such an order).

[236]*Duling v. Gristede's Operating Corp.*, 266 F.R.D. 66, 71 (S.D.N.Y. 2010).

[237]*Philadelphia Indem. Ins. Co. v. Federal Ins. Co.*, 215 F.R.D. 492 (E.D. Pa. 2003).

[238]*Manske v. UPS Cartage Services, Inc.*, __ F.Supp.2d __ (D.Me. 2011).

[239]*Kirschenman v. Auto-Owners Ins.*, 280 F.R.D. 474, 487 (D.S.D. 2012); *Medtronic Sofamor Danek, Inc. v. Michelson*, 229 F.R.D. 550 (W.D. Tenn.

discovery be conducted in a particular sequence.[240] The court may issue a stay of discovery.[241] The court may also modify any of the terms and conditions in subsequent orders.[242]

(3) *Method of Discovery:* The court may restrict discovery to a particular method (such as no depositions or depositions only upon written questions) under Rule 26(c)(1)(C). The general principle is that the parties may select their own discovery methods without unnecessary interference from the court.[243] Thus, most motions to restrict the discovery methods are denied unless the moving party shows special circumstances.[244]

(4) *Limit of Scope or Time:* The court may limit the scope of the automatic disclosures or discovery to specific areas of inquiry or to a specific time period.[245] The court may also stay discovery, either while a dispositive motion is pending,[246] or except with respect to a critical or threshold issue.[247] For example, if a jurisdictional dispute exists, the court may restrict discovery to the jurisdictional issues, then permit broad discovery if jurisdiction is found to exist.[248] Similarly, if liability and damages are to be tried separately, the court may restrict discovery to liability issues until the first phase of the case is complete.

(5) *Persons Present:* The court may exclude the public, the press, other witnesses, or other non-parties from a deposition or access to documents produced in discovery

---

2003).

[240]*Builders Ass'n of Greater Chicago v. City of Chicago*, 170 F.R.D. 435, 437 (N.D. Ill. 1996) (order setting the sequence of discovery appropriate when a potentially dispositive threshold issue has been raised).

[241]*Tradebay, LLC v. eBay, Inc.*, 278 F.R.D. 597 (D.Nev. 2011) (staying discovery pending resolution of dispositive motions).

[242]*Martin v. Reynolds Metals Corp.*, 297 F.2d 49 (9th Cir.1961).

[243]*National Life Ins. Co. v. Hartford Acc. and Indem. Co.*, 615 F.2d 595 (3d Cir. 1980).

[244]*Nguyen v. Excel Corp.*, 197 F.3d 200, 208–09 (5th Cir. 1999) (for "good cause shown," court may order discovery taken by a method other than that selected by the party seeking the discovery).

[245]*See CineTel Films, Inc. v. Does 1-1,052*, __ F.Supp.2d __ (D.Md. 2012); *Dilley v. Metropolitan Life Ins. Co.*, 256 F.R.D. 643, 644 (N.D.Cal. 2009).

[246]*Johnson v. New York Univ. School of Educ.*, 205 F.R.D. 433, 434 (S.D. N.Y. 2002); *GTE Wireless, Inc. v. Qualcomm, Inc.*, 192 F.R.D. 284, 285–86 (S.D. Cal. 2000) (before staying discovery, the court should "take a preliminary peek" at the merits to see if there is an "immediate and clear possibility" that the dispositive motion will be granted).

[247]*Vivid Technologies, Inc. v. American Science & Engineering, Inc.*, 200 F.3d 795, 804 (Fed. Cir. 1999) (staying discovery on all other issues until critical issue is resolved).

[248]*Orchid Biosciences, Inc. v. St. Louis University*, 198 F.R.D. 670 (S.D. Cal. 2001).

under Rule 26(c)(1)(E).[249] The court generally will not exclude the parties or their attorneys.

(6) *Sealed Transcript:* The court may order a deposition transcript sealed, and thus not part of the public record, under Rule 26(c)(1)(F).[250] Similar orders have been entered with respect to interrogatory answers or documents to be produced,[251] although such orders are not expressly authorized by 26(c)(1)(F).[252] Once a sealing order has been entered, parties are prohibited from disclosing to third persons information obtained pursuant to the court order. The prohibition does not apply, however, to information already in a party's possession when the order is entered.[253]

(7) *Confidential Information:* The court may enter an order restricting disclosure of private personal information[254] and trade secrets and confidential research, development, or commercial information[255] obtained during discovery.[256] Sealing a document is sometimes viewed as extraordinary relief, and there is a presumptive right to access to discovery in civil cases.[257] There is no absolute privilege or protection with respect to

---

[249]*Phillips ex rel. Estates of Byrd v. General Motors Corp.*, 307 F.3d 1206 (9th Cir. 2002) (the public generally, and the press in particular, are presumptively entitled to access to documents produced in discovery, and good cause must be demonstrated to shield document from such access).

[250]*Pintos v. Pacific Creditors Ass'n*, 565 F.3d 1106, 1115 (9th Cir. 2009) (once documents have been attached to a dispositive motion and become part of the public record, having them sealed involves a heightened burden); *In re Estate of Martin Luther King, Jr., Inc. v. CBS, Inc.*, 184 F. Supp. 2d 1353, 1362 (N.D. Ga. 2002) (only the court may seal documents; the parties cannot do so by stipulation).

[251]*U.S. v. $9,041,598.68 (Nine Million Forty One Thousand Five Hundred Ninety Eight Dollars and Sixty Eight Cents)*, 163 F.3d 238, 250 (5th Cir. 1998).

[252]*Morgan v. U.S. Dept. of Justice*, 923 F.2d 195 (D.C. Cir. 1991).

[253]*See Rodgers v. U.S. Steel Corp.*, 536 F.2d 1001 (3d Cir. 1976); *International Products Corp. v. Koons*, 325 F.2d 403, 408–09 (2d Cir. 1963).

[254]*Kuhns v. City of Allentown*, 264 F.R.D. 223, 227–28 (E.D.Pa. 2010).

[255]*R.C. Olmstead, Inc., v. CU Interface, LLC*, __ F.3d __ (6th Cir. 2010) (court may decide whether trade secrets are relevant and whether the need for discovery outweighs the harm of production); *Phillips v. General Motors Corp.*, 289 F.3d 1117 (9th Cir. 2002) (the enumerated categories of confidential information are not exclusive, and settlement information can be protected); *Jagex Ltd. v. Impulse Software*, __ F.R.D. __ (D.Mass. 2011) (source code deemed a trade secret).

[256]*Seattle Times Co. v. Rhinehart*, 467 U.S. 20, 104 S. Ct. 2199, 81 L. Ed. 2d 17 (1984); *Surfvivor Media, Inc. v. Survivor Productions*, 406 F.3d 625, 635 (9th Cir. 2005) (documents need not be privileged to be protected); *Pearson v. Miller*, 211 F.3d 57 (3d Cir. 2000).

[257]*In re Violation of Rule 28(D)*, 635 F.3d 1352, 1360 (Fed.Cir. 2011) (parties frequently abuse the confidentiality designation); *Keith H. v. Long Beach Unified School Dist.*, 228 F.R.D. 652 (C.D. Cal. 2005).

such matters.[258] The normal procedure is for the responding party to claim that certain information is confidential. Then, if the parties cannot agree to a confidentiality stipulation, the responding party can move for a protective order or the party seeking the discovery can move to compel under Rule 37(a). The party seeking the discovery will have the burden of showing that the information is relevant and needed.[259] In most cases, the discovery will be allowed, but under restricted conditions regarding further disclosure. The court can fashion any order it sees fit, limiting how the information may be used, who may see it, etc.[260] The court may also order disclosure of limited portions of confidential information, such as ordering disclosure of the ingredients of a product, but not the formula. The court can also designate an impartial third person to examine the confidential information.

(8) *Simultaneous Exchange:* The court may order the parties to simultaneously file designated documents or information in sealed envelopes, to be opened as directed by the court. This procedure is most common in patent cases, where it can be an advantage to know an opponent's claims.

Order Compelling Discovery

If the court denies a motion for a protective order, it may at the same time issue an order compelling the discovery. Such an order can facilitate obtaining sanctions under Rule 37.

Discovery While Motion for Protective Order Pending

Technically, a motion for protective order does not automatically stay the discovery that is the subject of the motion.[261] Thus, for example, a motion for protective order to prevent a deposition should not be filed on the day of the deposition, unless it was not practical to file it sooner. However, some local rules provide for an automatic stay of the subject discovery.[262]

Standing of Non-parties

In general, documents produced by private civil litigants, when the documents have not been filed, are not public, and

---

[258]*Federal Open Market Committee of Federal Reserve System v. Merrill,* 443 U.S. 340, 99 S. Ct. 2800, 61 L. Ed. 2d 587 (1979); *In re Violation of Rule 28(D),* 635 F.3d 1352, 1357 (Fed.Cir. 2011).

[259]*In re Cooper Tire & Rubber Co.,* 568 F.3d 1180 (10th Cir. 2009) (the burden then shifts to the party seeking the information to show that it is relevant and necessary); *Bruno &* *Stillman, Inc. v. Globe Newspaper Co.,* 633 F.2d 583 (1st Cir.1980).

[260]*See In re Violation of Rule 28(D),* 635 F.3d 1352, 1357 (Fed.Cir. 2011).

[261]*Creative Solutions Group, Inc. v. Pentzer Corp.,* 199 F.R.D. 443, 444 (D. Mass. 2001) (motion to stay discovery does not stay discovery).

[262]*Ecrix Corp. v. Exabyte Corp.,* 191 F.R.D. 611, 617 (D. Colo. 2000).

non-parties do not have a right to access the documents.[263]

Expenses and Attorney Fees

The court has discretion to require the party losing a motion for protective order to pay the expenses the opposing party incurred in connection with the motion, including reasonable attorney fees, under Rule 26(c) and Rule 37(a)(4).[264]

Motion to Vacate or Modify Protective Order

If circumstances change, a party may move to vacate or modify a protective order.[265]

Appeal of Discovery Order by Party

Discovery orders are normally interlocutory, not final, and thus not appealable until the end of the lawsuit.[266] A discovery order will be final if the underlying motion was the entire proceeding, such as with an order granting or denying a deposition to perpetuate testimony under Rule 27, an order denying discovery in aid of execution, an order granting or denying letters rogatory under Rule 28, or an order denying the deposition of a non-party that was entered in another district.[267]

Appeal of Discovery Order by Non-party

In general, non-parties cannot appeal discovery orders.[268] If the discovery is denied, they have no need to appeal. If the order is granted, their only recourse is to disobey, then appeal any contempt judgment. In limited circumstances, such as to protect the attorney client privilege, a non-party may be able to appeal a discovery order.[269]

RULE 26(d)—TIMING AND SEQUENCE OF DISCOVERY

CORE CONCEPT

Parties may not conduct discovery prior to their discovery conference meeting under Rule 26(f). Thereafter, each party may

---

[263]*Bond v. Utreras*, 585 F.3d 1061, 1065–66 (7th Cir. 2009) (older cases allowing access were based on the prior version of Rule 5(d), which generally required discovery documents to be filed).

[264]*Josendis v. Wall to Wall Residence Repairs, Inc.*, 662 F.3d 1292, 1304 (11th Cir. 2011).

[265]*In re Teligent, Inc.*, 640 F.3d 53, 58 (2nd Cir. 2011) (where there has been reasonable reliance on the protective order, the court should not modify it unless it was improvidently entered or there are compelling circumstances); *Rohrbough v. Harris*, 549 F.3d 1313, 1322 (10th Cir. 2008) (the

modification of a protective order, like its original entry, is left to the sound discretion of the court).

[266]*Cipollone v. Liggett Group, Inc.*, 785 F.2d 1108, 1116 (3d Cir. 1986).

[267]*U.S. v. Sciarra*, 851 F.2d 621, 628 (3d Cir. 1988).

[268]*National Super Spuds, Inc. v. New York Mercantile Exchange*, 591 F.2d 174 (2d Cir.1979). *See also In re Ford Motor Co.*, 110 F.3d 954 (3d Cir. 1997).

[269]*See U.S. v. Ryan*, 402 U.S. 530, 533, 91 S. Ct. 1580, 1582, 29 L. Ed. 2d 85 (1971); *Perlman v. U.S.*, 247 U.S. 7, 38 S. Ct. 417, 62 L. Ed. 950 (1918).

conduct whatever discovery that party chooses, in any sequence, regardless of the discovery undertaken by other parties. The various discovery devices may be used in any order or simultaneously.

APPLICATIONS

Commencement of Discovery

Parties may not conduct discovery prior to their discovery conference under Rule 26(f).[270] Expedited discovery may be conducted by court order for good cause shown or by stipulation.[271]

Court Orders

The court may order discovery in a specified sequence or according to a schedule "for the convenience of the parties and witnesses and in the interests of justice."[272] Such orders are authorized under Rule 26(c)(2), and are within the broad discretion of the court, but are reserved for unusual circumstances.[273]

No Set Sequence

Although interrogatories and document production typically precedes depositions, each party may conduct discovery in any sequence it chooses.[274]

Simultaneous Discovery

The parties may conduct discovery simultaneously. There is no obligation for any party to wait until others have completed their discovery.[275]

Failure to Answer by One Party

A party is not excused from answering discovery because another party has failed to answer discovery.[276] The proper remedy if another party fails to answer discovery is a motion to compel under Rule 37, not a refusal to comply with valid

---

[270]*Willis v. Town Of Marshall, N.C.*, 426 F.3d 251, 264, (4th Cir. 2005); *Alston v. Parker*, 363 F.3d 229, 236 n. 11 (3d Cir. 2004); *Apple Inc. v. Samsung Electronics Co., Ltd.*, __ F.Supp.2d __ (N.D.Cal. 2011).

[271]*See West Coast Prods., Inc. v. Does 1-1,434*, 280 F.R.D. 73, 74 (D.D.C. 2012); *Wilcox Indus. Corp. v. Hansen*, 279 F.R.D. 64, 67 (D.N.H. 2012).

[272]*Manske v. UPS Cartage Services, Inc.*, __ F.Supp.2d __ (D.Me. 2011); *Edgenet, Inc. v. Home Depot U.S.A., Inc.*, 259 F.R.D. 385 (E.D.Wis. 2009) (evaluating a request for expedited discovery).

[273]*See St. Louis Group, Inc. v. Metals and Additives Corp., Inc.*, __ F.R.D. __ (S.D.Tex. 2011) (discussing

the standards courts apply); *Ortiz-Rivera v. Municipal Government of Toa Alta*, 214 F.R.D. 51, 54 (D.P.R. 2003) (only the most obviously compelling reasons are sufficient to justify a departure from the rule).

[274]*Gabarick v. Laurin Maritime (America), Inc.*, __ F.R.D. __ (E.D.La. 2011).

[275]*George C. Frey Ready-Mixed Concrete, Inc. v. Pine Hill Concrete Mix Corp.*, 554 F.2d 551 (2d Cir.1977); *Gabarick v. Laurin Maritime (America), Inc.*, __ F.R.D. __ (E.D.La. 2011).

[276]*See Mulero-Abreu v. Puerto Rico Police Dept.*, 675 F.3d 88, 92 (1st Cir. 2012) ("In law as in life, two wrongs do not make a right.").

discovery requests.

No Mutuality

There is no requirement that a party conduct discovery in a manner like that used by other parties. Each party is free to conduct any authorized discovery in any sequence regardless of the discovery conducted by other parties.[277]

Excluded Proceedings

The moratorium on early discovery established by Rule 26(d) does not apply to the proceedings exempted from the initial disclosures and discovery conference process by Rule 26(a)(1)(E).[278]

RULE 26(e)—SUPPLEMENTING DISCLOSURES AND RESPONSES

CORE CONCEPT

Parties have a duty to supplement automatic disclosures and discovery responses under certain limited conditions set forth in Rule 26(e).[279] Otherwise, there is no general duty to supplement.[280]

APPLICATIONS

Impact of 2007 "Restyling" Amendments

Rule 26(e) was significantly restructured during the 2007 Federal Civil Rules "Restyling" Project. The 2007 amendments moved the provisions in Rule 26(e)(2) to Rule 26(e)(1)(A), and pulled the provisions regarding supplementing expert disclosures out of Rule 26(e)(1) and into Rule 26(e)(2). In researching current Rule 26(e), practitioners should be mindful of this repositioning.

Conditions Requiring Supplemental Responses

The following three conditions require supplemental answers:

(1) *Automatic Disclosures:* A party must at reasonable intervals supplement its initial,[281] expert,[282] and pretrial disclosures under Rule 26(a) if the party or its attorney learns that the information disclosed was incomplete or incorrect;[283]

(2) *Incorrect Response:* A party must supplement a re-

---

[277]*Keller v. Edwards*, 206 F.R.D. 412 (D. Md. 2002).

[278]*Durham v. IDA Grp. Ben. Trust*, 276 F.R.D. 259, 262 (N.D.Ind. 2011).

[279]*See, e.g., Rodowicz v. Massachusetts Mut. Life Ins. Co.*, 279 F.3d 36, 45, (1st Cir. 2002).

[280]*Alvariza v. Home Depot*, 240 F.R.D. 586, 590 (D. Colo. 2007), aff'd, 241 F.R.D. 663 (D. Colo. 2007) (no duty to supplement documents informally produced by agreement).

[281]*Harriman v. Hancock County*, 627 F.3d 22, 29 (1st Cir. 2010).

[282]*David E. Watson, P.C. v. U.S.*, 668 F.3d 1008, 1014 (8th Cir. 2012); *Gicla v. U.S.*, 572 F.3d 407, 410 (7th Cir. 2009).

[283]*Klonoski v. Mahlab*, 156 F.3d 255, 268 (1st Cir. 1998) (duty to

sponse to an interrogatory, request for production, or request for admission that the party or its attorney[284] learns was incorrect or incomplete when made and the information has not otherwise been made known to the other parties;[285] and

(3) *Court Order:* The duty to supplement may also arise by court order.[286]

Timing of Supplemental Responses

No specific time periods are established for the duty to supplement.[287] Instead, supplements are to be made "in a timely manner."[288] Supplements made after the close of discovery may not satisfy the Rules, particularly when the party had the documents or information in its possession, custody, or control prior to the close of discovery.[289]

No Request to Supplement Needed

The obligations to supplement under Rule 26(e) are self-effectuating; there is no need to serve a request to supplement.[290] Nonetheless, a party will sometimes serve a notice to supplement if it is concerned that another party has new information that it has not yet disclosed or produced.

Supplementing Expert Discovery

The obligations to supplement described above apply to both expert reports disclosed under Rule 26(a)(2)(B)[291] and depositions of such experts.[292] Supplemental expert information should be disclosed by the time the pretrial disclosures are made under Rule 26(a)(3), 30 days before trial unless otherwise

---

supplement is broad); *Robbins & Myers, Inc. v. J.M. Huber Corp.,* __ F.R.D. __ (W.D.N.Y. 2011) (duty includes documents created after initial response).

[284]*Ritchie Risk-Linked Strategies Trading (Ireland), Ltd. v. Coventry First LLC,* 280 F.R.D. 147, 156 (S.D.N.Y. 2012).

[285]*U.S. Aviation Underwriters, Inc. v. Pilatus Business Aircraft, Ltd.,* 582 F.3d 1131, 1145 (10th Cir. 2009); *Colon-Millin v. Sears Roebuck De Puerto Rico, Inc.,* 455 F.3d 30, 37 (1st Cir. 2006); *Robbins & Myers, Inc. v. J.M. Huber Corp.,* __ F.R.D. __ (W.D.N.Y. 2011) (duty includes documents created after initial response).

[286]*Chevron Corp. v. Salazar,* 275 F.R.D. 437, 449 (S.D.N.Y. 2011).

[287]*See AVX Corp. v. Cabot Corp.,* 252 F.R.D. 70, 77 (D.Mass. 2008) (parties should supplement at appropriate intervals **during the discovery pe-**riod); *Luma Corp. v. Stryker Corp.,* 226 F.R.D. 536, 539 (S.D. W. Va. 2005) (the absence of a court established deadline does not mean that the parties do not have to supplement).

[288]*R & R Sails, Inc. v. Ins. Co. of Pennsylvania,* 673 F.3d 1240, 1246 (9th Cir. 2012); *Kahle v. Leonard,* 563 F.3d 736, 740–41 (8th Cir. 2009).

[289]*In re Delta/AirTran Baggage Fee Antitrust Litig.,* 846 F.Supp.2d 1335, 1355 (N.D.Ga. 2012).

[290]*See Valley Entertainment, Inc. v. Friesen,* __ F.Supp.2d __ (N.D.Ill. 2010); *AVX Corp. v. Cabot Corp.,* 252 F.R.D. 70, 77 (D.Mass. 2008).

[291]*See Brainard v. American Skandia Life Assur. Corp.,* 432 F.3d 655, 664 (6th Cir. 2005); *Macaulay v. Anas,* 321 F.3d 45, 50 (1st Cir. 2003).

[292]*Osunde v. Lewis,* 281 F.R.D. 250, 257 (D.Md. 2012); *Trafton v. Sunbury Primary Care, P.A.,* __ F.Supp.2d __ (D.Me. 2010).

set by the court.[293] A party may not use the supplementing procedure to submit an amended or rebuttal report not based on new information.[294]

Information Already Provided

A party need not supplement a disclosure or discovery response if the other parties have already received the additional or corrective information in writing.[295]

No Other Duty

The duties described in Rule 26(e) are the only duties to supplement. Thus, an instruction in a set of interrogatories that the interrogatories are continuing or purporting to impose a duty to supplement is ineffective.

Sanctions

Failure to supplement a disclosure or discovery response is the equivalent of providing incorrect information in the initial disclosure or response. The court may exclude certain evidence[296] or claims,[297] may order a continuance and further discovery, or take any other action it deems appropriate[298] (*see* Rule 37 for a more detailed analysis of the available sanctions).

RULE 26(f)—CONFERENCE OF THE PARTIES; PLANNING FOR DISCOVERY

CORE CONCEPT

The parties must confer and develop a proposed discovery plan, to be submitted to the court in writing, addressing the discovery schedule and any modifications to the limits or scope of discovery.

APPLICATIONS

Impact of 2007 "Restyling" Amendments

Rule 26(f) was significantly restructured during the 2007 Federal Civil Rules "Restyling" Project. The 2007 amendments

---

[293]*U.S. S.E.C. v. Maxxon, Inc.*, 465 F.3d 1174, 1182, (10th Cir. 2006); *Sancom, Inc. v. Qwest Communications Corp.*, 683 F.Supp.2d 1043, 1062 (D.S.D. 2010) (Rule 26(e) is not to be used to delay disclosures until 30 days before trial by calling them supplements).

[294]*See, e.g., Avila v. Willits Environmental Remediation Trust*, 633 F.3d 828, 836 (9th Cir. 2011); *Diaz v. Con-Way Truckload, Inc.*, 279 F.R.D. 412, 421 (S.D.Tex. 2012).

[295]*Kapche v. Holder*, 677 F.3d 454, 468 (D.C. Cir. 2012); *U.S. Aviation Underwriters, Inc. v. Pilatus Business Aircraft, Ltd.*, 582 F.3d 1131, 1145 (10th Cir. 2009).

[296]*Osunde v. Lewis*, 281 F.R.D. 250, 257 (D.Md. 2012); *Quesenberry v. Volvo Group North America, Inc.*, ___ F.R.D. ___ (W.D.Va. 2010) (no need to show that bad faith was the cause of the nondisclosure).

[297]*U.S. v. Philip Morris USA, Inc.*, 219 F.R.D. 198, 200–01 (D.D.C. 2004); *Loral Fairchild Corp. v. Victor Co. of Japan, Ltd.*, 911 F. Supp. 76, 80 (E.D. N.Y. 1996).

[298]*Townsend v. Daniel, Mann, Johnson & Mendenhall*, 196 F.3d 1140, 1151 (10th Cir. 1999) (no sanction warranted where conduct not culpable and no harm to defendant).

broke the text of Rule 26(f) into 4 new subsections, some of which have as many as 6 subsections of their own. In researching current Rule 26(f), practitioners should be mindful of this repositioning.

Time for Conference

Rule 26(f) directs that the parties confer "as soon as practicable and in any event at least 21 days before a scheduling conference is held or a scheduling order is due under Rule 16(b)."[299] The timing of the discovery conference may be modified by local rule or court order, and specified actions may be exempted from the discovery conference requirement.

In Person Attendance

The rules do not require that the Rule 26(f) conference be conducted in person, and the parties may participate by telephone.[300] However, the court can order the parties to participate in person.

Agenda for Discovery Conference

At the discovery conference, the parties must discuss the nature and basis of their claims and defenses and the possibilities of prompt settlement or resolution of the case.[301] They must also make or arrange for the initial automatic disclosures required by Rule 26(a)(1), discuss orders that the court should enter,[302] issues relating to preserving discoverable information,[303] and develop a proposed discovery plan, as described below. The parties may also attempt to reach a consensus as to the disputed facts alleged in the pleadings with particularity for purpose of the disclosures under Rule 26(a).

Content of Discovery Plan

The discovery plan should indicate the parties' positions or proposals concerning:

    (1) *Automatic Disclosures*: Any changes to the timing, form, or requirement for disclosures under Rule

---

[299]*Apple Inc. v. Samsung Electronics Co., Ltd.*, __ F.Supp.2d __ (N.D.Cal. 2011); *Plumbers & Pipefitters Local 562 Pension Fund v. MGIC Investment Corp.*, 256 F.R.D. 620, 626 (E.D.Wis. 2009).

[300]The Advisory Committee Note to the 2000 Amendment to Rule 26(f) expresses a preference for in person meetings, but recognizes that the distances some counsel would have to travel and the resulting expenses may outweigh the benefits of an in person meeting.

[301]*See U.S. ex rel. FLFMC, LLC v. TFH Publ'ns., Inc.*, __ F.Supp.2d __

(D.N.J. 2012) (discussion of alternative dispute resolution required by local rules).

[302]*Mallinckrodt, Inc. v. Masimo Corp.*, 254 F. Supp. 2d 1140, 1157 (C.D. Cal. 2003).

[303]Although not specifically so limited, the 2006 Amendment to Rule 26(f) added information preservation to the agenda for the Rule 26 conference to address issues related to the preservation of electronically stored information. See the 2006 Amendment to the Advisory Committee Note to Rule 26(f) for a discussion of potential document preservation issues.

26(a).[304] The plan must explicitly state when the initial disclosures were or are to be made;

(2) *Discovery Scope and Schedule*: The likely subjects of discovery, the completion date for discovery, and any discovery that should be conducted in phases or limited to or focused on particular issues;[305]

(3) *Electronic Information*: Issues relating to the disclosure or production of electronically stored information, including the sources of such data, the form in which it should be produced (i.e., in paper or electronic form, and if electronic, how it will be made available), and the costs of such production;[306]

(4) *Privilege Issues*: Issues relating to claims of privilege or work product protection, including any procedures to be used in the event of the production of privileged information (to the extend that they differ from the procedures in Rule 26(b)(2)(B));[307]

(5) *Discovery Limits*: Any changes to the discovery limits established by the Rules or by local rule, plus any additional limits; and

(6) *Other Orders*: Any other case management or protective orders proposed to the court for consideration at the court's scheduling conference.

Submission of Plan

The parties should submit to the court a written report outlining the plan within 14 days of the discovery meeting.[308] The court may order that the discovery plan be submitted at a different time or that the plan be submitted orally at the Rule 16 conference with the court. Form 35 of the Appendix of Forms to the Rules (printed in Part IV) contains a sample report.

Good Faith Participation

Rule 26(f) places a joint obligation on the attorneys (and on unrepresented parties) to schedule the discovery conference and to attempt in good faith to agree on a proposed discovery

---

[304]*In re Bristol-Myers Squibb Securities Litigation*, 205 F.R.D. 437, 440–41 (D.N.J. 2002) (the discovery conference should include a discussion of what documents are available in electronic format, and the format to be used for disclosures and production of such documents).

[305]*Fiber Optic Designs, Inc. v. New England Pottery, LLC*, 262 F.R.D. 586, 599 (D.Colo. 2009).

[306]*Rodriguez-Torres v. Government Development Bank of Puerto Rico*, __ F.Supp.2d __ (D.Puerto Rico 2010);

Covad Communications Co. v. Revonet, Inc., 254 F.R.D. 147, 149 (D.D.C. 2008).

[307]See the 2006 Amendment to the Advisory Committee Note to Rule 26(f) for a discussion of possible agreements regarding inadvertently produced privileged material, such as the "quick peek" procedure and the "clawback" procedure.

[308]*Siems v. City of Minneapolis*, 560 F.3d 824, 825, n.2 (8th Cir. 2009); *Durham v. IDA Grp. Ben. Trust*, 276 F.R.D. 259, 262 (N.D.Ind. 2011).

plan and a report outlining the plan.[309]

Excluded Proceedings

A discovery conference and discovery plan are not required in proceedings listed in Rule 26(a)(1)(B) as exempted from initial disclosures.[310] Additionally, the parties may be excused from the discovery conference and plan requirements by court order.

RULE 26(g)—SIGNING DISCLOSURES AND DISCOVERY REQUESTS, RESPONSES, AND OBJECTIONS

CORE CONCEPT

Every disclosure, request for discovery, and response or objection must be signed by at least one attorney of record. The signature constitutes a certification that to the best of the signer's knowledge, information, and belief, the document is complete and correct, and is being served for proper purposes within the Rules.[311]

APPLICATIONS

Impact of 2007 "Restyling" Amendments

Rule 26(g) was significantly restructured during the 2007 Federal Civil Rules "Restyling" Project. The 2007 amendments moved much of the content of Rule 26(g)(2) up into Rule 26(g)(1), and only the trailing text from Rule 26(g)(2) remains in that subsection. In researching current Rule 26(g), practitioners should be mindful of this repositioning.

Signature

Every disclosure, discovery request, response, or objection must be signed by at least one attorney of record (or by the party, if unrepresented).[312] The document must also state the address, e-mail address, and telephone number of the signer.

Certification for Rule 26(a) Disclosures

For the initial disclosures under Rule 26(a)(1) and the pretrial disclosures under Rule 26(a)(3), the signature constitutes a certification to the best of the signer's knowledge, information, and belief formed after "reasonable inquiry" that the

---

[309]*See Siems v. City of Minneapolis*, 560 F.3d 824, 826–27 (8th Cir. 2009) (dismissal based, in part, on failure to participate in the Rule 26(f) conference).

[310]*See, e.g., Orbe v. True*, 201 F. Supp. 2d 671 (E.D. Va. 2002) (habeas corpus proceedings exempt from Rule 26(f)).

[311]*See Mulero-Abreu v. Puerto Rico Police Dept.*, 675 F.3d 88, 92 (1st Cir. 2012) ("it is axiomatic that parties must act in good faith during discovery.").

[312]*Dugan v. Smerwick Sewerage Co.*, 142 F.3d 398, 407 (7th Cir. 1998); *Mancia v. Mayflower Textile Servs. Co.*, 253 F.R.D. 354, 357 (D.Md. 2008).

disclosure is complete and correct.[313]

Certification for Other Discovery Documents

For discovery requests, responses, and objections, the signature constitutes a certification to the best of the signer's knowledge, information, and belief formed after "reasonable inquiry"[314] that:

(A) The document is consistent with the Rules and existing law, or with a nonfrivolous argument for extension, modification, or reversal of existing law, or for establishing new law;[315]

(B) The document is not imposed for any improper purpose, such as to harass, delay, or cause needless expense for an opponent;[316] and

(C) The discovery is not unreasonably or unduly burdensome or expensive, given the nature of the case, the discovery already conducted, the amount in controversy, and the importance of the issues at stake in the litigation.[317]

Duty of Inquiry

The signer of a discovery document is under an obligation to make a reasonable inquiry into the issues covered by his certification before signing the document.[318]

Unsigned Discovery Documents

If without substantial justification a discovery disclosure, request, response, or objection is unsigned, other parties should advise the party making the disclosure, request, response, or objection. If counsel for that party fails to sign the document

---

[313]*Moore v. Publicis Groupe*, — F.R.D. — (S.D.N.Y. 2012) (noting that the "complete and correct" certification only applies to disclosures, not discovery responses); *Covad Communications Co. v. Revonet, Inc.*, 267 F.R.D. 14 (D.D.C. 2009).

[314]*Guantanamera Cigar Co. v. Corporacion Habanos, S.A.*, 263 F.R.D. 1, 5 (D.D.C. 2009); *R & R Sails Inc. v. Insurance Co. of State of PA*, 251 F.R.D. 520 (S.D.Cal. 2008).

[315]*Victor Stanley, Inc. v. Creative Pipe, Inc.*, 250 F.R.D. 251 (D.Md. 2008) (filing a discovery response asserting a privilege without a factual basis to support each element of each privilege is sanctionable).

[316]*U.S. v. Kouri-Perez*, 187 F.3d 1, 6 (1st Cir. 1999); *In re Motion to Compel Compliance with Subpoena Direct to Dept. of Veterans Affairs*, 257 F.R.D. 12, 17 (D.D.C. 2009).

[317]*See Legault v. Zambarano*, 105 F.3d 24, 27 (1st Cir. 1997); *Lynn v. Monarch Recovery Mgmt., Inc.*, — F.Supp.2d — (D.Md. 2012) (duplicative interrogatories deemed a violation of Rule 26(g)).

[318]*Green Leaf Nursery v. E.I. DuPont De Nemours and Co.*, 341 F.3d 1292, 1305 (11th Cir. 2003) (the signature certifies that the lawyer has made a reasonable effort to assure that the client has provided all the information and documents available to him that are responsive to the discovery demand); *Legault v. Zambarano*, 105 F.3d 24, 28 (1st Cir. 1997) (certifying attorney must make a reasonable effort to ensure that the client has provided all responsive information and documents to a discovery request); *In re Delta/AirTran Baggage Fee Antitrust Litig.*, 846 F.Supp.2d 1335, 1349-50 (N.D.Ga. 2012).

promptly, the unsigned document will be stricken, no party is obligated to respond to the unsigned document,[319] and the attorney serving the unsigned discovery document may be subject to sanctions.[320]

Unsigned Deposition Transcript

Some courts do not allow the filing of unsigned Deposition Transcripts.[321]

Unrepresented Parties

An unrepresented party should sign disclosures, discovery requests, responses, and objections and should list the party's address.

Sanctions

If without a substantial justification[322] a certification is made in violation of Rule 26(g), the court will impose an appropriate sanction[323] on the party, the attorney, or both.[324] The sanction may include expenses incurred because of the violation, including attorney fees.[325] Generally, a discovery sanction is not a final appealable order.[326]

Additional Research References

Wright & Miller, *Federal Practice and Procedure* §§ 2001 to 2052
C.J.S., Federal Civil Procedure §§ 526 to 535
West's Key Number Digest, Federal Civil Procedure ☞1261 to 1278

---

[319]*Saria v. Massachusetts Mut. Life Ins. Co.*, 228 F.R.D. 536 (S.D. W. Va. 2005).

[320]*Walls v. Paulson*, 250 F.R.D. 48 (D.D.C. 2008).

[321]*See, e.g., Rohrbough v. Harris*, 549 F.3d 1313, 1328 (10th Cir. 2008); *Reisner v. General Motors Corp.*, 511 F.Supp. 1167 (S.D.N.Y. 1981).

[322]*Grider v. Keystone Health Plan Central, Inc.*, 580 F.3d 119, 139–40 (3rd Cir. 2009) (sanctions vacated because the court did not expressly consider whether the violators had substantial justification).

[323]*Mancia v. Mayflower Textile Servs. Co.*, 253 F.R.D. 354, 358 (D.Md. 2008) (Rule 26(g) is designed to curb discovery abuses); *Bernal v. All American Investment Realty, Inc.*, 479 F. Supp. 2d 1291, 1334 (S.D. Fla. 2007) (court may fashion an appropriate sanction).

[324]*Maynard v. Nygren*, 332 F.3d 462 (7th Cir.2003) (attorney may not be sanctioned absent a knowing improper certification or violation of the discovery Rules); *Cherrington Asia Ltd. v. A & L Underground, Inc.*, 263 F.R.D. 653, 657–58 (D.Kan. 2010) (Rule 66(g) sanctions apply only to written discovery requests, responses or objections); *McCoo v. Denny's Inc.*, 192 F.R.D. 675 (D. Kan. 2000) (sanctions should be assessed against counsel absent evidence that the party was aware of the wrongdoing).

[325]*In re Delta/AirTran Baggage Fee Antitrust Litig.*, 846 F.Supp.2d 1335, 1349-50 (N.D.Ga. 2012); *Mancia v. Mayflower Textile Servs. Co.*, 253 F.R.D. 354, 357 (D.Md. 2008).

[326]*U.S. v. Kouri-Perez*, 187 F.3d 1, 6 (1st Cir. 1999).

RULE 27
DEPOSITIONS TO PERPETUATE TESTIMONY

(a) Before an Action Is Filed.

(1) *Petition.* A person who wants to perpetuate testimony about any matter cognizable in a United States court may file a verified petition in the district court for the district where any expected adverse party resides. The petition must ask for an order authorizing the petitioner to depose the named persons in order to perpetuate their testimony. The petition must be titled in the petitioner's name and must show:

(A) that the petitioner expects to be a party to an action cognizable in a United States court but cannot presently bring it or cause it to be brought;

(B) the subject matter of the expected action and the petitioner's interest;

(C) the facts that the petitioner wants to establish by the proposed testimony and the reasons to perpetuate it;

(D) the names or a description of the persons whom the petitioner expects to be adverse parties and their addresses, so far as known; and

(E) the name, address, and expected substance of the testimony of each deponent.

(2) *Notice and Service.* At least 21 days before the hearing date, the petitioner must serve each expected adverse party with a copy of the petition and a notice stating the time and place of the hearing. The notice may be served either inside or outside the district or state in the manner provided in Rule 4. If that service cannot be made with reasonable diligence on an expected adverse party, the court may order service by publication or otherwise. The court must appoint an attorney to represent persons not served in

the manner provided in Rule 4 and to cross-examine the deponent if an unserved person is not otherwise represented. If any expected adverse party is a minor or is incompetent, Rule 17(c) applies.

(3) *Order and Examination.* If satisfied that perpetuating the testimony may prevent a failure or delay of justice, the court must issue an order that designates or describes the persons whose depositions may be taken, specifies the subject matter of the examinations, and states whether the depositions will be taken orally or by written interrogatories. The depositions may then be taken under these rules, and the court may issue orders like those authorized by Rules 34 and 35. A reference in these rules to the court where an action is pending means, for purposes of this rule, the court where the petition for the deposition was filed.

(4) *Using the Deposition.* A deposition to perpetuate testimony may be used under Rule 32(a) in any later-filed district-court action involving the same subject matter if the deposition either was taken under these rules or, although not so taken, would be admissible in evidence in the courts of the state where it was taken.

(b) Pending Appeal.

(1) *In General.* The court where a judgment has been rendered may, if an appeal has been taken or may still be taken, permit a party to depose witnesses to perpetuate their testimony for use in the event of further proceedings in that court.

(2) *Motion.* The party who wants to perpetuate testimony may move for leave to take the depositions, on the same notice and service as if the action were pending in the district court. The motion must show:

(A) the name, address, and expected substance of the testimony of each deponent; and

(B) the reasons for perpetuating the testimony.

(3) *Court Order.* If the court finds that perpetuating the testimony may prevent a failure or delay of

justice, the court may permit the depositions to be taken and may issue orders like those authorized by Rules 34 and 35. The depositions may be taken and used as any other deposition taken in a pending district-court action.

(c) Perpetuation by an Action. This rule does not limit a court's power to entertain an action to perpetuate testimony.

[Amended effective March 19, 1948; October 20, 1949; July 1, 1971; August 1, 1987; April 25, 2005, effective December 1, 2005; April 30, 2007, effective December 1, 2007; March 26, 2009, effective December 1, 2009.]

AUTHORS' COMMENTARY ON RULE 27

PURPOSE AND SCOPE

Sometimes it will be important to preserve or perpetuate testimony before an action is commenced or during the appeal of an action. Rule 27 provides one mechanism for perpetuating such testimony by taking a deposition.

RULE 27(a)—BEFORE AN ACTION IS FILED

CORE CONCEPT

Rule 27 is most commonly used to perpetuate testimony when there is a danger that important testimony will be lost, but for one reason or another a civil action cannot yet be commenced.

APPLICATIONS

Verified Petition

A request for a deposition under Rule 27 must be by *verified* petition (*i.e.,* a petition accompanied by a statement signed by the petitioner that the factual averments are accurate).[1]

Contents of Petition

A Rule 27 petition must contain the following:

(1) A statement that the petitioner expects to be a party to an action in federal court; *In re I-35W Bridge Collapse Site Inspection*, 243 F.R.D. 349, 352 (D. Minn. 2007) (anticipated action must be cognizable in a court of the United States), but is presently unable to bring the action;

(2) A description of the subject matter of the anticipated

---

[1] *In re Chester County Elec., Inc.,* 208 F.R.D. 545, 546–47 (E.D. Pa. 2002).

action and the petitioner's relationship to the action;

(3) The facts that the petitioner intends to establish by the testimony, and the petitioner's need for perpetuating it;[2]

(4) The identities and addresses[3] of the persons expected to be adverse parties in the action; and

(5) The identity of the deponent(s) and a detailed description of the substance of their testimony.[4]

The petition must also include a proposed order describing the procedure and scope of the deposition.

Testimony Only

The general rule appears to be that one may not obtain documents or interrogatory responses under Rule 27, only deposition testimony.[5]

Certainty of Litigation Unnecessary

A party need not demonstrate that litigation is absolutely certain in order to file a motion to perpetuate; instead, the party must be found to be acting in anticipation of litigation.[6]

Need to Perpetuate

It is not necessary to show that the deponents are on their death beds. Rather, one must show that there is a danger of the testimony or evidence being lost,[7] such as when circumstances indicate that memories may fade.[8] In making this determination, however, the deponent's age alone can present a

---

[2]*In re Yamaha Motor Corp., U.S.A.*, 251 F.R.D. 97, 99 (N.D.N.Y. 2008) (petition denied for failing to set forth the facts to be established).

[3]*Norex Petroleum Ltd. v. Access Industries, Inc.*, 620 F.Supp.2d 587 (S.D.N.Y. 2009) (petition defective because it did not include the witness's address).

[4]*Penn Mut. Life Ins. Co. v. U.S.*, 68 F.3d 1371, 1374, (D.C. Cir. 1995) (instructing the district court on remand of a Rule 27 ruling to require a "narrowly tailored showing of the substance" of the testimony); *In re Petition of Allegretti*, 229 F.R.D. 93, 97 (S.D. N.Y. 2005) (discussing the degree of detail required).

[5]*U.S. v. Van Rossem*, 180 F.R.D. 245, 247 (W.D. N.Y. 1998). *But see Application of Deiulemar Compagnia Di Navigazione S.p.A. v. M/V Allegra*, 198 F.3d 473, 478, (4th Cir. 1999); *Ashafa v. City of Chicago*, 146 F.3d 459, 461 (7th Cir. 1998) (Rule 27 peti-

tion for names of officers involved in an incident); *In re I-35W Bridge Collapse Site Inspection*, 243 F.R.D. 349, 351 (D. Minn. 2007) (Rule 27 allows inspections of property).

[6]*Calderon v. U.S. Dist. Court for Northern Dist. of California*, 144 F.3d 618 (9th Cir. 1998).

[7]*Calderon v. U.S. Dist. Court for Northern Dist. of California*, 144 F.3d 618 (9th Cir. 1998); *In re Yamaha Motor Corp., U.S.A.*, 251 F.R.D. 97, 100 (N.D.N.Y. 2008) (issues of geography, advanced age, seriously impaired health, and rapid turnover of staff have been accepted as reasons for the perpetuation of testimony); *In re Ramirez*, 241 F.R.D. 595 (W.D.Tex. 2006) (conclusory statement that the petitioner believes that testimony will be lost is not sufficient).

[8]*State of Arizona v. State of California*, 292 U.S. 341, 54 S. Ct. 735, 78 L. Ed. 1298 (1934).

sufficient risk the deponent will be unable to testify.[9]

Pre-Litigation Only

Once litigation has been commenced, Rule 27(a) may no longer be used to perpetuate testimony, and Rules 26 and 30 take over.[10]

Inability to Bring Suit

One requirement for petitions to perpetuate testimony under Rule 27(a) is that the movant not be able to bring a law suit.[11] One basis for such inability is a lack of sufficient information to draft the complaint under the constraints of Rule 11.[12] However, Rule 27 may not be used to uncover or discover testimony necessary to file suit,[13] and applies only where known testimony is to be preserved.[14]

Place of Filing

The petition may be filed in the district in which any of the adverse parties reside. If *all* adverse parties are both not American citizens and not residing in the United States, the petition may be filed in any district.

Hearing

The court must hold a hearing on a Rule 27 petition.[15]

Notice and Service

At least 21 days prior to the hearing, the petitioner must send notice and a copy of the petition to all expected adverse parties.[16] The notice may be served in the manner provided under Rule 4. If personal service cannot be made, the court can order service by publication or otherwise. In such cases, the court must appoint an attorney to represent those not person-

---

[9]*Penn Mut. Life Ins. Co. v. U.S.*, 68 F.3d 1371, 1375 (D.C. Cir. 1995); *In re Ramirez*, 241 F.R.D. 595 (W.D.Tex. 2006).

[10]*19th Street Baptist Church v. St. Peters Episcopal Church*, 190 F.R.D. 345, 348 (E.D. Pa. 2000).

[11]*In re Enable Commerce, Inc.*, 256 F.R.D. 527, 532 (N.D.Tex. 2009); *Lucas v. Judge Advocate General, Naval Criminal Investigative Services*, 245 F.R.D. 8, 9 (D.D.C. 2007), aff'd, 279 Fed. Appx. 11 (D.C. Cir. 2008) (petition denied based, in part, upon lack of showing of inability to initiate litigation); *In re Town of Amenia, NY*, 200 F.R.D. 200 (S.D. N.Y. 2001) (party can take a Rule 27 deposition when a declaratory judgment is technically possible but the parties are still negotiating).

[12]*Petition of Alpha Industries, Inc.*, 159 F.R.D. 456 (S.D. N.Y. 1995).

[13]*Application of Deiulemar Compagnia Di Navigazione S.p.A. v. M/V Allegra*, 198 F.3d 473, 485 (4th Cir. 1999); *In re I-35W Bridge Collapse Site Inspection*, 243 F.R.D. 349, 352–53 (D. Minn. 2007) (Rule 27 cannot be used to discover evidence for the purpose of filing a complaint).

[14]*In re Ramirez*, 241 F.R.D. 595 (W.D.Tex. 2006); *Petition of Ford*, 170 F.R.D. 504, 507 (M.D. Ala. 1997).

[15]*In re I-35W Bridge Collapse Site Inspection*, 243 F.R.D. 349, 351 (D. Minn. 2007).

[16]*In re Petition of Allegretti*, 229 F.R.D. 93, 96 (S.D. N.Y. 2005); *In re Chester County Elec., Inc.*, 208 F.R.D. 545, 546–47 (E.D. Pa. 2002); *In re Solorio*, 192 F.R.D. 709 (D. Utah 2000) (notice is a "condition precedent" to discovery under Rule 27).

ally served. If an expected party is a minor or incompetent, then the provisions of Rule 17(c) apply.

Standard for Ruling

The court will order the deposition if it is satisfied that the perpetuation of the testimony may prevent a future failure or delay of justice.[17] The court may also make orders of the type allowable under Rules 34 (production of documents) and 35 (mental examinations).[18]

Conduct of the Deposition

The court must designate the deponent(s), the subject matter of the examination, and whether the deposition will be oral or written.[19] The deposition is then taken in accordance with the court order and Rules pertaining to depositions (*see* Rule 30 and Rule 31).

Scope of Deposition

An inquiry under Rule 27 may include inspection of documents and mental and physical examinations. However, the scope of a deposition under Rule 27 is often more narrow than a typical discovery deposition, and generally will be governed by the court's order.[20] In general, courts have required that the evidence to be preserved be material and competent, not merely discoverable under general discovery provisions.[21]

Use of the Transcript

A deposition taken pursuant to Rule 27 may be used in any subsequent action in federal court involving the subject matter identified in the petition, under the general terms and conditions governing use of depositions in Rule 32(a).

Subject Matter Jurisdiction

A proceeding to perpetuate testimony is not a separate civil action, and does not require its own basis for jurisdiction.[22] However, the petition must demonstrate that the anticipated legal action will proceed in federal court.[23]

---

[17]*In re Charter Communications, Inc., Subpoena Enforcement Matter*, 393 F.3d 771, 784 (8th Cir. 2005); *Norex Petroleum Ltd. v. Access Industries, Inc.*, 620 F.Supp.2d 587 (S.D.N.Y. 2009) (determination to grant or deny a Rule 27 motion is left to the discretion of the court).

[18]*Lucas v. Riddle*, 2004 WL 1084719 (D. Conn. 2004).

[19]*Martin v. Reynolds Metals Corp.*, 297 F.2d 49, 55 (9th Cir. 1961).

[20]*State of Nev. v. O'Leary*, 63 F.3d 932, 936 (9th Cir. 1995); *In re Yamaha Motor Corp., U.S.A.*, 251 F.R.D. 97, 99

(N.D.N.Y. 2008).

[21]*In re Hopson Marine Transp., Inc.*, 168 F.R.D. 560, 565 (E.D. La. 1996).

[22]*Socha v. Pollard*, 621 F.3d 667, 671 (7th Cir. 2010).

[23]*Socha v. Pollard*, 621 F.3d 667, 671 (7th Cir. 2010); *In re Complaint of Financial Indem. Co.*, 173 F.R.D. 435, 437 (W.D. La. 1997) (implicit in showing that legal action will proceed in federal court is requirement that in diversity cases, petitioner must prove by a preponderance of the evidence that the amount in controversy ex-

Bankruptcy Proceedings

Rule 27 does not apply in contested matters before a bankruptcy court.[24]

Appeals

A grant or denial of a Rule 27 petition is appealable as a final order.[25]

RULE 27(b)—PENDING APPEAL

CORE CONCEPT

Rule 27 may be used while a case is on appeal, or while the period to appeal is running, to preserve testimony in the event that further proceedings are needed.[26] A request for a deposition pending an appeal is made by motion (not petition) to the district court where the action proceeded.[27] The motion must include the names and addresses of the deponents, the substance of their testimony, and the reasons for perpetuating their testimony.[28] Otherwise, a motion pursuant to Rule 27(b) is subject to the notice, service, and other requirements and conditions for a petition under Rule 27(a) described immediately above.

RULE 27(c)—PERPETUATION BY AN ACTION

CORE CONCEPT

Rule 27 is not the exclusive method of perpetuating testimony.[29] Thus, for example, a deposition that would be admissible in a subsequent proceeding in state court will also be admissible in federal court, even though the offering party may not have complied with Rule 27. Likewise, a party may preserve testimony under a method authorized by statute.

Additional Research References

Wright & Miller, *Federal Practice and Procedure* §§ 2071 to 2076. Lisnek & Kaufman, *Depositions: Procedure, Strategy and Technique*

---

ceeds the jurisdictional amount). *But see Application of Deiulemar Compagnia Di Navigazione S.p.A. v. M/V Allegra*, 198 F.3d 473, 479 (4th Cir. 1999) (allowing Rule 27 discovery to preserve evidence for an arbitration).

[24] *See In re Szadkowski*, 198 B.R. 140, 141 n. 1 (Bankr. D. Md. 1996). *See also* Fed.Rules Bankr.Proc.Rule 9014.

[25] *Martin v. Reynolds Metals Corp.*, 297 F.2d 49 (9th Cir.1961).

[26] *See Schreier v. Weight Watchers Northeast Region, Inc.*, 872 F. Supp. 1 (E.D. N.Y. 1994), aff'd, 57 F.3d 1064 (2d Cir. 1995).

[27] *U.S. v. Van Rossem*, 180 F.R.D. 245, 247 (W.D. N.Y. 1998) (motion to compel Rule 27 discovery denied because need to perpetuate testimony was not demonstrated).

[28] *Foy v. Dicks*, 1996 WL 745501 (E.D. Pa. 1996) (petitioners' Rule 27 motion denied for failure to assert reasons why perpetuation of evidence was necessary).

[29] *See Nissei Sangyo America, Ltd. v. U.S.*, 31 F.3d 435 (7th Cir. 1994) (action to perpetuate foreign bank records).

C.J.S., Federal Civil Procedure §§ 544 to 547
West's Key Number Digest, Federal Civil Procedure ⌖1291 to 1299

RULE 28
PERSONS BEFORE WHOM
DEPOSITIONS MAY BE TAKEN

(a) Within the United States.

(1) *In General.* Within the United States or a territory or insular possession subject to United States jurisdiction, a deposition must be taken before:

(A) an officer authorized to administer oaths either by federal law or by the law in the place of examination; or

(B) a person appointed by the court where the action is pending to administer oaths and take testimony.

(2) *Definition of "Officer."* The term "officer" in Rules 30, 31, and 32 includes a person appointed by the court under this rule or designated by the parties under Rule 29(a).

(b) In a Foreign Country.

(1) *In General.* A deposition may be taken in a foreign country:

(A) under an applicable treaty or convention;

(B) under a letter of request, whether or not captioned a "letter rogatory";

(C) on notice, before a person authorized to administer oaths either by federal law or by the law in the place of examination; or

(D) before a person commissioned by the court to administer any necessary oath and take testimony.

(2) *Issuing a Letter of Request or a Commission.* A letter of request, a commission, or both may be issued:

(A) on appropriate terms after an application and notice of it; and

(B) without a showing that taking the deposition in another manner is impracticable or inconvenient.

(3) *Form of a Request, Notice, or Commission.* When a letter of request or any other device is used according to a treaty or convention, it must be captioned in the form prescribed by that treaty or convention. A letter of request may be addressed "To the Appropriate Authority in [name of country]." A deposition notice or a commission must designate by name or descriptive title the person before whom the deposition is to be taken.

(4) *Letter of Request—Admitting Evidence.* Evidence obtained in response to a letter of request need not be excluded merely because it is not a verbatim transcript, because the testimony was not taken under oath, or because of any similar departure from the requirements for depositions taken within the United States.

(c) Disqualification. A deposition must not be taken before a person who is any party's relative, employee, or attorney; who is related to or employed by any party's attorney; or who is financially interested in the action.

[Amended December 27, 1946, effective March 19, 1948; January 21, 1963, effective July 1, 1963; April 29, 1980, effective August 1, 1980; March 2, 1987, effective August 1, 1987; April 22, 1993, effective December 1, 1993; April 30, 2007, effective December 1, 2007.]

AUTHORS' COMMENTARY ON RULE 28

PURPOSE AND SCOPE

Rule 28 specifies the type of person who must be present at a deposition to administer the oath and to record the testimony.

RULE 28(a)—WITHIN THE UNITED STATES

CORE CONCEPT

In the United States, or a territory or insular possession, depositions may be taken before an officer authorized to administer oaths under federal or state law.[1] Typically, a stenographer is such an officer. A deposition may also be taken before someone appointed by the court, or before a person designated by the parties pursuant to Rule 29.[2]

RULE 28(b)—IN A FOREIGN COUNTRY

CORE CONCEPT

The procedures for taking depositions in a foreign country depend upon the particular country. Some countries have treaties with the United States that facilitate such depositions. Other countries strictly prohibit such depositions altogether.

NOTE: In some countries, the taking of evidence under unauthorized procedures may subject the interrogator to severe—even criminal—sanctions. Before taking such evidence, a practitioner should consult the Hague Convention and all treaty supplements thereto.[3]

APPLICATIONS

Alternatives

Depending upon the laws of the foreign country, a deposition in a foreign country may be taken:

(1) Pursuant to any applicable treaty or convention (such as the Hague Convention described above);[4]

(2) Pursuant to a letter request (or letter rogatory), which is a formal communication between the court in which an action is proceeding and another court requesting that the testimony of a foreign witness be taken under the direction of the foreign court;[5]

(3) Upon a notice of deposition by any person authorized to administer oaths either by the laws of the foreign country or the United States; and

(4) Before persons commissioned by the court, who will have power to administer an oath and hear testimony by virtue of their oaths.

Method Optional

A party seeking to depose a witness in a foreign country

---

[1]*Hudson v. Spellman High Voltage*, 178 F.R.D. 29, 32 (E.D. N.Y. 1998).

[2]*Popular Imports, Inc. v. Wong's Intern., Inc.*, 166 F.R.D. 276, 279–80 (E.D. N.Y. 1996).

[3]The Hague Convention on the Taking of Evidence Abroad in Civil or Commercial Matters is reproduced as a note to 28 U.S.C.A. § 1781, and may also be found on WESTLAW in the IEL database, **ci(vii-b & text)**. *Also see* Lowenfeld, International Litigation

and Arbitration: Selected Treaties, Statutes and Rules, page 262 (1993). *See Societe Nationale Industrielle Aerospatiale v. U.S. Dist. Court for Southern Dist. of Iowa*, 482 U.S. 522, 107 S. Ct. 2542, 96 L. Ed. 2d 461 (1987).

[4]*International Ins. Co. v. Caja Nacional De Ahoroo Y Seguro*, 2004 WL 555618 (N.D. Ill. 2004).

[5]*See Murata Mfg. Co., Ltd. v. Bel Fuse, Inc.*, 242 F.R.D. 470 (N.D. Ill. 2007).

may use any of the methods listed in Rule 28(b) allowed by the foreign country's laws, and may even combine two or more methods.

Issuance of Letter Requests

All courts of the United States are authorized to issue letter requests or letters rogatory,[6] which are typically channeled through the United States Department of State.

Testimony Pursuant to a Letter Request

The evidence taken pursuant to a letter request varies according to the foreign country's laws. Sometimes the foreign judge examines the witness, then makes a written summary of the testimony, which is acknowledged as correct by the witness. The United States court will then decide on the weight to be given to the evidence depending upon the method of recording.

Compelling Attendance of Witness

If the witness is a party, then the witness is subject to the United States court's sanctions if the witness fails to appear as noticed. If the witness is a United States citizen, then the witness still may be subject to the United States court's subpoena power. However, if the witness is an alien, then the party will have to rely on a letter request.

RULE 28(c)—DISQUALIFICATION

CORE CONCEPT

The officer at a deposition may not be a relative, employee, attorney, or counsel of any of the parties,[7] or an employee or relative of an attorney for a party, or anyone with a financial interest in the action.[8]

APPLICATIONS

Objections

Objections to the officer must be raised before the deposition starts, or as soon thereafter as the interest of the officer becomes known or should have become known, with due diligence. Otherwise, the objection is waived.[9]

Additional Research References

Wright & Miller, *Federal Practice and Procedure* §§ 2081 to 2084
C.J.S., Federal Civil Procedure § 593

---

[6]*See U.S. v. Reagan*, 453 F.2d 165 (6th Cir. 1971).

[7]*See U.S. v. Washington*, 46 M.J. 477, 482 (C.A.A.F. 1997) (defendant objected to the appointment of a prosecutor on the basis that he had prior prosecutorial involvement in the case).

[8]*Ott v. Stipe Law Firm*, 169 F.R.D. 380, 381 (E.D. Okla. 1996) (plaintiff is not permitted to administer oath).

[9]See Rule 32(d)(2).

West's Key Number Digest, Federal Civil Procedure ☞1371

RULE 29
STIPULATIONS ABOUT DISCOVERY PROCEDURE

Unless the court orders otherwise, the parties may stipulate that:

   (a) a deposition may be taken before any person, at any time or place, on any notice, and in the manner specified—in which event it may be used in the same way as any other deposition; and

   (b) other procedures governing or limiting discovery be modified—but a stipulation extending the time for any form of discovery must have court approval if it would interfere with the time set for completing discovery, for hearing a motion, or for trial.

[Amended March 30, 1970, effective July 1, 1970; April 22, 1993, effective December 1, 1993; April 30, 2007, effective December 1, 2007.]

AUTHORS' COMMENTARY ON RULE 29

PURPOSE AND SCOPE

For their convenience, the parties may stipulate to modified procedures for taking depositions and for other discovery methods as long as the stipulation does not interfere with a hearing or trial date or the discovery deadline.

APPLICATIONS

Procedures

   Rule 29 states that stipulations must be in writing.[1] Although not expressly required by Rule 29, the stipulation

---

[1] *In re Carney*, 258 F.3d 415, 419 (5th Cir. 2001) (stipulation not effective if not in writing); *Venture Funding, Ltd. v. U.S.*, 190 F.R.D. 209, 212 (E.D. Mich. 1999) (oral agreement that only certain documents need to be ɼroduced is unenforceable); *Pescia v. Auburn Ford-Lincoln Mercury Inc.*, 177 F.R.D. 509, 510 (M.D. Ala. 1997) (oral agreement, even though confirmed in writing, did not satisfy the requirement of Rule 29 that stipulations must be in writing).

should be signed by the parties.[2] Stipulations under Rule 29 are self-effectuating, and do not need to be filed with the court unless they interfere with the close of discovery or any other case management deadline.[3]

Depositions

The parties may designate the person before whom a deposition will occur, and the time, location, notice requirements, and method of taking the deposition.[4] Thereafter, a deposition taken in accordance with the stipulation may be used as if taken in accordance with the provisions governing depositions in Rules 30 and 31.[5]

Other Discovery Methods

The parties may also stipulate to any other discovery method,[6] except that the parties need court approval to modify the time to respond to interrogatories, document requests, and requests for admission set forth in Rules 33, 34, and 36 if the extension would interfere with the court's discovery deadline or with a hearing or trial date.[7]

Court Override

The court can order that parties perform under the Rules as written, vitiating any stipulations.[8]

Additional Research References

Wright & Miller, *Federal Practice and Procedure* §§ 2091 to 2092
C.J.S., Federal Civil Procedure § 566
West's Key Number Digest, Federal Civil Procedure ☞1326

---

[2]*Land Ocean Logistics, Inc. v. Aqua Gulf Corp.*, 181 F.R.D. 229, 243 (W.D. N.Y. 1998) (competing unsigned stipulations are unenforceable).

[3]*In re DFI Proceeds, Inc.*, 441 B.R. 914, 916 (Bankr.N.D.Ind. 2011).

[4]*In re Angst*, 428 B.R. 776, 781 (Bankr.N.D.Ohio 2010); *Reder Enterprises, Inc. v. Loomis, Fargo & Co. Corp.*, 490 F. Supp. 2d 111 (D. Mass. 2007) (parties may stipulate that depositions be taken "at any . . . place").

[5]*See In re Angst*, __ B.R. __ (Bankr.N.D.Ohio 2010).

[6]*See Erie Ins. Property & Cas. Co. v. Johnson*, 272 F.R.D. 177, 182 (S.D.W.Va. 2010) (extension of time to respond to disclosures or discovery).

[7]*See Laborers' Pension Fund v. Blackmore Sewer Const., Inc.*, 298 F.3d 600, 605–06 (7th Cir. 2002); *In re DFI Proceeds, Inc.*, 441 B.R. 914, 916 (Bankr.N.D.Ind. 2011).

[8]The Advisory Note to the 1970 amendment of Rule 29.

RULE 30
DEPOSITIONS BY ORAL EXAMINATION

(a) When a Deposition May Be Taken.

(1) *Without Leave.* A party may, by oral questions, depose any person, including a party, without leave of court except as provided in Rule 30(a)(2). The deponent's attendance may be compelled by subpoena under Rule 45.

(2) *With Leave.* A party must obtain leave of court, and the court must grant leave to the extent consistent with Rule 26(b)(2):

   (A) if the parties have not stipulated to the deposition and:

      (i) the deposition would result in more than 10 depositions being taken under this rule or Rule 31 by the plaintiffs, or by the defendants, or by the third-party defendants;

      (ii) the deponent has already been deposed in the case; or

      (iii) the party seeks to take the deposition before the time specified in Rule 26(d), unless the party certifies in the notice, with supporting facts, that the deponent is expected to leave the United States and be unavailable for examination in this country after that time; or

   (B) if the deponent is confined in prison.

(b) Notice of the Deposition; Other Formal Requirements.

(1) *Notice in General.* A party who wants to depose a person by oral questions must give reasonable written notice to every other party. The notice must state the time and place of the deposition and, if known, the deponent's name and address. If the name is unknown, the notice must provide a general description sufficient to identify the

person or the particular class or group to which the person belongs.

(2) *Producing Documents.* If a subpoena duces tecum is to be served on the deponent, the materials designated for production, as set out in the subpoena, must be listed in the notice or in an attachment. The notice to a party deponent may be accompanied by a request under Rule 34 to produce documents and tangible things at the deposition.

(3) *Method of Recording.*

    (A) *Method Stated in the Notice.* The party who notices the deposition must state in the notice the method for recording the testimony. Unless the court orders otherwise, testimony may be recorded by audio, audiovisual, or stenographic means. The noticing party bears the recording costs. Any party may arrange to transcribe a deposition.

    (B) *Additional Method.* With prior notice to the deponent and other parties, any party may designate another method for recording the testimony in addition to that specified in the original notice. That party bears the expense of the additional record or transcript unless the court orders otherwise.

(4) *By Remote Means.* The parties may stipulate—or the court may on motion order—that a deposition be taken by telephone or other remote means. For the purpose of this rule and Rules 28(a), 37(a)(2), and 37(b)(1), the deposition takes place where the deponent answers the questions.

(5) *Officer's Duties.*

    (A) *Before the Deposition.* Unless the parties stipulate otherwise, a deposition must be conducted before an officer appointed or designated under Rule 28. The officer must begin the deposition with an on-the-record statement that includes:

        (i)   the officer's name and business address;

        (ii) the date, time, and place of the deposition;

        (iii) the deponent's name;

(iv) the officer's administration of the oath or affirmation to the deponent; and

(v) the identity of all persons present.

(B) *Conducting the Deposition; Avoiding Distortion.* If the deposition is recorded non-stenographically, the officer must repeat the items in Rule 30(b)(5)(A)(i)–(iii) at the beginning of each unit of the recording medium. The deponent's and attorneys' appearance or demeanor must not be distorted through recording techniques.

(C) *After the Deposition.* At the end of a deposition, the officer must state on the record that the deposition is complete and must set out any stipulations made by the attorneys about custody of the transcript or recording and of the exhibits, or about any other pertinent matters.

(6) *Notice or Subpoena Directed to an Organization.* In its notice or subpoena, a party may name as the deponent a public or private corporation, a partnership, an association, a governmental agency, or other entity and must describe with reasonable particularity the matters for examination. The named organization must then designate one or more officers, directors, or managing agents, or designate other persons who consent to testify on its behalf; and it may set out the matters on which each person designated will testify. A subpoena must advise a nonparty organization of its duty to make this designation. The persons designated must testify about information known or reasonably available to the organization. This paragraph (6) does not preclude a deposition by any other procedure allowed by these rules.

(c) Examination and Cross-Examination; Record of the Examination; Objections; Written Questions.

(1) *Examination and Cross-Examination.* The examination and cross-examination of a deponent proceed as they would at trial under the Federal

Rules of Evidence, except Rules 103 and 615. After putting the deponent under oath or affirmation, the officer must record the testimony by the method designated under Rule 30(b)(3)(A). The testimony must be recorded by the officer personally or by a person acting in the presence and under the direction of the officer.

(2) *Objections.* An objection at the time of the examination—whether to evidence, to a party's conduct, to the officer's qualifications, to the manner of taking the deposition, or to any other aspect of the deposition—must be noted on the record, but the examination still proceeds; the testimony is taken subject to any objection. An objection must be stated concisely in a nonargumentative and nonsuggestive manner. A person may instruct a deponent not to answer only when necessary to preserve a privilege, to enforce a limitation ordered by the court, or to present a motion under Rule 30(d)(3).

(3) *Participating Through Written Questions.* Instead of participating in the oral examination, a party may serve written questions in a sealed envelope on the party noticing the deposition, who must deliver them to the officer. The officer must ask the deponent those questions and record the answers verbatim.

(d) Duration; Sanction; Motion to Terminate or Limit.

(1) *Duration.* Unless otherwise stipulated or ordered by the court, a deposition is limited to 1 day of 7 hours. The court must allow additional time consistent with Rule 26(b)(2) if needed to fairly examine the deponent or if the deponent, another person, or any other circumstance impedes or delays the examination.

(2) *Sanction.* The court may impose an appropriate sanction—including the reasonable expenses and attorney's fees incurred by any party—on a person who impedes, delays, or frustrates the fair examination of the deponent.

(3) *Motion to Terminate or Limit.*

(A) *Grounds.* At any time during a deposition, the deponent or a party may move to terminate or limit it on the ground that it is being conducted in bad faith or in a manner that unreasonably annoys, embarrasses, or oppresses the deponent or party. The motion may be filed in the court where the action is pending or the deposition is being taken. If the objecting deponent or party so demands, the deposition must be suspended for the time necessary to obtain an order.

(B) *Order.* The court may order that the deposition be terminated or may limit its scope and manner as provided in Rule 26(c). If terminated, the deposition may be resumed only by order of the court where the action is pending.

(C) *Award of Expenses.* Rule 37(a)(5) applies to the award of expenses.

(e) Review by the Witness; Changes.

(1) *Review; Statement of Changes.* On request by the deponent or a party before the deposition is completed, the deponent must be allowed 30 days after being notified by the officer that the transcript or recording is available in which:

(A) to review the transcript or recording; and

(B) if there are changes in form or substance, to sign a statement listing the changes and the reasons for making them.

(2) *Changes Indicated in the Officer's Certificate.* The officer must note in the certificate prescribed by Rule 30(f)(1) whether a review was requested and, if so, must attach any changes the deponent makes during the 30-day period.

(f) Certification and Delivery; Exhibits; Copies of the Transcript or Recording; Filing.

(1) *Certification and Delivery.* The officer must certify in writing that the witness was duly sworn and that the deposition accurately records the witness's testimony. The certificate must accompany the record of the deposition. Unless the court orders otherwise, the officer must seal the deposition in an envelope or package bearing the

title of the action and marked "Deposition of [witness's name]" and must promptly send it to the attorney who arranged for the transcript or recording. The attorney must store it under conditions that will protect it against loss, destruction, tampering, or deterioration.

(2) *Documents and Tangible Things.*

   (A) *Originals and Copies.* Documents and tangible things produced for inspection during a deposition must, on a party's request, be marked for identification and attached to the deposition. Any party may inspect and copy them. But if the person who produced them wants to keep the originals, the person may:

      (i) offer copies to be marked, attached to the deposition, and then used as originals—after giving all parties a fair opportunity to verify the copies by comparing them with the originals; or

      (ii) give all parties a fair opportunity to inspect and copy the originals after they are marked—in which event the originals may be used as if attached to the deposition.

   (B) *Order Regarding the Originals.* Any party may move for an order that the originals be attached to the deposition pending final disposition of the case.

(3) *Copies of the Transcript or Recording.* Unless otherwise stipulated or ordered by the court, the officer must retain the stenographic notes of a deposition taken stenographically or a copy of the recording of a deposition taken by another method. When paid reasonable charges, the officer must furnish a copy of the transcript or recording to any party or the deponent.

(4) *Notice of Filing.* A party who files the deposition must promptly notify all other parties of the filing.

(g) Failure to Attend a Deposition or Serve a Subpoena; Expenses. A party who, expecting a deposition to be taken, attends in person or by an attorney may recover reasonable expenses for attending, including attorney's fees, if the noticing party failed to:

(1) attend and proceed with the deposition; or

(2) serve a subpoena on a nonparty deponent, who consequently did not attend.

[Amended January 21, 1963, effective July 1, 1963; March 30, 1970, effective July 1, 1970; March 1, 1971, effective July 1, 1971; November 20, 1972, effective July 1, 1975; April 29, 1980, effective August 1, 1980; March 2, 1987, effective August 1, 1987; April 22, 1993, effective December 1, 1993; April 17, 2000, effective December 1, 2000; April 30, 2007, effective December 1, 2007.]

AUTHORS' COMMENTARY ON RULE 30

PURPOSE AND SCOPE

Rule 30 sets forth the procedures for the taking of depositions by oral examination. Rule 30 must be considered in conjunction with the other discovery rules, and in particular Rule 26 governing the scope of discovery.

NOTE: Rule 30 was substantially revised in 1993, 2000, and 2007, and great care should be exercised when citing decisions pertaining to Rule 30.

RULE 30(a)—WHEN A DEPOSITION MAY BE TAKEN

CORE CONCEPT

In general, a party may take the deposition of up to 10 witnesses, party or otherwise, at any time after the parties have conducted the discovery conference under Rule 26(d).

APPLICATIONS

Persons Subject to Deposition

Rule 30 applies to parties and nonparties alike.[1] A party may even take the party's own deposition if, for example, the party will be unable to attend trial. One may also take the deposition of attorneys, including the attorneys for parties,[2] although the attorney-client privilege may protect most of an attorney's testimony. Depositions are also permitted of public officials, the United States, individual states, and other

---

[1] *CSC Holdings, Inc. v. Redisi*, 309 F.3d 988, 993 (7th Cir. 2002) (a party has a general right to compel any person to appear at a deposition).

[2] *Shelton v. American Motors Corp.*, 805 F.2d 1323 (8th Cir. 1986); *Sterne Kessler Goldstein & Fox, PLLC v. Eastman Kodak Co.*, 276 F.R.D. 376, 380 (D.D.C. 2011) (deposition of opposing counsel is disfavored).

governmental subdivisions.[3]

Number of Depositions

The plaintiffs as a group are limited to 10 depositions total, by written and/or oral examination, as are the defendants and third-party defendants.[4] Subpoenas to produce documents do not count towards the 10 deposition limit.[5] It is not clear whether expert depositions count toward the limit.[6] This number may be increased by stipulation or by order of court.[7]

Repeat Depositions

Leave of court or a stipulation of the parties is required to depose someone a second time (although leave of court is not required to reconvene and continue a deposition that was suspended or not completed the first day).[8] This restriction arguably applies to depositions of a corporate representative under Rule 30(b)(6).[9] Leave shall be granted subject to the principles in Rule 26(b)(2), such as when the sought-after information could not have been obtained in the first deposition.[10]

Counting Depositions of Rule 30(b)(6) Representatives

A notice to take the deposition of a corporate representative under Rule 30(b)(6) will count as one deposition toward the 10 deposition limit, regardless of the number of representatives designated to appear and testify.[11] The application of the limitation on repeat depositions of the same individual to Rule 30(b)(6) depositions are less clear. Some courts have held that it is impermissible to issue a second Rule 30(b)(6) notice without leave of court.[12] Other courts have held that leave of court is not required to take the deposition of a witness as a

---

[3]*U. S. v. Procter & Gamble Co.*, 356 U.S. 677, 78 S. Ct. 983, 2 L. Ed. 2d 1077 (1958).

[4]*O'Leary v. Accretive Health, Inc.*, 657 F.3d 625, 636 (7th Cir. 2011); *Byrd v. District of Columbia*, 259 F.R.D. 1, 4 (D.D.C. 2009).

[5]*Andamiro U.S.A. v. Konami Amusement of America, Inc.*, 2001 WL 535667 (C.D. Cal. 2001).

[6]*Express One Intern., Inc. v. Sochata*, 2001 WL 363073 (N.D. Tex. 2001).

[7]*O'Leary v. Accretive Health, Inc.*, 657 F.3d 625, 636 (7th Cir. 2011); *Raniola v. Bratton*, 243 F.3d 610, 628 (2d Cir. 2001).

[8]*Kleppinger v. Texas Dept. of Transp.*, __ F.R.D. __ (S.D.Tex. 2012); *Paige v. Consumer Programs, Inc.*, 248 F.R.D. 272, 275 (C.D. Cal. 2008) (when the party appears but the deposition does not occur, the party may be re-

noticed without violating the rule against second depositions); *In re Tutu Water Wells Contamination CERCLA Litig.*, 189 F.R.D. 153, 155 (D.V.I. 1999) (balancing need for testimony against burden of second deposition).

[9]*See Ameristar Jet Charter, Inc. v. Signal Composites, Inc.*, 244 F.3d 189 (1st Cir.2001).

[10]*Collins v. International Dairy Queen*, 189 F.R.D. 496, 498 (M.D. Ga. 1999).

[11]See The Advisory Committee Note to the 1993 amendment of Rule 30(a); *Quality Aero v. Telmetrie Elektronik*, 212 F.R.D. 313 (E.D.N.C. 2002).

[12]*See Ameristar Jet Charter, Inc. v. Signal Composites, Inc.*, 244 F.3d 189 (1st Cir. 2001); *In re Sulfuric Acid Antitrust Litigation*, 2005 WL 1994105 (N.D.Ill. 2005).

Rule 30(b)(6) representative even if the witness has already been deposed in his or her individual capacity.[13]

When Depositions May be Conducted

Depositions generally may be taken at any time after the Rule 26(d) discovery conference and before the cut-off date for discovery established by the court. Leave of court is generally required to depose someone prior to the time when the parties conduct the discovery conference under Rule 26(d).[14] An exception occurs when the deponent is expected to leave the United States. In such instances, the notice of deposition must contain a certification with the facts supporting the need for the early deposition.[15] Additionally, in proceedings listed in Rule 26(a)(1)(B) as exempt from initial disclosures, there is no preliminary waiting period for depositions.

Postjudgment Depositions

A judgment creditor is entitled to take depositions of the judgment debtor to inquire into the assets necessary to satisfy the judgment.[16]

Deponent in Prison

Leave of court must be obtained in order to take the deposition of a person confined in prison.[17]

RULE 30(b)(1)—NOTICE OF THE DEPOSITION; OTHER FORMAL REQUIREMENTS: NOTICE IN GENERAL

CORE CONCEPT

A party desiring to take a deposition must serve a written notice upon all other parties identifying the deponent and time and location of the deposition.[18] Depositions are only admissible against parties properly noticed or actually represented at the deposition.

---

[13]*See Beaulieu v. Board of Trustees of University of West Fla.*, 2007 WL 4468704 (N.D.Fla. 2007); *Quality Aero v. Telmetrie Elektronik*, 212 F.R.D. 313 (E.D.N.C. 2002).

[14]*St. Louis Group, Inc. v. Metals and Additives Corp., Inc.*, __ F.R.D. __ (S.D.Tex. 2011); *Dimension Data North America, Inc. v. NetStar-1, Inc.*, 226 F.R.D. 528, 531 (E.D. N.C. 2005).

[15]*19th Street Baptist Church v. St. Peters Episcopal Church*, 190 F.R.D. 345, 348 n. 5 (E.D. Pa. 2000).

[16]*Credit Lyonnais, S.A. v. SGC Intern., Inc.*, 160 F.3d 428, 430 (8th Cir. 1998).

[17]*Ashby v. McKenna*, 331 F.3d 1148 (10th Cir. 2003) (prisoner plaintiff sanctioned for refusing to participate in deposition without court order); *Davis v. Artuz*, 2001 WL 50887 (S.D. N.Y. 2001).

[18]*Pegoraro v. Marrero*, 281 F.R.D. 122, 128 (S.D.N.Y. 2012) (court cannot compel witnesses to attend deposition without proof of a proper deposition notice).

APPLICATIONS

Impact of 2007 "Restyling" Amendments

Rule 30(b) was significantly restructured during the 2007 Federal Civil Rules "Restyling" Project. The portion of Rule 30(b)(1) addressing subpoenas for the production of documents and things was combined with Rule 30(b)(5) to form new Rule 30(b)(2). The content of Rule 30(b)(2) and Rule 30(b)(3) pertaining to methods of recording a deposition were combined to form new Rule 30(b)(3). Rule 30(b)(7), pertaining to telephonic and remote depositions, was moved to Rule 30(b)(4). Old Rule 30(b)(4) became Rule 30(b)(5). Only Rule 30(b)(6) was immune from this reorganization. In researching current Rule 30(b), practitioners should be mindful of this repositioning.

Content of Notice

The notice must state the time and place of the deposition.[19] It must also state the name and address of the deponent, if known, or a general description sufficient to identify the deponent. If a subpoena duces tecum (seeking documents) is to be served under Rule 45, then the notice must include a description of the documents sought.[20] There is no need to state the subject of the inquiry.[21]

Filing of Notice

The notice need not be filed.

Notice to Party

Parties must comply with a notice of deposition or they are potentially subject to sanctions from the court.[22] A corporate party is required to produce directors, officers, and managing agents[23] pursuant to a notice of deposition; a subpoena is required for other employees.[24] Parties that believe that they should not be required to attend can file motions for protective orders.

Failure to Notify

If a party does not receive a notice of a deposition and does not appear, or is not represented at the deposition, the testimony cannot be used against that party, even if the party

---

[19]*Shockey v. Huhtamaki, Inc.*, 280 F.R.D. 598, 600 (D.Kan. 2012); *Nuskey v. Lambright*, 251 F.R.D. 3 (D.D.C. 2008).

[20]*Orleman v. Jumpking, Inc.*, 2000 WL 1114849 (D. Kan. 2000) (description of documents to be produced must be attached to or included in the notice).

[21]*Whitehead v. Hidden Tavern, Inc.*, __ F.Supp.2d __ (W.D.Tex. 2011).

[22]*Blazek v. Capital Recovery Associates, Inc.*, 222 F.R.D. 360, 361 (E.D. Wis. 2004) (a defaulting party deemed a party for purposes of a notice of deposition).

[23]*Murata Mfg. Co., Ltd. v. Bel Fuse, Inc.*, 242 F.R.D. 470 (N.D. Ill. 2007) (managing agents generally are current employees with control or authority over day-to-day business decisions).

[24]*U.S. Fidelity & Guar. Co. v. Braspetro Oil Services Co.*, 2001 WL 43607 (S.D. N.Y. 2001).

had actual knowledge.[25]

Notice to Non-party

A notice of deposition is not binding on a non-party. Instead, a subpoena must be issued pursuant to Rule 45 to force a non-party to attend a deposition.[26] However, the party taking the deposition must still serve a deposition notice upon the other parties.[27]

Reasonable Notice

Rule 30(b)(1) states that a party must give reasonable notice.[28] There is no bright line as to what is reasonable notice, and the determination is extremely fact-specific.[29] If the parties cannot agree on a mutually acceptable date, then unreasonable notice may be challenged by a motion to enlarge or shorten the time for taking the deposition by a motion for a protective order under Rule 26(c).

One Notice Sufficient for All Parties

Each party does not have to serve its own notice in order to examine the witness; all parties are entitled to conduct examination once a deposition has been noticed.[30]

Sanctions

The sanctions for failure to appear at a deposition depend upon whether the witness is a party. Non-party witnesses may be held in contempt of court for failure to obey a subpoena. Party witnesses are subject to the sanctions described in Rule 37(d).

Place of Examination

For a party deponent, one may select any location for the deposition, subject to the party's right to move for a protective order (but see the general rules below).[31] For a non-party witness, the witness must travel up to 100 miles from the place where the witness resides, is employed, or regularly transacts business.

---

[25]*Nuskey v. Lambright*, 251 F.R.D. 3, 12 (D.D.C. 2008) (a witness cannot be compelled to testify at a deposition until the witness fails to appear after being served a reasonable written notice stating the time and place of the deposition); *Lauson v. Stop-N-Go Foods, Inc.*, 133 F.R.D. 92 (W.D. N.Y. 1990).

[26]*Lefkoe v. Jos. A. Bank Clothiers, Inc.*, 577 F.3d 240, 246 (4th Cir. 2009).

[27]*Lefkoe v. Jos. A. Bank Clothiers, Inc.*, 577 F.3d 240, 246 (4th Cir. 2009).

[28]*Howard v. Everex Systems, Inc.*, 228 F.3d 1057, 1067 (9th Cir. 2000); *U.S. v. Philip Morris Inc.*, 312 F. Supp. 2d 27 (D.D.C. 2004) (3 days notice for busy professionals is not reasonable).

[29]*In re Sulfuric Acid Antitrust Litigation*, 231 F.R.D. 320, 327 (N.D. Ill. 2005) (10 days unreasonable in a complex case); *In re Stratosphere Corp. Securities Litigation*, 183 F.R.D. 684, 687 (D. Nev. 1999) (six days notice not reasonable).

[30]*FCC v. Mizuho Medy Co. Ltd.*, 257 F.R.D. 679, 681–82 (S.D.Cal. 2009).

[31]*New Medium Technologies LLC v. Barco N.V.*, 242 F.R.D. 460 (N.D. Ill. 2007).

General Rules for Deposition Location

The court has discretion to control the location of a deposition.[32] In general, however, plaintiffs will be required to travel to the district where the suit is pending for their depositions,[33] whereas defendants can have their depositions taken where they work or live.[34] Also, in general, the deposition of a corporation occurs at its principal place of business.[35] These general principles are, of course, subject to extenuating circumstances, such as a plaintiff who is too sick to travel.

Motion for Protective Order

If a notice of deposition is facially valid, then the witness must attend or file a motion for a protective order pursuant to Rule 26(c).[36] The motion must be made before the time scheduled for the deposition, and must show good reason for the requested protection. The motion must be accompanied by a certification that the parties met prior to the filing of the motion and attempted to resolve their dispute without intervention by the court.

RULE 30(b)(2)—PRODUCING DOCUMENTS

CORE CONCEPT

A witness may be compelled to bring documents to a deposition by including a description of the documents in the notice of deposition (for a party witness) or by issuing a subpoena duces tecum under Rule 45(a)(1)(A)(iii) and including a description in the notice (for a non-party witness).[37] However, if the witness is a party, then the witness must be accorded 30 days to interpose objections to the document request[38] (the rationale being that one should not be able to circumvent the 30-day period in the document request rules by issuing a notice of deposition).[39] A deposition notice to a party may also be accompanied by a document request under Rule 34.

---

[32]*In re Standard Metals Corp.*, 817 F.2d 625, 628 (10th Cir. 1987); *Estate of Gerasimenko v. Cape Wind Trading Co.*, 272 F.R.D. 385, 387 (S.D.N.Y. 2011).

[33]*Shockey v. Huhtamaki, Inc.*, 280 F.R.D. 598, 600 (D.Kan. 2012); *Estate of Gerasimenko v. Cape Wind Trading Co.*, 272 F.R.D. 385, 387 (S.D.N.Y. 2011).

[34]*Rapoca Energy Company, L.P. v. Amci Export Corp.*, 199 F.R.D. 191, 193 (W.D. Va. 2001).

[35]*U.S. ex rel. Barko v. Halliburton Co.*, 270 F.R.D. 26, 29 (D.D.C. 2010); *In re Outsidewall Tire Litiga-*tion, __ F.Supp.2d __ (E.D.Va. 2010).

[36]*Collins v. Wayland*, 139 F.2d 677 (C.C.A. 9th Cir. 1944).

[37]*Lee v. U.S. Dept. of Justice*, 287 F. Supp. 2d 15, 22 (D.D.C. 2003), aff'd, 413 F.3d 53 (D.C. Cir. 2005).

[38]*Dowling v. Cleveland Clinic Foundation*, 593 F.3d 472, 479 (6th Cir. 2010).

[39]*See Canal Barge Co. v. Commonwealth Edison Co.*, 2001 WL 817853 (N.D. Ill. 2001) (discussing the relationship between document requests under Rule 34 and requests to bring documents to depositions).

APPLICATIONS

Impact of 2007 "Restyling" Amendments

Rule 30(b) was significantly restructured during the 2007 Federal Civil Rules "Restyling" Project. The portion of Rule 30(b)(1) addressing subpoenas for the production of documents and things was combined with Rule 30(b)(5) to form new Rule 30(b)(2). The content of Rule 30(b)(2) and Rule 30(b)(3) pertaining to methods of recording a deposition were combined to form new Rule 30(b)(3). Rule 30(b)(7), pertaining to telephonic and remote depositions, was moved to Rule 30(b)(4). Old Rule 30(b)(4) became Rule 30(b)(5). Only Rule 30(b)(6) was immune from this reorganization. In researching current Rule 30(b), practitioners should be mindful of this repositioning.

RULE 30(b)(3)—THE DEPOSITION; METHOD OF RECORDING

CORE CONCEPT

The notice of deposition must specify the method for recording the deposition testimony.[40]

APPLICATIONS

Impact of 2007 "Restyling" Amendments

Rule 30(b) was significantly restructured during the 2007 Federal Civil Rules "Restyling" Project. The portion of Rule 30(b)(1) addressing subpoenas for the production of documents and things was combined with Rule 30(b)(5) to form new Rule 30(b)(2). The content of Rule 30(b)(2) and Rule 30(b)(3) pertaining to methods of recording a deposition were combined to form new Rule 30(b)(3). Rule 30(b)(7), pertaining to telephonic and remote depositions, was moved to Rule 30(b)(4). Old Rule 30(b)(4) became Rule 30(b)(5). Only Rule 30(b)(6) was immune from this reorganization. In researching current Rule 30(b), practitioners should be mindful of this repositioning.

Methods Available

The party taking the deposition may have it recorded by audio, audio visual, or stenographic means, unless the court orders otherwise.[41] Other parties may arrange for additional methods of recording under Rule 30(b)(3)(B).

---

[40]*Pioneer Drive, LLC v. Nissan Diesel America, Inc.*, 262 F.R.D. 552, 555, n.2 (D.Mont. 2009).

[41]*Planned Parenthood of Columbia/Willamette, Inc. v. American Coalition of Life Activists*, 290 F.3d 1058 (9th Cir. 2002) ("nonstenographic" means audio or visual); *Citizens for Responsibility and Ethics in Washington v. Cheney*, 580 F.Supp.2d 168, 183 (D.D.C. 2008) (while videotaping is normally permitted as a matter of course, it was denied when the limited issues before the court made videotape not helpful to the court); *Banks v. Office of the Senate Sergeant-At-Arms*, 241 F.R.D. 370 (D.D.C. 2007) (videotape of deposition not permitted because the party intended to use the tape for publicity,

Cost of Recording

The party taking the deposition bears the cost of the party's chosen method(s) of recording.[42]

Transcript

Any party may, at its own expense, arrange for a transcript to be made of a deposition recorded by nonstenographic means.[43]

Additional Methods of Recording

Any party may arrange for a method of recording a deposition in addition to that specified in the notice of deposition.[44] The party desiring such additional method of recording must send prior notice to all other parties and to the deponent,[45] and will bear the expense of the additional recording unless otherwise ordered by the court.[46] Any party may arrange to transcribe a deposition.

Use of Nonstenographic Depositions

In order to use a nonstenographically recorded deposition at trial or in connection with a dispositive motion, a party must submit a transcript of the portions to be introduced for the court's use.[47]

Objections

Objections to the nonstenographic recording of a deposition should be raised prior to the commencement of the deposition via a motion for protective order under Rule 26(c) or at the commencement of the deposition under Rule 30(c).[48]

RULE 30(b)(4)—NOTICE OF THE DEPOSITION; BY REMOTE MEANS

CORE CONCEPT

The parties may stipulate to, or move the court for an order

---

not for proper purposes).

[42]*Morrison v. Reichhold Chemicals, Inc.*, 97 F.3d 460, 464 (11th Cir. 1996); *Hudson v. Spellman High Voltage*, 178 F.R.D. 29 (E.D. N.Y. 1998). *See also Cherry v. Champion Intern. Corp.*, 186 F.3d 442, 448–49 (4th Cir. 1999) (discussing the recovery of alternative means of recording as costs under 28 U.S.C. § 1920).

[43]*Hudson v. Spellman High Voltage*, 178 F.R.D. 29 (E.D. N.Y. 1998).

[44]*Pioneer Drive, LLC v. Nissan Diesel America, Inc.*, 262 F.R.D. 552, 555 (D.Mont. 2009).

[45]*Ogden v. Keystone Residence*, 226 F. Supp. 2d 588, 605 (M.D. Pa. 2002).

[46]*See Craftsmen Limousine, Inc. v. Ford Motor Co.*, 579 F.3d 894, 897 (8th Cir. 2009) (discussing when the expenses of a videotaped deposition can be recovered as costs).

[47]Rule 26(a)(3)(A)(ii) and Rule 32(c); *But see Hudson v. Spellman High Voltage*, 178 F.R.D. 29 (E.D. N.Y. 1998) ("there is no requirement that a party taking a deposition by nonstenographic means provide a written transcript of the entire deposition to other parties.").

[48]*Fanelli v. Centenary College*, 211 F.R.D. 268 (D.N.J. 2002) (anxiety over videotaping not good cause sufficient to warrant a protective order).

that a deposition be taken by telephone, videoconference, or other remote means.[49] Generally, leave to take depositions by remote means will be granted liberally.[50] Such depositions are deemed to occur in the district where the deponent is located when answering the questions,[51] and the court reporter should be in the presence of the witness, not the attorneys.[52]

Although motions to take depositions remotely are typically filed by the noticing party seeking to avoid traveling to the witness, they can also be filed by the receiving party seeking to avoid traveling to the location of the deposition.[53] The provisions for remote depositions apply to depositions of party representatives under Rule 30(b)(6) as well as to depositions of specific individuals.[54]

APPLICATIONS

Impact of 2007 "Restyling" Amendments

Rule 30(b) was significantly restructured during the 2007 Federal Civil Rules "Restyling" Project. The portion of Rule 30(b)(1) addressing subpoenas for the production of documents and things was combined with Rule 30(b)(5) to form new Rule 30(b)(2). The content of Rule 30(b)(2) and Rule 30(b)(3) pertaining to methods of recording a deposition were combined to form new Rule 30(b)(3). Rule 30(b)(7), pertaining to telephonic and remote depositions, was moved to Rule 30(b)(4). Old Rule 30(b)(4) became Rule 30(b)(5). Only Rule 30(b)(6) was immune from this reorganization. In researching current Rule 30(b), practitioners should be mindful of this repositioning.

RULE 30(b)(5)—THE DEPOSITION; OFFICER'S DUTIES

CORE CONCEPT

At the beginning of a deposition, the officer shall place on the record administrative details identifying and describing the deposition. During the deposition, the demeanor of the witnesses shall not be distorted in the recording.

---

[49]*Shockey v. Huhtamaki, Inc.*, 280 F.R.D. 598, 600 (D.Kan. 2012) (allowing depositions by videoconference); *Brown v. Carr*, 236 F.R.D. 311 (S.D. Tex. 2006) (upon motion, the party seeking the telephone deposition has the initial burden of establishing a legitimate need for the motion; the burden then shifts to the other party to establish good cause why the deposition should not occur by telephone).

[50]*Brown v. Carr*, 253 F.R.D. 410, 412 (S.D.Tex. 2008).

[51]*Hudson v. Spellman High Voltage*, 178 F.R.D. 29, 32 (E.D. N.Y. 1998).

[52]*Aquino v. Automotive Service Industry Ass'n*, 93 F. Supp. 2d 922 (N.D. Ill. 2000).

[53]*See Estate of Gerasimenko v. Cape Wind Trading Co.*, 272 F.R.D. 385, 387 (S.D.N.Y. 2011).

[54]*See Estate of Gerasimenko v. Cape Wind Trading Co.*, 272 F.R.D. 385, 390 (S.D.N.Y. 2011).

APPLICATIONS

Impact of 2007 "Restyling" Amendments

Rule 30(b) was significantly restructured during the 2007 Federal Civil Rules "Restyling" Project. The portion of Rule 30(b)(1) addressing subpoenas for the production of documents and things was combined with Rule 30(b)(5) to form new Rule 30(b)(2). The content of Rule 30(b)(2) and Rule 30(b)(3) pertaining to methods of recording a deposition were combined to form new Rule 30(b)(3). Rule 30(b)(7), pertaining to telephonic and remote depositions, was moved to Rule 30(b)(4). Old Rule 30(b)(4) became Rule 30(b)(5). Only Rule 30(b)(6) was immune from this reorganization. In researching current Rule 30(b), practitioners should be mindful of this repositioning.

Statement at Deposition Beginning

The officer recording the deposition shall begin the record with a statement that includes:

A) the officer's name and business address;

B) the date, time, and place of deposition;

C) the name of the deponent;

D) the administration of the oath or affirmation to the deponent; and

E) an identification of all persons present.

If the deposition is recorded other than stenographically, then each separate tape or unit of recording must begin with the officer's name and business address, the date, time and place of the deposition, and the deponent's name.

Statement at Deposition End

The officer recording the deposition shall close the record by stating that the deposition is complete and setting forth any administrative stipulations regarding the deposition.

Witness Demeanor

The recording device should accurately and neutrally depict the witness's demeanor and appearance.[55]

RULE 30(b)(6)—THE DEPOSITION; NOTICE OR SUBPOENA DIRECTED TO AN ORGANIZATION

CORE CONCEPT

Rule 30(b)(6) allows a party to notice the deposition of a corporation, partnership,[56] association, governmental agency,[57] or

---

[55]*Pioneer Drive, LLC v. Nissan Diesel America, Inc.*, 262 F.R.D. 552, 555 (D.Mont. 2009) (deposition cannot be recorded in such a way that the appearance and demeanor of the deponent or attorneys are distorted).

[56]*Starlight Intern. Inc. v. Herlihy*, 186 F.R.D. 626, 638 (D. Kan. 1999) (Rule 30(b)(6) applies to partnerships and joint ventures).

other entity[58] and to specify the areas of inquiry. The named organization must then designate one or more representatives to testify as to the areas of inquiry.

APPLICATIONS

Subpoena

If the corporation or organization is not a party, then one must issue a subpoena to compel attendance.[59] If the corporation or organization is a party, a notice of deposition is sufficient.

Content of Notice

The notice (and the subpoena, if necessary) must state that the corporation has the duty to designate a representative, and must specify the areas of inquiry with reasonable particularity.[60] Notices that list too many topics or are otherwise too burdensome may not be enforceable.[61]

Selection of Representatives

The representative does not have to be an officer or director of the organization, and in fact does not even need to be employed by the organization.[62] Instead, the company has a duty to make a conscientious, good-faith effort to designate a knowledgeable representative.[63] Regardless of the status of the representative, however, the representative's testimony will be admissible against the organization and the organization must prepare the representative to testify as to the organization's collective knowledge and information.[64] If no single individual can provide the corporation's testimony as to all the designated

---

[57]*Watts v. S.E.C.*, 482 F.3d 501, 505 (D.C. Cir. 2007); *Great Socialist People's Libyan Arab Jamahiriya v. Miski*, 683 F.Supp.2d 1, 11–12 (D.D.C. 2010).

[58]Advisory Committee Notes to the 2007 Amendments (the phrase "other entity" is intended to capture any type of organization not specifically listed, such as limited liability companies).

[59]*See Mattel, Inc. v. Walking Mountain Productions*, 353 F.3d 792, 797 (9th Cir. 2003); *Cates v. LTV Aerospace Corp.*, 480 F.2d 620 (5th Cir.1973).

[60]*Whitehead v. Hidden Tavern, Inc.*, __ F.Supp.2d __ (W.D.Tex. 2011); *McBride v. Medicalodges, Inc.*, 250 F.R.D. 581 (D.Kan. 2008) (for Rule 30(b)(6) to function properly, areas of inquiry must be designated with "painstaking specificity"); *Tri-State*

Hosp. Supply Corp. v. U.S., 226 F.R.D. 118, 125 (D.D.C. 2005) (the phrase "including but not limited to" rendered the deposition topics overbroad).

[61]*See Edelen v. Campbell Soup Co.*, __ F.R.D. __ (N.D.Ga. 2010) (40 pages and 120 topics was too burdensome).

[62]*See Ecclesiastes 9:10-11-12, Inc. v. LMC Holding Co.*, 497 F.3d 1135, 1146–47 (10th Cir. 2007).

[63]*Ecclesiastes 9:10-11-12, Inc. v. LMC Holding Co.*, 497 F.3d 1135, 1146–47 (10th Cir. 2007) (organization must designate representatives, and cannot use lack of knowledgeable employees as an excuse); *Brazos River Authority v. GE Ionics, Inc.*, 469 F.3d 416, 433 (5th Cir. 2006).

[64]*FCC v. Mizuho Medy Co. Ltd.*, 257 F.R.D. 679 (S.D.Cal. 2009); *Sprint Communications Co., L.P. v. Theglobe. com, Inc.*, 236 F.R.D. 524 (D. Kan. 2006).

topics, the corporation must name more than one representative.[65] Sometimes, corporate counsel are selected as the corporate representative.[66]

Particular Officer

To depose a specific officer, director, or managing agent, there is no need to use Rule 30(b)(6); a notice of deposition may be sent indicating that the individual's testimony is sought in the individual's official capacity.[67] The corporation is then subject to sanctions if the named representative fails to appear.[68] The party moving for such sanctions has the burden of proving that the individual was an officer, director, or managing agent.

Officer vs. Employee

One cannot compel the attendance at a deposition of an employee who is not an officer, director, or managing agent of the organization merely by sending a notice.[69] Such an employee may be served with a subpoena,[70] and the employee is then subject to sanctions if the employee fails to appear. The corporation is not bound by the statements of such employees.[71]

Sanctions Against Organization

If the designated officer, director, or managing agent fails to appear for a deposition, the corporation or organization is subject to sanctions. Likewise, if a corporation provides witnesses who cannot answer questions listed in notice of deposition, then corporation has failed to comply with its obligations under the rule and may be subject to sanctions.[72] The organization can also be sanctioned for failing to designate representatives.[73]

[65]*QBE Ins. Corp. v. Jorda Enters., Inc.*, __ F.R.D. __ (S.D.Fla. 2012); *Covad Communications Co. v. Revonet, Inc.*, __ F.R.D. __ (D.D.C. 2010).

[66]*See In re Pioneer Hi-Bred Intern., Inc.*, 238 F.3d 1370, 1376 (Fed. Cir. 2001) (addressing the attorney client privilege issues when counsel is designated as the corporate representative); *Cartier, a Div. of Richemont North America, Inc. v. Bertone Group, Inc.*, 404 F. Supp. 2d 573 (S.D. N.Y. 2005).

[67]*Cummings v. General Motors Corp.*, 365 F.3d 944, 953 (10th Cir. 2004); *Simms v. Center for Correctional Health and Policy Studies*, 272 F.R.D. 36, 41 (D.D.C. 2011) (party may not use Rule 30(b)(6) to depose a former officer).

[68]*Bon Air Hotel, Inc. v. Time, Inc.*, 376 F.2d 118 (5th Cir. 1967); *Covad Communications Co. v. Revonet, Inc.*, __ F.R.D. __ (D.D.C. 2010).

[69]*See Folwell v. Hernandez*, 210 F.R.D. 169, 173 (M.D. N.C. 2002) (the definition of a managing agent is made on a case-by-case factual determination).

[70]*Philadelphia Indem. Ins. Co. v. Federal Ins. Co.*, 215 F.R.D. 492 (E.D. Pa. 2003).

[71]*Burns Bros. v. the B & O No. 177*, 21 F.R.D. 142 (E.D. N.Y. 1957).

[72]*Baker v. St. Paul Travelers Ins. Co.*, 670 F.3d 119, 124 (1st Cir. 2012); *Reilly v. Natwest Markets Group Inc.*, 181 F.R.D. 253 (2d Cir. 1999) (corporation precluded from offering testimony from witnesses not designated in response to Rule 30(b)(6) notice).

[73]*Ecclesiastes 9:10-11-12, Inc. v. LMC Holding Co.*, 497 F.3d 1135 (10th

Scope of Testimony

The corporation or organization must select an individual or individuals who can testify to the areas specified in the notice.[74] The individual(s) must testify to all matters known or reasonably available to the corporation,[75] which may necessitate some gathering of documents and interviewing witnesses and having the individual(s) review and become familiar with the documents and information.[76] Thus, the individual will often testify to matters outside the individual's personal knowledge.[77] The courts are divided as to whether the examination of the representative is limited to the areas of inquiry identified in the notice of deposition.[78] The testimony is not limited to facts, but can include beliefs and opinions held by the entity.[79]

Legal Claims and Theories

The courts are divided as to whether topics for a Rule 30(b)(6) deposition may include the party's contentions or facts supporting those contentions.[80] Many courts are reluctant to allow depositions of opposing counsel, and will closely examine notices under Rule 30(b)(6) that are "back door" attempts to depose opposing counsel.[81]

Duty to Prepare

If the representative(s) cannot testify as to the corporation's collective information on the matters requested, then the corporation has a duty to gather the information and prepare the representative(s) so that the representatives can give

---

Cir. 2007) (case dismissed after plaintiff delayed making designation, then the logical representative died).

[74]*Poole ex rel. Elliott v. Textron, Inc.*, 192 F.R.D. 494 (D. Md. 2000) (a corporation should make a "diligent inquiry" to determine the individual(s) best suited to testify).

[75]*QBE Ins. Corp. v. Jorda Enters., Inc.*, __ F.R.D. __ (S.D.Fla. 2012); *Great American Ins. Co. of New York v. Vegas Const. Co., Inc.*, 251 F.R.D. 534 (D.Nev. 2008).

[76]*Poole ex rel. Elliott v. Textron, Inc.*, 192 F.R.D. 494 (D. Md. 2000); *Alexander v. F.B.I.*, 186 F.R.D. 148 (D.D.C. 1999) (listing 5 obligations of recipient of a Rule 30(b)(6) notice).

[77]*PPM Finance, Inc. v. Norandal USA, Inc.*, 392 F.3d 889, 894–95 (7th Cir. 2004); *QBE Ins. Corp. v. Jorda Enters., Inc.*, __ F.R.D. __ (S.D.Fla. 2012).

[78]*See Philbrick v. eNom, Inc.*, 593 F.Supp.2d 352, 363 (D.N.H. 2009) (party does not vouch for the ability of the designate to speak to matters outside the notice); *FCC v. Mizuho Medy Co. Ltd.*, 257 F.R.D. 679 (S.D.Cal. 2009).

[79]*Brazos River Authority v. GE Ionics, Inc.*, 469 F.3d 416, 432 (5th Cir. 2006); *QBE Ins. Corp. v. Jorda Enters., Inc.*, __ F.R.D. __ (S.D.Fla. 2012). *But see U.S. ex rel. Tiesinga v. Dianon Systems, Inc.*, 240 F.R.D. 40 (D. Conn. 2006) (representative cannot be forced to endorse an expert opinion).

[80]*See Radian Asset Assur., Inc. v. College of the Christian Bros. of New Mexico*, __ F.Supp.2d __ (D.N.M. 2011) (discussing the split of authority).

[81]*See Sprint Communications Co., L.P. v. Theglobe.com, Inc.*, 236 F.R.D. 524 (D. Kan. 2006) (in order to avoid privilege issues, the party can designate a non-attorney and then prepare that designee to testify as to all non-privileged information); *S.E.C. v. Buntrock*, 217 F.R.D. 441, 445 (N.D. Ill. 2003), aff'd, 2004 WL 1470278 (N.D. Ill. 2004) (3 factor test for obtaining the deposition of opposing counsel).

complete, knowledgeable, and binding testimony.[82] Failure to adequately prepare the representative can result in sanctions.[83]

Effect of Testimony

Testimony by a Rule 30(b)(6) representative has the effect of an evidentiary admission, not a judicial admission, and thus may be controverted or explained by the party.[84] The organization may be prohibited from using theories or information not disclosed during the Rule 30(b)(6) deposition unless the information was unavailable at the time of the deposition.[85]

RULE 30(c)—EXAMINATION AND CROSS-EXAMINATION; RECORD OF THE EXAMINATION; OBJECTIONS; WRITTEN QUESTIONS

CORE CONCEPT

In general, the examination of witnesses at a deposition proceeds much like at trial,[86] except that most objections are reserved until the testimony is offered into evidence. Objections to questions must be stated in a non-suggestive and non-argumentative manner.

APPLICATIONS

Impact of 2007 "Restyling" Amendments

Rule 30(c) was significantly restructured during the 2007 Federal Civil Rules "Restyling" Project. The provisions of Rule 30(c) were broken into Rules 30(c)(1) and 30(c)(3). The provisions in Rule 30(d)(1) regarding statement of objections and instructions not to answer were moved to Rule 30(c)(2), together with some text from old Rule 30(c). The sanction provisions of Rule 30(d)(3) became Rule 30(d)(2). Finally, the provision of Rule 30(d)(4) became Rule 30(d)(3). In researching current Rule 30(c), practitioners should be mindful of this repositioning.

Oath or Affirmation

The officer before whom the deposition is to be taken (usu-

---

[82]*Brazos River Authority v. GE Ionics, Inc.*, 469 F.3d 416, 433 (5th Cir. 2006); *QBE Ins. Corp. v. Jorda Enters., Inc.*, __ F.R.D. __ (S.D.Fla. 2012).

[83]*Black Horse Lane Assoc., L.P. v. Dow Chemical Corp.*, 228 F.3d 275, 301–05 (3d Cir. 2000); *Pioneer Drive, LLC v. Nissan Diesel America, Inc.*, 262 F.R.D. 552, 559 (D.Mont. 2009) (producing an unprepared witness is tantamount to nonappearance).

[84]*State Farm Mut. Auto. Ins. Co. v. New Horizont, Inc.*, 250 F.R.D. 203, 212 (E.D.Pa. 2008) (the purpose behind Rule 30(b)(6) is to create testi-mony that will bind the corporation, but it is not a judicial admission); *U.S. ex rel Fago v. M & T Mort. Corp.*, 235 F.R.D. 11, 22 (D.D.C. 2006) ("the agents' testimony is generally admissible as a statement of the corporation.").

[85]*QBE Ins. Corp. v. Jorda Enters., Inc.*, __ F.R.D. __ (S.D.Fla. 2012); *Rainey v. American Forest and Paper Ass'n, Inc.*, 26 F. Supp. 2d 82, 94 (D.D.C. 1998).

[86]*Brincko v. Rio Props., Inc.*, 278 F.R.D. 576, 579 (D.Nev. 2011).

ally the stenographer) will put the witness on oath or affirmation at the beginning of the deposition.

Recording

The officer will also arrange to have the testimony recorded, either stenographically or otherwise (as discussed above under Rule 30(b)(3)).

Expense of Recording

The party noticing the deposition arranges for and pays the cost of recording but the other parties pay for their copies of the recording. If the party taking the deposition does not order a transcript, then any other party can order one, and the court then has discretion as to who bears the expense.[87]

Examination

Examination proceeds as at trial, with direct examination and cross-examination[88] except that examination proceeds irrespective of objections.[89] Unlike trial, cross-examination is not limited to matters raised on direct, although the admission at trial of the deposition transcript may be limited on that basis.

Witness's Rights

At a deposition, the witness has the same rights as at trial, and may refresh his recollection with former testimony.[90] The extent to which a witness has the right to confer with counsel during a deposition is unsettled.[91]

Refusal to Answer Question

If a witness refuses to answer a question, the examining party may suspend the proceedings to seek an order under Rule 37(a) compelling an answer or may reserve the right to move for an order to compel and proceed to other areas. The losing party to such a motion to compel may then be subject to sanctions under Rule 37(a)(5).

Objections to Questions

Some objections to questions must be raised at the time of the deposition or they are waived, others are reserved until trial. The way to determine whether an objection must be made is to determine whether the examiner could rephrase the ques-

---

[87]The Advisory Committee Note to the 1970 amendment of Rule 30(c).

[88]*Sperling v. City of Kennesaw Dept.*, 202 F.R.D. 325, 329 (N.D. Ga. 2001) (adverse party entitled to review and use writing used by witness to refresh recollection).

[89]*Rangel v. Gonzalez Mascorro*, — F.R.D. — (S.D.Tex. 2011).

[90]*See Magee v. Paul Revere Life Ins. Co.*, 172 F.R.D. 627, 637 (E.D.

N.Y. 1997) (deponent repeatedly consulted his notes to refresh his memory at the deposition).

[91]*See, e.g., In re Stratosphere Corp. Securities Litigation*, 182 F.R.D. 614, 620 (D. Nev. 1998) (witness not permitted to confer while a question is pending); *Hall v. Clifton Precision, a Div. of Litton Systems, Inc.*, 150 F.R.D. 525, 526 (E.D. Pa. 1993).

tion to cure the objection.[92] Thus, parties must object to leading questions in order to give the examiner an opportunity to ask the question in a non-leading fashion. Conversely, parties do not need to raise objections such as relevancy or competency that cannot be cured.

Stating Objections

Objections must be stated in a non-suggestive manner.[93] Attorneys should not use an objection to instruct the witnesses how to answer (or not answer) a question.[94] However, the specific nature of the objection should be stated so that the court later can rule on the objection (*i.e.* "objection, leading" or "objection, lack of foundation").[95]

Instruction Not to Answer

Directions to a witness not to answer a question are only allowed in three narrow circumstances:[96] to claim a privilege (*i.e.*, attorney client communication);[97] to enforce a court directive limiting the scope or length of the deposition;[98] or to suspend the deposition for purposes of a motion under Rule 30(d)(3) relating to improper harassing conduct.[99] Thus, it is inappropriate for counsel to instruct a witness not to answer a question on the basis of relevance,[100] on the basis that the question has

---

[92]*Quiksilver, Inc. v. Kymsta Corp.*, 247 F.R.D. 579, 582 (C.D. Cal. 2007) (objections waived as to errors that could be obviated, removed, or cured).

[93]*Banks v. Office of the Senate Sergeant-At-Arms*, 241 F.R.D. 370 (D.D.C. 2007); *Jones v. J.C. Penney's Dept. Stores, Inc.*, 228 F.R.D. 190, 197–98 (W.D. N.Y. 2005).

[94]*Board of Trustees of Leland Stanford Junior University v. Tyco Intern. Ltd.*, 253 F.R.D. 524 (C.D.Cal. 2008); *Calzaturficio S.C.A.R.P.A. s.p.a. v. Fabiano Shoe Co., Inc.*, 201 F.R.D. 33 (D. Mass. 2001); *Quantachrome Corp. v. Micromeritics Instrument Corp.*, 189 F.R.D. 697, 700 (S.D. Fla. 1999).

[95]*Moloney v. U.S.*, 204 F.R.D. 16, 20–21 (D. Mass. 2001) (certain privileges were waived because the objection did not identify those privileges).

[96]*Baker v. St. Paul Travelers Ins. Co.*, 670 F.3d 119, 123 (1st Cir. 2012); *GMAC Bank v. HTFC Corp.*, 248 F.R.D. 182, 191 n. 10 (E.D. Pa. 2008) (some courts allow a witness not to answer if the question is irrelevant, argumentative, or misleading).

[97]*Brincko v. Rio Props., Inc.*, 278 F.R.D. 576, 579 (D.Nev. 2011); *Baltimore Line Handling Co. v. Brophy*, __ F.Supp.2d __ (D.Md. 2011).

[98]*Baker v. St. Paul Travelers Ins. Co.*, 670 F.3d 119, 123 (1st Cir. 2012).

[99]*See Biovail Laboratories, Inc. v. Anchen Pharmaceuticals, Inc.*, 233 F.R.D. 648, 653 (C.D. Cal. 2006) (Rule 30(d)(4) is the only authority allowing the interruption of a deposition); *A.W. v. I.B. Corp.*, 224 F.R.D. 20, 22 (D. Me. 2004); *Cobell v. Norton*, 213 F.R.D. 16, 27 (D.D.C. 2003) (counsel may not instruct the witness not to answer because the question is harassing, but only to suspend the deposition to seek a court order protecting the witness from harassment); *Mathias v. Jacobs*, 167 F. Supp. 2d 606, 626 (S.D. N.Y. 2001) (Rule 30(d) is the only mechanism for redressing harassing conduct at a deposition).

[100]*Resolution Trust Corp. v. Dabney*, 73 F.3d 262, 266 (10th Cir. 1995); *GMAC Bank v. HTFC Corp.*, 248 F.R.D. 182, 190–91 (E.D. Pa. 2008).

been asked and answered,[101] is harassing,[102] or on the basis that the question is outside the areas of inquiry identified in the notice of deposition for a Rule 30(b)(6) deposition of a party representative.[103]

Objections to Officer or Procedures

All objections to the qualifications of the officer, to the manner of recording, or to any other procedure must be raised at the deposition and noted by the officer or they are waived.[104]

Objections to Exhibits

Exhibits that have been objected to are taken and appended to the transcript subject to a subsequent ruling on the objection.

Procedure after Objections

After an objection to the officer recording the deposition, the manner of taking the deposition, the evidence, the conduct of a party, or any other aspect of the deposition, the deposition should continue subject to such objections.[105] Exceptions to this principle are matters like questions seeking attorney-client information, as discussed under Rule 30(c)(2).

Attendance by Other Witnesses

Other witnesses are not excluded from observing deposition absent a court order under Rule 26(c)(1)(E).[106]

Written Questions

Instead of attending a deposition in person, a party can send written questions to the party taking the deposition, who will then ask the questions to the deponent on the record. This procedure is rarely used.

RULE 30(d)—DURATION; SANCTION; MOTION TO TERMINATE OR LIMIT

CORE CONCEPT

The Rules provide for a 7 hour time limit on depositions, which may be extended by court order. Rule 30(d) also provides protection from unreasonable or vexatious examination during a deposition.

---

[101]*Brincko v. Rio Props., Inc.*, 278 F.R.D. 576, 581 (D.Nev. 2011); *Athridge v. Aetna Cas. and Sur. Co.*, 184 F.R.D. 200, 208 (D.D.C. 1998).

[102]*Redwood v. Dobson*, 476 F.3d 462, 467–68 (7th Cir. 2007); *Brincko v. Rio Props., Inc.*, 278 F.R.D. 576, 581 (D.Nev. 2011).

[103]*Paparelli v. Prudential Ins. Co. of America*, 108 F.R.D. 727, 730–31 (D. Mass. 1985).

[104]*Pioneer Drive, LLC v. Nissan Diesel America, Inc.*, 262 F.R.D. 552,

556 (D.Mont. 2009) (the deposition continues after such depositions).

[105]*Morales v. Zondo, Inc.*, 204 F.R.D. 50 (S.D. N.Y. 2001).

[106]The Advisory Committee Note to the 1993 Amendment to Rule 30; *In re Terra Intern., Inc.*, 134 F.3d 302, 305–06 (5th Cir. 1998) (party moving to exclude other witnesses must show good cause why such witnesses should not attend); *Bell ex rel. Estate of Bell v. Board of Educ. of County of Fayette*, 225 F.R.D. 186, 195 (S.D. W. Va. 2004).

APPLICATIONS

Impact of 2007 "Restyling" Amendments

Rule 30(d) was significantly restructured during the 2007 Federal Civil Rules "Restyling" Project. The provisions of Rule 30(c) were broken into Rules 30(c)(1) and 30(c)(3). The provisions in Rule 30(d)(1) regarding statement of objections and instructions not to answer were moved to Rule 30(c)(2), together with some text from old Rule 30(c). The sanction provisions of Rule 30(d)(3) became Rule 30(d)(2). Finally, the provision of Rule 30(d)(4) became Rule 30(d)(3). In researching current Rule 30(d), practitioners should be mindful of this repositioning.

Duration of Depositions

Rule 30(d)(1) sets a time limit for depositions of 1 day of 7 hours. The time period includes only time spent examining the witness; lunch and other breaks are not counted.[107] The parties can extend or eliminate the time limitation by stipulation,[108] or can file a motion to extend the time limit for specified depositions[109] or for the case in general (discussed below).

Motion to Extend Time

A party may file a motion to extend the 1 day 7 hour limitation.[110] The court must allow additional time if needed for a "fair examination" of the witness or if the examination has been impeded or delayed by another person or by circumstances.[111] Examples of situations in which an extended deposition would be warranted include: witnesses who need interpreters; examinations covering long periods of time or numerous and/or lengthy documents (although the Advisory Committee suggests that a prerequisite might be sending the documents to the witness to review prior to the deposition); instances where documents were requested but not produced prior to the deposition; multi-party cases (if the parties have taken measures to avoid duplicative questioning); depositions in which the lawyer for the witness also wants to ask questions; depositions of expert witnesses; depositions interrupted by power outage, health emergency, or other like event; and depositions in which improper objections or other conduct by other attorneys or the witness has impeded the examination.[112] The court need not order an extended deposition if the extended

---

[107]The Advisory Committee Note to the 2000 Amendment to Rule 30(d).

[108]*Vazquez-Rijos v. Anhang*, 654 F.3d 122, 130 (1st Cir. 2011).

[109]*LaPlante v. Estano*, 226 F.R.D. 439, 439–40 (D. Conn. 2005) (deposition extended because party and attorney were recalcitrant and uncooperative during the deposition).

[110]*See Dunkin' Donuts Incorporated v. Mary's Donuts, Inc.*, 206 F.R.D. 518, 522 (S.D. Fla. 2002).

[111]*George v. City of Buffalo*, __ F.Supp.2d __ (W.D.N.Y. 2011); *Roberson v. Bair*, 242 F.R.D. 130 (D.D.C. 2007).

[112]*Kleppinger v. Texas Dept. of Transp.*, __ F.R.D. __ (S.D.Tex. 2012).

deposition would be cumulative or unreasonably burdensome, as provided by Rule 26(b)(2).[113] The burden will be on the party moving for an extension to show good cause why the extension is warranted.[114]

Designated Representatives

If a corporation or entity designates more than 1 representative in response to a deposition notice under Rule 30(b)(6), the 1 day 7 hour limitation will apply separately to each representative.[115]

Sanctions for Impediment or Delay

Parties or witnesses should not engage in conduct that unreasonably impedes, delays, or otherwise frustrates a deposition.[116] When such conduct occurs, the court may impose the costs of such conduct, including attorney fees, on the party or attorney[117] engaging in the obstructive behavior.[118] Nonparty witnesses are also subject to such sanctions.

Motion to Terminate or Limit Deposition

In order to prevail on a motion to terminate or limit an examination, the moving party must demonstrate that the examination was being conducted in bad faith or in an unreasonably annoying, embarrassing, or oppressive manner.[119] The court can then order the deposition concluded or can limit the time and/or scope of the deposition,[120] and may impose upon the losing party or attorney an appropriate sanction, including the reasonable costs and attorney's fees incurred by any parties as a result.[121]

Which Court for Motion to Terminate

A motion to terminate or limit the deposition under may be filed either in the court where the case is pending or in the district where the deposition is occurring.

Suspension of Deposition

A party desiring to make a motion to terminate or limit the

---

[113]*George v. City of Buffalo*, __ F.Supp.2d __ (W.D.N.Y. 2011).

[114]*Kleppinger v. Texas Dept. of Transp.*, __ F.R.D. __ (S.D.Tex. 2012).

[115]The Advisory Committee Note to the 2000 Amendment to Rule 30(d) (2).

[116]*Baker v. St. Paul Travelers Ins. Co.*, 670 F.3d 119, 123 (1st Cir. 2012).

[117]*GMAC Bank v. HTFC Corp.*, 252 F.R.D. 253 (E.D.Pa. 2008) (attorney sanctioned for sitting idly by while the client engaged in abusive conduct).

[118]*Pioneer Drive, LLC v. Nissan Diesel America, Inc.*, 262 F.R.D. 552,

556 (D.Mont. 2009) (sanctions imposed for improperly halting deposition); *GMAC Bank v. HTFC Corp.*, 248 F.R.D. 182, 194 (E.D. Pa. 2008) (sanctions imposed jointly on the party (for inappropriate conduct) and the attorney (for failing to curb the client's inappropriate conduct)).

[119]*Garland v. Torre*, 259 F.2d 545 (2d Cir. 1958); *Rangel v. Gonzalez Mascorro*, __ F.R.D. __ (S.D.Tex. 2011).

[120]*Brincko v. Rio Props., Inc.*, 278 F.R.D. 576, 581 (D.Nev. 2011); *Withers v. eHarmony, Inc.*, __ F.R.D. __ (C.D.Cal. 2010).

[121]*Rangel v. Gonzalez Mascorro*, __ F.R.D. __ (S.D.Tex. 2011).

deposition may suspend the deposition for the period of time necessary to make the motion.[122]

Expenses of Motion to Terminate

In ruling on a motion to terminate or limit the deposition, the court must consider awarding expenses to the prevailing party, in accordance with Rule 37(a)(3).[123]

Resuming Terminated Deposition

Once a deposition has been terminated by the court upon a Rule 30(d)(3) motion, it cannot be resumed or re-noticed without leave of court.

Parallel to Protective Order

A party may seek the same types of protection for a deposition under Rule 30(d) that are available under a protective order under Rule 26(c).[124] A motion for a protective order under Rule 26(c) provides similar protection before a deposition begins, at which point Rule 30(d) takes over.

RULE 30(e)—REVIEW BY THE WITNESS; CHANGES

CORE CONCEPT

The opportunity to review and correct the transcript is available upon timely request.

APPLICATIONS

Request to Review

To obtain an opportunity to review and correct the transcript, the deponent or a party must make a request prior to the completion of the deposition.[125]

Submission of Changes

If a review is requested, the court reporter will make the deposition transcript available to the witness, typically by sending a copy to the witness to review.[126] The witness must submit a signed statement describing any changes within 30 days of submission by the officer.[127] The statement should state the

---

[122]*McClelland v. Blazin'Wings, Inc.*, 675 F.Supp.2d 1074, 1081 (D.Colo. 2009).

[123]*Brincko v. Rio Props., Inc.*, 278 F.R.D. 576, 581 (D.Nev. 2011); *McClelland v. Blazin'Wings, Inc.*, 675 F.Supp.2d 1074, 1081 (D.Colo. 2009).

[124]*In re CFS-Related Securities Fraud Litigation*, 256 F. Supp. 2d 1227, 1240 (N.D. Okla. 2003) (a deposition transcript may be placed under seal under Rule 30(d)).

[125]*Rock River Commc'ns, Inc. v. Universal Music Grp.*, 276 F.R.D. 633, 635 (C.D.Cal. 2011) (the party taking the deposition cannot force the witness to review the transcript).

[126]*Parkland Venture, LLC v. City of Muskego*, 270 F.R.D. 439, 441 (E.D.Wis. 2010) (court reporter not required to send a copy to the witness, can make the copy available at the reporter's office).

[127]*Delaware Valley Floral Group,*

reasons for the changes[128] and be signed by the witness. The time for submission of changes may be extended by the court upon motion.[129] Any changes that are submitted are attached to the transcript.

Changes in Form

Changes in form, such as typographic errors, are entered into the transcript with an explanation as to the reason for the change.

Changes in Substance

The courts vary as to whether and when they will allow a witness to make changes in the substance of the testimony,[130] which are also entered into the transcript with an explanation as to the reason for the change.[131] With changes in substance, the deposition can be reconvened.[132] A deponent who changes the answers may be impeached with the former answers.[133]

Failure to Submit Changes

A witness who fails to submit any changes or return the signed errata sheet within the time period allowed waives the right to make corrections to the transcript.[134]

Inc. v. Shaw Rose Nets, LLC, 597 F.3d 1374, 1379–81 (Fed.Cir. 2010); *Margo v. Weiss*, 213 F.3d 55 (2d Cir.2000).

[128]*E.E.O.C. v. Skanska USA Bldg., Inc.*, 278 F.R.D. 407, 409–10 (W.D.Tenn. 2012); *E.I. du Pont de Nemours and Co. v. Kolon Inds., Inc.*, 277 F.R.D. 286, 295 (E.D.Va. 2011).

[129]*Statzer v. Town of Lebanaon, VA*, 2001 WL 604160 (W.D. Va. 2001).

[130]*See Norelus v. Denny's, Inc.*, 628 F.3d 1270, 1281 (11th Cir. 2010) ("novella-length errata sheet making a slew of material changes to their client's deposition testimony was improper"); *Carter v. Ford Motor Co.*, 561 F.3d 562, 568 (6th Cir. 2009) (Rule 30(e) authorizes changes "in form or substance"); *Garcia v. Pueblo Country Club*, 299 F.3d 1233 (10th Cir.2002) (a deposition is not a take home examination); *Hambleton Bros. Lumber Co. v. Balkin Enters., Inc.*, 397 F.3d 1217, 1225–26 (9th Cir.2005) (deponent may not make substantive changes offered solely to create a material factual dispute in to evade summary judgment).

[131]*Norelus v. Denny's, Inc.*, 628 F.3d 1270, 1295 (11th Cir. 2010); *Podell v. Citicorp Diners Club, Inc.*, 112 F.3d 98, 103 (2d Cir. 1997).

[132]*See Norelus v. Denny's, Inc.*, 628 F.3d 1270, 1294 (11th Cir. 2010); *Tingley Systems, Inc. v. CSC Consulting, Inc.*, 152 F. Supp. 2d 95, 120 (D. Mass. 2001).

[133]*Thorn v. Sundstrand Aerospace Corp.*, 207 F.3d 383, 388–89 (7th Cir. 2000); *Podell v. Citicorp Diners Club, Inc.*, 112 F.3d 98 (2d Cir.1997) (the changes made do not replace the deponent's original answers; the original information remains part of the record and may be introduced at trial).

[134]*E.I. du Pont de Nemours and Co. v. Kolon Inds., Inc.*, 277 F.R.D. 286, 296 (E.D.Va. 2011); *Dore v. Wormley*, __ F.Supp.2d __ (S.D.N.Y. 2010).

RULE 30(f)—CERTIFICATION AND DELIVERY; EXHIBITS; COPIES OF THE TRANSCRIPT OR RECORDING; FILING

CORE CONCEPT

The officer must certify that the witness was duly sworn and that the deposition transcript was a true record of the testimony given by the deponent.

APPLICATIONS

Impact of 2007 "Restyling" Amendments

Rule 30(f) was significantly restructured during the 2007 Federal Civil Rules "Restyling" Project. Rule 30(f)(1) was broken into Rule 30(f)(1) and Rule 30(f)(2). Rule 30(f)(2) was renumbered Rule 30(f)(3) and Rule 30(f)(3) was renumbered Rule 30(f)(4). In researching current Rule 30(f), practitioners should be mindful of this repositioning.

Certificate

The officer shall prepare a written certificate to accompany the record of the deposition.[135] The certificate should indicate that the witness was sworn, that the deposition is a true and accurate record of the testimony, and whether review of the record was requested.[136]

Uncertified Transcript

A deposition transcript that is not properly certified is inadmissible.[137]

Filing of Transcript

Ordinarily, deposition transcripts should not be filed. However, under Rule 5(d), once a deposition is used in a proceeding, the attorney must file it.

Original Transcript

The stenographer should supply the original transcript to the party noticing the deposition in a sealed envelope, which should be preserved for use at trial.[138]

---

[135]*Orr v. Bank of America, NT & SA*, 285 F.3d 764, 774 (9th Cir. 2002); (an affidavit of counsel is not sufficient to authenticate a deposition transcript); *Giulio v. BV CenterCal, LLC*, 815 F.Supp.2d 1162, 1169 (D.Or. 2011).

[136]*Del Toro-Pacheco v. Pereira-Castillo*, 662 F.Supp.2d 202, 211 (D.Puerto Rico 2009).

[137]*Batiz v. American Commercial Sec. Services*, __ F.Supp.2d __ (C.D.Cal. 2011).

[138]*Barton v. City and County of Denver*, 432 F. Supp. 2d 1178, 1199 n.6 (D. Colo. 2006), aff'd, 2007 WL 3104909 (10th Cir. 2007).

Copies of the Transcript

Any party or the deponent can obtain a copy of the recording of the deposition for a reasonable charge.[139] If the deposition was recorded stenographically and has not been transcribed, then the party seeking the transcript will normally have to pay the transcription costs, unless the court orders otherwise.

Exhibits

Upon the request of a party, a document produced at a deposition (or any other document) may be marked for identification and annexed to the deposition transcript. A copy of a document may be substituted for the original. If documents are produced at a deposition, any party has a right to inspect and copy them.

Retaining Recording

The officer should retain a copy of the transcript or recording of the deposition.

RULE 30(g)—FAILURE TO ATTEND A DEPOSITION OR SERVE SUBPOENA; EXPENSES

CORE CONCEPT

The court may award expenses, including attorney fees, to a party that appears for a deposition that does not occur because either: (1) the party noticing the deposition does not attend;[140] or (2) the party fails to subpoena a witness and that witness does not appear. In both cases, the party noticing the deposition may be ordered to pay the expenses of other parties incurred as a result of appearing for the deposition.

Additional Research References

Wright & Miller, *Federal Practice and Procedure* §§ 2101 to 2120
C.J.S., Federal Civil Procedure §§ 548 to 583 et seq., 600 to 644 et seq.
West's Key Number Digest, Federal Civil Procedure ⊱1311 to 1456

---

[139]*Rivera v. DiSabato*, 962 F. Supp. 38, 39–40 (D.N.J. 1997).

[140]*Albee v. Continental Tire North America, Inc.*, __ F.Supp.2d __ (E.D.Cal. 2011) (awarding fees based on the cancellation of a deposition the night before, when the witness had already prepared and traveled); *Frazier v. Layne Christensen Co.*, 486 F. Supp. 2d 831 (W.D. Wis. 2006), aff'd, 239 Fed. Appx. 604 (Fed. Cir. 2007).

RULE 31
DEPOSITIONS BY WRITTEN QUESTIONS

(a) When a Deposition May Be Taken.

(1) *Without Leave.* A party may, by written questions, depose any person, including a party, without leave of court except as provided in Rule 31(a)(2). The deponent's attendance may be compelled by subpoena under Rule 45.

(2) *With Leave.* A party must obtain leave of court, and the court must grant leave to the extent consistent with Rule 26(b)(2):

   (A) if the parties have not stipulated to the deposition and:

   (i) the deposition would result in more than 10 depositions being taken under this rule or Rule 30 by the plaintiffs, or by the defendants, or by the third-party defendants;

   (ii) the deponent has already been deposed in the case; or

   (iii) the party seeks to take a deposition before the time specified in Rule 26(d); or

   (B) if the deponent is confined in prison.

(3) *Service; Required Notice.* A party who wants to depose a person by written questions must serve them on every other party, with a notice stating, if known, the deponent's name and address. If the name is unknown, the notice must provide a general description sufficient to identify the person or the particular class or group to which the person belongs. The notice must also state the name or descriptive title and the address of the officer before whom the deposition will be taken.

(4) *Questions Directed to an Organization.* A public or private corporation, a partnership, an association, or a governmental agency may be deposed

by written questions in accordance with Rule 30(b)(6).

(5) *Questions from Other Parties.* Any questions to the deponent from other parties must be served on all parties as follows: cross-questions, within 14 days after being served with the notice and direct questions; redirect questions, within 7 days after being served with cross-questions; and recross-questions, within 7 days after being served with redirect questions. The court may, for good cause, extend or shorten these times.

(b) Delivery to the Officer; Officer's Duties. The party who noticed the deposition must deliver to the officer a copy of all the questions served and of the notice. The officer must promptly proceed in the manner provided in Rule 30(c), (e), and (f) to:

(1) take the deponent's testimony in response to the questions;

(2) prepare and certify the deposition; and

(3) send it to the party, attaching a copy of the questions and of the notice.

(c) Notice of Completion or Filing.

(1) *Completion.* The party who noticed the deposition must notify all other parties when it is completed.

(2) *Filing.* A party who files the deposition must promptly notify all other parties of the filing.

[Amended March 30, 1970, effective July 1, 1970; March 2, 1987, effective August 1, 1987; April 22, 1993, effective December 1, 1993; April 30, 2007, effective December 1, 2007.]

AUTHORS' COMMENTARY ON RULE 31

PURPOSE AND SCOPE

Rule 31 contains the procedures for taking depositions through written questions.

RULE 31(a)—WHEN A DEPOSITION MAY BE TAKEN

CORE CONCEPT

Any party may take depositions by serving written questions, which are asked by the deposition officer (stenographer) and answered orally by the witness. Depositions by written question are rarely used, and their only advantage seems to be that they may be less expensive than depositions by oral question.[1]

APPLICATIONS

Notice

A party seeking to take a deposition by written questions must serve a notice on all other parties stating the name and address of the deponent, if known, or a general description sufficient to identify the deponent and providing the name or title and address of the stenographer or officer before whom the deposition will be taken.[2]

Timing of Notice

The notice of written deposition may be served at any time after the parties have conducted the discovery conference under Rule 26(d), or earlier with leave of court. In proceedings listed in Rule 26(a)(1)(B) as exempt from initial disclosures, there is no preliminary waiting period for written depositions. The latest time to conduct a deposition upon written questions will be governed by the court's scheduling order.[3]

Subpoenas

Subpoenas must be used to compel the attendance of non-party witnesses. Party witnesses and representatives of corporations are compelled to attend by virtue of the notice alone.

Service of Direct-Examination

The written deposition questions for direct examination are served upon all parties with the notice.[4]

Cross, Redirect, and Recross

Within 14 days of service of the notice and direct examination questions, any other party may serve cross-examination questions. The noticing party may then serve redirect examina-

---

[1] *See Brown v. Carr*, 236 F.R.D. 311 (S.D. Tex. 2006) ("If plaintiff is unable to afford to take depositions via telephone, then he may take depositions upon written questions.").

[2] *Rahn v. Hawkins*, 464 F.3d 813, 821–22 (8th Cir. 2006).

[3] *See Summerville v. Local 77*, 369 F. Supp. 2d 648, 651 (M.D. N.C. 2005), aff'd, 142 Fed. Appx. 762 (4th Cir. 2005) (written deposition questions are treated like other written discovery, and must be served such that the responses are due before the close of written discovery).

[4] *In re Lenders Mortg. Services, Inc.*, 224 B.R. 707, 710 (Bankr. E.D. Mo. 1997).

tion questions within 7 days, and the other party may serve re-cross examination questions within 7 more days. The court may shorten or lengthen these time periods upon motion and for cause shown. All questions should be served on all parties.

Number of Depositions
The plaintiffs as a group are limited to 10 depositions total, by written and/or oral examination, as are the defendants and the third-party defendants. This number may be increased by stipulation or by leave of court.

Scope of Questions
The scope of the written deposition questions is the same as oral questions, and is controlled by Rule 26.

Persons Subject
Both parties and non-parties are subject to written depositions.[5]

Corporate Representative
A party may require a corporation or organization to designate a representative to respond to the questions, as described in detail under Rule 30(b)(6).

Repeat Depositions
Leave of court is required to depose someone a second time.[6]

Deponent in Prison
If the deponent is in prison, leave of court is required to take a written deposition.[7]

Objections
Objections to the form of a written question (*i.e.,* because it is leading) must be served in writing upon the party propounding the question within the time for serving succeeding questions and within 5 days of the last questions authorized.[8]

RULE 31(b)—DELIVERY TO THE OFFICER; OFFICER'S DUTIES

CORE CONCEPT
Once all the questions have been served, the party initiating the deposition provides all the questions to the deposition officer. The officer then promptly takes the deposition by reading the

---

[5]*New Hampshire Motor Transport Ass'n v. Rowe,* 324 F. Supp. 2d 231, 237 (D. Me. 2004) (written deposition questions, in contrast to interrogatories, can be served on non-parties).

[6]*Rahn v. Hawkins,* 464 F.3d 813,

821–22 (8th Cir. 2006).

[7]*Whitehurst v. U.S.,* 231 F.R.D. 500, 501 (S.D. Tex. 2005).

[8]*See* Rule 32(d)(3)(C); *Whitehurst v. U.S.,* 231 F.R.D. 500, 501 (S.D. Tex. 2005).

questions and recording the answers.[9] A transcript is then prepared and submitted to the witness as provided in Rule 30 governing oral depositions.

RULE 31(c)—NOTICE OF COMPLETION OR FILING

CORE CONCEPT

When the deposition has been completed, the party who noticed the deposition must provide notice to all other parties. Local rules usually determine whether the officer files a sealed transcript with the court. If so, the party noticing the deposition must promptly give notice of the filing of the transcript to all other parties.

Additional Research References

Wright & Miller, *Federal Practice and Procedure* §§ 2131 to 2133
C.J.S., Federal Civil Procedure §§ 591 to 592
West's Key Number Digest, Federal Civil Procedure ⚖1369 to 1370

---

[9]*See Estate of Ungar v. Palestinian Authority*, 451 F. Supp. 2d 607, 612 (S.D. N.Y. 2006).

RULE 32
USING DEPOSITIONS IN COURT PROCEEDINGS

(a) Using Depositions.

(1) *In General.* At a hearing or trial, all or part of a deposition may be used against a party on these conditions:

(A) the party was present or represented at the taking of the deposition or had reasonable notice of it;

(B) it is used to the extent it would be admissible under the Federal Rules of Evidence if the deponent were present and testifying; and

(C) the use is allowed by Rule 32(a)(2) through (8).

(2) *Impeachment and Other Uses.* Any party may use a deposition to contradict or impeach the testimony given by the deponent as a witness, or for any other purpose allowed by the Federal Rules of Evidence.

(3) *Deposition of Party, Agent, or Designee.* An adverse party may use for any purpose the deposition of a party or anyone who, when deposed, was the party's officer, director, managing agent, or designee under Rule 30(b)(6) or 31(a)(4).

(4) *Unavailable Witness.* A party may use for any purpose the deposition of a witness, whether or not a party, if the court finds:

(A) that the witness is dead;

(B) that the witness is more than 100 miles from the place of hearing or trial or is outside the United States, unless it appears that the witness's absence was procured by the party offering the deposition;

(C) that the witness cannot attend or testify because of age, illness, infirmity, or imprisonment;

(D) that the party offering the deposition could

not procure the witness's attendance by subpoena; or

(E) on motion and notice, that exceptional circumstances make it desirable—in the interest of
justice and with due regard to the importance
of live testimony in open court—to permit the
deposition to be used.

(5) *Limitations on Use.*

(A) *Deposition Taken on Short Notice.* A deposition must not be used against a party who,
having received less than 14 days' notice of
the deposition, promptly moved for a protective order under Rule 26(c)(1)(B) requesting
that it not be taken or be taken at a different
time or place—and this motion was still pending when the deposition was taken.

(B) *Unavailable Deponent; Party Could Not Obtain
an Attorney.* A deposition taken without leave
of court under the unavailability provision of
Rule 30(a)(2)(A)(iii) must not be used against
a party who shows that, when served with the
notice, it could not, despite diligent efforts,
obtain an attorney to represent it at the
deposition.

(6) *Using Part of a Deposition.* If a party offers in
evidence only part of a deposition, an adverse
party may require the offeror to introduce other
parts that in fairness should be considered with
the part introduced, and any party may itself
introduce any other parts.

(7) *Substituting a Party.* Substituting a party under
Rule 25 does not affect the right to use a deposition previously taken.

(8) *Deposition Taken in an Earlier Action.* A deposition lawfully taken and, if required, filed in any
federal-or state-court action may be used in a
later action involving the same subject matter
between the same parties, or their representatives or successors in interest, to the same extent
as if taken in the later action. A deposition previously taken may also be used as allowed by the
Federal Rules of Evidence.

(b) Objections to Admissibility. Subject to Rules 28(b) and 32(d)(3), an objection may be made at a hearing or trial to the admission of any deposition testimony that would be inadmissible if the witness were present and testifying.

(c) Form of Presentation. Unless the court orders otherwise, a party must provide a transcript of any deposition testimony the party offers, but may provide the court with the testimony in nontranscript form as well. On any party's request, deposition testimony offered in a jury trial for any purpose other than impeachment must be presented in nontranscript form, if available, unless the court for good cause orders otherwise.

(d) Waiver of Objections.

    (1) *To the Notice.* An objection to an error or irregularity in a deposition notice is waived unless promptly served in writing on the party giving the notice.

    (2) *To the Officer's Qualification.* An objection based on disqualification of the officer before whom a deposition is to be taken is waived if not made:

        (A) before the deposition begins; or

        (B) promptly after the basis for disqualification becomes known or, with reasonable diligence, could have been known.

    (3) *To the Taking of the Deposition.*

        (A) *Objection to Competence, Relevance, or Materiality.* An objection to a deponent's competence—or to the competence, relevance, or materiality of testimony—is not waived by a failure to make the objection before or during the deposition, unless the ground for it might have been corrected at that time.

        (B) *Objection to an Error or Irregularity.* An objection to an error or irregularity at an oral examination is waived if:

            (i) it relates to the manner of taking the deposition, the form of a question or answer, the oath or affirmation, a party's conduct, or other matters that might have been corrected at that time; and

    (ii)   it is not timely made during the deposition.

  (C) *Objection to a Written Question.* An objection to the form of a written question under Rule 31 is waived if not served in writing on the party submitting the question within the time for serving responsive questions or, if the question is a recross-question, within 7 days after being served with it.

 (4) *To Completing and Returning the Deposition.* An objection to how the officer transcribed the testimony—or prepared, signed, certified, sealed, endorsed, sent, or otherwise dealt with the deposition—is waived unless a motion to suppress is made promptly after the error or irregularity becomes known or, with reasonable diligence, could have been known.

[Amended March 30, 1970, effective July 1, 1970; November 20, 1972, effective July 1, 1975; April 29, 1980, effective August 1, 1980; March 2, 1987, effective August 1, 1987; April 22, 1993, effective December 1, 1993; April 30, 2007, effective December 1, 2007; March 26, 2009, effective December 1, 2009.]

AUTHORS' COMMENTARY ON RULE 32

PURPOSE AND SCOPE

Rule 32 specifies the circumstances in which a deposition is admissible at trial. Any analysis, however, must always include reference to the applicable rules of evidence.

RULE 32(a)—USING DEPOSITIONS

CORE CONCEPT

A deposition may be used at trial or hearing against any party who was present or represented at, or had reasonable notice of,[1] the deposition if admissible under the Federal Rules of Evidence and: it is used to impeach a witness or for any other purpose permitted by the Federal Rules of Evidence; the deposition was of an adverse party; or the witness is unavailable as defined by Rule 32(a)(4). If one party offers part of a deposition, other parties may introduce other parts.

---

[1]*Jackson v. United Artists Theatre Circuit, Inc.*, 278 F.R.D. 586, 596 (D.Nev. 2011) (deposition inadmissible where defendant was not notified).

APPLICATIONS

2009 "Time Computation" Amendments

To make the computation of federal time periods more consistent, more simple, and more clear, the 2009 amendments standardized most time periods into multiples of 7-days and enlarged very short time periods. The time period set in Rule 32(a)(5)(A) governing the use of depositions taken on short notice, formerly 11 days long, has now been enlarged to 14 days.

Impact of 2007 "Restyling" Amendments

Rule 32(a) was significantly restructured during the 2007 Federal Civil Rules "Restyling" Project. The 2007 amendments changed Rule 32(a) from 4 subsections to 8 subsections. In researching current Rule 32(a), practitioners should be mindful of this repositioning.

Impeachment

Rule 32(a)(2) allows the use of a deposition to impeach or contradict a witness. A party may use a deposition to impeach the party's own witness, if permitted by the applicable rules of evidence. The Federal Rules of Evidence allow the use of a prior inconsistent statement made at the deposition as substantive evidence (as opposed to for impeachment purposes only).[2]

Deposition of Adverse Party

Rule 32(a)(3) allows the deposition of an adverse party to be used for any purpose (*i.e.*, as substantive evidence or for impeachment).[3] Rule 32(a)(3) applies to the deposition of an officer, director, or managing agent of a party organization,[4] and to a representative of a party designated pursuant to a Rule 30(b)(6) deposition notice.[5]

Unavailable Non-party Witness

Under Rule 32(a)(4), the deposition of a witness may be used as substantive, non-impeachment evidence only under certain circumstances (but see Rules 801(d) and 801(d)(2) of the Federal Rules of Evidence relating to hearsay). The general requirement is that the witness be unavailable at the time of

---

[2]Fed.R.Evid. 801(d); *Fiber Systems Intern., Inc. v. Roehrs*, 470 F.3d 1150, 1160 (5th Cir. 2006).

[3]*Creative Consumer Concepts, Inc. v. Kreisler*, 563 F.3d 1070, 1080 (10th Cir. 2009) (no need to show that the witness is unavailable when introducing the testimony of a party opponent); *State Farm Mut. Auto. Ins. Co. v. Lincow*, 715 F.Supp.2d 617, 642 (E.D.Pa. 2010).

[4]*Shanklin v. Norfolk Southern Ry. Co.*, 369 F.3d 978 (6th Cir.2004); *Palmer Coal & Rock Company v. Gulf Oil Company*, 524 F.2d 884 (10th Cir. 1975).

[5]*SanDisk Corp. v. Kingston Tech. Co., Inc.*, __ F.Supp.2d __ (W.D.Wis. 2012); *Simms v. Center for Correctional Health and Policy Studies*, 272 F.R.D. 36, 41 (D.D.C. 2011).

trial.[6] More specifically, the party seeking to introduce the testimony must establish the existence of one of the following five conditions in Rule 32(a)(4):

(A) The witness is dead.[7] However, if the witness dies during the taking of the deposition, so that one party does not have a full opportunity to examine the witness, then the Court has discretion as to whether to admit the testimony;

(B) The witness is more than 100 miles from the courthouse (measured "as the crow flies")[8] or outside the United States, unless it appears that the party offering the testimony procured the absence of the witness;[9]

(C) The deponent is unable to attend trial because of age,[10] sickness,[11] infirmity, or imprisonment;[12]

(D) The party offering the deposition was unable to procure the deponent's attendance at trial by subpoena;[13] or

(E) Exceptional other circumstances.[14] In order to take advantage of the catchall in Rule 32(a)(4)(E), a party

---

[6]*Niver v. Travelers Indem. Co. of IL*, 430 F. Supp. 2d 852, 866 (N.D. Iowa 2006) (availability is evaluated at the time of the testimony).

[7]*See Dellwood Farms, Inc. v. Cargill, Inc.*, 128 F.3d 1122, 1128 (7th Cir. 1997).

[8]*Chrysler Intern. Corp. v. Chemaly*, 280 F.3d 1358, 1359 (11th Cir. 2002); *Ueland v. U.S.*, 291 F.3d 993, 996 (7th Cir. 2002); *Chao v. Tyson Foods, Inc.*, 255 F.R.D. 560, 562 (N.D.Ala. 2009) (witness who appears at trial will not be considered unavailable, regardless of how far away the witness lives); *Niver v. Travelers Indem. Co. of IL*, 430 F. Supp. 2d 852 (N.D. Iowa 2006) (distance should be measured at the time the deposition is offered).

[9]*Garcia-Martinez v. City and County of Denver*, 392 F.3d 1187, 1191–92 (10th Cir. 2004); *F.T.C. v. Asia Pacific Telecom, Inc.*, __ F.Supp.2d __ (N.D.Ill. 2011); *Culebra II, LLC v. River Cruises and Anticipation Yachts, LLC*, 564 F.Supp.2d 70, 79 (D.Me. 2008) (party seeking to admit its own testimony has the burden of proving it did not procure its unavailability).

[10]*U.S. v. Firishchak*, 468 F.3d 1015, 1023 (7th Cir. 2006).

[11]*Smith v. Pfizer Inc.*, __ F.R.D. __ (M.D.Tenn. 2010); *Pages-Ramirez v. Hospital Espanol Auxilio Mutuo de Puerto Rico, Inc.*, 553 F.Supp.2d 108 (D.Puerto Rico 2008) (declining to admit deposition based on insufficient evidence of illness).

[12]*Delgado v. Pawtucket Police Dept.*, 668 F.3d 42, 46 (1st Cir. 2012) (it is not enough to show the witness is in prison, the party must show that the witness is unavailable because of imprisonment).

[13]*Thomas v. Cook County Sheriff's Dept.*, __ F.3d __ (7th Cir. 2010) (knowledge of the witness's location is not dispositive if the party has exercised reasonable efforts to obtain the witness's attendance); *Griman v. Makousky*, 76 F.3d 151, 154 (7th Cir. 1996) (counsel must have used reasonable diligence to secure witness' attendance).

[14]*See Battle ex rel. Battle v. Memorial Hosp. at Gulfport*, 228 F.3d 544, 554 (5th Cir. 2000) (videotaped deposition of physician allowed); *Whyte v. U.S. Postal Serv.*, 280 F.R.D. 700, 701 (S.D.Fla. 2012) (denying request to allow admission of treating physician's deposition testimony); *Luster v. Ledbetter*, 665 F.Supp.2d 893, 896 (M.D.Ala. 2009) (counsel's inability to locate the plaintiff does not constitute exceptional other circumstances).

must give notice to the other party of its intent.[15] Note, however, that the general policy favoring live testimony leads to a restrictive reading of this "catch-all" clause.[16]

The admissibility analysis for an unavailable non-party witness becomes even more complex when the witness was a designated representative under Rule 30(b)(6).[17]

Otherwise Admissible Under the FRE

Rule 32(a)(1) authorizes the admission of deposition testimony that does not meet any of the three specific criteria in Rules 32(a)(1), (2), or (3), but is otherwise admissible under the Federal Rules of Evidence.[18]

Must Comply with Rules of Evidence

Once the criteria in Rule 32 for use of a deposition have been satisfied, the deposition must still be admissible under the rules of evidence.[19] The rules of evidence are applied as though the deponent were present and testifying.[20] Thus, the effect of Rule 32 is to negate the hearsay objection.[21] Furthermore, as with any evidence, the admission of deposition testimony is subject to the Court's discretion.[22]

Use of Part of a Deposition

If a party introduces only part of a deposition, any adverse party may require the offering party to introduce additional parts necessary to clarify the offered text.[23] Such adverse parties have the right to have the additional text introduced immediately following the admission of the offered testimony.[24] The admission of the additional parts is still subject to eviden-

---

[15]*In re Hayes Lemmerz Intern., Inc.*, 340 B.R. 461, 468 (Bankr. D. Del. 2006).

[16]*Griman v. Makousky*, 76 F.3d 151, 153 (7th Cir. 1996); *Whyte v. U.S. Postal Serv.*, 280 F.R.D. 700, 701 (S.D.Fla. 2012) (denying request to allow admission of treating physician's deposition testimony).

[17]*See Sara Lee Corp. v. Kraft Foods Inc.*, 276 F.R.D. 500, 503–04 (N.D.Ill. 2011).

[18]*Creative Consumer Concepts, Inc. v. Kreisler*, 563 F.3d 1070, 1080 (10th Cir. 2009) (statement of a party opponent admissible under the FRE); *Fiber Systems Intern., Inc. v. Roehrs*, 470 F.3d 1150, 1160 (5th Cir. 2006) (transcript admissible under FRE 801(d)(1)(A)).

[19]*Reeg v. Shaughnessy*, 570 F.2d 309 (10th Cir.1978).

[20]*Sara Lee Corp. v. Kraft Foods Inc.*, 276 F.R.D. 500, 502–03 (N.D.Ill. 2011); *S.E.C. v. Franklin*, 348 F. Supp. 2d 1159, 1162 (S.D. Cal. 2004).

[21]*Ueland v. U.S.*, 291 F.3d 993 (7th Cir. 2002); *Vandenbraak v. Alfieri*, 2005 WL 1242158 (D. Del. 2005).

[22]*Coletti v. Cudd Pressure Control*, 165 F.3d 767, 773 (10th Cir. 1999) (upholding trial court's refusal to admit deposition testimony as substantive evidence).

[23]*Lentomyynti Oy v. Medivac, Inc.*, 997 F.2d 364 (7th Cir.1993); *Hupp v. City of Walnut Creek*, 389 F. Supp. 2d 1229, 1231 n.2 (N.D. Cal. 2005).

[24]*Westinghouse Elec. Corp. v. Wray Equipment Corp.*, 286 F.2d 491, 494 (1st Cir. 1961); *Trepel v. Roadway Exp., Inc.*, 194 F.3d 708, 710 (6th Cir. 1999).

tiary objections.[25]

Deposition Taken in Another Matter

A deposition from another matter may be used if the witness is unavailable and if the party against whom the testimony is offered (or the party's predecessor in interest) had an opportunity and similar motive to examine the witness at the deposition.[26]

Documents Attached to Transcript

A document attached to a deposition transcript may be used under the same circumstances as the transcript itself.[27]

Who May Use

Deposition transcripts may be used by any party, regardless of who noticed the deposition.[28]

Use of One's Own Deposition

Parties may notice their own deposition for use at trial if they know they will be "unavailable" under the provisions of Rule 32(a)(4).[29] The court will evaluate whether the party truly was "unavailable."[30]

Against Whom/Reasonable Notice

The deposition may be used against any party who was present or represented at, or had reasonable notice of, the deposition.[31] A deposition cannot be used against a party who demonstrates that it was unable to obtain counsel to represent it at the deposition despite the exercise of diligence. Likewise, the deposition cannot be used against a party who received less than 14 days notice and who has filed a motion for a protective order that was pending at the time of the deposition.[32]

---

[25]*See Heary Bros. Lightning Protection Co., Inc. v. Lightning Protection Institute*, 287 F. Supp. 2d 1038, 1065 n.10 (D. Ariz. 2003), aff'd in part, rev'd in part, 262 Fed. Appx. 815 (9th Cir. 2008).

[26]*See* Fed.R.Evid. 804(b)(1); *Nippon Credit Bank, Ltd. v. Matthews*, 291 F.3d 738 (11th Cir.2002); *Arrowood Indem. Co. v. Hartford Fire Ins. Co.*, __ F.Supp.2d __ (D.Del. 2011).

[27]*Gore v. Maritime Overseas Corp.*, 256 F. Supp. 104, 119 (E.D. Pa. 1966), aff'd in part, rev'd in part, 378 F.2d 584 (3d Cir. 1967).

[28]*Savoie v. Lafourche Boat Rentals, Inc.*, 627 F.2d 722 (5th Cir. 1980).

[29]*Richmond v. Brooks*, 227 F.2d 490 (2d Cir.1955).

[30]*Vevelstad v. Flynn*, 16 Alaska 83, 230 F.2d 695 (9th Cir. 1956).

[31]*Creative Consumer Concepts, Inc. v. Kreisler*, 563 F.3d 1070, 1080 (10th Cir. 2009); *S.E.C. v. Phan*, 500 F.3d 895, 913 (9th Cir. 2007).

[32]*U.S. S.E.C. v. Talbot*, 430 F. Supp. 2d 1029 (C.D. Cal. 2006), rev'd on other grounds, 530 F.3d 1085 (9th Cir. 2008) (amended notice does not trigger the 11 day provision where the original notice put the party on notice of the date of the deposition).

Discovery Depositions

Rule 32 does not draw any distinctions between depositions taken for discovery purposes and those taken "for use at trial."[33]

Substitution of Parties

Substitution of parties pursuant to Rule 25 (such as upon the death of a party) does not affect the use of a deposition transcript unless the substitution significantly alters the nature of the claim.

Motion for Summary Judgment

Deposition transcripts may be used in support of or in opposition to motions for summary judgment.[34] The use of depositions in connection with summary judgment is governed by Rule 56(c).

RULE 32(b)—OBJECTIONS TO ADMISSIBILITY

CORE CONCEPT

Objections to the admissibility of a deposition under Rule 32 must be made at the time the testimony is offered at trial or the objections are waived.

APPLICATIONS

Rules of Evidence

A deposition admissible under Rule 32 must also be admissible under the rules of evidence.[35] Evidentiary rulings are made as though the deponent were present and testifying.

Compare to Objections at Deposition

Objections that can be cured by rephrasing the question, such as leading questions, must be raised at the deposition or they are waived. These objections are covered by Rule 32(d)(3). All other objections, such as relevance,[36] capacity, etc., are reserved until the testimony is offered at trial.[37]

Non-jury Trial

In a non-jury trial, the court can admit a deposition transcript subject to future rulings on objections.

---

[33]*Manley v. AmBase Corp.*, 337 F.3d 237, 247 (2d Cir. 2003); *Niver v. Travelers Indem. Co. of IL*, 430 F. Supp. 2d 852 (N.D. Iowa 2006).

[34]*Carmen v. San Francisco Unified School Dist.*, 237 F.3d 1026, 1028 (9th Cir. 2001); *Beiswenger Enterprises Corp. v. Carletta*, 46 F. Supp. 2d 1297 (M.D. Fla. 1999) (allowing the use of a deposition from another action to support a motion for summary judgment); *In re KZK Livestock, Inc.*, 221 B.R. 471, 475 (Bankr. C.D. Ill. 1998) (allowing the use of a deposition transcript that did not meet the requirements for use at trial, but did meet the requirements for an affidavit).

[35]*Marshall v. Planz*, 145 F. Supp. 2d 1258 (M.D. Ala. 2001).

[36]*In re Stratosphere Corp. Securities Litigation*, 182 F.R.D. 614, 618 (D. Nev. 1998).

[37]*Cronkrite v. Fahrbach*, 853 F. Supp. 257 (W.D. Mich. 1994).

RULE 32(c)—FORM OF PRESENTATION

CORE CONCEPT

Deposition testimony may be offered in stenographic or nonstenographic form. In jury trials, any party may require that the non-stenographic form be used if available.

APPLICATIONS

Nonstenographic Forms

A party expecting to use a nonstenographic form of deposition at trial must provide other parties with a transcript in advance of trial under Rule 26(a)(3)(A)(ii). When nonstenographic forms of testimony are offered, the offering party shall also provide the court a transcript.[38] Rule 32 does not authorize the submission of deposition summaries in lieu of the transcript.[39]

Jury Trials

In a jury trial, any party may require that depositions be offered in nonstenographic form if available unless the deposition is being used for impeachment or unless the court orders otherwise for good cause shown.

RULE 32(d)—WAIVER OF OBJECTIONS

CORE CONCEPT

Objections to the procedures at a deposition must be asserted as soon as practicable or they are waived.

APPLICATIONS

Defects in Notice

Objections to the notice must be made in writing to the party issuing the notice,[40] unless there was no opportunity to object.[41]

Disqualification of Officer

Objections to the qualifications of the officer (*e.g.,* stenographer), which are set forth in Rule 28, must be made before the start of the deposition or they are waived.

---

[38]*Tilton v. Capital Cities/ABC, Inc.*, 115 F.3d 1471, 1479 (10th Cir. 1997) (a party intending to use a videotape deposition must provide a transcript).

[39]*Planned Parenthood of Columbia/Willamette, Inc. v. American Coalition of Life Activists*, 290 F.3d 1058, 1117 (9th Cir. 2002).

[40]*State Farm Mut. Auto. Ins. Co. v. Dowdy ex rel. Dowdy*, 445 F. Supp. 2d 1289, 1293 (N.D. Okla. 2006).

[41]*Oates v. S. J. Groves & Sons Co.*, 248 F.2d 388 (6th Cir. 1957).

Objections to Testimony

Objections that can be cured by rephrasing the question, such as leading questions, must be raised at the deposition.[42] These objections are covered by Rule 32(d)(3). All other objections, such as relevance,[43] capacity, etc., are reserved until the testimony is offered at trial.[44]

Objections as to Oath

Objections as to the manner of the oath or affirmation administered must be made at the time of the deposition or they are waived.[45]

Objections to Written Deposition Questions

Objections to the form of a written question (*e.g.,* because it is leading) must be served in writing upon the party propounding the question within the time for serving succeeding questions and within 7 days of the last questions authorized.

Objections as to Manner of Transcription

Objections as to the manner of transcription or as to the procedures used in correcting and signing the transcript must be made in the form of a motion to suppress, which must be made with "reasonable promptness" after the defect is discovered or should have been discovered with due diligence.[46]

Additional Research References

Wright & Miller, *Federal Practice and Procedure* §§ 2142 to 2157
C.J.S., Federal Civil Procedure §§ 544 to 568, 633 to 638 et seq.
West's Key Number Digest, Federal Civil Procedure ⚷1297, 1298, 1334, 1432 to 1440

---

[42]*Whitehurst v. U.S.*, 231 F.R.D. 500, 501 (S.D. Tex. 2005) (a party who has not objected to a leading question at the deposition may not subsequently object to it when the deposition is introduced at trial); *Daubach v. Wnek*, 2001 WL 290181 (N.D. Ill. 2001); *Boyd v. University of Maryland Medical System*, 173 F.R.D. 143, 147 (D. Md. 1997) (containing a list of the ten most common objections to the form of the question).

[43]*Rangel v. Gonzalez Mascorro*, ___ F.R.D. ___ (S.D.Tex. 2011);

Quantachrome Corp. v. Micromeritics Instrument Corp., 189 F.R.D. 697, 700 (S.D. Fla. 1999).

[44]*State Farm Mut. Auto. Ins. Co. v. Dowdy ex rel. Dowdy*, 445 F. Supp. 2d 1289, 1293 (N.D. Okla. 2006) (such objections should not be made at the deposition).

[45]*Cabello v. Fernandez-Larios*, 402 F.3d 1148, 1160 (11th Cir. 2005).

[46]*Trade Development Bank v. Continental Ins. Co.*, 469 F.2d 35 (2d Cir.1972).

RULE 33
INTERROGATORIES TO PARTIES

(a) In General.

(1) *Number.* Unless otherwise stipulated or ordered by the court, a party may serve on any other party no more than 25 written interrogatories, including all discrete subparts. Leave to serve additional interrogatories may be granted to the extent consistent with Rule 26(b)(2).

(2) *Scope.* An interrogatory may relate to any matter that may be inquired into under Rule 26(b). An interrogatory is not objectionable merely because it asks for an opinion or contention that relates to fact or the application of law to fact, but the court may order that the interrogatory need not be answered until designated discovery is complete, or until a pretrial conference or some other time.

(b) Answers and Objections.

(1) *Responding Party.* The interrogatories must be answered:

(A) by the party to whom they are directed; or

(B) if that party is a public or private corporation, a partnership, an association, or a governmental agency, by any officer or agent, who must furnish the information available to the party.

(2) *Time to Respond.* The responding party must serve its answers and any objections within 30 days after being served with the interrogatories. A shorter or longer time may be stipulated to under Rule 29 or be ordered by the court.

(3) *Answering Each Interrogatory.* Each interrogatory must, to the extent it is not objected to, be answered separately and fully in writing under oath.

(4) *Objections.* The grounds for objecting to an interrogatory must be stated with specificity. Any ground not stated in a timely objection is waived

unless the court, for good cause, excuses the failure.

(5) *Signature.* The person who makes the answers must sign them, and the attorney who objects must sign any objections.

(c) Use. An answer to an interrogatory may be used to the extent allowed by the Federal Rules of Evidence.

(d) Option to Produce Business Records. If the answer to an interrogatory may be determined by examining, auditing, compiling, abstracting, or summarizing a party's business records (including electronically stored information), and if the burden of deriving or ascertaining the answer will be substantially the same for either party, the responding party may answer by:

(1) specifying the records that must be reviewed, in sufficient detail to enable the interrogating party to locate and identify them as readily as the responding party could; and

(2) giving the interrogating party a reasonable opportunity to examine and audit the records and to make copies, compilations, abstracts, or summaries.

[Amended December 27, 1946, effective March 19, 1948; March 30, 1970, effective July 1, 1970; April 29, 1980, effective August 1, 1980; April 22, 1993, effective December 1, 1993; April 12, 2006, effective December 1, 2006; April 30, 2007, effective December 1, 2007.]

AUTHORS' COMMENTARY ON RULE 33

PURPOSE AND SCOPE

Rule 33 sets forth the procedures for using interrogatories. It must be read in conjunction with Rule 26, which establishes the scope of all the discovery rules.

NOTE: Rule 33 was substantially revised in 1970, 1993, 2006, and 2007, and great care should be exercised when citing decisions pertaining to Rule 33.

RULE 33(a)—IN GENERAL

CORE CONCEPT

Any party may serve up to 25 interrogatories or questions on any other party. The scope of interrogatories is the broad discovery available under Rule 26.

APPLICATIONS

Impact of 2007 "Restyling" Amendments

Rule 33(a) was significantly restructured during the 2007 Federal Civil Rules "Restyling" Project. The 2007 amendments moved the "scope" provisions of Rule 33(c) to Rule 33(a)(2), and the provisions regarding responses by organizations from Rule 33(a) to Rule 33(b)(1)(B). In researching current Rule 33(a), practitioners should be mindful of this repositioning.

Who May Serve

Any party may serve interrogatories.

Who May Be Served

Interrogatories are limited to parties to the action,[1] although the party need not be an adverse party. The interrogatories must be addressed to the party. Thus, if the party is a corporation, interrogatories should be addressed to the corporation, not to a corporate officer or the attorney.[2] In a class action, the courts are split as to whether only the named representatives can be served.[3]

Time for Service

Interrogatories can be served after the parties have conducted the discovery conference under Rule 26(f),[4] or earlier with leave of court. In proceedings listed in Rule 26(a)(1)(B) as exempt from initial disclosures, there is no preliminary waiting period for interrogatories. The Rules do not set an outer limit on how late in the case interrogatories may be served, but many local rules or case management orders will set such a limit. Usually, when such a limit exists, interrogatories must be served so that the answers are due before the close of

---

[1]*U.S. v. Lot 41, Berryhill Farm Estates*, 128 F.3d 1386, 1397 (10th Cir. 1997); *New Hampshire Motor Transport Ass'n v. Rowe*, 324 F. Supp. 2d 231, 237 (D. Me. 2004) (but one may take the deposition by written examination of a non-party); *Alcon Laboratories, Inc. v. Pharmacia Corp.*, 225 F. Supp. 2d 340, 344 (S.D. N.Y. 2002).

[2]*Holland v. Minneapolis-Honeywell Regulator Co.*, 28 F.R.D.

595 (D. D.C. 1961).

[3]*Brennan v. Midwestern United Life Ins. Co.*, 450 F.2d 999 (7th Cir. 1971) (unnamed members of class required to respond); *Wainwright v. Kraftco Corp.*, 54 F.R.D. 532 (N.D. Ga. 1972) (unnamed members of class not required to respond).

[4]*Krause v. Buffalo and Erie County Workforce Development Consortium, Inc.*, 425 F. Supp. 2d 352 (W.D. N.Y. 2006).

discovery.[5]

Number

Each party may serve up to 25 interrogatories,[6] including subparts,[7] on each other party.[8] Additional interrogatories may be served pursuant to a court order or stipulation.[9]

Scope of Questions

The scope of interrogatories, and all other discovery forms, is controlled by Rule 26(b).[10] The information sought must be relevant to the issues in the case, but need not be admissible evidence. Privileged information is not discoverable, and discovery is limited with respect to expert witnesses and trial preparation materials.

Opinions or Contentions

Rule 33(a)(2) explicitly states that an interrogatory is not objectionable because it seeks an opinion or contention that relates to fact or the application of law to fact.[11] However, the court may order that a contention interrogatory not be answered until discovery is complete or until after the pre-trial conference is held.[12] Rule 33(a)(2) does not authorize a question that asks for a pure legal conclusion, without application to the

---

[5]*Thomas v. Pacificorp*, 324 F.3d 1176 (10th Cir. 2003); *Gofron v. Picsel Techs., Inc.*, 804 F.Supp.2d 1030, 1040 (N.D.Cal. 2011).

[6]*Allahverdi v. Regents of University of New Mexico*, 228 F.R.D. 696 (D.N.M. 2005) (answering some of the interrogatories is a waiver to the objection to the number of interrogatories); *Walker v. Lakewood Condominium Owners Ass'n*, 186 F.R.D. 584, 586–89 (C.D. Cal. 1999) (interrogatories count toward the limit of 25 even though the respondent objects instead of answering, and such interrogatories may not be withdrawn to allow for additional interrogatories).

[7]*Allen v. Mill-Tel, Inc.*, __ F.R.D. __ (D.Kan. 2012) (subparts counted as separate interrogatories if they pertain to discrete areas); *Pouncil v. Branch Law Firm*, 277 F.R.D. 642, 646 (D.Kan. 2011).

[8]The Advisory Committee Note to the 1993 Amendment to Rule 33; *Chudasama v. Mazda Motor Corp.*, 123 F.3d 1353, 1357 (11th Cir. 1997); *Nagele v. Electronic Data Systems Corp.*, 193 F.R.D. 94 (W.D. N.Y. 2000) (allowing more than 25 interrogatories where the recipient failed to object).

[9]*Weaver v. Mateer and Harbert, P.A.*, 277 F.R.D. 655, 659 (M.D.Fla. 2011) (answer should respond fully to the interrogatory, not just refer to a document); *Clean Earth Remediation and Const. Services, Inc. v. American Intern. Group, Inc.*, 245 F.R.D. 137, 138 n. 1 (S.D. N.Y. 2007) (stipulation not enforceable because not in writing or in open court).

[10]*Lynn v. Monarch Recovery Mgmt., Inc.*, __ F.Supp.2d __ (D.Md. 2012); *Gingerich v. City of Elkhart Probation Dept.*, __ F.R.D. __ (N.D.Ind. 2011).

[11]*In re Rail Freight Fuel Surcharge Antitrust Litig.*, 281 F.R.D. 1, 4 (D.D.C. 2011) (work product doctrine is not a valid objection to contention interrogatory); *Pouncil v. Branch Law Firm*, 277 F.R.D. 642, 650 (D.Kan. 2011).

[12]*See Huthnance v. District of Columbia*, 255 F.R.D. 297, 298, n.2 (D.D.C. 2008) (court expressly authorized to defer responses to contention interrogatories until much or all discovery has been completed); *Kartman v. State Farm Mut. Auto. Ins. Co.*, 247 F.R.D. 561, 566 (S.D. Ind. 2007) (the question is not whether the respon-

facts.[13]

Form

Parties have a great deal of latitude in framing interrogatories, as long as the responding party can reasonably determine the information to include in the answer. Only rarely will a question be so ambiguous that it does not require an answer, although the responding party can limit the scope of its answer.

Proceedings Where Interrogatories Available

Rule 33 applies to all civil actions in district court, including post-judgment proceedings (*i.e.*, interrogatories in aid-of-execution). Rule 33 does not apply to habeas proceedings.[14]

RULE 33(b)—ANSWERS AND OBJECTIONS

CORE CONCEPT

The responding party must answer interrogatories separately and in writing within 30 days after service. Objections must be stated with specificity, and objections are waived if not made timely. The responding party must sign the answers and the attorney must sign any objections.

APPLICATIONS

Impact of 2007 "Restyling" Amendments

Rule 33(b) was significantly restructured during the 2007 Federal Civil Rules "Restyling" Project. The 2007 amendments moved the provisions regarding responses by organizations from Rule 33(a) to Rule 33(b)(1)(B). The subsections of Rule 33(b) were also reorganized and renumbered. In researching current Rule 33(b), practitioners should be mindful of this repositioning.

Answers

Each interrogatory must be answered separately and fully[15] in writing,[16] unless an objection is interposed in lieu of an answer.[17] The answer must include all information within the

---

dent will answer the contention interrogatories, but when).

[13]*Gingerich v. City of Elkhart Probation Dept.*, __ F.R.D. __ (N.D.Ind. 2011); *U.S. v. Boyce*, 148 F. Supp. 2d 1069 (S.D. Cal. 2001), aff'd, 36 Fed. Appx. 612 (9th Cir. 2002).

[14]*Harris v. Nelson*, 394 U.S. 286, 293–94, 89 S. Ct. 1082, 1087, 22 L. Ed. 2d 281 (1969); *Sloan v. Pugh*, 351 F.3d 1319, 1322 (10th Cir. 2003).

[15]*See DCFS USA, LLC v. Dist. of Columbia*, 803 F.Supp.2d 29, 35 (D.D.C. 2011); *Covad Communications*

Co. v. Revonet, Inc., 258 F.R.D. 17 (D.D.C. 2009) (the answer must be true, explicit, responsive, complete, and candid).

[16]*Vazquez-Fernandez v. Cambridge College, Inc.*, 269 F.R.D. 150, 154 (D.Puerto Rico 2010); *Wsol v. Fiduciary Management Associates, Inc.*, 2000 WL 748143 (N.D. Ill. 2000) (oral answers are not permitted).

[17]*Vazquez-Fernandez v. Cambridge College, Inc.*, 269 F.R.D. 150, 154 (D.Puerto Rico 2010).

party's control or known by the party's agents.[18] This includes *facts* in an attorney's possession and information supplied to the party by others.[19] At the same time, a party does not have to obtain publically available information not in its possession, custody, or control.[20] If no such information is available, the answer may so state.[21] If only some information is available, that information must be provided, and may be prefaced with a statement placing the answer in context. Generally, incorporating the pleadings or other discovery will not be sufficient, although the answer to one interrogatory may incorporate information provided in another.[22]

Time to Answer

Answers and objections are due within 30 days of service.[23] Failure to serve a response in a timely manner (i.e. within 30 days of service) may constitute a waiver of all objections.[24] The time to answer may be extended by order of court or written agreement under Rule 29.[25]

Who Answers

The party must answer the interrogatories, not the party's attorney (although it is common practice for the attorney to draft the answers).[26] The attorney interposes the objections. If the party is a corporation or organization, an officer or agent will answer for the corporation.[27] In this case, the attorney may answer the interrogatories as agent for the corporation.[28] The answering officer or agent need not have first-hand knowledge

---

[18]*Costa v. Kerzner Intern. Resorts, Inc.*, 277 F.R.D. 468, 472–73 (S.D.Fla. 2011) (information held by affiliated corporation within the control of a party); *American Intern. Specialty Lines Ins. Co. v. NWI-I, Inc.*, 240 F.R.D. 401, 413 (N.D. Ill. 2007) (information held by former officers is not in the party's custody or control, and need not be gathered and produced).

[19]*Hickman v. Taylor*, 329 U.S. 495, 504, 67 S. Ct. 385, 390, 91 L. Ed. 451 (1947). *see also Gingerich v. City of Elkhart Probation Dept.*, __ F.R.D. __ (N.D.Ind. 2011)

[20]*Huthnance v. District of Columbia*, 255 F.R.D. 285, 292 (D.D.C. 2008).

[21]*Hansel v. Shell Oil Corp.*, 169 F.R.D. 303, 305 (E.D. Pa. 1996) (answer should set forth the efforts used to attempt to obtain the requested information).

[22]*Vazquez-Fernandez v. Cambridge College, Inc.*, 269 F.R.D. 150, 156 (D.Puerto Rico 2010).

[23]*See Verkuilen v. South Shore*

Bldg. and Mortg. Co., 122 F.3d 410, 411 (7th Cir. 1997); *Franco v. Bank of America Corp.*, __ F.Supp.2d __ (M.D.Fla. 2010).

[24]*See Mulero-Abreu v. Puerto Rico Police Dept.*, 675 F.3d 88, 90 (1st Cir. 2012); *McKissick v. Three Deer Ass'n Ltd. Partnership*, 265 F.R.D. 55, 57 (D.Conn. 2010) (delay of one month not sufficient to warrant waiver of objections).

[25]*See Underdog Trucking, L.L.C. v. Verizon Services Corp.*, __ F.R.D. __ (S.D.N.Y. 2011); *Huthnance v. District of Columbia*, 255 F.R.D. 297, 298 (D.D.C. 2008); *Walls v. Paulson*, 250 F.R.D. 48 (D.D.C. 2008).

[26]*Huthnance v. District of Columbia*, 255 F.R.D. 297, 300 (D.D.C. 2008).

[27]*General Dynamics Corp. v. Selb Mfg. Co.*, 481 F.2d 1204 (8th Cir. 1973); *Lynn v. Monarch Recovery Mgmt., Inc.*, __ F.Supp.2d __ (D.Md. 2012).

[28]*Wilson v. Volkswagen of America, Inc.*, 561 F.2d 494, 508 (4th

of the information being provided.[29] However, the responding agent's answers must provide the composite knowledge available to the party.[30] If the party is an infant, the infant's attorney or next friend may answer.[31]

Verification

When the party is an individual, the party, not the attorney,[32] must sign a verification or affidavit as to the accuracy of the answers.[33] This is one of the few exceptions to the general principle under the Federal Rules of Civil Procedure that the attorney may sign all pleadings and papers. A representative of a corporate party may verify interrogatory answers without personal knowledge of every response by furnishing the information available to the corporation.[34] The courts are divided as to whether an attorney can verify interrogatory answers for a corporation.[35]

Objections

If the responding party determines that a particular interrogatory is outside the scope of discovery, the party may object to the question in lieu of answering it. The objection must be made in writing, must state the grounds of the objection with specificity,[36] and must be signed by the attorney for the responding party.[37] In a motion, the burden will be on the party asserting the objection to demonstrate that the interrogatory

---

Cir. 1977).

[29]*Brown v. White's Ferry, Inc.*, 280 F.R.D. 238, 242–43 (D.Md. 2012); *Abrams v. Ciba Specialty Chemicals Corp.*, __ F.R.D. __ (S.D.Ala. 2010).

[30]*Law v. National Collegiate Athletic Ass'n*, 167 F.R.D. 464, 476 (D. Kan. 1996).

[31]*Hall v. Hague*, 34 F.R.D. 449 (D. Md. 1964).

[32]*Villareal v. El Chile, Inc.*, __ F.R.D. __ (N.D.Ill. 2010) (emails from counsel are not proper interrogatory responses); *Saria v. Massachusetts Mut. Life Ins. Co.*, 228 F.R.D. 536, 538–39 (S.D. W. Va. 2005) (verification by the attorney renders the attorney a witness).

[33]*Abrams v. Ciba Specialty Chemicals Corp.*, __ F.R.D. __ (S.D.Ala. 2010) (if the signature is not under oath, it does not satisfy Rule 33(b)); *Walls v. Paulson*, 250 F.R.D. 48 (D.D.C. 2008) (requirement that interrogatory answers be signed by the party is not optional).

[34]*Shepherd v. American*

Broadcasting Companies, Inc., 62 F.3d 1469, 1482 (D.C. Cir. 1995); *Gingerich v. City of Elkhart Probation Dept.*, __ F.R.D. __ (N.D.Ind. 2011) (the agent certifies that the responses contain the information that is available to the party).

[35]*Compare Sorrell v. District of Columbia*, 252 F.R.D. 37, 43 (D.D.C. 2008) (paralegal signature not permitted) *with Rea v. Wichita Mortg. Corp.*, 747 F.2d 567, 574, n.6 (10th Cir. 1984) (attorney signature allowed) *and Wilson v. Volkswagen of America, Inc.*, 561 F.2d 494, 508 (4th Cir. 1977) (same).

[36]*See Mulero-Abreu v. Puerto Rico Police Dept.*, 675 F.3d 88, 93 (1st Cir. 2012) (blanket objection improper); *Covington v. Sailormen Inc.*, __ F.R.D. __ (N.D.Fla. 2011) (general objection incorporated into every response not sufficient specificity).

[37]*Moreno Rivera v. DHL Global Forwarding*, 272 F.R.D. 50, 55 (D.Puerto Rico 2011); *Sorrell v. District of Columbia*, 252 F.R.D. 37, 43 (D.D.C. 2008).

was improper.[38] Some common objections are:

- *Overly broad, unduly vague, and ambiguous:* When a question is written broadly so that it extends to information not relevant to the complaint (such as a question not limited in time to the events relevant to the complaint), the question may be overly broad.[39] When a question is susceptible to numerous meanings, it may be unduly vague and ambiguous. In general, these objections are probably not justification for refusing to answer a question altogether, but the responding party can raise the objection, then expressly limit the scope of the response.

- *Burdensome and oppressive:* In general, the responding party must produce the information available without undue effort or expense. Thus, questions that require extensive research, compilation of data, or evaluation of data may be objectionable.[40] The responding party is not required to prepare the adverse party's case. Likewise, an interrogatory that seeks a high level of detail may be overly burdensome.[41] The reasonableness of an interrogatory is within the court's discretion.

- *Privileged information:* Questions that seek information protected by the attorney-client privilege or by another privilege are objectionable. When privileged information is withheld, the responding party must explicitly state the objection and describe the nature of the information not provided sufficiently to enable other parties to assess the applicability of the privilege. Care should be exercised in responding to such interrogatories, because the privilege may be waived by revealing part or all of the privileged communication.

- *Attorney work product:* Rule 26(b)(3) provides that trial preparation materials may be discovered only upon a showing that the party is unable to obtain the equivalent information through other means without undue hardship.[42]

- *Non-discoverable expert information:* Rule 26(b)(4) limits the scope of discovery directed towards experts. It gen-

---

[38]*Pegoraro v. Marrero*, 281 F.R.D. 122, 128-29 (S.D.N.Y. 2012); *Moreno Rivera v. DHL Global Forwarding*, 272 F.R.D. 50, 55 (D.Puerto Rico 2011).

[39]*Jewish Hospital Ass'n of Louisville, Ky. v. Struck Const. Co., Inc.*, 77 F.R.D. 59 (W.D. Ky. 1978).

[40]*IBP, Inc. v. Mercantile Bank of Topeka*, 179 F.R.D. 316, 321 (D. Kan. 1998) (interrogatory asking for every fact and application of law to fact supporting claim held burdensome).

[41]*See Ritchie Risk-Linked Strategies Trading (Ireland), Ltd. v. Coventry First LLC*, __ F.R.D. __ (S.D.N.Y. 2010) (requests for every fact, piece of evidence, and witness supporting the party's position is overly broad and unduly burdensome); *Cardenas v. Dorel Juvenile Group, Inc.*, 231 F.R.D. 616, 618 (D. Kan. 2005).

[42]*See* Rule 26(b)(3) (in-depth discussion of discovery of work product).

erally requires the responding party to provide an expert report for each expert it may call as a witness, and thereafter allows other parties to depose such experts. Further discovery with respect to such witnesses is available only upon motion. Rule 26(b)(4)(B) does not allow any discovery with respect to experts not intended to be called as witnesses, absent "exceptional circumstances."[43]

- *Not calculated to lead to the discovery of admissible evidence:* A party may object that an interrogatory seeks information that is not reasonably calculated to lead to the discovery of admissible evidence or is otherwise outside the scope of discovery allowed under Rule 26(b)(1).[44]

Failure to Object Is Waiver

All grounds for objection must be specifically stated in a timely response or they are waived,[45] unless excused by the court for good cause shown.[46]

Objection to Part of Interrogatory

If only part of an interrogatory is objectionable, the responding party must answer the interrogatory to the extent that it is not objectionable.[47] Thus, if an interrogatory is overly broad, it must be answered to the extent it is not overly broad.[48]

Motion for a Protective Order

As an alternative to making objections to individual questions, the responding party may make a motion for a protective order under Rule 26(c). A motion for a protective order is appropriate when most or all of a set of interrogatories is too burdensome or cumulative. The burden is on the moving party to show hardship or injustice.[49] The motion must be accompanied by a certification that the parties met prior to the filing of the motion and attempted to resolve their dispute without intervention by the court.

---

[43]*See* Rule 26(b)(4) (in-depth discussion of discovery directed toward experts).

[44]*See* Rule 26(b)(1) (in-depth discussion of the scope of discovery).

[45]*United Auto. Ins. Co. v. Veluchamy*, 747 F.Supp.2d 1021, 1027 (N.D.Ill. 2010); *Dine v. Metropolitan Life Ins. Co.*, 255 F.R.D. 534, 536 (C.D.Cal. 2009) (declining to find waiver despite lack of timely objection); *India Brewing, Inc. v. Miller Brewing Co.*, 237 F.R.D. 190, 194 (E.D. Wis. 2006) (each specific objection must be asserted or it is waived).

[46]*United Auto. Ins. Co. v. Veluchamy*, 747 F.Supp.2d 1021, 1027 (N.D.Ill. 2010); *Frontier-Kemper Constructors, Inc. v. Elk Run Coal Co., Inc.*, 246 F.R.D. 522 (S.D. W. Va. 2007) (discussing the good cause analysis).

[47]*Khadim v. Lab. Corp. of Am.*, 838 F.Supp.2d 448, 465 (W.D.Va. 2011); *Tequila Centinela, S.A. de C.V. v. Bacardi & Co. Ltd.*, 242 F.R.D. 1 (D.D.C. 2007).

[48]*See Walls v. International Paper Co.*, 192 F.R.D. 294 (D. Kan. 2000).

[49]*Roesberg v. Johns-Manville Corp.*, 85 F.R.D. 292 (E.D. Pa. 1980).

Motion to Compel

If the responding party fails to answer or objects to a question, the propounding party may file a motion to compel under Rule 37(a).[50] The court will award the prevailing party its reasonable expenses, including attorney fees, incurred in connection with the motion to compel, unless the conduct of the losing party was justified (*i.e.*, not frivolous). The motion must be accompanied by a certification that good faith attempts were made to resolve discovery disputes before relief was sought from the court. In a motion to compel, the burden is on the responding party (the non-moving party) to convince the court that an interrogatory is objectionable.[51]

Discretion of Court

The district court has extremely broad discretion in ruling on objections to interrogatories.[52] The court will balance the need and the burden, but will generally require an answer unless the administration of justice would be impeded.

Appeals

The court's rulings on objections to interrogatories are not final orders, and cannot be appealed until the conclusion of the case.

Sanctions for Failure to Answer

If a party files no response to an interrogatory, the court may impose certain sanctions specified in Rule 37(b)(2), such as deeming certain facts established or refusing to allow the party to oppose or support certain claims.[53] Furthermore, the court must award reasonable expenses, including attorney fees, caused by the responding party's failure to answer, unless the court finds that the failure to answer was justified.

Sanctions for Incomplete Answers or Improper Objections

A nonresponsive or incomplete answer or an improper objection will be treated as a failure to respond,[54] and the propounding party can make a motion to compel under Rule 37(a). The court will award the prevailing party its reasonable expenses, including attorney fees, incurred in connection with the motion to compel, unless the conduct of the losing party was justified.[55] If the motion is granted in part and denied in part, then the court will award expenses as it sees fit.

---

[50]*PCS Phosphate Co., Inc. v. Norfolk Southern Corp.*, 238 F.R.D. 555, 559 (E.D. N.C. 2006).

[51]*See Donahay v. Palm Beach Tours & Transp., Inc.*, 242 F.R.D. 685 (S.D. Fla. 2007).

[52]*Mack v. Great Atlantic and Pacific Tea Co., Inc.*, 871 F.2d 179, 186 (1st Cir. 1989).

[53]*See* Rule 37(d).

[54]*See Mulero-Abreu v. Puerto Rico Police Dept.*, 675 F.3d 88, 93 (1st Cir. 2012); *Mezu v. Morgan State University*, 269 F.R.D. 565, 573 (D.Md. 2010).

[55]*Lynn v. Monarch Recovery Mgmt., Inc.*, __ F.Supp.2d __ (D.Md. 2012).

Sanctions for Failure to Obey Order to Answer

If, in response to a motion to compel, the court orders an answer or a more complete answer, and if the responding party fails to comply, then the court can impose the sanctions specified in Rule 37(b)(2), such as deeming certain facts established or refusing to allow the party to oppose or support certain claims. Furthermore, the court must award reasonable expenses, including attorney fees, caused by the responding party's failure to answer, unless the court finds that the failure to answer was justified.

Sanctions for Untrue Answers

If an answer is untrue, either at the time it was made or subsequently, and is not supplemented, the court may exclude certain testimony or make whatever order justice requires.[56]

Duty to Supplement

Rule 26(e)(1)(A) provides that a party must supplement its response to an interrogatory if the party learns that the response is in some material respect incomplete or incorrect and if the additional or corrective information has not been provided to the other parties in writing or at a deposition.[57] Supplemental responses must be verified just like original responses.[58]

RULE 33(c)—USE

CORE CONCEPT

Interrogatory answers are not admissions, but generally may be used as though made in court by the party.

APPLICATIONS

Impact of 2007 "Restyling" Amendments

Rule 33(c) was significantly restructured during the 2007 Federal Civil Rules "Restyling" Project. The 2007 amendments moved the "scope" provisions of Rule 33(c) to Rule 33(a)(2). In researching current Rule 30(c), practitioners should be mindful of this repositioning.

Requests for Documents

Interrogatories may not be used to obtain documents.[59] Rather, a document request must be made under Rule 34. However, interrogatories may inquire about the existence of

---

[56]*Garcia v. Berkshire Life Ins. Co. of America*, 569 F.3d 1174, 1180 (10th Cir. 2009) (dismissing the case based on fabrications).

[57]*See Covad Communications Co. v. Revonet, Inc.*, 258 F.R.D. 17 (D.D.C. 2009) (because the responding party has a continuing duty to supplement, the party may state that it is unable to provide the information requested but will supplement its answers as information becomes available).

[58]*Knights Armament Co. v. Optical Systems Technology, Inc.*, 254 F.R.D. 463, 466 (M.D.Fla. 2008).

[59]*Alltmont v. U.S.*, 177 F.2d 971 (3d Cir. 1949); *Donahay v. Palm Beach Tours & Transp., Inc.*, 242 F.R.D. 685 (S.D. Fla. 2007).

documents and the facts contained therein. Furthermore, documents may, under certain circumstances, be produced in lieu of answering an interrogatory, as discussed below under Rule 33(d).

Use of Interrogatory Answers at Trial

Answers to interrogatories are treated like any other evidence, and may be offered[60] and admitted into evidence as allowed by the Federal Rules of Evidence.[61] However, the responding party is not bound by its answers, and generally may change the answers or offer evidence that is inconsistent with them,[62] although some courts hold that answers become binding where the other party relies on them and would be prejudiced by a late change.[63] They may be objected to as irrelevant, prejudicial, confusing, cumulative, or for any other applicable reason. Interrogatory answers are generally not hearsay with respect to the party making the answer because they are party admissions.[64] However, they may be hearsay if offered against another party. If only part of an answer is read, the responding party may require that other parts of the answer be admitted at the same time in order to clarify the portion offered.[65]

Answers Not Binding

Answers to interrogatories are not admissions, and a party is not bound by its answers.[66] Thus, a party can supplement or amend its answers, and is obligated to do so under certain circumstances discussed above. Even absent an amendment, a party may take a different position at trial unless it would prejudice another party.[67] Opposing parties may then impeach by questioning the reason for the changed answer.

Use of Interrogatory Answers in a Summary Judgment Motion

Interrogatory answers may be used in support of or in opposition to a motion for summary judgment, as provided in Rule 56(c).[68]

---

[60]*Cimino v. Raymark Industries, Inc.*, 151 F.3d 297, 309 (5th Cir. 1998) (interrogatory answers are not part of the record unless formally offered into evidence).

[61]*AMCO Ins. Co. v. Inspired Techs., Inc.*, 648 F.3d 875, 881 (8th Cir. 2011).

[62]*U.S. ex rel. Tyson v. Amerigroup Illinois, Inc.*, 230 F.R.D. 538, 541 (N.D. Ill. 2005).

[63]*See Hamelin v. Faxton-St. Luke's Healthcare*, __ F.R.D. __ (N.D.N.Y. 2011).

[64]*Underberg v. U.S.*, 362 F. Supp. 2d 1278, 1283 (D.N.M. 2005).

[65]*Grace & Co. v. City of Los Angeles*, 278 F.2d 771 (9th Cir.1960).

[66]*Bradley v. Allstate Ins. Co.*, 620 F.3d 509, 527, n.21 (5th Cir. 2010).

[67]The Advisory Committee Note to Rule 33(b).

[68]*Bradley v. Allstate Ins. Co.*, 620 F.3d 509, 527, n. 21 (5th Cir. 2010).

RULE 33(d)—OPTION TO PRODUCE BUSINESS RECORDS

CORE CONCEPT

A party may produce business records in lieu of answering an interrogatory when the burden of extracting the requested information would be substantially equal for either party.

APPLICATIONS

Business Records Only

Only business records of the responding party may be used in lieu of interrogatory answers.[69] Thus, one cannot produce pleadings[70] or deposition transcripts[71] or refer to the administrative record[72] instead of answering an interrogatory.

Documents Must Contain Information

In order to respond to an interrogatory by producing business records, a party must state that the documents contain the requested information.[73] It is not sufficient to state that the documents *may* contain the information.[74]

Identify Specific Documents

A party responding to an interrogatory by producing business records must provide sufficient detail so that the propounding party can identify which individual documents contain the information requested.[75]

Equal Burden

In order to respond to interrogatories by producing business records, the burden of deriving or ascertaining the answer must be substantially equal for the requesting party and the producing party.[76] If the sufficiency of the response is challenged, the producing party will bear the burden of making this showing.[77]

---

[69]*Covad Communications Co. v. Revonet, Inc.*, 258 F.R.D. 17, 20 (D.D.C. 2009) (responding party may not refer to the opposing party's records).

[70]*Melius v. National Indian Gaming Com'n*, 2000 WL 1174994 (D.D.C. 2000).

[71]*Starlight Intern., Inc. v. Herlihy*, 190 F.R.D. 587 (D. Kan. 1999).

[72]*Mullins v. Prudential Ins. Co. of America*, __ F.Supp.2d __ (W.D.Ky. 2010) (Rule 33(d) is not a procedural device for avoiding the duty to provide the information).

[73]*See Nature's Plus Nordic A/S v. Natural Organics, Inc.*, __ F.R.D. __ (E.D.N.Y. 2011) (documents in foreign language do not contain the information as contemplated by Rule 32(d)); *Mullins v. Prudential Ins. Co. of*

America, __ F.Supp.2d __ (W.D.Ky. 2010) (responding party is certifying that the information is found in the documents).

[74]*Daiflon, Inc. v. Allied Chemical Corp.*, 534 F.2d 221 (10th Cir. 1976).

[75]*Rainbow Pioneer No. 44-18-04A v. Hawaii-Nevada Inv. Corp.*, 711 F.2d 902 (9th Cir.1983); *Mullins v. Prudential Ins. Co. of America*, __ F.Supp.2d __ (W.D.Ky. 2010) (Rule 33(d) is not a procedural device for avoiding the duty to provide the information).

[76]*Lynn v. Monarch Recovery Mgmt., Inc.*, __ F.Supp.2d __ (D.Md. 2012); *Nature's Plus Nordic A/S v. Natural Organics, Inc.*, __ F.R.D. __ (E.D.N.Y. 2011) (burden of obtaining responsive information from documents in foreign language not equal).

[77]*U.S. S.E.C. v. Elfindepan, S.A.*,

871

Electronic Data

A party may provide access to electronically stored information instead of answering an interrogatory if, and only if, the burden of deriving the answer is equal on both parties and the responding party provides sufficient specificity such that the other party can locate the records containing the answer as easily as the responding party.[78]

Compilations, Abstracts, and Summaries

If a compilation, abstract, or summary exists of the documents containing the responsive information, then a party electing to refer to documents in lieu of answering an interrogatory must make available the compilation, abstract, or summary.[79]

Privileged Documents

A party cannot elect to produce business records and then withhold the documents as privileged in order to prevent a party from deriving an answer.[80]

Copies or Originals

The responding party may allow the propounding party to inspect and copy the originals or may make copies.[81]

Expense of Compiling Records

Under proper circumstances, the court will, upon motion for a protective order, require the propounding party to pay the cost of compiling the records.[82]

Motion to Compel

If the propounding party believes that its burden to find the answers from the records is substantially greater than that of the responding party, the propounding party can file a motion to compel an answer.[83] Note that the court may find the burden not substantially the same, yet nonetheless deny the motion to compel, if the court finds that the burden on the responding party to answer fully would be excessive or unreasonable.[84] The motion to compel must be accompanied by a certification that the parties met prior to the filing of the motion and attempted to resolve their dispute without intervention by the court.

---

206 F.R.D. 574, 577 (M.D. N.C. 2002).

[78]The 2006 Amendment to the Advisory Committee Note to Rule 33(d).

[79]*U.S. ex rel. Englund v. Los Angeles County*, 235 F.R.D. 675 (E.D. Cal. 2006).

[80]*Vazquez-Fernandez v. Cambridge College, Inc.*, 269 F.R.D. 150, 158 (D.Puerto Rico 2010); *Ampex Corp. v. Mitsubishi Elec. Corp.*, 937 F.

Supp. 352, 355 (D. Del. 1996).

[81]*Neal v. Siegel-Robert, Inc.*, 171 F.R.D. 264, 267 (E.D. Mo. 1996).

[82]*See* Rule 26(c) (detail on costs).

[83]*See Matthews v. USAir, Inc.*, 882 F. Supp. 274 (N.D. N.Y. 1995) (may not respond by producing documents that are unintelligible).

[84]The Advisory Committee Note to the 1970 amendment of Rule 33(c).

Additional Research References

Wright & Miller, *Federal Practice and Procedure* §§ 2161 to 2182
C.J.S., Federal Civil Procedure §§ 645 to 695 et seq.
West's Key Number Digest, Federal Civil Procedure ⚙1471 to 1542

RULE 34
PRODUCING DOCUMENTS, ELECTRONICALLY STORED INFORMATION, AND TANGIBLE THINGS, OR ENTERING ONTO LAND, FOR INSPECTION AND OTHER PURPOSES

(a) In General. A party may serve on any other party a request within the scope of Rule 26(b):

   (1) to produce and permit the requesting party or its representative to inspect, copy, test, or sample the following items in the responding party's possession, custody, or control:

      (A) any designated documents or electronically stored information—including writings, drawings, graphs, charts, photographs, sound recordings, images, and other data or data compilations—stored in any medium from which information can be obtained either directly or, if necessary, after translation by the responding party into a reasonably usable form; or

      (B) any designated tangible things; or

   (2) to permit entry onto designated land or other property possessed or controlled by the responding party, so that the requesting party may inspect, measure, survey, photograph, test, or sample the property or any designated object or operation on it.

(b) Procedure.

   (1) *Contents of the Request.* The request:

      (A) must describe with reasonable particularity each item or category of items to be inspected;

      (B) must specify a reasonable time, place, and manner for the inspection and for performing the related acts; and

      (C) may specify the form or forms in which electronically stored information is to be produced.

(2) *Responses and Objections.*

   (A) *Time to Respond.* The party to whom the request is directed must respond in writing within 30 days after being served. A shorter or longer time may be stipulated to under Rule 29 or be ordered by the court.

   (B) *Responding to Each Item.* For each item or category, the response must either state that inspection and related activities will be permitted as requested or state an objection to the request, including the reasons.

   (C) *Objections.* An objection to part of a request must specify the part and permit inspection of the rest.

   (D) *Responding to a Request for Production of Electronically Stored Information.* The response may state an objection to a requested form for producing electronically stored information. If the responding party objects to a requested form—or if no form was specified in the request—the party must state the form or forms it intends to use.

   (E) *Producing the Documents or Electronically Stored Information.* Unless otherwise stipulated or ordered by the court, these procedures apply to producing documents or electronically stored information:

     (i) A party must produce documents as they are kept in the usual course of business or must organize and label them to correspond to the categories in the request;

     (ii) If a request does not specify a form for producing electronically stored information, a party must produce it in a form or forms in which it is ordinarily maintained or in a reasonably usable form or forms; and

     (iii) A party need not produce the same electronically stored information in more than one form.

(c) Nonparties. As provided in Rule 45, a nonparty may be compelled to produce documents and

tangible things or to permit an inspection.

[Amended December 27, 1946, effective March 19, 1948; March 30, 1970, effective July 1, 1970; April 29, 1980, effective August 1, 1980; March 2, 1987, effective August 1, 1987; April 30, 1991, effective December 1, 1991; April 22, 1993, effective December 1, 1993; April 12, 2006, effective December 1, 2006; April 30, 2007, effective December 1, 2007.]

AUTHORS' COMMENTARY ON RULE 34

PURPOSE AND SCOPE

Rule 34 sets forth the procedures for obtaining access to documents and things within the control of other parties, and for gaining entry upon other parties' land for inspection. It must be read in conjunction with Rule 26, which establishes the scope of all discovery rules.

NOTE: Rule 34 was substantially revised in 1970, 1991, 1993, 2006, and 2007, and great care should be exercised when citing decisions pertaining to Rule 34.

RULE 34(a)—IN GENERAL

CORE CONCEPT

The scope of document requests and other discovery under Rule 34 is the broad discovery available under Rule 26.[1] Generally, any relevant, non-privileged document is discoverable unless it was prepared in anticipation of litigation, pertains to expert witnesses, or would be unreasonably burdensome to produce.

APPLICATIONS

Documents

"Documents" is broadly defined to include all forms of recorded information. Rule 34(a) specifically lists writings, drawings, graphs, charts, photographs, phonorecords, and other data compilations.

No Duty to Create Documents

Generally, a party is not required to create documents meeting the document requests, only to produce documents already in existence.[2]

---

[1]*Lynn v. Monarch Recovery Mgmt., Inc.*, __ F.Supp.2d __ (D.Md. 2012); *U.S. v. Approximately $7,400 in U.S. Currency*, __ F.Supp.2d __ (E.D.Wis. 2011).

[2]*Barnes v. Dist. of Columbia*, 281 F.R.D. 53, 54 (D.D.C. 2012); *Harris v. Koenig*, 271 F.R.D. 356, 371 (D.D.C.

Inspection, not Copying

The producing party is not required to make copies of the documents, just make them available for inspection.[3] The requesting party is entitled to inspect, copy, test, or sample discoverable documents. Frequently, however, the parties will agree to copy documents they are producing, particularly when each party is producing a roughly equivalent quantity of documents.

Electronic Data

Rule 34(a) specifically includes "electronically stored information" or "ESI" among the categories of documents and things that must be produced.[4] ESI is intended to be a broad and flexible term encompassing email and information "stored in any medium"[5] If the ESI is not stored in a form that is reasonably accessible, Rule 34(a) requires that the producing party translate it into a reasonably usable form.[6] Rule 34(a) allows a party to make a request to inspect, copy, test, or sample the ESI.[7] For more information about the discovery of ESI, see the Sedona Principles: Best Practices, Recommendations & Principles for Addressing Electronic Document Production, Second Edition,[8] upon which the courts have come to rely.[9]

Metadata

One particular form of electronically stored information that has drawn considerable attention in litigation is metadata (data about data), which describes the data that many programs store about the documents created in the program, such as the identity of the author, when the document was created, the identify of those editing the document, and when

---

2010); *but see Harris v. Athol-Royalston Regional School District Committee*, 200 F.R.D. 18 (D. Mass. 2001) (party required to create a handwriting exemplar for examination by the opposing party's expert).

[3]*Mezu v. Morgan State University*, __ F.Supp.2d __ (D.Md. 2011).

[4]*See Soto v. Castlerock Farming & Transp., Inc.*, __ F.R.D. __ (E.D.Cal. 2012); *Columbia Pictures, Inc. v. Bunnell*, 245 F.R.D. 443, 447 (C.D. Cal. 2007) (the 2006 amendments explicitly provide for the discovery of electronically stored information).

[5]The 2006 Amendment to the Advisory Committee Note to Rule 34(a). *See also Wynmoor Cmty. Council, Inc. v. QBE Ins. Corp.*, 280 F.R.D. 681,

685 (S.D.Fla. 2012) (deleted emails and files are discoverable); *Columbia Pictures, Inc. v. Bunnell*, 245 F.R.D. 443, 446–47 (C.D. Cal. 2007) (Rule 34(a)(1) is expansive and includes any type of information that is stored electronically, including information in RAM).

[6]The 2006 Amendment to the Advisory Committee Note to Rule 34(a).

[7]The 2006 Amendment to the Advisory Committee Note to Rule 34(a).

[8]Available at http://www.thesedo naconference.org/content/miscFiles/TS C__PRINCP__2nd__ed__607.pdf.

[9]*See, e.g., John B. v. Goetz*, 531 F.3d 448, 460 (6th Cir. 2008).

those edits occurred.[10] Metadata raises a host of issues (including preservation or destruction of metadata and potential attorney client privilege issues),[11] and should be discussed during the Rule 26(f) conference. Case law is evolving regarding when metadata is discoverable, and a party seeking metadata should specifically request it.[12]

Tangible Things

Rule 34 allows a party to inspect and copy, test, or sample real property[13] or tangible things relevant to the action (e.g., the allegedly defective product in a products liability case).[14]

Property

A party has the right to enter onto another party's land and inspect, measure, survey, photograph, test, or sample property or a designated object or operation thereon if relevant to the pending action.[15] The persons conducting the inspections are not permitted to question the representatives of the party whose property is being inspected.[16]

Parties Only

Only parties are obligated to respond to document requests.[17] "Party" is sometimes liberally construed, such as to include experts,[18] insurance companies,[19] and garnishees.[20] Note, however, that documents may be obtained from non-parties by

---

[10]The Sedona Principles: Best Practices, Recommendations & Principles for Addressing Electronic Document Production, Second Edition 11, 28 (The Sedona Conference Working Group Series, 2007), available at http:// www.thesedonaconference.org/content/miscFiles/ TSC_PRINCP_2nd_ed_607.pdf. *See also Race Tires Am., Inc. v. Hoosier Racing Tire Corp.,* 674 F.3d 158, 161, n.3 (3d Cir. 2012).

[11]*See, e.g., Southern New England Telephone Co. v. Global NAPs, Inc.,* 251 F.R.D. 82, 89 (D.Conn. 2008); *Williams v. Sprint/United Management Co.,* 230 F.R.D. 640, 653 (D. Kan. 2005).

[12]*See, e.g., Covad Communications Co. v. Revonet, Inc.,* __ F.R.D. __ (D.D.C. 2010) (native format, with metadata, is not the only acceptable form of production); *Autotech Technologies Ltd. Partnership v. Automationdirect.com, Inc.,* 248 F.R.D. 556 (N.D. Ill. 2008).

[13]*Lease v. Fishel,* __ F.Supp.2d __ (M.D.Pa. 2010).

[14]*Harris v. Athol-Royalston Regional School Dist. Committee,* 206

F.R.D. 30, 32–33 (D. Mass. 2002) (fingerprint samples may be obtained under either Rule 34 or Rule 35).

[15]*Albany Bank & Trust Co. v. Exxon Mobil Corp.,* 310 F.3d 969, 974 (7th Cir. 2002); *Hoewischer v. Deerwood Vill. Mall, LLC,* 281 F.R.D. 665, 665-66 (M.D.Fla. 2011) (limiting the inspection to areas of the property relevant to the litigation); *Baugus v. CSX Transp., Inc.,* 223 F.R.D. 469, 470 (N.D. Ohio 2004) (suggesting that it is improper to videotape the property of another party without going through the Rule 34 procedures).

[16]*U.S. v. Territory of the Virgin Islands,* 280 F.R.D. 232, 236-37 (D.Virgin Islands 2012).

[17]*See Hobley v. Burge,* 433 F.3d 946, 949 (7th Cir. 2006) (Rule 45 subpoena is the only way to get documents from a non-party); *In re Greenwood Air Crash,* 161 F.R.D. 387 (S.D. Ind. 1995) (discussion of who constitutes a "party" under Rule 34).

[18]*Alper v. U.S.,* 190 F.R.D. 281, 283 (D. Mass. 2000) (document request to the party's expert is deemed a document request to the party).

a subpoena under Rule 45.[21]

Documents Within Party's Possession, Custody, or Control

A party must produce all discoverable documents or things responsive to a request that are in the party's possession, custody, or control.[22] Documents are deemed to be within the possession, custody, or control of a party if the party has actual possession, custody, control, or the legal right to obtain the documents on demand.[23] Documents held by the party's attorney,[24] expert,[25] insurance company,[26] accountant,[27] spouse,[28] contractor,[29] officer,[30] or agent[31] are deemed to be within the party's control. Likewise, documents held by a subsidiary, affiliated corporation,[32] or branch office in another state may be within a party's control.[33] Moreover, documents owned by a third person but possessed by a party are within the party's

---

[19]See, e.g., Parrett v. Ford Motor Co., 47 F.R.D. 22, 24 (W.D. Mo. 1968).

[20]See, e.g., Conversion Chemical Corp. v. Dr.-Ing. Max Schloetter Fabrik Fur Galvanotechnik, 49 F.R.D. 126 (D. Conn. 1969).

[21]Hobley v. Burge, 433 F.3d 946, 949 (7th Cir. 2006) (Rule 45 subpoena is the only way to get documents from a non-party).

[22]Kissinger v. Reporters Committee for Freedom of the Press, 445 U.S. 136, 166, 100 S. Ct. 960, 976, 63 L. Ed. 2d 267 (1980); Wiwa v. Royal Dutch Petroleum Co., 392 F.3d 812, 821 (5th Cir. 2004) (having access to documents does not render them within a party's possession, custody, or control).

[23]In re Bankers Trust Co., 61 F.3d 465, 469 (6th Cir. 1995); Noaimi v. Zaid, __ F.R.D. __ (D.Kan. 2012).

[24]Hobley v. Burge, 433 F.3d 946, 949–50 (7th Cir. 2006) (documents held by former attorney are not within the party's control); Avocent Redmond Corp. v. Rose Electronics, 491 F. Supp. 2d 1000, 1010 (W.D. Wash. 2007) (documents held by former attorney are within the party's control); American Society For Prevention of Cruelty To Animals v. Ringling Brothers and Barnum & Bailey Circus, 233 F.R.D. 209, 212 (D.D.C. 2006) (documents held by attorney are within party's control, but subject to work product protection).

[25]Alper v. U.S., 190 F.R.D. 281, 283 (D. Mass. 2000) (documents held by the party's expert are within the party's control).

[26]Henderson v. Zurn Industries, Inc., 131 F.R.D. 560, 567 (S.D. Ind. 1990). But see Japan Halon Co., Ltd. v. Great Lakes Chemical Corp., 155 F.R.D. 626 (N.D. Ind. 1993) (subsidiary not required to obtain documents from parent in another country).

[27]Wardrip v. Hart, 934 F. Supp. 1282, 1286, 18 A.D.D. 447 (D. Kan. 1996) (financial records of defendant in possession of defendant's accountant are in defendant's control).

[28]Monroe's Estate v. Bottle Rock Power Corp., 2004 WL 737463 (E.D. La. 2004).

[29]Mercy Catholic Medical Center v. Thompson, 380 F.3d 142, 160 (3d Cir. 2004).

[30]Flagg v. City of Detroit, 252 F.R.D. 346, 353 (E.D.Mich. 2008).

[31]American Rock Salt Co., LLC v. Norfolk Southern Corp., 228 F.R.D. 426, 457 (W.D. N.Y. 2004).

[32]Shcherbakovskiy v. Da Capo Al Fine, Ltd., 490 F.3d 130, 138 (2d Cir. 2007) (documents held by a corporation held to be in the control of a board member).

[33]Goodman v. Praxair Services, Inc., 632 F.Supp.2d 494, 513 (D.Md. 2009); Steele Software Systems, Corp. v. DataQuick Information Systems, Inc., 237 F.R.D. 561, 564–65 (D. Md. 2006).

control.[34] Electronic documents on the server of a third party provider, such as text messages or emails, are within the control of the party.[35] The courts are divided as to whether a party will be deemed to have possession, custody or control of documents which the party may release by authorization, such as medical records.[36]

Duty to Search for Documents

A party must make a reasonable search of all sources reasonably likely to contain responsive documents.[37]

Documents Available From Another Source

The fact that documents are available from another source, such as public records, is not, by itself, a valid basis for objecting or refusing to produce such documents if they are within the possession, custody, or control of the responding party.[38] Depending on the circumstances, however, the availability of alternative sources for the requested documents may support an objection on the basis of undue burden.[39] A party that does not have the requested records in its possession, custody, or control will not be required to obtain those documents from public sources or third parties.[40]

Proceedings Where Requests Available

Document requests are available in all civil actions in

---

[34]*Societe Internationale Pour Participations Industrielles Et Commerciales, S. A. v. Rogers*, 357 U.S. 197, 78 S. Ct. 1087, 2 L. Ed. 2d 1255 (1958); *Commerce and Industry Ins. Co. v. Grinnell Corp.*, 2001 WL 96377 (E.D. La. 2001).

[35]*Flagg v. City of Detroit*, 252 F.R.D. 346, 352–53 (E.D.Mich. 2008) (text messages are within the party's control).

[36]*See Jackson v. United Artists Theatre Circuit, Inc.*, 278 F.R.D. 586, 593 (D.Nev. 2011) (party complies with Rule 34 by providing authorizations); *Vazquez-Fernandez v. Cambridge College, Inc.*, 269 F.R.D. 150, 165 (D.Puerto Rico 2010) (party not required to sign release for bank records); *Klugel v. Clough*, 252 F.R.D. 53, 55 (D.D.C. 2008) (Rule 34 does not compel a party to complete a medical records release); *Preservation Products, LLC v. Nutraceutical Clinical Laboratories Intern., Inc.*, 214 F.R.D. 494, 495 (N.D. Ill. 2003) (plaintiff must supply authorization for SEC testimony sought by defendant).

[37]*Tucker v. Am. Intern. Grp., Inc.*,

281 F.R.D. 85, 90-91 (D.Conn. 2012) (responding party makes the search; requesting party has no right to search responding party's documents); *Tequila Centinela, S.A. de C.V. v. Bacardi & Co. Ltd.*, 247 F.R.D. 198, 204 (D.D.C. 2008) (if a party has searched for, and been unable to locate, responsive documents, it should so state).

[38]*Sabouri v. Ohio Bureau of Employment Services*, 2000 WL 1620915 (S.D. Ohio 2000) (party required to produce a pleading that could also be obtained from the courthouse). *But see Bleecker v. Standard Fire Ins. Co.*, 130 F. Supp. 2d 726 (E.D. N.C. 2000) (discovery is not required when documents are readily obtainable by the party seeking a motion to compel).

[39]*See Tequila Centinela, S.A. de C.V. v. Bacardi & Co. Ltd.*, 242 F.R.D. 1 (D.D.C. 2007).

[40]*Shcherbakovskiy v. Da Capo Al Fine, Ltd.*, 490 F.3d 130, 138 (2d Cir. 2007); *Bush v. Ruth's Chris Steak House, Inc.*, __ F.Supp.2d __ (D.D.C. 2012).

federal court, subject to certain narrow exceptions listed in Rule 81. Document requests are available in bankruptcy proceedings.

Procedure to Perpetuate Testimony

A party may file a motion to obtain documents in connection with an action to perpetuate testimony under Rule 27.

Procedures in Aid of Execution

Document requests may be served following the entry of judgment, as part of procedures in aid of execution.

Motion for a Protective Order

As an alternative to making objections to individual document requests, the responding party may make a motion for a protective order under Rule 26(c).[41] A motion for a protective order is appropriate when most or all of a set of document requests is too burdensome or cumulative. The burden is on the moving party to show hardship or injustice. The motion must be accompanied by a certification that the parties met prior to the filing of the motion and attempted to resolve their dispute without intervention by the court.

Contractual Agreements

Parties sometimes have previously entered into agreements defining a right to inspect designated documents (such as an agreement restricting one party's right to inspect another party's financial records for one year). Such agreements may be upheld by the court, if reasonable.

RULE 34(b)—PROCEDURE

CORE CONCEPT

Any party may serve document requests on any other party, who must respond in writing within 30 days.

APPLICATIONS

Who May Serve

Any party may serve document requests.

Who May Be Served

Document requests are limited to parties to the action, although the party need not be an adverse party (documents are obtained from non-parties by a subpoena under Rule 45). The document requests must be addressed to the party. Thus, if the party is a corporation, document requests should be addressed to the corporation, not to a corporate officer or the attorney. In a class action, the courts are split as to whether only the named

---

[41]*Simms v. Center for Correctional Health and Policy Studies,* 272 F.R.D. 36, 40 (D.D.C. 2011) (motion for protective order to shift costs of production); *Minnesota Mining & Mfg. Co., Inc. v. Nippon Carbide Industries Co., Inc.,* 171 F.R.D. 246 (D. Minn. 1997).

representatives can be served.[42] Copies of the document requests should be served upon all parties.

Time for Service

Document requests can be served after the parties have conducted the discovery conference under Rule 26(f), or earlier with leave of court. In proceedings listed in Rule 26(a)(1)(B) as exempt from initial disclosures, there is no preliminary waiting period for document requests. The Rules do not set an outer limit on how late in the case document requests may be served, but many local rules or case management orders will set such a limit. Usually, when such a limit exists, document requests must be served so that the response is due before the close of discovery.[43]

Number

The Rule contains no limitation on the number of document requests.[44] Some districts have local rules limiting the number of document requests.[45]

Designation of Documents

Documents to be produced must be designated with "reasonable particularity."[46] Rule 34(b) permits requests for categories of documents as long as the category is described with reasonable particularity.[47] Essentially, the test is whether the responding party can determine what documents to produce.

Form of Requests

A request for inspection should be a formal document[48] setting forth the items to be inspected with "reasonable particularity."[49] What constitutes "reasonable particularity" depends on the circumstances. The request should also specify a reasonable time, place, and manner for the inspection.[50] The time designated should be after the time to respond has elapsed (30 days). As an alternative, the serving party may designate "a time and manner convenient to the parties," then reach an

---

[42]*Brennan v. Midwestern United Life Ins. Co.*, 450 F.2d 999 (7th Cir. 1971) (unnamed members of class required to respond); *Wainwright v. Kraftco Corp.*, 54 F.R.D. 532 (N.D. Ga. 1972) (unnamed members of class not required to respond).

[43]*Thomas v. Pacificorp*, 324 F.3d 1176, 1179 (10th Cir. 2003).

[44]*Bourguignon v. Spielvogel*, 2004 WL 743668 (D. Conn. 2004).

[45]*See Lurensky v. Wellinghoff*, 258 F.R.D. 27 (D.D.C. 2009).

[46]*Hager v. Graham*, __ F.R.D. __ (N.D.W.Va. 2010); *Hager v. Graham*, __ F.R.D. __ (N.D.W.Va. 2010).

[47]*Goosman v. A. Duie Pyle, Inc.*, 320 F.2d 45 (4th Cir.1963).

[48]*Suid v. Cigna Corp.*, 203 F.R.D. 227, 229–29 (D.V.I. 2001) (letters between counsel are not document requests under Rule 34).

[49]*Regan-Touhy v. Walgreen Co.*, 526 F.3d 641, 649–50 (10th Cir. 2008) (all-encompassing requests are not sufficiently particular); *Soto v. Castlerock Farming & Transp., Inc.*, __ F.R.D. __ (E.D.Cal. 2012).

[50]*Mezu v. Morgan State University*, __ F.Supp.2d __ (D.Md. 2011); *Southern Estate Services, Inc. v. Puritan Financial Services, Inc.*, 2000 WL 1725086 (E.D. La. 2000).

agreement with opposing counsel. If the request seeks electronic data, the request may, but is not required to, specify the form in which electronic data is to be produced.

Response

A party served with a document request must serve a written response[51] or move for a protective order under Rule 26(c). Otherwise, the party will be subject to the sanctions in Rule 37(d). The response should fairly respond to each request.[52] It may state that the request will be complied with in the manner requested. It may also state that the request will be complied with, but at some other time or place, or in some other manner. It is common to state in the response that responsive documents will be produced at a mutually convenient time and location.[53] The response may also raise objections to some or all of the requests. If the request does not specify the form for production of electronic data, or if the responding party has objected to the form specified in the request, then the response must specify the form in which electronic data will be produced. Finally, the response may advise that the party has no such documents in its possession, custody, or control.[54] The response is generally not required to be verified or under oath, in contrast to interrogatory answers.[55]

Time to Answer

A written response is due within 30 days of service.[56] The time to answer may be extended by written agreement under Rule 29.[57] If the responding party intends to object to some of the document requests, the stipulation should specify that the time is extended to answer and file objections.[58] The period for responding may also be shortened or lengthened by the court,

[51]*Starcher v. Correctional Medical Systems, Inc.*, 144 F.3d 418, 420–21 (6th Cir. 1998), aff'd, 527 U.S. 198, 119 S. Ct. 1915, 144 L. Ed. 2d 184 (1999); *Vazquez-Fernandez v. Cambridge College, Inc.*, 269 F.R.D. 150, 154 (D.Puerto Rico 2010).

[52]*Mulero-Abreu v. Puerto Rico Police Dept.*, 675 F.3d 88, 93 (1st Cir. 2012).

[53]*But see Mezu v. Morgan State University*, 269 F.R.D. 565, 574 (D.Md. 2010) (it is improper to state that documents will be produced at some unspecified time).

[54]*See Fishel v. BASF Group*, 175 F.R.D. 525, 531 (S.D. Iowa 1997) ("Even if there are no such documents, plaintiff is entitled to a response as required by Fed.R.Civ.P. 34(b) and the Court will so order.").

[55]*Swindell Dressler Intern. Co. v. Travelers Cas. & Sur. Co.*, 827 F.Supp.2d 498, 502 (W.D.Pa. 2011). *But see Vazquez-Fernandez v. Cambridge College, Inc.*, 269 F.R.D. 150, 154 (D.Puerto Rico 2010) (when the answer is something other than an objection or an agreement to produce, it must be verified).

[56]*Jayne H. Lee, Inc. v. Flagstaff Industries Corp.*, 173 F.R.D. 651, 654 (D. Md. 1997).

[57]*Tropix, Inc. v. Lyon & Lyon*, 169 F.R.D. 3 (D. Mass. 1996).

[58]*Coregis Ins. Co. v. Baratta & Fenerty, Ltd.*, 187 F.R.D. 528, 530 (E.D. Pa. 1999).

typically upon motion by one of the parties.[59]

Service of Response
The response must be served upon all parties.

Objections
If the responding party determines that a particular document request is outside the scope of discovery, the party may object to the request in lieu of producing the documents.[60] The objection must be made in writing, must state the grounds of the objection with specificity,[61] and must be signed by the attorney for the responding party.[62] Some common objections are:

- *Overly broad, unduly vague, and/or ambiguous:* When a document request is written broadly so that it extends to documents not relevant to the complaint (such as a request not limited in time to the events relevant to the complaint), the request may be overly broad.[63] When a request is susceptible to numerous meanings, it may be unduly vague and ambiguous. In general, these objections are probably not justification for refusing to provide documents altogether, but the responding party can raise the objection, then expressly limit the scope of the response.

- *Burdensome and oppressive:* In general, the responding party must produce the documents available without undue effort or expense. Thus, requests that require extensive research, compilation, or evaluation of documents may be objectionable.[64] The responding party is not required to prepare the adverse party's case. The reasonableness of a request is within the court's discretion.

- *Privileged information:* Requests that seek documents protected by the attorney-client privilege or by another privilege are objectionable.[65] When privileged documents are withheld, the responding party must explicitly state the objection and describe the nature of the documents

---

[59]*Brenford Environmental System, L.P. v. Pipeliners of Puerto Rico, Inc.*, 269 F.R.D. 143, 145 (D.Puerto Rico 2010); *Ellsworth Associates, Inc. v. U.S.*, 917 F. Supp. 841, 844 (D.D.C. 1996) (motion for expedited discovery is particularly appropriate with a claim for injunctive relief).

[60]*Lurensky v. Wellinghoff*, 258 F.R.D. 27 (D.D.C. 2009) (objections must be to specific requests — general objection that the requests are burdensome is insufficient).

[61]*U.S. v. Philip Morris Inc.*, 347 F.3d 951, 954 (D.C. Cir. 2003); *Sallah v. Worldwide Clearing LLC*, __

F.Supp.2d __ (S.D.Fla. 2012) (generic objections are meaningless).

[62]*Frontier-Kemper Constructors, Inc. v. Elk Run Coal Co., Inc.*, 246 F.R.D. 522, 527–28 (S.D. W. Va. 2007).

[63]*Westhemeco Ltd. v. New Hampshire Ins. Co.*, 82 F.R.D. 702 (S.D. N.Y. 1979).

[64]*Chambers (Robert) v. Capital Cities/ABC, Burke (Daniel), Callahan (Robert)*, 154 F.R.D. 63 (S.D. N.Y. 1994).

[65]*Tequila Centinela, S.A. de C.V. v. Bacardi & Co. Ltd.*, 242 F.R.D. 1 (D.D.C. 2007).

not produced sufficiently to enable other parties to assess the applicability of the privilege.[66] A log of the documents withheld on the basis of privilege should be provided to the requesting party, either at the time of the responses or at a mutually agreeable time.[67] Care should be exercised in responding to such requests, because the privilege may be waived by revealing part or all of the privileged documents.

- *Attorney work product:* Rule 26(b)(3) provides that trial preparation materials may be discovered only upon a showing that the party is unable to obtain the equivalent information through other means without undue hardship.[68]

- *Non-discoverable expert information:* Rule 26(b)(4) limits the scope of discovery directed towards experts. It generally requires the responding party to provide an expert report for each expert the party may call as a witness, and thereafter allows other parties to depose such experts. Further discovery with respect to such witnesses is available only upon motion. Rule 26(b)(4)(B) does not allow any discovery with respect to experts not intended to be called as witnesses, absent "exceptional circumstances."[69]

- *Not calculated to lead to the discovery of admissible evidence:* Rule 26 takes a very broad approach with respect to what information is discoverable. The requested information need not be admissible, only relevant. Information that is neither admissible nor reasonably calculated to lead to the discovery of admissible evidence, however, is not discoverable.[70]

- *Form of Electronic Data:* If the requesting party specifies a form for the production of electronic data that the responding party believes is burdensome or otherwise objectionable, Rule 34(b) specifically provides for objections to the request.

Failure to Object Is Waiver

In contrast to Rule 33 governing interrogatories, Rule 34 does not contain an explicit provision stating that failure to

---

[66]*U.S. v. Philip Morris Inc.*, 347 F.3d 951, 954 (D.C. Cir. 2003); *Tequila Centinela, S.A. de C.V. v. Bacardi & Co. Ltd.*, 242 F.R.D. 1 (D.D.C. 2007).

[67]*Burlington Northern & Santa Fe Ry. Co. v. U.S. Dist. Court for Dist. of Mont.*, 408 F.3d 1142, 1147 (9th Cir. 2005) (failure to produce a privilege log within 30 days is not a per se waiver of the privilege); *Universal City Development Partners, Ltd. v. Ride &* *Show Engineering, Inc.*, 230 F.R.D. 688, 695 (M.D. Fla. 2005); *Strougo v. BEA Associates*, 199 F.R.D. 515, 521 (S.D. N.Y. 2001).

[68]*See* Rule 26(b)(3) (discovery of work product).

[69]*See* Rule 26(b)(4) (in-depth discussion of discovery directed toward experts).

[70]*See* Rule 26(b)(1) (in-depth discussion of the scope of discovery).

serve timely objections results in a waiver of those objections, but many courts hold that such waiver is implied.[71] The court can excuse the waiver for good cause shown.[72]

Objection to Part of Request

If any part of a request is objectionable, the responding party must specify the objectionable part and respond to the remaining parts.[73]

Production of Documents

The responding party has the option of allowing the serving party to inspect, copy, test, or sample the documents as they are normally kept (*i.e.*, "There is our file room.").[74] The responding party may also produce selected responsive documents, in which case the party must organize and label them to correspond to the categories requested.[75] The responding party may make copies for the requesting party, but is not obligated to do so.[76] A party may generally produce copies of the requested documents, although the requesting party may insist on the original when colors or a signature are at issue.[77]

Use of Documents at Trial

Documents produced in response to document requests are treated like any other evidence, and are admissible as allowed by the rules of evidence. They may be objected to as irrelevant, prejudicial, confusing, cumulative, or any other applicable objection.

---

[71] *See, e.g., Wynmoor Cmty. Council, Inc. v. QBE Ins. Corp.*, 280 F.R.D. 681, 685 (S.D.Fla. 2012); *Cargill, Inc. v. Ron Burge Trucking, Inc.*, __ F.R.D. __ (D.Minn. 2012).

[72] *United Auto. Ins. Co. v. Veluchamy*, 747 F.Supp.2d 1021, 1027 (N.D.Ill. 2010).

[73] *Hager v. Graham*, __ F.R.D. __ (N.D.W.Va. 2010); *Aponte-Navedo v. Nalco Chemical Co.*, __ F.R.D. __ (D.Puerto Rico 2010).

[74] *Mezu v. Morgan State University*, __ F.Supp.2d __ (D.Md. 2011); *Mizner Grand Condominium Ass'n, Inc. v. Travelers Property Cas. Co. of America*, 270 F.R.D. 698, 701 (S.D.Fla. 2010) (records from a prior litigation are not kept in the ordinary course of business); *Doe v. District of Columbia*, 231 F.R.D. 27, 36–7 (D.D.C. 2005) (producing party does not have

to organize and label documents that are produced as they are kept); *but see Bonilla v. Trebol Motors Corp.*, 1997 WL 178844 (D.P.R. 1997) (responding party may not utilize a system of record-keeping which conceals rather than discloses relevant records or which makes production of the documents excessively burdensome and costly).

[75] *Go v. Rockefeller Univ.*, 280 F.R.D. 165, 169 (S.D.N.Y. 2012); *Mizner Grand Condominium Ass'n, Inc. v. Travelers Property Cas. Co. of America*, 270 F.R.D. 698, 700 (S.D.Fla. 2010).

[76] *Mezu v. Morgan State University*, 269 F.R.D. 565, 575 (D.Md. 2010).

[77] *Robinson-Reeder v. American Council on Educ.*, 262 F.R.D. 41, 45 (D.D.C. 2009).

Cost of Copying

The requesting party is responsible for the cost of copying the requested documents,[78] although parties sometimes agree (formally or informally) that the responding party pays copying costs.[79] The requesting party may inspect the produced documents before copying in order to avoid duplicative copying of documents already in the requesting party's possession.[80]

Production of Electronic Data

Rule 34(b) allows, but does not require, the requesting party to specify the form in which it is requesting electronic data.[81] If the requesting party wants the electronic data in a particular format (such as one that is compatible with a particular software application or one that includes metadata), the requesting party should so specify in the request.[82] The responding party can then produce it in that form or object and specify the form in which it will produce the electronic data.[83] If the requesting party does not specify the form, then the responding party must produce it in the form in which it is ordinarily maintained or in a form that is reasonably usable.[84] Unless the responding party is producing the data in the form specified by the requesting party, the responding party must specify the form it intends to use for production in its written response to the document request.[85] If the responding party objects to the form stated by the requesting party, or if the requesting party is not satisfied with the form specified by the responding party, then the parties must meet and confer under Rule 37(a)(2)(B).[86] Under any of these scenarios, a party need

---

[78]*LightGuard Sys., Inc. v. Spot Devices, Inc.*, __ F.R.D. __ (D.Nev. 2012); *Obiajulu v. City of Rochester, Dept. of Law*, 166 F.R.D. 293, 297 (W.D. N.Y. 1996) (plaintiff may copy documents by bringing in his own portable copying machine or by paying the defendant a reasonable copying cost).

[79]*LightGuard Sys., Inc. v. Spot Devices, Inc.*, __ F.R.D. __ (D.Nev. 2012) (parties may contractually alter the default presumption that the requesting party pays copying costs).

[80]*Stiller v. Arnold*, 167 F.R.D. 68, 70 (N.D. Ind. 1996).

[81]*Star Direct Telecom, Inc. v. Global Crossing Bandwidth, Inc.*, 272 F.R.D. 350, 359 (W.D.N.Y. 2011); *Covad Communications Co. v. Revonet, Inc.*, 254 F.R.D. 147, 149 (D.D.C. 2008).

[82]*See Autotech Technologies Ltd. Partnership v. Automationdirect.com, Inc.*, 248 F.R.D. 556, 558–59 (N.D. Ill. 2008) (requesting party did not specify metadata, and therefore cannot complaint when it did not receive the electronic files in a format that preserved metadata).

[83]*Ford Motor Co. v. Edgewood Properties, Inc.*, 257 F.R.D. 418 (D.N.J. 2009).

[84]*Automated Merchandising Sys. Inc. v. Crane Co.*, 279 F.R.D. 366, 373 (N.D.W.Va. 2011); *Covad Communications Co. v. Revonet, Inc.*, __ F.R.D. __ (D.D.C. 2010).

[85]The 2006 Amendment to the Advisory Committee Note to Rule 34(b).

[86]*Ford Motor Co. v. Edgewood Properties, Inc.*, 257 F.R.D. 418 (D.N.J. 2009).

not produce electronic data in more than one form.[87] Sometimes, the requesting party will seek to have the producing party's servers or hard drives imaged, so that the requesting party can conduct its own searches or forensic analysis, but the courts will require this only when the specific situation warrants.[88] The preservation and production of electronically stored information raises a host of issues, many of which are discussed in the Sedona Principles: Best Practices, Recommendations & Principles for Addressing Electronic Document Production.[89]

Limitations on Inspection

The responding party can set reasonable limitations on the time, place, and manner of an inspection.

Motion to Compel

If the responding party fails to respond to a document request or to allow an inspection, or objects to a document request, the propounding party may file a motion to compel under Rule 37(a).[90] The court will award the prevailing party its reasonable expenses, including attorney fees, incurred in connection with the motion to compel, unless the conduct of the losing party was justified (*i.e.,* not frivolous).

NOTE: Rule 37 requires the moving party to certify in writing that good faith attempts were made to resolve discovery disputes before relief was sought from the court.

Burden of Persuasion

In a motion to compel, the burden is on the responding party (the non-moving party) to convince the court that a document request is objectionable.[91]

Discretion of Court

The district court has extremely broad discretion in ruling on objections to document requests.[92] The court will balance the need for the documents and the burden of producing them, but

---

[87]*Automated Merchandising Sys. Inc. v. Crane Co.*, 279 F.R.D. 366, 373 (N.D.W.Va. 2011); *Covad Communications Co. v. Revonet, Inc.*, __ F.R.D. __ (D.D.C. 2010) (documents already produced in paper form need not be produced electronically).

[88]*See, e.g., John B. v. Goetz*, 531 F.3d 448, 460 (6th Cir. 2008) (referring to the Advisory Committee's warning not to turn every case into a forensic exercise).

[89]The Sedona Principles: Best Practices, Recommendations & Principles for Addressing Electronic Document Production, Second Edition 11, 28 (The Sedona Conference Working Group Series, 2007), available at http:// www.thesedonaconference.org/c ontent/miscFiles/ TSC__PRINCP__2n d__ed__607.pdf. *See also John B. v. Goetz*, 531 F.3d 448, 459 (6th Cir. 2008) (*citing* the Sedona Principles); *Ford Motor Co. v. Edgewood Properties, Inc.*, 257 F.R.D. 418, 424 (D.N.J. 2009).

[90]*Molski v. Franklin*, 222 F.R.D. 433, 435 (S.D. Cal. 2004); *U.S. v. Kattar*, 191 F.R.D. 33, 35–36 (D.N.H. 1999) (such a motion must comply with the requirements of Rule 37(a)).

[91]*Tequila Centinela, S.A. de C.V. v. Bacardi & Co. Ltd.*, 242 F.R.D. 1 (D.D.C. 2007).

[92]*McConnell v. Canadian Pac. Realty Co.*, 280 F.R.D. 188, 192 (M.D.Pa. 2011) (discretion extends to magistrate judges).

will generally require production unless the administration of justice would be impeded. The court may allow inspection under limited conditions, and may restrict further disclosure of sensitive documents. The court may also privately inspect the documents before ruling.

Appeals

The court's rulings on objections to document requests are not final orders, and cannot be appealed until the conclusion of the case.

Sanctions for Failure to Respond

If a party files no response to a document request, the court may impose certain sanctions under Rule 37(b)(2), such as deeming certain facts established or refusing to allow the party to oppose or support certain claims.[93] The court may also deem objections to the document request waived by the failure to file a timely response.[94] Furthermore, the court must award reasonable expenses, including attorney fees, caused by the responding party's failure to answer, unless the court finds that the failure to answer was justified.

RULE 34(c)—NONPARTIES

CORE CONCEPT

Although document requests or requests for inspection cannot be served on a non-party, documents or inspections can be obtained from a non-party by a subpoena under Rule 45.[95] Furthermore, Rule 34 does not preclude an independent action for production of documents or things or for permission to enter onto land (but such actions may be unnecessary under the expanded subpoena powers in Rule 45).[96]

Additional Research References

Wright & Miller, *Federal Practice and Procedure* §§ 2201 to 2218
C.J.S., Federal Civil Procedure §§ 696 to 740 et seq.
West's Key Number Digest, Federal Civil Procedure ⚷1551 to 1640

---

[93]*See* Rule 37(d); *Land Ocean Logistics, Inc. v. Aqua Gulf Corp.*, 181 F.R.D. 229, 235 (W.D. N.Y. 1998) (preclusion of evidence is a harsh sanction reserved for exceptional cases).

[94]*Scaturro v. Warren and Sweat Mfg. Co., Inc.*, 160 F.R.D. 44 (M.D. Pa. 1995).

[95]*Hobley v. Burge*, 433 F.3d 946, 949 (7th Cir. 2006) (Rule 45 subpoena is the only way to get documents from a non-party); *Tucker v. Am. Intern. Grp., Inc.*, 281 F.R.D. 85, 90-91 (D.Conn. 2012).

[96]*See Darbeau v. Library of Congress*, 453 F. Supp. 2d 168, 171 (D.D.C. 2006); the Advisory Committee Note to the 1970 amendment to Rule 34(c).

RULE 35
PHYSICAL AND MENTAL EXAMINATIONS

(a) Order for an Examination.

(1) *In General.* The court where the action is pending may order a party whose mental or physical condition—including blood group—is in controversy to submit to a physical or mental examination by a suitably licensed or certified examiner. The court has the same authority to order a party to produce for examination a person who is in its custody or under its legal control.

(2) *Motion and Notice; Contents of the Order.* The order:

(A) may be made only on motion for good cause and on notice to all parties and the person to be examined; and

(B) must specify the time, place, manner, conditions, and scope of the examination, as well as the person or persons who will perform it.

(b) Examiner's Report.

(1) *Request by the Party or Person Examined.* The party who moved for the examination must, on request, deliver to the requester a copy of the examiner's report, together with like reports of all earlier examinations of the same condition. The request may be made by the party against whom the examination order was issued or by the person examined.

(2) *Contents.* The examiner's report must be in writing and must set out in detail the examiner's findings, including diagnoses, conclusions, and the results of any tests.

(3) *Request by the Moving Party.* After delivering the reports, the party who moved for the examination may request—and is entitled to receive—from the party against whom the examination order was issued like reports of all earlier or

later examinations of the same condition. But those reports need not be delivered by the party with custody or control of the person examined if the party shows that it could not obtain them.

(4) *Waiver of Privilege.* By requesting and obtaining the examiner's report, or by deposing the examiner, the party examined waives any privilege it may have—in that action or any other action involving the same controversy—concerning testimony about all examinations of the same condition.

(5) *Failure to Deliver a Report.* The court on motion may order—on just terms—that a party deliver the report of an examination. If the report is not provided, the court may exclude the examiner's testimony at trial.

(6) *Scope.* This subdivision (b) applies also to an examination made by the parties' agreement, unless the agreement states otherwise. This subdivision does not preclude obtaining an examiner's report or deposing an examiner under other rules.

[Amended effective July 1, 1970; August 1, 1987; November 18, 1988; December 1, 1991; April 30, 2007, effective December 1, 2007.]

AUTHORS' COMMENTARY ON RULE 35

PURPOSE AND SCOPE

Rule 35 requires a party to submit to a mental or physical examination when the party's mental or physical condition is at issue in the action. In contrast to most other discovery procedures, mental or physical examinations are available only for "good cause."

RULE 35(a)—ORDER FOR AN EXAMINATION

CORE CONCEPT

Examination is compulsory only if ordered by the court. A court will order examination for good cause shown, which will generally exist in every case in which the plaintiff is claiming personal injuries.

APPLICATIONS

Motion

Technically, a request for examination must be made by motion, with a proposed order attached, served upon the person to be examined and all parties.[1] The motion should specify the time, place, manner, conditions, and scope of the examination and the person or persons by whom it is to be made, as well as the grounds supporting the motion.[2] Typically, however, examination is arranged by consent.

Order

If the court grants a motion for a Rule 35 examination, it must issue an order that specifies the time, place, manner, conditions, and scope of the examination and the examiner.[3] These topics are discussed individually below. The order may also include protective measures deemed appropriate by the court.[4]

Condition at Issue

Examinations for a particular condition are allowed only when that condition is in controversy.[5]

Good Cause

The court will order an examination "for good cause shown."[6] The burden of demonstrating good cause rests with the moving party.[7] The requirement of good cause is not a formality; the court must genuinely balance the need for the information with the right to privacy and safety of the party.[8] In a tort action where the plaintiff seeks to recover for personal injuries, good

---

[1] *Smith v. Koplan*, 215 F.R.D. 11, 12 (D.D.C. 2003).

[2] *See Doe v. Provident Life & Acc. Ins. Co.*, 247 F.R.D. 218, 221 (D.D.C. 2008); *Cabana v. Forcier*, 200 F.R.D. 9 (D. Mass. 2001) (the movant complied with Rule 35 by providing a time and place for the exam as well as the name of the examiner and a general idea of the exam's intended scope).

[3] *Schaeffer v. Sequoyah Trading & Transp.*, __ F.R.D. __ (D.Kan. 2011); *Ziemba v. Armstrong*, 2004 WL 834685 (D. Conn. 2004).

[4] *Schaeffer v. Sequoyah Trading & Transp.*, __ F.R.D. __ (D.Kan. 2011) (ordering videotaping of the examination); *Favale v. Roman Catholic Diocese of Bridgeport*, 235 F.R.D. 553, 555 (D. Conn. 2006).

[5] *Green v. Branson*, 108 F.3d 1296, 1304 (10th Cir. 1997) (denying motion by the plaintiff to have himself examined where purpose was for the plain-

tiff, a prisoner, to obtain treatment); *Diaz v. Con-Way Truckload, Inc.*, 279 F.R.D. 412, 419 (S.D.Tex. 2012) (examination may also be to explore changes in the party's condition); *Nuskey v. Lambright*, 251 F.R.D. 3, 6–7 (D.D.C. 2008) (discussing the split as to whether "garden variety" emotional distress puts the plaintiff's mental condition at issue).

[6] *Schlagenhauf v. Holder*, 379 U.S. 104, 85 S. Ct. 234, 13 L. Ed. 2d 152 (1964) (describing "good cause" as a determination that must be made on a case-by-case basis); *Diaz v. Con-Way Truckload, Inc.*, 279 F.R.D. 412, 423 (S.D.Tex. 2012).

[7] *Doe v. District of Columbia*, 229 F.R.D. 24, 26 (D.D.C. 2005); *Cauley v. Ingram Micro, Inc.*, 216 F.R.D. 241 (W.D. N.Y. 2003).

[8] *Schlagenhauf v. Holder*, 379 U.S. 104, 118, 85 S. Ct. 234, 242, 13 L. Ed. 2d 152 (1964); *Diaz v. Con-Way Truckload, Inc.*, 279 F.R.D. 412, 423

cause will almost always be found to exist.[9] It becomes less clear when the party has not put the party's own mental or physical condition at issue.[10]

Time for Filing Motion

There is no time limit on the filing of a motion for an examination, although the court can take the timing of the motion into account in considering the motion.[11]

Who Conducts Exam

Rule 35 states that the examination may be conducted by any suitably licensed or certified examiner or examiners.[12] It does not address the selection of a particular examiner. In general, the court will allow the movant to select the examiner unless the person to be examined raises a valid objection.[13] The court may reject a particular examiner upon a showing of bias[14] or, arguably, if a person requests a doctor of the same gender. Some local rules have provisions regarding the selection of a neutral examiner.[15] The court order must designate the examiner, and may be invalid if it fails to do so.

Testimony of Examiner

The party conducting the examination may call the examiner to testify as an expert witness (assuming the criteria for expert testimony are satisfied). The courts are split as to whether the party who was examined may call the examiner as

---

(S.D.Tex. 2012) (motion should be denied only if no additional relevant information could be gained by an examination).

[9]*See Chaney v. Venture Transport, Inc.*, 2004 WL 445134 (E.D. La. 2004); *Nyfield v. Virgin Islands Telephone Corp.*, 2001 WL 378858 (D.V.I. 2001).

[10]*See Bradford Felmly v. Hills*, 222 F.R.D. 257, 258–59 (D.V.I. 2004); *Ali v. Wang Laboratories, Inc.*, 162 F.R.D. 165, 11 A.D.D. 1333 (M.D. Fla. 1995).

[11]*Diaz v. Con-Way Truckload, Inc.*, 279 F.R.D. 412, 416–21 (S.D.Tex. 2012) (discussing the role of the deadline for expert reports in evaluating a Rule 35 motion).

[12]*Merritt v. Stolt Offshore, Inc.*, 2004 WL 224578 (E.D. La. 2004) (holding that the court may order more than one examiner, but noting that some states hold differently); *Fischer v. Coastal Towing Inc.*, 168 F.R.D. 199, 201 (E.D. Tex. 1996) (vocational-rehabilitation expert deemed a "suit-

ably licensed and/or certified examiner").

[13]*Douponce v. Drake*, 183 F.R.D. 565, 566 (D. Colo. 1998) (allowing the defendant's selected examiner despite allegations of bias); *Lahr v. Fulbright & Jaworski, L.L.P.*, 164 F.R.D. 196, 202–03 (N.D. Tex. 1995).

[14]*See O'Sullivan v. Rivera*, 229 F.R.D. 184 (D.N.M. 2004) (the fact that the expert regularly testifies for defendants does not disqualify the expert under Rule 35); *Nyfield v. Virgin Islands Telephone Corp.*, 2001 WL 378858 (D.V.I. 2001) ("There is no requirement that a Rule 35 examination be conducted by a physician wholly unconnected with either party and absent evidence of bias, Defendants should be allowed their chosen examiner.").

[15]*But see Hunt v. R & B Falcon Drilling USA, Inc.*, 2000 WL 1838327 (E.D. La. 2000) (a motion for a court appointed examiner is more properly brought under Federal Rule of Evidence 706).

an expert.[16]

Type of Exams

The type of exams allowable depends on the circumstances of the case. Exams can include blood tests, x-rays,[17] electrocardiograms, fingerprint analysis,[18] and other safe, medically accepted tests indicated by the condition at issue.[19] Vocational exams are also permissible under Rule 35.[20] The burden on the movant to show good cause will be greater if the tests are more invasive, painful, or burdensome, or if repeated examinations are sought. However, a party that objects to a particular test as too painful or invasive may be precluded from offering evidence of the type that would result from the test. A court may also limit testing to only those tests that have been specifically identified.[21]

Mental Examinations

Psychiatric examinations are allowable if a person's mental condition is at issue.[22] The examination may be conducted by a psychiatrist or psychologist. Courts are divided as to whether a claim for emotional distress places the plaintiff's mental condition at issue.[23]

Safety of Tests

In order to oppose a mental or physical exam on the grounds that the exam is unsafe, a party must demonstrate that the proposed test is potentially dangerous. Thereafter, the burden shifts to the party requesting the examination to show that it

---

[16]*Lehan v. Ambassador Programs, Inc.*, 190 F.R.D. 670 (E.D. Wash. 2000) (discussing the various positions taken by the courts on this issue).

[17]*Tarte v. U.S.*, 249 F.R.D. 856 (S.D.Fla. 2008) (x-rays and MRIs are routine procedures).

[18]*Harris v. Athol-Royalston Regional School Dist. Committee*, 206 F.R.D. 30, 32–33 (D. Mass. 2002) (fingerprint samples may be obtained under either Rule 34 or Rule 35).

[19]*See Jefferys v. LRP Publications, Inc.*, 184 F.R.D. 262, 263 (E.D. Pa. 1999) (allowing interview by vocational expert).

[20]*See Storms v. Lowe's Home Centers, Inc.*, 211 F.R.D. 296, 297 (W.D. Va. 2002); *Douris v. County of Bucks*, 2000 WL 1358481 (E.D. Pa. 2000).

[21]*Hirschheimer v. Associated Metals & Minerals Corp.*, 7 Nat'l Disability Law Rep. P 318, 1995 WL 736901 (S.D. N.Y. 1995); *contra Ragge*

v. MCA/Universal Studios, 165 F.R.D. 605, 609 (C.D. Cal. 1995).

[22]*Roberson v. Bair*, 242 F.R.D. 130 (D.D.C. 2007) (emotional distress claim places the plaintiff's condition at issue). *See also Smith v. J.I. Case Corp.*, 163 F.R.D. 229, 230 (E.D. Pa. 1995) (discussing four possible situations in which a party's mental condition is in controversy).

[23]*See E.E.O.C. v. Grief Bros. Corp.*, 218 F.R.D. 59, 61 (W.D. N.Y. 2003) (mental examinations may be obtained where a plaintiff's allegations of emotional distress amount to more than a claim for garden variety emotional distress damages); *Ford v. Contra Costa County*, 179 F.R.D. 579, 579–80 (N.D. Cal. 1998) (mere claim for emotional distress damages does not place mental condition at issue); *E.E.O.C. v. Old Western Furniture Corp.*, 173 F.R.D. 444, 445–46 (W.D. Tex. 1996); *Neal v. Siegel-Robert, Inc.*, 171 F.R.D. 264 (E.D. Mo. 1996).

is both necessary and safe.[24]

Second Examinations

When permanent injuries are claimed or under other appropriate circumstances, the court may allow a second examination just before trial.[25] A stronger showing of necessity is usually required for a second examination.[26]

Time and Location

The court will designate the time and location of the examination in the order. Usually, the plaintiff will be required to travel to the district where the action is pending to be examined.[27]

Cost of Examination

The moving party must pay the medical or professional expenses of the examination. The person to be examined is not compensated, however, for transportation costs[28] and lost time.

Who Is Present at Examination

The court has discretion to determine who may be present at the examination.[29] Some courts allow the person being examined by a doctor to bring his own physician, others do not.[30] It is also unsettled as to whether attorneys have a right to be present.[31]

Persons Subject to Examination

Any party is subject to examination upon motion by any other party, provided that the physical or mental condition of the party to be examined is at issue.[32] Additionally, a person who is within the control of a party is subject to examination. Thus, a parent suing on behalf of an injured child may have to

---

[24]*Pena v. Troup*, 163 F.R.D. 352, 353–54 (D. Colo. 1995).

[25]See *Galieti v. State Farm Mut. Auto. Ins. Co.*, 154 F.R.D. 262 (D. Colo. 1994).

[26]*Furlong v. Circle Line Statue of Liberty Ferry, Inc.*, 902 F. Supp. 65 (S.D. N.Y. 1995).

[27]*Landry v. Green Bay & Western R. Co.*, 121 F.R.D. 400 (E.D. Wis. 1988).

[28]*McCloskey v. United Parcel Service General Services Co.*, 171 F.R.D. 268, 270 (D. Or. 1997).

[29]See *Tarte v. U.S.*, 249 F.R.D. 856 (S.D.Fla. 2008) (presence of 3rd party or recording device are within the court's discretion); *Bethel v. Dixie Homecrafters, Inc.*, 192 F.R.D. 320 (N.D. Ga.2000).

[30]*Favale v. Roman Catholic Diocese of Bridgeport*, 235 F.R.D. 553, 555 (D. Conn. 2006) (Rule 35 does not provide for anyone to be present); *Shirsat v. Mutual Pharmaceutical Co., Inc.*, 169 F.R.D. 68, 71 (E.D. Pa. 1996).

[31]*Marsch v. Rensselaer County*, 218 F.R.D. 367, 371 (N.D. N.Y. 2003) (although attorneys are generally not permitted to be present during the examination, Fifth Amendment concerns dictated allowing counsel to be present); *Cabana v. Forcier*, 200 F.R.D. 9 (D. Mass. 2001) (the clear majority of federal courts have refused to permit third party observers at Rule 35 examinations); *Gensbauer v. May Dept. Stores Co.*, 184 F.R.D. 552 (E.D. Pa. 1999).

[32]*Schlagenhauf v. Holder*, 379 U.S. 104, 85 S. Ct. 234, 13 L. Ed. 2d 152 (1964).

produce the child for examination.[33] This principle has also been extended to a spouse when one spouse is suing for injuries to the other.[34] In such case, the party has a duty to make a good faith effort to obtain the person's presence.[35]

Sanctions

If a party fails to comply with the order, most of the sanctions in Rule 37(b)(2) are available, such as deeming certain facts established or refusing to allow the violator to oppose or support certain claims. However, contempt sanctions are not available for failure to submit to the examination.[36] If a person within the control of a party is to be examined, no sanctions apply to that person because he is not a party. The party's duty is to make a good faith effort to obtain the person's presence, and the party will be subject to the sanctions if the party fails to make the requisite good faith effort.[37]

Actions Applicable

Examinations are available in all civil actions in federal court,[38] subject to certain narrow exceptions in Rule 81. The court may also order an examination in connection with a deposition to perpetuate testimony under Rule 27.[39]

Appeal

The courts are split as to whether an order directing or refusing an examination is interlocutory, and thus generally not appealable until the end of the action or may be appealed immediately as a collateral order.[40]

RULE 35(b)—EXAMINER'S REPORT

CORE CONCEPT

Upon request by the party or person examined, the party moving for the examination must provide a copy of a detailed written report by the examiner, together with any reports of earlier

---

[33]The Advisory Committee Note to the 1970 amendment of Rule 35(a); *but see Caban ex rel. Crespo v. 600 E. 21st Street Co.*, 200 F.R.D. 176 (E.D. N.Y. 2001) (a guardian suing on behalf of a child is not the party or within the control of the party, and thus is not subject to examination under Rule 35).

[34]*In re Certain Asbestos Cases*, 112 F.R.D. 427, 434 (N.D. Tex. 1986).

[35]The Advisory Committee Note to the 1970 amendment of Rule 35(a).

[36]*Sibbach v. Wilson & Co.*, 312 U.S. 1, 312 U.S. 655, 61 S. Ct. 422, 85 L. Ed. 479 (1941).

[37]The Advisory Committee Note to the 1970 amendment of Rule 35(a).

[38]*Caban ex rel. Crespo v. 600 E. 21st Street Co.*, 200 F.R.D. 176 (E.D. N.Y. 2001) (Rule 35 governs in diversity cases even in the face of conflicting state rules regarding examinations of parties).

[39]*See* Rules 27(a)(3) and 27(b).

[40]*See Goodman v. Harris County*, 443 F.3d 464, 467–68 (5th Cir. 2006) (applying the factors for appeal of a collateral order to a Rule 35 order); *O'Malley v. Chrysler Corp.*, 160 F.2d 35 (C.C.A. 7th Cir. 1947).

examinations for the same condition.[41] Following the delivery of such a copy, the examined party must provide copies of reports of the results of any other examinations for the same condition, whether conducted before or after the Rule 35 examination.

APPLICATIONS

Examination by Agreement

The report exchanging provisions apply to examinations by agreement unless the agreement expressly provides otherwise.

Effect of Report

Testimony by the examiner will be limited to the opinions disclosed in the report.[42]

Waiver of Privilege

A request for a report under Rule 35 acts as a waiver of the doctor-patient or psychologist-patient privilege for other examinations for the same condition.[43] Thus, the examined party may not refuse to produce other reports on the basis of privilege once the party has requested a copy of the report of the Rule 35 examination. Note that the Rule 35 waiver may be avoided by attempting to obtain the reports via another discovery rule or another procedural device.

Other Discovery Procedures

The parties may use other discovery procedures in lieu of or in addition to the report exchange procedures in Rule 35, such as document requests or depositions of the examiner.[44]

Failure to Exchange

If either party fails to provide covered reports, the court can order production.

Failure to Draft Report

If the examiner fails to prepare or provide a report, the court may exclude the examiner's testimony.

Extraneous Material

If the report contains extraneous or unreasonably prejudicial material, the court can order certain portions excised.

Reports for Persons Under Control of Party

If a person is examined under Rule 35 because that person is in the control of a party, the party is entitled to the same reporting rights and obligations as the person would be.

---

[41]*See Grajales-Romero v. American Airlines, Inc.*, 194 F.3d 288, 298 (1st Cir. 1999) (duty to exchange applies to an examination voluntarily submitted to by the plaintiff).

[42]*Licciardi v. TIG Ins. Group*, 140 F.3d 357 (1st Cir. 1998) (testimony be-

yond the scope of the report excluded).

[43]*Cunningham v. Connecticut Mut. Life Ins.*, 845 F. Supp. 1403 (S.D. Cal. 1994).

[44]*Tarte v. U.S.*, 249 F.R.D. 856 (S.D.Fla. 2008).

Additional Research References

Wright & Miller, *Federal Practice and Procedure* §§ 2231 to 2239
C.J.S., Federal Civil Procedure §§ 752 to 755
West's Key Number Digest, Federal Civil Procedure ⟜1651 to 1664

RULE 36
REQUESTS FOR ADMISSION

(a) Scope and Procedure.

(1) *Scope.* A party may serve on any other party a written request to admit, for purposes of the pending action only, the truth of any matters within the scope of Rule 26(b)(1) relating to:

  (A) facts, the application of law to fact, or opinions about either; and

  (B) the genuineness of any described documents.

(2) *Form; Copy of a Document.* Each matter must be separately stated. A request to admit the genuineness of a document must be accompanied by a copy of the document unless it is, or has been, otherwise furnished or made available for inspection and copying.

(3) *Time to Respond; Effect of Not Responding.* A matter is admitted unless, within 30 days after being served, the party to whom the request is directed serves on the requesting party a written answer or objection addressed to the matter and signed by the party or its attorney. A shorter or longer time for responding may be stipulated to under Rule 29 or be ordered by the court.

(4) *Answer.* If a matter is not admitted, the answer must specifically deny it or state in detail why the answering party cannot truthfully admit or deny it. A denial must fairly respond to the substance of the matter; and when good faith requires that a party qualify an answer or deny only a part of a matter, the answer must specify the part admitted and qualify or deny the rest. The answering party may assert lack of knowledge or information as a reason for failing to admit or deny only if the party states that it has made reasonable inquiry and that the information it knows or can readily obtain is insufficient to enable it to admit or deny.

(5) *Objections.* The grounds for objecting to a request

must be stated. A party must not object solely on the ground that the request presents a genuine issue for trial.

(6) *Motion Regarding the Sufficiency of an Answer or Objection.* The requesting party may move to determine the sufficiency of an answer or objection. Unless the court finds an objection justified, it must order that an answer be served. On finding that an answer does not comply with this rule, the court may order either that the matter is admitted or that an amended answer be served. The court may defer its final decision until a pretrial conference or a specified time before trial. Rule 37(a)(5) applies to an award of expenses.

(b) Effect of an Admission; Withdrawing or Amending It. A matter admitted under this rule is conclusively established unless the court, on motion, permits the admission to be withdrawn or amended. Subject to Rule 16(e), the court may permit withdrawal or amendment if it would promote the presentation of the merits of the action and if the court is not persuaded that it would prejudice the requesting party in maintaining or defending the action on the merits. An admission under this rule is not an admission for any other purpose and cannot be used against the party in any other proceeding.

[Amended December 27, 1946, effective March 19, 1948; March 30, 1970, effective July 1, 1970; March 2, 1987, effective August 1, 1987; April 22, 1993, effective December 1, 1993; April 30, 2007, effective December 1, 2007.]

AUTHORS' COMMENTARY ON RULE 36

PURPOSE AND SCOPE

Rule 36 allows each party to require other parties to admit each relevant fact not in controversy, thereby eliminating the need to produce witnesses and evidence in support of these facts. It must be read in conjunction with Rule 26, which establishes the scope of all discovery rules.

RULE 36(a)—SCOPE AND PROCEDURE

CORE CONCEPT

Rule 36 establishes a procedure whereby one party serves requests for admission on another party, who must investigate and either admit, deny with specificity, or object to each requested admission.

APPLICATIONS

Who May Serve

Any party may serve requests for admission.

Who May Be Served

Requests for admission are limited to parties to the action, although the party need not be an adverse party.

Time for Service

Requests for admission can be served after the parties have conducted the discovery conference under Rule 26(f).[1] In proceedings listed in Rule 26(a)(1)(B) as exempt from initial disclosures, there is no preliminary waiting period for requests for admission. The Rules do not set an outer limit on how late in the case requests for admission may be served, and courts are split as to whether requests for admission are discovery devices subject to a general discovery cutoff.[2] However, many local rules or case management orders will set a limit for requests for admission. Usually, when such a time limit exists, requests for admission must be served so that the response is due before the specified deadline.[3]

Contents of Request

Each fact[4] or matter for which admission is requested should be set forth in a separate paragraph.[5] All facts that are part of the request should be set forth in the request—it is improper to incorporate facts by reference to other text. Requests for admission must be simple, direct, and concise so they may be admit-

---

[1] *DIRECTV, Inc. v. DeVries*, 302 F. Supp. 2d 837, 838 (W.D. Mich. 2004).

[2] *Kelly v. McGraw-Hill Cos., Inc.*, 279 F.R.D. 470, 472–73 (N.D.Ill. 2012) (rule 36 should not be construed inflexibly as a discovery technique); *See Freeman v. City of Detroit*, ___ F.Supp.2d ___ (E.D.Mich. 2011) (discussing the split); *Tequila Centinela, S.A. de C.V. v. Bacardi & Co. Ltd.*, 247 F.R.D. 198, 204–05 (D.D.C. 2008) (requests are governed by the discovery cut-off date).

[3] *Laborers' Pension Fund v. Blackmore Sewer Const., Inc.*, 298 F.3d 600,

605 (7th Cir. 2002).

[4] *See Fisher v. Baltimore Life Ins. Co.*, 235 F.R.D. 617 (N.D. W. Va. 2006) (a request for an admission that seeks the application of law to fact is proper); *Disability Rights Council v. Wash. Metro. Area*, 234 F.R.D. 1, 3 (D.D.C. 2006) (a request to admit a pure matter of law is improper).

[5] *See U.S. ex rel. Englund v. Los Angeles County*, 235 F.R.D. 675 (E.D. Cal. 2006) (requests for admission should not contain compound, conjunctive, or disjunctive statements).

ted or denied with little or no explanation or qualification.[6]

Scope

The scope of requests for admission is the broad discovery available under Rule 26.[7] The purpose of requests for admission, however, is to narrow the issues for trial, not to lead to the discovery of admissible evidence.[8] The requests may pertain to any issue that is or may be in the case, including the ultimate facts at issue,[9] the application of law to fact,[10] jurisdiction, or the statute of limitations, but may not seek an admission as to a pure conclusion of law.[11]

Number

Rule 36 contains no limitation on the number of requests for admission. Some districts have local rules limiting the number of requests.

Authenticity of Documents

A request may ask that the genuineness or authenticity of a document be admitted.[12] If so, a copy of the document should be attached, unless already provided.

Who Must Receive Copies

All parties must be served with a copy of the requests for admissions.

Time to Answer

A written response is due within 30 days of service.[13] The time to answer may be extended by written agreement under Rule 29.[14] Additionally, the court has discretion to lengthen or shorten the time in which a party must respond.[15]

---

[6]*United Coal v. Powell Construction*, 839 F.2d 958, 967–68 (3rd Cir. 1988); *Sommerfield v. City of Chicago*, 251 F.R.D. 353, 354 (N.D.Ill. 2008).

[7]*Johnson v. Royal Coal Co.*, 326 F.3d 421, 424 n.2 (4th Cir. 2003); *Lynn v. Monarch Recovery Mgmt., Inc.*, __ F.Supp.2d __ (D.Md. 2012).

[8]*Lynn v. Monarch Recovery Mgmt., Inc.*, __ F.Supp.2d __ (D.Md. 2012); *Erie Ins. Property & Cas. Co. v. Johnson*, 272 F.R.D. 177, 184 (S.D.W. Va. 2010).

[9]*In re Carney*, 258 F.3d 415, 419 (5th Cir. 2001). *But see North Louisiana Rehabilitation Center, Inc. v. U.S.*, 179 F. Supp. 2d 658, 663 (W.D. La. 2001) (allowing withdrawal of an admission because the ultimate issues are better decided on the merits).

[10]*Quasius v. Schwan Food Co.*,

596 F.3d 947, 950 (8th Cir. 2010); *In re Carney*, 258 F.3d 415, 419 (5th Cir. 2001).

[11]*In re Rail Freight Fuel Surcharge Antitrust Litig.*, 281 F.R.D. 1, 10-11 (D.D.C. 2011).

[12]*Booth Oil Site Administrative Group v. Safety-Kleen Corporation*, 194 F.R.D. 76, 80 (W.D. N.Y. 2000).

[13]*Zimmerman v. Cambridge Credit Counseling Corp.*, 529 F. Supp. 2d 254, 264 (D. Mass. 2008).

[14]*Tequila Centinela, S.A. de C.V. v. Bacardi & Co. Ltd.*, 247 F.R.D. 198, 204 (D.D.C. 2008).

[15]*Manatt v. Union Pacific R. Co.*, 122 F.3d 514, 517 (8th Cir. 1997); *A. Farber & Partners, Inc. v. Garber*, 237 F.R.D. 250, 257 (C.D. Cal. 2006) (responses served 2 days late deemed timely).

Service of Response

Copies of the response should be served on the propounding party and all other parties, unless the court has ordered otherwise.

Form of Response

The response should be in writing and signed by the party or the attorney.[16] It should be a single document organized in numbered paragraphs to correspond to the requests.

Responses

The responding party essentially has four possible responses to a request for admission. The party can admit the request (in part or in full), deny the request (in part or in full), set forth reasons why the party cannot admit or deny the request, or object to the request (by a specific objection or by a motion for a protective order).

Duty to Supplement

Rule 26(e) imposes a duty to supplement a denial or statement of inability to admit or deny if the party learns that the original response is in some material respect incomplete or incorrect, and if the additional or corrective information has not been provided to the other parties in writing or at a deposition.[17]

Denials

A denial must specifically address the substance of the requested admission.[18] The denial may be as simple as the single word "denied,"[19] or may be a longer sentence, but may not sidestep the request or be evasive.[20] If the propounding party feels that the denial is not sufficiently specific, the party can move the court to determine the sufficiency of the denial. If the court deems the denial not sufficiently specific, it can deem the denial an admission or order a more specific answer.

Partial Denial

If the responding party believes that part of a requested admission is accurate and part is not, the proper response is to

---

[16]The Advisory Committee Note to Rule 36(a).

[17]*See House v. Giant of Maryland LLC*, 232 F.R.D. 257, 259 (E.D. Va. 2005).

[18]The Advisory Committee Note to Rule 36(a); *Tequila Centinela, S.A. de C.V. v. Bacardi & Co. Ltd.*, 247 F.R.D. 198, 202 (D.D.C. 2008); *Fisher v. Baltimore Life Ins. Co.*, 235 F.R.D. 617 (N.D. W. Va. 2006) (the denial must "meet the substance of the requested admission").

[19]*Caruso v. Coleman Co.*, 1995 WL 347003 (E.D. Pa. 1995); *Wanke v. Lynn's Transp. Co.*, 836 F. Supp. 587 (N.D. Ind. 1993).

[20]*Asea, Inc. v. Southern Pac. Transp. Co.*, 669 F.2d 1242, 1245 (9th Cir. 1981) (evasive denial may be deemed an admission); *U.S. ex rel. Englund v. Los Angeles County*, 235 F.R.D. 675 (E.D. Cal. 2006) ("When the purpose and significance of a request are reasonably clear, courts do not permit denials based on an overly-technical reading of the request.").

admit the accurate portion and deny the balance.[21]

Inability to Admit or Deny

If the responding party is genuinely unable to admit or deny the requested admission, the party can so state, but must describe in detail why after reasonable inquiry the party cannot admit or deny.[22] A general statement that the responding party has insufficient information to respond will be treated as an insufficient answer, and upon motion the court will treat the answer as an admission or will order a further answer.[23]

Objections

Objections must be made in writing within the time allowed for answering. If answering some requests and objecting to others, the objections should be included in the document containing the answers. Typical grounds for objections to requests for admission are:

- *Privilege:* If a response requires the disclosure of privileged matters, it is objectionable.[24] *See* Rule 26 (discussion of commonly asserted privileges).
- *Vague or Ambiguous:* A request may be objectionable if it is so vague or ambiguous that the responding party cannot answer it.[25]
- *Outside the Scope of Discovery:* Rule 36 is limited to relevant matters, as defined by Rule 26. Thus, if a requested admission is irrelevant to the issues that are or may be in the case, it is objectionable.[26]

Improper Objections

An improper objection is not the same as an admission, and the proper response to an improper objection is to file a motion to compel a further response.[27] It is irrelevant who has the burden of proof with respect to the matter for which admission

---

[21]*ATD Corp. v. Lydall, Inc.*, 159 F.3d 534, 549 (Fed. Cir. 1998); *Harris v. Koenig*, 271 F.R.D. 356, 374 (D.D.C. 2010).

[22]*Lynn v. Monarch Recovery Mgmt., Inc.*, __ F.Supp.2d __ (D.Md. 2012); *Taborn v. Unknown Officers*, 2001 WL 138908 (N.D. Ill. 2001) (reasonable inquiry includes investigation and inquiry of any of defendant's officers, administrators, agents, employees, servants, enlisted or other personnel who may have information which may lead to or furnish the necessary and appropriate response).

[23]*Erie Ins. Property & Cas. Co. v. Johnson*, 272 F.R.D. 177, 184 (S.D.W. Va. 2010). *City of Rome v. U.S.*, 450 F. Supp. 378 (D.D.C. 1978), aff'd, 446 U.S. 156, 100 S. Ct. 1548, 64 L. Ed. 2d 119 (1980).

[24]*U.S. v. One Tract of Real Property Together With all Bldgs., Improvements, Appurtenances and Fixtures*, 95 F.3d 422, 428 (6th Cir. 1996).

[25]*See Erie Ins. Property & Cas. Co. v. Johnson*, 272 F.R.D. 177, 185 (S.D.W.Va. 2010).

[26]*But see Bell v. Domino's Pizza, Inc.*, 2000 WL 1780266 (D.D.C. 2000) (relevance concerns are diminished with requests for admission because they cannot be used in any other proceeding).

[27]*Butler v. Oak Creek-Franklin School Dist.*, 172 F. Supp. 2d 1102, 1122, (E.D. Wis. 2001).

is requested. Likewise, a party cannot refuse to answer a request on the basis that the serving party already knows the answer, that the subject matter is within the other party's own knowledge, that it invades the province of the jury, that it addresses a subject for expert testimony, that it presents a genuine issue for trial, that the document at issue speaks for itself, that the responding party is not the custodian of the document, or that it is more properly directed to another party.[28] Similarly, a party cannot refuse to answer a request on the basis that it pertains to ultimate facts in the case or facts for proof at trial.[29]

Opinions and Conclusions

Rule 36 explicitly states that a request for admission is not objectionable because it involves an opinion or contention that relates to fact or the application of law to fact.[30] Rule 36 does not authorize a request that requires a pure legal conclusion, without application to the facts.[31]

Motion for a Protective Order

As an alternative to making objections to individual requests for admission, the responding party may make a motion for a protective order under Rule 26(c). A motion for a protective order is appropriate when most or all of a set of requests is objectionable. The motion must be accompanied by a certification that the parties met prior to the filing of the motion and attempted to resolve their dispute without intervention of the court.

Failure to Respond

Failure to respond in a timely fashion is deemed an admission.[32] The court has discretion to allow a party to submit responses after the allowed time for a response.[33]

Motion to Determine Sufficiency

If a party believes that a response is insufficient or that an objection is improper, the party can move the court to determine the sufficiency of the answer or objection.[34] Note that "insufficient" refers to the specificity of the response, not whether the

---

[28]*Harris v. Koenig*, 271 F.R.D. 356, 374 (D.D.C. 2010); *Frontier-Kemper Constructors, Inc. v. Elk Run Coal Co., Inc.*, 246 F.R.D. 522, 531 (S.D. W. Va. 2007)

[29]*Sommerfield v. City of Chicago*, 251 F.R.D. 353, 356 (N.D.Ill. 2008); *Taborn v. Unknown Officers*, 2001 WL 138908 (N.D. Ill. 2001).

[30]*Marchand v. Mercy Medical Center*, 22 F.3d 933 (9th Cir.1994); *Lynn v. Monarch Recovery Mgmt., Inc.*, __ F.Supp.2d __ (D.Md. 2012).

[31]*Long v. Howard University*, 561

F.Supp.2d 85, 94 (D.D.C. 2008); *Miller v. Holzmann*, 240 F.R.D. 1, 4–5 (D.D.C. 2006).

[32]*In re Taylor*, 655 F.3d 274, 280 (3d Cir. 2011); *Quasius v. Schwan Food Co.*, 596 F.3d 947, 950–51 (8th Cir. 2010).

[33]*U.S. v. Petroff-Kline*, 557 F.3d 285, 293–93 (6th Cir. 2009) (responses 3 days late deemed timely); *Medina v. Donahoe*, __ F.Supp.2d __ (N.D.Cal. 2012) (late responses allowed for pro se party).

[34]*Praetorian Ins. Co. v. Site Inspec-*

response is correct or in good faith.[35] The burden will be on the party raising an objection to show that the objection was proper.[36] If the court determines that the answer was insufficient, it can deem the answer an admission or can order a more complete answer.[37] The court may also defer ruling until later in the pretrial proceedings.[38]

Expenses of Motion to Determine Sufficiency

The party losing a motion to determine the sufficiency of a response pays the other party's expenses, including a reasonable attorney fee, incurred in connection with the motion, pursuant to Rule 37(a)(5).[39]

Sanctions

The sanctions available depend upon the conduct of the responding party. The sanction for failure to respond is that the requests are deemed admitted.[40] The sanction for improperly denying a request is that the responding party will be required to pay the costs of the other party incurred in proving the matter, including attorney fees, under Rule 37(c).[41] The sanction for an insufficient answer or improper objection is that the response may be deemed an admission, plus the responding party will be liable for the other party's expenses in bringing the motion, including a reasonable attorney fee. The sanctions for failing to obey a court order to make a further response are the sanctions set forth in Rule 37(b)(2), such as deeming certain facts established or refusing to allow the party to oppose or support certain claims. Furthermore, the court must award reasonable expenses, including attorney fees, caused by the responding party's failure to comply with the order, unless the court finds that the failure was justified. Sanctions can be awarded against the party under Rule 37(c) and/or against the attorney under Rule 26(g).[42]

Appeals

The court's rulings on the sufficiency of and objections to requests for admissions are not final orders, and cannot be appealed until the conclusion of the case.

---

tion, LLC, 604 F.3d 509 (8th Cir. 2010); *Harris v. Koenig*, 271 F.R.D. 356, 372–73 (D.D.C. 2010).

[35]*Foretich v. Chung*, 151 F.R.D. 3 (D.D.C. 1993).

[36]*Moses v. Halstead*, 236 F.R.D. 667, 680 (D. Kan. 2006).

[37]*Harris v. Koenig*, 271 F.R.D. 356, 373 (D.D.C. 2010); *Tequila Centinela, S.A. de C.V. v. Bacardi & Co. Ltd.*, 247 F.R.D. 198, 202 (D.D.C. 2008).

[38]The Advisory Committee Note to Rule 36(a).

[39]*Epling v. UCB Films, Inc.*, 2000 WL 1466216 (D. Kan. 2000).

[40]*Microsoft Corp. v. EEE Business Inc.*, 555 F.Supp.2d 1051, 1058 (N.D.Cal. 2008); *Weiss v. National Westminster Bank, PLC*, 242 F.R.D. 33 (E.D. N.Y. 2007).

[41]*Lynn v. Monarch Recovery Mgmt., Inc.*, __ F.Supp.2d __ (D.Md. 2012); *Long v. Howard University*, 561 F.Supp.2d 85, 91 (D.D.C. 2008).

[42]*Johnson Intern. Co. v. Jackson Nat. Life Ins. Co.*, 19 F.3d 431 (8th Cir. 1994).

RULE 36(b)—EFFECT OF AN ADMISSION; WITHDRAWING OR AMENDING IT

CORE CONCEPT

An admission is deemed conclusively established unless the court permits withdrawal or amendment of the admission.[43]

APPLICATIONS

Proceedings Covered

An admission is only binding within the action in which the request was served.[44] An admission may be introduced at trial or in the context of a motion, such as a motion for summary judgment.[45]

Evidentiary Objections

Admissions are still subject to evidentiary objections at trial, such as hearsay.[46] However, adverse parties can use the exception to the hearsay rule for admissions of party opponents.[47]

Party Making Admission

The party making the admission may not introduce it at trial.[48]

Coparties Not Bound

An admission will only be binding on the admitting party and will not be binding on any coparties.[49]

Withdrawal

A party may move to withdraw or amend an admission.[50] The court may allow withdrawal or amendment when it will aid in the resolution of the matter on the merits and when the party who obtained the admission will not be prejudiced by the amendment or withdrawal.[51] Normally, changed circumstances

---

[43]*Pensacola Motor Sales Inc. v. Eastern Shore Toyota, LLC*, 684 F.3d 1211, 1230 (11th Cir. 2012); *Fabriko Acquisition Corporation v. Prokos*, 536 F.3d 605, 607 (7th Cir. 2008).

[44]*American Civil Liberties Union v. The Florida Bar*, 999 F.2d 1486 (11th Cir.1993); *Bell v. Domino's Pizza, Inc.*, 2000 WL 1780266 (D.D.C. 2000).

[45]*Quasius v. Schwan Food Co.*, 596 F.3d 947, 950–51 (8th Cir. 2010); *Presidio Advisors, LLC v. U.S.*, 101 Fed.Cl. 393, 398 (Fed.Cl. 2011).

[46]*Walsh v. McCain Foods Ltd.*, 81 F.3d 722, 726 (7th Cir. 1996); *Harris v. Koenig*, 271 F.R.D. 356, 373 (D.D.C. 2010).

[47]*Walsh v. McCain Foods Ltd.*, 81 F.3d 722, 726 (7th Cir. 1996).

[48]*In re Air Crash*, 982 F. Supp. 1060, 1067 (D.S.C. 1996).

[49]*Becerra v. Asher*, 921 F. Supp. 1538, 1544 (S.D. Tex. 1996), aff'd, 105 F.3d 1042 (5th Cir. 1997).

[50]*Quasius v. Schwan Food Co.*, 596 F.3d 947, 951–52 (8th Cir. 2010) (request to withdraw must be by motion); *In re Carney*, 258 F.3d 415, 419 (5th Cir. 2001) (discussing the standards for a motion to withdraw an admission).

[51]*Raiser v. Utah County*, 409 F.3d 1243, 1246 (10th Cir. 2005) (inconvenience does not constitute prejudice);

or honest error will be valid grounds.[52] Amendment or withdrawal will not be allowed where prejudice will result to the opponent from reliance on the admission.[53] The court has broad discretion in ruling on motions to withdraw or amend admissions.[54]

Binding Nature of Formal Admissions

A matter formally admitted under Rule 36 is conclusively established.[55] In contrast, an informal, extrajudicial admission is evidence, but not conclusive.[56]

Proof of Admission by Failure to Answer

In order to use the failure to answer as an admission, the offering party must prove service of the requests and the failure to answer.[57]

Additional Research References

Wright & Miller, *Federal Practice and Procedure* §§ 2251 to 2265
C.J.S., Federal Civil Procedure §§ 756 to 774 et seq.
West's Key Number Digest, Federal Civil Procedure ⊙1671 to 1686

Gallegos v. City of Los Angeles, 308 F.3d 987, 993 (9th Cir. 2002) (the prejudice relates to the difficulty a party may face in proving its case, such as problems caused by the unavailability of key witnesses, or the sudden need to obtain evidence with respect to the questions previously deemed admitted).

[52]*See ADM Agri-Industries, Ltd. v. Harvey*, 200 F.R.D. 467 (M.D. Ala. 2001) (courts should be reluctant to deny motions to withdraw or amend when final disposition of the case may result from mere discovery noncompliance rather than the merits).

[53]*Sonoda v. Cabrera*, 255 F.3d 1035, 1039 (9th Cir. 2001) (prejudice refers to the difficulty the non-moving party will have in proving its case, such as by the unavailability of witnesses related to the delay); *In re Durability Inc.*, 212 F.3d 551 (10th Cir. 2000) (the court's focus in a motion to withdraw an admission is the prejudice on the opposing party, not

on the excuse of the moving party); *Zimmerman v. Cambridge Credit Counseling Corp.*, 529 F. Supp. 2d 254, 264 (D. Mass. 2008).

[54]*Conlon v. U.S.*, 474 F.3d 616, 621 (9th Cir. 2007) (Rule 36(b) is permissive, not mandatory); *Raiser v. Utah County*, 409 F.3d 1243, 1245–46 (10th Cir. 2005).

[55]*Praetorian Ins. Co. v. Site Inspection, LLC*, 604 F.3d 509 (8th Cir. 2010) (admission under Rule 36 cannot be overcome by offering contradictory affidavits); *Central Admixture Pharmacy Services, Inc. v. Advanced Cardiac Solutions, P.C.*, 482 F.3d 1347, 1352 (Fed. Cir. 2007).

[56]*Murrey v. U.S.*, 73 F.3d 1448, 1455 (7th Cir. 1996); *Harrington v. Wilber*, 670 F.Supp.2d 958, 964, n.4 (S.D.Iowa 2009).

[57]*Gilbert v. General Motors Corporation*, 133 F.2d 997 (C.C.A. 2d Cir. 1943).

RULE 37

FAILURE TO MAKE DISCLOSURES OR TO COOPERATE IN DISCOVERY; SANCTIONS

(a) Motion for an Order Compelling Disclosure or Discovery.

(1) *In General.* On notice to other parties and all affected persons, a party may move for an order compelling disclosure or discovery. The motion must include a certification that the movant has in good faith conferred or attempted to confer with the person or party failing to make disclosure or discovery in an effort to obtain it without court action.

(2) *Appropriate Court.* A motion for an order to a party must be made in the court where the action is pending. A motion for an order to a nonparty must be made in the court where the discovery is or will be taken.

(3) *Specific Motions.*

(A) *To Compel Disclosure.* If a party fails to make a disclosure required by Rule 26(a), any other party may move to compel disclosure and for appropriate sanctions.

(B) *To Compel a Discovery Response.* A party seeking discovery may move for an order compelling an answer, designation, production, or inspection. This motion may be made if:

(i) a deponent fails to answer a question asked under Rule 30 or 31;

(ii) a corporation or other entity fails to make a designation under Rule 30(b)(6) or 31(a)(4);

(iii) a party fails to answer an interrogatory submitted under Rule 33; or

(iv) a party fails to respond that inspection will be permitted—or fails to permit inspection—as requested under Rule 34.

(C) *Related to a Deposition.* When taking an oral deposition, the party asking a question may complete or adjourn the examination before moving for an order.

(4) *Evasive or Incomplete Disclosure, Answer, or Response.* For purposes of this subdivision (a), an evasive or incomplete disclosure, answer, or response must be treated as a failure to disclose, answer, or respond.

(5) *Payment of Expenses; Protective Orders.*

(A) *If the Motion Is Granted (or Disclosure or Discovery Is Provided After Filing).* If the motion is granted—or if the disclosure or requested discovery is provided after the motion was filed—the court must, after giving an opportunity to be heard, require the party or deponent whose conduct necessitated the motion, the party or attorney advising that conduct, or both to pay the movant's reasonable expenses incurred in making the motion, including attorney's fees. But the court must not order this payment if:

(i) the movant filed the motion before attempting in good faith to obtain the disclosure or discovery without court action;

(ii) the opposing party's nondisclosure, response, or objection was substantially justified; or

(iii) other circumstances make an award of expenses unjust.

(B) *If the Motion Is Denied.* If the motion is denied, the court may issue any protective order authorized under Rule 26(c) and must, after giving an opportunity to be heard, require the movant, the attorney filing the motion, or both to pay the party or deponent who opposed the motion its reasonable expenses incurred in opposing the motion, including attorney's fees. But the court must not order this payment if the motion was substantially justified or other circumstances make an award of expenses unjust.

(C) *If the Motion Is Granted in Part and Denied in Part.* If the motion is granted in part and denied in part, the court may issue any protective order authorized under Rule 26(c) and may, after giving an opportunity to be heard, apportion the reasonable expenses for the motion.

(b) Failure to Comply with a Court Order.

(1) *Sanctions in the District Where the Deposition Is Taken.* If the court where the discovery is taken orders a deponent to be sworn or to answer a question and the deponent fails to obey, the failure may be treated as contempt of court.

(2) *Sanctions in the District Where the Action Is Pending.*

(A) *For Not Obeying a Discovery Order.* If a party or a party's officer, director, or managing agent—or a witness designated under Rule 30(b)(6) or 31(a)(4)—fails to obey an order to provide or permit discovery, including an order under Rule 26(f), 35, or 37(a), the court where the action is pending may issue further just orders. They may include the following:

(i) directing that the matters embraced in the order or other designated facts be taken as established for purposes of the action, as the prevailing party claims;

(ii) prohibiting the disobedient party from supporting or opposing designated claims or defenses, or from introducing designated matters in evidence;

(iii) striking pleadings in whole or in part;

(iv) staying further proceedings until the order is obeyed;

(v) dismissing the action or proceeding in whole or in part;

(vi) rendering a default judgment against the disobedient party; or

(vii) treating as contempt of court the failure to obey any order except an order to submit to a physical or mental examination.

(B) *For Not Producing a Person for Examination.* If a party fails to comply with an order under Rule 35(a) requiring it to produce another person for examination, the court may issue any of the orders listed in Rule 37(b)(2)(A)(i)–(vi), unless the disobedient party shows that it cannot produce the other person.

(C) *Payment of Expenses.* Instead of or in addition to the orders above, the court must order the disobedient party, the attorney advising that party, or both to pay the reasonable expenses, including attorney's fees, caused by the failure, unless the failure was substantially justified or other circumstances make an award of expenses unjust.

(c) Failure to Disclose, to Supplement an Earlier Response, or to Admit.

(1) *Failure to Disclose or Supplement.* If a party fails to provide information or identify a witness as required by Rule 26(a) or (e), the party is not allowed to use that information or witness to supply evidence on a motion, at a hearing, or at a trial, unless the failure was substantially justified or is harmless. In addition to or instead of this sanction, the court, on motion and after giving an opportunity to be heard:

(A) may order payment of the reasonable expenses, including attorney's fees, caused by the failure;

(B) may inform the jury of the party's failure; and

(C) may impose other appropriate sanctions, including any of the orders listed in Rule 37(b)(2)(A)(i)–(vi).

(2) *Failure to Admit.* If a party fails to admit what is requested under Rule 36 and if the requesting party later proves a document to be genuine or the matter true, the requesting party may move that the party who failed to admit pay the reasonable expenses, including attorney's fees, incurred in making that proof. The court must so order unless:

(A) the request was held objectionable under Rule 36(a);

(B) the admission sought was of no substantial importance;

(C) the party failing to admit had a reasonable ground to believe that it might prevail on the matter; or

(D) there was other good reason for the failure to admit.

(d) Party's Failure to Attend Its Own Deposition, Serve Answers to Interrogatories, or Respond to a Request for Inspection.

(1) *In General.*

(A) *Motion; Grounds for Sanctions.* The court where the action is pending may, on motion, order sanctions if:

(i) a party or a party's officer, director, or managing agent—or a person designated under Rule 30(b)(6) or 31(a)(4)—fails, after being served with proper notice, to appear for that person's deposition; or

(ii) a party, after being properly served with interrogatories under Rule 33 or a request for inspection under Rule 34, fails to serve its answers, objections, or written response.

(B) *Certification.* A motion for sanctions for failing to answer or respond must include a certification that the movant has in good faith conferred or attempted to confer with the party failing to act in an effort to obtain the answer or response without court action.

(2) *Unacceptable Excuse for Failing to Act.* A failure described in Rule 37(d)(1)(A) is not excused on the ground that the discovery sought was objectionable, unless the party failing to act has a pending motion for a protective order under Rule 26(c).

(3) *Types of Sanctions.* Sanctions may include any of the orders listed in Rule 37(b)(2)(A)(i)–(vi). Instead of or in addition to these sanctions, the court must require the party failing to act, the attorney advising that party, or both to pay the

reasonable expenses, including attorney's fees, caused by the failure, unless the failure was substantially justified or other circumstances make an award of expenses unjust.

(e) Failure to Provide Electronically Stored Information. Absent exceptional circumstances, a court may not impose sanctions under these rules on a party for failing to provide electronically stored information lost as a result of the routine, good-faith operation of an electronic information system.

(f) Failure to Participate in Framing a Discovery Plan. If a party or its attorney fails to participate in good faith in developing and submitting a proposed discovery plan as required by Rule 26(f), the court may, after giving an opportunity to be heard, require that party or attorney to pay to any other party the reasonable expenses, including attorney's fees, caused by the failure.

[Amended December 29, 1948, effective October 20, 1949; March 30, 1970, effective July 1, 1970; April 29, 1980, effective August 1, 1980; amended by Pub.L. 96-481, Title II, § 205(a), October 21, 1980, 94 Stat. 2330, effective October 1, 1981; amended March 2, 1987, effective August 1, 1987; April 22, 1993, effective December 1, 1993; April 17, 2000, effective December 1, 2000; April 12, 2006, effective December 1, 2006; April 30, 2007, effective December 1, 2007.]

AUTHORS' COMMENTARY ON RULE 37

PURPOSE AND SCOPE

Rule 37 contains the mechanisms for enforcing the provisions of the other discovery rules by imposing sanctions on parties who violate the Rules. In general, obtaining sanctions is a two-step process in which a party must first obtain an order compelling discovery under Rule 37(a), then move for sanctions under Rule 37(b) for failure to comply with the order. If, however, the responding party totally fails to respond to an entire discovery request, the sanctions may be available immediately.

NOTE: Rule 37 was revised in 1993, 2000, 2006, and 2007, and care should be exercised when citing case law pertaining to Rule 37.

RULE 37(a)—MOTION FOR AN ORDER COMPELLING DISCLOSURE OR DISCOVERY

CORE CONCEPT

The first step in obtaining sanctions is to make a motion for an order compelling the discovery sought.[1] A motion to compel is filed after the opponent fails to make the automatic disclosures required by Rule 26(a), fails to respond to discovery served pursuant to the discovery rules, or makes an improper or incomplete disclosure or discovery response.

APPLICATIONS

Basis for Motion to Compel

Generally, a motion to compel may be filed after a discovery request has been properly served and the opposing party has failed to respond.[2] A motion to compel may also be filed when the moving party disagrees with the objections interposed by the other party and wants to compel more complete answers.[3] A motion to compel may be filed after a witness improperly refuses to answer a deposition question.[4] A party cannot bring a motion to compel where the subject is not a discovery request to which the other party has not adequately responded.[5]

Procedures

Motions to compel are served on all parties and filed with the court. There is no set time limit for filing a motion to compel, and the court will consider delay in filing the motion and the procedural posture of the case in deciding whether a motion to compel is timely.[6]

Certification of Conference

The motion to compel must be accompanied by a certification that the movant has in good faith conferred or attempted

---

[1]*Helfand v. Gerson*, 105 F.3d 530, 536 (9th Cir. 1997) (failure to bring a motion to compel is a waiver of any future objections).

[2]*Ward v. Am. Pizza Co.*, 279 F.R.D. 451, 454 (S.D.Ohio 2012); *Wynmoor Cmty. Council, Inc. v. QBE Ins. Corp.*, 280 F.R.D. 681, 685 (S.D.Fla. 2012).

[3]*See Moreno Rivera v. DHL Global Forwarding*, 272 F.R.D. 50 (D.Puerto Rico 2011); *In re Heparin Products Liability Litigation*, __ F.R.D. __ (N.D.Ohio 2011).

[4]*See Bell v. Vill. of Streamwood*, 806 F.Supp.2d 1052, 1058 (N.D. Ill. 2011); *GMAC Bank v. HTFC Corp.*, 248 F.R.D. 182, 184 (E.D. Pa. 2008).

[5]*Ward v. Am. Pizza Co.*, 279 F.R.D. 451, 454 (S.D.Ohio 2012); *Mitchell v. National R.R. Passenger Corp.*, 217 F.R.D. 53, 57–58 (D.D.C. 2003) (prevailing party not entitled to expenses under Rule 37(a) where motion was to take additional depositions).

[6]*PCS Phosphate Co., Inc. v. Norfolk Southern Corp.*, 238 F.R.D. 555, 558 (E.D. N.C. 2006) (close of discovery often considered deadline for motions to compel where no deadline expressly set); *U.S. ex rel. Purcell v. MWI Corp.*, 232 F.R.D. 14, 17 (D.D.C. 2005) (motion to compel responses to discovery served 2 years earlier deemed timely where no motion for summary judgment pending and no trial date set).

to confer with the other party or person in an effort to resolve the dispute without court action.[7]

Which Court

The proper court in which to file a motion to compel depends on the location and status of the person that is the subject of the motion. If the individual or entity is a party, then a motion to compel must be filed in the court where the action is pending.[8] If the motion to compel pertains to a non-party witness, pursuant to a subpoena for deposition or to produce documents, then only the court issuing the subpoena can enforce it through the court's contempt powers.[9]

Expenses

In general, the victorious party in a motion to compel is entitled to recover its expenses in preparing the motion, including a reasonable attorney fee,[10] from the losing party, its attorney, or both.[11] The movant is also entitled to expenses if the respondent provides a disclosure or discovery response after the motion was filed.[12] The award of expenses by the court is mandatory unless the movant failed to confer with the respondent in good faith prior to filing the motion[13] or the losing party demonstrates that its conduct was "substantially justified,"[14] or

---

[7]*Naviant Marketing Solutions, Inc. v. Larry Tucker, Inc.*, 339 F.3d 180 (3d Cir. 2003); *LaFleur v. Teen Help*, 342 F.3d 1145, 1152 (10th Cir. 2003); *Madison v. Harford County, Md.*, 268 F.R.D. 563, 564 (D.Md. 2010) (statement that the movant tried to contact opposing counsel is insufficient); *but see Oleson v. Kmart Corp.*, 175 F.R.D. 570, 571 (D. Kan. 1997) (entertaining a motion for sanctions where the correspondence between the parties indicated that the dispute would not have been resolved by additional efforts to confer).

[8]*U.S. ex rel. Pogue v. Diabetes Treatment Centers of America, Inc.*, 444 F.3d 462, 468, (6th Cir. 2006).

[9]*U.S. ex rel. Pogue v. Diabetes Treatment Centers of America, Inc.*, 444 F.3d 462, 468 (6th Cir. 2006); *see also* Rule 45 (discussing subpoenas). *But see Platypus Wear, Inc. v. K.D. Co., Inc.*, 905 F. Supp. 808, 810 (S.D. Cal. 1995) (holding that a disputed claim of privilege should be presented to the court where the action is pending regardless of the location of the deposition).

[10]*Josendis v. Wall to Wall Residence Repairs, Inc.*, 662 F.3d 1292, 1313–14 (11th Cir. 2011); *Kister v. District of Columbia*, 229 F.R.D. 326, 330 (D.D.C. 2005) (attorney may only bill hours to the adversary that would properly be billed to the attorney's own client).

[11]*Josendis v. Wall to Wall Residence Repairs, Inc.*, 662 F.3d 1292, 1313 (11th Cir. 2011); *Interactive Products Corp. v. a2z Mobile Office Solutions, Inc.*, 326 F.3d 687, 700 (6th Cir. 2003) (motion for leave to take depositions deemed motion to compel, and expenses awarded against unsuccessful movant).

[12]*Underdog Trucking, L.L.C. v. Verizon Services Corp.*, __ F.R.D. __ (S.D.N.Y. 2011); *Tuszkiewicz v. Allen-Bradley Co., Inc.*, 172 F.R.D. 396, 398, 23 A.D.D. 985 (E.D. Wis. 1997).

[13]*Arnold v. ADT Sec. Services, Inc.*, 627 F.3d 716, 720 (8th Cir. 2010); *Board of Trustees of Leland Stanford Junior University v. Tyco Intern. Ltd.*, 253 F.R.D. 521 (C.D.Cal. 2008).

[14]*Josendis v. Wall to Wall Residence Repairs, Inc.*, 662 F.3d 1292, 1314 (11th Cir. 2011) (objections are substantially justified when reason-

if other circumstances render an award of expenses "unjust."[15] The award of sanctions does not depend on a finding of bad faith or willful misconduct by the sanctioned party.[16]

- *Substantially Justified:* Good faith generally does not equate to substantial justification; the losing party must demonstrate some unsettled issue of law or like circumstance.[17] The burden is on the losing party to show that the party's behavior was "substantially justified."

- *Opportunity to be Heard*: The court must provide the non-moving party with an opportunity to be heard, either orally or in writing.[18]

- *Who Pays Expenses:* The court may impose the expenses on the party, the attorney, or both.[19]

- *Motion Granted in Part:* If a motion to compel is granted in part and denied in part, the court may apportion the expenses as it sees fit.[20]

- *Non-parties:* The expense provisions apply only to certain motions involving non-parties.[21] Fees will be awarded in connection with a non-party making a motion to obtain a copy of the non-party's statement. A non-party may be required to pay expenses incurred because of the non-party's failure to attend a deposition if a court order had already been entered compelling the non-party's attendance.

- *Motion to Compel:* The expense provisions of Rule 37(a)

---

able people could differ as to the appropriateness of the contested action); *Arnold v. ADT Sec. Services, Inc.*, 627 F.3d 716, 721 (8th Cir. 2010).

[15]*Arnold v. ADT Sec. Services, Inc.*, 627 F.3d 716, 721 (8th Cir. 2010); *Rickels v. City of South Bend, Ind.*, 33 F.3d 785 (7th Cir.1994).

[16]*Underdog Trucking, L.L.C. v. Verizon Services Corp.*, __ F.R.D. __ (S.D.N.Y. 2011).

[17]*Pierce v. Underwood*, 487 U.S. 552, 565, 108 S. Ct. 2541, 2550, 101 L. Ed. 2d 490 (1988) (motion is substantially justified if it raises an issue about which there is a genuine dispute, or if reasonable people could differ as to the appropriateness of the contested action); *Doe v. Lexington-Fayette Urban County Government*, 407 F.3d 755, 765 (6th Cir. 2005).

[18]*Kister v. District of Columbia*, 229 F.R.D. 326, 329 n. 2 (D.D.C. 2005) (written submissions provide an opportunity to be heard); *Swackhammer*

v. Sprint Corp. PCS, 225 F.R.D. 658, 666–67 (D. Kan. 2004).

[19]*A. Farber & Partners, Inc. v. Garber*, 237 F.R.D. 250, 257 (C.D. Cal. 2006) (fees awarded jointly against party and attorney); *Hoffman v. United Parcel Service, Inc.*, 206 F.R.D. 506, 507 (D. Kan. 2002) (fees should be imposed on the person or entity responsible for the sanctionable conduct).

[20]*Josendis v. Wall to Wall Residence Repairs, Inc.*, 662 F.3d 1292, 1313–14 (11th Cir. 2011); *Kinetic Concepts, Inc. v. Convatec Inc.*, __ F.R.D. __ (M.D.N.C. 2010).

[21]*Athridge v. Aetna Cas. and Sur. Co.*, 184 F.R.D. 200, 208 (D.D.C. 1998); *Cuthbertson v. Excel Industries, Inc.*, 179 F.R.D. 599, 602 (D. Kan. 1998) (non-party who appeared voluntarily at a deposition without subpoena was not subject to the court's jurisdiction or to sanctions).

apply to motions to compel under Rule 26(c).[22]
- *Fees From United States:* Attorney fees can be awarded against the United States.[23]
- *Appeal of Fee Award:* An award of attorney fees under Rule 37(a)(5) is not a final, appealable order.[24]

Evasive or Incomplete Answer

Rule 37(a)(4) states that an evasive or incomplete answer or disclosure is treated as a failure to answer or disclose.[25]

Motion Denied

If a motion to compel is denied, the court can at the same time enter a protective order under Rule 26(c).[26] The court will award expenses to the party who obtained the protective order.[27]

RULE 37(b)—FAILURE TO COMPLY WITH A COURT ORDER

CORE CONCEPT

The sanctions listed in Rule 37(b) become available if a party or deponent fails to obey a court order regarding discovery. The court has broad discretion to impose one or more[28] of the listed sanctions or any other sanction it deems appropriate.[29]

APPLICATIONS

Order Prerequisite

The court may not impose sanctions under Rule 37(b) unless it has already issued an order to provide or permit discovery with which a party or deponent has failed to comply.[30] The order may be pursuant to a motion to compel under Rule

---

[22]*Josendis v. Wall to Wall Residence Repairs, Inc.*, 662 F.3d 1292, 1313 (11th Cir. 2011); *High Point SARL v. Sprint Nextel Corp.*, 280 F.R.D. 586, 597 (D.Kan. 2012).

[23]*U.S. v. Horn*, 29 F.3d 754 (1st Cir. 1994) (fees may be assessed against the United States as a sanction); *Cook v. Watt*, 597 F. Supp. 552 (D. Alaska 1984).

[24]*Cunningham v. Hamilton County, Ohio*, 527 U.S. 198, 200, 119 S. Ct. 1915, 1917, 144 L. Ed. 2d 184 (1999) (fee award against attorney is not immediately appealable even if attorney has withdrawn).

[25]*International Broth. of Elec. Workers, Local Union No. 545 v. Hope Elec. Corp.*, 380 F.3d 1084, 1105 (8th Cir. 2004); *Dotson v. Bravo*, 321 F.3d 663, 667 (7th Cir. 2003) (incomplete or evasive responses to interrogatories can support dismissal of the entire action).

[26]Rule 36(a)(5).

[27]*Rodriquez v. Parsons Infrastructure & Technology Group, Inc.*, 271 F.R.D. 620, 622–23 (S.D.Ind. 2010).

[28]*Young v. Office of U.S. Senate Sergeant at Arms*, 217 F.R.D. 61, 65, (D.D.C. 2003) (the sanctions are not mutually exclusive).

[29]*Anderson v. Foundation for Advancement, Educ. and Employment of American Indians*, 155 F.3d 500, 504 (4th Cir. 1998).

[30]*Smith & Fuller, P.A. v. Cooper Tire & Rubber Co.*, 685 F.3d 486, 488 (5th Cir. 2012); *Melendez-Garcia v. Sanchez*, 629 F.3d 25, 33 (1st Cir. 2010).

37(a), an order issued in a discovery conference under Rule 26(f), or an order requiring an examination under Rule 35).[31] Some courts authorize sanctions under Rule 37(b) for violations of protective orders issued under Rule 26(c).[32] Note, however, that the court may impose certain sanctions under Rules 37(c) and 37(d) without having first issued a discovery order, under the circumstances discussed below.

Exception to Order Prerequisite

Courts occasionally use Rule 37 to impose sanctions for egregious conduct in the absence of a violation of an order compelling discovery.[33]

Sanctions by Court Where Deposition to Occur

If a non-party witness fails to comply with an order to appear and be sworn in for a deposition or an order to answer a question at a deposition, the court in the district where the deposition was to occur may treat the failure as a contempt of court under Rule 37(b)(1).[34]

Sanctions by Court Where Action Pending

Rule 37(b)(2) lists specific categories of sanctions that may be imposed by the court where the action is pending on a party (or an officer, director, or managing agent of a party)[35] who fails to obey an order to permit or provide discovery. The court has broad discretion to impose any sanction or combination of sanctions it deems appropriate,[36] including the following listed sanctions:

- *Deem Facts Established:* The court may deem as established the facts that the moving party was seeking to establish.[37]

- *Prohibit Evidence:* The court may refuse to allow the

---

[31]*Smith & Fuller, P.A. v. Cooper Tire & Rubber Co.*, 685 F.3d 486, 488-90 (5th Cir. 2012); *Lipscher v. LRP Publications, Inc.*, 266 F.3d 1305, 1322–23 (11th Cir. 2001) (Rule 37(b) sanctions not available for violation of a protective order under Rule 26(c)).

[32]*See Smith & Fuller, P.A. v. Cooper Tire & Rubber Co.*, 685 F.3d 486, 489 (5th Cir. 2012) (discussing the split of authority on this issue).

[33]*Melendez-Garcia v. Sanchez*, 629 F.3d 25, 33, n.5 (1st Cir. 2010) (discussing case law allowing sanctions without an order to compel for serious disregard of discovery obligations); *Monsanto Co. v. Ralph*, 382 F.3d 1374, 1382 (Fed. Cir. 2004) (district court has the inherent power under Rule 37 to sanction abuses of the judicial process irrespective of the

existence of any particular order).

[34]*In re Sealed Case*, 141 F.3d 337 (D.C. Cir. 1998).

[35]*U.S. ex rel. Pogue v. Diabetes Treatment Centers of America, Inc.*, 444 F.3d 462, 468, (6th Cir. 2006).

[36]*Smith & Fuller, P.A. v. Cooper Tire & Rubber Co.*, 685 F.3d 486, 488 (5th Cir. 2012); *Benedict v. Super Bakery, Inc.*, 665 F.3d 1263, 1266 (Fed. Cir. 2011).

[37]*Insurance Corp. of Ireland, Ltd. v. Compagnie des Bauxites de Guinee*, 456 U.S. 694, 102 S. Ct. 2099, 72 L. Ed. 2d 492 (1982) (deeming personal jurisdiction established as a discovery sanction); *Fencorp, Co. v. Ohio Kentucky Oil Corp.*, 675 F.3d 933, 942 (6th Cir. 2012).

disobedient party to introduce certain matters into evidence, or to support or oppose certain claims.[38]

- *Strike Pleadings:* The court may strike any pleading or portion of a pleading.[39]
- *Issue Stay:* The court may stay further proceedings until the order is obeyed.[40]
- *Dispositive Ruling:* In extreme situations, the court may dismiss an action or portions of the action.[41] The court may also enter judgment against the disobedient party.[42]
- *Contempt:* The court may treat the failure to obey its order as a contempt of court,[43] with the exception of a failure to submit to a mental or physical examination (which is punishable by other sanctions, but not as contempt).[44]

List Not Exclusive

The court is not limited to the sanctions listed in Rule 37(b)(2), and may make any order that is "just."[45] In practice, however, courts generally have imposed only those sanctions listed.

Magistrate Judges

Magistrate Judges can impose sanctions under Rule 37(b).[46]

Sanctions Under 28 U.S.C. § 1927

Sanctions may also be available against a party who

---

[38]*E.E.O.C. v. CRST Van Expedited, Inc.*, 679 F.3d 657, 692 (8th Cir. 2012); *Paz v. Brush Engineered Materials, Inc.*, 555 F.3d 383, 390–91 (5th Cir. 2009).

[39]*See Smith & Fuller, P.A. v. Cooper Tire & Rubber Co.*, 685 F.3d 486, 488 (5th Cir. 2012); *Creative Gifts, Inc. v. UFO*, 235 F.3d 540, 544 (10th Cir. 2000).

[40]Rule 37(b)(2)(A)(iv).

[41]*Benedict v. Super Bakery, Inc.*, 665 F.3d 1263, 1266 (Fed. Cir. 2011); *Bay Fireworks, Inc. v. Frenkel & Co., Inc.*, 359 F. Supp. 2d 257, 262 (E.D. N.Y. 2005) (dismissal pursuant to Rule 37 deemed on the merits and with prejudice). *See also Atchison, Topeka and Santa Fe Ry. Co. v. Hercules Inc.*, 146 F.3d 1071, 1074 (9th Cir. 1998) (court may not dismiss a separate but related action).

[42]*Dreith v. Nu Image, Inc.*, 648 F.3d 779, 786–87 (9th Cir. 2011) (default judgment); *Connecticut General Life Ins. Co. v. New Images of Beverly Hills*, 482 F.3d 1091, 1096–96 (9th Cir. 2007).

[43]*Serra Chevrolet, Inc. v. General Motors Corp.*, 446 F.3d 1137 (11th Cir. 2006); *General Ins. Co. of America v. Eastern Consol. Utilities, Inc.*, 126 F.3d 215, 220 (3d Cir. 1997) (a nonparty may be held in contempt of court for violating an order requiring the nonparty to produce documents and attend a deposition); *Maynard v. Nygren*, 332 F.3d 462, 470 (7th Cir. 2003) (fines are permissible sanctions); *Jones v. J.C. Penney's Dept. Stores, Inc.*, 228 F.R.D. 190, 198 (W.D. N.Y. 2005) (attorney held in contempt for conduct during deposition in violation of order).

[44]Rule 37(b)(2)(A)(vii).

[45]*Valley Engineers Inc. v. Electric Engineering Co.*, 158 F.3d 1051, 1056 (9th Cir. 1998) (justice is the central factor in a sanctions order under rule 37(b)); *Harris v. City of Philadelphia*, 47 F.3d 1311 (3d Cir.1995); *Forsythe v. Brown*, 281 F.R.D. 577, 586 (D.Nev. 2012).

[46]*See Moore v. Napolitano*, 723 F.Supp.2d 167, 171–72 (D.D.C. 2010).

"multiplies the proceedings in any case unreasonably and vexatiously" under 28 U.S.C. § 1927.[47]

Failure to Produce Another for Examination

If a party fails to comply with an order to produce another for a mental or physical examination, the party is subject to the same sanctions that would apply if the party failed to appear, unless the party can show that the party was unable to produce the individual.[48]

Spoliation - Failure to Preserve Evidence

The importance of discovery of electronically stored information has led parties to seek orders requiring opposing parties to preserve electronically stored information. Sanctions are available under Rule 37(b) for failure to comply with such orders.[49] Courts also impose Rule 37 sanctions for spoliation of evidence in the absence of an order to preserve.[50]

Multiple Sanctions

The court may impose any combination of sanctions it deems appropriate.[51]

Expenses

The court will also require the party not complying with the court order and/or the party's attorney[52] to pay all expenses, including a reasonable attorney fee, incurred by the moving party as a result of the failure to comply.[53] This includes expenses incurred in the motion for sanctions, but not expenses incurred in obtaining the order compelling the discovery (although these expenses may be recoverable under Rule 37(a) as discussed above). The court must award such expenses unless it finds that the failure was "substantially justified" or that

---

[47]See *Atkins v. Fischer*, 232 F.R.D. 116, 127 (D.D.C. 2005).

[48]*Societe Internationale Pour Participations Industrielles Et Commerciales, S. A. v. Rogers*, 357 U.S. 197, 78 S. Ct. 1087, 2 L. Ed. 2d 1255 (1958).

[49]See *Turner v. Public Service Co. of Colorado*, 563 F.3d 1136, 1149 (10th Cir. 2009); *John B. v. Goetz*, 531 F.3d 448 (6th Cir. 2008).

[50]See, e.g., *E.E.O.C. v. Dillon Cos., Inc.*, 839 F.Supp.2d 1141, 1144 (D.Colo. 2011); *State Farm Mut. Auto. Ins. Co. v. Grafman*, __ F.R.D. __ (E.D.N.Y. 2011).

[51]See *O'Neill v. AGWI Lines*, 74 F.3d 93 (5th Cir.1996) (dismissing the action and imposing attorney's fees).

[52]*Stuart I. Levin & Associates, P.A. v. Rogers*, 156 F.3d 1135, 1140 (11th Cir. 1998); *Heath v. F/V ZOLOTOI*, 221 F.R.D. 545 (W.D. Wash. 2004).

[53]*Card Technology Corp. v. DataCard Inc.*, 249 F.R.D. 567, 570 (D. Minn. 2008) (court ***must*** award fees caused by the failure unless the failure was substantially justified or other circumstances make the award of fees unjust); *Ofoedu v. St. Francis Hosp.*, 234 F.R.D. 26, 33 (D. Conn. 2006) (expense reimbursement is the mildest sanction); *Knox v. Palestine Liberation Organization*, 229 F.R.D. 65 (S.D. N.Y. 2005) (party against whom expenses are sought must have an opportunity to challenge the expenses).

other circumstances exist that would make the award "unjust."[54] The amount of monetary damages must be related to the expenses incurred as a result of the violations.[55]

Corporate Representative

The court may also impose sanctions on a party that is a corporation or organization if its officer, director, managing agent, or designated representative fails to obey an order.[56] The party noticing the deposition will have the burden of showing that the person had the necessary relationship to the corporation.

Waiver of Sanctions

A party might be deemed to have waived its rights to sanctions by not strictly enforcing the order, such as by failing to make attempts to schedule a physical examination[57] or by failing to bring a motion for sanctions in a reasonable period of time.[58]

Conflicts with Regulations

Where compliance with a discovery order would force a party to violate a federal agency regulation, compliance with the discovery order will be excused.[59]

Appeals

Sanctions orders are normally interlocutory orders not immediately appealable, but sometimes may be appealed under the collateral order doctrine.[60]

RULE 37(c)—FAILURE TO DISCLOSE, TO SUPPLEMENT AN EARLIER RESPONSE, OR TO ADMIT

CORE CONCEPT

If a party improperly fails to make the automatic disclosures under Rule 26(a) or makes false or misleading disclosures, or if a party fails to supplement a prior discovery response as required by Rule 26(e)(1), the party generally will not be permitted to use

---

[54]*Novak v. Wolpoff & Abramson LLP*, 536 F.3d 175, 177, n.1 (2nd Cir. 2008) (award of expenses is mandatory unless the opposing party establishes one of the two exceptions); *U.S. v. One 1999 Forty Seven Foot Fountain Motor Vessel*, 240 F.R.D. 695, 697 (S.D. Fla. 2007).

[55]*Tollett v. City of Kemah*, 285 F.3d 357 (5th Cir. 2002) (discussing the method of proving attorney fees); *Martin v. Brown*, 63 F.3d 1252, 1263–64 (3d Cir. 1995).

[56]*Bon Air Hotel, Inc. v. Time, Inc.*, 376 F.2d 118 (5th Cir. 1967).

[57]*Hinson v. Michigan Mut. Liability Co.*, 275 F.2d 537 (5th Cir. 1960).

[58]*U.S. Fidelity & Guar. Co. v. Baker Material Handling Corp.*, 62 F.3d 24, 29 (1st Cir. 1995); *Tolliver v. Federal Republic of Nigeria*, 265 F. Supp. 2d 873 (W.D. Mich. 2003).

[59]*In re Bankers Trust Co.*, 61 F.3d 465, 469–70 (6th Cir. 1995).

[60]*U.S. ex rel. Pogue v. Diabetes Treatment Centers of America, Inc.*, 444 F.3d 462, 472 (6th Cir. 2006).

the information or documents not properly provided, and may be subject to a variety of additional sanctions. If a party improperly fails to admit a matter, Rule 37(c) imposes on that party the cost to the other party in proving the matter.

APPLICATIONS

Failure to Disclose

If a party fails to make the automatic disclosures under Rule 26(a)[61] in a timely manner[62] or makes false or misleading disclosures, the party will not be permitted to use at trial or in a motion[63] the documents, information,[64] expert testimony,[65] or witnesses[66] not properly disclosed,[67] unless the party had "substantial justification"[68] or the failure was harmless.[69] The exclusion of evidence or witnesses not properly disclosed is automatic, and there is no need to file a motion for sanctions.[70]

Failure to Supplement

If a party fails to supplement its automatic disclosures or to supplement a prior discovery response as required under Rule 26(e)(1), the party will not be permitted to use at trial the documents, information, opinions,[71] or witnesses not properly

---

[61]*Alvariza v. Home Depot*, 240 F.R.D. 586, 590 (D. Colo. 2007), aff'd, 241 F.R.D. 663 (D. Colo. 2007) (Rule 37(c) sanctions do not apply to informal agreements to disclose, only to the formal Rule 26(a) disclosure process).

[62]*Trost v. Trek Bicycle Corp.*, 162 F.3d 1004, 1008 (8th Cir. 1998) (failure to disclose in a timely manner is equivalent to failure to disclose); *Johnson v. United Parcel Service, Inc.*, 236 F.R.D. 376 (E.D. Tenn. 2006) (the exclusion of undisclosed evidence is automatic and mandatory unless nondisclosure was justified or harmless).

[63]*Shepard v. Frontier Communications Services, Inc.*, 92 F. Supp. 2d 279 (S.D. N.Y. 2000).

[64]*E.E.O.C. v. Serv. Temps Inc.*, 679 F.3d 323, 334 (5th Cir. 2012) (exclusion of damages information not disclosed); *R & R Sails, Inc. v. Ins. Co. of Pennsylvania*, 673 F.3d 1240, 1245–46 (9th Cir. 2012).

[65]*Frederick v. Swift Transp. Co.*, 616 F.3d 1074, 1083 (10th Cir. 2010); *Osunde v. Lewis*, 281 F.R.D. 250, 257-58 (D.Md. 2012).

[66]*Doe v. Young*, 664 F.3d 727, 734 (8th Cir. 2011); *Crispin-Taveras v. Municipality Of Carolina*, __ F.3d. __

(1st Cir. 2011).

[67]*Elion v. Jackson*, 544 F. Supp. 2d 1, 5 (D.D.C. 2008) (exclusion is self-executing sanction, and the motive or reason for failure is irrelevant).

[68]*Grider v. Keystone Health Plan Central, Inc.*, 580 F.3d 119, 141 (3rd Cir. 2009) (sanctions vacated because the court did not expressly evaluate substantial justification); *Gagnon v. Teledyne Princeton, Inc.*, 437 F.3d 188, 195–96 (1st Cir. 2006).

[69]*R & R Sails, Inc. v. Ins. Co. of Pennsylvania*, 673 F.3d 1240, 1247 (9th Cir. 2012) (burden to prove harmlessness is on the party seeking to avoid the sanction); *Crispin-Taveras v. Municipality Of Carolina*, __ F.3d. __ (1st Cir. 2011).

[70]*Goodman v. Staples The Office Superstore, LLC*, __ F.3d. __ (9th Cir. 2011); *but see Malik v. Falcon Holdings, LLC*, 675 F.3d 646, 649 (7th Cir. 2012) (defendant could not wait until discovery closed to raise its contention that the damages disclosure was inadequate).

[71]*Air Turbine Technology, Inc. v. Atlas Copco AB*, 410 F.3d 701, 711–12 (Fed. Cir. 2005); *Southern States Rack And Fixture, Inc. v. Sherwin-Williams*

disclosed,[72] unless the party had "substantial justification" or the failure was harmless.[73]

When Exclusion is a Dispositive Sanction

When exclusion of information or documents is effectively dispositive of a claim, the court will scrutinize the sanction more closely.[74]

Additional Sanctions

In addition to or in lieu of[75] precluding the evidence, upon motion and after an opportunity to be heard,[76] the court may impose additional sanctions, including:

- payment of reasonable expenses, including attorney and/or expert fees, caused by the failure;[77]
- informing the jury of the failure to make the disclosure;[78]
- deeming certain matters established;
- precluding the non-disclosing party from supporting or opposing designated claims or defenses;[79]
- striking pleadings or portions thereof;[80]
- staying the action pending proper disclosure; or
- dismissing or entering judgment as to part or all of the action.[81]

The court has broad discretion in awarding sanctions under

Co., 318 F.3d 592, 595–96 (4th Cir. 2003)

[72]Robbins & Myers, Inc. v. J.M. Huber Corp., __ F.R.D. __ (W.D.N.Y. 2011); Kinetic Concepts, Inc. v. Convatec Inc., __ F.R.D. __ (M.D.N.C. 2010).

[73]Harriman v. Hancock County, 627 F.3d 22, 29 (1st Cir. 2010) (although sanctions can vary depending on the circumstances, the required sanction in the ordinary case is mandatory preclusion); Shuck v. CNH America, LLC, 498 F.3d 868, 874 (8th Cir. 2007).

[74]R & R Sails, Inc. v. Ins. Co. of Pennsylvania, 673 F.3d 1240, 1247–48 (9th Cir. 2012); Samaan v. St. Joseph Hosp., 670 F.3d 21, 36–37 (1st Cir. 2012).

[75]Dura Automotive Systems of Indiana, Inc. v. CTS Corp., 285 F.3d 609, 615–16 (7th Cir. 2002) (additional sanctions may be imposed in lieu of evidence exclusion only if the failure to disclose was substantially justified).

[76]Paladin Associates, Inc. v. Montana Power Co., 328 F.3d 1145, 1164–65 (9th Cir. 2003) (the opportu-nity to submit briefs was an opportu-nity to be heard).

[77]Hicks v. Avery Drei, LLC, 654 F.3d 739, 745 (7th Cir. 2011); Clear-Value, Inc. v. Pearl River Polymers, Inc., 560 F.3d 1291, 1305–06 (Fed.Cir. 2009) (court should consider ability to pay in award of attorney fees).

[78]Hicks v. Avery Drei, LLC, 654 F.3d 739, 745 (7th Cir. 2011); Central States Indus. Supply, Inc. v. McCullough, 279 F. Supp. 2d 1005, 1025 (N.D. Iowa 2003).

[79]Patterson v. State Auto. Mut. Ins. Co., 105 F.3d 1251, 1252 (8th Cir. 1997) (expert's testimony about his unannounced second visit to site was precluded due to prejudice on oppos-ing party); Lodge v. United Homes, LLC, __ F.Supp.2d __ (E.D.N.Y. 2011) (the party seeking the sanctions bears the burden of proof).

[80]Second Chance Body Armor, Inc. v. American Body Armor, Inc., 177 F.R.D. 633, 637 (N.D. Ill. 1998).

[81]Vallejo v. Santini-Padilla, 607 F.3d 1, 6 (1st Cir. 2010); Wade v. Soo Line R.R. Corp., 500 F.3d 559, 562 (7th Cir. 2007).

Rule 37(c).[82]

Sanctions Apply at Trial, Hearing, or Motion

The information or witnesses not properly disclosed are most commonly excluded from trial, but also may be excluded from a hearing or motion for summary judgment.[83]

Failure to Admit

If a party fails to admit a matter that another party subsequently proves at trial,[84] the other party can move after trial for its reasonable expenses, including a reasonable attorney fee, incurred in proving the matter.[85] The court must[86] then award expenses unless one of the following four conditions exists:

(1) The request was objectionable;[87]

(2) The admission sought was of no substantial importance, such as when the proof of the matter was trivial;[88]

(3) The party refusing to admit had reasonable grounds to believe that it would be successful on the matter;[89] or

(4) Other good reasons exist for the failure to admit, such as a genuine inability to determine the truth of the matter.[90]

Party Only

Expenses and fees under Rule 37(c) may be awarded against the party only, not against the attorney, in contrast to other

---

[82]*Gagnon v. Teledyne Princeton, Inc.*, 437 F.3d 188, 191 (1st Cir. 2006); *Tisdale v. Federal Exp. Corp.*, 415 F.3d 516 (6th Cir.2005) (listing factors for abuse of discretion).

[83]*Gagnon v. Teledyne Princeton, Inc.*, 437 F.3d 188, 199 (1st Cir. 2006) (motion for summary judgment based on lack of any expert testimony following exclusion based on untimely expert disclosure); *Poulis-Minott v. Smith*, 388 F.3d 354, 358 (1st Cir. 2004).

[84]*Joseph v. Fratar*, 197 F.R.D. 20 (D. Mass. 2000) (motion for expenses for improper failure to admit may not be made until after trial).

[85]*Bradshaw v. Thompson*, 454 F.2d 75 (6th Cir. 1972); *House v. Giant of Maryland LLC*, 232 F.R.D. 257, 260 (E.D. Va. 2005) (party is not required to meet and confer or file a pre-trial motion in order to obtain sanctions for an improper failure to admit); *National Semiconductor Corp. v. Ramtron Intern. Corp.*, 265 F. Supp. 2d 71

(D.D.C. 2003).

[86]*Sparks v. Reneau Pub. Inc.*, 245 F.R.D. 583, 588 (E.D. Tex. 2007) (court has no discretion — it *shall* award fees unless one of the exceptions exists).

[87]*Russo v. Baxter Healthcare Corp.*, 51 F. Supp. 2d 70, 78 (D.R.I. 1999).

[88]*Read-Rite Corp. v. Burlington Air Express, Inc.*, 183 F.R.D. 545, 547 (N.D. Cal. 1998).

[89]*Mutual Service Ins. Co. v. Frit Industries, Inc.*, 358 F.3d 1312, 1326 (11th Cir. 2004) (the true test is not whether a party prevailed at trial, but whether it acted reasonably in believing that it might prevail); *Washington State Dept. of Transp. v. Washington Natural Gas Co., Pacificorp*, 59 F.3d 793, 805–06 (9th Cir. 1995).

[90]*Maynard v. Nygren*, 332 F.3d 462, 470 (7th Cir. 2003) (attorneys can be sanctioned for failure-to-disclose violations under Rule 26(g)(3)).

provisions of Rule 37.[91]

Improper Statement of Inability to Admit

The sanctions in Rule 37(c) apply to an improper statement of inability to admit or deny, as well as to an improper denial.

Failure to Respond to Requests for Admissions

The sanctions in Rule 37(c) do not apply to a failure to respond to a request for admissions because such a failure is deemed an admission.[92]

Explanation of Sanctions

The court order must state the basis for its decision to impose sanctions so that the appellate court can conduct a meaningful review.[93]

RULE 37(d)—PARTY'S FAILURE TO ATTEND ITS OWN DEPOSITION, SERVE ANSWERS TO INTERROGATORIES, OR RESPOND TO A REQUEST FOR INSPECTION

CORE CONCEPT

Rule 37(d) provides that upon motion sanctions are immediately available against a party who completely fails to participate in the discovery process.

APPLICATIONS

When Available

Sanctions under Rule 37(d) are available when a party fails to appear for the party's deposition after being served with proper notice,[94] fails to answer or object to properly-served interrogatories,[95] or fails to serve a written response to a properly-

---

[91]*Grider v. Keystone Health Plan Central, Inc.*, 580 F.3d 119, 141 (3rd Cir. 2009); *Wade v. Soo Line R.R. Corp.*, 500 F.3d 559, 564–65 (7th Cir. 2007); *but see Ritchie Risk-Linked Strategies Trading (Ireland), Ltd. v. Coventry First LLC*, 280 F.R.D. 147, 157 (S.D.N.Y. 2012) (sanctions allowed against party, attorney, or both).

[92]*West Ky. Coal Co. v. Walling*, 153 F.2d 582, 587 (C.C.A. 6th Cir. 1946).

[93]*Mutual Service Ins. Co. v. Frit Industries, Inc.*, 358 F.3d 1312, 1326 (11th Cir. 2004) ("[I]n cases invoking the sanction power of Rule 37 the district court must 'clearly state its reasons so that meaningful review

may be had on appeal.' "); *but see Umbenhower v. Copart, Inc.*, 222 F.R.D. 672, 675 (D. Kan. 2004) (court need not make explicit findings regarding substantial justification or harmlessness).

[94]*Wolters Kluwer Financial Services, Inc. v. Scivantage*, 564 F.3d 110, 118 (2nd Cir. 2009); *Rangel v. Gonzalez Mascorro*, __ F.R.D. __ (S.D.Tex. 2011) (a party cannot escape sanctions by telling the opponent that the party does not intend to appear).

[95]*Roney v. Starwood Hotels & Resorts Worldwide, Inc.*, 236 F.R.D. 346 (E.D. Mich. 2006); *Jayne H. Lee, Inc. v. Flagstaff Industries Corp.*, 173 F.R.D. 651, 653 (D. Md. 1997).

served request to inspect documents or things.[96] Thus, a court order is not a prerequisite to sanctions under Rule 37(d).[97] Rule 37(d) does not specify when the motion for sanctions must be filed, but some courts have held that the motion must be filed without "unreasonable delay,"[98] or before the entry of judgment.[99]

Parties Only

Rule 37(d) applies only to parties; a nonparty's failure to attend a deposition does not result in automatic sanctions under Rule 37(d).[100]

Certification of Conference

A motion for sanctions under Rule 37(d) for failure to respond to interrogatories or requests for inspection must include a certification that the movant has in good faith conferred or attempted to confer with the other party or person in an effort to obtain a response without court action.[101] Note that this requirement does not apply to the failure to appear for a deposition.[102]

Sanctions

Rule 37(d) states that the court may impose whatever sanctions as are "just,"[103] including those listed in Rule 37(b)(2)(A),[104] which are essentially the sanctions discussed above except for contempt of court sanctions.[105] The court has broad discretion

---

[96]*Alvariza v. Home Depot*, 240 F.R.D. 586, 590 (D. Colo. 2007), aff'd, 241 F.R.D. 663 (D. Colo. 2007) (Rule 37(c) sanctions do not apply to informal agreements to provide documents, only to properly served Rule 34 document requests); *Roney v. Starwood Hotels & Resorts Worldwide, Inc.*, 236 F.R.D. 346 (E.D. Mich. 2006).

[97]*Guidry v. Continental Oil Co.*, 640 F.2d 523, 533 (5th Cir. 1981); *Inmuno Vital, Inc. v. Telemundo Group, Inc.*, 203 F.R.D. 561, 566 (S.D. Fla. 2001).

[98]*See Lancaster v. Independent School Dist. No. 5*, 149 F.3d 1228, 1237 (10th Cir. 1998).

[99]*See Mercy v. Suffolk County, New York*, 748 F.2d 52, 55–56 (2d Cir. 1984).

[100]*Kamps v. Fried, Frank, Harris, Shriver & Jacobson L.L.P.*, __ F.R.D. __ (S.D.N.Y. 2011).

[101]*Black Horse Lane Assoc., L.P. v. Dow Chemical Corp.*, 228 F.3d 275, 301 (3d Cir. 2000).

[102]*Grand Oaks, Inc. v. Anderson*, 175 F.R.D. 247, 250 (N.D. Miss. 1997); *but see Simms v. Center for Correctional Health and Policy Studies*, 272 F.R.D. 36, 39 (D.D.C. 2011) (requiring a certification of conference even for failure to attend a deposition).

[103]*In re Hutter*, 207 B.R. 981, 986 (Bankr. D. Conn. 1997), aff'd, 2001 WL 34778750 (D. Conn. 2001).

[104]*Michael v. Liberty*, 547 F. Supp. 2d 43, 46 (D. Me. 2008); *Panaderia La Diana, Inc. v. Salt Lake City Corp.*, 342 F. Supp. 2d 1013, 1030 (D. Utah 2004), aff'd, 455 F.3d 1155 (10th Cir. 2006) (dismissal is an appropriate sanction when a plaintiff fails to appear for the plaintiff's deposition).

[105]*See Bishop v. First Mississippi Financial Group, Inc.*, 221 F.R.D. 461 (S.D. Miss. 2004) (dismissal for failure to appear at depositions and respond to motions); *Viswanathan v. Scotland County Bd. of Educ.*, 165 F.R.D. 50 (M.D. N.C. 1995), aff'd, 76 F.3d 377 (4th Cir. 1996) (dismissing action after claimant failed to appear at a

in deciding what sanction to impose.[106] The court can consider all the circumstances, such as whether the failure was accidental or in bad faith in determining the sanctions to impose.[107]

Expenses

The court must require that the party failing to participate in discovery and/or the party's attorney pay the resulting expenses of the other party, including a reasonable attorney fee.[108] The court must award such expenses unless it finds that the failure was "substantially justified"[109] or that other circumstances exist that would make the award "unjust."[110] The award of expenses can be in addition to or instead of other sanctions.

Objections to Discovery/Protective Order

It is not a defense to a motion for sanctions under Rule 37(d) to argue that the discovery request was objectionable.[111] The proper response to an objectionable discovery request is to file a motion for a protective order under Rule 26(c), not to ignore the discovery request.[112]

Court Order

Although a court order is not a prerequisite to a motion for sanctions under Rule 37(d), the motion may still be brought if the party failing to participate in discovery had been ordered to participate.[113]

Procedure

A motion for sanctions under Rule 37(d) is filed in the court in which the action is pending.

---

[106]*Black Horse Lane Assoc., L.P. v. Dow Chemical Corp.*, 228 F.3d 275, 301 (3d Cir. 2000); *Webb v. District of Columbia*, 146 F.3d 964 (D.C. Cir. 1998).

[107]*In re Sumitomo Copper Litigation*, 204 F.R.D. 58, 60–61 (S.D. N.Y. 2001) (case dismissed based on willful failure to appear at deposition).

[108]*Hyde & Drath v. Baker*, 24 F.3d 1162 (9th Cir.1994); *Surowiec v. Capital Title Agency, Inc.*, __ F.Supp.2d __ (D.Ariz. 2011) (pro se litigant, even if an attorney, cannot recover for his or her time).

[109]*Telluride Management Solutions, Inc. v. Telluride Inv. Group*, 55 F.3d 463 (9th Cir. 1995) (good faith but incorrect belief that the action had been dismissed was not sufficient to excuse absence from a deposition);

Kamps v. Fried, Frank, Harris, Shriver & Jacobson L.L.P., __ F.R.D. __ (S.D.N.Y. 2011) (objection to deposition notice does not excuse failure to attend unless motion for protective order was pending).

[110]*Miller v. International Paper Co.*, 408 F.2d 283, 292–94 (5th Cir. 1969).

[111]*International Broth. of Elec. Workers, Local Union No. 545 v. Hope Elec. Corp.*, 380 F.3d 1084, 1106 (8th Cir. 2004); *Kamps v. Fried, Frank, Harris, Shriver & Jacobson L.L.P.*, __ F.R.D. __ (S.D.N.Y. 2011).

[112]*Kamps v. Fried, Frank, Harris, Shriver & Jacobson L.L.P.*, __ F.R.D. __ (S.D.N.Y. 2011); *Amobi v. District of Columbia Dept. of Corrections*, 257 F.R.D. 8, 10–11 (D.D.C. 2009).

[113]*Independent Productions Corp. v. Loew's Inc.*, 283 F.2d 730 (2d Cir. 1960).

Corporate Representative

A corporation or organization that is a party is subject to the sanctions in Rule 37(d) if its officer, director, managing agent, or person designated to testify under Rule 30(b)(6) fails to appear for a deposition after being properly noticed.[114] Likewise, if a party refuses to designate a representative, the party will be subject to sanctions under Rule 37(d).[115] In extreme cases, a party who produces an unprepared or inappropriate representative may also be subject to sanctions under Rule 37(d).[116]

Refusal to Be Sworn In

A party appearing at the designated time but who refuses to be sworn in generally is not subject to Rule 37(d) sanctions.[117]

Refusal to Answer Specific Questions

A party who appears and is sworn in, but who then refuses to answer a specific question or questions is not subject to sanctions under Rule 37(d).[118] The proper procedure is for the party taking the deposition to move to compel answers under Rule 37(a), then move for sanctions under Rule 37(b) if the party still refuses to answer.[119] The same result is reached with respect to evasive or incomplete answers. However, if the party refuses to answer all or substantially all of the questions, Rule 37(d) will apply.[120]

Continuation of Deposition

Sanctions under Rule 37(d) do not apply to a party who fails to appear for the continuation of a deposition if the date of the

---

[114]*Ecclesiastes 9:10-11-12, Inc. v. LMC Holding Co.*, 497 F.3d 1135, 1147 (10th Cir. 2007) (corporation required to produce its directors, officers, and managing agents); *Atlantic Cape Fisheries v. Hartford Fire Ins. Co.*, 509 F.2d 577 (1st Cir.1975); *but see Stone v. Morton Intern., Inc.*, 170 F.R.D. 498, 503 (D. Utah 1997) (questioning the ability to sanction a corporation for failure of its officer to appear).

[115]*Ferko v. National Ass'n for Stock Car Auto Racing, Inc.*, 218 F.R.D. 125, 133 (E.D. Tex. 2003).

[116]*See Baker v. St. Paul Travelers Ins. Co.*, 670 F.3d 119, 124 (1st Cir. 2012); *Ferko v. National Ass'n for Stock Car Auto Racing, Inc.*, 218 F.R.D. 125, 142–43 (E.D. Tex. 2003) (if the representative is not knowledgeable about the designated subject matter, the appearance is, for all practical purposes, no appearance at all).

[117]*Aziz v. Wright*, 34 F.3d 587 (8th Cir. 1994).

[118]*See Baker v. St. Paul Travelers Ins. Co.*, 670 F.3d 119, 123 (1st Cir. 2012).

[119]*Independent Productions Corp. v. Loew's Inc.*, 283 F.2d 730 (2d Cir. 1960).

[120]*GMAC Bank v. HTFC Corp.*, 248 F.R.D. 182, 185 (E.D. Pa. 2008) (sanctions are available under Rule 37(d) if the deponent's conduct is so egregious that it impedes, delays, or frustrates the fair examination); *Black Horse Lane Assoc., L.P. v. Dow Chemical Corp.*, 228 F.3d 275, 301 (3d Cir. 2000) (producing an unprepared Rule 30(b)(6) corporate representative is tantamount to not producing a witness at all).

continuation was not specified in a notice.[121]

Incomplete Response to Interrogatories or Document Requests

Rule 37(d) only applies if the party fails altogether to serve a response to interrogatories or document requests. If the party serves an incomplete or evasive response, the proper procedure is a motion to compel under Rule 37(a), then a motion for sanctions under Rule 37(b) if the party does not comply with the court order.[122] Some courts allow sanctions under Rule 37(d) when the response to the discovery requests is so deficient as to be tantamount to no response at all.[123]

Failure to Preserve Evidence

Dismissal may be imposed as a sanction against parties who bring actions with knowledge that their own actions, or actions of a third party, have caused the spoliation or loss of key pieces of evidence which render defense of the action difficult.[124]

Compliance After Motion

Once a motion for sanctions has been filed, the non-participating party cannot avoid sanctions by responding to the discovery request. However, the court can consider that conduct in deciding what sanctions to impose.[125]

RULE 37(e)—FAILURE TO PROVIDE ELECTRONICALLY STORED INFORMATION

CORE CONCEPT

Rule 37(e) recognizes that certain types of electronically stored information are lost during the regular operation of a computer system. It prohibits the imposition of sanctions for failure to produce such lost information, in the absence of exceptional circumstances.

APPLICATIONS

Impact of 2007 "Restyling" Amendments

The 2007 "Restyling" Project deleted former abrogated Rule 37(e) and renumbered former Rule 37(f) as Rule 37(e).[126] In researching current Rule 37(e), practitioners should be mindful of this repositioning.

---

[121]*Miller v. International Paper Co.*, 408 F.2d 283, 292–294 (5th Cir. 1969).

[122]*Fjelstad v. American Honda Motor Co., Inc.*, 762 F.2d 1334 (9th Cir.1985).

[123]*See Melendez-Garcia v. Sanchez*, 629 F.3d 25, 33, n.5 (1st Cir. 2010).

[124]*Thiele v. Oddy's Auto and Marine, Inc.*, 906 F. Supp. 158, 161–62 (W.D. N.Y. 1995).

[125]*Antico v. Honda of Camden*, 85 F.R.D. 34, 36 (E.D. Pa. 1979).

[126]*Disability Rights Council of Greater Washington v. Washington Metropolitan Transit Authority*, 242 F.R.D. 139, 146 (D.D.C. 2007).

Data Lost Through Routine Operation

A party is generally protected from sanctions for data that is lost through the routine operation of a computer system.[127] An example of the type of data that is contemplated by this provision is the metadata (or data about data) that computers automatically store such as the last time a document was opened. Each time the document is opened, the information that was stored in that field is deleted and replaced by new data. A party would not likely be sanctioned for the loss of the data about when a document was last opened.[128]

Good Faith

The protections in Rule 37(e) are expressly limited to the good faith operation of the computer system.[129] Thus, a party cannot exploit the Rule 37(e) protections to deliberately delete relevant information.[130]

Suspending Routine Operation

Under certain circumstances, a party must suspend those features of its computer system that result in the routine loss of information.[131] A party wishing to require another party to preserve electronic data can write a letter to the party placing it on notice that the electronic data may be relevant and should be preserved, or can seek a preservation order from the court.[132]

RULE 37(f)—FAILURE TO PARTICIPATE IN FRAMING A DISCOVERY PLAN

CORE CONCEPT

If a party fails to participate in developing a proposed discovery plan as required by Rule 26(f), the court may, after opportunity for a hearing, require the party failing to participate to pay the expenses of the other party, including a reasonable attorney fee, caused by the failure.

APPLICATIONS

Impact of 2007 "Restyling" Amendments

The 2007 "Restyling" Project renumbered former Rule 37(g) as Rule 37(f). In researching current Rule 37(f), practitioners

---

[127]*Denim North America Holdings, LLC v. Swift Textiles, LLC*, 816 F.Supp.2d 1308, 1311 (M.D.Ga. 2011); *Disability Rights Council of Greater Washington v. Washington Metropolitan Transit Authority*, 242 F.R.D. 139, 146 (D.D.C. 2007).

[128]See The 2006 Amendment to the Advisory Committee Note to former Rule 37(f).

[129]*Peskoff v. Faber*, 244 F.R.D. 54, 60 (D.D.C. 2007).

[130]See *Peskoff v. Faber*, 244 F.R.D. 54, 60 (D.D.C. 2007).

[131]See *Disability Rights Council of Greater Washington v. Washington Metropolitan Transit Authority*, 242 F.R.D. 139, 146 (D.D.C. 2007); *Peskoff v. Faber*, 244 F.R.D. 54, 60 (D.D.C. 2007).

[132]See The 2006 Amendment to the Advisory Committee Note to former Rule 37(f).

should be mindful of this repositioning.

Additional Research References

Wright & Miller, *Federal Practice and Procedure* §§ 2281 to 2293
C.J.S., Federal Civil Procedure §§ 535 to 547, 640 to 644, 694, 695, 748 to 774
West's Key Number Digest, Federal Civil Procedure ⊶1278, 1299, 1451 to 1456, 1537 to 1542, 1636 to 1640, 1663 to 1664, 1685

VI. TRIALS

RULE 38
RIGHT TO A JURY TRIAL; DEMAND

(a) Right Preserved. The right of trial by jury as declared by the Seventh Amendment to the Constitution—or as provided by a federal statute—is preserved to the parties inviolate.

(b) Demand. On any issue triable of right by a jury, a party may demand a jury trial by:

(1) serving the other parties with a written demand—which may be included in a pleading—no later than 14 days after the last pleading directed to the issue is served; and

(2) filing the demand in accordance with Rule 5(d).

(c) Specifying Issues. In its demand, a party may specify the issues that it wishes to have tried by a jury; otherwise, it is considered to have demanded a jury trial on all the issues so triable. If the party has demanded a jury trial on only some issues, any other party may—within 14 days after being served with the demand or within a shorter time ordered by the court—serve a demand for a jury trial on any other or all factual issues triable by jury.

(d) Waiver; Withdrawal. A party waives a jury trial unless its demand is properly served and filed. A proper demand may be withdrawn only if the parties consent.

(e) Admiralty and Maritime Claims. These rules do not create a right to a jury trial on issues in a claim that is an admiralty or maritime claim under Rule 9(h).

[Amended February 28, 1966, effective July 1, 1966; March 2, 1987, effective August 1, 1987; April 22, 1993, effective December 1, 1993; April 30, 2007, effective December 1, 2007; March 26, 2009, effective December 1, 2009.]

AUTHORS' COMMENTARY ON RULE 38

PURPOSE AND SCOPE

Rule 38 governs the parties' right to a trial by jury and how the parties exercise their right to such a trial. Rule 38 essentially serves two functions: (1) Rules 38(a) and 38(e) describe the issues for which the parties have a right to a jury trial; and (2) Rules 38(b), 38(c), and 38(d) control the procedural aspects of making a jury trial demand and the consequences of failing to do so.

NOTE: The right to a jury trial is waived unless a jury trial demand is served within 14 days of the answer or last pleading.

RULE 38(a)—RIGHT PRESERVED

CORE CONCEPT

Rule 38 essentially codifies the Constitution's Seventh Amendment, which provides that the parties have a right to trial by jury for all suits at law with more than $20.00 in controversy.[1]

APPLICATIONS

Law vs. Equity

Under Rule 38, one has a right to a jury in all actions that historically would have been tried at law, such as actions for damages, but no right to a jury in actions that historically would have been tried in the courts of equity, such as actions for specific performance[2] or injunctive relief.[3]

Declaratory Judgment Actions

The right to a jury trial is preserved in declaratory judgment actions. If the issues would have been triable by a jury had something other than declaratory relief been sought, a right to a jury trial exists in a declaratory judgment action.[4]

Individual Issues

The right to a jury trial is evaluated claim by claim, not for

---

[1] *Jones v. United Parcel Serv., Inc.*, 674 F.3d 1187, 1203 (10th Cir. 2012); *U.S. ex rel. Drakeford v. Tuomey Healthcare Sys., Inc.*, 675 F.3d 394, 404 (4th Cir. 2012).

[2] *See Tull v. U.S.*, 481 U.S. 412, 417, 107 S. Ct. 1831, 1835, 95 L. Ed. 2d 365 (1987); *Parklane Hosiery Co., Inc. v. Shore*, 439 U.S. 322, 99 S. Ct. 645, 58 L. Ed. 2d 552 (1979).

[3] *U.S. v. Porath*, 764 F.Supp.2d 883 (E.D.Mich. 2011) (to assess eligibility for a jury trial, court must deter-

mine whether the matter would have been brought in a court of law or equity in 18th century England); *S.E.C. v. Kopsky*, 537 F. Supp. 2d 1023, 1025 (E.D. Mo. 2008).

[4] *See Simler v. Conner*, 372 U.S. 221, 83 S. Ct. 609, 9 L. Ed. 2d 691 (1963); *Beacon Theatres, Inc. v. Westover*, 359 U.S. 500, 79 S. Ct. 948, 3 L. Ed. 2d 988 (1959); *Esso Standard Oil Co. v. Zayas*, 352 F. Supp. 2d 165, 170 (D.P.R. 2005), aff'd, 445 F.3d 13 (1st Cir. 2006).

the entire case.[5] If one claim triable at law is present in the case, then the parties have a right to a jury trial on that claim; whether the primary or principal claim is legal or equitable is immaterial.[6]

Policy Favors Jury Trials

There is a strong policy in favor of jury trials, so courts will tend to allow jury trials if it is unclear whether an issue historically would have been triable at law.[7]

Governing Law

Federal law generally governs whether an issue is legal or equitable, not state law.[8] The determination of whether a party has a right to a jury trial is a legal determination subject to de novo review.[9]

Right Depends on Facts

The court bases its rulings on the issues raised by the *facts* alleged in the pleadings, not on the labels used by the parties.[10]

Jury Issues First

When there are jury and non-jury issues or claims present, typically the jury first determines the jury trial issues, then the court resolves any remaining issues. Any factual findings made by the jury are then binding on the court when trying the non-jury issues. The court may also conduct completely separate trials of jury and non-jury issues.[11] In any event, the court should endeavor not to let the right to a jury trial on legal issues be lost through a prior determination of the equitable issues.[12]

Procedural Posture

The procedural device by which the parties arrive at court is irrelevant; legal issues are tried by jury even if the claims are brought under the historically equitable joinder provisions

---

[5]*Bleecker v. Standard Fire Ins. Co.*, 130 F. Supp. 2d 726, 737 (E.D. N.C. 2000).

[6]*Beacon Theatres, Inc. v. Westover*, 359 U.S. 500, 79 S. Ct. 948, 3 L. Ed. 2d 988 (1959).

[7]*Beacon Theatres, Inc. v. Westover*, 359 U.S. 500, 79 S. Ct. 948, 3 L. Ed. 2d 988 (1959).

[8]*Simler v. Conner*, 372 U.S. 221, 83 S. Ct. 609, 9 L. Ed. 2d 691 (1963); *Jones v. United Parcel Serv., Inc.*, 674 F.3d 1187, 1206 (10th Cir. 2012) (federal procedural law controls the question of whether there is a right to a jury trial).

[9]*Indiana Lumbermens Mut. Ins. Co. v. Timberland Pallet and Lumber Co., Inc.*, 195 F.3d 368, 374 (8th Cir. 1999).

[10]*Dairy Queen, Inc. v. Wood*, 369 U.S. 469, 82 S. Ct. 894, 8 L. Ed. 2d 44 (1962); *California Scents v. Surco Products, Inc.*, 406 F.3d 1102, 1106 (9th Cir. 2005).

[11]*Beacon Theatres, Inc. v. Westover*, 359 U.S. 500, 79 S. Ct. 948, 3 L. Ed. 2d 988 (1959).

[12]*Beacon Theatres, Inc. v. Westover*, 359 U.S. 500, 79 S. Ct. 948, 3 L. Ed. 2d 988 (1959); *Starr Intern. Co., Inc. v. American Intern. Group, Inc.*, 623 F.Supp.2d 497 (S.D.N.Y. 2009).

such as class actions, derivative actions, and intervention.[13]

RULE 38(b)—DEMAND

CORE CONCEPT

Any party may make a jury trial demand. The demand then applies to all parties for the duration of the case.[14]

APPLICATIONS

Form of Demand

The jury trial demand should be in writing,[15] and can be part of pleading[16] or a separate signed document.[17] Rule 38 does not require any particular language or placement, so long as the intent to demand a jury is clear.[18] To avoid timing problems, it is advisable to include the jury demand on the complaint or answer. Note that it is probably not sufficient to indicate a jury trial on the civil coversheet or legal backer.[19] Likewise, a jury trial demand in a motion is probably not effective.[20]

Timing of Service and Filing

A party wishing a jury trial for an issue must *serve* a jury trial demand within 14 days after service of the last pleading raising or responding to that issue.[21] Normally, the last plead-

---

[13]*Ross v. Bernhard*, 396 U.S. 531, 90 S. Ct. 733, 24 L. Ed. 2d 729 (1970).

[14]*Kramer v. Banc of America Securities, LLC*, 355 F.3d 961, 967 (7th Cir. 2004).

[15]*Solis v. County of Los Angeles*, 514 F.3d 946, 954 n.11 (9th Cir. 2008) (confirming that the 2007 Amendments did not make any substantive changes to Rule 38); *U.S. Leather, Inc. v. Mitchell Mfg. Group, Inc.*, 276 F.3d 782, 790 (6th Cir. 2002) (oral jury demand during proceedings before a magistrate judge deemed insufficient).

[16]*Solis v. County of Los Angeles*, 514 F.3d 946, 953 (9th Cir. 2008) (the demand may be endorsed on a pleading); *Metzger v. City of Leawood*, 144 F. Supp. 2d 1225 (D. Kan. 2001) ("While it is not desirable to bury the demand in the text of the pleading, plaintiff is correct in stating that demand may be incorporated in a pleading.").

[17]*Davis v. Nationwide Mut. Fire Ins. Co.*, __ F.Supp.2d __ (E.D.Va. 2011) (jury demand in brief that was filed and served effective).

[18]*Lutz v. Glendale Union High School*, 403 F.3d 1061, 1063 (9th Cir. 2005) (local rule requiring a particular placement is unenforceable, test is whether a careful reader would understand that a jury trial had been demanded); *Duhn Oil Tool, Inc. v. Cooper Cameron Corp.*, 818 F.Supp.2d 1193, 1205 (E.D.Cal. 2011).

[19]*Johnson v. Dalton*, 57 F. Supp. 2d 958, 959 (C.D. Cal. 1999). *But see Wright v. Lewis*, 76 F.3d 57, 59 (2d Cir. 1996) (a jury trial demand on a civil cover sheet can satisfy Rule 38(b) if the cover sheet is served).

[20]*Bogosian v. Woloohojian Realty Corp.*, 323 F.3d 55, 62 (1st Cir. 2003); *In re Hunt*, 215 B.R. 505, 509 (Bankr. W.D. Tex. 1997) (jury trial demand contained in a motion to withdraw reference to bankruptcy court is not effective).

[21]*Marshall v. Knight*, 445 F.3d 965, 970 n. 5 (7th Cir. 2006) (jury demand may be made not later than 10 days after *service*); *Burns v. Lawther*, 44 F.3d 960 (11th Cir.1995) (look to Rule 7 for definition of pleading).

ing is the answer to the pleading raising the issue.[22] The party must also *file* the jury trial demand within a reasonable time, as provided in Rule 5(d).[23] If a jury trial demand is served after the 14th day, the court has discretion to consider the demand.[24]

Other Parties

Once one party has made a jury demand, the other parties may rely on that demand and do not need to file jury demands of their own.[25]

Amendments

An amended or supplemental pleading does not restart the jury trial demand clock for issues raised in the original pleading.[26] The focus is the issue, not the remedy.[27] Therefore, if the original complaint seeks specific performance of a breached contract and the amended complaint adds a damages claim arising out of the same breach, under the majority approach, the parties do not have the right to demand a jury trial 14 days after service of the amended complaint, unless the court directs the party to make such a demand.[28]

Removal

The removing party may make a jury trial demand within 14 days of filing the petition.[29] Others may make demands

---

[22]*See U.S. v. California Mobile Home Park Management Co.*, 107 F.3d 1374, 1378, 20 A.D.D. 658 (9th Cir. 1997) ("last pleading" is the answer to the intervenor's complaint, rather than the answer to the original complaint filed); *Winchester Industries, Inc. v. Sentry Ins.*, 630 F.Supp.2d 237, 240 (D.Conn. 2009).

[23]*Solis v. County of Los Angeles*, 514 F.3d 946, 954 n.11 (9th Cir. 2008) (confirming that the 2007 Amendments did not make any substantive changes to Rule 38); *Harrington v. Wilber*, 384 F. Supp. 2d 1321, 1324 (S.D. Iowa 2005).

[24]*Zivkovic v. Southern California Edison Co.*, 302 F.3d 1080 (9th Cir. 2002) (the district court's discretion is narrow and does not permit a court to grant relief when the failure to make a timely demand results from an oversight or inadvertence, such as a good faith mistake with respect to the deadline for demanding a jury trial); *Members v. Paige*, 140 F.3d 699 (7th Cir.1998) (district judge may require a litigant who requests an untimely jury trial to offer a reason for not meeting

the deadline); *Miller v. Merrill Lynch Credit Corp.*, 2004 WL 813029 (D. Conn. 2004) (a court's discretion to permit a late jury demand is somewhat broader in removed cases than original actions).

[25]*California Scents v. Surco Products, Inc.*, 406 F.3d 1102, 1106 (9th Cir. 2005); *Maraglia v. Maloney*, 499 F. Supp. 2d 93, 97 (D. Mass. 2007).

[26]*Mega Life and Health Ins. Co. v. Pieniozek*, 585 F.3d 1399, 1404 (11th Cir. 2009); *Huff v. Dobbins, Fraker, Tennant, Joy & Perlstein*, 243 F.3d 1086 (7th Cir.2001).

[27]*See Ramirez-Suarez v. Foot Locker Inc.*, 609 F.Supp.2d 181, 184 (D.Puerto Rico 2009). *Unidev, L.L.C. v. Housing Authority of New Orleans*, 250 F.R.D. 268 (E.D.La. 2008).

[28]*See, e.g., California Scents v. Surco Products, Inc.*, 406 F.3d 1102, 1106 (9th Cir. 2005); *Hostrop v. Board of Jr. College Dist. No. 515, Cook and Will Counties and State of Ill.*, 523 F.2d 569 (7th Cir. 1975).

[29]*Wilhelm v. Wilhelm*, 662 F.Supp.2d 424, 426 (D.Md. 2009).

within 14 days of service of the petition.[30] If a pleading is filed after the petition, then all parties have 14 days from service of the pleading.[31] If, prior to removal, a party has made a jury demand in accordance with state procedures or has made a jury demand that would satisfy federal requirements,[32] or if state procedures do not require an express demand, then no jury demand is necessary following removal.[33]

Objections to Jury Trial Demand

A party objecting to a jury trial demand may challenge it by filing a motion to strike. The Rules do not specify a time limit for moving to strike a jury trial demand.[34]

Appeals

A party that believes that the court has incorrectly denied its right to a jury trial may either seek a Writ of Mandamus or take an appeal after final judgment.[35]

RULE 38(c)—SPECIFYING ISSUES

CORE CONCEPT

A party may limit a jury trial demand to specific issues.[36] Other parties then have 14 days to make a jury trial demand for remaining issues.

APPLICATIONS

Demand Not Specifying Issues

A demand that does not specify individual issues is deemed a demand for a jury trial on all issues that are properly triable to a jury.[37]

RULE 38(d)—WAIVER; WITHDRAWAL

CORE CONCEPT

Failure to serve and file a timely jury trial demand is a waiver

---

[30]*Wilhelm v. Wilhelm*, 662 F.Supp.2d 424, 426 (D.Md. 2009).

[31]*See* Rule 81(c); *Lutz v. Glendale Union High School*, 403 F.3d 1061, 1063 (9th Cir. 2005).

[32]*Lutz v. Glendale Union High School*, 403 F.3d 1061, 1063 (9th Cir. 2005); *Wyatt v. Hunt Plywood Co., Inc.*, 297 F.3d 405, 415 n.26 (5th Cir. 2002).

[33]Rule 81(c); *Wilhelm v. Wilhelm*, 662 F.Supp.2d 424, 426 (D.Md. 2009).

[34]*Jones-Hailey v. Corporation of Tennessee Valley Authority*, 660 F. Supp. 551, 553 (E.D. Tenn. 1987) (motion to strike jury trial demand allowed one month before trial because

Rule 38 contains no time limit).

[35]*Dairy Queen, Inc. v. Wood*, 369 U.S. 469, 82 S. Ct. 894, 8 L. Ed. 2d 44 (1962); *California Scents v. Surco Products, Inc.*, 406 F.3d 1102, 1106 (9th Cir. 2005) (the erroneous denial of a jury trial is subject to harmless error analysis).

[36]*Athridge v. Iglesias*, 2003 WL 23100036 (D.D.C. 2003).

[37]*See Allison v. Citgo Petroleum Corp.*, 151 F.3d 402 (5th Cir. 1998); *Duhn Oil Tool, Inc. v. Cooper Cameron Corp.*, 818 F.Supp.2d 1193, 1205 (E.D.Cal. 2011).

of the right, even if the failure was inadvertent.[38]

APPLICATIONS

Participation in Bench Trial

A party making timely jury trial demand waives that right if the party participates in a non-jury trial without objecting.[39]

Withdrawal of Demand

Once a jury trial demand has been made, it cannot be withdrawn except with the consent of all parties.[40] Note, however, that if the case develops such that the right to a jury trial no longer exists, the court can designate the case as non-jury without the consent of the party initially making the jury demand.[41]

RULE 38(e)—ADMIRALTY AND MARITIME CLAIMS

CORE CONCEPT

Rule 38 does not create a right to a jury trial for admiralty or maritime claims.[42] However, jury trials in an admiralty claim are not forbidden.[43]

Additional Research References

Wright & Miller, *Federal Practice and Procedure* §§ 2301 to 2322
C.J.S., Admiralty §§ 216 to 218; Federal Civil Procedure §§ 943 to 950; Juries §§ 9, 11, 84 to 113 et seq.
West's Key Number Digest, Admiralty ⟐80; Jury ⟐9 to 37

---

[38]*Solis v. County of Los Angeles,* 514 F.3d 946, 955 (9th Cir. 2008) (local rule cannot create additional requirements resulting in waivers); *Bogosian v. Woloohojian Realty Corp.,* 323 F.3d 55, 62 (1st Cir. 2003) (cursory objection to bench trial cannot resurrect a waived jury trial right); *Garcia-Ayala v. Lederle Parenterals, Inc.,* 212 F.3d 638, 645 (1st Cir. 2000) (the right to a jury trial is constitutionally protected and casual waivers are not to be presumed).

[39]*U.S. v. Resnick,* 594 F.3d 562, 569 (7th Cir. 2010); *Bostic v. Goodnight,* 443 F.3d 1044, 1047 (8th Cir. 2006); *but see U.S. v. California Mobile Home Park Management Co.,* 107 F.3d 1374, 1379–80, 20 A.D.D. 658 (9th Cir. 1997) (plaintiff's filing a continuing demand for a jury trial and objecting several times prior to trial was sufficient to preserve her right to a jury trial even

though she went to bench trial and did not object at trial); *Jennings v. McCormick,* 154 F.3d 542, 545 (5th Cir. 1998) (participation in bench trial by a *pro se* party is not a waiver).

[40]*Lamex Foods, Inc. v. Audeliz Lebron Corp.,* 646 F.3d 100, 106 (1st Cir. 2011); *Palmer v. Valdez,* 560 F.3d 965, 969, n.5 (9th Cir. 2009).

[41]*Kramer v. Banc of America Securities, LLC,* 355 F.3d 961, 968 (7th Cir. 2004).

[42]*See Fitzgerald v. U. S. Lines Co.,* 374 U.S. 16, 83 S. Ct. 1646, 10 L. Ed. 2d 720 (1963); *Luera v. M/V Alberta,* 635 F.3d 181, 193 (5th Cir. 2011).

[43]*See Luera v. M/V Alberta,* 635 F.3d 181, 194 (5th Cir. 2011); *American River Transp. Co., Inc. v. Paragon Marine Services, Inc.,* 329 F.3d 946, 947 (8th Cir. 2003).

RULE 39
TRIAL BY JURY OR BY THE COURT

(a) When a Demand Is Made. When a jury trial has been demanded under Rule 38, the action must be designated on the docket as a jury action. The trial on all issues so demanded must be by jury unless:

(1) the parties or their attorneys file a stipulation to a nonjury trial or so stipulate on the record; or

(2) the court, on motion or on its own, finds that on some or all of those issues there is no federal right to a jury trial.

(b) When No Demand Is Made. Issues on which a jury trial is not properly demanded are to be tried by the court. But the court may, on motion, order a jury trial on any issue for which a jury might have been demanded.

(c) Advisory Jury; Jury Trial by Consent. In an action not triable of right by a jury, the court, on motion or on its own:

(1) may try any issue with an advisory jury; or

(2) may, with the parties' consent, try any issue by a jury whose verdict has the same effect as if a jury trial had been a matter of right, unless the action is against the United States and a federal statute provides for a nonjury trial.

[Amended April 30, 2007, effective December 1, 2007.]

AUTHORS' COMMENTARY ON RULE 39

PURPOSE AND SCOPE

Rule 39 describes the mechanisms for allocating issues for trial by jury or non-jury (other than by filing a jury trial demand pursuant to Rule 38). Rule 39 also covers advisory juries.

RULE 39(a)—WHEN A DEMAND IS MADE

CORE CONCEPT

Once a jury trial has been demanded, the docket will be so

designated and the claim will be tried to a jury unless the parties stipulate otherwise or the court determines that no right to a jury trial exists under the Constitution or federal statute.[1]

APPLICATIONS

Stipulations

The parties may stipulate to a non-jury trial, even if a timely jury trial demand has been filed.[2] The parties may also stipulate to trial by the court of specific issues.[3] Such a stipulation should be clear and unambiguous,[4] and must be made either:

- in writing and filed with the court;[5] or
- orally in open court and entered in the record.[6]

Striking Improper Jury Demand

When a party has filed a jury trial demand for an equity claim, the court should order a non-jury trial, either *sua sponte*[7] or upon motion.[8]

Jury Verdict Binding

If a trial occurs before a jury following a jury trial demand, the verdict is binding and may not be treated as advisory.

Contractual Waiver

The courts will enforce contractual agreements agreeing to waive the right to a jury trial.[9]

Waiver by Participation in Bench Trial

Participating in a bench trial without objection may constitute a waiver of the right to a jury trial, even if a timely

---

[1] *Solis v. County of Los Angeles*, 514 F.3d 946, 954 (9th Cir. 2008) (confirming that the 2007 Amendments did not make any substantive changes to Rule 39); *South Port Marine, LLC v. Gulf Oil Ltd. Partnership*, 234 F.3d 58, 62 (1st Cir. 2000).

[2] *Clark v. Runyon*, 218 F.3d 915, 917–18 (8th Cir. 2000).

[3] *Gaworski v. ITT Commercial Finance Corp.*, 17 F.3d 1104 (8th Cir. 1994).

[4] *Hupp v. Siroflex of America, Inc.*, 159 F.R.D. 29 (S.D. Tex. 1994) (failure to object is not a stipulation).

[5] *Solis v. County of Los Angeles*, 514 F.3d 946, 955 (9th Cir. 2008); *Garcia-Ayala v. Lederle Parenterals, Inc.*, 212 F.3d 638, 645 (1st Cir. 2000).

[6] *Solis v. County of Los Angeles*, 514 F.3d 946, 955 (9th Cir. 2008); *Fuller v. City of Oakland, Cal.*, 47 F.3d 1522 (9th Cir.1995).

[7] *Tegal Corp. v. Tokyo Electron America, Inc.*, 257 F.3d 1331, 1341 (Fed. Cir. 2001); *Kennedy v. Alabama State Bd. of Educ.*, 78 F. Supp. 2d 1246, 1259 (M.D. Ala. 2000).

[8] *Tracinda Corp. v. DaimlerChrysler AG*, 502 F.3d 212, 226–27 (3d Cir. 2007) (motion to strike can be filed at any time, even on the eve of trial); *Kramer v. Banc of America Securities, LLC*, 355 F.3d 961, 967–68 (7th Cir. 2004); *General Instrument Corp. of Delaware v. Nu-Tek Electronics & Mfg., Inc.*, 1996 WL 184794 (E.D. Pa. 1996) (holding that a party may unilaterally revoke a demand for a jury trial where a jury trial is not a matter of right).

[9] *Mowbray v. Zumot*, 536 F. Supp. 2d 617, 621 (D. Md. 2008).

demand has been filed.[10]

RULE 39(b)—WHEN NO DEMAND IS MADE

CORE CONCEPT

Claims for which no party has filed a jury trial demand are tried by the court.[11]

APPLICATIONS

No Jury Without Demand or Motion

The court may not impanel a jury without a demand or motion,[12] except in an advisory capacity.[13]

Rules Governing Trial by Court

Other Rules govern the procedures for trial by the court. *See* Rule 41(b) (pertaining to involuntary dismissal), Rule 43(c) (pertaining to offers of proof), Rule 52 (pertaining to findings of fact), Rules 53(b) and (e)(2) (pertaining to reference to a master), Rule 58 (pertaining to entry of judgments), and Rule 59(c) (pertaining to grounds for a new trial).

Motion for Jury Trial

When a jury demand is omitted or filed out-of-time, the court, upon motion[14] and in its discretion, may order a jury trial of claims for which a jury trial could properly have been made.[15] Courts are split on the standard for granting such motions.[16]

---

[10]*Solis v. County of Los Angeles*, 514 F.3d 946, 955–56 (9th Cir. 2008) (waiver only applies when the party is trying to get a second bite at the apple); *U.S. v. Rangel de Aguilar*, 308 F.3d 1134, 1138 (10th Cir. 2002) (allowing waiver of jury trial right by oral stipulation entered in the record).

[11]*Duhn Oil Tool, Inc. v. Cooper Cameron Corp.*, 818 F.Supp.2d 1193, 1205 (E.D.Cal. 2011); *Montanez-Baez v. Puerto Rico Ports Authority*, 509 F. Supp. 2d 152, 154 (D.P.R. 2007).

[12]*Sartin v. Cliff's Drilling Co.*, 2004 WL 551209 (E.D. La. 2004) (Rule 39(b) requires a motion by a party; the court may not employ Rule 39(b) of its own initiative).

[13]*Swofford v. B & W, Inc.*, 336 F.2d 406, 409 (5th Cir. 1964).

[14]*Ramirez-Suarez v. Foot Locker Inc.*, 609 F.Supp.2d 181, 185 (D.Puerto Rico 2009) ("on motion" requirement was inserted to prevent district courts from ordering a jury trial *sua sponte*

when the parties agreed to a bench trial).

[15]*U.S. S.E.C. v. Infinity Group Co.*, 212 F.3d 180 (3d Cir. 2000); *Duhn Oil Tool, Inc. v. Cooper Cameron Corp.*, 818 F.Supp.2d 1193, 1205 (E.D.Cal. 2011).

[16]*See Pacific Fisheries Corp. v. HIH Cas. & General Ins., Ltd.*, 239 F.3d 1000, 1002 (9th Cir. 2001) (discretion to grant an untimely jury trial is narrow, and does not permit a court to grant relief when the failure to make a timely demand results from an oversight or inadvertence); *Green Const. Co. v. Kansas Power & Light Co.*, 1 F.3d 1005 (10th Cir. 1993) (jury trial should be granted in the absence of strong and compelling reasons to the contrary); *Unidev, L.L.C. v. Housing Authority of New Orleans*, 250 F.R.D. 268 (E.D.La., 2008) (court should grant motion in absence of compelling reasons to the contrary); *Ruiz v. Rodriguez*, 206 F.R.D. 501 (E.D. Cal. 2002) (discussing the different standards ap-

RULE 39(c)—ADVISORY JURY; JURY TRIAL BY CONSENT

CORE CONCEPT

The judge may impanel an advisory jury if the case will not be tried to a binding jury.

APPLICATIONS

Verdict Non-binding

The judge is the ultimate trier of fact as to equitable claims,[17] and has complete discretion to adopt or reject the verdict of an advisory jury.[18]

Findings of Fact and Conclusions of Law

The court must make its own findings of fact and conclusions of law in cases tried with an advisory jury.[19]

Broad Discretion

The court has broad discretion as to whether to impanel an advisory jury.[20]

Binding Jury With Consent

If no claims at law are present, the judge still may impanel a normal, binding jury with the consent (either express or by failure to object) of *all* parties.[21] Consent of the parties does not require the judge to empanel a jury, it merely gives the court the discretion to do so.[22] The exception to this rule is that certain statutes prohibit jury trials in specified actions against the United States.[23]

Mixed Jury and Non-jury Issues

In a case in which a jury trial has been demanded as to some of the claims (or if the right to a jury trial exists as to only some of the claims), the court may consider the non-jury

---

plied by various courts).

[17]*The City of New York v. Mickalis Pawn Shop, LLC*, __ F.3d __ (2nd Cir. 2011) (judge sits as the finder of fact); *N.A.A.C.P. v. AcuSport, Inc.*, 271 F. Supp. 2d 435, 469 (E.D. N.Y. 2003) (the judge in an equitable action is the ultimate trier of fact even when the judge has invoked the discretionary right to empanel an advisory jury).

[18]*Schaffart v. ONEOK, Inc.*, 686 F.3d 461, 475 (8th Cir. 2012); *Hyde Properties v. McCoy*, 507 F.2d 301 (6th Cir.1974).

[19]Rule 52(a); *Kolstad v. American Dental Ass'n*, 108 F.3d 1431, 1440 (D.C. Cir. 1997).

[20]*Schaffart v. ONEOK, Inc.*, 686 F.3d 461, 475 (8th Cir. 2012); *Kramer v. Banc of America Securities, LLC*, 355 F.3d 961, 968 (7th Cir. 2004).

[21]*See Holland v. Gee*, 677 F.3d 1047, 1064, n.8 (11th Cir. 2012); *Broadnax v. City of New Haven*, 415 F.3d 265 (2d Cir. 2005) (failure to object to a trial before a jury is the equivalent of consenting).

[22]*Ed Peters Jewelry Co., Inc. v. C & J Jewelry Co., Inc.*, 215 F.3d 182 (1st Cir.2000).

[23]*See Palischak v. Allied Signal Aerospace Co.*, 893 F. Supp. 341, 342 (D.N.J. 1995).

claims as being submitted to the jury on an advisory basis.[24]

Advisory Jury With Legal Claims

Rule 39(c) states that a judge may impanel an advisory jury "[i]n an action not triable of right by a jury. . . ."[25] Some courts construe this language broadly to include any action for which the right has not been exercised.

Additional Research References

Wright & Miller, *Federal Practice and Procedure* §§ 2323 to 2350

C.J.S., Federal Civil Procedure §§ 933, 946, 1028 to 1030; Juries §§ 11, 91 to 98

West's Key Number Digest, Federal Civil Procedure ☜1991, 2251, 2252; Jury ☜25(1), 28(6)

---

[24]*AMW Materials Testing, Inc. v. Town of Babylon*, 584 F.3d 436, 441 (2nd Cir. 2009); *Everest Capital Ltd. v. Everest Funds Management, L.L.C.*, 393 F.3d 755, 762 (8th Cir. 2005).

[25]*Ernster v. Luxco, Inc.*, 596 F.3d 1000, 1006, n.5 (8th Cir. 2010) (only actions not triable as of right to a jury may be tried with an advisory jury); *Mota v. University of Texas Houston Health Science Center*, 261 F.3d 512, 526, (5th Cir. 2001) (although front pay was equitable remedy to be decided by the court, an advisory jury could be empaneled); *Epstein v. Kalvin-Miller Intern., Inc.*, 2000 WL 1761052 (S.D. N.Y. 2000) (court of its own initiative has the right to try issue with advisory jury where the claim was not triable of right by a jury, even when parties not given notice of the advisory jury in advance of trial).

RULE 40
SCHEDULING CASES FOR TRIAL

Each court must provide by rule for scheduling trials. The court must give priority to actions entitled to priority by a federal statute.

[Amended April 30, 2007, effective December 1, 2007.]

AUTHORS' COMMENTARY ON RULE 40

PURPOSE AND SCOPE

Rule 40 allows individual district courts to formulate their own rules for placing cases on the trial calendar.

APPLICATIONS

Broad Discretion

Individual judges have broad discretion in enforcing the district court's rules regarding assignment of cases. They may give precedence to cases of public importance or cases in which delay will cause hardship.[1]

Precedence by Statute

Some statutes provide for precedence for actions brought thereunder.

Motion for Continuance

The trial judge has great discretion in ruling on motions for continuance.[2]

Additional Research References

Wright & Miller, *Federal Practice and Procedure* §§ 2351 to 2352
C.J.S., Federal Civil Procedure § 934
West's Key Number Digest, Federal Civil Procedure ☞1993 to 1994

---

[1]*Clinton v. Jones*, 520 U.S. 681, 707–708, 117 S. Ct. 1636, 1650–51, 137 L. Ed. 2d 945 (1997) (the court abused its discretion in deferring trial until after president left office).

[2]*Clinton v. Jones*, 520 U.S. 681, 706–707, 117 S. Ct. 1636, 1650–51, 137 L. Ed. 2d 945 (1997).

RULE 41
DISMISSAL OF ACTIONS

(a) Voluntary Dismissal.

(1) *By the Plaintiff.*

(A) *Without a Court Order.* Subject to Rules 23(e), 23.1(c), 23.2, and 66 and any applicable federal statute, the plaintiff may dismiss an action without a court order by filing:

(i)   a notice of dismissal before the opposing party serves either an answer or a motion for summary judgment; or

(ii)   a stipulation of dismissal signed by all parties who have appeared.

(B) *Effect.* Unless the notice or stipulation states otherwise, the dismissal is without prejudice. But if the plaintiff previously dismissed any federal-or state-court action based on or including the same claim, a notice of dismissal operates as an adjudication on the merits.

(2) *By Court Order; Effect.* Except as provided in Rule 41(a)(1), an action may be dismissed at the plaintiff's request only by court order, on terms that the court considers proper. If a defendant has pleaded a counterclaim before being served with the plaintiff's motion to dismiss, the action may be dismissed over the defendant's objection only if the counterclaim can remain pending for independent adjudication. Unless the order states otherwise, a dismissal under this paragraph (2) is without prejudice.

(b) Involuntary Dismissal; Effect. If the plaintiff fails to prosecute or to comply with these rules or a court order, a defendant may move to dismiss the action or any claim against it. Unless the dismissal order states otherwise, a dismissal under this subdivision (b) and any dismissal not under this rule—except one for lack of jurisdiction, improper venue, or failure to join a party under Rule 19—

operates as an adjudication on the merits.

(c) Dismissing a Counterclaim, Crossclaim, or Third-Party Claim. This rule applies to a dismissal of any counterclaim, crossclaim, or third-party claim. A claimant's voluntary dismissal under Rule 41(a)(1)(A)(i) must be made:

(1) before a responsive pleading is served; or

(2) if there is no responsive pleading, before evidence is introduced at a hearing or trial.

(d) Costs of a Previously Dismissed Action. If a plaintiff who previously dismissed an action in any court files an action based on or including the same claim against the same defendant, the court:

(1) may order the plaintiff to pay all or part of the costs of that previous action; and

(2) may stay the proceedings until the plaintiff has complied.

[Amended effective March 19, 1948; July 1, 1963; July 1, 1966; July 1, 1968; August 1, 1987; December 1, 1991; April 30, 2007, effective December 1, 2007.]

AUTHORS' COMMENTARY ON RULE 41

PURPOSE AND SCOPE

Rule 41 controls the procedural aspects and effects of dismissals. It addresses both voluntary and involuntary dismissals, as well as the plaintiff's ability to initiate another action based on the same cause of action.

NOTE: The second voluntary dismissal by the plaintiff acts as an adjudication on the merits and will bar subsequent actions based on the same claims.

RULE 41(a)(1)—VOLUNTARY DISMISSAL; BY THE PLAINTIFF

CORE CONCEPT

The plaintiff may dismiss an action without consent of the court either by stipulation of all parties or unilaterally if the defendant has not yet filed an answer or motion for summary judgment.[1]

APPLICATIONS

Notice of Dismissal

Dismissal under Rule 41(a)(1) is achieved by filing a *notice of dismissal*, not by motion, and no court order is required.[2] The notice is effective when filed,[3] but must be served on all parties pursuant to Rule 5(a).

Timing of Notice

Unless stipulated to by all parties, a plaintiff may file a notice of dismissal under Rule 41(a)(1) only if the defendant has not yet served an answer or motion for summary judgment.[4] Otherwise, a plaintiff must file a motion under Rule 41(a)(2).[5]

Notice Unconditional

A notice of dismissal must be unconditional[6] and unequivocal[7] in both dismissals by the plaintiff and by stipulation, although the parties may privately impose conditions (such as the payment of a sum of money) on their participation in a stipulation for dismissal.

Stipulation

A stipulation for dismissal must be signed by all parties who have appeared in the action or it is not effective.[8]

---

[1]*In re September 11 Prop. Damage Litig.*, 650 F.3d 145, 150–51 (2d Cir. 2011); *Wilson v. City of San Jose*, 111 F.3d 688, 692 (9th Cir. 1997).

[2]*Michigan Surgery Inv., LLC v. Arman*, 627 F.3d 572, 575 (6th Cir. 2010); *Qureshi v. U.S.*, 600 F.3d 523, 525 (5th Cir. 2010).

[3]*Anago Franchising, Inc. v. Shaz, LLC*, 677 F.3d 1272, 1277 (11th Cir. 2012) (once the notice of dismissal is filed, the district court loses jurisdiction over the action); *Marques v. Federal Reserve Bank of Chicago*, 286 F.3d 1014, 1018 (7th Cir. 2002) (a judgment entered after a proper voluntary dismissal is void). *But see University of South Alabama v. American Tobacco Co.*, 168 F.3d 405, 409 (11th Cir. 1999) (dismissal not effective where court did not have subject matter jurisdiction and motion to remand was pending).

[4]*Michigan Surgery Inv., LLC v. Arman*, 627 F.3d 572, 575 (6th Cir. 2010) (motion incorrectly labeled motion for summary judgment did not terminate right to dismissal); *RFR*

Industries, Inc. v. Century Steps, Inc., 477 F.3d 1348, 1351–52 (Fed. Cir. 2007) (answer that had been filed and faxed but not properly served did not preclude a voluntary dismissal).

[5]*GF Gaming Corp. v. City of Black Hawk, Colo.*, 405 F.3d 876, 887–88 (10th Cir. 2005).

[6]*Hyde Const. Co. v. Koehring Co.*, 388 F.2d 501, 507 (10th Cir. 1968); *Scam Instrument Corp. v. Control Data Corp.*, 458 F.2d 885 (7th Cir. 1972).

[7]*Carter v. Beverly Hills Sav. and Loan Ass'n*, 884 F.2d 1186 (9th Cir. 1989).

[8]*See Garber v. Chicago Mercantile Exchange*, 570 F.3d 1361, 1365 (Fed.Cir. 2009); *Mutual Assignment and Indemnification Co. v. Lind-Waldock & Co., LLC*, 364 F.3d 858, 860 (7th Cir. 2004); *Camacho v. Mancuso*, 53 F.3d 48 (4th Cir.1995) (stipulation of dismissal ssigned by the plaintiff only is not effective even though all parties admit that they consented); *but see Role v. Eureka Lodge No. 434, I.A. of M & A.W.*

Effect of Dismissal

A voluntary dismissal leaves the situation as if the lawsuit had never been filed, unless the dismissal is specified as with prejudice.[9] A voluntary dismissal that is specified as with prejudice is given the same res judicata effect as any other judgment.[10] In general, a dismissal under Rule 41(a) deprives the court of any further jurisdiction.[11] If parties want the court to retain jurisdiction (such as to enforce a settlement agreement), they need to ask the court to enter an order to that effect before the dismissal is filed.[12]

Absolute Right

Generally, the right to voluntarily dismiss an action is considered absolute, not requiring assent by the court or opposing parties.[13] Likewise, the court cannot impose conditions in connection with a voluntary dismissal[14] (although it can do so under Rule 41(a)(2)).[15]

Dismissal Without Prejudice (Two Dismissal Rule)

Dismissals by stipulation are presumed without prejudice unless they specify otherwise.[16] Dismissals unilaterally by the plaintiff are governed by the Two Dismissal Rule: the first voluntary dismissal of a given claim is without prejudice; the second dismissal acts as a final adjudication on the merits and

---

AFL-CIO, 402 F.3d 314, 318 (2d Cir. 2005) ("a voluntary, clear, explicit, and unqualified stipulation of dismissal entered into by the parties in court and on the record is enforceable even if the agreement is never reduced to writing, signed, or filed").

[9]*Nelson v. Napolitano*, 657 F.3d 586, 587 (7th Cir. 2011); *Bailey v. Shell Western E&P, Inc.*, 609 F.3d 710, 719 (5th Cir. 2010); *Harvey Specialty & Supply, Inc. v. Anson Flowline Equipment Inc.*, 434 F.3d 320, 324 (5th Cir. 2005).

[10]*Norfolk Southern Corp. v. Chevron, U.S.A., Inc.*, 371 F.3d 1285 (11th Cir.2004); *but see Headwaters Inc. v. U.S. Forest Service*, 399 F.3d 1047 (9th Cir. 2005) (although dismissals under Rule 41 are commonly denominated adjudications "on the merits," only a judgment that actually passes directly on the substance of a particular claim before the court triggers the doctrine of *res judicata* or claim preclusion).

[11]*Anago Franchising, Inc. v. Shaz, LLC*, 677 F.3d 1272, 1277 (11th Cir. 2012); *Nelson v. Napolitano*, 657 F.3d

586, 588–89 (7th Cir. 2011) (although the court generally loses jurisdiction, it retains the supervisory power to consider collateral matters).

[12]*Anago Franchising, Inc. v. Shaz, LLC*, 677 F.3d 1272, 1280 (11th Cir. 2012).

[13]*Bailey v. Shell Western E&P, Inc.*, 609 F.3d 710, 719 (5th Cir. 2010); *Wolters Kluwer Financial Services, Inc. v. Scivantage*, 564 F.3d 110, 114 (2nd Cir. 2009) (the plaintiff has an "unfettered right" to voluntary dismissal, even where the reason is to flee the jurisdiction or the judge).

[14]*Commercial Space Management Co., Inc. v. Boeing Co., Inc.*, 193 F.3d 1074, 1076 (9th Cir. 1999); *Hester Industries, Inc. v. Tyson Foods, Inc.*, 160 F.3d 911, 916 (2d Cir. 1998).

[15]*Commercial Space Management Co., Inc. v. Boeing Co., Inc.*, 193 F.3d 1074, 1078 (9th Cir. 1999).

[16]*Cadkin v. Loose*, 569 F.3d 1142, 1149 (9th Cir. 2009); *Bowers v. National Collegiate Athletic Ass'n*, 346 F.3d 402, 413 (3d Cir. 2003).

will preclude a third action based on the same claim.[17]

Dismissal With Prejudice

A dismissal stipulation may specifically provide that dismissal is with prejudice.[18]

Actions in State Court

The Two Dismissal Rule applies to actions filed in state court on the first occasion. However, if the second action is filed and dismissed in state court, it will not trigger the Two Dismissal Rule[19] unless the state has a similar rule.[20] Once an action is barred in federal court by the Two Dismissal Rule, it will also be barred in state court.

Statute of Limitations

An action dismissed without prejudice does not toll the statute of limitations.[21]

Rules and Statutes Requiring Court Approval of Dismissals

Rule 41 is expressly subject to the provisions of Rule 23(e) (requiring court approval for the dismissal of a class action)[22] and Rule 66 (governing cases in which a receiver has been appointed). Rule 41 also may not apply in other statutorily controlled areas, such as *qui tam* actions[23] and stockholders' derivative actions.[24] Rule 41 does apply to appeals of certain proceedings to a federal court, such as an appeal of a decision by the Board of Veterans' Appeals.[25]

---

[17]*Anderson v. Aon Corp.*, 614 F.3d 361, 365 (7th Cir. 2010); *Murray v. Conseco, Inc.*, 467 F.3d 602, 605 (7th Cir. 2006) (dismissal for lack of subject matter does not implicate the Two Dismissal Rule); *American Cyanamid Co. v. Capuano*, 381 F.3d 6, 17 (1st Cir. 2004) (two dismissal rule applies only to the defendants of the dismissed actions or those in privity); *ASX Inv. Corp. v. Newton*, 183 F.3d 1265, 1267–68 (11th Cir. 1999) (Two Dismissal Rule does not count a dismissal by court order under Rule 41(a)(2)).

[18]*Norfolk Southern Corp. v. Chevron, U.S.A., Inc.*, 371 F.3d 1285 (11th Cir.2004) (a stipulation of dismissal with prejudice is given the same res judicata effect as any other judgment).

[19]*Rader v. Baltimore & O. R. Co.*, 108 F.2d 980 (C.C.A. 7th Cir. 1940).

[20]*Manning v. South Carolina Dept. of Highway and Public Transp.*, 914 F.2d 44 (4th Cir.1990).

[21]*Beck v. Caterpillar Inc.*, 50 F.3d 405 (7th Cir.1995).

[22]*Crawford v. F. Hoffman-La Roche Ltd.*, 267 F.3d 760, 764 (8th Cir. 2001); *In re Painewebber Limited Partnerships Litigation*, 147 F.3d 132, 137 (2d Cir. 1998).

[23]*Bailey v. Shell Western E&P, Inc.*, 609 F.3d 710, 719 (5th Cir. 2010); *Luka v. Procter and Gamble Co.*, — F.Supp.2d — (N.D.Ill. 2011).

[24]*Baker v. America's Mortg. Servicing, Inc.*, 58 F.3d 321 (7th Cir. 1995).

[25]*Graves v. Principi*, 294 F.3d 1350 (Fed. Cir. 2002).

Removal
Rule 41 applies with equal force to cases removed from state court.[26]

Rule 12 Motions
In general, a motion to dismiss pursuant to Rule 12(b) for failure to state a claim or for lack of jurisdiction or venue does not terminate the plaintiff's unilateral right to dismiss.[27] An exception may arise if the court has held extensive hearings on the motion,[28] or converted the motion to dismiss into a motion for summary judgment.[29]

Dismissal of Part of Action
Courts differ as to the proper procedural mechanism for voluntarily dismissing part of an action. Some courts allow voluntary dismissal of part of an action by notice pursuant to Rule 41.[30] Some courts require a motion to amend pursuant to Rule 15(a).[31] A third party plaintiff may voluntarily dismiss the third party complaint under Rule 41(a)(1).[32]

Costs and Fees
Following a voluntary dismissal under Rule 41, the district court retains jurisdiction over the matter such that the court may award costs to the defendant.[33] The defendant is not considered the prevailing party following a voluntary dismissal pursuant to Rule 41(a)(1) for purposes of statutes governing the award of attorney fees to the prevailing party.[34]

Enforcement of Settlement Agreement
Normally, a federal court does not have jurisdiction over an action to enforce the terms of a settlement agreement. In order to vest the court with such jurisdiction, the parties can include language in their Rule 41(a)(1)(ii) stipulation for dismissal

---

[26]*Grivas v. Parmelee Transp. Co.,* 207 F.2d 334 (7th Cir. 1953).

[27]*Manze v. State Farm Ins. Co.,* 817 F.2d 1062, 1066 (3d Cir. 1987).

[28]*Harvey Aluminum, Inc. v. American Cyanamid Co.,* 203 F.2d 105 (2d Cir. 1953).

[29]*In re Bath and Kitchen Fixtures Antitrust Litigation,* 535 F.3d 161, 166 (3d Cir. 2008) (motion to dismiss including new factual material does not cut off the right to voluntary dismissal until it is actually converted into a motion for summary judgment); *Swedberg v. Marotzke,* 339 F.3d 1139 (9th Cir. 2003); *Hamm v. Rhone-Poulenc Rorer Pharmaceuticals, Inc.,* 187 F.3d 941, 950 (8th Cir. 1999); *Finley Lines Joint Protective Bd. Unit 200 v. Norfolk Southern Corp.,* 109 F.3d 993 (4th Cir. 1997).

[30]*See Bowers v. National Collegiate Athletic Ass'n,* 346 F.3d 402, 413 (3d Cir. 2003); *Commercial Space Management Co., Inc. v. Boeing Co., Inc.,* 193 F.3d 1074, 1079 (9th Cir. 1999).

[31]*See Campbell v. Altec Industries, Inc.,* __ F.3d __ (11th Cir. 2010); *Ramirez v. Miami-Dade Cnty.,* 846 F.Supp.2d 1308, 1313 (S.D.Fla. 2012).

[32]*Century Mfg. Co., Inc. v. Central Transport Intern., Inc.,* 209 F.R.D. 647 (D. Mass. 2002).

[33]*Sequa Corp. v. Cooper,* 245 F.3d 1036, 1037 (8th Cir. 2001).

[34]*See RFR Industries, Inc. v. Century Steps, Inc.,* 477 F.3d 1348, 1351–52 (Fed. Cir. 2007) (the defendant not the prevailing party for purposes of 35 U.S.C. § 285).

providing that the court will retain jurisdiction for purposes of enforcing the settlement agreement.[35]

Appeals

The first voluntary dismissal under Rule 41(a)(1) is normally not considered a final order and thus not appealable.[36] The second dismissal, however, is a final, appealable order.[37]

RULE 41(a)(2)—BY COURT ORDER; EFFECT

CORE CONCEPT

Except as provided in Rule 41(a)(1) above (dismissal by stipulation or before an answer or motion for summary judgment has been filed), dismissal of an action must be by court order.[38]

APPLICATIONS

Prejudice

A dismissal by order of court can be with or without prejudice.[39] A court order granting voluntary dismissal is presumed to be without prejudice unless it explicitly specifies otherwise.[40]

Discretion of Court

The decision whether to grant or deny the plaintiff's motion for voluntary dismissal is within the sound discretion of the court,[41] although some courts hold that the court had no discretion to deny a motion to dismiss *with prejudice* (reasoning that it is unfair to force an unwilling plaintiff to go to trial).[42] A court should grant a Rule 41(a)(2) motion for voluntary dismissal unless a defendant can show that it will suffer some

---

[35]*Kokkonen v. Guardian Life Ins. Co. of America*, 511 U.S. 375, 378–81, 114 S. Ct. 1673, 1675–1677, 128 L. Ed. 2d 391 (1994); *Anago Franchising, Inc. v. Shaz, LLC*, 677 F.3d 1272, 1280 (11th Cir. 2012).

[36]*Versa Products, Inc. v. Home Depot, USA, Inc.*, 387 F.3d 1325 (11th Cir. 2004); *State Treasurer of State of Michigan v. Barry*, 168 F.3d 8, 11 (11th Cir. 1999).

[37]*Muzikowski v. Paramount Pictures Corp.*, 322 F.3d 918, 923–24 (7th Cir. 2003).

[38]*National Inspection & Repairs, Inc. v. George S. May Intern. Co.*, 600 F.3d 878, 883 (7th Cir. 2010); *Wilson v. City of San Jose*, 111 F.3d 688, 692 (9th Cir. 1997).

[39]*See, e.g., Minnesota Mining And Mfg. Co. v. Barr Laboratories, Inc.*, 289 F.3d 775, 779 (Fed. Cir. 2002).

[40]*Romoland School Dist. v. Inland Empire Energy Center, LLC*, 548 F.3d 738, 748 (9th Cir. 2008); *LeBlang Motors, Ltd. v. Subaru of America, Inc.*, 148 F.3d 680, 687 (7th Cir. 1998) (dismissal deemed with prejudice even though the defendant's motion only asked for dismissal without prejudice).

[41]*Walter Kidde Portable Equipment, Inc. v. Universal Sec. Instruments, Inc.*, 479 F.3d 1330, 1336 (Fed. Cir. 2007) (dismissal within the court's discretion as long as there is no impairment of the defendant's rights); *Camilli v. Grimes*, 436 F.3d 120, 123 (2d Cir. 2006).

[42]*Smoot v. Fox*, 340 F.2d 301 (6th Cir.1964).

plain legal prejudice as a result.[43] In general, courts are more likely to grant motions for voluntary dismissal at earlier stages of the litigation.[44]

Conditions

The court may include terms and conditions in its order granting voluntary dismissal in order to prevent prejudice to the defendant.[45] These conditions may be proposed by the parties or *sua sponte* by the court.[46] Examples of such conditions include the payment of costs[47] and/or attorney fees,[48] the production of specified documents,[49] making the dismissal with prejudice,[50] and an agreement not to assert specified claims in another action. If the plaintiff is unhappy with the conditions imposed by the court, the plaintiff may decline the dismissal.[51]

Defendant as Prevailing Party

For purposes of statutes that award costs or fees to the prevailing party, a defendant can be deemed the prevailing

---

[43]*WPP Luxembourg Gamma Three Sarl v. Spot Runner, Inc.*, 655 F.3d 1039, 1058, n.6 (9th Cir. 2011); *In re FEMA Trailer Formaldahyde Products Liability Litigation*, 628 F.3d 157, 163 (5th Cir. 2010).

[44]*See Thatcher v. Hanover Ins. Grp., Inc.*, 659 F.3d 1212, 1214 (8th Cir. 2011); *Jones v. Simek*, 193 F.3d 485, 491 (7th Cir. 1999).

[45]*In re FEMA Trailer Formaldahyde Products Liability Litigation*, 628 F.3d 157, 163 (5th Cir. 2010); *Bridgeport Music, Inc. v. Universal-MCA Music Pub., Inc.*, 583 F.3d 948, 953 (6th Cir. 2009) (the purpose of conditions is to avoid prejudice to the nonmoving party).

[46]*Brown v. Baeke*, 413 F.3d 1121, 1123 (10th Cir. 2005) (some conditions proposed by the plaintiff, and others added by the court).

[47]*Chavez v. Illinois State Police*, 251 F.3d 612 (7th Cir.2001); *Williams v. Peralta Community College Dist.*, 227 F.R.D. 538, 540 (N.D. Cal. 2005) (listing factors for deciding whether to award costs); *ACEquip, Ltd. v. Am. Eng'g Corp.*, 219 F.R.D. 44, 46 (D. Conn. 2003) (deciding not to award costs, but requiring that any future action be filed in the same court).

[48]*Steinert v. Winn Group, Inc.*, 440 F.3d 1214, 1222 (10th Cir. 2006) (when dismissal is *without* prejudice,

attorney fees should only be awarded in extreme circumstances); *Brown v. Local 58, Intern. Broth. of Elec. Workers, AFL-CIO*, 76 F.3d 762, 766–67 (6th Cir. 1996); *Hinfin Realty Corp. v. The Pittston Co.*, 212 F.R.D. 461, 462 (E.D. N.Y. 2002) (courts often grant fee awards when a plaintiff dismisses a suit without prejudice under Rule 41(a)(2)); *BD ex rel. Jean Doe v. DeBuono*, 193 F.R.D. 117 (S.D. N.Y. 2000) (attorney fees awarded only where conduct of the plaintiff was in bad faith or vexatious).

[49]*In re Vitamins Antitrust Litigation*, 198 F.R.D. 296 (D.D.C. 2000) (dismissal conditioned on the plaintiff responding to outstanding document requests and interrogatories).

[50]*Michigan Surgery Inv., LLC v. Arman*, 627 F.3d 572, 575 (6th Cir. 2010) (must give the plaintiff notice and an opportunity to withdraw the motion before making dismissal with prejudice); *Elbaor v. Tripath Imaging, Inc.*, 279 F.3d 314, 316 n.1 (5th Cir. 2002) (the court may require the dismissal to be with prejudice to protect the defendant, but not to punish the plaintiff).

[51]*Michigan Surgery Inv., LLC v. Arman*, 627 F.3d 572, 575 (6th Cir. 2010); *In re FEMA Trailer Formaldahyde Products Liability Litigation*, 628 F.3d 157, 163 (5th Cir. 2010).

party following a dismissal under Rule 41(a)(2).[52]

Counterclaims

If the defendant has filed a counterclaim, then the plaintiff cannot dismiss the action against the defendant's objections unless the counterclaim can remain pending for adjudication.[53] The defendant may dismiss its own counterclaim in the same manner that Rule 41 provides for dismissal of the plaintiff's claims.[54]

Dismissal of Part of Action

The plaintiff may dismiss some, but not all, of the defendants.[55] Courts differ as to the proper procedural mechanism for voluntarily dismissing part of an action after an answer or summary judgment motion has been filed.[56] Some courts allow voluntary dismissal by court order pursuant to Rule 41(a)(2).[57] Some courts require a motion to amend pursuant to Rule 15(a).[58]

Enforcement of Settlement Agreement

Normally, a federal court does not have jurisdiction over an action to enforce the terms of a settlement and stipulated dismissal.[59] In order to vest the district court with such jurisdiction, the court may, at its discretion, make the parties' compliance with a settlement agreement part of its dismissal order.[60]

Circumvention of Rule 39(b)

A district court may not use Rule 41(a)(2) to allow an untimely jury demand (by dismissal, then refiling a new com-

---

[52]*Riviera Distributors, Inc. v. Jones*, 517 F.3d 926, 928 (7th Cir. 2008); *Richardson v. Tex-Tube Co.*, 843 F.Supp.2d 699, 704-06 (S.D.Tex. 2012).

[53]*See Walter Kidde Portable Equipment, Inc. v. Universal Sec. Instruments, Inc.*, 479 F.3d 1330, 1336 (Fed. Cir. 2007); *Esso Standard Oil Co. (Puerto Rico) v. Rodriguez-Perez*, 455 F.3d 1 (1st Cir. 2006).

[54]*eCash Technologies, Inc. v. Guagliardo*, 127 F. Supp. 2d 1069, 1081–82 (C.D. Cal. 2000), aff'd, 35 Fed. Appx. 498 (9th Cir. 2002).

[55]*Disabled in Action of Pennsylvania v. Southeastern Pennsylvania Transp. Authority*, 224 F.R.D. 601, 605 (E.D. Pa. 2004); *Protocomm Corp. v. Novell, Inc.*, 171 F. Supp. 2d 459, 471 (E.D. Pa. 2001) (dismissal of some defendants is permissible even in the presence of cross-claims).

[56]*See Jet, Inc. v. Sewage Aeration Systems*, 223 F.3d 1360, 1364 (Fed. Cir. 2000) (Rule 41(a)(2) and Rule 15(a) are functionally interchangeable); *State Treasurer of State of Michigan v. Barry*, 168 F.3d 8, 18 (11th Cir. 1999).

[57]*See Transwitch Corp. v. Galazar Networks, Inc.*, 377 F. Supp. 2d 284 (D. Mass. 2005) (allowing motion for voluntary dismissal of all claims and substitution of new claims under Rule 42).

[58]*See Campbell v. Altec Industries, Inc.*, __ F.3d __ (11th Cir. 2010).

[59]*Solv-Ex Corp. v. Quillen*, 186 F.R.D. 313, 315 (S.D. N.Y. 1999); *Lee v. Runyon*, 18 F. Supp. 2d 649, 653 (E.D. Tex. 1998).

[60]*Kokkonen v. Guardian Life Ins. Co. of America*, 511 U.S. 375, 114 S. Ct. 1673, 128 L. Ed. 2d 391 (1994); *Bragg v. Robertson*, 54 F. Supp. 2d 653, 662–63 (S.D. W. Va. 1999).

plaint with a jury demand) if it would be prohibited from doing so under Rule 39(b), as that would introduce an unnecessary conflict between the two federal rules.[61]

Appeal

The Plaintiff normally cannot appeal the granting or denial of a motion for voluntary dismissal.[62] However, mandamus will lie if the motion was to dismiss with prejudice.[63] The plaintiff may be able to appeal the granting of its own motion to dismiss if the court imposes conditions on the dismissal that prejudice the plaintiff and to which the plaintiff has not acquiesced.[64] The plaintiff may not appeal prior rulings in an action if the action is dismissed without prejudice.[65] The defendant may appeal a notice of voluntary dismissal[66] or an order granting a motion for voluntary dismissal.[67]

RULE 41(b)—INVOLUNTARY DISMISSAL; EFFECT

CORE CONCEPT

Rule 41(b) governs two types of involuntary dismissals: dismissal for failure to prosecute; and dismissal for failure to comply with other Rules or with a court order.

APPLICATIONS

Disfavored

Involuntary dismissal is within the discretion of the court,[68] but is disfavored and is granted sparingly.[69]

---

[61]*Russ v. Standard Ins. Co.*, 120 F.3d 988, 990 (9th Cir. 1997); *but see Hoffmann v. Alside, Inc.*, 596 F.2d 822, 823 (8th Cir. 1979).

[62]*See Palka v. City of Chicago*, 662 F.3d 428, 436 (7th Cir. 2011); *Briseno v. Ashcroft*, 291 F.3d 377 (5th Cir.2002).

[63]*In re Intern. Business Machines Corp.*, 687 F.2d 591 (2d Cir. 1982).

[64]*See Versa Products, Inc. v. Home Depot, USA, Inc.*, 387 F.3d 1325 (11th Cir. 2004); *Chavez v. Illinois State Police*, 251 F.3d 612 (7th Cir.2001); *Belle-Midwest, Inc. v. Missouri Property & Cas. Ins. Guarantee Ass'n*, 56 F.3d 977 (8th Cir. 1995).

[65]*Martens v. Thomann*, 273 F.3d 159, 183 (2d Cir. 2001) ("interlocutory orders should not ordinarily merge with a final judgment dismissing an action for failure to prosecute"); *Chappelle v. Beacon Communications Corp.*, 84 F.3d 652, 654 (2d Cir. 1996).

[66]*Harvey Aluminum, Inc. v. American Cyanamid Co.*, 203 F.2d 105 (2d Cir. 1953).

[67]*Pontenberg v. Boston Scientific Corp.*, 252 F.3d 1253 (11th Cir.2001) (order granting dismissal is reviewed under the abuse of discretion standard).

[68]*Bishop v. Lewis*, 155 F.3d 1094, 1096 (9th Cir. 1998).

[69]*Garcia-Perez v. Hospital Metropolitano*, 597 F.3d 6, 7 (1st Cir. 2010); *Lewis v. Rawson*, 564 F.3d 569, 575–76 (2nd Cir. 2009).

Failure to Prosecute

The court may dismiss for failure to prosecute *sua sponte* or upon motion.[70] Local Rules frequently specify the conditions for dismissal based on inactivity (typically, lack of activity for a period of one year).[71]

Failure to Comply With Order

Upon motion or *sua sponte*, the court may dismiss an action based on the plaintiff's failure to comply with a court order.[72]

Failure to Comply with Rules

The court may dismiss an action for failure to comply with the Rules. For example, the plaintiff may risk involuntary dismissal by persistently refusing to file a pretrial statement. To determine whether dismissal is an appropriate sanction for violation of a particular Rule, the practitioner should also review the author commentary and case law discussing that Rule.[73]

With Prejudice

Involuntary dismissals are presumed to be with prejudice unless the court specifies otherwise.[74] Additionally, involuntary dismissal under Rule 41(b) and dismissals not under Rule 41 (other than dismissals for lack of jurisdiction,[75] lack of venue,[76] or failure to join a party under Rule 19) operate as adjudications on the merits for purposes of res judicata or collateral

---

[70]*Brown v. Columbia Sussex Corp.*, 664 F.3d 182, 190 (7th Cir. 2011) (should be a clear record of delay or contumacious conduct for dismissal for failure to prosecute); *Garcia-Perez v. Hospital Metropolitano*, 597 F.3d 6, 7 (1st Cir. 2010) (*sua sponte* dismissal vacated).

[71]*See Wagner v. Ashcroft*, 214 F.R.D. 78 (N.D. N.Y. 2003).

[72]*Slack v. McDaniel*, 529 U.S. 473, 120 S. Ct. 1595, 146 L. Ed. 2d 542 (2000); *Lewis v. School Dist. #£70*, __ F.3d __ (7th Cir. 2011) (dismissal appropriate when there is a clear record of delay or contumacious conduct or when less drastic sanctions have proven ineffective); *Peterson v. Archstone Communities LLC*, 637 F.3d 416, 418 (D.C.Cir. 2011) (court may dismiss sua sponte for failure to comply with its orders); *Wynder v. McMahon*, 360 F.3d 73, 78 (2d Cir. 2004) (court may not dismiss based on failure to comply with an order that imposes requirements greater than those authorized by the Rules).

[73]*See, e.g., Bowling v. Hasbro, Inc.*, 403 F.3d 1373, 1375–76 (Fed. Cir. 2005) (Rule 4(m) does not permit dismissal with prejudice); *Jackson v. City of New York*, 22 F.3d 71 (2d Cir.1994).

[74]*Kwan v. Schlein*, 634 F.3d 224, 230 (2nd Cir. 2011) (listing factors for deciding whether dismissal would be with prejudice); *Jones v. Horne*, 634 F.3d 588, 603 (D.C.Cir. 2011).

[75]*In re IFC Credit Corp.*, 663 F.3d 315, 320 (7th Cir. 2011); *Intera Corp. v. Henderson*, 428 F.3d 605, 620 (6th Cir. 2005) (rule applies with equal effect to personal and subject matter jurisdiction); *Matosantos Commercial Corp. v. Applebee's Intern., Inc.*, 245 F.3d 1203, 1209 (10th Cir. 2001) (noting that the first adjudication will have estoppel effect as to the jurisdictional issues actually determined by the court).

[76]*See Vasquez v. Bridgestone/Firestone, Inc.*, 325 F.3d 665, 678 (5th Cir. 2003) (dismissal for forum non conveniens is not dismissal for lack of venue, and this is a dismissal with prejudice).

estoppel.[77]

Motion Formalities

If the defendant makes the motion for involuntary dismissal at the close of plaintiff's case, it may be oral and without notice. Otherwise, the defendant must comply with the normal procedural formalities.

Dismissal Under Other Rules

Rule 41(b) governs only the two specified types of involuntary dismissal. Other types of dismissal are addressed elsewhere, such as in Rule 12(b), governing dismissal for reasons such as failure to state a claim and lack of jurisdiction.[78]

Appeal

The plaintiff may appeal an involuntary dismissal as a final order.[79]

RULE 41(c)—DISMISSING A COUNTERCLAIM, CROSSCLAIM, OR THIRD-PARTY CLAIM

CORE CONCEPT

The provisions of Rule 41 apply to counterclaims, crossclaims, and third-party claims with equal force.[80]

RULE 41(d)—COSTS OF A PREVIOUSLY DISMISSED ACTION

CORE CONCEPT

If a plaintiff who has already *voluntarily* dismissed an action commences another action on the same claim, the court, in its discretion, can stay the second action until the plaintiff[81] pays such costs of the first action as the court deems appropriate.[82] The courts are split as to whether an award of costs under Rule

---

[77]*See Semtek Intern. Inc. v. Lockheed Martin Corp.*, 531 U.S. 497, 121 S. Ct. 1021, 149 L. Ed. 2d 32 (2001) (Rule 41 determines that the dismissal is on the merits, but in diversity cases, state law then determines the preclusive effect of the dismissal on another action); *Hells Canyon Preservation Council v. U.S. Forest Service*, 403 F.3d 683, 687 (9th Cir. 2005); *Orca Yachts, L.L.C. v. Mollicam, Inc.*, 287 F.3d 316, 319 (4th Cir. 2002).

[78]*See Blue Cross and Blue Shield of Alabama v. Fondren*, 966 F. Supp. 1093, 1097 (M.D. Ala. 1997) (case due to be dismissed for lack of subject matter jurisdiction is due to be dismissed without prejudice).

[79]*Lal v. California*, 610 F.3d 518,

523 (9th Cir. 2010); *Wynder v. McMahon*, 360 F.3d 73, 76 (2d Cir. 2004) (a dismissal without prejudice that does not give leave to amend and closes the case is a final, appealable order).

[80]*Orca Yachts, L.L.C. v. Mollicam, Inc.*, 287 F.3d 316, 319 (4th Cir. 2002); *Amerimax Real Estate Partners, Inc. v. RE/MAX Intern., Inc.*, 600 F.Supp.2d 1003, 1006 (N.D.Ill. 2009).

[81]*Duffy v. Ford Motor Co.*, 218 F.3d 623, 636 (6th Cir. 2000) (Rule 41(d) discusses the imposition of costs upon the plaintiffs, not counsel).

[82]*Pontenberg v. Boston Scientific Corp.*, 252 F.3d 1253 (11th Cir.2001); *Rogers v. Wal-Mart Stores, Inc.*, 230 F.3d 868, 874 (6th Cir. 2000) (part of

41(d) may include attorneys fees.[83]

Additional Research References

Wright & Miller, *Federal Practice and Procedure* §§ 2361 to 2376
C.J.S., Federal Civil Procedure §§ 486, 775 to 819 et seq., 839 to 869 et seq.
West's Key Number Digest, Federal Civil Procedure ⬿1691 to 1715, 1721 to 1729, 1741, 1758 to 1765, 1821 to 1842

---

the purpose of Rule 41(d) is to avoid forum shopping; it is not necessary to show bad faith or vexatious conduct); *Labtest Intern., Inc. v. Centre Testing Intern. Corp.*, __ F.Supp.2d __ (N.D.Ill. 2011).

[83]*See Rogers v. Wal-Mart Stores, Inc.*, 230 F.3d 868, 875 (6th Cir. 2000) (noting the split and determining that fees are not available in the 6th Circuit); *Esposito v. Piatrowski*, 223 F.3d 497 (7th Cir.2000) (attorneys fees may be recovered only when an underlying statute defines costs as including attorneys fees); *Oteng v. Golden Star Resources, Ltd.*, 615 F.Supp.2d 1228 (D.Colo. 2009) (majority allow award of attorney fees).

RULE 42

CONSOLIDATION; SEPARATE TRIALS

(a) Consolidation. If actions before the court involve a common question of law or fact, the court may:

   (1) join for hearing or trial any or all matters at issue in the actions;

   (2) consolidate the actions; or

   (3) issue any other orders to avoid unnecessary cost or delay.

(b) Separate Trials. For convenience, to avoid prejudice, or to expedite and economize, the court may order a separate trial of one or more separate issues, claims, crossclaims, counterclaims, or third-party claims. When ordering a separate trial, the court must preserve any federal right to a jury trial.

[Amended effective July 1, 1966; April 30, 2007, effective December 1, 2007.]

AUTHORS' COMMENTARY ON RULE 42

PURPOSE AND SCOPE

Rule 42 allows the court to control the manner in which the cases on its docket are tried; the court may consolidate several actions into a single proceeding or may conduct separate trials of various issues within a single action.

RULE 42(a)—CONSOLIDATION

CORE CONCEPT

When actions pending before the court[1] share common issues of law or fact, the court can consolidate the actions, either completely or for limited proceedings or stages.[2]

---

[1]*Thermodyn Corp. v. 3M Co.*, 593 F.Supp.2d 972, 991 (N.D.Ohio 2008) (court must have jurisdiction over both cases); *Mourik Intern. B.V. v. Reactor Services Intern., Inc.*, 182 F. Supp. 2d 599, 602 (S.D. Tex. 2002) (the case must be properly pending before the court to be consolidated; an improperly removed case could not be consolidated).

[2]*Lewis v. ACB Business Services, Inc.*, 135 F.3d 389, 412 (6th Cir. 1998);

959

APPLICATIONS

Court's Discretion

In deciding whether to consolidate actions, the court should balance the savings to the judicial system against the possible inconvenience, delay, or prejudice to the parties.[3] The court has broad discretion in this balancing process,[4] and does not need the parties' consent.[5]

Common Issues Necessary

Although the court has broad discretion, it may not consolidate actions that do not share common issues of law or fact.[6] Identity of parties, however, is not necessary.[7]

Limited Consolidation

The court may consolidate actions for all purposes, for pretrial proceedings only, or for specified hearings or issues.

Actions in Different Districts

Actions in different districts may not be consolidated. However, if actions are pending in different districts that ought to be consolidated, the actions may be transferred to a single district, then consolidated, as provided in the Multidistrict Litigation or MDL procedures.[8]

Actions Remain Separate

In general, consolidated actions retain their separate identity.[9] Thus, the pleadings will remain separate and the court will enter separate judgments in each action.[10] However, the court can merge the cases or order that briefs and rulings

---

Stone v. Agnico-Eagle Mines Ltd., 280 F.R.D. 142, 143 (S.D.N.Y. 2012).

[3]*Arnold v. Eastern Air Lines, Inc.*, 681 F.2d 186, 193 (4th Cir. 1982); *In re Oreck Corp. Halo Vacuum & Air Purifiers Marketing and Sales Practices Litig.*, __ F.R.D. __ (C.D.Cal. 2012).

[4]*Blue Cross Blue Shield of Massachusetts, Inc. v. BCS Ins. Co.*, 671 F.3d 635, 640 (7th Cir. 2011); *Young v. City of Augusta, Ga. Through DeVaney*, 59 F.3d 1160, 1168 (11th Cir. 1995).

[5]*Connecticut General Life Ins. Co. v. Sun Life Assur. Co. of Canada*, 210 F.3d 771 (7th Cir. 2000); *Disher v. Citigroup Global Markets, Inc.*, 486 F. Supp. 2d 790 (S.D. Ill. 2007) (court can consolidate over the objections of the parties).

[6]*Malcolm v. National Gypsum Co.*, 995 F.2d 346 (2d Cir.1993); *Doug Brady, Inc. v. New Jersey Bldg. Laborers Statewide Funds*, 250 F.R.D. 171,

176 (D.N.J. 2008) (the existence of common facts is a prerequisite, but does not compel, consolidation); *Saudi Basic Industries Corp. v. Exxonmobil Corp.*, 194 F. Supp. 2d 378, 416 (D.N.J. 2002) (Rule 42(a) does not require that the cases be identical, merely that there be a common question of law or fact).

[7]*National Ass'n of Mortg. Brokers v. Board of Governors of Federal Reserve System*, __ F.Supp.2d __ (D.D.C. 2011).

[8]*In re Korean Air Lines Co., Ltd.*, 642 F.3d 685, 699–700 (9th Cir. 2011).

[9]*Horizon Asset Management Inc. v. H & R Block, Inc.*, 580 F.3d 755, 769 (8th Cir. 2009); *Boardman Petroleum, Inc. v. Federated Mut. Ins. Co.*, 135 F.3d 750, 752 (11th Cir. 1998).

[10]*Horizon Asset Management Inc. v. H & R Block, Inc.*, 580 F.3d 755, 769 (8th Cir. 2009) (plaintiffs are entitled to a decision on the merits of their

apply to all consolidated cases.[11]

Conflicts of Interest
Consolidation may be improper if it aligns parties who have conflicting interests.[12]

Arbitration
Many courts do not permit consolidation of arbitrations unless there is an express provision in the arbitration agreements providing for consolidation.[13]

Procedures
Consolidation is achieved by motion of any party or by the court *sua sponte*.[14] Local rules may determine to which judge a motion to consolidate should be presented if the matters are pending before different judges.[15] Once actions have been consolidated, the court manages the proceedings. In unusual circumstances, the court may appoint one counsel as lead or liaison counsel.

Appeals
An order granting or denying a motion for consolidation is not appealable as a final judgment,[16] although mandamus may be available under extreme circumstances.[17]

RULE 42(b)—SEPARATE TRIALS

CORE CONCEPT
The court may conduct separate trials of any claim or issue.[18]

---

claims even though their case has been consolidated).

[11]*In re Air Crash at Lexington, KY, AUGUST 27, 2006*, 251 F.R.D. 258, 260–61 (E.D.Ky. 2008); *Specht v. Netscape Communications Corp.*, 150 F. Supp. 2d 585, 586, (S.D. N.Y. 2001), aff'd, 306 F.3d 17 (2d Cir. 2002).

[12]*Dupont v. Southern Pac. Co.*, 366 F.2d 193 (5th Cir. 1966); *Atkinson v. Roth*, 297 F.2d 570 (3d Cir.1961).

[13]*Champ v. Siegel Trading Co., Inc.*, 55 F.3d 269, 274 (7th Cir. 1995); *but see Office & Professional Employees Intern. Union, AFL-CIO v. Sea-Land Service, Inc.*, 210 F.3d 117, 123 (2d Cir. 2000) (developing common law of labor contracts empowered district court to consolidate two arbitration proceedings without consideration of whether such consolidation was authorized by Fed.R.Civ.P. 42(a)).

[14]*National Ass'n of Mortg. Brokers v. Board of Governors of Federal Reserve System*, __ F.Supp.2d __ (D.D.C. 2011); *Tucker v. Kenney*, 994 F. Supp. 412 (E.D. N.Y. 1998).

[15]*Stewart v. O'Neill*, 225 F. Supp. 2d 16, 21 (D.D.C. 2002) (local rule providing that the motion to consolidate should be presented in the matter first filed).

[16]*National Ass'n for Advancement of Colored People of Louisiana v. Michot*, 480 F.2d 547, 548 (5th Cir. 1973).

[17]*In re Repetitive Stress Injury Litigation*, 11 F.3d 368 (2d Cir.1993).

[18]*Bridgeport Music, Inc. v. Justin Combs Pub.*, 507 F.3d 470, 481 (6th Cir. 2007); *Simon v. Philip Morris Incorporated*, 200 F.R.D. 21, 27 (E.D. N.Y. 2001) (the court may order a separate trial of any claim, cross-claim, counterclaim, or third-party claim, or of any separate issue or of any number of claims, cross-claims, counterclaims, third-party claims, or issues).

APPLICATIONS

Court's Discretion

In deciding whether to order separate trials, the court should balance the savings to the judicial system against the possible inconvenience, delay, or prejudice to the parties.[19] The court has broad discretion in this balancing process.[20]

Burden of Proof

The burden is on the moving party to demonstrate that bifurcation is justified even in cases where bifurcation is not uncommon.[21]

Single Action

A separation under Rule 42 separates aspects of the action for trial, but the aspects remain part of a single action, and result in a single judgment.[22] This contrasts with claims that are severed pursuant to Rule 21.[23]

Liability and Damages

The most common instance of separate trials is when the court first conducts a trial as to liability, then as to damages if necessary.[24]

Separate Trials for Each Defendant

The court may order separate trials for each defendant, particularly if one is in bankruptcy, as long as the defendants are not indispensable parties.[25]

Procedure

The court may order separate trials *sua sponte* or by motion of any party.

Federal Law Controls

Bifurcated trials are permissible under Rule 42 even when the state law would prohibit bifurcation.[26]

---

[19]*Athridge v. Aetna Cas. and Sur. Co.*, __ F.3d __ (D.C.Cir. 2010); *Thabault v. Chait*, 541 F.3d 512, 529 (3rd Cir. 2008).

[20]*U.S. ex rel. Bahrani v. ConAgra, Inc.*, 624 F.3d 1275, 1283 (10th Cir. 2010); *Athridge v. Aetna Cas. and Sur. Co.*, 604 F.3d 625, 635 (D.C.Cir. 2010).

[21]*Clark v. I.R.S.*, __ F.Supp.2d __ (D.Hawai'i 2009) (bifurcation is the exception, not the rule); *Svege v. Mercedes-Benz Credit Corporation*, 329 F. Supp. 2d 283, 284 (D. Conn. 2004).

[22]*White v. ABCO Engineering Corp.*, 199 F.3d 140, 145 (3d Cir. 1999); *Reid v. General Motors Corp.*, 240 F.R.D. 260, 263 (E.D. Tex. 2007); *Hecht v. City of New York*, 217 F.R.D. 148, 149–50 (S.D. N.Y. 2003).

[23]*Rice v. Sunrise Express, Inc.*, 209 F.3d 1008, 1014–16 (7th Cir. 2000); *Reid v. General Motors Corp.*, 240 F.R.D. 260, 263 (E.D. Tex. 2007) (explaining the distinction between Rule 42(b) and Rule 21).

[24]*See Gafford v. General Elec. Co.*, 997 F.2d 150 (6th Cir. 1993); *Colon ex rel. Molina v. BIC USA, Inc.*, 199 F. Supp. 2d 53, 97-98 (S.D. N.Y. 2001).

[25]*Hecht v. City of New York*, 217 F.R.D. 148, 150 (S.D. N.Y. 2003).

[26]*Oulds v. Principal Mut. Life Ins. Co.*, 6 F.3d 1431 (10th Cir. 1993).

Jury Trials

The procedures for separate trials do not affect the parties' rights to a jury trial.[27] Separate trials may be conducted before one jury or different juries.[28] If there are jury and non-jury claims present, the jury claims may have to be tried first, so that the court does not make factual findings that should properly have been made by the jury.[29]

State Law Claims

The court may conduct a separate trial of an issue over which it could not exercise independent jurisdiction.[30] Thus, if a court exercised supplemental jurisdiction over a state law claim that otherwise could not have been brought as a separate action, the court may at the trial stage conduct a separate trial for that state law claim.[31]

Appeals

An order granting or denying a motion for bifurcation is not appealable as a final judgment, although mandamus may be available under extreme circumstances.[32]

Additional Research References

Wright & Miller, *Federal Practice and Procedure* §§ 2381 to 2392
C.J.S., Federal Civil Procedure §§ 611, 916 to 918
West's Key Number Digest, Federal Civil Procedure ⊗8 to 9, 1953 to 1965

---

[27]*Shum v. Intel Corp.*, 499 F.3d 1272, 1276 (Fed. Cir. 2007) (trial court must ensure that the litigant's constitutional right to a jury is preserved); *Danjaq LLC v. Sony Corp.*, 263 F.3d 942, 961–62 (9th Cir. 2001).

[28]*See Reid v. General Motors Corp.*, 240 F.R.D. 260, 263 (E.D. Tex. 2007) (separate juries should not be allowed to pass on overlapping issues of fact because of the risk of inconsistent verdicts).

[29]*See Dairy Queen, Inc. v. Wood*, 369 U.S. 469, 479, 82 S.Ct. 894, 8 L.Ed.2d 44 (1962); *Beacon Theatres, Inc. v. Westover*, 359 U.S. 500, 79 S.Ct. 948, 3 L.Ed.2d 988 (1959).

[30]*Delaney v. District of Columbia*, 612 F.Supp.2d 38, 44 (D.D.C. 2009).

[31]*Travelers Indemnity Co. v. Miller Mfg. Co.*, 276 F.2d 955 (6th Cir. 1960).

[32]*See In re Repetitive Stress Injury Litigation*, 11 F.3d 368 (2d Cir.1993).

RULE 43
TAKING TESTIMONY

(a) In Open Court. At trial, the witnesses' testimony must be taken in open court unless a federal statute, the Federal Rules of Evidence, these rules, or other rules adopted by the Supreme Court provide otherwise. For good cause in compelling circumstances and with appropriate safeguards, the court may permit testimony in open court by contemporaneous transmission from a different location.

(b) Affirmation Instead of an Oath. When these rules require an oath, a solemn affirmation suffices.

(c) Evidence on a Motion. When a motion relies on facts outside the record, the court may hear the matter on affidavits or may hear it wholly or partly on oral testimony or on depositions.

(d) Interpreter. The court may appoint an interpreter of its choosing; fix reasonable compensation to be paid from funds provided by law or by one or more parties; and tax the compensation as costs.

[Amended effective July 1, 1966; July 1, 1975; August 1, 1987, December 1, 1996; April 30, 2007, effective December 1, 2007.]

AUTHORS' COMMENTARY ON RULE 43

PURPOSE AND SCOPE

Rule 43, formerly entitled "Evidence" was largely supplanted by the Federal Rules of Evidence. The remaining provisions govern the manner in which testimony is taken, the manner in which evidence is presented in support of motions, and the use of interpreters. A discussion of the Federal Rules of Evidence is beyond the scope of this book.

RULE 43(a)—IN OPEN COURT

CORE CONCEPT

There is a preference in federal court for testimony taken in open court.[1] All testimony shall be in such form unless otherwise authorized by the Federal Rules of Evidence,[2] federal statute, or Supreme Court rule, or if stipulated by the parties.[3]

APPLICATIONS

Live Testimony

The Rules place a strong emphasis on live testimony taken in open court.[4] Rule 43(a) reflects the permissible use of other forms of communication, such as writing or sign language, if the witness cannot speak.[5]

Remote Testimony

Rule 43(a) allows the transmitting of testimony from a different location.[6] However, the Rules continue to emphasize live testimony in court, and transmitted testimony is permitted only for good cause shown in compelling circumstances.[7] In cases where remote testimony is to be used, the court must employ appropriate safeguards to protect the procedure and the parties' interests.[8] Transmitted testimony might be allowed when unexpected circumstances, such as an accident or illness, render a witness unable to appear in court.[9]

---

[1]*In re Stevinson*, 194 B.R. 509, 511 (D. Colo. 1996) (approving use of written direct testimony and live cross-examination).

[2]*Kuntz v. Sea Eagle Diving Adventures Corp.*, 199 F.R.D. 665, 667 (D. Haw. 2001) (Federal Rules of Evidence authorize the submission of testimony by affidavit).

[3]*Charlton Memorial Hosp. v. Sullivan*, 816 F. Supp. 50 (D. Mass. 1993); *Saverson v. Levitt*, 162 F.R.D. 407, 408 (D.D.C. 1995).

[4]*Palmer v. Valdez*, 560 F.3d 965, 969, n.4 (9th Cir. 2009) (the importance of live testimony cannot be forgotten); *Rusu v. U.S. I.N.S.*, 296 F.3d 316 (4th Cir.2002).

[5]The Advisory Committee Note to the 1996 Amendment to Rule 43.

[6]*Parkhurst v. Belt*, 567 F.3d 995 (8th Cir. 2009) (testimony by closed circuit television allowed); *Beltran-Tirado v. I.N.S.*, 213 F.3d 1179, 1185–86 (9th Cir. 2000) (rejecting a due process challenge to telephonic testimony).

[7]*See El-Hadad v. United Arab Emirates*, 496 F.3d 658, 668–69 (D.C. Cir. 2007) (good cause demonstrated when witness could not get a visa to enter the United States); *In re Emanuel*, 406 B.R. 634, 636 (Bankr.S. D.N.Y. 2009) (fear of arrest in jurisdiction does not constitute good cause); *In re Vioxx Products Liability Litigation*, 414 F. Supp. 2d 574 (E.D. La. 2006) (listing the factors for considering remote testimony); *F.T.C. v. Swedish Match North America, Inc.*, 197 F.R.D. 1, 2 (D.D.C. 2000) (serious inconvenience to the witness constitutes good cause).

[8]*Parkhurst v. Belt*, 567 F.3d 995 (8th Cir. 2009); *F.T.C. v. Swedish Match North America, Inc.*, 197 F.R.D. 1 (D.D.C. 2000) (in assessing the safeguards of remote testimony, the courts focus on whether the testimony was made in open court, under oath, and whether the opportunity for cross examination was available).

[9]The Advisory Committee Note to the 1996 Amendment to Rule 43.

RULE 43(b)—AFFIRMATION INSTEAD OF AN OATH

CORE CONCEPT

A party who, for religious reasons or otherwise, chooses not to take an oath, may make a "solemn affirmation" instead.[10]

APPLICATIONS

Impact of 2007 "Restyling" Amendments

Warning: Rule 43 was restructured during the 2007 Federal Civil Rules "Restyling" Project. Former abrogated Rules 43(b) and (c) were deleted, and former Rule 43(d) was renumbered as Rule 43(b). In researching current Rule 43(b), practitioners should be mindful of this repositioning.

RULE 43(c)—EVIDENCE ON A MOTION

CORE CONCEPT

A party may submit affidavits in support of or in opposition to a motion in order to demonstrate facts not found in the record.[11] The court, in its discretion, may order oral evidence taken[12] or may request deposition transcripts when a motion is based on facts not of record.[13] The court may also consider a motion solely on the parties' written submissions.[14] The court may also consider preliminary injunction applications under Rule 43(c).[15]

APPLICATIONS

Impact of 2007 "Restyling" Amendments

Rule 43 was restructured during the 2007 Federal Civil Rules "Restyling" Project. Former abrogated Rules 43(b) and (c) were deleted, and former Rule 43(e) was renumbered as

---

[10]*Doe v. Phillips*, 81 F.3d 1204 (2d Cir. 1996).

[11]*Bryant v. Rich*, 530 F.3d 1368, 1377 n.16 (11th Cir. 2008); *Valentin v. Hospital Bella Vista*, 254 F.3d 358, 364 (1st Cir. 2001); *In re Chicago Invs., LLC*, 470 B.R. 32, 103 (D.Mass. 2012).

[12]*Bath Junkie Branson, L.L.C. v. Bath Junkie, Inc.*, 528 F.3d 556, 560 (8th Cir. 2008); *March v. Levine*, 249 F.3d 462 (6th Cir. 2001) (oral testimony is not favored in summary judgment proceedings due to the well founded reluctance to turn a summary judgment hearing into a trial); *Thompson v. Mahre*, 110 F.3d 716, 719 (9th Cir. 1997) (district courts may in their discretion "sparingly and with great care" take oral testimony under

Rule 43(c) on a summary judgment motion); *PAR Microsystems, Inc. v. Pinnacle Development Corp.*, 995 F. Supp. 655 (N.D. Tex. 1997) (oral testimony permitted only when a controlling credibility question is presented).

[13]*Smith v. Oakland County Circuit Court*, 344 F. Supp. 2d 1030, 1051 (E.D. Mich. 2004).

[14]*Sunseri v. Macro Cellular Partners*, 412 F.3d 1247, 1248 (11th Cir. 2005).

[15]*Johnson Service Grp., Inc. v. Olivia France*, 763 F.Supp.2d 819, 823, n.1 (N.D.Tex. 2011); *Jones v. Bush*, 122 F. Supp. 2d 713, 715 (N.D. Tex. 2000), aff'd, 244 F.3d 134 (5th Cir. 2000).

Rule 43(c).[16] In researching current Rule 43(c), practitioners should be mindful of this repositioning.

RULE 43(d)—INTERPRETER

CORE CONCEPT

The court may, in its discretion, appoint an interpreter,[17] who then should take an oath or affirmation that the translation will be accurate. If an interpreter is appointed, the court may determine the interpreter's fees. The court may order that one party pay the fees, and may award the fees as costs after the conclusion of the trial.

APPLICATIONS

Impact of 2007 "Restyling" Amendments

Rule 43 was restructured during the 2007 Federal Civil Rules "Restyling" Project. Former abrogated Rules 43(b) and (c) were deleted, and former Rule 43(f) was renumbered as Rule 43(d). In researching current Rule 43(d), practitioners should be mindful of this repositioning.

Additional Research References

Wright & Miller, *Federal Practice and Procedure* §§ 2401 to 2417
C.J.S., Courts § 1-110; Federal Civil Procedure §§ 368, 373, 935; Witnesses §§ 320 to 326
West's Key Number Digest, Courts ☞56; Federal Civil Procedure ☞921, 2011; West's Key Number Digest, Witnesses ☞227, 228, 230

---

[16]*Fener v. Belo Corp.*, 560 F.Supp.2d 502, 503 n.1 (N.D. Tex. 2008).

[17]*Pedraza v. Phoenix*, 1994 WL 177285 (S.D. N.Y. 1994) (no right to a court-ordered translation of pre-trial motions).

RULE 44
PROVING AN OFFICIAL RECORD

(a) Means of Proving.

(1) *Domestic Record.* Each of the following evidences an official record—or an entry in it—that is otherwise admissible and is kept within the United States, any state, district, or commonwealth, or any territory subject to the administrative or judicial jurisdiction of the United States:

(A) an official publication of the record; or

(B) a copy attested by the officer with legal custody of the record—or by the officer's deputy—and accompanied by a certificate that the officer has custody. The certificate must be made under seal:

    (i) by a judge of a court of record in the district or political subdivision where the record is kept; or

    (ii) by any public officer with a seal of office and with official duties in the district or political subdivision where the record is kept.

(2) *Foreign Record.*

(A) *In General.* Each of the following evidences a foreign official record—or an entry in it—that is otherwise admissible:

    (i) an official publication of the record; or

    (ii) the record—or a copy—that is attested by an authorized person and is accompanied either by a final certification of genuineness or by a certification under a treaty or convention to which the United States and the country where the record is located are parties.

(B) *Final Certification of Genuineness.* A final certification must certify the genuineness of the signature and official position of the attester or of any foreign official whose certificate of genuineness relates to the attestation or is in a chain of certificates of genuineness relating to the attestation. A final certification may be made by a secretary of a United States embassy or legation; by a consul general, vice consul, or consular agent of the United States; or by a diplomatic or consular official of the foreign country assigned or accredited to the United States.

   (C) *Other Means of Proof.* If all parties have had a reasonable opportunity to investigate a foreign record's authenticity and accuracy, the court may, for good cause, either:

     (i)   admit an attested copy without final certification; or

     (ii) permit the record to be evidenced by an attested summary with or without a final certification.

(b) Lack of a Record. A written statement that a diligent search of designated records revealed no record or entry of a specified tenor is admissible as evidence that the records contain no such record or entry. For domestic records, the statement must be authenticated under Rule 44(a)(1). For foreign records, the statement must comply with (a)(2)(C)(ii).

(c) Other Proof. A party may prove an official record—or an entry or lack of an entry in it—by any other method authorized by law.

[Amended effective July 1, 1966; August 1, 1987; December 1, 1991; April 30, 2007, effective December 1, 2007.]

AUTHORS' COMMENTARY ON RULE 44

PURPOSE AND SCOPE

Rule 44 describes certain methods for authenticating official records of the United States or foreign governments. It also provides methods to demonstrate the absence of a particular official document or record.

RULE 44(a)(1)—MEANS OF PROVING; DOMESTIC RECORD

CORE CONCEPT

An official record kept within the United States is authenticated if it is an official publication or if it is a copy of an official record which is attested to by the legal custodian and accompanied by a certificate made by a judge or public officer with a seal of office.

APPLICATIONS

Official Record

"Official record" is not a defined term, but includes such documents as weather bureau records, records of conviction, tax returns, marriage and birth certificates, and selective service files. "Official" does not mean "public"; the public need not have access to "official records."

No Summaries

The Rule applies only to the record itself, not to summaries of the contents of the record.

Authentication Only

Rule 44 only *authenticates* records. It does not render the records immune from other objections, such as hearsay (but see the exception to the hearsay rule for official records), nor does it govern the import of those records.[1]

Entries in Record

The Rule applies equally to entire records or individual entries.

Official Publication

When a document has been printed by government authority, its authenticity is established.

Documents Kept in the United States

Rule 44 applies to all official federal, state, or local records physically maintained within the United States or within territories subject to United States jurisdiction, not just to United States official records. Thus, it includes foreign government records maintained in the United States.

Attested Copy

A copy of an official record may be attested to by the officer having legal custody of the record or by the officer's deputy.[2]

---

[1] *Moreno v. Macaluso*, 844 F. Supp. 736 (M.D. Fla. 1994).

[2] *U.S. v. Estrada-Eliverio*, 583 F.3d 669, 672 (9th Cir. 2009).

Certificate

The attested copy must be accompanied by a certificate that the attesting individual has custody of the record.[3] The certificate must be made by a judge in the district or political subdivision in which the document is kept, or by a public official with duties in the district or political subdivision in which the document is kept, provided that the official has a seal of office and authenticates the certificate with that seal.[4]

RULE 44(a)(2)—MEANS OF PROVING; FOREIGN RECORD

CORE CONCEPT

A foreign official record may be authenticated in essentially the same manner as a domestic record (described immediately above), with some minor variations.

APPLICATIONS

Official Publication

As with a domestic official record, official publications of foreign official records are self-authenticating.[5]

Attested Copy With Certificate

A foreign official record may be attested to by any person authorized by the laws of that country to attest records if the signature is certified by a secretary of embassy or legation, consul general, consul, vice consul or consular agent of the United States, or a diplomatic or consular official of the foreign country assigned or accredited to the United States.[6] The certification will not be necessary if the United States and the foreign country are signatories to a treaty providing for proof of foreign records without a certification and the foreign record is submitted in accordance with the treaty.[7] In particular, see the Hague Public Documents Convention,[8] and the Convention Abolishing the Requirement of Legalization for Foreign Public Documents.[9]

---

[3]*U.S. v. Estrada-Eliverio*, 583 F.3d 669, 672 (9th Cir. 2009).

[4]*Espinoza v. I.N.S.*, 45 F.3d 308 (9th Cir. 1995).

[5]*Construction Drilling, Inc. v. Chusid*, 63 F. Supp. 2d 509 (D.N.J. 1999).

[6]*Starski v. Kirzhnev*, 682 F.3d 51, 53 (1st Cir. 2012); *U.S. v. Squillacote*, 221 F.3d 542 (4th Cir. 2000) (the certification may be a separate document—the Rule does not require that the document itself be signed).

[7]*Corovic v. Mukasey*, 519 F.3d 90, 93 n.2 (2d Cir. 2008) (verification by apostille); *U.S. v. Pintado-Isiordia*, 448 F.3d 1155, 1157 (9th Cir. 2006) (Mexican birth certificate self-authenticating).

[8]Reprinted in *Martindale Hubbell*, International Law Digests. *See also Jiang v. Gonzales*, 474 F.3d 25, 29 n. 4 (1st Cir. 2007).

[9]The Convention Abolishing the Requirement of Legalization for Foreign Public Documents may be found on WESTLAW in the IEL database,

Chain of Certificate

An attestation may also be certified via a chain of certifications, as long as the chain leads to one of the officials listed above.[10]

Attested Copy Without Certificate

The court has discretion to admit an attested copy of a foreign official record without a certificate if all parties have had a reasonable opportunity to investigate the authenticity and accuracy of the record, or for good cause.[11]

RULE 44(b)—LACK OF A RECORD

CORE CONCEPT

One may prove the absence of a particular record with a written statement that after diligent search, no record or entry of the specified nature exists. The statement must be authenticated in the same manner as for an official record.

RULE 44(c)—OTHER PROOF

CORE CONCEPT

The methods in Rule 44 are not exclusive.[12] Quite often, an official will testify as to the authenticity of an official record. Similarly, certain documents are self-authenticating under Rule 902 of the Federal Rules of Evidence. Additionally Rule 902 allows the court to relax the Rule 44 authentication requirements if the party so requesting show that it was unable to satisfy the rule's requirements for authentication despite reasonable efforts.[13]

Additional Research References

Wright & Miller, *Federal Practice and Procedure* §§ 2431 to 2437
C.J.S., Evidence §§ 634 et seq.
West's Key Number Digest, Evidence ☞366

---

ci(vii-c & text).

[10]*See U.S. v. Squillacote*, 221 F.3d 542 (4th Cir. 2000) (second official certified identity of first official and that first official was authorized to attest to the authenticity of the documents).

[11]*Zhanling Jiang v. Holder*, 658 F.3d 1118, 1120 (9th Cir. 2011); *Vatyan v. Mukasey*, 508 F.3d 1179, 1184 (9th Cir. 2007) (exception is only when it is shown that the party is unable to satisfy the basic requirements despite reasonable efforts).

[12]*U.S. v. Estrada-Eliverio*, 583 F.3d 669, 672 (9th Cir. 2009) (proof may be by any other means authorized by law).

[13]*Starski v. Kirzhnev*, 682 F.3d 51, 54 (1st Cir. 2012).

RULE 44.1
DETERMINING FOREIGN LAW

A party who intends to raise an issue about a foreign country's law must give notice by a pleading or other writing. In determining foreign law, the court may consider any relevant material or source, including testimony, whether or not submitted by a party or admissible under the Federal Rules of Evidence. The court's determination must be treated as a ruling on a question of law.

[Added effective July 1, 1966; amended effective July 1, 1975; August 1, 1987; April 30, 2007, effective December 1, 2007.]

AUTHORS' COMMENTARY ON RULE 44.1

PURPOSE AND SCOPE

Rule 44.1 contains the provisions for raising and determining issues concerning the law of a foreign country. A party must give notice of its intent to raise an issue of foreign law. Thereafter, the judge will determine the applicable law of the foreign country.

NOTE: Rule 44.1 (which became effective in 1966) presents a significant diversion from past law, so be wary of citing any authority before 1966.

APPLICATIONS

Notice of Foreign Law Issue

A party must give written notice to the court and all other parties of its intent to raise an issue concerning foreign law.[1] The notice should specify the issues or claims purportedly governed by foreign law, but need not state the specific provisions of the foreign law. Failure to provide the required notice of intent to raise an issue concerning foreign law can result in

---

[1]*In re Griffin Trading Co.*, 683 F.3d 819, 822 (7th Cir. 2012) (notice only need be reasonable to avoid unfair surprise); *DP Aviation v. Smiths Industries Aerospace and Defense Systems Ltd.*, 268 F.3d 829, 846 (9th Cir. 2001) (presenting a detailed analysis of what constitutes sufficient notice).

a waiver of the right to raise the issue.[2]

Form of Notice

The notice may be included in a pleading or may be a separate document.[3]

Timing for Notice

Rule 44.1 does not set a specific time for filing the notice. If the notice is a separate document, it should be served as soon as possible to give a reasonable opportunity to all parties to prepare.[4] If not already raised, issues of foreign law are sometimes raised at the pretrial conference.[5]

Party Giving Notice

Notice is normally given by the party whose claim or defense is based on foreign law, but may be raised by any party. If one party has given notice, other parties can rely on that notice and do not need to provide their own notices.[6] If parties believe that a different foreign law applies from the law raised by another party, they should issue separate notices.

Court Determines Foreign Law

The determination of foreign law is now considered a matter of law, not a matter of fact, and is therefore made by the court.[7]

Materials Used by the Court

The court may consider any relevant material or source to determine foreign law,[8] regardless of whether it is admissible.[9] Common methods of proving foreign law are through expert

---

[2]*In re Magnetic Audiotape Antitrust Litigation*, 334 F.3d 204 (2d Cir.2003); *In re Wachovia Equity Securities Litigation*, 753 F.Supp.2d 326, 380, n.49 (S.D.N.Y. 2011) (reservation of right to raise foreign law issue in a footnote insufficient notice).

[3]*In re Griffin Trading Co.*, 683 F.3d 819, 822 (7th Cir. 2012) (notice in the complaint is sufficient); *Melea, Ltd. v. Jawer SA*, 511 F.3d 1060, 1071 (10th Cir. 2007) (fair written notice provided by motion — point is to avoid unfair surprise); *Local 875 I.B.T. Pension Fund v. Pollack*, 992 F. Supp. 545 (E.D. N.Y. 1998) (raising issue of foreign law in reply papers is not sufficient notice under Rule 44.1).

[4]*See APL Co. Pte. Ltd. v. UK Aerosols Ltd.*, 582 F.3d 947, 955 (9th Cir. 2009) (listing factors to determine whether notice was reasonable); *Rationis Enterprises Inc. of Panama v. Hyundai Mipo Dockyard Co., Ltd.*, 426 F.3d 580 (2d Cir. 2005) (Rule 44.1 deliberately does not provide a specific time period); *Club Car, Inc. v. Club Car (Quebec) Import, Inc.*, 362 F.3d 775, 782 (11th Cir. 2004) (notice 2 weeks before trial held reasonable).

[5]*Mutual Service Ins. Co. v. Frit Industries, Inc.*, 358 F.3d 1312, 1321 (11th Cir. 2004) (notice at pretrial conference held reasonable); *but see Whirlpool Financial Corp. v. Sevaux*, 96 F.3d 216, 221 (7th Cir. 1996) (choice-of-law issue is waived if party brings it up after summary judgment is rendered).

[6]*In re Griffin Trading Co.*, 683 F.3d 819, 823 (7th Cir. 2012).

[7]*In re Griffin Trading Co.*, 683 F.3d 819, 822 (7th Cir. 2012); *U.S. Fidelity and Guar. Co. v. Braspetro Oil Services Co.*, 369 F.3d 34 (2d Cir. 2004).

[8]*McGee v. Arkel Intern., LLC*, 671 F.3d 539, 546 (5th Cir. 2012); *City of Harper Woods Employees' Retirement System v. Olver*, 589 F.3d 1292,

testimony,[10] affidavits from lawyers practicing in the foreign country,[11] and treatises.[12] The court may also do its own research[13] or seek the aid of an expert witness to help in the interpretation of foreign law,[14] but is under no obligation to do so.[15]

Absence of Proof

In the absence of proof of foreign law, the court may presume that the foreign law would be the same as local law.[16]

Summary Judgment

As an issue of law, a determination of foreign law is appropriate for summary judgment.[17]

Choice of Law

In diversity cases, the state conflict of law rules will determine which jurisdiction's laws apply. Rule 44.1 is implicated only after the court has determined that a foreign country's laws apply.

Appellate Review

A ruling as to foreign law is interlocutory, and cannot be immediately appealed.

1298 (D.C.Cir. 2009); *Ferrostaal, Inc. v. M/V Sea Phoenix*, 447 F.3d 212, 216 (3d Cir. 2006).

[9]*Tobar v. U.S.*, 639 F.3d 1191, 1200 (9th Cir. 2011); *Melea, Ltd. v. Jawer SA*, 511 F.3d 1060, 1071 (10th Cir. 2007).

[10]*Estate of Botvin v. Islamic Republic of Iran*, __ F.Supp.2d __ (D.D.C. 2012) (court need not accept expert testimony); *Strauss v. Credit Lyonnais, S.A.*, 249 F.R.D. 429 (E.D. N.Y. 2008).

[11]*Transportes Aereos Pegaso, S.A. de C.V. v. Bell Helicopter Textron, Inc.*, 623 F.Supp.2d 518, 534 (D.Del. 2009).

[12]*See Access Telecom, Inc. v. MCI Telecommunications Corp.*, 197 F.3d 694, 713 (5th Cir. 1999).

[13]*McGee v. Arkel Intern., LLC*, 671 F.3d 539, 546 (5th Cir. 2012); *Brockmeyer v. May*, 361 F.3d 1222, 1241 (9th Cir. 2004) (courts may reject even the uncontradicted conclusions of an expert witness and reach their own decisions on the basis of independent examination of foreign legal authorities).

[14]*In re Agent Orange Product Liability Litigation*, 373 F. Supp. 2d 7, 18 (E.D. N.Y. 2005), aff'd, 517 F.3d 104 (2d Cir. 2008) (court has broad discretion to rely on expert testimony to interpret foreign law); *ID Sec. Systems Canada, Inc. v. Checkpoint Systems, Inc.*, 198 F. Supp. 2d 598, 623 (E.D. Pa. 2002); *Thomson Consumer Electronics, Inc. v. Innovatron, S.A.*, 3 F. Supp. 2d 49 (D.D.C. 1998) (no express hierarchy of sources exists for questions of foreign law).

[15]*Bodum USA, Inc. v. La Cafetiere, Inc.*, 621 F.3d 624, 628 (7th Cir. 2010); *In re Vivendi Universal, S.A. Securities Litigation*, 618 F.Supp.2d 335, 340 (S.D.N.Y. 2009).

[16]*Ferrostaal, Inc. v. M/V Sea Phoenix*, 447 F.3d 212, 216 (3d Cir. 2006); *Harris v. Kellogg, Brown & Root Servs., Inc.*, 796 F.Supp.2d 642, 651 (W.D.Pa. 2011).

[17]*McKesson HBOC, Inc. v. Islamic Republic of Iran*, 271 F.3d 1101, 1108 (D.C. Cir. 2001); *In re Vitamin C Antitrust Litig.*, 810 F.Supp.2d 522, 540 (E.D.N.Y. 2011) (dispute among experts regarding foreign law does not create issue of fact precluding summary judgment).

Additional Research References

Wright & Miller, *Federal Practice and Procedure* §§ 2441 to 2447
C.J.S., Evidence §§ 12 to 26
West's Key Number Digest, Evidence ☞37, 51

RULE 45
SUBPOENA

(a) In General.

  (1) *Form and Contents.*

    (A) *Requirements—In General.* Every subpoena must:

      (i)   state the court from which it issued;

      (ii) state the title of the action, the court in which it is pending, and its civil-action number;

      (iii) command each person to whom it is directed to do the following at a specified time and place: attend and testify; produce designated documents, electronically stored information, or tangible things in that person's possession, custody, or control; or permit the inspection of premises; and

      (iv) set out the text of Rule 45(c) and (d).

    (B) *Command to Attend a Deposition—Notice of the Recording Method.* A subpoena commanding attendance at a deposition must state the method for recording the testimony.

    (C) *Combining or Separating a Command to Produce or to Permit Inspection; Specifying the Form for Electronically Stored Information.* A command to produce documents, electronically stored information, or tangible things or to permit the inspection of premises may be included in a subpoena commanding attendance at a deposition, hearing, or trial, or may be set out in a separate subpoena. A subpoena may specify the form or forms in which electronically stored information is to be produced.

    (D) *Command to Produce; Included Obligations.* A command in a subpoena to produce documents, electronically stored information, or tangible things requires the responding party to permit inspection, copying, testing, or sampling of the materials.

(2) *Issued from Which Court.* A subpoena must issue as follows:

(A) for attendance at a hearing or trial, from the court for the district where the hearing or trial is to be held;

(B) for attendance at a deposition, from the court for the district where the deposition is to be taken; and

(C) for production or inspection, if separate from a subpoena commanding a person's attendance, from the court for the district where the production or inspection is to be made.

(3) *Issued by Whom.* The clerk must issue a subpoena, signed but otherwise in blank, to a party who requests it. That party must complete it before service. An attorney also may issue and sign a subpoena as an officer of:

(A) a court in which the attorney is authorized to practice; or

(B) a court for a district where a deposition is to be taken or production is to be made, if the attorney is authorized to practice in the court where the action is pending.

(b) Service.

(1) *By Whom; Tendering Fees; Serving a Copy of Certain Subpoenas.* Any person who is at least 18 years old and not a party may serve a subpoena. Serving a subpoena requires delivering a copy to the named person and, if the subpoena requires that person's attendance, tendering the fees for 1 day's attendance and the mileage allowed by law. Fees and mileage need not be tendered when the subpoena issues on behalf of the United States or any of its officers or agencies. If the subpoena commands the production of documents, electronically stored information, or tangible things or the inspection of premises before trial, then before it is served, a notice must be served on each party.

(2) *Service in the United States.* Subject to Rule 45(c)(3)(A)(ii), a subpoena may be served at any

place:

(A) within the district of the issuing court;

(B) outside that district but within 100 miles of the place specified for the deposition, hearing, trial, production, or inspection;

(C) within the state of the issuing court if a state statute or court rule allows service at that place of a subpoena issued by a state court of general jurisdiction sitting in the place specified for the deposition, hearing, trial, production, or inspection; or

(D) that the court authorizes on motion and for good cause, if a federal statute so provides.

(3) *Service in a Foreign Country.* 28 U.S.C. § 1783 governs issuing and serving a subpoena directed to a United States national or resident who is in a foreign country.

(4) *Proof of Service.* Proving service, when necessary, requires filing with the issuing court a statement showing the date and manner of service and the names of the persons served. The statement must be certified by the server.

(c) Protecting a Person Subject to a Subpoena.

(1) *Avoiding Undue Burden or Expense; Sanctions.* A party or attorney responsible for issuing and serving a subpoena must take reasonable steps to avoid imposing undue burden or expense on a person subject to the subpoena. The issuing court must enforce this duty and impose an appropriate sanction—which may include lost earnings and reasonable attorney's fees—on a party or attorney who fails to comply.

(2) *Command to Produce Materials or Permit Inspection.*

(A) *Appearance Not Required.* A person commanded to produce documents, electronically stored information, or tangible things, or to permit the inspection of premises, need not appear in person at the place of production or inspection unless also commanded to appear for a deposition, hearing, or trial.

(B) *Objections.* A person commanded to produce

documents or tangible things or to permit inspection may serve on the party or attorney designated in the subpoena a written objection to inspecting, copying, testing or sampling any or all of the materials or to inspecting the premises—or to producing electronically stored information in the form or forms requested. The objection must be served before the earlier of the time specified for compliance or 14 days after the subpoena is served. If an objection is made, the following rules apply:

- (i)   At any time, on notice to the commanded person, the serving party may move the issuing court for an order compelling production or inspection.

- (ii)   These acts may be required only as directed in the order, and the order must protect a person who is neither a party nor a party's officer from significant expense resulting from compliance.

   (3) *Quashing or Modifying a Subpoena.*

     (A) *When Required.* On timely motion, the issuing court must quash or modify a subpoena that:

- (i)   fails to allow a reasonable time to comply;

- (ii)   requires a person who is neither a party nor a party's officer to travel more than 100 miles from where that person resides, is employed, or regularly transacts business in person—except that, subject to Rule 45(c)(3)(B)(iii), the person may be commanded to attend a trial by traveling from any such place within the state where the trial is held;

- (iii)   requires disclosure of privileged or other protected matter, if no exception or waiver applies; or

- (iv)   subjects a person to undue burden.

     (B) *When Permitted.* To protect a person subject to or affected by a subpoena, the issuing court may, on motion, quash or modify the subpoena if it requires:

- (i)   disclosing a trade secret or other confidential research, development, or commercial information;

(ii) disclosing an unretained expert's opinion or information that does not describe specific occurrences in dispute and results from the expert's study that was not requested by a party; or

(iii) a person who is neither a party nor a party's officer to incur substantial expense to travel more than 100 miles to attend trial.

(C) *Specifying Conditions as an Alternative.* In the circumstances described in Rule 45(c)(3)(B), the court may, instead of quashing or modifying a subpoena, order appearance or production under specified conditions if the serving party:

(i) shows a substantial need for the testimony or material that cannot be otherwise met without undue hardship; and

(ii) ensures that the subpoenaed person will be reasonably compensated.

(d) Duties in Responding to a Subpoena.

(1) *Producing Documents or Electronically Stored Information.* These procedures apply to producing documents or electronically stored information:

(A) *Documents.* A person responding to a subpoena to produce documents must produce them as they are kept in the ordinary course of business or must organize and label them to correspond to the categories in the demand.

(B) *Form for Producing Electronically Stored Information Not Specified.* If a subpoena does not specify a form for producing electronically stored information, the person responding must produce it in a form or forms in which it is ordinarily maintained or in a reasonably usable form or forms.

(C) *Electronically Stored Information Produced in Only One Form.* The person responding need not produce the same electronically stored information in more than one form.

(D) *Inaccessible Electronically Stored Information.* The person responding need not provide discovery of electronically stored information from sources that the person identifies as not reasonably accessible because of undue burden or cost. On motion to compel discovery or for a protective order, the person responding must show that the information is not reasonably accessible because of undue burden or cost. If that showing is made, the court may nonetheless order discovery from such sources if the requesting party shows good cause, considering the limitations of Rule 26(b)(2)(C). The court may specify conditions for the discovery.

(2) *Claiming Privilege or Protection.*

(A) *Information Withheld.* A person withholding subpoenaed information under a claim that it is privileged or subject to protection as trial-preparation material must:

(i) expressly make the claim; and

(ii) describe the nature of the withheld documents, communications, or tangible things in a manner that, without revealing information itself privileged or protected, will enable the parties to assess the claim.

(B) *Information Produced.* If information produced in response to a subpoena is subject to a claim of privilege or of protection as trial-preparation material, the person making the claim may notify any party that received the information of the claim and the basis for it. After being notified, a party must promptly return, sequester, or destroy the specified information and any copies it has; must not use or disclose the information until the claim is resolved; must take reasonable steps to retrieve the information if the party disclosed it before being notified; and may promptly present the information to the court under seal for a determination of the claim. The person who produced the information must preserve the information until the claim is resolved.

(e) Contempt. The issuing court may hold in contempt a person who, having been served, fails without adequate excuse to obey the subpoena. A nonparty's failure to obey must be excused if the subpoena purports to require the nonparty to attend or produce at a place outside the limits of Rule 45(c)(3)(A)(ii).

[Amended effective March 19, 1948; October 20, 1949; July 1, 1970; August 1, 1980; August 1, 1985; August 1, 1987; December 1, 1991; April 25, 2005, effective December 1, 2005; April 12, 2006, effective December 1, 2006; April 30, 2007, effective December 1, 2007.]

AUTHORS' COMMENTARY ON RULE 45

PURPOSE AND SCOPE

Rule 45 governs subpoenas, which are the mechanism for obtaining discovery and testimony from ***non-parties***. It addresses subpoenas *ad testificandum,* pertaining to testimony, and subpoenas *duces tecum,* pertaining to documents.

RULE 45(a)—IN GENERAL

CORE CONCEPT

Parties to legal proceedings have the power to obtain a subpoena compelling a non-party to appear and testify at a designated time and location,[1] produce documents or things, or permit the inspection of premises.

APPLICATIONS

Issued by Clerk

A subpoena may be issued by the clerk of court.[2] The clerk will issue subpoenas with the name of the recipient left blank, to be filled in by the party.[3]

Issued by Attorney

A subpoena may also be issued by an attorney, acting as an officer of the court.[4] To be effective, the subpoena must be

---

[1] *In re Boeh*, 25 F.3d 761 (9th Cir. 1994) ("when the subpoena is ad testificandum, there can be no pinch hitters.").

[2] *U.S. S.E.C. v. Hyatt*, 621 F.3d 687, 693 (7th Cir. 2010).

[3] *U.S. S.E.C. v. Hyatt*, 621 F.3d 687, 693 (7th Cir. 2010).

[4] *U.S. S.E.C. v. Hyatt*, 621 F.3d 687, 693 (7th Cir. 2010); *Allied World*

signed by the issuing attorney.[5] An attorney may issue a subpoena on behalf of any court before which the attorney is authorized to practice. An attorney may also issue a subpoena on behalf of a court where a deposition is to occur, provided that the deposition pertains to a matter pending in a court where the attorney is authorized to practice. This applies equally to attorneys admitted *pro hac vice* (for one matter only).

Which Court

A subpoena commanding attendance at a trial or hearing shall be issued from the court in which the trial is to occur. A subpoena for attendance at a deposition shall be issued from the court for the district in which the deposition is to occur, bearing the same case name and number as the case in the court where trial is to occur.[6] If the subpoena is issued from a court other than that where the action is pending, it is not necessary to open a new action with a miscellaneous docket number in the court issuing the subpoena unless it becomes necessary to move to enforce the subpoena. If a separate subpoena is issued commanding the production of documents or an inspection of premises (without an instruction to appear and testify at a deposition), the subpoena shall issue from the court for the district in which the production or inspection is to occur.[7] A subpoena issued by the wrong court will generally be considered void.[8]

Subject Matter Jurisdiction

In order to issue a valid, enforceable subpoena in a lawsuit, the lawsuit must properly be before a federal court with subject matter jurisdiction.[9]

Contents

Every subpoena should:

(1) state the name of the court issuing the subpoena;[10]

(2) state the name of the court where the action is pend-

Assur. Co. (U.S.), Inc. v. Lincoln Gen. Ins. Co., 280 F.R.D. 197, 200 (M.D.Pa. 2012).

[5]*Atlantic Inv. Management, LLC v. Millennium Fund I, Ltd.*, 212 F.R.D. 395, 397 (N.D. Ill. 2002) (lack of signature waived by conduct of recipient).

[6]*Hallamore Corp. v. Capco Steel Corp.*, 259 F.R.D. 76, 79 (D.Del. 2009); *Amgen Inc. v. Kidney Center of Delaware County, Ltd.*, 879 F. Supp. 878 (N.D. Ill. 1995).

[7]*Chevron Corp. v. Weinberg Grp.*, 682 F.3d 96, 97 (C.A.D.C. 2012); *Dynegy Midstream Services v. Trammochem*, 451 F.3d 89, 95 (2d Cir. 2006); *Cusumano v. Microsoft Corp.*, 162 F.3d 708, 711 (1st Cir. 1998) (motion to compel docketed as an independent matter in court where documents were to be produced); *Hallamore Corp. v. Capco Steel Corp.*, 259 F.R.D. 76, 79 (D.Del. 2009) (if a subpoena compels attendance at a deposition and production of documents, it should be issued from the court where the deposition is to occur).

[8]*Hallamore Corp. v. Capco Steel Corp.*, 259 F.R.D. 76, 80 (D.Del. 2009).

[9]*Olcott v. Delaware Flood Co.*, 76 F.3d 1538, 1552 (10th Cir. 1996).

[10]*Morris v. Sequa Corp.*, 275 F.R.D. 562, 565 (N.D.Ala. 2011).

ing;

  (3) contain the caption and civil action number of the case;[11]

  (4) command the recipient to appear and give testimony, to produce for inspection the documents, electronically stored information, or things described in the subpoena or in an attachment thereto,[12] or to permit inspection of premises, at a designated time and location;[13] and

  (5) recite the language in subsections (c) and (d) of Rule 45.[14]

NOTE: Blank subpoenas generally are available at the clerk's office and will include the requisite language.

Scope

The scope of documents or information that can be obtained by subpoena is the same as the scope of discovery generally under Rule 26.[15]

Multiple Commands

A subpoena to produce documents or to inspect premises may be issued separately or joined with a command to appear to testify.

Number

There is no limit on the number of subpoenas in a civil action.

Time

Subpoenas for trial testimony may be served at any time. The majority of the courts treat subpoenas for production of documents as discovery activities that must be issued prior to the discovery deadline.[16]

Documents

Witnesses may be compelled to produce all documents which they possess, have custody of, or control.[17] Thus, a corporation may have to produce documents in the possession of its agent,

---

[11]*U.S. v. Patiwana*, 267 F. Supp. 2d 301 (E.D. N.Y. 2003) (enforcing subpoena despite failure to include a civil action number).

[12]*Orleman v. Jumpking, Inc.*, 2000 WL 1114849 (D. Kan. 2000); *Insituform Technologies, Inc. v. Cat Contracting, Inc.*, 168 F.R.D. 630, 633 (N.D. Ill. 1996).

[13]*Kinetic Concepts, Inc. v. Convatec Inc.*, __ F.R.D. __ (M.D.N.C. 2010).

[14]*Bertrand v. Cordiner Enters., Inc.*, 2011 WL 3036128, (V.I.Super. 2011) (subpoena enforced despite omission of language from Rule 45(c) and

(d) based on absence of real prejudice); *Anderson v. Government of Virgin Islands*, 180 F.R.D. 284 (D.V.I. 1998).

[15]*Hendricks v. Total Quality Logistics, LLC*, __ F.R.D. __ (S.D.Ohio 2011); *S.E.C. v. Sassano*, __ F.R.D. __ (S.D.N.Y. 2011).

[16]*Buhrmaster v. Overnite Transp. Co.*, 61 F.3d 461, 464 (6th Cir. 1995); *Williamson v. Horizon Lines LLC*, 248 F.R.D. 79, 83 (D. Me. 2008); *Dreyer v. GACS Inc.*, 204 F.R.D. 120, 122–23 (N.D. Ind. 2001).

[17]*Hay Group, Inc. v. E.B.S. Acquisition Corp.*, 360 F.3d 404, 408 (3d Cir. 2004); *In re Citric Acid Litiga-*

attorney, or affiliate,[18] even if these documents are located outside the district.[19] See the coverage of Rule 26(b)(1) for a more full discussion of the meaning of "possession, custody, or control."

Electronic Data

Rule 45 expressly allows for the party issuing the subpoena to request to inspect, copy, sample, or test electronic data.[20]

- *Form of Electronic Data:* Rule 45(d)(1)(B) allows, but does not require, the requesting party to specify the form in which it is requesting electronic data (i.e., hard copy or electronic, and if electronic, the precise manner of production). If the requesting party does not specify the form, then the responding person must produce it in the form in which it is ordinarily maintained or in a form that is reasonably usable. In any event, a person need not produce electronic data in more than one form.

- *Undue Burden or Cost:* If the responding person believes that the production of electronic data from certain sources will cause undue burden or cost, the person can, in lieu of producing the documents, identify those sources.[21] If a motion to compel or quash is filed, the responding person will have the burden of showing that production would cause undue burden or cost. The burden would then shift to the requesting party to show good cause why the data should be produced nonetheless.

Inspection, Testing, or Sampling

A subpoena may be used to obtain inspection, testing, or sampling of the property, documents, or electronic data of a non-party.[22]

Asserting Privileges

The recipient of a subpoena *duces tecum* may refuse to pro-

---

tion, 191 F.3d 1090, 1106–07 (9th Cir. 1999) ("control" is defined as the legal right to obtain documents upon demand).

[18]*U.S. v. Deloitte & Touche USA LLP*, 623 F.Supp.2d 39, 41 (D.D.C. 2009) (the party must produce documents held by an affiliate if it has the legal right, authority, or ability to obtain the documents upon demand).

[19]*See In re Automotive Refinishing Paint*, 229 F.R.D. 482 (E.D. Pa. 2005) (documents outside the court's jurisdiction must be produced if the party is served within the court's jurisdiction); *Crafton v. U.S. Specialty*

Ins. Co., 218 F.R.D. 175, 177 (E.D. Ark. 2003) (quashing document subpoena served on a corporate agent in one state where documents and corporate headquarters were in a different state more than 100 miles from service).

[20]*Soto v. Castlerock Farming & Transp., Inc.*, __ F.R.D. __ (E.D.Cal. 2012).

[21]Rule 45(d)(1)(D).

[22]*Fitzpatrick v. Arco Marine, Inc.*, 199 F.R.D. 663, 664 (C.D. Cal. 2001) (allowing inspection of a non-party's ship).

duce privileged documents.[23] If the issuing party contests the asserted privilege, that party can request that the court conduct an *in camera* inspection of such documents.

Recalling Privileged Information

Rule 45(d)(2)(B) establishes a procedure to recall privileged information that has already been produced. Anyone believing that a person has produced privileged information in response to a subpoena may provide a notification to the parties who have received the information. After receiving such a notification, the receiving parties must return, sequester, or destroy the specified information and all copies (including taking reasonable steps to retrieve any information that the receiving party had already disclosed to other persons). If they do not agree with the privilege assertion, they can present the information to the court under seal for a determination of the privilege claim. During the pendency of the court's review of the privilege claim, the receiving parties are prohibited from using the information and the producing party must preserve it.

Challenge

The proper method for challenging a subpoena that requires personal attendance is by motion to quash. The court can modify or quash the subpoena if it is unreasonable or oppressive.[24] Expense is not a reason to quash, but the court may condition compliance on the advancement of the expenses of complying by the issuing party.[25] A motion to quash may only be brought by the witness; the parties do not have standing to bring the motion on behalf of the witness.[26] If the subpoena is issued in one district for an action pending in another district, a motion to quash should be brought in the court issuing the subpoena.[27] In addition, if the subpoena is for a deposition, the witness may move for a protective order under the discovery provisions in Rule 26(c). If the subpoena is for the production of documents only, the recipient may serve written objections on the issuer within 14 days of receipt of the subpoena, or before the date for production if sooner than 14 days from receipt of the subpoena.[28] After serving written objections, the recipient does not need to produce the documents unless the serving party successfully brings a motion to compel.

---

[23]*See In re Teligent, Inc.*, 459 B.R. 190, 199–200 (S.D.N.Y. 2011).

[24]*Ariel v. Jones*, 693 F.2d 1058 (11th Cir.1982).

[25]*Securities and Exchange Commission v. Arthur Young & Co.*, 584 F.2d 1018 (D.C. Cir. 1978).

[26]*Brown v. Braddick*, 595 F.2d 961, 967 (5th Cir. 1979).

[27]*In re Sealed Case*, 141 F.3d 337, 340 (D.C. Cir. 1998).

[28]*See* Rule 45(c) below.

Parties

A subpoena is not necessary to take the deposition of a party or an officer, director, or managing agent of a party,[29] or to compel a party to produce documents;[30] a notice of deposition pursuant to Rules 30(b) and 31(a) is sufficient.[31] A subpoena is necessary for all other employees of corporations.[32] Subpoenas may be used to require parties to appear and testify at trial.[33]

Corporations

In deposing a corporation, one may describe the information sought in the subpoena (or notice) and require the corporation to designate a representative qualified to testify about the designated issues.[34]

United States or States

As a general rule, agencies and representatives of the United States or a State must comply with subpoenas.[35]

RULE 45(b)—SERVICE

CORE CONCEPT

Subpoenas may be served by any non-party not under the age of 18.

APPLICATIONS

Personal Service

The courts are divided as to whether service of a subpoena must be personal, in-hand service, or can be accomplished by delivery to the recipient's residence or place of business.[36]

Proof of Service

If necessary, service can be proved by filing a statement of the date and manner of service, certified by the person making

---

[29]*E.I. DuPont de Nemours and Co. v. Kolon Industries, Inc.*, __ F.R.D. __ (E.D.Va. 2010) (the law is sketchy as to who is considered a managing agent).

[30]*Dixon v. Ford Motor Credit Co.*, 2000 WL 1182274 (E.D. La. 2000) (Rule 34, not Rule 45, provides the proper way for a party to obtain documents from another party).

[31]*COMSAT Corp. v. National Science Foundation*, 190 F.3d 269, 278 (4th Cir. 1999); but see *First City, Texas-Houston, N.A. v. Rafidain Bank*, 197 F.R.D. 250, 254 (S.D. N.Y. 2000) (nothing in the Rules prevents issuing a subpoena to a party).

[32]*Memory Bowl v. North Pointe Ins. Co.*, 280 F.R.D. 181, 187 (D.N.J. 2012).

[33]*See Chao v. Tyson Foods, Inc.*, 255 F.R.D. 556, 557–58 (N.D.Ala. 2009).

[34]*Price Waterhouse LLP v. First American Corp.*, 182 F.R.D. 56, 61 (S.D. N.Y. 1998).

[35]*Ott v. City of Milwaukee*, 682 F.3d 552, 557 (7th Cir. 2012) (state agencies are persons subject to subpoena); *Yousuf v. Samantar*, 451 F.3d 248, 251–53 (D.C. Cir. 2006) (agencies of the United States are persons who must respond to subpoenas).

[36]*See Ott v. City of Milwaukee*, 682 F.3d 552, 557 (7th Cir. 2012) (personal service not required); *Hall v. Sullivan*, 229 F.R.D. 501 (D. Md. 2005) (discussing the split in authority).

service, with the clerk of the court issuing the subpoena.

Deadline for Subpoenas

Rule 45 does not establish any cutoff or deadline for serving subpoenas. However, a subpoena for a deposition or for the production of documents may be governed by the discovery deadline.[37]

Not on Lawyer

Service upon the witness's lawyer is not sufficient.

Corporations

Service on the agent of a corporation is sufficient to obtain service on the corporation.[38]

Expenses

If the recipient's attendance is commanded, service must be accompanied by the tender of the fees and expenses for a 1-day appearance, unless the issuing party is the United States or officer or agency thereof.[39] There is no requirement to tender witness fees and expenses when the subpoena is only for the production of documents, and no witness is commanded to appear.[40] The amount of fees and expenses is controlled by 28 U.S.C.A. § 1821.[41]

Place of Service

A subpoena may be served at any place within the district,[42] at any place within 100 miles of the hearing, deposition, production, or trial,[43] or at any place within the state where a

---

[37]*See Alper v. U.S.*, 190 F.R.D. 281, 283 (D. Mass. 2000).

[38]*Sabatier v. Barnes*, 2001 WL 175234 (E.D. La. 2001) (service on a secretary or receptionist is technically sufficient, but not advisable); *In re Motorsports Merchandise Antitrust Litigation*, 186 F.R.D. 344 (W.D. Va. 1999) (look to Rule 4 to determine proper service on a corporation).

[39]*In re Dennis*, 330 F.3d 696, 704–05 (5th Cir. 2003) (Rule 45(b)(1) requires simultaneous tendering of witness fees and the reasonably estimated mileage allowed by law with service of a subpoena; mileage need not be precise, only a reasonable estimate); *In re Hunt*, 238 F.3d 1098, 1100 (9th Cir. 2001) (subpoena quashed because service not accompanied by witness fee and mileage).

[40]*U.S. E.E.O.C. v. Laidlaw Waste, Inc.*, 934 F. Supp. 286, 290 n.6 (N.D. Ill. 1996).

[41]28 U.S.C.A. § 1821 is reprinted in this book. *See also Fisher v. Ford Motor Co.*, 178 F.R.D. 195 (N.D. Ohio 1998).

[42]*In re Automotive Refinishing Paint*, 229 F.R.D. 482 (E.D. Pa. 2005) (the critical location is the place where the documents are to be produced, not where they are maintained).

[43]*See In re Security Life Ins. Co. of America*, 228 F.3d 865, 871 (8th Cir. 2000) (100 mile limitation does not apply to a subpoena for documents); *Gipson v. Wells Fargo Bank, N.A.*, 239 F.R.D. 280, 281 (D.D.C. 2006) (offer to take deposition by telephone does not allow subpoena of witness located more than 100 miles away); *In re Automotive Refinishing Paint*, 229 F.R.D. 482 (E.D. Pa. 2005) (the critical location is the place where the documents are to be produced, not where they are maintained).

subpoena could be served under state law.[44] The 100-mile limit is extended by statute under some circumstances,[45] such as in some bankruptcy proceedings.

Service in Multiparty, Multiforum Actions

When jurisdiction of the district court is based in whole or in part on the multiparty, multiforum statute,[46] a subpoena for attendance at a hearing or trial may, if authorized by the court upon motion for good cause shown, be served at any place within the United States, or anywhere outside the United States if otherwise permitted by law.[47] The court may impose terms and conditions on service under this provision.[48]

Foreign Countries

Under certain circumstances, a witness subject to the jurisdiction of the court may be in a foreign country. The procedure for issuing a subpoena to such a witness is governed by 28 U.S.C.A. § 1783 (The Walsh Act), which provides for the issuance of such a subpoena if the court finds that the witness's testimony or documents are "necessary in the interest of justice," and it is not possible to obtain the testimony or documents by other means. The person serving such a subpoena must advance the recipient estimated travel expenses.

NOTE: The Walsh Act, 28 U.S.C.A. § 1783, only governs issuing a subpoena to a trial witness. Rule 30 discusses when foreign witnesses may be deposed.

Service on Other Parties

If the subpoena is for a deposition, a notice of deposition must be served on all parties pursuant to Rule 30 or 31. If the subpoena requires the production of documents or inspection of premises, notice must be served upon all parties prior to service on the recipient so that they may assert any privileges or objections and may obtain the same or additional documents.[49]

Arbitrations

The federal courts can enforce subpoenas issued by arbitrators under the provisions of the Federal Arbitration Act, 9 U.S.C. §§ 1 et seq.[50]

RULE 45(c)—PROTECTING A PERSON

---

[44]*Chao v. Tyson Foods, Inc.*, 255 F.R.D. 556, 558 (N.D.Ala. 2009) (rejecting the majority view that the distance limitations do not apply to parties); *Brackett v. Hilton Hotels Corp.*, 619 F.Supp.2d 810, 821 (N.D.Cal. 2008).

[45]*Dynegy Midstream Services v. Trammochem*, 451 F.3d 89, 95 (2d Cir. 2006).

[46]28 U.S.C. § 1369.

[47]28 U.S.C. § 1783.

[48]28 U.S.C. § 1783.

[49]*Josendis v. Wall to Wall Residence Repairs, Inc.*, 662 F.3d 1292, 1303, n.17 (11th Cir. 2011); *Williams v. Thaler*, 602 F.3d 291, 311 (5th Cir. 2010).

[50]*Festus & Helen Stacy Foundation, Inc. v. Merrill Lynch, Pierce Fenner, & Smith Inc.*, 432 F. Supp. 2d 1375, 1377–78 (N.D. Ga. 2006).

SUBJECT TO A SUBPOENA

CORE CONCEPT

An attorney has a duty not to issue a subpoena for improper purposes or to impose undue burden on the recipient of the subpoena. Rule 45(c) also provides mechanisms for recipients of subpoenas to challenge the subpoenas.

NOTE: The cautionary language in Rule 45(c) *must* be reprinted on every subpoena.

APPLICATIONS

Duty to Avoid Undue Burden

An attorney issuing a subpoena has a duty to avoid causing undue burden or expense on the recipient.[51] The court will impose an appropriate sanction, which may include attorney fees and lost wages, on a party or attorney who fails to comply with this duty.[52]

Compensation for Respondent

If compliance with a subpoena would require the disclosure of an unretained expert's opinion or information,[53] or would cause undue burden[54] or expense, the court issuing the subpoena may shift some or all of the costs to the party issuing the subpoena,[55] or otherwise provide for reasonable compensation.[56] The compensation may include wages lost because of the improperly issued subpoena, and may also include attorney fees.[57]

---

[51]*Northwestern Memorial Hosp. v. Ashcroft*, 362 F.3d 923, 938 (7th Cir. 2004); *F.D.I.C. v. Garner*, 126 F.3d 1138, 1145–46 (9th Cir. 1997); *In re Subpoena Duces Tecum to AOL, LLC*, 550 F. Supp. 2d 606, 612 (E.D. Va. 2008) (an overbroad subpoena places an undue burden on the recipient); *Liberty Mut. Ins. Co. v. Diamante*, 194 F.R.D. 20, 23 (D. Mass. 2000) (good faith is not sufficient, but rather the issue is whether the issuing party took reasonable steps to avoid imposing undue burden or expense on the person subject to the subpoena).

[52]*Alberts v. HCA Inc.*, 405 B.R. 498, 502 (D.D.C. 2009).

[53]*Klay v. All Defendants*, 425 F.3d 977, 983–84 (11th Cir. 2005) (compensation could include the value of the intellectual property provided to the recipient).

[54]*Flatow v. Islamic Republic of Iran*, 201 F.R.D. 5, 8 (D.D.C. 2001) (describing test for evaluating undue burden).

[55]*Heidelberg Americas, Inc. v. Tokyo Kikai Seisakusho, Ltd.*, 333 F.3d 38 (1st Cir.2003) (a court "shall" quash or modify a subpoena if the subpoena subjects a person to undue burden); *Allied World Assur. Co. (U.S.), Inc. v. Lincoln Gen. Ins. Co.*, 280 F.R.D. 197, 205 (M.D.Pa. 2012).

[56]*Wells Fargo Bank, N.A. v. Konover*, 259 F.R.D. 206, 207 (D.Conn. 2009) (but the court has discretion not to award any compensation if circumstances warrant); *Dravo Corp. v. Liberty Mut. Ins. Co.*, 160 F.R.D. 123 (D. Neb. 1995).

[57]*Mattel, Inc. v. Walking Mountain Productions*, 353 F.3d 792, 814 (9th Cir. 2003); *Wells Fargo Bank, N.A. v. Konover*, 259 F.R.D. 206, 207 (D.Conn. 2009) (but the court has discretion not to award any fees if circumstances warrant).

Attendance by Person Producing Documents

A person subpoenaed to produce documents or things or to permit an inspection need not actually appear at the designated time, as long as the person complies with the subpoena.

Objection to Subpoena to Produce Documents

A person subpoenaed to produce documents or things or to permit an inspection may serve an objection to all or part of the subpoena within fourteen days after service of the subpoena (or before the time designated in the subpoena, if sooner).[58] Note that the objection procedure does not apply to testimonial subpoenas; those may only be challenged by a motion to quash or modify the subpoena.[59] Objections to subpoenas are customarily made by letter.[60] All grounds for objection should be asserted or they may be waived.[61] Once an objection has been served on the party issuing the subpoena, the subpoena recipient is not obligated to comply with the subpoena.[62] Failure to serve timely objections may constitute a waiver of objections to the subpoena other than objections relating to service.[63] Only non-parties may serve objections; parties must contest a subpoena by a motion to quash or modify.[64]

Motion to Compel

If a subpoena recipient serves an objection to the subpoena, the serving party may file a motion to compel in the court from which the subpoena was issued.[65] The motion must be served on the subpoena recipient. In ruling on such a motion, the court will protect non-parties from "significant" expense.[66] Respondents to motions to compel should raise the issue of ex-

---

[58]*Forsythe v. Brown*, 281 F.R.D. 577, 587 (D.Nev. 2012); *McCoy v. Southwest Airlines Co., Inc.*, 211 F.R.D. 381, 384 (C.D. Cal. 2002) (only the nonparty can prevent disclosure by objection; the party to whom the subpoenaed records pertain cannot simply object).

[59]*Ceroni v. 4Front Engineered Solutions, Inc.*, __ F.Supp.2d __ (D.Colo. 2011).

[60]*See Tuite v. Henry*, 98 F.3d 1411, 1416 (D.C. Cir. 1996).

[61]*Ott v. City of Milwaukee*, 682 F.3d 552, 558 (7th Cir. 2012) (recipient must raise all objections at once - reservation of right to assert additional objections ineffective); *In re DG Acquisition Corp.*, 151 F.3d 75, 81 (2d Cir. 1998).

[62]*U.S. S.E.C. v. Hyatt*, 621 F.3d 687, 694 (7th Cir. 2010); *Pamida, Inc. v. E.S. Originals, Inc.*, 281 F.3d 726, 732 (8th Cir. 2002).

[63]*Judicial Watch, Inc. v. U.S. Dept. of Commerce*, 196 F.R.D. 1, 2 (D.D.C. 2000).

[64]*Moon v. SCP Pool Corp.*, 232 F.R.D. 633, 636 (C.D. Cal. 2005)

[65]*U.S. ex rel. Pogue v. Diabetes Treatment Centers of America, Inc.*, 444 F.3d 462, 468 (6th Cir. 2006); *Ceroni v. 4Front Engineered Solutions, Inc.*, __ F.Supp.2d __ (D.Colo. 2011).

[66]*See Klay v. All Defendants*, 425 F.3d 977, 984 (11th Cir. 2005); *McCabe v. Ernst & Young, LLP*, 221 F.R.D. 423 (D.N.J. 2004); *In re First American Corp.*, 184 F.R.D. 234, 238 (S.D. N.Y. 1998) (respondent awarded expenses plus a portion of attorney's fees).

penses or risk waiver.[67] Some courts and local rules require counsel for the moving party to make a reasonable effort to confer with opposing counsel prior to filing a motion to compel.[68]

Motion to Quash or Modify

A subpoena recipient[69] may move to quash a subpoena in the court from which the subpoena was issued.[70] If the court finds the subpoena objectionable,[71] it may either quash it altogether or modify it to cure the objection.[72] The motion must be "timely" filed, and should certainly be filed before the subpoena's return date.[73] Failure to file a motion to quash may constitute a waiver of objections to the subpoena.[74] The moving party will have the burden of showing that the subpoena should be quashed.[75] A motion to quash is normally filed in the district where the subpoena was issued, but the court where the matter is pending also has the authority to issue protective orders and generally control the scope of discovery[76] and some courts allow the issuing court to transfer enforcement of the subpoena to the court where the case is pending.[77] Some courts and local rules require counsel for the moving party to make a reason-

---

[67]*In re First American Corp.*, 184 F.R.D. 234, 238–39 (S.D. N.Y. 1998).

[68]*See Boukadoum v. Hubanks*, 239 F.R.D. 427, 429–30 (D. Md. 2006); *Medical Components, Inc. v. Classic Medical, Inc.*, 210 F.R.D. 175, 178 (M.D. N.C. 2002).

[69]*Sterling Merchandising, Inc. v. Nestle, S.A.*, 470 F. Supp. 2d 77, 81 (D.P.R. 2006) (only the recipient of a subpoena may move to quash, unless the movant is asserting its privilege).

[70]*S.E.C. v. CMKM Diamonds, Inc.*, 656 F.3d 829, 831–32 (9th Cir. 2011); *Pamida, Inc. v. E.S. Originals, Inc.*, 281 F.3d 726, 729 n.3 (8th Cir. 2002).

[71]*Forsythe v. Brown*, 281 F.R.D. 577, 587 (D.Nev. 2012) (court may quash a subpoena that was not properly served); *Stock v. Integrated Health Plan, Inc.*, 241 F.R.D. 618 (S.D. Ill. 2007) (court had wide discretion as to what is objectionable, and can quash a subpoena seeking irrelevant information, as well as for the reasons listed in Rule 45(c)(3)(A)).

[72]*Wiwa v. Royal Dutch Petroleum Co.*, 392 F.3d 812, 818 (5th Cir. 2004) (modifying a subpoena is generally preferable to quashing it); *CSC Holdings, Inc. v. Redisi*, 309 F.3d 988, 993 (7th Cir. 2002).

[73]*See Centrifugal Acquisition*

Corp., Inc. v. Moon, 849 F.Supp.2d 814, 839 (E.D.Wis. 2012); *Sterling Merchandising, Inc. v. Nestle, S.A.*, 470 F. Supp. 2d 77, 81 (D.P.R. 2006) ("timely" is not defined in the Rule, and is subject to interpretation).

[74]*In re Flat Glass Antitrust Litigation*, 288 F.3d 83, 90 (3d Cir. 2002) (failure to file motion to quash constitutes waiver of objections to manner of service of subpoena).

[75]*Payne v. Dist. of Columbia*, __ F.Supp.2d __ (D.D.C. 2012); *Hendricks v. Total Quality Logistics, LLC*, __ F.R.D. __ (S.D.Ohio 2011).

[76]*GFL Advantage Fund, Ltd. v. Colkitt*, 216 F.R.D. 189 (D.D.C. 2003); *Static Control Components, Inc. v. Darkprint Imaging*, 201 F.R.D. 431, 437 (M.D. N.C. 2001); *Goodyear Tire & Rubber Co. v. Kirk's Tire & Auto Servicenter of Haverstraw, Inc.*, 211 F.R.D. 658, 660 (D. Kan. 2003) (it is within the discretion of the court that issued the subpoena to transfer motions involving the subpoena to the district in which the action is pending); *but see High Point SARL v. Sprint Nextel Corp.*, 280 F.R.D. 586, 593–94 (D.Kan. 2012) (only the issuing court may modify or quash a subpoena).

[77]*See In re Subpoena of American Nurses Association*, __ F.Supp.2d __ (D.Md. 2011).

able effort to confer with opposing counsel prior to filing a motion to quash.[78] Rule 45(c)(3) lists situations in which a subpoena will be quashed or modified:[79]

(1) *Time to Comply:* Rule 45(c)(3)(A)(i) requires that the subpoena recipient be provided reasonable time to comply.[80]

(2) *Distance to Travel:* Rule 45(c)(3)(A)(ii) provides for the quashing of a subpoena requiring a person not a party or officer of a party[81] to travel too far. For a deposition, a non-party may be compelled to travel up to 100 miles from any place that the person resides, is employed, or regularly transacts business in person.[82] When the subpoena is for trial, such a person must travel anywhere within the state.[83] Some courts hold that subpoenas for the production of documents are not subject to the distance limitation because the documents can be produced by mail and the Rule 45(c)(2)(A) does not require the subpoena recipient to appear in person at the place of production.[84]

(3) *Privileged Matters:* Rule 45(c)(3)(A)(iii) provides that a subpoena must be quashed if it requires the disclosure of privileged or other protected matters.[85]

(4) *Undue Burden:* Rule 45(c)(3)(A)(iv) provides that a

---

[78]*See Hill v. Wheatland Waters, Inc.,* 327 F. Supp. 2d 1294, 1298 n.5 (D. Kan. 2004); *In re Bennett Funding Group, Inc.,* 259 B.R. 243, 250 (N.D. N.Y. 2001); *Smith v. Midland Brake, Inc.,* 162 F.R.D. 683, 685 (D. Kan. 1995).

[79]*See Arista Records LLC v. Does 1–19,* 551 F. Supp. 2d 1, 7 (D.D.C. 2008) (suggesting that the court will not quash a subpoena for any reason other than those listed in Rule 45(c)(3)(A)).

[80]*Ott v. City of Milwaukee,* __ F.R.D. __ (E.D.Wis. 2011) (remedy for unreasonable notice is to allow more time to respond); *Hernandez v. Esso Standard Oil Co.,* 252 F.R.D. 118, 119 (D.Puerto Rico 2008) (11 days to produce documents reasonable); *Paul v. Stewart Enterprises, Inc.,* 2000 WL 1171120 (E.D. La. 2000) (one business day's notice is clearly unreasonable in light of the requirement in Rule 45(c)(2)(B) that a subpoenaed person be permitted 14 days to object).

[81]*See Chao v. Tyson Foods, Inc.,* 255 F.R.D. 556, 558 (N.D.Ala. 2009) (rejecting the majority view that the 100 mile rule does not apply to par-

ties); *In re Vioxx Products Liability Litigation,* 414 F. Supp. 2d 574 (E.D. La. 2006).

[82]*See In re Apple, Inc.,* 602 F.3d 909, 914, n.1 (8th Cir. 2010); *Cooper Tire & Rubber Co. v. Farese,* 423 F.3d 446, 452 (5th Cir. 2005); *Price Waterhouse LLP v. First American Corp.,* 182 F.R.D. 56, 62 (S.D. N.Y. 1998) (when the subpoena seeks a corporate representative, travel distance is measured for the representative, not the corporation).

[83]*In re Hoffmann-La Roche Inc.,* 587 F.3d 1333, 1337 (Fed.Cir. 2009); *Williams v. City of Cleveland,* 848 F.Supp.2d 646, 656 (N.D.Miss. 2012); *Zimmer Enterprises, Inc. v. Atlandia Imports, Inc.,* 478 F. Supp. 2d 983, 991–92 (S.D. Ohio 2007) (offer to pay travel expenses does not cure distance problem).

[84]*See U.S. Bank Nat. Ass'n v. James,* 264 F.R.D. 17, 19 (D.Me. 2010); *Walker v. Center for Food Safety,* 667 F.Supp.2d 133, 138 (D.D.C. 2009).

[85]*Zoltek Corp v. U.S.,* __ Fed.Cl. __ (Fed.Cl. 2012); *Arista Records, LLC v. Doe 3,* 604 F.3d 110, 118 (2nd Cir.

subpoena must be quashed if it subjects the recipient to undue burden.[86] This provision is sometimes used as justification for imposing the non-party's expenses on the party issuing the subpoena to cure the undue burden on the non-party.[87]

Substantial Need of Serving Party

Rule 45(c)(3)(B) lists circumstances in which a subpoena will be quashed unless the serving party shows a "substantial need" for the testimony, documents, or inspection. In such cases, the court will condition compliance on the serving party compensating the recipient. These circumstances are:

(1) *Trade Secrets:* Rule 45(c)(3)(B)(i) provides limited protection for trade secrets and other confidential research, development, and commercial information.[88]

(2) *Unretained Experts:* Rule 45(c)(3)(B)(ii) provides limited protection for experts who have not been retained, so that parties cannot obtain their testimony without paying their fees.[89]

(3) *Undue Travel:* Rule 45(c)(3)(B)(iii) provides limited protection to persons who are not parties or officers of parties who would incur substantial expenses to travel more than 100 miles to attend trial.[90]

RULE 45(d)—DUTIES IN RESPONDING TO A SUBPOENA

CORE CONCEPT

Documents may be produced as they are normally kept or may be separated and organized. When privileges are asserted, the privilege must be expressly described.

NOTE: The cautionary language in Rule 45(d) *must* be reprinted on every subpoena.

2010) (first amendment right to anonymous speech is a protectable interest).

[86] *Positive Black Talk Inc. v. Cash Money Records, Inc.*, 394 F.3d 357, 377–78 (5th Cir. 2004) (requiring an expert to testify in the face of a potential conflict of interest was an unreasonable burden); *Northwestern Memorial Hosp. v. Ashcroft*, 362 F.3d 923, 927 (7th Cir. 2004) (balancing the burden and the need for the information).

[87] *See Alberts v. HCA Inc.*, 405 B.R. 498, 502 (D.D.C. 2009); *Medical Components, Inc. v. Classic Medical, Inc.*, 210 F.R.D. 175, 179 (M.D. N.C. 2002).

[88] *Mattel, Inc. v. Walking Mountain Productions*, 353 F.3d 792, 814 (9th Cir. 2003); *Hobley v. Burge*, 223 F.R.D. 499, 505 (N.D. Ill. 2004) (newspaper reporter's notes are confidential research).

[89] *In re Smirman*, ___ F.R.D. ___ (E.D.Mich. 2010); *Express One Intern., Inc. v. Sochata*, 2001 WL 363073 (N.D. Tex. 2001) (witness was an employee who has not consented to serve as an expert and cannot be forced to testify as an expert).

[90] *Kisser v. Coalition for Religious Freedom*, 1995 WL 590169 (E.D. Pa. 1995) (ordering party to reimburse non-party for reasonable attorney's fees and travel expenses).

APPLICATIONS

Production of Documents

The scope of production under a subpoena is the same as the scope for discovery generally under Rule 26.[91] The responding party has the option of allowing the serving party to inspect and copy the documents where they are normally kept (*e.g.*, "There is our file room.")[92] The responding party may also collect the responsive documents and organize and label them to correspond to the categories requests.[93] The responding party may make copies for the requesting party, but is not obligated to do so.

Electronic Data

Rule 45 expressly allows for the party issuing the subpoena to request to inspect, copy, sample, or test electronic data.

- *Form of Electronic Data:* Rule 45(d)(1)(B) allows, but does not require, the requesting party to specify the form in which it is requesting electronic data (i.e., hard copy or electronic, and if electronic, the precise manner of production). If the requesting party does not specify the form, then the responding person must produce it in the form in which it is ordinarily maintained or in a form that is reasonably usable. In any event, a person need not produce electronic data in more than one form.

- *Undue Burden or Cost:* If the responding person believes that the production of electronic data from certain sources will cause undue burden or cost, the person can, in lieu of producing the documents, identify those sources.[94] If a motion to compel or quash is filed, the responding person will have the burden of showing that production would cause undue burden or cost.[95] The burden would then shift to the requesting party to show good cause why the data should be produced nonetheless.[96] In such cases, the court may specify conditions for the production, such as payment of the expenses of the production by the requesting party.[97]

---

[91]*Chevron Corp. v. Salazar*, 275 F.R.D. 437, 447, n.8 (S.D.N.Y. 2011); *Stock v. Integrated Health Plan, Inc.*, 241 F.R.D. 618 (S.D. Ill. 2007).

[92]*Kinetic Concepts, Inc. v. Convatec Inc.*, __ F.R.D. __ (M.D.N.C. 2010); *In re John Adams Associates, Inc.*, 255 F.R.D. 7, 8 (D.D.C. 2008).

[93]*Kinetic Concepts, Inc. v. Convatec Inc.*, __ F.R.D. __ (M.D.N.C. 2010).

[94]*Guy Chemical Co., Inc. v. Romaco AG*, 243 F.R.D. 310 (N.D. Ind.

2007).

[95]*Guy Chemical Co., Inc. v. Romaco AG*, 243 F.R.D. 310 (N.D. Ind. 2007).

[96]*Guy Chemical Co., Inc. v. Romaco AG*, 243 F.R.D. 310 (N.D. Ind. 2007) (good cause exists where no other source exists for the information).

[97]*Guy Chemical Co., Inc. v. Romaco AG*, 243 F.R.D. 310 (N.D. Ind. 2007).

Asserting a Privilege

When the subpoena recipient seeks to withhold information that is privileged, the recipient must expressly claim the privilege and describe the nature of the documents, communications, or things not produced in sufficient detail that the court and parties can assess the privilege.[98] The party asserting the privilege should provide a detailed privilege log at the time of asserting the privilege or within a reasonable time thereafter.[99]

Recalling Privileged Information

Rule 45(d)(2)(B) establishes a procedure to recall privileged information that has already been produced. Anyone believing that a person has produced privileged information in response to a subpoena may provide a notification to the parties who have received the information. After receiving such a notification, the receiving parties must return, sequester, or destroy the specified information and all copies (including taking reasonable steps to retrieve any information that the receiving party had already disclosed to other persons). If they do not agree with the privilege assertion, they can present the information to the court under seal for a determination of the privilege claim. During the pendency of the court's review of the privilege claim, the receiving parties are prohibited from using the information and the producing party must preserve it.

RULE 45(e)—CONTEMPT

CORE CONCEPT

Failure to obey a valid subpoena without adequate excuse is a contempt of the court issuing the subpoena.[100]

APPLICATIONS

Challenge to Subpoena

If a party believes that a subpoena is not valid, the proper response is a motion to quash or a motion for a protective order. *See* Rule 26(c). If the motion is unsuccessful and the party disobeys the subpoena nonetheless, the party can also raise validity grounds again at the contempt proceedings.[101] However, if the lawsuit is not before a federal court with subject matter

---

[98]*Ott v. City of Milwaukee*, 682 F.3d 552, 558 (7th Cir. 2012) (failure to assert detailed objection constitutes waiver); *In re Subpoena Duces Tecum Issued to Commodity Futures Trading Com'n*, 439 F.3d 740, 751 (D.C. Cir. 2006) (a privilege log generally satisfies Rule 45(d)(2)).

[99]*Perry v. Schwarzenegger*, ___ F.R.D. ___ (N.D.Cal. 2010) (court may waive log requirement to lessen burden on a non-party; *Horace Mann Ins.*

Co. v. Nationwide Mut. Ins. Co., 240 F.R.D. 44, 47 (D. Conn. 2007) (discussing what qualifies as a reasonable period of time).

[100]*Blackmer v. U.S.*, 284 U.S. 421, 52 S. Ct. 252, 76 L. Ed. 375 (1932); *S.E.C. v. CMKM Diamonds, Inc.*, 656 F.3d 829, 831–32 (9th Cir. 2011).

[101]*U.S. v. Ryan*, 402 U.S. 530, 533, 91 S. Ct. 1580, 1582, 29 L. Ed. 2d 85 (1971).

jurisdiction, the subpoena will not be enforceable and a disobedient recipient is not subject to contempt sanctions.[102]

Due Process

Before sanctions may be imposed on a person charged with contempt under Rule 45, due process requires that the person receive notice and an opportunity to be heard.[103] There is no prerequisite, however, of a motion to compel compliance; the court can issue contempt sanctions based on the failure to comply with the subpoena even if the subpoena is issued without court involvement.[104]

Adequate Excuse

Inability to comply is an adequate excuse.[105] The fact that the subpoena would require the recipient to travel greater distances than those listed in Rule 45(c)(3)(A)(iii) is also an adequate excuse.[106] Likewise, a timely objection to the subpoena is an adequate excuse.[107] Preferring to work instead of comply with the subpoena is not an adequate excuse.[108]

Appeal

Orders pertaining to subpoenas are ordinarily interlocutory, and thus not appealable. An exception exists when one district clerk issues a discovery subpoena for an action proceeding in another district, and that subpoena is quashed. Such an order is immediately appealable as a final order.[109]

Additional Research References

Wright & Miller, *Federal Practice and Procedure* §§ 2451 to 2463

C.J.S., Federal Civil Procedure §§ 582 to 583 et seq., 644; Witnesses §§ 13 to 27 et seq.

West's Key Number Digest, Federal Civil Procedure ☞1353 to 1354, 1456; Witnesses ☞7 to 16, 21

---

[102]*Olcott v. Delaware Flood Co.*, 76 F.3d 1538, 1552 (10th Cir. 1996).

[103]*U.S. S.E.C. v. Hyatt*, 621 F.3d 687, 694 (7th Cir. 2010); *In re Corso*, 328 B.R. 375 (E.D. N.Y. 2005).

[104]*U.S. S.E.C. v. Hyatt*, 621 F.3d 687, 694 (7th Cir. 2010).

[105]*U.S. S.E.C. v. Hyatt*, 621 F.3d 687, 693, 697 (7th Cir. 2010); *Fisher v. Marubeni Cotton Corp.*, 526 F.2d 1338, 1342 (8th Cir. 1975).

[106]*See Hillard v. Guidant Corp.*, 76 F. Supp. 2d 566, 570 (M.D. Pa. 1999); *National Property Investors VIII v. Shell Oil Co.*, 917 F. Supp. 324, 328 (D.N.J. 1995).

[107]*Flatow v. The Islamic Republic of Iran*, 196 F.R.D. 203, 208 (D.D.C. 2000).

[108]*Higginbotham v. KCS Intern., Inc.*, 202 F.R.D. 444, 455 (D. Md. 2001).

[109]*CF & I Steel Corp. v. Mitsui & Co. (U.S.A.), Inc.*, 713 F.2d 494 (9th Cir.1983); *Horizons Titanium Corp. v. Norton Co.*, 290 F.2d 421 (1st Cir. 1961).

RULE 46
OBJECTING TO A RULING OR ORDER

A formal exception to a ruling or order is unnecessary. When the ruling or order is requested or made, a party need only state the action that it wants the court to take or objects to, along with the grounds for the request or objection. Failing to object does not prejudice a party who had no opportunity to do so when the ruling or order was made.

[Amended effective August 1, 1987; April 30, 2007, effective December 1, 2007.]

AUTHORS' COMMENTARY ON RULE 46

PURPOSE AND SCOPE

Rule 46 abolishes the formality of noting "exceptions" when the court overrules an objection or takes some action contrary to a request.[1]

NOTE: An attorney still needs to voice an objection to a court's ruling in the first instance; Rule 46 only relieves the need to note exceptions to the court's ruling.

APPLICATIONS

Applies to All Stages

Rule 46 applies to all stages of a trial, from voir dire through jury instructions. The attorney must object even to questions asked by the judge, although the appeals court may be more lenient about the form and timing of such objections.

Form of Objection

In order to preserve an issue for appeal, an attorney must state the particular grounds upon which the objection rests.[2] It is not sufficient to state simply, "objection," or to make a general objection. The primary purpose of the specificity require-

---

[1]*Kasper v. Saint Mary of Nazareth Hosp.*, 135 F.3d 1170, 1175 (7th Cir. 1998).

[2]*Ramey v. District 141, Intern. Ass'n of Machinists and Aerospace Workers*, 378 F.3d 269, 281 (2d Cir. 2004) (a party seeking to preserve an objection must make known to the court the party's objection to the action of the court and the grounds therefore); *Kasper v. Saint Mary of Nazareth Hosp.*, 135 F.3d 1170, 1176 (7th Cir. 1998).

ment is to apprise the court of the litigant's position so that the court can correct its ruling if appropriate.[3] Consequently, if the grounds are obvious to the trial judge, an appellate court may overlook a lack of specificity.[4] If the judge's ruling is ambiguous, a party cannot challenge it on appeal without first attempting to have the judge clarify the ruling.[5]

Exceptions

It is not necessary to note an exception or take any other action to preserve a properly raised but overruled objection.[6]

Failure to Object

In general, failure to object to a ruling or issue constitutes a waiver of the ruling or issue.[7] Rule 46 provides that an attorney need not object if there is no opportunity to do so.[8] Additionally, the appeals court may consider on appeal an issue to which no objection was asserted when the basis was so clear that no objection was necessary, such as when the attorney has already objected to the same evidence.[9] Also, the appellate court may overlook the lack of an objection if the error was so fundamental that it caused a miscarriage of justice.[10]

Unsuccessful Motion in Limine

If a party files an unsuccessful motion in limine where the exclusion of certain evidence is sought, that party does not have to formally object at trial when the evidence in question is introduced as long as two conditions are met: (1) the party filed a written pre-trial motion setting forth reasons and case citations in support of the request that the evidence be excluded; and (2) the district court made a "definitive" ruling with no suggestion that it would reconsider the matter at trial.[11]

---

[3]*In re Sealed Case*, 552 F.3d 841, 852 (D.C.Cir. 2009); *Kasper v. Saint Mary of Nazareth Hosp.*, 135 F.3d 1170, 1176 (7th Cir. 1998).

[4]*New England Newspaper Pub. Co. v. Bonner*, 68 F.2d 880 (C.C.A. 1st Cir. 1934).

[5]*Kasper v. Saint Mary of Nazareth Hosp.*, 135 F.3d 1170, 1176 (7th Cir. 1998).

[6]*Jacques v. DiMarzio, Inc.*, 386 F.3d 192, 200–01 (2d Cir. 2004) (formal exceptions to rulings of the court are unnecessary as long as the party makes known its objection and the basis for it at the time the district court rules); *Fogarty v. Near North Ins. Brokerage, Inc.*, 162 F.3d 74, 81 (2d Cir. 1998).

[7]*See S.E.C. v. Diversified*

Corporate Consulting Group, 378 F.3d 1219, 1227 (11th Cir.2004); *Krieger v. Fadely*, 211 F.3d 134 (D.C. Cir. 2000).

[8]*Marlin v. Moody Nat. Bank, N.A.*, 533 F.3d 374, 380 (5th Cir. 2008); *Boeing Co. v. Cascade Corp.*, 207 F.3d 1177, 1191 (9th Cir. 2000).

[9]*Beech Aircraft Corp. v. Rainey*, 488 U.S. 153, 109 S. Ct. 439, 102 L. Ed. 2d 445 (1988).

[10]*Sibbach v. Wilson & Co.*, 312 U.S. 1, 16, 312 U.S. 655, 61 S. Ct. 422, 427, 85 L. Ed. 479 (1941).

[11]*Walden v. Georgia-Pacific Corp.*, 126 F.3d 506, 518 (3d Cir. 1997). *See also Inter Medical Supplies, Ltd. v. EBI Medical Systems, Inc.*, 181 F.3d 446, 455 (3d Cir. 1999) (objection unnecessary following motion in limine where the court has made a definitive

Additional Research References

Wright & Miller, *Federal Practice and Procedure* §§ 2471 to 2473
C.J.S., Federal Civil Procedure §§ 370 et seq., 941 to 942
West's Key Number Digest, Federal Civil Procedure ☞928, 2017 to 2019

---

ruling on the issue and is unlikely to   reconsider).

RULE 47
SELECTING JURORS

(a) Examining Jurors. The court may permit the parties or their attorneys to examine prospective jurors or may itself do so. If the court examines the jurors, it must permit the parties or their attorneys to make any further inquiry it considers proper, or must itself ask any of their additional questions it considers proper.

(b) Peremptory Challenges. The court must allow the number of peremptory challenges provided by 28 U.S.C. § 1870.

(c) Excusing a Juror. During trial or deliberation, the court may excuse a juror for good cause.

[Amended effective July 1, 1966; December 1, 1991; April 30, 2007, effective December 1, 2007.]

AUTHORS' COMMENTARY ON RULE 47

PURPOSE AND SCOPE

Rule 47 addresses the examination of prospective jurors (voir dire) and contains provisions for alternate jurors.

RULE 47(a)—EXAMINING OF JURORS

CORE CONCEPT

The court and/or the parties may ask prospective jurors questions in order to determine bias and to enable the parties to exercise their peremptory challenges in a meaningful manner.

APPLICATIONS

Scope of Examinations

The court has broad discretion with respect to the scope of voir dire.[1] It may conduct the examination itself or allow the

---

[1]*Csiszer v. Wren*, 614 F.3d 866, 875 (8th Cir. 2010); *Smith v. Vicorp, Inc.*, 107 F.3d 816, 817 (10th Cir. 1997).

parties to do so.[2] If the court conducts the examination, the parties may submit proposed questions, which the court may ask if it deems them proper.[3] In exercising its discretion, the court must allow sufficient questioning so that the selection process is meaningful.

Challenges for Cause

Challenges for cause are ruled on by the court. The party making the challenge has the burden of persuading the court. Partiality is the main grounds for such challenges. Parties can challenge the entire panel or the selection process. Such challenges should be made at the time of jury selection, not in a motion for new trial.[4]

Qualifications for Jurors

The qualifications for jurors is governed by the Jury Selection and Service Act of 1968, 28 U.S.C. §§ 1861 et seq. Essentially, jurors must be United States citizens, have resided in the district for at least one year, must meet minimum literacy requirements and be fluent in English, must be mentally and physically capable of service, and must be free from pending charges or past convictions of crimes punishable by imprisonment for more than 2 years.

Excluded Groups

The Jury Selection and Service Act of 1968 also provides for the establishment of certain groups who are precluded or excused from serving. Generally, these include: persons providing vital services (such as members of the armed services and policemen); persons for whom service would be a particular hardship (such as sole proprietors, mothers with young children, persons with gravely ill family members); and those excluded by the court for partiality or because they are likely to be disruptive.

Conduct of Jurors

The court has great latitude with respect to such issues as note taking by jurors, sequestration, questions by the jury, etc.

Alternate Jurors

Alternate jurors are no longer used in civil trials in federal court.[5]

RULE 47(b)—PEREMPTORY CHALLENGES

CORE CONCEPT

Rule 47(b) provides that peremptory challenges are governed

---

[2]*Csiszer v. Wren*, 614 F.3d 866, 875 (8th Cir. 2010).

[3]*Csiszer v. Wren*, 614 F.3d 866, 875 (8th Cir. 2010); *Smith v. Tenet Healthsystem SL, Inc.*, 436 F.3d 879, 884 (8th Cir. 2006).

[4]*Atlas Roofing Mfg. Co. v. Parnell*, 409 F.2d 1191 (5th Cir.1969).

[5]The Advisory Committee Note to the 1991 Amendments to Rule 47 and Rule 48; *Delaney v. Detella*, 2004 WL 525007 (N.D. Ill. 2004).

by 28 U.S.C.A. § 1870, which provides that each party has 3 peremptory challenges, and generally need not give any explanation for using those challenges. Peremptory challenges are not constitutionally protected fundamental rights, but are merely one means to the constitutional end of an impartial jury and a fair trial.[6] When there are multiple plaintiffs or defendants, the court may require them to exercise the challenges collectively or may allow additional challenges.[7]

APPLICATIONS

Improper Grounds

It is improper to use a peremptory challenge to exclude a juror on the basis of race[8] or gender.[9]

RULE 47(c)—EXCUSING A JUROR

CORE CONCEPT

The court may excuse a juror for reasons of sickness, family emergency, juror misconduct, or for other "good cause shown."[10] A juror's refusal to join the majority is not grounds for excuse.[11]

APPLICATIONS

Considerations for Excuse

Characteristics of a juror to be scrutinized pursuant to Rule 47(c) include not only spoken words, but gestures and attitudes in order to ensure the jury's impartiality and competence.[12]

Additional Research References

Wright & Miller, *Federal Practice and Procedure* §§ 2481 to 2485. Bennett & Hirschhorn, Bennett's *Guide to Jury Selection and Trial Dynamics in Civil and Criminal Litigation.*
C.J.S., Juries §§ 208 to 250 et seq., 251 to 285 et seq.
West's Key Number Digest, Jury ☞83 to 142

---

[6]*U.S. v. Allen-Brown*, 243 F.3d 1293, 1299 (11th Cir. 2001); *see also Rahn v. Hawkins*, 464 F.3d 813, 819 (8th Cir. 2006) (declining to vacate a verdict where trial court erroneously gave each side 2 peremptory challenges).

[7]*In re Air Crash Disaster*, 86 F.3d 498, 518–519 (6th Cir. 1996).

[8]*Edmonson v. Leesville Concrete Co., Inc.*, 500 U.S. 614, 111 S. Ct. 2077, 114 L. Ed. 2d 660 (1991).

[9]*Montanez v. Puerto Rico Police Dept.*, 33 F. Supp. 2d 106, 108 (D.P.R. 1999).

[10]*See Harris v. Folk Const. Co.*, 138 F.3d 365, 371 (8th Cir. 1998); *Interpool Ltd. v. Patterson*, 874 F. Supp. 616 (S.D. N.Y. 1995) (juror excused because of important business trip).

[11]*See Murray v. Laborers Union Local No. 324*, 55 F.3d 1445, 1450–51 (9th Cir. 1995).

[12]*Harris v. Folk Const. Co.*, 138 F.3d 365, 371 (8th Cir. 1998).

RULE 48
NUMBER OF JURORS; VERDICT

(a) Number of Jurors. A jury must begin with at least 6 and no more than 12 members, and each juror must participate in the verdict unless excused under Rule 47(c).

(b) Verdict. Unless the parties stipulate otherwise, the verdict must be unanimous and must be returned by a jury of at least 6 members.

(c) Polling. After a verdict is returned but before the jury is discharged, the court must on a party's request, or may on its own, poll the jurors individually. If the poll reveals a lack of unanimity or lack of assent by the number of jurors that the parties stipulated to, the court may direct the jury to deliberate further or may order a new trial.

[Amended effective December 1, 1991; April 30, 2007, effective December 1, 2007; March 26, 2009, effective December 1, 2009.]

AUTHORS' COMMENTARY ON RULE 48

PURPOSE AND SCOPE

The court may select any number of jurors from 6 to 12, inclusive. Unless the parties stipulate otherwise, the verdict must be unanimous.

APPLICATIONS

Number of Jurors

The court may select any number of jurors from 6 to 12, inclusive.[1]

Verdicts Normally Unanimous

Absent a stipulation, verdicts must be unanimous.[2] However, verdicts are considered unanimous even if 1 or more

---

[1] *See Show v. Ford Motor Co.*, 659 F.3d 584, 586 (7th Cir. 2011); *Wolfe v. Fayetteville, Arkansas Sch. Dist.*, 648 F.3d 860, 869 (8th Cir. 2011).

[2] *Jazzabi v. Allstate Ins. Co.*, 278 F.3d 979, 985 (9th Cir. 2002) (jury must be unanimous as to affirmative defense as well as ultimate verdict);

jurors reluctantly joins just to reach a verdict.[3] If a jury reports being unable to reach a unanimous verdict, the majority of the courts allow an instruction to the jury to deliberate further to attempt to break the deadlock.[4]

Polling the Jury

A party may demand that the jury be polled to verify that the verdict is unanimous. If 1 or more jurors dissents, the court may require the jury to deliberate further or may declare a mistrial. Polling must occur before the verdict is recorded and the jury is discharged.

Excused Jurors

If a juror is excused for illness or other reason under Rule 47(c), a unanimous verdict among the remaining jurors will be valid if at least 6 jurors remain.[5] If fewer than 6 remain, the parties may consent to allow the trial or deliberations to continue and to then be bound by the verdict.[6]

Stipulations

By stipulation, the parties can agree that a unanimous decision is not necessary, and that the decision of a specified majority will be taken as the decision of the jury.[7] The parties may also stipulate to fewer than 6 jurors.[8]

Alternate Jurors

Alternate jurors are not used in civil trials in federal court.[9]

Advisory Jury

It does not appear that the provisions of Rule 48 regarding unanimity pertain to advisory juries.[10]

Robinson v. Cattaraugus County, 147 F.3d 153, 161 (2d Cir. 1998).

[3]*See Cary v. Allegheny Technologies Inc.*, 267 F. Supp. 2d 442 (W.D. Pa. 2003) (allowing a charge to the jury about the benefits of reaching a verdict).

[4]*Cary v. Allegheny Technologies Inc.*, 267 F. Supp. 2d 442, 446 (W.D. Pa. 2003) (the "vast majority" of the courts allow supplemental "Allen" instructions to civil juries).

[5]*Weaver v. Blake*, 454 F.3d 1087 (10th Cir.2006).

[6]*Meyers v. Wal-Mart Stores, East, Inc.*, 257 F.3d 625, 633 (6th Cir. 2001) (approving a trial with 4 jurors based on the parties' stipulation, and noting that a bench trial is essentially a stipulation to trial before zero jurors);

N.A.A.C.P. v. Acusport Corp., 253 F. Supp. 2d 459 (E.D. N.Y. 2003).

[7]*Baxter Healthcare Corp. v. Spectramed, Inc.*, 49 F.3d 1575 (Fed. Cir. 1995); *Cook v. Rockwell Intern. Corp.*, 428 F. Supp. 2d 1152, 1154 (D. Colo. 2006); *N.A.A.C.P. v. AcuSport, Inc.*, 271 F. Supp. 2d 435 (E.D. N.Y. 2003).

[8]*Meyers v. Wal-Mart Stores, East, Inc.*, 77 F. Supp. 2d 826, 827 (E.D. Mich. 1999), aff'd, 257 F.3d 625 (6th Cir. 2001) (both parties stipulated to 4 jurors).

[9]The Advisory Committee Note to the 1991 Amendments to Rule 47 and Rule 48; *Delaney v. Detella*, 2004 WL 525007 (N.D. Ill. 2004).

[10]*N.A.A.C.P. v. Acusport Corp.*, 253 F. Supp. 2d 459 (E.D. N.Y. 2003).

Additional Research References

Wright & Miller, *Federal Practice and Procedure* §§ 2491 to 2492. Bennett & Hirschhorn, Bennett's *Guide to Jury Selection and Trial Dynamics in Civil and Criminal Litigation.*

C.J.S., Federal Civil Procedure §§ 995 et seq.; Juries § 4

West's Key Number Digest, Federal Civil Procedure ⚷2191; Jury ⚷4

RULE 49
SPECIAL VERDICT; GENERAL VERDICT AND QUESTIONS

(a) Special Verdict.

(1) *In General.* The court may require a jury to return only a special verdict in the form of a special written finding on each issue of fact. The court may do so by:

(A) submitting written questions susceptible of a categorical or other brief answer;

(B) submitting written forms of the special findings that might properly be made under the pleadings and evidence; or

(C) using any other method that the court considers appropriate.

(2) *Instructions.* The court must give the instructions and explanations necessary to enable the jury to make its findings on each submitted issue.

(3) *Issues Not Submitted.* A party waives the right to a jury trial on any issue of fact raised by the pleadings or evidence but not submitted to the jury unless, before the jury retires, the party demands its submission to the jury. If the party does not demand submission, the court may make a finding on the issue. If the court makes no finding, it is considered to have made a finding consistent with its judgment on the special verdict.

(b) General Verdict with Answers to Written Questions.

(1) *In General.* The court may submit to the jury forms for a general verdict, together with written questions on one or more issues of fact that the jury must decide. The court must give the instructions and explanations necessary to enable the jury to render a general verdict and answer the questions in writing, and must direct

the jury to do both.

(2) *Verdict and Answers Consistent.* When the general verdict and the answers are consistent, the court must approve, for entry under Rule 58, an appropriate judgment on the verdict and answers.

(3) *Answers Inconsistent with the Verdict.* When the answers are consistent with each other but one or more is inconsistent with the general verdict, the court may:

  (A) approve, for entry under Rule 58, an appropriate judgment according to the answers, notwithstanding the general verdict;

  (B) direct the jury to further consider its answers and verdict; or

  (C) order a new trial.

(4) *Answers Inconsistent with Each Other and the Verdict.* When the answers are inconsistent with each other and one or more is also inconsistent with the general verdict, judgment must not be entered; instead, the court must direct the jury to further consider its answers and verdict, or must order a new trial.

[Amended effective July 1, 1963; August 1, 1987; April 30, 2007, effective December 1, 2007.]

AUTHORS' COMMENTARY ON RULE 49

PURPOSE AND SCOPE

Rule 49 provides mechanisms for directing specific questions to the jury. There are 2 alternative methods: special verdicts, which allow the jury to make findings as to each issue of fact; and written interrogatories which, together with a general verdict, allow the parties to verify that the jury is applying the law to the facts in the manner instructed by the court.[1]

---

[1]*Black v. U.S.*, 130 S.Ct. 2963, 2969, 177 L.Ed.2d 695, 78 USLW 4732, (U.S. 2010).

RULE 49(a)—SPECIAL VERDICT

CORE CONCEPT

The court may require the jury to return special verdicts as to each factual issue, instead of a general verdict in favor of one party.[2]

APPLICATIONS

Comparison With General Verdict

A general verdict is a single statement disposing of the entire case ("We find in favor of the defendant.").[3] Special verdicts ask the jury to decide specific factual questions ("At the time of the accident, the vehicle was proceeding at an excessive rate of speed.").[4]

Court's Discretion

The court has virtually absolute discretion as to the use of special verdicts.[5] This discretion extends to determining the content and layout of the verdict form, and any interrogatories submitted to the jury, provided the questions asked are reasonably capable of an interpretation that would allow the jury to address all factual issues essential to judgment.[6] Generally, special verdicts are more appropriate in complex cases.[7] Special verdicts are also valuable when the status of the law is uncertain because if the trial court is reversed on the law, sufficient special verdicts may render a new trial unnecessary.

Scope of Questions

The special verdicts should fairly present the case, and should cover all factual issues.[8] Although special verdicts should not ask purely legal questions, they sometimes will contain a mixture of law and fact.

Form of Questions

Special verdicts may take different forms. Sometimes the questions will require the jury to write a brief answer (such as "yes" or "no"). Sometimes alternative special verdicts will be

---

[2]*Lee v. Coss*, 39 F. Supp. 2d 170 (D. Conn. 1999), aff'd, 201 F.3d 431 (2d Cir. 1999).

[3]*Mason v. Ford Motor Co., Inc.*, 307 F.3d 1271, 1274 (11th Cir. 2002).

[4]*Zhang v. American Gem Seafoods, Inc.*, 339 F.3d 1020, 1031 (9th Cir. 2003) (comparing special and general verdicts); *Lavin v. Emery Air Freight Corp.*, 980 F. Supp. 93, 98 (D. Conn. 1997), aff'd, 141 F.3d 1151 (2d Cir. 1998) (court looks to two factors when determining whether a verdict is general or special, its own intent and the substantive charge given).

[5]*See Ling Nan Zheng v. Liberty Apparel Co. Inc.*, 617 F.3d 182, 186 (2nd Cir. 2010); *International Ground Transp. v. Mayor And City Council Of Ocean City, MD*, 475 F.3d 214, 223 (4th Cir. 2007).

[6]*E.E.O.C. v. Mgmt. Hospitality of Racine, Inc.*, 666 F.3d 422, 439–40 (7th Cir. 2012); *U.S. v. Real Property Located at 20832 Big Rock Drive, Malibu, Cal. 902655*, 51 F.3d 1402, 1408 (9th Cir. 1995).

[7]*Dinco v. Dylex Ltd.*, 111 F.3d 964, 969 (1st Cir. 1997).

[8]*E.E.O.C. v. Mgmt. Hospitality of Racine, Inc.*, 666 F.3d 422, 440 (7th Cir. 2012); *Santos v. Posadas De Puerto Rico Associates, Inc.*, 452 F.3d 59, 65 (1st Cir. 2006).

written out, and the jury need only choose one alternative.

Instructions to Jury

Rule 49(a) requires the court to give the jury sufficient instructions so that they can determine each issue before them.[9] When an issue before the jury involves mixed questions of fact and law, the court must give instructions as to the applicable law.[10]

Omission of Issues

If the court submits special verdicts to the jury and omits a question of fact raised by the pleadings or evidence, each party must object to the omission before the jury retires or that party waives the right to a jury trial on that issue (note that one party cannot rely on the objection of another party).[11] As to issues not submitted to the jury and not objected to, the court may make a finding.[12] If the court merely issues a general verdict, the court will be deemed to have ruled in a consistent fashion on issues not submitted to the jury.[13]

Return of Verdict

The jury's verdicts must be certain, unequivocal, and consistent. If there is a construction of the verdicts that renders them consistent, it will be adopted.[14] Otherwise, the court may require the jury to deliberate further[15] or may declare a mistrial. The court may not, however, enter judgment contrary to the jury verdict.[16]

Failure to Find

If the jury fails to unanimously agree on some of the answers to special interrogatories, the judge has several available procedures prior to dismissing the jury. The judge can: resubmit the interrogatories to the jury for further delibera-

---

[9]*Romano v. Howarth*, 998 F.2d 101 (2d Cir.1993). *But see Aerotech Resources, Inc. v. Dodson Aviation, Inc.*, 191 F. Supp. 2d 1209, 1220 (D. Kan. 2002), aff'd, 91 Fed. Appx. 37 (10th Cir. 2004) (with special interrogatories, the jury makes findings of fact as to each contested fact, then the court applies the law to those facts, so instructions of the law to the jury are unnecessary).

[10]*Manufacturers Hanover Trust Co. v. Drysdale Securities Corp.*, 801 F.2d 13, 26 (2d Cir. 1986); *Tights, Inc. v. Acme-McCrary Corp.*, 541 F.2d 1047, 1061 (4th Cir. 1976).

[11]*See Ross v. Marshall*, 426 F.3d 745, 762 (5th Cir. 2005); *Becker v. Poling Transp. Corp.*, 356 F.3d 381, 390 (2d Cir. 2004); *Reynolds v. City of Chicago*, 296 F.3d 524 (7th Cir.2002).

[12]*Lore v. City of Syracuse*, 670 F.3d 127, 167 (2d Cir. 2012); *Patsy's Italian Restaurant, Inc. v. Banas*, 658 F.3d 254, 265 (2d Cir. 2011) (issue must be raised in the pleadings or evidence).

[13]*Ansin v. River Oaks Furniture, Inc.*, 105 F.3d 745, 756 (1st Cir. 1997).

[14]*Technical Resource Services, Inc. v. Dornier Medical Systems, Inc.*, 134 F.3d 1458, 1464 (11th Cir. 1998); *Riddle v. Tex-Fin, Inc.*, 719 F.Supp.2d 742, 746 (S.D.Tex. 2010).

[15]*Selgas v. American Airlines, Inc.*, 858 F. Supp. 316 (D.P.R. 1994).

[16]*Lore v. City of Syracuse*, 670 F.3d 127, 167 (2d Cir. 2012); *Ramos v. Davis & Geck, Inc.*, 224 F.3d 30, 32 (1st Cir. 2000).

tions; ask the parties if they would be willing to accept the majority responses; enter judgment on the basis of the unanimous interrogatory answers if they are dispositive; declare the entire case a mistrial; or order a partial retrial of the issues not unanimously agreed upon.[17]

Objections

Objections to the instructions to the jury should be made before the jury retires.[18] Objections to the jury's responses or to the verdict to be entered based on the jury's responses should be made, if possible, before the jury is discharged. Failure to do so may result in a waiver of the objections.[19]

Law Governing

The use of special verdicts or interrogatories is a procedural issue governed by federal law, not by state law.[20]

RULE 49(b)—GENERAL VERDICT WITH ANSWERS TO WRITTEN QUESTIONS

CORE CONCEPT

The court may submit to the jury a general verdict[21] and written interrogatories about specific factual issues.

APPLICATIONS

Purpose

Written interrogatories can serve 2 functions. First they focus the jury's attention on important factual issues and insure that the general verdict is consistent with the factual findings. Second, if the court is subsequently reversed on a legal issue, a new trial may be avoided if the interrogatories contain sufficient findings.

Court's Discretion

As with special verdicts, the court has virtually absolute discretion with respect to the use of written interrogatories to

---

[17]*Baxter Healthcare Corp. v. Spectramed, Inc.*, 49 F.3d 1575 (Fed. Cir. 1995).

[18]*Cash v. Cnty. of Erie*, 654 F.3d 324, 340 (2d Cir. 2011); *Shcherbakovskiy v. Da Capo Al Fine, Ltd.*, 490 F.3d 130, 141 (2d Cir. 2007).

[19]*L & W, Inc. v. Shertech, Inc.*, 471 F.3d 1311, 1319 (Fed. Cir. 2006); *Marcano-Rivera v. Pueblo Intern., Inc.*, 232 F.3d 245, 253 n.4 (1st Cir. 2000). *But see Johnson v. Ablt Trucking Co., Inc.*, 412 F.3d 1138, 1141 (10th Cir. 2005) (failure to object to inconsistent special verdicts before the jury is discharged is not a waiver); *Heno v.*

Sprint/United Management Co., 208 F.3d 847, 851 (10th Cir. 2000) (a party is not required to object to inconsistent special verdicts before the jury retires in order to preserve the issue for a subsequent motion to the court).

[20]*Affiliated FM Ins. Co. v. Neosho Const. Co., Inc.*, 192 F.R.D. 662, 673 (D. Kan. 2000); *Dewitt v. Smith*, 152 F.R.D. 162 (W.D. Ark. 1993).

[21]*Zhang v. American Gem Seafoods, Inc.*, 339 F.3d 1020 (9th Cir. 2003) (the Rules do not define general verdicts, but they imply that general verdicts do not involve factual findings but rather ultimate legal conclusions).

the jury and with respect to the format of the questions.[22] The court also has broad discretion in evaluating the consistency of the interrogatories and the general verdict, and in selecting the remedy for any inconsistencies as described below.[23]

Content of Interrogatories

Because there is a general verdict, the content of the interrogatories is not as critical as with special verdicts—every issue need not be covered. A special interrogatory should address an issue or issues of fact, the resolution of which is necessary to the verdict.[24]

Interrogatory Answers and Verdict Consistent

If the general verdict is consistent with the interrogatory answers, then the court will enter judgment accordingly. Any ambiguity will be resolved in favor of consistency.[25]

Interrogatory Answers and Verdict Not Consistent

If the interrogatory answers are internally consistent but not consistent with the general verdict,[26] the court has 3 options: it can order the jury to deliberate further;[27] it can enter judgment based on the interrogatories if they are sufficient;[28] or it can declare a mistrial.[29] The court may not enter judgment based on the general verdict in the face of inconsistent interrogatory answers (although judgment may be proper if the inconsistent interrogatory response goes to a different issue or is not necessary for the judgment).[30] If the interrogatory answers are internally inconsistent and inconsistent with the general verdict, the court can order further deliberations or de-

---

[22]*Micrel, Inc. v. TRW, Inc.*, 486 F.3d 866 (6th Cir. 2007); *JGR, Inc. v. Thomasville Furniture Indust., Inc.*, 370 F.3d 519 (6th Cir.2004); *Cruz v. Town of Cicero, Ill.*, 275 F.3d 579, 591 (7th Cir. 2001).

[23]*Radvansky v. City of Olmsted Falls*, 496 F.3d 609, 618 (6th Cir. 2007).

[24]*U.S. ex rel. Tyson v. Amerigroup Illinois, Inc.*, 488 F.Supp.2d 719, 724 (N.D.Ill. 2007).

[25]*Hundley v. District of Columbia*, 494 F.3d 1097, 1102 (D.C. Cir. 2007) (the court has a duty to harmonize the jury's answers if it is possible under a fair reading of them); *Turyna v. Martam Const. Co., Inc.*, 83 F.3d 178, 181 (7th Cir. 1996).

[26]*Wilbur v. Correctional Services Corp.*, 393 F.3d 1192, 1200 (11th Cir. 2004) (a verdict contains an inconsis-

tency if answers given by the jury may not fairly be said to represent a logical and probable decision on the relevant issues as submitted).

[27]*Kerman v. City of New York*, 261 F.3d 229, 244 (2d Cir. 2001).

[28]*Masters v. UHS of Delaware, Inc.*, 631 F.3d 464, 475 (8th Cir. 2011); *Zhang v. American Gem Seafoods, Inc.*, 339 F.3d 1020, 1038 (9th Cir. 2003).

[29]*See Masters v. UHS of Delaware, Inc.*, 631 F.3d 464, 475 (8th Cir. 2011); *Intermatic Inc. v. Lamson & Sessions Co.*, 273 F.3d 1355, 1369 (Fed. Cir. 2001).

[30]*Armstrong ex rel. Armstrong v. Brookdale University Hospital and Medical Center*, 425 F.3d 126, 135 (2d Cir. 2005); *Guam Top Builders, Inc. v. Tanota Partners*, 2011 WL 6937474 (Guam Terr. 2011).

clare a mistrial, but cannot enter judgment.[31] A party believing that the interrogatory answers are inconsistent with the general verdict should place an objection on the record to avoid waiving the objection.[32]

Inconsistent Interrogatories

When the interrogatory answers are internally inconsistent, the court may order the jury to deliberate further or may order a new trial.[33]

Inconsistent General Verdicts

When general verdicts on different claims are inconsistent, a court may not simply mold one of the two verdicts to be consistent with the other. Faced with inconsistent general verdicts, the court may take one of four approaches: (1) "in certain circumstances, . . . allow the verdict to stand;" (2) "attempt to read the verdict in a manner that will resolve the inconsistencies;" (3) "resubmit the question to the jury;" or (4) "order an entirely new trial."[34]

Waiver of Objection to Inconsistency

Failure to object to an inconsistency prior to the jury being excused can result in waiver of the objection.[35]

Additional Research References

Wright & Miller, *Federal Practice and Procedure* §§ 2501 to 2513. Bennett & Hirschhorn, *Bennett's Guide to Jury Selection and Trial Dynamics in Civil and Criminal Litigation.*
C.J.S., Federal Civil Procedure §§ 1009 to 1027 et seq.
West's Key Number Digest, Federal Civil Procedure ☞2211 to 2220, 2231 to 2242

---

[31]*Cash v. Cnty. of Erie*, 654 F.3d 324, 342 (2d Cir. 2011); *King v. Ford Motor Co.*, 209 F.3d 886 (6th Cir. 2000) (court has broad discretion as to whether to send the jury out for further deliberations or order a new trial).

[32]*Nolfi v. Ohio Kentucky Oil Corp.*, 675 F.3d 538, 552 (6th Cir. 2012); *Wilbur v. Correctional Services Corp.*, 393 F.3d 1192, 1200 (11th Cir. 2004) (formal objection not necessary when the court has already indicated that it recognizes the inconsistency).

[33]*Wilbur v. Correctional Services Corp.*, 393 F.3d 1192, 1204 (11th Cir. 2004) (court has wide discretion as to which option to employ); *Zhang v. American Gem Seafoods, Inc.*, 339 F.3d 1020, 1038 (9th Cir. 2003); *King v. Ford Motor Co.*, 209 F.3d 886, 895 (6th Cir. 2000) (the court has wide discretion as to which option to employ).

[34]*Mosley v. Wilson*, 102 F.3d 85, 90–91 (3d Cir. 1996) (quoting *City of Los Angeles v. Heller*, 475 U.S. 796, 106 S. Ct. 1571, 89 L. Ed. 2d 806 (1986)) (internal quotes omitted).

[35]*Nolfi v. Ohio Kentucky Oil Corp.*, 675 F.3d 538, 551–52 (6th Cir. 2012); *Correia v. Fitzgerald*, 354 F.3d 47, 57 (1st Cir. 2003) (failure to object to an alleged inconsistency while the jury is still in the box forfeits a party's objection, subject only to the possibility of relief for plain error).

RULE 50

JUDGMENT AS A MATTER OF LAW IN A JURY TRIAL; RELATED MOTION FOR A NEW TRIAL; CONDITIONAL RULING

(a) Judgment as a Matter of Law.

(1) *In General.* If a party has been fully heard on an issue during a jury trial and the court finds that a reasonable jury would not have a legally sufficient evidentiary basis to find for the party on that issue, the court may:

(A) resolve the issue against the party; and

(B) grant a motion for judgment as a matter of law against the party on a claim or defense that, under the controlling law, can be maintained or defeated only with a favorable finding on that issue.

(2) *Motion.* A motion for judgment as a matter of law may be made at any time before the case is submitted to the jury. The motion must specify the judgment sought and the law and facts that entitle the movant to the judgment.

(b) Renewing the Motion After Trial; Alternative Motion for a New Trial. If the court does not grant a motion for judgment as a matter of law made under Rule 50(a), the court is considered to have submitted the action to the jury subject to the court's later deciding the legal questions raised by the motion. No later than 28 days after the entry of judgment—or if the motion addresses a jury issue not decided by a verdict, no later than 28 days after the jury was discharged—the movant may file a renewed motion for judgment as a matter of law and may include an alternative or joint request for a new trial under Rule 59. In ruling on the renewed motion, the court may:

(1) allow judgment on the verdict, if the jury returned a verdict;

(2)　order a new trial; or

(3)　direct the entry of judgment as a matter of law.

(c) Granting the Renewed Motion; Conditional Ruling on a Motion for a New Trial.

(1) *In General.* If the court grants a renewed motion for judgment as a matter of law, it must also conditionally rule on any motion for a new trial by determining whether a new trial should be granted if the judgment is later vacated or reversed. The court must state the grounds for conditionally granting or denying the motion for a new trial.

(2) *Effect of a Conditional Ruling.* Conditionally granting the motion for a new trial does not affect the judgment's finality; if the judgment is reversed, the new trial must proceed unless the appellate court orders otherwise. If the motion for a new trial is conditionally denied, the appellee may assert error in that denial; if the judgment is reversed, the case must proceed as the appellate court orders.

(d) Time for a Losing Party's New-Trial Motion. Any motion for a new trial under Rule 59 by a party against whom judgment as a matter of law is rendered must be filed no later than 28 days after the entry of the judgment.

(e) Denying the Motion for Judgment as a Matter of Law; Reversal on Appeal. If the court denies the motion for judgment as a matter of law, the prevailing party may, as appellee, assert grounds entitling it to a new trial should the appellate court conclude that the trial court erred in denying the motion. If the appellate court reverses the judgment, it may order a new trial, direct the trial court to determine whether a new trial should be granted, or direct the entry of judgment.

[Amended January 21, 1963, effective July 1, 1963; March 2, 1987, effective August 1, 1987; April 30, 1991, effective December 1, 1991; April 22, 1993, effective December 1, 1993; April 27, 1995, effective December 1, 1995; April 12, 2006, effective December 1, 2006; April 30, 2007, effective December 1, 2007; March 26, 2009, effective December 1, 2009.]

AUTHORS' COMMENTARY ON RULE 50

―――――――――――― **PURPOSE AND SCOPE** ――――――――――――

Rule 50 contains the provisions governing motions for judgment as a matter of law during and following jury trials. These remedies are generally available when the evidence in the record could not reasonably support a particular verdict.

NOTE: A motion for judgment after trial must be filed within 10 days of entry of the verdict.

2006 AMENDMENTS: The 2006 Amendments refine the procedures under Rule 50 for asserting a motion for new trial. They eliminate the language requiring a party to renew a motion for judgment as a matter of law at the close of evidence as a prerequisite to filing a post trial motion under Rule 50(b). The 2006 Amendments also add a provision allowing a party 10 days from the discharge of the jury to file a post-trial motion under Rule 50(b) if the party's prior motion for judgment as a matter of law addressed an issue that was not decided by the verdict.

RULE 50(a)—JUDGMENT AS A MATTER OF LAW

CORE CONCEPT

Rule 50(a) allows the court to take a case away from the jury by entering a judgment if there is not sufficient evidence to raise a genuine factual controversy.[1]

APPLICATIONS

Content of Motion

A motion for judgment as a matter of law must state the judgment sought (*i.e.*, the counts or issues upon which judgment is sought[2]) and the law and facts supporting the judgment.[3]

―――――――

[1]*Wimmer v. Suffolk County Police Dept.*, 176 F.3d 125, 134 (2d Cir. 1999); *CVI/Beta Ventures, Inc. v. Tura LP*, 112 F.3d 1146, 1152 (Fed. Cir. 1997).

[2]*Laymon v. Lobby House, Inc.*, 613 F.Supp.2d 504, 512 (D.Del. 2009).

[3]*Wallace v. McGlothan*, 606 F.3d 410 (7th Cir. 2010); *Smith v. Northwest Financial Acceptance, Inc.*, 129 F.3d 1408, 1415 (10th Cir. 1997); *Zeigler v. Fisher-Price, Inc.*, 302 F. Supp. 2d 999, 1007 (N.D. Iowa 2004) (although the grounds do not have to be stated with technical precision, the movant must give fair notice to the court of the grounds for the motion).

Form and Timing of Motion

A motion for judgment as a matter of law may be made orally or in writing, but must be made on the record.[4] The motion may be made after the opposing party has been fully heard on an issue, at any time before submission of the case to the jury.[5] Such motions are typically made at the close of the plaintiff's case (by the defendant), at the close of the record, or both.

Subject of Motion

A motion for judgment as a matter of law may seek judgment on entire claims or defenses or on specific issues that are not wholly dispositive of a claim or defense.[6]

Opportunity to Cure

A major purpose of the motion is to call a deficiency in the evidence to the attention of the court so the opposing counsel may cure the defect.[7] The court then has a duty to apprise the non-moving party of the materiality of the dispositive fact and provide that party with an opportunity to present any available evidence.[8]

Standard

The sufficiency of the evidence is an issue of law to be determined by the judge.[9] The primary consideration is whether the evidence in the record could properly support a particular verdict.[10] The court must view all evidence in the light most favorable to the party opposing the motion;[11] it may not make credibility determinations or weigh the evidence.[12] However, the court may disregard testimony that is opposed to undis-

---

[4]*Ross v. Rhodes Furniture, Inc.*, 146 F.3d 1286, 1289 (11th Cir. 1998).

[5]*Maxwell v. Dodd*, 662 F.3d 418, 421 (6th Cir. 2011); *Bristol v. Board of County Com'rs of County of Clear Creek*, 281 F.3d 1148, 1163 (10th Cir. 2002).

[6]*Ross v. Rhodes Furniture, Inc.*, 146 F.3d 1286, 1289–90 (11th Cir. 1998) (grounds for motion must be clear from the record so that the appeals court can ensure that setting aside the verdict would not be a surprise to the non-movant); *Chesapeake Paper Products Co. v. Stone & Webster Engineering Corp.*, 51 F.3d 1229, 1236 (4th Cir. 1995).

[7]*See Hyundai Motor Finance Co. v. McKay Motors I, LLC*, 574 F.3d 637, 642 (8th Cir. 2009) (technical precision is not necessary so long as the court and opposing party are on notice of the issue); *Laborers' Pension Fund v. A & C Environmental, Inc.*, 301 F.3d 768, 775 (7th Cir. 2002).

[8]*Waters v. Young*, 100 F.3d 1437, 1441 (9th Cir. 1996) (adding that the court's duty is especially important when confronted with pro se litigants).

[9]*Lange v. Penn Mut. Life Ins. Co.*, 843 F.2d 1175, 1181 (9th Cir. 1988).

[10]*Anderson v. Liberty Lobby, Inc.*, 477 U.S. 242, 106 S. Ct. 2505, 91 L. Ed. 2d 202 (1986); *Linden v. CNH Am., LLC*, 673 F.3d 829, 834 (8th Cir. 2012).

[11]*Galloway v. U.S.*, 319 U.S. 372, 63 S. Ct. 1077, 87 L. Ed. 1458 (1943); *E.E.O.C. v. Go Daddy Software, Inc.*, 581 F.3d 951, 961 (9th Cir. 2009).

[12]*Reeves v. Sanderson Plumbing Prods., Inc.*, 530 U.S. 133, 150, 120 S.Ct. 2097, 147 L.Ed.2d 105 (2000); *E.E.O.C. v. Go Daddy Software, Inc.*, 581 F.3d 951, 961 (9th Cir. 2009).

puted physical facts.[13] Moreover, a "mere scintilla" of evidence is not sufficient.[14] The standard for a motion for judgment as a matter of law is the same as for a motion for summary judgment (making that substantial body of case law applicable).[15]

Inferences

The court must draw all reasonable inferences from the evidence that favor the party opposing the motion.[16] Thus, even if all the facts are undisputed, a motion for judgment as a matter of law will still be denied if the evidence is susceptible of conflicting inferences.[17] However, inferences created by statute or doctrine, such as *res ipsa loquitur,* may raise different issues requiring specific research.

Jury Trials Only

Rule 50 applies only to binding jury cases.[18] The appropriate motion in non-jury trials and trials with an advisory jury is a motion for judgment on partial findings under Rule 52(c).[19]

Motions Held Under Consideration

The court is under no obligation to grant a motion for judgment as a matter of law even if the record supports the motion. Courts often allow the jury to reach a verdict in order to minimize the likelihood of needing a new trial, if the court enters a judgment contrary to the verdict that is overturned on appeal, then enter judgment contrary to the verdict if the verdict is unsupported by sufficient evidence.[20]

Motion Granted

If the court grants a motion for judgment as a matter of

---

[13]*See, e.g., O'Connor v. Pennsylvania R. Co.,* 308 F.2d 911 (2d Cir. 1962) (testimony about snowfall disregarded when contrary to the records of the Weather Bureau); *Grant v. Cia Anonima Venezolana de Navegacion,* 228 F. Supp. 232 (E.D. La. 1964), aff'd, 343 F.2d 757 (5th Cir. 1965) (testimony that a winch was operated electrically disregarded when a physical inspection showed that the winch was operated hydraulically).

[14]*A.B. Small Co. v. Lamborn & Co.,* 267 U.S. 248, 254, 45 S. Ct. 300, 303, 69 L. Ed. 597 (1925); *Filipovich v. K & R Exp. Systems, Inc.,* 391 F.3d 859, 863 (7th Cir. 2004); *DP Solutions, Inc. v. Rollins, Inc.,* 353 F.3d 421, 427 (5th Cir. 2003).

[15]*See Linden v. CNH Am., LLC,* 673 F.3d 829, 834 (8th Cir. 2012).

[16]*Laxton v. Gap Inc.,* 333 F.3d 572, 577 (5th Cir. 2003). *Green v. Administrators of Tulane Educational Fund,* 284 F.3d 642, 652 (5th Cir. 2002).

[17]*Daniels v. Twin Oaks Nursing Home,* 692 F.3d 1321, 1325 (11th Cir. 1982); *but see Everett v. Verizon Wireless, Inc.,* 361 F. Supp. 2d 698 (N.D. Ohio 2005) (where there are two possible inferences and no factual basis to pick one over the other, the court may enter judgment against the party with the burden of proof).

[18]*Federal Ins. Co. v. HPSC, Inc.,* 480 F.3d 26, 32 (1st Cir. 2007); *Nieto v. Kapoor,* 268 F.3d 1208, 1217 (10th Cir. 2001).

[19]*Federal Ins. Co. v. HPSC, Inc.,* 480 F.3d 26, 32 (1st Cir. 2007); *Northeast Drilling, Inc. v. Inner Space Services, Inc.,* 243 F.3d 25, 37 (1st Cir. 2001).

[20]*Colonial Lincoln-Mercury, Inc. v. Musgrave,* 749 F.2d 1092, 1098 (4th Cir. 1984); *U.S. v. Singleton,* 702 F.2d 1159, 1172 (D.C. Cir. 1983).

law, it will enter the appropriate verdict without involvement of the jury.

Motion Denied

If the motion for judgment as a matter of law is denied, the defendant may put on evidence. However, if the plaintiff's case lacked a certain element and that element is brought out during the defendant's case, the deficiency will be cured.[21]

Who May Make Motion

Both defendants and plaintiffs may make motions for judgment as a matter of law. Thus, if the plaintiff enters evidence sufficient to support each element of the plaintiff's case and that evidence is not contradicted during the defendant's case, the plaintiff will be entitled to a judgment as a matter of law.[22] In addition, the judge may grant a judgment as a matter of law *sua sponte.*[23]

Prerequisite to Appeal

A motion for judgment as a matter of law at the close of the record is a prerequisite to challenging the sufficiency of the evidence on appeal.[24] Note, however, that appellate issues other than those relating to the sufficiency of the evidence are not affected.[25] An exception to this principle occurs if the verdict constitutes plain error on the face of the record, and a miscarriage of justice would result if the verdict remained in effect.[26]

Summary Judgment Motions

A party whose summary judgment motion was denied should raise the issue again as a Rule 50(a) motion if the summary judgment motion raised sufficiency of the evidence issues.[27] A party does not need to raise again summary judgment issues that are pure legal issues. If you are not sure which category your motion falls into, it is good practice to raise summary judgment motions as Rule 50 motions at the end of the evidence, and again before submission to the jury if necessary.[28]

RULE 50(b)—RENEWING THE MOTION AFTER

---

[21]*Trustees of University of Pennsylvania v. Lexington Ins. Co.,* 815 F.2d 890, 903 (3d Cir. 1987); *Peterson v. Hager,* 724 F.2d 851, 854 (10th Cir. 1984).

[22]*Hurd v. American Hoist and Derrick Co.,* 734 F.2d 495, 499 (10th Cir. 1984); *Walter E. Heller & Co. v. Video Innovations, Inc.,* 730 F.2d 50, 54 (2d Cir. 1984).

[23]*American and Foreign Ins. Co. v. Bolt,* 106 F.3d 155, 160 (6th Cir. 1997).

[24]*Unitherm Food Systems, Inc. v. Swift-Eckrich, Inc.,* 546 U.S. 394, 126

S. Ct. 980, 987, 163 L. Ed. 2d 974 (2006); *Federal Ins. Co. v. HPSC, Inc.,* 480 F.3d 26, 32 (1st Cir. 2007).

[25]*Linden v. CNH Am., LLC,* 673 F.3d 829, 832–33 (8th Cir. 2012); *Ruyle v. Continental Oil Co.,* 44 F.3d 837 (10th Cir. 1994).

[26]*Stephenson v. Doe,* 332 F.3d 68, 75–76 (2d Cir. 2003).

[27]*See Keup v. Hopkins,* 596 F.3d 899, 904 (8th Cir. 2010); *Haberman v. The Hartford Insurance Group,* 443 F.3d 1257 (C.A.10 2006).

[28]*Haberman v. The Hartford Insurance Group,* 443 F.3d 1257

TRIAL; ALTERNATIVE MOTION FOR A NEW TRIAL

CORE CONCEPT

The court can enter a judgment that is inconsistent with the jury's verdict if it determines that the verdict was not supported by the evidence.

APPLICATIONS

Content of Motion

A motion for judgment after trial must state the grounds for relief,[29] and may include only those grounds raised in the motion for judgment as a matter of law.[30]

Timing

The motion must be filed not later than 28 days after the *entry* of the judgment[31] (not the notice of entry of the judgment). If the jury is discharged without reaching a verdict, such as with a mistrial, the 28 day period begins to run with the discharge of the jury. If the jury does not return a verdict, such as with a mistrial, or if the subject of the motion for judgment as a matter of law was an issue not decided by the verdict, the parties have 28 days from the discharge of the jury. The courts are divided as to whether time limit can be enlarged.[32]

Failure to File is Waiver

Failure to file a postverdict motion under Rule 50(b) limits a party's right to appeal, because it deprives an appellate court of the power to direct the district court to enter judgment con-

---

(C.A.10 2006).

[29]*Andreas v. Volkswagen of America, Inc.*, 336 F.3d 789 (8th Cir.2003) (Rule 50(b) motion must put the court and the parties on notice of the issues being raised).

[30]*Wallace v. McGlothan*, __ F.3d __ (7th Cir. 2010) (responding to new issues raised in the Rule 50(b) motion waives the objection that they were not raised in the Rule 50(a) motion); *Ross v. Rhodes Furniture, Inc.*, 146 F.3d 1286, 1289–90 (11th Cir. 1998) (grounds for motion must be clear from the record so that the appeals court can ensure that setting aside the verdict would not be a surprise to the non-movant).

[31]*Hinz v. Neuroscience, Inc.*, 538 F.3d 979, 983 (8th Cir. 2008) (where motion filed timely but brief filed 1 day late, brief could not be considered); *Green v. Administrators of Tulane Educational Fund*, 284 F.3d 642, 652 (5th Cir. 2002) (Rule 50(b) motion timely when delivered to the clerk's office within 10 days even though the clerks did not file the motion until after 10 days).

[32]*Blue v. Int'l. Broth. of Elec. Workers Local Union 159*, 676 F.3d 579, 582–83 (7th Cir. 2012) (period cannot be expanded or waived); *Advanced Bodycare Solutions, LLC v. Thione Intern., Inc.*, 615 F.3d 1352, 1359, n.15 (11th Cir. 2010) (limit for filing Rule 50(b) motion cannot be enlarged, but it is not jurisdictional, so it can be waived); *Art Attacks Ink, LLC v. MGA Entertainment Inc.*, 581 F.3d 1138, 1142 (9th Cir. 2009) (discussing the split in authority).

trary to the one the jury rendered.[33]

Same Standard as Rule 50(a)

A renewed motion for judgment as a matter of law under Rule 50(b) is evaluated under the same standard as the initial motion under Rule 50(a) filed at the close of evidence;[34] the motion will be denied if the evidence in the record could properly support the verdict, viewing the evidence, and all inferences, in the light most favorable to the non-moving party.[35] This standard is discussed in more detail in the commentary to Rule 50(a) above.

Motion During Trial a Prerequisite

A party cannot make a motion for judgment after trial unless it filed a motion for judgment as a matter of law before the case was submitted to the jury.[36] Moreover, the post trial motion is limited to the issues raised in the pre-verdict motion.[37] If there was no motion for judgment as a matter of law but the evidence does not support the verdict, the court can order a new trial.[38]

Motion for a New Trial

A party may join a motion for a new trial with a motion for judgment after trial, or request a new trial in the alternative.[39] The standard is the same as with a motion for new trial under Rule 59; the motion will be granted if the verdict is contrary to

---

[33]*Oritz v. Jordan*, __ U.S. __, 131 S.Ct. 884, 178 L.Ed.2d 703 (2011); *Unitherm Food Sys. v. Swift-Eckrich, Inc.*, 546 U.S. 394, 407, 126 S.Ct. 980, 163 L.Ed.2d 974 (2006); *Copar Pumice Co., Inc. v. Morris*, 639 F.3d 1025, 1027 (10th Cir. 2011) (withdrawal of a pending Rule 50(b) motion leaves case as if motion never filed).

[34]*Chaney v. City of Orlando*, 483 F.3d 1221, 1227 (11th Cir. 2007); *Rice v. Dist. of Columbia*, 818 F.Supp.2d 47, 54 (D.D.C. 2011).

[35]*See Smart Marketing Group v. Publications Intern. Ltd.*, 624 F.3d 824, 829 (7th Cir. 2010); *Radvansky v. City of Olmsted Falls*, 496 F.3d 609, 614 (6th Cir. 2007) (motion will not be granted unless reasonable minds could only come to one conclusion, in favor of the moving party).

[36]*Tortu v. Las Vegas Metropolitan Police Dept.*, 556 F.3d 1075, 1081 (9th Cir. 2009); *Rinehimer v. Cemcolift, Inc.*, 292 F.3d 375 (3d Cir.2002); *but see Minnesota Supply Co. v. Raymond Corp.*, 472 F.3d 524, 535–36 (8th Cir.

2006) (failure to renew the motion not a waiver when the court advised the party that there was no need to renew the motion).

[37]*E.E.O.C. v. Go Daddy Software, Inc.*, 581 F.3d 951, 961 (9th Cir. 2009); *Hinz v. Neuroscience, Inc.*, 538 F.3d 979, 983–84 (8th Cir. 2008); *but see Learning Annex Holdings, LLC v. Rich Global, LLC*, __ F.Supp.2d __ (S.D.N.Y. 2012) (considering an issue not raised in a Rule 50(a) motion where it was raised at trial and non-moving party would not be prejudiced).

[38]*Johnson v. New York, N.H. & H.R. Co.*, 344 U.S. 48, 54, 73 S. Ct. 125, 128, 97 L. Ed. 77 (1952); *Pediatrix Screening, Inc. v. Telechem Intern., Inc.*, 602 F.3d 541, 546–47 (3rd Cir. 2010).

[39]*Pediatrix Screening, Inc. v. Telechem Intern., Inc.*, 602 F.3d 541, 546 (3rd Cir. 2010); *Willis v. State Farm Fire and Cas. Co.*, 219 F.3d 715 (8th Cir.2000) (moved for judgment as a matter of law and, in the alternative, for a new trial).

the clear weight of the evidence.[40] A new trial is favored over a judgment contrary to the verdict when it appears that the party could present sufficient evidence to support the verdict at a future date.

Rulings

If the jury returned a verdict, the court may allow the verdict to stand, order a new trial, or direct entry of judgment as a matter of law.[41] If no verdict was returned, the court may order a new trial or direct the entry of judgment as a matter of law. When a motion for new trial is joined with a motion for judgment after trial, Rule 50 specifically requires that the court rule on both motions.[42]

Appeals

Rulings on motions for judgment after trial are final, appealable orders. In contrast, an order granting a new trial may not be a final, appealable order.[43]

RULE 50(c)—GRANTING THE RENEWED MOTION; CONDITIONAL RULINGS ON A MOTION FOR A NEW TRIAL

CORE CONCEPT

If the court grants a motion for judgment as a matter of law after trial and a motion for a new trial was also filed, the court will make a conditional ruling on the motion for a new trial.[44]

APPLICATIONS

Impact of 2007 "Restyling" Amendments

Rule 50(c) was restructured during the 2007 Federal Civil Rules "Restyling" Project. Former Rule 50(c)(2) was renumbered as Rule 50(d). In researching Rules 50(c)(2) or (d), practitioners should be mindful of this repositioning.

Rulings Conditional on Reversal

The trial court's rulings on the motion for a new trial are applicable if the appeals court reverses the granting of the

---

[40]*Oritz v. Jordan*, __ U.S. __, 131 S.Ct. 884, 178 L.Ed.2d 703 (2011) (discussing the difference between insufficient evidence under Rule 50(b) and weight of the evidence under Rule 59); *Jennings v. Jones*, 587 F.3d 430, 436 (1st Cir. 2009) (discussing the difference between the standard for a motion for a new trial and the standard for a motion for judgment after trial).

[41]*Health Alliance Network, Inc. v. Continental Cas. Co.*, 245 F.R.D. 121,

125 (S.D. N.Y. 2007), aff'd, 2008 WL 4442493 (2d Cir. 2008).

[42]*See Jennings v. Jones*, 587 F.3d 430, 432 (1st Cir. 2009).

[43]*Binder v. Long Island Lighting Co.*, 57 F.3d 193 (2d Cir.1995).

[44]*Christopher v. Florida*, 449 F.3d 1360, 1365 (11th Cir. 2006); *Rhone Poulenc Rorer Pharmaceuticals Inc. v. Newman Glass Works*, 112 F.3d 695, 698 (3d Cir. 1997).

judgment after trial.[45] In that case, the appeals court will generally enter the original verdict or order a new trial, depending on the trial court's conditional ruling. However, the appeals court also may review the trial court's conditional ruling on the motion for a new trial.

Granting of Both Motions

If the trial court grants both a motion for judgment notwithstanding the verdict and a motion for a new trial, the ruling on the motion for a new trial is automatically deemed conditional.

Failure to Issue a Conditional Ruling

If a court fails to issue a conditional ruling, the appellate court has the authority to either remand to the trial court to decide the new trial motion or decide the new trial motion itself.[46]

RULE 50(d)—TIME FOR A LOSING PARTY'S NEW-TRIAL MOTION

CORE CONCEPT

If the court grants a motion for judgment after trial, the party against whom judgment was entered may file a motion for a new trial no later than 28 days after the entry of judgment, pursuant to Rule 59.

APPLICATIONS

Impact of 2007 "Restyling" Amendments

Rule 50(d) was restructured during the 2007 Federal Civil Rules "Restyling" Project. Former Rule 50(c)(2) was renumbered as Rule 50(d). In researching Rules 50(c)(2) or (d), practitioners should be mindful of this repositioning.

RULE 50(e)—DENYING THE MOTION FOR JUDGMENT AS A MATTER OF LAW; REVERSAL ON APPEAL

CORE CONCEPT

If the losing party appeals the denial of a motion for judgment after trial, the prevailing party may on appeal assert grounds for a new trial in the event that the court reverses the denial of the motion for judgment after trial. If the appellate court does reverse, it may order the entry of judgment, order a new trial, or

---

[45]*Fioto v. Manhattan Woods Golf Enterprises, LLC.*, 304 F. Supp. 2d 541 (S.D. N.Y. 2004), aff'd, 123 Fed. Appx. 26 (2d Cir. 2005).

[46]*Acosta v. City and County of San Francisco*, 83 F.3d 1143, 1149 (9th Cir. 1996); *but see Christopher v. Florida*, 449 F.3d 1360, 1365 n. 3 (11th Cir. 2006) (where the appellant fails to pursue a new trial on appeal, the court will consider the issue abandoned).

remand to the trial court to determine whether a new trial is warranted.

APPLICATIONS

Impact of 2007 "Restyling" Amendments

Rule 50 was restructured during the 2007 Federal Civil Rules "Restyling" Project. Former Rule 50(d) was renumbered as Rule 50(e). In researching Rules 50(d) and (e), practitioners should be mindful of this repositioning.

Additional Research References

Wright & Miller, *Federal Practice and Procedure* §§ 2521 to 2540
C.J.S., Federal Civil Procedure §§ 958 to 977 et seq.
C.J.S., Federal Civil Procedure § 1034, § 1089, § 1093, §§ 1219 to 1226 et seq.
West's Key Number Digest, Federal Civil Procedure ☞2111 to 2156, 2601 to 2610

RULE 51
INSTRUCTIONS TO THE JURY; OBJECTIONS; PRESERVING A CLAIM OF ERROR

(a) Requests.

    (1) *Before or at the Close of the Evidence.* At the close of the evidence or at any earlier reasonable time that the court orders, a party may file and furnish to every other party written requests for the jury instructions it wants the court to give.

    (2) *After the Close of the Evidence.* After the close of the evidence, a party may:

        (A) file requests for instructions on issues that could not reasonably have been anticipated by an earlier time that the court set for requests; and

        (B) with the court's permission, file untimely requests for instructions on any issue.

(b) Instructions. The court:

    (1) must inform the parties of its proposed instructions and proposed action on the requests before instructing the jury and before final jury arguments;

    (2) must give the parties an opportunity to object on the record and out of the jury's hearing before the instructions and arguments are delivered; and

    (3) may instruct the jury at any time before the jury is discharged.

(c) Objections.

    (1) *How to Make.* A party who objects to an instruction or the failure to give an instruction must do so on the record, stating distinctly the matter objected to and the grounds for the objection.

    (2) *When to Make.* An objection is timely if:

        (A) a party objects at the opportunity provided under Rule 51(b)(2); or

    (B) a party was not informed of an instruction or action on a request before that opportunity to object, and the party objects promptly after learning that the instruction or request will be, or has been, given or refused.

(d) Assigning Error; Plain Error.

  (1) *Assigning Error.* A party may assign as error:

    (A) an error in an instruction actually given, if that party properly objected; or

    (B) a failure to give an instruction, if that party properly requested it and—unless the court rejected the request in a definitive ruling on the record—also properly objected.

  (2) *Plain Error.* A court may consider a plain error in the instructions that has not been preserved as required by Rule 51(d)(1) if the error affects substantial rights.

[Amended effective August 1, 1987; March 27, 2003, effective December 1, 2003; April 30, 2007, effective December 1, 2007.]

AUTHORS' COMMENTARY ON RULE 51

PURPOSE AND SCOPE

Before the jury retires to deliberate, the judge must instruct the jury as to the law that they are to apply. The parties have an opportunity to request that certain instructions be given, and to object to the instructions given and to the instructions not given.

RULE 51(a)—REQUESTS

CORE CONCEPT

The parties may submit proposed jury instructions to the court. Proposed instructions are submitted at the close of the evidence, or at such earlier time as directed by the court.

APPLICATIONS

Timing of Requests

Requests for jury instructions are normally made at the close of the evidence, or earlier if the court so directs.[1] If the court has set a time before the close of evidence for submission of requests for instructions, a party may submit additional requests for instructions after the close of evidence on issues that could not have been anticipated when the requests were submitted.[2] Note, however, that local rules may set the time for making requests for jury instructions. The court, in its discretion, may consider untimely requests.[3]

Form and Content of Requests

Requests normally should be reasonably neutral statements of the law governing the case, and not overly argumentative. Requests are usually written, although they can be oral.

Service

Requests for instruction must be furnished to every other party.[4]

RULE 51(b)—INSTRUCTIONS

CORE CONCEPT

The court must inform the parties of its proposed instructions before instructing the jury and before the parties' final arguments to the jury, and must give the parties an opportunity to object on the record and out of the jury's hearing.

APPLICATIONS

Rulings on Requests

The court is required to inform the parties of its rulings on the jury instruction requests before the closing arguments,[5] so that the counsel may adjust their closings accordingly. Failure to do so, however, will not be grounds for a new trial unless it is prejudicial.[6]

---

[1] *Potthast v. Metro-North Railroad Co.*, 400 F.3d 143, 153 (2d Cir. 2005).

[2] *Potthast v. Metro-North Railroad Co.*, 400 F.3d 143, 153 (2d Cir. 2005); *Williams v. Dist. of Columbia*, 825 F.Supp.2d 88, 103 (D.D.C. 2011).

[3] Rule 51(a)(2)(B).

[4] Rule 51(a)(1).

[5] *DeCaro v. Hasbro, Inc.*, 580 F.3d 55, 64 (1st Cir. 2009) (the rule does not require the court to provide the parties with a written copy of the instructions).

[6] *Delano v. Kitch*, 542 F.2d 550 (10th Cir. 1976).

Form and Procedure for Instructions

Instructions are given to the jury in open court at any time after trial begins and before the jury is discharged.[7] The judge may repeat portions of the charge or give a supplemental charge at the jury's request, but must afford the parties notice and an opportunity to be present for such additional instruction. The judge may submit a written charge to the jury, although it is not commonly done.

Content of Instructions

The court should give an instruction on every material issue in the case.[8] The instruction should clearly and understandably convey the status of the applicable law.[9] There is no particular wording or order mandated,[10] and the judge need not use the language requested by the parties. Narrowly-tailored instructions are favored over broad statements of the law.

Deadlocked Jury

In the civil context, the judge may instruct a jury claiming to be deadlocked to make further attempts to reach a verdict. The judge may not, however, coerce reluctant jurors to join the majority.

Comments on Evidence

The court, in its discretion, may comment on the evidence and even focus the jury's attention on certain portions of the evidence. If the judge does so, the judge must make it clear to the jury that they, not the judge, are the ultimate fact finders.

Opportunity to Object

The court must give the parties an opportunity to raise objections to the instructions on the record and out of the hearing of the jury before the instructions and closing arguments are delivered.[11] If the court fails to give an opportunity to raise the objections, parties with objections should request such an opportunity. However, if instructions are reread or the jury is given additional instructions, an objection may be raised at that time.[12]

---

[7]*Heimlicher v. Steele*, 615 F.Supp.2d 884, 932 (N.D.Iowa 2009).

[8]*See Williams v. Dist. of Columbia*, 825 F.Supp.2d 88, 91 (D.D.C. 2011).

[9]*See Williams v. Dist. of Columbia*, 825 F.Supp.2d 88, 91 (D.D.C. 2011).

[10]*Williams v. Dist. of Columbia*, 825 F.Supp.2d 88, 91 (D.D.C. 2011).

[11]*Schandelmeier-Bartels v. Chicago Park Dist.*, 634 F.3d 372, 386 (7th Cir. 2011); *Lewis v. City of Chicago Police Dept.*, 590 F.3d 427, 434 (7th Cir. 2009).

[12]*Barrett v. Orange County Human Rights Com'n*, 194 F.3d 341, 349 (2d Cir. 1999).

RULE 51(c)—OBJECTIONS

CORE CONCEPT

Objections to the instructions must be made on the record[13] with a statement of the grounds when the court provides and opportunity for such objections.[14]

APPLICATIONS

Content of Objection

The objection must be stated with sufficient clarity and specificity that the judge can understand the nature of the objection and remedy the problem if the judge agrees.[15] Any appeal must be based upon issues so raised in an objection.[16]

Time of Objections

A party must object to the content of the instructions at the opportunity provided by the court before the instructions and closing arguments are delivered,[17] even if the party has previously raised and attempted to preserve the same objection.[18] If a party was not informed of an instruction or action on a request for an instruction prior to the opportunity to object provided by the court, the party may object promptly upon learning that the instruction was or would be given or refused.[19]

---

[13]*Colon-Millin v. Sears Roebuck De Puerto Rico, Inc.*, 455 F.3d 30 (1st Cir.2006) (judge's statement that the parties could rely on objections asserted earlier in chambers did not relieve them of the obligation to state the objections on the record); *Positive Black Talk Inc. v. Cash Money Records, Inc.*, 394 F.3d 357, 368 (5th Cir. 2004) (off the record objections, no matter how clear and detailed, cannot satisfy Rule 51).

[14]*Mullins v. TestAmerica, Inc.*, 564 F.3d 386, 411, n.11 (5th Cir. 2009).

[15]*Diaz v. Jiten Hotel Mgmt., Inc.*, 671 F.3d 78, 84, n.4 (1st Cir. 2012) (judge must be told precisely what the problem is and what the attorney proposes as a cure); *Bauer v. Curators of Univ. of Missouri*, 680 F.3d 1043, 1044–45 (8th Cir. 2012).

[16]*Bauer v. Curators of Univ. of Missouri*, 680 F.3d 1043, 1045 (8th Cir. 2012); *Galena v. Leone*, 638 F.3d 186, 201 (3rd Cir. 2011).

[17]*U.S. v. Bader*, 678 F.3d 858, 867 (10th Cir. 2012); *Schandelmeier-*

Bartels v. Chicago Park Dist., 634 F.3d 372, 386 (7th Cir. 2011).

[18]*Torres-Rivera v. O'Neill-Cancel*, 406 F.3d 43, 49–50 (1st Cir. 2005) (party must object at the time of the instructions even if the party previously proposed the instruction that the court declined to give); *Gray v. Genlyte Group, Inc.*, 289 F.3d 128, 134 (1st Cir. 2002) (it is not enough to refer back to previously raised objections); *Libbey-Owens-Ford Co. v. Insurance Co. of North America*, 9 F.3d 422 (6th Cir. 1993) (objections were waived even though the trial court told the parties that previously raised objections were preserved); *but see Vicor Corp. v. Vigilant Ins. Co.*, 674 F.3d 1, 8, n.4 (1st Cir. 2012) (reference to earlier overruled objection sufficient); *Lighting & Power Services, Inc. v. Roberts*, 354 F.3d 817, 820 (8th Cir. 2004) (finding that plaintiff's counsel's fully explained in-chambers objections satisfied Rule 51).

[19]*Booker v. Massachusetts Dept. of Public Health*, 612 F.3d 34, 41 (1st Cir. 2010).

Objection on the Record

Objections to jury instructions must be on the record; objections made off the record in chambers are not effective.[20] It is not sufficient to have proposed an instruction that the court does not give.[21]

Failure to Object

If a party fails to object to an instruction before the jury begins deliberations and the court has not already made a definitive ruling on the record regarding the subject instruction,[22] the party loses the right to challenge the instruction on appeal.[23] Some courts will undertake appellate review in the absence of a timely objection if the party never had an opportunity to object,[24] but most courts strictly require a timely objection on the record.[25] Similarly, some courts will undertake appellate review in the absence of a timely objection if an objection would have been a pointless formality.[26] Thus, as a general matter, if a party does not make a timely objection, it is limited to objections of plain error under Rule 51(d).

RULE 51(d)—ASSIGNING ERROR; PLAIN ERROR

[20]See Belk, Inc. v. Meyer Corp., U.S., 679 F.3d 146, 153, n.6 (4th Cir. 2012); Foradori v. Harris, 523 F.3d 477, 513 (5th Cir. 2008).

[21]Franklin Prescriptions, Inc. v. New York Times Co., 424 F.3d 336, 339 (3d Cir. 2005).

[22]The 2003 amendment to Rule 51 provided that a party need not object to an instruction if the court has made a definitive ruling on the issue on the record. See also Colon-Millin v. Sears Roebuck De Puerto Rico, Inc., 455 F.3d 30 (1st Cir.2006).

[23]Fox v. Hayes, 600 F.3d 819, 838 (7th Cir. 2010); Melford Olsen Honey, Inc. v. Adee, 452 F.3d 956 (8th Cir. 2006).

[24]Schmitz v. Canadian Pacific Ry. Co., 454 F.3d 678 (7th Cir.2006) (judge changed the instructions without notifying the parties).

[25]See Shcherbakovskiy v. Da Capo Al Fine, Ltd., 490 F.3d 130, 141 n.2 (2d Cir. 2007) (judge's assurance that the movant would be deemed to have made "every motion available" did not preserve objections); Colon-Millin v.

Sears Roebuck De Puerto Rico, Inc., 455 F.3d 30 (1st Cir.2006) (judge's statement that the parties could rely on objections asserted earlier in chambers did not relieve them of the obligation to state the objections on the record).

[26]See CollegeNet, Inc. v. ApplyYourself, Inc., 418 F.3d 1225 (Fed. Cir. 2005) (where the district court is aware of the party's concerns and further objection would be unavailing, a futile formal objection is not required); Riverwood Intern. Corp. v. R.A. Jones & Co., Inc., 324 F.3d 1346, 1353 (Fed. Cir. 2003) (no need to object when issue had already been briefed and objection would have been futile); Monroe v. City of Phoenix, Ariz., 248 F.3d 851, 858 (9th Cir. 2001) (overruled by, Acosta v. Hill, 504 F.3d 1323 (9th Cir. 2007)) (an objection may be a pointless formality when: (1) throughout the trial the party argued the disputed matter with the court; (2) it is clear from the record that the court knew the party's grounds for disagreement with the instruction; and (3) the party offered an alternative instruction).

CORE CONCEPT

A party may base an appeal on an instruction if the party made a proper objection pursuant to Rule 51(c) or upon plain error.

APPLICATIONS

Issues On Appeal

In general, a party may only raise on appeal issues regarding the instructions given that the party properly raised as objections pursuant to Rule 51(c).[27] A party may only raise on appeal an issue regarding an instruction not given if the party made a proper request for the instruction[28] and either the court made a definitive ruling on the record rejecting the request[29] or the party made a proper objection regarding the omitted instruction.[30]

Plain Error

The appeals court generally will review only issues to which there was a timely objection, but may, under extreme circumstances when justice demands, reverse even if no objections were made when an instruction contains plain error.[31] Additionally, the appeals court may consider an issue not preserved by objection where there has been a supervening change in the law.[32]

Additional Research References

Wright & Miller, *Federal Practice and Procedure* §§ 2551 to 2558. Devitt, Blackmar, Wolff & O'Malley, *Federal Jury Practice and Instructions.*
C.J.S., Federal Civil Procedure §§ 983 to 994 et seq.
West's Key Number Digest, Federal Civil Procedure ⊶2171 to 2185

---

[27]*Craig Outdoor Advertising, Inc. v. Viacom Outdoor, Inc.*, 528 F.3d 1001, 1016 (8th Cir. 2008); *Connelly v. Hyundai Motor Co.*, 351 F.3d 535, 544 (1st Cir. 2003) (an objection on one ground does not preserve appellate review of a different ground).

[28]*Microsoft Corp. v. i4i Ltd. Partnership*, __ U.S. __, 131 S.Ct. 2238, 180 L.Ed.2d 131 (2011); *Connick v. Thompson*, __ U.S. __, 131 S.Ct. 1350, 179 L.Ed.2d 417 (2011).

[29]*Colon-Millin v. Sears Roebuck De Puerto Rico, Inc.*, 455 F.3d 30, 40, (1st Cir. 2006).

[30]*Latin American Music Co. v. American Soc. of Composers Authors and Publishers*, 593 F.3d 95, 102 (1st Cir. 2010); *Lewis v. City of Chicago Police Dept.*, 590 F.3d 427, 434 (7th Cir. 2009) (plain error is one that probably changed the outcome of the trial).

[31]*Gregg v. Ham*, 678 F.3d 333, 338 (4th Cir. 2012); *Bauer v. Curators of Univ. of Missouri*, 680 F.3d 1043, 1045 (8th Cir. 2012).

[32]*See Cadena v. Pacesetter Corp.*, 224 F.3d 1203, 1212 (10th Cir. 2000); *Anixter v. Home-Stake Production Co.*, 77 F.3d 1215, 1230–31 (10th Cir. 1996).

RULE 52
FINDINGS AND CONCLUSIONS BY THE COURT; JUDGMENT ON PARTIAL FINDINGS

(a) Findings and Conclusions.

(1) *In General.* In an action tried on the facts without a jury or with an advisory jury, the court must find the facts specially and state its conclusions of law separately. The findings and conclusions may be stated on the record after the close of the evidence or may appear in an opinion or a memorandum of decision filed by the court. Judgment must be entered under Rule 58.

(2) *For an Interlocutory Injunction.* In granting or refusing an interlocutory injunction, the court must similarly state the findings and conclusions that support its action.

(3) *For a Motion.* The court is not required to state findings or conclusions when ruling on a motion under Rule 12 or 56 or, unless these rules provide otherwise, on any other motion.

(4) *Effect of a Master's Findings.* A master's findings, to the extent adopted by the court, must be considered the court's findings.

(5) *Questioning the Evidentiary Support.* A party may later question the sufficiency of the evidence supporting the findings, whether or not the party requested findings, objected to them, moved to amend them, or moved for partial findings.

(6) *Setting Aside the Findings.* Findings of fact, whether based on oral or other evidence, must not be set aside unless clearly erroneous, and the reviewing court must give due regard to the trial court's opportunity to judge the witnesses' credibility.

(b) Amended or Additional Findings. On a party's motion filed no later than 28 days after the entry of judgment, the court may amend its findings—or make additional findings—and may amend the judgment accordingly. The motion may accompany a motion for a new trial under Rule 59.

(c) Judgment on Partial Findings. If a party has been fully heard on an issue during a nonjury trial and the court finds against the party on that issue, the court may enter judgment against the party on a claim or defense that, under the controlling law, can be maintained or defeated only with a favorable finding on that issue. The court may, however, decline to render any judgment until the close of the evidence. A judgment on partial findings must be supported by findings of fact and conclusions of law as required by Rule 52(a).

[Amended December 27, 1946, effective March 19, 1948; January 21, 1963, effective July 1, 1963; April 28, 1983, effective August 1, 1983; April 29, 1985, effective August 1, 1985; April 30, 1991, effective December 1, 1991; April 22, 1993, effective December 1, 1993; April 27, 1995, effective December 1, 1995; April 30, 2007, effective December 1, 2007; March 26, 2009, effective December 1, 2009.]

AUTHORS' COMMENTARY ON RULE 52

PURPOSE AND SCOPE

Following a non-jury trial, Rule 52 requires that the trial judge make findings of fact and conclusions of law. Rule 52 also sets forth the standard of review for such findings, and allows the judge to enter judgment during the trial if a party fails to carry its burden of proof.

RULE 52(a)—FINDINGS AND CONCLUSIONS

CORE CONCEPT

The trial judge shall explicitly state findings of fact and conclusions of law upon which the judge bases the verdict. Findings of fact will not be disturbed on appeal unless clearly erroneous.[1] Conclusions of law are fully reviewable on appeal.[2]

---

[1]*King v. Zamiara*, 680 F.3d 686, 694 (6th Cir. 2012).

[2]*Wachovia Sec., LLC v. Banco Panamericano, Inc.*, 674 F.3d 743, 751 (7th Cir. 2012).

APPLICATIONS

Impact of 2007 "Restyling" Amendments

Rule 52 was restructured during the 2007 Federal Civil Rules "Restyling" Project. The 2007 amendments moved the text from Rule 52(b) providing that a party may challenge the sufficiency of the evidentiary support for the court's findings after the findings are made regardless of whether the party previously took any positions on the findings into new Rule 52(a)(5). In researching current Rule 52(a)(5), practitioners should be mindful of this repositioning.

Findings and Conclusions Mandatory

The requirement that the judge make findings of fact and conclusions of law is mandatory, and cannot be waived.[3] The parties do not need to request findings.

Content of Findings and Conclusions

The findings must be sufficient to indicate the factual basis for the ultimate conclusion,[4] and permit meaningful appellate review,[5] but need not address all the evidence presented at trial.[6] The court need not make findings on uncontested or stipulated facts.[7] The court should make separate findings of fact and conclusions of law.[8]

Standard for Findings of Fact

When making findings of fact, the court may accept or reject the testimony of witnesses and draw any inferences it deems appropriate.[9]

Proposed Findings and Conclusions

The court may require the parties to submit proposed find-

---

[3]See *Golden Blount, Inc. v. Robert H. Peterson Co.*, 365 F.3d 1054, 1060–61 (Fed. Cir. 2004); *Francis v. Goodman*, 81 F.3d 5, 8 (1st Cir. 1996).

[4]*Attorney General of Oklahoma v. Tyson Foods, Inc.*, 565 F.3d 769, 782 (10th Cir. 2009); *Arpin v. U.S.*, 521 F.3d 769, 776 (7th Cir. 2008) (court must explain the reasoning behind the damages calculation).

[5]*U.S. v. Alabama Dept. of Mental Health and Mental Retardation*, 673 F.3d 1320, 1329 (11th Cir. 2012); *Folger Coffee Co. v. Olivebank*, 201 F.3d 632, 635 (5th Cir. 2000).

[6]See *Lesch v. U.S.*, 612 F.3d 975, 981 (8th Cir. 2010); *Torres-Lazarini v. U.S.*, 523 F.3d 69 (1st Cir. 2008) (the judge need only make brief, definite, pertinent findings and conclusions upon the contested matters). *But see*

Kidd v. Illinois State Police, 167 F.3d 1084, 1101 (7th Cir. 1999) (court should address conflicting testimony in its findings); *League of United Latin American Citizens, Council No. 4434 v. Clements*, 986 F.2d 728 (5th Cir.1993) (the court should address all substantial evidence contrary to its opinion).

[7]*Simeonoff v. Hiner*, 249 F.3d 883, 891 (9th Cir. 2001) ("We will affirm the district court if . . . there can be no genuine dispute about omitted findings").

[8]*Giles v. Kearney*, 571 F.3d 318, 328 (3rd Cir. 2009); *Kurth v. Hartford Life & Acc. Ins. Co.*, 845 F.Supp.2d 1087, 1091 (C.D.Cal. 2012).

[9]*Diesel Props S.r.l. v. Greystone Business Credit II LLC*, 631 F.3d 42, 52 (2nd Cir. 2011).

ings of fact and conclusions of law,[10] although the court's wholesale adoption of the prevailing party's submission is discouraged.[11]

Proceedings Covered by Rule 52

Rule 52 requires findings of fact and conclusions of law in non-jury trials, trials with advisory juries,[12] proceedings for preliminary or permanent injunctions,[13] and when the court grants a motion for dismissal after the plaintiff has presented evidence pursuant to Rule 52(c).[14] Rule 52 does not apply to motions for summary judgment under Rule 56,[15] motions under Rule 12(b)[16] (such as motions to dismiss), motions for attorney fees,[17] or any other motion other than a motion for judgment on partial findings under Rule 52(c).[18] Likewise, findings are not required for actions before administrative agencies that submit reports and recommendations to the district court,[19] or in proceedings where the district court reviews rulings made by the bankruptcy court.

Findings in Jury Trials

In jury trials, Rule 52 applies to any issues decided by the court instead of the jury. The court must also make findings of fact and conclusions of law in a case tried before an advisory

---

[10]*American River Transp. Co. v. Kavo Kaliakra SS*, 148 F.3d 446, 449 (5th Cir. 1998) (proposed findings adopted by the court are entitled to the same deference as findings crafted by the court).

[11]*McLennan v. American Eurocopter Corp., Inc.*, 245 F.3d 403, 409 (5th Cir. 2001) ("the district court's decision to adopt one party's proposed findings and conclusions without change may cause us to approach such findings with greater caution, and as a consequence to apply the standard of review more rigorously"); *Counihan v. Allstate Ins. Co.*, 194 F.3d 357, 365 (2d Cir. 1999).

[12]*OCI Wyoming, L.P. v. Pacifi-Corp*, 479 F.3d 1199, 1203 (10th Cir. 2007).

[13]*See Ali v. Quarterman*, __ F.3d __ (5th Cir. 2010); *but see Dresser-Rand Co. v. Virtual Automation Inc.*, 361 F.3d 831, 847 (5th Cir. 2004) (findings not required at when addressing a request for a permanent injunction at the conclusion of a jury trial).

[14]*Nieto v. Kapoor*, 268 F.3d 1208, 1217 (10th Cir. 2001).

[15]*Barry v. Moran*, 661 F.3d 696, 702, n.9 (1st Cir. 2011); *Grossman v.* Berman, 241 F.3d 65, 68 (1st Cir. 2001); *but see Holly D. v. California Institute of Technology*, 339 F.3d 1158, 1180 (9th Cir. 2003) (Rule 52(a) does not relieve a court of the burden of stating its reasons somewhere in the record when its underlying holdings would otherwise be ambiguous).

[16]*Souza v. Pina*, 53 F.3d 423 (1st Cir.1995) (noting that, although not required, findings would be helpful).

[17]*W.G. v. Senatore*, 18 F.3d 60, 4 A.D.D. 493 (2d Cir. 1994) (suggesting that findings regarding attorney fees would have been helpful, even though not required); *but see Kelly v. Golden*, 352 F.3d 344, 352 (8th Cir. 2003) (when awarding attorney fees, the court must make findings).

[18]*Microfinancial, Inc. v. Premier Holidays Intern., Inc.*, 385 F.3d 72, 76 (1st Cir. 2004) (Rule 52 does not apply to a motion to stay); *Enzo Biochem, Inc. v. Calgene, Inc.*, 188 F.3d 1362, 1379 (Fed. Cir. 1999).

[19]*But see Muller v. First Unum Life Ins. Co.*, 341 F.3d 119, 124 (2d Cir. 2003) (findings are required in ruling on a motion for judgment on the administrative record).

jury.[20]

Injunctions

Findings of fact and conclusions of law are required for injunctions, but not necessarily at the same level of detail as other matters.[21] The court must make findings of fact and conclusions of law when ruling on a motion for a preliminary injunction.[22] If a temporary restraining order is to be extended beyond the period allowed by Rule 65, it becomes a preliminary injunction and findings are required.[23] In ruling on a permanent injunction, the court must make findings if the ruling hinges on factual issues,[24] but the court will not be bound by findings made at the preliminary injunction stage.[25] Findings are not required in ruling on a motion to dissolve an injunction.[26]

Form

The findings of fact may be a separate document or may be included in an opinion.[27] The court may also make its findings orally on the record.[28] If the court makes separate findings, then on appeal those findings control over any contradictory factual statements in an opinion.[29]

Challenges to Sufficiency of Evidence

A party may challenge the sufficiency of the evidence supporting the findings, regardless of whether the party requested the findings, objected to them, or moved to amend them.[30]

RULE 52(b)—AMENDED OR ADDITIONAL FINDINGS

CORE CONCEPT

Upon motion, the court may amend its findings and/or

---

[20]*Kolstad v. American Dental Ass'n*, 108 F.3d 1431, 1440 (D.C. Cir. 1997). *See also*, Rule 39(c) and the author commentary discussing advisory juries.

[21]*Osthus v. Whitesell Corp.*, 639 F.3d 841, 845 (8th Cir. 2011).

[22]*Gordon v. Holder*, 632 F.3d 722, 724 (D.C.Cir. 2011); *Ali v. Quarterman*, __ F.3d __ (5th Cir. 2010).

[23]*Hoechst Diafoil Co. v. Nan Ya Plastics Corp.*, 174 F.3d 411 (4th Cir. 1999).

[24]*Alberti v. Cruise*, 383 F.2d 268 (4th Cir.1967); *but see Dresser-Rand Co. v. Virtual Automation Inc.*, 361 F.3d 831, 847 (5th Cir. 2004) (findings not required at when addressing a request for a permanent injunction at the conclusion of a jury trial).

[25]*TEC Engineering Corp. v. Budget Molders Supply, Inc.*, 82 F.3d 542, 545 (1st Cir. 1996).

[26]*Baltimore & O. R. Co. v. Chicago River & I. R. Co.*, 170 F.2d 654 (7th Cir. 1948).

[27]*Attorney General of Oklahoma v. Tyson Foods, Inc.*, 565 F.3d 769, 782 (10th Cir. 2009).

[28]*Dexia Credit Local v. Rogan*, 602 F.3d 879, 884–85 (7th Cir. 2010); *Federal Trade Com'n v. Enforma Natural Products, Inc.*, 362 F.3d 1204, 1212 (9th Cir. 2004).

[29]*Snow Machines, Inc. v. Hedco, Inc.*, 838 F.2d 718, 727 (3d Cir. 1988).

[30]*Schaub v. VonWald*, 638 F.3d 905, 924 (8th Cir. 2011).

judgment.

APPLICATIONS

Impact of 2007 "Restyling" Amendments

Rule 52 was restructured during the 2007 Federal Civil Rules "Restyling" Project. The 2007 amendments moved the text from Rule 52(b) providing that a party may challenge the sufficiency of the evidentiary support for the court's findings after the findings are made regardless of whether the party previously took any positions on the findings into new Rule 52(a)(5). In researching Rule 52(b), practitioners should be mindful of this repositioning.

Timing

Motions to amend the findings must be filed no later than 28 days after entry of judgment.[31] This time period is absolute, and cannot be enlarged by the court.[32] The motion may be filed before entry of judgment.

Grounds

Proper grounds for a Rule 52(b) motion to amend include newly discovered evidence,[33] a change in the law, or a manifest error of fact or law by the trial court.[34] A Rule 52(b) motion to amend should not merely relitigate old issues or rehear the merits of the case.[35] A party may move to amend the findings of fact even if the modified or additional findings in effect reverse the judgment.[36] Once a motion to amend has been filed, the court can amend any findings it deems appropriate, regardless of the issues raised in the motion.[37]

Tolls Appeal Period

The filing of a motion to amend the findings tolls the running of the time to file an appeal.[38] The appeal clock starts over when the court enters an order granting or denying the motion to amend.

---

[31]*Golden Blount, Inc. v. Robert H. Peterson Co.*, 438 F.3d 1354, 1358 (Fed. Cir. 2006); *Gutierrez v. Johnson & Johnson*, 743 F.Supp.2d 418, 422 (D.N.J. 2010).

[32]*Martin v. Monumental Life Ins. Co.*, 240 F.3d 223, 237–38 (3d Cir. 2001).

[33]*See Gutierrez v. Johnson & Johnson*, 743 F.Supp.2d 418, 422 (D.N.J. 2010); *Draim v. Virtual Geosatellite Holdings, Inc.*, 241 F.R.D. 48, 50 (D.D.C. 2007) (evidence that was merely not offered into evidence does not support a Rule 52(b) motion to amend).

[34]*In re Heritage Org., L.L.C.*, 466 B.R. 862, 868 (N.D.Tex 2012); *Gutierrez v. Johnson & Johnson*, 743 F.Supp.2d 418, 422 (D.N.J. 2010).

[35]*In re Busch*, 369 B.R. 614, 621 (B.A.P. 10th Cir. 2007); *In re Heritage Org., L.L.C.*, 466 B.R. 862, 868 (N.D.Tex 2012).

[36]*Golden Blount, Inc. v. Robert H. Peterson Co.*, 438 F.3d 1354, 1358 (Fed. Cir. 2006) (if the trial court has entered an erroneous judgment, it should correct it).

[37]*Golden Blount, Inc. v. Robert H. Peterson Co.*, 438 F.3d 1354, 1358 (Fed. Cir. 2006).

[38]*Weyant v. Okst*, 198 F.3d 311, 314–15 (2d Cir. 1999).

RULE 52(c)—JUDGMENT ON PARTIAL FIND-INGS

CORE CONCEPT

At any time in a non-jury trial after a party has presented all its evidence with respect to a particular issue, the court may enter judgment against that party if the evidence failed to persuade the judge.[39]

APPLICATIONS

Proceedings Applicable

Rule 52(c) applies only in non-jury trials.[40] The parallel for jury trials is a judgment as a matter of law under Rule 50(a).[41]

Timing of Motion

A Rule 52(c) motion may be made at any time after all the evidence has been presented on a particular topic;[42] although motions for judgment on partial findings are typically made at the close of the opposing party's case,[43] the movant technically does not need to wait until the opposing party has rested.[44]

Standard for Granting

The trial judge rules on motions for judgment on partial findings as a final factfinder, reviewing all evidence presented thus far without presumptions in favor of either party.[45] The judge grants the motion if, upon the evidence already presented, the judge would find against the party that has already presented evidence and in favor of the moving party.[46]

Scope of Judgment

The judge will enter judgment on the claim or issue that is

---

[39]*Martin v. Harris*, 560 F.3d 210, 218 (4th Cir. 2009) (court has discretion to decline to enter judgment on partial findings).

[40]*Fillmore v. Page*, 358 F.3d 496, 502–03 (7th Cir. 2004); *Northeast Drilling, Inc. v. Inner Space Services, Inc.*, 243 F.3d 25, 35 (1st Cir. 2001).

[41]*Federal Ins. Co. v. HPSC, Inc.*, 480 F.3d 26, 32 (1st Cir. 2007) (motion for judgment as a matter of law in a non-jury trial treated as a motion for judgment on partial findings under Rule 52(c)).

[42]*First Virginia Banks, Inc. v. BP Exploration & Oil Inc.*, 206 F.3d 404, 407 (4th Cir. 2000) (Rule 52 does not create a right to introduce all the evidence on a topic that the party wishes; the court may exclude evidence if cumulative or not probative); *Pub.*

Patent Found., Inc. v. GlaxoSmithK-line Consumer Healthcare, L.P., 801 F.Supp.2d 249, 255 (S.D.N.Y. 2011).

[43]*See, e.g., Pinkston v. Madry*, 440 F.3d 879, 885–86 (7th Cir. 2006); *Pub. Patent Found., Inc. v. GlaxoSmithK-line Consumer Healthcare, L.P.*, 801 F.Supp.2d 249, 255 (S.D.N.Y. 2011).

[44]*Cajun Elec. Power Co-op., Inc. v. Gulf States Utilities Co.*, 848 F. Supp. 71 (M.D. La. 1994).

[45]*Ortloff v. U.S.*, 335 F.3d 652, 660 (7th Cir. 2003) (contrasting the standard under Rule 52(c) to the standard under Rule 52(a)); *Geddes v. Northwest Missouri State University*, 49 F.3d 426 (8th Cir.1995).

[46]*S.E.C. v. Razmilovic*, 822 F.Supp.2d 234, 257 (E.D.N.Y. 2011); *Cantwell & Cantwell v. Vicario*, 464 B.R. 776, 786 (N.D.Ill. 2011).

the subject of the motion and on any other claim, issue, counterclaim, crossclaim, or third-party claim that is determined by the outcome of the issue that is the subject of the motion.[47]

Findings of Fact

If the judge grants a motion for judgment on partial findings, the judge must make findings of fact pursuant to Rule 52(a).[48]

Deferred Ruling

The judge, in an exercise of discretion, may defer ruling until all evidence has been presented.[49] If the court defers ruling on a motion for judgment on partial findings and the non-moving party enters additional evidence regarding the subject of the motion, the court will consider all the evidence when it ultimately rules.[50]

Additional Research References

Wright & Miller, *Federal Practice and Procedure* §§ 2571 to 2591
C.J.S., Federal Civil Procedure §§ 1036 to 1056 et seq.
West's Key Number Digest, Federal Civil Procedure ☞2261 to 2293

---

[47]*See Cantwell & Cantwell v. Vicario*, 464 B.R. 776, 783 (N.D.Ill. 2011).

[48]*Burger v. New York Institute of Technology*, 94 F.3d 830, 835 (2d Cir. 1996) (explaining that a "one-sentence statement in no way constitutes the requisite findings under Rule 52"); *Akerley v. North Country Stone, Inc.*, 620 F.Supp.2d 591, 593 (D.Vt. 2009).

[49]*Cantwell & Cantwell v. Vicario*, 464 B.R. 776, 787 (N.D.Ill. 2011); *U.S. v. Davis*, 20 F. Supp. 2d 326, 331 (D.R.I. 1998).

[50]*S.E.C. v. Razmilovic*, 822 F.Supp.2d 234, 257–58 (E.D.N.Y. 2011); *TransCanada Pipelines Ltd. v. USGen New England, Inc.*, 458 B.R. 195, 214–15 (D.Md. 2011).

RULE 53
MASTERS

(a) Appointment.

   (1) *Scope.* Unless a statute provides otherwise, a court may appoint a master only to:

     (A) perform duties consented to by the parties;

     (B) hold trial proceedings and make or recommend findings of fact on issues to be decided without a jury if appointment is warranted by:

       (i) some exceptional condition; or

       (ii) the need to perform an accounting or resolve a difficult computation of damages; or

     (C) address pretrial and posttrial matters that cannot be effectively and timely addressed by an available district judge or magistrate judge of the district.

   (2) *Disqualification.* A master must not have a relationship to the parties, attorneys, action, or court that would require disqualification of a judge under 28 U.S.C. § 455, unless the parties, with the court's approval, consent to the appointment after the master discloses any potential grounds for disqualification.

   (3) *Possible Expense or Delay.* In appointing a master, the court must consider the fairness of imposing the likely expenses on the parties and must protect against unreasonable expense or delay.

(b) Order Appointing a Master.

   (1) *Notice.* Before appointing a master, the court must give the parties notice and an opportunity to be heard. Any party may suggest candidates for appointment.

   (2) *Contents.* The appointing order must direct the master to proceed with all reasonable diligence and must state:

     (A) the master's duties, including any investigation or enforcement duties, and any limits on the master's authority under Rule 53(c);

 (B) the circumstances, if any, in which the master may communicate ex parte with the court or a party;

 (C) the nature of the materials to be preserved and filed as the record of the master's activities;

 (D) the time limits, method of filing the record, other procedures, and standards for reviewing the master's orders, findings, and recommendations; and

 (E) the basis, terms, and procedure for fixing the master's compensation under Rule 53(g).

 (3) *Issuing.* The court may issue the order only after:

 (A) the master files an affidavit disclosing whether there is any ground for disqualification under 28 U.S.C. § 455; and

 (B) if a ground is disclosed, the parties, with the court's approval, waive the disqualification.

 (4) *Amending.* The order may be amended at any time after notice to the parties and an opportunity to be heard.

(c) Master's Authority.

 (1) *In General.* Unless the appointing order directs otherwise, a master may:

 (A) regulate all proceedings;

 (B) take all appropriate measures to perform the assigned duties fairly and efficiently; and

 (C) if conducting an evidentiary hearing, exercise the appointing court's power to compel, take, and record evidence.

 (2) *Sanctions.* The master may by order impose on a party any noncontempt sanction provided by Rule 37 or 45, and may recommend a contempt sanction against a party and sanctions against a nonparty.

(d) Master's Orders. A master who issues an order must file it and promptly serve a copy on each party. The clerk must enter the order on the docket.

(e) Master's Reports. A master must report to the

court as required by the appointing order. The master must file the report and promptly serve a copy on each party, unless the court orders otherwise.

(f) Action on the Master's Order, Report, or Recommendations.

 (1) *Opportunity for a Hearing; Action in General.* In acting on a master's order, report, or recommendations, the court must give the parties notice and an opportunity to be heard; may receive evidence; and may adopt or affirm, modify, wholly or partly reject or reverse, or resubmit to the master with instructions.

 (2) *Time to Object or Move to Adopt or Modify.* A party may file objections to—or a motion to adopt or modify—the master's order, report, or recommendations no later than 21 days after a copy is served, unless the court sets a different time.

 (3) *Reviewing Factual Findings.* The court must decide de novo all objections to findings of fact made or recommended by a master, unless the parties, with the court's approval, stipulate that:

  (A) the findings will be reviewed for clear error; or

  (B) the findings of a master appointed under Rule 53(a)(1)(A) or (C) will be final.

 (4) *Reviewing Legal Conclusions.* The court must decide de novo all objections to conclusions of law made or recommended by a master.

 (5) *Reviewing Procedural Matters.* Unless the appointing order establishes a different standard of review, the court may set aside a master's ruling on a procedural matter only for an abuse of discretion.

(g) Compensation.

 (1) *Fixing Compensation.* Before or after judgment, the court must fix the master's compensation on the basis and terms stated in the appointing order, but the court may set a new basis and terms after giving notice and an opportunity to be heard.

 (2) *Payment.* The compensation must be paid either:

  (A) by a party or parties; or

    (B) from a fund or subject matter of the action within the court's control.

    (3) *Allocating Payment.* The court must allocate payment among the parties after considering the nature and amount of the controversy, the parties' means, and the extent to which any party is more responsible than other parties for the reference to a master. An interim allocation may be amended to reflect a decision on the merits.

(h) Appointing a Magistrate Judge. A magistrate judge is subject to this rule only when the order referring a matter to the magistrate judge states that the reference is made under this rule.

[Amended February 28, 1966, effective July 1, 1966; April 28, 1983, effective August 1, 1983; March 2, 1987, effective August 1, 1987; April 30, 1991, effective December 1, 1991; April 22, 1993, effective December 1, 1993; March 27, 2003, effective December 1, 2003; April 30, 2007, effective December 1, 2007; March 26, 2009, effective December 1, 2009.]

AUTHORS' COMMENTARY ON RULE 53

PURPOSE AND SCOPE

Rule 53 provides the procedures governing the reference of designated aspects of an action to a master.

NOTE: Rule 53 was substantially revised in 2003 to reflect changing practices in using masters. The amendment recognizes that special masters are used for a variety of pretrial and post-trial functions as well as to conduct trials. The amendment also changes the standard of review for findings of fact by a master.

RULE 53(a)—APPOINTMENT

CORE CONCEPT

The court in which an action is pending may appoint a special master to conduct trials in limited circumstances and to conduct certain pretrial and post-trial functions.

APPLICATIONS

Functions Performed by Master

Rule 53 defines three categories of functions that a master may perform:

- Duties consented to by the parties;[1]
- Hold trial proceedings and make recommended findings of fact on non-jury issues if the appointment is warranted by an exceptional condition or by the need to perform an accounting or resolve a difficult computation of damages;[2] or
- address pretrial[3] or post-trial matters[4] if they cannot be addressed effectively and timely by the court.

Jury Trials

The court may not appoint a special master in matters to be tried to a jury unless the parties consent.[5]

Ineligible Persons

One cannot be master if related to the parties, the action, or the court under the same standards that govern disqualification of a judge set forth in 28 U.S.C. § 455.[6] The clerk of court and the clerk's deputies are also ineligible. The parties can waive this restriction with the court's approval.[7]

Court's Discretion—Fairness

In determining whether to appoint a master, the court must consider the fairness of imposing the cost of the master's compensation on the parties and the effects of delay.[8] The court has discretion as to whether to refer a matter to a master,[9] but reference should be the exception, not the rule.[10] The court also has discretion to refuse to appoint a master even if the parties have consented.[11]

Magistrate Judges

The court may appoint a United States Magistrate Judge to

---

[1]*See Gulf States Reorganization Grp., Inc. v. Nucor Corp.*, 822 F.Supp.2d 1201, 1205 (N.D.Ala. 2011); *Cremin v. Merrill Lynch, Pierce, Fenner & Smith, Inc.*, 328 F. Supp. 2d 865, 869 (N.D. Ill. 2004).

[2]*See Alvarez v. City of Chicago*, 605 F.3d 445 (7th Cir. 2010); *Beazer East, Inc. v. Mead Corp.*, 412 F.3d 429, 441 (3d Cir. 2005) (equitable allocation under CERCLA is not a computation of damages and thus may not be referred to a special master).

[3]*Rohrbough v. Harris*, 549 F.3d 1313, 1318 (10th Cir. 2008) (master attended depositions to rule on objections).

[4]*See* The Advisory Committee Note to the 2003 Amendment to Rule 53 (reliance on a master is appropriate when a complex decree requires ongoing policing).

[5]The Advisory Committee Note to the 2003 Amendments to Rule 53.

[6]*In re Kensington Intern. Ltd.*, 353 F.3d 211, 222 (3d Cir. 2003).

[7]*See U.S. v. Michigan*, 234 F.R.D. 636 (E.D. Mich. 2006).

[8]*See Gaddis v. U.S.*, 381 F.3d 444, 462 (5th Cir. 2004); *Taylor v. Islamic Republic of Iran*, 811 F.Supp.2d 1, 17 (D.D.C. 2011).

[9]*Middle Tennessee News Co., Inc. v. Charnel of Cincinnati, Inc.*, 250 F.3d 1077 (7th Cir.2001) ("The district court did not need the consent of the parties to refer" complicated "issues to an independent accountant under Rule 53."); *U.S. v. State of Wash.*, 157 F.3d 630, 660 (9th Cir. 1998).

[10]*U.S. v. State of Washington*, 135 F.3d 618, 646 (9th Cir. 1998).

[11]The Advisory Committee Note to the 2003 Amendments to Rule 53.

serve as a special master.[12] The provisions regarding compensation do not apply when a United States Magistrate Judge is designated to serve as a special master.

Common References

References are most common in patent, trademark, and copyright actions.[13] They are also used occasionally to supervise discovery, following summary judgment on liability when the damages are difficult to calculate, and to oversee compliance.[14]

RULE 53(b)—ORDER APPOINTING A MASTER

CORE CONCEPT

A master is appointed by an order setting forth the duties and parameters of the reference.

APPLICATIONS

Notice and Opportunity to Be Heard

The court must give notice of the proposed appointment of a master to the parties and provide an opportunity to be heard before appointing the master.[15] Written submissions will provide an "opportunity to be heard" unless the circumstances require live testimony.[16]

Candidates for Appointment

A party may suggest candidates for appointment as master.[17]

Contents of Order

The order appointing a master must:

- Direct the master to proceed with all reasonable diligence;[18]
- State the master's duties and any limits on the master's authority;[19]
- State the circumstances, if any, in which the master may communicate *ex parte* with the court or a party;[20]
- State the nature of the materials to be preserved and filed as the record of the master's activities;[21]

---

[12]*S.E.C. v. AMX, Intern., Inc.*, 872 F. Supp. 1541 (N.D. Tex. 1994).

[13]*See Absolute Software, Inc. v. Stealth Signal, Inc.*, 659 F.3d 1121, 1131 (Fed. Cir. 2011).

[14]*See U.S. v. Microsoft Corp.*, 147 F.3d 935 (D.C. Cir. 1998) (discussing the "well established tradition allowing use of special masters to oversee compliance.").

[15]Rule 53(b)(1). *See also Amgen, Inc. v. Hoechst Marion Roussel, Inc.*, 339 F. Supp. 2d 202, 221 (D. Mass. 2004).

[16]The Advisory Committee Note to the 2003 Amendment to Rule 53.

[17]Rule 53(b)(1).

[18]Rule 53(b)(2).

[19]Rule 53(b)(2)(A). *See also Horn v. McQueen*, 353 F. Supp. 2d 785, 850 (W.D. Ky. 2004).

[20]Rule 53(b)(2)(B). *See also* The Advisory Committee Note to the 2003 Amendment to Rule 53 (ordinarily, the order should prohibit *ex parte* communications).

[21]Rule 53(b)(2)(C). *See also* The Advisory Committee Note to the 2003

- State the time limits, methods of filing the record, other procedures, and standards for reviewing the master's orders, findings, and recommendations;[22] and
- State the basis, terms, and procedures for determining the master's compensation under Rule 53(g).[23]

Affidavit re Disqualification

Before the court can enter the order appointing the master, the master must file an affidavit disclosing whether there is any ground for disqualification under 28 U.S.C. § 455.[24] If a ground for disqualification is disclosed, the court may not enter the order unless the parties have consented with the court's approval to waive the disqualification.[25]

Amendment of Order

The order appointing the master may be amended at any time after notice to the parties and an opportunity to be heard.[26]

Challenging Reference

The proper method for contesting a reference is a motion to amend, vacate or revoke the reference.[27] Failure to make such a motion may be deemed a consent or waiver.[28] If the motion to vacate is denied, the disgruntled party may attempt to compel the court to vacate by a writ of mandamus.[29] Orders of reference are interlocutory, and may not be appealed directly, but may be appealed at the conclusion of the district court proceedings.[30]

RULE 53(c)—MASTER'S AUTHORITY

CORE CONCEPT

Absent specific limitations in the order appointing the master, the master has all powers necessary to perform the referred matters, including the powers necessary to regulate the proceedings, rule on evidentiary issues, place witnesses under oath, and examine witnesses.[31] The master has discretion as to what procedures to employ, with the only requirement being that when

---

Amendment to Rule 53 (a basic requirement is that the master must make and file a complete record of the evidence considered in making or recommending findings of fact).

[22]Rule 53(b)(2)(D).

[23]*In re Holocaust Victim Assets Litigation*, 528 F. Supp. 2d 109, 119, (E.D. N.Y. 2007).

[24]Rule 53(b)(3).

[25]Rule 53(b)(3).

[26]Rule 53(b)(4).

[27]*Fajardo Shopping Center, S.E. v. Sun Alliance Ins. Co. of Puerto Rico,*

Inc., 167 F.3d 1, 6 (1st Cir. 1999).

[28]*Fajardo Shopping Center, S.E. v. Sun Alliance Ins. Co. of Puerto Rico, Inc.*, 167 F.3d 1, 6 (1st Cir. 1999); *Spaulding v. University of Washington*, 740 F.2d 686, 693 (9th Cir. 1984).

[29]*La Buy v. Howes Leather Company*, 352 U.S. 249, 77 S. Ct. 309, 1 L. Ed. 2d 290 (1957); *U.S. v. Microsoft Corp.*, 147 F.3d 935 (D.C. Cir. 1998).

[30]*Sierra Club v. Clifford*, 257 F.3d 444 (5th Cir.2001).

[31]*U.S. v. Clifford Matley Family Trust*, 354 F.3d 1154, 1159 (9th Cir. 2004) (the order referring the case is

the master determines that a hearing is necessary, the master shall make a record of the evidence offered and excluded in the same manner and subject to the same limitations as provided in the Federal Rules of Evidence for a non-jury trial.[32] The court has the duty to oversee the special master's performance of his duties to ensure that they are appropriately discharged.[33]

APPLICATIONS

Impact of 2007 "Restyling" Amendments

Warning: Rule 53 was restructured during the 2007 Federal Civil Rules "Restyling" Project. The 2007 amendments moved the provisions of Rule 53(d) to Rule 53(c)(1)(C), and the provisions in the sections following former Rule 53(d) were renumbered accordingly. In researching Rules 53(c) and (d), practitioners should be mindful of this repositioning.

Sanctions

The master may impose on a party any non-contempt sanction provided by Rule 37 or 45. The master may also recommend contempt sanctions against a party and sanctions against a non-party.

Evidentiary Hearings

Unless otherwise limited by the order appointing the master, the master may exercise the powers of the court to compel (by subpoena under Rule 45), take, and record evidence.

RULE 53(d)—MASTER'S ORDERS

CORE CONCEPT

A master who makes an order must file the order with the clerk and promptly serve a copy on each party. The clerk must enter the order on the docket.

APPLICATIONS

Impact of 2007 "Restyling" Amendments

Rule 53 was restructured during the 2007 Federal Civil Rules "Restyling" Project. The 2007 amendments moved the provisions of Rule 53(d) to Rule 53(c)(1)(C), and the provisions in the sections following former Rule 53(d) were renumbered accordingly. Rule 53(e) was renumbered as Rule 53(d). In researching current Rule 53(d), practitioners should be mindful of this repositioning.

RULE 53(e)—MASTER'S REPORTS

the source and the limit of the master's duties and powers); *Laube v. Campbell*, 333 F. Supp. 2d 1234, 1240 (M.D. Ala. 2004).

[32]*U.S. v. Clifford Matley Family Trust*, 354 F.3d 1154, 1159 (9th Cir. 2004).

[33]*Cordoza v. Pacific States Steel Corp.*, 320 F.3d 989, 999 (9th Cir. 2003) (court has the duty to reduce special master's compensation if appropriate).

CORE CONCEPT

A master must prepare reports as directed by the order of appointment. The master must file such reports with the clerk and promptly serve a copy upon each party unless the court directs otherwise.[34]

APPLICATIONS

Impact of 2007 "Restyling" Amendments

Rule 53 was restructured during the 2007 Federal Civil Rules "Restyling" Project. The 2007 amendments moved the provisions of Rule 53(d) to Rule 53(c)(1)(C), and the subsequent sections were renumbered accordingly. Rule 53(f) was renumbered as Rule 53(e). In researching current Rule 53(e), practitioners should be mindful of this repositioning.

Supporting Materials

The master should provide all portions of the record that the master deems relevant to the report. The parties may seek to designate additional materials from the record, and may seek to supplement the record. The court may provide that additional materials from the record be filed.[35]

Sealed Report

Sealing of the report from public access may be appropriate, particularly with respect to pre-trial and post-trial masters. A report detailing a continuing or failed settlement effort is one example of a report that might be sealed.[36]

RULE 53(f)—ACTION ON THE MASTER'S ORDER, REPORT, OR RECOMMENDATIONS

CORE CONCEPT

Rule 53(f) sets forth the procedures for the court to act on the masters report and the standards by which the court should review the report.

APPLICATIONS

Impact of 2007 "Restyling" Amendments

Rule 53 was restructured during the 2007 Federal Civil Rules "Restyling" Project. The 2007 amendments moved the provisions of Rule 53(d) to Rule 53(c)(1)(C), and the subsequent sections were renumbered accordingly. Rule 53(g) was renumbered as Rule 53(f).[37] In researching current Rule 53(f), practitioners should be mindful of this repositioning.

---

[34]*See Schaefer Fan Co., Inc. v. J & D Mfg.*, 265 F.3d 1282, 1289 (Fed. Cir. 2001); *In re Latex Glove Products Liability Litigation*, 2004 WL 1118691 (E.D. Pa. 2004).

[35]The Advisory Committee Note to the 2003 Amendment to Rule 53.

[36]The Advisory Committee Note to the 2003 Amendment to Rule 53.

[37]*See In re Intel Corp. Microprocessor Antitrust Litigation*, 526 F.Supp.2d 461, 462 (D. Del. 2008).

Actions by the Court

When considering an order, report, or recommendation from a master, the court may adopt or affirm, modify, reject or reverse in whole or in part, or resubmit to the master with instructions.[38]

Opportunity to be Heard

Before taking action on an order, report, or recommendation from a master, the court must provide the parties with an opportunity to be heard.[39] Written submissions will provide an "opportunity to be heard" unless the circumstances require live testimony.[40]

Consideration of Additional Evidence

The court has discretion to consider additional evidence in connection with its review of the master's report, but is not required to do so.[41]

Time for Objections

A party may file objections to the master's order, report, or recommendations no later than 21 days from the time the order, report, or recommendations are served, unless the court sets a different time.[42] The parties may also file a motion to adopt or modify the order, report, or recommendations in the same time frame.[43] This time period is not jurisdictional, and the court has the authority to consider a late objection or motion.[44]

Findings of Fact

Absent a stipulation otherwise,[45] the court must decide *de novo* all objections to findings of fact made or recommended by a master.[46] The court may also review *de novo* findings of fact made or recommended by a master in the absence of an

---

[38]*Paone v. Microsoft Corp.*, __ F.Supp.2d __ (E.D.N.Y. 2011); *In re Intel Corp. Microprocessor Antitrust Litigation*, 526 F.Supp.2d 461, 463 (D.Del. 2008).

[39]*World Triathalon Corp. v. Dunbar*, 539 F. Supp. 2d 1270, 1275 (D. Haw. 2008); *U.S. v. Fairway Capital Corp.*, 433 F. Supp. 2d 226 (D.R.I. 2006), aff'd, 483 F.3d 34 (1st Cir. 2007).

[40]The Advisory Committee Note to the 2003 Amendment to Rule 53.

[41]*Commissariat à l'Energie Atomique v. Samsung Electronics Co.*, 245 F.R.D. 177, 179 (D. Del. 2007).

[42]*See Petties v. District of Columbia*, __ F.Supp.2d __ (D.D.C. 2011); *Skaaning v. Sorensen*, 679 F.Supp.2d

1220, 1222 (D.Hawai'i 2010).

[43]Rule 53(f)(2).

[44]*See Wallace v. Skadden, Arps, Slate, Meagher & Flom, LLP*, 362 F.3d 810, 816 (D.C. Cir. 2004); The Advisory Committee Note to the 2003 Amendment to Rule 53.

[45]*AgGrow Oils, L.L.C. v. National Union Fire Ins. Co. of Pittsburgh, PA*, 276 F. Supp. 2d 999, 1005 (D.N.D. 2003), aff'd, 420 F.3d 751 (8th Cir. 2005) (when the parties stipulate that a master's findings of fact shall be final, the district court shall only consider questions of law).

[46]*In re Refco Sec. Litig.*, 280 F.R.D. 102, 104 (S.D.N.Y. 2011); *City of Colton v. Am. Promotional Events, Inc.*, 277 F.R.D. 578, 580 (C.D.Cal. 2011).

objection.[47] The parties may stipulate, with the court's consent, that the master's findings of fact will only be reviewed for clear error.[48] The parties may also stipulate, with the court's consent, that the master's findings of fact will be final if the master was appointed by consent or was appointed to address pretrial or post-trial matters.[49] The court may withdraw its consent to a stipulation for clear error review or finality, may reopen the opportunity for the parties to object.[50]

Conclusions of Law

The court must decide *de novo* all objections to conclusions of law made or recommended by a master.[51]

Procedural Matters

In the absence of a different standard set by the order of appointment, the court reviews a master's ruling on a procedural matter for abuse of discretion.[52]

Appeals

The report of the master is not appealable until adopted by the court. Only issues that are raised in objections to the special master's report are preserved for appeal.[53]

RULE 53(g)—COMPENSATION

CORE CONCEPT

The court sets the compensation for a master. The master's compensation will be allocated among the parties or taken from the subject matter of the litigation.

APPLICATIONS

Impact of 2007 "Restyling" Amendments

Rule 53 was restructured during the 2007 Federal Civil Rules "Restyling" Project. The 2007 amendments moved the provisions of Rule 53(d) to Rule 53(c)(1)(C), and the subsequent sections were renumbered accordingly. Rule 53(h) was renum-

---

[47]The Advisory Committee Note to the 2003 Amendment to Rule 53.

[48]Rule 53(f)(3)(A). *See also* The Advisory Committee Note to the 2003 Amendment to Rule 53 (suggesting that clear error review is more likely to be appropriate with respect to findings that do not go to the merits of the claims or defenses, such as findings of fact going to a privilege issue); *Grace v. City of Detroit*, 341 F. Supp. 2d 709, 714 (E.D. Mich. 2004), aff'd, 216 Fed. Appx. 485 (6th Cir. 2007).

[49]Rule 53(f)(3)(B).

[50]The Advisory Committee Note to the 2003 Amendment to Rule 53.

[51]*In re Refco Sec. Litig.*, 280 F.R.D. 102, 104 (S.D.N.Y. 2011); *City of Colton v. Am. Promotional Events, Inc.*, 277 F.R.D. 578, 580 (C.D.Cal. 2011).

[52]*In re Refco Sec. Litig.*, 280 F.R.D. 102, 104, n.4 (S.D.N.Y. 2011) (court may set the standard of review for procedural matters); *Gulf States Reorganization Grp., Inc. v. Nucor Corp.*, 822 F.Supp.2d 1201, 1211 (N.D.Ala. 2011) (abuse of discretion standard for special master reports is "more searching" than an appellate court's review of district court).

[53]*Absolute Software, Inc. v. Stealth Signal, Inc.*, 659 F.3d 1121, 1131 (Fed. Cir. 2011).

bered as Rule 53(g). In researching current Rule 53(g), practitioners should be mindful of this repositioning.

Amount of Compensation

The court fixes the compensation for a master,[54] and the amount will not be disturbed on appeal absent an abuse of discretion.[55] The court may also require the posting of a bond to secure payment of the fee or require the payment of the fee into escrow.[56] The amount of compensation will be controlled by the order of appointment,[57] but the court may set a new basis and terms after notice to the parties and an opportunity to be heard.[58]

Source of Compensation

The court may impose the master's fee upon either party or may apportion it among the parties.[59] The court may also direct that the fee be paid from any fund[60] or subject matter of the action in the custody of the court.

Allocation Among Parties

If the compensation is to be paid by the parties, the court must allocate the compensation among the parties. The court should consider the nature and amount of the controversy, the parties' financial means, and the extent to which any party is more responsible for the reference to the master.[61] The court may make interim allocations and may adjust the interim allocation later to reflect the decision on the merits.[62]

Collection of Compensation

The master may obtain a writ of execution against a party not paying his share of the master's fee. The master may not withhold the report to obtain payment.

RULE 53(h)—APPOINTING A MAGISTRATE JUDGE

CORE CONCEPT

The provisions of Rule 53 do not pertain to matters referred to magistrate judges unless the order of reference specifically states

---

[54]*Cordoza v. Pacific States Steel Corp.*, 320 F.3d 989, 999 (9th Cir. 2003) (court has the duty to reduce special master's compensation if appropriate).

[55]*Roy v. County of Lexington, South Carolina*, 141 F.3d 533 (4th Cir. 1998).

[56]*Allapattah Services, Inc. v. Exxon Corp.*, 157 F. Supp. 2d 1291, 1325 (S.D. Fla. 2001), aff'd, 333 F.3d 1248 (11th Cir. 2003), aff'd, 545 U.S. 546, 125 S. Ct. 2611, 162 L. Ed. 2d 502 (2005).

[57]*Gaddis v. U.S.*, 381 F.3d 444, 462 (5th Cir. 2004).

[58]Rule 53(g)(1).

[59]*See Gaddis v. U.S.*, 381 F.3d 444, 462 (5th Cir. 2004); *Roy v. County of Lexington, South Carolina*, 141 F.3d 533, 549 (4th Cir. 1998).

[60]*See Six L's Packing Co., Inc. v. Post & Taback, Inc.*, 132 F. Supp. 2d 306, 309 (S.D. N.Y. 2001).

[61]Rule 53(g)(3).

[62]Rule 53(g)(3). *See also Kaplan v. First Hartford Corp.*, __ F.Supp.2d __ (D.Me. 2010).

that it is made pursuant to Rule 53.[63]

APPLICATIONS

Impact of 2007 "Restyling" Amendments

Rule 53 was restructured during the 2007 Federal Civil Rules "Restyling" Project. The 2007 amendments moved the provisions of Rule 53(d) to Rule 53(c)(1)(C), and the subsequent sections were renumbered accordingly. Rule 53(i) was renumbered as Rule 53(h). In researching current Rule 53(h), practitioners should be mindful of this repositioning.

Additional Research References

Wright & Miller, *Federal Practice and Procedure* §§ 2601 to 2615
C.J.S., Federal Civil Procedure §§ 890 to 904; United States Commissioners
  § 3
West's Key Number Digest, Federal Civil Procedure ⬦1871 to 1908; United
  States Magistrates ⬦14

---

[63]*See Wallace v. Skadden, Arps, Slate, Meagher & Flom, LLP*, 362 F.3d 810, 814–16 (D.C. Cir. 2004); *Gonzalez v. Rakkas*, 846 F. Supp. 229 (E.D. N.Y. 1994).

VII. JUDGMENT

RULE 54
JUDGMENT; COSTS

(a) Definition; Form. "Judgment" as used in these rules includes a decree and any order from which an appeal lies. A judgment should not include recitals of pleadings, a master's report, or a record of prior proceedings.

(b) Judgment on Multiple Claims or Involving Multiple Parties. When an action presents more than one claim for relief—whether as a claim, counterclaim, crossclaim, or third-party claim—or when multiple parties are involved, the court may direct entry of a final judgment as to one or more, but fewer than all, claims or parties only if the court expressly determines that there is no just reason for delay. Otherwise, any order or other decision, however designated, that adjudicates fewer than all the claims or the rights and liabilities of fewer than all the parties does not end the action as to any of the claims or parties and may be revised at any time before the entry of a judgment adjudicating all the claims and all the parties' rights and liabilities.

(c) Demand for Judgment; Relief to Be Granted. A default judgment must not differ in kind from, or exceed in amount, what is demanded in the pleadings. Every other final judgment should grant the relief to which each party is entitled, even if the party has not demanded that relief in its pleadings.

(d) Costs; Attorney's Fees.

   (1) *Costs Other Than Attorney's Fees.* Unless a federal statute, these rules, or a court order provides otherwise, costs—other than attorney's fees—should be allowed to the prevailing party. But costs against the United States, its officers, and its agencies may be imposed only to the

extent allowed by law. The clerk may tax costs on 14 days' notice. On motion served within the next 7 days, the court may review the clerk's action.

(2) *Attorney's Fees.*

(A) *Claim to Be by Motion.* A claim for attorney's fees and related nontaxable expenses must be made by motion unless the substantive law requires those fees to be proved at trial as an element of damages.

(B) *Timing and Contents of the Motion.* Unless a statute or a court order provides otherwise, the motion must:

(i) be filed no later than 14 days after the entry of judgment;

(ii) specify the judgment and the statute, rule, or other grounds entitling the movant to the award;

(iii) state the amount sought or provide a fair estimate of it; and

(iv) disclose, if the court so orders, the terms of any agreement about fees for the services for which the claim is made.

(C) *Proceedings.* Subject to Rule 23(h), the court must, on a party's request, give an opportunity for adversary submissions on the motion in accordance with Rule 43(c) or 78. The court may decide issues of liability for fees before receiving submissions on the value of services. The court must find the facts and state its conclusions of law as provided in Rule 52(a).

(D) *Special Procedures by Local Rule; Reference to a Master or a Magistrate Judge.* By local rule, the court may establish special procedures to resolve fee-related issues without extensive evidentiary hearings. Also, the court may refer issues concerning the value of services to a special master under Rule 53 without regard to the limitations of Rule 53(a)(1), and may refer a motion for attorney's fees to a magistrate judge under Rule 72(b) as if it were a dispositive pretrial matter.

(E) *Exceptions.* Subparagraphs (A)–(D) do not apply to claims for fees and expenses as sanctions for violating these rules or as sanctions under 28 U.S.C. § 1927.

[Amended December 27, 1946, effective March 19, 1948; April 17, 1961, effective July 19, 1961; March 2, 1987, effective August 1, 1987; April 22, 1993, effective December 1, 1993; amended April 29, 2002, effective December 1, 2002; March 27, 2003, effective December 1, 2003; April 30, 2007, effective December 1, 2007; March 26, 2009, effective December 1, 2009.]

AUTHORS' COMMENTARY ON RULE 54

PURPOSE AND SCOPE

Rule 54 defines the term "judgment", discusses the limits of recovery on a judgment, and allows the taxation of costs. The Rule also permits the federal court to enter judgment as to just one adjudicated claim or the adjudicated rights of just one party, and thus permit an immediate appeal from that otherwise incomplete judgment.

RULE 54(a)—DEFINITION AND FORM OF "JUDGMENT"

CORE CONCEPT

A judgment is any appealable decree or order.

APPLICATIONS

Definition

To be a "judgment" within the meaning of Rule 54(a), the court's order or decree must be a ruling from which an appeal can be taken.[1] Ordinarily, this requires "some clear and unequivocal manifestation" by the district court that, at least as far as that court is concerned, the case is closed.[2] (Preliminary injunctions often qualify as "judgments".[3]) A ruling that partially adjudicates a claim or is an otherwise non-final order will not usually qualify as a judgment.[4]

---

[1] See In re Metropolitan Gov't of Nashville & Davidson County, Tenn., 606 F.3d 855, 860 (6th Cir. 2010); Auto Services Co. v. KPMG, LLP, 537 F.3d 853, 856 (8th Cir. 2008).

[2] See Diaz-Reyes v. Fuentes-Ortiz, 471 F.3d 299, 301 (1st Cir. 2006).

[3] See People Against Police Violence v. City of Pittsburgh, 520 F.3d 226, 233 n.5 (3d Cir. 2008).

[4] See Auto Servs. Co. v. KPMG, LLP, 537 F.3d 853, 856 (8th Cir. 2008); DeJohn v. Temple University, 537 F.3d 301, 307 (3d Cir. 2008). See also Dishman v. UNUM Life Ins. Co. of America, 269 F.3d 974, 990–91 (9th

Appears Alone

To avoid confusion and uncertainty about what is (and is not) a "judgment", it should appear alone. It should not include recitals of the pleadings, a report from a master, or a record of prior proceedings.[5] It should, instead, be set forth in its own document containing nothing of substance other than the judgment.[6]

RULE 54(b)—JUDGMENT ON MULTIPLE CLAIMS OR INVOLVING MULTIPLE PARTIES

CORE CONCEPT

A judgment entered as to fewer than all claims or all parties in a lawsuit is not immediately appealable. Instead, the appeal must generally await the entry of judgment as to all remaining claims and parties. However, the district court can make a final adjudication of such claims or parties "final", and immediately appealable, by expressly determining that no just cause exists to delay the appeal and by directing the entry of judgment.

APPLICATIONS

Purpose

Separate, piecemeal appeals during a single litigation are often inefficient and uneconomical, and thus are contrary to the historic federal policy favoring one appeal on all issues at the conclusion of the lawsuit.[7] Rule 54(b) determinations allowing immediate appeal permit exceptions from this general policy for those infrequent instances where awaiting a final judgment would be unduly harsh or unjust.[8]

Cir. 2001) (holding that post-judgment interest does not begin to accrue when district court enters a partial or non-final judgment because the ruling doesn't qualify under Rule 54(a)). *But cf.* Rule 54(b); *infra* Authors' Commentary to Rule 54(b) (a judgment that fully adjudicates one distinct part of a lawsuit may qualify as an immediately-appealable judgment, even though the remainder of the lawsuit continues).

[5]*See* Rule 54(a).

[6]*See* Rule 58(a); *infra* Authors' Commentary to Rule 58(a).

[7]*See Reiter v. Cooper*, 507 U.S. 258, 263, 113 S. Ct. 1213, 1217, 122 L. Ed. 2d 604 (1993); *Curtiss-Wright*

Corp. v. General Elec. Co., 446 U.S. 1, 8, 100 S. Ct. 1460, 1464–65, 64 L. Ed. 2d 1 (1980). *Cf. Williams v. County of Westchester*, 171 F.3d 98, 102 (2d Cir. 1999) (holding that interlocutory orders are, by their nature, subject to modification or adjustment by the trial court prior to the entry of a final judgment adjudicating the claims to which they pertain).

[8]*See Williams v. County of Dakota*, 687 F.3d 1064, 1067–68 (8th Cir. 2012); *O'Bert ex rel. Estate of O'Bert v. Vargo*, 331 F.3d 29, 40–41 (2d Cir. 2003); *Oklahoma Turnpike Authority v. Bruner*, 259 F.3d 1236, 1241–42 (10th Cir. 2001).

Prerequisites to Rule 54(b) Judgments

In evaluating whether to grant a Rule 54(b) determination, the district courts function somewhat like a "dispatcher".[9] They must decide whether three prerequisites for an immediately appealable partial judgment exist:

- **1: Multiple Claims or Parties Fully Resolved:** To be eligible for immediate appeal under Rule 54(b), an adjudication must *either* (a) finally resolve at least one claim or (b) finally resolve the rights and liabilities of at least one party. A claim or a party's interest *must* be adjudicated to finality, such that there is nothing more to do on that claim or for that party but await the conclusion of the remaining portions of the litigation.[10] This limitation is a pivotal one. Rule 54(b) does not alter the normal rules of appellate finality for individual claims, and no appeal may be taken from district court rulings on any particular claim until the court finally resolves that claim.[11] Thus, for example, if an affirmative defense, an insurance coverage contest, or the amount of damages remains unresolved, the claim has not been finally resolved (even if all other issues are completely adjudicated), and an immediate appeal is improper.[12]

  - *"Claim Defined":* A "claim" has been defined to include all legal grounds based on closely related facts.[13] There are no bright-line rules for testing whether multiple claims are adequately "separate"; a simple variation in legal theory alone will not suffice,[14] nor will the mere fact that the al-

[9] *See Curtiss-Wright Corp. v. General Elec. Co.*, 446 U.S. 1, 8, 100 S. Ct. 1460, 1464, 64 L. Ed. 2d 1 (1980); *Lloyd Noland Foundation, Inc. v. Tenet Health Care Corp.*, 483 F.3d 773, 777–78 (11th Cir. 2007); *Berckeley Inv. Group, Ltd. v. Colkitt*, 455 F.3d 195, 202 (3d Cir. 2006).

[10] *See Curtiss-Wright Corp. v. General Elec. Co.*, 446 U.S. 1, 7, 100 S. Ct. 1460, 1464, 64 L. Ed. 2d 1 (1980); *MCI Constructors, LLC v. City of Greensboro*, 610 F.3d 849, 855 (4th Cir. 2010).

[11] *See Lee-Barnes v. Puerto Ven Quarry Corp.*, 513 F.3d 20, 25 (1st Cir. 2008); *Ultra-Precision Mfg. Ltd. v. Ford Motor Co.*, 338 F.3d 1353, 1357 (Fed. Cir. 2003); *Information Resources, Inc. v. Dun and Bradstreet Corp.*, 294 F.3d 447, 451–52 (2d Cir. 2002). *See also N.W. Enterprises Inc. v. City of Houston*, 352 F.3d 162, 179 (5th Cir. 2003) (Rule 54(b) judgment improper where district court only authorized appeal of elements of claims, and not entire claims).

[12] *See Kerr-McGee Chem. Corp. v. Lefton Iron & Metal Co.*, 570 F.3d 856, 857 (7th Cir. 2009); *Waldorf v. Shuta*, 142 F.3d 601, 611 (3d Cir. 1998).

[13] *See EJS Props., LLC v. City of Toledo*, 689 F.3d 535, 538 (6th Cir. 2012); *Jordan v. Pugh*, 425 F.3d 820, 827 (10th Cir. 2005); *Greenwell v. Aztar Indiana Gaming Corp.*, 268 F.3d 486, 490 (7th Cir. 2001).

[14] *See Marseilles Hydro Power, LLC v. Marseilles Land and Water Co.*, 518 F.3d 459, 464 (7th Cir. 2008).

legations were pleaded separately.[15] Multiple claims exist where each claim is factually separate and independent,[16] where each claim could be enforced separately,[17] where there is more than one potential recovery, or where different types of relief are requested.[18] If, however, only one recovery is possible (even though several legal theories are offered to support that same recovery) or if alternative recoveries either substantially overlap or are mutually exclusive, the partial adjudication of such claims cannot be immediately appealed under Rule 54(b).[19] One test of a claim's separability asks whether that claim so overlaps the claims that remain for trial such that an appeal at the end of the case on the retained claims would compel the court to retrace the same ground it would have addressed had the first claim received a Rule 54(b) determination; if so, then the Rule 54(b) determination should be denied.[20] Counterclaims are treated no differently, and are assessed using this same inquiry.[21] But this Rule applies only to multiple claims within a single action; thus, claims that have been severed under Rule 21 and are later dismissed will not

---

[15]*See EJS Props., LLC v. City of Toledo*, 689 F.3d 535, 538 (6th Cir. 2012).

[16]*See Seatrain Shipbuilding Corp. v. Shell Oil Co.*, 444 U.S. 572, 100 S. Ct. 800, 63 L. Ed. 2d 36 (1980); *Advanced Magnetics, Inc. v. Bayfront Partners, Inc.*, 106 F.3d 11, 16 (2d Cir. 1997). *See Lawyers Title Ins. Corp. v. Dearborn Title Corp.*, 118 F.3d 1157 (7th Cir.1997) (noting that test for "separate claims" is whether the claim at issue so overlaps the claims remaining that any appeal at the end of the case on the remaining claims would require the appellate court to cover the same ground addressed on the Rule 54(b) appeal).

[17]*See Advanced Magnetics, Inc. v. Bayfront Partners, Inc.*, 106 F.3d 11, 16 (2d Cir. 1997); *Rieser v. Baltimore and Ohio Railroad Company*, 224 F.2d 198 (2d Cir. 1955). *Cf. General Acquisition, Inc. v. GenCorp, Inc.*, 23 F.3d 1022, 1028 (6th Cir. 1994) (if the action seeks to vindicate only one legal right, but merely alleges several elements of damage, only one claim is presented and Rule 54(b) does not apply).

[18]*See Marseilles Hydro Power, LLC v. Marseilles Land and Water Co.*, 518 F.3d 459, 464 (7th Cir. 2008); *Advanced Magnetics, Inc. v. Bayfront Partners, Inc.*, 106 F.3d 11, 16 (2d Cir. 1997); *In re Southeast Banking Corp.*, 69 F.3d 1539, 1547 (11th Cir. 1995).

[19]*See Lloyd Noland Foundation, Inc. v. Tenet Health Care Corp.*, 483 F.3d 773, 780 (11th Cir. 2007); *Lowery v. Federal Exp. Corp.*, 426 F.3d 817, 820 (6th Cir. 2005); *Lottie v. West American Ins. Co., of Ohio Cas. Group of Ins. Companies*, 408 F.3d 935, 939 (7th Cir. 2005).

[20]*See Outdoor Cent., Inc. v. GreatLodge.com, Inc.*, 643 F.3d 1115, 1119 (8th Cir. 2011); *Lottie v. West American Ins. Co., of Ohio Cas. Group of Ins. Companies*, 408 F.3d 935, 938–39 (7th Cir. 2005).

[21]*See Curtiss-Wright Corp. v. General Elec. Co.*, 446 U.S. 1, 9, 100 S. Ct. 1460, 64 L. Ed 2d 1 (1980); *MCI Constructors, LLC v. City of Greensboro*, 610 F.3d 849, 855 n.5 (4th Cir. 2010).

need Rule 54(b) to allow their appeal.[22]

- *Multiple Parties:* As the text of Rule 54(b) makes clear, absent the determination allowed under this rule, the dismissal of one defendant in a multi-defendant case is not immediately appealable.[23] But Rule 54(b) is not just limited to defendants. If the criteria for Rule 54(b) is satisfied, the dismissal of any party (plaintiff or defendant) may be appealed.[24] A named, but unserved, defendant will typically not be considered a "party" for the purpose of applying this Rule.[25]

- *2: No Just Cause for Delay:* The district court must state, in clear and unmistakable language, that there is no just cause to delay the appeal of the adjudicated claim or the adjudicated rights and liabilities of a party. This determination requires a weighing of both the equities in the case and the judicial administrative interests (especially the interest in avoiding piecemeal appeals).[26] Ordinarily, this weighing will favor an immediate appeal only where delay in appealing presents some risk of hardship or injustice that would be avoided by an immediate review, where a plaintiff could be prejudiced by a delay in recovering a monetary judgment, or where an expensive, duplicative trial could be avoided by reviewing a dismissed claim promptly before the remaining claims reach trial.[27] Conversely, where multiple claims, even if separate, could again be subject to yet another review in a later appeal,[28] or where the claims—though discrete—are so interrelated as to form a single factual unit,[29] an immediate appeal would be improper. Whether "just cause" exists is a determination made on a case-by-case basis.[30] Certain criteria guide the court's consideration:

---

[22]*See Brooks v. District Hosp. Partners, L.P.*, 606 F.3d 800, 805–06 (D.C. Cir. 2010).

[23]*See Morton Intern., Inc. v. A.E. Staley Mfg. Co.*, 460 F.3d 470 (3d Cir. 2006).

[24]*See Brooks v. District Hosp. Partners, L.P.*, 606 F.3d 800, 805 n.2 (D.C.Cir. 2010) (although Rule's motivation was to permit plaintiffs to appeal dismissal of defendant in multiple-defendant cases, it applies to "all multiple party situations").

[25]*See Cambridge Holdings Group, Inc. v. Federal Ins. Co.*, 489 F.3d 1356, 1360–61 (D.C. Cir. 2007); *Raiser v. Utah County*, 409 F.3d 1243, 1245 n.2 (10th Cir. 2005); *Kane Enterprises v.*

MacGregor (USA) Inc., 322 F.3d 371, 374 n.1 (5th Cir. 2003).

[26]*See McAdams v. McCord*, 533 F.3d 924, 928 (8th Cir. 2008).

[27]*See Taco John's of Huron, Inc. v. Bix Produce Co.*, 569 F.3d 401, 402 (8th Cir. 2009); *Advanced Magnetics, Inc. v. Bayfront Partners, Inc.*, 106 F.3d 11, 16 (2d Cir. 1997).

[28]*See Transport Workers Union of America, Local 100, AFL-CIO v. New York City Transit Authority*, 505 F.3d 226, 230 (2d Cir. 2007).

[29]*See Novick v. AXA Network, LLC*, 642 F.3d 304, 311 (2d Cir. 2011).

[30]*See Sears, Roebuck & Co. v. Mackey*, 351 U.S. 427, 76 S. Ct. 895, 100 L. Ed. 1297 (1956); *McAdams v.*

- The relationship between adjudicated and unadjudicated claims;

- The possibility that the need for appellate review might be mooted by future developments in the district court;

- The possibility that the district court might be obligated to consider the same issue on a later occasion;

- The presence (or absence) of a claim or counterclaim that could result in a set-off against the judgment now sought to be made final and appealed; and

- Other factors, including delay, economic and solvency concerns, shortening of trial time, frivolity of competing claims, and expense.[31]

Thus, for example, a Rule 54(b) determination may be proper where, among other factors, the appellate resolution could facilitate a global settlement.[32] Conversely, a Rule 54(b) determination is likely to be improper where the litigation itself, and the contested claim resolution, is routine and would inevitably return to the trial court on essentially the same set of facts.[33]

- **3: *Entry of Judgment:*** In clear and unmistakable language, the district court must also direct that judgment is entered as to that one claim or one party.[34]

Use of "Magic Language"

Immediate appealability hinges on the district court "expressly" determining that there is no just reason for delay and directing entry of the partial final judgment.[35] There is, however, some authority that the court's failure to incant this language may be overlooked, so long as the trial judge's intent

---

McCord, 533 F.3d 924, 928 (8th Cir. 2008). *See also Doe v. City of Chicago*, 360 F.3d 667, 673 (7th Cir. 2004) (ruling that there was "just reason for delay" and, thus, Rule 54(b) relief was not available, where factual development of certain claim was necessary).

[31]*See MCI Constructors, LLC v. City of Greensboro*, 610 F.3d 849, 855 (4th Cir. 2010); *Brooks v. District Hosp. Partners, L.P.*, 606 F.3d 800, 806 (D.C.Cir. 2010).

[32]*See Lowery v. Federal Exp. Corp.*, 426 F.3d 817, 828 (6th Cir. 2005). *But see Taco John's of Huron, Inc. v. Bix Produce Co.*, 569 F.3d 401, 402 (8th Cir. 2009) (potential for resolving liability issue as to all other defendants, with similar defenses, not sufficient to warrant immediate appeal).

[33]*See Wood v. GCC Bend, LLC*, 422 F.3d 873, 878 (9th Cir. 2005). *See also Credit Francais Intern., S.A. v. Bio-Vita, Ltd.*, 78 F.3d 698, 707 (1st Cir. 1996) (early appeal is particularly suspect when the appellants remain litigants before the trial court).

[34]*Blackman v. District of Columbia*, 456 F.3d 167, 175–76 (D.C. Cir. 2006) (must be an express direction for entry of judgment); *Berckeley Inv. Group, Ltd. v. Colkitt*, 455 F.3d 195, 202 (3d Cir. 2006) (must be a final judgment on the merits); *Jordan v. Pugh*, 425 F.3d 820, 826 (10th Cir. 2005) (must be a final decision on at least one claim); *Wood v. GCC Bend, LLC*, 422 F.3d 873, 878 (9th Cir. 2005) (must render a final judgment).

[35]*See* Rule 54(b).

to proceed under Rule 54(b) is otherwise unmistakably clear.[36] But not all courts follow this approach.[37] But magic language or not, the determination must always be made "expressly".[38]

> *Abandoned Claims*: A district court's judgment that resolves some open claims, but leaves others unaddressed, may still be deemed to be final (even without the inclusion of the "magic language"), if the court concluded that the unaddressed claims were abandoned.[39]

Explanation by the District Court

In its order entering a Rule 54(b) judgment, the district court must clearly and cogently explain why it has concluded that an immediate appellate review of the order is advisable,[40] or those reasons must be readily apparent from the record.[41] the district court should not simply reprint, in boilerplate, the formula of the Rule.[42] The court of appeals may, in the absence of such a written explanation, dismiss the appeal as inappropriately allowed under Rule 54(b),[43] or at the very least

---

[36]*See Elliott v. Archdiocese of New York*, 682 F.3d 213, 227–28 (3d Cir. 2012); *Stewart v. Mississippi Transp. Com'n*, 586 F.3d 321, 327 (5th Cir. 2009); *Noel v. Hall*, 568 F.3d 743, 747 n.5 (9th Cir. 2009). *But cf. Berckeley Inv. Group, Ltd. v. Colkitt*, 259 F.3d 135, 141–42 (3d Cir. 2001). *See also Downie v. City of Middleburg Heights*, 301 F.3d 688, 693 (6th Cir. 2002) (district court need not enter partial final judgment in its certification, but it must recognize that such a partial final judgment has been entered).

[37]*See Joint Venture 1 v. Weyand*, 649 F.3d 310, 319–20 (5th Cir. 2011) (failure to make express determination required by Rule 54(b) means that judgment was appealable only if it disposed of all parties and claims); *Blackman v. District of Columbia*, 456 F.3d 167, 175–76 (D.C. Cir. 2006) (trial court must make *express* determination that there is no just reason for delay and *express* direction for the entry of judgment; absent such statements, Rule 54(b) treatment must be reversed on appeal).

[38]*See EJS Props., LLC v. City of Toledo*, 689 F.3d 535, 538 (6th Cir. 2012); *Elliott v. Archdiocese of N.Y.*, 682 F.3d 213, 224–25, 228–29 (3d Cir.2012)

[39]*See DIRECTV, Inc. v. Budden*, 420 F.3d 521 (5th Cir. 2005).

[40]*See Novick v. AXA Network, LLC*, 642 F.3d 304, 310 (2d Cir. 2011) (reasoned, even if brief, explanation required); *Lowery v. Federal Exp. Corp.*, 426 F.3d 817, 821–22 (6th Cir. 2005) (trial court must "spell out its reasons"); *Stockman's Water Co., LLC v. Vaca Partners, L.P.*, 425 F.3d 1263, 1265 (10th Cir. 2005) (trial court must "clearly articulate" its reasons and "make careful statements based on the record"); *Federal Home Loan Mortgage Corp. v. Scottsdale Ins. Co.*, 316 F.3d 431, 440 (3d Cir. 2003) (court should clearly articulate reasons and factors underlying decision to permit Rule 54(b) appeal).

[41]*See Brown v. Eli Lilly & Co.*, 654 F.3d 347, 355 (2d Cir. 2011); *Denson v. U.S.*, 574 F.3d 1318, 1335 n.52 (11th Cir. 2009); *Noel v. Hall*, 568 F.3d 743, 747 n.5 (9th Cir. 2009); *iLor, LLC v. Google, Inc.*, 550 F.3d 1067, 1072 (Fed. Cir. 2008).

[42]*See iLOR, LLC v. Google, Inc.*, 550 F.3d 1067, 1072 (Fed.Cir. 2008); *Akers v. Alvey*, 338 F.3d 491, 495 (6th Cir. 2003); *O'Bert ex rel. Estate of O'Bert v. Vargo*, 331 F.3d 29, 41 (2d Cir. 2003).

[43]*See Novick v. AXA Network, LLC*, 642 F.3d 304, 310 (2d Cir. 2011) (inadequate ruling is insufficient to confer appellate jurisdiction); *Clark v. Baka*, 593 F.3d 712, 714–15 (8th Cir.

subject the determination to special scrutiny.[44] Although dismissal of the appeal is permitted (and perhaps even likely) without a corresponding explanation from the trial court, dismissal is not compulsory; the failure to offer a written explanation is *not* a jurisdictional defect that *compels* the appeal's dismissal.[45]

Duty of Counsel in Explanation Requirement

In moving for a Rule 54(b) determination, the courts expect counsel, as officers of the court and advocates for an immediate appeal, to assist the district court by making appropriate submissions that express the reasons for and basis of a Rule 54(b) determination.[46] In fact, if the trial judge fails to offer a detailed explanation for the Rule 54(b) determination, the reasons offered by counsel can assume special significance.[47]

Burden of Proof

The moving party bears the burden of establishing that a partial judgment should be entered under Rule 54(b).[48]

Discretion of District Judge

The court is not *required* to enter a final judgment in an action involving multiple parties where the court resolves claims involving less than all parties or less than all claims.[49] To the contrary, whether to enter a judgment under Rule 54(b) is reserved for the sound discretion of the district judge.[50] Indeed, such judgments are contrary to the historic federal policy

---

2010) (without reasoning, immediate appeal rejected); *Smith ex rel. Smith v. Half Hollow Hills Cent. School Dist.*, 298 F.3d 168, 171 (2d Cir. 2002) (dismissing appeal, ruling that district courts must not "merely repeat the formulaic language" of Rule 54(b), but must offer "a brief, reasoned explanation" for the decision to allow an immediate appeal).

[44]*See Williams v. County of Dakota*, 687 F.3d 1064, 1068 (8th Cir. 2012).

[45]*See Brown v. Eli Lilly & Co.*, 654 F.3d 347, 355 (2d Cir. 2011) (order lacking supporting statement "is no less final"); *Carter v. City of Philadelphia*, 181 F.3d 339 (3d Cir. 1999) (not jurisdictional). *See also McAdams v. McCord*, 533 F.3d 924, 928 (8th Cir. 2008) (although detailed statement not required, without it appeals court review is more speculative and less circumscribed); *Smith ex rel. Smith v. Half Hollow Hills Cent. School Dist.*, 298 F.3d 168, 171 (2d Cir. 2002) (noting that, under rare certain circum-

stances, the reason for certification may be sufficiently obvious that no explanation is required and the court of appeals is able to provide meaningful review without an explanation from the trial judge of why certification was deemed appropriate).

[46]*See Federal Home Loan Mortgage Corp. v. Scottsdale Ins. Co.*, 316 F.3d 431, 441–42 (3d Cir. 2003).

[47]*See Williams v. County of Dakota*, 687 F.3d 1064, 1067–68 (8th Cir. 2012).

[48]*See Braswell Shipyards, Inc. v. Beazer East, Inc.*, 2 F.3d 1331, 1335 (4th Cir. 1993); *Anthuis v. Colt Industries Operating Corp.*, 971 F.2d 999, 1003 (3d Cir. 1992).

[49]*See generally Ruiz v. Blentech Corp.*, 89 F.3d 320, 323 (7th Cir. 1996) (court has two options in placing into final form individual orders in multiparty cases: Rule 54(b) finality order or final order disposing of all claims respecting all parties).

[50]*See Curtiss-Wright Corp. v.*

against piecemeal appeals, particularly during a period when the courts of appeals' caseload has grown faster than any other segment of the federal bench.[51] For this reason, Rule 54(b) orders are not granted routinely,[52] or merely with the hope of avoiding a trial,[53] or as an accommodation to counsel.[54] Instead, the district court must carefully balance the needs of the parties for an immediate appeal against the interest of efficient management of the litigation.[55] Rule 54(d) determinations are the exceptions, not the rule.[56]

Determination by Trial Judge Is *Not* Conclusive on Court of Appeals

That the district judge allowed a ruling for an immediate appeal under Rule 54(b) is not wholly dispositive. The courts of appeals will still review the matter to ensure that the trial judge allowed a ruling that was eligible for immediate review under the Rule.[57]

General Elec. Co., 446 U.S. 1, 100 S. Ct. 1460, 64 L. Ed. 2d 1 (1980). *See also Clark v. Baka*, 593 F.3d 712, 714–15 (8th Cir. 2010); *Noel v. Hall*, 568 F.3d 743, 747 (9th Cir. 2009). *See generally Sears, Roebuck & Co. v. Mackey*, 351 U.S. 427, 437, 76 S. Ct. 895, 900, 100 L. Ed. 1297 (1956) (noting that discretion lies primarily with the district court "as the one most likely to be familiar with the case and with any justifiable reasons for delay").

[51]*See In re Southeast Banking Corp.*, 69 F.3d 1539, 1548 (11th Cir. 1995). *See also Reiter v. Cooper*, 507 U.S. 258, 263, 113 S. Ct. 1213, 1218, 122 L. Ed. 2d 604 (1993); *Curtiss-Wright Corp. v. General Elec. Co.*, 446 U.S. 1, 8, 100 S. Ct. 1460, 1465, 64 L. Ed. 2d 1 (1980); *Soliday v. Miami County, Ohio*, 55 F.3d 1158, 1163 (6th Cir. 1995) (reiterating that Rule 54(b) does not permit the piecemeal review of claims, nor should it be used indiscriminately).

[52]*See Curtiss-Wright Corp. v. General Elec. Co.*, 446 U.S. 1, 10, 100 S. Ct. 1460, 1466, 64 L. Ed. 2d 1 (1980) (writing that sound judicial administration does not require that Rule 54(b) requests be granted routinely). *See also Williams v. County of Dakota*, 687 F.3d 1064, 1067 (8th Cir. 2012); *Novick v. AXA Network, LLC*, 642 F.3d 304, 310 (2d Cir. 2011).

[53]*See Credit Francais Intern., S.A. v. Bio-Vita, Ltd.*, 78 F.3d 698, 706 (1st Cir. 1996) (possibility of avoiding a trial is "rarely, if ever, a self-sufficient basis for a Rule 54(b) certification").

[54]*See Clark v. Baka*, 593 F.3d 712, 714–15 (8th Cir. 2010); *Braswell Shipyards, Inc. v. Beazer East, Inc.*, 2 F.3d 1331, 1335 (4th Cir. 1993).

[55]*See McAdams v. McCord*, 533 F.3d 924, 928 (8th Cir. 2008). *See also L.B. Foster Co. v. America Piles, Inc.*, 138 F.3d 81, 86 (2d Cir. 1998) (certification should be reserved for "the infrequent harsh case" where danger exists for hardship or injustice through delay, which could be alleviated by immediate appeal); *PYCA Industries, Inc. v. Harrison County Waste Water Management Dist.*, 81 F.3d 1412, 1421 (5th Cir. 1996) (certification should be granted only where some danger of hardship or injustice through delay exists).

[56]*See Elliott v. Archdiocese of New York*, 682 F.3d 213, 220 (3d Cir. 2012).

[57]*See Noel v. Hall*, 568 F.3d 743, 747 (9th Cir. 2009); *Gonzalez Figueroa v. J.C. Penney Puerto Rico, Inc.*, 568 F.3d 313, 318 n.3 (1st Cir. 2009); *Huggins v. FedEx Ground Package Sys., Inc.*, 566 F.3d 771, 774 (8th Cir. 2009); *Marseilles Hydro Power, LLC v. Marseilles Land and Water Co.*, 518 F.3d 459, 464 (7th Cir. 2008).

Procedure for Obtaining Rule 54(b) Determination

The Rule sets no defined procedure for obtaining a determination under Rule 54(b). The district court may grant such a determination *sua sponte* to accompany the order at issue. Alternatively, the parties may separately move the district court under Rule 54(b) to grant a determination. The time for making such a motion is not specified in the Rule. Prudent practitioners will seek a Rule 54(b) determination promptly, and within the 28-day period allotted for alterations or amendments to "judgments". Although Rule 54(b) motions are technically not motions seeking Rule 59 or Rule 60 relief (and, thus, might not fall within the ambit of the 28-day limit), this type of prompt action is consistent with the moving party's claim that the order qualifies as an immediate "judgment" under the Rule and comports with the Rule 54(b) objective of permitting some piecemeal appeals where delay would be unduly harsh or unjust.[58] If an appeal is taken prior to the district court's determination under Rule 54(b), most Circuits have ruled that the belated determination will "ripen" an otherwise improper appeal, so long as the determination issues prior to the date the court of appeals considers the appeal.[59]

Effect of Rule 54(b) Judgments

Once a Rule 54(b) judgment is entered, the time for appeal on that judgment begins to run,[60] as does post-judgment interest.[61] Note, however, that some courts have ruled that the time for appeal following a Rule 54(b) determination can begin to run even earlier, before entry on the docket—on the date the order granting Rule 54(b) relief was signed and mailed to the parties.[62] Accordingly, prudent counsel should file their appeal promptly after the Rule 54(b) order is served.

---

[58]There does not appear to be published case law resolving this issue, a factor that all the more urgently counsels in favor of prompt action by the moving party.

[59]*See, e.g., Barrett ex rel. Estate of Barrett v. U.S.*, 462 F.3d 28, 34–35 (1st Cir. 2006); *U.S. v. Brown*, 348 F.3d 1200, 1206 (10th Cir. 2003); *Lewis v. B.F. Goodrich Co.*, 850 F.2d 641 (10th Cir.1988); *Tidler v. Eli Lilly and Co., Inc.*, 824 F.2d 84, 85–87 (D.C. Cir. 1987)) (per curiam).

[60]*See Federal Deposit Ins. Corp. v. Tripati*, 769 F.2d 507 (8th Cir. 1985). *See also Brown v. Eli Lilly & Co.*, 654 F.3d 347, 354 (2d Cir. 2011) (appeal time began and ended, while counsel relied on errant conclusion that appeal right had not yet ripened).

[61]*See* 28 U.S.C.A. § 1961; *Hooks v. Washington Sheraton Corp.*, 642 F.2d 614 (D.C. Cir. 1980).

[62]*See Silivanch v. Celebrity Cruises, Inc.*, 333 F.3d 355, 364–65 (2d Cir. 2003) (commenting that "[t]here is no requirement that such a certification be docketed in order for it to become effective", and thus the order became effective, and the appeal period began to run, when the order "was signed and mailed to the parties"). *But cf. Brown v. Mississippi Valley State University*, 311 F.3d 328, 331–32 (5th Cir. 2002) (noting that, for purposes of Rule 4 of the Federal Rules of Appellate Procedure 4, judgment becomes final on the date Rule 54(b) determination is entered).

Effect of Improper Rule 54(b) Determinations

If the appeals court finds that the district court's Rule 54(b) determination was given or prepared improperly, appellate jurisdiction is lost.[63] Counsel are wise to take care before making this assessment themselves; if the determination contains an impropriety that the appeals court overlooks, a failure to take a prompt appeal could be disastrous.[64]

Effect of Dismissals Without Rule 54(b) Judgment

Unless the court enters a separate judgment under Rule 54(b), litigants in a multi-party case who are dismissed may technically remain in the case until the final resolution of all claims as to all parties. Dismissed litigants are, however, entitled to rely on the dismissal until notified that they have been rejoined as parties. Thus, until notified otherwise, dismissed litigants need not participate in discovery, in pretrial proceedings, or in the trial itself.[65]

Scope of "Determination"

On appeal following a Rule 54(b) determination, the court of appeals will confine its review only to those specific rulings for which determination was granted. All other rulings by the district court will not be examined during the interlocutory appeal.[66]

No Counsel-Manipulated Rule 54(b) Dismissals

After the district court dismisses one claim or one party, the litigants might not be able to *create* appealability by voluntarily dismissing the remaining claims and parties in order to obtain immediate appellate review.[67]

No "Tag-Along" Partial Appeals

A decision to permit an immediate appeal of one part of a litigation is not, by itself, sufficient justification to grant Rule 54(b) relief for another part.[68]

"Certification" Nomenclature

Often in the case law, the Rule 54(b) determination procedure is described as a "certification", a "misnomer born of

---

[63]*See EJS Props., LLC v. City of Toledo*, 689 F.3d 535, 538 (6th Cir. 2012); *Elliott v. Archdiocese of New York*, 682 F.3d 213, 220 & 224 (3d Cir. 2012).

[64]*See Brown v. Eli Lilly & Co.*, 654 F.3d 347, 355 (2d Cir. 2011).

[65]*See Bennett v. Pippin*, 74 F.3d 578, 587 (5th Cir. 1996).

[66]*See Monsanto Co. v. McFarling*, 363 F.3d 1336, 1343 n.1 (Fed. Cir. 2004); *New Castle County v. Hartford Acc. and Indem. Co.*, 933 F.2d 1162,

1178 (3d Cir. 1991).

[67]*See Robinson-Reeder v. American Council on Educ.*, 571 F.3d 1333, 1339–40 (D.C.Cir. 2009) (rejecting such maneuver as weakening the federal policy against piecemeal appeals and undermining the trial judge's independence).

[68]*See Edwards v. Prime, Inc.*, 602 F.3d 1276, 1288–89 (11th Cir. 2010); *O'Bert ex rel. Estate of O'Bert v. Vargo*, 331 F.3d 29, 43 (2d Cir. 2003).

confusion".[69] The term "certification" is used accurately to describe the procedure for seeking immediate appellate review of interlocutory orders under 28 U.S.C. § 1292(b). Conversely, a Rule 54(b) determination, if granted, effectively severs what becomes a *final* judgment (albeit as to one or more but fewer than all claims or parties) from the remaining claims and parties in the case.[70]

Appealability of Denials of Rule 54(b) Requests

Allowing immediate appellate review of "partial" final judgments is a practice that departs from the federal courts' traditional opposition to piecemeal appeals. Rule 54(b), thus, represents an unusual exception to this settled policy. Predictably, the courts reject attempts to immediately challenge denials of Rule 54(b) determinations as premature and unappealable until a final ruling is entered on the merits.[71]

Sua Sponte Review on Appeal

Even if the appealing litigants do not challenge a Rule 54(b) determination, the court of appeals lacks appellate jurisdiction if the determination was improper; consequently, the appeals court will consider the propriety of a Rule 54(b) determination *sua sponte*.[72]

Adversary Proceedings in Bankruptcy

The majority view holds that litigants who lose and then seek to immediately appeal from an adversary proceeding ruling in bankruptcy are required to obtain a Rule 54(b) determination from the trial court in order to press the appeal.[73]

Rule 54(b) and Tax Court Rulings

Although there is some division of authority on the point, recent case law supports the application of Rule 54(b) procedures to partial rulings by the United States Tax Court.[74]

RULE 54(c)—DEMAND FOR JUDGMENT; RELIEF TO BE GRANTED

CORE CONCEPT

The district court generally must grant all the relief to which

---

[69]*See James v. Price Stern Sloan, Inc.*, 283 F.3d 1064, 1067–68 n. 6 (9th Cir. 2002).

[70]*See James v. Price Stern Sloan, Inc.*, 283 F.3d 1064, 1067–68 n. 6 (9th Cir. 2002) ("Referring to a Rule 54(b) severance order as a 'certification' misleadingly brings to mind the kind of rigorous judgment embodied in the section 1292(b) certification process. In reality, issuance of a Rule 54(b) order is a fairly routine act that is reversed only in the rarest instances").

[71]*See United Industries, Inc. v. Eimco Process Equipment Co.*, 61 F.3d 445, 448 (5th Cir. 1995).

[72]*See Lowery v. Federal Exp. Corp.*, 426 F.3d 817, 820 (6th Cir. 2005).

[73]*See Settembre v. Fidelity & Guar. Life Ins. Co.*, 552 F.3d 438, 441 (6th Cir. 2009); *In re Boca Arena, Inc.*, 184 F.3d 1285 (11th Cir.1999).

[74]*See New York Football Giants, Inc. v. C.I.R.*, 349 F.3d 102, 106–07 (3d Cir. 2003) (so holding, and surveying division among Circuits).

the prevailing party is entitled, whether or not such relief was requested in the pleadings. Pleadings serve as "guides" to the nature of the case, but the lawsuit is ultimately measured by what is pleaded and proven, not merely by what was demanded.[75] In default judgments, however, the district court may not award relief beyond that sought in the complaint.

APPLICATIONS

Default Judgments

Because a defaulting defendant may be relying on the demand (or WHEREFORE) clause contained in the complaint, a plaintiff may not receive a default judgment for more than the amount sought in the complaint.[76] Courts are also unlikely to construe closing, boilerplate language in a pleading to expand the available remedies in a default situation.[77] Among the sparse exceptions to this rule are where the defendant originally appeared in the action and was placed on proper notice of the possible expanded relief[78] and where the complaint fairly identified the nature of the claimed loss and placed the defendant on notice that the value of that loss would continue to accrue during the litigation.[79]

- *"Defaulting" Party:* A party defaults within the meaning of Rule 54(b) by either failing to appear at all or defaulting following an appearance.[80]

Non-default Judgments

Where the defendant has answered or otherwise appeared to defend the lawsuit, a plaintiff may receive a judgment for an amount greater or less than that sought in the complaint,[81] as well as types of relief not mentioned in the complaint's demand clause.[82] It is the court's duty to grant generally all appropriate

---

[75]*See Minyard Enterprises, Inc. v. Southeastern Chemical & Solvent Co.*, 184 F.3d 373 (4th Cir. 1999); *Baker v. John Morrell & Co.*, 266 F. Supp. 2d 909, 929 (N.D. Iowa 2003), aff'd, 382 F.3d 816 (8th Cir. 2004).

[76]*See Hooper-Haas v. Ziegler Holdings, LLC*, 690 F.3d 34, 40 (1st Cir. 2012); *Silge v. Merz*, 510 F.3d 157, 160 (2d Cir. 2007).

[77]*See Silge v. Merz*, 510 F.3d 157, 160 (2d Cir. 2007) (unpleaded claim not encompassed within generic request for "such other and further relief which this Court deems just and proper").

[78]*See Silge v. Merz*, 510 F.3d 157, 161 n.5 (2d Cir. 2007).

[79]*See Finkel v. Triple A Group*,

Inc., 708 F.Supp.2d 277, 282 (E.D.N.Y. 2010).

[80]*See Hooper-Haas v. Ziegler Holdings, LLC*, 690 F.3d 34, 40 n.4 (1st Cir. 2012).

[81]*See Avitia v. Metropolitan Club of Chicago, Inc.*, 49 F.3d 1219, 1229 (7th Cir. 1995) (holding that, except for "special damages" under Rule 9(g), plaintiffs are not obligated to itemize their damages in their complaints); *Stineman v. Fontbonne College*, 664 F.2d 1082 (8th Cir.1981).

[82]*See Holt Civic Club v. City of Tuscaloosa*, 439 U.S. 60, 65–66, 99 S. Ct. 383, 387–388, 58 L. Ed. 2d 292 (1978) (federal courts should not dismiss meritorious constitutional claims because pleadings specify one remedy, rather than another). *See also People*

relief.[83]

Limitations on Awarding Additional Relief

The courts' ability to award unpleaded relief is not unbounded. They are not licensed with untethered roaming authority, permitting them to provide remedies for all wrongs.[84] Rather, this Rule is simply designed to protect against clumsy drafting and to prevent technical missteps from depriving the pleader of a deserved recovery; it is not, however, meant to allow the pleader to recover on *claims* never alleged.[85]

It will not permit a recovery on issues that were not actually litigated, or revive a right to relief lost in the pleadings or through a failure of proof.[86] It will not allow relief against a defendant from whom no relief has been sought,[87] or force upon the litigants a remedy none of them desires.[88] Litigants will be held bound to representations made during a pretrial conference or in a pretrial order that outlined the claims and relief in the case.[89] In short, this Rule will not permit an additional award that would be unfairly prejudicial or unjust.[90] For example, pleaders may not manipulatively "cap" their claims to

---

for Ethical Treatment of Animals, Inc. v. Gittens, 396 F.3d 416, 420–21 (D.C. Cir. 2005); *In re Bennett*, 298 F.3d 1059, 1069–70 (9th Cir. 2002).

[83] *See Felce v. Fiedler*, 974 F.2d 1484, 1501 (7th Cir. 1992) (noting that Rule 54(c) is to be liberally construed so that there is no doubt but that the court must grant whatever relief is appropriate). *See Feldman v. Philadelphia Housing Authority*, 43 F.3d 823, 832 (3d Cir. 1994) (commenting that nature of relief is "determined by the merits of the case, not by the pleadings").

[84] *See Knight v. Alabama*, 476 F.3d 1219, 1229 n.19 (11th Cir. 2007).

[85] *See USX Corp. v. Barnhart*, 395 F.3d 161, 165 (3d Cir. 2004).

[86] *See Old Republic Ins. Co. v. Employers Reinsurance Corp.*, 144 F.3d 1077, 1080 (7th Cir. 1998) (trial court may not award relief upon theory not properly raised at trial); *Gilbane Bldg. Co. v. Federal Reserve Bank*, 80 F.3d 895, 904 (4th Cir. 1996) (alternative relief only permitted where the factfinder has found all factual conclusions necessary to support that relief); *Rodriguez v. Doral Mortg. Corp.*, 57 F.3d 1168, 1173 (1st Cir. 1995) (commenting that the thesis of Rule 54(c) is "hollow at its core", because the Rule creates no entitle-

ment to any relief based on issues not presented to and tried before the factfinder).

[87] *See Powell v. National Bd. of Medical Examiners*, 364 F.3d 79, 86 (2d Cir. 2004); *N.A.A.C.P., Jefferson County Branch v. U.S. Sugar Corp.*, 84 F.3d 1432, 1438 (D.C. Cir. 1996).

[88] *See Minyard Enterprises, Inc. v. Southeastern Chemical & Solvent Co.*, 184 F.3d 373, 386 (4th Cir. 1999).

[89] *See Walker v. Anderson Elec. Connectors*, 944 F.2d 841, 844 (11th Cir. 1991) (limiting plaintiff to the relief demanded at the pretrial conference, and finding no conflict between Rule 54(c) and requirement that plaintiff set forth, at the pretrial conference, all relief sought). *See also Seven Words LLC v. Network Solutions*, 260 F.3d 1089, 1098 (9th Cir. 2001) (where damages claim was made years into litigation, after various representations that only declaratory and injunctive relief was sought, after a motion to dismiss, and only days before oral argument on appeal, court joins other courts of appeals in declining to read damages claim into complaint).

[90] *See Trim Fit, LLC v. Dickey*, 607 F.3d 528, 532 (8th Cir. 2010); *Powell v. National Bd. of Medical Examiners*, 364 F.3d 79, 86 (2d Cir. 2004). *See also United Phosphorus, Ltd. v. Midland*

achieve some tactical advantage, and then receive under this Rule the very same relief they earlier shunned.[91]

- • *Types of Unpleaded Relief Permitted:* Courts have permitted litigants to recover punitive damages,[92] attorney's fees,[93] and prejudgment interest[94] where those remedies were not expressly sought in the complaints, in appropriate cases.

RULE 54(d)—COSTS AND ATTORNEY'S FEES

CORE CONCEPT

The district court should ordinarily award "costs" to the prevailing party in a lawsuit; the clerk may tax such "costs" on 14 days' notice. Taxable "costs" are limited to those items set by statute. An award of attorney's fees must be on motion (filed not later than 14 days from entry of judgment), unless those fees were established, at trial, as an element of compensable damages under the controlling substantive law.

APPLICATIONS

"Prevailing Party" Defined

A prevailing plaintiff is one who succeeds on some significant issue in the litigation and thereby achieves some of the benefit sought in filing the lawsuit.[95] (At least one court has held that, for costs taxation purposes, there can be only one prevailing party.[96]) A plaintiff, thus, "prevails" by obtaining an

---

Fumigant, Inc., 205 F.3d 1219, 1235 (10th Cir. 2000) (although jury award exceeding relief requested does not invalidate jury's award, remittitur may be necessary to avoid a double recovery).

[91]*See Morgan v. Gay,* 471 F.3d 469, 476–77 (3d Cir. 2006), (construing Class Action Fairness Act of 2005(CAFA), Pub.L. No. 109-2, 119 Stat. 4 (2005) (codified in scattered sections of 28 U.S.C.)); *De Aguilar v. Boeing Co.,* 47 F.3d 1404, 1410 (5th Cir. 1995) (construing removal jurisdiction).

[92]*See Bowles v. Osmose Utilities Services, Inc.,* 443 F.3d 671, 675 (8th Cir. 2006). *Curtis v. TransCor America, LLC,* __ F. Supp. 2d __, __, 2012 WL 2524946, at *15–*16 (N.D.Ill. 2012).

[93]*See Sea-Land Service, Inc. v. Murrey & Son's Co. Inc.,* 824 F.2d 740, 745 (9th Cir. 1987); *Black v. O'Haver,* 567 F.2d 361, 370–71 (10th Cir. 1977) *Wachovia Bank, N.A. v. VCG Special*

Opportunities Master Fund, Ltd., __ F. Supp. 2d __, __, 2012 WL 3245420, at *3 (S.D.N.Y. 2012).

[94]*See, e.g., RK Co. v. See,* 622 F.3d 846, 853–54 (7th Cir. 2010); *Rathborne Land Co., L.L.C. v. Ascent Energy, Inc.,* 610 F.3d 249, 262 (5th Cir. 2010); *WOW Logistics Co. v. Pro-Pac, Inc.,* 477 B.R. 92, 98 (E.D.Wis. 2012). *But see Silge v. Merz,* 510 F.3d 157, 160 (2d Cir.2007) (award of prejudgment interest not permitted).

[95]*See Shum v. Intel Corp.,* 629 F.3d 1360, 1367 (Fed.Cir. 2010); *Smart v. Local 702 Int'l Bhd. of Elec. Workers,* 573 F.3d 523, 525 (7th Cir. 2009). *Cf. Texas State Teachers Ass'n v. Garland Indep. Sch. Dist.,* 489 U.S. 782, 791–92, 109 S. Ct. 1486, 1493–94, 103 L. Ed. 2d 866 (1989); *Hensley v. Eckerhart,* 461 U.S. 424, 433, 103 S. Ct. 1933, 1939, 76 L. Ed. 2d 40 (1983).

[96]*See Shum v. Intel Corp.,* 629 F.3d 1360, 1366–67 (Fed.Cir. 2010).

award of monetary damages (even nominal damages)[97] or some other relief that materially alters the parties' legal relationship by modifying the behavior of the defendant in a way that directly benefits the plaintiff.[98]

A prevailing defendant is one who defeats the litigation and obtains a denial of relief. Thus, a dismissal, with prejudice and on the merits, of all claims against a defendant will generally make that defendant a prevailing party.[99]

A litigant need not succeed on all issues to qualify as a prevailing party.[100] For example, a counterclaiming defendant may be deemed a prevailing party by defeating the larger primary claim even if losing on the smaller counterclaim.[101]

Generally, there are no prevailing parties if the case is dismissed for lack of jurisdiction[102] or *forum non conveniens*.[103] Similarly, if the prevailing parties at the trial court lose the case on appeal, their status has changed and their entitlement to costs is lost.[104]

A litigant who is deemed a "prevailing party" for purposes of awarding attorney's fees is likewise a "prevailing party" for purposes of taxing costs.[105]

Against Whom May Costs Be Taxed

Under Rule 54(d), costs may be taxed only against the non-prevailing party; costs may not be taxed under this Rule

---

[97]*See Farrar v. Hobby*, 506 U.S. 103, 111–13, 113 S. Ct. 566, 573, 121 L. Ed. 2d 494 (1992); *Barber v. T.D. Williamson, Inc.*, 254 F.3d 1223, 1234 (10th Cir. 2001).

[98]*See Buckhannon Bd. and Care Home, Inc. v. West Virginia Dept. of Health and Human Resources*, 532 U.S. 598, 605, 121 S. Ct. 1835, 1840, 149 L. Ed. 2d 855 (2001); *Farrar v. Hobby*, 506 U.S. 103, 111–13, 113 S. Ct. 566, 573, 121 L. Ed. 2d 494 (1992); *Dattner v. Conagra Foods, Inc.*, 458 F.3d 98 (2d Cir. 2006).

[99]*See Power Mosfet Technologies, L.L.C. v. Siemens AG*, 378 F.3d 1396 (Fed. Cir. 2004) (prevailing party is one who "wins completely on every claim at issue", and thus party who "had all claims against it dismissed with prejudice" so qualifies); *Weaver v. Toombs*, 948 F.2d 1004 (6th Cir.1991) (a dismissal, whether on the merits or not, makes defendant the prevailing party).

[100]*See Maker's Mark Distillery, Inc. v. Diageo North America, Inc.*, 679 F.3d 410, 425 (6th Cir. 2012); *Shum v.*

Intel Corp., 629 F.3d 1360, 1367–68 (Fed.Cir. 2010). *See also Fireman's Fund Ins. Co. v. Tropical Shipping and Const. Co., Ltd.*, 254 F.3d 987, 1012–13 (11th Cir. 2001) (noting precedent supporting an award of costs where the prevailing party obtains a judgment "on even a fraction of the claims advanced").

[101]*See Haynes Trane Serv. Agency, Inc. v. American Standard, Inc.*, 573 F.3d 947, 967 (10th Cir. 2009).

[102]*See Miles v. State of California*, 320 F.3d 986, 988 (9th Cir. 2003).

[103]*See Dattner v. Conagra Foods, Inc.*, 458 F.3d 98 (2d Cir. 2006).

[104]*See Solis v. County of Los Angeles*, 514 F.3d 946, 958–59 (9th Cir. 2008).

[105]*See Dattner v. Conagra Foods, Inc.*, 458 F.3d 98 (2d Cir. 2006); *Tunison v. Continental Airlines Corp., Inc.*, 162 F.3d 1187, 1189–90 (D.C. Cir. 1998); *Manildra Mill. Corp. v. Ogilvie Mills, Inc.*, 76 F.3d 1178, 1180 n. 1 (Fed. Cir. 1996).

against counsel for a litigant.[106]

Types of Taxable Costs

The types of costs that can be taxed in favor of the prevailing party in a federal litigation are set by statute,[107] and are comparably modest - often only a fraction of the expenses of litigation.[108] Though limited, those costs can nevertheless still be substantial[109] and often may constitute a substantial measure of discovery costs.[110] These statutorily permitted taxable costs are:

1. Clerk and U.S. Marshal fees,[111] which might even include *pro hac vice* admission fees;[112]

2. Deposition expenses, if "necessarily" obtained for use in the case (typically a broadly-defined concept: costs taxed if the transcript was received in evidence or otherwise necessary to be prepared for reasonable trial contingencies,[113] but not taxed for transcripts taken solely for discovery purposes, as a mere convenience to counsel or the court, or of witnesses withdrawn or precluded);[114] if allowed, costs can include videotape depositions[115] and perhaps even the stenographic

---

[106]*See In re Cardizem CD Antitrust Litigation*, 481 F.3d 355, 359–60 (6th Cir. 2007); *Wilder v. GL Bus Lines*, 258 F.3d 126, 127–31 (2d Cir. 2001).

[107]*See* 28 U.S.C.A. § 1920. *See also* 28 U.S.C.A. §§ 1911 to 31 (defining costs provisions generally). In addition, the Rules allow costs to be taxed in other instances: when an attorney violates Rule 11, conducts discovery improperly in violation of Rule 37, or rejects unwisely an offer of settlement under Rule 68.

[108]*See Taniguchi v. Kan Pacific Saipan, Ltd.*, __ U.S. __, __,132 S.Ct. 1997, 2006, 182 L.Ed.2d 903 (2012).

[109]*See In re Williams Secs. Litig.-WCG Subclass*, 558 F.3d 1144, 1147 (10th Cir. 2009) (affirming award of more than $600,000 in costs against non-prevailing plaintiff); *Tibble v. Edison Int'l*, 2011 WL 3759927, at *6–*8 (C.D.Cal. Aug. 22, 2011) (approving costs of $530,000, though ultimately applied only as an offset).

[110]*See Rundus v. City of Dallas*, 634 F.3d 309, 315–16 (5th Cir. 2011) (affirming taxation of substantial discovery costs against losing party); *Baisden v. I'm Ready Prods., Inc.*, 793 F.Supp. 2d 970, 987 (S.D.Tex. 2011)

(ordering reimbursement for costs of depositions of party's own witnesses and experts).

[111]*See Winniczek v. Nagelberg*, 400 F.3d 503, 504–05 (7th Cir. 2005) (allowing docketing fee to be taxed).

[112]*See Craftsmen Limousine, Inc. v. Ford Motor Co.*, 579 F.3d 894, 898 (8th Cir. 2009).

[113]*See In re Williams Secs. Litig.-WCG Subclass*, 558 F.3d 1144, 1147–48 (10th Cir. 2009); *Smith v. Tenet Health-system SL, Inc.*, 436 F.3d 879, 889–90 (8th Cir. 2006); *Summit Technology, Inc. v. Nidek Co., Ltd.*, 435 F.3d 1371, 1378–80 (Fed. Cir. 2006). *See also Virginia Panel Corp. v. Mac Panel Co.*, 887 F. Supp. 880, 886 (W.D. Va. 1995), aff'd, 133 F.3d 860 (Fed. Cir. 1997) (cost of daily copies of trial transcripts is recoverable if daily copy is "indispensable", and not a convenience for counsel).

[114]*See In re Williams Secs. Litig.-WCG Subclass*, 558 F.3d 1144, 1147–48 (10th Cir. 2009); *Marmo v. Tyson Fresh Meats, Inc.*, 457 F.3d 748 (8th Cir.2006).

[115]*See Craftsmen Limousine, Inc. v. Ford Motor Co.*, 579 F.3d 894, 897–98 (8th Cir. 2009); *Little v. Mitsubishi*

transcription of those videotapes.[116]

3a. Printing fees;

3b. Witness fees and witnesses' travel and subsistence expenses, where the witnesses' testimony was material, relevant, and reasonably necessary to the case;[117]

4a. Fees to "exemplify" documents (which may include reimbursement for many methods of illustration, including models, charts, graphs, and sometimes even computerized presentation systems[118]);

4b. Fees to print copies of papers necessary for use in the case[119] (which likely will not include electronic data preparation costs (e.g., gathering, preserving, processing, searching, and culling ESI),[120] might not include copying documents for discovery,[121] but likely will include conversion from native files to readable format,[122] and scanning and imaging of documents;[123] to recover costs, a copy-by-copy tracking might not be required, but a bill of costs showing a reasonably accurate calculation will be[124]);

Motors North America, Inc., 514 F.3d 699, 701 (7th Cir. 2008). But cf. Cherry v. Champion Intern. Corp., 186 F.3d 442 (4th Cir. 1999) (although costs of video depositions may be taxed, prevailing party must make a showing why *both* the transcript and the video deposition were "necessary").

[116]See Little v. Mitsubishi Motors North America, Inc., 514 F.3d 699, 701–02 (7th Cir. 2008); Tilton v. Capital Cities/ABC, Inc., 115 F.3d 1471, 1478 (10th Cir. 1997).

[117]See Marmo v. Tyson Fresh Meats, Inc., 457 F.3d 748 (8th Cir. 2006); Baisden v. I'm Ready Prods., Inc., 793 F.Supp.2d 970, 976–85 (S.D.Tex. 2011).

[118]See Cefalu v. Village of Elk Grove, 211 F.3d 416, 427–28 (7th Cir. 2000) (affirming reimbursement for cost of computerized, multi-media system used to present exhibits to jury). But cf. Race Tires America, Inc. v. Hoosier Racing Tire Corp., 674 F.3d 158, 166 (3d Cir. 2012) (noting, but not resolving, whether exemplification is legal authentication only or more broadly illustrating by example); Kohus v. Toys R Us, Inc., 282 F.3d 1355, 1357–61 (Fed. Cir. 2002) (reversing award of $12,950 for video model/animation as unauthorized under fed-

eral law); Arcadian Fertilizer, L.P. v. MPW Indus. Services, Inc., 249 F.3d 1293, 1297 (11th Cir. 2001) (refusing reimbursement for videotape exhibits and computer animation).

[119]See Little v. Mitsubishi Motors North America, Inc., 514 F.3d 699, 701 (7th Cir. 2008); BDT Products, Inc. v. Lexmark Intern., Inc., 405 F.3d 415, 419–20 (6th Cir. 2005); Concord Boat Corp. v. Brunswick Corp., 309 F.3d 494, 497–98 (8th Cir. 2002).

[120]See Race Tires America, Inc. v. Hoosier Racing Tire Corp., 674 F.3d 158, 168–72 (3d Cir. 2012).

[121]See Little Rock Cardiology Clinic PA v. Baptist Health, 591 F.3d 591, 601–02 (8th Cir. 2009) (noting various views, and finding no abuse of discretion in denial of such costs).

[122]See Race Tires America, Inc. v. Hoosier Racing Tire Corp., 674 F.3d 158, 166–68 (3d Cir. 2012).

[123]See BDT Products, Inc. v. Lexmark Intern., Inc., 405 F.3d 415, 420 (6th Cir. 2005).

[124]See In re Williams Secs. Litig.-WCG Subclass, 558 F.3d 1144, 1148 (10th Cir. 2009); Summit Technology, Inc. v. Nidek Co., Ltd., 435 F.3d 1371, 1378–80 (Fed. Cir. 2006).

5. Certain docket fees;[125] and

6. Fees for court-appointed experts (which often include guardians and special masters)[126] and interpreters (though limited to oral interpreters, not translators of written work).[127]

Types of Costs That Will Not Be Taxed

The district court may not tax costs under Rule 54(d) that are not authorized by statute or court rule.[128] Thus, in the absence of an express legal authority otherwise, courts generally may *not* tax as costs the fees and expenses of expert witnesses (beyond the modest travel and subsistence expenses noted above for witnesses generally);[129] computer-assisted legal research;[130] trial consultants who prepared computer animations, videos, powerpoint slides, and graphic illustrations;[131] postage, overnight courier, and similar messenger or delivery services;[132] telephone calls;[133] facsimile transmissions;[134] parale-

---

[125]*See BDT Products, Inc. v. Lexmark Intern., Inc.*, 405 F.3d 415, 419–20 (6th Cir. 2005).

[126]*See Gaddis v. United States*, 381 F.3d 444 (5th Cir. 2004); *Kollsman, a Div. of Segua Corp. v. Cohen*, 996 F.2d 702 (4th Cir. 1993). *But cf. Hull by Hull v. United States*, 971 F.2d 1499 (10th Cir. 1992) (may be taxed only depending upon role of guardian).

[127]*See Taniguchi v. Kan Pacific Saipan, Ltd.*, __ U.S. __, __,132 S.Ct. 1997, 1999-2007, 182 L.Ed.2d 903 (2012).

[128]*See Arlington Cent. School Dist. Bd. of Educ. v. Murphy*, 548 U.S. 291, 301, 126 S. Ct. 2455, 2461–62, 165 L. Ed. 2d 526 (2006); *Little Rock Cardiology Clinic PA v. Baptist Health*, 591 F.3d 591, 601 (8th Cir. 2009); *Little v. Mitsubishi Motors North America, Inc.*, 514 F.3d 699, 701 (7th Cir. 2008).

[129]*See Arlington Cent. School Dist. Bd. of Educ. v. Murphy*, 548 U.S. 291, 301, 126 S. Ct. 2455, 165 L. Ed. 2d 526 (2006); *West Virginia University Hospitals, Inc. v. Casey*, 499 U.S. 83, 102, 111 S. Ct. 1138, 113 L. Ed. 2d 68 (1991); *Crawford Fitting Co. v. J. T. Gibbons, Inc.*, 482 U.S. 437, 439, 107 S. Ct. 2494, 96 L. Ed. 2d 385 (1987).

[130]*See Jones v. Unisys Corp.*, 54 F.3d 624, 633 (10th Cir. 1995); *Garshman Co., Ltd. v. General Elec. Co., Inc.*,

993 F. Supp. 25, 29 (D. Mass. 1998), aff'd, 176 F.3d 1 (1st Cir. 1999). *But see Little v. Mitsubishi Motors North America, Inc.*, 514 F.3d 699, 701 (7th Cir. 2008) (ruling such costs authorized by § 1920).

[131]*See Summit Technology, Inc. v. Nidek Co., Ltd.*, 435 F.3d 1371, 1374–75 (Fed. Cir. 2006). *But see Marmo v. Tyson Fresh Meats, Inc.*, 457 F.3d 748 (8th Cir.2006) (taxing as "copying and exemplification" costs the expenses for graphic and visual aids, and other materials prepared for electronic display).

[132]*See Smith v. Tenet Healthsystem SL, Inc.*, 436 F.3d 879, 889–90 (8th Cir. 2006); *O'Bryhim v. Reliance Standard Life Ins. Co.*, 997 F. Supp. 728, 737–38 (E.D. Va. 1998), aff'd, 188 F.3d 502 (4th Cir. 1999).

[133]*See O'Bryhim v. Reliance Standard Life Ins. Co.*, 997 F. Supp. 728, 737–38 (E.D. Va. 1998), aff'd, 188 F.3d 502 (4th Cir. 1999); *Ortega v. IBP, Inc.*, 883 F. Supp. 558, 562–63 (D. Kan. 1995).

[134]*See O'Bryhim v. Reliance Standard Life Ins. Co.*, 997 F. Supp. 728, 737–38 (E.D. Va. 1998), *aff'd*, 188 F.3d 502 (4th Cir. 1999); *Garshman Co., Ltd. v. General Elec. Co., Inc.*, 993 F. Supp. 25, 29 (D. Mass. 1998), *aff'd*, 176 F.3d 1 (1st Cir. 1999).

gals;[135] travel, lodging, transportation, and parking;[136] mediation;[137] or post-trial / pre-appeal costs (like supersedeas bond premiums).[138] Courts are divided on whether the costs of private process servers are taxable.[139]

Attorney's Fees as Costs

In the absence of a federal statute to the contrary, attorney's fees may not be taxed as costs beyond the modest provisions set forth in 28 U.S.C.A. § 1923.[140]

> *Exceptions:* Attorney's fees, however, may be taxed against a common fund generated in a class action or shareholders' derivative action,[141] and where a party instituted, defended, or conducted litigation in bad faith.[142]

Burden of Proof

The burden of proving the amount of compensable costs and expenses lies with the party seeking those costs.[143] Once the prevailing party demonstrates the amount of its costs and that they fall within an allowable category of taxable costs, the prevailing party enjoys the "strong presumption" that its costs will be awarded "in full measure".[144] The party opposing the award of costs bears the burden of demonstrating that the award would be improper.[145]

Diversity Jurisdiction Cases

Federal law governs the taxation of costs in the district courts, even where the district court's jurisdiction is premised on diversity of citizenship.[146]

---

[135]*See Thomas v. Treasury Management Ass'n, Inc.*, 158 F.R.D. 364, 372 (D. Md. 1994).

[136]*See O'Bryhim v. Reliance Standard Life Ins. Co.*, 997 F. Supp. 728, 737–38 (E.D. Va. 1998), *aff'd*, 188 F.3d 502 (4th Cir. 1999); *Garshman Co., Ltd. v. General Elec. Co., Inc.*, 993 F. Supp. 25, 29 (D. Mass. 1998), *aff'd*, 176 F.3d 1 (1st Cir. 1999).

[137]*See Brisco-Wade v. Carnahan*, 297 F.3d 781, 782 (8th Cir. 2002).

[138]*See Republic Tobacco Co. v. North Atlantic Trading Co., Inc.*, 481 F.3d 442, 447–48 (7th Cir. 2007).

[139]*See Francisco v. Verizon South, Inc.*, 272 F.R.D. 436, 441–42 (E.D.Va. 2011) (discussing divided case law).

[140]*See Alyeska Pipeline Service Co. v. Wilderness Society*, 421 U.S. 240, 95 S. Ct. 1612, 44 L. Ed. 2d 141 (1975).

[141]*See Mills v. Electric Auto-Lite Co.*, 396 U.S. 375, 90 S. Ct. 616, 24 L. Ed. 2d 593 (1970).

[142]*See Chambers v. NASCO, Inc.*, 501 U.S. 32, 111 S. Ct. 2123, 115 L. Ed. 2d 27 (1991).

[143]*See In re Williams Secs. Litig.-WCG Subclass*, 558 F.3d 1144, 1148 (10th Cir. 2009).

[144]*See Shum v. Intel Corp.*, 629 F.3d 1360, 1370 (Fed.Cir. 2010); *Goldberg v. Pacific Indem. Co.*, 627 F.3d 752, 755 n.4 (9th Cir. 2010).

[145]*See In re Ricoh Co., Ltd. Patent Litig.*, 661 F.3d 1361, 1364 (Fed.Cir. 2011); *Quan v. Computer Sciences Corp.*, 623 F.3d 870, 888 (9th Cir. 2010); *In re Williams Secs. Litig.-WCG Subclass*, 558 F.3d 1144, 1148 (10th Cir. 2009).

[146]*See Humann v. KEM Elec. Co-op., Inc.*, 497 F.3d 810, 813 (8th Cir. 2007); *Gobbo Farms & Orchards v. Poole Chemical Co., Inc.*, 81 F.3d 122, 123 (10th Cir. 1996).

Discretion of District Court

Rule 54(d) provides that costs "should" be taxed.[147] The courts have interpreted this mandate to create a presumption in favor of the award of costs in favor of the prevailing party,[148] but reserving for the district judge the discretion to deny costs in appropriate circumstances.[149] A "sound basis" is needed to overcome this presumption,[150] since denying costs is essentially a "penalty" that deprives a litigant of an entitlement.[151] If the court chooses not to award costs to a prevailing party, the court must explain its good reasons for not doing so[152] (although a formal written opinion is not required either when costs are awarded[153] or denied).[154] An implied or implicit justification will ordinarily be insufficient to sustain the denial on appeal,[155] at least unless the reasons for denying costs are clear.[156]

Mandatory Reasons for Denying Costs

The district court must deny costs if a federal statute, another Rule, or a court order so commands.[157]

---

[147]See Stafford Invs., LLC v. Vito, 2009 WL 1362513, at *11 (E.D.Pa. May 14, 2009), aff'd, 375 Fed. Appx. 221 (3d Cir. 2010) (noting 2007 Restyling Amendments revision of syntax "as of course" to "should" retained pre-amendment meaning). See also Miles v. State of California, 320 F.3d 986, 988 (9th Cir. 2003); Concord Boat Corp. v. Brunswick Corp., 309 F.3d 494, 497–98 (8th Cir. 2002). See also In re Paoli R.R. Yard PCB Litigation, 221 F.3d 449 (3d Cir. 2000) (tracing history of award of costs from English inception).

[148]See Delta Air Lines, Inc. v. August, 450 U.S. 346, 352, 101 S. Ct. 1146, 1150, 67 L. Ed. 2d 287 (1981); Manderson v. Chet Morrison Contractors, Inc., 666 F.3d 373, 384 (5th Cir. 2012); Shum v. Intel Corp., 629 F.3d 1360, 1370 (Fed.Cir. 2010).

[149]See Crawford Fitting Co. v. J. T. Gibbons, Inc., 482 U.S. 437, 107 S. Ct. 2494, 96 L. Ed. 2d 385 (1987); Farmer v. Arabian Am. Oil Co., 379 U.S. 227, 85 S. Ct. 411, 13 L. Ed. 2d 248 (1964).

[150]See Mathews v. Crosby, 480 F.3d 1265, 1277 (11th Cir. 2007). See also Goldberg v. Pacific Indem. Co., 627 F.3d 752, 755 n.4 (9th Cir. 2010) ("limited discretion" to refuse to tax costs); Utah Animal Rights Coalition v. Salt Lake County, 566 F.3d 1236, 1245

(10th Cir. 2009) ("valid reason").

[151]See Reger v. Nemours Found., Inc., 599 F.3d 285, 288–89 (3d Cir. 2010); Rodriguez v. Whiting Farms, Inc., 360 F.3d 1180, 1190–91 (10th Cir. 2004).

[152]See Manderson v. Chet Morrison Contractors, Inc., 666 F.3d 373, 384 (5th Cir. 2012); Quan v. Computer Sciences Corp., 623 F.3d 870, 888 (9th Cir. 2010); Estate of Hevia v. Portrio Corp., 602 F.3d 34, 47 n.7 (1st Cir. 2010).

[153]See Craftsmen Limousine, Inc. v. Ford Motor Co., 579 F.3d 894, 896–97 (8th Cir. 2009).

[154]See Reger v. Nemours Found., Inc., 599 F.3d 285, 289 (3d Cir. 2010).

[155]See Holton v. City of Thomasville School Dist., 425 F.3d 1325, 1355–56 (11th Cir. 2005). See also Allison v. Bank One-Denver, 289 F.3d 1223, 1248–49 (10th Cir. 2002) (trial court abuses its discretion when it rests its ruling on an erroneous legal conclusion or where no rational basis supports the ruling).

[156]See Estate of Hevia v. Portrio Corp., 602 F.3d 34, 47 n.7 (1st Cir. 2010).

[157]See Rouse v. Law Offices of Rory Clark, 603 F.3d 699, 702 (9th Cir. 2010).

Discretionary Reasons for Denying Costs

The proper exercise of a trial court's discretion to deny costs may hinge on whether the costs are of a type authorized by law and whether the costs pay for materials necessarily obtained for use in the case.[158] Costs may be denied, for example, where both parties partially prevail in the litigation,[159] where a prevailing plaintiff fails to prove that federal jurisdiction was proper (either because plaintiff fails to recover the $75,000 jurisdictional minimum in a diversity case or because plaintiff fails to win on the federal question counts),[160] where the prevailing party needlessly prolongs the litigation or otherwise acts in bad faith,[161] or, perhaps, where the losing party is unable to pay or would be rendered indigent by paying,[162] or is incarcerated,[163] or where the prevailing party's recovery was nominal or

---

[158]See Allison v. Bank One-Denver, 289 F.3d 1223, 1248 (10th Cir. 2002).

[159]See Farrar v. Hobby, 506 U.S. 103, 115–16, 113 S. Ct. 566, 575, 121 L. Ed. 2d 494 (1992) (commenting that, having considered the amount and nature of the plaintiff's success on the merits, district courts may award modest fees or no fees at all); Estate of Hevia v. Portrio Corp., 602 F.3d 34, 46–47 (1st Cir. 2010) (courts commonly order such parties to bear their own costs); Kemin Foods, L.C. v. Pigmentos Vegetales Del Centro S.A. de C.V., 464 F.3d 1339, 1348 (Fed. Cir. 2006) (courts may apportion costs according to parties' relative success); Barber v. T.D. Williamson, Inc., 254 F.3d 1223, 1234–35 (10th Cir. 2001) (same); Perlman v. Zell, 185 F.3d 850 (7th Cir.1999) (plaintiff's modest recovery (in relation to original demand) implies that defendants won more of the dispute than they lost, and therefore award of costs could be refused); Cherry v. Champion Intern. Corp., 186 F.3d 442 (4th Cir. 1999) (same); AeroTech, Inc. v. Estes, 110 F.3d 1523, 1526 (10th Cir. 1997) (same); Amarel v. Connell, 102 F.3d 1494, 1523 (9th Cir. 1996) (district court may require each party to bear their own costs in the event of a mixed judgment); Testa v. Village of Mundelein, Ill., 89 F.3d 443, 447 (7th Cir. 1996) (same).

[160]See Miles v. State of California, 320 F.3d 986, 988 (9th Cir. 2003); Perlman v. Zell, 185 F.3d 850 (7th Cir. 1999).

[161]See Quan v. Computer Sciences Corp., 623 F.3d 870, 888 (9th Cir. 2010); Mother and Father v. Cassidy, 338 F.3d 704, 708 (7th Cir. 2003); In re Paoli R.R. Yard PCB Litigation, 221 F.3d 449, 468 (3d Cir. 2000).

[162]See Rivera v. City of Chicago, 469 F.3d 631, 634–35 (7th Cir. 2006) (indigency may be considered); Champion Produce, Inc. v. Ruby Robinson Co., Inc., 342 F.3d 1016, 1022 (9th Cir. 2003) (losing party's "limited financial resources" may be considered); Lampkins v. Thompson, 337 F.3d 1009, 1017 (8th Cir. 2003) (party's indigency properly considered); Chapman v. AI Transport, 229 F.3d 1012, 1039 (11th Cir. 2000) (noting that non-prevailing party's financial status is factor to be considered, but court must first require substantial documentation of true inability to pay costs); In re Paoli R.R. Yard PCB Litigation, 221 F.3d 449 (3d Cir. 2000) (commenting that "most important" factor is defeated party's indigency or inability to pay which may, but need not automatically, excuse taxation of costs). But see Rodriguez v. Whiting Farms, Inc., 360 F.3d 1180, 1190–91 (10th Cir. 2004) (finding no error in district court's rejection of party's indigency as possible justification to deny costs).

[163]See Lampkins v. Thompson, 337 F.3d 1009, 1017 (8th Cir. 2003).

"substantially less" than what was sought,[164] where a voluntarily dismissal is entered but only after first obtaining some modicum of relief,[165] or where there would be some other "injustice" in approving an award of costs.[166] Generally, a district court may not deny costs simply upon a finding that the case was brought and litigated in "good faith" and without a vexatious motive,[167] because a significant disparity exists between the parties' financial resources,[168] because a heavy taxation would deter the poor from seeking redress,[169] because the case was "complex" or a "close call",[170] because the prevailing party had rejected the defendant's Rule 68 offer of judgment,[171] or because the case involved significant matters in the public

---

[164]See Champion Produce, Inc. v. Ruby Robinson Co., Inc., 342 F.3d 1016, 1022–23 (9th Cir. 2003).

[165]See Knology, Inc. v. Insight Communications Co., L.P., 460 F.3d 722 (6th Cir. 2006).

[166]See Cherry v. Champion Intern. Corp., 186 F.3d 442 (4th Cir. 1999). See also Barber v. T.D. Williamson, Inc., 254 F.3d 1223, 1234–35 (10th Cir. 2001) (noting that courts have refused to award costs where neither side entirely prevailed, both sides prevailed, or litigation resulted from fault on both parties).

[167]See Pacheco v. Mineta, 448 F.3d 783, 794–95 (5th Cir. 2006) (surveying views from various circuits); In re Paoli R.R. Yard PCB Litigation, 221 F.3d 449, 454 (3d Cir. 2000); Cherry v. Champion Intern. Corp., 186 F.3d 442 (4th Cir. 1999). But see Champion Produce, Inc. v. Ruby Robinson Co., Inc., 342 F.3d 1016, 1022 (9th Cir. 2003) (whether losing party litigated in good faith could be considered).

[168]See Reger v. Nemours Found., Inc., 599 F.3d 285, 289 (3d Cir. 2010) (rejecting financial disparity as reason, holding this possibility should cause "pause" and calculation of risks of pressing marginal or meritless claims); In re Paoli R.R. Yard PCB Litigation, 221 F.3d 449 (3d Cir. 2000) (rejecting relative wealth of parties as relevant factor); Cherry v. Champion Intern. Corp., 186 F.3d 442 (4th Cir. 1999) (rejecting "comparative economic power" argument, noting that it would frequently favor defendant, thus ignoring plain language of Rule and undermining foundation of legal

system that justice is administered to all equally, regardless of wealth or status). But see Quan v. Computer Sciences Corp., 623 F.3d 870, 888–89 (9th Cir. 2010) (losing party's limited financial resources a proper consideration).

[169]See Smith v. Tenet Healthsystem SL, Inc., 436 F.3d 879, 889–90 (8th Cir. 2006).

[170]See In re Paoli R.R. Yard PCB Litigation, 221 F.3d 449 (3d Cir. 2000) (complexity or closeness of issues not appropriate factors for consideration); Klein v. Grynberg, 44 F.3d 1497, 1506 (10th Cir. 1995) (rejecting premise that costs may be denied because litigation was complex or lengthy). See also Rodriguez v. Whiting Farms, Inc., 360 F.3d 1180, 1190–91 (10th Cir. 2004) (finding no error in district court's rejection of claim that case involved "close and difficult call" as possible justification to deny costs). Note, however, that the case law in this area is not developing uniformly. See Quan v. Computer Sciences Corp., 623 F.3d 870, 888–89 (9th Cir. 2010) (whether issues were "close and difficult" a proper consideration); Cherry v. Champion Intern. Corp., 186 F.3d 442 (4th Cir. 1999) (closeness and difficulty of the issues may be considered); Luckey v. Baxter Healthcare Corp., 183 F.3d 730 (7th Cir. 1999) (district judge might require each side to bear its own costs when the case is close, or when the side with the better position loses on a technicality).

[171]See Champion Produce, Inc. v. Ruby Robinson Co., Inc., 342 F.3d 1016, 1022–24 (9th Cir. 2003).

interest.[172] In many cases, the district court will also be precluded from denying costs merely because the prevailing party failed to demand them in a pleading.[173]

Note, however, that the Circuits are not always uniform in their approaches to these various factors.[174]

Taxing Costs For or Against the United States

The United States may be awarded costs in the same manner as any prevailing party.[175] Costs may be taxed against the United States in accordance with the list set forth in 28 U.S.C.A. § 1920,[176] except that in non-tort actions, the district court may refuse to tax costs upon a finding that the United States' position was substantially justified or where special circumstances make an award of costs unjust.[177]

Taxing Costs Against States

Some courts have construed the Eleventh Amendment to the United States Constitution as prohibiting a district court's right to tax costs against a State.[178]

Costs in Pauper Actions

The district court may, in its discretion, permit a civil litigant, criminal defendant, or appellant to proceed without the prepayment of costs upon receiving an affidavit showing an in-

---

[172]See Mitchell v. City of Moore, Oklahoma, 218 F.3d 1190 (10th Cir.2000) (presumption in favor of awarding costs applies even where prevailing party is defendant in civil rights case); Cherry v. Champion Intern. Corp., 186 F.3d 442 (4th Cir. 1999) (holding that presumptive award of costs cannot be defeated on the basis of the nature of the underlying litigation). But see Quan v. Computer Sciences Corp., 623 F.3d 870, 888–89 (9th Cir. 2010) (whether case presented landmark issue of national importance a proper consideration); Stanley v. University of Southern California, 178 F.3d 1069, 1079 (9th Cir. 1999) (directing courts, in civil rights cases, to consider plaintiff's financial resources and amount of cost so as to avoid unnecessarily chilling civil rights litigation; "Without civil rights litigants who are willing to test the boundaries of our laws, we would not have made much of the progress that has occurred in this nation since Brown v. Board of Educ.").

[173]See Flynn v. AK Peters, Ltd., 377 F.3d 13, 26 (1st Cir. 2004) (right to attorney's fees not waived where prayer for fees not listed as "special damages" in complaint); Port of Stock-ton v. Western Bulk Carrier KS, 371 F.3d 1119, 1121–22 (9th Cir. 2004) (same effect).

[174]See Knology, Inc. v. Insight Communications Co., L.P., 460 F.3d 722 (6th Cir. 2006) (factors that may justify denying costs include losing party's good faith, difficulty of case, winning party's behavior, and necessity of costs); Rivera v. NIBCO, 701 F.Supp.2d 1135, 1135–45 (E.D.Cal. 2010) (denying costs in language-based discrimination claim contesting English-only tests because, although unsuccessful, dispute involved: (1) issues of substantial public importance, (2) great economic disparity between plaintiffs and defendants, (3) close and difficult issues, (4) some merit, and (5) risk that award of costs would seriously chill future civil rights litigants).

[175]See U.S. E.E.O.C. v. W&O, Inc., 213 F.3d 600, 620 (11th Cir. 2000); U.S. v. Lynd, 349 F.2d 785 (5th Cir. 1965).

[176]See 28 U.S.C.A. § 1920.

[177]See 28 U.S.C.A. § 2412.

[178]See Alyeska Pipeline Service Co. v. Wilderness Society, 421 U.S. 240, 269 n. 44, 95 S. Ct. 1612, 1627 n. 44, 44 L. Ed. 2d 141 (1975).

ability to pay costs.[179]

Procedure & Timing: Non-Attorney's Fee Costs

To obtain an award of costs, the prevailing party must file a "Bill of Costs" with the clerk (the district court may have a preprinted form for this purpose). The Bill of Costs must be verified by affidavit. The clerk may tax costs on 14-days notice. Within 7 days thereafter, a disappointed party may seek court review of the clerk's assessment. Some courts have ruled that a failure to seek review within this period waives the losing party's right to challenge the award.[180] Other courts have noted that the time period is not jurisdictional and untimely objections may, in the trial court's discretion, be considered.[181] The district court is authorized to conduct a *de novo* review of the clerk's assessments.[182] Costs may be taxed against multiple losing parties either in allocated amounts or jointly and severally.[183] The time for filing a Bill of Costs is typically regulated by local court rule, but usually is set after the court has rendered its decision in the case.[184]

- *2009 Amendments Note:* Effective December 2009, the Rule 54(d)(1) time periods were extended from 1 day and 5 days, respectively, to 14 days and 7 days, respectively, to conform to the new multiples-of-7-days standard for federal civil time periods.

Procedure & Timing: Attorney's Fees

Where an award of attorney's fees is appropriate, Rule 54(d)(2) fixes the procedure for obtaining an award of such fees and related non-taxable expenses.[185] This procedure does *not* apply to attorney's fees recoverable as an element of damages (*e.g.*, under terms of a contract) or to fees and expenses awarded as sanctions.[186] Courts are cautioned against permitting fees

---

[179]*See* 28 U.S.C.A. § 1915.

[180]*See Ahlberg v. Chrysler Corp.*, 481 F.3d 630, 638–39 (8th Cir. 2007); *Bloomer v. United Parcel Service, Inc.*, 337 F.3d 1220, 1221 (10th Cir. 2003); *Cooper v. Eagle River Memorial Hosp., Inc.*, 270 F.3d 456, 464 (7th Cir. 2001); *Walker v. California*, 200 F.3d 624, 626 (9th Cir. 1999); *Prince v. Poulos*, 876 F.2d 30, 34 (5th Cir. 1989).

[181]*See Corwin v. Walt Disney Co.*, 475 F.3d 1239, 1254 (11th Cir. 2007); *In re Paoli R.R. Yard PCB Litigation*, 221 F.3d 449 (3d Cir. 2000).

[182]*See In re Paoli R.R. Yard PCB Litigation*, 221 F.3d 449 (3d Cir. 2000).

[183]*In re Paoli R.R. Yard PCB Litigation*, 221 F.3d 449 (3d Cir. 2000).

[184]*See S.A. Healy Co. v. Milwaukee Metropolitan Sewerage Dist.*, 60 F.3d 305 (7th Cir. 1995) (commenting that because Rule 54(d) specifies no uniform national deadline for filing Bills of Costs, such timing is typically governed by local court rules).

[185]*See Riordan v. State Farm Mut. Auto. Ins. Co.*, 589 F.3d 999, 1005–06 (9th Cir. 2009) (ruling that such fees must be made by motion, and need not be pleaded).

[186]*See Carolina Power and Light Co. v. Dynegy Marketing and Trade*, 415 F.3d 354, 358–59 (4th Cir. 2005); *United Industries, Inc. v. Simon-Hartley, Ltd.*, 91 F.3d 762, 766 (5th Cir. 1996).

requests to spur a "second major litigation".[187] Typically, such motions are decided on affidavits alone, without additional discovery or evidentiary hearings.[188] The procedure follows:

1. *Motion Required:* The prevailing party must apply for such an award by motion. The motion must: (a) specify the judgment; (b) identify the legal source authorizing such an award of fees or expenses; and (c) state the amount, or a fair estimate of the amount, of the requested award.[189]

   Court-Implemented Settlements: In cases where a settlement must be implemented by the court, the district court may also require that the motion disclose any fee agreement affecting the litigation.

2. *Time for Filing:* Unless otherwise provided,[190] motions must be filed with the court "no later" than 14 days after entry of judgment.[191] This time trigger assumes a qualifying judgment (and may, therefore, be impacted by the separate document rule).[192] This deadline helps both to ensure that the opponent receives proper notice of the fees claim and to promote a prompt fees ruling from the district court, thus permitting simultaneous appellate review of both the merits and the fees award.[193] The deadline also forecloses the revival of disputes that adversaries long since thought were closed.[194] Failure to file within this allotted time constitutes a waiver of a party's right to recover such fees or expenses.[195] Nevertheless, because the 14-day time period is not jurisdic-

---

[187] *See Hensley v. Eckerhart*, 461 U.S. 424, 437, 103 S. Ct. 1933, 1941, 76 L. Ed. 2d 40 (1983).

[188] *See Menchise v. Akerman Senterfitt*, 532 F.3d 1146, 1153 (11th Cir. 2008).

[189] *See* Rule 54(d)(2)(A) to (2)(B). *See also In re Ferrell*, 539 F.3d 1186, 1192 (9th Cir. 2008); *Vanguard Environmental, Inc. v. Kerin*, 528 F.3d 756, 758 (10th Cir. 2008).

[190] Rule 54(b) has been interpreted to apply broadly. *See, e.g., Walker v. Astrue*, 593 F.3d 274, 274–80 (3d Cir. 2010) (noting Circuit split, but finding Rule 54(d) applies to certain fee petitions under Social Security Act).

[191] *See* Rule 54(d)(2)(B)(i). This Rule was amended in 2002 and 2007. The earlier 14-day time trigger was set to *service* of the motion as well, whereas the current trigger is set to *filing* of the motion alone. Because of the goal served by the time period, it

is unlikely that this change will relax the period's mandatory nature.

[192] *See Cardinal Health 110, Inc. v. Cyrus Pharm., LLC*, 560 F.3d 894, 902 (8th Cir. 2009) (period does not begin to run until separate judgment entered); *United Auto. Workers Local 259 Social Sec. Dept. v. Metro Auto Center*, 501 F.3d 283, 287 (3d Cir. 2007) (same).

[193] *See United Industries, Inc. v. Simon-Hartley, Ltd.*, 91 F.3d 762, 766 (5th Cir. 1996).

[194] *See Robinson v. City of Harvey*, 617 F.3d 915, 918–19 (7th Cir. 2010) ("Litigation must have its end.").

[195] *See Robinson v. City of Harvey*, 617 F.3d 915, 918–19 (7th Cir. 2010); *In re Veritas Software Corp. Secs. Litig.*, 496 F.3d 962, 972–74, (9th Cir. 2007); *United Indus., Inc. v. Simon-Hartley, Ltd.*, 91 F.3d 762, 767 (5th Cir. 1996). *But cf. Johnson v. Lafayette Fire Fighters Ass'n Local 472, Intern. Ass'n of*

tional, some courts have held that the district judge may exercise discretion to extend the time period.[196] Most courts also agree that this 14-day period does not begin to run until post-trial motions under Rules 50(b), 52(b), or 59 are resolved.[197]

- *Amended Judgments:* Amended judgments are "judgments" just the same, and the 14-day period will run from them as well.[198]

- *Local Rules & Standing Orders:* Practitioners must *carefully* consult the applicable local rules on Rule 54(d) attorneys fee motions. This 14-day period may be modified "by statute or order of the court".[199] Several courts have ruled that local rules which adopt longer periods for making attorney's fee motions qualify as "standing orders" and, thus, are authorized modifications of the 14-day period.[200]

3. *Time for Serving:* Originally, Rule 54(d) required that a motion for attorney's fees must be *both* served and filed within 14 days. This requirement was changed in the 2002 amendments to the Rule. Now, filing alone is the time trigger, although service remains required under Rule 5(a).[201]

4. *Opponent's Response:* Upon request, the court must provide the opponent with the opportunity to present evidence in opposition to the requested award.[202]

5. *Court's Delegation:* The court may enlist the help of a Special Master for setting the proper value to be

---

Fire Fighters, AFL-CIO-CLC, 51 F.3d 726, 729 (7th Cir. 1995) (holding that local court rule, as a uniform "order of court", modified the 14-day period set forth in Rule 54(d)(2)(B)).

[196] *See Green v. Administrators of Tulane Educ. Fund*, 284 F.3d 642, 664 (5th Cir. 2002); *Amarel v. Connell*, 102 F.3d 1494 (9th Cir.1996). *See also Tancredi v. Metropolitan Life Ins. Co.*, 378 F.3d 220, 227–28 (2d Cir. 2004) (before extension to 14-day deadline may be granted, trial court must find "excusable neglect").

[197] *See Bailey v. County of Riverside*, 414 F.3d 1023, 1024 (9th Cir. 2005); *Miltimore Sales, Inc. v. Int'l Rectifier, Inc.*, 412 F.3d 685, 689 (6th Cir. 2005); *Members First Federal Credit Union v. Members First Credit Union of Florida*, 244 F.3d 806, 807 (11th Cir. 2001); *Weyant v. Okst*, 198 F.3d 311, 314 (2d Cir. 1999).

[198] *See Quigley v. Rosenthal*, 427 F.3d 1232, 1236–37 (10th Cir. 2005).

[199] *See* Rule 54(d)(2)(B).

[200] *See Miltimore Sales, Inc. v. International Rectifier, Inc.*, 412 F.3d 685, 692 (6th Cir. 2005); *Planned Parenthood of Cent. New Jersey v. Attorney General of State of New Jersey*, 297 F.3d 253, 259–61 (3d Cir. 2002); *Green v. Administrators of Tulane Educational Fund*, 284 F.3d 642, 664 (5th Cir. 2002).

[201] *See* Rule 5(a). *See also* Rule 54(d)(2)(B) advisory committee note to 2002 amendments (noting deletion of 14-day service requirement "to establish a parallel with Rules 50, 52, and 59. Service continues to be required under Rule 5(a)").

[202] *See Sloane v. Equifax Information Services, LLC*, 510 F.3d 495, 507 (4th Cir. 2007).

awarded for the attorney services provided. The court may also refer the entire motion to a magistrate judge for a Report & Recommendation.

6. *Court's Ruling:* In ruling on a Rule 54(d)(2) motion, the court must issue findings of fact and conclusions of law as required under Rule 52(a), and must issue a separate judgment as required under Rule 58. The court may, at its option, bifurcate its consideration of the motion to resolve liability issues first, before considering the amount of an appropriate award.

7. *Additional Procedures By Local Rule:* Rule 54(d)(2) permits the district courts to promulgate local rules to govern procedures for claims without the need for extensive evidentiary hearings.[203]

Procedure: Costs Bonds

Collateral to the authority to award costs, courts also have the authority to require litigants to post a bond to safeguard against dissipation of funds needed to reasonably cover anticipated taxable costs. But cost bonds are not sanctions, and may not be imposed upon indigent parties in a manner that functionally denies them access to the federal courts.[204]

Effect of an Attorney's Fees Motion on "Finality"

The filing of a Rule 54(d)(2) motion for an award of attorney's fees does not ordinarily affect the finality of the underlying judgment.[205] However, when a *timely* motion for fees is made, and so long as no notice of appeal has yet been filed (or become effective), the district court may enter an order directing that the fees motion be deemed to have the same effect as a timely Rule 59 motion and, thereby, toll the time for taking an appeal until after the motion is resolved.[206] This extension option applies only to fees motions, not to the taxation of costs.[207]

Additional Research References

Wright & Miller, *Federal Practice and Procedure* §§ 2651 to 79
C.J.S., Federal Civil Procedure §§ 1105 to 1120 et seq., 1236; Federal Courts

---

[203]Local rules *must* be consulted on this point. The advisory committee notes suggest that, by local rule, the district courts may even adopt schedules listing customary attorney's fees or factors that affect attorney's fees within a particular legal community. *See* Rule 54(d)(2)(D) advisory committee note.

[204]*See Gay v. Chandra*, 682 F.3d 590, 594–95 (7th Cir. 2012).

[205]*See* Rule 58(c)(1). *See also Moody Nat. Bank of Galveston v. GE Life and Annuity Assur. Co.*, 383 F.3d 249 (5th Cir. 2004).

[206]*See* Rule 58(c)(2). *See also Moody Nat. Bank of Galveston v. GE Life and Annuity Assur. Co.*, 383 F.3d 249 (5th Cir. 2004).

[207]*See Moody Nat. Bank of Galveston v. GE Life and Annuity Assur. Co.*, 383 F.3d 249 (5th Cir. 2004).

§ 293(17)

West's Key Number Digest, Federal Civil Procedure ⬉2391 to 2399, 2571 to 2587, 2721 to 2742.5; Federal Courts ⬉660

RULE 55
DEFAULT; DEFAULT JUDGMENT

(a) Entering a Default. When a party against whom a judgment for affirmative relief is sought has failed to plead or otherwise defend, and that failure is shown by affidavit or otherwise, the clerk must enter the party's default.

(b) Entering a Default Judgment.

   (1) *By the Clerk.* If the plaintiff's claim is for a sum certain or a sum that can be made certain by computation, the clerk—on the plaintiff's request, with an affidavit showing the amount due—must enter judgment for that amount and costs against a defendant who has been defaulted for not appearing and who is neither a minor nor an incompetent person.

   (2) *By the Court.* In all other cases, the party must apply to the court for a default judgment. A default judgment may be entered against a minor or incompetent person only if represented by a general guardian, conservator, or other like fiduciary who has appeared. If the party against whom a default judgment is sought has appeared personally or by a representative, that party or its representative must be served with written notice of the application at least 7 days before the hearing. The court may conduct hearings or make referrals—preserving any federal statutory right to a jury trial—when, to enter or effectuate judgment, it needs to:

     (A) conduct an accounting;

     (B) determine the amount of damages;

     (C) establish the truth of any allegation by evidence; or

     (D) investigate any other matter.

(c) Setting Aside a Default or a Default Judgment. The court may set aside an entry of default for good cause, and it may set aside a default judgment under Rule 60(b).

(d) Judgment Against the United States. A default judgment may be entered against the United States, its officers, or its agencies only if the claimant establishes a claim or right to relief by evidence that satisfies the court.

[Amended effective August 1, 1987; April 30, 2007, effective December 1, 2007; March 26, 2009, effective December 1, 2009.]

AUTHORS' COMMENTARY ON RULE 55

PURPOSE AND SCOPE

Rule 55 sets the procedure for defaults and default judgments in the federal courts. Because default judgments are not favored by the courts, Rule 55 also defines the procedure for setting aside defaults and default judgments.

RULE 55(a)—ENTERING A DEFAULT

CORE CONCEPT

Upon motion of a party, the clerk of court may enter a default against a party who has failed to plead or otherwise defend.

APPLICATIONS

Distinguished From Default Judgment

The clerk's entry of a party's default is the official recognition that the party is in default.[1] The entry of default is a prerequisite for the entry of judgment upon that default.[2] It is, in effect, akin to a finding of liability with the entry of final judgment yet to come.[3] Thus, there are two stages in a default proceeding—the establishment of the default itself, followed by the entry of a default judgment.[4]

---

[1] *See City of New York v. Mickalis Pawn Shop, LLC*, 645 F.3d 114, 128 (2d Cir. 2011); *New York Life Ins. Co. v. Brown*, 84 F.3d 137, 141 (5th Cir. 1996).

[2] *See Heard v. Caruso*, 351 Fed.Appx. 1, 15–16 (6th Cir. 2009); *New York v. Green*, 420 F.3d 99, 104 (2d Cir. 2005); *Johnson v. Dayton Elec. Mfg. Co.*, 140 F.3d 781, 783 (8th Cir. 1998); *Rowley v. Morant*, 276 F.R.D. 669, 670–71 (D.N.M. 2011). *But see La*

Barbera v. Federal Metal & Glass Corp., 666 F.Supp.2d 341, 347 (E.D.N.Y. 2009) (although default should be sought before default judgment, courts may overlook this misstep).

[3] *See Alameda v. Secretary of Health, Ed. and Welfare*, 622 F.2d 1044, 1048 (1st Cir. 1980).

[4] *See City of New York v. Mickalis Pawn Shop, LLC*, 645 F.3d 114, 128 (2d Cir. 2011); *In re Catt*, 368 F.3d

Prerequisites

The party against whom the default is entered must have been properly served with process, and the district court must enjoy subject matter jurisdiction and either personal or quasi-in-rem/in-rem jurisdiction over the defaulting party.[5] The request for entry of default must be made promptly.[6] Additionally, the clerk must be satisfied, by the moving party's affidavit or otherwise, that the defaulting party has failed to plead or otherwise defend.[7]

Test

Entry of default is proper when a party fails to plead or to "otherwise defend." Courts have interpreted this phrase broadly, permitting entries of default for persistent lack of pretrial diligence or discovery misbehavior, failure to appear at an adjourned trial's resumption, dismissing counsel without an appointed replacement, and abandonment of an active defense.[8] But defaults are disfavored, and doubts should be resolved in the defaulting party's favor.[9] Thus, a failure to properly plead may be excused where the party is unquestionably "otherwise" defending.[10]

- *2007 "Restyling" Impact:* In 2007, the phrase "as provided by these rules" was stricken from Rule 55(a), confirming prior practice that an evinced "intent to defend" is sufficient to avoid a default even if it is manifested in a manner that does not comport strictly

---

789, 793 (7th Cir. 2004). *See also Rowley v. Morant*, 276 F.R.D. 669, 670 (D.N.M. 2011) (both steps are required; default judgment cannot be granted absent prior entry of default).

[5]*See Scott v. District of Columbia*, 598 F.Supp.2d 30, 36 (D.D.C. 2009) (no default is service of process was insufficient); *Maryland State Firemen's Ass'n v. Chaves*, 166 F.R.D. 353 (D. Md. 1996) ("axiomatic" that process must be properly served before default may be entered); *Dahl v. Kanawha Inv. Holding Co.*, 161 F.R.D. 673 (N.D. Iowa 1995) (proper service is precondition for entry of default).

[6]*See Harvey v. United States*, 685 F.3d 939, 946 (10th Cir. 2012) (actively litigating for more than two years before seeking default for a 1-day late filing forfeited the timeliness objection).

[7]*See New York Life Ins. Co. v. Brown*, 84 F.3d 137, 141 (5th Cir. 1996) (entry of default is made by clerk, once default established by affidavit or

otherwise); *Ortiz v. Lasker*, 590 F.Supp.2d 423, 425 (W.D.N.Y. 2008).

[8]*See City of New York v. Mickalis Pawn Shop, LLC*, 645 F.3d 114, 129–30 (2d Cir. 2011) (collecting cases); *United States v. $23,000 in U.S. Currency*, 356 F.3d 157, 163 (1st Cir. 2004) (refusal to file verified statement required by admiralty and maritime rules was failure to otherwise defend).

[9]*See Pacific M. Int'l Corp. v. Raman Int'l Gems, Ltd.*, __ F. Supp. 2d __, __, 2012 WL 3194968, at *4–*5 (S.D.N.Y. 2012). *But cf. J & J Sports Prods., Inc. v. Romenski*, 845 F.Supp.2d 703, 705 (W.D.N.C. 2012) (properly entered when adversary process has halted due to unresponsive opponent).

[10]*See Peters v. AstraZeneca LP*, 224 Fed.Appx. 503, 506 (7th Cir. 2007) (district judge had discretion—absent prejudice to plaintiff—to deny default judgment where defendants failed to file answer but were otherwise defending).

with the Rules.[11]

Entry by Clerk or Court

Although entry of default is typically a ministerial act undertaken by the clerk, the district judges themselves possess the power to enter default as well.[12]

Contested Motions for Entry of Default

Where a motion for entry of default is opposed by a party who has entered an appearance, the courts may, in considering the contested motion, apply the criteria guiding motions to set aside a default.[13]

Effect of Entry of Default

The entry of default provides formal notice to litigants that they are in default.[14] Upon entry, a defaulting party is deemed to have admitted all well-pleaded allegations of the complaint (except for the amount of damages);[15] allegations that are not well-pleaded, as well as conclusions of law, are not deemed admitted.[16] This greatly limits a defendant's ability to defend the lawsuit. A defendant in default is ordinarily foreclosed from raising any defenses other than a challenge to the legal sufficiency of the pleading to support a cognizable judgment, the adequacy of service of process, and the propriety of the court's jurisdiction.[17] The court, however, may nevertheless examine the pleaded allegations to confirm that they do, in fact, state a cognizable cause of action.[18]

---

[11]*See In re Clark*, 2010 WL 2639842, at *3 (W.D.Wash. June 28, 2010); *Hall v. Purky*, 2010 WL 1875713, at *1 (E.D.Tenn. May 10, 2010); *Siegel v. Deutsche Bank Nat'l Trust Co.*, 2009 WL 2868225, at *1 (D.Neb. Sept. 2, 2009).

[12]*See City of New York v. Mickalis Pawn Shop, LLC*, 645 F.3d 114, 128 (2d Cir. 2011); *Pacific M. Int'l Corp. v. Raman Int'l Gems, Ltd.*, __ F. Supp. 2d __, __, 2012 WL 3194968, at *4–*5 (S.D.N.Y. 2012).

[13]*See Rule 55(c). See also Schmir v. Prudential Ins. Co. of America*, 220 F.R.D. 4, 5 (D. Me. 2004) (applying Rule 55(c) factors, namely (1) whether default was willful, (2) prejudice to adversary, (3) whether meritorious defense is presented, (4) nature of explanation for default, (5) good faith of parties, (6) amount of money involved, (7) timing of motion, and (8) general philosophy favoring decisions on merits).

[14]*See Tweedy v. RCAM Title Loans, LLC*, 611 F.Supp.2d 603, 605 (W.D.Va. 2009).

[15]*See City of New York v. Mickalis Pawn Shop, LLC*, 645 F.3d 114, 128 (2d Cir. 2011); *DIRECTV, Inc. v. Hoa Huynh*, 503 F.3d 847, 851 (9th Cir. 2007); *In re The Home Restaurants, Inc.*, 285 F.3d 111, 114 (1st Cir. 2002).

[16]*See DIRECTV, Inc. v. Hoa Huynh*, 503 F.3d 847, 851 (9th Cir. 2007); *Gines v. D.R. Horton, Inc.*, __ F.Supp.2d __, __, 2012 WL 243309, at *3 (M.D.La. 2012).

[17]*See Tyco Fire & Sec., LLC v. Alcocer*, 218 Fed. Appx. 860, 863–64 (11th Cir. 2007); *J & J Sports Prods., Inc. v. Romenski*, 845 F.Supp.2d 703, 705 (W.D.N.C. 2012).

[18]*See Gines v. D.R. Horton, Inc.*, __ F.Supp.2d __, __, 2012 WL 243309, at *3 (M.D.La. 2012); *J & J Sports Prods., Inc. v. Romenski*, 845 F.Supp.2d 703, 705–06 (W.D.N.C. 2012); *Lang-Correa v. Diaz-Carlo*, 672 F.Supp.2d 265, 269 (D.P.R. 2009).

Appealability

Entry of default is an interlocutory order, from which an immediate appeal ordinarily cannot be taken.[19] However, in an appeal from entry of a default judgment, the appeals court may review both the interlocutory entry of default as well as the ensuing entry of default judgment.[20]

RULE 55(b)—ENTERING A DEFAULT JUDGMENT

CORE CONCEPT

Where the defendant has defaulted for failing to appear and the moving party has submitted evidence by affidavit establishing damages in a sum certain or in a sum that can be made certain by computation, the clerk of court may enter a default judgment upon motion. In all other cases, the *court* (and *not* the clerk of court) may enter a default judgment.

APPLICATIONS

Effect of a Default Judgment

A default judgment transforms a defendant's admissions (which occur upon entry of the default) into a final judgment; it usually terminates the litigation by entering a final award in favor of the pleader.[21]

Prerequisites

Before a default judgment may be granted, a "default" under Rule 55(a) must first have been entered.[22] The request for a default judgment must be made promptly.[23] The entering court must confirm that it has subject matter jurisdiction over the dispute,[24] and also may (some Circuits hold "must") confirm that it possesses personal jurisdiction over the defaulting defendant.[25] The Court must respect the Due Process rights of the defaulting party,[26] which requires minimally the 7-day notice to appearing defendants (see below) and the opportunity to

---

[19]*See City of New York v. Mickalis Pawn Shop, LLC*, 645 F.3d 114, 128 n. 15 (2d Cir. 2011); *Symantec Corp. v. Global Impact, Inc.*, 559 F.3d 922, 923 (9th Cir. 2009).

[20]*See City of New York v. Mickalis Pawn Shop, LLC*, 645 F.3d 114, 129 (2d Cir. 2011).

[21]*See City of New York v. Mickalis Pawn Shop, LLC*, 645 F.3d 114, 128 (2d Cir. 2011).

[22]*See Rowley v. Morant*, 276 F.R.D. 669, 670–71 (D.N.M. 2011).

[23]*See Harvey v. United States*, 685 F.3d 939, 946 (10th Cir. 2012) (actively litigating for more than two years before seeking a default judgment for a 1-day late filing forfeited the timeliness objection).

[24]*See Jennifer Matthew Nursing & Rehab. Ctr. v. U.S. Dep't of Health & Human Servs.*, 607 F.3d 951, 955 (2d Cir.2010).

[25]*See City of New York v. Mickalis Pawn Shop, LLC*, 645 F.3d 114, 133 (2d Cir. 2011) (surveying views on obligation to inquire).

[26]*See City of New York v. Mickalis Pawn Shop, LLC*, 645 F.3d 114, 132–33 (2d Cir. 2011).

be heard on the details and nature of the resulting default judgment.[27] Although defaulting defendants are precluded from contesting facts now deemed to be admitted, they may always challenge whether those admitted facts establish a cognizable claim for relief.[28]

The "Appearance" 7-Day Rule

If a default judgment is being sought against a party who has "appeared" (as that term is used in Rule 55(b)), that party must be served with *written* notice of the application for a default judgment at least 7 days before the hearing.[29] Such an appearance, obviously, must occur *before* the default judgment is entered in order to trigger the entitlement to written notice,[30] and that entitlement can be waived if an objection is not timely raised.[31]

- ***2009 Amendments Note:*** Effective December 2009, the Rule 55(b)(2) time period was extended from 3 days to 7 days, to conform to the new multiples-of-7-days standard for federal civil time periods.

Defining Defendant's "Appearance"

A defendant "appears" in the action by making some presentation or submission to the court (*e.g.*, serving a responsive pleading, filing an entry of appearance, serving a Rule 12 motion, or having counsel attend a conference on the client's behalf).[32] Some courts have taken an even wider view,[33] ruling that "appearing" within the meaning of Rule 55(b) is not necessarily limited to a formal event in court.[34] In those courts, informal acts such as correspondence or telephone calls be-

---

[27]*See City of New York v. Mickalis Pawn Shop, LLC*, 645 F.3d 114, 132 (2d Cir. 2011).

[28]*See Marshall v. Baggett*, 616 F.3d 849, 852 (8th Cir. 2010); *Finkel v. Romanowicz*, 577 F.3d 79, 84 (2d Cir.2009). *See also Ohio Cent. R. Co. v. Central Trust Co.*, 133 U.S. 83, 91, 10 S.Ct. 235, 33 L.Ed. 561 (1890) (defaulting defendant "is not precluded from contesting the sufficiency of the bill, or from insisting that the averments contained in it do not justify the decree").

[29]*See* Rule 55(b)(2).

[30]*See Jenkens & Gilchrist v. Groia & Co.*, 542 F.3d 114, 118 n.2 (5th Cir. 2008).

[31]*See U.S. v. Varmado*, 342 Fed. Appx. 437 (11th Cir. 2009) (unpublished opinion).

[32]*See Sun Bank of Ocala v. Pelican Homestead and Sav. Ass'n*, 874 F.2d 274, 276 (5th Cir. 1989) (filing motion to dismiss constitutes "appearing"); *Hudson v. State of N.C.*, 158 F.R.D. 78, 80 (E.D. N.C. 1994) (same); *Lutwin v. City of New York*, 106 F.R.D. 502, 504 n.1 (S.D. N.Y. 1985), aff'd, 795 F.2d 1004 (2d Cir. 1986) (Table).

[33]*See New York v. Green*, 420 F.3d 99, 105 (2d Cir. 2005) (noting division among the Circuits on the issue).

[34]*See Silverman v. RTV Communications Group, Inc.*, 2002 WL 483421, at *3 (S.D. N.Y. 2002) (holding that appearance "is broadly defined and is not limited to a formal court filing"). *See also Rogers v. Hartford Life and Acc. Ins. Co.*, 167 F.3d 933, 936–37 (5th Cir. 1999) (noting that Fifth Circuit does not construe "appeared" as requiring the filing of responsive papers or actual in-court actions by the defendant). *But see Zuelzke Tool & Engineering Co., Inc. v. Anderson Die Castings, Inc.*, 925 F.2d 226, 230 (7th

tween counsel can constitute the requisite appearance,[35] as can engaging in settlement negotiations under certain circumstances.[36] Given the judicial philosophy disfavoring default judgments, the courts may search to find that an appearance has occurred.[37] Nevertheless, merely accepting or waiving service of process will not qualify as "appearing" within the meaning of this Rule.[38]

Entry of Default Judgment by Clerk

The clerk may only enter a default judgment where the following three prerequisites are met:

1. The defendant was defaulted because of a failure to appear; *and*

2. The defendant is not a minor or incompetent person; *and*

3. The moving party submits an affidavit establishing that the amount due is either a sum certain or a sum that can be made certain by computation.

   - *"Sum Certain" Defined:* A claim is not a "sum certain" under Rule 55 unless there is no doubt as to the amount that must be awarded,[39] and the amount due is beyond question (such as actions on money judgments or negotiable instruments).[40] This standard is not met where some portion of damages, such as "reasonable" attorney's fees or punitive damages, still needs to be determined.[41]

Entry of Default Judgment by Court

In all other circumstances, the court may enter the default judgment:

1. Where the defendant has "appeared", in which case the

Cir. 1991) (rejecting informal contacts approach); *Town and Country Kids, Inc. v. Protected Venture Inv. Trust #1, Inc.*, 178 F.R.D. 453, 455 (E.D. Va. 1998) (holding that, for purposes of Rule 55(b), parties "appear" in action only where they make a presentation or submission to the court).

[35]*See Sun Bank of Ocala v. Pelican Homestead and Sav. Ass'n*, 874 F.2d 274, 276–77 (5th Cir. 1989). *See generally New York v. Green*, 420 F.3d 99 (2d Cir.2005) (noting prevailing view, that informal contacts, like telephone calls, may suffice provided there is "clear intention to defend").

[36]*See S.E.C. v. Getanswers, Inc.*, 219 F.R.D. 698, 700 (S.D. Fla. 2004).

[37]*See Franchise Holding II, LLC. v. Huntington Restaurants Group, Inc.*,

375 F.3d 922, 927 (9th Cir. 2004).

[38]*See Rogers v. Hartford Life and Acc. Ins. Co.*, 167 F.3d 933, 936–37 (5th Cir. 1999).

[39]*See Franchise Holding II, LLC. v. Huntington Restaurants Group, Inc.*, 375 F.3d 922, 928–29 (9th Cir. 2004); *KPS & Associates, Inc. v. Designs By FMC, Inc.*, 318 F.3d 1, 19–20 (1st Cir. 2003).

[40]*See KPS & Associates, Inc. v. Designs By FMC, Inc.*, 318 F.3d 1, 19–20 (1st Cir. 2003)

[41]*See Dailey v. R & J Comm'l Contracting*, 2002 WL 484988, at *3 (S.D. Ohio 2002) (error for clerk to enter requested judgment involving punitive damages); *Combs v. Coal & Mineral Mgmt. Services, Inc.*, 105 F.R.D. 472 (D.D.C. 1984).

appearing defendant must be served with written notice of the application for default judgment at least 7 days before any hearing on the application;[42]

2. Where the defendant is a minor or incompetent person, in which case a default judgment may be entered only if the minor or incompetent is represented;

3. Where the amount due is not certain, in which case the court may rely on the facts of record (if appropriate) or conduct a hearing, bench trial, or jury trial to assess damages;[43]

4. Where the defendant has been defaulted for a reason other than a failure to appear.

Default Judgment Hearings

When the damages amount is not a sum certain, the court may convene an evidentiary hearing[44] or simply rely on affidavits or other documentary evidence.[45] No evidentiary hearing is mandatory in all cases,[46] and, so long as a proper factual basis supports the court's award,[47] whether (and how) to conduct hearings is left to the trial judge's discretion.[48] Whether by hearing or otherwise, the party seeking the default judgment bears the burden of proving an entitlement to it.[49] Although the entry of default deprives the defendant of the right to contest most of the complaint's factual allegations (unless

---

[42]See Canal Ins. Co. v. Ashmore, 61 F.3d 15 (8th Cir. 1995) (abuse of discretion to fail to set aside default judgment where defendant never received notice); D.B. v. Bloom, 896 F. Supp. 166, 11 A.D.D. 760 (D.N.J. 1995) (court must be satisfied that party received notice of motion).

[43]See Campbell v. Humphries, 353 Fed.Appx. 334, 337 (11th Cir. 2009); Stephenson v. El-Batrawi, 524 F.3d 907, 915–16 (8th Cir. 2008). See also Wing v. East River Chinese Restaurant, 884 F. Supp. 663, 669 (E.D. N.Y. 1995) (unless amount of damages is certain, court required to make independent determination of sum to be awarded; factors for court's consideration include amount potentially involved, whether material factual issues exist, whether default is "largely technical", prejudice to the movant, harshness of judgment, likelihood that default would be set aside).

[44]See Finkel v. Romanowicz, 577 F.3d 79, 87 (2d Cir. 2009).

[45]See J & J Sports Prods., Inc. v. Romenski, 845 F.Supp.2d 703, 705 (W.D.N.C. 2012); Hounddog Prods., L.L.C. v. Empire Film Group, Inc., 826 F.Supp.2d 619, 627 (S.D.N.Y. 2011).

[46]See Tara Prods., Inc. v. Hollywood Gadgets, Inc., 449 Fed.Appx. 908, 911–12 (11th Cir. 2011); Marcus Food Co. v. DiPanfilo, 671 F.3d 1159, 1172 (10th Cir. 2011); Wecosign, Inc. v. IFG Holdings, Inc., 845 F.Supp.2d 1072, 1079 (C.D.Cal. 2012).

[47]See Marcus Food Co. v. DiPanfilo, 671 F.3d 1159, 1172 (10th Cir. 2011); Stephenson v. El-Batrawi, 524 F.3d 907, 917 n.11 (8th Cir. 2008); S.E.C. v. Smyth, 420 F.3d 1225, 1231–32 (11th Cir. 2005).

[48]See Campbell v. Humphries, 353 Fed.Appx. 334, 337 (11th Cir. 2009); Finkel v. Romanowicz, 577 F.3d 79, 87 (2d Cir. 2009); Stephenson v. El-Batrawi, 524 F.3d 907, 916 (8th Cir. 2008).

[49]See Stephenson v. El-Batrawi, 524 F.3d 907, 915–16 (8th Cir. 2008).

the default is set aside),[50] the defendant may contest the amount of damages. Thus, all the well-pleaded facts in the complaint (except those relating to the amount of damages) are presumed true,[51] but the moving party must prove damages[52] and the court must independently determine them.[53] In doing so, however, all reasonable inferences from the evidence are drawn in the moving party's favor.[54]

- *Jury Right:* Most courts that have considered the issue have ruled that defaulting defendants have no jury right in post-default hearings.[55]

Default in Multiple Defendant Cases

Where the plaintiff alleges joint liability against multiple defendants or the defendants have closely related defenses, the default of one defendant usually will not result in a judgment against another defendant. Instead, the court will allow the lawsuit to proceed as to the other, non-defaulting defendants. The result in the litigation (*e.g.*, judgment for plaintiff or judgment for defendants) will then simply be entered as to the defaulting defendant as well.[56]

Defaulting Defendants in the Military

The federal Soldiers' and Sailors' Civil Relief Act of 1940[57] prohibits the entry of any federal or State judgment by default against absent military defendants, unless the court first appoints counsel to represent the absent defendants' interests. Often, the court may simply stay a lawsuit against the absent military defendants until their return.

Note: In seeking a default judgment, a plaintiff ordinarily

---

[50]*See Ramos-Falcon v. Autoridad de Energia Electrica*, 301 F.3d 1, 2 (1st Cir. 2002).

[51]*See Finkel v. Romanowicz*, 577 F.3d 79, 84 (2d Cir. 2009); *In re Catt*, 368 F.3d 789, 793 (7th Cir. 2004).

[52]*See Stephenson v. El-Batrawi*, 524 F.3d 907, 915–16 (8th Cir. 2008); *La Barbera v. Tadco Const. Corp.*, 647 F. Supp. 2d 247, 250 (E.D.N.Y. 2009).

[53]*See J & J Sports Prods., Inc. v. Romenski*, 845 F.Supp.2d 703, 705 (W.D.N.C. 2012).

[54]*See Finkel v. Romanowicz*, 577 F.3d 79, 84 (2d Cir. 2009); *Pleitez v. Carney*, 594 F.Supp.2d 47, 48–49 (D.D.C. 2009); *Victoria Cruises, Inc. v. Changjiang Cruise Overseas Travel Co.*, 630 F.Supp.2d 255, 260 (E.D.N.Y. 2008).

[55]*See Olcott v. Del. Flood Co.*, 327 F.3d 1115, 1124 (10th Cir.2003); *Graham v. Malone Freight Lines, Inc.*,

314 F.3d 7, 16 (1st Cir.1999); *Dierschke v. O'Cheskey*, 975 F.2d 181, 185 (5th Cir.1992).

[56]*See Frow v. De La Vega*, 82 U.S. 552, 21 L. Ed. 60 (1872). *But see Whelan v. Abell*, 953 F.2d 663 (D.C. Cir. 1992) (construing *Frow* narrowly to hold that a default order that is inconsistent with a judgment on the merits must be set aside only where the liability is actually "joint" (i.e., where the theory of recovery would render all defendants (even the defaulting defendant) liable if any one of the defendants is liable)); *In re Uranium Antitrust Litigation*, 617 F.2d 1248, 1257–58 (7th Cir. 1980) (same); *Douglas v. Metro Rental Services, Inc.*, 827 F.2d 252 (7th Cir. 1987) (same); *Martin v. Coughlin*, 895 F. Supp. 39 (N.D. N.Y. 1995) (same, and noting Second Circuit view that it is "most unlikely" that *Frow* principle survived promulgation of Rule 54(b)).

[57]50 U.S.C.A.App. § 501.

must, by factual averment or affidavit, attest that the defaulting defendant is not in the military.

Limitation on Default Judgments

No judgment by default can be greater in amount or different in kind from the demand contained in the complaint.[58]

Discretion of District Court

Judgments by default are disfavored and are never granted as a matter of right.[59] Whether to enter a judgment by default is a decision entrusted to the sound discretion of the district court.[60] Thus, a defendant's default does not necessarily entitle the plaintiff to an automatic default judgment,[61] nor need the judge presume that the pleader's allegations constitute a valid cause of action.[62] Before exercising their discretion and entering a default judgment, courts may examine the standards for setting aside a default;[63] whether a responsive pleading has since (though belatedly) been received,[64] and a myriad of other factors, such as the clarity of the grounds for default, the adequacy of notice, the size of the claim; the facts in dispute, and prejudice to either party.[65] Nevertheless, and notwithstanding the preference for decisions on the merits, where the inquiry satisfies the court that a default judgment is proper, it will be entered.[66]

Appealability

The entry of a judgment by default is a final order, and is subject to immediate appeal.[67] Although often, upon the entry of a default judgment, the defaulted litigant will move the district court for relief from the default under Rule 55(c) and Rule 60(b), this is not required; because a default judgment is

---

[58]See Rule 54(c).

[59]See Harvey v. United States, 685 F.3d 939, 946 (10th Cir. 2012); Kauffman v. Cal Spas, 37 F. Supp. 2d 402, 404 (E.D. Pa. 1999).

[60]See Pacific M. Int'l Corp. v. Raman Int'l Gems, Ltd., __ F. Supp. 2d __, __, 2012 WL 3194968, at *4–*5 (S.D.N.Y. 2012); Bender Shipbuilding & Repair Co., Inc. v. Vessel DRIVE OCEAN V, 123 F. Supp. 2d 1201, 1208 (S.D. Cal. 1998), aff'd, 221 F.3d 1348 (9th Cir. 2000).

[61]See Philip Morris USA, Inc. v. Castworld Products, Inc., 219 F.R.D. 494, 498 (C.D. Cal. 2003).

[62]See Finkel v. Romanowicz, 577 F.3d 79, 84 (2d Cir. 2009).

[63]See Stout Street Funding LLC v. Johnson, __ F. Supp. 2d __, __, 2012

WL 1994800, at *3 (E.D.Pa. 2012); Philip Morris USA, Inc. v. Castworld Products, Inc., 219 F.R.D. 494, 498 (C.D. Cal. 2003).

[64]See Semler v. Klang, 603 F.Supp.2d 1211, 1218–19 (D.Minn. 2009).

[65]See Pacific M. Int'l Corp. v. Raman Int'l Gems, Ltd., __ F. Supp. 2d __, __, 2012 WL 3194968, at *5 (S.D.N.Y. 2012); Moroccanoil, Inc. v. Allstate Beauty Prods., Inc., 847 F.Supp.2d 1197, 1200 (C.D.Cal. 2012).

[66]See Swarna v. Al-Awadi, 607 F.Supp.2d 509, 527–29 (S.D.N.Y. 2009).

[67]See City of New York v. Mickalis Pawn Shop, LLC, 645 F.3d 114, 129 (2d Cir. 2011); Ackra Direct Marketing Corp. v. Fingerhut Corp., 86 F.3d 852, 855 n. 3 (8th Cir. 1996).

a final order, the defaulted litigant may appeal at once.[68]

RULE 55(c)—SETTING ASIDE DEFAULT OR A DEFAULT JUDGMENT

CORE CONCEPT

The court may set aside the entry of default for good cause, and may vacate a judgment by default in accordance with Rule 60(b) (which governs the grounds upon which a party may seek relief from a judgment).

APPLICATIONS

Policy and Liberality

Defaults and default judgments are disfavored, since they are inconsistent with the federal courts' preference for resolving disputes on their merits.[69] Accordingly, motions for relief from both defaults and default judgments are considered liberally[70] and are often granted.[71] Where only a default has been entered (without an accompanying default judgment), the standard for lifting the default is especially generous.[72]

Setting Aside a Default

Rule 55(c) authorizes the district courts, "for good cause", to set aside the entry of a default.[73] Not susceptible to a precise definition, "good cause" has been labeled a liberal and "mutable" standard, one that varies from situation to situation.[74] It is a standard applied generously, and more liberally where only a default has been entered (with no accompanying default

---

[68]*See City of New York v. Mickalis Pawn Shop, LLC*, 645 F.3d 114, 127–28 (2d Cir. 2011).

[69]*See Harvey v. United States*, 685 F.3d 939, 946 (10th Cir. 2012); *U.S. v. Signed Personal Check No. 730 of Yubran S. Mesle*, 615 F.3d 1085, 1091 (9th Cir. 2010); *United States v. $22,050.00 U.S. Currency*, 595 F.3d 318, 322 (6th Cir. 2010). *But see O'Brien v. R.J. O'Brien & Assoc., Inc.*, 998 F.2d 1394, 1401 (7th Cir.1993) ("this circuit no longer follows the earlier doctrine disfavoring defaults").

[70]*See Colleton Preparatory Academy, Inc. v. Hoover Universal, Inc.*, 616 F.3d 413, 417 (4th Cir. 2010); *United States v. $22,050.00 U.S. Currency*, 595 F.3d 318, 322 (6th Cir. 2010).

[71]*See Indigo America, Inc. v. Big Impressions, LLC*, 597 F.3d 1, 6 (1st Cir. 2010); *California Trout v. F.E.R.C.*, 572 F.3d 1003, 1027 n.1 (9th Cir. 2009).

[72]*See Colleton Preparatory Academy, Inc. v. Hoover Universal, Inc.*, 616 F.3d 413, 418 (4th Cir. 2010); *U.S. v. Signed Personal Check No. 730 of Yubran S. Mesle*, 615 F.3d 1085, 1091 n.1 (9th Cir. 2010); *Cracco v. Vitran Exp., Inc.*, 559 F.3d 625, 630–31 (7th Cir. 2009).

[73]*See Dassault Systemes, SA v. Childress*, 663 F.3d 832, 838–39 (6th Cir. 2011); *Brandt v. American Bankers Ins. Co.*, 653 F.3d 1108, 1111 (9th Cir. 2011); *Johnson v. Arden*, 614 F.3d 785, 798 (8th Cir. 2010).

[74]*See Compania Interamericana Export-Import, S.A. v. Compania Dominicana de Aviacion*, 88 F.3d 948, 951 (11th Cir. 1996).

judgment).[75] Ergo, entries of default are often set aside.[76] The requisite "good cause", however, is not "good cause" for the defendant's mistake, but rather "good cause" justifying the court's decision to set the default aside.[77]

In testing for "good cause", the courts generally consider some or all of the following factors: (1) proof that the default was not willful or culpable[78] (which typically requires more than mere inaction or negligence);[79] (2) swiftness of the action to remedy the default;[80] (3) existence of a meritorious defense[81] (which usually is not a very heavy burden but requires only the alleging of sufficient facts that, if true, would constitute a defense,)[82] and (4) whether the opponent would be prejudiced were the default lifted[83] (and prejudice means not merely delay or the obligation to have to prove the merits,[84] but some loss of evidence, unavailability of witnesses, or other impairment of the ability to prove the merits.)[85] In addition to these leading factors, courts have often considered other equitable criteria as

---

[75]See *Colleton Preparatory Academy, Inc. v. Hoover Universal, Inc.*, 616 F.3d 413, 420 (4th Cir. 2010); *Cracco v. Vitran Exp., Inc.*, 559 F.3d 625, 630–31 (7th Cir. 2009); *In re OCA, Inc.*, 551 F.3d 359, 370 (5th Cir. 2008).

[76]See *California Trout v. F.E.R. C.*, 572 F.3d 1003, 1027 n.1 (9th Cir. 2009).

[77]See *Sims v. EGA Products, Inc.*, 475 F.3d 865, 868 (7th Cir. 2007).

[78]See *Dassault Systemes, SA v. Childress*, 663 F.3d 832, 838–39 (6th Cir. 2011); *Brandt v. American Bankers Ins. Co.*, 653 F.3d 1108, 1111 (9th Cir. 2011); *Colleton Preparatory Academy, Inc. v. Hoover Universal, Inc.*, 616 F.3d 413, 417 (4th Cir. 2010).

[79]See *Garcia v. Sebelius*, __ F. Supp. 2d __, __, 2012 WL 2149559, at *10 (D.D.C. 2012); *U.S. v. Signed Personal Check No. 730 of Yurban S. Mesle*, 615 F.3d 1085, 1092 (9th Cir. 2010); *U.S. v. $22,050.00 U.S. Currency*, 595 F.3d 318, 324 (6th Cir. 2010).

[80]See *Colleton Preparatory Academy, Inc. v. Hoover Universal, Inc.*, 616 F.3d 413, 417 (4th Cir. 2010); *Indigo America, Inc. v. Big Impressions, LLC*, 597 F.3d 1, 3 (1st Cir. 2010); *Cracco v. Vitran Exp., Inc.*, 559 F.3d 625, 630–31 (7th Cir. 2009).

[81]See *Dassault Systemes, SA v. Childress*, 663 F.3d 832, 838–39 (6th

Cir. 2011); *Brandt v. American Bankers Ins. Co.*, 653 F.3d 1108, 1111 (9th Cir. 2011); *Colleton Preparatory Academy, Inc. v. Hoover Universal, Inc.*, 616 F.3d 413, 417 (4th Cir. 2010).

[82]See *U.S. v. Signed Personal Check No. 730 of Yurban S. Mesle*, 615 F.3d 1085, 1094 (9th Cir. 2010); *Indigo America, Inc. v. Big Impressions, LLC*, 597 F.3d 1, 6 (1st Cir. 2010); *U.S. v. $22,050.00 U.S. Currency*, 595 F.3d 318, 326 (6th Cir. 2010). See also *Mohamad v. Rajoub*, 634 F.3d 604, 606 (D.C.Cir. 2011) ("even a hint of a suggestion which, if proven, would constitute a complete defense" may suffice), *aff'd*, 132 S.Ct. 1702, 182 L.Ed.2d 720 (2012).

[83]See *Dassault Systemes, SA v. Childress*, 663 F.3d 832, 838–39 (6th Cir. 2011); *Brandt v. American Bankers Ins. Co.*, 653 F.3d 1108, 1111 (9th Cir. 2011); *Colleton Preparatory Academy, Inc. v. Hoover Universal, Inc.*, 616 F.3d 413, 417 (4th Cir. 2010).

[84]See *Colleton Preparatory Academy, Inc. v. Hoover Universal, Inc.*, 616 F.3d 413, 417 & 419 n.6 (4th Cir. 2010) *U.S. v. Signed Personal Check No. 730 of Yurban S. Mesle*, 615 F.3d 1085, 1092 (9th Cir. 2010); *Indigo America, Inc. v. Big Impressions, LLC*, 597 F.3d 1, 4 (1st Cir. 2010).

[85]See *East Coast Exp., Inc. v. Ruby, Inc.*, 162 F.R.D. 37 (E.D. Pa. 1995); *Mathon v. Marine Midland Bank, N.A.*, 875 F. Supp. 986, 992 (E.D.N.Y. 1995).

well, including: (a) whether the default resulted from a good faith mistake in following a rule of procedure;[86] (b) the nature of the defendant's explanation for defaulting;[87] (c) any history of dilatory conduct;[88] (d) the amount in controversy;[89] (e) the availability of effective alternative sanctions;[90] and (f) whether entry of a default would produce a harsh or unfair result.[91] For many courts, each particular consideration need not be satisfied,[92] and the list of criteria is seen as a non-exhaustive list of mere indicators.[93] For those courts, motions to set aside default are made in a "practical, commonsense manner, without rigid adherence to, or undue reliance upon, a mechanical formula".[94] Other courts take a different view, and consider the leading factors to be mandatory with a failure to meet any one of them sufficient alone to deny the motion.[95]

> *Note:* In practice, any of the grounds that justify vacating a default judgment will likely also constitute adequate "good cause" to warrant setting aside the entry of a default. This "good cause" test is more lenient than the Rule 60(b) standard,[96] however, and some circumstances that might not justify relief from judgment under Rule 60(b) could still permit the setting aside of the entry of default under Rule 55(c) (*e.g.,* illness of counsel, mistake of counsel).

---

[86]*See Indigo America, Inc. v. Big Impressions, LLC*, 597 F.3d 1, 3 (1st Cir. 2010).

[87]*See Indigo America, Inc. v. Big Impressions, LLC*, 597 F.3d 1, 3 (1st Cir. 2010).

[88]*See Colleton Preparatory Academy, Inc. v. Hoover Universal, Inc.*, 616 F.3d 413, 417 (4th Cir. 2010).

[89]*See Indigo America, Inc. v. Big Impressions, LLC*, 597 F.3d 1, 3 (1st Cir. 2010); *Compania Interamericana Export-Import, S.A. v. Compania Dominicana de Aviacion*, 88 F.3d 948, 951 (11th Cir. 1996).

[90]*See Colleton Preparatory Academy, Inc. v. Hoover Universal, Inc.*, 616 F.3d 413, 417 (4th Cir. 2010); *Agnew v. E*Trade Secs. LLC*, 811 F.Supp.2d 1177, 1183 (E.D.Pa. 2011).

[91]*See Richardson v. Nassau County*, 184 F.R.D. 497, 501 (E.D. N.Y. 1999); *Canfield v. VSH Restaurant Corp.*, 162 F.R.D. 431 (N.D. N.Y. 1995).

[92]*See U.S. v. $22,050.00 U.S. Currency*, 595 F.3d 318, 324–25 (6th Cir. 2010); *Agnew v. E*Trade Secs.*

LLC, 811 F.Supp.2d 1177, 1183 (E.D.Pa. 2011).

[93]*See Indigo America, Inc. v. Big Impressions, LLC*, 597 F.3d 1, 3 (1st Cir. 2010); *Effjohn Int'l Cruise Holdings, Inc. v. A&L Sales, Inc.*, 346 F.3d 552, 563 (5th Cir. 2003); *Fink v. Swisshelm*, 185 F.R.D. 353 (D. Kan. 1999).

[94]*See KPS & Associates, Inc. v. Designs By FMC, Inc.*, 318 F.3d 1, 12 (1st Cir. 2003).

[95]*See Lacy v. Sitel Corp.*, 227 F.3d 290, 291 (5th Cir. 2000); *U.S. v. Certain Real Property commonly known as 21105 116TH Street Bristol, Wis.*, 845 F.Supp.2d 961, 964 (E.D.Wis. 2012) (same). *Cf. Brandt v. American Bankers Ins. Co.*, 653 F.3d 1108, 1111–12 (9th Cir. 2011) (if any of leading factors is absent, court may—but is not compelled to—deny relief).

[96]*See Colleton Preparatory Academy, Inc. v. Hoover Universal, Inc.*, 616 F.3d 413, 420–21 (4th Cir. 2010); *Cracco v. Vitran Exp., Inc.*, 559 F.3d 625, 630–31 (7th Cir. 2009); *In re OCA, Inc.*, 551 F.3d 359, 370 (5th Cir. 2008).

Vacating a Judgment by Default

Once a judgment is entered upon a party's default, the task of vacating it becomes more difficult.[97] The court may vacate a default judgment if (1) the defaulting party meets the "good cause" test noted above, *and also* (2) satisfies one of the Rule 60(b) reasons for vacating a judgment (*i.e.*, mistake, inadvertence, surprise, excusable neglect, newly discovered evidence, misconduct by an adverse party, void judgment, or satisfied or discharged judgment).[98] Default judgments are "the biggest weapon in the district court's armory", and may be useful in reining in recalcitrant parties or penalizing prejudicial tactics.[99] Such judgments generally are not appropriate where the misstep does not prejudice the adversary but costs the erring party an otherwise certain victory.[100] Rather, this is an equitable inquiry that considers all relevant circumstances.[101] The time for filing such motions is set forth in Rule 60(b).

Burden of Proof

The burden of demonstrating that either a default or default judgment should be lifted lies with the moving party.[102]

Discretion of District Court

Because they clash with the federal courts' preference for decisions on the merits, defaulting a party is viewed as a drastic step and extreme sanction, and ought to be reserved for only rare occasions.[103] Accordingly, the "good faith" criteria are applied generously,[104] and doubts are resolved in favor of lifting the default.[105] Whether to set aside the entry of default or vacate a default judgment is left to the discretion of the district judge[106] Where it did not explain its reasoning, a district court's decision to vacate may nevertheless be upheld where the basis

---

[97]*See U.S. v. $22,050.00 U.S. Currency*, 595 F.3d 318, 324 (6th Cir. 2010); *Saunders v. Morton*, 269 F.R.D. 387, 401 (D.Vt. 2010); *Brand Scaffold Builders, Inc. v. Puerto Rico Elec. Power Authority*, 364 F. Supp. 2d 50, 54 (D.P.R. 2005).

[98]*See Brandt v. American Bankers Ins. Co.*, 653 F.3d 1108, 1111 (9th Cir. 2011); *Brien v. Kullman Industries, Inc.*, 71 F.3d 1073, 1077 (2d Cir. 1995).

[99]*See Mommaerts v. Hartford Life and Acc. Ins. Co.*, 472 F.3d 967, 967–69 (7th Cir. 2007).

[100]*See Mommaerts v. Hartford Life and Acc. Ins. Co.*, 472 F.3d 967, 969–69 (7th Cir. 2007).

[101]*See Brandt v. American Bankers Ins. Co.*, 653 F.3d 1108, 1112 (9th Cir. 2011).

[102]*See Indigo America, Inc. v. Big Impressions, LLC*, 597 F.3d 1, 4 (1st Cir. 2010).

[103]*See U.S. v. Signed Personal Check No. 730 of Yurban S. Mesle*, 615 F.3d 1085, 1091 (9th Cir. 2010); *Stewart v. Astrue*, 552 F.3d 26, 28 (1st Cir. 2009). *See also Martin v. Coughlin*, 895 F. Supp. 39, 42 (N.D. N.Y. 1995) (default judgment is "a weapon of last, and not first, resort").

[104]*See Martin v. Coughlin*, 895 F. Supp. 39 (N.D. N.Y. 1995).

[105]*See Budget Blinds, Inc. v. White*, 536 F.3d 244, 258 (3d Cir. 2008) *Powerserve Intern., Inc. v. Lavi*, 239 F.3d 508, 514 (2d Cir. 2001); *Lacy v. Sitel Corp.*, 227 F.3d 290, 291 (5th Cir. 2000).

[106]*See Brandt v. American Bankers Ins. Co.*, 653 F.3d 1108, 1112 (9th Cir. 2011); *Cracco v. Vitran Exp., Inc.*, 559 F.3d 625, 630 (7th Cir. 2009); *Payne*

for the ruling is apparent.[107]

Sua Sponte Set Asides

Although defaults and default judgments are set aside usually upon motion of a party, the district courts may do so *sua sponte*.[108]

RULE 55(d)—DEFAULT JUDGMENT AGAINST THE UNITED STATES

CORE CONCEPT

No default judgment may be entered against the United States or any federal agency or officer, unless the plaintiff establishes, by evidence satisfactory to the court, a claim or right to relief.

APPLICATIONS

Impact of 2007 "Restyling" Amendments

The 2007 amendments repositioned the content of former Rule 55(e) to its current location, in Rule 55(d). The former content of Rule 55(d) was deleted as unnecessary and incomplete. In researching current Rule 55(d), practitioners should be mindful of this repositioning.

Policy

The entry of default judgments against the United States is especially disfavored.[109] The courts reason that federal taxpayers (on whom the burden of paying the default judgment would ultimately fall) should not be called upon to pay a penalty imposed as the consequence of the neglect of some government official, if to do so would cause a windfall to the litigant.[110] Thus, Rule 55(d) is intended to prevent the entry of default judgments against the United States for mere procedural

---

ex rel. Estate of Calzada v. Brake, 439 F.3d 198, 204 (4th Cir. 2006).

[107]*See Mohamad v. Rajoub*, 634 F.3d 604, 606 (D.C.Cir. 2011), *cert. granted*, 80 U.S.L.W. 3059 & 3128 (U.S. Oct 17, 2011).

[108]*See Judson Atkinson Candies, Inc. v. Latini-Hohberger Dhimantec*, 529 F.3d 371, 385–86 (7th Cir. 2008) (approving *sua sponte* set asides of default; collecting cases).

[109]*See Harvey v. United States*, 685 F.3d 939, 946 (10th Cir. 2012); *Payne v. Barnhart*, 725 F.Supp.2d 113, 116 (D.D.C. 2010).

[110]*See Compania Interamericana Export-Import, S.A. v. Compania Dominicana de Aviacion*, 88 F.3d 948,

951 (11th Cir. 1996); *ABI Inv. Group v. F.D.I.C.*, 860 F. Supp. 911, 914 (D.N.H. 1994). The Foreign Sovereign Immunities Act, 28 U.S.C.A. § 1608(e), provides foreign sovereigns with this same protection against default judgments in federal courts. *See Commercial Bank of Kuwait v. Rafidain Bank*, 15 F.3d 238, 242 (2d Cir. 1994); *Nationsbank of Florida v. Banco Exterior de Espana*, 867 F. Supp. 167, 174 (S.D. N.Y. 1994) (commenting that court's preference for denying motion for default judgment is particularly strong where the defendant is a foreign sovereign; when foreign sovereign defaults, movant bears the burden to show sufficient evidence that default judgment is appropriate).

missteps.[111] Consequently, such defaults are frequently denied outright or set aside.[112] This "presumption-against-defaulting" the government is especially strong when the movant is seeking criminal habeas relief.[113]

Applies Only to Judgments, Not Defaults

Although default judgments may not be entered summarily against the United States, the default itself may be.[114]

Plaintiff's High Burden

To default the United States or federal officers or agencies, plaintiffs must carry the heavy burden of establishing a claim or right-to-relief.[115] They must do so by evidence that is satisfactory to the court.[116] This inquiry does not necessarily require a hearing, or either more or different evidence than would otherwise be received.[117] (However, at least one court has ruled that the burden for default against the United States requires a demonstration of an evidentiary basis that is legally sufficient for a reasonable jury to find for the plaintiff.[118]) Instead, the courts assume a flexible approach in determining the procedures necessary to conduct this inquiry.[119] If uncontroverted, a plaintiff's *evidence* may be accepted as true,[120] but if the government comes forward with a meritorious defense and a willingness to litigate, the default judgment will likely be denied.[121]

Foreign Governments

By statute, Congress requires that this same "satisfies-the-court" standard be applied in actions against foreign governments, foreign political subdivisions, and foreign agencies and

---

[111]*See Arevalo v. U.S.*, 2008 WL 3874795, at *6 (E.D. Pa. 2008).

[112]*See Payne v. Barnhart*, 725 F.Supp.2d 113, 116 (D.D.C. 2010).

[113]*See U.S. v. Dill*, 555 F. Supp. 2d 514, 521 (E.D. Pa. 2008).

[114]*See Alameda v. Secretary of Health, Ed. and Welfare*, 622 F.2d 1044, 1048 (1st Cir. 1980) (noting that default may be entered, and commenting that the exemption from default judgments "heightens" the United States' obligation to cooperate with the court). *See also Washington v. Astrue*, 2009 WL 1916238, at *1 (S.D.Fla. June 30, 2009); *Flowers v. U.S. Postal Serv.*, 2009 WL 691291, at *2 (N.D.Ill. Mar. 16, 2009).

[115]*See Campbell v. U.S.*, 375 Fed. Appx. 254 (3d Cir. 2010); *Willever v. United States*, 775 F.Supp.2d 771 (D.Md. 2011).

[116]*See Harvey v. United States*, 685 F.3d 939, 946–56 (10th Cir. 2012); *Campbell v. United States*, 375 Fed. Appx. 254 (3d Cir. 2010).

[117]*See Commercial Bank of Kuwait v. Rafidain Bank*, 15 F.3d 238, 242 (2d Cir. 1994).

[118]*See Smith ex rel. Smith v. Islamic Emirate of Afghanistan*, 262 F. Supp. 2d 217, 223–24 (S.D. N.Y. 2003).

[119]*See Jin v. Ministry of State Security*, 557 F. Supp. 2d 131, 139–40 (D.D.C. 2008); *Gadoury v. U.S.*, 187 B.R. 816, 822 (D.R.I. 1995).

[120]*See Estate of Botvin ex rel. Ellis v. Islamic Republic of Iran*, 772 F.Supp.2d 218, 227 (D.D.C. 2011).

[121]*See Stewart v. Astrue*, 552 F.3d 26, 28–29 (1st Cir. 2009).

instrumentalities.[122]

Additional Research References

Wright & Miller, *Federal Practice and Procedure* §§ 2681 to 2702
C.J.S., Federal Civil Procedure §§ 1122 to 1134 et seq.
West's Key Number Digest, Federal Civil Procedure ⟸2411 to 2455

---

[122]*See* 28 U.S.C.A. § 1608(e). *See*   2d 457, 491 n.28 (S.D. N.Y. 2006).
also Weininger v. Castro, 462 F. Supp.

RULE 56
SUMMARY JUDGMENT

(a) Motion for Summary Judgment or Partial Summary Judgment. A party may move for summary judgment, identifying each claim or defense--or the part of each claim or defense--on which summary judgment is sought. The court shall grant summary judgment if the movant shows that there is no genuine dispute as to any material fact and the movant is entitled to judgment as a matter of law. The court should state on the record the reasons for granting or denying the motion.

(b) Time to File a Motion. Unless a different time is set by local rule or the court orders otherwise, a party may file a motion for summary judgment at any time until 30 days after the close of all discovery.

(c) Procedures.

(1) *Supporting Factual Positions.* A party asserting that a fact cannot be or is genuinely disputed must support the assertion by:

(A) citing to particular parts of materials in the record, including depositions, documents, electronically stored information, affidavits or declarations, stipulations (including those made for purposes of the motion only), admissions, interrogatory answers, or other materials; or

(B) showing that the materials cited do not establish the absence or presence of a genuine dispute, or that an adverse party cannot produce admissible evidence to support the fact.

(2) *Objection That a Fact Is Not Supported by Admissible Evidence.* A party may object that the material cited to support or dispute a fact cannot be presented in a form that would be admissible in evidence.

(3) *Materials Not Cited.* The court need consider

only the cited materials, but it may consider other materials in the record.

(4) *Affidavits or Declarations.* An affidavit or declaration used to support or oppose a motion must be made on personal knowledge, set out facts that would be admissible in evidence, and show that the affiant or declarant is competent to testify on the matters stated.

(d) When Facts Are Unavailable to the Nonmovant. If a nonmovant shows by affidavit or declaration that, for specified reasons, it cannot present facts essential to justify its opposition, the court may:

(1) defer considering the motion or deny it;

(2) allow time to obtain affidavits or declarations or to take discovery; or

(3) issue any other appropriate order.

(e) Failing to Properly Support or Address a Fact. If a party fails to properly support an assertion of fact or fails to properly address another party's assertion of fact as required by Rule 56(c), the court may:

(1) give an opportunity to properly support or address the fact;

(2) consider the fact undisputed for purposes of the motion;

(3) grant summary judgment if the motion and supporting materials--including the facts considered undisputed--show that the movant is entitled to it; or

(4) issue any other appropriate order.

(f) Judgment Independent of the Motion. After giving notice and a reasonable time to respond, the court may:

(1) grant summary judgment for a nonmovant;

(2) grant the motion on grounds not raised by a party; or

(3) consider summary judgment on its own after identifying for the parties material facts that may not be genuinely in dispute.

(g) Failing to Grant All the Requested Relief. If

the court does not grant all the relief requested by the motion, it may enter an order stating any material fact--including an item of damages or other relief--that is not genuinely in dispute and treating the fact as established in the case.

(h) Affidavit or Declaration Submitted in Bad Faith. If satisfied that an affidavit or declaration under this rule is submitted in bad faith or solely for delay, the court--after notice and a reasonable time to respond--may order the submitting party to pay the other party the reasonable expenses, including attorney's fees, it incurred as a result. An offending party or attorney may also be held in contempt or subjected to other appropriate sanctions.

[Amended effective March 19, 1948; July 1, 1963; August 1, 1987; April 30, 2007, effective December 1, 2007; March 26, 2009, effective December 1, 2009; April 28, 2010, effective December 1, 2010.]

———— The 2010 Summary Judgment Amendments ————

Effective December 1, 2010, the federal summary judgment Rule underwent its most extensive revision since it was first adopted in 1938. The current version of Rule 56 appears above. Because courts, practitioners, and academics may have need, during this transitional period, to consult the prior language, the pre-amendment version of Rule 56 is reprinted below in reduced font. The *Authors' Commentary* for Rule 56 highlights the changes and effects of the 2010 Amendments throughout the discussions below.

Rule 56. Summary Judgment

[Former text of Rule 56]

(a) By a Claiming Party. A party claiming relief may move, with or without supporting affidavits, for summary judgment on all or part of the claim.

(b) By a Defending Party. A party against whom relief is sought may move, with or without supporting affidavits, for summary judgment on all or part of the claim.

(c) Time for a Motion, Response, and Reply; Proceedings.

(1) These times apply unless a different time is set by local rule or the court orders otherwise:

(A) a party may move for summary judgment at any time until 30 days after the close of all discovery;

(B) a party opposing the motion must file a response within 21 days after the motion is served or a responsive pleading is due, whichever is later; and

(C) the movant may file a reply within 14 days after the response is served.

(2) The judgment sought should be rendered if the pleadings, the discovery and disclosure materials on file, and any affidavits show that there is no genuine issue as to any material fact and that the movant is entitled to judgment as a matter of law.

(d) Case Not Fully Adjudicated on the Motion.

(1) *Establishing Facts.* If summary judgment is not rendered on the whole action, the court should, to the extent practicable, determine what material facts are not genuinely at issue. The court should so determine by examining the pleadings and evidence before it and by interrogating the attorneys. It should then issue an order specifying what facts—including items of damages or other relief—are not genuinely at issue. The facts so specified must be treated as established in the action.

(2) *Establishing Liability.* An interlocutory summary judgment may be rendered on liability alone, even if there is a genuine issue on the amount of damages.

(e) Affidavits; Further Testimony.

(1) *In General.* A supporting or opposing affidavit must be made on personal knowledge, set out facts that would be admissible in evidence, and show that the affiant is competent to testify on the matters stated. If a paper or part of a paper is referred to in an affidavit, a sworn or certified copy must be attached to or served with the affidavit. The court may permit an affidavit to be supplemented or opposed by depositions, answers to interrogatories, or additional affidavits.

(2) *Opposing Party's Obligation to Respond.* When a motion for summary judgment is properly made and supported, an opposing party may not rely merely on allegations or denials in its own pleading; rather, its response must—by affidavits or as otherwise provided in this rule—set out specific facts showing a genuine issue for trial. If the opposing party does not so respond, summary judgment should, if appropriate, be entered against that party.

(f) When Affidavits Are Unavailable. If a party opposing the motion shows by affidavit that, for specified reasons, it cannot present facts essential to justify its opposition, the court may:

(1) deny the motion;

(2) order a continuance to enable affidavits to be obtained, depositions to be taken, or other discovery to be undertaken; or

(3) issue any other just order.

(g) Affidavit Submitted in Bad Faith. If satisfied that an affidavit under this rule is submitted in bad faith or solely for delay, the court must order the submitting party to pay the other party the reasonable expenses, including attorney's fees, it incurred as a result. An offending party or attorney may also be held in contempt.

AUTHORS' COMMENTARY ON RULE 56

PURPOSE AND SCOPE

Rule 56 sets the procedure by which a party may request or oppose either full or partial summary judgment, and the standards the federal courts consider when ruling on motions for summary judgment.

COMPARISONS WITH OTHER RULES OF ADJUDICATION

Dismissals and Judgments on the Pleadings: Motions to

dismiss (under Rule 12(b)(6)) and for judgment on the pleadings (under Rule 12(c)) are *as-alleged* challenges. They test whether a pleading's averments of law and fact, if proven true, would be legally sufficient to sustain a claim or defense. In contrast, motions for summary judgment are *as-provable* challenges. They test whether, notwithstanding the allegations, evidence exists to establish a genuine factual dispute.

- *"Conversion"*: If, in ruling on a Rule 12(b)(6) motion to dismiss, the court is invited to, and does, consider extrinsic materials beyond the pleadings, the court will convert the motion into a summary judgment challenge.[1]

Judgments as a Matter of Law (JMOL): Motions for judgments as a matter of law (under Rule 50) are *as-proven* challenges - the federal equivalent of directed verdict and JNOV motions. They test whether, irrespective of the allegations and solely in light of the evidence presented at trial, a reasonable jury could return a verdict for the non-moving party. In this respect, both summary judgment motions and JMOL motions alike use the lens of the reasonable factfinder to test a party's case or defense.[2] The difference is timing. Summary judgment assessments are made pre-trial, and are supported by pleadings, discovery, affidavits, and other "cold" evidence. JMOL assessments are made during or after trial, with the judge having listened to the actual, live testimony and evidentiary presentation. In other words, Rule 50 motions for JMOL ask whether there is any need for the trial—then underway—to continue on to the jury deliberation stage; Rule 56 motions for summary judgment ask whether there is any need to convene a trial at all.

RULE 56(a) — MOTION FOR SUMMARY JUDGMENT OR PARTIAL SUMMARY JUDGMENT

CORE CONCEPT

Parties may move to summarily terminate all or part of a claim, defense, or entire lawsuit. If the court determines that an actual trial before a factfinder is unnecessary to resolve all or part of those claims or defenses (because no true dispute as to any fact of consequence exists), the court shall grant summary judgment.

---

[1]*See* Rule 12(d). *See also supra* Authors' Commentary to Rule 12(d).

[2]*See Anderson v. Liberty Lobby, Inc.*, 477 U.S. 242, 250–51, 106 S. Ct. 2505, 2511, 91 L. Ed. 2d 202 (1986) (noting that summary judgment standard "mirrors the standard for a directed verdict under Federal Rule of Civil Procedure 50(a), which is that the trial judge must direct a verdict if, under the governing law, there can be but one reasonable conclusion as to the verdict"); *In re Dana Corp.*, 574 F.3d 129, 151–52 (2d Cir. 2009) (principles governing Rule 50 and Rule 56 motions are the same).

APPLICATIONS

2010 Amendments — Amended Rule 56(a)

Former Rules 56(a) and 56(b) explained that both claiming parties and defending parties could move for summary judgment, and either could move with or without supporting affidavits. Although the 2010 Amendments give no indication that any aspect of that former practice has been altered,[3] those two separate Rules have been deleted. In their place, Amended Rule 56(a) now contains the standards for granting summary judgment (also unchanged from prior practice), express authorization for a moving party to seek "partial" summary judgment, and an obligation on the trial court to explain the reasons for its ruling on summary judgment motions.

Motions by Claiming Parties

Summary judgment is not only a defensive tool; claimants can move for summary judgment on their own claims as well.[4]

Motions by Defending Parties

Defending parties may move for summary judgment.[5] Note, however, that the case law is unclear whether moving for summary judgment tolls the time for defending parties to answer a complaint.[6] The filing of an answer is clearly not, however, a prerequisite for filing a summary judgment motion.[7]

Motions by Both Parties (Cross-Motions)

Both parties may seek summary judgment in the same ac-

---

[3]*See* Rule 56(a) (amended 2010) (prescribing broadly that "[a] party" may seek summary judgment); Rule 56(c)(1)(A) (amended 2010) (allowing motions to be supported by affidavits "or other materials"); Rule 56(c)(1)(B) (amended 2010) (allowing motions to be supported by a showing of what summary judgment record does not establish).

[4]*See Alexander v. CareSource*, 576 F.3d 551, 557–58 (6th Cir. 2009); *Bouchat v. Baltimore Ravens Football Club, Inc.*, 346 F.3d 514, 521 (4th Cir. 2003).

[5]*See Jefferson v. Chattanooga Pub. Co.*, 375 F.3d 461, 463 (6th Cir. 2004); *Alexander v. Pathfinder, Inc.*, 189 F.3d 735, 744 (8th Cir. 1999); *Mattei v. Mattei*, 126 F.3d 794, 807 (6th Cir. 1997); *Brill v. Lante Corp.*, 119 F.3d 1266 (7th Cir.1997).

[6]*Compare Poe v. Cristina Copper Mines, Inc*, 15 F.R.D. 85 (D. Del. 1953) (holding that summary judgment motion does not automatically toll the period for answering), and *Albert Levine Assocs., Inc. v. Kershner*, 45 F.R.D. 450, 451 (S.D. N.Y. 1968) (suggesting that belief that summary judgment motion tolled time to answer was "mistaken"), with *Parks v. Doan*, 2007 WL 757649, at *5 n.3 (N.D.Ga. Mar. 6, 2007) (summary judgment motion tolls time to answer) *and Rashidi v. Albright*, 818 F. Supp. 1354 (D. Nev. 1993) (holding that summary judgment motion will toll the period for answering) *aff'd*, 39 F.3d 1188 (9th Cir. 1994) (table). *See also Marquez v. Cable One, Inc.*, 463 F.3d 1118, 1120–21 (10th Cir. 2006) (Rule 12(b)(6) motion, though converted to summary judgment motion, tolls time to answer). *See generally* 10A Charles Alan Wright, Arthur R. Miller, Mary Kay Kane, *Federal Practice & Procedure* § 2718, at 303 to 04 (3d ed. 1998) (opining that Rule 12(a) tolling ought to apply to a pre-answer summary judgment motion).

[7]*See HS Resources, Inc. v. Wingate*, 327 F.3d 432, 440 (5th Cir. 2003).

tion, with "cross-motions" under Rule 56.[8]

Motions by Others

Summary judgment is available only when one party is formally asserting a claim against, or defending against a claim formally asserted by, another party. The rights of parties can only be resolved by summary judgment if claims or defenses are already pending.[9]

Partial Motions

Motions may seek summary judgment as to the entire claim or defense, or just parts of a claim or defense.[10] This entitlement is made explicit in the 2010 amendments to Rule 56(a).[11]

Purpose of Summary Judgment

The purpose of summary judgment is to isolate, and then terminate, claims and defenses that are factually unsupported.[12] It is not a disfavored technical shortcut, but rather an integral component of the Rules.[13] Summary judgment motions must be resolved not only with regard for the rights of those asserting claims and defenses to have their positions heard by a factfinder, but also with due regard for the rights of persons opposing such claims and defenses to demonstrate, under this Rule and *before* trial, that the claims and defenses have no factual basis.[14] Thus, a party moving for summary judgment forces the opponent to come forward with at least one sworn averment of fact essential to that opponent's claims or defenses, before the time-consuming process of litigation will continue.[15] The nonmoving party must do this by showing that there is a genuine dispute requiring a trial.[16] If that party is unable to make that showing, entry of a judgment in favor of the moving party "shall" be granted.[17] As one court has ably described it, a Rule 56 motion is "essentially 'put up or shut up' time for the non-

---

[8]*See infra* Authors' Commentary to Rule 56(a) ("**Stipulated Facts and Cross Motions**").

[9]*See Scottsdale Ins. Co. v. Knox Park Const., Inc.*, 488 F.3d 680, 685 (5th Cir. 2007).

[10]*See Lehr v. City of Sacramento*, 624 F.Supp.2d 1218, 1222–23 (E.D.Cal. 2009); *Leventhal v. Schaffer*, 612 F.Supp.2d 1026, 1037 (N.D.Iowa 2009); *Emigra Group, LLC v. Fragomen, Del Rey, Bernsen & Loewy, LLP*, 612 F.Supp.2d 330, 346 n.52 (S.D.N.Y. 2009).

[11]*See* Rule 56(a) (amended 2010). *See also* Rule 56(a) advisory committee note to 2010 amendments (revisions "make clear" that motions make seek summary judgment as to an entire claim or defense, or just part of

one).

[12]*See Celotex Corp. v. Catrett*, 477 U.S. 317, 323–24, 106 S. Ct. 2548, 2552–53, 91 L. Ed. 2d 265 (1986).

[13]*See Celotex Corp. v. Catrett*, 477 U.S. 317, 327, 106 S. Ct. 2548, 2554, 91 L. Ed. 2d 265 (1986).

[14]*See Celotex Corp. v. Catrett*, 477 U.S. 317, 327, 106 S. Ct. 2548, 2554, 91 L. Ed. 2d 265 (1986).

[15]*See Lujan v. National Wildlife Federation*, 497 U.S. 871, 888–89, 110 S. Ct. 3177, 3188–89, 111 L. Ed. 2d 695 (1990).

[16]*See Beard v. Banks*, 548 U.S. 521, 529, 126 S. Ct. 2572, 2578, 165 L. Ed. 2d 697 (2006).

[17]*See Beard v. Banks*, 548 U.S. 521, 529, 126 S. Ct. 2572, 2578, 165 L.

moving party."[18]

Standards for Granting or Denying Summary Judgment

The 2010 Amendments did *not* change the standard for granting summary judgment.[19] Accordingly, summary judgment shall be granted if the summary judgment record shows that: (1) there is no genuine dispute, (2) as to any material fact, and (3) the moving party is entitled to judgment.[20]

- *Genuine Dispute:*[21] A "genuine dispute" exists (and, thus, summary judgment is improper) when a rational factfinder, considering the evidence in the summary judgment record, could find in favor of the non-moving party.[22] A genuine dispute is not created by a mere "scintilla" of favorable evidence, or evidence that is only "colorable" or insufficiently probative.[23] Nor will summary judgment be defeated if the claim or defense poses a factual scenario that is plainly contradicted by the summary judgment record.[24] When a claim or defense is factually improbable, a more persuasive record will be

---

Ed. 2d 697 (2006).

[18]*See Harney v. Speedway Super-America, LLC*, 526 F.3d 1099, 1104 (7th Cir. 2008); *Berckeley Inv. Group, Ltd. v. Colkitt*, 455 F.3d 195, 201 (3d Cir. 2006).

[19]*See Newell Rubbermaid, Inc. v. Raymond Corp.*, 676 F.3d 521, 533 (6th Cir. 2012); *Del Toro Pacheco v. Pereira*, 633 F.3d 57, 62 n.6 (1st Cir. 2011); *Donnell v. Correctional Health Servs., Inc.*, 405 Fed.Appx. 617, 621 n.3 (3d Cir. 2010). *See generally* Rule 56 advisory committee note to 2010 amendments ("The standard for granting summary judgment remains unchanged."). *See also id.* ("The amendments will not affect continuing development of the decisional law construing and applying" these three inquiries).

[20]*See Beard v. Banks*, 548 U.S. 521, 529, 126 S. Ct. 2572, 2578, 165 L. Ed. 2d 697 (2006); *Department of Commerce v. U.S. House of Representatives*, 525 U.S. 316, 327, 119 S. Ct. 765, 772, 142 L. Ed. 2d 797 (1999); *Nebraska v. Wyoming*, 507 U.S. 584, 589, 113 S. Ct. 1689, 1694, 123 L. Ed. 2d 317 (1993); *Celotex Corp. v. Catrett*, 477 U.S. 317, 322, 106 S. Ct. 2548, 2552, 91 L. Ed. 2d 265 (1986).

[21]The 2010 Amendments replaced the phrase "genuine issue" with "genuine dispute," reasoning that it better reflected the focus of the Rule 56 determination. *See* Rule 56(a) advisory committee note to 2010 amendments.

[22]*See Ricci v. DeStefano*, 557 U.S. 557, 586, 129 S.Ct. 2658, 2677, 174 L.Ed.2d 490 (2009); *Scott v. Harris*, 550 U.S. 372, 380, 127 S. Ct. 1769, 167 L. Ed. 2d 686 (2007); *Anderson v. Liberty Lobby, Inc.*, 477 U.S. 242, 247–252, 106 S. Ct. 2505, 91 L. Ed. 2d 202 (1986); *Matsushita Elec. Indus. Co., Ltd. v. Zenith Radio Corp.*, 475 U.S. 574, 586–587, 106 S. Ct. 1348, 89 L. Ed. 2d 538 (1986).

[23]*See Anderson v. Liberty Lobby, Inc.*, 477 U.S. 242, 247–252, 106 S. Ct. 2505, 91 L. Ed. 2d 202 (1986).

[24]*See Scott v. Harris*, 550 U.S. 372, 380, 127 S. Ct. 1769, 167 L. Ed. 2d 686 (2007) (court should not adopt plaintiff's version of high-speed auto chase that was "blatantly contradicted" by unchallenged videotape evidence); *Carnaby v. City of Houston*, 636 F.3d 183, 187 (5th Cir. 2011) (same). *See also Coble v. City of White House*, 634 F.3d 865, 868–69 (6th Cir. 2011) (the *Scott* principle—no need to credit "visible fiction"—applies not just to conflicting videotape but to all types of objective conflicting evidence).

necessary to stave off summary judgment.[25] The court will test for a "genuine dispute" through the prism of whatever quantum and quality of proof will apply to the claims or defenses. Thus, if the claimant must prove its case by clear and convincing evidence, the court will examine whether the summary judgment record would allow a rational factfinder to find that the claim has been established by clear and convincing evidence.[26]

- *Material Fact:* A fact is "material" if it might affect the outcome of the case.[27] Ergo, whether a fact qualifies as "material" hinges on the substantive law at issue. Disputes (even if "genuine") over irrelevant or unnecessary facts will not defeat a motion for summary judgment.[28]

- *Appropriate As A Matter Of Law:* Judgment is appropriate "as a matter of law" when, in the absence of a genuine dispute of material fact, the moving party should prevail. Thus, the mere fact that the moving party's summary judgment record is uncontested,[29] or even unresponded to,[30] is not enough. But summary judgment is appropriate when the non-moving party fails to make an adequate showing on an essential element of its case, as to which that party has the burden of proof.[31]

District Court *"Shall"* Grant Summary Judgment

This choice of verb has proven controversial, as the drafters, courts, and practitioners debate the proper measure of discretion a district judge ought to retain in resolving a summary

---

[25]See *Matsushita Elec. Indus. Co., Ltd. v. Zenith Radio Corp.*, 475 U.S. 574, 587, 106 S. Ct. 1348, 1356, 89 L. Ed. 2d 538 (1986).

[26]See *Anderson v. Liberty Lobby, Inc.*, 477 U.S. 242, 254, 106 S. Ct. 2505, 2513, 91 L. Ed. 2d 202 (1986).

[27]See *Anderson v. Liberty Lobby, Inc.*, 477 U.S. 242, 248, 106 S. Ct. 2505, 2510, 91 L. Ed. 2d 202 (1986). *See also Wright ex rel. Trust Co. of Kansas v. Abbott Laboratories, Inc.*, 259 F.3d 1226, 1231–32 (10th Cir. 2001) ("material" if, under substantive law, fact is "essential to the proper disposition of the claim"); *Hoffman-Dombrowski v. Arlington Intern. Racecourse, Inc.*, 254 F.3d 644, 650 (7th Cir. 2001) ("material" if fact "might affect the outcome of the suit under the governing law").

[28]See *Anderson v. Liberty Lobby,*

Inc., 477 U.S. 242, 248, 106 S. Ct. 2505, 2510, 91 L. Ed. 2d 202 (1986). *See also Scott v. Harris*, 550 U.S. 372, 380, 127 S. Ct. 1769, 167 L. Ed. 2d 686 (2007); *State Automobile Ins. Co. v. Lawrence*, 358 F.3d 982, 985 (8th Cir. 2004).

[29]See *Edwards v. Aguillard*, 482 U.S. 578, 595, 107 S. Ct. 2573, 96 L. Ed. 2d 510 (1987).

[30]See *Torres-Rosado v. Rotger-Sabat*, 335 F.3d 1, 9 (1st Cir. 2003).

[31]See *Cleveland v. Policy Management Systems Corp.*, 526 U.S. 795, 804, 119 S. Ct. 1597, 1603, 143 L. Ed. 2d 966 (1999); *Celotex Corp. v. Catrett*, 477 U.S. 317, 323, 106 S. Ct. 2548, 2552, 91 L. Ed. 2d 265 (1986); *The News & Observer Publ'g Co. v. Raleigh-Durham Airport Auth.*, 597 F.3d 570, 576 (4th Cir. 2010).

judgment motion.[32] The 2010 Amendments did not settle this controversy, which remains guided only by case law. Ergo, a court *must* deny summary judgment when a genuine dispute of material fact remains to be tried, or where the moving party is not entitled to a judgment as a matter of law.[33] A court also may not decide the motion on the basis of clearly erroneous findings of fact, an improper application of the law, or an erroneous legal standard.[34] In all other contexts, a court enjoys some measure of discretion to grant or deny the motion.[35] Some case language suggests that this discretion might not be very broad.[36] Other precedent suggests differently. For example, summary judgment may be denied where the factual records are "disturbingly thin" or "contain gaps" that could be resolved by readily obtainable evidence,[37] where the court concludes that a fuller factual development is necessary,[38] or where there is some particular reason to believe that the wiser course would be to proceed to trial.[39] In a non-jury / bench trial, the district judge may have more discretion still.[40] Nevertheless, a meritorious summary judgment motion should generally be granted.[41]

---

[32]After many decades as "shall", this verb was changed to "should" during the 2007 "restyling" amendments. *See* Rule 56(c) advisory committee note to 2007 amendments. The 2010 Amendments originally considered changing it again to "must" but decided instead to restore it back to the original "shall" in fear of inadvertently altering the prevailing summary judgment standard. *See* Rule 56(a) advisory committee note to 2010 amendments.

[33]*See Ortiz v. Jordan*, __ U.S. __, __, 131 S.Ct. 884, 891, 178 L.Ed.2d 703 (2011). *See generally* Rule 56 advisory committee note to 2007 amendments.

[34]*See In re Brown*, 342 F.3d 620, 633 (6th Cir. 2003).

[35]*See* Rule 56 advisory committee note to 2007 amendments (citing *Kennedy v. Silas Mason Co.*, 334 U.S. 249, 256–57, 68 S. Ct. 1031, 92 L. Ed. 1347 (1948)). *But cf. Beard v. Banks*, 548 U.S. 521, 529, 126 S. Ct. 2572, 2578, 165 L. Ed. 2d 697 (2006) (noting that, if the non-moving party is unable to demonstrate a genuine issue of material fact, the law "requires" entry of a judgment in favor of the moving party).

[36]*See Beard v. Banks*, 548 U.S. 521, 529, 126 S. Ct. 2572, 2578, 165 L.

Ed. 2d 697 (2006) (if non-moving party fails to show genuine issue of material fact, "the law requires entry of judgment"); *Celotex Corp. v. Catrett*, 477 U.S. 317, 322, 106 S. Ct. 2548, 2552, 91 L. Ed. 2d 265 (1986) ("plain language of Rule 56(b) mandates the entry of summary judgment); *Everett v. Cook County*, 655 F.3d 723, 726 (7th Cir. 2011) (court "must" grant summary judgment if party fails to establishment essential element in party's case); *Bentkowski v. Scene Magazine*, 637 F.3d 689, 693 (6th Cir. 2011) (court "should" grant summary judgment for defendant if plaintiff cannot establish an element of claim).

[37]*See Spratt v. Rhode Island Dept. Of Corrections*, 482 F.3d 33, 43 (1st Cir. 2007).

[38]*See Kennedy v. Silas Mason Co.*, 334 U.S. 249, 68 S. Ct. 1031, 92 L. Ed. 1347 (1948).

[39]*See Anderson v. Liberty Lobby, Inc.*, 477 U.S. 242, 255, 106 S. Ct. 2505, 2513, 91 L. Ed. 2d 202 (1986).

[40]*See Johnson v. Diversicare Afton Oaks, LLC*, 597 F.3d 673, 676 (5th Cir. 2010) (has discretion to decide that evidence could not possibly persuade him or her to a different result).

[41]*See Weigel v. Broad*, 544 F.3d 1143, 1157 (10th Cir. 2008).

Doubts and Inferences

In ruling on a motion for summary judgment, the court will never weigh the evidence or find the facts.[42] Instead, the court's role under Rule 56 is narrowly limited to assessing the threshold issue of whether a genuine dispute exists as to material facts requiring a trial.[43] Thus, the evidence of the non-moving party will be believed as true, all doubts will be resolved against the moving party, all evidence will be construed in the light most favorable to the non-moving party, and all reasonable inferences will be drawn in the non-moving party's favor.[44]

"Reasonable" inferences are inferences reasonably drawn from all the facts then before the court, after sifting through the universe of all possible inferences the facts could support. "Reasonable" inferences need not be necessarily more probable or likely than other inferences that might tilt in the moving party's favor. Instead, so long as more than one reasonable inference can be drawn, and one inference creates a genuine dispute of material fact, the trier of fact is entitled to decide which inference to believe and summary judgment is not appropriate.[45]

Ordinarily, an appropriately supported summary judgment motion cannot be defeated by inferences that are unreasonable or improbable, allegations that are conclusory, or mere speculation and imagination.[46] Nor will a motion be defeated by a posited factual scenario that is clearly contradicted by the summary judgment record,[47] or by the mere promise from the non-moving party that he will later demonstrate the falsity of the

---

[42]See Anderson v. Liberty Lobby, Inc., 477 U.S. 242, 255, 106 S.Ct. 2505, 91 L.Ed.2d 202 (1986); Baranski v. Fifteen Unknown Agents of Bureau of Alcohol, Tobacco and Firearms, 452 F.3d 433, 451 (6th Cir. 2006).

[43]See Anderson v. Liberty Lobby, Inc., 477 U.S. 242, 249, 106 S. Ct. 2505, 2510, 91 L. Ed. 2d 202 (1986).

[44]See Crawford v. Metropolitan Gov't of Nashville & Davidson County, 555 U.S. 271, 274 n.1, 129 S.Ct. 846, 849 n.1, 172 L.Ed.2d 650 (2009); Beard v. Banks, 548 U.S. 521, 530–31, 126 S. Ct. 2572, 2578, 165 L. Ed. 2d 697 (2006); Hunt v. Cromartie, 526 U.S. 541, 550–55, 119 S. Ct. 1545, 1551–52, 143 L. Ed. 2d 731 (1999); Eastman Kodak Co. v. Image Technical Services, Inc., 504 U.S. 451, 456, 112 S. Ct. 2072, 2076, 119 L. Ed. 2d 265 (1992); Anderson v. Liberty Lobby, Inc., 477 U.S. 242, 255, 106 S. Ct. 2505, 2513, 91 L. Ed. 2d 202 (1986); Adickes v. S. H. Kress & Co., 398 U.S. 144, 157–59,

90 S. Ct. 1598, 1608–09, 26 L. Ed. 2d 142 (1970).

[45]See Hunt v. Cromartie, 526 U.S. 541, 552, 119 S. Ct. 1545, 1552, 143 L. Ed. 2d 731 (1999); Patterson & Wilder Const. Co., Inc. v. U.S., 226 F.3d 1269, 1273 (11th Cir. 2000).

[46]See Fabrikant v. French, 691 F.3d 193, 205 (2d Cir. 2012) ("conclusory statements or mere allegations" not sufficient); Linn Farms & Timber Ltd. P'ship v. Union Pac. R. Co., 661 F.3d 354, 357 (8th Cir. 2011) (only reasonable inferences, "without resort to speculation," will be drawn); Bonefont-Igaravidez v. Int'l Shipping Corp., 659 F.3d 120, 123 (1st Cir. 2011) (no deference to "unsupported, subjective, conclusory, or imaginative" statements).

[47]See Scott v. Harris, 550 U.S. 372, 380, 127 S. Ct. 1769, 167 L. Ed. 2d 686 (2007) (court should not adopt plaintiff's version of high-speed auto chase that was "blatantly contradicted" by unchallenged videotape evi-

moving party's facts.[48] "Evidence, not contentions, avoids summary judgment,"[49] and non-moving parties must arrive brandishing more than "a cardboard sword".[50] Alone, an "earnest hope" and "brash conjecture" are not enough.[51]

Credibility Questions

The court will not weigh the credibility of witnesses or other evidence in ruling on a motion for summary judgment.[52] Evaluating credibility, weighing evidence, and drawing factual inferences are all functions reserved for the jury.[53] However, simply lobbing broad, conclusory attacks on a witness's credibility is not enough to defeat summary judgment.[54]

State of Mind Questions

Summary judgment is not automatically foreclosed merely because a person's state of mind (such as motive, knowledge, intent, good faith or bad faith, malice, fraud, conspiracy, or consent) is at issue.[55] But such cases will seldom lend themselves to a summary disposition because questions of credibility will ordinarily abound.[56] Thus, summary judgment is used "sparingly" and "seldom granted" in cases involving peculiarly intensive state of mind questions such as employ-

---

dence).

[48]See *Cutting Underwater Techs. USA, Inc. v. Eni U.S. Operating Co.*, 671 F.3d 512, 517 (5th Cir. 2012); *Island Software and Computer Service, Inc. v. Microsoft Corp.*, 413 F.3d 257, 261–62 (2d Cir. 2005).

[49]See *Al-Zubaidy v. TEK Industries, Inc.*, 406 F.3d 1030, 1036 (8th Cir. 2005).

[50]See *Calvi v. Knox County*, 470 F.3d 422, 426 (1st Cir. 2006).

[51]See *Balser v. Int'l Union of Elec., Elec., Salaried, Mach. & Furniture Workers (IUE) Local 201*, 661 F.3d 109, 118 (1st Cir. 2011).

[52]See *Anderson v. Liberty Lobby, Inc.*, 477 U.S. 242, 255, 106 S.Ct. 2505, 91 L.Ed.2d 202 (1986); *Kaytor v. Electric Boat Corp.*, 609 F.3d 537, 546 (2d Cir. 2010). See also *Reeves v. Sanderson Plumbing Prods., Inc.*, 530 U.S. 133, 150–51, 120 S.Ct. 2097, 147 L.Ed.2d 105 (2000) (comparing Rule 50 standard).

[53]See *Anderson v. Liberty Lobby, Inc.*, 477 U.S. 242, 255, 106 S. Ct. 2505, 2513, 91 L. Ed. 2d 202 (1986).

[54]See *Deville v. Marcantel*, 567 F.3d 156, 165 (5th Cir. 2009); *Levesque*

v. Doocy, 560 F.3d 82, 87 (1st Cir. 2009); *Island Software and Computer Service, Inc. v. Microsoft Corp.*, 413 F.3d 257, 261–62 (2d Cir. 2005).

[55]See *S.E.C. v. Ficken*, 546 F.3d 45, 51 (1st Cir. 2008); *Ward v. Bechtel Corp.*, 102 F.3d 199, 202 (5th Cir. 1997); *Ennis v. National Ass'n of Bus. & Educ. Radio, Inc.*, 53 F.3d 55, 62, 10 A.D.D. 113 (4th Cir. 1995).

[56]See *Hutchinson v. Proxmire*, 443 U.S. 111, 99 S. Ct. 2675, 61 L. Ed. 2d 411 (1979). See also *Graham v. Long Island R.R.*, 230 F.3d 34, 38 (2d Cir. 2000) (commenting that summary judgment is used "sparingly" where intent and state of mind are implicated); *EMI Catalogue Partnership v. Hill, Holliday, Connors, Cosmopulos Inc.*, 228 F.3d 56, 61 (2d Cir. 2000) ("caution" must be observed with issues involving defendant's intent); *Seamons v. Snow*, 206 F.3d 1021, 1027–28 (10th Cir. 2000) (noting that grant of summary judgment is "especially questionable" in cases delving into party's state of mind); *U.S. ex rel. Cantekin v. University of Pittsburgh*, 192 F.3d 402, 411 (3d Cir. 1999) (noting "basic rule" that state of mind issues typically should not be decided on summary judgment).

ment discrimination actions,[57] antitrust cases,[58] and certain intellectual property disputes.[59]

Predominantly Legal Disputes

Summary judgment is often appropriate in cases where the remaining unresolved disputes are primarily legal, rather than factual in nature.[60]

Stipulated Facts and Cross-Motions

If the parties stipulate to the facts, obviously no genuine dispute as to material facts then exists for a factfinder to resolve.[61] Nevertheless, the summary judgment standard remains the same. The court must draw inferences from the stipulated facts, and resolve those inferences in favor of the non-moving party.[62] Cross-motions for summary judgment are also examined under the usual Rule 56 standards.[63] Each cross-

---

[57]*See Bagley v. Blagojevich*, 646 F.3d 378, 389 (7th Cir. 2011) (although no special rule exists for, and summary judgment can be proper in, discrimination cases, courts must not grant where intent is properly contested); *Gorzynski v. Jetblue Airways Corp.*, 596 F.3d 93, 101 (2d Cir. 2010) ("caution" needed in employment discrimination cases); *Peterson v. Scott County*, 406 F.3d 515, 521 (8th Cir. 2005) ("seldom" granted in employment discrimination cases).

[58]*See Smith Wholesale Co., Inc. v. R.J. Reynolds Tobacco Co.*, 477 F.3d 854, 862 (6th Cir. 2007) (disfavored, but not precluded, in antitrust litigation); *Ashley Creek Phosphate Co. v. Chevron USA, Inc.*, 315 F.3d 1245, 1253 (10th Cir. 2003) ("sparingly" in antitrust cases). *See also Southeast Missouri Hosp. v. C.R. Bard, Inc.*, 642 F.3d 608, 612 (8th Cir. 2011) (but "no different or heightened summary judgment standard" applies). *But cf. In re Publ'n Paper Antitrust Litig.*, 690 F.3d 51, 61 (2d Cir. 2012) (noting how summary judgment can serve a "vital function" in antitrust cases by avoiding a chilling effect on pro-competitive market forces).

[59]*See Zobmondo Entm't, LLC v. Falls Media, LLC*, 602 F.3d 1108, 1113 (9th Cir. 2010) ("disfavored in the trademark arena"); *Latimer v. Roaring Toyz, Inc.*, 601 F.3d 1224, 1232 (11th Cir. 2010) ("historically viewed . . . as inappropriate in the copyright infringement context").

[60]*See Thomas v. Metropolitan Life Ins. Co.*, 631 F.3d 1153, 1160 (10th Cir. 2011); *Koehn v. Indian Hills Community College*, 371 F.3d 394, 396 (8th Cir. 2004).

[61]*See Cincom Sys., Inc. v. Novelis Corp.*, 581 F.3d 431, 435 (6th Cir. 2009); *Centennial Ins. Co. v. Ryder Truck Rental, Inc.*, 149 F.3d 378 (5th Cir.1998); *Luden's Inc. v. Local Union No. 6 of Bakery, Confectionery and Tobacco Workers' Intern. Union of America*, 28 F.3d 347, 353 (3d Cir. 1994).

[62]*See Leebaert v. Harrington*, 332 F.3d 134, 138–39 (2d Cir. 2003); *Luden's Inc. v. Local Union No. 6 of Bakery, Confectionery and Tobacco Workers' Intern. Union of America*, 28 F.3d 347, 353 (3d Cir. 1994). *But see United Paperworkers Intern. Union Local 14, AFL-CIO-CLC v. International Paper Co.*, 64 F.3d 28, 31 (1st Cir. 1995) (noting that summary judgment standard may be modified where dispute arrives as a "case stated"; in that instance, trial judge is free to engage in certain factfinding, including the drawing of inferences). *But see also U.S. Fidelity and Guar. Co. v. Planters Bank & Trust Co.*, 77 F.3d 863, 866 (5th Cir. 1996) (noting that court of appeals recognizes a "hint of a distinction" between the standard applied in jury cases and an arguably more lenient standard in certain non-jury cases).

[63]*See Saieg v. City of Dearborn*, 641 F.3d 727, 733–34 (6th Cir. 2011);

motion must be evaluated on its own merits,[64] with the court viewing all facts and reasonable inferences in the light most favorable to the nonmoving party.[65] Thus, the mere fact that cross-motions have been filed does not, by itself, necessarily justify the entry of a summary judgment,[66] nor will the denial of one cross-motion compel the grant of the other cross-motion.[67]

Trial Court's Duty to Explain

Amended Rule 56(a) directs trial judges to set forth, "on the record," the reasons for their disposition of summary judgment motions, although the particular form and content of that explanation is left to the court's discretion.[68] This requirement was added to facilitate both subsequent trial-level proceedings and appeals.[69]

Supreme Court's Original Jurisdiction

These standards do not technically control summary judgment in cases where the Supreme Court is sitting in its original jurisdiction, but the Court has embraced them as a guide.[70]

Effect of Ruling—"Law Of The Case"

The "law of the case" doctrine holds that when a court decides upon a rule of law, that decision should generally control the same issues throughout the subsequent stages in the same case.[71] It is based on the sound, salutary policy of judicial finality—that all litigation should come to an end.[72] This is a prudential doctrine; it guides and influences the

---

Wells Real Estate Inv. Trust II, Inc. v. Chardon / Hato Rey P'ship, S.E., 615 F.3d 45, 51 (1st Cir. 2010); *Bronx Household of Faith v. Board of Educ. of City of New York*, 492 F.3d 89, 96–97 (2d Cir. 2007).

[64]*See Retail Ventures, Inc. v. National Union Fire Ins. Co.*, 691 F.3d 821, 826 (6th Cir. 2012); *Certain Interested Underwriters at Lloyd's, London v. Stolberg*, 680 F.3d 61, 65 (1st Cir. 2012); *Marcatante v. City of Chicago*, 657 F.3d 433, 438–39 (7th Cir. 2011).

[65]*See Edwards v. Briggs & Stratton Ret. Plan*, 639 F.3d 355, 359 (7th Cir. 2011); *Tidewater Inc. v. U.S.*, 565 F.3d 299, 302 (5th Cir. 2009); *Pichler v. UNITE*, 542 F.3d 380, 386 (3d Cir. 2008).

[66]*See Marcatante v. City of Chicago*, 657 F.3d 433, 438–39 (7th Cir. 2011); *Ferro Corp. v. Cookson Group, PLC*, 585 F.3d 946, 949 (6th Cir. 2009); *Atlantic Richfield Co. v. Farm Credit Bank of Wichita*, 226 F.3d 1138, 1148 (10th Cir. 2000).

[67]*See Christian Heritage Academy v. Oklahoma Secondary School Activities Ass'n*, 483 F.3d 1025, 1030 (10th Cir. 2007).

[68]*See* Rule 56(a) advisory committee note to 2010 amendments.

[69]*See* Rule 56(a) advisory committee note to 2010 amendments.

[70]*See* Sup. Ct. R. 17.2. *See also Alabama v. North Carolina*, __ U.S. __, __, 130 S.Ct. 2295, 2308, 176 L. Ed. 2d 1070 (2010).

[71]*See Arizona v. California*, 460 U.S. 605, 618, 103 S. Ct. 1382, 1391, 75 L. Ed. 2d 318 (1983); *Gander Mountain Co. v. Cabela's, Inc.*, 540 F.3d 827, 830 (8th Cir. 2008).

[72]*See Lyons v. Fisher*, 888 F.2d 1071 (5th Cir. 1989). *See also Gindes v. U.S.*, 740 F.2d 947, 949 (Fed. Cir. 1984) (commenting that doctrine rests upon important public policy litigants do not enjoy the right to cover the same ground twice, hoping that passage of time or changes in court's composition will alter outcome).

court's exercise of discretion, but it does not limit the court's jurisdiction or power.[73] It may not apply where intervening controlling authority warrants a revisiting of an earlier decision.[74] Because *denials* of summary judgment generally do nothing more than acknowledge that a genuine issue of material fact remains for trial, such denials are typically not accorded any preclusive effect nor do they become "law of the case".[75] The same is true for other interlocutory rulings that preceded the entry of summary judgment.[76]

Constitutionality of Summary Judgment

Only once has the Supreme Court examined the constitutionality of summary judgment, on a claim that the procedure deprives defeated claimants of their Seventh Amendment rights to a trial by jury. The Court rejected this argument, reasoning that any time summary judgment is granted, it is only because there *is* no triable issue for the jury.[77] No lower federal court has ever declared summary judgment unconstitutional.

Appealability

The general rule is that an order granting summary judgment is appealable only when (1) it constitutes the "final order" in the case,[78] or (2) it constitutes a partial summary judgment that resolves one claim (among multiple claims) or one party (among multiple parties) and is accompanied by a proper Rule 54(b) determination from the trial court.[79] The appealability of an order denying summary judgment is less simple. If the denial is based on the presence of genuinely disputed facts, that order decides merely that the case must continue; it nei-

---

[73]*See Arizona v. California*, 460 U.S. 605, 618, 103 S. Ct. 1382, 1391, 75 L. Ed. 2d 318 (1983); *Sejman v. Warner-Lambert Co., Inc.*, 845 F.2d 66, 68–69 (4th Cir. 1988).

[74]*See Marable v. Nitchman*, 511 F.3d 924, 930 n.11 (9th Cir. 2007).

[75]*See Switzerland Cheese Ass'n, Inc. v. E. Horne's Market, Inc.*, 385 U.S. 23, 25, 87 S. Ct. 193, 17 L. Ed. 2d 23 (1966); *Rigby v. Damant*, 486 F.3d 692, 692–93 (1st Cir. 2007); *Murphy v. Missouri Dept. of Corrections*, 372 F.3d 979, 986 (8th Cir. 2004); *Kovacevich v. Kent State University*, 224 F.3d 806 (6th Cir. 2000). *But see Federal Ins. Co. v. Scarsella Bros., Inc.*, 931 F.2d 599, 601 (9th Cir. 1991) (holding that doctrine is not amenable to such broad generalizations, and may apply to summary judgment denials when trial court intends to resolve definitively the legal questions in issue).

[76]*See Gander Mountain Co. v.* *Cabela's, Inc.*, 540 F.3d 827, 830–31 (8th Cir. 2008) (arguably inconsistent discovery rulings); *Elephant Butte Irr. Dist. of New Mexico v. U.S. Dept. of Interior*, 538 F.3d 1299, 1306 (10th Cir. 2008) (same).

[77]*See Fidelity & Deposit Co. v. U.S.*, 187 U.S. 315, 319–21, 23 S.Ct. 120, 47 L.Ed. 194 (1902). *See alsp J.R. Simplot v. Chevron Pipeline Co.*, 563 F.3d 1102 (10th Cir. 2009) (declaring Seventh Amendment question "well-settled"). *But see* Suja A. Thomas, *Why Summary Judgment is Unconstitutional*, 93 VA. L. REV. 139 (2007) (arguing why Rule 56 violates the Seventh Amendment).

[78]*See Santaella v. Metropolitan Life Ins. Co.*, 123 F.3d 456, 461 (7th Cir. 1997). *See also* 28 U.S.C.A. § 1291.

[79]*See* Rule 54(b). *See also Bonner v. Perry*, 564 F.3d 424, 427 (6th Cir. 2009).

ther finally settles nor tentatively resolves anything else about the merits.[80] For this reason, it is ordinarily not immediately appealable[81] (unless the effect of the denial is to fully resolve all issues and cause entry of a final judgment).[82] In fact, several courts hold that, once a trial on the merits occurs, the order can never be reviewed, because the "prediction" that denial represented has been rendered moot by the actual introduction of evidence at trial.[83] Other courts recognize an exception to this general prohibition, and permit a summary judgment denial to be reviewed on appeal if the denial was based on the interpretation of a pure question of law.[84] Other courts narrow the exception still further, permitting review when the denial was based on a pure question of law and the judge was the factfinder (non-jury, bench trial).[85] Other courts hold that, although such review is generally denied, an appeal might be tolerated were "extraordinary circumstances" to exist.[86] Mindful of the variety of these approaches and the uncertainty they introduce, prudent practitioners should always renew summary judgment motions with a Rule 50 motion for judgment as a matter of law at the close of the evidence (and, if rejected, again after the trial has concluded).[87]

- *Exceptions:* Practitioners must be wary. Exceptions to even these rules exist. For example, if the motion asserts questions of immunity from suit, a denial of summary judgment may be immediately appealable.[88] Similarly, a denial of a cross-motion for summary judg-

---

[80]*See Switzerland Cheese Ass'n, Inc. v. E. Horne's Market, Inc.*, 385 U.S. 23, 25, 87 S. Ct. 193, 195, 17 L. Ed. 2d 23 (1966).

[81]*See Ortiz v. Jordan,* __ U.S. __, __, 131 S.Ct. 884, 891, 178 L.Ed.2d 703 (2011).

[82]*See Karuk Tribe of Cal. v. U.S. Forest Serv.*, 640 F.3d 979, 987 (9th Cir. 2011);

[83]*See Varghese v. Honeywell Int'l, Inc.*, 424 F.3d 411, 420–23 (4th Cir. 2005); *Lind v. United Parcel Serv., Inc.*, 254 F.3d 1281, 1283–86 (11th Cir. 2001); *Mauser v. Raytheon Co. Pension Plan for Salaried Employees*, 239 F.3d 51, 55 (1st Cir. 2001); *Black v. J.I. Case Co.*, 22 F.3d 568, 570–72 (5th Cir. 1994). *Cf. Travelers Cas. & Sur. Co. v. Ins. Co. of N. America*, 609 F.3d 143, 167 n.32 (3d Cir. 2010) (court need not decide whether case presented "one of those rare instances" which permitted review of summary judgment denial following merits trial).

[84]*See HOK Sport, Inc. v. FC Des*

Moines, L.C., 495 F.3d 927, 942 (8th Cir. 2007); *Banuelos v. Construction Laborers' Trust Funds for So. Cal.*, 382 F.3d 897, 902–03 (9th Cir. 2004); *Rose v. Uniroyal Goodrich Tire Co.*, 219 F.3d 1216, 1221 n.3 (10th Cir. 2000).

[85]*See Becker v. Tidewater, Inc.*, 586 F.3d 358, 365 n.4 (5th Cir. 2009).

[86]*See Pahuta v. Massey-Ferguson, Inc.*, 170 F.3d 125, 132 (2d Cir. 1999).

[87]*See HOK Sport, Inc. v. FC Des Moines, L.C.*, 495 F.3d 927, 942 (8th Cir. 2007); *Chemetall GMBH v. ZR Energy, Inc.*, 320 F.3d 714, 718–19 (7th Cir. 2003); *Wolfgang v. Mid-America Motorsports, Inc.*, 111 F.3d 1515, 1521 (10th Cir. 1997).

[88]*See Ortiz v. Jordan,* __ U.S. __, __, 131 S.Ct. 884, 891, 178 L.Ed.2d 703 (2011); *Swint v. Chambers County Com'n*, 514 U.S. 35, 115 S. Ct. 1203, 131 L. Ed. 2d 60 (1995) *Mitchell v. Forsyth*, 472 U.S. 511, 530, 105 S. Ct. 2806, 2817, 86 L. Ed. 2d 411 (1985). *But cf. Jones v. City of Jackson*, 203 F.3d 875, 878 (5th Cir. 2000) (even

ment may be immediately appealable along with a challenge to that portion of the cross-motion that was granted.[89]

RULE 56(b) — TIME TO FILE A MOTION

CORE CONCEPT

Parties may move for summary judgment at any time until 30 days after the close of all discovery, absent a local rule or court order directing otherwise. The time for responding to motions is left undefined, to be set by local rule or court order.

APPLICATIONS

2010 Amendments — Amended Rule 56(b)

The Rules had earlier experimented with national "default" time periods for filing, opposing, and replying to summary judgment motions.[90] Presently, however, only the filing default period remains—all others were rescinded in 2009.

Time for Filing

A national timing procedure governs summary judgment motions, permitting their filing at any time "until 30 days after the close of discovery".[91] This procedure is only a "default" provision, however, and can be modified freely by local rule or court order.[92] Indeed, noting that timing rules specially tailored to the needs of a particular case "are likely to work better," the drafters anticipate that this default rule is likely to be modified "in most cases" by case-specific scheduling orders, periods proposed by the parties, case staging regimes, or local rules.[93] Under a former version of the Rule, a claimant had to wait 20-days after commencing the action before becoming eligible to file for summary judgment; that restriction, deemed "outmoded"

---

with immunity motions, summary judgment denials are not immediately appealable if disputed and material factual issues are present).

[89] *See Stilwell v. American Gen. Life Ins. Co.*, 555 F.3d 572, 576 (7th Cir. 2009); *Levy v. Sterling Holding Co., LLC*, 544 F.3d 493, 501 n.6 (3d Cir. 2008); *Barr v. Lafon*, 538 F.3d 554, 562 (6th Cir. 2008).

[90] *See* Rule 56(c)(1)(A) to (C) (amended 2009; deleted 2010).

[91] *See* Rule 56(b) (amended 2010). *Note:* the syntax of this Rule includes a somewhat ambiguous use of the word "until". Because "until" could connote the last of the permitted days, or the first of the forbidden days, this word choice is not ideal. When read in conjunction with the 2009 amend-

ments to Rule 6(a)(1)(C) and Rule 6(a)(4), however, the most reasonable reading seems to be that this "until" period runs to the close of the 30th day after the end of discovery.

[92] *See Hoffman v. Tonnemacher*, 593 F.3d 908, 911 (9th Cir. 2010) (case-specific, tailored scheduling orders "are likely to work better than default rules").

[93] *See* Rule 56(c)(1) advisory committee notes to 2009 amendments. *See also Moss v. Wyeth, Inc.*, ___ F. Supp. 2d ___, ___, 2012 WL 1802445, at *4 (D.Conn. 2012) (motion timely if comports with scheduling order); *Diez v. Washington Mut. Bank*, 2012 WL 601454, at *4 (E.D.N.Y. Feb. 23, 2012) (motion timely if comports with court-set schedule).

by the drafters, was deleted in 2009.[94] In current practice, unless local rules or scheduling orders provide otherwise, motions for summary judgment are timely even if filed before an answer or dismissal motion.[95]

Filing Too Quickly (or Before Discovery)

Early summary judgment motions (those filed at the time the lawsuit is commenced or otherwise before discovery) are clearly permitted, unless foreclosed by local rules or scheduling orders.[96] Such filings, though consistent with some prior case law,[97] seemed at odds with the Supreme Court's admonition in 1986 that summary judgment should be granted only after the nonmoving party had an "adequate time for discovery".[98] The drafters addressed this issue obliquely in 2009 and again in 2010, noting that motions filed at commencement, though permitted, may prove premature[99] and, if so, courts may readily extend the response time.[100] Seeking a deferral of a ruling pending further discovery also always remains an option for the nonmoving party.[101] In any event, in practice, pre-discovery summary judgment motions prove to be the exception, not the norm.[102]

---

[94]*See* Rule 56(c)(1) advisory committee notes to 2009 amendments. In current practice, unless local rules or scheduling orders provide otherwise, motions for summary judgment are timely even if filed before an answer or dismissal motion.

[95]*See Charvat v. ACO, Inc.*, 2012 WL 847328, at *4 (D.Neb. Mar. 13, 2012); *Taylor v. Lantagne*, 2012 WL 256170, at *2 (W.D.Mich. Jan. 27, 2012).

[96]*See* Rule 56(b) advisory committee note to 2010 amendments.

[97]*See, e.g., Alholm v. American Steamship Co.*, 144 F.3d 1172, 1177 (8th Cir. 1998) (noting that Rule 56 does not require that discovery be closed before motion can be heard); *G & G Fire Sprinklers, Inc. v. Bradshaw*, 136 F.3d 587 (9th Cir. 1998) (rejecting argument that plaintiff's motion for summary judgment was "premature" when it was filed more than 20 days after lawsuit was commenced and no motion under Rule 56(f) was pending); *Brill v. Lante Corp.*, 119 F.3d 1266, 1275 (7th Cir. 1997) (commenting that plaintiff's argument that summary judgment should not have been granted while discovery remained open is an argument that "hardly

concerns us because a party can file a motion for summary judgment at any time, indeed, even before discovery has begun").

[98]*Celotex Corp. v. Catrett*, 477 U.S. 317, 322, 106 S. Ct. 2548, 2552, 91 L. Ed. 2d 265 (1986).

[99]*See* Rule 56(b) advisory committee note to 2010 amendments.

[100]*See* Rule 56(c)(1) advisory committee note to 2009 amendments.

[101]*See* Rule 56(d) (formerly Rule 56(f)). *See also Koehnke v. City of McKeesport*, 350 Fed.Appx. 720, 723 (3d Cir. 2009).

[102]*See Doe v. Abington Friends Sch.*, 480 F.3d 252, 257 (3d Cir. 2007) ("well established" that opposing party must be given "adequate opportunity to obtain discovery"); *Information Handling Servs., Inc. v. Defense Automated Printing Servs.*, 338 F.3d 1024, 1032 (D.C. Cir. 2003) (summary judgment is ordinarily proper only when plaintiff has had adequate time for discovery); *Miller v. Wolpoff & Abramson, L.L.P.*, 321 F.3d 292, 303–04 (2d Cir. 2003) (pre-discovery summary judgment granted in only rarest cases); *Vaughn v. U.S. Small Business Admin.*, 65 F.3d 1322, 1325 n. 1 (6th Cir. 1995) (defendant's sum-

Time for Responding

The national 21-day time period for responding to summary judgment motions had a brief life, adopted in December 2009 and rescinded in December 2010.[103] The current response period, therefore, reverts back to the prior practice as adopted by local rule and chambers orders. Relying on prior Rule language, many courts had previously held that the response period must be at least 10-days long,[104] although this minimum could be excused if the non-moving party had sufficient opportunity to oppose the motion or if no further materials could have been developed during the period that would have defeated the motion.[105] Absent local rule or chambers order, it is as yet unclear whether courts will revert to this earlier approach.

RULE 56(c) — PROCEDURES

CORE CONCEPT

Several summary judgment procedures are nationally defined: the manner for factually supporting motions and oppositions; the method for objecting to improper support for motions or oppositions; the content of the summary judgment record; and the proper content for supporting or opposing affidavits and declarations. Other summary judgment procedures developed through case law over time.

APPLICATIONS

2010 Amendments — Amended Rule 56(c)

Former Rule 56(c) set out the national "default" time schedule for summary judgment practice and the legal standard for granting summary judgment. What remains of that timing schedule has now been relocated to amended Rule 56(b), and the legal standard now appears in amended Rule 56(a). The current content of Rule 56(c) includes the affidavit requirements (formerly in Rule 56(e)(1)), a recasting of the opposition requirements (formerly in Rule 56(e)(2) and as described in the Supreme Court's *Celotex* decision), and two new provisions addressing objections to improper factual support and the content of the summary judgment record.

Procedure #1: Supporting Factual Positions

Parties moving for summary judgment have the burden of

---

mary judgment motion cannot ordinarily be considered until the plaintiff has had the opportunity to conduct discovery).

[103]*See* Rule 56(c)(1)(B) (amended 2009; deleted 2010).

[104]*See* Rule 56(c) (rescinded 2007) ("The motion shall be served at least 10 days before the time fixed for the

hearing.").

[105]*See Moses v. Providence Hosp. & Med. Ctrs., Inc.*, 561 F.3d 573, 584 (6th Cir. 2009); *Celestine v. Petroleos de Venezuella SA*, 266 F.3d 343, 350 (5th Cir. 2001); *Restigouche, Inc. v. Town of Jupiter*, 59 F.3d 1208, 1213 (11th Cir. 1995).

"identifying" each claim, defense, or part thereof on which they seek summary judgment.[106] In addition, parties moving for, or resisting, summary judgment have the further burden to factually support their positions. They must discharge that obligation of factual support in either of two ways:

- *First*, they may cite the court to certain parts of the summary judgment record (which may contain depositions, documents, electronically stored information, affidavits or declarations, stipulations, admissions, interrogatory answers, and other materials). In doing so, their citation must be specific and to "particular parts" of the record materials.[107]

- *Second*, they may show either (a) that the materials cited by their opponent do not establish the absence or presence of a genuine dispute or (b) that the opponent cannot produce admissible evidence to support the claimed fact.[108]

This procedure seems to essentially codify the burden-shifting summary judgment procedure described by the Supreme Court in *Celotex Corp. v. Catrett*.[109] As the Court outlined it, the party moving for summary judgment always has the burden of persuasion on such a motion. The burden of going forward, however, shifts during the motion process.

The moving party must first make a prima facie showing that summary judgment is appropriate under Rule 56 — that is, the movant must properly "put the ball in play".[110] This does not require the moving party to disprove the opponent's claims or defenses.[111] Instead, this prima facie burden may be discharged simply by pointing out for the court an absence of evidence in support of the non-moving party's claims or defenses.[112] However, where the moving party is the party with the ultimate burden of proof at trial, the prima facie burden is often higher, requiring that party to show that it can, in fact,

---

[106] *See* Rule 56(a).

[107] *See* Rule 56(c)(1)(A). *See also Seng-Tiong Ho v. Taflove*, 648 F.3d 489, 496 (7th Cir. 2011). *See generally* Rule 56(c)(1)(A) advisory committee note to 2010 amendments.

[108] *See* Rule 56(c)(1)(B). *See also Seng-Tiong Ho v. Taflove*, 648 F.3d 489, 496 (7th Cir. 2011). *See generally* Rule 56(c)(1)(A) advisory committee note to 2010 amendments.

[109] *Celotex Corp. v. Catrett*, 477 U.S. 317, 106 S. Ct. 2548, 91 L. Ed. 2d 265 (1986). *See also* Rep. of Jud. Conf. Comm. on Rules of Practice & Procedure at 14 (Sept. 2009) ("The proposed amendments are not intended to

change the summary-judgment standard or burdens.") (available at http://www.uscourts.gov/uscourts/RulesAnd Policies/rules/Reports/Combined__S T__Report__Sept__2009.pdf).

[110] *See Evans Cabinet Corp. v. Kitchen In'l, Inc.*, 593 F.3d 135, 140 (1st Cir. 2010).

[111] *See Edwards v. Aguillard*, 482 U.S. 578, 595, 107 S. Ct. 2573, 96 L. Ed. 2d 510 (1987); *Celotex Corp. v. Catrett*, 477 U.S. 317, 323, 106 S. Ct. 2548, 2553, 91 L. Ed. 2d 265 (1986).

[112] *See Celotex Corp. v. Catrett*, 477 U.S. 317, 106 S. Ct. 2548, 2553, 91 L. Ed. 2d 265 (1986). *See also* Rule 56(c)(1)(B).

carry its burden of proving all essential elements of its claim or defense.[113] If the moving party meets its prima facie burden, then the burden of going forward shifts to the non-moving party to show, by affidavit or otherwise, that a genuine dispute of material fact remains for the factfinder to resolve.[114] The non-moving party must carry this burden as to each essential element on which it bears the burden of proof.[115] Thus, once this summary judgment stage arrives, the non-moving party is not saved by mere allegations or denials,[116] assertions in legal memoranda or argument,[117] speculation,[118] conclusory statements,[119] or simply recounting the generous notice-pleading standards of the federal courts.[120] Nor will an "earnest hope" to discover evidence,[121] or a promise to come forward later with proof, suffice.[122] The party must show evidence.[123] A party does *not* meet this burden simply by theorizing a "plausible scenario" in support of the party's claims, when that proffered scenario conflicts with direct, contrary evidence.[124]

Procedure #2: Objecting to Improper Support

Materials offered to support or oppose a fact during summary judgment briefing must be capable of being offered at trial in an admissible form.[125] (Generally, this does not mean that the materials themselves must be presented in an admissible form during the summary judgment briefing, only that an

---

[113]*See J.S. ex rel. Snyder v. Blue Mountain Sch. Dist.*, 650 F.3d 915, 925 (3d Cir. 2011); *Mauerhan v. Wagner Corp.*, 649 F. 3d 1180, 1185 (10th Cir. 2011); *VRV Dev't L.P. v. Mid-Continent Cas. Co.*, 630 F.3d 451, 455 (5th Cir. 2011).

[114]*See Celotex Corp. v. Catrett*, 477 U.S. 317, 106 S. Ct. 2548, 91 L. Ed. 2d 265 (1986). *See also Beard v. Banks*, 548 U.S. 521, 529, 126 S. Ct. 2572, 2578, 165 L. Ed. 2d 697 (2006).

[115]*See Wheeler v. Aventis Pharmaceuticals*, 360 F.3d 853, 857 (8th Cir. 2004).

[116]*See First Nat. Bank of Ariz. v. Cities Service Co.*, 391 U.S. 253, 289, 88 S. Ct. 1575, 1592, 20 L. Ed. 2d 569 (1968); *Seng-Tiong Ho v. Taflove*, 648 F.3d 489, 496–97 (7th Cir. 2011); *Rivera-Colon v. Mills*, 635 F.3d 9, 12 (1st Cir. 2011).

[117]*See Berckeley Inv. Group, Ltd. v. Colkitt*, 455 F.3d 195, 201 (3d Cir. 2006).

[118]*See Linn Farms & Timber Ltd. P'ship v. Union Pac. R. Co.*, 661 F.3d 354, 357 (8th Cir. 2011); *Rivera-Colon v. Mills*, 635 F.3d 9, 12 (1st Cir. 2011).

[119]*See Fabrikant v. French*, 691 F.3d 193, 205 (2d Cir. 2012); *Bonefont-Igaravidez v. Int'l Shipping Corp.*, 659 F.3d 120, 123 (1st Cir. 2011).

[120]*See Tucker v. Union of Needletrades, Industrial and Textile Employees*, 407 F.3d 784, 788 (6th Cir. 2005).

[121]*See Balser v. Int'l Union of Elec., Elec., Salaried, Mach. & Furniture Workers (IUE) Local 201*, 661 F.3d 109, 118 (1st Cir. 2011).

[122]*See Cutting Underwater Techs. USA, Inc. v. Eni U.S. Operating Co.*, 671 F.3d 512, 517 (5th Cir. 2012); *Island Software & Computer Serv., Inc. v. Microsoft Corp.*, 413 F.3d 257, 261–62 (2d Cir. 2005).

[123]*See Al-Zubaidy v. TEK Industries, Inc.*, 406 F.3d 1030, 1036 (8th Cir. 2005) ("Evidence, not contentions, avoids summary judgment").

[124]*See Scott v. Harris*, 550 U.S. 372, 380, 127 S. Ct. 1769, 1774–76, 167 L. Ed. 2d 686 (U.S. 2007); *Swanson v. Leggett & Platt, Inc.*, 154 F.3d 730, 733 (7th Cir. 1998).

[125]*See* Rule 56(c)(2). *See also Cooper v. AlliedBarton Sec. Servs.*, 422 Fed.Appx. 33, 34 (2d Cir. 2011);

admissible form exists by which those facts may be later introduced at trial.)[126] A party may object that the opponent has supported a position (either seeking or opposing summary judgment) by material that cannot be presented at trial in a form that would be admissible as evidence.[127] The objections must specifically explain what particular exhibit is improper and why.[128] Once made, the objection shifts the burden to the opponent to defend the contested material as admissible in its current form or to explain some other anticipated form by which it may be admitted.[129] Failure to make this objection does not forfeit a later objection to admissibility at time of trial.[130]

The objection contemplated by this section is narrow: that the relied upon material cannot be presented in an admissible form. Whether other objections are permitted under this Rule is unclear. Under prior practice, a party objecting to summary judgment materials on other grounds (*e.g.*, that an affiant lacked personal knowledge or was incompetent) was compelled to objected in a timely fashion or risk forfeiting the objection entirely.[131] This procedure developed, examined one court, to avoid the objecting party playing the game of "dog-in-the-manger" — fighting the summary judgment motion on its merits and only later, if unsuccessful, unveiling technical objections as a hidden "ace".[132] Prior to the 2010 Amendments, the courts were also divided as to whether an improper affidavit could be challenged on a motion to strike.[133] Those that allowed the practice often compelled it on risk of waiver,[134] though courts were admonished in ruling on such motions to use "a scalpel,

---

Hernandez v. Yellow Transp., Inc., 641 F.3d 118, 124–25 (5th Cir. 2011).

[126]*See Trevizo v. Adams*, 455 F.3d 1155, 1160 (10th Cir. 2006); *Miller v. Glenn Miller Productions, Inc.*, 454 F.3d 975, 988 (9th Cir. 2006); *Cottrill v. MFA, Inc.*, 443 F.3d 629, 635–36 (8th Cir. 2006); *Stinnett v. Iron Works Gym/Executive Health Spa, Inc.*, 301 F.3d 610, 613 (7th Cir. 2002). *See also Celotex Corp. v. Catrett*, 477 U.S. 317, 324, 106 S. Ct. 2548, 2553, 91 L. Ed. 2d 265 (1986) (commenting that party need not depose its own witnesses in order to defeat a summary judgment motion). Indeed, the most frequently submitted support on a summary judgment motion—affidavits—will rarely (if ever) be admissible at trial in the absence of the affiant.

[127]*See* Rule 56(c)(2).

[128]*See Haack v. City of Carson City*, 2012 WL 3638767, at *6 (D.Nev. Aug. 22, 2012); *Halebian v. Berv*, __ F.

Supp. 2d __, __ n.24, 2012 WL 3132683, at *16 n.24 (S.D.N.Y. 2012).

[129]*See* Rule 56(c)(2) advisory committee note to 2010 amendments. *See also Brown v. White's Ferry, Inc.*, 280 F.R.D. 238, 241 (D.Md. 2012); *Mitchell v. Zia Park, LLC*, 842 F.Supp.2d 1316, 1320 (D.N.M. 2012).

[130]*See* Rule 56(c)(2) advisory committee note to 2010 amendments.

[131]*See MSK EyEs Ltd. v. Wells Fargo Bank, Nat'l Ass'n*, 546 F.3d 533, 543 n.6 (8th Cir. 2008); *Capobianco v. City of New York*, 422 F.3d 47, 55 (2d Cir. 2005).

[132]*See Desrosiers v. Hartford Life and Acc. Co.*, 515 F.3d 87, 91–92 (1st Cir. 2008).

[133]*See supra* Authors' Commentary to Rule 12(f) ("**Striking Documents Other Than Pleadings**").

[134]*See Ruby v. Springfield R-12 Public School Dist.*, 76 F.3d 909, 912

not a butcher knife"[135] so as to strike off only those offending portions.[136]

Procedure #3: Content of Summary Judgment Record

In ruling on a summary judgment motion, the trial court is obliged to consider the materials cited by the parties in the motion papers[137] (though the court is also free to conduct an independent search of the record, if it so chooses).[138] In both its respects, this codifies the prior majority practice.[139] The fate of two earlier caveats to this practice remains unclear, however. Certain courts had commanded an independent record search in certain sensitive types of cases (like First Amendment disputes).[140] Other courts had cautioned that independent reviews of the record must be limited, and that trial judges remain vigilant to their limited, neutral roles and their duty to avoid partisan advocacy.[141]

(8th Cir. 1996) (absent motion to strike or other timely objection, district judge may consider a document which fails to conform to Rule 56's formal requirements); *In re Unisys Sav. Plan Litigation*, 74 F.3d 420, 437 (3d Cir. 1996), (party waived objection to form of affidavit by failing to move to strike or otherwise object); *Humane Soc. of U.S. v. Babbitt*, 46 F.3d 93, 96 (D.C. Cir. 1995) (agreeing with sister circuits that Rule 56 defects are deemed waived if motion to strike not filed in the district court); *Casas Office Machines, Inc. v. Mita Copystar America, Inc.*, 42 F.3d 668, 682 (1st Cir. 1994) (commenting that, absent motion to strike (which specifies objectionable portions of affidavit and grounds for challenge), objections to Rule 56 affidavit are deemed waived).

[135]*See Perez v. Volvo Car Corp.*, 247 F.3d 303, 315–16 (1st Cir. 2001).

[136]*See Perez v. Volvo Car Corp.*, 247 F.3d 303, 315–16 (1st Cir. 2001); *Hollander v. American Cyanamid Co.*, 172 F.3d 192, 198 (2d Cir. 1999); *Evans v. Technologies Applications & Service Co.*, 80 F.3d 954, 962 (4th Cir. 1996).

[137]*See* Rule 56(c)(3); *Phelps v. State Farm Mut. Auto. Ins. Co.*, 680 F.3d 725, 735 (6th Cir. 2012) (district court improperly failed to consider record evidence relied upon in motion briefing). *See also Seng-Tiong Ho v. Taflove*,

648 F.3d 489, 497 (7th Cir. 2011); *Hernandez v. Yellow Transp., Inc.*, 641 F.3d 118, 124 (5th Cir. 2011). *See generally* Rule 56(c)(3) advisory committee note to 2010 amendments.

[138]*See Lynn ex rel. Lynn v. Yamaha Golf-Car Co.*, __ F. Supp. 2d __, __, 2012 WL 3544774, at *10 (W.D.Pa. 2012) (district court may, but is not required to, consider uncited record materials); *In re WL Homes LLC*, 476 B.R. 830, 840 n.5 (D.Del. 2012) (same); *Bell v. Crowne Mgmt., LLC*, 844 F.Supp.2d 1222, 1225 n.2 (S.D.Ala. 2012) (same).

[139]*See RSR Corp. v. Int'l Ins. Co.*, 612 F.3d 851, 857 (5th Cir. 2010); *Satcher v. Univ. of Ark. at Pine Bluff Bd. of Trs.*, 558 F.3d 731, 735 (8th Cir. 2009); *Tucker v. Tennessee*, 539 F.3d 526, 531 (6th Cir. 2008). *But see Stepanischen v. Merchants Despatch Transp. Corp.*, 722 F.2d 922, 931 (1st Cir. 1983) (holding that Rule 56(c) imposes on trial courts the duty to examine all evidence "on file").

[140]*See Rohrbough v. Univ. of Colo. Hosp. Auth.*, 596 F.3d 741, 745 (10th Cir. 2010); *Clear Channel Outdoor, Inc. v. City of New York*, 594 F.3d 94, 103 (2d Cir. 2010), *cert. denied*, 131 S. Ct. 414, 178 L. Ed. 2d 323 (2010).

[141]*See Adler v. Wal-Mart Stores, Inc.*, 144 F.3d 664, 672 (10th Cir. 1998).

Procedure #4: Content of Affidavits / Declarations

Affidavits or declarations may be used to support or oppose a motion for summary judgment, if they meet four prerequisites: (1) sworn or otherwise subscribed as true under a risk of perjury; (2) made on personal knowledge; (3) set out facts that would be admissible in evidence; and (4) show that the maker is competent to testify on the matters expressed.[142] A court generally will not consider affidavits and declarations failing these prerequisites.[143]

- *Sworn*: An affidavit must be sworn[144] and a declaration must be made under penalty of perjury[145] to qualify. Thus, verified complaints (ordinarily not required under the Rules) may suffice,[146] while an attorney's statements at oral argument generally will not.[147]

- *Personal Knowledge*: The affidavit or declaration must be made upon personal knowledge.[148] Statements based on "information and belief" — facts the maker *believes* are true, but does not *know* are true — are not proper.[149] Likewise, inferences and opinions must be premised on

---

[142]*See* Rule 56(c)(4).

[143]*See Collins v. Seeman*, 462 F.3d 757, 760 n.1 (7th Cir. 2006); *Briggs v. Potter*, 463 F.3d 507, 512 (6th Cir. 2006); *Patterson v. County of Oneida, N.Y.*, 375 F.3d 206, 219 (2d Cir. 2004). *But see Ruby v. Springfield R-12 Public School Dist.*, 76 F.3d 909, 912 (8th Cir. 1996) (absent motion to strike or other timely objection, district judge may consider a document which fails to conform to Rule 56's formal requirements).

[144]*See Adickes v. S. H. Kress & Co.*, 398 U.S. 144, 158 n.17, 90 S. Ct. 1598, 1609 n.17, 26 L. Ed. 2d 142 (1970); *Southern Grouts & Mortars, Inc. v. 3M Co.*, 575 F.3d 1235, 1248 n.8 (11th Cir. 2009); *MSK EyEs Ltd. v. Wells Fargo Bank, Nat'l Ass'n*, 546 F.3d 533, 543 n.6 (8th Cir. 2008). *Cf. Collins v. Seeman*, 462 F.3d 757, 760 n.1 (7th Cir. 2006) (rejecting unsworn written witness summaries); *Watts v. Kroger Co.*, 170 F.3d 505, 508 (5th Cir. 1999) (same, for handwritten statements); *Chaiken v. VV Pub. Corp.*, 119 F.3d 1018 (2d Cir. 1997) (same, for unsworn letters do not meet prerequisites); *Berwick Grain Co., Inc. v. Illinois Dept. of Agriculture*, 116 F.3d 231, 234 (7th Cir. 1997) (same, for unsworn

transcript of witness interview).

[145]*See* Rule 56(c)(4) advisory committee note to 2010 amendments (noting that formal affidavits are "no longer required," and declarations under penalty of perjury pursuant to 28 U.S.C. § 1746 are sufficient).

[146]*See Josendis v. Wall to Wall Residence Repairs, Inc.*, 662 F.3d 1292, 1305 n.23 (11th Cir. 2011); *Monahan v. New York City Dept. of Corrections*, 214 F.3d 275, 292 (2d Cir. 2000). *But cf. Lantec, Inc. v. Novell, Inc.*, 306 F.3d 1003, 1019 (10th Cir. 2002) (district court properly refused to consider verified complaint as summary judgment affidavit where its allegations were merely conclusory).

[147]*See Lane v. Dep't of Interior*, 523 F.3d 1128, 1140 (9th Cir. 2008).

[148]*See Hexcel Corp. v. Ineos Polymers, Inc.*, 681 F.3d 1055, 1063 (9th Cir. 2012); *SCR Joint Venture L.P. v. Warshawsky*, 559 F.3d 133, 138 (2d Cir. 2009); *Livick v. Gillette Co.*, 524 F.3d 24, 28 (1st Cir. 2008).

[149]*See Automatic Radio Mfg. Co. v. Hazeltine Research*, 339 U.S. 827, 831, 70 S. Ct. 894, 896, 94 L. Ed. 1312 (1950); *Hicks v. Baines*, 593 F.3d 159, 167 (2d Cir. 2010).

first-hand observations or personal experience.[150] A statement will not be rejected merely because it is a self-serving recitation by the party (indeed, it would make little sense for a party to submit one that was not self-serving).[151] But the self-serving affirmations must be more than mere conclusions or unsupported inferences; in other words, such statements must aver specific facts and otherwise satisfy the requirements of this Rule.[152]

- *Specific Admissible Facts:* The affidavit or declaration must also contain specific facts[153] which, in turn, must be admissible in evidence at time of trial.[154] For most courts, it is not necessary that the evidence be submitted in a *form* that would be admissible at trial (indeed, most summary judgment motions are supported and opposed by affidavit evidence), so long as the offered evidence may ultimately be presented at trial in an admissible form.[155] Thus, hearsay statements,[156] conclusory averments,[157] unfounded self-serving declarations,[158]

---

[150]*See Briggs v. Potter*, 463 F.3d 507, 512 (6th Cir. 2006); *Argo v. Blue Cross and Blue Shield of Kansas, Inc.*, 452 F.3d 1193, 1200 (10th Cir. 2006). *See also Payne v. Pauley*, 337 F.3d 767, 772 (7th Cir. 2003) (personal knowledge may include reasonable inferences grounded in observation or other first-hand experience; they may not be "flights of fancy, speculations, hunches, intuitions, or rumors about matters remote from that experience").

[151]*See Berry v. Chicago Transit Auth.*, 618 F.3d 688, 691 (7th Cir. 2010); *S.E.C. v. Phan*, 500 F.3d 895, 913 (9th Cir. 2007); *Velazquez-Garcia v. Horizon Lines Of Puerto Rico, Inc.*, 473 F.3d 11, 18 (1st Cir. 2007).

[152]*See Gonzalez v. Secretary of Dep't of Homeland Sec.*, 678 F.3d 254, 263 (3d Cir. 2012); *Gander Mountain Co. v. Cabela's, Inc.*, 540 F.3d 827, 831 (8th Cir. 2008); *S.E.C. v. Phan*, 500 F.3d 895, 913 (9th Cir. 2007).

[153]*See Howard v. Kansas City Police Dep't*, 570 F.3d 984, 997 (8th Cir. 2009); *Ass'n of Flight Attendants-CWA, AFL-CIO v. U.S. Dep't of Transp.*, 564 F.3d 462, 465 (D.C.Cir. 2009); *Moore v. J.B. Hunt Transport, Inc.*, 221 F.3d 944 (7th Cir.2000); *Santiago-Ramos v. Centennial P.R. Wireless Corp.*, 217 F.3d 46, 53 (1st Cir. 2000).

[154]*See Ass'n of Flight Attendants-*

CWA, AFL-CIO v. U.S. Dep't of Transp., 564 F.3d 462, 465 (D.C.Cir. 2009); *McIntosh v. Partridge*, 540 F.3d 315, 322 (5th Cir. 2008); *Hardrick v. City of Bolingbrook*, 522 F.3d 758, 761 (7th Cir. 2008); *Trevizo v. Adams*, 455 F.3d 1155, 1160 (10th Cir. 2006).

[155]*See Alexander v. CareSource*, 576 F.3d 551, 558–59 (6th Cir. 2009); *Hardrick v. City of Bolingbrook*, 522 F.3d 758, 761 (7th Cir. 2008); *Trevizo v. Adams*, 455 F.3d 1155, 1160 (10th Cir. 2006).

[156]*See Gonzalez v. Secretary of Dep't of Homeland Sec.*, 678 F.3d 254, 262 (3d Cir. 2012); *Hernandez v. Yellow Transp., Inc.*, 641 F.3d 118, 124–25 (5th Cir. 2011); *Johnson v. Weld County*, 594 F.3d 1202, 1210 (10th Cir. 2010). *But see J.F. Feeser, Inc. v. Serv-A-Portion, Inc.*, 909 F.2d 1524, 1542 (3d Cir. 1990) (noting Third Circuit rule that hearsay evidence produced in an affidavit opposing summary judgment may be considered if the out-of-court declarant could later present the evidence through direct testimony at trial).

[157]*See SCR Joint Venture L.P. v. Warshawsky*, 559 F.3d 133, 138 (2d Cir. 2009); *Shakur v. Schriro*, 514 F.3d 878, 890 (9th Cir. 2008); *Scaife v. Cook County*, 446 F.3d 735, 740 (7th Cir. 2006). *See also Lujan v. National Wildlife Federation*, 497 U.S. 871, 888,

ambiguous statements,[159] speculation or conjecture,[160] and inadmissible expert opinions[161] are generally improper in summary judgment affidavits and declarations. A party's promise that he or she has certain unidentified "additional evidence", which will be produced at trial, is insufficient to avoid summary judgment.[162]

- *Competence:* The affidavit or declaration must demonstrate that the maker is competent to testify as to the facts contained in the document.[163] Competence to testify may be inferred from the documents themselves.[164] Ordinarily, statements of counsel in a memorandum of law are not competent to support or oppose that litigant's own summary judgment position.[165]

- *"Acquired" Competence:* In appropriate circumstances, the makers of affidavits and declarations can "acquire" competence and personal knowledge they otherwise lack by research and a proper review of records.[166]

---

110 S. Ct. 3177, 3188, 111 L. Ed. 2d 695 (1990) (noting that object of Rule 56 is not to replace conclusory averments in a pleading with conclusory allegations in an affidavit).

[158]*See Evans v. Technologies Applications & Service Co.*, 80 F.3d 954, 962 (4th Cir. 1996); *Hall v. Bellmon*, 935 F.2d 1106, 1111 (10th Cir. 1991). *See also In re Kaypro*, 218 F.3d 1070, 1075 (9th Cir. 2000) ("self-serving" affidavit is not necessarily disqualified, so long as foundation was adequate); *Delange v. Dutra Const. Co., Inc.*, 183 F.3d 916 (9th Cir. 1999) (when nonmoving party relies only on his own affidavit to oppose summary judgment, his affidavit may not be conclusory or unsupported by factual data).

[159]*See Archuleta v. Wal-Mart Stores, Inc.*, 543 F.3d 1226, 1234 (10th Cir. 2008).

[160]*See Stagman v. Ryan*, 176 F.3d 986, 995 (7th Cir. 1999).

[161]*See Bryant v. Farmers Ins. Exchange*, 432 F.3d 1114, 1122–23 (10th Cir. 2005) (expert opinion testimony may not be considered unless affiant has been designated as an expert for trial); *Ruffin v. Shaw Industries, Inc.*, 149 F.3d 294 (4th Cir. 1998) (because expert's opinions are inadmissible under Supreme Court's

Daubert test, expert's affidavits and deposition testimony cannot be considered on summary judgment motion).

[162]*See Geske & Sons, Inc. v. N.L.R. B.*, 103 F.3d 1366, 1376 (7th Cir. 1997); *Roche v. John Hancock Mut. Life Ins. Co.*, 81 F.3d 249, 253 (1st Cir. 1996).

[163]*See Security Ins. Co. of Hartford v. Old Dominion Freight Line Inc.*, 391 F.3d 77, 84–85 (2d Cir. 2004); *Lantec, Inc. v. Novell, Inc.*, 306 F.3d 1003, 1019 (10th Cir. 2002); *Markel v. Board of Regents of University of Wisconsin System*, 276 F.3d 906, 912 (7th Cir. 2002).

[164]*See Barthelemy v. Air Lines Pilots Ass'n*, 897 F.2d 999, 1018 (9th Cir. 1990) (noting that affiant's competence could be inferred from position with the company).

[165]*See Orson, Inc. v. Miramax Film Corp.*, 79 F.3d 1358, 1372 (3d Cir. 1996) (noting that legal memoranda and oral argument are not evidence and cannot independently create a genuine issue of disputed fact sufficient to preclude summary judgment); *Lopez v. Corporacion Azucarera de Puerto Rico*, 938 F.2d 1510, 1516 n. 11 (1st Cir. 1991).

[166]*See Nader v. Blair*, 549 F.3d 953, 963 (4th Cir. 2008) (affidavit from witness familiar with record-keeping practices). *But cf. Hernandez-Santiago v. Ecolab, Inc.*, 397 F.3d 30, 35 (1st

Affidavits and Declarations to Authenticate Summary Judgment Documents and Exhibits

Documents (even documents obtained through discovery) might not automatically become part of a summary judgment record merely because they are cited in a supporting memorandum.[167] Many courts have long required that every document used to support or oppose a summary judgment motion be authenticated through an affidavit or declaration, which must be made upon personal knowledge and must both identify and authenticate the offered document.[168] Documents that failed to satisfy this authentication requirement could be disregarded by the court in resolving the pending motion.[169] It remains unclear whether the 2010 Amendments altered this practice.[170] The drafters had deleted earlier Rule language on which this authentication practice may have been based,[171] but did so for apparently unrelated reasons.[172] Moreover, the 2010 drafters had earlier emphasized that the Rule 56(c) amendments were not intended to dislodge prevailing local practices on submission form.[173]

"Vouching" Risk with Summary Judgment Affidavits

At least one court has ruled that a party offering a summary judgment affidavit or declaration effectively concedes that it qualifies for consideration (that is, that the statements made are sworn, made upon personal knowledge, factually specific

---

Cir. 2005) (affidavit that represented merely the "review of relevant manufacturing and sales records" not sufficient, where affiant did not attest that he conducted or supervised review or had personal knowledge of results of review).

[167]See *Hoffman v. Applicators Sales and Serv., Inc.*, 439 F.3d 9, 15 (1st Cir. 2006).

[168]See *DG&G, Inc. v. FlexSol Packaging Corp. of Pompano Beach*, 576 F.3d 820, 825–26 (8th Cir. 2009); *Alexander v. CareSource*, 576 F.3d 551, 558–59 (6th Cir. 2009); *Bias v. Moynihan*, 508 F.3d 1212, 1224 (9th Cir. 2007).

[169]See *Scott v. Edinburg*, 346 F.3d 752, 759–60 n.7 (7th Cir. 2003); *Citizens for Better Forestry v. U.S. Dept. of Agriculture*, 341 F.3d 961, 972 n.7 (9th Cir. 2003); *Stuart v. General Motors Corp.*, 217 F.3d 621, 635 n.20 (8th Cir. 2000); *Carmona v. Toledo*, 215 F.3d 124, 131 (1st Cir. 2000).

[170]One court appears to believe that the 2010 amendments changed this practice. *See Warner Bros. Entm't, Inc. v. X One X Prods.*, 644 F.3d 584,

592 n.4 (8th Cir. 2011) ("The current version of Rule 56 no longer requires attachment of a sworn or certified copy of each paper referenced in an affidavit," in preference to the objection procedure set out in Rule 56(c)(2)).

[171]See Rule 56(e)(1) (rescinded 2010) ("If a paper or part of a paper is referred to in an affidavit, a sworn or certified copy must be attached to or served with the affidavit.").

[172]See Rule 56(c)(4) advisory committee notes to 2010 amendments ("The requirement that a sworn or certified copy of a paper referred to in an affidavit or declaration be attached to the affidavit or declaration is omitted as unnecessary given the requirement . . . that a statement or dispute of fact be supported by materials in the record.").

[173]See Rule 56(c)(1) advisory committee notes to 2010 amendments (noting that amended Rule 56(c)(1) "does not address the form for providing the required support," and that "[d]ifferent courts and judges have adopted different forms").

and admissible, and competent). The court may properly deny a party's later, pretrial *in limine* motion to strike testimony that the same moving party had earlier itself offered in support of a summary judgment brief.[174]

Contradictory Sworn Evidence from Same Party

Most courts have embraced the "sham affidavit" rule, which ordinarily prevents a party from defeating summary judgment by simply denying, in an affidavit or declaration, a statement that the party had earlier admitted in a sworn statement.[175] To create a genuine dispute for trial sufficient to defeat summary judgment, such a party must, in addition to the denial itself, offer an explanation for the inconsistency that the district court finds adequate to allow a reasonable juror to *both* accept the current denial and yet still assume either the truth of, or the party's good faith belief in, the earlier sworn statement.[176] Where the original statement was truly ambiguous, and the later affidavit or declaration serves to clarify the testimony, the subsequent statement may be accepted.[177]

Form of Motion

Motions for summary judgment generally must be in writing.[178] Local rules may prescribe the briefing requirements for summary judgment motions, and such requirements have been enforced strictly.[179] These rules should always be consulted before briefing. In some judicial districts, for example, the local rules require the moving parties to compile a list of all mate-

---

[174]*See Williams v. Trader Pub. Co.,* 218 F.3d 481, 485 (5th Cir. 2000) (in an employment case, party offered affidavits of certain male employees to support its summary judgment position, then later attempted to argue that the testimony of these same male employees was inadmissible because the male employees were not in situations "nearly identical" to the plaintiff; court ruled that the testimony was properly admitted because defendant, by introducing this same evidence at the summary judgment stage, contended that the evidence would be relevant and admissible at trial).

[175]*See In re Family Dollar FLSA Litig.,* 637 F.3d 508, 512–13 (4th Cir. 2011).

[176]*See Cleveland v. Policy Management Systems Corp.,* 526 U.S. 795, 804, 119 S. Ct. 1597, 1603, 143 L. Ed. 2d 966 (1999); *Meuser v. Federal Express Corp.,* 564 F.3d 507, 515 (1st Cir. 2009); *Galvin v. Eli Lilly and Co.,* 488 F.3d 1026, 1030 (D.C. Cir. 2007).

[177]*See Galvin v. Eli Lilly and Co.,* 488 F.3d 1026, 1030 (D.C. Cir. 2007); *Selenke v. Medical Imaging of Colorado,* 248 F.3d 1249, 1258 (10th Cir. 2001).

[178]*See National Fire Ins. v. Bartolazo,* 27 F.3d 518, 520 (11th Cir. 1994); *Hanson v. Polk County Land, Inc.,* 608 F.2d 129, 131 (5th Cir. 1979).

[179]*See, e.g., A.M. Capen's Co., Inc. v. American Trading and Production Corp.,* 202 F.3d 469, 472 (1st Cir. 2000) (finding that trial court properly admitted uncontested facts when non-moving party failed to comply with local rules in opposing motion with proper format); *Jackson v. Finnegan, Henderson, Farabow, Garrett & Dunner,* 101 F.3d 145, 154 (D.C. Cir. 1996) (citing local rule, deeming "admitted" all facts which the nonmoving party did not dispute when filing its counterstatement); *Johnson v. Gudmundsson,* 35 F.3d 1104, 1108 (7th Cir. 1994) (noting court's strict enforcement of local rule requiring statement).

rial facts they believe are not in dispute, and require non-moving parties to submit a counterstatement listing material facts they believe to be disputed.[180]

Miscellaneous Other Procedures

Over time, the federal courts have embraced various other local procedures for summary judgment practice, some local rule-based and some purely common law. Several of those are outlined below:

- *"Lodged", Not Filed Documents:* Documents attached to a submission that the court has refused to accept, although perhaps contained in the court clerk's official file, are not part of the summary judgment record.[181]

- *Party Admissions:* Admissions by a party—whether express (intentional acknowledgment) or through default (*e.g.*, where a party fails to deny Rule 36 requests for admission)—are considered conclusive as to the matters admitted, cannot be contradicted by affidavit or otherwise, and can support a grant of summary judgment.[182]

- *Transcribed Oral Testimony:* Deposition testimony may be used to support a motion for summary judgment, so long as the testimony meets the competence and admissibility requirements of Rule 56.[183]

- *Live Oral Testimony:* Entertaining live oral testimony in conjunction with a summary judgment motion is rare and problematic. Because the summary judgment procedure is intended to offer a speedy resolution when the material facts are undisputed, and because the trial court may not, under Rule 56, resolve any facts that remain disputed, oral testimony in summary judgment proceedings will only be granted "sparingly" and "with great care".[184]

- *Briefs:* The court may consider concessions in a party's brief or during oral argument in gauging whether a gen-

---

[180]*See, e.g.,* M.D. Pa. Loc. R. 56.1 ("Upon any motion for summary judgment pursuant to Fed.R.Civ.P. 56, there shall be filed with the motion a separate, short and concise statement of the material facts, in numbered paragraphs, as to which the moving party contends there is no genuine issue to be tried. The papers opposing a motion for summary judgment shall include a separate, short and concise statement of the material facts, responding to the numbered paragraphs set forth in the statement required in the foregoing paragraph, as to which it is contended that there exists a genuine issue to be tried."). *See also* D. Conn. Loc. R. 56(a) (same effect); M.D. Ga. Loc. R. 56 (same effect); W.D. Mo. Loc. R. 56.1(a) (same effect); M.D. Tenn. Loc. R. 56.01(b) to (c) (same effect).

[181]*See Nicholson v. Hyannis Air Serv., Inc.,* 580 F.3d 1116, 1127 & 1127 n.5 (9th Cir. 2009).

[182]*See In re Carney,* 258 F.3d 415, 420 (5th Cir. 2001).

[183]*See Carmen v. San Francisco Unified School Dist.,* 237 F.3d 1026, 1028 n.4 (9th Cir. 2001).

[184]*See Seamons v. Snow,* 206 F.3d 1021, 1025–26 (10th Cir. 2000).

uine issue of material fact exists; otherwise, however, the parties' briefs are not evidence.[185]

Submitting New Evidence in the Reply

If the moving party introduces new evidence in a reply brief or memoranda, the trial court should not accept and consider the new evidence without first affording the non-moving party an opportunity to respond.[186]

Hearings and Oral Argument

Although the district court may, in its discretion, entertain a hearing or oral argument on the Rule 56 motion, hearings and oral argument are not obligatory.[187]

Multiple Summary Judgment Motions

The district court may permit a second motion for summary judgment,[188] especially where there has been an intervening change in the controlling law, where new evidence has become available or the factual record has otherwise expanded through discovery, or where a clear need arises to correct a manifest injustice.[189]

---

[185] *See Orson, Inc. v. Miramax Film Corp.*, 79 F.3d 1358, 1372 (3d Cir. 1996) (legal memoranda and oral argument are not evidence and cannot create a factual dispute that prevents summary judgment); *American Title Ins. Co. v. Lacelaw Corp.*, 861 F.2d 224, 226–27 (9th Cir. 1988) (noting that district court, in its discretion, may consider statements of fact contained in summary judgment briefing as party admissions for Rule 56 purposes); *Stallard v. U.S.*, 12 F.3d 489, 496 (5th Cir. 1994) (noting same practice).

[186] *See Seay v. Tennessee Valley Authority*, 339 F.3d 454, 481–82 (6th Cir. 2003); *Beaird v. Seagate Technology, Inc.*, 145 F.3d 1159, 1163–65 (10th Cir. 1998).

[187] *See* Rule 78(b) (authorizing determination of motions without oral argument). *See Jones v. Secord*, 684 F.3d 1, 6 (1st Cir. 2012); *Johnson v. U.S.*, 460 F.3d 616, 620 (5th Cir. 2006); *AD/SAT, Div. of Skylight, Inc. v. Associated Press*, 181 F.3d 216, 226 (2d Cir. 1999).

[188] *See Hoffman v. Tonnemacher*, 593 F.3d 908, 910–12 (9th Cir. 2010); *Narducci v. Moore*, 572 F.3d 313, 324 (7th Cir.2009); *Sira v. Morton*, 380 F.3d 57, 68 (2d Cir.2004); *Enlow v. Tishomingo County*, 962 F.2d 501, 506–07 (5th Cir.1992).

[189] *Lexicon, Inc. v. Safeco Ins. Co. of America, Inc.*, 436 F.3d 662, 670 n.6 (6th Cir. 2006) (where factual record has expanded); *Enlow v. Tishomingo County, Miss.*, 962 F.2d 501, 506 (5th Cir. 1992) (when new facts were presented by amended pleading); *Williamsburg Wax Museum, Inc. v. Historic Figures, Inc.*, 810 F.2d 243, 251 (D.C. Cir. 1987) (premised upon expanded record); *Shearer v. Homestake Min. Co.*, 727 F.2d 707, 709 (8th Cir. 1984) (based upon substantial discovery of facts not previously before the court); *Geneva Int'l Corp. v. Petrof, Spol, S.R.O.*, 608 F.Supp.2d 993, 997–98 (N.D.Ill. 2009) (upon intervening change in controlling law, new evidence or expanded factual record, or need to correct a clear error or prevent manifest injustice). *See also Gann v. Fruehauf Corp.*, 52 F.3d 1320, 1324 (5th Cir. 1995) (reversing district court's sanctioning of counsel for filing a second motion for summary judgment where arguments presented in both motions differed).

RULE 56(d)—WHEN FACTS ARE UNAVAILABLE TO THE NONMOVANT

CORE CONCEPT

Once a motion for summary judgment is filed, the non-moving party must show to the court that a genuine and material factual dispute exists to defeat summary judgment. If the non-moving party is still conducting productive discovery or for some other reason is not yet ready or able to make that showing, the party may file an affidavit or declaration explaining why a ruling on summary judgment should be postponed. The court, in its discretion, may then grant a temporary reprieve if the reasons offered are persuasive.

APPLICATIONS

2010 Amendments — Amended Rule 56(d)

Former Rule 56(d) permitted courts that were unable to grant summary judgment to declare undisputed material facts as established for purposes of trial. That procedure has been revised and relocated to amended Rule 56(g). Amended Rule 56(d) now contains the content of former Rule 56(f), permitting a non-moving party to request that a court defer or deny a summary judgment motion pending further discovery or for other reasons. The earlier practice has been repositioned here, with no change in substance from prior practice.[190]

Purpose

The procedure created by Rule 56(d) serves a valuable purpose in summary judgment practice; it is the vehicle through which diligent litigants are assured a pre-ruling opportunity for fair discovery.[191] When properly invoked, Rule 56(d) serves as the "safety value" designed to abate a hasty swing of the "summary judgment axe".[192]

Affidavit Requirement for Motion

Some courts will not consider a Rule 56(d) request unless it is accompanied by a sworn affidavit or proper declaration.[193] Other courts, in appropriate circumstances, will excuse the

---

[190]See Rule 56(d) advisory committee note to 2010 amendments. *See also Michelman v. Lincoln Nat'l Life Ins. Co.*, 685 F.3d 887, 899 n.7 (9th Cir. 2012); *Jones v. Secord*, 684 F.3d 1, 5 n.2 (1st Cir. 2012).

[191]See *Cardinal v. Metrish*, 564 F.3d 794, 797 (6th Cir. 2009), *cert. denied*, 131 S. Ct. 2149, 179 L. Ed. 2d 951 (2011); *Six Flags, Inc. v. Westchester Surplus Lines Ins. Co.*, 565 F.3d 948, 963 (5th Cir. 2009); *Dennis v. Osram Sylvania, Inc.*, 549 F.3d 851, 860 (1st Cir. 2008).

[192]See *Rivera-Torres v. Rey-Hernandez*, 502 F.3d 7, 10–11 (1st Cir. 2007).

[193]See *Pa. Dep't of Public Welfare v. Sebelius*, 674 F.3d 139, 157 (3d Cir. 2012); *CareToLive v. Food & Drug Admin.*, 631 F.3d 336, 345 (6th Cir. 2011); *Marksmeier v. Davie*, 622 F.3d 896, 903 (8th Cir. 2010); *McKissick v. Yuen*, 618 F.3d 1177, 1190 (10th Cir. 2010). *See also Pastore v. Bell Telephone Co. of Pennsylvania*, 24 F.3d 508 (3d Cir. 1994) (noting that affidavit requirement ensures that Rule 56(f) protection is being invoked in good faith and provides trial court with the showing necessary to assess the merits of the party's opposition to the motion).

failure to submit a formal affidavit where all other necessary information has been supplied.[194] This liberality by the courts was not addressed by the 2010 Amendments.

Formal Request Requirement for Motion

A party seeking Rule 56(d) relief must make that request specifically, for example by plainly asking the trial court to deny the pending motion or to defer it until discovery is completed.[195] Neglecting to seek relief at all,[196] or making passing mention in a footnote to a brief,[197] will not trigger the protection of this Rule.

Substantive Requirements for Motion

Although relief under this Rule is often and liberally granted,[198] it does not come automatically.[199] Before the courts will postpone a summary judgment ruling pending further discovery, the courts will generally require a Rule 56(d) movant to make essentially three showings: (1) a description of the particular discovery the movant intends to seek; (2) an explanation showing how that discovery would preclude the entry of summary judgment; and (3) a statement justifying why this discovery had not been or could not have been obtained earlier.[200] Although the affidavit or declaration need not contain evidentiary facts,[201] the showing made must be specific—vague or baldly conclusory statements will not suffice.[202] Moreover, the affidavit or declaration containing these showings must be authoritative (that is, it must be taken by someone with first-

---

[194]*See Hernandez-Santiago v. Ecolab, Inc.*, 397 F.3d 30, 35 n.3 (1st Cir. 2005) (failure to comply with affidavit rule can, in appropriate circumstances, be excused as technical error); *Cacevic v. City of Hazel Park*, 226 F.3d 483, 488–89 (6th Cir. 2000) (noting practice by other courts to permit Rule 56(f) request by form other than affidavit); *Stults v. Conoco, Inc.*, 76 F.3d 651, 657–58 (5th Cir. 1996) (affidavit form not required).

[195]*See Been v. O.K. Industries, Inc.*, 495 F.3d 1217, 1235 (10th Cir. 2007); *Hackworth v. Progressive Casualty Ins. Co.*, 468 F.3d 722, 732 (10th Cir. 2006); *Velez v. Awning Windows, Inc.*, 375 F.3d 35, 40 (1st Cir. 2004).

[196]*See Jones v. Secord*, 684 F.3d 1, 6 (1st Cir. 2012).

[197]*See Allen v. Sybase, Inc.*, 468 F.3d 642, 662 (10th Cir. 2006).

[198]*See Murphy v. Millennium Radio Group LLC*, 650 F.3d 295, 309–10 (3d Cir. 2011); *Six Flags, Inc. v. Westchester Surplus Lines Ins. Co.*, 565 F.3d 948,

963 (5th Cir. 2009).

[199]*See Valley Forge Ins. Co. v. Health Care Mgmt. Partners, Ltd.*, 616 F.3d 1086, 1096 (10th Cir. 2010); *Mir-Yepez v. Banco Popular de Puerto Rico*, 560 F.3d 14, 15–16 (1st Cir. 2009); *Allen v. CSX Transp., Inc.*, 325 F.3d 768, 775 (6th Cir. 2003).

[200]*See Jones v. Secord*, 684 F.3d 1, 6 (1st Cir. 2012); *Pa. Dep't of Public Welfare v. Sebelius*, 674 F.3d 139, 157 (3d Cir. 2012); *Valley Forge Ins. Co. v. Health Care Mgmt. Partners, Ltd.*, 616 F.3d 1086, 1096 (10th Cir. 2010). *See also Siggers v. Campbell*, 652 F.3d 681, 696 (6th Cir. 2011) (listing five factors for consideration).

[201]*See Price ex rel. Price v. Western Resources, Inc.*, 232 F.3d 779, 783–84 (10th Cir. 2000).

[202]*See CareToLive v. Food & Drug Admin.*, 631 F.3d 336, 345 (6th Cir. 2011); *Raby v. Livingston*, 600 F.3d 552, 561 (5th Cir. 2010); *In re Dana Corp.*, 574 F.3d 129, 149 (2d Cir.2009).

hand knowledge of the statements made).[203] The court is unlikely to grant such a request where the moving party has not been diligent in beginning and pursuing discovery.[204] "Rule 56(d) is meant to minister to the vigilant, not to those who sleep upon perceptible rights."[205] If the moving party fails to adequately make any of these showings, the court may deny the requested postponement and rule upon the pending summary judgment motion.[206]

When Rule 56(d) Formalities May Not Be Required

Some courts have held that a postponement in entering summary judgment may still be appropriate, even in the absence of a Rule 56(d) affidavit or declaration, where the nonmoving party adequately notifies the trial court that summary judgment is premature and that additional discovery is necessary, and where the nonmoving party—through no fault— has had little or no opportunity for discovery.[207] Practitioners should be cautioned against relying on this case-specific liberalizing approach, however; even in those cases where this approach is followed, the court has "hasten[ed] to add that parties who ignore [the] affidavit requirement do so at their peril".[208]

Postponing Very Early Filed Motions for Summary Judgment

When a summary judgment motion is filed very early in the litigation, before a realistic opportunity for discovery, courts

---

[203]*See C.B. Trucking, Inc. v. Waste Management, Inc.*, 137 F.3d 41, 44 n. 2 (1st Cir. 1998). *But cf. Simas v. First Citizens' Federal Credit Union*, 170 F.3d 37, 46 (1st Cir. 1999) (although movant must attest to personal knowledge of recited grounds, statement need not be presented in form admissible at trial, so long as it rises sufficiently above mere speculation; thus, reliance on hearsay is not necessarily a dispositive defect under Rule 56(f)).

[204]*See Dennis v. Osram Sylvania, Inc.*, 549 F.3d 851, 860 (1st Cir. 2008); *Chance v. Pac-Tel Teletrac Inc.*, 242 F.3d 1151, 1161 n.6 (9th Cir. 2001); *Beattie v. Madison County Sch. Dist.*, 254 F.3d 595, 606 (5th Cir. 2001).

[205]*See Rivera-Torres v. Rey-Hernandez*, 502 F.3d 7, 12 (1st Cir. 2007).

[206]*See Nitro Distrib., Inc. v. Alitcor, Inc.*, 565 F.3d 417, 430 (8th Cir. 2009); *Family Home and Finance Center, Inc. v. Federal Home Loan Mortg. Corp.*, 525 F.3d 822, 827 (9th Cir. 2008); *Kelly*

v. Marcantonio, 187 F.3d 192 (1st Cir. 1999). *See also Cervantes v. Jones*, 188 F.3d 805 (7th Cir. 1999) (affirming denial of Rule 56(f) motion where excuse for failing to conduct the deposition earlier was a desire to refrain from beginning discovery in order to "foster an atmosphere conducive to settlement"); *Byrd v. U.S. E.P.A.*, 174 F.3d 239, 248 (D.C. Cir. 1999) (affirming denial where movant, without more, alleged merely that "there may well be" evidence helpful to the claim).

[207]*See Nader v. Blair*, 549 F.3d 953, 961 (4th Cir. 2008); *Harrods Ltd. v. Sixty Internet Domain Names*, 302 F.3d 214, 244 (4th Cir. 2002).

[208]*See Harrods Ltd. v. Sixty Internet Domain Names*, 302 F.3d 214, 246 (4th Cir. 2002) (making comment, and "reiterat[ing] that our court expects full compliance with Rule 56(f)"). *See also Bradley v. U.S.*, 299 F.3d 197, 207 (3d Cir. 2002) (noting "strong presumption against a finding of constructive compliance with Rule 56(f)").

generally grant Rule 56(d) postponements freely.[209] In such cases, summary judgment should be refused as a matter of course,[210] with exceptions permitted in only rare cases.[211] With such early filed motions, the courts recognize that the Rule 56(d) affiant or declarant may not be capable of framing a postponement request with great specificity.[212] Nevertheless, even with very early motions, Rule 56(d) relief may still be denied where the supporting affidavit or declaration is especially vague or conclusory or where additional discovery could not make a factual or legal difference to the outcome.[213]

Timing

A Rule 56(d) motion to postpone a summary judgment ruling must be made in a timely fashion, which generally means before the party files a response to the pending motion or, in any event, prior to any scheduled oral argument on the motion.[214] A party may not wait until after the court rules on the main Rule 56 motion. Thus, a party may not attempt to defeat the summary judgment motion on its merits and, only if an adverse ruling is entered, seek the Rule 56(d) extension for discovery in an effort to pursue reconsideration.[215]

Burden on the Movant

The party moving to postpone the summary judgment ruling bears the burden of demonstrating the requisite basis for relief under Rule 56(d).[216]

---

[209]See *Siggers v. Campbell*, 652 F.3d 681, 696 (6th Cir. 2011); *Burlington Northern Santa Fe R. Co. v. Assiniboine and Sioux Tribes of Fort Peck Reservation*, 323 F.3d 767, 773–74 (9th Cir. 2003).

[210]See *Anderson v. Liberty Lobby, Inc.*, 477 U.S. 242, 250 n.5, 106 S. Ct. 2505, 91 L. Ed. 2d 202 (1986); *Been v. O.K. Industries, Inc.*, 495 F.3d 1217, 1235 (10th Cir. 2007).

[211]See *CenTra, Inc. v. Estrin*, 538 F.3d 402, 420–21 (6th Cir. 2008); *Miller v. Wolpoff & Abramson, L.L.P.*, 321 F.3d 292, 303–04 (2d Cir. 2003).

[212]See *Burlington Northern Santa Fe R. Co. v. Assiniboine and Sioux Tribes of Fort Peck Reservation*, 323 F.3d 767, 773–74 (9th Cir. 2003) (noting that affiant cannot be expected to frame motion with great specificity as to nature of discovery likely to develop

useful information because ground for such specificity has not yet been laid).

[213]See *CenTra, Inc. v. Estrin*, 538 F.3d 402, 420 (6th Cir. 2008).

[214]See *Blough v. Holland Realty, Inc*, 574 F.3d 1084, 1091 n.5 (9th Cir. 2009); *Adorno v. Crowley Towing And Transp. Co.*, 443 F.3d 122, 127–28 (1st Cir. 2006).

[215]See *Been v. O.K. Industries, Inc.*, 495 F.3d 1217, 1235 (10th Cir. 2007); *Hackworth v. Progressive Casualty Ins. Co.*, 468 F.3d 722, 732–33 (10th Cir. 2006); *Rodriguez-Cuervos v. Wal-Mart Stores, Inc.*, 181 F.3d 15, 23 (1st Cir. 1999).

[216]See *Blough v. Holland Realty, Inc*, 574 F.3d 1084, 1091 n.5 (9th Cir. 2009); *Summers v. Leis*, 368 F.3d 881, 887 (6th Cir. 2004); *Stanback v. Best Diversified Products, Inc.*, 180 F.3d 903, 911 (8th Cir. 1999).

District Court's Discretion and Options

Whether to grant or deny a Rule 56(d) postponement is committed to the district court's discretion.[217] In ruling, the district court must balance the moving party's need for the requested discovery against the burden the discovery and delay will place on the opposing party.[218] Ordinarily, such requests are construed and granted liberally;[219] denying properly made and supported motions is "disfavored".[220] On the basis of a party's meritorious Rule 56(d) showings, the district court may: (1) deny the motion for summary judgment; (2) grant a continuance to allow affidavits to be prepared and submitted; (3) permit discovery; or (4) make any other order as is just. If the court is presented with a Rule 56(d) motion, it generally may not proceed to decide the summary judgment motion without first considering and ruling upon the Rule 56(d) request.[221]

RULE 56(e) — FAILING TO PROPERLY SUPPORT OR ADDRESS A FACT

CORE CONCEPT

When a party fails to properly support or oppose a motion for summary judgment, the court has several options. It may grant summary judgment (but only when such an order is proper and never merely because a party has procedurally defaulted on its burdens). It may grant the delinquent party a further opportunity to show its support or opposition. It may consider the unaddressed fact to be undisputed for the purpose of the motion. Or it may issue some other appropriate order.

APPLICATIONS

2010 Amendments — Amended Rule 56(e)

Former Rule 56(e) prescribed the requirements for a proper summary judgment affidavit and set out the opposing party's burden to respond. These provisions have been relocated, the affidavit requirements to amended Rule 56(c)(4) and the responding obligations to amended Rule 56(c)(1). The current content of Rule 56(e) outlines the trial court's options when confronted by a party who fails to either properly support or

---

[217]See In re Dana Corp., 574 F.3d 129, 148–49 (2d Cir.2009); Ball v. Union Carbide Corp., 376 F.3d 554, 561 (6th Cir. 2004); Chance v. Pac-Tel Teletrac Inc., 242 F.3d 1151, 1161 n.6 (9th Cir. 2001).

[218]See Harbert Intern., Inc. v. James, 157 F.3d 1271, 1280 (11th Cir. 1998).

[219]See Murphy v. Millennium Radio Group LLC, 650 F.3d 295, 309–10 (3d Cir. 2011); Culwell v. City of Fort Worth, 468 F.3d 868, 871 (5th Cir. 2006). See also Simas v. First Citizens' Federal Credit Union, 170 F.3d 37, 46 (1st Cir. 1999) (when all preconditions are met, a "strong presumption arises in favor of relief").

[220]See Ingle ex rel. Estate of Ingle v. Yelton, 439 F.3d 191, 196 (4th Cir. 2006).

[221]See Doe v. Abington Friends School, 480 F.3d 252, 257 (3d Cir. 2007).

properly oppose a summary judgment motion.

No Summary Judgments by "Default"

Summary judgment may not be entered automatically, upon the non-moving party's failure to respond at all or to respond properly.[222] Likewise, summary judgment may not be denied automatically, simply because the moving party failed to reply properly to the opponent's response.[223] The 2010 Amendments emphasize these points.[224] Instead, summary judgment may be granted only if it is appropriate to do so.[225] Consequently, although it is assuredly a dangerous practice to fail to oppose a summary judgment motion, even entirely uncontested motions must be examined carefully by the district court to determine whether no genuine dispute of material fact remains and whether judgment is appropriate as a matter of law.[226] The trial court may not accept as true the moving party's itemization of undisputed facts; instead, the court must satisfy itself that the evidence in the summary judgment record supports this relief.[227] This does not necessarily require the court to review all evidentiary materials on file, but it must at least review those materials supporting the motion itself.[228] Moreover, the district court's order should recount that it addressed the underlying motion on its merits.[229]

District Court's Options With Improper Responses

When confronting an improperly supported motion or an improperly supported opposition, the court has several choices in how to respond:

- *Another Chance:* The court may permit the delinquent party a further opportunity to file a proper motion or re-

---

[222]*See Fabrikant v. French*, 691 F.3d 193, 205 n.18 (2d Cir. 2012); *Reese v. Herbert*, 527 F.3d 1253, 1269 (11th Cir. 2008); *De La Vega v. San Juan Star, Inc.*, 377 F.3d 111, 115–16 (1st Cir. 2004).

[223]*See* Rule 56(e) advisory committee note to 2010 amendments.

[224]*See* Rule 56(e) advisory committee note to 2010 amendments ("summary judgment cannot be granted by default" upon either a complete failure to respond or a failure to respond properly).

[225]*See* Rule 56(a) (summary judgment entered only if no genuine dispute of material facts exists *and* movant is entitled to judgment). *See also Fabrikant v. French*, 691 F.3d 193, 205 n.18 (2d Cir. 2012); *Adams v. Travelers Indem. Co. of Connecticut*, 465 F.3d 156 (5th Cir. 2006); *U.S. v. One Piece of Real Prop. Located at 5800 SW 74th Ave., Miami, Fla.*, 363 F.3d 1099, 1101 (11th Cir.2004).

[226]*See Reese v. Herbert*, 527 F.3d 1253, 1269 (11th Cir. 2008); *Aguiar-Carrasquillo v. Agosto-Alicea*, 445 F.3d 19, 25 (1st Cir. 2006); *Vermont Teddy Bear Co., Inc. v. 1-800 Beargram Co.*, 373 F.3d 241, 244–46 (2d Cir. 2004).

[227]*See Vermont Teddy Bear Co., Inc. v. 1-800 Beargram Co.*, 373 F.3d 241, 244 (2d Cir. 2004).

[228]*See U.S. v. One Piece of Real Prop. Located at 5800 SW 74th Ave., Miami, Fla.*, 363 F.3d 1099, 1101–02 (11th Cir.2004).

[229]*See U.S. v. One Piece of Real Prop. Located at 5800 SW 74th Ave., Miami, Fla.*, 363 F.3d 1099, 1101–02 (11th Cir.2004).

sponse, with Rule 56(c)-qualifying support.[230] The drafters presume that this choice is likely to be a court's "preferred first step".[231]

- *"Deemed" Undisputed:* A fact improperly contested by the opponent in its response, or a fact improperly contested by the movant its reply, may be considered by the court to be undisputed.[232] The court is not compelled to do so, however, especially if it is aware that the summary judgment record shows the fact to be genuinely disputed.[233] If the court does treat the fact as undisputed, that consequence is limited to the summary judgment motion only; if the delinquent party survives summary judgment, he or she is not barred from contesting the fact in later proceedings.[234]

- *Grant Summary Judgment:* Because a party's delinquent response cannot, alone, compel summary judgment,[235] summary judgment is properly granted following a delinquent response only if the standards for summary judgment are otherwise satisfied.[236] As to those standards, the court must conduct a full, normal inquiry.[237]

- *Other Appropriate Order:* The court may also enter some other appropriate order, when designed to prompt a proper presentation of the record.[238] Special orders designed to spur forward *pro se* litigants are one such example.[239]

Pro Se Motions

In considering summary judgment motions involving *pro se* litigants, the courts construe liberally the *pro se* party's pleadings, but are not obligated to act as the party's advocate.[240]

Warning to *Pro Se* Litigants

Before summary judgment may be entered against unrepre-

---

[230]*See* Rule 56(e)(1). *See also Douglas v. Brookville Area Sch. Dist.*, 836 F.Supp.2d 329, 351 (W.D.Pa. 2011).

[231]*See* Rule 56(e)(1) advisory committee note to 2010 amendments.

[232]*See* Rule 56(e)(2). *See also Buntin v. City of Indianapolis*, 838 F.Supp.2d 849, 851 n.2 (S.D.Ind. 2011); *United States v. Sumpolec*, 811 F.Supp.2d 1349, 1353 (M.D.Fla. 2011).

[233]*See* Rule 56(e)(2) advisory committee note to 2010 amendments.

[234]*See* Rule 56(e)(2) advisory committee note to 2010 amendments.

[235]*See supra* Authors' Commentary to Rule 56(e) (**"No Summary Judgment by 'Default'"**).

[236]*See* Rule 56(e)(3).

[237]*See* Rule 56(e)(3) advisory committee note to 2010 amendments (noting that, even as to "deemed" undisputed facts, court "must determine the legal consequences of these facts and possible inferences from them").

[238]*See* Rule 56(e)(4).

[239]*See* Rule 56(e)(4) advisory committee note to 2010 amendments. *See also infra* Authors' Commentary to Rule 56(e) (**"Warning to *Pro Se* Litigants"**).

[240]*See Cardoso v. Calbone*, 490 F.3d 1194, 1197 (10th Cir. 2007). *See also supra* Authors' Commentary to Rule 8(e) (**"Pleadings Drafted by Laypersons"**).

sented litigants, some courts have required that the unrepresented party first be expressly informed of the consequences of failing to come forward with contradicting evidence (*e.g.*, the party must be told he or she cannot rely merely on the allegations of the pleadings, and risks dismissal in doing so).[241] Other courts adopt this special warning duty only in the context of incarcerated unrepresented parties;[242] as to nonprisoner unrepresented parties, those courts would require no special warning.[243]

RULE 56(f) — JUDGMENT INDEPENDENT OF THE MOTION

CORE CONCEPT

Provided the court gives the parties notice and a reasonable time to respond, it may grant summary judgment in favor of a party who has not sought it, grant summary judgment on different grounds than those requested by the litigants, or grant summary judgment *sua sponte*.

APPLICATIONS

2010 Amendments — Amended Rule 56(f)

Former Rule 56(f) contained the affidavit procedure by which parties could request a court to postpone ruling on a pending summary judgment motion until further discovery has been completed. That procedure has now been relocated to amended Rule 56(d). The current content of Rule 56(f) contains three special uses of the summary judgment device that have been often recognized by the courts but not formerly codified.

Summary Judgment for Non-Moving Parties

In resolving a pending motion for summary judgment, the court may grant summary judgment in favor of a party who has not requested it — so long as the court gives the parties notice and reasonable time to respond.[244] This might occur in at least two contexts. First, in a multi-defendant case where one co-defendant obtains summary judgment on motion, the court may enter a similar summary judgment *sua sponte* in favor of

---

[241]*See U.S. v. Ninety Three Firearms*, 330 F.3d 414, 427 (6th Cir. 2003) (collecting cases); *Rand v. Rowland*, 154 F.3d 952, 960–61 (9th Cir.1998) (en banc); *Bryant v. Madigan*, 84 F.3d 246, 248, (7th Cir. 1996) (Posner, J.).

[242]*See U.S. v. Ninety Three Firearms*, 330 F.3d 414, 427–28 (6th Cir. 2003).

[243]*See U.S. v. Ninety Three Firearms*, 330 F.3d 414, 428 (6th Cir.

2003) (citing other precedent in concluding that this distinction "was only fair because parties choosing to have counsel 'must bear the risk of their attorney's mistakes,' and thus, 'a litigant who chooses himself as a legal representative should be treated no differently' ").

[244]*See* Rule 56(f)(1). *See also* Rule 56(f) (requiring notice and response opportunity).

other similarly situated non-moving co-defendants.[245] Second, a court that denies a moving party's request for summary judgment may enter an unrequested summary judgment *against* that party and in favor of the non-moving party. Such judgments are generally only entered if the court is convinced that the factual record is fully developed, that the non-moving party is "clearly" entitled to judgment, and that entry of the judgment would not result in procedural prejudice to the moving party.[246] Before granting such relief, the court must find that entering summary judgment is both proper and is procedurally sound (that its entry does not offend fundamental fairness).[247]

Summary Judgment on Unrequested Grounds

In resolving a pending motion for summary judgment, the court may grant summary judgment on grounds not requested by the parties — so long as the court gives the parties notice and reasonable time to respond.[248] This is a change from prior practice, which had generally foreclosed such grants[249] or limited them to only situations that would suffice for *sua sponte* summary judgments.[250]

Summary Judgment *Sua Sponte*

The court may enter summary judgment *sua sponte*.[251] In doing so, the court will apply the usual summary judgment standards, resolving all ambiguities and drawing all factual inferences in the target party's favor.[252] But the case law cautions great care in the grant of *sua sponte* summary judgments.[253] In practice, *sua sponte* summary judgments should be unnecessary because the trial court may always

---

[245]See *Judson Atkinson Candies, Inc. v. Latini-Hohberger Dhimantec*, 529 F.3d 371, 384–85 (7th Cir. 2008).

[246]See *Faustin v. City and County of Denver, Colo.*, 423 F.3d 1192, 1198–99 (10th Cir. 2005); *E. C. Ernst, Inc. v. General Motors Corp.*, 537 F.2d 105, 109 (5th Cir. 1976).

[247]See *Caswell v. City of Detroit Housing Com'n*, 418 F.3d 615 (6th Cir. 2005); *John G. Alden, Inc. of Mass. v. John G. Alden Ins. Agency of Fla., Inc.*, 389 F.3d 21, 25 (1st Cir. 2004).

[248]See Rule 56(f)(2). *See also Gentry v. Harborage Cottages-Stuart, LLLP*, 654 F.3d 1247, 1261 (11th Cir.2011) (without advance notice, such summary judgments would be vacated); *Liberty Mut. Ins. Co. v. Pella Corp.*, 650 F.3d 1161, 1177–78 (8th Cir.2011) (same).

[249]See *Washburn v. Harvey*, 504 F.3d 505, 510 (5th Cir. 2007).

[250]See *Byars v. Coca-Cola Co.*, 517 F.3d 1256, 1264–65 (11th Cir. 2008).

[251]See Rule 56(f)(3). *See also Celotex Corp. v. Catrett*, 477 U.S. 317, 326, 106 S. Ct. 2548, 2554, 91 L. Ed. 2d 265 (1986) (noting district court's right to enter *sua sponte* motions under Rule 56); *Wells Real Estate Inv. Trust II, Inc. v. Chardon/Hato Rey P'ship, S.E.*, 615 F.3d 45, 51–52 (1st Cir. 2010); *Global Petromarine v. G.T. Sales & Mfg., Inc.*, 577 F.3d 839, 844 (8th Cir. 2009).

[252]See *NetJets Aviation, Inc. v. LHC Communications, LLC*, 537 F.3d 168, 178 (2d Cir. 2008).

[253]See *First American Kickapoo Operations, L.L.C. v. Multimedia Games, Inc.*, 412 F.3d 1166, 1170 (10th Cir. 2005) (practice is "not encourage[d]"); *Ramsey v. Coughlin*, 94 F.3d 71, 74 (2d Cir. 1996) ("great care"); *Goldstein v. Fidelity and Guar. Ins. Underwriters, Inc.*, 86 F.3d 749, 751

invite a party to file a summary judgment motion.[254]

Where the court considers entering a *sua sponte* judgment, it must first ensure that proper advance notice of this intention has been made.[255] A litigant must appreciate that he is the "target" of a summary judgment inquiry, and possess that motivation when preparing the response.[256] This notice must identify for the parties those material facts that the court believes might not be genuinely disputed.[257] The court must also confirm that the litigants have a full and fair opportunity to respond.[258] These notice-and-opportunity requirements apply even when the *sua sponte* summary judgment is entered against a party who, already, has moved for summary judgment.[259]

Prior to the 2010 Amendments, certain case law practices regarding *sua sponte* summary judgments had developed over time. Some courts had held that discovery must either be completed or clearly be of no further benefit, before *sua sponte* summary judgments could be granted.[260] Other courts had held that notice to the litigants need not be explicit, if the affected party is "fairly appraised" under the circumstances.[261] Previously, an order granting summary judgment *sua sponte* without notice was generally reversed unless the nonmoving party had waived this right or unless it was clear that the non-moving party suffered no prejudice (*e.g.*, because there was no additional evidence for the record or because none of the evidence would create a genuine issue of material fact).[262] Other courts had excused this notice and response requirement where three

---

(7th Cir. 1996) ("special caution" warranted with this "just a bit risky" practice, which the court of appeals does not want to encourage); *Employers Ins. of Wausau v. Petroleum Specialties, Inc.*, 69 F.3d 98, 105 (6th Cir. 1995) ("discourage[d]").

[254]*See Goldstein v. Fidelity and Guar. Ins. Underwriters, Inc.*, 86 F.3d 749, 751 (7th Cir. 1996).

[255]*See* Rule 56(f) (requiring notice and response opportunity). *See also Atkins v. Salazar*, 677 F.3d 667, 678–79 (5th Cir. 2011); *Global Petromarine v. G.T. Sales & Mfg., Inc.*, 577 F.3d 839, 844 (8th Cir. 2009); *Corales v. Bennett*, 567 F.3d 554, 570 (9th Cir. 2009). *But cf. Enowmbitang v. Seagate Technology, Inc.*, 148 F.3d 970 (8th Cir. 1998) (holding that trial court may grant *sua sponte* summary judgment without prior notice for failure to state claim upon which relief may be granted).

[256]*See John G. Alden, Inc. of Mass. v. John G. Alden Ins. Agency of Fla., Inc.*, 389 F.3d 21, 25 (1st Cir. 2004).

[257]*See* Rule 56(f)(3).

[258]*See* Rule 56(f) (requiring notice and response opportunity). *See also Whitfield v. Walker*, 438 Fed.Appx. 501, 504 (7th Cir. 2011); *Priestley v. Headminder, Inc.*, 647 F.3d 497, 504 (2d Cir. 2011); *Wells Real Estate Inv. Trust II, Inc. v. Chardon/Hato Rey P'ship, S.E.*, 615 F.3d 45, 51–52 (1st Cir. 2010).

[259]*See Bridgeway Corp. v. Citibank*, 201 F.3d 134, 139–40 (2d Cir. 2000).

[260]*See Priestley v. Headminder, Inc.*, 647 F.3d 497, 504 (2d Cir. 2011); *Puerto Rico Elec. Power Authority v. Action Refund*, 515 F.3d 57, 64–65 (1st Cir. 2008).

[261]*See Priestley v. Headminder, Inc.*, 647 F.3d 497, 504 (2d Cir. 2011); *U.S. v. 14.02 Acres of Land More or Less in Fresno County*, 530 F.3d 883, 894 (9th Cir. 2008).

[262]*See Atkins v. Salazar*, 677 F.3d 667, 678 (5th Cir. 2011); *Bondex Int'l, Inc. v. Hartford Acc. & Indem. Co.*, 667 F.3d 669, 684–85 (6th Cir. 2011); *Wells*

criteria were met: the summary judgment record was fully developed, there was no prejudice to the non-moving party, and the decision rested on a purely legal issue.[263]

Any objection to this notice-and-opportunity requirement must be appropriately preserved for appeal, however. Thus, filing a motion for reconsideration that contests a *sua sponte* grant of summary judgment, but that omits from that motion a challenge to the procedural propriety of the order, will be reviewed narrowly for "plain error" only.[264]

RULE 56(g) — FAILING TO GRANT ALL OF THE REQUESTED RELIEF

CORE CONCEPT

After considering the standards for summary judgment, the court may conclude that such a judgment is not appropriate at all or not appropriate as to every claim or defense for which it was sought. Nevertheless, the inquiry might have revealed that certain material facts are not genuinely disputed. The court may (but is not required to) declare those facts as established for purposes of the case.

APPLICATIONS

2010 Amendments — Amended Rule 56(g)

Former Rule 56(g) set forth the penalties for summary judgment affidavits made in bad faith. That provision has now been relocated to amended Rule 56(h). The current content of Rule 56(g) prescribes the trial court's ability to declare as undisputed those individual facts that the summary judgment inquiry showed to be not genuinely disputed. Former Rule 56(d) had set out this procedure previously. The amended Rule continues it, with one notable drafting revision. The prior language had seemed to urge the court to make such a ruling (using the verb "should"); the amended Rule is more permissive (with the verb "may").

Impact of the 2007 "Restyling" Amendments

Researching this "declaring-as-established" procedure is likely to prove frustrating. Although this procedure has been contained in Rule 56 for a great many years, it has recently moved around quite a bit. Portions of this procedure had earlier appeared in two places in the pre-2007 / pre-"Restyled" version of the Rule, namely former Rules 56(c) and 56(d). All portions were gathered into "restyled" Rule 56(d) in 2007. Those portions, reworded once more, have now been moved again to

---

Real Estate Inv. Trust II, Inc. v. Chardon/Hato Rey P'ship, S.E., 615 F.3d 45, 51–52 (1st Cir. 2010).

[263]*See DL Resources, Inc. v. FirstEnergy Solutions Corp.*, 506 F.3d 209, 223–24 (3d Cir. 2007).

[264]*See Love v. National Medical Enterprises*, 230 F.3d 765, 771 (5th Cir. 2000).

amended Rule 56(g). In researching current Rule 56(g), practitioners should be mindful of these repositionings.

Purpose of the "Declaring-As-Established" Procedure

The goal of this procedure is to allow trial courts to salvage some constructive result from their efforts in ruling upon otherwise denied (or partially denied) summary judgment motions.[265] Where the summary judgment inquiry demonstrates that certain material facts are not genuinely disputed, the court may declare them established for trial, even though summary judgment itself is being fully or partially denied.[266] Such declared-facts may accelerate litigations by winnowing down the number of issues that must be tried.[267]

Which Facts May Be Declared as Established

Provided the fact is a *material* one, any fact may be declared as undisputed by the court, including liability and damages facts (and even particular items of damages).[268]

Standard for Declaring Facts as Established

Because this procedure is in the nature of a collateral by-product of the summary judgment inquiry itself, the standard for declaring facts to be established is the same standard used in granting summary judgment.[269] The parties need not *agree* on which material facts are undisputed (or that any of them are).[270] Rather, the burden of demonstrating that a material fact is genuinely undisputed lies with the moving party, employing the same burden-of-going-forward shift used with summary judgment motions generally.[271]

District Court's Discretion

The 2010 Amendments make clear that the trial judge is not required to use this procedure to declare facts to be

---

[265]*See Mullaney v. Hilton Hotels Corp.*, 634 F.Supp.2d 1130, 1161 (D.Haw. 2009); *Geneva Int'l Corp. v. Petrof, Spol, S.R.O.*, 608 F.Supp.2d 993, 1004–05 (N.D.Ill. 2009); *McCollough v. Johnson, Rodenberg & Lauinger*, 587 F.Supp.2d 1170, 1177 (D.Mont. 2008).

[266]*See F.D.I.C. v. Massingill*, 24 F.3d 768 (5th Cir. 1994); *Singh v. George Washington Univ. Sch. of Med. & Health Sciences*, 508 F.3d 1097, 1106 (D.C. Cir. 2007); *City of Los Angeles v. County of Kern*, 509 F. Supp. 2d 865, 878 (C.D. Cal. 2007).

[267]*See Global Crossing Bandwidth, Inc. v. Locus Telecommc'n, Inc.*, 632 F.Supp.2d 224, 238 (W.D.N.Y. 2009); *Geneva Int'l Corp. v. Petrof, Spol, S.R.O.*, 608 F.Supp.2d 993, 1004–05 (N.D.Ill. 2009); *Megargee v. Wittman*, 550 F. Supp. 2d 1190, 1199 (E.D. Cal. 2008).

[268]*See* former Rule 56(d)(1) (facts); former Rule 56(d)(2) (liability).

[269]*See* Rule 56(g) advisory committee note to 2010 amendments. *See also California v. Campbell*, 138 F.3d 772, 780 (9th Cir. 1998); *Global Crossing Bandwidth, Inc. v. Locus Telecommc'n, Inc.*, 632 F.Supp.2d 224, 238 (W.D.N.Y. 2009); *Green v. Sun Life Assur. Co. of Canada*, 383 F. Supp. 2d 1224, 1226 (C.D. Cal. 2005).

[270]*See Global Crossing Bandwidth, Inc. v. Locus Telecommc'n, Inc.*, 632 F.Supp.2d 224, 238 (W.D.N.Y. 2009).

[271]*See Green v. Sun Life Assur. Co. of Canada*, 383 F. Supp. 2d 1224, 1226 (C.D. Cal. 2005).

established for trial. Instead, the decision lies entirely within the trial judge's discretion.[272] Thus, for example, the court may decide that the exercise of declaring facts to be established will be more costly than addressing those facts through other means (like trial), or may conclude that a full trial may better illuminate those facts.[273] This conforms with prior practice that, likewise, had acknowledged the court's discretion to use, or not use, this procedure.[274]

No Interference With Opposing Party's Strategy

The 2010 Amendments also make clear that parties opposing summary judgment may choose strategically to concede (or to not affirmatively dispute) a certain fact, and to do so for summary judgment motion purposes only. The court must take care to ensure that such strategic, procedural concessions are not used to declare a fact as established when, at trial, it will be contested.[275]

Making a Motion to Declare-As-Established

Under the earlier version of this procedure, courts were divided whether parties could file an independent motion seeking to have certain facts declared as established.[276] The current language of the Rule has not resolved this uncertainty. Some courts held that litigants could only seek full (or partial) summary judgments and not "declared-as-established" facts,[277] or alternatively, that any such independent motion be made only "in the wake" of such an unsuccessful full motion.[278] Other courts rejected this reasoning, and permitted the filing of

---

[272]*See* Rule 56(g) advisory committee note to 2010 amendments ("Even if the court believes that a fact is not genuinely in dispute it may refrain from ordering that the fact be treated as established."). *See also Triple H Debris Removal, Inc. v. Companion Prop. & Cas. Ins. Co.*, 647 F.3d 780, 785–86 (8th Cir. 2011).

[273]*See* Rule 56(g) advisory committee note to 2010 amendments. *See also Triple H Debris Removal, Inc. v. Companion Prop. & Cas. Ins. Co.*, 647 F.3d 780, 785–86 (8th Cir. 2011).

[274]*See Colasanto v. Life Ins. Co. of North America*, 100 F.3d 203, 210 (1st Cir. 1996); *Patrick Schaumburg Autos., Inc. v. Hanover Ins. Co.*, 452 F. Supp. 2d 857, 867 (N.D. Ill. 2006).

[275]*See also* Rule 56(g) advisory committee note to 2010 amendments. *See Triple H Debris Removal, Inc. v. Companion Prop. & Cas. Ins. Co.*, 647

F.3d 780, 785–86 (8th Cir. 2011).

[276]*See Beaty v. Republic of Iraq*, 480 F. Supp. 2d 60, 100 (D.D.C. 2007) (discussing division), *rev'd on other grounds*, 556 U.S. 848, 129 S.Ct. 2183, 173 L.Ed.2d 1193 (2009).

[277]*See, e.g., Mullaney v. Hilton Hotels Corp.*, 634 F.Supp.2d 1130, 1161 (D.Haw. 2009); *Patrick Schaumburg Autos., Inc. v. Hanover Ins. Co.*, 452 F. Supp. 2d 857, 867 (N.D. Ill. 2006); *Sears, Roebuck & Co. v. Sears Realty Co.*, 932 F. Supp. 392, 410 (N.D. N.Y. 1996). *See also Coffman v. Federal Labs.*, 171 F.2d 94, 98 (3d Cir. 1948) (motion not proper for a portion of a claim); *Biggins v. Oltmer Iron Works*, 154 F.2d 214, 216 (7th Cir. 1946) (same).

[278]*See Kendall McGaw Labs., Inc. v. Community Mem. Hosp.*, 125 F.R.D. 420, 421 (D.N.J. 1989).

distinct motions seeking "declared-as-established" rulings.[279]

Effect of Declared-As-Established Rulings

If the court chooses to grant them, "declared-as-established" rulings are not "judgments" and do not become "final orders" until the district court enters a judgment disposing of the entire case.[280] Nevertheless, such declarations are still rulings on a "dispositive motion",[281] and will be accorded treatment as "law of the case".[282] Thus, the parties are entitled to rely on the conclusiveness of the declaration[283] and, absent good reason for doing so, the district court will not generally revisit or alter the issues adjudicated under Rule 56(g).[284] Nevertheless, such declarations are not immutable and have no *res judicata* effect; they may, under appropriate circumstances, be revisited.[285] If the court later decides that good reasons exist to alter a "declared-as-established" ruling, the court must so inform the parties and permit them an opportunity to present evidence concerning any of the revisited issues.[286]

RULE 56(h)—AFFIDAVIT OR DECLARATION SUBMITTED IN BAD FAITH

CORE CONCEPT

If the district court concludes that an affidavit or declaration submitted in a summary judgment proceeding was presented in bad faith or solely for purposes of delay, the court may order the offending party to pay reasonable expenses incurred by the party's adversary (including attorney's fees) as a result of the

---

[279]See, e.g., Zapata Hermanos Sucesores, S.A. v. Hearthside Baking Co., Inc., 313 F.3d 385, 391 (7th Cir. 2002); McDonnell v. Cardiothoracic & Vascular Surgical Assocs., Inc., 2004 WL 1234138 (S.D. Ohio 2004); Northeast Illinois Reg'l Commuter R.R. Corp. v. Kiewit Western Co., 396 F. Supp. 2d 913, 921 (N.D. Ill. 2005).

[280]See Alberty-Velez v. Corporacion de Puerto Rico Para La Difusion Publica, 361 F.3d 1, 6 n.5 (1st Cir. 2004); Burkhart v. Washington Metropolitan Area Transit Auth., 112 F.3d 1207, 1215–16 (D.C. Cir. 1997).

[281]See Burkhart v. Washington Metropolitan Area Transit Auth., 112 F.3d 1207, 1215–16 (D.C. Cir. 1997).

[282]See Burge v. Parish of St. Tammany, 187 F.3d 452, 467 (5th Cir. 1999); Carr v. O'Leary, 167 F.3d 1124, 1126 (7th Cir. 1999); Palmer v. Fox Software, Inc., 107 F.3d 415, 419 (6th Cir. 1997).

[283]See Huss v. King Co., Inc., 338 F.3d 647, 650–51 (6th Cir. 2003); Leddy v. Standard Drywall, Inc., 875 F.2d 383, 386 (2d Cir. 1989).

[284]See Carr v. O'Leary, 167 F.3d 1124, 1126 (7th Cir. 1999).

[285]See Alberty-Velez v. Corporacion de Puerto Rico Para La Difusion Publica, 361 F.3d 1, 6 n.5 (1st Cir. 2004); Burge v. Parish of St. Tammany, 187 F.3d 452, 467 (5th Cir. 1999).

[286]See Alberty-Velez v. Corporacion de Puerto Rico Para La Difusion Publica, 361 F.3d 1, 6 n.5 (1st Cir. 2004); Huss v. King Co., Inc., 338 F.3d 647, 650–51 (6th Cir. 2003). See also Joseph P. Caulfield & Assocs., Inc. v. Litho Prods., Inc., 155 F.3d 883, 888 (7th Cir. 1998) (holding that proper procedure to seek a revisitation of the adjudicated issues is to file a motion to vacate the ruling and request either that the issues be added to the trial or that they be resolved as a matter of law in favor of the moving party).

improper affidavits or declarations.

APPLICATIONS

2010 Amendments — Repositioned as Rule 56(h)

Rule 56(h) sets forth the penalties for summary judgment affidavits and declarations made in bad faith. That content is repositioned here from its former location in Rule 56(g). Three substantive changes were made. Imposing sanctions is no longer mandatory, but discretionary. Before sanctions can be imposed, the offending party must have notice and a reasonable time to respond. Other sanctions, beyond counsel fees and contempt, are now authorized.

Purpose

The submission of bad faith affidavits and declarations derails, in an illegitimate way, the summary judgment process by creating the false impression of a genuine, material factual dispute that must await trial. Because the impression is not real, but dishonestly simulated, the maneuver forces the parties and the court to incur the time and costs of an unnecessary trial.[287] Rule 56(h) is intended to combat that abuse.

Express Requirements: Bad Faith or Delay

Less frequently invoked or granted,[288] this Rule permits the court to compensate a party who confronts summary judgment affidavits or declarations submitted either in bad faith or solely for purposes of delay.[289] One of those two situations must be proven[290] (or both may, because the bad faith motivation may be delay).[291] Thus, the mere disbelief by one party of the truth of an affidavit or declaration is not sufficient,[292] nor is the mere presence of a conflict between the affidavit or declaration and

---

[287]See U.S. v. Nguyen, 655 F. Supp. 2d 1203 (S.D.Ala. 2009).

[288]See Fort Hill Builders, Inc. v. National Grange Mut. Ins. Co., 866 F.2d 11, 16 (1st Cir. 1989); Abdelkhaleq v. Precision Door of Akron, 653 F. Supp. 2d 773, 787 (N.D.Ohio 2009).

[289]See In re Gioioso, 979 F.2d 956, 961–62 (3d Cir.1992).

[290]See Klein v. Stahl GMBH & Co. Maschinefabrik, 185 F.3d 98, 110 (3d Cir. 1999); Johnson & Johnson Consumer Cos. v. Aini, 2010 WL 986550, at *2 (E.D.N.Y. Mar. 17, 2010); Halmekangas v. State Farm Ins. Co., 2009 WL 982628, at *13 (E.D.La. Apr. 9, 2009); Murray v. Board of Educ. of City of New York, 111 F. Supp. 2d 349 (S.D. N.Y. 2000)

(same); Rogers v. AC Humko Corp., 56 F. Supp. 2d 972 (W.D. Tenn. 1999). But cf. Hunt v. Tektronix, Inc., 952 F. Supp. 998, 1010 (W.D. N.Y. 1997) (denying sanctions where affiant's actions, though "unfortunate", were not deliberately taken in bad faith); Feltner v. Partyka, 945 F. Supp. 1188, 1192 (N.D. Ind. 1996) (denying sanctions where affiant, although technically deficient, was not "willful[ly]" deficient).

[291]See U.S. v. Nguyen, 655 F. Supp. 2d 1203 (S.D.Ala. 2009).

[292]See Moorer v. Grumman Aerospace Corp., 964 F. Supp. 665, 676 (E.D. N.Y. 1997), aff'd, 162 F.3d 1148 (2d Cir. 1998).

other testimony.[293] Instead, the circumstances must be "egregious"[294] —a "deliberate or knowing act for an improper purpose"[295] —such as perjurious or blatantly false allegations or facts,[296] a contradiction without a bona fide explanation,[297] or a statement made without color, with dishonesty of belief or purpose, or asserted wantonly or to harass, delay, or for some other improper purpose.[298] The district courts have wide discretion in conducting this analysis.[299]

"Implied" Requirements: Prejudice and Causation

The Rule's language seems austere, yet some courts have implied additional prerequisites for relief under the Rule. Some courts require the moving party to show prejudice before sanctions are awarded,[300] and some courts will not award sanctions unless the offending document was actually considered by judge in resolving a summary judgment motion.[301]

District Court's Discretion

Sanctions for violating this Rule are now discretionary, not

[293]See Thoroughman v. Savittieri, 323 Fed.Appx. 548, 551 (9th Cir. 2009); Turner v. Baylor Richardson Medical Center, 476 F.3d 337, 349 (5th Cir. 2007); Becton v. Starbucks Corp., 491 F. Supp. 2d 737, 743 (S.D. Ohio 2007); Bausman v. Interstate Brands Corp., 50 F. Supp. 2d 1028 (D. Kan. 1999), aff'd in part, rev'd in part, 252 F.3d 1111 (10th Cir. 2001). See also Cleveland v. Policy Mgmt. Sys. Corp., 526 U.S. 795, 804, 119 S. Ct. 1597, 1603, 143 L. Ed. 2d 966 (1999) (party ordinarily cannot defeat summary judgment by simply denying, in an affidavit, a statement that the party had earlier admitted in a sworn statement unless an adequate explanation for the inconsistency is offered).

[294]See Fort Hill Builders, Inc. v. National Grange Mut. Ins. Co., 866 F.2d 11, 16 (1st Cir. 1989); Stern v. Regency Towers, LLC, __ F. Supp. 2d __, __, 2012 WL 3264363, at *10 (S.D.N.Y. 2012); James v. U.S. Bank Nat'l Ass'n, 272 F.R.D. 47, 48–49 (D.Me. 2011).

[295]See Raher v. Federal Bureau of Prisons, 2011 WL 4832574, at *8 (D.Or. Oct. 12, 2011).

[296]See Fort Hill Builders, Inc. v. National Grange Mut. Ins. Co., 866 F.2d 11, 16 (1st Cir. 1989); Abdelkhaleq v. Precision Door of Akron, 653 F. Supp. 2d 773, 787 (N.D.Ohio 2009); Boggs v. Die Fliedermaus, LLP, 286 F.

Supp. 2d 291, 302 (S.D. N.Y. 2003).

[297]See Ormesher v. Raskin, 2010 WL 2998800, at *1–*2 (C.D.Cal. July 28, 2010); GSS Salvage v. Alter Trading Corp., 2009 WL 1392073, at *3 (C.D.Ill. May 14, 2009).

[298]See Bowers v. University of Virginia, 2008 WL 2346033, at *4 (W.D. Va. 2008). See also Nuzzi v. St. George Cmty. Consol. Sch. Dist. No. 258, 688 F.Supp.2d 815, 834 (C.D. Ill. 2010) (finding 100-page-long rambling, unsupported, "ranting" affidavits violate Rule).

[299]See Turner v. Baylor Richardson Medical Center, 476 F.3d 337, 349 (5th Cir. 2007); nVision Global Tech. Solutions, Inc. v. Cardinal Health 5, LLC, __ F. Supp. 2d __, __, 2012 WL 3527376, at *16 (N.D.Ga. 2012); Horton v. Dobbs, 2011 WL 1899760, at *2-*3 (N.D.W.Va. May 19, 2011); Cobell v. Norton, 214 F.R.D. 13, 20 (D.D.C. 2003).

[300]See Trustees of Plumbers and Steamfitters Local Union No. 43 Health and Welfare Fund v. Crawford, 573 F. Supp. 2d 1023, 1039 (E.D. Tenn. 2008).

[301]See, e.g., Sutton v. U.S. Small Bus. Admin., 92 Fed.Appx. 112, 117–18 (6th Cir.2003); Abdelkhaleq v. Precision Door of Akron, 653 F. Supp. 2d 773, 787 (N.D.Ohio 2009); Wilson v. Maricopa County, 463 F. Supp. 2d 987, 1000 (D. Ariz. 2006).

mandatory.[302] This is a change from prior practice.[303] But no sanctions may be imposed until the offending party is first afforded notice and a reasonable time to respond.[304]

Available Sanctions

The district court enjoys an array of choices to address bad faith affidavits or declarations in summary judgment practice. The courts may strike the offending affidavits,[305] compel the offenders to reimburse their adversaries for reasonable expenses (including attorney's fees) incurred by the submission,[306] hold the offenders or their counsel in contempt,[307] and impose "other appropriate sanctions."[308] Moreover, false swearing could also expose the offending party to criminal prosecution.[309]

Submissions from *Pro Se* Litigants

Some courts apply the sanction rule more gently in cases involving affidavits and declarations submitted by *pro se* litigants.[310]

Submissions Made in Any Summary Judgment Setting

The Rule applies to all affidavits and declarations made in a summary judgment context, including those made by both the moving and non-moving parties under Rule 56(c), as well as affidavits and declarations under Rule 56(d) seeking to postpone a summary judgment ruling.[311]

---

[302]*See* Rule 56(h) advisory committee note to 2010 amendments. *See also Golden Wolf Partners v. BASF Corp.*, 2010 WL 5173197, at *10 n.2 (E.D.Cal. Dec. 13, 2010) (noting substantive nature of change).

[303]*See Scott v. Metropolitan Health Corp.*, 234 Fed. Appx. 341 (6th Cir. 2007); *In re Gioioso*, 979 F.2d 956, 961–62 (3d Cir. 1992); *Trustees of Plumbers and Steamfitters Local Union No. 43 Health and Welfare Fund v. Crawford*, 573 F.Supp. 2d 1023, 1039 (E.D. Tenn. 2008). The curious explanation for this shift from mandatory to discretionary imposition was the drafters' observation that "courts seldom invoke the independent Rule 56 authority to impose sanctions." *See* Rule 56(h) advisory committee note to 2010 amendments.

[304]*See* Rule 56(h).

[305]*See nVision Global Tech. Solutions, Inc. v. Cardinal Health 5, LLC*, __ F. Supp. 2d __, __, 2012 WL 3527376, at *16 (N.D.Ga. 2012); *Bausman v. Interstate Brands Corp.*, 50 F. Supp. 2d 1028 (D. Kan. 1999),

aff'd in part, rev'd in part, 252 F.3d 1111 (10th Cir. 2001).

[306]*See Klein v. Stahl GMBH & Co. Maschinefabrik*, 185 F.3d 98, 110 (3d Cir. 1999); *United States v. Nguyen*, 655 F.Supp.2d 1203, 1209–10 (S.D.Ala. 2009).

[307]*See Klein v. Stahl GMBH & Co. Maschinefabrik*, 185 F.3d 98, 110 (3d Cir. 1999).

[308]*See* Rule 56(h).

[309]*See* 18 U.S.C.A. § 1623 (prescribing that person who makes a knowingly false material declaration to a court is subject to a $10,000 fine, five years in prison, or both).

[310]*See Boggs v. Die Fliedermaus, LLP*, 286 F. Supp. 2d 291, 302 (S.D. N.Y. 2003) (finding sanctions inappropriate where litigant appeared *pro se*, no bad faith evidence existed, there had not been repeated unmeritorious filings, and no prior warnings to litigant had been given by the court).

[311]*See Range v. Brubaker*, 2009 WL 161699, at *2 (N.D.Ind. Jan. 21, 2009) (applies to Rule 56(f) affidavits).

Submissions Made in Non-Summary Judgment Settings

By its terms, this Rule applies only to affidavits and declarations presented in the summary judgment context. Affidavits and declarations submitted for other purposes, or in support of relief under other Rules, are not subject to Rule 56(h).[312]

Additional Research References

Wright & Miller, *Federal Practice and Procedure* §§ 2711 to 2742
C.J.S., Federal Civil Procedure §§ 1135 to 1187 et seq., §§ 1189 to 1216 et seq.
West's Key Number Digest, Federal Civil Procedure ☞2461 to 2559

---

[312]*See Lownsberry v. Lees*, 2008 WL 4852791, at *5 (E.D.Mich. Nov. 7, 2008); *McCarley v. Household Finance Corp. III*, 2007 WL 1100330, at *2 (M.D. Ala. 2007).

RULE 57
DECLARATORY JUDGMENT

These rules govern the procedure for obtaining a declaratory judgment under 28 U.S.C. § 2201. Rules 38 and 39 govern a demand for a jury trial. The existence of another adequate remedy does not preclude a declaratory judgment that is otherwise appropriate. The court may order a speedy hearing of a declaratory-judgment action.

[Amended effective October 20, 1949; April 30, 2007, effective December 1, 2007.]

AUTHORS' COMMENTARY ON RULE 57

PURPOSE AND SCOPE

Rule 57 permits parties to obtain a declaratory judgment to determine their rights and obligations in cases involving actual controversies. The Rule operates in conjunction with the federal Declaratory Judgment Act, 28 U.S.C.A. §§ 2201 to 02.

APPLICATIONS

Purpose

A declaratory judgment declares the rights and obligations of litigants. Its purpose is to afford litigants an early opportunity to resolve their federal disputes so as to avoid the threat of impending litigation,[1] and obtain both clarity in their legal relationships and the ability to make responsible decisions about their future.[2] Lacking an ultimately coercive effect capable of being remedied through contempt, it is considered a "milder" form of relief.[3] Nevertheless, it often provides very practical litigation solutions. It allows controversies to be settled before they mature into full-fledged violations of law or

[1] See Severe Records, LLC v. Rich, 658 F.3d 571, 580 (6th Cir. 2011); Biodiversity Legal Foundation v. Badgley, 309 F.3d 1166, 1172 (9th Cir. 2002).

[2] See Maytag Corp. v. Int'l Union, United Auto., Aerospace & Agricul-tural Implement Workers of Am., 687 F.3d 1076, 1081–82 (8th Cir. 2012); Surrick v. Killion, 449 F.3d 520, 529 (3d Cir. 2006).

[3] See Steffel v. Thompson, 415 U.S. 452, 471, 94 S.Ct. 1209, 39 L.Ed.2d 505 (1974).

breaches of duty.[4] It enables probable-defendants to terminate a non-litigation standstill where the very delay in filing the lawsuit is a plaintiff's strategy.[5] It permits defendants who are confronting multiple claims to pursue an adequate, expedient, and comparably inexpensive declaration of rights that may avoid a multiplicity of actions.[6] In each of these ways, and others, declaratory judgments provide a prudent procedural vehicle for "clearing the air".[7]

Relationship between Rule 57 and 28 U.S.C. § 2201

Courts have held that the federal Declaratory Judgment Act, 28 U.S.C.A. §§ 2201 to 02, is "mirrored by" and "functionally equivalent to" Rule 57.[8]

The Constitutional Requirements: Subject Matter Jurisdiction, Actual Controversy, and Ripeness

Subject Matter Jurisdiction. A plaintiff seeking declaratory relief must establish an independent basis for the district court's subject matter jurisdiction (*e.g.,* diversity of citizenship or federal question).[9] Neither Rule 57 nor the Declaratory Judgment Act expands the court's jurisdiction; these provisions only provide a declaratory remedy in cases properly brought in federal court.[10]

> *Note:* In diversity cases, the amount in controversy is measured by the value of the object of the litigation.[11] In federal question cases, the district courts will apply the "well-pleaded complaint" rule to assess whether the plaintiff's action involves a federal question. Thus, where the federal nature of plaintiff's claim comes only from plaintiff's anticipation that the defendant will assert a federal defense, the court is likely to find that the

---

[4]*See Maytag Corp. v. Int'l Union, United Auto., Aerospace & Agricultural Implement Workers of Am.,* 687 F.3d 1076, 1081–82 (8th Cir. 2012); *Vantage Trailers, Inc. v. Beall Corp.,* 567 F.3d 745, 748 (5th Cir. 2009).

[5]*See DeBartolo v. Healthsouth Corp.,* 569 F.3d 736, 741 (7th Cir. 2009); *BP Chemicals Ltd. v. Union Carbide Corp.,* 4 F.3d 975, 977 (Fed. Cir. 1993).

[6]*See Biodiversity Legal Foundation v. Badgley,* 309 F.3d 1166, 1172 (9th Cir. 2002).

[7]*See Microchip Technology Inc. v. Chamberlain Group, Inc.,* 441 F.3d 936, 943 (Fed. Cir. 2006).

[8]*See Ernst & Young v. Depositors Economic Protection Corp.,* 45 F.3d 530, 534 n.8 (1st Cir. 1995).

[9]For further discussion on this point, see Part II of this text §§ 2.10 to 2.13 on subject matter jurisdiction.

[10]*See Vaden v. Discover Bank,* 556 U.S. 49, 70 n.19, 129 S.Ct. 1262, 1278 n.19, 173 L.Ed.2d 206 (2009); *Schilling v. Rogers,* 363 U.S. 666, 677, 80 S. Ct. 1288, 1295, 4 L. Ed. 2d 1478 (1960); *Aetna Life Ins. Co. of Hartford, Conn. v. Haworth,* 300 U.S. 227, 240, 57 S. Ct. 461, 463, 81 L. Ed. 617 (1937).

[11]*See Hunt v. Wash. State Apple Adver. Comm'n,* 432 U.S. 333, 347, 97 S.Ct. 2434, 53 L.Ed.2d 383 (1977); *Northup Props., Inc. v. Chesapeake Appalachia, L.L.C.,* 567 F.3d 767, 770 (6th Cir. 2009).

plaintiff's claim lacks subject matter jurisdiction.[12] Likewise, where the declaratory judgment action is an "inverted" one (*i.e.*, the natural defendant filing against the natural plaintiff), it is the true claim, and not the defense, that vests subject matter jurisdiction.[13]

Actual Controversy. The district court may only enter a declaratory judgment where the dispute between the parties is definite and concrete, affecting the parties' adverse legal interests with sufficient immediacy as to justify relief.[14] No declaratory judgment may be entered where the parties' dispute is hypothetical, abstract, or academic.[15] Whether an actual controversy exists will be measured at the time the complaint was filed; post-filing events are not sufficient.[16]

Note: The Supreme Court has confirmed that declaratory relief is available where the plaintiff is threatened by adverse government action, and has noted (without criticism) that the lower federal courts have long agreed that declaratory relief is available where the plaintiff is threatened by adverse action from a private party.[17]

Ripeness. The actual controversy requirement obligates the court to determine that the case is "ripe" for adjudication.[18] This "ripeness" must remain throughout the lawsuit. Thus, the district court must decide at the time it is about to enter judgment whether an actual controversy still exists between the parties. Thus, even if an actual controversy existed at the time the lawsuit was filed, the court will not enter a declaratory judgment if later events ended the controversy and the dispute

---

[12]*See Public Service Commission of Utah v. Wycoff Co., Inc.*, 344 U.S. 237, 73 S. Ct. 236, 97 L. Ed. 291 (1952). *See also Skelly Oil Co. v. Phillips Petroleum Co.*, 339 U.S. 667, 673, 70 S. Ct. 876, 880, 94 L. Ed. 1194 (1950) ("It would turn into the federal courts a vast amount of litigation indubitably arising under State law, in the sense that the right to be vindicated was State-created, if a suit for a declaration of rights could be brought into the federal courts merely because an anticipated defense derived from federal law").

[13]*See DeBartolo v. Healthsouth Corp.*, 569 F.3d 736, 741 (7th Cir. 2009).

[14]*See MedImmune, Inc. v. Genentech, Inc.*, 549 U.S. 118, 127, 127 S. Ct. 764, 771, 166 L. Ed. 2d 604 (2007); *Maryland Cas. Co. v. Pacific Coal & Oil Co.*, 312 U.S. 270, 61 S. Ct. 510, 85 L. Ed. 826 (1941); *Aetna Life Ins. Co. of Hartford, Conn. v. Haworth*, 300 U.S. 227, 57 S. Ct. 461, 81 L. Ed. 617

(1937). *Cf. Calderon v. Ashmus*, 523 U.S. 740, 118 S. Ct. 1694, 140 L. Ed. 2d 970 (1998) (holding that declaratory judgments cannot be sought merely for the purpose of testing the validity of a defense that a State may possibly raise in some future, as yet unfiled habeas proceeding).

[15]*See MedImmune, Inc. v. Genentech, Inc.*, 549 U.S. 118, 127, 127 S. Ct. 764, 771, 166 L. Ed. 2d 604 (2007).

[16]*See Vantage Trailers, Inc. v. Beall Corp.*, 567 F.3d 745, 748 (5th Cir. 2009).

[17]*See MedImmune, Inc. v. Genentech, Inc.*, 549 U.S. 118, 129–30, 127 S. Ct. 764, 772–73, 166 L. Ed. 2d 604 (2007).

[18]*See Pittsburgh Mack Sales & Service, Inc. v. Int'l Union of Operating Eng'rs, Local Union No. 66*, 580 F. 3d 185, 190 (3d Cir. 2009); *Pic-A-State Pa., Inc. v. Reno*, 76 F.3d 1294, 1298 (3d Cir. 1996).

has become moot.[19]

> *Note:* The courts recognize an exception to this mootness limitation where the plaintiff is able to show a substantial likelihood that the dispute will re-occur in the future.[20]

The Prudential Concerns: Exercise of Discretion

Declaratory relief is never automatic. The courts have no "unflagging duty" to hear declaratory judgment cases.[21] Whether to grant or deny declaratory relief is vested in the sound discretion of the district court.[22] Likewise, the court has the discretion in fashioning the relief, and its extent.[23] This discretion, though wide, is not boundless; the district court may not refuse on "whim or personal disinclination" to hear a declaratory judgment action, but must instead base its refusal on good reason[24] (such as when the declaration would serve no useful purpose).[25] If the court decides not to entertain the declaratory proceeding, it may either stay or dismiss the federal action, and may enter such an order before trial or after all arguments come to a close.[26]

Factors for Court's Consideration

To decide whether to entertain a declaratory judgment action, courts may consider various factors, including whether

---

[19]*See Preiser v. Newkirk*, 422 U.S. 395, 95 S. Ct. 2330, 45 L. Ed. 2d 272 (1975); *Golden v. Zwickler*, 394 U.S. 103, 89 S. Ct. 956, 22 L. Ed. 2d 113 (1969).

[20]*See Super Tire Engineering Co. v. McCorkle*, 416 U.S. 115, 94 S. Ct. 1694, 40 L. Ed. 2d 1 (1974); *Malowney v. Federal Collection Deposit Group*, 193 F.3d 1342, 1347 (11th Cir. 1999) (holding that declaratory judgment remedy is only proper where plaintiffs assert a reasonable expectation that injury will continue or will be repeated in the future).

[21]*See Diaz-Fonseca v. Puerto Rico*, 451 F.3d 13, 39 (1st Cir. 2006).

[22]*See MedImmune, Inc. v. Genentech, Inc.*, 549 U.S. 118, 136, 127 S. Ct. 764, 776, 166 L. Ed. 2d 604 (2007); *Provident Tradesmens Bank & Trust Co. v. Patterson*, 390 U.S. 102, 88 S. Ct. 733, 19 L. Ed. 2d 936 (1968). *See also Wilton v. Seven Falls Co.*, 515 U.S. 277, 281, 115 S. Ct. 2137, 2140, 132 L. Ed. 2d 214 (1995) (noting that, even when subject matter jurisdiction prerequisites are otherwise satisfied, district courts enjoy discretion to determine whether, in what circumstances, to entertain declaratory judg-

ment action); *Hewitt v. Helms*, 482 U.S. 755, 762, 107 S. Ct. 2672, 2676, 96 L. Ed. 2d 654 (1987) ("The fact that a court can enter a declaratory judgment does not mean that it should"); *Public Service Commission of Utah v. Wycoff Co., Inc.*, 344 U.S. 237, 241, 73 S. Ct. 236, 239, 97 L. Ed. 291 (1952) (noting that the declaratory judgment statute "is an enabling act, which confers a discretion on the courts rather than an absolute right upon the litigant"); *Brillhart v. Excess Ins. Co. of America*, 316 U.S. 491, 494, 62 S. Ct. 1173, 1175, 86 L. Ed. 1620 (1942) (vesting discretion).

[23]*See Strawberry Water Users Ass'n v. U.S.*, 576 F.3d 1133, 1142 (10th Cir. 2009).

[24]*See Public Affairs Associates, Inc. v. Rickover*, 369 U.S. 111, 112, 82 S. Ct. 580, 7 L. Ed. 2d 604 (1962); *Nautilus Ins. Co. v. Winchester Homes, Inc.*, 15 F.3d 371, 375 (4th Cir. 1994).

[25]*See Cincinnati Indem. Co. v. A & K Const. Co.*, 542 F.3d 623, 625 (8th Cir. 2008).

[26]*See Wilton v. Seven Falls Co.*, 515 U.S. 277, 287, 115 S. Ct. 2137, 2143, 132 L. Ed. 2d 214 (1995).

the declaratory judgment proceeding will resolve the controversy, whether such a proceeding would serve a useful purpose in clarifying the legal relations in dispute, whether the proceeding is being initiated for the purpose of forum shopping, "racing to res judicata", or to procedurally "fence" with the opponent, whether the declaratory judgment action would be inequitable to the allegedly injured party, whether a State court action is already pending in which the controversy could be fully litigated, whether the district court would increase friction between federal and State court systems by hearing the case or would otherwise encroach upon State jurisdiction, whether some alternate relief might be better or more effective, and whether the federal court is a convenient forum for parties and witnesses and would otherwise serve the interests of judicial economy.[27]

> *Note:* When another lawsuit involving the same dispute is pending in state court, the district judge may defer to the State forum, particularly where the State case was filed first.[28]

Statement of Circumstances Supporting Declaratory Judgment

If a party contests the prudence of the district court's exercise of discretion to hear a declaratory judgment claim, the court must articulate the factual circumstances supporting the award of declaratory relief.[29]

Realignment of the Parties

In determining whether to grant a declaratory judgment, the courts may realign the parties in order to reflect the nature

---

[27] *See, e.g., Niagara Mohawk Power Corp. v. Hudson River-Black River Regulating Dist.*, 673 F.3d 84, 105 (2d Cir. 2012) (listing several factors); *Savoie v. Martin*, 673 F.3d 488, 495–96 (6th Cir. 2012) (same); *St. Paul Fire and Marine Ins. Co. v. Runyon*, 53 F.3d 1167, 1169 (10th Cir. 1995) (same). *See Igartua-De La Rosa v. U.S.*, 417 F.3d 145, 149 (1st Cir. 2005) (cautioning that declaratory relief to be exercised with "great circumspection" when matters of public moment are involved); *Ameritas Variable Life Ins. Co. v. Roach*, 411 F.3d 1328, 1330–32 (11th Cir. 2005) (noting concern for abstention on state-law claims in face of parallel State court litigation); *International Ass'n of Entrepreneurs of America v. Angoff*, 58 F.3d 1266, 1270 (8th Cir. 1995) (noting reluctance to grant such relief where the action is filed to obtain a "tactical advantage" over an opponent or to open an otherwise closed avenue into federal court by asserting what is essentially a defensive action, reactive to State court litigations); *BASF Corp. v. Symington*, 50 F.3d 555, 558–59 (8th Cir. 1995) (emphasizing that declaratory judgment actions may merit closer inspection to ensure that the plaintiff is not simply forum shopping, and such proceedings may be refused where the plaintiff asserts principally an affirmative defense in a declaratory judgment action brought to deny an injured party its otherwise proper choice of forum and time for suit).

[28] *See Geni-Chlor Intern., Inc. v. Multisonics Development Corp.*, 580 F.2d 981 (9th Cir. 1978).

[29] *See Government Employees Ins. Co. v. Dizol*, 133 F.3d 1220, 1225 (9th Cir. 1998).

of the actual, underlying controversy.[30] In making this determination, the courts may consider the underlying purposes of declaratory relief, the parties' respective burdens of proof, and the best, clearest method for presenting evidence to the jury.[31] Where both sides will carry proof burdens at trial, realignment may properly be refused.[32]

Burden of Proof

A party seeking a declaratory judgment bears the burden of proving the existence of an actual case or controversy.[33] But the courts are divided on the question of the merits burden of proof in declaratory judgment actions. Because a declaratory judgment plaintiff often seeks a determination that the defendant lacks some type of right that, had defendant filed suit first, the defendant would bear the burden of proving, some courts permit a shift in the burden of proof.[34] Practitioners should consult their local rules and substantive case law on this issue.

Type of Relief Available

The court may grant a successful plaintiff whatever relief is warranted by the evidence, regardless of the demand in the plaintiff's complaint. The Declaratory Judgment Act provides that further relief can be awarded after reasonable notice and hearing. The courts, for example, possess "broad power" to make damages awards in declaratory judgment actions where appropriate.[35]

> *Note:* The Eleventh Amendment ordinarily does not preclude declaratory judgment proceedings instituted against State officials.[36]

Effect on Later Lawsuit For Different Remedy

Courts often recognize an exception to claim preclusion theory where the only relief sought in an original lawsuit is

---

[30]*See BASF Corp. v. Symington,* 50 F.3d 555, 557 (8th Cir. 1995).

[31]*See Fresenius Medical Care Holdings, Inc. v. Baxter Int'l, Inc.,* 2006 WL 1646110, at *1 (N.D. Cal. 2006).

[32]*See Anheuser-Busch, Inc. v. John Labatt Ltd.,* 89 F.3d 1339, 1344 (8th Cir. 1996); *L-3 Commc'ns Corp. v. OSI Systems, Inc.,* 418 F. Supp. 2d 380, 383 (S.D. N.Y. 2005).

[33]*See Cardinal Chemical Co. v. Morton Int'l Inc.,* 508 U.S. 83, 94, 113 S. Ct. 1967, 1974, 124 L. Ed. 2d 1 (1993); *Streck, Inc. v. Research & Diagnostic Sys., Inc.,* 665 F.3d 1269, 1281–82 (Fed.Cir. 2012).

[34]*See Reliance Life Ins. Co. v. Burgess,* 112 F.2d 234 (C.C.A. 8th Cir.

1940). *See also American Eagle Ins. Co. v. Thompson,* 85 F.3d 327, 331 (8th Cir. 1996) (burden remains on the party asserting the affirmative on an issue); *Utah Farm Bureau Ins. Co. v. Dairyland Ins. Co.,* 634 F.2d 1326 (10th Cir.1980) (noting divergent views on burden of proof in declaratory judgment actions); *Fireman's Fund Ins. Co. v. Videfreeze Corp.,* 540 F.2d 1171 (3d Cir. 1976).

[35]*See United Teacher Assocs. Ins. Co. v. Union Labor Life Ins. Co.,* 414 F.3d 558, 570 (5th Cir. 2005); *BancInsure, Inc. v. BNC Nat. Bank, N.A.,* 263 F.3d 766, 772 (8th Cir. 2001).

[36]*See Native Village of Noatak v. Blatchford,* 38 F.3d 1505, 1513–14 (9th Cir. 1994).

declaratory; in such cases, the plaintiff is often permitted to pursue a second claim for either injunctive relief or damages.[37]

The Existence of Other Possible Remedies

With one exception, declaratory relief is not foreclosed merely by showing that an adequate remedy other than a declaratory judgment exists.[38] A declaratory judgment may be entered whether or not further relief is sought or could have been awarded.[39] However, the existence of another, adequate remedy may convince the district court to exercise its discretion to deny declaratory relief in favor of some better or more effective remedy.[40] Moreover, where declaratory relief will not terminate the controversy, but further remedies will be sought in a different or subsequent proceeding, the declaratory judgment can be refused.[41]

> *Exception:* Where a special statutory proceeding has been provided to adjudicate a special type of case, declaratory relief may not be awarded.[42]

Partial Remedy

If it exercises its discretion to hear a declaratory judgment case, the trial court is not obligated to rule on every issue presented. The court may, instead, properly choose to decide some of the issues raised and decline to decide others.[43]

Declaratory *versus* Injunctive Remedies

As between a declaratory or injunctive remedy, the district court enjoys discretion. Although a declaratory judgment cannot be enforced in contempt, it is "a real judgment, not just a bit of friendly advice"; it fixes the litigants' legal rights.[44] Nevertheless, it is likely to be a more simple and less elaborate or-

---

[37]See *Allan Block Corp. v. County Materials Corp.*, 512 F.3d 912, 916–17 (7th Cir. 2008).

[38]See *Exxon Shipping Co. v. Airport Depot Diner, Inc.*, 120 F.3d 166 (9th Cir.1997). *But see National Private Truck Council, Inc. v. Oklahoma Tax Com'n*, 515 U.S. 582, 589, 115 S. Ct. 2351, 2356, 132 L. Ed. 2d 509 (1995) (commenting that the availability of an adequate remedy at law makes declaratory relief unwarranted).

[39]See *Powell v. McCormack*, 395 U.S. 486, 89 S. Ct. 1944, 23 L. Ed. 2d 491 (1969); *Nautilus Ins. Co. v. Winchester Homes, Inc.*, 15 F.3d 371, 379 (4th Cir. 1994).

[40]See *Pateley Assocs. I, LLC v. Pitney Bowes, Inc.*, 704 F. Supp. 2d 140, 151–52 (D.Conn. 2010); *Universal Underwriters Service Corp. v. Melson*, 953 F. Supp. 385, 388 (M.D. Ala. 1996).

[41]See Rule 57 advisory committee note ("A declaratory judgment is appropriate when it will 'terminate the controversy' giving rise to the proceeding. . . . When declaratory relief will not be effective in settling the controversy, the court may decline to grant it.").

[42]See *Katzenbach v. McClung*, 379 U.S. 294, 296, 85 S.Ct. 377, 13 L.Ed.2d 290 (1964); *Lac D'Amiante du Quebec, Ltee v. American Home Assur. Co.*, 864 F.2d 1033, 1042 n.11 (3d Cir.1988).

[43]See *Henglein v. Colt Industries Operating Corp.*, 260 F.3d 201, 210–11 (3d Cir. 2001).

[44]See *Badger Catholic, Inc. v. Walsh*, 620 F.3d 775, 782 (7th Cir. 2010).

der than an injunction.[45]

Any Party May Seek Declaratory Judgment

Any party who has an interest in an actual controversy has standing to seek a declaratory judgment.

Who Declaratory Judgments Benefit

Ordinarily, a declaratory judgment is effective only as to the plaintiffs who obtained it. Often, however, such relief has far broader ramifications (such as in cases declaring the invalidity of a statute or patent).

Rules of Procedure

All rules of procedure applicable generally to civil lawsuits apply in a declaratory judgment action.[46] Thus, for example, a declaratory judgment remedy cannot be entered without first filing an action for relief; requests for declaratory relief must be asserted by complaint, not by mere motion.[47]

Expedited Treatment

The district court may order a speedy hearing in declaratory judgment cases, and may move such cases to the top of the court's calendar.

Jury Trial

The right to a jury trial is preserved in declaratory judgment actions. If the issues would have been triable by a jury had something other than declaratory relief been sought, a right to a jury trial exists.[48]

Common Uses

Classically, declaratory judgments are often useful in insurance cases, to resolve policy coverage and interpretation disputes,[49] and in intellectual property cases, to resolve questions

---

[45]*See Badger Catholic, Inc. v. Walsh*, 620 F.3d 775, 782 (7th Cir. 2010).

[46]*See Cloverland-Green Spring Dairies, Inc. v. Pennsylvania Milk Marketing Bd.*, 298 F.3d 201, 210 (3d Cir. 2002) (noting that standards for granting summary judgment in declaratory judgment case are same as for all other types of relief).

[47]*See Thomas v. Blue Cross & Blue Shield Ass'n*, 594 F.3d 823, 830 (11th Cir. 2010); *Kam-Ko Bio-Pharm Trading Co. Ltd-Australasia v. Mayne Pharma (USA) Inc.*, 560 F.3d 935, 943 (9th Cir. 2009).

[48]*See Simler v. Conner*, 372 U.S. 221, 83 S. Ct. 609, 9 L. Ed. 2d 691 (1963); *Beacon Theatres, Inc. v. Westo-ver*, 359 U.S. 500, 79 S. Ct. 948, 3 L. Ed. 2d 988 (1959). *See also Marseilles Hydro Power, LLC v. Marseilles Land and Water Co.*, 299 F.3d 643, 649 (7th Cir. 2002) (if declaratory judgment action fits into none of existing equitable patterns, but is instead an "inverted law suit") (a claim by a litigant who, at common law, would have been a defendant, then a jury right exists; if, however, the action is the counterpart of an equity suit, no jury right exists); *Owens-Illinois, Inc. v. Lake Shore Land Co., Inc.*, 610 F.2d 1185, 1189 (3d Cir. 1979) (same).

[49]*See, e.g., Aetna Life Ins. Co. of Hartford, Conn. v. Haworth*, 300 U.S. 227, 57 S. Ct. 461, 81 L. Ed. 617 (1937).

of validity and infringement.[50] But declaratory judgments have a far broader range. For example, they may be useful in deciding the constitutionality of government laws,[51] immunity questions,[52] land title and property rights,[53] competition and trade claims,[54] scope of entitlements to beneficiaries,[55] and prisoner rights.[56]

Cautious Uses

The district court frequently will refrain from declaratory relief in cases involving important public issues, where the concreteness of a monetary or injunctive dispute is more advisable.[57] The district judge will also often deny declaratory relief that would act to interfere with a State criminal prosecution.[58]

Improper Uses

Declaratory relief is generally not available to merely adjudicate past conduct or to proclaim that one litigant is liable to another.[59] It is also not available where a special statutory proceeding has been provided to adjudicate a special type of case.[60] And it is often not available in federal and State tax cases, particularly where State law provides for efficient tax challenges and remedies, and where the action contests the constitutionality of a State tax provision.

Appealability

Whether a declaratory judgment order is immediately appealable depends upon the nature of the court's ruling. Once the court disposes of all the issues presented in the declaratory judgment action (either by ruling upon them or by declining to rule upon them), the resulting declaratory judgment becomes

---

[50]*See, e.g., CLS Bank Int'l v. Alice Corp. Pty. Ltd.*, 685 F.3d 1341 (Fed.Cir. 2012).

[51]*See, e.g., Greater Baltimore Ctr. for Pregnancy Concerns, Inc. v. Mayor of Baltimore*, 683 F.3d 539 (4th Cir. 2012).

[52]*See, e.g., Aetna Life Ins. Co. of Hartford, Conn. v. Haworth*, 300 U.S. 227, 57 S. Ct. 461, 81 L. Ed. 617 (1937).

[53]*See, e.g., Nixon v. AgriBank, FCB*, 686 F.3d 912 (8th Cir.2012).

[54]*See, e.g., Pensacola Motor Sales Inc. v. Eastern Shore Toyota, LLC*, 684 F.3d 1211 (11th Cir. 2012).

[55]*See, e.g., Fleisher v. Standard Ins. Co.*, 679 F.3d 116 (3d Cir. 2012) (ERISA dispute).

[56]*See, e.g., McFaul v. Valenzuela*, 684 F.3d 564 (5th Cir. 2012).

[57]*See Public Affairs Associates, Inc. v. Rickover*, 369 U.S. 111, 82 S. Ct. 580, 7 L. Ed. 2d 604 (1962).

[58]*See Samuels v. Mackell*, 401 U.S. 66, 91 S. Ct. 764, 27 L. Ed. 2d 688 (1971).

[59]*See Corliss v. O'Brien*, 200 Fed. Appx. 80, 84–85 (3d Cir. 2006); *Tapia v. U.S. Bank, N.A.*, 718 F.Supp.2d 689, 695 (E.D.Va. 2010).

[60]*See The New York Times Co. v. Gonzales*, 459 F.3d 160, 166 (2d Cir. 2006) (such proceedings include petitions for habeas corpus and motions to vacate criminal sentences, proceedings under the Civil Rights Act of 1964, and certain administrative proceedings).

complete, final, and appealable.[61] Conversely, if the court enters
an order resolving certain of the issues presented, but expressly
leaves open for later resolution other issues in the case, the order is merely interlocutory and, therefore, not immediately appealable under the final order doctrine.[62]

Additional Research References:

Wright & Miller, *Federal Practice and Procedure* §§ 2751 to 2771, §§ 2781 to
2787

C.J.S., Declaratory Judgments §§ 1 to 24 et seq., §§ 25 to 75, §§ 76 to 126,
§§ 127 to 142 et seq., §§ 143 to 165; Federal Civil Procedure §§ 1227 to
1231 et seq.

West's Key Number Digest, Declaratory Judgment ⬗1 to 395; Federal Civil
Procedure ⬗2621 to 2628

---

[61]*See Henglein v. Colt Industries
Operating Corp.*, 260 F.3d 201, 211 (3d
Cir. 2001).

[62]*See Henglein v. Colt Industries
Operating Corp.*, 260 F.3d 201, 211 (3d
Cir. 2001).

RULE 58
ENTERING JUDGMENT

(a) Separate Document. Every judgment and amended judgment must be set out in a separate document, but a separate document is not required for an order disposing of a motion:

(1) for judgment under Rule 50(b);

(2) to amend or make additional findings under Rule 52(b);

(3) for attorney's fees under Rule 54;

(4) for a new trial, or to alter or amend the judgment, under Rule 59; or

(5) for relief under Rule 60.

(b) Entering Judgment.

(1) *Without the Court's Direction.* Subject to Rule 54(b) and unless the court orders otherwise, the clerk must, without awaiting the court's direction, promptly prepare, sign, and enter the judgment when:

(A) the jury returns a general verdict;

(B) the court awards only costs or a sum certain; or

(C) the court denies all relief.

(2) *Court's Approval Required.* Subject to Rule 54(b), the court must promptly approve the form of the judgment, which the clerk must promptly enter, when:

(A) the jury returns a special verdict or a general verdict with answers to written questions; or

(B) the court grants other relief not described in this subdivision (b).

(c) Time of Entry. For purposes of these rules, judgment is entered at the following times:

(1) if a separate document is not required, when the judgment is entered in the civil docket under Rule 79(a); or

(2) if a separate document is required, when the

judgment is entered in the civil docket under Rule 79(a) and the earlier of these events occurs:

(A) it is set out in a separate document; or

(B) 150 days have run from the entry in the civil docket.

(d) Request for Entry. A party may request that judgment be set out in a separate document as required by Rule 58(a).

(e) Cost or Fee Awards. Ordinarily, the entry of judgment may not be delayed, nor the time for appeal extended, in order to tax costs or award fees. But if a timely motion for attorney's fees is made under Rule 54(d)(2), the court may act before a notice of appeal has been filed and become effective to order that the motion have the same effect under Federal Rule of Appellate Procedure 4(a)(4) as a timely motion under Rule 59.

[Amended December 27, 1946, effective March 19, 1948; January 21, 1963, effective July 1, 1963; April 22, 1993, effective December 1, 1993; April 29, 2002, effective December 1, 2002; April 30, 2007, effective December 1, 2007.]

AUTHORS' COMMENTARY ON RULE 58

PURPOSE AND SCOPE

Rule 58 sets the procedure by which the district court enters judgments on its docket records. The date a judgment is "entered" on the district court docket triggers the time for making post-trial motions, for taking an appeal, and for executing on the relief awarded.

RULE 58(a)—SEPARATE DOCUMENT

CORE CONCEPT

To avoid uncertainty about when the clock for taking an appeal begins to tick, the district courts are required to set forth most judgments (and amended judgments) in a "separate document".

APPLICATIONS

Impact of 2007 "Restyling" Amendments

In 2007, former Rule 58(a) was divided into two sub-rules. Current Rule 58(a) now contains only the separate document rule. Current Rule 58(b) contains the remaining content of former Rule 58(a) (namely, the procedure for entering judgments).

In researching current Rules 58(a) and (b), practitioners should be mindful of this repositioning.

The "Old" Separate Document Rule

Prior to 2002, a judgment was required to be (1) set forth in writing, (2) in a "separate document", and (3) entered on the docket. These requirements were intended to create a "bright line" for litigants and the courts in determining when finality attached and, thus, when the period for seeking an appeal began.[1] To abate any uncertainty as to when the appeal "clock" would start ticking, the courts generally applied these requirements mechanically.[2] Until each requirement was met, the judgment was not deemed to have been entered[3] and the time for filing an appeal would not begin to run.[4]

What resulted was a significant body of interpretative case law construing the "separate document" requirement, and deciding what, if any, effect it would have on the appeal period. Some cases explained how rulings orally announced from the bench[5] or included within the text of a minute-order, a memorandum, or a written opinion[6] could not qualify as "judgments" under Rule 58. Other cases explained how a little, but not much, collateral discussion by the trial court might be overlooked when included on the "judgment" document.[7] Still other cases explained that the "separate document" requirement could be waived because it was not jurisdictional.[8] Some courts determined that waiver could occur by express agreement of the parties[9] or by failing to timely object.[10] In still other instances, the courts would simply excuse a "separate document" failure entirely where the circumstances made it plain that the court's

[1]See Fogade v. ENB Revocable Trust, 263 F.3d 1274, 1285–86 (11th Cir. 2001); U.S. v. Haynes, 158 F.3d 1327, 1329 (D.C. Cir. 1998).

[2]See Trotter v. Regents of University of New Mexico, 219 F.3d 1179 (10th Cir. 2000).

[3]See U.S. v. Indrelunas, 411 U.S. 216, 93 S. Ct. 1562, 36 L. Ed. 2d 202 (1973); Miller v. Marriott Int'l, Inc., 300 F.3d 1061, 1064–65 (9th Cir. 2002).

[4]See Fogade v. ENB Revocable Trust, 263 F.3d 1274, 1286 (11th Cir. 2001); Trotter v. Regents of University of New Mexico, 219 F.3d 1179 (10th Cir. 2000).

[5]Atlantic Richfield Co. v. Monarch Leasing Co., 84 F.3d 204 (6th Cir. 1996).

[6]See U.S. v. Johnson, 254 F.3d 279, 285 (D.C. Cir. 2001); Transit Management of Southeast Louisiana, Inc. v. Group Ins. Admin., Inc., 226 F.3d 376, 382 (5th Cir. 2000).

[7]See Kidd v. District of Columbia, 206 F.3d 35, 39 (D.C. Cir. 2000); Pacific Employers Ins. Co. v. Domino's Pizza, Inc., 144 F.3d 1270, 1278 (9th Cir. 1998).

[8]See Bankers Trust Co. v. Mallis, 435 U.S. 381, 98 S. Ct. 1117, 55 L. Ed. 2d 357 (1978); Henglein v. Colt Industries Operating Corp., 260 F.3d 201, 209 n.5 (3d Cir. 2001).

[9]See Pohl v. United Airlines, Inc., 213 F.3d 336, 338 (7th Cir. 2000).

[10]See American Disability Ass'n, Inc. v. Chmielarz, 289 F.3d 1315, 1318 (11th Cir. 2002); Puerto Rico Aqueduct & Sewer Authority v. Constructora Lluch, Inc., 169 F.3d 68, 76 (1st Cir. 1999).

decision was final.[11]

Ultimately, a split developed among the Circuits over how to address the nagging spectre of an appeal period being postponed indefinitely by the failure to meet the requirements of a "separate document" judgment.[12]

The Current Separate Document Rule

The underlying purpose of the current Rule 58 remains the same: the separate document requirement is designed to ensure that litigants are alerted to the entry of judgment and to the starting of the clock for post-verdict motions or an appeal.[13] The Rule is designed to resolve finally the long-haunting question of "when is a judgment a judgment".[14] As before, the Rule achieves this goal by insisting on a "clear line of demarcation" between a judgment and an opinion or memorandum.[15] The Rule mandates an extraordinarily austere approach to drafting judgments: the body of the proper judgment should state the relief granted and little else.[16] This austerity should make clear for the parties when the appeal time has begun.[17] In the cause of preserving appeal periods, the current version of the "separate document" rule is applied mechanically as well.[18] When extraneous text offends the separate document requirement, and when it does not, remains a question for the courts.[19] But

---

[11]See *Allison v. Bank One-Denver*, 289 F.3d 1223, 1232–33 (10th Cir. 2002); *First Ins. Funding Corp. v. Federal Ins. Co.*, 284 F.3d 799, 804 n. 3 (7th Cir. 2002). *See also Quinn v. Haynes*, 234 F.3d 837, 843 (4th Cir. 2000) (separate-document requirement may be excused where (1) trial court evidenced its intent that order constituted final decision in the case, (2) judgment was docketed by the clerk, and (3) no objection was made to the procedural violation).

[12]*Compare White v. Fair*, 289 F.3d 1, 6 (1st Cir. 2002) (noting court rule that waiver will be inferred where a party fails to act within 3 months to resolve a separate document failure) *with Hammack v. Baroid Corp.*, 142 F.3d 266, 270 (5th Cir. 1998) (rejecting First Circuit's 3-month inferred waiver rule); *U.S. v. Haynes*, 158 F.3d 1327, 1330–31 (D.C. Cir. 1998) (same); *Rubin v. Schottenstein, Zox & Dunn*, 143 F.3d 263, 270 (6th Cir. 1998) (en banc) (same).

[13]See *Bankers Trust Co. v. Mallis*, 435 U.S. 381, 384, 98 S. Ct. 1117, 55 L. Ed. 2d 357 (1978) (per curiam); *Kunz*

v. DeFelice, 538 F.3d 667, 673 (7th Cir. 2008); *In re Taumoepeau*, 523 F.3d 1213, 1217 (10th Cir. 2008).

[14]See *United Auto. Workers Local 259 Social Sec. Dept. v. Metro Auto Center*, 501 F.3d 283, 287 n.1 (3d Cir. 2007).

[15]See *In re Cendant Corp. Securities Litigation*, 454 F.3d 235, 243 (3d Cir. 2006).

[16]See *In re Cendant Corp. Securities Litigation*, 454 F.3d 235, 245 (3d Cir. 2006).

[17]See *In re Cendant Corp. Securities Litigation*, 454 F.3d 235, 245 (3d Cir. 2006).

[18]See *In re Taumoepeau*, 523 F.3d 1213, 1217 (10th Cir. 2008); *United Auto. Workers Local 259 Social Sec. Dept. v. Metro Auto Center*, 501 F.3d 283, 286–87 (3d Cir. 2007).

[19]See Rule 58 advisory committee notes to 2002 amendment (noting that Forms 31 and 32 "provide examples" of a proper separate document judgment). The Appendix of Forms is reprinted in Part IV of this text.

the postponement period for the appeals clock is now capped.[20] The "separate document" requirement applies to many categories of judgments, including declaratory judgments[21] and summary judgments.[22]

When a "Separate Document" is *Not* Required

A separate document is not required for an order "disposing" of a Rule 50(b) renewed motion for judgment after trial, a Rule 52(b) motion to amend or make additional findings of fact, a Rule 54(d) motion for attorney's fees, a Rule 59 motion for new trial or to alter or amend a judgment, or a Rule 60 motion for relief from a judgment or order.[23] These exceptions create grave risks for the unwary—because a "separate document" is not required for these dispositions, the time for taking an appeal *will begin to run immediately*. Dispositions by Rule 41 dismissals also might not require a separate document.[24] Two nuances have arisen in the case law. First, it is unclear whether *amended* judgments require a "separate document" (the Rule's use of the phrase "disposing of" suggests possibly not).[25] Some courts navigate this uncertainty by requiring a "separate document" when an amended judgment is granted, but not when one is denied.[26] Second, it is unclear how to treat a ruling on a mis-labeled motion. One court chose to abide by the moving party's choice of labeling (even if errant); thus, a motion mislabeled as one filed under Rule 60 will be treated for Rule 58(a) purposes as a Rule 60 motion, and the "separate document" requirement will not apply.[27]

What Qualifies as a "Separate Document"?

Except for the five exempted instances set out in the Rule's text,[28] every judgment (as well as partial dispositions under Rule 54(b)[29]) must be labeled "judgment" and must be set forth on a separate document.[30] Neither a judicial memorandum or

---

[20]*See infra* Authors' Commentary to Rule 58(c).

[21]*See Specialized Seating, Inc. v. Greenwich Indus., LP*, 616 F.3d 722, 725–26 (7th Cir. 2010).

[22]*See Perry v. Sheet Metal Workers' Local No. 73 Pension Fund*, 585 F.3d 358, 360–61 (7th Cir. 2009).

[23]*See* Rule 58(a)(1).

[24]*See Federated Towing & Recovery, LLC v. Praetorian Ins. Co.*, __ F.R.D. __, __ n.4, 2012 WL 1944618, at *4 (D.N.M. 2012); *Advance Capital, Inc. v. M/V ANGIE, Official No. 249544*, 273 F.R.D. 660, 661 (W.D. Wash. 2011).

[25]*See Kunz v. DeFelice*, 538 F.3d

667, 673–74 (7th Cir. 2008).

[26]*See Kunz v. DeFelice*, 538 F.3d 667, 673–74 (7th Cir. 2008); *Employers Ins. of Wausau v. Titan Intern., Inc.*, 400 F.3d 486, 489 (7th Cir. 2005).

[27]*See Lawuary v. United States*, 669 F.3d 864, 865–67 (7th Cir. 2012).

[28]*See* Rule 58(a)(1) to (a)(5). *See also supra* Authors' Commentary to Rule 58(a) ("**When a 'Separate Document' is *Not* Required**").

[29]*See In re Cendant Corp. Securities Litigation*, 454 F.3d 235, 240 n.2 (3d Cir. 2006).

[30]*See* Rule 58(a). *See also Silivanch v. Celebrity Cruises, Inc.*, 333 F.3d 355, 363 (2d Cir. 2003) (must be

opinion,[31] nor marginal entry orders,[32] nor minute orders,[33] nor electronic docket notations[34] satisfy this requirement; indeed, even an otherwise qualifying order that is mistakenly stapled to the end of a memorandum opinion will fail this separateness requirement.[35] Likewise, a judgment that is encumbered with extraneous text, such as an "extensive" recitation of legal reasoning, analysis, facts, or procedural history, fails the separateness requirement.[36] Thus, to qualify as a "separate document", the judgment must (1) be a self-contained, separate document, (2) state the relief granted, and (3) omit the reasoning used by the district court to dispose of pending motions (which should, instead, be contained in the court's opinion).[37]

- *Two Documents?:* The majority view holds that the separate document requirement can, in appropriate circumstances, be met even if there is only one document (such as when the court's reasoning and analysis was conveyed orally, during oral argument or a hearing).[38]

- *Actual or Implied Clarity:* The fact that the litigants knew, or should have known, that the contested order was intended to serve as a final judgment will not excuse a failure to meet the separateness requirement.[39] Debating over a "known-or-should-have-known" standard is precisely what Rule 58 is designed to avoid. As one court wrote: "Rule 58 is a touch-the-base requirement that

---

labeled a "judgment"). *But see LeBoon v. Lancaster Jewish Community Center Ass'n*, 503 F.3d 217, 224 (3d Cir. 2007) ("No magic words are necessary").

[31]*See Bullock v. Sloane Toyota Inc.*, 415 Fed.Appx. 386, 387 n.1 (3d Cir. 2011); *Constien v. United States*, 628 F.3d 1207, 1211–12 (10th Cir. 2010); *Specialized Seating, Inc. v. Greenwich Indus., LP*, 616 F.3d 722, 725–26 (7th Cir. 2010).

[32]*See Inland Bulk Transfer Co. v. Cummins Engine Co.*, 332 F.3d 1007, 1015 n.7 (6th Cir. 2003).

[33]*See ABF Capital Corp., a Delaware Corp. v. Osley*, 414 F.3d 1061, 1065 (9th Cir. 2005). *But see Perry v. Sheet Metal Workers' Local No. 73 Pension Fund*, 585 F.3d 358, 361 (7th Cir. 2009) (some minute-entries may qualify).

[34]*See Barber v. Shinseki*, 660 F.3d 877, 879 (5th Cir. 2011).

[35]*See Alinsky v. U.S.*, 415 F.3d 639, 643 (7th Cir. 2005).

[36]*See In re Cendant Corp. Securities Litigation*, 454 F.3d 235, 243 (3d Cir. 2006).

[37]*See LeBoon v. Lancaster Jewish Community Center Ass'n*, 503 F.3d 217, 224 (3d Cir. 2007); *Selkridge v. United of Omaha Life Ins. Co.*, 360 F.3d 155, 160 n.2 (3d Cir. 2004). *See also Local Union No. 1992 of Intern. Broth. of Elec. Workers v. Okonite Co.*, 358 F.3d 278, 284–85 (3d Cir. 2004) (separate document requirement satisfied where order was self-contained and separate from opinion, had separate caption, was separately (not consecutively) paginated, was separately signed, was separately file-stamped, and was separately docketed).

[38]*See In re Taumoepeau*, 523 F.3d 1213, 1217 (10th Cir. 2008); *In re Cendant Corp. Secs. Litig.*, 454 F.3d 235, 241–42 (3d Cir. 2006).

[39]*See In re Cendant Corp. Secs. Litig.*, 454 F.3d 235, 241 n.4 (3d Cir. 2006).

lays perception aside".[40]

- *Using the "Order" Label:* The Circuits are divided as to whether a document marked "Order" can ever qualify under this Rule as a judgment, even if the "separate document" requirements are otherwise met.[41]
- *Using the "Judgment" Label:* Although Rule 58 ordinarily requires that a qualifying judgment be labeled "Judgment", the inverse is not necessarily true. If a court's order does not qualify as a judgment under Rule 58, labeling it that way will not rescue it.[42]

Waiving the "Separate Document" Requirement

The "separate document" requirement is designed to create protection, not traps.[43] An appellant can always waive the right to receive a judgment on a "separate document", and file an early appeal from a judgment that fails to meet this requirement.[44] Choosing not to wait until full compliance with the "separate document" requirement will not affect the validity of the appeal.[45] In other words, the "clock" for a timely appeal does not begin running until the judgment is placed in a "separate document" (unless, of course, the judgment is exempt from this requirement), or the capped outside time period set by the Rule expires.[46] During this time, the district court would

---

[40]*See In re Cendant Corp. Secs. Litig.*, 454 F.3d 235, 241 n.4 (3d Cir. 2006).

[41]*See Local Union No. 1992 of Intern. Broth. of Elec. Workers v. Okonite Co.*, 358 F.3d 278, 285–86 (3d Cir. 2004) (finding "order" may qualify, and discussing case law); *U.S. v. Johnson*, 254 F.3d 279, 285–86 & 286 n.7 (D.C. Cir. 2001) (same); *Mirpuri v. ACT Mfg., Inc.*, 212 F.3d 624, 628–29 (1st Cir. 2000) (same). *See also* Rule 54(a) (defining "judgment" to include "a decree and any order from which an appeal lies"). *But see Kanematsu-Gosho, Ltd. v. M/T Messiniaki Aigli*, 805 F.2d 47, 48–49 (2d Cir. 1986) (per curiam) ("order" does not qualify as judgment).

[42]*See Riley v. Kennedy*, 553 U.S. 406, 419 128 S. Ct. 1970, 1981, 170 L. Ed. 2d 837 (2008).

[43]*See Bankers Trust Co. v. Mallis*, 435 U.S. 381, 386, 98 S. Ct. 1117, 55 L. Ed. 2d 357 (1978) (per curiam) (requirement is to be "interpreted to prevent loss of the right of appeal, not to facilitate loss"); *Bailey v. Potter*, 478 F.3d 409, 411 (D.C. Cir. 2007) (same).

[44]*See Bankers Trust Co. v. Mallis*, 435 U.S. 381, 384, 98 S. Ct. 1117, 1119, 55 L. Ed. 2d 357 (1978); *Constien v. United States*, 628 F.3d 1207, 1211–12 (10th Cir. 2010); *LeBoon v. Lancaster Jewish Community Center Ass'n*, 503 F.3d 217, 225 (3d Cir. 2007); *Long v. County of Los Angeles*, 442 F.3d 1178, 1184 n.3 (9th Cir. 2006).

[45]*See Turner v. McGee*, 681 F.3d 1215, 1218 (10th Cir. 2012); *Meilleur v. Strong*, 682 F.3d 56, 60–61 (2d Cir. 2012); *Bravo v. City of Santa Maria*, 665 F.3d 1076, 1089 n.5 (9th Cir. 2011).

[46]*See Shalala v. Schaefer*, 509 U.S. 292, 113 S. Ct. 2625, 125 L. Ed. 2d 239 (1993) (decided under pre-2002 amendment, but noting that trial court's failure to enter judgment on a separate document kept the time for appeal open). *See also Perry v. Sheet Metal Workers' Local No. 73 Pension Fund*, 585 F.3d 358, 361–62 (7th Cir. 2009); *Cambridge Holdings Group, Inc. v. Federal Ins. Co.*, 489 F.3d 1356, 1364 (D.C. Cir. 2007); *In re Cendant Corp. Secs. Litig.*, 454 F.3d 235, 245 (3d Cir. 2006).

never lose its jurisdiction over the case.[47] Nevertheless, while appellants are permitted to wait (until either the "separate document" requirement is met or the outside time period runs), they are not obligated to wait.[48]

- *Appellee Cannot Stop Appeal:* An appellee cannot oppose an appellant's early appeal in order to insist that the appellant first return to the district court to demand compliance with the ministerial act of preparing a "separate document" judgment.[49] If the appellant elects to waive the right to a "separate document" and immediately appeal, the appellee cannot stop it.

- *Other Means of Waiver:* Other conduct, like filing a Rule 60 motion for relief from a non-separate-document judgment, may also constitute a waiver of the "separate document" requirement.[50]

- *Practitioners' Safe Harbor:* Because these early appeals are permitted, the effect grants the appellant a safe harbor. Consequently, when in doubt whether a "separate document" has been filed or not, the practitioner may always file an appeal.[51]

RULE 58(b)—ENTERING JUDGMENT

CORE CONCEPT

Judgments on a general verdict, for sums certain or costs, or that deny relief may be entered by the clerk. All other judgments must be entered by the court.

APPLICATIONS

Impact of 2007 "Restyling" Amendments

Current Rule 58(b) now contains the procedure for entering judgments (which, formerly, was the second part of old Rule 58(a)). The displaced former content of Rule 58(b) has been repositioned to Rule 58(c). In researching current Rules 58(a), (b), and (c), practitioners should be mindful of this repositioning.

Manner of Entering the Judgment

Unless it is a "partial" final judgment under Rule 54(b),[52] all federal judgments are entered either by the clerk or by the

---

[47]*See Fogade v. ENB Revocable Trust*, 263 F.3d 1274, 1286 (11th Cir. 2001).

[48]*See* Rule 58(c); *see also infra* Authors' Commentary to Rule 58(c).

[49]*See Bailey v. Potter*, 478 F.3d 409, 411 (D.C. Cir. 2007); *Peng v. Mei Chin Penghu*, 335 F.3d 970, 975 n.4 (9th Cir. 2003) (9th Cir. 2003).

[50]*See Casey v. Albertson's Inc*, 362

F.3d 1254, 1256–59 (9th Cir. 2004).

[51]*See In re Cendant Corp. Secs. Litig.*, 454 F.3d 235, 245 (3d Cir. 2006); *Borrero v. City of Chicago*, 456 F.3d 698, 701 (7th Cir. 2006).

[52]*See* Rule 54(b) (permitting court to direct the entry of final judgment "as to one or more but fewer than all of the claims or parties only upon an express determination that there is no just reason for delay and upon an

court:

- *By The Clerk:* Unless the court otherwise orders,[53] the clerk of court must, without awaiting any further direction from the court, promptly prepare, sign, and enter judgment when (i) the jury returns a general verdict, (ii) the court awards only costs or a sum certain, or (iii) the court denies all relief.[54]
- *By The Court:* The court must review and promptly approve the form of judgment (which the clerk then must promptly enter) when (i) the jury returns a special verdict or a general verdict accompanied by interrogatories, or (ii) the court grants other relief not described above.[55] The district court's obligation to personally "approve" the judgment may be critical. The text of judgments are often drafted by clerks and, while often satisfactory in form, they are likely to prove troublesome when the case's disposition is complicated and a non-attorney clerk is left "at sea" without judicial guidance.[56]

Contents of Judgment

The judgment document must clearly state which parties are entitled to what relief.[57]

Transferring Judgments to Another Judicial District

A judgment for money or property entered by one federal district court may be transferred to, and executed upon in, another district court. Such transfers are accomplished by filing a certified copy of the judgment in the new district court *after* the judgment has become final after appeal, by the expiration of time for appeal, or when, still pending appeal, the court so orders for good cause.[58] The transferred judgment will have the same effect as any other judgment entered in the new district.[59]

RULE 58(c)—TIME OF ENTRY

CORE CONCEPT

Judgments are deemed to be entered when they are placed on the civil docket, unless a "separate document" is required. In those cases, the judgments are deemed entered *either* when the

---

express direction for the entry of judgment").

[53]*See Passananti v. Cook County,* 689 F.3d 655, 660 (7th Cir. 2012).

[54]*See* Rule 58(b)(1). *See also Otis v. City of Chicago,* 29 F.3d 1159, 1163 (7th Cir. 1994) (observing that Rule 58 places on clerk of court the onus of preparing the judgment).

[55]*See* Rule 58(b)(2).

[56]*See Rush University Medical Center v. Leavitt,* 535 F.3d 735, 737–38

(7th Cir. 2008).

[57]*See U.S. v. Marrocco,* 578 F.3d 627, 631 n.3 (7th Cir. 2009) (document ineffectual if omits "who is entitled to what from whom") (citation omitted); *Citizens Elec. Corp. v. Bituminous Fire & Marine Ins. Co.,* 68 F.3d 1016, 1021 (7th Cir. 1995) (proper judgments say who is liable for how much, then stop).

[58]*See Stanford v. Utley,* 341 F.2d 265 (8th Cir.1965).

[59]*See* 28 U.S.C.A. § 1963.

"separate document" requirement is met *or* 150-days after placement on the civil docket (whichever is earlier).

APPLICATIONS

Impact of 2007 "Restyling" Amendments

Current Rule 58(c) now contains the timing principles for entered judgments (which, formerly, was found in old Rule 58(b)). The displaced former content of Rule 58(c) has been repositioned to Rule 58(e). In researching current Rules 58(b), (c), and (e), practitioners should be mindful of this repositioning.

Triggering "Entry of Judgment" Date

The date the clerk enters the judgment "in the civil docket" is the trigger for calculating time under Rule 58(c). The clerk is obligated by Rule 79(a) to make this entry.[60] This ministerial, administrative duty is distinct from the Rule 58(b)(2) duty of the court to approve a "separate document" judgment before it is deemed a true Rule 58 judgment. Though ministerial, this event is still vulnerable to a surprising amount of confusion. *First*, there may be a flurry of docketing dates associated with any given order (*e.g.*, date of signing, date of filing, date of entry); only the date of entry controls for Rule 58(c) purposes.[61] *Second*, the clerk may, properly, record a "judgment" in the civil docket, even though the document so recorded fails the "separate document" requirement; in such cases, the time for appeal will not begin ticking until the 150-day cap expires.[62] *Third,* the syntax used by the clerk in making the entry may be ambiguous, such as a local clerk's office practice to omit the term "ENTERED" when the entry date is the same as the filed date; in those instances, the date of entry — albeit identified with uncertainty — controls.[63] *Fourth,* the clerk may neglect to give notice of entry, or the notice given may fail to reach the litigants; because counsel are under an affirmative duty to monitor the official dockets, failure to discover such judgment entries may have calamitous consequences on post-trial motions and appeals.[64]

---

[60]*See* Rule 79(a)(1) (clerk must maintain the civil docket); Rule 79(a)(2)(C) (judgments must be entered chronologically in the civil docket).

[61]*See United States v. Fiorelli,* 337 F.3d 282, 287 (3d Cir.2003).

[62]*See Burnley v. City of San Antonio,* 470 F.3d 189, 194–96 (5th Cir. 2006).

[63]*See Vargas Torres v. Toledo,* 672 F.Supp.2d 261, 262–65 (D.P.R. 2009).

[64]*See United States ex rel. McAllan v. New York*, 248 F.3d 48, 53 (2d Cir. 2001) (untimely notice of appeal not rescued by clerk's office docketing problems, "because parties have an obligation to monitor the docket sheet to inform themselves of the entry of orders they wish to appeal"); *Bortugno v. Metro-North Commuter RR,* 905 F.2d 674, 676–77 (2d Cir.1990) (extension of appeal period not warranted by failure of clerk to send counsel notice of entry of judgment).

Computing "Entry of Judgment" Date

A judgment must always be entered on the docket.[65] To avoid the uncertainty created by the old "separate document" requirement (which could, theoretically, have allowed months or years to pass before the appeals clock might begin to run),[66] the current Rule now imposes an outside time limit for triggering the appeal period:

- *When Separate Document Required:* If a separate document is required, the judgment is deemed to be entered when (1) it is entered in the civil docket *and* (2) it is actually set forth on a qualifying separate document *or* 150 days passes after the entry in the civil docket, whichever occurs earlier.[67] Thus, the time for a civil appeal is either 30 days (the normal appeal period, assuming a Rule 58-qualifying judgment has been entered) or 180 days (the normal appeal period plus 150-days, if no Rule 58-qualifying judgment was entered).[68] Of course, at any point during the first 150 days, if the court were to discover that it had entered a deficient order, and then were the court to correct it with a proper Rule 58-qualifying judgment, presumably a normal 30-day appeal period would begin to run from that entry.

- *When Separate Document Not Required:* If a separate document is not required (*i.e.*, involving a qualifying Rule 50(b), 52(b), 54(d), 59, or 60 motion), the judgment is deemed to be entered when it is entered in the civil docket.[69]

Inapplicability of the 150-Day Cap

The 150-day outside time limit is only implicated when the order in question is a final one; absent a Rule 54(b) determination, an order disposing of less than all claims or less than all parties will not become a judgment merely because 150 days has passed since its entry.[70]

Disregarding the 150-Day Cap

The 150-day outside time limit should be disregarded where

---

[65]*See* Rule 79 (providing for entries on the official court docket).

[66]*See Burnley v. City of San Antonio*, 470 F.3d 189, 195 (5th Cir. 2006) (noting that 2002 amendments to Rule 58 were designed to ensure that appeal time "does not linger on indefinitely").

[67]*See* Rule 58(c)(2). *See Harmston v. City and County of San Francisco*, 627 F.3d 1273, 1280–81 (9th Cir. 2010); *Robinson v. Livingston*, 565 F.3d 343, 344 (6th Cir. 2009); *Goldberg & Connolly v. New York Cmty. Bancorp,*

Inc., 565 F.3d 66, 71 n.3 (2d Cir. 2009).

[68]*See Harmston v. City and County of San Francisco*, 627 F.3d 1273, 1280 (9th Cir. 2010); *Perry v. Sheet Metal Workers' Local No. 73 Pension Fund*, 585 F.3d 358, 362 (7th Cir. 2009); *In re Taumoepeau*, 523 F.3d 1213, 1216–17 (10th Cir. 2008).

[69]*See* Rule 58(c)(1). *See also Kunz v. DeFelice*, 538 F.3d 667, 673–74 (7th Cir. 2008).

[70]*See In re Metropolitan Gov't of Nashville & Davidson County*, 606 F.3d 855, 860–61 (6th Cir. 2010).

it serves no purpose to apply it.[71] Thus, for example, assessing the propriety of an appeal from a collateral order should *not* be complicated by the separate document requirement.[72] To the contrary, appeal periods for collateral orders should start to run when the collateral order is entered, and should not await either the creation of a separate document or the passing of 150 days.[73]

RULE 58(d)—REQUEST FOR ENTRY

CORE CONCEPT

Because entry of judgment in a "separate document" has serious procedural consequences (for, among other things, the time for appealing), a party may request the court to prepare one.

APPLICATIONS

Former Prohibition on Attorney-Prepared Judgments

Before the 2002 amendments, Rule 58 prohibited attorneys from drafting and submitting proposed forms of judgment, unless directed to do so by the court.[74] This prohibition was designed to avoid delays encountered by such drafting and submission and to avoid occasionally inept drafting results.[75]

Party's Request to Prompt a "Separate Document"

A party may now request the district court to enter a "separate document" judgment. Allowing such requests was intended to help protect a party's need to ensure that timing periods are promptly triggered for motions, appeals, and enforcement procedures.[76] Thus, a party may make such a request in order to cure a "separate document" problem with an existing judgment (and, thus, trigger the running of the appeals clock),[77] to seek a Rule 54(b) determination that would permit an immediate partial judgment appeal,[78] or to quicken the pace for

---

[71]*See* Rule 58 advisory committee notes to 2002 amendments.

[72]*See* Rule 58 advisory committee notes to 2002 amendments.

[73]*See* Rule 58 advisory committee notes to 2002 amendments.

[74]*See* Rule 58 (former language: "Attorneys shall not submit forms of judgment except upon direction of the court, and these directions shall not be given as a matter of course").

[75]*See* Rule 58 advisory committee notes to 2002 amendment. *See also Matteson v. U.S.*, 240 F.2d 517, 519 (2d Cir. 1956) (commenting that earlier practice of having lawyers prepare

form of judgment caused delay in the entry of judgment and forced the court to sift through "the normal excess of detail supplied by zealous advocates in their natural desire to press home all conceivable ad hoc advantages from the judgment").

[76]*See* Rule 58(d) advisory committee notes to 2002 amendment.

[77]*See Perry v. Sheet Metal Workers' Local No. 73 Pension Fund*, 585 F.3d 358, 362 (7th Cir. 2009); *In re Carolina Tobacco Co.*, 2007 WL 1541507, at *1 (D. Or. 2007).

[78]*See Cook v. Avi Casino Enterprise, Inc.*, 2006 WL 3694859, at *1 (D. Ariz. 2006).

enforcement.[79] Such a request can also be made by a party who suffers a dismissal *without prejudice*, and who wishes to appeal that dismissal rather than attempt to re-plead.[80]

RULE 58(e)—COST OR FEE AWARDS

CORE CONCEPT

To facilitate a single, consolidated appeal from both a merits ruling and a ruling on an award of attorney's fees, the district court may allow the pending (but yet undecided) attorney's fees motion to suspend the time for finality.

APPLICATIONS

Impact of 2007 "Restyling" Amendments

Current Rule 58(e) now contains the costs or fees award provision, which, formerly, was found in old Rule 58(c)). In researching current Rule 58(e), practitioners should be mindful of this repositioning.

Purpose

Generally, the entry of final judgment (and, thus, the triggering of the clock for taking an appeal) is neither delayed nor extended while the district court considers requests to tax costs or award attorney's fees.[81] A Rule 58(e) motion offers an exception to this practice, which enhances judicial efficiency by allowing the appeals court to review a fees award appeal at the same time as it reviews the merits.[82]

Effect of a Rule 58(e) Order

In order to allow a consolidated appeal of both its merits judgment and its ruling on attorney's fees, the district court may, in its discretion,[83] enter an order under Rule 58(e) that treats a pending motion for an award of attorney's fees as the equivalent of a Rule 59 motion.[84] (*Note:* the court may only enter such an order if the fees motion has already been filed.[85]) If the court enters such an order, the time for appealing will not begin to run until the court decides the pending fees

---

[79]*See Uhl v. Komatsu Forklift Co., Ltd.*, 466 F. Supp. 2d 899, 911 (E.D. Mich. 2006), aff'd, 512 F.3d 294 (6th Cir. 2008).

[80]*See Parker v. Google, Inc.*, 242 Fed. Appx. 833 (3d Cir. 2007).

[81]*See* Rule 58(e). *See also Richards v. Government of Virgin Islands*, 579 F.2d 830 (3d Cir. 1978).

[82]*See Kira, Inc. v. All Star Maintenance, Inc.*, 294 Fed.Appx. 139, 141 n.2 (5th Cir. 2008).

[83]*See Electronic Privacy Info. Ctr. v. U.S. Dep't of Homeland Sec.*, 811 F.Supp.2d 216, 225 n.2 (D.D.C. 2011).

[84]*See* Rule 58(e). *See also Burnley v. City of San Antonio*, 470 F.3d 189, 199 (5th Cir. 2006) (noting purpose); *Gilda Marx, Inc. v. Wildwood Exercise, Inc.*, 85 F.3d 675, 680 (D.C. Cir. 1996) (from the perspective of the appellate courts, it is obviously desirable to have merits appeals and fees order appeals decided together).

[85]*See Robinson v. City of Harvey*, 489 F.3d 864, 868 (7th Cir. 2007) (finding it "clear that the time for appeal cannot be extended in anticipation of a fee petition").

motion.[86] The court must, however, actually enter the Rule 58(e) order; the mere fact that a litigant has asked the court to enter such an order is not sufficient to toll.[87] If the district court elects not to grant the order, it retains jurisdiction over the fee motion even while the merits appeal is pending,[88] which in turn deprives the appeals court of jurisdiction over that issue pending the district court's ruling.[89]

Prerequisites for a Rule 58(e) Order

The court may enter a Rule 58(e) order only if: (1) the motion for fees is pending and has been timely made (*i.e.*, within 14 days after entry of judgment),[90] (2) no effective notice of appeal has yet been made, and (3) a timely notice of appeal is still possible (*i.e.*, the time for appealing has not already expired).[91] An order under Rule 58(e) must satisfy the "separate document" requirement.[92]

When the Order is *Not* Proper

The practical effect of a Rule 58(e) motion is to delay the arrival of finality and, with it, the time for taking an appeal from the court's order. The reason why district courts are authorized to grant this postponement is efficiency: to permit a simultaneous, joint appeal from both the trial court's judgment on the merits and its ruling on attorney's fees.[93] If that goal cannot be attained, no Rule 58(e) postponement order is proper. Thus, if an appeal has already been taken from the merits ruling, if the attorney's fees motion has already been ruled upon, or if the merits judgment has already become unappealable (*e.g.*, if the appeal time has already expired), the district court has no reason or authority to issue such a postponement order.[94]

---

[86]*See Mahach-Watkins v. Depee*, 593 F.3d 1054, 1059 (9th Cir. 2010); *Wikol ex rel. Wikol v. Birmingham Public Schools Bd. of Educ.*, 360 F.3d 604, 607–08 (6th Cir. 2004); *Deboard v. Sunshine Min. and Refining Co.*, 208 F.3d 1228, 1236 (10th Cir. 2000).

[87]*See Stephanie-Cardona LLC v. Smith's Food and Drug Centers, Inc.*, 476 F.3d 701, 705 (9th Cir. 2007). *See also Wikol ex rel. Wikol v. Birmingham Public Schools Bd. of Educ.*, 360 F.3d 604, 609–10 (6th Cir. 2004) (6th Cir. 2004) (criticizing confusing former language of Rule 58).

[88]*See Kira, Inc. v. All Star Maint., Inc.*, 294 Fed.Appx. 139, 141 n.2 (5th Cir. 2008).

[89]*See McCarter v. Ret. Plan for Dist. Mngrs. of Am. Family Ins. Group*, 540 F.3d 649, 652–53 (7th Cir. 2008).

[90]*See Cooper v. Pentecost*, 77 F.3d 829 (5th Cir.1996) (noting that 14-day period for petitioning for fee award does not begin to run until judgment is entered in a separate document).

[91]*See Mendes Junior Intern. Co. v. Banco do Brasil, S.A.*, 215 F.3d 306 (2d Cir. 2000) (the filing of a fees-and-costs motion cannot rescue an otherwise out-of-time appeal; if the 30-day appeal clock has run, a ruling on the fees-and-costs motion will not revive the time to appeal).

[92]*See Deboard v. Sunshine Min. and Refining Co.*, 208 F.3d 1228, 1237 (10th Cir. 2000).

[93]*See Burnley v. City of San Antonio*, 470 F.3d 189, 199 (5th Cir. 2006).

[94]*See Burnley v. City of San Antonio*, 470 F.3d 189, 199 (5th Cir.

Order Cannot Apply When Fees Are Part of Claim Itself

The district court may not grant a Rule 58(e) postponement when the fees are an integral part of the underlying substantive claim, such as where the fees are sought as an element of damages pursuant to a contract that authorizes fees. Ordinarily, no final judgment is even possible in such a case until the fees issue (considered to be core damages) is resolved.[95]

Order Applies Only to Fees, Not Costs

A postponement of finality under Rule 58(e) is, by its terms, only applicable to attorney's fee awards; finality cannot be suspended while costs are being taxed.[96]

Additional Research References

Wright & Miller, *Federal Practice and Procedure* §§ 2781 to 2787
C.J.S., Federal Civil Procedure §§ 1227 to 1231 et seq.
West's Key Number Digest, Federal Civil Procedure ⚖2621 to 2628

2006); *Electronic Privacy Info. Ctr. v. U.S. Dep't of Homeland Sec.*, 811 F.Supp.2d 216, 225 n.2 (D.D.C. 2011). *See also Robinson v. City of Harvey*, 489 F.3d 864, 868–69 (7th Cir. 2007) (appeal period must still be live at time of order; order may not "revive" an already-expired appeal period).

[95]*See Carolina Power and Light Co. v. Dynegy Marketing and Trade*, 415 F.3d 354, 359 (4th Cir. 2005) (holding that unresolved claim for *substantive* attorneys fees prevents entry of judgment); *Maristuen v. National States Ins. Co.*, 57 F.3d 673, 678 (8th

Cir. 1995) (8th Cir. 1995) (award of specific sum in attorney's fees required for final order where such award was integral part of claim, such as bad faith claim).

[96]*See Moody Nat. Bank of Galveston v. GE Life and Annuity Assur. Co.*, 383 F.3d 249, 253 (5th Cir. 2004). *See also Mahach-Watkins v. Depee*, 593 F.3d 1054, 1059 (9th Cir. 2010), *cert. denied*, 131 S. Ct. 898, 178 L. Ed. 2d 747 (2011) (court's withholding of final decision on costs had no effect on resolution of attorney's fees motion).

RULE 59
NEW TRIAL; ALTERING OR AMENDING A JUDGMENT

(a) In General.

   (1) *Grounds for New Trial.* The court may, on motion, grant a new trial on all or some of the issues—and to any party—as follows:

     (A) after a jury trial, for any reason for which a new trial has heretofore been granted in an action at law in federal court; or

     (B) after a nonjury trial, for any reason for which a rehearing has heretofore been granted in a suit in equity in federal court.

   (2) *Further Action After a Nonjury Trial.* After a nonjury trial, the court may, on motion for a new trial, open the judgment if one has been entered, take additional testimony, amend findings of fact and conclusions of law or make new ones, and direct the entry of a new judgment.

(b) Time to File a Motion for a New Trial. A motion for a new trial must be filed no later than 28 days after the entry of judgment.

(c) Time to Serve Affidavits. When a motion for a new trial is based on affidavits, they must be filed with the motion. The opposing party has 14 days after being served to file opposing affidavits. The court may permit reply affidavits.

(d) New Trial on the Court's Initiative or for Reasons Not in the Motion. No later than 28 days after the entry of judgment, the court, on its own, may order a new trial for any reason that would justify granting one on a party's motion. After giving the parties notice and an opportunity to be heard, the court may grant a timely motion for a new trial for a reason not stated in the motion. In either event, the court must specify the reasons in its order.

(e) Motion to Alter or Amend a Judgment. A motion to alter or amend a judgment must be filed no later than 28 days after the entry of the judgment.

[Amended effective March 19, 1948; July 1, 1966; April 27, 1995, effective December 1, 1995; April 30, 2007, effective December 1, 2007; March 26, 2009, effective December 1, 2009.]

AUTHORS' COMMENTARY ON RULE 59

PURPOSE AND SCOPE

When appropriate to prevent a miscarriage of justice, the district court may set aside a verdict and order a new trial or, alternatively, alter or amend a judgment. Effective December 1, 2009, a party moving for either a new trial or an order altering or amending a judgment must file such a motion no later than 28 days after the judgment is entered. The district court may *not* extend this period.

RULE 59(a)—NEW TRIALS, GENERALLY

CORE CONCEPT

In both jury and bench trials, the court may grant a new trial for any reason for which new trials (jury trials) or rehearings (bench trials) were formerly granted, such as where the verdict is against the weight of the evidence or is either excessive or inadequate, where probative evidence is newly discovered, or where conduct by the court, counsel, or the jury improperly influenced the deliberative process.

APPLICATIONS

Procedure

Motions for new trial are usually made in writing and must state with particularity the grounds for relief.

Discretion of District Court

Whether the circumstances justify the granting of a new trial is a decision left to the sound discretion of the trial judge,[1] and this discretion is far greater than the court's authority to grant a motion for judgment as a matter of law.[2] So broad is this discretion in certain contexts, that one court has described

---

[1]*See Gasperini v. Center for Humanities, Inc.*, 518 U.S. 415, 433, 116 S. Ct. 2211, 2222, 135 L. Ed. 2d 659 (1996) ("the authority of trial judges to grant new trials . . . is large"); *Allied Chemical Corp. v. Daiflon, Inc.*, 449 U.S. 33, 101 S. Ct. 188, 66 L. Ed. 2d 193 (1980) (noting that the authority to grant a new trial "is confided almost entirely to the exercise of discretion on the part of the trial court").

[2]*See Jennings v. Jones*, 587 F.3d 430, 436 (1st Cir. 2009); *Tatum v.*

it as "virtually unassailable on appeal".[3] In exercising this discretion, the trial judge may reopen a judgment, hear additional testimony, and amend (or make new) findings of fact and conclusions of law.[4] Although there is some dispute on the point,[5] the majority view prescribes that a trial judge is not bound to view the evidence in the light most favorable to the verdict winner,[6] and may reweigh the evidence, accepting or rejecting evidence, witnesses, and other proof that the jury considered.[7] But the court must proceed carefully, and avoid merely substituting its judgment for the jury's without good reason.[8] (Some courts even describe motions for new trial as "disfavored").[9] Nevertheless, in long, complicated trials involving topics beyond the ken of ordinary jurors, the judge ought to be especially vigilant in examining the verdict.[10] The task of assessing whether to grant a new trial is, obviously, a highly fact-dependent one.[11]

Grounds for New Trials

Rule 59(a) provides no list of proper reasons for which new trials may be granted, and relies instead upon historical practice.[12] What historically justified a new trial in an action at law in the federal courts, today warrants a new trial following

---

Jackson, 668 F.Supp.2d 584, 598 (S.D.N.Y. 2009).

[3]*See Children's Broadcasting Corp. v. Walt Disney Co.*, 357 F.3d 860, 867 (8th Cir. 2004). *See also Gasperini v. Center for Humanities, Inc.*, 518 U.S. 415, 433, 116 S. Ct. 2211, 2222, 135 L. Ed. 2d 659 (1996) ("the authority of trial judges to grant new trials . . . is large").

[4]*See Defenders of Wildlife v. Bernal*, 204 F.3d 920, 928–29 (9th Cir. 2000).

[5]*See Robinson v. McNeil Consumer Healthcare*, 671 F.Supp.2d 975, 989 n.4 (N.D.Ill. 2009) (noting apparent division within panels of the Seventh Circuit); *Tatum v. Jackson*, 668 F.Supp.2d 584, 598 n.10 (S.D.N.Y. 2009) (same, within the Second Circuit). *But cf. Paradigm Alliance, Inc. v. Celeritas Techs., LLC*, 722 F.Supp.2d 1250, 1258 (D.Kan. 2010) (must view evidence most favorably to verdict winner).

[6]*See Allied Chem. Corp. v. Daiflon, Inc.*, 449 U.S. 33, 36, 101 S.Ct. 188, 66 L.Ed.2d 193 (1980); *Jennings v. Jones*, 587 F.3d 430, 439 (1st Cir. 2009) (following "general rule in the circuits", and citing cases); *Robinson*

v. McNeil Consumer Healthcare, 671 F.Supp.2d 975, 989 n.4 (N.D.Ill. 2009) (describing majority view as one endorsed by Professors Wright and Miller in their treatise). *See also Raedle v. Credit Agricole Indosuez*, 670 F.3d 411, 418–19 (2d Cir. 2012).

[7]*See Raedle v. Credit Agricole Indosuez*, 670 F.3d 411, 418–19 (2d Cir. 2012); *Kode v. Carlson*, 596 F.3d 608, 612 (9th Cir.2010).

[8]*See Armisted v. State Farm Mut. Auto. Ins. Co.*, 675 F.3d 989, 995 (6th Cir. 2012); *Raedle v. Credit Agricole Indosuez*, 670 F.3d 411, 418–19 (2d Cir. 2012); *Rodriguez v. Senor Frog's de la Isla, Inc.*, 642 F.3d 28, 37 (1st Cir. 2011).

[9]*See Guidance Endodontics, LLC v. Dentsply Int'l, Inc.*, 749 F.Supp.2d 1235, 1256 (D.N.M. 2010).

[10]*See Lind v. Schenley Indus. Inc.*, 278 F.2d 79, 90–91 (3d Cir.1960); *ZF Meritor, LLC v. Eaton Corp.*, 769 F.Supp.2d 684, 690 (D.Del. 2011).

[11]*See Heimlicher v. Steele*, 615 F.Supp.2d 884, 899 (N.D.Iowa 2009).

[12]*See Molski v. M.J. Cable, Inc.*, 481 F.3d 724, 729 (9th Cir. 2007); *Cal-Agrex, Inc. v. Tassell*, 258 F.R.D. 340, 343 (N.D.Cal. 2009).

a jury verdict; what historically justified a rehearing in a suit in equity in the federal courts, today warrants a new trial following a bench decision.[13] The courts have recognized that new trials may be properly granted in at least the following circumstances:

- *Verdict Against the Weight of Evidence:* when the district court concludes that the factfinder's verdict is against the "clear" or "great" weight of the evidence, and a new trial is therefore necessary to prevent a miscarriage of justice.[14] This ground—often premised entirely on a court's disagreement with a jury's credibility assessments—is a "rare occurrence,"[15] and ought to be considered with great restraint.[16]

- *Verdict is Excessive or Inadequate:* when the district court determines that the amount of the verdict is so unreasonable that it shocks the conscience;[17]

    - *"Remittitur":* If the court decides that the verdict is excessive, the court may offer the verdict winner a reduction—called a "remittitur"—in exchange for the court's denial of a motion for a new trial.[18] If the verdict winner accepts the court's of-

---

[13]*See* Rule 59(a)(1).

[14]*See Byrd v. Blue Ridge Rural Elec. Co-op., Inc.*, 356 U.S. 525, 540, 78 S. Ct. 893, 902, 2 L. Ed. 2d 953 (1958); *Molski v. M.J. Cable, Inc.*, 481 F.3d 724, 729–30 (9th Cir. 2007); *Mitchell v. Boelcke*, 440 F.3d 300, 303 (6th Cir. 2006). *See also Latino v. Kaizer*, 58 F.3d 310, 314 (7th Cir. 1995) (ruling that jury's verdict should be accorded greater deference under Rule 59 in cases involving simple issues with highly disputed facts, than in cases involving complex issues with facts that are not as disputed).

[15]*See Armisted v. State Farm Mut. Auto. Ins. Co.*, 675 F.3d 989, 994–95 (6th Cir. 2012).

[16]*See Raedle v. Credit Agricole Indosuez*, 670 F.3d 411, 418–19 (2d Cir. 2012).

[17]*See Mitchell v. Boelcke*, 440 F.3d 300, 303 (6th Cir. 2006). *See also Rivera Castillo v. Autokirey, Inc.*, 379 F.3d 4, 13 (1st Cir. 2004) (exceed "any rational appraisal or estimate of the damage that could be based on the evidence before the jury"); *Eiland v. Westinghouse Elec. Corp.*, 58 F.3d 176, 183 (5th Cir. 1995) ("contrary to right rea-

son" or "entirely disproportionate to the injury sustained"); *Reynolds v. Univ. of Pa.*, 684 F.Supp.2d 621, 627 (E.D.Pa. 2010) (high standard respects jury's factfinding function). *But see Gasperini v. Center for Humanities, Inc.*, 518 U.S. 415, 116 S. Ct. 2211, 135 L. Ed. 2d 659 (1996) (citing the *Erie* doctrine in applying New York's state law standard for judging "excessiveness", where state standard differed from federal "shocks the conscience" benchmark).

[18]*See Linn v. United Plant Guard Workers of America, Local 114*, 383 U.S. 53, 65–66, 86 S. Ct. 657, 664–65, 15 L. Ed. 2d 582 (1966) (if damages award is excessive, trial judge has the "duty" to require a remittitur or grant a new trial); *Cortez v. Trans Union, LLC*, 617 F.3d 688, 715–18 (3d Cir. 2010) (describing remittitur procedure, and distinguishing from constitutionally-reduced verdicts); *Atlas Food Systems and Services, Inc. v. Crane Nat. Vendors, Inc.*, 99 F.3d 587, 593 (4th Cir. 1996) (noting remittitur's history). Note, however, that the court ordinarily may not reduce plaintiff's damages award without first offering plaintiff a new trial. *See Hetzel*

fer, the verdict winner waives the right of appeal.[19] If remitted, the jury's verdict will usually be reduced to the maximum amount the jury could have awarded without being excessive.[20] A trial court's decision on remittitur is accorded wide discretion, given that judge's ability to hear the testimony and assess the demeanor of the witnesses; a trial court's ruling that denies remittitur will be overturned on appeal only where the verdict is found to be so grossly excessive that the outcome is "monstrous or shocking".[21] Noneconomic damages (such as pain and suffering) are usually remitted in only extraordinary circumstances.[22] Properly done, remittitur will generally not offend the Seventh Amendment's entitlement to a jury trial,[23] and may serve the laudable ends of avoiding delay and expense and limiting judicial intrusion into the jury's domain.[24]

- *"Additur"*: If the court finds that the verdict is inadequate, the court may *not* offer the verdict winner an increase in verdict size—called an "additur"—in exchange for the court's denial of a motion for new trial, due to Seventh Amendment concerns.[25] Where the verdict is inadequate, the court's only option is ordering a new trial.

- *Newly Discovered Evidence:* when the district court learns of a party's newly discovered evidence. To entitle the moving party to a new trial, the "newly discovered evidence" generally: (1) must have existed as of the time of trial; (2) must have been excusably overlooked by the

---

v. *Prince William Cnty.*, 523 U.S. 208, 211, 118 S.Ct. 1210, 140 L.Ed.2d 336 (1998) (per curiam).

[19]See *Donovan v. Penn Shipping Co., Inc.*, 429 U.S. 648, 97 S. Ct. 835, 51 L. Ed. 2d 112 (1977) (per curiam).

[20]See *Sloane v. Equifax Information Services, LLC*, 510 F.3d 495, 502–03 (4th Cir. 2007); *Eiland v. Westinghouse Elec. Corp.*, 58 F.3d 176, 183 (5th Cir. 1995). *See also Earl v. Bouchard Transp. Co., Inc.*, 917 F.2d 1320, 1328–30 (2d Cir. 1990) (adopting same rule, but discussing the three views on remittitur and scholarly commentary's preferences).

[21]See *Hite v. Vermeer Mfg. Co.*, 446 F.3d 858, 869–70 (8th Cir. 2006).

[22]See *Rodriguez v. Senor Frog's de la Isla, Inc.*, 642 F.3d 28, 39 (1st Cir. 2011).

[23]See *Gasperini v. Center for Humanities, Inc.*, 518 U.S. 415, 433, 116 S. Ct. 2211, 135 L. Ed. 2d 659 (1996); *Dimick v. Schiedt*, 293 U.S. 474, 486–87, 55 S. Ct. 296, 301, 79 L. Ed. 603 (1935). *See also Casey v. Long Island R. Co.*, 406 F.3d 142, 149 (2d Cir. 2005) (emphasizing that constitutionality of remittitur hinges on being given the choice between remittitur and new trial).

[24]See *Dwyer v. Deutsche Lufthansa, AG*, 686 F.Supp.2d 216, 218 (E.D.N.Y. 2010).

[25]See *Gasperini v. Center for Humanities, Inc.*, 518 U.S. 415, 433, 116 S. Ct. 2211, 135 L. Ed. 2d 659 (1996); *Dimick v. Schiedt*, 293 U.S. 474, 486–87, 55 S. Ct. 296, 301, 79 L. Ed. 603 (1935).

moving party, notwithstanding the moving party's due diligence in attempting to discover it; (3) must be admissible; and (4) must be likely to alter the trial's outcome.[26] In addition to a new trial under Rule 59, newly discovered evidence may also entitle the moving party to relief from judgment under Rule 60(b)(2).

- *Improper Conduct by Counsel or the Court:* when improper conduct by either an attorney or the court unfairly influenced the verdict.[27]

- *Improper Conduct Affecting the Jury:* when the jury verdict was not unanimous or was facially inconsistent,[28] or when the jury was improperly influenced,[29] or when an erroneous jury instruction likely misled or confused the jury.[30] Note, however, that after the verdict is returned, jurors may not impeach or alter their verdict except to testify as to improper, extrinsic influences.[31]

Prejudice

Trial errors may only give rise to a new trial if they affect the substantive rights of the parties and are not cured by the trial judge's cautionary instructions to the jury.[32] (Consequently, appeals from new trial rulings should almost always be accompanied by the trial transcript.[33])

District Court Findings and Conclusions

In granting a new trial, the district court is ordinarily under

---

[26]*See Colon-Millin v. Sears Roebuck De Puerto Rico, Inc.*, 455 F.3d 30, 36 n.4 (1st Cir. 2006); *Advanced Display Systems, Inc. v. Kent State University*, 212 F.3d 1272, 1284 (Fed. Cir. 2000); *Defenders of Wildlife v. Bernal*, 204 F.3d 920, 928–29 (9th Cir. 2000).

[27]*See Wharf v. Burlington Northern R. Co.*, 60 F.3d 631 (9th Cir.1995) (granting new trial where counsel permitted district court to read to the jury an untruthful stipulated fact concerning plaintiff); *Aggarwal v. Ponce School of Medicine*, 837 F.2d 17 (1st Cir. 1988) (before conduct of judge will warrant a new trial, the moving party must be "so seriously prejudiced as to be deprived of a fair trial"); *City of Cleveland v. Peter Kiewit Sons' Co.*, 624 F.2d 749 (6th Cir.1980) (moving for new trial where counsel injected into trial notion that insurance company would pay any award).

[28]*See Monaco v. City of Camden*, 366 Fed.Appx. 330, 331–32 (3d Cir. 2010); *Babby v. Wilmington Dep't of Police*, 614 F.Supp.2d 508, 512 (D.Del.

2009).

[29]*Cf. Parker v. Gladden*, 385 U.S. 363, 87 S. Ct. 468, 17 L. Ed. 2d 420 (1966) (per curiam)(statement by bailiff that defendant was a "wicked fellow" who was guilty, and that the higher courts would correct a guilty verdict if it was wrong).

[30]*See Susan Wakeen Doll Co., Inc. v. Ashton Drake Galleries*, 272 F.3d 441, 452 (7th Cir. 2001).

[31]*See Carson v. Polley*, 689 F.2d 562 (5th Cir.1982); *Smallwood v. Pearl Brewing Co.*, 489 F.2d 579 (5th Cir. 1974).

[32]*See* Rule 61 (directing that harmless errors are to be disregarded). *See also Rodriguez v. Senor Frog's de la Isla, Inc.*, 642 F.3d 28, 37–38 (1st Cir. 2011); *Krippelz v. Ford Motor Co.*, 750 F.Supp.2d 938, 942–43 (N.D.Ill. 2010); *Reynolds v. Univ. of Pa.*, 747 F.Supp.2d 522, 533–34 (E.D.Pa. 2010).

[33]*See Rodriguez v. Senor Frog's de la Isla, Inc.*, 642 F.3d 28, 37–39 (1st Cir. 2011); *Giron v. McFadden*, 746 F.Supp.2d 5, 7 n.5 (D.D.C. 2010).

no obligation to set out supporting findings of fact and conclusions of law.[34]

Burden of Proof

The burden of proving the necessity of a new trial lies with the party seeking it.[35]

Preservation and Waiver

A party may not seek a new trial on grounds not brought contemporaneously to the trial judge's attention.[36] The courts recognize a narrow exception to this waiver rule where a trial error is so fundamental that gross injustice would result were it not corrected. Beyond this obligation of general preservation, motions for new trials (unlike Rule 50 motions for judgment on the pleadings) do not require a further pre-verdict motion, nor is a new trial motion at the district court level essential to preserving a right of appeal[37] (although when the motion attacks sufficiency of the trial evidence, this point has been cast into some doubt).[38]

Bench Trials

If a new trial is awarded following a bench trial, the district court may, upon retrial, open a judgment already entered, hear additional testimony, revise or add findings of fact and conclusions of law, and direct the entry of a new judgment.[39] But such motions are usually not proper platforms for new evidence which could have been offered earlier, new theories, or a rehearing on the merits.[40] Moreover, trial courts may refuse a reopening upon examining the probative value of the evidence at issue, the justification for the failure to offer it earlier, and the likelihood that the reopening will inflict undue prejudice.[41]

---

[34]*See Jennings v. Jones*, 587 F.3d 430, 441 n.11 (1st Cir. 2009).

[35]*See ZF Meritor, LLC v. Eaton Corp.*, 769 F.Supp.2d 684, 690 (D.Del. 2011); *Guidance Endodontics, LLC v. Dentsply Int'l, Inc.*, 749 F.Supp.2d 1235, 1256 (D.N.M. 2010). *See also Czekalski v. Secretary of Transp.*, 577 F.Supp.2d 120, 122–23 (D.D.C. 2008) (noting burden is "heavy").

[36]*See U.S. v. Walton*, 909 F.2d 915 (6th Cir. 1990); *Guidance Endodontics, LLC v. Dentsply Int'l, Inc.*, 728 F.Supp.2d 1170, 1185 (D.N.M. 2010). *But cf. Pulla v. Amoco Oil Co.*, 72 F.3d 648, 656 (8th Cir. 1995) (party may move for new trial under Rule 59 "based on the overwhelming evidence contrary to the verdict without ever previously raising such an objection").

[37]*See Pediatrix Screening, Inc. v. Telechem Int'l., Inc.*, 602 F.3d 541, 546–47 (3d Cir. 2010); *Fuesting v. Zimmer, Inc.*, 448 F.3d 936, 940–42 (7th Cir. 2006).

[38]*But see Pediatrix Screening, Inc. v. Telechem Int'l., Inc.*, 602 F.3d 541, 546–47 (3d Cir. 2010) (rejecting suggestion that Supreme Court's decision in *Unitherm Food Systems, Inc. v. Swift-Eckrich, Inc.*, 546 U.S. 394, 126 S.Ct. 980, 163 L.Ed.2d 974 (2006), demands further preservation); *Fuesting v. Zimmer, Inc.*, 448 F.3d 936, 940–42 (7th Cir. 2006) (same point, citing Fed. R. Evid. 103(a)).

[39]*See* Rule 59(a)(2).

[40]*See Chavez v. City of Albuquerque*, 640 F. Supp. 2d 1340, 1343 (D.N.M. 2008).

[41]*See Precision Pine & Timber, Inc. v. United States*, 596 F.3d 817,

Partial New Trials

The court may grant a partial new trial limited only to certain issues, provided the error justifying the new trial did not affect the determination of the remaining issues,[42] and provided that the singular issue for retrial is so clearly distinct and separate from all other issues that a retrial of it alone will not be unjust.[43] When a partial new trial is granted, those portions of the original judgment that were not set aside by the court become part of the single, ultimate judgment following the new trial. Most commonly, courts have granted partial new trials on damages, following an error-free trial on liability issues, but partial new trials can be granted as to any "separable matter".[44] If, however, the trial court concludes that passion influenced the jury, a partial new trial on the issue of damages alone is ordinarily improper; the court must instead order a new trial on all issues.[45]

Appealability

An order granting a new trial is generally interlocutory and not immediately appealable, absent a showing that the court lacked authority to enter the order.[46] An order denying a new trial is also usually not immediately appealable,[47] or appealable at all;[48] rather, the party's proper appeal is typically an appeal from the final judgment itself, not from the mere denial of a new trial (at least absent new matters arising after entry of the judgment).[49] Note that even ultimate appellate review of denials of new trials may be further limited by Seventh Amendment constitutional concerns.[50]

RULE 59(b)—TIME TO FILE A MOTION FOR A

833–34 (Fed.Cir. 2010).

[42] See Anderson v. Siemens Corp., 335 F.3d 466, 475–76 (5th Cir. 2003); Eximco, Inc. v. Trane Co., 737 F.2d 505 (5th Cir.1984).

[43] See Gasoline Products Co. v. Champlin Refining Co., 283 U.S. 494, 500, 51 S. Ct. 513, 515, 75 L. Ed. 1188 (1931); East Tex. Med. Ctr. Reg'l Healthcare Sys. v. Lexington Ins. Co., 575 F.3d 520, 532 (5th Cir. 2009).

[44] See Rice v. Community Health Ass'n, 203 F.3d 283, 290 (4th Cir. 2000).

[45] See Sanford v. Crittenden Memorial Hosp., 141 F.3d 882, 885 (8th Cir. 1998).

[46] See Allied Chemical Corp. v. Daiflon, Inc., 449 U.S. 33, 101 S. Ct. 188, 66 L. Ed. 2d 193 (1980); Schudel v. General Elec. Co., 120 F.3d 991, 994–95 (9th Cir. 1997).

[47] See Clark By and Through Clark v. Heidrick, 150 F.3d 912 (8th Cir. 1998).

[48] See Youmans v. Simon, 791 F.2d 341, 349 (5th Cir. 1986).

[49] See Johansen v. Combustion Eng'g, Inc., 170 F.3d 1320, 1329 n.12 (11th Cir. 1999); Bether v. McAllister Bros., 81 F.3d 376, 382 (3d Cir. 1996); Youmans v. Simon, 791 F.2d 341, 349 (5th Cir. 1986). But see Fiore v. Washington County Cmty. Mental Health Ctr., 960 F.2d 229, 232–33 & 233 n.8 (1st Cir. 1992) (noting conflict with other courts, but holding that denials of new trial motions are appealable independently from appeal of judgment itself).

[50] See Jocks v. Tavernier, 316 F.3d 128, 137 (2d Cir. 2003) (commenting that district court's determination that jury's verdict was not against weight of evidence is not reviewable on ap-

NEW TRIAL

CORE CONCEPT

A party must file a motion for a new trial within 28 days after entry of the judgment (prior to December 2009, this period had been 10 days).

APPLICATIONS

Impact of 2009 "Time Computation" Amendments

Deemed unrealistically short, the longstanding 10-day period for filing motions for new trials was extended to 28 days, effective December 2009.

28-Day Period to *File* Motion for New Trial

This time period is for *filing*, not merely service.[51] Thus, a party seeking a new trial must *file* the Rule 59 motion within 28 days after the district court enters judgment on the docket.

Amended Judgments

Where an amended judgment is filed and alters the legal rights or obligations of the parties, a new time period for filing Rule 59 motions might be triggered.[52]

Early Motions

A party may move for a new trial before the formal entry of judgment and at any time during the 28 days following the entry of judgment. Originally, a notice of appeal, filed prematurely before the trial court had ruled upon a pending motion for a new trial, would have been deemed a "nullity".[53] Under recent amendments to Federal Rule of Appellate Procedure 4(a)(4), a prematurely filed appeal is now treated as filed as of the date the trial court ultimately disposes of the pending Rule 59 motion.[54]

Each Party Seeking Relief Must File

In a multi-party case, a motion by one litigant under Rule 59 will not excuse the non-filing by another litigant; each party

---

peal due to limitations imposed by Seventh Amendment).

[51]*See Schudel v. General Elec. Co.*, 120 F.3d 991 (9th Cir. 1997) (noting that Rule 59, as amended in 1995, requires that such motions be timely filed, not served).

[52]*See Walker v. Bain*, 257 F.3d 660, 670 (6th Cir. 2001).

[53]*See Griggs v. Provident Consumer Discount Co.*, 459 U.S. 56, 61, 103 S. Ct. 400, 403, 74 L. Ed. 2d 225 (1982) (per curiam). *Accord Acosta*

v. Louisiana Dept. of Health and Human Resources, 478 U.S. 251, 254, 106 S. Ct. 2876, 2877, 92 L. Ed. 2d 192 (1986).

[54]*See* Fed. R. App. P. 4(a)(4)(B). *See also New Windsor Volunteer Ambulance Corps, Inc. v. Meyers*, 442 F.3d 101, 120 (2d Cir. 2006); *Leader Nat. Ins. Co. v. Industrial Indem. Ins. Co.*, 19 F.3d 444 (9th Cir. 1994) (noting that, after 1993 amendment, appeal is no longer a nullity but is merely held in abeyance).

seeking relief under this Rule must move for it.[55]

No Extensions

This 28-day period may not be extended by court order.[56] Over the years, two common law exceptions were recognized to this prohibition, though only one persists.[57] If an out-of-time Rule 59 motion is filed, but not objected to, the court may, in its discretion, consider the untimely motion (though the ramifications for a later appeal remain uncertain).[58] In any event, courts may treat an untimely Rule 59 motion as one made under Rule 60 and assess it under that Rule.[59]

3-Day Service Extension Does *Not* Apply

Rule 6(d) extends a party's time for acting by 3 days if the relevant time period is dated from service by mail, electronic service, or certain other service methods. Because Rule 59(b) requires *filing* (not service) no later than 28 days after entry of judgment, this 3-day service extension does not apply.[60]

Timely Motion Tolls Appeal Period

A timely-filed motion for a new trial delays the finality of the underlying judgment and tolls the time for appeal.[61]

- *Tolling Applies to All Parties:* A timely filed Rule 59 motion tolls the time for appeal for all parties.[62]

Motion Filed After Notice of Appeal

The filing of a notice of appeal is jurisdictional; once filed, the district court is divested of jurisdiction over those aspects of the case implicated in the appeal, and jurisdiction is conferred upon the court of appeals.[63] Consequently, a party seeking to move the district court for a new trial after a notice of appeal has been filed must file a motion with the district

---

[55]*See Hertz Corp. v. Alamo Rent-A-Car, Inc.*, 16 F.3d 1126 (11th Cir. 1994).

[56]*See* Rule 6(b)(2). *See also Blue v. Int'l Bhd. of Elec. Workers Local Union 159*, 676 F.3d 579, 584–85 (7th Cir. 2012); *Schneider ex rel. Estate of Schneider v. Fried*, 320 F.3d 396, 402–03 (3d Cir. 2003).

[57]*See supra* Authors' Commentary to Rule 6(b) (**"No Extensions"**).

[58]*See Blue v. Int'l Bhd. of Elec. Workers Local Union 159*, 676 F.3d 579, 584–85 (7th Cir. 2012); *Lizardo v. United States*, 619 F.3d 273, 277–80 (3d Cir. 2010).

[59]*See Blue v. Int'l Bhd. of Elec. Workers Local Union 159*, 676 F.3d 579, 585 (7th Cir. 2012); *Feathers v. Chevron U.S.A., Inc.*, 141 F.3d 264, 268 (6th Cir. 1998).

[60]*See Cavaliere v. Allstate Ins. Co.*, 996 F.2d 1111, 1112–14 (11th Cir. 1993). *See also Adams v. Trustees of New Jersey Brewery Employees' Pension Trust Fund*, 29 F.3d 863, 870–71 (3d Cir. 1994) (applying same reasoning in construing Rule 59(e)); *Derrington-Bey v. District of Columbia Dept. of Corrections*, 39 F.3d 1224, 1225 (D.C. Cir. 1994) (same).

[61]*See* Fed. R. App. P. 4(a)(4)(A)(v). *See also York Group, Inc. v. Wuxi Taihu Tractor Co.*, 632 F.3d 399, 401 (7th Cir. 2011).

[62]*See New Windsor Volunteer Ambulance Corps, Inc. v. Meyers*, 442 F.3d 101, 120 (2d Cir. 2006).

[63]*See Griggs v. Provident Consumer Discount Co.*, 459 U.S. 56, 58, 103 S. Ct. 400, 402, 74 L. Ed. 2d 225 (1982) (per curiam).

judge, and the judge may then request a remand of the case from the court of appeals.[64]

RULE 59(c)—TIME TO SERVE AFFIDAVITS

CORE CONCEPT

A party may support a motion for new trial with affidavits. In such a case, the supporting affidavits must be filed with the motion. Opposing affidavits may be filed 14 days thereafter.

Impact of 2009 "Time Computation" Amendments

Effective December 2009, the Rule 59(c) time period for filing affidavits opposing new trial motions was extended from 10 days to 14 days, to conform to the new multiples-of-7-days standard for federal civil time periods.

RULE 59(d)—NEW TRIAL ON THE COURT'S INITIATIVE OR FOR OTHER REASONS NOT IN THE MOTION

CORE CONCEPT

The court may grant a new trial entirely on its own initiative, or, upon reviewing a party's motion, may grant a new trial for a reason not stated in the moving papers.

APPLICATIONS

Impact of 2009 "Time Computation" Amendments

Deemed unrealistically short, the longstanding 10-day period for *sua sponte* grants of new trials was extended to 28 days, effective December 2009.

Grounds

The court may grant a new trial for any reason that a party could have permissibly requested by motion.[65]

Timing

A court that intends to grant a new trial on its own initiative must do so within 28 days after the entry of judgment. When a court receives a motion, but decides to grant a new trial for reasons not specified in the motion, the timing is less clear. One court has held that the timing requirement does not apply to such rulings;[66] another court has held the opposite.[67]

Granting on Different Grounds

When a court decides to grant a new trial for reasons differ-

---

[64]*See Hattersley v. Bollt*, 512 F.2d 209 (3d Cir.1975). *See also* Rule 62.1 (permitting "indicative rulings").

[65]*See Park West Galleries, Inc. v. Hochman*, 692 F.3d 539, 544 (6th Cir. 2012); *Pryer v. C.O. 3 Slavic*, 251 F.3d

448, 453 (3d Cir. 2001).

[66]*See Kelly v. Moore*, 376 F.3d 481, 484 (5th Cir. 2004).

[67]*See Demeretz v. Daniels Motor Freight, Inc.*, 307 F.2d 469, 472–73 (3d Cir.1962).

ent from those set forth in the moving party's papers, the court must give the parties notice of this intention and an opportunity to be heard.[68]

Specifying Grounds for New Trial

When the court grants a motion for a new trial on its own initiative or on grounds different from those stated in a party's motion papers, the order must specify the grounds for the court's decision.

Other *Sua Sponte* Revisions to Judgments

Although Rule 59(d) does not expressly contemplate it, one court has approved use of the Rule to substantively amend a judgment.[69]

RULE 59(e)—MOTION TO ALTER OR AMEND A JUDGMENT

CORE CONCEPT

The court may alter or amend its judgment upon motion by a party.

APPLICATIONS

Impact of 2009 "Time Computation" Amendments

Deemed unrealistically short, the longstanding 10-day period for motions to alter or amend a judgment was extended to 28 days, effective December 2009.

Purpose

The purpose of Rule 59(e) is to provide the district court with a means for correcting errors that may have "crept into the proceeding", while that court still holds jurisdiction over the case.[70] It thus gives the trial court the opportunity to cure its own mistakes (if it believes it made any).[71]

Grounds

No listing of proper grounds for altering or amending a judgment is included in the language of Rule 59(e), and federal case law has been left to fill in that void.[72] Broadly, a motion to alter or amend a judgment is appropriate where it seeks a reexamination of matters properly encompassed within the trial

---

[68]*See Capitol Records, Inc. v. Thomas*, 579 F.Supp.2d 1210, 1213 (D.Minn. 2008) (court gave notice of possible alternative grounds, accepted additional briefing, and heard oral argument).

[69]*See HyperQuest, Inc. v. N'Site Solutions, Inc.*, 632 F.3d 377, 386 (7th Cir. 2011).

[70]*See Sosebee v. Astrue*, 494 F.3d 583, 589 (7th Cir. 2007).

[71]*See Howard v. U.S.*, 533 F.3d 472, 475 (6th Cir. 2008); *Zinkand v. Brown*, 478 F.3d 634, 637 (4th Cir. 2007).

[72]*See Sloas v. Ass'n of Am. R.R.s.*, 616 F.3d 380, 385 n.2 (4th Cir. 2010).

court's decision on the merits.[73] The case law acknowledges four grounds that justify altering or amending a judgment: to incorporate an intervening change in the law,[74] to reflect new evidence not available at the time of trial,[75] to correct a clear legal error,[76] and to prevent a manifest injustice.[77] Thus, for example, a Rule 59(e) motion was appropriate where the court misunderstood the facts, a party's arguments, or the controlling law,[78] where the original judgment failed to provide that relief which the court found a party entitled to receive,[79] or where the party seeks a post-judgment award of prejudgment interest.[80]

District Court's Discretion

The decision whether to alter or amend a judgment is generally committed to the discretion of the trial judge.[81] Exercis-

---

[73]*See White v. New Hampshire Dept. of Employment Sec.*, 455 U.S. 445, 451, 102 S. Ct. 1162, 1166, 71 L. Ed. 2d 325 (1982).

[74]*See Somerlott v. Cherokee Nation Distribs., Inc.*, 686 F.3d 1144, 1153 (10th Cir. 2012); *Patton Boggs LLP v. Chevron Corp.*, 683 F.3d 397, 403 (D.C.Cir. 2012); *Nolfi v. Ohio Ky. Oil Corp.*, 675 F.3d 538, 551–52 (6th Cir. 2012).

[75]*See Patton Boggs LLP v. Chevron Corp.*, 683 F.3d 397, 403 (D.C.Cir. 2012); *Nolfi v. Ohio Ky. Oil Corp.*, 675 F.3d 538, 551–52 (6th Cir. 2012); *Mayfield v. Nat'l Ass'n for Stock Car Auto Racing, Inc.*, 674 F.3d 369, 378–79 (4th Cir. 2012). *See generally Devon Energy Prod. Co., L.P. v. Mosaic Potash Carlsbad, Inc.*, 693 F.3d 1195, 1213 (10th Cir. 2012) (must show newly discovered or diligent (though) unsuccessful efforts to obtain it, and how evidence would have prevented dismissal); *Greyhound Lines, Inc. v. Wade*, 485 F.3d 1032, 1036 (8th Cir. 2007) (party must show that (1) the evidence was discovered after trial; (2) the movant exercised due diligence to discover it before the end of trial; (3) the evidence is material and not merely cumulative or impeaching; and (4) the evidence would probably produce a different result).

[76]*See Somerlott v. Cherokee Nation Distribs., Inc.*, 686 F.3d 1144, 1153 (10th Cir. 2012); *Patton Boggs LLP v. Chevron Corp.*, 683 F.3d 397, 403 (D.C.Cir. 2012); *Nolfi v. Ohio Ky. Oil*

Corp., 675 F.3d 538, 551–52 (6th Cir. 2012).

[77]*See Patton Boggs LLP v. Chevron Corp.*, 683 F.3d 397, 403 (D.C.Cir. 2012); *Nolfi v. Ohio Ky. Oil Corp.*, 675 F.3d 538, 551–52 (6th Cir. 2012); *Mayfield v. Nat'l Ass'n for Stock Car Auto Racing, Inc.*, 674 F.3d 369, 378–79 (4th Cir. 2012). *See also Ford Motor Credit Co. v. Bright*, 34 F.3d 322, 324 (5th Cir. 1994) (in considering Rule 59(e) motion, court may take into account attorney's conduct).

[78]*See Barber ex rel. Barber v. Colorado Dep't of Revenue*, 562 F.3d 1222, 1228 (10th Cir. 2009).

[79]*See Continental Cas. Co. v. Howard*, 775 F.2d 876 (7th Cir. 1985).

[80]*See Osterneck v. Ernst & Whinney*, 489 U.S. 169, 109 S. Ct. 987, 103 L. Ed. 2d 146 (1989). *But see Buchanan v. Stanships, Inc.*, 485 U.S. 265, 108 S. Ct. 1130, 99 L. Ed. 2d 289 (1988) (seeking an allowance of costs under Rule 54(d) is not appropriate for a Rule 59(e) motion, because such costs are collateral to the merits of the action); *White v. New Hampshire Dept. of Employment Sec.*, 455 U.S. 445, 102 S. Ct. 1162, 71 L. Ed. 2d 325 (1982) (seeking an award of attorney's fees is not appropriate for a Rule 59(e) motion).

[81]*See Sipp v. Astrue*, 641 F.3d 975, 981 (8th Cir. 2011); *Barber ex rel. Barber v. Colorado Dep't of Revenue*, 562 F.3d 1222, 1228 (10th Cir. 2009); *Betts v. Costco Wholesale Corp.*, 558 F.3d 461, 467 (6th Cir. 2009).

ing this discretion calls upon the court to balance two competing interests—the need to bring litigation to a close and the
need to render just rulings based on all the facts.[82] However,
this liberal discretion standard does not apply to Rule 59(e)
motions seeking review of a grant of summary judgment; as to
those motions, a *de novo* standard applies.[83] Reconsideration of
a judgment is an extraordinary remedy that is used only sparingly,[84] and a remedy "exceedingly difficult" for the moving
party to obtain.[85]

28-Day Period to *File* Motion to Alter or Amend

The Rule 59(e) time period is for *filing*, not merely service.[86]
Thus, a party seeking to alter or amend a judgment must *file*
that Rule 59(e) motion with 28 days after the district court
enters judgment on the docket.[87]

No Extensions

The court may not grant a party any extensions to this time
period.[88] An untimely Rule 59(e) motion may be deemed a nullity,[89] or, in an appropriate case, treated as a Rule 60(b) motion
for relief from a judgment.[90] However, there is developing case
law that when an untimely Rule 59(e) motion is filed, but not
objected to by the non-moving party, the timeliness objection
may be deemed forfeited through waiver.[91] This is a dangerous
gamble, though; if the trial court grants the motion, the ag-

---

[82]*See Templet v. HydroChem Inc.*, 367 F.3d 473, 478–79 (5th Cir. 2004).

[83]*See Cockrel v. Shelby County School Dist.*, 270 F.3d 1036, 1047 (6th Cir. 2001).

[84]*See Mayfield v. Nat'l Ass'n for Stock Car Auto Racing, Inc.*, 674 F.3d 369, 378–79 (4th Cir. 2012); *Templet v. HydroChem Inc.*, 367 F.3d 473, 479 (5th Cir. 2004).

[85]*See Soto-Padro v. Public Bldgs. Auth.*, 675 F.3d 1, 9 (1st Cir. 2012).

[86]*See Schudel v. General Elec. Co.*, 120 F.3d 991 (9th Cir. 1997), (noting that Rule 59, as amended in 1995, requires that such motions be filed, not served, within 10 days following entry of judgment). *See also Life Ins. Co. of North America v. Von Valtier*, 116 F.3d 279, 282–83 (7th Cir. 1997) (considering motion to be timely filed where it was delivered to district court, as required by standing chambers order, but trial judge delayed in transmitting motion to clerk's office for formal filing).

[87]*See Keith v. Bobby*, 618 F.3d 594, 597–99 (6th Cir. 2010) (period

runs from date order was entered, not date it became final).

[88]*See* Rule 6(b). *See also Keith v. Bobby*, 618 F.3d 594, 598–99 (6th Cir. 2010); *Green v. Drug Enforcement Admin.*, 606 F.3d 1296, 1299 (11th Cir. 2010); *Fisher v. Kadant, Inc.*, 589 F.3d 505, 511 (1st Cir. 2009).

[89]*See Fisher v. Kadant, Inc.*, 589 F.3d 505, 511 (1st Cir. 2009).

[90]*See Lora v. O'Heaney*, 602 F.3d 106, 111 (2d Cir. 2010); *Walker v. Astrue*, 593 F.3d 274, 279 (3d Cir. 2010); *Benson v. St. Joseph Reg'l Health Ctr.*, 575 F.3d 542, 546–47 (5th Cir. 2009).

[91]*See National Ecological Foundation v. Alexander*, 496 F.3d 466, 474–75 (6th Cir. 2007) (relying on two recent Supreme Court cases, *Eberhart v. U.S.*, 546 U.S. 12, 126 S. Ct. 403, 163 L. Ed. 2d 14 (2005) (per curiam) and *Kontrick v. Ryan*, 540 U.S. 443, 124 S. Ct. 906, 157 L. Ed. 2d 867 (2004)). *See also Obaydullah v. Obama*, 688 F.3d 784, 787–91 (D.C.Cir. 2012); *Lizardo v. United States*, 619 F.3d 273, 276–78 (3d Cir. 2010).

grieved party may receive meaningful relief, but it the trial
court denies the motion, the aggrieved party's time for taking
an appeal may well be already long lost.[92]

3-Day Service Extension Does Not Apply

Rule 6(e) extends a party's time for acting by 3 days if the
relevant time period is to begin upon service by mail, electronic
service, or certain other means of service. Because Rule 59(e)
requires *filing* (not service) no later than 28 days after entry of
judgment, this 3-day service extension does not apply.[93]

Prisoner Plaintiffs

The prisoner "mailbox rule" has been adopted by some
courts for Rule 59(e) motions. Consequently, a *pro se* prisoner's
papers may be deemed filed when deposited with the post
office.[94]

Motion Tolls Appeal Period

Like Rule 59 motions for new trial, a timely-filed Rule 59(e)
motion to alter or amend the judgment tolls the time for
appeal.[95] A prematurely filed appeal during the pendency of a
Rule 59(e) motion is held in abeyance until the date the district
court resolves the pending motion.[96] An untimely Rule 59(e)
motion generally will not toll the time for appeal,[97] nor, generally, will a second or later Rule 59(e) motion.[98] However, in
rare instances, the trial court's ruling on a Rule 59(e) motion
will change "matters of substance" or resolve a "genuine ambiguity" in court's original order and, in those infrequent cases, a
new judgment is recognized, from which a new Rule 59(e) mo-

---

[92]*See Lizardo v. United States*,
619 F.3d 273, 276–80 (3d Cir. 2010)
(Rule 59(e) is "claim processing rule",
and timeliness requirement may be
forfeited, but for appeal purposes,
untimely Rule 59(e) motions do not toll
appeal period, which begins to run
from judgment); *Green v. Drug Enforcement Admin.*, 606 F.3d 1296, 1302
(11th Cir. 2010) (same effect). *But see
Nat'l Ecological Found. v. Alexander*,
496 F.3d 466, 476 (6th Cir. 2007)
(discerning no reason why motion that
was properly considered by trial court
because timeliness objection was
waived would fail to extend appeal period).

[93]*See Albright v. Virtue*, 273 F.3d
564, 567 (3d Cir. 2001); *FHC Equities,
L.L.C. v. MBL Life Assur. Corp.*, 188
F.3d 678 (6th Cir.1999). *See also
Cavaliere v. Allstate Ins. Co.*, 996 F.2d
1111, 1112–14 (11th Cir. 1993) (applying same reasoning in construing Rule
59(b)).

[94]*See Long v. Atlantic City Police
Dep't*, 670 F.3d 436, 440–45 (3d Cir.
2012); *Edwards v. U.S.*, 266 F.3d 756,
758 (7th Cir. 2001).

[95]*See, e.g., Green v. Drug Enforcement Admin.*, 606 F.3d 1296, 1299
(11th Cir. 2010); *Auto Servs. Co. v.
KPMG, LLP*, 537 F.3d 853, 856 (8th
Cir. 2008).

[96]*See* Fed. R. App. P. 4(a)(4) (as
amended Dec. 1, 1993); *Moses v.
Howard Univ. Hosp.*, 606 F.3d 789,
796 (D.C.Cir. 2010); *Andrews v. E.I.
Du Pont De Nemours and Co.*, 447
F.3d 510, 515 (7th Cir. 2006).

[97]*See Garcia-Velazquez v. Frito
Lay Snacks Caribbean*, 358 F.3d 6, 9
(1st Cir. 2004); *Panhorst v. U.S.*, 241
F.3d 367, 370 (4th Cir. 2001); *Wight v.
BankAmerica Corp.*, 219 F.3d 79, 84
(2d Cir. 2000).

[98]*See Benson v. St. Joseph Reg'l
Health Ctr.*, 575 F.3d 542, 546–47 (5th
Cir. 2009); *Acevedo-Villalobos v.
Hernandez*, 22 F.3d 384 (1st Cir. 1994).

tion (with appeal-period tolling effect) may be filed.[99]

"Particularity" Requirement for Motion

All Rule 59(e) motions must satisfy the "particularity" requirement of Rule 7(b)(1).[100] Failure to do so may have dire consequences, including a loss of appeal-period tolling. Thus, a "skeleton" motion that fails to alert the court or the other litigants of the grounds for which an alteration or amendment is sought may be deemed improper and, thus, ineffective in tolling the appeal period.[101]

> *Appeal Must Name Correct Order:* The filing of a timely, proper Rule 59(e) motion can toll the time for filing an appeal from the original underlying *merits* ruling, and not just from the court's disposition of the Rule 59(e) motion itself.[102] However, to benefit from that *merits* tolling effect, the litigant must list the *merits* ruling on the Notice of Appeal (in addition to any other orders from which the appeal is taken).[103] Although the appellate courts will liberally construe the Notice of Appeal to give effect to the parties' intentions if clearly obvious (and in the absence of prejudice to the adversary),[104] litigants have been cautioned by the courts "that such rescue missions are not automatic, and litigants will do well to draft notices of appeal with care".[105]

Motions for "Reconsideration"

The Rules do not expressly recognize motions for "reconsideration".[106] When "reconsideration" is sought from an interlocutory order (*e.g.*, a denial of a motion to dismiss or for

---

[99]*See Andrews v. E.I. Du Pont De Nemours and Co.*, 447 F.3d 510, 516 (7th Cir. 2006) (noting exception, and stating that test is "whether the district court disturbed or revised legal rights settled in the original . . . order").

[100]*See Intera Corp. v. Henderson*, 428 F.3d 605, 611 (6th Cir. 2005).

[101]*See Talano v. Northwestern Medical Faculty Foundation, Inc.*, 273 F.3d 757, 760–61 (7th Cir. 2001) ("if a party could file a skeleton motion and later fill it in, the purpose of the time limitation would be defeated").

[102]*See Andrews v. Columbia Gas Transmission Corp.*, 544 F.3d 618, 623 n.4 (6th Cir. 2008); *Chamorro v. Puerto Rican Cars, Inc.*, 304 F.3d 1, 3 (1st Cir. 2002).

[103]*See Chamorro v. Puerto Rican Cars, Inc.*, 304 F.3d 1, 3 (1st Cir. 2002) (an appeal taken only from the order denying the Rule 59(e) motion will generally not be considered an appeal from the underlying merits judgment); *Correa v. Cruisers, a Div. of KCS Intern., Inc.*, 298 F.3d 13, 21 n. 3 (1st Cir. 2002) (same).

[104]*See Chamorro v. Puerto Rican Cars, Inc.*, 304 F.3d 1, 3 (1st Cir. 2002) (commenting that "formalism is not obligatory", and Notice will be construed liberally and examined in the context of the record as a whole, "with a recognition that the core purpose of a notice of appeal is to 'facilitate a proper decision on the merits' "); *Correa v. Cruisers, a Div. of KCS Intern., Inc.*, 298 F.3d 13, 21 n. 3 (1st Cir. 2002) (same effect).

[105]*See Chamorro v. Puerto Rican Cars, Inc.*, 304 F.3d 1, 3 (1st Cir. 2002).

[106]*See Katyle v. Penn Nat'l Gaming, Inc.*, 637 F.3d 462, 470 n.4 (4th Cir. 2011); *Auto Services Co., Inc. v. KPMG, LLP*, 537 F.3d 853, 856 (8th Cir. 2008);

summary judgment), that motion is not properly considered under Rule 59(e) but, instead, as simply a request for the district court to revisit its earlier ruling.[107] When "reconsideration" is sought from a true judgment or other final order, such a motion will be treated *either* as one under Rule 59(e) *or* as one under Rule 60(b),[108] a classification typically dependent on the date the motion is filed. If filed within the 28-day period set for Rule 59(e) motions, the "reconsideration" will generally be treated under Rule 59(e).[109] Otherwise, the courts will ordinarily examine the motion under Rule 60(b).[110] In either case, however, the applicable legal analysis will depend on the grounds asserted for the relief requested.[111]

Motions for "reconsideration" will not be granted absent "highly unusual circumstances."[112] Such motions do not provide litigants with an opportunity for a "second bite at the apple"[113] or allow them, like Emperor Nero, to "fiddle as Rome burns",[114] or to "ante up and play a new hand,"[115] or license a litigation "game of hopscotch" in which parties switch from one legal theory to a new one "like a bee in search of honey".[116] In other words, motions for reconsideration are not vehicles for relitigat-

---

Computerized Thermal Imaging, Inc. v. Bloomberg, L.P., 312 F.3d 1292, 1296 n.3 (10th Cir. 2002).

[107]*See Jones v. Bernanke*, 557 F.3d 670, 677–78 (D.C.Cir. 2009).

[108]*See Commonwealth Prop. Advocates, LLC v. Mortgage Elec. Registration Sys., Inc.*, 680 F.3d 1194, 1200 (10th Cir. 2011); *Auto Services Co., Inc. v. KPMG, LLP*, 537 F.3d 853, 856 (8th Cir. 2008).

[109]*See Katyle v. Penn Nat'l Gaming, Inc.*, 637 F.3d 462, 470 n.4 (4th Cir. 2011); *Negron-Almeda v. Santiago*, 528 F.3d 15, 20 (1st Cir. 2008); *Carrascosa v. McGuire*, 520 F.3d 249, 253 n.3 (3d Cir. 2008).

[110]*See U.S. v. Comprehensive Drug Testing, Inc.*, 513 F.3d 1085, 1098 (9th Cir. 2008); *Allender v. Raytheon Aircraft Co.*, 439 F.3d 1236, 1242 (10th Cir. 2006); *Texas A&M Research Foundation v. Magna Transp., Inc.*, 338 F.3d 394, 400 (5th Cir. 2003).

[111]*See Negron-Almeda v. Santiago*, 528 F.3d 15, 20 (1st Cir. 2008); *Obriecht v. Raemisch*, 517 F.3d 489, 493–94 (7th Cir. 2008); *Jennings v. Rivers*, 394 F.3d 850, 855 (10th Cir. 2005).

[112]*See McDowell v. Calderon*, 197 F.3d 1253, 1255 (9th Cir. 1999). *See*

also *U.S. ex rel. Becker v. Westinghouse Savannah River Co.*, 305 F.3d 284, 290 (4th Cir. 2002) (simple disagreement with the court's ruling will not support Rule 59(e) relief).

[113]*See Sequa Corp. v. GBJ Corp.*, 156 F.3d 136 (2d Cir.1998); *Bhatnagar v. Surrendra Overseas Ltd.*, 52 F.3d 1220, 1231 (3d Cir. 1995); *Senza-Gel Corp. v. Seiffhart*, 803 F.2d 661, 664 (Fed. Cir. 1986).

[114]*Vasapolli v. Rostoff*, 39 F.3d 27, 36 (1st Cir. 1994) (Selya, J.)("Unlike the Emperor Nero, litigants cannot fiddle as Rome burns. A party who sits in silence, withholds potentially relevant information, allows his opponent to configure the summary judgment record, and acquiesces in a particular choice of law does so at his peril").

[115]*See Markel Am. Ins. Co. v. Diaz-Santiago*, 674 F.3d 21, 33 (1st Cir. 2012) (especially when the movant is "long past being a day late and well over a dollar short").

[116]*See Cochran v. Quest Software, Inc.*, 328 F.3d 1, 11 (1st Cir. 2003) (noting that litigants "frame the issues in a case before the trial court rules" and, once framed, should not be permitted to switch from theory to theory thereafter).

ing old issues.[117] But nor are they motions for "initial consideration".[118] Courts properly decline to consider new arguments or new evidence on reconsideration where those arguments or evidence were available earlier.[119]

Motions to Include Prejudgment Interest

Generally, motions to amend to include an award of either mandatory or discretionary prejudgment interest are treated under this Rule and, thus, must be sought within 28 days of entry of the judgment or be deemed waived.[120] However, for some courts, such a motion will be deemed untimely if the request for prejudgment interest is being raised for the first time on the Rule 59(e) motion.[121]

Additional Research References

Wright & Miller, Federal Practice and Procedure §§ 2801 to 21
C.J.S., Federal Civil Procedure §§ 1061 to 1103 et seq., §§ 1233 to 1251 et seq.
West's Key Number Digest, Federal Civil Procedure ⊂⇒2311 to 2377, ⊂⇒2641 to 2662

---

[117]See Prescott v. Higgins, 538 F.3d 32, 45 (1st Cir. 2008); Arthur v. King, 500 F.3d 1335, 1343 (11th Cir. 2007); Sigsworth v. City of Aurora, Ill., 487 F.3d 506, 512 (7th Cir. 2007); Templet v. HydroChem Inc., 367 F.3d 473, 478–79 (5th Cir. 2004).

[118]See GSS Group Ltd v. Nat'l Port Auth., 680 F.3d 805, 812 (D.C.Cir. 2012); Markel Am. Ins. Co. v. Diaz-Santiago, 674 F.3d 21, 32 (1st Cir. 2012); National Ecological Foundation v. Alexander, 496 F.3d 466, 477 (6th Cir. 2007).

[119]See Patton Boggs LLP v. Chevron Corp., 683 F.3d 397, 403 (D.C.Cir. 2012); Soto-Padro v. Public Bldgs.

Auth., 675 F.3d 1, 9 (1st Cir. 2012); Rosenblatt v. United Way of Greater Houston, 607 F.3d 413, 419 (5th Cir. 2010).

[120]See Osterneck v. Ernst & Whinney, 489 U.S. 169, 173–78, 109 S. Ct. 987, 989–92, 103 L. Ed. 2d 146 (1989) (mandatory prejudgment interest); McCalla v. Royal MacCabees Life Ins. Co., 369 F.3d 1128, 1130–34 (9th Cir. 2004) (mandatory prejudgment interest); Crowe v. Bolduc, 365 F.3d 86, 92–93 (1st Cir. 2004) (mandatory or discretionary prejudgment interest).

[121]See First State Bank of Monticello v. Ohio Cas. Ins. Co., 555 F.3d 564, 572 (7th Cir. 2009).

RULE 60
RELIEF FROM A JUDGMENT OR ORDER

(a) Corrections Based on Clerical Mistakes; Oversights and Omissions. The court may correct a clerical mistake or a mistake arising from oversight or omission whenever one is found in a judgment, order, or other part of the record. The court may do so on motion or on its own, with or without notice. But after an appeal has been docketed in the appellate court and while it is pending, such a mistake may be corrected only with the appellate court's leave.

(b) Grounds for Relief from a Final Judgment, Order, or Proceeding. On motion and just terms, the court may relieve a party or its legal representative from a final judgment, order, or proceeding for the following reasons:

   (1) mistake, inadvertence, surprise, or excusable neglect;

   (2) newly discovered evidence that, with reasonable diligence, could not have been discovered in time to move for a new trial under Rule 59(b);

   (3) fraud (whether previously called intrinsic or extrinsic), misrepresentation, or misconduct by an opposing party;

   (4) the judgment is void;

   (5) the judgment has been satisfied, released or discharged; it is based on an earlier judgment that has been reversed or vacated; or applying it prospectively is no longer equitable; or

   (6) any other reason that justifies relief.

(c) Timing and Effect of the Motion.

   (1) *Timing.* A motion under Rule 60(b) must be made within a reasonable time—and for reasons (1), (2), and (3) no more than a year after the entry of the judgment or order or the date of the proceeding.

(2) *Effect on Finality.* The motion does not affect the judgment's finality or suspend its operation.

(d) Other Powers to Grant Relief. This rule does not limit a court's power to:

(1) entertain an independent action to relieve a party from a judgment, order, or proceeding;

(2) grant relief under 28 U.S.C. § 1655 to a defendant who was not personally notified of the action; or

(3) set aside a judgment for fraud on the court.

(e) Bills and Writs Abolished. The following are abolished: bills of review, bills in the nature of bills of review, and writs of coram nobis, coram vobis, and audita querela.

[Amended effective March 19, 1948; October 20, 1949; August 1, 1987; April 30, 2007, effective December 1, 2007.]

AUTHORS' COMMENTARY ON RULE 60

PURPOSE AND SCOPE

The district judge may grant relief from a judgment or order to correct clerical errors or in circumstances justifying an alteration of the judgment or order. Motions to correct clerical errors may be made at any time. Motions for relief from judgment founded on other reasons must be made within a "reasonable" time after the judgment is entered and, in some cases, no later than 1 year after the judgment is entered. Motions for relief on the basis that the judgment is void may be made at any time.

RULE 60(a)—CORRECTION BASED ON CLERICAL MISTAKES; OVERSIGHTS AND OMISSIONS

CORE CONCEPT

The district court, on its own initiative or on motion of a party, may correct clerical errors in judgments, orders, or other parts of the record, as well as errors arising from oversight or omission.

APPLICATIONS

Procedure

Motions to correct clerical errors are made to the district court that rendered the judgment sought to be corrected, rather than to any court where such a judgment may have been transferred.

Sua Sponte Corrections

The court *sua sponte* may raise clerical errors for correction.[1] Before doing so, however, the court must provide the parties with fair notice of its intention, allow them the opportunity to present their positions, and assure itself that no significant prejudice would follow from correcting the errors.[2]

Types of Qualifying Errors

Rule 60(a) is reserved for "clerical mistakes" or "mistakes arising from oversight or omission." Because the district courts enjoy the broadest discretion in correcting these types of mistakes,[3] accurately defining them is essential. Most simply, the distinction lies with intent. Where the judgment, as entered, fails to reflect the original intention of the court, the error can be corrected with Rule 60(a).[4] Conversely, where the judgment was entered accurately, but ought to have been done differently, Rule 60(a) does not apply.[5] Rule 60(a) errors are minor and ministerial ones, not substantively factual or legal.[6] This is a distinction between "blunders in execution" and "a change of

---

[1]*See Matter of West Texas Marketing Corp.*, 12 F.3d 497, 503 (5th Cir. 1994).

[2]*See Day v. McDonough*, 547 U.S. 198, 210, 126 S. Ct. 1675, 1684, 164 L. Ed. 2d 376 (2006).

[3]*See Agro Dutch Indus. Ltd. v. U.S.*, 589 F.3d 1187, 1192 (Fed.Cir. 2009).

[4]*See Companion Health Serv., Inc. v. Kurtz*, 675 F.3d 75, 87 (1st Cir. 2012); *Rivera v. PNS Stores, Inc.*, 647 F.3d 188, 193–94 (5th Cir. 2011); *Agro Dutch Indus. Ltd. v. U.S.*, 589 F.3d 1187, 1192 (Fed.Cir. 2009).

[5]*See Blue Cross and Blue Shield Ass'n v. American Express Co.*, 467 F.3d 634, 637 (7th Cir. 2006) (noting that Rule 60(a) "cannot be used to change language that was poorly chosen, as opposed to incorrectly transcribed", and instead "allows a court to correct records to show what *was* done, rather than change them to reflect what *should have been* done").

[6]*See Matter of West Texas Marketing Corp.*, 12 F.3d 497, 504–05 (5th Cir. 1994) ("As long as the intentions of the parties are clearly defined and all the court need do is employ a judi-

cial eraser to obliterate a mechanical or mathematical mistake, the modification will be allowed" under Rule 60(a)). *See, e.g. Pfizer Inc. v. Uprichard*, 422 F.3d 124, 129–30 (3d Cir. 2005) (inclusion of prejudgment interest proper, but order to sign settlement agreement was not); *U.S. v. Mosbrucker*, 340 F.3d 664, 665–67 (8th Cir. 2003) (permitting correction to note true status of easement tract); *Big Bear Lodging Ass'n v. Snow Summit, Inc.*, 182 F.3d 1096 (9th Cir. 1999) (to clarify whether court ruled on pending state law claims); *Rezzonico v. H & R Block, Inc.*, 182 F.3d 144 (2d Cir. 1999) (used to correct district court's omission of word "not" from judgment); *Hale Container Line, Inc. v. Houston Sea Packing Co., Inc.*, 137 F.3d 1455, 1474 (11th Cir. 1998) (correcting damages award containing erroneous mathematical computation); *McNamara v. City of Chicago*, 138 F.3d 1219, 1221 (7th Cir. 1998) (replacing "Chicago Police Department" with "Chicago Fire Department" in one sentence of opinion); *Kosnoski v. Howley*, 33 F.3d 376, 379 (4th Cir. 1994) (correcting a calculation, based upon earlier determined formula, to fix the total amount of judgment).

mind".[7] Thus, the Rule provides a remedy for clerical mistakes, inaccurate transcriptions, inadvertent omissions, mathematical errors, and similar flaws in recitation, but not for missteps in judgment or reasoning.[8] Where the error lies in accurately reducing the court's original intentions to paper, a Rule 60(a) motion is appropriate; however, where the written order accurately captures the court's intentions, but that ruling is allegedly in error, a Rule 60(a) motion is not proper.[9] Nevertheless, Rule 60(a) is not limited to simple typographical error correction; the Rule may also be used to clarify an unambiguous original order by inserting the original order's "necessary implications" and by otherwise ensuring the original order's full implementation and enforcement.[10]

Whose Errors

Relief under Rule 60(a) is not limited to clerical mistakes committed only by the clerk; the Rule applies to mistakes by the court, the parties, and the jury as well.[11] Most inadvertent errors may be corrected under Rule 60(a), if the correction would cause the ruling to reflect not a new and later intention of the court, but merely to conform the order to the court's original intention.[12]

Mislabeled "Substantive" Motions

An incorrectly labeled Rule 60(a) motion that actually seeks substantive alterations of a judgment may, in the court's discretion, be treated as a request seeking Rule 59(e) relief (and, then, would be tested under Rule 59(e)).[13]

Omission of Interest Award

Correction under Rule 60(a) might be available for omitted

---

[7]See Harman v. Harper, 7 F.3d 1455, 1457 (9th Cir. 1993). See also In re Walter, 282 F.3d 434, 440–41 (6th Cir. 2002) (citing quotation with approval).

[8]See Rivera v. PNS Stores, Inc., 647 F.3d 188, 193–94 (5th Cir. 2011).

[9]See Rivera v. PNS Stores, Inc., 647 F.3d 188, 195–96 (5th Cir. 2011) (not for correction of deliberate choices); Lowe v. McGraw-Hill Companies, Inc., 361 F.3d 335, 341 (7th Cir. 2004) ("defining element" is that litigants knew error "was by pure inadvertence, rather than a mistaken exercise of judgment"); U.S. v. Mosbrucker, 340 F.3d 664, 666 (8th Cir. 2003) (to reflect "what was understood, intended, and agreed upon by parties and court"); In re Craddock, 149 F.3d 1249, 1254 (10th Cir. 1998) (where "the thing spoken, written or

recorded is not what the person intended to speak, write or record"; Rule may not be used "to correct something that was deliberately done but later discovered to be wrong").

[10]See Garamendi v. Henin, 683 F.3d 1069, 1077–80 (9th Cir. 2012).

[11]See Day v. McDonough, 547 U.S. 198, 210–11, 126 S. Ct. 1675, 1684, 164 L. Ed. 2d 376 (2006); In re Walter, 282 F.3d 434, 440–41 (6th Cir. 2002); Matter of West Texas Marketing Corp., 12 F.3d 497, 503–04 (5th Cir. 1994); Pattiz v. Schwartz, 386 F.2d 300 (8th Cir.1968).

[12]See Robert Lewis Rosen Associates, Ltd. v. Webb, 473 F.3d 498, 505 n.11 (2d Cir. 2007).

[13]See Companion Health Serv., Inc. v. Kurtz, 675 F.3d 75, 87 (1st Cir. 2012).

awards of interest, but only where the court had earlier announced the award and merely neglected to fix the amount.[14] If the court was previously silent on the question of an interest award, a motion under Rule 60(a) would likely be improper.[15]

Time for Correction

The district court may correct clerical errors at any time, even after an appeal is taken;[16] however, once the case is docketed in the appellate court the district court may correct clerical errors only upon leave of the court of appeals.[17]

Implications for Appeal

Timely filing a Rule 60(a) motion to correct clerical mistakes, oversights, or omissions will toll the time for filing an appeal.[18] But the implications of this tolling are significant. To obtain appellate review of the underlying merits ruling, litigants must file within the post-trial motion period; delaying an appeal until after the district court decides the Rule 60(a) motion may limit the scope of that appeal to *only* the correctness of the Rule 60(a) ruling.[19]

Nature of Appellate Review

An appeal from a district court order denying relief under Rule 60(a) implicates only the propriety of that denial, and not the underlying merits of the contested judgment itself.[20]

RULE 60(b)—OTHER GROUNDS FOR RELIEF

CORE CONCEPT

In its discretion, the district court may grant relief from a final judgment, order, or proceeding for various enumerated reasons.

---

[14]*See Stryker Corp. v. XL Ins. America Inc.*, 726 F.Supp.2d 754, 789 (W.D.Mich. 2010).

[15]*See Osterneck v. Ernst & Whinney*, 489 U.S. 169, 109 S.Ct. 987, 103 L.Ed.2d 146 (1989) (ruling that Rule 59(e), not Rule 60(a), is implicated in such instances). *See also Winslow v. F.E.R.C.*, 587 F.3d 1133, 1135–36 (D.C.Cir. 2009) (same, citing cases following this interpretation).

[16]*See Rivera v. PNS Stores, Inc.*, 647 F.3d 188, 193 (5th Cir. 2011); *Winslow v. F.E.R.C.*, 587 F.3d 1133, 1135 (D.C.Cir. 2009); *Morrison Knudsen Corp. v. Ground Improvement Techniques, Inc.*, 532 F.3d 1063, 1085 (10th Cir. 2008).

[17]*See* Rule 62.1. *See also Home Prods. Int'l, Inc. v. United States*, 633 F.3d 1369, 1377 n.9 (Fed.Cir. 2011); *Thomas v. iStar Fin., Inc.*, 629 F.3d 276, 280 (2d Cir. 2010).

[18]*See Catz v. Chalker*, 566 F.3d 839, 841–42 (9th Cir. 2009); *Dudley ex rel. Estate of Patton v. Penn-Am. Ins. Co.*, 313 F.3d 662, 665 (2d Cir. 2002); *Internet Fin. Servs., LLC v. Law Firm of Larson-Jackson, P.C.*, 394 F.Supp.2d 1, 4–5 (D.D.C. 2005). *See also* Fed. R. App. P. 4(a)(4)(A)(vi) and advisory committee notes to 1993 amendment.

[19]*See Garamendi v. Henin*, 683 F.3d 1069, 1077–81 (9th Cir. 2012); *Rivera v. PNS Stores, Inc.*, 647 F.3d 188, 201 n.55 (5th Cir. 2011).

[20]*See Rivera v. PNS Stores, Inc.*, 647 F.3d 188, 201 n.55 (5th Cir. 2011); *Paddington Partners v. Bouchard*, 34 F.3d 1132, 1147 (2d Cir. 1994).

APPLICATIONS

Impact of 2007 "Restyling" Amendments

In 2007, former Rule 60(b) was divided into four sub-rules. The very long first sentence of the former Rule remains as current Rule 60(b). The rest of the former Rule was repositioned to Rules 60(c), (d), and (e). In researching current Rule 60(b), practitioners should be mindful of this repositioning.

Purpose

The purpose of permitting substantive relief from a judgment or order is to allow the federal courts to strike the proper balance between two often conflicting principles—that litigation must be brought to a final close and that justice must be done.[21] Rule 60(b) is not a substitute for a timely appeal.[22] Because upsetting a settled judgment clashes with this finality objective,[23] the relief is considered "extraordinary" and generally reserved for only exceptional circumstances.[24] Broadly stated, relief under Rule 60(b) is not available for deliberate choices later shown to be unwise ones.[25]

Reasons for Granting Substantive Relief

Rule 60(b) provides five specified reasons for which substantive (non-clerical) relief may be granted, and adds a sixth catch-all category for reasons not otherwise specifically listed. Ordinarily, proper post-judgment relief under Rule 60(b) will not be denied simply because the moving party failed to invoke the proper reason or Rule sub-part[26]—provided, of course, that the substantive argument for relief is apparent.[27]

Reason 1—Mistake, Inadvertence, Surprise, or Excusable Neglect

Relief from a judgment or order may be granted for mistakes by any person, not just a party,[28] and even legal errors by the

---

[21]See United Student Aid Funds, Inc. v. Espinosa, __ U.S. __, __, 130 S.Ct. 1367, 1380, 176 L.Ed.2d 158 (2010) (Rule 60(b) represents an "exception to finality"); Gonzalez v. Crosby, 545 U.S. 524, 529, 125 S. Ct. 2641, 2646, 162 L. Ed. 2d 480 (2005) (Rule 60(b)'s "whole purpose is to make an exception to finality").

[22]See Lowry Dev't, L.L.C. v. Groves & Assocs. Ins., Inc., 690 F.3d 382, 387 (5th Cir. 2012).

[23]See United Student Aid Funds, Inc. v. Espinosa, __ U.S. __, __, 130 S.Ct. 1367, 1376, 176 L.Ed.2d 158 (2010) (Rule 60(b) represents an "exception to finality").

[24]See Wehrs v. Wells, 688 F.3d 886, 890 (7th Cir. 2012); Dronsejko v. Thornton, 632 F.3d 658, 670 (10th Cir. 2011).

[25]See Park West Galleries, Inc. v. Hochman, 692 F.3d 539, 545 (6th Cir. 2012).

[26]See Fisher v. Kadant, Inc., 589 F.3d 505, 513 (1st Cir. 2009).

[27]See Nelson v. Napolitano, 657 F.3d 586, 589–90 (7th Cir. 2011) (noting mistaken belief that courts are "obliged to research and construct legal arguments for parties").

[28]See Associates Discount Corp. v. Goldman, 524 F.2d 1051 (3d Cir.1975).

court.[29] This category may permit relief where the order or judgment results from such circumstances as an inability to consult with counsel,[30] a misunderstanding regarding the duty to appear,[31] a failure to receive service,[32] or, in some circumstances, an attorney's negligent failure to meet a deadline.[33] (Note, however, that not all courts recognize attorney negligence as capable of qualifying under this category, and those that do impose a heavy standard .[34]) This category also permits relief when the district court had made a substantive error of law or fact in the its judgment or order.[35]

The standard for relief under this category is a demanding one.[36] Whether relief is appropriate is assessed on a case-by-case analysis: not every error or omission in the course of litigation will qualify as "excusable neglect",[37] nor will routine carelessness,[38] a lack of diligence,[39] a confusion concerning the Rules or the law,[40] or a party's misunderstanding of the consequences of her actions (even after advice of counsel) qualify for relief.[41] Moreover, otherwise careful clients can be penalized for omis-

---

[29]*See United Airlines, Inc. v. Brien*, 588 F.3d 158, 175 (2d Cir. 2009).

[30]*See Falk v. Allen*, 739 F.2d 461 (9th Cir.1984).

[31]*See Ellingsworth v. Chrysler*, 665 F.2d 180 (7th Cir.1981).

[32]*See Blois v. Friday*, 612 F.2d 938 (5th Cir.1980).

[33]*See Ahanchian v. Xenon Pictures, Inc.*, 624 F.3d 1253, 1261–62 (9th Cir. 2010); *U.S. v. $23,000 in U.S. Currency*, 356 F.3d 157, 164 (1st Cir. 2004).

[34]*See Latshaw v. Trainer Wortham & Co., Inc.*, 452 F.3d 1097, 1101 (9th Cir. 2006) (surveying other Circuits, and ruling that Rule 60(b)(1) does not remedy erroneous legal advice (even innocent carelessness) of counsel, explaining that "[s]uch mistakes are more appropriately addressed through malpractice claims"); *Robb v. Norfolk & Western Ry. Co.*, 122 F.3d 354, 361–63 (7th Cir. 1997) (noting that Circuit discontinues its "hard-and-fast" rule barring application of Rule to attorney negligence, but sternly cautioning counsel against expecting such relief to be granted automatically). *See also Acevedo-Garcia v. Vera-Monroig*, 368 F.3d 49, 54 (1st Cir. 2004); *McCurry ex rel. Turner v. Adventist Health System / Sunbelt, Inc.*, 298 F.3d 586, 595 (6th Cir. 2002).

[35]*See Utah ex rel. Div. of Foresty, Fire & State Lands v. U.S.*, 528 F.3d 712, 722–23 (10th Cir. 2008); *Manning v. Astrue*, 510 F.3d 1246, 1249 (10th Cir. 2007).

[36]*See U.S. v. $23,000 in U.S. Currency*, 356 F.3d 157, 164 (1st Cir. 2004).

[37]*See Rodgers v. Wyoming Atty. Gen.*, 205 F.3d 1201, 1206 (10th Cir. 2000) (party who simply misunderstands the legal consequences of his deliberate acts might not be deemed excusably neglectful). *See also Robinson v. Armontrout*, 8 F.3d 6, 7 (8th Cir. 1993) (party's and attorney's failure to object does not justify relief).

[38]*See Robinson v. Wix Filtration Corp. LLC*, 599 F.3d 403, 413 (4th Cir. 2010); *Noah v. Bond Cold Storage*, 408 F.3d 1043, 1045 (8th Cir. 2005); *Easley v. Kirmsee*, 382 F.3d 693, 698 (7th Cir. 2004).

[39]*See Aguiar-Carrasquillo v. Agosto-Alicea*, 445 F.3d 19, 28 (1st Cir. 2006).

[40]*See United States v. Davenport*, 668 F.3d 1316, 1324–25 (11th Cir. 2012); *Noah v. Bond Cold Storage*, 408 F.3d 1043, 1045 (8th Cir. 2005).

[41]*See Cashner v. Freedom Stores, Inc.*, 98 F.3d 572, 577–78 (10th Cir. 1996).

sions of their careless attorneys.[42] As a threshold showing, the moving party must demonstrate that the error made did not result from his or her own culpable conduct,[43] and instead that the party has behaved with appropriate diligence.[44] To qualify as "excusable neglect", the conduct is tested against an equitable standard, one that weighs the totality of the circumstances;[45] among the factors[46] the courts consider in this analysis are: (1) prejudice to the opponent; (2) length of delay and impact on the proceedings; (3) reason for the delay; and (4) the moving party's good faith.[47] The "reason-for-delay" factor is characterized as the "key" factor for this analysis,[48] although no *per se* rule, which elevates one factor to a singularly dispositive level, is usually proper.[49]

> *Note:* This provision has been applied for seeking relief under Rule 60(b) from default judgments, and, so applied, generally obligates the moving party to show good cause for defaulting, quick action in correcting the default, and the existence of a meritorious defense.[50] But the burden on the movant increases under Rule 60(b), since concerns of finality and repose are then implicated.[51] Courts may also consider whether the case implicates the public interest or would impose an especially significant financial loss on the defendant.[52]

Reason 2—Newly Discovered Evidence

Relief from an order or judgment may also be granted on the basis of new evidence where: (1) the evidence has been newly discovered since trial, (2) the moving party was diligent in discovering the new evidence, (3) the new evidence is not

---

[42]*See United States v. Davenport,* 668 F.3d 1316, 1324–25 (11th Cir. 2012); *Easley v. Kirmsee,* 382 F.3d 693, 698 (7th Cir. 2004).

[43]*See Yeschick v. Mineta,* 675 F.3d 622, 628–28 (6th Cir. 2012); *Ungar v. Palestine Liberation Org.,* 599 F.3d 79, 85 (1st Cir. 2010).

[44]*See Robinson v. Wix Filtration Corp. LLC,* 599 F.3d 403, 413 (4th Cir. 2010).

[45]*See Brandt v. American Bankers Ins. Co.,* 653 F.3d 1108, 1111 (9th Cir. 2011); *Connecticut State Dental Ass'n v. Anthem Health Plans, Inc.,* 591 F.3d 1337, 1355 (11th Cir. 2009).

[46]Note that some courts require that each of these four factors *must* be considered and weighed before ruling. *See Ahanchian v. Xenon Pictures, Inc.,* 624 F.3d 1253, 1261–62 (9th Cir. 2010).

[47]*See United States v. Davenport,* 668 F.3d 1316, 1324–25 (11th Cir. 2012); *Ahanchian v. Xenon Pictures, Inc.,* 624 F.3d 1253, 1261–62 (9th Cir. 2010).

[48]*See In re Guidant Corp. Implantable Defibrillators Products Liability Litigation,* 496 F.3d 863, 867 (8th Cir. 2007).

[49]*See Ahanchian v. Xenon Pictures, Inc.,* 624 F.3d 1253, 1261–62 (9th Cir. 2010).

[50]*See supra* Authors' Commentary to Rule 55(c). *See also Wehrs v. Wells,* 688 F.3d 886, 890 (7th Cir. 2012); *Brandt v. American Bankers Ins. Co.,* 653 F.3d 1108, 1111 (9th Cir. 2011).

[51]*See Colleton Preparatory Academy, Inc. v. Hoover Universal, Inc.,* 616 F.3d 413, 420–21 (4th Cir. 2010).

[52]*See In re OCA, Inc.,* 551 F.3d 359, 369 (5th Cir. 2008).

merely cumulative or impeaching, (4) the new evidence is material, and (5) in view of the new evidence, a new trial would probably produce a different result.[53] Implicit in these elements is the recognition that the evidence must be evidence of facts that were in existence at the time of trial (though not discovered until after trial).[54] Moreover (and implicitly), the newly discovered evidence must be both admissible and credible.[55] These requirements are strictly enforced.[56] If the movant fails to meet *any* of these prerequisites, the Rule 60(b)(2) motion may be denied.[57]

> *Note:* The same principles apply whether relief is sought for this reason under Rule 59 or Rule 60(b).[58]

Reason 3—Fraud, Misrepresentation, Other Adversary Misconduct

Relief from a judgment or order may be permitted on the basis of misconduct where: (1) the moving party possessed a meritorious claim at trial, (2) the adverse party engaged in fraud, misrepresentation, or other misconduct, and (3) the adverse party's conduct prevented the moving party from fully and fairly presenting its case during trial.[59] This category is the "lineal descendant" of the rule in equity that a court, finding fraud or undue influence, may alter or negate a written instrument.[60] Relief is reserved for judgments that were unfairly obtained, not at those that are claimed to be just factually in error.[61] Indeed, an actual factual error in the judgment

---

[53]*See Dronsejko v. Thornton*, 632 F.3d 658, 670 (10th Cir. 2011); *Thermacor Process, L.P. v. BASF Corp.*, 567 F.3d 736, 744 (5th Cir. 2009); *Liquidation Com'n of Banco Intercontinental, S.A. v. Renta*, 530 F.3d 1339, 1357–58 (11th Cir. 2008). *See also Ins. Co. of N. Am. v. Pub. Serv. Mut. Ins. Co.*, 609 F.3d 122, 131 (2d Cir. 2010) (must be truly newly discovered and impossible to find by due diligence); *Serafinn v. Local 722, Int'l Bhd. of Teamsters, Chauffeurs, Warehousemen & Helpers of Am.*, 597 F.3d 908, 917 (7th Cir. 2010) (must be non-cumulative).

[54]*See General Universal Systems, Inc. v. Lee*, 379 F.3d 131 (5th Cir. 2004); *Betterbox Communications Ltd. v. BB Technologies, Inc.*, 300 F.3d 325 (3d Cir. 2002).

[55]*See Goldstein v. MCI WorldCom*, 340 F.3d 238, 257 (5th Cir. 2003).

[56]*See Waddell v. Hendry County Sheriff's Office*, 329 F.3d 1300, 1309 (11th Cir. 2003).

[57]*See Jones v. Lincoln Elec. Co.*, 188 F.3d 709 (7th Cir. 1999) (commenting that if any of these prerequisites is not satisfied, Rule 60(b)(2) motion must fail); *McCormack v. Citibank, N.A.*, 100 F.3d 532, 542 (8th Cir. 1996) (commenting that even if movant could meet many prerequisites, he would fail to meet at least one).

[58]*See Jones v. Aero/Chem Corp.*, 921 F.2d 875 (9th Cir. 1990).

[59]*See Willis v. Lepine*, 687 F.3d 826, 833 (7th Cir. 2012); *Thomas v. Parker*, 609 F.3d 1114, 1119–20 (10th Cir. 2010); *Hutchins v. Zoll Medical Corp.*, 492 F.3d 1377, 1385–86 (Fed. Cir. 2007). *See also Assmann v. Fleming*, 159 F.2d 332 (C.C.A. 8th Cir. 1947) (noting possibility of relief, irrespective of whether the fraud is considered "extrinsic" or "intrinsic").

[60]*See Ty Inc. v. Softbelly's, Inc.*, 517 F.3d 494, 498 (7th Cir. 2008).

[61]*See General Universal Systems, Inc. v. Lee*, 379 F.3d 131, 156 (5th Cir.

may not even be required.[62] This provision is remedial, and is liberally construed.[63] The rule does not define "fraud", and the definition is unlikely to be borrowed from State law, prompting one court to pronounce the "general common law understanding" of fraud to be: "the knowing misrepresentation of a material fact, or concealment of the same when there is a duty to disclose, done to induce another to act to his or her detriment."[64] In appropriate cases, relief under this category may be granted to remedy belatedly uncovered misconduct during discovery, but only where the challenged behavior substantially interfered with the moving party's ability to fully and fairly try the case.[65] Ordinarily, relief under this category is reserved for instances where the fraud was committed by the adversary (and not by the party's own counsel or other non-adversaries).[66] Further, the fraud must generally have been perpetrated in the course of litigation, and not, for example, during the course of an underlying commercial transaction.[67] A party's entitlement to relief must be proven by clear and convincing evidence.[68]

> *Note:* Some courts will presume or infer the third element (substantial interference with the ability to fully and fairly prepare) where the misconduct is proven to be knowing or deliberate.[69]

Reason 4—Void Judgment

Relief may also be granted where the judgment or order is void, whether because the court lacked jurisdiction over the subject matter, lacked personal jurisdiction over the parties, acted in some manner inconsistent with constitutional due process, or otherwise acted beyond the powers granted to it under the law.[70] When a motion challenges a judgment as void, the district court lacks discretion: either the judgment is void (in

---

2004).

[62]*See Hesling v. CSX Transp., Inc.,* 396 F.3d 632, 641 (5th Cir. 2005) (proof that withheld information would have altered outcome is not required, because Rule "is aimed at judgments which were unfairly obtained, not at those which are factually incorrect").

[63]*See Hesling v. CSX Transp., Inc.,* 396 F.3d 632, 641 (5th Cir. 2005).

[64]*See Info-Hold, Inc. v. Sound Merch., Inc.,* 538 F.3d 448, 455–56 (6th Cir. 2008).

[65]*See General Universal Systems, Inc. v. Lee,* 379 F.3d 131 (5th Cir. 2004); *Summers v. Howard University,* 374 F.3d 1188, 1193 (D.C. Cir. 2004); *Cummings v. General Motors Corp.,* 365 F.3d 944, 955 (10th Cir. 2004).

[66]*See Latshaw v. Trainer Wortham*

& *Co., Inc.,* 452 F.3d 1097, 1102 (9th Cir. 2006).

[67]*See Roger Edwards, LLC v. Fiddes & Son Ltd.,* 427 F.3d 129, 134 (1st Cir. 2005).

[68]*See Arnold v. ADT Sec. Servs., Inc.,* 627 F.3d 716, 722 (8th Cir. 2010); *Wickens v. Shell Oil Co.,* 620 F.3d 747, 759 (7th Cir. 2010); *Thomas v. Parker,* 609 F.3d 1114, 1119–20 (10th Cir. 2010).

[69]*See Aguiar-Carrasquillo v. Agosto-Alicea,* 445 F.3d 19, 28 (1st Cir. 2006).

[70]*See Northridge Church v. Charter Tp. of Plymouth,* 647 F.3d 606, 611 (6th Cir. 2011); *City of New York v. Mickalis Pawn Shop, LLC,* 645 F.3d 114, 138 (2d Cir. 2011); *Oldfield v. Pueblo De Bahia Lora, S.A.,* 558 F.3d 1210, 1215 n.13 (11th Cir. 2009).

which case relief must be granted) or it is not.[71] As interpreted by the courts, however, the definition of a "void" judgment is a narrow one. A ruling alleged to be simply wrong is not "void",[72] nor is a judgment that is merely "voidable" (based on the existence of a particular defense or objection).[73] Relief under Rule 60(b)(4) is not a substitute for a timely appeal.[74] Instead, a judgment is deemed "void" only when the judgment is a "legal nullity" — premised on a fundamental jurisdictional or due process error.[75] As other courts have restated it, a "void" judgment is one where the rendering court was powerless to enter it[76] or contravened due process by entering it,[77] or where the exercise of jurisdiction was otherwise "egregious" and a "clear usurpation of power", lacking even an arguable ground for jurisdiction.[78] Courts are divided on which party bears the burden of proof in Rule 60(b)(4) challenges: some courts impose the burden on the party who invoked the court's jurisdiction originally,[79] while others vest the burden with the movant.[80]

Reason 5—Changed Circumstances

Relief from a judgment or order may also be granted where the circumstances justifying the ruling have changed, such as (1) when the judgment is satisfied, released, or discharged, (2) where a prior judgment on which the present judgment is based has been reversed or otherwise vacated, or (3) in any other circumstance where the continued enforcement of the judg-

---

[71] See *Marcus Food Co. v. DiPanfilo*, 671 F.3d 1159, 1166 (10th Cir. 2011); *Philos Techs., Inc. v. Philos & D, Inc.*, 645 F.3d 851, 854–55 (7th Cir. 2011); *City of New York v. Mickalis Pawn Shop, LLC*, 645 F.3d 114, 138 (2d Cir. 2011).

[72] See *United Student Aid Funds, Inc. v. Espinosa*, __ U.S. __, __, 130 S.Ct. 1367, 1377, 176 L.Ed.2d 158 (2010); *Northridge Church v. Charter Tp. of Plymouth*, 647 F.3d 606, 611 (6th Cir. 2011).

[73] See *Days Inns Worldwide, Inc. v. Patel*, 445 F.3d 899, 906–08 (6th Cir. 2006) (distinguishing between void ab initio and voidable).

[74] See *United Student Aid Funds, Inc. v. Espinosa*, __ U.S. __, __, 130 S.Ct. 1367, 1377, 176 L.Ed.2d 158 (2010); *Northridge Church v. Charter Tp. of Plymouth*, 647 F.3d 606, 611 (6th Cir. 2011).

[75] See *United Student Aid Funds, Inc. v. Espinosa*, __ U.S. __, __, 130 S.Ct. 1367, 1377, 176 L.Ed.2d 158 (2010); *Northridge Church v. Charter*

Tp. of Plymouth, 647 F.3d 606, 611 (6th Cir. 2011).

[76] See *Karsner v. Lothian*, 532 F.3d 876, 886 (D.C. Cir. 2008).

[77] See *Baldwin v. Credit Based Asset Servicing and Securitization*, 516 F.3d 734, 737 (8th Cir. 2008).

[78] See *Wendt v. Leonard*, 431 F.3d 410, 412–13 (4th Cir. 2005); *Central Vermont Public Service Corp. v. Herbert*, 341 F.3d 186, 190 (2d Cir. 2003); *In re G.A.D., Inc.*, 340 F.3d 331, 336 (6th Cir. 2003). See also *United Student Aid Funds, Inc. v. Espinosa*, __ U.S. __, __, 130 S.Ct. 1367, 1377, 176 L.Ed.2d 158 (2010) (noting the no-arguable-ground prediction of lower courts, but finding no need to discuss it).

[79] See *Craig v. Ontario Corp.*, 543 F.3d 872, 876 (7th Cir. 2008).

[80] See *"R" Best Produce, Inc. v. DiSapio*, 540 F.3d 115, 126 (2d Cir. 2008) (in collateral challenge to personal jurisdiction, defendant bears burden if it had notice of original lawsuit).

ment would be inequitable (*e.g.*, a change in legislative or decisional law, or a change in critical facts).[81] These three grounds are disjunctive; the presence of any one is sufficient to justify relief.[82] This encompasses the traditional power invested in a court of equity to modify its decree when appropriate in view of changed circumstances.[83] In evaluating such motions, the courts consider whether a substantial change in circumstances or law has occurred since the contested order was entered, whether complying with the contested order would cause extreme and unexpected hardship, and whether a good reason for modification exists.[84] The party seeking relief bears the burden of proving changed circumstances warranting relief, but once that entitlement is shown, the court must modify the order.[85] The proposed modification must be "suitably tailored" to meet the new legal or factual circumstances.[86] Relief under the "changed circumstances" category is only available where there is a prospective effect to the challenged judgment;[87] the mere fact that a ruling will have future collateral estoppel effect (something obviously common to many rulings)[88] or

---

[81]*See Agostini v. Felton*, 521 U.S. 203, 117 S. Ct. 1997, 138 L. Ed. 2d 391 (1997) (allowing relief under Rule 60(b)(5) to alter permanent injunction in light of Supreme Court's decision to overrule earlier constitutional precedent on which injunction was based); *Rufo v. Inmates of Suffolk County Jail*, 502 U.S. 367, 112 S. Ct. 748, 116 L. Ed. 2d 867 (1992) (parties seeking a modification of an order entered by consent bear the burden of demonstrating a "significant change" in circumstances to warrant relief from the decree). *See also Reynolds v. McInnes*, 338 F.3d 1221, 1227 (11th Cir. 2003) (modification may be warranted where significant time has passed since order was entered and, despite defendants' efforts, objectives of original agreement have not been met); *Maraziti v. Thorpe*, 52 F.3d 252, 254 (9th Cir. 1995) (noting that nearly every court order causes some reverberations into the future, and mere "continuing consequences" do not equate with the "prospective application" required under Rule 60(b)(5); instead, standard for Rule 60(b)(5) is whether judgment is "executory" or implicates "supervision of changing conduct or conditions"); *Valentine Sugars, Inc. v. Sudan*, 34 F.3d 320, 321–22 (5th Cir. 1994) (modification under Rule 60(b)(5) is

granted cautiously and only when dangers have almost disappeared, moving party is experiencing significantly extreme and unexpected hardship and oppression, and movant's case is unanswerable).

[82]*See Horne v. Flores*, 557 U.S. 433 454, 129 S.Ct. 2579, 2597, 174 L.Ed.2d 406 (2009).

[83]*See Frew ex rel. Frew v. Hawkins*, 540 U.S. 431, 441–42, 124 S. Ct. 899, 905–06, 157 L. Ed. 2d 855 (2004).

[84]*See U.S. v. Kayser-Roth Corp.*, 272 F.3d 89, 95 (1st Cir. 2001); *Parton v. White*, 203 F.3d 552, 555 (8th Cir. 2000).

[85]*See Horne v. Flores*, 557 U.S. 433, 447, 129 S.Ct. 2579, 2593–95, 174 L.Ed.2d 406 (2009); *U.S. v. Texas*, 601 F.3d 354, 373 (5th Cir. 2010).

[86]*See Reynolds v. McInnes*, 338 F.3d 1221 (11th Cir. 2003).

[87]*See Baum v. Blue Moon Ventures, LLC*, 513 F.3d 181, 190 (5th Cir. 2008); *Prudential Ins. Co. of America v. National Park Medical Center, Inc.*, 413 F.3d 897, 903 (8th Cir. 2005).

[88]*See Coltec Industries, Inc. v. Hobgood*, 280 F.3d 262, 271–72 (3d Cir. 2002) ("If this [collateral estoppel argument] were enough to satisfy Rule

otherwise causes "some reverberations into the future"[89] does not provide the requisite "prospective" effect necessary for relief under this provision. Ordinarily, money judgments will not possess the required "prospective" effect because the set nature of the monetary outlay provides the finality.[90] However, the "satisfied, released, or discharged" clause is often invoked by parties seeking to have a judgment satisfied by the court, due to an ongoing dispute with the judgment holder over the judgment.[91] The "based-on-earlier-judgment" alternative usually requires that the prior judgment have a preclusionary (res judicata or collateral estoppel) effect, and not a mere precedential impact.[92] The courts are divided whether such relief may be granted *sua sponte*.[93]

> *Note:* The Supreme Court has confirmed that the lower courts should not apply Rule 60(b)(5) in *anticipation* of the Supreme Court's overruling of an earlier precedent. To the contrary, the Supreme Court instructs that where one of its precedents applies directly to the circumstances at hand, even though the precedent's reasoning has been undermined by other opinions, the lower courts should follow the precedent and leave to the Supreme Court the prerogative of overruling its own decisions.[94]

Reason 6—In the Interests of Justice

Finally, relief from a judgment or order may be permitted to further the interests of justice. This "catch-all" category is reserved for extraordinary circumstances.[95] Relief under this Rule is "exceedingly rare".[96] It does not offer an unsuccessful

---

60(b)(5)'s threshold requirement, then the Rule's requirement of 'prospective application' would be meaningless").

[89]*See Kalamazoo River Study Group v. Rockwell Intern. Corp.*, 355 F.3d 574, 587–88 (6th Cir. 2004).

[90]*See Kalamazoo River Study Group v. Rockwell Intern. Corp.*, 355 F.3d 574, 587–88 (6th Cir. 2004).

[91]*See BUC Intern. Corp. v. International Yacht Council Ltd.*, 517 F.3d 1271, 1274–75 (11th Cir. 2008); *Zamani v. Carnes*, 491 F.3d 990, 995–96 (9th Cir. 2007).

[92]*See Manzanares v. City of Albuquerque*, 628 F.3d 1237, 1240 (10th Cir. 2010).

[93]*See Baum v. Blue Moon Ventures, LLC*, 513 F.3d 181, 190 (5th Cir. 2008) (*sua sponte* grants permitted); *Dr. Jose S. Belaval, Inc. v. Perez-Perdomo*, 465 F.3d 33, 37 (1st Cir. 2006) (discussing Circuit split).

[94]*See Agostini v. Felton*, 521 U.S. 203, 117 S. Ct. 1997, 138 L. Ed. 2d 391 (1997). *See also Cano v. Baker*, 435 F.3d 1337, 1341–43 (11th Cir. 2006) (rejecting, on similar grounds, Rule 60(b)(5)'s use by former abortion plaintiff who sought to revisit her earlier abortion rights decision as wrongly decided in light of intervening medical evidence).

[95]*See, e.g., Gonzalez v. Crosby*, 545 U.S. 524, 535, 125 S. Ct. 2641, 2649, 162 L. Ed. 2d 480 (2005); *Marino v. Drug Enforcement Admin.*, 685 F.3d 1076, 1079 (D.C.Cir. 2012); *Mackey v. Hoffman*, 682 F.3d 1247, 1251 (9th Cir. 2012).

[96]*See In re Guidant Corp. Implantable Defibrillators Products Liability Litigation*, 496 F.3d 863, 868 (8th Cir. 2007). *See also Kramer v. Gates*, 481 F.3d 788, 791–92 (D.C. Cir. 2007) (used "sparingly").

litigant an opportunity "to take a mulligan".[97] Seeking relief under this Rule also generally requires a showing of actual injury and the presence of circumstances beyond the movant's control that prevented timely action to protect her interests.[98] There is also some authority for the conclusion that this Rule is limited to setting aside a judgment or order, and may not be used to grant affirmative relief.[99] This "catch-all" category and the preceding five specific categories are mutually exclusive. If the reason for which relief is sought fits within one of the five specific categories (even though the facts fail to meet the prerequisites for that relief (*e.g.*, the neglect is not truly excusable, the time period for seeking relief under that Rule provision has passed, etc.)), the catch-all category will not permit relief.[100] "Something more" is required, and, given the breadth of the reasons captured by Rule 60(b)(1) through (b)(5), there is an understandably thin volume of cases explaining when that "something more" will be present to warrant relief under Rule 60(b)(6).[101] Note, however, that some cases have ruled that Rule 60(b)(6) may be proper where a defaulted client seeks relief from judgment on the basis of extremely gross negligence of counsel.[102]

Burden of Proof

The party seeking relief from a judgment or order bears the burden of demonstrating that the prerequisites for such relief are satisfied.[103] Because this relief is not intended to be a substitute for appeal, some courts have elevated the level of proof required for recovery.[104] Because the relief is fundamentally equitable, equitable defenses against the moving party (*e.g.*, unclean hands) may foreclose it.[105]

Discretion of District Judge

Whether to grant relief under Rule 60(b) is left to the broad

---

[97]*See Kramer v. Gates*, 481 F.3d 788, 792 (D.C. Cir. 2007).

[98]*See Gardner v. Martino*, 563 F.3d 981, 992 (9th Cir. 2009).

[99]*See Delay v. Gordon*, 475 F.3d 1039, 1044–45 (9th Cir. 2007).

[100]*See Liljeberg v. Health Services Acquisition Corp.*, 486 U.S. 847, 108 S. Ct. 2194, 100 L. Ed. 2d 855 (1988). *See also Aikens v. Ingram*, 652 F.3d 496, 500 (4th Cir. 2011); *East Brooks Books, Inc. v. City of Memphis*, 633 F.3d 459, 465 (6th Cir. 2011); *Salazar ex rel. Salazar v. District of Columbia*, 633 F.3d 1110, 1116 (D.C.Cir. 2011).

[101]*See East Brooks Books, Inc. v. City of Memphis*, 633 F.3d 459, 465 (6th Cir. 2011). *See generally Lopez v. Ryan*, 678 F.3d 1131, 1135–37 (9th Cir. 2012) (applying 6-factor test for habeas relief under Rule 60(b)(6)).

[102]*See Marino v. Drug Enforcement Admin.*, 685 F.3d 1076, 1080 (D.C.Cir. 2012); *Mackey v. Hoffman*, 682 F.3d 1247, 1251 (9th Cir. 2012); *Shepard Claims Service, Inc. v. William Darrah & Associates*, 796 F.2d 190, 195 (6th Cir. 1986).

[103]*See Gates v. Syrian Arab Republic*, 646 F.3d 1 (D.C.Cir. 2011); *U.S. v. Texas*, 601 F.3d 354, 373 (5th Cir. 2010).

[104]*See Info-Hold, Inc. v. Sound Merch., Inc.*, 538 F.3d 448, 454 (6th Cir. 2008).

[105]*See Motorola Credit Corp. v. Uzan*, 561 F.3d 123, 127 (2d Cir. 2009).

discretion of the trial court.[106] In the case of "void" judgments attacked under Rule 60(b)(4), however, the district court's discretion is almost illusory, if it exists at all. True "void" judgments are "legal nullities", and the court's refusal to vacate such judgments is a *per se* abuse of discretion.[107]

Jurisdiction

No new independent basis for the court's jurisdiction is necessary to support a Rule 60(b) motion or ruling. Rather, such a proceeding is deemed to be a continuation of the original action, and jurisdiction to consider a later Rule 60(b) motion is not divested by subsequent events.[108]

Procedure

Motions under this Rule should be made to the court that rendered the judgment.[109] Absent a local rule dictating otherwise, the court is not required to convene a hearing on Rule 60(b) motions, but may choose to do so in its discretion.[110] The court generally does not need to enter findings of fact and conclusions of law to grant Rule 60(b) relief,[111] although a careful articulation of its analysis is advised as "helpful" and aiding appellate review.[112]

Who May Seek Relief

Relief under this Rule may be requested by a party, the party's legal representative,[113] or one in privity with a party.[114]

Relief Only from Final Judgments

Rule 60(b) relief is only available from final, appealable judgments.[115]

---

[106]*See Wehrs v. Wells*, 688 F.3d 886, 890 (7th Cir. 2012); *Motorola Credit Corp. v. Uzan*, 561 F.3d 123, 126 (2d Cir. 2009); *Jones v. Swanson*, 512 F.3d 1045, 1048 (8th Cir. 2008).

[107]*See, e.g., Marcus Food Co. v. DiPanfilo*, 671 F.3d 1159, 1166 (10th Cir. 2011); *Johnson v. Arden*, 614 F.3d 785, 798–99 (8th Cir. 2010); *Central Vermont Pub. Serv. Corp. v. Herbert*, 341 F.3d 186, 189 (2d Cir. 2003).

[108]*See D'Ambrosio v. Bagley*, 656 F.3d 379, 388 (6th Cir. 2011); *East Brooks Books, Inc. v. City of Memphis*, 633 F.3d 459, 465 (6th Cir. 2011).

[109]*See Board of Trustees, Sheet Metal Workers' Nat. Pension Fund v. Elite Erectors, Inc.*, 212 F.3d 1031, 1034 (7th Cir. 2000).

[110]*See Atkinson v. Prudential Property Co., Inc.*, 43 F.3d 367, 374 (8th Cir. 1994).

[111]*See Atkinson v. Prudential Property Co., Inc.*, 43 F.3d 367, 374 (8th Cir. 1994).

[112]*See Lemoge v. U.S.*, 587 F.3d 1188, 1194 (9th Cir. 2009).

[113]*See Matter of El Paso Refinery, LP*, 37 F.3d 230, 234 (5th Cir. 1994) (defining phrase "party's legal representative" as person standing in the place, and in the stead, of another (such as an heir at law), who either holds position tantamount to that of the party, or whose legal rights were so tied to the party that his or her rights were directly affected by final judgment).

[114]*See Eyak Native Village v. Exxon Corp.*, 25 F.3d 773 (9th Cir. 1994).

[115]*See Dassault Systemes, SA v. Childress*, 663 F.3d 832, 840 (6th Cir. 2011).

Sua Sponte Motions

The Circuits are divided on whether a district court may, on its own initiative, grant relief from a judgment or order under Rule 60(b).[116] When such *sua sponte* relief is permitted, the courts generally demand that the parties receive notice and an opportunity to be heard before the relief is ordered.[117]

Vacating Judgments Entered by Other Courts

One court should attempt to vacate a judgment entered by a different court under Rule 60(b) only in extraordinary circumstances, but there is disputed case support for the proposition that courts may have the authority to do so in an appropriate case.[118]

Nature of Appellate Review

An appeal from a district court order denying relief under Rule 60(b) implicates only the propriety of that denial, and not the underlying judgment's merits (which ordinarily are reviewed only through a direct appeal of that judgment itself).[119]

RULE 60(c)—TIMING AND EFFECT OF MOTION

CORE CONCEPT

Relief under Rule 60(b) must be sought within a "reasonable" time after entry of the challenged judgment or order, except for three grounds which specify a 1-year time limit (from which no extensions may be granted). Making a motion under this Rule has no effect on finality.

APPLICATIONS

Impact of 2007 "Restyling" Amendments

In 2007, former Rule 60(b) was divided into four sub-rules.

---

[116]*See Pierson v. Dormire*, 484 F.3d 486, 491–92 (8th Cir. 2007) (describing Circuit split). *Compare U.S. v. Pauley*, 321 F.3d 578, 581 (6th Cir. 2003) (no *sua sponte* relief, *and Dow v. Baird*, 389 F.2d 882, 884–85 (10th Cir. 1968) (same), *with Baum v. Blue Moon Ventures, LLC*, 513 F.3d 181, 190 (5th Cir. 2008) (*sua sponte* relief permitted), *and Pierson v. Dormire*, 484 F.3d 486, 491–92 (8th Cir. 2007) (*sua sponte* relief permitted); *Fort Knox Music Inc. v. Baptiste*, 257 F.3d 108, 111 (2d Cir. 2001) (same), *and Kingvision Pay-Per-View Ltd. v. Lake Alice Bar*, 168 F.3d 347, 351 (9th Cir. 1999) (same) *and U.S. v. Jacobs*, 298 F.2d 469, 472 (4th Cir. 1961) (same).

[117]*See Pierson v. Dormire*, 484 F.3d 486, 492 (8th Cir. 2007); *Fort Knox Music Inc. v. Baptiste*, 257 F.3d 108, 111 (2d Cir. 2001); *Kingvision Pay-Per-View Ltd. v. Lake Alice Bar*, 168 F.3d 347, 352 (9th Cir. 1999) (9th Cir. 1999).

[118]*See Budget Blinds, Inc. v. White*, 536 F.3d 244, 251–55 (3d Cir. 2008). *But see Board of Trustees, Sheet Metal Workers' Nat. Pension Fund v. Elite Erectors, Inc.*, 212 F.3d 1031, 1034 (7th Cir. 2000) (ruling that courts do not have that authority).

[119]*See Browder v. Director, Dep't of Corrections of Illinois*, 434 U.S. 257, 263, 98 S. Ct. 556, 54 L. Ed. 2d 521 (1978); *Bailey v. Cain*, 609 F.3d 763, 767 (5th Cir. 2010); *Lora v. O'Heaney*, 602 F.3d 106, 111 (2d Cir. 2010).

The second and third sentences of the former Rule are now Rule 60(c). In researching current Rule 60(c), practitioners should be mindful of this repositioning.

The "Reasonable" Time Grounds

Relief from a judgment or order that is sought under either Reason 5 ("changed circumstances") or Reason 6 ("interests of justice") must be made "within a reasonable time" after entry of the judgment or order being challenged.[120] The courts determine whether the time of filing is "reasonable" on a case-by-case basis.[121] It is not assessed merely by the length of time that passes between discovery and filing,[122] and the period is not necessarily *more* than a year (and might be less than one).[123] Rather, the courts consider the length of delay along with its explanation, any resulting prejudice, any circumstances favoring relief, the nature of the dispute, and whether the public interest is implicated.[124] For some courts, prejudice is a pivotal inquiry.[125] Moreover, to prevail under the catch-all category of Rule 60(b)(6), the moving party must also generally demonstrate faultlessnes in the delay.[126]

The "Void" Judgment Ground

Relief from a "void" judgment or order can be sought at any time.[127] Laches and similar finality principles generally have no effect on void judgments; the courts have held that the mere passage of time will not convert a void judgment into a proper one.[128] However, if a party attacks the court's jurisdiction and loses on that issue, the question of jurisdiction becomes *res judicata* and, accordingly, the judgment is not void; the party's only recourse in such a case is a proper, timely merits appeal, not relief under Rule 60(b).[129]

---

[120]*See* Rule 60(c)(1). *See also Baum v. Blue Moon Ventures, LLC*, 513 F.3d 181, 190 (5th Cir. 2008) (noting that 1-year limitation period does not restrict power to modify a continuing injunction).

[121]*See Lemoge v. U.S.*, 587 F.3d 1188, 1194, 1196–97 (9th Cir. 2009); *U.S. v. $670,706.55*, 367 Fed.Appx. 532, 535 (5th Cir. 2010); *Thompson v. Bell*, 580 F.3d 423, 452 (6th Cir. 2009).

[122]*See Doe v. Briley*, 562 F.3d 777, 781 (6th Cir. 2009).

[123]*See Massi v. Walgreen Co.*, 337 Fed.Appx. 542, 545 (6th Cir. 2009).

[124]*See Lemoge v. U.S.*, 587 F.3d 1188, 1194, 1196–97 (9th Cir. 2009); *U.S. v. $670,706.55*, 367 Fed.Appx. 532, 535 (5th Cir. 2010); *Thompson v. Bell*, 580 F.3d 423, 452 (6th Cir. 2009);

Venture Indus. Corp. v. Autoliv ASP, Inc., 457 F.3d 1322, 1328 (Fed. Cir. 2006).

[125]*See Salazar ex rel. Salazar v. District of Columbia*, 633 F.3d 1110, 1118–19 (D.C.Cir. 2011).

[126]*See Amado v. Microsoft Corp.*, 517 F.3d 1353, 1363 (Fed. Cir. 2008).

[127]*See "R" Best Produce, Inc. v. DiSapio*, 540 F.3d 115, 123–24 (2d Cir. 2008); *Jackson v. FIE Corp.*, 302 F.3d 515, 523–24 (5th Cir. 2002); *Hertz Corp. v. Alamo Rent-A-Car, Inc.*, 16 F.3d 1126, 1130 (11th Cir. 1994).

[128]*See Jackson v. FIE Corp.*, 302 F.3d 515, 523–24 (5th Cir. 2002); *U.S. v. One Toshiba Color Television*, 213 F.3d 147, 157–58 (3d Cir. 2000).

[129]*See Durfee v. Duke*, 375 U.S. 106, 84 S. Ct. 242, 11 L. Ed. 2d 186

The 1-Year Time Grounds

Seeking relief from a judgment or order under any one of the three remaining Rule 60(b) grounds for relief must be done within a reasonable time, but in no event later than 1 year from the entry of the challenged ruling.[130] Thus, this 1-year time limit applies to Reason 1 ("mistake, inadvertence, surprise"),[131] Reason 2 ("newly discovered evidence"),[132] and Reason 3 ("fraud, misrepresentation, other adversary misconduct").[133]

No Extensions

Where the 1-year time limit is specified in Rule 60(c), the period is "absolute" and the district court lacks the authority to extend the time for bringing a motion.[134] However, there is developing case law that when an untimely Rule 60(b) motion is filed, but not objected to by the non-moving party, the timeliness objection may be deemed forfeited through waiver.[135]

Enforceability of Judgment

Rule 60(b) provides that a judgment challenged under that Rule remains valid and enforceable unless and until the Rule 60(b) motion is granted.[136]

Effect of Appeals

A motion for relief under Rule 60 will not affect the finality of the underlying judgment nor suspend its operation.[137] Consequently, the filing of such a motion will ordinarily not suspend the time for taking an appeal.[138] There is one exception, however. If the motion is filed immediately—during the 28-days after judgment post-trial motions period—the time for appealing will be tolled.[139] Once an appeal is taken, the district court's ability to act on any then-pending Rule 60(b) motion is

---

(1963); *American Surety Co. v. Baldwin*, 287 U.S. 156, 53 S. Ct. 98, 77 L. Ed. 231 (1932).

[130]*See Greene v. District of Columbia*, 575 F.3d 716 (D.C.Cir. 2009); *CFA Inst. v. Inst. of Chartered Fin. Analysts of India*, 551 F.3d 285, 290 n.11 (4th Cir. 2009).

[131]*See The Tool Box, Inc. v. Ogden City Corp.*, 419 F.3d 1084 (10th Cir.2005) (noting one-year time limit is "absolute"). *See also In re G.A.D., Inc.*, 340 F.3d 331, 334 (6th Cir. 2003).

[132]*See In re G.A.D., Inc.*, 340 F.3d 331, 334 (6th Cir. 2003).

[133]*See In re G.A.D., Inc.*, 340 F.3d 331, 334 (6th Cir. 2003).

[134]*See* Rule 60(c)(1). *See also Wilburn v. Robinson*, 480 F.3d 1140, 1147–48 (D.C. Cir. 2007) (noting that court may not extend); *Martha Graham*

Sch. & Dance Found., Inc. v. Martha Graham Ctr. for Contemporary Dance, Inc., 466 F.3d 97, 100 (2d Cir.2006) (period is "absolute"); *The Tool Box, Inc. v. Ogden City Corp.*, 419 F.3d 1084, 1088 (10th Cir. 2005) (same).

[135]*See Wilburn v. Robinson*, 480 F.3d 1140, 1147–48 (D.C. Cir. 2007).

[136]*See* Rule 60(c)(2). *See also Balark v. City of Chicago*, 81 F.3d 658, 663 (7th Cir. 1996) (Rule 60(b) order "operates prospectively only").

[137]*See* Rule 60(c)(2).

[138]*See Carpenter v. Williams*, 86 F.3d 1015 (10th Cir.1996) (Rule 60(b) motion filed more than ten days after district court dismissed case does not toll time for filing notice of appeal).

[139]*See* Fed. R. App. P. 4(a)(4)(A) (vi). *See also York Group, Inc. v. Wuxi Taihu Tractor Co.*, 632 F.3d 399,

limited. Although the district court might be able to *deny* such motions, it may not *grant* them without a remand from the court of appeals.[140]

RULE 60(d)—OTHER POWERS TO GRANT RELIEF

CORE CONCEPT

Although Rule 60(a) and Rule 60(b) give the district courts specific Rule-based authority to grant relief from judgments and orders, the courts also enjoy other vehicles for granting such relief as well.

APPLICATIONS

Impact of 2007 "Restyling" Amendments

In 2007, former Rule 60(b) was divided into four sub-rules. The fourth sentence of the former Rule is now Rule 60(d). In researching current Rule 60(d), practitioners should be mindful of this repositioning.

Relief by an Independent Action

Litigants may also seek relief from a judgment or order by filing an "independent action", a proceeding that sounds in equity.[141] Independent actions are completely distinct from a motion under Rule 60.[142] They are permitted in only exceptional cases to prevent grave miscarriages of justice.[143] An independent action may be maintained where:

(1) the judgment should not, in good conscience, be enforced;

(2) a good defense exists to the plaintiff's lawsuit;

(3) fraud, accident, or mistake prevented the defendant from obtaining the benefit of the good defense;

(4) the defendant is free of fault and negligence; *and*

401–02 (7th Cir. 2011); *Wilburn v. Robinson,* 480 F.3d 1140, 1144 (D.C. Cir. 2007). The Federal Rules of Appellate Procedure set the length of appeal-tolling post-trial motions. Prior to the 2009 "time computation" amendments, this period was 10-days from date of entry; after December 1, 2009, the period is extended to 28-days from date of entry. *See* Fed. R. App. P. 4(a)(4)(A)(vi).

[140]*See* Rule 62.1. *See also Home Prods. Int'l, Inc. v. United States,* 633 F.3d 1369, 1377 n.9 (Fed.Cir. 2011); *Brooks v. Celeste,* 16 F.3d 104, 108 (6th Cir. 1994) (noting that once notice of appeal is filed, district court will gen-

erally lack jurisdiction to consider Rule 60(b) motions).

[141]*See U.S. v. Beggerly,* 524 U.S. 38, 118 S. Ct. 1862, 141 L. Ed. 2d 32 (1998); *Mitchell v. Rees,* 651 F.3d 593, 594 (6th Cir. 2011).

[142]*See Herring v. U.S.,* 424 F.3d 384, 389 (3d Cir. 2005).

[143]*See U.S. v. Beggerly,* 524 U.S. 38, 118 S. Ct. 1862, 141 L. Ed. 2d 32 (1998); *Park West Galleries, Inc. v. Hochman,* 692 F.3d 539, 545 (6th Cir. 2012); *Superior Seafoods, Inc. v. Tyson Foods, Inc.,* 620 F.3d 873, 878, (8th Cir. 2010).

(5) there is no adequate remedy at law.[144]

The Rule 60(c) time limits do not apply to independent actions in equity[145] (although courts are wary—but not necessarily prohibitive—of litigants using independent actions to evade timeliness problems in what would otherwise be a Rule 60(b) motion).[146] If the independent action is filed in the same court that granted the judgment, supplemental jurisdiction exists—regardless of diversity or federal question jurisdiction.[147] Absent prejudice, a mislabeled independent action may be treated as a Rule 60(b) motion, and vice versa.[148]

Relief by Section 1655 of the Judiciary Code

Congress has, by statute, created a procedure for the enforcement and the removal of liens, incumbrances, and clouds upon the title to real or personal property. The statute provides a means for notifying the affected defendant of the pending proceeding. If, however, the defendant does not receive proper notification, he may act within 1 year to have the judgment lifted and appear to defend (provided he pays costs assessed by the court).[149]

Relief due to Fraud on the Court

Finally, the district court also possesses the inherent power to grant relief where the judgment or order is obtained through a fraud on the court.[150] No time limits apply,[151] provided relief is sought within a reasonable time.[152] The court may grant the relief on its own initiative or on motion. Such fraud must be proven by clear and convincing evidence.[153] To constitute a fraud on the court, the alleged misconduct must be something

---

[144]*See Mitchell v. Rees*, 651 F.3d 593, 595 (6th Cir. 2011); *Superior Seafoods, Inc. v. Tyson Foods, Inc.*, 620 F.3d 873, 878 (8th Cir. 2010); *LinkCo, Inc. v. Naoyuki Akikusa*, 367 Fed.Appx. 180, 182 (2d Cir. 2010).

[145]*See Park West Galleries, Inc. v. Hochman*, 692 F.3d 539, 545 (6th Cir. 2012); *Robinson v. Volkswagenwerk AG*, 56 F.3d 1268, 1274 (10th Cir. 1995).

[146]*See Turner v. Pleasant*, 663 F.3d 770, 775–76 (5th Cir. 2011); *Mitchell v. Rees*, 651 F.3d 593, 597 (6th Cir. 2011).

[147]*See U.S. v. Beggerly*, 524 U.S. 38, 118 S. Ct. 1862, 141 L. Ed. 2d 32 (1998); *Cresswell v. Sullivan & Cromwell*, 922 F.2d 60, 70 (2d Cir. 1990).

[148]*See Mitchell v. Rees*, 651 F.3d 593, 595 (6th Cir. 2011); *United States v. Demjanjuk*, 838 F.Supp.2d 616, 626 (N.D.Ohio 2011).

[149]*See* 28 U.S.C.A. § 1655.

[150]*Universal Oil Products Co. v. Root Refining Co.*, 328 U.S. 575, 66 S. Ct. 1176, 90 L. Ed. 1447 (1946); *Hazel-Atlas Glass Co. v. Hartford-Empire Co.*, 322 U.S. 238, 64 S. Ct. 997, 88 L. Ed. 1250 (1944).

[151]*See United States v. Chapman*, 642 F.3d 1236, 1240 n.3 (9th Cir. 2011); *King v. First American Investigations, Inc.*, 287 F.3d 91, 95 (2d Cir. 2002).

[152]*See Apotex Corp. v. Merck & Co.*, 507 F.3d 1357, 1361 (Fed.Cir.2007).

[153]*See Wickens v. Shell Oil Co.*, 620 F.3d 747, 759 (7th Cir. 2010); *King v. First American Investigations, Inc.*, 287 F.3d 91, 95 (2d Cir. 2002).

more than fraud among the litigants.[154] Instead, the misconduct must be an assault on the integrity of the judicial process, which defiles the court itself or is perpetrated by officers of the court in such a manner that the impartial system of justice fails to function.[155] It must also have caused prejudice to the moving party,[156] such that it would be manifestly unconscionable to permit the judgment to remain.[157] Fraud in the discovery process, to the extent it meets this standard, can support relief.[158]

RULE 60(e)—BILLS AND WRITS ABOLISHED

CORE CONCEPT

The old common law writs of coram nobis, coram vobis, audita querela, and bills of review are abolished in civil proceedings.[159] Filings under these ancient writs may be treated by the courts as motions for relief under Rule 60(b).[160]

Impact of 2007 "Restyling" Amendments

In 2007, former Rule 60(b) was divided into four sub-rules. The last sentence of the former Rule is now Rule 60(e). In researching current Rule 60(e), practitioners should be mindful of this repositioning.

Many Such Writs Preserved in Criminal Cases

Although abolished by the Rules for civil cases, many such

---

[154]See *Superior Seafoods, Inc. v. Tyson Foods, Inc.*, 620 F.3d 873, 878 (8th Cir. 2010).

[155]See *LinkCo, Inc. v. Naoyuki Akikusa*, 367 Fed.Appx. 180, 182 (2d Cir. 2010); *U.S. v. Smiley*, 553 F.3d 1137, 1144–45 (8th Cir. 2009); *Apotex Corp. v. Merck & Co., Inc.*, 507 F.3d 1357, 1360–61 (Fed. Cir. 2007). *See also Baltia Air Lines, Inc. v. Transaction Mgmt., Inc.*, 98 F.3d 640, 642 (D.C. Cir. 1996) (citing bribery of a judge or an attorney's knowing participation in the presentation of perjured testimony).

[156]See *Wickens v. Shell Oil Co.*, 620 F.3d 747, 759 (7th Cir. 2010).

[157]See *Superior Seafoods, Inc. v. Tyson Foods, Inc.*, 620 F.3d 873, 878 (8th Cir. 2010).

[158]See *Appling v. State Farm Mut. Auto. Ins. Co.*, 340 F.3d 769, 780 (9th Cir. 2003).

[159]At the old common law, a writ of coram nobis (if sought at the King's Bench) or writ of coram vobis (if sought in the Courts of Common Pleas) were the procedural tools to correct errors of fact by petitioning to bring before the court certain facts which, if known earlier, would have prevented the entry of judgment. *See* 18 Am. Jur. 2d Coram Nobis & Allied Statutory Remedies §§ 1 to 2 (1985). A person against whom execution has issued or was about to issue could seek a writ of audita querela to prevent execution where the execution would be contrary to justice. *See* 7 Am. Jur. 2d Audita Querela § 1 (1997). Finally, a bill of review was a new action, filed in equity, that sought the correction, reversal, alteration, or explanation of a decree issued in an earlier proceeding. *See* 27A Am. Jur. 2d Equity § 256 (1996). Each of these ancient writs—in civil actions only—have been abolished by the Federal Rules. *See U.S. v. Silva*, 423 Fed.Appx. 809 n.2 (10th Cir. 2011).

[160]See *Green v. White*, 319 F.3d 560, 563 n.1 (3d Cir. 2003) (treating request for writ in the nature of a writ of coram nobis as motion under Rule 60(b)).

writs exist in criminal proceedings.[161]

Additional Research References

Wright & Miller, *Federal Practice and Procedure* §§ 2851 to 73
C.J.S., Federal Civil Procedure § 368, § 373, §§ 1233 to 1251 et seq.
West's Key Number Digest, Federal Civil Procedure ⚷921, ⚷2641 to 2662

---

[161]*See Massey v. U.S.*, 581 F.3d 172, 174 (3d Cir. 2009) (audita querela preserved in criminal cases); *Trenkler v. U.S.*, 536 F.3d 85 (1st Cir. 2008) (same, coram nobis).

RULE 61
HARMLESS ERROR

Unless justice requires otherwise, no error in admitting or excluding evidence—or any other error by the court or a party—is ground for granting a new trial, for setting aside a verdict, or for vacating, modifying, or otherwise disturbing a judgment or order. At every stage of the proceeding, the court must disregard all errors and defects that do not affect any party's substantial rights.

[Amended April 30, 2007, effective December 1, 2007.]

AUTHORS' COMMENTARY ON RULE 61

PURPOSE AND SCOPE

Rule 61 codifies the principle that "harmless" errors by the district court—those errors that do not affect the parties' substantial rights—will not justify a new trial, setting aside a verdict, or vacating, modifying, or otherwise disturbing the court's order.

APPLICATIONS

Standard for "Harmlessness"

Rule 61 defines a harmless error as one that does not affect the substantial rights of the parties or does not defeat substantial justice.[1] But an error will not be discounted as harmless if the court is left with a grave doubt as to whether the error had a substantial influence in the ultimate result.[2] A more exacting definition is probably impossible, just as it is

---

[1] Rule 61. *See Brandt v. Vulcan, Inc.*, 30 F.3d 752 (7th Cir.1994) (harmless error calls into question the fundamental fairness of the trial).

[2] *See Krulewitch v. U.S.*, 336 U.S. 440, 444–45, 69 S. Ct. 716, 718–19, 93 L. Ed. 790 (1949) (defining harmlessness in criminal context); *Hearn v. McKay*, 603 F.3d 897, 904 n.11 (11th Cir. 2010) (not harmless if error had (or court has "grave doubt" whether it

had) substantial influence on outcome); *Sims v. Great American Life Ins. Co.*, 469 F.3d 870, 886 (10th Cir. 2006) (reverse unless jury's verdict more probably than not was unaffected by error); *General Motors Corp. v. New A.C. Chevrolet, Inc.*, 263 F.3d 296, 329 (3d Cir. 2001) (non-constitutional legal errors harmless if it is "highly probable that the error did not affect the judgment"); *Nieves-Villanueva v.*

impossible to ignore the subjectivity inherent in the inquiry itself.[3] Some baseline principles exist, however. In testing for harmlessness, the court considers the entire record, and applies the standard on a case-by-case basis.[4] Every reasonable possibility of prejudice need not be disproved.[5] At its core, the harmless error inquiry asks whether the trial error could (or did) affect "the outcome of a case to the substantial disadvantage of the losing party".[6] Unsurprisingly, this risk is considered greater in close cases, than in more one-sided cases.[7]

Burden of Proof

The party moving for relief bears the burden of establishing that a trial error affected that party's substantial rights and, thus, was not harmless.[8] (Note, however, that the standard for harmlessness (as articulated by some courts) seems to suppose that harm is presumed, rather than proved.[9])

Applies to All Errors

The harmless error rule applies to all types of errors, including most constitutional errors. The courts of appeals review rulings of the district courts under this standard as well.[10]

Soto-Rivera, 133 F.3d 92, 102 (1st Cir. 1997) (court assumes error affected the verdict if court is in "grave doubt" about its effect on verdict).

[3]*See U.S. v. O'Keefe*, 169 F.3d 281, 287 n. 5 (5th Cir. 1999) (citing formulations by Judge Traynor and Justice Rutledge as among the clearest formulations) (citing 11 Charles Alan Wright, Arthur R. Miller, & Mary Kay Kane, *Federal Practice & Procedure* § 2883, at 445 to 47 (2d ed. 1995)). *Cf.* Roger Traynor, The Riddle of Harmless Error 35 (1970) ("[U]nless the appellate court believes it highly probable that the error did not affect the judgment, it should reverse"); *Kotteakos v. U.S.*, 328 U.S. 750, 760, 66 S. Ct. 1239, 1245, 90 L. Ed. 1557 (1946) (Rutledge, J.) ("Do not be technical, where technicality does not really hurt the party whose rights in the trial and in its outcome the technicality affects").

[4]*See Sims v. Great American Life Ins. Co.*, 469 F.3d 870, 886 (10th Cir. 2006); *Nieves-Villanueva v. Soto-Rivera*, 133 F.3d 92, 102 (1st Cir. 1997); *Brewer v. Jeep Corp.*, 724 F.2d 653 (8th Cir.1983).

[5]*See General Motors Corp. v. New A.C. Chevrolet, Inc.*, 263 F.3d 296,

329 (3d Cir. 2001).

[6]*See U.S. v. O'Keefe*, 169 F.3d 281, 287 n. 5 (5th Cir. 1999). *See also Muldrow ex rel. Estate of Muldrow v. Re-Direct, Inc.*, 493 F.3d 160, 168 (D.C. Cir. 2007); *Pelletier v. Main Street Textiles, LP*, 470 F.3d 48, 52–53 (1st Cir. 2006).

[7]*See Sims v. Great American Life Ins. Co.*, 469 F.3d 870, 886 (10th Cir. 2006).

[8]*See Palmer v. Hoffman*, 318 U.S. 109, 116, 63 S. Ct. 477, 481–82, 87 L. Ed. 645 (1943) (moving party bears the burden of showing resulting prejudice); *Morgan v. Covington Tp.*, 648 F.3d 172, 179 (3d Cir. 2011); *MMG Fin. Corp. v. Midwest Amusements Park, LLC*, 630 F.3d 651, 658 (7th Cir. 2011).

[9]*See Sims v. Great American Life Ins. Co.*, 469 F.3d 870, 886 (10th Cir. 2006) (court must reverse unless it finds that jury's verdict was, more probably than not, unaffected by error).

[10]*See* 28 U.S.C.A. § 2111 (fixing harmlessness standard for appeals). *See also McDonough Power Equipment, Inc. v. Greenwood*, 464 U.S. 548, 554, 104 S. Ct. 845, 849, 78 L. Ed. 2d 663 (1984) (noting that appellate

Federal Law Controls

Under *Erie* principles,[11] the federal (not State) construction of the harmless error rule usually controls where the federal and State standards are inconsistent.[12]

Errors in Rulings on Pleadings

Technical errors in pleadings will generally be discounted as harmless.[13] Likewise, errors in granting parties the right to intervene are not overturned unless they affected the substantial rights of the parties.[14]

Errors in Ruling on Motions

The same "substantial rights" standard applies to errors in ruling upon motions.[15] Thus, an improper striking of an amended complaint was harmless if the proposed amendment would not have prevented a dismissal,[16] an improper dismissal of a claim was harmless if, in light of later discovery, it would not have survived summary judgment,[17] an improper preclusion was harmless if similarly situated plaintiffs were also properly dismissed,[18] an improper dismissal of co-defendants was harmless if the plaintiffs were already barred from a recovery,[19] an improper dismissal of counterclaims was harmless when those claims could be asserted in another proceeding,[20] and an improper consideration (or exclusion) of summary judgment affidavits and exhibits was harmless where, in context, the effect could not have been prejudicial.[21]

---

courts must act in accordance with the salutary policy embodied in Rule 61); *General Motors Corp. v. New A.C. Chevrolet, Inc.*, 263 F.3d 296, 329 n.18 (3d Cir. 2001) (same).

[11] *See Erie R. Co. v. Tompkins*, 304 U.S. 64, 58 S. Ct. 817, 82 L. Ed. 1188 (1938) (in diversity cases, the federal courts will apply federal rules of procedure but State substantive law). *See* discussion of the *Erie* Doctrine in Part II of this text.

[12] *See Sokol Crystal Products, Inc. v. DSC Communications Corp.*, 15 F.3d 1427 (7th Cir. 1994); *Smith v. Chesapeake & Ohio Ry. Co.*, 778 F.2d 384 (7th Cir. 1985).

[13] *See Toth v. Corning Glass Works*, 411 F.2d 912 (6th Cir.1969) (refusal to strike a pleading's claim deemed harmless).

[14] *See Prete v. Bradbury*, 438 F.3d 949, 959–60 (9th Cir. 2006).

[15] *See, e.g., Lore v. City of Syracuse*, 670 F.3d 127, 150 (2d Cir. 2012) (motions for judgment as a matter of law);

Henning v. Union Pacific R. Co., 530 F.3d 1206, 1216–17 (10th Cir. 2008) (motions for new trial); *California Valley Miwok Tribe v. U.S.*, 515 F.3d 1262, 1268 (D.C. Cir. 2008) (motions for leave to supplement claims); *Applied Information Sciences Corp. v. eBAY, Inc.*, 511 F.3d 966, 969 n.1 (9th Cir. 2007) (motions for summary judgment).

[16] *See Lopez v. Target Corp.*, 676 F.3d 1230, 1232 n.3 (11th Cir. 2012).

[17] *See Quinn v. St. Louis County*, 653 F.3d 745, 750 (8th Cir. 2011).

[18] *See Ellis v. CCA of Tennessee LLC*, 650 F.3d 640, 652 (7th Cir. 2011).

[19] *See Lippoldt v. Cole*, 468 F.3d 1204, 1221 (10th Cir. 2006).

[20] *See Walter Kidde Portable Equipment, Inc. v. Universal Sec. Instruments, Inc.*, 479 F.3d 1330, 1340 (Fed. Cir. 2007).

[21] *See S.E.C. v. Smart*, 678 F.3d 850, 856 (10th Cir. 2012); *Romero v. Drummond Co.*, 552 F.3d 1303, 1324 (11th Cir. 2008); *Carter v. Lindgren*,

Errors in Admitting or Excluding Evidence

The district court enjoys broad discretion to admit or exclude evidence.[22] Errors in such rulings are harmless if the party raises no objection,[23] if the evidence wrongfully admitted or excluded was cumulative,[24] if adequate curative instructions are given,[25] or if the rulings are otherwise determined not to have caused substantial prejudice or to have substantially influenced the jury.[26] However, evidentiary rulings that affected the substantial rights of a party are *not* harmless, and the rulings must be reversed.[27] Thus, if the trial evidence is not sufficient to support the verdict without the wrongfully admitted evidence, the ruling is prejudicial.[28] Likewise, an improper decision to admit (or exclude) evidence of an invocation of Fifth Amendment rights can be prejudicial.[29] In making this "harmlessness" evaluation, the court considers the centrality of the evidence and the prejudicial effect of the inclusion or exclusion of the evidence.[30] The court also examines whether other evidence is "sufficiently strong" to support a conclusion that the

---

502 F.3d 26, 33 (1st Cir. 2007).

[22]*See Jones v. Nat'l Am. Univ.*, 608 F.3d 1039, 1044 (8th Cir. 2010); *Nimely v. City of New York*, 414 F.3d 381, 399–400 (2d Cir. 2005); *U.S. v. Kim*, 111 F.3d 1351, 1363 (7th Cir. 1997).

[23]*See Abrams v. Lightolier Inc.*, 50 F.3d 1204, 1213 (3d Cir. 1995); *Sokol Crystal Products, Inc. v. DSC Communications Corp.*, 15 F.3d 1427, 1435 (7th Cir. 1994).

[24]*See In re Air Crash Disaster*, 86 F.3d 498, 531 (6th Cir. 1996); *La Crosse County v. Gershman, Brickner & Bratton, Inc.*, 982 F.2d 1171, 1175 (7th Cir. 1993).

[25]*See Grizzle v. Travelers Health Network, Inc.*, 14 F.3d 261, 269 (5th Cir. 1994) (court must consider curative instructions when assessing harmlessness). In ruling on the effect of the curative instructions, a court will assume that the jury obeyed the court and followed its instructions. *Trademark Research Corp. v. Maxwell Online, Inc.*, 995 F.2d 326, 340 (2d Cir. 1993). *Compare Davidson v. Smith*, 9 F.3d 4 (2d Cir.1993) (improper testimony not cured by trial instructions) *with Trademark Research Corp. v. Maxwell Online, Inc.*, 995 F.2d 326 (2d Cir.1993) (trial error deemed cured by

court's instructions).

[26]*See Meyer Intellectual Props. Ltd. v. Bodum, Inc.*, 690 F.3d 1354, 1376 (Fed.Cir. 2012); *Abraham v. BP America Prod. Co.*, 685 F.3d 1196, 1202 (10th Cir. 2012); *Jones v. Nat'l Am. Univ.*, 608 F.3d 1039, 1044 (8th Cir. 2010). *See also Hynes v. Coughlin*, 79 F.3d 285, 291 (2d Cir. 1996) (tests for whether improperly admitted evidence substantially influenced the jury include: examining whether evidence was unimportant in relation to all other issues jury considered, whether evidence bore on an issue that was plainly critical to the jury's deliberations, and whether the evidence was emphasized during jury argument).

[27]*See Florek v. Village of Mundelein*, 649 F.3d 594, 602 (7th Cir. 2011); *English ex rel. Estate of Taft v. District of Columbia*, 651 F.3d 1, 3 (D.C.Cir. 2011); *United States v. Yarrington*, 634 F.3d 440, 447 (8th Cir. 2011).

[28]*See S.E.C. v. Happ*, 392 F.3d 12, 28 (1st Cir. 2004); *Havrum v. U.S.*, 204 F.3d 815, 818 (8th Cir. 2000).

[29]*See Hinojosa v. Butler*, 547 F.3d 285, 292–95 (5th Cir. 2008).

[30]*See Nieves-Villanueva v. Soto-Rivera*, 133 F.3d 92, 102 (1st Cir. 1997).

evidentiary error had no effect on the outcome.[31] The courts often begin with a "presumption of prejudice"[32] — thus, only if the court can say with fair assurance that the judgment was not substantially affected by the wrongfully admitted or excluded evidence, the error will be considered harmless.[33] The courts are particularly careful in discounting an error as harmless in close cases,[34] or where it is substantively important, inflammatory, repeated, emphasized, or unfairly self-serving.[35]

- *Expert Testimony:* This same harmless error standard applies to challenges to expert testimony as well.[36]
- *Rebuttal Testimony:* The harmlessness standard applies to the decision to exclude (or limit) rebuttal evidence.[37]
- *Effect of Multiple Errors:* Although each individual evidentiary error might not, standing alone, have affected a party's substantial rights, the court may find that the collective effect of multiple evidentiary errors deprived the moving party of a fair trial.[38]

Errors in Seating Jurors

Errors in striking or refusing to strike prospective jurors are also measured under the harmless error standard.[39]

Errors in Jury Instructions

Jury instructions must be considered in their entirety.[40] If the charging errors would not have changed the trial result,[41]

---

[31]*See Goebel v. Denver and Rio Grande Western R.R. Co.*, 215 F.3d 1083, 1089 (10th Cir. 2000).

[32]*See Jerden v. Amstutz*, 430 F.3d 1231, 1240–41 (9th Cir. 2005).

[33]*See Guillemard-Ginorio v. Contreras-Gomez*, 585 F.3d 508, 534 (1st Cir. 2009); *Hirst v. Inverness Hotel Corp.*, 544 F.3d 221, 228 (3d Cir. 2008); *Tesser v. Board of Educ. of City School Dist. of City of New York*, 370 F.3d 314, 319–20 (2d Cir. 2004). *See also Mihailovich v. Laatsch*, 359 F.3d 892, 913–14 (7th Cir. 2004) (errors in evidence satisfy standard only if significant chance exists that errors affected trial's outcome).

[34]*See Sims v. Great Am. Life Ins. Co.*, 469 F.3d 870, 886 (10th Cir. 2006); *Nimely v. City of New York*, 414 F.3d 381, 400 (2d Cir. 2005).

[35]*See Doty v. Sewall*, 908 F.2d 1053, 1057 (1st Cir.1990).

[36]*See Dresser-Rand Co. v. Virtual Automation Inc.*, 361 F.3d 831, 842 (5th Cir. 2004).

[37]*See Peals v. Terre Haute Police Dept.*, 535 F.3d 621, 630 (7th Cir. 2008).

[38]*See Jerden v. Amstutz*, 430 F.3d 1231, 1240–41 (9th Cir. 2005); *Gomez v. Rivera Rodriguez*, 344 F.3d 103, 118 (1st Cir. 2003); *Phoenix Associates III v. Stone*, 60 F.3d 95, 105 (2d Cir. 1995).

[39]*See Avichail ex rel. T.A. v. St. John's Mercy Health Sys.*, 686 F.3d 548, 553 (8th Cir. 2012).

[40]*See Gonzales v. Duran*, 590 F.3d 855, 862 (10th Cir. 2009); *Costa-Urena v. Segarra*, 590 F.3d 18, 24 (1st Cir. 2009).

[41]*See Czekalski v. LaHood*, 589 F.3d 449, 453 (D.C.Cir. 2009) (must be prejudicial); *Richards v. Relentless, Inc.*, 341 F.3d 35, 48 (1st Cir. 2003) (new trial necessary only if instruction error could have affected jury's deliberation); *Elwell v. University Hospitals Home Care Services*, 276 F.3d 832, 844 (6th Cir. 2002) (assessing ruling in context of instructions as a whole, ruling "harmless because risk of jury confusion was minimal"); *Dadian v.*

or if the parties waived the errors by failing to timely object,[42] challenges to jury instructions will be rejected as harmless.[43] Conversely, if the jury may have based their verdict on an erroneous instruction,[44] or if the instruction was otherwise prejudicially misleading, confusing, or legally incorrect,[45] a new trial is warranted.

Errors in Jury Verdict Form Interrogatories

Whether mistakes in crafting jury interrogatories on the verdict form is deemed reversible error will also be measured under the harmless error standard.[46]

Errors in Ruling on Counsel's Conduct During Trial

Misconduct by counsel during trial will be deemed harmless unless the court determines that the misconduct affected the verdict,[47] as will errors in permitting inappropriate counsel invitations for jury participation in a trial demonstration.[48]

Errors in Bench Judgments

In bench trials, errors are harmless if the record shows that

---

Village of Wilmette, 269 F.3d 831, 839 (7th Cir. 2001) (testing whether instructions, as a whole, sufficiently informed jury correctly as to applicable law and thus did not affect substantial rights of parties).

[42]*See Foley v. Commonwealth Elec. Co.*, 312 F.3d 517, 520 (1st Cir. 2002) (if party properly objects to jury instruction, harmless error Rule 61 applies; if proper objection not made, plain error rule applies which requires proof of: (1) error, (2) that error was plain, (3) that error likely altered outcome, and (4) that error was sufficiently fundamental to threaten fairness, integrity, or public reputation of judicial proceedings).

[43]*See Terminate Control Corp. v. Horowitz*, 28 F.3d 1335 (2d Cir. 1994) (jury instructions warrant a new trial only if the court is persuaded, based on the record as a whole, that the error was prejudicial or the charge was highly confusing).

[44]*See Biegas v. Quickway Carriers, Inc.*, 573 F.3d 365, 377 (6th Cir. 2009) (not harmless because could have impacted deliberations); *Dossett v. First State Bank*, 399 F.3d 940, 950 (8th Cir. 2005) (not harmless where it eliminated potentially viable avenue to establish liability); *S.E.C. v. Yun*, 327 F.3d 1263, 1282 (11th Cir. 2003) (granting new trial due to court's er-

roneous jury instruction, reinforced in counsel's closing argument); *Jannotta v. Subway Sandwich Shops, Inc.*, 125 F.3d 503, 515 (7th Cir. 1997) (not harmless if it provided jury with inadequate understanding of the law and caused prejudice to the complaining party); *Coleman v. B-G Maintenance Management of Colorado, Inc.*, 108 F.3d 1199, 1204–05 (10th Cir. 1997) (because the jury, in all probability, based its verdict on erroneous instruction, jury's verdict must be reversed).

[45]*See Costa-Urena v. Segarra*, 590 F.3d 18, 24 (1st Cir. 2009).

[46]*See Happel v. Walmart Stores, Inc.*, 602 F.3d 820, 826–28 (7th Cir. 2010); *Desmond v. Mukasey*, 530 F.3d 944, 967 (D.C. Cir. 2008).

[47]*Cf.* Rule 39(c) (relating to advisory juries). *See Peterson v. Willie*, 81 F.3d 1033, 1036 (11th Cir. 1996) (noting that statements made during oral arguments will not constitute reversible error unless they are plainly unwarranted and clearly injurious); *Westfarm Associates Ltd. Partnership v. Washington Suburban Sanitary Com'n*, 66 F.3d 669, 685 (4th Cir. 1995) (inappropriate allusion made during closing argument, followed by proper instructions from the court, is not basis for reversal).

[48]*See Noel v. Artson*, 641 F.3d 580, 592 (4th Cir. 2011).

the district judge would have reached the same judgment regardless of the error.[49] Thus, a judge's mistaken application of a certain method of damages valuation (one to which there was no testimony or other record basis) will be deemed harmless if the effect of the error caused no prejudice.[50]

Error in Granting or Denying Jury Trial

The court's mistaken decision to grant a jury trial is generally harmless error,[51] but an improper denial of a jury trial is usually grounds for reversal.[52]

Additional Research References

Wright & Miller, *Federal Practice and Procedure* §§ 2881 to 88
C.J.S., Federal Civil Procedure §§ 1062 to 1100 et seq., §§ 1241 to 1247 et seq.
West's Key Number Digest, Federal Civil Procedure ⚫➡2333 to 2353, ⚫➡2651 to 2656

---

[49]*See Barber v. Ruth*, 7 F.3d 636, 641 (7th Cir. 1993).

[50]*See U.S. v. 191.07 Acres of Land*, 482 F.3d 1132, 1137 (9th Cir. 2007) (finding valuation error was harmless as to appellants because it resulted in a higher award than appellants (using other method) would otherwise have received).

[51]*See Mateyko v. Felix*, 924 F.2d 824, 828 (9th Cir. 1990). *See also Venture Properties, Inc. v. First Southern Bank*, 79 F.3d 90, 92 (8th Cir. 1996) (movant demonstrated no prejudice from court's decision to conduct a jury trial rather than a bench trial).

[52]*See Burns v. Lawther*, 53 F.3d 1237, 1241–42 (11th Cir. 1995) (harmless error rule may be applied to improper denials of trial by jury, but only if the issues could have been resolved by summary judgment or judgment as a matter of law); *King v. United Ben. Fire Ins. Co.*, 377 F.2d 728, 731 (10th Cir. 1967) (denial will be deemed harmless where only a question of law is involved or where a verdict for the movant would have been set aside). *See also Sailor v. Hubbell, Inc.*, 4 F.3d 323 (4th Cir.1993) (denial of jury trial harmless if it did not affect party's rights, such as where no reasonable jury could have found in that party's favor).

RULE 62
STAY OF PROCEEDINGS TO ENFORCE A JUDGMENT

(a) **Automatic Stay; Exceptions for Injunctions, Receiverships, and Patent Accountings.** Except as stated in this rule, no execution may issue on a judgment, nor may proceedings be taken to enforce it, until 14 days have passed after its entry. But unless the court orders otherwise, the following are not stayed after being entered, even if an appeal is taken:

(1) an interlocutory or final judgment in an action for an injunction or a receivership; or

(2) a judgment or order that directs an accounting in an action for patent infringement.

(b) **Stay Pending the Disposition of a Motion.** On appropriate terms for the opposing party's security, the court may stay the execution of a judgment—or any proceedings to enforce it—pending disposition of any of the following motions:

(1) under Rule 50, for judgment as a matter of law;

(2) under Rule 52(b), to amend the findings or for additional findings;

(3) under Rule 59, for a new trial or to alter or amend a judgment; or

(4) under Rule 60, for relief from a judgment or order.

(c) **Injunction Pending an Appeal.** While an appeal is pending from an interlocutory order or final judgment that grants, dissolves, or denies an injunction, the court may suspend, modify, restore, or grant an injunction on terms for bond or other terms that secure the opposing party's rights. If the judgment appealed from is rendered by a statutory three-judge district court, the order must be made either:

(1) by that court sitting in open session; or

(2) by the assent of all its judges, as evidenced by

their signatures.

(d) Stay with Bond on Appeal. If an appeal is taken, the appellant may obtain a stay by supersedeas bond, except in an action described in Rule 62(a)(1) or (2). The bond may be given upon or after filing the notice of appeal or after obtaining the order allowing the appeal. The stay takes effect when the court approves the bond.

(e) Stay Without Bond on an Appeal by the United States, Its Officers, or Its Agencies. The court must not require a bond, obligation, or other security from the appellant when granting a stay on an appeal by the United States, its officers, or its agencies or on an appeal directed by a department of the federal government.

(f) Stay in Favor of a Judgment Debtor Under State Law. If a judgment is a lien on the judgment debtor's property under the law of the state where the court is located, the judgment debtor is entitled to the same stay of execution the state court would give.

(g) Appellate Court's Power Not Limited. This rule does not limit the power of the appellate court or one of its judges or justices:

(1) to stay proceedings—or suspend, modify, restore, or grant an injunction—while an appeal is pending; or

(2) to issue an order to preserve the status quo or the effectiveness of the judgment to be entered.

(h) Stay with Multiple Claims or Parties. A court may stay the enforcement of a final judgment entered under Rule 54(b) until it enters a later judgment or judgments, and may prescribe terms necessary to secure the benefit of the stayed judgment for the party in whose favor it was entered.

[Amended effective March 19, 1948; October 20, 1949; July 19, 1961; August 1, 1987; April 30, 2007, effective December 1, 2007; March 26, 2009, effective December 1, 2009.]

AUTHORS' COMMENTARY ON RULE 62

———————— **PURPOSE AND SCOPE** ————————

Rule 62 provides for stays to prevent the enforcement of judgments pending post-trial motions and appeals.

The "Restyling" and "Time Computation" Amendments

The Rules have undergone dramatic changes in the past few years. Every Rule was "restyled" in 2007; nearly every time period set by the Rules was revised in 2009. The Rule text above, and the commentary below, reflect the current language of the Rules. These two amendments are discussed in Detail in Part III-A of this text.

———

RULE 62(a)—AUTOMATIC STAY; EXCEPTIONS FOR INJUNCTIONS, RECEIVERSHIPS, AND PATENT ACCOUNTINGS

CORE CONCEPT

The automatic stay postpones enforcement of a judgment for fourteen days from the date of entry of the judgment.[1] However, Rule 62(a) provides no automatic stay in three circumstances: (1) an interlocutory or final judgment in an action for an injunction;[2] (2) an interlocutory or final judgment in a receivership action; and (3) a judgment or order directing an accounting in an action for infringement of letters patent.

APPLICATIONS

Effect

An automatic stay will prevent the enforcement of the judgment, but the stay will not affect the appealability of the judgment or the running of the appeal time.[3] Additionally, the judgment has *res judicata* effect during the pendency of the appeal.[4]

———

[1] *See, e.g., In re High Sulfur Content Gasoline Products Liability Litigation*, 517 F.3d 220, 231 (5th Cir. 2008) (in context of attorneys' fees, purpose of Rule is both to forestall fee disputes and prevent obstacles to reallocation of fees if court decides later to alter award).

[2] *See, e.g., Ogden Fire Co. No. 1 v. Upper Chichester TP.*, 504 F.3d 370, 377 n.3 (3d Cir. 2007) ("Inasmuch as the district court's order was in the form of an injunction, it remains in effect and must be complied with during the pendency of this appeal.").

[3] FED.R.APP.P. 4(a).

[4] *See, e.g., Fish Market Nominee Corp. v. Pelofsky*, 72 F.3d 4, 7 (1st Cir. 1995) (noting distinction between bar to enforcing judgment and absence of bar to *res judicata*).

Judgments Covered

The automatic stay applies to any judgment defined in Rule 54(a).[5]

Expiration of Stay Period

Once the automatic stay period expires, a party may seek enforcement of the judgment.[6]

Armed Services Personnel

The Soldiers and Sailors Civil Relief Act of 1940, 50 U.S.C.A. §§ 203 to 04, Appendix §§ 523 to 24, provides that a court may stay the execution of any judgment entered against a person in the military service, or vacate or stay an attachment or garnishment.

Relation to Rule 6(a)

Although there is little authority on point, it appears that for purposes of 14-day stays under Rule 62(a), time shall be computed under the standards of Rule 6(a).[7]

RULE 62(b)—STAY PENDING THE DISPOSITION OF A MOTION

CORE CONCEPT

After judgment, a court has discretion to order a stay while it considers post-trial motions. The court also has discretion to establish conditions for the security of the adverse party during the pendency of the stay.

APPLICATIONS

Security

The court has discretion not only to order a stay pending post-trial motions, but may order the movant to post security, including the amount of the judgment and interest, during the period of the stay. The court may also require the bond to include costs and damages for delay or any other loss that may result during the period of the stay. Additionally, the court may order the movant to provide written notice to the opposing parties of any material disposition of the movant's assets.

Effect of Denial

When the court denies a stay pending disposition of a post trial motion, judgment is binding (and may be enforced) until

---

[5]*But cf., Arnold v. Garlock, Inc.,* 278 F.3d 426, 437 (5th Cir. 2001) (remand of pending case to state court is not final judgment and therefore Rule 62 has no applicability to remands).

[6]*See, e.g., Acevedo-Garcia v. Vera-Monroig,* 368 F.3d 49, 58 (1st Cir. 2004) ("The federal rules contemplate that, absent a stay, a victorious plain-tiff may execute on the judgment even while an appeal of that judgment is pending.").

[7]*See, e.g., KRW Sales, Inc. v. Kristel Corp.,* 154 F.R.D. 186, 188 (N.D. Ill. 1994) (computing time limit for purposes of Rule 62(a) under standards of Rule 6(a)).

vacated by the court or reversed on appeal.

Procedure

The filing of post-trial motions does not stay execution of the judgment or the proceeding in execution. Hence, a party should assert the motion for stay before the end of the automatic stay period, provided under Rule 62(a). Once the motion for stay is made, the court has discretion to stay execution or enforcement of the judgment pending disposition of the post-trial motions.

RULE 62(c)—INJUNCTION PENDING AN APPEAL

CORE CONCEPT

Rule 62(c) authorizes the district judge or a district court of three judges, having granted, dissolved, or denied a preliminary or final injunction to stay its decision or grant other interim relief pending appeal.[8]

NOTE: There are no automatic stays in injunction actions. Injunction actions may be stayed only by court order. The district court has discretion to determine whether to grant a stay.[9]

APPLICATIONS

Scope

Rule 62(c) expressly covers interlocutory as well as final judgments in injunction cases and applies to cases where the court has denied an injunction as well as granted an injunction. However, the district court may not dissolve an injunction that has been appealed. Instead, the court may only modify the injunction while it is being appealed, with the purpose of maintaining the status quo.[10]

---

[8]*See, e.g., Baum v. Blue Moon Ventures, LLC*, 513 F.3d 181, 190 (5th Cir. 2008) ("While the validity of an injunction is on appeal, the district court's power is limited to 'maintaining the status quo.' "). *See also A&M Records, Inc. v. Napster, Inc.*, 284 F.3d 1091, 1099 (9th Cir. 2002) (Rule 62(c) "authorizes a district court to continue supervising compliance with the injunction." Affirming district court's decision to continue to supervise defendant's compliance with injunction.).

[9]*See, e.g., LiButti v. U.S.*, 178 F.3d 114, 121 (2d Cir. 1999) ("It has been long-established law that simply filing an appeal from the grant or denial of an injunction—absent a stay of further proceedings—does not enjoin the operative effect of the trial court's ruling from which the appeal is taken.").

[10]*See, e.g., Mayweathers v. Newland*, 258 F.3d 930, 935 (9th Cir. 2001) (filing of notice of appeal generally strips district court of jurisdiction over case, but Rule 62(c) is exception; under Rule 62(c) district court may issue second injunction while first injunction is under appeal-provided that new injunction does not change status quo); *Natural Resources Defense Council, Inc. v. Southwest Marine Inc.*, 242 F.3d 1163, 1166 (9th Cir. 2001) (Rule 62(c) gives district court authority only to take steps to maintain status quo while case is pending on appeal; district court has no authority to re-visit the merits of case on appeal).

Time for Motion

A party should make a motion to stay an injunction immediately after the notice of appeal has been filed and may make this motion at any time while the appeal is pending.[11]

Which Court

The movant should first assert the motion in the district court. If the district court denies relief or the district court provides inadequate relief, the movant may assert the motion in the court of appeals.[12] Where submission to a panel would prejudice the movant, the motion can be made to a single judge of the court of appeals.[13] In extraordinary circumstances, pending disposition of an application for writ of certiorari and during the pendency of an appeal to the court of appeals[14] or from a final judgment of the court of appeals,[15] a single justice of the Supreme Court, sitting as a single Circuit Justice, may take any action provided in Rule 62(g).[16] In addition, a judge of the court rendering the judgment may grant a stay on application for writ of certiorari to the Supreme Court.[17]

Requirements

Rule 62(c) authorizes the court to issue a stay to maintain the status quo or the effectiveness of the final judgment during the pendency of an appeal. When a party makes a motion under Rule 62(c), the courts will require the movant to show the following elements:[18] (a) a strong likelihood of success on the merits of the appeal; (b) that unless the motion is granted the movant will suffer irreparable injury; (c) no substantial harm will come to other interested parties; and (d) a grant of the motion will not harm the public interest. The courts have often

---

[11]*See, e.g., Credit Suisse First Boston Corp. v. Grunwald*, 400 F.3d 1119, 1124 (9th Cir. 2005) (motion may be made "at any time before entry of a final judgment"); *Minnesota Humane Society v. Clark*, 184 F.3d 795, 797 (8th Cir. 1999) (denial of preliminary injunction that was sought to bar removal and killing of geese should have caused plaintiff to seek prompt appeal under 28 U.S.C. § 1292 and request for injunction pending appeal).

[12]FED.R.APP. 8(a). *See Rakovich v. Wade*, 834 F.2d 673, 675 (7th Cir. 1987) (movant should first seek relief in district court; if district court denies relief, movant may then seek stay in court of appeals).

[13]FED.R.APP. 8(a).

[14]*Atiyeh v. Capps*, 449 U.S. 1312, 101 S. Ct. 829, 66 L. Ed. 2d 785 (1981) (per Justice Rehnquist).

[15]*Graddick v. Newman*, 453 U.S. 928, 102 S. Ct. 4, 69 L. Ed. 2d 1025 (1981); *Holtzman v. Schlesinger*, 414 U.S. 1304, 94 S. Ct. 1, 38 L. Ed. 2d 18 (1973) (per Justice Marshall).

[16]28 U.S.C.A. § 1651(a); U.S.Sup. Ct.R. 23.

[17]28 U.S.C.A. 2101(f).

[18]*Hilton v. Braunskill*, 481 U.S. 770, 776, 107 S. Ct. 2113, 95 L. Ed. 2d 724 (1987). *See, e.g., Cuomo v. U.S. Nuclear Regulatory Com'n*, 772 F.2d 972, 974 (D.C. Cir. 1985) (per curiam) (citing same four factors; also noting "[A] movant need not always establish a high probability of success on the merits. Probability of success is inversely proportional to the degree of irreparable injury evidenced. A stay may be granted with either a high probability of success and some injury, or *vice versa*.").

balanced the irreparable injury to the movant if the court did not issue the stay, against the harm the stay would cause to the other parties and to the public. The governing considerations are the same whether the party applies to the district court or to the appellate courts under Rule 62(g).

Requirements of Order

An injunctive order issued pursuant to Rule 62(c) must set forth the reasons for its issuance and be specific in its terms in compliance with the requirements of Rule 65(d).

Security for Stay

The court will usually order the movant to post security during the period of the stay or the injunction.[19]

Three Judge District Court

When a district court of three judges, sitting by statute, renders judgment in an injunction case, a motion to that judgment should be addressed to all three judges. Such a court may only issue a stay pending an appeal in open court or by signature of all three judges.

RULE 62(d)—STAY WITH BOND UPON APPEAL

CORE CONCEPT

The act of appealing a judgment does not automatically create a stay of the judgment pending appeal.[20] However, a party may obtain a stay by filing a supersedeas bond with the court (*i.e.*, a bond posted as security against an appeal) that is approved by the court.[21] Unless state law provides otherwise (as described in Rule 62(f)),[22] Rule 62(d) governs the only circumstances in which a party may obtain a stay of enforcement of a money judgment pending appeal,[23] beyond the automatic 14-day period provided by Rule 62(a).

---

[19]*See, e.g., Roche Diagnostics Corp. v. Medical Automation Systems, Inc.*, ___ F.3d ___ (7th Cir. 2011) ("Normally an injunction bond or equivalent security is essential." Bond should be sufficient to cover losses caused by erroneously issued injunction.).

[20]*See, e.g., Correa v. Cruisers, a Div. of KCS Intern., Inc.*, 298 F.3d 13, 29 (1st Cir. 2002) ("[T]here is no requirement that the judgment become final before it can be enforced.").

[21]*See, e.g., Alphas Co. v. Dan Tudor & Sons Sales, Inc.*, 679 F.3d 35, 38 n.2 (1st Cir. 2012) (noting general applicability of Rule 62(d); *ACLU v. Masto*, 670 F.3d 1046, 1067 (9th Cir. 2012) (appellant who appeals and posts supersedeas bond with district court is entitled to stay "as a matter of right;" otherwise, stay is within district court's discretion).

[22]*But cf., Vacation Village, Inc. v. Clark County, Nev*, 497 F.3d 902, 913 (9th Cir. 2007) (where state law requires appellant to pay full value of judgment into court, but Rule 62(d) requires a supersedeas bond, court applies Rule 62(d); not mentioning Rule 62(f).

[23]*See, e.g., Cleveland Hair Clinic, Inc. v. Puig*, 104 F.3d 123, 125 (7th Cir. 1997) (Rule 62(d) stay may also prevent enforcement of final decision to sanction parties and attorney for misconduct in case; applicability of

APPLICATIONS

Stay as of Right

By posting a supersedeas bond with the court and upon approval of the bond by the court, a party may obtain a stay upon appeal as a matter of course.[24]

Amount of Bond

The amount of the bond will usually be an amount sufficient to satisfy the judgment plus interest.[25] The court may also require the bond to include costs,[26] plus any damages for delay. The court has the discretion to provide a lesser amount or other types of security.[27] Local rule may provide the amount required.

Alternatives to Bond

Although Rule 62(d) speaks only of bonds, courts may permit "other forms of judgment guarantee."[28]

Deadline for Posting Bond

Rule 62(d) permits the bond to be posted at the time a party files a notice of appeal (or receives permission to appeal), or later. However, because the stay does not become effective until the court approves the bond, it is wise to post the bond within the 14-day period of the automatic stay provided by Rule

---

Rule 62(d) not limited to circumstances involving only judgments).

[24] *See, e.g., Exxon Valdez v. Exxon Mobil Corp.*, 568 F.3d 1077 (9th Cir. 2009) (bond stays enforcement of judgment pending appeal). *But see, N.L.R.B. v. Westphal*, 859 F.2d 818, 819 (9th Cir. 1988) (Rule 62(d) stay as of right limited to money judgments; no right to stay order enforcing subpoenas).

[25] *See, e.g., Strong v. Laubach*, 443 F.3d 1297, 1299 (10th Cir. 2006) (bond "is usually for the full amount of the judgment").

[26] F.R.A.P. 7.

[27] *See, e.g., Olcott v. Delaware Flood Co.*, 76 F.3d 1538, 1559 (10th Cir. 1996) (bond normally equals amount of judgment; trial court, however, has discretion to require lesser amount; but no discretion, apparently to require bond in amount greater than judgment). *Dillon v. City of Chicago*, 866 F.3d 902 (7th Cir.1988) (identifying circumstances when other guarantees are appropriate).

[28] *See, e.g., Arban v. West Pub. Corp.*, 345 F.3d 390, 409 (6th Cir. 2003) (bond that meets requirements of Rule

62(d) entitles party to stay as of right; however, even in absence of bond, court has discretion to issue stay); *Dale M. ex rel. Alice M. v. Board of Educ.*, 237 F.3d 813, 815 (7th Cir. 2001) (judgment debtor who pays judgment and does not choose to post bond under Rule 62(d) has not rendered appeal moot and is entitled to repayment of judgment if reversed); *In re Carlson*, 224 F.3d 716, 719 (7th Cir. 2000) (waiver of bond requirement "is appropriate only if the appellant has a clearly demonstrated ability to satisfy the judgment if the appeal is unsuccessful and there is no other concern that the appellee's rights will be compromised by a failure adequately to secure the judgment"); *Olympia Equipment Leasing Co. v. Western Union Telegraph Co.*, 786 F.2d 794, 796 (7th Cir. 1986) ("[A]n inflexible requirement of a bond would be inappropriate in two sorts of case: where the defendant's ability to pay the judgment is so plain that the cost of the bond would be a waste of money; and the opposite case, one of increasing importance in an age of titanic damage judgments-where the requirement would put the defendant's other creditors in undue jeopardy.").

62(a).[29]

Actions Not Stayed

Rule 62(d), by its own terms, does not apply to the three circumstances enunciated in Rule 62(a). Those circumstances are: judgments in injunction actions;[30] judgments in receivership actions; and judgments requiring an accounting in patent infringement cases. In such cases an appealing party may not post a bond and obtain a stay of judgment under Rule 62(d).

Judgments for Damages and Injunctions

If a party seeks to use Rule 62(d) to stay a judgment by which the court ordered both money damages and equitable relief, the stay under Rule 62(d) is effective only to stop enforcement of the damage award.[31] Unless the appealing party can persuade the court to stay the injunction under Rule 62(c), the injunction portion of the judgment may be enforced pending appeal.

Failure to Post Bond

Failure to post bond under Rule 62(d) does not affect a party's right to appeal.[32] However, in the absence of a stay ordered pursuant to Rule 62(d), an adverse party may enforce a judgment while the appeal is pending,[33] which sometimes may render the appeal moot.[34]

It should be noted that while Rule 62(d) mandates a stay when an appropriate supersedeas bond is filed, some courts

---

[29]*But see, E.E.O.C. v. Clear Lake Dodge*, 25 F.3d 265, 273 (5th Cir. 1994) (Rule 62(d) permits posting of bond at or after filing notice of appeal; thus, to post bond prior to appealing is inappropriate).

[30]*See, e.g., Solis v. Malkani*, 638 F.3d 269, 275 (4th Cir. 2011) (Rule 62(d) applies only to monetary judgments, not to injunctive relief); *Hebert v. Exxon Corp.*, 953 F.2d 936, 938 (5th Cir. 1992) ("Courts have restricted the application of Rule 62(d)'s automatic stay to judgments for money because a bond may not adequately compensate a non-appealing party for loss incurred as a result of the stay of a non-money judgment.").

[31]*N.L.R.B. v. Westphal*, 859 F.2d 818 (9th Cir.1988) (Rule 62(d) cannot stay injunctions).

[32]*See, e.g., Porco v. Trustees of Indiana University*, 453 F.3d 390, 394 (7th Cir. 2006) (failure to obtain stay under Rule 62(d) does not ordinarily moot appeal); *In re American President Lines, Inc.*, 779 F.2d 714, 718 (D.C. Cir. 1985) (per curiam)(failure to post bond leaves appellant vulnerable to enforcement of judgment, but does not forfeit right of appeal).

[33]*See, e.g., Eurasia Intern., Ltd. v. Holman Shipping, Inc.*, 411 F.3d 578, 585 (5th Cir. 2005) (failure to post bond means no automatic stay may issue; bond requirement not met by filing motion to stay that was contingent on filing bond); *In re American President Lines, Inc.*, 779 F.2d 714, 718 (D.C. Cir. 1985) (per curiam) (failure to post bond leaves appellant vulnerable to enforcement of judgment, but does not forfeit right of appeal).

[34]*But see Strong v. Laubach*, 443 F.3d 1297, 1299 (10th Cir. 2006) (judgment debtor who does not post bond may nonetheless appeal; upon successful appeal, district court may (on motion or sua sponte) order disgorgement of benefit previously obtained by judgment creditor; but in such circumstances, risk that judgment creditor is insolvent falls on judgment debtor).

may grant stays notwithstanding the absence of a bond.[35] To determine which courts follow this practice, attorneys are advised to consult local practice.

Impact of Appeal by Prevailing Party

If the prevailing party also appeals some facet of a district court's judgment, there is some conflict in the cases as to whether the judgment debtor must post a bond to stay execution of judgment pending the judgment debtor's appeal.[36] Attorneys are urged to consult local precedent.

Relation to Rule 11

Inappropriate use of Rule 62(d) bonds may be grounds for sanctions under Rule 11.

RULE 62(e)—STAY WITHOUT BOND ON AN APPEAL BY THE UNITED STATES, ITS OFFICERS, OR ITS AGENCIES

CORE CONCEPT

The United States is not required to post a bond to obtain a stay of the enforcement of a judgment pending appeal. This exemption also extends to officers and agents of the United States government, and any party acting under the direction of any department or agency of the government, as provided by 28 U.S.C.A. § 2408.

RULE 62(f)—STAY IN FAVOR OF A JUDGMENT DEBTOR UNDER STATE LAW

CORE CONCEPT

When the judgment creates a lien upon the debtor's property and the judgment debtor is entitled to a stay under applicable state law, the district court shall stay the enforcement of the judgment to the same extent that state law directs a state court

---

[35]*See, e.g., In re Diet Drugs Product Liability Litigation*, 582 F.3d 524, 552 (3d Cir. 2009) (Rule 62(d) governs stays granted as of right, but does not prohibit a grant of a stay as a matter of judicial discretion); *Federal Prescription Service, Inc. v. American Pharmaceutical Ass'n*, 636 F.2d 755, 759 (D.C. Cir. 1980) ("[The Rule] speaks only to stays granted as a matter of right, it does not speak to stays granted by the court in accordance with its discretion;" collecting cases).

[36]*Compare Tennessee Valley Authority v. Atlas Mach. & Iron Works, Inc.*, 803 F.2d 794, 797 (4th Cir. 1986) (appeal by prevailing party suspends judgment; thus losing party need not post supersedeas bond to prevent execution on judgment while losing party's appeal is pending), *with Trustmark Ins. Co. v. Gallucci*, 193 F.3d 558, 559 (1st Cir. 1999) (noting split of authority; concluding that appeal by prevailing party eliminates obligation of judgment debtor to post bond under Rule 62(d) to stay execution of money judgment only when basis of prevailing party's appeal is inconsistent with enforcement of judgment; requiring bond when prevailing party's appeal was only for denial of pre-judgment interest, which is not inconsistent with immediate enforcement of judgment).

to enter a stay.[37] The court has no discretion to deny such a stay.[38] Moreover, while the normal practice anticipates that the judgment debtor will file a motion for a stay, there appears to be no requirement for such a motion and the stay can become effective even in the absence of a motion.[39]

RULE 62(g)—APPELLATE COURT'S POWER NOT LIMITED

CORE CONCEPT

The provisions of Rule 62 apply only to district courts, and do not limit appellate courts.

RULE 62(h)—STAY WITH MULTIPLE CLAIMS OR PARTIES

CORE CONCEPT

When a court issues a partial judgment under Rule 54(b), it may allow immediate enforcement of the partial judgment or it may stay enforcement of the partial judgment pending a further adjudication.

APPLICATIONS

Time for Filing

A party must make a motion for stay upon partial judgment after the entry of the partial judgment and during the fourteen-day automatic stay period.

Standards for Granting a Stay

The court has discretion to decide a motion for stay, balancing the equities of the parties and considering the administration of the case.[40]

---

[37]*See, e.g., Hoban v. Washington Metropolitan Area Transit Authority,* 841 F.2d 1157, 1159 (D.C. Cir. 1988) (per curiam)(if state law authorizes stay without requiring a supersedeas bond, stay imposed under rule 62(f) must also be unencumbered by bond). *But cf., Vacation Village, Inc. v. Clark County, Nev,* 497 F.3d 902, 913 (9th Cir. 2007) (where state law requires appellant to pay full value of judgment into court, but Rule 62(d) requires a supersedeas bond, court applies Rule 62(d); not mentioning Rule 62(f)).

[38]*Cf., Rodriguez-Vazquez v. Lopez-Martinez,* 345 F.3d 13, 14 (1st Cir. 2003) ("Our own inclination is to think that where a lien can be procured [under state law] by minor ministerial

acts, this minor burden on the judgment-creditor should not preclude a stay under Rule 62(f)." Citing conflicting authority in district courts).

[39]*See, e.g., Whitehead v. Food Max of Mississippi, Inc.,* 332 F.3d 796, 804–05 (5th Cir. 2003) (en banc) (no requirement for a formal motion to grant a Rule 62(f) stay; if sanctions under Rule 11 are appropriate because prevailing party violated stay, the absence of a Rule 62(f) motion does not prevent imposition).

[40]*See, e.g., North Penn Transfer, Inc. v. Maple Press Co.,* 176 B.R. 372, 375–77 (M.D. Pa. 1995) (judgment for plaintiff on unpaid shipping charges stayed under Rule 62(h) so that defendant can challenge reasonableness of

Independent Actions

When a court consolidates several independent actions and renders judgment on one of the independent actions, this is not considered a partial judgment under Rule 54(b), and a stay will not be granted under Rule 62(h).[41]

Posting of Security

When issuing a stay of a particular judgment, the court may require security to be posted to secure that part of the judgment.[42]

Additional Research References

Wright & Miller, Federal Practice and Procedure: Civil 2d §§ 2901 to 20
C.J.S., Federal Civil Procedure § 1263; Federal Courts § 294(1 to 5) et seq.
West's Key Number Digest, Federal Civil Procedure ⚹2700; Federal Courts ⚹684 to 687

---

shipping rates before regulatory agency; citing possibility that immediate enforcement of judgment would make defendant insolvent).

[41]*In re Massachusetts Helicopter Airlines, Inc.*, 469 F.2d 439, 442 (1st Cir. 1972) (Rule 62(h) applicable only to circumstances governed by Rule 54(b); independent actions cannot be stayed under Rule 62(h)).

[42]*Curtiss-Wright Corp. v. General Elec. Co.*, 446 U.S. 1, 13, 100 S. Ct. 1460, 64 L. Ed. 2d 1 (1980) ("[W]e assume it would be within the power of the District Court to protect all parties by having the losing party deposit the amount of the judgment with the court.").

RULE 62.1
INDICATIVE RULING ON A MOTION FOR RELIEF THAT IS BARRED BY A PENDING APPEAL

(a) Relief Pending Appeal. If a timely motion is made for relief that the court lacks authority to grant because of an appeal that has been docketed and is pending, the court may:

(1) defer considering the motion;

(2) deny the motion; or

(3) state either that it would grant the motion if the court of appeals remands for that purpose or that the motion raises a substantial issue.

(b) Notice to the Court of Appeals. The movant must promptly notify the circuit clerk under Federal Rule of Appellate Procedure 12.1 if the district court states that it would grant the motion or that the motion raises a substantial issue.

(c) Remand. The district court may decide the motion if the court of appeals remands for that purpose.

[Added March 26, 2009, effective December 1, 2009.]

AUTHORS' COMMENTARY ON RULE 62.1

PURPOSE AND SCOPE

Rule 62.1 governs some circumstances when a motion has been made to a district court in a case that has been docketed and is pending on appeal. If the district court lacks authority to grant the motion because the appeal is pending, Rule 62.1 provides the district court with several options to indicate the way in which it might act if the appellate court remands the case for the district court to deal with the subject matter of the motion.

RULE 62.1(a) RELIEF PENDING APPEAL

CORE CONCEPT

Rule 62.1(a) with a district court with some limited authority to announce how it would deal with a pending motion that it cannot address because the case is now subject to the jurisdiction of an appellate court. In that sense, a district court's decision to exercise its authority under Rule 62.1 is "indicative" only.

APPLICATIONS

Requirement of Timeliness

A district court has whatever authority Rule 62.1 may provide only in situations where the motion before the court was filed in a timely way. If the motion is untimely, Rule 62.1 is inapplicable.

Applicability: Exception for Motions Which District Court May Grant: Appellate Rule 4

Federal Rule of Appellate Procedure 4(a)(4) identifies six motions that, if timely filed with the district court, have the effect of stopping the appellate process (including the time limit for filing a notice of appeal) until the district court disposes of all such motion(s),[1] through, e.g., granting or denying them. In other words, notwithstanding that a party may already have filed a notice of appeal (or not), Appellate Rule 4 permits the district court to decide those motions before the appeal may proceed further. Because the application of Rule 62.1 is expressly limited to circumstances in which a district court may be prevented from granting a motion in a case pending on appeal, Rule 62.1 has no applicability to motions that fall within the scope of Appellate Rule 4.

Applicability: District Court's Authority to Deny a Motion

The applicability of Rule 62.1 is limited to circumstances in which the district court has no authority to grant a motion due to the pending appeal. However, if the court is inclined to deny the motion, Rule 62.1 is not a barrier. This point is discussed further immediately below.

Scope of District Court's Options

When Rule 62.1 is applicable, it provides the court with the following options. First, the court may choose to defer consideration of the motion pending outcome of the appeal. Second the court may deny the motion. Thus, notwithstanding the existence of a pending appeal, a district court is normally free to deny any motion made during the pendency of an appeal even if the court might not have had authority to grant the motion (if the court was so inclined). Third, the court may express its view that the motion would be granted if the appellate court chooses to remand the case for that purpose. Fourth, the district court may state simply that the motion raises a substanstantial issue.

---

[1]Fed.R.App.P. 4(a)(4).

RULE 62.1(b) NOTICE TO THE COURT OF APPEALS

CORE CONCEPT

Rule 62.1 establishes a requirement for the party that filed the motion to notify the appellate court if the district court stated that it would either grant the motion or that the motion raises a substantial issue.

APPLICATIONS

Notice: Relation to Appellate Rule 12.1

Rule 62.1(b) expressly provides that if a movant is obligated to notify an appellate court that the district court indicated it might either grant the motion or, at least, that the motion raises a substantial issue, the manner of notification is governed by Federal Rule of Appellate Procedure 12.1[2] Rule 12.1 is a new addition to the Federal Rules of Appellate Procedure. It should be noted that if the district court has indicated that it would either defer consideration of the motion or deny the motion, Rule 62.1(b) imposes no obligation on the movant to notify the appellate court.

RULE 62.1(c) REMAND

CORE CONCEPT

Rule 62.1(c) provides the district court with authority to decide the motion if the court of appeals has remanded the case for that purpose.[3]

---

[2]Fed.R.App.P. 12.1

[3]See, e.g., Arlington Industries v. Bridgeport Fittings, Inc., 632 F.3d 1246 (Fed.Cir. 2011) (noting district court's authority to provide "indicative" ruling).

RULE 63
JUDGE'S INABILITY TO PROCEED

If a judge conducting a hearing or trial is unable to proceed, any other judge may proceed upon certifying familiarity with the record and determining that the case may be completed without prejudice to the parties. In a hearing or a nonjury trial, the successor judge must, at a party's request, recall any witness whose testimony is material and disputed and who is available to testify again without undue burden. The successor judge may also recall any other witness.

[Amended effective August 1, 1987; December 1, 1991; April 30, 2007, effective December 1, 2007.]

AUTHORS' COMMENTARY ON RULE 63

PURPOSE AND SCOPE

When a judge withdraws after a trial or hearing begins, any other judge of the court may proceed with the case. The successor judge will read the pertinent portions of the record, certify familiarity with that record, and then decide whether he or she may proceed with the case without causing prejudice to the parties. In a non-jury hearing or trial format, if the successor judge proceeds with the case, he or she must recall any witnesses requested by the parties, if their testimony is material and disputed and where the witnesses are available to testify again without undue burden. In addition, the successor judge may recall any witnesses in order to become more familiar with the record.

APPLICATIONS

Caution in Relying on Pre-1992 Case Law

Rule 63 was substantially amended in late 1991 to expand the Rule's scope and to alter certain interpretations given to the Rule by the courts. Decisions that predate the 1991 amendment should be cited with due care.[1]

---

[1]*But see Zand v. C.I.R. Service,* 143 F.3d 1393, 1400 (11th Cir. 1998) (court may look to pre-1991 decisions for guidance given facts of particular

Conditions for Inability to Proceed

A judge's withdrawal must rest on compelling reasons, such as sickness, death, or other disability, including recusal and disqualification.[2] A judge may not withdraw for personal convenience.[3]

Statement of Grounds for Withdrawal

The withdrawing judge must state on the record the reasons for his or her withdrawal.[4]

Only Applicable *After* Hearing or Trial Begins

The certification obligation of Rule 63 is only triggered if the substitution is made *after* a hearing or trial has begun; before that time, a substitution may be made without any requirement of certification by the substituting judge.[5]

Timing of Substitution

The original text of Rule 63 implied that, once a trial or hearing had begun, district judges could not be substituted unless the departing judge had already filed findings of fact and conclusions of law. The courts embraced this implication and, unless the parties stipulated otherwise, required new trials where the departing judge had not filed the findings and conclusions.[6]

This "negative inference" mandate ascribed to Rule 63 was abolished in 1991. Citing the increasing length of trials in federal court and the expected concomitant increase in the number of trials interrupted by a judge's disability,[7] the drafters provided that a substitution may be made after trial commences and even in the absence of filed findings and conclusions, if the replacement judge (1) can certify his or her familiarity with the proceedings in the case to date, and (2) can continue the proceedings without prejudicing the parties.

---

case).

[2] *See* Rule 63 advisory committee notes to 1991 amendment. *See also* 28 U.S.C. §§ 144 & 455 (providing for disqualification of judges).

[3] *See* Rule 63 advisory committee notes to 1991 amendment.

[4] *See* Rule 63 advisory committee notes to 1991 amendment.

[5] *See Beck v. Dileo*, 2010 WL 4875685, at *1 (E.D.Cal. Nov. 23, 2010); *Houston v. Encinitas Union School Dist.*, 2008 WL 2220414, at *4 (S.D. Cal. 2008).

[6] *See, e.g., In re Higginbotham*, 917 F.2d 1130, 1132 (8th Cir. 1990); *Olle v. Henry & Wright Corp.*, 910 F.2d 357, 361 (6th Cir. 1990); *Home Place-*

ment Service, Inc. v. Providence Journal Co., 819 F.2d 1199, 1202 (1st Cir. 1987); *Whalen v. Ford Motor Credit Co.*, 684 F.2d 272, 274 (4th Cir. 1982); *Thompson v. Sawyer*, 678 F.2d 257, 268–69 (D.C. Cir. 1982); *Arrow-Hart, Inc. v. Philip Carey Co.*, 552 F.2d 711, 713 (6th Cir. 1977).

[7] *See* Rule 63 advisory committee notes to 1991 amendment. *See also Mergentime Corp. v. Washington Metropolitan Area Transit Authority*, 166 F.3d 1257, 1262 (D.C. Cir. 1999) (noting motivation for Rule change, and commenting that successor judges may now take over at any point after the trial begins, subject to certain additional responsibilities imposed upon the successor judges).

Certifying Familiarity With the Record

Once a trial or hearing has begun, no substitute judge can replace a departing judge without first "certifying familiarity with the record".[8] It is this certification procedure that ensures that Due Process is not violated when the case resumes.[9] Although an express "certification" is plainly preferred,[10] the court of appeals will likely not reverse in the absence of an express certification so long as the successor judge's statements confirm compliance with the record familiarity requirement.[11] Nor will the appeals court likely reverse for unfortunate, though non-prejudicial, misstatements in the certification.[12] This certification requirement obligates the substitute judge to read and consider all relevant portions of the record.[13] What portions of the record the successor judge is required to learn depends upon the nature of the successor judge's role in the case. For example, if the successor judge inherits a jury trial before the evidence has closed, the judge must become familiar with the entire record so as to properly rule upon relevance-based evidentiary objections; but if the successor judge inherits the case after the entry of verdict or judgment, the judge need only review those portions of the record relevant to the particular issues challenged by post-trial motions.[14]

Prerequisite for Substitution

In order for a judge to be substituted, there must be an available transcript or a videotape to permit the replacement judge to become familiar with the proceedings that occurred prior to the substitution. The Committee Notes encourage the prompt preparation of the trial or videotape transcript, so as to

---

[8]*See In re Reale*, 584 F.3d 27, 32 (1st Cir. 2009); *Maritimes & Northeast Pipeline, L.L.C. v. 0.714 Acres of Land, More or Less, in Danvers, Mass.*, 2007 WL 2461054, at *1 (D. Mass. 2007).

[9]*See Patelco Credit Union v. Sahni*, 262 F.3d 897, 905 (9th Cir. 2001).

[10]*See, e.g., Vescio v. Merchants Bank*, 272 B.R. 413, 420 (D. Vt. 2001), aff'd, 54 Fed. Appx. 513 (2d Cir. 2002) ("The Court hereby certifies pursuant to Fed.R.Civ.P. 63 that it has reviewed the transcript of the trial, together with the exhibits, and that the proceedings in this case may be completed without prejudice to the parties").

[11]*See Bisbal-Ramos v. City of Mayaguez*, 467 F.3d 16, 26 (1st Cir. 2006); *Mergentime Corp. v. Washington Metropolitan Area Transit Authority*, 166 F.3d 1257, 1265 (D.C. Cir. 1999).

See also United States v. Washington, 653 F.3d 1057, 1064 (9th Cir. 2011) ("ministerial" failure to certify "does not cast doubt on the proceeding's integrity").

[12]*See In re Reale*, 584 F.3d 27, 32 n.2 (1st Cir. 2009) (finding certification's confirmation that successor judge had considered witnesses' demeanor "unfortunate" but, given the record evidence, not prejudicial).

[13]*See Mergentime Corp. v. Washington Metropolitan Area Transit Authority*, 166 F.3d 1257, 1265 (D.C. Cir. 1999); *Canseco v. U.S.*, 97 F.3d 1224, 1226 (9th Cir. 1996) (as amended Dec. 18, 1996).

[14]*See Mergentime Corp. v. Washington Metropolitan Area Transit Authority*, 166 F.3d 1257, 1265 (D.C. Cir. 1999).

prevent delaying the jury longer than necessary.[15]

Jury Trials

In a jury trial, the parties do not have the right to insist that a witness be recalled.[16] Instead, if the successor judge can certify familiarity with the record and can determine that the proceedings are able to be completed without prejudice to the parties, nothing more is required.[17] Should the judge choose to do so, however, the successor judge has the discretion to recall a witness.[18]

Bench Trials

In a non-jury trial, the parties can insist that the successor judge recall a witness whose testimony is material and disputed *and* who is available to testify again:[19]

(1) *Testimony of Available Witness:* When a witness is available, the successor judge may decide to hear the witness' testimony if the testimony is material or disputed. It may be error for the new judge to decline to hear the testimony of a witness whose credibility is material to a finding of fact, particularly if a party so requests.[20]

(2) *Testimony of Unavailable Witness:* If a witness has become unavailable, such that a subpoena to compel testimony at trial is unavailable, the successor judge can consider the testimony recorded at trial or, if the testimony was not material or not disputed, may choose not to hear the testimony at all.[21]

Previously Litigated Issues

Unless the controlling law has changed, the successor judge

---

[15]*See* Rule 63 advisory committee notes to 1991 amendment.

[16]*See Jackson v. State of Alabama State Tenure Com'n*, 405 F.3d 1276, 1286–87 (11th Cir. 2005).

[17]*See Jackson v. State of Alabama State Tenure Com'n*, 405 F.3d 1276, 1287 (11th Cir. 2005).

[18]*See* Rule 63.

[19]*See* Rule 63. *See also In re Reale*, 584 F.3d 27, 32 (1st Cir. 2009); *Jackson v. State of Alabama State Tenure Com'n*, 405 F.3d 1276, 1286–87 (11th Cir. 2005); *New York v. Shinnecock Indian Nation*, 523 F. Supp. 2d 185, 193 n.3 (E.D. N.Y. 2007).

[20]*See* Rule 63 advisory committee notes to 1991 amendment. *See also In re Karten*, 293 Fed.Appx. 734, 736 (11th Cir. 2008) (successor judge should not make credibility determinations, but should retry the case); *Mergentime Corp. v. Washington Metropolitan Area Transit Authority*, 166 F.3d 1257, 1266 (D.C. Cir. 1999) (holding that, upon request of party, district court must recall any witness whose testimony is material and disputed and who, without undue burden, is available to testify again); *Canseco v. U.S.*, 97 F.3d 1224, 1227 (9th Cir. 1996) (as amended Dec. 18, 1996) (where credibility of witness is questioned, and where sufficiency of the evidence hinges on that witness's testimony and credibility cannot be determined from the record, substitute judge must recall the witness, if available without undue burden, and make own credibility determination); *Universal Furniture Int'l, Inc. v. Collezione Europa, USA, Inc.*, 599 F.Supp.2d 648, 651 (M.D.N.C. 2009) (absent parties' consent, successor judge should not make credibility determinations of witnesses).

[21]*See* Rule 63 advisory committee notes to 1991 amendment.

will not ordinarily revisit rulings made by the withdrawing judge. However, the successor judge is required to consider and rule upon allegations of trial error properly raised in post-trial motions.[22]

Option To Enter Summary Judgment

If, after reviewing the trial transcript, the successor judge decides that no credibility determinations are required and that one party is entitled to a judgment as a matter of law, summary judgment can be entered as an alternative to the successor judge "stepping into the shoes" of the unavailable trial judge.[23]

Removed Cases

Where the parties or issues permit a belated removal of a State court proceeding, the federal court may enter judgment upon the State court jury's verdict.[24]

Waiver of Right to Object to New Judge

Following the departure of the original judge, the litigants may be deemed to have waived any objection to the case's reassignment to a new judge if the litigants fail either to timely seek a new trial or timely object to a reassignment,[25] or fail to timely insist upon the recall of witnesses.[26] Minimally, a failure to object will likely relegate the appellate court to the very forgiving "plain error" standard of review.[27]

Additional Research References

Wright & Miller, *Federal Practice and Procedure: Civil 2d* §§ 2921 to 30
C.J.S., Judges §§ 35 to 68
West's Key Number Digest, Judges ⟐21, ⟐32

---

[22]*See Mergentime Corp. v. Washington Metropolitan Area Transit Authority*, 166 F.3d 1257, 1263 (D.C. Cir. 1999) (holding that successor judge may not refuse to consider post-trial motions out of deference to the original judge).

[23]*See Patelco Credit Union v. Sahni*, 262 F.3d 897, 906 (9th Cir. 2001).

[24]*See Sweeney v. Resolution Trust Corp.*, 16 F.3d 1, 5–6 (1st Cir. 1994).

[25]*See See Littleton v. Pilot Travel Ctrs., LLC*, 568 F.3d 641, 648 (8th Cir. 2009) (party may not "sit back and await decision" before objecting); *Zand v. C.I.R. Service*, 143 F.3d 1393, 1400 (11th Cir. 1998) (ruling that parties had "cleverly tiptoe[d]" across a "procedural tightrope", refusing to consent to a reassignment while, simultaneously, failing to seek the added expense of a retrial; therefore, an unfavorable verdict by the successor judge could not be challenged under Rule 63).

[26]*See Marantz v. Permanente Med. Group, Inc. Long Term Disability Plan*, 687 F.3d 320, 327 (7th Cir. 2012); *In re Reale*, 584 F.3d 27, 32–33 (1st Cir. 2009).

[27]*See Bisbal-Ramos v. City of Mayaguez*, 467 F.3d 16, 26 (1st Cir. 2006).

VIII. PROVISIONAL AND FINAL REMEDIES

RULE 64
SEIZING A PERSON OR PROPERTY

(a) Remedies Under State Law—In General. At the commencement of and throughout an action, every remedy is available that, under the law of the state where the court is located, provides for seizing a person or property to secure satisfaction of the potential judgment. But a federal statute governs to the extent it applies.

(b) Specific Kinds of Remedies. The remedies available under this rule include the following—however designated and regardless of whether state procedure requires an independent action:

- arrest;
- attachment;
- garnishment;
- replevin;
- sequestration; and
- other corresponding or equivalent remedies.

[Amended April 30, 2007, effective December 1, 2007.]

AUTHORS' COMMENTARY ON RULE 64

PURPOSE AND SCOPE

After the commencement of an action and until the time of judgment, Rule 64 provides means by which a claimant may seek an order of court to seize a person or property in order to secure satisfaction of the eventual judgment. Relief under Rule 64 is infrequently granted and should be infrequently sought.

RULE 64(a)—REMEDIES UNDER STATE LAW—IN GENERAL

CORE CONCEPT

Rule 64(a) provides that federal courts possess the same remedies for seizing a person or property that are available to a state court in the state where the federal court is located.[1] However, Rule 64(a) provides that if a federal statute is applicable, it governs in place of state law.[2]

APPLICATIONS

Time to Seek an Order

At any time after the commencement of an action and until the time of judgment,[3] a party may assert an ancillary claim in the pending action or file an independent action to seize property under Rule 64.

Application: Comparison to Rule 70

Rule 64, where applicable, permits prejudgment relief. Rule 70, by contrast, is applicable to circumstances arising after a judgment is entered.[4]

Sources of Remedies

The claimant must seek the applicable federal remedy, if a specific federal remedy exists.[5] The Advisory Committee Notes to Rule 64 list some of the federal remedies. Otherwise, the movant may choose any provisional remedy under applicable state law.[6]

RULE 64(b)—SPECIFIC KINDS OF REMEDIES

CORE CONCEPT

Rule 64(b) provides a non-exclusive list of remedies available to a federal court, without regard to how a state may designated those remedies. It also provides that a district court may use those remedies without the need to follow state rules that may otherwise require an independent enforcement action.

---

[1]*See, e.g., Lee-Barnes v. Puerto Ven Quarry Corp.*, 513 F.3d 20, 23 n.1 (1st Cir. 2008) (applying Puerto Rican law governing prejudgment security bond).

[2]*See, e.g., United States v. Witham*, 648 F.3d 40, 44 (1st Cir. 2011) (noting that federal law governs, if applicable).

[3]*See, e.g., Rosen v. Cascade Intern., Inc.*, 21 F.3d 1520, 1530 (11th Cir. 1994) (Rule 64 authorizes prejudgment attachment in some situations); *But see, Credit Managers Ass'n of Southern California v. Kennesaw Life and Acc. Ins. Co.*, 25 F.3d 743, 750 (9th Cir. 1994) (permitting use of Rule 64 to satisfy existing judgment; but Rule 64 deferred to state law, which prohibited satisfaction on instant facts).

[4]*See, e.g., Deegan v. Strategic Azimuth LLC*, 768 F.Supp.2d 107, 115 n.1 (D.D.C. 2011) (comparing Rule 64 and Rule 70).

[5]*See, e.g., Hoult v. Hoult*, 373 F.3d 47, 54 (1st Cir. 2004) ("federal statute governs to the extent applicable").

[6]*See, e.g., Goya Foods, Inc. v. Wallack Management Co.*, 290 F.3d 63, 70 (1st Cir. 2002) ("By its terms [Rule 64] allows a federal court to borrow provisional remedies created by state law."); *Stephens v. National Distillers and Chemical Corp.*, 69 F.3d 1226, 1228 n. 2 (2d Cir. 1995) (noting that Rule 64 incorporates state remedies).

APPLICATIONS

Method for Obtaining Relief

Where a federal remedy exists, the procedure for obtaining relief will be provided by the relevant statute and the Rules. When relief is sought under a state remedy, state law generally supplies the procedures, except to the extent that the Rules apply. The method for obtaining relief will vary from state to state and district to district. However, in all cases a U.S. Marshal rather than a state officer would seize the goods or property.

Jurisdiction

Procedures under Rule 64 whether asserted in a pending action or in an independent action do not require a separate basis of subject matter jurisdiction.[7]

Constitutional Limitations

The seizure of a person or property without notice or a prior hearing may often be a violation of constitutional due process.[8]

Relation to Rule 65

It now appears settled that in cases involving only money damages on an unsecured claim, a party may not use Rule 65 (governing preliminary injunctions and temporary restraining orders) to obtain a prejudgment injunction aimed at preventing dissipation of assets. Instead, such relief must be sought under other provisions, such as Rule 64's authorization to use state law prejudgment attachment provisions.[9] However, if the lawsuit also seeks equitable relief, the district court is not restricted by Rule 64 and may still grant a prejudgment injunction that freezes specific assets that are the subject of a restitution or recission claim or that preserves the power of the court to grant final injunctive relief.[10]

---

[7]*Cf., Skevofilax v. Quigley*, 810 F.2d 378 (3d Cir. 1987).

[8]*North Georgia Finishing, Inc. v. Di-Chem, Inc.*, 419 U.S. 601, 95 S. Ct. 719, 42 L. Ed. 2d 751 (1975) (*Fuentes v. Shevin* is weakened); *Mitchell v. W. T. Grant Co.*, 416 U.S. 600, 94 S. Ct. 1895, 40 L. Ed. 2d 406 (1974); *Fuentes v. Shevin*, 407 U.S. 67, 92 S. Ct. 1983, 32 L. Ed. 2d 556 (1972).

[9]*Grupo Mexicano de Desarrollo S.A. v. Alliance Bond Fund, Inc.*, 527 U.S. 308, 330–31, 119 S. Ct. 1961, 1968–75, 144 L. Ed. 2d 319 (1999) (in case involving only general creditor seeking damages at law and with no lien in specific property of defendant, Rule 65 may not be used to obtain prejudgment injunction because, *inter alia,* such use of Rule 65 would render Rule 64 "a virtual irrelevance. Why go through the trouble of complying with local attachment and garnishment standards when this all-purpose prejudgment injunction is available?"). *See also TMTV Corp. v. Mass Productions, Inc.*, 645 F.3d 464, 475 (1st Cir. 2011) (where prejudgment interest is appropriate, there is no uniform federal interest rate; use of state rate may be appropriate).

[10]*See, e.g., U.S. ex rel. Rahman v. Oncology Associates*, 198 F.3d 489, 495–97 (4th Cir. 1999) (explaining relationship of *Grupo Mexicano* to earlier Supreme Court precedent authorizing use of prejudgment injunction in eq-

Armed Services Personnel

Provisional relief under Rule 64 is subject to the Soldiers' and Sailors' Civil Relief Act of 1940, 50 U.S.C.A. §§ 203, 204, Appendix §§ 523, 524, which prohibits seizure of the assets of absent military personnel in many circumstances.

Execution

A plaintiff who recovers judgment is entitled to an execution sale of the previously seized property in satisfaction of the judgment.

Additional Research References

Wright & Miller, *Federal Practice and Procedure: Civil 2d* §§ 2931 to 40
C.J.S., Federal Civil Procedure §§ 233 to 241, § 1271
West's Key Number Digest, Federal Civil Procedure ☞581 to 590, ☞601 to 610

---

uity cases; also noting that equity court "has enhanced authority when the public interest is involved"). *See also De Beers Consol. Mines v. U.S.,* 325 U.S. 212, 219, 65 S. Ct. 1130, 1133–34, 89 L. Ed. 1566 (1945) ("A preliminary injunction is always appropriate to grant intermediate relief of the same character as that which may be granted finally"; however, in instant case property affected by injunction lies outside issues of case; also noting, *inter alia,* that relief government requested was not available under Rule 64).

RULE 65
INJUNCTIONS AND RESTRAINING ORDERS

(a) Preliminary Injunction.

(1) *Notice.* The court may issue a preliminary injunction only on notice to the adverse party.

(2) *Consolidating the Hearing with the Trial on the Merits.* Before or after beginning the hearing on a motion for a preliminary injunction, the court may advance the trial on the merits and consolidate it with the hearing. Even when consolidation is not ordered, evidence that is received on the motion and that would be admissible at trial becomes part of the trial record and need not be repeated at trial. But the court must preserve any party's right to a jury trial.

(b) Temporary Restraining Order.

(1) *Issuing Without Notice.* The court may issue a temporary restraining order without written or oral notice to the adverse party or its attorney only if:

(A) specific facts in an affidavit or a verified complaint clearly show that immediate and irreparable injury, loss, or damage will result to the movant before the adverse party can be heard in opposition; and

(B) the movant's attorney certifies in writing any efforts made to give notice and the reasons why it should not be required.

(2) *Contents; Expiration.* Every temporary restraining order issued without notice must state the date and hour it was issued; describe the injury and state why it is irreparable; state why the order was issued without notice; and be promptly filed in the clerk's office and entered in the record. The order expires at the time after entry—not to exceed 14 days—that the court sets, unless before that time the court, for good

cause, extends it for a like period or the adverse party consents to a longer extension. The reasons for an extension must be entered in the record.

(3) *Expediting the Preliminary-Injunction Hearing.* If the order is issued without notice, the motion for a preliminary injunction must be set for hearing at the earliest possible time, taking precedence over all other matters except hearings on older matters of the same character. At the hearing, the party who obtained the order must proceed with the motion; if the party does not, the court must dissolve the order.

(4) *Motion to Dissolve.* On 2 days' notice to the party who obtained the order without notice—or on shorter notice set by the court—the adverse party may appear and move to dissolve or modify the order. The court must then hear and decide the motion as promptly as justice requires.

(c) Security. The court may issue a preliminary injunction or a temporary restraining order only if the movant gives security in an amount that the court considers proper to pay the costs and damages sustained by any party found to have been wrongfully enjoined or restrained. The United States, its officers, and its agencies are not required to give security.

(d) Contents and Scope of Every Injunction and Restraining Order.

(1) *Contents.* Every order granting an injunction and every restraining order must:

(A) state the reasons why it issued;

(B) state its terms specifically; and

(C) describe in reasonable detail—and not by referring to the complaint or other document—the act or acts restrained or required.

(2) *Persons Bound.* The order binds only the following who receive actual notice of it by personal service or otherwise:

(A) the parties;

(B) the parties' officers, agents, servants, employees, and attorneys; and

(C) other persons who are in active concert or

participation with anyone described in Rule 65(d)(2)(A) or (B).

(e) Other Laws Not Modified. These rules do not modify the following:

(1) any federal statute relating to temporary restraining orders or preliminary injunctions in actions affecting employer and employee;

(2) 28 U.S.C. § 2361, which relates to preliminary injunctions in actions of interpleader or in the nature of interpleader; or

(3) 28 U.S.C. § 2284, which relates to actions that must be heard and decided by a three-judge district court.

(f) Copyright Impoundment. This rule applies to copyright-impoundment proceedings.

[Amended effective March 19, 1948; October 20, 1949; July 1, 1966; August 1, 1987; April 23, 2001, effective December 1, 2001; April 30, 2007, effective December 1, 2007; March 26, 2009, effective December 1, 2009.]

AUTHORS' COMMENTARY ON RULE 65

PURPOSE AND SCOPE

Rule 65 establishes the procedural requirements for obtaining a temporary restraining order or a preliminary injunction. It is important to note that although a party must satisfy the procedures of Rule 65 before a court will grant such injunctive relief, the substantive requirements for an injunction are separate from and additional to Rule 65, and they must also be satisfied.[1]

The substantive requirements for injunctions are found predominantly in federal case law, as well as federal statutes authorizing injunctions in certain circumstances and limiting their applicability in others.[2] Although there can be substantial variations in the requirements from one circuit to another, courts deciding whether to grant an injunction generally weigh some or all of the following factors: (1) whether the potential harm to the

---

[1]See, e.g. U.S. v. Cohen, 152 F.3d 321, 324 (4th Cir. 1998) ("[Rule] 65 is not a source of power for a district court to enter an injunction. Rather, it regulates the issuance of injunctions otherwise authorized.").

[2]See, e.g., Muffley ex rel. N.L.R.B.

v. Spartan Mining Co., 570 F.3d 534 (4th Cir. 2009) (in cases seeking injunctive relief pursuant to National Labor Relations Act, 29 U.S.C. § 160(j), court notes "three competing standards" for determining appropriateness of injunctive relief).

person seeking injunctive relief is irreparable,[3] *i.e.,* whether such harm could be cured through an award of money damages instead of an injunction;[4] (2) whether the person against whom an injunction would be entered would be harmed excessively by the injunction; (3) whether, and to what extent, the grant or denial of an injunction would affect interests of third persons, including public interests; and (4) when a motion for a temporary restraining order or a preliminary injunction is before the court, whether the person seeking such relief is likely to prevail on the merits when the case comes to trial.[5]

NOTE: It is important to keep in mind that most of Rule 65 applies only to requests for preliminary relief. With the exception of Rule 65(d), discussed below, Rule 65 has no application to grants or denials of permanent injunctions.[6]

---

[3]*See, e.g., Rodriguez ex rel. Rodriguez v. DeBuono,* 175 F.3d 227, 235 (2d Cir. 1999) (per curiam) (noting that both preliminary and permanent injunction require a showing of irreparable harm; however, standard for obtaining preliminary injunction is nevertheless more stringent, because moving party must also demonstrate "imminence" of harm, which is not required for grant of permanent injunction). *But cf., Prayze FM v. F.C.C.,* 214 F.3d 245, 250 (2d Cir. 2000) (where government seeks preliminary injunction for violation of statute irreparable nature of injury is rebuttably presumed; distinguishing private injunction claims).

[4]*Cf., Grupo Mexicano de Desarrollo S.A. v. Alliance Bond Fund, Inc.,* 527 U.S. 308, 119 S. Ct. 1961, 144 L. Ed. 2d 319 (1999) (in action for money damages on contract claim district court lacks jurisdiction to issue preliminary injunction preventing defendants' transfer of assets prior to judgment). *See also Lakeview Technology, Inc. v. Robinson,* 446 F.3d 655 (7th Cir.2006) (if issue is whether the person to be enjoined will be able to pay damages in the absence of an injunction, the issue may be neutralized if that person provides a "non-injunction" bond that will compensate opponent if no injunction is granted and opponent is thereby damaged).

[5]*See, e.g., Prairie Band of Potawatomi Indians v. Pierce,* 253 F.3d 1234 (10th Cir.2001) (citing all four factors, but observing that if party seeking preliminary relief can establish last three factors, application of first factor is "less strict"); *U.S. v. Power Engineering Co.,* 191 F.3d 1224, 1230 (10th Cir. 1999) (citing use of all four factors; also noting that "[a] mandatory preliminary injunction (*i.e.,* one that directs a party to act) imposes an even heavier burden on [the movant] of showing that the four factors . . . weigh heavily and compellingly in movant's favor"). *But cf., Heideman v. South Salt Lake City,* 348 F.3d 1182, 1189 (10th Cir. 2003) (if movant can show that latter three "harm" factors tip *decidedly* in its favor, it is entitled to a "somewhat relaxed" burden on probability of success standard; however, no such leniency applies to application for injunction against government action undertaken in public interest); *New Comm Wireless Services, Inc. v. SprintCom, Inc.,* 287 F.3d 1, 9 (1st Cir. 2002) ("The sine qua non of this four-part inquiry is likelihood of success on the merits: if the moving party cannot demonstrate that he is likely to succeed in his quest, the remaining factors become matters of idle curiosity.").

[6]*See, e.g., U.S. v. Criminal Sheriff, Parish of Orleans,* 19 F.3d 238 (5th Cir. 1994) (Rule 65 does not apply to permanent injunctions).

RULE 65(a)—PRELIMINARY INJUNCTION

CORE CONCEPT

Rule 65(a) contains two distinct concepts. The first portion of the Rule ensures that courts will not grant applications for preliminary injunctions until affected parties receive notice and an opportunity to oppose the proposed preliminary injunction. The second part of Rule 65(a) provides that the court may consolidate an application for a preliminary injunction with a trial on the merits, to the extent that consolidation is feasible under the facts of the particular case.

APPLICATIONS

Purpose

The purpose of a preliminary injunction is usually to maintain the status quo until the merits of a case can be decided.[7] Courts grant preliminary injunctions ordering an alteration of the status quo only in unusual circumstances where the merits clearly favor one party over another.[8] A preliminary injunction can only apply during the pendency of the case, at the end of which the court may consider whether to enter a permanent injunction.

Relation to Rule 64

It now appears settled that in cases involving only money damages on an unsecured claim, a party may not use Rule 65 (governing preliminary injunctions and temporary restraining orders) to obtain a prejudgment injunction aimed at preventing dissipation of assets. Instead, such relief must be sought under other provisions, such as Rule 64's authorization to use state law prejudgment attachment provisions.[9] However, if the lawsuit also seeks equitable relief, the district court is not

---

[7]*See, e.g., Resolution Trust Corp. v. Cruce,* 972 F.2d 1195, 1198 (10th Cir. 1992) (primary purpose of preliminary injunction is to preserve status quo). *Cf., U.S. Philips Corp. v. KBC Bank, N.V.,* 590 F.3d 1091, 1093 (9th Cir. 2010) ("A preliminary injunction [pursuant to Rule 65] . . . dissolves *ipso facto* when a final judgment is entered in the cause.").

[8]*See, e.g., Dominion Video Satellite, Inc. v. EchoStar Satellite Corp.,* 269 F.3d 1149, 1154–55 (10th Cir. 2001) (movant has "heightened burden of showing that the traditional four factors weigh heavily and compellingly in its favor before obtaining a preliminary injunction. . . . The heightened burden applies to preliminary injunctions that (1) disturb the status quo, (2) mandatory rather than prohibitory, or (3) provide the movant substantially

all the relief it could feasibly attain after a full trial on the merits. . . . This court disfavors such injunctions."); *Aoude v. Mobil Oil Corp.,* 862 F.2d 890, 893 (1st Cir. 1988) ("[On] the peculiar facts of this case, the preliminary injunction is not vulnerable to attack even if it is seen as changing the status quo.").

[9]*Grupo Mexicano de Desarrollo S.A. v. Alliance Bond Fund, Inc.,* 527 U.S. 308, 330–31, 119 S. Ct. 1961, 1968–75, 144 L. Ed. 2d 319 (1999) (in case involving only general creditor seeking damages at law and with no lien in specific property of defendant, Rule 65 may not be used to obtain prejudgment injunction because, *inter alia,* such use of Rule 65 would render Rule 64 "a virtual irrelevance. Why go through the trouble of complying with local attachment and garnishment standards when this all-purpose pre-

restricted by Rule 64 and may still grant a prejudgment injunction that freezes specific assets that are the subject of a restitution or recission claim or that preserves the power of the court to grant final injunctive relief.[10]

Comparison With Temporary Restraining Order

A temporary restraining order is also directed at freezing circumstances in place until further action can be taken. However, in certain circumstances discussed below, Rule 65(b) permits a temporary restraining order to issue without notice to the opposing party. Temporary restraining orders issued without notice are effective for no more than fourteen days, and may be extended without the consent of the opposing party only once, for a maximum of fourteen additional days. Courts often use temporary restraining orders to maintain the status quo until there is an opportunity for a fuller hearing on a motion for a preliminary injunction.[11]

Appeal

A court's decision to grant, deny, dissolve, continue, or modify a preliminary injunction is immediately appealable of right pursuant to 28 U.S.C.A. § 1292(a)(1).[12]

(1) NOTICE

Contents of Notice

Rule 65(a)(1) prohibits issuance of a preliminary injunction without notice to the opposing party.[13] However, the Rule contains no provisions governing what constitutes adequate notice. The amount of time that must be provided to a party opposing a preliminary injunction is not clear. Moreover, there is little guidance as to which documents (if any) must be

---

judgment injunction is available?").

[10]*See, e.g., U.S. ex rel. Rahman v. Oncology Associates*, 198 F.3d 489, 495–97 (4th Cir. 1999) (explaining relationship of *Grupo Mexicano* to earlier Supreme Court precedent authorizing use of prejudgment injunction in equity cases; also noting that equity court "has enhanced authority when public interest is involved"). *See also De Beers Consol. Mines v. U.S.*, 325 U.S. 212, 219, 65 S. Ct. 1130, 1133–34, 89 L. Ed. 1566 (1945) ("A preliminary injunction is always appropriate to grant intermediate relief of the same character as that which may be granted finally"; however, in instant case property affected by injunction lies outside issues of case; also noting, *inter alia*, that relief government requested was not available under Rule 64); *Deckert v. Independence Shares*

Corp., 311 U.S. 282, 289, 61 S. Ct. 229, 233, 85 L. Ed. 189 (1940) (in case where equitable remedy of recission is sought, district court has authority to issue prejudgment injunction freezing assets as means of preserving status quo pending final outcome of case).

[11]*See, e.g., Hospital Resource Personnel, Inc. v. U.S.*, 860 F. Supp. 1554, 1556 (S.D. Ga. 1994) (granting restraining order so that court can "conduct a thorough inquiry" on injunction).

[12]*See, e.g., Nutrasweet Co. v. Vit-Mar Enterprises, Inc.*, 112 F.3d 689 (3d Cir.1997).

[13]*Cf., Western Water Management, Inc. v. Brown*, 40 F.3d 105, 109 (5th Cir. 1994) (prohibiting modification of injunction in absence of notice).

served.[14] Attorneys must therefore consult the local practice.

Scope of Hearing

Rule 65 requires that the court hold a hearing before granting or refusing a preliminary injunction.[15] However, the scope of such a hearing is subject to the discretion of the trial court.[16]

Timing of Service

A motion for a preliminary injunction should meet the timeliness requirements of Rule 6(d).[17]

(2) CONSOLIDATION OF HEARING WITH TRIAL ON MERITS

Standard for Consolidation

The court has discretion to consolidate the preliminary injunction hearing with the trial on the merits.[18] Parties seeking a quick decision in the case may consent to consolidation, because Rule 65(a)(2) provides that the schedule for the trial will be advanced to the date of the preliminary injunction hearing. However, the tactical consequences that can follow

---

[14]*See, e.g., Wyandotte Nation v. Sebelius*, 443 F.3d 1247, 1253 (10th Cir. 2006) (rejecting need to give minimum five days notice, but holding that failure of district court to give notice that injunction was being considered was "obvious violation of Rule 65 and is a clear abuse of discretion"). *But cf., Dominion Video Satellite, Inc. v. EchoStar Satellite Corp.*, 269 F.3d 1149, 1154 (10th Cir. 2001) (noting that most circuits have not incorporated Rule 6(d)'s notice requirement into Rule 65(a)(1)); holding that three days was sufficient in circumstances of instant case.

[15]*See, e.g., Hunter v. Hamilton County Board of Elections*, 635 F.3d 219, 246 (6th Cir. 2011). *But cf., Certified Restoration Dry Cleaning Network, L.L.C. v. Tenke Corp.*, 511 F.3d 535, 552 (6th Cir. 2007) (Rule 65 "does not explicitly require the court to conduct an evidentiary hearing" but implies that result; in Sixth Circuit, hearing is required only for factual issues, not "when the issues are primarily questions of law").

[16]*See, e.g., McDonald's Corp. v. Robertson*, 147 F.3d 1301, 1311–13 (11th Cir. 1998) ("Rule 65 does not [always] require an evidentiary hearing;" undisputed material facts require no hearing, but "bitterly disputed"

facts do; in cases where facts are clear but dispute exists as to which important inferences to draw, trial court has substantial discretion as to whether to hold evidentiary hearing); *Campbell Soup Co. v. Giles*, 47 F.3d 467 (1st Cir.1995) (sometimes it is acceptable to consider documentary evidence only; evidentiary hearing may be curtailed or eliminated when speedy decision is required); *Schulz v. Williams*, 38 F.3d 657, 658 (2d Cir. 1994) (per curiam) (parties entitled only to "reasonable opportunity" to contest evidence).

[17]*Cf., e.g., Gomperts v. Chase*, 404 U.S. 1237, 92 S. Ct. 16, 30 L. Ed. 2d 30 (1971) (Douglas, J., in chambers) (three days insufficient to prepare for or implement preliminary injunction).

[18]*See, e.g., American Train Dispatchers Dept. of Intern. Broth. of Locomotive Engineers v. Fort Smith R. Co.*, 121 F.3d 267, 270 (7th Cir. 1997) (noting also that district court must provide parties with "clear and unambiguous notice" of intent to do so). *See also Teva Pharmaceuticals USA, Inc. v. Food & Drug Admin.*, 441 F.3d 1, 3 (D.C. Cir. 2006) (permitting consolidation of hearing on preliminary injunction with motion for summary judgment).

from such an approach should not be overlooked.[19] If the case on the merits is not yet ripe for trial, as when discovery is not yet completed, courts will not consolidate the trial with the preliminary injunction hearing.[20]

Timing of Order to Consolidate

Rule 65(a)(2) permits the court to order consolidation before or after commencement of the hearing on the preliminary injunction. This authorization is construed to mean that courts will not order consolidation unless all parties had adequate warning of the possibility of consolidation and a reasonable opportunity to prepare their positions on the merits.[21]

Preliminary Injunction Evidence

If the court decides not to consolidate the preliminary injunction hearing with trial on the merits, evidence presented at the hearing is nonetheless preserved as part of the record. Significantly, Rule 65(a)(2) provides that the evidence need not be repeated for trial and may be used as it was inserted in the record of the hearing, consistent with the rules of evidence.[22]

Trial by Jury

Rule 65(a)(2) directs that it be construed so that consolidation and/or preservation of evidence for trial does not interfere with a party's right to a jury trial.[23] Thus, if the court decides a motion for a preliminary injunction by ruling on some issues of fact, evidence presented on those issues of fact is preserved for

---

[19]*See, e.g., Rodriguez ex rel. Rodriguez v. DeBuono*, 175 F.3d 227, 235 (2d Cir. 1999) (per curiam) (standard for permanent injunction is less stringent than standard for preliminary injunction because, *e.g.,* motion for permanent injunction does not have to demonstrate potential for "imminent" irreparable harm, while motion for preliminary injunction must make such a showing).

[20]*Pughsley v. 3750 Lake Shore Drive Co-op. Bldg.*, 463 F.2d 1055, 1057 (7th Cir. 1972) ("A litigant applying for a preliminary injunction should seldom be required either to forego discovery in order to seek emergency relief, or to forego a prompt application for an injunction in order to prepare adequately for trial.").

[21]*University of Texas v. Camenisch*, 451 U.S. 390, 101 S. Ct. 1830, 68 L. Ed. 2d 175, 1 A.D.D. 76 (1981) (parties entitled to clear notice of intent to consolidate so that parties can prepare). *See also, American Train Dispatchers Dept. of Intern. Broth. of Locomotive Engineers v. Fort Smith R.*

Co., 121 F.3d 267 (7th Cir. 1997) ("Because different standards of proof may apply in the hearing than in the trial, parties must be given a clear chance to object or to propose special procedures for the consolidation."). *But cf., Campaign for Family Farms v. Glickman*, 200 F.3d 1180, 1186 (8th Cir. 2000) (When dealing "with a purely legal issue on a fixed administrative standard . . . a district court may properly reach the merits in such a case without expressly ordering consolidation under Rule 65 and without giving the parties adequate notice.").

[22]*See, e.g., Attorney General of Oklahoma v. Tyson Foods, Inc.*, 565 F.3d 769, 776 (10th Cir. 2009) ("[E]vidence presented at a preliminary injunction hearing need not be repeated at trial.").

[23]*See, e.g., New Windsor Volunteer Ambulance Corps v. Meyers*, 442 F.3d 101, 120 (2d Cir. 2006) (agreement to consolidation with trial on merits "in no way amounts to a waiver of the right to jury trial").

trial. However, the trier of fact at trial is not bound by the previous findings of fact made by the court in the preliminary injunction hearing.[24]

Modifying or Dissolving a Preliminary Injunction

Although Rule 65(a) is silent on the matter, a preliminary injunction can be modified or dissolved on motion of party who demonstrates that the purpose of the injunction has been fulfilled.[25] Thus, a preliminary injunction not to interfere with the destruction of a derelict building is fulfilled when the building is destroyed.

RULE 65(b)—TEMPORARY RESTRAINING OR-DER

CORE CONCEPT

Rule 65(b) provides the procedure for obtaining a temporary restraining order. Although the Rule permits a party to obtain a temporary restraining order without first providing notice to opposing parties, it restricts such relief to circumstances where it is clear that notice was not feasible, and limits the duration of such restraining orders to a maximum of twenty-eight days (including a single renewal).

APPLICATIONS

Purpose

The purpose of a temporary restraining order is generally to hold the status quo in place until the court has an opportunity to hear a request for fuller relief, such as a preliminary injunction.[26]

Comparison With Preliminary Injunction

A preliminary injunction is also usually directed at freezing circumstances in place until there is greater opportunity to hear the merits of a case.[27] However, a preliminary injunction cannot be issued unless all parties are provided with notice of the motion for such relief, whereas it is possible in some circumstances to obtain a temporary restraining order without

---

[24]*University of Texas v. Camenisch*, 451 U.S. 390, 395, 101 S. Ct. 1830, 1834, 68 L. Ed. 2d 175 (1981) ("[F]indings of fact and conclusions of law made by a court granting a preliminary injunction are not binding at trial on the merits.").

[25]*U.S. v. United Shoe Machinery Corp.*, 391 U.S. 244, 88 S. Ct. 1496, 20 L. Ed. 2d 562 (1968). See also, *Favia v. Indiana University of Pennsylvania*, 7 F.3d 332, 337 (3d Cir. 1993) (modification proper only when change of circumstances makes continuation of original order inequitable).

[26]*See, e.g., Hospital Resource Personnel, Inc. v. U.S.*, 860 F. Supp. 1554, 1556 (S.D. Ga. 1994) (granting temporary restraining order to preserve status quo until hearing on preliminary or permanent injunction).

[27]*See, e.g., CMM Cable Rep., Inc. v. Ocean Coast Properties, Inc.*, 48 F.3d 618, 620 (1st Cir. 1995) ("The purpose of a preliminary injunction is to preserve the status quo," pending full adjudication later).

first providing notice to opposing parties. Preliminary injunctions may be effective for the pendency of the case, whereas temporary restraining orders issued without notice are effective, with a single renewal, for a maximum of twenty-eight days.[28] Normally a longer extension would require the consent of the opposing party.[29] When courts grant temporary restraining orders, it is often with an eye to holding a prompt hearing on a motion for a preliminary injunction.[30] In one respect, temporary restraining orders are identical to preliminary injunctions, i.e., the substantive requirements for both (discussed above) are identical.[31]

Order Without Notice to Opposing Party

Although much of Rule 65(b) is devoted to the circumstances in which a party may obtain a temporary restraining order without first notifying opponents of the motion, it is important to note that such ex parte temporary restraining orders are disfavored.[32] Before granting one, the court will search the facts carefully to ascertain the need for ex parte relief, and will require that the party seeking relief satisfy *all* the requirements in Rule 65 for a temporary restraining order, as well as substantive prerequisites in case law governing such equitable remedies as restraining orders and injunctions.[33]

Oral Notice

The preferred method of notice for a temporary restraining order is formal service of written documents upon the opposing party. However, the court has substantial discretion to approve lesser notice.[34] Additionally, Rule 65(b) provides that if written notice is impractical, a party seeking relief under the Rule should attempt to notify the adversary orally.

---

[28]*See also Miller v. Mitchell*, 598 F.3d 139, __ (3d Cir. 2010) (order designated as temporary restraining order can be a preliminary injunction if it is entered for an indefinite period with notice to defendant and an appropriate hearing). *Cf., Bennett v. Medtronic, Inc.*, 285 F.3d 801, 804 (9th Cir. 2002) (if district court's order exceeds time limits of temporary restraining order, order should be reviewed under standards of preliminary injunction).

[29]Fed. R. Civ. P. 65(b)(2).

[30]*Granny Goose Foods, Inc. v. Brotherhood of Teamsters and Auto Truck Drivers Local No. 70 of Alameda County*, 415 U.S. 423, 94 S. Ct. 1113, 39 L. Ed. 2d 435 (1974).

[31]*See, e.g., Bieros v. Nicola*, 857 F. Supp. 445, 446 (E.D. Pa. 1994) ("The standards for a temporary re-

straining order are the same as those for a preliminary injunction.").

[32]*See, e.g., Reno Air Racing Ass'n., Inc. v. McCord*, 452 F.3d 1126, 1131 (9th Cir. 2006) ("[C]ircumstances justifying the issuance of an ex parte order are extremely limited."); *Redken Laboratories, Inc. v. Levin*, 843 F.2d 226, 228 (6th Cir. 1988) (Ex parte temporary restraining orders "often [exact] manifest injustices.").

[33]*See, e.g., Phillips v. Charles Schreiner Bank*, 894 F.2d 127, 131 (5th Cir. 1990) (noting "stringent restrictions" of Rule 65(b) on ex parte temporary restraining orders).

[34]*Cf., People of State of Ill. ex rel. Hartigan v. Peters*, 871 F.2d 1336, 1340 (7th Cir. 1989) ("[w]e leave the question of what constitutes sufficient notice primarily to the district court's discretion.").

Orders Issuing Without Prior Notice

Rule 65(b) permits issuance of a temporary restraining order without prior notice to the opposing party, but imposes two additional requirements before such an order is granted: proof of irreparable injury and a statement of the efforts made to notify the opposing party.

Irreparable Injury

Rule 65(b)(1) requires a party to show by affidavit or verified complaint the irreparable injury that will occur if the order is not granted until the opposing parties are notified and have an opportunity to appear.[35]

(1) *Affidavit or Complaint:* The quality and detail required in an affidavit or complaint vary substantially, but the explanation should be sufficient for the court to understand the risk of irreparable injury, along with other relevant facts that will help the court understand the need for prompt action.[36]

(2) *Irreparable Injury:* The concept of what constitutes irreparable injury is so flexible as to be elusive. However, it seems clear that a party can demonstrate that the loss likely to occur if an ex parte temporary restraining order is not issued is an irreparable loss when the damages will be of a nature as are difficult to calculate.[37] Thus, substantial risk of lost future profits or business reputation might constitute irreparable injury. Alternatively, if the loss will be of a nature that the courts normally consider beyond compensation by money, however calculated, the injury is likely to be irreparable. Thus, risk of damage to unique property, such as land, might also meet the standard of irreparable injury.

Efforts to Notify Adversary

Rule 65(b)(2) requires that an applicant for a temporary restraining order explain, in writing, whatever efforts have been made to notify the opposing party, and the reasons why no further efforts at notification before issuance of the order are justified. Although the Rule does not literally require that an applicant make efforts to notify an adversary, the court may treat failure to make efforts that would have been reasonable as a ground for denying the motion for a temporary restraining order.[38]

Date and Time of Issuance

If a party is able to obtain a temporary restraining order

---

[35]*See, e.g., American Can Co. v. Mansukhani*, 742 F.2d 314, 321–24 (7th Cir. 1984) (failure to comply with Rule 65(b)(1) is abuse of discretion).

[36]*See, e.g., Id.*

[37]*Cf., In re Arthur Treacher's Franchisee Litigation*, 689 F.2d 1137, 1145 (3d Cir. 1982) ("we have never upheld an injunction where the claimed injury constituted a loss of money, a loss capable of recoupment in a proper action at law.").

[38]*See, e.g., American Can Co. v. Mansukhani*, 742 F.2d 314, 321–24 (7th Cir. 1984) (failure to make reasonable efforts make grant of order an abuse of discretion).

without first providing notice to opposing parties, Rule 65(b) requires that the order be indorsed with the date and time it was issued. This indorsement is significant because it begins the running of the fourteen-day period, discussed below, for which the order is effective.

Filing With Clerk

Once an order is issued without prior notice, it must be filed "forthwith" with the clerk of court and entered as part of the record of the case.[39]

Explanation of Injury and Lack of Notice

The court's temporary restraining order will explain the apprehended irreparable injury in detail sufficient to inform an appellate court,[40] and will also explain the reasons why the court found it necessary to issue the order without first hearing from opposing parties.

Duration of Temporary Restraining Order

If an order issues under Rule 65(b) without prior notice to opposing parties, the order will expire no later than fourteen days after issuance.[41] The court may provide for expiration of the order in a lesser period. Additionally, even temporary restraining orders issued with notice cannot continue indefinitely unless they meet the standards required for preliminary injunctions.[42]

Consent to Extension

If the opposing party consents to an extension of the temporary restraining order, the order may be extended for any length of time to which the parties agree.[43]

---

[39]*See, e.g., Garcia v. Yonkers School District*, 561 F.3d 97, 106 (2d Cir. 2009) (noting requirements of filing with clerk and entry in record).

[40]*See, e.g., Ben David v. Travisono*, 495 F.2d 562, 564–65 (1st Cir. 1974) ("Expansive" injunction against "brutalization" of prisoners must be based on "express findings that the prohibited conduct is likely").

[41]*Cf., CVI/Beta Ventures, Inc. v. Custom Optical Frames, Inc.*, 859 F. Supp. 945, 948 (D. Md. 1994) (but if order issues only after notice to opponent, order may extend for longer period; order is then analogous to preliminary injunction).

[42]*See, e.g., In re Criminal Contempt Proceedings Against Gerald Crawford, Michael Warren*, 329 F.3d 131, 137 (2d Cir. 2003) (where tempo-

rary restraining order was unambiguous as to its continuing nature and was originally granted only upon notice and hearing, it properly continued beyond time limit as a preliminary injunction). *But cf., Chicago United Industries, Ltd. v. City of Chicago*, 445 F.3d 940, 946 (7th Cir. 2006) (notwithstanding the literal language of Rule 65(b), all temporary restraining orders are subject to the time limit, not merely "without notice" temporary restraining orders; but "without notice" restraining orders are subject to additional restrictions; citing other cases).

[43]*See, e.g., In re Arthur Treacher's Franchise Litigation*, 689 F.2d 1150 (3d Cir.1982); *Cf., Hudson v. Barr*, 3 F.3d 970, 973 (6th Cir. 1993) (noting that temporary restraining order can be extended beyond time limit only

Judicial Extension of Time

Temporary restraining orders issued without prior notice may be extended by judicial order for an additional period not greater than the length of time in the original order, and in no event for more than fourteen additional days.[44]

Obtaining an Extension

A party seeking judicial extension of an order must move for the extension within the time limitation of the original order, and must show good cause for the extension. Good cause might be a continuation of the circumstances of irreparable injury that justified the original order, or such new circumstances as the temporary restraining order produced. For example, if the court is considering issuance of a preliminary injunction, extension of a temporary restraining order might be appropriate to allow the court more time to decide the preliminary injunction question.[45]

Recording of Reasons for Extension

If a temporary restraining order is extended, Rule 65(b) provides that the court must record its reasons for granting the extension.[46]

Timing of Hearing on Preliminary Injunction

If the court grants a temporary restraining order without prior notice to opposing parties, Rule 65(b) directs that a hearing on a motion for a preliminary injunction will be held "at the earliest possible time." The preliminary injunction hearing must move to the head of the court's docket, second only to preliminary injunction matters that are already pending.

Failure to Seek a Preliminary Injunction

If a party obtained a temporary restraining order without prior notice, and then fails to pursue an application for a preliminary injunction at the scheduled hearing, the court will terminate the temporary restraining order.

Motion to Modify or Dissolve Order

Like preliminary injunctions, temporary restraining orders may be modified or dissolved on motion of a party. Grounds for dissolution include a demonstration that the purpose of the order has been fulfilled. An order may also be modified or dis-

---

with consent of parties).

[44]*See, e.g., Belbacha v. Bush*, 520 F.3d 452, 455 (D.C. Cir. 2008) (where case will require more time before decision can be reached, "preserving the status quo required a preliminary injunction rather than a temporary restraining order.").

[45]*See, e.g., Joseph v. Hell Oil Virgin Islands Corp.*, ___ F.3d ___ (3d Cir. 2011) (good cause means a "legally

sufficient reason").

[46]*But cf., Reliance Ins. Co. v. Mast Const. Co.*, 159 F.3d 1311, 1316 (10th Cir. 1998) (extension of expiration date of order does not require that operative language of order must be restated; it is sufficient that extension incorporated by reference such language as was previously laid out when order was originally granted).

solved if the court is persuaded that the circumstances requiring the order have changed.

Notice

A party subject to a temporary restraining order issued without prior notice may move to dissolve or modify the order. Rule 65(b) requires that the moving party provide other parties at least two days notice of a hearing on the motion to dissolve, unless the court permits less notice.

Timing of Hearing

Rule 65(b) establishes no time limit within which the court must hear a motion to dissolve or modify a temporary restraining order, but the Rule clearly encourages a prompt hearing, "as expeditiously as the ends of justice require."

Appeal

Generally, a court's decision to grant, deny, modify, continue, or dissolve a temporary restraining order is not appealable.[47]

RULE 65(c)—SECURITY

CORE CONCEPT

Rule 65(c) requires that, as a condition of granting a preliminary injunction or temporary restraining order, the court must impose a bond or other security.[48] The party bound by the injunction or order is entitled to recover damages from the posted security if the injunction or order is subsequently found to have been erroneously granted. The court retains substantial discretion to determine the amount of the security.

APPLICATIONS

Mandatory Security

Although the language of Rule 65(c) seems to direct a court to impose a bond, many cases treat the decision to impose a bond as a matter of discretion for the court.[49]

---

[47]*See, e.g., In re Lorillard Tobacco Co.*, 370 F.3d 982, 986 (9th Cir. 2004) (temporary restraining orders "are generally not appealable as of right"); *Robinson v. Lehman*, 771 F.2d 772, 782 (3d Cir. 1985) (temporary restraining order not appealable unless denial of order effectively decides the case).

[48]*Cf., Mead Johnson & Co. v. Abbott Laboratories*, 209 F.3d 1032, 1033 (7th Cir. 2000) (per curiam) (posting bond may be required to obtain preliminary injunction, but "posting a bond is [still] voluntary"; if party

chooses to do so, party can decline to pay bond and drop the suit).

[49]*Snider v. Temple University*, 502 U.S. 1032, 112 S. Ct. 873, 116 L. Ed. 2d 778 (1992) (sometimes a strict reading of bond requirement may be "inappropriate"). *See, e.g., Roda Drilling Co. v. Siegal*, 552 F.3d 1203, 1215 (10th Cir. 2009) (noting wide latitude of trial courts in determining whether to require bond); *Moltan Co. v. Eagle-Picher Industries, Inc.*, 55 F.3d 1171, 1176 (6th Cir. 1995) ("While we recognize that the language of Rule 65(c)

Timing

If a bond is required, it must be posted when the court grants a preliminary injunction or temporary restraining order.[50] There is no requirement to post security when a party initially seeks such relief.

Amount of Security

The maximum amount of security that may be required is the court's estimate of the potential loss to a party proximately caused by erroneous issuance of the injunction or order.[51] The court has discretion to require posting of lesser amounts than the bound party's estimated potential loss.[52] In practice, that means in some cases the court may limit security to a nominal amount, if such a small sum is in the interest of justice.[53]

---

appears to be mandatory, and that many circuits have so interpreted it, the rule in our circuit has long been that the district court possesses discretion over whether to require the posting of security"). *But see Nichols v. Alcatel USA, Inc.*, 532 F.3d 364 (5th Cir. 2008) (failure to require bond is reversible error); *Sprint Communications Co. L.P. v. CAT Communications Intern., Inc.*, 335 F.3d 235 (3d Cir. 2003) (suggesting that exceptions to bond requirement are rare). *See also Ty, Inc. v. Publications Intern. Ltd.*, 292 F.3d 512, 516 (7th Cir. 2002) (bond requirement of Rule 65(c) applies only to temporary restraining order or preliminary injunction, . . . "not for a permanent injunction").

[50]*But Compare Kos Pharmaceuticals, Inc. v. Andrx Corp.*, 369 F.3d 700, 728 (3d Cir. 2004) (court should determine amount of bond by evaluation of potential financial damages; however, decision to grant injunction should be separate from determination of bond amount), *with Corning Inc. v. PicVue Electronics, Ltd.*, 365 F.3d 156, 158 (2d Cir. 2004) ("While it might have been within the discretion of the district court to decide that, under the circumstances, no security was required, . . . the district court was required to make this determination before it entered the preliminary injunction.").

[51]*See, e.g., Hoechst Diafoil Co. v. Nan Ya Plastics Corp.*, 174 F.3d 411, 421 (4th Cir. 1999) (court must impose bond of an amount that considers magnitude of both defendant's potential loss and plaintiff's potential enrichment, as well as likelihood that harm will actually occur; citing authority for bond amount of zero if no evidence supported likelihood of harm). *But cf., Connecticut General Life Ins. Co. v. New Images of Beverly Hills*, 321 F.3d 878, 883 (9th Cir. 2003) (party affected by injunction has obligation to present evidence that bond in a particular amount is needed).

[52]*See, e.g., GoTo.com, Inc. v. Walt Disney Co.*, 202 F.3d 1199, 1211 (9th Cir. 2000) (refusing to raise bond from $25,000 to $20,000,000; noting discretion of district court and practical result); *International Ass'n of Machinists and Aerospace Workers v. Eastern Airlines, Inc.*, 925 F.2d 6 (1st Cir. 1991) (district court has "substantial discretion" to set terms of bond).

[53]*See, e.g., Davis v. Mineta*, 302 F.3d 1104 (10th Cir.2002) ("Ordinarily, where a party is seeking to vindicate the public interest served by [federal environmental law], a minimal bond amount should be considered."); *Cronin v. U.S. Dept. of Agriculture*, 919 F.2d 439, 445 (7th Cir. 1990) (citing circuits that require only nominal bonds in environmental cases). *But see, Mead Johnson & Co. v. Abbott Laboratories*, 201 F.3d 883, 888 (7th Cir. 2000) ("When setting the amount of security, district courts should err on the high side"; partly because bond acts to limit damages recoverable); *MacDonald v. Chicago Park Dist.*, 132 F.3d 355, 358 (7th Cir.

Requests for Increase in Bond

If a party believes the amount designated for the bond is insufficient to cover damages, the party may seek an increase in the bond during the time when the preliminary relief is in effect—or when the preliminary remedy has been lifted, but might still be re-imposed. However, once an injunction or restraining order has been reversed and will not be replaced, the amount of the bond cannot be increased.[54]

Standard for "Wrongfully Enjoined"

A party has been wrongfully enjoined "if it is ultimately found that the enjoined party had at all times the right to do the enjoined act."[55]

Damages Recoverable

An injured party's maximum recovery is generally limited to the amount of the bond.[56] However, a party may pursue an independent action for malicious prosecution in the unusual cases where the elements of that tort are satisfied.[57]

Actions Involving the United States

Rule 65(c) exempts the United States, its officers, and agencies from the obligation to post security.

Relation to Rule 65.1

Rule 65.1 governs the procedure by which a party may seek recovery against security posted pursuant to Rule 65(c).

1997) (per curiam) (finding error in imposition of $100 bond on plaintiff of modest means; loss to defendant is potentially much larger).

[54]*See, e.g., Mead Johnson & Co. v. Abbott Laboratories*, 209 F.3d 1032, 1033 (7th Cir. 2000) (per curiam) ("To permit changes in the bond after an injunction's reversal would be to overturn the rule [that recoverable damages are limited to amount of the bond] in fact, if not in name.").

[55]*Blumenthal v. Merrill Lynch, Pierce, Fenner & Smith, Inc.*, 910 F.2d 1049, 1054 (2d Cir. 1990). *See also Global Naps, Inc. v. Verizon New England, Inc.*, 489 F.3d 13, 22 (1st Cir. 2007) (adopting majority view; rejecting contrary view that injunction is wrongful only if grant of injunction was abuse of discretion); *Milan Exp., Inc. v. Averitt Exp., Inc.*, 254 F.3d 966 (11th Cir. 2001) (elements are: (1) wrongfully enjoined; and (2) proximately caused damage). *But see H & R Block, Inc. v. McCaslin*, 541 F.2d

1098, 1099–1100 (5th Cir. 1976) (per curiam) (where injunction issued on basis of good faith claims and district court did not abuse discretion, later finding that injunction wrongfully issue did not establish liability on bond for party that obtained injunction).

[56]*W.R. Grace and Co. v. Local Union 759, Intern. Union of United Rubber, Cork, Linoleum and Plastic Workers of America*, 461 U.S. 757, 770, 103 S. Ct. 2177, 2185, 76 L. Ed. 2d 298 (1983) ("A party injured by the issuance of an injunction later determined to be erroneous has no action for damages in the absence of a bond."). *See, e.g., Coyne-Delany Co., Inc. v. Capital Development Bd. of State of Ill.*, 717 F.2d 385, 393–94 (7th Cir. 1983) (bond is a ceiling on damages, except where plaintiff acted in bad faith).

[57]*Meyers v. Block*, 120 U.S. 206, 211, 7 S. Ct. 525, 528, 30 L. Ed. 642 (1887) (bond sets limit of recovery, in absence of suit for malicious prosecution).

"Non-Injunction" Bonds

As is explained immediately above, Rule 65(c) governs the circumstances in which a bond requirement may be imposed as a prerequisite to the imposition of a preliminary injunction or temporary restraining order. A "non-injunction" bond, by contrast, addresses a very different situation.

One of the underlying elements a court considers in determining if it should grant equitable relief is whether, in the absence of such relief, irreparable harm may be done to the unsuccessful moving party. Such harm may arise in a number of circumstances—including the possibility that while activities by one party may cause damage to the other that would normally give rise to monetary relief, such relief is unobtainable because the wrongdoer is penniless or, at least, unlikely to be able to pay the damages that might arise.[58] When such a possibility is before a district court, therefore, the court is entitled to consider whether harm that could arise from its refusal to grant injunctive relief is "irreparable," notwithstanding that a legal remedy is nominally available. That would, of course, weigh in favor of granting the injunction or temporary restraining order.

A "non-injunction" bond is one possible response to that situation by the party opposing a motion for injunctive relief. As a means of establishing that potential damage to the moving party is not irreparable because the opposing party is impoverished or unable to pay for damages, the opposing party may offer a "non-injunction" bond or other financial guarantee that would compensate the moving party if the motion for injunctive relief is denied and the moving party later suffers monetary loss. Thus, the "non-injunction" bond may play almost the opposite role of a bond issued pursuant to Rule 65(c).[59]

RULE 65(d)—CONTENTS AND SCOPE OF EVERY INJUNCTION AND RESTRAINING ORDER

CORE CONCEPT

Rule 65(d) governs the information that must be contained in injunctions and temporary restraining orders.[60] The Rule also describes categories of persons who are bound by an injunction or order.

---

[58]*See generally Lakeview Technology, Inc. v. Robinson*, 446 F.3d 655 (7th Cir.2006). *See also* Author's Commentary on Rule 65.

[59]*See, e.g., Lakeview Technology, Inc. v. Robinson*, 446 F.3d 655 (7th Cir.2006) ("A 'non-injunctive' bond . . . is the flip side of an injunction bond

under Rule 65(c).").

[60]*But cf., S.E.C. v. Homa*, 514 F.3d 661, 673–74 (7th Cir. 2008) ("Rule 65(d) . . . must be regarded as a codification rather than a limitation on a federal court's inherent power to protect its ability to render a binding judgment.").

Impact of 2007 "Restyling" Amendments

Most changes to Rule 65 were minor. However, in Rule 65(d), changes were made to clarify that a party or its agents could only be bound by an injunction after they had received actual notice. Further, clarity was added to the established rule that non-parties and non-agents could also be bound by an injunction if they acted in concert with parties or agents and received actual notice.

APPLICATIONS

Reasons for Issuance

The injunction or order must contain an explanation of the reasons for its issuance. However, failure of a district court to provide such an explanation does not, of itself, mandate reversal of the grant of the injunction.[61] A sufficient explanation will state specifically the facts found by the court as well as the conclusions of law upon which the court's decision is based.[62] An explanation of the reason for the court's action is usually direct, without excessive detail.

Relation to Rule 52

Alongside the Rule 65(d) requirement of reasons for issuance of an injunction or restraining order, Rule 52(a) provides that district courts must make findings of fact and conclusions of law when granting or denying a request for an interlocutory injunction.[63] This issue is discussed in greater detail under Rule 52.

Description of Acts Proscribed: Requirement of Writing

Rule 65(d) ordinarily requires that the injunction or order describe the prohibited acts with sufficient detail and clarity so that a layperson who was bound by the order could distinguish between acts that were permitted and acts the injunction or or-

---

[61]See, e.g., Test Masters Educational Services, Inc. v. Singh, 428 F.3d 559, 577 (5th Cir. 2005) (failure to make express findings does not require reversal or vacation of injunction, but it does force circuit court to examine record "to determine if sufficient evidence supports the issuance of injunctive relief").

[62]Schmidt v. Lessard, 414 U.S. 473, 476, 94 S. Ct. 713, 715, 38 L. Ed. 2d 661 (1974) ("The specificity provisions of Rule 65(d) are no mere technical requirements. The Rule was designed to prevent uncertainty and confusion on the part of those faced with injunction orders, and to avoid

the possible founding of a contempt citation on a decree too vague to be understood."). *But cf., E.E.O.C. v. Severn Trent Services, Inc.*, 358 F.3d 438, 442 (7th Cir. 2004) ("The explanation can be oral rather than written . . . and the absence of explanation can be forgiven when the justification for the injunction is clear from the record.").

[63]See, e.g., Prairie Band of Potawatomi Indians v. Pierce, 253 F.3d 1234 (10th Cir.2001) ("[W]ithout adequate findings of fact and conclusions of law, appellate review is in general not possible.").

der prohibited.[64] Thus, a court will ordinarily not use highly technical language unless there is no other way to describe the acts and the parties affected are likely to be uniquely capable of understanding such language.[65]

The scope of the order depends on the circumstances of the case, and can be extended to legitimate activity where such a reach is necessary to protect against unlawful conduct.[66]

Part of the requirement of describing with reasonable precision the prohibited conduct is a companion requirement that the court's order must be reduced to writing.[67]

Relation to Rule 23(b)(2)

Rule 23(b)(2) identifies some of the requirements for certification of a case as a class action potentially eligible for injunctive relief applicable to the class as a whole. There is authority that the specificity requirements of Rule 23(b)(2) mirror the specificity requirements that Rule 65(d) imposes for a grant of injunctive relief.[68]

---

[64]*See, e.g., Francisco Sanchez v. Esso Standard Oil Co.*, 572 F.3d 1 (1st Cir. 2009) (requirements of Rule 65(d)(1) applicable even to emergency situations); *Nuxoll ex rel. Nuxoll v. Indian Prairie School Dist. # 204*, 523 F.3d 668, 675 (7th Cir. 2008) ("A litigant has a feeble claim for a preliminary injunction when he can't articulate what he wants enjoined."); *Fortyune v. American Multi-Cinema, Inc.*, 364 F.3d 1075, 1087 (9th Cir. 2004) (district court has no duty to explain *how* to enforce injunction, only to explain what must or must not be done); *Prairie Band of Potawatomi Indians v. Pierce*, 253 F.3d 1234 (10th Cir.2001) (finding sufficient specificity in order barring state from enforcing state motor vehicle registration and titling laws against vehicles registered and titled under tribal motor vehicle code; use of words "applying" and "enforcing" in instant context are clear; "Rule 65(d) does not require the impossible."); *Power v. Summers*, 226 F.3d 815, 819 (7th Cir. 2000) (prohibition on "retaliation" against plaintiffs who are suing for alleged violation of free speech rights is not unduly vague); *Reliance Ins. Co. v. Mast Const. Co.*, 159 F.3d 1311, 1316 (10th Cir. 1998) (temporary restraining order blocking transfer of assets of bank account in which "defendants have or maintain an interest" is sufficiently

specific under Rule 65(d); "interest" is not ambiguous "when used to describe rights in a bank account"); *Cf., Dupuy v. Samuels*, 465 F.3d 757, 759 (7th Cir. 2006) (where injunction violates Rule 65(b), but its "core . . . is clear enough to be enforceable," injunction can be enforced as to prohibitions within injunction that are clear).

[65]*See, e.g., Reno Air Racing Association, Inc. v. McCord*, 452 F.3d 1126, 1134 (9th Cir. 2006) ("The benchmark for clarity and fair notice is not lawyers and judges [but] the lay person, who is the target of the injunction.").

[66]*McComb v. Jacksonville Paper Co.*, 336 U.S. 187, 192, 69 S.Ct. 497, 93 L.Ed. 599 (1949) (approving broad injunction if "a proclivity for unlawful conduct has been shown"). *See, e.g., Russian Media Group, LLC v. Cable America, Inc.*, 598 F.3d 302, 307 (7th Cir. 2010) ("The district court may even enjoin certain otherwise lawful conduct when the defendant's conduct has demonstrated that prohibiting only unlawful conduct would not effectively protect the plaintiff's rights against future encroachment.").

[67]*See, e.g., Lau v. Meddaugh*, 229 F.3d 121, 123 (2d Cir. 2000) (failure to memorialize order is reversible error).

[68]*See, e.g., Vallario v. Vandehey*, 554 F.3d 1259, 1268 (10th Cir. 2009)

Incorporation by Reference

The Rule specifically provides that prohibited acts *may not* be described only by reference to the complaint or other documents in the action.[69] However, some courts hold that Rule 65(d) is satisfied if a document specifically describing the prohibited acts is "physically appended" to the injunction order.[70]

Persons Bound

Rule 65(d) describes the categories of persons subject to an injunction or order: (1) parties;[71] (2) their officers, agents, servants, employees, and attorneys;[72] and (3) other persons "in active concert or participation with [parties]."[73]

Successors in Office: Relation to Rule 25

It appears settled that an injunction against a public official also binds successors in office.[74] This view is reinforced by Federal Rule of Civil Procedure 25(d), governing replacement

---

(explaining similarity of specificity requirements); *Shook v. Board of County Commissioners of El Paso County*, 543 F.3d 597, 604 (10th Cir. 2008) (cohesiveness required for Rule 23(b)(2) includes specificity requirement of Rule 65(d)).

[69]*See, e.g., Advent Electronics, Inc. v. Buckman*, 112 F.3d 267 (7th Cir.1997) (order must state reasons for issuance and specific terms "without reference to another document"); *Dunn v. New York State Dept. of Labor*, 47 F.3d 485 (2d Cir. 1995) (unacceptable to incorporate consent decree from related case; because consent decree can be modified, incorporation of such decree risks confusion in instant case).

[70]*LeBlanc-Sternberg v. Fletcher*, 143 F.3d 748 (2d Cir.1998). *See also Reno Air Racing Ass'n., Inc. v. McCord*, 452 F.3d 1126, 1132–33 (9th Cir. 2006) (permitting incorporation by reference in "limited scenarios" where document is physically attached to injunction).

[71]*See, e.g., U.S. v. Vitek Supply Corp.*, 151 F.3d 580 (7th Cir. 1998) (Rule 65(d) extends scope of injunction to bind alter egos); *Hernandez v. O'Malley*, 98 F.3d 293, 294 (7th Cir. 1996) (injunction against public official also applies to successor in office).

[72]*See, e.g., Whiting v. Marathon County Sheriff's Dept.*, 382 F.3d 700, 704 (7th Cir. 2004) (attorney bound by no-contact order issued against client); *Planned Parenthood of Columbia/*

Willamette, Inc. v. American Coalition of Life Activists, 290 F.3d 1058, 1088 n. 19 (9th Cir. 2002) (en banc) (individual employee/agent of party is appropriately within scope of injunction); *American Civil Liberties Union v. Johnson*, 194 F.3d 1149 (10th Cir.1999) (preliminary injunction against enforcement by governor and attorney general of criminal statute also binds state's district attorneys). *But cf., Medical Mutual Insurance Co. of Maine v. Indian Harbor Insurance Co.*, 583 F.3d 57, 63–64 (1st Cir. 2009) (agents of company can be enjoined, but they are not personally liable if they are not parties to lawsuit).

[73]*Regal Knitwear Co. v. N.L.R.B.*, 324 U.S. 9, 65 S. Ct. 478, 89 L. Ed. 661 (1945). *See, e.g., Marshak v. Treadwell*, 595 F.3d 478 (3d Cir. 2009) (Rule 65(d)(2)(C) extends the binding effect of an injunction beyond "parties and their privies" to include non-parties who knowingly abet violation of injunction). *Additive Controls & Measurement Systems, Inc. v. Flowdata, Inc.*, 96 F.3d 1390, 1395 (Fed. Cir. 1996) ("Having a relationship to an enjoined party of the sort set forth in Rule 65(d) exposes a non-party to contempt for assisting the party to violate the injunction, but does not justify granting injunctive relief against the non-party in its separate capacity.").

[74]*See, e.g., Salt River Agricultural Improvement & Power District v. Lee*,

in office while a lawsuit is pending. Rule 25(d) provides that in such circumstances the successor in office automatically replaced the predecessor, and the lawsuits proceeds to its conclusion.[75]

Notice to Persons Bound

No one is bound by an injunction or order until that person receives fair notice of the judicial act.[76] However, formal notice, in the form of service of documents, is not necessarily required to bind a party or those in privity with a party. A party or a person in a close relationship with a party may be bound if they simply have actual knowledge of the injunction or order.[77]

Personal Jurisdiction

Persons outside the jurisdiction of the court are not subject to its orders.[78] For a further discussion of jurisdiction over persons and things, see §§ 2.2 to 2.10.

Persons in Active Concert

This broad category of persons who may be subject to an injunction or order is necessarily fact-specific in application.[79] Generally, however, assignees who take an interest from a party with actual or constructive notice of an injunction or order prohibiting that party from performing a certain act relating to the interest may also be barred from performing the act.[80] Similarly, an injunction can run in favor of any unnamed member of a group, provided that the group is sufficiently identified.[81]

Another way of describing the binding effect of an injunction

---

672 F.3d 1176, 1180 (9th Cir. 2012) (injunction "remains in force against the officer's successors"; also citing other authority).

[75]Fed.R.Civ.P. 25(d).

[76]*See, e.g., Citizens for Smart Growth v. Secretary of DOT*, 669 F.3d 1203, 1210 n.1 (11th Cir. 2012) (noting requirement of notice).

[77]*Spallone v. U.S.*, 493 U.S. 265, 110 S. Ct. 625, 107 L. Ed. 2d 644 (1990).

[78]*See, e.g., R.M.S. Titanic, Inc. v. Haver*, 171 F.3d 943, 957–58 (4th Cir. 1999) ("[A] party cannot obtain injunctive relief against another without first obtaining in personam jurisdiction over that person or someone in legal privity with that person."); *Parker v. Ryan*, 960 F.2d 543, 546 (5th Cir. 1992) (nonparty acting independently of defendant is not subject to court's jurisdiction under Rule 65(d)). *But see, Waffenschmidt v. MacKay*, 763 F.2d

711, 714 (5th Cir. 1985) (nonparties residing outside territorial jurisdiction are nevertheless subject to court's jurisdiction if they intentionally and knowingly aid and abet violation of court's order).

[79]*See, e.g., Reliance Ins. Co. v. Mast Const. Co.*, 84 F.3d 372 (10th Cir. 1996) (nonparties bound include alter egos, and also those "with actual notice" who assist defendant or privy in violation of order); *U.S. v. International Broth. of Teamsters, Chauffeurs, Warehousemen and Helpers of America, AFL-CIO*, 964 F.2d 180, 184 (2d Cir. 1992) (whether a person is bound "always depends on the precise relationship of that person to the underlying litigation").

[80]*Regal Knitwear Co. v. N.L.R.B.*, 324 U.S. 9, 65 S. Ct. 478, 89 L. Ed. 661 (1945).

[81]*See, e.g., Zamecnik v. Indian Prairie School District No. 204*, 636 F.3d 874, 879 (7th Cir. 2011) (no re-

on non-parties is to identify two important categories of such non-parties. The first categories is comprised of non-parties who are "legally identified" with an enjoined party. Such persons are bound if they were identified in the injunction.[82] The second category is made up of persons who act in concert with named parties in violation of an injunction. However, non-parties in this group are not bound if they acted for their own purposes wholly independent of the named party.[83]

Permanent Injunctions

Unlike other provisions of Rule 65, Rule 65(d) does not refer only to preliminary injunctions or temporary restraining orders. Thus, Rule 65(d)'s provisions for a satisfactory explanation of the court's decision, an adequate description of prohibited acts, and the categories of persons bound by an injunction or order apply equally to permanent injunctions.[84]

Standing to Enforce Permanent Injunction

As is described above, there are many circumstances in which persons who are not parties may nonetheless be bound by an injunction. However, only those who are parties to a lawsuit have standing to seek enforcement of a final injunction.[85]

Failure to Comply with Injunction or Order

Persons within the categories of Rule 65(d) who have notice of an injunction or order and who do not comply are subject to the court's power of contempt.[86]

RULE 65(e)—OTHER LAWS NOT MODIFIED

CORE CONCEPT

Rule 65(e) provides that nothing in Rule 65 shall be construed to modify statutes relating to labor relations, interpleader actions, or actions subject to the jurisdiction of a three-judge court.

APPLICATION

Alterations to Courts' Injunctive Power

In each of the three areas of law addressed by Rule 65(e)—

---

quirement to name parties who may enforce injunction; students at school may enforce injunction against school).

[82]*See, e.g., Merial, Ltd. v. Cipia Ltd.*, 681 F.3d 1283, 1304-05 (Fed. Cir. 2012).

[83]*Id.*

[84]*See, e.g., Reich v. ABC/York-Estes Corp.*, 64 F.3d 316, 320 (7th Cir. 1995) (holding that failure to comply with Rule 65(d) meant no permanent injunction existed).

[85]*See, e.g., Planned Parenthood of Idaho, Inc. v. Wasden*, 376 F.3d 908 (9th Cir. 2004) ("Only a proper party to an action can enforce an injunction that results from a final judgment.").

[86]*Gunn v. University Committee to End War in Viet Nam*, 399 U.S. 383, 90 S. Ct. 2013, 26 L. Ed. 2d 684 (1970). *See also, Reliance Ins. Co. v. Mast Const. Co.*, 84 F.3d 372, 376 (10th Cir. 1996) ("Generally speaking, a person who violates an injunction or temporary restraining order during its pendency is subject to a compensatory civil contempt judgment.").

labor law, statutory interpleader, and three-judge courts—federal statutes alter the typical power of courts to issue injunctions and restraining orders. Rule 65(e) makes clear that when those statutes are applicable to a case and conflict with a provision of Rule 65, the statute governs.

RULE 65(f)—COPYRIGHT IMPOUNDMENT

CORE CONCEPT

Rule 65(f) provides that other provisions of Rule 65 apply to copyright impoundment proceedings.

Additional Research References

Wright & Miller, *Federal Practice and Procedure* §§ 2941 to 62
C.J.S., Injunctions §§ 4 to 54, §§ 60 to 110, §§ 111 to 158, §§ 160 to 206, §§ 213 to 263, §§ 264 to 314, §§ 320 to 341
West's Key Number Digest, Injunction ⊙132 to 188

RULE 65.1
PROCEEDINGS AGAINST A SURETY

Whenever these rules (including the Supplemental Rules for Admiralty or Maritime Claims and Asset Forfeiture Actions) require or allow a party to give security, and security is given through a bond or other undertaking with one or more sureties, each surety submits to the court's jurisdiction and irrevocably appoints the court clerk as its agent for receiving service of any papers that affect its liability on the bond or undertaking. The surety's liability may be enforced on motion without an independent action. The motion and any notice that the court orders may be served on the court clerk, who must promptly mail a copy of each to every surety whose address is known.

[Added effective July 1, 1966; amended effective August 1, 1987; April 12, 2006, effective December 1, 2006; April 30, 2007, effective December 1, 2007.]

AUTHORS' COMMENTARY ON RULE 65.1

PURPOSE AND SCOPE

Rule 65.1 provides a summary procedure by which parties can enforce their rights against a surety who has posted security.

APPLICATIONS

Scope

Rule 65.1 applies to proceedings to enforce a surety's liability on an appeal bond, a supersedeas bond, or an injunction bond posted pursuant to Rule 65(c). The Rule also applies when the Supplemental Rules for Certain Admiralty and Maritime Claims require the posting of bond. Finally, Rule 65.1 applies to the satisfaction of provisional remedies under Rule 64, when state law requires a bond.

Injunction Bonds: Rebuttable Presumption

The majority of courts hold that a party wrongfully enjoined under Rule 65 enjoys a rebuttable presumption in favor of recovering provable damages up to the limit of any bond required under Rule 65(c). Only in "rare cases" will the wrongfully enjoined party not be entitled to recovery on the bond.[1]

Alternative Procedures

Rule 65.1 is not the only means by which a party can seek to collect on a bond. Instead of employing the Rule, a party may bring an independent action against the surety in a state or federal court.[2]

Motion for Judgment

The appropriate method for seeking to collect from a surety under Rule 65.1 is a motion for judgment on the bond.[3]

Timing

Generally, a party may seek recovery under Rule 65.1 once the court has terminated or altered the relief that the bond secured. Thus, if a court determines that a preliminary injunction was improvidently granted, or was of excessive scope, the party previously enjoined may then move against the bond for damages.[4]

Consent to Personal Jurisdiction

Rule 65.1 provides that when a surety posts a bond or other security, the surety submits to the personal jurisdiction of the court for purposes of any litigation relating to liability on the bond.[5] Personal jurisdiction is discussed in more detail earlier in this text.

Service of Process

Upon posting bond, a surety also irrevocably appoints the clerk of court as the surety's agent to receive service of process in matters relating to liability on the bond.

Notice

A party seeking to collect on a bond should serve the motion on the clerk of court, along with such other notice as the court may require. Rule 65.1 requires that the clerk shall "forthwith"

---

[1]*Nintendo of America, Inc. v. Lewis Galoob Toys, Inc.*, 16 F.3d 1032, 1039 (9th Cir. 1994) (presumption in favor of recovery of proven damages). *But cf., Bass v. First Pacific Networks, Inc.*, 219 F.3d 1052, 1053 (9th Cir. 2000) (attorney's fees allegedly incurred in collecting on bond under Rule 65.1 cannot be recovered under that Rule; contrary state law is irrelevant to bond enforcement under Rule 65.1).

[2]*See, e.g., State of Ala. ex rel. Siegelman v. U.S. E.P.A.*, 925 F.2d 385, 388 (11th Cir. 1991) (permitting independent action when bond is unavailable).

[3]*See, e.g., Global Naps, Inc. v. Verizon New England, Inc.*, 489 F.3d 13, 20 (1st Cir. 2007) (enforcement on motion is appropriate; no need to file independent action); *Lyrick Studios, Inc. v. Big Idea Productions, Inc.*, 420 F.3d 388 (5th Cir. 2005) (noting that motion is appropriate, obviating need for separate actions).

[4]*See, e.g., American Bible Soc. v. Blount*, 446 F.2d 588, 595 n. 12 (3d Cir. 1971) (liability on bond arises after defendant prevails on merits).

[5]*See, e.g., Instant Air Freight Co. v. C.F. Air Freight, Inc.*, 882 F.2d 797, 804 (3d Cir. 1989) (noting that Rule 65.1 requires that surety submit to jurisdiction of court).

mail copies of the documents to all affected sureties whose addresses are known.

Injunction Staying Enforcement

Although Rule 65.1 is intended to provide an expeditious means of recovering damages from a bond, there are situations in which Rule 65.1 proceedings will be stayed. In particular, if a court enjoins proceedings against the bond, the injunction must be obeyed until it is modified or dissolved.[6]

Collecting From Principals

Although Rule 65.1 addresses the means by which a party may seek damages on a surety's bond or other undertaking, courts also permit the use of Rule 65.1 for similar relief against a surety's principal.[7]

Subject Matter Jurisdiction

If a party seeks in the original action to collect against a bond under Rule 65.1, the court will have supplemental jurisdiction over the claim.[8] If a party seeks to enforce a bond in an independent action, the court has subject matter jurisdiction under 28 U.S.C.A. § 1352, governing independent actions on bonds posted pursuant to federal law.[9] Subject matter jurisdiction is discussed further at §§ 2.10 to 2.13.

Additional Research References

Wright & Miller, *Federal Practice and Procedure* §§ 2971 to 74
C.J.S., Federal Civil Procedure §§ 1273 to 1295
West's Key Number Digest, Federal Civil Procedure ⟐2732 to 2733

---

[6]*Celotex Corp. v. Edwards*, 514 U.S. 300, 115 S. Ct. 1493, 131 L. Ed. 2d 403 (1995) (notwithstanding Rule 65.1, a bankruptcy court's injunction may stay collection from a debtor's surety until injunction is modified or dissolved).

[7]*See, e.g., Willis v. Celotex Corp.*, 970 F.2d 1292 (4th Cir.1992) (Rule 65.1 permits recovery against both surety and principal). *See also Lyrick Studios, Inc. v. Big Idea Productions, Inc.*, 420 F.3d 388, 396–97 (5th Cir. 2005) (party had enforced surety's liability on motion without filing independent action; held, when party later lost on appeal, surety also had no need to file separate action and could instead recover

on motion).

[8]*See, e.g., Buddy Systems, Inc. v. Exer-Genie, Inc.*, 545 F.2d 1164, 1166 (9th Cir. 1976) (jurisdiction over collection against bond exists until bond is discharged).

[9]*See, e.g., Milan Exp., Inc. v. Averitt Exp., Inc.*, 208 F.3d 975, 980 (11th Cir. 2000) (28 U.S.C. § 1352 provides jurisdiction over claims against injunction bond issued under Rule 65; further, claim for damages in excess of bond, based on allegation of bad faith, could be heard under supplemental jurisdiction of court, 28 U.S.C. § 1367).

RULE 66
RECEIVERS

These rules govern an action in which the appointment of a receiver is sought or a receiver sues or is sued. But the practice in administering an estate by a receiver or a similar court-appointed officer must accord with the historical practice in federal courts or with a local rule. An action in which a receiver has been appointed may be dismissed only by court order.

[Amended effective March 19, 1948; October 20, 1949; April 30, 2007, effective December 1, 2007.]

AUTHORS' COMMENTARY ON RULE 66

PURPOSE AND SCOPE

Rule 66 provides that, when appointed by district courts, federal equity receivers shall administer estates in accordance with prior federal practice and local court rules. Once an equity receiver is appointed in a particular lawsuit, the action may not thereafter be dismissed without the court's prior approval.

APPLICATIONS

Role of Federal Equity Receiver

Receivership is an extraordinary equitable remedy, justified only in extreme circumstances.[1] It is not a substantive entitlement, but an ancillary remedy used to facilitate the primary relief sought in a lawsuit.[2] Federal courts appoint equity receivers to assume custody, control, and management of property that either is presently involved or is likely to become involved in litigation.[3] The receiver is charged to preserve the property, and any rents or profits the property earns, until a final dispo-

---

[1]See *United States v. Bradley,* 644 F.3d 1213, 1310 (11th Cir. 2011); *Canada Life Assur. Co. v. LaPeter,* 563 F.3d 837, 844 (9th Cir. 2009).

[2]See *U.S. Bank Nat'l Ass'n v. Nesbitt Bellevue Prop. LLC,* __ F. Supp. 2d __, __, 2012 WL 1965341, at *6–*8 (S.D.N.Y. 2012). *See also Roberts*

v. American Bank & Trust Co., Inc., 835 F.Supp.2d 183, 205 (E.D.La. 2011) (receivership request denied until plaintiff first establishes valid claim for relief).

[3]See *Gilchrist v. General Elec. Capital Corp.,* 262 F.3d 295, 302 (4th Cir. 2001) (noting that federal courts

sition by the court.[4] Although typically appointed only to care for property, a federal equity receiver may be appointed where other, extraordinary circumstances compel intimate judicial supervision.[5]

- *Officer of the Court:* An equity receiver is not an agent of any of the parties to the litigation. Instead, the receiver is deemed to be an officer of the court.[6]

- *Auxiliary Remedy Only:* The appointment of a receiver is not permitted as an end in itself; receivers are only appointed as an auxiliary remedy necessary to some other, primary requested relief.[7]

Administration of Estates By Receivers

Traditional federal practice and, where promulgated, local court rules guide a federal equity receiver in administering the receivership property.[8]

- *State Law:* The substantive law of the State in which the receivership property is located dictates the manner in which the receiver must manage and operate the receivership property.[9]

Federal Rules Control Litigations Involving Receivers

The Rules govern all actions in which a party seeks the appointment of a federal equity receiver, as well as all actions brought by or against the receiver once appointed.[10]

Appointment of Receivers

Rule 66 does not create a substantive right to the appoint-

---

have equity power to appoint receivers and administer receiverships).

[4]*See S.E.C. v. Vescor Capital Corp.*, 599 F.3d 1189, 1194 (10th Cir. 2010); *Liberte Capital Group, LLC v. Capwill*, 462 F.3d 543, 551 (6th Cir. 2006).

[5]*See Morgan v. McDonough*, 540 F.2d 527 (1st Cir. 1976) (affirming appointment of federal receiver for public high school, to implement desegregation orders). *See also De Boer Structures (U.S.A.), Inc. v. Shaffer Tent and Awning Co.*, 187 F. Supp. 2d 910, 925 (S.D. Ohio 2001) (noting that appointment of receiver is extraordinary remedy justified only in extreme situations).

[6]*See Liberte Capital Group, LLC v. Capwill*, 462 F.3d 543, 551 (6th Cir. 2006); *Gaskill v. Gordon*, 27 F.3d 248, 251 (7th Cir.1994).

[7]*See Gordon v. Washington*, 295 U.S. 30, 37 n. 4, 55 S. Ct. 584, 588 n. 4, 79 L. Ed. 1282 (1935) ("A receiver-

ship is only a means to reach some legitimate end sought through the exercise of the power of a court of equity. It is not an end in itself"); *See also Kelleam v. Maryland Cas. Co. of Baltimore*, 312 U.S. 377, 381, 61 S.Ct. 595, 85 L.Ed. 899 (1941) (same).

[8]*See S.E.C. v. Vescor Capital Corp.*, 599 F.3d 1189, 1193–94 (10th Cir. 2010); *Liberte Capital Group, LLC v. Capwill*, 462 F.3d 543, 551 (6th Cir. 2006).

[9]*See* 28 U.S.C.A. § 959(b). *See also S.E.C. v. Vescor Capital Corp.*, 599 F.3d 1189, 1193–94 (10th Cir. 2010); *Gilchrist v. General Elec. Capital Corp.*, 262 F.3d 295, 302 (4th Cir. 2001).

[10]*See Canada Life Assur. Co. v. LaPeter*, 563 F.3d 837, 842–43 (9th Cir. 2009); *Phelan v. Middle States Oil Corp.*, 210 F.2d 360 (2d Cir. 1954); *Terry v. June*, 359 F. Supp. 510, 518–19 (W.D. Va. 2005).

ment of a receiver; a statute or general principle of equity must first justify the appointment. Federal law controls whether an equity receiver should be appointed, even in a diversity case.[11] But the Rule provides little guidance other than requiring that a receiver's appointment and work "accord with the historical practice in federal courts or with a local rule."[12] Absent explicit consent from the defendant, the plaintiff ordinarily bears the burden of making an adequate showing that a receiver should be appointed.[13]

- *Who May Seek An Appointment:* The appointment of a receiver may be requested by any person having a legally recognized right to the property—a mere interest or claim to the property will not be sufficient to justify the appointment of a receiver.[14] Receivers are appointed frequently at the request of secured creditors, mortgagees, judgment creditors, and plaintiffs in shareholder derivative actions.[15]

- *Prerequisites for Appointment:* The appointment of a receiver is an extraordinary remedy, available only upon a clear showing that no remedy at law is available or adequate,[16] and that a receivership is essential to protect the property from some threatened loss or injury pending a final disposition by the court.[17] Although no precise formula exists for assessing whether a receiver ought to be appointed,[18] the courts consider various factors, including:

  - the existence of a valid claim by the party seek-

---

[11]*See Canada Life Assur. Co. v. LaPeter*, 563 F.3d 837, 842–43 (9th Cir. 2009); *National Partnership Inv. Corp. v. National Housing Development Corp.*, 153 F.3d 1289, 1291–92 (11th Cir. 1998); *Aviation Supply Corp. v. R.S.B.I. Aerospace, Inc.*, 999 F.2d 314, 317 (8th Cir. 1993); *But see Office Depot Inc. v. Zuccarini*, 596 F.3d 696, 701 (9th Cir. 2010) (proper location for appointment of receiver in aid of execution of a judgment is assessed by looking to state law).

[12]*See Rule 66. See also U.S. Bank Nat'l Ass'n v. Nesbitt Bellevue Prop. LLC*, __ F. Supp. 2d __, __, 2012 WL 1965341, at *6 (S.D.N.Y. 2012); *New York Cmty. Bank v. Sherman Ave. Assocs., LLC*, 786 F.Supp.2d 171, 175 (D.D.C. 2011).

[13]*See U.S. Bank Nat'l Ass'n v. Nesbitt Bellevue Prop. LLC*, __ F. Supp. 2d __, __, 2012 WL 1965341, at *2 (S.D.N.Y. 2012).

[14]*See Santibanez v. Wier McMahon & Co.*, 105 F.3d 234, 241 (5th Cir. 1997) (appointments sought by judgment creditors); *Piambino v. Bailey*, 757 F.2d 1112 (11th Cir. 1985); *Mintzer v. Arthur L. Wright & Co.*, 263 F.2d 823 (3d Cir.1959).

[15]*See Santibanez v. Wier McMahon & Co.*, 105 F.3d 234, 241 (5th Cir. 1997) (appointments sought by judgment creditors).

[16]*See United States v. Bradley*, 644 F.3d 1213, 1310 (11th Cir. 2011).

[17]*See Gordon v. Washington*, 295 U.S. 30, 55 S. Ct. 584, 79 L. Ed. 1282 (1935); *Aviation Supply Corp. v. R.S.B.I. Aerospace, Inc.*, 999 F.2d 314, 317 (8th Cir. 1993); *Sumpter v. U.S.*, 314 F. Supp. 2d 684, 690 (E.D. Mich. 2004).

[18]*See Canada Life Assur. Co. v. LaPeter*, 563 F.3d 837, 844 (9th Cir. 2009); *First Bank Bus. Capital, Inc. v. Agriprocessors, Inc.*, 602 F.Supp.2d 1076, 1094 (N.D.Iowa 2009).

ing the appointment;

- the imminent nature of any danger to the property, to its concealment or removal, or to its value;
- the adequacy of other legal remedies;
- the lack of a less drastic equitable remedy;
- the plaintiff's probable success in the lawsuit and the risk of irreparable injury to the property;
- whether the defendant has engaged, or may engage, in any fraudulent actions with respect to the property;
- the likelihood that appointing the receiver will do more good than harm; *and*
- whether the potential harm to the plaintiff outweighs the injury to others.[19]

Each factor need not be satisfied, so long as the court determines that its review favors the receiver's appointment.[20] Courts have held that the existence of an express contractual right to the appointment of a receiver, along with adequate *prima facie* evidence of default, can suffice to justify appointment.[21]

Consent to Appointment

The court may appoint a receiver where the defendant both admits liability for the claim asserted in the litigation and consents to the appointment of a receiver—provided that there has been no improper attempt by the parties to collusively manufacture federal jurisdiction.[22]

Discretion of the District Court

Whether to appoint a receiver lies within the district judge's sound discretion.[23]

Who May Be Appointed

The court may appoint as the receiver any person deemed capable of serving in that capacity. Ordinarily, this requires the appointment of someone who is indifferent between the

---

[19]*See Canada Life Assur. Co. v. LaPeter*, 563 F.3d 837, 844 (9th Cir. 2009); *Santibanez v. Wier McMahon & Co.*, 105 F.3d 234, 241–42 (5th Cir. 1997); *Aviation Supply Corp. v. R.S.B.I. Aerospace, Inc.*, 999 F.2d 314, 317 (8th Cir. 1993); *Consolidated Rail Corp. v. Fore River Ry. Co.*, 861 F.2d 322, 326–27 (1st Cir.1988).

[20]*See Fleet Business Credit, L.L.C. v. Wings Restaurants, Inc.*, 291 B.R. 550, 556 (N.D. Okla. 2003) (appointing receiver where "several of the factors weigh in favor of the propriety of appointing a receiver").

[21]*See Pioneer Capital Corp. v. Environamics Corp.*, 2003 WL 345349, at *9 (D. Me. 2003), *aff'd*, 2003 WL 1923765 (D. Me. 2003).

[22]*See In re Reisenberg*, 208 U.S. 90, 28 S. Ct. 219, 52 L. Ed. 403 (1908).

[23]*See S.E.C. v. Vescor Capital Corp.*, 599 F.3d 1189, 1194 (10th Cir. 2010); *Santibanez v. Wier McMahon & Co.*, 105 F.3d 234, 241 (5th Cir. 1997); *Roberts v. American Bank & Trust Co., Inc.*, 835 F.Supp.2d 183, 205 (E.D.La. 2011).

parties.[24] Federal law prevents the judge from appointing as a receiver any person related to the judge by consanguinity within the fourth degree,[25] a clerk or deputy of the court (absent special circumstances),[26] or a federal employee or person employed by the appointing judge.[27]

Place of Appointment

Because the appointment of a receiver is a type of *in rem* proceeding, the appointing court must enjoy a strong relationship to the contemplated receivership: a substantial portion of the defendant's business must be conducted in the host district, or a substantial portion of the anticipated receivership property must be located within the host district.

- *Conflicting Claims to Jurisdiction:* If two courts of concurrent and coordinate jurisdiction (*e.g.,* two federal courts) attempt to assert a claim to the same property, the court where the legal papers are first filed assumes exclusive jurisdiction, irrespective of whether its receiver is the first to obtain physical possession of the property.

  If the two courts are not of the same or concurrent jurisdiction (*e.g.,* one State and one federal court), and where the subject matter in the one litigation is not the same as in the other litigation, or where no constructive possession of the property is obtained through the filing, the court whose receiver first obtains actual possession of the property assumes exclusive jurisdiction.[28]

Notice of Appointment

Generally, the court gives notice to all parties before appointing an equity receiver. But where notice is impractical or self-defeating, or where the appointment must be made immediately, the court enjoys the power to appoint a receiver *ex parte.*[29]

Effect of Appointment

Once a receiver is appointed and gives the bond required by the court, the court and the receiver obtain exclusive jurisdiction of all of the defendant's property, no matter where it is kept.[30] To obtain such jurisdiction over property outside the appointing district, the receiver must first file a copy of the com-

---

[24]*See Liberte Capital Group, LLC v. Capwill*, 462 F.3d 543, 551 n.2 (6th Cir. 2006).

[25]28 U.S.C.A. § 458; 18 U.S.C.A. § 1910.

[26]28 U.S.C.A. § 957.

[27]28 U.S.C.A. § 958.

[28]*See Harkin v. Brundage*, 276 U.S. 36, 48 S. Ct. 268, 72 L. Ed. 457 (1928).

[29]*See Arkansas Louisiana Gas Co. v. Kroeger*, 303 F.2d 129 (5th Cir. 1962).

[30]*See Liberte Capital Group, LLC v. Capwill*, 462 F.3d 543, 551 (6th Cir. 2006).

plaint and appointment order in that foreign district.[31]

Actions by Receivers

A federal equity receiver is authorized to commence and prosecute any action necessary to accomplish the objectives of the receivership.[32] The receiver may be directed to bring suit on specific instructions from the court, or the receiver may independently institute lawsuits pursuant to the receiver's general duties of receiving, controlling, and managing the receivership property.

- *May Sue In Any Jurisdiction:* The receiver may bring suit in any federal district, including those districts outside the court in which the receiver was formally appointed.[33]
- *Equitable Defenses*: Receivers are deemed to have stepped into the shoes of the persons or entities for whom they act. Thus, absent statutory provisions dictating otherwise, defenses that could be asserted against the original plaintiff are equally available against the plaintiff's equity receiver. However, equitable defenses (such as unclean hands) that could be asserted against the original plaintiff might not be effective against the receiver.[34]

Actions Against Receivers

A person may sue an equity receiver, without leave of court, for any of the receiver's actions taken after the receiver was appointed and during the receiver's management and operation of the receivership property.[35]

- *Leave of Court Needed:* Leave of court is required before the receiver may be sued for claims that arise from the property owner's actions or for claims that do not challenge the receiver's actions since appointment.[36] To protect the assets (and to avoid their diminution by the costs of defending lawsuits), the receivership court may issue a blanket injunction staying all litigation against

---

[31]28 U.S.C.A. § 754.

[32]*See Gilchrist v. General Elec. Capital Corp.*, 262 F.3d 295, 302 (4th Cir. 2001) (noting that, when appointed, federal equity receivers may sue and be sued as provided by federal law).

[33]28 U.S.C.A. § 754.

[34]*See F.D.I.C. v. O'Melveny & Myers*, 61 F.3d 17, 19 (9th Cir. 1995) (commenting that while party may be denied right or defense due to its misdeeds, the same punishment should not be imposed upon innocent

receiver who assumes control pursuant to court order or by operation of law).

[35]28 U.S.C.A. § 959(a). *See Gilchrist v. General Elec. Capital Corp.*, 262 F.3d 295, 301 (4th Cir. 2001) (noting that, when appointed, federal equity receivers may sue and be sued as provided by federal law).

[36]*See Barton v. Barbour*, 104 U.S. 126, 128, 26 L.Ed. 672 (1881); *In re VistaCare Group, LLC*, 678 F.3d 218, 225 (3d Cir. 2012); *McDaniel v. Blust*, 668 F.3d 153, 156 (4th Cir. 2012).

the receiver and entities under the receiver's control.[37] Although claimants are entitled to have their claims heard, the court enjoys broad control over the time and manner of those proceedings.[38] Intentionally interfering with a receivership in violation of such an injunction is punishable as contempt.[39]

- *Subject to Court's General Equity Power:* Suits against receivers remain subject to the court's general equity powers, which the court may exercise to achieve the ends of justice.

Jurisdiction in Actions Involving Receivers

Receivers may only sue or be sued when the district court would enjoy subject matter jurisdiction over the dispute.

- *Diversity Cases:* In diversity jurisdiction cases, the citizenship of the appointed receiver is examined to determine whether complete diversity exists.[40]
- *Federal Question Cases:* The district court's act of appointing a federal receiver probably will suffice to vest that district court with subject matter jurisdiction over actions brought by or against the receiver in that district.[41] Thus, when instituted in the appointing district, suits by the receiver intended to accomplish the objectives of the receivership are deemed ancillary to the appointing court's subject matter jurisdiction.[42] Likewise, suits may be maintained against the receiver in the receiver's appointing district even though no independent basis for subject matter jurisdiction is present.[43]
- *Outside Appointing District:* Suits by or against receivers instituted outside the appointing district will generally require an independent basis for federal subject matter jurisdiction.[44]

Dismissal of Actions Involving Receivers

After the court appoints a receiver in a litigation, the parties may not thereafter dismiss the litigation without first

---

[37]*See Liberte Capital Group, LLC v. Capwill*, 462 F.3d 543, 551–52 (6th Cir. 2006).

[38]*See Liberte Capital Group, LLC v. Capwill*, 462 F.3d 543, 552 (6th Cir. 2006).

[39]*See Liberte Capital Group, LLC v. Capwill*, 462 F.3d 543, 552 (6th Cir. 2006).

[40]*See Barber v. Powell*, 135 F.2d 728, 729 (C.C.A. 4th Cir. 1943).

[41]*See Gay v. Ruff*, 292 U.S. 25, 54 S. Ct. 608, 78 L. Ed. 1099 (1934).

[42]*See Pope v. Louisville, N.A. & C. Ry. Co.*, 173 U.S. 573, 19 S. Ct. 500, 43 L. Ed. 814 (1899); *Haile v. Henderson Nat. Bank*, 657 F.2d 816 (6th Cir. 1981).

[43]*See Rouse v. Hornsby*, 161 U.S. 588, 16 S. Ct. 610, 40 L. Ed. 817 (1896); *Robinson v. Michigan Consol. Gas Co. Inc.*, 918 F.2d 579 (6th Cir. 1990).

[44]*See U.S. v. Franklin National Bank*, 512 F.2d 245 (2d Cir. 1975).

obtaining the court's approval.[45] This requirement protects against a waste of the court's time in unnecessarily establishing a receivership.

Vacating or Terminating the Receivership

The district court may vacate the order appointing the receiver or terminate the receivership when the objectives of the receivership have been obtained or the need for the receiver has abated.[46]

Appeals

The district court's decision to appoint a receiver may be immediately appealed.[47] The court of appeals will review the appointment under the lenient abuse of discretion standard. If the appointment is found to have been improvident, the court of appeals may reverse and tax the costs and expenses incurred in the receivership on the persons who procured the receivership.[48]

Orders refusing to wind up the receivership or that otherwise have the effect of either ousting persons from their property or injuring the property may also be immediately appealed.[49]

All other orders involving receivers may only be appealed after entry of a final order.

Additional Research References

Wright & Miller, *Federal Practice and Procedure* §§ 2981 to 86
C.J.S., Mechanics Liens § 214; Receivers §§ 1 to 30 et seq., §§ 52 to 103 et seq., §§ 105 to 150 et seq., §§ 163 to 208 et seq., §§ 227 to 256 et seq., §§ 283 to 325 et seq., §§ 365 to 411 et seq., §§ 418 to 431 et seq.
West's Key Number Digest, Receivers ☞1 to 220

---

[45] *See* Rule 66.

[46] *See SEC v. An-Car Oil Co.*, 604 F.2d 114, 119–20 (1st Cir. 1979).

[47] 28 U.S.C.A. § 1292(a)(2).

[48] *See Tucker v. Baker*, 214 F.2d 627 (5th Cir.1954).

[49] 28 U.S.C.A. § 1292(a)(2).

RULE 67
DEPOSIT INTO COURT

(a) Depositing Property. If any part of the relief sought is a money judgment or the disposition of a sum of money or some other deliverable thing, a party—on notice to every other party and by leave of court—may deposit with the court all or part of the money or thing, whether or not that party claims any of it. The depositing party must deliver to the clerk a copy of the order permitting deposit.

(b) Investing and Withdrawing Funds. Money paid into court under this rule must be deposited and withdrawn in accordance with 28 U.S.C. §§ 2041 and 2042 and any like statute. The money must be deposited in an interest-bearing account or invested in a court-approved, interest-bearing instrument.

[Amended effective October 20, 1949; August 1, 1983; April 30, 2007, effective December 1, 2007.]

AUTHORS' COMMENTARY ON RULE 67

PURPOSE AND SCOPE

Rule 67 governs the circumstances in which a court may accept deposits of money and other personal assets pending the outcome of a case.

RULE 67(a)—DEPOSITING PROPERTY

CORE CONCEPT

Rule 67(a) authorizes the court, in its discretion, to accept deposits of money or some other deliverable property in cases where such assets are genvinely at issue in the case.[1]

---

[1]*See, e.g., Alstom Caribe, Inc. v. Geo. P. Reintjes Co.*, 484 F.3d 106, 113 (1st Cir. 2007) ("The core purpose of Rule 67 is to relieve a party who holds a contested fund from responsibility for disbursement of that fund among those claiming some entitlement thereto.").

APPLICATIONS

Common Uses

Parties have used Rule 67 in cases concerning Rule 22 and statutory interpleader[2] and when Rule 62 provides for security as a condition of a stay pending appeal.[3] Rule 67 has no applicability to payments permitted or ordered in criminal cases.[4]

Time for Deposit

A party may move pursuant to Rule 67 at any time during an action.

Stakeholder's Decision

Rule 67 provides the holder of a disputed asset with an opportunity to seek relief from the burden of safeguarding the asset. However, it provides no authority for another party to demand surrender of the asset.[5]

Leave of Court

Deposits may only be made with leave of court, on motion and with notice to all other parties.[6] If funds are actually deposited with the court, one effect may be to stop a party's liability for the accrual of interest on claims until the case is decided.[7]

Content of Motion

In the motion, the movant should state that opposing parties dispute the ownership of the property or money as well as the particular reasons for making the deposit, such as to avoid responsibility for the property or money.

Method of Deposit

When the court grants leave to make the deposit, the party must serve the order on the clerk of court at the time of making the deposit.

---

[2]See, e.g., Gulf State Utilities Co. v. Alabama Power Co., 824 F.2d 1465, 1474 (5th Cir. 1987) (Rule 67 suitable for use in interpleader case).

[3]Cf., e.g., Kotsopoulos v. Asturia Shipping Co., 467 F.2d 91, 94 (2d Cir. 1972) (by paying amount of judgment into court, party can stop running of interest against that party during pendency of appeal).

[4]See, e.g., U.S. v. Sun Growers of California, 212 F.3d 603, 606 (D.C. Cir. 2000) (Rule 67 applies "only to civil actions.").

[5]See, e.g., Cajun Elec. Power Co-op., Inc. v. Riley Stoker Corp., 901 F.2d 441, 444–45 (5th Cir. 1990) ("The . . . purpose [of Rule 67] is to relieve the depositor of responsibility for the fund in dispute while the parties hash out their differences with respect to it.").

[6]See, e.g., Alstom Caribe, Inc. v. Geo. P. Reintjes Co., Inc., 484 F.3d 106, 113–14 (1st Cir. 2007) (noting court's discretion to accept deposit is limited to cases where there is genuine dispute as to entitlement to funds, and dispute is still alive at time of motion to make deposit; deposit with court may be appropriate even when some claimants to funds are not parties to action).

[7]See, e.g., Cordero v. De Jesus-Mendez, 922 F.2d 11, 18 (1st Cir. 1990) (refusing to charge interest against party who deposited money under rule 67, because once deposit was made duty fell on clerk of court to place money in interest bearing account).

RULE 67(b)—INVESTING AND WITHDRAWING FUNDS

CORE CONCEPT

Rule 67(b) identifies the relevant statutes governing deposits and withdrawals, and also provides that money paid into court under Rule 67 must be deposited in a court-approved interest bearing account.

Administration of Deposit

The clerk of court must invest any money paid into the court in an interest-bearing account or in an interest-bearing instrument approved by the court in the name and to the credit of the court.

Withdrawal of Deposit

A person seeking the money deposited in court must make a motion asserting a judgment or any other document establishing that person's judicially defined interest in the deposit. The court may not disburse any deposit until it establishes ownership by court order, unless the parties have stipulated to the ownership of the property under the direction of the court.[8]

The Merits

Rule 67 provides a potential safe haven for an asset until a court determines rights in the asset. However, Rule 67 does not of itself offer a forum for adjudicating such rights. The question of the merits is reserved for some separate proceeding.[9]

Deposit Not Claimed

If the deposit is not claimed by the person entitled to the deposit for five years from the date of adjudication or from the date of deposit when the asset deposited is not in dispute, the asset will be transferred to the U.S. Treasury in the name of and to the credit of the United States.[10]

Additional Research References

Wright & Miller, *Federal Practice and Procedure* §§ 2991 to 3000
C.J.S., Deposits in Court §§ 1 to 9
West's Key Number Digest, Deposits in Court ⊙1 to 12

---

[8]*But cf., In re Craig's Stores of Texas, Inc.*, 402 F.3d 522, 524 (5th Cir. 2005) (where money was deposited in court in a proceeding in which court was subsequently found to be lacking in jurisdiction, court could not distribute funds as it deemed just; instead, court had to return funds to party who made deposit).

[9]*See, e.g., LTV Corp. v. Gulf States Steel, Inc. of Alabama*, 969 F.2d 1050, 1063 (D.C. Cir. 1992) (Rule 67 " 'provides a place of safekeeping for disputed funds pending the resolution of a legal dispute, but it cannot be used as a means of altering the contractual relationships and legal duties of the parties.' ").

[10]28 U.S.C.A. § 2042.

RULE 68
OFFER OF JUDGMENT

(a) Making an Offer; Judgment on an Accepted Offer. At least 14 days before the date set for trial, a party defending against a claim may serve on an opposing party an offer to allow judgment on specified terms, with the costs then accrued. If, within 14 days after being served, the opposing party serves written notice accepting the offer, either party may then file the offer and notice of acceptance, plus proof of service. The clerk must then enter judgment.

(b) Unaccepted Offer. An unaccepted offer is considered withdrawn, but it does not preclude a later offer. Evidence of an unaccepted offer is not admissible except in a proceeding to determine costs.

(c) Offer After Liability Is Determined. When one party's liability to another has been determined but the extent of liability remains to be determined by further proceedings, the party held liable may make an offer of judgment. It must be served within a reasonable time—but at least 14 days—before the date set for a hearing to determine the extent of liability.

(d) Paying Costs After an Unaccepted Offer. If the judgment that the offeree finally obtains is not more favorable than the unaccepted offer, the offeree must pay the costs incurred after the offer was made.

[Amended effective March 19, 1948; July 1, 1966; August 1, 1987; April 30, 2007, effective December 1, 2007; March 26, 2009, effective December 1, 2009.]

AUTHORS' COMMENTARY ON RULE 68

–––––––––– **PURPOSE AND SCOPE** ––––––––––

Rule 68 governs the circumstances in which a party defending against a claim for money damages or property may seek to resolve the claim by offering to allow judgment against that party for a specified amount of money or property. The Rule also establishes the consequences when a party does not accept an offer of judgment.

RULE 68(a)—MAKING AN OFFER; JUDGMENT ON AN ACCEPTED OFFER

CORE CONCEPT

Rule 68(a) establishes the time limit for making an offer of judgment. It also provides that the offer and proof of service will be filed with the court only if the opposing party accepts the offer. Finally, it provides that an accepted offer requires the clerk of court to enter judgment.

APPLICATIONS

Contents of Offer

An offer of judgment must be for a specified dollar amount or specified property.[1] Rule 68 provides that the offer must include an offer to pay costs accrued by the claiming party prior to receipt of the offer of judgment.[2] In practice, however, if the offer provides a specified amount for costs or provides that costs are included, the offer satisfies the requirements of the Rule.[3] The court may add an amount for costs only when the offer does not provide for costs.[4]

Relation to Rule 54

Rule 54(d) provides that the party who prevails in a lawsuit is entitled to costs "as of course" unless some other provision of

---

[1]*See, e.g., Basha v. Mitsubishi Motor Credit of America, Inc.*, 336 F.3d 451 (5th Cir.2003) (offer that proposed to settle all claims but did not quantify damages could not meet Rule 68 requirements); *Marryshow v. Flynn*, 986 F.2d 689, 691 (4th Cir. 1993) (offer must be for "specified amount").

[2]*See, e.g., McCain v. Detroit II Auto Finance Center*, 378 F.3d 561 (6th Cir.2004) (defendant's silence on costs means they are recoverable by plaintiff).

[3]*See, e.g., Utility Automation 2000, Inc. v. Choctawhatchee Elec. Co-op., Inc.*, 298 F.3d 1238, 1241 (11th Cir. 2002) (offer of judgment proper as long as it does not explicitly exclude costs).

[4]*Marek v. Chesny*, 473 U.S. 1, 105 S. Ct. 3012, 87 L. Ed. 2d 1 (1985). *But compare, Stewart v. Professional Computer Centers, Inc.*, 148 F.3d 937 (8th Cir.1998) (defendant made offer to cover "any and all counts;" plaintiff had sought attorneys' fees and costs in complaint; held, facts were open to more than one interpretation, and therefore no valid offer and acceptance had occurred; judgment based on Rule 68 must therefore be vacated), *with Webb v. James*, 147 F.3d 617 (7th Cir.1998) (defendants' offer did not mention costs; held, plaintiff entitled to attorneys' fees and costs under applicable law; principles of contract recission should not apply to situations involving Rule 68). *See also Hennessy v. Daniels Law Office*, 270 F.3d 551, 553–54 (8th Cir. 2001) (where accepted offer is silent as to attorney's fees and no parol evidence exists to resolve ambiguity, defendant is liable for attorney's fees; using contract principle to construe ambiguity against offeror).

federal law or the federal rules intervenes.[5] When Rule 68 is applicable, it is a provision of the federal rules that overrides Rule 54(d) and can create a situation where a non-prevailing party may recover costs.[6]

Offering Judgment

The appropriate method of offering judgment is to serve a written offer upon the party whose claim is at issue.[7] Although the Rule does not strictly require it, standard practice is to serve copies of the offer upon all other parties to the case. However, until an offer is accepted by the claiming party, it is inappropriate to file a copy of the offer with the clerk's office.[8]

Settlement Offers

Settlement offers are not offers of judgment under Rule 68. Thus Rule 68 has no applicability to offers of settlement.[9]

Ambiguities: Ordinary Contract Analysis

In accordance with ordinary rules of contract law, ambiguities in Rule 68 offers are construed against the offeror.[10]

Timing of Offer

To be effective under Rule 68, an offer of judgment must be served on the party prosecuting a claim more than 14 days before the date set for the beginning of a trial.[11] However, if the trial is a bifurcated proceeding, in which liability only is established in a first hearing, a timely offer of judgment may be served after a determination of liability but not less than 14

---

[5]Fed.R.Civ.P. 54(d).

[6]*See, e.g., Payne v. Milwaukee County*, 288 F.3d 1021, 1027 (7th Cir. 2002).

[7]*See, e.g., Driver Music Co., Inc. v. Commercial Union Ins. Companies*, 94 F.3d 1428, 1432 (10th Cir. 1996) (Rule 68 contemplates that offer will be in writing); *Magnuson v. Video Yesteryear*, 85 F.3d 1424, 1429 (9th Cir. 1996) (absent demonstrated special need or consent of opposing party, service by fax or federal express is ineffective service).

[8]*See, e.g., Kason v. Amphenol Corp.*, 132 F.R.D. 197 (N.D. Ill. 1990) ("[N]o filing is permitted at the time of tender.").

[9]*See, e.g., Menchise v. Senterfitt*, 532 F.3d 1146, 1152 (11th Cir. 2008) (offers of settlement do not require entry of a judgment and are therefore outside the scope of Rule 68).

[10]*See, e.g., Andretti v. Borla Performance Industries, Inc.*, 426 F.3d 824, 837 (6th Cir. 2005) ("[W]e should apply general contract principles to interpret Rule 68 offers of judgment."); *Arbor Hill Concerned Citizens Neighborhood Ass'n v. County of Albany*, 369 F.3d 91, 95 (2d Cir. 2004) (mere promise that is dependent on will or inclination of promisor is not an offer of a mutually binding contract and therefore cannot be an offer of judgment); *Gavoni v. Dobbs House, Inc.*, 164 F.3d 1071, 1077 (7th Cir. 1999) (unapportioned offer of $10,000 to three defendants is ineffective to trigger Rule 68; burden is on defendant to make offer with precision); *Herrington v. County of Sonoma*, 12 F.3d 901 (9th Cir.1993) (additionally, extrinsic evidence is admissible to clarify ambiguities).

[11]*See also Horowitch v. Diamond Aircraft Industries, Inc.*, ___ F.3d ___ n.2 (11th Cir. 2011) ("Rule 68 instructs the parties not to file an offer of judgment with the court at the time of service.").

day the date set for a damages hearing.[12]

Method of Accepting an Offer

The appropriate method for accepting an offer of judgment is by written notice of acceptance to the party who made the offer. It is standard practice to serve copies of such notice on all other parties to the case.

Terms of Acceptance

The offer must be accepted in its entirety, or it is deemed rejected.[13]

Trap for the Unwary

Although Rule 68 is intended to, and often does, serve as an efficient, relatively peaceful means of resolving some cases, it may sometimes become an unanticipated problem for a defendant. The problem can arise if a plaintiff accepts a Rule 68 offer, leading the defendant to believe the case is ended — only to learn that, pursuant to a statutory allowance of, *e.g.,* attorney's fees and costs,[14] a large sum is still owing to the plaintiff.[15] Probably the best solution for a defendant who wishes to make a Rule 68 offer is to include in the offer a clear statement that the offer includes fees and costs. An offer that is silent on that point will frequently result in additional expenses for the defendant.[16]

RULE 68(b)—UNACCEPTED OFFER

CORE CONCEPT

Rule 68(b) provides that unaccepted offers are deemed withdrawn, though it remains possible for a party to make a subsequent offer. Unaccepted offers are not admissible in court, except in a proceeding to determine costs,[17] or to challenge subject matter jurisdiction.

Timing of Acceptance

A party has 14 days after receipt of service of the written of-

---

[12]*Delta Air Lines, Inc. v. August,* 450 U.S. 346, 101 S. Ct. 1146, 67 L. Ed. 2d 287 (1981).

[13]*See, e.g., Whitcher v. Town of Matthews,* 136 F.R.D. 582, 585 (W.D. N.C. 1991) (plaintiffs cannot both accept offer as to money damages and continue action as to equitable relief). *But cf., Gordon v. Gouline,* 81 F.3d 235 (D.C. Cir. 1996) (acceptance is effective even when conditioned upon approval of bankruptcy court).

[14]*See, e.g.,* 42 U.S.C. § 1988.

[15]*See, e.g., Lima v. Newark Police Department,* 645 F.3d 1254, 1259 (3d Cir. 2011) (describing this "trap for the unwary").

[16]*See, e.g., Lima v. Newark Police Department,* ___ F.3d ___ (3d Cir. 2011) (offer silent as to fees and costs creates additional vulnerability for defendant); *Bosley v. Mineral County Commission,* ___ F.3d ___ (4th Cir. 2011) (same analysis and result).

[17]*See, e.g., O'Brien v. Ed Donnelly Enterprises, Inc.,* 575 F.3d 567, 574 (6th Cir. 2009) (offer of judgment cannot be used to support or challenge merits of claim; it can be used to determine costs or challenge subject matter jurisdiction).

fer to accept the offer of judgment.[18] If the offer is not accepted within the 14-day period, Rule 68 treats the offer as withdrawn, and it cannot thereafter be accepted. However, it is possible for the party that made the offer to renew the offer, or make a different offer, in which event the 14-day period for acceptance begins to run again.

Offers by Plaintiff

Unless a plaintiff is defending against a counterclaim or a crossclaim, as described in Rules 13 and 14, a plaintiff cannot make an offer of judgment.[19] Only parties defending against claims may use Rule 68 to make offers of judgment.[20]

Offer for Full Amount of Claim

It is settled that if a Rule 68 offer of judgment is made for the full amount of relief sought or for the full amount of recovery authorized by statute, the case is ended.[21] Courts differ only as to whether the plaintiff should simply be forced to accept the offer[22] or whether the outcome is mandated by the resulting disappearance of subject matter jurisdiction (for lack of a case or controversy).[23]

Entering Final Judgment: Judicial Discretion

If the party prosecuting a claim accepts the offer of judgment, Rule 68 permits either party to file the offer and notice of acceptance, along with proof of service, with the clerk of

---

[18]*See, e.g., Perkins v. U.S. West Communications*, 138 F.3d 336 (8th Cir. 1998) (defendant filed motion for summary judgment; while motion was pending, defendant made offer of judgment under Rule 68; two days after offer of judgment was made, court granted defendant's summary judgment motion; plaintiff, upon notice of grant of summary judgment, accepted Rule 68 offer; held, acceptance bound defendant, notwithstanding grant of summary judgment; possible different result if defendant had conditioned offer of judgment on court's denial of summary judgment motion).

[19]*Delta Air Lines, Inc. v. August*, 450 U.S. 346, 101 S. Ct. 1146, 67 L. Ed. 2d 287 (1981).

[20]*See, e.g., Garcia v. Wal-Mart Stores, Inc.*, 209 F.3d 1170, 1176 (10th Cir. 2000) ("Rule 68 governs only defendants' costs."). *Cf., Amati v. City of Woodstock*, 176 F.3d 952, 958 (7th Cir. 1999) ("A plaintiff has no right to demand a Rule 68 offer."). *But cf., S.A. Healy Co. v. Milwaukee Metropolitan Sewerage Dist.*, 60 F.3d 305, 310–12 (7th Cir. 1995) (Rule 68 permits offers only by parties defending claims, but in diversity case, state law permitting plaintiff's offer of settlement may be applied).

[21]*See, e.g., Warren v. Sessoms & Rogers, P.A.*, 676 F.3d 365, 371 (4th Cir. 2012) (if offer includes all relief plaintiff sought, offer makes lawsuit moot; but such offer must be unequivocal); *Zimmerman v. Bell*, 800 F.2d 386, 390 (4th Cir. 1986) (dismissing securities fraud claim where defendant offered full amount of relief sought); *But cf., Lucero v. Bureau of Collection Recovery, Inc.*, 639 F.3d 1239, 1243 (10th Cir. 2011) (accepting general rule, but questioning its applicability to class actions governed by Rule 23; citing numerous cases).

[22]*See, e.g., Wilner v. OSI Collection Services, Inc.*, 198 F.R.D. 393, 395 (S.D. N.Y. 2001) (asserting power to compel plaintiff to accept offer).

[23]*See, e.g., Abrams v. Interco Inc.*, 719 F.2d 23, 32–33 (2d Cir. 1983) (asserting lack of subject matter jurisdiction).

court. Rule 68 then directs that the clerk shall enter judgment consistent with the offer and acceptance.[24]

Once the offer, notice of acceptance and proof of service are filed with the court, the court must normally enter judgment.[25] Except in circumstances where the literal language of Rule 68 conflicts with some other requirement of federal law, the court has no discretion to refuse to enter judgment.[26]

Determining Whether Judgment is "More Favorable"

In cases involving only money damages, it is usually not difficult to calculate whether the judgment a party won is more favorable than an earlier offer of judgment. However, where a party obtains an injunction as part of a favorable judgment, the calculation can be more challenging.[27] Nevertheless, it appears settled that in determining whether a judgment is more favorable than an earlier offer of judgment, the value of an injunction granted should be included in the calculation.[28]

Equitable Claims

Rule 68 generally applies to offers of specific sums or specific property. Typically the Rule is not used to resolve claims in equity where a party seeks only an injunction, but Rule 68 itself does not expressly prohibit such an application.[29]

Revocation

It appears settled that except in exceptional circumstances a Rule 68 offer cannot be revoked during the 14 days provided

---

[24]*See, e.g., Parental Guide of Texas, Inc. v. Thomson, Inc.*, 446 F.3d 1265, 1270 (Fed. Cir. 2006) ("[T]he entry of judgment 'is generally a ministerial act and can be performed by the clerk without any input from the court or a jury.' ").

[25]*See, e.g., Webb v. James*, 147 F.3d 617, 621 (7th Cir. 1998).

[26]*See, e.g., Parental Guide of Texas, Inc. v. Thomson, Inc.*, 446 F.3d 1265, 1270 (Fed. Cir. 2006) ("[U]nder Rule 68, the terms of a judgment are agreed upon by the parties; the court has no input or discretion to alter or modify any of the terms."); *Ramming v. Natural Gas Pipeline Co. of America*, 390 F.3d 366, 371 (5th Cir. 2004) (duty of court to review settlement of class action under Rule 23 provides exception to Rule 68; same result, slightly different reasoning, when case involves plea for injunctive relief).

[27]*See, e.g., Andretti v. Borla Performance Industries, Inc.*, 426 F.3d 824,

837 (6th Cir. 2005) ("comparing the value of damages to an injunction is like comparing apples and oranges," but courts must sometimes do so in situations governed by Rule 68).

[28]*See, e.g., Reiter v. MTA New York City Transit Authority*, 457 F.3d 224 (2d Cir. 2006) ("Nothing in the language of Rule 68 suggests that a final judgment that contains equitable relief is inherently less favorable than a Rule 68 offer that contains monetary relief."); *Andretti v. Borla Performance Industries, Inc.*, 426 F.3d 824, 837 (6th Cir. 2005) ("[M]oney damages [need not be] the only measure of whether a plaintiff has obtained a 'more favorable' judgment under Rule 68.").

[29]*See, e.g., Chathas v. Local 134 Intern. Broth. of Elec. Workers*, 233 F.3d 508, 511 (7th Cir. 2000) ("Rule 68 offers are much more common in money cases than in equity cases, but nothing in the rule forbids its use in the latter type of case.").

by the Rule.[30] This conclusion is an exception to the general rule that principles of contract law apply to construe a Rule 68 offer and acceptance.[31]

Offer of Judgment as Evidence

Rule 68 provides that if an offer of judgment is not accepted, the offer may not be used as evidence at trial. The only use to which a nonaccepted offer of judgment may be put is to establish the consequences, if any, to the nonaccepting party when final judgment is entered in the case.

Consequences of Nonacceptance

The consequences of nonacceptance of an offer under Rule 68 depend on the outcome of the litigation. Once final judgment is entered, if the party that did not accept the offer has won a judgment greater than the amount in the offer of judgment, the refusal of the offer has no consequence whatever.[32] If, however, the nonaccepting party receives a favorable final judgment, but for less than the amount in the offer of judgment— Rule 68 requires the nonaccepting party to pay the offering party's costs incurred after the offer was made.[33] Rule 68 may thus permit a party that has made an offer of judgment, and then loses the case, to recover some costs from the prevailing party. To that extent, Rule 68 provides a possible exception to Rule 54(d), which provides that the prevailing party ordinarily will collect costs from the losing party.

---

[30]*See, e.g., Richardson v. National R.R. Passenger Corp.*, 49 F.3d 760, 764 (D.C. Cir. 1995) (noting that courts treat offers as irrevocable for [14] days.). *Cf., Perkins v. U.S. West Communications*, 138 F.3d 336 (8th Cir. 1998) (revocation permitted only for "good cause").

[31]*See, e.g., Herrington v. County of Sonoma*, 12 F.3d 901, 907 (9th Cir. 1993) (Rule 68 is subject to standard rules of contract construction).

[32]*See, e.g., Brown v. Cox*, 286 F.3d 1040, 1047 (8th Cir. 2002) (plaintiff refused offer of judgment and then won judgment greater than offer; held, plaintiff's right to attorney's fees established by applicable federal civil rights law was therefore unaffected by refusal).

[33]*See, e.g., UMG Recordings, Inc. v. Shelter Capital Partners, Inc.*, 667 F.3d 1022, 1047–48 (9th Cir. 2011) (purpose of Rule 68 is to force plaintiff to "think very hard" about continuing litigation and to "compensate defen-

dants for costs they ought not have had to incur"); *Payne v. Milwaukee County*, 288 F.3d 1021, 1025 (7th Cir. 2002) (civil rights case; prevailing plaintiff who won less than offer of judgment is not entitled to recovery attorney's fees that would otherwise have been available under federal civil rights law); *Haworth v. State of Nev.*, 56 F.3d 1048 (9th Cir. 1995) (plaintiff recovering less than offer of judgment cannot recover costs incurred after offer, and must pay defendant's post-offer costs). *See also Pouillon v. Little*, 326 F.3d 713, 715 (6th Cir. 2003) (Rule 68 offer that was not accepted retains cost-shifting effect after plaintiff got reversal on appeal of original loss and won nominal amount upon remand). *Cf., Berkla v. Corel Corp.*, 302 F.3d 909, 922 (9th Cir. 2002) (prevailing party won less than rejected offer, but offer did not satisfy elements of Rule 68; held, prevailing party could not be denied costs that would otherwise have been awarded if no offer had been made).

Relation to Rule 23

Rule 23 governs class actions. If a plaintiff has sought to have a case certified as a class action, there is substantial authority holding that a Rule 68 offer of judgment for the full statutory amount of the individual plaintiff's claim cannot be used to render the putative class action moot.[34] Contrary authority now exists, however, and attorneys must consult local authority.[35]

Additionally, when an offer of judgment is made in a case that has been certified as a class action, it may appear that the authority of a district judge to review and approve proposed settlements (found in Rule 23) is in conflict with the provision of Rule 68 that the court has no authority to approve or reject an offer of judgment that meets the requirements of Rule 68. However, the case law seems to establish clearly that, when applicable, Rule 23 is an exception to the limitations Rule 68 imposes on a court.[36]

When Defendant Prevails

If an opponent of a claim makes an offer of judgment that is not accepted, and if the offeror then wins the case, Rule 68 has *no* effect. Rule 68 is applied, if at all, only when an offer is not accepted, and then the offeree obtains judgment—but for less than the amount of the offer.[37]

---

[34]*See, e.g., Carroll v. United Compucred Collections, Inc.*, 399 F.3d 620, 625 (6th Cir. 2005) (in instant case motion for class certification was pending but not yet decided when offer of judgment was made; if complaint could be rendered moot by use of Rule 68, court could never reach class action even in cases where class certification would be appropriate); *Weiss v. Regal Collections*, 385 F.3d 337, 348 (3d Cir. 2004) (same, but making exception for "undue delay" in filing motion for class certification).

[35]*See, e.g., Damascus v. Clearwire Corp.*, 662 F.3d 891, 896 (7th Cir. 2011) (generally rejecting majority view; concluding that offer of judgment for full amount can negate subsequent motion for class certification).

[36]*See, e.g., Ramming v. Natural Gas Pipeline Co. of America*, 390 F.3d 366, 371 (5th Cir. 2004) (duty of court to review settlement of class actions under Rule 23 provides exception to Rule 68; same result when case involves plea for injunctive relief).

[37]*Delta Air Lines, Inc. v. August*, 450 U.S. 346, 352, 101 S. Ct. 1146, 1150, 67 L. Ed. 2d 287 (1981). *See also, Payne v. Milwaukee County*, 288 F.3d 1021, 1025 (7th Cir. 2002) ("Had [plaintiff] not prevailed in some significant sense, [defendant] would be confined to Rule 54(d), and rule 68 would simply have no application."). *MRO Communications, Inc. v. American Tel. & Tel. Co.*, 197 F.3d 1276, 1280 (9th Cir. 1999) (under *Delta Air Lines* "Rule 68 is inapplicable in a case in which the defendant obtains judgment"); *Amati v. City of Woodstock*, 176 F.3d 952, 957 (7th Cir. 1999) ("Rule 68 bites only when the plaintiff wins but wins less than the defendant's offer of judgment."); *Louisiana Power & Light Co. v. Kellstrom*, 50 F.3d 319, 333 (5th Cir. 1995) ("If a plaintiff takes nothing . . . Rule 68 does not apply." (citing *Delta Air Lines*)). *But see McCauley v. Trans Union, L.L.C.*, 402 F.3d 340, 341–42 (2d Cir. 2005) (where plaintiff has rejected offer of judgment that included full dollar amount at issue but also included a denial of liability of defendant, proper remedy is to enter default judgment for full dol-

RULE 68(c)—OFFER AFTER LIABILITY IS DETERMINED

CORE CONCEPT

Rule 68(c) permits an offer after liability is determined, but the amount of liability has not been established. Such an offer must be served at least fourteen days before the date set for a hearing on the extent of liability.

Offer to Multiple Plaintiffs

If a defendant makes an offer of judgment to more than one plaintiff in the same case, the offer must itemize the proposed payment to each plaintiff. If the offer does not identify the proposed allocation of money among the plaintiffs, the defendant will not collect costs even if the plaintiffs' final judgment is for less than the offer.[38]

Joint Offer from Multiple Defendants

When more than one defendant makes an offer of judgment to a plaintiff, the defendants should be careful to make clear the proportion of the offer being made by each defendant. Failure to provide more than an unapportioned joint offer creates a significant possibility that, if one of the defendants is somehow excused but another is found liable, the offeror/defendants will not meet their burden of demonstrating that the offer was more favorable than the judgment the plaintiff later obtained.[39]

Settled Cases

The literal language of Rule 68 bars its use to award costs in cases that settle without going to judgment. Less certain is

---

lar amount, plus costs; judgment will contain no record of liability of defendant).

[38] *See, e.g., Gavoni v. Dobbs House, Inc.*, 164 F.3d 1071, 1075–77 (7th Cir. 1999) (defendant has burden of showing that offer was more favorable than final judgment; defendant also has burden of making offer clear, and plaintiffs are entitled to "a clear baseline from which [they] may evaluate the merits of their case relative to the value of the offer").

[39] *See, e.g., Harbor Motor Co., Inc. v. Arnell Chevrolet-Geo, Inc.*, 265 F.3d 638, 647–49 (7th Cir. 2001) (one defendant won at trial, but other lost; held, plaintiff could not have estimated with any confidence what portion of offer was attributable to losing defendant, so offer was ineffective; acknowledging possibility that on different facts court might be able to calculate the share of an unapportioned offer to

ascribe to each of several defendants; "We need not go so far as to conclude . . . that Rule 68 always requires an exact delineation of the manner in which damages are to be apportioned among multiple parties."); *Johnston v. Penrod Drilling Co.*, 803 F.2d 867, 870 (5th Cir. 1986) (plaintiff settled with one defendant, won judgment against another; held, offer of judgment and judgment actually obtained could not be compared because "settlement may have . . . had an effect on the damage award;" noting different result if plaintiff's judgment had been won against both defendants). *Cf., Le v. University of Pennsylvania*, 321 F.3d 403, 408 (3d Cir. 2003) (distinguishing results in other cases where it was not as clear as in instant case that all payments, whether pursuant to Rule 68 or judgment on merits, would be made by one defendant who had duty of indemnification to other defendant).

the result when the parties settle, and the court enters judgment on the settlement.[40] Attorneys are advised to consult local practice.

RULE 68(d)—PAYING COSTS AFTER AN UNACCEPTED OFFER

CORE CONCEPT

Rule 68(d) establishes the consequences when an offer has been rejected and the offeree subsequently obtains a judgment that is not more favorable than the offer. In that circumstance the offeree must pay costs incurred by the offering party after the offer was made. As is noted under Rule 68(b) above, however, the offeree has no obligation to pay costs if the offeree loses the case.

Attorney Fees

Rule 68 is silent as to whether a nonaccepting party may be required to pay another party's attorney fees as part of the other party's "costs". However, it is settled that Rule 68 does not itself create a right to recover attorney fees.[41] There is uncertainty as to whether Rule 68 authorizes recovery of attorney fees from a nonaccepting party—who subsequently received a final judgment less favorable than the offer of judgment—if some other provision of federal law permits recovery of attorney fees. Thus, if a defendant who was sued on a federal civil rights claim made an offer of judgment that was not accepted, and the defendant then lost on the merits (but for less than the offer of judgment), the defendant might be entitled to recover costs that included attorney fees if federal civil rights law included attorney fees within the range of recoverable costs.[42] Moreover, if the statute normally awarded fees to a prevailing plaintiff (who recovered less than the offer), the

---

[40]*Compare, e.g., E.E.O.C. v. Hamilton Standard Div., United Technologies Corp.*, 637 F. Supp. 1155, 1158 (D. Conn. 1986) (refusing to apply Rule 68 to case ending in settlement and stipulated dismissal), *with Lang v. Gates*, 36 F.3d 73, 77 (9th Cir. 1994) (approving application of Rule 68 to order enforcing settlement).

[41]*See, e.g., McCain v. Detroit II Auto Finance Center*, 378 F.3d 561 (6th Cir.2004) ("[T]he only way in which Rule 68 directly implicates awards of attorney's fees is in situations where such fees are made an element of 'costs'—whether by statute . . . or as a matter of contract."); *Poteete v. Capital Engineering, Inc.*, 185 F.3d 804, 807 (7th Cir. 1999) ("Rule 68 does not entitle a defendant to recover his

attorneys' fees." (citing extensive authority)).

[42]*Marek v. Chesny*, 473 U.S. 1, 105 S. Ct. 3012, 87 L. Ed. 2d 1 (1985). *Harbor Motor Co., Inc. v. Arnell Chevrolet-Geo, Inc.*, 265 F.3d 638, 646 (7th Cir. 2001) (agreeing with *Crossman*, infra, that in cases controlled by fee provision of copyright law "only prevailing parties can receive attorney's fees pursuant to rule 68;" defendant who lost case for less than offer of judgment therefore cannot recover attorney's fees; acknowledging different result in *Jordan v. Time, Inc.*, infra); *Crossman v. Marcoccio*, 806 F.2d 329, 333–34 (1st Cir. 1986) (where underlying copyright statute awards attorney's fees only to prevailing party, defendant who lost case—but for amount less than offer of judg-

court has authority to reduce the attorney fees award to the plaintiff.[43]

Multiple Offers

Rule 68 explicitly permits a party whose previous offer of judgment was not accepted to continue making offers, provided that the offers are served more than 14 days before the beginning of a trial.

Additional Research References

Wright & Miller, *Federal Practice and Procedure* §§ 3001 to 10. Lisnek, *Effective Negotiation and Mediation, A Lawyer's Guide.*
C.J.S., Federal Civil Procedure § 1276
West's Key Number Digest, Federal Civil Procedure ☞2725

---

ment—cannot recover attorney's fee because defendant did not prevail in case). *But see Jordan v. Time, Inc.*, 111 F.3d 102, 105 (11th Cir. 1997) (requiring plaintiff in copyright case who obtained judgment for less than offer of judgment to pay defendant's costs and fees incurred after offer was made).

[43]*See, e.g., Dalal v. Alliant Techsystems, Inc.*, 182 F.3d 757 (10th Cir.1999) (affirming reduced award of attorney fees for legal work done between date of offer of judgment and date of judgment; acknowledging lack of precise formula for making calculation); *Haworth v. State of Nev.*, 56 F.3d 1048 (9th Cir. 1995) (reducing plaintiff's recovery of attorney fees because judgment was for less than the offer of judgment).

RULE 69
EXECUTION

(a) In General.

(1) *Money Judgment; Applicable Procedure.* A money judgment is enforced by a writ of execution, unless the court directs otherwise. The procedure on execution—and in proceedings supplementary to and in aid of judgment or execution—must accord with the procedure of the state where the court is located, but a federal statute governs to the extent it applies.

(2) *Obtaining Discovery.* In aid of the judgment or execution, the judgment creditor or a successor in interest whose interest appears of record may obtain discovery from any person—including the judgment debtor—as provided in these rules or by the procedure of the state where the court is located.

(b) Against Certain Public Officers.
When a judgment has been entered against a revenue officer in the circumstances stated in 28 U.S.C. § 2006, or against an officer of Congress in the circumstances stated in 2 U.S.C. § 118, the judgment must be satisfied as those statutes provide.

[Amended effective October 20, 1949; July 1, 1970; August 1, 1987; April 30, 2007, effective December 1, 2007.]

AUTHORS' COMMENTARY ON RULE 69

PURPOSE AND SCOPE

Rule 69 provides a mechanism for executing money judgments entered by a federal court. Rule 69 also provides for the execution of judgments entered against district directors of the Internal Revenue Service and officers of Congress.

RULE 69(a)—IN GENERAL

CORE CONCEPT

Rule 69(a) provides for the enforcement of money judgments generally through a writ of execution. If enforcement of a money judgment requires ancillary litigation, state law will usually control such litigation unless a federal statute otherwise provides.[1] However, discovery to enforce a money judgment may be conducted pursuant to either the federal discovery rules or the discovery rules of the forum state.

APPLICATIONS

Scope

Rule 69 only applies to an execution of a money judgment entered by a federal court[2] and has no application to state court judgments or other types of judgments.

Subject Matter Jurisdiction

Efforts to collect judgments under Rule 69 fall within the supplemental jurisdiction of district courts.[3]

Supplementing or Supplanting State Procedure

Although Rule 69(a) directs a district court to use state procedure,[4] to enforce money judgments,[5] it also provides that the court may "direct otherwise." At the same time, federal courts apparently have authority to supplement such procedure with

---

[1]*See, e.g., U.S. v. Little*, 52 F.3d 495 (4th Cir. 1995) (holding that Rule 69(a) requires application of state law governing enforcement of judgments). *But cf., Laborers' Pension Fund v. Pavement Maintenance, Inc.*, 542 F.3d 189, 194 (7th Cir. 2008) ("State rules of procedure cannot negate subject-matter jurisdiction arising from a federal statute and federal question."); *Apparel Art Intern., Inc. v. Amertex Enterprises Ltd.*, 48 F.3d 576 (1st Cir. 1995) (Rule 69 requires application of state procedure on execution; however, Rule 69 does not require use of "general state procedural law," such as state doctrine on res judicata).

[2]*See, e.g., U.S. v. Timilty*, 148 F.3d 1, 4 (1st Cir. 1998) (enforcement of judgment imposing criminal fine in favor of United States is also controlled by, *inter alia*, Rule 69(a)). *See also Ziino v. Baker*, 613 F.3d 1326,1328 (11th Cir. 2010) (prerequisite to use of Rule 69 is existence of a *money* judgment; final judgments that are not money judgments are not subject to Rule 69).

[3]*See, e.g., Kokkonen v. Guardian Life Ins. Co. of America*, 511 U.S. 375, 379, 114 S. Ct. 1673, 1676, 128 L. Ed. 2d 391 (1994) (ancillary jurisdiction permits district court, *inter alia*, to "vindicate its authority, and effectuate its decrees"); *Yang v. City of Chicago*, 137 F.3d 522, 525 (7th Cir. 1998) (citing to extensive authority). *But cf., Sandlin v. Corporate Interiors Inc.*, 972 F.2d 1212, 1217 (10th Cir. 1992) (if enforcement proceeding is an attempt to collect judgment from non-party on theory distinct from theory underlying judgment, "an independent basis for federal jurisdiction must exist").

[4]*Peacock v. Thomas*, 516 U.S. 349, 359, 116 S. Ct. 862, 133 L. Ed. 2d 817 (1996) ("Rule 69(a) . . . permits judgment creditors to use any execution method consistent with [state] practice and procedure.").

[5]*See, e.g., Bergmann v. Michigan State Transportation Commission*, 665 F.3d 681, 684 (6th Cir. 2011) (but also noting, under Rule 70(a), no requirement to use state law to perform "spe-

federal practice when necessary.[6] Indeed, if state law is an obstacle to enforcement, federal courts may even be able to disregard state practice.[7] Finally, Rule 69(a) explicitly provides that any applicable federal statute supplants state law.[8]

Stay of Enforcement

Rule 62(a) directs that a federal money judgment may not be executed upon until 10 days after entry of judgment. The court may further stay execution of the final judgment when an appeal is properly taken or when the court reviews post-trial motions, as provided by Rule 62.[9]

Time for Enforcement

State law will determine the time limitation of the writ of execution and how the time limitation may be extended.

Source of Remedies

A party seeking execution of a money judgment may use any applicable federal statute. Federal remedies for executions in aid of judgments are listed at 28 U.S.C.A. §§ 2001 et seq. See also the Advisory Committee Notes to Rule 69. Additionally, a party may use any of the provisional remedies of the forum state at the time the remedy is sought, such as garnishment, arrest, mandamus, contempt, or the appointment of a receiver. When a state remedy is utilized, a party need only

---

cific act").

[6]*See, e.g., U.S. v. Harkins Builders, Inc.*, 45 F.3d 830, 833 (4th Cir. 1995) (Rule 69(a) permits use of federal procedure to further "the federal policy of affording judgment creditors the right to a writ of execution to enforce money judgments in federal courts."). *But see, Credit Suisse v. U.S. Dist. Court for Cent. Dist. of California*, 130 F.3d 1342, 1344 (9th Cir. 1997) (Rule 69(a) authorizes only a writ of execution; it provides no authority for court to order payment into court); *Aetna Cas. & Sur. Co. v. Markarian*, 114 F.3d 346, 349 (1st Cir. 1997) ("The 'otherwise' clause is narrowly construed. . . . It does not authorize enforcement of a civil money judgment by methods other than a writ of execution, except [in unusual circumstances];" vacating writ that required judgment debtor to surrender passport).

[7]*See, e.g., Hankins v. Finnel*, 964 F.2d 853, 860 (8th Cir. 1992) ("Where state law fails to supply the necessary

procedure, or actually stands in the way of enforcement, the district court may take the necessary steps to ensure compliance with its judgment."). *But see, Credit Suisse v. U.S. Dist. Court for Cent. Dist. of California*, 130 F.3d 1342, 1344 (9th Cir. 1997) (where state law requires service of a notice of levy on the branch office where defendant holds account—and that branch is not within state—service is ineffective).

[8]*See, e.g., Walters v. Industrial and Commercial Bank of China, Ltd.*, ___ F.3d ___ (2d Cir. 2011) (Foreign Sovereign Immunities Act, 28 U.S.C. §§ 1604 et seq., may block application of Rule 69); *Office Depot, Inc., v. Zuccarini*, 596 F.3d 696, 701 (9th Cir. 2010) ("The federal rules, including Rule 66, qualify as federal statutes under Rule 69(a).").

[9]*Cf., Acevedo-Garcia v. Vera-Monroig*, 296 F.3d 13 (1st Cir.2002) ("Absent a stay on some ground, plaintiffs are free to seek execution of the judgment pursuant to Fed. R. Civ. P. 69.").

comply substantially with the provisions of the state remedy.[10]

Registering a Judgment in District Outside Forum State

A judgment for money or property entered by any district court may be registered in any other district court by filing a certified copy of such judgment in the other district after the judgment has become final.[11] A judgment that has been registered has the same effect as the original judgment and may be enforced as would any other judgment. However, a potentially important result of registering a judgment in federal court that was previously awarded in a different federal court in a different state is that the law of the enforcing state—not the judgment state—will normally control.[12]

Writ of Execution

A writ of execution is a writ to enforce a judgment by the seizure and sale of property of the debtor in satisfaction of the judgment.

Enforcement of Judgment

Upon obtaining the writ of execution, the judgment creditor may serve the writ on the U.S. Marshal or state officer, who will then execute, by attachment or otherwise, the property of the judgment debtor in the possession of third parties, and may have the judgment debtor's property sold at an execution sale. The specific procedures for obtaining a writ of execution and executing on the property of the judgment debtor will depend upon the remedy sought and will vary from state to state and district to district.

Comparison with Rule 70

In general, Rule 69 provides mechanisms for enforcement of money judgments. By contrast, Rule 70 authorizes the district court to issue orders to ensure that equitable relief is provided.[13]

---

[10]*Duchek v. Jacobi*, 646 F.2d 415, 417 (9th Cir. 1981) (state law requiring that enforcement proceedings be held in state court may properly be disregarded).

[11]28 U.S.C.A. § 1963.

[12]*See, e.g., Condaire, Inc. v. Allied Piping, Inc.*, 286 F.3d 353, 357–58 (6th Cir. 2002) (collecting other cases on point). *Cf., Gagan v. Monroe*, 269 F.3d 871, 873 (7th Cir. 2001) (judgment in Indiana federal district court; when defendant did not pay, plaintiff sought Rule 69 enforcement in Indiana district court; held, because property to be executed upon was in Arizona, Indiana state law required use of Arizona law to determine whether property was subject to execution).

[13]*See, e.g., Board of Com'rs of Stark County, OH v. Cape Stone Works, Inc.*, 206 F. Supp. 2d 100, 102 (D. Mass. 2002) (default judgment that contained award of money damages could be enforced under Rule 69(a); but where judgment made no reference to specific performance that complaint had sought, not such relief was available under Rule 70).

Discovery

A party seeking to enforce a judgment may use either the federal or the state discovery rules[14] to uncover information concerning assets of the debtor and to aid in execution of the judgment. Rule 69(a) expressly provides that such discovery may be directed toward "any person," including persons not parties to the lawsuit.[15]

Property Subject to Levy

State law will designate the property of the judgment debtor which may be levied upon in satisfaction of the judgment.

Foreign Sovereign Immunity

The Foreign Sovereign Immunities Act provides substantial immunity for foreign sovereigns from the jurisdiction of American courts.[16] The Act also immunizes the property of foreign states from attachment and execution on their property.[17] It appears settled, therefore, that Rule 69 can be applied only to circumstances where the Act does not provide immunity against a judgment creditor's attempt to execute against property.[18]

Fees and Costs

Fees for writs, subpoenas, keeping attached property, seizing or levying on property, and for the sale of property may be taxed as costs.[19]

RULE 69(b)—AGAINST CERTAIN PUBLIC OFFICERS

CORE CONCEPT

If a district director of the Internal Revenue Service—a "collector" of revenue—or an officer of Congress has obtained a certificate of probable cause, a judgment entered against such district

---

[14]*See, e.g., Natural Gas Pipeline Co. of America v. Energy Gathering, Inc.*, 2 F.3d 1397, 1403 (5th Cir. 1993) (post-judgment discovery may follow federal pre-trial discovery or applicable state discovery law).

[15]*See, e.g., Credit Lyonnais, S.A. v. SGC Intern., Inc.*, 160 F.3d 428, 430 (8th Cir. 1998) (Under Rule 69(a) and applicable state procedure, "[a] party may depose almost anyone, including corporations, who may provide relevant information."); *F.D.I.C. v. LeGrand*, 43 F.3d 163, 172 (5th Cir. 1995) ("The scope of postjudgment discovery is very broad.").

[16]28 U.S.C. § 1604. *See, e.g., Walters v. Industrial & Commercial Bank of China, Ltd.*, 651 F.3d 280, 292 (2d Cir. 2011) (under Rule 69 court must consider, where applicable, issues of foreign sovereign immunity before permitting execution against property).

[17]28 U.S.C. § 1609.

[18]*See, e.g., Walters v. Industrial and Commercial Bank of China, Ltd.*, ___ F.3d ___ (2d Cir. 2011); *Rubin v. Islamic Republic of Iran*, 637 F.3d 783, 799 (7th Cir. 2011) (scope of liability under FSIA is broader than scope of allowable execution on judgments).

[19]28 U.S.C.A. § 1921.

director[20] or officer[21] for damages resulting from any of the individual's official acts, or for the recovery of any money exacted by or paid to the individual and subsequently paid into the Treasury may only be executed against the United States Treasury, and not against the individual's property.

APPLICATIONS

District Director

"District director" is defined as any district director of the Internal Revenue Service, former district director, or personal representative of a deceased district director.

Obtaining Certificate of Probable Cause

When a judgment creditor seeks to enforce a judgment, the district director or the officer of Congress may apply to the court for a certificate of probable cause. Upon such application, the court will determine whether the director or officer acted with probable and reasonable cause in performing their proper governmental duties. If the court so finds, the court will issue a certificate of probable cause.

Effect of Certificate

The certificate of probable cause converts the action to one against the United States, extinguishing the personal liability of the individual. Subsequently, the judgment creditor may serve the certificate of probable cause, along with the judgment, on the United States Treasury. The Treasury will pay the amount of the judgment.

Additional Research References

Wright & Miller, *Federal Practice and Procedure* §§ 3011 to 3020
C.J.S., Federal Civil Procedure §§ 1254 to 1272 et seq.
West's Key Number Digest, Federal Civil Procedure ⬤⟿2691 to 2714

---

[20]28 U.S.C.A. § 2006 (Internal Revenue Officer).

[21]2 U.S.C.A. § 118 (18 Stat. 401) (Officer of Congress).

RULE 70
ENFORCING A JUDGMENT FOR A SPECIFIC ACT

(a) Party's Failure to Act; Ordering Another to Act. If a judgment requires a party to convey land, to deliver a deed or other document, or to perform any other specific act and the party fails to comply within the time specified, the court may order the act to be done—at the disobedient party's expense—by another person appointed by the court. When done, the act has the same effect as if done by the party.

(b) Vesting Title. If the real or personal property is within the district, the court—instead of ordering a conveyance—may enter a judgment divesting any party's title and vesting it in others. That judgment has the effect of a legally executed conveyance.

(c) Obtaining a Writ of Attachment or Sequestration. On application by a party entitled to performance of an act, the clerk must issue a writ of attachment or sequestration against the disobedient party's property to compel obedience.

(d) Obtaining a Writ of Execution or Assistance. On application by a party who obtains a judgment or order for possession, the clerk must issue a writ of execution or assistance.

(e) Holding in Contempt. The court may also hold the disobedient party in contempt.

[April 30, 2007, effective December 1, 2007.]

AUTHORS' COMMENTARY ON RULE 70

—————— PURPOSE AND SCOPE ——————

Rule 70 provides that the court may convey property or perform any other specific actj, pursuant to a judgment when a party ordered to convey property or perform a specific act fails to comply.

RULE 70(a)—PARTY'S FAILURE TO ACT; ORDERING ANOTHER TO ACT

CORE CONCEPT

Rule 70(a) provides that if a judgment includes a requirement that a party transfer property or perform some other act, the court may appoint a person to do the act if the party fails to do so. Such appointment will be at the expense of the non-performing party and will carry the same legal result as if the party had performed the act.

APPLICATIONS

Scope

Rule 70 "applies only to parties who have failed to perform specific acts pursuant to a judgment."[1] In the absence of a judgment, Rule 70 has no applicability.[2]

Comparison with Rule 69

In general, Rule 69 provides mechanisms for enforcement of money judgments, but in most cases the means of enforcement must accord with state procedure.[3] By contrast, Rule 70 authorizes the district court to issue orders to ensure that equitable relief is provided,[4] but unlike Rule 69, Rule 70 does not require deference to state law.[5]

---

[1]See, e.g., Analytical Engineering, Inc. v. Baldwin Filters, Inc., 425 F.3d 443, 449 (7th Cir. 2005) ("Rule 70 gives the district court a discrete and limited power to deal with parties who thwart final judgments by refusing to comply with orders to perform specific acts."); Westlake North Property Owners Ass'n v. City of Thousand Oaks, 915 F.2d 1301, 1304 (9th Cir. 1990) (party's attorneys cannot be sanctioned under Rule 70). Cf., McAlpin v. Lexington 76 Auto Truck Stop, Inc., 229 F.3d 491, 504 (6th Cir. 2000) (where judgment contained only one term of twenty-page settlement and otherwise dismissed case, court had no authority under Rule 70 to enforce terms of settlement not incorporated in judgment). But see Peterson v. Highland Music, Inc., 140 F.3d 1313, 1323 (9th Cir. 1998) (non-parties who aid parties in defying judgment are also subject to Rule 70; upholding contempt citation).

[2]See, e.g., Deegan v. Strategic Azimuth LLC, 768 F.Supp.2d 107, 115 n.1 (D.D.C. 2011) (noting applicability of Rule 64, not Rule 70, to prejudgment relief).

[3]See, e.g., Bergmann v. Michigan State Transportation Commission, 665 F.3d 681, 684 (6th Cir. 2011) (noting difference between Rules 69 and 70).

[4]See, e.g., Board of Com'rs of Stark County, OH v. Cape Stone Works, Inc., 206 F. Supp. 2d 100, 102 (D. Mass. 2002) (default judgment that contained award of money damages could be enforced under Rule 69(a); but where judgment made no reference to specific performance that complaint had sought, no such relief was available under Rule 70).

[5]See, e.g., Bergmann v. Michigan State Transportation Commission, 665 F.3d 681, 681 (6th Cir. 2011) (no deference to state law, unlike Rule 69).

RULE 70(b)—VESTING TITLE

CORE CONCEPT

Rule 70(b) provides that if property to be transferred pursuant to judgment is located within the district where the court sits, the court may simply enter judgment transferring title, without going through the process of appointing a person to do the act.

Property Within the District

If a party has failed to obey a court order pertaining to real or personal property physically located within the district in which the court sits, the court may order title transferred directly from the disobedient party to the prevailing party.

Property Outside the District

If the real or personal property is not physically located within the district in which the court sits, the court must appoint a person to convey the property. The act performed by the appointed party has the full effect as it if it were executed by the disobedient party.

Timing

Rule 70 applies to the enforcement of court orders after the entry of judgment and after the time for performing the ordered action has elapsed.[6]

Content of Motion

In a written motion, the movant should allege with specificity the disobedient party's noncompliance, as well as the relief sought to remedy noncompliance.

RULE 70(c)—OBTAINING A WRIT OF ATTACHMENT OR SEQUESTRATION

CORE CONCEPT

Rule 70(c) provides that a party entitled to performance of an act may obtain a writ of sequestration or attachment to ensure performance.

Alternative Enforcement Remedies

The court may enforce a judgment by requiring a party to convey property or perform a specific act through the following remedies.

Upon proper motion to the clerk of court, a prevailing party may obtain a writ of attachment or sequestration authorizing seizure of the disobedient party's property or money until that party complies with a judgment.

Costs Against Disobedient Party

A court may tax against the disobedient party the costs of

---

[6]*See, e.g., Barmat, Inc. v. U.S.,* 159 F.R.D. 578, 582 (N.D. Ga. 1994) (Rule 70 "is operative only after entry of judgment").

transferring the property or performing the specific act.

RULE 70(d)—OBTAINING A WRIT OF EXECUTION OR ASSISTANCE

CORE CONCEPT

Rule 70(d) provides that a party who has obtained a judgment or order for possession of property may apply for a write of execution or assistance. Upon proper application, it is the duty of the clerk to issue such a writ.

Upon a proper motion to the clerk of court, a party may obtain a writ of assistance to enforce the delivery of property to the person entitled to the property under a judgment against a party who refuses to surrender possession.

RULE 70(e)—HOLDING IN CONTEMPT

CORE CONCEPT

Rule 70(e) provides that in addition to other remedies available under Rule 70, the court has authority to hold disobedient parties in contempt.[7]

Additional Research References

Wright & Miller, *Federal Practice and Procedure* §§ 3021 to 3030
C.J.S., Assistance, Writ of § 3, § 4; Contempt § 12; Federal Civil Procedure §§ 1254 to 1260 et seq.
West's Key Number Digest, Assistance, Writ of ☞2; Contempt ☞20; Federal Civil Procedure ☞2691, ☞2695

---

[7] *See, e.g., McMahan & Co. v. Po Folks, Inc.*, 206 F.3d 627, 634 (6th Cir. 2000) ("[U]nder Fed.R.Civ.P. 70, a party may be held in civil contempt for violating a garnishment order.").

RULE 71
ENFORCING RELIEF FOR OR
AGAINST A NONPARTY

When an order grants relief for a nonparty or may be enforced against a nonparty, the procedure for enforcing the order is the same as for a party.
[Amended effective August 1, 1987; April 30, 2007, effective December 1, 2007.]

AUTHORS' COMMENTARY ON RULE 71

PURPOSE AND SCOPE

Rule 71 provides for the enforcement of a court order by any person (including a non-party) in whose favor an order has been entered. Additionally, Rule 71 provides for the enforcement of a court order against a non-party when such enforcement is otherwise lawful.

APPLICATIONS

In Favor of a Non-party

A court order may be enforced by a non-party when that person shares an identity of interest with a prevailing party or is an intended beneficiary of the court order with the right to enforce it.[1] Thus, an assignee of a party who prevailed in a dispute concerning the title of property is entitled under Rule 71 to enforce a judgment in the same manner as the assignor.[2]

Against a Non-party

A court order may be enforced against a non-party when that person's interests are so closely related to a losing party's

---

[1]*See, e.g., Brennan v. Nassau County*, 352 F.3d 60, 65 (2d Cir. 2003) (suggesting that motion to compel may be suitable means of employing Rule 71; but also noting that non-parties must be able to meet requirements of standing); *Beckett v. Air Line Pilots Ass'n*, 995 F.2d 280, 287–88 (D.C. Cir. 1993) (Rule 71 permits intended beneficiaries of consent decree to sue to enforce decree; incidental third-party beneficiaries do not have such standing). *See also, Washington Hosp. v. White*, 889 F.2d 1294, 1299 (3d Cir. 1989) (third-party beneficiary has standing under Rule 71 to enforce court-ordered stipulation of dismissal).

[2]*See, e.g., Peterson v. Highland Music, Inc.*, 140 F.3d 1313 (9th Cir. 1998) (citing rule 71 as authority to hold non-parties in contempt).

interests that enforcement against that non-party is not unfair.[3] When enforcing a judgment against non-parties, Rule 71 is explicitly restricted to circumstances where enforcement does not violate due process or is otherwise lawful.[4]

Additional Research References

Wright & Miller, *Federal Practice and Procedure* §§ 3031 to 3040
C.J.S., Federal Civil Procedure § 1107
West's Key Number Digest, Federal Civil Procedure ⟜2394

---

[3]*See, e.g., Irwin v. Mascott*, 370 F.3d 924, 931–32 (9th Cir. 2004) (Rule 71 permits use of contempt power of court to enforce order against non-party who has notice of injunction).

[4]*See, e.g., LiButti v. U.S.*, 178 F.3d 114 (2d Cir. 1999) (enforcement of a judgment against a person who is a successor in interest to a party requires that the court first obtain personal jurisdiction over the successor in interest).

IX. SPECIAL PROCEEDINGS

RULE 71.1
CONDEMNING REAL OR PERSONAL PROPERTY

(a) Applicability of Other Rules. These rules govern proceedings to condemn real and personal property by eminent domain, except as this rule provides otherwise.

(b) Joinder of Properties. The plaintiff may join separate pieces of property in a single action, no matter whether they are owned by the same persons or sought for the same use.

(c) Complaint.

   (1) *Caption.* The complaint must contain a caption as provided in Rule 10(a). The plaintiff must, however, name as defendants both the property—designated generally by kind, quantity, and location—and at least one owner of some part of or interest in the property.

   (2) *Contents.* The complaint must contain a short and plain statement of the following:

     (A) the authority for the taking;

     (B) the uses for which the property is to be taken;

     (C) a description sufficient to identify the property;

     (D) the interests to be acquired; and

     (E) for each piece of property, a designation of each defendant who has been joined as an owner or owner of an interest in it.

   (3) *Parties.* When the action commences, the plaintiff need join as defendants only those persons who have or claim an interest in the property and whose names are then known. But before any hearing on compensation, the plaintiff must add as defendants all those persons who have or claim an interest and whose names have become known or can be found by a reasonably diligent

search of the records, considering both the property's character and value and the interests to be acquired. All others may be made defendants under the designation "Unknown Owners."

(4) *Procedure.* Notice must be served on all defendants as provided in Rule 71.1(d), whether they were named as defendants when the action commenced or were added later. A defendant may answer as provided in Rule 71.1(e). The court, meanwhile, may order any distribution of a deposit that the facts warrant.

(5) *Filing; Additional Copies.* In addition to filing the complaint, the plaintiff must give the clerk at least one copy for the defendants' use and additional copies at the request of the clerk or a defendant.

(d) Process.

(1) *Delivering Notice to the Clerk.* On filing a complaint, the plaintiff must promptly deliver to the clerk joint or several notices directed to the named defendants. When adding defendants, the plaintiff must deliver to the clerk additional notices directed to the new defendants.

(2) *Contents of the Notice.*

(A) *Main Contents.* Each notice must name the court, the title of the action, and the defendant to whom it is directed. It must describe the property sufficiently to identify it, but need not describe any property other than that to be taken from the named defendant. The notice must also state:

(i)   that the action is to condemn property;

(ii)   the interest to be taken;

(iii) the authority for the taking;

(iv)   the uses for which the property is to be taken;

(v)   that the defendant may serve an answer on the plaintiff's attorney within 21 days after being served with the notice;

(vi)   that the failure to so serve an answer constitutes consent to the taking and to the court's authority to proceed with the action and fix the compensation; and

(vii) that a defendant who does not serve an answer may file a notice of appearance.

(B) *Conclusion.* The notice must conclude with the name, telephone number, and e-mail address of the plaintiff's attorney and an address within the district in which the action is brought where the attorney may be served.

(3) *Serving the Notice.*

(A) *Personal Service.* When a defendant whose address is known resides within the United States or a territory subject to the administrative or judicial jurisdiction of the United States, personal service of the notice (without a copy of the complaint) must be made in accordance with Rule 4.

(B) *Service by Publication.*

(i) A defendant may be served by publication only when the plaintiff's attorney files a certificate stating that the attorney believes the defendant cannot be personally served, because after diligent inquiry within the state where the complaint is filed, the defendant's place of residence is still unknown or, if known, that it is beyond the territorial limits of personal service. Service is then made by publishing the notice—once a week for at least three successive weeks—in a newspaper published in the county where the property is located or, if there is no such newspaper, in a newspaper with general circulation where the property is located. Before the last publication, a copy of the notice must also be mailed to every defendant who cannot be personally served but whose place of residence is then known. Unknown owners may be served by publication in the same manner by a notice addressed to "Unknown Owners."

(ii) Service by publication is complete on the

date of the last publication. The plaintiff's attorney must prove publication and mailing by a certificate, attach a printed copy of the published notice, and mark on the copy the newspaper's name and the dates of publication.

(4) *Effect of Delivery and Service.* Delivering the notice to the clerk and serving it have the same effect as serving a summons under Rule 4.

(5) *Proof of Service; Amending the Proof or Notice.* Rule 4(l) governs proof of service. The court may permit the proof or the notice to be amended.

(e) Appearance or Answer.

(1) *Notice of Appearance.* A defendant that has no objection or defense to the taking of its property may serve a notice of appearance designating the property in which it claims an interest. The defendant must then be given notice of all later proceedings affecting the defendant.

(2) *Answer.* A defendant that has an objection or defense to the taking must serve an answer within 21 days after being served with the notice. The answer must:

    (A) identify the property in which the defendant claims an interest;

    (B) state the nature and extent of the interest; and

    (C) state all the defendant's objections and defenses to the taking.

(3) *Waiver of Other Objections and Defenses; Evidence on Compensation.* A defendant waives all objections and defenses not stated in its answer. No other pleading or motion asserting an additional objection or defense is allowed. But at the trial on compensation, a defendant—whether or not it has previously appeared or answered— may present evidence on the amount of compensation to be paid and may share in the award.

(f) Amending Pleadings. Without leave of court, the plaintiff may—as often as it wants—amend the complaint at any time before the trial on compensation. But no amendment may be made if it would result in a dismissal inconsistent with Rule 71.1(i)(1) or (2). The plaintiff need not serve a copy of an amendment, but must serve notice of the filing, as provided in Rule 5(b), on every affected party who has appeared and, as provided in Rule 71.1(d), on every affected party who has not appeared. In addition, the plaintiff must give the clerk at least one copy of each amendment for the defendants' use, and additional copies at the request of the clerk or a defendant. A defendant may appear or answer in the time and manner and with the same effect as provided in Rule 71.1(e).

(g) Substituting Parties. If a defendant dies, becomes incompetent, or transfers an interest after being joined, the court may, on motion and notice of hearing, order that the proper party be substituted. Service of the motion and notice on a nonparty must be made as provided in Rule 71.1(d)(3).

(h) Trial of the Issues.

(1) *Issues Other Than Compensation; Compensation.* In an action involving eminent domain under federal law, the court tries all issues, including compensation, except when compensation must be determined:

(A) by any tribunal specially constituted by a federal statute to determine compensation; or

(B) if there is no such tribunal, by a jury when a party demands one within the time to answer or within any additional time the court sets, unless the court appoints a commission.

(2) *Appointing a Commission; Commission's Powers and Report.*

(A) *Reasons for Appointing.* If a party has demanded a jury, the court may instead appoint a three-person commission to determine compensation because of the character, location, or quantity of the property to be condemned or for other just reasons.

(B) *Alternate Commissioners.* The court may appoint up to two additional persons to serve as alternate commissioners to hear the case and replace commissioners who, before a decision is filed, the court finds unable or disqualified to perform their duties. Once the commission renders its final decision, the court must discharge any alternate who has not replaced a commissioner.

(C) *Examining the Prospective Commissioners.* Before making its appointments, the court must advise the parties of the identity and qualifications of each prospective commissioner and alternate, and may permit the parties to examine them. The parties may not suggest appointees, but for good cause may object to a prospective commissioner or alternate.

(D) *Commission's Powers and Report.* A commission has the powers of a master under Rule 53(c). Its action and report are determined by a majority. Rule 53(d), (e), and (f) apply to its action and report.

(i) Dismissal of the Action or a Defendant.

(1) *Dismissing the Action.*

(A) *By the Plaintiff.* If no compensation hearing on a piece of property has begun, and if the plaintiff has not acquired title or a lesser interest or taken possession, the plaintiff may, without a court order, dismiss the action as to that property by filing a notice of dismissal briefly describing the property.

(B) *By Stipulation.* Before a judgment is entered vesting the plaintiff with title or a lesser interest in or possession of property, the plaintiff and affected defendants may, without a court order, dismiss the action in whole or in part by filing a stipulation of dismissal. And if the parties so stipulate, the court may vacate a judgment already entered.

(C) *By Court Order.* At any time before compensation has been determined and paid, the court may, after a motion and hearing, dismiss the action as to a piece of property. But if the plaintiff has already taken title, a lesser interest, or possession as to any part of it, the court must award compensation for the title, lesser interest, or possession taken.

(2) *Dismissing a Defendant.* The court may at any time dismiss a defendant who was unnecessarily or improperly joined.

(3) *Effect.* A dismissal is without prejudice unless otherwise stated in the notice, stipulation, or court order.

(j) Deposit and Its Distribution.

(1) *Deposit.* The plaintiff must deposit with the court any money required by law as a condition to the exercise of eminent domain and may make a deposit when allowed by statute.

(2) *Distribution; Adjusting Distribution.* After a deposit, the court and attorneys must expedite the proceedings so as to distribute the deposit and to determine and pay compensation. If the compensation finally awarded to a defendant exceeds the amount distributed to that defendant, the court must enter judgment against the plaintiff for the deficiency. If the compensation awarded to a defendant is less than the amount distributed to that defendant, the court must enter judgment against that defendant for the overpayment.

(k) Condemnation Under a State's Power of Eminent Domain. This rule governs an action involving eminent domain under state law. But if state law provides for trying an issue by jury—or for trying the issue of compensation by jury or commission or both—that law governs.

(l) Costs. Costs are not subject to Rule 54(d).

[Adopted April 30, 1951, effective August 1, 1951; amended January 21, 1963, effective July 1, 1963; April 29, 1985, effective August 1, 1985; March 2, 1987, effective August 1, 1987; April 25, 1988, effective August 1, 1988; amended by Pub.L. 100-690, Title VII, § 7050, November 18, 1988, 102 Stat. 4401 (although amendment by Pub.L. 100-690 could not be executed due to prior amendment by Court order which made the same change effective August 1, 1988); amended April 22, 1993, effective December 1, 1993; March 27, 2003, effective December 1, 2003; April 30, 2007, effective December 1, 2007; March 26, 2009, effective December 1, 2009.]

AUTHORS' COMMENTARY ON RULE 71.1

——— PURPOSE AND SCOPE ———

Rule 71.1 provides a uniform set of rules for the condemnation of real and personal property under the federal and state powers of eminent domain.

RULE 71.1(a)—APPLICABILITY OF OTHER RULES

CORE CONCEPT

Rule 71.1(a) directs that, unless specifically otherwise provided in Rule 71.1, the General Civil Rules govern the procedure for the condemnation of real and personal property under the power of eminent domain.

APPLICATIONS

Condemnation of Personal Property

Rule 71.1 applies to the condemnation of personal property as an appurtenance to real property or as the sole object of the proceeding.[1]

Inverse Condemnation Proceedings

Rule 71.1 does not apply to inverse condemnation proceedings. An inverse condemnation "is a cause of action by which a landowner recovers just compensation from the government for a taking of his or her property when condemnation proceedings have not been instituted."[2] An important difference between an inverse condemnation and a direct condemnation governed by Rule 71.1 is that there is no right to a jury trial on any issue—not even compensation—in an inverse condemnation proceeding.[3]

Supplementary Condemnation Statutes

Rule 71.1 does not affect supplementary condemnation statutes, such as the Declaration of Taking Act,[4] which permit the Federal Government to take private property for public use under the power of eminent domain.

Uniformity of Procedure

Rule 71.1 makes the procedure for condemnation of prop-

---

[1] *See,* 42 U.S.C.A. §§ 1805, 1811, 1813 (Atomic Energy Act); 50 U.S.C.A. § 79 (nitrates); 50 U.S.C.A. §§ 161 to 166 (helium gas).

[2] *KLK, Inc. v. U.S. Dept. of Interior,* 35 F.3d 454, 455 n. 1 (9th Cir. 1994) (Rule 71.1 applicable only to

"traditional" condemnation, not inverse condemnation).

[3] *See, e.g., U.S. v. 191.07 Acres of Land,* 482 F.3d 1132, 1136 (9th Cir. 2007) (in inverse proceeding, compensation is determined by bench trial).

[4] 40 U.S.C.A. §§ 248a to 258e.

erty under all statutes uniform.

Choice of Law

Federal condemnation is strictly governed by federal law and precedent. State law only defines the nature of the real or personal property interest, such as the meaning of property, defining what is taken, or determining the ownership of land.

Condemnation Under State Law

A district court may entertain condemnation proceedings under state law, as provided by Rule 71.1(k).

Jurisdiction and Venue

The district courts have original jurisdiction over proceedings to condemn real property for the use of the United States, its agencies, or departments.[5] Venue will be in the district court of the district in which the real property is located or, if located in different districts in the same state, in any such districts.[6]

Rule 71.1 and the Other Rules

In cases where Rule 71.1 does not provide a procedure concerning litigation, the court will apply other applicable Rules, such as the discovery Rules.[7]

RULE 71.1(b)—JOINDER OF PROPERTIES

CORE CONCEPT

Rule 71.1(b) permits condemnation of separate properties, including properties belonging to different owners, or properties for different public uses in the same court action.[8] Only in exceptional circumstances is the court required to conduct separate trials. To eliminate jury confusion over the relative value of properties, the court may separate the evidence concerning the damages sustained by each owner.

RULE 71.1(c)—COMPLAINT

CORE CONCEPT

The requirements for a complaint under Rule 71.1(c) are different from those in an ordinary civil action. In the complaint's caption, Rule 71.1(c) requires the plaintiff to name as defendants both the property and at least one of the owners. Rule 71.1(c) does not require the plaintiff to serve a summons and a complaint on the defendants; rather the clerk of court arranges for

---

[5] 28 U.S.C.A. § 1358.

[6] 28 U.S.C.A. § 1403.

[7] *See also East Tennessee Natural Gas Co. v. Sage*, 361 F.3d 808, 828–29 (4th Cir. 2004) (approving use of Rule 65 to obtain preliminary injunction enabling early occupation of land).

[8] *See, e.g., McLaughlin v. Mississippi Power Co.*, 376 F.3d 344 (5th Cir.2004) (also noting that joinder of properties under Rule 71.1 is "much broader" than joinder of parties under Rules 19 and 20 and joinder of claims under Rule 18).

notice to all defendants as provided in Rule 71.1(d). However, prior to a hearing on compensation, the plaintiff must join all defendants who can be ascertained from a reasonably diligent search of the records.

APPLICATIONS

Caption

The complaint's caption must include the name of the court, the title of the action, the docket number, and the name of the type of pleading being presented.[9] The caption must name as defendants both the property and at least one of the owners. The plaintiff will name the property as the defendant by stating the kind, quantity, and location of the property.

Contents of Complaint

The complaint must contain a short and plain statement of:
(1) the authority for the taking;
(2) the use for which the property is to be taken;[10]
(3) a description of the property sufficient for identification;[11]
(4) the interests to be acquired; and
(5) for each separate piece of property, the owners who have been joined as defendants or who have some interest.

Filing of Complaint and Notice

The plaintiff must file the complaint with the clerk and provide the clerk with at least one copy for the defendants. Upon the request of the clerk or the defendants, the plaintiff must furnish additional copies. This practice differs from the normal practice under Rule 4, which requires the plaintiff to serve a summons and a copy of the complaint on the defendants.

Joining Parties at Commencement

At the commencement of an action, the condemnor must join as defendants all persons or entities of title record having or claiming an interest in the property whose names are then known. All other persons unascertained or unknown shall be made parties as defendants by description if their names are unknown.

Joining of Interested Parties Prior to Hearing

Prior to a hearing involving compensation, the condemnor must add as defendants all persons who have an interest whose

---

[9]*See* Official Form 29.

[10]*See, e.g., City of Arlington, Tex. v. Golddust Twins Realty Corp.*, 41 F.3d 960, 964 (5th Cir. 1994) (Rule 71.1(c) requires condemning authority to state purpose for which condemnation is sought).

[11]*See, e.g., Southern Natural Gas Co. v. Land, Cullman County*, 197 F.3d 1368, 1375 (11th Cir. 1999) (a legal description and plat map showing location of pipeline and related easements "easily" satisfies Rule 71A(c)(2)).

identities can be ascertained by a reasonably diligent search of the records,[12] and also those whose names have been learned. "Reasonably diligent" search means the type of search a title searcher would undertake, but the extent of the search required will depend upon the character and value of the property involved and the interests to be acquired. Property owners joined after the commencement of the action must be served with notice by the clerk and allowed to answer.

Failure to Join a Party

There are no indispensable parties in a condemnation action. Therefore, the failure to join a party will not defeat the condemnor's title to the land because a condemnation action is an action *in rem*.[13] If the condemnor fails to join a party, the omitted party may have the right to sue for compensation in the Claims Court after the condemnation is completed.[14]

RULE 71.1(d)—PROCESS

CORE CONCEPT

Rule 71.1(d) directs that the clerk will deliver a notice of the complaint to a marshal or specially appointed person who will make personal service on the defendants.

APPLICATIONS

Content of Notice

Each notice must state:

(1)   the court;

(2)   the title of the action;

(3)   the name of the defendant to whom it is directed;

(4)   the nature of the action (condemning property);

(5)   a description of the property sufficient for its identification;

(6)   the interest to be taken;

(7)   the authority for the taking;

(8)   the uses for which the property is being taken;

(9)   the time for answering the complaint (the defendant may serve an answer upon the plaintiff's attorney within twenty-one days after the service of the notice);

---

[12]*See, e.g., Cadorette v. U.S.*, 988 F.2d 215, 224 (1st Cir. 1993) (Rule 71A(c) requires government to make an affirmative search for "lost" heirs).

[13]*Fulcher v. U.S.*, 632 F.2d 278, 282 (4th Cir. 1980); ("Persons not identified . . . can be impleaded as unknown.").

[14]*See, e.g., U.S. v. 194.08 Acres of Land*, 135 F.3d 1025, 1035 n. 8 (5th Cir. 1998) (failure to join party or give required notice does not invalidate taking; such failure only preserves right of unjoined interested party to challenge taking). *Cadorette v. U.S.*, 988 F.2d 215, 225 (1st Cir. 1993) (person not joined may seek compensation in Claims Court through the device of a takings claim).

(10) the penalty for failing to answer (a consent to the taking, permitting the court to proceed to hear the action and fix compensation); and

(11) that any defendant who chooses not to file an answer may nevertheless file a notice of appearance.

The notice must, finally, include the name, telephone number, and e-mail address of the plaintiff's attorney as well as an address within the district in which the suit is brought where that attorney may be served.

Preparation of Notice

The plaintiff may prepare joint or separate notices. However, one notice must be delivered to each named defendant and need contain a description of only that property taken from the particular defendant to whom it is directed.

Filing of Notice

The plaintiff's attorney will prepare a notice and deliver it to the clerk with the complaint. Subsequently, the clerk will file and enter the complaint in the record and deliver a notice of the complaint (but not a copy of the complaint itself) to the marshal or specially-appointed person for service.

Persons Requiring Notice

At the commencement of the case, the clerk need only provide notice to persons whose names are in the complaint. Property owners joined after the filing of the complaint must be served with notice and allowed to answer.

Service

Personal service of the notice (but without copies of the complaint) shall be made in accordance with Rule 4 upon each defendant who resides within the United States or its territories or insular possessions and whose residence is known.

Service By Publication

(1) *Persons Served by Publication:* A plaintiff may make service by publication on three types of defendants:[15]

(a) owners who do not reside in the United States, its territories, or insular possessions, and who, therefore, are beyond the territorial limits of personal service;

(b) owners within the state in which the complaint is filed whose place of residence is unknown after a diligent search of the records; and

(c) unknown owners.

(2) *Publication:* The plaintiff must publish the notice in a newspaper in the county where the land is located. When no newspaper exists in the county where the land is located, the

---

[15]*See, e.g., U.S. v. 499.472 Acres of Land More or Less in Brazoria County, Tex.,* 701 F.2d 545, 551 (5th Cir. 1983) (publication service permissible only in the explicit circumstances described in Rule 71.1(d)).

plaintiff must publish the notice in a newspaper having a circulation in the area where the land is located. The plaintiff must publish the notice once a week for at least three successive weeks.

(3) *Proof of Publication:* When a plaintiff wishes to make proof of service by publication, the plaintiff's attorney must file with the court a certificate stating that the defendant cannot be served personally because the defendant's residence is beyond the personal service limits or after diligent inquiry defendant's residence is unknown. The plaintiff's attorney must attach to the certificate a printed copy of the published notice marked with the name of the newspaper and the dates of publication.

(4) *Defendants Who Cannot Be Served But Residence Known:* A defendant who cannot be personally served but whose place of residence is known must be mailed a copy of the notice prior to the date of the last publication. Service is complete on the date of the last publication.

RULE 71.1(e)—APPEARANCE OR ANSWER

CORE CONCEPT

A defendant may respond to a condemnation complaint in two ways. If the defendant intends to either contest the taking or make objections to the complaint, the defendant must file an answer. Alternatively, if the defendant has no defenses or objections to the taking, the defendant simply serves a notice of appearance designating the property in which the defendant has an interest. Filing a notice of appearance requires that the defendant be given notice of all subsequent proceedings that affect that defendant's interest.[16] However, regardless of whether the defendant files an answer or an appearance, a defendant may present evidence at the hearing on compensation and share in the award.[17]

APPLICATIONS

Answer

The answer is the only document in which defenses or objections may be asserted.[18] Unlike most answers to complaints in ordinary civil actions, the defendant must make specific allegations. In the answer the defendant must identify the property, the defendant's interest in the property, and the de-

---

[16]*Cf., U.S. v. 14.02 Acres of Land,* 547 F.3d 943, 954 (9th Cir. 2008) (Rule 71.1(e) overrides requirement of Rule 5 that all post-complaint filings be served on all parties).

[17]*See, e.g., Bank One Texas v. U.S.,* 157 F.3d 397 (5th Cir. 1998).

[18]*See, e.g., Washington Metropolitan Area Transit Authority v. Precision Small Engines,* 227 F.3d 224, 228 n. 2 (4th Cir. 2000) (except for amount of compensation, defenses or objections not raised in answer are waived; "Simply put, no other pleading besides the answer is contemplated.").

fenses to the taking. After filing an answer, the defendant is entitled to receive notice of all of the proceedings affecting the defendant.

Counterclaims and Crossclaims

An answer may not contain a counterclaim or crossclaim.[19] A counterclaim must be brought in a separate action in the district court or the Court of Claims.

Timing of Answer

Within 21 days of service of the notice, the defendant must answer the complaint. This response period may be enlarged by motion, as provided by Rule 6(b).

Appearance

When the defendant has no defenses or objections to the taking or to the complaint, the defendant may serve a notice of appearance. The notice of appearance should designate the property in which the defendant claims an interest. When a defendant has filed an appearance, the defendant is entitled to receive notice of all of the proceedings affecting the defendant.[20]

RULE 71.1(f)—AMENDING PLEADINGS

CORE CONCEPT

Before the trial on the issue of just compensation, a plaintiff may amend the complaint multiple times without leave of court. However, except as provided by Rule 71.1(i), the plaintiff may not amend the complaint to remove the names of defendants or claims. Within 20 days of the notice of each amended complaint, the defendant is entitled to file one amended answer as of right.

APPLICATIONS

Procedure for Amending Complaint

The plaintiff may amend the complaint by filing with the clerk the amended pleading and by serving notice of the amended pleading on each defendant. The plaintiff need not serve a copy of the amended pleading itself on defendants, a practice that differs from normal civil actions. Instead, if a defendant or the clerk requests additional copies of the amended complaint, the plaintiff must provide the clerk with additional copies.

Service to Persons Who Have Not Entered an Appearance

The plaintiff should serve notice of an amended complaint

---

[19]*See, e.g., U.S. v. Certain Land Situated in City of Detroit*, 361 F.3d 305, 308 (6th Cir. 2004) ("A district court lacks jurisdiction to hear counterclaims against the United States in condemnation cases.").

[20]*See, e.g., Columbia Gas Transmission, LLC v. Crawford*, 746 F.Supp.2d 905, 909–10 (N.D. Ohio 2010) (but defendant retains right to offer evidence on compensation).

on persons who have not entered an appearance.[21]

RULE 71.1(g)—SUBSTITUTING PARTIES

CORE CONCEPT

Upon proper motion and notice of hearing, the court may order the substitution of parties when a defendant dies or becomes incompetent, or transfers an interest after the defendant's joinder. If a new party is substituted, the plaintiff must serve a copy of the motion and notice of hearing on the new party, as provided by Rule 71.1(d). Rule 25, governing substitution of parties in most civil actions, does not apply to condemnation actions.

RULE 71.1(h)—TRIAL OF THE ISSUES

CORE CONCEPT

All issues other than the issue of compensation will be decided by the court.[22] The issue of compensation will be decided by either a special tribunal, a commission, a jury, or the court, in condemnation actions instituted by the federal or state government under powers of eminent domain. Federal law may require the issue of compensation to be decided by a tribunal specially constituted by Congress. When any party demands a trial by jury, the court will decide whether to conduct a jury trial or to appoint a commission to decide the issue of compensation.

NOTE: If a commission is appointed to decide the issue of compensation, the commission must issue a report. Within 10 days after service of the commission report, parties must make and serve on the other parties and the court their objections to the report.

APPLICATIONS

Trial by Jury

When any party demands a trial by jury, the court may conduct a jury trial or may appoint a commission to decide the issue of compensation. However, there is no constitutional right to a trial by jury in condemnation cases,[23] and the jury in such

---

[21]*See*, Rule 71.1(d).

[22]*See, e.g., U.S. v. 480.00 Acres of Land*, 557 F.3d 1297, 1312 (11th Cir. 2009) ("A district judge has a much broader role in a condemnation proceeding than he does in a conventional jury trial, and except for the single issue of the amount of just compensation, the trial judge decides all issues, legal and factual."). *See also United States v. 33.92356 Acres of Land*, 585 F.3d 1, 10 (1st Cir. 2009) (unity of use is issue for court to decide, but absent

timely objection court may submit issue to advisory jury).

[23]*U.S. v. Reynolds*, 397 U.S. 14, 18, 90 S. Ct. 803, 806, 25 L. Ed. 2d 12 (1970). ("[I]t has long been settled that there is no constitutional right to a jury in eminent domain cases."). *See, e.g., U.S. v. Certain Land Situated in the City of Detroit, Wayne County*, 450 F.3d 205 (6th Cir. 2006) (no constitutional right to trial by jury in eminent domain proceedings; instead, Rule 71.1(h) authorizes, but does not re-

cases may decide only the issue of compensation.[24]

(1) *Time for Demand:* Within the time allowed for the answer to the condemnation complaint (20 days of service of the notice of the complaint, unless an enlargement of time has extended the period) or a further time fixed by the court, any party may demand a trial by jury.

(2) *Procedure for Trial by Jury:* The trial of a condemnation action is similar to any other civil proceeding involving a trial by jury. However, the judge will determine all issues other than the amount of compensation.[25]

Trial by Commission

(1) *Appointment of Commission:* When a party demands a trial by jury, the court has discretion to appoint a commission to decide the issue of compensation rather than conducting a trial by jury.[26] Although the court is not required to make findings of fact to support its determination to appoint a commission, for purposes of appellate review the court will often state in writing its reasons for appointing a commission.

(a) *Conditions for Reference to Commission:* Courts have appointed commissions for such reasons as: local preference or habit, the preference of the Justice Department, the distance of the property from the courthouse, the complexity of the issues, the character of the land, the nature of the interest or the number of tracts taken, the need for numerous jury trials, the desirability of uniform awards, or to prevent discrimination.

(2) *Number of Commissioners:* A commission is generally composed of three persons. The court may appoint two alternate commissioners to sit at the hearing with the other

---

quire, the district court to convene a jury to decide the single issue of just compensation; other issues, such as whether certain property was within the original scope of a project, are to be decided by the judge). *See also Southern Natural Gas Co. v. Land, Cullman County,* 197 F.3d 1368, 1373 (11th Cir. 1999) (condemnation action pursuant to Natural Gas Act, 15 U.S.C. §§ 717 et seq.; notwithstanding provision in Natural Gas Act providing that condemnation procedure shall conform as closely as possible to state law, Rule 71.1(h) permits district court to appoint commission in place of jury; held, Rule 71.1(h) supercedes applicable provisions of Natural Gas Act).

[24]*See, e.g., U.S. v. Certain Land Situated in the City of Detroit, Wayne County,* 450 F.3d 205, 208 (6th Cir. 2006) (jury decides only narrow issue of compensation). *See also U.S. v.*

191.07 Acres of Land, 482 F.3d 1132, 1136 (9th Cir. 2007) (in inverse proceeding compensation is determined by bench trial).

[25]*See, e.g., U.S. v. 4.0 Acres of Land,* 175 F.3d 1133 (9th Cir. 1999) (jury's sole function is to determine amount of compensation).

[26]*But cf., U.S. v. 320.0 Acres of Land, More or Less in Monroe County, State of Fla.,* 605 F.2d 762, 828 (5th Cir. 1979) (acknowledging some contrary authority but holding that "a commission is to be used only for exceptional cases" such as large tracts of land held by many small landowners or tracts too distant for jury to view); *Questar Southern Trails Pipeline Co. v. 4.26 Acres of Land,* 194 F. Supp. 2d 1192, 1193 (D.N.M. 2002) (in 10th Circuit "jury trial is . . . still the standard").

commissioners.

(3) *Appointment of Commissioners:* Usually, the court will appoint commissioners and alternate commissioners. Often, the court will appoint a lawyer or ex-judge as chair of the commission and one real estate person as a member. After appointing the commissioners, the court will advise the parties of the identity and qualifications of each prospective commissioner and alternate commissioner. The parties may examine the commissioners and may, for valid cause, object to the appointment of any commissioner.[27]

(4) *Reformation and Revocation of Commission:* When the court believes the judgment of the commission has been affected by bias, the court may reform the commission by replacing some or all of the commissioners.[28] When justice so requires, such as instances of undue delay, the court may vacate the reference to the commission.

(5) *Procedure for Trial by Commission:*

(a) *Powers:* The commission will only try the issue of compensation; all other issues will be decided by the court. The commission has the same powers as a master in a non-jury trial. Proceedings before the commission are governed by Rule 53(c). The commission may regulate its proceedings, require the production of all documents, rule on the admissibility of evidence, call and examine witnesses, and permit the witnesses to be examined by the parties. These powers will be regulated indirectly by the court through its instructions to the commission in the order of reference.

(b) *Instructions:* In its order of reference, the trial judge will instruct the commissioners as to such issues as: the qualifications of expert witnesses, the weight to be given to other opinions of evidence, competent evidence of value, the best evidence of value, the manner of the hearing and the method of conducting it, the right to view the property, the limited purpose of viewing, and the kind of evidence which is inadmissible and the manner of ruling on the admissibility of evidence.

(c) *Admission of Evidence:* Although the court will control the kind of evidence which is admissible, the commission will apply the Federal Rules of Evidence when ruling on the admissibility of the evidence.

(1) *View of Property:* When necessary or conducive to a

---

[27]*But cf., Guardian Pipeline, L.L.C. v. 950.80 Acres of Land,* 525 F.3d 554, 557–58 (7th Cir. 2008) (litigant who does not examine proposed commissioner at outset forgoes opportunity to make post-proceeding challenge to commissioner).

[28]*But cf., City of Stilwell, Okl. v. Ozarks Rural Elec. Co-op. Corp.,* 166 F.3d 1064, 1069 (10th Cir. 1999) (commissioners need not have "complete and absolute impartiality;" no error in appointment of either customer of cooperative's competitor (owned by city) or owner-members of cooperative, especially when virtually every resident in area used utility services of one or another of the parties).

proper determination of compensation and when not inconvenient or the cause of undue delay or expense, the commission may view the property.

(6) *Findings and Report of Commission:* A majority of the commissioners will decide the amount of compensation to award, and the commission will submit a report. The findings and the report of the commission will follow the provisions of Rule 53(e)(2). In its report, the commission must clearly show a factual basis for its finding, but need not make detailed findings. A suitable commission report will state what evidence and what measure of damages the commission accepted and why the commission reached its award.[29]

(7) *Objection to Commission Report:* Within 10 days after service of the commission's report, a party must make and file with the court and serve on all other parties objections to the report.[30] The party objecting to the report retains the burden of demonstrating that the report is erroneous.

(8) *Trial Court Review of Commission Report:* The trial court must adopt the report of the commission unless it finds the report to be clearly erroneous.[31] A trial court may find the report clearly erroneous when there was a substantial error in the proceedings, when the report is unsupported by substantial evidence, against the clear weight of the evidence,[32] or involves a misapplication of law. Courts have also found commission reports clearly erroneous when the award was grossly inadequate. When the trial court finds the report clearly erroneous, the court may examine the testimony and make its own judgment or it may recommit the matter to the commission with instructions.[33]

(9) *Commissioners' Compensation:* Commissioners will be compensated in reasonable relation to the services rendered (i.e., the bar association's minimum fee schedule). The commissioners' compensation will be charged to the condemnor and may be included in the damage award, not taxed as costs against the award.

(10) *Appellate Court Review of Commission or Court Decision:* An appellate court reviews the judgment of a trial

[29]See, *U.S. v. Merz*, 376 U.S. 192, 198, 84 S. Ct. 639, 643, 11 L. Ed. 2d 629 (1964) (conclusory findings are unacceptable; commissioners should explain reasoning, what evidence was used, etc.).

[30]See, Rule 53(e)(2).

[31]*U.S. v. Merz*, 376 U.S. 192, 198, 84 S. Ct. 639, 643, 11 L. Ed. 2d 629 (1964) (adopting "clearly erroneous" standard).

[32]*Georgia Power Co. v. 138.30 Acres of Land*, 596 F.2d 644 (5th Cir. 1979).

[33]See, e.g., *Southern Natural Gas Co. v. Land, Cullman County*, 197 F.3d 1368, 1375 (11th Cir. 1999) (district court has discretion to recommit matter to commission or to hear additional evidence itself).

court under a clearly erroneous standard.[34]

RULE 71.1(i)—DISMISSAL OF THE ACTION OR A DEFENDANT

CORE CONCEPT

The procedures for dismissal depend on the posture of the proceedings. Prior to a hearing or declaration of taking, the action may be dismissed as of right. Where the government files a declaration of taking, acquires an interest, acquires title, or takes possession of the property before the entry of judgment, neither the plaintiff nor the court may dismiss an action, except by stipulation of the parties.[35] After the entry of judgment the court has discretion to vacate the judgment upon the stipulation of the parties.

APPLICATIONS

Dismissal

(1) *As of Right:* Before a hearing on compensation has begun and before the plaintiff has filed a declaration of taking as provided by statute, acquired title, acquired an interest, or taken possession of the property, the plaintiff may dismiss the action by filing a notice of dismissal stating a brief description of the property.

(2) *By Stipulation:* Before the entry of a judgment vesting plaintiff with title, an interest, or possession of the property, the parties may stipulate to a dismissal in whole or in part without an order of the court. After judgment, the parties may stipulate to a dismissal and the court may vacate the judgment and revest title in the defendant.

(3) *By Court Order:* When the hearing on compensation has begun, but the plaintiff has not filed a declaration of taking, acquired title, acquired an interest, or taken possession, the court will decide whether to grant a voluntary dismissal.[36] However, when the hearing has begun and the plaintiff has filed a declaration of taking, acquired title, acquired an interest, or taken possession, the court must award just compensa-

---

[34]*See, e.g., U.S. v. 179.26 Acres of Land in Douglas County, Kansas*, 644 F.2d 367, 373 (10th Cir. 1981) (applying clearly erroneous standard).

[35]*Kirby Forest Industries, Inc. v. U.S.*, 467 U.S. 1, 12, n. 18, 104 S. Ct. 2187, 2195 n. 18, 81 L. Ed. 2d 1 (1984) (Rule 71.1(i)(1)(C) bars dismissal by court if government has acquired interest in property—court must first hold compensation hearing).

[36]*See, e.g., U.S. v. 4,970 Acres of Land*, 130 F.3d 712, 714–15 (5th Cir.

1997) (if jury has returned verdict but government has not yet engaged in specified acts, government may buy property by tendering the amount of the verdict or may move to dismiss condemnation action; if government sought dismissal of action, court then would have discretion to dismiss; "Condemnation is a means by which the sovereign may find out what any piece of property will cost.").

tion for the possession, title, or the interest taken, unless stipulated otherwise by the parties.[37]

Dismissal of Improperly and Unnecessarily Joined Parties

At any time, upon a motion or *sua sponte,* the court may dismiss a defendant who has no interest but has been unnecessarily or improperly joined.

Dismissal Without Prejudice

Unless stated in the order or the stipulation, a dismissal of a condemnation proceeding is without prejudice.

RULE 71.1(j)—DEPOSIT AND ITS DISTRIBUTION

CORE CONCEPT

Rule 71.1(j) describes the procedure for the deposit of money with the court when required or permitted by statute. State substantive law will determine the amount to be deposited in state eminent domain actions, while federal substantive law will determine the amount to be deposited in federal eminent domain actions.

APPLICATIONS

The Declaration of Taking Act

The Declaration of Taking Act supplements the procedure under Rule 71.1(j), relating to the deposit and distribution in eminent domain cases. Under the Act, upon the filing of a declaration of taking and a deposit of the estimated compensation with the court, title immediately vests in the federal government.

(1) *Time for Filing:* A declaration of taking may be brought at the commencement of the condemnation action and at any time before a judgment.

(2) *Certification:* The chief of the government department or bureau acquiring the land will certify that the land is within the value prescribed by Congress.

(3) *Surrender of Possession; Encumbrances:* Upon the filing of a declaration of taking, the court will fix the time and the terms upon which the parties in possession will surrender possession of the property to the plaintiff. The court may also make orders concerning encumbrances, liens, rents, taxes, assessments, insurance, etc.

(4) *Amount of Award:* The judgment will include 6 percent interest from the date of the taking to the date of the award. However, no interest will be ordered on money paid into the court. When the court or the jury awards an amount greater

---

[37]*See, e.g., Id. at* 715.

than the deposit, the court will enter judgment against the plaintiff and in favor of the defendant for the difference plus 6 percent interest.[38] When the court or the jury awards an amount less than the deposit, the court will enter judgment against the defendant and in favor of the plaintiff for the amount of overpayment. When the deposit exceeds the award the plaintiff will obtain the excess deposit from the clerk.[39]

(5) *Deposit and Distribution:* At the time of the taking and the deposit into the court, the court may order distribution of the deposit to the known defendants.[40]

(6) *Appellate Review:* A transfer of title is not a final appealable judgment until a final judgment on compensation has been entered.[41]

RULE 71.1(k)—CONDEMNATION UNDER A STATE'S POWER OF EMINENT DOMAIN

CORE CONCEPT

Although most federal court eminent domain cases will involve the federal power of eminent domain, a state may institute an eminent domain action in a federal district court when diversity of citizenship exists between the plaintiff (condemnor) and the defendant (landowner) and the amount in controversy exceeds $75,000, exclusive of interest and costs. Similarly, a defendant (landowner) may remove a state eminent domain action to federal district court when the condemnor initiates the suit and the defendant (landowner) is not a citizen of the state in which the action is brought, and the amount in controversy exceeds $75,000, exclusive of interest and costs.[42] These state eminent domain actions must be brought in the federal district court for the district in which the land is situated.

APPLICATIONS

Choice of Law

The federal court will apply the procedure described in Rule

---

[38] *U.S. v. 9.20 Acres of Land, More or Less, Situated in Polk County, State of Iowa*, 638 F.2d 1123 (8th Cir. 1981) (deposit insufficient). *See also,* 40 U.S.C.A. § 258a.

[39] *U.S. v. Featherston*, 325 F.2d 539, 541 (10th Cir. 1963) (if deposit exceeds award, government can get excess from the clerk or sue landowner if landowner received excess).

[40] *See,* Rule 71A(c)(2). *See also,* 40 U.S.C.A. § 258a. *Cf., U.S. v. 8.0 Acres of Land*, 197 F.3d 24, 29 n. 1 (1st Cir. 1999) (when United States has taken title to condemned land, it has no standing to participate in proceedings relating to distribution of compensation award once amount of award has been determined; however, when other parties initiate appeal, United States may properly seek to have district court judgment affirmed and to offer government's advice on distribution; citing Rule 71.1(j) provision dealing with expediting distribution of money deposited).

[41] *Catlin v. U.S.*, 324 U.S. 229, 65 S. Ct. 631, 89 L. Ed. 911 (1945) (appeal must await final judgment).

[42] 28 U.S.C.A. § 1441(a), (b).

71.1. The court will apply state substantive condemnation law.[43]

Trial by Jury

In state eminent domain cases, the court will follow state law provisions for trial by jury or a commission.[44]

Collateral Attack of State Court Judgment

A party may not bring a federal court action challenging a state court judgment in a state eminent domain action.

RULE 71.1(*l*)—COSTS

CORE CONCEPT

Rule 71.1(l) governs the assessment of costs in condemnation proceedings decided pursuant to Rule 71.1. The normal expenses of the proceeding will be charged to the condemnor. Expenses incurred in the distribution of the award are charged to the condemnee.

APPLICATIONS

Costs Paid by Condemnor

The condemnor shall pay the normal expenses such as the bills for publication of notice, commissioners' fees, the cost of transporting commissioners and jurors for a view, fees for attorneys representing defendants who have failed to answer, and witness' fees. These expenses shall be charged to the government and, when required, be included as damages in the award but will not be taxed against the award, except to the extent permitted by law.[45] In addition, the condemnor shall pay for the expenses of a commissioner who records the deed and executes the conveyance.

Expenses of Distribution

Expenses incurred in the distribution of the award, such as ascertaining the identity of the distributees and deciding between conflicting claimants, are chargeable against the award.[46]

Additional Research References

Wright & Miller, *Federal Practice and Procedure* §§ 3041 to 3056
C.J.S., Eminent Domain §§ 209 to 251 et seq., §§ 267 to 315 et seq., §§ 319 to

---

[43]*See, e.g., Donovan v. Town of Edgartown*, 568 F.Supp.2d 134, 135 (D. Mass. 2008) ("[A] federal court applies the substantive law of the State in which the taking occurs."). *But cf., Donovan v. Town of Edgartown*, 570 F.Supp.2d 174, 175 (D. Mass. 2008) (if state confers right to jury trial, district court "must respect it;" but size of jury, unanimity requirement and *voir dire*

are governed by federal law).

[44]*West, Inc. v. U.S.*, 374 F.2d 218, 224 n. 3 (5th Cir. 1967) (Rule 71.1(k) applies when state has condemned property and diversity jurisdiction causes case to be in federal court).

[45]*See,* Advisory Committee Note to Rule 71.1(l).

[46]*See,* Advisory Committee Note to Rule 71.1(l).

366 et seq., §§ 373 to 386 et seq.
West's Key Number Digest, Eminent Domain ⊙166 to 265(5)

RULE 72
MAGISTRATE JUDGES: PRETRIAL ORDER

(a) Nondispositive Matters. When a pretrial matter not dispositive of a party's claim or defense is referred to a magistrate judge to hear and decide, the magistrate judge must promptly conduct the required proceedings and, when appropriate, issue a written order stating the decision. A party may serve and file objections to the order within 14 days after being served with a copy. A party may not assign as error a defect in the order not timely objected to. The district judge in the case must consider timely objections and modify or set aside any part of the order that is clearly erroneous or is contrary to law.

(b) Dispositive Motions and Prisoner Petitions.

(1) *Findings and Recommendations.* A magistrate judge must promptly conduct the required proceedings when assigned, without the parties' consent, to hear a pretrial matter dispositive of a claim or defense or a prisoner petition challenging the conditions of confinement. A record must be made of all evidentiary proceedings and may, at the magistrate judge's discretion, be made of any other proceedings. The magistrate judge must enter a recommended disposition, including, if appropriate, proposed findings of fact. The clerk must promptly mail a copy to each party.

(2) *Objections.* Within 14 days after being served with a copy of the recommended disposition, a party may serve and file specific written objections to the proposed findings and recommendations. A party may respond to another party's objections within 14 days after being served with a copy. Unless the district judge orders otherwise, the objecting party must promptly arrange for transcribing the record, or whatever portions of it the parties agree to or

the magistrate judge considers sufficient.

(3) *Resolving Objections.* The district judge must determine de novo any part of the magistrate judge's disposition that has been properly objected to. The district judge may accept, reject, or modify the recommended disposition; receive further evidence; or return the matter to the magistrate judge with instructions.

[Former Rule 72 abrogated December 4, 1967, effective July 1, 1968; new Rule 72 adopted April 28, 1983, effective August 1, 1983; amended April 30, 1991, effective December 1, 1991; April 22, 1993, effective December 1, 1993; April 30, 2007, effective December 1, 2007; March 26, 2009, effective December 1, 2009.]

AUTHORS' COMMENTARY ON RULE 72

PURPOSE AND SCOPE

Rule 72 provides that a district judge may refer pretrial, trial, and post-trial matters to a magistrate judge without the consent of the parties under the court's additional duties jurisdiction, as provided by 28 U.S.C.A. § 636(b)(3). A district judge may also refer prisoner petitions challenging conditions of confinement for consideration by a magistrate judge.

RULE 72(a)—NONDISPOSITIVE MATTERS

CORE CONCEPT

A district judge may refer, without the consent of the parties,[1] pretrial matters nondispositive of a claim or a defense to a magistrate judge. Such decisions of the magistrate judge may be appealed to the district court for review on a standard of clear error or contrary to law.

NOTE: A party must file written objections to the magistrate judge's order within 14 days after being served with a copy of the order. Failure to make a timely objection may constitute a waiver of appellate review of the magistrate judge's order.[2]

---

[1]*Holder v. Holder*, 392 F.3d 1009, 1022 (9th Cir. 2004) (noting absence of requirement for consent).

[2]*See, e.g., Phinney v. Wentworth Douglas Hosp.*, 199 F.3d 1, 4 (1st Cir. 1999) (Rule 72(a) objection to magistrate judge's order must contain all claims of error; claims of error not raised before district judge cannot be raised in circuit court); *Simpson v. Lear Astronics Corp.*, 77 F.3d 1170, 1174 (9th Cir. 1996) ("[A] party who fails to file timely objections to a magistrate judge's nondispositive order . . . forfeits its right to appellate review."). *But see Spence v. Superin-*

APPLICATIONS

Nondispositive Pretrial Matters

A nondispositive pretrial matter is a matter which is collateral and nonessential to a full disposition of the petitioner's claim and the defendant's liability, such as: (1) motions relating to discovery matters; (2) a motion for sanctions for noncompliance with a discovery order;[3] (3) motions to add claims; and (4) a motion to join a counterclaim. It is unclear whether a magistrate judge may impose sanctions under Rule 72(a) for violations of Rule 11 (governing sanctions for inappropriate pleadings, motions and other papers) or may only recommend such sanctions to the district court pursuant to Rule 72(b).[4]

Dispositive Sanction Not Imposed

If a motion seeks a sanction that would be dispositive, but the magistrate judge denies the motion, the matter is not considered dispositive. Instead, the standard of review is provided by Rule 72(a) (clearly erroneous or contrary to law), rather than Rule 72(b) (de novo review upon the record).[5]

Magistrate Judge's Authority

When appropriate, and to aid further proceedings, Rule 72 authorizes a magistrate judge to enter a written order on the record that constitutes a final adjudication regarding nondispositive pretrial matters, subject to review on appeal by the district court.

Magistrate Judge's Ruling

A magistrate judge's ruling on a pretrial matter on referral from a district judge will follow the Rules. When a magistrate judge decides a nondispositive pretrial matter, the order becomes effective when made, and requires no further action by the district judge.

---

tendent, Great Meadow Correctional Facility, 219 F.3d 162, 174 (2d Cir. 2000) (exception to time limit for arguments with "substantial merit" or existence of plain error in magistrate judge's ruling); *Kruger v. Apfel*, 214 F.3d 784, 786–87 (7th Cir. 2000) (time limit is not jurisdictional; where appeal is only a few days late and opposing party experienced no unfair prejudice, district court should consider objections to magistrate judge's recommendation de novo; moreover, separate from party's objection, district court should examine recommendation of magistrate judge for clear error).

[3]*See, e.g., Hutchinson v. Pfeil*, 105 F.3d 562, 566 (10th Cir. 1997)

(magistrate judge may impose sanctions in discovery as nondispositive matter).

[4]*See, e.g., Alpern v. Lieb*, 38 F.3d 933, 935 (7th Cir. 1994) (citing conflicting cases; holding that Rule 72(a) does not confer such authority on magistrate judges). *But cf., Hutchinson v. Pfeil*, 208 F.3d 1180, 1184 n. 7 (10th Cir. 2000) (refusing to decide issue).

[5]*See, e.g., Gomez v. Martin Marietta Corp.*, 50 F.3d 1511 (10th Cir.1995) (decision not to impose dispositive sanction alters standard of review).

Review of Nondispositive Pretrial Matter

The district judge who assigned the case retains ultimate authority over the case and shall modify or set aside any portion of the magistrate judge's order found to be clearly erroneous or contrary to law.[6] Even if no objections are presented, the district judge may rehear or reconsider the matter *sua sponte.*

Implicit Affirmation of Magistrate Judge's Decision

If a party objects to the ruling of a magistrate judge, but the district court does not expressly rule on some part of the objections, in appropriate circumstances the district court's action may be treated as a denial of those objections.[7]

Failure to Object

When a party fails to file a timely objection to a magistrate judge's ruling under Rule 72(a), that party's right to seek review of the magistrate judge's ruling is greatly curtailed. However, it is uncertain whether such a failure to object terminates the possibility of review completely.[8]

Review by Court of Appeals

A party may not appeal directly to the Court of Appeals from a magistrate judge's nondispositive pretrial order.[9]

RULE 72(b)—DISPOSITIVE MOTIONS AND PRISONER PETITIONS

CORE CONCEPT

When a dispositive matter is referred to a magistrate judge,

---

[6]*See, e.g., Hall v. Norfolk Southern Ry. Co.*, 469 F.3d 590, 595 (7th Cir. 2006) ("[D]istrict judges are to review nondispositive motions for clear error."). *But cf., PowerShare, Inc. v. Syntel, Inc.*, 597 F.3d 10, 15 (1st Cir. 2010) (for pure issues of law, "there is no practical difference between review" under Rule 72(a) and 72(b)); *Williams v. Beemiller, Inc.*, 527 F.3d 259, 265 (2d Cir. 2008) (magistrate judge's order to remand case to state court is dispositive matter and therefore is not reviewed by district court under the lenient "clearly erroneous or contrary to law" standard of Rule 72(a)).

[7]*See, e.g., Fielding v. Tollaksen*, 510 F.3d 175, 179 (2d Cir. 2007) (when district court "enters an order disposing of a case without expressly ruling on a pending [and timely] objection filed pursuant to [Rule 72(a)], the judgment . . . functions as a final order overruling the objection"); *Miller v. Automobile Club Of New Mexico, Inc.*, 420 F.3d 1098, 1117 (10th Cir. 2005) (where record indicated district court had considered all materials, "we may properly construe a district court's failure to address arguments raised in a Rule 72(a) objection 'as an implicit denial of those arguments' and a refusal to overrule the magistrate judge's order.").

[8]*See, e.g., Solis v. Malkani*, 638 F.3d 269, 274 (4th Cir. 2011) (failure to object "waives further review").

[9]*See, e.g., U.S. v. Gonzalez-Ramirez*, 350 F.3d 731, 733 (8th Cir. 2003) (no right to appeal to circuit court unless district court has already reviewed magistrate judge's order after objection to order); *Simpson v. Lear Astronics Corp.*, 77 F.3d 1170, 1173–74 (9th Cir. 1996) (if party does not object to district court, and if district court does not therefore hear the issue, finding of magistrate judge under Rule 72(a) cannot be appealed to circuit court).

the magistrate judge will conduct evidentiary hearings and submit a recommendation, and when appropriate, submit proposed findings of fact to the district judge. If a party makes a timely written objection to the proposed findings and recommendation of the magistrate judge, the district judge must make a *de novo* review of the record.[10]

NOTE: A party must file specific, written objections to the magistrate judge's findings and recommendation within 14 days after being served with a copy of the recommended disposition. Failure to make timely objection constitutes a waiver of the right to review of the magistrate judge's findings and recommendation.[11]

APPLICATIONS

Matters Considered Dispositive

The following matters are deemed dispositive by statute:[12] (1) a motion for injunctive relief; (2) a motion for judgment on the pleadings; (3) a motion for summary judgment; (4) a motion to dismiss or permit maintenance of a class action; (5) a motion to dismiss for failure to state a claim upon which relief may be granted; or (6) a motion for involuntary dismissal.[13] The following matters may also be considered dispositive: (1) an application to proceed *in forma pauperis*;[14] (2) a motion to amend a pleading;[15] (3) a motion for attorney's fees;[16] and (4) an order

---

[10] 28 U.S.C.A. § 636(b)(1)(C). *See also, Rajaratnam v. Moyer*, 47 F.3d 922, 925 n. 8 (7th Cir. 1995) (de novo review does not require new trial; only a fresh look at issues to which objection has been raised). *But cf., Taylor v. Farrier*, 910 F.2d 518, 521 (8th Cir. 1990) ("in conducting [de novo] review, the district court must, at a minimum, listen to a tape recording or read a transcript of the evidentiary hearing.").

[11] *See Banco Del Atlantico, S.A. v. Woods Industries Inc.*, 519 F.3d 350, 354 (7th Cir. 2008) ("We have determined that a failure to file objections with the district judge waives the right to appeal the issues."); *International Surplus Lines Ins. Co. v. Wyoming Coal Refining Systems, Inc.*, 52 F.3d 901, 904 (10th Cir. 1995) (failure to make timely objection constitutes waiver). *But see Small v. Secretary of Health and Human Services*, 892 F.2d 15, 16 (2d Cir. 1989) (per curiam) (pro se litigant's failure to object does not waive right to appellate review of

district court's decision "unless the magistrate's report explicitly states that failure to object to the report . . . will preclude appellate review and specifically cites [*inter alia*, Rule 72]").

[12] 28 U.S.C.A. § 636(b)(1)(A).

[13] *See, e.g., Bennett v. General Caster Service of N. Gordon Co., Inc.*, 976 F.2d 995, 997 (6th Cir. 1992) (identifying similar list and noting that list is "nonexhaustive").

[14] *See, e.g., Woods v. Dahlberg*, 894 F.2d 187, 187 (6th Cir. 1990) (per curiam)(motion to proceed in forma pauperis is dispositive, and therefore magistrate judge may only make recommendation).

[15] *Lundy v. Adamar of New Jersey, Inc.*, 34 F.3d 1173, 1183 (3d Cir. 1994) (motion to amend is dispositive of statute of limitations defense).

[16] *See, e.g., Massey v. City of Ferndale*, 7 F.3d 506 (6th Cir.1993) (motion for attorney's fees is dispositive; *but see Merritt v. International Broth. of Boilermakers*, 649 F.2d 1013,

remanding a removed case to state court.[17] It is unclear whether sanctions for violations of Rule 11 (governing pleadings, motions and other papers) is within a magistrate judge's authority under Rule 72(a), or whether the magistrate judge may only make a recommendation to the district judge under Rule 72(b).[18]

Dispositive Sanction Not Imposed

If a motion seeks a sanction that would be dispositive, but the magistrate judge denies the motion, the matter is not considered dispositive. Instead, the standard of review is provided by Rule 72(a) (clearly erroneous or contrary to law), rather than Rule 72(b) (de novo review upon the record).[19]

Habeas Corpus

Rule 72(b) does not extend to habeas corpus petitions. Habeas corpus petitions are governed by specific statutes.[20]

Procedure for Dispositive Pretrial Matters

A magistrate judge has substantial discretion to conduct hearings on dispositive matters. The magistrate judge shall make a record of all evidentiary proceedings, but has discretion whether to keep a record of non-evidentiary proceedings. The magistrate judge shall submit a recommendation for disposition of the matter to the district judge who assigned the case to the magistrate judge. When appropriate, the magistrate judge shall submit proposed findings of fact with the recommendation. The clerk of the court is required to mail copies of the magistrate judge's recommendation and findings of fact to all parties.

Obligation to Order Transcript

A party objecting to the magistrate judge's recommended disposition should promptly arrange for the transcription of the record or portions of the record agreed upon by the parties or as directed by the magistrate judge, unless directed otherwise by the district judge.

Response to Objections

A party may respond to another party's objections within 14

1016–18 (5th Cir. 1981) (post-judgment award of attorney's fees as sanction for misconduct in pre-trial discovery is non-dispositive; held, pre-trial discovery issues are inherently non-dispositive matters).

[17]*Vogel v. U.S. Office Products Co.*, 258 F.3d 509, 515 (6th Cir. 2001) (also collecting other examples of dispositive motions); *First Union Mortg. Corp. v. Smith*, 229 F.3d 992, 996 (10th Cir. 2000).

[18]*See, e.g., Alpern v. Lieb*, 38 F.3d 933, 935 (7th Cir. 1994) (citing conflict-

ing cases; holding that Rule 72(a) does not confer such authority on magistrate judges). *But cf., Hutchinson v. Pfeil*, 208 F.3d 1180, 1184 n. 7 (10th Cir. 2000) (refusing to decide issue).

[19]*See, e.g., Gomez v. Martin Marietta Corp.*, 50 F.3d 1511 (10th Cir.1995) (decision not to impose dispositive sanction alters standard of review).

[20]28 U.S.C.A. §§ 2254, 2255.

days after service of a copy of the objections.[21]

De Novo Review of Dispositive Motions by District Judge

Upon proper objection, the district judge who assigned the motion to the magistrate judge shall make a *de novo* determination. After making a *de novo* review of the ruling, a district judge may accept, reject, or modify the recommended disposition or recommit the matter to the magistrate judge with instructions.

A district judge, under the *de novo* review standard, is not required to conduct a new hearing, but is required to make a new examination of the issues upon which specific, written objections were based, either on the record, through the recall of witnesses, or by receiving additional testimony.[22]

Failure to Object and Untimely Objections

The courts are split on whether and to what extent the district judge is obligated to review a magistrate judge's recommendation absent a timely objection.[23]

Waiver of Right to Appeal

A party who fails to file a timely objection to the district judge regarding the magistrate judge's findings or recommendations waives the party's right to appeal the issue to the court of

---

[21]*See, e.g., U.S. v. Mora*, 135 F.3d 1351, 1357 (10th Cir. 1998).

[22]*See, e.g., Arista Records LLC v. Doe*, 604 F.3d 110, 116 (2d Cir. 2010) (usually Rule 72(b) involves "motions for injunctive relief and motions for dismissal;" noting district court's duty to conduct *de novo* review). *See also Garcia v. City of Albuquerque*, 232 F.3d 760, 766 (10th Cir. 2000) (Rule 72(b) does not require district court to make specific findings, only a de novo review of record); *Hynes v. Squillace*, 143 F.3d 653, 656 (2d Cir. 1998) (district court has discretion to deny supplementation of record upon *de novo* review); *Borden v. Secretary of Health and Human Services*, 836 F.2d 4, 6 (1st Cir. 1987) ("We hold categorically that an unsuccessful party is not entitled as of right to de novo review by the judge of an argument never seasonably raised before the magistrate."). *But see U.S. v. George*, 971 F.2d 1113, 1118 (4th Cir. 1992) ("[A] district court is required to consider all arguments directed to that issue, regardless of whether they were raised before the magistrate.").

[23]*See, e.g., Conetta v. National Hair Care Centers, Inc.*, 236 F.3d 67, 73 (1st Cir. 2001) (even in absence of timely objection to final action by magistrate judge, Rule 72(b) requires district court to "adapt, reject, or modify the recommendation before there is any final judgment"). *See also United States v. Overseas Shipholding Group, Inc.*, 625 F.3d 1, 7 n.3 (1st Cir. 2010) ("[T]he failure to timely file an objection is not jurisdictional."). *But see Diamond v. Colonial Life & Acc. Ins. Co.*, 416 F.3d 310 (4th Cir. 2005) ("[I]n the absence of a timely filed objection, a district court need not conduct a de novo review, but instead must 'only satisfy itself that there is no clear error on the fact of the record in order to accept the recommendation.' "); *F.D.I.C. v. Hillcrest Associates*, 66 F.3d 566, 569 (2d Cir. 1995) (failure to make timely objection acts as waiver; very narrow exception to that general rule in pro se cases); *Douglass v. United Services Auto. Ass'n*, 79 F.3d 1415 (5th Cir. 1996) (court need only determine absence of clear error).

appeals.[24]

Additional Research References

Wright & Miller, *Federal Practice and Procedure* §§ 3076.1 to 3076.9
C.J.S., United States Commissioners § 3
West's Key Number Digest, United States Magistrates ⇔15 to 31

---

[24]*See, e.g., Phillips ex rel. Estates of Byrd v. General Motors Corp.*, 307 F.3d 1206, 1210 (9th Cir. 2002) (failure to file timely appeal is waiver of right to appeal to appellate court).

RULE 73

MAGISTRATE JUDGES: TRIAL BY CONSENT; APPEAL

(a) Trial by Consent. When authorized under 28 U.S.C. § 636(c), a magistrate judge may, if all parties consent, conduct a civil action or proceeding, including a jury or nonjury trial. A record must be made in accordance with 28 U.S.C. § 636(c)(5).

(b) Consent Procedure.

(1) *In General.* When a magistrate judge has been designated to conduct civil actions or proceedings, the clerk must give the parties written notice of their opportunity to consent under 28 U.S.C. § 636(c). To signify their consent, the parties must jointly or separately file a statement consenting to the referral. A district judge or magistrate judge may be informed of a party's response to the clerk's notice only if all parties have consented to the referral.

(2) *Reminding the Parties About Consenting.* A district judge, magistrate judge, or other court official may remind the parties of the magistrate judge's availability, but must also advise them that they are free to withhold consent without adverse substantive consequences.

(3) *Vacating a Referral.* On its own for good cause—or when a party shows extraordinary circumstances—the district judge may vacate a referral to a magistrate judge under this rule.

(c) Appealing a Judgment. In accordance with 28 U.S.C. § 636(c)(3), an appeal from a judgment entered at a magistrate judge's direction may be taken to the court of appeals as would any other appeal from a district-court judgment.

[Former Rule 73 abrogated December 4, 1967, effective July 1, 1968; new Rule 73 adopted April 28, 1983, effective August 1, 1983; amended March 2, 1987, effective August 1, 1987; April 22, 1993, effective December 1, 1993, April 11, 1997, effective December 1, 1997; April 30, 2007, effective December 1, 2007.]

AUTHORS' COMMENTARY ON RULE 73

PURPOSE AND SCOPE

Rule 73 provides that, upon consent of the parties, a district judge may refer cases to a magistrate judge for trial or final disposition. Rule 73 also provides for the district judge to vacate the reference to the magistrate judge's ruling.

RULE 73(a)—TRIAL BY CONSENT

CORE CONCEPT

By local rule or by order of court, and with the consent of the parties, a magistrate judge may be designated with case-dispositive or final judgment authority to conduct any or all of the proceedings in a jury or non-jury case.[1] In such cases, the magistrate judge has all of the powers of a district judge, except the power of contempt. A local rule providing that magistrate judges may hear case-dispositive proceedings may not restrict the types of cases a magistrate judge may hear.

APPLICATIONS

Preserving the Record

The magistrate judge must decide by what means the record should be preserved, such as verbatim by a court reporter, by electronic sound, or by shorthand. When deciding the means of preservation of the record, the magistrate judge may consider the complexity of the case, the likelihood of appeal, the costs of the record, and time constraints.

Contempt

Magistrate judges may not hold contempt hearings. Instead, the magistrate judge will certify the facts of the contempt to the district judge and serve an order to show cause why a contempt citation should not be issued upon the alleged disobedient party. Subsequently, the district judge in a summary proceeding will hear the evidence of the contemptuous act and may punish the disobedient party.[2]

RULE 73(b)—CONSENT PROCEDURE

CORE CONCEPT

The clerk of court handles the procedures for obtaining the

---

[1] *See, e.g., Holt-Orsted v. City of Dickson*, 641 F.3d 230, 233 (6th Cir. 2011) (noting requirement of unanimous consent).

[2] 28 U.S.C.A. § 636(e).

parties' consent to trial before a magistrate judge, isolating the district judge from the consenting process. All parties must make a free and voluntary consent to having a magistrate judge preside over their trial.[3]

APPLICATIONS

Consent Procedure

To prevent the district judge from exercising any influence over the decision by the parties and to prevent the district judge from knowing who may have opposed the reference, the clerk of court administers the complete consent procedure.

Notification

At the time the action is filed, the clerk of court notifies the parties in writing of their option to proceed before a magistrate judge.[4]

Time for Consent

The time for indicating a party's consent or lack of consent is set generally by local rule or court order.[5]

Acceptance

Parties indicate their consent by submitting completed consent forms supplied by the clerk of court.[6]

Voluntariness of Consent

Most courts have local rules to ensure the voluntariness and willingness of consent, such as preventing the clerk of court from notifying litigants that their case will be heard sooner by a magistrate judge or that they will receive an experienced magistrate judge. Neither the district judge, the magistrate judge, nor the clerk of court may attempt to persuade the parties to consent to a trial before a magistrate judge. The parties must clearly and unambiguously consent to a magistrate judge.[7] A mere acquiescence or failure to object

---

[3]28 U.S.C.A. § 636(c)(2).

[4]28 U.S.C.A. § 636(c)(2).

[5]*See, e.g., Rembert v. Apfel*, 213 F.3d 1331, 1335 n. 1 (11th Cir. 2000) ("Parties can consent even after judgment."); *Drake v. Minnesota Min. & Mfg. Co.*, 134 F.3d 878, 883 (7th Cir. 1998) (good consent even after appellate oral argument). *But see Hajek v. Burlington Northern R.R. Co.*, 186 F.3d 1105, 1108 (9th Cir. 1999) (consent in appellate brief is ineffective); *Archie v. Christian*, 808 F.2d 1132 (5th Cir.1987) (en banc) (consent must be given before trial begins—rule of 5th Circuit).

[6]*But see Roell v. Withrow*, 538 U.S. 580, 581, 123 S. Ct. 1696, 1699, 155 L. Ed. 2d 775 (2003) (noting normal requirement of written consent, but holding that where non-consenting parties appear before magistrate without making further objection, magistrate has jurisdiction; fact of inferred consent satisfies requirement of Rule 73(b)).

[7]*See, e.g., Hajek v. Burlington Northern R.R. Co.*, 186 F.3d 1105, 1108 (9th Cir. 1999) (party's response to proposed referral to magistrate judge that " 'at this time the Defendant does not believe any special procedures are required or are appropri-

does not constitute consent.[8]

Consequence of Failure to Consent

If a magistrate judge hears a case without the consent of the parties, the resulting judgment is a "nullity."[9]

Additional Parties and Consent

In general, local rules will control the time within which new parties must exercise their right to consent. The clerk of court will notify new parties of their right to consent in the same manner as the original parties. When an additional party is joined who does not consent to the participation of the magistrate judge, the district judge must hear the case.[10]

Vacating the Reference to a Magistrate by the District Judge

The court may, for good cause shown on its own motion, or under extraordinary circumstances shown by any party, vacate its reference of a civil matter to a magistrate judge.[11] For example, it has been held that a district judge may vacate a proceeding from a magistrate judge when the magistrate judge is faced with extraordinary questions of law with possibly wide precedential effect.[12] This power may not be used routinely to vacate certain categories of cases from a magistrate judge.[13] The court retains this power, notwithstanding the consent of all parties to trial before a magistrate judge.

---

ate' " is "far from 'clear and unambiguous' "). *Alaniz v. California Processors, Inc.*, 690 F.2d 717, 720 (9th Cir. 1982) (per curiam) (holding that consent must be clear and unambiguous). *But see Wilhelm v. Rotman*, 680 F.3d 1113, 1119 (9th Cir. 2012) (requirement to advise party that withholding consent is free of consequence applies only to "repeated communications" regarding consent, not to initial communication advising party about potential of using magistrate judge);*Kadonsky v. U.S.*, 216 F.3d 499, 502 (5th Cir. 2000) (sufficient consent where party signed document "evincing his willingness to proceed before a magistrate judge;" use of particular written form is not required for consent); *Rembert v. Apfel*, 213 F.3d 1331, 1335 (11th Cir. 2000) ("Although consent must be 'express and on the record,' it need not necessarily be written.").

[8]*See, e.g., Hajek v. Burlington Northern R.R. Co.*, 186 F.3d 1105, 1108 (9th Cir. 1999) (local rule provided that failure to object to referral to magistrate judge was consent to referral; held, local rule is invalid);

Nasca v. Peoplesoft, 160 F.3d 578, 579 (9th Cir. 1998) (" 'consent by failure to object' " does not provide magistrate judge with authority under Rule 73(b); appellate court raised issue *sua sponte*); *Caprera v. Jacobs*, 790 F.2d 442, 444 (5th Cir. 1986) (consent cannot be inferred from parties' conduct; "consent to proceed before a magistrate [must] be explicit").

[9]*Binder v. Gillespie*, 184 F.3d 1059, 1063 (9th Cir. 1999).

[10]*See, e.g., New York Chinese TV Programs, Inc. v. U.E. Enterprises, Inc.*, 996 F.2d 21, 24 (2d Cir. 1993) (intervenors must also consent, even when joined after magistrate judge begins to hear case).

[11]28 U.S.C.A. § 636(c)(6).

[12]*Gomez v. Harris*, 504 F. Supp. 1342, 1345 (D. Alaska 1981) (reference vacated in case with "controlling question of law and a thicket of procedural difficulties").

[13]*See,* S.Report No. 74, 96th Cong., 1st Sess. 14 (1979) (WESTLAW: LH database, **ti(senate + 5 96-74)**).

RULE 73(c)—APPEALING A JUDGMENT

CORE CONCEPT

The appeal procedure provides that a party make a direct appeal of a magistrate judge's final judgment to the Court of Appeals in the same manner as a judgment from the district court.[14]

Additional Research References

Wright & Miller, *Federal Practice and Procedure* §§ 3077.1 to 3077.5
C.J.S., United States Commissioners § 3
West's Key Number Digest, United States Magistrates ⬚12 to 13, ⬚24 to 31

---

[14]*See, e.g., Holt-Orsted v. City of Dickson*, 641 F.3d 230, 233 (6th Cir. 2011) (appeal is directly to circuit court); *Dluhos v. Floating and Abandoned Vessel, Known as New York*, 162 F.3d 63, 67 (2d Cir. 1998) (consent to trial before magistrate judge waives any appeal to district judge; appeal is to circuit court).

RULE 74[1]
METHOD OF APPEAL FROM MAGISTRATE TO DISTRICT JUDGE UNDER TITLE 28, U.S.C. § 636(C)(4) AND RULE 73(D)

---

[1]Rules 73(d) and 74 to 76 provided that when a magistrate judge hears a case, the parties could choose to appeal to either the district court or the court of appeals. However, in 1997 the so-called "optional appeal route" to the district court was abolished by Congress. Accordingly, the Supreme Court abrogated Rules 73(d) and 74 to 76 effective in December, 1997. Henceforth appeals from trials conducted by magistrate judges shall be made only to the appropriate court of appeals.

RULE 75[1]
PROCEEDINGS ON APPEAL FROM MAGISTRATE TO DISTRICT JUDGE UNDER RULE 73(D)

[1]Rules 73(d) and 74 to 76 provided that when a magistrate judge hears a case, the parties could choose to appeal to either the district court or the court of appeals. However, in 1997 the so-called "optional appeal route" to the district court was abolished by Congress. Accordingly, the Supreme Court abrogated Rules 73(d) and 74 to 76 effective in December, 1997. Henceforth appeals from trials conducted by magistrate judges shall be made only to the appropriate court of appeals.

RULE 76[1]
JUDGMENT OF THE DISTRICT JUDGE ON THE APPEAL UNDER RULE 73(D) AND COSTS

[1]Rules 73(d) and 74 to 76 provided that when a magistrate judge hears a case, the parties could choose to appeal to either the district court or the court of appeals. However, in 1997 the so-called "optional appeal route" to the district court was abolished by Congress. Accordingly, the Supreme Court abrogated Rules 73(d) and 74 to 76 effective in December, 1997. Henceforth appeals from trials conducted by magistrate judges shall be made only to the appropriate court of appeals.

X. DISTRICT COURTS AND CLERKS

RULE 77
CONDUCTING BUSINESS; CLERK'S AUTHORITY; NOTICE OF AN ORDER OR JUDGMENT

(a) When Court Is Open. Every district court is considered always open for filing any paper, issuing and returning process, making a motion, or entering an order.

(b) Place for Trial and Other Proceedings. Every trial on the merits must be conducted in open court and, so far as convenient, in a regular courtroom. Any other act or proceeding may be done or conducted by a judge in chambers, without the attendance of the clerk or other court official, and anywhere inside or outside the district. But no hearing—other than one ex parte—may be conducted outside the district unless all the affected parties consent.

(c) Clerk's Office Hours; Clerk's Orders.

    (1) *Hours.* The clerk's office—with a clerk or deputy on duty—must be open during business hours every day except Saturdays, Sundays, and legal holidays. But a court may, by local rule or order, require that the office be open for specified hours on Saturday or a particular legal holiday other than one listed in Rule 6(a)(4)(A).

    (2) *Orders.* Subject to the court's power to suspend, alter, or rescind the clerk's action for good cause, the clerk may:

      (A) issue process;

      (B) enter a default;

      (C) enter a default judgment under Rule 55(b)(1); and

      (D) act on any other matter that does not require the court's action.

(d) Serving Notice of an Order or Judgment.

(1) *Service.* Immediately after entering an order or judgment, the clerk must serve notice of the entry, as provided in Rule 5(b), on each party who is not in default for failing to appear. The clerk must record the service on the docket. A party also may serve notice of the entry as provided in Rule 5(b).

(2) *Time to Appeal Not Affected by Lack of Notice.* Lack of notice of the entry does not affect the time for appeal or relieve—or authorize the court to relieve—a party for failing to appeal within the time allowed, except as allowed by Federal Rule of Appellate Procedure (4)(a).

[Amended effective March 19, 1948; July 1, 1963; July 1, 1968; July 1, 1971; August 1, 1987; December 1, 1991; April 23, 2001, effective December 1, 2001; April 30, 2007, effective December 1, 2007.]

AUTHORS' COMMENTARY ON RULE 77

PURPOSE AND SCOPE

Rule 77 contains a variety of provisions pertaining to the operations of the district court and the clerk's office. It provides that the court is always "open," and sets forth the times that the clerk's office is open. It also states that trials and hearings shall be conducted in the courtroom. Finally, Rule 77 controls notice of judgments and orders.

RULE 77(a)—WHEN COURT IS OPEN

CORE CONCEPT

The district courts are deemed open at all times for the purposes of filing papers, issuing process, and the like.[1] This does not mean that the clerk's office will be manned and open at all times.[2] Rather, papers may be filed after hours by delivering them to the clerk or a deputy clerk, depositing them in a designated receptacle provided by the clerk and authorized by lo-

---

[1] *In re Bradshaw*, 283 B.R. 814, 817 (B.A.P. 1st Cir. 2002) (the guiding principle is that clerks of court must be available in some fashion twenty-four hours a day); *In re Papst Licensing GMBH & Co. KG Litigation*, 631 F.Supp.2d 42, 46 (D.D.C. 2009).

[2] *Stone Street Capital, Inc. v. McDonald's Corp.*, 300 F. Supp. 2d 345, 348 n. 4 (D. Md. 2003); *In re Bradshaw*, 283 B.R. 814, 818 (B.A.P. 1st Cir. 2002); *McIntosh v. Antonino*, 71 F.3d 29, 35 (1st Cir. 1995).

cal rule,[3] or even leaving them with a judge under exceptional circumstances.[4] However, filing is not accomplished merely by delivery to the clerk's office without delivering the paper to a proper officer or otherwise using an established method of after-hours filing.[5]

RULE 77(b)—PLACE FOR TRIAL AND OTHER PROCEEDINGS

CORE CONCEPT

All trials must be conducted in open court, and in a regular courtroom to the extent practicable.[6] Other proceedings, such as status conferences, pretrial conferences, etc., may be conducted in chambers or some other location.[7] However, no hearing, other than one *ex parte,* may be held outside the district without consent of all parties.

RULE 77(c)—CLERK'S OFFICE HOURS; CLERK'S ORDERS

CORE CONCEPT

The clerk's office must be open at minimum during working hours on all days except weekends and holidays. The hours may be expanded by local rule. The clerk's office has the power to take certain acts, such as entering default judgments and process to execute judgments.[8] Such actions by the clerk's office are reviewable by the court and may be suspended, altered, or rescinded upon cause shown.[9]

RULE 77(d)—SERVING NOTICE OF AN ORDER OR JUDGMENT

CORE CONCEPT

The clerk's office must send notice of the entry of judgment to all parties who have entered appearances in the manner set forth

---

[3]*Ticketmaster Corp. v. Tickets. Com, Inc.*, 2000 WL 525390, 2000 (C.D. Cal. 2000) (a drop box is one method to accommodate the fact that the court shall be deemed always open).

[4]*Turner v. City of Newport*, 887 F. Supp. 149 (E.D. Ky. 1995) (deposit in post office box of clerk deemed filing).

[5]*McIntosh v. Antonino*, 71 F.3d 29, 35 (1st Cir. 1995); *In re Fisherman's Wharf Fillet, Inc.*, 83 F. Supp. 2d 651, 657 (E.D. Va. 1999) (after hours facsimile is not adequate filing).

[6]*National Ass'n of Waterfront*

Employers v. Chao, 587 F.Supp.2d 90, 98, n.5 (D.D.C. 2008).

[7]*B.H. v. McDonald*, 49 F.3d 294 (7th Cir.1995); *Crumrine v. NEG Micon USA, Inc.*, 104 F. Supp. 2d 1123, 1126 (N.D. Iowa 2000) (court could be held at any courthouse within the district even without the consent of the parties).

[8]*U.S. v. Laws*, 352 F. Supp. 2d 707, 709 (E.D. Va. 2004) (writ of garnishment).

[9]*Brady v. U.S.*, 211 F.3d 499 (9th Cir. 2000) (clerk's entry of default may be set aside for cause shown).

in Rule 5(b).[10] However, the failure of the clerk to do so does not necessarily increase the time for appeal[11] (but note that the appellate courts may extend the time for appeal and may consider the failure of the clerk to send notice,[12] and that the district court may reopen and extend the time for appeal[13]). A party who wants to insure that all parties have notice of the judgment (and thus that the time for appeal has commenced running) may serve the notice by mail[14] as provided in Rule 5.[15]

Additional Research References

Wright & Miller, *Federal Practice and Procedure* §§ 3081 to 3084
C.J.S., Courts § 236; Federal Civil Procedure §§ 915 et seq., § 1213; Federal Courts §§ 302 et seq.
West's Key Number Digest, Clerk of Courts ☞1; Federal Civil Procedure ☞1951, ☞2628; Federal Courts ☞971

---

[10]*Khor Chin Lim v. Courtcall Inc.*, 683 F.3d 378, 380 (7th Cir. 2012); *Mackey v. Hoffman*, 682 F.3d 1247, 1252 (9th Cir. 2012); *Dempster v. Dempster*, 404 F. Supp. 2d 445, 448 (E.D. N.Y. 2005) (service by email pursuant to electronic docketing system is sufficient).

[11]*Maples v. Thomas*, __ U.S. __, 132 S. Ct. 912, 933, 181 L. Ed. 2d 807 (2012); *Ultimate Appliance CC v. Kirby Co.*, 601 F.3d 414, 416 (6th Cir. 2010).

[12]*Maples v. Thomas*, __ U.S. __, 132 S. Ct. 912, 933, 181 L. Ed. 2d 807 (2012) (but appellate Rule 4(a)(6) establishes an outside limit of 180 days after entry of judgment).

[13]*Bowles v. Russell*, 127 S. Ct. 2360, 168 L. Ed. 2d 96 (U.S. 2007); *Mackey v. Hoffman*, 682 F.3d 1247, 1252 (9th Cir. 2012) (motion must be filed within the earlier of 14 days after notice and 180 days after entry of judgment).

[14]*Ryan v. First Unum Life Ins. Co.*, 174 F.3d 302, 304–05 (2d Cir. 1999) (service must be by mail, not by hand delivery).

[15]*Resendiz v. Dretke*, 452 F.3d 356, 358, (5th Cir. 2006) (only formal service pursuant to Rule 5(b) constitutes notice); *Bass v. U.S. Dept. of Agriculture*, 211 F.3d 959 (5th Cir. 2000); *Nunley v. City of Los Angeles*, 52 F.3d 792 (9th Cir.1995).

RULE 78
HEARING MOTIONS; SUBMISSION ON BRIEFS

(a) Providing a Regular Schedule for Oral Hearings. A court may establish regular times and places for oral hearings on motions.

(b) Providing for Submission on Briefs. By rule or order, the court may provide for submitting and determining motions on briefs, without oral hearings.

[Amended effective August 1, 1987; April 30, 2007, effective December 1, 2007.]

AUTHORS' COMMENTARY ON RULE 78

SCOPE AND PURPOSE

Rule 78 allows each district to enact local rules establishing regular motion days for the presentation of motions requiring a hearing. However, judges may conduct oral arguments on motions at other times. Furthermore, the districts or individual judges may also provide that motions are to be determined on briefs only, without oral argument.

RULE 78(a)—PROVIDING A REGULAR SCHEDULE FOR ORAL HEARINGS

CORE CONCEPT

The court may establish regular times for hearing arguments, but also may hear arguments at any time or place on notice that the court considers reasonable.

RULE 78(b)—PROVIDING FOR SUBMISSION ON BRIEFS

CORE CONCEPT

The court may decide motions on the papers, without oral argument.[1]

---

[1]*U.S. v. Peninsula Communica-* *tions, Inc.*, 287 F.3d 832, 839 (9th Cir.

Additional Research References

Wright & Miller, *Federal Practice and Procedure* §§ 3091
C.J.S., Federal Civil Procedure § 933
West's Key Number Digest, Federal Civil Procedure 1991

2002); *Willis v. Pacific Maritime Ass'n,*
244 F.3d 675, 684 n. 2 (9th Cir. 2001);

Memory Bowl v. North Pointe Ins. Co.,
280 F.R.D. 181, 183 (D.N.J. 2012).

RULE 79
RECORDS KEPT BY THE CLERK

(a) Civil Docket.

(1) *In General.* The clerk must keep a record known as the "civil docket" in the form and manner prescribed by the Director of the Administrative Office of the United States Courts with the approval of the Judicial Conference of the United States. The clerk must enter each civil action in the docket. Actions must be assigned consecutive file numbers, which must be noted in the docket where the first entry of the action is made.

(2) *Items to be Entered.* The following items must be marked with the file number and entered chronologically in the docket:

(A) papers filed with the clerk;

(B) process issued, and proofs of service or other returns showing execution; and

(C) appearances, orders, verdicts, and judgments.

(3) *Contents of Entries; Jury Trial Demanded.* Each entry must briefly show the nature of the paper filed or writ issued, the substance of each proof of service or other return, and the substance and date of entry of each order and judgment. When a jury trial has been properly demanded or ordered, the clerk must enter the word "jury" in the docket.

(b) Civil Judgments and Orders. The clerk must keep a copy of every final judgment and appealable order; of every order affecting title to or a lien on real or personal property; and of any other order that the court directs to be kept. The clerk must keep these in the form and manner prescribed by the Director of the Administrative Office of the United States Courts with the approval of the Judicial Conference of the United States.

(c) Indexes; Calendars. Under the court's direction, the clerk must:

(1) keep indexes of the docket and of the judgments and orders described in Rule 79(b); and

(2) prepare calendars of all actions ready for trial, distinguishing jury trials from nonjury trials.

(d) Other Records. The clerk must keep any other records required by the Director of the Administrative Office of the United States Courts with the approval of the Judicial Conference of the United States.

[Amended effective March 19, 1948; October 20, 1949; July 1, 1963; April 30, 2007, effective December 1, 2007.]

AUTHORS' COMMENTARY ON RULE 79

PURPOSE AND SCOPE

Rule 79 governs the record keeping duties of the district court clerk's office.

RULE 79(a)—CIVIL DOCKET

CORE CONCEPT

The clerk shall keep a civil docket, which is a descriptive, chronological listing of each pleading, motion, order, etc., filed in the case.[1] The docket may be maintained manually or electronically.[2]

APPLICATIONS

Description

The docket should contain a brief description of each entry.[3] Entries should be entered chronologically[4] and should show the dates on which orders or judgments are entered.[5]

---

[1] *Harmston v. City and County of San Francisco*, 627 F.3d 1273, 1279 (9th Cir. 2010).

[2] *Active Products Corp. v. A.H. Choitz & Co. Inc.*, 163 F.R.D. 274, 280–81 (N.D. Ind. 1995).

[3] *U.S. v. Alcantara*, 396 F.3d 189, 200 (2d Cir. 2005) (even a motion filed under seal should be reflected in the docket).

[4] *Casey v. Long Island R. Co.*, 406 F.3d 142, 148 (2d Cir. 2005); *Goode v.*

Winkler, 252 F.3d 242 (2d Cir.2001) (criticizing the district court for not arranging the docket strictly chronologically).

[5] *Connecticut ex rel. Blumenthal v. Crotty*, 346 F.3d 84, 92 (2d Cir. 2003) (the operative date is the date the order is entered onto the docket, not the date the order is signed or dated); *Houston v. Greiner*, 174 F.3d 287 (2d Cir. 1999) (computerized docketing system that did not list a date for each entry violates Rule 79).

Jury vs. Non-jury

The docket should indicate if the case is to be tried before a jury.

Judgments

Judgments are not effective until entered on the docket.[6] Under Rule 58, a judgment must be a separate document.[7]

Briefs

In general, briefs are not part of the record, so they are not filed and are not entered on the docket.

Time of Entry

Rule 79 does not specify the time for making entries in the docket. However, the parties' rights will not be prejudiced by a delay in entry on the docket.

RULE 79(b)—CIVIL JUDGMENTS AND ORDERS

CORE CONCEPT

Rule 79(b) requires the clerk's office to retain a copy of every final judgment, appealable order, order creating a lien on property, and any other order as directed by the court.

RULE 79(c)—INDEXES; CALENDARS

CORE CONCEPT

Rule 79(c) requires the clerk's office to maintain an index or indices of the civil docket and of every civil judgment, appealable order, order creating a lien on property, and other order as directed by the court. The clerk's office must also maintain a calendar of all actions ready for trial. This calendar will indicate whether the matter is to be tried jury or non-jury.

RULE 79(d)—OTHER RECORDS

CORE CONCEPT

The Administrative Office of the United States may direct that the clerk's offices maintain other books and records.

Additional Research References

Wright & Miller, *Federal Practice and Procedure* §§ 3101 to 3107
C.J.S., Federal Civil Procedure § 933, §§ 1227 et seq.
West's Key Number Digest, Federal Civil Procedure ⟷1991, ⟷2621

---

[6]*Constien v. U.S.*, 628 F.3d 1207, 1211 (10th Cir. 2010); *U.S. v. Fiorelli*, 337 F.3d 282 (3d Cir. 2003) (although an order may be signed by the district court, received by the clerk, and entered in the docket on different days, the entry date controls).

[7]*Bravo v. City of Santa Maria*, 665 F.3d 1076, 1089, n.5 (9th Cir. 2011); *Constien v. U.S.*, 628 F.3d 1207, 1211 (10th Cir. 2010).

RULE 80
STENOGRAPHIC TRANSCRIPT AS EVIDENCE

If stenographically reported testimony at a hearing or trial is admissible in evidence at a later trial, the testimony may be proved by a transcript certified by the person who reported it.

[Amended effective March 19, 1948; April 30, 2007, effective December 1, 2007.]

AUTHORS' COMMENTARY ON RULE 80

PURPOSE AND SCOPE

Rule 80 pertains to the use of testimony at one trial or hearing as evidence at a subsequent hearing or trial. The rule provides that a transcript certified by an official court reporter is proof of the prior testimony.[1]

Additional Research References

Wright & Miller, *Federal Practice and Procedure* §§ 3121 to 3122
C.J.S., Evidence §§ 629 to 633 et seq., §§ 652 et seq.
West's Key Number Digest, Evidence ⚷332(1), (4), ⚷340

---

[1] *Orr v. Bank of America, NT & SA*, 285 F.3d 764, 776 (9th Cir. 2002) (transcripts not properly certified not admitted).

XI. GENERAL PROVISIONS

RULE 81
APPLICABILITY OF THE RULES IN GENERAL; REMOVED ACTIONS

(a) Applicability to Particular Proceedings.

    (1) *Prize Proceedings.* These rules do not apply to prize proceedings in admiralty governed by 10 U.S.C. §§ 7651 to 7681.

    (2) *Bankruptcy.* These rules apply to bankruptcy proceedings to the extent provided by the Federal Rules of Bankruptcy Procedure.

    (3) *Citizenship.* These rules apply to proceedings for admission to citizenship to the extent that the practice in those proceedings is not specified in federal statutes and has previously conformed to the practice in civil actions. The provisions of 8 U.S.C. § 1451 for service by publication and for answer apply in proceedings to cancel citizenship certificates.

    (4) *Special Writs.* These rules apply to proceedings for habeas corpus and for quo warranto to the extent that the practice in those proceedings:

      (A) is not specified in a federal statute, the Rules Governing Section 2254 Cases, or the Rules Governing Section 2255 Cases; and

      (B) has previously conformed to the practice in civil actions.

    (5) *Proceedings Involving a Subpoena.* These rules apply to proceedings to compel testimony or the production of documents through a subpoena issued by a United States officer or agency under a federal statute, except as otherwise provided by statute, by local rule, or by court order in the proceedings.

    (6) *Other Proceedings.* These rules, to the extent applicable, govern proceedings under the following laws, except as these laws provide other

procedures:

(A) 7 U.S.C. §§ 292, 499g(c), for reviewing an order of the Secretary of Agriculture;

(B) 9 U.S.C., relating to arbitration;

(C) 15 U.S.C. § 522, for reviewing an order of the Secretary of the Interior;

(D) 15 U.S.C. § 715d(c), for reviewing an order denying a certificate of clearance;

(E) 29 U.S.C. §§ 159, 160, for enforcing an order of the National Labor Relations Board;

(F) 33 U.S.C. §§ 918, 921, for enforcing or reviewing a compensation order under the Longshore and Harbor Workers' Compensation Act; and

(G) 45 U.S.C. § 159, for reviewing an arbitration award in a railway-labor dispute.

(b) Scire Facias and Mandamus. The writs of scire facias and mandamus are abolished. Relief previously available through them may be obtained by appropriate action or motion under these rules.

(c) Removed Actions.

(1) *Applicability.* These rules apply to a civil action after it is removed from a state court.

(2) *Further Pleading.* After removal, repleading is unnecessary unless the court orders it. A defendant who did not answer before removal must answer or present other defenses or objections under these rules within the longest of these periods:

(A) 21 days after receiving—through service or otherwise—a copy of the initial pleading stating the claim for relief;

(B) 21 days after being served with the summons for an initial pleading on file at the time of service; or

(C) 7 days after the notice of removal is filed.

(3) *Demand for a Jury Trial.*

(A) *As Affected by State Law.* A party who, before removal, expressly demanded a jury trial in accordance with state law need not renew the demand after removal. If the state law did not require an express demand for a jury trial, a party need not make one after removal unless the court orders the parties to do so within a specifed time. The court must so order at a party's request and may so order on its own. A party who fails to make a demand when so ordered waives a jury trial.

   (B) *Under* Rule 38. If all necessary pleadings have been served at the time of removal, a party entitled to a jury trial under Rule 38 must be given one if the party serves a demand within 14 days after:

   (i)   it files a notice of removal; or

   (ii) it is served with a notice of removal filed by another party.

(d) Law Applicable.

   (1) *"State Law" Defined.* When these rules refer to state law, the term "law" includes the state's statutes and the state's judicial decisions.

   (2) *"State" Defined.* The term "state" includes, where appropriate, the District of Columbia and any United States commonwealth or territory.

   (3) *"Federal Statute" Defined in the District of Columbia.* In the United States District Court for the District of Columbia, the term "federal statute" includes any Act of Congress that applies locally to the District.

[Amended effective December 28, 1939; March 19, 1948; October 20, 1949; August 1, 1951; July 1, 1963; July 1, 1966; July 1, 1968; July 1, 1971; August 1, 1987; April 23, 2001, effective December 1, 2001; April 29, 2002, effective December 1, 2002; April 30, 2007, effective December 1, 2007; March 26, 2009, effective December 1, 2009.]

AUTHORS' COMMENTARY ON RULE 81

PURPOSE AND SCOPE

Rule 81 specifies whether the Federal Rules of Civil Procedure apply in various proceedings. It also specifies how the Rules operate in the District of Columbia, contains some provisions governing removed actions, abolishes the Writs of Mandamus and Scire Facias, and defines "Officer of the United States."

RULE 81(a)—APPLICABILITY TO PARTICULAR PROCEEDINGS APPLICABLE

CORE CONCEPT

Rule 81(a) lists specific proceedings to which the Rules apply and identifies specific proceedings to which the Rules do not apply.

APPLICATIONS

Not Applicable[1]

Rule 81(a) provides that the Rules do not apply to:

- Prize Proceedings in Admiralty;[2]
- Proceedings to Review Orders of the Secretary of Agriculture;[3]
- Proceedings to Review Orders of the Secretary of the Interior;[4]
- Proceedings to Review Orders of the Petroleum Control Boards;[5] and
- Proceedings to Enforce Orders of the National Labor Relations Board.[6]

Applicable

The Rules supplement the statutory procedures for the following:

- Bankruptcy Proceedings, to the extent provided by the Bankruptcy Rules;[7]
- Admission to Citizenship Proceedings;[8]
- Habeas Corpus Proceedings;[9]
- Quo Warranto Proceedings;[10]
- Proceedings for Enforcement or Review of Compensation Orders under the Longshoremen's and Harbor Workers' Compensation Act;[11] and
- Proceedings to enforce subpoenas to testify or to pro-

---

[1] Rule 81(a) exempted copyright proceedings and mental health proceedings in the United States District Court for the District of Columbia from the Rules. These exemptions were removed by the 2001 amendments to Rule 81(a).

[2] Rule 81(a)(1).

[3] Rule 81(a)(6)(A). *Riccelli's Produce, Inc. v. Horton Tomato Co., Inc.*, 155 F.R.D. 411 (N.D. N.Y. 1994).

[4] Rule 81(a)(6)(C).

[5] Rule 81(a)(6)(D).

[6] Rule 81(a)(6)(E).

[7] *Chrysler Financial Corp. v. Powe*, 312 F.3d 1241, 1243 n. 1 (11th Cir. 2002); *In re Appleseed's Intermediate Holdings, LLC*, 470 B.R. 289, 304 (D.Del. 2012).

[8] *Chan v. Gantner*, 464 F.3d 289, 295 (2d Cir. 2006); *Moore v. James*, __ F.Supp.2d __ (E.D.Va. 2011).

[9] *Mayle v. Felix*, 545 U.S. 644, 125 S. Ct. 2562, 2569, 162 L. Ed. 2d 582 (2005); *U.S. v. MacDonald*, 641 F.3d 596, 616, n.12 (4th Cir. 2011).

[10] Rule 81(a)(4).

[11] Rule 81(a)(6)(F); *Galle v. Director, Office of Workers' Compensation Programs*, 246 F.3d 440, 447 (5th Cir. 2001); *Pleasant-El v. Oil Recovery Co., Inc.*, 148 F.3d 1300, 1302 (11th Cir. 1998).

duce documents issued by agencies of the United States.[12]

Arbitrations

In proceedings arbitrated under federal statute, the Rules generally act as default provisions, applying when no arbitration rule addresses the procedural issue.[13]

Habeas Corpus

Prior to the 2002 Amendments, Rule 81(a)(2) contained specific procedures relating to writs of habeas corpus. Those procedures were eliminated by the 2002 Amendments to eliminate the inconsistency between the procedures in Rule 81(a)(2) and in Sections 2254 and 2255.[14]

RULE 81(b)—SCIRE FACIAS AND MANDAMUS

CORE CONCEPT

Rule 81(b) abolishes the Writs of Scire Facias (a writ with a variety of functions such as reviving a judgment[15] or effecting execution) and Mandamus (a writ compelling an official to take an action).[16]

APPLICATIONS

District Court Only

Rule 81(b) abolishes the Writs in the district court only.[17] Thus, a Court of Appeals, under appropriate circumstances, may issue a Writ of Mandamus to a district judge under Rule 21 of the Federal Rules of Appellate Procedure.[18]

---

[12]*Martin v. Bally's Park Place Hotel & Casino*, 983 F.2d 1252 (3d Cir. 1993); *U.S. v. Omega Solutions, LLC*, __ F.Supp.2d __ (E.D.Mich. 2012).

[13]*AIG Baker Sterling Heights, LLC v. American Multi-Cinema, Inc.*, 579 F.3d 1268, 1276 (11th Cir. 2009); *D.H. Blair & Co., Inc. v. Gottdiener*, 462 F.3d 95, 108 (2d Cir. 2006).

[14]The Advisory Committee Note to the 2002 Amendment to Rule 81. *See also Gonzalez v. Crosby*, 545 U.S. 524, 125 S. Ct. 2641, 2646, 162 L. Ed. 2d 480 (2005); *U.S. v. Nelson*, 465 F.3d 1145, 1147 (10th Cir. 2006); *Harris v. U.S.*, 522 F. Supp. 2d 199, 202 (D.D.C. 2007).

[15]*TDK Electronics Corp. v. Draiman*, 321 F.3d 677, 680 (7th Cir. 2003) (although the writ of *scire facias* is abolished, revival or reentry of a judgment is obtainable by a more modern motion).

[16]*U.S. v. Choi*, 818 F.Supp.2d 79, 85 (D.D.C. 2011); *Badier v. Gonzales*, 475 F. Supp. 2d 1294, 1298 (N.D. Ga. 2006).

[17]*U.S. v. Choi*, 818 F.Supp.2d 79, 84–85 (D.D.C. 2011).

[18]*In re Nagy*, 89 F.3d 115, 116–17 (2d Cir. 1996); *U.S. v. Choi*, 818 F.Supp.2d 79, 84–85 (D.D.C. 2011). *But see In re Campbell*, 264 F.3d 730, 731 (7th Cir. 2001) (declining to issue writ of mandamus to state court).

Relief Not Abolished

Only the Writs themselves are abolished. The relief sought may be available through some other motion or proceeding.[19]

RULE 81(c)—REMOVED ACTIONS

CORE CONCEPT

Rule 81(c) provides that the Rules apply to actions commenced in state court and removed to federal court.[20] It also contains procedures governing removed actions.

APPLICATIONS

Rules Apply After Removal

The Rules apply to pleadings or motions filed after the removal.[21] Thus, Rules governing the form of pleadings would not apply to pleadings filed in state court prior to removal.[22]

Time for Service of Complaint

The 120-day deadline for service of the complaint for defendants not served with the complaint prior to removal is calculated from the date of removal.[23]

Time to Answer

If the defendant has not yet answered at the time of removal, the defendant may file an answer or responsive motion either by 7 days from the date of removal,[24] or 21 days from service of the original pleading, if the pleading has been filed, whichever is later.[25] Note, however, that the act of removal alone does not trigger an obligation to answer a complaint that

---

[19]*In re Cheney*, 406 F.3d 723, 728–29 (D.C. Cir. 2005) (mandamus like relief can be obtained through a mandatory injunction); *Simmat v. U.S. Bureau of Prisons*, 413 F.3d 1225, 1235 (10th Cir. 2005) (mandamus relief otherwise available); *TDK Electronics Corp. v. Draiman*, 321 F.3d 677, 680 (7th Cir. 2003) (although the writ of *scire facias* is abolished, revival or reentry of a judgment is obtainable by a more modern motion).

[20]*Wallace v. Microsoft Corp.*, 596 F.3d 703, 706 (10th Cir. 2010); *S. Wallace Edwards & Sons, Inc. v. Cincinnati Ins. Co.*, 353 F.3d 367, 374, (4th Cir. 2003).

[21]*Christiansen v. West Branch Cmty. Sch. Dist.*, 674 F.3d 927, 939 (8th Cir. 2012); *Price v. Wyeth Holdings Corp.*, 505 F.3d 624, 628 (7th Cir. 2007) (applying state law to pre-removal conduct).

[22]*See Romo v. Gulf Stream Coach,*

Inc., 250 F.3d 1119 (7th Cir. 2001) ("The Federal Rules make clear that they do not apply to filings in state court, even if the case is later removed to federal court."); *Griffen v. City of Oklahoma City*, 3 F.3d 336 (10th Cir. 1993) (holding that Rule 11 sanctions do not apply to a complaint filed in state court and removed to federal court); *but see Christiansen v. West Branch Cmty. Sch. Dist.*, 674 F.3d 927, 939 (8th Cir. 2012) (complaint filed in state court subject to federal standards after removal).

[23]*Cardenas v. City of Chicago*, 646 F.3d 1001, 1004 (7th Cir. 2011); *Wallace v. Microsoft Corp.*, 596 F.3d 703, 706 (10th Cir. 2010).

[24]*D.H. Blair & Co., Inc. v. Gottdiener*, 462 F.3d 95, 102 (2d Cir. 2006); *Norsyn, Inc. v. Desai*, 351 F.3d 825, 828 (8th Cir. 2003).

[25]*Murphy Bros., Inc. v. Michetti Pipe Stringing, Inc.*, 526 U.S. 344, 346,

has not yet been properly served.[26]

Repleading Unnecessary

Unless the court orders otherwise, pleadings filed while the action was in state court do not need to be repleaded after removal to federal court.[27]

Jury Demand

If a jury trial demand has been properly made in state court, no new demand is necessary.[28] If no jury trial demand was made in state court and if all pleadings were filed in state court, the parties may nonetheless make a jury trial demand within 14 days of removal to federal court.[29] The 14 days are measured from filing the removal petition in the case of the petitioner and from service of the petition for all other parties. If no express jury trial demand is required under state law, none will be required in the removed action unless the court so directs.[30] If a jury demand was made in the state court proceedings that does not meet the state requirements but does satisfy federal requirements, it can be accepted by the federal court.[31] There remain some scenarios that are not covered by Rule 81(c). In New York, jury demands may be made shortly before trial. In such cases, the court will have discretion to allow a late jury demand.[32]

RULE 81(d)—LAW APPLICABLE

CORE CONCEPT

Rule 81(d) provides that, in general, when the Rules refer to "states," they include the District of Columbia.[33] Thus, when the Rules refer to the law of the state in which the court sits, the United States District Court for the District of Columbia uses the law applied in the District of Columbia. Rule 81(d) also defines

---

119 S. Ct. 1322, 1325, 143 L. Ed. 2d 448 (1999); *Boyle v. American Auto Service, Inc.*, 571 F.3d 734, 743, n.5 (8th Cir. 2009) (party may answer or assert other defenses within the specified time periods); *Silva v. City of Madison*, 69 F.3d 1368, 1371 (7th Cir. 1995) (only proper service triggers the 20 day period to answer).

[26]*Norsyn, Inc. v. Desai*, 351 F.3d 825, 829 (8th Cir. 2003).

[27]*Wasserman v. Rodacker*, 557 F.3d 635, 639 (D.C.Cir. 2009).

[28]*Lutz v. Glendale Union High School*, 403 F.3d 1061, 1063–64 (9th Cir. 2005); *Winter v. Minnesota Mut. Life Ins. Co.*, 199 F.3d 399, 406 (7th Cir. 1999).

[29]*Lutz v. Glendale Union High School*, 403 F.3d 1061, 1063–64 (9th

Cir. 2005); *Wilhelm v. Wilhelm*, 662 F.Supp.2d 424, 426 (D.Md. 2009).

[30]*Bruns v. Amana*, 131 F.3d 761, 762 (8th Cir. 1997); *Wilhelm v. Wilhelm*, 662 F.Supp.2d 424, 426 (D.Md. 2009).

[31]*Wyatt v. Hunt Plywood Co., Inc.*, 297 F.3d 405, 415 (5th Cir. 2002).

[32]*See* Rule 38(b); *Felix-Hernandez v. American Airlines, Inc.*, 539 F. Supp. 2d 511, 512 (D.P.R. 2007); *Ajnoha v. JC Penney Life Ins. Co.*, 480 F. Supp. 2d 663, 676–77 (E.D. N.Y. 2007). *Breedlove v. Cabou*, 296 F. Supp. 2d 253, 278 (N.D. N.Y. 2003).

[33]*Wasserman v. Rodacker*, 557 F.3d 635, 639 (D.C.Cir. 2009); *U.S. Intern. Trade Com'n v. ASAT, Inc.*, 411 F.3d 245, 250 (D.C. Cir. 2005).

the phrase "law of a state" as including statutes and judicial decisions.

APPLICATIONS

Impact of 2007 "Restyling" Amendments

Rule 81 was restructured during the 2007 Federal Civil Rules "Restyling" Project. The 2007 amendments eliminated abrogated Rule 81(d), and Rule 81(e) was renumbered as Rule 81(d). In researching current Rule 81(d), practitioners should be mindful of this repositioning.

Additional Research References

Wright & Miller, *Federal Practice and Procedure* §§ 3131 to 3134
C.J.S., Federal Civil Procedure §§ 7 to 23 et seq.
West's Key Number Digest, Federal Civil Procedure ⬦31 to 44

RULE 82
JURISDICTION AND VENUE UNAFFECTED

These rules do not extend or limit the jurisdiction of the district courts or the venue of actions in those courts. An admiralty or maritime claim under Rule 9(h) is not a civil action for purposes of 28 U.S.C. §§ 1391 to 1392.

[Amended effective October 20, 1949; July 1, 1966; April 23, 2001, effective December 1, 2001; April 30, 2007, effective December 1, 2007.]

AUTHORS' COMMENTARY ON RULE 82

PURPOSE AND SCOPE

Jurisdiction and venue are determined by statute (as discussed in separate sections of this book) and are not affected by the Rules.[1]

APPLICATIONS

Subject Matter Jurisdiction Only

As a general matter, the Rules do not extend the court's subject matter jurisdiction.[2] This principle is limited to *subject matter* jurisdiction (*i.e.,* the type of case a district court can hear), not *personal* jurisdiction (*i.e.,* which parties must appear and defend themselves).[3] Likewise, the Rules contain timing requirements that are often described as "jurisdictional" but do not affect the court's subject matter jurisdiction.[4]

---

[1] *Henderson v. U.S.*, 517 U.S. 654, 116 S. Ct. 1638, 134 L. Ed. 2d 880 (1996); *Laborers' Pension Fund v. Pavement Maintenance, Inc.*, 542 F.3d 189, 193 (7th Cir. 2008).

[2] *Freedom From Religion Foundation, Inc. v. Geithner*, __ F.3d __ (9th Cir. 2011); *Bright v. U.S.*, 603 F.3d 1273, 1281–82 (Fed.Cir. 2010).

[3] *See Chambers Medical Foundation v. Chambers*, 236 F.R.D. 299

(W.D. La. 2006), aff'd, 2006 WL 1895462 (W.D. La. 2006) and aff'd, 221 Fed. Appx. 349 (5th Cir. 2007); *In re National Century Financial Enterprises, Inc., Inv. Litigation*, 323 F. Supp. 2d 861 (S.D. Ohio 2004).

[4] *Kontrick v. Ryan*, 540 U.S. 443, 124 S. Ct. 906, 157 L. Ed. 2d 867 (2004) ("the filing deadlines prescribed in Bankruptcy Rules 4004 and 9006(b)(3) are claim-processing rules that do not delineate what cases bankruptcy

Joinder

Intervention will not create subject matter jurisdiction where none existed before the intervention[5] or defeat diversity jurisdiction where it existed prior to the intervention.[6] However, the Rules actually do affect subject matter jurisdiction in the sense that they govern the joinder of ancillary claims and parties.[7]

Admiralty and Maritime Cases

Rule 82 also provides that admiralty and maritime cases are not considered civil actions for purposes of the venue statutes.[8] Admiralty and maritime cases generally have separate venue provisions to facilitate suing seamen wherever they may be found.[9]

Additional Research References

Wright & Miller, *Federal Practice and Procedure* §§ 3141 to 3142
C.J.S., Federal Civil Procedure § 19
West's Key Number Digest, Federal Civil Procedure ⊙⇒40

---

courts are competent to adjudicate"); *Brickwood Contractors, Inc. v. Datanet Engineering, Inc.*, 369 F.3d 385 (4th Cir.2004) (courts are said to be without jurisdiction to consider an untimely motion under Rule 59); *American Canoe Ass'n, Inc. v. City Of Attalla*, 363 F.3d 1085, 1088 (11th Cir. 2004) (application of Rule 6(a)'s computational rules presents no offense to Rule 82).

[5] *Disability Advocates, Inc. v. New York Coalition for Quality Assisted Living, Inc.*, 675 F.3d 149, 160 (2d Cir. 2012) (intervention by the United States does not create jurisdiction).

[6] *Freedom from Religion Found., Inc. v. Geithner*, 644 F.3d 836, 843 (9th Cir. 2011).

[7] *See Lunney v. U.S.*, 319 F.3d 550, 556–57 (2d Cir. 2003).

[8] *See Sunbelt Corp. v. Noble, Denton & Associates, Inc.*, 5 F.3d 28 (3d Cir.1993); *Empty Barge Lines II, Inc. v. DREDGE LEONARD FISHER*, 441 F. Supp. 2d 786 (E.D. Tex. 2006); *Holmes v. Energy Catering Services, LLC*, 270 F. Supp. 2d 882 (S.D. Tex. 2003).

[9] *See Empty Barge Lines II, Inc. v. DREDGE LEONARD FISHER*, 441 F. Supp. 2d 786 (E.D. Tex. 2006); *Holmes v. Energy Catering Services, LLC*, 270 F. Supp. 2d 882, 885 (S.D. Tex. 2003); *Denson v. U.S.*, 99 F. Supp. 2d 792, 793 (S.D. Tex. 2000).

RULE 83
RULES BY DISTRICT COURTS; JUDGE'S DIRECTIVES

(a) Local Rules.

(1) *In General.* After giving public notice and an opportunity for comment, a district court, acting by a majority of its district judges, may adopt and amend rules governing its practice. A local rule must be consistent with—but not duplicate— federal statutes and rules adopted under 28 U.S.C. §§ 2072 and 2075, and must conform to any uniform numbering system prescribed by the Judicial Conference of the United States. A local rule takes effect on the date specified by the district court and remains in effect unless amended by the court or abrogated by the judicial council of the circuit. Copies of rules and amendments must, on their adoption, be furnished to the judicial council and the Administrative Office of the United States Courts and be made available to the public.

(2) *Requirement of Form.* A local rule imposing a requirement of form must not be enforced in a way that causes a party to lose any right because of a nonwillful failure to comply.

(b) Procedure When There Is No Controlling Law.
A judge may regulate practice in any manner consistent with federal law, rules adopted under 28 U.S.C. §§ 2072 and 2075, and the district's local rules. No sanction or other disadvantage may be imposed for noncompliance with any requirement not in federal law, federal rules, or the local rules unless the alleged violator has been furnished in the particular case with actual notice of the requirement.

[Amended effective August 1, 1985; April 27, 1995, effective December 1, 1995; April 30, 2007, effective December 1, 2007.]

AUTHORS' COMMENTARY ON RULE 83

PURPOSE AND SCOPE

Rule 83 authorizes the districts to develop local rules that are "consistent" with the Federal Rules.

RULE 83(a)—LOCAL RULES

CORE CONCEPT

Rule 83(a) provides that each district court can develop local rules.[1] These local rules must be consistent with the federal rules, both in substance and in numbering. Local rules pertaining to matters of form cannot be enforced in a manner that prejudices the substantive rights of a party.

APPLICATIONS

Consistent with Federal Rules

Local rule must be consistent with, and not duplicative of,[2] Acts of Congress[3] and the Federal Rules.[4] Additionally, numbering must be consistent with the Federal Rules.

Typical Local Rules

Local rules can cover a wide variety of topics, and vary greatly in number and scope from district to district. Some typical local rules address:

- Admission to practice before the district courts;[5]
- Admission *Pro Hac Vice;*
- Procedures for disbarment;
- Security for court costs;
- Creation of divisions within the district;
- Form and number of copies of pleadings and briefs;
- Period of time for process;
- Manner for presentation of motions;[6]
- Notice for constitutional challenges to acts of Congress;

---

[1] *Hollingsworth v. Perry*, 130 S.Ct. 705, 710 (U.S. 2010).

[2] *U.S. v. Galiczynski*, 44 F. Supp. 2d 707 (E.D. Pa. 1999), aff'd, 203 F.3d 818 (3d Cir. 1999); *Guidance Endodontics, LLC v. Dentsply Intern., Inc.*, __ F.Supp.2d __ (D.N.M. 2011).

[3] *In re Ricoh Co., Ltd. Patent Litig.*, 661 F.3d 1361, 1370, n.5 (Fed. Cir. 2011) (local rule cannot render disallowable costs allowed under statute); *D'Iorio v. Majestic Lanes, Inc.*, 370 F.3d 354 (3d Cir.2004).

[4] *Law Co., Inc. v. Mohawk Const. and Supply Co., Inc.*, 577 F.3d 1164, 1170, n.5 (10th Cir. 2009); *Auto Services Co., Inc. v. KPMG, LLP*, 537 F.3d 853, 857 (8th Cir. 2008).

[5] *See In re Poole*, 222 F.3d 618, 621 (9th Cir. 2000).

[6] *Miltimore Sales, Inc. v. International Rectifier, Inc.*, 412 F.3d 685, 693 (6th Cir. 2005) (motions for attorneys fees); *Jetton v. McDonnell Douglas Corp.*, 121 F.3d 423, 426 (8th Cir. 1997); *Goltz v. University of Notre*

- Continuances;
- Discovery procedures;
- Pretrial and status conferences, including pretrial statements;
- Impartial medical examinations;
- Courtroom rules and regulations, including the use of cameras and recording equipment;
- Size, selection, and instruction of the jury;
- Handling and marking of exhibits;
- Entry of judgment; and
- Motions for new trials.

Effect of Local Rule

A valid local rule has the effect of law,[7] and must be obeyed.[8] The court has authority to impose sanctions when a party violates the court's local rules.[9] However, a local rule imposing a requirement of form (as opposed to substance) may not be enforced in a manner that causes a party to lose rights for a "nonwillful" violation.[10] Thus, a party should not be deprived of a right to a jury trial because it is unaware of or forgets a local rule requiring jury demands to be noted in the caption of pleadings.[11]

Promulgation of Local Rules

Local rules are adopted pursuant to the procedures in the Rules Enabling Act.[12]

Dame du Lac, 177 F.R.D. 638 (N.D. Ind. 1997) (one purpose of local rules is to further the administration of justice by mandating that motions for summary judgment be properly briefed).

[7]*Hollingsworth v. Perry*, 130 S.Ct. 705, 710 (U.S. 2010); *Nahno-Lopez v. Houser*, 625 F.3d 1279, 1284 (10th Cir. 2010); *Jetton v. McDonnell Douglas Corp.*, 121 F.3d 423, 426 (8th Cir. 1997) (local rule has "the force of law" and the parties are charged with knowledge of the district court's rules the same as with knowledge of the Federal Rules and all federal law).

[8]*Weil v. Neary*, 278 U.S. 160, 169, 49 S. Ct. 144, 148, 73 L. Ed. 243 (1929); *Benuzzi v. Bd. of Educ. of City of Chicago*, 647 F.3d 652, 654 (7th Cir. 2011).

[9]*Carmona v. Wright*, 233 F.R.D. 270, 275 (N.D. N.Y. 2006); *Nick v. Morgan's Foods, Inc.*, 99 F. Supp. 2d 1056, 1061 (E.D. Mo. 2000).

[10]*Yancick v. Hanna Steel Corp.*, 653 F.3d 532, 537 (7th Cir. 2011) (requirement to attach evidentiary support to a brief is more than a matter of form); *Transportes Navieros and Terrestres S.A. De C.V. v. Fairmount Heavy Transport, N.V*, 572 F.3d 96 (2nd Cir. 2009).

[11]The Advisory Committee Note to the 1995 amendment to Rule 83.

[12]28 U.S.C. § 2071(b); *In re Dorner*, 343 F.3d 910, 913 (7th Cir. 2003); *see also Hollingsworth v. Perry*, 130 S.Ct. 705, 710 (U.S. 2010) (local rules may not be amended unless the district court gives public notice and an opportunity for comment).

Public Comment

Before a local rule may be enacted, it must be published for comment by the public.[13]

Copies

Local rules are included in West's court rules pamphlets for most states. A copy of the local rules can also be obtained from the clerk's office for a nominal fee. Additionally, Rule 83 provides that the district must submit a copy of the local rules to the Administrative Office of the United States Courts.[14]

Bankruptcy

Local rules do not apply to proceedings in Bankruptcy.[15]

RULE 83(b)—PROCEDURE WHEN THERE IS NO CONTROLLING LAW

CORE CONCEPT

In the absence of a federal or local rule of procedure, the judges may regulate proceedings before them as they see fit, so long the court's rules are consistent with federal law, the Federal Rules, and local rules.[16]

APPLICATIONS

Orders Consistent with Other Rules

Individual judges' standing orders or requirements must be consistent with Acts of Congress, the Federal Rules, and local rules.[17]

Parties Must have Actual Notice of Court Requirements

The court may not sanction or "disadvantage" a party for noncompliance with a requirement not found in federal law, federal rules, or local rules unless that party has been furnished in the particular case with actual notice of the requirement.[18] Actual notice can be provided with a copy of the judge's requirements, by an order referencing the judge's stand-

---

[13]*In re Dorner*, 343 F.3d 910, 913 (7th Cir. 2003). *Antoine v. Atlas Turner, Inc.*, 66 F.3d 105, 108 (6th Cir. 1995).

[14]*Dais v. Lane Bryant, Inc.*, 2000 WL 869489 (S.D. N.Y. 2000).

[15]*In re Flanagan*, 999 F.2d 753 (3d Cir.1993).

[16]*See Carnes v. Zamani*, 488 F.3d 1057, 1059 (9th Cir. 2007) (the judge's power under Rule 83(b) to regulate the practice in the court only applies where there is no other controlling law); *Amnesty America v. Town of West Hartford*, 288 F.3d 467, 470–71 (2d Cir. 2002) (district court may regulate motion practice in any man-

ner consistent with federal law and the federal rules).

[17]*In re Dorner*, 343 F.3d 910, 913 (7th Cir. 2003).

[18]*Massachusetts Institute of Technology and Electronics For Imaging, Inc. v. Abacus Software*, 462 F.3d 1344, 1359 (Fed. Cir. 2006); *Amnesty America v. Town of West Hartford*, 288 F.3d 467, 471 (2d Cir. 2002); *Carroll v. Jaques Admiralty Law Firm, P.C.*, 110 F.3d 290, 293 (5th Cir. 1997) (but, the rule does not eliminate a court's inherent power to sanction for intentional disruption of the discovery process).

ing order and indicating how copies can be obtained, or by oral notice at a Rule 16 conference.[19]

Additional Research References

Wright & Miller, *Federal Practice and Procedure* §§ 3151 to 3155
C.J.S., Federal Civil Procedure § 21
West's Key Number Digest, Federal Civil Procedure ⊶25

---

[19]*See Tyco Fire Products LP v. Victaulic Co.*, __ F.Supp.2d __ (E.D.Pa. 2011) (notice at status conference deemed sufficient); the Advisory Committee Note to the 1995 amendment to Rule 83.

RULE 84
FORMS

The forms in the Appendix suffice under these rules and illustrate the simplicity and brevity that these rules contemplate.

[Amended effective March 19, 1948; April 30, 2007, effective December 1, 2007.]

AUTHORS' COMMENTARY ON RULE 84

PURPOSE AND SCOPE

The Rules contain an Appendix of Forms that contains 82 forms, including complaints, answers, motions, discovery requests, and notices of appeal. The forms were completely rewritten in the 2007 amendments, and are intended to indicate the simplicity and brevity that are sufficient and acceptable under in federal court.[1] The official forms cannot be challenged under the Rules[2] (although they can be challenged with substantive legal defenses, such as immunities).[3]

Additional Research References

Wright & Miller, *Federal Practice and Procedure* §§ 3161 to 3162
C.J.S., Federal Civil Procedure § 251
West's Key Number Digest, Federal Civil Procedure ☞625 to 627

---

[1] *In re Bill of Lading Transmission and Processing Sys. Patent Litig.*, 681 F.3d 1323, 1334 (Fed.Cir. 2012); *McCauley v. City of Chicago*, 671 F.3d 611, 623–24 (7th Cir. 2011) (questioning whether the forms still suffice after the recent Supreme Court decisions regarding pleading).

[2] *In re Bill of Lading Transmis-sion and Processing Sys. Patent Litig.*, 681 F.3d 1323, 1334 (Fed.Cir. 2012); *McZeal v. Sprint Nextel Corp.*, 501 F.3d 1354, 1360 (Fed. Cir. 2007) (bare allegation consistent with Form 16 meets the requirements of Rule 8).

[3] *See Atchinson v. District of Columbia*, 73 F.3d 418, 423 (D.C. Cir. 1996).

RULE 85
TITLE

These rules may be cited as the Federal Rules of Civil Procedure.

[Amended April 30, 2007, effective December 1, 2007.]

AUTHORS' COMMENTARY ON RULE 85

PURPOSE AND SCOPE

The full title of the Rules is the "Federal Rules of Civil Procedure." The Rules should be cited as "Fed.R.Civ.P. ___."

Additional Research References

Wright & Miller, *Federal Practice and Procedure* § 3171
C.J.S., Federal Civil Procedure §§ 7 et seq.
West's Key Number Digest, Federal Civil Procedure ⟜31

RULE 86
EFFECTIVE DATES

(a) In General. These rules and any amendments take effect at the time specified by the Supreme Court, subject to 28 U.S.C. § 2074. They govern:

   (1) proceedings in an action commenced after their effective date; and

   (2) proceedings after that date in an action then pending unless:

      (A) the Supreme Court specifies otherwise; or

      (B) the court determines that applying them in a particular action would be infeasible or work an injustice.

(b) December 1, 2007 Amendments. If any provision in Rules 1–5.1, 6–73, or 77–86 conflicts with another law, priority in time for the purpose of 28 U.S.C. § 2072(b) is not affected by the amendments taking effect on December 1, 2007.

[Amended effective March 19, 1948; October 20, 1949; July 19, 1961; July 1, 1963; April 30, 2007, effective December 1, 2007.]

AUTHORS' COMMENTARY ON RULE 86

———— PURPOSE AND SCOPE ————

Rule 86 lists the effective dates of the Rules and certain of the amendments. Amendments typically become effective 90 days after transmittal to Congress.

APPLICATIONS
RULE 86(a)—IN GENERAL

CORE CONCEPT

In general, amendments to the Rules will apply to all actions filed after the effective date of the amendments, and to proceedings in actions filed before the effective date unless the Supreme Court has specified otherwise or if the court determines that application of an amended provision would not be feasible or would work an injustice.[1]

RULE 86(b)—DECEMBER 1, 2007 AMEND-MENTS

CORE CONCEPT

Rule 86(b) addresses the interplay between the 2007 amendments to the Rules and the supersession clause in 28 U.S.C. § 2072(b). The supersession clause says that laws in conflict with one or more of the Rules shall have no further force and effect after such Rules have taken effect. In essence, the Rules are deemed to have superseded existing inconsistent laws. Because the supersession clause focuses on priority in time between the Rules and other laws, Rule 86(b) provides that the non-substantive changes to every Rule in the 2007 amendments do not affect the priority in time analysis.

Additional Research References

Wright & Miller, *Federal Practice and Procedure* §§ 3181 to 3182
C.J.S., Federal Civil Procedure §§ 7 et seq.
West's Key Number Digest, Federal Civil Procedure ⟵31

---

[1]*In re Harwell*, 628 F.3d 1312, 1317, n.4 (11th Cir. 2010); *In re Application of Republic of Ecuador*, 280 F.R.D. 506, 510–11 (N.D.Cal. 2012).

SUPPLEMENTAL RULES FOR ADMIRALTY OR MARITIME CLAIMS AND ASSET FORFEITURE ACTIONS

Adopted February 28, 1966, effective July 1, 1966

The former Rules of Practice in Admiralty and Maritime Cases, promulgated by the Supreme Court on December 6, 1920, effective March 7, 1921, as revised, amended and supplemented, were rescinded, effective July 1, 1966.

Including Amendments effective December 1, 2009

RULE A
SCOPE OF RULES

(1)   These Supplemental Rules apply to:
   (A) the procedure in admiralty and maritime claims within the meaning of Rule 9(h) with respect to the following remedies:
      (i)   maritime attachment and garnishment,
      (ii) actions in rem,
      (iii) possessory, petitory, and partition actions, and
      (iv) actions for exoneration from or limitation of liability;
   (B) forfeiture actions in rem arising from a federal statute; and
   (C) the procedure in statutory condemnation proceedings analogous to maritime actions in rem, whether within the admiralty and maritime jurisdiction or not. Except as otherwise provided, references in these Supplemental Rules to actions in rem include such analogous statutory condemnation proceedings.

(2)   The Federal Rules of Civil Procedure also apply to the foregoing proceedings except to the extent that they are inconsistent with these Supplemental Rules.

[Added Feb. 28, 1966, eff. July 1, 1966; April 12, 2006, effective December 1, 2006.]

RULE B
IN PERSONAM ACTIONS:
ATTACHMENT AND GARNISHMENT

(1) When Available; Complaint, Affidavit, Judicial Authorization, and Process. In an in personam action:

(a) If a defendant is not found within the district when a verified complaint praying for attachment and the affidavit required by Rule B(1)(b) are filed, a verified complaint may contain a prayer for process to attach the defendant's tangible or intangible personal property—up to the amount sued for—in the hands of garnishees named in the process.

(b) The plaintiff or the plaintiff's attorney must sign and file with the complaint an affidavit stating that, to the affiant's knowledge, or on information and belief, the defendant cannot be found within the district. The court must review the complaint and affidavit and, if the conditions of this Rule B appear to exist, enter an order so stating and authorizing process of attachment and garnishment. The clerk may issue supplemental process enforcing the court's order upon application without further court order.

(c) If the plaintiff or the plaintiff's attorney certifies that exigent circumstances make court review impracticable, the clerk must issue the summons and process of attachment and garnishment. The plaintiff has the burden in any post-attachment hearing under Rule E(4)(f) to show that exigent circumstances existed.

(d) (i) If the property is a vessel or tangible property on board a vessel, the summons, process, and any supplemental process must be delivered to the marshal for service.

(ii) If the property is other tangible or intangible property, the summons, process, and any supplemental process must be delivered to a person or organization authorized to serve it, who may be (A) a marshal; (B) someone under contract with the United States; (C) someone specially appointed by the court for that purpose; or, (D) in an action brought by the United States, any officer or employee of the United States.

(e) The plaintiff may invoke state-law remedies under Rule 64 for seizure of person or property for the purpose of securing satisfaction of the judgment.

(2) Notice to Defendant. No default judgment may be entered except upon proof—which may be by affidavit—that:

(a) the complaint, summons, and process of attachment or garnishment have been served on the defendant in a manner authorized by Rule 4;

(b) the plaintiff or the garnishee has mailed to the defendant the complaint, summons, and process of attachment or garnishment, using any form of mail requiring a return receipt; or

(c) the plaintiff or the garnishee has tried diligently to give notice of the action to the defendant but could not do so.

(3) Answer.

(a) By Garnishee. The garnishee shall serve an answer, together with answers to any interrogatories served with the complaint, within 21 days after service of process upon the garnishee. Interrogatories to the garnishee may be served with the complaint without leave of court. If the garnishee refuses or neglects to answer on oath as to the debts, credits, or effects of the defendant in the garnishee's hands, or any interrogatories concerning such debts, credits, and effects that may be propounded by the plaintiff, the court may award compulsory process against the garnishee. If the garnishee admits any debts, credits, or effects, they shall be held in the garnishee's hands or paid into the registry of the court, and shall be held in either case subject to the further order of the court.

(b) By Defendant. The defendant shall serve an answer within 30 days after process has been executed, whether by attachment of property or service on the garnishee.

[Added Feb. 28, 1966, eff. July 1, 1966, and amended Apr. 29, 1985, effective Aug. 1, 1985; Mar. 2, 1987, effective Aug. 1, 1987; April 17, 2000, effective December 1, 2000; April 25, 2005, effective December 1, 2005; amended March 26, 2009, effective December 1, 2009.]

RULE C
IN REM ACTIONS: SPECIAL PROVISIONS

(1) When Available. An action in rem may be brought:

    (a) To enforce any maritime lien;

    (b) Whenever a statute of the United States provides for a maritime action in rem or a proceeding analogous thereto.

Except as otherwise provided by law a party who may proceed in rem may also, or in the alternative, proceed in personam against any person who may be liable.

Statutory provisions exempting vessels or other property owned or possessed by or operated by or for the United States from arrest or seizure are not affected by this rule. When a statute so provides, an action against the United States or an instrumentality thereof may proceed on in rem principles.

(2) Complaint. In an action in rem the complaint must:

    (a) be verified;

    (b) describe with reasonable particularity the property that is the subject of the action; and

    (c) state that the property is within the district or will be within the district while the action is pending.

(3) Judicial Authorization and Process.

    (a) Arrest Warrant.

        (i) The court must review the complaint and any supporting papers. If the conditions for an in rem action appear to exist, the court must issue an order directing the clerk to issue a warrant for the arrest of the vessel or other property that is the subject of the action.

        (ii) If the plaintiff or the plaintiff's attorney certifies that exigent circumstances make court review impracticable, the clerk must promptly issue a summons and a warrant for the arrest of the vessel or other property that is the subject of the action. The plaintiff has the burden in any post-arrest hearing under Rule E(4)(f) to show that exigent circumstances existed.

(b) Service.

  (i) If the property that is the subject of the action is a vessel or tangible property on board a vessel, the warrant and any supplemental process must be delivered to the marshal for service.

  (ii) If the property that is the subject of the action is other property, tangible or intangible, the warrant and any supplemental process must be delivered to a person or organization authorized to enforce it, who may be: (A) a marshal; (B) someone under contract with the United States; (C) someone specially appointed by the court for that purpose; or, (D) in an action brought by the United States, any officer or employee of the United States.

(c) Deposit in Court. If the property that is the subject of the action consists in whole or in part of freight, the proceeds of property sold, or other intangible property, the clerk must issue—in addition to the warrant—a summons directing any person controlling the property to show cause why it should not be deposited in court to abide the judgment.

(d) Supplemental Process. The clerk may upon application issue supplemental process to enforce the court's order without further court order.

(4) Notice. No notice other than execution of process is required when the property that is the subject of the action has been released under Rule E(5). If the property is not released within 14 days after execution, the plaintiff must promptly—or within the time that the court allows—give public notice of the action and arrest in a newspaper designated by court order and having general circulation in the district, but publication may be terminated if the property is released before publication is completed. The notice must specify the time under Rule C(6) to file a statement of interest in or right against the seized property and to answer. This rule does not affect the notice requirements in an action to foreclose a preferred ship mortgage under 46 U.S.C. §§ 31301 et seq., as amended.

(5) Ancillary Process. In any action in rem in which process has been served as provided by this rule, if any part of the property that is the subject of the action has not been brought within the control of the court because it has been removed or sold, or because it is intangible property in the hands of a person who has not been served with process, the court may, on motion, order any person having possession or control of such property or its proceeds to show cause why it should not be delivered into the custody of the marshal or other person or organization having a warrant for the arrest of the property, or paid into court to abide the judgment; and, after hearing, the court may enter such judgment as law and justice may require.

(6) Responsive Pleading; Interrogatories.

   (a) Statement of Interest; answer. In an action in rem:

     (i) a person who asserts a right of possession or any ownership interest in the property that is the subject of the action must file a verified statement of right or interest:

       (A) within 14 days after the execution of process, or

       (B) within the time that the court allows;

     (ii) the statement of right or interest must describe the interest in the property that supports the person's demand for its restitution or right to defend the action;

     (iii) an agent, bailee, or attorney must state the authority to file a statement of right or interest on behalf of another; and

     (iv) a person who asserts a right of possession or any ownership interest must serve an answer within 21 days after filing the statement of interest or right.

(b) Interrogatories. Interrogatories may be served with the complaint in an in rem action without leave of court. Answers to the interrogatories must be served with the answer to the complaint.

[Added Feb. 28, 1966, eff. Jul. 1, 1966, and amended Apr. 29, 1985, effective Aug. 1, 1985; Mar. 2, 1987, effective Aug. 1, 1987; Apr. 30, 1991, effective Dec. 1, 1991; April 17, 2000, effective December 1, 2000; April 29, 2002, effective December 1, 2002; April 25, 2005, effective December 1, 2005; April 12, 2006, effective December 1, 2006; amended March 26, 2009, effective December 1, 2009.]

RULE D
POSSESSORY, PETITORY, AND PARTITION ACTIONS

In all actions for possession, partition, and to try title maintainable according to the course of the admiralty practice with respect to a vessel, in all actions so maintainable with respect to the possession of cargo or other maritime property, and in all actions by one or more part owners against the others to obtain security for the return of the vessel from any voyage undertaken without their consent, or by one or more part owners against the others to obtain possession of the vessel for any voyage on giving security for its safe return, the process shall be by a warrant of arrest of the vessel, cargo, or other property, and by notice in the manner provided by Rule B(2) to the adverse party or parties.

[Added Feb. 28, 1966, eff. Jul. 1, 1966.]

RULE E
ACTIONS IN REM AND QUASI IN REM: GENERAL PROVISIONS

(1) Applicability. Except as otherwise provided, this rule applies to actions in personam with process of maritime attachment and garnishment, actions in rem, and petitory, possessory, and partition actions, supplementing Rules B, C, and D.

(2) Complaint; Security.

(a) *Complaint.* In actions to which this rule is applicable the complaint shall state the circumstances from which the claim arises with such particularity that the defendant or claimant will be able, without moving for a more definite statement, to commence an investigation of the facts and to frame a responsive pleading.

(b) *Security for Costs.* Subject to the provisions of Rule 54(d) and of relevant statutes, the court may, on the filing of the complaint or on the appearance of any defendant, claimant, or any other party, or at any later time, require the plaintiff, defendant, claimant, or other party to give security, or additional security, in such sum as the court shall direct to pay all costs and expenses that shall be awarded against the party by any interlocutory order or by the final judgment, or on appeal by any appellate court.

(3) Process.

(a) In admiralty and maritime proceedings process in rem or of maritime attachment and garnishment may be served only within the district.

(b) Issuance and Delivery. Issuance and delivery of process in rem, or of maritime attachment and garnishment, shall be held in abeyance if the plaintiff so requests.

(4) Execution of Process; Marshal's Return; Custody of Property; Procedures for Release.

(a) *In General.* Upon issuance and delivery of the

process, or, in the case of summons with process of attachment and garnishment, when it appears that the defendant cannot be found within the district, the marshal or other person or organization having a warrant shall forthwith execute the process in accordance with this subdivision (4), making due and prompt return.

(b) *Tangible Property.* If tangible property is to be attached or arrested, the marshal or other person or organization having the warrant shall take it into the marshal's possession for safe custody. If the character or situation of the property is such that the taking of actual possession is impracticable, the marshal or other person executing the process shall affix a copy thereof to the property in a conspicuous place and leave a copy of the complaint and process with the person having possession or the person's agent. In furtherance of the marshal's custody of any vessel the marshal is authorized to make a written request to the collector of customs not to grant clearance to such vessel until notified by the marshal or deputy marshal or by the clerk that the vessel has been released in accordance with these rules.

(c) *Intangible Property.* If intangible property is to be attached or arrested the marshal or other person or organization having the warrant shall execute the process by leaving with the garnishee or other obligor a copy of the complaint and process requiring the garnishee or other obligor to answer as provided in Rules B(3)(a) and C(6); or the marshal may accept for payment into the registry of the court the amount owed to the extent of the amount claimed by the plaintiff with interest and costs, in which event the garnishee or other obligor shall not be required to answer unless alias process shall be served.

(d) *Directions With Respect to Property in Custody.* The marshal or other person or organization having the warrant may at any time apply to the court for directions with respect to property that has been attached or arrested, and shall give notice of such application to any or all of the parties as the court may direct.

(e) *Expenses of Seizing and Keeping Property; Deposit.* These rules do not alter the provisions of Title 28, U.S.C., § 1921, as amended, relative to the expenses of seizing and keeping property attached or arrested and to the requirement of deposits to cover such expenses.

(f) *Procedure for Release From Arrest or Attachment.* Whenever property is arrested or attached, any person claiming an interest in it shall be entitled to a prompt hearing at which the plaintiff shall be required to show why the arrest or attachment should not be vacated or other relief granted consistent with these rules. This subdivision shall have no application to suits for seamen's wages when process is issued upon a certification of sufficient cause filed pursuant to Title 46, U.S.C. §§ 603 and 604 or to actions by the United States for forfeitures for violation of any statute of the United States.

(5) Release of Property.

(a) *Special Bond.* Whenever process of maritime attachment and garnishment or process in rem is issued the execution of such process shall be stayed, or the property released, on the giving of security, to be approved by the court or clerk, or by stipulation of the parties, conditioned to answer the judgment of the court or of any appellate court. The parties may stipulate the amount and nature of such security. In the event of the inability or refusal of the parties so to stipulate the court shall fix the principal sum of the bond or stipulation at an amount sufficient to cover the amount of the plaintiff's claim fairly stated with accrued interest and costs; but the principal sum shall in no event exceed (i) twice the amount of the plaintiff's claim or (ii) the value of the property on due appraisement, whichever is smaller. The bond or stipulation shall be conditioned for the payment of the principal sum and interest thereon at 6 per cent per annum.

(b) *General Bond.* The owner of any vessel may file

a general bond or stipulation, with sufficient surety, to be approved by the court, conditioned to answer the judgment of such court in all or any actions that may be brought thereafter in such court in which the vessel is attached or arrested. Thereupon the execution of all such process against such vessel shall be stayed so long as the amount secured by such bond or stipulation is at least double the aggregate amount claimed by plaintiffs in all actions begun and pending in which such vessel has been attached or arrested. Judgments and remedies may be had on such bond or stipulation as if a special bond or stipulation had been filed in each of such actions. The district court may make necessary orders to carry this rule into effect, particularly as to the giving of proper notice of any action against or attachment of a vessel for which a general bond has been filed. Such bond or stipulation shall be indorsed by the clerk with a minute of the actions wherein process is so stayed. Further security may be required by the court at any time.

If a special bond or stipulation is given in a particular case, the liability on the general bond or stipulation shall cease as to that case.

(c) *Release by Consent or Stipulation; Order of Court or Clerk; Costs.* Any vessel, cargo, or other property in the custody of the marshal or other person or organization having the warrant may be released forthwith upon the marshal's acceptance and approval of a stipulation, bond, or other security, signed by the party on whose behalf the property is detained or the party's attorney and expressly authorizing such release, if all costs and charges of the court and its officers shall have first been paid. Otherwise no property in the custody of the marshal, other person or organization having the warrant, or other officer of the court shall be released without an order of the court; but such order may be entered as of course by the clerk, upon the giving of approved security as provided by law and these rules, or upon the dismissal or discontinuance of the action; but the marshal or other person or organization having the warrant shall not deliver any property so released until the costs and charges of the officers of the court shall first have been paid.

(d) *Possessory, Petitory, and Partition Actions.* The foregoing provisions of this subdivision (5) do not apply to petitory, possessory, and partition actions. In such cases the property arrested shall be released only by order of the court, on such terms and conditions and on the giving of such security as the court may require.

(6) Reduction or Impairment of Security. Whenever security is taken the court may, on motion and hearing, for good cause shown, reduce the amount of security given; and if the surety shall be or become insufficient, new or additional sureties may be required on motion and hearing.

(7) Security on Counterclaim.

(a) When a person who has given security for damages in the original action asserts a counterclaim that arises from the transaction or occurrence that is the subject of the original action, a plaintiff for whose benefit the security has been given must give security for damages demanded in the counterclaim unless the court for cause shown, directs otherwise. Proceedings on the original claim must be stayed until this security is given unless the court directs otherwise.

(b) The plaintiff is required to give security under Rule E(7)(a) when the United States or its corporate instrumentality counterclaims and would have been required to give security to respond in damages if a private party but is relieved by law from giving security.

(8) Restricted Appearance. An appearance to defend against an admiralty and maritime claim with respect to which there has issued process in rem, or process of attachment and garnishment, may be expressly restricted to the defense of such claim, and in that event is not an appearance for the purposes of any other claim with respect to which such process is not available or has not been served.

(9) Disposition of Property; Sales.

(a) Interlocutory Sales; Delivery.

(i) On application of a party, the marshal, or other person having custody of the property, the court may order all or part of the property sold—with the sales proceeds, or as much of them as will satisfy the judgment, paid into court to await further orders of the court—if:

(A) the attached or arrested property is perishable, or liable to deterioration, decay, or injury by being detained in custody pending the action;

(B) the expense of keeping the property is excessive or disproportionate; or

(C) there is an unreasonable delay in securing release of the property.

(ii) In the circumstances described in Rule E(9)(a)(i), the court, on motion by a defendant or a person filing a statement of interest or right under Rule C(6), may order that the property, rather than being sold, be delivered to the movant upon giving security under these rules.

(b) *Sales; Proceeds.* All sales of property shall be made by the marshal or a deputy marshal, or by other person or organization having the warrant, or by any other person assigned by the court where the marshal or other person or organization having the warrant is a party in interest; and the proceeds of sale shall be forthwith paid into the registry of the court to be disposed of according to law.

(10) Preservation of Property. When the owner or another person remains in possession of property attached or arrested under the provisions of Rule E(4)(b) that permit execution of process without taking actual possession, the court, on a party's motion or on its own, may enter any order necessary to preserve the property and to prevent its removal.

[Added Feb. 28, 1966, eff. Jul. 1, 1966, and amended Apr. 29, 1985, effective Aug. 1, 1985; Mar. 2, 1987, effective Aug. 1, 1987; Apr. 30, 1991, effective Dec. 1, 1991; April 17, 2000, effective December 1, 2000; April 12, 2006, effective December 1, 2006.]

RULE F
LIMITATION OF LIABILITY

(1) Time for Filing Complaint; Security. Not later than six months after receipt of a claim in writing, any vessel owner may file a complaint in the appropriate district court, as provided in subdivision (9) of this rule, for limitation of liability pursuant to statute. The owner (a) shall deposit with the court, for the benefit of claimants, a sum equal to the amount or value of the owner's interest in the vessel and pending freight, or approved security therefor, and in addition such sums, or approved security therefor, as the court may from time to time fix as necessary to carry out the provisions of the statutes as amended; or (b) at the owner's option shall transfer to a trustee to be appointed by the court, for the benefit of claimants, the owner's interest in the vessel and pending freight, together with such sums, or approved security therefor, as the court may from time to time fix as necessary to carry out the provisions of the statutes as amended. The plaintiff shall also give security for costs and, if the plaintiff elects to give security, for interest at the rate of 6 percent per annum from the date of the security.

(2) Complaint. The complaint shall set forth the facts on the basis of which the right to limit liability is asserted and all facts necessary to enable the court to determine the amount to which the owner's liability shall be limited. The complaint may demand exoneration from as well as limitation of liability. It shall state the voyage if any, on which the demands sought to be limited arose, with the date and place of its termination; the amount of all demands including all unsatisfied liens or claims of lien, in contract or in tort or otherwise, arising on that voyage, so far as known to the plaintiff, and what actions and proceedings, if any, are pending thereon; whether the vessel was damaged, lost, or abandoned, and, if so, when and where; the value of the vessel at the close of the voyage or, in case of wreck, the value of her wreckage, strippings, or proceeds, if any, and where and in whose possession they are; and the amount of any pending freight recovered or recoverable. If the plaintiff elects to transfer the plaintiff's interest in the vessel to a trustee, the complaint must further show any prior paramount liens thereon, and what voyages or trips, if any, she has made since the voyage or trip on which the claims sought to be limited arose, and any existing liens arising upon any such subsequent voyage or trip, with the amounts and causes thereof, and the names and addresses of the lienors, so far as known; and whether the vessel sustained any injury upon or by reason of such subsequent voyage or trip.

(3) Claims Against Owner; Injunction. Upon compliance by the owner with the requirements of subdivision (1) of this rule all claims and proceedings against the owner or the owner's property with respect to the matter in question shall cease. On application of the plaintiff the court shall enjoin the further prosecution of any action or proceeding against the plaintiff or the plaintiff's property with respect to any claim subject to limitation in the action.

(4) Notice to Claimants. Upon the owner's compliance with subdivision (1) of this rule the court shall issue a notice to all persons asserting claims with respect to which the complaint seeks limitation, admonishing them to file their respective claims with the clerk of the court and to serve on the attorneys for the plaintiff a copy thereof on or before a date to be named in the notice. The date so fixed shall not be less than 30 days after issuance of the notice. For cause shown, the court may enlarge the time within which claims may be filed. The notice shall be published in such newspaper or newspapers as the court may direct once a week for four successive weeks prior to the date fixed for the filing of claims. The plaintiff not later than the day of second publication shall also mail a copy of the

notice to every person known to have made any
claim against the vessel or the plaintiff arising out
of the voyage or trip on which the claims sought to
be limited arose. In cases involving death a copy of
such notice shall be mailed to the decedent at the
decedent's last known address, and also to any
person who shall be known to have made any claim
on account of such death.

(5) Claims and Answer. Claims shall be filed and
served on or before the date specified in the notice
provided for in subdivision (4) of this rule. Each
claim shall specify the facts upon which the claimant relies in support of the claim, the items thereof,
and the dates on which the same accrued. If a
claimant desires to contest either the right to
exoneration from or the right to limitation of liability the claimant shall file and serve an answer
to the complaint unless the claim has included an
answer.

(6) Information to Be Given Claimants. Within 30
days after the date specified in the notice for filing
claims, or within such time as the court thereafter
may allow, the plaintiff shall mail to the attorney
for each claimant (or if the claimant has no attorney to the claimant) a list setting forth (a) the
name of each claimant, (b) the name and address
of the claimant's attorney (if the claimant is known
to have one), (c) the nature of the claim, i.e.,
whether property loss, property damage, death,
personal injury etc., and (d) the amount thereof.

(7) Insufficiency of Fund or Security. Any claimant may by motion demand that the funds deposited in court or the security given by the plaintiff
be increased on the ground that they are less than
the value of the plaintiff's interest in the vessel
and pending freight. Thereupon the court shall
cause due appraisement to be made of the value of
the plaintiff's interest in the vessel and pending
freight; and if the court finds that the deposit or
security is either insufficient or excessive it shall
order its increase or reduction. In like manner any
claimant may demand that the deposit or security
be increased on the ground that it is insufficient to

carry out the provisions of the statutes relating to claims in respect of loss of life or bodily injury; and, after notice and hearing, the court may similarly order that the deposit or security be increased or reduced.

(8) Objections to Claims: Distribution of Fund. Any interested party may question or controvert any claim without filing an objection thereto. Upon determination of liability the fund deposited or secured, or the proceeds of the vessel and pending freight, shall be divided pro rata, subject to all relevant provisions of law, among the several claimants in proportion to the amounts of their respective claims, duly proved, saving, however, to all parties any priority to which they may be legally entitled.

(9) Venue; Transfer. The complaint shall be filed in any district in which the vessel has been attached or arrested to answer for any claim with respect to which the plaintiff seeks to limit liability; or, if the vessel has not been attached or arrested, then in any district in which the owner has been sued with respect to any such claim. When the vessel has not been attached or arrested to answer the matters aforesaid, and suit has not been commenced against the owner, the proceedings may be had in the district in which the vessel may be, but if the vessel is not within any district and no suit has been commenced in any district, then the complaint may be filed in any district. For the convenience of parties and witnesses, in the interest of justice, the court may transfer the action to any district; if venue is wrongly laid the court shall dismiss or, if it be in the interest of justice, transfer the action to any district in which it could have been brought. If the vessel shall have been sold, the proceeds shall represent the vessel for the purposes of these rules.

[Added Feb. 28, 1966, eff. Jul. 1, 1966, and amended Mar. 2, 1987, effective Aug. 1, 1987.]

RULE G
FORFEITURE ACTIONS IN REM

(1) Scope. This rule governs a forfeiture action in rem arising from a federal statute. To the extent that this rule does not address an issue, Supplemental Rules C and E and the Federal Rules of Civil Procedure also apply.

(2) Complaint. The complaint must:

  (a) be verified;

  (b) state the grounds for subject-matter jurisdiction, in rem jurisdiction over the defendant property, and venue;

  (c) describe the property with reasonable particularity;

  (d) if the property is tangible, state its location when any seizure occurred and—if different—its location when the action is filed;

  (e) identify the statute under which the forfeiture action is brought; and

  (f) state sufficiently detailed facts to support a reasonable belief that the government will be able to meet its burden of proof at trial.

(3) Judicial Authorization and Process.

  (a) Real Property. If the defendant is real property, the government must proceed under 18 U.S.C. § 985.

  (b) Other Property; Arrest Warrant. If the defendant is not real property:

  (i) the clerk must issue a warrant to arrest the property if it is in the government's possession, custody, or control;

  (ii) the court—on finding probable cause—must issue a warrant to arrest the property if it is not in the government's possession, custody, or control and is not subject to a judicial restraining order; and

  (iii) a warrant is not necessary if the property is subject to a judicial restraining order.

(c) Execution of Process.

    (i) The warrant and any supplemental process must be delivered to a person or organization authorized to execute it, who may be: (A) a marshal or any other United States officer or employee; (B) someone under contract with the United States; or (C) someone specially appointed by the court for that purpose.

    (ii) The authorized person or organization must execute the warrant and any supplemental process on property in the United States as soon as practicable unless:

        (A) the property is in the government's possession, custody, or control; or

        (B) the court orders a different time when the complaint is under seal, the action is stayed before the warrant and supplemental process are executed, or the court finds other good cause.

    (iii) The warrant and any supplemental process may be executed within the district or, when authorized by statute, outside the district.

    (iv) If executing a warrant on property outside the United States is required, the warrant may be transmitted to an appropriate authority for serving process where the property is located.

(4) Notice.

  (a) Notice by Publication.

    (i) **When Publication Is Required.** A judgment of forfeiture may be entered only if the government has published notice of the action within a reasonable time after filing the complaint or at a time the court orders. But notice need not be published if:

        (A) the defendant property is worth less than $1,000 and direct notice is sent under Rule G(4)(b) to every person the government can reasonably identify as a potential claimant; or

        (B) the court finds that the cost of publication exceeds the property's value and that other means of notice would satisfy due process.

(ii) Content of the Notice. Unless the court orders otherwise, the notice must:

    (A) describe the property with reasonable particularity;

    (B) state the times under Rule G(5) to file a claim and to answer; and

    (C) name the government attorney to be served with the claim and answer.

(iii) Frequency of Publication. Published notice must appear:

    (A) once a week for three consecutive weeks; or

    (B) only once if, before the action was filed, notice of nonjudicial forfeiture of the same property was published on an official internet government forfeiture site for at least 30 consecutive days, or in a newspaper of general circulation for three consecutive weeks in a district where publication is authorized under Rule G(4)(a)(iv).

(iv) Means of Publication. The government should select from the following options a means of publication reasonably calculated to notify potential claimants of the action:

    (A) if the property is in the United States, publication in a newspaper generally circulated in the district where the action is filed, where the property was seized, or where property that was not seized is located;

    (B) if the property is outside the United States, publication in a newspaper generally circulated in a district where the action is filed, in a newspaper generally circulated in the country where the property is located, or in legal notices published and generally circulated in the country where the property is located; or

    (C) instead of (A) or (B), posting a notice on an official internet government forfeiture site for at least 30 consecutive days.

(b) Notice to Known Potential Claimants.

  (i) Direct Notice Required. The government must

send notice of the action and a copy of the complaint to any person who reasonably appears to be a potential claimant on the facts known to the government before the end of the time for filing a claim under Rule G(5)(a)(ii)(B).

(ii) Content of the Notice. The notice must state:

(A) the date when the notice is sent;

(B) a deadline for filing a claim, at least 35 days after the notice is sent;

(C) that an answer or a motion under Rule 12 must be filed no later than 21 days after filing the claim; and

(D) the name of the government attorney to be served with the claim and answer.

(iii) Sending Notice.

(A) The notice must be sent by means reasonably calculated to reach the potential claimant.

(B) Notice may be sent to the potential claimant or to the attorney representing the potential claimant with respect to the seizure of the property or in a related investigation, administrative forfeiture proceeding, or criminal case.

(C) Notice sent to a potential claimant who is incarcerated must be sent to the place of incarceration.

(D) Notice to a person arrested in connection with an offense giving rise to the forfeiture who is not incarcerated when notice is sent may be sent to the address that person last gave to the agency that arrested or released the person.

(E) Notice to a person from whom the property was seized who is not incarcerated when notice is sent may be sent to the last address that person gave to the agency that seized the property.

(iv) When Notice Is Sent. Notice by the following means is sent on the date when it is placed in the mail, delivered to a commercial carrier, or sent by electronic mail.

(v) Actual Notice. A potential claimant who had

actual notice of a forfeiture action may not oppose or seek relief from forfeiture because of the government's failure to send the required notice.

(5) Responsive Pleadings.

(a) Filing a Claim.

(i) A person who asserts an interest in the defendant property may contest the forfeiture by filing a claim in the court where the action is pending. The claim must:

(A) identify the specific property claimed;

(B) identify the claimant and state the claimant's interest in the property;

(C) be signed by the claimant under penalty of perjury; and

(D) be served on the government attorney designated under Rule G(4)(a)(ii)(C) or (b)(ii)(D).

(ii) Unless the court for good cause sets a different time, the claim must be filed:

(A) by the time stated in a direct notice sent under Rule G(4)(b);

(B) if notice was published but direct notice was not sent to the claimant or the claimant's attorney, no later than 30 days after final publication of newspaper notice or legal notice under Rule G(4)(a) or no later than 60 days after the first day of publication on an official internet government forfeiture site; or

(C) if notice was not published and direct notice was not sent to the claimant or the claimant's attorney:

(1) if the property was in the government's possession, custody, or control when the complaint was filed, no later than 60 days after the filing, not counting any time when the complaint was under seal or when the action was stayed before execution of a warrant issued under Rule G(3)(b); or

(2) if the property was not in the govern-

ment's possession, custody, or control
when the complaint was filed, no later
than 60 days after the government complied with 18 U.S.C. § 985(c) as to real
property, or 60 days after process was executed on the property under Rule G(3).

(iii) A claim filed by a person asserting an interest
as a bailee must identify the bailor, and if filed
on the bailor's behalf must state the authority
to do so.

(b) Answer. A claimant must serve and file an
answer to the complaint or a motion under Rule
12 within 21 days after filing the claim. A claimant waives an objection to in rem jurisdiction or
to venue if the objection is not made by motion
or stated in the answer.

(6) Special Interrogatories.

(a) Time and Scope. The government may serve
special interrogatories limited to the claimant's
identity and relationship to the defendant property without the court's leave at any time after
the claim is filed and before discovery is closed.
But if the claimant serves a motion to dismiss
the action, the government must serve the interrogatories within 21 days after the motion is
served.

(b) Answers or Objections. Answers or objections
to these interrogatories must be served within
21 days after the interrogatories are served.

(c) Government's Response Deferred. The government need not respond to a claimant's motion
to dismiss the action under Rule G(8)(b) until 21
days after the claimant has answered these
interrogatories.

**(7) Preserving, Preventing Criminal Use, and
Disposing of Property; Sales.**

**(a) Preserving and Preventing Criminal Use of
Property.** When the government does not have
actual possession of the defendant property the
court, on motion or on its own, may enter any order necessary to preserve the property, to prevent
its removal or encumbrance, or to prevent its use

in a criminal offense.

(b) Interlocutory Sale or Delivery.

   (i) Order to Sell. On motion by a party or a person having custody of the property, the court may order all or part of the property sold if:

      (A) the property is perishable or at risk of deterioration, decay, or injury by being detained in custody pending the action;

      (B) the expense of keeping the property is excessive or is disproportionate to its fair market value;

      (C) the property is subject to a mortgage or to taxes on which the owner is in default; or

      (D) the court finds other good cause.

   (ii) Who Makes the Sale. A sale must be made by a United States agency that has authority to sell the property, by the agency's contractor, or by any person the court designates.

   (iii) Sale Procedures. The sale is governed by 28 U.S.C. §§ 2001, 2002, and 2004, unless all parties, with the court's approval, agree to the sale, aspects of the sale, or different procedures.

   (iv) Sale Proceeds. Sale proceeds are a substitute res subject to forfeiture in place of the property that was sold. The proceeds must be held in an interest-bearing account maintained by the United States pending the conclusion of the forfeiture action.

   (v) Delivery on a Claimant's Motion. The court may order that the property be delivered to the claimant pending the conclusion of the action if the claimant shows circumstances that would permit sale under Rule G(7)(b)(i) and gives security under these rules.

(c) Disposing of Forfeited Property. Upon entry of a forfeiture judgment, the property or proceeds from selling the property must be disposed of as provided by law.

(8) Motions.

(a) Motion To Suppress Use of the Property as Evidence. If the defendant property was seized, a party with standing to contest the lawfulness of the seizure may move to suppress use of the property as evidence. Suppression does not affect forfeiture of the property based on independently derived evidence.

(b) Motion To Dismiss the Action.

   (i) A claimant who establishes standing to contest forfeiture may move to dismiss the action under Rule 12(b).

   (ii) In an action governed by 18 U.S.C. § 983(a)(3)(D) the complaint may not be dismissed on the ground that the government did not have adequate evidence at the time the complaint was filed to establish the forfeitability of the property. The sufficiency of the complaint is governed by Rule G(2).

(c) Motion To Strike a Claim or Answer.

   (i) At any time before trial, the government may move to strike a claim or answer:

   (A) for failing to comply with Rule G(5) or (6), or

   (B) because the claimant lacks standing.

   (ii) The motion:

   (A) must be decided before any motion by the claimant to dismiss the action; and

   (B) may be presented as a motion for judgment on the pleadings or as a motion to determine after a hearing or by summary judgment whether the claimant can carry the burden of establishing standing by a preponderance of the evidence.

(d) Petition To Release Property.

   (i) If a United States agency or an agency's contractor holds property for judicial or nonjudicial forfeiture under a statute governed by 18 U.S.C. § 983(f), a person who has filed a claim to the property may petition for its release under § 983(f).

   (ii) If a petition for release is filed before a judicial forfeiture action is filed against the property, the petition may be filed either in the district where the property was seized or in the district where a warrant to seize the property issued. If a judicial forfeiture action against the property is later filed in another district—or if the government shows that the action will be filed in another district—the petition may be transferred to that district under 28 U.S.C. § 1404.

(e) Excessive Fines. A claimant may seek to mitigate a forfeiture under the Excessive Fines Clause of the Eighth Amendment by motion for summary judgment or by motion made after entry of a forfeiture judgment if:

(i) the claimant has pleaded the defense under Rule 8; and

(ii) the parties have had the opportunity to conduct civil discovery on the defense.

(9) Trial. Trial is to the court unless any party demands trial by jury under Rule 38.

(Added Apr. 12, 2006, eff. Dec. 1, 2006; amended March 26, 2009, effective December 1, 2009.)

PART IV
APPENDIX OF FORMS

(See Rule 84)

Table of Forms

Introductory Statement.

Form

1. Caption.
2. Date, Signature, Address, E-Mail Address, and Telephone Number.
3. Summons.
4. Summons an a Third-Party Complaint.
5. Notice of a Lawsuit and Request to Waive Service of a Summons.
6. Waiver of the Service of Summons.
7. Statement of Jurisdiction.
8. Statement of Reasons for Omitting a Party.
9. Statement Noting a Party's Death.
10. Complaint to Recover a Sum Certain.
11. Complaint for Negligence.
12. Complaint for Negligence When the Plaintiff Does Not Know Who is Responsible.
13. Complaint for Negligence Under the Federal Employers' Liability Act.
14. Complaint for Damages Under the Merchant Marine Act.
15. Complaint for Damages Under the Merchant Marine Act.
16. Third-Party Complaint.
17. Complaint for Specific Performance of a Contract to Convey Land.
18. Complaint for Patent Infringement.
19. Complaint for Copyright Infringement and Unfair Competition.
20. Complaint for Interpleader and Declaratory Relief.
21. Complaint On a Claim for a Debt and to Set Aside a Fraudulent Conveyance Under Rule 18(b).
30. Answer Presenting Defenses Under Rule 12(b).
31. Answer to a Complaint for Money Had and Received With a Counterclaim for Interpleader.
40. Motion to Dismiss Under Rule 12(B) for Lack of Jurisdiction, Improper Venue, Insufficient Service of Process, or Failure to State a Claim.
41. Motion to Bring In a Third-Party Defendant.
42. Motion to Intervene as a Defendant Under Rule 24.
50. Request to Produce Documents and Tangible Things, or to Enter Onto Land Under Rule 34.
51. Request for Admissions Under Rule 36.
52. Report of the Parties' Planning Meeting.
60. Notice of Condemnation.
61. Complaint for Condemnation.
70. Judgment On a Jury Verdict.
71. Judgment By the Court Without a Jury.
80. Notice of a Magistrate Judge's Availability.

81.   Consent to An Assignment to a Magistrate Judge.

82.   Order of Assignment to a Magistrate Judge.

INTRODUCTORY STATEMENT

1. The following forms are intended for illustration only. They are limited in number. No attempt is made to furnish a manual of forms. Each form assumes the action to be brought in the Southern District of New York. If the district in which an action is brought has divisions, the division should be indicated in the caption.

2. Except where otherwise indicated each pleading, motion, and other paper should have a caption similar to that of the summons, with the designation of the particular paper substituted for the word "Summons". In the caption of the summons and in the caption of the complaint all parties must be named but in other pleadings and papers, it is sufficient to state the name of the first party on either side, with an appropriate indication of other parties. See Rules 4(b), 7(b)(2), and 10(a).

3. In Form 3 and the forms following, the words, "Allegation of jurisdiction," are used to indicate the appropriate allegation in Form 2.

4. Each pleading, motion, and other paper is to be signed in his individual name by at least one attorney of record (Rule 11). The attorney's name is to be followed by his address as indicated in Form 3. In forms following Form 3 the signature and address are not indicated.

5. If a party is not represented by an attorney, the signature and address of the party are required in place of those of the attorney.

FORM 1
CAPTION

(Use on every summons, complaint, answer, motion, or other document.)

**United States District Court
for the
_____ District of _____**

A B, Plaintiff

v.

C D, Defendant

Civil Action No.

_____

v.   )
)
E F, Third-Party Defendant   )
     (Use if needed.)   )

(Name of Document)
(Added Apr. 20, 2007, eff. Dec. 1. 2007.)

FORM 2
DATE, SIGNATURE, ADDRESS, E-MAIL ADDRESS, AND TELEPHONE NUMBER

(Use at the conclusion of pleadings and other papers that require a signature.)

Date _____   _____
                              (Signature of the attorney
                              or unrepresented party)

                              _____

                              (Printed name)

                              _____

                              (Address)

                              _____

                              (E-mail address)

                              _____

                              (Telephone number)

(Added Apr. 20, 2007, eff. Dec. 1. 2007.)

FORM 3
SUMMONS

(Caption—See Form 1.)

To <u>name the defendant</u>:

A lawsuit has been filed against you.

Within 21 days after service of this summons on you (not counting the day you received it), you must serve on the plaintiff an answer to the attached complaint or a motion under Rule 12 of the Federal Rules of Civil Procedure. The answer or motion must be served on the plaintiff's attorney, _____, whose address is _____. If you fail to do so, judgment by default will be entered against you for the relief demanded in the complaint. You also must file your answer or motion with the court.

Date ———   ————————————
                            Clerk of Court

(Court Seal)

(Use 60 days if the defendant is the United States or a United States agency, or is an officer or employee of the United States allowed 60 days by Rule 12(a)(3).)

(Added Apr. 20, 2007, eff. Dec. 1. 2007; amended March 26, 2009, effective December 1, 2009.)

FORM 4
SUMMONS ON A THIRD-PARTY COMPLAINT

(Caption—See Form 1.)

To *name the third-party defendant*:

A lawsuit has been filed against defendant ———, who as third-party plaintiff is making this claim against you to pay part or all of what [he] may owe to the plaintiff ———.

Within 21 days after service of this summons on you (not counting the day you received it), you must serve on the plaintiff and on the defendant an answer to the attached third-party complaint or a motion under Rule 12 of the Federal Rules of Civil Procedure. The answer or motion must be served on the defendant's attorney, ———, whose address is ———, and also on the plaintiff's attorney, ———, whose address is ———. If you fail to do so, judgment by default will be entered against you for the relief demanded in the third-party complaint. You also must file the answer or motion with the court and serve it on any other parties.

A copy of the plaintiff's complaint is also attached. You may—but are not required to—respond to it.

Date ———   ————————————
                            Clerk of Court

(Court Seal)

(Added Apr. 20, 2007, eff. Dec. 1. 2007; amended March 26, 2009, effective December 1, 2009.)

FORM 5
NOTICE OF A LAWSUIT AND REQUEST TO WAIVE SERVICE OF A SUMMONS

(Caption—See Form 1.)

To *(name the defendant—or if the defendant is a corporation, partnership, or association name an officer or agent authorized to receive service)*:

Why are you getting this?

A lawsuit has been filed against you, or the entity you represent, in this court under the number shown above. A copy of the complaint is attached.

This is not a summons, or an official notice from the court. It is a request that, to avoid expenses, you waive formal service of a summons by signing and returning the enclosed waiver. To avoid these expenses, you must return the signed waiver within (*give at least 30 days or at least 60 days if the defendant is outside any judicial district of the United States*) from the date shown below, which is the date this notice was sent. Two copies of the waiver form are enclosed, along with a stamped, self-addressed envelope or other prepaid means for returning one copy. You may keep the other copy.

What happens next?

If you return the signed waiver, I will file it with the court. The action will then proceed as if you had been served on the date the waiver is filed, but no summons will be served on you and you will have 60 days from the date this notice is sent (see the date below) to answer the complaint (or 90 days if this notice is sent to you outside any judicial district of the United States).

If you do not return the signed waiver within the time indicated, I will arrange to have the summons and complaint served on you. And I will ask the court to require you, or the entity you represent, to pay the expenses of making service.

Please read the enclosed statement about the duty to avoid unnecessary expenses.

I certify that this request is being sent to you on the date below.

(Date and sign—See Form 2.)

(Added Apr. 20, 2007, eff. Dec. 1. 2007.)

FORM 6
WAIVER OF THE SERVICE OF SUMMONS

(Caption—See Form 1.)

To *name the plaintiff's attorney or the unrepresented plaintiff*:

I have received your request to waive service of a summons in this action along with a copy of the complaint, two copies of this waiver form, and a prepaid means of returning one signed copy of the form to you.

I, or the entity I represent, agree to save the expense of serving a summons and complaint in this case.

I understand that I, or the entity I represent, will keep all defenses or objections to the lawsuit, the court's jurisdiction, and the venue of the action, but that I waive any objections to the absence of a summons or of service.

I also understand that I, or the entity I represent, must file and serve an answer or a motion under Rule 12 within 60 days from _____, the date when this request was sent (or 90 days if it was sent outside the United States). If I fail to do so, a default judgment will be entered against me or the entity I represent.

(Date and sign—See Form 2.)

(Attach the following to Form 6.)

Duty to Avoid Unnecessary Expenses of Serving a Summons

Rule 4 of the Federal Rules of Civil Procedure requires certain defendants to cooperate in saving unnecessary expenses of serving a summons and complaint. A defendant who is located in the United States and who fails to return a signed waiver of service requested by a plaintiff located in the United States will be required to pay the expenses of service, unless the defendant shows good cause for the failure.

"Good cause" does *not* include a belief that the lawsuit is groundless, or that it has been brought in an improper venue, or that the court has no jurisdiction over this matter or over the defendant or the defendant's property.

If the waiver is signed and returned, you can still make these and all other defenses and objections, but you cannot object to the absence of a summons or of service.

If you waive service, then you must, within the time specified on the waiver form, serve an answer or a motion under Rule 12 on the plaintiff and file a copy with the court. By signing and returning the waiver form, you are allowed more time to respond than if a summons had been served.

(Added Apr. 20, 2007, eff. Dec. 1. 2007.)

FORM 7

STATEMENT OF JURISDICTION

a. *(For diversity-of-citizenship jurisdiction.)* The plaintiff is [a citizen of *Michigan*] [a corporation incorporated under the laws of *Michigan* with its principal place of business in *Michigan*]. The defendant is [a citizen of *New York*] [a corporation incorporated under the laws of *New York* with its principal place of business in *New York*]. The amount in controversy, without interest and costs, exceeds the sum or value specified by 28 U.S.C. § 1332.

b. *(For federal-question jurisdiction.)* This action arises under [the United States Constitution, *specify the article or amendment and the section*] [a United States treaty *specify*] [a federal statute, __ U.S.C. § ___].

c. *(For a claim in the admiralty or maritime jurisdiction.)* This is a case of admiralty or maritime jurisdiction. *(To invoke admiralty status under* Rule 9(h) *use the following:* This is an

admiralty or maritime claim within the meaning of Rule 9(h).)
(Added Apr. 20, 2007, eff. Dec. 1. 2007.)

FORM 8
STATEMENT OF REASONS FOR OMITTING A PARTY

(If a person who ought to be made a party under Rule 19(a) is not named, include this statement in accordance with Rule 19(c).)

This complaint does not join as a party *name* who [is not subject to this court's personal jurisdiction] [cannot be made a party without depriving this court of subject-matter jurisdiction] because *state the reason*.
(Added Apr. 20, 2007, eff. Dec. 1. 2007.)

FORM 9
STATEMENT NOTING A PARTY'S DEATH

(Caption—See Form 1.)

In accordance with Rule 25(a) *name the person*, who is [a party to this action] [a representative of or successor to the deceased party], notes the death during the pendency of this action of *name*, [*describe as party* in this action].

(Date and sign—See Form 2.)
(Added Apr. 20, 2007, eff. Dec. 1. 2007.)

FORM 10
COMPLAINT TO RECOVER A SUM CERTAIN

(Caption—See Form 1.)

1. (Statement of Jurisdiction—See Form 7.)

(Use one or more of the following as appropriate and include a demand for judgment.)

(a) On a Promissory Note

2. On *date*, the defendant executed and delivered a note promising to pay the plaintiff on *date* the sum of $_____ with interest at the rate of ____ percent. A copy of the note [is attached as Exhibit A] [is summarized as follows: _____].

3. The defendant has not paid the amount owed.

(b) On an Account

2. The defendant owes the plaintiff $_____ according to the account set out in Exhibit A.

(c) For Goods Sold and Delivered

2. The defendant owes the plaintiff $_____ for goods sold and delivered by the plaintiff to the defendant from *date* to *date*.

(d) For Money Lent

2. The defendant owes the plaintiff $_____ for money lent by

the plaintiff to the defendant on *date*.

(e) For Money Paid by Mistake

2. The defendant owes the plaintiff $_____ for money paid by mistake to the defendant on *date* under these circumstances: *describe with particularity in accordance with Rule 9(b)*.

(f) For Money Had and Received

2. The defendant owes the plaintiff $_____ for money that was received from *name* on *date* to be paid by the defendant to the plaintiff.

Demand for Judgment

Therefore, the plaintiff demands judgment against the defendant for $_____, plus interest and costs.

(Date and sign—See Form 2.)

(Added Apr. 20, 2007, eff. Dec. 1. 2007.)

FORM 11
COMPLAINT FOR NEGLIGENCE

(Caption—See Form 1.)

1. (Statement of Jurisdiction—See Form 7.)
2. On *date*, at *place*, the defendant negligently drove a motor vehicle against the plaintiff.
3. As a result, the plaintiff was physically injured, lost wages or income, suffered physical and mental pain, and incurred medical expenses of $_____.

Therefore, the plaintiff demands judgment against the defendant for $_____, plus costs.

(Date and sign—See Form 2.)

(Added Apr. 20, 2007, eff. Dec. 1. 2007.)

FORM 12
COMPLAINT FOR NEGLIGENCE WHEN THE PLAINTIFF DOES NOT KNOW WHO IS RESPONSIBLE

(Caption—See Form 1.)

1. (Statement of Jurisdiction—See Form 7.)
2. On *date*, at *place*, defendant *name* or defendant *name* or both of them willfully or recklessly or negligently drove, or caused to be driven, a motor vehicle against the plaintiff.
3. As a result, the plaintiff was physically injured, lost wages or income, suffered mental and physical pain, and incurred medical expenses of $_____.

Therefore, the plaintiff demands judgment against one or both defendants for $_____, plus costs.

(Date and sign—See Form 2.)

(Added Apr. 20, 2007, eff. Dec. 1. 2007.)

FORM 13
COMPLAINT FOR NEGLIGENCE UNDER THE FEDERAL EMPLOYERS' LIABILITY ACT

(Caption—See Form 1.)

1. (Statement of Jurisdiction—See Form 7.)
2. At the times below, the defendant owned and operated in interstate commerce a railroad line that passed through a tunnel located at _____.
3. On *date*, the plaintiff was working to repair and enlarge the tunnel to make it convenient and safe for use in interstate commerce.
4. During this work, the defendant, as the employer, negligently put the plaintiff to work in a section of the tunnel that the defendant had left unprotected and unsupported.
5. The defendant's negligence caused the plaintiff to be injured by a rock that fell from an unsupported portion of the tunnel.
6. As a result, the plaintiff was physically injured, lost wages or income, suffered mental and physical pain, and incurred medical expenses of $_____.

Therefore, the plaintiff demands judgment against the defendant for $_____, and costs.

(Date and sign—See Form 2.)

(Added Apr. 20, 2007, eff. Dec. 1. 2007.)

FORM 14
COMPLAINT FOR DAMAGES UNDER THE MERCHANT MARINE ACT

(Caption—See Form 1.)

1. (Statement of Jurisdiction—See Form 7.)
2. At the times below, the defendant owned and operated the vessel *name* and used it to transport cargo for hire by water in interstate and foreign commerce.
3. On *date*, at *place*, the defendant hired the plaintiff under seamen's articles of customary form for a voyage from _____ to _____ and return at a wage of $_____ a month and found, which is equal to a shore worker's wage of $_____ a month.
4. On *date*, the vessel was at sea on the return voyage. (*Describe the weather and the condition of the vessel.*)
5. (*Describe as in Form 11 the defendant's negligent conduct.*)
6. As a result of the defendant's negligent conduct and the unseaworthiness of the vessel, the plaintiff was physically injured, has been incapable of any gainful activity, suffered

mental and physical pain, and has incurred medical expenses of $_____.

Therefore, the plaintiff demands judgment against the defendant for $_____, plus costs.

(Date and—sign See Form 2.)

(Added Apr. 20, 2007, eff. Dec. 1. 2007.)

FORM 15

COMPLAINT FOR THE CONVERSION OF PROPERTY

(Caption—See Form 1.)

1. (Statement of Jurisdiction—See Form 7.)
2. On *date*, at *place*, the defendant converted to the defendant's own use property owned by the plaintiff. The property converted consists of *describe*.
3. The property is worth $_____.

Therefore, the plaintiff demands judgment against the defendant for $_____, plus costs.

(Date and sign—See Form 2.)

(Added Apr. 20, 2007, eff. Dec. 1. 2007.)

FORM 16

THIRD-PARTY COMPLAINT

(Caption—See Form 1.)

1. Plaintiff *name* has filed against defendant *name* a complaint, a copy of which is attached.
2. *(State grounds entitling defendant's name to recover from third-party defendant's name for (all or an identified share) of any judgment for plaintiff's name against defendant's name.)*

Therefore, the defendant demands judgment against *third-party defendant's name* for *all or an identified share* of sums that may be adjudged against the defendant in the plaintiff's favor.

(Date and sign—See Form 2.)

(Added Apr. 20, 2007, eff. Dec. 1. 2007.)

FORM 17

COMPLAINT FOR SPECIFIC PERFORMANCE OF A CONTRACT TO CONVEY LAND

(Caption—See Form 1.)

1. (Statement of Jurisdiction—See Form 7.)
2. On *date*, the parties agreed to the contract [attached as Exhibit A] [summarize the contract].
3. As agreed, the plaintiff tendered the purchase price and

requested a conveyance of the land, but the defendant refused to accept the money or make a conveyance.

4. The plaintiff now offers to pay the purchase price.

Therefore, the plaintiff demands that:

   (a) the defendant be required to specifically perform the agreement and pay damages of $———, plus interest and costs, or

   (b) if specific performance is not ordered, the defendant be required to pay damages of $———, plus interest and costs.

(Date and sign—See Form 2.)

(Added Apr. 20, 2007, eff. Dec. 1. 2007.)

FORM 18
COMPLAINT FOR PATENT INFRINGEMENT

(Caption—See Form 1.)

1. (Statement of Jurisdiction—See Form 7.)

2. On *date*, United States Letters Patent No. ——— were issued to the plaintiff for an invention in an *electric motor*. The plaintiff owned the patent throughout the period of the defendant's infringing acts and still owns the patent.

3. The defendant has infringed and is still infringing the Letters Patent by making, selling, and using *electric motors* that embody the patented invention, and the defendant will continue to do so unless enjoined by this court.

4. The plaintiff has complied with the statutory requirement of placing a notice of the Letters Patent on all *electric motors* it manufactures and sells and has given the defendant written notice of the infringement.

Therefore, the plaintiff demands:

   (a) a preliminary and final injunction against the continuing infringement;

   (b) an accounting for damages; and

   (c) interest and costs.

(Date and sign—See Form 2.)

(Added Apr. 20, 2007, eff. Dec. 1. 2007.)

FORM 19
COMPLAINT FOR COPYRIGHT INFRINGEMENT AND UNFAIR COMPETITION

(Caption—See Form 1.)

1. (Statement of Jurisdiction—See Form 7.)

2. Before *date*, the plaintiff, a United States citizen, wrote a book entitled ———.

3. The book is an original work that may be copyrighted under

United States law. A copy of the book is attached as Exhibit A.

4. Between _date_ and _date_, the plaintiff applied to the copyright office and received a certificate of registration dated _____ and identified as _date, class, number_.

5. Since _date_, the plaintiff has either published or licensed for publication all copies of the book in compliance with the copyright laws and has remained the sole owner of the copyright.

6. After the copyright was issued, the defendant infringed the copyright by publishing and selling a book entitled _____, which was copied largely from the plaintiff's book. A copy of the defendant's book is attached as Exhibit B.

7. The plaintiff has notified the defendant in writing of the infringement.

8. The defendant continues to infringe the copyright by continuing to publish and sell the infringing book in violation of the copyright, and further has engaged in unfair trade practices and unfair competition in connection with its publication and sale of the infringing book, thus causing irreparable damage.

Therefore, the plaintiff demands that:

   (a) until this case is decided the defendant and the defendant's agents be enjoined from disposing of any copies of the defendant's book by sale or otherwise;

   (b) the defendant account for and pay as damages to the plaintiff all profits and advantages gained from unfair trade practices and unfair competition in selling the defendant's book, and all profits and advantages gained from infringing the plaintiff's copyright (but no less than the statutory minimum);

   (c) the defendant deliver for impoundment all copies of the book in the defendant's possession or control and deliver for destruction all infringing copies and all plates, molds, and other materials for making infringing copies;

   (d) the defendant pay the plaintiff interest, costs, and reasonable attorney's fees; and

   (e) the plaintiff be awarded any other just relief.

                    (Date and sign—See Form 2.)

(Added Apr. 20, 2007, eff. Dec. 1. 2007.)

FORM 20

COMPLAINT FOR INTERPLEADER AND DECLARATORY RELIEF

                    (Caption—See Form 1.)

1. (Statement of Jurisdiction—See Form 7.)

2. On _date_, the plaintiff issued a life insurance policy on the life of _name_ with _name_ as the named beneficiary.

3. As a condition for keeping the policy in force, the policy required payment of a premium during the first year and then

annually.

4. The premium due on *date* was never paid, and the policy lapsed after that date.

5. On *date*, after the policy had lapsed, both the insured and the named beneficiary died in an automobile collision.

6. Defendant *name* claims to be the beneficiary in place of *name* and has filed a claim to be paid the policy's full amount.

7. The other two defendants are representatives of the deceased persons' estates. Each defendant has filed a claim on behalf of each estate to receive payment of the policy's full amount.

8. If the policy was in force at the time of death, the plaintiff is in doubt about who should be paid.

Therefore, the plaintiff demands that:

    (a) each defendant be restrained from commencing any action against the plaintiff on the policy;

    (b) a judgment be entered that no defendant is entitled to the proceeds of the policy or any part of it, but if the court determines that the policy was in effect at the time of the insured's death, that the defendants be required to interplead and settle among themselves their rights to the proceeds, and that the plaintiff be discharged from all liability except to the defendant determined to be entitled to the proceeds; and

    (c) the plaintiff recover its costs.

(Date and sign—See Form 2.)

(Added Apr. 20, 2007, eff. Dec. 1. 2007.)

FORM 21

COMPLAINT ON A CLAIM FOR A DEBT AND TO SET ASIDE A FRAUDULENT CONVEYANCE UNDER RULE 18(B)

(Caption—See Form 1.)

1. (Statement of Jurisdiction—See Form 7.)

2. On *date*, defendant *name* signed a note promising to pay to the plaintiff on *date* the sum of $_____ with interest at the rate of __ percent. [The pleader may, but need not, attach a copy or plead the note verbatim.]

3. Defendant *name* owes the plaintiff the amount of the note and interest.

4. On *date*, defendant *name* conveyed all defendant's real and personal property *if less than all, describe it fully* to defendant *name* for the purpose of defrauding the plaintiff and hindering or delaying the collection of the debt.

Therefore, the plaintiff demands that:

    (a) judgment for $_____, plus costs, be entered against defendant(s) *name(s)*; and

(b) the conveyance to defendant _name_ be declared void and any judgment granted be made a lien on the property.

(Date and sign—See Form 2.)

(Added Apr. 20, 2007, eff. Dec. 1. 2007.)

FORM 30
ANSWER PRESENTING DEFENSES UNDER RULE 12(B)

(Caption—See Form 1.)

Responding to Allegations in the Complaint

1. Defendant admits the allegations in paragraphs _____.
2. Defendant lacks knowledge or information sufficient to form a belief about the truth of the allegations in paragraphs _____.
3. Defendant admits *identify part of the allegation* in paragraph _____ and denies or lacks knowledge or information sufficient to form a belief about the truth of the rest of the paragraph.

Failure to State a Claim

4. The complaint fails to state a claim upon which relief can be granted.

Failure to Join a Required Party

5. If there is a debt, it is owed jointly by the defendant and _name_ who is a citizen of _____. This person can be made a party without depriving this court of jurisdiction over the existing parties.

Affirmative Defense—Statute of Limitations

6. The plaintiff's claim is barred by the statute of limitations because it arose more than _____ years before this action was commenced.

Counterclaim

7. *(Set forth any counterclaim in the same way a claim is pleaded in a complaint. Include a further statement of jurisdiction if needed.)*

Crossclaim

8. *(Set forth a crossclaim against a coparty in the same way a claim is pleaded in a complaint. Include a further statement of jurisdiction if needed.)*

(Date and sign—See Form 2.)

(Added Apr. 20, 2007, eff. Dec. 1. 2007.)

FORM 31
ANSWER TO A COMPLAINT FOR MONEY HAD AND RECEIVED WITH A COUNTERCLAIM FOR INTERPLEADER

(Caption—See Form 1.)
Response to the Allegations in the Complaint

(See Form 30.)

Counterclaim for Interpleader

1. The defendant received from *name* a deposit of $_____.
2. The plaintiff demands payment of the deposit because of a purported assignment from *name*, who has notified the defendant that the assignment is not valid and who continues to hold the defendant responsible for the deposit.

Therefore, the defendant demands that:
- (a) *name* be made a party to this action;
- (b) the plaintiff and *name* be required to interplead their respective claims;
- (c) the court decide whether the plaintiff or *name* or either of them is entitled to the deposit and discharge the defendant of any liability except to the person entitled to the deposit; and
- (d) the defendant recover costs and attorney's fees.

(Date and sign—See Form 2.)

(Added Apr. 20, 2007, eff. Dec. 1. 2007.)

FORM 40

MOTION TO DISMISS UNDER RULE 12(B) FOR LACK OF JURISDICTION, IMPROPER VENUE, INSUFFICIENT SERVICE OF PROCESS, OR FAILURE TO STATE A CLAIM

(Caption—See Form 1.)

The defendant moves to dismiss the action because:
1. the amount in controversy is less than the sum or value specified by 28 U.S.C. § 1332;
2. the defendant is not subject to the personal jurisdiction of this court;
3. venue is improper (this defendant does not reside in this district and no part of the events or omissions giving rise to the claim occurred in the district);
4. the defendant has not been properly served, as shown by the attached affidavits of _____; or
5. the complaint fails to state a claim upon which relief can be granted.

(Date and sign—See Form 2.)

(Added Apr. 20, 2007, eff. Dec. 1. 2007.)

FORM 41
MOTION TO BRING IN A THIRD-PARTY DEFENDANT

(Caption—See Form 1.)

The defendant, as third-party plaintiff, moves for leave to serve on *name* a summons and third-party complaint, copies of which are attached.

(Date and sign—See Form 2.)

(Added Apr. 20, 2007, eff. Dec. 1. 2007.)

FORM 42
MOTION TO INTERVENE AS A DEFENDANT UNDER RULE 24

(Caption—See Form 1.)

1. *name* moves for leave to intervene as a defendant in this action and to file the attached answer.

    (State grounds under Rule 24(a) or (b).)

2. The plaintiff alleges patent infringement. We manufacture and sell to the defendant the articles involved, and we have a defense to the plaintiff's claim.
3. Our defense presents questions of law and fact that are common to this action.

    (Date and sign—See Form 2.)

[*An Intervener's Answer must be attached. See Form 30.*]

(Added Apr. 20, 2007, eff. Dec. 1. 2007.)

FORM 50
REQUEST TO PRODUCE DOCUMENTS AND TANGIBLE THINGS, OR TO ENTER ONTO LAND UNDER RULE 34

(Caption—See Form 1.)

The plaintiff *name* requests that the defendant *name* respond within __ days to the following requests:

1. To produce and permit the plaintiff to inspect and copy and to test or sample the following documents, including electronically stored information:

    (Describe each document and the electronically stored information, either individually or by category.)

    (State the time, place, and manner of the inspection and any related acts.)

2. To produce and permit the plaintiff to inspect and copy—and to test or sample—the following tangible things:

    (Describe each thing, either individually or by category.)

(State the time, place, and manner of the inspection and any related acts.)

3. To permit the plaintiff to enter onto the following land to inspect, photograph, test, or sample the property or an object or operation on the property.

(Describe the property and each object or operation.)

(State the time and manner of the inspection and any related acts.)

(Date and sign—See Form 2.)

(Added Apr. 20, 2007, eff. Dec. 1. 2007.)

FORM 51
REQUEST FOR ADMISSIONS UNDER RULE 36

(Caption—See Form 1.)

The plaintiff *name* asks the defendant *name* to respond within 30 days to these requests by admitting, for purposes of this action only and subject to objections to admissibility at trial:

1. The genuineness of the following documents, copies of which [are attached] [are or have been furnished or made available for inspection and copying].

(List each document.)

2. The truth of each of the following statements:

(List each statement.)

(Date and sign—See Form 2.)

(Added Apr. 20, 2007, eff. Dec. 1. 2007.)

FORM 52
REPORT OF THE PARTIES' PLANNING MEETING

(Caption—See Form 1.)

1. The following persons participated in a Rule 26(f) conference on *date* by *state the method of conferring*:
2. Initial Disclosures. The parties [have completed] [will complete by *date*] the initial disclosures required by Rule 26(a)(1).
3. Discovery Plan. The parties propose this discovery plan:

(Use separate paragraphs or subparagraphs if the parties disagree.)

   (a) Discovery will be needed on these subjects: (*describe.*)
   (b) Disclosure or discovery of electronically stored information should be handled as follows: (*briefly describe the parties' proposals, including the form or forms for production.*)
   (c) The parties have agreed to an order regarding claims of privilege or of protection as trial-preparation material as-

serted after production, as follows: (*briefly describe the provisions of the proposed order.*)

(d) (Dates for commencing and completing discovery, including discovery to be commenced or completed before other discovery.)

(e) (Maximum number of interrogatories by each party to another party, along with dates the answers are due.)

(f) (Maximum number of requests for admission, along with the dates responses are due.)

(g) (Maximum number of depositions for each party.)

(h) (Limits on the length of depositions, in hours.)

(i) (Dates for exchanging reports of expert witnesses.)

(j) (Dates for supplementations under Rule 26(e).)

4. Other Items:

(a) (A date if the parties ask to meet with the court before a scheduling order.)

(b) (Requested dates for pretrial conferences.)

(c) (Final dates for the plaintiff to amend pleadings or to join parties.)

(d) (Final dates for the defendant to amend pleadings or to join parties.)

(e) (Final dates to file dispositive motions.)

(f) (State the prospects for settlement.)

(g) (Identify any alternative dispute resolution procedure that may enhance settlement prospects.)

(h) (Final dates for submitting Rule 26(a)(3) witness lists, designations of witnesses whose testimony will be presented by deposition, and exhibit lists.)

(i) (Final dates to file objections under Rule 26(a)(3).)

(j) (Suggested trial date and estimate of trial length.)

(k) (Other matters.)

(Date and sign—See Form 2.)

(Added Apr. 20, 2007, eff. Dec. 1. 2007; April 28, 2010, effective December 1, 2010.)

FORM 60
NOTICE OF CONDEMNATION

(Caption—See Form 1.)

To *name the defendant.*

1. A complaint in condemnation has been filed in the United States District Court for the _____ District of _____, to take property to use for *purpose*. The interest to be taken is *describe*. The court is located in the United States courthouse at this address: _____.

2. The property to be taken is described below. You have or claim an interest in it.

(Describe the property.)

3. The authority for taking this property is *cite*.
4. If you want to object or present any defense to the taking you must serve an answer on the plaintiff's attorney within 21 days [after being served with this notice] [from <u>(insert the date of the last publication of notice)</u>]. Send your answer to this address: _____.
5. Your answer must identify the property in which you claim an interest, state the nature and extent of that interest, and state all your objections and defenses to the taking. Objections and defenses not presented are waived.
6. If you fail to answer you consent to the taking and the court will enter a judgment that takes your described property interest.
7. Instead of answering, you may serve on the plaintiff's attorney a notice of appearance that designates the property in which you claim an interest. After you do that, you will receive a notice of any proceedings that affect you. Whether or not you have previously appeared or answered, you may present evidence at a trial to determine compensation for the property and share in the overall award.

(Date and sign—See Form 2.)

(Added Apr. 20, 2007, eff. Dec. 1. 2007; amended March 26, 2009, effective December 1, 2009.)

FORM 61
COMPLAINT FOR CONDEMNATION

(Caption—See Form 1; name as defendants the property and at least one owner.)
1. (Statement of Jurisdiction—See Form 7.)
2. This is an action to take property under the power of eminent domain and to determine just compensation to be paid to the owners and parties in interest.
3. The authority for the taking is _____.
4. The property is to be used for _____.
5. The property to be taken is (*describe in enough detail for identification—or attach the description and state "is described in Exhibit A, attached"*).
6. The interest to be acquired is _____.
7. The persons known to the plaintiff to have or claim an interest in the property are: _____. (*For each person include the interest claimed.*)
8. There may be other persons who have or claim an interest in the property and whose names could not be found after a reasonably diligent search. They are made parties under the designation "Unknown Owners."

Therefore, the plaintiff demands judgment:
  (a) condemning the property;

(b) determining and awarding just compensation; and

(c) granting any other lawful and proper relief.

(Date and sign—See Form 2.)

(Added Apr. 20, 2007, eff. Dec. 1. 2007.)

FORM 70
JUDGMENT ON A JURY VERDICT

(Caption—See Form 1.)

This action was tried by a jury with Judge _____ presiding, and the jury has rendered a verdict.

It is ordered that:

[the plaintiff *name* recover from the defendant *name* the amount of $_____ with interest at the rate of ____%, along with costs.]

[the plaintiff recover nothing, the action be dismissed on the merits, and the defendant *name* recover costs from the plaintiff *name*.]

Date _____

_____
Clerk of Court

(Added Apr. 20, 2007, eff. Dec. 1. 2007.)

FORM 71
JUDGMENT BY THE COURT WITHOUT A JURY

(Caption—See Form 1.)

This action was tried by Judge _____ without a jury and the following decision was reached:

It is ordered that [the plaintiff *name* recover from the defendant *name* the amount of $_____, with prejudgment interest at the rate of ____%, postjudgment interest at the rate of ____%, along with costs.] [the plaintiff recover nothing, the action be dismissed on the merits, and the defendant *name* recover costs from the plaintiff *name*.]

Date _____

_____
Clerk of Court

(Added Apr. 20, 2007, eff. Dec. 1. 2007.)

FORM 80
NOTICE OF A MAGISTRATE JUDGE'S AVAILABILITY

1. A magistrate judge is available under title 28 U.S.C. § 636(c) to conduct the proceedings in this case, including a jury or nonjury trial and the entry of final judgment. But a magis-

trate judge can be assigned only if all parties voluntarily consent.

2. You may withhold your consent without adverse substantive consequences. The identity of any party consenting or withholding consent will not be disclosed to the judge to whom the case is assigned or to any magistrate judge.

3. If a magistrate judge does hear your case, you may appeal directly to a United States court of appeals as you would if a district judge heard it.

A form called *Consent to an Assignment to a United States Magistrate Judge* is available from the court clerk's office.
(Added Apr. 20, 2007, eff. Dec. 1. 2007.)

FORM 81
CONSENT TO AN ASSIGNMENT TO A MAGISTRATE JUDGE

(Caption—See Form 1.)

I voluntarily consent to have a United States magistrate judge conduct all further proceedings in this case, including a trial, and order the entry of final judgment. (Return this form to the court clerk—not to a judge or magistrate judge.)

Date ———

———————————————

Signature of the Party

(Added Apr. 20, 2007, eff. Dec. 1. 2007.)

FORM 82
ORDER OF ASSIGNMENT TO A MAGISTRATE JUDGE

With the parties' consent it is ordered that this case be assigned to United States Magistrate Judge ——— of this district to conduct all proceedings and enter final judgment in accordance with 28 U.S.C. § 636(c).

Date ———

———————————————

United States District Judge

(Added Apr. 20, 2007, eff. Dec. 1. 2007.)

PART V
MULTIDISTRICT LITIGATION

Table of Sections

Sec.
5.1   Introduction.
5.2   The Federal Multidistrict Litigation Statute, 28 U.S.C.A. § 1407.

§ 5.1 Introduction

Congress created the Judicial Panel on Multidistrict Litigation in the late 1960's in response to the challenge of efficiently and effectively managing related, protracted, and complex civil cases that were being filed in various federal courts throughout the Nation.[1] At that time, nearly 2,000 separate but related electrical equipment antitrust cases were pending in 36 different federal judicial districts.[2] To manage these numerous distinct but related antitrust cases, Chief Justice Earl Warren appointed an advisory "Coordinating Committee for Multiple Litigation" which invited counsel and district court judges to attend hearings on how to economically supervise these electrical equipment litigations.[3]

The Committee prepared and recommended more than 40 "national pretrial orders" for the cases, which were then entered voluntarily by the judges in most of the districts where these electrical equipment antitrust cases were pending.[4] The orders established a coordinated system of national pretrial discovery, including a central document depository available to all parties and the conduct of depositions on a coordinated, nationwide schedule.[5]

This voluntary, advisory procedure was so successful that Congress established a statutory, national multidistrict litigation court in 1968 with affirmative authority to direct the transfer of multidistrict civil cases that involve one or more common questions of fact to a single federal district for the purpose of consolidated or coordinated nationwide pretrial proceedings.[6] This specialized court, entitled the "Judicial Panel on Multidistrict Litigation", comprises 7 circuit and district court judges, designated from time to time by the Chief Justice, no 2 of whom

---

[1] *See* 28 U.S.C. § 1407.

[2] *See* Robert A. Cahn, *A Look at the Judicial Panel on Multidistrict Litigation*, 72 F.R.D. 211, 211 (1976).

[3] *See id.* at 211–12.

[4] *See id.* at 212.

[5] *See id.*

[6] *See* 28 U.S.C. § 1407(a).

may come from the same Circuit.[7] The Judicial Panel is authorized to transfer cases for pretrial multidistrict litigation—or
"MDL"—treatment upon three findings: (a) that civil cases, then
pending in different federal judicial districts, involve one or more
common questions of fact, and that coordinated or consolidated
pretrial proceedings, centralized before a single district court, (b)
will be for the convenience of parties and witnesses and (c) will
promote the just and efficient conduct of the lawsuits.[8] Once these
prerequisite findings have been made, MDL transfer to a central
judicial district is appropriate, even if federal diversity jurisdiction, personal jurisdiction, or venue would otherwise be improper
there over the transferred cases.[9]

MDL treatment may be initiated by the Judicial Panel on its
own initiative or upon motion by a party in any action believed to
qualify for this type of coordination or consolidation.[10] If MDL
treatment is granted by the Judicial Panel, the general procedure
is as follows: a single judicial district and federal judge is selected
by the Judicial Panel as the MDL court for all the cases; all
qualifying federal lawsuits are then transferred to that federal
judge for pretrial purposes;[11] the MDL judge presides over and
manages a nationwide, coordinated discovery and pretrial
procedures program; and, in the event the cases are not disposed
of or settled by the MDL judge by the close of the pretrial stage,
the lawsuits are each transferred back to their original districts
for trial.[12] The MDL judge may rule on case-dispositive motions,
and consequently may grant motions to dismiss both on substantive grounds[13] and for failures to abide by court scheduling orders
and procedures.[14] The MDL judge may also rule on motions to file
amended complaints and superseding omnibus complaints, motions to otherwise amend or adjust pleadings, motions to enforce
venue requirements, discovery motions, and other pretrial mo-

---

[7]See 28 U.S.C. § 1407(d).

[8]See 28 U.S.C. § 1407(a). See also
Pinney v. Nokia, Inc., 402 F.3d 430,
451 (4th Cir.2005).

[9]See   Howard   v.   Sulzer
Orthopedics, Inc., 382 Fed. Appx. 436,
441–42 (6th Cir. 2010); Pinney v. Nokia,
Inc., 402 F.3d 430, 451–52 (4th Cir.
2005).

[10]See 28 U.S.C. § 1407(c).

[11]See Boomer v. AT & T Corp.,
309 F.3d 404, 413 (7th Cir.2002) (noting that multidistrict transfer order is
effective only when filed in the office of
the clerk in the transferee district).

[12]See 28 U.S.C. § 1407(a). See also
Lexecon Inc. v. Milberg Weiss Bershad
Hynes & Lerach, 523 U.S. 26, 32, 118
S.Ct. 956, 961, 140 L.Ed.2d 62 (1998)

(holding that MDL judge cannot ordinarily "self-transfer" unresolved MDL
cases to herself for post-pretrial resolution on the merits); Armstrong v.
LaSalle Bank Nat'l Ass'n, 552 F.3d
613, 614 (7th Cir. 2009) (noting normal
remand procedure); In re Collins, 233
F.3d 809 (3d Cir.2000) (refusing to
disturb MDL practice of transferring
back only compensatory damage asbestos claims to origination district, while
retaining punitive damages claims in
MDL).

[13]See In re African-American Slave
Descendants Litig., 471 F.3d 754,
754–57 & 763 (7th Cir. 2006).

[14]See In re Guidant Corp. Implantable Defibrillators Prods. Liab. Litig.,
496 F.3d 863, 867 (8th Cir. 2007).

tions, and may order attendance at settlement conferences.[15] (In diversity cases, the MDL judge will ordinarily apply both the substantive law[16] and the choice-of-law rules[17] of the various originating transferor jurisdictions.) The extent to which a transferor court, following remand, may overrule the MDL transferee judge remains unsettled; but because routine revisitations of the MDL judge's rulings would deal MDL litigants a "Return To Go" card[18] and thereby frustrate the intended goals of the MDL process,[19] the courts tend to affix law-of-the-case deference to the MDL judge's orders.[20]

Remands are made by the Judicial Panel (not by the transferee judge), although the transferee judge retains a vital role in the remand back to the original forum by notifying the Judicial Panel (typically through a "*Suggestion to Remand*") that the coordinated or consolidated proceedings have been concluded.[21] The parties do not need to assert their intention to seek remand in order to preserve it; rather, a remand at the close of all pretrial proceedings is presumed.[22] The Judicial Panel *must* remand when the coordinated or consolidated proceedings have concluded, but *may*, in its "unusually broad discretion", remand when all that remains to be accomplished is case-specific.[23] (If, however, the parties properly consent to a relinquishment of their entitlement to remand, the case may remain with the transferee judge.[24]) Thus, this MDL treatment is usually a vehicle for pretrial—and only pretrial—coordination and consolidation.[25]

The MDL procedure endeavors to achieve the economical use of the federal judiciary and the resolution of similar complex civil

---

[15]*See In re Korean Air Lines Co.*, 642 F.3d 685, 699 (9th Cir. 2011) (collecting cases).

[16]*See Chang v. Baxter Healthcare Corp.*, 599 F.3d 728, 732 (7th Cir. 2010).

[17]*See Anschutz Corp. v. Merrill Lynch & Co.*, 690 F.3d 98, 112 (2d Cir. 2012); *In re Volkswagen, Audi Warranty Extension Litig.*, 692 F.3d 4, 13 (1st Cir. 2012).

[18]*See In re Pharmacy Benefit Managers Antitrust Litig.*, 582 F.3d 432, 440 (3d Cir. 2009).

[19]*In re Ford Motor Co.*, 591 F.3d 406, 411 (5th Cir. 2009) (consequently, transferor courts should rarely overturn MDL judge's rulings).

[20]*See In re Ford Motor Co.*, 591 F.3d 406 (5th Cir. 2009) (applying law-of-the-case, but overturning transferee judge's forum non conveniens ruling); *In re Pharmacy Benefit Managers Antitrust Litig.*, 582 F.3d 432 (3d Cir.

2009) (applying law-of-the-case, and upholding transferee judge's arbitrability ruling).

[21]*See In re Wilson*, 451 F.3d 161, 165 & 165 n.5 (3d Cir.2006).

[22]*See Armstrong v. LaSalle Bank Nat'l Ass'n*, 552 F.3d 613, 616 (7th Cir. 2009).

[23]*See In re Wilson*, 451 F.3d 161, 172–73 (3d Cir.2006).

[24]*See Armstrong v. LaSalle Bank Nat'l Ass'n*, 552 F.3d 613, 616-17 (7th Cir. 2009); *In re Carbon Dioxide Industry Antitrust Litigation*, 229 F.3d 1321 (11th Cir.2000).

[25]*See In re Patenaude*, 210 F.3d 135, 142 (3d Cir.2000) (noting that MDL statute limits transferee court to only proceedings that are (1) coordinated or consolidated and (2) pretrial). *See also id.* at 144 (commenting that "pretrial" is interpreted broadly to mean all judicial proceedings that occur before trial).

cases with the least cost and disruption to the parties and witnesses.[26] During the coordinated or consolidated pretrial MDL proceedings, the MDL judge will typically look to the Federal Judicial Center's *Manual for Complex Litigation* as a primary resource for guiding the nationwide proceedings.[27] With those guidelines in mind, documents are generally produced only once for hundreds or thousands of cases, with responsive documents made available to all parties at a centralized document depository. Interrogatories and requests for admissions are served on behalf of an entire series of related cases. Witnesses and parties, whose testimony is relevant to perhaps thousands of different cases, are deposed only once (or at least far less often than otherwise would be the case) by a select group of lead or liaison counsel. Throughout the MDL process, the transferee judge generally possesses the power to act not only on behalf of the transferee district, but also with the powers of a district judge in every district from which the consolidated cases have been transferred.[28]

The MDL judge's discretion is broad and commensurate with the enormous task of managing a large litigation involving numerous litigants from across the country and posing substantial legal questions implicating pleading, discovery, expert, timeliness, choice of law, cognizable claim, and causation issues.[29] This authority encompasses the power to rule on motions relating to subpoenas issued from other judicial districts, including motions to quash.[30] But, although broad, the MDL judge's discretion is not unbounded; the judge may not, in the cause of efficiency and docketing progress, engage in "assembly-line justice".[31]

Appeals from the MDL judge's pretrial orders are often (but not always) heard by the Court of Appeals for the Circuit that encompasses the MDL judge's district.[32] Sometimes, for instance, the Judicial Panel on Multidistrict Litigation may, in its discretion, elect not to permit Rule 54(b) immediate appeals (to the

---

[26] *See In re Korean Air Lines Co.*, 642 F.3d 685, 698-99 (9th Cir. 2011).

[27] For an excellent annotated and commentary-laden version of this essential MDL resource, see David Herr's *Annotated Manual for Complex Litigation Third* (Thomson West, revised annually). Multidistrict litigation under § 1407 is also discussed in detail in Wright, Miller & Cooper, *Federal Practice and Procedure* §§ 3861 to 68 (West Group).

[28] *See In re Korean Air Lines Co.*, 642 F.3d 685, 699 (9th Cir. 2011); *In re Flat Glass Antitrust Litig.*, 288 F.3d 83, 90 n. 12 (3d Cir.2002).

[29] *See In re Korean Air Lines Co.*, 642 F.3d 685, 698-99 (9th Cir. 2011); *In re Guidant Implantable Defibrilla-*

tors Prods. Liab. Litig., 496 F.3d 863, 867 (8th Cir. 2007).

[30] *See In re Clients & Former Clients of Baron & Budd, P.C.*, 478 F.3d 670 (5th Cir. 2007) (per curiam).

[31] *See In re Korean Air Lines Co.*, 642 F.3d 685, 700-01 (9th Cir. 2011) (although broad, discretion does not permit court to disregard normal standards for assessing critical motions); *In re Phenylpropanolamine (PPA) Prods. Liab. Litig.*, 460 F.3d 1217, 1250 (9th Cir.2006) (affirming in part and reversing in part dismissals for non-compliance with discovery orders).

[32] *See United States ex rel. Pogue v. Diabetes Treatment Ctrs. of America, Inc.*, 444 F.3d 462, 467 (6th Cir.2006).

MDL judge's Court of Appeals) but, instead, to remand back to the originating transferor courts (with appeals, if any, to be taken to those various Courts of Appeals).[33] Likewise, when the MDL judge's order implicates a ruling compelling or sanctioning a non-party located outside the MDL judge's district, the appeal is generally taken to the Court of Appeals for the Circuit embracing the district of the foreign discovery event.[34] The preclusive effects of MDL litigation can be complicated. For example, the decision to appeal an MDL ruling as to some consolidated defendants (and not all) will likely be preclusive once a final judgment is entered on the appeal, but perhaps not before.[35]

Over the years, MDL pretrial treatment has been granted in many different types of lawsuits,[36] including national products liability cases,[37] airplane disaster and other large calamity cases,[38] antitrust cases,[39] trade practices and consumer fraud cases,[40] patent cases,[41] copyright cases, trademark cases, and a variety of other cases.[42] In its first 27 years of use, the statutory multidistrict litigation procedure had been applied to more than 39,000

[33]See FedEx Ground Package Sys., Inc. v. U.S. Judicial Panel on Multidistrict Litig., 662 F.3d 887, 890-91 (7th Cir. 2011).

[34]See United States ex rel. Pogue v. Diabetes Treatment Ctrs. of America, Inc., 444 F.3d 462, 467–68 (6th Cir. 2006).

[35]See In re Cygnus Telecommc'ns Tech., LLC, Patent Litig., 536 F.3d 1343, 1349–51 & 1350 n.1 (Fed.Cir. 2008).

[36]See Robert A. Cahn, A Look at the Judicial Panel on Multidistrict Litigation, 72 F.R.D. 211, 214 (1976).

[37]See, e.g., In re Pet Food Prods. Liab. Litig., 499 F.Supp.2d 1346 (J.P.M.L. 2007) (MDL No. 1850); In re Fosamax Prods. Liab. Litig., 444 F.Supp.2d 1347 (J.P.M.L. 2006) (MDL No. 1789); In re Diet Drugs (Phentermine, Fenfluramine, Dexfenfluramine) Prods. Liab. Litig., 990 F.Supp. 834 (J.P.M.L.1998) (MDL No. 1203); In re Pantopaque Prods. Liab. Litig., 787 F.Supp. 229 (J.P.M.L.1992) (MDL No. 920).

[38]See, e.g., In re Air Crash Near Peixoto De Azeveda, Brazil on Sept. 29, 2006, 493 F.Supp.2d 1374 (J.P.M.L. 2007) (MDL No. 1844); In re Air Crash Disaster at Sioux City, Iowa, on July 19, 1989, 128 F.R.D. 131 (J.P.M.L. 1989) (MDL No. 817); In re Air Disaster at Lockerbie, Scotland, on Dec. 21, 1988, 709 F.Supp. 231 (J.P.M.L.1989) (MDL No. 799), aff'd, 16 F.3d 513 (2d Cir.1994); In re Air Crash Disaster At Stapleton Int'l Airport, Denver Colo. on Nov. 15, 1987, 683 F.Supp. 266 (J.P.M.L.1988) (MDL No. 751); In re Fire Disaster at Dupont Plaza Hotel, San Juan, Puerto Rico, on Dec.31, 1986, 660 F.Supp. 982 (J.P.M.L.1987) (MDL No. 721).

[39]See, e.g., In re Ins. Brokerage Antitrust Litig., 360 F.Supp.2d 1371 (J.P.M.L. 2005) (MDL No. 1663); In re Western States Wholesale Natural Gas Antitrust Litig., 290 F.Supp.2d 1376 (J.P.M.L. 2003) (MDL No. 1566); In re Baseball Bat Antitrust Litig., 112 F.Supp.2d 1175 (2000) (MDL No. 1249); In re Professional Hockey Antitrust Litig., 369 F.Supp. 1117 (J.P.M.L.1974) (MDL No. 119).

[40]See In re Long-Distance Tel. Serv. Fed. Excise Tax Refund Litig., 469 F.Supp.2d 1348 (J.P.M.L. 2006) (MDL No. 1798); In re Columbia/HCA Healthcare Corp. Billing Practices Litig., 93 F.Supp.2d 876 (M.D.Tenn. 2000) (MDL No. 1227).

[41]See, e.g., In re Phonometrics, Inc., Elec. Long Distance Call Cost Computers & Recorder Patent Litig., 1997 WL 83673 (J.P.M.L.1997) (MDL No. 1141).

[42]See, e.g., In re South African Apartheid Litig., 238 F.Supp.2d 1379 (J.P.M.L. 2002) (MDL No. 1499).

federal civil cases, of which more than 90% were resolved in the MDL and prior to trial.[43] All told, well over a thousand MDL's have occurred, involving some of the most challenging litigations in the history of the federal judiciary.[44] Indeed, some recent scholarship suggests MDL treatment has "supplemented and perhaps displaced the class action device as a procedural mechanism for large settlements."[45]

For a more extensive treatment of MDL practice, see David F. Herr, *Multidistrict Litigation Manual: Practice Before The Judicial Panel On Multidistrict Litigation* (Thompson-West, revised annually).

§ 5.2 The Federal Multidistrict Litigation Statute, 28 U.S.C.A. § 1407

1407. Multidistrict Litigation

(a) When civil actions involving one or more common questions of fact are pending in different districts, such actions may be transferred to any district for coordinated or consolidated pretrial proceedings. Such transfers shall be made by the judicial panel on multidistrict litigation authorized by this section upon its determination that transfers for such proceedings will be for the convenience of parties and witnesses and will promote the just and efficient conduct of such actions. Each action so transferred shall be remanded by the panel at or before the conclusion of such pretrial proceedings to the district from which it was transferred unless it shall have been previously terminated: *Provided, however*, That the panel may separate any claim, cross-claim, counter-claim, or third-party claim and remand any of such claims before the remainder of the action is remanded.

(b) Such coordinated or consolidated pretrial proceedings shall be conducted by a judge or judges to whom such actions are assigned by the judicial panel on multidistrict litigation. For this purpose, upon request of the panel, a circuit judge or a district judge may be designated and assigned temporarily for service in the transferee district by the Chief Justice of the United States or the chief judge of the circuit, as may be required, in accordance with the provisions of chapter 13 of this title. With the consent of the transferee district court, such actions may be assigned by the panel to a judge or judges of such district. The judge or judges to whom such actions are assigned, the members

---

[43]*See Lexecon Inc. v. Milberg Weiss Bershad Hynes & Lerach*, 523 U.S. 26, 32, 118 S.Ct. 956, 961, 140 L.Ed.2d 62 (1998).

[44]*See FedEx Ground Package Sys., Inc. v. U.S. Judicial Panel on Multidistrict Litig.*, 662 F.3d 887, 891 (7th Cir. 2011).

[45]*See Sullivan v. DB Invs., Inc.*, 667 F.3d 273, 334 (3d Cir. 2011) (Scirica, J., concurring) (citing Thomas E. Willging & Emery G. Lee III, From Class Actions to Multidistrict Consolidations: Aggregate Mass–Tort Litigation after Ortiz, 58 U. KAN. L. REV. 775, 801 (2010)).

of the judicial panel on multidistrict litigation, and other circuit and district judges designated when needed by the panel may exercise the powers of a district judge in any district for the purpose of conducting pretrial depositions in such coordinated or consolidated pretrial proceedings.

(c) Proceedings for the transfer of an action under this section may be initiated by—

(i) the judicial panel on multidistrict litigation upon its own initiative, or

(ii) motion filed with the panel by a party in any action in which transfer for coordinated or consolidated pretrial proceedings under this section may be appropriate. A copy of such motion shall be filed in the district court in which the moving party's action is pending.

The panel shall give notice to the parties in all actions in which transfers for coordinated or consolidated pretrial proceedings are contemplated, and such notice shall specify the time and place of any hearing to determine whether such transfer shall be made. Orders of the panel to set a hearing and other orders of the panel issued prior to the order either directing or denying transfer shall be filed in the office of the clerk of the district court in which a transfer hearing is to be or has been held. The panel's order of transfer shall be based upon a record of such hearing at which material evidence may be offered by any party to an action pending in any district that would be affected by the proceedings under this section, and shall be supported by findings of fact and conclusions of law based upon such record. Orders of transfer and such other orders as the panel may make thereafter shall be filed in the office of the clerk of the district court of the transferee district and shall be effective when thus filed. The clerk of the transferee district court shall forthwith transmit a certified copy of the panel's order to transfer to the clerk of the district court from which the action is being transferred. An order denying transfer shall be filed in each district wherein there is a case pending in which the motion for transfer has been made.

(d) The judicial panel on multidistrict litigation shall consist of seven circuit and district judges designated from time to time by the Chief Justice of the United States, no two of whom shall be from the same circuit. The concurrence of four members shall be necessary to any action by the panel.

(e) No proceedings for review of any order of the panel may be permitted except by extraordinary writ pursuant to the provisions of title 28, section 1651, United States Code. Petitions for an extraordinary writ to review an order of the panel to set a transfer hearing and other orders of the panel issued prior to the order either directing or denying transfer shall be filed only in the court of appeals having jurisdiction over the district in which a hearing is to be or has been held. Petitions for an extraordinary writ to review an order to transfer or orders subsequent to transfer shall be filed only in the court of appeals having jurisdiction over the transferee district. There shall be no appeal or review of an order of the panel denying a motion to transfer for consolidated or coordinated proceedings.

(f) The panel may prescribe rules for the conduct of its business not inconsistent with Acts of Congress and the Federal Rules of Civil Procedure.

(g) Nothing in this section shall apply to any action in which the United States is a complainant arising under the antitrust laws. "Antitrust laws" as used herein include those acts referred to in the Act of October 15, 1914, as amended (38 Stat. 730; 15 U.S.C. 12), and also include the Act of June 19, 1936 (49 Stat. 1526; 15 U.S.C. 13, 13a, and 13b) and the Act of September 26, 1914, as added March 21, 1938 (52 Stat. 116, 117; 15 U.S.C. 56); but shall not include section 4A of the Act of October 15, 1914, as added July 7, 1955 (69 Stat. 282; 15 U.S.C. 15a).

(h) Notwithstanding the provisions of section 1404 or subsection (f) of this section, the judicial panel on multidistrict litigation may consolidate and transfer with or without the consent of the parties, for both pretrial purposes and for trial, any action brought under section 4C of the Clayton Act.

(Added Pub.L. 90-296, § 1, Apr. 29, 1968, 82 Stat. 109, and amended Pub.L. 94-435, Title III, § 303, Sept. 30, 1976, 90 Stat. 1396.)

PART VI
APPELLATE PROCEDURE

Table of Sections

Sec.
6.1   Introduction.
6.2   Step One: Appealability.
6.3   Step Two: Time for Taking an Appeal.
6.4   Step Three: Procedure for Taking an Appeal.
6.5   Step Four: Stays Pending Appeal.
6.6   Step Five: The Appeal Process.
6.7   Step Six: Appeals to the United States Supreme Court
6.8   *Federal Rules of Appellate Procedure.*
6.9   Appendix of Forms to the *Federal Rules of Appellate Procedure.*

§ 6.1 Introduction

The rules and procedures for appealing a district court's judgment or order are no longer included in the Federal Rules of Civil Procedure, as they once were. Since 1968, these rules and procedures have been set forth in the "Federal Rules of Appellate Procedure", as supplemented by local rules. In-depth, rule-by-rule commentary regarding the federal appeals rules is beyond the scope of this text. The following preview of federal appellate procedure is included only to orient the practitioner to the general procedures governing appeals in the federal courts.

§ 6.2 Step One: Appealability

CORE CONCEPT

Litigants are generally required to wait until a lawsuit is completed in the district court—until there is a "final order" in the case—before an appeal from any of the district court's rulings may be taken.[1] This "finality" doctrine was designed to limit the expense, delays, burdens, and inefficiencies of repeated, successive appeals in a single case.[2] Important exceptions to this finality or "final order" doctrine exist, however.

---

[1] *See Digital Equip. Corp. v. Desktop Direct, Inc.*, 511 U.S. 863, 868, 114 S.Ct. 1992, 1996, 128 L.Ed.2d 842 (1994) (litigants are entitled to only a single appeal in their case, which is usually deferred until the district court enters its final judgment, and may include claims of trial error from every stage of the litigation).

[2] *See generally Firestone Tire & Rubber Co. v. Risjord*, 449 U.S. 368, 374, 101 S.Ct. 669, 673, 66 L.Ed.2d 571 (1981); *DiBella v. U.S.*, 369 U.S. 121, 124, 82 S.Ct. 654, 7 L.Ed.2d 614

NOTE: Practitioners must exercise great care in determining an order's immediate appealability. When an order is immediately appealable, a delay in taking the appeal may forever foreclose the right of appeal. When an order is not immediately appealable, the premature filing of an appeal may be dismissed summarily.

APPLICATIONS

Threshold Nature of Appellate Jurisdiction

The right to a federal appeal is a "creature of statute", and exists only to that extent granted by Congress.[3] Federal appellate jurisdiction is not assumed, nor can it be conferred by waiver or consent.[4] Instead, federal appellate courts have an independent obligation to confirm the presence of their jurisdiction, even where the parties to the appeal are prepared to concede it.[5] Moreover, if the appellate court determines that the trial court lacked subject matter jurisdiction over the dispute, the court of appeals has jurisdiction over the appeal for the limited purpose of correcting the jurisdictional error only.[6]

Final Orders

Congress has vested the courts of appeals with jurisdiction to hear appeals from "final orders" of the district courts.[7] Final orders are, thus, immediately appealable to the courts of appeals. A final order is a ruling that "ends the litigation on the merits and leaves nothing for the court to do but execute the judgment."[8] It is usually the order by which the trial court "disassociates" itself from the case.[9] The "final order" rule has

---

(1962). *See also Cobbledick v. U.S.,* 309 U.S. 323, 325, 60 S.Ct. 540, 541, 84 L.Ed. 783 (1940) (judicial administration's "momentum would be arrested by permitting separate reviews of the component elements in a unified cause").

[3]*See Abney v. U.S.,* 431 U.S. 651, 656, 97 S.Ct. 2034, 52 L.Ed.2d 651 (1977).

[4]*See New York ex rel. Bryant v. Zimmerman,* 278 U.S. 63, 66, 49 S.Ct. 61, 73 L.Ed. 184 (1928); *Barnett v. Kunkel,* 264 U.S. 16, 19, 44 S.Ct. 254, 68 L.Ed. 539 (1924); *General Ins. Co. of America v. Clark Mall Corp.,* 644 F.3d 375, 378 (7th Cir. 2011).

[5]*See Bender v. Williamsport Area Sch. Dist.,* 475 U.S. 534, 541, 106 S.Ct. 1326, 1331, 89 L.Ed.2d 501 (1986).

[6]*See Bender v. Williamsport Area Sch. Dist.,* 475 U.S. 534, 541, 106 S.Ct. 1326, 1331, 89 L.Ed.2d 501 (1986).

[7]*See* 28 U.S.C.A. § 1291.

[8]*See Van Cauwenberghe v. Biard,* 486 U.S. 517, 521–22, 108 S.Ct. 1945, 1949, 100 L.Ed.2d 517 (1988) (quoting *Catlin v. U.S.,* 324 U.S. 229, 233, 65 S.Ct. 631, 633, 89 L.Ed. 911 (1945)). *See also Riley v. Kennedy,* 553 U.S. 406, 419, 128 S.Ct. 1970, 1981, 170 L.Ed.2d 837 (2008) (holding that orders that resolve liability without addressing relief are not final); *Cunningham v. Hamilton County,* 527 U.S. 198, 201–03, 119 S.Ct. 1915, 1919–20, 144 L.Ed.2d 184 (1999) (order imposing sanctions on attorney for discovery abuses was not a final order); *Behrens v. Pelletier,* 516 U.S. 299, 304, 116 S.Ct. 834, 838, 133 L.Ed.2d 773 (1996) (commenting that finality prevents consideration of rulings that remain subject to revision).

[9]*See Mohawk Indus., Inc. v. Carpenter,* 558 U.S. 100, 130 S.Ct. 599, 604–05, 175 L.Ed.2d 458 (2009);

been described as "pragmatic", not rigid.[10] Thus, a district court's dismissal that is technically denominated as "without prejudice" may qualify as a "final order" if, in the particular circumstances, the trial judge is "finished" with the case.[11]

Partial Final Orders (Rule 54(b))

Ordinarily, a judgment as to less than all claims in a lawsuit, or as to less than all parties in a lawsuit, is not immediately appealable until all other claims affecting all other parties are finally resolved. However, the district court may, in the exercise of its discretion, convert such "partial" judgments into immediately appealable final orders by (a) finally resolving at least one claim or the rights and liabilities of at least one party, (b) expressly declaring that no just cause exists to delay the appeal from such a ruling, and (c) directing the entry of judgment on the ruling.[12] The purpose, prerequisites, and procedure for such immediately appealable "partial" judgments are discussed earlier in this text.[13]

Interlocutory Orders

Interlocutory orders are all other interim rulings by the district courts—rulings that do not end the litigation and that contemplate some type of further action by the trial judge. Interlocutory orders are generally not appealable immediately to the courts of appeals.[14] Review of interlocutory orders must ordinarily wait until the district court enters its final order on the merits of the litigation. Under well-settled appellate tenets, litigants may, while appealing a final order, challenge many of the preceding interlocutory rulings previously entered by the trial court.[15]

Permitted Interlocutory Appeals (28 U.S.C. § 1292(a))

Certain rulings involving federal injunctions, receiverships, and admiralty orders are immediately appealable, notwithstanding that the rulings do not qualify as "final orders":

- *Injunctions:* Interlocutory orders that grant, continue,

Swint v. Chambers County Comm'n, 514 U.S. 35, 42, 115 S.Ct. 1203, 131 L.Ed.2d 60 (1995).

[10]*See* Mohawk Indus., Inc. v. Carpenter, 558, U.S. 100, 130, S.Ct. 599, 605, 175 L.Ed.2d 458 (2009); *GO Computer, Inc. v. Microsoft Corp.,* 508 F.3d 170, 176 (4th Cir. 2007).

[11]*See GO Computer, Inc. v. Microsoft Corp.,* 508 F.3d 170, 176 (4th Cir. 2007); *Hill v. Potter,* 352 F.3d 1142, 1144 (7th Cir.2003). *See also Frederico v. Home Depot,* 507 F.3d 188, 192 (3d Cir. 2007) (dismissals with leave to amend will be deemed "final orders" if plaintiff elects to stand on her original pleading).

[12]*See* Rule 54(b).

[13]*See supra* Authors' Commentary to Rule 54(b).

[14]*See Ortiz v. Jordan,* __ U.S. __, __, 131 S.Ct. 884, 891, 178 L.Ed.2d 703 (2011) (summary judgment denial is interlocutory and, thus, usually not immediately appealable); *Ashcroft v. Iqbal,* 556 U.S. 662, 672, 129 S.Ct. 1937, 1946, 173 L.Ed.2d 868 (2009) (interlocutory appeals "are the exception, not the rule"); *In re Carco Elecs.,* 536 F.3d 211, 213 (3d Cir. 2008) ("axiomatic" that discovery rulings are not "final orders").

[15]*See Koch v. City of Del City,* 660 F.3d 1228, 1237 (10th Cir. 2011); *Exxon Corp. v. St. Paul Fire & Marine Ins. Co.,* 129 F.3d 781, 784 (5th Cir.1997).

modify, refuse, or dissolve injunctions, or that refuse to dissolve or modify injunctions are appealable immediately.[16] This is considered a "narrowly tailored exception" to the general policy disfavoring piecemeal appeals,[17] and is construed strictly.[18] This means, at a threshold level, that the order must actually constitute an injunction, regardless of the specific nomenclature chosen by the district court to describe it.[19] Because of their brief duration, temporary restraining orders may not ordinarily be immediately appealed.[20] Rather, qualifying injunctive orders must generally possess three attributes: (1) a clearly defined, understandable directive that a party act or refrain from acting, (2) enforceable through contempt, and (3) gives some or all of the substantive relief sought in the complaint.[21] An order that has the "practical effect" of denying an injunction will not automatically trigger appellate review, unless its consequence is serious and only effectively challenged through immediate review.[22] Nor will an order "interpreting" an injunction permit an immediate appeal.[23] If, however, appellate jurisdiction exists over an injunctive ruling, that jurisdiction may extend to all matters inextricably bound up with that ruling.[24]

● *Receivers:* Interlocutory orders that appoint receivers, or refuse orders to wind up receiverships or take steps to accomplish those purposes (*i.e.,* directing disposals of property) are appealable immediately,[25] although this exception, too, is construed narrowly.[26]

● *Admiralty:* Decrees that determine the rights and liabilities of parties to admiralty cases in which appeals from

---

[16]28 U.S.C.A. § 1292(a)(1). *See also Crowe & Dunlevy, P.C. v. Stidham,* 640 F.3d 1140, 1147 (10th Cir. 2011); *Bacon v. Neer,* 631 F.3d 875, 877–78 (8th Cir. 2011).

[17]*See Sahu v. Union Carbide Corp.,* 475 F.3d 465, 467 (2d Cir. 2007). *See also Carson v. Am. Brands, Inc.,* 450 U.S. 79, 84, 101 S.Ct. 993, 67 L.Ed.2d 59 (1981) (interlocutory appeals prohibited unless litigants can show that district court's interlocutory order might have "serious, perhaps irreparable, consequence" and that only effective challenge to order is by immediate appeal).

[18]*See American River Transp Co. v. Ryan,* 579 F.3d 820, 824 (7th Cir. 2009).

[19]*See Turtle Island Restoration Network v. U.S. Dep't of Commerce,* 672 F.3d 1160, 1164–65 (9th Cir. 2012); *U.S. Fidelity & Guar. Co. v.* *Arch Ins. Co.,* 578 F.3d 45, 54 n.13 (1st Cir. 2009).

[20]*Service Employees Int'l Union v. Nat'l Union of Healthcare Workers,* 598 F.3d 1061, 1067 (9th Cir. 2010).

[21]*See Alabama v. United States Army Corps of Eng'rs,* 424 F.3d 1117, 1128–29 (11th Cir.2005).

[22]*See Carson v. American Brands, Inc.,* 450 U.S. 79, 83–84, 101 S.Ct. 993, 67 L.Ed.2d 59 (1981); *Salazar ex rel. Salazar v. District of Columbia,* 671 F.3d 1258, 1261–67 (D.C.Cir. 2012).

[23]*See American River Transp. Co. v. Ryan,* 579 F.3d 820, 824 (7th Cir. 2009).

[24]*See Amador v. Andrews,* 655 F.3d 89, 95 (2d Cir. 2011).

[25]28 U.S.C.A. § 1292(a)(2).

[26]*See Canada Life Assur. Co. v. LaPeter,* 563 F.3d 837, 841 (9th Cir. 2009).

final decrees are allowed, are appealable immediately.[27]

Discretionary Interlocutory Appeals (28 U.S.C. § 1292(b))

The district court may, in the exercise of its discretion,[28] choose to certify certain non-final, interlocutory orders as eligible for immediate appellate review.[29] Such certification by the district court does not require the court of appeals to hear the immediate appeal; rather, the courts of appeals also have discretion to reject interlocutory appeals,[30] and may do so for almost any reason (including docket congestion).[31]

Certification by the district judge is not routinely granted ("hen's teeth rare"[32]), and is reserved for "exceptional" cases.[33] Litigants seeking such certification bear a heavy burden.[34] Liberal grants of interlocutory appeals are "bad policy", and threaten the appropriate division of responsibility between federal trial and appellate courts.[35] The purpose of the procedure is to avoid protracted litigation, to assure the quick resolution of complicated legal issues, and to allow appellate review of ephemeral questions of law that could be lost in the context of a complete and final record.[36] The procedure was not intended to serve a mere error-correction function.[37]

To qualify for certification, the district court must state in writing:[38]

(1) That the order in question involves a "controlling question of law" (which generally means a question of "pure law", which can be resolved "quickly and cleanly" without laboring

---

[27] 28 U.S.C.A. § 1292(a)(3). *See also Wajnstat v. Oceania Cruises, Inc.*, 684 F.3d 1153, 1155–57 (11th Cir. 2012); *Chem One, Ltd. v. M/V RICKMERS GENOA*, 660 F.3d 626, 638–42 (2d Cir. 2011).

[28] *See Swint v. Chambers County Comm'n*, 514 U.S. 35, 47, 115 S.Ct. 1203, 1210, 131 L.Ed.2d 60 (1995) (noting that Congress conferred upon district courts the "first line discretion to allow interlocutory appeals").

[29] *See* 28 U.S.C.A. § 1292(b).

[30] *See* 28 U.S.C.A. § 1292(b). *See also Van Cauwenberghe v. Biard*, 486 U.S. 517, 530, 108 S.Ct. 1945, 1953, 100 L.Ed.2d 517 (1988); *Coopers & Lybrand v. Livesay*, 437 U.S. 463, 475, 98 S.Ct. 2454, 2461, 57 L.Ed.2d 351 (1978); *Tidewater Oil Co. v. U.S.*, 409 U.S. 151, 173 n. 50, 93 S.Ct. 408, 421 n. 50, 34 L.Ed.2d 375 (1972).

[31] *Coopers & Lybrand v. Livesay*, 437 U.S. 463, 475, 98 S.Ct. 2454, 2461, 57 L.Ed.2d 351 (1978).

[32] *See Camacho v. Puerto Rico Ports Auth.*, 369 F.3d 570, 573 (1st Cir. 2004).

[33] *See Caterpillar Inc. v. Lewis*, 519 U.S. 61, 74, 117 S.Ct. 467, 475, 136 L.Ed.2d 437 (1996) ("[r]outine resort to § 1292(b) requests would hardly comport with Congress' design to reserve interlocutory review for 'exceptional' cases while generally retaining for the federal courts a firm final judgment rule"); *Coopers & Lybrand v. Livesay*, 437 U.S. 463, 475, 98 S.Ct. 2454, 2461, 57 L.Ed.2d 351 (1978) ("exceptional circumstances" must exist).

[34] *See OFS Fitel, LLC v. Epstein, Becker & Green, P.C.*, 549 F.3d 1344, 1358-59 (11th Cir. 2008); *Union County v. Piper Jaffray & Co.*, 525 F.3d 643, 646 (8th Cir. 2008).

[35] *See Moorman v. UnumProvident Corp.*, 464 F.3d 1260, 1272 (11th Cir. 2006).

[36] *See Weber v. U.S.*, 484 F.3d 154, 159 (2d Cir. 2007).

[37] *See Weber v. U.S.*, 484 F.3d 154, 159 n.3 (2d Cir. 2007).

[38] *Couch v. Telescope Inc.*, 611 F.3d 629, 633 (9th Cir. 2010).

over the record[39]—such as the meaning of a regulatory, statutory, or constitutional provision or common law doctrine,[40] the resolution of which is *likely* (although not necessarily certain) to affect the future course of the litigation[41]); and

(2) There is "substantial ground for difference of opinion" on the legal issue the order resolves (which generally means either that there is conflicting legal authority on the disputed issue or that the issue is a particularly difficult or uncertain one of first impression);[42] and

(3) An immediate appeal from the interlocutory order may "materially advance" the ultimate termination of the litigation (which generally means that immediate appeal may avoid expensive and protracted litigation,[43] not that it must have a final, dispositive effect[44]).

The moving party must satisfy *all* of these criteria; unless

---

[39]*See McFarlin v. Conseco Servs., LLC*, 381 F.3d 1251, 1258 (11th Cir. 2004); *id.* at 1259 ("The legal question must be stated at a high enough level of abstraction to lift the question out of the details of the evidence or facts of a particular case and give it general relevance to other cases in the same area of law.").

[40]*See Ahrenholz v. Board of Trustees of Univ. of Ill.*, 219 F.3d 674, 676 (7th Cir.2000).

[41]*See Sokaogon Gaming Enter. Corp. v. Tushie-Montgomery Assocs., Inc.*, 86 F.3d 656, 659 (7th Cir.1996) ("controlling" if issue's resolution is "quite likely" to affect further course of litigation); *In re Baker & Getty Fin. Servs., Inc.*, 954 F.2d 1169, 1172 n. 8 (6th Cir.1992) ("controlling" if issue's resolution on appeal could materially affect outcome in trial court); *Klinghoffer v. S.N.C. Achille Lauro Ed Altri-Gestione Motonave Achille Lauro in Amministrazione Straordinaria*, 921 F.2d 21, 24 (2d Cir.1990) ("controlling" if reversal on appeal would terminate lawsuit). *See also Katz v. Carte Blanche Corp.*, 496 F.2d 747, 755 (3d Cir.1974) ("controlling" means "serious to the conduct of the litigation, either practically or legally", and saving of district court's time and litigants' money are "highly relevant" factors).

[42]*See Reese v. BP Exploration (Alaska) Inc.*, 643 F.3d 681, 688 (9th Cir. 2011) (actual case split not necessary, so long as "fair-minded jurists might reach contradictory conclusions"); *McFarlin v. Conseco Servs.,*

LLC, 381 F.3d 1251, 1258 (11th Cir. 2004); (not shown when appeals court is in "complete and unequivocal" agreement with district court); *White v. Nix*, 43 F.3d 374, 378 (8th Cir.1994) (shown by sufficient number of conflicting and contradictory opinions); *In re Baker & Getty Fin. Servs., Inc.*, 954 F.2d 1169, 1172 (6th Cir.1992) (shown by split among Circuits on issue); *Klinghoffer v. S.N.C. Achille Lauro Ed Altri-Gestione Motonave Achille Lauro in Amministrazione Straordinaria*, 921 F.2d 21, 25 (2d Cir.1990) (shown by difficult issues of first impression).

[43]*See McFarlin v. Conseco Servs., LLC*, 381 F.3d 1251, 1259 (11th Cir. 2004) (resolution would "avoid a trial or otherwise substantially shorten the litigation"). *See also White v. Nix*, 43 F.3d 374, 378–79 (8th Cir.1994) (when case will proceed in substantially similar manner regardless of decision on appeal, Court of Appeals' review will not "materially advance" termination of litigation); *Klinghoffer v. S.N.C. Achille Lauro Ed Altri-Gestione Motonave Achille Lauro in Amministrazione Straordinaria*, 921 F.2d 21, 25 (2d Cir.1990) (if Court of Appeals rules that jurisdiction is absent over one defendant, ruling would greatly assist litigation's ultimate termination).

[44]*See Sterk v. Redbox Automated Retail, LLC*, 672 F.3d 535, 536–37 (7th Cir. 2012); *Reese v. BP Exploration (Alaska) Inc.*, 643 F.3d 681, 688 (9th Cir. 2011).

each criterion is meet, the trial judge cannot grant the Rule 1292(b) certification.[45] If certification is granted, the trial judge generally should specify what question of law it finds to be "controlling"—although a failure to do so is not necessarily dispositive.[46] Certification is jurisdictional; if certification is not granted, the court of appeals lacks authority to hear the appeal under Section 1292(b).[47]

A party may move the district court for such a certification. There is no express time limit for seeking the trial judge to grant a Section 1292(b) certification, although unreasonably dilatory requests may be denied by the trial judge or refused by the courts of appeals.[48] If granted by the district judge, the party may petition the court of appeals within 10 days thereafter for permission to immediately appeal the certified question.[49] The scope of the appellate review is limited to the certified order. The court may not reach beyond that order to consider other, uncertified rulings by the trial judge.[50] But the court of appeals may address any issue that is "fairly included" within the certified order itself; review is limited by the order that is certified, not by the precise question found to be controlling.[51] Other issues that are "inextricably intertwined" with the certi-

---

[45]See Couch v. Telescope Inc., 611 F.3d 629, 633 (9th Cir. 2010); Estate of Storm v. Northwest Iowa Hosp. Corp., 548 F.3d 686, 687-88 (8th Cir. 2008); Ahrenholz v. Board of Trustees of Univ. of Ill., 219 F.3d 674, 676 (7th Cir.2000).

[46]See McFarlin v. Conseco Servs., LLC, 381 F.3d 1251, 1264 (11th Cir. 2004) ("Given our caseload, when the district court hands us an entire case to sort through for ourselves we are likely to hand it right back. If the district court is unsure about which of the questions, if any, that are answered by its order qualify for certification under § 1292(b), it should not certify the order for review. If convinced that a particular question does qualify, the district court should tell us which question it is.").

[47]See In re Ford Motor Co., Bridgestone/Firestone North American Tire, LLC, 344 F.3d 648, 654–55 (7th Cir. 2003) (noting jurisdictional nature, and how most courts hold that mandamus is not proper to compel district court to certify).

[48]See Richardson Elecs., Ltd. v. Panache Broad. of Pa., Inc., 202 F.3d 957, 958 (7th Cir.2000). See also Ahrenholz v. Board of Trustees of Univ. of Ill., 219 F.3d 674, 675–76 (7th Cir.2000) (commenting that petitions for certification must be filed in the district court within a "reasonable time" after the contested order is entered).

[49]See 28 U.S.C.A. § 1292(b); Fed. R. App. P. 5. The district court may, in certain circumstances, rescue a party's failure to petition within 10 days by vacating and re-entering the certification order. Generally, this is permitted when the moving party is blameless and the delay is caused by the court itself or by a failure to timely receive the certification order. See In re City of Memphis, 293 F.3d 345, 348–50 (6th Cir.2002) (discussing process and National case law on point).

[50]See Yamaha Motor Corp., U.S.A. v. Calhoun, 516 U.S. 199, 205, 116 S.Ct. 619, 623, 133 L.Ed.2d 578 (1996).

[51]See Yamaha Motor Corp. v. Calhoun, 516 U.S. 199, 205, 116 S.Ct. 619, 623, 133 L.Ed.2d 578 (1996) ("it is the order that is appealable, and not the controlling question identified by the district court"). Accord Moorman v. UnumProvident Corp., 464 F.3d 1260, 1272 (11th Cir. 2006); NVE, Inc. v. Dep't of Health & Human Servs., 436 F.3d 182, 196 (3d Cir.2006).

fied issue may be reached as well.[52]

Collateral Order Doctrine

In addition to the Rule and statutory exceptions to the "final order" limitation, the Supreme Court has developed the common law "collateral order" doctrine, which recognizes that certain important legal rulings—collateral to the litigation's underlying merits—may nevertheless be deemed "final" and eligible for immediate appellate review. To qualify under the collateral order doctrine, the district court's order must:

(1) Be conclusive on the issue sought to be immediately appealed; and

(2) Resolve an "important question" that is completely separate from the underlying merits; and

(3) Be effectively unreviewable if the appeal were to await a final order on the merits.[53]

A failure to satisfy even one of these three requirements defeats the use of the collateral order doctrine.[54]

The collateral order exception represents a narrow, common law construction of the final order doctrine.[55] It is applied stringently and is never permitted to "swallow" the general prohibition against piecemeal appeals.[56] Although collateral orders typically involve a claimed right to "avoid" trial (a right which would be lost and effectively unappealable later), the Supreme Court has rejected the notion that this characteristic alone justifies collateral order treatment.[57] Instead, the Court has ruled that true collateral orders are those that would imperil "a substantial public interest" or some high order value if not immediately reviewed.[58]

---

[52]*See Murray v. Metropolitan Life Ins. Co.*, 583 F.3d 173, 176 (2d Cir. 2009).

[53]*See Will v. Hallock*, 546 U.S. 345, 349, 126 S.Ct. 952, 956, 163 L.Ed.2d 836 (2006); *Coopers & Lybrand v. Livesay*, 437 U.S. 463, 468–69, 98 S.Ct. 2454, 2457–58, 57 L.Ed.2d 351 (1978); *Cohen v. Beneficial Indus. Loan Corp.*, 337 U.S. 541, 546, 69 S.Ct. 1221, 1226, 93 L.Ed. 1528 (1949). *Accord Sell v. U.S.*, 539 U.S. 166, 176, 123 S.Ct. 2174, 2182, 156 L.Ed.2d 197 (2003); *Cunningham v. Hamilton County*, 527 U.S. 198, 201–203, 119 S.Ct. 1915, 1919–20, 144 L.Ed.2d 184 (1999).

[54]*See Gulfstream Aerospace Corp. v. Mayacamas Corp.*, 485 U.S. 271, 276, 108 S.Ct. 1133, 99 L.Ed.2d 296 (1988).

[55]*See Houston Cmty. Hosp. v. Blue Cross & Blue Shield of Tex., Inc.*, 481 F.3d 265, 268 (5th Cir. 2007).

[56]*See Mohawk Indus., Inc. v. Carpenter*, 558 U.S. 100, __, 130 S.Ct. 599, 605, 175 L.Ed.2d 458 (2009); *Digital Equip. Corp. v. Desktop Direct, Inc.*, 511 U.S. 863, 868, 114 S.Ct. 1992, 1996, 128 L.Ed.2d 842 (1994).

[57]*See Will v. Hallock*, 546 U.S. 345, 350–51, 126 S.Ct. 952, 958, 163 L.Ed.2d 836 (2006).

[58]*See Mohawk Indus., Inc. v. Carpenter*, 558 U.S. 100, __, 130 S.Ct. 599, 605 & 606–07, 175 L.Ed.2d 458 (2009) (appealing denial of attorney-client privilege assertion does not qualify); *Will v. Hallock*, 546 U.S. 345, 352, 126 S.Ct. 952, 959, 163 L.Ed.2d 836 (2006) (offering, as examples, the need to respect the separation of powers, to preserve the efficiency of government and the initiative of its officials, to respect a State's dignitary interests, and to mitigate the govern-

Other Exceptions

Orders may be deemed immediately appealable for other special, common law reasons. For example, certain interlocutory orders may also be appealable immediately where they resolve the rights of one party to the potentially irreparable injury of another party.[59] The extensive case law that explains and defines the precise reach of these other, common law exceptions to the final order doctrine is beyond the scope of this text.

ADDITIONAL RESEARCH REFERENCES

C.J.S. Federal Courts §§ 290(1) to 291(5) et seq.
West's Key Number Digest, Federal Courts ⟂551 to 600

§ 6.3 Step Two: Time for Taking an Appeal

CORE CONCEPT

In civil cases, an appeal generally must be taken within 30 days after the entry of the disputed judgment or order, although if the United States is a party this period is extended to 60 days. Except for a few narrow exceptions, this time period may not be waived or extended. A failure to file a timely appeal will forfeit that party's right of appeal.

APPLICATIONS

When United States Is a Party

When the United States or a federal officer, employee, or agency is a party to the litigation, the parties have 60 days after the entry of the disputed judgment or order in which to take an appeal.[60] This 60-day period applies to all parties in the case—the federal parties as well as all others. However, the federal entity must be an actual party (not a mere potential party) for the longer period to apply.[61]

When United States Is *Not* a Party

In all other cases, the parties have 30 days after the entry of the disputed judgment or order in which to take an appeal.[62]

When Opponent Appeals

After one party takes an appeal, all other parties to the litigation have at least 14 days thereafter in which to take their

---

ment's advantage over the individual).

[59] *See Forgay v. Conrad*, 47 U.S. (6 How.) 201, 201, 12 L.Ed. 404 (1848) (allowing immediate appeal from order directing delivery of property to appellee).

[60] Fed. R. App. P. 4(a)(1)(B).

[61] *See U.S. ex rel. Eisenstein v. City of New York*, 556 U.S. 928, 931,

129 S.Ct. 2230, 2233, 173 L.Ed.2d 1255 (2009) (although aware of all Federal Claim Act lawsuits, United States is not a "party" (and 60-day period does not apply) unless it actually intervenes).

[62] Fed. R. App. P. 4(a)(1)(A).

own appeals.[63] The parties receive the benefit of this 14-day "extension" period even if the original notice of appeal is defective or otherwise is dismissed.[64] But that benefit only follows from an appeal by *another* party (and cannot be used to bootstrap a second, corrective appeal by the same party).[65]

Some courts of appeals have ruled that this 14-day period is mandatory and jurisdictional—if the time period lapses, the right to cross-appeal is irretrievably lost.[66] Other courts of appeals view the 14-day period as "proper procedure", but not jurisdictional; if appellate jurisdiction was already properly invoked with the filing of the *original* notice of appeal (*i.e.*, the one to which the cross-notice would be filed) the court may permit the 14-day period to be excused in a proper circumstance.[67]

Appeal Time is Mandatory and Jurisdictional

The applicable time period for taking an appeal is mandatory and jurisdictional.[68] It cannot be waived, even for good cause shown.[69] It also may not be extended, absent the few narrow exceptions discussed below.

Dated From "Entry" of Judgment or Order

For purposes of timeliness on appeal, the appeal period begins to run when the order is "entered" on the docket, after being filed by the district judge (and not when the parties or their attorneys receive a copy).[70]

> *Note:* When the "separate document" requirement of Rule 58 applies, the time for appeal will not begin to run until the "separate document" prerequisite is satisfied or the 150-day period expires.[71]

---

[63]Fed. R. App. P. 4(a)(3) (party may file notice of appeal within 14 days after first notice of appeal was filed or within the 30 or 60 day period prescribed in Rule 4(a), whichever period is longer).

[64]*See In re Julien Co.*, 146 F.3d 420, 423 (6th Cir.1998) (applying 14-day extension rule even where first appeal was dismissed for lack of standing).

[65]*See Cruz v. Int'l Collection Corp.*, 673 F.3d 991, 1002 (9th Cir. 2012).

[66]*See Johnson v. Teamsters Local 559*, 102 F.3d 21, 29 (1st Cir.1996); *EF Operating Corp. v. American Bldgs.*, 993 F.2d 1046, 1049 n. 1 (3d Cir.1993); *Francis v. Clark Equip. Co.*, 993 F.2d 545, 552–53 (6th Cir.1993).

[67]*See Mendocino Env'l Ctr. v. Mendocino County*, 192 F.3d 1283, 1297 (9th Cir.1999); *Texport Oil Co. v.*

M/V Amolyntos, 11 F.3d 361, 366 (2d Cir.1993).

[68]*Bowles v. Russell*, 551 U.S. 205, 214, 127 S.Ct. 2360, 2366, 168 L.Ed.2d 96 (2007); *Browder v. Director, Dep't of Corrections*, 434 U.S. 257, 98 S.Ct. 556, 54 L.Ed.2d 521 (1978).

[69]*See Bowles v. Russell*, 551 U.S. 205, 214, 127 S.Ct. 2360, 2366, 168 L.Ed.2d 96 (2007); *Benn v. First Judicial Dist. of Pa.*, 426 F.3d 233, 237 (3d Cir. 2005).

[70]*See* Fed. R. App. P. 4(a)(7). *See also Lemos v. Holder*, 636 F.3d 365, 367 (7th Cir. 2011).

[71]*See* Rule 58. *See also supra* Authors' Commentary to Rule 58. *See also Meilleur v. Strong*, 682 F.3d 56, 60–61 (2d Cir. 2012); *In re Lupron Mktg. & Sales Practices Litig.*, 677 F.3d 21, 28 (1st Cir. 2012).

Computing Time For Taking Appeal

The period within which an appeal must be taken is calculated according to the counting method set in the federal appellate rules.[72] Those rules were revised, effective December 1, 2009, and will apply unless a different method for computing time is specified.[73] In counting periods stated in units of time measured in days or longer (e.g., days, months, or years), the day that triggers the period is excluded and then every other day is included. If the period ends on a weekend, a legal holiday, or a day when the clerk's office is inaccessible, the period is extended to the end of the next day that is not a weekend, a legal holiday, or a clerk's-office-inaccessible day.[74] Unless otherwise specified, a day "ends" for electronic filing at midnight in the time zone of the court's principal office, and for most other filings when the clerk's office is scheduled to close.[75] The 2009 amendments also addressed time periods set in hours,[76] as well as the proper adjustments for federal and State holidays[77] and courthouse inaccessibility.[78]

WARNING: Old Less-Than-11-Day Counting Rule

Formerly, time periods of less than 11 days were given a special computation method (*i.e.*, intervening weekends and legal holidays were excluded). To simplify time computation, this approach was abolished, effective December 1, 2009, and time periods that were formerly less than 11 days have been expanded to compensate.[79]

Extensions – By Filing Post-Trial Motions

The timely filing of certain post-trial motions will suspend the time for appeal.[80] The post-trial motions that qualify for this suspension effect are:

- Motions for judgment as a matter of law, under Federal Rule of Civil Procedure 50(b);
- Motions to alter or supplement findings of fact, under Federal Rule of Civil Procedure 52(b);
- Motions for attorney's fees, under Federal Rule of Civil Procedure 54(d), but only if the district court extends the time for appeal in accordance with Federal Rule of Civil Procedure 58; and
- Motions to alter or amend the judgment, under Federal Rule of Civil Procedure 59;
- Motions for a new trial, under Federal Rule of Civil Pro-

---

[72]*See* Fed. R. App. P. 26(a).

[73]*See* Fed. R. App. P. 26(a).

[74]*See* Fed. R. App. P. 26(a)(1). *See generally Chao Lin v. U.S. Atty. Gen.*, 677 F.3d 1043, 1044–46 (11th Cir. 2012) (clerk's office not inaccessible when inclement weather delayed opening until 10:30 a.m., and FedEx delivered appellate petition next day).

[75]*See* Fed. R. App. P. 26(a)(4).

[76]*See* Fed. R. App. P. 26(a)(2).

[77]*See* Fed. R. App. P. 26(a)(6).

[78]*See* Fed. R. App. P. 26(a)(3).

[79]*See* Fed. R. App. P. 26(a)(1) advisory committee note to 2009 amendment.

[80]*See* Fed. R. App. P. 4(a)(4)(A).

cedure 59; and

- Motions for relief from a judgment or order, under Federal Rule of Civil Procedure 60, but only if such motion is served within 28 days after entry of judgment.

These motions need not be successful in order to extend the appeal period.[81] But the motions must be filed timely; an untimely filed post-trial motion will *not* suspend the appeal time.[82] (Although the trial court may hear an untimely post-trial motion, if the non-moving party waives its timeliness objection, many courts of appeals consider the motion still untimely and, therefore, as having no tolling effect on the time for appeal.)[83] Once the district court grants or denies the post-trial motion, the time for appeal begins to run.

Triggering the Appeals Clock After Post-Trial Motions

The courts of appeals are divided on whether the district court must *expressly* rule on all pending post-trial motions before the appeal clock resumes ticking. The majority rule holds that the appeal time remains tolled until the trial court explicitly grants or denies the pending post-trial motions.[84] The minority view holds that the appeal period can begin to run as soon as the district court enters the judgment (interpreting the entry as an implicit denial of the post-trial motions).[85]

Successive Post-Trial Motions

Most courts of appeals have ruled that after the time for appeal has been *once* extended by the filing of a tolling post-trial motion, the appeal period can not be suspended *again* by the filing of a *subsequent* post-trial motion.[86]

---

[81]*See Urso v. U.S.*, 72 F.3d 59, 61 (7th Cir.1995).

[82]*See Panhorst v. U.S.*, 241 F.3d 367, 370 (4th Cir.2001).

[83]*See Blue v. Int'l Bhd. of Elec. Workers Local Union 159*, 676 F.3d 579, 582–85 (7th Cir. 2012) (untimely post-trial motions forfeited right to appeal underlying judgment, though timely appeal from post-trial rulings permitted review limited to those rulings alone); *Lizardo v. U.S.*, 619 F.3d 273, 275–80 (3d Cir. 2010) (timeliness requirement may be forfeited, but for appeal purposes, untimely Rule 59(e) motions do not toll appeal period, which begins to run from judgment); *Green v. Drug Enforcement Admin.*, 606 F.3d 1296, 1302 (11th Cir. 2010) (same effect). *But see Obaydullah v. Obama*, 688 F.3d 784, 787–92 (D.C. Cir. 2012) (given opponent's waiver of timeliness objection, appeal was

proper); *Nat'l Ecological Found. v. Alexander*, 496 F.3d 466, 476 (6th Cir. 2007) (discerning no reason why motion that was properly considered by trial court because timeliness objection was waived would fail to extend appeal period).

[84]*See Havird Oil Co. v. Marathon Oil Co.*, 149 F.3d 283 (4th Cir.1998) (holding that district court must explicitly dispose of all outstanding post-trial motions before appeal period resumes).

[85]*See Dunn v. Truck World, Inc.*, 929 F.2d 311, 313 (7th Cir.1991) (holding that entry of judgment is implicitly the order denying a post-trial motion).

[86]*See York Group, Inc. v. Wuxi Taihu Tractor Co.*, 632 F.3d 399, 401 (7th Cir. 2011); *Benson v. St. Joseph Reg'l Health Ctr.*, 575 F.3d 542, 546–57 (5th Cir. 2009); *Johnson v. Teamsters Local 559*, 102 F.3d 21, 29–30 (1st Cir.

Abandoned Post-Trial Motions

If a party files timely post-trial motions, but then abandons them, the filing of those motions can be ignored; if the appeal period lapsed while those now-withdrawn motions were pending, appellate jurisdiction will likely be deemed lost.[87]

Extensions — By District Court (Neglect or Good Cause)

Upon a showing of either excusable neglect or good cause, the district court may briefly extend the time for appeal.[88] To obtain such an extension, the movant *must* seek the extension within the original 30-day appeal period itself or within 30 days after the original appeal period expires.[89] The district court may only extend the time for appeal for 30 days after the original appeal period expires, or for 14 days after the order granting the motion for extension is granted, whichever time is later.[90] The moving party must prove *either* excusable neglect or good cause.[91]

- *Excusable Neglect Defined:* Excusable neglect applies in circumstances involving fault, and seeks an extension typically made necessary by something that should have been within the movant's control.[92] It is not a "toothless" standard nor a merciless one—equitable considerations drive the inquiry.[93] Whether the neglect is "excusable" is a determination vested to the district court's discretion.[94] In evaluating whether "excusable neglect" exists, the courts will assess the risk of prejudice to the non-moving party, the length of the delay, the delay's potential impact on the proceedings, the reason for the delay and (especially whether that reason was within the reasonable control of the moving party), and the moving party's

1996).

[87]*See Vanderwerf v. SmithKline Beecham Corp.*, 603 F.3d 842, 845–46 (10th Cir.2010).

[88]*See* Fed. R. App. P. 4(a)(5).

[89]*See* Fed.R.App.P. 4(a)(5). *See also Cohen v. Empire Blue Cross & Blue Shield*, 142 F.3d 116, 118 (2d Cir.1998) (holding that district court lacks jurisdiction to grant extension that is not filed within 30-day grace period).

[90]Fed.R.App.P. 4(a)(5)(C) (This 14-day period becomes effective on December 1, 2009; until that time, the period was 10-days.).

[91]*See* Fed. R. App. P. 4(a)(5)(A). *See also id.* advisory committee notes to 2002 amendments. *See also Sherman v. Quinn*, 668 F.3d 421, 424–25 (7th

Cir. 2012) (noting former misunderstanding that "good cause" applied only to extensions sought before time expired, and "excusable neglect" to requests thereafter; now, either showing is sufficient); *Gibbons v. U.S.*, 317 F.3d 852, 854 n.3 (8th Cir.2003) (same).

[92]*See* Fed. R. App. P. 4(a)(5)(A) advisory committee notes to 2002 amendments. *See also Sherman v. Quinn*, 668 F.3d 421, 425 (7th Cir. 2012).

[93]*See Abuelyaman v. Illinois State Univ.*, 667 F.3d 800, 808 (7th Cir. 2011).

[94]*See Sherman v. Quinn*, 668 F.3d 421, 425 (7th Cir. 2012); *Gibbons v. U.S.*, 317 F.3d 852, 853–54 (8th Cir. 2003).

good faith.[95] These factors are not mechanically given equal weight, and the actual balance may depend on the circumstances.[96] "Excusable neglect" generally requires something more than an attorney's busy caseload or an oversight in consulting or a misreading of the procedural rules.[97]

- *Good Cause Defined:* Good cause applies in circumstances where there is no fault (excusable or otherwise), and seeks an extension typically made necessary by something that was not within the movant's control.[98]

Extensions — By District Court (Non-Receipt)

If the district court determines that a party entitled to notice of the entry of a judgment or order did not timely receive that notice, the court may extend the time for appeal, but only under the following conditions:

- *Party's non-receipt within 21 days:* The court must first find that the party did not receive formal Rule 77(d) notice within 21 days after entry of the judgment or order;[99] *and*
- *Party promptly moved to reopen the appeal period*: The

---

[95] *See Pioneer Inv. Servs. Co. v. Brunswick Assocs. Ltd. P'ship*, 507 U.S. 380, 395, 113 S.Ct. 1489, 1498, 123 L.Ed.2d 74 (1993) (assessing "excusable neglect" in bankruptcy rules context). *See also Treasurer, Trs. of Drury Indus., Inc. Health Care Plan & Trust v. Goding*, 688 F.3d 784, 787–92 (8th Cir. 2012); *Sherman v. Quinn*, 668 F.3d 421, 425–26 (7th Cir. 2012).

[96] *See Treasurer, Trs. of Drury Indus., Inc. Health Care Plan & Trust v. Goding*, 688 F.3d 784, 787–92 (8th Cir. 2012) (excuse for delay given greatest weight); *Abuelyaman v. Illinois State Univ.*, 667 F.3d 800, 808 (7th Cir. 2011) (degree of prejudice to opponent and good faith of movant given greatest weight).

[97] *See Sherman v. Quinn*, 668 F.3d 421, 426–27 (7th Cir. 2012) (overloaded with work not excusable neglect); *Midwest Employers Cas. Co. v. Williams*, 161 F.3d 877, 879–80 (5th Cir.1998) (where the Rule at issue is unambiguous, district court's determination that neglect was inexcusable is "virtually unassailable"); *Advanced Estimating Sys., Inc. v. Riney*, 130 F.3d 996, 998 (11th Cir.1997) (counsel's misunderstanding of a procedural rule's plain language cannot qualify as such excusable neglect); *U.S. v. Vaccaro*, 51 F.3d 189, 191 (9th Cir.1995) (inadvertence or mistake by counsel will not qualify as excusable neglect); *Weinstock v. Cleary, Gottlieb, Steen & Hamilton*, 16 F.3d 501, 503 (2d Cir.1994) ("excusable neglect" is never satisfied by a showing of an inability or refusal to read and comprehend the plain language of Rules). *Cf. Zipperer v. School Bd. of Seminole County*, 111 F.3d 847, 849–50 (11th Cir.1997) (finding excusable neglect where notice was filed one-day late, having been mailed to the Court, by in-State mailing, six days before filing, noting that normal mail delivery is three days).

[98] *See* Fed. R. App. P. 4(a)(5)(A) advisory committee notes to 2002 amendments. *See also Bishop v. Corsentino*, 371 F.3d 1203, 1207 (10th Cir.2004).

[99] *See* Fed. R. App. P. 4(a)(6)(A). This 21-day trigger requires actual, formal notice under Rule 77(d). Thus, if no formal Rule 77(d) notice was served within 21 days, but the party nevertheless receives informal notice of the entry, an extension of the appeal time may still be sought. *See* Fed. R. App. P. 4(a)(6)(A) advisory committee note (2005). *See also Benavides v. Bureau of Prisons*, 79 F.3d 1211, 1214

non-noticed party must promptly move the district court to reopen the appeal period within 14 days after receiving or observing written notice of the entry from any source;[100] *and*

- *Party moved no later than 180 days after entry:* The maximum window for an appeal extension can never last longer than 180 days (thus obligating practitioners to routinely check the court dockets, even when no formal notice has been received);[101] *and*

- *No party is prejudiced by the extension:* The court must find that no party would be prejudiced by granting an appeal period extension;[102] *and*

- *Actual extension may last only 14 days:* If an extension is granted, it will compel the non-noticed party to file the appeal within 14 days.[103]

The burden of demonstrating non-receipt rests with the moving party.[104] Evidence that the order was properly mailed or transmitted over a court's official electronic filing system creates a presumption of receipt; if contested, the district court will, as factfinder, assess the evidence and determine the question of receipt or non-receipt.[105] Motions for extensions due to non-receipt are committed to the district court's discretion.[106] In exercising that discretion, the district court may deny this extension even where the litigant otherwise satisfies the technical elements of the extension rule (provided, of course, that the basis for the court's denial is something other than the district court's own assessment of the merits of the appeal[107] or that the party failed to learn of the entry of judgment independently through its own means.)[108] The moving party is ordinarily not required to demonstrate "excusable neglect" in order to

---

(D.C. Cir. 1996) (same effect).

[100]*See* Fed. R. App. P. 4(a)(6)(B) (This 14-day period became effective on December 1, 2009; until that time, the period was 7-days.). The extension window will start to run on the day the party receives or observes "written" notice from "any source" (*e.g.*, by fax, e-mail, viewing a website entry, etc.), and will last for only 14 days. *See* Fed. R. App. P. 4(a)(6)(B) advisory committee note (2005) (as revised in 2009). Oral notice, "no matter how specific, reliable, or unequivocal", will not start the period running. *Id.*

[101]*See* Fed. R. App. P. 4(a)(6)(B).

[102]*See* Fed. R. App. P. 4(a)(6)(C).

[103]*See* Fed. R. App. P. 4(a)(6).

[104]*See Nunley v. City of Los Angeles*, 52 F.3d 792, 795 (9th Cir.1995).

[105]*See American Boat Co., Inc. v.*

Unknown Sunken Barge, 567 F.3d 348, 352-53 (8th Cir. 2009) (official email notices of a court's CM/ECF system are *presumed* received; absent evidence to disprove it, court may rely on presumption). *But see Nunley v. City of Los Angeles*, 52 F.3d 792, 796 (9th Cir.1995) (once specific factual denial of receipt is made, district court can give no further weight to presumption of receipt).

[106]*See* Fed. R. App. P. 4(a)(6) ("The district court . . . *may* extend the time for filing a notice of appeal . . .")(emphasis added).

[107]*See Kuhn v. Sulzer Orthopedics, Inc.*, 498 F.3d 365, 369–70 (6th Cir. 2007); *Arai v. American Bryce Ranches Inc.*, 316 F.3d 1066, 1069–71 (9th Cir. 2003).

[108]*See U.S. v. Withers*, 618 F.3d 1008, 1014–15 (9th Cir. 2010).

justify such relief.[109]

> *Note:* Seeking relief from orders under other rules, such as Rule 60(b), cannot be used to circumvent this 180-day limitation.[110]

Extensions — By District Court (Fee Motions)

When a party makes a timely attorneys' fees motion under Rule 54(d), the district court may suspend the time for taking an appeal until the fees motion is resolved.[111]

Extensions – By Court of Appeals

The courts of appeals may not grant litigants an extension of the time for appeal under any circumstances.[112]

Premature Appeals

A notice of appeal is *not* necessarily fatally defective merely because it is filed too quickly. If the notice is filed after the district court announces its decision, but before the judgment or order is formally entered, the notice of appeal will be deemed "filed" on the day the district court formally enters the judgment or order (at least as to orders that would be immediately appealable upon entry).[113] This rule, however, will not apply to orders that are clearly interlocutory and, thus, would not be immediately appealable upon entry[114] — unless the otherwise interlocutory order is thereafter given a Rule 54(b) determination.[115]

If the notice of appeal is filed after the district court formally enters the judgment or order, but before the district court rules upon those types of post-trial motions that suspend the time

---

[109]*See Benavides v. Bureau of Prisons*, 79 F.3d 1211, 1214 (D.C.Cir. 1996) (showings of excusable neglect and good cause are not required because the court supposes that the party's tardiness is not his or her fault; if the party is at fault (e.g., by negligently failing to notify the clerk of a change of address), the court may deny relief).

[110]*See Vencor Hosps., Inc. v. Standard Life & Acc. Ins. Co.*, 279 F.3d 1306, 1310 (11th Cir.2002).

[111]*See* Rule 58(e). *See also supra* Authors' Commentary to Rule 58(e).

[112]Fed. R. App. P. 26(b). *See In re Fischer*, 554 F.3d 656, 657 (7th Cir. 2009); *Burnley v. City of San Antonio*, 470 F.3d 189, 192–93 (5th Cir. 2006).

[113]Fed. R. App. P. 4(a)(2). *See FirsTier Mortg. Co. v. Investors Mortg. Ins. Co.*, 498 U.S. 269, 276, 111 S.Ct. 648, 112 L.Ed.2d 743 (1991); *Meilleur v. Strong*, 682 F.3d 56, 60–61 (2d Cir. 2012); *Bielskis v. Louisville Ladder,*

Inc., 663 F.3d 887, 892–93 (7th Cir. 2011).

[114]*See FirsTier Mortg. Co. v. Investors Mortg. Ins. Co.*, 498 U.S. 269, 276, 111 S.Ct. 648, 652, 112 L.Ed.2d 743 (1991); *Feldman v. Olin Corp.*, 692 F.3d 748, 757 (7th Cir. 2012); *Robinson-Reeder v. American Council on Educ.*, 571 F.3d 1333, 1337 (D.C.Cir. 2009). *But cf. Bonner v. Perry*, 564 F.3d 424, 427-29 (6th Cir. 2009) (notice of appeal filed after a partial disposition (that might have qualified for Rule 54(b) determination) may properly be treated as filed upon final disposition of all remaining claims).

[115]*See Brown v. Columbia Sussex Corp.*, 664 F.3d 182, 189–90 (7th Cir. 2011); *Nat'l Ass'n of Bds. of Pharmacy v. Bd. of Regents of Univ. Sys. of Ga.*, 633 F.3d 1297, 1306–07 (11th Cir. 2011). *But cf. Bielskis v. Louisville Ladder, Inc.*, 663 F.3d 887, 893 (7th Cir. 2011) (entry of Rule 58 judgment "obviates" unfiled Rule 54(b) determination).

for appeal, the notice is deemed to lie dormant. The notice will become effective on the date the trial court rules on the outstanding post-trial motions.[116]

ADDITIONAL RESEARCH REFERENCES

C.J.S., Federal Courts §§ 293(5 to 17) et seq.
West's Key Number Digest, Federal Courts ⊸652 to 660.40

§ 6.4 Step Three: Procedure for Taking an Appeal

CORE CONCEPT

A federal appeal is taken by filing a notice of appeal with the district court. Thus, there are essentially two "modest tasks" that must be completed before an appeal is properly taken: the appellants must give proper "notice" of their intent to appeal and they must deliver that notice "in time".[117]

APPLICATIONS

Contents of Notice of Appeal

A notice of appeal is typically a simple, one-page form. Its essential contents are: (1) naming the party or parties taking the appeal; (2) naming the court to which the appeal is taken; and (3) naming the order that is being appealed.[118] It need not name the appellees,[119] nor should it contain the appellant's legal arguments.

- *Naming All Parties:* The parties to the appeal should each be individually named.[120] Appeals are permitted only by those parties whose names appear on the notice of appeal itself (or whose intent to appeal is otherwise "objectively clear" from the notice).[121] Although the

---

[116]Fed. R. App. P. 4(a)(4)(B). *See Moses v. Howard Univ. Hosp.*, 606 F.3d 789, 796 (D.C.Cir. 2010); *Casanova v. Ulibarri*, 595 F.3d 1120, 1123 (10th Cir. 2010). This Rule represents a change in earlier practice, which before 1993 held that a notice of appeal was a "nullity" if prematurely filed while post-trial motions remained pending. *See Leader Nat'l Ins. Co. v. Industrial Indem. Ins. Co.*, 19 F.3d 444, 445 (9th Cir.1994) (noting 1993 amendment's change to practice).

[117]*See Isert v. Ford Motor Co.*, 461 F.3d 756, 758 (6th Cir.2006).

[118]*See* Fed. R. App. P. 3(c)(1). *See also Bennett v. Gaetz*, 592 F.3d 786,

790 (7th Cir. 2010); *Sines v. Wilner*, 609 F.3d 1070, 1074–75 (10th Cir. 2010); *Isert v. Ford Motor Co.*, 461 F.3d 756, 758 (6th Cir.2006).

[119]*See MIF Realty L.P. v. Rochester Assocs.*, 92 F.3d 752, 758 (8th Cir.1996) (Rules do not require specific listing of all appellees called upon to respond to the appeal); *Crawford v. Roane*, 53 F.3d 750, 752 (6th Cir.1995) (same).

[120]*See* Fed. R. App. P. 3(c)(1)(A).

[121]*See* Fed. R. App. P. 3(c)(4) & advisory committee note to 1993 amendment. *See also Raley v. Hyundai Motor Co.*, 642 F.3d 1271, 1277 (10th Cir. 2011) (party's intent to appeal be objectively clear from notice itself);

phrase "et al."[122] and other shorthand expressions[123] may, in some limited contexts, be sufficient, an express designation is always the safer course.[124] Where that clarity is missing, the appeal may be lost.[125]

- *Naming All Parts of Order Appealed From:* Each part of a separable judgment or separable order appealed from must be named.[126] Ordinarily, an appeal taken from the final judgment itself will support appellate review of most earlier interlocutory orders in the case,[127] so long as the intent to appeal from each particular interlocutory order is clear.[128] However, if a party chooses to name in the notice of appeal a particular order or ruling (*e.g.*, appealing from the order of November 10 granting summary judgment), the court of appeals may rule that the party has *not* also appealed from other rulings in the same case.[129] Some courts of appeals, however, will allow added information supplied in the party's other filings to supplement (and, perhaps, rescue) an otherwise

---

S.E.C. v. Wealth Mgmt. LLC, 628 F.3d 323, 331 (7th Cir. 2010) (holders of trust entitled to appeal where no confusion existed as to their identity); *Lamboy-Ortiz v. Ortiz-Velez*, 630 F.3d 228, 243–44 (1st Cir. 2010) (attorney's intent to appeal sanction rulings clear, though not separately listed as appellant); *Vivendi SA v. T-Mobile USA Inc.*, 586 F.3d 689, 690 n.2 (9th Cir. 2009) (explanatory statement in Civil Appeals Docketing Statement sufficed to allow co-appellant's appeal); *Pugh v. Goord*, 345 F.3d 121, 124 n.2 (2d Cir. 2003) (although all names all did not appear in caption, their names did appear in notice and, thus, were "objectively clear").

[122]*See Massie v. U.S. Dep't of Housing & Urban Dev't*, 620 F.3d 340, 348–49 (3d Cir. 2010) (though discouraged, use of "et al." preserved appeal by class members); *Olenhouse v. Commodity Credit Corp.*, 42 F.3d 1560, 1572 (10th Cir. 1994) (same). *But cf. Murphy v. Keystone Steel & Wire Co.*, 61 F.3d 560 (7th Cir. 1995) (only named class members could appeal, because intent of unnamed class members was unclear). Note, this rule reversed prior practice, which held that the failure to specifically name all appealing parties forfeited their right of appeal. *Cf. Torres v. Oakland Scavenger Co.*, 487 U.S. 312, 108 S.Ct. 2405, 101 L.Ed.2d 285 (1988).

[123]*See Air Line Pilots Ass'n v. Continental Airlines*, 125 F.3d 120 (3d Cir.1997) (finding term "the LPP Claimants" sufficient to adequately identify appellants).

[124]*See Olenhouse v. Commodity Credit Corp.*, 42 F.3d 1560, 1572 n. 19 (10th Cir.1994).

[125]*See Valadez-Lopez v. Chertoff*, 656 F.3d 851, 859 n.2 (9th Cir. 2011); *Raley v. Hyundai Motor Co.*, 642 F.3d 1271, 1274 (10th Cir. 2011).

[126]*See* Fed. R. App. P. 3(c)(1)(B).

[127]*See Bentkowski v. Scene Magazine*, 637 F.3d 689, 696 (6th Cir. 2011); *Cortez v. Trans Union, LLC*, 617 F.3d 688, 695 n.2 (3d Cir. 2010).

[128]*See Lolli v. County of Orange*, 351 F.3d 410, 414–15 (9th Cir. 2003) (appellant presumed to appeal from merits of summary judgment motion, and not just denial of reconsideration). *Cf. C & S Acquisitions Corp. v. Northwest Aircraft, Inc.*, 153 F.3d 622 (8th Cir.1998) (principle did not apply where notice failed to give sufficient notice of intent to appeal separate, distinct issues).

[129]*See White v. State Farm Fire & Cas. Co.*, 664 F.3d 860, 863–64 (11th Cir. 2011); *Parkhill v. Minnesota Mut. Life Ins. Co.*, 286 F.3d 1051, 1058 (8th Cir.2002). *Newman v. Federal Exp. Corp.*, 266 F.3d 401, 404 (6th Cir. 2001).

insufficiently detailed notice of appeal.[130] An order not listed in the notice of appeals may, nevertheless, be reviewed if it has a connection with the listed orders, the intention to appeal from it is clear, and the opponent has not been prejudiced.[131]

- *Naming Court of Appeals:* The notice of appeal must identify the specific court to which the appeal is being taken[132] (unless only one proper court is possible).[133]

Errors in Notice of Appeal

Although jurisdictional in nature,[134] the rules prescribing the proper contents of a notice of appeal are construed liberally,[135] and not hyper-technically.[136] A "technical variance" from the rules may be excused, if the rule requirements are "functionally" satisfied.[137] That function is notice, both to the court and the adversaries, of the appealing parties and the rulings to be reviewed.[138] If the appellant's intent is clear (or fairly inferred) and the appellee is not prejudiced by a technical error (generally, through ensuring a full opportunity to brief the issue), such mistakes may be overlooked.[139] This liberality may even permit a party's brief to substitute for an unfiled notice of appeal, where it provides all the requisite notice.[140] Pro se appeals

---

[130]*See Employers Mut. Cas. Co. v. Bartile Roofs, Inc.*, 618 F.3d 1153, 1164 n.9 (10th Cir. 2010) (docketing statement clarified intent to appeal venue issue); *One Indus., LLC v. Jim O'Neal Distrib., Inc.*, 578 F.3d 1154, 1159, (9th Cir. 2009) (opening brief's extensive discussion sufficed to preserve issue missing from notice of appeal); *Trotter v. Regents of Univ. of N.M.*, 219 F.3d 1179, 1184 (10th Cir.2000) (docketing statement accepted as the "functional equivalent" of a proper notice of appeal).

[131]*See Harvey v. Town of Merrill-ville*, 649 F.3d 526, 528 (7th Cir. 2011); *Cortez v. Trans Union, LLC*, 617 F.3d 688, 695 n.2 (3d Cir. 2010).

[132]*See* Fed. R. App. P. 3(c)(1)(C). *See also Bradley v. Work*, 154 F.3d 704 (7th Cir.1998). *But cf. U.S. v. Treto-Haro*, 287 F.3d 1000, 1002 n.1 (10th Cir.2002) (failure to name correct court will not warrant dismissal where intention may be reasonably inferred).

[133]*See In re Jones*, 680 F.3d 640, 642 (6th Cir. 2012); *In re Capco Energy, Inc.*, 669 F.3d 274, 278 n.2 (5th Cir. 2012).

[134]*See Smith v. Barry*, 502 U.S. 244, 248, 112 S.Ct. 678, 681, 116 L.Ed.2d 678 (1992).

[135]*See Employers Mut. Cas. Co. v. Bartile Roofs, Inc.*, 618 F.3d 1153, 1164 n.9 (10th Cir. 2010); *USCOC of Greater Mo. v. City of Ferguson*, 583 F.3d 1035, 1040 (8th Cir. 2009); *One Indus., LLC v. Jim O'Neal Distrib., Inc.*, 578 F.3d 1154, 1159 (9th Cir. 2009).

[136]*See Sines v. Wilner*, 609 F.3d 1070, 1074–75 (10th Cir. 2010); *Hudson v. District of Columbia*, 558 F.3d 526, 529 (D.C.Cir. 2009).

[137]*See Smith v. Barry*, 502 U.S. 244, 248, 112 S.Ct. 678, 681, 116 L.Ed.2d 678 (1992); *Torres v. Oakland Scavenger Co.*, 487 U.S. 312, 316–17, 108 S.Ct. 2405, 2408, 101 L.Ed.2d 285 (1988).

[138]*See Smith v. Barry*, 502 U.S. 244, 248, 112 S.Ct. 678, 682, 116 L.Ed.2d 678 (1992).

[139]*See Harvey v. Town of Merrill-ville*, 649 F.3d 526, 528 (7th Cir. 2011); *Employers Mut. Cas. Co. v. Bartile Roofs, Inc.*, 618 F.3d 1153, 1164 n.9 (10th Cir. 2010).

[140]*See Taylor v. Johnson*, 257 F.3d 470, 474 (5th Cir.2001).

will be assessed with special liberality.[141] Nevertheless, an appellant's subjective intentions are not enough,[142] and if the notice demanded by the rules is not satisfied either literally or functionally, the appeal will fail.[143]

Privacy Protection for Personal Data Identifiers

The vulnerability of electronically-accessible court files to privacy and security mischief prompted the adoption of special redaction and sealing privileges for certain civil cases.[144] In cases where these privileges applied at the district court level, the privileges will extend to the appeal as well.[145]

Notice Must Be *Filed* Timely

The notice of appeal must be actually *filed* with the clerk of court within the time allotted for taking an appeal.[146] Mailing the notice to the court or serving the notice on other parties is not sufficient. However, a notice of appeal is deemed to be "filed" when a *pro se* prisoner deposits the notice into the prison's internal mail system.[147]

Place of Filing

A notice of appeal is filed with the clerk of the district court from which the appeal is taken.[148] However, mistakenly filing the notice with the court of appeals will *not* defeat the appeal. If the notice is filed timely, albeit with the court of appeals, the appeals court clerk will note the date of filing and send the notice to the clerk of the district court.[149]

Electronic Filing

Each individual court of appeals may (but is not obligated to) permit the electronic filing of appeal papers.[150] In fact, the Appellate Rules now authorize a court of appeals to *require* electronic filing, so long as reasonable exceptions are allowed for litigants for whom such electronic filing would impose a hardship.[151]

Service Not Required

The appealing party need not serve the notice of appeal on all other parties; this service is made by the clerk of court.[152] The clerk's failure to serve the notice, however, does not defeat

---

[141]*See Sines v. Wilner*, 609 F.3d 1070, 1074–75 (10th Cir. 2010); *Smith v. Grams*, 565 F.3d 1037, 1041-42 (7th Cir. 2009).

[142]*See Smith v. Barry*, 502 U.S. 244, 248, 112 S.Ct. 678, 682, 116 L.Ed.2d 678 (1992).

[143]*See Smith v. Barry*, 502 U.S. 244, 248, 112 S.Ct. 678, 682, 116 L.Ed.2d 678 (1992).

[144]*See Rule 5.2. See also supra* Authors' Commentary to Rule 5.2.

[145]*See* Fed. R. App. P. 25(a)(5).

[146]*See* Fed. R. App. P. 3(a)(1) & 4(a)(1).

[147]Fed. R. App. P. 4(c) (requiring accompanying notarized statement or declaration).

[148]Fed. R. App. P. 3(a).

[149]Fed. R. App. P. 4(d).

[150]*See* Fed. R. App. P. 25(a)(2)(D).

[151]*See* Fed. R. App. P. 25(a)(2)(D) and advisory committee note to 2006 amendments.

[152]Fed. R. App. P. 3(d)(1).

the appeal.[153]

> *Service Copies to the Court:* Although the appellant does not actually serve the notice of appeal on the other parties, the appellant is required to provide the clerk's office with sufficient copies of the notice for service.[154]

Joint Appeals

Joint appeals may be taken by two or more parties whose similar interests make such joinder practicable.[155] Each plaintiff, however, must file a timely notice of appeal. The fact that some similarly situated plaintiffs timely appealed is immaterial; the appeal of each plaintiff must be appropriately noticed to the court.[156]

Consolidated Appeals

Upon its own motion or by motion of a party, the court of appeals may consolidate the appeals of different parties.[157]

Fees

The appealing party must pay to the district court both the district court fee for appeal and the court of appeals' docket fee.[158]

ADDITIONAL RESEARCH REFERENCES

C.J.S. Federal Courts §§ 282 to 301(48) et seq.
West's Key Number Digest, Federal Courts ⟜521 to 956

§ 6.5 Step Four: Stays Pending Appeal

CORE CONCEPT

A party may seek a stay of judgment by filing such an application with the district court. In applications *not* involving stays of injunctions, receiverships, or accountings in patent infringement actions, a party may request a stay pending appeal by filing a supersedeas bond. Stay applications must be filed timely and, generally, initially in the district court.

APPLICATIONS

14-Day "Automatic" Stay

For a period of 14 days after a judgment is entered, the parties are barred from executing upon the judgment or pursuing further proceedings for its enforcement.[159] This automatic stay does *not* apply to judgments involving injunctions, judgments

---

[153]Fed. R. App. P. 3(d)(3).

[154]Fed. R. App. P. 3(a)(1).

[155]Fed. R. App. P. 3(b)(1).

[156]*See Wooden v. Board of Regents of Univ. Sys. of Ga.*, 247 F.3d 1262, 1273 (11th Cir.2001).

[157]Fed. R. App. P. 3(b)(2).

[158]Fed. R. App. P. 3(e).

[159]*See* Rule 62(a) (This 14-day period became effective on December 1,

in receivership actions, or judgments or orders directing accountings in patent infringement actions.

Time to Apply for Stay

Applications for stay generally should be filed at the earliest possible opportunity. Because the automatic stay does not apply in certain injunction, receivership, and patent infringement circumstances, appellants in those cases do not enjoy the automatic 14-day[160] stay period and the time for execution and enforcement will immediately arrive. Even in automatic stay cases, supersedeas bonds must first be approved by the court before any stay is effective.[161] Consequently, a delay in seeking a stay will expose the defeated party to execution and enforcement of the judgment.

Where to Apply for Stay

Ordinarily, stays pending appeal must be filed first with the district court.[162] Only in those circumstances where applying in the district court is not practicable, or where the district court has denied the request or failed to grant all the relief requested, may a party request a stay in the court of appeals.[163]

Procedure for Stay Applications in the District Court

In cases that do not involve injunctions, receivers, or accountings in patent infringement cases, the posting of a supersedeas bond—after it has been approved by the court—will stay execution and enforcement of the judgment.[164]

In cases involving injunctions, the district court may, in its discretion, grant a stay of the injunction pending appeal.[165] To obtain such a stay, the moving party must generally make the traditional showing required for any injunction: strong likelihood of success on the merits, irreparable injury, no substantial harm to others, and no damage to the public interest.[166] The court may condition such a stay upon the posting of a bond or other appropriate security.[167]

Procedure for Stay Applications in the Court of Appeals

In applying for a stay in the court of appeals, the moving party must make several showings in the motion papers:[168]

    a. *Proceedings Before Trial Court:* The motion must show why a stay application cannot be practicably directed to the district judge, or that the district judge has denied a stay or failed to grant all the relief requested (the district court's reasons must be set forth); *and*

2009; until that time, the period was 10-days.).

[160]This 14-day period became effective on December 1, 2009; until that time, the period was 10-days.

[161]*See* Rule 62(d).

[162]*See* Fed. R. App. P. 8(a)(1).

[163]*See* Fed. R. App. P. 8(a)(2).

[164]*See* Rule 62(d).

[165]*See* Rule 62(c).

[166]*See supra* Author's Commentary to Rule 62(c).

[167]*See* Rule 62(c).

[168]*See* Fed. R. App. P. 8(a)(2)(A) to (2)(D).

b. *Reasons for Relief:* The motion must show the reasons for the relief requested, and set forth the facts relied upon in support of that showing. Relevant parts of the record shall be included and, where the facts relied upon are subject to dispute, supporting affidavits or other sworn statements shall also be included; *and*

c. *Reasonable Notice:* Reasonable notice of the motion shall be given to the non-moving party; *and*

d. *Disposition:* The motion will ordinarily be resolved by a panel or division of the court, unless exceptional circumstances justify submitting the motion to a single judge; *and*

e. *Bond or Security:* If the motion is granted, the court of appeals can condition the stay upon the filing in the district court of a bond or other appropriate security.[169]

§ 6.6 Step Five: the Appeal Process

CORE CONCEPT

Once the appeal is timely filed, the court of appeals will mail to each party a briefing notice that will schedule the filing of an Appellant's Brief, an Appellee's Brief, and an Appellant's Reply Brief. Thereafter, the court of appeals may schedule oral argument, the case will be submitted, and a written disposition on appeal will be filed.

APPLICATIONS

Effect of Appeal

Once the appeal is taken, jurisdiction over the case passes from the district court to the court of appeals.[170] The district court thereafter generally enjoys only the narrow power to preform ministerial functions, issues stays, and injunctions pending appeal, and, in certain instances, award counsel fees. However, under the new "indicative ruling" procedure, if the district court (after being divested of jurisdiction by an appeal) states that it would grant a trial-level motion or considers such a motion to raise a "substantial issue", the court of appeals may remand back to the district judge for further proceedings.[171]

Compliance With Schedule and Procedures

Failure to comply with the court of appeals' schedule and procedures is ground for such action as the court of appeals deems appropriate, including denial of right to participate in

---

[169]*See* Fed. R. App. P. 8(a)(2)(E).

[170]*See Griggs v. Provident Consumer Discount Co.*, 459 U.S. 56, 58, 103 S.Ct. 400, 402, 74 L.Ed.2d 225 (1982) (noting that notice of appeal is an event of jurisdictional significance, conferring jurisdiction on the Court of Appeals and divesting the district court of control over those aspects of the litigation involved in the appeal).

[171]*See* Fed. R. App. P. 12.1 (effective Dec. 1, 2009); *see also* Rule 62.1 (effective Dec. 1, 2009) (parallel district court provision).

oral argument or even dismissal of the appeal itself.[172]

Designation of the Record and Statement of Issues

The "record" on appeal consists of (1) the original papers and exhibits filed in the trial court, (2) the transcript, and (3) a certified copy of docket entries.[173] The "record" encompasses not just those exhibits admitted into evidence, but may include items presented for admission and denied by the district court.[174] Within 14 days after filing the notice of appeal, the appealing party must order those portions of the transcript that are necessary for the appeal.[175] Unless the appellant orders the entire transcript, the appellant must, during this same 14-day period,[176] file a statement of the issues for appeal and a list of the intended contents of the Appendix. The appellee may thereafter serve a counter-designation of additional portions of the transcript to be included.[177]

> *Note*: Some districts have promulgated Local Rules requiring the appellant to transcribe the entire proceedings.[178] Practitioners should be diligent in consulting their local rules for guidance on this point.

Briefing Procedures

Briefing procedures are generally set in the Federal Rules of Appellate Procedure,[179] but additional provisions vary by Local Rules among the different courts of appeals. The practitioner should always consult the Local Rules for these additional procedures.

Briefing Privacy

Special redaction and sealing privileges may be applied to certain civil cases in the district court (*e.g.*, social security numbers, taxpayer identification numbers, financial account numbers, birth years, and full names of minors may be presented in an abbreviated form).[180] In cases where these privileges applied at the district court level, the privileges will extend to the appeal as well.[181]

---

[172]*See* Fed. R. App. P. 3(a)(2).

[173]*See Morton Int'l, Inc. v. A.E. Staley Mfg. Co.*, 343 F.3d 669, 682 (3d Cir.2003).

[174]*See Morton Int'l, Inc. v. A.E. Staley Mfg. Co.*, 343 F.3d 669, 682 (3d Cir.2003).

[175]This 14-day period became effective on December 1, 2009; until that time, the period was 10-days.

[176]This 14-day period became effective on December 1, 2009; until that time, the period was 10-days.

[177]*See* Fed. R. App. P. 10, 11, & 30.

[178]*See* E.D.Pa. Loc. R. 7.1(e) (requiring moving party to order "a transcript of the trial"); *Bongard v. Korn*, 1993 WL 39267 (E.D.Pa.1993) ("the whole transcript is to be ordered rather than a mere portion of the trial transcript as the particular party requesting post-trial relief unilaterally deems necessary").

[179]*See* Fed. R. App. P. 25, 28, 28,1, 30, 31, 32.

[180]*See* Rule 5.2. *See also supra* Authors' Commentary to Rule 5.2.

[181]*See* Fed. R. App. P. 25(a)(5).

Briefing Reminders

The "Do's" and "Don't's" of effective appellate briefing could fill volumes. Several common oversights, however, are worth special mention:

Corporate Disclosure Statement: The Appellate Rules require each non-governmental corporate party in every civil case to file a statement identifying each of its parent corporations and all publicly-held companies that own 10% or more of the party's stock, and to supplement that statement whenever the necessary information changes.[182] The Rules require that this Statement be reprinted in front of the Table of Contents in that party's opening brief, even if the Statement has already been filed with the Court of Appeals.[183]

Footnote Restrictions: Some courts of appeals have adopted local rules that severely limit the use of footnotes in appellate briefs.[184] Practitioners should be careful to consult their court of appeals' local rules to be certain their briefs comply with these restrictions.

Citing "Unpublished" Decisions: For years, many courts of appeals forbade the citation of "unpublished", "non-precedential", "not-for-publication", or similarly labeled decisions. Effective January 1, 2007, the Appellate Rules invalidated this local practice. Courts of appeals may no longer prohibit or discourage the citation of such decisions[185] (although litigants citing such opinions that are not publicly accessible through a commercial, legal research service, or court database must file and serve copies).[186] The amendment, however, is a narrow one; it does not restrict a court of appeals from *issuing* decisions bearing those labels, nor does it prescribe what effect the court must give (or not give) to such decisions.[187] The amendment merely addresses the question of citation.

Oral Argument

Oral argument is permitted generally unless the appeal is frivolous, the dispositive issues were authoritatively decided, or the decisional process would not be significantly aided by argument because the facts and legal arguments are adequately set forth in the briefs.[188] The length, scheduling, and location of argument is set by the particular court of appeals.

Note: The parties cannot postpone oral argument by stipulation; postponement can occur only upon court order.

§ 6.7 Step Six: Appeals to the United States Supreme

---

[182]Fed. R. App. P. 26.1(a).

[183]Fed. R. App. P. 26.1(b).

[184]*See* 3d Cir. Loc. App. R. 32.2(a) ("Excessive footnotes in briefs are discouraged. Footnotes shall be printed in the same size type utilized in the text.").

[185]Fed. R. App. P. 32.1(a). *See also id.* advisory committee note to 2006 amendment.

[186]Fed. R. App. P. 32.1(b). *See also id.* advisory committee note to 2006 amendment.

[187]Fed. R. App. P. 32.1. *See also id.* advisory committee note to 2006 amendment.

[188]Fed. R. App. P. 34(a)(2).

Court

CORE CONCEPT

A party enjoys an appeal as of right to the United States Supreme Court in only very few circumstances. In all other cases, the Supreme Court has the discretion whether to permit or refuse appeals to the Court. In practice, only a small handful of the many thousands of requests for Supreme Court review are granted each year.

APPLICATIONS

Appeals As Of Right; Time to File

Whenever a specially convened three-judge district court panel declares any Act of Congress to be unconstitutional, a direct appeal may be taken to the Supreme Court.[189] Such appeals must be filed within 30 days of the date the district court's order is entered.[190] Congress may permit other direct appeals from the district courts, and such appeals must also be filed within 30 days of the district court's action.[191]

Discretionary Appeals; Time to File

The Supreme Court may, in its discretion, grant a party appellate review from other federal and State court rulings. Supreme Court review of federal appellate court decisions may be sought by petitioning for a Writ of Certiorari[192] or by seeking a certification from the court of appeals.[193] The Supreme Court may, in its discretion, also grant a Writ of Certiorari to review of decisions from the highest court of any State, but only where (a) a federal treaty or statute is drawn into question, (b) a State statute is drawn into question on federal grounds, or (c) any title, right, privilege, or immunity is specially set up or claimed under federal law.[194]

Petitions for Writs of Certiorari from federal court of appeals rulings must be filed with the Supreme Court within 90 days after the entry of the disputed judgment or decree.[195] Petitions for Writs from qualifying State court rulings must also be filed with the Supreme Court within 90 days after the entry of the disputed judgment or decree.[196]

---

[189] *See* 28 U.S.C.A. § 1253.

[190] *See* 28 U.S.C.A. § 2102(a).

[191] *See* 28 U.S.C.A. § 2102(b).

[192] *See* 28 U.S.C.A. § 1254(1). In Latin, "certiorari" means "to be informed of"; such writs of certiorari are of common law origin, and were (and are) issued by a higher court to a lower court requiring that the certified record in a case be delivered for review. *See Black's Law Dictionary* 207 (5th

ed. 1979).

[193] *See* 28 U.S.C.A. § 1254(2).

[194] *See* 28 U.S.C.A. § 1257.

[195] *See* 28 U.S.C.A. § 2101(c); U.S. S. Ct. R. 13(1), (3). *See also id.* (permitting Supreme Court, for good cause shown, to extend this 90-day period for another 60 days); U.S. S. Ct. R. 13(5) (same).

[196] *See* 28 U.S.C. § 2101(d); U.S. S. Ct. R. 13(1), (3).

Considerations in Granting Writs of Certiorari

The Supreme Court Rules provide a non-controlling, non-exhaustive list of the types of "compelling reasons" that may prompt the Supreme Court to grant a Writ of Certiorari:

(1) A conflict among the federal Circuits on an "important matter";

(2) A conflict between a federal court of appeals and the highest court of a State on an "important federal question";

(3) A ruling by a court of appeals that "so far departed from the accepted and usual course of judicial proceedings" (or that sanctions such a departure by a lower court) that the Supreme Court's "supervisory power" is called for;

(4) A ruling by the highest court of a State that conflicts with the decision of another State's highest court or a federal court of appeals on an "important federal question"; or

(5) A ruling by a State court or a federal court of appeals that decides "an important question of federal law that has not been, but should be," settled by the Supreme Court, or that decides "an important federal question in a way that conflicts with relevant decisions" of the Supreme Court.[197]

§ 6.8 *Federal Rules of Appellate Procedure* (Effective July 1, 1968; amendments effective December 1, 2011)

Rule

1. Scope of Rules; Title.

2. Suspension of Rules.

3. Appeal as of Right—How Taken.

3.1 Appeal from a Judgment of a Magistrate Judge in a Civil Case [Abrogated].

4. Appeal as of Right—When Taken.

5. Appeal by Permission.

5.1 Appeal By Leave Under 28 U.S.C. § 636(c)(5) [Abrogated].

6. Appeal in a Bankruptcy Case From a Final Judgment, Order, or Decree of a District Court or Bankruptcy Appellate Panel.

7. Bond for Costs on Appeal in a Civil Case.

8. Stay or Injunction Pending Appeal.

9. Release in a Criminal Case.

10. The Record on Appeal.

11. Forwarding the Record.

12. Docketing the Appeal; Filing a Representation Statement; Filing the Record.

12.1 Remand After an Indicative Ruling by the District Court on a Motion for Relief That Is Barred by a Pending Appeal

13. Review of a Decision of the Tax Court.

14. Applicability of Other Rules to the Review of a Tax Court Decision.

15. Review or Enforcement of an Agency Order—How Obtained; Intervention.

---

[197] *See* U.S. S. Ct. R. 10(a) to (c).

15.1	Briefs and Oral Argument in a National Labor Relations Board Proceeding.
16.	The Record on Review or Enforcement.
17.	Filing the Record.
18.	Stay Pending Review.
19.	Settlement of a Judgment Enforcing an Agency Order in Part.
20.	Applicability of Rules to the Review or Enforcement of an Agency Order.
21.	Writs of Mandamus and Prohibition, and Other Extraordinary Writs.
22.	Habeas Corpus and Section 2255 Proceedings.
23.	Custody or Release of a Prisoner in a Habeas Corpus Proceeding.
24.	Proceeding In Forma Pauperis.
25.	Filing and Service.
26.	Computing and Extending Time.
26.1	Corporate Disclosure Statement.
27.	Motions.
28.	Briefs.
28.1	Cross-Appeals.
29.	Brief of an Amicus Curiae.
30.	Appendix to the Briefs.
31.	Serving and Filing Briefs.
32.	Form of Briefs, Appendices, and Other Papers.
32.1	Citing Judicial Dispositions.
33.	Appeal Conferences.
34.	Oral Argument.
35.	En Banc Determination.
36.	Entry of Judgment; Notice.
37.	Interest on Judgment.
38.	Frivolous Appeal—Damages and Costs.
39.	Costs.
40.	Petition for Panel Rehearing.
41.	Mandate: Contents; Issuance and Effective Date; Stay.
42.	Voluntary Dismissal.
43.	Substitution of Parties.
44.	Case Involving a Constitutional Question When the United States or the Relevant State Is Not a Party.
45.	Clerk's Duties.
46.	Attorneys.
47.	Local Rules by Courts of Appeals.
48.	Masters.

TITLE I. APPLICABILITY OF RULES

RULE 1. SCOPE OF RULES; DEFINITION; TITLE

(a) Scope of Rules.

(1) These rules govern procedure in the United States courts of appeals.

(2) When these rules provide for filing a motion or other document in the district court, the procedure must comply with the practice of the district court.

(b) Definition. In these rules, "state" includes the District of Columbia and any United States commonwealth or territory.

(c) Title. These rules are to be known as the Federal Rules of Appellate Procedure.

RULE 2. SUSPENSION OF RULES

On its own or a party's motion, a court of appeals may—to expedite its decision or for other good cause—suspend any provision of these rules in a particular case and order proceedings as it directs, except as otherwise provided in Rule 26(b).

TITLE II. APPEAL FROM A JUDGMENT OR ORDER OF A DISTRICT COURT

RULE 3. APPEAL AS OF RIGHT—HOW TAKEN

(a) Filing the Notice of Appeal.

(1) An appeal permitted by law as of right from a district court to a court of appeals may be taken only by filing a notice of appeal with the district clerk within the time allowed by Rule 4. At the time of filing, the appellant must furnish the clerk with enough copies of the notice to enable the clerk to comply with Rule 3(d).

(2) An appellant's failure to take any step other than the timely filing of a notice of appeal does not affect the validity of the appeal, but is ground only for the court of appeals to act as it considers appropriate, including dismissing the appeal.

(3) An appeal from a judgment by a magistrate judge in a civil case is taken in the same way as an appeal from any other district court judgment.

(4) An appeal by permission under 28 U.S.C. § 1292(b) or an appeal in a bankruptcy case may be taken only in the manner prescribed by Rules 5 and 6, respectively.

(b) Joint or Consolidated Appeals.

(1) When two or more parties are entitled to appeal from a district-court judgment or order, and their interests make joinder practicable, they may file a joint notice of appeal. They may then proceed on appeal as a single appellant.

(2) When the parties have filed separate timely notices of appeal, the appeals may be joined or consolidated by the court of appeals.

(c) Contents of the Notice of Appeal.

(1) The notice of appeal must:

(A) specify the party or parties taking the appeal by naming each one in the caption or body of the notice, but an attorney representing more than one party may describe those parties with such terms as "all plaintiffs," "the defendants," "the plaintiffs A, B, et al.," or "all defendants except X";

(B) designate the judgment, order, or part thereof being appealed; and

(C) name the court to which the appeal is taken.

(2) A pro se notice of appeal is considered filed on behalf of the signer and the signer's spouse and minor children (if they are parties), unless the notice clearly indicates otherwise.

(3) In a class action, whether or not the class has been certified, the notice of appeal is sufficient if it names one person qualified to bring the appeal as representative of the class.

(4) An appeal must not be dismissed for informality of form or title of the notice of appeal, or for failure to name a party whose intent to appeal is otherwise clear from the notice.

(5) Form 1 in the Appendix of Forms is a suggested form of a notice of appeal.

(d) Serving the Notice of Appeal.

(1) The district clerk must serve notice of the filing of a notice of appeal by mailing a copy to each party's counsel of record—excluding the appellant's—or, if a party is proceeding pro se, to the party's last known address. When a defendant in a criminal case appeals, the clerk must also serve a copy of the notice of appeal on the defendant, either by personal service or by mail addressed to the defendant. The clerk must promptly send a copy of the notice of appeal and of the docket entries—and any later docket entries—to the clerk of the court of appeals named in the notice. The district clerk must note, on each copy, the date when the notice of appeal was filed.

(2) If an inmate confined in an institution files a notice of appeal in the manner provided by Rule 4(c), the district clerk must also note the date when the clerk docketed the notice.

(3) The district clerk's failure to serve notice does not affect the validity of the appeal. The clerk must note on the docket the names of the parties to whom the clerk mails copies, with the date of mailing. Service is sufficient despite the death of a party or the party's counsel.

(e) Payment of Fees. Upon filing a notice of appeal, the appellant must pay the district clerk all required fees. The district clerk receives the appellate docket fee on behalf of the court of appeals.

RULE 3.1. APPEAL FROM A JUDGMENT OF A MAGISTRATE JUDGE IN A CIVIL CASE [ABROGATED]

RULE 4. APPEAL AS OF RIGHT—WHEN TAKEN

(a) Appeal in a Civil Case.

(1) Time for Filing a Notice of Appeal.

(A) In a civil case, except as provided in Rules 4(a)(1)(B),

4(a)(4), and 4(c), the notice of appeal required by Rule 3 must be filed with the district clerk within 30 days after entry of the judgment or order appealed from.

(B) The notice of appeal may be filed by any party within 60 days after entry of the judgment or order appealed from if one of the parties is:

(i) the United States;

(ii) a United States agency;

(iii) a United States officer or employee sued in an official capacity; or

(iv) a current or former United States officer or employee sued in an individual capacity for an act or omission occurring in connection with duties performed on the United States' behalf — including all instances in which the United States represents that person when the judgment or order is entered or files the appeal for that person.

(C) An appeal from an order granting or denying an application for a writ of error *coram nobis* is an appeal in a civil case for purposes of Rule 4(a).

(2) **Filing Before Entry of Judgment.** A notice of appeal filed after the court announces a decision or order—but before the entry of the judgment or order—is treated as filed on the date of and after the entry.

(3) **Multiple Appeals.** If one party timely files a notice of appeal, any other party may file a notice of appeal within 14 days after the date when the first notice was filed, or within the time otherwise prescribed by this Rule 4(a), whichever period ends later.

(4) **Effect of a Motion on a Notice of Appeal.**

(A) If a party timely files in the district court any of the following motions under the Federal Rules of Civil Procedure, the time to file an appeal runs for all parties from the entry of the order disposing of the last such remaining motion:

(i) for judgment under Rule 50(b);

(ii) to amend or make additional factual findings under Rule 52(b), whether or not granting the motion would alter the judgment;

(iii) for attorney's fees under Rule 54 if the district court extends the time to appeal under Rule 58;

(iv) to alter or amend the judgment under Rule 59;

(v) for a new trial under Rule 59; or

(vi) for relief under Rule 60 if the motion is filed no later than 28 days after the judgment is entered.

(B) (i) If a party files a notice of appeal after the court announces or enters a judgment—but before it disposes of any motion listed in Rule 4(a)(4)(A)—the notice becomes effective to appeal a judgment or order, in whole or in part, when the order disposing of the last such remaining motion is entered.

(ii) A party intending to challenge an order disposing of any motion listed in Rule 4(a)(4)(A), or a judgment's alteration or amendment upon such a motion, must file a notice of appeal, or an amended notice of appeal—in compliance with Rule 3(c)—within the time prescribed by this Rule measured from the entry of the order disposing of the last such remaining motion.

(iii) No additional fee is required to file an amended notice.

(5) Motion for Extension of Time.

(A) The district court may extend the time to file a notice of appeal if:

(i) a party so moves no later than 30 days after the time prescribed by this Rule 4(a) expires; and

(ii) regardless of whether its motion is filed before or during the 30 days after the time prescribed by this Rule 4(a) expires, that party shows excusable neglect or good cause.

(B) A motion filed before the expiration of the time prescribed in Rule 4(a)(1) or (3) may be ex parte unless the court requires otherwise. If the motion is filed after the expiration of the prescribed time, notice must be given to the other parties in accordance with local rules.

(C) No extension under this Rule 4(a)(5) may exceed 30 days after the prescribed time or 14 days after the date when the order granting the motion is entered, whichever is later.

(6) Reopening the Time to File an Appeal. The district court may reopen the time to file an appeal for a period of 14 days after the date when its order to reopen is entered, but only if all the following conditions are satisfied:

(A) the court finds that the moving party did not receive notice under Federal Rule of Civil Procedure 77(d) of the entry of the judgment or order sought to be appealed within 21 days after entry;

(B) the motion is filed within 180 days after the judgment or order is entered or within 14 days after the moving party receives notice under Federal Rule of Civil Procedure 77(d) of the entry, whichever is earlier; and

(C) the court finds that no party would be prejudiced.

(7) Entry Defined.

(A) A judgment or order is entered for purposes of this Rule 4(a):

(i) if Federal Rule of Civil Procedure 58(a) does not require a separate document, when the judgment or order is entered in the civil docket under Federal Rules of Civil

Procedure 79(a); or

(ii) if Federal Rule of Civil Procedure 58(a) requires a separate document, when the judgment or order is entered in the civil docket under Federal Rule of Civil Procedure 79(a) and when the earlier of these events occurs:

- the judgment or order is set forth on a separate document, or

- 150 days have run from entry of the judgment or order in the civil docket under Federal Rule of Civil Procedure 79(a).

(B) A failure to set forth a judgment or order on a separate document when required by Federal Rule of Civil Procedure 58(a) does not affect the validity of an appeal from that judgment or order.

(b) Appeal in a Criminal Case.

(1) Time for Filing a Notice of Appeal.

(A) In a criminal case, a defendant's notice of appeal must be filed in the district court within 14 days after the later of:

(i) the entry of either the judgment or the order being appealed; or

(ii) the filing of the government's notice of appeal.

(B) When the government is entitled to appeal, its notice of appeal must be filed in the district court within 30 days after the later of:

(i) the entry of the judgment or order being appealed; or

(ii) the filing of a notice of appeal by any defendant.

(2) Filing Before Entry of Judgment. A notice of appeal filed after the court announces a decision, sentence, or order—but before the entry of the judgment or order—is treated as filed on the date of and after the entry.

(3) Effect of a Motion on a Notice of Appeal.

(A) If a defendant timely makes any of the following motions under the Federal Rules of Criminal Procedure, the notice of appeal from a judgment of conviction must be filed within 14 days after the entry of the order disposing of the last such remaining motion, or within 14 days after the entry of the judgment of conviction, whichever period ends later. This provision applies to a timely motion:

(i) for judgment of acquittal under Rule 29;

(ii) for a new trial under Rule 33, but if based on newly discovered evidence, only if the motion is made no later than 14 days after the entry of the judgment; or

(iii) for arrest of judgment under Rule 34.

(B) A notice of appeal filed after the court announces a decision, sentence, or order—but before it disposes of any of the motions referred to in Rule 4(b)(3)(A)—becomes effective upon the later of the following:

(i) the entry of the order disposing of the last such remaining motion; or

(ii) the entry of the judgment of conviction.

(C) A valid notice of appeal is effective—without amendment—to appeal from an order disposing of any of the motions referred to in Rule 4(b)(3)(A).

(4) Motion for Extension of Time. Upon a finding of excusable neglect or good cause, the district court may—before or after the time has expired, with or without motion and notice—extend the time to file a notice of appeal for a period not to exceed 30 days from the expiration of the time otherwise prescribed by this Rule 4(b).

(5) Jurisdiction. The filing of a notice of appeal under this Rule 4(b) does not divest a district court of jurisdiction to correct a sentence under Federal Rule of Criminal Procedure 35(c), nor does the filing of a motion under 35(c) affect the validity of a notice of appeal filed before entry of the order disposing of the motion. The filing of a motion under Federal Rule of Criminal Procedure 35(a) does not suspend the time for filing a notice of appeal from a judgment of conviction.

(6) Entry Defined. A judgment or order is entered for purposes of this Rule 4(b) when it is entered on the criminal docket.

(c) Appeal by an Inmate Confined in an Institution.

(1) If an inmate confined in an institution files a notice of appeal in either a civil or a criminal case, the notice is timely if it is deposited in the institution's internal mail system on or before the last day for filing. If an institution has a system designed for legal mail, the inmate must use that system to receive the benefit of this rule. Timely filing may be shown by a declaration in compliance with 28 U.S.C. § 1746 or by a notarized statement, either of which must set forth the date of deposit and state that first-class postage has been prepaid.

(2) If an inmate files the first notice of appeal in a civil case under this Rule 4(c), the 14-day period provided in Rule 4(a)(3) for another party to file a notice of appeal runs from the date when the district court dockets the first notice.

(3) When a defendant in a criminal case files a notice of appeal under this Rule 4(c), the 30-day period for the government to file its notice of appeal runs from the entry of the judgment or order appealed from or from the district court's docketing of the defendant's notice of appeal, whichever is later.

(d) Mistaken Filing in the Court of Appeals. If a notice of appeal in either a civil or a criminal case is mistakenly filed in the court of appeals, the clerk of that court must note on the notice the date when it was received and send it to the district clerk. The notice is then considered filed in the district court on the date so noted.

RULE 5. APPEAL BY PERMISSION

(a) Petition for Permission to Appeal.

(1) To request permission to appeal when an appeal is within the court of appeals' discretion, a party must file a petition for permission to appeal. The petition must be filed with the circuit clerk with proof of service on all other parties to the district-court action.

(2) The petition must be filed within the time specified by the statute or rule authorizing the appeal or, if no such time is specified, within the time provided by Rule 4(a) for filing a notice of appeal.

(3) If a party cannot petition for appeal unless the district court first enters an order granting permission to do so or stating that the necessary conditions are met, the district court may amend its order, either on its own or in response to a party's motion, to include the required permission or statement. In that event, the time to petition runs from entry of the amended order.

(b) Contents of the Petition; Answer or Cross-Petition; Oral Argument.

(1) The petition must include the following:

(A) the facts necessary to understand the question presented;

(B) the question itself;

(C) the relief sought;

(D) the reasons why the appeal should be allowed and is authorized by a statute or rule; and

(E) an attached copy of:

(i) the order, decree, or judgment complained of and any related opinion or memorandum, and

(ii) any order stating the district court's permission to appeal or finding that the necessary conditions are met.

(2) A party may file an answer in opposition or a cross-petition within 10 days after the petition is served.

(3) The petition and answer will be submitted without oral argument unless the court of appeals orders otherwise.

(c) Form of Papers; Number of Copies.

All papers must conform to Rule 32(c)(2). Except by the court's permission, a paper must not exceed 20 pages, exclusive of the disclosure statement, the proof of service, and the accompanying documents required by Rule 5(b)(1)(E). An original and 3 copies must be filed unless the court requires a different number by local rule or by order in a particular case.

(d) Grant of Permission; Fees; Cost Bond; Filing the Record.

(1) Within 14 days after the entry of the order granting permission to appeal, the appellant must:

(A) pay the district clerk all required fees; and

(B) file a cost bond if required under Rule 7.

(2) A notice of appeal need not be filed. The date when the order granting permission to appeal is entered serves as the date of the notice of appeal for calculating time under these rules.

(3) The district clerk must notify the circuit clerk once the petitioner has paid the fees. Upon receiving this notice, the circuit clerk must enter the appeal on the docket. The record must be forwarded and filed in accordance with Rules 11 and 12(c).

RULE 5.1. APPEAL BY LEAVE UNDER 28 U.S.C. § 636(C)(5) [ABROGATED]

RULE 6. APPEAL IN A BANKRUPTCY CASE FROM A FINAL JUDGMENT, ORDER, OR DECREE OF A DISTRICT COURT OR BANKRUPTCY APPELLATE PANEL

(a) Appeal From a Judgment, Order, or Decree of a District Court Exercising Original Jurisdiction in a Bankruptcy Case. An appeal to a court of appeals from a final judgment, order, or decree of a district court exercising jurisdiction under 28 U.S.C. § 1334 is taken as any other civil appeal under these rules.

(b) Appeal From a Judgment, Order, or Decree of a District Court or Bankruptcy Appellate Panel Exercising Appellate Jurisdiction in a Bankruptcy Case.

(1) Applicability of Other Rules. These rules apply to an appeal to a court of appeals under 28 U.S.C. § 158(d) from a final judgment, order, or decree of a district court or bankruptcy appellate panel exercising appellate jurisdiction under 28 U.S.C. § 158(a) or (b). But there are 3 exceptions:

(A) Rules 4(a)(4), 4(b), 9, 10, 11, 12(b), 13-20, 22–23, and 24(b) do not apply;

(B) the reference in Rule 3(c) to "Form 1 in the Appendix of Forms" must be read as a reference to Form 5; and

(C) when the appeal is from a bankruptcy appellate panel, the term "district court," as used in any applicable rule, means "appellate panel."

(2) Additional Rules. In addition to the rules made applicable by Rule 6(b)(1), the following rules apply:

(A) Motion for rehearing.

(i) If a timely motion for rehearing under Bankruptcy Rule 8015 is filed, the time to appeal for all parties runs from the entry of the order disposing of the motion. A notice of appeal filed after the district court or bankruptcy appellate panel announces or enters a judgment, order, or decree—but before disposition of the motion for rehearing—becomes effective when the order disposing of the motion for rehearing is entered.

(ii) Appellate review of the order disposing of the motion requires the party, in compliance with Rules 3(c) and 6(b)(1)(B), to amend a previously filed notice of appeal. A party intending to challenge an altered or amended judgment, order, or decree must file a notice of appeal or amended notice of appeal within the time prescribed by Rule 4—excluding Rules 4(a)(4) and 4(b)—measured from the entry of the order disposing of the motion.

(iii) No additional fee is required to file an amended notice.

(B) The record on appeal.

(i) Within 14 days after filing the notice of appeal, the appellant must file with the clerk possessing the record assembled in accordance with Bankruptcy Rule 8006—and serve on the appellee—a statement of the issues to be presented on appeal and a designation of the record to be certified and sent to the circuit clerk.

(ii) An appellee who believes that other parts of the record are necessary must, within 14 days after being served with the appellant's designation, file with the clerk and serve on the appellant a designation of additional parts to be included.

(iii) The record on appeal consists of:

- the redesignated record as provided above;
- the proceedings in the district court or bankruptcy appellate panel; and
- a certified copy of the docket entries prepared by the clerk under Rule 3(d).

(C) Forwarding the record.

(i) When the record is complete, the district clerk or bankruptcy appellate panel clerk must number the documents constituting the record and send them promptly to the circuit clerk together with a list of the documents correspondingly numbered and reasonably identified. Unless directed to do so by a party or the circuit clerk, the clerk will not send to the court of appeals documents of unusual bulk or weight, physical exhibits other than documents, or other parts of the record designated for omission by local rule of the court of appeals. If the exhibits are unusually bulky or heavy, a party must arrange with the clerks in advance for their transportation and receipt.

(ii) All parties must do whatever else is necessary to enable the clerk to assemble and forward the record. The court of appeals may provide by rule or order that a certified copy of the docket entries be sent in place of the redesignated record, but any party may request at any time during the pendency of the appeal that the redesignated record be sent.

(D) Filing the record. Upon receiving the record—or a certified copy of the docket entries sent in place of the redesignated record—the circuit clerk must file it and immediately notify all parties of the filing date.

RULE 7. BOND FOR COSTS ON APPEAL IN A CIVIL CASE

In a civil case, the district court may require an appellant to file a bond or provide other security in any form and amount necessary to ensure payment of costs on appeal. Rule 8(b) applies to a surety on a bond given under this rule.

RULE 8. STAY OR INJUNCTION PENDING APPEAL

(a) Motion for Stay.

(1) Initial Motion in the District Court. A party must ordinarily move first in the district court for the following relief:

(A) a stay of the judgment or order of a district court pending appeal;

(B) approval of a supersedeas bond; or

(C) an order suspending, modifying, restoring, or granting an injunction while an appeal is pending.

(2) Motion in the Court of Appeals; Conditions on Relief. A motion for the relief mentioned in Rule 8(a)(1) may be made to the court of appeals or to one of its judges.

(A) The motion must:

(i) show that moving first in the district court would be impracticable; or

(ii) state that, a motion having been made, the district court denied the motion or failed to afford the relief requested and state any reasons given by the district court for its action.

(B) The motion must also include:

(i) the reasons for granting the relief requested and the facts relied on;

(ii) originals or copies of affidavits or other sworn statements supporting facts subject to dispute; and

(iii) relevant parts of the record.

(C) The moving party must give reasonable notice of the motion to all parties.

(D) A motion under this Rule 8(a)(2) must be filed with the circuit clerk and normally will be considered by a panel of the court. But in an exceptional case in which time requirements make that procedure impracticable, the motion may be made to and considered by a single judge.

(E) The court may condition relief on a party's filing a bond or other appropriate security in the district court.

(b) Proceeding Against a Surety. If a party gives security in the form of a bond or stipulation or other undertaking with one or more sureties, each surety submits to the jurisdiction of the district court and irrevocably appoints the district clerk as the surety's agent on whom any papers affecting the surety's liability on the bond or undertaking may be served. On motion, a surety's liability may be enforced in the district court without the necessity of an independent action. The motion and any notice that the district court prescribes may be served on the district clerk, who must promptly mail a copy to each surety whose address is known.

(c) Stay in a Criminal Case. Rule 38 of the Federal Rules of Criminal Procedure governs a stay in a criminal case.

RULE 9. RELEASE IN A CRIMINAL CASE

(a) Release Before Judgment of Conviction.

(1) The district court must state in writing, or orally on the record, the reasons for an order regarding the release or detention of a defendant in a criminal case. A party appealing from the order must file with the court of appeals a copy of the district court's order and the court's statement of reasons as soon as practicable after filing the notice of appeal. An appellant who questions the factual basis for the district court's order must file a transcript of the release proceedings or an explanation of why a transcript was not obtained.

(2) After reasonable notice to the appellee, the court of appeals must promptly determine the appeal on the basis of the papers, affidavits, and parts of the record that the parties present or the court requires. Unless the court so orders, briefs need not be filed.

(3) The court of appeals or one of its judges may order the defendant's release pending the disposition of the appeal.

(b) Release After Judgment of Conviction. A party entitled to do so may obtain review of a district-court order regarding release after a judgment of conviction by filing a notice of appeal from that order in the district court, or by filing a motion in the court of appeals if the party has already filed a notice of appeal from the judgment of conviction. Both the order and the review are subject to Rule 9(a). The papers filed by the party seeking review must include a copy of the judgment of conviction.

(c) Criteria for Release. The court must make its decision regarding release in accordance with the applicable provisions of 18 U.S.C. §§ 3142, 3143, and 3145(c).

RULE 10. THE RECORD ON APPEAL

(a) Composition of the Record on Appeal. The following items constitute the record on appeal:

(1) the original papers and exhibits filed in the district court;

(2) the transcript of proceedings, if any; and

(3) a certified copy of the docket entries prepared by the district clerk.

(b) The Transcript of Proceedings.

(1) Appellant's Duty to Order. Within 14 days after filing the notice of appeal or entry of an order disposing of the last timely remaining motion of a type specified in Rule 4(a)(4)(A), whichever is later, the appellant must do either of the following:

(A) order from the reporter a transcript of such parts of the proceedings not already on file as the appellant considers necessary, subject to a local rule of the court of appeals and with the following qualifications:

(i) the order must be in writing;

(ii) if the cost of the transcript is to be paid by the United States under the Criminal Justice Act, the order must so state; and

(iii) the appellant must, within the same period, file a copy of the order with the district clerk; or

(B) file a certificate stating that no transcript will be ordered.

(2) Unsupported Finding or Conclusion. If the appellant intends to urge on appeal that a finding or conclusion is unsupported by the evidence or is contrary to the evidence, the appellant must include in the record a transcript of all evidence relevant to that finding or conclusion.

(3) Partial Transcript. Unless the entire transcript is ordered:

(A) the appellant must—within the 14 days provided in Rule 10(b)(1)—file a statement of the issues that the appellant intends to present on the appeal and must serve on the appellee a copy of both the order or certificate and the statement;

(B) if the appellee considers it necessary to have a transcript of other parts of the proceedings, the appellee must, within 14 days after the service of the order or certificate and the statement of the issues, file and serve on the appellant a designation of additional parts to be ordered; and

(C) unless within 14 days after service of that designation the appellant has ordered all such parts, and has so notified the appellee, the appellee may within the following 14 days either order the parts or move in the district court for an order requiring the appellant to do so.

(4) Payment. At the time of ordering, a party must make satisfactory arrangements with the reporter for paying the cost of the transcript.

(c) Statement of the Evidence When the Proceedings Were Not Recorded or When a Transcript Is Unavailable. If the transcript of a hearing or trial is unavailable, the appellant may prepare a statement of the evidence or proceedings from the best available means, including the appellant's recollection. The statement must be served on the appellee, who may serve objections or proposed amendments within 14 days after being served. The statement and any objections or proposed amendments must then be submitted to the district court for settlement and approval. As settled and approved, the statement must be included by the district clerk in the record on appeal.

(d) Agreed Statement as the Record on Appeal. In place of the record on appeal as defined in Rule 10(a), the parties may prepare, sign, and submit to the district court a statement of the case showing how the issues presented by the appeal arose and were decided in the district court. The statement must set forth only those facts averred and proved or sought to be proved that are essential to the court's resolution of the issues. If the statement is truthful, it—together with any additions that the district court may consider necessary to a full presentation of the issues on appeal—must be approved by the district court and must then be certified to the court of appeals as the record on appeal. The district clerk must then send it to the circuit clerk within the time provided by Rule 11. A copy of the agreed statement may be filed in place of the appendix required by Rule 30.

(e) Correction or Modification of the Record.

(1) If any difference arises about whether the record truly discloses what occurred in the district court, the difference must be submitted to and settled by that court and the record conformed accordingly.

(2) If anything material to either party is omitted from or misstated in the record by error or accident, the omission or misstatement may be corrected and a supplemental record may be certified and forwarded:

(A) on stipulation of the parties;

(B) by the district court before or after the record has been forwarded; or

(C) by the court of appeals.

(3) All other questions as to the form and content of the record must be presented to the court of appeals.

RULE 11. FORWARDING THE RECORD

(a) Appellant's Duty. An appellant filing a notice of appeal must comply with Rule 10(b) and must do whatever else is necessary to enable the clerk to assemble and forward the record. If there are multiple appeals from a judgment or order, the clerk must forward a single record.

(b) Duties of Reporter and District Clerk.

(1) Reporter's Duty to Prepare and File a Transcript. The reporter must prepare and file a transcript as follows:

(A) Upon receiving an order for a transcript, the reporter

must enter at the foot of the order the date of its receipt and the expected completion date and send a copy, so endorsed, to the circuit clerk.

(B) If the transcript cannot be completed within 30 days of the reporter's receipt of the order, the reporter may request the circuit clerk to grant additional time to complete it. The clerk must note on the docket the action taken and notify the parties.

(C) When a transcript is complete, the reporter must file it with the district clerk and notify the circuit clerk of the filing.

(D) If the reporter fails to file the transcript on time, the circuit clerk must notify the district judge and do whatever else the court of appeals directs.

(2) District Clerk's Duty to Forward. When the record is complete, the district clerk must number the documents constituting the record and send them promptly to the circuit clerk together with a list of the documents correspondingly numbered and reasonably identified. Unless directed to do so by a party or the circuit clerk, the district clerk will not send to the court of appeals documents of unusual bulk or weight, physical exhibits other than documents, or other parts of the record designated for omission by local rule of the court of appeals. If the exhibits are unusually bulky or heavy, a party must arrange with the clerks in advance for their transportation and receipt.

(c) Retaining the Record Temporarily in the District Court for Use in Preparing the Appeal. The parties may stipulate, or the district court on motion may order, that the district clerk retain the record temporarily for the parties to use in preparing the papers on appeal. In that event the district clerk must certify to the circuit clerk that the record on appeal is complete. Upon receipt of the appellee's brief, or earlier if the court orders or the parties agree, the appellant must request the district clerk to forward the record.

(d) [Abrogated.]

(e) Retaining the Record by Court Order.

(1) The court of appeals may, by order or local rule, provide that a certified copy of the docket entries be forwarded instead of the entire record. But a party may at any time during the appeal request that designated parts of the record be forwarded.

(2) The district court may order the record or some part of it retained if the court needs it while the appeal is pending, subject, however, to call by the court of appeals.

(3) If part or all of the record is ordered retained, the district clerk must send to the court of appeals a copy of the order and the docket entries together with the parts of the original record allowed by the district court and copies of any parts of the record designated by the parties.

(f) Retaining Parts of the Record in the District Court by Stipulation of the Parties. The parties may agree by written stipulation filed in the district court that designated parts of the record be retained in the district court subject to call by the court of appeals or request by a party. The parts of the record so designated remain a part of the record on appeal.

(g) Record for a Preliminary Motion in the Court of Appeals. If, before the record is forwarded, a party makes any of the following motions in the court of appeals:

- for dismissal;
- for release;
- for a stay pending appeal;
- for additional security on the bond on appeal or on a supersedeas bond; or
- for any other intermediate order—

the district clerk must send the court of appeals any parts of the record designated by any party.

RULE 12. DOCKETING THE APPEAL; FILING A REPRESENTATION STATEMENT; FILING THE RECORD

(a) Docketing the Appeal. Upon receiving the copy of the notice of appeal and the docket entries from the district clerk under Rule 3(d), the circuit clerk must docket the appeal under the title of the district-court action and must identify the appellant, adding the appellant's name if necessary.

(b) Filing a Representation Statement. Unless the court of appeals designates another time, the attorney who filed the notice of appeal must, within 14 days after filing the notice, file a statement with the circuit clerk naming the parties that the attorney represents on appeal.

(c) Filing the Record, Partial Record, or Certificate. Upon receiving the record, partial record, or district clerk's certificate as provided in Rule 11, the circuit clerk must file it and immediately notify all parties of the filing date.

RULE 12.1. REMAND AFTER AN INDICATIVE RULING BY THE DISTRICT COURT ON A MOTION FOR RELIEF THAT IS BARRED BY A PENDING APPEAL

(a) Notice to the Court of Appeals. If a timely motion is made in the district court for relief that it lacks authority to grant because of an appeal that has been docketed and is pending, the movant must promptly notify the circuit clerk if the district court states either that it would grant the motion or that the motion raises a substantial issue.

(b) Remand After an Indicative Ruling. If the district court states that it would grant the motion or that the motion raises a substantial issue, the court of appeals may remand for further proceedings but retains jurisdiction unless it expressly dismisses the appeal. If the court of appeals remands but retains jurisdiction, the parties must promptly notify the circuit clerk when the district court has decided the motion on remand.

TITLE III. REVIEW OF A DECISION OF THE UNITED STATES TAX COURT

RULE 13. REVIEW OF A DECISION OF THE TAX COURT

(a) How Obtained; Time for Filing Notice of Appeal.

(1) Review of a decision of the United States Tax Court is commenced by filing a notice of appeal with the Tax Court clerk within 90 days after the entry of the Tax Court's decision. At the time of filing, the appellant must furnish the clerk with enough copies of the notice to enable the clerk to comply with Rule 3(d). If one party files a timely notice of appeal, any other party may file a notice of appeal within 120 days after the Tax Court's decision is entered.

(2) If, under Tax Court rules, a party makes a timely motion to vacate or revise the Tax Court's decision, the time to file a notice of appeal runs from the entry of the order disposing of the motion or from the entry of a new decision, whichever is later.

(b) Notice of Appeal; How Filed. The notice of appeal may be filed either at the Tax Court clerk's office in the District of Columbia or by mail addressed to the clerk. If sent by mail the notice is considered filed on the postmark date, subject to § 7502 of the Internal Revenue Code, as amended, and the applicable regulations.

(c) Contents of the Notice of Appeal; Service; Effect of Filing and Service. Rule 3 prescribes the contents of a notice of appeal, the manner of service, and the effect of its filing and service. Form 2 in the Appendix of Forms is a suggested form of a notice of appeal.

(d) The Record on Appeal; Forwarding; Filing.

(1) An appeal from the Tax Court is governed by the parts of Rules 10, 11, and 12 regarding the record on appeal from a district court, the time and manner of forwarding and filing, and the docketing in the court of appeals. References in those rules and in Rule 3 to the district court and district clerk are to be read as referring to the Tax Court and its clerk.

(2) If an appeal from a Tax Court decision is taken to more than one court of appeals, the original record must be sent to the court named in the first notice of appeal filed. In an appeal to any other court of appeals, the appellant must apply to that other court to make provision for the record.

RULE 14. APPLICABILITY OF OTHER RULES TO THE REVIEW OF A TAX COURT DECISION

All provisions of these rules, except Rules 4–9, 15–20, and 22–23, apply to the review of a Tax Court decision.

TITLE IV. REVIEW OR ENFORCEMENT OF AN ORDER OF AN ADMINISTRATIVE AGENCY, BOARD, COMMISSION, OR OFFICER

RULE 15. REVIEW OR ENFORCEMENT OF AN AGENCY ORDER—HOW OBTAINED; INTERVENTION

(a) Petition for Review; Joint Petition.

(1) Review of an agency order is commenced by filing, within the time prescribed by law, a petition for review with the clerk of a court of appeals authorized to review the agency order. If their interests make joinder practicable, two or more persons may join in a petition to the same court to review the same order.

(2) The petition must:

(A) name each party seeking review either in the caption or the body of the petition—using such terms as "et al.," "petitioners," or "respondents" does not effectively name the parties;

(B) name the agency as a respondent (even though not named in the petition, the United States is a respondent if required by statute); and

(C) specify the order or part thereof to be reviewed.

(3) Form 3 in the Appendix of Forms is a suggested form of a petition for review.

(4) In this rule "agency" includes an agency, board, commission, or officer; "petition for review" includes a petition to enjoin, suspend, modify, or otherwise review, or a notice of appeal, whichever form is indicated by the applicable statute.

(b) Application or Cross-Application to Enforce an Order; Answer; Default.

(1) An application to enforce an agency order must be filed with the clerk of a court of appeals authorized to enforce the order. If a petition is filed to review an agency order that the court may enforce, a party opposing the petition may file a cross-application for enforcement.

(2) Within 21 days after the application for enforcement is filed, the respondent must serve on the applicant an answer to the application and file it with the clerk. If the respondent fails to answer in time, the court will enter judgment for the relief requested.

(3) The application must contain a concise statement of the proceedings in which the order was entered, the facts upon which venue is based, and the relief requested.

(c) Service of the Petition or Application. The circuit clerk must serve a copy of the petition for review, or an application or cross-application to enforce an agency order, on each respondent as prescribed by Rule 3(d), unless a different manner of service is prescribed by statute. At the time of filing, the petitioner must:

(1) serve, or have served, a copy on each party admitted to participate in the agency proceedings, except for the respondents;

(2) file with the clerk a list of those so served; and

(3) give the clerk enough copies of the petition or application to serve each respondent.

(d) Intervention. Unless a statute provides another method, a person who wants to intervene in a proceeding under this rule must file a motion for leave to intervene with the circuit clerk and serve a copy on all parties. The motion—or other notice of intervention authorized by statute—must be filed within 30 days after the petition for review is filed and must contain a concise statement of the interest of the moving party and the grounds for intervention.

(e) Payment of Fees. When filing any separate or joint petition for review in a court of appeals, the petitioner must pay the circuit clerk all required fees.

RULE 15.1. BRIEFS AND ORAL ARGUMENT IN A NATIONAL LABOR RELATIONS BOARD PROCEEDING

In either an enforcement or a review proceeding, a party adverse to the National Labor Relations Board proceeds first on briefing and at oral argument, unless the court orders otherwise.

RULE 16. THE RECORD ON REVIEW OR ENFORCEMENT

(a) Composition of the Record. The record on review or enforcement of an agency order consists of:

(1) the order involved;

(2) any findings or report on which it is based; and

(3) the pleadings, evidence, and other parts of the proceedings before the agency.

(b) Omissions From or Misstatements in the Record. The parties may at any time, by stipulation, supply any omission from the record or correct a misstatement, or the court may so direct. If necessary, the court may direct that a supplemental record be prepared and filed.

RULE 17. FILING THE RECORD

(a) Agency to File; Time for Filing; Notice of Filing. The agency must file the record with the circuit clerk within 40 days after being served with a petition for review, unless the statute authorizing review provides otherwise, or within 40 days after it files an application for enforcement unless the respondent fails to answer or the court orders otherwise. The court may shorten or extend the time to file the record. The clerk must notify all parties of the date when the record is filed.

(b) Filing—What Constitutes.

(1) The agency must file:

(A) the original or a certified copy of the entire record or parts designated by the parties; or

(B) a certified list adequately describing all documents, transcripts of testimony, exhibits, and other material constituting the record, or describing those parts designated by the parties.

(2) The parties may stipulate in writing that no record or certified list be filed. The date when the stipulation is filed with the circuit clerk is treated as the date when the record is filed.

(3) The agency must retain any portion of the record not filed with the clerk. All parts of the record retained by the agency are a part of the record on review for all purposes and, if the court or a party so requests, must be sent to the court regardless of any prior stipulation.

RULE 18. STAY PENDING REVIEW

(a) Motion for a Stay.

(1) Initial Motion Before the Agency. A petitioner must ordinarily move first before the agency for a stay pending review of its decision or order.

(2) Motion in the Court of Appeals. A motion for a stay may be made to the court of appeals or one of its judges.

(A) The motion must:

(i) show that moving first before the agency would be impracticable; or

(ii) state that, a motion having been made, the agency denied the motion or failed to afford the relief requested and state any reasons given by the agency for its action.

(B) The motion must also include:

(i) the reasons for granting the relief requested and the facts relied on;

(ii) originals or copies of affidavits or other sworn statements supporting facts subject to dispute; and

(iii) relevant parts of the record.

(C) The moving party must give reasonable notice of the motion to all parties.

(D) The motion must be filed with the circuit clerk and normally will be considered by a panel of the court. But in an exceptional case in which time requirements make that procedure impracticable, the motion may be made to and considered by a single judge.

(b) Bond. The court may condition relief on the filing of a bond or other appropriate security.

RULE 19. SETTLEMENT OF A JUDGMENT ENFORCING AN AGENCY ORDER IN PART

When the court files an opinion directing entry of judgment enforcing the agency's order in part, the agency must within 14 days file with the clerk and serve on each other party a proposed judgment conforming to the opinion. A party who disagrees with the agency's proposed judgment must within 10 days file with the clerk and serve the agency with a proposed judgment that the party believes conforms to the opinion. The court will settle the judgment and direct entry without further hearing or argument.

RULE 20. APPLICABILITY OF RULES TO THE REVIEW OR ENFORCEMENT OF AN AGENCY ORDER

All provisions of these rules, except Rules 3–14 and 22–23, apply to the review or enforcement of an agency order. In these rules, "appellant" includes a petitioner or applicant, and "appellee" includes a respondent.

TITLE V. EXTRAORDINARY WRITS

RULE 21. WRITS OF MANDAMUS AND PROHIBITION, AND OTHER EXTRAORDINARY WRITS

(a) Mandamus or Prohibition to a Court: Petition, Filing, Service, and Docketing.

(1) A party petitioning for a writ of mandamus or prohibition directed to a court must file a petition with the circuit clerk with proof of service on all parties to the proceeding in the trial court. The party must also provide a copy to the trial-court judge. All parties to the proceeding in the trial court other than the petitioner are respondents for all purposes.

(2) (A) The petition must be titled "In re [name of petitioner]."

(B) The petition must state:

(i) the relief sought;

(ii) the issues presented;

(iii) the facts necessary to understand the issue presented by the petition; and

(iv) the reasons why the writ should issue.

(C) The petition must include a copy of any order or opinion or parts of the record that may be essential to understand the matters set forth in the petition.

(3) Upon receiving the prescribed docket fee, the clerk must docket the petition and submit it to the court.

(b) Denial; Order Directing Answer; Briefs; Precedence.

(1) The court may deny the petition without an answer. Otherwise, it must order the respondent, if any, to answer within a fixed time.

(2) The clerk must serve the order to respond on all persons directed to respond.

(3) Two or more respondents may answer jointly.

(4) The court of appeals may invite or order the trial-court judge to address the petition or may invite an amicus curiae to do so. The trial-court judge may request permission to address

the petition but may not do so unless invited or ordered to do so by the court of appeals.

(5) If briefing or oral argument is required, the clerk must advise the parties, and when appropriate, the trial-court judge or amicus curiae.

(6) The proceeding must be given preference over ordinary civil cases.

(7) The circuit clerk must send a copy of the final disposition to the trial-court judge.

(c) Other Extraordinary Writs. An application for an extraordinary writ other than one provided for in Rule 21(a) must be made by filing a petition with the circuit clerk with proof of service on the respondents. Proceedings on the application must conform, so far as is practicable, to the procedures prescribed in Rule 21(a) and (b).

(d) Form of Papers; Number of Copies. All papers must conform to Rule 32(c)(2). Except by the court's permission, a paper must not exceed 30 pages, exclusive of the disclosure statement, the proof of service, and the accompanying documents required by Rule 21(a)(2)(C). An original and 3 copies must be filed unless the court requires the filing of a different number by local rule or by order in a particular case.

TITLE VI. HABEAS CORPUS; PROCEEDINGS IN FORMA PAUPERIS

RULE 22. HABEAS CORPUS AND SECTION 2255 PROCEEDINGS

(a) Application for the Original Writ. An application for a writ of habeas corpus must be made to the appropriate district court. If made to a circuit judge, the application must be transferred to the appropriate district court. If a district court denies an application made or transferred to it, renewal of the application before a circuit judge is not permitted. The applicant may, under 28 U.S.C. § 2253, appeal to the court of appeals from the district court's order denying the application.

(b) Certificate of Appealability.

(1) In a habeas corpus proceeding in which the detention complained of arises from process issued by a state court, or in a 28 U.S.C. § 2255 proceeding, the applicant cannot take an appeal unless a circuit justice or a circuit or district judge issues a certificate of appealability under 28 U.S.C. § 2253(c). If an applicant files a notice of appeal, the district clerk must send to the court of appeals the certificate (if any) and the statement described in Rule 11(a) of the Rules Governing Proceedings Under 28 U.S.C. § 2254 or § 2255 (if any), along with the notice of appeal and the file of the district-court proceedings. If the district judge has denied the certificate, the applicant may request a circuit judge to issue it.

(2) A request addressed to the court of appeals may be considered by a circuit judge or judges, as the court prescribes. If no express request for a certificate is filed, the notice of appeal constitutes a request addressed to the judges of the court of appeals.

(3) A certificate of appealability is not required when a state or its representative or the United States or its representative appeals.

RULE 23. CUSTODY OR RELEASE OF A PRISONER IN A HABEAS CORPUS PROCEEDING

(a) Transfer of Custody Pending Review. Pending review of a decision in a habeas corpus proceeding commenced before a court, justice, or judge of the United States for the release of a prisoner, the person having custody of the prisoner must not transfer custody to another unless a transfer is directed in accordance with this rule. When, upon application, a custodian shows the need for a transfer, the court, justice, or judge rendering the decision under review may authorize the transfer and substitute the successor custodian as a party.

(b) Detention or Release Pending Review of Decision Not to Release. While a decision not to release a prisoner is under review, the court or judge rendering the decision, or the court of appeals, or the Supreme Court, or a judge or justice of either court, may order that the prisoner be:

(1) detained in the custody from which release is sought;

(2) detained in other appropriate custody; or

(3) released on personal recognizance, with or without surety.

(c) Release Pending Review of Decision Ordering Release. While a decision ordering the release of a prisoner is under review, the prisoner must—unless the court or judge rendering the decision, or the court of appeals, or the Supreme Court, or a judge or justice of either court orders otherwise—be released on personal recognizance, with or without surety.

(d) Modification of the Initial Order on Custody. An initial order governing the prisoner's custody or release, including any recognizance or surety, continues in effect pending review unless for special reasons shown to the court of appeals or the Supreme Court, or to a judge or justice of either court, the order is modified or an independent order regarding custody, release, or surety is issued.

RULE 24. PROCEEDING IN FORMA PAUPERIS

(a) Leave to Proceed in Forma Pauperis.

(1) Motion in the District Court. Except as stated in Rule 24(a)(3), a party to a district-court action who desires to appeal in forma pauperis must file a motion in the district court. The party must attach an affidavit that:

(A) shows in the detail prescribed by Form 4 of the Appendix of Forms, the party's inability to pay or to give security for fees and costs;

(B) claims an entitlement to redress; and

(C) states the issues that the party intends to present on appeal.

(2) Action on the Motion. If the district court grants the motion, the party may proceed on appeal without prepaying or giving security for fees and costs, unless a statute provides otherwise. If the district court denies the motion, it must state its reasons in writing.

(3) Prior Approval. A party who was permitted to proceed in forma pauperis in the district-court action, or who was determined to be financially unable to obtain an adequate defense in a criminal case, may proceed on appeal in forma pauperis without further authorization, unless:

(A) the district court—before or after the notice of appeal is filed—certifies that the appeal is not taken in good faith or finds that the party is not otherwise entitled to proceed in forma pauperis and states in writing its reasons for the certification or finding; or

(B) a statute provides otherwise.

(4) Notice of District Court's Denial. The district clerk must immediately notify the parties and the court of appeals when the district court does any of the following:

(A) denies a motion to proceed on appeal in forma pauperis;

(B) certifies that the appeal is not taken in good faith; or

(C) finds that the party is not otherwise entitled to proceed in forma pauperis.

(5) Motion in the Court of Appeals. A party may file a motion to proceed on appeal in forma pauperis in the court of appeals within 30 days after service of the notice prescribed in Rule 24(a)(4). The motion must include a copy of the affidavit filed in the district court and the district court's statement of reasons for its action. If no affidavit was filed in the district court, the party must include the affidavit prescribed by Rule 24(a)(1).

(b) Leave to Proceed in Forma Pauperis on Appeal or Review of an Administrative-Agency Proceeding. When an appeal or review of a proceeding before an administrative agency, board, commission, or officer (including for the purpose of this rule the United States Tax Court) proceeds directly in a court of appeals, a party may file in the court of appeals a motion for leave to proceed on appeal in forma pauperis with an affidavit prescribed by Rule 24(a)(1).

(c) Leave to Use Original Record. A party allowed to proceed on appeal in forma pauperis may request that the appeal be heard on the original record without reproducing any part.

TITLE VII. GENERAL PROVISIONS

RULE 25. FILING AND SERVICE

(a) Filing.

(1) Filing with the Clerk. A paper required or permitted to be filed in a court of appeals must be filed with the clerk.

(2) Filing: Method and Timeliness.

(A) In general. Filing may be accomplished by mail addressed to the clerk, but filing is not timely unless the clerk receives the papers within the time fixed for filing.

(B) A brief or appendix. A brief or appendix is timely filed, however, if on or before the last day for filing, it is:

(i) mailed to the clerk by First-Class Mail, or other class of mail that is at least as expeditious, postage prepaid; or

(ii) dispatched to a third-party commercial carrier for delivery to the clerk within 3 days.

(C) Inmate filing. A paper filed by an inmate confined in an institution is timely if deposited in the institution's internal mailing system on or before the last day for filing. If an institution has a system designed for legal mail, the inmate must use that system to receive the benefit of this rule. Timely filing may be shown by a declaration in compliance with 28 U.S.C. § 1746 or by a notarized statement, either of which must set forth the date of deposit and state that first-class postage has been prepaid.

(D) Electronic filing. A court of appeals may by local rule permit or require papers to be filed, signed, or verified by electronic means that are consistent with technical standards, if any, that the Judicial Conference of the United States establishes. A local rule may require filing by electronic means only if reasonable exceptions are allowed. A paper filed by electronic means in compliance with a local rule constitutes a written paper for the purpose of applying these rules.

(3) Filing a Motion with a Judge. If a motion requests relief that may be granted by a single judge, the judge may permit the motion to be filed with the judge; the judge must note the filing date on the motion and give it to the clerk.

(4) Clerk's Refusal of Documents. The clerk must not refuse to accept for filing any paper presented for that purpose solely because it is not presented in proper form as required by these rules or by any local rule or practice.

(5) Privacy Protection. An appeal in a case whose privacy protection was governed by Federal Rule of Bankruptcy Procedure 9037, Federal Rule of Civil Procedure 5.2, or Federal Rule of Criminal Procedure 49.1 is governed by the same rule on appeal. In all other proceedings, privacy protection is governed by Federal Rule of Civil Procedure 5.2, except that

Federal Rule of Criminal Procedure 49.1 governs when an extraordinary writ is sought in a criminal case.

(b) Service of All Papers Required. Unless a rule requires service by the clerk, a party must, at or before the time of filing a paper, serve a copy on the other parties to the appeal or review. Service on a party represented by counsel must be made on the party's counsel.

(c) Manner of Service.

(1) Service may be any of the following:

(A) personal, including delivery to a responsible person at the office of counsel;

(B) by mail;

(C) by third-party commercial carrier for delivery within 3 days; or

(D) by electronic means, if the party being served consents in writing.

(2) If authorized by local rule, a party may use the court's transmission equipment to make electronic service under Rule 25(c)(1)(D).

(3) When reasonable considering such factors as the immediacy of the relief sought, distance, and cost, service on a party must be by a manner at least as expeditious as the manner used to file the paper with the court.

(4) Service by mail or by commercial carrier is complete on mailing or delivery to the carrier. Service by electronic means is complete on transmission, unless the party making service is notified that the paper was not received by the party served.

(d) Proof of Service.

(1) A paper presented for filing must contain either of the following:

(A) an acknowledgment of service by the person served; or

(B) proof of service consisting of a statement by the person who made service certifying:

(i) the date and manner of service;

(ii) the names of the persons served; and

(iii) their mail or electronic addresses, facsimile numbers, or the addresses of the places of delivery, as appropriate for the manner of service.

(2) When a brief or appendix is filed by mailing or dispatch in accordance with Rule 25(a)(2)(B), the proof of service must also state the date and manner by which the document was mailed or dispatched to the clerk.

(3) Proof of service may appear on or be affixed to the papers filed.

(e) Number of Copies. When these rules require the filing or furnishing of a number of copies, a court may require a different number by local rule or by order in a particular case.

RULE 26. COMPUTING AND EXTENDING TIME

(a) Computing Time. The following rules apply in computing any time period specified in these rules, in any local rule or court order, or in any statute that does not specify a method of computing time.

(1) **Period Stated in Days or a Longer Unit.** When the period is stated in days or a longer unit of time:

(A) exclude the day of the event that triggers the period;

(B) count every day, including intermediate Saturdays, Sundays, and legal holidays; and

(C) include the last day of the period, but if the last day is a Saturday, Sunday, or legal holiday, the period continues to run until the end of the next day that is not a Saturday, Sunday, or legal holiday.

(2) **Period Stated in Hours.** When the period is stated in hours:

(A) begin counting immediately on the occurrence of the event that triggers the period;

(B) count every hour, including hours during intermediate Saturdays, Sundays, and legal holidays; and

(C) if the period would end on a Saturday, Sunday, or legal holiday, the period continues to run until the same time on the next day that is not a Saturday, Sunday, or legal holiday.

(3) **Inaccessibility of the Clerk's Office.** Unless the court orders otherwise, if the clerk's office is inaccessible:

(A) on the last day for filing under Rule 26(a)(1), then the time for filing is extended to the first accessible day that is not a Saturday, Sunday, or legal holiday; or

(B) during the last hour for filing under Rule 26(a)(2), then the time for filing is extended to the same time on the first accessible day that is not a Saturday, Sunday, or legal holiday.

(4) **"Last Day" Defined.** Unless a different time is set by a statute, local rule, or court order, the last day ends:

(A) for electronic filing in the district court, at midnight in the court's time zone;

(B) for electronic filing in the court of appeals, at midnight in the time zone of the circuit clerk's principal office;

(C) for filing under Rules 4(c)(1), 25(a)(2)(B), and 25(a)(2)(C)--and filing by mail under Rule 13(b)--at the latest time for the method chosen for delivery to the post office, third-party commercial carrier, or prison mailing system; and

(D) for filing by other means, when the clerk's office is scheduled to close.

(5) **"Next Day" Defined.** The "next day" is determined by continuing to count forward when the period is measured after

an event and backward when measured before an event.

(6) **"Legal Holiday" Defined.** "Legal holiday" means:

(A) the day set aside by statute for observing New Year's Day, Martin Luther King Jr.'s Birthday, Washington's Birthday, Memorial Day, Independence Day, Labor Day, Columbus Day, Veterans' Day, Thanksgiving Day, or Christmas Day;

(B) any day declared a holiday by the President or Congress; and

(C) for periods that are measured after an event, any other day declared a holiday by the state where either of the following is located: the district court that rendered the challenged judgment or order, or the circuit clerk's principal office.

(b) Extending Time. For good cause, the court may extend the time prescribed by these rules or by its order to perform any act, or may permit an act to be done after that time expires. But the court may not extend the time to file:

(1) a notice of appeal (except as authorized in Rule 4) or a petition for permission to appeal; or

(2) a notice of appeal from or a petition to enjoin, set aside, suspend, modify, enforce, or otherwise review an order of an administrative agency, board, commission, or officer of the United States, unless specifically authorized by law.

(c) Additional Time after Service. When a party may or must act within a specified time after service, 3 days are added after the period would otherwise expire under Rule 26(a), unless the paper is delivered on the date of service stated in the proof of service. For purposes of this Rule 26(c), a paper that is served electronically is not treated as delivered on the date of service stated in the proof of service.

RULE 26.1. CORPORATE DISCLOSURE STATEMENT

(a) Who Must File. Any nongovernmental corporate party to a proceeding in a court of appeals must file a statement that identifies any parent corporation and any publicly held corporation that owns 10% or more of its stock or states that there is no such corporation.

(b) Time for Filing; Supplemental Filing. A party must file the Rule 26.1(a) statement with the principal brief or upon filing a motion, response, petition, or answer in the court of appeals, whichever occurs first, unless a local rule requires earlier filing. Even if the statement has already been filed, the party's principal brief must include the statement before the table of contents. A party must supplement its statement whenever the information that must be disclosed under Rule 26.1(a) changes.

(c) Number of Copies. If the Rule 26.1(a) statement is filed before the principal brief, or if a supplemental statement is filed, the party must file an original and 3 copies unless the court requires a different number by local rule or by order in a particular case.

RULE 27. MOTIONS

(a) In General.

(1) Application for Relief. An application for an order or other relief is made by motion unless these rules prescribe another form. A motion must be in writing unless the court permits otherwise.

(2) Contents of a Motion.

(A) Grounds and relief sought. A motion must state with particularity the grounds for the motion, the relief sought, and the legal argument necessary to support it.

(B) Accompanying documents.

(i) Any affidavit or other paper necessary to support a motion must be served and filed with the motion.

(ii) An affidavit must contain only factual information, not legal argument.

(iii) A motion seeking substantive relief must include a copy of the trial court's opinion or agency's decision as a separate exhibit.

(C) Documents barred or not required.

(i) A separate brief supporting or responding to a motion must not be filed.

(ii) A notice of motion is not required.

(iii) A proposed order is not required.

(3) Response.

(A) Time to file. Any party may file a response to a motion; Rule 27(a)(2) governs its contents. The response must be filed within 10 days after service of the motion unless the court shortens or extends the time. A motion authorized by Rules 8, 9, 18, or 41 may be granted before the 10-day period runs only if the court gives reasonable notice to the parties that it intends to act sooner.

(B) Request for affirmative relief. A response may include a motion for affirmative relief. The time to respond to the new motion, and to reply to that response, are governed by Rule 27(a)(3)(A) and (a)(4). The title of the response must alert the court to the request for relief.

(4) Reply to Response. Any reply to a response must be filed within 7 days after service of the response. A reply must not present matters that do not relate to the response.

(b) Disposition of a Motion for a Procedural Order. The court may act on a motion for a procedural order—including a motion under Rule 26(b)—at any time without awaiting a response, and may, by rule or by order in a particular case, authorize its clerk to act on specified types of procedural motions. A party adversely affected by the court's, or the clerk's, action may file a motion to reconsider, vacate, or modify that action. Timely opposition filed after the motion is granted in whole or in part does not constitute a request to reconsider, vacate, or modify the disposition; a motion requesting that relief must be filed.

(c) Power of a Single Judge to Entertain a Motion. A circuit judge may act alone on any motion, but may not dismiss or otherwise determine an appeal or other proceeding. A court of appeals may provide by rule or by order in a particular case that only the court may act on any motion or class of motions. The court may review the action of a single judge.

(d) Form of Papers; Page Limits; and Number of Copies.

(1) Format.

(A) Reproduction. A motion, response, or reply may be reproduced by any process that yields a clear black image on light paper. The paper must be opaque and unglazed. Only one side of the paper may be used.

(B) Cover. A cover is not required but there must be a caption that includes the case number, the name of the court, the title of the case, and a brief descriptive title indicating the purpose of the motion and identifying the party or parties for whom it is filed. If a cover is used, it must be white.

(C) Binding. The document must be bound in any manner that is secure, does not obscure the text, and permits the document to lie reasonably flat when open.

(D) Paper size, line spacing, and margins. The document must be on $8^{1}/_{2}$ by 11 inch paper. The text must be double-spaced, but quotations more than two lines long may be indented and single-spaced. Headings and footnotes may be single-spaced. Margins must be at least one inch on all four sides. Page numbers may be placed in the margins, but no text may appear there.

(E) Typeface and type styles. The document must comply with the typeface requirements of Rule 32(a)(5) and the type-style requirements of Rule 32(a)(6).

(2) Page Limits. A motion or a response to a motion must not exceed 20 pages, exclusive of the corporate disclosure statement and accompanying documents authorized by Rule 27(a)(2)(B), unless the court permits or directs otherwise. A reply to a response must not exceed 10 pages.

(3) Number of Copies. An original and 3 copies must be filed unless the court requires a different number by local rule or by order in a particular case.

(e) Oral Argument. A motion will be decided without oral argument unless the court orders otherwise.

RULE 28. BRIEFS

(a) Appellant's Brief. The appellant's brief must contain, under appropriate headings and in the order indicated:

(1) a corporate disclosure statement if required by Rule 26.1;

(2) a table of contents, with page references;

(3) a table of authorities—cases (alphabetically arranged), statutes, and other authorities—with references to the pages of the brief where they are cited;

(4) a jurisdictional statement, including:

(A) the basis for the district court's or agency's subject-matter jurisdiction, with citations to applicable statutory provisions and stating relevant facts establishing jurisdiction;

(B) the basis for the court of appeals' jurisdiction, with citations to applicable statutory provisions and stating relevant facts establishing jurisdiction;

(C) the filing dates establishing the timeliness of the appeal or petition for review; and

(D) an assertion that the appeal is from a final order or judgment that disposes of all parties' claims, or information establishing the court of appeals' jurisdiction on some other basis;

(5) a statement of the issues presented for review;

(6) a statement of the case briefly indicating the nature of the case, the course of proceedings, and the disposition below;

(7) a statement of facts relevant to the issues submitted for review with appropriate references to the record (see Rule 28(e));

(8) a summary of the argument, which must contain a succinct, clear, and accurate statement of the arguments made in the body of the brief, and which must not merely repeat the argument headings;

(9) the argument, which must contain:

(A) appellant's contentions and the reasons for them, with citations to the authorities and parts of the record on which the appellant relies; and

(B) for each issue, a concise statement of the applicable standard of review (which may appear in the discussion of the issue or under a separate heading placed before the discussion of the issues);

(10) a short conclusion stating the precise relief sought; and

(11) the certificate of compliance, if required by Rule 32(a)(7).

(b) Appellee's Brief. The appellee's brief must conform to the requirements of Rule 28(a)(1)–(9) and (11), except that none of the following need appear unless the appellee is dissatisfied with the appellant's statement:

(1) the jurisdictional statement;

(2) the statement of the issues;

(3) the statement of the case;

(4) the statement of the facts; and

(5) the statement of the standard of review.

(c) Reply Brief. The appellant may file a brief in reply to the appellee's brief. Unless the court permits, no further briefs may be filed. A reply brief must contain a table of contents, with page references, and a table of authorities—cases (alphabetically arranged), statutes, and other authorities—with references to the pages of the reply brief where they are cited.

(d) References to Parties. In briefs and at oral argument, counsel should minimize use of the terms "appellant" and "appellee." To make briefs clear, counsel should use the parties' actual names or the designations used in the lower court or agency proceeding, or such descriptive terms as "the employee," "the injured person," "the taxpayer," "the ship," "the stevedore."

(e) References to the Record. References to the parts of the record contained in the appendix filed with the appellant's brief must be to the pages of the appendix. If the appendix is prepared after the briefs are filed, a party referring to the record must follow one of the methods detailed in Rule 30(c). If the original record is used under Rule 30(f) and is not consecutively paginated, or if the brief refers to an unreproduced part of the record, any reference must be to the page of the original document. For example:

- Answer p. 7;
- Motion for Judgment p. 2;
- Transcript p. 231.

Only clear abbreviations may be used. A party referring to evidence whose admissibility is in controversy must cite the pages of the appendix or of the transcript at which the evidence was identified, offered, and received or rejected.

(f) Reproduction of Statutes, Rules, Regulations, etc. If the court's determination of the issues presented requires the study of statutes, rules, regulations, etc., the relevant parts must be set out in the brief or in an addendum at the end, or may be supplied to the court in pamphlet form.

(g) [Reserved]

(h) [Reserved]

(i) Briefs in a Case Involving Multiple Appellants or Appellees. In a case involving more than one appellant or appellee, including consolidated cases, any number of appellants or appellees may join in a brief, and any party may adopt by reference a part of another's brief. Parties may also join in reply briefs.

(j) Citation of Supplemental Authorities. If pertinent and significant authorities come to a party's attention after the party's brief has been filed—or after oral argument but before decision—a party may promptly advise the circuit clerk by letter, with a copy to all other parties, setting forth the citations. The letter must state the reasons for the supplemental citations, referring either to the page of the brief or to a point argued orally. The body of the letter must not exceed 350 words. Any response must be made promptly and must be similarly limited.

RULE 28.1. CROSS-APPEALS

(a) Applicability. This rule applies to a case in which a cross-appeal is filed. Rules 28(a)–(c), 31(a)(1), 32(a)(2), and 32(a)(7)(A)–(B) do not apply to such a case, except as otherwise provided in this rule.

(b) Designation of Appellant. The party who files a notice of appeal first is the appellant for the purposes of this rule and Rules 30 and 34. If notices are filed on the same day, the plaintiff in the proceeding below is the appellant. These designations may be modified by the parties' agreement or by court order.

(c) Briefs. In a case involving a cross-appeal:

(1) Appellant's Principal Brief. The appellant must file a principal brief in the appeal. That brief must comply with Rule 28(a).

(2) Appellee's Principal and Response Brief. The appellee must file a principal brief in the cross-appeal and must, in the same brief, respond to the principal brief in the appeal. That appellee's brief must comply with Rule 28(a), except that the brief need not include a statement of the case or a statement of the facts unless the appellee is dissatisfied with the appellant's statement.

(3) Appellant's Response and Reply Brief. The appellant must file a brief that responds to the principal brief in the cross-appeal and may, in the same brief, reply to the response in the appeal. That brief must comply with Rule 28(a)(2)–(9) and (11), except that none of the following need appear unless the appellant is dissatisfied with the appellee's statement in the cross-appeal:

(A) the jurisdictional statement;

(B) the statement of the issues;

(C) the statement of the case;

(D) the statement of the facts; and

(E) the statement of the standard of review.

(4) Appellee's Reply Brief. The appellee may file a brief in reply to the response in the crossappeal. That brief must comply with Rule 28(a)(2)–(3) and (11) and must be limited to the issues presented by the cross-appeal.

(5) No Further Briefs. Unless the court permits, no further briefs may be filed in a case involving a cross-appeal.

(d) Cover. Except for filings by unrepresented parties, the cover of the appellant's principal brief must be blue; the appellee's principal and response brief, red; the appellant's response and reply brief, yellow; the appellee's reply brief, gray; an intervenor's or amicus curiae's brief, green; and any supplemental brief, tan. The front cover of a brief must contain the information required by Rule 32(a)(2).

(e) Length.

(1) Page Limitation. Unless it complies with Rule 28.1(e)(2) and (3), the appellant's principal brief must not exceed 30 pages; the appellee's principal and response brief, 35 pages; the appellant's response and reply brief, 30 pages; and the appellee's reply brief, 15 pages.

(2) Type-Volume Limitation.

(A) The appellant's principal brief or the appellant's response and reply brief is acceptable if:

(i) it contains no more than 14,000 words; or

(ii) it uses a monospaced face and contains no more than 1,300 lines of text.

(B) The appellee's principal and response brief is acceptable if:

(i) it contains no more than 16,500 words; or

(ii) it uses a monospaced face and contains no more than 1,500 lines of text.

(C) The appellee's reply brief is acceptable if it contains no more than half of the type volume specified in Rule 28.1(e)(2)(A).

(3) Certificate of Compliance. A brief submitted under Rule 28.1(e)(2) must comply with Rule 32(a)(7)(C).

(f) Time to Serve and File a Brief. Briefs must be served and filed as follows:

(1) the appellant's principal brief, within 40 days after the record is filed;

(2) the appellee's principal and response brief, within 30 days after the appellant's principal brief is served;

(3) the appellant's response and reply brief, within 30 days after the appellee's principal and response brief is served; and

(4) the appellee's reply brief, within 14 days after the appellant's response and reply brief is served, but at least 7 days before argument unless the court, for good cause, allows a later filing.

RULE 29. BRIEF OF AN AMICUS CURIAE

(a) When Permitted. The United States or its officer or agency or a state, may file an amicus-curiae brief without the consent of the parties or leave of court. Any other amicus curiae may file a brief only by leave of court or if the brief states that all parties have consented to its filing.

(b) Motion for Leave to File. The motion must be accompanied by the proposed brief and state:

(1) the movant's interest; and

(2) the reason why an amicus brief is desirable and why the matters asserted are relevant to the disposition of the case.

(c) Contents and Form. An amicus brief must comply with Rule 32. In addition to the requirements of Rule 32, the cover must identify the party or parties supported and indicate whether the brief supports affirmance or reversal. An amicus brief need not comply with Rule 28, but must include the following:

(1) if the amicus curiae is a corporation, a disclosure statement like that required of parties by Rule 26.1;

(2) a table of contents, with page references;

(3) a table of authorities—cases (alphabetically arranged), statutes, and other authorities—with references to the pages of the brief where they are cited;

(4) a concise statement of the identity of the amicus curiae, its interest in the case, and the source of its authority to file;

(5) unless the amicus curiae is one listed in the first sentence of Rule 29(a), a statement that indicates whether:

(A) a party's counsel authored the brief in whole or in part;

(B) a party or a party's counsel contributed money that was intended to fund preparing or submitting the brief; and

(C) a person—other than the amicus curiae, its members, or its counsel—contributed money that was intended to fund preparing or submitting the brief and, if so, identifies each such person;

(6) an argument, which may be preceded by a summary and which need not include a statement of the applicable standard of review; and

(7) a certificate of compliance, if required by Rule 32(a)(7).

(d) Length. Except by the court's permission, an amicus brief may be no more than one-half the maximum length authorized by these rules for a party's principal brief. If the court grants a party permission to file a longer brief, that extension does not affect the length of an amicus brief.

(e) Time for Filing. An amicus curiae must file its brief, accompanied by a motion for filing when necessary, no later than 7 days after the principal brief of the party being supported is filed. An amicus curiae that does not support either party must file its brief no later than 7 days after the appellant's or petitioner's principal brief is filed. A court may grant leave for later filing, specifying the time within which an opposing party may answer.

(f) Reply Brief. Except by the court's permission, an amicus curiae may not file a reply brief.

(g) Oral Argument. An amicus curiae may participate in oral argument only with the court's permission.

RULE 30. APPENDIX TO THE BRIEFS

(a) Appellant's Responsibility.

(1) **Contents of the Appendix.** The appellant must prepare and file an appendix to the briefs containing:

(A) the relevant docket entries in the proceeding below;

(B) the relevant portions of the pleadings, charge, findings, or opinion;

(C) the judgment, order, or decision in question; and

(D) other parts of the record to which the parties wish to direct the court's attention.

(2) Excluded Material. Memoranda of law in the district court should not be included in the appendix unless they have independent relevance. Parts of the record may be relied on by the court or the parties even though not included in the appendix.

(3) Time to File; Number of Copies. Unless filing is deferred under Rule 30(c), the appellant must file 10 copies of the appendix with the brief and must serve one copy on counsel for each party separately represented. An unrepresented party proceeding in forma pauperis must file 4 legible copies with the clerk, and one copy must be served on counsel for each separately represented party. The court may by local rule or by order in a particular case require the filing or service of a different number.

(b) All Parties' Responsibilities.

(1) Determining the Contents of the Appendix. The parties are encouraged to agree on the contents of the appendix. In the absence of an agreement, the appellant must, within 14 days after the record is filed, serve on the appellee a designation of the parts of the record the appellant intends to include in the appendix and a statement of the issues the appellant intends to present for review. The appellee may, within 14 days after receiving the designation, serve on the appellant a designation of additional parts to which it wishes to direct the court's attention. The appellant must include the designated parts in the appendix. The parties must not engage in unnecessary designation of parts of the record, because the entire record is available to the court. This paragraph applies also to a cross-appellant and a cross-appellee.

(2) Costs of Appendix. Unless the parties agree otherwise, the appellant must pay the cost of the appendix. If the appellant considers parts of the record designated by the appellee to be unnecessary, the appellant may advise the appellee, who must then advance the cost of including those parts. The cost of the appendix is a taxable cost. But if any party causes unnecessary parts of the record to be included in the appendix, the court may impose the cost of those parts on that party. Each circuit must, by local rule, provide for sanctions against attorneys who unreasonably and vexatiously increase litigation costs by including unnecessary material in the appendix.

(c) Deferred Appendix.

(1) Deferral Until After Briefs Are Filed. The court may provide by rule for classes of cases or by order in a particular case that preparation of the appendix may be deferred until after the briefs have been filed and that the appendix may be filed 21 days after the appellee's brief is served. Even though the filing of the appendix may be deferred, Rule 30(b) applies; except that a party must designate the parts of the record it wants included in the appendix when it serves its brief, and need not include a statement of the issues presented.

(2) References to the Record.

(A) If the deferred appendix is used, the parties may cite in their briefs the pertinent pages of the record. When the appendix is prepared, the record pages cited in the briefs must be indicated by inserting record page numbers, in brackets, at places in the appendix where those pages of the record appear.

(B) A party who wants to refer directly to pages of the appendix may serve and file copies of the brief within the time required by Rule 31(a), containing appropriate references to pertinent pages of the record. In that event, within 14 days after the appendix is filed, the party must serve and file copies of the brief, containing references to the pages of the appendix in place of or in addition to the references to the pertinent pages of the record. Except for the correction of typographical errors, no other changes may be made to the brief.

(d) Format of the Appendix. The appendix must begin with a table of contents identifying the page at which each part begins. The relevant docket entries must follow the table of contents. Other parts of the record must follow chronologically. When pages from the transcript of proceedings are placed in the appendix, the transcript page numbers must be shown in brackets immediately before the included pages. Omissions in the text of papers or of the transcript must be indicated by asterisks. Immaterial formal matters (captions, subscriptions, acknowledgments, etc.) should be omitted.

(e) Reproduction of Exhibits. Exhibits designated for inclusion in the appendix may be reproduced in a separate volume, or volumes, suitably indexed. Four copies must be filed with the appendix, and one copy must be served on counsel for each separately represented party. If a transcript of a proceeding before an administrative agency, board, commission, or officer was used in a district-court action and has been designated for inclusion in the appendix, the transcript must be placed in the appendix as an exhibit.

(f) Appeal on the Original Record Without an Appendix. The court may, either by rule for all cases or classes of cases or by order in a particular case, dispense with the appendix and permit an appeal to proceed on the original record with any copies of the record, or relevant parts, that the court may order the parties to file.

RULE 31. SERVING AND FILING BRIEFS
(a) Time to Serve and File a Brief.

(1) The appellant must serve and file a brief within 40 days after the record is filed. The appellee must serve and file a brief within 30 days after the appellant's brief is served. The appellant may serve and file a reply brief within 14 days after service of the appellee's brief but a reply brief must be filed at least 7 days before argument, unless the court, for good cause, allows a later filing.

(2) A court of appeals that routinely considers cases on the merits promptly after the briefs are filed may shorten the time to serve and file briefs, either by local rule or by order in a particular case.

(b) Number of Copies. Twenty-five copies of each brief must be filed with the clerk and 2 copies must be served on each unrepresented party and on counsel for each separately represented party. An unrepresented party proceeding in forma pauperis must file 4 legible copies with the clerk, and one copy must be served on each unrepresented party and on counsel for each separately represented party. The court may by local rule or by order in a particular case require the filing or service of a different number.

(c) Consequence of Failure to File. If an appellant fails to file a brief within the time provided by this rule, or within an extended time, an appellee may move to dismiss the appeal. An appellee who fails to file a brief will not be heard at oral argument unless the court grants permission.

RULE 32. FORM OF BRIEFS, APPENDICES, AND OTHER PAPERS
(a) Form of a Brief.

(1) Reproduction.

(A) A brief may be reproduced by any process that yields a clear black image on light paper. The paper must be opaque and unglazed. Only one side of the paper may be used.

(B) Text must be reproduced with a clarity that equals or exceeds the output of a laser printer.

(C) Photographs, illustrations, and tables may be reproduced by any method that results in a good copy of the original; a glossy finish is acceptable if the original is glossy.

(2) Cover. Except for filings by unrepresented parties, the cover of the appellant's brief must be blue; the appellee's, red; an intervenor's or amicus curiae's, green; any reply brief, gray; and any supplemental brief, tan. The front cover of a brief must contain:

(A) the number of the case centered at the top;

(B) the name of the court;

(C) the title of the case (see Rule 12(a));

(D) the nature of the proceeding (e.g., Appeal, Petition for Review) and the name of the court, agency, or board below;

(E) the title of the brief, identifying the party or parties for whom the brief is filed; and

(F) the name, office address, and telephone number of counsel representing the party for whom the brief is filed.

(3) Binding. The brief must be bound in any manner that is secure, does not obscure the text, and permits the brief to lie reasonably flat when open.

(4) Paper Size, Line Spacing, and Margins. The brief must be on 8½ by 11 inch paper. The text must be double-spaced, but quotations more than two lines long may be indented and single-spaced. Headings and footnotes may be single-spaced. Margins must be at least one inch on all four sides. Page numbers may be placed in the margins, but no text may appear there.

(5) Typeface. Either a proportionally spaced or a monospaced face may be used.

(A) A proportionally spaced face must include serifs, but sans-serif type may be used in headings and captions. A proportionally spaced face must be 14-point or larger.

(B) A monospaced face may not contain more than 10½ characters per inch.

(6) Type Styles. A brief must be set in a plain, roman style, although italics or boldface may be used for emphasis. Case names must be italicized or underlined.

(7) Length.

(A) Page limitation. A principal brief may not exceed 30 pages, or a reply brief 15 pages, unless it complies with Rule 32(a)(7)(B) and (C).

(B) Type-volume limitation.

(i) A principal brief is acceptable if:

- it contains no more than 14,000 words; or

- it uses a monospaced face and contains no more than 1,300 lines of text.

(ii) A reply brief is acceptable if it contains no more than half of the type volume specified in Rule 32(a)(7)(B)(i).

(iii) Headings, footnotes, and quotations count toward the word and line limitations. The corporate disclosure statement, table of contents, table of citations, statement with respect to oral argument, any addendum containing statutes, rules or regulations, and any certificates of counsel do not count toward the limitation.

(C) Certificate of compliance.

(i) A brief submitted under Rules 28.1(e)(2) or 32(a)(7)(B) must include a certificate by the attorney, or an unrepresented party, that the brief complies with the type-volume limitation. The person preparing the certificate may rely on the word or line count of the word-processing system used to prepare the brief. The certificate must state either:

- the number of words in the brief; or
- the number of lines of monospaced type in the brief.

(ii) Form 6 in the Appendix of Forms is a suggested form of a certificate of compliance. Use of Form 6 must be regarded as sufficient to meet the requirements of Rules 28.1(e)(3) and 32(a)(7)(C)(i).

(b) Form of an Appendix. An appendix must comply with Rule 32(a)(1), (2), (3), and (4), with the following exceptions:

(1) The cover of a separately bound appendix must be white.

(2) An appendix may include a legible photocopy of any document found in the record or of a printed judicial or agency decision.

(3) When necessary to facilitate inclusion of odd-sized documents such as technical drawings, an appendix may be a size other than 8½ by 11 inches, and need not lie reasonably flat when opened.

(c) Form of Other Papers.

(1) Motion. The form of a motion is governed by Rule 27(d).

(2) Other Papers. Any other paper, including a petition for panel rehearing and a petition for hearing or rehearing en banc, and any response to such a petition, must be reproduced in the manner prescribed by Rule 32(a), with the following exceptions:

(A) A cover is not necessary if the caption and signature page of the paper together contain the information required by Rule 32(a)(2). If a cover is used, it must be white.

(B) Rule 32(a)(7) does not apply.

(d) Signature. Every brief, motion, or other paper filed with the court must be signed by the party filing the paper or, if the party is represented, by one of the party's attorneys.

(e) Local Variation. Every court of appeals must accept documents that comply with the form requirements of this rule. By local rule or order in a particular case a court of appeals may accept documents that do not meet all of the form requirements of this rule.

RULE 32.1. CITING JUDICIAL DISPOSITIONS

(a) Citation Permitted. A court may not prohibit or restrict the citation of federal judicial opinions, orders, judgments, or other written dispositions that have been:

(i) designed as "unpublished," "not for publication," "non-precedential," "not precedent," or the like; and

(ii) issued on or after January 1, 2007.

(b) Copies Required. If a party cites a federal judicial opinion, order, judgment, or other written disposition that is not available in a publicly accessible electronic database, the party must file and serve a copy of that opinion, order, judgment, or disposition with the brief or other paper in which it is cited.

RULE 33. APPEAL CONFERENCES

The court may direct the attorneys—and, when appropriate, the parties—to participate in one or more conferences to address any matter that may aid in disposing of the proceedings, including simplifying the issues and discussing settlement. A judge or other person designated by the court may preside over the conference, which may be conducted in person or by telephone. Before a settlement conference, the attorneys must consult with their clients and obtain as much authority as feasible to settle the case. The court may, as a result of the conference, enter an order controlling the course of the proceedings or implementing any settlement agreement.

RULE 34. ORAL ARGUMENT

(a) In General.

(1) *Party's Statement.* Any party may file, or a court may require by local rule, a statement explaining why oral argument should, or need not, be permitted.

(2) *Standards.* Oral argument must be allowed in every case unless a panel of three judges who have examined the briefs and record unanimously agrees that oral argument is unnecessary for any of the following reasons:

(A) the appeal is frivolous;

(B) the dispositive issue or issues have been authoritatively decided; or

(C) the facts and legal arguments are adequately presented in the briefs and record, and the decisional process would not be significantly aided by oral argument.

(b) Notice of Argument; Postponement. The clerk must advise all parties whether oral argument will be scheduled, and, if so, the date, time, and place for it, and the time allowed for each side. A motion to postpone the argument or to allow longer argument must be filed reasonably in advance of the hearing date.

(c) Order and Contents of Argument. The appellant opens and concludes the argument. Counsel must not read at length from briefs, records, or authorities.

(d) Cross-Appeals and Separate Appeals. If there is a cross-appeal, Rule 28.1(b) determines which party is the appellant and which is the appellee for purposes of oral argument. Unless the court directs otherwise, a cross-appeal or separate appeal must be argued when the initial appeal is argued. Separate parties should avoid duplicative argument.

(e) Nonappearance of a Party. If the appellee fails to appear for argument, the court must hear appellant's argument. If the appellant fails to appear for argument, the court may hear the appellee's argument. If neither party appears, the case will be decided on the briefs, unless the court orders otherwise.

(f) Submission on Briefs. The parties may agree to submit a case for decision on the briefs, but the court may direct that the case be argued.

(g) Use of Physical Exhibits at Argument; Removal. Counsel intending to use physical exhibits other than documents at the argument must arrange to place them in the courtroom on the day of the argument before the court convenes. After the argument, counsel must remove the exhibits from the courtroom, unless the court directs otherwise. The clerk may destroy or dispose of the exhibits if counsel does not reclaim them within a reasonable time after the clerk gives notice to remove them.

RULE 35. EN BANC DETERMINATION

(a) When Hearing or Rehearing En Banc May Be Ordered. A majority of the circuit judges who are in regular active service and who are not disqualified may order that an appeal or other proceeding be heard or reheard by the court of appeals en banc. An en banc hearing or rehearing is not favored and ordinarily will not be ordered unless:

(1) en banc consideration is necessary to secure or maintain uniformity of the court's decisions; or

(2) the proceeding involves a question of exceptional importance.

(b) Petition for Hearing or Rehearing En Banc. A party may petition for a hearing or rehearing en banc.

(1) The petition must begin with a statement that either:

(A) the panel decision conflicts with a decision of the United States Supreme Court or of the court to which the petition is addressed (with citation to the conflicting case or cases) and consideration by the full court is therefore necessary to secure and maintain uniformity of the court's decisions; or

(B) the proceeding involves one or more questions of exceptional importance, each of which must be concisely stated; for example, a petition may assert that a proceeding presents a question of exceptional importance if it involves an issue on which the panel decision conflicts with the authoritative decisions of every other United States Court of Appeals that has addressed the issue.

(2) Except by the court's permission, a petition for an en banc hearing or rehearing must not exceed 15 pages, excluding material not counted under Rule 32.

(3) For purposes of the page limit in Rule 35(b)(2), if a party files both a petition for panel rehearing and a petition for rehearing en banc, they are considered a single document even if they are filed separately, unless separate filing is required

by local rule.

(c) Time for Petition for Hearing or Rehearing En Banc. A petition that an appeal be heard initially en banc must be filed by the date when the appellee's brief is due. A petition for a rehearing en banc must be filed within the time prescribed by Rule 40 for filing a petition for rehearing.

(d) Number of Copies. The number of copies to be filed must be prescribed by local rule and may be altered by order in a particular case.

(e) Response. No response may be filed to a petition for an en banc consideration unless the court orders a response.

(f) Call for a Vote. A vote need not be taken to determine whether the case will be heard or reheard en banc unless a judge calls for a vote.

RULE 36. ENTRY OF JUDGMENT; NOTICE

(a) Entry. A judgment is entered when it is noted on the docket. The clerk must prepare, sign, and enter the judgment:

(1) after receiving the court's opinion—but if settlement of the judgment's form is required, after final settlement; or

(2) if a judgment is rendered without an opinion, as the court instructs.

(b) Notice. On the date when judgment is entered, the clerk must serve on all parties a copy of the opinion—or the judgment, if no opinion was written—and a notice of the date when the judgment was entered.

RULE 37. INTEREST ON JUDGMENT

(a) When the Court Affirms. Unless the law provides otherwise, if a money judgment in a civil case is affirmed, whatever interest is allowed by law is payable from the date when the district court's judgment was entered.

(b) When the Court Reverses. If the court modifies or reverses a judgment with a direction that a money judgment be entered in the district court, the mandate must contain instructions about the allowance of interest.

RULE 38. FRIVOLOUS APPEAL—DAMAGES AND COSTS

If a court of appeals determines that an appeal is frivolous, it may, after a separately filed motion or notice from the court and reasonable opportunity to respond, award just damages and single or double costs to the appellee.

RULE 39. COSTS

(a) Against Whom Assessed. The following rules apply unless the law provides or the court orders otherwise:

(1) if an appeal is dismissed, costs are taxed against the appellant, unless the parties agree otherwise;

(2) if a judgment is affirmed, costs are taxed against the appellant;

(3) if a judgment is reversed, costs are taxed against the appellee;

(4) if a judgment is affirmed in part, reversed in part, modified, or vacated, costs are taxed only as the court orders.

(b) Costs For and Against the United States. Costs for or against the United States, its agency, or officer will be assessed under Rule 39(a) only if authorized by law.

(c) Costs of Copies. Each court of appeals must, by local rule, fix the maximum rate for taxing the cost of producing necessary copies of a brief or appendix, or copies of records authorized by Rule 30(f). The rate must not exceed that generally charged for such work in the area where the clerk's office is located and should encourage economical methods of copying.

(d) Bill of Costs: Objections; Insertion in Mandate.

(1) A party who wants costs taxed must—within 14 days after entry of judgment—file with the circuit clerk, with proof of service, an itemized and verified bill of costs.

(2) Objections must be filed within 14 days after service of the bill of costs, unless the court extends the time.

(3) The clerk must prepare and certify an itemized statement of costs for insertion in the mandate, but issuance of the mandate must not be delayed for taxing costs. If the mandate issues before costs are finally determined, the district clerk must—upon the circuit clerk's request—add the statement of costs, or any amendment of it, to the mandate.

(e) Costs on Appeal Taxable in the District Court. The following costs on appeal are taxable in the district court for the benefit of the party entitled to costs under this rule:

(1) the preparation and transmission of the record;

(2) the reporter's transcript, if needed to determine the appeal;

(3) premiums paid for a supersedeas bond or other bond to preserve rights pending appeal; and

(4) the fee for filing the notice of appeal.

RULE 40. PETITION FOR PANEL REHEARING

(a) Time to File; Contents; Answer; Action by the Court if Granted.

(1) Time. Unless the time is shortened or extended by order or local rule, a petition for panel rehearing may be filed within 14 days after entry of judgment. But in a civil case, unless an order shortens or extends the time, the petition may be filed by any party within 45 days after entry of judgment if one of the parties is:

(A) the United States;

(B) a United States agency;

(C) a United States officer or employee sued in an official

capacity; or

(D) a current or former United States officer or employee sued in an individual capacity for an act or omission occurring in connection with duties performed on the United States' behalf — including all instances in which the United States represents that person when the court of appeals' judgment is entered or files the petition for that person.

(2) Contents. The petition must state with particularity each point of law or fact that the petitioner believes the court has overlooked or misapprehended and must argue in support of the petition. Oral argument is not permitted.

(3) Answer. Unless the court requests, no answer to a petition for panel rehearing is permitted. But ordinarily rehearing will not be granted in the absence of such a request.

(4) Action by the Court. If a petition for panel rehearing is granted, the court may do any of the following:

(A) make a final disposition of the case without reargument;

(B) restore the case to the calendar for reargument or resubmission; or

(C) issue any other appropriate order.

(b) Form of Petition; Length. The petition must comply in form with Rule 32. Copies must be served and filed as Rule 31 prescribes. Unless the court permits or a local rule provides otherwise, a petition for panel rehearing must not exceed 15 pages.

RULE 41. MANDATE: CONTENTS; ISSUANCE AND EFFECTIVE DATE; STAY

(a) Contents. Unless the court directs that a formal mandate issue, the mandate consists of a certified copy of the judgment, a copy of the court's opinion, if any, and any direction about costs.

(b) When Issued. The court's mandate must issue 7 days after the time to file a petition for rehearing expires, or 7 days after entry of an order denying a timely petition for panel rehearing, petition for rehearing en banc, or motion for stay of mandate, whichever is later. The court may shorten or extend the time.

(c) Effective Date. The mandate is effective when issued.

(d) Staying the Mandate.

(1) On Petition for Rehearing or Motion. The timely filing of a petition for panel rehearing, petition for rehearing en banc, or motion for stay of mandate, stays the mandate until disposition of the petition or motion, unless the court orders otherwise.

(2) Pending Petition for Certiorari.

(A) A party may move to stay the mandate pending the filing of a petition for a writ of certiorari in the Supreme Court. The motion must be served on all parties and must show that the certiorari petition would present a substantial question and that there is good cause for a stay.

(B) The stay must not exceed 90 days, unless the period is extended for good cause or unless the party who obtained the stay files a petition for the writ and so notifies the circuit clerk in writing within the period of the stay. In that case, the stay continues until the Supreme Court's final disposition.

(C) The court may require a bond or other security as a condition to granting or continuing a stay of the mandate.

(D) The court of appeals must issue the mandate immediately when a copy of a Supreme Court order denying the petition for writ of certiorari is filed.

RULE 42. VOLUNTARY DISMISSAL

(a) Dismissal in the District Court. Before an appeal has been docketed by the circuit clerk, the district court may dismiss the appeal on the filing of a stipulation signed by all parties or on the appellant's motion with notice to all parties.

(b) Dismissal in the Court of Appeals. The circuit clerk may dismiss a docketed appeal if the parties file a signed dismissal agreement specifying how costs are to be paid and pay any fees that are due. But no mandate or other process may issue without a court order. An appeal may be dismissed on the appellant's motion on terms agreed to by the parties or fixed by the court.

RULE 43. SUBSTITUTION OF PARTIES

(a) Death of a Party.

(1) After Notice of Appeal Is Filed. If a party dies after a notice of appeal has been filed or while a proceeding is pending in the court of appeals, the decedent's personal representative may be substituted as a party on motion filed with the circuit clerk by the representative or by any party. A party's motion must be served on the representative in accordance with Rule 25. If the decedent has no representative, any party may suggest the death on the record, and the court of appeals may then direct appropriate proceedings.

(2) Before Notice of Appeal Is Filed—Potential Appellant. If a party entitled to appeal dies before filing a notice of appeal, the decedent's personal representative—or, if there is no personal representative, the decedent's attorney of record—may file a notice of appeal within the time prescribed by these rules. After the notice of appeal is filed, substitution must be in accordance with Rule 43(a)(1).

(3) Before Notice of Appeal Is Filed—Potential Appellee. If a party against whom an appeal may be taken dies after entry of a judgment or order in the district court, but before a notice of appeal is filed, an appellant may proceed as if the death had not occurred. After the notice of appeal is filed, substitution must be in accordance with Rule 43(a)(1).

(b) Substitution for a Reason Other Than Death. If a party needs to be substituted for any reason other than death, the procedure prescribed in Rule 43(a) applies.

(c) Public Officer: Identification; Substitution.

(1) Identification of Party. A public officer who is a party to an appeal or other proceeding in an official capacity may be described as a party by the public officer's official title rather than by name. But the court may require the public officer's name to be added.

(2) Automatic Substitution of Officeholder. When a public officer who is a party to an appeal or other proceeding in an official capacity dies, resigns, or otherwise ceases to hold office, the action does not abate. The public officer's successor is automatically substituted as a party. Proceedings following the substitution are to be in the name of the substituted party, but any misnomer that does not affect the substantial rights of the parties may be disregarded. An order of substitution may be entered at any time, but failure to enter an order does not affect the substitution.

RULE 44. CASE INVOLVING A CONSTITUTIONAL QUESTION WHEN THE UNITED STATES OR THE RELEVANT STATE IS NOT A PARTY

(a) Constitutional Challenge to Federal Statute. If a party questions the constitutionality of an Act of Congress in a proceeding in which the United States or its agency, officer, or employee is not a party in an official capacity, the questioning party must give written notice to the circuit clerk immediately upon the filing of the record or as soon as the question is raised in the court of appeals. The clerk must then certify that fact to the Attorney General.

(b) Constitutional Challenge to State Statute. If a party questions the constitutionality of a statute of a State in a proceeding in which that State or its agency, officer, or employee is not a party in an official capacity, the questioning party must give written notice to the circuit clerk immediately upon the filing of the record or as soon as the question is raised in the court of appeals. The clerk must then certify that fact to the attorney general of the State.

RULE 45. CLERK'S DUTIES

(a) General Provisions.

(1) Qualifications. The circuit clerk must take the oath and post any bond required by law. Neither the clerk nor any deputy clerk may practice as an attorney or counselor in any court while in office.

(2) When Court Is Open. The court of appeals is always open for filing any paper, issuing and returning process, making a motion, and entering an order. The clerk's office with the clerk or a deputy in attendance must be open during business hours on all days except Saturdays, Sundays, and legal holidays. A court may provide by local rule or by order that the clerk's office be open for specified hours on Saturdays or on legal holidays other than New Year's Day, Martin Luther King, Jr.'s Birthday, Washington's Birthday, Memorial Day, Independence Day, Labor Day, Columbus Day, Veterans' Day, Thanksgiving Day, and Christmas Day.

(b) Records.

(1) The Docket. The circuit clerk must maintain a docket and an index of all docketed cases in the manner prescribed by the Director of the Administrative Office of the United States Courts. The clerk must record all papers filed with the clerk and all process, orders, and judgments.

(2) Calendar. Under the court's direction, the clerk must prepare a calendar of cases awaiting argument. In placing cases on the calendar for argument, the clerk must give preference to appeals in criminal cases and to other proceedings and appeals entitled to preference by law.

(3) Other Records. The clerk must keep other books and records required by the Director of the Administrative Office of the United States Courts, with the approval of the Judicial Conference of the United States, or by the court.

(c) Notice of an Order or Judgment. Upon the entry of an order or judgment, the circuit clerk must immediately serve a notice of entry on each party, with a copy of any opinion, and must note the date of service on the docket. Service on a party represented by counsel must be made on counsel.

(d) Custody of Records and Papers. The circuit clerk has custody of the court's records and papers. Unless the court orders or instructs otherwise, the clerk must not permit an original record or paper to be taken from the clerk's office. Upon disposition of the case, original papers constituting the record on appeal or review must be returned to the court or agency from which they were received. The clerk must preserve a copy of any brief, appendix, or other paper that has been filed.

RULE 46. ATTORNEYS

(a) Admission to the Bar.

(1) Eligibility. An attorney is eligible for admission to the bar of a court of appeals if that attorney is of good moral and professional character and is admitted to practice before the Supreme Court of the United States, the highest court of a state, another United States court of appeals, or a United States district court (including the district courts for Guam, the Northern Mariana Islands, and the Virgin Islands).

(2) Application. An applicant must file an application for admission, on a form approved by the court that contains the applicant's personal statement showing eligibility for membership. The applicant must subscribe to the following oath or affirmation: "I, _____, do solemnly swear [or affirm] that I will conduct myself as an attorney and counselor of this court, uprightly and according to law; and that I will support the Constitution of the United States."

(3) Admission Procedures. On written or oral motion of a member of the court's bar, the court will act on the application. An applicant may be admitted by oral motion in open court. But, unless the court orders otherwise, an applicant need not appear before the court to be admitted. Upon admission, an applicant must pay the clerk the fee prescribed by local rule or court order.

(b) Suspension or Disbarment.

(1) Standard. A member of the court's bar is subject to suspension or disbarment by the court if the member:

(A) has been suspended or disbarred from practice in any other court; or

(B) is guilty of conduct unbecoming a member of the court's bar.

(2) Procedure. The member must be given an opportunity to show good cause, within the time prescribed by the court, why the member should not be suspended or disbarred.

(3) Order. The court must enter an appropriate order after the member responds and a hearing is held, if requested, or after the time prescribed for a response expires, if no response is made.

(c) Discipline. A court of appeals may discipline an attorney who practices before it for conduct unbecoming a member of the bar or for failure to comply with any court rule. First, however, the court must afford the attorney reasonable notice, an opportunity to show cause to the contrary, and, if requested, a hearing.

RULE 47. LOCAL RULES BY COURTS OF APPEALS

(a) Local Rules.

(1) Each court of appeals acting by a majority of its judges in regular active service may, after giving appropriate public notice and opportunity for comment, make and amend rules governing its practice. A generally applicable direction to parties or lawyers regarding practice before a court must be in a local rule rather than an internal operating procedure or standing order. A local rule must be consistent with—but not duplicative of—Acts of Congress and rules adopted under 28 U.S.C. § 2072 and must conform to any uniform numbering system prescribed by the Judicial Conference of the United States. Each circuit clerk must send the Administrative Office of the United States Courts a copy of each local rule and internal operating procedure when it is promulgated or amended.

(2) A local rule imposing a requirement of form must not be enforced in a manner that causes a party to lose rights because of a nonwillful failure to comply with the requirement.

(b) Procedure When There Is No Controlling Law. A court of appeals may regulate practice in a particular case in any manner consistent with federal law, these rules, and local rules of the circuit. No sanction or other disadvantage may be imposed for noncompliance with any requirement not in federal law, federal rules, or the local circuit rules unless the alleged violator has been furnished in the particular case with actual notice of the requirement.

RULE 48. MASTERS

(a) Appointment; Powers. A court of appeals may appoint a special master to hold hearings, if necessary, and to recommend factual findings and disposition in matters ancillary to proceedings in the court. Unless the order referring a matter to a master specifies or limits the master's powers, those powers include, but are not limited to, the following:

(1) regulating all aspects of a hearing;

(2) taking all appropriate action for the efficient performance of the master's duties under the order;

(3) requiring the production of evidence on all matters embraced in the reference; and

(4) administering oaths and examining witnesses and parties.

(b) Compensation. If the master is not a judge or court employee, the court must determine the master's compensation and whether the cost is to be charged to any party.

§ 6.9 Appendix of Forms to the *Federal Rules of Appellate Procedure*

1. Notice of Appeal to a Court of Appeals From a Judgment or Order of a District Court.
2. Notice of Appeal to a Court of Appeals From a Decision of the United States Tax Court.
3. Petition for Review of Order of an Agency, Board, Commission or Officer.
4. Affidavit Accompanying Motion for Permission to Appeal In Forma Pauperis.
5. Notice of Appeal to a Court of Appeals from a Judgment or Order of a District Court or a Bankruptcy Appellate Panel.
6. Certificate of Compliance With Rule 32(a).

Form 1. Notice of Appeal to a Court of Appeals From a Judgment or Order of a District Court

United States District Court for the _____ District of _____

File Number _____

A.B., Plaintiff　　　)
　　　　　　　　　　)
　　　v　　　　　　　)　Notice of Appeal
　　　　　　　　　　)
C.D., Defendant　　)

Notice is hereby given that *[(here name all parties taking the appeal),* _____, *(plaintiffs) (defendants) in the above named case,*[1] *]* hereby appeal to the United States Court of Appeals for the _____ Circuit (from the final judgment) (from an order (describing it)) entered in this action on the _____ day of _____, 20___.

　　　　　　　　　　　　　　　　　(s) _____

　　　　　　　　　　　　　　　　　Attorney for [_____]

　　　　　　　　　　　　　　　　　[Address: _____]

----

[1] See Rule 3(c) for permissible ways of identifying appellants.

Form 2. Notice of Appeal to a Court of Appeals From a Decision of the United States Tax Court

UNITED STATES TAX COURT Washington, D.C.

A.B., Petitioner　　　　　　)
　　　　　　　　　　　　　　)
　　　v.　　　　　　　　　　)　Docket No.
　　　　　　　　　　　　　　　　_____
　　　　　　　　　　　　　　)
Commissioner of Internal　)
Revenue,
Respondent　　　　　　　　)

Notice of Appeal

Notice is hereby given that *[here name all parties taking the appeal*[1] *]*, hereby appeals to the United States Court of Appeals for the _____ Circuit from (that part of) the decision of this court entered in the above captioned proceeding on the _____ day of _____, 20___ (relating to _____).

(s) _____

Counsel for [_____]

[Address: _____]

_____

[1] See Rule 3(c) for permissible ways of identifying appellants.

Form 3. Petition for Review of Order of an Agency, Board, Commission or Officer

United States Court of Appeals for the _____ Circuit

A.B., Petitioner)
)
v.) Petition for Review
)
XYZ Commission,)
Respondent

[(here name all parties bringing the petition [1]*)]* hereby petitions the court for review of the Order of the XYZ Commission (describe the order) entered on _____, 20____.

[(s)] _____

Attorney for Petitioners

Address: _____

_____

[1] See Rule 15.

Form 4. Affidavit Accompanying Motion for Permission to Appeal in Forma Pauperis

United States District Court for the _____ District of _____

A.B., Plaintiff

v.   **Case No.** _____

C.D., Defendant

Affidavit in Support of Motion
I swear or affirm under penalty of perjury that, because of my

poverty, I cannot prepay the docket fees of my appeal or post a bond for them. I believe I am entitled to redress. I swear or affirm under penalty of perjury under United States laws that my answers on this form are true and correct. (28 U.S.C. § 1746; 18 U.S.C. § 1621.)

Instructions

Complete all questions in this application and then sign it. Do not leave any blanks: if the answer to a question is "0," "none," or "not applicable (N/A)," write in that response. If you need more space to answer a question or to explain your answer, attach a separate sheet of paper identified with your name, your case's docket number, and the question number.

Signed: _____ Date: _____ _____

My issues on appeal are:

1. For both you and your spouse estimate the average amount of money received from each of the following sources during the past 12 months. Adjust any amount that was received weekly, biweekly, quarterly, semiannually, or annually to show the monthly rate. Use gross amounts, that is, amounts before any deductions for taxes or otherwise.

Income source	Average monthly amount during the past 12 months	Amount expected next month
	You	**You**
Employment	$_____	$_____
Self-employment	$_____	$_____
Income from real property (such as rental income)	$_____	$_____
Interest and dividends	$_____	$_____
Gifts	$_____	$_____
Alimony	$_____	$_____
Child support	$_____	$_____
Retirement (such as social security, pensions, annuities, insurance)	$_____	$_____
Disability (such as social security, insurance payments)	$_____	$_____
Unemployment payments	$_____	$_____

Income source	Average monthly amount during the past 12 months	Amount expected next month
	You	You
Public-assistance (such as welfare)	$_____	$_____
Other (specify):_____	$_____	$_____
Total monthly income:	$_____	$_____

2. *List your employment history, most recent employer first. (Gross monthly pay is before taxes or other deductions.)*

Employer	Address	Dates of employment	Gross monthly pay
_____	_____	_____	_____
_____	_____	_____	_____
_____	_____	_____	_____

3. *List your spouse's employment history, most recent employer first. (Gross monthly pay is before taxes or other deductions.)*

Employer	Address	Dates of employment	Gross monthly pay
_____	_____	_____	_____
_____	_____	_____	_____
_____	_____	_____	_____

4. *How much cash do you and your spouse have?* $_____

Below, state any money you or your spouse have in bank accounts or in any other financial institution.

Financial institution	Type of account	Amount you have	Amount your spouse has
_____	_____	$_____	$_____
_____	_____	$_____	$_____
_____	_____	$_____	$_____

If you are a prisoner, you must attach a statement certified by the appropriate institutional officer showing all receipts, expenditures, and balances during the last six months in your institutional accounts. If you have multiple accounts, perhaps because you have been in multiple institutions, attach one certified statement of each account.

5. *List the assets, and their values, which you own or your spouse owns. Do not list clothing and ordinary household furnishings.*

Home (Value)	**Other real estate** (Value)	**Motor vehicle #1** (Value)
_____	_____	Make & year:_____
_____	_____	Model:_____
_____	_____	Registration #:_____

Motor vehicle #2 (Value) Make & year:___	**Other assets** (Value)	**Other assets** (Value)
Model: _____	_____	_____
Registration #:_	_____	_____

6. *State every person, business, or organization owing you or your spouse money, and the amount owed.*

Person owing you or your spouse money	**Amount owed to you**	**Amount owed to your spouse**
_____	_____	_____
_____	_____	_____
_____	_____	_____

7. *State the persons who rely on you or your spouse for support.*

Name [or, if under 18, initials only]	**Relationship**	**Age**
_____	_____	_____

Name [or, if under 18, initials only]	Relationship	Age
————	————	————
————	————	————

8. *Estimate the average monthly expenses of you and your family. Show separately the amounts paid by your spouse. Adjust any payments that are made weekly, biweekly, quarterly, semiannually, or annually to show the monthly rate.*

	You	**Your Spouse**
Rent or home-mortgage payment (include lot rented for mobile home)	$———	$———
Are real-estate taxes included? — Yes — No		
Is property insurance included? — Yes — No		
Utilities (electricity, heating fuel, water, sewer, and Telephone)	$———	$———
Home maintenance (repairs and upkeep)	$———	$———
Food	$———	$———
Clothing	$———	$———
Laundry and dry-cleaning	$———	$———
Medical and dental expenses	$———	$———
Transportation (not including motor vehicle payments)	$———	$———
Recreation, entertainment, newspapers, magazines, etc.	$———	$———
Insurance (not deducted from wages or included in Mortgage payments)	$———	$———
Homeowner's or renter's	$———	$———
Life	$———	$———
Health	$———	$———
Motor Vehicle	$———	$———
Other: ————————	$———	$———
Taxes (not deducted from wages or included in Mortgage payments) (specify): ————————	$———	$———
Installment payments	$———	$———

	You	**Your Spouse**
Motor Vehicle	$_____	$_____
Credit card (name): _____	$_____	$_____
Department store (name): _____	$_____	$_____
Other: _____	$_____	$_____
Alimony, maintenance, and support paid to others	$_____	$_____
Regular expenses for operation of business, profession, or farm (attach detailed statement)	$_____	$_____
Other (specify): _____	$_____	$_____
Total monthly expenses:	$_____	$_____

9. *Do you expect any major changes to your monthly income or expenses or in your assets or liabilities during the next 12 months?*

____ Yes ____ No If yes, describe on an attached sheet.

10. *Have you paid—or will you be paying—an attorney any money for services in connection with this case, including the completion of this form?* ____ Yes ____ No

If yes, how much? $_____

If yes, state the attorney's name, address, and telephone number:

_____

_____

_____

11. *Have you paid—or will you be paying—anyone other than an attorney (such as a paralegal or a typist) any money for services in connection with this case, including the completion of this form?*

____ Yes ____ No

If yes, how much? $_____

If yes, state the person's name, address, and telephone number:

_____

_____

_____

12. *Provide any other information that will help explain why you cannot pay the docket fees for your appeal.*

13. *State the city and state of your legal residence.*

_____

Your daytime phone number: (____) _____

Your age: _____ Your years of schooling: _____

Last four digits of your social-security number: _____

Form 5. Notice of Appeal to a Court of Appeals from a Judgment or Order of a District Court or a Bankruptcy Appellate Panel

United States District Court for the ....
District of ....

In re	)
	)
_____,	)
Debtor	)
	) File No. _____
_____,	)
Plaintiff	)
	)
v.	)
	)
_____,	)
Defendant	)

Notice of Appeal to United States Court of
Appeals for the .... Circuit

....................., the plaintiff [or defendant or other party] appeals to the United States Court of Appeals for the .... Circuit from the final judgment [or order or decree] of the district court for the district of .... [or bankruptcy appellate panel of the .... circuit], entered in this case on ...., 20 ..... [here describe the judgment, order, or decree] ....

The parties to the judgment [or order or decree] appealed from and the names and addresses of their respective attorneys are as follows:

Dated _____

Signed _____

Attorney for Appellant
Address: _____

_____

Form 6. Certificate of Compliance with Rule 32(a)

Certificate of Compliance With Type-Volume Limitation,
Typeface Requirements, and Type Style Requirements

1. This brief complies with the type-volume limitation of Fed. R. App. P. 32(a)(7)(B) because:

☐ this brief contains [*state the number of*] words, excluding the parts of the brief exempted by Fed. R. App. P. 32(a)(7)(B)(iii), or

☐ this brief uses a monospaced typeface and contains [*state the number of*] lines of text, excluding the parts of the brief exempted by Fed. R. App. P. 32(a)(7)(B)(iii).

2. This brief complies with the typeface requirements of Fed. R. App. P. 32(a)(5) and the type style requirements of Fed. R. App. P. 32(a)(6) because:

☐ this brief has been prepared in a proportionally spaced typeface using [*state name and version of word processing program*] in [*state font size and name of type style*], or

☐ this brief has been prepared in a monospaced typeface using [*state name and version of word processing program*] with [*state number of characters per inch and name of type style*].

(s)_____

Attorney for _____
Dated: _____

ADDITIONAL RESEARCH REFERENCES

David G. Knibb, *Federal Court of Appeals Manual: A Manual on Practice in the United States Court of Appeals*
Charles A. Wright, Arthur R. Miller, & Edward H. Cooper, *Federal Practice and Procedure* §§ 3945 to 4000
C.J.S. Federal Courts §§ 291(1) to 301(48) et seq.
West's Key Number Digest, Federal Courts ⊸741 to 956

PART VII
TITLE 28, JUDICIARY AND JUDICIAL PROCEDURE—SELECTED PROVISIONS
Including Amendments Received to October 1, 2011

Table of Sections

Sec.

144. Bias or Prejudice of Judge.
451. Definitions.
452. Courts Always Open; Powers Unrestricted by Expiration of Sessions.
455. Disqualification of Justice, Judge, or Magistrate.
636. Jurisdiction, Powers, and Temporary Assignment.
1251. Original Jurisdiction.
1253. Direct Appeals From Decisions of Three-Judge Courts.
1254. Courts of Appeals; Certiorari; Certified Questions.
1257. State Courts; Certiorari.
1291. Final Decisions of District Courts.
1292. Interlocutory Decisions.
1331. Federal Question.
1332. Diversity of Citizenship; Amount in Controversy; Costs.
1333. Admiralty, Maritime and Prize Cases.
1334. Bankruptcy Cases and Proceedings.
1335. Interpleader.
1337. Commerce and Antitrust Regulations; Amount in Controversy, Costs.
1338. Patents, Plant Variety Protection, Copyrights, Mask Works, Trademarks, and Unfair Competition
1339. Postal Matters.
1340. Internal Revenue; Customs Duties.
1343. Civil Rights and Elective Franchise.
1345. United States as Plaintiff.
1346. United States as Defendant.
1349. Corporation Organized Under Federal Law as Party.
1357. Injuries Under Federal Laws.
1359. Parties Collusively Joined or Made.
1361. Action to Compel an Officer of the United States to Perform His Duty.
1367. Supplemental Jurisdiction.
1369. Multiparty, Multiforum Jurisdiction.
1390. Scope.
1391. Venue Generally.
1397. Interpleader.
1400. Patents and Copyrights, Mask Works, and Designs
1401. Stockholder's Derivative Action.
1402. United States as Defendant.

1404.	Change of Venue.
1406.	Cure of Waiver of Defects.
1407.	Multidistrict Litigation.
1412.	Change of Venue.
1441.	Actions Removable Generally.
1442.	Federal Officers or Agencies Sued or Prosecuted.
1442a.	Members of Armed Forces Sued or Prosecuted.
1443.	Civil Rights Cases.
1445.	Nonremovable Actions.
1446.	Procedure for Removal.
1447.	Procedure After Removal Generally.
1448.	Process After Removal.
1449.	State Court Record Supplied.
1451.	Definitions.
1453.	Removal of Class Actions.
1631.	Transfer to Cure Want of Jurisdiction.
1651.	Writs.
1652.	State Laws as Rules of Decision.
1653.	Amendment of Pleadings to Show Jurisdiction.
1654.	Appearance Personally or by Counsel.
1657.	Priority of Civil Actions.
1658.	Time Limitations on the Commencement of Civil Actions Arising Under Acts of Congress.
1691.	Seal and Teste of Process.
1692.	Process and Orders Affecting Property in Different Districts.
1695.	Stockholder's Derivative Action.
1696.	Service in Foreign and International Litigation.
1697.	Service in Multiparty, Multiforum Actions.
1731.	Handwriting.
1732.	Record Made in Regular Course of Business; Photographic Copies.
1733.	Government Records and Papers; Copies.
1734.	Court Record Lost or Destroyed, Generally.
1735.	Court Record Lost or Destroyed Where United States Interested.
1738.	State and Territorial Statutes and Judicial Proceedings; Full Faith and Credit.
1739.	State and Territorial Nonjudicial Records; Full Faith and Credit.
1746.	Unsworn Declarations Under Penalty of Perjury.
1781.	Transmittal of Letter Rogatory or Request.
1782.	Assistance to Foreign and International Tribunals and to Litigants Before Such Tribunals.
1783.	Subpoena of Person in Foreign Country.
1784.	Contempt.
1785.	Subpoenas in Multiparty, Multiforum Actions.
1821.	Per Diem and Mileage Generally; Subsistence.
1826.	Recalcitrant Witnesses.
1914.	District Court; Filing and Miscellaneous Fees; Rules of Court.
1915.	Proceedings in Forma Pauperis.
1917.	District Courts; Fee on Filing Notice of or Petition for Appeal.
1920.	Taxation of Costs.

1924.	Verification of Bill of Costs.
1927.	Counsel's Liability for Excessive Costs.
1961.	Interest.
1963.	Registration of Judgments for Enforcement in Other Districts.
1964.	Constructive Notice of Pending Actions.
2071.	Rule-Making Power Generally.
2072.	Rules of Procedure and Evidence; Power to Prescribe.
2101.	Supreme Court; Time for Appeal of Certiorari; Docketing; Stay.
2104.	Reviews of State Court Decisions.
2106.	Determination.
2107.	Time for Appeal to Court of Appeals.
2111.	Harmless Error.
2201.	Creation of Remedy.
2202.	Further Relief.
2283.	Stay of State Court Proceedings.
2284.	Three-Judge Court; When Required; Composition; Procedure.
2361.	Process and Procedure.
2401.	Time for Commencing Action Against United States.
2402.	Jury Trial in Actions Against United States.
2403.	Intervention by United States or a State; Constitutional Question.
2404.	Death of Defendant in Damage Action.
2408.	Security not Required of United States.
2411.	Interest.
2412.	Costs and Fees.
2413.	Executions in Favor of United States.
2414.	Payment of Judgments and Compromise Settlements.
2415.	Time for Commencing Actions Brought by the United States.
2416.	———— Exclusions.

§ 144. Bias or Prejudice of Judge

Whenever a party to any proceeding in a district court makes and files a timely and sufficient affidavit that the judge before whom the matter is pending has a personal bias or prejudice either against him or in favor of any adverse party, such judge shall proceed no further therein, but another judge shall be assigned to hear such proceeding.

The affidavit shall state the facts and the reasons for the belief that bias or prejudice exists, and shall be filed not less than ten days before the beginning of the term at which the proceeding is to be heard, or good cause shall be shown for failure to file it within such time. A party may file only one such affidavit in any case. It shall be accompanied by a certificate of counsel of record stating that it is made in good faith.

§ 451. Definitions

As used in this title:

The term "court of the United States" includes the Supreme Court of the United States, courts of appeals, district courts constituted by chapter 5 of this title, including the Court of International Trade and any court created by Act of Congress the judges of which are entitled to hold office during good behavior.

The terms "district court" and "district court of the United States" mean the courts constituted by chapter 5 of this title.

The term "judge of the United States" includes judges of the courts of appeals, district courts, Court of International Trade and any court created by Act of Congress, the judges of which are entitled to hold office during good behavior.

The term "justice of the United States" includes the Chief Justice of the United States and the associate justices of the Supreme Court.

The term "district" and "judicial district" mean the districts enumerated in Chapter 5 of this title.

The term "department" means one of the executive departments enumerated in section 1 of Title 5, unless the context shows that such term was intended to describe the executive, legislative, or judicial branches of the government.

The term "agency" includes any department, independent establishment, commission, administration, authority, board or bureau of the United States or any corporation in which the United States has a proprietary interest, unless the context shows that such term was intended to be used in a more limited sense.

§ 452. Courts Always Open; Powers Unrestricted by Expiration of Sessions

All courts of the United States shall be deemed always open for the purpose of filing proper papers, issuing and returning process, and making motions and orders.

The continued existence or expiration of a session of court in no way affects the power of the court to do any act or take any proceeding.

§ 455. Disqualification of Justice, Judge, or Magistrate

(a) Any justice, judge, or magistrate of the United States shall disqualify himself in any proceeding in which his impartiality might reasonably be questioned.

(b) He shall also disqualify himself in the following circumstances:

(1) Where he has a personal bias or prejudice concerning a party, or personal knowledge of disputed evidentiary facts concerning the proceeding;

(2) Where in private practice he served as lawyer in the matter in controversy, or a lawyer with whom he previously practiced law served during such association as a lawyer concerning the matter, or the judge or such lawyer has been a material witness concerning it;

(3) Where he has served in governmental employment and in

such capacity participated as counsel, adviser or material witness concerning the proceeding or expressed an opinion concerning the merits of the particular case in controversy;

(4) He knows that he, individually or as a fiduciary, or his spouse or minor child residing in his household, has a financial interest in the subject matter in controversy or in a party to the proceeding, or any other interest that could be substantially affected by the outcome of the proceeding;

(5) He or his spouse, or a person within the third degree of relationship to either of them, or the spouse of such a person:

> **(i)** Is a party to the proceeding, or an officer, director, or trustee of a party;

> **(ii)** Is acting as a lawyer in the proceeding;

> **(iii)** Is known by the judge to have an interest that could be substantially affected by the outcome of the proceeding;

> **(iv)** Is to the judge's knowledge likely to be a material witness in the proceeding.

(c) A judge should inform himself about his personal and fiduciary financial interests, and make a reasonable effort to inform himself about the personal financial interests of his spouse and minor children residing in his household.

(d) For the purposes of this section the following words or phrases shall have the meaning indicated:

(1) "proceeding" includes pretrial, trial, appellate review, or other stages of litigation;

(2) the degree of relationship is calculated according to the civil law system;

(3) "fiduciary" includes such relationships as executor, administrator, trustee, and guardian;

(4) "financial interest" means ownership of a legal or equitable interest, however small, or a relationship as director, adviser, or other active participant in the affairs of a party, except that:

> **(i)** Ownership in a mutual or common investment fund that holds securities is not a "financial interest" in such securities unless the judge participates in the management of the fund;

> **(ii)** An office in an educational, religious, charitable, fraternal, or civic organization is not a "financial interest" in securities held by the organization;

> **(iii)** The proprietary interest of a policyholder in a mutual insurance company, of a depositor in a mutual savings association, or a similar proprietary interest, is a "financial interest" in the organization only if the outcome of the proceeding could substantially affect the value of the interest;

> **(iv)** Ownership of government securities is a "financial interest" in the issuer only if the outcome of the proceeding

could substantially affect the value of the securities.

(e) No justice, judge, or magistrate shall accept from the parties to the proceeding a waiver of any ground for disqualification enumerated in subsection (b). Where the ground for disqualification arises only under subsection (a), waiver may be accepted provided it is preceded by a full disclosure on the record of the basis for disqualification.

(f) Notwithstanding the preceding provisions of this section, if any justice, judge, magistrate, or bankruptcy judge to whom a matter has been assigned would be disqualified, after substantial judicial time has been devoted to the matter, because of the appearance or discovery, after the matter was assigned to him or her, that he or she individually or as a fiduciary, or his or her spouse or minor child residing in his or her household, has a financial interest in a party (other than an interest that could be substantially affected by the outcome), disqualification is not required if the justice, judge, magistrate judge, bankruptcy judge, spouse or minor child, as the case may be, divests himself or herself of the interest that provides the grounds for the disqualification.

§ 636. Jurisdiction, Powers, and Temporary Assignment

(a) Each United States magistrate judge serving under this chapter shall have within the district in which sessions are held by the court that appointed the magistrate judge, at other places where that court may function, and elsewhere as authorized by law—

(1) all powers and duties conferred or imposed upon United States commissioners by law or by the Rules of Criminal Procedure for the United States District Courts;

(2) the power to administer oaths and affirmations, issue orders pursuant to section 3142 of title 18 concerning release or detention of persons pending trial, and take acknowledgements, affidavits, and depositions;

(3) the power to conduct trials under section 3401, title 18, United States Code, in conformity with and subject to the limitations of that section;

(4) the power to enter a sentence for a petty offense; and

(5) the power to enter a sentence for a class A misdemeanor in a case in which the parties have consented.

(b) (1) Notwithstanding any provision of law to the contrary—

(A) a judge may designate a magistrate judge to hear and determine any pretrial matter pending before the court, except a motion for injunctive relief, for judgment on the pleadings, for summary judgment, to dismiss or quash an indictment or information made by the defendant, to suppress evidence in a criminal case, to dismiss or to permit maintenance of a class action, to dismiss for failure to state a claim upon which relief can be granted, and to involuntarily dismiss an action. A judge of the court may reconsider any pretrial matter under this subparagraph (A) where it has been shown that the magistrate judge's order is clearly erroneous or contrary to law.

(B) a judge may also designate a magistrate judge to conduct hearings, including evidentiary hearings, and to submit to a judge of the court proposed findings of fact and recommendations for the disposition, by a judge of the court, of any motion excepted in subparagraph (A), of applications for posttrial[1] relief made by individuals convicted of criminal offenses and of prisoner petitions challenging conditions of confinement.

(C) the magistrate judge shall file his proposed findings and recommendations under subparagraph (B) with the court and a copy shall forthwith be mailed to all parties.

Within fourteen days after being served with a copy, any party may serve and file written objections to such proposed findings and recommendations as provided by rules of court. A judge of the court shall make a de novo determination of those portions of the report or specified proposed findings or recommendations to which objection is made. A judge of the court may accept, reject, or modify, in whole or in part, the findings or recommendations made by the magistrate judge. The judge may also receive further evidence or recommit the matter to the magistrate judge with instructions.

(2) A judge may designate a magistrate judge to serve as a special master pursuant to the applicable provisions of this title and the Federal Rules of Civil Procedure for the United States district courts. A judge may designate a magistrate judge to serve as a special master in any civil case, upon consent of the parties, without regard to the provisions of rule 53(b) of the Federal Rules of Civil Procedure for the United States district courts.

(3) A magistrate judge may be assigned such additional duties as are not inconsistent with the Constitution and laws of the United States.

(4) Each district court shall establish rules pursuant to which the magistrate judges shall discharge their duties.

(c) Notwithstanding any provision of law to the contrary—

(1) Upon the consent of the parties, a full-time United States magistrate judge or a part-time United States magistrate judge who serves as a full-time judicial officer may conduct any or all proceedings in a jury or nonjury civil matter and order the entry of judgment in the case, when specially designated to exercise such jurisdiction by the district court or courts he serves. Upon the consent of the parties, pursuant to their

---

[1]So in original. Probably should   be "post-trial".

specific written request, any other part-time magistrate judge may exercise such jurisdiction, if such magistrate judge meets the bar membership requirements set forth in section 631(b)(1) and the chief judge of the district court certifies that a full-time magistrate judge is not reasonably available in accordance with guidelines established by the judicial council of the circuit. When there is more than one judge of a district court, designation under this paragraph shall be by the concurrence of a majority of all the judges of such district court, and when there is no such concurrence, then by the chief judge.

(2) If a magistrate judge is designated to exercise civil jurisdiction under paragraph (1) of this subsection, the clerk of court shall, at the time the action is filed, notify the parties of the availability of a magistrate judge to exercise such jurisdiction. The decision of the parties shall be communicated to the clerk of court. Thereafter, either the district court judge or the magistrate judge may again advise the parties of the availability of the magistrate judge, but in so doing, shall also advise the parties that they are free to withhold consent without adverse substantive consequences. Rules of court for the reference of civil matters to magistrate judges shall include procedures to protect the voluntariness of the parties' consent.

(3) Upon entry of judgment in any case referred under paragraph (1) of this subsection, an aggrieved party may appeal directly to the appropriate United States court of appeals from the judgment of the magistrate judge in the same manner as an appeal from any other judgment of a district court. The consent of the parties allows a magistrate judge designated to exercise civil jurisdiction under paragraph (1) of this subsection to direct the entry of a judgment of the district court in accordance with the Federal Rules of Civil Procedure. Nothing in this paragraph shall be construed as a limitation of any party's right to seek review by the Supreme Court of the United States.

(4) The court may, for good cause shown on its own motion, or under extraordinary circumstances shown by any party, vacate a reference of a civil matter to a magistrate judge under this subsection.

(5) The magistrate judge shall, subject to guidelines of the Judicial Conference, determine whether the record taken pursuant to this section shall be taken by electronic sound recording, by a court reporter, or by other means.

(d) The practice and procedure for the trial of cases before officers serving under this chapter shall conform to rules promulgated by the Supreme Court pursuant to section 2072 of this title.

(e) Contempt authority.—

(1) In general.—A United States magistrate judge serving under this chapter shall have within the territorial jurisdiction prescribed by the appointment of such magistrate judge the power to exercise contempt authority as set forth in this subsection.

(2) Summary criminal contempt authority.—A magistrate judge shall have the power to punish summarily by fine or imprisonment, or both, such contempt of the authority of such magistrate judge constituting misbehavior of any person in the magistrate judge's presence so as to obstruct the administration of justice. The order of contempt shall be issued under the Federal Rules of Criminal Procedure.

(3) Additional criminal contempt authority in civil consent and misdemeanor cases.—In any case in which a United States magistrate judge presides with the consent of the parties under subsection (c) of this section, and in any misdemeanor case proceeding before a magistrate judge under section 3401 of title 18, the magistrate judge shall have the power to punish, by fine or imprisonment, or both, criminal contempt constituting disobedience or resistance to the magistrate judge's lawful writ, process, order, rule, decree, or command. Disposition of such contempt shall be conducted upon notice and hearing under the Federal Rules of Criminal Procedure.

(4) Civil contempt authority in civil consent and misdemeanor cases.—In any case in which a United States magistrate judge presides with the consent of the parties under subsection (c) of this section, and in any misdemeanor case proceeding before a magistrate judge under section 3401 of title 18, the magistrate judge may exercise the civil contempt authority of the district court. This paragraph shall not be construed to limit the authority of a magistrate judge to order sanctions under any other statute, the Federal Rules of Civil Procedure, or the Federal Rules of Criminal Procedure.

(5) Criminal contempt penalties.—The sentence imposed by a magistrate judge for any criminal contempt provided for in paragraphs (2) and (3) shall not exceed the penalties for a Class C misdemeanor as set forth in sections 3581(b)(8) and 3571(b)(6) of title 18.

(6) Certification of other contempts to the district court.— Upon the commission of any such act—

(A) in any case in which a United States magistrate judge presides with the consent of the parties under subsection (c) of this section, or in any misdemeanor case proceeding before a magistrate judge under section 3401 of title 18, that may, in the opinion of the magistrate judge, constitute a serious criminal contempt punishable by penalties exceeding those set forth in paragraph (5) of this subsection, or

(B) in any other case or proceeding under subsection (a) or (b) of this section, or any other statute, where—

(i) the act committed in the magistrate judge's presence may, in the opinion of the magistrate judge, constitute a serious criminal contempt punishable by penalties exceeding those set forth in paragraph (5) of this subsection,

    (ii) the act that constitutes a criminal contempt occurs outside the presence of the magistrate judge, or

    (iii) the act constitutes a civil contempt,

the magistrate judge shall forthwith certify the facts to a district judge and may serve or cause to be served, upon any person whose behavior is brought into question under this paragraph, an order requiring such person to appear before a district judge upon a day certain to show cause why that person should not be adjudged in contempt by reason of the facts so certified. The district judge shall thereupon hear the evidence as to the act or conduct complained of and, if it is such as to warrant punishment, punish such person in the same manner and to the same extent as for a contempt committed before a district judge.

(7) *Appeals of magistrate judge contempt orders.*—The appeal of an order of contempt under this subsection shall be made to the court of appeals in cases proceeding under subsection (c) of this section. The appeal of any other order of contempt issued under this section shall be made to the district court.

(f) In an emergency and upon the concurrence of the chief judges of the districts involved, a United States magistrate judge may be temporarily assigned to perform any of the duties specified in subsection (a), (b), or (c) of this section in a judicial district other than the judicial district for which he has been appointed. No magistrate judge shall perform any of such duties in a district to which he has been temporarily assigned until an order has been issued by the chief judge of such district specifying (1) the emergency by reason of which he has been transferred, (2) the duration of his assignment, and (3) the duties which he is authorized to perform. A magistrate judge so assigned shall not be entitled to additional compensation but shall be reimbursed for actual and necessary expenses incurred in the performance of his duties in accordance with section 635.

(g) A United States magistrate judge may perform the verification function required by section 4107 of title 18, United States Code. A magistrate judge may be assigned by a judge of any United States district court to perform the verification required by section 4108 and the appointment of counsel authorized by section 4109 of title 18, United States Code, and may perform such functions beyond the territorial limits of the United States. A magistrate judge assigned such functions shall have no authority to perform any other function within the territory of a foreign country.

(h) A United States magistrate judge who has retired may, upon the consent of the chief judge of the district involved, be recalled to serve as a magistrate judge in any judicial district by the judicial council of the circuit within which such district is located.

Upon recall, a magistrate judge may receive a salary for such service in accordance with regulations promulgated by the Judicial Conference, subject to the restrictions on the payment of an annuity set forth in section 377 of this title or in subchapter III of chapter 83, and chapter 84, of title 5 which are applicable to such magistrate judge. The requirements set forth in subsections (a), (b)(3), and (d) of section 631, and paragraph (1) of subsection (b) of such section to the extent such paragraph requires membership of the bar of the location in which an individual is to serve as a magistrate judge, shall not apply to the recall of a retired magistrate judge under this subsection or section 375 of this title. Any other requirement set forth in section 631(b) shall apply to the recall of a retired magistrate judge under this subsection or section 375 of this title unless such retired magistrate judge met such requirement upon appointment or reappointment as a magistrate judge under section 361.

§ 1251. Original Jurisdiction

(a) The Supreme Court shall have original and exclusive jurisdiction of all controversies between two or more States.

(b) The Supreme Court shall have original but not exclusive jurisdiction of:

> **(1)** All actions or proceedings to which ambassadors, other public ministers, consuls, or vice consuls of foreign states are parties;

> **(2)** All controversies between the United States and a State;

> **(3)** All actions or proceedings by a State against the citizens of another State or against aliens.

§ 1253. Direct Appeals from Decisions of Three-Judge Courts

Except as otherwise provided by law, any party may appeal to the Supreme Court from an order granting or denying, after notice and hearing, an interlocutory or permanent injunction in any civil action, suit or proceeding required by any Act of Congress to be heard and determined by a district court of three judges.

§ 1254. Courts of Appeals; Certiorari; Certified Questions

Cases in the courts of appeals may be reviewed by the Supreme Court by the following methods:

> **(1)** By writ of certiorari granted upon the petition of any party to any civil or criminal case, before or after rendition of judgment or decree;

> **(2)** By certification at any time by a court of appeals of any question of law in any civil or criminal case as to which instructions are desired, and upon such certification the Supreme Court may give binding instructions or require the entire rec-

ord to be sent up for decision of the entire matter in controversy.

§ 1257. State Courts; Certiorari

(a) Final judgments or decrees rendered by the highest court of a State in which a decision could be had, may be reviewed by the Supreme Court by writ of certiorari where the validity of a treaty or statute of the United States is drawn in question or where the validity of a statute of any State is drawn in question on the ground of its being repugnant to the Constitution, treaties, or laws of the United States, or where any title, right, privilege, or immunity is specially set up or claimed under the Constitution or the treaties or statutes of, or any commission held or authority exercised under, the United States.

(b) For the purposes of this section, the term "highest court of a State" includes the District of Columbia Court of Appeals.

§ 1291. Final Decisions of District Courts

The courts of appeals (other than the United States Court of Appeals for the Federal Circuit) shall have jurisdiction of appeals from all final decisions of the district courts of the United States, the United States District Court for the District of the Canal Zone, the District Court of Guam, and the District Court of the Virgin Islands, except where a direct review may be had in the Supreme Court. The jurisdiction of the United States Court of Appeals for the Federal Circuit shall be limited to the jurisdiction described in sections 1292(c) and (d) and 1295 of this title.

§ 1292. Interlocutory Decisions

(a) Except as provided in subsections (c) and (d) of this section, the courts of appeals shall have jurisdiction of appeals from:

(1) Interlocutory orders of the district courts of the United States, the United States District Court for the District of the Canal Zone, the District Court of Guam, and the District Court of the Virgin Islands, or of the judges thereof, granting, continuing, modifying, refusing or dissolving injunctions, or refusing to dissolve or modify injunctions, except where a direct review may be had in the Supreme Court;

(2) Interlocutory orders appointing receivers, or refusing orders to wind up receiverships or to take steps to accomplish the purposes thereof, such as directing sales or other disposals of property;

(3) Interlocutory decrees of such district courts or the judges thereof determining the rights and liabilities of the parties to admiralty cases in which appeals from final decrees are allowed.

(b) When a district judge, in making in a civil action an order not otherwise appealable under this section, shall be of the opinion that such order involves a controlling question of law as to which there is substantial ground for difference of opinion and that an immediate appeal from the order may materially advance the ultimate termination of the litigation, he shall so state in writing in such order. The Court of Appeals which would have jurisdiction of an appeal of such action may thereupon, in its discretion, permit an appeal to be taken from such order, if application is made to it within ten days after the entry of the order: *Provided, however,* that application for an appeal hereunder shall not stay proceedings in the district court unless the district judge or the Court of Appeals or a judge thereof shall so order.

(c) The United States Court of Appeals for the Federal Circuit shall have exclusive jurisdiction—

(1) of an appeal from an interlocutory order or decree described in subsection (a) or (b) of this section in any case over which the court would have jurisdiction of an appeal under section 1295 of this title; and

(2) of an appeal from a judgment in a civil action for patent infringement which would otherwise be appealable to the United States Court of Appeals for the Federal Circuit and is final except for an accounting.

(d) (1) When the chief judge of the Court of International Trade issues an order under the provisions of section 256(b) of this title, or when any judge of the Court of International Trade, in issuing any other interlocutory order, includes in the order a statement that a controlling question of law is involved with respect to which there is a substantial ground for difference of opinion and that an immediate appeal from that order may materially advance the ultimate termination of the litigation, the United States Court of Appeals for the Federal Circuit may, in its discretion, permit an appeal to be taken from such order, if application is made to that Court within ten days after the entry of such order.

(2) When the chief judge of the United States Court of Federal Claims issues an order under section 798(b) of this title, or when any judge of the United States Court of Federal Claims, in issuing an interlocutory order, includes in the order a statement that a controlling question of law is involved with respect to which there is a substantial ground for difference of opinion and that an immediate appeal from that order may materially advance the ultimate termination of the litigation, the United States Court of Appeals for the Federal Circuit may, in its discretion, permit an appeal to be taken from such order, if application is made to that Court within ten days after the entry of such order.

(3) Neither the application for nor the granting of an appeal under this subsection shall stay proceedings in the Court of International Trade or in the Court of Federal Claims, as the case may be, unless a stay is ordered by a judge of the Court of International Trade or of the Court of Federal Claims or by the United States Court of Appeals for the Federal Circuit or a judge of that court.

(4) (A) The United States Court of Appeals for the Federal Circuit shall have exclusive jurisdiction of an appeal from an interlocutory order of a district court of the United States, the District Court of Guam, the District Court of the Virgin Islands, or the District Court for the Northern Mariana Islands, granting or denying, in whole or in part, a motion to transfer an action to the United States Court of Federal Claims under section 1631 of this title.

(B) When a motion to transfer an action to the Court of Federal Claims is filed in a district court, no further proceedings shall be taken in the district court until 60 days after the court has ruled upon the motion. If an appeal is taken from the district court's grant or denial of the motion, proceedings shall be further stayed until the appeal has been decided by the Court of Appeals for the Federal Circuit. The stay of proceedings in the district court shall not bar the granting of preliminary or injunctive relief, where appropriate and where expedition is reasonably necessary. However, during the period in which proceedings are stayed as provided in this subparagraph, no transfer to the Court of Federal Claims pursuant to the motion shall be carried out.

(e) The Supreme Court may prescribe rules, in accordance with section 2072 of this title, to provide for an appeal of an interlocutory decision to the courts of appeals that is not otherwise provided for under subsection (a), (b), (c), or (d).

§ 1331. Federal Question

The district courts shall have original jurisdiction of all civil actions arising under the Constitution, laws, or treaties of the United States.

§ 1332. Diversity of Citizenship; Amount in Controversy; Costs

(a) The district courts shall have original jurisdiction of all civil actions where the matter in controversy exceeds the sum or value of $75,000, exclusive of interest and costs, and is between—

(1) citizens of different States;

(2) citizens of a State and citizens or subjects of a foreign state, except that the district courts shall not have original jurisdiction under this subsection of an action between citizens of a State and citizens or subjects of a foreign state who are lawfully admitted for permanent residence in the United States and are domiciled in the same State;

(3) citizens of different States and in which citizens or subjects of a foreign state are additional parties; and

(4) a foreign state, defined in section 1603(a) of this title, as plaintiff and citizens of a State or of different States.

(b) Except when express provision therefor is otherwise made in a statute of the United States, where the plaintiff who files the case originally in the Federal courts is finally adjudged to be entitled to recover less than the sum or value of $75,000, computed without regard to any setoff or counterclaim to which the defendant may be adjudged to be entitled, and exclusive of interest and costs, the district court may deny costs to the plaintiff and, in addition, may impose costs on the plaintiff.

(c) For the purposes of this section and section 1441 of this title—

    (1) a corporation shall be deemed to be a citizen of every State and foreign state by which it has been incorporated and of the State or foreign state where it has its principal place of business, except that in any direct action against the insurer of a policy or contract of liability insurance, whether incorporated or unincorporated, to which action the insured is not joined as a party-defendant, such insurer shall be deemed a citizen of—

        (A) every State and foreign state of which the insured is a citizen;

        (B) every State and foreign state by which the insurer has been incorporated; and

        (C) the State or foreign state where the insurer has its principal place of business; and

    (2) the legal representative of the estate of a decedent shall be deemed to be a citizen only of the same State as the decedent, and the legal representative of an infant or incompetent shall be deemed to be a citizen only of the same State as the infant or incompetent.

(d) (1) In this subsection—

    (A) the term "class" means all of the class members in a class action;

    (B) the term "class action" means any civil action filed under rule 23 of the Federal Rules of Civil Procedure or similar State statute or rule of judicial procedure authorizing an action to be brought by 1 or more representative persons as a class action;

    (C) the term "class certification order" means an order issued by a court approving the treatment of some or all aspects of a civil action as a class action; and

    (D) the term "class members" means the persons (named or unnamed) who fall within the definition of the proposed or certified class in a class action.

(2) The district courts shall have original jurisdiction of any civil action in which the matter in controversy exceeds the sum or value of $5,000,000, exclusive of interest and costs, and is a class action in which—

    (A) any member of a class of plaintiffs is a citizen of a State different from any defendant;

(B) any member of a class of plaintiffs is a foreign state or a citizen or subject of a foreign state and any defendant is a citizen of a State; or

(C) any member of a class of plaintiffs is a citizen of a State and any defendant is a foreign state or a citizen or subject of a foreign state.

(3) A district court may, in the interests of justice and looking at the totality of the circumstances, decline to exercise jurisdiction under paragraph (2) over a class action in which greater than one-third but less than two-thirds of the members of all proposed plaintiff classes in the aggregate and the primary defendants are citizens of the State in which the action was originally filed based on consideration of—

(A) whether the claims asserted involve matters of national or interstate interest;

(B) whether the claims asserted will be governed by laws of the State in which the action was originally filed or by the laws of other States;

(C) whether the class action has been pleaded in a manner that seeks to avoid Federal jurisdiction;

(D) whether the action was brought in a forum with a distinct nexus with the class members, the alleged harm, or the defendants;

(E) whether the number of citizens of the State in which the action was originally filed in all proposed plaintiff classes in the aggregate is substantially larger than the number of citizens from any other State, and the citizenship of the other members of the proposed class is dispersed among a substantial number of States; and

(F) whether, during the 3-year period preceding the filing of that class action, 1 or more other class actions asserting the same or similar claims on behalf of the same or other persons have been filed.

(4) A district court shall decline to exercise jurisdiction under paragraph (2)—

(A) (i) over a class action in which—

(I) greater than two-thirds of the members of all proposed plaintiff classes in the aggregate are citizens of the State in which the action was originally filed;

(II) at least 1 defendant is a defendant—

(aa) from whom significant relief is sought by members of the plaintiff class;

(bb) whose alleged conduct forms a significant basis for the claims asserted by the proposed plaintiff class; and

(cc) who is a citizen of the State in which the action was originally filed; and

(III) principal injuries resulting from the alleged

conduct or any related conduct of each defendant were incurred in the State in which the action was originally filed; and

(ii) during the 3-year period preceding the filing of that class action, no other class action has been filed asserting the same or similar factual allegations against any of the defendants on behalf of the same or other persons; or

(B) two-thirds or more of the members of all proposed plaintiff classes in the aggregate, and the primary defendants, are citizens of the State in which the action was originally filed.

(5) Paragraphs (2) through (4) shall not apply to any class action in which—

(A) the primary defendants are States, State officials, or other governmental entities against whom the district court may be foreclosed from ordering relief; or

(B) the number of members of all proposed plaintiff classes in the aggregate is less than 100.

(6) In any class action, the claims of the individual class members shall be aggregated to determine whether the matter in controversy exceeds the sum or value of $5,000,000, exclusive of interest and costs.

(7) Citizenship of the members of the proposed plaintiff classes shall be determined for purposes of paragraphs (2) through (6) as of the date of filing of the complaint or amended complaint, or, if the case stated by the initial pleading is not subject to Federal jurisdiction, as of the date of service by plaintiffs of an amended pleading, motion, or other paper, indicating the existence of Federal jurisdiction.

(8) This subsection shall apply to any class action before or after the entry of a class certification order by the court with respect to that action.

(9) Paragraph (2) shall not apply to any class action that solely involves a claim—

(A) concerning a covered security as defined under 16(f)(3)[1] of the Securities Act of 1933 (15 U.S.C. 78p(f)(3)) and section 28(f)(5)(E) of the Securities Exchange Act of 1934 (15 U.S.C. 78bb(f)(5)(E));

(B) that relates to the internal affairs or governance of a corporation or other form of business enterprise and that arises under or by virtue of the laws of the State in which such corporation or business enterprise is incorporated or organized; or

(C) that relates to the rights, duties (including fiduciary duties), and obligations relating to or created by or pursuant to any security (as defined under section 2(a)(1) of the Securities Act of 1933 (15 U.S.C. 77b(a)(1)) and the regulations issued thereunder).

(10) For purposes of this subsection and section 1453, an unincorporated association shall be deemed to be a citizen of the State where it has its principal place of business and the State under whose laws it is organized.

(11) (A) For purposes of this subsection and section 1453, a mass action shall be deemed to be a class action removable under paragraphs (2) through (10) if it otherwise meets the provisions of those paragraphs.

(B) (i) As used in subparagraph (A), the term "mass action" means any civil action (except a civil action within the scope of section 1711(2)) in which monetary relief claims of 100 or more persons are proposed to be tried jointly on the ground that the plaintiffs' claims involve common questions of law or fact, except that jurisdiction shall exist only over those plaintiffs whose claims in a mass action satisfy the jurisdictional amount requirements under subsection (a).

(ii) As used in subparagraph (A), the term "mass action" shall not include any civil action in which—

(I) all of the claims in the action arise from an event or occurrence in the State in which the action was filed, and that allegedly resulted in injuries in that State or in States contiguous to that State;

(II) the claims are joined upon motion of a defendant;

(III) all of the claims in the action are asserted on behalf of the general public (and not on behalf of individual claimants or members of a purported class) pursuant to a State statute specifically authorizing such action; or

(IV) the claims have been consolidated or coordinated solely for pretrial proceedings.

(C) (i) Any action(s) removed to Federal court pursuant to this subsection shall not thereafter be transferred to any other court pursuant to section 1407, or the rules promulgated thereunder, unless a majority of the plaintiffs in the action request transfer pursuant to section 1407.

(ii) This subparagraph will not apply—

(I) to cases certified pursuant to rule 23 of the Federal Rules of Civil Procedure; or

(II) if plaintiffs propose that the action proceed as a class action pursuant to rule 23 of the Federal Rules of Civil Procedure.

(D) The limitations periods on any claims asserted in a mass action that is removed to Federal court pursuant to this subsection shall be deemed tolled during the period that the action is pending in Federal court.

(e) The word "States", as used in this section, includes the Territories, the District of Columbia, and the Commonwealth of Puerto Rico.

§ 1333. Admiralty, Maritime and Prize Cases

The district courts shall have original jurisdiction, exclusive of the courts of the States, of:

    (1) Any civil case of admiralty or maritime jurisdiction, saving to suitors in all cases all other remedies to which they are otherwise entitled.

    (2) Any prize brought into the United States and all proceedings for the condemnation of property taken as prize.

§ 1334. Bankruptcy Cases and Proceedings

(a) Except as provided in subsection (b) of this section, the district courts shall have original and exclusive jurisdiction of all cases under title 11.

(b) Except as provided in subsection (e)(2), and notwithstanding any Act of Congress that confers exclusive jurisdiction on a court or courts other than the district courts, the district courts shall have original but not exclusive jurisdiction of all civil proceedings arising under title 11, or arising in or related to cases under title 11.

(c) (1) Except with respect to a case under chapter 15 of title 11, nothing in this section prevents a district court in the interest of justice, or in the interest of comity with State courts or respect for State law, from abstaining from hearing a particular proceeding arising under title 11 or arising in or related to a case under title 11.

    (2) Upon timely motion of a party in a proceeding based upon a State law claim or State law cause of action, related to a case under title 11 but not arising under title 11 or arising in a case under title 11, with respect to which an action could not have been commenced in a court of the United States absent jurisdiction under this section, the district court shall abstain from hearing such proceeding if an action is commenced, and can be timely adjudicated, in a State forum of appropriate jurisdiction.

(d) Any decision to abstain or not to abstain made under subsection (c) (other than a decision not to abstain in a proceeding described in subsection (c)(2)) is not reviewable by appeal or otherwise by the court of appeals under section 158(d), 1291, or 1292 of this title or by the Supreme Court of the United States under section 1254 of this title. Subsection (c) and this subsection shall not be construed to limit the applicability of the stay provided for by section 362 of title 11, United States Code, as such section applies to an action affecting the property of the estate in bankruptcy.

(e) The district court in which a case under title 11 is commenced or is pending shall have exclusive jurisdiction—

(1) of all the property, wherever located, of the debtor as of the commencement of such case, and of property of the estate; and

(2) over all claims or causes of action that involve construction of section 327 of title 11, United States Code, or rules relating to disclosure requirements under section 327.

§ 1335. Interpleader

(a) The district courts shall have original jurisdiction of any civil action of interpleader or in the nature of interpleader filed by any person, firm, or corporation, association, or society having in his or its custody or possession money or property of the value of $500 or more, or having issued a note, bond, certificate, policy of insurance, or other instrument of value or amount of $500 or more, or providing for the delivery or payment or the loan of money or property of such amount or value, or being under any obligation written or unwritten to the amount of $500 or more, if

(1) Two or more adverse claimants, of diverse citizenship as defined in subsection (a) or (d) of section 1332 of this title, are claiming or may claim to be entitled to such money or property, or to any one or more of the benefits arising by virtue of any note, bond, certificate, policy or other instrument, or arising by virtue of any such obligation; and if (2) the plaintiff has deposited such money or property or has paid the amount of or the loan or other value of such instrument or the amount due under such obligation into the registry of the court, there to abide the judgment of the court, or has given bond payable to the clerk of the court in such amount and with such surety as the court or judge may deem proper, conditioned upon the compliance by the plaintiff with the future order or judgment of the court with respect to the subject matter of the controversy.

(b) Such an action may be entertained although the titles or claims of the conflicting claimants do not have a common origin, or are not identical, but are adverse to and independent of one another.

§ 1337. Commerce and Antitrust Regulations; Amount in Controversy, Costs

(a) The district courts shall have original jurisdiction of any civil action or proceeding arising under any Act of Congress regulating commerce or protecting trade and commerce against restraints and monopolies: Provided, however, That the district courts shall have original jurisdiction of an action brought under section 11706 or 14706 of title 49, only if the matter in controversy for each receipt or bill of lading exceeds $10,000, exclusive of interest and costs.

(b) Except when express provision therefor is otherwise made in a statute of the United States, where a plaintiff who files the case under section 11706 or 14706 of title 49, originally in the Federal courts is finally adjudged to be entitled to recover less than the sum or value of $10,000, computed without regard to any setoff or counterclaim to which the defendant may be adjudged to be entitled, and exclusive of any interest and costs, the district court may deny costs to the plaintiff and, in addition, may impose costs on the plaintiff.

(c) The district courts shall not have jurisdiction under this section of any matter within the exclusive jurisdiction of the Court of International Trade under chapter 95 of this title.

§ 1338. Patents, Plant Variety Protection, Copyrights, Mask Works, Designs, Trademarks, and Unfair Competition

(a) The district courts shall have original jurisdiction of any civil action arising under any Act of Congress relating to patents, plant variety protection, copyrights and trademarks. No State court shall have jurisdiction over any claim for relief arising under any Act of Congress relating to patents, plant variety protection, or copyrights. For purposes of this subsection, the term "State" includes any State of the United States, the District of Columbia, the Commonwealth of Puerto Rico, the United States Virgin Islands, American Samoa, Guam, and the Northern Mariana Islands.

(b) The district courts shall have original jurisdiction of any civil action asserting a claim of unfair competition when joined with a substantial and related claim under the copyright, patent, plant variety protection or trademark laws.

(c) Subsections (a) and (b) apply to exclusive rights in mask works under chapter 9 of title 17, and to exclusive rights in designs under chapter 13 of title 17, to the same extent as such subsections apply to copyrights.

§ 1339. Postal matters

The district courts shall have original jurisdiction of any civil action arising under any Act of Congress relating to the postal service.

§ 1340. Internal Revenue; Customs Duties

The district courts shall have original jurisdiction of any civil action arising under any Act of Congress providing for internal revenue, or revenue from imports or tonnage except matters within the jurisdiction of the Court of International Trade.

§ 1343. Civil Rights and Elective Franchise

(a) The district courts shall have original jurisdiction of any civil action authorized by law to be commenced by any person:

  (1) To recover damages for injury to his person or property, or because of the deprivation of any right or privilege of a citizen

1539

of the United States, by any act done in furtherance of any conspiracy mentioned in section 1985 of Title 42;

(2) To recover damages from any person who fails to prevent or to aid in preventing any wrongs mentioned in section 1985 of Title 42 which he had knowledge were about to occur and power to prevent;

(3) To redress the deprivation, under color of any State law, statute, ordinance, regulation, custom or usage, of any right, privilege or immunity secured by the Constitution of the United States or by any Act of Congress providing for equal rights of citizens or of all persons within the jurisdiction of the United States;

(4) To recover damages or to secure equitable or other relief under any Act of Congress providing for the protection of civil rights, including the right to vote.

(b) For purposes of this section—

(1) the District of Columbia shall be considered to be a State; and

(2) any Act of Congress applicable exclusively to the District of Columbia shall be considered to be a statute of the District of Columbia.

§ 1345. United States As Plaintiff

Except as otherwise provided by Act of Congress, the district courts shall have original jurisdiction of all civil actions, suits or proceedings commenced by the United States, or by any agency or officer thereof expressly authorized to sue by Act of Congress.

§ 1346. United States As Defendant

(a) The district courts shall have original jurisdiction, concurrent with the United States Court of Federal Claims, of:

(1) Any civil action against the United States for the recovery of any internal-revenue tax alleged to have been erroneously or illegally assessed or collected, or any penalty claimed to have been collected without authority or any sum alleged to have been excessive or in any manner wrongfully collected under the internal-revenue laws;

(2) Any other civil action or claim against the United States, not exceeding $10,000 in amount, founded either upon the Constitution, or any Act of Congress, or any regulation of an executive department, or upon any express or implied contract with the United States, or for liquidated or unliquidated damages in cases not sounding in tort, except that the district courts shall not have jurisdiction of any civil action or claim against the United States founded upon any express or implied contract with the United States or for liquidated or unliquidated damages in cases not sounding in tort which are subject to sections 7104(b)(1) and 7107(a)(1) of title 41. For the purpose of this paragraph, an express or implied contract with the Army and Air Force Exchange Service, Navy Exchanges, Marine Corps Exchanges, Coast Guard Exchanges, or Exchange Councils of the National Aeronautics and Space Administration shall be considered an express or implied contract with the United States.

(b) (1) Subject to the provisions of chapter 171 of this title, the district courts, together with the United States District Court for the District of the Canal Zone and the District Court of the Virgin Islands, shall have exclusive jurisdiction of civil actions on claims against the United States, for money damages, accruing on and after January 1, 1945, for injury or loss of property, or personal injury or death caused by the negligent or wrongful act or omission of any employee of the Government while acting within the scope of his office or employment, under circumstances where the United States, if a private person, would be liable to the claimant in accordance with the law of the place where the act or omission occurred.

(2) No person convicted of a felony who is incarcerated while awaiting sentencing or while serving a sentence may bring a civil action against the United States or an agency, officer, or employee of the Government, for mental or emotional injury suffered while in custody without a prior showing of physical injury.

(c) The jurisdiction conferred by this section includes jurisdiction of any set-off, counterclaim, or other claim or demand whatever on the part of the United States against any plaintiff commencing an action under this section.

(d) The district courts shall not have jurisdiction under this section of any civil action or claim for a pension.

(e) The district courts shall have original jurisdiction of any civil action against the United States provided in section 6226, 6228(a), 7426, or 7428 (in the case of the United States district court for the District of Columbia) or section 7429 of the Internal Revenue Code of 1986.

(f) The district courts shall have exclusive original jurisdiction of civil actions under section 2409a to quiet title to an estate or interest in real property in which an interest is claimed by the United States.

(g) Subject to the provisions of chapter 179, the district courts of the United States shall have exclusive jurisdiction over any civil action commenced under section 453(2) of title 3, by a covered employee under chapter 5 of such title.

§ 1349. Corporation Organized under Federal Law As Party

The district courts shall not have jurisdiction of any civil action by or against any corporation upon the ground that it was incorporated by or under an Act of Congress, unless the United

States is the owner of more than one-half of its capital stock.

§ 1357. Injuries under Federal Laws

The district courts shall have original jurisdiction of any civil action commenced by any person to recover damages for any injury to his person or property on account of any act done by him, under any Act of Congress, for the protection or collection of any of the revenues, or to enforce the right of citizens of the United States to vote in any State.

§ 1359. Parties Collusively Joined or Made

A district court shall not have jurisdiction of a civil action in which any party, by assignment or otherwise, has been improperly or collusively made or joined to invoke the jurisdiction of such court.

§ 1361. Action to Compel an Officer of the United States to Perform His Duty

The district courts shall have original jurisdiction of any action in the nature of mandamus to compel an officer or employee of the United States or any agency thereof to perform a duty owed to the plaintiff.

§ 1367. Supplemental Jurisdiction

(a) Except as provided in subsections (b) and (c) or as expressly provided otherwise by Federal statute, in any civil action of which the district courts have original jurisdiction, the district courts shall have supplemental jurisdiction over all other claims that are so related to claims in the action within such original jurisdiction that they form part of the same case or controversy under Article III of the United States Constitution. Such supplemental jurisdiction shall include claims that involve the joinder or intervention of additional parties.

(b) In any civil action of which the district courts have original jurisdiction founded solely on section 1332 of this title, the district courts shall not have supplemental jurisdiction under subsection (a) over claims by plaintiffs against persons made parties under Rule 14, 19, 20, or 24 of the Federal Rules of Civil Procedure, or over claims by persons proposed to be joined as plaintiffs under Rule 19 of such rules, or seeking to intervene as plaintiffs under Rule 24 of such rules, when exercising supplemental jurisdiction over such claims would be inconsistent with the jurisdictional requirements of section 1332.

(c) The district courts may decline to exercise supplemental jurisdiction over a claim under subsection (a) if—

    (1) the claim raises a novel or complex issue of State law,

    (2) the claim substantially predominates over the claim or claims over which the district court has original jurisdiction,

(3) the district court has dismissed all claims over which it has original jurisdiction, or

(4) in exceptional circumstances, there are other compelling reasons for declining jurisdiction.

(d) The period of limitations for any claim asserted under subsection (a), and for any other claim in the same action that is voluntarily dismissed at the same time as or after the dismissal of the claim under subsection (a), shall be tolled while the claim is pending and for a period of 30 days after it is dismissed unless State law provides for a longer tolling period.

(e) As used in this section, the term "State" includes the District of Columbia, the Commonwealth of Puerto Rico, and any territory or possession of the United States.

§ 1369. Multiparty, Multiforum Jurisdiction

(a) In general. —The district courts shall have original jurisdiction of any civil action involving minimal diversity between adverse parties that arises from a single accident, where at least 75 natural persons have died in the accident at a discrete location, if—

(1) a defendant resides in a State and a substantial part of the accident took place in another State or other location, regardless of whether that defendant is also a resident of the State where a substantial part of the accident took place;

(2) any two defendants reside in different States, regardless of whether such defendants are also residents of the same State or States; or

(3) substantial parts of the accident took place in different States.

(b) Limitation of jurisdiction of district courts. —The district court shall abstain from hearing any civil action described in subsection (a) in which—

(1) the substantial majority of all plaintiffs are citizens of a single State of which the primary defendants are also citizens; and

(2) the claims asserted will be governed primarily by the laws of that State.

(c) Special rules and definitions. —For purposes of this section—

(1) minimal diversity exists between adverse parties if any party is a citizen of a State and any adverse party is a citizen of another State, a citizen or subject of a foreign state, or a foreign state as defined in section 1603(a) of this title;

(2) a corporation is deemed to be a citizen of any State, and a citizen or subject of any foreign state, in which it is incorporated or has its principal place of business, and is deemed to be a resident of any State in which it is incorporated or licensed to do business or is doing business;

    (3) the term "injury" means—

        (A) physical harm to a natural person; and

        (B) physical damage to or destruction of tangible property, but only if physical harm described in subparagraph (A) exists;

    (4) the term "accident" means a sudden accident, or a natural event culminating in an accident, that results in death incurred at a discrete location by at least 75 natural persons; and

    (5) the term "State" includes the District of Columbia, the Commonwealth of Puerto Rico, and any territory or possession of the United States.

(d) Intervening parties. —In any action in a district court which is or could have been brought, in whole or in part, under this section, any person with a claim arising from the accident described in subsection (a) shall be permitted to intervene as a party plaintiff in the action, even if that person could not have brought an action in a district court as an original matter.

(e) Notification of judicial panel on multidistrict litigation. —A district court in which an action under this section is pending shall promptly notify the judicial panel on multidistrict litigation of the pendency of the action.

§ 1390. Scope

(a) **Venue defined**.—As used in this chapter, the term "venue" refers to the geographic specification of the proper court or courts for the litigation of a civil action that is within the subject-matter jurisdiction of the district courts in general, and does not refer to any grant or restriction of subject-matter jurisdiction providing for a civil action to be adjudicated only by the district court for a particular district or districts.

(b) **Exclusion of certain cases**.—Except as otherwise provided by law, this chapter shall not govern the venue of a civil action in which the district court exercises the jurisdiction conferred by section 1333, except that such civil actions may be transferred between district courts as provided in this chapter.

(c) **Clarification regarding cases removed from state courts**.—This chapter shall not determine the district court to which a civil action pending in a State court may be removed, but shall govern the transfer of an action so removed as between districts and divisions of the United States district courts.

§ 1391. Venue Generally

(a) **Applicability of section**.—Except as otherwise provided by law—

    (1) this section shall govern the venue of all civil actions brought in district courts of the United States; and

    (2) the proper venue for a civil action shall be determined

without regard to whether the action is local or transitory in nature.

(b) **Venue in general**.—A civil action may be brought in—

(1) a judicial district in which any defendant resides, if all defendants are residents of the State in which the district is located;

(2) a judicial district in which a substantial part of the events or omissions giving rise to the claim occurred, or a substantial part of property that is the subject of the action is situated; or

(3) if there is no district in which an action may otherwise be brought as provided in this section, any judicial district in which any defendant is subject to the court's personal jurisdiction with respect to such action.

(c) **Residency**.—For all venue purposes—

(1) a natural person, including an alien lawfully admitted for permanent residence in the United States, shall be deemed to reside in the judicial district in which that person is domiciled;

(2) an entity with the capacity to sue and be sued in its common name under applicable law, whether or not incorporated, shall be deemed to reside, if a defendant, in any judicial district in which such defendant is subject to the court's personal jurisdiction with respect to the civil action in question and, if a plaintiff, only in the judicial district in which it maintains its principal place of business; and

(3) a defendant not resident in the United States may be sued in any judicial district, and the joinder of such a defendant shall be disregarded in determining where the action may be brought with respect to other defendants.

(d) **Residency of corporations in states with multiple districts**.—For purposes of venue under this chapter, in a State which has more than one judicial district and in which a defendant that is a corporation is subject to personal jurisdiction at the time an action is commenced, such corporation shall be deemed to reside in any district in that State within which its contacts would be sufficient to subject it to personal jurisdiction if that district were a separate State, and, if there is no such district, the corporation shall be deemed to reside in the district within which it has the most significant contacts.

(e) **Actions where defendant is officer or employee of the united states**.—(1) **IN GENERAL**.—A civil action in which a defendant is an officer or employee of the United States or any agency thereof acting in his official capacity or under color of legal authority, or an agency of the United States, or the United States, may, except as otherwise provided by law, be brought in any judicial district in which (A) a defendant in the action resides, (B) a substantial part of the events or omissions giving rise to the claim occurred, or a substantial part of property that is the subject of the action is situated, or (C) the plaintiff resides if no real property is involved in the action. Additional persons may be joined as parties to any such action in accordance with the Federal Rules of Civil Procedure and with such other venue requirements as would be applicable if the United States or one of its officers, employees, or agencies were not a party.

(2) **Service**.—The summons and complaint in such an action shall be served as provided by the Federal Rules of Civil Procedure except that the delivery of the summons and complaint to the officer or agency as required by the rules may be made by certified mail beyond the territorial limits of the district in which the action is brought.

(f) **Civil actions against a foreign state**.—A civil action against a foreign state as defined in section 1603(a) of this title may be brought—

    (1) in any judicial district in which a substantial part of the events or omissions giving rise to the claim occurred, or a substantial part of property that is the subject of the action is situated;

    (2) in any judicial district in which the vessel or cargo of a foreign state is situated, if the claim is asserted under section 1605(b) of this title;

    (3) in any judicial district in which the agency or instrumentality is licensed to do business or is doing business, if the action is brought against an agency or instrumentality of a foreign state as defined in section 1603(b) of this title; or

    (4) in the United States District Court for the District of Columbia if the action is brought against a foreign state or political subdivision thereof.

(g) **Multiparty, multiforum litigation**.—A civil action in which jurisdiction of the district court is based upon section 1369 of this title may be brought in any district in which any defendant resides or in which a substantial part of the accident giving rise to the action took place.

§ 1397. Interpleader

Any civil action of interpleader or in the nature of interpleader under section 1335 of this title may be brought in the judicial district in which one or more of the claimants reside.

§ 1400. Patents and Copyrights, Mask Works, and Designs

(a) Civil actions, suits, or proceedings arising under any Act of Congress relating to copyrights or exclusive rights in mask works or designs may be instituted in the district in which the defendant or his agent resides or may be found.

(b) Any civil action for patent infringement may be brought in the judicial district where the defendant resides, or where the defendant has committed acts of infringement and has a regular and established place of business.

§ 1401. Stockholder's Derivative Action

Any civil action by a stockholder on behalf of his corporation may be prosecuted in any judicial district where the corporation might have sued the same defendants.

§ 1402. United States As Defendant

(a) Any civil action in a district court against the United States under subsection (a) of section 1346 of this title may be prosecuted only:

(1) Except as provided in paragraph (2), in the judicial district where the plaintiff resides;

(2) In the case of a civil action in a district court by a corporation under paragraph (1) of subsection (a) of section 1346, in the judicial district in which is located the principal place of business or principal office or agency of the corporation; or if it has no principal place of business or principal office or agency in any judicial district (A) in the judicial district in which is located the office to which was made the return of the tax in respect of which the claim is made, or (B) if no return was made, in the judicial district in which lies the District of Columbia. Notwithstanding the foregoing provisions of this paragraph a district court, for the convenience of the parties and witnesses, in the interest of justice, may transfer any such action to any other district or division.

(b) Any civil action on a tort claim against the United States under subsection (b) of section 1346 of this title may be prosecuted only in the judicial district where the plaintiff resides or wherein the act or omission complained of occurred.

(c) Any civil action against the United States under subsection (e) of section 1346 of this title may be prosecuted only in the judicial district where the property is situated at the time of levy, or if no levy is made, in the judicial district in which the event occurred which gave rise to the cause of action.

(d) Any civil action under section 2409a to quiet title to an estate or interest in real property in which an interest is claimed by the United States shall be brought in the district court of the district where the property is located or, if located in different districts, in any of such districts.

§ 1404. Change of Venue

(a) For the convenience of parties and witnesses, in the interest of justice, a district court may transfer any civil action to any other district or division where it might have been brought or to any district or division to which all parties have consented.

(b) Upon motion, consent or stipulation of all parties, any action, suit or proceeding of a civil nature or any motion or hearing thereof, may be transferred, in the discretion of the court, from the division in which pending to any other division in the same district. Transfer of proceedings in rem brought by or on behalf of the United States may be transferred under this section without the consent of the United States where all other parties request transfer.

(c) A district court may order any civil action to be tried at any place within the division in which it is pending.

(d) Transfers from a district court of the United States to the District Court of Guam, the District Court for the Northern Mariana Islands, or the District Court of the Virgin Islands shall not be permitted under this section. As otherwise used in this section, "district court" includes the District Court of Guam, the District Court for the Northern Mariana Islands, and the District Court of the Virgin Islands, and the term "district" includes the territorial jurisdiction of that court.

§ 1406. Cure or Waiver of Defects

(a) The district court of a district in which is filed a case laying venue in the wrong division or district shall dismiss, or if it be in the interest of justice, transfer such case to any district or division in which it could have been brought.

(b) Nothing in this chapter shall impair the jurisdiction of a district court of any matter involving a party who does not interpose timely and sufficient objection to the venue.

(c) As used in this section, "district court" includes the District Court of Guam, the District Court for the Northern Mariana Islands, and the District Court of the Virgin Islands, and the term "district" includes the territorial jurisdiction of that court.

§ 1407. Multidistrict Litigation

[Note to Reader: See Part V of this text.]

§ 1412. Change of Venue

A district court may transfer a case or proceeding under title 11 to a district court for another district, in the interest of justice or for the convenience of the parties.

§ 1441. Removal of civil actions

(a) Generally.— Except as otherwise expressly provided by Act of Congress, any civil action brought in a State court of which the district courts of the United States have original jurisdiction, may be removed by the defendant or the defendants, to the district court of the United States for the district and division embracing the place where such action is pending.

(b) Removal based on diversity of citizenship.—(1) In determining whether a civil action is removable on the basis of the jurisdiction under section 1332(a) of this title, the citizenship of defendants sued under fictitious names shall be disregarded.

(2) A civil action otherwise removable solely on the basis of the jurisdiction under section 1332(a) of this title may not be removed if any of the parties in interest properly joined and served as defendants is a citizen of the State in which such action is brought.

(c) Joinder of federal law claims and state law claims.—**(1)** If a civil action includes—

    (A) a claim arising under the Constitution, laws, or treaties of the United States (within the meaning of section 1331 of this title), and

    (B) a claim not within the original or supplemental jurisdiction of the district court or a claim that has been made nonremovable by statute,

the entire action may be removed if the action would be removable without the inclusion of the claim described in subparagraph (B).

(2) Upon removal of an action described in paragraph (1), the district court shall sever from the action all claims described in paragraph (1)(B) and shall remand the severed claims to the State court from which the action was removed. Only defendants against whom a claim described in paragraph (1)(A) has been asserted are required to join in or consent to the removal under paragraph (1).

(d) Actions against foreign states.—Any civil action brought in a State court against a foreign state as defined in section 1603(a) of this title may be removed by the foreign state to the district court of the United States for the district and division embracing the place where such action is pending. Upon removal the action shall be tried by the court without jury. Where removal is based upon this subsection, the time limitations of section 1446(b) of this chapter may be enlarged at any time for cause shown.

(e) Multiparty, multiforum jurisdiction.—**(1)** Notwithstanding the provisions of subsection (b) of this section, a defendant in a civil action in a State court may remove the action to the district court of the United States for the district and division embracing the place where the action is pending if—

    (A) the action could have been brought in a United States district court under section 1369 of this title; or

    (B) the defendant is a party to an action which is or could have been brought, in whole or in part, under section 1369 in a United States district court and arises from the same accident as the action in State court, even if the action to be removed could not have been brought in a district court as an original matter.

The removal of an action under this subsection shall be made in accordance with section 1446 of this title, except that a notice of removal may also be filed before trial of the action in State court within 30 days after the date on which the defendant first becomes a party to an action under section 1369 in a United States district court that arises from the same accident as the action in State court, or at a later time with leave of the district court.

(2) Whenever an action is removed under this subsection and the district court to which it is removed or transferred under section 1407(j) has made a liability determination requiring further proceedings as to damages, the district court shall remand the action to the State court from which it had been removed for the determination of damages, unless the court finds that, for the convenience of parties and witnesses and in the interest of justice, the action should be retained for the determination of damages.

(3) Any remand under paragraph (2) shall not be effective until 60 days after the district court has issued an order determining liability and has certified its intention to remand the removed action for the determination of damages. An appeal with respect to the liability determination of the district court may be taken during that 60-day period to the court of appeals with appellate jurisdiction over the district court. In the event a party files such an appeal, the remand shall not be effective until the appeal has been finally disposed of. Once the remand has become effective, the liability determination shall not be subject to further review by appeal or otherwise.

(4) Any decision under this subsection concerning remand for the determination of damages shall not be reviewable by appeal or otherwise.

(5) An action removed under this subsection shall be deemed to be an action under section 1369 and an action in which jurisdiction is based on section 1369 of this title for purposes of this section and sections 1407, 1697, and 1785 of this title.

(6) Nothing in this subsection shall restrict the authority of the district court to transfer or dismiss an action on the ground of inconvenient forum.

(f) DERIVATIVE REMOVAL JURISDICTION.—The court to which a civil action is removed under this section is not precluded from hearing and determining any claim in such civil action because the State court from which such civil action is removed did not have jurisdiction over that claim.

§ 1442. Federal Officers or Agencies Sued or Prosecuted

(a) A civil action or criminal prosecution that is commenced in a State court and that is against or directed to any of the following may be removed by them to the district court of the United States for the district and division embracing the place wherein it is pending:

(1) The United States or any agency thereof or any officer (or any person acting under that officer) of the United States or of any agency thereof, in an official or individual capacity, for or relating to any act under color of such office or on account of any right, title or authority claimed under any Act of Congress for the apprehension or punishment of criminals or the collection of the revenue.

(2) A property holder whose title is derived from any such officer, where such action or prosecution affects the validity of any law of the United States.

(3) Any officer of the courts of the United States, for or relating to any act under color of office or in the performance of his duties;

(4) Any officer of either House of Congress, for or relating to any act in the discharge of his official duty under an order of such House.

(b) A personal action commenced in any State court by an alien against any citizen of a State who is, or at the time the alleged action accrued was, a civil officer of the United States and is a nonresident of such State, wherein jurisdiction is obtained by the State court by personal service of process, may be removed by the defendant to the district court of the United States for the district and division in which the defendant was served with process.

(c) As used in subsection (a), the terms "civil action" and "criminal prosecution" include any proceeding (whether or not ancillary to another proceeding) to the extent that in such proceeding a judicial order, including a subpoena for testimony or documents, is sought or issued. If removal is sought for a proceeding described in the previous sentence, and there is no other basis for removal, only that proceeding may be removed to the district court.

§ 1442a. Members of Armed Forces Sued or Prosecuted

A civil or criminal prosecution in a court of a State of the United States against a member of the armed forces of the United States on account of an act done under color of his office or status, or in respect to which he claims any right, title, or authority under a law of the United States respecting the armed forces thereof, or under the law of war, may at any time before the trial or final hearing thereof be removed for trial into the district court of the United States for the district where it is pending in the manner prescribed by law, and it shall thereupon be entered on the docket of the district court, which shall proceed as if the cause had been originally commenced therein and shall have full power to hear and determine the cause.

§ 1443. Civil Rights Cases

Any of the following civil actions or criminal prosecutions, commenced in a State court may be removed by the defendant to the district court of the United States for the district and division embracing the place wherein it is pending:

(1) Against any person who is denied or cannot enforce in the courts of such State a right under any law providing for the equal civil rights of citizens of the United States, or of all persons within the jurisdiction thereof;

(2) For any act under color of authority derived from any law providing for equal rights, or for refusing to do any act on the ground that it would be inconsistent with such law.

§ 1445. Nonremovable Actions

(a) A civil action in any State court against a railroad or its receivers or trustees, arising under sections 1-4 and 5-10 of the Act of April 22, 1908 (45 U.S.C. 51 to 54, 55 to 60), may not be removed to any district court of the United States.

(b) A civil action in any State court against a carrier or its receivers or trustees to recover damages for delay, loss, or injury of shipments, arising under section 11706 or 14706 of title 49, may not be removed to any district court of the United States unless the matter in controversy exceeds $10,000, exclusive of interest and costs.

(c) A civil action in any State court arising under the workmen's compensation laws of such State may not be removed to any district court of the United States.

(d) A civil action in any State court arising under section 40302 of the Violence Against Women Act of 1994 may not be removed to any district court of the United States.

§ 1446. Procedure for removal of civil actions

(a) Generally.—A defendant or defendants desiring to remove any civil action from a State court shall file in the district court of the United States for the district and division within which such action is pending a notice of removal signed pursuant to Rule 11 of the Federal Rules of Civil Procedure and containing a short and plain statement of the grounds for removal, together with a copy of all process, pleadings, and orders served upon such defendant or defendants in such action.

(b) Requirements; generally.—**(1)** The notice of removal of a civil action or proceeding shall be filed within 30 days after the receipt by the defendant, through service or otherwise, of a copy of the initial pleading setting forth the claim for relief upon which such action or proceeding is based, or within 30 days after the service of summons upon the defendant if such initial pleading has then been filed in court and is not required to be served on the defendant, whichever period is shorter.

(2) (A) When a civil action is removed solely under section 1441(a), all defendants who have been properly joined and served must join in or consent to the removal of the action.

(B) Each defendant shall have 30 days after receipt by or service on that defendant of the initial pleading or summons described in paragraph (1) to file the notice of removal.

(C) If defendants are served at different times, and a later served defendant files a notice of removal, any earlier-served defendant may consent to the removal even though that earlier-served defendant did not previously initiate or consent to removal.

(3) Except as provided in subsection (c), if the case stated by the initial pleading is not removable, a notice of removal may be filed within thirty days after receipt by the defendant, through service or otherwise, of a copy of an amended pleading, motion, order or other paper from which it may first be ascertained that the case is one which is or has become removable.

(c) Requirements; removal based on diversity of citizenship.—**(1)** A case may not be removed under subsection (b)(3) on the basis of jurisdiction conferred by section 1332 more than 1 year after commencement of the action, unless the district court finds that the plaintiff has acted in bad faith in order to prevent a defendant from removing the action. **(2)** If removal of a civil action is sought on the basis of the jurisdiction conferred by section 1332(a), the sum demanded in good faith in the initial pleading shall be deemed to be the amount in controversy, except that—

    (A) the notice of removal may assert the amount in controversy if the initial pleading seeks—

        (i) nonmonetary relief; or

        (ii) a money judgment, but the State practice either does not permit demand for a specific sum or permits recovery of damages in excess of the amount demanded; and

    (B) removal of the action is proper on the basis of an amount in controversy asserted under subparagraph (A) if the district court finds, by the preponderance of the evidence, that the amount in controversy exceeds the amount specified in section 1332(a).

    (3) (A) If the case stated by the initial pleading is not removable solely because the amount in controversy does not exceed the amount specified in section 1332(a), information relating to the amount in controversy in the record of the State proceeding, or in responses to discovery, shall be treated as an "other paper" under subsection (b)(3).

    (B) If the notice of removal is filed more than 1 year after commencement of the action and the district court finds that the plaintiff deliberately failed to disclose the actual amount in controversy to prevent removal, that finding shall be deemed bad faith under paragraph (1).

(d) Notice to adverse parties and state court.—Promptly Promptly after the filing of such notice of removal of a civil action the defendant or defendants shall give written notice thereof to all adverse parties and shall file a copy of the notice with the clerk of such State court, which shall effect the removal and the

State court shall proceed no further unless and until the case is remanded.

(e) Counterclaim in 337 proceeding.—With respect to any counterclaim removed to a district court pursuant to section 337(c) of the Tariff Act of 1930, the district court shall resolve such counterclaim in the same manner as an original complaint under the Federal Rules of Civil Procedure, except that the payment of a filing fee shall not be required in such cases and the counterclaim shall relate back to the date of the original complaint in the proceeding before the International Trade Commission under section 337 of that Act.

*(g) (1) Where the civil action or criminal prosecution that is removable under section 1442(a) is a proceeding in which a judicial order for testimony or documents is sought or issued or sought to be enforced, the 30-day requirement of subsection (b) of this section and paragraph (1) of section 1455(b) is satisfied if the person or entity desiring to remove the proceeding files the notice of removal not later than 30 days after receiving, through service, notice of any such proceeding.

ED. NOTE:

Effective January 2012, revisions to Section 1446 repositioned subpart (f), leaving that subpart empty in the current statute.

§ 1447. Procedure after Removal Generally

(a) In any case removed from a State court, the district court may issue all necessary orders and process to bring before it all proper parties whether served by process issued by the State court or otherwise.

(b) It may require the removing party to file with its clerk copies of all records and proceedings in such State court or may cause the same to be brought before it by writ of certiorari issued to such State court.

(c) A motion to remand the case on the basis of any defect other than lack of subject matter jurisdiction must be made within 30 days after the filing of the notice of removal under section 1446(a). If at any time before final judgment it appears that the district court lacks subject matter jurisdiction, the case shall be remanded. An order remanding the case may require payment of just costs and any actual expenses, including attorney fees, incurred as a result of the removal. A certified copy of the order of remand shall be mailed by the clerk to the clerk of the State court. The State court may thereupon proceed with such case.

(d) An order remanding a case to the State court from which it was removed is not reviewable on appeal or otherwise, except that an order remanding a case to the State court from which it was removed pursuant to section 1442 or 1443 of this title shall be reviewable by appeal or otherwise.

(e) If after removal the plaintiff seeks to join additional defendants whose joinder would destroy subject matter jurisdiction, the court may deny joinder, or permit joinder and remand the action to the State court.

§ 1448. Process after Removal

In all cases removed from any State court to any district court of the United States in which any one or more of the defendants has not been served with process or in which the service has not been perfected prior to removal, or in which process served proves to be defective, such process or service may be completed or new process issued in the same manner as in cases originally filed in such district court.

This section shall not deprive any defendant upon whom process is served after removal of his right to move to remand the case.

§ 1449. State Court Record Supplied

Where a party is entitled to copies of the records and proceedings in any suit or prosecution in a State court, to be used in any district court of the United States, and the clerk of such State court, upon demand, and the payment or tender of the legal fees, fails to deliver certified copies, the district court may, on affidavit reciting such facts, direct such record to be supplied by affidavit or otherwise. Thereupon such proceedings, trial, and judgment may be had in such district court, and all such process awarded, as if certified copies had been filed in the district court.

§ 1451. Definitions

For purposes of this chapter—

(1) The term "State court" includes the Superior Court of the District of Columbia.

(2) The term "State" includes the District of Columbia.

§ 1453. Removal of Class Actions

(a) **Definitions**. —In this section, the terms "class", "class action", "class certification order", and "class member" shall have the meanings given such terms under section 1332(d)(1).

(b) **In general**. —A class action may be removed to a district court of the United States in accordance with section 1446 (except that the 1-year limitation under section 1446(c)(1) shall not apply), without regard to whether any defendant is a citizen of the State in which the action is brought, except that such action may be removed by any defendant without the consent of all defendants.

(c) **Review of remand orders**. —

(1) **In general**. —Section 1447 shall apply to any removal of a case under this section, except that notwithstanding section 1447(d), a court of appeals may accept an appeal from an order of a district court granting or denying a motion to remand

a class action to the State court from which it was removed if application is made to the court of appeals not more than 10 days after entry of the order.

(2) Time period for judgment. —If the court of appeals accepts an appeal under paragraph (1), the court shall complete all action on such appeal, including rendering judgment, not later than 60 days after the date on which such appeal was filed, unless an extension is granted under paragraph (3).

(3) Extension of time period. —The court of appeals may grant an extension of the 60-day period described in paragraph (2) if—

(A) all parties to the proceeding agree to such extension, for any period of time; or

(B) such extension is for good cause shown and in the interests of justice, for a period not to exceed 10 days.

(4) Denial of appeal. —If a final judgment on the appeal under paragraph (1) is not issued before the end of the period described in paragraph (2), including any extension under paragraph (3), the appeal shall be denied.

(d) Exception. —This section shall not apply to any class action that solely involves—

(1) a claim concerning a covered security as defined under section 16(f) (3) of the Securities Act of 1933 (15 U.S.C. 78p(f) (3)) and section 28(f)(5)(E) of the Securities Exchange Act of 1934 (15 U.S.C. 78bb(f)(5)(E));

(2) a claim that relates to the internal affairs or governance of a corporation or other form of business enterprise and arises under or by virtue of the laws of the State in which such corporation or business enterprise is incorporated or organized; or

(3) a claim that relates to the rights, duties (including fiduciary duties), and obligations relating to or created by or pursuant to any security (as defined under section 2(a)(1) of the Securities Act of 1933 (15 U.S.C. 77b(a)(1)) and the regulations issued thereunder).

§ **1631.** Transfer to Cure Want of Jurisdiction

Whenever a civil action is filed in a court as defined in section 610 of this title or an appeal, including a petition for review of administrative action, is noticed for or filed with such a court and that court finds that there is a want of jurisdiction, the court shall, if it is in the interest of justice, transfer such action or appeal to any other such court in which the action or appeal could have been brought at the time it was filed or noticed, and the action or appeal shall proceed as if it had been filed in or noticed for the court to which it is transferred on the date upon which it was actually filed in or noticed for the court from which it is transferred.

§ 1651. Writs

(a) The Supreme Court and all courts established by Act of Congress may issue all writs necessary or appropriate in aid of their respective jurisdictions and agreeable to the usages and principles of law.

(b) An alternative writ or rule nisi may be issued by a justice or judge of a court which has jurisdiction.

§ 1652. State Laws As Rules of Decision

The laws of the several states, except where the Constitution or treaties of the United States or Acts of Congress otherwise require or provide, shall be regarded as rules of decision in civil actions in the courts of the United States, in cases where they apply.

§ 1653. Amendment of Pleadings to Show Jurisdiction

Defective allegations of jurisdiction may be amended, upon terms, in the trial or appellate courts.

§ 1654. Appearance Personally or by Counsel

In all courts of the United States the parties may plead and conduct their own cases personally or by counsel as, by the rules of such courts, respectively, are permitted to manage and conduct causes therein.

§ 1657. Priority of Civil Actions

(a) Notwithstanding any other provision of law, each court of the United States shall determine the order in which civil actions are heard and determined, except that the court shall expedite the consideration of any action brought under chapter 153 or section 1826 of this title, any action for temporary or preliminary injunctive relief, or any other action if good cause therefor is shown. For purposes of this subsection, "good cause" is shown if a right under the Constitution of the United States or a Federal Statute (including rights under section 552 of title 5) would be maintained in a factual context that indicates that a request for expedited consideration has merit.

(b) The Judicial Conference of the United States may modify the rules adopted by the courts to determine the order in which civil actions are heard and determined, in order to establish consistency among the judicial circuits.

§ 1658. Time Limitations on the Commencement of Civil Actions Arising under Acts of Congress

(a) Except as otherwise provided by law, a civil action arising under an Act of Congress enacted after the date of the enactment of this section may not be commenced later than 4 years after the cause of action accrues.

(b) Notwithstanding subsection (a), a private right of action that involves a claim of fraud, deceit, manipulation, or contrivance in contravention of a regulatory requirement concerning the securities laws, as defined in section 3(a)(47) of the Securities Exchange Act of 1934 (15 U.S.C. 78c(a)(47)), may be brought not later than the earlier of—

   (1) 2 years after the discovery of the facts constituting the violation; or

   (2) 5 years after such violation.

§ 1691. Seal and Teste of Process

All writs and process issuing from a court of the United States shall be under the seal of the court and signed by the clerk thereof.

§ 1692. Process and Orders Affecting Property in Different Districts

In proceedings in a district court where a receiver is appointed for property, real, personal, or mixed, situated in different districts, process may issue and be executed in any such district as if the property lay wholly within one district, but orders affecting the property shall be entered of record in each of such districts.

§ 1695. Stockholder's Derivative Action

Process in a stockholder's action in behalf of his corporation may be served upon such corporation in any district where it is organized or licensed to do business or is doing business.

§ 1696. Service in Foreign and International Litigation

(a) The district court of the district in which a person resides or is found may order service upon him of any document issued in connection with a proceeding in a foreign or international tribunal. The order may be made pursuant to a letter rogatory issued, or request made, by a foreign or international tribunal or upon application of any interested person and shall direct the manner of service. Service pursuant to this subsection does not, of itself, require the recognition or enforcement in the United States of a judgment, decree, or order rendered by a foreign or international tribunal.

(b) This section does not preclude service of such a document without an order of court.

§ 1697. Service in Multiparty, Multiforum Actions

When the jurisdiction of the district court is based in whole or in part upon section 1369 of this title, process, other than subpoenas, may be served at any place within the United States, or anywhere outside the United States if otherwise permitted by law.

§ 1731. Handwriting

The admitted or proved handwriting of any person shall be admissible, for purposes of comparison, to determine genuineness of other handwriting attributed to such person.

§ 1732. Record Made in Regular Course of Business; Photographic Copies

If any business, institution, member of a profession or calling, or any department or agency of government, in the regular course of business or activity has kept or recorded any memorandum, writing, entry, print, representation or combination thereof, of any act, transaction, occurrence, or event, and in the regular course of business has caused any or all of the same to be recorded, copied, or reproduced by any photographic, photostatic, microfilm, micro-card, miniature photographic, or other process which accurately reproduces or forms a durable medium for so reproducing the original, the original may be destroyed in the regular course of business unless its preservation is required by law. Such reproduction, when satisfactorily identified, is as admissible in evidence as the original itself in any judicial or administrative proceeding whether the original is in existence or not and an enlargement or facsimile of such reproduction is likewise admissible in evidence if the original reproduction is in existence and available for inspection under direction of court. The introduction of a reproduced record, enlargement, or facsimile does not preclude admission of the original. This subsection shall not be construed to exclude from evidence any document or copy thereof which is otherwise admissible under the rules of evidence.

§ 1733. Government Records and Papers; Copies

(a) Books or records of account or minutes of proceedings of any department or agency of the United States shall be admissible to prove the act, transaction or occurrence as a memorandum of which the same were made or kept.

(b) Properly authenticated copies or transcripts of any books, records, papers or documents of any department or agency of the United States shall be admitted in evidence equally with the originals thereof.

(c) This section does not apply to cases, actions, and proceedings to which the Federal Rules of Evidence apply.

§ 1734. Court Record Lost or Destroyed, Generally

(a) A lost or destroyed record of any proceeding in any court of the United States may be supplied on application of any interested party not at fault, by substituting a copy certified by the clerk of any court in which an authentic copy is lodged.

(b) Where a certified copy is not available, any interested person not at fault may file in such court a verified application for an order establishing the lost or destroyed record.

Every other interested person shall be served personally with a copy of the application and with notice of hearing on a day stated, not less than sixty days after service. Service may be made on any nonresident of the district anywhere within the jurisdiction of the United States or in any foreign country.

Proof of service in a foreign country shall be certified by a minister or consul of the United States in such country, under his official seal.

If, after the hearing, the court is satisfied that the statements contained in the application are true, it shall enter an order reciting the substance and effect of the lost or destroyed record. Such order, subject to intervening rights of third persons, shall have the same effect as the original record.

§ 1735. Court Record Lost or Destroyed Where United States Interested

(a) When the record of any case or matter in any court of the United States to which the United States is a party, is lost or destroyed, a certified copy of any official paper of a United States attorney, United States marshal or clerk or other certifying or recording officer of any such court, made pursuant to law, on file in any department or agency of the United States and relating to such case or matter, shall, on being filed in the court to which it relates, have the same effect as an original paper filed in such court. If the copy so filed discloses the date and amount of a judgment or decree and the names of the parties thereto, the court may enforce the judgment or decree as though the original record had not been lost or destroyed.

(b) Whenever the United States is interested in any lost or destroyed records or files of a court of the United States, the clerk of such court and the United States attorney for the district shall take the steps necessary to restore such records or files, under the direction of the judges of such court.

§ 1738. State and Territorial Statutes and Judicial Proceedings; Full Faith and Credit

The Acts of the legislature of any State, Territory, or Possession of the United States, or copies thereof, shall be authenticated by affixing the seal of such State, Territory or Possession thereto.

The records and judicial proceedings of any court of any such State, Territory or Possession, or copies thereof, shall be proved or admitted in other courts within the United States and its Territories and Possessions by the attestation of the clerk and seal of the court annexed, if a seal exists, together with a certificate of a judge of the court that the said attestation is in proper form.

Such Acts, records and judicial proceedings or copies thereof, so authenticated, shall have the same full faith and credit in every court within the United States and its Territories and Possessions as they have by law or usage in the courts of such State,

Territory or Possession from which they are taken.

§ 1739. State and Territorial Nonjudicial Records; Full Faith and Credit

All nonjudicial records or books kept in any public office of any State, Territory, or Possession of the United States, or copies thereof, shall be proved or admitted in any court or office in any other State, Territory, or Possession by the attestation of the custodian of such records or books, and the seal of his office annexed, if there be a seal, together with a certificate of a judge of a court of record of the county, parish, or district in which such office may be kept, or of the Governor, or secretary of state, the chancellor or keeper of the great seal, of the State, Territory, or Possession that the said attestation is in due form and by the proper officers.

If the certificate is given by a judge, it shall be further authenticated by the clerk or prothonotary of the court, who shall certify, under his hand and the seal of his office, that such judge is duly commissioned and qualified; or, if given by such Governor, secretary, chancellor, or keeper of the great seal, it shall be under the great seal of the State, Territory, or Possession in which it is made.

Such records or books, or copies thereof, so authenticated, shall have the same full faith and credit in every court and office within the United States and its Territories and Possessions as they have by law or usage in the courts or offices of the State, Territory, or Possession from which they are taken.

§ 1746. Unsworn Declarations under Penalty of Perjury

Wherever, under any law of the United States or under any rule, regulation, order, or requirement made pursuant to law, any matter is required or permitted to be supported, evidenced, established, or proved by the sworn declaration, verification, certificate, statement, oath, or affidavit, in writing of the person making the same (other than a deposition, or an oath of office, or an oath required to be taken before a specified official other than a notary public), such matter may, with like force and effect, be supported, evidenced, established, or proved by the unsworn declaration, certificate, verification, or statement, in writing of such person which is subscribed by him, as true under penalty of perjury, and dated, in substantially the following form:

(1) If executed without the United States: "I declare (or certify, verify, or state) under penalty of perjury under the laws of the United States of America that the foregoing is true and correct. Executed on (date).

(Signature)".

(2) If executed within the United States, its territories, possessions, or commonwealths: "I declare (or certify, verify, or state)

under penalty of perjury that the foregoing is true and correct. Executed on *(date)*.

(Signature)".

§ 1781. Transmittal of Letter Rogatory or Request

(a) The Department of State has power, directly, or through suitable channels—

(1) to receive a letter rogatory issued, or request made, by a foreign or international tribunal, to transmit it to the tribunal, officer, or agency in the United States to whom it is addressed, and to receive and return it after execution; and

(2) to receive a letter rogatory issued, or request made, by a tribunal in the United States, to transmit it to the foreign or international tribunal, officer, or agency to whom it is addressed, and to receive and return it after execution.

(b) This section does not preclude—

(1) the transmittal of a letter rogatory or request directly from a foreign or international tribunal to the tribunal, officer, or agency in the United States to whom it is addressed and its return in the same manner; or

(2) the transmittal of a letter rogatory or request directly from a tribunal in the United States to the foreign or international tribunal, officer, or agency to whom it is addressed and its return in the same manner.

§ 1782. Assistance to Foreign and International Tribunals and to Litigants before Such Tribunals

(a) The district court of the district in which a person resides or is found may order him to give his testimony or statement or to produce a document or other thing for use in a proceeding in a foreign or international tribunal, including criminal investigations conducted before formal accusation. The order may be made pursuant to a letter rogatory issued, or request made, by a foreign or international tribunal or upon the application of any interested person and may direct that the testimony or statement be given, or the document or other thing be produced, before a person appointed by the court. By virtue of his appointment, the person appointed has power to administer any necessary oath and take the testimony or statement. The order may prescribe the practice and procedure, which may be in whole or part the practice and procedure of the foreign country or the international tribunal, for taking the testimony or statement or producing the document or other thing. To the extent that the order does not prescribe otherwise, the testimony or statement shall be taken, and the document or other thing produced, in accordance with the Federal Rules of Civil Procedure.

A person may not be compelled to give his testimony or statement or to produce a document or other thing in violation of any legally applicable privilege.

(b) This chapter does not preclude a person within the United States from voluntarily giving his testimony or statement, or producing a document or other thing, for use in a proceeding in a foreign or international tribunal before any person and in any manner acceptable to him.

§ 1783. Subpoena of Person in Foreign Country

(a) A court of the United States may order the issuance of a subpoena requiring the appearance as a witness before it, or before a person or body designated by it, of a national or resident of the United States who is in a foreign country, or requiring the production of a specified document or other thing by him, if the court finds that particular testimony or the production of the document or other thing by him is necessary in the interest of justice, and, in other than a criminal action or proceeding, if the court finds, in addition, that it is not possible to obtain his testimony in admissible form without his personal appearance or to obtain the production of the document or other thing in any other manner.

(b) The subpoena shall designate the time and place for the appearance or for the production of the document or other thing. Service of the subpoena and any order to show cause, rule, judgment, or decree authorized by this section or by section 1784 of this title shall be effected in accordance with the provisions of the Federal Rules of Civil Procedure relating to service of process on a person in a foreign country. The person serving the subpoena shall tender to the person to whom the subpoena is addressed his estimated necessary travel and attendance expenses, the amount of which shall be determined by the court and stated in the order directing the issuance of the subpoena.

§ 1784. Contempt

(a) The court of the United States which has issued a subpoena served in a foreign country may order the person who has failed to appear or who has failed to produce a document or other thing as directed therein to show cause before it at a designated time why he should not be punished for contempt.

(b) The court, in the order to show cause, may direct that any of the person's property within the United States be levied upon or seized, in the manner provided by law or court rules governing levy or seizure under execution, and held to satisfy any judgment that may be rendered against him pursuant to subsection (d) of this section if adequate security, in such amount as the court may direct in the order, be given for any damage that he might suffer should he not be found in contempt. Security under this subsection may not be required of the United States.

(c) A copy of the order to show cause shall be served on the person in accordance with section 1783(b) of this title.

(d) On the return day of the order to show cause or any later day to which the hearing may be continued, proof shall be taken. If the person is found in contempt, the court, notwithstanding any limitation upon its power generally to punish for contempt, may fine him not more than $100,000 and direct that the fine and costs of the proceedings be satisfied by a sale of the property levied upon or seized, conducted upon the notice required and in the manner provided for sales upon execution.

§ 1785. Subpoenas in Multiparty, Multiforum Actions

When the jurisdiction of the district court is based in whole or in part upon section 1369 of this title, a subpoena for attendance at a hearing or trial may, if authorized by the court upon motion for good cause shown, and upon such terms and conditions as the court may impose, be served at any place within the United States, or anywhere outside the United States if otherwise permitted by law.

§ 1821. Per Diem and Mileage Generally; Subsistence

(a) (1) Except as otherwise provided by law, a witness in attendance at any court of the United States, or before a United States Magistrate, or before any person authorized to take his deposition pursuant to any rule or order of a court of the United States, shall be paid the fees and allowances provided by this section.

(2) As used in this section, the term "court of the United States" includes, in addition to the courts listed in section 451 of this title, any court created by Act of Congress in a territory which is invested with any jurisdiction of a district court of the United States.

(b) A witness shall be paid an attendance fee of $40 per day for each day's attendance. A witness shall also be paid the attendance fee for the time necessarily occupied in going to and returning from the place of attendance at the beginning and end of such attendance or at any time during such attendance.

(c) (1) A witness who travels by common carrier shall be paid for the actual expenses of travel on the basis of the means of transportation reasonably utilized and the distance necessarily traveled to and from such witness's residence by the shortest practical route in going to and returning from the place of attendance. Such a witness shall utilize a common carrier at the most economical rate reasonably available. A receipt or other evidence of actual cost shall be furnished.

(2) A travel allowance equal to the mileage allowance which the Administrator of General Services has prescribed, pursuant to section 5704 of title 5, for official travel of employees of the Federal Government shall be paid to each witness who travels by privately owned vehicle. Computation of mileage under this paragraph shall be made on the basis of a uniformed table of distances adopted by the Administrator of General Services.

(3) Toll charges for toll roads, bridges, tunnels, and ferries, taxicab fares between places of lodging and carrier terminals, and parking fees (upon presentation of a valid parking receipt), shall be paid in full to a witness incurring such expenses.

(4) All normal travel expenses within and outside the judicial district shall be taxable as costs pursuant to section 1920 of this title.

(d) (1) A subsistence allowance shall be paid to a witness when an overnight stay is required at the place of attendance because such place is so far removed from the residence of such witness as to prohibit return thereto from day to day.

(2) A subsistence allowance for a witness shall be paid in an amount not to exceed the maximum per diem allowance prescribed by the Administrator of General Services, pursuant to section 5702(a) of title 5, for official travel in the area of attendance by employees of the Federal Government.

(3) A subsistence allowance for a witness attending in an area designated by the Administrator of General Services as a high-cost area shall be paid in an amount not to exceed the maximum actual subsistence allowance prescribed by the Administrator, pursuant to section 5702(c)(B) of title 5, for official travel in such area by employees of the Federal Government.

(4) When a witness is detained pursuant to section 3144 of title 18 for want of security for his appearance, he shall be entitled for each day of detention when not in attendance at court, in addition to his subsistence, to the daily attendance fee provided by subsection (b) of this section.

(e) An alien who has been paroled into the United States for prosecution, pursuant to section 212(d)(5) of the Immigration and Nationality Act (8 U.S.C. 1182(d)(5)), or an alien who either has admitted belonging to a class of aliens who are deportable or has been determined pursuant to section 240 of such Act (8 U.S.C. 1252(b)) to be deportable, shall be ineligible to receive the fees or allowances provided by this section.

(f) Any witness who is incarcerated at the time that his or her testimony is given (except for a witness to whom the provisions of section 3144 of title 18 apply) may not receive fees or allowances under this section, regardless of whether such a witness is incarcerated at the time he or she makes a claim for fees or allowances under this section.

§ 1826. Recalcitrant Witnesses

(a) Whenever a witness in any proceeding before or ancillary to any court or grand jury of the United States refuses without just cause shown to comply with an order of the court to testify or provide other information, including any book, paper, document, record, recording or other material, the court, upon such refusal, or when such refusal is duly brought to its attention, may summarily order his confinement at a suitable place until such time as the witness is willing to give such testimony or provide such information. No period of such confinement shall exceed the life of—

(1) the court proceeding, or

(2) the term of the grand jury, including extensions,

before which such refusal to comply with the court order occurred, but in no event shall such confinement exceed eighteen months.

(b) No person confined pursuant to subsection (a) of this section shall be admitted to bail pending the determination of an appeal taken by him from the order for his confinement if it appears that the appeal is frivolous or taken for delay. Any appeal from an order of confinement under this section shall be disposed of as soon as practicable, but not later than thirty days from the filing of such appeal.

(c) Whoever escapes or attempts to escape from the custody of any facility or from any place in which or to which he is confined pursuant to this section or section 4243 of title 18, or whoever rescues or attempts to rescue or instigates, aids, or assists the escape or attempt to escape of such a person, shall be subject to imprisonment for not more than three years, or a fine of not more than $10,000, or both.

§ 1914. District Court; Filing and Miscellaneous Fees; Rules of Court

(a) The clerk of each district court shall require the parties instituting any civil action, suit or proceeding in such court, whether by original process, removal or otherwise, to pay a filing fee of $350, except that on application for a writ of habeas corpus the filing fee shall be $5.

(b) The clerk shall collect from the parties such additional fees only as are prescribed by the Judicial Conference of the United States.

(c) Each district court by rule or standing order may require advance payment of fees.

§ 1915. Proceedings in Forma Pauperis

(a) (1) Subject to subsection (b), any court of the United States may authorize the commencement, prosecution or defense of any suit, action or proceeding, civil or criminal, or appeal therein, without prepayment of fees or security therefor, by a person who submits an affidavit that includes a statement of all assets such prisoner possesses that the person is unable to pay such fees or give security therefor. Such affidavit shall state the nature of the action, defense or appeal and affiant's belief that the person is entitled to redress.

(2) A prisoner seeking to bring a civil action or appeal a judgment in a civil action or proceeding without prepayment of fees or security therefor, in addition to filing the affidavit filed under paragraph (1), shall submit a certified copy of the trust fund account statement (or institutional equivalent) for the prisoner for the 6-month period immediately preceding the filing of the complaint or notice of appeal, obtained from the appropriate official of each prison at which the prisoner is or was confined.

(3) An appeal may not be taken in forma pauperis if the trial court certifies in writing that it is not taken in good faith.

(b) (1) Notwithstanding subsection (a), if a prisoner brings a civil action or files an appeal in forma pauperis, the prisoner shall be required to pay the full amount of a filing fee. The court shall assess and, when funds exist, collect, as a partial payment of any court fees required by law, an initial partial filing fee of 20 percent of the greater of—

    (A) the average monthly deposits to the prisoner's account; or

    (B) the average monthly balance in the prisoner's account for the 6-month period immediately preceding the filing of the complaint or notice of appeal.

(2) After payment of the initial partial filing fee, the prisoner shall be required to make monthly payments of 20 percent of the preceding month's income credited to the prisoner's account. The agency having custody of the prisoner shall forward payments from the prisoner's account to the clerk of the court each time the amount in the account exceeds $10 until the filing fees are paid.

(3) In no event shall the filing fee collected exceed the amount of fees permitted by statute for the commencement of a civil action or an appeal of a civil action or criminal judgment.

(4) In no event shall a prisoner be prohibited from bringing a civil action or appealing a civil or criminal judgment for the reason that the prisoner has no assets and no means by which to pay the initial partial filing fee.

(c) Upon the filing of an affidavit in accordance with subsections (a) and (b) and the prepayment of any partial filing fee as may be required under subsection (b), the court may direct payment by the United States of the expenses of (1) printing the record on appeal in any civil or criminal case, if such printing is required by the appellate court; (2) preparing a transcript of proceedings before a United States magistrate in any civil or criminal case, if such transcript is required by the district court, in the case of proceedings conducted under section 636(b) of this title or under section 3401(b) of title 18, United States Code; and (3) printing the record on appeal if such printing is required by the appellate court, in the case of proceedings conducted pursuant to section 636(c) of this title. Such expenses shall be paid when authorized by the Director of the Administrative Office of the United States Courts.

(d) The officers of the court shall issue and serve all process, and perform all duties in such cases. Witnesses shall attend as in other cases, and the same remedies shall be available as are provided for by law in other cases.

(e) (1) The court may request an attorney to represent any person unable to afford counsel.

(2) Notwithstanding any filing fee, or any portion thereof, that may have been paid, the court shall dismiss the case at any time if the court determines that—

(A) the allegation of poverty is untrue; or

(B) the action or appeal—

(i) is frivolous or malicious;

(ii) fails to state a claim on which relief may be granted; or

(iii) seeks monetary relief against a defendant who is immune from such relief.

(f) (1) Judgment may be rendered for costs at the conclusion of the suit or action as in other proceedings, but the United States shall not be liable for any of the costs thus incurred. If the United States has paid the cost of a stenographic transcript or printed record for the prevailing party, the same shall be taxed in favor of the United States.

(2) (A) If the judgment against a prisoner includes the payment of costs under this subsection, the prisoner shall be required to pay the full amount of the costs ordered.

(B) The prisoner shall be required to make payments for costs under this subsection in the same manner as is provided for filing fees under subsection (a)(2).

(C) In no event shall the costs collected exceed the amount of the costs ordered by the court.

(g) In no event shall a prisoner bring a civil action or appeal a judgment in a civil action or proceeding under this section if the prisoner has, on 3 or more prior occasions, while incarcerated or detained in any facility, brought an action or appeal in a court of the United States that was dismissed on the grounds that it is frivolous, malicious, or fails to state a claim upon which relief may be granted, unless the prisoner is under imminent danger of serious physical injury.

(h) As used in this section, the term 'prisoner' means any person incarcerated or detained in any facility who is accused of, convicted of, sentenced for, or adjudicated delinquent for, violations of criminal law or the terms and conditions of parole, probation, pretrial release, or diversionary program.

§ 1917. District Courts; Fee on Filing Notice of or Petition for Appeal

Upon the filing of any separate or joint notice of appeal or application for appeal or upon the receipt of any order allowing, or notice of the allowance of, an appeal or of a writ of certiorari $5 shall be paid to the clerk of the district court, by the appellant or petitioner.

§ 1920. Taxation of Costs

A judge or clerk of any court of the United States may tax as costs the following:

(1) Fees of the clerk and marshal;

(2) Fees for printed or electronically recorded manuscripts necessarily obtained for use in the case;

(3) Fees and disbursements for printing and witnesses;

(4) Fees for exemplification and the costs of making copies of any materials where copies are necessarily obtained for use in the case;

(5) Docket fees under section 1923 of this title;

(6) Compensation of court appointed experts, compensation of interpreters, and salaries, fees, expenses, and costs of special interpretation services under section 1828 of this title.

A bill of costs shall be filed in the case and, upon allowance, included in the judgment or decree.

§ 1924. Verification of Bill of Costs

Before any bill of costs is taxed, the party claiming any item of cost or disbursement shall attach thereto an affidavit, made by himself or by his duly authorized attorney or agent having knowledge of the facts, that such item is correct and has been necessarily incurred in the case and that the services for which fees have been charged were actually and necessarily performed.

§ 1927. Counsel's Liability for Excessive Costs

Any attorney or other person admitted to conduct cases in any court of the United States or any Territory thereof who so multiplies the proceedings in any case unreasonably and vexatiously may be required by the court to satisfy personally the excess costs, expenses, and attorneys' fees reasonably incurred because of such conduct.

§ 1961. Interest

(a) Interest shall be allowed on any money judgment in a civil case recovered in a district court. Execution therefor may be levied by the marshal, in any case where, by the law of the State in which such court is held, execution may be levied for interest on judgments recovered in the courts of the State. Such interest shall be calculated from the date of the entry of the judgment, at a rate equal to the weekly average 1-year constant maturity Treasury yield, as published by the Board of Governors of the Federal Reserve System, for the calendar week preceding the date of the judgment. The Director of the Administrative Office of the United

States Courts shall distribute notice of that rate and any changes in it to all Federal judges.

(b) Interest shall be computed daily to the date of payment except as provided in section 2516(b) of this title and section 1304(b) of title 31, and shall be compounded annually.

(c) (1) This section shall not apply in any judgment of any court with respect to any internal revenue tax case. Interest shall be allowed in such cases at the underpayment rate or overpayment rate (whichever is appropriate) established under section 6621 of the Internal Revenue Code of 1986.

(2) Except as otherwise provided in paragraph (1) of this subsection, interest shall be allowed on all final judgments against the United States in the United States Court of Appeals for the Federal circuit,[1] at the rate provided in subsection (a) and as provided in subsection (b).

(3) Interest shall be allowed, computed, and paid on judgments of the United States Court of Federal Claims only as provided in paragraph (1) of this subsection or in any other provision of law.

(4) This section shall not be construed to affect the interest on any judgment of any court not specified in this section.

§ **1963. Registration of Judgments for Enforcement in Other Districts**

A judgment in an action for the recovery of money or property entered in any court of appeals, district court, bankruptcy court, or in the Court of International Trade may be registered by filing a certified copy of the judgment in any other district or, with respect to the Court of International Trade, in any judicial district, when the judgment has become final by appeal or expiration of the time for appeal or when ordered by the court that entered the judgment for good cause shown. Such a judgment entered in favor of the United States may be so registered any time after judgment is entered. A judgment so registered shall have the same effect as a judgment of the district court of the district where registered and may be enforced in like manner.

A certified copy of the satisfaction of any judgment in whole or in part may be registered in like manner in any district in which the judgment is a lien.

The procedure prescribed under this section is in addition to other procedures provided by law for the enforcement of judgments.

§ **1964. Constructive Notice of Pending Actions**

Where the law of a State requires a notice of an action concerning real property pending in a court of the State to be registered,

---

[1]So in original. Probably should   be "Circuit,".

recorded, docketed, or indexed in a particular manner, or in a certain office or county or parish in order to give constructive notice of the action as it relates to the real property, and such law authorizes a notice of an action concerning real property pending in a United States district court to be registered, recorded, docketed, or indexed in the same manner, or in the same place, those requirements of the State law must be complied with in order to give constructive notice of such an action pending in a United States district court as it relates to real property in such State.

§ 2071. Rule-Making Power Generally

(a) The Supreme Court and all courts established by Act of Congress may from time to time prescribe rules for the conduct of their business. Such rules shall be consistent with Acts of Congress and rules of practice and procedure prescribed under section 2072 of this title.

(b) Any rule prescribed by a court, other than the Supreme Court, under subsection (a) shall be prescribed only after giving appropriate public notice and an opportunity for comment. Such rule shall take effect upon the date specified by the prescribing court and shall have such effect on pending proceedings as the prescribing court may order.

(c) (1) A rule of a district court prescribed under subsection (a) shall remain in effect unless modified or abrogated by the judicial council of the relevant circuit.

(2) Any other rule prescribed by a court other than the Supreme Court under subsection (a) shall remain in effect unless modified or abrogated by the Judicial Conference.

(d) Copies of rules prescribed under subsection (a) by a district court shall be furnished to the judicial council, and copies of all rules prescribed by a court other than the Supreme Court under subsection (a) shall be furnished to the Director of the Administrative Office of the United States Courts and made available to the public.

(e) If the prescribing court determines that there is an immediate need for a rule, such court may proceed under this section without public notice and opportunity for comment, but such court shall promptly thereafter afford such notice and opportunity for comment.

(f) No rule may be prescribed by a district court other than under this section.

§ 2072. Rules of Procedure and Evidence; Power to Prescribe

(a) The Supreme Court shall have the power to prescribe general rules of practice and procedure and rules of evidence for cases in the United States district courts (including proceedings before magistrates thereof) and courts of appeals.

(b) Such rules shall not abridge, enlarge or modify any substantive right. All laws in conflict with such rules shall be of no further force or effect after such rules have taken effect.

(c) Such rules may define when a ruling of a district court is final for the purposes of appeal under section 1291 of this title.

§ 2101. Supreme Court; Time for Appeal or Certiorari; Docketing; Stay

(a) A direct appeal to the Supreme Court from any decision under section 1253 of this title, holding unconstitutional in whole or in part, any Act of Congress, shall be taken within thirty days after the entry of the interlocutory or final order, judgment or decree. The record shall be made up and the case docketed within sixty days from the time such appeal is taken under rules prescribed by the Supreme Court.

(b) Any other direct appeal to the Supreme Court which is authorized by law, from a decision of a district court in any civil action, suit or proceeding, shall be taken within thirty days from the judgment, order or decree, appealed from, if interlocutory, and within sixty days if final.

(c) Any other appeal or any writ of certiorari intended to bring any judgment or decree in a civil action, suit or proceeding before the Supreme Court for review shall be taken or applied for within ninety days after the entry of such judgment or decree. A justice of the Supreme Court, for good cause shown, may extend the time for applying for a writ of certiorari for a period not exceeding sixty days.

(d) The time for appeal or application for a writ of certiorari to review the judgment of a State court in a criminal case shall be as prescribed by rules of the Supreme Court.

(e) An application to the Supreme Court for a writ of certiorari to review a case before judgment has been rendered in the court of appeals may be made at any time before judgment.

(f) In any case in which the final judgment or decree of any court is subject to review by the Supreme Court on writ of certiorari, the execution and enforcement of such judgment or decree may be stayed for a reasonable time to enable the party aggrieved to obtain a writ of certiorari from the Supreme Court. The stay may be granted by a judge of the court rendering the judgment or decree or by a justice of the Supreme Court, and may be conditioned on the giving of security, approved by such judge or justice, that if the aggrieved party fails to make application for such writ within the period allotted therefor, or fails to obtain an order granting his application, or fails to make his plea good in the Supreme Court, he shall answer for all damages and costs which the other party may sustain by reason of the stay.

(g) The time for application for a writ of certiorari to review a decision of the United States Court of Appeals for the Armed Forces shall be as prescribed by rules of the Supreme Court.

§ 2104. Reviews of State Court Decisions

A review by the Supreme Court of a judgment or decree of a State court shall be conducted in the same manner and under the same regulations, and shall have the same effect, as if the judgment or decree reviewed had been rendered in a court of the United States.

§ 2106. Determination

The Supreme Court or any other court of appellate jurisdiction may affirm, modify, vacate, set aside or reverse any judgment, decree, or order of a court lawfully brought before it for review, and may remand the cause and direct the entry of such appropriate judgment, decree, or order, or require such further proceedings to be had as may be just under the circumstances.

§ 2107. Time for Appeal to Court of Appeals

(a) Except as otherwise provided in this section, no appeal shall bring any judgment, order or decree in an action, suit or proceeding of a civil nature before a court of appeals for review unless notice of appeal is filed, within thirty days after the entry of such judgment, order or decree.

(b) In any such action, suit, or proceeding, the time as to all parties shall be 60 days from such entry if one of the parties is—

(1) the United States;

(2) a United States agency;

(3) a United States officer or employee sued in an official capacity; or

(4) a current or former United States officer or employee sued in an individual capacity for an act or omission occurring in connection with duties performed on behalf of the United States, including all instances in which the United States represents that officer or employee when the judgment, order, or decree is entered or files the appeal for that officer or employee.

(c) The district court may, upon motion filed not later than 30 days after the expiration of the time otherwise set for bringing appeal, extend the time for appeal upon a showing of excusable neglect or good cause. In addition, if the district court finds—

(1) that a party entitled to notice of the entry of a judgment or order did not receive such notice from the clerk or any party within 21 days of its entry, and

(2) that no party would be prejudiced,

the district court may, upon motion filed within 180 days after entry of the judgment or order or within 14 days after receipt of such notice, whichever is earlier, reopen the time for appeal for a period of 14 days from the date of entry of the order reopening the time for appeal.

(d) This section shall not apply to bankruptcy matters or other proceedings under Title 11.

§ 2111. Harmless Error

On the hearing of any appeal or writ of certiorari in any case, the court shall give judgment after an examination of the record without regard to errors or defects which do not affect the substantial rights of the parties.

§ 2201. Creation of Remedy

(a) In a case of actual controversy within its jurisdiction, except with respect to Federal taxes other than actions brought under section 7428 of the Internal Revenue Code of 1986, a proceeding under section 505 or 1146 of title 11, or in any civil action involving an antidumping or countervailing duty proceeding regarding a class or kind of merchandise of a free trade area country (as defined in section 516A(f)(10) of the Tariff Act of 1930), as determined by the administering authority, any court of the United States, upon the filing of an appropriate pleading, may declare the rights and other legal relations of any interested party seeking such declaration, whether or not further relief is or could be sought. Any such declaration shall have the force and effect of a final judgment or decree and shall be reviewable as such.

(b) For limitations on actions brought with respect to drug patents see section 505 or 512 of the Federal Food, Drug, and Cosmetic Act, or section 351 of the Public Health Service Act.

§ 2202. Further Relief

Further necessary or proper relief based on a declaratory judgment or decree may be granted, after reasonable notice and hearing, against any adverse party whose rights have been determined by such judgment.

§ 2283. Stay of State Court Proceedings

A court of the United States may not grant an injunction to stay proceedings in a State court except as expressly authorized by Act of Congress, or where necessary in aid of its jurisdiction, or to protect or effectuate its judgments.

§ 2284. Three-Judge Court; When Required; Composition; Procedure

(a) A district court of three judges shall be convened when otherwise required by Act of Congress, or when an action is filed challenging the constitutionality of the apportionment of congressional districts or the apportionment of any statewide legislative body.

(b) In any action required to be heard and determined by a district court of three judges under subsection (a) of this section, the composition and procedure of the court shall be as follows:

(1) Upon the filing of a request for three judges, the judge to

whom the request is presented shall, unless he determines that three judges are not required, immediately notify the chief judge of the circuit, who shall designate two other judges, at least one of whom shall be a circuit judge. The judges so designated, and the judge to whom the request was presented, shall serve as members of the court to hear and determine the action or proceeding.

(2) If the action is against a State, or officer or agency thereof, at least five days' notice of hearing of the action shall be given by registered or certified mail to the Governor and attorney general of the State.

(3) A single judge may conduct all proceedings except the trial, and enter all orders permitted by the rules of civil procedure except as provided in this subsection. He may grant a temporary restraining order on a specific finding, based on evidence submitted, that specified irreparable damage will result if the order is not granted, which order, unless previously revoked by the district judge, shall remain in force only until the hearing and determination by the district court of three judges of an application for a preliminary injunction. A single judge shall not appoint a master, or order a reference, or hear and determine any application for a preliminary or permanent injunction or motion to vacate such an injunction, or enter judgment on the merits. Any action of a single judge may be reviewed by the full court at any time before final judgment.

§ 2361. Process and Procedure

In any civil action of interpleader or in the nature of interpleader under section 1335 of this title, a district court may issue its process for all claimants and enter its order restraining them from instituting or prosecuting any proceeding in any State or United States court affecting the property, instrument or obligation involved in the interpleader action until further order of the court. Such process and order shall be returnable at such time as the court or judge thereof directs, and shall be addressed to and served by the United States marshals for the respective districts where the claimants reside or may be found.

Such district court shall hear and determine the case, and may discharge the plaintiff from further liability, make the injunction permanent, and make all appropriate orders to enforce its judgment.

§ 2401. Time for Commencing Action Against United States

(a) Except as provided by chapter 71 of title 41, every civil action commenced against the United States shall be barred unless the complaint is filed within six years after the right of action first accrues. The action of any person under legal disability or beyond the seas at the time the claim accrues may be commenced within three years after the disability ceases.

(b) A tort claim against the United States shall be forever barred unless it is presented in writing to the appropriate Federal agency within two years after such claim accrues or unless action is begun within six months after the date of mailing, by certified or registered mail, of notice of final denial of the claim by the agency to which it was presented.

§ 2402. Jury Trial in Actions Against United States

Subject to chapter 179 of this title, any action against the United States under section 1346 shall be tried by the court without a jury, except that any action against the United States under section 1346(a)(1) shall, at the request of either party to such action, be tried by the court with a jury.

§ 2403. Intervention by United States or a State; Constitutional Question

(a) In any action, suit or proceeding in a court of the United States to which the United States or any agency, officer or employee thereof is not a party, wherein the constitutionality of any Act of Congress affecting the public interest is drawn in question, the court shall certify such fact to the Attorney General, and shall permit the United States to intervene for presentation of evidence, if evidence is otherwise admissible in the case, and for argument on the question of constitutionality. The United States shall, subject to the applicable provisions of law, have all the rights of a party and be subject to all liabilities of a party as to court costs to the extent necessary for a proper presentation of the facts and law relating to the question of constitutionality.

(b) In any action, suit, or proceeding in a court of the United States to which a State or any agency, officer, or employee thereof is not a party, wherein the constitutionality of any statute of that State affecting the public interest is drawn in question, the court shall certify such fact to the attorney general of the State, and shall permit the State to intervene for presentation of evidence, if evidence is otherwise admissible in the case, and for argument on the question of constitutionality. The State shall, subject to the applicable provisions of law, have all the rights of a party and be subject to all liabilities of a party as to court costs to the extent necessary for a proper presentation of the facts and law relating to the question of constitutionality.

§ 2404. Death of Defendant in Damage Action

A civil action for damages commenced by or on behalf of the United States or in which it is interested shall not abate on the death of a defendant but shall survive and be enforceable against his estate as well as against surviving defendants.

§ 2408. Security Not Required of United States

Security for damages or costs shall not be required of the United

States, any department or agency thereof or any party acting under the direction of any such department or agency on the issuance of process or the institution or prosecution of any proceeding.

Costs taxable, under other Acts of Congress, against the United States or any such department, agency or party shall be paid out of the contingent fund of the department or agency which directed the proceedings to be instituted.

§ 2411. Interest

In any judgment of any court rendered (whether against the United States, a collector or deputy collector of internal revenue, a former collector or deputy collector, or the personal representative in case of death) for any overpayment in respect of any internal-revenue tax, interest shall be allowed at the overpayment rate established under section 6621 of the Internal Revenue Code of 1986 upon the amount of the overpayment, from the date of the payment or collection thereof to a date preceding the date of the refund check by not more than thirty days, such date to be determined by the Commissioner of Internal Revenue. The Commissioner is authorized to tender by check payment of any such judgment, with interest as herein provided, at any time after such judgment becomes final, whether or not a claim for such payment has been duly filed, and such tender shall stop the running of interest, whether or not such refund check is accepted by the judgment creditor.

§ 2412. Costs and Fees

(a) (1) Except as otherwise specifically provided by statute, a judgment for costs, as enumerated in section 1920 of this title, but not including the fees and expenses of attorneys, may be awarded to the prevailing party in any civil action brought by or against the United States or any agency or any official of the United States acting in his or her official capacity in any court having jurisdiction of such action. A judgment for costs when taxed against the United States shall, in an amount established by statute, court rule, or order, be limited to reimbursing in whole or in part the prevailing party for the costs incurred by such party in the litigation.

(2) A judgment for costs, when awarded in favor of the United States in an action brought by the United States, may include an amount equal to the filing fee prescribed under section 1914(a) of this title. The preceding sentence shall not be construed as requiring the United States to pay any filing fee.

(b) Unless expressly prohibited by statute, a court may award reasonable fees and expenses of attorneys, in addition to the costs which may be awarded pursuant to subsection (a), to the prevailing party in any civil action brought by or against the United States or any agency or any official of the United States acting in his or her official capacity in any court having jurisdiction of such action. The United States shall be liable for such fees and expenses to the same extent that any other party would be liable under the common law or under the terms of any statute which specifically provides for such an award.

(c) (1) Any judgment against the United States or any agency and any official of the United States acting in his or her official capacity for costs pursuant to subsection (a) shall be paid as provided in sections 2414 and 2517 of this title and shall be in addition to any relief provided in the judgment.

(2) Any judgment against the United States or any agency and any official of the United States acting in his or her official capacity for fees and expenses of attorneys pursuant to subsection (b) shall be paid as provided in sections 2414 and 2517 of this title, except that if the basis for the award is a finding that the United States acted in bad faith, then the award shall be paid by any agency found to have acted in bad faith and shall be in addition to any relief provided in the judgment.

(d) (1) (A) Except as otherwise specifically provided by statute, a court shall award to a prevailing party other than the United States fees and other expenses, in addition to any costs awarded pursuant to subsection (a), incurred by that party in any civil action (other than cases sounding in tort), including proceedings for judicial review of agency action, brought by or against the United States in any court having jurisdiction of that action, unless the court finds that the position of the United States was substantially justified or that special circumstances make an award unjust.

(B) A party seeking an award of fees and other expenses shall, within thirty days of final judgment in the action, submit to the court an application for fees and other expenses which shows that the party is a prevailing party and is eligible to receive an award under this subsection, and the amount sought, including an itemized statement from any attorney or expert witness representing or appearing in behalf of the party stating the actual time expended and the rate at which fees and other expenses were computed. The party shall also allege that the position of the United States was not substantially justified. Whether or not the position of the United States was substantially justified shall be determined on the basis of the record (including the record with respect to the action or failure to act by the agency upon which the civil action is based) which is made in the civil action for which fees and other expenses are sought.

(C) The court, in its discretion, may reduce the amount to be awarded pursuant to this subsection, or deny an award, to the extent that the prevailing party during the course of the proceedings engaged in conduct which unduly and unreasonably protracted the final resolution of the matter in controversy.

(D) If, in a civil action brought by the United States or a proceeding for judicial review of an adversary adjudication described in section 504(a)(4) of title 5, the demand by the United States is substantially in excess of the judgment finally obtained by the United States and is unreasonable when compared with such judgment, under the facts and circumstances of the case, the court shall award to the party the fees and other expenses related to defending against the excessive demand, unless the party has committed a willful violation of law or otherwise acted in bad faith, or special circumstances make an award unjust. Fees and expenses awarded under this subparagraph shall be paid only as a consequence of appropriations provided in advance.

(2) For the purposes of this subsection—

(A) "fees and other expenses" includes the reasonable expenses of expert witnesses, the reasonable cost of any study, analysis, engineering report, test, or project which is found by the court to be necessary for the preparation of the party's case, and reasonable attorney fees (The amount of fees awarded under this subsection shall be based upon prevailing market rates for the kind and quality of the services furnished, except that (i) no expert witness shall be compensated at a rate in excess of the highest rate of compensation for expert witnesses paid by the United States; and (ii) attorney fees shall not be awarded in excess of $125 per hour unless the court determines that an increase in the cost of living or a special factor, such as the limited availability of qualified attorneys for the proceedings involved, justifies a higher fee.);

(B) "party" means (i) an individual whose net worth did not exceed $2,000,000 at the time the civil action was filed, or (ii) any owner of an unincorporated business, or any partnership, corporation, association, unit of local government, or organization, the net worth of which did not exceed $7,000,000 at the time the civil action was filed, and which had not more than 500 employees at the time the civil action was filed; except that an organization described in section 501(c)(3) of the Internal Revenue Code of 1986 (26 U.S.C. 501(c)(3)) exempt from taxation under section 501(a) of such Code, or a cooperative association as defined in section 15(a) of the Agricultural Marketing Act (12 U.S.C. 1141j(a)), may be a party regardless of the net worth of such organization or cooperative association or for purposes of subsection (d)(1)(D), a small entity as defined in section 601 of Title 5;

(C) "United States" includes any agency and any official of the United States acting in his or her official capacity;

(D) "position of the United States" means, in addition to the position taken by the United States in the civil action, the action or failure to act by the agency upon which the civil action is based; except that fees and expenses may not be awarded to a party for any portion of the litigation in which the party has unreasonably protracted the proceedings;

(E) "civil action brought by or against the United States" includes an appeal by a party, other than the United States, from a decision of a contracting officer rendered pursuant to a disputes clause in a contract with the Government or pursuant to chapter 71 of title 41;

(F) "court" includes the United States Court of Federal Claims and the United States Court of Appeals for Veterans Claims;

(G) "final judgment" means a judgment that is final and not appealable, and includes an order of settlement;

(H) "prevailing party", in the case of eminent domain proceedings, means a party who obtains a final judgment (other than by settlement), exclusive of interest, the amount of which is at least as close to the highest valuation of the property involved that is attested to at trial on behalf of the property owner as it is to the highest valuation of the property involved that is attested to at trial on behalf of the Government; and

(I) "demand" means the express demand of the United States which led to the adversary adjudication, but shall not include a recitation of the maximum statutory penalty (i) in the complaint, or (ii) elsewhere when accompanied by an express demand for a lesser amount.

(3) In awarding fees and other expenses under this subsection to a prevailing party in any action for judicial review of an adversary adjudication, as defined in subsection (b)(1)(C) of section 504 of title 5, United States Code, or an adversary adjudication subject to chapter 71 of title 41, the court shall include in that award fees and other expenses to the same extent authorized in subsection (a) of such section, unless the court finds that during such adversary adjudication the position of the United States was substantially justified, or that special circumstances make an award unjust.

(4) Fees and other expenses awarded under this subsection to a party shall be paid by any agency over which the party prevails from any funds made available to the agency by appropriation or otherwise.

[**(5)** Repealed. Pub.L. 104-66, Title I, § 1091(b), Dec. 21, 1995, 109 Stat. 722]

(e) The provisions of this section shall not apply to any costs, fees, and other expenses in connection with any proceeding to which section 7430 of the Internal Revenue Code of 1986 applies (determined without regard to subsections (b) and (f) of such section). Nothing in the preceding sentence shall prevent the awarding under subsection (a) of section 2412 of title 28, United

States Code, of costs enumerated in section 1920 of such title (as in effect on October 1, 1981).

(f) If the United States appeals an award of costs or fees and other expenses made against the United States under this section and the award is affirmed in whole or in part, interest shall be paid on the amount of the award as affirmed. Such interest shall be computed at the rate determined under section 1961(a) of this title, and shall run from the date of the award through the day before the date of the mandate of affirmance.

§ 2413. Executions in Favor of United States

A writ of execution on a judgment obtained for the use of the United States in any court thereof shall be issued from and made returnable to the court which rendered the judgment, but may be executed in any other State, in any Territory, or in the District of Columbia.

§ 2414. Payment of Judgments and Compromise Settlements

Except as provided by chapter 71 of title 41, payment of final judgments rendered by a district court or the Court of International Trade against the United States shall be made on settlements by the Secretary of the Treasury. Payment of final judgments rendered by a State or foreign court or tribunal against the United States, or against its agencies or officials upon obligations or liabilities of the United States, shall be made on settlements by the Secretary of the Treasury after certification by the Attorney General that it is in the interest of the United States to pay the same.

Whenever the Attorney General determines that no appeal shall be taken from a judgment or that no further review will be sought from a decision affirming the same, he shall so certify and the judgment shall be deemed final.

Except as otherwise provided by law, compromise settlements of claims referred to the Attorney General for defense of imminent litigation or suits against the United States, or against its agencies or officials upon obligations or liabilities of the United States, made by the Attorney General or any person authorized by him, shall be settled and paid in a manner similar to judgments in like causes and appropriations or funds available for the payment of such judgments are hereby made available for the payment of such compromise settlements.

§ 2415. Time for Commencing Actions Brought by the United States

(a) Subject to the provisions of section 2416 of this title, and except as otherwise provided by Congress, every action for money damages brought by the United States or an officer or agency thereof which is founded upon any contract express or implied in law or fact, shall be barred unless the complaint is filed within six years after the right of action accrues or within one year after final decisions have been rendered in applicable administrative proceedings required by contract or by law, whichever is later: *Provided*, That in the event of later partial payment or written acknowledgment of debt, the right of action shall be deemed to accrue again at the time of each such payment or acknowledgment: *Provided further,* That an action for money damages brought by the United States for or on behalf of a recognized tribe, band or group of American Indians shall not be barred unless the complaint is filed more than six years and ninety days after the right of action accrued: *Provided further,* That an action for money damages which accrued on the date of enactment of this Act in accordance with subsection (g) brought by the United States for or on behalf of a recognized tribe, band, or group of American Indians, or on behalf of an individual Indian whose land is held in trust or restricted status, shall not be barred unless the complaint is filed sixty days after the date of publication of the list required by section 4(c) of the Indian Claims Limitation Act of 1982: *Provided*, That, for those claims that are on either of the two lists published pursuant to the Indian Claims Limitation Act of 1982, any right of action shall be barred unless the complaint is filed within (1) one year after the Secretary of the Interior has published in the Federal Register a notice rejecting such claim or (2) three years after the date the Secretary of the Interior has submitted legislation or legislative report to Congress to resolve such claim or more than two years after a final decision has been rendered in applicable administrative proceedings required by contract or by law, whichever is later.

(b) Subject to the provisions of section 2416 of this title, and except as otherwise provided by Congress, every action for money damages brought by the United States or an officer or agency thereof which is founded upon a tort shall be barred unless the complaint is filed within three years after the right of action first accrues: *Provided*, That an action to recover damages resulting from a trespass on lands of the United States; an action to recover damages resulting from fire to such lands; an action to recover for diversion of money paid under a grant program; and an action for conversion of property of the United States may be brought within six years after the right of action accrues, except that such actions for or on behalf of a recognized tribe, band or group of American Indians, including actions relating to allotted trust or restricted Indian lands, may be brought within six years and ninety days after the right of action accrues, except that such actions for or on behalf of a recognized tribe, band or group of American Indians, including actions relating to allotted trust or restricted Indian lands, or on behalf of an individual Indian whose land is held in trust or restricted status which accrued on the date of enactment of this Act in accordance with subsection (g) may be brought on or before sixty days after the date of the publication of the list required by section 4(c) of the Indian Claims Limitation Act of 1982: *Provided*, That, for those claims that are on either of the two lists published pursuant to the Indian Claims Limitation Act of 1982, any right of action shall be barred unless the complaint is filed within (1) one year after the Secretary of the Interior has published in the Federal Register a notice rejecting such claim or (2) three years after the Secretary of the Interior has submitted legislation or legislative report to Congress to resolve such claim.

(c) Nothing herein shall be deemed to limit the time for bringing an action to establish the title to, or right of possession of, real or personal property.

(d) Subject to the provisions of section 2416 of this title and except as otherwise provided by Congress, every action for the recovery of money erroneously paid to or on behalf of any civilian employee of any agency of the United States or to or on behalf of any member or dependent of any member of the uniformed services of the United States, incident to the employment or services of such employee or member, shall be barred unless the complaint is filed within six years after the right of action accrues: *Provided*, That in the event of later partial payment or written acknowledgment of debt, the right of action shall be deemed to accrue again at the time of each such payment or acknowledgment.

(e) In the event that any action to which this section applies is timely brought and is thereafter dismissed without prejudice, the action may be recommenced within one year after such dismissal, regardless of whether the action would otherwise then be barred by this section. In any action so recommenced the defendant shall not be barred from interposing any claim which would not have been barred in the original action.

(f) The provisions of this section shall not prevent the assertion, in an action against the United States or an officer or agency thereof, of any claim of the United States or an officer or agency thereof against an opposing party, a co-party, or a third party that arises out of the transaction or occurrence that is the subject matter of the opposing party's claim. A claim of the United States or an officer or agency thereof that does not arise out of the transaction or occurrence that is the subject matter of the opposing party's claim may, if time-barred, be asserted only by way of offset and may be allowed in an amount not to exceed the amount of the opposing party's recovery.

(g) Any right of action subject to the provisions of this section which accrued prior to the date of enactment of this Act shall, for purposes of this section, be deemed to have accrued on the date of enactment of this Act.

(h) Nothing in this Act shall apply to actions brought under the Internal Revenue Code or incidental to the collection of taxes imposed by the United States.

(i) The provisions of this section shall not prevent the United States or an officer or agency thereof from collecting any claim of the United States by means of administrative offset, in accordance with section 3716 of title 31.

§ 2416. Time for Commencing Actions Brought by the United States—Exclusions

For the purpose of computing the limitations periods established in section 2415, there shall be excluded all periods during which—

(a) the defendant or the res is outside the United States, its territories and possessions, the District of Columbia, or the Commonwealth of Puerto Rico; or

(b) the defendant is exempt from legal process because of infancy, mental incompetence, diplomatic immunity, or for any other reason; or

(c) facts material to the right of action are not known and reasonably could not be known by an official of the United States charged with the responsibility to act in the circumstances; or

(d) the United States is in a state of war declared pursuant to article I, section 8, of the Constitution of the United States.

PART VIII

THE CONSTITUTION OF THE UNITED STATES*

1787**

Preamble

We the People of the United States, in Order to form a more perfect Union, establish Justice, insure domestic Tranquility, provide for the common defence,

* Adapted, with permission, from United States Code Annotated, Constitution of the United States, Annotated (West Publishing Co. 1968).

** In May, 1785, a committee of Congress made a report recommending an alteration in the Articles of Confederation, but no action was taken on it, and it was left to the State Legislatures to proceed in the matter. In January, 1786, the Legislature of Virginia passed a resolution providing for the appointment of five commissioners, who, or any three of them, should meet such commissioners as might be appointed in the other States of the Union, at a time and place to be agreed upon, to take into consideration the trade of the United States; to consider how far a uniform system in their commercial regulations may be necessary to their common interest and their permanent harmony; and to report to the several States such an act, relative to this great object, as, when ratified by them, will enable the United States in Congress effectually to provide for the same. The Virginia commissioners, after some correspondence, fixed the first Monday in September as the time, and the city of Annapolis as the place for the meeting, but only four other States were represented, viz.: Delaware, New York, New Jersey, and Pennsylvania; the commissioners appointed by Massachusetts, New Hampshire, North Carolina, and Rhode Island failed to attend. Under the circumstances of so partial a representation, the commissioners present agreed upon a report, (drawn by Mr. Hamilton of New York,) expressing their unanimous conviction that it might essentially tend to advance the interests of the Union if the States by which they were respectively delegated would concur, and use their endeavors to procure the concurrence of the other States, in the appointment of commissioners to meet at Philadelphia on the second Monday of May following, to take into consideration the situation of the United States; to devise such further provisions as should appear to them necessary to render the

Constitution of the Federal Government adequate to the exigences of the Union; and to report such an act for that purpose to the United States in Congress assembled as, when agreed to by them, and afterwards confirmed by the Legislatures of every State, would effectually provide for the same.

Congress, on the 21st of February, 1787, adopted a resolution in favor of a convention, and the Legislatures of those States which had not already done so (with the exception of Rhode Island) promptly appointed delegates. On the 25th of May, seven States having convened, George Washington, of Virginia, was unanimously elected President, and the consideration of the proposed constitution was commenced. On the 17th of September, 1787, the Constitution as engrossed and agreed upon was signed by all the members present, except Mr. Gerry, of Massachusetts, and Messrs. Mason and Randolph, of Virginia. The president of the convention transmitted it to Congress, with a resolution stating how the proposed Federal Government should be put in operation, and an explanatory letter. Congress, on the 28th of September, 1787, directed the Constitution so framed, with the resolutions and letter concerning the same, to "be transmitted to the several Legislatures in order to be submitted to a convention of delegates chosen in each State by the people thereof, in conformity to the resolves of the convention."

On the 4th of March, 1789, the day which had been fixed for commencing the operations of Government under the new Constitution, it had been ratified by the conventions chosen in each State to consider it, as follows: Delaware, December 7, 1787; Pennsylvania, December 12, 1787; New Jersey, December 18, 1787; Georgia, January 2, 1788; Connecticut, January 9, 1788; Massachusetts, February 6, 1788; Maryland, April 28, 1788; South Carolina, May 23, 1788; New Hampshire, June 21, 1788; Virginia, June 26, 1788; and New York, July 26, 1788.

promote the general Welfare, and secure the Blessings of Liberty to ourselves and our Posterity, do ordain and establish this Constitution for the United States of America.

Article I

Section 1. All legislative Powers herein granted shall be vested in a Congress of the United States, which shall consist of a Senate and House of Representatives.

Section 2. [1] The House of Representatives shall be composed of Members chosen every second Year by the People of the several States, and the Electors in each State shall have the Qualifications requisite for Electors of the most numerous Branch of the State Legislature.

[2] No Person shall be a Representative who shall not have attained to the Age of twenty five Years, and been seven Years a Citizen of the United States, and who shall not, when elected, be an Inhabitant of that State in which he shall be chosen.

[3] [Representatives and direct Taxes shall be apportioned among the several States which may be included within this Union, according to their respective Numbers, which shall be determined by adding to the whole Number of free Persons, including those bound to Service for a Term of Years, and excluding Indians not taxed, three fifths of all other Persons.] The actual Enumeration shall be made within three Years after the first Meeting of the Congress of the United States, and within every subsequent Term of ten Years, in such Manner as they shall by Law direct. The Number of Representatives shall not exceed one for every thirty Thousand, but each State shall have at Least one Representative; and until such enumeration shall be made, the State of New Hampshire shall be entitled to chuse three, Massachusetts eight, Rhode Island and Providence Plantations one, Connecticut five, New York six, New Jersey four, Pennsylvania eight, Delaware one, Maryland six, Virginia ten, North Carolina five, South Carolina five, and Georgia three.

The clause of this paragraph inclosed in brackets was amended, as to the mode of apportionment of representatives among the several states, by the Fourteenth Amendment, § 2, and as to taxes on incomes without apportionment, by the Sixteenth Amendment.

[4] When vacancies happen in the Representation from any State, the Executive Authority thereof shall issue Writs of Election to fill such Vacancies.

[5] The House of Representatives shall chuse their Speaker and other Officers; and shall have the sole Power of Impeachment.

Section 3. [1] [The Senate of the United States shall be composed of two Senators from each State, chosen by the Legislature thereof, for six Years; and each Senator shall have one Vote.]

This paragraph and the clause of following paragraph inclosed in brackets were superseded by the Seventeenth Amendment.

[2] Immediately after they shall be assembled in Consequence of the first Election, they shall be divided as equally as may be into three Classes. The Seats

The President informed Congress, on the 28th of January, 1790, that North Carolina had ratified the Constitution November 21, 1789; and he informed Congress on the 1st of June, 1790, that Rhode Island had ratified the Constitution May 29, 1790. Vermont, in convention, ratified the Constitution January 10, 1791, and was on March 4, 1791, by an act of Congress approved February 18, 1791, "received and admitted into this Union as a new and entire member of theUnited States".

of the Senators of the first Class shall be vacated at the Expiration of the Second Year, of the second Class at the Expiration of the fourth Year, and of the third Class at the Expiration of the sixth Year, so that one third may be chosen every second Year; [and if Vacancies happen by Resignation, or otherwise, during the Recess of the Legislature of any State, the Executive thereof may make temporary Appointments until the next Meeting of the Legislature, which shall then fill such Vacancies.]

See note to preceding paragraph of this section.

[3] No Person shall be a Senator who shall not have attained to the Age of thirty Years, and been nine Years a Citizen of the United States, and who shall not, when elected, be an Inhabitant of that State for which he shall be chosen.

[4] The Vice President of the United States shall be President of the Senate, but shall have no Vote, unless they be equally divided.

[5] The Senate shall chuse their other Officers, and also a President pro tempore, in the Absence of the Vice President, or when he shall exercise the Office of President of the United States.

[6] The Senate shall have the sole Power to try all Impeachments. When sitting for that Purpose, they shall be on Oath or Affirmation. When the President of the United States is tried, the Chief Justice shall preside: And no Person shall be convicted without the Concurrence of two thirds of the Members present.

[7] Judgment in Cases of Impeachment shall not extend further than to removal from Office, and disqualification to hold and enjoy any Office of honor, Trust, or Profit under the United States: but the Party convicted shall nevertheless be liable and subject to Indictment, Trial, Judgment, and Punishment, according to Law.

Section 4. [1] The Times, Places and Manner of holding Elections for Senators and Representatives, shall be prescribed in each State by the Legislature thereof; but the Congress may at any time by Law make or alter such Regulations, except as to the Places of chusing Senators.

[2] The Congress shall assemble at least once in every Year, and such Meeting shall be on the first Monday in December, unless they shall by Law appoint a different Day.

Section 5. [1] Each House shall be the Judge of the Elections, Returns, and Qualifications of its own Members, and a Majority of each shall constitute a Quorum to do Business; but a smaller Number may adjourn from day to day, and may be authorized to compel the Attendance of absent Members, in such Manner, and under such Penalties as each House may provide.

[2] Each House may determine the Rules of its Proceedings, punish its Members for disorderly Behaviour, and, with the Concurrence of two thirds, expel a Member.

[3] Each House shall keep a Journal of its Proceedings, and from time to time publish the same, excepting such Parts as may in their Judgment require Secrecy; and the Yeas and Nays of the Members of either House on any question shall, at the Desire of one fifth of those Present, be entered on the Journal.

[4] Neither House, during the Session of Congress, shall, without the Consent of the other, adjourn for more than three days, nor to any other Place than that in which the two Houses shall be sitting.

Section 6. [1] The Senators and Representatives shall receive a Compensation for their Services, to be ascertained by Law, and paid out of the Treasury of the United States. They shall in all Cases, except Treason, Felony and Breach of the Peace, be privileged from Arrest during their Attendance at the Session of their respective Houses, and in going to and returning from the same; and for any Speech or Debate in either House, they shall not be questioned in any other Place.

[2]   No Senator or Representative shall, during the Time for which he was elected, be appointed to any civil Office under the Authority of the United States, which shall have been created, or the Emoluments whereof shall have been increased during such time; and no Person holding any Office under the United States, shall be a Member of either House during his Continuance in Office.

Section 7. [1] All Bills for raising Revenue shall originate in the House of Representatives; but the Senate may propose or concur with Amendments as on other Bills.

[2]   Every Bill which shall have passed the House of Representatives and the Senate, shall, before it become a Law, be presented to the President of the United States; If he approve he shall sign it, but if not he shall return it, with his Objections to the House in which it shall have originated, who shall enter the Objections at large on their Journal, and proceed to reconsider it. If after such Reconsideration two thirds of that House shall agree to pass the Bill, it shall be sent together with the Objections, to the other House, by which it shall likewise be reconsidered, and if approved by two thirds of that House, it shall become a Law. But in all such Cases the Votes of both Houses shall be determined by Yeas and Nays, and the Names of the Persons voting for and against the Bill shall be entered on the Journal of each House respectively. If any Bill shall not be returned by the President within ten Days (Sundays excepted) after it shall have been presented to him, the Same shall be a Law, in like Manner as if he had signed it, unless the Congress by their Adjournment prevent its Return in which Case it shall not be a Law.

[3]   Every Order, Resolution, or Vote, to Which the Concurrence of the Senate and House of Representatives may be necessary (except on a question of Adjournment) shall be presented to the President of the United States; and before the Same shall take Effect, shall be approved by him, or being disapproved by him, shall be repassed by two thirds of the Senate and House of Representatives, according to the Rules and Limitations prescribed in the Case of a Bill.

Section 8. [1] The Congress shall have Power to lay and collect Taxes, Duties, Imposts and Excises, to pay the Debts and provide for the common Defence and general Welfare of the United States; but all Duties, Imposts and Excises shall be uniform throughout the United States;

[2]   To borrow money on the credit of the United States;

[3]   To regulate Commerce with foreign Nations, and among the several States, and with the Indian Tribes;

[4]   To establish an uniform Rule of Naturalization, and uniform Laws on the subject of Bankruptcies throughout the United States;

[5]   To coin Money, regulate the Value thereof, and of foreign Coin, and fix the Standard of Weights and Measures;

[6]   To provide for the Punishment of counterfeiting the Securities and current Coin of the United States;

[7]   To Establish Post Offices and Post Roads;

[8] To promote the Progress of Science and useful Arts, by securing for limited Times to Authors and Inventors the exclusive Right to their respective Writings and Discoveries;

[9] To constitute Tribunals inferior to the supreme Court;

[10] To define and punish Piracies and Felonies committed on the high Seas, and Offenses against the Law of Nations;

[11] To declare War, grant Letters of Marque and Reprisal, and make Rules concerning Captures on Land and Water;

[12] To raise and support Armies, but no Appropriation of Money to that Use shall be for a longer Term than two Years;

[13] To provide and maintain a Navy;

[14] To make Rules for the Government and Regulation of the land and naval Forces;

[15] To provide for calling forth the Militia to execute the Laws of the Union, suppress Insurrections and repel Invasions;

[16] To provide for organizing, arming, and disciplining, the Militia, and for governing such Part of them as may be employed in the Service of the United States, reserving to the States respectively, the Appointment of the Officers, and the Authority of training the Militia according to the discipline prescribed by Congress;

[17] To exercise exclusive Legislation in all Cases whatsoever, over such District (not exceeding ten Miles square) as may, by Cession of particular States and the Acceptance of Congress, become the Seat of the Government of the United States, and to exercise like Authority over all Places purchased by the Consent of the Legislature of the State in which the Same shall be, for the Erection of Forts, Magazines, Arsenals, dock-Yards, and other needful Buildings;—And

[18] To make all Laws which shall be necessary and proper for carrying into Execution the foregoing Powers, and all other Powers vested by this Constitution in the Government of the United States, or in any Department or Officer thereof.

Section 9. [1] The Migration or Importation of Such Persons as any of the States now existing shall think proper to admit, shall not be prohibited by the Congress prior to the Year one thousand eight hundred and eight, but a Tax or duty may be imposed on such Importation, not exceeding ten dollars for each Person.

[2] The privilege of the Writ of Habeas Corpus shall not be suspended, unless when in Cases of Rebellion or Invasion the public Safety may require it.

[3] No Bill of Attainder or ex post facto Law shall be passed.

[4] No Capitation, or other direct, Tax shall be laid, unless in Proportion to the Census or Enumeration herein before directed to be taken.

[5] No Tax or Duty shall be laid on Articles exported from any State.

[6] No Preference shall be given by any Regulation of Commerce or Revenue to the Ports of one State over those of another: nor shall Vessels bound to, or from, one State be obliged to enter, clear, or pay Duties in another.

[7] No money shall be drawn from the Treasury, but in Consequence of Appropriations made by Law; and a regular Statement and Account of the Receipts and Expenditures of all public Money shall be published from time to time.

[8] No Title of Nobility shall be granted by the United States: And no Person holding any Office of Profit or Trust under them, shall, without the

Consent of the Congress, accept of any present, Emolument, Office, or Title, of any kind whatever, from any King, Prince, or foreign State.

Section 10. [1] No State shall enter into any Treaty, Alliance, or Confederation; grant Letters of Marque and Reprisal; coin Money; emit Bills of Credit; make any Thing but gold and silver Coin a Tender in Payment of Debts; pass any Bill of Attainder, ex post facto Law, or Law impairing the Obligation of Contracts, or grant any Title of Nobility.

[2]   No State shall, without the Consent of the Congress, lay any Imposts or Duties on Imports or Exports, except what may be absolutely necessary for executing it's inspection Laws: and the net Produce of all Duties and Imposts, laid by any State on Imports or Exports, shall be for the Use of the Treasury of the United States; and all such Laws shall be subject to the Revision and Controul of the Congress.

[3]   No State shall, without the Consent of Congress, lay any Duty of Tonnage, keep Troops, or Ships of War in time of Peace, enter into any Agreement or Compact with another State, or with a foreign Power or engage in War, unless actually invaded, or in such imminent Danger as will not admit of delay.

Article II

Section 1. [1] The executive Power shall be vested in a President of the United States of America. He shall hold his Office during the Term of four Years, and, together with the Vice President, chosen for the same Term, be elected, as follows:

[2]   Each State shall appoint, in such Manner as the Legislature thereof may direct, a Number of Electors, equal to the whole Number of Senators and Representatives to which the State may be entitled in the Congress; but no Senator or Representative, or Person holding an Office of Trust or Profit under the United States, shall be appointed an Elector.

[3]   [The Electors shall meet in their respective States, and vote by Ballot for two Persons, of whom one at least shall not be an Inhabitant of the same State with themselves. And they shall make a List of all the Persons voted for, and of the Number of Votes for each; which List they shall sign and certify, and transmit sealed to the Seat of the Government of the United States, directed to the President of the Senate. The President of the Senate shall, in the Presence of the Senate and House of Representatives, open all the Certificates, and the Votes shall then be counted. The Person having the greatest Number of Votes shall be the President, if such Number be a Majority of the whole Number of Electors appointed; and if there be more than one who have such Majority, and have an equal Number of Votes, then the House of Representatives shall immediately chuse by Ballot one of them for President; and if no Person have a Majority, then from the five highest on the List the said House shall in like Manner chuse the President. But in chusing the President, the Votes shall be taken by States, the Representation from each State having one Vote; A quorum for this Purpose shall consist of a Member or Members from two thirds of the States, and a Majority of all the States shall be necessary to a Choice. In every Case, after the Choice of the President, the Person having the greater Number of Votes of the Electors shall be the Vice President. But if there should remain two or more who have equal Votes, the Senate shall chuse from them by Ballot the Vice President.]

This paragraph, inclosed in brackets, was superseded by the Twelfth Amendment, post.

[4]   The Congress may determine the Time of chusing the Electors, and the Day on which they shall give their Votes; which Day shall be the same throughout the United States.

[5]   No person except a natural born Citizen, or a Citizen of the United States, at the time of the Adoption of this Constitution, shall be eligible to the Office of President; neither shall any Person be eligible to that Office who shall not have attained to the Age of thirty five Years, and been fourteen Years a Resident within the United States.

[6]   In case of the removal of the President from Office, or of his Death, Resignation or Inability to discharge the Powers and Duties of the said Office, the Same shall devolve on the Vice President and the Congress may by Law provide for the Case of Removal, Death, Resignation or Inability, both of the President and Vice President, declaring what Officer shall then act as President, and such Officer shall act accordingly, until the Disability be removed, or a President shall be elected.

[7]   The President shall, at stated Times, receive for his Services, a Compensation, which shall neither be increased nor diminished during the Period for which he shall have been elected, and he shall not receive within that Period any other Emolument from the United States, or any of them.

[8]   Before he enter on the Execution of his Office, he shall take the following Oath or Affirmation: "I do solemnly swear (or affirm) that I will faithfully execute the Office of President of the United States, and will to the best of my Ability, preserve, protect and defend the Constitution of the United States."

Section 2. [1] The President shall be Commander in Chief of the Army and Navy of the United States, and of the militia of the several States, when called into the actual Service of the United States; he may require the Opinion, in writing, of the principal Officer in each of the Executive Departments, upon any Subject relating to the Duties of their respective Offices and he shall have Power to grant Reprieves and Pardons for Offenses against the United States, except in Cases of Impeachment.

[2]   He shall have Power, by and with the Advice and Consent of the Senate, to make Treaties, provided two thirds of the Senators present concur; and he shall nominate, and by and with the Advice and Consent of the Senate, shall appoint Ambassadors, other public Ministers and Consuls, Judges of the supreme Court, and all other Officers of the United States, whose Appointments are not herein otherwise provided for, and which shall be established by Law; but the Congress may by Law vest the Appointment of such inferior Officers, as they think proper, in the President alone, in the Courts of Law, or in the Heads of Departments.

[3]   The President shall have Power to fill up all Vacancies that may happen during the Recess of the Senate, by granting Commissions which shall expire at the End of their next Session.

Section 3. He shall from time to time give to the Congress Information of the State of the Union, and recommend to their Consideration such Measures as he shall judge necessary and expedient; he may, on extraordinary Occasions, convene both Houses, or either of them, and in Case of Disagreement between them, with Respect to the Time of Adjournment, he may adjourn them to such Time as he shall think proper; he shall receive Ambassadors and other public

Ministers; he shall take Care that the Laws be faithfully executed, and shall Commission all the Officers of the United States.

Section 4. The President, Vice President and all civil Officers of the United States, shall be removed from Office on Impeachment for, and Conviction of, Treason, Bribery, or other high Crimes and Misdemeanors.

Article III

Section 1. The judicial Power of the United States, shall be vested in one supreme Court, and in such inferior Courts as the Congress may from time to time ordain and establish. The Judges, both of the supreme and inferior Courts, shall hold their Offices during good Behaviour, and shall, at stated Times, receive for their Services a Compensation, which shall not be diminished during their Continuance in Office.

Section 2. [1] The judicial Power shall extend to all Cases, in Law and Equity, arising under this Constitution, the Laws of the United States, and Treaties made, or which shall be made, under their Authority;—to all Cases affecting Ambassadors, other public Ministers and Consuls;—to all Cases of admiralty and maritime Jurisdiction;—to Controversies to which the United States shall be a Party;—to Controversies between two or more States;— between a State and Citizens of another State;—between Citizens of different States;—between Citizens of the same State claiming Lands under the Grants of different States, and between a State, or the Citizens thereof, and foreign States, Citizens or Subjects.

[2] In all Cases affecting Ambassadors, other public Ministers and Consuls, and those in which a State shall be a Party, the supreme Court shall have original Jurisdiction. In all the other Cases before mentioned, the supreme Court shall have appellate Jurisdiction, both as to Law and Fact, with such Exceptions, and under such Regulations as the Congress shall make.

[3] The trial of all Crimes, except in Cases of Impeachment, shall be by Jury; and such Trial shall be held in the State where the said Crimes shall have been committed; but when not committed within any State, the Trial shall be at such Place or Places as the Congress may by Law have directed.

Section 3. [1] Treason against the United States, shall consist only in levying War against them, or, in adhering to their Enemies, giving them Aid and Comfort. No Person shall be convicted of Treason unless on the Testimony of two Witnesses to the same overt Act, or on Confession in open Court.

[2] The Congress shall have Power to declare the Punishment of Treason, but no Attainder of Treason shall work Corruption of Blood, or Forfeiture except during the Life of the Person attainted.

Article IV

Section 1. Full Faith and Credit shall be given in each State to the public Acts, Records, and judicial Proceedings of every other State. And the Congress may by general Laws prescribe the Manner in which such Acts, Records and Proceedings shall be proved, and the Effect thereof.

Section 2. [1] The Citizens of each State shall be entitled to all Privileges and Immunities of Citizens in the several States.

[2] A Person charged in any State with Treason, Felony, or other Crime, who shall flee from Justice, and be found in another State, shall on demand of

the executive Authority of the State from which he fled, be delivered up, to be removed to the State having Jurisdiction of the Crime.

[3] No Person held to Service or Labour in one State, under the Laws thereof, escaping into another, shall, in Consequence of any Law or Regulation therein, be discharged from such Service or Labour, but shall be delivered up on Claim of the Party to whom such Service or Labour may be due.

Section 3. [1] New States may be admitted by the Congress into this Union; but no new State shall be formed or erected within the Jurisdiction of any other State; nor any State be formed by the Junction of two or more States, or Parts of States, without the Consent of the Legislatures of the States concerned as well as of the Congress.

[2] The Congress shall have Power to dispose of and make all needful Rules and Regulations respecting the Territory or other Property belonging to the United States; and nothing in this Constitution shall be so construed as to Prejudice any Claims of the United States, or of any particular State.

Section 4. The United States shall guarantee to every State in this Union a Republican Form of Government, and shall protect each of them against Invasion; and on Application of the Legislature, or of the Executive (when the Legislature cannot be convened) against domestic Violence.

Article V

The Congress, whenever two thirds of both Houses shall deem it necessary, shall propose Amendments to this Constitution, or, on the Application of the Legislatures of two thirds of the several States, shall call a Convention for proposing Amendments, which, in either Case, shall be valid to all Intents and Purposes, as part of this Constitution, when ratified by the Legislatures of three fourths of the several States, or by Conventions in three fourths thereof, as the one or the other Mode of Ratification may be proposed by the Congress; Provided that no Amendment which may be made prior to the Year One thousand eight hundred and eight shall in any Manner affect the first and fourth Clauses in the Ninth Section of the first Article; and that no State, without its Consent, shall be deprived of its equal Suffrage in the Senate.

Article VI

[1] All Debts contracted and Engagements entered into, before the Adoption of this Constitution, shall be as valid against the United States under this Constitution, as under the Confederation.

[2] This Constitution, and the Laws of the United States which shall be made in Pursuance thereof; and all Treaties made, or which shall be made, under the Authority of the United States, shall be the supreme Law of the Land; and the Judges in every State shall be bound thereby, any Thing in the Constitution or Laws of any State to the Contrary notwithstanding.

[3] The Senators and Representatives before mentioned, and the Members of the several State Legislatures, and all executive and judicial Officers, both of the United States and of the several States, shall be bound by Oath or Affirmation, to support this Constitution; but no religious Test shall ever be required as a Qualification to any Office or public Trust under the United States.

Article VII

The Ratification of the Conventions of nine States shall be sufficient for the Establishment of this Constitution between the States so ratifying the Same. DONE in Convention by the Unanimous Consent of the States present the Seventeenth Day of September in the Year of Our Lord one thousand seven hundred and Eighty seven and of the Independence of the United States of America the Twelfth. IN WITNESS whereof We have hereunto subscribed our Names,

Go. WASHINGTON—
Presidt.
and deputy from
Virginia

New Hampshire

JOHN LANGDON   NICHOLAS GILMAN

Massachusetts

NATHANIEL GORHAM   RUFUS KING

Connecticut

WM. SAML. JOHNSON   ROGER SHERMAN

New York

ALEXANDER HAMILTON

New Jersey

WIL: LIVINGSTON   WM. PATERSON
DAVID BREARLEY   JONA: DAYTON

Pennsylvania

B. FRANKLIN   THOS. FITZSIMONS
THOMAS MIFFLIN   JARED INGERSOLL
ROBT. MORRIS   JAMES WILSON
GEO. CLYMER   GOUV MORRIS

Delaware

GEO: READ   RICHARD BASSETT
GUNNING BEDFORD JUN   JACO: BROOM
JOHN DICKINSON

Maryland

JAMES MCHENRY   DANL. CARROLL
DAN OF ST THOS. JENIFER

Virginia

JOHN BLAIR   JAMES MADISON, JR.

North Carolina

WM. BLOUNT   HU WILLIAMSON
RICHD. DOBBS SPAIGHT

South Carolina

J. RUTLEDGE   CHARLES PINCKNEY
CHARLES COTESWORTH PINCKNEY   PIERCE BUTLER

Georgia

WILLIAM FEW   ABR BALDWIN
Attest   WILLIAM JACKSON
                                              Secretary

ARTICLES IN ADDITION TO, AND AMENDMENT OF, THE CONSTITU-
TION OF THE UNITED STATES OF AMERICA, PROPOSED BY CON-
GRESS, AND RATIFIED BY THE LEGISLATURES OF THE SEVERAL
STATES PURSUANT TO THE FIFTH ARTICLE OF THE ORIGINAL

CONSTITUTION.[1]

Amendment [I] [1791][2]

Congress shall make no law respecting an establishment of religion, or prohibiting the free exercise thereof; or abridging the freedom of speech, or of the press; or the right of the people peaceably to assemble, and to petition the Government for a redress of grievances.

Amendment [II] [1791]

A well regulated Militia, being necessary to the security of a free State, the right of the people to keep and bear Arms, shall not be infringed.

Amendment [III] [1791]

No Soldier shall, in time of peace be quartered in any house, without the consent of the Owner, nor in time of war, but in a manner to be prescribed by law.

Amendment [IV] [1791]

The right of the people to be secure in their persons, houses, papers, and effects, against unreasonable searches and seizures, shall not be violated, and no Warrants shall issue, but upon probable cause, supported by Oath or affirmation, and particularly describing the place to be searched, and the persons or things to be seized.

Amendment [V] [1791]

No person shall be held to answer for a capital, or otherwise infamous crime, unless on a presentment or indictment of a Grand Jury, except in cases arising in the land or naval forces, or in the Militia, when in actual service in time of War or public danger; nor shall any person be subject for the same offence to be twice put in jeopardy of life or limb; nor shall be compelled in any criminal case to be a witness against himself, nor be deprived of life, liberty, or property, without due process of law; nor shall private property be taken for public use, without just compensation.

Amendment [VI] [1791]

In all criminal prosecutions, the accused shall enjoy the right to a speedy and public trial, by an impartial jury of the State and district wherein the crime

1. All of the Amendments except the 13th, 14th, 15th, and 16th, were not specifically assigned a number in the resolution proposing the Amendment. Brackets enclose the number for such Amendments. The 13th, 14th, 15th, and 16th Amendments were ratified by number and thus no brackets enclose such Amendment numbers.

2. The first ten amendments to the Constitution of the United States were proposed to the legislatures of the several States by the First Congress, on the 25th of September 1789. They were ratified by the following States, and the notifications of ratification by the governors thereof were successively communicated by the President to Congress: New Jersey, November 20, 1789; Maryland, December 19, 1789; North Carolina, December 22, 1789; South Carolina, January 19, 1790; New Hampshire, January 25, 1790; Delaware, January 28, 1790; Pennsylvania, March 10, 1790; New York, March 27, 1790; Rhode Island, June 15, 1790; Vermont, November 3, 1791, and Virginia, December 15, 1791. The legislatures of Connecticut, Georgia, and Massachusetts ratified them on April 19, 1939, March 24, 1939, and March 2, 1939, respectively.

Note: other amendments have also been ratified by states after the amendment has been announced as ratified; these other, after-the-fact ratifications are not usually noted in this appendix.

shall have been committed, which district shall have been previously ascertained by law, and to be informed of the nature and cause of the accusation; to be confronted with the witnesses against him; to have compulsory process for obtaining witnesses in his favor, and to have the Assistance of Counsel for his defence.

Amendment [VII] [1791]

In Suits at common law, where the value in controversy shall exceed twenty dollars, the right of trial by jury shall be preserved, and no fact tried by jury, shall be otherwise re-examined in any Court of the United States, than according to the rules of the common law.

Amendment [VIII] [1791]

Excessive bail shall not be required, nor excessive fines imposed, nor cruel and unusual punishments inflicted.

Amendment [IX] [1791]

The enumeration in the Constitution, of certain rights, shall not be construed to deny or disparage others retained by the people.

Amendment [X] [1791]

The powers not delegated to the United States by the Constitution, nor prohibited by it to the States, are reserved to the States respectively, or to the people.

Amendment [XI] [1798]

The Judicial power of the United States shall not be construed to extend to any suit in law or equity, commenced or prosecuted against one of the United States by Citizens of another State, or by Citizens or Subjects of any Foreign State.

Historical Note

This amendment was proposed to the legislatures of the several States by the Third Congress, on the 5th September, 1794, and was declared in a message from the President to Congress, dated the 8th of January, 1798, to have been ratified by the legislatures of three-fourths of the States.

Amendment [XII] [1804]

The Electors shall meet in their respective states and vote by ballot for President and Vice–President, one of whom, at least, shall not be an inhabitant of the same state with themselves; they shall name in their ballots the person voted for as President, and in distinct ballots the person voted for as Vice–President, and they shall make distinct lists of all persons voted for as President, and of all persons voted for as Vice–President, and of the number of votes for each, which lists they shall sign and certify, and transmit sealed to the seat of the government of the United States, directed to the President of the Senate;— The President of the Senate shall, in the presence of the Senate and House of Representatives, open all the certificates and the votes shall then be counted;— The person having the greatest number of votes for President, shall be the President, if such number be a majority of the whole number of Electors appointed; and if no person have such majority, then from the persons having the highest numbers not exceeding three on the list of those voted for as President, the House of Representatives shall choose immediately, by ballot, the President. But in choosing the President, the votes shall be taken by states, the representation from each state having one vote; a quorum for this purpose shall consist of a member or members from two-thirds of the states, and a majority of all the states shall be necessary to a choice. And if the House of Representatives shall not choose a President whenever the right of choice shall devolve upon them before the fourth day of March next following, then the Vice–President shall act as President, as in the case of the death or other constitutional disability of the President.—The person having the greatest number of votes as Vice–President, shall be the Vice–President, if such number be a majority of the whole number of Electors appointed, and if no person have a majority, then from the two highest numbers on the list, the Senate shall choose the Vice–President; a quorum for the purpose shall consist of two-thirds of the whole number of Senators, and a majority of the whole number shall be necessary to a choice. But no person constitutionally ineligible to the office of President shall be eligible to that of Vice–President of the United States.

Historical Note

This amendment was proposed to the legislatures of the several States by the Eighth Congress, on the 12th of December, 1803, in lieu of the original third paragraph of the first section of the second article, and was declared in a proclamation of the Secretary of State, dated the 25th of September, 1804, to have been ratified by the legislatures of three-fourths of the States.

Amendment XIII [1865]

Section 1. Neither slavery nor involuntary servitude, except as a punishment for crime whereof the party shall have been duly convicted, shall exist within the United States, or any place subject to their jurisdiction.

Section 2. Congress shall have power to enforce this article by appropriate legislation.

Historical Note

This amendment was proposed to the legislatures of the several States by the Thirty-eighth Congress, on the 1st of February, 1865, and was declared, in a proclamation of the Secretary of State, dated the 18th of December, 1865, to have been ratified by the legislatures of twenty-seven of the thirty-six States, viz: Illinois, Rhode Island, Michigan, Maryland, New York, West Virginia, Maine, Kansas, Massachusetts, Pennsylvania, Virginia, Ohio, Missouri, Nevada, Indiana, Louisiana, Minnesota, Wisconsin, Vermont, Tennessee, Arkansas, Connecticut, New Hampshire, South Carolina, Alabama, North Carolina, and Georgia.

Amendment XIV [1868]

Section 1. All persons born or naturalized in the United States, and subject to the jurisdiction thereof, are citizens of the United States and of the State wherein they reside. No State shall make or enforce any law which shall abridge the privileges or immunities of citizens of the United States; nor shall any State deprive any person of life, liberty, or property, without due process of law; nor deny to any person within its jurisdiction the equal protection of the laws.

Section 2. Representatives shall be apportioned among the several States according to their respective numbers, counting the whole number of persons in each State, excluding Indians not taxed. But when the right to vote at any election for the choice of electors for President and Vice President of the United States, Representatives in Congress, the Executive and Judicial officers of a State, or the members of the Legislature thereof, is denied to any of the male inhabitants of such State, being twenty-one years of age, and citizens of the United States, or in any way abridged, except for participation in rebellion, or other crime, the basis of representation therein shall be reduced in the proportion which the number of such male citizens shall bear to the whole number of male citizens twenty-one years of age in such State.

Section 3. No person shall be a Senator or Representative in Congress, or elector of President and Vice President, or hold any office, civil or military, under the United States, or under any State, who having previously taken an oath, as a member of Congress, or as an officer of the United States, or as a member of any State legislature, or as an executive or judicial officer of any State, to support the Constitution of the United States, shall have engaged in insurrection or rebellion against the same, or given aid or comfort to the enemies thereof. But Congress may by a vote of two-thirds of each House, remove such disability.

Section 4. The validity of the public debt of the United States, authorized by law, including debts incurred for payment of pensions and bounties for services in suppressing insurrection or rebellion, shall not be questioned. But neither the United States nor any State shall assume or pay any debt or obligation incurred in aid of insurrection or rebellion against the United States, or any claim for the loss or emancipation of any slave; but all such debts, obligations and claims shall be held illegal and void.

Section 5. The Congress shall have power to enforce, by appropriate legislation, the provisions of this article.

Historical Note

This amendment was proposed to the legislatures of the several States by the Thirty-ninth Congress, on the 16th of June, 1866. On the 21st of July, 1868, Congress adopted and transmitted to the Department of State a concurrent resolution, declaring that "the legislatures of the States of Connecticut, Tennessee, New Jersey, Oregon, Vermont, New York, Ohio, Illinois, West Virginia, Kansas, Maine, Nevada, Missouri, Indiana, Minnesota, New Hampshire, Massachusetts, Nebraska, Iowa, Arkansas, Florida, North Carolina, Alabama, South Carolina, and Louisiana, being three-fourths and more of the several States of the Union, have ratified the fourteenth article of amendment to the Constitution of the United States, duly proposed by two-thirds of each House of the Thirty-ninth Congress: Therefore, Resolved, That said fourteenth article is hereby declared to be a part of the Constitution of the United States, and it shall be duly promulgated as such by the Secretary of State." The Secretary of State accordingly issued a proclamation, dated the 28th of July, 1868, declaring that the proposed fourteenth amendment had been ratified, in the manner hereafter mentioned by the legislatures of thirty of the thirty-six States, viz: Connecticut, June 30, 1866; New Hampshire, July 7, 1866; Tennessee, July 19, 1866; New Jersey, September 11, 1866, (and the legislature of the same State passed a resolution in April, 1868, to withdraw its consent to it); Oregon, September 19, 1866; Vermont, November 9, 1866; Georgia re-

1598

jected it November 13, 1866, and ratified it July 21, 1868; North Carolina rejected it December 4, 1866, and ratified it July 4, 1868; South Carolina rejected it December 20, 1866, and ratified it July 9, 1868; New York ratified it January 10, 1867; Ohio ratified it January 11, 1867, (and the legislature of the same State passed a resolution in January, 1868, to withdraw its consent to it); Illinois ratified it January 15, 1867; West Virginia, January 16, 1867; Kansas, January 18, 1867; Maine, January 19, 1867; Nevada, January 22, 1867; Missouri, January 26, 1867; Indiana, January 29, 1867; Minnesota, February 1, 1867; Rhode Island, February 7, 1867; Wisconsin, February 13, 1867; Pennsylvania, February 13, 1867; Michigan, February 15, 1867; Massachusetts, March 20, 1867; Nebraska, June 15, 1867; Iowa, April 3, 1868; Arkansas, April 6, 1868; Florida, June 9, 1868; Louisiana, July 9, 1868; and Alabama, July 13, 1868. Georgia again ratified the amendment February 2, 1870. Texas rejected it November 1, 1866, and ratified it February 18, 1870. Virginia rejected it January 19, 1867, and ratified October 8, 1869. The amendment was rejected by Kentucky January 10, 1867; by Delaware February 8, 1867; by Maryland March 23, 1867.

Amendment XV [1870]

Section 1. The right of citizens of the United States to vote shall not be denied or abridged by the United States or by any State on account of race, color, or previous condition of servitude.

Section 2. The Congress shall have power to enforce this article by appropriate legislation.

Historical Note

This amendment was proposed to the legislatures of the several States by the Fortieth Congress, on the 27th of February, 1869, and was declared, in a proclamation of the Secretary of State, dated March 30, 1870, to have been ratified by the legislatures of twenty-nine of the thirty-seven States. The dates of these ratifications (arranged in the order of their reception at the Department of State) were: from North Carolina, March 5, 1869; West Virginia, March 3, 1869; Massachusetts, March 12, 1869; Wisconsin, March 9, 1869; Maine, March 12, 1869; Louisiana, March 5, 1869; Michigan, March 8, 1869; South Carolina, March 16, 1869; Pennsylvania, March 26, 1869; Arkansas, March 30, 1869; Connecticut, May 19, 1869; Florida, June 15, 1869; Illinois, March 5, 1869; Indiana, May 14, 1869; New York, April 14, 1869, (and the legislature of the same State passed a resolution January 5, 1870, to withdraw its consent to it); New Hampshire, July 7, 1869; Nevada, March 1, 1869; Vermont, October 21, 1869; Virginia, October 8, 1869; Missouri, January 10, 1870; Mississippi, January 17, 1870; Ohio, January 27, 1870; Iowa, February 3, 1870; Kansas, January 19, 1870; Minnesota, February 19, 1870; Rhode Island, January 18, 1870; Nebraska, February 17, 1870; Texas, February 18, 1870. The State of Georgia also ratified the amendment February 2, 1870.

Amendment XVI [1913]

The Congress shall have power to lay and collect taxes on incomes, from whatever source derived, without apportionment among the several States, and without regard to any census or enumeration.

Historical Note

This Amendment was proposed to the legislatures of the several states by the Sixty–First Congress, on the 31st of July, 1909, and was declared, in a proclamation by the Secretary of State, dated the 25th of February, 1913, to have been ratified by the legislatures of the states of Alabama, Kentucky, South Carolina, Illinois, Mississippi, Oklahoma, Maryland, Georgia, Texas, Ohio, Idaho, Oregon, Washington, California, Montana, Indiana, Nevada, North Carolina, Nebraska, Kansas, Colorado, North Dakota, Michigan, Iowa, Missouri, Maine, Tennessee, Arkansas, Wisconsin, New York, South Dakota, Arizona, Minnesota, Louisiana, Delaware, and Wyoming, in all, thirty-six. The legislatures of New Jersey and New Mexico also passed resolutions ratifying the said proposed amendment.

Amendment [XVII] [1913]

[1] The Senate of the United States shall be composed of two Senators from each State, elected by the people thereof, for six years; and each Senator shall have one vote. The electors in each State shall have the qualifications requisite for electors of the most numerous branch of the State legislatures.

[2] When vacancies happen in the representation of any State in the Senate, the executive authority of such State shall issue writs of election to fill such vacancies: *Provided, that the legislature of any State may empower the executive thereof to make temporary appointments until the people fill the vacancies by election as the legislature may direct.*

[3] This amendment shall not be so construed as to affect the election or term of any Senator chosen before it becomes valid as part of the Constitution.

Historical Note

This amendment was proposed to the legislatures of the several states by the Sixty–Second Congress, on the 16th of May, 1912, in lieu of the original first paragraph of section 3 of article I, and in lieu of so much of paragraph 2 of the same section as related to the filling of vacancies, and was declared, in a proclamation by the Secretary of State, dated the 31st of May, 1913, to have been ratified by the legislatures of the states of Massachusetts, Arizona, Minnesota, New York, Kansas, Oregon, North Carolina, California, Michigan, Idaho, West Virginia, Nebraska, Iowa, Montana, Texas, Washington, Wyoming, Colorado, Illinois, North Dakota, Nevada, Vermont, Maine, New Hampshire, Oklahoma, Ohio, South Dakota, Indiana, Missouri, New Mexico, New Jersey, Tennessee, Arkansas, Connecticut, Pennsylvania, and Wisconsin, said states constituting three-fourths of the whole number of states.

Amendment [XVIII] [1919]

Section 1. After one year from the ratification of this article the manufacture, sale, or transportation of intoxicating liquors within, the importation thereof into, or the exportation thereof from the United States and all territory subject to the jurisdiction thereof for beverage purposes is hereby prohibited.

Section 2. The Congress and the several States shall have concurrent power to enforce this article by appropriate legislation.

Section 3. This article shall be inoperative unless it shall have been ratified as an amendment to the Constitution by the legislatures of the several States, as provided in the Constitution, within seven years from the date of the submission hereof to the States by the Congress.

Historical Note

This amendment was proposed to the legislatures of the several states by the Sixty–Fifth Congress, on the 19th day of December, 1917, and was declared, in a proclamation by the Acting Secretary of State, dated on the 29th day of January, 1919, to have been ratified by the legislatures of the states of Alabama, Arizona, California, Colorado, Delaware, Florida, Georgia, Idaho, Illinois, Indiana, Kansas, Kentucky, Louisiana, Maine, Maryland, Massachusetts, Michigan, Minnesota, Mississippi, Montana, Nebraska, New Hampshire, North Carolina, North Dakota, Ohio, Oklahoma, Oregon, South Dakota, South Carolina, Texas, Utah, Virginia, Washington, West Virginia, Wisconsin, and Wyoming.

Amendment [XIX] [1920]

[1]   The right of citizens of the United States to vote shall not be denied or abridged by the United States or by any State on account of sex.

[2]   Congress shall have power to enforce this article by appropriate legislation.

Historical Note

This amendment was proposed to the legislatures of the several states by the Sixty–Sixth Congress, on the 5th day of June, 1919, and was declared, in a proclamation by the Secretary of State, dated on the 26th day of August, 1920, to have been ratified by the legislatures of the states of Arizona, Arkansas, California, Colorado, Idaho, Illinois, Indiana, Iowa, Kansas, Kentucky, Maine, Massachusetts, Michigan, Minnesota, Missouri, Montana, Nebraska, Nevada, New Hampshire, New Jersey, New Mexico, North Dakota, New York, Ohio, Oklahoma, Oregon, Pennsylvania, Rhode Island, South Dakota, Tennessee, Texas, Utah, Washington, West Virginia, Wisconsin and Wyoming.

Amendment [XX] [1933]

Section 1. The terms of the President and Vice President shall end at noon on the 20th day of January, and the terms of Senators and Representatives at noon on the 3d day of January, of the years in which such terms would have ended if this article had not been ratified; and the terms of their successors shall then begin.

Section 2. The Congress shall assemble at least once in every year, and such meeting shall begin at noon on the 3d day of January, unless they shall by law appoint a different day.

Section 3. If, at the time fixed for the beginning of the term of the President, the President elect shall have died, the Vice President elect shall become President. If the President shall not have been chosen before the time fixed for the beginning of his term, or if the President elect shall have failed to qualify, then the Vice President elect shall act as President until a President shall have qualified; and the Congress may by law provide for the case wherein neither a President elect nor a Vice President elect shall have qualified, declaring who shall then act as President, or the manner in which one who is to act shall be selected, and such person shall act accordingly until a President or Vice President shall have qualified.

Section 4. The Congress may by law provide for the case of the death of any of the persons from whom the House of Representatives may choose a President whenever the right of choice shall have devolved upon them, and for the case of the death of any of the persons from whom the Senate may choose a Vice President whenever the right of choice shall have devolved upon them.

Section 5. Sections 1 and 2 shall take effect on the 15th day of October following the ratification of this article.

Section 6. This article shall be inoperative unless it shall have been ratified as an amendment to the Constitution by the legislatures of three-fourths of the several States within seven years from the date of its submission.

Historical Note

This amendment was proposed to the legislatures of the several states by the Seventy–Second Congress, on March 3, 1932, and was declared, in a proclamation by the Secretary of State, dated Feb. 6, 1933, to have been ratified by the legislatures of the states of Alabama, Arizona, Arkansas, California, Colorado, Connecticut, Delaware, Georgia, Idaho, Illinois, Indiana, Kansas, Kentucky, Louisiana, Maine, Massachusetts, Michigan, Minnesota, Mississippi, Missouri, Montana, Nebraska, New Jersey, New York, North Carolina, North Dakota, Ohio, Oklahoma, Pennsylvania, Rhode Island, South Carolina, South Dakota, Texas, Utah, Virginia, Washington, West Virginia, Wisconsin, and Wyoming.

Amendment [XXI] [1933]

Section 1. The eighteenth article of amendment to the Constitution of the United States is hereby repealed.

Section 2. The transportation or importation into any State, Territory, or possession of the United States for delivery or use therein of intoxicating liquors, in violation of the laws thereof, is hereby prohibited.

Section 3. This article shall be inoperative unless it shall have been ratified as an amendment to the Constitution by conventions in the several States, as provided in the Constitution, within seven years from the date of the submission hereof to the States by the Congress.

Historical Note

This amendment was proposed to the several states by the Seventy–Second Congress, on Feb. 20, 1933, and was declared, in a proclamation by the Secretary of State, dated Dec. 5, 1933, to have been ratified by conventions in the States of Arizona, Alabama, Arkansas, California, Colorado, Connecticut, Delaware, Florida, Idaho, Illinois, Indiana, Iowa, Kentucky, Maryland, Massachusetts, Michigan, Minnesota, Missouri, Nevada, New Hampshire, New Jersey, New Mexico, New York, Ohio, Oregon, Pennsylvania, Rhode Island, Tennessee, Texas, Utah, Vermont, Virginia, Washington, West Virginia, Wisconsin and Wyoming.

Amendment [XXII] [1951]

Section 1. No person shall be elected to the office of the President more than twice, and no person who has held the office of President, or acted as President, for more than two years of a term to which some other person was elected President shall be elected to the office of President more than once. But this Article shall not apply to any person holding the office of President when this Article was proposed by the Congress, and shall not prevent any person who may be holding the office of President, or acting as President, during the term within which this Article becomes operative from holding the office of President or acting as President during the remainder of such term.

Section 2. This article shall be inoperative unless it shall have been ratified as an amendment to the Constitution by the legislatures of three-fourths of the several States within seven years from the date of its submission to the States by the Congress.

Historical Note

Proposal and Ratification. This amendment was proposed to the legislatures of the several States by the Eightieth Congress on Mar. 24, 1947 by House Joint Res. No. 27, and was declared by the Administrator of General Services on Mar. 1, 1951, to have been ratified. The legislatures ratified this Amendment on the following dates: Maine, Mar. 31, 1947; Michigan, Mar. 31, 1947; Iowa, Apr. 1, 1947; Kansas, Apr. 1, 1947; New Hampshire, Apr. 1, 1947; Delaware, Apr. 2, 1947; Illinois, Apr. 3, 1947; Oregon, Apr. 3, 1947; Colorado, Apr. 12, 1947; California, Apr. 15, 1947; New Jersey, Apr. 15, 1947; Vermont, Apr. 15, 1947; Ohio, Apr. 16, 1947; Wisconsin, Apr. 16, 1947; Pennsylvania, Apr. 29, 1947; Connecticut, May 21, 1947; Missouri, May 22, 1947; Nebraska, May 23, 1947; Virginia, Jan. 28, 1948; Mississippi, Feb. 12, 1948; New York, Mar. 9, 1948; South Dakota, Jan. 21, 1949; North Dakota, Feb. 25, 1949; Louisiana, May 17, 1950; Montana, Jan. 25, 1951; Indiana, Jan. 29, 1951; Idaho, Jan. 30, 1951; New Mexico, Feb. 12, 1951; Wyoming, Feb. 12, 1951; Arkansas, Feb. 15, 1951; Georgia, Feb. 17, 1951; Tennessee, Feb. 20, 1951; Texas, Feb. 22, 1951; Utah, Feb. 26, 1951; Nevada, Feb. 26, 1951; Minnesota, Feb. 27, 1951, and North Carolina, Feb. 28, 1951.

Subsequent to the proclamation, Amendment XXII was ratified by South Carolina on Mar. 13, 1951; Maryland, Mar. 14, 1951; Florida, Apr. 16, 1951, and Alabama, May 4, 1951.

Certification of Validity. Publication of the certifying statement of the Administrator of General Services that the Amendment had become valid was made on Mar. 1, 1951, F.R.Doc. 51–2940, 16 F.R. 2019.

Amendment [XXIII] [1961]

Section 1. The District constituting the seat of Government of the United States shall appoint in such manner as the Congress may direct:

A number of electors of President and Vice President equal to the whole number of Senators and Representatives in Congress to which the District would be entitled if it were a State, but in no event more than the least populous state; they shall be in addition to those appointed by the states, but they shall be considered, for the purposes of the election of President and Vice President, to be electors appointed by a state; and they shall meet in the District and perform such duties as provided by the twelfth article of amendment.

Section 2. The Congress shall have power to enforce this article by appropriate legislation.

Historical Note

Proposal and Ratification. This amendment was proposed by the Eighty-sixth Congress on June 16, 1960 and was declared by the Administrator of General Services on Apr. 3, 1961, to have been ratified.

The amendment was ratified by the following States: Hawaii, June 23, 1960; Massachusetts, Aug. 22, 1960; New Jersey, Dec. 19, 1960; New York, Jan. 17, 1961; California, Jan. 19, 1961; Oregon, Jan. 27, 1961; Maryland, Jan. 30, 1961; Idaho, Jan. 31, 1961; Maine, Jan. 31, 1961; Minnesota, Jan. 31, 1961; New Mexico, Feb. 1, 1961; Nevada, Feb. 2, 1961; Montana, Feb. 6, 1961; Colorado, Feb. 8, 1961; Washington, Feb. 9, 1961; West Virginia, Feb. 9, 1961; Alaska, Feb. 10, 1961; Wyoming, Feb. 13, 1961; South Dakota, Feb. 14, 1961; Delaware, Feb. 20, 1961; Utah, Feb. 21, 1961; Wisconsin, Feb. 21, 1961; Pennsylvania, Feb. 28, 1961; Indiana, Mar. 3, 1961; North Dakota, Mar. 3, 1961; Tennessee, Mar. 6, 1961; Michigan, Mar. 8, 1961; Connecticut, Mar. 9, 1961; Arizona, Mar.

10, 1961; Illinois, Mar. 14, 1961; Nebraska, Mar. 15, 1961; Vermont, Mar. 15, 1961; Iowa, Mar. 16, 1961; Missouri, Mar. 20, 1961; Oklahoma, Mar. 21, 1961; Rhode Island, Mar. 22, 1961; Kansas, Mar. 29, 1961; Ohio, Mar. 29, 1961, and New Hampshire, Mar. 30, 1961.

Certification of Validity. Publication of the certifying statement of the Administrator of General Services that the Amendment had become valid was made on Apr. 3, 1961, F.R.Doc. 61–3017, 26 F.R. 2808.

Amendment [XXIV] [1964]

Section 1. The right of citizens of the United States to vote in any primary or other election for President or Vice President, for electors for President or Vice President, or for Senator or Representative in Congress, shall not be denied or abridged by the United States or any State by reason of failure to pay any poll tax or other tax.

Section 2. The Congress shall have power to enforce this article by appropriate legislation.

Historical Note

Proposal and Ratification. This amendment was proposed by the Eighty-seventh Congress by Senate Joint Resolution No. 29, which was approved by the Senate on Mar. 27, 1962, and by the House of Representatives on Aug. 27, 1962. It was declared by the Administrator of General Services on Feb. 4, 1964, to have been ratified.

This amendment was ratified by the following States: Illinois, Nov. 14, 1962; New Jersey, Dec. 3, 1962; Oregon, Jan. 25, 1963; Montana, Jan. 28, 1963; West Virginia, Feb. 1, 1963; New York, Feb. 4, 1963; Maryland, Feb. 6, 1963; California, Feb. 7, 1963; Alaska, Feb. 11, 1963; Rhode Island, Feb. 14, 1963; Indiana, Feb. 19, 1963; Utah, Feb. 20, 1963; Michigan, Feb. 20, 1963; Colorado, Feb. 21, 1963; Ohio, Feb. 27, 1963; Minnesota, Feb. 27, 1963; New Mexico, Mar. 5, 1963; Hawaii, Mar. 6, 1963; North Dakota, Mar. 7, 1963; Idaho, Mar. 8, 1963; Washington, Mar. 14, 1963; Vermont, Mar. 15, 1963; Nevada, Mar. 19, 1963; Connecticut, Mar. 20, 1963; Tennessee, Mar. 21, 1963; Pennsylvania, Mar. 25, 1963; Wisconsin, Mar. 26, 1963; Kansas, Mar. 28, 1963; Massachusetts, Mar. 28, 1963; Nebraska, Apr. 4, 1963; Florida, Apr. 18, 1963; Iowa, Apr. 24, 1963; Delaware, May 1, 1963; Missouri, May 13, 1963; New Hampshire, June 12, 1963; Kentucky, June 27, 1963; Maine, Jan. 16, 1964; South Dakota, Jan. 23, 1964.

Certification of Validity. Publication of the certifying statement of the Administrator of General Services that the Amendment had become valid was made on Feb. 5, 1964, F.R.Doc. 64–1229, 29 F.R. 1715. President Johnson and the Administrator signed this certificate on Feb. 4, 1964.

Amendment [XXV] [1967]

Section 1. In the case of the removal of the President from office or of his death or resignation, the Vice President shall become President.

Section 2. Whenever there is a vacancy in the office of the Vice President, the President shall nominate a Vice President who shall take office upon confirmation by a majority vote of both Houses of Congress.

Section 3. Whenever the President transmits to the President pro tempore of the Senate and the Speaker of the House of Representatives his written declaration that he is unable to discharge the powers and duties of his office, and until he transmits to them a written declaration to the contrary, such powers and duties shall be discharged by the Vice President as Acting President.

Section 4. Whenever the Vice President and a majority of either the principal officers of the executive departments or of such other body as Congress may by law provide, transmit to the President pro tempore of the Senate and the Speaker of the House of Representatives, their written declaration that the President is unable to discharge the powers and duties of his office, the Vice President shall immediately assume the powers and duties of the office as Acting President.

Thereafter, when the President transmits to the President pro tempore of the Senate and the Speaker of the House of Representatives his written declaration that no inability exists, he shall resume the powers and duties of his office unless the Vice President and a majority of either the principal officers of the executive department or of such other body as Congress may by law provide, transmit within four days to the President pro tempore of the Senate and the Speaker of the House of Representatives their written declaration that the President is unable to discharge the powers and duties of his office. Thereupon Congress shall decide the issue, assembling within forty-eight hours for that purpose if not in session. If the Congress, within twenty-one days after receipt of the latter written declaration, or, if Congress is not in session, within twenty-one days after Congress is required to assemble, determines by two-thirds vote of both Houses that the President is unable to discharge the powers and duties of his office, the Vice President shall continue to discharge the same as Acting President; otherwise, the President shall resume the powers and duties of his office.

Historical Note

Proposal and Ratification. This amendment was proposed by the Eighty-ninth Congress by Senate Joint Resolution No. 1, which was approved by the Senate on Feb. 19, 1965, and by the House of Representatives, in amended form, on Apr. 13, 1965. The House of Representatives agreed to a Conference Report on June 30, 1965, and the Senate agreed to the Conference Report on July 6, 1965. It was declared by the Administrator of General Services, on Feb. 23, 1967, to have been ratified.

This amendment was ratified by the following States: Nebraska, July 12, 1965; Wisconsin, July 13, 1965; Oklahoma, July 16, 1965; Massachusetts, Aug. 9, 1965; Pennsylvania, Aug. 18, 1965; Kentucky, Sept. 15, 1965; Arizona, Sept. 22, 1965; Michigan, Oct. 5, 1965; Indiana, Oct. 20, 1965; California, Oct. 21, 1965; Arkansas, Nov. 4, 1965; New Jersey, Nov. 29, 1965; Delaware, Dec. 7, 1965; Utah, Jan. 17, 1966; West Virginia, Jan. 20, 1966; Maine, Jan. 24, 1966; Rhode Island, Jan. 28, 1966; Colorado, Feb. 3, 1966; New Mexico, Feb. 3, 1966; Kansas, Feb. 8, 1966; Vermont, Feb. 10, 1966; Alaska, Feb. 18, 1966; Idaho, Mar. 2, 1966; Hawaii, Mar. 3, 1966; Virginia, Mar. 8, 1966; Mississippi, Mar. 10, 1966; New York, Mar. 14, 1966; Maryland, Mar. 23, 1966; Missouri, Mar. 30, 1966; New Hampshire, June 13, 1966; Louisiana, July 5, 1966; Tennessee, Jan. 12, 1967; Wyoming, Jan. 25, 1967; Washington, Jan. 26, 1967; Iowa, Jan. 26, 1967; Oregon, Feb. 2, 1967; Minnesota, Feb. 10, 1967; Nevada, Feb. 10, 1967; Connecticut, Feb. 14, 1967; Montana, Feb. 15, 1967; South Dakota, Mar. 6, 1967; Ohio, Mar. 7, 1967; Alabama, Mar. 14, 1967; North Carolina, Mar. 22, 1967; Illinois, Mar. 22, 1967; Texas, Apr. 25, 1967; Florida, May 25, 1967.

Certification of Validity. Publication of the certifying statement of the Administrator of General Services that the Amendment had become valid was made on Feb. 25, 1967, F.R.Doc. 67–2208, 32 F.R. 3287, and signed on July 23, 1967.

Amendment [XXVI] [1971]

Section 1. The right of citizens of the United States, who are eighteen years of age or older, to vote shall not be denied or abridged by the United States or by any State on account of age.

Section 2. The Congress shall have power to enforce this article by appropriate legislation.

Historical Note

Proposal and Ratification. This amendment was proposed by the Ninety-second Congress by Senate Joint Resolution No. 7, which was approved by the Senate on Mar. 10, 1971, and by the House of Representatives on Mar. 23, 1971. It was declared by the Administrator of General Services on July 5, 1971, to have been ratified.

This amendment was ratified by the following States: Connecticut, Mar. 23, 1971; Delaware, Mar. 23, 1971; Minnesota, Mar. 23, 1971; Tennessee, Mar. 23, 1971; Washington, Mar. 23, 1971; Hawaii, Mar. 24, 1971; Massachusetts, Mar. 24, 1971; Idaho, Mar. 30, 1971; Montana, Mar. 31, 1971; Arkansas, Apr. 1, 1971; Iowa, Apr. 1, 1971; Nebraska, Apr. 2, 1971; Kansas, Apr. 7, 1971; Michigan, Apr. 7, 1971; Indiana, Apr. 8, 1971; Maine, Apr. 9, 1971; Vermont, Apr. 16, 1971; California, Apr. 19, 1971; South Carolina, Apr. 28, 1971; West Virginia, Apr. 28, 1971; Pennsylvania, May 3, 1971; New Jersey, May 4, 1971; Texas, May 5, 1971; Maryland, May 6, 1971; New Hampshire, May 13, 1971; Arizona, May 17, 1971; Colorado, May 24, 1971; Louisiana, May 27, 1971; Rhode Island, May 27, 1971; New York, June 2, 1971; Oregon, June 5, 1971; Missouri, June 14, 1971; Wisconsin, June 18, 1971; Illinois, June 29, 1971; Alabama, June 30, 1971; Ohio, June 30, 1971; North Carolina, July 1, 1971; Oklahoma, July 1, 1971.

Certification of Validity. Publication of the certifying statement of the Administrator of General Services that the Amendment had become valid was made on July 7, 1971, F.R.Doc. 71–9691, 36 F.R. 12725, and signed on July 5, 1971.

Amendment [XXVII] [1992]

No law, varying the compensation for the services of the Senators and Representatives, shall take effect, until an election of Representatives shall have intervened.

Historical Note

Proposal and Ratification. This amendment was one of twelve that the first Congress proposed on September 25, 1789. Ten of these twelve became the first ten amendments, often called the Bill of Rights. A sufficient number of states did not ratify until 203 years later.

This amendment was ratified by the following States: Maryland, Dec. 19, 1789; North Carolina, Dec. 22, 1789; South Carolina, Jan. 19, 1790; Delaware, Jan. 28, 1790; Vermont, Nov. 3, 1791; Virginia, Dec. 15, 1791; Ohio, May 6, 1873; Wyoming, Mar. 3, 1978; Maine, Apr. 2, 1983; Colorado, Apr. 18, 1984; South Dakota, Feb. 21, 1985; New Hampshire, Mar. 7, 1985; Arizona, Apr. 3, 1985; Tennessee, May 23, 1985; Oklahoma, July 10, 1985; New Mexico, Feb. 14, 1986; Indiana, Feb. 24, 1986; Utah, Feb. 26, 1986; Arkansas, Mar. 5, 1987; Montana,

Mar. 17, 1987; Connecticut, May 13, 1987; Wisconsin, June 30, 1987; Georgia, Feb. 2, 1988; West Virginia, Mar. 10, 1988; Louisiana, July 6, 1988; Iowa, Feb. 7, 1989; Idaho, Mar. 23, 1989; Nevada, Apr. 26, 1989; Alaska, May 5, 1989; Oregon, May 19, 1989; Minnesota, May 22, 1989; Texas, May 25, 1989; Kansas, Apr. 4, 1990; Florida, May 31, 1990; North Dakota, Mar. 25, 1991; Missouri, May 5, 1992; Alabama, May 5, 1992; Michigan, May 7, 1992; New Jersey, May 7, 1992; Illinois, May 12, 1992.

Certification of Validity. On May 13, 1992, the Archivist of the United States announced that he would accept this amendment as valid once he received formal notice pursuant to 1 U.S.C.A. § 106b.